PHRS. **27. it is proven,** *probatum est* [L.], there is nothing more to be said, it must follow; **O.E.D.,** *quod erat demonstrandum* [hich was to be demonstrated].

---

505. DISPROOF

NOUNS **1. disproof,** disproval, **invalidation,** falsification, explosion, negation; exposure, exposition, exposé; *reductio ad absurdum* [L., a reduction to the absurd]

2. refutation, confutation, refutal, **rebuttal, answer,** complete answer; **contradiction,** opposition, controversion, contravention, traversal, **denial,** gainsaying; **overthrowal,** upset, subversion.

3. conclusive argument, knockdown argument, floorer, sockdolager [slang, U.S.], corker [slang]; **clincher,** crusher, **settler,** finisher, squelcher [all coll.].

VERBS **4. disprove, invalidate,** discredit, falsify, belie, give the lie to; **negate,** negative; **expose, show up; explode,** blow up, blow sky-high, **puncture, shoot full of holes; knock the bottom out of** [coll.], knock the props out from under, take the ground from under, cut the ground from under one's feet, not leave a leg to stand on.

5. refute, confute, rebut, parry, answer, **answer conclusively,** dismiss, dispose of; **contradict,** controvert, contravene, traverse, oppose, **dispute, deny,** impugn, gainsay; **overthrow,** overturn, overwhelm, throw over, upset, subvert, defeat, **confound,** gravel [coll.], floor, finish [chiefly coll.]; settle, squash [chiefly coll.], squelch [chiefly coll.], crush, smash all opposition; **silence,** put or reduce to silence, shut up, stop the mouth of.

ADJS. **6. refuting, confuting,** confutative, refutative, refutatory; contradictory, contrary, negatory.

7. disproved, invalidated, negated, discredited, falsified, belied; **exposed,** shown up; **punctured, exploded; refuted,** confuted; contradicted, disputed, denied, impugned; **upset, overthrown,** overturned; dismissed, discarded, rejected.

8. unproved, unproven, **undemonstrated,** unshown, **untried,** untested; **unfounded** 482.12; **unestablished,** unfixed, **unsettled, undetermined,** unascertained; **unconfirmed, unsubstantiated,** unattested, **unauthenticated,** unvalidated, uncertified, **unverified, uncorroborated,** unsustained, **unsupported,** unsupported by evidence;

inconclu[...], consequ[...]

9. un[...], undemonstrable, undemonstratable, unattestable, **unconfirmable,** unsubstantiatable, **unsupportable,** unsustainable, unverifiable.

10. refutable, confutable, **disprovable,** defeasible.

---

506. QUALIFICATION

NOUNS **1. qualification, limitation,** restriction, **modification,** coloring, **allowance, concession,** cession, grant, consideration, grain of salt; **reservation,** exception, exemption; **mental reservation,** *arrière-pensée* [F.]; extenuating circumstances.

2. condition, provision, proviso, stipulation, specification, arrangement, situation, circumstance, case; **string,** a string to it [both coll.]; **requisite, prerequisite,** obligation; postulate, postulation; *sine qua non, conditio sine qua non* [both L.]; joker [U.S.]; clause; saving clause; escalator clause; **terms,** provisions, etc., grounds; ultimatum.

VERBS **3. qualify, modify, limit, restrict,** restrain, narrow; affect, give a color to, take color from; adjust to, regulate by; **temper, season,** leaven, soften, modulate, moderate, assuage, **mitigate,** palliate, abate, reduce, diminish.

4. condition, make it a condition; **stipulate,** postulate, **specify,** define, fix, determine; insist upon, make a point of; bind, tie; have a string to it [coll.].

5. allow for, make allowance for, provide for, take account of, **take into account or consideration, consider,** reckon with, allow, **grant, concede,** acknowledge, admit, admit exceptions; disregard, leave out of account; **discount,** consider the source, **take with a grain of salt.**

6. depend, hang, rest, hinge; **depend on or upon, hang on or upon, rest on or upon,** rest with, repose upon, lie on, lie with, stand on or upon, be based on, be dependent on, be contingent on; **hinge on or upon,** turn on or upon, revolve on or upon, revolve around, hang around.

ADJS. **7. qualifying,** qualificative, qualificatory; **modifying,** modificatory; **limiting, restricting,** limitative, restrictive; **exceptional,** exceptionable; **extenuating,** extenuatory; **mitigating,** mitigative, mitigatory, modulatory, palliative, assuasive, lenitive.

P. M. Roget

PETER MARK ROGET

1779–1869

PETER MARK ROGET was the only son of John Roget, who hailed from Geneva and later had oversight of the French Protestant Church in Threadneedle Street, London, where Peter was born in 1779. His father died a few years later, and his mother removed to Edinburgh, where the son entered the university at the age of fourteen. He was graduated M.D. from the medical school at the early age of nineteen and distinguished himself by valuable research work on such subjects as consumption and the effects of laughing gas. In 1802 he went to Geneva, his father's home, in company with the sons of a wealthy merchant of Manchester, to whom he acted as tutor. The disturbances caused by the breach of the Peace of Amiens interrupted their tour and Roget was for a time held a prisoner at Geneva. He succeeded in getting away, however, at the end of 1803 and became private physician to the Marquis of Lansdowne.

In 1805 he became physician to the Manchester Infirmary and made a name for himself there by giving courses of lectures on scientific subjects. He combined in an unusual degree exact knowledge with a power of apt and vivid presentation, and this work he continued for well-nigh fifty years after his removal to London in 1808. He became physician to the Northern Dispensary in 1810 and lectured assiduously on medical and other subjects in various parts of the metropolis. A testimony to his versatility is afforded by the fact that he was asked by the Government to make an inquiry into the water supply of London, and in 1828 he published a report on the subject. For three years he held the post of Fullerian Professor of Physiology at the London Institution.

Dr. Roget was made a Fellow of the Royal Society in 1815, and served as secretary of the organization for over twenty years. He was appointed Examiner in Physiology in the University of London. He wrote various papers on physiology and health, among them *On Animal and Vegetable Physiology*, a Bridgewater treatise, 1834; a work on phrenology in two volumes, 1838; and *Electricity, Galvanism*, 1848.

These activities would be more than enough for most men, but Roget's insatiable thirst for knowledge and his appetite for work led him into yet other fields. He was no high-and-dry scientist who thought that learning was the prerogative of the elect; his aim was to broadcast it as widely as possible. He was a founder of the Society for the Diffusion of Knowledge and wrote for it a series of popular manuals. He devised a slide rule and spent much time in attempting to perfect a calculating machine. He showed remarkable ingenuity in inventing and solving chess problems and designed a pocket chessboard called the "Economic Chessboard."

However, the work that extended and perpetuated his fame on two continents was one which he regarded as a mere avocation. In the year 1852 he brought out his *Thesaurus of English Words and Phrases Classified and Arranged so as to Facilitate the Expression of Ideas and Assist in Literary Composition*. A second edition followed the next year, a third two years later, and still others in the next few years. The work was extended and corrected by his son. In 1911 the THOMAS Y. CROWELL COMPANY published the first edition prepared by the noted lexicographer and orientalist C. O. Sylvester Mawson. The edition of 1922—virtually a new book—was again the work of Dr. Mawson and the first to be called "International Edition." The long series of subsequent improved and enlarged editions finds its climax in the present third INTERNATIONAL, in which the Publishers and Editors have spared neither effort nor expense to live up to and even better the standards of so remarkable a tradition.

Peter Roget died in West Malvern, on September 12, 1869, at the age of ninety.

ROGET'S INTERNATIONAL THESAURUS

ROGET'S
INTERNATIONAL
THESAURUS

THIRD EDITION

THOMAS Y. CROWELL COMPANY

New York · Established 1834

CONTENTS

CONTENTS

HOW TO USE THIS BOOK

In a dictionary you start with a word and look for its meaning. In ROGET'S INTER-
NATIONAL THESAURUS you start with your idea and find the words to express it.

1. Look up your idea in the index and find beneath it the closest synonym.
2. Turn to the numbered section you choose and find dozens of synonyms and
   associated words.

Suppose, for example, you want a word meaning "to shade from light."

1. You look up the verb *shade* in the
index and select the closest synonym, or guide word, beneath it.

shackle
  nouns 758.4
  verbs 758.10
shade
  nouns ~ of difference
    16.2
  degree 29.1
  small amount 35.4
  tinge 44.7
  cover 227.2
  roof 227.6,42
  umbrella 227.7
  tent 227.8,43
  hat 230.25,59
  shadow 336.3
  shader 337.1
  types of ~ 337.8
  color 361.1
  illusion 518.4
  protection 697.1
  specter 1015.1
  soul 1032.17
  IN THE SHADE
  inferior 37.6
  concealed 613.12
  verbs ~ off 29.4
  ~ into 52.3
  cover 227.21
  darken 336.10
  screen 337.5
  color 361.13
  blacken 364.7
  cloud 403.7
  conceal 613.7
shaded
  shadowy 336.17
  sheltered 337.7
shader 337.1

337. SHADE

A Thing That Shades.—NOUNS **1. shade, shader, shelter, screen, shield, protection, curtain, veil,** purdah [India]; cover 227.2; shadow 336.3.

2. eyeshade, eyeshield, opaque; blinkers, blinds, blinders; blindfold; goggles, colored spectacles, smoked glasses, sunglasses.

3. lamp shade; moonshade; globe, light globe; light shield; fin, blinker, ear, gobo, nigger [all motion picture].

4. light filter, filter, diffusing screen; butterfly, silk, gauze [all motion picture]; gelatin filter, jelly [motion picture]; celluloid filter, cello [motion picture]; frosted lens, frost [motion picture].

VERBS **5. shade, shelter, protect; screen, shield, veil, curtain;** shutter; draw the curtains, put up or close the shutters; cover 227.21; overshadow 336.10.

ADJS. **6. shading, sheltering, protecting; screening, shielding, veiling, curtaining; covering** 227.37.

7. shaded, sheltered, protected; screened, shielded, veiled, curtained; shady 336.17.

8. shades

awning	screen
baldachino	shield
bamboo shade or	shutter
screen	smoke screen
blind	[mil.]
canopy	sunbonnet
curtain	sun hat
hat 230.25, 59	sun helmet
jalousie [F.]	sunshade
lamp shade	tent 227.8, 43
occulter, occulting	umbrella 227.7
screen	veil
panoply	Venetian blind
parasol	visor
pith helmet	window curtain
portiere	window screen
roof 227.6, 42	window shade
sash curtain	window shutter

2. You turn to the numbered section and find all the synonyms and associated words you need: *screen, shield, veil, curtain,* etc.

Here are five more time-saving features:

1. The most commonly used words are printed in heavy type: **shade, shelter.**
2. Cross-references will help you find more synonyms if you need them: "overshadow 336.10"
3. Alphabetical lists of specific things supply concrete examples for your use.
4. In the index, careful distinctions are made for each meaning of a word.
5. The index lists abundant phrases to help you find closer meanings.

If you don't find the word you want, try another guide word in the index. For example, "darken 336.10" may contain more words that you can use. Antonyms are in nearby categories. SHADE follows LIGHT (334) and LUMINARY (335).

PUBLISHER'S PREFACE

This *Third Edition* of ROGET'S INTERNATIONAL THESAURUS is a complete revision and resetting of the *New Edition* of 1946. It is the product of more than seventy-five years of development by the Thomas Y. Crowell Company of the original Thesaurus of Dr. Peter Mark Roget, and it is by far the largest and finest such book that has ever been produced.

A number of new features have been perfected and embodied in this *Third Edition*:

1. For the first time Dr. Roget's original 1,000 categories have been increased. Modern science and technology require that new categories be added, and now there is a total of 1,040.

2. New words have been added and outmoded words have been dropped. More than 45,000 words have been included that never appeared in the Thesaurus before.

3. The most commonly needed words are printed in heavy type, for rapid reference.

4. Word lists of specific objects have been added. Thus, names and nomenclature of plants, animals, tools, weapons, vehicles, and many other subjects are alphabetically arranged and shown in distinguishing type.

5. Both text and index pages have been redesigned for greater readability and efficiency. Electra and Electra Bold typefaces, designed by D. A. Dwiggins, have been used.

6. Parts of speech are now clearly designated in both text and index.

7. More phrases and idiomatic expressions, as well as more individual words, are now indexed for the first time.

The valuable features of previous editions have been retained. Foremost among these is Dr. Roget's basic principle of grouping words according to ideas, rather than alphabetically, as in a dictionary. This principle—the secret of the book's usefulness—has been preserved in the Crowell editions for three quarters of a century, while the amount and variety of material have steadily increased. ROGET'S INTERNATIONAL THESAURUS is the only thesaurus that has constantly enlarged its scope while retaining the original Roget system. As a result, it is the most nearly complete, up-to-date, and convenient thesaurus available.

The *Thesaurus of English Words and Phrases Classified and Arranged so as to Facilitate the Expression of Ideas and Assist in Literary Composition*, published in 1852, derived from a catalog of words that Peter Mark Roget had begun to compile solely for his own use as early as 1805. It was an instant success and a year later, in 1853, a second edition was published. A third "cheaper edition enlarged and improved" followed in 1855. By Roget's death in 1869, his Thesaurus had gone through twenty-eight editions.

Subsequently, the responsibility of revising and expanding was taken over by his son, Dr. John Lewis Roget, and in 1879 a greatly enlarged edition appeared from which this present INTERNATIONAL edition was ultimately derived. The Thomas Y. Crowell Company's first edition in 1886 initiated a policy of improvement and expansion that has produced a reference book of international renown. The edition of 1911—practically a new book—was the work of the noted lexicographer and orientalist, the late C. O. Sylvester Mawson, Revising Editor of *Webster's New International Dictionary*. This edition was completely revised and reset in 1922 as the INTERNATIONAL edition, which was further enlarged and improved in 1930, 1932, 1936,

1938, and 1939. In 1946 a complete overhauling produced the distinguished ROGET'S INTERNATIONAL THESAURUS: *New Edition.* Immediately, plans for another edition were made and the process of revision begun. After more than ten years of continuous revision, the present ROGET'S INTERNATIONAL THESAURUS: *Third Edition* takes its place among its famous predecessors.

The usefulness of the Thesaurus has been enhanced in other ways than the increase in its size. It has been brought up to date in two respects: (1) new words and idioms that the modern user will need have been added, and (2) words and phrases which, in our constantly changing language, have become obsolete since the previous edition have been removed. In particular, a whole new scientific and technical vocabulary has been added. The omission of the sections of quotations that appeared in previous editions, but now seem of limited usefulness, has made possible the inclusion of about fifty pages of new material. In all, the new edition contains about 30 per cent new material. The index has been expanded to include more phrases and expressions, which permit the user to single out more precise definitions than before.

ROGET'S INTERNATIONAL THESAURUS: *Third Edition* is, then, the most modern thesaurus on the market, and at the same time retains the best features of the classic reference work on which it is based. Complete, up-to-date, with all the advantages of modern design and type, it holds to its originator's simple, logical, and convenient system, which has never been equaled.

This edition of ROGET'S INTERNATIONAL THESAURUS was prepared by the staff of the Thomas Y. Crowell Company, which acknowledges with gratitude the help of Lester V. Berrey, who assisted with the preparation of previous editions as well as with this one. The revision of a great reference work is continuous, and preparation for a future edition began the moment this edition was completed.

THOMAS Y. CROWELL COMPANY

LESTER V. BERREY, *Revising Editor*   **GORTON CARRUTH,** *Reference Editor*

PETER ROGET'S PREFACE

to the First Edition

(1852)

It is now nearly fifty years since I first projected a system of verbal classification similar to that on which the present work is founded. Conceiving that such a compilation might help to supply my own deficiencies, I had, in the year 1805, completed a classed catalog of words on a small scale, but on the same principle, and nearly in the same form, as the Thesaurus now published. I had often during that long interval found this little collection, scanty and imperfect as it was, of much use to me in literary composition, and often contemplated its extension and improvement; but a sense of the magnitude of the task, amidst a multitude of other avocations, deterred me from the attempt. Since my retirement from the duties of Secretary of the Royal Society, however, finding myself possessed of more leisure, and believing that a repertory of which I had myself experienced the advantage might, when amplified, prove useful to others, I resolved to embark in an undertaking which, for the last three or four years, has given me incessant occupation, and has, indeed, imposed upon me an amount of labor very much greater than I had anticipated. Notwithstanding all the pains I have bestowed on its execution, I am fully aware of its numerous deficiencies and imperfections, and of its falling far short of the degree of excellence that might be attained. But, in a work of this nature, where perfection is placed at so great a distance, I have thought it best to limit my ambition to that moderate share of merit which it may claim in its present form; trusting to the indulgence of those for whose benefit it is intended, and to the candor of critics who, while they find it easy to detect faults, can at the same time duly appreciate difficulties.

P. M. Roget

April 29, 1852

SYNOPSIS OF CATEGORIES

CLASS ONE: ABSTRACT RELATIONS

CLASS ONE (Continued)

CLASS TWO: SPACE

CLASS SIX (Continued)

513. Uncertainty
514. Gamble
L. Conformity to Fact
515. Truth
516. Maxim
517. Error
518. Illusion
519. Disillusionment
M. Acceptance
520. Assent
520a. Dissent
521. Affirmation
522. Negation, Denial

II. STATES OF MIND

A. Mental Attitudes
523. Mental Attitude
524. Broad-mindedness
525. Narrow-
mindedness
526. Curiosity
527. Incuriosity
528. Attention
529. Inattention
530. Distraction
531. Care
532. Neglect
B. Creative Thought
533. Imagination
534. Unimaginative-
ness
C. Recollection
535. Memory
536. Forgetfulness
D. Anticipation
537. Expectation
538. Inexpectation
539. Disappointment
540. Foresight
541. Prediction
542. Foreboding

III. COMMUNICATION OF
IDEAS

A. Nature of Ideas Com-
municated
543. Meaning

544. Latency
545. Meaninglessness
546. Intelligibility
547. Unintelligibility
548. Ambiguity
549. Figure of Speech
550. Interpretation
551. Misinterpretation
B. Modes of Communica-
tion
552. Communication
553. Manifestation
554. Disclosure
555. Information
556. News
557. Publication
558. Communications
559. Messenger
C. Education
560. Teaching
561. Misteaching
562. Learning
563. Teacher
564. Student
565. School
D. Indication
566. Indication
567. Insignia
568. Record
569. Recorder
E. Representation
570. Representation
571. Misrepresentation
F. Arts of Design
572. Art
573. Sculpture
574. Ceramics
575. Photography
576. Engraving
577. Artist
G. Language
578. Language
579. Letter
580. Word
581. Nomenclature
582. Anonymity
583. Phrase

H. Grammar
584. Grammar
585. Ungrammatical-
ness
I. Style; Mode of
Expression
586. Diction
587. Elegance
588. Inelegance
589. Plain Speech
590. Conciseness
591. Diffuseness
J. Spoken Language
592. Speech
593. Imperfect Speech
594. Talkativeness
595. Conversation
596. Soliloquy
597. Elocution, Public
Speaking
598. Eloquence
599. Grandiloquence
K. Written Language
600. Writing
601. Printing
602. Correspondence
603. Book, Periodical
604. Treatise
605. Compendium
L. Linguistic Repre-
sentation
606. Description
607. Poetry
608. Prose
609. Drama
610. Actor
M. Uncommunicative-
ness; Secrecy
611. Uncommunica-
tiveness
612. Secrecy
613. Concealment
N. Falsehood
614. Falseness
615. Exaggeration
616. Deception
617. Deceiver
618. Dupe

CLASS SEVEN: VOLITION

I. VOLITION IN GENERAL

A. Will
619. Will
620. Willingness
621. Unwillingness
B. Resolution; Determina-
tion
622. Resolution
623. Perseverance
624. Obstinacy
C. Irresolution; Caprice
625. Irresolution
626. Tergiversation
627. Caprice

628. Impulse
D. Evasion
629. Avoidance
630. Escape
631. Abandonment
E. Inclination
632. Desire
633. Eagerness
634. Indifference
F. Choice
635. Choice
636. Rejection
637. Necessity
638. Predetermination
639. Prearrangement

G. Custom
640. Custom, Habit
641. Unaccus-
tomedness
642. Fashion
643. Convention
644. Formality
645. Informality
H. Motive
646. Motivation,
Inducement
647. Pretext
648. Allurement
649. Bribery
650. Dissuasion

CLASS SEVEN (Continued)

802. Pacification
803. Mediation
F. Mid-course
804. Neutrality
805. Compromise

VI. POSSESSIVE RELATIONS

A. Possession
806. Possession
807. Possessor
808. Property
809. Acquisition
810. Loss
811. Retention
812. Relinquishment
B. Sharing
813. Participation
814. Apportionment
C. Transfer of Property
815. Transfer of Property or Right

816. Giving
817. Receiving
818. Lending
819. Borrowing
D. Appropriation
820. Taking
821. Restitution
822. Theft
823. Thief
824. Illicit Business
E. Interchange of Property
825. Commerce
826. Purchase
827. Sale
828. Businessman, Merchant
829. Merchandise
830. Market
831. Stock Market
832. Securities

F. Monetary Relations
833. Money
834. Finance and Investment
835. Wealth
836. Poverty
837. Credit
838. Debt
839. Payment
840. Nonpayment
841. Expenditure
842. Receipts
843. Accounts
844. Price
845. Discount
846. Dearness
847. Cheapness
848. Gratuitousness
849. Economy
850. Parsimony
851. Liberality
852. Prodigality

CLASS EIGHT: AFFECTIONS

I. PERSONAL AFFECTIONS

A. Emotion
853. Feelings
854. Lack of Feelings
B. Excitability
855. Excitement
856. Inexcitability
857. Nervousness
858. Unnervousness
859. Patience
860. Impatience
C. Pleasure and Pleasureableness
861. Pleasantness
862. Unpleasantness
863. Pleasure
864. Displeasure
865. Dislike
866. Content
867. Discontent
868. Cheerfulness
869. Solemnity
870. Sadness
871. Regret
872. Unregretfulness
873. Lamentation
874. Rejoicing
875. Celebration
876. Amusement
877. Dancing
878. Humorousness
879. Wit and Humor
880. Banter
881. Dullness
882. Tedium
883. Aggravation
884. Relief
885. Comfort
D. Anticipative Emotions
886. Hope

887. Hopelessness
E. Concern
888. Anxiety
889. Fear
890. Cowardice
891. Courage
892. Rashness
893. Caution
F. Discriminative Affections
894. Fastidiousness
895. Taste
896. Vulgarity
897. Ugliness
898. Beauty
899. Ornamentation
900. Simplicity
901. Affectation
902. Ostentation
G. Pride
903. Pride
904. Humility
905. Servility
906. Modesty
907. Vanity
908. Boasting
909. Bluster
910. Arrogance
911. Insolence
H. Esteem
912. Repute
913. Disrepute
914. An Honor
915. Title
916. Nobility
917. Commonalty
I. Contemplative Emotions
918. Wonder
919. Unastonishment

II. SYMPATHETIC AFFECTIONS

A. Social Relations
920. Sociability
921. Unsociability
922. Seclusion
923. Hospitality, Welcome
924. Inhospitality
B. Social Affections
925. Friendship
926. Friend
927. Enmity
928. Hate
929. Love
930. Love-making, Endearment
931. Marriage
932. Celibacy
933. Divorce, Widowhood
C. Civility
934. Courtesy
935. Discourtesy
D. Benevolence
936. Kindness, Benevolence
937. Unkindness, Malevolence
938. Misanthropy
939. Public Spirit
940. Benefactor
941. Evildoer
E. Sympathy
942. Pity
943. Pitilessness
944. Condolence
945. Forgiveness
946. Congratulation
F. Gratefulness
947. Gratitude

ROGET'S
INTERNATIONAL
THESAURUS

THESAURUS
OF ENGLISH WORDS
AND PHRASES

1. EXISTENCE

NOUNS **1. existence,** subsistence, **being;** entity, essence; **occurrence, presence; life** 406.

2. reality, actuality, factuality; **truth** 515; **authenticity** 515.5; sober or grim reality, no joke, not a dream; ultimate reality, thing-in-itself [philos.].

3. fact, the case, the real know [slang], what's what [coll.]; **matter of fact,** plain matter of fact, "plain, plump fact" [Browning]; **bare fact,** naked fact, bald fact; **cold fact,** hard fact, **stubborn fact,** sober fact; **brutal fact,** brute fact [coll.], bitter fact, cruel fact, sordid fact, ugly fact, revolting fact; **actual fact,** positive fact, absolute fact; **accepted fact,** conceded fact, admitted fact, well-known fact, established fact, inescapable fact, indisputable fact, undeniable fact; **salient fact,** significant fact; accomplished fact, *fait accompli* [F.].

4. the facts, the dope [slang], the stuff [slang], the scoop [slang, U.S.], the score [slang]; the picture [coll.], the sketch [slang]; the facts in the matter, the facts of the case, the whole story [coll.]; essentials, basic or essential facts, brass tacks (as, to get down to *brass tacks* [coll.]).

5. self-existence, aseity, innascibility.

6. vegetable existence, vegetation, stagnation, inertia, mere existence, just being.

7. (science of existence) ontology, metaphysics, cosmology.

VERBS **8. exist, be,** have being; **live** 406.6; **subsist, stand,** obtain, hold, prevail, be the case; **occur,** be present, be there, be found, be met with, have place, happen to be.

9. live on, endure 110.6.

10. vegetate, stagnate, pass the time, merely exist, just be, live the life of a clam.

11. exist in, consist in, subsist in, lie in, rest in, repose in, stand in, reside in, abide in, dwell in, **inhere in,** be present in, be comprised in, be contained in, be constituted by.

12. become, come to be, get to be, turn out to be.

ADJS. **13. existent, existing,** in existence, that is; **subsistent,** subsisting; **being, in being; living** 406.10; **present, extant, prevalent, current,** afloat, on foot, under the sun, on the face of the earth.

14. self-existent, self-existing, innascible; uncreated, unoriginated, unbegotten.

15. real, actual, factual, veritable; positive, absolute; unideal, unimagined; **true** 515.11; **authentic** 515.13; **substantial** 3.4.

ADVS. **16. really, actually; truly** 515.16; **in reality, in actuality,** in effect, **in fact,** *de facto* [L.], in point of fact, as a matter of fact; positively, absolutely; no buts about it [coll.], nothing else but [slang]; *ipso facto* [L.], by the very fact.

2. NONEXISTENCE

NOUNS **1. nonexistence,** nonsubsistence; **nonentity, nonbeing,** not-being; **nothingness,** nullity, nihility; vacuity 186.2; negativeness, negation, negativity; nonoccurrence; **unreality,** nonreality, unactuality.

2. nothing, nil, *nihil* [L.], *nichts* [G.], nix [slang], **naught** or nought, **aught** or ought; **zero,** cipher; goose egg, duck egg, duck [all sports slang]; scratch; nothing whatever, nothing at all, nothing on earth *or* under the sun, no such thing; void 186.3; thing of naught 4.2.

3. **none,** not a one, not a blessed one [coll.]; never a one, ne'er a one, nary one [dial.]; **not any, not a bit,** not a whit, not a smitch *or* smidgen [dial.], not a speck, not a mite, not a particle, not an iota, not a jot, not a scrap, not a trace, not a lick [coll.], not a lick or smell [coll.], not a suspicion, not a shadow of a suspicion, neither hide nor hair.

VERBS 4. **not exist,** not be met with, not occur, not be found.

5. **cease,** cease to be, **perish, expire, die; vanish, disappear,** go phut [slang, U.S.], evaporate, fade, **fade away** *or* out, fly, dissolve, melt away, die out *or* away, pass, **pass away,** pass out of the picture [coll.], **come to nothing** *or* naught; peter out [coll.], peg out [slang]; **go,** be no more, leave no trace, "leave not a rack behind" [Shakespeare].

6. **nullify,** annihilate 691.13.

ADJS. 7. **nonexistent,** nonsubsistent, existless, unexisting, nowhere to be found; **minus, missing;** not a sign of, not a sign of life; **null, void,** devoid; vacuous 186.12; negative.

8. **unreal,** unactual, not real; nominal; **unsubstantial** 4.4; **fanciful** 533.19–22; unrealistic; illusory 518.9.

9. **unmade,** uncreated, unborn, unbegotten, unconceived, unproduced.

10. **no more,** napoo [slang]; **extinct, defunct, dead,** expired, passed away; vanished, gone phut [slang, U.S.]; perished, annihilated; **gone,** all gone; all over with, all up with [coll.], all up [slang], done for [coll.], dead and done for [coll.].

ADVS. 11. **none, no,** not at all, in no way, to no extent.

3. SUBSTANTIALITY

NOUNS 1. substantiality, substantialness; materiality 375; **substance, body,** mass; **solidity,** concreteness; **tangibility,** palpability, ponderability; **sturdiness, stability,** soundness, firmness, steadiness, stoutness, **strength; durability,** endurance

2. **substance, stuff, material,** metal; **matter** 375.2; tangible, ponderable.

3. **something, thing;** an existence, **being, entity,** individual, individuality; person, personality; creature, organism, life, body; **object** 375.4; objective.

ADJS. 4. **substantial,** substantive; **solid, concrete; tangible,** sensible, appreciable,

palpable, ponderable; **material** 375.9; **real** 1.15.

5. **sturdy,** stable, **solid,** sound, firm, steady, stout, **strong,** rugged; **durable,** lasting, enduring; **well-made,** well-constructed, well-built; **well-founded,** wellgrounded; **massive,** bulky, heavy, as big as life [coll.].

ADVS. 6. **substantially,** essentially 5.10.

4. UNSUBSTANTIALITY

NOUNS 1. unsubstantiality, unsubstantialness; **immateriality** 376; bodilessness, unsolidity, unconcreteness; **intangibility,** impalpability, imponderability; **tenuousness,** tenuity, subtlety, subtility, airiness, ethereality, **unreality;** fatuity, inanity; **flimsiness** 159.2.

2. thing of naught, nullity, nihility, **nonentity,** obscurity; cipher, "an O without a figure" [Shakespeare]; man of straw, jackstraw, lay figure, puppet, dummy; flash in the pan, dud [slang]; **trifle** 671.5, 6; nothing 2.2.

3. **intangible,** impalpable, imponderable; shadow, air, **thin air,** smoke, vapor, **bubble,** "such stuff as dreams are made on" [Shakespeare]; illusion 518; phantom 1015.

ADJS. 4. **unsubstantial,** nonsubstantial, unsubstanced; **immaterial** 376.7; **bodiless,** unsolid, unconcrete; **intangible,** impalpable, imponderable; weightless 352.10.

5. **tenuous,** subtile, subtle; **rarefied,** rare; **ethereal,** airy, windy, vaporous, gaseous; air-built, cloud-built; **chimerical,** gossamery, shadowy, phantomlike 1015.7; dreamlike, **illusory, unreal;** fatuous, fatuitous; fanciful 533.20–22.

6. **flimsy,** unsound, infirm 159.14–16.

7. **baseless, groundless,** ungrounded, **without foundation,** not well-founded, built on sand.

8. **nonobjective, abstract,** nonrepresentational.

5. INTRINSICALITY

NOUNS 1. intrinsicality, internality, innerness, **inwardness; inherence,** immanence, **inbeing,** indwelling; innateness, indigenousness; essentiality, fundamentality; **subjectivity,** nonobjectivity.

2. essence, substance, stuff; quid, quiddity; **quintessence,** elixir, flower; **essential, principle,** fundamental, hypostasis; gist, chat [coll.], jet, **nub** [coll., U.S.], nucleus, center, kernel, **core, pith,** meat, sap, marrow, **heart,** soul, spirit.

3. **nature, character, quality, property,** crasis, suchness; **constitution,** make-up, mold, fiber; **temperament,** temper; **disposition, mood, humor,** spirit, genius; tenor, way, habit, frame, cast, cue, tone, grain, vein, streak, stripe, stamp; kind 61.3; **characteristic** 80.3; **tendency** 173; the nature of, the way of, the nature of the beast [slang].

4. **inner nature,** inside, internal, inner *or* esoteric reality, true being, essential nature, true inwardness, center of life, vital principle; **spirit, soul, heart, breast, bosom, inner man;** heart of hearts, inmost heart *or* soul, secret *or* innermost recesses of the heart, heart's core, bottom of the heart, cockles of the heart; vitals, quick.

VERBS 5. **inhere,** indwell, **belong to;** run in the blood, run in the family, be born so, be built that way [slang].

ADJS. 6. **intrinsic, internal,** inner, inward; **inherent,** resident, implicit, immanent, indwelling; **inalienable; ingrained,** in the grain; infixed, implanted, inwrought, deep-seated; **subjective,** nonobjective.

7. **innate,** ingenerate, indigenous; **native, natural,** natural to, connatural; **constitutional,** temperamental, organic; born (as, a *born* athlete); **inborn, inbred,** bred in the bone, in the blood, running in the blood, born with one, "to the manner born" [Shakespeare]; congenital, genetous, genetic; connate, connatal, coeval with birth; **hereditary,** inherited; **instinctive,** instinctual.

8. **essential, fundamental; primary,** primitive, elementary, elemental, original, radical; **basic,** basal, underlying; substantive, substantial, material; virtual, practical, moral.

ADVS. 9. **intrinsically, inherently,** innately; internally, **inwardly;** originally; **naturally,** by birth, by nature.

10. **essentially, fundamentally, primarily, basically; at bottom,** *au fond* [F.], at heart; in essence, in effect, in substance, in the main; substantially, materially; practically, virtually, morally; per se, of *or* in itself.

6. EXTRINSICALITY

NOUNS 1. **extrinsicality,** externality, **outwardness; extraneousness,** foreignness; **objectivity,** nonsubjectivity, impersonality.

2. **nonessential,** unessential; **accessory,** extra, collateral; **appendage,** appurtenance, auxiliary, supplement, adjunct; secondary, subsidiary; **contingency,** contingent, incidental; accident, accidental.

ADJS. 3. **extrinsic, external, outward,** outside, outlying; **extraneous,** foreign; **objective,** nonsubjective, impersonal.

4. **unessential,** nonessential; **accessory, extra,** collateral, auxiliary; adventitious, ad-scititious, ascititious, additional, supplementary, supervenient; secondary, subsidiary; **incidental,** circumstantial, contingent; accidental, fortuitous, casual.

7. STATE

NOUNS 1. **state,** estate, **status, situation, position,** posture, place, station, standing, footing; **condition, circumstance,** circumstances; **case, lot; predicament, plight,** pass.

2. **the state of affairs,** the nature of things, the shape of things, the way it shapes up [coll.], how things stack up [slang], **how things stand,** the way of things, the way it is, **the way things are,** the way things go, how it goes, how she goes [slang], **how it is,** the how of it, the size of it [coll.]; how the land lies, the lay of the land [coll.].

3. **fettle, condition, commission** [coll.], **kilter** *or* kelter [dial. & coll.], **order,** repair, **fix** [slang], **whack** [slang], **shape** [coll.], trim, fig [coll.], form, way [coll.]; working order, adjustment, gear.

4. **mode, manner, way,** fashion, style, form, shape, guise, complexion, tenor, tone, turn.

5. (as in the capacity of a doctor, in quality of a friend) **capacity, character, role,** part, cue, quality, relation, status, rank, position, condition.

VERBS 6. **fare, do, go,** sagaciate [slang, U.S.], **get on** *or* **along,** come on *or* along [coll.]; **manage** [coll.], **contrive, make out** [coll.], come through, get by; **turn out,** come out, stack up [slang], shape up [coll.]; find oneself.

ADJS. 7. **conditional,** modal, formal; provisional 8.6.

8. CIRCUMSTANCE

NOUNS 1. **circumstance, occurrence, occasion, event, incident;** juncture, conjuncture, contingency, eventuality; **condition** 7.

2. **particular, instance, item, detail,** point, count, case, fact, matter, article, thing; respect, regard; **full particulars,** ins and outs; minutia, minutiae; incidentals, minor details.

3. circumstantiality, particularity, specialty.

4. circumstantiation, itemization, particularization, specification.

VERBS 5. **circumstantiate, itemize,** specialize, specify, particularize, **detail,** go or enter into detail, descend to particulars, give full particulars, spell out [coll.]; instance, cite, document, quote chapter and verse; **substantiate** 504.12.

ADJS. 6. **circumstantial,** conditional, provisional; **incidental,** occasional, contingent, adventitious, accidental, casual, nonessential.

7. **detailed,** detaily [coll.], **minute, full,** particular, fussy, nice, precise, exact, specific, special.

ADVS. 8. **thus, thusly** [coll.], in such wise, thuswise, this way, this-a-way [dial.], thus and thus, thus and so, **so,** so fashion [dial., U.S.], like this, like that, just like that; similarly 20.18.

9. **accordingly, in that case, in that event, at that rate,** that being the case, such being the case, that being so, **by the same token,** by the same sign, **under the circumstances,** according to circumstances, the condition being such, as it is, as matters stand, as the matter stands, **as the case may be,** as it may be, as it may happen or turn out, as things go, as times go, as the wind blows; **therefore** 154.6; **consequently** 153.9.

10. **circumstantially,** conditionally, provisionally; provided 506.11, 12.

11. **fully, in full, in detail,** minutely, particularly, in particular; at large, **at length,** in extenso [L.]; chapter and verse.

9. RELATION

NOUNS 1. **relation, relationship, kinship; affinity,** rapport; **connection,** tie-in [coll.], association, alliance, affiliation; cognation, agnation; **propinquity,** proximity, approximation, nearness; homology; blood relationship 11; marital affinity 12; correlation 13.

2. **relevance, pertinence; appositeness,** apposition; application, applicability; **connection,** reference, **bearing,** concern, concernment, interest, respect, regard; relativity.

VERBS 3. **relate to,** refer to, **apply to, bear on** or **upon,** respect, regard, concern, involve, touch, affect, interest; **pertain to,** appertain to, belong to, answer to, correspond to; **have to do with,** have business with, deal with, treat of, touch upon; connect, tie in with [coll.].

4. **relate, associate, connect,** ally, link, tie, couple, bracket, identify with; bring into relation with, bring to bear upon, apply; parallel, parallelize, draw a parallel; correlate 13.4.

ADJS. 5. **relative,** relational; connective, associative; **relating to,** pertaining to, referring to; **relative to,** referable or referrible to, pertinent or appurtenant to; in relation with, in common with; **comparative,** comparable; proportional, proportionate, proportionable; correlative 13.9.

6. **related, kindred, akin,** affinitive; **connected,** implicated, **affiliated, associated, allied,** in touch with; associate, affiliate; connate, cognate, agnate, connatural, congenerous, equiparant; **of that ilk** [coll.], of that kind or sort, in the same category; correlated 13.9; homologous; conjugate, paronymous; collateral; consanguineous 11.7.

7. **approximate,** approximating, approximative; **near,** close, something like; **comparable,** much at one, much of a muchness [coll.]; **similar** 20.10.

8. **relevant, pertinent,** appurtenant, germane, **apposite,** admissible, applicable, applying to, pertaining to, belonging to, bearing upon, **apropos** or à propos [F.], to the purpose, **to the point,** in point, ad rem [L.].

ADVS. 9. **relatively,** comparatively, proportionately, not absolutely; **relevantly,** pertinently, appositely.

PREPS. etc. 10. **with relation to,** with reference to, with regard to, with respect to, in respect to or of, relative to, in relation to, **in connection with,** à propos [F.] or apropos of, speaking of; **as to,** as for, as respects, as regards; **in the matter of,** on the subject of, in point of, on the part of, on the score of; re, in re [L.]; in that respect, in that regard.

11. **concerning, touching, respecting, regarding;** concerning which, in regard to which, in which, on which; whereon, whereupon, wherein, whereof, whereto, whereunto; thereon, thereupon, thereof, therein, thereto, thereunto, thereover, thereby; hereon, hereupon, hereof, hereinto, hereunto; quoad hoc [L., concerning this].

12. **about,** anent, of, on, upon, over, after.

10. IRRELATION

NOUNS 1. **irrelation**, unrelatedness; **irrelevance**, impertinence, inappositeness, inapplicability; inconnection, inconsequence, independence; disconnection, dissociation, disassociation.

2. misrelation, **misapplication**, misapplicability, misreference; misalliance, *mésalliance* [F.].

VERBS 3. **not concern**, have no concern with, have no relation to, **have no connection with**, **have no bearing upon**, have no business with *or* there, have nothing to do with.

4. **foist in, drag in, lug in**, work in, worm in, smuggle in, run in, drag *or* lug in by the head and shoulders.

ADJS. 5. **unrelated**, irrelative, no relation; **unconnected**, unallied, unassociated, unaffiliated; disrelated, disconnected, dissociated, detached, removed, separated, separate, segregate, apart, independent; isolated, insular; **foreign**, alien, strange, exotic, outlandish, extraneous.

6. **irrelevant**, irrelative; **impertinent, inapposite**, inconsequent, inapplicable, inappropriate, inadmissible; **without connection**, adrift, away from the point, *nihil ad rem* [L., nothing to the point], **beside the point**, beside the mark, **beside the question**, off the subject, not to the purpose, out of the way, traveling out of the record; bye, by; **unessential**, nonessential; incidental, parenthetical.

7. **farfetched, remote**, distant, out-of-the-way, forced, neither here nor there, quite another thing, something else again.

ADVS. 8. **irrelevantly**, irrelatively, impertinently, inappositely; without connection, without reference *or* regard to.

11. BLOOD RELATIONSHIP

NOUNS 1. **blood relationship**, blood, ties of blood, consanguinity, **kinship**, kindred, **relation, relationship**, sibship; propinquity; cognation; agnation; filiation, affiliation; alliance, connection, **family connection** *or* tie; brotherhood, brothership, fraternity; sisterhood, sistership; cousinhood, cousinship.

2. **kinsmen, kinsfolk**, kinfolk [dial.], kinfolks [dial.], kinspeople [U.S.], **kindred**, kinnery [slang], **kin**, kith and kin, kith and kind [dial.], sib, **relatives, relations, people**, folks [coll.], connections, belongings [coll.]; **blood relation** *or* **relative**, flesh,

blood, one's own flesh and blood, consanguinean; cognate; agnate; sib, sibling; german, germane; near relation, distant relation; next of kin; collateral relative, collateral; distaff *or* spindle side, distaff *or* spindle kin; spear side, spear kin.

3. (relatives) **brother**, bub [coll., U.S.], bud [dial. and coll.], buddy [coll., U.S.], br'er [dial., South. U.S.], frater; **sister**, sis [coll.], sissy [coll.]; brethren, sistern [dial.]; kid brother *or* sister; blood brother *or* sister, brother-german, sister-german; half brother *or* sister, foster brother *or* sister, stepbrother, stepsister; **aunt**, auntie, aunty; **uncle**, unc *or* uncs [slang], nunks *or* nunky [slang], nuncle [dial.]; **nephew, niece; cousin**, cousin-german, first ~, second cousin, etc., cousin once (twice etc.) removed, country cousin; great-uncle, granduncle; great-aunt, grandaunt; grandnephew, grandniece; **father, mother** 169.8–12; **son, daughter** 170.3.

4. **race, people, folk, family, house, clan, tribe, nation; lineage**, line, strain, stock, stem, stirps, **breed**, brood, kind; biological species, physiological race; **ethnic group**, ethnicon; **culture**, *Kultur* [G.]; nationality, gentility; races, peoples 417.

5. **tribesman**, clansman.

6. **family**, brood, **house, household**, ménage, people, folks [coll.], homefolks [coll.], belongings [coll.].

ADJS. 7. **related, kindred, akin**; consanguineous, consanguine, consanguinean, of the blood; cognate; agnate; sib, sibling; allied, affiliated; german, germane; collateral; foster; avuncular; intimately *or* closely related, remotely *or* distantly related.

8. **racial, tribal, national, family**, clannish, **lineal; ethnic**; phyletic, phylogenetic; gentile, gentilic.

12. AFFINITY

Relationship by Marriage.—NOUNS 1. **affinity**, marital affinity; connection, family connection, marriage connection.

2. **in-laws** [coll.], **relatives-in-law**, wrecking crew [joc.]; brother-in-law, sister-in-law, father-in-law.

3. **mother-in-law**; lawma, ersatz mother, back-seat driver [wit and slang].

ADJS. 4. **affinal**, affined.

13. CORRELATION

Reciprocal or Mutual Relation.—NOUNS 1. **correlation**, corelation; correlativity, correlativism; **reciprocation**, reciprocity, reciprocality; mutuality, commutuality; **correspondence,** equivalence, equipollence, coequality.

2. interrelation, interrelationship; **interconnection,** interassociation, interaffiliation, interdependence.

3. interaction, interworking, **interplay;** interlocking, interdigitation; meshing, intermeshing, mesh, engagement (as of gears).

4. correlate, correlative; **correspondent,** analogue; reciprocator, reciprocatist; each other, one another.

VERBS **5. correlate,** corelate.

6. interrelate, interconnect, interassociate, interlink, intertie, interjoin, interdepend.

7. interact, interwork, **interplay;** mesh, intermesh, engage (as gears), gear; interdigitate, interlock, dovetail.

8. reciprocate, correspond, answer, complement, coequal.

ADJS. **9. correlative,** corelative, correlational; **correlated,** corelated.

10. interrelated, interconnected, interassociated, interallied, interaffiliated, interlinked, intertied, interdependent.

11. interacting, interactive, interworking, interplaying; in gear, in mesh.

12. reciprocal, reciprocative; **corresponding,** correspondent, answering, analogous, homologous, equipollent, equiparant, equivalent, coequal; **complementary,** complemental.

13. mutual, commutual, **common, joint,** conjoint; respective.

ADVS. **14. reciprocally,** back and forth, to and fro.

15. mutually, commonly, jointly; respectively, each to each.

14. IDENTITY

NOUNS **1. identity,** identicalness; **sameness,** selfsameness; no difference, not a bit of difference; **coincidence,** correspondence, agreement; **equivalence,** equality 30; **synonymousness,** synonymity, synonymy, poecilonymy; **oneness, unity,** individuality; selfness, selfhood, self-identity; homoousia.

2. identification, unification, coalescence, combination, union, synthesis.

3. the same, selfsame, very same, one and the same, identical same, no other, very *or* actual thing; **equivalent** 20.5; **synonym,** poecilonym; *idem* [L.], *id.* [L.]; *ipsissima verba* [L., the very words].

VERBS **4. coincide, correspond,** agree, match, tally, ditto [coll.].

5. identify, make one, **unify,** unite, join, combine, coalesce, synthesize.

ADJS. **6. identical,** identic; **same, selfsame, one, one and the same,** all the same, all one, of the same kidney; undifferent, without difference; **alike,** just alike, exactly like, six of one and half a dozen of the other [coll.]; duplicate, twin; homoousian.

7. coinciding, coincident, coincidental; **corresponding,** correspondent; **synonymous,** synonymic(al), poecilonymic; **equivalent,** equal 30.8, 9; indistinguishable, without distinction.

ADVS. **8. identically,** synonymously, alike; coincidentally, correspondently, correspondingly; **equally** 30.12; on the same footing, on all fours with; **likewise,** the same way, just the same, as is, ditto, same here [coll.]; *ibidem* [L.], *ibid.* [L.].

15. CONTRARIETY

NOUNS **1.** contrariety, **oppositeness,** opposition, opposure; **antithesis, contrast,** contraposition, contradiction, contradistinction; antagonism, repugnance, oppugnance, hostility, inimicalness, antipathy, clashing, collision, conflict; polarity.

2. the contrary, contra, counter, **opposite, antithesis, reverse,** inverse, converse, obverse; the other side, the other side of the picture *or* coin; the direct opposite, the other extreme; antipode, antipodes (pl. used as sing.); antipole, counterpole, counterpoint; vis-à-vis; offset, setoff, foil; **antonym,** counterterm.

VERBS **3. go contrary to, run counter to,** counter, **contradict,** contravene, fly in the face of, be *or* play at cross-purposes; **oppose,** be opposed to, go *or* run in opposition to; **conflict with,** come in conflict with, conflict, clash; contrast with, antithesize; **offset,** set off; **counteract,** counterwork.

4. reverse, transpose 219.5.

ADJS. **5. contrary, opposite,** antithetic(al), **contradictory,** counter, contrapositive, contrasted, vis-à-vis; **converse, reverse,** obverse, inverse, adverse; **opposing, opposed,** oppositional; anti [coll.], dead against; **antagonistic,** repugnant, oppugnant, hostile, inimical, antipathetic(al), discordant, conflicting, clashing, at cross-purposes; contradistinct; antonymous.

6. **diametrically opposite,** diametric-(al), antipodal; as opposite as black and white, ~ as light and darkness, ~ as day and night, ~ as fire and water, ~ as the poles, etc., "Hyperion to a satyr" [Shakespeare].

ADVS. 7. **contrarily,** contra, **contrariwise, conversely,** inversely, in reverse English [coll., U.S.], **vice versa, on the other hand,** *per contra* [L.], **on** or **to the contrary,** *tout au contraire* [F.], rather, nay rather, quite the contrary, otherwise 16.11, just the other way, just the other way around, **oppositely,** just the opposite or reverse, no such thing; by contraries, by way of opposition; against the grain, *à rebours* [F.].

16. DIFFERENCE

NOUNS 1. **difference,** diff [slang], otherness, separateness, distinctness, **distinction; dissimilarity** 21; **variation,** variance, variety, heterogeneity, diversity; **deviation,** divergence, departure; **disparity,** inequality 31; odds; **discrepancy,** inconsistency, inconsonance, incongruity, discontinuity, unconformity, incompatibility, irreconcilability; **disagreement,** disaccord, disaccordance, inaccordance, discordance, dissonance, inharmoniousness, inharmony; **contrariety** 15; vast difference, a far cry, a whale of a difference [slang].

2. **nicety, subtlety,** refinement, delicacy, nice ~, fine ~, delicate or **subtle distinction,** fine point; shade of difference, **nuance,** hairline; differentia, differential.

3. **different thing,** different story [coll.], **something else,** something else again [coll.], *tertium quid* [L., a third something]; apple off another tree, another pair of shoes, another order of cat [slang], horse of a different color, bird of another feather; **nothing of the kind,** no such thing, no such a thing [dial. or coll.], **quite another thing; other, another;** this, that, or the other.

4. **differentiation, discrimination,** distinguishment, **distinction,** demarcation; **separation,** division, segregation, severance, severalization; modification, variation, diversification; specialization, particularization, individualization; disequalization, desynonymization, despecification.

VERBS 5. **differ, vary,** mismatch, stand apart, be distinguished from; **deviate from,** diverge from, divaricate from, depart from; **disagree with,** disaccord with, conflict with, clash with, jar with; bear no resemblance 21.2.

6. **differentiate,** difference; **distinguish, make a distinction,** mark, **discriminate; separate,** sever, severalize, segregate, divide; set off, set apart; modify, vary, diversify; specialize, particularize, individualize; disequalize, desynonymize, despecificate; split hairs, make a nice or subtle distinction.

ADJS. 7. **different,** differing; **dissimilar** 21.4; **distinct,** distinguished, **separate,** widely apart; **various,** variant, varying, varied, heterogeneous; **several,** many; **diverse,** divers; diversified 19.4; **divergent,** deviative, diverging, deviating, departing; **disparate,** unequal 31.4; **discrepant,** inconsistent, inconsonant, incongruous, incongruent, unconformable, incompatible, irreconcilable; **disagreeing,** in disagreement; at variance, at odds; inaccordant, disaccordant, discordant, dissonant, inharmonious; **contrary** 15.5.

8. **other, another,** else, otherwise, other than or from; not the same, not the type [coll.], not that sort, of another sort; of a sort, of sorts [both coll.].

9. **differentiative,** differential; **distinguishing,** discriminating, discriminative, separative; diagnostic, diacritical; **distinctive,** characteristic, peculiar.

ADVS. 10. **differently,** diversely, variously; in a different manner, in another way, with a difference.

11. **otherwise,** otherways [dial.], in other ways, **in other respects;** elsewise, elseways, elsehow [dial.]; else, or else; than, then [dial.], other than; **on the other hand; contrarily** 15.7; alias.

PHRS. 12. **what's the difference?,** what's the diff? [slang], **what's the odds?, so what?,** who cares?; it makes me no difference [slang], it's all one to me, it's one by me [slang].

17. UNIFORMITY

NOUNS 1. **uniformity,** evenness, equability; **steadiness,** steadfastness, persistence, continuity; **consistency,** consonance, correspondence, accordance, unity, homogeneity.

2. **regularity, constancy,** even tenor; sameness, **sameliness,** samesomeness, [dial.]; **monotony,** monotonousness, the same old thing; unvariation, undeviation, invariability; clockwork precision.

VERBS 3. persist, prevail, run through; run true to form or type.

4. uniform, uniformize; regulate, regularize; even, equalize, symmetrize, harmonize, balance; level, smooth, flatten; homogenize.

ADJS. 5. uniform, equable, equal, even; level, flat, smooth; regular, constant, steady, steadfast, persistent, continuous; unvaried, unbroken, undiversified, unchanged; invariable, unchangeable; unvarying, undeviating, unchanging; ordered, balanced, measured, stated; orderly, methodic(al), systematic(al); consistent, consonant, correspondent, accordant, homogeneous, alike, of a piece.

6. samely, samesome [dial.]; monotonous, humdrum, dingdong, singsong, jog trot [coll.].

ADVS. 7. uniformly, equably, evenly; samely, monotonously; in a rut or groove.

8. regularly, regular [chiefly dial.]; constantly, steadily, continually, right along [coll., U.S.]; invariably, without exception, at every turn, never otherwise; always 112.11; like clockwork, with clockwork precision.

18. UNUNIFORMITY

NOUNS 1. ununiformity, unevenness, irregularity, inconstancy, inequality, variability; variation, deviation, divergence, divarication.

ADJS. 2. ununiform, uneven, irregular, inconstant, unsteady; unequal, unequable; variable, changeable; varying, changing; deviative, deviatory, divergent; erose.

ADVS. 3. ununiformly, unequally, unevenly, irregularly, inconstantly, unsteadily; in all manner or ways, every which way or everwhichway [coll., U.S.], all over the shop; here, there, and everywhere.

19. MULTIFORMITY

NOUNS 1. multiformity, multifariousness, variety, diversity, diversification, variation, variegation, heterogeneity; omniformity, omnifariousness, polymorphism, heteromorphism; allotropy, allotropism [chem.].

VERBS 2. diversify, vary, variate, variegate, motley.

ADJS. 3. multiform, diversiform, "of every shape that was not uniform" (Lowell); manifold, multifold, multiplex, multifarious, multiphase, many-sided; polymorphous, polymorphic; heteromorphous, heteromorphic; metamorphic, meta-

morphotic; protean, proteiform; allotropic(al) [chem.].

4. diversified, varied, assorted, sorty [coll.], of sorts [coll.], heterogeneous; variegated, motley, checked, checkered, spotted, spotty, mosaic, daedal; various, divers, diverse, sundry, several, many; all sorts of, toutes sortes de [F.], all kinds of, all manner of, of every description, of every color and description; eclectic.

5. omniform, omnifarious, omnigenous.

ADVS. 6. variously, severally, sundrily.

20. SIMILARITY

NOUNS 1. similarity, likeness, alikeness, sameness, similitude; resemblance, semblance; analogy, correspondence, accordance, agreement, comparability, comparison, parallelism, parity, community, alliance, consimilarity; approximation, approach, closeness, nearness; homogeneity; homoiousia; identicalness 14.

2. connaturalness, connature, connateness, congeneracy; congeniality, affinity; family likeness, family favor.

3. assonance, alliteration, rhyme or rime; jingle, clink; pun, paronomasia.

4. a similar, the like, the like or likes of [coll.]; suchlike, such; analogue, analogon; parallel, parallelism; ally, associate; cognate, congener.

5. counterpart, complement, correspondent, pendant, like, similitude, tally, coordinate, reciprocal, obverse, equivalent, equal; correlate, correlative; duplicate, double, dub [slang, U.S.]; match, fellow, mate, companion, twin, brother, sister; second self, alter ego [L.]; couple, pair, team; two of a kind, birds of a feather; chip of or off the old block, second edition.

6. close resemblance, striking resemblance, startling resemblance, marked resemblance, decided resemblance; perfect likeness, lifelikeness, speaking likeness; image, very image, portrait, photograph, picture, very picture, living picture [coll.], dead rap [slang], fetch [dial.], dead or very fetch [dial.], moral [slang], ringer or dead ringer [slang]; spitting image, ~ picture or likeness, spit and image, spit, dead spit [all dial. & slang].

VERBS 7. resemble, be like, bear resemblance; put one in mind of [chiefly coll.], remind one of, bring to mind; look like, favor [coll.], feature [dial.]; take after, partake of, follow, appear like, seem like, sound like; savor or smack of, be redolent of; **have all the earmarks of,** have every appearance of, have all the features of, have all the signs of, have every sign *or* indication of; **approximate,** approach, near, come near, come close; **compare with,** stack up with [slang]; **correspond,** match, span [U.S.], **parallel;** not tell apart, not tell one from the other, not tell which from tother *or* tother from which [coll.].

8. similarize, assimilate, approximate, bring near; connaturalize.

9. assonate, alliterate, rhyme *or* rime, pun.

ADJS. **10. similar, like, alike,** something like, not unlike; **resembling,** following, favoring [coll.], savoring *or* smacking of, **on the order of;** consimilar; homogeneous; homoiousian; identical 14.6.

11. **analogous,** comparable; **corresponding,** correspondent; **parallel,** paralleling; **matching,** of a kind, of a size, of a piece; **duplicate, twin.**

12. **such as,** suchlike *or* such like, so; -like (as, crazy-*like* [dial.]).

13. connatural, connate, cognate, agnate, conspecific, correlative; congenerous, congeneric(al); congenial, affinitive; **akin, allied, connected;** brothers *or* sisters under the skin, tarred with the same brush [coll.].

14. **approximating,** approximative, approximate; **near, close;** much the same, much at one, much of a muchness [coll.], nearly the same, same but different [joc.], "like—but oh! how different" [Wordsworth]; *quasi* [L.], near- (as, *near*-silk [coll.]).

15. **very like, mighty like,** powerful like [dial.], uncommonly like, remarkably like, extraordinarily like, strikingly like, **ridiculously like, for all the world like,** as like as it can stare, **the very picture** *or* **image of;** a lot alike, pretty much the same, damned little difference [coll.]; as like as two peas, "as lyke as one pease is to another" [Lyly], "as like as eggs" [Shakespeare], *comme deux gouttes d'eau* [F., like two drops of water]; of a type, the same type, cast in the same mold; just like one, one all over [slang].

16. **lifelike,** speaking, faithful, living, to the life, **true to life** *or* nature; **realistic, natural.**

17. assonant, assonantal, alliterative, allilteral; rhyming *or* riming.

ADVS. *etc.* **18. similarly,** correspondingly, **like, likewise;** as, like as; in the manner of,

à la [F.]; **in like manner,** in kind; in that way, like that, like this; **thus** 8.8; so, so fashion [dial., U.S.], thus and so; by the same token, by the same sign; identically 14.8.

19. as if, *quasi* [L.], just as, just as if, like [coll.], like if [dial.]; **so to speak,** in a manner of speaking [coll.]; **as though,** though, **as it were,** as if *or* though it were; in a manner, in a way; kind of, sort of [both coll.].

21. DISSIMILARITY

NOUNS **1. dissimilarity,** unsimilarity; **dissimilitude,** dissemblance, **unresemblance; unlikeness,** unsameness; **difference** 16; incomparability, incommensurability; dissimilation.

VERBS **2. bear no resemblance,** not look like, **not compare with; differ** 16.5; tell apart, tell one from the other, tell which from tother *or* tother from which [coll.].

3. dissimilate; vary 139.6.

ADJS. **4. dissimilar,** unsimilar, unresembling; **unlike, unalike,** unsame, unidentical; **different** 16.7; scarcely like, hardly like, hardly what you'd call; a bit different, a mite different, a wee different; out of line with, a bit on the off side; unmatched, odd, out (as, *out* sizes).

5. **nothing like,** not a bit alike, not a bit of it, **nothing of the sort,** nothing of the kind, quite another thing, not the same thing at all, not so you could tell it, not that you would know it; **far from it,** far other [coll.]; way off, away off, a mile off; no such thing, no such a thing [coll.]; as like a dock as a daisy, "very like a whale" [Shakespeare], "no more like than an apple to an oyster" [Sir Thomas More]; as different as chalk from cheese, as different as Macedon and Monmouth.

6. **not to be compared with,** not comparable to; incomparable, incommensurable.

22. IMITATION

An Imitating. — NOUNS **1. imitation, copying,** repetition; **emulation,** following; simulation 614.3; copy 24.

2. **mimicry,** mockery, apery, parrotry; protective coloration *or* mimicry, aggressive mimicry, aposematic mimicry, cryptic mimicry.

3. **reproduction,** duplication, reduplication; **transcription;** tracing; mimeography.

4. imitator, mimic, mimicker, mimer, **mocker**; mockingbird, cuckoo; **parrot**, polly, poll-parrot *or* polly-parrot [coll.]; **ape**, monkey; echo, echoer, echoist; **copier**, copyist, **copycat** [coll.]; counterfeiter.

VERBS **5. imitate, copy, repeat**, ditto [coll.]; do like, do a [slang, U.S.], act like, go like; **mirror, reflect**, glass; **echo**, re-echo, chorus; **borrow**, steal one's stuff [slang, U.S.], take a leaf out of one's book; **simulate** 614.22.

6. mimic, mime, mock; ape, parrot, copycat [coll.]; take off, hit off, pipe off [slang], **hit** *or* **take off on**.

7. emulate, follow, follow in the steps *or* footsteps of, walk in the shoes of, put yourself in another's shoes, follow in the wake of, follow the example of, follow suit [coll.]; **copy after**, model after, pattern after, take after, take a leaf out of one's book.

8. (make a copy) **copy, reproduce; duplicate**, dupe [printers' slang], reduplicate; **double, dub** [slang, U.S.]; **transcribe**; trace; triplicate, quadruplicate; manifold, multigraph, mimeograph, photostat; facsimile, squeeze [cant].

ADJS. **9. imitation, mock, sham** 614.27; **pseudo**, quasi, near- (as, *near*-silk [coll., U.S.], ape- (as, *ape*-ware [slang, U.S.]), trick (as, *trick* decorations [slang]); borrowed, secondhand.

10. imitative, simulative; mimic, mimetic, **apish**; emulative.

11. imitable, copiable.

PREPS. **12. in imitation of**, after; in duplicate, in triplicate.

23. ORIGINALITY

Nonimitation.—NOUNS **1. originality, novelty**, freshness, uniqueness; **authenticity** 515.5.

2. original, sulphite [slang]; prototype 25.

ADJS. **3. original**, sulphitic *or* sulphidic [slang]; **novel**, fresh, unique; underived, firsthand; authentic 515.13.

4. unimitated, uncopied, **unduplicated, unreproduced**, unprecedented, unexampled.

24. COPY

NOUNS **1. copy, representation, image, likeness, resemblance**, semblance, similitude, simulacrum; ectype; *pasticcio* [It.]; fair copy, faithful copy; certified copy.

2. imitation, counterfeit 614.13; take-off [coll.], hit-off [slang]; **parody** 965.6; near-silk, near-leather, near-antique [all coll., U.S.]; ape-ware [slang, U.S.].

3. duplicate, duplication, dupe [printers' slang], ditto [coll.]; **double, dub** [slang, U.S.]; **reproduction, replica**, model [dial.], **counterpart**, tally; chip of *or* off the old block; triplicate, quadruplicate.

4. transcript, transcription, apograph, tenor [law]; **transfer**, tracing, counterscript; **carbon copy**, carbon; manifold; microcopy; recording, electrical transcription.

5. print, offprint; **impression**, impress; **reprint**, second edition; photostatic copy, photostat, stat [slang].

6. cast, casting; mold, **molding**; facsimile, squeeze [cant].

7. reflection, reflex; **shadow**, adumbration; echo.

ADJS. **8. faithful**, close, exact, strict, conscientious, servile.

25. MODEL

Thing Copied. — NOUNS **1. model, pattern, standard, criterion**, rule, original, mirror, paradigm; **prototype**, archetype, antitype; **precedent**, lead; representative, epitome; fugler, fugleman *or* flugleman; imitatee.

2. example, exemplar; representative, type, symbol, emblem; **exponent; exemplification**, illustration, demonstration, explanation; instance, relevant instance, case, case in point; object lesson.

3. sample, specimen, piece; taste, taster; swatch.

4. ideal, beau ideal; apotheosis; **shining example**, "the observed of all observers" [Shakespeare].

5. artist's model, dressmaker's model; dummy, lay figure; clay model; mock-up.

6. mold, form, cast, template, matrix, negative; die, punch, stamp, intaglio, seal, mint; last, shoe last.

VERBS **7. set an example**, set the pace, lead the way.

ADJS. **8. model, exemplary**, precedential, typical, paradigmatic; ideal.

9. prototypal, protypical, archetypal, primordial.

26. AGREEMENT

NOUNS **1. agreement, accord, accordance; concord**, concordance; **harmony**, *rapport* [F.], concert, consonance, assonance, concinnity; **unison**, union, oneness; **correspondence**, coincidence, parallelism, tally; congeniality, compatibility, affinity; **conformity,** conformance, conformation; **line, keeping;** congruity, congruence *or* congruency; **consistency,** self-consistency, coherence, compatibility; synchronization, sync [motion-picture slang], synchronism; assent 520.8.

2. understanding, entente; mutual *or* cordial understanding, *entente cordiale* [F.]; compact 769.

3. (general agreement) **consensus,** consentaneity, *consensus omnium* [L.], **unanimity; like-mindedness,** meeting of minds; unanimity 520.5.

4. adjustment, adaptation, coaptation, **regulation,** attunement, harmonization, coordination, accommodation, assimilation; reconciliation, reconcilement; readjustment, readaptation.

5. fitness, suitability, appropriateness, propriety, admissibility; **aptness,** aptitude, felicity, appositeness, apposition, applicability.

6. the thing, just the thing, the very thing, quite the thing; the article [slang, U.S.], the idea [coll.], the ticket [coll.], the card [slang & coll.].

VERBS **7. agree, accord, harmonize,** chime, fall *or* chime in with; **correspond,** coincide, match, tally, check, respond, **answer to;** gee [slang & dial.], jibe [coll., U.S.], hitch [coll.]; hit it off with, cotton, hitch horses [all coll.]; assent 520.8; come to an agreement 520.10.

8. suit, fit, benefit, become; serve, do, answer, answer the purpose; satisfy, please, be agreeable to, be O.K. [slang]; suit one's book, suit down to the ground [coll.], be just the thing, hit the spot [slang], be right down one's alley [slang].

9. go together, go with, conform with, adapt to, square *or* quadrate with, sort with, assort with, consort with, comport with; fit together, dovetail; fit like a glove, fit to a T *or* tittle.

10. be consistent, consist with, cohere, stand together; hang *or* hold together, **hold up, hold water,** wash, hold up in the wash [all coll.].

11. (make agree) **harmonize, accord,** agree, coordinate; similarize, assimilate; homologize; homologate; **synchronize,** sync [motion-picture slang].

12. fit, suit, accommodate, reconcile, **adapt;** tailor; dovetail, fadge, square.

13. adjust, set, regulate, fix, rectify, true, right, set right; tune, attune, put in

tune; measure, proportion; adjust to, gear to, key to; readjust, reset, readapt.

ADJS. **14. agreeing, in agreement; in accord,** in step; in rapport, *en rapport* [F.]; **in harmony with,** in accordance with, in unison with; **harmonious, accordant, concordant;** agreeable, congenial, compatible; **corresponding,** correspondent, coincident, conformable, answerable, reconcilable; commensurate, proportionate; **congruous,** congruent.

15. consistent, self-consistent, logically consistent, consonant, consequent, compatible, coherent, **of a piece.**

16. at one, at one with, **on all fours with,** of one mind, of the same mind, **like-minded;** consentient, consentaneous; **unanimous** 520.15.

17. synchronous, synchronized, in synchronization, in sync [motion-picture slang].

18. apt, apposite, applicable; **pat,** happy, neat, felicitous; in point, **to the point,** to the purpose, *ad rem* [L.], *à propos* [F.] *or* **apropos.**

19. fit, fitted, **suited,** adapted, geared to; **appropriate, suitable,** likely, sortable, seasonable, opportune; **fitting,** befitting, suiting, **becoming.**

PREPS. **20. in agreement, with,** right with, in there with, right along there with; **in line with,** in keeping with; together, together on.

27. DISAGREEMENT

NOUNS **1. disagreement, discord,** discordance *or* discordancy; **disaccord,** disaccordance, inaccordance; disunity, disunion; **disharmony,** unharmoniousness; dissonance, dissidence; jarring, clashing; **difference, variance,** divergence, diversity; **disparity,** discrepancy, inequality; antagonism, repugnance; dissent 520a; dissension 793.

2. inconsistency, incongruity, inconsonance, incoherence; **incompatibility,** irreconcilability, incommensurability; disproportion, disproportionateness; self-contradiction, paradox.

3. unfitness, inappropriateness, unsuitability, impropriety; **inaptness,** inaptitude, **inappositeness,** infelicity, uncongeniality, inconcinnity, inapplicability, inadmissibility; misjoining, misjoinder; **mismatch,** mismatchment; misalliance, *mésalliance* [F.].

4. misfit, ass in lion's skin, jackdaw in

peacock's feathers, fish out of water, square peg in a round hole.

VERBS 5. disagree, **differ,** vary, be *or* run at cross-purposes, **disaccord, conflict,** clash, jar, jostle, collide, swear at [slang]; come amiss; mismatch, mismate; dissent 520a.4; differ in opinion 793.9.

ADJS. 6. disagreeing, **differing; discordant,** disaccordant; dissonant, dissident; **inharmonious,** unharmonious, disharmonious; discrepant, disproportionate; divergent, variant; at variance, **at odds,** at war; antagonistic, repugnant; inaccordant, out of accord, out of whack [slang]; clashing, clashy [coll.], jarring.

7. **inapt,** unapt, inept; **inappropriate,** malapropos, *mal à propos* [F.]; **unfit,** unfitting, unbefitting; **unsuitable,** improper, **unbecoming,** unseemly; **inapposite,** infelicitous, inapplicable, inadmissible; **unseasonable,** ill-timed, untimely; **out of place,** out of keeping, out of character, out of proportion, out of joint, out of tune, out of time, out of season, out of its element.

8. **unsuited,** ill-suited; **unfitted,** ill-fitted; unadapted, **ill-adapted; ill-sorted,** ill-assorted; **ill-matched,** ill-mated; **mismatched,** mismated, misjoined, misplaced; uncongenial.

9. **inconsistent, incongruous, inconsonant,** inconsequent, incoherent, **incompatible,** irreconcilable; incommensurable, incommensurate; disproportionate, out of proportion; self-contradictory, paradoxical.

PREPS. 10. **in disagreement with,** in defiance of, in contempt of, in opposition to; **at odds,** at variance, **at loggerheads, at sixes and sevens;** out of line with, not in keeping with.

28. QUANTITY

NOUNS 1. **quantity, amount,** quantum, feck [Scot. & dial.], mass, **bulk,** substance, matter, magnitude, amplitude, **extent, sum; measure,** measurement; strength, force, numbers.

2. **a quantity, amount, sum, number, measure, portion,** lot, deal; batch, bunch, heap [coll.], pack, mess, grist [coll., U.S.], gob [dial. & slang], boiling [slang], jag [dial., U.S.], swad [slang, U.S.], budget, chance [dial., U.S.]; dose; lump sum.

3. **some,** somewhat, something; **aught,** ought; **any,** anything.

VERBS 4. **quantify,** rate, fix; modify, qualify; measure 489.11.

ADJS. 5. **quantitative,** quantitive, quantified.

6. **some,** certain, one; a, an; **any,** airy *or* ary [dial.]; more or less, *plus ou moins* [F.].

ADVS. 7. **to the amount of,** to the tune of [coll.]; as much as, all of [coll., U.S.], no less than.

8. quantities

armful	keg(ful)
bag(ful)	kettle(ful)
barrel(ful)	lapful
basin(ful)	mouthful
basket(ful)	mug(ful)
bin(ful)	pail(ful)
bottle(ful)	pitcher(ful)
bowl(ful)	plate(ful)
box(ful)	pocketful
bucket(ful)	pot(ful)
can(ful)	roomful
capful	sack(ful)
carton(ful)	scoop(ful)
case(ful)	shovel(ful)
crate(ful)	spoon(ful)
cup(ful)	tablespoon(ful)
flask(ful)	tank(ful)
glass(ful)	teacup(ful)
handful	teaspoon(ful)
jar(ful)	

29. DEGREE

Relative Quantity.—NOUNS 1. **degree, grade, step,** *pas* [F.]; round, rung, stair; **point,** mark, peg; **notch,** cut, hole [all coll.]; plane, level; **period,** space, interval; **extent, measure,** amount, ratio, proportion, stint *or* stent, standard, height, pitch, reach, remove, compass, range, scale, scope, caliber; **shade,** shadow.

2. **rank, standing, footing, status, station,** stage, position, place, sphere, order, echelon, precedence, condition; rate, rating; class, caste; brevet rank [mil.].

3. **gradation,** graduation, shading.

VERBS 4. **graduate, grade,** shade off.

ADJS. 5. **gradual,** gradational; regular, progressive.

ADVS. 6. **by degrees,** degreewise [mus.]; **gradually,** gradatim; **step by step,** grade by grade, *di grado in grado* [It.], **bit by bit, little by little,** inch by inch, drop by drop; by slow degrees, by inches, by little and little, a little at a time; **inchmeal,** by inchmeal; slowly 269.13.

7. **to a degree, to some extent,** in a way, in a measure, **in some measure; somewhat,** some [coll.], something, something like [coll.]; **kind of** [coll.], sort of [coll.]; **rather,** ratherish [coll.]; **pretty,** quite [coll.], fairly.

8. (to such an extent) inasmuch, insomuch, so, in such wise; for so much, *pro tanto* [L.].

9. (to whatever extent) whatever, whatsoever, to whatever; however, howe'er, howsoever, howsomever [dial.], soever.

30. EQUALITY

NOUNS **1.** equality, parity, par, parallelism; evenness, **level**; **balance**, poise, symmetry; equilibrium, equiponderance, equipoise; owelty [law].

2. equivalence or equivalency, correspondence, equipollence, coequality; **sameness** 14; distinction without a difference, six of one and half a dozen of the other, not a pin to choose.

3. equalization, equation; equilibration, co-ordination, integration, accommodation, adjustment.

4. tie, draw, standoff [coll.], level, even Stephen [slang, U.S.], even break [slang]; dead heat, neck-and-neck race, nose finish [turf slang], photo finish; tied score, knotted score [slang].

5. equal, match, fellow, like, equivalent, equipollent, coequal, parallel, ditto [coll.]; peer, compeer, rival.

VERBS **6.** equal, match, rival, fellow with, correspond, reach, touch; keep pace or step with, run abreast; amount to, come to, run to; measure up to, come up to, check with or up with [coll.], stack up with [slang], match up with; lie on a level with, balance, parallel, come or amount to the same thing, ditto [coll.]; even, even off, break even [slang]; tie, draw, knot the score [slang].

7. equalize, equate; even, square, level; balance, strike a balance, poise; co-ordinate, integrate, proportion; fit, accommodate, adjust; handicap, give points, give cards and spades.

ADJS. **8.** equal, even, level, par, on or upon a par; commensurate, proportionate; even with, level with, on the same level, on the same plane, on the same footing; on terms of equality, on even terms, on even ground; on a par with, on a level with, on a footing with, in the same boat; square, hunky [slang, U.S.], quits, even Stephen [slang, U.S.]; nip and tuck, hank and hank [naut.], horse and horse [slang]; equalized, drawn, tied.

9. equivalent, tantamount, equiparant, equipollent, coequal, co-ordinate; identical 14.6; corresponding, correspondent; convertible, resolvable into; much at one, much the same, as broad as long, neither more nor less; fifty-fifty [slang, U.S.], half-and-half, on or to the halvers [slang]; all one, all the same; tantamount to, as good as, as much as to say.

10. balanced, poised, apoise, on an even keel; equibalanced, equiponderant, equiponderous; symmetric(al).

11. equisized, equidimensional, equiproportional, equispaced; equiangular, isogonic; equilateral, equisided.

ADVS. **12.** equally, correspondingly, proportionately, equivalently, evenly; identically 14.8; without distinction, indifferently; in proportion, *pro rata* [L.]; at the same rate, *pari passu* [L.]; to the same degree, *ad eundem* [L.]; as, so; equally with, as well as; to all intents and purposes, other things being equal.

13. to a standoff [coll.], to a tie or draw.

31. INEQUALITY

NOUNS **1.** inequality, unevenness, disparity, odds; irregularity 18.1; disproportion, asymmetry; unbalance, imbalance, overbalance, inclination of the balance; inadequacy, insufficiency, shortcoming.

VERBS **2.** disequalize, disproportion.

3. unbalance, disbalance, overbalance, throw off balance; turn the scale.

ADJS. **4.** unequal, disparate, uneven; irregular 18.2; disproportionate, out of proportion, asymmetrical; disquiparant; ill-matched, ill-sorted; inadequate, insufficient; odd.

5. ill-balanced, unbalanced, overbalanced, off balance; top-heavy, topsided [dial.], lopsided; unstable, unsteady.

ADVS. **6.** unequally, disproportionately, unevenly.

32. MEAN

NOUNS **1.** mean, middle state, middle ground; golden mean, *juste-milieu* [F.]; medium, happy medium; average, balance, normal, rule, run, generality; middle term [logic], *mezzo termine* [It.].

VERBS **2.** average, split the difference, take the average, strike a balance, pair off; do on an average.

ADJS. **3.** medium, mean, intermediate, intermediary, medial; average, ordinary, normal, standard.

ADVS. **4.** mediumly, intermediately, in the mean.

5. on an average, in the long run; taking one thing with another, taking all things together, taking all in all, taking it for all in all, all things considered; generally 79.15; in round numbers.

33. COMPENSATION

A Making Up For.—NOUNS 1. compensation, recompense, indemnity, indemnification, measure for measure; commutation, substitution; offsetting, balancing, counterbalancing.

2. offset, setoff; counterbalance, counterpoise, equipoise, counterweight, makeweight, casting weight; balance, ballast; equivalent, *quid pro quo* [L., something for something].

3. counterclaim, counterdemand.

VERBS 4. compensate, make compensation, make good, make up for; recompense, indemnify; cover, fill up; give and take, get it coming and going [slang]; rob Peter to pay Paul.

5. offset, set off, counteract, countervail, counterbalance, counterweigh, counterpoise, balance, equiponderate; overbalance, outbalance; hedge; square, square up; lean over backwards.

ADJS. 6. compensating, compensatory; recompensive, amendatory, indemnificatory, reparative; offsetting, counteracting, countervailing, balancing, counterbalancing; in the opposite scale.

ADVS. 7. in compensation, in return, back; in consideration, for a consideration.

ADVS. *etc.* 8. notwithstanding, but, all the same [coll.], still, yet, even; however, howe'er; nevertheless, none the less; although, when, though; howbeit, albeit; at all events, in any event, in any case, at any rate; be that as it may, for all that, even so, on the other hand, rather, again, at the same time, just the same, however that may be; after all, after all is said and done.

9. in spite of, spite of [coll.], despite, in despite of, with, after.

10. regardless of, regardless, irregardless [erron.], irrespective of, without respect *or* regard to; cost what it may, *cueste lo que cueste* [Span.], regardless of cost, at any cost, at all costs.

34. GREATNESS

In Amount or Degree.—NOUNS 1. greatness, magnitude, muchness; amplitude, fullness; grandeur, grandness; immensity, enormity, vastness, tremendousness, stupendousness, prodigiousness; might, intensity; bigness (in size) 194.

2. eminence, loftiness, prominence, distinction, consequence, notability, nobility, sublimity, majesty.

3. (large amount) quantity, quantities, much, abundance, profusion, volume, mass, mountain, load; peck, bushel; bags, barrels, tons; world, worlds, ocean, oceans, sea; flood, spring tide; large number 101.3.

4. (colloquialisms) lot, lots, deal, good *or* great deal, considerable, sight, heap, heaps, pile, piles, stack, stacks, loads, raft, rafts, slew, slews, whole slew, wad, wads, batch, mess, mint, peck, pack, pot, hunk, plenty, galore, tidy sum, quite a little.

5. (slang) oodles, oodlins, gob, gobs, slather, slathers, scads, swad, lump, smear, whole smear, fat lot, dead loads, quite a shucks [U.S.].

6. (dialect) lashings, power, lavish, might, chance, quite a chance, right smart chance, heap sight, passel.

VERBS 7. loom, bulk, loom large, stand out; tower, rear; tower above, rise above.

ADJS. 8. great, grand, tall [slang], considerable, consequential, powerful [coll.], much, mighty, almighty [coll., U.S.], intense, goodly, precious; full, plenary; grave, serious, heavy, deep, sad; big (in size) 194.16.

9. eminent, prominent, high, elevated, exalted, lofty, sublime, august, majestic, noble, distinguished.

10. remarkable, marked, of mark, pointed, signal, conspicuous, striking; notable, noticeable, noteworthy; marvelous, wonderful, astonishing, appalling, fabulous, incredible, egregious [joc.].

11. vast, immense, prodigious, stupendous, enormous, huge, colossal, monumental; cosmic, astronomical; mammoth 194.20, 21.

12. (colloquialisms) tremendous, terrific, terrible, horrible, dreadful, awful, fearful, frightful, deadly.

13. (slang) whacking, banging, thumping, thundering, roaring, slapping, swingeing, rousing, whooping, spanking, howling, whaling, staving.

14. downright, outright, out-and-out, straight-out [coll., U.S.]; absolute, utter, perfect, consummate, positive [coll.], pronounced, decided, regular [coll.], proper [slang], precious, profound, blank, stark; thorough, thoroughgoing, thoroughpaced; unmitigated, unqualified, unequivocal;

flagrant, arrant, egregious, glaring, stark-staring, **rank**, crass, gross.

15. extreme, radical, thoroughgoing, forward; **greatest**, furthest, **most, utmost,** uttermost, outside [coll.]; **ultra,** ultra-ultra [slang]; at its height.

16. undiminished, unabated, unreduced, unrestricted, unretarded.

ADVS. **17. greatly, largely,** to a large *or* great extent, in great measure, on a large scale; **much,** muchly [slang], pretty much, very much, so, so very much, ever so much, ever so, never so; **considerably,** considerable [dial.]; abundantly, plenty [coll.], no end of, no end [coll., U.S.], not a little, **a lot,** a deal [coll.], **a great deal,** *beaucoup* [F.]; highly, to the skies; like *or* as all creation [coll.], like *or* as all get-out [slang, U.S.].

18. vastly, immensely, enormously, hugely, tremendously [coll.], prodigiously, stupendously.

19. by far, far, **far and away,** far and wide, by a long way, by a great deal, by a long chalk [coll.], by a long shot [slang], out and away.

20. very, exceedingly, quite, just, so, **real** [coll.], **right** [dial. & coll.], right smart [dial., U.S.], **pretty,** jolly [coll., Eng.], gallows [dial.], parlous [coll.], monstrous [coll.], mortal [chiefly dial.], mortally [coll.], proper [dial. & coll.], properly [chiefly slang], only too, a bit of [coll.]; mightily, **mighty** [chiefly coll.], almightily *or* almighty [slang], powerfully [dial. & coll.], powerful [dial.]; **intensely,** acutely, exquisitely, preciously, precious [coll.].

21. (in a positive degree) **positively, decidedly,** purely, appointedly [dial.], **absolutely, utterly, perfectly,** unequivocally, unconditionally, essentially, fundamentally, radically, downright, dead, quite; **certainly,** actually, really, truly, verily, assuredly, **indeed,** for a certainty, for fair [slang], fairly, seriously, in all conscience.

22. (in an extreme degree) **extremely,** in the extreme, **most,** *à outrance* [F., to the utmost], *à toute outrance* [F., to the very utmost]; immeasurably, incalculably, indefinitely, infinitely; beyond compare *or* comparison, beyond measure, beyond all bounds, all out [coll.]; excessively 661.23.

23. (in a marked degree) **remarkably,** markedly, **notably, strikingly,** signally, emphatically, pointedly, prominently, famously, glaringly; **particularly,** singularly, peculiarly; uncommonly, uncommon [dial.

& coll.], extraordinarily, unusually; **wonderfully** [coll.], wonderful [dial.], wondrous, amazingly, amazing [dial.], surprisingly, astonishingly, marvelously, incredibly.

24. (in a violent degree) **violently,** furiously, severely, **terrifically** [coll.], **desperately,** desperate [dial. & coll.], madly, **like mad,** like *or* as all possessed [coll., U.S.], **with a vengeance;** all to pieces, all to stick *or* sticks and staves, all to smash, all to smithereens [all coll.].

25. (in a distressing degree) **sadly, sorely, bitterly,** piteously, grievously, miserably, **cruelly,** woefully, lamentably, balefully, dolorously, distressingly, shockingly; **terribly** [coll.], terrible [dial. & slang], badly [coll.], **awfully** [coll.], awful [dial. & coll.], **dreadfully** [coll.], dreadful [dial. & coll.], **frightfully** [coll.], **horribly** [coll.], horrible [slang], abominably [coll.], deathly [coll.], deadly [coll.], something awful, ∼ fierce *or* terrible [slang], the worst way [slang].

26. (in an infamous degree) **cursedly, confoundedly, damnably, deucedly** [slang], dashedly [coll.], darned [coll.], blamed *or* blame [coll.], plaguily [coll.], plaguy [coll.], devilishly [coll.], **infernally** [coll.], hellishly, hell-firedly *or* hell-fired [slang], allfiredly *or* all-fired [slang], **bally** [slang, Eng.], bloody [slang, Eng.], bleeding [slang, Eng.], beastly [coll.].

35. SMALLNESS

In Amount or Degree.—NOUNS **1. smallness, insignificance,** inconsiderableness, inconsequentiality; slightness, scantiness, puniness, picayunishness [U.S.]; daintiness, delicacy, tenuity; minuteness; littleness (in size) 195.

2. (small amount) **modicum,** minim; **minimum; little, bit,** little bit [coll.], **particle, speck,** flyspeck, fleck, point, dot, jot, tittle, **iota,** hoot [slang], hooter [dial. & slang], **dab** [dial. & coll.], **dablet** [coll.], drab [coll.], canch [dial.], **mote, mite** [chiefly coll.], dight [dial.], **whit, ace,** hair, scruple, cantle, cantlet, scantling, **pittance,** dole, scrimption [dial.], smidge *or* **smidgen** [dial., U.S.], smitch [coll.], snitch [coll.], gobbet, dram; grain, granule; molecule, atom; vanishing point, material point; infinitesimal; thimbleful, spoonful, handful; nutshell; minutiae.

3. scrap, tatter, flitter [coll.], fritter, smither [coll.], shiver [dial. & coll.], shiv-een [Scot. & North Eng.], smithereen [coll.], patch, smatter [Scot.], **stitch, shred,** screed [Scot.], rag, tag; **snatch,** snack [dial.], snip, snippet, snick, slip, chip, nip; splinter, sliver, shive; **morsel,** *morceau* [F.], **crumb.**

4. **soupçon** [F.], **suspicion, suggestion,** hint, intimation; **trace, touch, dash,** cast, sprinkling; tinge, tincture; **taste, lick, smack,** sip, sup, spice, **smell;** look, **thought,** idea; **shade,** shadow; gleam, glim [Scot.], spark, scintilla.

5. **hardly anything, mere nothing,** next to nothing, just enough to swear by, **a drop in the bucket** or **ocean;** the shadow of a shade, the suspicion of a suspicion.

VERB 6. lie in a nutshell.

ADJS. 7. **small, insignificant, inconsiderable, inconsequential,** no great shakes [coll.]; puny, dinky [slang], poky, pindling, picayunish [U.S.]; minute; moderate, modest; **slight,** light, slender, **negligible;** scant, scanty; shallow, depthless, cursory, superficial, skin-deep; short, brief, low; little (in size) 195.9.

8. **dainty, delicate,** tender, cute [coll., U.S.], cunning [coll., U.S.]; subtle, subtile, tenuous.

9. **mere, sheer,** stark, bare, plain, simple.

ADVS. 10. (in a small degree) **slightly,** lightly, scantily, inconsequentially, **insignificantly, negligibly,** imperfectly, little; faintly, weakly, feebly; to a small extent, on a small scale; ever so little, *tant soit peu* [F.], as little as may be.

11. (in a certain or limited degree) **to a certain extent,** to such an extent, *pro tanto* [L.]; **partially,** partly, part, in part; comparatively, relatively; **merely,** simply, purely, only; **at least,** at the least, leastwise, leastways [coll.], at worst, at any rate; **at most,** at the most, at best, at the outside [coll.]; in a manner, in a manner of speaking [coll.], in a way, after a fashion; so far, thus far.

12. **scarcely, hardly, barely,** only just, no more than.

13. (in an uncertain degree) **about, just about,** thereabouts, somewhere about or near, **nearly,** near, **pretty near,** prett-near [dial.], near to, nigh, nigh about, nigh on or upon [dial.], near or close upon, **around,** *circa* [L.], **in the vicinity of,** in the neighborhood of [coll.], bordering on, **upwards of** [coll.], **approximately,** say, the same more or less.

14. (in no degree) **noway,** noways, no-

wise, in no wise, in no case, in no respect, **by no means,** by no manner of means, **on no account, under no circumstances,** at no hand, nohow [coll.], **not in the least,** not much [coll.], not at all, never; not by a darn sight, not by a long shot [both slang]; not nearly, nowhere near; **not a bit,** not a bit of it, not a whit, not a speck, not a jot, not an iota.

36. SUPERIORITY

NOUNS 1. **superiority, pre-eminence, lead,** transcendence or transcendency, **ascendancy** or ascendency, prestige, prepotence or prepotency, preponderance; predominance, predomination; **precedence, priority,** right of way; inimitability, incomparability; majority, seniority (personal superiority); psychological ascendancy.

2. **advantage,** vantage, odds, forehand, inside track [coll.]; **upper hand,** whip hand; start, head start; **edge,** bulge, jump, drop, deadwood, pull over [all slang]; **card up one's sleeve,** ace in the hole [both coll.]; vantage ground, ~ point or ~ post, coign of vantage.

3. **supremacy,** primacy, paramountcy, **first place;** maximum, most, *ne plus ultra* [L., the highest degree]; headship, **leadership;** championship, record, new high.

4. **a superior, higher-up** [slang], senior; superior being, superman, Triton among the minnows; ace, crackajack [slang, U.S.], heavyweight [coll., U.S.]; one's betters.

VERBS 5. **excel, surpass, exceed, transcend,** best, better, rival; **cap,** trump; top, overtop, o'ertop; **predominate,** prevail, preponderate; **outweigh,** overbalance, overbear.

6. **beat,** beat hollow or all hollow [coll.], beat all to pieces or smithereens [slang], beat all creation [coll.], beat the Dutch [coll.], beat the band [slang], skin [slang], skin a mile [slang], cut out [coll.], go one better [coll.], have it on [slang], have it all over [coll.], come it all over [slang], lay it over or all over [slang]; bear the palm, bear away the bell, take the cake [slang, U.S.], bring home the bacon [coll., U.S.].

7. **eclipse, overshadow, throw into the shade,** extinguish, take the shine out of [coll.]; put to shame, show up [coll.], put one's nose out of joint.

8. **outrival, outvie, outclass, outshine,** overmatch; outrank, rank; **outdo, outstrip,** outgo, outpoint, **outperform;** outplay, overplay; outrun, outstep, outpace, out-

march, run rings or circles around [coll.];
outride, override; outjump, overjump; out-
leap, overleap; out-Tory, out-Herod Herod.

9. **outdistance, distance; pass,** overpass; **get ahead of,** shoot ahead of; leave
behind, leave in the lurch; come to the
front, have a healthy lead [slang], come
through to a big lead [slang], drop, lap,
spread-eagle the field [turf slang, U.S.];
hold the field; steal a march upon.

10. **take precedence,** precede, **come** or
rank first, come to the front, lead, **take the
lead,** lead the way, lead the dance; play
first fiddle.

11. **have the advantage** or ascendancy,
have the better or **best of, have the upper** or **whip hand, have the edge on,**
~ bulge on, ~ deadwood on, ~ jump on
or drop on [all slang], have the pull over
[slang], have on the hip, have the inside
track [coll.]; **have a card up one's sleeve,**
have an ace in the hole, hold aces [all
coll.]; have at a disadvantage, get the drop
on [slang], beat to the draw [slang, U.S.];
turn the tables, turn the scale or balance.

12. **give an advantage,** give points,
give cards and spades [coll.], give an edge,
give the lead.

ADJS. 13. **superior, greater,** better, major, **higher,** upper, over, above; ascendant,
in the ascendant, in ascendancy; eminent,
distinguished, marked.

14. **surpassing, exceeding, excelling,
rivaling, eclipsing,** capping, topping,
transcending, transcendent or transcendental; ahead of, ahead of the game, a
jump ahead of, a cut or stroke above, one up
on [slang]; more than a match for.

15. **supreme,** superlative, **greatest,
highest,** maximal, maximum, most, utmost, last; top, topmost, **uppermost,** tip-
top, top-notch [coll.], top-hole [slang,
chiefly Eng.].

16. **chief, main, principal,** paramount,
foremost, headmost, **leading, dominant,**
crowning, capital, cardinal; great, arch,
banner [chiefly coll.], master, central;
prime, **primary,** primal, first; **pre-eminent,**
supereminent; **predominant,** preponderant, prevailing, hegemonic(al); ruling, overruling; sovereign, suzerain; topflight, ranking; star, stellar; champion [chiefly coll.].

17. **peerless, matchless; unmatched,**
unrivaled, unparagoned, unparalleled, nonpareil, **unequaled,** unpeered, unexampled,
unapproached, **unsurpassed, unexcelled;
unbeatable,** unsurpassable; inimitable, **in-**

comparable, beyond compare or comparison, unique; without equal or parallel,
sans pareil [F.]; easily first, *facile princeps*
[L.]; second to none, *nulli secundus* [L.];
ne plus ultra [L., no more beyond].

ADVS. 18. **superlatively, exceedingly,
surpassingly;** eminently, egregiously [joc.],
prominently; **supremely,** paramountly,
pre-eminently, **the most,** to crown all, *par
excellence* [F., of the highest degree]; inim-
itably, incomparably.

19. **chiefly, mainly, in the main,** in
chief; dominantly, **predominantly;** mostly,
for the most part; principally, especially,
particularly, peculiarly; **primarily, in the
first place,** first of all, **above all;** even, yea,
still more, more than ever, all the more,
a fortiori [L.]; ever so, never so.

PREPS. 20. **exceeding, beyond,** over,
past, **more than,** in advance of, **over and
above,** over or above the mark, above par;
at the top of the scale, at its height.

PHRS. 21. have to hand it to, have to tip
the hat to [both slang].

37. INFERIORITY

NOUNS 1. **inferiority, subordinacy, subordination,** secondariness; deficiency, inadequacy, imperfection; smallness, littleness, meanness, baseness, shabbiness; back
seat [coll.], second fiddle.

2. (personal inferiority) juniority, **minority;** subservience, subjection; inferiority
complex.

3. **an inferior, underling, understrapper, subordinate,** subsidiary, subaltern,
sub [coll.], **secondary,** second-stringer
[slang, U.S.], second fiddle, bottom sawyer
[coll.]; junior.

VERBS 4. **not come up to, not measure
up to,** fall or come short of; want, be
found wanting, kick the beam; **not compare with,** have nothing on [slang], **not
hold a candle to** [coll.], not approach, not
come near; play second fiddle, take a back
seat [coll.], eat or take one's dust [coll.].

5. (concede superiority) **bow to, hand it
to** [slang], tip the hat to [slang], yield the
palm; retire into the shade, hide its diminished head.

ADJS. 6. **inferior, subordinate,** subaltern, sub, **secondary,** second; **lesser, less,
lower,** baser, smaller; minor, junior; low,
lowly, humble; in the shade, thrown into
the shade; weighed in the balance and
found wanting.

7. **not to be compared with,** not com-

parable to, not a circumstance to [coll., U.S.], not a patch on [coll.], not a marker on or to [slang]; not able to touch, not able to reach [coll.], not able to come near, not fit to hold a candle to; not in it, not in the same street with, out of it, out of the picture, out of the running, left a mile [all coll.].

8. least, smallest, littlest, slightest, lowest, shortest; minimum, minim.

ADVS. *etc.* 9. least, less, least of all; under; below, short of; under par, below the mark, at a low ebb; at the bottom of the scale, at the bottom of the heap [slang, U.S.].

38. INCREASE

In Amount or Degree.—NOUNS 1. increase, gain, augmentation, enlargement, amplification, growth, extension, aggrandizement, access, accession, increment, accretion, accumulation; addition 40; expansion 196; accruement, accrual, accumulation; advance, appreciation, rise or raise (as in price), boost [slang, U.S.], hike [slang], heist [slang, U.S.], up [coll.], build-up; upturn, uptrend, upswing; leap, jump; boom [U.S.].

2. intensification, heightening, deepening, strengthening, enhancement, magnification, exaggeration, aggravation, concentration, condensation, consolidation, reinforcement, redoubling; pickup, step-up [both coll.].

3. gains, profits 809.3.

VERBS 4. (make greater) increase, enlarge, largify [dial.], biggen [chiefly dial., Eng.], aggrandize, amplify, augment, extend, add to; expand 196.4; lengthen, broaden, thicken; raise, exalt, boost [slang], hike or hike up [slang], heist [slang, U.S.], jack up [coll.], jump up [slang], put up, up [coll.]; build, build up; pyramid, parlay.

5. intensify, heighten, deepen, enhance, strengthen, aggravate, exaggerate, magnify; whet, sharpen; reinforce, double, redouble, triple; concentrate, condense, consolidate; give a boost to, step up [coll.], key up, hop up [slang], soup up [slang, U.S.], jazz up [slang]; add fuel to the flame.

6. (become greater) increase, advance, appreciate [coll. exc. in value], look up [coll.], gain, get ahead; grow, wax, swell, mount, rise, go up; intensify, gain strength, strengthen; accrue, accumulate; multiply, spread, prolificate; run or shoot up, boom [U.S.].

ADJS. 7. increased, heightened, intensified; enlarged, extended; larger, bigger; grown, full-grown.

8. increasing, crescent, growing, waxing, swelling, lengthening, multiplying; intensive, intensifying; incremental; on the increase, crescendo.

ADVS. 9. increasingly, growingly, more, more and more, on and on, greater and greater, ever more; crescendo.

39. DECREASE

In Amount or Degree.—NOUNS 1. decrease, decrescence, diminishment, diminution, reduction, lessening, lowering, step-down [coll.]; letup [coll.], abatement; alleviation, mitigation; attenuation, extenuation, weakening, languishment; depreciation, deflation; deduction 42; abridgement 202.3; contraction 197.

2. decline, declension, subsidence, slump [coll.], lapse, wane, ebb; downturn, downtrend; fall, decline and fall; decrescendo, diminuendo; catabasis [med.].

3. decrement, waste, loss, dissipation, wear and tear, erosion, consumption, shrinkage.

4. curtailment, retrenchment, cut, cutback, rollback (as in price [coll.]).

5. minimization, minification, belittling, belittlement.

VERBS 6. (grow less) decrease, diminish, lessen; let up, bate, abate; decline, subside, wane, ebb, dwindle, languish, die away, tail off, drop off, fall, fall off, fall away, fall to a low ebb, run low; waste, wear, waste or wear away, crumble, erode, consume, consume away; melt away, deliquesce.

7. reduce, decrease, diminish, lessen, take from; lower, depress, step down [coll.], tune down [coll.], scale down [U.S.]; downgrade; depreciate, deflate; curtail, retrench; cut, cut down, cut back, roll back (as prices [coll.]); shorten 202.6; compress 197.7.

8. abate, bate; weaken, attenuate, extenuate; alleviate, mitigate, ease, slacken, remit.

9. minimize, minify, belittle; dwarf, bedwarf.

ADJS. 10. reduced, decreased, diminished, lowered, dropped, fallen; lower, less, lesser, smaller, shorter.

11. decreasing, diminishing, lessening, subsiding, declining, languishing, dwindling, waning, on the wane; decres-

cent, reductive, deliquescent, contractive; diminuendo, decrescendo.

ADVS. **12. decreasingly,** less, **less and less;** decrescendo, diminuendo.

40. ADDITION

NOUNS **1. addition,** accession, annexation, affixation, attachment, joining, uniting; **increase** 38; **augmentation,** reinforcement; superaddition, superposition, superjunction, superfetation; adjunct 41.

2. computation, adding 87.3; plus sign, plus.

VERBS **3. add,** plus [coll.], put with, **join** *or* **unite with, affix, attach,** annex, append, subjoin, postfix, tag, tag on, **tack on,** tuck on [slang], clap on, slap on [coll.], saddle on, hitch on [coll.], superimpose, superpose, superadd; burden, encumber, saddle with.

4. add to, augment, supplement; increase 38.4; **reinforce,** restrengthen, fortify; recruit, swell the ranks of.

5. compute, add up 87.11, 12.

6. advene, supervene.

ADJS. **7. additive,** additory; cumulative, accumulative.

8. added, affixed, **attached,** appended, appendant.

9. additional, supplementary, supplemental; extra, plus, further, farther, fresh, **more,** new, **other,** another, ulterior; auxiliary, ancillary, supernumerary, contributory, accessory, collateral; **surplus,** spare.

ADVS. **10. additionally, in addition, also,** and also, and all [coll.], and so, **as well, too,** else, beside, **besides, to boot, into the bargain,** at that [coll.], on top of, over, above, over and above, past, beyond, plus, overplus, extra, on the side [slang], more, moreover, *au reste* [F.], farther, further, **furthermore,** then, again, yet, similarly, likewise, by the same token, by the same sign; item.

PREPS. *etc.* **11. with, including,** inclusive of, **along** *or* **together with,** coupled with, **in conjunction with; as well as,** not to mention, to say nothing of, let alone [coll.]; therewith, therewithal; all included, altogether; among other things, *inter alia* [L.].

CONJS. *etc.* **12. and,** also [coll.], and also, **in addition to,** added *or* linked to, along *or* together with, **as well as,** at the same time, in addition to being, with the addition of, attended by.

PHRS. **13. et cetera, and so forth, and**

so on, et al., *et alii* [L.], and all [coll.], and others, and other things, *cum multis aliis* [L., with many others], and ever [dial.], and everything else, and more of the same, and the rest, **and the like,** and suchlike, and all that sort of thing, and all that [coll.], and all like that [slang], and stuff like that [slang], **and what not, and what have you** [slang], and I don't know what [coll.], and God knows what [coll.], and then some [coll.]; and the following, *et sequens* [L.], *et seq.*

41. ADJUNCT

Thing Added.—NOUNS **1. adjunct,** addition, *additum* [L.], additament, additory, addendum (*pl.* addenda); plus, and [coll.]; **affix,** accession, increment, **attachment,** fixture; **annex,** *annexe* [F.], annexation; **appendage,** appendant, pendant, appanage; augment, augmentation, reinforcement; appurtenance, appurtenant; **accessory,** adjective; **supplement,** complement, expletive; continuation, extension; offshoot, side issue, corollary; rider, allonge; subscript, postscript; prefix, **suffix;** appendix, codicil; application, patch.

2. tab, tag, flap, apron, fly, tuck, skirt; lug, ear; lap, lappet, lapel.

3. (building) **wing, addition, annex,** extension, ell *or* L.

4. extra, more, another; bonus, boot [dial.], premium; supernumerary, super [slang].

ADJS. **5. winged,** alate, alated.

42. DEDUCTION

NOUNS **1. deduction, subtraction,** subduction, **removal;** abstraction, ablation; retrenchment.

2. (mathematics) **subtraction,** takeaway [slang]; subtrahend, minuend; negative; minus sign, minus.

3. excision, abscission, extirpation; deletion, erasure, **cancellation; editing,** bluepencilling; amputation, mutilation; truncation, detruncation, obtruncation; circumcision.

4. expurgation, censorship, bowdlerization, castration, emasculation.

5. castration, gelding, cutting, spaying (a female), alteration [coll.], emasculation.

6. (thing deducted) **deduction,** eduction, decrement, offtake, take-off [slang]; **discount;** tare; reprise [law]; **rebate,** rebatement.

VERBS **7. deduct,** deduce, reduct [dial.],

subduct, **subtract**, detract, minus [coll.], **take from,** take away, **remove, withdraw,** abstract, take off, **strike off,** knock off [coll.]; discount.

8. **excise,** cut, **cut out,** extirpate, strike off, **strike out,** scratch out, cross out, **cross off,** cross off the lists; **expunge, erase,** wipe out, rub out, blot out; rule out; **cancel, write off,** kill; edit, **edit out,** blue-pencil; **delete,** dele; thin, thin out, weed.

9. **expurgate, censor,** censure, **bowdlerize,** castrate, emasculate.

10. **cut off,** retrench, **amputate,** mutilate; truncate, detruncate, obtruncate; **prune,** pare, peel, **clip, crop,** bob (hair), poll, dock, lop, nip, snub, shear, shave, skive, mow; abrade, scrape off, file off, grind off, rub off; pollard; circumcise.

11. **castrate, geld,** cut [dial. & coll.], alter [coll.], spay (a female), capon or caponize (a cock); emasculate, unman, demasculinize, effeminize, eunuchize; **sterilize,** poulardize (a pullet).

ADJS. 12. deductive, subtractive.

PREPS. 13. **off, away, from.**

14. **minus,** less, short of, out [slang], without, lacking, leaving out, excepting.

43. REMAINDER

NOUNS 1. **remainder, remains,** relics [poetic], **remanence,** remnant, **residue,** residual, residuum (*pl.* residual), rest, **balance** [coll.]; **leavings, leftovers;** oddments, odds and ends, scraps, rags, orts, candle ends; scourings, offscourings; parings, scobs, raspings, filings, shavings, sawdust; chaff, straw, stubble; debris, detritus, ruins; end, **fag end;** stump, butt (as of a cigar), rump; remainders, plugs [publishers' slang]; vestige, trace, shadow; fossil.

2. **dregs,** sordes, **grounds, lees,** dross, sprue, slag, draff, recrement, scoria, feces or faeces; **sediment,** settlement, **settlings,** deposit, deposition; bottoms, heeltap or heeltaps; precipitate, precipitation, sublimate [chem.]; alluvium, alluvion, diluvium; silt, loess, moraine; scum, offscum, froth; ash, ember, cinder, sinter, clinker, coal, carbon, charcoal, lava; soot, smut.

3. **survivor,** survival, remainer.

VERBS 4. **remain, be left, survive,** subsist.

5. **leave,** leave over, leave behind.

ADJS. 6. **remaining, surviving,** over, left, **leftover, remanent,** odd; **spare,** to spare; unused, unconsumed; **surplus,** over and above; outstanding, outlying; net (remaining after deductions), neat.

7. **residual,** residuary; sedimental, sedimentary.

44. MIXTURE

NOUNS 1. **mixture,** mixing, blending; **admixture,** commixture, immixture, intermixture; **minglement,** interminglement, interlardment; **fusion,** interfusion; amalgamation, coalescence; **combination** 52.

2. **imbuement, impregnation, infusion,** suffusion, transfusion, infiltration, instillment, instillation, permeation, pervasion, penetration.

3. **adulteration, corruption,** contamination, denaturalization, sophistication, **doctoring** [coll.]; fortification, lacing (as tea); medication, **doping** [slang], drugging; **dilution,** cutting [coll.], watering; adulterant.

4. **crossbreeding,** crossing, **interbreeding,** miscegenation; **hybridism,** hybridization; touch of the tar brush [coll.].

5. **compound, mixture, admixture,** intermixture, immixture, commixture, **composite, blend;** composition, compo [slang, U.S.]; **combination,** combo [slang, U.S.]; amalgam, alloy; paste, magma.

6. **hodgepodge,** hotchpotch, hotchpot; **medley,** rhapsody, **miscellany,** mélange [F.], *pasticcio* [It.], **conglomeration, assortment,** olio, olla-podrida, **scramble, jumble,** mingle-mangle, mix [chiefly coll.], mix-up [coll.], mixty-maxty [Scot.], mux, **mess,** mash, hash, patchwork, chowchow, salad, gallimaufry, salmagundi, **potpourri,** stew [slang], omnium-gatherum [coll.], Noah's ark, **odds and ends,** all sorts, what the cat brought in [coll., U.S.].

7. (slight admixture) **tinge, tincture, touch, dash, smack,** taint, trace, vestige, hint, suggestion, thought, shade; sprinkling, seasoning, spice, infusion.

8. **crossbreed,** cross, mixblood, **halfbreed,** half-bred, half blood, half-caste, **mongrel, hybrid,** *ladino* [Sp.]; mustee or mestee [India & W. Ind.], *mestizo* [Sp.], *mestiza* (*fem.* [Sp.]), *métis* [F.], *métisse* (*fem.* [F.]); Eurasian, Americanadian; zebrule, zebrass, cattalo, mule; pomato, tangelo, citrange, plumcot.

9. **mulatto, high yellow** [coll., U.S.], sepian [slang, U.S.], kelt or keltch [dial. & slang, U.S.]; quadroon, quintroon, octoroon; *sambo, zambo* [Sp.], *cafuso* [Brazil], fustee [W. Ind.], dustee, *sacatra* [F.], mara-

bou [Louisiana], griqua [South Africa]; griffe, *grifado* [Sp.], griffado.

10. **mixer, blender,** beater, agitator; cement mixer, egg beater, churn.

VERBS 11. **mix,** admix, commix, immix, **intermix, mingle,** bemingle, commingle, immingle, **intermingle,** interlard; **blend,** interblend; **amalgamate,** coalesce, **fuse, merge,** compound; **combine** 52.3; mix up, hash up [chiefly coll.], stir up, **scramble,** conglomerate, shuffle, **jumble,** minglemangle, throw together; knead, work; brew.

12. **imbue,** imbrue, **infuse,** suffuse, transfuse, breathe, **instill,** infiltrate, **impregnate, permeate,** pervade, penetrate, leaven; **tinge, tincture,** entincture, color, dye, flavor, season; saturate, steep, dredge.

13. **adulterate, corrupt,** contaminate, debase, denaturalize, sophisticate, **tamper with,** doctor *or* doctor up [coll.], hocus [coll.], dash; alloy; **fortify** (a beverage), spike [slang, U.S.], lace (as tea), medicate, drug, **dope** *or* dope up [slang]; **dilute,** cut [coll.], water, irrigate [slang].

14. **crossbreed, cross, interbreed, hybridize,** miscegenate.

ADJS. 15. **mixed, mingled,** blended, compounded, amalgamated; **combined** 52.5; **composite,** compound, complex; **conglomerate,** heterogeneous, varied, **miscellaneous,** medley, chowchow, linsey-woolsey, promiscuous, indiscriminate, **scrambled, jumbled,** mixty-maxty [Scot.], thrown together; half-and-half, fifty-fifty [slang, U.S.]; amphibious.

16. **hybrid, mongrel,** interbred, **crossbred,** crossed, cross; **half-breed,** half-bred, half-blooded, half-caste.

17. miscible, mixable.

PREPS. 18. **among,** amongst, 'mongst; **amid,** mid *or* 'mid, amidst, midst *or* 'midst, **in the midst of, in the thick of;** with, together with.

45. SIMPLICITY

Freedom from Mixture or Complexity.
NOUNS 1. **simplicity, purity,** simpleness, **plainness,** unmixedness; **unadulteration,** unsophistication; **singleness,** uniformity, homogeneity.

2. **simplification,** streamlining; **disentanglement,** unscrambling, unsnarling.

VERBS 3. **simplify,** streamline.

4. **disinvolve,** disintricate, disembroil, **disentangle,** untangle, **unscramble, unsnarl,** unknot, untwist, unbraid, unweave,

untwine, unwind, uncoil, unthread, unravel, ravel, feaze [dial.]; comb, card.

ADJS. 5. **simple, plain,** bare, mere; **single,** uniform, homogeneous, of a piece; **pure,** simon-pure; pure and simple, *pur et simple* [F.]; Attic; elementary, elemental [both chem.].

6. **unmixed, unmingled,** unblended, **uncombined,** uncompounded; unleavened; **unadulterated,** uncorrupted, unsophisticated, unalloyed, untinged, undiluted, unfortified; **neat, straight,** absolute, sheer, naked.

7. **uncomplicated, uninvolved,** incomplex.

8. simplified, streamlined.

ADVS. 9. **simply, plainly, purely;** merely, barely; **singly, solely,** only, **alone,** simply and solely.

46. COMPLEXITY

NOUNS 1. **complexity, complication,** involvement, involution, tanglement, **entanglement,** perplexity, **intricacy,** intricateness, complexness, crabbedness; inextricability.

2. **complex,** complexus, involute; **tangle,** tangled skein, sleave, skein, kink, twist, intertwist, ravel, snarl, gnarl; knot, Gordian knot; **maze,** meander, **labyrinth,** "wild inextricable maze" [Blackmore]; webwork, mesh; wilderness, jungle, Hyrcanian wood; clockworks, wheels within wheels.

VERBS 3. **complicate, involve, perplex, confound, confuse,** muddle, **mix up,** ball up [slang], foul up [coll.], snarl up, implicate; **tangle,** entangle, embrangle, **snarl,** ravel [dial. & poetic], knot; foul, befoul, bedevil.

ADJS. 4. **complex, complicated,** complicate, complexed, perplexed, **confused,** confounded, **involved,** implicated, crabbed, **intricate,** elaborate, involute, involutional; **mixed up,** balled up [slang], fouled up; **tangled,** entangled, tangly, embrangled, **snarled,** gnarled, knotted, matted, twisted, convoluted; **mazy,** daedal, **labyrinthine,** labyrinthian, meandering.

5. **inextricable,** irreducible, unsolvable.

47. JUNCTION

NOUNS 1. **junction, joining,** joinder; **connection, union,** conjunction, conjugation, liaison, marriage, hookup [spec. coll.], tie-up [coll.], tie-in [coll.]; **combination** 52; **coupling,** copulation [chem.], accouplement, bracketing; **linking,** linkage, concatenation; **meeting,** confluence, concurrence, concourse; communication, intercommunication; **reunion,** reune [coll.].

2. interconnection, interjoinder, **interlinking,** interlocking, interdigitation; **interassociation,** interaffiliation.

3. fastening, attachment, affixation; ligation, astriction; binding, tieing, lashing, trussing, girding, hooking, clasping, buckling, buttoning; bond, fastener 48.

4. joint, jint [dial.], join, joining, **juncture, union, connection;** node [bot.]; articulation [anat. & bot.], diarthrosis [anat.]; pivot, **hinge;** knee, elbow, wrist, ankle, knuckle; ball-and-socket joint, pivot joint, hinged **joint,** gliding joint; toggle, toggle joint; **seam,** suture, stitch, raphe [anat. & bot.], closure, commissure; mortise, miter, dovetail, rabbet, weld.

VERBS **5.** (put together) **join,** conjoin, **unite, connect,** associate, league, band; **combine** 52.3; **couple,** accouple, copulate [chem.], conjugate, marry, **link,** yoke, bracket; **put together,** fix together, lay together, piece together, clap together, tack together, stick together, lump together, hang together; bridge, bridge over, span; reunite, reune [coll.].

6. interconnect, interjoin, intertie, **interassociate, interlink,** interlock, interdigitate.

7. fasten, attach, fix, affix, put to; set to; graft, ingraft; **secure,** anchor, cement, knit, set, grapple, **make fast;** clinch, clamp, cramp; tighten, trice up, screw up; cinch, cinch up [both U.S.].

8. hook, hitch; **clasp,** hasp, clip, snap; **button,** buckle, zipper; lock, latch; **pin,** skewer, peg, nail, tack, staple, toggle, screw, bolt, rivet; **sew,** stitch; **wedge,** jam, rabbet, mortise, miter, dovetail; batten, batten down; cleat; hinge; joint, articulate.

9. bind, tie, brace, truss, **lash,** leash, string, cord, rope, strap, lace, wire, cable, chain; belay [naut.]; splice, bend [naut. slang]; **gird,** girt, belt, girth, girdle, band, cinch; **tie up,** bind up, do up; **wrap,** wrap up; **bandage,** tape, band up [local, U.S.]; swathe, swaddle; garter.

10. yoke, poke [coll., U.S.]; **hitch up,** hook up [coll.]; harness, harness up [coll.]; halter, bridle; saddle.

11. (be joined) **join, connect, unite, meet, come together;** communicate, intercommunicate; knit, grow together; hang or hold together.

ADJS. **12. joint, conjoint,** conjunct, corporate, compact, concurrent, coincident, correal [civil law].

13. joined, united, connected, copulate, **coupled,** linked, bracketed, associated, leagued, banded together; hand-in-hand, hand-in-glove, intimate; unseparated, undivided.

14. fast, fastened, **fixed, secure,** firm, close, tight, set, sound.

15. inseparable, impartible, indivisible, undividable, indissoluble, indisceptible, inseverable, bound up in or with.

16. joining, connecting, meeting; **communicating,** intercommunicating; **connective,** connectional; conjunctive, combinative, copulative [gram.]; binding.

17. jointed, articulate.

ADVS. **18. securely, firmly, fast, close,** firm.

48. BOND, FASTENING

Connecting Medium.—NOUNS **1. bond,** bond of union, privity [law], **connection, union, tie, link, connecting link,** connective, interconnection, intermedium, vinculum, nexus, liaison; **coupling,** copula, coupler, couple; bridge, steppingstone; ligature, ligament, ligation; hyphen, dash.

2. fastening, fastener, fast, **attachment.**

3. knot, bend, **tie,** hitch; Gordian knot.

4. (anatomy) ligament, tendon, sinew, thew; hamstring; umbilical cord, spermatic cord.

5. neck [anat.], cervix, cervical region, scrag [slang], hals or halse [Scot. & dial., Eng.]; **nape,** scruff, scrag, nucha; auchenium [zool.]; **throat,** jugulum [zool.], gula [zool.]; clod (of beef).

6. adhesive, cement, glue, mucilage, paste, gluten, binder, stickum [slang].

7. fasteners

anchor	brace
band	braces [Eng.]
bandage	brad
bar	braid
barrette	buckle
bellyband	button
belt	cable
bind	carpet tack
binding	catch
binding stone	chain
binding twine	cinch
bobby pin	cincture
bollard	clamp
bolt	clasp
bonder [masonry]	cleat
bondstone	clevis
box hook	click

clinch
clip
clothespin
corking pin [dial.]
cotter
cotter pin
detent
dowel
drawing pin [Eng.]
duledge [mil.]
fillet
fishhook
funicle
garter
girder
girdle
girth
grab
grapnel
grappler
grappling or grapple iron or hook
guy
guy rope
hairpin
hank [naut.]
hasp
hawser
haywire
hitch
hitching post
holdfast
hook
hook and eye
inkle
interlocker
kevel [naut.]
kingbolt
kingpin
lace
lacing
lariat
latch
latchet
leader
line
lock
loop
moorings
nail
noose
nut

oxreim [South Africa]
padlock
paper clip
pawl
peg
pin
pintle
reata [Sp., lariat]
ring
rivet
roller
rope
safety pin
screw
seal
sennit [naut.]
setscrew
skewer
snap
snubbing post
spike
splice
staple
strap
string
strop
stub tenon
suspenders
tack
tag
terret
thole
tholepin
thong
thumbtack
tie
tie beam
toggle [naut.]
towline
treenail or trenail
tug
twine
vise
whang [Scot., thong]
wire
with or withe
withy
wrist pin
zipper

8. knots

anchor knot
becket knot
Blackwall hitch
bow
bowknot
bowline
bowline knot
builder's knot
carrick bend
cat's paw
clinch
clinch inside or outside
clove hitch
cuckold's neck
diamond knot
double hitch

Englishman's tie
figure-of-eight knot
fisherman's bend
flat knot
Flemish knot
French shroud knot
German knot
granny knot
half crown
half hitch
harness hitch
hawser bend
hawser fastening
heaving-line bend
inside clinch
lanyard knot

loop knot
magnus hitch
manrope knot
marlinespike hitch
marling hitch
Matthew Walker knot
mesh knot
midshipman's hitch
netting knot
open hand knot
outside clinch
overhand knot
prolonge knot
reef knot
reeving-line bend
rolling hitches
rope-yarn knot
round seizing
round turn and half hitch

running bowline
running knot
sheepshank
sheet bend
shroud knot
single knot
slide knot
slipknot
square knot
stevedore's knot
stopper knot
studding-sail halyard bend
stunner hitch
surgeon's knot
tack bend
timber knot or hitch
truckman's knot
wall knot
weaver's hitch or knot

9. adhesives

birdlime
fish glue
gum
library paste
lime
lute
mastic
putty

rabbitskin glue
sealing wax
size
solder
viscin
viscum
wafer

49. DISJUNCTION

NOUNS 1. disjunction, disjointure, **disconnection**, disengagement, **disunion**, disassociation; **separation, parting,** detachment, abstraction; divorce, divorcement; **division,** subdivision; section, resection; segmentation; dislocation, luxation; separability, partibility; separatism.

2. **severance,** disseverance, **sunderance,** scission, fission, cleavage; **cutting, slitting, splitting,** splitment [slang]; **rending, tearing;** laceration, dilaceration, discerption; mangling, mutilation; abscission, abstriction, adjunction; avulsion, divulsion; disruption, abruption, cataclasm; elision, syncope.

3. **break,** breakage, **breach, burst, rupture, fracture; crack,** snap; **fissure,** scissure; **cut, split,** slit; slash; **rift, rent,** rip, tear; chip; craze, check, crackle; chap.

4. **dissection, analysis, resolution,** breakdown, breakup, diaeresis; anatomy, anat [med. slang].

5. **disassembly, dismantlement,** dismemberment, dismounting, undoing, unbuilding.

6. **separator,** sieve, centrifuge; creamer, cream separator.

VERBS 7. **come apart,** fly apart, come unstuck, come undone, **come or fall to** pieces; come *or* fall off, peel off; get loose, give way; start, come apart at the seams.

8. disjoin, disunite, dissociate, **disconnect;** uncouple, unyoke; **separate, divide,** part, dispart, divorce, detach, remove; cut off, cut adrift.

9. unfasten, undo, unattach, unfix, **disengage,** open; **unloose,** loose, unloosen; **unhook,** unhitch, unclasp, unbuckle, unbutton, unsnap, unscrew, unpin; unbolt, unbar; unlock, unlatch; **untie,** unbind, unbandage, unlace, unstrap, unchain; unstick, unglue.

10. sever, dissever, sunder, **cleave, split,** fissure, cut in two; **cut,** incise, carve, slice, slash, slish [dial.], slit, snip, nip, lance, scissor; **chop, hew,** hack, whack [coll.], hackle, haggle, gash, whittle; saw, jigsaw; **tear, rend,** rive, discerp, rend asunder.

11. break, burst, bust [dial. & inelegant]; **fracture, rupture; crack,** split, fissure; snap; chip; craze, crackle, check; chap.

12. shatter, splinter, shiver, shivereen [dial.], break to pieces, break into shivereens [dial.], smithereen [coll.], break to smithers *or* smithereens [coll.], flinderate [slang], break to flinderation *or* all to flinderation [slang]; **smash,** crash, crush, crunch, cranch, craunch; break up, smash up; **fragment,** fritter, fission, atomize; pulverize 330.6; mince, make mincemeat of; hash, make a hash of.

13. tear apart, take ~, pull ~, pick *or* **tear to pieces,** pull in pieces, tear piecemeal, tear to rags *or* tatters; **lacerate,** mangle, mutilate, maim.

14. disassemble, take apart; take down, tear down, pull down; **dismantle,** dismount, unrig [chiefly naut.], undo, unbuild, unmake, unfurnish; dismast.

15. dismember, limb, dislimb, disbranch, **tear limb from limb.**

16. disjoint, joint, unjoint, unhinge; **dislocate,** throw out of joint *or* gear.

17. dissect, analyze, anatomize, decompose, break down, cut to pieces.

18. partition, parcel, portion, section, segment, lot; **divide,** divide up, divvy *or* divvy up [slang], **split,** split up, **cut up,** whack up [coll.]; subdivide, divide and redivide; plot (land); district, zone, chapter, canton.

19. part company, part, separate, split up, split out [coll.], break up, break it up [slang], leave, take leave, quit, go away, **go separate ways.**

ADJS. **20. unjoined,** disjoined, disjoint, disjunct; **unconnected,** disconnected, disengaged, **unattached,** detached, **disunited,** unassociated, **divided, separated,** removed, **apart,** asunder, **in two,** far between; **separate,** distinct, discrete; isolated, insular; disjointed, dislocated; bipartite, multipartite, multisegmental.

21. unfastened, uncaught, unfixed, **undone, loose, clear, free;** untied, unbound; unanchored, adrift, afloat, floating.

22. severed, cut, cleft, cracked, **split,** slit, reft; **rent, torn;** lacerated, lacerate, mangled, mutilated.

23. broken, busted [dial. & inelegant], **burst, ruptured;** sprung; crazed; shattered, in smithereens [coll.].

24. separating, dividing, parting; separative, disjunctive; cutting, secant.

25. separable, severable, **divisible,** cleavable, partible; **fissionable,** fissile, scissile; dissoluble, dissolvable.

ADVS. **26. separately,** severally, one by one; **apart,** adrift, asunder, **in two,** in twain; apart from, away from, aside from; abstractly, in the abstract.

27. to pieces, all to pieces, piecemeal, **to bits,** to flinders, to flinderation [slang], to smithers [coll.], **to smithereens** [coll.], to splinters, to sticks, to sticks and staves, to shreds, to smash, **all to smash.**

50. COHERENCE

A Sticking Together.—NOUNS **1. coherence, cohesion, adherence, adhesion,** sticking, cling; **consistency;** cementation, conglutination, agglutination; concretion, accretion, solidification, set, congelation, coagulation; conglomeration, agglomeration, consolidation.

2. tenacity, tenaciousness, **adhesiveness,** cohesiveness, stick-to-itiveness [coll.], stay [coll.], stay-putness [slang]; **stickiness,** tackiness, glueyness, gummyness, **viscidity,** viscosity, glutinosity, toughness.

3. (something adhesive or tenacious) **adherent,** adherer, **adhesive;** bulldog, barnacle, leech, remora; bur *or* burr, cocklebur, clotbur, bramble, brier, prickle, thorn, sticker [coll.]; plaster, adhesive plaster; sirup, molasses; glue 48.6.

4. conglomerate, conglomeration; agglomerate, agglomeration; concrete, concretion.

VERBS **5. cohere, adhere, stick, cling, cleave,** hold, close with; stay, stay put; cling to, freeze to [coll., U.S.]; hang on, hold on; take hold of, clasp, grasp, hug; **stick together, hang** or **hold together;** grow to, grow together.

6. **hold fast, stick close,** stick like wax, stick like the paper on the wall, stick like a wet shirt, stick closer than a brother, stick to like a barnacle or leech, cling like ivy, cling like a bur, adhere like Dejanira's shirt, hold on like a bulldog, hold on like old Billy Hell [slang].

7. **cement, stick together, bind, paste, glue,** agglutinate, conglutinate, solution; gum, lute; **weld, fuse,** burn on or together; **solder,** braze.

ADJS. 8. **coherent, cohesive, consistent;** cohering, adhering, **sticking, clinging,** cleaving, holding together; stuck, agglutinate.

9. **adhesive, adherent,** stickable, stick-to-itive [coll.], **tenacious,** clingy; **sticky,** tacky, gluey, gummy, **viscid,** glutinous, tough.

51. INCOHERENCE

A Want of Cohesion.—NOUNS 1. **incoherence, inconsistency,** noncohesion, nonadhesion, unadhesiveness, uncohesiveness, unadherence, untenacity; immiscibility; rope of sand.

2. **looseness, slackness, laxness,** laxity, laxation, relaxation.

VERBS 3. **slacken, loosen, relax,** laxate; slack, slack off; ease, ease off, let up.

ADJS. 4. **incoherent,** uncoherent, noncoherent, **inconsistent, uncohesive, unadhesive,** nonadhesive, noncohesive, nonadherent, **untenacious;** disconnected, unconnected, broken, detached; segregated, segregate; like grains of sand; immiscible.

5. **loose, slack, lax, relaxed,** easy; flapping, streaming; hanging, drooping, dangling; bagging, baggy.

52. COMBINATION

NOUNS 1. **combination,** combo [slang, U.S.]; **union, unification,** incorporation, embodiment, aggregation, coadunation, **amalgamation, consolidation,** solidification; **junction** 47; conjunction, conjugation; **alliance,** affiliation, association, hook-up [slang], tie-up [slang]; federation, confederation, federalization; **fusion,** blend, blending; inosculation, anastomosis; coalescence, coalition; synthesis, synizesis, synaeresis; syndication; crasis [gram.]; package deal.

2. mixture 44, compound 44.5.

VERBS 3. **combine, unite, unify,** incorporate, embody, coadunate, **amalgamate, consolidate,** solidify, coalesce, compound, put or lump together, roll into one, make one; **join** 47.5; **mix** 44.11; **merge, meld, blend,** shade into, **fuse, flux,** melt into one; interfuse, interblend; inosculate, anastomose; synthesize, syncretize; syndicate; re-embody.

4. **league, ally, affiliate** [U.S.], **associate,** consociate; unionize, cement a union; federate, confederate, federalize; **join forces,** join or unite with, join together, join up with [coll.], hook up with [slang], tie up or in with [slang], hitch horses [coll.], **throw in with** [slang], stand up with, go cahoots or in cahoots [slang], **pool one's interests, join fortunes with,** stand together, make common cause with; **band together,** club together [coll.], bunch, bunch up [coll.], gang up [coll.], gang, club; team with, **team up with** [coll.], couple, pair, pair off, partner; go in partnership, go in partners [coll.].

ADJS. 5. **combined, united, amalgamated, incorporated, consolidated,** coadunate, one; joint, conjoint; conjunctive, conjugate; **merged,** blended, fused; **mixed** 44.15.

6. **leagued,** enleagued, **allied, affiliated** [U.S.], affiliate, **ascociated,** associate, corporate; federated, confederated, federate, confederate; **in league,** in cahoots [slang], in with; partners with, in partnership; teamed, coupled, paired.

7. **combining, uniting,** incorporating; merging, blending, fusing; **combinative, combinatory;** associative; federative, federal; corporative, incorporative, corporational.

53. DISINTEGRATION

NOUNS 1. **disintegration, decomposition, dissolution,** resolution, disorganization, breakup, atomization; **erosion,** corrosion, crumbling, wear, wear and tear, ravages of time.

2. (chemistry) dissociation; catalysis, dialysis, hydrolysis, proteolysis, thermolysis; catalyst, hydrolyst; hydrolyte.

VERBS 3. **disintegrate, decompose,** dissolve, disorganize, **break up,** atomize, **come** or **fall to pieces; erode,** corrode, consume, consume ~, wear or waste away, crumble, crumble into dust.

4. (chemistry) dissociate; catalyze, dialyze, hydrolyze.

ADJS. **5. disintegrative,** disintegrating, decomposing; **erosive,** corrosive; resolvent, solvent, separative.

6. (chemistry) dissociative; catalytic, dialytic, hydrolytic, proteolytic, thermolytic.

54. WHOLE

NOUNS **1. whole, totality,** teetotality *or* T-totality [coll.], **entirety,** integrity, collectivity; complex, *complexus* [L.]; integration, embodiment; organic unity, compages; integer, integral [spec. math.].

2. total, teetotal *or* T-total [coll.], tote [coll.], tot, tottle; **sum,** sum total, **the amount,** whole *or* gross amount, the stick [sporting slang], grand total.

3. all, the whole, the entirety, everything, aggregate, assemblage, one and all, all and sundry, each and every [coll.], the devil and all [coll.], altogether, **ensemble,** *tout ensemble* [F.]; **be-all,** be-all and end-all, beginning and end, alpha and omega, length and breadth; lock, stock and barrel.

4. (slang terms) **whole boodle** *or* **caboodle,** the boodle, the caboodle, **whole kit** *or* **kit and caboodle,** the kit and caboodle, whole jimbang *or* jingbang, **whole shoot** *or* **shooting match,** the shooting match, whole boiling, **whole smear,** the shebang, **whole shebang,** whole business *or* works, the business, the works, whole toot and scramble *or* stumble, whole show, whole squeeze.

5. (main part) **best part,** better part, most; **majority,** generality; **bulk,** heft [coll., U.S.], **mass,** lump, gross, tissue, staple, body, main body; **lion's share,** Benjamin's mess, big *or* long end [slang].

VERBS **6. form a whole,** constitute a whole; **integrate,** embody, amass.

7. total, tottle [dial.], **amount to, come to, run to** *or* **into,** mount up to, **add up to,** tot *or* tot up to [coll.], tote *or* tote up to [coll.], reckon up to [coll.], pile up to, aggregate [coll.]; number, comprise, contain.

ADJS. **8.** (not partial) **whole, total,** teetotal *or* T-total (coll.], **entire,** aggregate, gross, all; integral, integrate; **one,** one and indivisible.

9. intact, undamaged 675.7, 8.

10. undivided, uncut, unsevered, unclipped, uncropped, unshorn; **undiminished,** unreduced.

11. unabridged, uncondensed.

ADVS. **12.** (not partially) **wholly,** entirely, all; **totally,** *in toto* [L.]; **altogether, all put together,** in its entirety; **in all,** on all counts, at large; **as a whole, in the aggregate,** in the lump, in the gross, in bulk, in the mass, *en masse* [F.], *en bloc* [F., in the block], by wholesale; collectively, bodily, in a body.

13. on the whole, in the long run, all in all, to all intents and purposes, **by and large,** in all respects; **in the main,** mainly, mostly, chiefly, substantially, effectually, **for the most part.**

14. for all, for all in all.

55. PART

NOUNS **1. part, portion, fraction, division,** parcel [law], dole [dial., Eng.], ward, sector, **segment, section,** cantle, cantlet, moiety, tithe; **fragment,** shard; **item,** detail, particular; installment; **subdivision,** detachment, contingent; cross section; **component** 58.2.

2. (part of writing) section, chapter, verse, article, clause, phrase, paragraph, passage, number, book, fascicle; serial, *livraison* [F.].

3. piece, particle, bit, item [coll.], **scrap,** morsel, **crumb,** canch [dial.], snatch, snack, whack [slang], cut, cutting, clip, clipping, paring, shaving, rasher, snip, chip, slice, collop, scale, jag [dial., U.S.]; **tatter, shred,** stitch; **splinter,** sliver; **flinder,** flitter [coll.], fritter; **shiver,** shivereen [Scot. & North Eng.], **smither** [coll.], **smithereen** [coll.]; **lump,** gob [coll.], hunch, hank [dial.], **hunk,** whang [Scot. & dial.]; **stump,** butt, end.

4. member, organ; limb, branch, bough, twig, sprig, spray, switch; runner, tendril, sarmentum; **offshoot,** ramification, scion, spur; **arm, leg; wing,** pinion; lobe, lobule; joint, link.

5. dose, go [coll.], slug [slang], rare [slang, U.S.]; homeopathic dose [coll.].

ADJS. **6. partial,** part; **fractional,** sectional; segmentary, segmental; **fragmentary,** scrappy, snippy; aliquot [math.]; multifid.

ADVS. **7. partly, partially,** part, **in part.**

8. piecemeal, inchmeal, by inchmeal; **piece by piece, bit by bit,** part by part, **little by little,** inch by inch, foot by foot, drop by drop; **by degrees,** by inches; **by** *or* **in snatches,** by *or* in installments, in lots, in small doses, in driblets, dribs-like [dial. & slang]; in detail.

56. COMPLETENESS

NOUNS 1. **completeness, wholeness, entireness, entirety, totality; unity, integrity;** solidity, solidarity; **thoroughness,** exhaustiveness, comprehensiveness, universality.

2. **fullness, full; amplitude, plenitude;** impletion, **repletion,** plethora [med.]; saturation, congestion; overfullness 661.3; high water, high tide, flood tide, springtide.

3. **fill,** full [coll.], **full measure,** "good measure, pressed down, and shaken together, and running over" (Bible); **load,** lading, **charge,** jag [chiefly dial.], lug [coll.]; bumper, brimmer; bellyful [vulgar], skinful [coll.], mouthful (in *say a mouthful;* slang); **crush,** cram [coll.], jam-up [slang].

4. **consummation, limit,** frozen limit [slang], **extremity,** extreme, **acme,** apogee, climax, **maximum,** optimum, ceiling; **utmost,** uttermost, utmost extent, highest degree, the nines [coll.], the nth [coll.], nth degree or power, *ne plus ultra* [L., no more beyond]; the outside; the whole length or way, the whole figure [coll.], the whole hog [slang], whole hog or none [slang], all or nothing; all creation, all forty, all get out [all slang].

5. **complement, supplement,** makeweight; supplementation.

VERBS 6. (make whole) **complete,** fulfill; **complement, supplement,** fill in, **fill out,** piece out, eke out, round out; **make up,** make good; replenish, refill.

7. **fill, charge, load,** lade, freight, weight; pile, heap; **stuff, wad,** pad, **pack,** crowd, **cram,** jam, jam-pack, ram in, chock, chuck full [dial.]; **fill up,** fill to the brim, brim, fill to overflowing, fill the measure of, capacitate [coll.]; supercharge, saturate; congest; overfill 661.16.

8. (be thorough) **go all lengths, go all out, go the limit** [coll.], go the whole way, **go the whole hog** [slang], go the whole figure [slang]; **see it through** [coll.], follow out or up, follow or prosecute to a conclusion; leave nothing undone, not overlook a bet [coll.]; **move heaven and earth, leave no stone unturned.**

ADJS. 9. **complete, whole, entire, solid;** all-sided, well-rounded.

10. **thorough, thoroughgoing,** thorough-paced, exhaustive, intensive, comprehensive, radical, sweeping; **unmitigated, unqualified,** unconditional, unrestricted, unreserved, all-out, total (as *total* or *all-out* war), whole-hog [slang]; **out-and-out,** **through-and-through,** outright, downright, straight, straight-out [coll., U.S.]; **consummate,** perfect [chiefly coll.], precious [chiefly coll.]; deep-dyed, dyed-in-the-wool [U.S.].

11. **utter, absolute, total; sheer,** clear, clean, **pure,** plumb [chiefly coll.], **plain,** regular [coll.], veritable, dead, blue [slang].

12. **full,** filled, **replete,** ample, good, plump, plenary, pleny [naut.], pregnant, flush, round (as, a *round* sum); **brimful, brimming, chuck-full,** chuck-full, chokefull, chug-full [dial.], chock or chuck [coll.], **cram-full,** topfull; **jam-full,** cramp-full, cram-jam-full, **jam-packed,** pack-jammed, jam-up, full-up [all slang]; **stuffed, packed, crammed;** bursting, ready to burst, fit to bust [slang]; **as full as a tick,** as full as a vetch, as full as an egg is of meat, packed like sardines or herrings; replete with, crawling or oozing with; saturated, capacitated [coll.]; congested; overfull 661.21.

13. **fraught, laden, loaded, charged;** heavy-laden; full-laden, full-fraught, full-charged, supercharged.

14. **completing,** filling, fulfilling; completive, completory; **complementary,** complemental; **supplementary,** supplemental; adscititious, ascititious, adventitious.

ADVS. 15. **completely, entirely, wholly, fully,** roundly, **altogether,** all over [coll.], outright, *tout à fait* [F.]; **thoroughly,** inside out [coll.]; in full, in full measure.

16. **absolutely, perfectly, totally;** quite, right, stark, stock [coll.], fair [dial.], clean, sheer, plumb [chiefly coll., U.S.], plain or just plain [dial. & coll.].

17. **utterly, to the utmost,** *à outrance* [F.], *à toute outrance* [F.], **to the full, to the limit,** to the backbone, to or up to the nines [coll.], to the nth [coll.], to the nth degree or power, to the sky or skies, to the top of one's bent, for all there is in it [coll.], for fair [slang], **to a fare-you-well** or fare-ye-well [coll.], as far as possible, *a más no poder* [Sp.], out of sight [slang, U.S.], as ... as can be, than which there is no whicher [slang]; with a vengeance, with a witness [coll.]; hollow, all hollow [both coll.].

18. **throughout, all out, clear out, over, all over,** over all, **inside and out, through and through,** through thick and thin, down to the ground [coll.], **from the ground up,** from the word go [coll.], **to the end,** to the end of the chapter, throughout the length and breadth of, at full length, *in extenso* [L.]; every inch, every whit, every bit; root

and branch, head and shoulders, neck and
heels *or* crop [coll.], hide and hair, body
and breeches [slang], heart and soul; up to
the brim, up to the crop, up to the hilt, up
to the handle [coll., U.S.], up to the
knocker [slang], up to the hub [U.S.], up to
the ears, up to the eyes, over head and ears;
in every respect, in all respects, *sous tous
les rapports* [F.], **on all counts,** at all
points, for good and all; lock, stock and
barrel [coll.].

19. **from beginning to end,** from end
to end, **from first to last, from A to Z,** from
A to Izzard [slang], from out to out, **from
here out** [coll.], from Dan to Beersheba,
from hell to breakfast [slang, U.S.], from
cover to cover; **from top to bottom,** *de fond
en comble* [F.]; from top to toe, **from head
to foot,** *a capite ad calcem* [L.], cap-a-pie;
from stem to stern, from clew to earing,
fore and aft; from soup to nuts [slang], *ab
ovo usque ad mala* [L., from egg to apples].

57. INCOMPLETENESS

NOUNS 1. **incompleteness,** incompletion;
deficiency, inadequacy, scant sufficiency
[coll.]; sketchiness, patchiness; short measure *or* weight, half-weight.

2. (part wanting) **deficiency, want, lack,
need, deficit,** defect, **shortage,** short [coll.],
wantage, ullage; defalcation, **omission;**
missing link.

VERBS 3. fall short 312.2.

ADJS. 4. **incomplete, deficient,** defective,
inadequate; wanting, lacking, needing,
failing; in default, in arrear *or* arrears; short,
in short supply; short of, shy *or* shy on
[slang]; sketchy, patchy; half-and-half.

5. **mutilated,** garbled, hashed, **mangled,
butchered,** docked, lopped, truncated, cut
short.

ADVS. 6. **incompletely,** by halves, by *or*
in half measures, with divided effort.

58. COMPOSITION

Manner of Being Composed.—NOUNS
1. **composition, constitution, construction, formation,** organization, consist; embodiment, incorporation; make, **make-up,**
getup [coll.], setup [coll.]; synthesis, synizesis, synaeresis.

2. **component, constituent, ingredient,**
integrant, **element, factor, part** 55, part
and parcel; leaven; appurtenance, adjunct;
feature, aspect; contents, makings [coll.],
fixings [coll., U.S.].

VERBS 3. **compose, constitute,** incorporate, embody, **form, enter into,** go into,
make, **make up, consist of,** be a feature of,
form a part of, combine *or* unite in, merge
in.

ADJS. 4. **composed of,** formed of, **made
of,** made up of, compact of, consisting of,
contained in, embodied in.

5. **component, constituent,** integrant,
integral.

59. ORDER

NOUNS 1. **order, arrangement, disposition,** disposal, formation, array, line-up,
setup, layout; **system, method;** routine,
even tenor; **regularity,** uniformity, symmetry, **harmony;** "the eternal fitness of
things" [Samuel Clark], "the foundation
of all good things" [Edmund Burke],
"Heav'n's first law" [Pope], the music of
the spheres.

2. sequence 65.

3. **orderliness, trimness, tidiness, neatness;** good shape [coll.], good condition,
fine fettle, fine fig [coll.], fine whack [slang],
apple-pie order [coll.], "a place for everything and everything in its place" [Samuel
Smiles].

VERBS 4. **form, take form,** take order,
take shape, crystallize, **shape up;** arrange
or range itself, place itself, take its place,
fall in, **fall into place,** fall into line, fall
into rank, take rank; come together, draw
up, gather around, rally round.

5. put in order 60.7.

ADJS. 6. **orderly, regular, well-regulated, well-ordered, methodic(al),** formal,
uniform, **systematic,** symmetrical, **harmonious,** businesslike; normal, habitual,
usual, *en règle* [F., according to rule]; **arranged** 60.13.

7. **in order, in trim,** to rights [coll.], in
apple-pie order [coll.]; **in condition,** in
good condition, in kilter *or* kelter [coll. &
dial.], in whack *or* fine whack [slang], **in
shape,** in good shape [coll.], **in good form,
in fine fettle,** in fine fig [coll.], in the pink
[coll.], in the pink of condition; **in repair,**
in commission [coll.], in adjustment, in
working order, fixed; up to scratch, up to
snuff [both slang].

8. **trim, tidy, neat,** spruce, sleek, jimp
[Scot. & dial., Eng.], trig [dial.], smug, snug,
tight [dial.], **shipshape; well-kept,** well-
cared-for, well-groomed; neat as a bandbox
or pin [coll.], like a cat in pattens.

ADVS. 9. **methodically, systematically,**

regularly, uniformly, harmoniously, like clockwork.

10. **in order, in turn, in sequence, in succession,** in series, *seriatim* [L.]; step by step, by stages.

60. ARRANGEMENT

Reduction to Order.—NOUNS 1. **arrangement, ordering,** "confusion unconfused" [Young]; **disposition, disposal,** disposure; **distribution,** collocation, allocation, allotment, apportionment; formation, form, lay, array; regimentation; taxis [tech.], syntaxis; order 59.

2. **organization, methodization,** regulation, **adjustment,** harmonization, **systematization,** ordination, co-ordination; **grouping,** groupage; classification 61.

3. **sorting,** assortment; **sifting, screening.**

4. **sorter,** sifter, **sieve,** riddle, **screen,** bolter, colander, grate, grating.

5. (act of making neat) **cleanup,** red-up [dial.]; tidy-up, trim-up, police-up, muck-up [all slang].

6. **rearrangement, reorganization,** readjustment.

VERBS 7. **arrange,** order, reduce to order, **put** *or* **set in order,** right, **put** *or* **set to rights,** put in *or* into shape, whip into shape.

8. **dispose, distribute, fix, place,** set out, collocate, allocate, **compose,** space, **marshal,** rally, array, size, **group;** align, line, **line up,** rank, range; regiment, brigade, echelon; **allot, apportion,** parcel out, deal, **deal out,** cast *or* assign the parts.

9. **organize,** methodize, **systematize, harmonize,** regulate, adjust, co-ordinate, fix, settle; classify 61.6.

10. **sort,** assort; **separate,** divide; **sift,** sieve, **screen,** bolt, riddle.

11. tidy, **tidy up,** neat, neaten, trim, **put in trim,** trim up, trig up [chiefly dial.], **straighten up,** fix up [coll.], do up [chiefly coll.], **clean up,** police *or* police up [coll.], fettle *or* fettle up [dial.], groom, spruce *or* spruce up [coll.], pick up [U.S.], **clear up,** clear the decks.

12. **rearrange, reorganize,** readjust.

ADJS. 13. **arranged, ordered, disposed,** composed, fixed, placed, aligned, ranged, grouped, ranked, graded; **organized,** methodized, **systematized,** regulated; sorted, assorted; orderly 59.6.

14. **organizational,** formational.

61. CLASSIFICATION

NOUNS 1. **classification,** analysis, **categorization,** placement, **pigeonholing,** sorting, **grouping,** ranking, rating, **grading;** division, subdivision; **cataloguing,** codification, digestion; taxonomy, biotaxy [biol.]; organization 60.2.

2. **class, category, head, order, division,** branch, set, **group,** grouping, bracket, pigeonhole; **grade,** rank, rating, status, estate; predicament [logic]; caste; sept; **subdivision,** subgroup, suborder.

3. **kind, sort, ilk, type,** tap [chiefly coll.], lot [coll.], **variety, species, genus,** *genre* [F.], denomination, designation, number [coll.], description, style, manner, **nature, character,** persuasion, the like *or* likes of [coll.]; **stamp, brand,** feather, color, stripe [usu. derog.], grain, kidney; **make,** cast, form, mold; tribe, breed.

4. **kingdom,** animal kingdom, vegetable kingdom, mineral kingdom.

5. (botanical and zoological classifications, in descending order) **kingdom;** subkingdom, **phylum** [zool.], branch [bot.]; superclass, **class,** subclass, superorder, **order,** suborder, superfamily, **family,** subfamily, tribe, subtribe, **genus,** subgenus, series, section, superspecies, **species;** subspecies, **variety.**

VERBS 6. **classify,** class; **categorize, pigeonhole,** place, **group,** rank, rate, **grade; sort,** assort; **divide,** subdivide, break down; **catalogue,** list, file, tabulate, index, alphabetize, digest, codify; organize 60.9.

ADJS. 7. **classificational,** classific, classificatory; **categoric(al),** taxonomic(al), ordinal; divisional, divisionary, divisive; subdivisional, subdivisive; sectary, sectarian, sectarial; denominational, denominative; sortal, sorty; typic(al), typal; special, specific.

8. **classified, catalogued, pigeonholed,** sorted, assorted, **graded, grouped,** placed; filed, on file; tabular, tabulate.

ADVS. 9. of any kind *or* sort, **of any description, at all,** whatever, soever, whatsoever.

62. DISORDER

NOUNS 1. **disorder, disorderliness, disarrangement,** derangement, **disorganization, discomposure, dishevelment, disarray;** topsy-turvy, topsy-turvydom; **irregularity,** ununiformity, unsymmetry, disharmony; promiscuity, promiscuousness, haphazardness, "fortuitous concourse of atoms" [Cicero]; "most admired disorder" [Shakespeare], "inharmonious harmony" [Horace].

2. confusion, chaos, anarchy; **muddle, mix-up** [coll.], foul-up [coll.], snafu [slang], hassle [slang], ruffle; pretty kettle of fish, pretty piece of business, nice piece of work.

3. jumble, scramble, tumble, huddle, **mess,** holy mess [slang], muss [coll., U.S.], mix [coll.], mux [dial.], mash, mishmash, hash, farrago, higgledy-piggledy, **clutter,** litter, lumber, rummage [chiefly dial.], omnium-gatherum [coll.], hurrah's nest [coll., U.S.], kettle of fish, what the cat brought in [coll., U.S.], "rough and disorderly mass" [Ovid]; hodgepodge 44.6

4. commotion, hubbub, tumult, turmoil, **uproar, racket,** riot, **disturbance, rumpus** [coll.], ruckus [dial. & slang], ruction [chiefly dial.], **fracas,** fraction [dial.], shindy [slang], shine [slang], rampage, randan or rantan [slang], razzle-dazzle [slang], **ado,** to-do [coll.], trouble, bother, pother, pudder [dial.], callithump [U.S.], hoopla [slang], bluster, stour [dial.], stir [coll.], breeze [coll.], squall [coll.], dust [slang], **fuss,** foofaraw, [orig. dial.], touse [chiefly dial.], **row** [coll.], rowdydow [coll.], brawl, broil, embroilment, melee, scramble; helter-skelter, pell-mell, spill and pelt; **roughhouse, rough-and-tumble.**

5. pandemonium, "confusion worse confounded" [Milton], **hell** or **Bedlam broke loose;** Babel, confusion of tongues; bear garden, saturnalia, Donnybrook Fair; bull in a china shop.

6. slovenry, slipshodness, carelessness, negligence; **untidiness,** unneatness, messiness [coll.], **sloppiness, dowdiness,** slouchiness [coll.], seediness, **shabbiness,** shoddiness, grubbiness [coll.], frowsiness, blowziness; **slatterliness,** frumpishness, sluttishness; **squalor,** squalidness, sordidness.

7. slattern, sloven, slob [coll.], **frump** [coll.], drab, dowdy, slubberer [chiefly dial.], slubberdegullion [dial.], drabbletail, draggletail, slammock or slummock [dial.], malkin [dial., Eng.], **slut, trollop,** traipse [dial.], bitch, alley cat [slang]; **pig,** swine, hog [all coll.]; litterbug [slang].

VERBS **8. create a disturbance, make a commotion,** make trouble, **make an ado** or **to-do** [coll.], raise a rumpus [coll.], raise a storm [coll.], create a riot, **cut loose,** run wild, **run riot,** run amuck, go on a rampage.

9. (slang terms) **kick up a row,** kick up a shindy, kick up or raise a dust, raise a breeze or squall, **raise the devil,** raise the deuce or dickens, raise Cain or Ned, **raise hell,** raise Hail Columbia, raise sand, **cut a shine,** raise the roof, whoop it or her up, hell around, tear up jack, go on the randan or rantan; **carry on,** go on; **cut up,** cut up rough, roughhouse.

10. disarrange 63.2.

ADJS. **11. orderless,** unordered, **unorganized, unarranged; unmethodical,** immethodical, informal; **unsystematic,** systemless, nonsystematic; **irregular, haphazard,** desultory, fitful, promiscuous, indiscriminate, casual, random, undirected, aimless, straggling, straggly.

12. disorderly, in disorder, disordered, **disorganized, disarranged, discomposed,** dislocated, deranged; **out of order,** out of place, out of sorts, **out of kilter** or **kelter** [coll.], **out of whack** [slang], out of gear, out of joint, out of tune; **awry,** amiss, askew, sky-west and crooked [slang, U.S.].

13. disheveled, mussed up [coll.], messed up [coll.], **rumpled,** ruffled; **tousled,** tously, tousy [coll. or dial.]; uncombed, shaggy, matted.

14. slovenly, slipshod, careless, negligent; **untidy, unneat, unkempt; messy** [coll.], mussy [coll., U.S.], **sloppy** [coll.], **dowdy,** slouchy [coll.], poky, seedy [coll.], **shabby,** shoddy, grubby [coll.], **frowzy, blowzy,** tacky [coll.], clatty [dial.], clatchy [dial.]; **slatternly,** slammocky or slummocky [dial.], **frumpish,** frumpy, sluttish; draggletailed, drabbletailed, draggled, bedraggled; down at the heel or heels, out at the heels, out at the elbows, in rags; **squalid,** sordid.

15. confused, chaotic, mommixed [dial.], **muddled, jumbled,** scattered, helter-skelter [coll.], higgledy-piggledy, huggermugger, ramble-scramble [slang], in a mess; **topsy-turvy,** upside-down; anyhow, all anyhow; **mixed up, balled up** [slang], screwed up [slang], **fouled-up** [slang], snafu [slang, U.S.], **haywire** [slang].

ADVS. **16. in disorder, in disarray, in confusion,** in a jumble, in a tumble, in a muddle, in a mess; **higgledy-piggledy,** helter-skelter [coll.], huggermugger, ramble-scramble [slang], harum-scarum [coll.], willy-nilly [coll.], all anyhow [coll.], which way or every which way [coll., U.S.]; all over, all over hell [slang], **all over the place, all over the shop** [coll.].

17. haphazardly, irregularly, desultorily, promiscuously, indiscriminately, aimlessly, randomly, fitfully; by or at intervals, by fits, by fits and starts, by or in snatches, in spots [coll.]; every now and then, every once in a while [both coll.]; at random, at haphazard, by chance, hit or miss.

63. DISARRANGEMENT

Bringing into Disorder.—NOUNS 1. disarrangement, derangement, misarrangement; disorganization, deorganization; discomposure, disturbance, perturbation; disorder 62.

VERBS 2. disarrange, derange, misarrange; disorder, disorganize, disarray, dishevel, rumple, ruffle; tousle [coll.], touse [dial.]; muss or muss up [coll., U.S.], mess or mess up [coll.], mux or mux up [dial.]; litter, clutter, scatter.

3. confuse, muddle, jumble, tumble, huddle, hustle, fumble, pie, mommick or mommix [dial.]; shuffle, riffle; mix up, snarl up, ball up [slang], foul up [slang], snafu [slang, U.S.]; make a hash or mess of it [slang], play horse with [slang, U.S.].

4. discompose, throw into confusion, upset, unsettle, disturb, perturb, trouble, agitate, toss, convulse, embroil.

ADJS. 5. disarranged 62.12.

64. PRECEDENCE

In Order.—NOUNS 1. precedence, antecedence, anteposition, anteriority; the lead, le pas [F.]; priority, preference; top priority.

VERBS 2. precede, antecede, come first, come or go before, go ahead of, go in advance, stand first, stand at the head, head, head up [slang], front, lead, take the lead, take precedence, have the pas [F.]; rank, outrank.

3. (place before) prefix, preface, premise, prelude, prologize, preamble, introduce.

ADJS. 4. preceding, precedent, prior, antecedent, anterior; preliminary, precursory, prevenient, prefatory, exordial, prelusive, preludial, proemial, preparatory, inaugural.

5. former, foregoing, afore-going; aforesaid, afore-mentioned, before-mentioned, above-mentioned, aforenamed, aforesighted, aforethought, forenamed, forementioned, said, named, same.

ADVS. 6. before 239.13; hereinbefore, hereinabove.

65. SEQUENCE

NOUNS 1. sequence, succession, successiveness, consecution, consecutiveness, following, coming after; order, order of succession; progression, procession, rotation; continuation, prolongation, extension.

2. series 71.2.

VERBS 3. come or go after, come next, come on, succeed, follow, ensue.

4. (place after) suffix, append, subjoin.

ADJS. 5. succeeding, successive, following, ensuing, sequent, sequential, sequacious, subsequent, consequent, proximate, next; appendant, appendent.

66. PRECURSOR

NOUNS 1. precursor, forerunner, foregoer, voorlooper [Du.], forelooper [South Africa], avant-courier; pioneer, voortrekker [Du.], frontiersman, bushwhacker; scout, scouter; leader 746.5; herald, messenger, harbinger; predecessor, precedent, antecedent, ancestor.

2. prelude, preamble, preface, prologue, foreword, introduction, avant-propos [F.], protasis, proem, proemium, prolegomenon, exordium; prefix, prefixture; frontispiece; preliminary, prelim [slang. U.S.]; overture, voluntary, ritornel, ritornello [It.], descant; premise, presupposition, postulate, prolepsis.

67. SEQUEL

NOUNS 1. sequel, sequela, sequelant, sequent, sequitur; continuation, continuance, follow-up [coll.]; supplement, addendum, appendix; postfix, suffix; postscript, P.S., subscript, postface, postlude, epilogue, conclusion, peroration, codicil, colophon, tag, more last words; afterthought, second thought, arrière-pensée [F.].

2. afterpart, afterpiece, aftercome [Scot.]; wake, trail, train, queue; tail, tailpiece; tab, tag.

3. aftermath, afterclap, afterglow, aftertaste; aftergrowth, aftercrop, aftergrass, rowen; arrish, eddish [both dial., Eng.]; afterbirth, placenta, secundines; afterpain.

68. BEGINNING

NOUNS 1. beginning, commencement, start, starting point, outstart, outset, setout; onset, oncoming; dawn; opening, rising of the curtain; first beginning, first rattle out of the box, go-off, first go-off, kick-off, jump-off, send-off, start-off, take-off [all coll.]; fresh start, new departure.

2. **first, prime, initial, alpha; initiative,** first move, **first step,** le premier pas [F.], first stage; first blush, first glance, first sight, first impression.

3. **origin,** origination, **genesis, inception,** incipience or incipiency, inchoation; **birth,** nascency, nativity; **infancy,** incunabula, beginnings, cradle.

4. **inauguration,** installation, installment, **institution, introduction,** initiation; embarkment, **launching,** floating, flotation, unveiling [coll.]; debut, coming out [coll.]; opener [coll.], curtain raiser or lifter; maiden speech, inaugural address.

5. **rudiments, elements, principles,** principia, outlines, grammar, alphabet, A B C's; first principles, first steps.

VERBS 6. **begin, commence, start; start in, start off, start out, set out,** set in, set to or about, get to, **turn to,** fall to, pitch in [coll.], dig in [slang], strike in, dive in [slang], plunge into, head in [slang], **go ahead,** fire away [coll.], take off [coll.], jump off [slang], kick off [slang, U.S.], hit the ball [slang, U.S.], get the show on the road [slang]; take up (as school).

7. **make a beginning,** make a move [coll.], **start up,** get going [coll.], get off, **get under way,** get in there [slang]; get leveled off [slang], **get squared away** [coll.]; make an auspicious beginning, auspicate, **get off to a good start,** get in on the ground floor [coll.].

8. enter, **enter on** or **upon, embark in,** take up, go into; make one's debut, come out [coll.].

9. **initiate, originate,** inchoate, induct, handsel; **take the initiative, take the first step,** take the lead, pioneer, **lead,** lead off, lead the way; **head,** head up [coll.], stand at the head, stand first; **break the ice,** break ground, cut the first turf, lay the first stone.

10. **inaugurate, institute, install, introduce,** broach; **launch,** float; christen [coll.]; **usher in,** ring in [coll.]; set up, **set on foot,** set abroach, set agoing, start up, start going, start the ball rolling [coll.].

11. **open,** open up, open the ball [slang], open the door to; open fire, apply the match to a train.

12. **originate, take origin,** be born, take birth, come into the world, **become,** come to be, get to be, see the light of day, rise, **arise,** take rise, take its rise, **come forth,**

issue forth, come out, spring or crop up; burst forth, break out.

ADJS. 13. **beginning, initial,** initiatory, initiative; **incipient, introductory,** inchoate; inaugural, inauguratory; prime, primal, **primary,** primitive; primogenial, primigenial; **original,** aboriginal; **elementary,** elemental; rudimentary, rudimental, abecedarian; embryonic, in embryo, in the bud, in its infancy; infant, infantile, incunabular.

14. **natal,** nascent; prenatal, antenatal; postnatal.

15. **first, foremost,** front, **head, chief, principal,** premier, **leading, main;** maiden.

ADVS. 16. **first,** firstly, at first, first off, first thing, **in the first place,** first and foremost, before everything; **principally,** mainly, chiefly; **primarily,** initially; **in the beginning,** in limine [L.], **at the start,** at the first go-off [coll.], at the drop of the hat or handkerchief [coll.]; from the beginning, **from the word go** [coll.], ab origine [L.], ab initio [L.]; ab ovo [L.].

69. MIDDLE

NOUNS 1. **middle,** middlement [dial.], median, **midmost, midst;** thick; **center** 225.2; interior 224.2; midriff, diaphragm; waist, waistline; equator; diameter.

2. **mid-distance,** middle distance; **equidistance;** halfway point or place, halfway house; bisection.

VERBS 3. middle, bisect; double, fold.

ADJS. 4. **middle, medial,** median, mesial, **middling** [dial.], medium, mezzo [music], mean, mid; **midmost,** middlemost; **central** 225.12; **intermediate,** intermediary; equidistant; equatorial; midland, mediterranean; midship, amidship.

ADVS. 5. **midway, halfway, in the middle,** halfway in the middle [coll.]; plump-, smack-, slap-, slab-dab or smack-dab in the middle [all slang]; medially, mediumly; in the mean, in medias res [L.]; **in the midst of,** in the thick of; midships, amidships.

70. END

NOUNS 1. **end,** ending, **termination, terminus, terminal,** term, period, apodosis, **expiration,** expiry, consummation, culmination, **conclusion, finish, finis, finale,** finality, stoppage, windup [coll.], blowoff [slang, U.S.], payoff [slang, U.S.], thirty [teleg. & slang], fall of the curtain, end of the book or chapter [coll.], end of the line [slang]; **last,** what the shoemaker threw at his wife [slang]; omega, izzard [slang], Z;

goal, destination; denouement, catastrophe; fate, destiny, doom.

2. extremity, extreme; limit, frozen limit [slang]; **tip,** point, nib, neb; tail, **tail end,** butt end, tag, tag end [coll.], fag end; bitter end; stub, butt; bottom dollar [coll.].

3. close, closing; cessation 144; decline, lapse; **homestretch, last lap** [coll.], last stage; beginning of the end, *commencement de la fin* [F.].

4. finishing stroke, ender, **end-all, quietus,** stopper, **deathblow,** death stroke, *coup de grâce* [F.]; **finisher,** clincher, **settler,** flattener, graveler, knockout or knockout blow [all coll.]; K.O. or kayo, kayo punch, sockdolager [U.S.], cincher, clapper, corker, capper, calker [all slang].

VERBS **5. end, terminate,** determine, **close, finish, conclude,** over [dial. & slang], finish up, wind up [coll.]; **stop, cease** 144.6, 11.

6. come to an end, draw to a close, expire, lapse [Law], become void, run out, run its course, pass, **pass away,** die away, wear off or away, go out, blow over, be all over, be no more.

7. put an end to, put a period to, **make an end of,** bring to an end, end off [dial.]; **get it over,** get through with; drop or ring down the curtain, ring down on [coll.]; put the lid on, put the clip on, fold up, wash up [all slang]; call off [coll.], call all bets off [slang]; **dispose of,** polish off [slang]; kibosh, put the kibosh on [both slang]; **give the quietus,** put the finisher or settler on [slang], knock on or in the head, knock out [coll.].

ADJS. **8. ended, at an end, terminated, concluded, finished,** fini [slang], settled, decided, set at rest; **over, all over,** all up or U.P. [slang]; all off [coll.], all bets off [slang]; **done,** done with, through or through with [coll.]; wound up [coll.], washed up [slang]; all over but the shouting [coll.].

9. ending, closing, concluding, finishing, terminating, crowning.

10. final, terminal, terminational, terminative, determinative, definitive, **conclusive; last,** eventual, farthest, extreme, **endmost,** ultimate; caudal; penultimate, last but one.

ADVS. **11. finally,** in fine; **ultimately, eventually; lastly, last, at last,** at the last, at length, at long last; in conclusion; **conclusively,** once for all.

12. to the end, to the bitter end, to the last extremity, **to a finish,** *à outrance* [F.], to the end of the chapter, through thick and thin, until the last cat is hung [slang].

PHRS. **13. that's final, that's that,** and that goes [slang], that's the end of the matter, so much for that, enough said; the subject is closed, the matter is ended, the deal is off [slang], the proposition is cold [slang].

71. CONTINUITY

Uninterrupted Sequence.—NOUNS **1. continuity, uninterruption, uninterruptedness,** unintermittedness, unbrokenness; **consecutiveness,** successiveness; continuousness, **endlessness, ceaselessness,** incessancy; constancy, constant flow 135.2; continuum.

2. series, succession, run, sequence, consecution, progression, course, gradation; connection, nexus; **train,** range, rank, **file, line, string,** thread, queue, **row,** bank, tier; windrow, swath; single file, Indian file; array; round, cycle; gamut, scale.

3. concatenation, catenation, **chain,** catena; concatenation of circumstances, chain reaction.

4. procession, train, column, line, string, cortege; cavalcade, caravan, motorcade [U.S.]; parade, pomp; dress parade; promenade, review, march past; funeral; skimmington, skimmington ride [both Eng.]; pack train [U.S.].

VERBS **5. connect up,** catenate; **string together,** string, thread.

6. line, align, line up, string out, rank, range; row, bank.

7. get in line, line up, form a line, get in formation, **fall in,** fall in or into line, fall into rank, take rank, take one's place; queue, **queue up.**

8. file, defile, file off; **parade,** go on parade, promenade, march past.

ADJS. **9. continuous,** continued, **continual,** continuing; **uninterrupted, unintermittent,** unintermitted, connected, **unbroken,** unstopped; unintermitting, unremitting; **incessant, constant, ceaseless,** unceasing, **endless,** unending, never-ending, **interminable,** perennial; straight, running, **nonstop; round-the-clock,** twentyfour-hour; immediate, direct.

10. consecutive, successive, successional, progressive; **serial,** ordinal; sequent, **sequential;** linear, lineal.

ADVS. **11. continuously, continually; un-interruptedly, unintermittently; without** cease, without stopping, without a break, together (as *for days together*), on end; **incessantly, constantly, ceaselessly,** unceasingly, **endlessly,** perennially, **interminably,** on and on, at or on a stretch; round the clock.

12. **consecutively, progressively,** sequentially, **successively, in succession,** one after the other, **in turn,** turn about, turn and turn about; step by step; running, hand running [coll.]; **serially,** in a series, *seriatim* [L.]; **in a line,** in a row, in column, in file; in single file, in Indian file.

72. DISCONTINUITY

Interrupted Sequence.—NOUNS 1. **discontinuity,** discontinuousness, noncontinuance; **disconnectedness,** disconnection; **intermittence,** fitfulness 138.1; episode, parenthesis; broken thread.

2. **interruption, suspension, break,** breach, caesura; **interval, pause,** letup [coll.], **intermission.**

VERBS 3. **discontinue, interrupt** 144.6, 10.

ADJS. 4. **discontinuous,** noncontinuous, unsuccessive, discontinued, **disconnected,** unconnected, *décousu* [F.], **broken;** broken off, **interrupted,** suspended; disjunctive, discrete, discretive; **intermittent, fitful** 138.3; scrappy, snatchy, spotty; choppy, chopped-off.

ADVS. 5. **discontinuously, disconnectedly,** brokenly; at intervals, *longo intervallo* [L.]; **by fits and starts,** by fits, by snatches, by catches, by jerks, by skips, skippingly, *per saltum* [L., by a leap]; willy-nilly, **here and there, in spots; intermittently, fitfully** 138.4.

73. ACCOMPANIMENT

NOUNS 1. **accompaniment,** concomitance or concomitancy, coefficiency.

2. **company, association,** consociation, **society; companionship, fellowship,** consortship, partnership.

3. **attendant,** concomitant, **accessory,** appendage; obbligato; coefficient.

4. **accompanier, accompanist,** accompanyist; **attendant, companion, fellow, mate,** co-mate, consort, **partner;** companion piece.

5. **escort, conductor, usher,** shepherd; **squire, esquire,** cavalier; **chaperon,** duenna, gooseberry [slang], third person; **bodyguard,** burkundaz [India], safe-conduct, **convoy.**

6. **attendance, following,** cortege, ret-

inue, **entourage,** suite, rout, train, trail, body of retainers; court.

VERBS 7. **accompany,** bear one company, **keep company with,** companion, companionize [coll.], go with, **go along with, attend,** wait on or upon; **associate with,** assort with, sort with, **consort with,** couple with, hang around with [coll.], go hand in hand with, row in the same boat; flock together, herd together, hunt or run in couples.

8. **escort, conduct,** marshal, **usher,** shepherd, **guide, lead; convoy; squire,** esquire, **attend,** wait on or upon [coll.], **take out,** carry [dial.], tote [coll., U.S.]; hustle [U.S.], chase [U.S.], drag [U.S.], flame [all slang]; **chaperon,** play gooseberry [slang].

ADJS. 9. **accompanying, attending, attendant,** concomitant, accessory, collateral, obbligato [chiefly mus.], associated or coupled with; **fellow, twin, joint,** conjoint, mutual.

ADVS. etc. 10. **in company with, with,** along [U.S.], **along with, together with,** coupled with, in conjunction with; hand in hand or glove, arm in arm, **side by side,** cheek by jowl, shoulder to shoulder; therewith, therewithal, herewith.

11. **together, collectively,** mutually, in conjunction, en masse, **in a body,** all at once, ensemble.

74. ASSEMBLAGE

NOUNS 1. **assemblage, assembly, collection, gathering,** ingathering, **congregation;** concourse, conflux, confluence; mobilization, muster, *attroupement* [F.]; roundup, rodeo [both West. U.S.]; reassembly, reunion.

2. **assembly** (of persons), *assemblée* [F.], **gathering,** forgathering, **congregation,** congress, convocation, concourse, **meeting,** meet, **get-together** [coll.], turnout [coll.]; convention, conventicle [relig.], synod, diet, conclave, levee [Eng.]; caucus; mass meeting, rally; **session,** séance, sitting, eisteddfod [Welsh]; plenum, quorum; rendezvous.

3. **company, group, party, band,** bund [slang, U.S.], **gang, crew,** outfit, pack, cohort, **troop,** troupe, tribe, **body,** corps, bunch [coll.], mob [slang], crowd [coll.]; push, shove [both crim. slang, U.S.]; squad, platoon, battalion, brigade, fleet, team, string; covey, bevy; posse, detachment, detail, *posse comitatus* [law]; phalanx.

4. **throng, multitude, horde,** host, heap

[coll.], army, legion, body, force, swad [slang, U.S.], posse, array, flock, covey, bevy, galaxy; **crowd**, press, crush, cram [coll.], jam, squeeze [coll.], push [slang, U.S.], shove [crim. slang, U.S.]; **mob**, rabble, rout, *cohue* [F.]; flight, cloud, storm, shower, volley.

5. **flock, bunch, pack**, drift [dial.]; covey, bevy, tribe, flight; **swarm**, hive, colony; **school**, shoal; kennel, pride (of lions); **herd, drove**, drive; *mulada, remuda* [both Sp. & West. U.S.].

6. **bunch, group**, crop, **cluster, clump**; grove, thicket; batch, lot; boodle [U.S.], caboodle, boiling, kit, kit and boiling [all slang]; tuft, wisp; tussock, hassock; shock, hattock [dial., Eng.], stook; fascicle, fasciculus.

7. **bundle**, bindle [tramp slang, U.S.], **pack, package**, packet, budget, **parcel**, fardel [dial.], bale, truss, seroon; **roll**, rouleau, bolt; fagot, fascine; sheaf.

8. **accumulation**, cumulation, **amassment**, congeries, acervation; agglomeration, conglomeration, glomeration, conglomerate, agglomerate; aggregation, aggregate; conglobation; **mass, lump**, gob [dial. & slang], **batch**, bulk, budget; snowball; stockpile, stockpiling.

9. **heap, pile, stack**, bing [dial.]; **mound, hill**; molehill, anthill; bank, embankment; haystack, hayrick, haymow, haycock, cock, mow, rick; drift, snowdrift; pyramid.

10. **collection**, collectanea; corpus, **body**; compilation; ana; symposium; chrestomathy, Americana.

11. **set, suit, suite, series**, string, stand, kit [coll.], pack, block, battery.

12. **miscellany**, miscellanea; **assortment**, variety, medley, mob [coll.], conglomerate, **conglomeration**, omnium-gatherum [coll.]; **sundries**, oddments, **odds and ends**.

13. (a putting together, as parts of a machine) **assembly**, assemblage; assembly line, production line; assembly-line production.

14. **collector**, gatherer, accumulator; whip, whipper-in; collection agent, bill collector; tax collector, exciseman [Eng.], tithing man, gauger, *douanier* [F.]; collector; stamp collector, philatelist.

VERBS 15. (come together) **assemble, congregate, collect**, muster, **meet, gather, forgather, come together**, gang up [coll.], round in [slang]; flock together, herd together, pig together; **throng, crowd**, swarm,

surge, stream, horde; **cluster**, bunch, bunch up; gather around, gang around [slang]; rally, rally around; huddle, go into a huddle [slang]; rendezvous.

16. **convene**, open, take up; hold a meeting, hold a session, sit; **convoke**, summon, call together.

17. (bring or gather together) **assemble, gather**; muster, rally, mobilize; **collect**, raise, take up; **accumulate**, cumulate, amass, mass, bulk, batch; agglomerate, conglomerate, aggregate; **bring together**, get together, **gather together**, draw together, lump together, batch together, bunch together; **bunch**, bunch up; **cluster, clump**; **group**, aggroup; gather in, get in, whip in; scrape together, rake up, dredge up; round up, drive together; **put together**, make up, compile.

18. **heap, pile, stack**, heap up, pile up, stack up; mound, hill, bank, bank up; rick; pyramid; drift.

19. **bundle**, bundle up, **package**, parcel, **pack**, truss; bale; **wrap up**, do up, tie up, bind up; roll up.

20. **reassemble**, reunite, reune [slang], rejoin.

ADJS. 21. **assembled, collected, gathered**; congregate, congregated; meeting, in session; **accumulated**, cumulate, massed, amassed; heaped, stacked, piled; glomerate, agglomerate, conglomerate, aggregate; clustered, bunched; fascicled, fasciculated.

22. **crowded, packed, crammed**; jampacked, pack-jammed [both slang]; **compact**, firm, solid, dense, close, serried, all of a heap [coll.]; **teeming, swarming, crawling**, bristling, populous, thickly set; crowded to suffocation, packed like sardines, as thick as hops, ~ flies *or* thieves, swarming like maggots.

23. **cumulative**, accumulative.

75. DISPERSION

NOUNS 1. **dispersion, scattering**, scatterment, scatteration [coll.]; **distribution, spreading**, strewing, sowing, broadcasting, **broadcast, spread, dissemination**, propagation, dispensation; diffusion, dissipation; circumfusion; sprinkling, spattering; peppering.

2. **decentralization**, deconcentration.

3. **disbandment**, dispersion, separation, parting; breakup, split-up [coll.]; **demobilization**, deactivation, release, detachment; dismissal 308.5; dissolution, disorganization, disintegration.

4. **distributor,** broadcaster, spreader; sower, seeder, planter.

VERBS 5. **disperse, scatter, distribute, broadcast, sow,** disseminate, propagate, diffuse, **spread,** dispread, ted, strew, bestrew; **issue, deal out,** retail, utter, dispense; sow broadcast, scatter to the winds; overscatter, overspread, oversow; circumfuse.

6. **dispel, dissipate,** dissolve; drive away, clear away, cast forth, blow off.

7. **sprinkle,** besprinkle, **spatter,** squatter [dial.]; **dot,** spot, speck, speckle, stud; **pepper,** powder, dust; flour, crumb, bread; dredge.

8. **decentralize,** deconcentrate.

9. **disband, disperse, scatter, separate, part,** break up, split up; part company, go separate ways; **demobilize,** demob [slang], deactivate, muster out [U.S.], release, detach, let go; dismiss 308.18; **dissolve,** disorganize, disintegrate.

ADJS. 10. **dispersed, scattered, distributed,** dissipated, disseminated, strown, strewn, broadcast, **spread,** dispread; **widespread,** diffuse, sparse, sporadic; straggling, straggly; all over the place, all over the shop [slang].

11. **sprinkled,** spattered, **peppered,** spotted, dotted, specked, speckled, **studded.**

12. dispersive, **scattering, spreading, distributive,** diffusive, dissipative.

ADVS. 13. **scatteringly,** diffusely, sparsely *sparsim* [L.], **here and there,** in places, **in spots** [coll.].

76. INCLUSION

NOUNS 1. **inclusion, comprisal, comprehension,** embracement, incorporation, embodiment; admission, reception.

2. **entailment, involvement, implication.**

VERBS 3. **include, comprise, contain, comprehend,** hold, **take in; cover,** occupy, take up, fill; **embrace,** encompass, enclose, encircle, incorporate, embody, admit, receive, subsume; **reckon in,** reckon with, reckon among, count in, **number among,** take into account *or* consideration.

4. (include as a necessary circumstance *or* consequence) **entail, involve, implicate,** imply, affect, take in, contain, comprise, **call for, require,** take, bring, lead to.

ADJS. 5. **inclusive, including, containing, comprising, covering, embracing,** encompassing, enclosing, encircling.

6. **comprehensive, sweeping; all-comprehensive,** all-inclusive 79.13; **over-all,** blanket, omnibus, across-the-board; encyclopedic; bird's-eye, panoramic.

77. EXCLUSION

NOUNS 1. **exclusion, barring,** debarring, debarment, preclusion, exception, omission, nonadmission; **rejection,** repudiation; relegation; prohibition, embargo, blockade; lockout; inadmissibility.

2. **elimination, riddance,** shut [dial.], quit, withdrawal, **removal,** discard, eradication, clearance, **ejection,** expulsion; disposal, disposition; **liquidation, purge.**

3. **segregation, separation,** division; **isolation,** insulation, insularity, seclusion; quarantine; racial segregation, apartheid [Afrikaan], color bar.

VERBS 4. **exclude, bar,** debar, bar out, lock out, **shut out, keep out,** count out [chiefly coll.], cut off, preclude; reject, repudiate; **leave out,** omit, pass over; relegate; blockade, embargo.

5. **eliminate, get rid of, get quit of,** get shut of [dial.], get shet of [dial.], **dispose of, remove,** abstract, eject, expel, cast off, chuck [slang], bilge [sea slang], throw over *or* overboard [coll.], clear, clear out, clear away, clear the decks; **weed out,** pick out; **cut out,** strike off *or* out, elide; eradicate, root up *or* out; **purge, liquidate.**

6. **segregate, separate,** divide; **isolate,** insulate, seclude; **set apart,** keep apart; quarantine; **set aside,** lay aside, put aside, keep aside; **sort** *or* **pick out,** sift, screen, sieve, bolt, riddle, winnow; thresh, thrash, gin.

ADJS. 7. **excluded,** precluded, **barred,** debarred, **shut out, left out,** left out in the cold [slang]; not included, not in it, not in the picture [coll.].

8. **exclusive, excluding,** exclusory; seclusive, preclusive, exceptional, inadmissible, prohibitive, preventive; separative, segregative; select, selective.

PREPS. *etc.* 9. **barring, bar, excluding,** exclusive of, precluding, omitting, **leaving out; excepting,** except, **except for,** with the exception of, outside of [coll., U.S.], save, saving, save and except, let alone; **besides,** beside, **aside from** [coll., U.S.], than; unless, without, ex.

78. EXTRANEOUSNESS

1. **extraneousness, foreignness;** alienism, alienage.

2. foreign body, foreign element.

3. **alien, stranger, foreigner,** furriner [dial.], **outsider,** outlander, uitlander [S. Africa], tramontane, ultramontane, barbarian, foreign devil [Chinese], gringo [Span.-Amer.].

4. **newcomer, new arrival,** *novus homo* [L.], Johnny Newcomer [slang, U.S.], Johnny-come-lately [slang, U.S.], new chum [coll., Austral.]; **tenderfoot,** maverick [slang, West. U.S.], shorthorn [slang, West. U.S.], jackaroo [coll., Austral.], griffin [Anglo-Ind.]; recruit, rookie [slang].

ADJS. 5. **extraneous, foreign,** furrin [dial.], foreignistic [coll.], **alien,** strange, exotic; **external,** exterior, ulterior, outside; outland, outlandish; barbarian, barbarous, barbaric; foreign-born; ecdemic [med.].

ADVS. 6. **abroad,** in foreign parts; oversea, overseas, beyond seas; on one's travels.

79. GENERALITY

NOUNS 1. **generality, universality,** worldwideness, ecumenicity; catholicity, catholicism; generalization.

2. **prevalence, commonness,** usualness; currency, reign, run; **extensiveness,** widespreadness, sweepingness, rifeness, rampantness.

3. **the generality, average,** ruck, **run,** general ∼, common ∼, average *or* **ordinary run.**

4. **everyone, everybody, each and every one,** each and every [dial.], **one and all,** all hands [coll.], all hands and the cook [slang], every man Jack [coll.], every mother's son [coll.], **all the world,** *tout le monde* [F.], all the world and his brother *or* wife, the devil and all [coll.]; whole boodle *or* caboodle, whole kit, whole kit and caboodle, whole toot and scramble *or* stumble [all slang].

5. **any,** anything, **aught,** ought; anybody, anyone, any one.

6. **whatever,** whate'er, **whatsoever,** whatsoe'er, what so *or* whatso [dial.], whatsomeover [dial.], what, **whichever,** anything soever which, no matter what *or* which.

7. **whoever,** whoso, **whosoever, whomever,** whomso, whomsoever, any one, no matter who.

VERBS 8. **generalize, universalize,** catholicize; **broaden, widen, expand,** extend, spread; make a generalization, deal in generalities.

9. **prevail, predominate,** reign, rule, rage; go about, stalk about; **obtain,** subsist.

ADJS. 10. **general,** nonspecific, generic; **indefinite,** indeterminate, vague, unspecified; **broad, wide;** collective.

11. **prevalent, prevailing, common,** popular, **current,** running; regnant, reigning, ruling, predominating; **rife, rampant,** epidemic, besetting.

12. **extensive, broad, wide,** liberal, diffuse, large-scale, **sweeping; wide-spread,** far-spread, far-stretched, **far-reaching,** far-going, far-embracing, far-extending, far-spreading, far-flying, far-ranging, **far-flung,** wide-flung, wide-reaching, wide-extending, wide-extended, wide-ranging, wide-stretching; wholesale, indiscriminate.

13. **universal,** heaven-wide, **world-wide, global; all-inclusive,** all-including, **all-embracing,** all-comprehensive, all-comprehending, all-filling, all-pervading, all-covering, covered with, **all over;** catholic, pandemic, ecumenic(al), **cosmopolitan;** country-wide, state-wide.

14. **every, all,** any; **each,** each one; every one, each and every [coll.], **each and all, one and all, all and sundry,** all and some.

14a. Pan-American, Pan-Pacific, Panhellenic, etc.

ADVS. 15. **generally, in general; generally** speaking, speaking generally, roughly speaking; **usually** 84.9, **as a rule,** as a matter of course; **by and large,** at large, altogether, **all things considered,** taking one thing with another, taking all things together, **all in all,** taking all in all, taking it for all in all, **on the whole,** as a whole, **in the long run,** for the most part, for better or for worse.

16. **universally, everywhere, all over,** the world over; in every instance, without exception, **invariably, always,** never otherwise.

80. SPECIALITY

Special Character.—NOUNS 1. **speciality, specialness,** specialty, **specificality, specificness,** definiteness, distinctiveness.

2. **the specific, the special, the particular.**

3. **characteristic, peculiarity, singularity,** particularity, specialty, **individualism,** character, nature, trait, trick, **feature,** distinctive feature, lineament; **mark, earmark,** index; badge, token; **type,** brand, cast, stamp, impress, impression; differen-

tial, differentia; **idiosyncrasy**, idiocrasy; **quality, property, attribute;** savor, flavor, aroma, smack, tang, taint.

4. individuality, individualism; **particularity**, singularity, originality, identity; **personality**, personship, personal identity; **selfness**, selfhood, **egohood**, self-identity; oneness 89.1.

5. self, ego; oneself, I, I myself, me, myself, number one [coll.], your Uncle Dudley [slang], yours truly [coll.]; yourself, himself, herself, itself; ourselves, yourselves; themselves, theirselves [dial.], theirsens [dial.]; you, you-all [dial.]; he, she; him, her; they, them; it; **inner self, inner man; subliminal self,** subliminal; **superego,** ethical self; **alter ego,** *alter, alterum* [both L.].

6. specification, designation, stipulation, signification, determination, denomination, fixing, selection, assignment.

7. particularization, specialization; individualization, personalization.

8. characterization, distinction, differentiation, definition, description; keynote [coll.].

VERBS **9. specify,** specialize, **designate, stipulate,** determine, **fix,** set, assign, **name,** denominate, state, mention, select, pick out, mark, tick off [slang], **signify,** point out, put *or* lay one's finger on.

10. particularize, specialize; individualize, personalize; **descend to particulars,** get down to brass tacks [coll.], get down to cases [slang, U.S.], come to the point; itemize 8.5.

11. characterize, distinguish, differentiate, define, describe; mark, earmark, mark off, mark out, **set apart;** keynote [coll.], sound the keynote, set the tone *or* mood, set the pace; be characteristic, **be a feature of;** be just like one, be one all over [slang], be the nature of the beast [slang], run true to form.

ADJS. **12. special, especial, specific, particular, express,** precise; **singular, individual,** individualist(ic); **personal,** private, intimate, esoteric; respective, several; **fixed, definite,** determinate, certain, exclusive; distinguished, noteworthy.

13. characteristic, peculiar, singular, typical, quintessential, **representative, distinctive,** marked, distinguished, appropriate, proper, endemic; original; idiocratic(al); **in character, true to form,** true to type, just like one, the nature of the beast [slang].

14. this, this here [dial.], **these.**

15. that, that there [dial.], **those;** yon, yond, yonder, yander [dial.].

ADVS. **16. specially, especially, specifically, expressly,** precisely, **particularly, in particular,** to be specific.

17. personally, privately, **individually; in person,** in the flesh, *in propria persona* [L., in one's own person]; **for all me, for my part,** as far as I am concerned.

18. namely, nominally, that is to say, *videlicet* [L.], viz., scilicet, scil., sc., **to wit.**

19. each, apiece; severally, respectively, one by one, each to each.

PREPS. **20. per, for each;** per annum, per diem, per capita.

81. SPECIALTY

Object of Special Attention.—NOUNS **1. specialty,** speciality, **line, pursuit, pet subject,** main interest; **vocation** 654.6; **forte,** *métier or* metier, **strong point,** long suit; specialism, specialization.

2. special, feature, main feature; **leader** [com.], lead item, leading card; special edition, special order, special study, special student, special correspondent, special train, etc.

3. specialist, specializer.

VERBS **4. specialize, feature; narrow, restrict,** limit, confine; specialize in, **go in for,** follow, pursue, **make it one's business;** major in, minor in.

ADJS. **5. specialized,** specialist, specialistic; **restricted, limited,** confined; **featured,** feature [U.S.].

82. CONFORMITY

NOUNS **1. conformity, conformance,** conformation; **compliance,** acquiescence, obedience, observance; **accordance,** accord, **correspondence,** harmony, agreement, uniformity; **consistency,** congruity; **line, keeping;** accommodation, adaptation, adaption, adjustment; reconciliation, reconcilement; **conventionality** 643; other-direction.

2. conformist, conformer; **conventionalist,** conventional; bromide *or* bromidite [slang], Babbitt [U.S.], Philistine; **formalist,** methodologist, precisianist, precisian; pedant.

VERBS **3. conform, comply, correspond,** accord, harmonize; **adapt, adjust, accommodate,** meet, suit, fit, shape; **comply with,** agree with, tally with, chime *or* fall in with, go by, be guided *or* regulated by, observe, follow; **adapt to,** adjust to, gear to, assimilate to, accommodate with; **reconcile**, settle, compose; rub off corners.

4. follow the rule, go according to Hoyle [coll.], play the game [coll.]; **follow the crowd,** follow the fashion, swim *or* go with the stream, ~ tide *or* current, follow the beaten path, **do as others do,** do in Rome as the Romans do, *hurler avec les loups* [F., howl with the wolves], **get in line,** fall into line, fall in with; **keep in step,** come to time; **toe the mark,** walk the chalk, walk the chalk mark *or* line [all coll.]; keep up to standard, pass muster, come up to scratch [coll.]; keep in countenance.

ADJS. **5. conformable, adaptable,** adaptive, adjustable; **compliant,** acquiescent, other-directed, submissive, tractable, obedient; in accord, in keeping, in line, in step; **conventional** 643.7.

6. conformable to, adapted to, adjusted to, proper to, suitable to, **according to,** agreeable to, answerable to; **consistent with,** congruent with, uniform with; **corresponding,** accordant, concordant, harmonious.

ADVS. *etc.* **7. conformably, in conformity with, in compliance with, in obedience to, in accordance with, in line with,** in step with, **in keeping with,** in agreement with, in harmony with, in uniformity with, consistently with, uniformly with.

8. according to, in correspondence to, agreeably to; by, after.

9. according to rule, *en règle* [F.], according to regulations, *selon les règles* [F.], **according to Hoyle,** ~ Cocker *or* Gunter [coll.]; by the card, **by the book.**

83. UNCONFORMITY

NOUNS **1. unconformity, inconsistency,** incongruity; **inaccordance,** disaccord, disaccordance.

2. nonconformity, nonconformance, disconformity; **nonobservance, noncompliance,** nonconcurrence, **dissent** 520a, disagreement, recusance *or* recusancy; unorthodoxy 1023.

3. unconventionality, unorthodoxy, originality, informality, Bohemianism.

4. nonconformist, unconformist, **original,** sulphite [slang], maverick [coll., U.S.], Bohemian, beatnik; **dissenter** 520a.3; **heretic** 1023.5; sectary, sectarian; nonjuror.

VERBS **5. not conform,** not comply; **get out of line** [coll.], **leave the beaten path, go out of bounds,** break bounds, have no

business there; stretch a point, drive a coach and six through; **dissent** 520a.4.

ADJS. **6. unconformable,** unconforming, nonconforming, unadaptable, unadjustable; **uncompliant,** unsubmissive; **nonobservant;** recusant, **dissentient** 520a.6.

7. out of line, out of keeping, out of order *or* place, misplaced, **out of step,** out of turn [slang], out of tune, out of one's element.

8. unconventional, unorthodox, unfashionable, not being done; offbeat [coll.], **out of the way; original,** sulphidic *or* sulphitic [slang], Bohemian, beat; **informal,** on the free and easy [slang].

84. NORMALITY

NOUNS **1. normality,** normalcy, **normalness, naturalness;** naturalism, realism.

2. usualness, ordinariness, commonness, commonplaceness; **prevalence,** currency.

3. the normal, a natural; **the usual, the ordinary, the common,** the commonplace.

4. rule, law, principle, standard, criterion; **norm,** norma; **form, formula,** formulary, formality, prescribed *or* set form; standing order; **hard and fast rule,** Procrustean law, law of the Medes and Persians; ground rules.

5. normalization, standardization.

VERBS **6. normalize,** standardize.

ADJS. **7. normal, natural,** typical, unexceptional; analogical; naturalistic, realistic.

8. usual, regular; customary, accustomed, wonted; standard, regulation, conventional; **common, commonplace, ordinary, everyday,** familiar, household, vernacular, stock; prevailing, current, popular, universal.

ADVS. **9. normally, naturally; usually,** commonly, ordinarily, customarily, **generally,** regularly, for the most part, most often *or* frequently; **as a rule,** as a matter of course; **as usual,** as per usual [coll.]; **as may be expected,** to be expected.

85. ABNORMALITY

NOUNS **1. abnormality,** abnormity; **unnaturalness,** unnaturalism; anomaly, anomalousness, anomalism; aberration, aberrance *or* aberrancy; **irregularity,** deviation, divergence; eccentricity, erraticism; teratism [med.], amorphism, heteromorphism; **subnormality.**

2. unusualness, uncommonness, unordinariness, unwontedness, exceptionality; **rar-**

ity, rareness, **uniqueness; extraordinariness,** prodigiousness, marvelousness, remarkableness, stupendousness; incredibility, inconceivability; the unusual, the abnormal.

3. oddity, queerness, curiousness, quaintness, **peculiarity,** singularity; **strangeness,** outlandishness; bizarreness, *bizarrerie* [F.]; freakishness, grotesqueness, weirdness, monstrousness, monstrosity.

4. (odd person) **oddity, character** [coll.], **card,** [coll.], **case** [slang], **caution** [coll., U.S.]; odd fellow, queer specimen [coll. or slang]; **oddball,** odd stick, odd *or* queer fish, queer duck, queer potato, rum customer, rum one, rummy [all slang]; **codger,** duffer [both coll.]; **guy; geezer,** galoot, gink, goof, goop, geke, coot, bird, duck [all slang]; **eccentric** 473.3.

5. (odd thing) **oddity, curiosity; abnormality,** anomaly; nonesuch, nondescript; **rarity,** *rara avis* [L., rare bird]; exception, one in a thousand, one in a way; prodigy, prodigiosity.

6. monstrosity, monster, miscreation, abortion, teratism [med.]; **freak,** freak of nature, *lucus naturae* [L.]; Mongolian monster; teratology, teratogeny [both med.].

7. supernaturalism, supernaturalness, supernaturality, supranaturalism, supernormalness, **preternaturalism,** supersensibleness, superphysicalness, superhumanity, **unearthliness,** unworldliness, **otherworldliness,** transcendentalism; the supernatural, the supersensible; supernature, supranature.

8. miracle, sign, prodigy, wonder, wonderwork.

ADJS. **9. abnormal, unnatural;** anomalous, anomalistic; **irregular,** eccentric, erratic, deviative, divergent; aberrant, stray, straying, wandering; heteroclite, heteromorphic, adelomorphic [biol.], amorphous; **subnormal.**

10. unusual, unordinary, **uncustomary,** unwonted, **uncommon, unfamiliar,** unheard-of, *recherché* [F.]; rare, unique, *sui generis* [L., of its own kind]; **out of the ordinary,** out of the way, out of the common, out of the pale, **off the beaten track;** unexpected, not to be expected, unthought-of, undreamt-of.

11. odd, outré [F.], **queer, peculiar, singular, curious,** quaint, funny [coll.], comical [coll.], rum [slang]; **strange,** outlandish, passing strange, "wondrous strange" [Shakespeare]; weird, unearthly; bastard (as, *bastard* type), off (as, *off* color), out (as, *out* sizes).

12. fantastic, fanciful; **incredible,** unimaginable, inconceivable, unaccountable; **freakish,** freak [coll.]; **monstrous,** teratogenic, teratoid; **grotesque, bizarre, baroque,** rococo.

13. extraordinary, exceptional, remarkable, noteworthy, **wonderful, marvelous,** stupendous, prodigious, portentous, phenomenal; unprecedented, unexampled, unparalleled, not within the memory of man; indescribable, nondescript.

14. supernatural, supranatural, preternatural; **supernormal,** hypernormal, preternormal; **superphysical,** hyperphysical; **supersensible,** supersensual, pretersensual; **superhuman,** preterhuman, unhuman, nonhuman; **supramundane,** extramundane, transmundane; **unearthly, unworldly, otherworldly; psychic(al), spiritual; transcendental.**

15. miraculous, wonder-working, thaumaturgic(al), **prodigious,** incomprehensible, *tombé des nues* [F., fallen from the clouds].

ADVS. **16. unusually, uncommonly, unnaturally,** abnormally, unordinarily, **uncustomarily,** unexpectedly; **rarely,** hardly, hardly ever.

17. extraordinarily, exceptionally, remarkably, wonderfully, marvelously, prodigiously, phenomenally, stupendously.

18. oddly, queerly, peculiarly, singularly, curiously, quaintly, **strangely,** outlandishly, fantastically, fancifully, grotesquely, monstrously.

PHRS. **19. what on earth,** what in the world, what under the sun, what in hell [coll.].

20. mythical monsters

ant lion	manticore *or*
basilisk	manticora
centaur	mermaid
Cerberus	merman
chimera	Minotaur
cockatrice	phoenix
Cyclops	Python
dipsas	ogre
dragon	ogress
drake	roc
griffin	Sagittary
Gorgon	salamander
hippocampus	sea horse
hippocentaur	sea serpent
hippocerf	simurgh
hippogriff *or* hip-	sphinx
pogryph	unicorn
hircocervus	wivern
Hydra	xiphopagus
kraken	zombi [U.S.]

21. humorous mythical creatures

gaboon   sidehill badger
gazook   sidewinder
gollywog   swamp gaboon
gyascutus   tree squeak
high-behind   wampus
 splintercat   wampus cat
hoofenpoofer   whangdoodle
oink   whiffle-bird
prock

86. NUMBER

NOUNS 1. **number, numeral, numero,**
No. *or* no. [abbr.], **figure,** figger [dial.],
digit, cipher, character, symbol; astronomical figure, boxcar number [slang].

2. (numbers) Arabic numerals, Roman numerals; cardinal number, cardinal; ordinal number, ordinal; integer, whole number; round number, abbreviated number; perfect number, imperfect number, deficient *or* defective number, abundant number; prime number, mixed number, serial number, figurate numbers, pyramidal numbers, polygonal numbers; binary digit, bit.

3. **sum,** summation, difference, product, **number, count,** account, cast, **score, reckoning, tally,** tale, the story *or* whole story [coll.], **aggregate, amount,** stick [sporting slang]; **total** 54.2; box score [U.S.].

4. permutation, combination, alternation; election.

5. variation, variation of a function, variation of an integral, variation of constants *or* parameters.

6. **ratio, rate, proportion; quota,** quotum; **percentage,** per cent *or* percent; geometric ratio *or* proportion, arithmetical proportion, harmonic proportion; rule of three.

7. **series, progression;** arithmetical progression, geometrical progression, harmonical progression.

ADJS. 8. **numeric(al), numeral,** numerary, numerative; figural, **figurate,** figurative; **digital;** aliquot, submultiple, reciprocal, prime, fractional, decimal, exponential, logarithmic, logometric, differential, fluxional, integral, totitive; positive, negative; rational, irrational; surd, radical; real, imaginary; possible, impossible.

9. mathematical elements

aliquot part   complement
antecedent   consequent
antilogarithm   cube
base   cube root
circulating   decimal
 decimal   denominator
coefficient   difference quotient
common measure   differential

dividend   multiplicand
divisor   multiplicator
exponent   multiplier
factor   number field
fluent   numerator
fluxion   power
formula   quotient
fraction   radix
increment   reciprocal
index   repetend
integral   root
logarithm   square root
minuend   submultiple
mixed decimal   subtrahend
modulus   totient
multiple   variable

87. NUMERATION

NOUNS 1. **numeration, enumeration, numbering, counting,** telling; pagination, foliation; dactylonomy.

2. **mathematics,** math [coll.], mathematic, **numbers, figures;** pure mathematics, abstract mathematics, applied mathematics, higher mathematics, elementary mathematics; trigonometry, trig [slang].

3. **calculation, computation, estimation, reckoning;** adding, footing, casting, totaling; dead reckoning.

4. (operations) notations, **addition, subtraction, multiplication, division,** proportion, practice, equations, extraction of roots, reduction, involution, evolution, approximation, interpolation, differentiation, integration.

5. **summation,** summary, **summing up,** recount, recounting, rehearsal, capitulation, **recapitulation,** statement, **reckoning,** count, account.

6. (as to keep account of) **account,** count, **reckoning, tab** [coll.], tally, check.

7. **statistics,** statistology; vital statistics; statistician.

8. calculator, computer, estimator.

9. **mathematician, arithmetician;** geometer, geometrician; algebraist, trigonometrician, abacist, geodesist, mathematical physicist, actuary.

VERBS 10. **number,** numerate, **enumerate, count,** tell, "tell his tale" [Milton], tell of, call off [U.S.], name *or* call over, run over; **count noses** [coll.], call the roll, census, poll; page, paginate, foliate.

11. **calculate, compute, estimate, reckon, figure,** cipher, cast, tally, score; **figure out,** dope out [slang]; figure in [coll.]; lump off [coll.]; **add, subtract, multiply, divide,** algebraize, extract roots.

12. **sum up,** sum, summate; **figure up,**

cipher up, reckon up [coll.], **count up, add up,** foot up, cast up, score up; **total,** tottle [dial.], total up, tot up [coll., Eng.]; **summarize, recapitulate, recount,** rehearse, recite, relate; detail, itemize, inventory.

13. keep account of, keep count of, **keep track of, keep tab** or **tabs** [coll.], keep tally, keep cases [coll], keep a check on.

14. check, verify 512.12; **prove,** demonstrate; balance, balance the books; audit, overhaul; take stock, inventory.

ADJS. **15. numerative, enumerative; calculative,** computive, estimative; **calculating,** computing, estimating; statistic(al).

16. calculable, computable, reckonable, estimable, countable, numberable; commensurable, commensurate.

17. mathematical, arithmetic(al), algebraic(al), trigonometrical(al), analytic-(al).

18. mathematics

algebra	infinitesimal
algebraic geometry	calculus
algorism	integral calculus
algorithm	intuitional
analysis	geometry
analytic geometry	invariant sub-
arithmetic	algebra
associative algebra	inverse geometry
binary arithmetic	line geometry
Boolian algebra	linear algebra
calculus	mathematical
calculus of	physics
differences	matrix algebra
circle geometry	metageometry
commutative	multiple algebra
algebra	natural geometry
complex or	nilpotent algebra
double algebra	noncommutative
denumerative	algebra
geometry	n-tuple linear
descriptive	algebra
geometry	plane trigonometry
differential	political arithmetic
calculus	projective geometry
division algebra	proper subalgebra
elementary	quadratics
arithmetic	quaternion algebra
elementary or	reducible algebra
ordinary algebra	Riemannian
equivalent algebras	geometry
Euclidean	semisimple algebra
geometry	simple algebra
geodesic geometry	speculative
geodesy	geometry
geometry	spherical
graphic algebra	trigonometry
higher algebra	subalgebra
higher arithmetic	trigonometry
hyperalgebra	universal algebra
hyperbolic	universal geometry
geometry	vector algebra
	zero algebra

19. calculators

abacus	listing machine
adding machine	Napier's bones
arithmograph	or rods
arithmometer	pari-mutuel
calculating	(machine)
machine	rule
cash register	slide rule, sliding
Comptometer	scale
counter	suan pan [Chin.]
difference engine	tabulator
electronic	totalizator
computer 348.16	

88. LIST

NOUNS **1. list, enumeration,** *tableau* [F.], scroll, screed; **schedule,** line-up [coll.]; **register,** registry; **inventory,** terrier; cadastre or cadaster, cadre; check list; tally sheet; active list, retired list, sick list.

2. table, contents, table of contents; **chart; index,** thumb index, card index.

3. catalogue; classified catalogue, *catalogue raisonné* [F.]; card catalogue [U.S.]; **file,** filing system, letter file, catalogue file, pigeonholes; pamphlet file, pam file [library cant]; **calendar,** calends or kalends.

4. bill, statement, account; **bill of fare,** menu, carte; waybill.

5. roll, roster, rota; **roll call,** muster, **census,** nose count [coll.], **poll,** returns, census report or returns; panel; muster roll; checkroll, check list; beadroll; roll of honor.

6. listing, tabulation; **cataloguing,** filing, indexing; **registration,** registry, enrollment, matriculation.

VERBS **7. list, enumerate, tabulate, catalogue,** tally; **register,** post, enter, enroll, matriculate, book; empanel, impanel; **file,** pigeonhole; **index;** inventory; calendar; score, keep score; **schedule,** line up [coll.].

ADJS. **8. inventorial;** cadastral.

89. UNITY

State of Being One.—NOUNS **1. unity, oneness, singleness,** singularity, **individuality,** identity, selfsameness; uniqueness; integrity, solidity, solidarity, undividedness; organic unity.

2. aloneness, loneness, loneliness, lonesomeness; solitariness; **solitude;** separateness, detachment, **isolation,** "splendid isolation" [Sir William Goschen].

3. one, unit, ace, monad; none else, no other, nought beside.

4. integer, entity, individual, singleton, item, article, point, module.

VERBS **5. unify,** make one; unite 52.3.

6. **stand alone**, stand apart.

ADJS. 7. **one, single, singular, individual, sole, solitary, lone;** exclusive, undivided; an, any, any one.

8. **alone, solitary,** solo, *solus* [L.]; **isolated,** insular, **apart, separate, separated,** detached, removed; **lone, lonely, lonesome;** friendless, kithless, homeless; companionless, **unaccompanied,** unattended; **unaided,** unassisted, unabetted, unsupported, unseconded, **singlehanded.**

9. **unique, sole,** singular, odd, unrepeated, azygous, **alone, only,** onliest [dial.], only-begotten, **one and only,** first and last.

10. **unitary, integrated,** integral, integrant, composite, undivided.

11. **unipartite,** unipart, **one-piece;** monad, monadic(al); unilateral, one-sided; uniangulate, unibivalent, unibranchiate, unicameral, unicellular, unicuspid, unidentate, unidigitate, unidimensional, unidirectional, uniflorous, unifoliate, unifoliolate, unigenital, uniglobular, unilinear, uniliteral, unilobed, unilobular, unilocular, unimodular, unimolecular, uninuclear, uniocular, unipolar, univalent, univocal.

12. **unific, unifying, uniting; combining,** combinative, combinatory; connective, connecting, connectional; conjunctive, conjunctival; coalescing, coalescent.

ADVS. 13. **singly, individually,** particularly, severally, one by one, one at a time; **singularly,** in the singular; **alone,** by itself, *per se* [L.]; **by oneself,** all by one's lonesome [coll.], **singlehandedly;** separately, apart.

14. **solely, exclusively, only,** merely, simply; **entirely,** wholly.

90. DUALITY

NOUNS 1. **duality, dualism, duplicity,** duplexity, **twoness;** biformity; polarity; conjugation.

2. **two,** twain [chiefly poetic]; **couple, pair, twosome** [spec. golf], brace, team, span, yoke, match, mates; **couplet,** distich [pros.], doublet; duad, dyad; the two, **both.**

3. (cards and dice) **deuce,** deucer [slang], dace [slang, U.S.]; **snake eyes** [slang], crabs, **craps** [all dice].

4. **twins,** pair of twins [coll.]; Siamese twins; Twin Stars, Castor and Pollux, Gemini.

VERBS 5. **pair, couple, bracket, team,** yoke, span [U.S.], mate, match, conjugate; **pair off,** couple up, team up.

ADJS. 6. **two,** twain [chiefly poetic]; **dual,** dualistic; dyadic; duadic; diphyletic [biol.]; tête-à-tête.

7. **both,** the two; both two, both twain, all both, all two [all dial.].

8. **coupled, paired,** yoked, matched, mated, bracketed; **conjugate,** conjugated; biconjugate, bigeminate; bijugate, unijugate [both bot.].

91. DUPLICATION

NOUNS 1. **duplication, reduplication,** conduplication, **reproduction, doubling;** gemination, ingemination; **repetition** 103; **copying** 22; **duplicate** 24.3.

VERBS 2. **duplicate, dupe** [print. slang], ditto [coll.]; **double,** dub [slang, U.S.]; geminate, ingeminate; **reduplicate, reproduce,** redouble; **repeat** 103.7; **copy** 22.8.

ADJS. 3. **duplicate, double,** duple, **dual, duplex, twofold,** bifold, binary, binate [bot.]; geminate, geminated; second, secondary; twin, biparous; biform, disomatous; two-sided, bilateral; two-faced, double-faced, bifacial; two-ply; conduplicate [bot.].

ADVS. 4. **doubly,** dually, **twofold,** as much again, twice as much; twice, two times.

5. **secondly,** second, secondarily, **in the second place** or instance.

6. **again,** another time, **once more,** once and again, over again; **anew,** afresh, new, freshly, newly.

92. BISECTION

NOUNS 1. **bisection, bipartition, bifidity,** dichotomy, **halving, division,** subdivision.

2. **half,** halver or halvers [dial. & slang]; moiety, mediety [law]; hemisphere, semisphere; **fifty percent,** fifty per [coll.]; half-and-half, fifty-fifty [slang].

VERBS 3. **bisect, halve, divide,** subdivide, cleave, split, **cut in two,** dimidiate, dichotomize.

ADJS. 4. **halved, bisected, divided,** dimidiate, split, cloven, cleft, asunder, **in half,** in halves, **in two,** in twain; half-and-half, fifty-fifty [slang].

5. **bipartite,** bifid; bicuspid, biaxial, bicameral, binocular, binomial, binominal, biped, bipetalous, bipinnate, bivalent.

6. **semi-, demi-, hemi-.**

93. THREE

NOUNS 1. **three, trio, threesome** [spec. golf], leash (as of hares); **triad, trilogy,** trinity, ternary, ternion; **triplet,** tercet [poetry], terzetto [mus.]; spike team [U.S.], three-up [coll., West. U.S.]; trefoil, shamrock, clover; tripod, trivet; triangle, trihedron, trident, trisul, triennium, trinomial, trionym, triplopy, trireme, triseme, triskelion, triumvirate.

2. (cards and dice) **trey**, deuce-ace [dice], little trey [dice slang]; tierce [cards].

3. threeness, triplicity; triunity, trinity.

ADJS. 4. **three**; trinal, trial [both gram.]; triadic(al); triune, three in one, *tria juncta in uno* [L.]; triform.

94. TRIPLICATION

NOUNS 1. triplicaton, triplicity, trebleness, **threefoldness**; triplicate, second carbon.

VERBS 2. **triplicate, triple, treble**, threefold; cube.

ADJS. 3. triplicate, **triple, treble, threefold**, triplex, trinal, tern, ternary, ternal, ternate; three-ply; trilogic(al).

4. **third**, tertiary.

ADVS. 5. **triply**, trebly, trinely, **threefold; thrice**, three times.

6. **thirdly**, in the third place, again and yet again.

95. TRISECTION

NOUNS 1. **trisection**, tripartition, trichotomy; triangulation.

2. **third**, tierce, third part, one third.

VERBS 3. **trisect, third**, trichotomize; triangulate.

ADJS. 4. trisected, **tripartite**, triparted, **three-parted**, trichotomous; three-sided, trilateral; three-forked, three-pronged, trifurcate; trident, tridental, tridentate *or* tridentated, trifid; tricuspid; three-footed, tripodic, tripedal; trifoliate, trifloral, triflorate, triflorous, tripetalous, triadelphous, triarch [all bot.]; trimerous, 3-merous [coll., both bot. & zool.]; three-cornered, tricornered, tricorn; trigonal, trigonoid; triquetrous, triquetral; trigrammatic, triliteral; triangular, triangulate, deltoid.

96. FOUR

NOUNS 1. **four**, tetrad, quatern, quaternion, quaternary, quaternity, **quartet** *or* quartette, **quadruplet**, foursome [esp. golf]; Little Joe (from Kokomo) [dice slang]; tetralogy; tetrapody [poetry]; tetraphony, four-part diaphony [both mus.]; quatrefoil *or* quadrifoil [bot.], four-leaf clover; tetragram, tetragrammaton; biquadrate [math.]; quadrinomial [algebra]; quadrilateral 250.14.

2. **fourness**, quaternity, quadruplicity.

VERBS 3. **square, quadrate;** cube, dice.

ADJS. 4. **four**; quaternary, quartile [tech.], quartic, quadric [tech.], quadratic; tetrad, tetradic; quadrinomial, biquadratic [both math.]; tetractinal, four-rayed [both zool.]; quadruped, four-legged; quadrivalent, tetravalent; quadrilateral 250.9.

97. QUADRUPLICATION

NOUNS 1. **quadruplication**, quadruplicature.

VERBS 2. **quadruplicate**, quadruple, fourfold, biquadrate [math.], quadruplex [teleg.].

ADJS. 3. **quadruplicate, quadruple**, quadrible, quadrable, **quadruplex, four-fold**, tetraploid, quadrigeminal [tech.], biquadratic [math.].

4. **fourth, quarter.**

ADVS. 5. **fourthly**, in the fourth place; **quarterly**, by quarters.

98. QUADRISECTION

NOUNS 1. **quadrisection**, quadripartition, **quartering.**

2. **fourth**, one fourth, **quarter**, quartern; quart; farthing.

VERBS 3. **quadrisect, quarter.**

ADJS. 4. quadrisected, **quartered**, quarter-cut; quadripartite, quadrifid; quadrifoliate, quadrigeminal, quadripinnate, quadriplanar, quadriserial, quadrivial, quadrifurcate, quadrumanal, quadrumanous.

99. FIVE, ETC.

NOUNS 1. **five**, fiver [slang], cinque, [spec. cards & dice], quint [cards & dice], quincunx, **quintet** *or* quintette [spec. mus.], **fivesome, quintuplet**, pentad; fin, finf, finnif, half saw *or* sawbuck, V, vee, one V [all slang, U.S.]; Phoebe, Little Phoebe, fever in the South [all dice slang]; pentagon, pentagram [both geom.]; pentapody, pentameter, pentastich [all pros.]; pentarchy, Pentateuch [Bible], pentathlon [athletics], pentacle, pentalpha; mullet, estoile [both her.].

2. **six**, sixer [slang], sise [dice], Captain Hicks [dice slang], **half a dozen, sextet** *or* sextette, sestet [pros.], **sextuplet**, hexad; hexagon, hexahedron, hexacosihedroid, hexagram [all geom.]; hexameter, hexapody, hexastich [all pros.]; hexavalent [chem.], hexapod, hexarchy, Hexateuch [Bible], hexastyle [arch.], hexachord [mus.], Hexabiblos, hexabromide.

3. seven, sevener [slang], heptad; seven-out [dice]; heptagon, heptahedron [both geom.]; heptameter, heptastich [both pros.]; heptarchy, Heptateuch [Bible], septet [spec. mus.], septuor, septennate.

4. eight, eighter [slang]; Ada Ross the stable hoss, eighter from Decatur [both dice slang]; octagon, octahedron [both geom.]; octave, octavo; octad [spec. chem.]; ogdoad, octonary; octet, octameter [both pros.]; octastyle [arch.], utas [eccl.], Octateuch [Bible], octosyllable.

5. nine, niner [slang], ennead; quinine (the bitter dose), Carolina nine [both dice slang]; nonage, novena [both eccl.]; nonagon [geom.], nonuplet [mus.], enneastyle [arch.].

6. ten, tenner [slang], X, **decade,** dicker [spec. of hides]; dews, double fin, saw, sawbuck [all slang, U.S.]; Big Dick, Big Dick from Boston [both dice slang]; decagon, decahedron [both geom.]; decagram, decigram, decaliter, deciliter, decare, decameter, decimeter, decastere [all metric meas.];decapod, decastyle [arch.], decasyllable, decemvir or decemvirate [spec. Rom. antiq.], decennium, decennary, Decalogue [Bible].

7. (eleven to ninety) **eleven,** 'leven [dial.]; **twelve, dozen,** boxcar or boxcars [dice slang]; **teens; thirteen,** long dozen, baker's dozen, devil's dozen; **fifteen,** quindecima [mus.], quindene [church hist.], quindecim [hist. & eccl.], quindecennial; **twenty, score,** double saw or sawbuck [crim. slang, U.S.]; **twenty-four,** four and twenty, two dozen; **twenty-five,** five and twenty, quarter of a hundred or century; **forty, twoscore; fifty,** half a hundred, L, half C or century [crim. slang, U.S.]; **sixty,** sexagenary, **threescore; seventy, threescore and ten; eighty, fourscore; ninety, fourscore and ten.**

8. hundred, century, C, one C [crim. slang, U.S.], centred [hist.], centrev or centref [hist., Welsh]; centennium, centennial, centenary; cental, centigram, centiliter, centimeter, centiare, centistere [all metric meas.]; hundred-weight, cwt.; hecatomb [Gr. antiq.]; centipede; centumvir [Rom. antiq.], centumvirate, centurion; bicentenary, bicentennial; tercentenary, tercentennial; great or long hundred (one hundred and twenty [coll.]); gross (twelve dozen).

9. five hundred, five centuries; five C's, half G or grand [both crim. slang, U.S.].

10. thousand, M, chiliad; **millennium;** G, grand, one G or grand, thou, yard [all crim. slang, U.S.]; chiliagon, chiliahedron or chiliaëdron [both geom.]; chiliarchia or chiliarch [Gr. antiq.]; millepede [zool.]; milligram, milliliter, millimeter, kilogram, kiloliter, kilometer [all metric meas.]; kilocycle (radio); **myriad,** ten thousand; one hundred thousand, lac or lakh [Ind.].

11. million; ten million, crore [Ind.].

12. billion, thousand million, milliard, great or long million [coll.].

13. (trillion, etc.) trillion, quadrillion, quintillion, sextillion, septillion, octillion, nonillion, decillion, undecillion, duodecillion, tredecillion, quattuordecillion, quindecillion, sexdecillion, septemdecillion, octodecillion, novemdecillion, vigintillion; zillion, jillion [both slang].

14. (division into five or more parts) quinquesection, quinquepartition, sextipartition, etc.; **decimation,** decimalization; fifth, sixth, etc.; **tenth, tithe,** decima.

VERBS **15.** (divide by five, etc.) quinquesect; **decimate,** decimalize.

16. (multiply by five, etc.) fivefold, sixfold, etc.; quintuple, quintuplicate; sextuple, sextuplicate; centuple, centuplicate.

ADJS. **17. fifth,** quinary; **fivefold, quintuple,** quintuplicate; quinquepartite, quinquefid; quincuncial [spec. bot.], pentastyle [arch.]; pentad, pentavalent [both chem.]; quin-, penta-.

18. sixth, senary; **sixfold, sextuple;** sexpartite, sextipartite, hexapartite; hexagonal, hexahedral, hexangular [all geom.]; hexad [chem.], sextuplex [teleg.], hexastyle [arch.], sexennial, hexatomic [chem.]; hexamerous [bot.]; hex-, hexa-, sex-.

19. seventh, septimal; **sevenfold, septuple,** septenary; septempartite [bot.], septemfid; heptagonal, heptahedral, heptangular [all geom.]; heptamerous [bot.]; sept-, hept-, hepta-.

20. eighth, octonary; **eightfold, octuple,** octofid, octaploid; octagonal, octahedral, octan, octangular [all geom.]; octastyle [arch.]; oct-, octa-, octo-.

21. ninth, novenary, nonary; **ninefold, nonuple;** enneahedral [geom.], enneastyle [arch.]; noven-, nona-, non-, ennea-, enne-.

22. tenth, denary, **decimal,** tithe; **tenfold, decuple;** decagonal, decahedral [both geom.]; decasyllabic; dec-, deci-, deca-, deka-.

23. eleventh, undecennial, undecennary.

24. twelfth, duodenary, duodenal; duodecimal.

25. thirteenth, fourteenth, etc.; 'steenth [coll.]; eleventeenth, umpteenth [both slang]; in one's teens.

26. **twentieth,** vicenary, vicennial, vigesimal, vicesimal.

27. **sixtieth,** sexagesimal, sexagenary.

28. **seventieth,** septuagesimal, septuagenary.

29. **hundredth,** centesimal, **centennial,** centenary, centurial; **hundredfold, centuple,** centuplicate; secular; centigrado; cent-, centi-, hecto-.

30. **sesquicentennial;** tercentenary.

31. **thousandth,** millenary, **millennial; thousandfold;** kilo-, milli-.

32. **millionth, billionth, trillionth,** etc.

100. PLURALITY

More Than One.—NOUNS 1. **plurality,** pluralism, pluralness; a greater number, more; the plural [gram.]; plurality of causes.

2. **majority,** plurality, more than half, the greater number, the greatest number, **most,** preponderance *or* preponderancy, **bulk, mass;** lion's share, Benjamin's mess; excess of votes.

3. pluralization, plurification.

4. **multiplication,** multiplying, proliferation, **spread;** multiple, multiplier, multiplicand; tables, multiplication table.

VERBS 5. pluralize, plurify.

6. **multiply, increase,** proliferate, **spread.** ADJS. 7. **plural,** more, more than one; some, certain; plurative [logic.].

8. **multiple,** multiplied, multifold, **manifold;** multinomial, polynomial [both math.].

9. majority, most, the greatest number. ADVS. 10. in majority, **in the majority.**

101. NUMEROUSNESS

NOUNS 1. **numerousness, multiplicity, manyness,** multitudinousness, rifeness, profuseness, profusion; **abundance** 659.2; **countlessness,** innumerability.

2. (indefinite number) **a number,** a certain number, one or two, two or three, **a few, several;** eleventeen, X-teen, umpteen, umptyum, forty-eleven [all slang].

3. (large number) **multitude,** plurality, **many; numbers, quantities,** flocks, **scores;** all kinds *or* sorts of, good *or* great few, quite a few, tidy sum [all coll.]; large amount 34.3–6; **host, army,** legion, all the world and his brother *or* wife [joc.]; **swarm, flock,** flight, cloud, bevy, covey, shoal, hive, nest, pack, bunch; throng, crowd 74.4.

4. (immense number) **a myriad,** a thousand, **a thousand and one,** a million, a billion, a quadrillion, a nonillion; a jillion, a zillion [both slang].

VERBS 5. **teem with,** overflow with, **abound with,** bristle with, **swarm with,** throng with, creep with, **crawl with, be alive with.**

6. outnumber.

ADJS. 7. **numerous, many,** not a few, no few; **very many,** full many, **ever so many,** quite some [slang], considerable [coll.]; **multitudinous,** multitudinal; **myriad,** thousand, million, billion; zillion, jillion [both slang]; **thousands of,** millions of, billions of; **worlds of,** a world of; numerous as the stars in the firmament, numerous as the sands on the seashore, numerous as the hairs on the head, "numerous as glittering gems of morning dew" [Young].

8. **several, divers, sundry,** various; fivish, sixish, etc.; some five or six, etc.; upwards of, uppards of [dial.].

9. **abundant,** copious, plentiful 659.7.

10. **teeming, swarming, crowding,** thronging, **crawling, alive with,** populous, crowded, thronged, studded, bristling, **rife, profuse,** in profusion, thick, **thick with,** thick-coming, thick as hops, ~ hail *or* flies; "thick as autumnal leaves that strow the brooks in Vallombrose" [Milton].

11. **innumerable, numberless, countless,** uncounted, untold; more than one can tell, more than you can shake a stick at [coll.], no end of *or* to.

12. **and many more,** *cum multis aliis* [L., with many others], and what not, and heaven knows what.

ADVS. 13. **numerously, multitudinously, profusely,** thickly; in throngs, in crowds, *en foule* [F.]; in heaps, *acervatim* [L.]; countlessly, **innumerably,** no end [coll., U.S.].

102. FEWNESS

NOUNS 1. **fewness,** infrequency, **sparsity,** sparseness, **scantiness, meagerness,** scrimpness, scrimpiness [coll.], skimpiness [coll.], rarity, exiguity.

2. **a few,** only a few, **small number,** scrimption [dial.], **handful, scattering,** sprinkling.

3. **minority,** least; the minority, the few; minority group.

ADJS. 4. **few, not many,** hardly *or* scarcely any, precious little [coll.], middling of [dial.], of small number, to be counted on one's fingers.

5. **sparse, scant, scanty, exiguous, infrequent,** thin, slim, **meager,** scrimp, scrimpy [coll.], skimp or skimpy [coll.], skimping [chiefly coll.], **scattered,** sprinkled, **few and far between;** rare, seldom met with, seldom seen.

6. **fewer,** smaller, less, not so much or many.

7. **minority,** least.

ADVS. 8. **sparsely,** sparsim [L.], **scantily, meagerly,** scrimp, scrimpily [coll.], skimpily [coll.], thinly, infrequently; **scatteringly, here and there,** in places, in spots [coll.], dribs-like [dial.].

103. REPETITION

NOUNS 1. **repetition, reproduction,** duplication, reduplication, redoubling; **recurrence,** reoccurrence, return, reappearance; **echo,** re-echo; quotation.

2. **iteration, reiteration, recapitulation,** recap [coll.], retelling, recounting, recountal, **recital, rehearsal,** restatement, rehash [chiefly coll.], review, summary, résumé, summing up; reassertion, reaffirmation; elaboration, dwelling upon.

3. battology, redundancy, tautology, tautologism, pleonasm; tautophony; macrology, dilogy, padding, expletive.

4. **repetitiousness,** repetitiveness; harping; **monotony,** monotone; **tedium** 882; **humdrum,** dingdong, singsong, pitter-patter; repeated sounds 454.

5. repetend, repeat, bis, ditto [coll.]; **refrain,** burden of a song, undersong, chorus, bob; bob wheel, bob and wheel; ritornel or ritornelle [mus.], ritornello [It.].

6. **encore, curtain call,** curtain [theat. cant], bow; repeat performance [coll.].

VERBS 7. **repeat, reproduce, duplicate,** dupe [slang], reduplicate, redouble, ditto [coll.], **echo,** re-echo; come again [slang], cut and come again; repeat oneself, do again; **quote,** give word for word; ring the changes on.

8. **iterate, reiterate, rehearse, recapitulate, recount,** rehash [chiefly coll.], **recite, retell,** retail, restate, reword, review, run over, sum up, summarize, resume; do or say over again, **go over,** say over, go over the same ground, go the same round, fight one's battles over again; battologize, tautologize; reaffirm, reassert.

9. **dwell on** or **upon,** insist upon, **harp upon,** harp on one or the same string,

mount or ride a hobby [coll.], sing the same old song or tune, never hear the last of; **thrash** or **thresh over,** go over again and again, go over and over; **elaborate,** dwell on at length; conjugate in all its moods, tenses and inflections.

10. **din, ding** [coll.], drum, beat, hammer, pound; **din in the ear,** say over and over.

11. (be repeated) **repeat,** do again, do a repeat; **recur,** reoccur, **come again,** come up again, **return,** reappear, resume, revert, turn or go back; keep coming, come again and again, happen over and over.

ADJS. 12. **repeated,** reproduced, redoubled; duplicated, reduplicated; **echoed,** re-echoed; **iterated, reiterated,** reiterate; retold, **twice-told;** warmed up or over, réchauffé [F.].

13. **recurrent, recurring, returning,** reappearing, ever-recurring, thick-coming, frequent, incessant.

14. **repetitious,** repetitive, repeating; **duplicative,** reduplicative; echoing, reechoing; **iterative, reiterative,** reiterant; recapitulative, recapitulatory; battological, tautological, redundant; tautophonic(al).

15. **monotonous,** monotone; **tedious** 882.8; harping; **humdrum,** singsong, dingdong [coll.], jogtrot.

ADVS. 16. **repeatedly, often, frequently, again and again, over and over,** over and over again, many times over, time and again, **time after time,** times without number; year after year, day after day, day by day, "tomorrow and tomorrow and tomorrow" [Shakespeare]; **many times,** several times, a number of times, many a time, full many a time; every now and then, every once in a while [both coll.].

17. **again,** over, over again, **once more,** two times, twice over, ditto; **anew,** de novo [L.], afresh; from the beginning, da capo [It.].

INTS. 18. encore!, bis!, once more!, again!

104. INFINITY

NOUNS 1. **infinity,** infiniteness, infinitude, immensity; **boundlessness, limitlessness, endlessness;** illimitability, interminability; **immeasurability,** incalculability, innumerability, incomprehensibility; measurelessness, countlessness, numberlessness; exhaustlessness, inexhaustibility; **all-inclusiveness,** all-comprehensiveness; **eternity** 112.2; olam, "a dark illimitable ocean, without bound" [Milton].

VERBS 2. **have no limit** or **bounds,** have or know no end, be without end, **go on and on,** go on forever, never cease or end.

ADJS. 3. **infinite,** olamic, immense; **boundless, endless, limitless,** termless, shoreless; unbounded, **unlimited,** illimited, without bound, without limit or end, no end of or to; illimitable, interminable, interminate, indefinite, indeterminate; **immeasurable,** incalculable, innumerable, incomprehensible, unfathomable; measureless, countless, sumless; **unmeasured,** unplumbed, untold, unnumbered, without measure; without number; exhaustless, inexhaustible; **all inclusive,** all comprehensive 79.13; **eternal** 112.7; "void and infinite" [Blackmore], "as boundless as the sea" [Shakespeare].

ADVS. 4. **infinitely,** immensely; **illimitably,** limitlessly, **interminably,** indefinitely, indeterminately; **immeasurably,** measurelessly, incalculably, innumerably, incomprehensibly; **endlessly,** without end, world without end; **eternally** 112.10; *ad infinitum* [L., to infinity.]

105. TIME

NOUNS 1. **time, duration,** term, while, space; **period** 107; cosmic time; space-time 178.6; time machine [science fiction].

2. Time, **Father Time,** "Old Time, that greatest and longest established spinner of all" [Dickens], "that old bald cheater, Time" [Jonson], "Old Time, the clocksetter, that bald sexton Time" [Shakespeare], "that old common arbitrator, Time" [ibid.], "the nurse and breeder of all good" [ibid.], "the soul of the world" [Pythagoras], "the Life of the soul" [Longfellow], "the author of authors" [Bacon], "the greatest innovator" [ibid.], "the devourer of things" [Ovid], "the illimitable, silent, never-resting thing called Time" [Carlyle], "a short parenthesis in a long period" [John Donne], "a sandpile we run our fingers in" [Sandburg].

3. tract of time, corridors of time, whirligig of time, glass of time, ravages of time, noiseless foot of Time, scythe of Time, "the tooth of time" [Shakespeare].

4. **course of time, passage of time, lapse of time,** progress of time, process of time, succession of time, flow of time, flux of time, stream of time, sweep of time, current of time, tide of time, march of time, step of time, flight of time, "Time's revolving wheels" [Petrarch].

VERBS 5. **elapse,** lapse, **pass, expire,** run its course, run out, go or pass by; flow, run, proceed, advance, roll or press on, flit, fly, slip, slide, glide.

6. **pass time, spend time, put in time,** employ or use time, fill or occupy time, consume time, **take time,** take up time, while away the time; spend (a specified time), pass, lead, put in, employ, use; talk against time, work against time; week-end, winter, summer; Sunday, Monday, Christmas, etc. [coll.].

ADVS. etc. 7. **when, at which time,** at which moment or instant, on which occasion, **upon which, whereupon,** at which, in which time, at what time, in what period, on what occasion, whenever or when ever [coll.]; **at that time,** on that occasion, at the same time as, at the same time or moment that, then.

8. **during,** pending, during the time or while; **in the course of,** in the process of, in the middle of [coll.]; **in the time of,** in the consulship of [joc.]; over, through, **throughout,** throughout the course of, **for the period of;** until the conclusion of, for the duration; at a stretch; during pleasure; during good behavior, *quamdiu se bene gesserit* [L., law].

9. **while,** whilst, whiles [dial.], the while; **during the time that,** at the time of, at the time that, at the same time that, at or during which time; **whereas, as long as.**

10. **until, till,** to, unto [poetic], **up to,** up to the time of, as far as, **down to,** to the time when, by the time that, pending.

11. **then,** thereat, **at that time,** at that moment or instant, in that case or instant, on that occasion; **again,** at another time, at some other time, anon.

12. **whenever,** whene'er [poetic], whensoever, whensoe'er [poetic], **at whatever time,** at anytime, anywhen [dial.], no matter when; if ever, once.

13. *anno Domini* [L.], A.D.; *ante Christum* [L.], A.C.; before Christ, B.C.; *anno urbis conditae* [L.], A.U.C.; *anno regni* [L.], A.R.

PHRS. 14. **time flies,** *tempus fugit* [L.], time runs out, time marches on, "Time rolls his ceaseless course" [Scott], time and tide wait for no man.

106. TIMELESSNESS

NOUNS 1. **timelessness, neverness,** no time, no time at all; *dies non juridicus* [both L. law; day on which no business is conducted].

2. (a time that will never come) Greek calends, Tib's or St. Tib's Eve, blue moon [slang], the 30th of February.

ADJS. 3. timeless, dateless.

ADVS. 4. never, ne'er [poetic], not ever, at no time, on no occasion, not at all; nevermore, "quoth the raven, 'Nevermore' " [Poe]; never in the world, never on earth; never in all one's born days [coll.], never in my life, jamais de ma vie [F.]; sine die [L., law, without any set day].

107. PERIOD

Portion or Point of Time.—NOUNS 1. period, point, juncture, stage; interval, space, span, stretch; time, while, hour, day, season; spell 108; ghurry [India].

2. (periods) moment, second, millisecond, microsecond; minute; hour, man-hour; day, sun; weekday; week; fortnight; month, moon, lunation; lunar month; quarter; semester; year, annum, sun, twelvemonth; light-year, solar or astronomical year, fiscal year; quinquennium, lustrum, luster; decade, decennium, decennary; century, age; millennium.

3. term, time, duration, tenure; tenure of office; enlistment, hitch [slang], bit [coll.], trick [slang].

4. (term of imprisonment) time [coll.]; hitch, stretch, jolt, lag [all slang].

5. age, generation, time, day, date, cycle; aeon; Kalpa, Yuga, Manvantara [all Hind.].

6. era, epoch, age; Ice Age, glacial epoch; Stone Age, Bronze Age, Iron Age, Steel Age; Middle Ages, Dark Ages; Depression Era; Prohibition Era [U.S.].

7. 1890's, Gay Nineties, Yellow Nineties, Moulting Nineties, Naughty Nineties, Mauve Decade, Golden Age, Gilded Age.

8. 1920's, Roaring Twenties, Golden Twenties, Mad Decade, Age of the Red-Hot Mama.

9. (modern age) Technological Age, Air Age, Jet Age, Supersonic Age, Atomic Age, Space Age; Jazz Age, Age of Jazz and Jitters.

10. geological ages

Archeozoic	Cretaceous
Azoic	Devonian
Cambrian	Eocene
Carboniferous	Jurassic
Cenozoic	Mesozoic
Comanchean	Miocene

Mississippian	Pleistocene
Oligocene	Pliocene
Ordovician	Pre-Cambrian
Paleozoic	Proterozoic
Pennsylvanian	Silurian
Permian	Triassic

11. historic eras

Abraham	Julian
Actian	Kali Yuga
Alexandrian	Kings
Armenian	the Maccabees
Augustan	Macedonian
Babylonian	the Martyrs
Byzantine	Mayan
Caesarean	Mohammedan
Caesarean Era of Antioch	Mundane Era of Alexandria
Chinese Era of Yao	Mundane Era of Antioch
Christian	Mundane Era of Constantinople
Common	
Constantinople	Nabonassar
Contracts	Olympic
Eastern Church	Persian
French Republic	Roman
Greek	Seleucidan
Greek Church	Sidonian
the Hegira	Spanish
Hindu Era of the Deluge	Syro-Macedonian Tyrian
Jalalaean or Gelalaean	Varro Vikramaditya
Japanese	Vulgar
Jewish Mundane	Yao

108. SPELL

Period of Duty, etc.—NOUNS 1. spell, fit, stretch, go [coll.].

2. turn, bout, round, inning, innings [esp. Eng.], time, time at bat, place, say, whack [slang], go [coll.]; opportunity, chance; relief, spell; one's turn, one's move [coll.], one's say.

3. shift, work shift, tour, tour of duty, watch, trick, time, turn, swing [coll.], relay, spell or turn of work; day shift, night shift, swing shift, graveyard shift [coll., U.S.]; dogwatch, anchor watch [both naut.]; lobster trick or tour, sunrise watch [both newspaper]; split shift, split schedule; overtime, golden hours [slang].

VERBS 4. take one's turn, take turns, alternate, turn and turn about; time off, spell [coll.], spell off [coll.], relieve, fill in for.

109. INTERIM

Intermediate Period.—NOUNS 1. interim, interval, interlude, intermission, intermittence, pause, break, interruption; respite 709.2; entr'acte; interregnum.

2. meantime, meanwhile, while, the while.

VERBS 3. **intervene,** interlude, interval, intermit.

ADJS. 4. **interim, temporary,** tentative, provisional, provisory.

ADVS. 5. **meanwhile, meantime,** whiles [dial. & Scot.], **in the meanwhile** or **meantime,** in the interim, *ad interim* [L.], *en attendant* [F.], in the intervening time, during the interval, at the same time, for the meantime, **for the time being,** for the nonce, for a time or season; *pendente lite* [L., law, while the suit is pending].

110. DURABILITY

Long Duration.—NOUNS 1. **durability, endurance,** duration, durableness, **lastingness,** abidingness, long-lastingness, perdurability; **continuance,** maintenance, **steadfastness,** constancy, persistence, **permanence,** standing, long standing; **longevity,** long-livedness; survival, survivance; everlastingness 112.

2. **protraction, prolongation,** continuation, extension, lengthening, lingering.

3. **length of time,** distance of time, vista of time.

4. **long time,** long while, long; **age** or **ages** [coll.], **aeon, century, eternity, years, years on end,** blue moon [coll.], coon's age [coll.], donkey's years [slang], month or week of Sundays [coll.], right smart spell [dial.].

5. **lifetime, life,** life's duration, period of existence; **generation, age;** (all) one's born days, (all) one's natural life [both coll.].

VERBS 6. **endure, last,** bide, **abide,** dwell, perdure, **continue,** run, extend, **go on,** carry on, hold on, keep on, stay on, run on, live, **live on,** continue to be, subsist, exist, **persist,** maintain, sustain, **remain, stay,** keep, hold, stand, prevail, last long, go far, hold out, brave a thousand years; perennate [bot.]; live through, tide over.

7. **linger on,** linger, tarry, go on, **go on and on, wear on,** crawl, creep, drag, **drag on,** drag along, drag its slow length along, drag a lengthening chain.

8. **outlast,** outwear, **outlive;** survive, live to light again.

9. **protract, prolong,** continue, **extend, lengthen,** lengthen out, **draw out, spin out,** drag out, string out [coll., U.S.], eke out; linger on, dwell on.

ADJS. 10. **durable,** perdurable, **lasting,** lasty [coll. & dial.], **enduring,** perduring, **abiding, continuing,** remaining, staying, persisting, persistent, **steadfast, constant, permanent,** perennial; **long-lasting,** long-standing, of long duration or standing; **long-lived,** longevous, macrobiotic; chronic; everlasting 112.7.

11. **protracted, prolonged,** extended, lengthened; long, overlong; lasting, **lingering,** languishing; long-continued, long-continuing, long-pending; spun-out, dragged-out, long-drawn, **long-drawn-out;** longwinded.

12. **daylong, nightlong,** weeklong, monthlong, yearlong.

13. **lifelong,** livelong, lifetime, for life.

ADVS. 14. **long, for long, for a long time,** for a right smart spell [dial.], for ever so long, for many a long day, for an age [coll.], for ages [coll.], for a coon's or dog's age [coll.], for a month or week of Sundays [coll.], **for ever and a day, for years on end;** all the year round, all the day long, the livelong day, as the day is long; morning, noon and night; hour after hour, day after day, month after month, year after year; day in day out, month in month out, year in year out.

111. TRANSIENCE

Short Duration.—NOUNS 1. **transcience** or **transiency,** transientness, **impermanence** or impermanency, transitoriness, **temporariness,** fleetingness, **momentariness; ephemerality;** evanescence, volatility, fugacity, short-livedness; mortality, perishability, corruptibility.

2. **brevity, briefness,** shortness, fleetness.

3. **short time, little while,** little, small space, span, spurt, **short spell;** no time, less than no time; bit or **little bit,** couple of winks, **two two's** [all coll.]; **two shakes,** couple or brace of shakes, shake of a lamb's tail, two shakes of a dead sheep's tail or brass monkey's tail [all slang].

4. **transient,** transient guest or boarder, temporary lodger.

5. **ephemeron** (*pl.* ephemera), ephemeral; ephemerid [zool.], shad fly, May fly; bubble, smoke; nine days' wonder.

VERBS 6. (be transient) **flit, fly,** fleet; pass, **pass away, vanish, evaporate,** fade, melt, sink; fade like a shadow, vanish like a dream, burst like a bubble, **go up in smoke.**

ADJS. 7. **transient, transitory,** transitive, transeunt; **temporary,** temporal; **impermanent,** unenduring, unendurable, undurable, nondurable, nonpermanent; **short-**

lived, **ephemeral,** evanescent, volatile, **momentary,** unstable, deciduous; **passing,** fleeting, flitting, flying; fugitive, fugacious; perishable, mortal, corruptible; "as transient as the clouds" [Ingersoll], here today and gone tomorrow.

8. **brief, short,** quick, brisk, fleet, "short and sweet" [T. Lodge]; **meteoric,** cometary, flashing; short-term, short-termed.

ADVS. 9. **temporarily,** for the moment, for the time, *pro tempore* [L.], *pro tem,* for the nonce, for the time being, for a time, awhile.

10. **briefly, shortly,** quickly, **in a little while,** in a short time, at short notice, **in no time,** in less than no time; **in a bit** *or* **little bit, in two two's,** in a couple of winks, in quick order, in nothing flat [all coll.]; **in two shakes,** in a couple *or* brace of shakes, in a shake of a lamb's tail, in two shakes of a dead sheep's tail *or* brass monkey's tail [all slang]; **momentarily,** momently, for a moment; fleetingly, flittingly; between cup and lip.

112. PERPETUITY

Endless Duration.—NOUNS 1. **perpetuity,** perpetualness; everness, foreverness, **everlastingness,** eternalness; **permanence,** ever-duringness, perdurability; **constancy,** continuance, continualness, perenniality; **ceaselessness,** unceasingness, incessancy; **endlessness,** never-endingness, **interminability.**

2. **eternity, infinity,** olam, everlasting, **forever,** sempiternity, endless time, **time without end;** "a moment standing still for ever" [James Montgomery], "a short parenthesis in a long period" [John Donne], "the stiller sea that stretches everlastingly" [W. W. Gibson], "the wide, th' unbounded prospect" [Addison]; coeternity.

3. **immortality, deathlessness,** imperishability, incorruptibility, athanasy *or* athanasia.

4. **perpetuation,** preservation, eternalization, immortalization.

VERBS 5. **perpetuate,** preserve from oblivion, perennialize, eternalize, eternize, **immortalize;** monumentalize.

6. last *or* endure forever, **go on forever,** go on and on, **have no end,** have no limits *or* bounds, never cease, never end, never die.

ADJS. 7. **perpetual, everlasting,** everliving, ever-being, ever-abiding, ever-during, ever-durable, **permanent,** perdurable; eter-

nal, eterne [poetic], **infinite,** olamic; sempiternal; dateless, ageless; **endless,** unending, never-ending, without end, **interminable; continual,** continuous, **constant, ceaseless,** unceasing, **incessant,** unremitting, unintermitting, uninterrupted, "continuous as the stars that shine" [Wordsworth] coeternal.

8. **perennial,** indeciduous, **evergreen,** ever-new; ever-blooming, ever-bearing.

9. **immortal,** everlasting, **deathless,** undying, never-dying, **imperishable,** incorruptible, amaranthine; fadeless, **unfading,** never-fading.

ADVS. 10. **perpetually,** in perpetuity, everlastingly, everly [dial.], **eternally,** permanently, perennially, **constantly,** continually, **ceaselessly,** unceasingly, **incessantly; endlessly,** unendingly, **interminably,** without end, world without end, time without end, "from everlasting to everlasting" [Bible].

11. **always, all along, all the time,** all the while, at all times, *semper et ubique* [L., always and everywhere]; **invariably,** without exception, never otherwise, *semper eadem* [L., always the same].

12. **forever, forevermore, for ever and ever,** forever and aye, forever and amen [coll.], forever and a day [coll.], now and forever, *ora e sempre* [It.], "yesterday and today and forever" [Bible]; ever, **evermore,** ever and anon, ever and again; aye, for aye; **for good,** for keeps [coll.], for good and all, for all time; throughout the ages, from age to age, in all ages, "for ages of ages" [Vulgate]; **to the end of time,** "to the last syllable of recorded time" [Shakespeare], to the crack of doom, till doomsday; till all is blue [coll.], till hell freezes over [slang], till the cows come home [slang].

13. **for life,** for all one's natural life [coll.], in all one's born days [coll.]; from the cradle to the grave, from the womb to the tomb; **till death,** till death do us part.

113. INSTANTANEOUSNESS

Imperceptible Duration.—NOUNS 1. **instantaneousness,** instantaneity, momentariness, **immediateness,** immediacy.

2. **suddenness,** suddenty [chiefly Scot. and law], sudden (as, all of a *sudden*), **abruptness,** precipitance *or* precipitancy; **unexpectedness,** unanticipation.

3. **instant, moment, second,** sec [slang], split second, half a second, minute, **trice,** twinkle, **twinkling, twinkling** *or* **twinkle of an eye,** twink, wink, bat of an eye [coll.],

flash, flash of lightning, crack, tick, stroke, breath, shake or half a shake [slang]; **jiffy**, jiff, half a jiffy [all coll.].

ADJS. **4. instantaneous**, instant, momentary, **immediate**, presto, quick as thought or lightning.

5. sudden, abrupt; precipitant, precipitate, precipitous; **hasty**, headlong, impetuous; speedy, swift, quick; **unexpected**, unanticipated, unforeseen, unlooked for.

ADVS. **6. instantly**, instanter, instant [poetic], momently, **instanteously, immediately**, presto, subito [It., music]; **on the instant**, on the spot, on the dot [coll.], on the nail; just then, just now; no sooner said than done.

7. in an instant, in a trice, in a second, in a moment, in a jiff or jiffy [coll.], in a flash, in a twink, **in a twinkling, in the twinkling of an eye**, in a shake or half a shake [slang], before you can say "Jack Robinson," ~ "knife" or "scat" [coll.]; in no time, in less than no time, in nothing flat [coll.]; like a shot, like a shot out of hell [slang].

8. at once, at once and on the spot, **then and there**, now, right now, right away, **right off**, bang-off [slang], this minute, this very minute, **without delay**, without the least delay; at the same instant, in the same breath; **all at once**, at one time, at a stroke, at one stroke, at a blow, at one blow, at one swoop, "at one fell swoop" [Shakespeare]; at one jump, per saltum [L.], uno saltu [L.].

9. suddenly, sudden, of a sudden, on a sudden, on a suddenty, **all of a sudden, all at once**, in a bang [slang]; **abruptly**, sharp (as, pull up sharp); **precipitously**, precipitately, precipitantly; slap-bang [coll.], slapdash; smack, bang, slap, plop, plunk, plump, pop; **unexpectedly**, unawares; like a thunderbolt or thunderclap, like a bolt from the blue.

114. CHRONOLOGY

Measurement of Time.—NOUNS **1. chronology**, horology, chronometry, horometry, chronoscopy.

2. the time, time of day; **hour**, minute; stroke of the hour, time signal, bell [naut.].

3. standard time, civil time, zone time [naut.]; mean time, solar time, mean solar time, sidereal time, apparent time, Greenwich time; local time, Eastern time, Central time, Mountain time, Pacific time [all U.S. & Can.]; Atlantic time [Can.]; Alaska standard time; daylight-saving time, fast time [coll.], summer time [chiefly Eng.].

4. date, point of time, time, **day**; postdate, antedate; datemark; date line, International Date Line.

5. epact, annual epact, monthly or menstrual epact.

6. timepiece, timekeeper, **timer**, chronometer, ghurry [India]; horologe, horologium; **clock**, ticker; **watch**, turnip [slang], souper [slang, U.S.]; clockworks, watchworks.

7. almanac, Almanach de Gotha, Ephemeris and Nautical Almanac, Information Please Almanac, Nautical Almanac, Poor Richard's Almanac, Whitaker's Almanack, World Almanac.

8. calendar, calends or kalends, style, fasti [L., pl.]; chronogram; astronomical calendar or almanac, ephemeris; perpetual calendar; Chinese calendar, Cotsworth calendar, Gregorian calendar, international fixed calendar, Jewish calendar, Julian calendar, Roman calendar, Swiss plan.

9. chronicle, chronology, register, registry, record; annals, journal, diary; time sheet, time book; timecard, time ticket; timetable.

10. chronologist, chronologer, chronographer, horologist, horologer; **chronicler**, annalist.

VERBS **11. time, fix or set the time**, mark the time; **keep time**, mark time, measure time, beat time; clock, stop-watch [both coll.].

12. punch the clock, punch in, punch out [all slang]; **time in, time out**; ring in, ring out.

13. date, be dated, date at or from, bear date; fix or set the date, make a date; **predate**, antedate; **postdate**; **update**, bring up to date; datemark.

14. chronologize, chronicle, calendar, intercalate.

ADJS. **15. chronologic(al)**, temporal; chronometric(al), chronoscopic, chronographic(al), chronogrammatic(al), horologic(al), horometric(al); metronomic(al); calendric(al), intercalary; dated.

ADVS. etc. **16. o'clock**, of the clock, by the clock; half past, half after [Eng.], half [Scot.; as, half six o'clock]; half past the corner, half past kissing time [both slang]; a quarter of or to, a quarter past or after.

17. timepieces

alarm clock	box chronometer
atomic clock	calendar watch

chronograph	pendulum clock
chronometer	pneumatic clock
chronopher	pocket chronom-
chronoscope	eter
clepsydra	program clock
cuckoo clock	repeater
egg glass	sandglass
electric clock	sidereal clock
electronic clock	split-second watch
dial	stemwinder [coll.]
gnomon	stop watch
grandfather clock	sundial
half-hour glass	telechron clock
half-minute glass	telltale
hourglass	three minute glass
independent-	time ball
seconds watch	time clock
isochronon	time recorder
journeyman	turret clock
marine	watchman's clock
chronometer	water clock
metronome	wristwatch
pendule	

115. ANACHRONISM

False Estimation of Time.—NOUNS 1. anachronism, mistiming, misdating, misdate; parachronism (a chronological error, esp. after the correct date), metachronism (after the correct date), prochronism (before the correct date); prolepsis, anticipation.

VERBS 2. mistime, misdate.

ADJS. 3. anachronous, anachronistic, parachronistic; mistimed, misdated; ahead of time, beforehand; behind time, behindhand; overdue.

116. PRIORITY

Previous Time.—NOUNS 1. priority, previousness, antecedence or antecedency, anteriority, precedence or precedency, precession; pre-existence; postdate, antedate; past time 119.

2. antecedent, premise.

VERBS 3. be prior, precede, antecede, precurse, forerun, come or go before; herald, usher in, proclaim, announce; antedate, predate; pre-exist.

ADJS. 4. prior, earlier, previous, cidevant [F.], former, fore, first, preceding, foregoing, anterior, antecedent; pre-existent.

5. prewar, ante-bellum, before the war.

ADVS. 6. prior to, previous to, hitherto, heretofore, theretofore, before, afore [dial.], earlier, ere, erenow, ere then or now, or ever; already, yet; formerly 119.10.

117. POSTERIORITY

Later Time.—NOUNS 1. posteriority, subsequence, sequence, succession, fol-lowing, coming after; supervenience, supervention; remainder, hangover [coll., U.S.].

VERBS 2. follow, come or go after, succeed, supervene; ensue, issue, emanate, attend, result.

ADJS. 3. subsequent, later, after, posterior, following, succeeding, successive, sequent, consecutive, ensuing, attendant; junior (of later date).

4. post-, after-; posthumous, after-death; postprandial, postcenal, after-dinner; postwar, post-bellum, after the war; postdiluvian, postdiluvial, after the flood.

ADVS. 5. subsequently, later, after, afterwards, after that, next, since; thereafter, thereon, thereupon, therewith, then; ex post facto [L., from what is done afterwards, after the offense has been committed.].

6. after which, on or upon which, whereupon, whereon, whereat, whereto, whereunto, wherewith, wherefore, on, upon; hereinafter.

PREPS. 7. after, subsequent to, later than, past, beyond, behind.

118. SIMULTANEOUSNESS

NOUNS 1. simultaneousness, simultaneity, coincidence, concurrence, concomitance, coexistence; contemporaneousness, contemporaneity, coetaneousness, coevality; synchronism, synchronization; isochronism.

2. contemporary, coexistent, coeval.

VERBS 3. synchronize, contemporize; coincide, concur, coexist; accompany, go hand in hand, keep pace with, keep in step; isochronize.

ADJS. 4. simultaneous, coinstantaneous, concurrent, concomitant, collateral; coexistent, coexisting; contemporaneous, contemporary, coetaneous, coeval; coterminous, conterminous; isochronous, isochronal; coeternal.

5. synchronous, synchronized, in sync [motion-picture slang]; in time, in step, in tempo.

ADVS. 6. simultaneously, concurrently, coinstantaneously; together, all together, at the same time, at one and the same time, as one, as one man, in concert with, in chorus, with one voice, una voce [L.], in the same breath; at one time, at a clip [coll., U.S.].

119. THE PAST

NOUNS **1. the past, heretofore, foretime,** former times, times past, **days gone by, bygone times** or **days, yesterday, yesteryear;** the years that are past, "the days that are no more" [Tennyson], "the irrevocable Past" [Longfellow], "thou unrelenting past" [Bryant], "the eternal landscape of the past" [Tennyson].

2. old or **olden times,** early times, **old days,** the olden time, times of old, **days of old, days of yore,** yore, yoretime, eld [poetic], good old times or days, langsyne or auld lang syne [chiefly Scot.], way back [dial. & coll.], **long ago,** the dear days beyond recall.

3. antiquity, ancient times, time immemorial, remote age or time, remote or **distant past,** distance of time, "the dark backward and abysm of time" [Shakespeare]; ancientness 123.

VERBS **4. be past, be a thing of the past,** be all over, have run its course, have run out, have had its day.

ADJS. **5. past, gone,** by, **gone-by, bygone,** bypast, ago, agone [dial.], **over,** departed, passed, passed away, elapsed, lapsed, expired, run out, blown over, exploded, forgotten, extinct, no more, irrecoverable, never to return.

6. (grammar) past, preterit or preterite; pluperfect, past perfect; aorist, aoristic.

7. former, fore, past, **previous,** late, recent, **once, one-time,** sometime, **erstwhile,** then, quondam; prior 116.4.

8. foregoing, afore-going, **preceding,** last, latter.

9. back, backward, into the past; early; retrospective, retroactive, ex post facto.

ADVS. **10. formerly, previously, earlier, before,** before now, ere now, erenow, **hitherto, heretofore,** aforetime, beforetime, **in the past,** in times past; then; prior to 116.6.

11. once, once upon a time, one day, one fine morning, time was.

12. ago, agone [dial.], apast [dial.], **since,** gone by; back, back when; backward, to or into the past; retrospectively, retroactively.

13. long ago, long since, a long while or **time ago,** right smart ago [dial.], some time ago or since, some time back, a way or away back [dial. & coll.], ages ago, **years ago,** donkey's years ago [slang]; **in times past,** in times gone by, in the old days, in the good old days; **anciently, of old, of yore,** in ancient times, in olden times, in the olden time, **in days of yore,** "in yore agone" [W. Morris]; early, in the memory of man, time out of mind.

14. since, ever since, until now.

15. since long ago, long since, from away back [dial. & coll.], since days of yore, **from time immemorial,** from time out of mind, since the world was made, since the world was young, since the days of Methuselah, since Adam, since Adam was a boy, since Heck or Hector was a pup [slang], since God knows when [slang].

120. THE PRESENT

NOUNS **1. the present,** the present juncture or occasion, the present hour or moment, **the present day** or **time,** the present age, **today,** this day, **this day and age,** this hour, **now,** the now, the nonce, the **time being;** the times, our times, these days; the historical present, the hysterical present [joc.]; "the living sum-total of the whole Past" [Carlyle].

ADJS. **2. present, immediate,** instant, **latest, current,** running, extant, existent, **existing,** actual, being, that is; **present-day,** present-time, present-age; **contemporary,** contemporaneous.

ADVS. **3. now, at present,** on the present occasion, **at this time,** at this time of day, at the present time, "upon this bank and shoal of time" [Shakespeare]; **today,** in these days, **in this day and age,** in our time, hereadays, **nowadays,** nowanights; tonight; here, hereat, **here and now,** even now, but now, just now, as of now; on the spot, on the dot [coll.], on the nail; for the nonce, for the time being; for this occasion, *pro hac vice* [L.]; on the spur of the moment or occasion, prompted by the occasion.

4. until now, till now, **hereunto,** until this time, by this time, **up to now,** up to the present, up to this time, to this day, **so far,** thus far, **as yet, to date,** yet, already, still, now or then as previously.

121. THE FUTURE

NOUNS **1. the future, futurity, hereafter,** aftertime, after years, **time to come,** the morrow, **tomorrow,** *mañana* [Sp.]; remote or distant future; **by-and-by,** the sweet by-and-by [coll.]; the womb of time, "the past again, entered through another gate" [Pinero], "the never-ending flight of future days" [Milton].

2. **the hereafter,** the great hereafter, "the good hereafter" [Whittier], **after-world,** other world, **next world,** world to come, life *or* world beyond the grave, **the beyond,** the great beyond, the unknown, the great unknown, **the grave,** home, abode *or* world of the dead, eternal home, "the great world of light, that lies behind all human destinies" [Longfellow]; **after-life, postexistence,** future state, **life to come,** life after death.

3. **doomsday,** doom, day of doom, crack of doom; **Judgment Day,** Day of Judgment, the Judgment; eschatology [theol.].

4. **futurity,** futureness; ultimateness, eventuality.

5. **advent,** coming, **approach of time,** time drawing on.

VERBS 6. **come,** come on, **approach,** near, **draw on** *or* near, await, stare one in the face.

7. **postexist,** live on.

ADJS. 8. **future,** later, hereafter; **coming,** forthcoming, approaching, nearing, prospective, eventual, ultimate, to-be, **to come.**

ADVS. 9. **in the future,** in after time, **afterwards,** later, at a later time, after a time *or* while, anon; **by and by,** in the sweet by-and-by [coll.]; **tomorrow,** *mañana* [Sp.], the day after tomorrow; *proximo* [L., in the next month], *prox.* [abbr.].

10. **in future, hereafter,** hereafterward [dial.], thereafter, **henceforth,** henceforwards, thence, **thenceforth,** thenceforward, thenceforwards, from this *or* that time, from then on, **from here** *or* **now on, from now on in** [coll.], from here in *or* out [coll.], as of now.

11. **in time, in due time,** in due season, in due course, all in good time, **in the fullness of time,** in the course *or* process of time, **eventually, ultimately,** in the long run.

12. **sometime,** somewhen, **someday, some of these days,** one of these days, some fine day *or* morning, one fine day *or* morning, some sweet day [coll.], sometime or other, **sooner or later.**

PREPS. 13. **about to,** at *or* **on the point of,** on the eve of, on the brink *or* verge of, near to, close upon, in the act of.

122. NEWNESS

NOUNS 1. **newness,** freshness, brandnewness; **recentness,** recency, lateness; **novelty,**

novelness, gloss of novelty, newfangledness; **uniqueness,** originality; **uncommonness,** unusualness, strangeness, unfamiliarity.

2. **a novelty, innovation,** newfangle [dial. & coll.], newfandangle [slang], newfangled device, contraption [coll.], newfangled contraption [coll.], new wheeze [slang], **new** *or* **latest wrinkle** [slang], **the last word** [slang], the latest thing, the latest scream [slang], *dernier cri* [F., the latest cry].

3. **modernity,** modernness; modernism, futurism; modernization.

4. **modern,** modern man; modernist; futurist; modernizer; neologist, neoterist, neoteric; modern generation, rising generation.

VERBS 5. **renew,** renovate 692.17.

6. **modernize,** streamline; update, **bring up to date;** futurize.

ADJS. 7. **new,** young, neoteric; **fresh,** fresh as paint [coll.], fresh as the morning's dew; **unused, firsthand, original;** untried, untouched, unhandled, unhandseled, untrodden, unbeaten; virgin, virginal; green, vernal; ever-new, evergreen.

8. **fresh** (as, a *fresh* start), **additional, further,** other, another; **renewed.**

9. **new-made,** new-built, new-wrought, new-begotten, new-grown, new-laid; **newborn,** new-fledged; **new-model,** late-model.

10. **brand-new,** bran-new, fire-new, span-new, spick-and-span, spick-and-span new; spit-and-spang new, brand spit-and-spang new, brand spick-and-span new, brand spank-fire new, brand spanking, **brand-spanking new,** brand splinterfire new, brand splinter new, spanking, spanking new, spank-fire new, splinterfire new, splinternew, spitnew, splitnew [all coll., slang or dial.]; **just out,** hot off the fire, hot off the press, hot off [coll.].

11. **novel, original, unique, different;** strange, unusual, uncommon; unfamiliar, unheard-of.

12. **newfangled,** newfangle [dial. & coll.]; newfandangled, newfandangle, newwrinkled [all slang].

13. **recent,** late, newly come, of yesterday; latter, later.

14. **modern, contemporary, present-day,** present-time, twentieth-century; **new-fashioned,** new-fashion [dial.]; **up-to-date,** up-to-datish, **up-to-the-minute,** up-to-dick [slang], up [coll.], abreast of the times; **advanced,** progressive, forward-looking, *fin-de-siècle* [F.]; **ultramodern,** ultra-

ultra; **modernistic,** futuristic; modernized, streamlined.

15. **newest,** last, **latest,** most recent.

ADVS. 16. **newly,** freshly, new, **anew,** *de novo* [L.], **afresh, again.**

17. **recently, lately, latterly, of late,** not long ago, a short time ago, the other day, only yesterday; just now, right now [chiefly coll.].

123. OLDNESS

Versus Modernness or Newness.—NOUNS
1. **oldness, age,** eld [poetic]; elderliness, old age 126.5; **ancientness, antiquity,** "hoar antiquity" [Thomas Warren], rust *or* cobwebs of antiquity; venerableness, great *or* hoary age, "the ancient and honourable" [Bible]; **primitiveness,** primordialism, primordiality, aboriginality.

2. **tradition, custom,** common law, **immemorial usage,** Sunna [Moham.]; traditionalism, traditionality; legend, lore, folklore.

3. **antiquation, superannuation,** staleness, disuse; **old-fashionedness,** unfashionableness, out-of-dateness; **old-fogyishness,** fogyishness, stuffiness, stodginess.

4. **antiquarianism,** archaism; medievalism, Pre-Raphaelitism; **archaeology** 123.22.

5. **antiquarian,** antiquary, *laudator temporis acti* [L., praiser of times past], "critics in rust" [Addison]; dryasdust, the Rev. Dr. Dryasdust [Scott], Jonathan Oldbuck [ibid.], Herr Teufelsdroeckh [Carlyle]; **archaeologist** 123.23; medievalist, Pre-Raphaelite; antique dealer.

6. **antiquities,** archaisms; **relics,** relics of the past, reliquiae; **remains,** survival, vestige, ruins; **fossil,** petrification; petrified wood, petrified forest; fossil man; prehuman, missing link, ape-man; **artifact,** eolith, mezzolith, microlith, neolith, paleolith, plateaulith; Egyptian, Assyrian, Babylonian, Sanskrit; ancient manuscripts 600.12; **antique.**

7. **ancient,** man of old; preadamite, antediluvian; **primitive, aboriginal,** aborigine, binghi [slang, Australia], autochthon; cave man, cave dwellers; Ice Age man, Stone Age man, Bronze Age man, Iron Age man.

8. (antiquated person) **back number** [coll., U.S.], dodo *or* old dodo [coll.], fossil [coll.], antique [joc.], **mossback** [slang], **longhair** [slang], square [slang], **mid-Victorian,** antediluvian; fogy, **old fogy,** regu-

lar old fogy, fogram *or* fogrum [coll.], **fuddy-duddy,** granny [coll.], old woman.

VERBS 9. **age,** grow old 126.10; **antiquate,** fossilize; **superannuate,** outdate; obsolesce, become obsolete *or* extinct.

ADJS. 10. **old** (not modern), ole [dial.], auld [dial. & Scot.], olden [chiefly poetic], old-time; **ancient, antique,** venerable, hoary; yore [dial.], of old, of yore; dateless, ageless; **immemorial,** whereof the memory of man runneth not to the contrary; old as Methuselah *or* Adam, old as history, old as the hills; **elderly** 126.15.

11. **primitive,** prime, **primeval,** primigenial, primordial, pristine; **aboriginal,** autochthonous; primoprimitive; ancestral, patriarchal; **prehistoric,** protohistoric, preadamite, ante-patriarchal; prehuman.

12. **traditional,** traditive; **legendary,** unwritten, handed down; **prescriptive,** customary, conventional, understood, admitted, recognized, acknowledged, received; **time-honored,** immemorial; **longstanding, of long standing,** long-established, established, fixed, inveterate, rooted.

13. **antiquated,** grown old, **superannuated, antique, archaic,** of other times, old-world, afterage; Victorian, mid-Victorian; medieval, Gothic; antediluvian, Noachian, arky [slang], Noarchaic [slang]; fossil, fossilized.

14. **stale, fusty, musty,** rusty, dusty, moldy, mildewed; **worn, timeworn; moth-eaten,** mossgrown, crumbling, moldering, gone to seed.

15. **passé, obsolete, extinct,** gone out, gone-by, dead, disused, past, run out, **outworn.**

16. **old-fashioned,** old-fashion [dial.], oldfangled, old-timy [coll.], **out-of-date, dated,** outdated, **outmoded,** out of fashion, out of season, **unfashionable,** styleless, offbeat, **behind the times,** of the old school, old hat [coll.], back-number [coll.], black-letter, has-been [coll.], tintype [slang], model-T [slang].

17. **old-fogyish,** fogyish, old-fogy; fuddy-duddy, **stuffy, stodgy.**

18. **secondhand, used,** worn, **unnew,** not new; hand-me-down, reach-me-down [both slang].

19. **older,** elder; **oldest,** eldest, eldermost [dial.]; former 119.7.

20. **archaeological,** paleological, etc. 123.22; antiquarian; paleolithic, eolithic, neolithic, mezzolithic.

ADVS. 21. anciently 119.13.

22. archaeology

Assyriology	paleoglaciology
Egyptology	paleography
epigraphy	paleoherpetology
fossilology	paleohistology
human	paleohydrography
paleontology	paleolatry
micropaleontology	paleolimnology
palaeosophy	paleolithy
palaeotypography	paleology
palaeziology	paleometeorology
paleechnology	paleontography
paleoanthropog-	paleontology
raphy	paleopathology
paleoanthropology	paleophysiography
paleobiogeography	paleophysiology
paleobiology	paleophytology
paleobotany	paleopotamology
paleochorology	paleopsychology
paleoclimatology	paleornithology
paleocosmology	paleozoology
paleodendrology	prehistoric
paleoecology	anthropology
paleoeremology	prehistoric
paleoethnography	archaeology
paleoethnology	prehistory
paleogeography	protohistory

23. archaeologists

Assyriologist	paleoethnologist
Egyptologist	paleoglaciologist
epigrapher,	paleographer,
epigraphist	paleographist
fossilologist	paleoherpetologist
palaeotypographist	paleolithist
palaetiologist	paleologist
paleethnographer	paleometeorologist
paleethnologist	paleontologist
paleoanthropologist	paleophysiologist
paleobiologist	paleophytologist
paleobotanist	paleornithologist
paleochorologist	paleozoologist
paleoclimatologist	prehistorian
paleodentrologist	protohistorian
paleoecologist	

24. Stone Age cultures

Acheulean	Magdalenian
Aurignacian	Mousterian
Azilian	Neolithic
Chellean	Paleolithic
Combe-Capelle	Pre-Chellean
Cro-Magnon	Solutrean
Eolithic	

25. prehistoric men and manlike primates

Aurignacian man	Grimaldi man
Australopithecus	Heidelberg man
Brunn race	Iberian race
cave man	Ice Age man
Cro-Magnon man	Java man
Dawn man (the	Meganthropus
Piltdown hoax)	Neanderthal man
eolithic man	neolithic man
Florisbad man	paleolithic man
Furfooz or	Peking man
Grenelle man	Piltdown man
Galley Hill man	(a hoax)

Pithecanthropus	Rhodesian man
Plesianthropus	Stone Age Man
pre-Incan	Swanscombe man

26. prehistoric animals

Brontops	ornithosaur
dinothere	phytosaur
Dinotheres	Phytosauria
Dinotheriidae	pterodactyl
Dinotherium	pterosaur
giant ground sloth	Pterosauria
ichthyosaur,	saber-toothed
ichthyosaurus	tiger or cat
Ichthyosauria	Smilodon
imperial mammoth	Stegodon
Machairodus	titanothere
mammoth	Titantotheriidae
mastodon	Titantotherium
megathere	wooly or northern
Megatheriidae	mammoth
Megatherium	

27. dinosaurs

Allosaurus	Ornithomimidae
Atlantosaurus	Ornithomimus
Brontosaurus	ornithopod
Ceratops	Ornithopoda
Ceratopsia	palaeosaur
Ceratopsidae	Palaeosaurus
Ceratosaurus	Predentata
Compsognathus	pterodactyl
Dinosauria	Saurischia
Diplodocus	sauropod
Gigantosaurus	Sauropoda
Iguanodon	Scelidosaurus
megalosaur	stegosaur
Megalosauridae	Stegosauria
Megalosaurus	Stegosaurus
Megatherium	theropod
Morosaurus	Theropoda
Ornithischia	Triceratops

124. YOUTH

NOUNS 1. **youth**, youthhood, youthhead [chiefly Scot.], **youthfulness**, youthiness [Scot.], **juvenility**, **youngness**, tenderness, tender age, early years, "the days of thy youth" [Bible]; prime of life, flower of life, "flower of youth" [Livy], springtide of life, seedtime of life, "the May of life" [Schiller], "the very May-morn of his youth" [Shakespeare], "the summer of your youth" [Edward Moore], "life's morning march" [Thomas Campbell], golden season of life, "the glad season of life" [Carlyle], heyday of youth, "**salad days**" [Shakespeare], calf days [coll.].

2. **childhood**, "childhood's careless days" [Bryant]; **boyhood**; **girlhood**, maidenhood, maidenhead, flapperhood [coll.].

3. **immaturity**, **undevelopment**, inexperience, **callowness**, unripeness, greenness, rawness, sappiness; **minority**, juniority, infancy [law], nonage.

4. **childishness**, childlikeness, **puerility**;

boyishness, boylikeness; **girlishness**, girl-likeness, maidenliness.

5. infancy, babyhood, incunabula, the cradle, the nursery.

6. adolescence, pubescence, **puberty**, goslings or gosling patch [slang].

7. teens, teen age, **awkward age**, age of growing pains [coll.].

VERBS **8.** make young, youthify, youthen; juvenilify, juvenilize; **rejuvenate**, reinvigorate.

ADJS. **9. young**, youngling, **juvenile, youthful**, youthy [chiefly Scot.], youthsome [dial.], youthlike, "in my flower of youth" [Milton].

10. immature, unadult, inexperienced; unseasoned, unfledged, newfledged, **callow, unripe**, unmellowed, raw, green, vernal, sappy, budding, tender, **undeveloped**, unformed, unlicked, not dry behind the ears; **minor**, underage.

11. childish, childlike, kiddish [coll.], **puerile; boyish**, boylike, beardless; **girlish**, girllike, maiden, maidenly, flapperish [coll., 1920's], frying size [slang].

12. infant, infantine, **infantile; babyish**, babish, baby; dollish, doll-like; kittenish, kittenlike; **newborn;** in the cradle, in swaddling clothes, in long clothes, in arms, in leading strings, at the breast.

13. adolescent, pubescent, hebetic.

14. teen-age, teen-aged, **in one's teens;** sweet sixteen [slang].

15. junior, Jr. or jr.; **younger**, puisne [law].

125. YOUNGLING

NOUNS **1. youngling, youngster**, younker [coll.], young person, **youth, juvenile;** stripling, slip, sprig, sapling; fledgling, chicken [chiefly coll.]; hopeful, young hopeful; **minor**, infant [law]; **adolescent**, pubescent; **teenager**, teenster; junior, younger; baby (the youngest of a family or group).

2. young people, youth, gilded youth, young, **younger generation**, rising generation, young blood, young fry [coll.], modern crop [coll.]; **children**, childkind, small fry, "pretty buds unblown" [Cowper]; boyhood, girlhood; babyhood, infantry [joc.].

3. child, urchin, bairn [Scot.], butcha [Ind.], kid [slang], punk [slang], punk kid [slang], **little one**, little fellow, little feller [dial.], little bugger [slang], shaver or little shaver [coll.], little squirt [slang], **tot, little tot**, tad or little tad [U.S.], mite, chit [coll.], scrap, scrap of a child, chunk of a

kid [dial. & slang]; innocent, little innocent; darling, cherub, lamb, **lambkin**, kitten, chick, chickabiddy, bantling, pullet, duckling; curled darling [coll.]; pickaninny; offspring 170.3.

4. brat, bratling, **minx, imp**, puck, elf, bratling elf, little monkey, **whippersnapper**, young whippersnapper, enfant terrible [F., terrible infant], unspanked child [coll.].

5. boy, lad, laddie, **youth**, garçon [F.], muchacho [Sp.], callant or callan [Scot. & North. Eng.], hobbledehoy; **fellow** 419.5; pup, puppy, whelp, cub, colt; master; sonny, sonny boy; bud, buddy [both coll.]; bub, bubby, bubby boy [all slang]; schoolboy.

6. girl, girlie [coll.], **maid, maiden, lass, lassie, damsel**, damoiselle, demoiselle, muchacha [Sp.], miss, missy, little missy, puss, pussy, wench [dial. & slang], jill or Jill; colleen, girleen [both Anglo-Ir.]; gal, dame, chicken, flapper [1920's], babe, baby, broad [U.S.], curve [U.S.], frail [U.S.], doll, cutie, fluff [U.S.], filly, heifer [all slang]; **schoolgirl**, schoolmaid, schoolmiss; subdebutante, **subdeb** [coll.]; bobbysocker or **bobbysoxer** [coll.]; **tomboy**, hoyden, romp; virgin.

7. infant, baby, babe, weanie [Scot.], bambino [It.], bouncing baby, puling infant, mewling infant, babykins [coll.], baby bunting; papoose; **toddler**, toddlekins [slang]; **suckling**, nursling, bottle-boy [dial.]; weanling; neonate; yearling, year-old; premature baby; incubator baby.

8. (animals) **fledgling**, birdling, nestling; **chick**, chicky, chickling; **pullet**, fryer or frier; **duckling; kitten**, kit, kitling [dial.], catling; **pup**, puppy, whelp; **cub; calf**, dogie (motherless calf [West. U.S.]), weaner (weaned calf [West. U.S.]); **colt**, foal; **lamb**, lambkin, kid, yeanling; **tadpole**, polliwog, pollywiggle [dial.], pollyfrog [dial. & slang].

9. larva, chrysalis, aurelia, **cocoon**, pupa; nymph, nympha; wriggler, wiggler; caterpillar, maggot, grub.

126. AGE

Time of Life.—NOUNS **1. age**, years, "the days of our years" [Bible], "measure of my days" [ibid.], "slow-consuming age" [Gray], "a tyrant, which forbids the pleasures of youth on pain of death" [La Rochefoucauld].

2. maturity, majority, adulthood, adultness, mature age, ripe age, full age, full

growth, full bloom, flower of age, age of responsibility, age *or* years of discretion;
manhood, manlihood; **womanhood**, wom-
anlihood.

3. seniority, eldership, deanship, primogeniture.

4. middle age, middle life, meridian of
life, the middle years, *mezzo cammin* [It.],
dangerous age [joc.].

5. old age, oldness, elderliness, senec-
titude, advanced age *or* years, **ripe old age**,
hoary age, vale of years, "an incurable disease" [Seneca]; **decline of life**, declining
years, "the downward slope" [Seneca], the
shady side [coll.]; gray hairs, "the sere, the
yellow leaf" [Shakespeare], "the silver livery of advised age" [ibid.], "a crown of
glory" [Bible]; autumn, winter; three score
years and ten; **decrepitude**, infirm old age,
infirmity of age, infirmity, feebleness; senility 468.10.

6. maturation, development, mellowing, ripening, seasoning; **aging**, senescence.

7. change of life, menopause, climacteric, grand climacteric.

8. (science of old age) nostology, gerontology, gerocomy.

VERBS **9. mature**, grow, **develop, ripen**,
mellow, season; feather, fledge, grow feathers; **come of age**, come to maturity, attain
majority, **reach one's majority**, reach manhood, write oneself a man, come to *or* into
man's estate, put on long trousers, assume
the *toga virilis* [L.], come into years of discretion, cut one's wisdom teeth, cut one's
eyeteeth [coll.], have sown one's wild oats.

10. age, grow old, get on *or* along, **get
on** *or* **along in years**; decline, wane, fade,
sink, waste away, fall "into the sere, the
yellow leaf" [Shakespeare]; wither, wrinkle,
shrivel, wizen; **live to a ripe old age**, make
old bones [coll.].

11. have had one's day, have seen one's
day *or* best days, **have seen better days;
show one's age**, show marks of age, look
around the clock [coll.].

ADJS. **12. adult, mature**, old, **of age**,
out of one's teens, of full *or* ripe age, big,
grown, **grown-up, developed**, fully developed, **full-grown**, full-fledged, full-blown,
in full bloom, ripe, mellow; old enough to
know better; marriageable, marriable, nubile; maturescent.

13. middle-aged, mid-life, *entre deux
âges* [F., between two ages], in one's prime.

14. past one's prime, no chicken [coll.],
on the shady side [coll.].

15. aged, elderly, old, grown old, in
years, **along in years**, years old, advanced,
advanced in life *or* years, **at an advanced
age, ancient**, senectuous, **venerable**, old
as Methuselah *or* as the hills; patriarchal;
hoary, hoar, gray, gray-headed, gray-haired,
gray-crowned, gray-bearded, gray with age;
wrinkled, with crow's feet, marked with the
crow's foot.

16. aging, senescent, growing old, **getting on** *or* **along**, getting on *or* along in
years; **declining**, sinking, waning, fading,
wasting, doting.

17. stricken in years, decrepit, infirm,
feeble, effete, gerontic [biol.], timeworn,
the worst for wear, rusty, moth-eaten [joc.],
mossbacked [slang], fossilized [joc.], run to
seed; **doddering**, doddery, tottering, tottery; on one's last legs, with one foot in the
grave; **senile** 468.23.

18. senior, Sr., **elder, older**, major;
eldest, eldermost [dial.], **oldest; first-born**,
primogenitary.

127. ADULT

NOUNS **1. adult, grownup**, no chicken
[coll.]; **man, woman**; major [law.].

2. elder, older, oldster [coll.]; **old man**,
old chap, **old gentleman**, old gent [coll.],
old codger [coll.], geezer *or* old geezer
[slang], gaffer, old duffer [coll.], old dog
[coll.]; **patriarch**, graybeard, reverend sir;
grandfather 169.11; Father Time, Methuselah, Nestor, Old Paar; sexagenarian, octo-
genarian, nonagenarian, centenarian.

3. old woman, old lady, granny, old
granny, dame, **grandam** *or* grandame,
gammer [dial., Eng.], trot *or* old trot [dial.];
old dame, old hen, old heifer, old girl [all
slang]; old battle-axe [slang], war horse
[coll.]; **crone**, hag, witch, beldam *or* beldame, frump [coll.], old wife; grandmother
169.12.

4. (classical elderly couples) Darby and
Joan, Baucis and Philemon [Gr. & Rom.
myth.].

5. senior, Sr., **elder**, older; dean, *doyen*
[F.]; father; firstling, first-born.

128. SEASON

Time of Year.—NOUNS **1. season**, season
of the year, "the measure of the year"
[Keats], period, annual period; dry ∼, rainy
or cold season, dead *or* off season, strawberry season, theatrical season; **social sea-
son**, the season [Eng.]; big season, little
season [both U.S.]; seasonality.

2. **spring**, springtide, **springtime**, seed-time, grass, prime, prime of the year, "the boyhood of the year" [Tennyson], "the time of the singing of birds" [Bible], "the tassel-time of Spring" [R. U. Johnson], "when the hounds of spring are on winter's traces" [Swinburne].

3. **summer**, summertide, **summertime**, good old summer time; midsummer; **dog days**, canicular days.

4. **autumn, fall** [esp. U.S.], fall of the year, fall of the leaf, harvest, harvest time.

5. **Indian summer**, St. Martin's summer, St. Luke's summer, little summer of St. Luke, St. Austin's summer, St. Augustine's summer, "the dead Summer's soul" [Mary Clemmer].

6. **winter**, wintertide, **wintertime**, "ruler of th' inverted year" [Cowper]; midwinter.

7. **equinox**, vernal equinox, autumnal equinox; **solstice**, summer solstice, winter solstice; Aries, Cancer, Libra, Capricorn or Capricornus.

ADJS. 8. **seasonal**, in or out of season, in season and out of season; **spring**, spring-like, vernal; **summer**, summery, summerly, summerlike, canicular, estival; midsummer; **autumn**, autumnal; **winter**, wintry, wintery, hibernal, hiemal, brumal, winterlike; midwinter; equinoctial, solstitial.

129. TIMELINESS

NOUNS 1. **timeliness**, **seasonableness**, opportuneness, convenience; **expedience**, meetness, fitness, appropriateness, suitability; **favorableness**, propitiousness, auspiciousness, felicitousness.

2. **opportunity**, **chance**, show [coll., U.S.], **time**, **occasion**; **opening**, room, scope, place, liberty; clear stage, fair field; opportunism, opportunist.

3. **good opportunity**, **good chance**, good or some show [coll., U.S.], golden opportunity, well-timed opportunity; suitable occasion, proper occasion, suitable or proper time, **good time**, high time, due season.

4. **crisis**, **critical point**, crucial period, climacteric; **turning point**, hinge, turn, turn of the tide; **emergency**, **exigency**, juncture, conjuncture, critical juncture; **pinch**, clutch [slang], squeeze [coll.], rub, push, pass, strait, extremity.

5. **crucial moment**, critical moment, decisive moment, **psychological moment**; nick of time, eleventh hour, the scratch [coll.].

6. **zero hour**, H-hour, D-day [all mil. & fig.]; A-day [mil.].

VERBS 7. **be timely**, suit or befit the time, ~ season or occasion.

8. **take the opportunity**, use the occasion, take the chance; take the bit in the teeth, *prendre la balle au bond* [F.].

9. **improve the occasion**, improve the shining hour; **turn to account** or good account, avail oneself of, **take advantage of**, put to advantage, profit by; take time by the forelock, seize the present hour, make hay while the sun shines; strike the iron while it is hot, *battre le fer sur l'enclume* [F.].

ADJS. 10. **timely**, **well-timed**, **seasonable**, **opportune**, convenient; **expedient**, meet, fit, fitting, befitting, suitable, sortable, appropriate; **favorable**, propitious, auspicious, lucky, providential, fortunate, happy, felicitous.

11. **critical**, **crucial**, climacteric(al), decisive.

12. **incidental**, **occasional**, **casual**, accidental; parenthetical, by-the-way.

ADVS. 13. **opportunely**, **seasonably**, in proper time or season, in due time or course, in the fullness of time, **in good time**, all in good time; in the nick of time, just in time, at the eleventh hour; now or never.

14. **by the way**, **by the by**; **incidentally**, while on the subject, speaking of, *à propos* [F.] or apropos of; **in passing**, *en passant* [F.], *obiter* [L.], *obiter dictum* [L., said in passing]; **parenthetically**, by way of parenthesis, *par parenthèse* [F.]; for example, *par exemple* [F.].

130. UNTIMELINESS

NOUNS 1. **untimeliness**, **unseasonableness**, inopportuneness, inopportunity, inconvenience, intempestivity; **inexpedience**, unappropriateness, unsuitability; **unfavorableness**, unfortunateness, inauspiciousness, infelicity; **prematurity** 131.2; **lateness** 132.

2. **wrong time**, **bad time**, unsuitable time, unfortunate time; evil hour; off year.

VERBS 3. **not have the time**, have other things to do, be otherwise occupied, **have other fish to fry**.

4. **ill-time, mistime**.

5. **speak inopportunely**, **put one's foot in one's mouth** [coll.], **talk out of turn** [slang], beat up one's gums off time [slang, U.S.]; **go off half-cocked** or at half cock [coll.].

6. **miss an opportunity, miss the chance, miss the boat** or **bus,** lose the opportunity, lose the chance, blow the chance [slang], throw away or waste the opportunity, neglect the opportunity, allow the occasion to go by, let slip through the fingers, lock the stable door after the horse is stolen.

ADJS. 7. **untimely, unseasonable, inopportune, ill-timed,** ill-seasoned, mistimed, too late or soon; inconvenient, unhandy; **inappropriate,** unsuitable, **inexpedient,** unfitting, unbefitting, untoward, malapropos, *mal à propos* [F.]; **unfavorable,** unfortunate, infelicitous, inauspicious, unpropitious, unhappy, unlucky; premature 131.8; **late** 132.15.

131. EARLINESS

NOUNS 1. **earliness,** time to spare; head start, running start; **anticipation,** prevenience; a stitch in time.

2. **prematurity,** prematureness; **untimeliness** 130; precocity, **precociousness,** forwardness; precipitation, hastiness, **overhastiness; unpreparedness,** unpremeditation.

3. **promptness, promptitude, punctuality,** punctualness, readiness, immediateness, immediacy, summariness, **alacrity, quickness,** speediness, swiftness, expeditiousness, expedition, dispatch.

4. **early bird,** early riser.

VERBS 5. **be early,** be ahead of time, take time by the forelock; gain time, draw on futurity or on the future.

6. **anticipate, foresee,** foreglimpse, foretaste; **forestall,** forerun, go before, **get ahead of,** get the start of, get a head start, steal a march upon; take the words out of one's mouth.

ADJS. 7. **early,** bright and early [coll.], **beforetime,** in good time or season; **forehand,** forehanded; **anticipative,** anticipatory, prevenient.

8. **premature, too early, too soon,** oversoon; previous, a bit or trifle previous [all coll.]; **untimely** 130.7; **precipitate,** hasty, **overhasty; unprepared,** unripe, unmatured; unpremeditated, unmeditated; **halfcocked,** half-baked [both coll.]; **precocious, forward,** advanced, far ahead, born before one's time.

9. **prompt, punctual, immediate, instant,** pronto [coll., U.S.], **quick,** speedy, swift, expeditious, summary, apt, alert, ready, Johnny on the spot [slang].

10. **earlier,** previous 116.4.

ADVS. 11. **early, beforehand,** aforehand [dial.], **beforetime,** betimes, **ahead of time, in advance,** in anticipation, ahead, before, **with time to spare.**

12. **in time,** in due time or season, **in good time,** in pudding time [chiefly dial.], **soon enough,** early enough; just in time, **in the nick of time,** with no time to spare, without a minute to spare.

13. **prematurely, oversoon, too soon,** too early, before its or one's time; **precipitately,** hastily, **overhastily;** at half cock [coll.].

14. **punctually, precisely,** exactly, sharp; **on time,** on the minute or instant, on or to the tick [coll.]; **on the dot, on the nose,** right on the nail [all slang].

15. **promptly,** prompt [coll.], **without delay,** without further delay, directly, **immediately,** immediately if not sooner [joc.], **instantly,** instanter, on the instant, on the spot, **at once,** right off, **right away, straightway,** straightaway, **forthwith,** forthright, pronto [coll., U.S.], big and pronto [slang, U.S.], **P.D.Q.** (pretty damned quick [slang]), **quickly,** swiftly, speedily, with all speed, **summarily,** expeditiously, apace, in no time, in less than no time; no sooner said than done.

16. **soon, presently, directly, shortly,** in a short time or while, right short [dial.], **before long,** ere long, in no long time, in a while, **in a little while, after a while, by and by,** anon, betimes, *bientôt* [F.], in due time, in due course, at the first opportunity; in a moment or minute, *tout à l'heure* [F.].

132. LATENESS

NOUNS 1. **lateness, tardiness, belatedness, unpunctuality;** untimeliness 130.

2. **delay,** delayage; **retardation,** retardance; **detention,** suspension, holdup [coll.]; **wait, halt, stay, stop,** pause, respite; reprieve, stay of execution; moratorium; red tape, red-tapery, red-tapism, pink ribbons [slang].

3. **waiting, tarriance,** tarrying, **lingering,** dawdling, dalliance, dallying, dillydallying.

4. **postponement, deferment,** deferral, prorogation, put-off [chiefly coll.]; **prolongation,** protraction, continuation, extension of time; **adjournment,** adjournal.

5. **procrastination,** vacillation, hesitation; **temporization,** a play for time, stall

[slang], standoff [coll.], hold-off [coll.]; Micawberism, Fabian policy; **dilatoriness,** slowness, backwardness, remissness, slackness, laxness.

VERBS 6. **be late, show up late, not be on time,** arrive in an armchair [coll.], be like a cow's or donkey's tail—always behind [joc.]; keep banker's hours; keep one waiting, hold up, stand up [slang].

7. **delay, detain, retard,** slacken, slow down, **hold up** [coll.], hold or keep back, check, stay, stop, arrest, impede, obstruct, confine; tie up with red tape.

8. **postpone, delay,** defer, **put off,** stave off, shift off, hold off or up [coll.], reserve, waive, suspend, hang up, stay, wait [coll.], protract, **prolong, extend,** continue, prorogate; **hold over,** lay over, stand over, let the matter stand; **put aside,** lay ~, set or push aside, side [coll.], lay or set by, **table,** lay on the table, pigeonhole, **shelve,** put on the shelf, put on the rack [coll.], put on ice [slang]; consult one's pillow, sleep upon.

9. **adjourn, prorogue,** suspend; recess, take a recess; break up, **dissolve;** adjourn to [coll.].

10. **procrastinate,** be dilatory, vacillate, hesitate, hang, hang back, hang fire; **dally, dillydally,** fiddle-faddle [coll.], **dawdle,** linger; **temporize,** gain or make time, **play for time,** stand off [chiefly coll.], hold off [coll.]; **stall,** stall off, **stall for time,** stall along or around [all slang]; talk against time, filibuster [U.S. polit.], speak for Buncombe [coll., U.S. polit.].

11. **wait, delay, stay,** bide, abide, bide or abide one's time, take one's time, take time, mark time; **tarry, linger, loiter,** dawdle, dally, dillydally; hang around or about [coll.], stick around [slang]; **hold on** [coll.], sit tight [coll.], hold one's breath; wait a minute or second, wait a shake [slang]; hold everything, hold your horses, keep your shirt on [all slang]; wait or stay up, sit up; wait and see, see which way the cat jumps; wait for something to turn up; **await** 537.6.

12. wait impatiently, sweat it out [slang], champ or chomp at the bit [slang].

13. be kept waiting, be stood up [slang], kick or cool one's heels [coll.].

14. overstay, overtarry.

ADJS. 15. **late, belated, tardy,** slow, behindhand, backward, back, **overdue; untimely** 130.7; **unpunctual,** unready; latish; delayed, detained, held up [coll.], in abeyance; delayed-action; moratory.

16. **dilatory, delaying,** Micawberish; **procrastinating,** procrastinative, procrastinatory; **lingering,** loitering, lagging, dallying, dillydallying, dillydally [dial.]; **slow,** sluggish, laggard, backward; easygoing, **lackadaisical; remiss,** slack, lax.

17. later 117.5.

ADVS. 18. **late, behindhand, behind,** backward, **slow, behind time,** after time, like a cow's or donkey's tail—always behind [joc.]; far on, deep in (as *deep in* the night); late in the day, at the eleventh hour.

19. **tardily, slowly,** deliberately, leisurely, at one's leisure.

133. MORNING, NOON

NOUNS 1. **morning,** morn, morningtide [poetic], morning time, morntime, matins [eccl.], **forenoon,** foreday; *ante meridiem* [L.], a.m., **A.M.,** Ack Emma [slang, Eng.]; "dewy morn" [Byron], "incense-breathing morn" [Gray], "genial morn" [T. Campbell], "grey-eyed morn" [Shakespeare], "rosy-finger'd morn" [Homer], "rich unfolding morn" [Keble]; this morning, this A.M. [coll.].

2. Morning, Aurora, Eos; "daughter of the dawn" [Homer], "mild blushing goddess" [Logan Pearsall Smith].

3. **dawn,** the dawn of day, dawning, **daybreak,** dayspring, day-peep, **sunrise, sunup** [coll., U.S.], cockcrow, cockcrowing, cocklight [dial., Eng.], light, daylight, aurora; **break of day,** peep of day, **crack of dawn,** prime, prime of the morning, first blush or flush of the morning, brightening or first brightening [dial.]; "the opening eyelids of the morn" [Milton], "vestibule of Day" [Bayard Taylor], "golden exhalations of the dawn" [Schiller], "the purple mystery of dawn" [F.W.H. Myers], "the white, still dawn" [Edwin Markham].

4. **foredawn, twilight,** cocklight [dial., Eng.], dawnlight, dawn's early light, crepuscle or crepuscule, aurora; **the small hours,** the wee sma' hours [Scot.], the wee and small [slang].

5. **noon, noonday,** noontide, nooning [dial., U.S.], noontime, **midday,** meridian, *meridiem* [L.], twelve o'clock; noonlight.

ADJS. 6. **morning,** matin, matinal, matutinal, **antemeridian.**

7. **noon,** noonday, **midday,** meridian, twelve-o'clock; noonlit.

ADVS. 8. **in the morning,** mornings [chiefly dial.]; at sunrise, **at the crack of dawn;** with the sun, with the lark.

134. EVENING, NIGHT

NOUNS 1. afternoon, after [coll.], aft [slang], evening [local Eng. & South. U.S.]; *post meridiem* [L.], p.m., **P.M.**, pip emma [slang, Eng.]; this afternoon, this after [coll.], this aft [slang], this P.M. [coll.].

2. evening, eve [poetic], even [poetic], eventide [poetic], vesper; close of day, decline *or* fall of day, shut of day [dial. & coll.], evening's close, when day is done; nightfall, sunset, sundown, sun-go-down [chiefly dial.], going down of the sun, cockshut [dial.]; shank of the afternoon *or* evening [coll.]; "the expiring day" [Dante], "the death-bed of a day" [P.J. Bailey], "evening's calm and holy hour" [S.G. Bulfinch], "the gray-hooded Ev'n" [Milton], "the pale child, Eve, leading her mother, Night" [Alexander Smith].

3. dusk, duskingtide, dusk-down [dial.], twilight, crepuscle *or* crepuscule, crepuscular light, gloam [poetic], **gloaming**, glooming [poetic], darkening [Scot. & North. Eng.; dial., U.S.], dimpsy [dial., Eng.], candlelight, candlelighting, owllight *or* owl's light, cocklight [dial. Eng.], "the pale dusk of the impending night" [Longfellow].

4. night, nighttime, nighttide, darky [slang], darkmans [crim. slang, Eng.]; "dusky night" [Milton], "sable-vested Night" [ibid.], "sable night" [Shakespeare], "dark-eyed night" [ibid.], "cowléd night" [F. Thompson], "empress of silence, and the queen of sleep" [Marlowe]; dark of night, "the suit of night" [Shakespeare].

5. eleventh hour, curfew, bedtime.

6. midnight, dead of night, hush of night, witching hour of the night; "the very witching time of night" [Shakespeare], "noonday night" [Longfellow], "outpost of advancing day" [Longfellow].

ADJS. 7. afternoon, postmeridian.

8. evening, vesper, vespertine; twilight, twilighty, crepuscular; dusk, dusky; sunsetty.

9. nocturnal, night, nightly, nighttime; night-fallen; midnight.

10. benighted, night-overtaken.

ADVS. 11. nightly, nights [dial. exc. U.S.], at *or* by night; overnight, through the night.

135. FREQUENCY

NOUNS 1. frequency, frequence, oftenness; commonness, usualness, prevalence, common occurrence.

2. constancy, continualness, steadiness, steadfastness, regularity, uninterruption, unintermission, incessancy, ceaselessness, constant flow; perpetuity 112.

VERBS 3. continue 143.3; recur 137.6.

ADJS. 4. frequent, oftentime, many, many times, recurrent, oft-repeated, thick-coming; common, prevalent, usual, ordinary, everyday; frequentative [gram.].

5. constant, continual, perennial; steady, steadfast, regular; incessant, ceaseless, unceasing, unintermitting, unintermittent, unintermitted, unremitting, unchanging, unvarying, uninterrupted, unstopped, unbroken; perpetual 112.7.

ADVS. 6. frequently, commonly, usually, ordinarily; often, oftens [dial.], oft [poetic], oftentimes, ofttimes; repeatedly 103.16; most often *or* frequently, in many instances, many times, many a time, full many a time, many a time and oft; in quick *or* rapid succession; often enough, not infrequently, not seldom, unseldom.

7. constantly, continually, steadily, steadfastly, regularly, right along [coll.], unvaryingly, uninterruptedly, unintermittently, incessantly, unceasingly, ceaselessly, without cease *or* ceasing, perennially, at all times, ever, ever and anon, on and on, without stopping; perpetually, always 112.10–12; every day, every hour, every moment; daily, hourly, daily and hourly; night and day, day and night; morning, noon and night; hour after hour, day after day, month after month, year after year; day in day out, month in month out, year in year out; "tomorrow and tomorrow and tomorrow" [Shakespeare].

136. INFREQUENCY

NOUNS 1. infrequency, infrequence, unfrequentness, seldomness; occasionalness; rarity, rareness, uncommonness, unusualness; sparsity 102.1.

ADJS. 2. infrequent, unfrequent, scarce, rare, uncommon, unusual, almost unheard-of, seldom met with, seldom seen; sparse 102.5; spasmodic 138.3.

3. occasional, casual, incidental; odd (as, *odd* jobs, *odd* moments), extra, side, off, out-of-the-way, spare, spare-time, part-time; semioccasional [coll., U.S.].

ADVS. 4. infrequently, unfrequently, seldom, rarely, uncommonly, scarcely, hardly, scarcely *or* hardly ever, seldom ever [now illit.], very seldom, not often, unoften; sparsely 102.8.

5. occasionally, semioccasionally [coll., U.S.], on occasion, **sometimes, at times,** betimes [dial.], at various times, on divers occasions, **now and then,** every now and then [coll.], **once in a while,** every once in a while [coll.], once in a way, once and again, once or twice, between times *or* whiles, at intervals, **from time to time,** there being times when; once in a blue moon, once in a coon's *or* dog's age [both coll.].

6. once, one time, on one occasion, just *or* only once, once for all, once and for all *or* always, for the nonce, *pro hac vice* [L., for this occasion].

137. REGULARITY OF RECURRENCE

NOUNS **1. regularity, methodicalness,** systematicalness; **uniformity** 17; **constancy** 135.2.

2. periodicity, periodicalness; **rhythm** 462.22; **recurrence,** reoccurrence, reappearance, return; **intermittence** *or* intermittency, alternation.

3. round, revolution, rotation, cycle, circle, **circuit, beat,** course, series, **bout, turn;** indiction, cycle of indiction.

4. anniversary, commemoration; biennial, triennial, quadrennial, quinquennial, sextennial, septennial, octennial, decennial, tricennial, jubilee (fiftieth anniversary); centennial, centenary; sesquicentennial; bicentennial, bicentenary; tercentennial, tercentenary; quincentennial, quincentenary; **wedding anniversary,** golden wedding anniversary, silver wedding anniversary; **birthday,** natal day; saint's day; leap year, a woman's year [coll.], bissextile day.

5. Christmas, Xmas, Merry Christmas, Noël, Yule, the Nativity; Yuletide, Christmastide; Christmas Day, Christmas Eve.

VERBS **6.** (occur periodically) **recur, reoccur, return,** reappear, **come again,** come up again, be here again, **come round** *or* **around,** come round again, come in its turn; **rotate, revolve, cycle, roll around,** wheel around; **intermit,** alternate, **come and go.**

ADJS. **7. regular, systematic(al), methodical,** ordered, orderly, regular as clockwork; **uniform** 17.5; **constant** 135.5.

8. periodic(al), seasonal, epochal, cyclic(al), serial, isochronal; **rhythmic(al)** 462.27; **recurrent,** recurring, reoccurring; **intermittent,** alternate, every other.

ADJS., ADVS. **9. momently,** momentarily; **hourly; daily,** diurnal, quotidian; **weekly,** tertian, hebdomadal, hebdomadary; biweekly, semiweekly; fortnightly; **monthly,** menstrual, catamenial; bimonthly, semimonthly; quarterly; biannual, biennial, semiannual, semiyearly, semestral; **yearly, annual;** triennial, decennial, etc. (*above* 137.4); centennial, centenary, secular.

ADVS. **10. regularly,** regular [chiefly dial.], **systematically, methodically,** like clockwork, at regular intervals; **uniformly** 17.7, 8; **constantly** 135.7.

11. periodically, recurrently, seasonally, epochally; **hourly, daily,** etc. (*above* 137.9); every hour, every day, etc.; hour by hour, day by day, etc.; from hour to hour, from day to day, *de die in diem* [L.].

12. by turns, in turns, in rotation, turn about, **turn and turn about, alternately,** every other, one after the other; off and on, ride and tie, hitch and hike, round and round.

13. anniversaries

holy days 1038.15	General Election
Admission Day	Day [U.S.]
[U.S.]	ground-hog *or*
April Fools' *or*	woodchuck day
All Fools' Day	[U.S.]
Arbor Day [U.S.]	Hallowe'en
Armistice Day	Holi [India]
[U.S.]	Inauguration Day
Army Day [U.S.]	[U.S.]
Bairam [Moham.]	Independence Day
Bastile Day	[U.S.]
[Canal Zone]	Kamehameha Day
Bird Day [U.S.]	[Hawaii]
Bloody Sunday	King's Birthday
[U.S.S.R.]	[Eng.]
Boxing Day [Eng.]	Labor Day [U.S.]
Christmas	Lenin Memorial
Columbus Day	Day [U.S.S.R.]
[U.S.]	Lincoln's Birthday
Decoration Day	[U.S.]
[U.S.]	May Day
Derby day [Eng.]	Memorial Day
Dewali [India]	[U.S.]
Discovery Day	Midsummer Day
[Puerto Rico]	[Eng.]
Dominion Day	Mother's Day
[Can.]	[U.S.]
Easter	Murharram
Emancipation Day	[Moham.]
[Puerto Rico]	National Aviation
Empire Day [Eng.]	Day [U.S.]
Fast Day	Navy Day [U.S.]
Father's Day	New Year's Day
[U.S.]	New Year's Eve
Flag Day [U.S.]	Orangemen's Day
Forefathers' Day	[Ir.]
[New Eng.]	Pan American Day
Foundation Day	[U.S.]
[Canal Zone]	Patriots' Day
Fourth of July	[Maine and
[U.S.]	Mass.]

Ramadan
[Moham.]
Remembrance
Day [Can.]
Saint Patrick's Day
Saint Swithin's
Day
Saint Valentine's
Day
San Jacinto Day
[Texas]
Sovereign's
Birthday [Can.]
State Day [U.S.]

Texas Independ-
ence Day
Thanksgiving
[U.S.]
Three Kings' Day
[Virgin Islands]
V–E Day
Veterans' Day
[U.S.]
Victoria Day
[Can.]
Victory Day [U.S.]
V–J Day
Washington's
Birthday [U.S.]

138. IRREGULARITY OF RECURRENCE

NOUNS 1. irregularity, unmethodical-
ness, unsystematicalness; inconstancy, unevenness, unsteadiness, uncertainty, desultoriness; variability, capriciousness, eccentricity, erraticness; fitfulness, sporadi-
calness, spottiness, choppiness, brokenness,
disconnectedness; intermittence, fluctuation.

VERBS 2. intermit, fluctuate, come and
go, go off and on, go by fits and starts.

ADJS. 3. irregular, unregular, unsystematic, unmethodical or immethodical; inconstant, unsteady, uneven, unequal, uncertain, unsettled; variable, deviative, heteroclite; capricious, erratic, eccentric; fitful,
spasmodic, spastic [med.], sporadic(al),
spotty, scrappy, snatchy, catchy, choppy,
broken, disconnected; intermittent, in-
termitting, desultory, fluctuating, wavering, flickering.

ADVS. 4. irregularly, unsystematically,
unmethodically; inconstantly, unsteadily,
unevenly, uncertainly; variably, capriciously, erratically; intermittently, disconnectedly, brokenly, desultorily, spottily,
in spots, in snatches; by fits and starts, by
fits, by jerks, by snatches, by catches; fitfully, sporadically, spasmodically; off
and on, on and off, in and out; at intervals, longo intervallo [L.]; every now and
then, every once in a while, "like angel
visits, few and far between" [T. Campbell].

139. CHANGE

NOUNS 1. change, alteration, modification; variation, variety, difference, diversity, diversification; deviation, diversion,
shift, turn; modulation, qualification;
"the ever whirling wheels of Change"
[Spenser], "Nature's mighty law" [Burns],
"the ringing grooves of change" [Tenny-

son], "the changes and chances of this mortal life" [Book of Common Prayer].

2. transformation, transmogrification
[coll.], metastasis; metamorphosis, metamorphism; mutation, transmutation, permutation; transfiguration, transfigure-
ment; metathesis, transposition, translocation, displacement, heterotopia [biol.];
transubstantiation, consubstantiation;
transanimation, transmigration, metempsychosis, avatar; metasomatism, metasomato-
sis [both geol.]; metabolism, metabola or
metabole [med. & zool.]; metagenesis
[biol.]; transformism.

3. innovation, introduction; neologism;
new phase; novelty 122.2; innovator, inno-
vationist, introducer.

4. alterant, alterer, alterative; transformer, transmogrifier [coll.]; modifier,
modificator; alembic.

VERBS 5. (be changed) change, undergo a change, go through a change, alter;
mutate; modulate, merge into; vary,
checker, diversify; deviate, turn, shift, veer,
jibe, jib, tack, chop, chop and change,
swerve, warp; turn aside, take a turn, turn
the corner; come about, come round or
around, haul around; flop, break.

6. (make a change) change, work a
change, alter; mutate; modify; adapt;
modulate, qualify; vary, diversify, ring the
changes; give a turn to, give a color to; turn
the tide, turn the tables, turn the scale or
balance; shift the scene; shuffle the cards;
turn over a new leaf.

7. transform, transfigure, transmute,
transmogrify [coll.], transubstantiate, convert, resolve, metamorphose; deform, denature; revamp [chiefly coll.], vamp, vamp
together or up; metabolize [physiol.].

8. innovate, make innovations, novate,
introduce, introduce new blood; neologize.

ADJS. 9. changed, altered, modified,
transformed.

10. innovational, innovative.

140. PERMANENCE

NOUNS 1. permanence or permanency,
changelessness, unchangingness; fixedness, constancy, persistence or persistency,
lastingness, abidingness, endurance, duration, standing; durability 110; perpetualness
112; stability 142; unchangeability 142.4.

2. maintenance, preservation, conservation; status quo [L., the existing state],
status in quo [L.], static condition, things

as they are; standing dish; law of the Medes
and Persians.

3. conservatism, opposition to change,
**unprogressivism, reactionaryism, modera-
tion,** moderationism, fogyism, standpatism
[coll.], standstillism, bitter-enderism *or*
bitter-endism [coll.], irreconcilability; intransigence, *intransigeance* [F.], intransigentism; right-wingism, Toryism [Eng.],
Hunkerism [U.S.]; ultraconservatism; laissez-faireism 704; old shool tie; "adherence
to the old and tried, against the new and
untried" [Lincoln], "an unhappy crossbreed, the mule of politics that engenders
nothing" [Disraeli].

4. conservative, conservatist; **unprogressive,** unprogressivist; **reactionary,** reactionist; **moderate,** moderatist, moderationist; **rightist,** right-winger; **die-hard, bitter-
ender** [coll.], standpat *or* standpatter
[coll.], uncompromiser, irreconcilable; intransigent, *intransigeant* [F.], intransigentist; **old fogy,** fogy, fogram *or* fogrum [coll.],
stick-in-the-mud [coll.], mossback [slang],
longhair [slang]; Hardshell [coll., U.S.],
Hunker [U.S.], Bourbon, Tory [Eng.]; *laudator temporis acti* [L., praiser of times
past], "a person who has something to conserve" [Edward Young], "the leftover progressive of an earlier generation" [Edmund
Fuller]; old school, right wing.

VERBS **5. remain, endure** 110.6.

6. be conservative, oppose change,
stand on ancient ways, *stare super antiquas
vias* [L.]; stand pat [coll.], stand still; **let
things take their course,** leave things as
they are, let be, let *or* leave alone, let well
enough alone, do nothing.

ADJS. **7. permanent, changeless, unchanging,** unvarying, unshifting; **unchanged,** unvaried, **unaltered,** inviolate,
undestroyed, intact; **constant, persistent,**
sustained, fixed, unchecked, unfailing, unfading; **lasting, enduring,** abiding, remaining, staying, continuing; durable 110.10;
perpetual 112.7; stable 142.13; **unchangeable** 142.18.

8. conservative, preservative, old-line,
hard-shell [coll., U.S.], **uncompromising,**
irreconcilable, intransigent, **die-hard,** bitter-end [coll.], standpat [coll.], standstill,
opposed to change; **unprogressive,** nonprogressive; **reactionary,** reactionist; **right-
wing,** right of center; **moderate,** not extreme; fogyish, **old-fogyish,** long-haired
[slang], stick-in-the-mud [coll.]; ultracon-
servative.

ADVS. **9. permanently,** changelessly,
unchangingly; **perpetually, always** 112.10–
12.

10. *in statu quo* [L., in the existing
state], **as is, as usual,** as per usual [coll.]; at
a stand *or* standstill, without a shadow of
turning.

141. CHANGEABLENESS

NOUNS **1. changeableness,** changeful-
ness, **changeability, alterability,** modifiability; mutability, permutability; mobility,
movability, plasticity, fluidity.

2. inconstancy, instability, unstable-
ness, **unsteadiness,** unsteadfastness, unfix-
edness, unsettledness; **uncertainty,** undependability, unreliability; **variability,** deviability; irregularity 138; **desultoriness,**
waywardness, wantonness; **erraticism, eccentricity;** freakishness, freakery; **capriciousness, fickleness** 627.2, 3.

3. fluctuation, vicissitude, **variation,** alternation, oscillation, vacillation, pendulation; **wavering,** shifting, shuffling, teetering, tottering, seesawing, teeter-tottering.

4. (comparisons) Proteus, kaleidoscope,
chameleon, shifting sands, rolling stone,
Cynthia of the minute, April showers, wheel
of fortune; mercury, quicksilver; weathercock, weather vane; moon, phases of the
moon.

VERBS **5. fluctuate, vary, alternate,
vacillate,** oscillate, pendulate; **waver,**
shift, shuffle, swing, sway, wobble, wabble,
wamble [dial.], flounder, stagger, dacker
[Scot. & dial., Eng.], teeter, totter, **seesaw,
teeter-totter;** keep off and on, back and fill,
turn and turn about, blow hot and cold,
play *or* play at fast and loose, say one thing
and mean another, ring the changes, have
as many phases as the moon.

ADJS. **6. changeable, alterable,** alterative, modifiable; mutable, permutable; **variable,** checkered, ever-changing, many-
sided, kaleidoscopic; mobile, movable, plastic, fluid; protean, proteiform; metamorphic.

7. inconstant, changeable, changeful,
uncertain, unreliable, undependable, **unstable, unfixed,** restless, **unsettled,** unstaid, **unsteady,** unsteadfast, unstable as
water; **variable,** deviable; vicissitudinous,
vicissitudinary; **capricious, fickle** 627.5, 7;
erratic, eccentric, freakish; volatile, mercurial; **fluctuating,** alternating, **vacillating, wavering,** wavery, shifting, shuffling;
irregular, spasmodic 138.3; **desultory,** ram-

bling, roving, vagrant, wanton, wayward; afloat, adrift; unrestrained, undisciplined, uncontrolled, fast and loose.

ADVS. 8. changeably, variably, **inconstantly**, uncertainly, **unsteadily**, unsteadfastly, capriciously, desultorily, erratically, waveringly; back and forth, to and fro, in and out, off and on, on and off, round and round.

142. STABILITY

NOUNS 1. **stability, firmness, soundness, substantiality, solidity;** security, secureness, fastness; reliability 512.4; **steadiness**, steadfastness; constancy, invariability, undeflectability; **equilibrium**, balance, aplomb or *à plomb* [F.].

2. **fixity**, fixedness, fixture, fixation; infixion, implantation, embedment; **establishment**, stabilization, confirmation, entrenchment; inveteracy, deep-rootedness, **deep-seatedness.**

3. **immobility**, immovability, unmovability, immovableness, irremovability; inextricability; **firmness**, unyieldingness; **inflexibility** 355.3; inertia, vis inertiae; immobilization.

4. **unchangeableness, unchangeability**, unalterability, unmodifiability, **immutability,** incommutability; **permanence** 140; irrevocability, indefeasibility, irreversibility; irretrievability, unreturnableness, unrestorableness; intransmutability.

5. **indestructability, imperishability,** incorruptibility, inextinguishability, **deathlessness;** ineradicability, indelibility, ineffaceability, inerasableness.

6. **constant, invariable.**

7. (comparisons) rock, pillar, tower, foundation; leopard's spots, Ethiopian's skin; law of the Medes and Persians.

VERBS 8. **stabilize**, stabilitate; firm, firm up; **steady, balance,** counterbalance, ballast; **immobilize**, freeze; **transfix,** stick, hold; set on its feet, set on its legs [coll.].

9. **secure,** make sure or secure, **make fast, fasten,** fasten down; **anchor,** moor; batten, batten down.

10. **fix,** define, set, settle; **establish,** found, ground, lodge, seat, **entrench,** confirm, **root; infix, ingrain,** plant, implant, ingraft, bed, imbed; **print,** engraft, imprint, **stamp,** inscribe, **etch,** engrave; impress, impact, pack, jam, **wedge;** intrench, embed; deep-dye, **dye in the wool;** stereotype.

11. (become firmly fixed) **root, take root,** strike root; build's one's house on a rock; **stick,** stick fast, **catch, jam, lodge.**

12. **stand fast,** remain firm, **stand pat** [coll.], stay put [chiefly coll.], hold fast, **stand** or **hold one's ground,** hold one's own, take one's stand, **stick to one's guns,** put one's foot down [coll.]; **hold out,** stick it out [coll.]; hold up, hold up in the wash [coll.]; weather, weather the storm, ride through.

ADJS. 13. **stable, substantial, firm, solid, sound;** firm as Gibraltar, solid as a rock; **fast, secure; steady,** steadfast; **reliable** 512.17; fiducial.

14. **established,** stabilized, **entrenched,** vested (as *vested interests*), firmly established; **well-established,** well-founded, **well-grounded,** on a rock; old-line, long-established; **confirmed, inveterate;** settled, set; well-settled, well-set; **rooted,** well-rooted; **deep-rooted, deep-seated,** deep-set, deep-settled, deep-fixed, deep-dyed, deep-engraven, deep-grounded, deep-laid; **infixed, ingrained,** implanted, ingrafted, imbedded, ingrown, inwrought; engraved, etched, graven; **dyed-in-the-wool.**

15. **fixed,** fastened, riveted; **set, settled, stated;** staple (as, a *staple* trade); straight (as, ten cents *straight* [slang, U.S.]).

16. **immovable,** unmovable, **immobile,** immotile, immotive, unmoving, **irremovable, stationary,** frozen, not to be moved, at a standstill; **firm, unyielding,** adamant; **inflexible** 355.12; pat, standpat [coll.].

17. **stuck, fast,** stuck fast, **fixed, transfixed, caught,** fastened, held, inextricable; **jammed,** impacted, packed, wedged; aground, grounded, stranded, high and dry.

18. **unchangeable,** not to be changed, **unalterable,** unalterative, **immutable,** incommutable, unmodifiable; unsusceptible, insusceptible of change; **constant, invariable,** undeviating, undeflectable; **permanent** 140.7; irrevocable, indefeasible, irreversible, nonreversible, reverseless; irretrievable, unrestorable, unreturnable, nonreturnable; intransmutable.

19. **indestructible,** undestroyable, **imperishable,** nonperishable, incorruptible; **deathless,** undying; **ineradicable,** indelible, ineffaceable, inerasable; **inextinguishable,** unquenchable, quenchless.

PHRS. 20. stet [print.], **let it stand,** let it go, keep, retain.

21. stabilizers

balance	balance rudder
balance piston	[sea]
balancer	balance wheel

balancing
  condenser [radio]
balancing flap
  [aero.]
ballast
counterbalance
counterweight
fixative
gyroscope
gyrostabilizer

hairspring
mordant
pendulum
pendulum wheel
shock absorber
springs
stabilizator [aero.]
stiffening
tail plane [aero.]

143. CONTINUANCE

Continuance in Action.—NOUNS 1. continuance, continuation; prolongation, extension, protraction, lengthening; maintenance, sustenance; pursuance; run; persistence, perseverance 623; endurance 110; continuity 71.

2. resumption, recommencement, rebeginning, renewal, reopening, re-entrance; fresh start, new beginning.

VERBS 3. continue, remain, bide, abide, stay, tarry, linger; go on, go along, keep on, keep going, carry on, stay on, hold on, run on, jog on, drag on; never cease, cease not; endure 110.6.

4. sustain, protract, prolong, extend, lengthen; maintain, keep, hold, retain, preserve; keep up, keep on foot, keep going, keep alive; maintain one's course, pursue the even tenor of one's way.

5. persist, persevere, keep at it 623.2.

6. resume, recommence, rebegin, renew, re-enter, reopen, return to, go back to, begin again, take up again, go on, go on with, go on with the show [coll.]; make a new beginning, make a fresh start, start all over.

ADJS. 7. continuing, abiding 110.10; continuous 71.9.

144. CESSATION

NOUNS 1. cessation, discontinuance, discontinuation; desistance, desinence, cease [obs. exc. in without cease], ceasing, stopping; end, ending; close, closing, shutdown (as of a factory), abandonment.

2. stop, stoppage, halt, stay, arrest, check; stand, standstill, stillstand; full stop, dead stop.

3. pause, rest, break, caesura, recess, intermission, intermittance, interval, interlude, respite, letup [coll.], interruption, hesitation, remission, suspense, suspension, abeyance, stay, drop, lull, lapse; truce; short shrift.

4. (punctuation) stop, point, period; comma, colon, semicolon, caesura.

5. (in debate) closure, cloture, clôture

[F.]; closure by compartment, kangaroo closure.

VERBS 6. cease, discontinue, end, stop, halt, hold, quit, stay, stow [slang], belay [naut. or coll.]; desist, refrain, leave off, lay off [slang], give over, have done with, hold or stay one's hand; cut out, drop it, drop everything [all slang]; come to an end 70.6.

7. come to a stop or halt, halt, stop in one's tracks; bring up, pull up, draw up, fetch up; stop short, come up short, bring up short, bring up with a round turn [coll.], come to a full stop, come to a stand or standstill, fetch up all standing; stall, stick, hang fire.

8. (stop work) lay off, knock off [coll.], call it a day [coll.], call it quits [coll.]; hang up one's ax, hang up the fiddle [both coll.]; shut up shop, close shop, shut down, close down, abandon.

9. pause, hesitate, rest, let up [coll.], rest on one's oars; recess, take a recess.

10. interrupt, suspend, intermit; break, break off, cut off, break or snap the thread.

11. put a stop to, put an end to 70.7, stop, stay, halt, arrest, check, stall, shut down on or upon [coll.]; stem, stem the tide or current; pull up, draw rein, pull the checkstring; bring to a stand or standstill, put to a stand, bring to, bring up short, stop short, cut short, check in full career.

12. turn off, shut off, shut, close; kill the engine, cut the gun [slang], turn off the juice [slang].

INTERJS. 13. cease!, stop!, halt!, halte [F.], hold!, stay!, desist!, let up!, leave off!, arrêtez! [F.], avast! [naut.], belay that or there! [coll.], have done!, hold!, tenez [F.], hold on! [coll.], hold hard!, whoa! enough!, a truce to!

14. (slang terms) cut it out!, can it! cheese it!, chuck it!, stow it!, drop it!, lay off!, come off!, come off of it!, knock it off! nix!, nix on it!

145. CONVERSION

Change to Something Different.—NOUNS 1. conversion, reconversion, change-over; change, transformation 139; transition, transit, passage; shift, lapse; growth, progress; resolution, reduction, assimilation, assumption; alchemy.

2. reformation, reform, regeneration, reclamation, redemption, amendment, renewal, rebirth, new birth, change of heart, change of mind, conviction, persuasion

3. rehabilitation, reconditioning, readjustment, reclamation; **re-education,** reinstruction; **repatriation;** indoctrination, **reindoctrination,** counterindoctrination; **brainwashing,** menticide; nazification.

4. proselytization, proselytism; Christianization, Protestantization; Catholicization, Romanization.

5. convert, proselyte, neophyte, catechumen, disciple.

6. converter, proselyter, proselytizer.

7. (instruments) melting pot, crucible, alembic, caldron, retort, mortar, potter's wheel, anvil, lathe, blowpipe.

VERBS **8. convert,** reconvert; **change over,** make over; **change, transform** 139.6, 7; **change into, turn into,** resolve into, assimilate to, bring to, reduce to; make, render.

9. reform, remodel, reshape, refashion; **renew,** new-model; **regenerate, reclaim,** redeem, amend, set straight, make a new man of, restore self-respect; mend or change one's ways, **turn over a new leaf,** put on the new man.

10. rehabilitate, recondition, reclaim; **re-educate,** reinstruct; **repatriate;** indoctrinate, **reindoctrinate,** counterindoctrinate; nazify.

11. convict, persuade, wean, bring over, **win over;** proselyte, **proselytize,** disciple; Christianize, Protestantize; Catholicize, Romanize.

12. be converted into, **turn to** or **into,** run into, fall into, pass into, slide or glide into, **grow into,** merge or blend into, melt into, open into, resolve itself into, settle into, come round to; **become,** go, get, **get to be;** wax, grow; mature, mellow, ripen into; melt, blend, merge, lapse, glide, shift.

ADJS. **13. convertible, resolvable into,** transmutable, transformable, transitional, modifiable.

146. REVERSION

Change to a Former State.—NOUNS **1. reversion,** reverting, retroversion, retrogradation, **retrogression,** retrocession, **regression,** revulsion; reconversion; **reverse,** reversal; **return,** returning; turn, turnabout; lapse, escheat [law]; relapse 694.

2. throwback, atavism [biol.].

3. reversioner, reversionist [both law].

VERBS **4. revert,** retrovert, **regress, retrogress,** retrograde, retrocede, **reverse, return;** lapse, escheat [law]; relapse 694.4.

5. turn back, change back, go back, hark back, cry back, break back.

6. revert to, return to, recur to, go back to, hark back to, cry back to.

ADJS. **7. reversionary,** reversional, **regressive,** recessive, retrogressive, retrograde, reactionary, revulsionary; retroverse, retrorse; atavistic [biol.].

8. revertible, returnable, reversible.

147. REVOLUTION

Sudden or Radical Change.—NOUNS **1. revolution, radical change,** striking alteration, sweeping change, clean sweep; revulsion, transilience; **overthrow,** overturn, upset, *bouleversement* [F.], convulsion, subversion, *coup d'état* [F.]; breakup, breakdown; cataclysm, catastrophe, debacle, *débâcle* [F.]; technological revolution; counterrevolution; **revolt** 765.4.

2. revolutionism, anarchism; Bolshevism or Bolshevikism [Russia], Carbonarism [Italy], Sinn Feinism [Ireland], Jacobinism [France]; sans-culottism [France], *sans-cullotterie* [F.].

3. revolutionist, revolutionary, revolutioner, revolutionizer; **rebel** 765.5; anarchist, anarch; red, Red; Red Republican [France], *bonnet rouge* [F.]; Jacobin [France], sansculotte, sans-cullottist; Bolshevik [Russia] Bolshevist, Bolshie [coll.]; *Carbonaro* [It.], Carbonarist; Sinn Feiner [Ireland], Fenian.

VERBS **4. revolutionize,** revolution, revoulte [slang], **make a radical change,** make a clean sweep, break with the past; **overthrow,** overturn, upset; revolt 765.8.

ADJS. **5. revolutionary,** revolutional; revulsive, revulsionary; transilient; cataclysmic, catastrophic; **radical,** sweeping 56.10; **insurrectionary** 765.12.

6. revolutionist, anarchic(al), "agin the government" [coll.]; Bolshevist(ic), Bolshevik; sans-cullottic, sans-cullottish; Jacobinic, Carbonarist, Fenian.

148. SUBSTITUTION

Change of One Thing for Another.—NOUNS **1. substitution, change, exchange,** switch, commutation, subrogation; **supplanting,** supplantment, supplantation; **replacement,** displacement; supersedence, supersedure, supersession.

2. substitute, sub [coll.], **substitution, replacement,** change, exchange, changeling, secondary, succedaneum, ersatz, surrogate; **alternate,** alternative, alternator; supplanter, superseder; **proxy,** dummy;

deputy 779; locum tenens, locum [coll.], warming pan [chiefly coll.]; **relief, fill-in, stand-in** [motion-picture], **understudy, pinch hitter** [coll.]; double, dub [slang, U.S.]; equivalent, equal; ringer, ring-in [both slang]; ghost, ghost writer; substituent [chem.]; makeshift 668.2.

3. scapegoat, goat [slang], fall guy [slang, U.S.], **whipping boy.**

VERBS **4. substitute, change, exchange,** switch, **replace,** displace, ring in [coll.], subrogate; **put in the place of,** change for, make way for, give place to; commute, redeem, compound for; borrow of Peter to pay Paul; dub in [motion-picture].

5. substitute for, sub for [coll.], **act for,** double for, fill in for, pinch-hit [coll.]; **relieve,** spell [coll.], **spell off** [coll.], time off; ghost, ghostwrite; **represent** 779.13.

6. supplant, supersede, succeed, **replace,** displace, take the place of, crowd out, cut out [coll.], change places with, swap places with [coll.], stand in the stead of, step into the shoes of, fill one's shoes.

7. cover up for, front for, go to the front for, take the rap for, be the goat [all slang].

ADJS. **8. substitute, alternate, alternative,** equivalent, token, dummy, secondary, vicarious, ersatz, proxy [petrographic]; makeshift, temporary, provisional, tentative.

9. substitutional, substitutionary, substitutive; supersessive.

10. replaceable, substitutable, supersedable, expendable.

ADVS. **11. instead,** in lieu, in behalf, in the place, rather, **rather than,** *faute de mieux* [F., for lack of something better].

PREPS. **12. instead of,** in stead of, in the stead of, **for, in place of,** in the place of, in the room of [dial.], **in behalf of, in lieu of,** in its stead *or* place; in one's stead, in one's behalf, in one's place, in one's shoes; **by proxy,** as proxy for, as a substitute for, as representing, as an alternative; vice; *in loco parentis* [L., law, in the place of a parent].

149. INTERCHANGE

Double or Mutual Change.—NOUNS **1. interchange, exchange,** counterchange; commutation, permutation, intermutation; alternation; **reciprocation,** reciprocality, reciprocity; **give-and-take,** something for something, *quid pro quo* [L.], a Roland for an Oliver, measure for measure, tit for tat, an eye for an eye, "an eye for an eye and a

tooth for a tooth" [Bible]; cross fire; battledore and shuttlecock.

2. trading, swapping [coll.]; trade, swap [coll.], switch; barter 825.2.

3. interchangeability, exchangeability, changeability; commutability, permutability.

VERBS **4. interchange, exchange,** change, counterchange; alternate; commute, permute; **trade, switch;** bandy, play at battledore and shuttlecock; **reciprocate,** respond; **give and take,** give a Roland for an Oliver, give as much as one takes, give as good as was sent, return the compliment, pay back, requite, return.

ADJS. **5. interchangeable, exchangeable,** changeable; returnable, convertible, fungible, commutable, permutable; commutative; **reciprocative,** reciprocal; mutual, give-and-take.

6. intercurrent; international, interstate, intertribal, interracial, interurban; interscholastic, intercollegiate; interdenominational.

ADVS. **7. interchangeably, exchangeably; in exchange, in return; reciprocally,** mutually; **in turn,** each in its turn, every one in his turn, by turns, turn about, turn and turn about; back and forth, backward and forward, backwards and forwards, forward and back, to and fro.

150. EVENTUALITY

NOUNS **1. eventuality, eventuation;** contingency, contingent; accident 155.6.

2. event, occurrence, incidence (as of a disease), **incident,** episode, **experience, adventure,** hap, **happening,** happenstance [coll., U.S.], **phenomenon,** fact, particular, circumstance, occasion; go, go-off, come-off [all coll.]; do, bloody do [both slang, Eng.].

3. affair, matter, thing, **concern,** concernment, interest, **business, job** [coll.], **transaction,** proceeding, doing.

4. affairs, matters, concerns, circumstances, relations, **dealings, proceedings,** doings, goings on [chiefly coll.]; course *or* run of things, current of events, march of events; the world, life, the times; order of the day.

VERBS **5. occur,** hap, **happen,** eventuate, **take place, transpire** [U.S.], **come, come off, come about,** come true, **come to pass,** pass, pass off, go off, fall, **befall,** betide; **be found,** be met with.

6. turn up, show up [coll.], crop up,

spring up, cast up [Scot. & dial., Eng.], arise, come forth, come or draw on, appear, materialize, present itself.

7. turn out, become of 153.5.

8. experience, have, know, feel, taste; encounter, meet, meet with, meet up with [slang], run up against [coll.]; undergo, go through, pass through, be subjected to, be exposed to, stand under, labor under, endure, suffer, sustain, pay, spend.

ADJS 9. happening, occurring, passing, doing, taking place, on, going on; current, prevalent, prevailing, in the wind, afloat, on foot.

10. eventful, momentous, stirring, bustling, full of incident; phenomenal.

11. eventual, coming, final, last, ultimate; contingent, collateral, secondary, indirect.

ADVS. etc. 12. eventually, ultimately, finally, in the long run; in the course of things, as things go, as times go, as the world goes, as the tree falls, as the cat jumps [coll.], as things turn out, as it may be.

13. in the event of, in case, in case of, in the contingency of, in case that, if it should happen that.

151. IMMINENCE

NOUNS 1. imminence or imminency, impendence or impendency, forthcomingness; forthcoming, coming, approach, loom.

VERBS 2. be imminent, impend, overhang, hang or lie over, hang over one's head, hover, threaten, menace, lower or lour; brew, gather; come or draw on, draw near, forthcome, approach, near, await, loom, stare one in the face, be in store for.

ADJS 3. imminent, impending, impendent, overhanging, hanging over one's head, threatening, lowering, menacing, "in danger imminent" [Spenser]; brewing, gathering, preparing; coming, forthcoming, upcoming, to come, about to be, about or going to happen, approaching, nearing, looming, looming in the distance or future; near, close, immediate, instant, at hand, near-at-hand, close at hand; in the offing, on the horizon, in prospect, in view, in one's eye, in store, in reserve, in the wind, in the womb of time, on the knees or lap of the gods, in the cards [coll.]; that will be, that is to be.

ADVS. 4. imminently, impendingly; any time, any time now, any moment, any min-

ute, any hour, any day; to be expected, as may be expected, as may be.

152. CAUSE

NOUNS 1. cause, occasion, call, ground, grounds, base, basis, element, principle, factor; determinant, determinative; causation, causality.

2. reason, reason why, rationale, rational, rational ground, explanation, the why, the wherefore, the whatfor [coll.], the whyfor [dial.], the why and wherefore, the idea [slang], the big idea [slang], the because of.

3. ultimate cause, causing cause, causa causans [L.], Great First Cause; final cause, causa finalis [L.]; provocation, last straw, straw that broke the camel's back, match in the powder barrel.

4. author, agent, originator, generator, creator, mover; parent, mother, father, sire; prime mover, primum mobile [L.].

5. source, origin, original, origination, derivation, rise, beginning, inception, commencement, head; provenance, provenience; root, grass roots; stem, stock.

6. fountainhead, headwater, headstream, riverhead, springhead, headspring, mainspring, wellspring, wellhead, well, spring, fountain, fount, font, fons et origo [L., fount and origin].

7. rudiment, anlage; egg, germ, nucleus, seed; embryo, bud.

8. birthplace, breeding place, rookery, hatchery; hotbed; incubator, brooder; nest, nidus; cradle, nursery.

9. womb, matrix, uterus, venter [law].

10. (a principle or movement) cause, principle, interest, issue, burning issue, great cause; movement, mass movement, activity; drive, campaign, crusade.

VERBS 11. cause, be the cause of, lie at the root of; bring about, bring to pass, effect, bring to effect, occasion, make, create, generate, produce, breed, work, do; originate, give origin to, give occasion to, give rise to, give birth to; author, father, sire, sow the seeds of; gestate, conceive; set up, set afloat, set on foot.

12. induce, lead, procure, get, obtain, contrive, effect, bring, bring on, draw on, call forth, elicit, evoke, provoke, draw down, open the door to; determine, decide, turn the scale, have the last word; superinduce.

13. contribute to, lead to, conduce to,

redound to; **advance, forward,** influence, subserve.

14. (espouse a cause) **campaign, crusade,** put on a drive; **espouse,** advocate; carry the banner of, march under the banner of; fight the good fight.

ADJS. **15. causal,** causative; occasional; originative, institutive, constitutive; **at the bottom of,** behind the scenes; etiological.

16. original, primary, primal, primitive, pristine, primordial, primeval, aboriginal, **elementary,** elemental, **basic,** basal, **rudimentary,** radical, **fundamental;** embryonic, in embryo, *in ovo* [L.], germinal; protogenic.

153. EFFECT

NOUNS **1. effect, result,** resultant, **consequence,** consequent, sequent, sequence, event, eventuality, eventuation, **upshot, outcome,** outgrowth, offshoot, offspring, issue, **fruit,** harvest, development, corollary; derivative, derivation.

2. conclusion, end, **end result, consummation, culmination,** denouement, catastrophe, termination, completion, finale, climax, pay-off [slang].

3. impact, force, **repercussion,** reaction, impress, impression.

4. aftereffect, aftermath, aftergrowth, aftercrop, **afterclap,** aftercome [Scot.], aftertaste.

VERBS **5. result, issue, ensue, follow,** attend; **turn out, come out,** fall out, **work out,** pan out [coll.], fare; turn out to be, prove, prove to be; **become of,** come of, come about; **eventuate,** terminate, end.

6. result from, be the effect of, be due to, originate in, **come from,** come out of, grow from, **grow out of,** follow from, proceed from, issue from, ensue from, emanate from, flow from, **derive from,** accrue from, rise or arise from, take its rise from, **spring from, stem from** [U.S.], sprout from, bud from, germinate from.

ADJS. **7. resultant, resulting, following,** ensuing; **consequent,** consequential, sequent, sequential; derivative, derivational.

8. resulting from, coming from, arising from; **owing to, due to;** caused by, occasioned by, **at the bottom of.**

ADVS. **9. consequently, as a result,** as a consequence, in consequence, of consequence [coll.], naturally, *naturellement* [F.], necessarily, of necessity, inevitably, of course, as a matter of course, and so, it follows that; **therefore** 154.6; **accordingly** 8.9.

154. ATTRIBUTION

Assignment of Cause.—NOUNS **1. attribution, assignment,** assignation, **ascription, imputation,** arrogation, placement, application, attachment, saddling, **charge, blame;** accounting for, reference to, derivation from, connection with; etiology; palaetiology.

VERBS **2. attribute, assign, ascribe, impute,** give, place, put, apply, attach.

3. attribute to, ascribe to, impute to, assign to, **lay to,** put or set down to, apply to, refer to, point to; **pin on,** fix on or upon, attach to, connect with, fasten upon, hang on [slang], **saddle on or upon,** place upon, **father upon,** settle upon, saddle with; blame, **blame for,** blame on or upon [coll.], charge on or upon, place or put the blame on, place the blame or responsibility for, **fix the responsibility for,** fix the burden of, **charge to,** lay to one's charge, place to one's account, set to the account of, account for, lay at the door of, bring home to; put words in one's mouth.

4. trace to, trace down, track down, **derive from,** trace the origin or derivation of; affiliate, filiate, father, fix the paternity of.

ADJS. **5. attributable, assignable,** ascribable, **imputable,** traceable, referable, accountable, explicable; owing, due to; derivable from, derivative, derivational; putative.

ADVS. **6. hence, therefore,** therefor, **wherefore,** wherefrom, whence, then, *ergo,* for which reason, by reason of; **consequently** 153.9; **accordingly** 8.9; **because of that,** for that, by reason of that, for that reason, from or for that cause, **on that account,** on that ground, to that end, thereat; **because of this, on this account,** on account of this, *propter hoc* [L.], for this reason, hereat; thus, thusly [coll.], thuswise.

7. why, why ever or whyever [coll.], whyfor [dial.], for why [dial.], **wherefore, what for,** for which, **on what account,** on account of what or which; **how,** for what or whatever reason, from what cause; because why, 'cause why [both coll. or dial.].

CONJS. *etc.* **8. since, as, whereas,** inasmuch as, in as much as, for as much as, **forasmuch as,** in so far as, **insofar as,** insomuch as, as things go; **in view of,** in view of the fact that, taking into account that, **seeing that,** seeing as how [dial. & coll.], being as how [dial.]; **considering**, in consideration of.

9. because, 'cause [dial. or coll.], *parce que* [F.], for why *or* forwhy [dial.]; because of, for the cause that, for the reason that, for, after, in that, **by reason of,** as a result of, by *or* in virtue of, **on account of,** on the score of, for the sake of, **owing to, due to,** thanks to.

155. CHANCE

Absence of Assignable Cause.—NOUNS
1. chance, hap, "heedless hap" [Spenser]; **luck,** joss [Pidgin Eng. & slang]; **fortune, fate, lot;** fortuity, fortuitousness, adventitiousness, indeterminateness, flukiness [slang], casualness, accidentality; **break** [coll.], the breaks [slang, U.S.]; the way things fall, the way the cards fall, how they fall; **risk, gamble** 514; **opportunity** 129.2.

2. Chance, Frank Chance; Fortune, Fortuna; Luck, Lady Luck; "blind Chance" [Lucan], "fickle Chance" [Milton], "a nickname of Providence" [de Chamfort], "that Power which erring men call Chance" [Milton], "the pseudonym of God when He did not want to sign" [Anatole France].

3. purposelessness, **causelessness,** designlessness, aimlessness.

4. haphazard, chance-medley, **random;** random shot; potluck.

5. vicissitudes, vicissitudes of fortune, ins and outs, ups and downs, ups and downs of life, chapter of accidents, "the various turns of chance" [Dryden]; **chain of circumstances,** concatenation of events, chain reaction, vicious circle.

6. (chance event) happening, hap, **happenstance** [coll., U.S.], happen-so [dial. & slang]; fortuity, **accident,** casualty, adventure, hazard; **contingent, contingency;** fluke [slang], scratch hit *or* shot [coll.].

7. even chance, even break [chiefly coll.], even *or* square odds, touch and go, odds, six-two-and-even [cant]; **half a chance,** half a show [coll.]; **toss, tossup.**

8. good chance, sporting chance, 1-2-3 chance [slang], good opportunity, good *or* some show [coll.], good possibility, fair shake [slang, U.S.]; **likelihood, possibility,** probability, show [coll.], favorable prospect, well-grounded hope; **sure bet,** good thing [coll.], good thing on ice [slang, U.S.], likely card [slang]; best bet, main chance.

9. small chance, little chance, small show [coll.], **poor prospect,** poor lookout [coll.], little opportunity, poor possibil-

ity, **unlikelihood, improbability,** hardly a chance, not half a chance, not half a show [coll.]; **off chance, outside chance** [coll.], **remote possibility,** bare possibility, a ghost of a chance, **fighting chance** [coll.]; poor bet, off bet [coll.]; long odds, long shot [slang], hundred-to-one shot [slang].

10. no chance, no show [coll.], not the ghost of a chance, not a fighting chance [coll.], not a Chinaman's *or* dog's chance [slang], not a prayer, not a snowball's chance in hell [slang]; **impossibility,** hopelessness.

VERBS **11. chance, bechance,** come by chance, hap, **happen,** come, **turn up, befall;** fall to one's lot, be one's fate.

12. risk, take a chance 514.18.

13. have a chance *or* an opportunity, **stand a chance,** have *or* stand a show [coll.], **run a good chance, bid** *or* **stand fair to,** admit of; be in it [slang], be in the running; have a chance at, have a fling *or* shot at [slang].

14. not have a chance, have no chance *or* opportunity, not stand a show [coll.], not have a prayer, not have a Chinaman's chance [slang], not stand a snowball's chance in hell [slang]; not be in it [slang], be out of it [slang], **be out of the running.**

ADJS. **15. chance,** chancy [coll.]; **fortuitous, accidental, casual,** adventitious, incidental, **contingent; causeless, uncaused;** indeterminate, undetermined; **unexpected, unforeseen;** fluky [slang], scratch [coll.].

16. purposeless, causeless, designless, **aimless,** driftless, undirected; **haphazard, random,** promiscuous, indiscriminate, casual.

17. unintentional, unintended, **unmeant,** undesigned, unpurposed, unthought-of; **unpremeditated,** unmeditated, unprompted, unguided, unguarded; **unwitting, unthinking,** unconscious, involuntary.

ADVS. **18. by chance,** perchance, **by accident, accidentally, casually,** incidentally, **fortuitously;** by a piece of luck, by a fluke [slang], by good fortune; **as it chanced, as luck would have it,** as it may happen, as it may be, as the case may be, as it may chance, as it may turn up *or* out.

19. purposelessly, aimlessly; haphazardly, randomly, promiscuously, indiscriminately, casually, **at haphazard, at random.**

20. without design, unintentionally, unwittingly, unthinkingly, unexpectedly, unconsciously, involuntarily.

156. POWER, POTENCY

Effective Force.—NOUNS 1. **power, potence** or **potency,** potentiality, **force, might, vigor,** puissance [poetic]; dint, virtue; powder, soup, steam [all slang]; powerfulness, forcefulness; **strength** (inherent power) 158; **energy** 160; cogence or cogency, effect, effectiveness, effectuality; power pack; main force, brute force; strong arm; full force, full blast; superpower; armipotence.

2. **ability,** ableness, **capability,** capableness, **capacity,** caliber, **competence,** adequacy, sufficiency, efficiency, efficacy; **proficiency** 731; the stuff, the goods, what it takes [all slang]; susceptibility.

3. **omnipotence, almightiness, all-powerfulness.**

4. horsepower, man power; electric power, electropower, hydroelectric power; hydraulic power, water power; solar power; atomic power, nuclear power, thermonuclear power; rocket power, jet power.

5. force of inertia, *vis inertiae* [L.]; dead force, *vis mortua* [L.]; living force, *vis viva* [L.]; force of life, *vis vitae* [L.].

6. centrifugal force or action, centripetal force or action.

7. (science of forces) dynamics, statics.

8. **empowerment, enablement;** investment, endowment.

VERBS 9. **empower, enable;** invest, clothe, invest or clothe with power; endue, endow; arm.

10. **be able,** be up to [coll.], **lie in one's power; can,** may, can do; come it, make it, make the grade [all coll.]; make out to [dial.], cut the mustard [slang].

ADJS. 11. **potent, powerful,** power-packed, **mighty, forceful,** forcible, dynamic, **vigorous,** puissant; **cogent,** striking, telling, effective; **strong** 158.13; high-powered, high-geared, high-pressure, high-potency; armipotent, mighty in battle.

12. **omnipotent, almighty, all-powerful;** plenipotentiary, abolute, unlimited.

13. **able, capable, equal to,** up to, **competent,** adequate, effective, effectual, efficient, efficacious; **proficient** 731.20–22.

ADVS. 14. **powerfully, potently, forcefully,** forcibly, mightily, vigorously, dynamically; **cogently,** strikingly, tellingly; **effectively,** with telling effect, to good account, to good purpose, with a vengeance.

15. **ably, capably, competently,** adequately, effectively, effectually, efficiently,

well; **to the best of one's ability,** as lies in one's power, so far as one can, as best one can; with all one's might, with everything that is in one.

16. **by force,** by main or brute force, with the strong arm, with a high hand; **forcibly,** amain, with might and main; by force of arms, at the point of the sword, by storm.

17. by dint of, by virtue of.

PHR. 18. can do [slang].

157. IMPOTENCE

NOUNS 1. **impotence** or impotency, **powerlessness,** forcelessness; **weakness** 159.

2. **inability, incapability, incapacity,** incapacitation, **incompetence** or incompetency, inadequacy, insufficiency, inefficiency, unfitness, imbecility; disability, disablement, disqualification.

3. **ineffectualness,** ineffectuality, **ineffectiveness,** inefficaciousness, **inefficacy,** invalidity, futility, fatuity, inanity.

4. **helplessness, defenselessness,** unprotection; invalidism.

5. **emasculation,** demasculinization, effeminization; castration 42.5.

6. **impotent, incapable, incompetent;** flash in the pan, blank cartridge, dud [slang]; eunuch.

VERBS 7. **be impotent, not have a leg to stand on;** be ineffective, not take [slang].

8. **cannot,** can't, caun't [affected]; can't come it, not cut the mustard, not make the grade [all slang].

9. **disable, disenable, incapacitate; cripple,** becripple, maim, lame, hamstring, hock; wing, clip the wings of; **inactivate,** put out of action, put *hors de combat* [F.]; **put out of order,** put out of commission [coll.], throw out of gear; bugger [slang], queer, queer the works [slang], gum up the works [slang], throw a wrench or monkey wrench in the machinery [coll.]; kibosh, put the kibosh on [both slang]; spike, spike one's guns, put a spoke in one's wheels.

10. **disqualify, unfit,** invalidate, knock the bottom out of [coll.].

11. (render powerless) **paralyze,** prostrate, knock out [slang], break the neck or back of; handcuff, tie the hands of, hogtie [coll., U.S.], **tie hand and foot;** throttle, strangle, get a strangle hold on; muzzle, gag, silence; **disarm,** pull one's teeth, draw the teeth of; **take the wind out of one's sails,** knock the props from under, cut the

ground from under, not leave a leg to
stand on.

12. **unman, unnerve, enervate, devitalize; emasculate,** demasculinize, effeminize;
castrate 42.11.

ADJS. 13. **impotent, powerless, forceless; weak** 159.12; rudderless, tillerless.

14. **unable, incapable, incompetent,**
inefficient, ineffective; **unqualified,** unendowed, **unfit,** unfitted; unable to, incapable
of.

15. **ineffectual, ineffective, inefficacious,**
feckless, **invalid, inoperative,** of no force;
nugatory, nugacious; fatuous, fatuitous;
vain, futile, unavailing, bootless, fruitless;
empty, inane, effete, barren, sterile.

16. **disabled, incapacitated; crippled,**
hamstring; disqualified, invalidated; disarmed; paralyzed; hog-tied [coll., U.S.];
done for, done brown, done up brown [all
coll.].

17. **out of action, out of commission**
[coll.], out of gear; *hors de combat* [F.],
out of the battle, off the field, out of the
running; laid on the shelf.

18. **helpless, defenseless, unprotected;**
aidless, friendless, unfriended; fatherless,
motherless; leaderless, guideless; prostrate,
on one's back, on one's beam-ends.

19. **unmanned, unnerved, enervated,**
devitalized; nerveless, sinewless, marrowless, pithless, lustless; **emasculate,** emasculated, demasculinized, effeminized.

PREPS. 20. **beyond one,** beyond, past, beyond the ability, beyond one's power or
capacity, beyond one's depth, above one's
head, too much for.

158. STRENGTH

Inherent Power.—NOUNS 1. **strength,**
might, mightiness, powerfulness; **potency,**
power 156; **energy** 160; **vigor, vitality,** vigorousness, heartiness, lustiness, lustihood;
stoutness, sturdiness, stalwartness, robustness, huskiness [coll.], hardiness, ruggedness; **stamina, guts** [slang], fortitude, endurance.

2. **muscularity,** brawniness, beefiness
[coll.], thewiness, sinewiness; **brawn, beef**
[coll.]; **muscle, thew,** sinew, thews, sinews;
musculature; voluntary muscles, involuntary muscles; flexor, tensor, extensor,
sphincter; biceps, triceps.

3. **soundness, firmness,** stanchness,
staunchness, stoutness, **sturdiness,** stability, solidity.

4. **impregnability,** impenetrability, in-

vulnerability, inexpugnability, inviolability; **unassailability,** unattackableness; resistlessness, irresistibility; **invincibility,** indomitability, insuperability, unconquerableness, unbeatableness.

5. **strengthening, invigoration,** fortification; hardening, casehardening; **restrengthening,** reinforcement; **reinvigoration,** refreshment, revivification.

6. **strong man, stalwart, tower of**
strength; powerhouse, roarer, snorter, muscle man, man mountain, big bruiser, big
beef [all slang]; **giant,** giant refreshed;
Hercules, Goliath, Atlas, Antaeus, Samson,
Cyclops, Briareus, colossus, Polyphemus,
Titan, Brobdingnagian, Tarzan; the strong,
the mighty.

7. (comparisons) horse, ox, lion; oak,
heart of oak; rock, Gibraltar; iron, steel,
nails.

VERBS 8. **be strong;** have the goods or
stuff, have what it takes, have the makings
or makin's [all slang].

9. **not weaken,** not flag; **bear up, hold**
up, keep up, stand up; **hold out,** stay it
out, stick it out [slang], stay the distance
[slang, U.S.], not give up, **never say die;**
not let it get one down, take it, stand up
and take it [all slang].

10. **exert strength,** muscle [dial., move
by muscular force], put plenty of beef into
[slang]; use force, strongarm [coll.].

11. **strengthen, invigorate, fortify,**
brace, buttress; brace up, screw up, set up,
set on one's legs or feet [coll.]; gird, gird up
one's loins; steel, harden, caseharden; confirm, sustain; **restrengthen,** reinforce; **reinvigorate,** refresh, recruit one's strength.

12. **proof,** insulate, weatherproof, soundproof, fireproof, waterproof, etc.

ADJS. 13. **strong,** strengthy [Scot. &
North Eng.], **mighty, powerful; potent**
156.11; **stout, sturdy, stalwart, rugged,**
hale, husky [coll.], strapping, hefty [coll.],
doughty [arch. or joc.], **hardy, hard,** hard
as nails; **robust,** robustious [joc.]; **vigorous,**
hearty, nervy, **lusty,** bouncing, fullblooded [U.S.]; sturdy as an ox, strong as a
lion, ∼ ox or horse, strong as brandy,
strong as strong.

14. **able-bodied, well-built,** well-set,
well-set-up [coll.], well-knit, broadshouldered, **athletic; muscular,** beefy [coll.],
brawny, thewy, sinewy, wiry.

15. **Herculean, Briarean, Brobdingnag-**
ian, Cyclopean, Atlantean, titanic.

16. **sound, firm, stout, sturdy, stanch,**

staunch, **stable**, solid; sound as a roach, solid as a rock, firm as Gibraltar, made of iron; in fine or high feather [coll.], like a giant refreshed.

17. impregnable, impenetrable, **invulnerable,** inviolable, inexpugnable; **unassailable,** unattackable, insuperable, unsurmountable; resistless, irresistible; **invincible,** indomitable, **unconquerable,** unsubduable, unbeatable, more than a match for.

18. proof, tight, resistant; proof against, impervious to; foolproof; weatherproof; watertight, leakproof, drop-dry [naut.]; airproof, airtight; soundproof, noiseproof; punctureproof, holeproof; bulletproof, ballproof, shellproof, bombproof; fireproof, flameproof, fire-resisting; burglarproof.

19. unweakened, undiminished, unallayed, unfaded, unwithered, unshaken, unworn, unexhausted; **unweakening, unflagging;** in full force or swing, **going strong** [slang]; in the plenitude of power.

ADVS. **20. strongly, stoutly, sturdily,** stalwartly, robustly, ruggedly; **mightily, powerfully; vigorously, heartily,** lustily; **soundly, firmly,** stanchly, staunchly.

159. WEAKNESS

NOUNS **1. weakness,** weakliness, **feebleness, strengthlessness,** unstrength [dial.]; **impotence** 157; **debility,** debilitation; faintness, gone feeling; languor, lassitude, languishment, dullness, sluggishness; atony, asthenia, adynamia, cachexia [all med.].

2. frailty, slightness, **delicacy, daintiness; flimsiness, unsubstantiality,** gimcrackiness [coll.]; **fragility,** frangibility, breakability, destructibility; human frailty, "amiable weakness" [Fielding].

3. infirmity, unsoundness, unsturdiness, **instability, unsubstantiality;** decrepitude; **unsteadiness, shakiness,** ricketiness, wobbliness, dottiness [coll.], grogginess, weewows [dial.].

4. weak side; weak point, vulnerable point, heel of Achilles.

5. weakening, enfeeblement, debilitation; languishment; **devitalization,** enervation, evisceration; fatigue (as of a metal); attenuation, extenuation; blunting, deadening, dulling; **dilution,** reduction, thinning.

6. weakling, weak soul, weak sister [coll.], softy [slang, U.S.], **jellyfish,** invertebrate, **baby,** big baby, chicken [coll.], canary [slang], milquetoast, sop, **milksop, namby-pamby, mollycoddle,** cream puff [slang, U.S.], ladyfinger [slang], pantywaist [slang], push-over [slang, U.S.], lightweight, poor or weak tool [coll.], doormat; droop, sad sack [both slang]; weathercock; the weak.

7. (comparisons) reed, thread, hair, rope of sand; house of cards, house built on sand; water, milk and water, gruel, cambric tea.

VERBS **8.** (be weak) **shake,** tremble, totter, teeter, dodder; halt, limp; be on one's last legs, have one foot in the grave.

9. (become weak) **weaken,** grow weak or weaker, go soft [slang]; **languish, droop,** drop, **sink, decline, flag, pine, fade, fail;** go downhill, hit the skids [slang, U.S.], go on the toboggan [slang, U.S.]; give way, break, cave in [coll.]; give out, conk out [slang, U.S.], fizzle out [coll.], peg out [slang], peter out [coll.], play out, poop out [slang]; die on the vine [coll.].

10. (render weak) **weaken, enfeeble, debilitate,** unstrengthen, unsinew; **devitalize,** enervate, eviscerate; **sap,** sap the strength of, exhaust, gruel, take it out of [coll.]; shake, unstring; reduce, lay low; attenuate, extenuate; blunt, deaden, dull, take the edge off.

11. dilute, cut [coll.], **reduce, thin,** attenuate, rarefy; **water,** irrigate [slang], baptize [slang].

ADJS. **12. weak,** weakly, **feeble, debilitated,** imbecile, unstrong [dial.]; **strengthless,** sapless, marrowless, pithless, sinewless, lustless; **impotent, powerless** 157.13; faint, faintish, gone (as a gone feeling); dull, slack; **soft** [coll.], flabby, flaccid, unhardened; limp, limber, limp or limber as a dishrag; **languorous,** languid, **drooping,** droopy; asthenic [med.] adynamic [tech.]; not what one used to be.

13. "weak as water" [Bible], weak as milk and water, weak as a drink of water, weak as a child or baby, weak as a chicken, weak as a mouse, "weak as a rained-on bee" [Torrence].

14. frail, slight, delicate, dainty, "delicately weak" [Pope]; puny, pindling [coll., U.S.]; **fragile,** frangible, **breakable,** destructible, shattery; **unsubstantial, flimsy,** slimsy [coll., U.S.], sleazy, gossamery, papery, pasteboardy; gimcrack, gimcracky [coll.]; gingerbread, gingerbready; jerrybuilt, jerry [builders' cant].

15. unsound, infirm, unstable, unsubstantial, unsturdy, unsolid, decrepit; poor, poorish; rotten, rotten at the core.

16. **unsteady, shaky, rickety,** ricketish, teetery, tottery, tottlish [coll.], tottering, doddering [coll.], jiggety [coll.], joggly [coll.], cogglety [dial.], dotty [coll.], rocky [slang], groggy, wobbly, wambly [dial.]; weewow, weewowy [both dial.]; cranky, craichy [dial.].

17. **wishy-washy,** washy, **namby-pamby, insipid,** watery, milky, milk-and-water, mushy.

18. **weakened, enfeebled; devitalized,** enervated, eviscerated; **wasted, run-down,** worn, worn to a shadow, reduced to a skeleton, "weakened and wasted to skin and bone" [Du Bartas].

19. **diluted, cut** [coll.], **reduced, thinned,** rarefied, attenuated; watered, watered down.

20. **weakening, debilitating, enfeebling; devitalizing,** enervating, sapping, exhausting, grueling.

21. **languishing, drooping, sinking, declining, flagging, pining, fading, failing.**

ADVS. 22. **weakly, feebly,** strengthlessly; faintly, dully; delicately, daintily; infirmly, unsoundly, unstably, unsubstantially, unsturdily, flimsily; shakily, unsteadily, teeteringly, totteringly.

160. ENERGY

NOUNS 1. **energy, vigor, force, intensity; potency** 156; **strength** 158; actual or kinetic energy; dynamic energy; potential energy; ergal [phys.].

2. **vim, verve,** fire, starch, snap [coll.], bang, **punch, dash, drive,** push [coll.], git [slang], get [slang], go [coll.]; **pep,** pepper, ginger, kick, zip, zing, zizz [all slang].

3. **animation, vivacity,** liveliness, spiritedness, **life, spirit;** activity 705.

4. **acrimony,** acridity, acerbity, acidity, bitterness, tartness, **causticity,** mordancy, mordacity, virulence; **harshness,** roughness, **severity,** stringency, astringency; **sharpness, keenness, poignancy,** trenchancy; edge, point; bite, sting.

5. **energizer, stimulant, stimulus,** stimulator, arouser; **activator,** motivating force, motive power; **animater,** spark plug [coll., U.S.], human dynamo [coll.]; life, life of the party.

6. (units of energy) atomerg, dinamode, dyne, erg, energid, foot-pound, horsepower, horsepower-hour, horsepower-year, joule, kilogrammeter, kilowatt-hour, photon, poundal, quantum.

7. **energizing, invigoration, animation,**

enlivenment, quickening, vitalization, **exhilaration, stimulation.**

8. **activation,** reactivation.

VERBS 9. **energize, dynamize; invigorate, animate, enliven,** liven, vitalize, quicken, **exhilarate, stimulate; pep up,** snap up, jazz up, zip up, whoop it up, punch it up, put pep, ∼ zip, etc. into [all slang].

10. **activate,** reactivate.

ADJS. 11. **energetic, vigorous, strenuous, forceful, forcible, strong, dynamic,** kinetic, **intense,** acute, keen, incisive, trenchant, vivid, vibrant; **active, lively,** living, **animated, spirited, vivacious,** brisk, spanking, smacking; snappy, zippy, peppy, full of pep [all slang].

12. **acrimonious, acrid,** acridulous, acid, **bitter,** tart, **caustic,** escharotic [med.], mordant, mordacious, virulent, vitriolic; **harsh, severe,** rough, stringent, astringent; **sharp, keen,** incisive, trenchant, **cutting,** biting, stinging, **scathing,** stabbing, **piercing, poignant,** edged, double-edged.

13. **energizing,** vitalizing, **enlivening,** quickening; **invigorating,** invigorative; **animating,** animative; **exhilarating,** exhilarative; **stimulating,** stimulative.

ADVS. 14. **energetically, vigorously, strenuously,** forcefully, forcibly, intensely, keenly; **actively,** briskly; **animatedly, spiritedly,** vivaciously, with pep [slang].

161. VIOLENCE

Vehement Action.—NOUNS 1. **violence, vehemence, furiousness, force,** rigor, impetuosity, inclemency, **severity, intensity,** acuteness, sharpness; **fierceness, ferociousness,** viciousness, savagery.

2. **turbulence, turmoil, fury, furor,** *furore* [It.], **rage, frenzy,** tempestuousness, tumultuousness, **tumult, uproar,** hubbub, **commotion, disturbance, agitation,** bluster, broil, brawl, embroilment, ferment, fume, ebullition, fomentation.

3. **unruliness, disorderliness,** obstreperousness; **riot, rioting.**

4. **storm, tempest,** war of the elements, "Nature's elemental din" [Thomas Campbell], "tempestuous rage" [Shakespeare], "groans of roaring wind and rain" [ibid.]; stormy weather, rough weather, foul weather, dirty weather, dirt [coll., naut.]; rainstorm 393.2; thunderstorm 393.3; windstorm 402.13–15; snowstorm 332.9.

5. **upheaval, convulsion,** cataclysm;

orgasm, aphrodisia; **earthquake,** quake, shake [coll.], temblor [U.S.]; diastrophism [geol.].

6. outburst, outbreak, eruption, eructation, flare-up; **burst,** bounce, dissiliency; **torrent,** rush, gust, tornado, stream, strain; **volcano,** volcan, burning mountain.

7. explosion, discharge, blowout, blowup, detonation, fulmination, **blast, burst;** flash, flare, fulguration; bang, boom 455; backfire.

8. concussion, shock; percussion, repercussion.

9. (violent person) **violent,** berserk *or* berserker; **hothead, madcap,** hotspur; **demon, fiend,** shaitan *or* sheitan [coll.], hellhound, hellcat, hellion [coll.], **beast,** wild beast, tiger, dragon, roarer *or* hellroarer [slang], ring-tailed roarer [slang, U.S.], terror [coll.], holy terror [slang], fireeater [coll.], spitfire, ugly customer [slang], **fury** [spec. female]; virago, vixen, termagent, beldam, she-wolf, tigress, witch [all female].

VERBS **10. rage, storm, rant, rave,** roar; **rampage,** ramp, **tear,** tear around; go on, carry on [both coll.]; come in like a lion.

11. seethe, boil, fume, foam, simmer, stew, ferment, stir, churn.

12. erupt, burst forth, break out, blow out, eruct, belch, **vomit,** spout, spew, disgorge, **discharge,** eject, throw *or* hurl forth.

13. explode, go off, blow out, blow up, blast, burst, bust [dial. & inelegant]; **detonate,** fulminate; **touch off,** set off, let off; **discharge,** fire, shoot; backfire.

14. run amuck, go berserk, go on a rampage, cut loose, run riot, run wild.

ADJS. **15. violent, vehement, severe, rigorous, furious, fierce, intense;** sharp, acute, keen, cutting, splitting, piercing; rough, tough [coll.]; **drastic,** extreme, extravagant, great.

16. unmitigated, unsoftened, untempered, unallayed, unsubdued, unquelled; unquenched, unextinguished.

17. turbulent, tumultuous, raging, storming, stormy, **tempestuous,** troublous, **frenzied, wild, frantic, furious,** infuriate, mad, angry, ravening, raving; **blustering,** blustery, blusterous; **uproarious,** riproaring [slang, U.S.]; pandemoniac; orgastic.

18. unruly, disorderly, obstreperous; **unbridled** 760.22; **riotous, wild, rampant.**

19. rampageous, rampacious [coll.]; **rambunctious** [U.S.], rambustious, rum-

bustious, rumbumptious [all slang]; **boisterous,** roisterous, wild, rollicking, **rowdy,** rough, harum-scarum [coll.]; knockabout, rough-and-tumble, knock-down-drag-out [coll.].

20. savage, fierce, ferocious, vicious; brutal, brutish, **bestial,** inhuman; feral, ferine; **wild,** untamed, tameless, ungentle; **barbarous,** barbaric; **uncivilized,** noncivilized.

21. fiery, heated, inflamed, flaming, scorching, hot, red-hot; ardent, passionate; **hotheaded,** madcap.

22. convulsive, upheaving; **spasmodic,** paroxysmal, spastic [med.].

23. explosive, bursting, detonating, fulminating; **volcanic,** eruptive; explosible, explodable.

ADVS. **24. violently, vehemently, rigorously, severely, fiercely; furiously,** wildly, madly, **like mad,** like fury [coll.], like blazes; all to pieces, all to smash *or* smithereens, all to sticks and staves [all coll.]; with a vengeance.

25. turbulently, tumultuously, uproariously, stormily, tempestuously, troublously, **frenziedly, frantically, furiously,** madly, angrily.

26. savagely, fiercely, ferociously, viciously, brutally, bestially, barbarously, inhumanly; **tooth and nail,** *bec et ongles* [F.].

162. MODERATION

NOUNS **1. moderation,** moderateness; **restraint,** constraint, control; **temperateness,** temperance, sobriety; **mildness,** gentleness; **unexcessiveness,** unextremeness, unextravagance, *meden agan* [Gr., nothing to excess]; **happy medium, golden mean,** *juste-milieu* [F.]; moderationism, **conservatism.**

2. modulation, abatement, remission, mitigation, diminution, **reduction,** lessening, falling off; **relaxation,** slackening, **easing,** loosening, letup [coll.], letdown, **alleviation,** assuagement, allayment, palliation, lightening, **tempering, softening,** subduement; deadening, dulling, blunting, **pacification, tranquilization,** mollification, demulsion, dulcification, **quieting,** quietening, lulling, **soothing, calming,** hushing.

3. mitigator, modulator, **moderator,** temperer, assuager; **alleviator,** alleviative, palliative, lenitive; **pacifier, soother,** mollifier, **tranquilizer,** calmative; **sedative** 685.11; balm, salve; cushion, shock absorber

4. **moderate,** moderatist, moderationist, conservative.

VERBS 5. **be moderate, keep within bounds,** strike a balance, keep a happy medium, keep the golden mean, steer or preserve an even course; keep the peace; sober down, settle down; remit, relent; take in sail; go out like a lamb.

6. **moderate, restrain,** constrain, control, **keep within bounds; modulate, mitigate,** abate, weaken, **diminish, reduce,** lessen, slow down; **alleviate,** assuage, swage [dial.], allay, lay, lighten, palliate; **temper,** attemper; **soften, subdue,** tame, chasten, tone or tune down; deaden, dull, blunt, obtund, take the edge off; smother, suppress, stifle; damp, dampen, throw cold water on, throw a wet blanket on; sober, sober down.

7. **calm,** becalm, **tranquilize, pacify,** mollify, appease, dulcify; **quiet,** hush, still, rest, compose, **lull, soothe,** cool, subdue, quell; smooth, smooth over, smooth down; pour oil on the troubled waters, pour balm into.

8. **cushion,** absorb the shock, **soften the blow,** deaden, soften, suppress, neutralize, offset.

9. **relax,** unlax [coll.], unbend; ease, **ease up,** ease off, **let up,** let down; abate, bate, remit, mitigate; **slacken,** slack, slake, slack off, slack up; loose, **loosen;** unbrace, unstrain, unstring.

ADJS. 10. **moderate, temperate,** sober; **mild,** soft, bland, **gentle,** tame; mild as milk or mother's milk, mild as milk and water, gentle as a lamb.

11. **restrained,** constrained, limited, controlled; tempered, **softened,** hushed, **subdued,** quelled, chastened.

12. **unexcessive,** unextreme, unextravagant, conservative; reasonable (as in price).

13. **equable,** even; tranquil, calm 267.10.

14. **mitigating,** assuaging, abating, **diminishing, reducing,** lessening, allaying, **alleviating, relaxing, easing;** tempering, **softening,** chastening, **subduing;** deadening, dulling, blunting, dampening, cushioning.

15. **tranquilizing,** pacifying, mollifying, appeasing; **calming,** lulling, quietening, hushing, stilling; **soothing,** soothful, restful; dreamy, drowsy.

16. **palliative,** assuasive, **alleviative,** lenitive, **calmative,** calmant, **sedative,** demulcent, anodyne; antiorgastic, anaphrodisiac.

ADVS. 17. **moderately, in moderation,** in reason, within bounds or compass; temperately, soberly; conservatively.

163. OPERATION

NOUNS 1. **operation, functioning, action, performance,** exercise, play, work, **working,** workings; function, office, agency; **management, conduct,** running; driving, steering; handling, manipulation.

2. **process, procedure,** proceeding, course; act, motion; step, measure.

3. **workability, operability,** actability, performability, negotiability [coll.], manipulatability, maneuverability; practicability.

4. **operator,** operative, operant; **handler,** manipulator; **driver,** runner, steersman, pilot, engineer; conductor.

VERBS 5. **operate, work, run, manage,** conduct, carry on, make go; **handle,** manipulate, maneuver; deal with; **drive,** steer, pilot; perform on, play; militate, militate for or against.

6. (produce as an effect) **bring about, work, act, produce,** carry out or through.

7. operate on, **act on** or **upon, work on,** treat; bring to bear upon.

8. (be operative) **operate, function, work, act, perform, go, run;** percolate, perk, tick [all slang]; play (applied to a musical instrument); be effective, have effect, take effect; have play, have free play.

9. **function as,** work as, **act as,** act or play the part of.

ADJS. 10. **operative,** operational, **functional, practical; effective,** effectual, efficient, efficacious.

11. **workable, operable,** operatable, **performable,** actable, **doable,** negotiable [coll.], manipulatable, maneuverable; **practicable,** practical.

12. **operating, working, functioning,** acting, active, running, **going,** going on; **in operation,** in action, **in practice, in force,** in play, in exercise, at work, on foot; in the act of, in the course of; **in process,** in the works, on the fire.

164. PRODUCTIVENESS

NOUNS 1. **productiveness,** productivity, **fruitfulness, fertility,** fecundity, pregnancy [fig.]; richness, luxuriance, prolificacy, generousness, bountifulness, plentifulness, plenteousness, copiousness.

2. proliferation, prolification, pullulation, multiplication.

3. fertilization, enrichment, fecundation; impregnation 168.4.

4. fertilizer, dressing, enrichener; organic fertilizer, manure, muck, night soil, guano, compost, castor bean meal; commercial fertilizer, inorganic fertilizer, chemical fertilizer, phosphate, superphosphate, ammonia, nitrogen.

5. (gods of fertility) Demeter [Gr. myth.], Ceres [Rom. myth.], Frey [Norse myth.], Isis [Egyptian myth.], Baal [Semitic myth.], Astarte or Ashtoreth [Phoenician myth.].

6. (comparisons) milk cow, rabbit, Hydra, warren, seed plot, hotbed, rich soil, land flowing with milk and honey, mustard.

VERBS 7. proliferate, pullulate, multiply, teem.

8. fertilize, enrich, fatten; fructify, fecundate, fecundify, prolificate; impregnate 168.11; dress, manure.

ADJS. 9. productive, fruitful, fecund; fertile, pregnant [fig.], rich, fat; prolific, proliferous, uberous, teeming, plenteous, plentiful, copious, generous, bountiful, abundant, luxuriant, exuberant; creative 166.23.

10. bearing, yielding, producing; fruitbearing, fructiferous.

11. fertilizing, enriching, richening, fattening, fecundative.

165. UNPRODUCTIVENESS

NOUNS 1. unproductiveness, unproductivity, unfruitfulness, barrenness, sterileness, sterility, unfertileness, infertility, infecundity; impotence; ineffectualness 157.3.

2. waste, wasteland, desolation, barren or barrens, barren land, "weary waste" [Southey], heath; desert, Sahara, "a barren waste, a wild of sand" [Addison]; karroo or karoo [S. Africa]; wilderness, howling wilderness, wild, wilds; bush, brush.

VERBS 3. be unproductive, come to nothing, hang fire, flash in the pan, fizzle out [coll.]; lie fallow.

ADJS. 4. unproductive, nonproductive, nonproducing; unfertile, nonfertile; unfruitful, sterile, impotent, acarpous [bot.], infecund, unprolific, ineffectual 157.15; barren, desert, arid, dry, jejune; childless, issueless, fruitless, teemless [poetic], without issue, sine prole [L., law]; fallow.

5. uncreative, noncreative; uninventive, unoriginal.

166. PRODUCTION

NOUNS 1. production, performance, execution, effectuation; through-put; overproduction.

2. mass production, volume production, assembly-line production; production line, assembly line.

3. creation, manufacture, making, fashioning, framing, forming, formation, formulation, preparation, composition, elaboration; construction, building, erection, architecture; fabrication, prefabrication; workmanship, craftsmanship, handiwork, handicraft.

4. establishment, foundation, constitution, institution, installation, formation, organization.

5. origination, invention, fabrication, concoction, coinage, devising, hatching, contriving, contrivance; improvisation; authorship; creative effort.

6. generation, genesis; development; procreation 168.2; abiogenesis, archigenesis, biogenesis, blastogenesis, digenesis, dysmerogenesis, epigenesis, eumerogenesis, heterogenesis, histogenesis, homogenesis, isogenesis, merogenesis, metagenesis, monogenesis, oögenesis, orthogenesis, pangenesis, parthenogenesis, phytogenesis, sporogenesis, xenogenesis; spontaneous generation.

7. incubation, gestation, hatching, maturation; brooding, sitting, covering.

8. bearing, yielding; fruition, fruiting, fructification.

9. birth, genesis, nativity, nascency, childbirth, childbearing, parturition, delivery; hatching (from the egg); act of God [joc.], blessed event [slang, U.S.]; the Nativity; multiparity; abortion, miscarriage; confinement, lying-in, childbed, accouchement [F.]; labor, travail, birth throe; birth control, contraception, contraceptive; birth rate; stork.

10. producer, maker; manufacturer, industrialist; creator, begetter, author, mother, father, sire; generator, mover; originator, initiator, inaugurator, introducer, institutor, beginner, prime mover; founder, organizer; inventor, deviser; builder, constructor, artificer, architect; executor, executrix; grower, raiser.

VERBS 11. produce, perform, do, execute, effectuate, bring about; cause 152.11; raise, rear, grow; mass-produce, volume-produce; overproduce.

12. create, make, manufacture, form, formulate, evolve, elaborate, fashion, forge, fabricate, frame; construct, build, erect, put up, set up, run up, raise, rear; make up, get up, prepare, compose, devise, concoct, compound; put together, piece together, patch together, fudge together; mill, machine; carve, chisel; prefabricate, prefab [U.S.].

13. establish, found, constitute, institute, install, form, set up, organize.

14. originate, invent, make up, devise, contrive, concoct, fabricate, coin, frame, hatch, hatch up, cook up, strike out; improvise; think up [U.S.], think out, dream up [U.S.], set one's wits to work, strain or crack one's invention.

15. generate, develop; breed, engender, beget, spawn, hatch [all fig.]; bring forth, give rise to, give being to, bring or call into being; procreate 168.9.

16. incubate, hatch; brood, sit, set, cover.

17. bear, yield, teem [dial.], produce, furnish; bring forth, usher into the world; fruit, bear fruit, fructify.

18. lay (eggs), deposit, drop; spawn, spat.

19. give birth, bear young, born [dial.], teem [dial.], kindle [chiefly dial.], come in [coll., U.S.], find [dial.], have, have young; drop, spring, cast, throw [all of animals]; bear a child, have a baby, baby [slang]; pup, whelp, cub, kitten, foal, calve, fawn; lamb, yean, ean [dial.]; litter; miscarry, abort, slink, sling, cast; lie in; labor.

20. be born, have birth, come forth, issue forth, come into the world; hatch; be born on the wrong side of the blanket, come in through a side door [both slang].

ADJS. **21.** productional, creational, formational; manufacturing, manufactural, industrial.

22. constructional, structural, edificial; architectural, architectonic.

23. creative, originative, causative, productive 164.9, constructive, formative, fabricative, demiurgic.

24. generative, genial, gametic; genital, genitive; genetic, abiogenetic, biogenetic, blastogenetic, digenetic, dysmerogenetic, epigenetic, eumerogenetic, heterogenetic, histogenetic, homogenetic, isogenetic, merogenetic, metagenetic, monogenetic, oögenetic, orthogenetic, pangenetic, parthenogenetic, phytogenetic, sporogenous, xenogenetic.

25. produced, caused, brought about; effectuated, executed, performed, done; grown, raised; mass-produced, volume-produced.

26. born, given birth; hatched; "born naked" [Robert Burton], "cast naked upon the naked earth" [Pliny the Elder]; nee; newborn; stillborn.

27. made, manufactured, created, formed, fashioned, built, constructed, fabricated; well-made, well-built, well-constructed; homemade, homespun, handmade, selfmade; machine-made; custom-made, custom-built, custom, made to order; ready-made, ready-formed, ready-prepared, ready-to-wear, ready-for-wear; prefabricated, prefab [coll.].

28. invented, fabricated, coined, made-up, made out of whole cloth.

29. producible, productible, causable.

ADVS. **30.** in production, under construction, in the works.

167. PRODUCT

NOUNS **1.** product, result, end product; work, œuvre [F.], handiwork, manufacture, production, creation, creature; offspring, child, fruit; issue, outgrowth, outcome, outgo; invention, origination, coinage, brain child; concoction, composition; opus (pl. opera), opuscule; consumer products.

2. produce, proceeds, yield, output; crop, harvest.

3. by-product, outgrowth, offshoot, side issue.

4. (amount made) make, making; batch, lot.

5. products

basketwork	lacework
beadwork	leadwork
bobbinwork	leafwork
bodywork	leatherwork
bolsterwork	masonry
brasswork	masonwork
brickwork	metalwork
bridgework	millwork
brushwork	needlework
cabinetwork	panelwork
chainwork	patchwork
checkerwork	pinwork
fancywork	plasterwork
featherwork	potwork
firework	rockwork
flowerwork	scrollwork
frostwork	sheetwork
glasswork	shellwork
goldwork	silkwork
ironwork	silverwork
knitwork	splatterwork

steelwork	toolwork
stonework	velvetwork
strapwork	waxwork
stuccowork	wickerwork
timberwork	wirework
tinwork	

168. REPRODUCTION

NOUNS 1. **reproduction, remaking, re-creation**, refashioning, reformation, **reconstruction**, rebuilding; re-establishment, reorganization; regeneration, regenesis, palingenesis; duplication (imitation) 22, (copy) 24, (repetition) 103.

2. **procreation, generation, begetting, breeding; propagation, multiplication;** proliferation; line breeding; inbreeding, endogamy; outbreeding, xenogamy; dissogeny.

3. **copulation,** copula [chiefly law], coupling, mating, **coition,** coitus, venery, **intercourse,** commerce, congress, **sexual intercourse,** sexual commerce, sexual congress, sexual union, sexual relations, relations, intimacy, connection, carnal knowledge, aphrodisia; fornication; love 930.

4. **fertilization,** fecundation; **impregnation,** insemination; **pollination,** pollinization; cross-fertilization, cross-pollination; self-fertilization, heterogamy, orthogamy; isogamy.

5. **conception,** coming with child; superfetation, superimpregnation.

6. **pregnancy, gestation,** parturiency, gravidness, gravidity, heaviness, greatness, bigness, awkwardness [dial.], the family way [coll.].

7. **birth** 166.9.

VERBS 8. **reproduce, remake,** make over, **recreate,** regenerate, reform, refashion, **reconstruct,** rebuild; re-establish, refound, reorganize; duplicate (copy) 22.8, (repeat) 103.7.

9. **procreate, generate, breed, beget,** get, engender; **propagate, multiply;** proliferate; mother; father, sire; reproduce in kind, reproduce after one's kind; breed true; inbreed, breed in and in; outbreed; crossbreed 44.14; line-breed.

10. **copulate, couple,** mate, unite in sexual intercourse, **have sexual relations,** come together; sleep with, lay with, go to bed with; **cover,** mount, board [slang], serve (of animals); fornicate; love 930.13.

11. **fertilize,** fructify, fecundate, fecundify; **impregnate, inseminate,** spermatize; **get with child** or **young,** big [dial.]; **pollinate,** pollinize, pollen; cross-fertilize,

cross-pollinate, cross-pollenize, cross-pollen.

12. **conceive, catch, come with child,** get in the family way [coll.]; superfetate.

13. **be pregnant, be with child** or **young,** be in the family way [coll.]; be expecting, anticipate a blessed event [slang, U.S.]; **gestate,** breed, teem [dial.], carry, carry young.

14. give birth 166.19.

ADJS. 15. **reproductive, recreative, regenerative, reconstructive,** reformative, progenitive; renascent, resurgent, reappearing; Hydra-headed.

16. **procreative,** procreant, **propagative,** life-giving; spermatic; fertilizing, fecundative; multiparous.

17. **bred, impregnated,** inseminated; inbred, endogamic, endogamous; outbred, exogamic, exogamous; crossbred 44.16; linebred.

18. **pregnant,** enceinte [F.], **with child** or **young, in the family way** [coll.], gestating, breeding, teeming, parturient; heavy with child or young, great or big with child or young, gravid, heavy, great, big, laden, awkward [dial.]; **expecting,** expectant, anticipating, anticipating a blessed event [slang, U.S.]; superfetate, superimpregnated.

169. ANCESTRY

NOUNS 1. **ancestry,** progenitorship; parentage, parenthood; grandparentage, grandfatherhood, grandmotherhood.

2. **paternity,** fatherhood, fathership; fatherliness, paternalness.

3. **maternity,** motherhood, mothership; motherliness, maternalness.

4. **lineage, line, bloodline, descent,** line of descent, succession, **extraction,** derivation, birth, blood, breed, **family,** house, **strain,** sept, **stock,** stirps, seed; direct line, phylum; branch, stem; filiation, affiliation; side; male line, spear side; female line, distaff or spindle side.

5. **genealogy, pedigree,** stemma, genealogical tree, **family tree,** tree; genealogist.

6. **heredity, heritage, inheritance, birth;** patrocliny (from the father), matrocliny (from the mother); inheritability, heritability, hereditability; Mendel's Law, Mendelism; Weismann theory, Weismannism; Altmann theory, De Vries theory, Galtonian theory, Verworn theory, Wiesner theory; **genetics,** genesiology, eugenics; **gene,** factor, inheritance factor, determiner, determinant; chromatin, id.

7. **ancestors, antecedents, predecessors,** ascendants, fathers, **forefathers,** foreparents [dial.], **forebears,** progenitors, primogenitors; grandparents, grandfathers; patriarchs, elders; ancestress, progenitress, progenitrix.

8. **parent, progenitor,** procreator, begetter; grandparent.

9. **father, sire,** paternal ancestor [joc. or affected], pater [coll. or affected], the old man [slang], governor [slang], abba; **papa, pa,** pap, pappy, pop, pops, **dad, daddy,** daddums [all affectionate or familiar]; patriarch, paterfamilias; stepfather; foster father.

10. **mother,** genetrix, dam, maternal ancestor [joc. or affected], the old woman [slang]; **mamma,** mama, mammy, mam, **ma,** mom, mommy, mummy, mumsy, motherkin, motherkins [all affectionate or familiar]; matriarch, materfamilias; stepmother; foster mother.

11. **grandfather; grandpa,** grampa, gramp, grandpapa, grandpap, grandpappy, granddad or grandad, granddaddy or grandaddy, granddada or grandada [all affectionate or familiar]; grandsire, gramfer, granther [all dial.]; old man 127.2; great-grandfather.

12. **grandmother,** grandame, grandam, granddam (of animals), grannam [dial.], gammer [dial., Eng.]; **grandma,** granma, grandmamma, grandmammy, **granny,** grammy, gammy [all affectionate or familiar]; old woman 127.3; great-grandmother.

ADJS. 13. **ancestral,** ancestorial, patriarchal; **parental,** parent; **paternal,** fatherly, fatherlike; **maternal,** mother, motherly; motherlike; grandparental; grandmotherly, grandmaternal; grandfatherly, grandpaternal.

14. **lineal,** family, genealogical; direct, in a direct line; phyletic, phylogenetic; diphyletic.

15. **hereditary,** patrimonial, **inherited; innate** 5.7; genetic, genic; patroclinous, matroclinous.

16. in heritable, heritable, hereditable.

170. POSTERITY

NOUNS 1. **posterity, progeny, issue,** offspring, fruit, seed, brood, breed, family, descent, succession; lineage 169.4; **descendants,** heirs, sons, **children;** grandchildren, great-grandchildren; rising generation.

2. **young, brood,** breed [dial.], get; spawn, spat, fry, **litter,** farrow; hatching, clutch, cletch [dial.].

3. **descendant, offspring, child, scion,** olive branch [fig.]; **son,** sonny; **daughter;** grandchild, grandson, granddaughter; stepchild, stepson, stepdaughter; foster child; chip of or off the old block.

4. (derived or collateral descendant) **offshoot,** offset, **branch,** sprout, shoot, filiation.

5. **bastard,** bantling, **illegitimate,** illegitimate child, natural child [chiefly dial.], *nullius filius* [L., law, the son of nobody].

6. sonship, sonhood; daughtership, daughterhood.

ADJS. 7. **filial,** sonly, sonlike; **daughterly,** daughterlike.

171. INFLUENCE

NOUNS 1. **influence,** influentiality; **power,** force, potency, pressure, effect; **prestige, weight,** moment, consequence, importance, eminence; **authority,** control, domination, hold; **sway,** swing, reign, rule; **mastery,** ascendancy, supremacy, dominance, predominance, preponderance; upper hand, whip hand; leverage, purchase.

2. **favor,** special favor, **interest; pull,** drag, suction, in, stand-in [all slang]; inside track [coll.].

3. **backstairs influence,** intrigues; **wires, strings,** ropes [all coll.]; **wirepulling** [coll.]; influence peddling; lobbying, lobbyism.

4. **sphere of influence,** orbit, ambit.

5. **influenceability,** swayableness, movability; **persuadability,** openness, openmindedness, perviousness, accessibility, receptiveness, responsiveness, amenableness; **suggestibility,** susceptibility, impressionability.

6. (influential person or thing) **influence,** good influence, bad influence; influencer, wirepuller [coll.]; **power behind the throne,** friend at or in court, kingmaker; **influence peddler,** four-percenter, lobbyist; **pressure group,** special-interest group, special interests; lobby.

VERBS 7. **influence,** make oneself felt, **affect,** weigh with; **sway,** bias, bend, incline, dispose, predispose, **move,** prompt, lead; **induce, persuade** 646.23; **work,** work or bend to one's will; wear down, soften up; win friends and influence people.

8. (exercise a governing or determining influence over) **govern, rule, control,** order, **regulate,** direct, guide; **determine,** decide, dispose.

9. **exercise** or **exert influence,** use one's influence, bring pressure to bear

upon, act on, **work on,** bear upon, throw one's weight into the scale; draw, draw on, lead on, magnetize; approach [U.S.], make advances, make overtures, make up to [coll.]; reach, get at [coll.]; **pull the strings,** ~ **wires** or **ropes,** wirepull [coll.]; lobby [chiefly U.S.], lobby through.

10. have influence, **be influential, carry weight, weigh, tell, count,** draw water [slang, U.S.]; have a way with one, be persuasive; have the or an in [slang, U.S.], stand in with [slang], have the inside track [coll.]; have full play.

11. have influence over, have the pull over [slang], have it all over [coll.], come it all over [slang], come over [coll.], come it over [slang]; **lead by the nose, twist ~, turn** or **wind around one's little finger,** keep under one's thumb, make lie down and turn over; dominate **739.14.**

12. gain influence, **get in with** [coll.], gain a footing, take hold, take root, strike root in; gain a hearing, make one's voice heard, be listened to, be recognized; get the mastery of, get control of, gain a hold upon; change the preponderance, turn the scale or balance, turn the tables.

ADJS. **13. influential, authoritative, powerful,** potent, strong; **effective,** effectual, efficacious, telling; **weighty,** momentous, important, consequential, substantial.

14. (in a position of influence) **dominant, predominant,** preponderant, prepotent, prepollent, regnant, ruling, swaying, prevailing; **ascendant,** in the ascendant, in ascendancy.

15. influenceable, swayable, movable; persuadable, persuasible, suasible, open, open-minded, pervious, accessible, receptive, responsive, amenable; **plastic, pliant,** pliable, dough-faced [coll.]; **suggestible,** susceptible, impressionable.

172. UNINFLUENTIALITY

NOUNS **1.** uninfluentiality, **unauthoritativeness,** powerlessness, forcelessness, impotence; **ineffectiveness,** inefficaciousness, inefficacy, ineffectuality.

2. uninfluenceability, unswayableness, unmovability; **unpersuadability,** impersuadability, impersuasibility, unreceptiveness, imperviousness, unresponsiveness; unsuggestibility, unsusceptibility, unimpressionability.

ADJS. **3. uninfluential, unauthoritative, powerless,** forceless, impotent; **ineffec-**tive, ineffectual, inefficacious; without any weight.

4. uninfluenceable, unswayable, unmovable; unpliable, unyielding, inflexible; **unpersuadable,** impersuadable, impersuasible, unreceptive, unresponsive, unamenable; impervious, closed to; **unsuggestible,** unsusceptible, unimpressionable.

5. uninfluenced, unmoved, unaffected, unswayed.

173. TENDENCY

NOUNS **1. tendency, inclination, leaning,** penchant, proneness, readiness, aptness, aptitude, disposition, **proclivity, propensity,** predisposition, predilection, conduciveness, diathesis, conatus; **bent, turn, bias,** cast, warp, twist.

2. trend, drift, course, current, movement, motion, run, **tenor,** tone, **set,** swing, bearing, line, direction, the general tendency, the main course, the course of events, the way things go, the way it looks.

VERBS **1. tend,** have a tendency, **incline,** dispose, **lean,** trend, set, go, head, lead, point, verge, turn, warp, bend to, work or gravitate toward; show a tendency, point to, look to; **conduce,** contribute, serve, redound to.

ADJS. **4. tending,** tendent, tendentious, tendential; **leaning, inclining,** inclinatory, inclinational.

5. tending to, conducive to, leading to, inclined towards, inclining towards, heading towards, working towards.

6. inclined to, prone to, disposed to, predisposed to, given to; **apt to, likely to, liable to 174.5,** calculated to, minded to, ready to, in a fair way to.

174. LIABILITY

NOUNS **1. liability, likelihood, aptitude, possibility,** probability; contingency, chance, eventuality; **proneness 173.1;** obligation **960.**

2. susceptibility, susceptivity, **openness,** exposure.

VERBS **3. be liable,** be subjected to, lie under; **expose oneself to, lay oneself open to,** open the door to; stand a chance, run the chance or risk; **admit of,** be in the way of, bid or stand fair to.

4. incur, contract, run, **bring on, bring down,** bring upon, bring down upon, bring upon oneself, bring down upon oneself; fall into, fall in with; get, gain, acquire.

ADJS. **5. liable to, subject to,** incident

to; **susceptible to,** susceptive to, **open to, exposed to,** in danger of, within range of, at the mercy of; **capable of,** ready for; likely to, **apt to** 173.6.

6. contingent, incidental, occasional, eventual, dependent, possible, in the cards. CONJS. 7. **lest, that, for fear that.**

175. IMPLICATION

NOUNS 1. **implication, involvement,** involution, **entanglement,** enmeshment, engagement, embarrassment.

VERBS 2. **implicate, involve,** tangle, **entangle,** embarrass, enmesh, engage, **draw in,** drag into, catch up in, **make a party to;** interest, concern.

ADJS. 3. **implicated, involved;** interested, concerned, a party to.

4. **implicated in, involved in,** tangled or entangled in, enmeshed in, **caught up in,** tied up in, wrapped up in, all wound up in; deeply involved, **up to one's neck or ears in,** up to one's elbows in, head over heels in, immersed or submerged in, far gone.

176. CONCURRENCE

NOUNS 1. **concurrence,** coaction, **coworking,** combined effort, united action, concert, synergy; **co-operation** 784; **coincidence,** synchronism; concomitance, accompaniment; **union,** junction, **conjunction,** combination, association, alliance; concourse, confluence; **accordance,** concordance, correspondence, consilience.

VERBS 2. **concur, coact, cowork,** synergize; **co-operate** 784.4; conspire; **combine, unite,** coadunate, join, conjoin, hitch horses [coll.]; **coincide,** synchronize, happen together; **accord,** correspond.

3. go with, **go along with, go hand in hand with,** be hand in glove with; keep pace with, run parallel to.

ADJS. 4. **concurrent,** concurring; **coacting,** coactive, **coworking,** co-operant, synergetic; **co-operative** 784.7; **united,** joint, conjoint, **combined,** concerted, associated, associate, coadunate; **coincident,** synchronous, co-ordinate; concomitant, accompanying, meeting, uniting, combining; **accordant,** concordant, consilient, at one with.

ADVS. 5. **concurrently,** coactively, **jointly, conjointly,** concertedly, with, **together; with one accord,** with one voice, as one, as one man; hand in hand, hand in glove, shoulder to shoulder.

177. COUNTERACTION

NOUNS 1. **counteraction, counterworking; opposition,** opposure, contradiction; **antagonism,** repugnance, oppugnance or oppugnancy, antipathy, conflict, friction, interference, clashing, collision; resistance, renitency.

2. **neutralization, nullification,** annulment, canceling, invalidation, vitiation, frustration, undoing; **offsetting,** counterbalancing.

3. **counteractant,** counteractive, **counteragent;** counterirritant; **antidote,** remedy, preventive, preventative, prophylactic; **neutralizer,** nullifier, offset; antacid, alkalizer.

4. **counterforce,** counterinfluence; counterpoise, counterbalance, counterweight; countercurrent, crosscurrent, undercurrent; counterblast; head wind, dead wind.

5. **countermeasure,** counterstep; **counterblow,** counterstroke, counterbuff; backfire.

VERBS 6. **counteract, counterwork,** countervail; **oppose,** antagonize, **go in opposition to,** go or **run counter to,** go **against,** run against, beat against, militate against, resist, cross, traverse, contradict, contravene, oppugn, conflict, interfere or conflict with, come in conflict with, clash.

7. **neutralize, nullify, annul, cancel,** cancel out, negative, invalidate, vitiate, frustrate, undo; **offset,** counterbalance 33.5.

ADJS. 8. **counteractive, counteractant, counteracting, counterworking,** countervailing; **opposing,** oppositional; contradicting, contradictory; **antagonistic,** oppugnant, repugnant, conflicting, clashing; reactionary; resistant, renitent.

9. **neutralizing, nullifying,** annulling, canceling, invalidating, vitiating; **offsetting,** counterbalancing; antacid, alkaline.

10. **counter-, anti-.**

ADVS. 11. **counteractively,** antagonistically, opposingly, **in opposition to, counter to.**

178. SPACE

Indefinite Space.—NOUNS 1. **space,** extent, extension; **expanse,** expansion; spread, breadth; **measure,** volume; **dimension,** proportion; area, tract, field, sphere; acreage; continuum.

2. **range, compass, scope, reach, stretch,**

sweep, carry; **gamut, scale,** register (of the voice), diapason [music].

3. **room, latitude,** swing, play, way; spare room, room to spare, **elbowroom, margin, leeway;** seaway, headway.

4. **open space,** clear space; **clearing,** clearance, opening [U.S.]; glade; open country, wide open spaces.

5. **spaciousness, roominess,** commodiousness, capaciousness, amplitude; extensiveness, expansiveness.

6. **fourth dimension, space-time,** time-space, space-time continuum, four-dimensional space; space-world; other continuums; **relativity,** theory of relativity, Einstein theory, principle of relativity, principle of equivalence, general theory of relativity, special or restricted theory of relativity, continuum theory; four-dimensional geometry; cosmic constant; time machine [science fiction].

VERBS 7. **reach, extend, stretch,** sweep, spread, run, go, cover, carry, **range,** lie; **reach out,** stretch out, hold out, stick out, thrust out; outreach, outstretch, outthrust; **reach forth,** put forth; stretch forth one's arm, make a long arm [slang].

ADJS. 8. **spatial,** space; **dimensional,** proportional; two-dimensional; three-dimensional, stereoscopic, 3-D; fourth-dimensional; space-time, spatiotemporal or spaciotemporal.

9. **spacious, roomy, commodious, capacious,** ample; **extensive,** expansive, extended; broad, wide; widespread 79.12.

ADVS. 10. **extensively, widely,** broadly, abroad; **far and wide,** far and near; **right-and-left,** a diestra y siniestra [Span.]; on all sides, on every side.

11. **everywhere,** everywheres [dial. & coll.]; here, there and everywhere; **in every place,** in all places, in every quarter, in all quarters; **all over,** all around, all over hell [slang], all over the map [coll.], all over the world, the world over, throughout the world, throughout the length and breadth of the land; from end to end, from pole to pole, "from China to Peru" [Johnson], "from Indus to the pole" [Pope], from Dan to Beersheba, from hell to breakfast [slang, U.S.]; **high and low,** upstairs and downstairs, inside and out, in every hole and corner; universally, in all creation.

12. **everywhence,** "from the four corners of the earth" [Shakespeare], from all points of the compass; everywhither, to the four winds, to the uttermost parts of the earth, to hell and back [slang].

179. REGION

NOUNS 1. **region, area, zone,** belt, **territory,** terrain; **place** 183; **country, land,** ground, soil; **district, quarter, section,** department, compartment, division; part, parts; **neighborhood,** vicinity, vicinage, purlieus; premises, confines; diggings [coll.], digs [slang, Eng.].

2. **sphere,** hemisphere, **orb, orbit,** ambit, circle; **circuit, beat, round,** walk; **realm,** demesne, **domain,** dominion, jurisdiction; **province,** precinct, department; **field,** pale, arena.

3. **latitude, zone; climate,** clime [poetic]; longitude, longitude in arc, longitude in time; meridian, prime meridian; equator, the line; tropic, Tropic of Cancer, Tropic of Capricorn; tropics, subtropics, Torrid Zone; Temperate or Variable Zones; Frigid Zones, Arctic Zone or Circle, Antarctic Zone or Circle; horse latitudes.

4. **plot,** plot of ground or land, parcel of land, plat, **patch, tract, field;** lot; block, square; section (square mile); close, enclave, enceinte [F.], croft [Eng.].

5. (territorial divisions) arrondissement [F.], bailiwick, canton, commune, county, diocese, district, hundred, lathe [Kent, Eng.], magistracy, metropolis, mofussil [India], parish, precinct, riding, shire, soke [hist.], state, tithing, township, wapentake, [hist.], ward.

6. (geographic regions) **Old World,** the old country; **New World,** America; **Western Hemisphere, Occident,** West; **Eastern Hemisphere, Orient,** Levant, East, eastland; Far East, Middle East, Near East; Asia, Eurasia, Asia Major, Asia Minor; antipodes, down under, Australasia, Oceania.

7. (geographic quarters) West, westland, wild West [U.S.]; Northwest, Southwest, Middle West; East, eastland; Northeast, Southeast; North, northland; South, southland; Dixie, Dixieland [both U.S.]; New England, down East [U.S.], Yankeeland [coll., U.S.].

ADJS. 8. **regional, territorial,** sectional, zonal, topographic(al); locational 183.20.

9. **local,** topical, vernacular, parochial, provincial, insular, limited, confined.

180. COUNTRY

NOUNS 1. **country,** land; **nation,** nationality, **state,** polity, **body politic;** power;

republic, commonwealth; kingdom, kingship; empire, empery; realm, dominion,
domain; principality, principate; duchy,
dukedom; grand duchy, archduchy, earldom, palatinate, seneschalty; chieftaincy,
chieftainry; toparchy, *toparchia* [L.]; city-
state, free city; province, territory, possession; colony, settlement; protectorate, mandate; mandatory; buffer state; ally, satellite;
free nations; captive nations, iron-curtain
countries.

2. fatherland, *Vaterland* [G.], motherland, mother country, native land or soil,
one's native heath, home, homeland,
God's country, the old country (Europe),
Auld Sod (Scotland), Blighty (England
[slang]).

3. United States, United States of America, U.S., U.S.A., America, Columbia, the
States, Yankeeland [coll.], Land of Liberty, the melting pot.

4. England, Britain, Great Britain, Britannia, Albion, Blighty [slang, Eng.],
Limeyland [slang, U.S.], Tight Little Island, Land of the Rose, Sovereign of the
Seas; British Empire, United Kingdom,
Commonwealth of Nations, British Commonwealth of Nations.

5. (national personifications) Uncle
Sam (U.S.), John Bull (England), Jean
Crapaud (France).

6. nationality, nationalism, statehood;
internationality, internationalism; Americanism; Briticism, Anglicism, Englishism;
Russianism, etc.

7. nationalization, internationalization.
VERBS 8. nationalize, internationalize.

9. countries

Afghanistan	Congo
Albania	(Leopoldville)
Andorra	Costa Rica
Argentina	Chad
Australia	Chile
Austria	China
Bahrein	Cuba
Belgium	Cyprus
Bhutan	Czechoslovakia
Bolivia	Dahomey
Brazil	Denmark
Bulgaria	Dominican
Burma	Republic
Cambodia	Ecuador
Cameroun	Eire (Ireland)
Canada	El Salvador
Central African	Estonia
Republic	Ethiopia
Ceylon	Federation of
Colombia	Malaya
Congo	Finland
(Brazzaville)	France
	Gabon

Germany	Norway
Ghana	Pakistan
Greece	Panama
Guatemala	Paraguay
Guinea	Peru
Haiti	Philippines
Honduras	Poland
Hungary	Portugal
Iceland	Qatar
India	Rumania
Indonesia	San Marino
Iran	Saudi Arabia
Iraq	Senegal
Israel	Sikkim
Italy	Somalia
Ivory Coast	Spain
Japan	Sudan
Jordan	Sweden
Korea	Switzerland
Kuwait	Taiwan
Laos	(Formosa)
Latvia	Thailand (Siam)
Lebanon	Tibet
Liberia	Togo
Libya	Trucial Oman
Liechtenstein	Tunisia
Lithuania	Turkey
Luxemburg	Union of South
Malagasy Republic	Africa
(Madagascar)	Union of Soviet
Maldive Islands	Socialist
Mali	Republics
Mauritania	United Arab
Mexico	Republic (Egypt,
Monaco	Syria)
Mongolian	United Kingdom
People's Republic	United States of
Morocco	America
Muscat and Oman	Upper Volta
Nepal	Uruguay
Netherlands	Vatican City
New Zealand	Venezuela
Nicaragua	Vietnam
Niger	Yemen
Nigeria	Yugoslavia

181. THE COUNTRY

NOUNS 1. the country, rural district,
rustic region, hoosier belt [slang], province
or provinces, countryside, the soil [poetic],
the clods [slang], the sticks [slang], grass
roots, yokeldom; hickdom, hoosierdom
[both slang]; cotton belt, tobacco belt, corn
belt, wheat belt, citrus belt; dust bowl;
highlands, uplands; lowlands, low veld
[Africa]; wide open spaces.

2. hinterland, back country, back
veld [Africa], upcountry [coll.], bundu
[Africa], boondock or boondocks [slang];
the bush, bush country, bush veld [Africa];
woods, woodlands, backwoods, forests,
timbers, brush; frontier, borderland, outpost; wild West.

3. rusticity, inurbanity, ruralism, agrarianism, bucolicism, provincialism, pro-
vinciality, pastorality; yokelism, hickishness

[slang], backwoodsiness; **boorishness,** churlishness, unrefinement, uncultivation.

4. ruralization, rustication, countrification, pastoralization.

VERBS **5. ruralize, rusticate, countrify,** pastoralize.

ADJS. **6. rustic, rural, country, provincial, pastoral, bucolic,** Arcadian [poetic], landward [Scot.], agrarian, agrestic; agricultural 412.20; **hick,** hoosier, rube, hayseed, chinwhisker [all slang]; lowland, upland.

7. countrified, inurbane; country-born, country-bred, from the sticks [slang]; **yokel, yokelish,** farmerish, hobnailed, clodhopping; **hickish,** hickified, hoosierified [all slang]; **boorish,** clownish, loutish, lumpish, cloddish, clodpolish, churlish, carlish [literary]; **uncouth,** unpolished, uncultivated, uncultured, unrefined; country-style, country-fashion.

8. hinterland, back, **back-country,** up-country [coll.]; backwood or backwoods, backwoodsy; woodland, silvan.

182. TOWN

NOUNS **1. town,** township, **metropolis, municipality,** municipium [Rom. antiq.], **city,** borough, **burg** [coll., U.S.], bourg, burgh [Scot.]; suburb, suburbia; exurb, exurbia; market town [Eng.]; boom town [U.S.]; ghost town.

2. village, hamlet, ham [arch. exc. in compounds], dorp [Dutch & S. Africa], thorp or thorpe [now chiefly in compounds], wick [rare exc. in compounds], kraal [S. Africa], bustee [India], bourgade [F.], clachan [Scot.], pueblo [Amer. Indian], rancho [Sp. Amer.]; country town, yokel town, oppidum [Rom. antiq.]; crossroads, wide place in the road; "a little one-eyed, blinking sort o' place" [Hardy], "a hive of glass, where nothing unobserved can pass" [C. H. Spurgeon].

3. (slang terms, chiefly U.S.] **one-horse town,** jerk-water town, **tank town** or station, **whistle stop,** jumping-off-place; **hick town,** rube town, hoosier town.

4. capital, capital city, **seat,** seat of government; county seat, county town, courthouse [local U.S.].

5. (city districts) East Side or End, West Side or End; downtown [U.S.], uptown; suburbs, suburbia, residential district; business district, shopping center; Tin Pan alley; ghetto, Jewry; Chinatown [U.S.], Little Italy, ~ Hungary etc., the other side of the tracks; slums; tenderloin [U.S.], red-light district, skid row or road [slang, U.S.].

6. block, city block, square.

7. square, plaza, place [F.], piazza [It.], campo [It.], polygon [mil.]; piazzetta [It.]; **market place,** market, forum [Rom. antiq.], agora [Gr. antiq.].

8. circle, circus [Eng.]; crescent.

ADJS. **9. urban, metropolitan, municipal,** burghal, **civic,** oppidan; city, town, village; citified; suburban; interurban; downtown [U.S.], uptown.

10. principal cities of the world
(* denotes capital)
*Accra, Ghana
*Addis Ababa, Ethiopia
Adelaide, Australia
Ahmedabad, India
Akron, Ohio
Aleppo, Syria
Alexandria, Egypt
*Amman, Jordan
*Amsterdam, Netherlands
*Andorra la Vieja, Andorra
*Ankara, Turkey
Antwerp, Belgium
*Asunción, Paraguay
*Athens, Greece
Atlanta, Ga.
Auckland, New Zealand
Avellaneda, Argentina
*Baghdad, Iraq
Baku, U.S.S.R.
Baltimore, Md.
Bandung, Indonesia
Bangalore, India
*Bangkok, Thailand
Barcelona, Spain
Barranquilla, Colombia
Basel, Switzerland
*Beirut, Lebanon
*Belfast, Northern Ireland
*Belgrade, Yugoslavia
Belo Horizonte, Brazil
*Bengasi, Libya
Berlin, Germany
*Bern, Switzerland
Birmingham, Ala.
Birmingham, England
*Bogotá, Colombia
Bombay, India
*Bonn, Germany (Federal Republic)

Bordeaux, France
Boston, Mass.
*Brasília, Brazil
Bratislava, Czechoslovakia
*Brazzaville, Congo
Brisbane, Australia
Brno, Czechoslovakia
*Brussels, Belgium
*Bucharest, Rumania
*Budapest, Hungary
*Buenos Aires, Argentina
Buffalo, N. Y.
*Cairo, Egypt
Calcutta, India
Calgary, Canada
Cali, Colombia
*Canberra, Australia
Canton, China
Capetown, Union of South Africa
*Caracas, Venezuela
Casablanca, Morocco
Charleroi, Belgium
Chicago, Ill.
Chungking, China
Cincinnati, Ohio
*Ciudad Trujillo, Dominican Republic
Cleveland, Ohio
Cologne, Germany
*Colombo, Ceylon
Columbus, Ohio
*Copenhagen, Denmark
Córdoba, Argentina
Dacca, Pakistan
*Dakar, French West Africa
Dallas, Texas
*Damascus, Syria
Dayton, Ohio
Debrecen, Hungary
Delhi, India
Denver, Colo.
Detroit, Mich.
*Doha, Qatar

Dresden, Germany
*Dublin, Ireland
Durban, Union of
South Africa
*Edinburgh, Scot-
land
Edmonton,
Canada
Essen, Germany
Fez, Morocco
Fortaleza, Brazil
Fort Worth, Texas
Frankfurt am
Main, Germany
Fukuoka, Japan
Gdańsk, Poland
Geneva, Switzer-
land
Genoa, Italy
George Town,
Federation of
Malaya
Ghent, Belgium
Glasgow, Scotland
Gorki, U.S.S.R.
Göteborg, Sweden
Graz, Austria
Guadalajara,
Mexico
*Guatemala City,
Guatemala
Guayaquil,
Ecuador
The Hague,
Netherlands
Halle am der
Saale, Germany
Hamburg, Ger-
many
Hamilton, Canada
*Hanoi, North
Vietnam
Harbin, China
*Havana, Cuba
*Helsinki, Finland
Honolulu, Hawaii
Houston, Texas
Hyderabad, India
Hyderabad,
Pakistan
Ibadan, Nigeria
Inchon, Korea
Indianapolis, Ind.
Innsbruck, Austria
Istanbul, Turkey
Jacksonville, Fla.
*Jakarta, Indonesia
Jersey City, N.J.
*Jerusalem, Israel
Johannesburg,
Union of South
Africa
*Kabul, Afghani-
stan
Kanpur, India
Kansas City, Mo.
Kaohsiung, Tai-
wan
*Karachi, Pakistan

Karl-Marxstadt,
Germany
*Katmandu, Nepal
Kharkov, U.S.S.R.
*Khartoum, Sudan
Kiev, U.S.S.R.
Kobe, Japan
Kraków, Poland
*Kuala Lumpur,
Federation of
Malaya
Kuybyshev,
U.S.S.R.
Kyoto, Japan
*Lagos, Nigeria
Lahore, Pakistan
Lanús, Argentina
La Paz, Bolivia
La Plata, Argentina
Leeds, England
Leipzig, Germany
Leningrad,
U.S.S.R.
*Léopoldville,
Congo
*Lhasa, Tibet
Liége, Belgium
*Lima, Peru
Linz, Austria
*Lisbon, Portugal
Liverpool, England
Lódz, Poland
*Lomé, Togo
*London, England
Long Beach, Calif.
Los Angeles, Calif.
Louisville, Ky.
*Luxemburg,
Luxemburg
Lyons, France
Madras, India
*Madrid, Spain
Magdeburg, Ger-
many
Makassar,
Indonesia
Málaga, Spain
*Malé, Maldive
Islands
Malmö, Sweden
*Managua,
Nicaragua
*Manama, Bahrein
Manchester, Eng-
land
Mandalay, Burma
Manila, Philippines
Maracaibo,
Venezuela
Marrakech,
Morocco
Marseilles, France
Mecca, Saudi
Arabia
Medan, Indonesia
Medellín, Colom-
bia
Melbourne, Aus-
tralia
Memphis, Tenn.

*Mexico City,
Mexico
Miami, Fla.
Milan, Italy
Milwaukee, Wis.
Minneapolis,
Minn.
Miskolc, Hungary
*Mogadiscio,
Somalia
*Monrovia, Liberia
Monte Carlo,
Monaco
Monterrey, Mexico
*Montevideo,
Uruguay
Montreal, Canada
*Moscow, U.S.S.R.
Mosul, Iraq
Mukden, China
Munich, Germany
*Muscat, Muscat
and Oman
Nagoya, Japan
Nanking, China
Nantes, France
Naples, Italy
Newark, N.J.
*New Delhi, India
New Orleans, La.
New York, N.Y.
Nice, France
Norfolk, Va.
*Nouakchott,
Mauritania
Novosibirsk,
U.S.S.R.
Oakland, Calif.
Oklahoma City,
Okla.
Omaha, Nebr.
Oporto, Portugal
Osaka, Japan
*Oslo, Norway
Ostrava, Czecho-
slovakia
*Ottawa, Canada
Palermo, Italy
*Panamá City,
Panama
*Paris, France
Pécs, Hungary
*Peiping, China
Perth, Australia
Philadelphia, Pa.
Pittsburgh, Pa.
*Pnompenh, Cam-
bodia
Port Arthur, China
Port-au-Prince,
Haiti
Port Elizabeth,
Union of South
Africa
Portland, Oreg.
Pôrto Alegre,
Brazil
Port Said. Egypt
Poznan, Poland

*Prague, Czecho-
slovakia
*Pretoria, Union of
South Africa
Providence, R.I.
Puebla, Mexico
*Punakha, Bhutan
Pusan, Korea
*Pyongyang, Korea
Quebec, Canada
*Quezon City,
Philippines
*Quito, Ecuador
*Rabat, Morocco
*Rangoon, Burma
Rawalpindi,
Pakistan
Recife, Brazil
*Reykjavik, Iceland
Richmond, Va.
*Riga, Latvia
Rio de Janeiro,
Brazil
*Riyadh, Saudi
Arabia
Rochester, N.Y.
*Rome, Italy
Rosario, Argentina
Rotterdam,
Netherlands
*Saigon, South
Vietnam
Salonika, Greece
Salvador, Brazil
Salzburg, Austria
*Sana, Yemen
San Antonio,
Texas
San Diego, Calif.
San Francisco,
Calif.
*San José, Costa
Rica
San Juan, Puerto
Rico
*San Marino, San
Marino
*San Salvador, El
Salvador
*Santiago, Chile
São Paulo, Brazil
Saragossa, Spain
Seattle, Wash.
Szczecin, Poland
Semarang, Indo-
nesia
Sendai, Japan
*Seoul, Korea
Seville, Spain
Shanghai, China
Sheffield, England
Sian, China
Singapore, Singa-
pore
Smyrna, Turkey
*Sofia, Bulgaria
Stalingrad, U.S.S.R.
Stalino, U.S.S.R.
St. Louis, Mo.

*Stockholm,
  Sweden
St. Paul, Minn.
*Sucre, Bolivia
Surabaja, Indonesia
Surakarta, Indo-
  nesia
Sverdlovsk,
  U.S.S.R.
Sydney, Australia
Syracuse, N.Y.
Szeged, Hungary
Tabriz, Iran
Taegu, Korea
Tainan, Taiwan
*Taipei, Taiwan
*Tallinn, Estonia
Tangier, Morocco
Tashkent, U.S.S.R.
Tbilisi, U.S.S.R.
*Tegucigalpa, Hon-
  duras
*Teheran, Iran
Tel Aviv, Israel
Tientsin, China
*Tirana, Albania
*Tokyo, Japan
Toledo, Ohio
Toronto, Canada
Toulouse, France
Tripoli, Lebanon
*Tripoli, Libya
Tsingtao, China

Turin, Italy
*Ulan Bator, Mon-
  golian People's
  Republic
Utrecht, Nether-
  lands
*Vaduz, Liechten-
  stein
Valencia, Spain
Valparaíso, Chile
Vancouver, Can-
  ada
Victoria, Hong
  Kong
*Vienna, Austria
*Vientiane, Laos
*Vilnius, Lithuania
*Warsaw, Poland
*Washington, D.C.
*Wellington, New
  Zealand
Winnipeg, Canada
Worcester, Mass.
Wroclaw, Poland
Wuhan, China
*Yaoundé,
  Cameroun
Yokohama, Japan
Zagreb, Yugo-
  slavia
Zürich, Switzer-
  land

183. LOCATION

NOUNS 1. **location, situation, place,** placement, emplacement, **position,** hole [slang], stead [dial.]; region 179; **locality,** locale, *locus* [L.]; **site,** situs; spot, point; bearings, latitude and longitude.

2. where, **whereabouts,** whereabout; here, there.

3. **station,** status, **stand, standing,** standpoint, footing, **seat, post,** base, ground, venue; railroad station, **depot** [U.S.], station house, *gare* [F.]; way station [U.S.]; terminus, terminal [U.S.].

4. **posture, pose, position,** lay, lie, set, **attitude,** aspect, **bearing;** port, carriage, air, mien, demeanor, presence; exposure, frontage (position fronting, as southern *exposure*).

5. **stead, place,** lieu, room [dial.].

6. (act of placing) **placement,** emplacement, **situation, location,** localization, locating, placing, putting; **allocation,** collocation, disposition; deposition, reposition, deposit; **stowage,** storage, loading, lading, packing.

7. **establishment, foundation,** settlement, plantation; lodgment, fixation; **installation,** installment.

8. topography, geography, chorography.

VERBS 9. **have place,** be there; have its place, **belong, go** (as, the book *goes* on the shelf).

10. **be situated, lie,** bear, rest, repose; lie in, have its seat in.

11. **locate, situate, place;** emplace, spot [slang], put in place; **allocate, collocate,** dispose; **localize,** identify, fix in, assign *or* consign to a place; pinpoint, spearhead.

12. **place, put, set,** seat, stick [coll.], station, post; park; pose, posture.

13. (put violently) **clap, slap, thrust, fling, hurl,** throw, cast, chuck, toss; **plump,** plunk [chiefly coll.], plank [coll.], plop.

14. (as to place confidence in) **place, put, set,** lodge, fix; **repose,** rest, lay, **vest in.**

15. **deposit,** reposit, lay, lodge; **put down,** set down, lay down, come down with [slang]; **plump down,** plunk down [chiefly coll.], plank down [coll.], plop down, slap down.

16. (put in or on) **load, lade,** freight; fill 56.7; **stow,** store, steeve, stive [chiefly Scot.]; **pack,** pack away; ship; stevedore; pile, heap, stack, mass; bag, sack, pocket; can, bottle, box, crate, barrel.

17. **establish, fix, plant,** pitch, seat, **set, settle,** ensconce; **found, base,** build, ground, lay the foundation; **install,** put in, put up, set up.

18. **settle, settle down,** sit down, locate [coll., U.S.], park [slang, U.S.], take up one's abode *or* quarters, drive stakes [coll.], residence [coll.], establish residence, **take up residence,** take residence at, put up at, put up one's horses at, hang up one's hat [slang]; take *or* strike root, plant oneself, get a footing; anchor, drop anchor, come to anchor, moor; squat, perch, roost; nest, hive, burrow; domesticate, **set up housekeeping,** keep house; set up in business, hang up one's shingle [coll.].

ADJS. 19. **located, placed, situated,** situate, set, seated, stationed, posited, bestead; **established,** fixed, **settled,** planted, ensconced, embosomed.

20. locational, positional, situational, situal; postural, attitudinal; regional 179.8.

ADVS. 21. **in place,** in position, *in situ* [L.], *in loco* [L.].

22. **where, whither,** whereabouts, whereaway [chiefly Scot.], to what *or* which place.

23. **wherever,** where'er [poetic], **wheresoever,** wheresoe'er [poetic], whitherso-

ever, wherever it may be; **anywhere,** anyplace [coll.].

24. **here,** hereat, in this place, on the spot; hereabout, **hereabouts,** in this vicinity; somewhere about *or* near, somewheres about [dial.], somewhere abouts [dial.], somewhere near; aboard, on board; **hither,** hitherward, hitherwards, hereto, hereunto, hereinto, to this place.

25. **there,** thereat, in that place; thereabout, **thereabouts,** in that vicinity; **thither,** thitherward, thitherwards, to that place.

26. **here and there,** in various places, **in places,** in spots, *passim* [L.].

27. **somewhere,** somewheres [dial.], someplace, in some place, someplace or other.

PREPS. 28. **at,** in, on, by, near; to, toward; from.

29. **over** (as, to travel *over*), here and there on *or* in, roundabout, through, **all through,** throughout.

184. DISLOCATION

NOUNS 1. **dislocation, displacement,** disjointing, unjointing, unhinging, luxation; heterotopia [biol.].

2. **unplacement,** dislodgment; **unseating,** unsaddling, unhorsing.

3. **misplacement,** misputting, mislaying.

VERBS 4. **dislocate, displace, disjoint,** unjoint, luxate, unhinge, put out of place, **put out of joint,** throw out of gear.

5. **unplace,** dislodge; **unseat,** unsaddle; **unhorse,** dismount; throw off, buck off.

6. **misplace,** misput, **mislay.**

ADJS. 7. **dislocatory,** dislocating, heterotopic [biol.].

8. **dislocated, displaced, disjointed,** unjointed, unhinged; out, **out of joint,** out of gear.

9. **unplaced,** unestablished, unsettled; unhoused, unharbored, houseless, homeless.

10. **misplaced,** misput, **mislayed; out of place,** out of its element; in the wrong place, in the wrong box *or* pew [coll.], in the right church but the wrong pew [coll.].

185. PRESENCE

NOUNS 1. **presence,** hereness, thereness; whereness, ubiety; **occurrence,** existence.

2. **omnipresence,** all-presence, ubiquity, infinity, everywhereness.

3. **pervasion, permeation,** penetration; **suffusion,** transfusion, diffusion, imbue-

ment; **overrunning,** overspreading, overswarming.

4. **attendance,** frequence; turnout [coll.], draw [theat. slang, U.S.]; standing room only, S.R.O. [theat.].

5. **attender,** attendant, attendee [coll.]; **visitor,** goer, **patron; frequenter,** habitué; spectator 441; theatergoer 609.42; audience 447.6.

VERBS 6. **be present,** be there, be found, be met with; **occur,** exist; lie, stand, remain; fall in the way of.

7. **pervade, permeate,** penetrate; **suffuse,** transfuse, diffuse, leaven, imbue; **fill,** occupy; **overrun,** overswarm, overspread, bespread, run through, meet one at every turn; creep with, crawl with, swarm with; honeycomb.

8. **attend,** be present at, find oneself at, **go to;** appear, turn up, show up [coll.], show one's face, make *or* put in an appearance; **visit, take in,** do [coll.]; catch an act [theat. cant]; witness, look on, *assister* [F.].

9. **revisit,** return to, go back to, come again.

10. **frequent, haunt,** resort to, hang around *or* about at, hang out at [slang]; affect (frequent habitually).

11. **present oneself, report;** report for duty.

ADJS. 12. **present,** attendant; **on hand,** on deck [coll.], on board; **at hand,** in view, within reach, ~ sight *or* call; **all present and accounted for.**

13. **omnipresent, all-present,** ubiquitous, infinite; everywhere 178.11.

ADVS. 14. **here, there.**

15. **in person,** personally, bodily, **in the flesh** [slang], in one's own person, *in propria persona* [L.].

16. **in the presence of,** in the face of, under the eyes *or* nose of, **before.**

186. ABSENCE

NOUNS 1. **absence,** nonpresence, awayness; nowhereness, **nonexistence** 2; **want, lack.**

2. **vacancy,** vacuity, voidness, **emptiness,** hollowness, inanition; **bareness,** barrenness, desolateness, bleakness, desertedness; depletion, exhaustion; **nonoccupance,** nonoccupation, noninhabitance, nonresidence; opening (as a job *opening*).

3. **void, vacuum,** blank; *tabula rasa* [L.], clean slate; nothing 2.2.

4. **absentation,** nonattendance, nonappearance; **truancy, hooky, French leave,**

Dutch leave, cut [coll.]; **absence without leave,** A.W.O.L. [mil.]; absenteeism, truantism.

5. absentee, truant.

6. **nobody,** no one, no man, nix [slang], **not a soul,** not a blessed soul, never a one, ne'er a one [poetic], nary one [dial.], nobody on earth *or* under the sun, nobody present.

VERBS 7. **absent oneself, stay away,** keep away, keep out of the way, make oneself scarce [coll.], not come, not show up [coll.], turn up missing [joc.]; slip off *or* away, slip out.

8. **play truant, play hooky,** absent oneself without leave, **go A.W.O.L.** [mil.], **take French leave** *or* Dutch leave, *filer à l'anglaise* [F.], cut [coll.], ditch [slang, U.S.], skip [slang], jump, duck [coll.], mooch [dial. & slang].

ADJS. 9. **absent,** not present, nonattendant, **away, gone;** out of sight; **missing,** wanting, lacking, minus [coll.], omitted, nowhere to be found; **nonexistent** 2.7; conspicuous by its absence.

10. **nonresident,** from home, **away from home;** on tour, on the road; abroad, oversea.

11. **truant,** absent without leave, **A.W.O.L.** [mil.], awol [coll.].

12. **vacant, empty,** hollow, **bare,** jejune, **vacuous, void,** devoid, null, null and void; **blank,** clear, white; **barren,** desert, **desolate,** bleak, gaunt, arid, dry, drained.

13. **unoccupied,** unfilled, **uninhabited,** untenanted, unpopulated, unpeopled, occupantless, tenantless; **deserted,** abandoned, forsaken, Godforsaken [coll.].

14. (as a position open) **open, available,** free, vacant, untaken, unfilled, unoccupied, untenanted.

ADVS. 15. **absently;** vacantly, emptily, hollowly, vacuously, blankly.

16. **nowhere,** nowheres [dial., U.S.], nowhither, no place [dial., U.S.], in no place, neither here nor there.

17. **away,** hence, thence; **elsewhere,** elsewhither, somewhere else, not here.

PREPS. 18. **void of,** without 660.11.

187. HABITATION

An Inhabiting.—NOUNS 1. **habitation,** inhabiting, inhabitation, habitancy, inhabitancy, occupancy, **occupation, residence,** residing, **dwelling,** lodging; cohabitation; abode 190.

2. **peopling, population,** inhabiting; **colonization,** settlement, plantation.

3. **housing,** domiciliation; lodgment, **lodging,** lodgings, houseroom; **quartering,** billeting; functional housing; **housing development,** subdivision, tract; assembly-line housing.

4. **camping,** tenting, **encampment;** castramentation [mil.]; bivouac; camp 190.25.

5. **sojourn,** sojournment; **stay, stop;** stopover, stop-off, layover.

6. **habitability,** inhabitability, livability.

7. **unhabitability,** uninhabitability, unlivability.

VERBS 8. **inhabit,** indwell, **occupy,** tenant; **reside, live, dwell,** lodge, stay, remain, abide, hang out [slang], keep [coll., U.S.]; home, house, cabin, domicile, domiciliate; **room,** bunk, berth; perch, roost [dial. or coll.]; nest, nide; cohabit.

9. **sojourn,** stop, stay, **stop over,** stay over.

10. **people, populate, inhabit,** denizen; colonize, settle, settle in, plant.

11. **house,** domicile, domiciliate, hovel; provide with a roof, shelter, harbor; **lodge, quarter,** put up, billet, canton, room [U.S.], bed, berth; stable.

12. **camp, encamp,** tent; pitch, **pitch camp,** pitch one's tent, drive stakes [coll.]; bivouac; camp out, sleep out, rough it.

ADJS. 13. **inhabited, occupied,** tenanted; **peopled, populated;** populous.

14. **resident,** residentiary, **in residence;** **residing, living, dwelling,** lodging, staying, remaining, abiding, indwelling, inmate, commorant.

15. **housed,** cabined, domiciled, domiciliated.

16. **habitable,** inhabitable, occupiable, lodgeable, tenantable, livable, **fit to live in.**

17. **unhabitable,** uninhabitable, nonhabitable, unoccupiable, untenantable, unlivable, **unfit to live in,** not fit for man or beast.

ADVS. 18. **at home,** to home [dial.], in the bosom of one's family; in one's element; back home, down home [both coll.].

188. NATIVITY

NOUNS 1. **nativity;** nativeness, indigenousness; nationality.

2. **citizenship,** citizenhood, citizenism, civism.

3. **domesticity,** domesticality, home-lovingness; housewifery, **housekeeping, home-making;** householding, householdry.

4. domestication, domiciliation; **taming,** breaking, housebreaking; **naturalization,** nationalization, denization, denizenation, adoption, admission, affiliation, assimilation; Americanization, Anglicization, Frenchification, Chinafication, Germanization, Gallicization, Russianization, Russification, Bolshevization, Europeanization; papers, citizenship papers.

VERBS **5. domesticate,** domesticize, domiciliate; **tame,** gentle [coll. & dial.], **break,** break in, bust [slang, U.S.]; housebreak; **naturalize,** nationalize, citizenize, denizenize, denizen, endenizen, adopt, admit, affiliate, assimilate; Americanize, Anglicize, Englishize, Frenchify, Germanize, Gallicize, Russianize, Russify, Bolshevize, Europeanize.

6. go native, go Hollywood, etc.

ADJS. **7. native,** natal, **indigenous,** endemic, autochthonous, vernacular; original, aboriginal, primitive; native-born, homebred; all-American.

8. domestic, household, family, home, homely [chiefly dial.]; **home-loving; housekeeping,** homemaking; **internal,** interior, inland, intestine; **homemade,** home-grown.

9. domesticated, domiciliated, **naturalized; tame,** tamed, broken, housebroken; familiar.

189. INHABITANTS, NATIVES

NOUNS **1. population, inhabitants,** habitancy, inhabitancy; **populace,** people, folk; public, general public; community, society, commonwealth.

2. inhabitant, inhabiter, habitant; **occupant,** occupier, **dweller, tenant,** commorant, **denizen,** indweller, inmate; **resident,** residencer, residenter [chiefly Scot. & dial., U.S.], residentiary, resider; intern [spec. med.]; incumbent, *locum tenens* [L.]; sojourner; addressee.

3. native, indigene, indigena, autochthon; primitive; **aborigine,** aboriginal, original, binghi [slang, Australia]; **old-timer** [coll.], sourdough [coll., West. U.S., Can. & Alaska], longhorn [slang, West. U.S.]; shorthorn [slang, West. U.S.]; wog (Middle Eastern native [slang]), gook (So. Pacific, Oriental or African native [slang]), gugu (So. Pacific native [slang]), dago (So. European native [slang]); Sudanese, fuzzy-wuzzy [slang].

4. citizen, national; naturalized citizen, denizen. hyphenated American, hyphenate;

all-American; cosmopolitan, cosmopolite, citizen of the world; citizenry.

5. fellow citizen, fellow countryman, **compatriot, countryman,** countrywoman; fellow townsman, home towner [slang].

6. townsman, towny *or* townee [slang], towner [slang], **villager,** oppidan, gillie [circus slang, U.S.]; city man, cit [derog.], **city slicker** [slang, U.S.]; urbanite; suburbanite; exurbanite; burgher, burgess; villein [hist.]; townswoman, villageress; townspeople, townfolks, townfolk.

7. householder; cottager, cotter, cottier [Eng. & Ir.]; villein, bordar, collibert [all feudal].

8. lodger, roomer [U.S.], paying guest; **boarder,** board-and-roomer [U.S.]; **transient,** transient guest *or* boarder; renter, lessee, underlessee.

9. settler, habitant [Can. & Louisiana], metic [Gr. antiq.]; **colonist,** colonizer, colonial, planter; **homesteader; squatter,** nester [West. U.S.]; **pioneer;** sooner [slang, West. U.S.].

10. backsettler, hinterlander [slang], bushman [Australia]; **frontiersman; backwoodsman,** woodlander, woodsman, woodman, forester; **mountaineer, hillbilly** [coll.], ridge-runner [slang], brush ape [slang, U.S.], briar-hopper [dial., U.S.], cracker [So. U.S.]; desert rat [West. U.S.].

11. (regional inhabitants) **easterner,** eastlander; **westerner,** westlander; **southerner,** southlander; **northener,** northlander, Yankee [coll., U.S.]; Northman; New Englander, down-Easter [U.S.], Yankee [coll., U.S.].

190. ABODE

Place of Habitation or Resort.—NOUNS **1. abode, habitation,** inhabitancy, **dwelling,** dwelling place, **residence; domicile,** *domus* [L.]; **lodging,** lodgment, lodging place; seat, nest, tabernacle [fig.], cantonment; place, address.

2. quarters, living quarters; **lodgings,** lodging, lodgment; **diggings** [coll.], digs [slang, Eng.]; **rooms,** berth, roost, sleeping place; **housing,** shelter, *gîte* [F.], resting place; chummery [Anglo-Ind.].

3. home, home sweet home, homestead, homestall [Eng.], home roof, place where one hangs his hat [joc.]; **fireside, hearth,** hearthstone, chimney corner, ingleside, inglenook; **household,** ménage; **paternal**

domicile, the ancestral halls; teacherage, deanery, embassy; love nest [coll.].

4. habitat, home, range, locality, native environment.

5. house, *casa* [Sp., Pg., It.]; **building, structure, edifice,** erection; roof, dome [poetic]; lodge; manor house, hall [esp. Eng.]; town house, *rus in urbe* [L.]; country house, countryseat; ranch house, farmhouse, farm; outhouse, outbuilding; pavilion, kiosk; rotunda; sod house, adobe, dobe [dial., West. U.S.]; lake dwelling 397.3; cliff dwelling; penthouse; split-level.

6. house and grounds, house and lot [U.S.], **homestead,** homecroft [Eng.], messuage, **hacienda** [Sp. Amer.], toft [Scot. & dial. Eng.; formerly *toft and croft*]; grange, barton [Eng.], pen [Jamaica], mains [Scot.]; cote [Eng. hist.].

7. mansion, dome [poetic], **villa, chateau,** *hôtel* [F.], **castle,** tower; **palace,** *palais* [F.], *palazzo* [It.], court.

8. cottage, cot, cote [dial.], **bungalow,** box; **cabin,** cabaña [U.S., orig. S.W.]; log cabin, blockhouse; chalet; bower.

9. hut, hutch, **shack** [coll.], **shanty,** crib, **shed;** lean-to, linter [dial., U.S.]; booth, bothy *or* boothy [Scot.], stall; wigwam, hogan, wichiup, tupek, igloo, jacal, [Southwest U.S.]; bunkhouse, boar's nest [slang, U.S.]; hooden [West. U.S.], rancho [Sp. Amer.]; Quonset hut, Nissen hut [both mil.].

10. hovel, dump [slang], hole, sty, pigsty, pigpen, tumble-down shack.

11. summerhouse; arbor, **bower,** pergola, kiosk, pandal [Ceylon & India], alcove.

12. apartment house, flat house; tenement, rent [coll., U.S.]; duplex, duplex house *or* apartment.

13. inn, hotel, hostel, **tavern,** cabaret [original use], ordinary, *posada* [Sp.]; **roadhouse,** caravansary, resthouse [chiefly India & Ceylon], dak bungalow [India], khan [Near East]; **hospice,** hospital [hist.]; **lodginghouse, rooming house,** lodgment, kip [slang]; **flophouse,** doss house [both slang]; **boardinghouse,** *pension* [F.]; public house, public [coll., Eng.], **pub** [slang, Eng.].

14. motel, motor court, **auto court;** trailer court.

15. hall; assembly hall, assembly [U.S.], **meetinghouse; auditorium,** aud [college slang, U.S.], audience hall, hall of audience, durbar [India]; lecture hall, lyceum;

concert hall; town hall, guildhall, tollhouse [local, Eng.], tolbooth *or* tollbooth [chiefly Scot.]; city hall [U.S.]; community center [U.S.]; clubhouse, club; gymnasium, gym [coll.].

16. barn, stable, stall; **cowbarn,** cowhouse, cowshed, cow byre, byre, shippon [Scot. & dial., Eng.]; mews.

17. (for vehicles) **garage,** carport; coach house; carbarn; roundhouse; hangar; boathouse.

18. kennel, doghouse, doghole, dogwam [joc.]; pound, dog pound.

19. chicken house, henhouse, hencote, hennery.

20. aviary, birdhouse, bird cage; dovecote, dovecot, pigeon house, columbary, columbarium [Rom. antiq.]; roost, perch, roosting place.

21. nest, nidus; aerie, eyrie; clutch (nest of eggs), cletch [dial., Eng.]; hornet's nest, bike [Scot.]; wasp's nest, vespiary.

22. lair, den, cave, hole, covert, mew, form; **burrow,** tunnel, pipe, earth, run, couch (otter's burrow), lodge (of a beaver or otter).

23. resort, haunt, purlieu, **hangout** [slang, U.S.], **stamping ground** [slang]; concourse [U.S.]; gathering place, rallying point, meeting place, meet; nest, den (as of thieves); health resort 687.31; **spa,** baths, springs, watering place.

24. (low resort) **dive** [chiefly U.S.], **den;** hole [U.S.], dump, **joint,** place [all slang]; scatter, drum [both crim. slang, U.S.].

25. camp, encampment, laager [South Africa], leaguer [hist.]; **bivouac; barrack** *or* **barracks,** casern, cantonment; jungle *or* jungles, bo camp [both tramp slang, U.S.]; tourist camp [U.S.]; trailer camp; detention camp, concentration camp; campground [U.S.].

26. (gods of the household) lares, penates [both Rom. myth.]; Vesta [Rom. myth.], Hestia [Gr. myth.].

ADJS. **27. residential,** residentiary; domiciliary, domal; **home, household;** mansional, palatial.

28. homelike, homish, homey [coll.], **homely;** comfortable, friendly, cheerful, peaceful, cozy, snug, intimate; simple, plain, unpretending.

191. ROOM

Compartment.—NOUNS **1. room,** chamber, *chambre* [F.], *salle* [F.], cubicle, roomlet; by-room.

2. **compartment,** chamber; **cavity,** hollow, hole; **cell,** cellule; **booth,** stall, crib, manger; box, pew; crypt, vault, hold.

3. **rook, corner, cranny, niche, recess,** hole [chiefly dial., Eng.]; cove, alcove; cubby, **cubbyhole;** pigeonhole; glory hole [coll.].

4. **apartment, flat,** tenement, chambers [Eng.]; **suite,** suite or set of rooms; walk-up, walk-back, walk-down [all U.S.]; cold-water flat; dormitory, dorm [slang]; penthouse.

5. **parlor, living room, sitting room, drawing room, front room,** best room [coll.], keeping room [dial., Eng.]; salon, saloon [esp. Eng.]; sun parlor, solarium.

6. **library, study,** studio, office.

7. **bedroom, boudoir,** chamber, **bedchamber;** kip, doss [both crim. slang, U.S.]; cubicle, cubiculum; dormitory; nursery.

8. (private chamber) **sanctum,** sanctum sanctorum, holy of holies, adytum, **den,** closet, cabinet.

9. (ships) cabin, stateroom.

10. (railways) drawing room, saloon, stateroom.

11. **dining room,** salle à manger [F.], spense [chiefly Scot.], dining saloon [naut.; esp. Eng.]; dinette [U.S.]; dining hall, refectory, mess hall [mil.]; commons.

12. **playroom,** recreation room, game room, **rumpus room** [slang, U.S.]; billiard room.

13. **utility room,** laundry room, sewing room.

14. kitchen 329.3, storeroom 658.6, lavatory 679.8, water closet 680.13, smoking room 433.14.

15. **closet,** clothes closet, cloakroom; linen closet.

16. **attic,** attic room, **garret, loft,** sky parlor; cockloft.

17. **cellar, basement,** underground [Eng.]; serdab [Near East]; subbasement; wine cellar; potato cellar, spud hole [dial. U.S.]; storm cellar, cyclone cellar, fraid hole [slang, U.S.], funk hole [slang, chiefly Eng.]; hold, hole [both naut.].

18. **corridor, hall, hallway;** passage, passageway; **gallery,** loggia; arcade, colonnade, cloister, peristyle [Gr. arch.]; areaway [U.S.]; breezeway.

19. **vestibule,** portal, **portico,** entry, entrance, **entrance hall,** entranceway, threshold; **lobby, foyer;** propylaeum [classical arch.], stoa [Gr. arch.]; narthex, galilee [both eccl.].

20. **anteroom,** antechamber; **waiting room,** salle d'attente [F.]; **reception room,** presence chamber or room; lounge, swing room [slang, U.S.].

21. **porch,** stoop [U.S.], **veranda,** piazza [U.S.], lanai [Hawaiian], levee [South. & West. U.S.], gallery [South. U.S.], side-kicker [dial., West. U.S.]; sun porch, solarium; sleeping porch.

22. **balcony,** gallery.

23. **floor,** level, **story;** first floor or story, ground or street floor, rez-de-chaussée [F.]; mezzanine, mezzanine floor, entresol [F.]; clerestory or clearstory.

24. (Rom. antiq.) atrium, peristyle, peristylium, tablinum.

192. RECEPTACLE

NOUNS 1. **receptacle, container,** holder, **vessel,** utensil; receiver, **recipient;** dish, plate; tableware.

2. **bag, sack,** sac [bot. & anat.], poke [dial.], pocket, pouch, pod, budget [dial.]; bladder, sound, air bladder.

3. **belly, stomach,** tummy [childish], **abdomen,** venter, bag [Scot. & dial. Eng.], wame [Scot. & dial.], **crop** [dial. exc. zool.], ingluvies [zool.], gorge [dial.], **craw,** maw, gizzard [coll. & joc. exc. zool.]; breadbasket, kitchen, little Mary, the inner man [all slang]; **paunch,** pod [orig. dial.], tun, bay window [slang], corporation [slang], potbelly, **pot** [slang], swagbelly [chiefly dial.]; underbelly; first stomach, rumen; second stomach, reticulum, honeycomb stomach; third stomach, psalterium, omasum, manyplies; fourth stomach, abomasum, rennet bag.

4. **basket,** wisket or whisket [dial., Eng.], skippet [dial.], kit [Eng.]; hamper, maund or maun [Scot. & dial.].

5. **can,** tin [Eng.], tin can.

6. **bucket, pail,** skeel [dial.]; scuttle, coal scuttle, hod.

7. **ladle, dipper,** bail, scoop.

8. **tray,** waiter, salver; ashtray; coaster.

ADJS. 9. **vascular, vesicular;** camerated, capsular, cellular, cystic, locular, marsupial, saccular, siliquose.

10. **abdominal,** ventral, coeliac; stomachal, stomachic(al), gastric, ventricular.

11. **receptacles**

autoclave	bucket
billy or billycan	caddy
[orig. Austral.]	cage
boat (as, gravy	can
boat)	canister

cannikin
casserole
catchall
coal scuttle
compote [U.S.]
creamer [U.S.]
crock
dinner pail
gallipot
garbage can
G.I. can [army
 slang]
hod
holdall
hopper
magazine

milk pail
pail
patera [L.]
piggin [chiefly
 dial.]
pipkin
pitcher
platter
porringer
powder horn
saucer
scuttle
slop pail
tray
trencher [hist.]

12. basins

bathtub
bowl
catch basin or
 drain
cistern
punch bowl
tank

terrine
tub
tureen
vat
washbasin
washtub

13. pots

amphora
biggin
boiler
caldron
chatty [India]
coffeepot
coffee urn
cuspidor
demijohn
flowerpot
jardiniere
jug

kettle
kitchen boiler
olla [U.S.]
patella [archaeol.]
pipkin
spittoon
tazza [It.]
teakettle
teapot
tea urn
urn
vase

14. pans

ashpan
bakepan
bedpan
boiler
brazier
bread pan
broiler
cake pan
dishpan
double boiler
dustpan

frying pan
pan boiler
piepan
posnet [dial.]
roaster
saucepan
skillet
spider
stewpan
warming pan

15. cups, drinking vessels

beaker
beer glass
blackjack
bowl
cannikin
chalice
coffee cup
demitasse
fifth
glass
goblet
highball glass
horn
jigger [U.S.]
jorum [coll.]

magnum
mazer
mug
noggin
pony [coll., U.S.]
rummer
schooner
shot glass
stein
tankard
teacup
Toby
tumbler
tyg, tig
wineglass

16. ladles

calabash
chopsticks
cyathus [Gr.
 antiq.]
gourd
labis [eccl.]

spatula
spoon
tablespoon
teaspoon
trowel

17. bottles

calabash
canteen
carafe
carboy
caster
cruet
cruse
decanter
ewer
flacon
flagon
flask

flasket
gourd
jar
lota [India]
mussuk [India]
olla
phial
pocket flask
stoup
thermos
vacuum bottle
vial

18. casks

barrel
butt
drum
firkin
harness cask or
 tub [naut.]
keg

kilderkin
pipe
puncheon
rundlet
tun
water butt

19. cases

ammunition box
bandbox
bandoleer
bin
boot
box
bunker
caisson
canister
capsule, capsula
cardcase
carton
casket
cedar chest
chest
coffer
crate
crib
file
filing box or case
folio
hatbox

holster
hope chest
housewife, huswife,
 hussy [dial.]
hutch
kit [chiefly Scot. &
 dial. Eng.]
letter file
pillbox
pod
portfolio
powder box
quiver
rack
scabbard
sheath
skippet
socket
tinderbox
vanity case
vasculum

20. baskets

bassinet
buck basket
bushel
clothesbasket
clothes hamper or
 bin
corbeil
crane [Scot.]
creel
dosser
fruit basket

flower basket
hamper
pannier
reed basket
rush basket
splint basket
stave basket
washbasket
wicker basket
wire basket
wooden basket

21. bags

caddie bag
fob

gamebag
golf bag

gunny, gunny sack | pouch
handbag | purse
kyack [West. U.S.] | reticule
mail pouch | sack
moneybag | saddlebag
net | school bag
nose bag | sleeping bag
pack sack | wineskin
pocket |

22. luggage, baggage

bag | kit bag
barracks bag [mil.] | knapsack
boodle bag [slang] | portmanteau
Boston bag [U.S.] | [chiefly Eng.]
brief case | rucksack
carpetbag [chiefly | *sac de nuit* [F.,
U.S.] | night bag]
ditty bag or box | Saratoga trunk
duffel bag | satchel
Gladstone, Glad- | sea bag [naut.]
stone bag | suitcase
go-away bag [dial., | traveling bag
U.S.] | trunk
grab-all [coll.] | tucker bag
grip [U.S.] | [Austral.]
gripsack [U.S.] | turkey [slang U.S.
grouch bag [slang, | & Can.]
U.S.] | valise
handbag | war bag or sack
haversack | [army slang]
holdall | yannigan bag
kit | [slang, U.S.]

23. botany, anatomy

bladder | pocket
bleb | pod
blister | sac
boll | saccule
bursa | sacculus
calyx | scrotum
cancelli | seedcase
capsule | silique
cell | sinus
cyst, cystis | sound
follicle | theca
gall bladder | udder
legume | utricle
loculus | vasculum
marsupium | ventricle
musk bag | *vesica*
pericarp | vesicle

24. cupboards

buffet | escritoire
bunker | *étagère* [F.]
bureau | highboy [U.S.]
cabinet | kitchen cabinet
Canterbury | locker
cellaret | lowboy [U.S.]
chest | press
chest of drawers | safe
chiffonier | *secrétaire* [F.]
chifforobe [U.S.] | secretary
closet | shelf
clothespress | shelves
commode | sideboard
davenport | vargueno
desk | vitrine
drawer | whatnot
dresser |

193. CONTENTS

NOUNS 1. contents, content; insides, innards [dial. & slang], inwards [coll.], inners [coll. & dial.], guts [slang]; filling, stuffing, stuffings, filler, inlay [dentistry]; stuffing, stuffings, wadding, padding, packing, lining.

2. load, lading, cargo, freight, charge, burden, bale, lug [coll.], jag [chiefly dial.]; boatload, busload, carload, cartload, shipload, trainload, truckload, vanload, wagonload; payload.

3. (contents of a container) cup, cupful etc. 28.8.

4. (essential content) substance, stuff, matter; sum and substance, gist, meat, marrow, pith, sap; heart, soul, spirit.

5. enclosure, the enclosed.

194. SIZE

NOUNS 1. size, largeness, bigness, magnitude, amplitude; mass, bulk, volume, body; dimensions, proportions, dimension, proportion; measure, measurement, gauge, scale; extent, expanse, expansion, scope, range, spread, area; breadth, width; girth (size around).

2. capacity, volume, content, accommodation, room, space, measure, limit, burden [naut.]; poundage, tonnage, cordage; stowage, tankage.

3. full size, full growth; life size.

4. large size, economy size, king size.

5. oversize, outsize; overlargeness, overbigness; overgrowth, overdevelopment; overweight, overheaviness; overstoutness, overfatness, overplumpness.

6. sizableness, largeness, bigness, greatness, grandness; largishness, biggishness; voluminousness, capaciousness, generousness, ampleness; broadness, wideness; extensiveness, expansiveness, comprehensiveness; spaciousness 178.5.

7. hugeness, vastness, enormousness, immenseness, enormity, immensity, tremendousness, prodigiousness, stupendousness, mountainousness, giantlikeness, monumentalism; monstrousness, monstrosity.

8. corpulence, corporosity [joc., U.S.], obesity, stoutness, *embonpoint* [F.]: fatness, fattishness, adiposis [med.], adiposity, fleshiness, beefiness, grossness; plumpness, rotundity, tubbiness [coll.], roly-poliness; pudginess, podginess; chubbiness, chumpiness [coll.], chunkiness [coll.], stockiness, stodginess; portliness; paunchiness; hippiness [coll.]; fat, adipose tissue.

9. **bulkiness,** hulkiness, **massiveness,** lumpishness, clumpishness; **ponderousness,** combrousness, cumbersomeness; **clumsiness,** awkwardness, unwieldiness.

10. **lump,** clump, clunk [dial., U.S.], hunch, **hunk** [coll.], hank [dial.], **chunk** [coll.], chump, whang [Scot. & dial.]; **mass,** bulk, **gob** [dial. & slang], batch, **wad,** swad [slang, U.S.], block, loaf; pat (as of butter); clod; nugget.

11. (something large) **whopper,** whapper, whacker, bumper [all coll.]; thumper, spanker, **slapper, strapper,** banger, lolloper, whaler, whale [all slang]; jumbo [chiefly coll.]; hulk.

12. (corpulent person) corporosity [joc., U.S.], lump [coll.], **heavyweight,** heavy [slang], human or man mountain [slang]; **fat man,** fatty [slang], humpty-dumpty, roly-poly, **tubby** [slang], squab, dumpling [coll.], grampus [coll.], porpoise [coll.], pudge [coll.], pudgy [slang], blimp [slang], **potbelly.**

13. **giant,** giantess [fem.], **colossus, titan;** Aegir, Antaeus, Briareus, Brobdingnagian, Cyclops, Fafnir, Fenrir, Gargantua, Gerth, Goliath, Grendel, Gymir, Hercules, Hler, Hymir, Jotunn, Loki, Mimir, Norm, Polyphemus, Ran, Titan, Titaness, Wade, Ymir; Gog and Magog.

14. **behemoth,** leviathan, **monster; mammoth,** mastodon; elephant, hathi [India], jumbo [chiefly coll.]; whale; hippopotamus, **hippo** [coll.], river horse; mammoths, dinosaurs 123.26, 27.

VERBS 15. **size,** adjust, **grade,** group, range, rank, graduate, sort, match; gauge, measure, proportion.

ADJS. 16. **large,** sizable, sizely [coll.], **big, great, grand,** tall [slang, U.S.], **considerable, goodly,** tidy [coll.], substantial, bumper (as, a bumper crop), astronomic(al) (as, an astronomical figure); largish, biggish; large-scale; man-sized [slang]; bull.

17. **voluminous, capacious, generous, ample,** broad, wide, extensive, expansive, comprehensive; spacious 178.9.

18. **stout, corpulent, fat,** fattish, **obese,** gross, **fleshy,** beefy; paunchy 196.13; **plump,** full, rotund, **tubby** [coll.], roly-poly; **pudgy,** podgy; **heavy-set, thickset, chubby,** chumpy [coll.], chunky [coll.], **stocky,** stodgy; lusty, strapping [coll.], chopping, bouncing, stalwart, brawny, burly; **portly,** imposing; well-fed, corn-fed, grain-fed; chubby-faced, round-faced, **moonfaced;** hippy [coll.], full-buttocked, **broad in the beam** [slang];

plump as a dumpling or partridge, fat as a quail, fat as a pig or hog, "fat as a pork hog" [Malory], "fat as a porpoise" [Swift], "fat as a fool" [Lyly], "fat as butter" [Shakespeare], fat as brawn or bacon [coll.].

19. **bulky, hulky,** hulking, lumpish, lumping [coll.], clumpish; **massive,** massy; elephantine, hippopotamic; **ponderous,** cumbrous, cumbersome; **clumsy,** awkward, **unwieldy.**

20. **huge,** hugeous [joc. or coll.], **immense, vast, enormous,** tremendous, prodigious, stupendous; great big [redundant], mighty, **titanic, colossal, monumental,** heroic(al), towering, mountainous; monster, monstrous; **mammoth,** mastodon; **gigantic,** gigantean; **giant,** giantlike; Cyclopean, Brobdingnagian, Gargantuan, Herculean, Atlantean; elephantine, jumbo [chiefly coll.]; dinosaurian, dinotherian.

21. (slang and colloquialisms) **whopping, whaling, whacking,** spanking, slapping, lolloping, thumping, thundering, bumping, banging.

22. **full-sized,** full-size, full-scale; **full-grown,** full-fledged, full-blown; full-formed, full-fashioned (as hose); **life-sized,** large as life, large as life and twice as natural [joc.].

23. **oversize,** oversized; **outsize,** outsized, **kingsize; overlarge,** overbig, too big; **overgrown,** overdeveloped; **overweight,** overheavy; overfleshed, overstout, overfat, overplump, overfed.

ADVS. 24. largely, on a large scale, in a big way; in the large.

195. LITTLENESS

Small Size.—NOUNS 1. **littleness, smallness,** smallishness, **diminutiveness,** slightness, exiguity; puniness, pokiness, dinkiness [slang]; **tininess, minuteness;** undersize; petiteness; dapperness; shortness 202.

2. **infinitesimalness, microdimensions,** atomity; inappreciability, insensibility, evanescence; intangibility, impalpability, imponderability; imperceptibility, invisibility.

3. (small place) **tight spot,** tight squeeze, **pinch** [all coll.]; hole, pigeonhole; hole in the wall; cubby, cubbyhole; cubbyhouse, dollhouse, playhouse, doghouse.

4. **diminutive, runt, shrimp,** wart [slang], wisp, chit, slip, **peewee** [slang], jitney [slang], fingerling, small fry [chiefly coll.]; lightweight, featherweight; bantam, banty [coll.]; pony; minnow, minny [coll.];

mouse, tit, titmouse, tomtit [Eng.]; nubbin [chiefly U.S.], button (stunted growth of horn).

5. miniature, minny [slang]; subminiature; microcosm, microcosmos; baby; doll, puppet; microvolume; Elzevir, Elzevir edition; duodecimo, twelvemo [coll.].

6. dwarf, dwarfling, **midget,** midge, **pygmy,** droich [Gael.], manikin, homunculus, atomy, micromorph [zool.], hop-o'-my-thumb; elf, gnome, brownie; dapperling; **runt,** shrimp, wart [slang], peewee [dial., U.S.]; Negrito, Negrillo; Lilliputian, Pigwiggen, Tom Thumb, Alberich, Alviss, Andvari, Nibelung, Reginn.

7. (minute thing) **minutia** (*pl.* minutiae) minim, **mite** [chiefly coll.]; **point,** vanishing point, mathematical point, point of a pin, pin point, **dot,** mote, fleck, **speck,** flyspeck, jot, tittle, iota; **particle,** crumb, scrap, snip, snippet; grain, grain of sand; millet seed, mustard seed; midge, mite, gnat; atom, atomy, monad; molecule; electron, ion; microbe, microorganism; animalicule, microzoan, microzoa [*pl.*].

8. (minute measures) micron, millimicron; mite, grain, barleycorn.

ADJS. **9. little, small,** smallish, **slight,** exiguous; **puny,** poky, pindling [coll., U.S.], **dinky** [slang]; cramped, limited; one-horse, two-by-four [both coll.]; pint-sized, half-pint; petite; dapper; short 202.8.

10. tiny, teeny [coll.], teeny-weeny [coll.], **wee** [coll.], peewee [slang], little-bitsy [dial. or slang]; **minute,** fine.

11. diminutive, miniature, minikin, small-scale, pony; bantam, banty [coll.]; baby, baby-sized; pocket, pocket-sized; duodecimo, twelvemo [coll.]; subminiature.

12. dwarf, dwarfed, dwarfish; **pygmy,** nanoid, elfin; Lilliputian, Tom Thumb; **undersized,** undersize; **stunted,** runty [U.S.]; scrubby, scraggy; Negritic.

13. infinitesimal, microscopic, evanescent; inappreciable, insensible; impalpable, imponderable, intangible; imperceptible, indiscernible, invisible, unseeable; atomic; molecular; corpuscular; microcosmic(al).

14. microbic, microbial, **microorganic;** animalcular, microzoic; embryonic, germinal, incipient, rudimentary, rudimental; bacterial; amoebic, amoeboid.

ADVS. **15.** smally, small, little, slightly; **on a small scale,** in a small compass, in a small way; **in miniature,** in the small; in a nutshell.

16. microscopy

electrophoto	micrometry
micrography	micromineralogy
microbiology	micropaleontology
microchemistry	micropathology
microcosmography	micropetrography
microcosmology	micropetrology
microcrystallog-	microphotography
raphy	microphysics
microgeology	microphysiography
micrography	microscopics
micrology	microspectroscopy
micromechanics	microtechnic
micrometallog-	microzoology
raphy	photomicrography
micrometallurgy	photomicroscopy

17. microorganisms

amoeba	microzoa
animalcule	microzyme
arthrospore	monad
bacillus	moner, moneron
bacteria	paramecium
culture	Phytozoa
diatom	Phytozoaria
dyad	protozoa
entozoa	radiolarian
filterable virus	rhizopod
foraminifer	rotifer
germ	schizomycete
gonidium	tetrad
gregarine	triad
Infusoria	virus
mastigophoran	zoogloea
mastigopod	zoogonidium
microbe	zoospore
micrococcus	zygospore
microphyte	zygote
microspore	

196. EXPANSION, GROWTH

Increase in Size.—NOUNS **1. expansion, extension, enlargement, increase,** magnification, aggrandizement, amplification, ampliation; broadening, widening; **spread,** spreading, flare, splay; deployment [chiefly mil.].

2. distension, stretching; **inflation,** sufflation, tympany; **dilation,** dilatation, diastole [physiol. & biol.]; **swelling,** swellage; swell 255.4; puffing, puff, bloating; **flatulence,** flatulency, flatus, gassiness, windiness; turgidness, turgidity, turgescence; tumidness, tumidity, tumefaction; tumescence, intumescence; **swollenness, puffiness,** bloatedness; dropsy, edema; tympanites, tympany, tympanism, meteorism.

3. growth, development, upgrowth; vegetation 410.30; germination, pullulation; burgeoning, sprouting; budding, gemmation; outgrowth, excrescence.

VERBS **4.** (make larger) **enlarge,** largify [dial.], **expand, extend, widen, broaden,** biggen [chiefly dial., Eng.], aggrandize, amplify, **magnify, increase,** augment, develop, bulk; **stretch, distend, dilate,** swell, **inflate, blow up,** puff up, huff, puff, bloat; pump, pump up; rarefy.

5. (become larger) **enlarge, expand, extend, increase,** develop, **widen, broaden,** bulk; **stretch, distend, dilate,** swell, balloon, puff up, fill out.

6. **spread,** spread out, outspread, outstretch; **expand, extend,** widen; open, **open up,** unfold; **flare, flue,** splay; sprawl; bush, branch, branch out; fan, fan out; mantle [spread the wings]; deploy [chiefly mil.]; spread like wildfire; overrun, overgrow.

7. **grow, develop, wax, increase;** gather, brew; **grow up,** spring up, **shoot up,** sprout up, upshoot, upspring, upsprout, upspear; burgeon, put forth, burst forth; **sprout,** shoot; bud, gemmate; germinate, pullulate; vegetate 410.31; flourish, thrive, grow like a weed; mushroom; outgrow (surpass in growing; grow too large for; grow out of).

8. **fatten,** fat, plump, pinguefy; **gain weight,** gather flesh, take or put on weight.

ADJS. 9. **expansive, extensive;** expansional, extensional; expansile, extensile, elastic; expansible, inflatable; distensive, dilatant; inflationary.

10. **expanded, extended, enlarged,** increased, amplified, widened, broadened.

11. **spread, spreading,** patulous; sprawling, sprawly; **outspread, outstretched,** spread out, stretched out; open, unfolded; widespread, wide-open; flared, flued, splayed; flaring, fluing, splaying; splay, flue [dial.]; fanned, fanning; fanlike, fanshaped, fan-shape, flabelliform, rhipidate.

12. **distended, dilated, inflated, puffed up, swollen,** swelled, **bloated,** turgid, tumid, plethoric, incrassate [bot. & zool.]; **puffy,** pursy; flatulent, gassy, windy, ventose; dropsical, edematous; enchymatous [biol.].

13. **big-bellied,** full-bellied, abdominous; **paunchy,** paunched; **potbellied,** swagbellied [chiefly dial.]; thick-bodied, thick-girthed.

197. CONTRACTION

Decrease in Size.—NOUNS 1. **contraction,** systole [physiol. & biol.]; **compression,** condensation, concentration; narrowing; reduction 39; shortening 202.3; **constric-** tion, stricture, striction, astriction; astringency, constringency; puckering, pursing; knitting, wrinkling.

2. **squeezing,** compression, tightening; pressure, press, crush; **squeeze, pinch, tweak, nip;** strangulation, stranglement.

3. **shrinking,** shrinkage; **shriveling, withering;** searing, parching; wasting, consumption; preshrinking, preshrinkage, Sanforization.

4. **collapse,** prostration, cave-in; **deflation.**

5. contractibility, compressibility, condensability; collapsibility.

6. contractor, constrictor, compressor; **astringent,** styptic; alum, astringent bitters, styptic pencil.

VERBS 7. **contract, compress,** cramp, compact, condense, concentrate; **reduce** 39.7; **shorten** 206.6; **narrow,** draw, draw in or together; **constrict,** constringe; **pucker,** pucker up, **purse,** cockle; **knit, wrinkle.**

8. **squeeze,** compress, tighten; **press,** crush; **pinch, tweak, nip;** strangle, strangulate.

9. **shrink, shrivel, wither,** warp [poetic]; sear, parch, dry up; **wizen,** wizzen [dial.], weazen; waste, waste away; preshrink, Sanforize.

10. **collapse, cave in,** fall in; fold, fold up; **deflate,** let the air out of; puncture, puncture one's balloon.

ADJS. 11. **contractive,** contractional, contractible, contractile; **astringent,** constringent, styptic; **compressible,** condensable; **collapsible,** foldable; deflationary.

12. **contracted, compressed,** cramped, compact, concentrated, condensed; puckered, pursed, cockled.

13. **shrunk,** shrunken; **shriveled,** shriveled up; **withered,** sear, parched, corky; dried up; **wizened,** wizen, weazened; wizenfaced; preshrunk, Sanforized.

14. **deflated, flat.**

198. DISTANCE

NOUNS 1. **distance, remoteness,** farness; **extent, length,** space, **reach,** stretch, range, compass, span, stride; way, ways [dial. & coll.]; piece [dial.], chance [dial., U.S.], spell [coll.]; perspective.

2. **long way,** good ways [dial. & coll.], **great distance,** right smart chance [dial., U.S.], long chalk [coll.], **far cry,** far piece [dial.]; long step, tidy step [coll.], giant's stride; long range.

3. the distance, **remote distance; offing,** horizon, background.

4. (remote region) jumping-off-place [coll.], Godforsaken place [coll.], the back of beyond [slang]; outpost, outskirt.

VERBS **5. reach out, stretch out,** extend out; outreach, outstretch, outlie.

6. extend to, stretch to, stretch away to, **reach to,** lead to, go to, get to, come to, run to, carry to.

7. keep one's distance, remain at a distance, keep at a respectful distance, **keep away from,** stand off or away, keep or stand clear of, **steer clear of** [coll.], keep out of the way of, keep at arm's length, keep or stand aloof.

ADJS. **8. distant,** distal, **remote, removed, far, far off,** away, **faraway,** at a distance, right smart off [dial.]; separated, apart, asunder; long-distance.

9. out-of-the-way, God-forsaken [coll.], back of beyond [slang]; **out of reach,** inaccessible, unapproachable, intouchable.

10. thither, ulterior; **yonder,** yon [chiefly dial.], yond [dial.]; **farther, further,** remoter, more distant.

11. trans-, tra-, ultra-, over-; transoceanic, transmarine, ultramarine, oversea, overseas; transatlantic, transpacific; tramontane, transmontane, ultramontane, transalpine; transarctic, transcontinental, transequatorial, transpolar, transpontine, ultramundane.

12. farthest, furthest, farthermost, furthermost, extreme, remotest, most distant.

ADVS. **13. yonder,** yander [dial.], yon [now dial.], yond [dial.].

14. in the distance, in the remote distance; **in the offing,** on the horizon, in the background.

15. at a distance, off, away, aloof, at arm's length; distantly, remotely.

16. far, far off, far away, **afar,** afar off, a long way off, a good ways off [dial. & coll.], a long cry to, "over the hills and far away" [Gay], as far as the eye can see, clear to hell and gone [slang].

17. far and wide, far and near, distantly and broadly, wide, **widely,** broadly, abroad.

18. apart, aside, away, wide apart, wide away, "as wide asunder as pole and pole" [Froude], "as far as the east is from the west" [Bible].

19. wide of, clear of; wide of the mark, abroad, all abroad, astray, afield, far afield.

PREPS. **20. to, as far as.**

21. beyond, yond [dial.], yonder or yonder of [dial.]; **past, over, across;** farther, further, farther off, further away.

22. out of reach, beyond reach, **out of range,** beyond the bounds, out of the way, out of the sphere of; out of sight, à perte de vue [F.]; out of hearing, out of earshot or earreach.

199. NEARNESS

NOUNS **1. nearness,** closeness; **proximity,** propinquity, immediacy; approximation, approach; **vicinity,** vicinage, **neighborhood,** precinct.

2. short distance, short way, little ways [dial. & coll.], a few ways [dial., U.S.], **step,** short step, brief span, piece [dial.], spell [coll.], little; close quarters, close range; **stone's throw,** spitting distance [joc.], bowshot, gunshot, pistol shot; earshot, earreach, mouth shot [dial.]; whoop, whoop or two whoops and a holler or hello [all slang]; ace, bit [coll.], crack, spot [slang], hair, hairbreadth or hairsbreadth, inch, span.

3. juxtaposition, apposition, adjacency; contiguity, contiguousness; abuttal, abutment; junction, connection, union; **conjunction,** conjugation; appulse, syzygy [both astron.].

4. meeting, joining, **encounter;** rencounter, recontre.

5. contact, touch, touching, taction, tangency, contingence; impingement, impingence; osculation [geom.].

6. neighbor, neighborer; borderer; abutter, joiner; bystander; tangent; perihelion [astron.].

VERBS **7. near,** approach 295.3.

8. be near, be in the vicinity or neighborhood of, approximate, approach; be warm or hot, burn [all coll.]; come near, begin to (as, it doesn't begin to fit).

9. (lie contiguous to) **adjoin,** join [coll.], conjoin, **connect,** butt, **abut,** abut on or upon, **neighbor,** neighbor by, border, **border on** or **upon,** trench on, verge upon; lie by, stand by; go with, march with.

10. come in contact, contact, touch, impinge, hit; osculate [geom.]; **graze,** rub, brush, scrape, skim.

11. meet, encounter; come across, run across, fall across, cross the path of; **come upon,** run upon, fall upon, light or alight on or upon; come among, fall among; **meet with,** meet up with [coll.], hit up with [coll.], come face to face with; **run into,**

bump **into** [coll.], come or run up against [coll.], run or fall foul of; burst upon, pitch upon; pop upon, bounce upon, plump upon [all coll.].

12. **stay near, keep close to;** stand by, lie by; follow close upon, tread on the heels of; hang about, hang upon the skirts of, hover over; **cling to,** clasp, hug, huddle [chiefly dial.]; hug the shore or land, keep hold of the land, make free with the land [sea slang].

13. **juxtapose,** juxtaposit, **appose, join, adjoin, abut,** neighbor; bring near, put with, place side by side.

ADJS. 14. **near, nigh, close,** intimate; approximate, proximate, proximal; **in the vicinity** or **neighborhood of,** vicinal; near the mark; warm, hot, burning [all coll.].

15. **nearby, close by,** at hand, **close at hand,** near at hand, **handy;** at one's elbow, at one's feet, at one's fingers' ends or finger tips, under one's nose; **convenient,** convenient to [both coll.].

16. **adjacent, next to,** immediate, contiguous, **adjoining, abutting; neighboring,** neighbor; juxtaposed, juxtapositive, juxtapositional; bordering, **bordering upon,** conterminous; in connection with, in touch with; end to end, endways, endwise.

17. **in contact, touching, meeting,** contingent; impinging, impingent; tangent, tangential; osculatory [geom.].

18. **nearer, nigher, closer,** near [dial.].

19. **nearest, nighest, closest,** nearmost [chiefly dial.]; next, immediate.

ADVS., PREPS. 20. **near, nigh;** anigh, anear [both dial.]; close upon, hard, hard upon, **close to,** at close quarters; near by, **nearby, close by,** hard by, fast by, by; nearabout, nearabouts, nigh about [all dial.]; about, around [coll., U.S.], close about, along towards (of time [coll., U.S.]); **not far from,** at no great distance, but a step; in an inch of, within an ace of, as near as no matter [coll.]; **within reach** or **range,** within call or hearing, within earshot or earreach, in sight of, within a whoop or two whoops and a holler or hello [slang], within a stone's throw, in spitting distance [joc.].

21. **in juxtaposition, in conjunction,** in apposition; beside 241.11, 12; fornent, fornint, fornenst, feninst [all dial.].

22. **bordering upon, verging on,** on the confines of, at the threshold of, **on the brink** or **verge of,** on the edge of, at or on the point of, on the skirts of; next door to, at one's door.

23. **against,** on, upon, over against, in contact with.

ADVS. 24. **closely,** near, close.

25. **nearly,** near; near to, **close to,** near by [Scot.]; pretty near, prett-near [dial.]; **almost,** most [coll. & dial.], all but, not quite, as good as; **well-nigh, just about;** nigh, nigh about, nearabout, nigh on or upon, nigh onto [all dial.].

26. **approximately,** approximatively, practically [coll.], much, more or less; **roughly, roundly,** in round numbers; generally, generally speaking, roughly speaking, say; **about** [coll.], around [coll., U.S.], *circa* [L.], somewhere about or near, near or close upon, upwards of [coll.], **in the neighborhood** or **vicinity of** [coll.]; thereabout or thereabouts, hereabout or hereabouts.

200. INTERVAL

Space Between.—NOUNS 1. **interval, space, interspace,** interstice, intersection; interruption, interregnum; hiatus, caesura, lacuna.

2. **cleft, crack,** cranny, creek [dial.], chink, chap, **crevice,** fissure, scissure, incision, cut, gash, slit, split, **rift,** rent, rime; **opening,** hole; **gap,** gape, yawn; **gulf,** chasm; **breach, break,** fracture, rupture; fault, flaw; leak.

3. (geographic) **gap,** notch [U.S.], cut; ravine, gorge, dell, flume [U.S.], nullah [Anglo-Ind.], wadi [Near East & N. Africa], donga [S. Africa]; **canyon** or cañon, couloir [F.], coulee [West. U.S.]; **gully, gulch** [U.S.], arroyo, draw [U.S.]; clough, cleuch or cleugh [Scot.]; **gulf, chasm, abyss,** abysm; crevasse; chimney; **defile,** pass, passage, col.

VERBS 4. **space, interspace, interval,** set at intervals, separate, part, dispart, set or keep apart, remove.

ADJS. 5. **intervallic, interstitial;** interregnal.

6. **spaced, interspaced,** intervaled, separated, parted, removed.

7. **cleft, cut, cloven, rift, rent, slit, split;** gaping, dehiscent; fissured, fissury, rimose, rimulose [bot. & zool.]; chinky.

201. LENGTH

NOUNS 1. **length,** longness, lengthiness, longitude [joc.]; **extent, measure, span, reach, stretch;** distance 198; footage, yardage, mileage.

2. oblongness, oblongitude.

3. (a length) **piece, portion,** part; coil; roll; run.

4. line, strip; stripe 566.5; string 71.2.

5. lengthening, prolongation, elongation, production, protraction, **extension,** stretching; stretch, tension, strain.

6. linear measures 489.17.

7. (length of a step in walking) step, footstep, pace, stride.

VERBS **8. stretch out,** extend out, reach out; outstretch, outreach; sprawl, spread; "drag its slow length along" [Pope].

9. lengthen, prolong, prolongate, **elongate, extend,** produce [geom.], **protract,** continue; lengthen out, let out, **draw out,** drag out, string out [coll., U.S.], spin out; **stretch,** draw; tense, strain.

10. look along, view in perspective.

ADJS. **11. long, lengthy;** longish, longsome [dial.]; tall 206.21; **extensive, far-reaching,** fargoing, far-flung; sesquipedalian, sesquipedal; as long as my arm, a mile long; interminable, without end, no end of or to.

12. lengthened, prolonged, prolongated, **elongated, extended, protracted; drawn out,** dragged out, spun out, strung out [coll., U.S.], **stretched,** drawn; tense, strained.

13. oblong, oblongated, oblongitudinal, **elongated;** rectangular; elliptical.

ADVS. **14.** lengthily, extensively.

15. lengthwise, lengthways, **longwise,** longways, longitudinally, along, at length; **endwise,** endways, endlong.

202. SHORTNESS

NOUNS **1. shortness,** briefness, **brevity; succinctness,** curtness, summariness, compendiousness, compactness; **conciseness** 590; littleness 195; lowness 207.

2. stubbiness, stumpiness [coll.], **stockiness,** stodginess, chubbiness, chumpiness [coll.], chunkiness [coll.], blockiness, squattiness, dumpiness, squabbiness; pudginess, podginess; snubbiness, snubbishness.

3. shortening, abbreviation; reduction 39; **abridgment, condensation,** compression, epitomization; **curtailment,** retrenchment; elision, ellipsis, syncope, apocope; foreshortening [drawing].

4. abridger, epitomizer, epitomist.

5. short cut, cut, cutoff, crosscut, shortest way; **beeline,** air line.

VERBS **6. shorten, abbreviate;** reduce 39.7; **abridge, condense,** compress, **boil down,** abstract, epitomize, capsulize; cur-

tail, retrench, take in; elide, **cut short,** cut, off short, cut back; clip, snub, nip; pollard; stunt, check the growth of; telescope; foreshorten [drawing].

7. take a short cut, short-cut; **cut across,** crosscut, cut through, cut across lots; **cut a corner,** cut corners; **make a beeline,** take the air line.

ADJS. **8. short, brief, abbreviatory,** "short and sweet" [T. Lodge]; **concise** 590.4; **curt,** curtal, curtate, decurtate; **succinct,** summary, compendious, compact, compacted; synoptic(al); little 195.9; low 207.6.

9. shortened, abbreviated; abridged, compressed, condensed, epitomized; capsule, capsulized; **curtailed,** cut short; shortcut; elided, elliptic(al).

10. stubby, stubbed, stumpy [coll.], **thickset, stocky,** stodgy, stuggy [dial., Eng.], blocky, **chunky** [coll.], chumpy [coll.], **chubby,** tubby [coll.], spuddy [dial. & coll.], punchy [coll.], dumpy; **squat,** squatty, squattish; squab, squabby, squabbish; **pudgy,** podgy; scrubby, scrub; snubby, snubbish, snub, **snubbed;** pug, **pugged;** pug-sed, snub-nosed; turned-up, *retroussé* [F.].

11. short-legged, breviped; short-winged, brevipennate.

ADVS. **12. shortly, briefly,** summarily, curtly, succinctly; **concisely** 590.5, 6.

13. short (as, to stop *short*), **abruptly,** suddenly, all of a sudden.

203. BREADTH, THICKNESS

NOUNS **1. breadth, width,** depth, broadness, wideness, amplitude, extent, **span, expanse, spread;** beam [naut.].

2. thickness, the third dimension, breadth and depth; **mass, bulk, body;** corpulence, bodily size; **coarseness** (opposed to *fineness*), grossness, fatness.

3. diameter, bore, caliber, module [numis]; **radius,** semidiameter, chord; ray, spoke.

VERBS **4. broaden, widen,** deepen; **expand,** extend; **spread,** spread out, outspread, outstretch.

5. thicken, thick.

ADJS. **6. broad, wide,** deep; extensive, **expansive;** spacious, **roomy** 178.9; ample, full; widespread 79.12; wide-spaced, wideset, wide-wayed, wide-spanned; broad-gauge or -gauged; "broad as the world" [Lowell], "wide as a church door" [Shakespeare].

7. broad-beamed, broad-sterned, beamy

[naut.]; broad-ribbed, wide-ribbed, laticostate; broad-toothed, wide-toothed, latidentate.

8. **thick,** three-dimensional; **thickset, heavy-set,** thick-bodied, broad-bodied, thick-girthed; **massive, bulky,** corpulent; **coarse** (opposed to *fine*), heavy, gross, fat; full (of wines, etc.); dense 353.12; thick-necked, bullnecked.

ADVS. 9. **breadthwise,** breadthways; **widthwise,** widthways; broadwise, broadways; broadside, broad side foremost.

10. **broad**

broad-backed	broad-winged
broad-based	wide-arched
broad-billed	wide-armed
broad-bladed	wide-banked
broad-bosomed	wide-branched
broad-bottomed	wide-breasted
broad-breasted	wide-brimmed
broad-brimmed	wide-eared
broad-chested	wide-eyed
broad-eyed	wide-faced
broad-faced	wide-framed
broad-gauge *or*	wide-hipped
-gauged	wide-leaved
broad-headed	wide-lipped
broad-leaved *or*	wide-nosed
-leafed	wide-petaled
broad-lipped	wide-ribbed
broad-mouthed	wide-rimmed
broad-nosed	wide-streeted
broad-roomed	wide-tracked
broad-shouldered	wide-winged
broad-tailed	

11. **thick**

thick-ankled	thick-leaved
thick-barked	thick-legged
thick-barred	thick-lipped
thick-bottomed	thick-ribbed
thick-cheeked	thick-stalked
thick-coated	thick-stemmed
thick-eared	thick-tailed
thick-fingered	thick-toed
thick-footed	thick-toothed
thick-jawed	thick-walled
thick-kneed	thick-wristed

204. NARROWNESS, THINNESS

NOUNS 1. **narrowness, slenderness;** closeness, nearness; restriction, limitation, confinement; incapaciousness, incommodiousness; tightness, tight squeeze; hair, hairbreadth *or* hairsbreadth; finger's breadth.

2. **narrowing, tapering,** taper; **contraction** 197; stricture, constriction, coarctation [all med.].

3. narrow, **narrows, strait;** neck, isthmus; channel, canal; pass, defile, ghat [India].

4. **thinness, slenderness, slimness,** slimth [dial.]; **frailty,** delicacy, flimsiness;

fineness; **tenuity, rarity,** subtility, extility, exiguity; attenuation, extenuation; wateriness, weakness.

5. **leanness, skinniness,** fleshlessness, spareness, meagerness, **scrawniness** [U.S.], gauntness, lankness, **lankiness,** gawkiness, boniness, skin and bones; haggardness, poorness, peakedness [coll.], "lean and hungry look" [Shakespeare]; underweight; hatchet face, lantern jaws.

6. **emaciation,** attenuation, atrophy, tabes [med.], marasmus [med.].

7. (comparisons) paper, wafer, lath, slat, rail, rake, splinter, slip, shaving, streak, vein; shadow, mere shadow; skeleton.

8. (thin person) **skinny** [slang], **slim** [slang], lanky [slang], scrag, **shadow, skeleton,** walking skeleton, study in anatomy, corpse, barebone, bag *or* stack of bones, **rackabones** [coll., U.S.], rattlebones [coll.], spareribs [coll.], slab-sides [dial. & slang], spindleshanks [coll.], spindlelegs [coll.], gangleshanks [slang], lathlegs [slang], **bean pole,** beanstalk, broomstick, clothes pole.

9. **reducing, slenderizing;** Bantingism.

VERBS 10. **narrow,** diminish, draw in, go in; **taper,** snape; **contract** 197.7.

11. **thin,** thinnen [dial.], thin down, thin away, ~ off *or* out; **rarefy,** attenuate, extenuate; **emaciate,** macerate.

12. **slenderize, reduce,** reduce weight, lose weight, lose flesh; slim, **slim down,** thin down, gaunt down [dial.], leanen [dial.], meager; bantingize, bant [coll.].

ADJS. 13. **narrow, slender;** narrowish, narrowy; **close,** near; **tight,** strait, closefitting; **restricted,** limited, circumscribed, confined, constricted; **cramped,** cramp; incapacious, incommodious; **meager,** scant, scanty; narrow-gauge *or* -gauged; angustifoliate, angustirostrate, angustiseptal, angustisellate.

14. **tapered,** taper, tapering.

15. **thin, slender, slim,** slimmer [Scot.], gracile; thin-bodied, thin-set, narrowwaisted; **svelte;** thinnish, slenderish, slimmish; **slight,** slight-made; **frail,** delicate; flimsy, slimsy [coll., U.S.], **fine; finespun,** thin-spun, fine-drawn, wiredrawn; threadlike, slender as a thread; **tenuous,** subtle, rare, **rarefied;** attenuated, attenuate, extenuated; **watery, weak,** small.

16. **lean,** lean-looking, **skinny,** fleshless, lean-fleshed, thin-fleshed, **spare,** meager; **scrawny** [U.S.], scraggy, weedy [coll.], lathy [coll.], ribby [coll.], thin-bellied, her-

ring-gatted [coll.]; **gaunt,** gaunted, gaunty; **lank, lanky; gangling** [coll.], gangly [coll. & dial.]; gawky, gawkward [slang, U.S.]; **spindling,** spindly [coll.]; slink, slinky [both dial.]; **bony, rawboned,** rattleboned [slang], skeletal, **mere skin and bones;** flat-sided [coll.], slab-sided [slang, U.S.], slap-sided [dial. & slang, U.S.]; **underweight;** thin or skinny as a lath or rail, "lean as a rake" [Chaucer].

17. lean-limbed, thin-legged, lath-legged [coll.], spindle-legged, spindle-shanked, gangle-shanked [slang].

18. lean-faced, thin-faced, thin-featured, **hatchet-faced;** wizen-faced, weazen-faced; lean-cheeked, thin-cheeked; lean-jawed, **lantern-jawed.**

19. **haggard, poor, peaked** [coll.], **pinched;** shriveled, withered; **wizened,** wizen, wizzen [dial.], weazened, weazen [dial.], weazeny; **emaciated,** emaciate, wasted, attenuated, cadaverous; tabetic, tabid [both med.]; marantic, marasmic [both med.]; **starved,** starveling, starved-looking; **undernourished,** underfed; worn to a shadow, "worn to the bones" [Shakespeare], "weakened and wasted to skin and bone" [Du Bartas].

20. **slenderizing,** reducing, slimming.

ADVS. 21. **narrowly,** closely, nearly, barely, hardly, only just, **by the skin of one's teeth.**

22. **thinly,** thin; meagerly, sparsely, sparingly, scantily.

205. FILAMENT

NOUNS 1. **filament, fiber, thread;** threadlet, filamentule; fibril, fibrilla; capillament [bot.]; cilium, ciliolum; tendril, cirrus, flagellum; gossamer, web, cobweb, spider or spider's web; skein; denier (unit of thread size).

2. **cord, line, string,** strand; ligament, ligature, ligation; twine, rope, wire, cable; strap, strop; braid, twist, inkle, oxreim [S. Africa]; thong, whang [Scot. & dial.], boondoggle [slang, U.S.], brail [falconry].

3. **cordage,** cording, **ropework,** roping; tackle, tack, gear, service or serving [naut.]; ship's ropes 273.30.

4. **strip,** shred, slip, list, spill; **band,** fillet, fascia, taenia; **ribbon,** ribband; tape, tapeline, ticker tape; slat, lath; ligule, ligula [both tech.].

5. **spinner;** silkworm, spider; spinning wheel, spinning jenny, jenny, mule, mule-jenny; throstle; spinning frame, bobbin and

fly frame; spinnerette [rayon mfg.]; spinneret [zool., spinning organ].

VERBS 6. (make threads) **spin;** filament, shred.

ADJS. 7. **threadlike,** thready; **stringy,** ropy, wiry; filamentary, filiform; fibrous, fibry, fibroid, fibrilliform; ligamental; capillary, capilliform; cirrose, cirrous; funicular, funiculate; flagelliform; taeniate, taeniform; ligulate, ligular; gossamery, flossy, silky.

8. **fibers, threads**

acetate rayon	near-silk [chiefly
Acrilon	coll.]
Aralac	nylon
Avisco	oakum
batting	orlon
Celanese	packthread
Chemstrand	Polyfibre
cotton	protein fibers
cotton batting	raffia
Dacron	raw silk
darning cotton	rayon
Dynelo	Rexenite
Fiberfrax	Sarelon
flax	sericin gum
floss, floss silk	sewing thread
Fortisan	silk
harl	sisal, sisal hemp
hemp	soybean fibers
horsehair	spun rayon
jute	tussah
Lastex	Velon
linen	Vicara
manila, manila	Vinyon
hemp	wool
merino	yarn
	zephyr, zephyr yarn

9. **cords**

binding twine	rope
catgut	sennit
clothesline	ship's ropes 273.10
fast	shoelace
gut	shoestring
guy	sinew
guy rope	spermatic cord
hamstring	stay
lace	string
lacing	tendon
lariat	thew
lasso	towline
lead	trace
leader [fishing]	tug
pack twine	twine
pepper-and-salt	umbilical cord
rope [coll.]	whipcord
rein	wire rope

206. HEIGHT

NOUNS 1. **height,** heighth [dial.]; **highness, loftiness, tallness; altitude,** elevation, exaltation, eminence, prominence; stature.

2. **a height, elevation,** eminence, alto [Sp. Amer.], steep; **rise, raise, uprise, lift,** rising ground, vantage point or ground;

heights, soaring *or* towering heights, aerial heights, dizzy height.

3. **highland, upland; highlands, uplands.**

4. **plateau, tableland,** table, bench.

5. **hill, down,** moor [dial., Eng.], brae [Scot. & dial. Eng.], knap, kop [S. Africa], barrow (now only in proper names), fell [Scot. & North. Eng.; now only in proper names]; **hillock,** monticle, monticule, **knoll, hummock,** tummock [Scot. & dial., Eng.], tump [dial., Eng.], kopje [S. Africa]; **mound, swell,** knob; anthill, molehill; **dune,** sand dune; butte [U.S.], picacho [Sp.; Southwest. U.S.], loma [Southwest. U.S.]; drumlin [geol.]; foothills.

6. **ridge,** *arete* [F.], chine, spine, kame [Scot. & North. Eng.], comb [Scot. & dial.], esker; saddle, saddleback; horseback, hogback, hog's-back.

7. **mountain, mount, alp,** hump [aeronaut.]; lofty mountains, towering alps; "the wooded mountains" [Vergil], "the hills, rock-ribbed, and ancient as the sun" [Bryant], "earth's undying monuments" [Hawthorne], "the palaces of Nature" [Byron], "bare steeps where desolation stalks" [Wordsworth], "mountains with hills at their knees" [Leigh Buckner Hanes]; table mountain.

8. **peak,** pike [chiefly North. Eng.], *pico* [Sp.], **pinnacle,** point, **crest,** tor; **mountaintop; hilltop,** knoll [dial., Eng.]; summit 210.2; lofty peak, cloud-capped *or* cloud-topped peak, snowclad peak, "sunbright summit" [Campbell].

9. range, **mountain range, chain,** cordillera [West. U.S.], sierra [U.S.]; "alps on alps" [Pope], hill heaped upon hill.

10. **watershed,** water parting, **divide;** Great Divide.

11. **tower; turret,** *tourelle* [F.]; campanile, bell tower, belfry; cupola; dome; martello, martello tower; barbican; **derrick,** windmill tower, observation tower, fire tower; **spire,** pinnacle; **steeple,** *flèche* [F.]; minaret; stupe, tope, pagoda; pyramid; pylon; sikhara, vimana, gopura [all India]; mole [Rome. antiq.]; shaft, pillar, column; pilaster; obelisk; monument; colossus; skyscraper.

12. (tall person) **longlegs,** longshanks, daddy longlegs, granddaddy longlegs, highpockets, lengthy, long drink of water [all slang or joc.]; bean pole, etc. (tall, thin person) 204.8; six-footer, seven-footer, etc. [coll.].

13. high water, **high tide,** flood tide, spring tide.

14. (measurement of height) altimetry, hypsometry, hypsography; altimeter, hypsometer.

VERBS 15. **tower, spire, soar,** "buss the clouds" [Shakespeare]; rise, **uprise,** ascend, mount, **rear;** stand on tiptoe.

16. **rise above, tower above** *or* **over,** overtop, o'ertop, top, surmount; **overlook,** look over; **command,** dominate, command a view of.

17. (become higher) **grow,** grow up, upgrow; uprise, **rise up,** mount.

18. **heighten,** height [Scot. & dial. Eng.]; elevate 315.5.

ADJS. 19. **high,** high-reaching, **lofty, elevated,** eminent, exalted, prominent, steep, supernal; **towering,** towery, **soaring,** spiring, aspiring, airy, aerial; monumental, colossal; higher than a cat's back [slang], high as a steeple; topless; breast-high, knee-high; high-set, high-pitched.

20. **skyscraping, sky-high,** heaven-reaching, heaven-kissing, "as high as Heaven and as deep as Hell" [Beaumont and Fletcher]; cloud-touching, cloud-surmounting; cloud-topped, cloud-capped.

21. **tall, lengthy** [chiefly coll.]; long 201.11; **rangy, lanky,** lank; **gangling** [coll.], gangly [coll. & dial.]; **long-legged,** long-limbed, leggy, lathy [coll.], lath-legged [coll.], gangle-shanked [slang], spindle-shanked, spindle-legged.

22. **highland,** upland; hill-dwelling, mountain-dwelling.

23. **hilly,** knobby [U.S.]; **mountainous,** mountained, **alpine,** alpen, alpestrine, alpigene; subalpine; monticuline, monticulous, montigeneous, montiform.

24. **higher,** superior, greater; **over,** above, supra; upper, uppermost.

25. highest 210.9.

26. altimetric(al), hypsometric(al), hypsographic(al).

ADVS. 27. **on high,** high up, high; **aloft,** aloof; **up,** upward, upwards; **above, over,** o'er [poetic]; **overhead;** above one's head, over head and ears; skyward, airward, in the air, in the clouds; upstairs, abovestairs; tiptoe, on tiptoe; on stilts; on the shoulders of.

28. **mountains, peaks**

Aconcagua	Batu
Ancohuma	Blackburn
Aneto	Bona
Annapurna	Bonete

Carstensz	Manaslu
Cho Oyu	Markham
Citlaltepec	Matterhorn
Dent Blanche	McKinley
Dhaulagiri	Mercedario
Dom	Meru
Dykh Tau	Mont Blanc
Elbrus	Monte Rosa
Elgon	Nadelhorn
Erebus	Nanga Parbat
Everest	Ojos del Salado
Falso Azufre	Perdido
Foraker	Pissis
Godwin Austen	Popocatepetl
(K2)	Posets
Grand Combin	Ras Dashan
Huascarán	Ruwenzori
Iderburg	Sajama
Iztaccihuatl	Sanford
Kanchenjunga	Shkara
Karisimbi	Steele
Kashtan Tau	St. Elias
Kenya	Täschhorn
Kilimanjaro	Tocorpuri
King	Toubkal
Kirkpatrick	Vancouver
Lenzspitze	Wade
Logan	Weisshorn
Lucania	Wood
Makalu	

29. mountain ranges

Alps	Pamirs
Andes	Pyrenees
Cascades	Rockies
Caucasus	Ruwenzori
Cordillera	Sierra Madre
Elburz	Sierra Nevada
Himalayas	Simen
Hindu Kush	St. Elias
Kamchatka	Ural
Kurlun	Wrangell

207. LOWNESS

NOUNS 1. **lowness, shortness** (as opposed to *tallness*); squatness, squattiness; depression, debasement; subjacency.

2. **low water, low tide,** ebb tide, neap tide, neap.

3. **lowland, lowlands.**

VERBS 4. **lie low,** squat, crouch, couch; lie under, underlie.

5. **lower, depress** 316.4.

ADJS 6. **low, unelevated, short** [as opposed to *tall*]; **squat,** squatty; debased, depressed; **low-lying,** low-set, low-hung; **low-built,** low-sized, low-statured, low-bodied; low-level, low-leveled; neap; knee-high to a grasshopper, ~ duck or jack rabbit [slang], knee-high to a chaw of tobacco [dial.].

7. **low-necked, low-cut, décolleté.**

8. **lower,** inferior, **under, nether,** subjacent; down; less advanced [biol.]; earlier [geol.]

9. **lowest** 211.7.

ADVS. 10. **low,** near the ground; at a low ebb.

ADVS., PREPS. 11. **below,** alow [now chiefly naut.]; **under, underneath, beneath,** 'neath [poetic], aneath [Scot. & dial., Eng.]; belowstairs, downstairs, below deck; underfoot; at the foot of, at the base of; below par, below the mark.

208. DEPTH

NOUNS 1. **depth, deepness,** profoundness, profundity; deep-seatedness, deep-rootedness; bottomlessness, plumblessness, fathomlessness.

2. **pit, deep, depth, hole,** hollow, **cavity,** shaft, well, **gulf, chasm, abyss,** abysm, yawning abyss; crater; crevasse; bowels, bowels of the earth; bottomless pit; infernal pit, hell; dark depths, unknown depths, unfathomed deeps.

3. **ocean depths, deep sea, deep, deeps, depths,** Bassalia [biogeog.], abyss; bottom waters; abyssal zone, bathyal zone, pelagic zone; **bottom of the sea,** "bosom of the Deep" [Milton], "the bottom of the monstrous world" [ibid.], ocean bottom, floor, bed, ground, benthos, benthon, Davy Jones's locker [coll.].

4. **sounding** or **soundings** [naut.], sound, depth sounding; **echo sounding,** echolation; Sonar [sound navigation and ranging], Sofar [sound fixing and ranging]; bathometry, bathymetry; fathomage, water (depth of water).

5. **draft** or **draught** [naut.], submergence, submersion, sinkage, **displacement.**

6. **deepening, lowering, depression;** sinking, sinkage.

VERBS 7. **deepen, lower, depress, sink;** countersink.

8. **sound, take soundings,** make a sounding, heave ~, cast or sling the lead, **fathom, plumb,** plumb-line, plumb the depths.

ADJS. 9. **deep, profound,** deep-down; deepish, deepsome [poetic]; deep-going, deep-lying, deep-reaching; **deep-set,** deep-laid; deep-sunk, deep-sunken, deep-sinking; **deep-seated, deep-rooted,** deep-fixed, deep-settled; deep-cut, deep-engraven; knee-deep, ankle-deep.

10. **abysmal,** abyssal, yawning; **bottomless,** soundless, plumbless, **fathomless,** unfathomed, unfathomable; deep as a well, deep as the sea.

11. **subterranean,** subterraneous, **underground;** buried, deep-buried.

12. underwater, subaqueous; **submarine, undersea;** submerged, submersed, immersed, buried, engulfed, inundated.

13. deep-sea, dipsey [naut.]; bathyal, bathysmal, bathybic [biol.]; benthal, benthonic; abyssal, Bassalian [biogeog.]; bathyorographic(al), bathymetric(al); bathypelagic, benthopelagic.

14. deep-bosomed, bathycolpian, bathycolpic.

15. deepest, deepmost.

ADVS. **16. beyond one's depth,** out of one's depth; over one's head, over head and ears.

17. sounders

bathometer	plummet
bathymeter	probe [surg.]
bob	sonic depth
depth sounder	sounder
dipsey or deep-sea	sound
line or lead	sounding bottle
echo sounder	sounding lead
fathomer	sounding line
fathometer	sounding machine
Kelvin machine	sounding rod
lead	sounding tube
plumb	Tanner-Blish
plumb bob	machine
plumb line	

209. SHALLOWNESS

NOUNS **1. shallowness, depthlessness;** shoalness, shoaliness; **superficiality,** triviality, **cursoriness,** slightness; surface, superficies; veneer, gloss; pinprick, scratch, mere scratch.

2. shoal, shallow, shallows, shallow or shoal water, flat, shelf; **bank, bar,** sandbank, sand bar; **reef,** coral reef; ford.

VERBS **3. shallow,** shoal; fill in or up, silt up.

4. scratch the surface, touch upon, hardly touch, skim, skim over, skim the surface.

5. shallow, shoal, depthless, not deep, unprofound, fleet [chiefly dial., Eng.], ebb [dial.]; **surface,** on the surface; **superficial, cursory,** slight, trivial; skin-deep, ankle-deep, knee-deep; shallow-rooted, shallow-rooting; shallow-draft, shallow-hulled; shallow-sea.

6. shoaly, shelfy; reefy.

210. TOP

NOUNS **1. top,** top side, upper side, upside; surface 223.2; topside [naut.]; upper story, top floor; clerestory or clearstory.

2. summit, top, **tip-top,** peak, pinnacle, **crest, brow,** edge, **crown,** cap, **tip,** point, spire, height, pitch, fastigium, topgallant [fig.]; **apex,** vertex, **acme, zenith, climax,** apogee; **culmination,** culmen; extremity, **maximum, limit,** upper extremity, highest point, very top, extreme limit, utmost height, "the very acme and pitch" [Pope]; meridian, noon [both fig.]; mountaintop 206.8.

3. (top part) **head,** heading, **headpiece,** cap, *caput* [L.], capsheaf [fig.], **crown,** crest; topknot; pinhead, nailhead.

4. capital [arch.], head, crown, cap; bracket capital.

5. head [anat.], headpiece, **pate,** poll [dial. or joc.], crown, top [as in, from *top* to toe]; sconce, noddle [both coll.]; **noodle, noggin,** chump, knob, nob, **bean,** dome, attic, loft, garret, upper story, belfry, bun, cocoa, conk, crumpet, nut, [all slang]; "the dome of Thought, the palace of the Soul" [Byron].

6. skull, cranium; pericranium, epicranium; brainpan, brain box, brain case; think tank, phrenology box [both slang].

7. topping, icing, frosting.

VERBS **8. top, crown, cap,** crest, head, tip, peak, surmount; culminate, consummate, climax; ice, frost (a cake).

ADJS. **9. top,** topmost, **uppermost,** upmost, overmost, **highest;** tiptop, tip-crowning, topgallant [fig.]; **maximum,** maximal; summital, apical, vertical, zenithal, climatic(al); acmic, acmatic; meridian, meridional; **head,** headmost, capital, chief, paramount, supreme, pre-eminent.

10. topping, crowning, capping, heading, surmounting; culminating, consummating, climaxing.

11. topped, headed, **crowned, capped,** crested; tipped, peaked.

12. topless, headless, crownless.

13. cephalic, encephalic.

ADVS., PREPS. **14. atop, on, upon,** at or on the top, **on top of,** topside [coll.]; at the top of the tree or ladder, on top of the roost.

15. architectural toppings

architrave	frontispiece
capstone	gable end
coping	head
coping stone	headboard
corona	header
crown	headmold
drip	head molding
entablature	headpiece
epistyle	headpost
fastigium	headsill
frieze	hoodmold

larmier
lintel
pediment

sconce
tympanum
zoophorus

16. capital styles

Byzantine
Corinthian
Doric
Gothic
Greek
Greek Corinthian
Greek Ionic

Ionic
Moorish
Roman Corinthian
Roman Doric
Romanesque
Roman Ionic
Tuscan

17. capital parts

abacus
antefix
astragal
bell
console
corbel
corona
cymatium
dentil

echinus
gorgerin
gutta
metope
modillion
mutule
taenia
triglyph

211. BOTTOM

NOUNS **1. bottom,** bottom side, under side, **underside,** nether side, lower side, downside, **underneath;** belly, underbelly [both fig.]; breech; **rock bottom, bedrock,** hardpan [chiefly U.S.].

2. base, basement, **foot,** sole; nadir (lowest point); **foundation** 215.6; baseboard mopboard [U.S.]; wainscot.

3. (ground part) **ground,** earth, *terra firma* [L.]; **floor,** flooring; parquet; **deck; pavement,** pave [chiefly U.S.], *pavé* [F.], paving; carpet.

4. bed [of water], **bottom, floor,** ground, **basin, channel,** coulee [U.S.]; ocean bottom 208.3.

5. foot [anat.], sole [chiefly poetic], extremity [affected or joc.], pes [*pl.* pedes], pedal [affected or joc.], *pied* [F.], hand (as of an ape or hawk), **trotter** [joc. exc. zool.], pedal extremity, **dog** [U.S.], beetle-crusher, dew-beater, kick, kicker, tootsy [all slang]; **hoof** [joc. exc. zool.], ungula; **paw, pad,** *patte* [F., her.], pat [slang], pud [coll.]; forefoot, forepaw; harefoot, splayfoot, clubfoot; toe, tootsy [slang]; heel; sole; instep, arch; pastern; fetlock.

VERBS **6. base on, found on, ground on, build on,** bottom on, bed on.

ADJS. **7. bottom,** bottommost, **undermost,** nethermost, lowermost, **lowest; rock-bottom,** bedrock [coll.]; ground.

8. basic, basal, basilar; **underlying, fundamental,** radical, essential, elementary, elemental, primary, primal, primitive, rudimentary, original; nadiral.

9. based on, founded on, grounded on, bedded on, built on.

NOUNS **1. verticalness,** verticality; **erectness,** uprightness, up-and-downness; **perpendicularity,** plumbness, aplomb; rightangledness, right-angularity, orthogonality.

2. vertical, upright, perpendicular, plumb, normal [geom.]; right angle, orthodiagonal; vertical circle, azimuth circle.

3. precipice, cliff, steep, *peña* [Sp., Southwest. U.S.], **bluff,** wall, scar, krans [S. Africa]; crag, craig [Scot. & North. Eng.]; scarp, escarpment; **palisade,** palisades.

4. erection, erecting, **elevation;** rearing, raising; **uprearing,** upraising, upraisal, uplifting.

5. rising, uprising, uprisal; rise, uprise.

6. (instruments) square, T square, try square, set square, carpenter's square; plumb, plumb line, plumb rule, plummet, bob, plumb bob, lead.

VERBS **7. rise, arise, uprise, rise up, get up,** get to one's feet; **stand up,** stand erect *or* upright; stand up straight, **stand on end; stick up,** cock up; bristle; **rear,** uprear, rear up, rise on the hind legs; upheave; sit up, sit bolt upright; jump up, spring to one's feet.

8. erect, elevate, rear, raise, pitch, **set up,** raise up, lift up, cast up; uprear, upraise, uplift, upheave; upright; **upend,** stand on end; set on its feet.

9. plumb, plumb-line, set *à plomb* [F.]; **square.**

ADJS. **10. vertical, upright,** bolt upright, **erect,** upstanding, standing up, stand-up; **upended,** upraised, upreared; **downright.**

11. perpendicular, sheer, plumb, plum, straight-up, straight-up-and-down, **up-and-down,** rampant [her.]; precipitous 217.12; **right-angled,** right-angle, right-angular, orthogonal, orthodiagonal.

ADVS. **12. vertically, erectly,** upstandingly, uprightly, **upright,** up; **on end,** up on end, right on end, endwise, endways; on one's feet *or* legs, on one's hind legs [coll.].

13. perpendicularly, perpendicular [careless]; sheer, sheerly; up and down, **straight up and down; plumb,** plum, *à plomb* [F.]; at right angles, square.

213. HORIZONTALNESS

NOUNS **1. horizontalness,** horizontality, horizontalism; **levelness, flatness,** evenness, flushness.

2. recumbency, decumbency, accum-

bency, accubation; **prostration, proneness;**
supineness, supination; reclining, reclination; lying, lounging, **repose;** sprawl, loll.

3. horizontal, plane, level, flat, homaloid [math.], dead level *or* flat; horizontal plane, level plane; horizontal line, level line; horizontal projection; horizontal parallax; horizontal axis; horizontal fault; water level, sea level, mean sea level; parterre; esplanade; ground, earth, floor; bowling green, table, billiard table.

4. horizon, sky line, rim of the horizon; **sea line, offing;** apparent ∼, local *or* visible horizon, sensible horizon, celestial ∼, rational ∼, geometrical *or* true horizon, artificial *or* false horizon; azimuth.

VERBS **5. lie, lie down, recline, repose,** lounge, couch; lie flat *or* prostrate, lie on its face *or* back, lie on a level; sprawl, loll.

6. level, flatten, even, equalize, align *or* aline, flush; grade [U.S.], bulldoze; lay, lay down, lay out; **raze** *or* rase, fell, lay level, lay level with the ground.

7. prostrate, supinate, prone [South. U.S.]; fell 316.5.

ADJS. **8. horizontal, level, flat, even, flush,** homaloidal [math.]; **plane,** plain; flat as a pancake, "flat as a cake" [Erasmus], flat as a billiard table *or* bowling green, flat as a board, "flat as a flounder" [John Fletcher], "flat as a prairie" [Lowell].

9. recumbent, accumbent, procumbent, decumbent; **prostrate, prone,** flat; supine, resupine; couchant, *couché* [F.]; **lying, reclining,** reposing; sprawling, lolling; on one's back; on all fours.

ADVS. **10. horizontally, flat,** flatly, flatways, flatwise; **evenly,** flush; **level, on a level;** lengthwise, lengthways, at full length.

214. PENDENCY

NOUNS **1. pendency,** pendulousness, pendulosity, pensility; **hanging, suspension,** suspense, dependence *or* dependency.

2. hang, droop, dangle, swing, fall; sag, bag.

3. overhang, overhanging, impendence *or* impendency, **projection,** beetling, jutting.

4. pendant, pendle [dial.], *pendeloque* [F.]; hanger; **hanging,** drape; lobe, lobule, lobation, lappet, ear lobe.

5. suspender, hanger, supporter; **suspenders,** pair of suspenders, braces [Eng.], galluses [dial.], gallows [chiefly dial.].

VERBS **6. hang,** hang down, fall; de-

pend, pend [chiefly dial.]; **dangle,** swing, flap, flop [coll.]; flow; drape (fall in folds); **droop,** lop; **sag,** swag [dial.], bag; **trail,** drag, **draggle,** drabble, daggle.

7. overhang, hang over, hang out, **impend,** impend over, **project over, beetle, jut,** beetle *or* jut over, stick out over.

8. suspend, hang, **hang up,** put up, fasten up; sling.

ADJS. **9. pendent,** pendulous, pendulant, pendular, penduline [zool.], pensile; **suspend,** hung; **hanging,** pending, depending, dependent; dangling, swinging; weeping (as a willow), cernuous (as a flower), nodding [bot.]; flowing.

10. drooping, droopy, limp, loose, floppy [coll.], loppy, lop; **sagging,** saggy [chiefly dial.]; **bagging,** baggy; lop-eared.

11. overhanging, overhung; **impending,** impendent; incumbent, superincumbent; pendulous, pending; **projecting, jutting; beetling,** beetle; beetle-browed.

12. lobular, lobar, lobate, lobated.

13. pendants

bell rope	queue
drop	skirt
eardrop	tail
earring	tailpiece
flap	tassel
hangnail	tippet
lavaliere	tossel [dial.]
liripipe [hist.]	trail
lobe	train
pendulum	wattle
pigtail	

14. suspenders, hangers

belt	knob
button	nail
clothes hanger	peg
clotheshorse	pendant post
clothesline	[arch.]
clothespin	pendant tackle
clothes tree	[naut.]
coat hanger	pothanger
gallows	pothook
garter	ring
gibbet	sock suspenders
hanger bolt	spar
hanging post	stud
hook	tenterhook
horse	

215. SUPPORT

NOUNS **1. support, backing, upholding,** upkeep, maintenance, sustainment, sustenance, sustentation.

2. supporter, support, upholder, sustainer, maintainer, staff [fig.], stave [fig.], crutch [fig.], stay, **prop,** fulcrum, **brace,** bracer, buttress [fig.], shoulder [fig.], arm [fig.]; **mainstay,** backbone, reliance, dependerce; reinforcement, reinforce, strengthener; back, backing; rest, resting place.

3. (mythology) Altas, Hercules, tortoise that supports the earth.

4. **buttress,** buttressing; abutment, shoulder; **bulwark,** rampart; **embankment,** bank; **breakwater,** sea wall, mole, jetty, jutty, groin; **pier,** pier buttress, buttress pier; flying buttress, *arc-boutant* [F.]; hanging buttress.

5. **footing, foothold, toehold,** hold, purchase; **standing,** stand, stance, standing place, *locus standi* [L.]; footrest, footrail; footstool, cricket, ottoman.

6. **foundation,** *fond* [F.], **base, basis,** basement, pavement, **ground,** grounds, **groundwork, seat,** sill, fundament; bed, bedding; **substructure,** substruction, substratum, **understructure,** understruction, underbuilding, underpinning; stereobate, stylobate; hypostasis, anlage, fundamental, principle, radical, rudiment; solid ground, *terra firma* [L.]; solid rock or bottom, rock bottom, bedrock; riprap [U.S.].

7. **foundation stone,** footstone; **cornerstone, keystone,** headstone, first stone, quoin.

8. **pedestal, base; stand,** standard; dado, die; plinth, subbase; surbase; socle.

9. **sill,** groundsill, groundsel; mudsill; window sill; doorsill, threshold; doorstone.

10. **mounting,** mount, **backing, setting,** frame.

11. **handle, hold,** grip, grasp, haft, helve.

12. **scaffold,** scaffolding, *échafaudage* [F.]; stage, staging.

13. **platform,** flatform [dial.]; **stage,** estrade, dais, floor; **rostrum, podium, pulpit** [church], suggestum [Rom. antiq.], **soapbox** [chiefly coll.]; hustings [polit.], stump [U.S.]; tribune, tribunal; emplacement (gun platform); catafalque (funeral scaffold platform); landing stage, landing; terrace, step terrace; **balcony, gallery.**

14. **shelf,** shelve, **ledge;** settle; shoulder; mantel, mantelshelf, mantelpiece; retable, superaltar, gradin, *gradino* [It.], predella [all eccl.]; hob (on a fireplace).

15. **table,** board, **stand;** dining table, the mahogany [coll.]; tea table, teapoy; bench, workbench, worktable; **counter, bar,** buffet.

16. **desk,** writing table, **secretary,** *secrétaire* [F.], escritoire; **lectern,** ambo, reading desk.

17. **trestle,** trest [Scot. & dial.], **horse;** sawhorse, buck [U.S.]; clotheshorse; trestle board or table, trestle and table; trestlework, trestling.

18. **seat, chair,** sill; **bench,** form.

19. **saddle,** cack or kack [slang, U.S.]; montura, hull, leather, wood, pine [all West. U.S.]; **pommel,** horn; apple, biscuit, nubbin [all slang]; cantle; saddle skirts, bastos [West. U.S.]; jockey; girth, girt, surcingle, bellyband; cinch, latigo [West. U.S.]; stirrup.

20. **bed, couch, bunk,** kip [dial. & slang]; doss, hay [U.S.], downy, the feathers, flop [U.S.], roost [all slang]; shakedown, breakdown [slang, U.S.]; bedstead; **litter, stretcher.**

21. **bedding,** underbed, underbedding; **mattress,** paillasse, pallet; innerspring mattress; pad, mat, rug; litter, bedstraw; **pillow,** cushion, bolster; **springs,** bed springs, box springs.

VERBS 22. **support, bear,** carry, **hold, sustain, maintain, bolster,** back, shoulder, give ~, furnish ~, afford ~, supply or lend support; **hold up, bear up, bolster** up, keep up, back up; **uphold,** upbear, upkeep; **brace, prop,** crutch, buttress; shore, shore up; stay, mainstay; underbrace, underprop, underpin, underset; cradle; cushion, pillow.

23. **rest on,** bear on, **stand on, lie on,** recline on, repose on, **lean on,** abut on; sit on, perch, ride; **straddle,** bestraddle, stride, bestride; underlie, be based on, be at the bottom of, form the foundation of.

ADJS. 24. **supporting, bearing, holding,** upholding, maintaining, sustaining, sustentative, suspensory; bracing, propping, bolstering, buttressing.

25. **supported,** borne, upborne, held, **upheld, sustained,** maintained; braced, propped, bolstered, buttressed; based on 211.9.

ADVS. 26. **astride, astraddle,** straddle, straddle-legged, straddleback, on the back of; horseback, on horseback; pickaback.

27. **supports**

anvil	maulstick
back rest	music stand
bandage	prop
block	raker
brace	ratline
cue rest	rib
easel	shoe
guy	shore
heel	shoring
hod	shroud
lap	skid

sole
splint
stand
stay
stilts

stirrup
strut
tripod
trivet
umbrella **stand**

28. handles

bail
bow
brace
brake
crank
crop
doorknob
handle bar
handstaff
helm
hilt
knob
knocker
loom
lug
panhandle

pull
rounce
rudder
sally
shaft
shank
snatch
snead [chiefly
  Scot. & dial.]
spindle
stock
tiller
tote
trigger
withe

29. brackets

ancon
angle
angle iron
brace
cantilever
cheek
consol

corbel
cul-de-lampe [F.]
gusset
modillion
shoulder
strut

30. tables

captain's table
coffee table
console *or* console
  table
dinette table
dining table
dresser
dressing table
drop-leaf table
extension table
gate-leg *or* gate-

legged table
kitchen table
lampstand
round table
sideboard
side table
taboret
tea table
tea wagon
trivet table
turntable

31. seats, chairs

armchair
armless chair
back seat
barrel chair
bar stool
basket chair
bed chair
bicycle seat
Boston rocker
boudoir chair
bow-back chair
bucket seat
campaign chair
camp chair
campstool
captain's chair
channel-back chair
club chair
club lounge chair
cocktail chair
comb-back chair
contour chair
cricket chair

deck chair
dining chair
draft chair
easy chair
elbowchair
fan-back chair
fauteuil [F.]
folding chair
foldstool
gaddi [India]
garden chair
hassock
high chair
horse
howdah
ladder-back chair
lawn chair
long chair
long-sleeve chair
  [Anglo-Ind.]
lounge chair
milking stool
Morris chair

musnud [Oriental]
occasional chair
ottoman
overstuffed chair
pew
platform rocker
Priscilla rocker
pull-up chair
railroad chair
raj-gaddi [India]
recliner
reclining lounge
  chair
rocker
rocking chair
rumble seat
saddle

saddle seat
sedan chair
snack stool
steamer chair
step stool
stool
straight chair
swing
swing chair
swivel chair
taboret
throne
tub chair
TV chair
Windsor chair
wing chair

32. saddles

aparejo [West.
  U.S.]
bridal saddle
cavalry saddle
cowboy saddle
English cavalry
  saddle
English riding
  saddle
English saddle

jockey saddle
packsaddle
panel
pillion
racing saddle
riding saddle
sidesaddle
stock saddle
U.S. cavalry saddle
Western saddle

33. sofas

causeuse [F.]
chaise longue [F.]
couch
dais [Scot.]
davenport
day bed
divan
lounge
love seat

ottoman
settee
settle
spoonholder
  [local, U.S.]
squab
studio couch
tête-à-tête [F.]

34. beds

bassinet
bed-davenport
berth
bunk
bunk bed
Colonial bed
cot
cradle
crib
day bed
door bed
double bed
double bunk
duplex bed
feather bed
fold-away bed
folding bed
four-poster

French bed
hammock
Hollywood bed
hospital bed
lower [R.R.]
nest (birds)
pallet
panel bed
poster bed
roll-away bed
single bed
sofa-bed
tester bed
three-quarter bed
trestle bed
truckle bed
trundle bed
upper [R.R.]

216. SHAFT

NOUNS **1. shaft, pole, bar, rod, stick;
stalk, stem;** thill; tongue, wagon tongue,
nib [dial., Eng.], neap [U.S.], disselboom
[S. Africa]; reach, wagon reach, perch; flag-
pole, flagstaff; totem pole; Maypole; telephone pole, telegraph pole; tent pole.

2. staff, stave; **cane, stick, walking**

stick, handstaff; Malacca cane; swagger
stick, swanking stick; pilgrim's staff, bourdon [hist.]; pastoral staff, shepherd's staff,
crook; crosier, cross-staff, cross, paterissa;
pikestaff, alpenstock; quarterstaff, lathee
[Anglo-Ind.]; cowlstaff [hist. & dial.]; lituus
[Rom. antiq.]; thyrsus [Gr. rel.]; **crutch**,
crutch-stick [dial. U.S.].

3. **beam, timber,** caber, pole, spar
[dial.].

4. **post, standard, upright;** king post,
crown post; newel; banister, baluster; balustrade, balustrading; gatepost, swinging
or hinging post, shutting post; doorpost,
jamb, doorjamb; stile, mullion; stanchion,
stanchel [Scot.], stancher [Scot. & North.
Eng.]; hitching post, snubbing post.

5. **pillar, column,** post, pier; pilaster;
colonnette, columella; caryatid; atlas [pl.
atlantes], telamon [pl. telamones]; colonnade, arcade, pilastrade, portico, peristyle.

6. **leg,** shank; legs [anat.] 272.16.

7. **stake,** stob [dial.], peg; pile, spile;
picket, pale, palisade.

8. **beams**

angle rafter	ridge strut
balk	scantling
batten	sill
boom	sleeper
box girder	spar
breastsummer	sprit
corbel	stringpiece
crossbeam	strut
crosstie	stud
footing beam	studding
girder	summer
hammer beam	summertree
H beam	tie
hip rafter	tie beam
I beam	transom
joist	transverse
lattice girder	trave
lintel	traverse
plate girder	truss
rafter	truss beam
ridgepole	

217. PARALLELISM

Physically Parallel Direction or State.—
NOUNS 1. **parallelism, coextension,** collaterality, concurrence, equidistance; col-
lineation, collimation [physics & astron.];
parallelization; parallelotropism.

2. **parallel,** paralleler; parallel line, par-
allel dash, parallel bar, parallel file, par-
allel series, parallel columns, parallel trench
[mil.]; parallelogram, parallel vectors, parallelepiped, parallelepipedon [all geom.].

3. (instruments) parallel rule or ruler,
parallelograph, parallelometer.

VERBS 4. **parallel, coextend,** run parallel, go alongside, go beside, run abreast;
match, equal.

5. **parallelize,** place parallel to, equidistance; line up, align; collineate, collimate
[physics & astron.]; match; correspond, follow, equate.

ADJS. 6. **parallel,** paralleling, **coextend-
ing,** coextensive, **equidistant,** equispaced,
collateral, concurrent; **alongside, abreast;**
lined up, aligned; equal, even; parallelo-
grammic(al), parallelogrammatic(al); parallelepipedal [geom.]; parallelotropic; parallelodrome, parallelinervate [both bot.].

218. OBLIQUITY

NOUNS 1. **obliquity,** obliqueness; **deviation,** divergence, digression, excursion,
declination; deflection, deflexure; diagonality; bevel, bezel.

2. **inclination, leaning,** lean; **slant,**
slaunch [dial.], **slope,** rake; **tilt, tip,** pitch,
list, cant, swag, sway; leaning tower, tower
of Pisa.

3. **bias, bend,** bent, crook, **warp, twist,
turn,** skew, slue, veer, sheer, swerve.

4. **incline,** inclination, **slope, grade,**
gradient [chiefly Eng.], pitch, ramp, bank
[dial.], talus, sideling [chiefly dial.]; gentle
or easy slope, glacis; rapid or steep slope,
stiff climb, scarp, chute; helicline (curving ramp); hillside, side; hanging gardens;
shelving beach.

5. **declivity, descent,** dip, drop, fall,
decline; hang, hanging; **downgrade,** downgate [Scot.], **downhill.**

6. **acclivity, ascent,** climb, **rise,** rising,
uprise, uprising, rising ground; **upgrade,
uphill,** upgo, upclimb, uplift, upwith
[chiefly Scot.]; steepness, precipitousness,
abruptness.

7. **diagonal,** oblique, transverse, bias.

8. **zigzag,** zig, zag; zigzaggery, flexuosity
[bot.]; chevron [spec. arch.].

VERBS 9. **oblique, deviate, diverge,** deflect, **bear off;** angle, **angle off; swerve,**
veer, sheer, sway, slue, skew, **twist, turn,**
bend, bias; crook, crooken, crump [dial.].

10. **incline, lean; slope, slant,** slaunch
[dial.], rake, pitch, bank, shelve; **tilt, tip,
list,** cant, careen, keel, sidle, swag, sway;
ascend, rise, uprise, climb, **go uphill;**
descend, decline, dip, drop, fall, **go downhill;** retreat (slope backwards).

11. **catercorner,** cater [dial.], diagonalize.

12. **zigzag,** zig, zag, **stagger,** crankle, wind in and out.

ADJS. 13. **oblique, devious,** deviative, **indirect,** side, sidelong; left-handed, sinister; backhand, backhanded; circuitous 319.7.

14. **askew,** skew, skewed; **awry,** wry; **askance,** askant, asquint; skew-jawed, skewgee, askewgee, agee *or* ajee, agee-jawed, wamper-jawed, catawampous, catawamptious, yaw-ways [all dial. *or* slang]; cockeyed, screwy [both slang, U.S.]; **crooked** 248.11.

15. **inclining,** inclined, inclinatory, inclinational; **leaning,** recumbent; **sloping,** sloped, aslope; raking, pitched; **slanting,** slanted, slant, aslant, slantways, slantwise; bias, biased; shelving, shelvy; **tilting,** tilted, atilt, tipped, **tipping,** listing, canting, careening; sideling, sidelong; out of the perpendicular, slantidicular [joc.]; bevel, beveled.

16. (sloping downward) **downhill, downgrade; descending,** falling, dropping, dipping; **declining,** declined; declivous, declivitous, declivate, declive; hanging (as, *hanging* gardens), pendent (as, a *pendent* hillside); anticlinal; synclinal.

17. (sloping upward) **uphill, upgrade; rising,** uprising, **ascending,** climbing; acclivous, acclivitous, acclinate.

18. **steep, precipitous, bluff,** abrupt, bold, **sheer,** sharp, rapid; headlong, breakneck; stiff, arduous, heavy.

19. **transverse,** across 220.9.

20. **diagonal,** bendwise [her.], antigodlin *or* antigoglin [dial., U.S.]; **catercorner** *or* **catercornered,** catacorner *or* catacornered, cattycorner *or* cattycornered, kittycorner *or* kittycornered [U.S.], capercorner *or* capercornered [dial., U.S.]; bias, biased, catabiased [dial.].

21. **zigzag,** zigzagged, zigzaggy, zigzagwise, zigzagways; flexuous [bot.], staggered, crankled; chevrony, chevronwise, chevronways [all spec. arch.].

ADVS. 22. **obliquely, deviously,** deviately, **indirectly; sideways,** sidewise, sidelong, sideling, on *or* to one side, by a side wind; at an angle; akimbo, hand on hip.

23. **askew, awry; askance,** askant, asquint.

24. **slantingly, slopingly,** aslant, aslope, atilt, slopewise, slopeways, slantwise, slantways, aslantwise; slaunchwise, slaunchways [both dial.]; **downhill, downgrade; uphill, upgrade.**

25. **transversely,** across 220.13.

26. **diagonally,** diagonalwise; **on the bias,** bias, biaswise; **cornerwise,** cornerways; catercornerways, catacornerways, **catercorner,** catacorner, cattycorner, kittycorner [U.S.], capercorner [dial., U.S.], cater [dial.].

219. INVERSION

NOUNS 1. **inversion,** resupination [bot.]; eversion, ectropion [med.]; introversion, retroflexion; reverse, **reversal,** reversion, revulsion; transposition, transposal; topsy-turvy, topsy-turvydom, topsy-turvyhood.

2. **overturn, upset,** overset, **overthrow,** upturn, **turnover,** spill [coll.]; subversion, subversal; **capsizal,** capsize; **somersault,** somerset, *culbute* [F.]; cart wheel.

3. (grammar and rhetoric) metastasis, metathesis; anastrophe, chiasmus, hypallage, hyperbaton, hysteron proteron, palindrome, parenthesis, synchysis, tmesis.

4. inverse, reverse, opposite 15.2.

VERBS 5. **invert,** inverse; introvert; **turn down; turn inside out,** turn out, evert; **reverse,** transpose, convert; put the cart before the horse; turn the tables, turn the scale *or* balance.

6. **overturn, turn over, turn upside down,** turn bottom side up, upturn, **upset,** overset, **overthrow,** subvert, *culbuter* [F.]; turn a somersault, go head over heels; **turn turtle,** turn topsy-turvy, topsy-turvy, topsy-turvify; **tip over,** keel over, topple over; **capsize.**

ADJS. 7. **inverted,** inversed; **reversed,** transposed; **inside out,** outside in, wrong side out; **upside-down, topsy-turvy;** hyperbatic, palindromic(al) [both gram.]; resupinate [bot.]; introverted.

ADVS. 8. **upside down,** over, **topsy-turvy;** topside-turfway, topside-totherway, topside-the-other-way [all slang]; **bottom up,** bottom side up; head over heels, heels over head.

220. CROSSING

NOUNS 1. **crossing, intercrossing,** intersecting, **intersection;** decussation, chiasma [anat. & biol.]; traversal, transversion; cruciation.

2. **crossway, crossing, crosswalk, crossroad,** crosspoint [Eng.], *carrefour* [F.], **intersection,** intercrossing; level crossing [Eng.], grade crossing [U.S.]; overcrossing, undercrossing; traffic circle, rotary; cloverleaf.

3. **network, webwork, meshwork,** tis-

sue, texture, reticulum; reticulation, cancellation; **net**, netting; **mesh**, meshes, moke [dial., Eng.]; **web,** webbing; weave, weft; lace, lacery, lacing, lacework; screen, screening; sieve, riddle; wicker, wickerwork; basketwork, basketry; lattice, latticework; trellis, trelliswork; grate, grating; grill, grille, grillwork; grid, gridiron; tracery, fretwork, fret, filigree; plexus, plexure; reticle, reticule [both optics]; wattle.

4. cross, crux [spec. her.], cruciform; crucifix, rood; **crisscross,** christcross; X, ex; T, tau; crossbones, skull and crossbones.

5. crosspiece, traverse, transverse, cross bitt [naut.]; **crossbar,** crossarm; swingletree, singletree, whiffletree, whippletree; doubletree.

VERBS **6. cross, crisscross; intersect,** intercross, decussate; **cut across,** crosscut; **traverse,** lie across; crossbar.

7. net, web, mesh; lattice, trellis; grate, grid.

ADJS. **8. cross, crossing, crossed; crisscross, crisscrossed; intersecting, intersected,** intersectional; crosscut, cut across; decussate, decussated; chiasmal, chiasmic [both anat. & biol.]; secant [geom.].

9. transverse, transversal, traverse; **across, cross,** crossway, **crosswise,** thwart; overthwart; oblique 218.13.

10. crucial, cruciate, **cruciform, crosslike,** cross-shaped, x-shaped, cross, crossed; cruciferous.

11. netlike, retiform, plexiform; reticular, reticulate, reticulated; cancellate, cancellated; **netted,** netty; **meshed,** meshy; laced, lacy, lacelike; latticed, latticelike; grated, gridded; barred, crossbarred; streaked, striped.

12. webbed, webby, weblike; webfooted, palmiped.

ADVS. **13. crosswise,** crossways, crossway, **cross, crisscross, across,** thwart, thwartly, thwartways, **athwart,** athwartwise, overthwart; **traverse,** traversely; transverse, transversely, transversally; obliquely 218.22; **sideways,** sidewise; contrariwise, contrawise; cross-grained, across the grain; athwartship, athwartships.

221. WEAVING

NOUNS **1. weaving,** texture; **interweaving,** interweavement, intertexture; **interlacing,** interlacement, interlacery; **intertwining,** intertwinement; intertieing, interknitting, interthreading, intertwisting; **lacing,** enlacement; **twining,** entwining, enwinement; wreathing, knitting, twisting; **braiding,** plaiting.

2. web 220.3; fabric 377.5.

3. braid, plait, plat [dial.]; **wreath,** wreathwork.

4. warp; woof, weft, filling; shoot, pick.

5. weaver; weaverbird, weaver finch, whirligig beetle.

6. loom, weaver; hand loom; knitting machine.

VERBS **7. weave,** loom, tissue; **interweave, interlace, intertwine,** interknit, interthread, intertissue, intertie, intertwist; inweave, intort; web, net; **lace,** enlace; **twine,** entwine; **braid,** plait, pleat [dial., Eng.], plat; **wreath,** raddle, knit, twist, mat, wattle; twill; loop, noose; splice.

ADJS. **8. woven,** textile; **interwoven, interlaced,** interthreaded, **intertwined,** interknit, intertissued, intertied, intertwisted; **laced,** enlaced; **wreathed,** fretted, raddled, knit; **twined,** entwined; **braided,** plaited, platted.

9. twining, entwining; **intertwining, interlacing,** interweaving.

222. SEWING

NOUNS **1. sewing, needlework,** stitching, stitchery, suture; **fancywork;** garment making 230.31.

2. sewer, needleworker; **seamstress,** sempstress, needlewoman; embroider, embroideress; knitter; garmentmaker 230.33–35.

3. sewing machine, sewer.

VERBS **4. sew, stitch,** needle; sew up; tailor.

5. sew

backstitch	overcast
baste	overhand
bind	purl
buttonhole	quilt
chain-stitch	renter
crochet	run
cross-stitch	saddle-stitch
double-stitch	seam
embroider	single-stitch
fell	tack
finedraw	tat
hemstitch	whip
knit	whipstitch
machine-stitch	

6. needlework

basting	cross-stitching
binding	embroidery
buttonholing	felling
chain-stitching	finedrawing
crochet	hemming
crocheting	hemstitching
crochet work	knitting

knitwork	quilting
machine stitching	tacking
netting	tatting
overcasting	whipstitching
purling	

7. stitches

carpet stitch	needle point
chain stitch	over-and-over
coral stitch	stitch
cord stitch	saddleback stitch
cross-stitch	saddle stitch
damask stitch	saddle wire stitch
double stitch	side stitch
glover's stitch	side thread stitch
half stitch	side wire stitch
hemstitch	single stitch
lace stitch	suture [surgery]
machine stitch	twist stitch
	whipstitch

8. needles

between	knitting wire
blunt	long-eyed sharp
crochet hook	sacking needle
darner	sewing-machine
darning needle	needle
embroidery needle	sewing needle
ground-down	sharp
knitting needle	tacking needle
knitting pin	

223. EXTERIORITY

NOUNS 1. exteriority, externality, **outwardness**, outerness; extraterritoriality, extrality [coll.].

2. **exterior, external, outside; surface,**
superficies, top; disk [bot.]; **face, facet;**
extrados [arch.].

3. **outdoors,** outside, **the out-of-doors,**
the great out-of-doors, the open, **the open
air.**

4. externalization, exteriorization; objectification, actualization.

VERBS 5. **externalize,** exteriorize; **objectify,** actualize.

ADJS. 6. **exterior, external; outer, outside, out, outward,** outlying, outstanding;
outermost, outmost; surface, superficial;
peripheral, round about; exomorphic
[geol.].

7. **outdoor, out-of-door,** out-of-doors,
outside; open-air, alfresco.

8. extraterritorial, exterritorial; extraterrestrial, exterrestrial, extramundane; extralateral, extraliminal, extramural, extrapolar,
extrasolar, extraprovincial, extratribal.

ADVS. 9. **externally, outwardly,** exte-
riorly; **without, outside,** outwards, out.

10. **outdoors, out of doors, outside,**
abroad; in the open, **in the open air,** alfresco.

224. INTERIORITY

NOUNS 1. interiority, internality, **inwardness,** innerness, inness; internalization.

2. **interior, inside,** inner, inward, internal, interne or intern [poetic]; innermost,
inner recess, recesses, **innermost recesses,**
penetralia; bosom; intrados [arch.]; center
225.2.

3. **inland,** inlands, **interior,** incountry
[Scot.], upcountry [coll.]; **midland,** mid-
lands; hinterland 181.2.

4. (inside parts) **insides, innards** [dial.
& slang], inwards, inners [coll. & dial.], internals; **guts** [slang], entrails, **bowels,**
vitals, viscera [all fig.].

5. (vital organs) **vitals, viscera,** internals, inners [coll. & dial.], insides [coll.],
innards [dial. & slang], inwards [coll.], inner man [joc.]; **giblets** (of a fowl); **heart,**
ticker [slang]; **brain, lungs, liver, kidneys,
gizzard** (of a fowl); stomach, abdomen
192.3.

6. **intestines, entrails, bowels, guts,**
tripes [dial.], gizzard [joc. & coll.], chitterlings (of animals), stuffings [slang], puddings [dial. & slang]; large intestine, small
intestine; blind gut, caecum; fore-gut, hind-
gut; mid-gut, mesogaster; colon; duodenum,
jejunum, ileum; appendix, vermiform appendix or process; rectum, anus.

7. enterology, enterography, splanchnology.

VERBS 8. internalize, put in, keep within.

ADJS. 9. **interior, internal, inner, inside,
inward,** intestine; **innermost,** inmost, intimate; indoor.

10. **inland, interior,** upcountry [coll.];
hinterland 181.8; **midland,** mediterranean;
inshore.

11. intramarginal, intramural, intramundane, intramontane, intraterritorial, intracoastal, intragroupal.

12. **visceral,** splanchnic; **intestinal,** enteric; colonic, colic; caecal, duodenal, ileac,
jejunal, mesogastric, appendical; rectal,
anal; cardiac; pneumonic, pulmonic.

ADVS. 13. **internally, inwardly,** inte-
riorly, inly; under the surface.

14. **in, inside, within,** withinside
[Scot.], ben [Scot.]; herein, therein, wherein.

15. **inward, inwards, inwardly,** with-
inward, withinwards; inland, inshore.

16. **indoors,** indoor, withindoors.

PREPS. 17. **in, into; within,** at, inside,
inside of, in the limits of.

225. CENTRALITY

NOUNS **1. centrality,** centralness; centricity, centricality; concentricity; eccentricity.

2. center, middle, centrum, centry; centroid; **heart, core, nucleus, kernel; pith, marrow,** medulla [anat. & bot.]; **hub,** nave, axis, pivot; **navel,** umbilicus, omphalos; bull's-eye; dead center; metacenter; epicenter [geol.]; center of gravity, center of mass.

3. (biology) central body, centriole, centrosome, centrosphere.

4. focus, focal point; **center of interest** or attention, focus of attention, center of consciousness; **center of attraction,** cynosure; polestar, lodestar.

5. nerve center, ganglion [fig.], center of activity.

6. headquarters, H.Q., central station, main office, seat, base, **base of operations,** center of authority; general headquarters, **G.H.Q.;** company headquarters, orderly room [mil.]; SHAEF (Supreme Headquarters, Allied Expeditionary Forces), SHAFE (Supreme Headquarters, Allied Forces in Europe).

7. metropolis (principal center), seat, base.

8. art center, medical center, shopping center, shipping center, railroad center, etc.

9. centralization, centering; **focalization,** focusing; convergence 297; **concentration,** concentralization; centralism; decentralization.

VERBS **10. centralize, center,** middle; center round, center on or in; decentralize.

11. focus, focalize, come to a point or focus, bring into focus; **concentrate,** concentralize, concenter; converge 297.2.

ADJS. **12. central,** centric(al), **middle;** centermost, middlemost, **midmost;** umbilical, omphalic; axial, pivotal; centroidal; centrosymmetric; geocentric(al) [astron.].

13. nuclear, nucleal, nucleary, nucleate.

14. focal, confocal [math.]; converging 290.3; centrolineal, centripetal.

15. concentric(al), homocentric(al); coaxial, coaxal.

16. eccentric, off-center, off-balanced, unbalanced, uncentered.

ADVS. **17. centrally,** in the center or middle of, at the heart of.

226. LAYER

NOUNS **1. layer,** thickness; **level, tier,** stage, story, deck, dess [Scot. & North. Eng.]; **stratum, seam** [geol.], belt, **bed, course,** measure [geol.]; zone [geol.]; shelf; **overlayer, superstratum,** overstory [forestry]; **underlayer, substratum,** understratum, understory [forestry]; floor, bedding.

2. lamina, lamella; **sheet,** leaf, foil; wafer, disk; **plate,** plating; **coat,** coating, veneer, film, scum, membrane, pellicle, peel, skin; slice, cut, rasher, collop; **slab,** slat, tablet, table; panel, pane; **fold,** lap, flap, ply, plait; laminated glass, safety glass; laminated wood, plywood.

3. flake, fleck, flag [Scot. & North. Eng.], flock, floccule, flocculus; **scale,** shale [dial.]; scurf, dandruff; chip; shaving, paring; shive, shove; snowflake.

4. stratification, lamination, lamellation; foliation; delamination, exfoliation; desquamation [med.], furfuration; flakiness, scaliness.

VERBS **5. layer, stratify, laminate;** flake, scale; delaminate, desquamate [med.], exfoliate.

ADJS. **6. layered,** in layers; **laminated,** laminate, laminous; lamellated, lamellate, lamellar, lamelliform; two-ply, three-ply, etc.; **stratified,** stratiform; foliated, foliaceous, leaflike, leafy; spathic, spathose; filmy, scummy; membranous; tabular, tabloid.

7. flaky, flocculent; **scaly,** scurfy, squamous, lentiginous, furfuraceous, lepidote [bot.]; scabby, scabious, scabrous, asperous [bot.].

227. COVERING

NOUNS **1. covering** (act of covering), coverage; **coating,** cloaking; **screening,** shielding, curtaining, **veiling,** shrouding, blanketing; **wrapping,** sheathing, envelopment; **overlaying,** overspreading; superimposition, superposition; superincumbence; upholstering, upholstery; plasterwork, stuccowork, cementwork, pargeting.

2. cover, kiver [dial.], covering, coverage, covert, coverture, **shelter, screen,** shroud, shield, veil, pall, mantle, housing, **coat,** cloak, mask, guise; vestment, investment, vestiture, investiture; canopy, cope, awning, tent, pavilion, blanket [all fig.]; shade 337.

3. integument, tegument, tegmen, tegmentum [anat. & bot.].

4. overlayer, overlay; **lap, overlap,** overlapping, imbrication.

5. lid, led [dial.], **top,** cover, **cap;** operculum [bot. & zool.]; stopper 265.4.

6. roof, roofing, top, **housetop;** deck [R.R.]; eaves; **ceiling,** *plafond* [F.], planchment [local, U.S.]; dome, cupola.

7. umbrella, 'brella [dial.], brolly [slang, Eng.], bumbershoot [slang, U.S.], **sunshade,** *en-tout-cas* [F.], mush or mushroom [slang, Eng.], chatta [India], gingham [coll.]; gamp; **parasol,** bumbersoll [slang].

8. tent, pavilion, canvas; top, whitetop, round top, big top [all circus cant]; tentage, canvas [collective].

9. rug, carpet; mat, doormat; carpeting.

10. coverlet, coverlid [chiefly dial.], **cover, spread, robe, blanket,** rug [Eng.]; lap robe, buffalo robe [U.S.].

11. bedcover, bedspread; counterpane, counterpin [dial.]; comfort, comforter, comfortable [all U.S.]; quilt, eiderdown [quilt]; patchwork quilt, rildy [local, U.S.]; **bedding, bedclothes,** clothes; linen, bed linen; sheets, sheeting; pillowcase, pillow slip, case, slip.

12. horsecloth, horse blanket; caparison, housing; **saddle blanket,** saddlecloth, apishamore [Northwest. U.S.], tilpah [Southwest. U.S.], namda [India].

13. coating, coat; veneer, facing; pellicle, **film, scum,** skin, scale; fur (coating on the tongue); paint 361.7.

14. plating, plate; nickel plate, silver plate, gold plate, copper plate, chromium plate; electroplating, electrocoating.

15. incrustation, crust, shell; piecrust, pastry shell; stalactite, stalagmite; scale, shale [dial.]; scab, eschar [med.].

16. shell, lorication, lorica [zool.]; test, testa [both bot. & zool.], episperm [bot.]; pericarp [bot.]; scute, scutum [both zool.]; armor, nail, shield, carapace, plate, chitin [all zool.]; **protective covering,** cortex [fig.], thick skin.

17. hull, shell; **husk, shuck;** cornhusk, corn shuck [U.S.]; chaff, bran, palea [bot.], flight [dial., Eng.].

18. case, casing, incasement; **sheath,** sheathing.

19. wrapper, wrapping, wrap; **binder,** binding; **bandage,** bandaging; **envelope,** envelopment; **jacket,** jacketing; dust jacket.

20. lining, liner; **interlining,** interlineation; inlayer, inlay, inlaying; padding, wadding, stuffing, packing; facing; doubling, doublure; bushing, bush; wainscot; insole.

VERBS **21. cover,** cover up; **put on,** lay on; **superimpose,** superpose; **lay over,** overlay; **spread over,** overspread; **clothe, cloak,** mantle, blanket, canopy, cope, cowl, **veil,** curtain, **screen, shield,** mask; film, scum.

22. wrap, enwrap or inwrap, wrap up, wrap about or around; **envelop, sheathe;** surround, embrace, invest; shroud, enshroud; swathe, swaddle.

23. top, cap, tip, crown; hood, hat, coif, bonnet; roof; ceil; dome, endome.

24. floor; carpet; pave, causeway, cobblestone, flag, pebble; cement, concrete; blacktop, tar, asphalt, macadamize.

25. face, veneer; sheathe; board, plank, weatherboard, clapboard, lath; shingle, shake; tile, stone, brick, slate; thatch; glass, glaze; paper, wallpaper.

26. coat, spread on, **spread with;** smear, **smear on,** besmear, dab, daub, bedaub; lay it on thick; enamel, gild, gloss; butter; tar.

27. plaster, parget, stucco, cement, concrete, mortar; roughcast.

28. plate, chromium-plate, copper-plate, gold-plate, nickel-plate, silver-plate; **electroplate, galvanize;** metal, iron, steel, copper, brass, braze, silver, zinc, tin, lead.

29. incrust, encrust, **crust;** loricate; effloresce.

30. line, interline, interlineate; inlay; face; wainscot, ceil; pad, wad, stuff, pack; fettle [metal.]; feather, fur.

31. upholster, overstuff.

32. re-cover, reupholster, recap (a tire).

33. overlie, lie over; **overlap,** lap, **lap over,** override [chiefly med.], imbricate, shingle; **extend over,** span, bridge; arch over, overarch.

ADJS. **34. covered,** covert, under cover; **cloaked,** mantled, blanketed, canopied, coped, cowled, **shrouded, veiled,** curtained, **screened,** shielded, masked; tented, under canvas; **wrapped,** enwrapped, **enveloped,** sheathed, swathed; **coated,** filmed, scummed; loricate, loricated.

35. plated, chromium-plated, copper-plated, gold-plated, nickel-plated, silver-plated; electroplated, galvanized.

36. upholstered, overstuffed.

37. covering, coating; cloaking, blanketing, shrouding, **veiling, screening,** shielding; wrapping, **enveloping,** sheathing.

38. overlying, incumbent, superincumbent, superimposed; **overlapping,** lapping, shingled, equitant [bot.]; imbricate, imbricated; lapstreak, clinker-built; spanning, bridging; overarched, overarching.

39. integumental, integumentary, tegumentary, tegumental, tegmental; vaginal, thecal [both zool.].

PREPS. **40. on, upon, over,** o'er [poetic], **above, on top of.**

41. covers

altar cloth *or* carpet	marquee, marquise
antimacassar	mask
awning	pall
balcachin	pavilion
blind	pledget [med.]
canopy	purdah [India]
centerpiece	pyx cloth *or* veil
cerecloth	scarf
cerement	screen
chrismal [eccl.]	shamianah
cloth	(canopy [India])
corporal, corporale [eccl.]	sheet
	shield
cozy, cosy	shroud
curtain	shutters
doily	smoke screen
dossil [med.]	tablecloth
elyton [zool.]	tarpaulin, tarp
fannel [eccl.]	tester
fanon [eccl.]	tidy
fingerstall	veil
housing	veiling
mantle	venetian blinds

42. roofs

barrack roof [local, U.S.]	mansard roof
bulkhead [Eng.]	M roof
curb roof	pantile roof
flat roof	penthouse roof
French roof	pitched roof
gable roof	pyramidal roof
gambrel roof	shed roof
hip-and-valley roof	shingle roof
hip roof	slate roof
jerkin-head roof	thatched roof
lean-to roof	tile roof

43. tents

A tent	pup tent [coll.]
bell tent	shelter tent
canoe tent	Sibley tent
dog tent [slang]	*tente d'abri*
field tent	[F., shelter tent]
fly tent	tepee
kibitka [Russian]	tupek
lean-to tent	wall tent
marquee, marquise	wigwam
praetorium [Rom. antiq.]	

44. rugs, carpets

bearskin rug	hooked rug
body Brussels	imperial Brussels
Brussels carpet	Indian rug
camel's hair rug	linoleum
Caucasian rug	mohair rug
Chinese rug	namda [India]
Congoleum	nammad [Persia]
drugget	numdah rug
East Indian rug	Oriental rug

Persian rug	tapestry Brussels
scatter rug	throw rug
shag rug	Turkish rug
steamer rug	Turkoman rug

45. shells

armadillo shell	nutshell
clam shell	oyster shell
cockleshell	sea shell
cocoa shell	snail shell
conch (shell)	turtle shell
eggshell	winkle (shell)
marine shell	

46. covering materials

brick	sheeting
carpeting	shingle
clapboard	shingling
cobblestone	siding
flag	slate
flagging	slating
flagstone	stone
flooring	tar paper
pantile	thatch
paper	tile
pavement	tilestone
pavestone	tiling
paving	veneer
plasterboard	wainscoting
roofing, roofage	wallboard
roofing paper	walling
roofing tile	wallpaper
shake	weatherboard
sheathing board	wood

47. plasters

adobe	mortar
cement	parget
chinking	plaster of Paris
clay	Portland cement
composition, compo	roughcast
daubing	scagliola
grout	stucco

228. SKIN

NOUNS **1. skin, cuticle, rind;** integument, tegument; **pelt, hide, coat, jacket, fell, fur** [all of animals]; hide, leather, pelt, bark, jacket [all joc. of persons]; leather (dressed hide); rawhide; peltry [collective]; furring.

2. peel, peeling, rind, skin, epicarp; bark; cork, phellum; cortex, cortical tissue; periderm, phelloderm; peridium; dermatogen.

3. membrane, membrana, pellicle; basement membrane, membrana propria; serous membrane, serosa, membrana serosa; tympanic membrane, tympanum, membrana tympani, eardrum; mucous membrane, peritoneum, pleura, pericardium, meninges, conjunctiva, maidenhead.

4. (skin layers) epidermis, scarfskin, ecderon; hypodermis, hypoderma; dermis, derma, corium, cutis, *cutis vera* [L.]; epithelium, pavement epithelium, endothelium; endoderm, entoderm; blastoderm; ectoderm, epiblast, ectoblast; enderon; connective tissue.

5. (castoff skin) slough, cast, desquamation, exuviae [*pl.*].

ADJS. 6. **cutaneous**, cuticular; skinlike, skinny; epidermal, epidermic, ecderonic; hypodermic, hypodermal, subcutaneous; dermal, dermic; ectodermal, ectodermic; endermic, endermatic; cortical; epicarpal; testaceous.

7. **leather**, leathern; buff.

8. pelts, furs, hides

Alaska sable	Hudson Bay seal
Australian seal	kolinsky
Baltic leopard	krimmer
Baltic tiger	lambskin
bearskin	lapin
beaver	leopard
beaverette	leopardskin
beaverskin	marmink
black fox	marmot
black marten	marten
black sable	merino
brook mink	miniver
buckskin	mink
calf	mole
calfskin	moleskin
caracul	monkey
cat	muskrat
catskin	New Zealand seal
chinchilla	nutria
chinchillette	otter
coast seal	Persian lamb
Coney leopard	polar seal
Coney mole	rabbit
cony	rabbitskin
cowhide	raccoon
deerskin	red fox
doeskin	red sable
electric beaver	Roman seal
electric mole	sable
electric seal	seal
ermine	sealskin
erminette	shagreen
fleece	skunk
fox	Tartar sable
fox hair	tiger
genet	water mink
goatskin	white fox
golden sable	wool
horsehide	

9. leathers

buff	Morocco
chamois, chammy	patent leather
chamoisskin	sheepskin
cordovan	shoe leather
cup leather	suède
hat leather	tawed leather
kid	whitleather, white
Mocha	leather

229. HAIR, FEATHERS

NOUNS 1. **hairiness**, hirsuteness, hirsuties, pilosity, crinosity, hispidity; pubescence; hirsutism, pilosis [both med.]; pilosism [bot.].

2. **hair**, pile, crine; **fur**, coat; pelt 228.1; **fleece**, wool; camel's hair, horsehair; mane; shag, mat of hair; pubescence, pubes [both bot. & zool.]; pubic hair, pubes; hairlet, villus [bot.], capillament [bot.], cilium [bot. & zool.], ciliolum [biol.]; seta, setula [both biol.]; bristle 260.3.

3. gray hair, grizzle, "hoary hair" [Thomas Gray], "the silvery livery of advised age" [Shakespeare], "a crown of glory" [Bible].

4. **head of hair**, head, crine; **crop**, crop of hair, mat, **thatch**, mop, **shock**, shag, **mane; locks, tresses;** "her native ornament of hair" [Ovid], "amber-dropping hair" [John Milton], "the red-gold cataract of her streaming hair" [Stephen Phillips].

5. **lock, tress; curl, ringlet,** "wanton ringlets wav'd" [Milton]; earlock; lovelock, beaucatcher [coll.], heartbreaker [coll.], kiss curl *or* kiss-me-quick [coll.]; spit curl [coll.], drop curl, swing curl, pin curl; frizz, frizzle; crimp; elflocks, scolding locks [coll.], follow-me-lads [slang].

6. **tuft, flock,** fleck; forelock, fetlock, cowlick.

7. **braid,** plait, twist; **pigtail,** rat's-tail *or* rattail [joc.], tail; **queue,** cue; coil, knot; topknot; bun, rat's nest [joc.]; chignon, waterfall [coll.].

8. **beard, whiskers;** beaver, muff, wind tormentors [all slang]; chin whiskers, side whiskers; **sideburns** [U.S.], burnsides [coll., U.S.]; **goatee,** tuft; **mutton chops,** imperial, Charley, **Vandyke,** Galways [slang, U.S.]; adolescent beard, pappus, down, "the soft down of manhood" [Callimachus], "his phoenix down" [Shakespeare]; stubble, bristles.

9. (plant beard) awn, brush [bot.], arista, pile, pappus.

10. (animal and insect whiskers) tactile process, tactile hair, feeler, vibrissa; barb, barbel, barbule; cat whiskers.

11. **mustache,** mustachio, soup-strainer [joc.]; handle bars, handle-bar mustache [both slang].

12. **eyelashes,** lashes, cilia, eyewinkers, winkers [coll.], blinkers [slang]; **eyebrows,** brows.

13. hairpiece, switch, rat [coll., U.S.].

14. **wig, peruke,** jasey [coll.]; **toupee,** scalp doily [joc.]; **periwig,** frizz, front, Brutus, *Chedreux* [F.], Gregorian, Ramillie, grizzle.

15. hairdo, haircut, coiffure, head-dress; wave; **marcel**, marcel wave; **permanent**, permanent wave; home permanent; cold wave; Toni; bob, shingle.

16. **feather, plume**, pinion; **quill**; pinfeather; down feather, plumule; filoplume; hackle; scapular; **crest**, tuft, topknot, panache [spec. of a helmet]; beard; vibrissa, seta.

17. (parts of feathers) quill, calamus, barrel; barb, shaft, barbule, barbicel, cilium, filament, filamentule.

18. **plumage, feathers**, feather, feathering; contour feathers; breast feathers, mail (of a hawk); hackle; flight feathers; remiges, primaries, secondaries, tertiaries; covert, tectrices; speculum, wing bay.

19. **down, fluff**, flue, **fuzz**, fur (as of a peach), pile; eiderdown, eider; swansdown; thistledown; lint.

VERBS 20. hair [coll.], grow hair; whisker, **bewhisker**, beard.

21. **feather, fledge**, feather out; sprout wings.

22. **coiffure**; pompadour, roach [coll., U.S.], wave, marcel; bob, shingle, bang.

ADJS. 23. **hairlike**, trichoid, capillary; filamentous, filamentary, filiform; bristle-like 260.10.

24. **hairy**, hirsute, barbigerous, crinose, crinite [bot. & zool.], pubigerous, pubescent [bot.]; pilose, pilous, pileous; **furry**, furred; villous; villose; ciliate [bot. & zool.]; cirrose [zool.]; hispid, hispidulous [bot. & zool.]; **woolly**, fleecy, lanate, lanated, flocky, flocculent, floccose; woolly-headed, woolly-haired, ulotrichous; bushy, shaggy, shagged; unshorn; bristly 260.9; fuzzy.

25. **bearded**, whiskered, **bewhiskered**, barbate, barbigerous; awned, awny, pappose [all bot.]; goateed; unshaved, unshaven; stubbled, stubbly.

26. **wigged**, periwigged, peruked, toupeed.

27. **feathery, plumy**; hirsute; featherlike, plumelike, pinnate; **downy**, fluffy.

28. **feathered, plumaged**, flighted, pinioned, plumed, plumate, plumose.

29. **tufted**, crested, topknotted.

30. **women's hairdos**

Andalusian swirl	debutante bob
bangs	feathercut
bob	Flemish bob
bohemian bob	French knot
boyish bob	Italian bob
chignon bob	long bob
contour bob	long mane
coquette bob	mannish bob

mannish wavy	shingle
shingle	short bob
page-boy	shortcut
personality bob	straight hair shingle
pompadour	swirl
pony tail	swirl bob
Psyche knot	ultramannish bob
new moon bob	updo [coll.]
rat	upswept hairdo
roach [coll., U.S.]	windblown bob
Romanesque bob	

31. **boys' haircuts**

boogie	flattop
butch	fuzz cut
crewcut	pachuco
d.a.	

230. CLOTHING

NOUNS 1. **clothing, clothes, apparel**, wear, wearing apparel, **dress**, dressing, **raiment**, garmenture, **garb, attire**, array, habit, habiliment (chiefly pl.), guise, costume, gear, clobber [slang, Eng.], fig [coll.], toilette, trim, bedizenment; **vestment**, vesture, investment, investiture; **garments, raiments**, robes, robing, rags [derog.], drapery, feathers; wearables, toggery, togs, **duds** [all coll.]; sportswear; work clothes, fatigues.

2. **wardrobe**, furnishings, things, accouterments, trappings, traps [coll.], duds [coll.]; **outfit**, livery, harness, caparison, turnout, layout [slang], get-up [coll.], rig [coll.], rigging, rig-out [slang]; trousseau.

3. **garment, raiment**, vestment, vesture, robe, frock, gown, rag [derog.], fig leaf [slang]; tog, dud, wearable [all coll.].

4. **ready-mades**, store clothes [dial.], slops, confections [Gallicism], hand-me-downs [slang].

5. **rags, tatters**, duds [chiefly dial.], old clothes.

6. **suit**, suit of clothes, **frock, dress**, rig [coll.], **costume, habit**, bib and tucker [coll.].

7. **uniform, livery**, harness [crim. slang, U.S.].

8. **mufti**, civvies [slang], cits [slang], plain clothes.

9. **costume**, character dress; masquerade, disguise; theatricals, scenery [theat. slang]; hawbuck harness (medieval court costume); tights; dots (clown's costume [circus slang]); motley, cap and bells; buskin, sock.

10. **finery, frippery**, gaudery, flashery [slang], flash [slang], war paint [coll.], fo-farrow [slang], lugs [coll., U.S.], fine or full feather; **best clothes**, best bib and tucker

[coll.], **Sunday best** or black [coll.], Sunday clothes [joc. or slang], Sunday-go-to-meeting clothes or Sunday-go-to-meetings [both joc. or slang], **glad rags** [slang, U.S.], dress-ups [slang].

11. formals, formal dress, **evening dress, full dress,** fair winds [slang], **soup-and-fish** [slang]; dinner clothes; dress suit, full-dress suit, tails [coll.]; Tuxedo, Tux [coll.]; dress uniform, full-dress uniform, special full-dress uniform, social full-dress uniform [all mil.]; evening gown, dinner dress or gown.

12. cloak, mantle, robe, overgarment; **wrap,** wrapper.

13. coat, jacket; **overcoat,** greatcoat, **topcoat,** topper [coll.], surcoat, surtout; benjamin, benny [both thieves' slang].

14. waistcoat, weskit [dial.], **vest,** benjy [crim. slang], pitticoat [dial., Eng.].

15. waist, shirt, shirtwaist, intimate [slang], sark [hist. & dial.], shift [dial.]; **blouse,** blou [slang, Eng.]; bodice, body [now chiefly dial.], corsage; dickey, bosom [U.S.].

16. dress, gown, frock; skirt, jupe [chiefly Scot.], jupon.

17. apron, *tablier* [F.]; pinafore, gaberdine [local, Eng.], tier [local, U.S.]; bib; smock.

18. trousers, pair of trousers, trews [Scot.], **breeches,** britches [dial.], **pantaloons, pants** [coll.], jeans [chiefly, U.S.], galligaskins [now joc.], kicks [slang], kickseys or kicksies [slang, Eng.], strides [slang], sit-upons [coll.].

19. breechcloth, waistcloth, **loincloth, G string,** dhoti [India], moocha [S. Africa], *pagne* [F.]; **diaper,** dydee [coll.], hipping or hippen [Scot. & dial., Eng.].

20. dishabille, *déshabillé* [F.], **undress,** something comfortable; **negligee,** *négligé* [F.].

21. nightwear, night clothes; **nightdress, nightgown,** nightie [coll.], bedgown; nightshirt; **pajamas** or pyjamas, P.J.'s [slang].

22. underclothes, underclothing, undergarments, **underwear,** U-wear [slang], skivvies [U.S. Navy], body clothes, smallclothes, intimates [slang], unmentionables [joc.]; **lingerie,** underlinen; flannels, woolens.

23. corset, stays, jupes [Scot.]; corselet; **girdle,** undergirdle, two-way stretch; panty girdle; corset cover, underbody [dial., U.S.].

24. brassiere, bra [coll.]; bandeau; half

bra [coll.]; uplift brassiere; falsies [slang].

25. headdress, headgear, headwear, headclothes, headtire; **haberdashery, millinery;** headpiece, **chapeau, cap, hat;** lid, dicer, tile, benny, skimmer, katy [all slang]; headcloth, **kerchief,** coverchief, handkerchief.

26. veil, veiling, veiler; yashmak [Moham.]; mantilla [Sp.]; fall.

27. footwear, footgear, *chaussure* [F.]; **shoes, boots;** dogs, kicks, clodhoppers [all slang]; wooden shoes, sabots, pattons.

28. hosiery, hose, stockings; socks, half hose.

29. bathing suit, swim suit; trunks; bikini.

30. children's wear, shortclothes, smallclothes, smalls [coll.]; rompers, jumpers; creepers; layette, baby linen; swaddling clothes, swaddle.

31. garment making, **tailoring; dressmaking; haberdashery, millinery;** shoemaking, bootmaking, **cobbling.**

32. clothier, mercer [Eng.], outfitter; costumier, costumer; glover; hosier; furrier; draper, linen draper.

33. garmentmaker, garmentworker.

34. tailor, tailoress [fem.], *tailleur* [F.], darzee [India], sartor [joc.], stitch [joc.], snip [slang], habit maker; busheler, bushelman [both U.S.].

35. dressmaker, modiste, *couturière* [*fem.*, F.], *couturier* [*masc.*, F.]; seamstress 222.2.

36. haberdasher, hatter, hatmaker, **milliner.**

37. shoemaker, bootmaker, **cobbler,** Crispin; snob, souter [both Scot. & dial.].

VERBS **38. clothe,** enclothe, **dress, garb, attire,** array, **apparel,** raiment, garment, tog [coll.], dud [slang], robe, enrobe, invest, endue [fig.], deck, bedeck, rag out or up [slang, U.S.]; drape, bedrape; wrap, enwrap, envelop, sheathe, shroud, enshroud; wrap up, bundle up, muffle up; swathe, swaddle.

39. cloak, mantle; coat, jacket; gown, frock; breech, pant [South. U.S.]; shirt; coif, bonnet, cap, hat, hood; boot, shoe; stocking, sock.

40. outfit, equip, **accouter,** caparison, rig, rig out or up, fit, **fit out,** turn out, **costume,** habit, suit.

41. dress up, put on the dog [coll.], **get up, fix up** [coll., U.S.], **doll up** [slang, U.S.], **spruce up** [coll.], **primp up,** prink up, prank up, spiff up [slang, U.S.], smarten up, slick up [slang, U.S.], buck up [coll.], pretty up [dial.], deck out, dike out or up [dial.], trick out or up, tog out or up [coll.], rag out or up [slang, U.S.], fig out or up; **primp**, prink, prank, titivate or tittivate [joc.]; dizen, bedizen; overdress.

42. don, put on, slip on, get on, huddle on, assume, dress in; change.

43. wear, have on, be dressed in, bear, carry, sport [coll.].

ADJS. **44. clothed, clad, dressed**, attired, arrayed, **garbed**, garmented, vestmented, robed, raimented, appareled, decent [theat. slang]; invested, endued [fig.]; liveried; costumed, in costume, *costumé* [F.]; breeched, trousered, pantalooned; coifed, capped, bonneted, hatted, hooded; shod, shoed, booted, *chaussé* [F.].

45. dressed up, fixed up [coll., U.S.], **dolled up** [slang, U.S.], spiffed up [slang, U.S.], **spruced up** [coll.]; spruce, sprucy [slang]; dressed to advantage, dressed to the nines, dressed fit to kill [slang]; in Sunday best, *endimanché* [F.], in one's best bib and tucker [coll.], in fine or high feather; *en grande tenue* or *toilette* [F.], in full dress, in full feather, in tails [coll.].

46. in dishabille, *en déshabillé* [F.], **in undress**, in negligee; décolleté.

47. vestmental; sartorial.

48. suits

business suit	sports suit
combination	sun suit
ensemble	town-and-country
one-piece suit	suit
riding habit	two-piece suit
separates	zoot suit
shirtwaist suit	

49. uniforms

blues	olive-drab
brass buttons	regimentals
[slang]	sailor suit
continentals	square rig [coll.,
[Amer. hist.]	Eng.]
fore-and-aft rig	stripes (prison uni-
[coll., Eng.]	form)
khaki	whites
nauticals	

50. cloaks, overgarments

afghan	chuddar [Anglo-
blouse	Ind.]
burnoose or bur-	frock
nous [N. Africa]	gaberdine
caftan [Levant]	haik [N. Africa]
cape	houppelande [hist.]
capote	huke [hist.]
cardinal	jubbah [Moham.]
cashmere, Cash-	kimono
mere shawl	kirtle [hist.]
chlamys [Gr.	manta
antiq]	mantelet

mantelletta [eccl.]	serape
mantellone [eccl.]	shawl
mantilla	slop
mantle	smock
pelerine	smock frock
pelisse	tabard [hist.]
plaid [Scot.]	talma
poncho [Sp.	tunic
Amer.]	wrap-around, wrap-
robe	round
roquelaure [hist.]	wrapper
sagum [Roman]	wrap-up

51. coats, jackets

blazer	nor'wester [U.S.]
blouse [U.S. Army]	parka
bolero	peacoat, pea jacket
capuchin	pilot jacket
chaqueta [Sp.]	Prince Albert
chesterfield	redingote
claw-hammer coat,	reefer
claw hammer	sack, sacque
coach coat	sack coat
coatee	shad-bellied coat,
cutaway coat,	shadbelly [both
cutaway [coll.]	coll.]
dinner coat or	shell jacket
jacket	shooting jacket
dolman	ski jacket
doublet	sleeve waistcoat
dress coat	smoking jacket
dressing jacket	spencer
fingertip coat	spiketail coat,
fitted coat	spiketail [both
frock coat, frock	slang, U.S.]
jerkin [hist. or	sports coat or
dial.]	jacket
jumper	swagger coat [coll.]
jupe [Scot.]	swallow-tailed coat,
lounging jacket	swallowtail
Mackinaw, Mack-	tabard [hist.]
inaw coat [local,	tail coat, tails
U.S.]	[coll.]
mantevil [hist.]	Tuxedo coat or
mess jacket [mil.]	jacket
monkey jacket	windbreaker [U.S.]
[coll.]	wooly (woolen
Norfolk jacket	jacket)

52. sweaters

bolero	shoulderette
bulky	ski sweater
cardigan, cardigan	slip-on
jacket	slipover
crew-neck sweater	sloppy Joe [slang]
desk sweater	sweat shirt
fisherman's sweater	topper
hand-knit	turtle-neck sweater
jersey	V-neck sweater
knittie	windbreaker
pull-on sweater	wooly
pull-over	

53. overcoats

capote	mackintosh
chesterfield	oilskins
dreadnought	paletot
duster [U.S.]	raglan
fearnought	raincoat
Inverness, Inver-	slicker [U.S.]
ness cape	slip-on

tarpaulin
trench coat
ulster
waterproof

wet weathers
  [coll.]
wrap-around
wraprascal

54. waists, shirts

basque
blaze-faced shirt
  [slang]
blouse
coat shirt
dickey
doublet [hist.]
dress shirt
gipon [hist.]
habit shirt
hair shirt
halter

hickory shirt
jupe [Scot.]
middy blouse
O.D. or olive-drab
  shirt
overblouse
polo shirt
pourpoint [hist.]
pull-over
sport shirt
T-shirt

55. dresses, skirts

crinoline
culottes
dinner dress or
  gown
dirndl
evening gown
farthingale
filibeg, philabeg
hoop skirt
jumper
kilt
kirtle [hist.]
mantua [hist.]

Mother Hubbard
muu-muu
overdress
overskirt
pannier
peplum
petticoat
pinafore
sack
sari
sarong
sheath
shirtdress

56. trousers

bags
bell-bottoms
Bermuda shorts
bloomers
blue jeans [chiefly
  U.S.]
buckskins
clam diggers
corduroys, cords
denims
ducks
dungarees
flannels
gabardines
gym pants
high-water pants
  [slang]
Jamaica shorts
jodhpurs
knee breeches
knee pants [coll.]
knickerbockers,
  knickers

Levi's [U.S.]
overalls
pajamas, pyjamas
  [India & Persia]
pantalets
pedal-pushers
pegtops
plus-fours
riding pants
rompers
sacks
shintiyan
  [Moslem]
shorts
ski pants
slacks
smallclothes [hist.]
tights
toreador pants
trouserettes
trunks
tweeds
whites

57. dishabille

bathrobe
bed jacket
brunch coat
dressing gown
dressing sack or
  jacket
housecoat
kimono
lounging pajamas

lounging robe
morning dress
peignoir [F.]
robe
robe-de-chambre
  [F.]
smoking jacket
tea gown
wrapper

58. undergarments

Balmoral
bloomers
brassière
bustle
B.V.D.'s
camisole
chemise
combination
corset
crinoline
drawers
foundation gar-
  ment
long underwear
pannier
panties [coll.]
pants [coll.]

petticoat
scanties [coll.]
shift
shorts
skivvie shirt
  [U.S. Navy]
slip
smock
step-ins [1920's]
tournure [F.]
underpants [coll.]
undershirt
underskirt
undervest
union suit
wrapper [coll.]

59. hats, caps

bearskin
beaver
beret
billycock hat, billy-
  cock [Eng.]
bonnet
boudoir cap
bowler
busby
calash [hist.]
campaign hat
  [mil.]
capote
castor
chapeau bras [F.]
cloche
cock-and-pinch
  [slang]
cocked hat
coif
coxcomb
crush hat
derby
dress cap [mil.]
dunce cap
Dutch cap
fantail [Eng.]
fedora [U.S.]
felt hat
fez
forage cap [mil.]
fore-and-aft or
  -after [coll., naut.]
helmet
homburg
hood
kaffiyeh [Arab]
kelly [slang, U.S.]
kepi [mil.]
leghorn
mobcap
nightcap
opera hat
overseas cap [mil.]
Panama hat,
  panama

picture hat
pillbox
pith hat or helmet
plug hat, plug
  [slang, chiefly
  U.S.]
poke bonnet, poke
porkpie
puggree [India]
riding hood
rumal [India]
sailor
Salvation-Army
  bonnet
scraper [slang]
shako [mil.]
silk hat
skullcap
snood
sola topee [India]
sombrero
sou'wester
stovepipe hat,
  stovepipe [coll.,
  U.S.]
straw hat
sunbonnet
sundown
sun hat
sun helmet
tam-o'-shanter, tam
tarboosh
ten-gallon hat
  [coll., U.S.]
three-cornered hat
topee [India]
top hat, topper
  [slang]
toque
turban
wide-awake hat,
  wide-awake
wimple
wind-cutter [slang]

60. shoes

arctics
bootees

bootikins
boots

Blucher boots or
  shoes, bluchers
brogues, brogans
buskins
button shoes
campus shoes
clogs
creepers [slang]
field shoes [mil.]
gaiters
galoshes
gum shoes, gums
gymnasium shoes
half boots
Hessian boots, hes-
  sians
high-button shoes
high-lows
high-topped shoes
hip boots
hobnailed shoes
horseshoes
jackboots
lace shoes
loafers
loungers

moccasins
mules
overshoes
Oxfords, Oxford
  shoes or ties
pattens
pumps
riding boots
rubbers
sandals
scuffs
ski boots
slippers
sneakers
snowshoes
socks [theat.]
stogies
tennis shoes
top boots
veldschoens [S.
  Africa]
wedgies
Wellington boots,
  wellingtons
wooden shoes
work shoes

61. hosiery

anklets
argyles
athletic socks
bobbysocks [coll.]
boothose
boot socks
crew socks
dress sheers
full-fashioned
  stockings
garter stockings
knee socks

nylons
seamless stockings
sheer stockings,
  sheers
stocking hose
stretch stockings
sweat socks
tights
trunk hose
varsity socks
work socks

62. leggings, gaiters

antigropelos
chaps. chaparajos,
  chaparejos
[Southwest. U.S.;
  Sp. Amer.]
chivarras, chivarros
[Mex. & South-
  west. U.S.]
galligaskins [dial.,
  Eng.]

gamashes [hist. exc.
  Scot. & North.
  Eng.]
gambados
greaves
leg armor
puttees, putts
  [slang]
spats
spatterdashes

63. handwear, gloves

boxing gloves
gauntlets, gantlets
kid gloves, kids
mittens, mitts
mousquetaire

gloves, mous-
  quetaires
muff
suède gloves,
  suèdes

64. neckwear

ascot, Ascot tie
band [eccl.]
bertha
boa
celluloid collar
chemisette
choke [slang],
  choker [coll.]
collar
comforter

cravat
fichu
four-in-hand, four-
  in-hand tie
fur
guimpe
kerchief
muffler
neckband
neckcloth

neckerchief
neckpiece
necktie
plunging neckline
rebato [hist.]
ruff

scarf
stock
tie
tippet
tucker
Windsor tie [U.S.]

65. waistbands

baldric
band
bellyband
belt
cincture
cestus [Gr. & Rom.
  antiq.]
cummerbund
  [India]

fascia
girdle
girt
girth
sash
waist belt
waistcloth

66. garment parts

arm
armhole
armlet
bosom
coattail
collar
collarband
cuff
fly
French cuff
lap

leg
neck
neckband
pocket
seat
shirttail
sleeve
stomacher
waist
wristband

231. DIVESTMENT

NOUNS 1. divestment, divestiture, divesture; removal; stripping, denudation; de-
cortication, excoriation; desquamation, exfoliation; exuviation, ecdysis [both zool.].

2. disrobement, undressing, uncloth-
ing; strip-tease [theat.].

3. nudity, nakedness, bareness; the
nude, the altogether [coll.], l'ensemble
[F.], tout ensemble [F.], the buff [coll.],
the raw [slang]; state of nature, nature in
the raw [joc.], nature's garb, birthday suit
[joc.]; not a stitch, not a stitch to one's
name or back; nudism; nudist.

4. hairlessness, baldness, acomia, alopecia; beardlessness; bald-headedness, bald-
patedness; baldhead, baldpate, baldy [coll.];
depilation; hair remover, depilatory.

VERBS 5. divest, strip, remove; uncover,
uncloak, expose, lay open, bare, lay bare,
denude; fleece, shear; pluck, displume; un-
coif.

6. take off, remove, doff, douse [coll.],
off with, put off; cast off, throw off; unwrap, undo.

7. undress, unclothe, undrape, ungar-
ment, unapparel, unarray, disarray; disrobe, dismantle; strip, strip to the buff
[coll.], do a strip-tease [theat.].

8. peel, pare, skin, strip, flay, excoriate,
decorticate, bark; scalp.

9. husk, hull, pod, shell.

10. shed, cast, throw off, slough, molt, exuviate [zool.].

11. scale, flake, scale or flake off, desquamate, exfoliate.

ADJS. 12. divested, stripped, denuded.

13. unclad, undressed, unclothed, unattired, ungarmented, undraped, ungarbed, unappareled; clothesless, garbless, garmentless, raimentless, leafless [poetic]; not decent, indecent [both theat.].

14. naked, nude, bare, bald, raw [slang], in the raw [slang], in puris naturalibus [L., in a state of nature], in a state of nature, in nature's garb, in one's birthday suit [joc.], in the buff [coll.], in native buff [coll.], stripped to the buff [coll.], in the altogether [coll.], en l'ensemble [F.], with nothing on, without a stitch, without a stitch to one's name or back, wearing a smile [joc.], sky-clad [joc.]; stark-naked, start-naked [dial.]; bare as the back of one's hand, naked as the day one was born, "naked as a worm" [Chaucer], "naked as a needle" [Wm. Langland], "naked as my nail" [J. Heywood], "naked and bare as a shorn sheep" [Edmund Gayton], "in naked beauty more adorned" [Milton].

15. barefoot, barefooted, unshod; discalced, discalceate.

16. bare-ankled, bare-armed, barebacked, bare-chested, barefaced, barehanded, bareheaded, bare-kneed, barelegged, barenecked, bare-throated.

17. hairless, depilous; bald, acomous; bald as a coot, bald as an egg; bald-headed, bald-pated, tonsured; beardless, whiskerless, shaven, clean-shaven, smooth-shaven, smooth-faced; smooth, glabrous.

18. exuvial, sloughy; desquamative, exfoliatory.

ADVS. 19. nakedly, barely, baldly.

232. ENVIRONMENT

NOUNS 1. environment, surroundings, environs, entourage, circumjacencies, circumambiencies, circumstances, alentours [F.]; precincts, purlieus, milieu; neighborhood, vicinity, vicinage; suburbs, faubourgs [F.], banlieues [F.] or banlieus; outskirts, outposts, borderlands; context (associative surroundings).

2. setting, scene (as, a change of scene); background, backdrop, ground, back, rear, hinterland, distance; stage, stage setting, stage-set, mise en scène [F.].

3. (surrounding influence or condition) atmosphere, climate, air, aura; feeling, feel, quality.

4. (natural or suitable environment) element, medium.

5. surrounding, encompassment, environment, circumambience or circumambiency, circumjacence or circumjacency; enclosure 235; encirclement, cincture, encincture, circumcincture, circling, girdling; girding; envelopment, infoldment or enfoldment, embracement; circumposition; circumflexion.

VERBS 6. surround, environ, compass, encompass, enclose or inclose, close; go round or around, compass about; hem, hedge, hem or hedge in; beset, besiege, beleaguer, blockade; envelop, infold or enfold, wrap, enwrap or inwrap, embrace, enclasp, embosom, embay, involve, invest.

7. encircle, circle, ensphere; cincture, encincture; girdle, gird, begird, engird; belt, ring, band; loop; wreathe.

ADJS. 8. environmental, environal.

9. surrounding, environing, encompassing, enclosing or inclosing; enveloping, wrapping, infolding, embracing; encircling, circling; circumjacent, circumferential, circumambient, ambient; circumfluent, circumfluous; circumflex; roundabout, suburban, neighboring.

10. all-around, all-round [U.S.].

11. surrounded, environed, compassed, encompassed, enclosed or inclosed; enveloped, wrapped, infolded.

12. circled, encircled, ringed, cintured, encinctured, belted, girdled, girt, begirt.

ADVS., PREPS. 13. around, round, about, round about; in the neighborhood or vicinity of, close about.

14. all round or around, all about, on every side, on all sides, on all hands, right-and-left.

233. CIRCUMSCRIPTION

NOUNS 1. circumscription, bounding, demarcation, delimitation, definition, determination, specification.

2. limitation, restriction, confinement, restraint, qualification; bounds 234.

3. limit, frozen limit [slang]; utmost extent 56.4; termination, terminal, end, period; deadline [U.S.], target date.

VERBS 4. circumscribe, bound, compass, encompass, encircle, enclose or inclose, surround; mark off, lay off; rope off; demarcate, delimit, delimitate, define, determine, fix.

5. **limit, restrict, restrain, bound, confine**; straiten, narrow; specialize; stint, scant; number (limit in number; as, his days are *numbered*); fix, specify, define, determine, condition, qualify; draw the line.

6. **hem in** 235.5.

ADJS 7. **circumscribed**, circumscript; **encircled, surrounded**, ringed about, circled about, **hemmed in**, hedged in, fenced in, in a ring fence.

8. **limited, restricted**, bound, bounded, finite; **confined**, confining, cramped, strait, straitened, narrow; conditioned, qualified; fixed, definite, determinate, determined, defined, specific, precise, exact; partial, partway, half-way.

9. (military) restricted, out of bounds, off limits.

10. **limiting, restricting**, defining, confining; limitative, limitary, restrictive, definitive, exclusive.

11. **limital**, terminal; limitable, terminable.

234. BOUNDS

NOUNS 1. **bounds, limits, limitations, confines, pale,** marches, outlines, skirts, outskirts, fringes, metes, metes and bounds; periphery, perimeter; compass, circumference, circumscription.

2. **outline, coutour,** *tournure* [F.], delineation, lines, lineaments, *galbe* [F.; art]; figure, figuration, configuration; features, main features; profile, silhouette; relief; skeleton, framework.

3. **boundary, bound, limit,** limitation, hedge, confine, march, mark [hist.], mete, compass, circumscription; **boundary line,** line, **border line,** division line, **line of demarcation** or circumvallation, deadline [U.S.]; landmark.

4. **border,** bordure, board, **edge, verge, brink,** brow, **brim, rim, margin, skirt, fringe, hem,** list, selvage [fig.], side; side line; wayside; lip, labium [tech.], labrum [zool.], labellum [bot.]; flange; ledge; frame, enframement; feather-edge; ragged edge.

5. **frontier, border, borderland,** border ground, marchland, march, marches; outskirt, outpost; iron curtain, bamboo curtain.

6. **curb,** kerb [Eng.], curbing; border stone, curbstone, kerbstone [Eng.], edgestone.

7. **edging, bordering,** bordure, **trimming,** binding, skirting; fringe, fimbriation,

fimbria [tech.]; hem, selvage, list, welt; frill, frilling; beading, flounce, furbelow, galloon, motif, ruffle, valance.

VERBS 8. **bound,** limit 233.4, 5.

9. **outline,** contour; **delineate** 652.12; silhouette, profile.

10. **border, edge, bound, rim, skirt, hem, fringe,** befringe, list, margin, marge [poetic], marginate, march, verge, line, side, frontier; adjoin 199.9; frame, enframe; trim, bind; purl; purfle.

ADJS 11. **bordering, fringing, rimming,** skirting; **marginal, borderline,** frontier; coastal, littoral.

12. **bordered,** edged; margined, marginate, marginated; **fringed,** befringed, fimbriate, fimbriated, laciniate, laciniated.

13. lipped, labial, labiate.

14. outlinear, delineatory; peripheral, perimetric(al), circumferential; outlined, **in outline.**

ADVS. 15. **on the verge, on the brink,** on the point, on the edge, on the ragged edge.

235. ENCLOSURE

NOUNS 1. **enclosure** or inclosure, closure, **confinement,** immurement, inclusion; surrounding 232.5.

2. **packaging, packing,** package; boxing, crating, incasement or encasement; canning, tinning [Eng.]; bottling.

3. (enclosed place) **enclosure,** close, **confine,** pale, paling, list, cincture; **pen, coop,** fold; **yard,** court, courtyard, curtilage, wynd [chiefly dial.]; square, quadrangle, quad [coll.]; patio [U.S.].

4. **fence,** boundary, **barrier; wall;** rail, railing; balustrade, balustrading.

VERBS 5. **enclose** or inclose, close, bound, include, contain; compass, encompass; **surround,** encircle 232.7; **shut in, pen in, coop in; fence in,** wall in, rail in; **hem in, hedge in,** box in, pocket; shut up, coop up, mew up; pen, coop, corral, cage, impound, mew, blockade; yard, yard up; house in; chamber; stable, kennel, shrine, enshrine.

6. **confine, immure;** cramp, straiten; cloister, closet, cabin, crib; entomb, coffin, casket; bottle up or in, box up or in.

7. **fence, wall,** pale, rail, bar; hem, hedge; picket, palisade; bulkhead in.

8. parenthesize, bracket.

9. **package, pack, parcel;** box, box up, case, encase or incase, crate, carton; can, tin [chiefly Eng.]; bottle, jar, pot; barrel,

cask, tank; sack, bag; basket, hamper; capsule, encyst.

ADJS. **10. enclosed** or **inclosed, closed; confined,** bound, immured, cloistered, "cabined, cribbed, confined" [Shakespeare]; **shut-in** [U.S.], pent-up, penned, cooped, mewed; fenced, walled, paled, railed, barred; hemmed, hedged.

11. enclosures

barnyard	keddah [India]
barton [Eng.]	kraal [So. Africa]
bull pen	manger
cage	paddock
cattlefold	pasture
chicken coop	pigpen, pigsty
chicken yard	pinfold
compound	polygon [mil.]
corral	pound
crib	run
croft [Eng.]	runway
dog pound	sheepcote
dooryard [U.S.]	sheepfold
farmyard	stall
hen coop	stockyard
henyard	sty
hutch	

12. fences, walls

contravallation	perpend wall
countervallation	picket fence
[fort.]	rampart
dead wall	ring fence
dike [Scot. & dial.,	scarp wall
Eng.]	stockade
espalier	stone wall
garden wall	sunk fence
ha-ha (sunk fence)	quickset hedge
hedge, hedgerow	trellis
hoarding [Eng.]	vallation
paling	weir
palisade	zigzag fence
parapet	

236. INTERPOSITION

A Placing or Coming Between.—NOUNS **1. interposition,** interposure, interlocation, interjacence; intervention, intervenience, intercurrence; intrusion 237.

2. interjection, interpolation, introduction, injection, insinuation, intercalation; insertion 303; interlocution, remark, parenthetical or side remark, aside, parenthesis; episode.

3. interspersion, interfusion, interlardment, interpenetration.

4. intermediary, intermedium, mediary, medium; link, **connecting link,** connection, go-between; mediator 803.3.

5. partition, dividing wall, division, separation, *cloison* [F.]; septum, interseptum, septulum, dissepiment; wall, barrier; panel; paries [biol.]; brattice, brattish; bulk-

head; diaphragm, midriff; dividing line, midrib [fig.], party line or wall.

VERBS **6. come between, interpose, intervene;** interlie.

7. interject, interpose, interpolate, intercalate, interjaculate; put between, sandwich; **insert in,** introduce in, insinuate in, inject in, implant in; **foist in,** fudge in, work in, drag in, lug in, worm in, smuggle in, throw in, run in, thrust in, edge in, wedge in; intrude 237.5.

8. intersperse, interfuse, interlard, interpenetrate; intersow, intersprinkle.

9. partition, set apart, separate, divide; **wall off,** fence off; panel.

ADJS. **10. interjectional, interpolative,** intercalary; parenthetical, episodic.

11. intervening, intervenient, **interjacent,** intercurrent; **intermediate,** intermediary, medial, mean, medium, mesne [law], median, middle.

12. intercolumnar, intercontinental, interfacial, interlineal, interlinear, intermundane, intermural, interoceanic, interplanetary, interpolar, intersectional, interstellar, interradial, interstitial.

13. partitioned, walled; mural; septal.

PREPS. **14. between,** atween [dial.], **betwixt,** 'twixt, atwixt [dial.], betwixt and between [coll.]; **among, amongst,** 'mongst; **amid, amidst,** mid, 'mid, midst, 'midst; in the midst of, in the thick of.

237. INTRUSION

NOUNS **1. intrusion,** obtrusion, **interloping;** interposition, interposure, imposition, insinuation, **interference,** intervention, interruption; **encroachment,** entrenchment, **infringement,** invasion, incursion, inroad.

2. meddling, intermeddling; kibitzing [coll.]; **meddlesomeness, intrusiveness, forwardness; officiousness,** pragmatism; inquisitiveness 526.1.

3. intruder, interloper, trespasser, buttinsky [slang]; crasher, gate crasher [both slang, U.S.].

4. meddler, intermeddler; **busybody,** busy [slang]; **pry,** Paul Pry, snoop or snooper [U.S.]; **kibitzer** [coll.], back-seat driver [joc.]; pragmatist.

VERBS **5. intrude,** obtrude, **interlope; interpose, intervene, interfere,** insinuate, impose; **encroach, infringe, trespass,** trench, entrench, invade; **break in upon,** break in, bust in [slang], **barge in** [coll.], **cut in,** thrust in, push in, press in, crowd in, squeeze in; **butt in, horn in,** chisel in, muscle in [all slang]; crash, crash in, crash the gates [all slang, U.S.]; **foist in,** worm *or* work in, edge in, put *or* shove in one's oar; **foist oneself upon,** thrust oneself upon; put on *or* upon, impose on *or* upon.

6. **interrupt, put in, cut in, break in;** chime in [coll.], chip in [coll., U.S.].

7. **meddle, intermeddle,** busybody, not mind one's business; **meddle with, tamper with,** mix oneself up with, monkey with, fool with *or* around with [coll.], mess with *or* around with [slang]; **pry,** Paul-Pry, snoop [U.S.], nose, **stick** *or* **poke one's nose in,** stick one's long nose into; have a finger in, have a finger in the pie; kibitz [coll.].

ADJS. 8. **intrusive,** obtrusive, **interfering,** interverient, invasive, interruptive.

9. **meddlesome,** meddling; **officious,** overofficious, pragmatic(al); **busybody,** busy, pushing, forward; **prying,** nosy [coll.], snoopy [coll., U.S.]; inquisitive 526.5.

PHRS. 10. **none of your business,** that's my pigeon, what's it to you?

11. **mind your own business,** keep your nose out of this, ~ butt out of this, I'm skinning this cat, go soak your head, go sit on a tack, go roll your hoop, go peddle your fish, go lay an egg, go fry an egg, go fly a kite, go chase yourself, go jump in the lake, go blow your nose.

238. CONTRAPOSITION

A Placing Over Against.—NOUNS 1. contraposition, anteposition; **opposition,** opposure; antithesis, contrast; confrontment, confrontation; polarity, polarization.

2. **opposites,** antipodes; **poles,** opposite poles, antipoles, counterpoles, North Pole, South Pole; antipodal points, antipoints [both math.]; contrapositives, contraposita [both logic].

3. the opposite side, the other side, the other side of the picture *or* coin; **reverse, inverse, obverse, converse;** heads, tails (of a coin).

VERBS 4. contrapose, oppose, contrast, match, set over against, put in opposition, set *or* pit against one another; **confront,** face, front; subtend; polarize; contraposit [logic].

ADJS. 5. contrapositive, **opposite,** antithetic(al); reverse, **inverse, obverse, converse;** antipodal; polar, polaric.

PREPS., ADVS. 6. **opposite to,** in opposition to, against, over against; contra, counter; versus, *vs.;* **facing, fronting,** confronting, **in front of,** abreast of, toward; **face to face,** vis-à-vis, *front à front* [F.], nose to nose.

239. FRONT

NOUNS 1. **front, fore,** fore part *or* forepart, foreside, forefront, forehand; priority, anteriority; foreland; foreground, proscenium; frontage; frontispiece; head, heading; **face,** façade, frontal; facet, *facette* [F.]; facia; obverse (of a medal), head (of a coin); forequarter; lap [anat.].

2. **van, vanguard,** advance guard, avant-garde, outguard; front [mil.], first line, first line of battle; **outpost,** forepost, Cossack post; **spearhead, bridgehead,** beachhead, airhead, railhead [all mil.].

3. **prow,** prore [poetic], **stem,** rostrum [Rom. antiq.]; nose, beak; bowsprit, jib boom.

4. **face** [anat.], **visage,** physiognomy [often joc.]; phiz, phizog [both slang]; **countenance,** features, lineaments, favor, façade [joc.], jib [dial. & slang]; **mug,** mush, pan, index, kisser, lug, map, puss [all slang].

5. **forehead, brow.**

6. **chin,** mentum [anat.], whiskers [slang]; point of the chin, button [slang], knockout *or* sleep button [boxing slang].

7. physiognomy, metoposcopy, phrenology, craniology; physiognomist, metoposcopist, phrenologist, craniologist.

VERBS 8. **confront, front,** affront, **face,** envisage; **meet, encounter,** meet squarely, meet face to face, come face to face with, look in the face.

9. **confront with, face with,** bring face to face with, tell one to one's face, cast *or* throw in one's teeth, present to, **put** *or* **bring before,** set *or* place before, lay before; bring up, bring forward; put it to, put it up to; **challenge,** dare, defy.

10. **front on, face upon, give upon,** face *or* look toward, look out upon, look over, **overlook.**

ADJS. 11. **front, frontal, anterior; fore,** foreward, forehand; **foremost,** headmost, leading, first, chief, head, prime, primary.

12. **head-on, headlong.**

ADVS. 13. **before, ahead, in front,** in the front, in the lead, in the van, in advance, in the lee of, in the foreground; **to the fore,** to the front; **foremost,** headmost, first; before one's face *or* eyes, under one's nose.

14. **frontward**, frontwards, **forward**, forwards, vanward, **headward**, headwards, **onward**, onwards.

240. REAR

NOUNS 1. **rear, rear end, hind end**, hind part, hinder part, after part *or* afterpart, **posterior, behind**, breech, stern, tail, tail end; **afterpiece**, tailpiece, heelpiece, heel; **back**, back side, reverse (of a coin or medal), tail (of a coin); back door, postern, postern door; back seat, rumble seat; hindhead, occiput [tech.].

2. rear guard, rear.

3. **back** [anat.], dorsum, tergum [zool.]; ridge; dorsal region, lumbar region; hindquarter; loin.

4. **rump, buttocks**, butt [vulgar exc. of meat], **hips, posteriors**, fundament, **bottom** [coll.], arse [now vulgar], ass [vulgar], fud [Scot. & North. Eng.], **rear** [coll.], stern [coll.], tail [coll.], **backside** [coll.], **hind end** [vulgar], behind [coll.], bum [now vulgar], **fanny** [slang, U.S.], prat [slang], breech, **seat**, seater [slang], croup (of a quadruped; joc. of a person), crupper (of a horse), podex [zool.]; **haunches**, hunkers [Scot. & dial.], hunkies [dial. & slang]; gluteal region; nates [anat., zool.].

5. **tail**, cauda [tech.], caudation, caudal appendage, train [poetic], pole [sporting slang]; tailpiece, appendage [both joc.]; bunt [Scot. & Eng.], fud [Scot. & North. Eng.], scut (all of a hare); single (of a deer), brush (of a fox), fantail (of fowls); *empennage* [F., aeronaut.]; rattail, rat's-tail; dock, stub; **queue**, cue, **pigtail**.

6. **stern** [naut.], heel; poop, counter, tail end; sternpost, rudderpost.

VERBS 7. (be behind) **bring up the rear**, come last, **follow**, come after; trail, trail behind, lag behind; fall behind, fall back, fall astern.

ADJS. 8. **rear**, rearward, **back, posterior**, postern, tail; after, aft [naut.]; **hind, hinder; hindmost**, hindermost, hindhand, posteriormost, **aftermost**, aftmost [naut.], rearmost.

9. (anatomy) posterial, dorsal, tergal, neural, lumbar, gluteal, sciatic, occipital.

10. caudal, caudate, caudated, tailed; taillike, caudiform.

11. backswept, swept-back.

ADVS. 12. **behind**, ahind [dial.], **in the rear, in back of**; in the background; behind the scenes; behind one's back; back to back; tandem.

13. **after; aft**, abaft, abaff, baft, baff, astern [all naut.].

14. **rearward**, rearwards, **hindward**, hindwards, **backward**, backwards, tailward, tailwards.

241. SIDE

NOUNS 1. **side, flank, hand**; border 234.4; pleuron [zool.]; flitch (as of bacon); beam; broadside; quarter [naut.]; hip, haunch; cheek, jowl, chop; temple; hypotenuse [geom.].

2. **lee side, lee**, leeward; lee shore; lee tide; lee wheel, lee helm, lee anchor, lee sheet, lee tack.

3. **weather side**, weather, weatherboard, **windward side, windward**, windwards; weather wheel, weather helm, weather anchor, weather sheet, weather tack, weather rail, weather bow, weather deck; weather roll; windward tide, weather-going tide, windward ebb, windward flood.

VERBS 4. **side, flank**; border 234.10.

5. **sidle**, lateralize, **edge, veer, skew**; crabsidle [coll.]; sideslip, skid.

ADJS. 6. **side, lateral; sidelong**, sideling, **sidewise**, sideway, **sideways**, sideward, **sidewards**; leeward, lee; windward, weather.

7. **sided, flanked; one-sided**, unilateral; **two-sided, bilateral**, dihedral [geom.], bifacial; **three-sided, trilateral**, trihedral [geom.], triquetrous [tech.]; **four-sided, quadrilateral**, tetrahedral [geom.]; **many-sided, multilateral**, polyhedral [geom.].

ADVS. 8. **laterally**, laterad [anat.]; **sideways**, sideway, **sidewise, sidewards**, sideward, sideling, sidling, sidelings *or* sidelins [Scot. & dial., Eng.], sidelong, aside; **edgeways**, edgeway, **edgewise**; **askance**, askant, asquint; broadside, **broadside on**, on the beam; on the other hand; right-and-left.

9. **leeward**, to leeward, alee; **windward**, to windward, weatherward, aweather.

10. **aside**, on one side, **to one side**, to the side, away.

PREPS. 11. **beside**, aside [dial.], **alongside, abreast**, on one side, on the side, by, along by, **by the side of**, along the side of, sidelong; fornent, fernint, fornenst, ferninst [all dial.]; near by, in juxtaposition 199.20, 21.

12. **side by side**, tête à tête, cheek to cheek, cheek by cheek, cheek by jowl, shoulder to shoulder, back to back, yardarm to yardarm.

242. RIGHT SIDE

NOUNS **1. right,** right side, **right hand,** right-hand side, dexter, off side (of a horse or vehicle), starboard [naut.]; Epistle side [eccl.], decanal side (of a choir [eccl.]), recto (of a book); right-hand division [mil.]; right field [baseball]; starboard tack [naut.].

2. rightness, dextrality; **dexterity, right handedness;** dextroversion, dextrocularity, dextroduction; dextrorotation, dextrogyration.

3. ambidexterity, ambidexterousness.

ADJS. **4. right, right-hand,** dextral, dexter, off. starboard [naut.]; dextrorse [bot.]; dextropedal; dextrocardial [anat.]; dextrocerebral [neurol.]; dextrocular; **clockwise,** dextrorotary, dextrogyrate, dextrogyratory.

5. right-handed, dextromanual, dexterous or dextrous, orthodox [baseball slang].

6. ambidextrous, ambidextral, ambidexter; dextrosinistral, sinistrodextral.

ADVS. **7. rightward,** rightwards, rightwardly, **right, to the right,** dextrally, dextrad [anat.]; starboard [naut.].

243. LEFT SIDE

NOUNS **1. left,** left side, **left hand,** left-hand side, wrong side [coll.], near or nigh side (of a horse or vehicle), portside [chiefly slang exc. naut.], port [naut.], larboard [naut.]; Gospel side [eccl.], cantorial side [eccl.], verso (of book); port tack [naut.].

2. leftness, sinistrality, **left-handedness;** sinistration; levoversion, levoduction; levorotation, sinistrogyration.

3. left hand, southpaw [slang], portside flinger [baseball slang], sinistra or sinistra mano [It.; mus.].

4. left-handed person) **left-hander,** lefty [slang], sinistral, portsider [slang, U.S.], **southpaw** [slang].

ADJS. **5. left, left-hand,** sinister, sinistral, near, nigh; **larboard, port** [both naut.]; sinistrorse [bot.]; sinistrocerebral [neurol.]; sinistrocular; **counterclockwise,** levorotatory, sinistrogyrate.

6. left-handed, sinistromanual, sinistral, southpaw [slang], unorthodox [baseball slang]; dextrosinistral, sinistrodextral.

ADVS. **7. leftward,** leftwards, leftwardly, **left, to the left,** sinistrally, sinistrad; larboard, port, aport [all naut.].

244. STRUCTURE

NOUNS **1. structure, construction,** architecture. frame, make, build, fabric, texture, arrangement, organization, **constitution, composition; make-up,** getup [coll.], setup, stack-up [slang]; formation, conformation, format; anatomy; **form** 245.

2. a structure, building, edifice, construction, construct, erection, establishment, architecture, fabric; house 190.5; tower, pile, pyramid, skyscraper; prefabrication, prefab [U.S.], packaged house; superstructure; jerry-building.

3. understructure, understruction, underbuilding, **substructure,** substruction.

4. frame, framing; **framework, skeleton** [fig.], fabric, cadre; lattice, latticework; sash, casement, case, casing [U.S.]; window case or frame, doorframe; picture frame.

5. skeleton, anatomy, atomy [joc.], **carcass,** frame [dial.], **bones;** endoskeleton, exoskeleton; axial skeleton, appendicular skeleton.

6. bone; ossicle.

7. (science of structure) **anatomy;** morphology, geomorphology, promorphology; tectology; histology; zootomy, anthropotomy; organology, organography; myology, myography; splanchnology, splanchnography; angiology, angiography; osteology, osteography.

VERBS **8.** construct 166.12.

ADJS. **9. structural,** formal, edificial, tectonic, textural; anatomic(al), organic; **architectural,** archetectonic; superstructural, substructural.

10. skeleton, skeletal.

11. bone, osteal; **bony,** osseous, ossiferous; ossicular; ossified.

12. bones

aitchbone	frontal
anklebone	funny bone
astragalus	hallux
backbone	haunch bone
breastbone	hipbone
calcaneus	heel bone
cannon bone [zool.]	humerus
carpal	ilium
carpus	incus
cheekbone	inferior maxillary
chine [zool.]	innominate bone
clavicle	ischium
coccyx	jawbone
collarbone	kneecap
costal	kneepan
cuboid	lachrymal
cranium	malleus
edgebone	mandible
ethmoid	mastoid
femoral	maxilla
femur	maxillary
fibula	metacarpal
floating ribs	metacarpus
	metatarsal

metatarsus	spinal
nasal	spinal column
occipital	spine
parietal	stapes
patella	sternum
pelvis	stirrup bone
phalanges	superior maxillary
phalanx	talus
pubis	tarsal
rachidial	tarsus
rachis	temporal
radius	thighbone
ribs	tibia
sacrum	ulna
scaphoid	ulnar
scapula	vertebrae
sesamoid bones	vertebral
shinbone	vertebral column
shoulder blade	vomer
skull	wishbone
soup bone	wristbone
sphenoid	zygomatic

245. FORM

NOUNS 1. form, shape, figure; figuration, configuration; formation, conformation; structure 244; build, make, frame; cut, set, stamp, type, turn, cast, mold, impression, pattern, model; style, fashion.

2. contour, *tournure* [F.], *galbe* [F.; art]; outline 234.2.

3. appearance, lineaments, features (outward form) 445.2–4.

4. (human form) figure, form, shape, frame, physique, build, person; body 375.3.

5. forming, shaping, molding, fashioning; formation, formature, conformation, figuration; sculpture.

VERBS 6. form, formalize, shape, fashion, tailor, frame, figure, lick into shape; work, knead; set, fix; forge, drop-forge, hammer out; mold, model, sculpture; cast, found; stamp, mint; carve, cut, chisel, hew; roughhew, roughcast, rough out, block out, hammer or knock out.

7. (be formed) form, shape, shape up, take shape.

ADJS. 8. formative, formal, formational, plastic, morphotic.

9. (in biology) plasmatic, plasmic, protoplasmic, plastic, metabolic.

246. FORMLESSNESS

NOUNS 1. formlessness, shapelessness; amorphism, amorphia [med.]; chaos, orderlessness; indeterminateness, indefiniteness, indecisiveness, vagueness, unclearness, obscurity.

2. (person) unlicked cub, diamond in the rough.

VERBS 3. unform, unshape.

ADJS. 4. formless, shapeless, featureless, inform; amorphous, amorphic; chaotic, orderless, unordered, unorganized; indeterminate, indefinite, undefined, indecisive, vague, unclear, obscure.

5. unformed, unshaped, unshapen, unfashioned, unlicked; uncut, unhewn.

247. SYMMETRY

NOUNS 1. symmetry, symmetricalness, proportion, proportionality, balance; regularity, uniformity, evenness; finish; harmony, congruity, consistency, conformity, correspondence, keeping; eurythmy, eurythmics; dynamic symmetry; bilateral ~, trilateral *or* multilateral symmetry.

2. shapeliness, good figure, good shape; comeliness 898.3.

3. symmetrization, regularization, balancing, harmonization; evening, equalization; co-ordination, integration.

VERBS 4. symmetrize, regularize, balance, harmonize; proportion, proportionate; even, equalize; co-ordinate, integrate.

ADJS. 5. symmetric(al), balanced, proportioned; regular, uniform, even, equal; coequal, co-ordinate; well-balanced, well-set, well-set-up [coll.]; finished.

6. shapely, well-shaped, well-proportioned, well-made, well-formed, well-favored; comely 898.17; trim, neat, clean, clean-cut.

248. DISTORTION

NOUNS 1. distortion, detorsion, contortion, crookedness; asymmetry, unsymmetry; irregularity, deviation; twist, quirk, turn, screw, wring, wrench, wrest; warp, buckle; knot, gnarl; anamorphosis, anamorphism.

2. perversion, corruption, misdirection, misrepresentation, misinterpretation, misconstruction, false coloring; misuse 665.

3. deformity, deformation, malformation, malconformation, monstrosity, misproportion, misshape; disfigurement, defacement; mutilation, truncation; humpbackedness, kyphosis [med.]; humpback, hunchback, crookback, camel back; swayback; clubfoot, talipes [med.], flatfoot, splayfoot; knock-knee; bowlegs; harelip; teratology [med.].

4. grimace, wry face, wry mouth, mouth, face [coll.], mug [slang], mop, "mops and mowes" [Fletcher].

VERBS 5. distort, contort, turn awry; twist, turn, screw, wring, wrench, wrest;

writhe; warp, buckle; knot, gnarl; **crook, crooken.**

6. **pervert, garble, put a false construction upon, give a false coloring,** color, varnish; misrepresent, misconstrue, misinterpret, misrender, misdirect; misuse 665.4.

7. **deform,** misshape; **disfigure, deface;** mutilate, truncate; blemish, mar.

8. **grimace, make faces** [coll.], **make a face** [coll.], make a wry face or wry mouth, pull a face, **screw up one's face,** mug [slang], mouth, make a mouth, mop, mow, mop and mow.

ADJS. 9. **distortive, contortive, contortional.**

10. **distorted, contorted, warped, twisted; perverted,** garbled; **unsymmetric(al),** asymmetric(al), nonsymmetric(al); irregular, deviative; one-sided; askew 218.14.

11. **crooked,** turning, curved, **twisted, bent,** bendified [slang], crump [dial.]; thrawart, thraw or thrawn [all Scot.]; weewow [dial.], weewaw [dial., U.S.]; galley-west, galley-west and crooked, skywest, skywest and crooked [all slang]; six ways from Sunday [slang, U.S.]; crooked as a ram's horn, crooked as a dog's hind leg, crooked as a Virginia fence [U.S.].

12. **deformed, malformed, misshapen,** misbegotten, misproportioned, ill-proportioned, ill-made, ill-shaped, **out of shape,** curtailed of one's fair proportions; **disfigured,** defaced, blemished, marred; mutilated, truncated; grotesque, monstrous; sway-back(ed); round-shouldered; bowlegged, bandy-legged, bandy; knock-kneed; club-footed, taliped(ic) [med.]; flatfooted, splayfoot(ed); pug-nosed, snub-nosed, simous.

13. **humpbacked, hunchbacked,** bunchbacked, crookbacked, crookedbacked, camel-back, humped, gibbous, kyphotic [med.].

249. STRAIGHTNESS

NOUNS 1. **straightness,** directness, lineality, rectilinearity; verticalness 212; horizontalness 213.

2. **straight line,** straight, right line, direct line, straight course, straightaway; **bee-line,** airline; **short cut** 202.5; great-circle track [naut.]; streamline; secant, chord [both geom.].

VERBS 3. have no turning; go straight 289.11.

4. **straighten, set** or **put straight,** rectify; **unbend,** unfold, unwrap, unkink, un-

curl; disentangle 45.4; straighten up, stand or sit up; straighten out, extend; streamline.

ADJS. 5. **straight,** straight-lined, even, right, true, straight as an arrow; **rectilinear,** rectilineal; linear, lineal, in a line; **direct, undeviating, unswerving,** unbending; **unbent, unbowed,** unturned, uncurved, undistorted; **uninterrupted, unbroken;** streamlined, streamline; straight-side, straight-front, straight-cut; vertical 212.10; horizontal 213.8.

ADVS. 6. **straight,** straightly, on the straight; **directly** 289.25.

7. down the alley, in the groove, on the beam [all slang, U.S.].

250. ANGULARITY

NOUNS 1. **angularity,** angularness; orthogonality, right-angledness, right-angularity, rectangularity.

2. **angle,** point, bight; **corner,** quoin, coin, nook; **crook, hook,** crotchet; **bend,** inflection; el or ell, L; cant; fork 298.4; zigzag, zig, zag; elbow, knee; crank; sickle, scythe; cube, die, dice; lozenge, diamond; wedge, cuneus; pyramid, pyramidion; prism, prismoid.

3. (angular measurement) goniometry; trigonometry, trig [school slang].

4. (instruments) goniometer, radiogoniometer; altimeter, pantometer, clinometer, graphometer, astrolabe; theodolite, transit theodolite, transit, transit instrument; sextant, quadrant; bevel, bevel square; protractor, bevel protractor.

VERBS 5. **angle, crook, hook, bend, elbow;** corner [U.S.]; crank; angle off or away, go off on a tangent; fork 298.7; zigzag, zig, zag.

ADJS. 6. **angular,** cornered, **crooked, hooked, bent,** akimbo; geniculate, geniculated; crotched, Y-shaped, V-shaped; forked 298.10; sharp-cornered, **sharp, pointed,** edgy, abrupt; dovetailed; prismed, prismal, prismatic(al); pyramided, pyramidal, pyramidic(al).

7. **right-angled,** right-angular, right-angle; orthogonal, orthodiagonal, orthometric.

8. **triangular, trilateral,** trigonal, deltoid; wedge-shaped, cuneiform, cuneate, cuneated.

9. **quadrangular, quadrilateral,** quadrate, quadriform; **rectangular, square,** foursquare, orthogonal; tetragonal, tetra-

hedral; **oblong;** rhombic(al), rhomboid(al).

10. **cubic**(al), cubiform, cuboid, cube-shaped, cubed, diced.

11. decagonal, dodecagonal, dodecahedral, heptagonal, hexagonal, hexahedral, icosahedral, octagonal, octahedral, oxygonal, pentagonal, pentahedral, rhombohedral, trapezoid(al), trapezohedral.

12. multiangular, multilateral; polygonal, polyhedral.

13. angles

acute angle	right angle
oblique angle	salient angle
obtuse angle	spherical angle
re-entering angle	straight angle
reflex angle	

14. geometric figures

acute-angled triangle	Platonic bodies
	polygon
cube	polyhedron
cuboid	quadrangle
cusp	quadrant
decagon	quadrature
dodecagon	quadrilateral
dodecahedron	rectangle
equilateral triangle	rhombohedron
foursquare	rhombus, rhomb,
heptagon	rhomboid
hexagon	right-angled triangle
hexahedron	angle
icosahedron	right triangle
isosceles triangle	scalene triangle
oblong	square
obtuse-angled triangle	trapezium, trapeze
	trapezohedron
octagon	trapezoid
octahedron	tetragon
oxygon	tetragram
parallelepiped,	tetrahedroid
parallelepipedon	tetrahedron
parallelogram	triangle
pentagon	trigon
pentahedron	trilateral

251. CURVATURE

NOUNS 1. **curvature,** curving, curvation; incurvature, incurvation; excurvature, excurvation; decurvature, decurvation; **arching, vaulting,** arcuation, concameration; aduncity, aquilinity; circularity 252; convolution 253; rotundity 254.

2. **curve,** sinus, bought [dial.]; **bow, arc; crook, hook;** parabola, hyperbola [both geom.]; caustic, catacaustic, diacaustic [all optical]; catenary [math.], festoon; tracery; circle 252.2; curl 253.2.

3. **bend,** bending; **bow,** bowing; **turn,** turning, sweep; **flexure,** flex, **flection,** flexion, inflection, deflection; reflection; geanticline, geosyncline [both geol.].

4. **arch, span, vault,** vaulting, concam-

eration, fornix [anat. & bot.]; camber; ogive; apse; **dome,** cupola, concha; cove; arched roof, ceilinged roof; **arcade, archway,** arcature; voussoir, keystone, skewback.

5. **crescent, semicircle,** meniscus; crescent moon, half-moon; lunula, lunule [zool.]; horseshoe.

VERBS 6. **curve, turn,** sweep; **crook, hook;** incurve, incurvate; recurve, decurve; sag, swag [dial.]; **bend,** flex; deflect, inflect; reflect, reflex; **bow,** embow; **arch, vault;** dome; **hump,** hunch; wind, curl 253.4, 5; round 254.8.

ADJS. 7. **curved,** curve, curvate, curvated, **curving,** curvy, curvaceous [coll.], curvesome, curviform; curvilinear, curvilineal; **bent,** bendified [slang]; incurved, incurving, incurvate, incurvated; recurved, recurving, recurvate, recurvated; geosynclinal, geanticlinal [both geol.].

8. **hooked, crooked, aquiline,** aduncous; **hook-shaped,** hooklike; uncate, uncinal, unciform; hamulate, hamate, hamiform; clawlike, unguiform; **hook-nosed,** acquiline-nosed, Roman-nosed, crooknosed, crookbilled.

9. **beaked,** billed; **beak-shaped,** beaklike; bill-shaped, bill-like; rostrate, rostriform; rhamphoid.

10. **bowed,** embowed, bandy; bowlike, bow-shaped; convex, convexed; convexo-concave; arcuate, arcuated, arcual, arciform, arclike; **arched,** vaulted; **humped,** hunched, humpy, hunchy; gibbous, gibbose; humpbacked 248.13.

11. **crescent-shaped,** crescentlike, crescent, crescentiform; meniscoid(al), menisciform; sigmoid; **semicircular,** semilunar; horn-shaped, hornlike, horny, horned, corniform; bicorn, two-horned.

12. boat-shaped, boatlike; navicular, naviform; cymbiform, scaphoid.

13. sickle-shaped, sicklelike; falcate, falciform.

14. lens-shaped, lenticular, lentiform.

15. moon-shaped, moonlike, lunar, lunate, lunular, luniform; Cynthian.

16. bell-shaped, bell-like; campanular, campanulate, campaniform.

17. pear-shaped, pearlike, pyriform, obconic(al).

18. heart-shaped, heartlike; cordate, cardioid, cordiform.

19. kidney-shaped, kidneylike, reniform.

20. turnip-shaped, turniplike, napiform.

21. shell-shaped, shell-like; conchate, conchiform.

22. shield-shaped, shieldlike, peltate; scutate, scutiform; clypeate, clypeiform.

23. helmet-shaped, helmetlike, galeiform, cassideous.

24. **arches**

fixed arch	round arch
flat arch	rowlock arch
four-centered or	segmental arch
Tudor arch	shouldered arch
horseshoe arch	three-centered or
lancet arch	basket-handle
ogee arch	arch
primitive arch	trefoil arch
rampant arch	

252. CIRCULARITY

Simple Circularity.—NOUNS **1. circularity, roundness,** annularity.

2. circle, ring, annulus, orb [poetic], O; **circumference,** radius; **round,** roundel, rondelle [tech.]; **cycle, circuit;** wheel 320.4, 18; disk; loop, looplet; noose, lasso; crown, diadem, coronet, corona; garland, wreath; halo, areola or areole, aureole; washer.

3. (thing encircling) **band, belt, cincture,** cingulum [tech.], **girdle, girth,** girt, zone, fascia, fillet; waistband, bellyband, baldric, cestus [Gr. & Rom. antiq.], sash, cummerbund [India]; collar, collarband, neckband; necklace, chaplet; bracelet, armlet, wristlet, wristband, anklet; ring, earring, nose ring; hoop, hoople [local, U.S.]; zodiac, baldric [poetic]; cordon.

4. rim, felly, tire; pneumatic tire, pneumatic; balloon tire, balloon; tubeless tire, safety tire, nonskid tire; retread, recap; flat tire, flat casing [U.S.]; tread; tube, inner tube.

5. circlet, ringlet, roundlet, annulet, eye, **eyelet,** grommet.

6. oval, ovule, ovoid; ellipse, ellipsoid; spheroid oblate spheroid, prolate spheroid.

7. cycloid; epicycloid, epicycle.

8. semicircle, half circle, hemicycle; crescent 251.5; quadrant, sextant, sector.

VERBS **9. circle, round;** circularize; **encircle** 232.7.

ADJS. **10. circular, round,** rounded, annular, ringlike; disklike, discoid; cyclic(al), cycloid(al); coronary, crownlike.

11. oval, ovate, ovoid, oviform; eggshaped; elliptic(al), ellipsoidal; oblate, prolate; obovate, obovoid [both bot.].

253. CONVOLUTION

Complex Circularity.—NOUNS **1. convolution,** involution, circumvolution, wind-ing, **twisting, turning; meander,** meandering; crinkle, crinkling; ambagiousness, ambages; tortuousness, tortuosity, tortility; torsion, intorsion; sinuousness, sinuosity, sinuation; flexuousness, flexuosity; undulation, wave, waving; rivulation.

2. coil, quoil [dial.], **whorl,** roll, **curl,** curlique, **spiral,** helix, volute; **kink, twist, twirl;** screw, corkscrew; tendril, cirrus; snake, serpent, viper, worm, eel.

3. curler, curling iron; curlpaper, papillote.

VERBS **4.** convolve, **wind, twine, twirl, twist, turn, twist and turn, meander,** crinkle; serpentine, snake, worm; screw, corkscrew [coll.]; whorl; scallop, escallop; wring; intort; contort.

5. curl, coil, quoil [dial.]; crisp, kink, crimp; friz or frizz, frizzle; marcel.

ADJS. **6. convolutional, winding, twisting, turning; meandering,** meandrous; **serpentine,** screwy, anfractuous; **sinuous,** sinuose, sinuate; **tortuous,** torsional, tortile; flexuous, flexuose; involutional, involute, involuted; rivose, rivulose [chiefly bot.]; sigmoid(al); wreathy, wreathlike; ruffled, crêpé [F.]; whorled.

7. snakelike, snaky, snake-shaped, **serpentine,** serpentile, serpentoid; serpentiform; anguine, anguiform; eellike, eel-shaped, anguilliform; wormlike, vermiform, lumbriciform.

8. spiral, spiroid; helical, helicoid(al); anfractuous; screw-shaped, screwy, corkscrew, corkscrewy; cochlear, cochleate; turbinal, turbinate [both zool.].

9. curly, curled; **kinky,** kinked; **frizzly,** frizzy, frizzed; crispy, crisp, crisped.

10. wavy, undulatory, undulative, undulating, undulate, undulated; **billowy,** surgy, rolling; flamboyant.

ADVS. **11. windingly, twistingly,** sinuously, tortuously, serpentinely, meanderingly, meandrously; **in-and-out,** round and round.

254. ROTUNDITY

NOUNS **1. rotundity, roundness,** rotundness, orbicularity; **sphericalness,** sphericality; globularity, globosity; spheroidity, spheroidicity; cylindricality.

2. sphere, ball, orb, orbit, **globe;** geoid; spheroid, globoid; spherule, globule, globelet, orblet; blob; **pellet;** bulb, bulbil [bot. & anat.], bulblet; knob, knot; football, pigskin [coll.]; spherulite [petrog.].

3. **drop**, droplet; dewdrop, raindrop; tear; bead, pearl.

4. **cylinder**, cylindroid; pillar, column; barrel, drum; roll, rouleau, roller, rolling pin.

5. **cone**, conoid, conelet; complex cone, cone of a complex; funnel, pyramid, ice-cream cone, pine cone, cornet, cop.

VERBS 6. **round**, rotund; **round out, fill out**; cone, pyramid.

7. **ball, snowball**; sphere, spherify, globe; bead.

ADJS. 8. **rotund, round,** rounded, rounded out, round as a ball.

9. **spheric(al)**, sphere, spheriform, spherelike; **globular, global,** globed, globous, globose, globate, globelike, globe-shaped; **orbic(al)**, orbicular, orbiculate, orbed, orb, orby, orblike; spheroid(al), globoid; hemispheric(al).

10. **beady**, beaded, bead-shaped, bead-like; moniliform, monilated, moniloid [all bot. & zool.].

11. **cylindric(al)**, cylindroid(al); **columnar**, columnal, columned, columelliform.

12. **conic(al)**, coned, cone-shaped, cone-like; conoid(al); spheroconic; funnel-shaped, funnellike, funnelled, funnelform [bot.], infundibuliform, infundibular; pyramidal, pyramidical.

13. **balls**

ball bearing	golf ball
baseball	handball
basketball	medicine ball
billiard ball	ping-pong ball
bowling ball, bowl	polo ball
cannon ball	pushball
clew	shot
cricket ball	snowball
croquet ball	soft ball
eight ball	tennis ball
football	volleyball

14. **pellets**

BB	pea
bead	pearl
buckshot	pebble
bullet	pill
marble	shot

255. CONVEXITY, PROTUBERANCE

NOUNS 1. **convexity**, convexness, convexedness; excurvature, excurvation; camber.

2. **protuberance** or protuberancy, **projection, protrusion, extrusion**; prominence, salience, boldness; gibbousness, gibbosity; excrescence or excrescency; tuberousness, tuberosity, flange, lip; jog, joggle; shoulders, withers; salient [mil.].

3. **bulge**, bilge, bow, convex; **bump**, thank-you-ma'am [U.S.], cahot [chiefly Can.]; **hump**, hunch; **lump**, clump; nubbin; mole, nevus [med.]; wart, verruca [med.]; **knob**, boss, bulla, button, stud; **knot**, knur, knurl, gnarl, burl; **ridge**, rib, chine, spine; welt [coll.], whelp [dial., U.S.], wale; bleb, blob [chiefly dial.]; blister, vesicle [med.]; bubble.

4. **swelling, swell**, swollenness; **rising, lump, bump**, pimple [fig.], pustule [fig.]; dilation, dilatation; tumescence, intumescence; tumor, tumefaction; distention 196.2; pustule 655.16.

5. **node**, nodule, nodulus, nodulation, nodosity.

6. **breast, bosom, bust, chest**, crop [dial.], brisket [zool.]; thorax; bubby [vulg.], booby [slang], mamma; **teat**, tit [vulgar exc. zool.], titty [familiar], dug [derog. exc. zool.]; **nipple**, papilla, pap [dial.], mammilla, mamelon [F.]; mammillation, mamelonation.

7. **nose**, nese [Scot.], olfactory organ, **snout** [chiefly coll. exc. zool.], snoot [coll.], nozzle [slang exc. zool.], muzzle [zool.]; **proboscis** [joc. exc. zool.], antlia [zool.], trunk (of an elephant); **beak; bill,** pecker [all slang exc. zool.]; nib, neb [Scot.]; smeller, beezer, bugle, schnozzle, conk [all slang]; muffle, rhinarium [both zool.]; nostrils, noseholes [dial., Eng.], nares.

8. (point of land) **point**, hook, spur, **cape**, tongue, bill; **promontory**, foreland, **headland**, head, mull [Scot.]; naze, ness (chiefly in place names); **neck, isthmus; peninsula**, chersonese; **delta; spit**, sandspit; **reef**, coral reef; breakwater 215.4.

VERBS 9. **protrude, protuberate, project, extrude; stick out,** jut out, poke out, stand out, shoot out; **stick up**, bristle up, start up, cock up, shoot up.

10. **bulge**, bilge, bouge, **belly**, bag, **pouch**, pooch [dial.]; pout; **goggle**, bug [coll., U.S.], pop; **swell, dilate, distend**, billow; swell out, belly out, round out.

11. **boss, emboss**, chase, raise; ridge.

ADJS. 12. **convex**, convexed; excurved, excurvate, excurvated [all zool.]; bowed, arched 251.10; gibbous, gibbose; humped 251.10.

13. **protruding, protrusive**, protrudent; **protuberant**, protuberating; **projecting, extruding**, outstanding; prominent, eminent, salient, bold; prognathous; excrescent, excrescential; protrusile.

14. bulging, swelling, bellying, pouching; bagging, baggy; billowing, billowy; bumpy, bumped; bunchy, bunched; bulbous, bulbose; warty, verrucose, verrucated.

15. bulged, bulgy; swollen 196.12; bellied, ventricose; pouched, pooched [dial.]; goggled, goggle; bug-eyed [slang], pop-eyed [coll.].

16. knobbed, knobby, knoblike, torose; knotty, knotted; gnarled, knurled, knurly, gnarly; noded, nodal, nodiform; noduled, nodular, nodulated; tuberculous, tubercular; tuberous, tuberose.

17. in relief, in bold or high relief, bold, raised, repoussé [F.]; chased, bossed, embossed, bossy.

18. pectoral, bosom; mammary, mammillary, mammiform; mammalian, mammate; papillary, papillose, papulous; breasted, bosomed, chested; teated, nippled.

19. peninsular; isthmic, isthmian; deltaic, deltal.

256. CONCAVITY

NOUNS 1. concavity, hollowness; incurvature, incurvation.

2. cavity, concavity, concave, hollow, hole, pit, depression, dip, sink; scoop, pocket; basin, bowl, cup; crater, crump hole [army slang]; antrum, sinus [anat. & zool.]; lacuna; alveola, alveolus, alveolation [all tech.]; vug or vugg, vugh [all min.]; follicle, crypt [anat.]; armpit; socket.

3. pothole, sinkhole, pitchhole, chuckhole [U.S.], mudhole, cahot [chiefly Can.], thank-you-ma'am [coll., U.S.], Yankee bump [dial., U.S.], love-hole [dial.], dips-and-ducks.

4. pit, well, shaft; chasm, gulf, abyss, abysm; excavation, grave [chiefly dial.], groove [dial.]; diggings, workings; mine 382.6.

5. cave. cavern, cove [Scot. & North. Eng.], hole, grotto, subterrane; lair 190.22; tunnel, burrow; subway, underground [Eng.], tube; dugout, abri [F.].

6. indentation, indent, indention, indenture, dent, dint; dimple; pit, pockmark; impression, impress; imprint, print; alveolus, alveolation; honeycomb; notch 261.

7. recess, recession, niche, nook; cove, alcove; bay; pitchhole.

8. (a hollow in the side of a mountain) coomb, cwm, cirque, corrie [all geol.].

9. valley, vale [poetic], dale, dell;

glen, coomb, bottom, bottoms, bottom glade, intervale [local U.S. & Can.], strath [Scot.], gill, ghyll [Scot. & dial., Eng.], dingle, wadi [Near East & N. Africa], grove [dial.], park [U.S.]; ravine 200.3.

10. excavator, digger; sapper [mil.]; miner 382.8; tunneler, sand hog [slang], ground hog [min.]; driller; steam shovel, navvy; dredge, dredger.

11. excavation, digging; mining.

VERBS 12. (be concave) dish, cup, bowl, hollow; retreat, retire.

13. hollow, hollow out, concave, dish, dish out, cup, bowl; cave, cave in.

14. indent, dent, dint, depress; impress, imprint; pit; pock, pockmark; dimple; recess, set back; set in; notch 261.4.

15. excavate, dig, dig out, scoop, scoop out, gouge, gouge out, grub, delve [now chiefly dial.], grave [dial.]; dredge; tunnel, burrow; drive [min.], sink, lower; mine, sap; quarry; drill.

ADJS. 16. concave, incurved, incurving, incurvous; sunk, sunken; retreating, retiring; hollow, hollowed; dished, dishing; cupped, cup-shaped, scyphate, scyphiform, calathiform; cavernous.

17. indented, dented, depressed; dimpled; pitted; pocked, pock-marked; honeycombed, alveolar, alveolate, faveolate; notched 261.5.

257. SHARPNESS

NOUNS 1. sharpness, keenness, edge; acuteness, acuity; pointedness, acumination; spinosity, mucronation.

2. (sharp edge) edge, knife-edge, razor-edge, featheredge.

3. edged tools 347.2, 10; side arms 799.22.

4. point, tip, cusp, acumination; nib, neb; spike, pike; prong, tine, tang [Scot. & dial., Eng.]; prick, prickle; spearhead.

5. (pointed projection) projection, jag; snag, snaggle; tooth, fang; denticulation, denticle, dentil [arch.], dent [tech.]; cog, sprocket, ratchet; saw tooth; comb, harrow, rake.

6. teeth [anat.], game [Scot.], picket fence [slang]; denture, false teeth, set of teeth, plate, bridgework, dental bridge, uppers and lowers; crown; gums.

7. tooth [anat.], pearl, ivory [slang], dental [joc.], poose [childish]; fang, tang [dial.]; tusk, tush [dial.], scrivello; snag, snaggletooth, peg; bucktooth, gagtooth or gang tooth [dial.]; cuspid, bicuspid; canine tooth, canine, dogtooth, eyetooth; molar,

grinder; premolar; incisor, cutter, fore tooth; wisdom tooth; milk tooth; crown.

8. **thorn, bramble, brier, nettle,** bur *or* burr, prickle, sticker [coll.]; **spike,** spikelet; **spine; needle,** pine, pine needle; thistle, catchweed, cleavers, goose grass, cactus; beggar's-lice, beggar's-ticks; yucca, Adam's-needle.

VERBS 9. come to a point, acuminate.

10. **sharpen, edge,** acuminate; **whet, hone,** file, grind; strop, strap; set, reset; point, cuspidate; barb.

ADJS. 11. **sharp, keen, edged, acute,** poignant [fig.], fine, **cutting,** knifelike; sharp-edged, keen-edged, razor-edged, knife-edged, featheredged; two-edged, double-edged; sharp as a razor, sharp as a needle, sharp as a tack, "sharp as a two-edged sword" [Bible], "sharper than a serpent's tooth" [Shakespeare]; sharpened, set.

12. **pointed,** acuminate; tapered, tapering; cusped, cuspidate; **sharp-pointed,** aculeate; **needlelike,** acicular; **spiked,** spiky, spiculate; **barbed, tined, pronged; horned,** horny, cornuted, corniculate, cornified [anat.]; **spined,** spiny, spinous, mucronate, "like quills upon the fretful porpentine" [Shakespeare].

13. **prickly,** pricky [dial.], muricate, echinate, acanaceous [bot.]; pricking, stinging; **thorny,** brambly, briery, thistly.

14. **arrowlike,** arrowy, arrowheaded; sagittal, sagittate, sagittiform.

15. **spearlike,** hastate; lancelike, lanciform.

16. **swordlike,** gladiate, ensate, ensiform.

17. **toothlike,** dentiform, dentoid, odontoid; dental; molar; bicuspid; **toothed, fanged, tusked;** snaggle-toothed, snaggled.

18. **star-shaped, starlike,** starry, stellar, stellate, stellular, stelliform.

19. points

antler	hat pin
awl	hook
barb	horn
barblet	lance
barbule	nail
barbwire, barbed wire	needle 222.8
	pike
bodkin	pin
carpet tack	pitchfork
cheval-de-frise	prong
fishhook	quill
fork	rowel
gaff	skewer
gimlet	spear
harpoon	spicule

spiculum [zool.]	staple
spike	tack
spine	thumbtack
spit	tine
spur	

20. sharpeners

carborundum	oilstone
emery	rubstone
emery wheel	steel
file	strap, strop
grindstone	whetrock [dial.]
hone	whetstone
novaculite	

258. BLUNTNESS

NOUNS 1. **bluntness, dullness,** unsharpness, obtuseness, obtundity; bluffness; abruptness; dullification [coll.].

VERBS 2. **blunt, dull,** dullify [coll.], obtund, **take the edge off;** turn, turn the edge *or* point of; weaken, repress.

ADJS. 3. **blunt, dull,** obtuse; bluntish, dullish; **unsharp,** unsharpened; **unedged,** edgeless; **unpointed,** pointless; blunted, dulled; blunt-edged, dull-edged; blunt-pointed, dull-pointed, blunt-ended; **bluff,** abrupt.

4. **toothless,** teethless, edentate, edental.

259. SMOOTHNESS

NOUNS 1. **smoothness, levelness, flatness,** evenness, uniformity, regularity; **sleekness,** glossiness; **slickness,** slipperiness; silkiness, velvetiness.

2. **polish, gloss, glaze, burnish, shine,** luster; patina.

3. (smooth surface) smooth, **plane, level, flat;** slide; glass, ice; marble, alabaster, ivory; silk, satin, velvet.

4. **smoother,** smooth; sleeker, slicker; polish, burnish; **abrasive,** abradant.

VERBS 5. **smooth, flatten, plane,** planish, **level,** even, equalize; **dress,** dub, dab; smooth down, lay; plaster, plaster down; harrow, drag; grade; mow, shave.

6. **press,** hot-press, **iron, mangle,** calender; roll.

7. **polish, shine** [coll.], **burnish,** furbish, sleek, slick [coll.], gloss, glaze, glance (metal work), luster; **rub,** scour, buff; wax.

8. **grind, file, sand,** sandpaper, emery, pumice; sandblast.

ADJS. 9. **smooth, even, level, plane, flat,** regular, uniform, **unbroken;** unrough, unroughened, unruffled, unwrinkled; glabrous, glabrate [bot. & zool.]; smooth-shaven 231.17.

10. **sleek, slick, glossy;** silky, silken,

satiny, velvety; **polished,** burnished, furbished; glazed, *glacé* [F.]; glassy, smooth as glass.

11. slippery, slippy, **slick,** slithery [chiefly dial.], sliddery [dial.], slippery as an eel.

ADVS. **12. smoothly, evenly,** regularly, uniformly; **like clockwork,** on wheels.

13. smoothers

buff	ironing board
buffer	mangle
burnisher	plane 347.14
calender	planisher
chamois	polisher
drag	press
electric iron	presser
flatiron	roller
floor polisher	rolling pin
glazer	sadiron
goose	smoothing iron
grader	steam roller
harrow	trowel 347.13
iron	

14. polishes, abrasives

aluminum oxide	pumice stone
auto polish	quartz sand
corundum	rasp
emery	rottenstone
emery board	sandpaper
emery paper	scouring pad
file	shoe polish
furniture polish	silicon carbide
garnet	silver polish
nail file	tripoli
pumice	wax

260. ROUGHNESS

NOUNS **1. roughness, unsmoothness, unevenness,** irregularity, ununiformity, inequality, asperity; **ruggedness,** rugosity; **raggedness,** raggedness, cragginess, scraggliness; **bumpiness; choppiness;** granulation; hispicity.

2. (rough surface) **rough,** broken ground; **corrugation,** ripple, washboard; washboard road, corduroy road, corduroy.

3. bristle, barb [bot.], striga [bot.]; setule, setula, seta [biol. & bot.]; **stubble.**

VERBS **4. roughen,** rough, rough up; coarsen; granulate; gnarl.

5. ruffle, rumple, bristle; **rub the wrong way,** go the wrong way of the goods, **go against the grain,** set on edge.

ADJS. **6. rough, unsmooth, uneven,** ununiform, unlevel, inequal, **broken,** irregular; **bumpy; choppy;** ruffled, unkempt; **shaggy,** shagged; **coarse,** rank, unrefined; unpolished; rough-grained, coarse-grained; cross-grained; granulated; rough-hewn, rough-cast; homespun, linsey-woolsey.

7. rugged, ragged; **jagged,** jaggy;

snaggy, snagged, snaggled; **scraggy,** scragged, scraggly; **craggy,** cragged; **rocky,** stony; rock-bound, ironbound.

8. gnarled, gnarly; **knurled,** knurly; **knotted,** knotty.

9. bristly, bristling, bristled, hispid, hirsute, barbellate [bot.], glochidiate [bot.]; setaceous, setose; strigal, strigose, strigate [all bot.]; studded; **stubbled,** stubbly; hairy 229.24.

10. bristlelike, setiform, aristate, setarious.

ADVS. **11. roughly,** rough, **in the rough;** unsmoothly, brokenly, unevenly, irregularly.

12. cross-grained, **against the grain,** the wrong way, the wrong way of the goods.

261. NOTCH

NOUNS **1. notch, nick,** nitch [dial.], nock (as of an arrow), **cut,** cleft, **incision, gash,** hack, blaze, scotch, **score,** kerf, crena, depression, jag; **jog, joggle; indentation** 256.6.

2. notching, serration; denticulation, dentil [arch.], dentil band [arch.]; crenation, crenelation, crenulation; scallop, escallop; rickrack; picot edge, Vandyke edge; cockscomb, crest; saw, saw teeth.

3. battlement, embrasure, castellation, machicolation.

VERBS **4. notch, nick,** nitch [dial.], **cut, incise, gash,** crimp, scotch, **score,** blaze, jag, scarify; **indent** 256.14; scallop, escallop; serrate, pink, mill (as coins), tooth, Vandyke.

ADJS. **5. notched, nicked,** incised, gashed, scotched, scored, blazed; **indented** 256.17; serrate, serrated; crenate, crenated; scalloped, escalloped; dentate, dentated; toothed; saw-toothed, **sawlike;** lacerate, lacerated; **jagged,** jaggy; erose [bot.].

262. FURROW

NOUNS **1. furrow, groove,** scratch, crack, cranny, chink, score, **cut,** gash, gouge, slit, chase, incision; sulcus, sulcation; **rut,** ruck [dial., Eng.], well-worn groove; wrinkle 263.3; **corrugation;** flute, fluting; microgroove.

2. trench, trough, channel, ditch, dike, fosse, grave [chiefly dial.], **canal,** cut, graff [hist.]; gutter, grip [chiefly dial., Eng.]; moat [fort.]; levee; ha-ha; aqueduct 395; entrenchment [mil.] 797.5; canalization.

VERBS **3. furrow, groove,** score, scratch, incise, cut, carve, chisel, gash, gouge, slit, crack; plow; **channel, trough, flute,** chamfer; **trench,** canal [U.S.], canalize, **ditch,** dike, gully [U.S.], **rut; corrugate;** wrinkle 263.6.

ADJS. **4. furrowed, grooved,** scored, scratched, incised, cut, gashed, gouged, slit; **channeled, troughed, fluted;** sulcate, sulcated; canaliculate, canaliculated; **rutted; corrugated,** corrugate; corduroy, corduroyed; wrinkled 263.8; ribbed, costate [bot. & zool.].

263. FOLD

NOUNS **1. fold, double,** doubling, duplicature; ply; plication, plica, plicature; flection, flexure; **crease,** creasing; crimp; **tuck, gather;** ruffle, frill; flounce; lappet; lapel; dog's-ear, dog-ear.

2. pleat, plait, plat [dial.]; accordion pleat, box pleat, knife pleat.

3. wrinkle, corrugation, ridge, **furrow, crease,** crimp, ruck, **pucker,** cockle; **crinkle,** crankle, rimple, ripple; crumple, rumple; crow's-feet.

4. folding, infolding, **infoldment** or enfoldment; plication, plicature.

VERBS **5. fold,** infold or enfold, **double,** ply, plicate; fold over, double over, lap over, turn over or under; **crease, crimp;** crisp; **pleat,** plait, plat [dial.]; **tuck, gather;** ruffle, ruff, frill; flounce; twill, quill, flute; dog-ear, dog's-ear; interfold.

6. wrinkle, corrugate, shirr, ridge, **furrow, crease,** crimp, crimple [dial., Eng.], cockle, cocker [dial.], **pucker, purse; knit,** knot; ruck, ruckle [Eng.]; **crumple,** rumple; **crinkle,** rimple, ripple; curl, crisp, kink, frizz, frizzle.

ADJS. **7. folded, doubled,** enfolden [poetic]; plicate, plicated; **pleated,** plaited; **creased,** crimped; tucked, gathered; flounced; twilled, quilled, fluted; dog-eared.

8. wrinkled, wrinkly; **corrugated,** corrugate; **creased, furrowed,** ridged; cockled, cockly [dial.]; puckered, puckery; pursed, pursy; **knitted,** knotted; rugged, rugose, rugous; **crinkled,** crinkly, crankelty [dial.], rimpled, rippled; crisped, crispy; frizzled, frizzly; crimped, crimpy; **crumpled,** rumpled.

264. OPENING

NOUNS **1. opening, aperture, hole, orifice,** slot (esp. elongated); passageway 655.4; inlet 301.5; outlet 302.9; **gap, gape,** yawn, hiatus, **chasm, gulf;** cleft 200.2; fontanel; foramen, fenestra; stoma; pore.

2. gaping, yawning, oscitation, oscitancy, dehiscence, pandiculation; **gape, yawn** (in physiological sense); the gapes.

3. perforation, penetration, piercing, puncture, broach, transforation [surg.]; terebration; acupuncture, acupunctuation; **impalement,** transfixion, transfixation; bore, borehole, drill hole.

4. (holes) armhole, bunghole, keyhole, knothole, loophole, manhole, mousehole, peephole, pigeonhole, pinhole, porthole; placket, placket hole; vent, venthole; air hole, blowhole, spiracle; eye, eyelet, eye of a needle.

5. mouth [anat.], mouthpiece [joc.], gob [dial. or vulgar], gab [Scot.]; **muzzle** [joc. exc. zool.], jaw, lips; bazoo, kisser, mug, mush, trap, yap [all slang]; **jaws,** mandibles, chops, chaps, jowls; maxilla; premaxilla.

6. (mouthlike aperture) **orifice, mouth** bouche [F.]; embouchure, embouchement [F.]; mouthpiece; estuary, influx, firth, frith; jaws, cheeks (as of a vice); muzzle, nozzle.

7. window, casement [poetic]; porthole, port; bull's-eye, œil-de-bœuf [F.]; casement window; bay window, bow window, bay, window bay, oriel, dormer; picture window; grille, wicket, lattice; fanlight, fan window; skylight, lantern; **windowpane,** window glass, pane, light.

8. porousness, porosity; sievelikeness, cribriformity; screen, sieve, riddle, net, honeycomb; sponge.

9. perviousness, permeability, accessibility.

10. opener; can opener, tin opener [Eng.]; corkscrew, bottle screw; latchstring, key, screw [thieves' slang], clavis; latchkey, passkey, passe partout [F.], master key, skeleton key; open-sesame.

VERBS **11. open,** ope [poetic], **open up,** lay open, throw open; fly open, spring open, swing open; **tap, broach;** cut open, cut, cleave, split, slit, crack, chink, fissure, crevasse, incise; rift, rive; tear open, rent, tear, rip; part, dispart, separate, divide, divaricate; spread, spread out.

12. unclose, unshut; **unfold,** unwrap, unroll; **unstop, unclog, unblock,** deobstruct; **unplug,** uncork; **unlock,** unlatch, undo; unseal, unclench, unclutch; **uncover,** uncase, unsheathe, unveil, undrape, uncurtain; **disclose,** expose, reveal, bare.

13. make an opening, find an opening, make place, **make way, make room.**

14. **breach, rupture; break open,** force open, pry open, crack open; break into, break through; break in, burst in, bust in [dial. & inelegant], stave in, cave in.

15. **perforate, pierce, penetrate, puncture,** punch, prick, bite, hole; **tap, broach; stab, stick,** pink, run through; **transfix,** transpierce, **impale,** spit; spear, lance, spike, needle; **bore,** drill, auger; **ream,** rime [Eng.]; gouge, gouge out; trepan, trephine [both surg.]; punch full of holes, **riddle, honeycomb.**

16. **gape,** gap [dial.], **yawn,** oscitate, dehisce, hang open.

ADJS. 17. **open, unclosed,** uncovered; **unobstructed, unstopped, unclogged;** clear, free; wide-open, unrestricted; bare, exposed. naked, bald.

18. **gaping, yawning,** oscitant, dehiscent, ringent; agape, ajar.

19. **apertured,** slotted, **holey;** perforated, perforate; honeycombed, riddled.

20. **porous,** porose; sievelike, cribriform; spongy, spongelike.

21. **pervious, permeable, penetrable,** openable, accessible.

22. orificial, **mouthlike, oral;** mandibular, maxiliary.

INTERJS. 23. **open up!,** open sesame!, gangway!, passageway!, make way!

265. CLOSURE

NOUNS 1. **closure, closing, shutting,** occlusion; **shutdown;** blockade.

2. **imperviousness, impermeability, impenetrability,** impassability; imperforation.

3. **obstruction, clog, block,** blockade, **blockage, stoppage** stop, bar, barrier, obstacle, impediment; **congestion,** jam; gorge; constipation, obstipation [med.], costiveness; infarct, infarction; embolism, embolus [both med.]; bottleneck.

4. **stopper,** stop, **stopple,** stopgap; **plug,** cork, bung, spike, spill, spile, tap, spigot, peg, pin; lid 227.5.

5. **stopping, wadding, stuffing,** padding, **packing;** gasket.

VERBS 6. **close, shut,** occlude; close up, shut up; fold, fold up; **fasten,** secure; **lock,** lock up, key, padlock, latch, bolt, bar, barricade; **seal,** seal up, plumb; button, button up; snap; zipper, zip up; batten, batten down; shut the door, slam, clap, bang.

7. **stop, stop up; obstruct,** bar; **block,** block up; **clog,** clog up, foul; **choke,** choke up; **fill,** fill up; **stuff,** pack, jam; **congest,** stuff up; **plug,** plug up; stopper, stopple, cork, bung, spile; cover; **dam,** dam up; stanch, staunch, stench [Scot.]; chink; calk or caulk; blockade; constipate, bind.

8. **shut up shop,** close shop, close up, shut up, **shut down,** close down [U.S.], shutter [slang], put up the shutters.

ADJS. 9. **closed, shut, unopen,** unopened; unvented, unventilated; blank; blind, caecal, dead; dead-end, blind-alley.

10. **unpierced,** pierceless, **unperforated,** imperforate, infarcted; **untrodden,** pathless, wayless, trackless.

11. **stopped, stopped up; obstructed, blocked; plugged,** plugged up; **clogged,** clogged up; foul, fouled; **choked,** choked up; **full, stuffed,** packed, jammed; **congested,** stuffed up; constipated, costive, bound.

12. **close, tight, compact, fast,** shut fast, **snug,** stanch, firm; sealed; hermetic(al), hermetically sealed; airtight, dust-tight, gastight, light-tight, oiltight, raintight, smoketight, storm-tight, watertight, windtight.

13. **impervious, impenetrable, impermeable; impassable,** unpassable; unpierceable, unperforable; **punctureproof,** nonpuncturable.

266. MOTION

Motion in General.—NOUNS 1. **motion, movement,** moving, move, stir; activity 705; kinesis; actuation; mobilization.

2. **course, career,** set, **passage,** flow, flux, flight, **stream, current,** run, rush, onrush, ongoing; drift, driftage.

3. **motivity,** motive power, motility, movableness; motorium.

VERBS 4. **move, budge, stir;** go, travel 272.17; move over, mooch over [slang], get over; shift, change, shift or change place.

5. **set in motion, move, actuate,** impel, propel; mobilize.

ADJS. 6. **moving, stirring, in motion;** transitional; motive, motile, motor; traveling 272.35; active 705.16.

ADVS. 7. **under way,** under sail.

267. QUIESCENCE

Being at Rest; Absence of Motion.—NOUNS 1. **quiescence** or quiescency, **stillness,** quietness, **quiet,** quietude; **calmness,** restfulness, **peacefulness, placidness,** placidity, **tranquillity, serenity, peace,** composure; **rest, repose,** silken repose, statuelike repose.

2. **motionlessness, immobility;** inactivity, inaction; fixity, fixation.

3. **standstill, stand,** stillstand; **stop, halt;** dead stop, dead stand [So. U.S.], full stop; deadlock, lock, dead set.

4. **inertness, dormancy; inertia,** vis inertia; passiveness, passivity; suspense, abeyance, latency; torpor, languor; **stagnation,** stagnancy, **vegetation,** stasis [physics]; backwater.

5. **calm,** "the stilly hour when storms are gone" [T. Moore]; **lull,** lull before the storm; dead calm, deathlike calm; up-and-down wind, Irishman's hurricane, soldier's wind [all joc., naut.]; doldrums; anticyclone.

6. **airlessness, closeness, oppressiveness,** oppression, **stuffiness.**

VERBS 7. **be still, keep quiet,** lie still; **rest, repose; remain, stay,** tarry; remain motionless, freeze [coll.]; stand, **stand still,** be at a standstill; stand or stick fast, stick, stand firm, stay put [chiefly coll.]; stand like a post, stand like a stuck pig [coll.]; **not stir,** not stir a step; not breathe, hold one's breath; abide, abide one's time, mark time; rest on one's oars, rest and be thankful.

8. (be inert) **stagnate, vegetate;** sleep, slumber; smolder, hang fire; idle [mach.].

9. **becalm,** take the wind out of one's sails; calm, tranquilize 162.7.

ADJS. 10. **quiescent, quiet, still,** stilly [poetic], stillish, hushed; **at rest,** resting, reposing; restful, reposeful; **calm, tranquil, peaceful,** peaceable, pacific, halcyon; **placid, smooth; unruffled, untroubled,** undisturbed, unagitated, unmoved, unstirring; nothing doing [slang]; calm as a mill pond; still as death, "quiet as a street at night" [Rupert Brooke].

11. **motionless, unmoving,** moveless, **immobile,** immotive, **still, fixed, stationary,** at a standstill; **stock-still,** dead-still; still as a statue, statuelike; still as a mouse; at anchor, riding at anchor.

12. **inert, inactive, static, dormant,** passive, latent, suspended, abeyant, in suspense or abeyance; sleeping, slumbering, smoldering; **stagnant,** standing, foul; **torpid, languorous, languid; sluggish, logy** [U.S.], heavy, leaden, leaded, **dull,** flat, slack, tame, **dead, lifeless.**

13. **untraveled, stay-at-home.**

14. **airless, breathless,** breezeless, windless; close, **stuffy, oppressive, stifling, suffocating;** not a breath of air, not a leaf stirring, "not wind enough to twirl the one red leaf" [Coleridge]; ill-ventilated, unventilated, unvented.

15. **becalmed, in** a dead calm.

ADVS. 16. quiescently, **quietly,** stilly, still; **calmly, tranquilly, peacefully;** placidly, smoothly.

17. **motionlessly,** movelessly, stationarily, fixedly.

18. **inertly, inactively,** statically, dormantly, passively, latently; stagnantly; **torpidly, languorously, languidly; sluggishly,** heavily, dully, lifelessly.

268. VELOCITY

NOUNS 1. **velocity, speed, rapidity, celerity, swiftness, fastness, quickness,** snappiness [slang], speediness, gow [slang, U.S.]; **haste, hurry;** dispatch, expedition; flight, flit; eagle speed, lightning speed; fast or swift rate, smart or lively pace, round pace, tall stepping [slang]; air speed [aero.].

2. **rate, gait, pace,** tread, step, stride, pelt, bat [coll.], clip [coll.], lick [coll.], legs [slang, chiefly naut.]; **travel, progress,** career; revolutions per minute, r.p.m.

3. **speed of sound, sonic speed;** Mach, Mach one, Mach two, etc.; subsonic speed; supersonic ~, ultrasonic ~, hypersonic or transsonic speed.

4. **run, sprint; dash, rush,** brash, plunge, **race, scurry, scamper,** scud, scuttle, scuddle [Scot.], scour, scorch [coll.]; **spurt,** spurtle, burst, **burst of speed,** flutter [coll.]; canter, gallop, lope; high lope, hand gallop, full gallop; dead run; trot, fox trot [U.S.], round trot; dog trot, jog trot.

5. **acceleration, quickening, pickup;** step-up, speed-up [both coll.]; accelerator.

6. **speeder,** scorcher [slang], clipper [coll.], flier, goer, stepper, hot-shot [slang, U.S.], hummer [slang], hustler [coll.], sizzler [slang], **speed demon** or maniac [coll.]; **racer, runner;** horse racer, turfman, jockey.

7. (comparisons) lightning, greased lightning [slang], thunderbolt, streak of lightning, streak, blue streak [coll.], bat out of hell [slang], light, electricity, wind, shot, cannon ball, rocket, arrow, dart, hydrargyrum, quicksilver, mercury, express train, torrent, eagle, swallow, antelope, courser, barb, gazelle, greyhound, hare.

8. **speedometer,** velocimeter, accelerometer; cyclometer; Mach meter [aero.], log, log line, patent log, taffrail log, harpoon log, ground log [all naut.].

VERBS 9. **speed, go fast, got it,** come it [coll.], clip [coll.], spank, cut along [coll.], tear along, bowl along, bundle on or along, breeze or breeze along [slang], split the breeze or wind [slang], hit or burn the breeze [slang], scorch [coll.], sizzle [slang]; zip, whiz, whisk, sweep, brush, skim; fly, flit, fleet, wing one's way, fly on the wings of the wind, outstrip the wind; highball [coll., U.S.], ball the jack [slang, U.S.], barrel [slang, U.S.], bundle, powder [coll.], railroad [slang, U.S.], pour it on [slang, U.S.], hit the high spots [coll.]; dig, get out and dig [both slang]; ride hard, clap spurs to one's horse; boom, zoom; break the sound barrier.

10. rush, tear, dash, dart, shoot, bolt, fling, scamper, scurry, chevy, skedaddle [slang], scoot, scour, scud, scuttle, scuddle, [Scot.], scramble, race, chase [coll.], career; hasten, haste [literary], make haste, hurry, hie [poetic], post; step on it [slang], step on the gas [slang], hump or hump it [slang, U.S.], stir one's stumps [slang]; march in quick or double-quick time [mil.].

11. run, sprint, trip, spring, bound, peg [coll.], hotfoot [coll.], high-tail [coll.], make tracks [coll., U.S.], step lively [coll.], step or step along [coll.], do some tall stepping [slang], run along, hop or hop along [slang], get [slang, U.S.], git [dial., U.S.], get up or out and get [slang]; gallop, lope, canter; trot, fox-trot.

12. go like the wind, go like a shot, go like lightning or a streak of lightning, go like greased lightning [slang], go like a bat out of hell [slang], run like mad [coll.], go hell-bent for election [slang, U.S.].

13. make time, make good time, cover ground, get over the ground, make strides or rapid strides, make the best of one's way, put one's best foot foremost.

14. go at full blast [coll.], go all out [slang], run wide open, go full speed ahead, let her out [slang], open her up [slang].

15. accelerate, speed up, gear up, step up [coll.], hurry up [coll.], quicken; hasten 707.4; crack on, put on, put on steam, put on more speed, quicken one's pace, mend one's licks [slang]; pick up speed, gain ground; give her the gas, step on her tail, gun the motor, give her the gun [all slang]; race (the motor), rev [coll.].

16. (nautical and figurative) put on sail, crack or pack on sail, crowd sail, give her beans [naut. slang].

17. spurt, spurtle, make a spurt or dash, dash ahead, dart ahead, shoot ahead, rush ahead, put on or make a burst of speed.

18. keep up with, keep pace with, run neck and neck.

ADJS. 19. fast, swift, speedy, rapid, quick, double-quick, express, fleet, hasty, expeditious, snappy [slang], dashing; spanking, smacking, splitting [all coll.]; agile, nimble, nimble-footed, light-footed, light-legged, light of heel; winged, eagle-winged; mercurial; quick as lightning, quick as thought, swift as an arrow, "swifter than arrow from the Tartar's bow" [Shakespeare], "as swift as swallow flies" [ibid.].

20. supersonic, transsonic, ultrasonic, hypersonic, faster than sound.

ADVS. 21. swiftly, rapidly, quickly, snappily [slang], speedily, with speed, fast, quick, apace, amain, alive [coll.], on eagle's wings, ventre à terre [F., belly to the ground]; at a great rate, at a good bat or clip [coll.], with rapid strides, with giant strides, à pas de geant [F.], in seven-league boots, by leaps and bounds, trippingly; lickety-split, lickety-cut, lickety-brindle [all slang, U.S.]; hell-bent, hell-bent for election or leather, hell for leather [all slang, U.S.]; posthaste, post, hastily, expeditiously, with great or all haste, whip and spur, hand over hand or fist; double-quick, in double time, in double-quick time, on the double or double-quick [coll.]; in high, in high gear; under press of sail, under press of sail and steam [all naut.].

22. like a shot, like a flash, like a streak, like a blue streak [coll.], like a streak of lightning, like lightning, like greased lightning [coll.], like a bat out of hell [slang], like a house afire [coll.]; like sixty [coll.], like all forty [slang]; like mad, like fury [coll.], like all possessed [coll., U.S.], like sin [slang]; to beat the band, to beat the Dutch, to beat the deuce or devil [all slang].

23. in short order, in no time, in less than no time, in nothing flat [coll.]; in a jiff or jiffy [coll.], in a flash, in a twink, in a twinkling, "in the twinkling of an eye" [Bible], "in the twinkling of a bed-staff" [Thomas Shadwell], "in the squeezing of a lemon" [Goldsmith]; P.D.Q. [slang], pronto [Sp. & coll., U.S.].

24. at full speed, with all speed, at the top of one's bent, for all one is worth [coll.], as fast as one's legs will carry one, as fast as one can lay feet to the ground; at full blast, ~ drive, ~ bat, ~ butt, ~ pelt or chisel; under full steam, in full

sail; **all out** [slang], **wide open;** full speed ahead.

269. SLOWNESS

NOUNS 1. **slowness, leisureliness,** poki-ness, slackness; sluggishness, languor, lenti-tude; deliberateness, deliberation; drawl.

2. **slow motion, leisurely gait,** snail's *or* tortoise's pace; **creep, crawl; walk,** saunter, stroll; slouch, shuffle, shamble; dog trot, jog trot; jog, rack; mincing steps; slow march, dead *or* funeral march.

3. **dawdling, lingering, loitering,** tar-rying, dalliance, **dallying,** dillydallying; lag, lagging.

4. **retardation,** retardment; **slowing,** slackening, slowing down; **slow-down, slow-up, letup, letdown, slack-up, slack-off,** ease-off, ease-up [all coll.]; **decelera-tion,** negative *or* minus acceleration [all mech.]; **delay, detention, setback, hold-up** [coll.], check, arrest, obstruction; lag, drag.

5. **slowpoke** [coll.], poke [slang, U.S.], **slow coach** [coll.], slow goer, **slow-foot,** slowbelly, **lingerer, loiterer, dawdler,** dawdle, **laggard,** stiff [slang], stick-in-the-mud [coll.], drone, slug, sluggard, Weary Willie [coll.], dead one *or* 'un [slang]; tor-toise, snail.

VERBS 6. **go slow** *or* **slowly,** go at a snail's pace, get no place fast [slang]; **drag,** drag out; **creep, crawl;** inch, inch along; worm, worm along; poke, **poke along;** slug, slug along; shuffle along, stagger along, tot-ter along, toddle along; drag one's feet, drag one's freight [slang]; walk, traipse [dial.], **mosey** [slang, U.S.]; saunter, stroll, toddle [slang]; jog-trot, dogtrot.

7. **plod,** plug [slang], peg, **trudge,** stump, lumber; plod along, plug along [slang]; rub on, jog on.

8. **dawdle,** dander [dial.], **linger, loiter, tarry, delay, dally, dillydally, take one's time,** take one's own sweet time [coll.]; lag, drag, trail; flag, falter, halt.

9. **slow, slow down** *or* **up, let down** *or* **up, ease off** *or* **up, slack off** *or* **up, slacken,** relax, moderate; **decelerate** [mech.], throttle down; **retard, delay, de-tain,** impede, obstruct, arrest, stay, check, curb, **hold up** [coll.], **hold back,** keep back, set back, hold in check; draw rein, rein in; brake, **put on the brakes,** put on the drag; reef, take in sail [naut.]; back water, backpedal; lose ground; clip the wings.

ADJS. 10. **slow, leisurely,** slack, moder-ate, gentle, easy, deliberate, gradual; **creep-ing, crawling; poking,** poky, slow-poky [coll.]; sluggish, languid, languorous; **slow-going, slow-moving,** slow-creeping, slow-crawling, slow-running, slow-sailing; **slow-footed,** slow-foot, slow-legged, slow-gaited, slow-paced, easy-paced, slow-stepped, slow-winged; snaillike, tortoiselike, turtlelike, "creeping like snail" [Shakespeare]; slow as slow, slow as molasses, slow as death, slower than the seven-year itch [coll.], too slow to grow fast [slang].

11. **dawdling, lingering, loitering, tarrying, dallying, dillydallying,** dillydally [dial.]; **lagging, dragging.**

12. **retarded,** slowed down, **delayed, detained,** checked, **arrested,** impeded, set back, backward, behind.

ADVS. 13. **slowly, slow, leisurely,** easily, moderately, gently; creepingly, crawlingly; pokingly, pokily; sluggishly, languidly, lan-guorously; deliberately, with deliberation; **lingeringly,** loiteringly, tarryingly; **in slow motion,** at a funeral pace, with faltering *or* halting steps; at a snail's *or* turtle's pace, "in haste like a snail" [J. Heywood]; in slow tempo, in march time; in low gear; under easy sail [naut.].

14. **gradually,** little by little 29.6.

270. TRANSFERENCE

Removal from One Place to Another. —NOUNS 1. **transference, transfer; trans-mission,** transmittal, transmittance; trans-position, transposal; **translocation, trans-plantation,** translation; **transit,** transition, **passage;** communication; metastasis, me-tathesis; conduction, convection [both physics]; transfusion; transfer of property *or* right 815; delivery 816.1.

2. **removal, movement,** moving, shift, removement, remotion, amotion; displace-ment, delocalization.

3. **transportation, conveyance,** con-vection, conduction; **carrying,** bearing, packing [chiefly West. U.S.], toting [coll., U.S.], lugging [coll.]; **carriage,** carry [U.S. & Can.], haulage, portage, porterage, waft-age; **cartage, truckage,** drayage; ferriage; telpherage; **freightage,** freight, expressage; air-freight, air express; **shipment,** shipping, transshipment; asportation.

4. **transferability,** conveyability; trans-missibility, transmittability; movability, removability; portability, transportability; communicability, impartibility.

5. **carrier, conveyer,** transporter, **bear-er, porter,** cargador [P.I.], boy; common carrier; redcap [U.S.]; coolie; gun bearer; water carrier or bearer, water boy, bheesty [India]; the Water-Bearer, Aquarius; letter carrier 559.5; bus boy, omnibus; expressman, express; freighter; stevedore; carrier pigeon, homing pigeon.

6. **beast of burden; pack animal,** pack horse or mule, sumpter, sumpter horse or mule; horse, ass, mule 413.12–23; ox; camel, ship of the desert, oont [Anglo-India], dromedary, llama; reindeer; ele-phant, *hathi* [India]; sledge dog, husky.

7. **freight,** freightage; **shipment, con-signment,** goods [Eng.]; **cargo,** payload; lading, load, jag [chiefly dial.], lug [coll.], haul, tote [coll.], pack; **baggage** [chiefly U.S. & Can.], **luggage** [chiefly Eng.]; ex-press [U.S.].

8. (geology) **deposit,** sediment; drift, silt, loess, moraine, sinter; alluvium, allu-vion, diluvium; detritus, debris.

VERBS 9. **transfer, transmit, transpose,** translocate, **transplant,** translate; **pass,** pass over, **hand over,** turn over, carry over; **deliver** 816.13; pass on, hand on, relay; com-municate, impart; transfuse; transfer prop-erty or right 815.3.

10. **remove, move, shift,** change [coll.], shunt; displace, delocalize, dislodge; **take away,** cart away, carry off or away; man-handle; set ∼, lay or put aside, put or set to one side, side.

11. **transport, convey,** conduct, **take; carry, bear,** pack [chiefly West. U.S.], tote [coll., U.S.], lug [coll.], buck, jag [chiefly dial.]; shoulder, back [coll.], hump [slang, Australia], ride [coll.], horse; waft, whisk, wing.

12. **haul,** vehicle; **cart,** dray, truck, van, wagon, coach, wheelbarrow; railroad [U.S.], train [coll.]; sled [chiefly U.S.], sledge; ship, boat, barge, ferry; raft, float; chair.

13. (convey through a channel) **chan-nel,** put through channels; **pipe,** tube, pipe-line [U.S.], flume [U.S.], **siphon, funnel.**

14. **send,** send off or away, send forth; dispatch, transmit, forward; expedite; **ship, freight,** embark, **express** [chiefly U.S.]; **post, mail,** air-mail, drop a letter; export.

15. **fetch, bring, go get,** go and get, go to get, **go after,** go fetch, **go for,** call for; **get,** obtain, procure, secure; **bring back, retrieve;** chase after, run after, shag, shack [coll., U.S.]; fetch and carry.

16. **ladle,** lade; **dip, scoop;** bail, buck-

et; dish, dish out or up; cup; shovel, spade, fork; spoon.

ADJS. 17. **transferable, conveyable; transmittable,** transmissible, transmissive; **movable,** removable; **portable,** portative; transportable, transportative, transportive; conductive, conductional; **communicable,** impartible; metastatic(al), metathetic(al); mailable, expressable; assignable 815.5.

ADVS. 18. from hand to hand, from pil-lar to post.

19. by transfer [U.S.], by freight, by express; by rail, by trolley, by bus, by steam-er, by airplane; by mail, by special delivery.

20. **on the way,** along the way, on the road or high road, **en route, in transit,** *in transitu* [L.], on the wing, as one goes; in passing, *en passant* [F.]; in mid-progress.

271. VEHICLE

Means of Conveyance.—NOUNS 1. **vehi-cle, conveyance,** carriage, bus [slang], chariot [joc. exc. spec.], machine.

2. **wagon,** waggon [Eng.], wain; van, caravan; covered wagon, prairie schooner [U.S.], Conestoga wagon or wain.

3. **cart,** two-wheeler; dumpcart, coup-cart [chiefly Scot.]; jinrikisha, ricksha [coll.].

4. **carriage,** four-wheeler, *voiture* [F.], gharry [India]; chaise, chay [corruption], shay [dial.], "one hoss shay" [Holmes].

5. **rig, equipage,** turnout [coll.], coach-and-four; team, pair, span; tandem, ran-dem; spike [U.S.], spike team, unicorn; three-in-hand, four-in-hand, etc.; three-up, four-up, etc., [U.S.].

6. **baby carriage,** wagon [coll.]; per-ambulator, pram [chiefly Eng.]; gocart; stroller, walker.

7. **wheel chair,** Bath chair.

8. **cycle,** wheel [coll.]; **bicycle,** bike [slang], jigger, boneshaker [slang]; **tricycle,** trike [slang]; **motorcycle,** motocycle, mo-torbike [slang].

9. **automobile, auto, motorcar,** moto-car, autocar, **car, machine,** motor, motor vehicle, motorized vehicle; bus, buggy, boat, crate, tub [all slang]; **flivver** [slang, U.S.]; jalopy [coll., U.S.], wreck [coll.]; hoopie, clunker, dog, heap [all slang, U.S.]; coupé, coop [slang]; electromobile, electric [coll.].

10. **patrol car; prowl car,** squad car, cruiser [all U.S.]; **police van,** patrol wagon [U.S.], wagon [coll.], Black Maria [coll., U.S.], carryall.

11. (public vehicles) stage, stage-coach, *diligence* [F.]; mail coach, post coach, post car, postcart; bus, omnibus; autobus, motorbus, motor coach, jitney [coll.]; double-decker [coll.]; cab, taxicab, taxi [coll.], autocab; nighthawk [slang, U.S.].

12. train, railroad train; choo-choo, choo-choo train [both childish]; passenger train; local, way train, accommodation train [all U.S.]; shuttle train, shuttle [both U.S.]; express train, express; lightning express, flier, cannon-ball express [slang], manifest [railroad cant]; local express; special, limited [U.S.]; parliamentary train, parliamentary [both Eng.]; freight train [U.S. & Can.], goods train [Eng.], freight, freighter, rattler [tramp slang, U.S.]; baggage train [U.S. & Can.], luggage train [Eng.]; electric train, electric [coll.]; interurban; subway [U.S.], underground [Eng.]; streamliner; rolling stock.

13. railway car, car; passenger car, coach, carriage [Eng.]; chair car, day coach [U.S.]; sleeping car, sleeper; Pullman, Pullman car; drawing-room car, palace car, parlor car [U.S.]; drawing room [U.S.], roomette; caravan [Eng.]; dining car *or* compartment, diner; smoking car *or* compartment, smoker; freight car [U.S. & Can.], waggon [Eng.], goods waggon [Eng.], rattler [tramp slang, U.S.]; boxcar [U.S.], box waggon [Eng.], covered waggon [Eng.]; flatcar, flat, truck [Eng.]; gondola car [U.S.], gondola [U.S.], open waggon [Eng.]; baggage car [U.S. & Can.], luggage van [Eng.], van [Eng.]; mail car, mail van [Eng.]; refrigerator car, reefer [tramp slang, U.S.]; tank car, tank; stockcar; coal car; tender; caboose, buggy [U.S.]; dinghy; way car, local; cable car [U.S.].

14. streetcar [U.S.], trolley *or* trolley car [U.S. & Can.], tram *or* tramcar [Eng.]; electric car, electric [coll.]; trolley bus, trackless trolley; horsecar [U.S.], horse box [Eng.], jigger [cant, U.S.]; Jim Crow *or* Jim Crow car [coll., South. U.S.].

15. handcar (railway), go-devil; push car, trolley, truck car, rubble car.

16. tractor, traction engine; caterpillar tractor, caterpillar, cat [slang]; amphibian [mil.], amphib [coll.]; amphibian tractor, amtrac [coll.]; bulldozer, dozer [coll.].

17. trailer, trail car; house trailer, truck trailer.

18. sled, sledge, sleigh, *traîneau* [F.]; skis; snowshoes; runner, blade.

19. skates, ice skates, roller skates, boh skates.

ADJS. **20.** vehicular, curricular.

21. carriages

araba	hackney, hackney
barouche	coach
berlin	hansom, hansom
break	cab
britska	jaunting *or* jaunty
brougham	car
buckboard [U.S.]	jigger
buggy [U.S.]	jinrikisha
bullock cart	kibitka
cabriolet	kitereen [W.
calash	Indies]
calèche [F.;	landau
Quebec]	limber [mil.]
Cape cart [S.	mail phaeton
Africa]	outside jaunting
cariole	car
carryall [U.S.]	oxcart
cart	phaeton
chaise	post chaise [hist.]
charabanc	road cart
chariot	rockaway
chariotee	runabout
charrette [F.]	shandrydan [Scot.
clarence	& Ir.]
coach	sidecar [Ir.]
Concord buggy	sociable, sociable
[U.S.]	coach
coupé	spring wagon
curricle	stanhope
dearborn [U.S.]	sulky
desobligeant	surrey [U.S.]
dogcart	tallyho, tallyho
dormeuse [F.]	coach
drag	tandem
dray	tilbury
droshky	tonga [India]
ekka [India]	trap [coll.]
fiacre	troika
fly [Eng.]	trolley
four-in-hand coach	tumbrel, tumbril
gig	*vettura* [It.]
glass coach	victoria
growler [slang,	vis-à-vis
Eng.]	voiturette
hack	wagonette
hackery [India]	whisky [hist.]
	Whitechapel cart

22. automobiles

ambulance	command car
armored car	[mil.]
autobolide	convertible
beach wagon	convertible coupé
berline, berlin	convertible sedan
berline-landaulet	coupé
blitzbuggy [slang,	coupelet
U.S. army]	crash wagon
bloodmobile	[aero.]
bookmobile	dragster [slang,
brougham	U.S.]
cabriolet	electric brougham
clubmobile	electromobile
coach	fire engine
combat car [mil.]	hardtop
	hearse

hot rod [slang, U.S.]
jeep [mil.]
landau
landaulet
limousine
locomobile
• phaeton
racer
roadster
rocker car
runabout
scout car [mil.]

23. auto parts

accelerator
ammeter
bearings
bonnet [Eng.]
brake
bumpers
camshaft
carburetor
chassis
choke
clutch
connecting rod
convertible top
cowl
crank
crankcase
crankshaft
cutout
cylinder
cylinder head
dashboard, dash
differential
distributor
exhaust, exhaust pipe
fan
fender
flywheel
gear
gearbox
gearshift
generator
headlights

24. trucks

auto carrier [Eng.]
autotruck
carryall
cart
delivery truck
dolly
dray
duck [mil.]
dump truck
electric truck
float
four-by-four [coll.]
freighter
garbage truck
hand truck
lorry [esp. Eng.]
motor truck

25. tractors

amphibian [mil.]
amtrac [coll., mil.]

sedan
sedan limousine
staff car [mil.]
station wagon
steamer
stock car
torpedo
touring car
touring coupé
tow car
tractor
wrecker

hood [U.S.]
horn
ignition
intake, intake manifold
klaxon
landau
magneto
manifold
muffler
oil gauge
piston
primer
radiator
radius rod
rear-view mirror
rumble seat
running board
self-starter
shock absorber
spark plug
speedometer
starter
steering wheel
taillights
tonneau
top
transmission
turret top
universal joint
valve
windscreen [Eng.]
windshield [U.S.]

moving van
pickup [U.S.]
quad [coll.]
railroad truck
refrigerator truck
semi [coll.]
six-by-six [coll.]
sloven [E. Can. & Newfound.]
stake truck
tongue truck
transfer [local, U.S.]
van
wagon truck
warehouse truck

bulldozer
caterpillar, caterpillar tractor

caterpillar tank
combat car [mil.]
crawler, crawler tractor
creeper, creeper tractor
duck, DUKW [U.S. mil.]
go-devil

26. handcarts

barrow
handbarrow
push car

27. cycles

bicycle
dandy horse
draisine
hobby
hydrocycle
monocycle
motorcycle, motocycle
motor scooter

28. litters

brancard
cacolet [F.]
camel litter
dandy [India]
doolie [India]
gocart
handbarrow
horse litter
jampan [India]

29. sleds

autosled
belly-bumper [slang]
bobsled, bobsleigh [both U.S.]
cariole [Can.]
coaster [U.S.]
cutter
double-ripper, double-runner [U.S.]

grader
halftrack [U.S. mil.]
LVT (landing vehicle tracked [U.S. mil.])
scraper
tank [mil.]
tracklayer

pushcart
teacart
wheelbarrow

push bicycle
quadricycle
safety bicycle
scooter
tandem, tandem bicycle
tricycle
velocipede

kajawah [India]
lectica [Rom. antiq.]
norimon [Jap.]
palanquin
polki [India]
sedan, sedan chair
stretcher
tonjon [Ceylon]

drag
dray
jumper [U.S. & Can.]
pigsticker [slang]
pung [U.S.]
scoot [logging]
skid
toboggan
troika

272. TRAVEL

NOUNS **1. travel**, traveling, going, moving, **movement, motion, locomotive, transit, progress, passage,** course; commutation; world travel, globe-trotting [coll.]; tourism, touristry.

2. travels, journeys, **journeyings, wanderings,** peregrinations, peripatetics [joc.]; odyssey.

3. wandering, roving, roaming, rambling, gadding, traipsing [dial.], gallivanting, peregrination; roam, rove, ramble, gad [coll.]; **itineracy,** itinerancy; **nomadism,** nomadization, **vagabondism,** vagabondage; **vagrancy,** hoboism [U.S.]; the open road; wanderyear, Wanderjahr [G.]; wanderlust.

4. migration, transmigration, passage, trek; run (of fish), flight (of birds and insects); swarm, swarming (both of bees; also fig.]; **immigration,** in-migration; **emigration**; remigration; intermigration.

5. journey, jornada [Sp. & S.W. U.S.], **trip,** peregrination, sally, **trek,** gait [Scot. & dial.]; progress, course, run; jump [chiefly coll.], hop [slang]; **tour,** grand tour; round trip, circuit, turn, whirl [coll.]; **expedition,** campaign; safari [in E. Africa], hunting expedition; **pilgrimage,** hadj [Arab.]; **excursion, jaunt, junket** [U.S.], **outing,** pleasure trip; sightseeing trip, rubberneck tour [slang, U.S.]; package tour; **voyage** 274.6.

6. riding, driving; motoring, automobiling; motorcycling, bicycling; **horseback riding,** equitation; horsemanship, manège.

7. ride, drive; spin, whirl [both coll.]; joy ride [coll.]; straw ride [coll., U.S.]; lift [coll.], pickup [slang].

8. gliding, sliding, slipping, slithering, coasting, sweeping, flowing, sailing; **skating, skiing, tobogganing, sledding;** glide, slide, slither, sweep, skim, flow.

9. creeping, crawling; sneaking, stealing; tiptoeing, tiptoe; creep, crawl, scramble, scrabble; all fours.

10. walking, ambulation, perambulation, pedestrianism; footwork, legwork [both coll.]; strolling, sauntering; **tramping, marching, hiking** [coll.]; **hitchhiking** [coll.]; jaywalking [coll., U.S.].

11. nightwalking, noctambulation, noctambulism; night-wandering, noctivagation; **sleepwalking,** somnambulation, somnambulism; sleepwalk.

12. walk, ramble, **hike** [coll.], **march, tramp,** traipse or trapes [dial.], mush [N.W. Amer.]; **stroll,** saunter; parade; **promenade,** pasear [Sp. Amer. & coll., U.S.]; jaunt, airing; **constitutional** [coll.], stretch; turn, whirl [coll.]; peripatetic journey or exercise, peripateticism; forced march.

13. step, pace, stride, straddle; **footstep,** footfall, tread; hoofbeat, clop; hop; jump; skip, hippety-hop [coll.].

14. gait, pace, walk, step, stride, tread; saunter, strolling gait; shuffle, shamble, hobble, limp, hitch; totter, stagger; toddle, paddle; slouch, droop; mincing steps, scuttle, prance, flounce, stalk, strut, swagger; jog; swing, roll; amble, pace, singlefoot [U.S.], rack, piaffer [all of horses]; trot, gallop 268.4; lock step, the one-two

[crim. slang]; velocity 268; slowness 269.

15. (military steps) march; quick or quickstep march, quickstep, quick time; double march, double-quick, double time; slow march, slow time; half step [U.S.], goose step.

16. legs, limbs, shanks, hind legs [joc. exc. zool.], podites [zool.]; stumps, pegs, **pins** [all coll.]; stems, props, **gams,** trotters, ponies, shanks' mares, ~ mules or horses, underpins, underpinnings, locomotives, propellers [all slang]; gamb or gambe, jamb [all esp. her.]; foreleg, hind leg; bowlegs, baker's legs, scissor-legs; bayonet legs; gangleshanks, longshanks, spindlelegs, spindleshanks, lath legs [all slang]; shin; ankle, tarsus; hock, gambrel; calf; knee; thigh, hock [dial.], popliteal space, ham, drumstick (of a fowl); gigot (as of lamb).

VERBS **17. travel, go,** gang [Scot. & dial., Eng.], **move, pass,** fare, fetch [chiefly naut.], hie, locomote [coll.], sashay [slang, U.S.], cover ground; **progress** 293.2; move on or along, go along, mog [dial.]; wend, **wend one's way;** betake oneself, direct one's course, bend one's steps or course; course, run, flow, stream; roll, roll on; commute.

18. (go at a given speed) **go, go at, make, do,** hit [slang].

19. traverse, travel over, go or **pass over, cover,** measure [poetic], track, course, do, perambulate, peregrinate, overpass, go over the ground; patrol; scour the country.

20. journey, go a journey, go on a journey, **take a trip,** fare, **wayfare, trek, jaunt,** peregrinate; **tour,** tourist [coll.]; hit the trail [slang], take the road, go on the road [theat.]; **voyage** 274.13; go abroad; globe-trot [coll.]; pilgrimage, pilgrim, go on or make a pilgrimage; campaign, go on an expedition; go on a sightseeing trip, sightsee.

21. migrate, transmigrate, trek; flit, take wing; run (of fish), swarm (of bees); **emigrate; immigrate,** in-migrate; remigrate; intermigrate.

22. wander, roam, rove, range, nomadize, **gad,** gad about, go on the gad [coll.], traipse or trapes [dial.], gallivant, haze, haze around or about [coll.], bat around or about [slang], mooch [dial. & slang], prowl, **drift, stray,** straggle, **meander, ramble,** stroll, saunter, jaunt, peregrinate, go or run about, go the rounds; **tramp,** hobo [U.S.], vagabond, vagabondize, vag it [tramps' slang, U.S.], take to the road, "travel the open road" [Whitman], beat one's way; hit the road or trail, pound the pavement [all tramp slang]; walk the tracks, count ties [tramp slang].

23. go for an outing or **airing**, take the air; go for a walk 272.28; go for a ride 272.32.

24. go to, repair to, resort to, hie to, direct one's course to, bend one's steps to, betake oneself to, **visit**.

25. creep, **crawl**, scramble, scrabble, grovel, **go on hands and knees**, go on all fours; worm, worm along, worm one's way; inch, inch along; **sneak**, **steal**, steal along; pussyfoot [slang], gumshoe [slang, U.S.]; **tiptoe**, **go on tiptoe**.

26. walk, ambulate, peripateticate, pedestrianize, traipse or trapes [dial.]; **step**, **tread**, **pace**, track [slang, U.S.], pad; foot, foot it; leg, leg it; hoof it, beat or pad the hoof, ankle, go on the heel and toe [U.S.], go on the marrowbone stage, ride shanks' mare, ~ mules or horses, take or ride the shoe-leather or hobnail express, mope, stump it, walk the chalks [all slang]; peg ~, jog ~, wag or shuffle on or along; perambulate; circumambulate; jaywalk [coll., U.S.].

27. (paces) stroll, saunter; shuffle, scuff, scuffle, shamble; stride, straddle; trudge, plod, peg, traipse or trapes [dial.], clump, stump [coll.], slog, lumber, barge; stamp, stomp [dial.]; swing, roll, lunge; hobble, halt, limp, hitch; totter, stagger; toddle, paddle; waddle, wobble, wabble, wamble; slouch; stalk; strut, swagger; mince, sashay [slang, U.S.], scuttle, prance, flounce, trip, skip, foot; hop, jump, hippety-hop [coll.]; jog, jolt; bundle, bowl along; amble, pace; single-foot [U.S.], rack; piaffe, piaffer.

28. go for a walk, **take a walk**, take one's constitutional [coll.], take a stretch, stretch the legs; **promenade**, **parade**, perambulate, pasear [Sp. Amer. & coll., U.S.].

29. march, mush [N.W. Amer.], footslog [slang], **tramp**, hike [coll.]; file, defile, file off; **parade**, go on parade; goose-step [coll.], do the goose step; do the lock step, do the one-two [crim. slang].

30. hitchhike [coll.], hitch rides [slang], beat one's way, **thumb one's way** [slang]; catch a ride; hitch a ride, hook a ride, bum a ride, thumb a ride [all slang].

31. nightwalk, noctambulate; **sleepwalk**, somnambulate, walk in one's sleep.

32. ride, **go for a ride**, or **drive**; spin, go for a spin [both coll.]; **drive**, **chauffeur**;

motor, auto [coll.], automobile; cab, taxicab, taxi; cycle [coll.], wheel [coll.], **motorcycle**, **bicycle**; go by rail, railroad [U.S.]; trolley [coll.], tram [Eng.]; joy-ride, take a joy ride [both coll.]; catch a ride, hook a ride [slang]; catch a train, make a train [coll.]; ride and tie.

33. take horse, **go on horseback**; ride bareback, ride in the slick [West. U.S.]; hack; lark [coll.]; ride hard, clap spurs to one's horse; trot; canter, gallop, lope; prance, frisk; caracole.

34. glide, **coast**, **skim**, sweep, flow; sail, fly, flit, kite [coll.]; volplane; **slide**, **slip**, slither, glissade; skate, ice-skate, roller-skate; ski; toboggan, sled, sleigh; belly-whop [dial.].

ADJS. **35. traveling**, **going**, **moving**, passing; **progressing** 293.5; **itinerant**, itinerary; **journeying**, **wayfaring**; peripatetic; ambulant, ambuling, ambulatory; ambulative; perambulating, perambulatory; **walking**, **pedestrian**, gradient; mincing; **touring**, on tour; touristic(al), touristry [coll.]; expeditionary.

36. wandering, **roving**, **roaming**, ranging, **rambling**, **meandering**, strolling, **drifting**, **straying**, straggling, shifting, landlouping, errant, discursive, circumforaneous; **gadding**, traipsing or trapesing [dial.], gallivanting; **nomad**, nomadic; **transient**, fugitive; **migratory**, migrational, transmigratory; **vagrant**, vagabond; **foot-loose**, footloose and fancy-free.

37. nightwalking, noctambulant, noctambulous; night-wandering, noctivagant; **sleepwalking**, somnambulant, somnambular.

38. creeping, **crawling**, **on hands and knees**, **on all fours**; reptant, repent, reptile, reptatorial; **on tiptoe**, atiptoe, tiptoeing, tiptoe.

39. traveled, well-traveled.

40. wayworn, way-weary, **travel-worn**, travel-weary, travel-tired; travel-sated, travel-jaded; travel-soiled, travel-stained.

ADVS. **41. on the move** or **go**, on the wing or fly; on the run, on the jump [coll.], on the hop [slang]; on the tramp or march; on or upon the gad [coll.], on the drift [slang, U.S.].

42. on foot, afoot, by foot, footback [dial.], on footback; on the heel and toe [U.S.], on the marrowbone stage, on shanks' mares, ~ mules or horses, on the shoe-leather or hobnail express [all slang].

43. on horseback, horseback, by horse.

273. TRAVELER

NOUNS 1. traveler, goer, comers and goers; wayfarer, journeyer, trekker; tourist, tourer, tripper [coll., esp. Eng.], dude [slang, West. U.S.], visiting fireman; excursionist, sight-seer, rubberneck or rubbernecker [slang, U.S.]; voyager, voyageur [F.], cruiser, sailor; globe-trotter [coll.], globe-girdler; pilgrim, palmer, hadji [Arab.]; passenger, fare; commuter, straphanger [coll.]; transient; passer-by; adventurer; explorer; camper.

2. wanderer, rover, roamer, rambler, stroller, straggler, mover; gad [coll.], gadabout [coll.], runabout, go-about [chiefly dial.]; itinerant, peripatetic [joc.], bird of passage; drifter [coll.], floater [coll.]; Wandering Jew, Ahasuerus, Ancient Mariner, Flying Dutchman.

3. vagabond, vagrant, vag [slang, U.S.]; bum or bummer [slang, U.S.], loafer, wastrel, losel [archaic & dial.], lazzarone [Naples]; tramp, turnpiker, piker, knight of the road [joc.], hobo [U.S.], bo [slang, U.S.], stiff [slang, U.S.], landlouper, sundowner [coll., Austral.], prog or progger [dial., U.S.]; bindle stiff [slang, U.S.], swagman or swagsman [Austral.]; beggar 772.8; waif, stray, waifs and strays; ragamuffin, tatterdemalion; gamin, Arab, street Arab, mud lark, guttersnipe [coll.]; beachcomber; ragman, ragpicker.

4. nomad, Bedouin, Arab, Saracen; gypsy, Romany, zingaro [It.].

5. migrant, migrator, trekker; immigrant, in-migrant; wetback [coll.]; emigrant, emigree, émigré [F.]; evacuee, évacué [F.], vackie [slang, Eng.].

6. pedestrian, walker, walkist, foot traveler, foot passenger, hoofer [slang], peripatetic [joc.]; hiker [coll.], tramper, tramp; hitch-hiker [slang]; jaywalker [coll.].

7. nightwalker, noctambulist, noctambule, sleepwalker, somnambulist, somnambulator, somnambule.

8. rider, equestrian, horseman, horseback rider, horsebacker, caballero [S.W. U.S.], cavalier; horsewoman, equestrienne; cowboy, cowgirl, puncher or cowpuncher [coll., U.S.], vaquero [Sp. Amer.], Gaucho [So. Amer.]; broncobuster [slang, U.S.], buckaroo [S.W. U.S.]; postilion, postboy; roughrider; jockey.

9. driver, reinsman, whip, Jehu [joc.], skinner [slang]; coachman, coachy [coll.],

cocher [F.], cochero [Sp.], voiturier [F.], vetturino [It.], gharry-wallah [India]; stage coachman; charioteer; cab-driver, cabman, cabby [coll.]; hackman, hacky [coll.], jarvey [slang, Eng.]; wagoner, drayman, truckman; carter, cartman, carman; teamster, four-up driver [West. U.S.]; muleteer, mule skinner [slang, U.S.]; bullwhacker (oxen driver [U.S.]); mahout (elephant driver [E. Indies]); cameleer.

10. motorist, automobilist, autoist [coll.]; chauffeur, chauffeuse [F., fem.], James [slang]; truck driver, truckman, trucker; bus driver, busman; cabdriver 273.9; jitney driver, jitneur, jitneuse [fem.]; speed demon or maniac [coll.], speeder, racer; road hog [slang], Sunday driver [joc.]; joyrider [coll.]; hit-and-run driver; back-seat driver, co-pilot [both joc.].

11. cyclist, cycler; bicyclist, bicycler; motorcyclist, motorcycler.

12. engineer, engineman, engine driver; hogger, hoghead, boiler head, lokey man [all R.R. slang, U.S.]; Casey Jones; motorman; cat skinner [slang].

13. trainman, railroad man, railroader [U.S.], rail [slang, U.S.; chiefly in old rail]; conductor, guard [Eng.]; brakeman, guard [U.S.], brakie [slang, U.S.]; fireman, stoker; smoke agent, bakehead [both R.R. slang, U.S.]; switchman; yardman; yardmaster; trainmaster, dispatcher; stationmaster; lineman; baggage man, baggagesmasher [slang, U.S.]; porter, redcap [U.S.]; trainboy, butcher [slang].

274. NAVIGATION

Travel by Water.—NOUNS 1. navigation, navigating, seafaring, sailing, voyaging, cruising; boating, yachting; circumnavigation, periplus; navigability; sea legs.

2. (methods) celestial navigation; coastal navigation, dog-barking navigation [derog.]; Sonar (sound navigation and ranging), Sofar (sound fixing and ranging); plane ~, traverse ~, spherical ~, parallel ~, middle ~, latitude ~, Mercator ~, great-circle or composite sailing.

3. seamanship, shipmanship; seamanliness, seamanlikeness.

4. pilotship, pilotry, pilotage, steerage; proper piloting.

5. embarkation 300.3; disembarkation 299.2.

6. voyage, ocean trip, cruise, sail; course, run, passage; crossing; shake-down cruise; leg.

7. **maneuvers,** tactical maneuvers, tactics; for nation cruising; fleet work.

8. (submarines) **surfacing,** breaking water; **submergence, dive;** stationary dive, running dive, crash dive.

9. **way, progress; headway,** steerage-way, sternway, leeway, driftway.

10. **seaway, waterway,** fairway, ocean or sea lane, ship route, steamer track.

11. **aquatics, swimming, bathing,** natation, balneation; **swim, bathe** [esp. Eng.]; crawl, Australian crawl, breast stroke, side stroke, backstroke; floating; diving 318.3; wading; fin; flipper, flapper; fishtail.

12. **swimmer, bather,** natator, merman; bathing girl, mermaid; bathing beauty; Frogman [U.S. mil.]; diver 318.4.

VERBS 13. **navigate, sail, cruise,** seafare, **voyage,** ply, go by ship, go on or take a voyage, "go down to the sea in ships" [Bible]; sail the sea, sail the ocean blue; **boat, yacht;** steam, steamer, steamboat; bear or carry sail; cross, traverse, hop the drink [slang]; sail round, circumnavigate; ran a blockade, run the gantlet.

14. **pilot,** helm, coxswain, **steer,** guide, direct, manage, handle, run, operate, **conn** or cond, be at the conn; shape or chart a course.

15. **embark** 300.17; **disembark** 299.8.

16. **anchor,** come to anchor, lay anchor, cast anchor, let go the anchor, heave the hook [naut. slang]; carry out the anchor; **dock; moor,** run out a warp or rope; lash, lash and tie; snub the chain; foul the anchor; back an anchor.

17. **ride at anchor,** ride, lie, rest; ride easy; ride hawse full; lie athwart.

18. **lay** or **lie to,** lay or lie by; lie near or close to the wind, head to wind or windward, be under the sea; lie off, lie off the land; lay or lie up.

19. **weigh anchor,** up-anchor, bring the anchor home, break ground, loose for sea; raise the dead, heave and raise the dead [both naut. slang]; **unmoor,** cast off, ~ loose or get away.

20. **get under way,** get under weigh [erroneous], put or have way upon, **put or shove off;** hoist the blue Peter; **put to sea,** put out to sea, go to sea; **sail,** sail away; embark 300.17.

21. **set sail,** hoist sail, unfurl or spread sail, heave out a sail, make sail, **trim sail,** deck [cant]; hang out the washing, give her muslin [both naut. slang]; square away, square the yards.

22. **clap** ~, **crack** or **pack on sail,** put on (more) sail; clap on, crack on, pack on; crowd sail, give her beans [naut. slang]; keep them rap-full; bagpipe a sail, bagpipe the mizzen [both cant]; sneer (a ship), make all sneer again [both cant].

23. **make way, gather way,** freshen the way [cant], make headway or sternway; go full speed ahead or astern.

24. **run, run** or **sail before the wind,** sail bunt fair [cant], run or sail with the wind, run or sail down the wind, sail off the wind, sail free, sail with the wind aft, sail with the wind abaft the beam; tack down wind; run or sail with the wind quartering.

25. **bring off the wind,** bear off or away, put the helm to leeward, bear or head to leeward, pay off the head.

26. **sail against the wind,** sail on the wind, sail by the wind, sail to windward, bear or head to windward; **bring in** or **into the wind,** bring by or on the wind, haul the wind or one's wind; uphelm, put the helm up; haul, haul off, haul up; **haul to, bring to, heave to,** heave to on starboard or port tack; sail in or into the wind's eye, sail in the teeth of the wind [both cant]; sail to the windward of, weather.

27. **sail near the wind,** sail close to the wind, lie near or close to the wind, hold a close wind, sail close-hauled, close-haul; work ~, beat or eat to windward, **beat, ply, luff;** sail too close to the wind, sail fine, touch the wind, pinch, luff and lie or touch her [cant].

28. **gain to windward of,** eat to windward of, eat the wind out of, have the wind of, be to windward of.

29. **course,** take or follow a course, fetch; **shape a course for,** lay or lie a course for, lay or lie up for; **keep** or **hold the course** or **a course,** hold on the course or a course, stand on or upon a course, stand on a straight course, maintain or keep the bearing, keep pointed, cape [cant]; keep or put the rudder amidships.

30. **go, come, bring, put, fetch, haul.**

31. **drift off course,** discourse, yaw, yaw off, bear off, drift, sag, bag on a bowline [cant]; sag ~, bear ~, ride or drive to leeward, make leeway, drive, fetch away; drift with the current, fall down.

32. **change course,** change the bearing, bear off or away (spec. to leeward), bear to starboard or port; sheer, swerve; **tack,** busk, cast, **jib, jibe,** break, yaw, shift, **turn; cant,**

cant round or across; **beat, ply; veer, wear, wear ship; put about,** come ~, go ~, bring or fetch about, beat about, cast or throw about; bring ~, swing ~, heave or haul round; **about-ship,** turn or put back, turn on her heel, wind; swing the stern; box off; back and fill; stand off and on; double or round a point; miss stays.

33. put the rudder hard left or right, put the rudder or helm hard over, put the rudder amidships, ease the rudder or helm, give her more rudder, etc. (orders) 274.80; starboard, port.

34. veer or **wear short,** bring by the lee, **broach to,** build a chapel [cant].

35. fetch up, haul up, fetch up all standing.

36. back water, go astern; go full speed astern; make sternway.

37. sail for, put away for, make for or toward, make at, run for, stand for, head or steer toward, lay for, lay a course or one's course for, bear up for; bear up to, **bear down on** or **upon,** run or bear in with, close with; close with the land, run or bear in with the land; heave or go alongside, lay (a ship) aboard, go aboard and board; lay or lie in; put in or into, put into port, approach anchorage.

38. sail away from, head or steer away from, run from, stand from, lay away or off from; stand off, bear off, put off, shove off, haul off; stand off and on.

39. clear the land, bear off the land, lay or settle the land, make sea room.

40. make land, reach land; close with the land 274.37; sight land.

41. coast, range the coast, skirt the shore, lie along the shore, **hug the shore** or **land,** keep hold of the land [cant], make free with the land [naut. slang].

42. weather the storm, weather, ride, **ride out,** outride, ride or ride out a storm, make heavy or bad weather.

43. sail into, run down, run in or into, **run foul** or **afoul of, collide,** fall aboard; nose or head into, run prow ~, end or head on, run head and head; run broadside on.

44. shipwreck, wreck, pile up [coll.], be sewed up, cast away; **go aground,** ground, beach, strand, run on the rocks; ground hard and fast.

45. careen, list, heel, keel, tip, cant, heave or lay down, lie along; be on her beam ends; broach to 274.34.

46. capsize, upset, overset, **overturn,** turn over, upset the boat, keel or heel over; **sink, founder,** go down, go to the bottom, go to Davy Jones's locker [slang]; scuttle.

47. go overboard, go by the board, go over the board or side.

48. (battleships) **maneuver,** execute a maneuver; heave in together, keep in formation, maintain position, **keep station,** keep pointed, steam in line, steam in line of bearing; convoy.

49. (submarines) **surface,** break water; **submerge, dive,** go below; rig for diving, etc. (orders) 274.82.

50. (activities aboard ship) lay, lay aloft, lay forward, etc.; traverse a yard, brace a yard fore and aft; heave, haul, bouse [cant]; kedge; warp; boom; heave round, heave short, heave apeak; log, heave the log; haul down, board; spar down; ratline down, clap on ratlines; batten down the hatches; unlash, cut or cast loose; clear hawse.

51. trim ship, trim, trim up; trim by the head or stern, put in proper fore-and-aft trim, give greater draft fore and aft, **put on an even keel;** shift ballast, wing up ballast; break out ballast, break bulk, shoot ballast; **clear the decks,** clear for action.

52. reduce sail, shorten or take in sail, snug down [cant], **reef,** reef one's sails; double-reef; lower sail, dowse sail [cant]; run under bare poles.

53. take bearings, cast a traverse; correct distance and maintain the bearings; run down the latitude, **take a sight,** shoot Charley Noble [naut. slang], shoot the sun [cant], bring down the sun; **box the compass.**

54. take soundings 208.8.

55. signal, speak, hail and speak; cheer ship; unfurl or hoist a banner, unfurl an ensign, **break out a flag;** hoist the blue Peter; show one's colors, **exchange colors;** salute, dip; make her number; jibber the kibber [cant].

56. row, paddle, ply the oar, **pull, scull, punt;** give way, row away; catch or cut a crab or lobster [coll.]; feather, feather an oar; sky an oar [coll.]; row dry [coll., Eng.]; pace, shoot; ship oars.

57. float, ride, drift; **sail, scud,** run, shoot; skim, *effleurer* [F.]; ride the sea, plow the deep, walk the waters.

58. pitch, toss, tumble, toss and tumble, pitch and toss, **plunge, rear, rock, roll, reel, swing, sway, lurch, heave,** scend, flounder welter, wallow; buffet the waves, bruise the sea [naut. slang].

59. swim, bathe, go in swimming or bathing; float, float on one's back; wade, go in wading; dive 318.6.

ADJS. 60. nautical, marine, maritime, naval, navigational; seafaring, seagoing, ocean-going, water-borne; seamanly, seamanlike; oceanic 396.7.

61. aquatic, water-dwelling, water-living, water-growing, water-loving; swimming, natant, natatory, natatorial; grallatorial [zool.].

62. navigable, boatable.

63. sailing; fluking, afluking, all afluking [all coll.]; close-hauled; outboard.

64. floating, afloat, awash, watching (of a buoy), water-borne.

65. adrift, afloat, unmoored, unanchored, aweigh.

ADVS. 66. on board, on shipboard, on board ship, aboard, all aboard, afloat; on deck, topside; aloft; in sail; before the mast; athwart the hawse, athwarthawse.

67. under way, under weigh [erroneous], with way on; at sea, on the high seas; under sail or canvas, with sails spread; under press of sail, ~ canvas or steam; under steam; under bare poles; on or off the bearing or course; in soundings, homeward bound.

68. before the wind, with the wind, down the wind, off the wind, with the wind aft, with the wind abaft the beam, bunt fair [cant]; running free; wing and wing, wung-out [cant]; under the wind, under the lee.

69. against the wind, on the wind, in or into the wind, up the wind, by the wind, head to wind; in or into the wind's eye, in the teeth of the wind [both cant].

70. near the wind, close to the wind, close-hauled, on a bowline.

71. coastward, landward, to landward; coastwise, coastways.

72. at anchor, riding at anchor; lying leeward, windward 241.9.

73. aft, abaft, abaff, baft, baff, astern; fore and aft.

74. alongside, board and board, yardarm to yardarm.

75. at anchor, riding at anchor; lying to.

76. afoul, foul, in collision; head and head, head ~, end or prow on; broadside on.

77. aground, on the rocks; hard and fast.

78. overboard, over the board or side, by the board; aft the fantail.

INTERJS. 79. (orders, calls) ahoy!, ahoy there!, ship ahoy!; avast!, hold fast!; belay!, belay that or there!; aye, aye!, aye, aye, sir!; heave!, heave ho!, yo-heave-ho!, heave and awash!; lend a hand!, lend us your pound! [slang]; keep one hand for yourself and one for the ship!; stand by!, stand by to weigh anchor!, stand by the main sheet!, etc.; anchors aweigh!; aloft!, aloft there!; turn out!, show a leg!, rise and shine!; man overboard!; aboard!, all aboard!, take ship!, up oars!, give way!, row away!; way enough!, ship oars!

80. (orders to the helm) up helm!, down helm!, port!, larboard!, starboard!, helm aport!, helm astarboard!, helm alee!, helm aweather!, hard aport!, hard alee!, hard astarboard!, hard aweather!, hard over!, right!, left!, right or left rudder!, right or left standard rudder!, right or left five (ten etc.) degrees rudder!, right or left half rudder!, right or left full rudder!, right or left handsomely!, give her more rudder!, shift the rudder!, meet her!, ease the helm or rudder!, rudder amidships!, nothing to the right or left!, no nearer!, how is your rudder?, how does she head?, keep her so!, steady!, steady so!, steady as you go!, about ship!

81. (orders to the engine room) starboard or port engine!, all engines!, ahead!, back!, astern!, starboard or port engine ahead!, full speed ahead! or astern!, slow ahead!, slow astern!, all engines ahead!, ~ ahead one-third!, ~ ahead two-thirds!, ~ ahead standard!, ~ ahead full!, ~ back one-third!, ~ back two-thirds!, ~ back full!

82. (submarine orders) rig for diving!, ventilate inboard!, shift the control!, stations for diving!, secure the engines!, secure the main induction!, close the conning tower hatch!, ahead both motors!, flood the tank!, blow the tank!, flood main ballast!, close main vents!, flood 2000 etc., pounds in after trim!

275. MARINER

NOUNS 1. mariner, seaman, sailor, sailorman, navigator, seafarer, seafaring man, sea dog [coll.], water dog [coll.], shipman [poetic], Jack, jacky, Jack afloat, jacktar, tar, salt [coll.], hearty, lobscouser [slang], matelot [F.], windjammer (on sailing vessel [coll.]); limey or limejuicer (English sailor [slang, U.S.]), lascar [East

Indies]; common *or* ordinary seaman, O.D.; able *or* able-bodied seaman, A.B. *or* a.b.; deep-sea man, salt-water sailor, blue-water sailor; fresh-water sailor; fair-weather sailor [derog.]; pirate; Ancient Mariner, Flying Dutchman.

2. (novice) **lubber, landlubber.**

3. (veteran) **old salt,** old sea dog [both coll.]; shellback, barnacle-back, tall-water sailor [all slang]; master mariner.

4. **navy man,** man-of-war's man, **blue-jacket, gob** [slang, U.S.], galiongee [Turk.]; **marine, leatherneck** [slang], **gyrene** (G.I. marine [slang, U.S.]), devil dog [slang, U.S.], jolly [slang, Eng.]; horse marine; boot [slang, U.S.]; **midshipman,** middy [coll.]; cadet, naval cadet; coast-guardsman, Naval Reservist, Seabee [U.S.], frogman [U.S.]; navy 798.27.

5. **boatman,** boatsman, **boater,** water-man; **oarsman,** oar, rower; **yachtsman,** yachter; **ferryman,** ferrier, ferryer; **barge-man,** barger, bargee [Eng.], bargemaster; lighterman; **gondolier,** *gondoliere* [It.].

6. (ship's crew) hand, **deck hand,** deckie [Eng.]; stoker, bakehead [slang]; black gang (stokehold crew [slang]); cabin boy, drudge [slang]; yeoman, ship's writer; purser; ship's carpenter, chips [slang]; ship's cooper, bungs *or* Jimmy Bungs [slang]; ship's tailor, snip *or* snips [slang]; steward, stewardess, commissary steward, mess steward, hospital steward; commissary clerk; mail orderly; navigator; landing signalman; gunner, gun loader, torpedoman; after-guard.

7. (ship's officers) **captain, shipmaster,** sailing master, **skipper, commander,** old man [coll.], *patron* [F.]; navarch [Gr. antiq.]; navigating officer; deck officer, officer of the deck; **mate,** first *or* chief mate, second mate, third mate, boatswain's mate; **boatswain,** bos'n, pipes [slang]; naval officers 747.24.

8. **steersman,** helmsman, wheelsman, boat steerer; **coxswain,** cox [coll.]; **pilot,** conner.

9. (malingering sailor) sham Abram *or* Abraham, galley stoker, lead swinger, soldier, sojer [all slang *or* derog.].

10. **longshoreman** [U.S.], wharf *or* dock hand, docker, **dock-walloper** [slang]; **stevedore,** loader; **roustabout** [U.S.], lumper.

276. WATERCRAFT

NOUNS **1. marine, ships, shipping,** "wooden walls" [Themistocles]; mercan-tile *or* merchant marine; **fleet,** flotilla, argosy; fishing fleet, whaling fleet, etc.; **navy** 798.27; rum row [coll., U.S.].

2. **watercraft,** craft, **vessel,** water vessel, **boat,** bateau [chiefly Can. & Louisiana]; pair-oar, four-oar, eight-oar, etc.; motor boat, powerboat.

3. **ship, boat, bottom, bark** [poetic], **hulk,** timber [poetic], tub [slang], bucket [slang], shipboard, packet, hooker [derog]; leviathan; "that packet of assorted miseries which we call a ship" [Kipling], "the ship, a fragment detached from the earth" [Conrad], "a goodly vessel that shall laugh at all disaster" [Longfellow].

4. **steamer, steamboat, steamship;** excursion steamer, hurrah boat [slang]; paddle boat *or* steamer, inside walkee [pidgin Eng.]; side-wheeler [coll.], side-kicker [slang, U.S.], sidewinder [slang, U.S.]; stern-wheeler [coll., U.S.], stem-winder [slang], kickup [slang, U.S.].

5. **liner,** ocean liner, ocean greyhound [coll.], passenger steamer, floating hotel *or* palace.

6. **sailing vessel, sailboat,** sailing boat, sailing ship, sail, sailer, **windjammer** [coll.]; galleon; three-master, four-master, etc.; three-sticker, four-sticker, etc. [coll.].

7. **warship,** war vessel, **man-of-war,** man-o'-war, ship of war, armored vessel; U.S.S., United States Ship; H.M.S. [Eng.], His Majesty's Ship; line-of-battle ship, ship of the line; **battleship,** battlewagon [slang], capital ship; **destroyer,** can *or* tin can [slang]; submarine chaser, subchaser, eagle boat [U.S.], E-boat [coll.]; **navy** 798.27.

8. **carrier,** aircraft carrier, shipplane carrier, seaplane carrier, **flattop** [U.S.]; flight deck, landing deck, island, runway.

9. **submarine, sub,** submersible, **U-boat,** *U-boot* [G.], *Unterseeboot* [G.], pig boat [slang]; minisub; snorkel, schnorkel.

10. **hydroplane,** hydroglider, gliding boat, glider.

11. **float, raft,** balsa; life raft; boom; pontoon; buoy, life buoy; surfboard; cork; bob [fishing].

12. **rigging, rig, tackle,** tackling, **gear,** ropework, roping, hempen bridle [slang]; service, serving; standing rigging, running rigging.

13. **spars,** timber; **mast,** pole, stick [coll.], tree [coll.]; bare poles, soldier's masts [coll.].

14. **sail, canvas,** muslin, cloth, rag

[coll.]; skysail, skyscraper [coll.], cloud cleaner [slang]; moonsail, moonraker; kites, flying kites, lady's pocket handkerchief [slang], sail teaser [slang]; luff; leech; crowd of sail.

15. **oar, paddle,** scull, sweep, pole.

16. **anchor,** hook [slang], mud hook [slang]; anchorage, moorings; mooring buoy.

ADJS. 17. **rigged,** decked, trimmed; square-rigged, lateen-rigged, monkey-rigged [hist.].

18. **seaworthy,** sea-kindly, fit for sea, snug, bold; **watertight,** waterproof, drop-dry [cant]; **A1,** A one, A1 at Lloyd's.

19. **trim,** in trim; apoise, on an even keel.

ADJS., ADVS. 20. **shipshape,** Bristol fashion, shipshape and Bristol fashion, ataunt, all ataunto [cant], bungup and bilge-free [cant].

21. boats

airboat	gig
almadia, almadie	glider
ark	gliding boat
auxiliary, auxiliary	gondola
boat	houseboat
barge	hoy
broadhorn [West.	hydroglider
U.S.]	hydroplane
bunder boat	iceboat
[India]	ice canoe
bungo	ice yacht
cabin cruiser	jolly, jolly boat
caïque	kayak, kaiak
canalboat	launch
canoe	lerret [Eng.]
cargo boat	lifeboat
catamaran	lighter
catboat, cat	log canoe
coble	longboat
cockboat	mail boat, mailer
cockle	motorboat
cockleboat	motor launch
cockleshell	nuggar [Egypt]
cog	outboard
coracle	motorboat
cruiser	pair-oar
cutter	pilot, pilot boat
dahabeah [Egypt]	pinnace
dinghy	piragua
dispatch boat	pirogue
dory [U.S.]	pontoon
dugout	post boat
eight-oar	powerboat
faltboat	praam
ferry, ferryboat	punt [chiefly Eng.]
fireboat	racer
fishing boat	racing shell
fishing dory	radio-controlled
flatboat	lifeboat
flyboat	randan
foldboat	rowboat, rowing
four-oar	boat
funny [Eng.]	runabout
galley [Eng.]	sailboat 276.23

sampan	steam launch
scooter	towboat
scow	trawler,
scull	trawlboat
sea sled	tug, tugboat
shallop	umiak [Eskimo]
shell	wanigan [U.S.]
showboat	whaleboat
skiff	wherry
small boat	yawl
speedboat	

22. ships

argosy	revenue cutter
ark	[U.S.]
battleship 276.24	rotor, rotor ship
cabin boat	sailing vessel
caravel	276.23
coaler, collier	screw steamer
coaster	side-wheeler [coll.]
coast guard cutter	slaver
[U.S.]	spar-decker, spar-
derelict	deck vessel
excursion steamer	stage boat
fishing boat or	steamboat
vessel	steamer
freighter	steam schooner
galley 276.25	steamship
lightship	stern-wheeler
liner	[coll., U.S.]
mail steamer	storeship
merchant ship,	tanker
merchantman	tender
ocean liner	tramp
packet, packet	transport
boat or ship	trawler
paddle boat or	turbine
steamer	turbine steamer
passenger steamer	whaleback [U.S.]
refrigeration ship	whaler

23. sailing vessels

baggala	frigate
bark	galiot
barkentine	galleass
bastard schooner	galleon [hist.]
bilander	hermaphrodite
brig	brig
brigantine	hooker
bully	junk
[Newfoundland]	keelboat
buss	ketch
caravel	knockabout [U.S.]
carrack [hist.]	lateen, lateener
cat	lorcha
catboat	lugger
chasse-marée [F.]	outrigger
clipper	pinnace [hist. or
corsair	poetic]
corvette, corvet	piragua
cutter	pirogue
dandy	polacre, polacca
dhow	praam
dogger	proa [Malaysia]
felucca	rigger
fishing schooner	saic
fishing smack	sailboat, sailing
fore-and-aft, fore-	boat
and-after [coll.]	sailing barge
four-masted bark	sailing canoe
four-master	sailing launch

sailing packet
sailing trawler
sailing yacht
sampan
schooner
scooter [local, U.S.]
shallop [hist.]
shipentine
sloop
smack

smack boat
snow
square-rigger
tartan
three-master
topsail schooner
well smack
xebec
yacht
yawl

24. naval vessels

aircraft carrier
aircraft tender
AKA boat (auxiliary cargo attack)
ammunition ship
APA boat (auxiliary personnel attack)
armored or protected cruiser
assault boat
assault transport
battle cruiser
battleship
blockship
bomb ketch or vessel [hist.]
caravel [Turk.]
carrier
coast guard cutter [U.S.]
convoy
corvette, corvet
crash boat
cruiser
cutter [U.S.]
depot ship
destroyer
destroyer leader
destroyer tender
dreadnought
eagle boat [U.S.]
E-boat [coll.]
escort carrier
fireboat
fire ship
first-rate
flagship
flattop [U.S.]
floating battery
frigate
fuel ship
guard ship or boat
gunboat
heavy cruiser
hospital ship
ironclad
ironclad ram
ironsides
landing craft
LC (landing craft)
LCC (landing craft, control)
LCI (landing craft, infantry)
LCM (landing craft, mechanized)

LCP (landing craft, personnel)
LCT (landing craft, tank)
LCV (landing craft, vehicle)
LCVP (landing craft, vehicle-personnel)
light cruiser
line-of-battle ship
LSD (landing ship, dock)
LSM (landing ship, medium)
LST (landing ship, tank)
mine layer, mine ship
mine sweeper
minisub
monitor
mosquito boat
motor torpedo boat
MTB (motor torpedo boat)
naval auxiliary
patrol boat
patrol torpedo boat
PC (patrol craft)
PCE (patrol craft, escort)
PCS (patrol craft, sweeper)
picketboat
pig boat [slang]
pocket battleship
privateer
protected cruiser
PT boat (patrol torpedo boat)
ram
receiving ship
repair ship
river gunboat
rocket boat
SC (scouting craft)
scout
scout cruiser
seaplane carrier
second-line battleship
second-line destroyer
ship of the line
ship of war

shipplane carrier
sloop of war
storeship
storm boat
submarine
submarine chaser, subchaser
submarine patrol boat
submarine tender
submersible
superdreadnought
supply ship
sweeper

tanker
target boat
tender
torpedo boat
torpedo-boat destroyer or catcher
transport, transport ship or vessel
troopship
turret ship
U-boat
warship

25. galleys [hist.]

bireme
foist
galiot
galleass
galley foist
half galley
hepteris
hexeris
penteconter

quadrireme
quarter galley
quinquereme
tessaraconter
triaconter
trireme
Venetian galley
war galley

26. parts of ships

back
balance rudder
beak, beakhead
beam
bilge keel
bilge keelson
bitt
board
bollard
bow
bridge
bull's-eye
bulwarks
casemate
centerboard
companion
companion ladder
companionway
conning tower
conning tower hatch
counter
crow's-nest
cutwater
davit
entrance
false keel
forefoot
foresheets
foretop
freeboard
futtock
gangplank
gangway
garboard strake
gunwale, gunnel
hatch
hatchway
hawse, hawsehole
hawsepiece
hawsepipe
hawse timber
head

heel
island
keel
keel and keelson
keelson
kevel
larboard
lee, leeside, leeward
leeboard
limber board
limber hole
maintop
mizzentop
monkey rail
nose
paddle wheel
poop
port, portside
porthole
post
propeller
prow
rail
rudder
rudderpost
rudderstock
run
scuttle
scuttlebutt
sheave hole
sheets
shelf, shelfpiece
sister or side keelson
snorkel, schnorkel
spirketing
stanchion
starboard
stem
stern
sternpost
stern sheets

strake
superstructure
tail end
tail shaft
water line
waterway

weather, weather
  side
weatherboard
windward,
  windward side

dolphin striker
boom
mast
masthead
mizzen,
  mizzenmast
mizzen-royal mast
mizzen-royal yard
mizzen-skysail
  mast
mizzen-skysail yard
mizzen-topgallant
  mast
mizzen-topgallant
  yard
mizzen-topmast

mizzen-topsail yard
sheer pole
skysail mast
skysail yard
spanker boom
spanker gaff
sprit
tack bumpkin
topgallant mast
topgallant yard
topmast
trysail gaff
whisker boom
yard
yardarm

27. compartments

below
between-decks,
  'tween-decks
brig
bunker
cabin
caboose, camboose
galley
head
hold, hole

officers' country
  [cant, U.S. Navy]
pilothouse
quarters
roundhouse
sail loft
sick bay
stateroom
stokehold
topside
wardroom

28. decks

after deck
anchor deck
boat deck
bridge deck
flight deck
forecastle,
  fo c'sle
forward deck
gun deck
half deck
hurricane deck
landing deck
lower deck
main deck
middle deck
monkey deck or
  forecastle

orlop deck
partial hold deck
platform, platform
  deck
poop, poop deck
promenade deck
protective deck
quarterdeck
shelter deck
spar deck
splinter deck
superstructure
  deck
upper or top deck
weather deck

30. sails

baby jib topsail
balance or French
  lug
balloon sail,
  ballooner
club topsail
crossjack
dipping lug
fly-by-night
flying jib
flying kites
fore gaff-topsail
foreroyal
foreroyal studding
  sail
foresail
fore-skysail
forestaysail
fore topgallant sail
fore-topgallant
  studding sail
fore-topmast
  staysail
fore-topmast
  studding sail
fore-topsail
inner jib
jib
jimbo [cant]
jolly jumper
kites
lateen sail
lower studding sail
  lug
lugsail
main gaff-topsail
main royal
main-royal staysail
main-royal
  studding sail
mainsail

main skysail
main staysail
main-topgallant
  sail
main-topgallant
  studding sail
main-topmast
  staysail
main-topmast
  studding sail
main-topsail
mizzen
mizzen royal
mizzen-royal
  staysail
mizzen sail
mizzen skysail
mizzen staysail
mizzen-topgallant
  sail
mizzen-topgallant
  staysail
mizzen-topmast
  staysail
moonraker
moonsail
outer jib
reef
royal
skysail
skyscraper [coll.]
spanker
spritsail
square sail
standing lug
staysail
stern staysail
studding sail
topgallant sail
topsail
trysail

29. spars

boom
bowsprit
brace bumpkin
bumpkin, bumkin,
  boomkin
crossjack yard
crosstree
flying jib boom
fore jack
foremast
foreroyal mast
foreroyal-studding-
  sail boom
foreroyal yard
fore-skysail mast
fore-skysail yard
fore-topgallant
  mast
fore-topgallant-
  studding-sail
  boom
fore-topgallant
  yard
fore-topmast
fore-topmast-
  studding-sail
  boom
fore-topsail yard
foretrysail gaff
foreyard
gaff

jack
jib boom
jigger mast
lower boom
lower mizzen-
  topsail yard
main-brace
  bumpkin
mainmast
main-royal mast
main-royal-
  studding-sail
  boom
main-royal yard
main-skysail mast
main-skysail yard
main-topgallant
  mast
main-topgallant-
  studding-sail
  boom
main-topgallant
  yard
main-topmast
main-topmast-
  studding-sail
  boom
main-topsail yard
main-trysail gaff
main yard
martingale or

31. ropes, rigging

after shroud
backropes
backstay
boat line
bobstay
boltrope
bow fast
bowline
bowsprit shroud
brace

brail
breast fast
buntline
crossjack brace
crossjack lift
downhaul
earing
fast
Flemish horse
flying jib guy

flying jib
  martingale
flying-jib stay
footropes
forebrace
foreganger
fore lift
foreroyal backstay
foreroyal brace
foreroyal lift
foreroyal shroud
foreroyal stay
forerunner
foresheet
fore-skysail
  backstay
fore-skysail brace
fore-skysail lift
fore-skysail shroud
fore-skysail stay
forestay
foretack
fore-topgallant
  backstay
fore-topgallant
  brace
fore-topgallant lift
fore-topgallant
  shroud
fore-topgallant
  stay
fore-topmast
  backstay
fore-topmast stay
fore-topmast
  staysail stay
fore-topsail lift
fore-trysail peak
  halyard
fore-trysail vang
futtock shroud
gasket
grab rope [U.S.]
guess-rope
guess-warp
guest rope
guy
halyard
harbor gasket
hawser
head earing
head fast
Jacob's ladder
jib guy
jib martingale
jibstay
lanyard
lee sheet
lee tack
life line
lift
lower-boom
  topping lift
main brace
main lift
main-royal brace

32. anchors

Baldt anchor
bower
center anchor

main-royal lift
main-royal stay
mainsheet
main-skysail brace
main-skysail lift
main-skysail stay
mainstay
main-topgallant
  brace
main-topgallant
  lift
main-topgallant
  stay
main-topmast stay
main-topsail lift
main-trysail peak
  halyard
main-trysail vang
marline
martingale
messenger
mizzen-royal brace
mizzen-royal lift
mizzen-royal stay
mizzen-skysail
  brace
mizzen-skysail lift
mizzen-skysail stay
mizzen stay
mizzen-topgallant
  brace
mizzen-topgallant
  lift
mizzen-topgallant
  stay
mizzen-topmast
  stay
mizzen-topsail lift
mooring pendant
painter
quarter fast
ratline, ratlin
reef earing
roband, raband,
  robbin
ropeband
sea gasket
sheet
shroud
span
spanker peak
  halyard
spanker sheet
spanker vang
spring
starboard or port
  tack
stay
stern fast
stirrup
swifter
tack
timenoguy
vang
weather sheet
whisker jumper

drag anchor
Dunn anchor
floating anchor

grapnel
kedge, kedge
  anchor
killick
Martin's anchor
mushroom anchor
port anchor

sacred anchor [Gr.
  & Rom. antiq.]
sea anchor
sheet anchor
starboard anchor
stern anchor
stream anchor
Trotman's anchor

33. helms

electrohydraulic
  steering gear
gyroscopic pilot
hand gear
lee helm
lever pilot

servo-pilot
steering gear
telemotor
tiller
weather helm

34. equipment

anemometer
anemoscope
barograph
barometer
belaying pin
bilge pump
binnacle
boat hook
calking iron
capstan
compass
grapnel
grappling iron

hawse bag
hawse hook
holystone
hygrograph
mooring swivel or
  shackle
nigger [U.S.]
pump
sounders 208.17
tackle 286.10
thermograph
toggle

277. AERONAUTICS

NOUNS 1. **aeronautics, aviation,** airplaning, planing [coll.], skyriding, **flying,**
flight, winging, soaring; volation, volita-
tion; aeronautism, aerodromics; cruising;
gliding, volplaning; ballooning, balloonery;
barnstorming [coll.]; heavy or ironhanded
flying [cant]; high-altitude flying; blind or
instrument flying; contact flying, pilotage;
sky writing; cloud seeding; in-flight training, ground school; airline; astronautics 281;
air service 798.29, 30.

2. (allied sciences) aerocartography,
aerodonetics, aerodynamics, aerography,
aerology, aeromechanics, aerometry, aeronautical engineering, aeronautical meteorology, aerophotography, aerophysics, aeroscopy, aerostatics, aerostation, aerotechnics,
aircraft hydraulics, avionics, climatology,
hydrostatics, jet engineering, kinematics,
kinetics, meteorology, micrometry, photometry, pneumatics, rocket engineering; supersonics, supersonic aerodynamics; aviation
medicine, Air Force School of Aviation
Medicine, Air Force Department of Space
Medicine.

3. **airmanship,** pilotship; aerophobia,
aeropathy; airsickness; air legs; washout
(failure in flight training [slang]).

4. **navigation, avigation,** aerial navigation; celestial navigation; electronic naviga-

tion, automatic electronic navigation; navar (navigation and ranging), teleran (television radar air navigation), loran (long range aid to navigation), shoran (short range aid to navigation); omnidirectional range, omnirange, VAR (visual-aural range).

5. (aeronautical organizations) Civil Aeronautics Administration, C.A.A.; Bureau of Aeronautics, BuAer; National Advisory Committee for Aeronautics, NACA; Office of Naval Research, ONR; Civil Air Patrol, CAP; Aircraft Recognition Society, A.R.S.; Air Force 798.30.

6. take-off, hopoff [slang]; taxiing, take-off run; daisy-clipping, grass-cutting [both slang]; ground loop; level-off; ATO (assisted take-off [Eng.]), JATO (jet-assisted take-off); booster rocket, take-off rocket; catapult, electropult.

7. flight, trip, run; hop, jump, air jump [all slang]; powered flight; solo flight, solo; nolo flight (pilotless); inverted flight; supersonic flight; test flight, test hop [slang]; airlift; airdrop; shuttle; shuttle service, shuttle trip; weather or meteorological reconnaissance; in-flight refueling; radius of action, navigation radius.

8. (Air Force) mission, flight operation; training mission; gunnery mission; combat rehearsal, dry run [coll.]; transition mission; reconnaissance mission, reconnaissance, observation flight, search mission; milk run [coll.]; box-top mission [slang]; combat flight; sortie; air raid; shuttle raid; bombing mission; bombing, strafing 796.7, 8; air support (for ground troops), air cover, cover, umbrella, air umbrella; briefing, brief, flight plan, run-down [slang].

9. formation flying, formation; close formation, loose formation, wing formation; V formation, echelon.

10. (maneuvers) acrobatic or tactical evolutions or maneuvers, acrobatics, aerobatics; stunting, stunt flying [both coll.]; rolling, crabbing, banking, porpoising, fishtailing, diving; dive, nose dive, power dive; zoom, chandelle; stall, whip stall; glide, volplane; spiral, split "S", lazy eight, sideslip, push-down, pull-up, pull-out.

11. roll, barrel roll, aileron roll, outside roll, snap roll.

12. spin, autorotation, tail spin, flat spin, inverted spin, normal spin, power spin, uncontrolled spin, falling leaf.

13. loop, spiral loop, ground loop, nor-mal loop, outside loop, inverted normal or outside loop, dead-stick loop [cant], wing-over, looping the loop; Immelmann turn, reverse turn, reversement; flipper turns.

14. buzzing, flathatting [slang]; hedge-hopping, roadhopping, carhopping [all slang, U.S.].

15. landing, landfall, perch [slang], arrival; landing run; ballooning in, parachute approach; blind or instrument landing, dead-stick landing [cant], glide landing, stall landing, fishtail landing, sideslip landing, level or two-point landing, normal or three-point landing, Chinese landing (one wing low [slang]), tail-high landing, tail-low landing, thumped-in landing [slang], pancake landing, belly landing, crash landing, nose-over, nose-up; practice landing, bounce drill [Air Force].

16. (flying and landing guides) marker, pylon; beacon; radio beacon, radio marker; fan marker; radar beacon, racon; beam, radio beam; beacon lights 335.10; wind indicator, wind cone or sock, air sleeve; I.L.S. (Instrument Landing System); TRODI (Touchdown Rate of Descent Indicator); G.C.A. (Ground-Controlled Approach); talking-down system, talking down.

17. crash, crack-up, crock-up [Eng.], prang [slang, Eng.]; crash landing.

18. blackout; gray-out; anoxia; useful consciousness; pressure suit, antiblackout suit.

19. airport, airfield, airdrome, aero-drome [esp. Eng.], drome [coll.], port, air harbor [Can.], aviation field, landing field, landing, field, airship station; air base [mil.], nest [slang]; airpark; heliport, helidrome; control tower; Air Route Traf-fic Control Center [U.S.]; FIDO (Fog Investigation Dispersal Operations).

20. runway, taxiway, strip, landing strip, airstrip, flight strip, take-off strip; fairway, launching way; stopway; clearway; transition strip; apron; flight deck, landing deck, island.

21. hangar, housing, dock, shed, airship shed; mooring mast.

22. (technical) aerocurve, aerodynamic or air volume, airplane heading, amplitude, aspect ratio, bearing, beam direction, cam-ber, décalage [F.], direction of relative wind, equivalent monoplane, fineness ratio, flight path, margin of power, positive direction of roll, propulsive efficiency, resultant force, righting or restoring moment, skin friction, slip, stagger, sweepback, tail force.

23. (angle) aileron angle, blade angle, coning angle, dihedral angle, drift angle, downwash angle, elevator angle, flapping angle, flight path angle, gliding angle, helix angle, landing angle, rudder angle, trim angle, zero-lift angle, angle of attack, angle of dead rise, angle of heel, angle of incidence or wing setting, angle of pitch, angle of roll or bank, angle of sideslip, angle of stabilizer setting, angle of yaw.

24. (center) aerodynamic center, elastic center, center of buoyancy, center of gravity, center of mass, center of pressure, center-of-pressure coefficiency.

25. (axis) horizontal or longitudinal axis, fore-and-aft axis, X axis; lateral axis, Y axis; normal axis, Z axis; elastic axis, wing axis, drag axis, positive lift axis; yawing, yaw, positive direction of yaw.

26. (stability) automatic stability, directional stability, dynamic stability, inherent stability, lateral stability, longitudinal stability, static stability.

27. (load) basic load, design load, full load, normal load, ultimate load, useful load; payload, offensive load; power loading, span loading, unsymmetrical loading, wing loading.

28. (pressure) altitude or height pressure, dynamic pressure, impact pressure, manometer pressure, superpressure; center of pressure; stress, working stress, breathing stresses; torsion, torsional stress, torque, propeller torque; structural fatigue.

29. thrust, propeller thrust, static propeller thrust, line of thrust or flight; thrust augmenter, rocket assist.

30. (propulsion) rocket propulsion, rocket power; jet propulsion, jet power; turbojet propulsion, pulse-jet propulsion, ram-jet propulsion, resojet propulsion; constant or ram pressure, air ram; reaction propulsion, reaction, action and reaction; GALCIT (Jet Propulsion Laboratory of the Guggenheim Aeronautical Laboratory of the California Institute of Technology).

31. pitch, pitch ratio, aerodynamic pitch, effective pitch, geometrical pitch, zero-thrust pitch; angle of pitch, positive direction of pitch.

32. lift, lift ratio, lift force or component, lift direction; aerostatic lift, dynamic lift, gross lift, useful lift, margin of lift.

33. drag, resistance; drag ratio, drag force or component, induced drag, wing drag, parasite or structural drag, profile drag, head resistance, drag direction, cross-wind force.

34. drift, drift angle; lateral drift, leeway.

35. flow, air flow, laminar flow.

36. wash, wake, stream; down-wash; backwash, slipstream, propeller race, prop-wash [cant]; blow wash (jet [cant]); vapor trail, condensation trail, contrail, vortex.

37. (speed) air speed, true air speed, operating or flying speed, minimum flying speed, hump speed, peripheral speed, pitch speed, terminal speed, sinking speed, getaway or take-off speed, landing speed, ground speed; speed of sound, sonic speed, zone of no signal, Mach; Mach one, Mach two, etc.; Mach cone; Mach meter; subsonic speed; supersonic ∼, ultrasonic ∼, hypersonic or transsonic speed; sound barrier, sonic barrier or wall; escape velocity.

38. (air, atmosphere) airspace, navigable airspace; troposphere, tropopause, substratosphere, stratosphere, stratopause, ionosphere; space, empty space; ceiling, ballonet ceiling, service ceiling, static ceiling, absolute ceiling, ceiling zero; visibility, visibility zero; overcast, undercast; fog, soup [slang]; high-pressure area, low-pressure area; trough, trough line; air pocket or hole, air bump, pocket, hole, bump; head wind, tail wind; atmospheric tides.

39. airway, air lane, air line, air route, skyway, corridor, lane, path.

40. course, heading, vector; compass heading or course, compass direction (of flight), magnetic heading, true heading or course.

41. (altitude) altitude of flight, absolute, altitude, critical altitude, density altitude, pressure altitude, sextant altitude; clearance; ground elevation.

VERBS 42. fly, flit, wing, take wing, make wing, wing one's way, take a flight, take to the air, take the air, volitate, be wafted; aviate, airplane, aeroplane, aero, plane [coll.], go by plane [coll.], navigate the air, go by air, take to the airways, ride the skies; hop [coll.]; soar, drift, hover; cruise; glide, volplane; hydroplane; balloon; ferry; airlift; break the sound barrier; navigate, avigate.

43. pilot, control, be at the controls, fly, manipulate, drive, herd [slang]; copilot; solo; barnstorm [coll.]; fly blind, fly by the seat of one's pants [slang]; follow the beam, ride the beam [cant]; fly in formation, take position; peel off.

44. take off, hop off [slang], get off the

ground take to the air, go *or* fly aloft; **taxi.**

45. ascend, climb, mount; zoom, hoick [cant], chandelle.

46. (maneuver) **stunt** [coll.], perform aerobatics; crab, crab the wind; fishtail, kick her tail around [slang]; spin, go into a tail spin; loop, loop the loop; roll, wingover, spiral, undulate, porpoise, feather, yaw, sideslip, skid, bank, dip, nose down, nose up, pull up, push down, pull out, plow, mush through.

47. dive, nose-dive, power-dive, pique.

48. buzz, flathat [slang]; **hedgehop,** roadhop, carhop [all slang, U.S.].

49. land, set her down [cant], **alight, light,** touch down; **descend,** come down, fly down; come in for a landing; **level off,** flatten out; up-wind, down-wind; overshoot, undershoot; make a dead-stick landing [cant]; pancake a landing, thump in [slang]; bellyland, settle down, balloon in; fishtail down; **crash-land;** ditch [slang]; nose up, nose over; talk down.

50. crash, crack up, crock up [Eng.]; spin in fail to pull out.

51. stall, conk out [slang].

52. black out, gray out.

53. bail out, parachute, make a parachute jump, make a brolly-hop [slang, Eng.].

54. brief, give a briefing, give the rundown [slang].

ADJS **55. aeronautic(al),** aeropleustic, aerial; **aviatorial,** aviatory, aviatic; aerodonetic, aerotechnical, aerostatic(al), aeromechanic(al), aerodynamic(al), aerophysical; aeromarine; aerobatic; airworthy, airminded, air-conscious; air-wise; airsick.

56. flying flitting, winging; volant, volitant, volitational; **air-borne;** jet-propelled, rocket-propelled.

ADVS. **57. in flight, on the wing** *or* fly. INTERJS. **58. switch off!,** contact!

59. instruments

accelerometer
aerial
  reconnaissance
  camera
aerograph
aerometer
aeroscope
air controls
air log
air-speed head
air-speed indicator
altigraph
altimeter
altitude mixture
  control

ammeter
anemograph
anemometer
anemoscope
aneroid
automatic boost
  control
automatic *or* robot
  pilot
autopilot
autosyn
bank *or* banking
  indicator
barometer
bearing plate

bombing locator
bombsight
Bourdon tube
calorimeter
carburetor altitude
  control
card compass
card magnetic
  compass
ceiling-height
  indicator
chronometer
climatometer
compass
control rod *or*
  column
controls
control stick
directional gyro
direction finder
direction
  indicator
drift meter
dual controls
earth inductor *or*
  induction compass
electrical capacity
  altimeter
engine controls
engine gauge
evaporimeter
flight recorder
fuel-flow meter
fuel quantity
  indicator
galvanometer
gosport, gosport
  tube
gyrocompass
gyro horizon
gyropilot
gyrosyn
horn
hub dynamometer
hygrograph
hygrometer
hypsometer
inclinometer
induction compass
instrument board
  or panel
intervalometer
Joyce stick
joy stick [slang]
macaviator
Mach meter
magnetic compass
manifold pressure
  gauge

meteorograph
micrometer
nephoscope
octant
optical altimeter
ozonometer
pelorus
photometer
pitch *or* pitching
  indicator
Pitot-static tube
pluviometer
polymeter
position indicator
potentiometer
pressure altimeter
pyrometer
quadrant
radar
radio
radio altimeter
radio compass
radio direction
  finder
radiogoniometer
rate-of-climb
  indicator
recording altimeter
recording
  anemometer
recording
  hygrometer
sextant
sound-ranging
  altimeter
Sperry Antiaircraft
  Director
spirit level
static tube
stick, stick control
sting
strike radar scanner
sun compass
tachometer
terrain clearance
  indicator
thermograph
thermometer
thermostat
throttle
transit instrument
turn-and-bank
  indicator
turnmeter
variometer
Venturi tube
viscosimeter
yawmeter

278. AERONAUT

NOUNS **1. aeronaut, aviator,** aeroplaner, airplaner, aeroplanist, airplanist, **airman, flier** *or* flyer, **pilot,** wingman; bird, birdman, man-bird [all coll.]; copilot; jet pilot, jet jockey [slang]; volplanist; test pilot; bush pilot [U.S.]; astronaut 281.8; cloud seeder, rainmaker; barnstormer [coll.]; stunt man, stunt flier [both coll.]; flying circus.

2. **aviatrix**, aviatrice, aviatress, **air-woman**, birdwoman [coll.].

3. **air serviceman**, war bird [coll.], **eagle** or American eagle [slang, U.S.]; Flying Cadet; fighter pilot; bomber pilot; suicide pilot; observer, spotter, scout; ace; air force 798.29.

4. crew, **aircrew**; aircrewman, airedale [slang]; navigator, avigator; bombardier; gunner, machine gunner, belly gunner, tail gunner; aerial photographer; meteorologist; stewardess.

5. **ground crew**, chairborne troops [U.S. Air Force]; landing crew, plane handlers; nonflier, groundhog [slang], kiwi [slang, Eng.], dodo [slang].

6. **aircraftsman**; aeromechanic; rigger; aeronautical engineer, jet engineer, rocket engineer 280.6; ground tester, flight tester.

7. **balloonist**, ballooner.

8. **parachutist**, chutist or chuter [coll.], parachute jumper; **paratrooper**; paradoctor, para-medic; jumpmaster.

9. (mythological fliers) Daedalus, Icarus.

279. AIRCRAFT

NOUNS 1. **aircraft**, aerocraft, **airplane, aeroplane, plane**, aero [coll.], aeronef, **ship**, boat [slang], **flying machine**, avion [F.]; aerodyne, heavier-than-air craft; jalopy [coll., U.S.]; planform.

2. **propeller plane**, single-prop, double-prop, multi-prop; tractor, tractor plane; pusher, pusher plane.

3. **jet plane, jet; turbojet, ramjet, pulsejet**; single-jet, twin-jet, multi-jet; delta-planform jet, tailless jet, twin-tailboom jet; subsonic jet, supersonic jet; stratojet.

4. **rocket plane**, repulsor; rocket ship, spaceship 281.2; rocket 280.1.

5. **rotor, plane**, rotocraft; **gyroplane,** gyro, **autogiro**, windmill [slang]; **helicopter,** copter [coll.]; whirlybird, puddle jumper, flying eggbeater [all slang]; convertiplane, planicopter; gyrodine.

6. **orthopter, ornithopter**, wind flapper [slang], mechanical bird.

7. **flying platform**, flying ring, Hiller-CNR machine; flying crow's nest, flying motorcycle, flying bathtub [all slang].

8. **seaplane**, waterplane, **hydroplane,** aerohydroplane, aeroboat, duck [slang]; **floatplane**, float seaplane; **flying boat,** boat seaplane; **amphibian,** triphibian.

9. **warplane, battleplane**, combat plane; suicide plane, kamikaze; bogey, unidentified object; fleet, armada.

10. **trainer;** Link Trainer, jeep [slang]; flight simulator, penguin; dual-control trainer; basic or primary trainer, intermediate trainer, advanced trainer; crew trainer, flying classroom; navigator-bombardier trainer, radio-navigational trainer, etc.

11. **aerostat,** lighter-than-air craft; **airship,** ship, aeronat, **dirigible, blimp** [coll.]; **zeppelin,** Graf Zeppelin [World War I]; **balloon,** ballon [F.].

12. **glider,** gliding machine, aerodone; sailplane; aviette; rocket glider; student glider.

13. **parachute, chute** [coll.], umbrella [slang], brolly [slang, Eng.]; pilot parachute; rip cord, safety loop, shroud lines, harness, pack, vent; parachute jump, brolly-hop [slang, Eng.].

14. **kite,** box kite, Eddy kite, Hargrave or cellular kite, tetrahedral kite.

15. **airplanes**

aeroboat	cargo transport
aerobus [coll.]	carrier-based plane
aerodone	carrier fighter
aerohydroplane	casualty-evacuation
air coach	plane
air cruiser	clipper
airfreighter	club plane
airliner	commercial
air scout	transport
air-sea rescue	constant-chord-
amphibian	rotor helicopter
air-sea rescue plane	convertiplane
all-weather fighter	cruiser
ambulance	cub
amphibian	delta planform jet
amphibian	dive bomber
transport	double-prop
anti-submarine	drone
patrol	escort fighter
anti-submarine	evacuation
plane	ambulance
arctic rescue	evacuation plane
helicopter	executive plane
assault transport	feeder liner
assault-troop plane	fighter
atom-liner	fighter-bomber
atom-plane	floatplane
attack bomber	flying banana
attack plane	flying bedstead
attack transport	[slang]
autogiro	flying boat
aviette	flying platform
avion-canon [F.]	flying tanker
battleplane	flying wing
biplace [F., two-	freighter
seater]	freight transport
biplane	general
boat seaplane	reconnaissance
bomber	glider
cabin plane	grasshopper
canard	ground-attack
cargo plane	fighter

ground-support
  aircraft
gyrodine
gyroplane
heavy bomber
heavy transport
helibus
helicopter
helivector
high-altitude
  reconnaissance
  plane
high-altitude
  research aircraft
high-wing
  monoplane
hunter
hydroplane
in-flight refuelling
  tanker
interceptor
intermeshing-rotor
  helicopter
jet, jet plane
jet bomber
jet fighter
killer
landplane
liaison plane
light bomber
light transport
liner [U.S.]
long-range attack
  aircraft
long-range bomber
long-range medium
  or heavy bomber
long-range patrol
  bomber
low-wing mono-
  plane
mail plane
maritime recon-
  naissance plane
medium bomber
meteorological re-
  connaissance
  plane
midwing mono-
  plane
military transport
mobile command
  post
monoplace [F.,
  single-seater]
monoplane
mosquito
multi-jet
multi-prop
multipurpose plane
naval bomber
naval fighter
naval interceptor
night fighter
observation plane
ornithopter
orthopter
passenger plane
pathfinder
patrol bomber
patrol plane

photo-reconnais-
  sance plane
picket patrol plane
planicopter
precision bomber
pulsejet
pulsejet helicopter
pursuit plane
pusher, pusher
  plane
ramjet
reconnaissance
  plane
repulsor
rescue plane
research plane
robot plane
rocket-firing plane
rocket plane
rotorcraft
rotor plane
sailplane
scout, scout plane
seaplane
search plane
service aircraft
sesquiplane
shipboard inter-
  ceptor
shipboard plane
shipplane
single-jet
single-prop
sky truck
stratofreighter
stratojet
strike plane
subsonic jet
supersonic com-
  bat plane
supersonic jet
supersonic research
  plane
tactical support
  bomber
tailless jet
tandem plane
tandem-rotor
  helicopter
target-tug or -tower
taxiplane
torpedo bomber
torpedo strike
  aircraft
tractor, tractor
  plane
trainer
trainer-bomber
trainer-fighter
transport
triphibian
troop transport
turbojet
turboprop
twin-jet
twin-prop
twin-tailboom jet
utility plane
V.I.P. transport
  [Very Important
  Persons]

warplane
waterplane

16. plane parts

adjustable propel-
  ler
aerothermo-
  dynamic duct
afterburner
aileron
air brake
air control
airfoil, aerofoil
airframe
air intake
air scoop
airscrew [Eng.]
antidrag wire
antilift or landing
  wire
arresting gear
arrestor hook
astrodome
athodyd
axial flow unit
balancing flap
ball turret
bay
beaching gear
belly tank
blister
blister canopy
body
bomb bay
bomb rack
bomb release
bonnet
booster rocket unit
bow
brace wire
bubble
bubble canopy
bubble hood
bucket seat
bumper bag
butterfly tail
cabin
canopy
cat strip
channel patch
chassis
chin
coaxial propellers
cockpit
contraprops
contra-rotating
  airscrews
controls 272.59
control surface
control wires
cowl
crew compartment
dead stick [cant]
deceleron
deck
de-icer
delta wings
dihedral
diving rudder
dorsal airdome
dorsal blister

weather recon-
  naissance plane
double-bubble
drag strut
drag wire
drift wire
ejection seat
ejector
elevating rudder
elevator
elevon
emergency landing
  gear
empennage
fin
finger patch
flame trap
flap
float
flotation gear
fuel injector
fuselage
gas-shaft hood
gore
gun mount
hatch
hood
instruments 277.59
interceptor
intermeshing rotors
jackstay
jet pipe
jury skid
keel
landing gear
landing skis
launching gear
launching tube
leading edge
lift wire
longeron
monocoque [F.]
nacelle
nose
nose radiator
nose turret
nosewheel
nosewheel under-
  carriage
oleo gear
oleo leg
pants, wheel pants
  [slang]
perspex "chin"
  housing
pilot plane
pontoon
projector tube
prop [cant]
propeller
propulsive duct
radar nacelle
radar nose
radar scanner
radome
retractable landing
  gear
rocket launcher
rotors

rudder
rudder bar
rudder pedals
runners (for snow
  or ice)
safety wire
skid fin
skid landing gear
ski landing gear
spinner
spoiler
spray strip
stabilizer, stabiliza-
  tor
stagger or inci-
  dence wire
stay
stringers
strut
stub-wing stabilizer
supersonic wings
tail
tail boom
tail fin
tailpipe
tailplane
tail rotor
tail skid

tail stinger
tail unit
tail wheel
tandem rotors
tandem seat
tractor airscrew
trailing edge
truss
turbine nozzle
turboprops
turret
turtleback
twin tail wheel
undercarriage
ventral airdome
ventral radome
vertical fin
V-tail
waist gun blister
walking beam
wheel cowlings
wing
wing radiator
wing rib
wing root air intake
wing roots
wing skid
wing truss

17. aeromotors

axial-flow turbojet
axial-type
cam engine
compound engine
compression-igni-
  tion engine
double-row radial
  engine
gas jet
gas turbine jet
  engine
impulse duct en-
  gine
intermittent duct
  engine
inverted engine
jet
pancake engine
propeller-drive gas
  turbine
propeller-jet engine
pulsejet
radial engine

ramjet
reaction motor
reciprocating en-
  gine
resojet
resonance duct jet
  engine
resonance jet en-
  gine
rocket motor
rotary engine
supercharged en-
  gine
turbine
turbojet
turboprop
turboprop-jet
turbo-ram-jet
twin-engines
vertical engine
V-type
W-type
X-type

18. balloons

ballon-sonde
barrage balloon
blimp [coll.]
captive balloon
ceiling balloon
dirigible balloon
fire balloon
free balloon
kite balloon or
  sausage

montgolfier
observation balloon
pilot balloon
rockoon (rocket-
  balloon)
sausage, sausage
  balloon
sounding balloon
stratosphere
  balloon

19. aerostat parts

ballonet
basket
car
catwalk
envelope

gas chamber or cell
gondola
landing or mooring
  line
mooring harness

observation car
observation plat-
  form

side or wing car
subcloud car

280. ROCKETS AND
FLYING MISSILES

NOUNS 1. **rocket,** repulsor; **spaceship** 281.2.

2. **flying missile,** projectile rocket, ballistic missile, ordnance rocket, combat rocket, military rocket, war rocket, **missile,** bird [slang]; **guided** missile, servo-controlled missile; manned missile; countermissile, antimissile; warhead.

3. **rocket bomb,** flying bomb or torpedo, cruising missile; **robot bomb,** robomb, P-plane, *Vergeltungswaffe* [G.]; **buzzbomb,** bumblebomb, doodlebug, Chase-Me-Charlie [all slang; World War II].

4. **multistage rockets, step rockets;** two or three stage rockets, two or three step rockets; single-stage rocket, one-step rocket; **booster,** booster unit, booster rocket, take-off booster or rocket; piggyback rocket [slang].

5. **test rocket,** research rocket, high-altitude research rocket, registering rocket, instrument rocket, instrument carrier, test instrument vehicle, rocket laboratory.

6. **rocket man,** missile man, **rocket engineer,** rocketeer, rocketer, rocketor.

7. **rocketry,** rocket engineering; rocket research, missile research; atmospheric exploration, high-altitude research; ground test; firing test, static firing; guided missile project or program, ORDCIT project (Ordnance and California Institute of Technology); payload (research equipment).

8. **proving ground,** testing ground; White Sands; firing area; impact area; control center; radar tracking station, visual tracking station; meteorological tower.

9. **rocket propulsion,** reaction propulsion, blast propulsion; charge, propelling or propulsion charge, powder charge or grain, high-explosive charge; thrust, constant thrust; exhaust, jet blast, backflash, "rocket's red glare."

10. **rocket fire, launching;** shot, shoot [slang]; guided or automatic control, programming; flight, trajectory; burnout, end of burning; velocity peak, Brennschluss; altitude peak, ceiling; descent; airburst; impact.

11. **launcher,** projector; launching platform or rack, firing table, take-off ramp;

tower projector, launching tower; launching mortar, launching tube, projector tube, firing tube; rocket gun, bazooka; superbazooka; multiple projector, calliope, Stalin organ [slang; World War II]; anti-submarine projector, Mark 10, hedgehog [slang]; Minnie Mouse launcher, mousetrap [slang]; Meilewagon.

VERBS **12. rocket, skyrocket.**

13. launch, project, shoot, fire.

14. rockets and flying missiles

AAM (air-to-air missile)	incendiary antiaircraft rocket
AA target rocket	incendiary rocket
airborne rocket	IRBM (intermediate range ballistic missile)
antiaircraft rocket	
anti-mine rocket	
antimissile	liquid-fuel rocket
anti-radar rocket	long-range rocket
anti-submarine or	loon
anti-sub rocket	piggyback rocket [slang]
anti-tank rocket	
ASM (air-to-surface missile)	ram rocket
	retro-float light
ATA missile (air-to-air)	retro-rocket
	SAM (surface-to-air missile)
ATG rocket (air-to-ground)	
	smoke rocket
atom-rocket	snake (anti-mine)
AUM (air-to-underwater missile)	solid-fuel rocket
	spinner
barrage rocket	spin-stabilized rocket
bat bomb	
bazooka rocket	SSM (surface-to-surface missile)
bombardment rocket	STS rocket (ship-to-shore)
chemical rocket	
combat high-explosive rocket	submarine killer
	supersonic rocket
countermissile	target missile
demolition rocket	torpedo rocket
fin-stabilized rocket	training rocket or missile
flying tank	
GAPA (ground-to-air pilotless aircraft)	trajectory missile
	transoceanic rocket
glide bomb	window rocket (anti-radar)
GTA rocket (ground-to-air)	winged rocket
GTG rocket (ground-to-ground)	XAAM (experimental air-to-air missile)
guided missile	XASM (experimental air-to-surface missile)
high-altitude rocket	
homing rocket	XAUM (experimental air-to-underwater missile)
HVAR (high velocity aircraft rocket)	
	XSAM (experimental surface-to-air missile)
ICBM (intercontinental ballistic missile)	XSSM (experimental surface-to-surface missile)

15. rocket names

Aerobee	Asp
Aerojet	Asroc

Astor	Nike Ajax
Atlas	Nike Hercules
Bomarc	Nike Zeus
Bullpup	Pershing
Cajun	Petrel
Corporal	Pofo
Corvus	Polaris
Crossbow	Private A
Dart	Private F
Davy Crockett	Quail
Deacon	Ram
Ding-Dong	Rascal
Dove	Redeye
Falcon	Redstone
Firebee	Regulus I
Genie	Sergeant
Hawk	Shillelagh
Holy Moses	Sidewinder
Honest John	Skybolt
Hound Dog	SLAM
Jupiter	Snark
Lacrosse	Spaerobee
Lark	Sparrow
Little John	SS-10, SS-11
Lobber	Subroc
Loki	Super Talos
Loon	Talos
Mace	Tartar
Matador	Terrier
Mauler	Thor
Minnie Mouse	Tiny Tim
Minuteman	Titan
NATIV (North American test instrument vehicle)	V-1, V-2
	Viking
	WAC-Corporal
Navaho	Wagtail
Nike	Zuni

16. powder rockets

fireworks rocket	signal rocket
flare rocket	skyrocket
harpoon rocket	smokeless powder rocket
line-throwing rocket	

281. ASTRONAUTICS

NOUNS **1. astronautics,** cosmonautics, astronavigation, **space travel,** navigation of empty space; interplanetary travel, interglobe-trotting [slang]; space exploration, interplanetary reconnaissance; space patrol; space flight, multistage flight, step flight, shuttle flights; trip to the moon, trip to Mars; round trip, one-way trip; space terminal, target planet; spaceites, the rocket bug [slang]; space fiction, space opera [radio & TV slang]; science fiction.

2. spaceship, space rocket, space "hotrod," **rocket ship,** manned rocket, interplanetary rocket; **rocket 280;** moon ship, Mars ship, etc.; deep-space ship; exploratory ship, reconnaissance rocket; ferry rocket, tender rocket, tanker ship, fuel ship; step rockets, multistage or multistep rockets, shuttle rockets, single-step rocket; dusk rocket, dawn rocket; solar rocket (solar-powered), atom-rocket (atomic-powered); robot rocket, remote-controlled spaceship; crash rocket, moon messenger.

3. flying saucer, flying disk, flying flapjack, unidentified flying object, UFO, foo fighter [World War II].

4. rocket engine, solar engine, cosmic-ray power plant, atomic power plant; solar battery.

5. space station, astro station, **space island,** island base, cosmic steppingstone, halfway station, advance base; manned station; triple station, inner station, outer station, transit station; space airport, **spaceport,** spaceport station, space dock, launching base; research station, space laboratory, space observatory; radar station, radio station; radio relay station, radio mirror; space mirror, solar mirror; moon station, moon base, lunar base, lunar city, observatory on the moon.

6. artificial satellite, satellite rocket, space satellite, robot satellite, unmanned satellite, baby satellite, orbital rocket, **artificial moon** or moonlet, manmade moon, MOUSE (minimum orbital unmanned satellite of earth), MOUSE-moon, space-go-round [slang]; *Sputnik* [Russ.]; satellite station; robot laboratory, listening post, telemetering post.

7. (satellite telemetered recorders) micro-instrumentation; aurora particle counter, cosmic ray counter, gamma ray counter, heavy particle counter, impulse recorder, magnetometer, solar ultraviolet detector, solar X-ray detector, telecamera.

8. astronaut, astronavigator, cosmonaut, **spaceman,** space traveller, **rocket man,** rocketeer, rocket pilot; space crew; planetary colony, lunar colony; extraterrestrial visitor, **saucerman, man from Mars,** Martian; space enthusiast, rocket bug [slang]; space doctor, Air Force Department of Space Medicine.

9. rocket society, American Rocket Society, American Interplanetary Society, British Interplanetary Society, German Society for Space Research.

10. cosmic space 374.3.

11. (space hazards) cosmic particles, intergalactic matter, aurora particles, cosmic ray bombardment; meteors, meteorites; meteor dust impacts, meteoric particles, space bullets; bends, blackout, weightlessness; gravity insulator, cavorite.

12. space suit, pressure suit, G suit, anti-G suit; space helmet.

13. space gun, moon gun; disintegrator.

14. (flight mechanics) vertical or horizontal take-off, powered climb, coasting, synergic ascent, descending ellipse, aerodynamic landing; air braking, atmospheric braking, atmosphere bumping, grazing the atmosphere; power braking, rocket braking; exhaust velocity, transition velocity, circular velocity, orbital velocity, ideal velocity; escape velocity, velocity of liberation or escape; voyage orbit, free orbit; orbital refueling, refueling in free orbit; gravitational field, pit.

VERBS **15. astronavigate,** sail the heavens, sail or soar through space; **escape earth,** break free, leave the atmosphere, shoot into space; rocket to the moon, vacation on the moon; park in space, hang or float in space.

ADJS. **16. astronautical,** cosmonautical, astronavigational, space-traveling; rocket-borne, spaceborne.

282. IMPULSE

Driving Force.—NOUNS **1. impulse,** impulsion, impelling force; **impetus; momentum;** moment [tech.], moment of force.

2. thrust, push, shove, boost [coll., U.S.]; press, **pressure, stress,** bearing; **prod, poke, punch, jab,** dig, nudge; **bump,** jog, jolt; **jostle,** hustle; **butt,** bunt; head (pressure of water, steam, etc.).

3. collision, clash, appulse, encounter, meeting, **impact,** impingement, **bump, crash;** carom [esp. billiards], cannon; sideswipe [coll.]; smash, smashup, **crack-up** [all coll.]; **shock, brunt;** percussion, concussion.

4. blow, stroke, hit, knock, rap, pound, bat [coll.], slam, bang, crack [coll.], **whack, smack, thwack,** smash, dash, wipe [dial. & slang], belt [slang], **clout** [coll.], squash, douse [dial. & slang], whop [dial.], **swat** [slang], **punch, poke, jab,** dig, drub, thump, pelt, yerk [dial.], plug [slang], cut, chop, **clip** [coll.], **lick** [coll.], peg [dial. & coll.], soak [slang], **sock** [slang], **biff** [coll., U.S.], dint, slog, slug [dial. & coll.], bash [dial. & slang]; beating 1008.4.

5. (boxing blows) backhander, backhand, backstroke; sidewinder [slang]; hook; short-arm blow; swing, round-arm blow, roundhouse, Long Melford; uppercut, bolo punch; haymaker.

6. tap, rap, pat, dab, chuck, bob; **snap, flick, flip,** fillip, flirt; bunt [baseball, U.S.].

7. peck, pick.

8. slap, smack, flap; **box, cuff,** buffet; spank; whip, lash, cut, stripe.

9. kick, boot; punt, drop kick [both football]; kicking, calcitration.

10. stamp, stomp [dial.], drub, clump, clop.

VERBS 11. impel, give an impetus, **set going** or agoing, put or set in motion, drive, move, animate, actuate, forward; propel 284.10; motivate, incite 646.12–21.

12. thrust, push, shove, boost [coll., U.S.]; press, stress, bear, bear upon, bring pressure to bear upon; ram, jam, crowd, cram; drive, force, run; prod, goad, poke, punch, jab, dig, nudge; bump, jog, jolt; jostle, hustle, hurtle; elbow, shoulder; butt, bunt, buck [coll., U.S.], put [dial., Eng.], run ~, bump or butt against, knock or run one's head against; nose.

13. collide, come into collision, clash, meet, encounter, impinge; bump, hit, strike, knock, bang; run into, bump into, bang into, slam into, smack into, crash into, smash into, dash into, carom into; hit against, strike against, knock against; foul, fall or run foul or afoul of; hurtle, hurt; carom [esp. billiards], cannon; graze, sideswipe [coll.]; crash, smash; smash up, crack up.

14. strike, hit, smite, knock, clobber [slang], belt [slang], bat [coll.], bang, slam, dash, bash [dial. & slang], biff [coll., U.S.], paste [slang], poke, punch, pink [boxing cant], jab, thwack, smack, clap, crack [coll.], wipe [dial. & slang], whack, whop [dial.], wallop [slang], clip [slang], cut, plunk [coll.], plug [slang], swat [slang], peg [dial. & coll.], soak [slang], sock [slang], slog, slug, lam [slang], clout [dial. & coll.], douse [dial. & slang], yerk [dial.]; deal, fetch, deal or fetch a blow, hit a clip [coll], let have it; thump, snap; hook [boxing]; conk [slang]; strike at 796.17.

15. pound, beat, hammer, knock, rap, bang, thump, drub, buffet, batter, patter, pommel, pummel, pelt, wallop [dial. & coll.], larrup [coll.], baste, lambaste [slang]; thresh, thrash; flail, frail [dial.]; spank, flap; tamp; whip 1008.14.

16. tap, rap, pat, dab, chuck, bob; snap, flick, flip, flirt; bunt [baseball, U.S.].

17. peck, pick, beak.

18. slap, smack, flap; box, cuff, buffet; spank; whip 1008.14.

19. club, cudgel, blackjack [U.S.], sandbag.

20. kick, boot, calcitrate; punt, drop-kick [both football].

21. stamp, stomp [dial.], drub, clump, clop.

ADJS. 22. impelling, impellent, impulsive, pulsive, **moving**, animating, actuating, **driving.**

283. REACTION

NOUNS 1. **reaction**, retroaction; response, respondence, reply, answer, rise [slang]; reflex, reflection, **reflex action**; return, revulsion; reflux, refluence; action and reaction; conditioned reflex.

2. **recoil, rebound**, resilience, repercussion, *contrecoup* [F.]; **bounce, bound, spring**; repulse, rebuff; backlash, backlashing; **kickback,** kick, recalcitration; **backfire, boomerang,** the biter bit; ricochet.

3. (a drawing back) **retreat**, fallback; flinch, wince, cringe; **side step,** shy; **dodge**, duck [coll.].

4. **reactionary**, reactionist, recalcitrant.

VERBS 5. react, respond, reply, answer; rise to the fly, take the bait.

6. **recoil, rebound**, resile; **bounce, bound, spring; spring** or **fly back,** bounce or bound back, snap back; kick, kick back, recalcitrate; **backfire, boomerang**; backlash; ricochet.

7. **pull** or **draw back**, retreat, **fall back,** reel back, hang back, start back, shrink back; **shrink, flinch, wince, cringe,** blink, blench, quail; **shy,** start aside; **dodge,** duck [coll.]; jib, swerve, sheer off.

8. **get a reaction** or response, strike fire, strike or hit home, **get a rise out of** [slang].

ADJS. 9. **reactive**, reacting; **responsive**, responent, responding; reactionary; retroactionary, retroactive; revulsive; refluent.

10. recoiling, rebounding, **resilient; bouncing,** bounding, springing; repercussive; recalcitrant.

ADVS. 11. **on the rebound,** on the return, on the bounce.

284. PROPULSION

Motion Given to an Object Situated in Front.—NOUNS 1. **propulsion**, pulsion, **propelling,** propelment; **pushing, shoving;** push, shove; butt, bunt; shunt.

2. steam propulsion, gas propulsion, diesel propulsion, jet propulsion, turbojet propulsion, pulse-jet propulsion, ram-jet propulsion, resojet propulsion, rocket propulsion, reaction propulsion.

3. **projection,** trajection, jaculation; **throwing,** flinging, slinging, **pitching,** casting, hurling, heaving; **shooting,** firing, gunnery; trapshooting; archery.

4. **throw, fling, sling, cast, hurl,** chuck, chunk [chiefly U.S.], heave, shy, **pitch, toss,** peg [coll.]; **flip,** flirt, fillip; put, shotput; pass [football], forward pass, lateral pass, lateral; serve, service [tennis]; bowl [cricket]; curve [baseball], screwball [slang.], incurve, outcurve, upcurve, downcurve.

5. **shot,** discharge; detonation 455.3; gunfire 796.9; bullet 799.14; **salvo, volley,** spray; bowshot, gunshot, stoneshot, potshot; bull's-eye, carton.

6. **projectile,** trajectile; **missile** 799.12; ball 254.13; discus, quoit.

7. **propeller,** prop [aero.], airscrew [aero. Eng.]; propellant, propulsor, driver; screw, screw propeller, twin screws; turbine; pedal, treadle.

8. **thrower, pitcher,** hurler, flinger, slinger, chucker; shot-putter; javelin thrower; discus thrower, discobolus.

9. **shooter,** shot; **gunner, gun, gunman; rifleman,** musketeer, carbineer; artilleryman 798.11; Nimrod, hunter 653.5; trapshooter; archer, bowman, toxophilite; **marksman,** markswoman, **sharpshooter;** good shot, dead shot, **crack shot.**

VERBS 10. **propel,** impel, **drive,** forward; **push, shove;** butt, bunt; shunt; pole, boom [naut.]; pedal, treadle; **roll,** troll, bowl, trundle.

11. **project,** traject.

12. **throw, fling, sling, pitch, toss,** cast, hurl, heave, chuck, chunk [chiefly U.S.], chug [dial.], peg [coll.], shy, fire [coll.], launch, dash, bung, let fly; catapult; **flip,** flirt, fillip; snap, jerk; bowl [cricket]; pass [football]; serve [tennis]; put, put the shot; dart, lance, tilt; fork, pitchfork; pelt 796.29, 30.

13. **shoot, fire,** fire off, let off, let fly, **discharge;** detonate 455.8; gun [coll.], pistol; strike, hit, plug [slang]; shoot down, fell, drop, stop in one's tracks; **riddle,** pepper, pelt, pump full of lead [slang]; snipe, pick off; flight; torpedo; hull; pot; potshoot, potshot, take a potshot; shoot at 796.23; load, prime, charge; cock.

14. **start,** start off, start up, give a start, **put** or **set in motion,** set on foot, set going or agoing, start going, **start the ball rolling** [coll.]; **launch,** float, set afloat; send, send off or forth; bundle, bundle off.

ADJS. 15. **propulsive,** propulsory, pulsive; propellant, propelling; **driving, pushing, shoving.**

16. **projectile,** trajectile, jaculatory; **ballistic,** missile.

17. jet-propelled, rocket-propelled, steam-propelled, gas-propelled, diesel-propelled.

285. TRACTION

Motion Given to an Object Situated Behind.—NOUNS 1. **traction, drawing, pulling,** tugging; towing, towage; **hauling,** haulage.

2. **pull, draw,** draft or draught, **heave, haul,** lug [coll.], **tug,** strain; "a long pull, a strong pull, and a pull altogether" [Dickens].

3. **jerk,** yerk [dial.], **yank** [coll.]; **twitch,** tweak, pluck, hitch, wrench, start, bob; **flip,** flick, flirt, flounce; jig, **jiggle;** jog, joggle.

VERBS 4. **draw, pull, heave, haul,** hale, trek [S. Africa], lug, **tug, tow,** take in tow; trail, train; **drag,** draggle, snake [coll., U.S.]; troll, trawl.

5. **jerk,** yerk [dial.], **yank** [coll., U.S.]; **twitch,** tweak, pluck, snatch, hitch, wrench, chap, bob, snake [coll., U.S.]; **flip,** flick, flirt, flounce; **jiggle,** jig, jigget [coll.], jigger [coll.]; jog, joggle.

ADJS. 6. **tractional,** tractive, **drawing, pulling,** hauling, tugging, towing.

286. LEVERAGE, PURCHASE

Mechanical Advantage Applied to Moving or Raising, as by a Lever, Tackle, or Windlass.—NOUNS 1. **leverage,** fulcrumage; **pry,** prize [dial.].

2. **purchase, hold,** advantage; **foothold,** toehold, footing; differential purchase; collier's purchase.

3. **fulcrum, axis, pivot,** bait [U.S.], bearing, rest, resting point, *point d'appui* [F.]; thole, tholepin; rowlock, oarlock; gimbal, gimmal.

4. **lever,** leever [dial.]; **pry,** prize [dial.]; **bar, crowbar,** crow, iron crow, gavelock [dial.]; **jimmy,** jemmy; handspike, marlinespike; boom, outrigger; pedal, treadle.

5. **arm, limb,** soupbone [slang, U.S.]; **wing,** pinion [both joc. exc. zool.]; **fin** [slang exc. zool.]; flipper [slang exc. zool.], flapper [zool.]; forearm; wrist; elbow.

6. **tackle,** purchase.

7. **windlass; capstan,** nigger [U.S.]; **winch,** crab; reel; Chinese windlass.

VERBS 8. **pry**, prize, lever; **jimmy**, crowbar.

9. **reel in**, wind in, draw in, pull in; windlass, winch.

10. **tackle**

Bell's tackle or	luff, luff tackle
purchase	pulley
block	pulley tackle
block and tackle	runner
burton	runner and tackle
cat	single tackle
chain block	single-whip tackle
collier's purchase	snatch block
deck tackle	Spanish burton
double or twofold	stay tackle
tackle	tackle block
duplex purchase	threefold, fourfold,
fore-and-aft tackle	etc., tackle
foretackle	top burton
gun tackle	yard tackle
hatch tackle	

287. ATTRACTION

A Drawing Toward.—NOUNS 1. **attraction**, traction, attractiveness, attractivity; pulling power, **pull**, draw; magnetism 341.7; gravity, gravitation; capillarity, capillary attraction; adduction [physiol.]; **allurement** 648.

2. attractor, attractant, attrahent; **lure** 648.2.

3. **magnet**, artificial magnet, field magnet, bar magnet, horseshoe magnet, electromagnet, paramagnet, electromagnetic lifting magnet, magnetic battery; magnetic needle; loadstone, magnetite; lodestar, polestar.

VERBS 4. **attract, pull, draw,** pull or draw towards; **magnetize,** magnet; **lure** 648.4, 5; adduct [physiol.].

ADJS. 5. attracting, drawing, pulling; **attractive, magnetic,** attrahent; **alluring** 648.7; adductive, adducent [physiol.].

288. REPULSION

A Thrusting Away.—NOUNS 1. **repulsion**, repulse, rebuff, repellence or repellency, **repelling**; magnetic repulsion, diamagnetism.

VERBS 2. **repulse, repel, rebuff,** put back, beat back, drive ~, push or thrust back; drive away, chase, chase off or away; send off or away, send about one's business, **send packing,** pack off, send away with a flea in one's ear [coll.], send to the right-about [coll.]; **ward off,** hold off, keep off, fend off, keep at arm's length.

ADJS. 3. **repulsive,** repellent, **repelling;** diamagnetic.

289. DIRECTION

Compass Direction or Course.—NOUNS 1. **direction, quarter, line,** line of direction, **point, aim, way,** range, **bearing, heading, course,** current, stretch, set, tendency, inclination, bent, trend, tenor, run, drift; lay, lie; steering, steerage; line of march.

2. (nautical and aviation) bearing, heading, course, vector [aero.], tack [naut.]; compass direction, compass bearing or heading, magnetic heading, true heading or course; lee side, weather side 241.2, 3.

3. **points of the compass,** cardinal points; rhumb [naut.]; **north,** nor', northward; **south,** southward; **east,** eastward, orient, sunrise; **west,** westward, occident, sunset; southeast, southwest, northeast, northwest; azimuth, magnetic azimuth.

4. easting, westing, northing, southing.

5. **orientation, bearings;** adaptation, adjustment, accommodation; disorientation.

VERBS 6. **direct, point, aim, turn, bend, train,** present, fix, set, determine; point to or at, aim at, level at, turn or train upon; take aim; cover, have one covered, get the drop on [slang, U.S.].

7. **direct to,** lead or conduct to, point out to, show or **point the way,** put on the track, put on the right track, set straight, set or put right.

8. (have or take a direction) **bear, head, turn, point, aim, lead, go; incline, tend,** trend, set, dispose, verge, tend to go.

9. **wester, west, western; easter, east; norther, north, northern;** south.

10. **head for, bear for, go for,** make for, hit for [coll.], steer for, put for, **set out** or **off for,** strike out for, take off for [coll.], bend one's steps for, lay for [naut.], bear up for [naut.], bear up to, make up to, set in towards; direct or shape one's course for, set one's compass for; align one's march; **break for** [U.S.], make a break for [coll.], run for, make a dash for.

11. **go directly, go straight,** go straight on, **head straight for,** go straight to the point, steer a straight course, follow a course, keep or hold one's course, keep pointed [naut.]; **make a beeline,** take the air line.

12. **orient,** orientate, **get the bearings,** get the lay or lie of the land, see which way the land lies, see which way the wind blows, see which way the cat jumps [coll.]; orient

oneself, **get one's bearings;** adapt, adjust, accommodate.

ADJS. **13. direct,** immediate, **straight, straightforward, straightaway,** straightway; undeviating, unswerving; uninterrupted, unbroken; one-way.

14. directable, directive; aimable, determinable; **steerable, dirigible,** guidable, leadable.

15. directional, directive; **northern,** boreal, hyperborean; **southern,** austral; **eastern,** oriental; **western,** occidental; arctic, antarctic.

16. northbound, southbound, eastbound, westbound.

ADJS., ADVS. **17. north,** N, nor', northern, northerly, northward, north'ard, norward [poetic], northwards, northwardly; northernmost; north about [naut.].

18. south, S, southern, southerly, southward, south'ard, southwards, southwardly; southernmost; south about [naut.].

19. east, E, eastern, easterly, eastward, eastwards, eastwardly; easternmost, eastermost; eastabout [naut.].

20. west, W, western, westerly, westernly, westward, westwards, westwardly; westernmost; westabout [naut.].

21. northeast, NE, nor'east, northeastern, northeasterly, northeastward, northeastwards, northeastwardly; north-northeast, NNE; northeast by east, N by E; northeast by north, NE by N.

22. northwest, NW, nor'west, northwestern, northwesterly, northwestward, northwestwards, northwestwardly; northnorthwest, NNW; northwest by west, NW by W; northwest by north, NW by N.

23. southeast, SE, southeastern, southeasterly, southeastward, southeastwards, southeastwardly; south-southeast, SSE; southeast by east, SE by E; southeast by south, SE by S.

24. southwest, SW, southwestern, southwesterly, southwestward, southwestwards, southwestwardly; south-southwest, SSW; southwest by south, SW by S.

ADVS. **25. directly, direct, straight,** straightly, **straightforward,** straightforwards, **straight ahead,** dead ahead; due, dead, due north, etc.; right, forthright; in a direct or straight line, in line with, **in a beeline, as the crow flies,** straight across, across lots [coll.]; straight as an arrow; full tilt at.

26. squarely, square, right, straight, flush, full, point-blank; **plump,** caplump [sl.], plumb, plunk, plop, smack, smackdab, spang [coll.]; **exactly,** precisely.

27. in every direction, in all directions, in all manner of ways, every which way [coll., U.S.], everywhither, **every-way, everywhere,** everywheres [dial. & coll.], in every quarter, on every side; forty ways, six ways from Sunday [both slang, U.S.]; from every quarter, everywhence; from or to the four corners of the earth, from or to the four winds.

PREPS., ADVS. **28. toward,** towards, **in the direction of, to,** up, on, upon, against; headed for, on the way to, on the road or high road to; homeward, landward, seaward, earthward, heavenward; leeward, windward 241.9.

PREPS. **29. through,** by, **by way of,** by the way of, **via;** over, around, roundabout, here and there in, all through.

290. DEVIATION

Indirect Course.—NOUNS **1. deviation, departure, digression,** diversion, **divergence,** divarication, divagation, declination, aberration, **variation,** indirection, exorbitation; excursion, excursus; circuity 319; **wandering,** rambling, **straying;** drift, drifting; turning, shifting, swerving; **turn,** bend, swerve, veer, sheer, sweep; shift, double; tack [naut. & fig.], yaw [naut.].

2. deflection, deflexure; **refraction, diffraction,** diffusion, dispersion.

VERBS **3. deviate, depart from, vary, diverge,** divaricate, **digress,** divagate, **turn aside,** go out of the way; **swerve, veer,** sheer, **shift, turn,** trend, bend, heel, bear off; tack [naut.] 274.32; alter one's course, change the bearing.

4. stray, go astray, lose one's way; drift, go adrift; **wander,** ramble, rove, straggle, divagate; meander, wind, twist, twist and turn.

5. deflect, deviate, **divert,** diverge, **turn,** bend, crook; **warp,** bias, twist, skew; refract, diffract, **diffuse, disperse.**

6. turn aside or **to the side,** draw aside, side, **turn away,** avert; gee (turn right), haw (turn left); **sidetrack,** shove aside, shunt, switch [U.S.]; **head off,** turn back; **step aside,** move aside or to the side; **steer clear of,** make way for, get out of the way of; go off, bear off, ease off, edge off; fly off, go or fly off at a tangent; glance, glance off.

ADJS. **7. deviative,** deviatory, deviating,

departing, shifting, turning, swerving; **digressive**, discursive, excursive; **devious**, indirect, out-of-the-way; errant, **wandering**, rambling, roving, winding, twisting, meandering, vagrant, stray, desultory, erratic, planetary, undirected; aberrant.

8. **deflective**, inflective, diffractive, refractive; refractile, refrangible.

291. PRECEDING

Going Before.—NOUNS **1. preceding**, precession, **leading**, **heading**, foregoing; anteposition, the lead, *le pas* [F.]; precedence 64; front, van 239; leader 66.1.

VERBS **2. precede**, **go before**, go ahead, go in the van, **go in advance**, forerun, **head**, spearhead, stand at the head, stand first; **lead**, take the lead, go in the lead, **lead the way**; lead the dance, lead the cotillon [U.S.], lead the german [U.S.]; **light the way**, beacon, guide; get before, get ahead or in front of, come to the front; pace, set the pace; get or have the start, get a head start, steal a march upon.

ADJS. **3. preceding**, **leading**, precessional, precedent, precursory, foregoing; first, foremost, headmost; antecedent 64.4.

ADVS. **4. before**, in advance 239.13.

292. FOLLOWING

Going After.—NOUNS **1. following**, heeling, **trailing**, tailing [coll.], shadowing; hounding, dogging; sequence 65.

2. follower, heeler [coll.], successor, tagtail, tail [slang], shadow; **pursuer**, pursuivant **attendant**, **satellite**, **hanger-on**, dangler, adherent, appendage, dependent; **henchman**, ward heeler [polit., U.S.]; partisan, votary, sectary; courtier, *homme de cour* [F., man of the court], *cavalier servente* [F.]; trainbearer; accompanier, following 73.4–6; disciple 564.2.

VERBS **3. follow**, **go after**, move behind, **pursue**, shadow, tail [coll.], **trail**, trail after, follow in the trail of, camp on the trail of, **heel**, follow or tread on the heels of, follow in the steps of, tread close upon, follow in the wake of, hang on the skirts of, go in the rear of, bring up the rear, take or swallow one's dust; tag, **tag after**, tag along [all coll.]; string along [slang]; **dog**, bedog, **hound**; succeed 65.3.

4. lag, **lag behind**, drag, trail, **trail behind**, hang back, loiter, linger, **loiter** or **linger behind**, get behind, fall behind or behindhand.

ADJS. **5. following**, trailing; succeeding 64.5.

ADVS. **6. behind**, **after**, in the train or wake of; in back of 240.12.

293. PROGRESSION

Motion Forwards.—NOUNS **1. progression**, **progress**, progressiveness, **passage**, course, march; **advance**, advancing, **advancement**, **furtherance**; **ongoing**, on-go, go-ahead [coll.], onward course; **headway**, way; travel 272.

VERBS **2. progress**, **advance**, **proceed**, **go**, go or move forward, step forward, go on, **go ahead**, go along, pass on or along; move, travel 272.17; **make progress**, come on, **get along**, come along [coll.], **get ahead**; **make headway**, gather head, gather way; make strides or rapid strides, cover ground, get over the ground, make good time, make the best of one's way; make up for lost time, gain ground, make up leeway.

3. rub on, **jog on**, wag on, roll on; drift along, go with the stream.

4. make one's way, **work one's way**, weave ~, worm or thread one's way, carve one's way; push or force one's way, fight one's way; **forge ahead**, drive on or ahead, **push** or **press on** or **onward**, push or press forward, push, crowd.

ADJS. **5. progressive**, progressing, advancing, proceeding, **ongoing**, oncoming, onward, forward, **forward-looking**, go ahead [coll.]; moving 272.35.

ADVS. **6. in progress**, in mid-progress; going on.

7. forwards, forward, **onwards**, onward, forth, **on**, along, **ahead**; on the way to, on the road or high road to, en route for.

INTERJS. **8. forward!**, onward!, *en avant!* [F.]; forward, march!

294. REGRESSION

Motion Backwards.—NOUNS **1. regression**, regress; **retrogression**, retrocession, retrogradation, retroaction, retrusion; return; **backwardization**; **setback**, backwardation, backset, throwback [coll.], rollback.

2. retreat, *reculade* [F.], **withdrawal**, withdrawment, **retirement**, fallback; recession (motion from) 296.

3. reverse, reversal, reversion; **backing**, backing up, backup; **about-face**, *volte-face* [F.], rightabout, rightabout-face, turn to the rightabout, turnaround; back track, back trail.

4. **countermotion,** countermovement; countermarching, countermarch.

VERBS 5. **regress,** recede, return, revert; **retrogress,** retrograde, retrocede; **fall behind,** go behind, lose ground.

6. **retreat,** sound or beat a retreat, **withdraw, retire; fall back,** move back, go back, stand back; run back; **draw back,** draw off; **back out** or **out of** [coll.], back down; crawfish [coll., U.S.], crawdad [dial.]; crawl, crawl out of [both slang, U.S.]; give ground, give place.

7. **reverse,** go into reverse; back, **back up,** back off or away, **back water; backtrack,** back-trail, take the back track; retrace one's steps, dance the back step; counter march.

8. **turn back, put back** [chiefly naut.]; double, double back; turn one's back upon.

9. **turn round** or **around,** turn, **come** or **go about,** put about [naut.], fetch about; veer, veer around; swivel, pivot, pivot about, swing, round, swing round; wheel, wheel about; heel, turn upon one's heel.

10. **about-face,** *volte-face,* rightabout-face, **do an about-face** or a rightabout-face, perform a *volte face,* **face about,** turn or face to the rightabout, do a turn to the rightabout.

ADJS. 11. **regressive,** recessive; **retrogressive,** retrograde; retroactive.

12. **reversed,** reflex, **turned around,** back, **backward.**

ADVS., PREPS. 13. **backwards,** backward, **hindwards,** hindward, **rearwards,** rearward, arear, astern [naut.]; **back,** away, from, fro, *à reculons* [F.]; in reverse; against the grain, *à rebours* [F.]; counterclockwise.

295. APPROACH

Motion Towards.—NOUNS 1. **approach,** approaching, access, nearing; approximation, proximation; **advance,** oncoming; **advent, coming,** forthcoming; appulse [astron.]; nearness 199; imminence 151.

2. **approachability, accessibility,** access, get-at-ableness, come-at-ableness [coll.], attainability.

VERBS 3. **approach, near, draw near** or nigh, go or come near, come closer or nearer, come to close quarters; approximate, proximate; **advance, come, come forward,** come on, come up, bear up, step up; ease ~, edge or sidle up to; bear down

on or upon, follow close upon, tread on the heels of, gain upon.

ADJS. 4. **approaching, nearing,** advancing; **coming, oncoming, forthcoming,** upcoming, to come; approximate, proximate, approximative.

5. **approachable, accessible,** get-at-able, come-at-able [coll.], attainable.

INTERJS. 6. **approach!,** come!, come near!, **come on!,** come here!, come hither!, here!, forward!, advance!

296. RECESSION

Motion From.—NOUNS 1. **recession,** recedence, retrocedence; **retreat, retirement, withdrawal;** retraction.

VERBS 2. **recede,** retrocede; **retreat, retire, withdraw;** move off or away, standoff or away; go, go away; **die away,** fade away, drift away; **diminish,** decline, sink, dwindle, fade, ebb, wane; go out with the tide.

3. **retract, withdraw, draw** or **pull back,** draw or pull in; draw in one's claws or horns.

ADJS. 4. **recessive,** recessional; recedent, retrocedent.

5. **receding, retreating, retiring;** diminishing, declining, sinking, dwindling, ebbing, waning; fading, dying.

6. **retractile,** retractable.

297. CONVERGENCE

Approach Together.—NOUNS 1. **convergence,** confluence, concourse, conflux; **meeting,** congress, concurrence; **concentration,** concentralization; **focalization** 225.9; focus 225.4; asymptote [math.].

VERBS 2. **converge, come together,** run together, **meet,** unite, fall in with, close with, close, close up, close in upon; funnel; centralize, center, **come to a center;** concentralize, concenter, **concentrate,** come or tend to a point; **come to a focus** 225.11.

ADJS. 3. **converging,** convergent; **meeting,** uniting; concurrent, confluent; connivent [biol.]; **focal,** confocal [math.]; centrolineal, centripetal; asymptotic(al) [math.].

298. DIVERGENCE

Recession from Each Other.—NOUNS 1. **divergence,** divarication, aberration; **separation,** division; spread, spreading.

2. **radiation, irradiation,** ray; radi-

ance, irradiance; diffusion, dispersion, emanation.

3. **forking,** furcation, bifurcation, biforking, divarication; **branching, ramification;** arborescence, arborization, treelikeness.

4. **fork,** prong; Y, V; **branch, ramification,** stem, offshoot; **crotch,** crutch; groin, inguen; furcula, furculum [both anat.].

VERBS 5. **diverge,** divaricate, aberrate; **separate,** divide; spread, **spread out,** outspread: go off or away, **fly or go off at a tangent.**

6. **radiate, irradiate,** ray, diffuse, emanate, shed, spread, disperse, scatter.

7. **fork,** furcate, bifurcate, divaricate; **branch,** stem, ramify, branch off or out.

ADJS. 8. **diverging,** divergent; divaricate, divaricating; palmate, palmated; centrifugal.

9. **radiant,** radial, radiate, radiated; radiative; **irradiant,** irradiate, irradiated, irradiative.

10. **forked, forking,** furcate, biforked, bifurcate, bifurcated, forklike; **crotched,** Y-shaped, V-shaped; **branched, branching;** arborescent, arboreal, arboriform, treelike, tree-shaped, dendriform; branchlike, ramous.

299. ARRIVAL

NOUNS 1. **arrival, coming, advent,** approach, reaching, showup [coll.]; attainment, achievement.

2. **landing,** landfall; **disembarkation,** disembarkment, debarkation.

3. **return, homecoming;** re-entrance, re-entry; remigration.

4. **welcome, greetings** 923.2–4.

5. **destination, goal,** bourn or bourne, port, **journey's end;** terminus, terminal, terminal point; stop, stopping place, last stop.

VERBS 6. **arrive,** arrive at, arrive in, **come,** get, **come or get to,** approach, **reach, hit** [coll., U.S.], strike [coll.], find, gain, attain, attain to, achieve, make, fetch, fetch up at, get there, reach one's destination, come to one's journey's end; make or put in an appearance, show up [coll.], turn up, pop up [coll.]; **get in, come in,** blow in [slang], pull in, roll in; **check in,** punch or ring in [coll.], weigh in [coll.]; hit town [coll., U.S.]; come to hand, be received.

7. (as to arrive at a solution, a method, the truth) **arrive at, come at, get at,**

reach, arrive upon, come upon, **hit upon,** strike upon, fall upon, light upon, pitch upon, stumble on or upon.

8. **land,** come to land, set foot on dry land; reach land, make land; put in or into, put into port; go ashore, **disembark,** debark, unboat; **detrain, debus** [coll.], **disemplane;** alight 314.7; land [aero.] 277.49.

9. **overtake, overhaul,** overget [dial.], catch, reach, catch up, **catch up with,** come up with or to, gain upon; ride down.

ADJS. 10. **arriving,** approaching, entering, **coming,** incoming; inbound, inward-bound; homeward, homeward-bound.

INTERJS. 11. welcome!, greetings!, 923.14, 15.

300. DEPARTURE

NOUNS 1. **departure, leaving, going,** passing, **parting; exit,** exodus; egress 302; **withdrawal,** removal, retreat, retirement; evacuation, abandonment; decampment; flight 629.4.

2. **outset,** outsetting, setout, outstart, **start,** starting, start-off, setoff, go-off [coll.], take-off [coll.].

3. **embarkation,** embarkment; entrainment; take-off [aero.], hopoff [aero. slang].

4. **leave-taking, leave, parting; send-off** [coll.], valediction, Godspeed; **adieu,** farewell, good-by or good-bye; valedictory address, valedictory, valediction, parting words; valedictorian.

5. **point of departure, starting place** or **point,** takeoff, start, base, basis; starting post [turf]; port of embarkation.

VERBS 6. **depart,** take one's departure or leave, **leave, go,** up and go [dial. & coll.], **go away, go off, get off or away,** come away, go one's way, go or get along, be getting along [coll.], gang along [Scot. & dial.], go on, get on; **shove on,** heave on, trot along, **toddle along,** stagger along [all slang]; mosey, sashay, mosey or sashay off or along [all slang, U.S.]; **buzz off** or along, pipe off [both slang]; move off or away, march off or away; **pull out;** leave home, go from home; exit 302.11; break or tear oneself away.

7. **set forth,** put forth, go forth, **sally forth,** sally, issue, issue forth, set forward, **set out or off,** outset, start, **start out or off, strike out,** get off, take off or out [slang], push off, shove off [slang], hit the trail [coll.].

8. **quit, vacate,** evacuate, abandon, turn one's back on; **withdraw,** retreat, **beat a**

retreat, retire, remove; **bow out** [coll.], make one's exit.

9. begone, get gone [slang], **get out, be off,** take oneself off *or* away, pack, pack off *or* away, get *or* git [slang & dial., U.S.]; **clear out,** wag, pike [all coll.].

10. (slang terms: begone) **beat it,** scram [U.S.], **skiddoo** [U.S., circa 1904+], **skedaddle** [U.S., circa 1861+], **blow** [U.S.], **vamoose** [U.S.], vamos [U.S.], **lam,** take it on the lam [U.S.], **absquatulate** [U.S., circa 1830+], pull *or* drag one's freight [U.S.], **make oneself scarce,** get the hell out.

11. make off, decamp, skip *or* **skip out** [coll.], slope [slang, U.S.; circa 1830+], mizzle [slang, Eng.; circa 1781+], guy [slang, Eng.; circa 1874+], dust [slang, U.S.; circa 1860+], scoot [coll.], cut stick *or* one's stick [slang], walk one's chalks [slang].

12. hasten off, hurry away; **scamper off,** skelter off [coll.], scaddle [dial.], **dash off,** whizz off, whip off *or* away, nip *or* nip off [slang], tear off *or* out, **light out** [slang, U.S.], dig out [slang, U.S.], skin out [slang], get up *or* out and get *or* git [slang], go on the double *or* double-quick [coll.], set off at a score, go off like a shot.

13. fling out *or* **off, flounce out** *or* **off.**

14. run off *or* **away,** run along [coll.], chase along [slang], **flee, fly, take to one's heels,** pull foot [slang], put [slang], cut [coll.], **cut and run** [coll.], leg it [slang], stump it [slang], hook it [slang & dial.], shin out [coll., U.S.], hike *or* hike out [dial.], hightail it out [slang, U.S.], light a shuck [dial.], **make tracks** [coll., U.S.]; run for one's life; run away from 629.10.

15. check out, ring *or* punch out, weigh out [all coll. in fig. sense].

16. decamp, break camp, strike camp *or* tent, **pull up stakes.**

17. embark, go aboard, board, go on board; go on ship board, take ship; **entrain, emplane, embus;** weigh anchor, put to sea 274.19, 20.

18. take leave, say *or* bid good-by *or* farewell, **bid farewell;** bid Godspeed, cheer, give a send-off [coll.], "speed the parting guest" [Pope].

ADJS. **19. departing, leaving; parting,** last, final, farewell; valedictory; **outward-bound.**

20. departed, left, gone, gone off *or* away.

ADVS., PREPS. **21. hence,** thence, whence; **away, from,** frae [Scot.], **away from,** therefrom, thereof, out, out of, forth, off.

INTERJS. **22.** begone! 308.27, 28.

23. all aboard!, aboard!, 'board!

24. to horse!, to boot!, to saddle!

25. farewell!, fare you *or* ye well!, **adieu!, good-by** *or* good-bye!, bye-bye! [coll.], **good-day!,** so **long!** [slang], **cheerio!,** *au revoir!* [F.], *¡adios!* [Span.], *auf Wiedersehen!* [G.], *vale!* [L.], *vive valeque!* [L., live and farewell], *aloha!* [Hawaiian], **until we meet again!,** until tomorrow!, *à demain!* [F.], **see you later!,** see you!, I'll be seeing you!, *à bientôt!* [F.], *au plaisir de vous revoir!* [F., to the pleasure of seeing you again], **be good!,** keep in **touch!,** come again!, *bon voyage!* [F., pleasant journey!], *glücklicke Reise!* [G.], **happy landing!; Godspeed!,** good luck!; peace be with you!, *pax vobiscum!* [L.], all good go with you!, God bless you!

26. good night!, *bonne nuit!* [F.], *gute Nacht!* [G.].

301. INGRESS, ENTRANCE

NOUNS **1.** (act of entering) **ingress,** ingression, introgression; **entrance,** entrancement, **entry,** entree, *entrée* [F.]; **ingoing, incoming,** income; **input, intake,** take-in [coll.]; penetration, interpenetration; infiltration; insertion 303; reception 305.

2. influx, influxion, **inflow,** indraft *or* indraught, inpour, inrun, inrush.

3. immigration, in-migration, incoming population, foreign influx.

4. incomer, entrant, comer, arrival; **visitor,** visitant; **immigrant,** in-migrant; newcomer 78.4; settler 189.9; **intruder** 237.3.

5. (place for entering) **entrance,** entry, **entranceway,** entryway; **inlet,** ingress, intake, adit, approach, **access,** means of access, ingate [North. Eng.], in [slang, U.S.], way in; **opening,** aperture, orifice, mouth; **passageway,** passage, way; vestibule 191.19.

6. portal, postern, **threshold; door, doorway; gate, gateway,** pylon; front door, back door, side door; carriage entrance, porte-cochere; cellar door, cellarway; bulkhead [U.S.]; hatch, hatchway; storm door, dingle [North. U.S.]; trap door, trap; barway; tollgate; stile, turnstile, turnpike.

VERBS **7. enter, go in** *or* **into, come in,** find one's way into, put in *or* into [chiefly naut.]; **set foot in,** step in; **get in,** jump in, hop in; **drop in,** pop in [both coll.]; **breeze in,** come breezing in; break *or* burst in, bust in [dial. & inelegant], come busting in [dial. & slang]; **barge in,** come barging in [both coll.]; thrust in, push or press in, crowd in, squeeze in; slip or creep in, wriggle or worm oneself into, edge in, work in, insinuate oneself.

8. insert 303.2.

9. **penetrate,** interpenetrate, **pierce,** pass or go through, get through, get into, make way into, make an entrance, gain entree.

10. **flow in,** inflow, inpour, inrush, **pour in.**

11. **filter in,** infiltrate, seep in, percolate into.

12. **immigrate,** in-migrate.

ADJS. 13. **entering,** ingressive, **incoming, ingoing;** in, inward; **inbound,** inward-bound; inflowing, inpouring, inrushing; ingrowing.

ADVS., PREPS. 14. **into,** to, in, inward, inwards, inwardly.

302. EGRESS, EMERGENCE

NOUNS 1. (act of coming out) **egress,** egression; **exit, exodus; outgoing,** outgo; outcoming, outcome, forthcoming; departure 300.

2. **emergence,** emersion; **issue, issuance;** emission, emanation, vent, discharge.

3. outburst 161.6.

4. **outflow,** outflowing; **outpour,** outpouring; effluence, effusion; **efflux,** effluxion, defluxion; **runoff,** flowoff; drainage, drain; gush 394.4.

5. **leakage,** leaking, leak; **dripping,** dripping, **drip,** dribble, drop, trickle; distillation.

6. **exudation,** transudation; **filtration,** exfiltration, filtering; straining; **percolation,** percolating; leaching, lixiviation; effusion [physiol.], extravasation; seepage, seep; **oozing,** ooze; excretion 309.

7. **emigration;** remigration.

8. **export,** exportation.

9. **outlet,** egress, exit, outgo, outcome, outgate [Scot. & North. Eng.], out [slang, U.S], way out; loophole [fig.]; **opening,** orifice; mouth (as of a stream) 264.6; **vent,** ventage, venthole; avenue, channel; debouch [mil.], débouché [F.]; door 301.6; outgate, sally port [mil. & naut.]; vomitory; emunctory [physiol.]; pore.

10. **outgoer,** goer, leaver, departer; **emigrant,** émigré [F.].

VERBS 11. **exit,** make an exit, **make one's exit;** egress, go out, get out, pass out, bow out [coll.]; depart 300.6.

12. **emerge, come out,** issue, issue forth, **come forth,** sally, sally forth; emanate, effuse, arise, come; debouch, disembogue; burst forth, break forth; break cover, **come out in the open.**

13. **run out,** empty, find vent; **drain,** drain out; **flow out,** outflow, outpour, **pour out,** well out, gush or spout out, flow, pour, well, surge, gush, jet, spout, vomit forth.

14. **leak, leak out, drip,** dribble, drop, trickle, trill, weep, distill.

15. **exude,** exudate, transude, reek; **emit,** discharge, give off; **filter,** filtrate, exfiltrate; strain; **percolate;** leach, lixiviate; effuse [physics], extravasate [physiol.]; seep, ooze; bleed; weep; excrete 309.10.

16. **emigrate;** remigrate.

17. **export,** send abroad.

ADJS. 18. **emerging,** emergent; **issuing,** arising, coming, forthcoming; emanating, emanent, emanative.

19. **outgoing, outbound,** outwardbound; **outflowing,** outpouring, effusive, effluent.

20. exudative, transudative; percolative; porous, pervious, leaky; excretory 309.17.

ADVS., PREPS. 21. **out of,** ex; **forth, from;** out, outward, outwards, outwardly.

303. INSERTION

Putting In.—NOUNS 1. **insertion, entrance, introduction,** insinuation, injection, inoculation, intromission; interjection 236.2; infixion, implantation; embedment.

2. **insert,** insertion; **inset,** inlay.

VERBS 3. **insert, enter, introduce,** insinuate, inject, inoculate, intromit; **put in, stick in,** set in, throw in, pop in, tuck in, whip in; interject 236.7.

4. **inset, inlay; embed** or imbed, bed, bed in.

5. **graft,** ingraft or engraft; bud; inarch.

6. **thrust in, drive in, run in, plunge in,** force in, push in, ram in, press in, stuff in, crowd in, squeeze in, cram in, jam in, pack in, wedge in.

7. **implant,** infix 142.10.

304. EXTRACTION

Taking or Drawing Out.—NOUNS 1. **extraction, withdrawal,** removal; **drawing, pulling,** drawing out; eradication, uprooting, unrooting, deracination; avulsion, evulsion; extrication, evolvement; excavation.

2. **drafting** or draughting, **drawing;** sucking, **suction,** aspiration; pumping; tap-

ping, broaching; milking; drainage, draining, emptying.

3. **evisceration**, gutting, **disembowelment.**

4. **elicitation**, education; **evocation**, calling forth; arousal.

5. **extortion**, **exaction**, claim, demand; **wresting, wrenching, wringing, rending;** wrest, wrench, wring.

6. (obtaining an extract) **squeezing, pressing,** expression; **distillation;** decoction; **rendering,** rendition; steeping, soaking, infusion; concentration.

7. **extract,** extraction; **essence, quintessence, spirit, elixir;** floressence; decoction; **distillate,** distillation; **concentrate,** concentration; infusion.

8. **extractor,** separator; press, wringer; corkscrew; forceps, pliers.

VERBS 9. **extract, take out,** get out, **withdraw, remove;** pull, draw; **pull out, draw out,** tear out, pluck out, pick out, weed out, rake out; **pull up,** pluck up; **root up** or **out,** uproot, unroot, eradicate, deracinate, pull up by the roots; avulse, evulse; extricate, evolve; **dig up** or **out,** grub up or out, excavate, unearth.

10. **draft** or **draught off, draw off,** draft, draw, draw from; **suck,** suck out or up; **siphon off;** pump, pump out; tap, broach; let, let out; bleed; milk; **drain,** decant; exhaust, empty.

11. **eviscerate, gut, disembowel.**

12. **elicit,** educe, deduce, induce, derive, obtain, procure, secure; **get from,** get out of; **evoke, call up, summon up,** call or summon forth, call out; rouse, arouse; **draw out** or **forth,** bring out or forth, drag out, worm out, bring to light; wangle, wangle out of, worm out of.

13. **extort, exact,** claim, demand; **wrest, wring** ∼, **wrench** ∼, **rend** ∼, **wrest** ∼, tear from.

14. (obtain an extract) **squeeze** or **press out,** express, wring, wring out; **distill;** decoct; **render,** melt down; steep, soak, infuse; concentrate.

ADJS. 15. **extractive,** eductive; **eradicative,** uprooting; elicitory, **evocative,** arousing; **exacting,** exactive; **extortionate,** extortionary, extortive.

16. **essential,** quintessential.

17. **alcohols**

absolute alcohol	ethanol
amyl alcohol	ethyl alcohol
dehydrated alcohol	grain alcohol
denatured alcohol	industrial alcohol
methyl alcohol	rubbing alcohol
primary alcohol	wood alcohol

305. RECEPTION

Taking In.—NOUNS 1. **reception,** receipt, recipience.

2. **admission,** admittance; immission, intromission; **installation,** instatement, inauguration, initiation.

3. (free admission) **entree,** *entrée* [F.], entry, entrance, **access,** opening, **open door.**

4. **ingestion,** imbibition; engorgement, ingurgitation, engulfment; **swallowing,** gulping; swallow, gulp.

5. (drawing in) **suction,** suck, sucking; **inhalation,** inhalement, **inspiration;** snuff, snuffle.

6. **absorption,** sorption, engrossment, **assimilation,** infiltration; **sponging, blotting;** seepage, percolation; **osmosis,** endosmosis, exosmosis, electroosmosis; absorbency; **absorbent,** adsorbent, sponge, blotter, blotting paper.

7. (bringing in) **introduction;** import, **importation.**

8. readmission; reabsorption, resorbence.

9. **receptivity,** receptiveness, admissibility.

VERBS 10. **receive, take in; admit, let in,** immit, intromit, give entrance or admittance to, give an entree, open the door to, throw open to; **install,** instate, inaugurate, initiate.

11. **ingest,** imbibe; **swallow, devour,** ingurgitate; **engulf,** engorge; **gulp,** gulp down.

12. **draw in, suck,** suckle, suck in or up; **inhale, inspire,** breathe in; **snuff,** snuffle, snuff in or up.

13. **absorb,** adsorb, assimilate, engross, drink, imbibe, take up or in, drink up or in; blot, **blot up, soak up,** sponge; osmose; infiltrate, filter in; **soak in, seep in,** percolate in; chemisorb.

14. **bring in,** induct, **introduce, import.**

15. readmit; reabsorb, resorb.

ADJS. 16. **receptive,** recipient; introceptive; **admissive,** admissory, admissible; intromissive, intromittent; ingestive, imbibitory.

17. **absorbent,** adsorbent, **assimilative,** bibulous, imbibitory, thirsty, soaking, blotting; spongy, spongeous; osmotic, endosmotic, exosmotic; resorbent.

18. **introductory,** introductive; **initiatory,** initiative.

306. EATING

NOUNS **1. eating, feeding, dining;** ingestion, consumption, devourment, deglutition; discussion [coll.]; chewing, mastication, manducation, rumination; feasting, epulation; gluttony 992; carnivorousness, carnivorism; vegetarianism, phytophagy; omnivorousness, pantophagy.

2. bite, morsel; mouthful, gob [dial. & slang]; cud, quid; bolus; **chew, chaw** [dial.]; nip, nibble; munch, crunch, craunch, scrunch [coll.]; gnash; champ, chomp [dial.] snap.

3. drinking, imbibing, potation; compotation, symposium [Gr. antiq.]; drunkenness 994.

4. drink, potion, potation, libation [joc.]; **draft** or draught, dram, drench, swig [coll.], swill [coll.], guzzle [vulg.], quaff, **sip, sup,** suck, pull [coll.], lap, gulp; nip, peg; beverage 306a.47.

5. meal, repast, feed [coll.], scoff [slang], mess, spread [coll.], table, board, meat; **refreshment,** refection, regalement, entertainment, treat.

6. (meals) **breakfast,** déjeuner [F.], déjeuné or dejeune, petit déjeuner [F.]; chota hazri [Anglo-Ind.]; meat breakfast, déjeuner à la fourchette [F.]; **brunch** [coll.]; **lunch, luncheon,** tiffin [Anglo-Ind.]; hot luncheon, dinette [Eng.]; **dinner,** diner or dîné [F.]; **supper,** souper or soupé [F.]; buffet supper or lunch; TV dinner; picnic, junket [U.S.]; coffee break.

7. light repast, lunch, luncheon, light lunch, spot of lunch [slang], collation, **snack** [coll.], piece [dial., U.S.], bever [chiefly dial.], bait [dial.], bite [coll.], bite to eat [coll.], a lick and a smell [slang].

8. hearty meal, healthy meal [coll.], full or substantial meal, **square meal** [coll.], square (as, three squares [slang]), man-sized meal, large order.

9. feast, banquet, junket, festa [It.], fiesta [Sp.], festal board; feed, big feed, spread [all coll.]; blowout, tuck, tuck-in, tuck-out [all slang].

10. serving, service; **helping,** help; second helping; **course;** dish, plate; antepast; entree, entrée [F.], entremets; relevé [F.]; remove [Eng.]; dessert.

11. (manner of service) service, table service, counter service, self-service; table d'hote, ordinary; à la carte; cover, couvert [F.]; cover charge; American plan, European plan.

12. menu, bill of fare, carte.

13. eater, consumer, devourer; **diner,** luncher; mouth, hungry mouth; diner-out, eater-out; boarder, board-and-roomer; omnivore, pantophagist; flesh eater, meat eater, carnivore, omophagist, predacean; man-eater, cannibal; vegetarian, lactovegetarian; plant-eater, herbivore, phytophagan; grass-eater, graminivore; grain-eater, granivore; glutton, gourmand, trencherman 992.3, 4.

14. restaurant, eating house, dining room; eatery, beanery, hashery, hash house [all slang]; **lunchroom,** lunchery [slang], luncheonette; **café,** caffe [It.]; **tearoom; coffeehouse,** coffeeroom, **coffee shop,** estaminet [F.]; tavern 190.13; chophouse; grill, grillroom; cookshop; buffet, **lunch counter,** quick-lunch counter; hot-dog stand [slang, U.S.]; drive-in; **snack bar,** bistro [coll., Fr.]; **cafeteria** [U.S.], luncheteria [slang, U.S.]; automat; mess hall, dining hall; canteen; cookhouse, cookshack [slang, U.S.]; lunch wagon, chuck wagon [slang, West. U.S.]; diner, dining car, dining saloon [Eng.].

VERBS **15. feed, dine;** satisfy, gratify; regale; bread, meat; breakfast, lunch, dinner, supper; board; pasture, put out to pasture, graze, grass; forage, fodder; provision 657.9.

16. nourish, nurture, foster; **nurse, suckle,** lactate, breast-feed, wet-nurse; dry-nurse.

17. eat, feed, fare, take, partake of, break bread; discuss [coll.]; refresh or entertain the inner man, appease or feed the animal, feed one's tapeworm [all joc.]; fall to, pitch in [coll.].

18. (slang terms) scoff, chuck [U.S.], chuck up [U.S.], grub [U.S.], grub up [U.S.], feed one's face, grease the gills, line the jacket.

19. dine, dinner; **sup,** supper; breakfast; lunch, luncheon; snack, piece [coll.]; picnic; eat out, dine out; board; mess with, break bread with.

20. devour, swallow, ingest, **consume,** take in, tuck in [slang], down, take down, get down, put away [coll.], tuck away [slang]; **eat up,** dispatch [coll.], dispose of, get away with [coll., U.S.]; surround, put oneself outside of [both slang].

21. gobble, gulp, bolt, wolf, gobble ~, gulp ~, bolt or wolf down, whale down [coll.].

22. feast, banquet, regale; eat heartily,

eat like a horse, eat one's head off [coll.], do oneself proud [coll.], do one's duty, do justice to, polish the platter, play a good knife and fork [dial., Eng.]; eat out of house and home.

23. stuff, gorge, engorge, glut, guttle, cram, eat one's fill.

24. pick, peck [coll.], nibble; pick at, peck at [coll.], eat like a bird.

25. chew, chaw [dial.]; **masticate,** manducate; **ruminate,** chew the cud; champ, chomp [dial.], chonk [dial.]; munch, crunch, craunch, scrunch [coll.], scranch [dial.]; gnash; nibble, gnaw; mouth, mumble; gum.

26. feed on or **upon, feast upon,** batten upon, fatten upon; prey on or upon; pasture on, browse, graze, crop.

27. drink, drink in, **imbibe,** wet one's clay, ~ whistle or swallow [coll. or joc.]; **quaff,** sip, sup, bib, swig [coll.], swill [coll.], guzzle [vulg.]; **suck,** suckle, suck in or up; drink off or up, toss off or down, drain the cup; wash down; tipple 994.29.

28. lap up, lick, lap.

ADJS. **29. eating,** gastronomic(al); omnivorous, pantophagous; flesh-eating, meat-eating, carnivorous, omophagous, predaceous or predacious; man-eating, cannibal, cannibalistic; insect-eating, insectivorous; vegetable-eating, vegetarian, lactovegetarian; plant-eating, herbivorous, phytivorous, phytophagous; grass-eating, graminivorous; grain-eating, granivorous.

30. masticatory, manducatory, chewing; ruminant, ruminating, cud-chewing.

31. edible, eatable, comestible, gustable, esculent.

32. drinkable, potable.

INTERJS. **33.** chow down!, soup's on!, grub's on!, come and get it!

306a. FOOD

NOUNS **1. food,** foodstuff, **victuals** [coll.], vittles [dial.], **comestibles, edibles,** eatables, viands, **cuisine,** tucker [chiefly Austral.], bouche [F.], ingesta, fare, cheer, creature comfort, creature; provision, provender [coll.]; meat [fig.], bread [fig.], daily bread; board, table.

2. (slang terms) **grub,** grubbery, **eats, chow,** chuck, scoff, peck, prog.

3. nutriment, nourishment, nurture; pabulum, aliment; **refreshment,** refection; sustenance, support, keep.

4. feed, fodder, provender; forage, pasturage; grain, corn, oats, barley, wheat;

meal, bran, chop; **hay, straw;** ensilage, silage; chicken feed, scratch, scratch feed, mash; slops, swill.

5. provisions, provender, supplies, food supply, commissariate; **groceries,** grocery; viaticum.

6. rations, commons, allowance, allotment, tucker [chiefly Austral.], tommy [mil. slang, Eng.]; short commons; emergency rations, iron rations [mil. cant]; K-ration, D-ration [both U.S. mil.]; garrison ~, travel ~, field ~, reserve or Filipino rations [all U.S. mil.].

7. dish, preparation, concoction; casserole; grill, broil, boil, roast, fry; main dish, pièce de résistance [F.].

8. delicacy, dainty, goody [coll.], kickshaw, luxury; **titbit,** tidbit [U.S.]; **morsel,** choice morsel, bonne bouche [F.]; tasty dish, dish fit for a king; savory; ambrosia, nectar, manna, nightingale's tongue.

9. appetizer, whet, **apéritif** [F.]; foretaste, antepast, antipasto [It.]; **hors d'oeuvre;** smorgasbord; canapé.

10. soup, pottage, potage [F.]; consommé, gravy soup; purée; broth, bouillon, stock; vegetable soup, potage aux herbes [F.]; tomato soup, potage au tomate [F.]; julienne, potage à la julienne [F.]; chicken soup, potage à la reine [F.]; turtle soup, potage à la tortue [F.]; mock turtle soup, potage à la téte de veau [F.]; bisque, borsch or borscht, gumbo, minestrone, mulligatawny, petite marmite [F.].

11. stew. olla, olio, olla-podrida; meat stew, etuvée [F.]; Irish stew, mulligan stew or mulligan [slang, U.S.]; goulash, Hungarian goulash; ragout; salmi; bouillabaisse; chowder, clam chowder; salmagundi; fricassee; curry.

12. meat, flesh, viande [F.]; butcher's meat, viande de boucherie [F.]; game, menue viande [F.]; venison; roast, joint, rôti [F.]; pot roast; barbecue, shish kebab [Armen.]; boiled meat, bouilli [F.]; forcemeat; mincemeat, mince; hash, hachis [F.]; meat loaf; meat balls; croquettes; fricandel, fricandelle, fricandeau, fricando; jugged hare, civet [F.]; pemmican; scrapple; aspic.

13. beef, bœuf [F.]; roast beef, rosbif [F.]; chuck roast; short ribs; hamburger [U.S.]; corned beef, corned Willie [slang], Admiralty ham [naut. slang]; bully, bully beef; chipped beef; salt beef; jerky, charqui; pastrami; beef extract, beef tea.

14. veal, veau [F.]; breast of veal, poitrine de veau [F.]; calf's head, tête de *veau* [F.]; calf's liver, *foie de veau* [F.]; sweetbread, *ris de veau* [F.]; calf's brains.

15. **mutton,** *mouton* [F.]; **lamb,** *agneau* [F.]; breast of lamb, *poitrine d'agneau* [F.]; leg of lamb, leg of mutton, *gigot* [F.], *jambe de mouton* [F.]; saddle of mutton; baked sheep's head, jimmy; lamb fries, mountain oysters [joc.].

16. **pork,** *porc* [F.], pig; sucking pig, *cochon de lait* [F.]; **ham,** *jambon* [F.]; small ham, *jambonneau* [F.]; picnic ham; **bacon,** *lard* [F.]; Canadian bacon; rasher of bacon, *barde* [F.], *tranche de lard* [F.]; side of bacon, flitch, *flèche de lard* [F.]; gammon; salt pork *or* bacon, sowbelly [coll.], side meat [South. U.S.]; spareribs; hog jowl; pigs' knuckles, pigs' feet, trotters, *pieds de cochon* [F.]; chitterlings; cracklings; headcheese.

17. (cuts of meat) brisket, chuck, flank, knuckle, round, rump, saddle, shank, shoulder; loin, sirloin, tenderloin; clod, shoulder clod; plate, plate piece; cold cuts.

18. **steak,** *tranche* [F.]; **beefsteak,** *bifteck* [F.], *tranche de boeuf* [F.]; club steak, flank steak, planked steak, porterhouse steak, round steak, rump steak, sirloin steak, Swiss steak, tenderloin steak; Hamburg steak, hamburg, hamburger [U.S.].

19. **chop, cutlet,** *côtelette* [F.]; pork chop, *côtelette de porc frais* [F.]; mutton chop, *côtelette de mouton* [F.]; veal cutlet, *côtelette de veau* [F.].

20. (edible viscera) kidneys, heart, liver, tongue.

21. **sausage,** *saucisson* [F.]; sossinger, sassinger [both dial.]; **frankfurter,** frank, **hot dog** [slang, U.S.]; **wienerwurst, wiener,** wienie [slang]; **bologna,** boloney; salami; liverwurst; Bratwurst [G.]; blood pudding.

22 **fowl,** *oiseau* [F.]; broiler, fryer, roaster; chicken, *poulet* [F.]; capon, *chapon* [F.]; duck, *canard* [F.]; duckling, *caneton* [F.]; wild duck, *canard sauvage* [F.]; goose, *oie* [F.]; turkey, *dindon* [F.]; pheasant, *faisan* [F.]; partridge, *perdrix* [F.]; grouse, *coq de bruyère* [F.]; quail, *caille* [F.]; pigeon; squab, *pigeonneau* [F.]; *pâté de foie gras* [F.].

23. (parts of fowl) drumstick, leg, wing, wishbone, breast; white meat, *viande blanche* [F.]; dark meat, *viande noire* [F.]; giblets, liver, heart, gizzard.

24. **fish** 413.55, *poisson* [F.]; seafood, surf food; finnan haddie *or* haddock; kipper, kippered salmon *or* herring; smoked herring, red herring; fillet of sole, *filet de sole* [F.]; fried sole, *sole frite* [F.]; codfish balls; eel, *anguille* [F.]; fish eggs, roe, caviar *or* caviare.

25. **shellfish,** *coquillage* [F.]; clam, mussel, limpet, periwinkle, scallop, whelk; oyster, *huître* [F.]; blue point; pickled oysters, *huîtres marinées* [F.]; oysters on *or* in the half shell, *huîtres à l'écaille* [F.]; shrimp, prawn, *crevette* [F.]; crab, *crabe* [F.]; softshell crab; crayfish [usu. Eng.], crawfish [usu. U.S. & Ir.], *écrevisse* [F.]; lobster, *homard* [F.]; *écrevisse de mer* [F.]; lobster Newburg, lobster à la king.

26. **eggs,** *œufs* [F.]; fried eggs, *œufs sur le plat* [F.]; boiled eggs, *œufs à la coque* [F.]; poached eggs, *œufs pochés* [F.]; buttered eggs, *œufs brouillés* [F.]; addled eggs, *œufs couvi* [F.]; scrambled eggs, dropped eggs, shirred eggs, stuffed eggs, deviled eggs; omelet, omelette; soufflé.

27. **bread,** *pain* [F.]; staff of life; breadstuff; white bread, dark bread, whole-wheat bread, rye bread, pumpernickel bread, graham bread; sourbread, sourcake [dial., Eng.]; unleavened bread, matzoth [Jewish]; loaf of bread, tommy [Scot. & dial., Eng.]; ashcake, hoecake, [South., U.S.]; damper [Austral.]; toast, Melba toast, French toast; crust.

28. **corn bread;** pone, corn pone, corn tash, johnnycake [all South. U.S.]; dodger, corn dodger, corn dab [all South. U.S.]; cracklin' bread [dial., U.S]; *tortilla* [Sp. Amer.].

29. **biscuit;** hardtack, hard tommy [mil. slang, Eng.], pantile [naut. slang], sea biscuit, ship biscuit, pilot biscuit *or* bread; cracker, soda cracker, graham cracker; wafer; rusk, zwieback, Brussels biscuit; pretzel.

30. **bun,** roll, muffin, gem, popover [U.S.], scone; cross bun, hot cross bun.

31. **sandwich,** hamburger [coll., U.S.], hot dog [slang, U.S.].

32. **Italian paste,** *pasta* [It.], paste; macaroni, spaghetti, vermicelli, noodles, ravioli.

33. **dumpling,** doughboy [coll.], sinker [slang, U.S.]; apple dumpling, apple slump, apple grunt [dial., U.S.].

34. **cereal, breakfast food;** porridge, pease porridge, etc.; gruel, loblolly; mush, hasty pudding [U.S.], supawn [local, U.S.]; oatmeal, rolled oats; farina, millet, hominy [U.S.], samp [U.S.], frumenty, flummery, atole [Sp. Amer.], crowdy [Scot. & dial., Eng.].

35. vegetables, truck [U.S.], *légumes* [F.]; potherbs; greens; beans, frijoles [Mex. & Span. Amer.], *haricots* [F.]; potato, spud [coll.], *pomme de terre* [F.]; Irish potato, white potato, bog apple [slang]; tomato, love apple, *pomme d'amour* [F.]; eggplant, mad apple; rhubarb, pieplant [U.S.]; sauerkraut, kraut.

36. salad, *salade* [F.]; green salad, combination salad, tossed salad, potato salad, Waldorf salad, fruit salad; slaw, coleslaw.

37. dressing; salad dressing, mayonnaise, French dressing, Russian dressing, Thousand Island dressing; sauce, sass [dial.]; gravy; stuffing, forcemeat, farce.

38. nuts, *noisettes* [F.]; kernel, meat; Brazil nut, niggertoe [chiefly U.S.]; peanut, goober or goober pea [South. U.S.], pinder [dial.], ground-pea [dial.]; salted peanuts; almond, *amande* [F.]; burnt almond, *amande pralinée* [F.]; bitter almond, *amande amère* [F.]; sweet almond, *amande douce* [F.]; shelled almonds, *amandes cassées* [F.]; almond paste, *pâte d'amande* [F.]; peanut butter.

39. sweets, sweet stuff, **confectionery,** confetti, tuck [slang]; **sweet, sweetmeat; confection,** confectionary; candy; comfit, confiture; preserve, conserve; jelly, jam; marmalade, squish [slang]; jujube; Bar-le-Duc; gelatin, Jello; compote; mousse; blancmange; tutti-frutti; maraschino cherries; honey; icing, frosting; meringue; whipped cream.

40. pastry, patisserie; French pastry, Danish pastry; tart; turnover; **pie,** *pâté* [F.]; pasty; patty, patty-cake; patty shell, *vol-au-vent* [F.]; dowdy, pandowdy [U.S.]; trifle; strudel; *petits fours* [F.]; puff, cream puff; éclair, chocolate éclair.

41. cake, *gâteau* [F.]; angel cake, angel food cake; devil's food cake, fruitcake, pound cake, marble cake, sponge cake, shortcake, shortbread, cupcake, coffee cake, tea cake, cheesecake, layer cake, jumble.

42. cooky [U.S.], biscuit [Eng.]; brownie, gingersnap, macaroon, ladyfinger, fruit bar, date bar, sugar cookie.

43. friedcake, boil cake [dial., U.S.]; **doughnut,** sinker [slang, U.S.]; French doughnut, raised doughnut; **cruller;** twister; bismarck, olycook or olykoek, cymbal or simball, fasnacht [all local, U.S.]; fritter, flitter [dial.], *beignet* [F.]; apple fritter, *beignet de pommes* [F.].

44. griddlecake, pancake, hot cake, battercake, flapcake, **flapjack,** slapjack [U.S.]; chapatty [India]; **waffle;** blintz, cheese blintz.

45. pudding, plum pudding, tapioca pudding, etc.; charlotte, charlotte russe; brown Betty, custard, junket, duff, hasty pudding, Yorkshire pudding.

46. ice, *glacé* [F.], frozen dessert; **sherbet,** water ice [esp. Eng.]; **ice cream,** *crème glacée*[F.] ; French ice cream; parfait; sundae, ice-cream sundae, college ice [all U.S.]; ice-cream soda, frappé, banana split, ice-cream cone, frozen pudding.

47. beverage, drink, potation, **potable,** drinkable [coll.], liquor, liquid; soft drink, nonalcoholic beverage; cold drink; carbonated water, soda water, soda, pop, soda pop; Coca-Cola, Coke [coll., U.S.]; malted milk, malt [coll.]; buttermilk, sourdook [Scot.]; alcoholic drink 994.12–21.

48. beverages

ade	ice water
alcoholic beverages	juice
994.48–51	kumiss
ambrosia	lemonade
beef tea	lemon juice
birch beer	limeade
buttermilk	maté
café au lait	malted milk
café espresso	mead
chicory	metheglin
chocolate	milk
cider	milk shake
cocktail	mineral water
cocoa	Mocha, mocha
coffee	nectar
cream	orangeade
eggnog	orange juice
evaporated milk	phosphate
frappé	pineapple juice
fruit juice	pomegranate juice
ginger ale	punch
ginger beer	root beer
ginger pop	sarsaparilla
ginger punch	Seltzer
grape juice	tea
hydromel	Turkish coffee
ice-cream soda	water
iced coffee	whey
iced tea	

49. vegetables

acorn squash	cabbage
artichoke	carrot
asparagus	cauliflower
beans	celery
beet, beetroot	chard
[Eng.]	chick-peas
beet greens	chicory
bell pepper	chili pepper
Bermuda onion	chive
black-eyed peas	chive garlic
broccoli	collards, collard
Brussels sprouts	greens
butter beans	corn

cos, Cos lettuce
cowpeas
cress
cucumber
dandelion greens
eggplant
endive
escarole
fennel, *finocchio*
  [It.]
French beans
garbanzos [Sp.]
garlic
green beans
green peas
green pepper
gumbo
hominy
horse-radish
Hubbard squash
kale
kidney beans
kohlrabi
leek
lentils
lettuce
Lima beans
maize
mushroom
mustard greens
navy beans
okra
onion
oyster plant
parsley
parsnip

peas
pepper
pimento, pimiento
pinto beans
pomato
popcorn
pumpkin
radish
red pepper
rhubarb
rice
romaine
rutabaga
salsify
scallion
scarlet runners
shallot
snap beans
soy, soya
soybeans, soya
  beans
spinach
squash
string beans
succory
sugar beet
summer squash
sweet corn
sweet potato
tomato
truffle
turnip
water cress
yam
zucchini

50. fruits

akee
alligator pear
ananas
apple
apricot
avocado
banana
barberry
bearberry
berry
bilberry
blackberry
blueberry
boysenberry
breadfruit
cacao
candleberry
canistel
cantaloupe
caprifig
capulin
casaba, casaba
  melon
Catawba
checkerberry
cherimoya
cherry
citrange
citron
citrus, citrus fruit
civet fruit
cranberry
currant

custard apple
date
dewberry
durian
elderberry
feijoa
fig
gooseberry
granadilla
grape
grapefruit
guanabana
guava
hagberry
honeydew melon
huckleberry
icaco
ilama
imbu
jaboticaba
jackfruit
jujube
kumquat, cumquat
lemon
lime
lingonberry
litchi
loganberry
loquat
mamey or mam-
  mee apple
mango
mangosteen

manzanilla
marang
May apple
medlar
melon
mombin
mulberry
muscadine
muscat, muscatel
muskmelon
nectarine
nutmeg melon
olive
orange
papaw, pawpaw
papaya
passion fruit
peach
pear
Persian melon
persimmon
pineapple
pitanga
plantain
plum

51. nuts

acorn
almond
beechnut
ben nut
betel nut
black walnut
bonduc nut
Brazil nut
butternut
candle nut
cashew, cashew
  nut
chestnut
chinquapin, chin-
  capin, chinkapin
cobnut
coconut, cocoanut
cola or kola nut
corozo nut
cumara nut
dika nut

52. cheeses

American cheese
appetitost
Bel Paese cheese
bleu, blue cheese
box cheese
Brie cheese
Camembert, Cam-
  embert cheese
Cheddar, Cheddar
  cheese
Cheshire cheese
cottage cheese
cream cheese
Dutch cheese
Edam, Edam
  cheese
Emmental, Em-
  mentaler cheese
gjetost
Gorgonzola, Gor-
  gonzola cheese

plumcot
pomegranate
pond apple
prickly pear
prune
pulasan
quince
raisin
rambutan
raspberry
red currant
rose-apple
sapodilla
sapote
soursop
strawberry
sugar apple
sugarplum
sweetsop
tamarind
tangelo
tangerine
water lemon
watermelon
whortleberry

English walnut
filbert
groundnut
grugru nut
hazelnut
hickory nut
horse chestnut
kola, kola nut
litchi or lychee nut
palm nut
peanut
pecan
physic nut
pine nut
piñon
pistachio, pistachio
  nut
sassafras nut
souari or suwarrow
  nut
walnut

Gouda, Gouda
  cheese
grated cheese
Gruyère, Gruyère
  cheese
hand cheese
jack cheese
Leyden cheese
Liederkranz
Limburger, Lim-
  burg or Lim-
  burger cheese
mozzarella cheese
Münster cheese
Neufchâtel, Neuf-
  châtel cheese
New York cheese
oka cheese
Parmesan cheese
Pecorino cheese

Port du Salut
  cheese
pot cheese
process cheese
Provolone cheese
ricotta cheese
Romano cheese
Roquefort, Roque-
  fort cheese

schweizerkäse,
  schweizer
smearcase [U.S.]
Stilton cheese
Swiss cheese
Tilsiter cheese
Wensleydale
  cheese
Wisconsin cheese

chop suey [U.S.]
chow mein
compote
corned beef and
  cabbage
fish and chips
fondue
galantine
ham and eggs
kidney pie
liver and onions
macaroni and
  cheese

meat pie
pilau [Oriental]
poi [Hawaiian]
pork and beans
pork pie
potpie
spaghetti and meat
  balls
succotash [U.S.]
tamale
Welsh rabbit,
  Welsh rarebit
  [erron.]

53. candies

bonbon
brittle
butterscotch
caramel
chocolate
chocolate bar
chocolate drop
cream
divinity
fondant
fudge
glacé
gumdrop
honey crisp
horehound
jujube
licorice
lollipop
lozenge

marshmallow
marzipan, march-
  pane
mint
nougat
panocha
peanut bar
peanut brittle
peppermint
popcorn balls
praline
rock candy
Scotch kisses
sugar candy
sugarplum
taffy
toffee, toffy
tutti-frutti

54. condiments

allspice
applesauce
bell pepper
black pepper
capsicin
capsicum
cardamon, carda-
  mum
catchup
cayenne, cayenne
  pepper
chili
chili pepper
chili sauce
chili vinegar
chive
chive garlic
chutney
dill
dillseed, dill seeds
dressing
garlic
ginger
green pepper
hedge garlic
horseradish
cinnamon
clove
cubeb
leek
mace
marjoram
mayonnaise

mint
mustard
nutmeg
onion
paprika
parsley
pepper
peppermint
piccalilli
pickle 431.3
pimento, pimiento
pimpernel
potherb
radish
red pepper
relish
sage
salad dressing
salt
sauce
sauce-alone
savory
shallot
soy, soy sauce
spice
tabasco, tabasco
  sauce
tartar sauce
thyme
turmeric
vanilla
vinegar
white pepper

55. dishes

bacon and eggs
boiled dinner
Boston baked
  beans

bubble and squeak
chili, chile, chile
  con carne
chili and beans

56. manners of cooking or serving [F. and quasi F.]

à la béarnaise
à la bonne femme
à la bordelaise
à la bourgeoise
à la carte
à la casserole
à la Châteaubriand
à la cocotte
à la coque
à la Crécy
à la créole
à la Croissy
à la dauphine
à la dauphinoise
à la diable
à la florentine
à la française
à la godiveau
à la jardinière
à la julienne
à la king
à l'allemande
à la lyonnaise
à la macédoine
à la Maintenon
à la maître d'hôtel
à la Marengo
à la Maryland
à la matelote
à l'américaine
à la milanaise
àlamode, à la mode
à la mode de Caen
à la napolitaine
à la Newburg

à l'anglaise
à la normande
à la parisienne
à la Périgord
à la polonaise
à la printanière
à la ravigote
à la reine
à la russe
à la serviette
à la Soubise
à la suisse
à la tartare
à l'aurore
à la vinaigrette
à l'espagnole
à l'estragon
à l'italienne
au beurre fondu
au beurre roux
au fromage
au gras
au gratin
au jus
au kirsch
au maigre
au naturel
au vert pré
au vin blanc
aux fines herbes
aux petits pois
en casserole
maître d'hôtel
table d'hôte

307. NUTRITION

NOUNS **1. nutrition, nourishment;** alimentation; ingestion, digestion, assimilation, absorption; eutrophy [med.]; **food value.**

2. nutritiousness, digestibility; innutritiousness, indigestibility.

3. nutrient, nutritive, nutriment; aliment, pabulum; food **306a.**

4. vitamin, nutramin; provitamin; vitamer.

5. carbohydrate, saccharide; starches, sugars.

6. protein, proteide; protide, protid; holoproteide, simple proteide, derived proteide; heteroproteide, conjugated proteide; **amino acid.**

7. **digestion,** primary digestion, secondary digestion; predigestion; salivary digestion, gastric *or* peptic digestion, pancreatic digestion, intestinal digestion; digestive system, alimentary canal, gastro-intestinal tract; salivary glands, gastric glands, liver, pancreas; digestive secretions, saliva, gastric juice, pancreatic juice, intestinal juice, bile.

8. **digestant,** digester, digestive; **enzyme.**

9. **metabolism,** basal metabolism, acid-base metabolism, energy metabolism; anabolism, assimilation; catabolism, disassimilation; cholesterol.

10. **diet,** dietary; **regimen,** regime; bland diet; soft diet, pap, spoon food *or* meat, spoon victuals [dial.]; gruel, caudle; balanced diet; diabetic diet, allergy diet, etc.; reducing diet, obesity diet; high-caloric diet, low-caloric diet; high-protein diet; high-vitamin diet, vitamin-deficiency diet; acid-ash diet, alkaline-ash diet; low-salt diet, salt-free diet; elimination diet, Rowe diet; Coleman diet, Karrell diet, Lenhartz diet, Mayo diet, Meulengracht diet, Minot-Murphy diet, Sippy diet; diet book, vitamin chart, calory chart, calorie counter.

11. **dietary deficiency, malnutrition;** vitamin deficiency, vitamin A deficiency, vitamin B deficiency, etc.; mineral deficiency, fatty acid deficiency, etc.

12. **vitaminization, fortification, enrichment,** restoration.

13. **nutritionist, dietician, biochemist,** vitaminologist, enzymologist.

14. (science of nutrition) **dietetics,** dietotherapeutics, dietotherapy; **biochemistry, biochemy,** biochemics; vitaminology; enzymology.

VERBS 15. **nourish,** nutrify; **sustain, strengthen.**

16. **digest,** appropriate, **assimilate,** absorb; metabolize; predigest.

17. **diet,** go on a diet.

18. **vitaminize, fortify, enrich,** restore.

ADJS. 19. **nutritious,** nutritive, nutrient, **nourishing;** alimentary, alimental; digestible.

20. **innutritious,** uncongenial; indigestible.

21. **digestive,** assimilative; peptic.

22. **dietary,** dietal, dietetic; regiminal.

23. vitamins

alpha carotin	beta carotin
alpha tocopherol	beta tocopherol
ascorbic acid	biotin

calciferol	P-P factor (pellagra-preventing)
cholercalciferol	
choline	pterolglutamic acid
cobalamin	pyridoxal
cyanocobalamin	pyridoxamine
folic acid	pyridoximer
gamma carotin	pyridoxine
gamma tocopherol	riboflavin
hydroxocobalamin	thiamine
inositol	tocopherol
lactoflavin	vitamin A, A₁, A₂
menadione	vitamin B *or* B complex
neovitamin A	
niacin	vitamin B₁ to B₁₅
niacinamide	vitamin C, C₂
nicotinamide	vitamin D₁, D₂, D₃
nicotinic acid	vitamin E
nitrosocobalamin	vitamin J
PABA	vitamin K, K₁, K₂, K₃
pangamic acid	
pantothen	vitamin L₁, L₂ (undetermined)
pantothenic acid	
para-aminobenzoic acid	vitamins R to Y (undetermined)
phylloquinone	

24. carbohydrates

albose	lactose
altrose	levulose
arbinose	lyxose
beet sugar	maltose
cane sugar	malt sugar
cellobiose	mannose
cellulose	maple sugar
dextrin	melibiose
dextro-glucose	milk sugar
dextrose	pentosan
erythrose	raffinose
fructose	ribose
fruit sugar	saccharose
galactose	sorbose
glucose	starch
glycogen	sucrose
grape sugar	tagarose
gulose	talose
idose	trehalose
inulin	xylose

25. proteins

albumin	histone
albuminoid	ichthulin
amandin	keratin
bynin	lactalbumin
casein	lecithin
caseinogen	lecithoprotein
chlorophyll	lipide
chromoprotein	lipoprotein
clupeine	metaprotein
coagulated protein	mucin
collagen	nucleohistone
cytoglobulin	nucleoprotein
edestin	ordein
elastin	oryzenin
gliadin	osseomucoid
globin	ovalbumin
globulin	ovoglobulin
glutelin	ovovitellin
glutenin	peptide
glycoprotein	peptone
helicoprotein	phosphoaminolipide
hemoglobin	

phospholipide
phosphoprotein
prolamine
protamine
proteose
salmine
serum albumin

serum globulin
sturine
tendomucin
thymus histone
vegetable albumin
vitellin
zein

26. amino acids (basic units)

alanine
arginine
aspartic acid
cystine
glutamic acid
glycine
histidine
isoleucine
leucine
lysine

methionine
phenylalanine
proline
sarcosine
serine
threomine
tryosine
tryptophane
valine

27. digestive enzymes

amidase
aminopeptidase
aminopolypepti-
  dase
amylase
arginase
carbohydrase
carboxypeptidase
chymotrypsin
esterase
glutaminase

lactase
lipase
nuclease
nucleotidase
pepsin
peptidase
polynucleotidase
protease
rennin
saccharase
trypsin

28. health foods

blackstrap
  molasses
brewer's yeast
buckwheat flour
cottonseed flour
fortified flour
fortified milk
fruits
grits
liver
middlings
nonfat milk

nuts
peanut flour
powdered milk
raw vegetables
rice polish
soybeans
soy flour
unrefined flour
wheat germ
whole wheat
whole wheat flour
yogurt

308. EJECTION

NOUNS 1. ejection, ejectment, expulsion, discharge, extrusion, ousting, removal; the bounce [U.S.], the chuck [Eng.], the boot, the bum's rush, the 1-2-3, the old heave-ho [all slang]; rejection; dispatch, expedition.

2. eviction, ousting, dislodgment, dispossession; ouster [law]; rogue's march.

3. depopulation, dispeoplement; devastation, desolation.

4. banishment, relegation, exclusion, excommunication, disfellowship, expatriation; exile, exilement; ostracism, ostracization; deportation, transportation, extradition; rustication.

5. dismissal, discharge, congé [F.]; firing [slang], cashiering; disemployment, layoff, removal, retirement; the

bounce [U.S.], the chuck [Eng.], the boot, the order of the boot, the gate, the sack, the can, the axe [all slang]; walking papers or ticket, pink slip, mittimus [all coll.]; deposal 781; bumping [slang], backtracking; dishonorable discharge, bobtail [mil. slang].

6. evacuation, voidance; elimination, removal; clearance, clearage; exhaustion, emptying, depletion; draining, drainage; excretion, defecation 309.

7. disgorgement, disemboguement, expulsion, ejaculation [chiefly physiol.], discharge, emission; eruption, eructation, extravasation [geol.], blowout, outburst; outpour, jet, spout, squirt, spurt.

8. vomiting, vomition, disgorgement, regurgitation, emesis [med.], pukes [coll.], heaves [slang]; retching, heaving, gagging; nausea 684.22; vomit, puke [vulg.], spew.

9. belch, burp [coll.], ructation, eructation.

10. ejector, expeller; ouster, evictor; bouncer [U.S.], chucker, chucker-out, boot-giver [all slang].

11. dischargee, expellee; evict [coll., Eng.], evictee.

VERBS 12. eject, expel, discharge, extrude, obtrude, exclude, cast, remove; oust, bounce [coll.], give the hook [coll.], put out, turn out, thrust out; throw out, cast out, chuck out, toss out, heave out, kick downstairs; kick out, boot out, give the bum's rush, give the old heave-ho, give the 1-2-3, throw out on one's ear [all slang].

13. drive out, run out, chase out, rout out; drum out; freeze out [coll., U.S.]; force out; hunt out, ~ away or from, harry out; smoke out, drive into the open; run out of town, ride on a rail.

14. evict, oust, dislodge, dispossess, put out, turn out, turn out of doors, turn out of house and home, turn or put out bag and baggage; unhouse, unkennel.

15. depopulate, dispeople, unpeople; devastate, desolate.

16. banish, expel, cast out, relegate, ostracize, disfellowship, exclude, excommunicate, exile, expatriate, send to Coventry; deport, transport, extradite, lag [slang]; outlaw, ban, proscribe; rusticate.

17. dismiss, send off or away, turn off or away, bundle, bundle off or out, pack off, send packing, send about one's business, put ~, send or turn to the right-

about [coll.], send away with a flea in one's ear [coll.], send to Jericho [coll.], send to the showers [sport slang, U.S.], see the behind of [slang]; bow out, **show the door** *or* **gate; give the gate,** give the air [both slang].

18. **dismiss, discharge, expel, cashier, disemploy, lay off,** turn off, release, let go, let out, turn out, remove, displace, replace, strike off the rolls, take up one's badge, give the pink slip; give one his mittimus, give one his walking papers *or* ticket [all coll.]; **fire,** fire out, dejob, **sack,** give the sack, **can,** give the can, **bump, bounce** [U.S.], kick, boot, give the order of the boot, give the ax, give the gate [all slang]; depose, disbar, **781.2; break, bust** [slang]; **retire,** put on the retired list; pension off, superannuate; read out of.

19. **get rid of,** get quit of, get shut *or* shet of [dial.], rid oneself of; **dispose of, do away with;** exterminate, purge, liquidate; **shake off,** dispel; **throw off,** fling off, cast off; eliminate, eradicate **77.5;** throw away **666.7.**

20. **evacuate, void; eliminate;** remove; **empty,** empty out, deplete, exhaust, drain; **purge,** clean out, clear off, ~ out *or* away, sweep out, make a clean sweep, clear the decks; defecate **309.11.**

21. **unload, unlade, unpack, disburden,** unburden, **discharge, dump** [chiefly U.S.]; unship, break bulk [naut.].

22. **let out,** give vent to, give out *or* off, throw off, **emit,** exhaust, **evacuate; exhale,** expire, breathe out, let one's breath out; open the sluices *or* floodgates, turn on the tap.

23. **disgorge,** debouch, disembogue, **discharge, exhaust, expel, ejaculate** [chiefly physiol.], throw out, cast forth, send out *or* forth; **erupt, eruct, blow out,** extravasate [geol.]; **pour out** *or* **forth,** pour, outpour; **spew,** jet, spout, squirt, spurt.

24. **vomit, spew, disgorge, regurgitate,** puke [vulg.], **throw up** [coll.], bring up, cast [chiefly dial.], cast *or* heave the gorge, cast up one's accounts [joc.]; unswallow, upchuck, urp, put, shoot the cat, shoot one's cookies [all slang]; **retch, keck, heave, gag;** reject; be seasick, feed the fish [joc.].

25. **belch, burp** [coll.], eruct, eructate.

ADJS. 26. **ejective, expulsive, ejaculative, emissive, extrusive; eliminate,** eliminant; vomitive, vomitory.

INTERJS. 27. **away with!, off with!**

28. **begone!,** get you gone!, go away!,

go along!, get along!, **run along!,** get **along with you!,** away!, away with you!, **off with you!,** have off with you!, off you go!, on your way!, go your way!, go about your business!, be off!, avaunt!, *allez!* [F.], *allez-vous-en!* [F.], *va-t'en!* [F.], **shoo!,** scat!, get *or* git! [slang & dial., U.S.]; that door works both ways!, don't slam the door after you!, here's your hat—what's your hurry?; "get thee behind me, Satan" [Bible], "stand not on the order of your going, but go at once" [Shakespeare].

29. (slang terms) **beat it!, scram!, skiddoo!, skedaddle!, vamoose!,** cheese it!, make yourself scarce!, get lost!, go chase yourself!, walk your chalks!; shove in your clutch! [U.S. Army slang].

309. EXCRETION

Bodily Discharge.—NOUNS 1. **excretion,** egestion, **elimination, discharge;** emission; eccrisis [med.]; **exudation,** transudation; extravasation, effusion, flux; ejaculation; secretion **310.**

2. **defecation,** dejection, **evacuation,** voidance; movement, **bowel movement, stool; diarrhea,** flux, trots [slang], backdoor trot [slang], summer complaint [coll.]; lientery [med.]; **dysentery,** bloody flux; coeliac flux *or* passion [med.]; catharsis, purgation, purge.

3. **excrement,** dejection, dejecture, discharge, ejection; waste, waste matter; **excreta,** excretes, egesta, ejecta, ejectamenta, dejecta; exudation, exudate; transudation, transudate; extravasation, extravasate.

4. **feces** *or* **faeces,** feculence, defecation, movement, **stool,** turd [now vulgar], ordure, jakes [dial., Eng.]; **manure, dung, droppings;** cow chips [West. U.S.], argol [Mongol.]; coprolite, coprolith; **sewage,** sewerage.

5. **urine,** water [euphemistic], piss [now vulgar], pee, pee-pee, stale [zool.]; **urination,** micturition; urea.

6. **peccant humor, pus, matter,** corruption [dial.], ichor, sanies; pussiness, purulence; **suppuration,** maturation, **festering, rankling,** mattering, running, weeping [coll.].

7. **sweat, perspiration,** water; exudation, exudate; diaphoresis, sudor [both med.]; honest sweat, the sweat of one's brow; beads of sweat, beaded brow; cold sweat; **lather,** swelter, muck of sweat [coll.], streams of sweat; sudoresis [med.]; body odor, **B.O.**

8. **hemorrhage,** hemorrhea, **bleeding;** nosebleed.

9. **menstruation,** menstrual discharge, ~flow *or* flux, catamenia, catamenial discharge, sickness, curse of Eve; **menses, monthlies,** courses, period(s), that time.

VERBS 10. **excrete,** egest, **eliminate, discharge,** emit, pass, give off; **exude,** exudate, transude; weep; effuse, extravasate; ejaculate; **secrete 310.5.**

11. **defecate, evacuate,** void, **stool,** dung, have a bowel movement.

12. **urinate,** micturate [erron.], **make water, wet,** stale [dial.], piss [now vulg.], pee, pee-pee.

13. **suppurate, matter, fester, rankle,** run, weep [coll.]; ripen, maturate, come *or* draw to a head.

14. **sweat, perspire,** wet [chiefly dial.], exude; break out in a sweat, get in a muck of sweat [coll.], **get all in a lather** [coll.]; sweat like a trooper, sweat like an ox; swelter, cook [coll.], wilt.

15. **bleed,** lose blood, **shed blood,** spill blood; bloody.

16. **menstruate,** fly the red flag [slang], come sick, come around.

ADJS. 17. **excretory,** excretive, excretionary; eliminative, egestive; exudative, transudative; **secretory 310.7.**

18. **excremental,** excrementary; **fecal,** feculent, dungy; **urinary,** urinative, uric.

19. suppurative, maturative, **festering, rankling,** mattering; pussy, purulent.

20. **sweaty, perspiry** [coll.]; sweating, perspiring; wet with sweat, beaded with sweat, **sticky** [coll.], **clammy;** bathed in sweat, drenched with sweat, wilted; **in a sweat, in a muck of sweat** [coll.]; sudatory, sudoric, sudorific, diaphoretic [all med.].

21. **menstrual,** catamenial.

310. SECRETION

NOUNS 1. **secretion,** secreta, secernment; **excretion 309;** external secretion, internal secretion; lactation.

2. (Internal secretions) digestive secretions *or* juices, salivary secretion, gastric juice, pancreatic juice, intestinal juice; bile, gall; endocrine; thyroxin; autacoid, hormone, chalone..

3. **saliva, spittle, sputum, spit,** expectoration; salivation, ptyalism; **slobber,** slabber, slaver, **drivel,** dribble, **drool.**

4. (science of secretions) eccrinology, endocrinology, hormonology.

VERBS 5. **secrete,** secern; **excrete 309.10;** water; lactate.

6. **salivate,** ptyalize; **slobber,** slabber, slaver, **drool, drivel,** dribble; **expectorate, spit,** spew; hawk, clear the throat.

ADJS. 7. **secretory,** secretive, secretional, secretionary; **excretory 309.17;** watery, watering; salivary, salivant, salivous; mouth-watering.

8. **glandular,** glandulous; adrenal, pancreatic, etc. **310.9;** gonadal, ovarian, splenetic, thymic.

9. **glands**

adrenal (gland)	pituitary (gland)
breast	prostate (gland)
ductless gland	salivary gland
endocrine (gland)	sebaceous gland
gonad	spermary
hermaphrodite	spleen
gland	suprarenal (gland)
lymph gland	sweat gland
mamma	testicle
mammary gland	testis
ovaries	thymus (gland)
pancreas	thyroid (gland)
parathyroid (gland)	

10. **hormones**

adrenosterone	hydroxydehydro-
adrenotrophin	corticosterone
androgen	hydroxydesoxycor-
cholecystokinin	ticosterone
corticosterone	insulin
cortisone	lactogenic hormone
dehydrocorti-	lipocaic
costerone	parathyrin
desoxycorticoster-	progesterone
one	progestin
diiodotyrosine	prolactin
enterocrinin	secretin
enterogastrone	somatrophin
estradiol	testosterone
estriol	thyroglobulin
estrogen	thyrotrophin
gonadotrophin	thyroxin
hydroxycorticoster-	
one	

311. OVERRUNNING

NOUNS 1. **overrunning, overgoing, overpassing;** overrun, overpass; **overspreading,** overgrowth; overflowing **394.6.**

2. **infestation,** infestment; invasion, ravage, plague; **overrunning, overswarming,** overspreading; lousiness, pediculosis [med.].

3. **overstepping, transgression, trespass,** inroad, advancement, incursion, intrusion, entrenchment *or* intrenchment, **encroachment,** infraction, **infringement.**

VERBS 4. **overrun, overgo, overpass,** overreach; overstep, overstride; overleap, overjump; **overshoot,** overshoot the mark, overshoot the field [aeronaut.].

5. overspread, bespread, spread over; overgrow, grow over, run riot.

6. infest, beset, invade, ravage, plague; overrun, overswarm, overspread; creep with, crawl with, swarm with.

7. run over, overrun; ride over, override, run down, ride down; trample, trample on or upon, tread upon, trample underfoot, ride roughshod over; hit and run; overflow 394.18.

8. pass, go or pass by, get or shoot ahead of; by-pass; pass over, cross, go across, ford; step over, overstride, bestride.

9. overstep, transgress, trespass, intrude encroach, infringe, invade, advance upon, trench on, entrench or intrench on; strain, stretch, force, strain or stretch a point.

ADJS. **10.** overrun, overspread, overgrown.

11. infested, beset, ravaged, plagued; lousy, pediculous, pedicular; wormy, grubby; ratty.

312. SHORTCOMING

Motion Short Of.—NOUNS **1.** shortcoming, falling short, shortfall, shortage, fallshortage [coll.]; deficiency 57.1; insufficiency 660; delinquency; default, defalcation; arrear, arrears, arrearage; decline, slump; imperfection 676.

VERBS **2.** fall short, come short, run short, stop short, not reach, not make the grade [coll.]; want, lack, be found wanting, kick the beam; decline, lose ground, slump, fall away.

3. fall through, fall down [coll.], fall to the ground, fall flat, flat out [coll., U.S.], collapse, come to nothing, end or go up in smoke, fizzle out [coll.].

4. miss, miscarry, go amiss, go astray, miss the mark; miss stays [naut.]; miss one's mooring.

ADJS. **5.** short of, short; deficient, inadequate, lacking, wanting, minus; unreached.

ADVS. **6.** behind, behindhand, in arrears or arrear.

7. amiss, astray, beside the mark, far from it, to no purpose.

313. ASCENT

Motion Upwards.—NOUNS **1.** ascent, ascension; rise, rising, uprising, uprise, uprisal; upgoing, upgo, upgang [dial.]; upcoming, upcome [Scot.]; mount, mount-

ing; climb, upclimb, clamber, escalade; upsurgence, uprush; updraft; upswing; upgrowth; upgrade 218.6; elevation 315.

2. upturn, uptrend, upcast, upsweep, upbend.

3. stairs, stairway, staircase, escalier [F.], steps, flight of steps; spiral staircase, winding staircase; companionway, companion; stile; back stairs, escalier dérobé [F.]; perron; fire escape; landing, landing stage.

4. ladder, scale, Jacob [slang]; stepladder; extension ladder; Jacob's ladder, companion ladder, accommodation ladder, side ladder, gangway ladder, quarter ladder, stern ladder [all naut.].

5. step, stair, footstep, rest, footrest; rung, round, rundle, spoke, stave, scale; doorstep; tread; riser; bridgeboard, string.

6. climber, mountain climber, mountaineer; Alpine Club, Himalayan Club.

7. (comparisons) rocket, skyrocket; lark, skylark, eagle.

VERBS **8.** ascend, mount, rise, arise, uprise, upcome, upgo, go up, rise up, come up; go onwards and upwards, go up and up; upsurge, surge, upstream; swarm up, upswarm; upwind, upspin, spiral, spire, curl upwards; upgrow, grow up.

9. shoot up, spring up, start up, fly up, pop up, bob up; upshoot, upstart, upspring, upspear (as grass); rocket, skyrocket.

10. soar, plane, kite [coll.], fly aloft; aspire; spire, tower; hover, hang, poise, float, float in the air.

11. climb, climb up, upclimb, mount, clamber, clamber up, scramble or scrabble up, shin or shin up [coll.], coon [dial., U.S.], ramp [dial.], work one's way up; scale, escalade, scale the heights; climb over, surmount.

12. get on, climb on, mount, back; bestride, bestraddle; board, go aboard, go on board; get in, jump in, hop in, pile in [slang].

13. upturn, turn up; upcast, upsweep, upbend.

ADJS. **14.** ascending, mounting, rising, uprising, upgoing, upcoming; ascendant or ascendent, ascensional, ascensive; upward, uppard [dial.]; uphill, uphillward; climbing, scandent, scansorial [zool.].

15. upturned, upcast, uplifted, turnedup, retroussé.

ADVS. **16.** up, upward, upwards, uppard or uppards [dial.], upwith [Scot.];

skyward, heavenward; uplong, upalong; upstream, upstreamward; uphill; uphillward; upstairs, upstair; up attic, up garret, up steps [all dial.]; uptown; up north.

INTERJS. **17. excelsior!**, onward and upward!; **alley-oop!**, up-a-daisy!, upsy-daisy!

314. DESCENT

Motion Downward.—NOUNS **1. descent,** downcome, comedown, down; **dropping, falling; drop, fall, downfall;** downrush, downflow, **downpour,** defluxion; downturn, downtrend; declension, declination, inclination; gravitation; downgrade 218.5.

2. sinkage, lowering, **decline, slump,** subsidence, lapse, decurrence or decurrency; cadence; **droop, sag,** swag.

3. tumble, fall, *culbute* [F.], cropper [coll.], mucker [slang], **flop** [slang], spill [coll.], forced landing [joc.]; precipitation, **header** [coll.]; **sprawl;** pratfall [slang]; **stumble,** trip.

4. slide, slidder [Scot. & dial., Eng.]; **slip,** slippage; **glide,** coast, glissade (on snow); glissando [mus.]; slither; **skid,** sideslip; **landslide,** landslip [Eng.]; **snowslide,** snowslip [Eng.]; **avalanche.**

VERBS **5. descend, go** or **come down, down;** gravitate; **fall, drop,** fall or drop down; **pitch, plunge;** cascade, cataract; parachute; come down a peg [coll.]; **fall off,** drop off.

6. sink, go down, sink down; **set, settle,** settle down; **decline,** lower, subside, lapse; **droop, sag, swag; slump,** slump down; flump, flump down; flop, flop down [both coll.]; plump, plop, plump or plop down; founder 318.8.

7. get down, alight, light; land, settle, perch; **dismount, get off,** unhorse, light and rest one's saddle [South. U.S.]; climb down.

8. tumble, fall, fall down, come ~, fall or get a cropper [coll.], come a mucker [slang], take a fall or tumble, take a flop [slang], take a spill [coll.], precipitate oneself; **sprawl,** spread-eagle [coll.], measure one's length; fall headlong, **take a header** [coll.]; fall prostrate, fall flat, fall on one's face; **fall over,** topple down or over, nod to its fall; **topple,** lurch, pitch; **stumble,** trip, founder.

9. slide, slip, slidder [dial.], slip or slide down; **glide,** coast, glissade (on snow); slither; **skid,** sideslip; avalanche.

10. light on, alight on, settle on; descend upon, come down on, fall on, drop on, hit or strike upon.

ADJS. **11. descending,** descendent; **down,** downward; **downgoing,** downcoming; down-reaching; **dropping, falling,** downfalling; **sinking,** downsinking; setting; declining, subsiding; drooping, sagging; downhill 218.16.

12. downcast, downturned; hanging, downhanging.

ADVS. **13. down, downward, downwards,** downwith [Scot.], adown; downright; downhill, downgrade; downstreet; downline [railroad]; downstream; downstairs, downstair; downtown; down south.

315. ELEVATION

Act of Raising.—NOUNS **1. elevation, raising, lifting, rearing, erection,** sublevation; **uplift,** upheaval, upthrow, upcast, upthrust; **exaltation,** sublimation; height 206.

2. lift, boost [coll., U.S.], hoist [coll.], heist [slang, U.S.], heave; a leg up.

3. lifter, erector; crane, derrick, crab; jack, jackscrew; lever 286.4; windlass 286.7; tackle 286.10.

4. elevator, *ascenseur* [F.], **lift** [chiefly Eng.]; escalator, moving staircase or stairway; dumbwaiter.

VERBS **5. elevate, raise, rise, rear, erect,** sublevate; **heighten,** height [Scot. & dial., Eng.]; **lift,** boost [coll., U.S.], **hoist,** heist [slang, U.S.], heft, heave; raise up, rear up, lift up, hold up, set up, stick up, perk up; **upraise, uplift,** uphold, uprear, uphoist; upheave, upthrow, upcast; throw up, cast up; knock up, loft; sky [coll.].

6. exalt, sublimate, pinnacle, put on a pedestal.

7. give a lift, give a boost [coll., U.S.], give a leg up [coll.], **help up,** put on; mount, horse.

8. pick up, take up, **gather up;** draw up, fish up, drag up; dredge, dredge up.

ADJS. **9. raised, lifted, elevated;** upraised, **uplifted,** upcast; upreared, rampant; upthrown, upflung; exalted, sublimated; stilted, on stilts; "like a lily lifted high and white" [C. Rosetti]; erect, upright 212.10; high 206.19.

10. elevating, elevatory; **lifting, uplifting;** erective, erectile.

316. DEPRESSION

Act of Lowering.—NOUNS **1. depression, lowering, sinking,** debasement; detrusion; reduction, diminution; hollow 256.2.

2. **downthrow,** downcast; **overthrow,** overturn 219.2; **precipitation,** prostration.

3. **crouch, stoop,** bend, squat.

VERBS 4. **depress, lower,** let or take down, debase, **sink,** bring low, reduce, couch; take down a peg [coll.]; bear down, downbear; thrust ~, press or push down, detrude; indent 256.14.

5. **fell, drop, precipitate, bring down,** fetch down, down [coll.], take down, lay low; **raze** or rase, raze to the ground; **level,** lay level; pull down, pull about one's ears; **cut down,** chop down, hew down, whack down [coll.], mow down; **knock down,** dash down, **floor,** ground, **gravel** [coll.], grass [slang], **bowl down** or over [coll.], lay out [slang]; **prostrate,** supinate, prone [South. U.S.]; **throw,** throw ~, fling or cast down; bulldog [U.S.]; spread-eagle [coll.]; blow over or down, overblow.

6. **overthrow,** overturn 219.6.

7. **drop,** let drop or fall.

8. **crouch, couch, cower; stoop,** bend, **squat,** get down; hunch, hunch down; scrootch, scrouch, scrootch or scrouch down [all dial.]; grovel, wallow, welter.

9. **sit, sit down** [dial.], **be seated,** seat oneself; squat, get down on one's hunkers [Scot. & dial.]; perch, roost.

ADJS. 10. **depressed, lowered,** debased, reduced, **fallen;** sunk, **sunken;** downcast, downthrown; prostrate 213.9; low, at a low ebb.

317. LEAP

NOUNS 1. **leap, jump, hop, spring, bound,** bounce; **pounce;** upleap, upspring; **hurdle; vault,** pole vault, demivolt; curvet, capriole [both manège]; standing ~, running or flying jump; broad jump, standing or running broad jump; high jump, standing or running high jump; handspring; buck, buckjump; skip; hippety-hop [coll.]; hop, skip and jump.

2. **caper,** dido [coll., U.S.], antic, **gambol, frisk,** curvet, cavort [U.S.], capriole; **prance,** prink [dial.]; caracole or caracol; gambade [F.], gambado; falcade.

3. **leaping, jumping,** bouncing, bounding, hopping, springing, saltation; **vaulting,** pole vaulting; **hurdling,** the hurdles, hurdle race, timber topping [slang], steeplechase; leapfrogging.

4. **jumper, leaper, hopper;** broad jumper, high jumper; **vaulter,** pole vaulter; **hurdler,** hurdle racer, timber topper [slang];

bucking bronco, buckjumper, sunfisher [slang]; jumping bean.

VERBS 5. **leap, jump, vault, spring, hop, bound,** bounce; upleap, upspring, updive; leap ~, jump etc. over, overleap, overjump, overskip; **hurdle,** clear, negotiate [cant]; leapfrog; curvet, capriole [both manège]; buck, buckjump; start, start up, start aside; **pounce,** pounce on or upon; hippety-hop [coll.].

6. **caper,** cut capers [coll.], cut a dido [coll., U.S.], antic, curvet, cavort [U.S.], capriole, **gambol,** gambado, **frisk,** flounce, **trip, skip,** bob, bounce, jump about; **romp,** ramp [dial.]; **prance,** prank [dial.]; caracole or caracol.

ADJS. 7. **leaping, jumping,** springing, hopping, bouncing, bounding; saltant, saltatory, saltatorial.

318. PLUNGE

NOUNS 1. **plunge, dive, pitch, drop, fall;** header [coll.]; **swoop, pounce;** swan dive, gainer, jackknife; belly-buster, belly-whopper [both dial.]; nose dive, power dive [both aeronaut.]; crash dive, stationary dive, running dive [all submarine].

2. **submergence, submersion, immersion,** immergence, engulfment, **inundation,** burial; **dipping, ducking, dousing,** sousing, sinking; **dip, duck, souse;** baptism.

3. **diving, plunging;** fancy diving, high diving, skin diving, pearl diving, deep-sea diving.

4. **diver, plunger;** high diver, skin diver, pearl diver, deep-sea diver, frogman [U.S. mil.].

5. (diving equipment) diving bell, diving chamber, bathysphere, bathyscaphe, benthoscope, aquascope; diving boat; diving suit; diving helmet, diving hood; snorkel or schnorkel, periscope.

VERBS 6. **plunge, dive, pitch, plummet, drop, fall;** plump, plunk, plop; **swoop,** swoop down, **pounce,** pounce on or upon; nose-dive, make a nose dive, pique [all aeronaut.]; skin-dive; sound; take a header [coll.].

7. **submerge,** submerse, **immerse,** immerge, merge, **sink,** bury, engulf, **inundate,** deluge, drown, overwhelm, whelm; **dip, duck, dunk** [coll., U.S.], douse, **souse,** plunge in water; baptize.

8. **sink, scuttle** [naut.], send to the bottom, send to Davy Jones's locker [slang], feed the fish; **founder, go down,** go to the

bottom, go down like a stone; get out of one's depth.

ADJS. **9. submersible,** submergible, immersible, sinkable.

319. CIRCUITY

NOUNS **1. circuity,** circuitousness, circulation; **roundaboutness,** indirection; **deviation, digression** 290; **excursion,** excursus; circumvention, circumambulation, circumambience *or* circumambiency, circumflexion, circumnavigation, circummigration.

2. circuit, round, revolution, **circle, cycle,** orbit, ambit, **beat, walk,** tour, turn, lap, loop.

3. detour, by-pass, roundabout way, roundabout, circuit, circumbendibus [joc.], digression, deviation, excursion, ambages.

VERBS **4. circuit,** make a circuit, describe a circle, move in a circle, circulate; **go round** *or* **around,** go about; **circle,** encircle; **compass,** encompass; skirt, flank; go the round, make the round of; circumvent, circumambulate, circummigrate; circumnavigate, "put a girdle round about the earth" [Shakespeare].

5. round, go around, turn, turn *or* round a corner, double *or* round a point [naut.].

6. detour, make a detour, **go around,** go round about, go out of one's way, **by-pass;** deviate 290.3.

ADJS. **7. circuitous, roundabout, out-of-the-way, devious, oblique, indirect,** backhanded, ambagious; **deviating,** digressive, discursive, excursive; crooked, twisted, curved; **winding, twisting,** turning, flexuous, sinuous, tortuous, serpentine; wandering, rambling, vagrant, errant; mazy, labyrinthine.

8. circumambient, curcumambulatory, circumforaneous, circumfluent, circumvolant, circumnavigatory.

ADVS. **9. circuitously, deviously, obliquely, indirectly, round about,** about it and about, in a roundabout way, by a side door, by a side wind.

320. ROTATION

NOUNS **1. rotation, revolution,** volution, roll, **gyration,** circulation, turbination; circumrotation, circumgyration; **turning, whirling,** swirling, spinning, wheeling, reeling; swiveling, pivoting, swinging; **rolling,** trolling, trundling, bowling.

2. whirl, wheel, reel, **spin, turn,** round, gyre; pirouette; **swirl,** twirl, **eddy,** gurge, surge; vortex; merry-go-round, whirligig, whirlabout [all fig.]; dizzy round.

3. revolutions, revs [coll.]; revolutions per minute, r.p.m.

4. rotator, rotor; **roller,** rundle; **whirler,** whirligig, whirlabout; merry-go-round, carrousel, roundabout; **wheel,** disk; Ixion's wheel; rolling stone.

5. axle, axis, pivot, gudgeon, trunnion, swivel, spindle, arbor, pole, radiant; pin, pintle; **hub,** hubble [U.S.], **nave;** axle shaft, axle spindle, axle bar, axle-tree; disstaff; mandrel; gimbal; **hinge,** hingle [dial.]; rowlock, oarlock.

6. axle box, journal, journal box; hotbox.

7. bearing, ball bearing, roller bearing, bevel bearing, bushing, jewel.

8. (science of rotation) **trochilics,** gyrostatics.

VERBS **9. rotate, revolve, turn,** round, **go round,** turn round; **gyrate,** gyre; circumrotate, circumvolute; **circle,** circulate; **swivel, pivot, wheel,** swing; pirouette, turn a pirouette; wind (as a watch), twist, screw, crank.

10. roll, trundle, troll, **bowl;** goggle (roll the eyes); roll up, **furl.**

11. whirl, whirligig, twirl, **wheel, reel, spin,** spin like a top *or* teetotum; **swirl,** gurge, surge, **eddy,** whirlpool.

12. (move around in confusion) **seethe,** stir, moil; mill, **mill around** (as cattle).

13. (roll about in) **wallow,** welter, grovel, roll, flounder, tumble.

ADJS. **14. rotating, revolving, turning,** gyrating; **whirling, swirling,** twirling, **spinning,** wheeling, **reeling; rolling,** trolling, bowling.

15. rotary, rotatory, rotational, rotative; trochilic, vertiginous; circumrotatory, circumvolutory, circumgyratory; **gyral,** gyratory, gyrational; whirly, swirly, gulfy; whirlabout, whirligig; vortical; whirlwindy, whirlwindish; gyrostatic, gyroscopic.

ADVS. **16. round,** around [esp. U.S.], round about, **in a circle; round and round,** in circles, like a horse in a mill; in a whirl, in a spin; head over heels, heels over head; clockwise, counterclockwise.

17. rotators

bobbin	jack
gyro [coll.]	propeller
gyroplane	reel
gyroscope	revolving door
gyrostat	revolving lever

roller	top
rolling pin	treadmill
rotary drill	turbine
screw	windmill
spit	whirl drill
spool	whirling table
teetotum	

18. wheels

balance wheel	paddle wheel
bevel gear	pinion
cart wheel	pinwheel
caster, castor	potter's wheel
cog	spinning wheel
cogwheel	sprocket wheel
contrate wheel	spur gear
crown wheel	spur pinion
Ferris wheel	spur wheel
flywheel	vortex wheel
gear	wagon wheel
gearwheel	wheel of fortune
gyrowheel	worm wheel or
mill wheel	gear

321. EVOLUTION

NOUNS 1. **evolution,** evolvement; **unfoldment,** unfolding, unrolling, opening.

2. **development, growth,** rise; flowering, blossoming; ripening; maturation; advance, advancement, furtherance; **progress,** progression; **elaboration,** enlargement, amplification, **expansion,** explication.

3. (biology) **genesis;** phylogeny, phylogenesis; ontogeny, ontogenesis; physiogeny, physiogenesis.

4. **evolutionism,** theory of evolution; **Darwinism,** Neo-Darwinism, Haeckelism, Lamarckism, Neo-Lamarckism, Weismannism, **Spencerianism;** natural selection, adaptation.

VERBS 5. **evolve,** evolute [coll.]; **unfold,** unroll, unfurl, unwind, unreel, uncoil; open, **open up.**

6. **develop, grow, progress, advance;** ripen, mature; flower, blossom; **elaborate,** labor, **work out,** enlarge upon, amplify, enlarge, **expand,** detail, go or enter into detail, go into, labor the point.

ADJS. 7. **evolutionary,** evolutional; evolving, developing, unfolding; **progressing, advancing;** phylogenetic, ontogenetic, physiogenetic.

322. OSCILLATION

Motion To and Fro.—NOUNS 1. **oscillation, vibration,** libration; pendulation; fluctuation, vacillation, wavering; libration of the moon, libration in latitude or longitude; vibratility.

2. **waving, undulation,** undulancy; brandishing, flourishing, flaunting, shaking; brandish, flaunt, flourish; wave 394.14.

3. **pulsation, pulse, beat, throb;** beating, throbbing; drumming 454.1; **palpitation,** pitter-patter, pitapat, pitapatation [joc.]; heartbeat, heartthrob.

4. **alternation,** reciprocation; **coming and going,** to-and-fro, ebb and flow, flux and reflux, systole and diastole, ups and downs; **seesawing,** teetering, tottering, **teeter-tottering;** seesaw, teeter, teeter-totter, wigwag.

5. **swing, sway, swag, rock, lurch, roll,** reel; wag, waggle; wave, waver; lilt, rhythm.

6. **seismicity, seismism; seismology,** seismography, seismometry.

7. (instruments) **oscilloscope,** oscillograph, oscillometer; vibroscope, vibrograph; seismoscope, seismograph, seismometer.

8. **oscillator, vibrator;** pendulum, pendulum wheel; swing; seesaw, teeter [U.S.], teeter-totter, teeterboard, teetery-bender; shuttle; rocker, rocking chair; rocking stone, logan or loggan stone.

VERBS 9. **oscillate, vibrate,** librate; pendulate; **fluctuate,** vacillate, waver, wave; **swing, sway, swag,** dangle, **reel, rock, lurch, roll,** toss, pitch; wag, waggle; **wobble,** wabble, wamble [dial.], coggle [dial.]; **bob,** bobble [coll.]; shake, flutter 323.10–12.

10. **wave, undulate; brandish, flourish,** flaunt, shake, swing, wield; float, fly (as a flag); **flap, flutter;** wag, wigwag.

11. **pulsate, pulse, beat, throb,** pant, palpitate, go pitapat; drum 454.4.

12. **alternate,** reciprocate, swing, **go to and fro,** to-and-fro, **come and go,** pass and repass, ebb and flow, ride and tie, hitch and hike, back and fill; **seesaw,** teeter, **teeter-totter;** shuttle, shuttlecock; wigwag, wibble-wabble [coll.]; zigzag.

13. (move up and down; as, to *pump* one's hand) **pump, shake.**

ADJS. 14. **oscillating,** oscillatory; **vibrating,** vibratory, vibratile, libratory; pendulous; **fluctuating,** wavering; vacillating, vacillatory.

15. **waving, undulating,** undulatory, undulant.

16. **swinging, swaying,** dangling, **reeling, rocking, lurching, rolling,** tossing, pitching.

17. pulsative, pulsatory, pulsatile; pulsating, **pulsing, beating, throbbing, palpitating,** palpitant, pitapat.

18. **alternate,** reciprocal, reciprocative; **back-and-forth, to-and-fro,** up-and-down, seesaw.

19. seismatic(al), seismological, seismographic, seismometric.

ADVS. 20. **to and fro, back and forth,** backward and forward, backwards and forwards, **in and out, up and down,** seesaw, shuttlewise, from side to side, from pillar to post, off and on, ride and tie, hitch and hike, round and round, like buckets in a well.

323. AGITATION

Irregular Motion.—NOUNS 1. **agitation, perturbation, trepidation,** trepidity, **unrest,** restlessness, **disquiet,** disquietude, inquietude, **stir, churn, ferment,** fermentation, foment, seethe, seething, ebullition, embroilment, roil, turbidity, fume, **disturbance, commotion,** moil, **turmoil, turbulence, tumult,** hubbub, rout, fuss, bluster, fluster, flurry, bustle, hurly-burly; maelstrom; **excitement** 855.

2. **shaking, quaking, quivering, quavering, shivering, trembling, vibration;** succussion, succussation; jactation, jactitation [med.]; shakes [dial., U.S.], shivers or cold shivers [coll.], ague.

3. **shake, quake, quiver, quaver,** falter, **tremor, tremble, shiver,** twitter, didder, dither; **wobble,** wabble; **bob,** bobble [coll.]; **jog, joggle; jolt,** jar, jostle; **bounce,** bump; **jerk,** twitch; jig, jiggle, jigget [coll.].

4. **flutter,** flitter, flit, **flicker, waver,** dance; shake, quiver 323.3; **sputter, splutter; flap,** flop [coll.]; **beat,** beating; **palpitation,** pitapatation [joc.], pitapat, pitter-patter.

5. **twitching, jerking,** vellication; **fidgets,** fidgetiness, all-overs [dial. U.S.].

6. **spasm, convulsion,** convulse [poetic], **paroxysm,** throe; epitasis, eclampsia [both med.]; **seizure,** grip, stroke, attack, **fit,** ictus [med.].

7. **wriggle, wiggle;** wag, **waggle;** writhe, **squirm.**

8. **flounder, flounce,** stagger, totter, stumble, falter; wallow, welter; **roll, rock, reel, lurch, swing, sway;** toss, tumble, pitch, plunge.

9. (instruments) **agitator,** shaker, vibrator; beater, paddle, whisk, eggbeater; churn.

VERBS 10. **agitate, shake, disturb, perturb,** perturbate, **disquiet, discompose, trouble, stir,** flurry, fret, roughen, ruffle, ripple, ferment, convulse; **churn,** whip, whisk, beat, paddle; **stir up,** work up, shake up, churn up, whip up, beat up; roil, rile [coll., chiefly U.S.], excite 855.11.

11. **shake, quake, vibrate; tremble, quiver, quaver,** falter, **shiver,** twitter, didder; shake in one's boots or shoes, shake or tremble like an aspen leaf; **wobble,** wabble; **bob,** bobble [coll.]; **jog, joggle; jolt,** jar, jostle, hustle, jounce, **bounce,** jump, bump.

12. **flutter,** flitter, flit, **flick, flicker,** bicker, wave, **waver,** dance; shake, quiver 323.11; **sputter, splutter; flap, flop** [coll.], flip, beat; **palpitate,** pitter-patter, go pitapat.

13. **twitch, jerk,** vellicate; jig, **jiggle,** jigger [coll.], jigget [coll.]; **fidget,** have the fidgets.

14. **wriggle, wiggle;** wag, **waggle;** writhe, **squirm,** twist and turn.

15. **flounder, flounce, stagger, totter,** stumble, falter, blunder, wallop; **struggle,** labor; **wallow, welter; roll, rock, reel, lurch, swing, sway;** toss, **tumble, pitch, plunge,** pitch and plunge, toss and tumble, toss and turn, be the sport of winds and waves.

16. seethe 161.11.

ADJS. 17. **agitated, disturbed, perturbed, disquieted, discomposed, troubled, ruffled,** flurried; stirred up, shaken up; **troublous,** restless, uneasy, unquiet, unpeaceful; all of a twitter [coll.], all of a flutter; **turbulent** 161.17; **excited** 855.21–28.

18. **shaking, vibrating; quivering, quavering, quaking, shivering, trembling, tremulous,** aspen; **successive,** succussatory; **shaky,** quivery, quavery, shivery, trembly; wobbly, wabbly.

19. **fluttering, flickering, wavering,** dancing; sputtering, spluttering, **sputtery,** fluttery, flickery, flicky [coll.], wavery, **unsteady,** desultory.

20. **jerky,** twitchy or twitchety [coll.], jerking, **twitching, fidgety, jumpy,** jigety [coll.], vellicative.

21. **jolting,** jolty [coll.], **joggling,** joggly [coll.], jogglety [coll.], **bouncy, bumpy,** choppy, rough; jarring.

22. **wriggly, wriggling; wiggly,** wiggling; squirmy, squirming; writhy, writhing.

ADVS. 23. **agitatedly, troublously, restlessly,** uneasily, unquietly, unpeacefully.

24. **shakily,** quiveringly, quaveringly, **quakingly, tremblingly,** tremulously; flutteringly, waveringly, unsteadily, desultorily; **jerkily,** fitfully, by jerks, by snatches, by fits and starts, "with many a flirt and flutter" [Pope].

324. PHYSICS

NOUNS **1. physics,** natural *or* physical science, natural philosophy; applied physics, aerophysics, astrophysics, basic conductor physics, biophysics, cytophysics, electrophysics, geophysics, hyperphysics, iatrophysics [hist.], macrophysics, mathematical physics, mechanics 346, microphysics, molecular physics, nuclear physics 325, physicologic, physicomathematics, psychophysics, radiation physics 326.7, solar physics, stereophysics, zoophysics; physical chemistry, physicochemistry, chemicophysics; electron physics, electrophysics.

2. physicist, aerophysicist, astrophysicist, biophysicist, electronic physicist, geophysicist, iatrophysicist [hist.], nuclear physicist 325.3, physicochemist, physicomathematician, radiation physicist 326.8.

ADJS. **3. physical,** aerophysical, astrophysical, biophysical, cytophysical, electrophysical, geophysical, iatrophysical [hist.], physiological, physicomathematical, zoophysical; chemicophysical, physicochemical, physiochemical.

325. ATOMICS

NOUNS **1. atomics,** atomistics, atomology, atomic science; **nucleonics, nuclear physics;** atomic *or* nuclear chemistry; atomechanics, quantum mechanics, wave mechanics; molecular physics; radiology 326.7.

2. (atomic theory) quantum theory, Bohr theory, Rutherford theory, Schroedinger theory, Lewis-Langmuir *or* octet theory, Thompson's hypothesis; law of conservation of mass, law of definite proportions, law of multiple proportions, law of Dulong and Petit, correspondence principle; atomism [philos.].

3. atomic scientist, nuclear physicist, atomologist; radiologist 326.8.

4. atom, carbon atom, hydrogen atom, etc.; radical, simple radical, compound radical; tracer, tracer atom, tagged atom; atomic model, nuclear atom.

5. isotope, isotope of lead, ~ lithium, etc.; protium, isotope of hydrogen; deuterium, heavy hydrogen; deuteride, deuterium oxide, heavy water; tritium, triple heavy water; isotone; radioisotope; artificial isotope; pleiad.

6. atomic nucleus, nuclear particles, elementary particles, subatomic particles, subatoms; nucleons (neutrons and protons), deuterons (deuterium nuclei), tri-

tons (tritium nuclei); nuclear isomer, nuclear isomerism; shell, planetary shell; valence shell, valence electrons.

7. (atomic cluster) chain, straight chain, branched chain, side chain; ring, closed chain, cycle; homocycle, heterocycle; benzene ring *or* nucleus, Kekule's formula; lattice, space-lattice.

8. nuclear fission, fission reaction, atomic disintegration, **atom-smashing,** atom-chipping, **splitting the atom;** atomic reaction: stimulation, dissociation, photodisintegration, ionization, nucleization, cleavage, fission; neutron reaction, proton reaction, etc.; reversible reaction, nonreversible reaction; **chain reaction;** exchange reaction; substitution, monosubstitution, disubstitution, trisubstitution; breeding; disintegration series; bombardment, bullet, target; proton gun.

9. nuclear fusion, fusion reaction, thermonuclear reaction, thermonuclear fusion.

10. fissionable material, nuclear fuel; fertile material; **critical mass,** noncritical mass; parent element, daughter element; end product.

11. atomic accelerator, atom smasher, atomic cannon.

12. reactor, nuclear reactor, **pile,** atomic pile, reactor pile, chain-reacting pile, chain reactor, **furnace,** atomic *or* nuclear furnace, neutron factory; power reactor, breeder reactor, power-breeder reactor; homogeneous reactor, heterogeneous reactor; plutonium reactor, uranium reactor, etc.; fast pile, intermediate pile, slow pile; lattice; bricks; rods.

13. atomic engine, atomic *or* nuclear power plant, reactor engine.

14. atomic energy, nuclear energy *or* power, thermonuclear power; activation energy, binding energy, mass energy; energy level; atomic research, atomic project; Atomic Energy Commission, AEC.

15. atomic explosion, atom blast, A-blast; hydrogen blast, **H-blast;** blast wave, Mach stem; Mach front; mushroom cloud; **fallout,** airborne radioactivity, fission particles, dust cloud, radioactive dust; flash burn; A-bomb shelter, fallout shelter.

VERBS **16. atomize,** nucleize; activate, accelerate; bombard, cross-bombard; cleave, fission, **split** *or* smash the atom.

ADJS. **17. atomic,** atomatic, atomistic; atomiferous; monatomic, diatomic, triatomic, tetratomic, pentatomic, hexatomic, heptatomic; heteroatomic, heteroatomic;

subatomic; dibasic, tribasic; cyclic, isocyclic, homocyclic, heterocyclic; isotopic, isobaric, isoteric.

18. nuclear, thermonuclear, isonuclear, homonuclear, heteronuclear, extranuclear.

19. fissionable, fissile, scissile.

20. atoms

acceptor atom	hot atom
asymmetric carbon	impurity atom
atom	isobar
discrete atom	isotere
excited atom	isotopic isobar

21. theoretic atoms

Bohr atom	Rutherford atom
cubical atom	Schroedinger atom
Lewis-Langmuir atom	Thomson atom

22. univalent, bivalent, etc., atoms or elements

monad	pentad
dyad	hexad
triad	heptad
tetrad	octad

23. subatomic particles

alpha particle	neutrino
antiparticle	neutron
beta particle	photon
electron	pion, pi-meson
meson	positron
mesotron	proton
muon, mu-meson	"w" particles

24. neutrons

fast neutron	resonance neutron
monoenergetic neutron	slow neutron
photoneutron	thermal neutron

25. atomic units and constants

atom [coll.]	kiloton
atomic mass	magnetic quantum number
atomic number	magneton
atomic weight	mass number
crystal-lattice constant	Petit's constant
Dulong's constant	Planck's constant
elementary quantum of action	quantum
	quantum number
gram atom	Rydberg number or constant
gram-atomic weight	valence
	valence number

26. accelerators

betatron	linear accelerator
bevatron	microwave linear accelerator
cascade transformer	positive-ion accelerator
charge-exchange accelerator	synchrotron
cosmotron	synchrocyclotron
cyclotron	swindletron [joc.]
electron accelerator	Van de Graaf generator
electrostatic generator	

27. atomic power applications

atomic battery	atom-plane
atomic factory	atom-rocket
atomic generator	atom-sub
atom-liner	

326. RADIATION AND RADIOACTIVITY

NOUNS **1. radiation,** radiant energy; **radioactivity,** activity, radioactive radiation *or* emanation, atomic *or* nuclear radiation; natural radioactivity, artificial radioactivity; specific activity, high specific activity; radiotransparency, radiolucency; radiopacity; radiosensitivity, radiosensibility; contamination, decontamination; saturation point; fallout 325.15.

2. radioluminescence, autoluminescence; cathode luminescence.

3. radiorays, nuclear rays; alpha ray, beta ray, gamma ray; alpha radiation, beta radiation, gamma radiation; X ray, Roentgen ray, X radiation; cathode ray, anode ray; Lenard ray; actinic ray; Becquerel ray; positive ray, canal ray; cosmic ray, cosmic radiation; cosmic ray bombardment, electron shower.

4. radioactive particles, radions, Geigers [coll.]; alpha particles, beta particles, gamma particles; heavy particles; mesons, mesotrons; cosmic particles, solar particles, aurora particles, V-particles.

5. (radioactive substance) **radiator;** alpha radiator, beta radiator, gamma radiator; fluorescent paint, radium paint; radium dial; fission products; radiocarbon, radiocopper, radioiodine, radiothorium, etc; mesothorium; **radioelement;** polonium, radioactive bismuth; radon, radium emanation; radioisotope; tracer, tracer element, tracer atom.

6. radioscope, counter, radiodetector, **atom-tagger** (slang).

7. radiology, radiatics, radiation physics, radiological physics; radiobiology, radiochemistry, radiometallography, radiography, roentgenography, roentgenology, radiometry, radiotechnology, radiopathology; radiotherapy 687.8; radioscopy, curiescopy, roentgenoscopy, radiostereoscopy, fluoroscopy, photofluorography, orthodiagraphy; tracer investigation, atom-tagging [slang].

8. radiologist, radiation physicist, atom-tagger [slang]; radiobiologist, radiochemist.

VERBS **9. radioactivate,** activate, irradiate, charge; radiumize; **contaminate,** poison, infect; decontaminate.

ADJS. **10. radioactive,** activated, radioactivated, irradiated, charged, **hot; contaminated,** infected, poisoned; radiferous; radioluminescent, autoluminescent.

11. **radiable;** radiotransparent, radioparent, radiolucent; radiopaque, radiumproof; radiosensitive.

12. **radioactive elements**

actinium	neptunium
americium	nobelium
astatine	plutonium
berkelium	polonium
californium	promethium
curium	protactinium
einsteinium	radium
fermium	radon
francium	technetium
mendelevium	thorium
	uranium

13. **radioscopes**

alpha pulse	ion counter
analyzer	ionization chamber
atom counter	kicksorter
atom-tracing	mine detector
spectrometer	minometer
aurora particle	particle counter
counter	proportional
beta-ray	counter
spectrograph *or*	pulse analyzer
spectrometer	radiation
cloud chamber	pyrometer
cosmic ray counter	radiometer
counting tube	radiomicrometer
crystal counter	Rutherford-Geiger
electronic counter	counter
expansion chamber	scintillator
gamma ray counter	scintillometer
Geiger counter	screen-wall counter
Geiger-counter	solar gamma ray
telescope	counter
Geiger-Müller	solar X-ray counter
counter	spectroradiometer
heavy particle	spinthariscope
counter	tube counter

14. **radioactive units**

curie	millicurie
half-life	multicurie
megacurie	photon
microcurie	roentgen

327. HEAT

NOUNS **1. heat, hotness,** hot [dial.]; **warmth,** warmness; **fervor,** fervency, fervidity, **ardor;** radiant heat, induction heat, convector heat, gas heat, steam heat, electric heat, solar heat, dielectric heat, ultraviolet heat, atomic heat, molecular heat; animal heat, body heat, blood heat; fever heat, fever 684.6; heating, burning 328.

2. temperature; boiling point, melting point, recalescence point [steel mfg.]; absolute zero.

3. lukewarmness, tepidness, **tepidity.**

4. torridness, torridity; intense heat,

torrid heat, red heat, white heat, tropical heat, Afric heat, Indian heat, Bengal heat, summer heat.

5. sultriness, stuffiness, closeness, oppressiveness; humidity, **humidness, mugginess,** stickiness [coll.], swelter.

6. hot weather, sunny *or* sunshiny weather; sultry weather, stuffy weather, humid weather, muggy weather, sticky weather [coll.]; summer, midsummer; dog days, canicular days; **heat wave,** hot wave, monkeys [slang]; broiling sun, midday sun; vertical rays.

7. hot day, summer day; **scorcher, roaster,** broiler, sizzler, swelterer [all coll.].

8. hot air, superheated air.

9. hot water, boiling water; **steam,** vapor; volcanic water; hot *or* warm springs, thermae; geyser; Old Faithful.

10. (hot place) **oven, furnace,** fiery furnace, hell; **tropics,** subtropics, Torrid Zone; equator.

11. glow, incandescence; **flush, blush, bloom,** redness, whiteness, rubicundity; hectic, hectic flush.

12. fire, blaze, flame, ingle, devouring element; **combustion, ignition; conflagration;** flicker 334.8, wavering *or* flickering flame, "lambent flame" [Dryden]; smoldering fire, sleeping fire; **cheerful fire,** cozy fire, crackling fire, "bright-flaming, heat-full fire" [Du Bartas]; **roaring fire,** blazing fire; **raging fire,** sheet of fire, sea of flames, "whirlwinds of tempestuous fire" [Milton]; bonfire, bonner [slang, Eng.], tandle [Scot.]; balefire; beacon fire, beacon, signal beacon, watch fire; alarm fire, two-alarm ~, three-alarm, etc., fire; wildfire, prairie fire, forest fire; backfire [U.S.]; open fire; campfire; smudge fire, smudge [both U.S.]; death fire, pyre, funeral pile; fiery cross.

13. flare, flare-up, **flash, blaze,** burst, outburst.

14. spark, sparkle; **scintillation,** scintilla.

15. coal, live coal, **ember, cinder.**

16. fireworks *or* firework, **pyrotechnics.**

17. (perviousness to heat) transcalency; adiathermancy, athermancy.

18. thermal unit; British thermal unit, B.T.U.; Board of Trade unit, B.O.T; centigrade thermal unit; centigrade scale, Fahrenheit scale; **calorie,** mean calorie, centuple *or* rational calorie, small calorie; large *or* great calorie, kilocalorie, kilogram-calorie; therm.

19. **thermometer,** mercury, glass.

20. (science of heat) **thermology,** thermotics, thermodynamics; volcanology; pyrology, pyrognostics; pyrotechnics, pyrotechny; calorimetry.

VERBS 21. (be hot) **burn, scorch,** parch, scald, **swelter, roast,** toast, cook, bake, fry, broil, boil, seethe, simmer, stew; **blaze, flame,** flame up, **flare,** flare up; **flicker** 334.25; **glow,** incandesce, flush, bloom; smolder; steam; sweat 309.14; gasp, pant; **suffocate, stifle,** smother, choke.

22. **smoke, fume,** reek, funk [slang]; smudge.

23. heat, burn 328.17–24.

ADJS. 24. **warm,** calid, thermal, mild, genial; **toasty** [coll.], warm as toast; **sunny,** sunshiny; summery; **temperate,** warmish; **tropical,** subtropical; **tepid, lukewarm,** luke; blood-warm, blood-hot; unfrozen.

25. **hot, heated, torrid; sweltering,** sweltry, swelty [dial.]; **burning,** parching, scorching, searing, scalding, blistering, baking, roasting, toasting, broiling, simmering; **boiling,** seething, ebullient; **piping hot,** scalding hot, burning hot, roasting hot, scorching hot, sizzling hot, smoking hot; **red-hot,** white-hot; **fervid, fervent, ardent,** flushed; overwarm, overhot, overheated; hot as fire, hot as pepper *or* red pepper, hot as hell *or* blazes, hotter than the hinges of hell, hot enough to roast an ox, like a furnace *or* oven; feverish 684.43.

26. **fiery,** igneous, firelike; combustive, conflagrative.

27. **burning, ignited,** blazing, ablaze, flaring, flaming, aflame, inflamed, alight, **afire, on fire,** in flames, in a blaze; conflagrant, comburent; live, living; **glowing,** aglow, in a glow, incandescent, candescent, candent; **flickering,** aflicker; unquenched, unextinguished; slow-burning; **smoldering; smoking,** fuming, reeking.

28. **sultry, stifling, suffocating, stuffy,** close, oppressive; **humid, sticky** [coll.], **muggy.**

29. warm-blooded, hot-blooded.

30. thermal, thermic; isothermal, isothermic; centigrade, Fahrenheit.

31. diathermic, diathermal, transcalent; adiathermic, adiathermal, athermanous.

32. pyrological, pyrotechnic(al); pyrogenic, pyrogenous; thermodynamic(al).

33. fireworks

bomb	cannon cracker
candlebomb	cap

Catherine wheel	rocket
cracker	Roman candle
cracker bonbon	serpent
firecracker	skyrocket
fizgig	snake
flare	sparkler
flowerpot	squib
girandole	torpedo
ladyfinger	whiz-bang, whizz-
pinwheel	bang

34. thermometers

black-bulb	platinum
thermometer	thermometer
calorimeter	pyrometer
centigrade	register *or* self-
thermometer	registering
clinical	thermometer
thermometer	resistance
dry-bulb	thermometer
thermometer	telethermometer
electric	thermoelectrom-
thermometer	eter
Fahrenheit	thermometrograph
thermometer	thermopile
galvanothermom-	thermoregulator
eter	thermostat
gas thermometer	wet-bulb
metallic	thermometer
thermometer	

328. HEATING

NOUNS 1. **heating, warming,** calefaction, torrefaction; tepefaction; preheating; stove heating, furnace heating; radiant heating, panel heating; central heating; induction heating, gas heating, steam heating, electric heating, electronic heating, dielectric heating; solar heating, insolation; cooking 329.

2. **boiling, seething, stewing,** ebullition, ebullience *or* ebulliency, coction; decoction; simmering; boil; simmer; ebullioscope, ebulliometer.

3. **melting, fusion,** running; **thawing,** thaw; liquation [metal.]; fusibility.

4. **ignition, lighting, kindling,** firing, inflammation.

5. **burning, combustion,** blazing, flaming; **scorching,** parching, singeing; **searing,** branding; **blistering,** vesication; **cauterization,** cautery; **incineration,** cineration; **cremation,** concremation; suttee, self-cremation, self-immolation; the stake, burning at the stake, auto-da-fé; scorification; carbonization; oxidation, oxidization; calcination; cupellation; deflagration [chem.]; **spontaneous combustion,** thermogenesis.

6. **burn,** scald, scorch, singe; sear; brand; sunburn, sunscald; mat burn.

7. **incendiarism, arson; pyromania.**

8. incendiary, arsonist, arsonite; pyromaniac, firebug [coll. U.S.], pétroleur [F.], pétroleuse [F.; fem.].

9. inflammability, combustibility.

10. heater, warmer; stove; furnace, fiery furnace, volcano [fig.]; cooker, cookery; firebox; tuyère, tewel; burner, jet, gas jet, pilot light or burner.

11. fireplace, hearth, ingle; fireside, ingleside, inglenook, ingle cheek [Scot. & Ir.], chimney corner; hearthstone; hob, hub; fireguard, fireboard, fire screen, fender.

12. incinerator, cinerator, burner; crematory, cremator, crematorium, burning ghat [India]; calcinatory.

13. blowtorch, blast lamp, torch; blowpipe; burner; welder, 347.21; acetylene torch or welder, oxyacetylene blowpipe or torch, welding blowpipe or torch.

14. cauterant, cauterizer, cauter, cautery; hot iron, branding iron, brand iron, brand; caustic, corrosive, mordant, escharotic; acid 378.12; lunar caustic; radium.

15. fire iron; andiron, firedog, tongs, pair of tongs, fire tongs, coal tongs; poker, stove poker, salamander [chiefly dial., Eng.], fire hook; lifter, stove lifter; pothook, crook, crane, chain; trivet, tripod; spit, turnspit; grate, grating; gridiron, grid, griddle [dial.], grill, griller; damper.

16. (products of combustion) scoria, slag, dross; ashes, ash; cinder, clinker, coal; coke, charcoal, brand, lava, carbon, calx; soot, smut, culm, coom or coomb [Scot. & dial., Eng.]; smoke, smudge, fume, reek [dial. & literary].

VERBS 17. heat, hot [dial.], warm, fire, chafe; tepefy; gas-heat, steam-heat, electric-heat; superheat; overheat; preheat; reheat, recook, warm over; mull (as wine); steam; foment; digest [chem.]; cook 329.4.

18. insolate, sun; bask, bask in the sun, sun oneself; sun-dry.

19. boil, bile [dial.], stew, simmer, seethe.

20. melt, run, colliquate [med.], fuse, flux; smelt; thaw, thaw out, unfreeze; defrost, deice.

21 ignite, fire, set fire to, set on fire, build a fire, kindle, enkindle, inflame, light, light up, strike a light, apply the match or torch to, burn, conflagrate; rekindle, relight, relume; backfire [U.S.]; feed, feed the fire, stoke, stoke the fire, add fuel to the flame; bank; poke or stir up the fire, blow up the fire, fan the flame.

22. catch on fire, catch fire, catch, take, burn, flame, blaze, blaze up, burst into flame.

23. burn, torrefy, scorch, parch, sear; singe, swinge [dial.]; blister, vesicate; cauterize, brand, burn in; char, coal, carbonize; scorify; calcine; oxidize, oxidate; deflagrate [chem.]; cupel; burn off, nigger off [local U.S. & Can.]; blaze, flame 327.21.

24. burn up, incinerate, cremate, consume, burn or reduce to ashes, burn to a cinder; burn down, burn to the ground, go up in smoke.

ADJS. 25. heating, warming, chafing, calorific; calefactory, calefactive, calefacient; burning 327.25, 27; cauterant, cauterizing; calcinatory.

26. inflammatory, inflammative, inflaming, kindling, enkindling, lighting; incendiary.

27. inflammable, combustible, burnable, accendible, fiery.

28. heated, het or het up [dial.], warmed; gas-heated, steam-heated, electric-heated; superheated; overheated; reheated, recooked, warmed-over, réchauffé [F.]; hot 327.25.

29. burnt, burned; scorched, blistered, parched, singed, seared, charred, adust; sunburned, sunburnt; burnt up, incinerated, cremated, consumed, consumed by fire; ashen, ashy.

30. molten, melted, fused; meltable, fusible.

31. heaters

bedpan	infrared heater
bloom heater	infrared lamp
brazier	ingot heater
brick oven	iron heater
Bunsen burner	kiln 574.5
calefactory [eccl.]	oven
defroster	plate heater
deicer	preheater
dielectric heater	radiator
dielectric preheater	radio-frequency
Dutch oven	heater
electric blanket	register
electric heater	rivet heater
electric pad	solar heater
electronic heater	steam heater
fireless heater	steam radiator
foot warmer	sun lamp
forge	superheater
gas heater	tire heater
heat lamp	warming house
high-frequency	[eccl.]
heater	warming pad
induction heater	warming pan
induction heating	water heater
machine	water oven

32. stoves, furnaces

athanor [alchemy]	kitchener [Eng.]
Bessemer furnace	kitchen range
blast furnace	Norwegian stove
calefactor	oil stove
coal stove	open-hearth
coke oven	furnace
cookstove	potbellied stove
Dutch stove	range
electric-arc furnace	reverberatory,
electric furnace	reverbatory
electric range	furnace
electric stove	salamander,
footstove	salamander stove
Franklin stove	scorifier
gas range	smelter
gas stove	

33. cookers

baker [U.S.]	grill
barbecue	griller
boiler	infrared broiler
broiler	infrared cooker
chafer	percolator
chafing dish or pan	pots, pans 192.13,
coffee maker	14
corn popper	pressure cooker
Dutch oven	roaster
electric cooker	samovar
electric roaster	toaster
electric toaster	waffle iron
fireless cooker	waterless cooker
fry-cooker	

329. COOKING

NOUNS 1. **cooking, cookery, cuisine, culinary art**; baking, toasting, roasting, frying, boiling, stewing, basting, braising, poaching, shirring [U.S.], barbecuing, brewing, grilling, broiling, pan-broiling; broil.

2. **cook**, kitchener; **chef**, *chef de cuisine* [F.]; fry cook.

3. **kitchen, cookroom,** cookery, scullery, cuisine; kitchenette [U.S.]; **galley,** caboose or camboose; cookhouse; **bakery,** bakehouse.

VERBS 4. **cook,** do, prepare; boil, stew, simmer, parboil; brew; poach, coddle; bake, fire, oven-bake; scallop, escallop; shirr [U.S.]; roast; toast; fry, griddle, pan; sauté; frizz, frizzle; sear, braise, brown; broil, grill, pan-broil; barbecue; fricassee; steam; devil; curry; baste, jipper [naut. slang]; **do to a turn,** do to rags [coll.].

ADJS. 5. **cooking, culinary.**

6. **cooked,** stewed, fried, barbecued, curried, fricasseed, deviled, sautéd, shirred [U.S.], toasted; roasted, roast; broiled, grilled, pan-broiled; seared, braised, browned; boiled, biled [dial.]; parboiled; poached, coddled; baked, fired, oven-baked; scalloped, escalloped.

7. **done, well-done, well-cooked,** *bien cuit* [F.]; overcooked, **overdone.**

8. **underdone,** undercooked, not done, rare, *saignant* [F.]; sodden, sad [dial.], fallen.

330. FUEL

NOUNS 1. **fuel, firing; combustible, inflammable;** coal, coke, charcoal, briquette, fireball; peat, turf; carbon, gas carbon; dope, fuel dope; oils 379; gas 400.10.

2. **slack,** coal dust, coom or comb, culm.

3. **firewood,** stovewood, wood; **kindling,** kindlings, kindling wood; brush, brushwood; fagot, bavin [Eng.]; log, backlog, yule log or clog.

4. **lighter,** light, igniter, sparker; pocket lighter, cigar or cigarette lighter; **torch,** flambeau, mussal [India], taper, spill; brand, **firebrand;** portfire; **flint,** flint and steel.

5. **match,** lucifer; lights [chiefly Eng.]; friction match, safety match, vesuvian, vesta, fusee; Congreve, Congreve match.

6. **tinder,** touchwood; **punk, spunk,** German tinder, amadou; tinder fungus; pyrotechnic sponge; tinderbox.

7. **detonator,** exploder; **cap,** blasting cap; electric detonator or exploder; detonating powder; **primer,** priming; **fuse,** squib [chiefly mining].

VERBS 8. **fuel;** refuel; **coal; stoke,** feed, add fuel to the flame.

ADJS. 9. **coaly,** carbonaceous, carboniferous; anthracite, bituminous, lignitic.

10. coal

anthracite or	flaxseed coal
hard coal	glance coal
bituminous or soft	grate coal
coal	lignite
blind coal	lump coal
broken coal	mustard-seed coal
brown coal	nut coal
buckwheat coal	pea coal
cannel, cannel coal	steamboat coal
chestnut coal	stove coal
egg coal	

11. fuses

base fuse	friction fuse
chemical fuse	point fuse
concussion or	proximity fuse
percussion fuse	time fuse
detonating fuse	variable-time or
electric fuse	VT fuse

331. INCOMBUSTIBILITY

NOUNS 1. **incombustibility, uninflammability,** unburnableness.

2. **extinguishment,** extinction, anni-

hilation, **quenching**, dousing [coll. & dial.], **snuffing**, putting out; **choking, damping, stifling, smothering,** smotheration; fire fighting.

3. **extinguisher,** *extincteur* [F.], **fire extinguisher;** fire apparatus, fire engine, hook-and-ladder truck; carbon tetrachloride, carbon tet; water, soda, acid, foam, wet blanket.

4. **fire fighter, fireman,** fire eater [coll., U.S.]; forest fire fighter; fire department, fire brigade.

5. **fireproofing;** asbestos; amianthus, earth flax, mountain flax; asbestos curtain, fire wall.

VERBS 6. **fireproof,** flameproof.

7. **extinguish, put out, quench,** annihilate, out, dout [dial., Eng.], douse [coll. & dial.], **snuff,** snuff out, blow out, stamp out; **choke, damp, smother, stifle,** slack.

8. **go out, burn out, die,** die out or away; fizzle, **fizzle out** [both coll.].

ADJS. 9. **incombustible, uninflammable,** noninflammable, unburnable; asbestine, asbestic; amianthine.

10. **fireproof, flameproof,** fire-resisting, fire-resistant.

11. **extinguished,** quenched, snuffed, **out.**

332. COLD

NOUNS 1. **cold, coldness, coolness,** coolth [dial. or joc.], **chilliness; chill, nip,** sharp air; **crispness,** briskness, nippiness; **frigidity, iciness,** gelidity, algidity; rawness, bleakness, keenness, sharpness, bitterness, severity, inclemency, rigor, "a hard, dull bitterness of cold" [Whittier]; cool (as, the *cool* of the evening); freezing point.

2. (sensation of cold) **chill,** chilliness, chilling; shivering, **shivers, cold shivers,** didders, dithers [chiefly dial.], chattering of the teeth; creeps, **cold creeps** [both coll.]; goose flesh, goose pimples, goose or duck bumps [dial.], horripilation; ache, aching.

3. **cold weather,** bleak weather, raw weather, wintry weather, **freezing weather,** zero weather, subzero weather; **cold wave,** snap, **cold snap;** freeze, frost; winter, depth of winter, hard winter; wintry wind 402.8.

4. **cold front,** polar front, wind-shift line, squall line [all meteorol.].

5. (cold place) Siberia, Novaya Zemlya, Alaska, Iceland, Greenland, Greenland's icy mountains; North Pole, South Pole; Frigid Zones; arctic, Arctic Circle or Zone; antarctic, Antarctic Circle or Zone.

6. **ice,** frozen water; ice needle or crystal; **icicle,** iceshockle or iceshogle [Scot. & dial., Eng.]; ice sheet, ice field; **floe, ice floe,** ice raft, ice pack; **iceberg,** berg; calf; snowberg; **icecap,** jokul [Iceland]; **glacier,** glacieret, glaciation, "motionless torrents, silent cataracts" [Coleridge]; Piedmont glacier; icefall; **sleet, glaze,** glazed frost; snow ice; firm, névé, granular snow; ground ice, anchor ice, frazil [Can. & North. U.S.]; lolly; sludge, slob; ice cubes; dry ice; icequake.

7. **hail,** hailstone; soft hail, graupel [meteorol.]; **hailstorm,** ice storm [meteorol.].

8. **frost,** Jack Frost; **hoarfrost,** hoar, rime, rime frost, white frost; black frost; hard frost, sharp frost; frost smoke.

9. **snow,** "the soft and slumbrous snow" [Elizabeth Akers Allen], "the frolic architecture of the snow" [Emerson]; **snowfall,** "feather'd rain" [Wm. Strode], "the whitening shower" [James Thomson], "a flaky torrent" [George Crabbe]; **snowstorm,** snow blast, snow squall, flurry, blizzard; **snowflake,** flake, crystal; snow dust; **snowdrift,** snowbank, snow wreath [Eng.], snow roller, driven snow; snowcap; snow blanket, snow bed, snow field, mantle of snow; snowscape; snowland; snowball; snowslide, snowslip; snow slush, **slush,** slosh.

VERBS 10. **be cold, shiver, quiver,** quake, shake, tremble, shudder, didder, dither [chiefly dial.]; **chatter; chill,** have a chill, have the cold shivers; **freeze,** freeze to death, perish with cold, starve [dial.]; horripilate.

11. (make cold) **chill,** chill to the bone or marrow, make one shiver, make one's teeth chatter; **nip,** bite, cut, **pierce,** penetrate, go through; **freeze,** freeze to death; numb, benumb; refrigerate 333.10.

12. **hail, sleet, frost, snow;** snow in [U.S.]; snow under.

ADJS. 13. **cool,** coolish; chill, **chilly; fresh,** bracing, **invigorating,** stimulating; cool as a cucumber, cool as custard.

14. **unheated,** unwarmed; unmelted, unthawed.

15. **cold, crisp, brisk,** nipping, **nippy,** snappy [coll.], **raw, bleak, keen, sharp,** bitter, biting, pinching, cutting, **piercing,** penetrating, inclement, severe, rigorous; snow-cold; **icy,** icelike, **ice-cold,** glacial; **frigid,** gelid, algid; below zero, subzero; **freezing,** freezing cold, numbing; **wintry,**

wintery, winterlike, hiemal, brumal, hibernal; arctic, Siberian, boreal, hyperborean; cold as ice, cold as marble, cold as a frog, cold as charity, cold as Christmas, colder than blixens, cold enough to freeze the tail off a brass monkey.

16. (feeling cold) **cold, cool, chilly; shivering,** shivery, shaky, dithery [chiefly dial.]; aguish, aguey; chattering, with chattering teeth; **frozen,** half-frozen, frozen to death, starved [dial.], *transi de froid* [F., overcome with cold], so cold one could spit ice cubes.

17. **frosty,** frostlike; **frosted,** frost-beaded, frost-chequered, **hoary,** hoar-frosted, rime-frosted; frost-riven, frost-rent; frosty-faced, frosty-whiskered; frost-bound, frost-fettered.

18. **snowy,** snowlike; snow-blown, snow-drifted, snow-driven; **snow-covered,** snow-clad, snow-mantled, snow-robed, snow-sprinkled, snow-lined, snow-encircled, snow-laden, snow-loaded, snow-hung; **snow-capped,** snow-crested, snow-crowned, snow-tipped, snow-topped; snow-feathered; snow-bearded; snow-still.

19. frozen out *or* in, **snowbound, icebound.**

20. **cold-blooded,** heterothermic, poikilothermic.

333. REFRIGERATION

Reduction of Temperature.—NOUNS 1. **refrigeration,** infrigidation; **cooling, chilling; freezing,** glacification, glaciation, congelation, congealment; refreezing, regelation; mechanical refrigeration, electric refrigeration, electronic refrigeration, gas refrigeration; quick freezing, deep freezing, sharp freezing, dehydrofreezing; air cooling.

2. **frostbite, chilblains,** kibe.

3. **cooler,** chiller; water cooler, air cooler; ventilator 401.11; surface cooler; ice pail, wine cooler; ice bag, ice pack, cold pack.

4. **refrigerator,** refrigeratory, **icebox,** ice chest; Frigidaire [trade name], frigidaire [coll.]; electric refrigerator, electronic refrigerator, gas refrigerator; refrigerator car, reefer [tramp slang, U.S.].

5. **freezer, deep-freeze,** deep-freezer, quick-freezer, sharp-freezer; ice-cream freezer; ice machine, freezing machine, refrigerating machine *or* engine; **ice plant,** icehouse, refrigerating plant.

6. **cold storage; frozen food locker,** locker, freeze locker, locker plant; frigidarium; coolhouse.

7. (cooling agent) **coolant; refrigerant;** ice, dry ice, ice cubes; freezing mixture, liquid air, ammonia, carbon dioxide, ether.

8. antifreeze.

9. refrigerating engineering, refrigerating engineer.

VERBS 10. **refrigerate,** infrigidate; **cool, chill;** refresh, freshen; ice, ice-cool; water-cool, air-cool; ventilate 401.12.

11. **freeze,** ice, glacify, glaciate, congeal; **deep-freeze,** quick-freeze, sharp-freeze; **freeze to death,** starve [dial.]; **nip,** blight, blast; frost, frostbite; refreeze, regelate; be cold 332.10, 11.

ADJS. 12. **refrigerative,** refrigeratory, refrigerant, frigorific(al), algific; **cooling, chilling; freezing,** congealing; quick-freezing, deep-freezing, sharp-freezing; freezable, glaciable.

13. **cooled, chilled;** iced, ice-cooled; air-cooled, water-cooled.

14. **frozen,** froze, glacial, gelid, congealed; **icy,** ice, icelike; deep-froze *or* ~ frozen, quick-froze *or* ~ frozen, sharp-froze *or* ~ frozen; frostbitten, frostnipped.

15. antifreeze, antifreezing.

334. LIGHT

NOUNS 1. **light,** radiant *or* luminous energy [phys.], **illumination, radiation, radiance** *or* radiancy, irradiance *or* irradiancy, irradiation, emanation; "the light of Heaven" [Homer], "God's first creature" [Bacon], "God's eldest daughter" [Fuller], "offspring of Heav'n firstborn" [Milton], "the first of painters" [Emerson], "the prime work of God" [Milton]; highlight; side light; photosensitivity; luminary 335.

2. **shine,** shininess, **luster, sheen, gloss,** glint; **glow, gleam; incandescence,** candescence; shining light; afterglow.

3. **lightness, luminousness,** luminosity; **lucidity,** lucence *or* lucency, translucency.

4. **brightness, brilliance** *or* brilliancy, **splendor,** radiant splendor, **radiance** *or* radiancy, resplendence *or* resplendency, **vividness,** flamboyance; effulgence, refulgence *or* refulgency, fulgor *or* fulgour; **glare,** blare, blaze; bright light, brilliant light, blazing light, glaring light, dazzling light, blinding light; streaming light, flood of light.

5. **ray,** radiation, **beam, gleam,** leam [Scot. & North. Eng.], **stream, streak, pencil, glade, patch,** ray ~, beam etc. of light; streamer, stream of light; violet ray, ultraviolet ray, infrared ray; actinic ray *or*

light, actinism; atomic beam, atomic ray; solar rays; radiorays 326.3.

6. **flash, blaze, flare, flame,** coruscation, **gleam, glint, glance;** flash ~, gleam ~ of light, flashlight; facula [astron.].

7. **glitter, glimmer, shimmer, twinkle, blink;** sparkle, spark; **scintillation,** scintilla; **glisten,** glister; glittering, glimmering, shimmering, twinkling, blinking.

8. **flicker, flutter, dance, quiver;** flickering, fluttering, dancing, quivering, lambency; wavering or flickering light, "lambent flame" [Dryden], "the lambent easy light" [ibid.].

9. **reflection,** reflectance; blink, iceblink snowblink, water blink.

10. **daylight,** dayshine, light of day; day, daytime, daytide [poetic]; **sunlight, sunshine,** shine; noonlight, midday sun, noonday or noontide light; broad daylight, full sun; twilight 134.3; dawn 133.3, 4; sunburst. **sunbeam,** sun spark, ray of sunshine.

11 **moonlight, moonshine,** moonglow; **moonbeam,** moonglade [poetic].

12. **starlight,** starshine.

13. **luminescence,** autoluminescence, cathode luminescence, chemiluminescence or chemicoluminescence, crystalloluminescence, electroluminescence, photoluminescence, radioluminescence, thermoluminescence, triboluminescence; bioluminescence, noctiluscence; **fluorescence,** tribofluorescence; **phosphorescence,** tribophosphorescence; *ignis fatuus* [L.], will-o'-the-wisp, will-with-the-wisp, wisp, jack-o'-lantern; friar's lantern; fata morgana; fox fire; St. Elmo's light or fire, corposant; double corposant, Castor and Pollux [naut.]; ectoplasm, exteriorized protoplasm.

14. **halo, nimbus,** aura, aureole, **aureola,** circle, ring, glory, *vesica piscis* [L.; eccl. art]; solar halo, lunar halo; **corona,** solar corona, lunar corona; parhelion, parhelic circle or ring, mock son, sun dog; anthelion, antisun, countersun; paraselene, mock moon, moon dog.

15. (nebulous light) nebula 374.14; zodiacal light, Gegenschein, counterglow.

16. **polar lights,** aurora; northern lights, **aurora borealis,** merry dancers; southern lights, **aurora australis;** aurora polaris; aurora glory; streamer, polar ray.

17. **lightning,** flash or stroke of lightning, fulmination, bolt, **bolt of lightning,** bolt from the blue, **thunderbolt,** thunderstroke, thunderball, firebolt, levin bolt or

brand; "flying flame" [Tennyson], "the lightning's gleaming rod" [Joaquin Miller], "oak-cleaving thunderbolts" [Shakespeare]; fork or forked lightning, chain lightning, globular or ball lightning, summer or heat lightning, sheet lightning, dark lightning [meteorol.]; Jupiter Fulgur or Fulminator [Rom. myth.].

18. (artificial illumination) candlelight, candleshine, rushlight; lamplight, lantern light, torchlight; midnight oil; firelight; incandescent light, electric light, fluorescent light, zircon light; gaslight; spotlight, limelight, footlights.

19. **lighting, illumination,** enlightenment; radiation, irradiation; gaslighting, electric lighting, incandescent lighting, fluorescent lighting, glow lighting, arc lighting; direct lighting, indirect lighting; floodlighting, overhead lighting, stage lighting, decorative lighting, festoon lighting, strip lighting, spot lighting, diffused lighting, cove lighting.

20. **illuminant,** luminant; electricity; gas, illuminating gas; oil, petroleum, benzine; gasoline, petrol [chiefly Eng.]; kerosene, coal oil; luminary 335.

21. (measurement of light) **candle power,** luminous power, luminous flux, flux, intensity, light; quantum, **light quantum,** photon; unit of light, unit of flux; candle, international candle, British candle, hefner candle; foot-candle, candle-foot, decimal candle, bougie decimale [F.]; lux, candle-meter; lumen, candle lumen; candle-hour, lamp-hour, lumen-hour.

22. (science of light) **photics,** photology, photometry; **optics,** geometrical optics, physical optics; dioptrics, catoptrics; actinology, actinometry; heliology, heliometry, heliography.

VERBS 23. **shine,** shine forth, **burn, give light,** incandesce; **glow,** gloze, beam, **gleam,** glint, glance; **flash, flare, blaze, flame,** fulgurate; **radiate,** spread light; be bright, shine brightly, beacon; **glare;** daze, dazzle, bedazzle.

24. **glitter, glimmer, shimmer, twinkle, blink,** spangle, coruscate; **sparkle,** spark, scintillate; **glisten,** glister, glisk [chiefly Scot.].

25. **flicker,** bicker, **flutter, waver, dance,** quiver.

26. **luminesce,** phosphoresce, fluoresce.

27. **grow light,** grow bright, light, lighten, brighten; dawn, break.

28. **illuminate, illumine, illume** [po-

etic], luminate, **light, light up, lighten,** enlighten, brighten, irradiate; **shed light upon,** cast or throw light upon, shine upon, overshine; spotlight, highlight; floodlight; beacon.

29. light, strike a light, turn or **switch on the light;** relight, reilluminate, reillumine, relume.

ADJS. **30. luminous,** luminant, luminative, luminificent, luminiferous, illuminant; **incandescent,** candescent; **lustrous,** orient; **radiant,** irradiative; **shining,** shiny, burning, lamping, streaming; **beaming,** beamy; **gleaming,** gleamy, glinting; **glowing,** aglow; rutilant, rutilous; **sunny, sunshiny,** bright and sunny, light as day; starry, starlike, starbright.

31. light, lightish, lightsome; **lucid,** lucent, luculent, relucent; **translucent,** translucid, pellucid, transparent [poetic]; **clear,** serene; **cloudless,** unclouded, unobscured.

32. bright, brilliant, vivid, splendid, splendrous or splendorous, splendent, **resplendent,** bright and shining; fulgid, fulgent, effulgent, refulgent; **flamboyant,** flaming; **glaring,** glary, garish; **dazzling,** bedazzling.

33. shiny, shining, lustrous, **glossy,** glassy, glacé [F.], **sheeny, polished,** burnished, shined.

34. flashing, flashy, blazing, flaming, flaring, fulgurant, fulgurating, meteoric.

35. glittering, glimmering, shimmering, twinkling, blinking, glistening, glistering; glittery, glimmery, glimmerous, shimmery, twinkly, blinky, spangly; **sparkling, scintillating,** scintillant, scintillescent.

36. flickering, bickering, **fluttering, wavering, dancing,** quivering, lambent; flickery, flicky [coll.], aflicker, fluttery, wavery, quivery.

37. luminescent, photogenic; **electroluminescent,** photoluminescent, radioluminescent, thermoluminescent, triboluminescent; chemiluminescent, chemicoluminescent; **phosphorescent,** tribophosphorescent; **fluorescent,** tribofluorescent; autoluminescent, self-luminous, self-luminescent; bioluminescent, noctilucent.

38. illuminated, luminous, **lightened,** enlightened, **lighted, lit, lit up;** irradiated, irradiate; **alight,** aglow, ablaze, in a blaze; lamplit, lanternlit, candlelit, torchlit, gaslit, firelit; sunlit, moonlit, starlit; spangled, bespangled, studded; star-spangled, starstudded.

39. illuminating, illumining, **lighting, lightening,** enlightening, brightening.

40. luminary, photic; photologic(al), photometric(al); heliological, heliographic; actinic, photoactinic; catoptric(al); luminal.

41. photosensitive.

42. light meters

actinometer	polarimeter
fluorometer	pyrheliometer
heliometer	radiometer
illuminometer	reflectometer
interferometer	refractometer
lucimeter	spectrophotometer
photometer	

335. LUMINARY

Source of Light.—NOUNS **1. luminary,** illuminator, luminant, illuminant, **light, glim** [slang], luster or lustre; lamp, lantern, candle, taper, torch [all fig.]; "a lamp unto my feet, and a light unto my path" [Bible]; fire 327.12; sun, moon, stars 374.

2. candle, taper; dip, farthing dip, tallow dip [coll.]; tallow, tallow candle; wax, wax candle, bougie; bayberry candle; rush candle, rushlight; corpse candle, death light.

3. torch, flaming torch, flambeau, lamp [poetic], brand [poetic], mussal [India], link.

4. traffic lights, stop-and-go lights; stop or red light, go or green light.

5. firefly, fire beetle, glowfly, lampfly, lightning bug [U.S.]; candle fly, lantern fly; **glowworm,** fireworm.

6. chandelier, gaselier, gasoliery, electrolier, luster; corona, corona lucis, crown, circlet.

7. wick, taper; candlewick, lampwick.

8. lamps, lights

aphlogistic lamp	electric arc
arc lamp	electric candle
Argand lamp	electric light or
baby spotlight	lamp
barn lantern	electric torch
battery lamp	filament lamp
bed lamp	Finsen light or
bridge lamp	lamp
broadside	flame lamp
bull's-eye, bull's-	flaming arc
eye lantern	flash
calcium lamp	flash bulb
carbon light or	flasher
lamp	flash gun
Carcel lamp	flashing lamp
Chinese lantern	[motion pictures]
cresset	flash lamp
dark lantern	flashlight, flashing
daylight lamp	light
desk light	

floodlight, flood
  lamp
floor lamp
fluorescent light
focus lamp
gaslight, gas lamp
glow light or lamp
headlight, head
  lamp
Hefner lamp
incandescent
  electric lamp
incandescent light
  or lamp
jack-o'-lantern
Japanese lantern
klieg light
lampion
lamplet
lantern
light bulb
limelight
magic lantern
magnetite arc lamp
mercury-arc lamp
mercury lamp
mercury-vapor
  lamp
miner's lamp
moderator lamp
Moore light, lamp
  or tube
neon light or lamp
Nernst lamp
night light or
  lamp
oil lamp

osmium lamp
petane lamp
photoflash lamp
photoflood lamp
pilot light or
  lamp
pin-up light
police lantern
projector lamp
quartz lamp
railroad lantern
reading lamp
safety lamp
searchlight, search
  lamp
searchlight lantern
Sheringham
  daylight lamp
shunt lamp
side lamp
side light
spotlight, spot
stop light
sun arc
sun lamp
sun or sunlight
  burner
sun spot
table lamp
taillight, tail lamp
tantalum lamp
tungsten lamp
uviol lamp
vanity lamp
vapor lamp
veilleuse [F.]
zircon lamp

9. beacons, signal lights

balefire
beacon fire
candlebomb
flare
flare light
flare-up
fusee, fuzee
lighthouse
lightship
pharos

rocket
Roman candle
signal beacon
signal lamp
signal lantern
signal light
signal rocket
skyrocket
watchfire

10. aviation beacons

airport beacon
airway beacon
anchor light
approach light
blinker light
boundary light
ceiling light or
  projector
course light
fixed light
flashing light

identification light
landing-direction
  light
landing light
landmark beacon
Lindbergh light
marker
navigation light
obstruction light
position light

11. light holders

candelabra lamp
  holder
candelabrum
candleholder
candlestand
candlestick

chandelier
gas fixture
girandole
lamp holder
lamp socket
lampstand

light fixture
light socket
sconce

torch holder
torch staff

12. burners

Argand burner
filament
fishtail burner
gas burner
gas jet
gas mantle

incandescent
  mantle
jet
mantle
moderator
Welsbach mantle

336. DARKNESS

Absence of Light.—NOUNS 1. darkness, dark, lightlessness; obscurity, obscure; tenebrity, tenebrousness; sunlessness, moonlessness, starlessness; pitch-darkness, pitch-blackness, intense darkness, Cimmerian darkness, Stygian darkness, Egyptian darkness, darkness invisible; "obscure darkness" [Bible], "the palpable obscure" [Milton], "the suit of night" [Shakespeare], "darkness which may be felt" [Bible]; blackness, swarthiness (dark color) 364; night 134.4.

2. gloom, gloomth, gloominess, dismalness, dreariness, luridness; somberness, sombrousness, somber; bleakness, desolation.

3. shadow, shade, shadiness, umbra, "shadows numberless" [Keats]; thick shade, gloom; mere shadow, "the shadow of a shade" [Aeschylus]; penumbra; moonshade; silhouette.

4. darkishness, darksomeness, duskiness; duskness; murkiness, murk [chiefly dial.]; semidarkness, semidark, partial darkness, half-light, demi-jour [F.]; dusk 134.3; twilight 133.4, 134.3.

5. dimness, dim; faintness, paleness; indistinctness, vagueness; blurriness, bleariness; mistiness, haziness, fogginess, filminess, cloudiness, nebulousness; blur, blear, film, mist, haze, fog; dimmer.

6. dullness, deadness, flatness, lifelessness, coldness, drabness, leadenness, glassiness; lackluster, lacklusterness, lusterlessness; mat, mat finish.

7. darkening, dimming; obscuration, obfuscation; shadowing, shading, overshadowing, overshading, overshadowment, adumbration; clouding, overclouding, nubilation, gathering of the clouds; misting, fogging; blurring, blearing; blackening 364.5; extinguishment 331.2.

8. blackout, dimout, brownout.

9. eclipse, occultation; total eclipse, partial eclipse, central eclipse, annular eclipse; solar eclipse, lunar eclipse.

VERBS 10. **darken**, bedarken; **obscure**, obfuscate; **eclipse**, occultate; **black out**, blot out; **overcast**, darken over; **shadow**, **shade**, cast a shadow, spread a shadow *or* shade over, encompass with shadow, overshadow, adumbrate; **cloud**, becloud, encloud, cloud over, overcloud, nubilate; **gloom**, somber, cast a gloom over; murk; blacken 364.7.

11. **dim**, bedim; **fog**, befog; **mist**, enmist, bemist; **cloud**, cloud over; **blur**, blear; **dull**, mat; **tone down.**

12. **extinguish** 331.7; **turn out** *or* **off**, turn *or* switch off the light, kill the light [motion-picture cant].

13. **grow dark**, **darken**, darkle, lower *or* lour; gloom, gloam [chiefly Scot.]; dusk; **dim**, fade, pale, "pale his uneffectual fire" [Shakespeare]; cloud over, etc. 336.10, 11.

ADJS. 14. **dark**, **black**, darksome, darkling; **lightless**, unlighted, **unilluminated**, unlit, shorn of its beams; **obscure**, caliginous, clothed *or* shrouded in darkness; tenebrous, tenebrious, tenebrose; **pitchdark**, pitch-black, pitchy; dark as pitch, "dark as a wolf's mouth" [Scott], dark as the inside of a black cat; night-dark, nightblack, dark *or* black as night; night-clad, night-cloaked, night-enshrouded, nightmantled, night-veiled, night-hid, nightfilled; sunless, moonless, starless; black (color) 364.8.

15. **gloomy**, gloomful, dark and gloomy, **dismal**, drear, **dreary**, **somber**, sombrous, gray, black, lowering *or* louring, lurid, dusky, swart [poetic], **funereal**, **melancholy**, uncheerful; **bleak**, desolate; Cimmerian, Stygian; cloudy, clouded, overcast; ill-lighted, ill-lit.

16. **darkish**, darksome, **semidark**; **dusky**, dusk; **murky**, murkish, murk [poetic & dial.]; dark-colored 364.9.

17. **shadowy**, **shady**, bosky, shaded; overshadowed, overshaded, umbrageous.

18. **dim**, dimmish, dimmy, dimpsy [dial., Eng.]; **faint**, **weak**, **pale**; obscure, **indistinct**, vague, shadowed forth; nebulous, nubilous; **overcast**, **cloudy**, hazy, **filmy**, **misty**, **foggy**; clouded, filmed, misted, fogged; **blurred**, blurry, bleared, bleary, blear.

19. **lackluster**, lacklustrous, **lusterless**; **dull**, **dead**, deadened, **lifeless**, somber, drab, cold, **glassy**, glazed, **leaden**, dun, **flat**, mat.

20. obscuring, obscurant.

ADVS. 21. **in the dark**, darkling, in darkness; in the night, in the dark of night, in the dead of night, at *or* by night.

337. SHADE

A Thing That Shades.—NOUNS 1. **shade**, shader, **shelter**, **screen**, **shield**, protection, **curtain**, veil, purdah [India]; cover 227.2; shadow 336.3.

2. **eyeshade**, eyeshield, opaque; blinkers, **blinds**, blinders; **blindfold**; goggles, colored spectacles, smoked glasses, sunglasses.

3. **lamp shade**; moonshade; globe, light globe; **light shield**; fin, blinker, ear, gobo, nigger [all motion picture].

4. **light filter**, filter, diffusing screen; butterfly, silk, gauze [all motion picture]; gelatin filter, jelly [motion picture]; celluloid filter, cello [motion picture]; frosted lens, frost [motion picture].

VERBS 5. **shade**, **shelter**, **protect**; **screen**, **shield**, veil, curtain; shutter; draw the curtains, put up *or* close the shutters; cover 227.21; overshadow 336.10.

ADJS. 6. **shading**, **sheltering**, **protecting**; **screening**, **shielding**, veiling, curtaining; covering 227.37.

7. **shaded**, **sheltered**, **protected**; **screened**, **shielded**, veiled, curtained; shady 336.17.

8. **shades**

awning	screen
baldachino	shield
bamboo shade *or*	shutter
screen	smoke screen
blind	[mil.]
canopy	sunbonnet
curtain	sun hat
hat 230.25, 59	sun helmet
jalousie [F.]	sunshade
lamp shade	tent 227.8, 43
occulter, occulting	umbrella 227.7
screen	veil
panoply	Venetian blind
parasol	visor
pith helmet	window curtain
portiere	window screen
roof 227.6, 42	window shade
sash curtain	window shutter

338. TRANSPARENCY

NOUNS 1. **transparency**, transparence, perviousness, show-through; **translucence** *or* translucency, lucence *or* lucency, translucidity; **lucidity**, pellucidity, **clearness**, clarity, limpidity; **crystallinity**, crystalclearness; **glassiness**, glasslikeness, vitreosity, hyalescence; **diaphanousness**, sheerness, thinness; **gossameriness**, gauziness.

2. **glass, glassware, glasswork, vitrics;** stemware; pane, windowpane.

VERBS 3. be transparent, show through.

ADJS. 4. **transparent,** pervious; **translucent,** lucent, translucid; **lucid,** pellucid, **clear,** limpid; **crystalline,** crystal, **crystalclear,** clear as crystal; **diaphanous,** diaphane; sheer, thin; **gossamery,** gossamer, gossamered, gauzy.

5. **glass, glassy,** glasslike; vitreous, vitreal, vitrean, vitriform; hyaline, hyalescent; hyalinocrystalline [min.].

6. transparent things

beryl	Lucite
Cellophane	mica
celluloid	moonstone
chalcedony	oilpaper
chiffon	oil silk
chrysolite	onionpeel
citrine	onionskin
Clearsite	quartz
crystal	sheers
Crystalite	silk
diamond	tissue
diaphane	tissue paper
gossamer	veil
hyaline	water
hyalite	window
isinglass	

7. glass

blown glass	opal glass
Celo-Glass	opaline
CM-glass	ornamental glass
CF-glass	plastic glass
crown glass	plate glass
cryolite glass	Plexiglas
crystal	porcelain glass
crystal glass	pressed glass
cut glass	Pyrex
etched glass	safety glass
Fiberglas	Sandwich glass
flint glass	sheet glass
Fostoria	stained glass
frosted glass	Steuben glass
glass brick	Swedish glass
hobnail glass	uranium glass
Lalique glass	Venetian glassware
laminated glass	Vitaglass
milk glass	wire or wired glass

339. SEMITRANSPARENCY

NOUNS 1. **semitransparency,** semipellucidity, semidiaphaneity; semiopacity.

2. **pearliness, opalescence, milkiness;** pearl, opal, mother-of-pearl, nacre.

VERBS 3. **frost,** frost over.

ADJS. 4. **semitransparent,** semitranslucent, semipellucid, semidiaphanous; semiopaque; frosty, frosted.

5. **pearly,** nacreous, **milky, opalescent,** opaline, opaloid.

340. OPAQUENESS

NOUNS 1. **opaqueness,** opacity, intransparency, nontranslucency, imperviousness, adiaphonousness; thickness, density; **darkness, obscurity;** obfuscation, nubilation; **cloudiness,** fogginess, mistiness, haziness, filminess; smokiness, fuliginousness; **murkiness,** muddiness, dirtiness; turbidity, turbidness; opaque.

VERBS 2. opaque, **darken, obscure,** obfuscate; **cloud,** becloud, mist, bemist, fog, haze, smoke, film; murk, muddy.

ADJS. 3. **opaque,** intransparent, nontranslucent, adiaphanous, impervious; thick, dense; **dark, obscure,** obfuscated; **cloudy,** nubilous, foggy, misty, hazy, filmy; smoky, fuliginous; **murky,** murkish, muddy, dirty, turbid.

341. ELECTRICITY

NOUNS 1. **electricity,** pyroelectricity, photoelectricity, piezoelectricity, thermoelectricity, faradic electricity, animal electricity, atmospheric electricity; static electricity, friction electricity, franklinic electricity; voltaic electricity, voltaelectricity, dynamic or current electricity; voltaism, galvanism; magnetic electricity, magnetoelectricity; positive electricity, negative electricity.

2. **electric current,** electric stream, electric fluid, juice [slang]; direct current, D.C.; alternating current, A.C.; free alternating current, single-phase alternating current, three-phase alternating current; multiphase current, rotary current; high-frequency current, low-frequency current; galvanic current, voltaic current; magnetizing current, exciting current; active current, watt current; reactive current, wattless or idle current; absorption current, conduction current, convection current, displacement current, dielectric displacement current, ionization current, oscillating current, thermoelectric current; cycle.

3. **electric field,** static field, electrostatic field; magnetic field, magnetic field of currents.

4. **circuit,** path; galvanic circuit or circle, complete circuit, loop [cant], closed circuit, live circuit, hot circuit; open or broken circuit, break, dead circuit; branch or lateral circuit, leg [slang]; multiple circuit or connection, multiple series, series multiple or parallel; multiplex circuit, mux

[slang]; circuital field, vector field; short circuit, short.

5. **charge,** electric charge, unit quantity; live wire.

6. **discharge,** electric discharge; aperiodic discharge, arc discharge, brush discharge, disruptive discharge, electrodeless discharge, glow discharge, oscillatory discharge, silent discharge, stratified discharge; **arc,** A.C. arc, Poulsen arc, arc column; **spark,** electric spark; spark gap; **shock,** electric shock, galvanic shock.

7. **magnetism, electromagnetism,** magnetic attraction; magnetization; diamagnetism, paramagnetism, ferromagnetism; residual magnetism, magnetic remanence; magnetic memory, magnetic retentiveness; magnetic elements, magnetic dip *or* inclination, magnetic variation *or* declination, magnetic intensity; hysteresis, magnetic hysteresis, magnetic friction, magnetic lag *or* retardation, magnetic creeping; permeability, magnetic permeability, magnetic conductivity; magnetic circuit, magnetic curves, magnetic figures, magnetic flux, magnetic moment, magnetic potential, magnetic viscosity; magnetics.

8. **polarity,** polarization; **pole,** positive pole, negative pole; magnetic pole, magnetic axis.

9. electroaffinity, electric attraction; electric repulsion.

10. (electrical or magnetic force) electromotive force, magnetomotive force; electromotivity, magnetomotivity; magnetic force *or* intensity, magnetic flux density; tube of electric force, electrostatic tube of force, magnetic tube of force; line of force.

11. (electric measures) **amperage, ohmage, voltage, wattage;** amperes, amps [cant]; electron volt, equivalent volt.

12. **resistance,** electric resistance; surface resistance, volume resistance; insulation resistance; **reluctance,** magnetic reluctance *or* resistance; specific reluctance, reluctivity; **reactance,** inductive reactance, capacitive reactance; **impedance.**

13. **conduction,** electric conduction; **conductance,** conductivity; gas conduction, ionic conduction, metallic conduction, liquid conduction, photoconduction; **conductor,** semiconductor, superconductor; **nonconductor,** dielectric.

14. **induction,** electrostatic induction, magnetic induction, electromagnetic induction, electromagnetic induction of currents; self-induction, mutual induction; **inductance,** inductivity.

15. **capacitance,** capacity; collector junction capacitance, emitter junction capacitance, resistance capacitance.

16. **gain,** available gain, current gain, operational gain.

17. **electric power,** electropower; electric horsepower; hydroelectric power, hydroelectricity; power load.

18. **powerhouse,** power station, power plant, central station; hydroelectric plant.

19. **electrician,** electric man, **electrotechnician;** radiotrician 343.27; juicer, juice hand, sparks [all slang]; electragist; circuitman; **maintenance man,** faultsman, trouble man, **trouble shooter** [coll.]; **lineman,** rigger; **groundman,** grunt *or* grunter [slang]; juice gang [slang].

20. **electrotechnologist,** electrobiologist, electrochemist, electrometallurgist, electrophysicist, electrophysiologist, electrical engineer, galvanist.

21. **electrification,** electrization.

22. **electrolysis;** ionization; galvanization, electrogalvanization; electrocoating, electroplating, electrogilding, electrograving, electroetching; ion, cation, anion, thermion; ionogen; electrolyte, nonelectrolyte.

VERBS 23. **electrify,** electricize, electrize, **galvanize;** shock; energize, **charge; generate,** oscillate [cant]; step up, amplify, stiffen; step down; plug in, loop in [cant]; switch on *or* off, turn on *or* off, turn on *or* off the juice [slang]; short-circuit, short.

24. **magnetize, electromagnetize;** demagnetize, degauss.

25. **electrolyze;** ionize; galvanize, electrogalvanize; electroplate, electrogild.

26. insulate, isolate; ground.

ADJS. 27. **electric(al),** electrifying; **galvanic,** voltaic; dynamoelectric, hydroelectric, photoelectric, piezoelectric, pyroelectric, magnetoelectric, voltaelectric; thermoelectric, electrothermal; chemicoelectric, electrochemical; dynamic, electrodynamic, static, electrostatic; electromotive, magnetomotive; electrokinetic; electromechanical; electropneumatic; electroscopic, galvanoscopic; electrometric, galvanometric, voltametric; electroreceptive.

28. **magnetic, electromagnetic;** diamagnetic, paramagnetic, ferromagnetic; **polar,** electropolar.

29. **electrolytic,** hydrolytic; ionic, anionic, cationic, thermionic; ionogenic.

30. electrotechnical, electroballistic, electrobiological, electrochemical, electrometallurgical, electrophysiological.

31. charged, electrified, live, hot; high-tension, low-tension.

32. positive, electropositive, plus; **negative,** electronegative, minus.

33. nonconducting, nonconductive, dielectric.

34. electrics

electrical engineering
electroballistics
electrobiology
electrochemistry
electrodynamics
electrokinematics
electrokinetics
electromechanics
electrometallurgy
electrometry
electronics 342
electrooptics
electrophoto
micrography
electrophysiology
electrophysics
electrostatics
electrotechnics
electrotechnology
electrothermics
galvanism
ionics
magnetics
magnetometry
thermionics
voltaism

35. practical electric units

abampere
abcoulomb
abfarad
abhenry
abmho
abohm
abvolt
ampere
coulomb
erg
farad
henry
joule
kilovolt
kilovolt-ampere
kilowatt
megacoulomb
megafarad
megajoule
megampere
megavolt
megawatt
megohm
mho
milliampere
millihenry
millivolt
ohm
statampere
statcoulomb
statfarad
statvolt
volt
volt-coulomb
watt

36. practical magnetic units

gauss
gilbert
maxwell
oersted
weber

37. rational units

ampere-foot
ampere-hour
ampere-minute
ampere-second
ampere-turn
kilowatt-hour
ohm-mile
volt-second
watt-hour

38. electrical parts and devices

alternator
anode
armature
autoconverter
autostarter
autotransformer
battery charger
brush
cap, plug cap
capacitor
cathode
charger
choking coil
circuit breaker
coil
commutator
compensator
condenser
controller
converter
coupling
cutout
distributor
dynamo
dynamotor
electric column
electric switch
electrode
electrolytic interrupter
electrophorus
electroscope
fuse
galvanoscope
generator
grid
ground
ignition
inductor
inductoscope
insulator
interrupter
jumper
lightning rod or arrester
magnet 287.3
magneto, magneto-electric machine
magnetoscope
oscillator
oscilloscope
outlet
pile
plug
pocket
points
push button
reactor
rectifier
relay
resistance box
resistor
rheoscope
rheostat
rotary gap
self-starter
selsyn
shunt
socket
spark plug
starter
step-down transformer
step-up transformer
switch
synchronous converter
tap
terminal
thermistor
timer
transformer
trickle charger
voltage changer
voltage regulator
voltage transformer
voltaic or galvanic pile

39. batteries

accumulator
atomic battery
cell
dry battery
dry cell
electronic battery
Leyden battery
Leyden jar
primary battery
secondary battery
solar battery
storage battery
storage cell
voltaic battery
wet cell

40. electric meters

ammeter
amperemeter, amperometer
capillary electrometer
coulometer, coulomb meter
dynameter
dynamometer
electrodyna-mometer
electroergometer
electrometer
ergometer
expansion ammeter
faradmeter
galvanometer
magnetometer
megohmmeter
mhometer
milliammeter
millivoltmeter
ohm-ammeter
ohmmeter
potentiometer
quadrant electrometer
rheometer
thermal ammeter
thermocouple
thermocouple meter
thermoelectrometer
thermoelement
variometer
voltameter
voltammeter
voltmeter
voltmeter-milliameter
volt-ohm-milliameter, VOM
watt-hour meter
wattmeter

41. electric wire

battery cable
coaxial cable
electric cable
electric cord

high line
ignition cable
lead
line
power line

telegraph line
telephone line
transmission line
way wire
wire line

342. ELECTRONICS

NOUNS **1. electronics,** radionics; electron physics, electrophysics; avionics, basic conductor physics, electron dynamics, electronic engineering, electron microscopy, electron optics, infrared spectroscopy, mass spectrometry, mass spectroscopy, radiogoniometry, **radiometry,** radioscopy, spectrophotometry, **spectroradiometry,** thermionics, **transistor** physics; X-ray photometry, X-ray spectrometry; photelectronics, photoelectricity, radio **343**; television **344**; radar **345**; automation **348**.

2. (electron theory) electron theory of atoms, electron theory of electricity, electron theory of solids.

3. electron, negatron, cathode particle; positron, positive electron; heavy electron, meson, mesotron or mesoton, barytron; photoelectron; thermion; primary electron, secondary electron; recoil electron; bound electron, surface-bound electron; free electron, wandering electron; spinning electrons, planetary electrons; electron spin; electron pair, lone pair, sharing pair, duplet; shells, electron layers; valence shell, valence electrons, subvalent electrons; electron affinity, relative electron affinity.

4. electronic effect, Edison effect, photoelectric effect.

5. electron emission, thermionic emission, photoelectric emission, collision emission, bombardment emission, secondary emission, field emission; electron ray, cathode ray, anode ray; positive ray, canal ray; glow discharge, cathode luminescence, cathodoluminescence, cathodofluorescence; electron diffraction, crystal diffraction, ring diffraction.

6. electron current, electron flow, electron stream, electron beam; photoelectric current; thermionic current; cathode current, plate current; input current, output current; base current, base signal current; collector current, collector signal current; emitter current, emitter signal current; saturation current.

7. electron volt, equivalent volt; input voltage, output voltage; base signal voltage, collector signal voltage, emitter signal voltage; battery supply voltage; screen-grid voltage; inverse peak voltage; voltage saturation.

8. electronic circuit, equivalent circuit, coupling circuit, flip-flop circuit, trigger circuit, back-to-back switching circuit; rectifier circuit, amplifier circuit, etc.; sinusoidal circuit, nonsinusoidal circuit; astable circuit, monostable circuit, bistable circuit; small signal short circuit, small signal hybrid short circuit; small signal open circuit, small signal hybrid open circuit; printed circuit, wireless circuit.

9. conductance, input conductance, feedback conductance, transfer conductance, output conductance; transconductance, inversion transconductance.

10. resistance, base resistance, collector resistance, emitter resistance; input resistance, output resistance; image-matched input resistance, image-matched output resistance; reverse transfer resistance, forward transfer resistance; load resistance.

11. electron tube, tube, **radio tube, valve,** thermionic tube or valve; **vacuum tube** or valve, discharge tube or valve, vacuum discharge valve.

12. photoelectric tube or cell, phototube, photocell; electron-ray tube, **electric eye.**

13. transistor, germanium triode, germanium crystal triode; photo-transistor.

14. electronic engineer, electronic physicist.

ADJS. **15. electronic;** photoelectronic, **photoelectric;** autoelectronic; thermionic; anodic, cathodic.

16. electron tubes

audion	heptode
beam tetrode	ignitron
Braun tube	kenotron
cathode-ray tube	klystron
cavity magnetron	magnetron
Crookes tube	mercury-vapor tube
diode	monoscope
disk-seal tube	multigrid tube
duodiode	multiplex tube
duodiode-triode	pentagrid
dynatron	pentode
electron-ray tube	phanotron
excitron	phasitron
field-emission X-ray	pliotron
tube	resnatron
gas-filled tube	strobotron
Geissler tube	tetragrid
glow-discharge	tetrode
tube	thyratron
glow tube	trigger tube
grid-glow tube	triode
grid-seal tube	triode-heptode
heptagrid	twin triode

vacuum tube
vapor tube
varistor

X-ray diffraction
  tube
X-ray tube

17. photoelectric tubes and cells

electron-image tube
photoconductive
  cell
photoelectric mul-
  tiplier tube

photomultiplier
  tube
photovoltaic cell
photronic cell

18. special-purpose tubes

amplifier
audio-frequency
  tube
ballast regulator
ballast tube
converter
crystal detector
current regulator
detector
discriminator
doubler
focus tube
generator
iconoscope 344.19
inverter
limiter
mixer

modulator
multiplier
multipurpose tube
multivibrator
oscillator
phase inverter
picture tube
344.18
pulse generator
rectifier
regulator
repeater
transducer
tripler
TR tube (transmit-
  receive)

19. vacuum tube components

anode
cathode
electrode
electron gun
filament
grid
photocathode,

photoelectric
  cathode
plate
screen grid
thermionic cathode
trigatron

20. electronic devices

airborne controls
automatic or robot
  pilot
calutron
cathode-ray oscil-
  lograph
cathode-ray oscil-
  loscope
cytoanalyzer
depth sounder
dielectric heater
dielectric pre-
  heater
electric eye
electrocardiograph
electroencephalo-
  graph
electrograph
electron-diffraction
  camera
electronic air con-
  ditioner
electronic air filter
electronic altimeter
electronic battery
electronic clock
electronic com-
  puter 348.16
electronic detector
electronic drum

electronic fuel
  gauge
electronic heater
electronic nut-
  cracker
electronic oscillator
electronic pilot
electronic precipi-
  tator
electronic recorder
electronic refrigera-
  tor
electronic stencil-
  ing machine
electronic stetho-
  scope
electronic switch
electronic timer
electronic type-
  writer
electron image
  projector
electron lens
electron magnetic
  spectroscope
electron micro-
  graph
electron micro-
  scope
flexowriter type-
  writer

fluorescent tube
  or lamp
germicidal lamp
hearing aid
high-frequency
  heater
image dissector
induction heater
infrared cooker
isotron
magnetic drum
  recorder
magnetic recorder
magnetic tape
  recorder
magnetic wire
  recorder
mass spectrograph
mass spectrometer
mass spectroscope
microwave dia-
  thermy machine
neon tube or light
oscillograph

oscilloscope
photo flash bulb
polarizing micro-
  scope
radio direction
  finder
radio-frequency
  heater
radiosonde
radio telescope
short-wave dia-
  thermy machine
spectroradiometer
thermal timing
  relay
time-delay relay
TR box (transmit-
  receive switch)
ultrasonic elec-
  tronic machine
  tools
video tape recorder
X-ray microscope

21. electronic meters

count-rate meter
duodial
electronic
  chronometer
electronic limit
  gauge
electronic
  potentiometer
electronic
  pyrometer
electronic
  voltmeter
events-per-unit-
  time meter

illuminometer
interferometer
ionization gauge
pH meter
radiomicrometer
sanguinometer
telemeter
tensiometer
thermionic instru-
  ment
time-interval meter
vacuum-tube
  electrometer

22. photosensitive devices

electrophotometer
Geiger counter
  X-ray spectrom-
  eter
infrared beam
  projector
infrared telescope
photoelectric
  colorimeter

photoelectric
  image converter
photoelectric pin-
  hole detector
photoelectric sorter
spectrophotometer
X-ray photometer
X-ray spectrometer

343. RADIO

NOUNS 1. radio, wireless [Eng.]; high
fidelity, hi-fi [slang]; full fidelity, true fidelity; radiophony, radiotelegraphy 558.4.

2. radio electronics, radiotechnology, radio engineering, communication engineering; radiodynamics, radiogoniometry, ra-
dioacoustics; conelrad (Control of Electromagnetic Radiation for Civil Defense).

3. radio set, receiver, receiving set,
radio, wireless [Eng.], wireless set [Eng.],
set; wrist radio, Dick Tracy [slang]; cabinet, console, housing.

4. speaker, loudspeaker, amplifier, bull-

horn [esp. Navy]; high-fidelity speaker, full-fidelity speaker; **tweeter,** high-frequency speaker; **woofer,** low-frequency speaker, cone, diaphragm; horn.

5. **transmitter,** broadcaster, radiator; AM transmitter, FM transmitter, short-wave transmitter; **beacon,** radio beacon, radio range beacon; radio marker, fan marker; radiosonde, radiometeorograph.

6. **microphone, mike** [slang], radiomicrophone; mobile microphone, jeep mike [slang].

7. **public-address system,** P.A.

8. **radiomobile,** remote-pickup unit; sound truck.

9. **radio station,** transmitting station, **studio,** studio plant; AM station, FM station, short-wave station, ultrahigh-frequency station, clear-channel station, direction-finder station; relay station, microwave relay station; amateur station, ham shack [slang].

10. **control room,** mixing room; monitor room, monitoring booth; **control desk,** console; master control desk, throne [slang]; instrument panel, control panel or board, mixer [slang].

11. **network,** netting [slang], radio links, **hookup,** circuit, network stations, network affiliations, affiliated stations; coaxial network, circuit network, coast-to-coast hookup.

12. **circuit,** radio-frequency circuit, audio-frequency circuit, amplifying circuit, regenerative circuit, self-heterodyne circuit; electronic circuit 342.8; feedback, inverse feedback.

13. **radio signal,** direct signal, short-wave signal, AM signal, FM signal; reflected signal, bounce; unidirectional signal, beam; signal-noise ratio.

14. **radio wave,** electric wave, electromagnetic wave, hertzian wave; short wave, "long" wave, microwave, high-frequency wave, low-frequency wave; carrier, carrier wave; wave length.

15. **frequency;** radio frequency, R.F.; audio frequency, A.F.; high frequency, H.F.; very high frequency, V.H.F.; ultrahigh frequency, U.H.F.; superhigh frequency, S.H.F.; medium frequency, M.F.; intermediate frequency, I.F.; low frequency, L.F.; very low frequency, V.L.F.; upper frequencies, lower frequencies; carrier, carrier frequency; spark frequency; spectrum, frequency spectrum; kilocycles, megacycles.

16. **band,** frequency band, standard band, short-wave band, FM band; **channel,** radio channel, broadcast channel.

17. **modulation;** amplitude modulation, AM; frequency modulation, FM; phase modulation, P.M.

18. **amplification,** radio-frequency amplification, audio-frequency amplification, high-frequency amplification.

19. **broadcasting, radiobroadcasting, radiocasting;** standard broadcasting, AM broadcasting, FM broadcasting, shortwave broadcasting; direction or beam transmission, assymetric or vestigial transmission; mixing, volume control, sound or tone control, fade-in, fadeout.

20. **pickup,** outside pickup, **remote pickup,** spot pickup.

21. **broadcast,** radio broadcast, **radiobroadcast, radiocast,** aircast [slang], **program;** rebroadcast, rerun; newscast, sportscast, timecast; radio fare, network show; commercial program, commercial; sustaining program, sustainer; serial, soap opera [slang, U.S.]; electrical transcription, E.T.; sound effects.

22. **signature, station identification,** call letters; **theme song;** station break, pause for station identification.

23. **commercial,** commercial announcement, **spot announcement,** plug [slang].

24. **reception,** full-fidelity reception, high-fidelity reception; **fading,** fadeout; **drift,** creeping, crawling; **interference,** noise interference, station interference; **static,** atmospherics, noise; line noise; scratches, shredding, hum, hissing, howling, blurping, blooping, woomping, wowwows, squeals, **whistles,** birdies (tweet-tweet sounds), motorboating (putt-putt sounds); blasting, blaring; blind spot.

25. **radio listener, listener-in** [coll.], tuner-inner [slang]; **hi-fi fan** [slang], audiophile.

26. **broadcaster,** radio broadcaster, **radiobroadcaster, radiocaster,** aircaster [slang], etherizer [slang]; newscaster, sportscaster; commentator; announcer, spieler [slang]; disk jockey [slang]; master of ceremonies, M.C., emcee [slang]; program director, programmer; sound-effects man, sound man; American Federation of Radio Artists, AFRA.

27. **radioman,** radio technician, radio engineer; **radiotrician,** radio electrician; **radioperator,** control engineer, volume engineer; mixer, knob twister [slang], but-

ton duster [slang]; **ham,** ham operator, radio amateur; monitor; radiotelegrapher 558.18.

VERBS **28. broadcast, radiobroadcast, radiocast,** aircast [slang], **radio, wireless** [Eng.], radiate, transmit, send, release; shortwave; beam; newscast, sportscast, put or go on the air, sign on; go off the air, sign off.

29. monitor, check.

30. listen in, tune in; tune up, tune down, tune out, tune off.

ADJS. **31. radio,** radial, **wireless** [esp. Eng.]; radiosonic; neutrodyne; heterodyne; superheterodyne, supersonic; short-wave; radio-frequency, audio-frequency; high-frequency, low-frequency; high-fidelity, hi-fi [slang]; radiogenic.

32. radios

all-wave receiver	radio-phonograph
AM-FM receiver	railroad radio
AM receiver	rechargeable-bat-
auto radio	tery radio
aviation radio	short-wave receiver
battery radio	superheterodyne
combination record	supersonic hetero-
player	dyne
FM receiver	table radio
hancie-talkie [coll.]	three-way or three-
high-fidelity or	power receiver
high-fi set	transceiver
intercom [coll.]	transistor radio
mobile radio	transmit-receiver
neutrodyne	two-way radio
pocket radio	walkie-talkie [coll.]
portable radio	wrist radio
radiophone 558.6	

33. receiver units

amplitude control	phase control
baffle	power pack
by-pass	power plug
capacitor	preamplifier
chassis	preselector
choke	program discrim-
coil	inator
condenser	radio tubes
dial	342.16–18
exciter	resistor
filter	rheostat
frequency control	selector
frequency divider	selsyn
heater	speaker
heterodyne	tone control
inductor	transformer
knob	transistor
lead-in wire	trimmer
on-off switch	variable condenser
parasitic suppres-	volume control
sor	wave trap

34. transmitter units

amplifier chain	coaxial cable
broadcast loop	fader
carrier amplifier	frequency changer

frequency	power amplifier
converter	program feed
frequency doubler	resonance fre-
frequency meter	quency control
litz	signal generator
mixer	signal multiplier
modulator	volume control
monitor	volume indicator
oscillator	wave changer

35. aerials, antennas

artificial antenna	omnidirectional
auto antenna	antenna
beam antenna	open aerial
colinear beam	parabolic antenna
antenna	printed antenna
condenser antenna	rabbit ears
dipole	reflector
directional antenna	resonance wave
doublet	coil
dummy antenna	rhombic antenna
eight-ball antenna	rotary-beam an-
FM antenna	tenna
frame aerial	short-wave antenna
free-space aerial	telescope antenna
hank-type antenna	tower
loop aerial	tuned antenna
mast	universal antenna
mobile antenna	vertical radiator
nondirectional	antenna
antenna	wave antenna
	yagi

36. testing equipment

ammeter	regenerative wave-
audio-frequency	meter
oscillator	standing-wave in-
audio-IF oscillator	dicator
field-strength meter	sweep generator
frequency meter	variable-frequency
grid-dip meter	audio-IF oscillator
grid-dip oscillator	vertical amplifier
Lecher wires	voltmeter
milliameter	voltmeter-milliam-
modulation	eter
monitor	volt-ohm-miliam-
ohmmeter	eter, VOM
oscilloscope	wavemeter
RC oscillator	

344. TELEVISION

NOUNS **1. television, TV,** teevee, **video,** radiovision, lookies [slang]; color television, telecolor; stereo or stereoscopic television, three-dimensional television, 3-D; ultrasonic system, scophony.

2. television broadcast, telecast, TV show; direct broadcast, live or flesh show [slang]; telemovies [slang], telefilm, film pickup; colorcast; simulcast [coll.].

3. televising, telecasting; facsimile broadcasting; monitoring, mixing, shading, blanking, switching; scanning, parallel-line scanning, interlaced scanning.

4. (transmission) photoemission, audioemission; television channel, TV band; video or picture channel, audio or sound channel; picture carrier, sound carrier; beam, scanning beam, return beam; triggering pulse, voltage pulse, output pulse, timing pulse, equalizing pulse; synchronizing pulse, vertical synchronizing pulse, horizontal synchronizing pulse; video signal, audio signal; IF video signal, IF audio signal; synchronizing signal, blanking signal.

5. (reception) telepicture, teleview, picture, image; definition, blacker than black synchronizing; shading, black spot, hard shadow; test pattern, scanning pattern, grid; vertical interference, rain; granulation, scintillation, snow, snowstorm; flare, bloom, woomp; picture shifts, blooping; double image, ghost; video static, noise, picture noise; signal-to-noise ratio; fringe area.

6. television studio, TV station.

7. mobile unit, TVmobile; video truck, audio truck, transmitter truck.

8. transmitter, televisor; audio transmitter, video transmitter.

9. relay links, boosters, booster amplifiers, relay transmitters, **booster** or **relay stations;** microwave link; aeronautical relay, stratovision.

10. television camera, telecamera, pickup camera, pickup; mobile camera, jeep camera [slang]; creepie-peepie, walkie-lookie [both slang].

11. television receiver, television radio receiver, **television** or **TV set,** televisor,

12. televiewer, radiobserver, radio spectator, looker-in [slang].

13. television technician, TV man, television engineer; monitor, sound or audio monitor, picture or video monitor; pickup unit, cameraman, sound man.

VERBS **14. televise, telecast;** colorcast.

15. teleview.

ADJS. **16. televisional,** televisual, televisionary, **video;** telegenic, videogenic; in synchronization, in sync [slang], locked in.

17. receiver units

audio amplifier	limiter
audio detector	mixer
audio-frequency detector	photocathode
blanking amplifier	photoelectric cells 342.17
contrast control	picture control
converter	picture detector
deflection generator	radio units 343.33
electron tubes 342.16–18	screen
	shading amplifier
FM detector	signal separator
horizontal deflector	sound limiter
horizontal synchronizer	synchronizing separator
	vertical deflector

vertical synchronizer

video amplifier
video detector

18. picture tubes

cathode-ray tube	monoscope
direct-viewing tube	Oscilight
Kinescope	projection tube

19. camera tubes

dissector tube	image orthicon
iconoscope	orthicon
image dissector	pickup tube
image iconoscope	vidicon

20. transmitter units

adder	reproducing element
antenna filter	signal generator
camera deflection generator	sound units 343.34
channel filter	synchronizing generator
encoder	Tel-Eye
exploring element	TV-Eye
monitor screen	

345. RADAR AND RADIOLOCATORS

NOUNS **1. radar,** pulse radar, microwave radar, continuous wave or CW radar; radar fence or screen.

2. airborne radar, aviation radar; **navar** (navigation and ranging), **teleran** (television radar air navigation); H$_2$S (height to surface [Eng.]), Stinky [slang], H$_2$X, [U.S. equivalent], Mickey [slang]; bombing locator, GH [Eng.], gee box [slang]; radar bombsight, K-1 bombsight; radome, bathtub [slang].

3. loran (long range aid to navigation), **shoran** (short range aid to navigation).

4. direction finder, radio direction finder, radiogoniometer, sniffer [slang]; high-frequency direction finder, huff-duff [slang]; height finder, super-duper [slang]; radio compass, wireless compass [esp. Eng.].

5. radar speed meter, electronic cop [slang]; radar highway patrol.

6. radar station, control station, nerve center; Combat Information Center, CIC; Air Route Traffic Control Center, ART-CC; beacon station, display station; fixed station, home station; portable field unit, mobile trailer unit; tracking station; direction-finder station, radio compass station; triangulation stations, cat and mouse [slang].

7. radar beacon, racon; transponder; radar beacon buoy, marker buoy, radar marked beacon, ramark.

8. (radar operations) data transmission, scanning, scan conversion, flector tuning, signal modulation, triggering signals;

phase adjustment, locking signals; triangulation, three-pointing; mapping, ground painting [slang]; range finding, strobbing blips [slang]; tracking, automatic tracking, locking on; precision focusing, pinpointing; radar-telephone relay, plotting and telling [slang]; radar navigation, screwdriver navigation [slang], knob twisting [slang].

9. applications) detection, interception, ranging, ground control, blind flying, blind landing, storm tracking.

10. pulse, radio-frequency *or* RF pulse, high-frequency *or* HF pulse, intermediate-frequency *or* IF pulse, trigger pulse, echo pulse.

11. signal, radar signal; transmitter signal, output signal; return signal, echo signal, video signal, reflection, picture, target image, display, signal display, trace, reading, return, **echo, bounces, blips, pips;** spot, CRT spot; three-dimensional *or* 3D display, double-dot display; deflection-modulated *or* DM display, intensity-modulated *or* IM display; radio-frequency *or* RF echoes, intermediate-frequency *or* IF signal, beat signal, doppler signal, local oscillator signal; beam, beavertail beam.

12. deflection, refraction, superrefraction; atmospheric attenuation, signal fades, blind spots, false echoes; clutter, ground clutter, sea clutter.

13. (radar countermeasure) **jamming,** spoofing [slang]; tinfoil, aluminum foil, chaff [U.S.], window [Eng.], Dueppel [Ger.].

14. radar technician, radar engineer, radar man, knob twister [slang]; ground controller.

VERBS **15. transmit, send,** radiate, beam.

16. reflect, return, echo, bounce back.

17. receive, tune in, pick up, spot, home on; pinpoint; identify, trigger [slang]; lock on; sweep, scan; map, paint [slang].

18. jam, spoof [slang].

19. radars

AGCA radar (automatic ground control approach)
AI radar (aircraft interception)
antiaircraft *or* AA radar
antisubmarine radar
ASV radar (air to surface vessel)
CCA radar (close control of aircraft)
DEW Line (distant early warning line)
DME (distance measuring equipment)
DVOP (doppler velocity and position)
FC radar (fire control)
GCA radar (ground control approach)
GCI radar (ground control of interception)
H₂S (height to surface [Eng.])
H₂X (height to surface [U.S.])
IFF radar (identification, friend or foe)
interception radar
LAW (long-range aircraft warning)
MAD (magnetic airborne detection)
MEW (microwave early warning)
MTI radar (moving target indication)
Navaglobe
Oboe (beacon bombing system)
PAR (precision approach radar)
RAWIN (radio automatic wind recording)
SARAH (search rescue and homing)
SCR (Signal Corps radar)
search radar
surface *or* ground radar
surveillance radar
taxi radar (airport surface detection)
TRW (tornado radar warning)
Volscan

20. radiolocators

automatic gun director, AGD
automatic range finder, ARF
bombing locator
depth sounder
gun director
height finder
microwave height finder, MHF
position finder
range finder

21. radar assembly

AFC mixer
altimeter
amplifier
analyzer
ATR box (anti-transmit-receive)
ATR switch
automatic frequency control, AFC
cascade screen
cathode-ray tube, CRT
continuous wave *or* CW oscillator
demodulator
detector
discriminator
frequency meter
hard-tube pulser
indicator
limiter
local oscillator
magnetron
microwave mixer
mixer
modulator
network pulser
oscillator
plan position indicator, PPI
position data transmitter
position tracker
potentiometer
pulse generator
pulser
pulse transformer
range-marker generator
range-sweep amplifier
range-sweep generator
receiver
reference-voltage generator
scan converter
screen
second detector
square-wave generator
synchronizer
tracker
transmit-receive *or* TR unit
transmitter
TR box (transmit-receive)
TR switch
trigatron

22. oscilloscopes

A-scope
B-scope
J-scope
PPI-scope (plan position indicator scope)

23. antennas

bedspring type	omnidirectional
directional antenna	antenna
feed-and-reflector	scanner
unit	sontenna
mattress type	strike radar scan-
	ner (airborne)

24. reflectors

beaver-tail reflector	orange peel reflec-
corner reflector	tor
dish reflector	parabolic reflector
horn reflector	Venetian blind
	reflector

346. MECHANICS

NOUNS **1. mechanics,** mechanology, machine technology; theoretical *or* analytical mechanics, pure *or* abstract mechanics, rational mechanics; practical mechanics, mechanical arts; applied mechanics; statistical mechanics; matrix mechanics; aeromechanics.

2. statics, biostatics, electrostatics, geostatics, graphostatics, gyrostatics, psychostatics, rheostatics, stereostatics, thermostatics.

3. dynamics, kinetics, kinematics.

4. hydraulics, hydromechanics, hydrokinetics, hydrodynamics, hydrostatics; hydrology, hydrography, hydrometry, fluviology.

5. pneumatics, pneumatology, pneumatonomy, pneumatostatics; aeromechanics, aerophysics, aerology, aerometry, aerography, aeroscopy, aerotechnics, aerodynamics; aerostatics, aerostation.

6. engineering, mechanical engineering, jet engineering, etc. [*see* engineer] 716.9.

7. mechanic, mechanician; artisan, artificer; **machinist,** machiner; auto mechanic; aeromechanic.

8. mechanization; motorization.

VERBS **9. mechanize;** motorize.

10. machine, mill.

ADJS. **11. mechanical,** mechanistic; machinal, machinelike; mechanized; power-driven, motor-driven; locomotive, locomotor; aeromechanical.

12. dynamic(al), kinetic(al), kinematic(al).

13. pneumatic, pneumatological; aeromechanical, aerophysical, aerologic(al), aerotechnical, aerodynamic, areostatic, aeroscopic, aerographic(al).

14. hydrologic(al), hydrometric(al), hydromechanic(al), hydrodynamic, hydrostatic.

347. TOOLS AND MACHINERY

NOUNS **1. tool, instrument, implement, utensil; apparatus, device,** contrivance, contraption [coll.], gadget, gimcrack, gimmick [slang, U.S.]; **appliance,** convenience, facility, utility, commodity; fixture; power tools. machine tools; speed tools; precision tools *or* instruments; labor-saving device; instrumentology.

2. cutlery, edge tools; **knife, blade,** cutter, whittle [Scot. & dial., Eng.]; steel, cold steel, naked steel; pigsticker, toad stabber *or* sticker [all slang]; perforator, piercer, puncturer.

3. tableware, dining utensils; **silverware,** silver; **flatware,** flat silver [U.S.]; hollow ware; **cutlery,** knives, forks, spoons; tablespoon, teaspoon; chopsticks.

4. machinery, enginery; **machine,** mechanical device; **engine, motor;** power plant.

5. mechanism, machinery, **movement,** movements, **action, motion,** works, workings, inner workings; wheelwork, **wheelworks,** wheels, gear, wheels within wheels, epicyclic train; clockworks, watchworks; servomechanism 348.13, 30.

6. gear, gearing; gearwheel, cogwheel 320.18; rack; **gearshift;** low, intermediate, high, neutral, reverse; differential, differential gear *or* gearing; transmission, gearbox; selective transmission; fluid drive, overdrive, freewheeling, hydromatic, Dyna-Flow.

7. instrumentation, implementation, tooling; retooling; industrial instrumentation; servo instrumentation.

VERBS **8. implement,** instrument, **tool;** retool.

9. tools

awl	flail
bar	forceps
battering ram	fork
belt punch	grapnel
bevel, bevel square	grappling *or* grap-
bodkin	ple iron *or* hook
bradawl	grease gun
buffer	grindstone
calipers	hawk
cant hook	header
crowbar	jack
dibble	jackscrew
dividers	jointer
drum sander	lathe
edger	level
electric riveter	miter box
electric sander	monkey
emery wheel	nail file
file	nail puller

palette knife
pincers, pinchers
pitchfork
planer
pliers
power sander
puller
punch
puncheon
punch pliers
puncher
ram
rammer
ramrod
screwdriver
shaper
spatula

square
stapler
tackle 286.10
tamp, tamper
tamping iron
tamping pick
tamping stick
tap
tapper
T-bevel
tire iron
tire tool
tongs
tweezers
vise
wrecking bar

10. edge tools

adz, adze
ax axe
belduque [South-
  west. U.S.]
bill, billhook
bistoury
bowie knife
bread knife
broadax
bushwhacker
  [U.S.]
butcher knife
carving knife
case knife
chaser
chisel
cleaver, cleave
clipper, clippers
cold chisel
colter
cutoff
cutting pliers
drawing knife,
  drawknife
drawshave
electric razor
gouge
groover
hack
hatchet
hedge trimmer
hoe
jackknife

knife
lance
lancet
linoleum knife
machete
mattock
nippers
panga [E. Africa]
paring knife
penknife
pick
pickax
plowshare
pocketknife
razor
rip chisel
safety razor
scalpel
scissors
scoop
scraper
scythe
share
shears
sickle
slotter
snips
spoke shave
surgical knife
table knife
tin snips
tomahawk
wedge

11. saws

back saw
band saw
bow saw
bucksaw
butcher's saw
buzz saw
chain saw
circular saw
compass saw
coping saw
cordwood saw
crosscut saw
double-cut saw
dovetail saw
electric saw
hacksaw
handsaw

helicoidal saw
jigsaw
keyhole saw
kitchen saw
lightning or M saw
lumberman's saw
mill or milling saw
panel saw
pit saw
portable saw
power saw
pruning saw
ripsaw
saw knife
saw machine
scroll saw
splitsaw

surgeon's saw
table saw
two-handed saw

12. shovels

air shovel
coal shovel
drain spade
garden spade
irrigating shovel
loy [Ir. & U.S.]
peat spade
posthole spade

13. trowels

brick trowel
circle or cove
  trowel
corner trowel
curbing trowel

14. planes

beading plane
bench plane
block plane
bullnose
chamfer plane
circular plane
combination plane
core-box plane
dado plane
dovetail plane
edge plane
filletster plane
fore plane
grooving plane
head
jack plane
jointer, jointer

15. borers

air drill
auger
automatic drill
bench drill
bit
bore
bore bit
bow drill
brace
brace and bit
broach
burr
cockscrew
cross bit
disk drill
drill
drill press
electric drill
flat drill

16. hammers

air hammer
ball-peen hammer
beetle
blacksmith's ham-
  mer
boilermaker's
  hammer
brick hammer
chipping hammer
claw hammer

vertical saw
whipsaw
wood saw

scoop
scoop shovel
slick
spade
split shovel
spud
stump spud

garden trowel
guttering trowel
plastering trowel
pointing trowel
radius trowel

plane
match plane
planer
planing machine
rabbet plane
reed plane
routing plane
sash plane
scraper plane
scrub plane
smooth or smooth-
  ing plane
thumb plane
tonguing plane
toothing plane
trying plane

gimlet
hand drill
portable drill
posthole auger
power drill
pump drill
push drill
ratchet drill
reamer, rimer
rotary drill
shell drill
spike bit
star drill
strap drill
trepan
trephine
twist drill
wimble

cross-peen hammer
die hammer
drop hammer
electric hammer
engineer's ham-
  mer
machinist's
  hammer
maul
mallet

peen hammer
pneumatic hammer
raising hammer
riveting hammer
rubber mallet
sledge, sledgeham-
mer

spalling hammer
steam hammer
stone hammer
tack hammer
tile setter's ham-
mer
triphammer

17. wrenches

alligator wrench
box wrench
carriage wrench
lug wrench
monkey wrench
open-end wrench
pin wrench

pipe wrench
screw key
socket wrench
spanner
Stillson wrench
tappet wrench

18. machinery

adding machine
addressing machine
automobile 271.9,
22
bulldozer
carryall
compressor
crab
crane
crimping machine
cutting machine
cutting press
derrick
dishwasher
dredge, dredger,
dredging machine
dumping machine
edger
elevator dredge
flying machine 279
folding machine
gin
grader
hoist, hoisting
machine
hydraulic press
lawn mower
machine drill
mailing machine
milling cutter

motorcycle 271.8,
27
mower
navvy
packager
pile driver
planing machine
power shovel
press
printing machine
pulp machine
punching machine
pusher
roller
ruling machine or
engine
saw machine
scraper
screwing machine
sewing machine,
sewer
snowplow
solar machine
steam hammer
steam roller
steam shovel
tractor 271.16, 25
typing machine
washing machine
water wheel
windlass 286.7

19. farm machinery

all-crop harvester
baler
bean harvester
beet harvester
binder
breaker
cast plow
combine
corn picker
cotton gin
cotton picker
cultivator
disk
disk harrow
disk plow
drag
drill
drill plow
four-bottom plow
gang plow

gin
grain harvester
harrow
harvester
hayrake
header
hoe drill
lister
lister drill
middle-breaker or
-buster
moldboard plow
mowing machine
peg-tooth harrow
planter
plow, plough
plow drill
prairie breaker
press drill
rake

roller gin
rotary plow
saw gin
scooter
seeder
seed plow
shovel plow
snap machine
sprayer
spring-tooth har-
row
stag gang
subsoil plow
sulky lister

sulky plow
swather
swivel plow
tedder
three-bottom plow
thresher, thrasher
threshing machine
trencher
turnplow
two-bottom plow
vineyard plow
walking plow
windrower

20. mills

arrastra
bone mill
cane mill
cider mill
coffee mill
cotton mill
drag-stone mill
flour mill
grinding mill
gristmill
lapidary mill

milling machine
planing mill
powder mill
rolling mill
sawmill
stamp
stamp mill
stone mill
treadmill
water mill
windmill

21. welders

acetylene welder
AC welder
arc welder
blowtorch 328.13
DC welder
electric soldering
iron
electric torch
electric welder

gas welder
oxyacetylene
welder
soldering gun
three-phase resist-
ance welder
welding blowpipe
or torch

22. pumps

air lift
air pump
aspirator
bicycle pump
bucket pump
centrifugal pump
displacement
pump
donkey pump
force pump
forcer
hydraulic ram

jet pump
lift or lifting pump
piston pump
pulsometer
pumping engine
rotary pump
sand pump
shell pump
suction pump
turbine centrifugal
pump
vacuum pump

23. engines, motors

aeromotor 279.17
air engine or motor
alternating current
or AC motor
beam engine
blowing engine
caloric or heat
engine
cam engine
capacitor motor
commutator motor
compensated
motor
compound motor
compression-
ignition engine
condensing engine
Corliss engine

diagonal engine
Diesel engine
dinkey
direct-acting or
-action engine
direct current or
DC motor
donkey, donkey
engine
double-acting or
-action engine
double-row radial
engine
dynamo
dynamotor
electric motor,
electromotor

external-
combustion
engine
fire engine
gas engine
gas jet
generator
horizontal engine
hot-air engine
hydraulic engine
hydro-jet
impulse duct
  engine
inclined engine
induction motor
intermittent duct
  engine
internal-
  combustion
  engine
inverted engine
jet, jet engine
locomotive
locomotor
marine engine
mill-type motor
mule
noncondensing
  engine
oil engine
oscillation-cylinder
  engine
oscillation engine
outboard motor
pancake engine
phase-wound rotor
  motor
piston engine

piston-valve engine
portable engine
pulsejet
pumping engine
radial engine
ramjet
reaction motor
reciprocating
  engine
refrigerating
  engine
resojet
rocket motor
rose engine
rotary engine
rotor motor
series motor
servomotor
shunt motor
side-valve engine
single-acting or
  -action engine
single-phase motor
solar engine
squirrelcage rotor
  motor
stationary engine
steam engine
supercharged
  engine
synchronous
  motor
triple-expansion
  engine
trunk engine
turbine
turbojet
vertical engine

24 engine parts

bearings
boiler
cam
camshaft
connecting rod
crankcase
crankshaft
cylinder
cylinder head
differential

electrical parts
  341.38
flywheel
gearbox
gears 320.18
piston
piston rod
transmission
universal joint

348. AUTOMATION

NOUNS 1. automation, automatism; self-action, self-activity; self-movement, self-propulsion, self-impulsion; self-control, self-direction, self-government, self-regulation: automaticity; spontaneousness, spontaneity; automatization; servo instrumentation.

2. automatics, automatic technology, automatic electronics, automatic engineering, automatic control engineering, servo engineering, servomechanics, system engineering, feedback system engineering; cybernetics; radiodynamics, radio control; ultrasonics; systems planning; circuit analysis.

3. automatic control, servo control, robot control; cybernetic control; electronic control, electronic-mechanical control; feedback control, digital feedback control, analogue feedback control; cascade control, "piggyback" control; supervisory control; action, control action; derivative or rate action, reset action; control agent; control means.

4. semiautomatic control; remote control, push-button control, remote handling, tele-action; telemechanics; telemechanism.

5. control system, automatic control system, servo system, robot system; closed-loop system; open-sequence system; linear system, nonlinear system; carrier-current system; integrated system, complex control system; data system, data-handling system, data-reduction system, data-input system, data-interpreting system, digital data reducing system; process-control system, annunciator system, flow-control system, motor-speed control system, etc.; automanual system [R.R.]; automatic telephone system; electrostatic spraying system; automatic or robot factory, push-button plant; servo laboratory, servolab.

6. feedback, closed sequence, closed loop; multiple-feed closed loop; process loop, quality loop; feedback circuit, current-control circuit, direct-current circuit, alternating-current circuit, calibrating circuit, switching circuit, flip-flop circuit, peaking circuit; multiplier channels; open sequence, linear operation; negative feedback; reversed feedback, degeneration.

7. (functions) accounting, analysis, automatic electronic navigation, automatic guidance, comparison of variables, computation, coordination, corrective action, fact distribution, forecasts, impedance matching, inspection, linear or nonlinear calibrations, manipulation, measurement of variables, missile guidance, output measurement, processing, rate determination, record keeping, statistical communication, system stabilization, ultrasonic or supersonic flow detection.

8. process control, bit-weight control, color control, density control, dimension control, diverse control, end-point control, flavor control, flow control, fragrance control, hold control, humidity control, light-intensity control, limit control, liquid-level control, load control, pressure control, precision-production control, proportional control, quality control, quantity control, revo-

lution control, temperature control, time control, weight control.

9. **variables,** process variables; temperature, pressure, flow, liquid level, humidity, weight, color, etc.; simple variable, complex variable; manipulated variable; steady state, transient state.

10. **values,** target values; set point; differential gap; proportional band; dead band, dead zone; neutral zone.

11. **time constants;** time lead, gain; time delay, dead time; lag, process lag, hysteresis, hold-up, output lag; through-put.

12. (automatic device) **automatic;** semiautomatic; self-actor, self-mover; **robot, automaton,** mechanical man; televox.

13. **servomechanism,** servo; cybernion, automatic machine; servomotor; synchro, synchronous motor.

14. **regulator, control,** controller, **governor;** servo control, servo regulator; control element.

15. **control panel,** console; coordinated panel, graphic panel; panelboard, set-up board.

16. **electronic brain,** electric brain, **electronic computer** or **calculator,** electrocomputer **87.19, lightning calculator,** giant calculator, **information machine,** thinking machine, **brain machine,** electronic mastermind, **master control,** director, the Professor [slang].

17. **storage** system or unit, **memory,** high-speed memory; random access memory, RAM; memory tubes; magnetic tape, magnetic drum.

18. (read-in, read-out media) summing register, relay register; reader, tape reader; magnetic tape, punched tape; punched cards, punch-cards; microcards, microfilm; recorder, magnetic recorder; alphabetical printer; teletypewriter, Flexowriter typewriter; oscilloscope, oscillograph recorder; digital graph plotter, Teleplotter.

19. (data fed to or delivered by a computer) **data,** information, message, instructions, commands; single messages, multiple messages; **input data, output data;** random data, unorganized data; numeric data, alphabetic data; film data, punch-card data, oscillograph data; visible-speech data, sound-level data; angular data, rectangular data, polar data; quantity (the quantity to be controlled), input quantity, output quantity, reference quantity, controlled quantity; **signals,** control signals, block signals, checking signals, error signals, correct-

ing signals, feedback signals; command pulses, feedback pulses; error (deviation from setting); play, noise (element in message not put there intentionally); binary scale or system; binary digit, bit.

20. **data processing,** high-speed data handling, data reduction, machine computation, telecomputing; computing, scanning, analyzing, sorting, collating, integrating, classifying, reporting.

21. **process,** digital process, analogue process; behavior pattern; oscillatory behavior, self-excitation; input oscillation, output oscillation; hunting, feeling; correction of error; overcorrection of error, overshoot; offset (the difference between value desired and attained).

22. **control engineer,** servo engineer, system engineer, automatic control system engineer, feedback system engineer, automatic technician, robot specialist; computer engineer; cybernetic technologist, cyberneticist.

VERBS 23. **automatize,** robotize; robot-control, servo-control.

24. **self-govern,** self-control, **self-regulate,** self-direct.

ADJS. 25. **automatic,** automatous, **spontaneous; self-acting,** self-active; **self-operating,** self-operative, self-working; **self-regulating,** self-regulative, self-governing, self-directing; **self-regulated, self-controlled,** self-governed, self-directed, self-steered; self-adjusting, self-closing, self-cocking, self-cooking, self-dumping, self-emptying, self-lighting, self-loading, self-opening, self-priming, self-rising, self-sealing, self-starting, self-winding, automanual [R.R.]; semiautomatic.

26. **self-propelled,** self-moved, horseless; **self-propelling,** self-moving, self-propellent; self-driven, self-drive; **automotive,** automobile, automechanical; **locomotive,** locomobile.

27. **servomechanical,** servo-controlled; **cybernetic;** isotronic.

28. **remote-control,** remote-controlled, telemechanic; by remote control.

29. **automatic devices**

airborne controls	-jointer, etc.
anti-aircraft gun positioner	automatic gun
artificial feedback	automatic gun director
kidney	automatic heater
automat	automatic iron
automatic block signal [R.R.]	automatic piano
automatic drill,	automatic or robot pilot

automatic
  pinspotter
  [bowling]
automatic pistol
automatic printer
automatic rifle
automatic sight
automatic
  sprinkler
automatic stop
  [R.R.]
automatic
  telegraph
automatic
  telephone
automatic
  telephone
  exchange
automaton

autopilot
  [aeronaut.]
chess-playing
  machine
guided missile
gyroscopic pilot
  [naut.]
laundromat
lever pilot [naut.]
mechanical heart
Multiple-Stylus
  Electronic Printer
radar controls
robot plane
robot submarine
self-starter
speedometer
televox
watcher [R.R.]

UNIVAC
  (Universal
  Automatic
  Computer)

versatile digit
  computer

30. servomechanisms

alternating-current
  servo
automatic feed
  mechanism
direct-current servo
electronic servo
hemostat
hydraulic servo
instrument servo
motor-generator
  servo

pneumatic servo
power servo
selsyn
servomotor
sine mechanism
synchro
synchro receiver
synchro transmitter
telemechanism

31. electronic computers

analogue computer
Audrey (Automatic
  Digit Recognizer)
automatic plotter
BINAC (Binary
  Automatic
  Computer)
data processor
decimal digital
  differential
  analyzer
decoding servo-
  mechanism
differential
  analyzer
digital computer
digital differential
  analyzer
digital general
  purpose computer
digital graph
  plotter
direct-reading
  computer
Electronic Data
  Processing
  Machine "701"
ENIAC (Electronic
  Numerical
  Integrator and
  Computer)
ENIAD (Elec-
  tronic Numerical
  Integrating and
  Analyzing Device)
equation solver

ERMA (Electronic
  Recording
  Machine
  —Accounting)
high-speed digit
  computer
IBM "702"
IDA (Integro-
  Differential
  Analyzer)
IDP machine
  (Integrated Data
  Processing)
Magnetronic
  Reservisor
OARAC (Office of
  Air Research
  Automatic
  Computer)
printing calculator
Production-Control
  Quantometer
RAYDAC
  (Raytheon Data
  Calculator)
selective calculator
Selective Sequence
  Electronic
  Calculator
square root
  planimeter
telecomputer
Teleplotter
Telereader
tristimulus
  computer

32. computer units

adder
analytical control
  unit
analyzer
coder
coefficient
component
collator
decoder
detector
differential
divider
electrostatic
  storage unit
FOSDIC (Film

Optical Sensing
Device for Input
to Computers)
integrator
memory tubes
multiplier
phase discriminator
position code
  converter
position coder
receptor
relay
selector
storage unit
transmitter

33. system components

actuator
amplifier
amplifying
  generator
calibrating unit
capacitor
clock
control relay
control resistor
converter
discriminating
  relay
effector
electro-pneumatic
  transducer
feedback amplifier
generator
inductor
load-indicating
  resistor
magnetic amplifier
magnetic relay

meter relay
modulator
oscillator
oscillator relay
actuator
phase-discriminat-
  ing amplifier
pressure transducer
reactor
records-pulse
  generator
regenerator
relay
reluctance amplifier
resistor
servo amplifier
thermal timing
  relay
transducer
transmitter
uncommitted
  amplifier

34. control mechanisms

automatic switch
  or trip
channel selector
check valve
contour follower
control transformer
control valve
diaphragm motor
  valve
electrical governor
electro-mechanical
  controller
electronic control
electro-pneumatic
  valve positioner
emergency control
finder switch
flowmanostat
flow valve
indicating control
  switch
internal selector
limit switch
line switch or

breaker
manostat
manual control
oscillator relay
  control
overload breaker
overload switch
  or circuit
phase advancer
positioning
  mechanism
pressure
  transmitter
proportioning lever
rectifier
register regulator
safety control
safety fuse
safety stop
safety switch
safety valve
selector switch
sequence switch
servo valve

speed regulator
thermoswitch
timer

voltage regulator
voltage stabilizer

35. detectors, inspectors

chemical detector
electronic counter
electronic detector
error corrector
error detector
liquid-level sensor
mercury-vapor
　detector
metal detector
photoelectric
　detector
photoelectric

inspection
machine
photoelectric
pinhole detector
photoelectric sorter
sensor
temperature sensor
ultrasonic detector
　or inspector
ultrasonic flow
　detector

36. analyzers

Agtron (judges
　ripeness of
　tomatoes)
analytical
　spectrometer
color gauge or
　checker
comparator
CO_2 recorder
data analyzer
dewpoint recorder
direct-reading
　spectrometer
electronic
　comparator

gas analyzer
infrared gas and
　liquid analyzer
mass spectrograph
mass spectrometer
oxygen recorder
recording analyzer
scanner
stigmatic grating
　spectrograph
surface analyzer
vibration and stress
　analyzer

37. indicators and correctors

control indicator
count-rate meter
current indicator
density indicator
detonation
　indicator
differential pressure
　gauge
events-per-unit-
　time meter
fault lamp
filled-system
　thermometer
flowmeter
galvanometer
humidity indicator
hygrometer
integrating
　flowmeter
interferometer
ionization gauge
light-intensity
　indicator
liquid-level
　indicator
load indicator

logger
moisture meter
pH meter
potentiometer
pressure indicator
proximity meter
psychometer
pyrometer
radiation
　pyrometer
resistance
　thermometer
square-root
　flowmeter
strain gauge
tensiometer
thermistor
thermocouple
thermocouple
　pyrometer
time-interval
　meter
turns-indicating
　duodial
vibration meter
voltage indicator

349. FRICTION

NOUNS 1. friction, affrication, confrication; rubbing, rub, elbow grease [joc.]; scrubbing, scrub; scouring, burnishing, polishing.

2. abrasion, attrition detrition, limation; grinding, filing, rasping, chafing,

fretting, galling; scraping, grazing, scratching, scuffing; scrape, scratch, scuff; abrasive 259.14.

3. massage, massaging, kneading, rub-down; anatripsis [med.]; facial [coll.], facial massage, massage facial [F.].

4. massager, massagist, masseur, masseuse [fem.], massageuse [fem.], masser, rubber.

5. (mechanics) force of friction, internal friction, magnetic friction, starting friction, rolling friction, sliding friction, force of viscosity; coefficient of friction, friction factor; resistance, frictional resistance [both naut.]; friction loss, friction-head.

VERBS 6. rub, frictionize, affricate, scrub, scour, buff, burnish, polish, rub up; massage, knead, rub down.

7. abrade, abrase; grind, rasp, file, grate, chafe, fret, gall; scrape, graze, raze, scratch, scuff, bark, skin; fray, frazzle.

8. gnash, grind the teeth; crunch, craunch, scranch [now chiefly dial.], scrunch [coll. & dial.]; gnaw.

ADJS. 9. frictional, friction; fricative [phonet. & music]; rubbing, anatriptic [med.].

10. abrasive, abradant, attritive; grinding, rasping, chafing, fretting, galling; gnawing, arrosive.

350. TEXTURE

Surface Quality.—NOUNS 1. texture, contexture, intertexture, fabric; surface, finish, feel; grain, fineness or coarseness of grain, grit (of stone), ingrain; tooth; fiber, woof, wale, warp and woof or weft; nap, pile, shag; roughness 260; smoothness 259; structure 244.

2. coarseness, grossness, unrefinement; coarse-grainedness, cross-grainedness; graininess, granularity, granulation, grittiness.

3. fineness, refinement, fine-grainedness; delicacy, daintiness; subtility, subtlety; gossameriness, filminess.

VERBS 4. coarsen; grain, ingrain, granulate; tooth; roughen 260.4.

ADJS. 5. textural, textile, textured.

6. coarse, gross, unrefined; coarse-grained, cross-grained; ingrained, ingrain; grained, grainy; granular, granulated; gritty; linsey-woolsey, homespun; rough 260.6.

7. nappy, pily, shaggy; downy, fluffy; velvety, velutinous.

8. fine, refined, fine-grained; delicate, dainty; subtile, subtle; finespun, thin-

spun, fine-drawn, wiredrawn; attenuated, attenuate; gossamery, gossamer, gauzy, filmy; smooth 259.9.

351. WEIGHT

NOUNS 1. **weight, gravity, heaviness, weightiness,** heftiness [coll.], heft [coll.]; avoirdupois [coll., U.S.], beef [coll.]; poundage, tonnage; ponderability; gross weight, gr. wt.; net weight, neat weight, nt. wt., net; scant weight, lazy weight [coll.]. underweight; overweight, overbalance; overweightage.

2. **ponderousness,** ponderosity, onerousness, **burdensomeness, oppressiveness, cumbersomeness,** combrousness, massiveness, lumpishness, unwieldiness.

3. (sports) bantamweight, catchweight, featherweight, flyweight, heavyweight, lightweight, middleweight, welterweight.

4. **counterbalance** 33.2; makeweight, casting weight; **ballast,** ballasting.

5. (physics) **gravity, gravitation,** G; specific gravity; Baumé gravity; geotropism, positive geotropism, negative geotropism; G suit, anti-G suit.

6. (a weight) **weight,** ponderable; paperweight, letterweight; sinker, lead, plumb, plummet, bob; sandbag.

7. **burden,** pressure, **oppression,** charge, **load,** lading, freight, bale, cumber, cumbrance, **encumbrance** or incumbrance, incubus; incumbency, superincumbency; handicap [racing], impost [slang]; millstone; surcharge; **overload** 351.7.

8. (systems of weight) avoirdupois weight, troy weight, apothecaries' weight, molecular weight.

9. **weighing,** ponderation, hefting [coll.], balancing.

VERBS 10. **weigh,** weight [coll.], heft [coll.]; **balance,** poise, weigh in the balance, strike a balance, hold the scales; **counterbalance** 33.5; overweigh; weigh in, weigh out; be heavy, have weight, carry weight; kick the beam.

11. **weigh on** or **upon,** rest on or upon, bear on or upon, lie on.

12. **weight, weigh down;** ballast, poise; lead, sandbag.

13. **burden, load,** lade, cumber, **encumber** or incumber, charge, **freight,** tax, handicap, hamper, saddle; oppress, **weigh down, weigh on** or **upon, weigh heavy on,** bear or rest hard upon, lie hard or heavy upon, press hard upon; **overburden** 661.16; pile Ossa upon Pelion.

14. **outweigh,** overweigh, overweight, overbalance, **outbalance,** weigh down; outpoise, overpoise [both chiefly fig.].

15. **gravitate, descend,** drop, plunge, precipitate, sink, settle, subside; **tend,** tend to go, **incline,** point, head, lead, lean.

ADJS. 16. **heavy,** hefty [coll.], **weighty;** heavyweight; overweight.

17. **ponderous, onerous, oppressive, burdensome, cumbersome,** cumbrous, massive, lumpish, **unwieldy,** unwieldly; incumbent, superincumbent.

18. **weighted, weighed down;** burdened, oppressed, loaded, **laden,** cumbered, **encumbered** or incumbered, charged, freighted, taxed, hampered.

19. **ponderable,** weighable; **appreciable,** palpable, sensible.

20. **gravitate,** gravitational.

ADVS. 21. **heavily,** heavy, weightily; burdensomely, onerously; oppressively; **ponderously,** cumbersomely, cumbrously, unwieldily.

22. weighing instruments

alloy balance	pair of scales
analytical balance	plate fulcrum scale
assay balance	precision scale
automatic-	Roman balance
indicating scale	scale, scales
balance	scale beam
balance of	scale of precision
precision	short-arm balance
barrel scale	spiral balance
beam	spring balance
bullion balance	spring scale
counter scale	steelyard
cylinder drum	weigh beam
scale	weighbridge
Danish balance	weighing machine
fan scale	weighing scales
flexure plate scale	weightometer
long-arm balance	weight scale
Nicholson's	weight voltameter
balance	

23. weights

assay ton, AT	weight, grm. mol.
carat, crt.	gross hundred-
carat grain, crt. gr.	weight, gross cwt.
centigram, cg. or	gross ton, gr. tn.
cgm.	hectogram, hg.
decagram,	hundredweight,
dekagram, dkg.	cwt.
decigram, dg.	kilogram, kg. or
denier	kilo.
dram, dr.	kiloton, ktn.
dram apothecaries',	long hundred-
dr. ap.	weight, l. cwt.
dram avoirdupois,	long ton, l. tn.
dr. avdp.	megaton, mgtn.
grain, g. or gr.	metric carat, met.
gram, grm.	crt.
gram molecule	metric ton, met.
gram-molecular	tn.

millier, mr.
milligram, mgrm.
mole, m.
myriagram, myg.
net hundred-
weight, net cwt.
net ton, net tn.
ounce, oz.
ounce apothe-
caries', oz. ap.
ounce avoirdupois,
oz. avdp.
ounce troy, oz. t.
pennyweight, dwt.
pound, lb.

pound apothe-
caries', lb. ap.
pound avoirdupois,
lb. avdp.
pound mole, lb.
m.
pound troy, lb. t.
quintal, q.
scruple, s. or s. ap.
short hundred-
weight, sh. cwt.
short ton, sh. tn.
stone, st.
ton, tn.
tonneau, t.

352. LIGHTNESS

Lack of Weight.—NOUNS 1. **lightness, levity, weightlessness,** unheaviness; imponderability, impalpability; **buoyancy,** floatability, levitation; **volatility**; airiness, ethereality; softness, gentleness, delicacy, daintiness, tenderness.

2. **imponderable,** impalpable; imponderables, imponderabilia [NL.].

3. (comparisons) feather, down, thistledown, flue, fluff, gossamer, cobweb, straw, chaff, dust, mote, cork, bubble, air, ether.

4. **lightening,** easing, **easement, softening, alleviation,** relief; disburdening, **disencumberment,** unburdening, unloading, unlading.

5. **leavening, fermentation; leaven, ferment.**

VERBS 6. **lighten,** ease, **alleviate, relieve,** soften; **disburden, disencumber,** unburden, unload, unlade.

7. **leaven,** raise, **ferment.**

8. **buoy,** buoy up, float; **sustain, hold up,** bear up, uphold, upbear, uplift, upraise.

9. **levitate** (opposed to gravitate), **rise, soar,** hover, **float,** swim, waft, sail, fly, plane.

ADJS. 10. **light, weightless,** unheavy, imponderous; **imponderable,** impalpable; **airy, ethereal,** frothy, foamy, gossamery, feathery; light as air, ∼ a feather, etc. 352.3.

11. **gentle, soft, delicate,** dainty, tender, **easy.**

12. **lightweight,** bantamweight, featherweight; underweight, "weighed in the balance and found wanting" [Bible].

13. **buoyant, volatile,** corky [coll.], floaty, floatable; floating, superfluent, supernatant.

14. levitative, levitational.

15. **lightening,** easing, alleviating, alleviative, relieving, softening.

16. **leavening,** raising; **fermenting,** fermentative, working; yeasty, barmy; enzymic, zymic, diastatic, peptic(al).

17. leavens, ferments

bacteria
baking powder
baking soda
barm
beaten egg
buttermilk
carbon dioxide
cream of tartar
diastase

enzyme
mother, mother of
vinegar
pepsin
soda
sour milk
yeast
zyme

353. DENSITY

NOUNS 1. **density, denseness, solidity,** thickness, compactness, closeness, spissitude, crassitude; impenetrability, impermeability, imporosity; incompressibility; specific gravity, relative density.

2. **indivisibility, inseparability,** impartibility, infrangibility, indiscerptibility; insolubility, indissolubility; infusibility.

3. densification, **condensation, compression, concentration,** consolidation; **solidification** 355.5.

4. **thickening,** inspissation, incrassation; **congelation,** congealment, **coagulation,** setting, concretion; gelatinization, gelatination, jellification, **jellying,** gelling; **curdling,** clabbering, caseation.

5. **precipitation,** condensation, deposit; precipitate 43.2.

6. **solid,** solid body, body, mass; lump; block, cake, knot; concrete, concretion; conglomerate, conglomeration.

7. **clot,** grume, coagulum, crassamentum; casein, caseinogen, paracasein, legumin; **curd, clabber,** lopper [Scot.], bonnyclabber, clotted cream, Devonshire cream.

8. (instruments) densimeter, densitometer; aerometer, hydrometer, lactometer, urinometer.

VERBS 9. **densify,** densen; **condense, compress,** compact, **consolidate, concentrate,** squeeze, press, crowd, cram, ram down; **solidify** 355.8.

10. **thicken,** thick; inspissate, incrassate; **congeal, coagulate, clot,** set, concrete; gelatinize, gelatinate, **jelly,** jellify, jell [coll.], gel; **curdle,** cruddle [dial.], curd, clabber, lopper [dial.]; cake, lump, knot.

11. **precipitate,** condense, deposit.

ADJS. 12. **dense, compact, close,** serried, **thick, heavy,** thickset, thick-packed, thick-growing, thick-coming, thick-spread, thick-spreading; **condensed, compressed,** compacted, consolidated, concentrated;

solid, firm, substantial, massive; impenetrable, impermeable, imporous, nonporous;
incompressible.

13. indivisible, nondivisible, undividable, inseparable, impartible, infrangible,
indiscerptible; insoluble, indissoluble, undissolvable; infusible.

14. thickened, inspissated, incrassated;
congealed, coagulated, clotted, knotted,
grumous; curdled, curded, clabbered, caseous; jellied, gelatinized; lumped, lumpy,
lumpish; caked, caky.

ADVS. 15. densely, compactly, close,
closely, thick, thickly, heavily; solidly,
firmly.

354. RARITY

Opposite of Density.—NOUNS 1. rarity,
rareness; tenuousness, tenuity; subtlety,
subtility, subtilty; fineness, thinness, exil-
ity; slightness, flimsiness, unsubstantiality;
ethereality, airiness.

2. rarefaction, rarification, attenuation,
subtilization.

3. refinement, clarification, purification, cleansing, defecation, depuration;
straining, draining, elutriation; filtering,
filtration; percolation, leaching, lixiviation;
sifting, separation, screening, sieving, bolting, riddling, winnowing; sublimation, spiritualization.

4. refiner, refinery; clarifier, defecator;
filter, filterer; strainer, colander, colatorium, Hippocrates' sleeve; percolator, lixiviator; sifter, sieve, screen, riddle, cribble; winnow, winnower; cradle, rocker.

VERBS 5. rarefy, rarify, attenuate, thin;
subtilize, etherealize; expand 196.4.

6 refine, clarify, clear, purify, rectify,
cleanse, defecate, depurate, decrassify;
strain, drain, elutriate; filter, filtrate; percolate, leach, lixiviate; sift, separate, sieve,
screen, bolt, riddle, winnow; sublimate,
sublime, spiritualize.

ADJS. 7. rare, rarefied; subtle, subtile;
thin, attenuated, attenuate; fine, refined;
tenuous, flimsy, slight, unsubstantial; airy,
ethereal, vaporous, gaseous, windy; uncom-
pact, uncompressed.

8. rarefactive, rarefactional.

355. HARDNESS, RIGIDITY

NOUNS 1. hardness, solidity, durity, induration; callousness, callosity; stoniness,
flintiness.

2. rigidity, rigidness, rigor; firmness,
fixedness, renitence or renitency; stiffness,

starchiness, consistency; tension, tensity,
tenseness, tautness, tightness.

3. inflexibility, unpliability, unmalle-
ability, intractability, unbendingness, un-
limberness, unyieldingness, stubbornness,
toughness; unalterability, immutability;
immovability 142.3; inelasticity, irresili-
ence or irresiliency; inextensibility, unexten-
sibility, unextendibility, inductility.

4. temper, chisel temper, die temper,
razor temper, saw-file temper, set temper,
spindle temper, tool temper.

5. hardening, induration, stiffening;
tempering, casehardening; solidification,
setting, concretion; crystallization; granulation; callusing; callus, callosity; lithi-
fication; lapidification; petrification, petrifaction; fossilization, fossilation; fossil; ossification; cornification, hornification; horn;
cartilaginification, chondrification; calcification; calculus; glaciation; vitrification, vitrifaction.

6. (comparisons) stone, rock, adamant,
granite, flint, marble, diamond; steel, iron,
nails; concrete, cement; brick; oak, heart of
oak; bone, cartilage.

VERBS 7. harden, indurate, toughen;
callous; temper, anneal, caseharden;
petrify, lapidify, fossilize; mineralize; lith-
ify [geol.]; vitrify; glacify; calcify; ossify;
cornify, hornify.

8. solidify, concrete, cement, fix, set,
take a set, cake; condense, thicken 353.9, 10;
crystallize, granulate, kern [chiefly dial.],
candy.

9. stiffen, rigidify; tense, tighten, brace,
trice up, screw up.

ADJS. 10. hard, solid; stony, rocky,
stonelike, rocklike, lapideous, lithoid(al);
flinty, flintlike; marble, marblelike; granitic,
granitelike; concrete, cement, cemental;
horny, corneous; bony, osseous; cartilaginous, chondric; hard-boiled; hard as nails,
~ a rock, etc. 355.6, "as firm as a stone; yea,
as hard as a piece of the nether millstone"
[Bible].

11. rigid, rigorous, stiff, fixed, stark,
firm, renitent; tense, taut, tight, unrelaxed; virgate, rodlike; ramroddy, pokerish
[both coll.]; stiff as a poker, stiff as buckram; starched, starchy.

12. inflexible, unflexible, unpliable,
unpliant, unmalleable, intractable, un-
tractable, intractile, unbending, unlimber,
unyielding, stubborn, tough; unalterable,
immutable; immovable 142.16; adamant,
adamantine; inelastic, nonelastic, irresili-

ent; inextensile, inextensible, unextensible, inextensional, unextendible, nonstretchable, inductile.

13. **hardened**, indurate, indurated; **casehardened; callous**, calloused; **solidified**, fixed, set; crystallized, granulated; petrified, lapidified, fossilized; vitrified; ossified; cornified, hornified; crusted, crusty, incrusted.

14. **hardening**, indurative; petrifying, petrifactive.

356. SOFTNESS, PLIANCY

NOUNS 1. **softness, gentleness**, easiness, delicacy, tenderness; mellowness; fluffiness, flossiness, downiness; velvetiness, silkiness; sponginess, pithiness.

2. **pliancy, pliability, plasticity, flexibility**, flexility, flexuousness, ductility, ductibility, tractility, **tractability**, facility, **elasticity**, give, bendability; **suppleness**, willowiness, **litheness, limberness; malleability**, moldability, fictility, sequacity; **impressionability**, susceptibility, responsiveness, receptiveness, sensitiveness; formability, formativeness; extensibility, extendibility.

3. **flaccidity**, flaccidness, **flabbiness, limpness, limberness**, flimsiness; **looseness**, laxness, laxity, laxation.

4. (comparisons) putty, clay, dough, wax, butter, pudding; velvet, satin, silk; wool, fleece; kapok; puff; fluff, floss, flue; down, eiderdown, swansdown, thistledown.

5. **softening, easing**, mollification, dulcification, demulsion, assuagement; mollescence; **relaxation**, laxation; mellowing; padding, wadding; pad, cushion, pillow.

VERBS 6. **soften, ease, subdue**, mollify, dulcify, assuage, milden, tone or tune down; mellow; **relax**, laxate, loosen; **limber**, limber up, supple; **mash, smash, squash** [coll.].

7. (be pliant) **yield, give**, relent, relax, bend, unbend, give way.

ADJS. 8. **soft**, nonrigid; **gentle, easy, delicate, tender**; mellow, mellowy; whisper-soft, soft as a kiss, soft as a sigh, "soft as woman's love" [Hammond], "soft as sinews of the new-born babe" [Shakespeare], soft as butter.

9. **pliant, pliable, flexible**, flexile, flexuous, **plastic, elastic, ductile** facile, tractile, **tractable**, waxy, **dough-faced** [coll.]; **yielding**, giving, bending; **malleable**, moldable, fictile, sequacious; **impressionable, impressible**, susceptible, responsive,

receptive, sensitive; **formable**, formative; **bendable**, bendsome; **supple**, willowy, **limber; lithe**, lithesome, lissome, "as lissome as a hazel wand" [Tennyson]; extensile, extensible; like putty, like wax, like dough.

10. **flaccid, flabby, limp, limber**, flimsy; **loose**, lax, relaxed.

11. **spongy, pithy**, medullary [tech.], edematous.

12. **pasty, doughy**; loamy, clayey, argillaceous.

13. **squashy**, squshy [dial.], squdgy [dial.], squishy, **squelchy**, pulpy.

14. **fluffy**, flossy; **downy**, feathery; fleecy, woolly, furry.

15. **velvety**, velvetlike, velutinous; **satiny**, satinlike; cottony; **silky**, silken, silklike, sericeous, soft as silk.

16. **softening, easing**, subduing, mollifying, dulcifying, assuaging; assuasive, demulcent, lenitive, lenient; **relaxing**, loosening; mollient, emollient, mollescent.

ADVS. 17. **softly, gently**, easily, delicately, tenderly.

357. ELASTICITY

NOUNS 1. **elasticity, resilience** or resiliency, **give; buoyance** or buoyancy, verve, snap, bounce; tone, tonicity; renitence or renitency; **spring**, springiness; rebound 283.2; **stretch**, stretchability; ductility, tensility, tensibility; extensibility, extendibility, protractility; **flexibility**, flexility; **adaptability**, responsiveness; vulcanization.

2. **stretching**; extension 201.5; distension 196.2; **stretch, tension, strain**.

3. **elastic**; rubber, gum, gum elastic; rubber elastic, rubber band; gum, chewing gum; whalebone, baleen; spring; racket, battledore.

VERBS 4. **stretch**; extend 201.9; distend 196.4.

5. give, yield 356.7; spring back 283.6.

6. elasticize; rubberize, rubber; vulcanize.

ADJS. 7. **elastic, resilient, buoyant** [fig.], **springy**; renitent; **stretchable**, stretchy [coll.]; **ductile**, tensile, tensible; extensile, extensible, extendible; protractile, protractible; **flexible**, flexile; **adaptable**, adaptive, responsive.

8. rubber, **rubbery**, rubberlike; rubberized.

9. **rubbers**

buna [synthetic]	caucho
caoutchouc	Ceará rubber

cold rubber
crepe rubber
crude rubber
elastic rubber
foam latex
foam rubber
hard rubber
India rubber,
  ir diarubber
Lastex
methyl rubber
native or wild
  rubber

neoprene
  [synthetic]
Pará rubber
plantation rubber
raw rubber
reclaimed rubber
rubber tissue
sponge rubber
synthetic rubber
Vinylite [synthetic]
vulcanite
vulcanized rubber

10. springs

bedspring
Bréquet spring
bumper spring
coil spring
elliptic spring
flat spring
hairspring

leaf spring
mainspring
shock absorber
spiral spring
springboard
volute spring
wire spring

358. TOUGHNESS

NOUNS 1. **toughness, resistance, strength, stiffness; unbreakableness,** infrangibility; **tenacity, viscidity** 50.2; **hardness** 355; leatheriness, leatherlikeness; stringiness, ropiness.

2. (comparisons) leather, whitleather; gristle, cartilage.

VERBS 3. **toughen, harden, stiffen, strengthen.**

ADJS. 4. **tough, resistant, stiff, strong,** vigorous; **tenacious, viscid** 50.9; **hard** 355.10; chewy [coll.]; leathery, leatherlike, coriaceous, tough as leather or whitleather; grisly, cartilaginous; stringy, ropy, fibrous.

5. **unbreakable, nonbreakable, infrangible,** unshatterable.

359. BRITTLENESS, FRAGILITY

NOUNS 1. **brittleness, crispness,** crispiness; **fragility, frailty,** delicacy; **breakableness,** frangibility, fracturableness, crackableness, crushableness, lacerability; fissility; friability 360.3.

VERBS 2. **crisp, crackle.**

3. break, shatter 49.11, 12.

ADJS. 4. **brittle,** brash [U.S.]; **crisp,** crispy; **fragile,** fractile, **frail,** delicate; **breakable,** frangible, crushable, crackable, fracturable, lacerable; **shatterable,** shattery, shivery, splintery; friable 360.13; fissile, scissile; brittle as glass, crisp as celery.

5. **short,** cold-short, hot-short, redshort [l metal.].

360. POWDERINESS, CRUMBLINESS

NOUNS 1. **powderiness,** pulverulence, **dustiness;** chalkiness; **mealiness,** flouriness, branniness; efflorescence [chem.].

2. **granularity, graininess,** granulation; sandiness, grittiness, arenosity, sabulosity.

3. **friability,** pulverableness, crispness, **crumbliness;** brittleness 359.

4. **pulverization,** comminution, disintegration, trituration, tripsis [med.], levigation; atomization, micronization; **powdering, crumbling;** abrasion 349.2; granulation, granulization; **beating, pounding, thrashing** or threshing; **mashing, smashing, crushing.**

5. **powder, dust,** attritus; cosmetic powder, face powder; efflorescence [chem.]; **crumb, crumble; meal,** bran, flour, farina; grits, groats; filings, raspings, scobs, sawdust; detritus, debris; soot, smut.

6. **grain,** granule, granulet; **grit, sand, gravel,** shingle.

7. **pulverizer,** comminutor, triturator, levigator; **mill** 347.20; **grinder;** granulater; grater, nutmeg grater; pestle, pestle and mortar; **masher,** potato masher; millstone, quernstone, quern, kern [dial.]; roller, steam roller.

8. koniology; konimeter, koniscope.

VERBS 9. **pulverize, powder,** comminute, triturate, contriturate, levigate, bray, disintegrate, reduce to powder or dust; atomize, micronize; **crumble,** crumb; **granulate,** granulize, grain; **grind, grate;** abrade 349.7; **mill,** flour; **beat, pound, thrash** or thresh, bruise; **mash, smash, crush,** squash, crunch, craunch, scranch [chiefly dial.], scrunch [coll. & dial.].

10. (be reduced to powder) **powder,** come or fall to dust, **crumble,** crumble to or into dust, **disintegrate,** fall to pieces, break up; effloresce; granulate, grain.

ADJS. 11. **powdery, dusty;** pulverulent, pulverous, pulvereous, pulveraceous; **pulverized,** powdered, disintegrated, comminute, gone to dust, reduced to powder; **fine,** impalpable; **chalky,** chalklike; **mealy,** floury, farinaceous; branny, furfuraceous; detrited, detrital; efflorescent [chem.].

12. **granular, grainy,** granulate, granulated; **sandy, gritty,** sabulous, sabulose, sabuline, arenose, psammous; **pebbled,** pebbly.

13. **pulverable, pulverizable,** pulverulent, triturable; **friable,** crimp, short, crisp, **crumbly,** chalky, shivery.

361. COLOR

NOUNS 1. **color, hue; tint,** tinct [poetic], tincture [poetic], **tinge, shade;** tone, cast; **dye, stain; coloring, coloration;** complexion, schoolgirl complexion; undercolor; local color; technicolor; colorama.

2. **warmth,** warmth of color, warm color; **blush, flush, glow.**

3. **colorfulness,** color, bright color, **brightness, vividness,** intensity; **richness,** gorgeousness, gaiety *or* gayety; riot of color.

4. **gaudiness** 902.3; loud *or* screaming color [coll.]; shocking pink, jaundiced yellow, arsenic green.

5. **color** quality, colorimetric quality, **value; chroma,** chromaticity; **tone,** key, note; keeping [art]; chromatism, chromism; achromaticity, achromatism.

6. chromatic color, achromatic *or* neutral color; **spectrum,** color spectrum, chromatic spectrum; hue cycle, color cycle *or* gamut; color circle, chromatic circle; fundamental colors; primary *or* primitive color, primary; secondary color, secondary; tertiary color, tertiary; complimentary color; spectral color; spectrum color, pure *or* full color; broken color; monochrome; demitint, half tint, half tone.

7. (coloring matter) **color, coloring, colorant,** tinction, tincture, **pigment, stain; paint; dye,** dyestuff; opaque color, transparent color; chromogen; *gouache* [F.]; medium, vehicle; distemper, tempera; drier; thinner; turpentine, turps [coll.].

8. (persons according to hair coloring) **brunet** [masc.], brunette [fem.]; **blond** [masc.], blonde [fem.], blondine, goldilocks; blondie, dizzy blonde [both slang]; peroxide blonde, drugstore blonde [slang]; **towhead; redhead;** carrottop, red, sandy [all slang].

9. (science of colors) colorifice, chromatology; chromatics, chromatography, chromatoscopy, colorimetry; spectrum analysis, spectrology.

10. (applying color) **coloring,** coloration; **staining, dyeing; tinting,** tinging, tinction; pigmentation; illumination, emblazonry.

11. **painting,** coating, covering; **enameling,** glossing, glazing; **varnishing,** japanning, lacquering, shellacking; **calcimining, whitewashing;** gilding; stippling; frescoing, fresco; undercoating, priming.

12. **coat,** coating, **coat of paint; undercoat,** undercoating, **primer,** priming, prime coat, **ground, flat coat,** dead-color; wash, wash coat, flat wash.

VERBS 13. **color,** hue; **tinge, tint,** tinct [poetic], **tincture,** tone, complexion; pigment; **stain, dye;** imbue; imbrue; deep-dye,

fast-dye, double-dye, dye in the wool; ingrain, grain; shade, shadow; illuminate, emblazon.

14. **paint,** sling paint [slang]; **coat,** cover, face; dab, daub, bedaub, smear, besmear; slick, slick on [both coll.]; slapdash [coll.], slap-dab [slang]; **enamel,** gloss, glaze; **varnish,** japan, lacquer, **shellac; calcimine, whitewash;** wash; gild, begild, engild; stipple; fresco; parget; distemper; undercoat, prime, dead-color, flat; turpentine, turp [slang].

15. (be inharmonious) **clash,** collide [coll.], swear at [slang]; cut (be too prominent [art]).

ADJS. 16. **chromatic,** colorific, colorative, tinctorial; colorable, tingible; monochrome, monochromic, monochromatic; dichromatic; polychromatic; prismatic; pigmentary; warm; cool, cold.

17. **colored,** hued; **tinged, tinted,** tinctured, tinct [poetic], toned; **stained, dyed;** imbued, imbrued; complexioned, complected [dial., U.S.]; full-colored, full; deep, deep-colored; wash-colored.

18. **deep-dyed, fast-dyed,** double-dyed, **dyed-in-the-wool;** ingrained, ingrain; fast, fadeless, unfading, indelible.

19. **colorful,** colory [coll.]; **bright, vivid,** intense, **rich,** exotic, **gorgeous, gay,** florid; bright-colored, rich-colored, gay-colored, high-colored.

20. **gaudy** 902.20.

21. **off-color,** off-tone; **inharmonious,** discordant, incongruous, harsh, clashing, colliding [coll.].

22. soft-colored, **soft,** softened, **subdued,** mellow, delicate, tender, sweet.

23. **dyes**

acid color *or* dye	*garanceux* [F.]
alizarin, alizarin dye *or* color	lake
	madder
aniline, aniline dye	madder bloom
anthracene	madder extract
artificial *or* synthetic dye	methylene
	mineral pigment
azo dye	mordant dye
basic dye	naphthol
chromotrope	natural dye *or* dyestuff
crocein	
developing dye	pincoffin
direct cotton dye	sulphoncyanine
fast dye	vat dye
garance	wood fast dye

24. **paints**

animé	cosmetics 898.11
calcimine	elemi
Chinese lacquer	enamel
copal	engobe
copalite, copaline	gilt, gilding

glaze
japan
lac
lacquer
megilp or megilph
oils, oil paints or colors

shellac
synthetic lacquer
varnish
water colors
water glass
whitewash

25. instruments

chromatograph
chromatometer
chromatoscope
chromatrope,
  chromotrope
chromometer

chromoscope
colorimeter
kaleidoscope
prism
spectroscope
442.15

362. COLORLESSNESS

NOUNS 1. **colorlessness,** huelessness, tonelessness; achromatism, achromaticity; dullness, lackluster 336.6.

2. **paleness, dimness,** weakness, **faintness;** lightness, fairness; **pallor,** pallidity; **wanness, sallowness,** pastiness, ashiness; **anemia** [med.], bloodlessness; achroma, achromasia [both med.]; **ghastliness, haggardness,** luridness, sickliness; pastel.

3. **decoloration,** decolorization, discoloration, achromatization; **fading, paling; whitening,** blanching, etiolation; **bleaching,** bleach, dealbation; market bleach, madder bleach, Turkey-red bleach.

4. **bleach,** bleacher; decolorant, decolorizer.

VERBS 5. **decolor, decolorize,** discolor, achromatize, etiolate; **fade, wash out; dim, dull,** tarnish, tone down; **pale, whiten,** blanch; **bleach,** peroxide, fume.

6. **lose color, fade,** fade out, vanish, fly, go; **bleach,** bleach out; **pale, turn pale,** grow pale, **change color,** turn white, **whiten,** blanch, wan.

ADJS 7. **colorless, hueless,** toneless, uncolored, decolorate, achromic, achromatic; neutral; dull, lackluster 336.19.

8. **faded, washed-out,** dimmed, discolored, etiolated.

9. **pale, dim,** weak, **faint; pallid, wan, sallow,** fallow; **white,** white as a sheet; **pasty,** mealy; **ashen,** ashy; **anemic,** bloodless, chlorotic; **ghastly,** lurid, **haggard,** cadaverous, sickly, deadly or deathly pale; pale as death, ~ a ghost, ~ a witch, ~ a corpse, "pale as a forpined ghost" [Chaucer], "pale as his shirt" [Shakespeare]; pale-faced, tallow-faced.

10. **light, fair,** light-colored, light-hued; pastel; whitish 363.9.

11. bleaches

bleaching clay or earth

bleaching powder
bleach liquor

chlorine
chlorine water
Clorox
dilute acid
eau de Javelle [F.]
gray sour
hydrochloric acid
hydrogen peroxide
Javelle water
lime

lye boil
oxalic acid
peroxide
Purex
sodium
  hypochlorite
sour
sulphuric acid
white sour

363. WHITENESS

NOUNS 1. **whiteness, whitishness,** albescence; **white,** silver; **lightness, fairness;** paleness 362.2; silveriness, snowiness, frostiness, chalkiness, pearliness, creaminess, blondness; hoariness, grizzliness, canescence; milkiness, lactescence; leucoderma [med.]; albinism, albinoism; albino.

2. (comparisons) chalk, lily, milk, pearl, sheet, silver, snow, driven snow.

3. **white man, Caucasian,** paleface; buckra, fay, kelt [all Negro dial.]; white trash.

4. **whitening,** albification, albication, etiolation, dealbation; **whitewashing; bleaching** 362.3; silvering, frosting, grizzling.

5. **whiting,** whitening, **whitewash.**

VERBS 6. **whiten,** white, etiolate, **blanch; bleach** 362.5; white out [printing]; silver, grizzle, frost, besnow; chalk.

7. **whitewash,** white; gloss, gloze, gloss over [all fig.].

ADJS 8. **white,** pure white; **snow-white,** snowy, niveous, white as snow, "white as driven snow" [Shakespeare], "whiter than new snow on a raven's back" [ibid.]; frosty, frosted; **hoary,** hoar; **grizzled,** grizzly, canescent; silver, **silvery,** silvered; argent, argentine; platinum; chalky, cretaceous; milk-white, milky, lactescent; marble, marmoreal; lily-white, white as a lily, "white as the whitest lily on a stream" [Longfellow]; white as a sheet.

9. **whitish,** whity, albescent; **light, fair;** pale 362.9; off-white; eggshell; pearl, pearly, pearl-white; alabaster, alabastrine; ivory, ivory-white; gray-white, dun-white; lint-white.

10. **blond** or blonde, ash-blond, platinum blond; artificial blond, peroxide blond, drugstore blond [joc.]; blond-headed, blond-haired; **towheaded,** tow-haired; golden-haired 369.5.

11. **albinic,** albinistic.

12. colors, pigments

alabaster
blanc d'argent [F.]

blanc d'Espagne [F.]

blanc de fard [F.]
blanc fixe
barium sulphate
baryta white
blond, blonde
carbonate of lead
Chinese white
Dutch white
eggshell
flake white
indigo white
ivory

off white
Paris white
pearl
pearl white
permanent white
platinum
silver
snow white
white lead
zinc oxide
zinc sulphide
zinc white

364. BLACKNESS

NOUNS 1. blackness, nigritude, nigrescence; black, sable, ebony; ink black, etc. 364.13; lividness, lividity; pitch-blackness, pitch-darkness; nigrities [med.].

2. darkness, darkishness, darksomeness, blackishness; swarthiness, swartness, swarth; duskiness, duskness; murkiness, murk [chiefly dial.]; soberness, somberness, graveness, sadness; lightlessness, gloominess, dimness, dullness 336.

3. dinginess, griminess, smokiness, sootiness, smudginess, smuttiness, blotchiness, dirtiness, muddiness; fuliginousness, fuliginosity.

4. (comparisons) ebony, ebon [poetic]; jet, ink, sloe, pitch, tar, coal, smoke, soot, smut, raven, crow, night, ace of spades.

5. blackening, darkening, denigration; shading; smudging, smutching, smirching; smudge, smutch, smirch, smut.

6. blacking, blackening; blackwash; blackface; charcoal, burnt cork, black ink; lampblack, carbon black, gas black, soot.

VERBS 7. blacken, black; nigrify, negroize, denigrate; darken, bedarken; shade, shadow; blackwash, ink, charcoal, cork; smudge, smutch, smirch, besmirch, murk, blotch, blot, dinge [coll. & dial., Eng.]; smut, soot; smoke, oversmoke.

ADJS. 8. black, sable, dhu [Celtic]; negro, nigrous, nigrine; ebony, "black as ebony" [Shakespeare]; deep black, of the deepest dye; pitch-black, pitch-dark, pitchy, black or dark as pitch; night-black, night-dark, black or dark as night; midnight, black as midnight; inky, inky-black, ink-black, black as ink; jet-black, jetty; coal-black, coaly, black as coal; shoe, sloe-black, sloe-colored; raven, raven-black, black as a crow, "cyprus black as e'er was crow" [Shakespeare]; black as my hat, black as a shoe, black as the ace of spades, black as a stack of black cats, "black as hell" [Shakespeare], "black as the pit from pole to pole" [W.E. Henley], "more black than

ash-buds in the front of March" [Tennyson].

9. dark, dark-colored, darkish, darksome, blackish; nigrescent, nigricant; swarthy, swart [poetic]; dusky, dusk; murky, murkish, murk [poetic & dial.]; somber, sombrous; sober, grave, sad; lightless, gloomy, dim, dull 336.14–19.

10. dark-skinned, black-skinned, dark-complexioned, colored.

11. dingy, grimy, smoky, sooty, smudgy, smutty, blotchy, dirty, muddy, fuliginous; smirched, besmirched.

12. livid, black and blue.

13. colors, pigments

alizarin cyanine	ink black
aniline black	ivory black
anthracite (black)	japan
blue black	lampblack
bone black	naphthol black
Brunswick black	naphthylamine
cachou de Laval	black
diphenyl black	nigrosine
direct deep black	raven black
drop black	soot black
Frankfort black	sulphur black
immedial black	ungreenable black

365. GRAYNESS

NOUNS 1. grayness, grayishness, gray, neutral tint; taupe, iron gray, etc. 365.5; pearliness, silveriness, smokiness, mousiness, slatiness, leadenness; dullness, soberness, somberness.

VERBS 2. gray or grey, grizzle, silver, dapple.

ADJS. 3. gray or grey, grayish, gray-colored, gray-hued, gray-toned; dull, dingy; somber, sober, sad, dreary; iron-gray; Quaker-gray, quaker-colored; dove-gray, dove-colored; pearl-gray, pearl, pearly; silver-gray, silver, silvery, silvered; grizzly, grizzled; ash-gray, ashen, ashy; cinerous, cinereal; dusty, dust-gray; smoky, smoke-gray; slaty, slate-colored; stone-colored; leaden, livid, lead-gray; mousy, mouse-gray, mouse-colored; taupe; dapple-gray, dappled-gray, dappled; gray-spotted, gray-speckled; pepper-and-salt; gray-white, gray-black, gray-blue, gray-brown, gray-green, etc.

4. gray-haired, gray-headed, silver-headed; hoary, hoary-haired, hoaryheaded; gray-bearded, silver-bearded.

5. colors, pigments

acier	cadet gray
ash	cinder gray
ash gray	crystal gray
bat	diaminogen
battleship gray	dove gray

field gray	Payne's gray
French gray	pearl
gray induline	pearl gray
gun metal	pepper and salt
iron gray	Quaker gray
lead gray	silver gray
mole (gray)	smoke gray
moleskin	steel gray
mouse gray	taupe
neutral tint	zinc gray
Oxford gray	

366. BROWNNESS

NOUNS 1. **brownness, brownishness, brown;** chocolate, cinnamon, etc. 366.5.

VERBS 2. **brown,** embrown; rust; **tan, bronze;** suntan, sunburn, burn.

ADJS. 3. **brown, brownish;** cinnamon, hazel, puce, fuscous, **brunet** or brunette; tawny, fulvous; tan, tan-colored; tan-faced, tan-skinned, sun-tanned; khaki, khaki-colored; drab, olive-drab; dun, dun-brown, dun-drab, dun-olive; chocolate, chocolate-colored, chocolate-brown; cocoa, cocoa-colored, cocoa-brown; coffee, coffee-colored, coffee-brown; toast, toast-brown; nut-brown; walnut, walnut-brown; seal, seal-brown; fawn, fawn-colored; snuff-colored, mummy-brown; umber, umber-colored, umber-brown; olive, olive-brown; yellowish-brown, brownish-yellow; brown as a berry.

4. **reddish-brown,** brownish-red; sepia, roan, sorrel, henna, terra-cotta, rufous, foxy; livid-brown, lurid; mahogany, mahogany-brown; auburn, titian or Titian; russet, russety; rust, rust-colored, rusty, ferruginous, rubiginous; liver-colored, liver-brown; bronze, bronze-colored, bronzed, brazen; copper, coppery, copperish, cupreous, copper-colored; chestnut, chestnut-colored, chestnut-brown, castaneous; bay, bay-colored, bayard; sunburned, sunburnt.

5. **colors, pigments**

acid brown	chocolate (brown)
acorn	chrysamine
adust	cocoa (brown)
alesan	coconut brown
Argos brown	coffee (brown)
aurin	Cologne brown
autumn leaf	Cyprus earth or
azoflavine	umber
biscuit	dead leaf
Bismarck brown	direct brown
bister	drab
Bordeaux	dun
brown madder	fawn
brown ocher	feuille-morte [F.]
brunet, brunette	foliage brown
burnt almond	French nude
café au lait	hazel
café noir	khaki
Castilian brown	leather

madder brown	Roman umber
Manchester brown	seal (brown)
manganese brown	Sicilian umber
Mars brown	snuff color
meadow lark	sulphoncyanine
Merida	suntan
mummy (brown)	tan
nut brown	Tanagra
old cedar	tawny
olive (brown)	tenné
olive drab	terra umbra
oriole	toast (brown)
otter brown	topaz
partridge	Turkey umber
philamot	umber
pickaninny	Vandyke brown
raw umber	Verona brown
resorcin brown	walnut (brown)

6. **reddish brown**

auburn	raw sienna
bay	roan
bronze	russet
burnt sienna	rust
burnt umber	sepia
chestnut (brown)	sienna (brown)
copper	sorrel
henna	terra cotta
liver brown	terra sienna
mahogany (brown)	titian

367. REDNESS

NOUNS 1. **redness, reddishness,** rubescence, erubescence, rubicundity, rubricity, floridity; **ruddiness,** color; **red,** *rouge* [F.], rubelle, gules [her.]; scarlet, crimson, etc. 367.13; reddish brown 366.6.

2. **pinkness, pinkishness, pink;** rose, flesh, etc. 367.14; *couleur de rose* [F.].

3. **reddening,** rubefaction, rubification, rubrication, rubescence, erubescence; **coloring,** mantling, crimsoning, **blushing, flushing;** blush, flush, glow, bloom; hectic, hectic flush.

VERBS 4. (make red) **redden, rouge,** ruddle, rubricate, rubricize; warm, inflame; crimson, encrimson; vermilion, madder, henna, rust, carmine; incarnadine, pinkify; red-ink, lipstick.

5. (become red) **redden,** turn or grow red, **color,** color up, **mantle, blush, flush, crimson;** flame, glow.

ADJS. 6. **red, reddish,** red-colored, red-hued, red-dyed, red-looking; **ruddy,** ruddied; rubicund, rubric(al), rubiate, rubricate, rubricose; rufous, rufulous; warm, hot, glowing; fiery, flaming, flame-colored, flame-red, fire-red, red as fire, red as a hot or live coal; reddened, inflamed.

7. scarlet, vermillion, crimson, maroon, damask, puce, stammel, murrey, magenta, cerise, iron-red; cardinal, cardinal-red; cherry, cherry-colored, cherry-red; carmine,

incarmined; ruby, ruby-colored, ruby-red; wine, wine-colored, wine-red, claret-colored, vinaceous; carnation, carnation-red; brick-red, brick-colored, bricky, tile-red, lateritious; lake-colored, laky; lobster-red, red as a lobster; copper-red, carnelian; Titian or titian, Titian-red; infrared; reddish-amber, reddish-gray, etc.; reddish-brown 366.4.

8. **sanguine,** sanguineous, **blood-red,** blood-colored, bloody-red, bloody, gory, red as blood.

9. **pink,** pink-colored, **pinkish,** pinky; **rose, rosy,** rose-colored, rose-hued, rose-red, roseate; primrose; flesh-color, flesh-colored, flesh-pink, incarnadine; coral, coral-colored, coral-red, coralline; salmon, salmon-colored, salmon-pink.

10. **red-complexioned,** ruddy-complexioned, warm-complexioned, red-fleshed, red-faced, ruddy-faced; **ruddy,** rubicund, **florid,** sanguine, full-blooded; blowzy, blowzed; rosy, **rosy-cheeked;** glowing, blooming; hectic, flushed, flush; burnt, sunburned, sunburnt.

11. **redheaded,** red-haired, red-polled; red-crested, red-crowned, red-tufted; sandy, carroty, chestnut, auburn, Titian or titian.

12. reddening, blushing, flushing, coloring; rubescent, erubescent, rubificative, rubrific.

13. colors, pigments

Adrianople red	flame red
alizarin, alizarine	fuchsin, fuchsine
amidonaphthol red	hellebore red
annatto	Indian red
azogrenadine	infrared
blood red	iron red
burnt carmine	Japanese red
burnt crimson lake	lake
burnt lake	light red
cardinal (red)	lobster
carmine	madder
carmine lake	madder carmine
carminette	madder crimson
carnation (red)	madder red
carnelian	madder scarlet
cerise	magenta
cherry (red)	Majolica earth
Chinese red	maroon
chrome red	minium
chrome scarlet	murrey
cinnabar	Naples red
claret red	palladium red
cochineal	Persian earth
Congo rubine	Persian red
copper (red)	Pompeian red
coquelicot	ponceau
cresol red	poppy (red)
crimson	Prussian red
crimson madder	puce
damask	Quaker drab
fire red	realgar

red lead	solferino (red)
red ocher	stammel
roccellin	terra rosa
rubiate	tile red
rubine, rubin	toluidine red
ruby	Turkey red
ruddle	Vandyke red
sanguine	Venetian red
scarlet	vermilion
scarlet madder	vermilionette
scarlet ocher	wine (red)
Siena	

14. pink colors

annatto	mallow pink
burnt rose	moonlight
cameo pink	opera pink
carnation rose	Pompeii
chrome primrose	primrose
Dutch pink	red pink
English pink	rose
flesh, flesh color	rose bengale
flesh red or pink	rose madder
incarnadine	salmon (pink)
Italian pink	shocking pink
livid pink	stil-de-grain yellow
madder lake or	tea rose
pink	yellow madder
madder yellow	

368. ORANGENESS

NOUNS 1. **orangeness,** oranginess, **orange;** tangerine, marigold, etc. 368.3.

ADJS. 2. **orange, orangeish,** orangey [coll.], orange-colored, orange-hued, reddish-yellow; ocherous, ochery; old-gold; apricot, peach; carroty, carrot-colored; orange-red, orange-yellow, reddish-orange, yellowish-orange.

3. colors, pigments

apricot	ocher
burnt orange	old gold
burnt Roman	orange chrome
ocher	yellow
cadmium	orange lead
cadmium orange	orange madder
cadmium yellow	orange mineral or
carrot	minium
chrome orange	orange ocher
helianthin	orange vermilion
madder orange	orange shellac
mandarin (orange)	peach
marigold	Spanish ocher
marigold yellow	tangerine
Mars orange	Tangier
methyl orange	zinc orange

369. YELLOWNESS

NOUNS 1. **yellowness, yellowishness, yellow,** or [her.]; lemon, saffron, etc. 369.7; sallowness, fallowness.

2. (medical) xanthochroia, xanthosis, xanthoderma, xanthocyanopia, xanthochromia; **jaundice,** yellow jaundice, icterus.

VERBS 3. yellow, turn yellow; **gild,** be-gild, engild; chrome; sallow; **jaundice.**

ADJS. 4. **yellow, yellowish;** lutescent, luteous, luteolous; xanthic, xanthous; **gold, golden,** gold-colored, golden-yellow, gilt, gilded aureate; canary, canary-yellow; citron, citron-colored, citron-yellow, citrine, citreous; lemon, lemon-colored, lemon-yellow; sulphur-colored, sulphur-yellow; pale-yellow, **sallow,** fallow; cream, creamy, cream-colored; straw, straw-colored; flaxen, flaxen-colored, flax-colored; sandy, sand-colored; ocherous, ochery; buff, buff-colored, buff-yellow; beige, ecru; saffron, saffron-colored, saffron-yellow; apricot, peach; primrose, primrose-yellow; topaz-yellow.

5. **golden-haired,** flaxen-haired, auricomous, blond 363.10.

6. yellow-faced, yellow-complexioned, yellow-cheeked; **jaundiced,** icterine, icterous, **icteroid.**

7. colors, pigments

acid yellow	jonquil (yellow)
amber	justic
apricot	king's yellow
auramine	lemon
aureolin	lemon chrome
aurin	lemon yellow
barium chrome *or* chromate	madder yellow
barium yellow	maize
baryta yellow	massicot
beige	metanil yellow
buff	mikado yellow
butter (yellow)	naphthol yellow
cadmium yellow	orpiment
canarin	Paris yellow
canary (yellow)	peach
Cassel yellow	peanut
champagne	pebble
chrome	permanent yellow
chrome lemon	phosphine
chrome yellow	primrose (yellow)
chrysophenin	primuline yellow
citron (yellow)	purree
Claude tint	pyrethrum yellow
cream	quince yellow
crocus	saffron
dandelion	sand
ecru	snapdragon
euxanthin	stil-de-grain yellow
fast yellow	straw (yellow)
flax	sunflower yellow
gamboge	sulphur (yellow)
gold	tartrazine
golden pheasant	yellow madder
goldenrod	yellow ocher
golden yellow	yolk yellow
immedial yellow	xanthein
Indian yellow	xanthin
	xanthophyll

370. GREENNESS

NOUNS 1. greenness, greenishness, greenhood; **verdantness,** verdancy, **verdure,** virescence, viridescence, viridity; **green, verte** [her.]; emerald, jade, etc. 370.6; chlorophyll.

2. **verdigris, patina;** patination.

VERBS 3. **green;** verdigris, patinate, patinize.

ADJS. 4. **green, verdant,** verdurous; **greenish,** virescent; grass-green, chlorine, green as grass; citrine, citrinous; olive, olive-green, olivaceous; beryl-green, berylline; leek-green, porraceous; emerald, emerald-green, smaragdine; chartreuse; yellow-green, yellowish-green, greenish-yellow; glaucous, glaucous-green; blue-green, bluish-green, greenish-blue; apple-green, pea-green, etc. 370.6.

5. verdigrisy, verdigrised; patinous, patinated.

6. colors, pigments

absinthe (green)	Kelly green
acid fuchsine	leaf green
apple green	leek green
aquagreen	malachite green
aquamarine, aqua marina	marine green
	meadow brook
benzoyl green	methyl green
beryl green	mignonette
bice	milori green
bottle green	Mitis green
Brunswick green	Mittler's green
celadon	Montpellier green
celadonite	moss (green)
chartreuse	myrtle (green)
chrome *or* chromium green	Nile (green)
chrome oxide green	olive (green)
	Paris green
chromic oxide	patina green
chrysoidine	pea green
chrysolite green	phenosafranine
chrysoprase green	Quaker green
cobalt green	reseda
corbeau	sap green
cucumber green	Schweinfurt green
duck green	sea *or* sea-water green
Egyptian green	serpentine green
emerald (green)	shamrock (green)
emeraude	Spanish green
fir (green)	terre-verte
gallein	turquoise (green)
galloflavine	verdant green
glauconite	verdet
glaucous green	verdigris (green)
grass green	verditer (green)
green ocher	Veronese green
Guignet's green	Vienna green
Guinea green	viridian
Irish green	viridine green
jade (green)	yew green
Janus green	zinc green

371. BLUENESS

NOUNS 1. blueness, bluishness; azureness, azurineness; **blue, azure;** turquoise, peacock blue, etc. 371.4; bluing.

VERBS 2. **blue**, azure.

ADJS. 3. **blue**, blue-colored; **bluish**, azury, cerulescent; cyanic, cyaneous, cyanean; cerulean, ceruleous; **azure**, azurine, azurean, azurous, azured, azure-blue, azure-colored, azure-tinted; sky-blue, sky-colored, sky-dyed; light-blue, lightish-blue, light-bluish, pale-blue; dark-blue, deep-blue; peacock-blue, pavonine, pavonian; beryl-blue, berylline; turquoise, turquoise-blue; sapphire, sapphire-blue, sapphirine; garter-blue; navy-blue, baby-blue, etc. 371.4.

4. colors, pigments

aniline blue	indanthrene blue
aquamarine, aqua	indigo
marina	isamine blue
azo blue	Italian blue
azure (blue)	jouvence blue
azurite blue	lacmoid
baby blue	lavender blue
benzoazurine	Leitch's blue
beryl (blue)	leucocyan
bice (blue)	madder blue
bleu céleste [F.]	marine (blue)
bleu d'azur [F.]	methyl or methyl-
bleu de Lyon [F.]	ene blue
bleu de Saxe [F.]	midnight blue
bleu Louise [F.]	milori blue
bleu lumière [F.]	national blue
bleu passé [F.]	navy (blue)
blue turquoise	new blue
Brunswick blue	old blue
cadet blue	peacock blue
calamine blue	Persian blue
cerulean (blue)	powder blue
ceruleum	Prussian blue
ciba blue	robin's-egg blue
cobalt	sapphire (blue)
cornflower (blue)	sea blue
cyan (blue)	sky (blue)
cyanin, cyanine	smalt
cyanine blue	steel (blue)
cyanogen	syenite blue
dahlia	trypan blue
direct blue	turquoise (blue)
Dresden blue	sea blue
electric (blue)	ultramarine (blue)
émail [F.]	water blue
French blue	wisteria blue
hyacinth (blue)	zaffer

372. PURPLENESS

NOUNS 1. **purpleness**, **purplishness**, purpliness; **purple**, purplure [her.]; lavender, violet, etc. 372.4; lividness, lividity.

VERBS 2. **purple**, empurple.

ADJS. 3. **purple**, purpie [Scot.], purple-colored; **purplish**, purply, purplescent; violet, violaceous; plum-colored, plum-purple; amethystine, lavender, lavender-blue, lilac, magenta, mauve, mulberry, orchid, pansy-purple, pansy-violet, raisin-colored; livid.

4. colors, pigments

amethyst	magenta
bishop's purple	mallow
Burgundy	Mars violet
damson	mauve
fluorite violet	mulberry
grape	orchid
gridelin	pansy
heliotrope	pansy purple
hyacinth	pansy violet
hyacinth violet	plum
lavender	raisin
lilac	raisin black
livid purple	raisin purple
livid violet	solferino
madder violet	violet

373. VARIEGATION

Diversity of Colors.—NOUNS 1. **variegation**, **motley**, **multicolor**, parti-color or party-color, polychrome; dichroism, trichroism; harlequin.

2. **iridescence**, iridization, irisation, **opalescence**, play of colors.

3. **spottiness**, maculation; **fleck**, **speck**, **speckle**; freckle; **spot**, dot, blotch, splotch, patch, splash; **mottle**, **dapple**.

4. **check**, **checker**; **plaid**, tartan; checkerwork, patchwork; parquet, parquetry, marquetry, mosaic, tesserae, tessellation; chessboard, checkerboard.

5. **striation**, striature, striae; striola [biol.], striga; **streak**, streaking, **stripe**, striping, bar, band, belt, list; brindle.

6. (comparisons) spectrum, rainbow, iris; chameleon; leopard, panther, jaguar, cheetah, ocelot, zebra; peacock, butterfly; mother-of-pearl, nacre, tortoise shell, opal, cymophane, marble, ophite; mackerel, mackerel sky; confetti; Joseph's coat.

VERBS 7. **variegate**, motley; polychrome, polychromize; **mottle**, **dapple**, stipple; **fleck**, flake; **speck**, **speckle**, bespeckle; freckle; **spot**, bespot, dot, sprinkle, pepper, stud, maculate; blotch, splotch; tattoo, stigmatize; **check**, **checker**; tessellate; **streak**, **stripe**, **striate**, band, bar, vein; marble, marbleize; rainbow, iris.

8. **iridesce**, iridize, iris; **opalesce**, opalize.

ADJS. 9. **variegated**, **many-colored**, many-hued, divers-colored; **multicolored**, multicolor, multicolorous; **varicolored**, varicolorous; versicolored, versicolor, versicolorate, versicolorous; polychrome, polychromic, polychromatic; parti-colored or party-colored, parti-color or party-color; colorful, colory [coll.]; of all manner of colors, of all the colors of the rainbow, daedal, kaleidoscopic(al); prismatic(al), prismal; shot, shot through; bicolored, bicolor, dichromic, dichromatic; tricolored, tricolor, trichromic, trichromatic.

10. **iridescent,** iridal, iridial, iridian; irised, irisated; **rainbowy,** rainbowlike; **opalescent,** opaline, opaloid; nacreous, nacrous, nacry, *nacré* [F.], nacred; **pearly,** pearlish; mother-of-pearl; tortoise-shell; pavonine, pavonian; cymophanous, chatoyant.

11. **chameleonlike,** chameleonic.

12. **mottled, motley; pied, piebald,** skewbald, pinto; **dappled,** dapple; calico; marbled; clouded; pepper-and-salt.

13. **spotted, dotted,** sprinkled, peppered, studded; **spotty,** dotty, patchy; **speckled, specked,** speckledy, speckly, specky; **flecked,** fleckered; maculate, maculated; macular; punctate, punctated; freckled, freckly; blotched, blotchy; flea-bitten.

14. **checked, checkered,** check; **plaid,** plaided; tessellated, tessellate; mosaic.

15. **streaked,** streaky; **striated,** striate, striatal, striolate; strigate, strigose; **striped,** barred, banded, listed, veined; **brindle,** brindled, brinded; tabby; watered.

374. UNIVERSE

NOUNS 1. **universe, world, cosmos** or kosmos, creation, **all creation,** olam, nature system; wide world, whole wide world, "world without end" [Bible]; plenum; macrocosm, macrocosmos, megacosm; "but a small parenthesis in eternity" [Sir Thomas Browne], "a great factory or shop of power, with its rotating constellations, times, and tides" [Emerson]; the expanding universe.

2. **heavens,** heaven, **sky, firmament,** empyrean, welkin, *caelum* [L.], lift or lifts [now chiefly dial.]; **the blue,** blue sky, azure, cerulean, the blue yonder, the blue serene; ether, air, hyaline, "the ambient ether" [Mortimer Collins], "the clear hyaline, the glassy sea" [Milton]; **vault,** cope, canopy, vault or canopy of heaven, "the vault on high" [J.R. Drake], "the arch of heaven" [Vergil], "that inverted bowl they call the sky" [Omar Khayyám], "heaven's ebon vault" [Shelley], "starry cope" [ibid.], starry heaven or heavens, "this majestical roof fretted with golden fire" [Shakespeare], "this gorgeous arch with golden worlds inlay'd" [Young], "infinite meadows of heaven" [Longfellow]; Caelus (deified sky [Rom. myth.]).

3. **cosmic space, outer space,** empty space, ether space, pressureless space, celestial spaces, aerial region, interplanetary ~, interstellar ~, intergalactic or intercosmic space, **the void,** void of the ether space, the void above, ocean of emptiness; chaos; outermost reaches of space; zone of terrestrial attraction; temperate belt; light year; parsec, secpar.

4. **stars,** starry host, "the glorious host of night" [Bryant], "these blessed candles of the night" [Shakespeare], "the burning tapers of the sky" [ibid.], "the mystical jewels of God" [Robert Buchanan], "golden fruit upon a tree all out of reach" [G. Eliot], "flowers of the sky" [Erasmus Darwin], "the forget-me-nots of the angels" [Longfellow], "bright sentinels of the sky" [Wm. Habington], "the pale populace of Heaven" [Browning]; music or harmony of the spheres.

5. **star, heavenly body,** celestial body or sphere, **luminary, orb, sphere;** fixed star, variable star; radio stars; comet; **morning star,** daystar, Lucifer, Phosphor, Phosphorus; **evening star,** Vesper, Hesper, Hesperus, Venus; **North Star,** polestar, polar star, lodestar, Polaris, Cynosure, *l'Etoile du Nord* [F.]; Dog Star, Sirius, Canicula, Canis Majoris; Bull's Eye, Aldebaran.

6. **planet,** terrestrial planet, inferior planet, superior planet, secondary planet, major planet; minor planet, planetoid, asteroid; **satellite;** Earth, Jupiter, Mars, Mercury, Neptune, Pluto, Saturn, Uranus, Venus; solar system.

7. **earth, world,** *terra* [L.], **globe,** terrestrial globe, sphere, orb; vale, vale of tears; "this pendent world" [Shakespeare], "the little O, the earth" [ibid.], "this goodly frame, the earth" [ibid.], "a stage where every man must play a part" [ibid.], "a seat where gods might dwell" [Milton], "but the frozen echo of the silent voice of God" [Hageman], "only a ball-bearing in the hub of the universe" [Christopher Morley]; mother earth, Gaea (deified earth [Gr. myth.]), Terra [Rom. myth.]; whole wide world, four corners of the earth, the length and breadth of the land.

8. **moon,** parish lantern [dial., Eng.], piece of green cheese [joc.], orb of night, queen of heaven, queen of night; "the wat'ry star" [Shakespeare], "the governess of floods" [ibid.], "the lantern of the night" [Butler], "a ghostly galleon tossed upon cloudy seas" [A. Noyes], "Maker of sweet poets" [Keats], "the wandering Moon" [Milton], "bright wanderer, fair coquette

of Heaven" [Shelley], "that orbèd maiden with white fire laden" [ibid.], "fair regent of the night" [Erasmus Darwin], "that huntress of the silver bow" [Hood], "Queen and huntress, chaste and fair" [Jonson], "sovereign mistress of the true melancholy" [Shakespeare], "a ruined world, a globe burnt out, a corpse upon the road of night" [Sir Richard Burton]; silvery moon; **new moon,** wet moon; **crescent moon,** crescent, increscent moon, increscent, waxing moon; decrescent moon, decrescent, waning moon; **half-moon,** demilune; **full moon,** plenilune [poetic], **harvest moon,** hunter's moon; the man in the moon.

9. (moon goddess, the moon personified) Diana, Phoebe, Cynthia, Artemis, Hecate or Hekate, Selene [all Gr. & Rom. myth.]; Luna [Rom. myth.]; Astarte [Phoenician myth.].

10. **sun,** orb of day, daystar [poetic]; "the lamp of day" [Falconer], "the glorious lamp of Heav'n, the radiant sun" [Dryden], "centre and sire of light" [P.J. Bailey], "God's crest upon His azure shield" [ibid.], "that orbèd continent, the fire that severs day from night" [Shakespeare], "of this great world both eye and soul" [Milton], "the God of life and poesy and light" [Byron]; photosphere, chromosphere.

11. (sun god, the sun personified) Sol [Rom. myth.]; Helios, Hyperion, Titan, Phaëthon, Phoebus, Phoebus Apollo, Apollo [all Gr. myth.]; Ra or Amen-Ra [Egyptian myth.]; Shamash [Semitic myth.]; Surya, Savitar [both Hindu myth.].

12. **constellation, configuration,** asterism; zodiacal parallel.

13. **galaxy, island universe,** spiral; Milky Way, galactic circle, Via Lactea [L.].

14. **nebulae,** galactic nebulae, anagalactic nebulae, planetary nebulae, diffuse nebulae, spiral nebulae, dark nebulae; nebula of Andromeda, ~ Lyra or Orion; coalsack; the Coalsack, Black Magellanic Cloud; nebulous stars.

15. **meteor,** falling or shooting star, meteoroid, aerolite, fireball, bolide; **meteorite,** meteorolite; meteoric shower; meteor dust, cosmic dust.

16. **orbit, circle, trajectory;** circle of the sphere, great circle, small circle; ecliptic; **zodiac;** zone; meridian, celestial meridian; colures, equinoctial colure, solstitial colure; equator, celestial equator, equinoctial, equinoctial circle or line; equinox, vernal

equinox, autumnal equinox; longitude, celestial longitude, geocentric longitude, heliocentric longitude, galactic longitude, astronomical longitude, geographic or geodetic longitude; apogee, perigee.

17. **observatory; planetarium,** orrery; eidouranion.

18. **cosmology,** cosmography, cosmogony, cosmometry, cosmical physics, cosmic(al) geology; cosmism, cosmic philosophy, cosmic evolution; nebular hypothesis.

19. **astronomy, stargazing;** astrochemistry, astrophysics, astrography, astrophotography, astrophotometry, astroscopy, radio astronomy, solar physics; celestial mechanics, mechanical astronomy, gravitational astronomy; astrogeny, astrogony; uranology, uranography, uranometry; meteorology, meteoritics, meteoroscopy.

20. **astrology,** stargazing, astromancy, astrognosy, **horoscopy;** astrodiagnosis; natural astrology; judicial or mundane astrology; genethlialogy, genethliacs, genethliac astrology; **horoscope,** nativity; zodiac, **signs of the zodiac; house,** mansion; house of life, mundane house, planetary house or mansion; aspect.

21. **cosmologist;** cosmogonist, cosmogoner; cosmographer, cosmographist.

22. **astronomer,** stargazer; astrochemist, astrophysicist, astrophotographer, meteorologist; uranologist, uranographer, uranographist.

23. **astrologer,** astrologian, astrologaster [derog.], astromancer, stargazer, Chaldean; astroalchemist; horoscoper, horoscopist.

ADJS. 24. **cosmic(al),** kosmic(al), **universal;** cosmogonal, cosmogonic(al); cosmographic(al).

25. **celestial, heavenly, empyrean,** empyreal; **astronomical,** uranic; **astral, starry, stellar,** stellary, sphery; star-spangled, star-studded; sidereal, sideral [spec. astrol.]; **astrologic(al),** astrologistic, astrologous; **planetary,** planetarian, planetal; planetoidal, planetesimal, asteroidal; **solar,** heliac(al); **lunar,** lunular, lunate, lunulate, lunary, Cynthian [poetic]; semilunar; meteoric, meteoritic; nebular, nebulous, nebulose; zodiacal; equinoctial; interstellar, intersidereal; interplanetary; intercosmic.

26. **extraterrestrial,** exterrestrial, extraterrene, extramundane, **transmundane, otherworldly,** transcendental; extrasolar.

27. **earthly, earthy, worldly, mundane, terrestrial,** terrene, planetary, "of the earth,

earthy" [Bible]; telluric, tellurian; temporal; subastral, sublunar, under the sun.

ADVS. **28. universally,** the world over 178.11.

29. on earth, on the face of the earth *or* globe, in the world, in the wide world, in the whole wide world; **under the sun,** *sub Jove* [L.], under the stars, beneath the sky, *à la belle étoile* [F.], under heaven, below, here below.

30. constellations

Andromeda, the Chained Lady	the Northern Crown	Orion's Belt
Antlia, the Air Pump	Corvus, the Crow	Orion's Sword
Apus, the Bird of Paradise	Crater, the Cup	Pavo, the Peacock
Aquarius, the Water Bearer	Crux, the Cross, the Southern Cross	Pegasus, the Winged Horse

Andromeda, the
Chained Lady
Antlia, the Air
Pump
Apus, the Bird of
Paradise
Aquarius, the
Water Bearer
Aquila, the Eagle
Ara, the Altar
Argo (Navis), the
Ship Argo
Aries, the Ram
Auriga, the
Wagoner, the
Charioteer
Big Dipper
Boötes, the Herdsman
Caelum, the Sculptor's Tool
Camelopardalis,
Camelopardus,
the Giraffe
Cancer, the Crab
Canes Venatici,
the Hunting Dogs
Canis Major, the
Dog, Orion's
Hound
Canis Minor, the
Lesser Dog
Capricorn, the
Goat
Carina, the Keel
Cassiope, Cassiopeia's Chair
Cassiopeia, the
Lady in the Chair
Centaurus, the
Centaur
Cepheus, the
Monarch
Cetus, the Sea
Monster
Chamaeleon, the
Chameleon
Circinus, the
Compasses
Columba (Noae),
Noah's Dove
Coma Berenices,
Berenice's Hair
Corona Australis,
the Wreath, the
Southern Crown
Corona Borealis,

the Northern
Crown
Corvus, the Crow
Crater, the Cup
Crux, the Cross,
the Southern
Cross
Cygnus, the Swan
Delphinus, the
Dolphin
Dipper, Charles's
Wain
Dorado, the Goldfish, the Swordfish
Draco, the Dragon
Equuleus, the Foal
Eridanus, the
River Eridanus
Fornax, the Furnace
Gemini, the Twins
Grus, the Crane
Hercules
Horologium, the
Clock
Hyades, Hyads
Hydra, the Sea
Serpent
Hydrus, the
Water Snake
Indus, the Indian
Lacerta, the Lizard
Leo, the Lion
Leo Minor, the
Lesser Lion
Lepus, the Hare
Libra, the Balance
Little Dipper
Lupus, the Wolf
Lynx, the Lynx
Lyra, the Lyre,
the Harp
Malus, the Mast
Mensa, the Table
Mountain
Microscopium, the
Microscope
Monoceros, the
Unicorn
Musca, the Fly
Norma, the Rule
Octans, the Octant
Ophiuchus, the
Serpent Bearer
Orion, the Giant
Hunter

Orion's Belt
Orion's Sword
Pavo, the Peacock
Pegasus, the
Winged Horse
Perseus, the
Rescuer, the
Champion
Phoenix, the
Phoenix
Pictor, the
Painter's Easel
Pisces, the Fishes
Piscis Australis,
the Southern Fish
Pleiades, Atlantides
Puppis, the Poop
Reticulum, the
Net
Sagitta, the Arrow
Sagittarius, the
Archer
Scorpio, the
Scorpion
Sculptor, the
Sculptor's Workshop

Scutum, the Shield
of Sobieski
Serpens, the Serpent
Sextans, the
Sextant
Taurus, the Bull
Telescopium, the
Telescope
Triangulum, the
Triangle
Triangulum Australe, the (Southern) Triangle
Tucana, the
Toucan
Ursa Major, the
Great Bear
Ursa Minor, the
Lesser Bear
Vela, the Sails
Virgo, the Virgin
Volans, Piscis
Volans, the Flying Fish
Vulpecula, the
Little Fox

375. MATERIALITY

NOUNS **1. materiality,** materialness; **corporeity,** corporality, corporeality; **substantiality** 3; **physicalness,** physicality, flesh, flesh and blood.

2. matter, material, materiality, **substance, stuff,** hyle [philos.]; brute matter; elements, constituents; hypostasis, substratum [philos.].

3. body, physical body, corpus [chiefly joc. of a person], anatomy [joc.], person, **figure, form, frame, physique,** carcass [joc. exc. of a dead body], bones, flesh, clay, clod; hulk (of a vessel); **torso, trunk;** soma [tech.].

4. object, article, thing, affair, something; gadget 347.1; thingum, **thingumabob,** thingumadad, thingumadoodle, **thingumajig,** thingumajigger, thingumaree, thingummy, **doodad,** dofunny, **dojigger,** dojiggy, domajig, domajigger, **dohickey,** dowhacky, flumadiddle, gigamaree, **gimmick, gismo,** dingus, hickey, jigger, hootmalalie, hootnanny, whatchy, widgit [all slang]; what's-its-name 582.2; something or other, I don't know what, *je ne sais quoi* [F.].

5. materialism, physicism, somatism, substantialism; naturalism; hylism, hylicism; hylotheism; physicalism, animalism; **worldliness, earthliness;** positivism, positive philosophy, *philosophie positive* [F.]; atomism; mechanism; panpsychism; monism, philosophical unitarianism; historical materialism, dialectical materialism.

6. materialist, physicist, somatist, substantialist, hylicist; hylotheist; positivist; atomist.

7. materialization, corporealization; substantialization, substantiation; **embodiment, incorporation,** personification, **incarnation; reincarnation,** re-embodiment, transmigration, metempsychosis.

VERBS **8. materialize,** corporealize; substantialize, substantify, substantiate; **embody,** body, **incorporate,** corporify, personify, **incarnate; reincarnate,** re-embody, transmigrate.

ADJS. **9. material,** materiate; **substantial 3.4; corporeal,** corporeous, corporal, **bodily; physical,** somatic(al), hylic, **fleshly; unspiritual,** nonspiritual.

10. embodied, bodied, **incorporated, incarnate.**

11. **materialistic(al),** naturalistic; **worldly, earthly;** hylotheistic, atomistic, monistic.

376. IMMATERIALITY

NOUNS **1. immateriality,** immaterialness; incorporeity, incorporality, incorporeality, **bodilessness; unsubstantiality,** unsubstantialness; **intangibility,** impalpability, imponderability; inextension, nonextension; nonexteriority, nonexternality; **unearthliness, unworldliness;** supernaturalism 85.7; **spirituality,** spiritualness, spirituosity, spirituousness, inwardness; spirit world, astral plane.

2. (something immaterial) incorporeal, incorporeity, immateriality, unsubstantiality; intangible 4.3.

3. immaterialism, idealism, Berkeleianism; Platonism, Platonic Idea or Ideal; psychism, panpsychism; animism, animatism; hylozoism; **spiritualism,** metaphysical idealism.

4. immaterialist; idealist; Berkelian, Platonist; spiritualist, psychist 1032.13, 14; panpsychist, hylozoist, animist.

5. dematerialization; **disembodiment,** disincarnation; **spiritualization.**

VERBS **6.** dematerialize, immaterialize, unsubstantialize; **disembody,** disincarnate; **spiritualize,** spiritize.

ADJS. **7. immaterial,** nonmaterial, asomatous; **unsubstantial, intangible,** impalpable, imponderable; **incorporeal,** incorporal, incorporate, incorporeous; **bodiless,** unembodied; disembodied, discarnate, de-

carnate, decarnated; **unphysical,** nonphysical, **unfleshly; spiritual,** psychic(al), internal; **unearthly, unworldly,** extramundane, transmundane; supernatural 85.14.

8. animistic, animative, animatistic; hylozoistic.

377. MATERIALS

NOUNS **1. materials,** substances, stuff; **raw material, staple, stock;** strategic materials.

2. (building materials) sticks and stones, lath and plaster, bricks and mortar; roofing, roofage; walling, siding; flooring, pavement, paving; roofing and paving materials 227.46; plasters 227.47; cement, concrete, cyclopeon concrete, reinforced concrete; brick, firebrick, clinker, adobe; tile, tiling.

3. wood, lumber, timber; hardwood, softwood; **stick,** stick of wood, stave; billet; pole, post, beam 216; **board,** plank; deal; two-by-four, three-by-four, etc.; slab, puncheon; slat, splat, lath; boarding, timbering, timberwork; lathing, lathwork; sheeting; panelling, panel board, panelwork; sheathing, sheathing board; siding, sideboard; weatherboard, clapboard; shingle, shake; log, clog [Scot. & N. of Eng.]; driftwood; firewood, stovewood; cordwood; cord.

4. cane, bamboo, rattan.

5. fabric, cloth, rag, textile, textile fabric, texture, tissue, weave, weft, woof, web, **material, goods,** drapery; napery, table linen.

6. paper, *papier* [F.]; sheet, leaf, page; quire, ream; stationery 600.30.

7. plastic, synthetic; thermoplastic, thermosetting plastic; resin plastics, cellulose plastics, protein plastics; synthetic fabrics, synthetic rubbers; cast plastics, molded plastics; molding compounds; laminates; adhesives; plasticizer; polymer.

ADJS. **8. wooden,** wood, woody, ligneous; log; cedar, oak, etc. 377.13; oaken.

9. cloth, rag, **textile,** woven; homespun; cotton, wool, etc. 377.15; woolen, woolly; silken, silky; chintzy, cottony, gauzy, gossamery, linsey-woolsey, plushy, satiny, tweedy, velvety; lacy, lacelike; shoddy.

10. paper, paperlike, papery; pasteboard, cardboard.

11. plastic, synthetic.

12. waxen, wax, waxy.

13. woods

acacia	ash
alder	balsa

bass basswood
beech, beech-
   wood
birch
briarwood, briar-
   wood
burl
buttonwood
cedar, cedarwood
cherry
chestnut
cork
cottonwood
cypress
dogwood
ebony
elm, elmwood
eucalyptus
fir
fruit wood
gum, gumwood
hazel, hazelwood
hemlock
hickory
incense wood
ironwood
juniper
knotty pine

14. panelings

Celotex
Cotwood
Compoboard
compreg
fiberboard
Formica
hardboard
impreg
Lamicoid
laminated wood
Masonite

15. fabrics

acetate rayon
Acrilan
alpaca
Aralac
arras
astrakhan,
   astrachan
Avisco
awning cloth
Axminster
baize
balbriggan
batik
batiste
bouclé
broadcloth
broadloom
brocade
brocatel
bunting
burlap
byssus
calico
cambric
cambric muslin
camel's hair
Canton flannel
canvas

lancewood
larch
lignum vitae
linden
locust
logwood
magnolia
mahogany
maple
oak
olive
pine
Philippine
   mahogany
poplar
redwood
rosewood
sandalwood
satinwood
spruce
sumac
sycamore
teak, teakwood
tulipwood
tupelo
walnut
yew
zebrawood

Panelyte
pegboard
plasterboard
plastic plywood
plywood
Pregwood
pressed hardboard
Reziwood
wallboard
Weldwood

carpeting
casheen
cashmere
cassimere
castor
Celanese
Celanese acetate
challis, challie
chambray [U.S.]
cheesecloth
Chemstrand
chenille
chenille Axminster
cheviot
chiffon
China silk
chinchilla
chintz
coating
cord
corduroy
corseting
cotton
cotton cambric
covert (cloth)
crash
crepe, crape
crepe de Chine

cretonne
crinoline
Dacron
damask
denim
dimity
doeskin
drap d'or [F.]
drill
drilling
drugget
duck
duffel
dungaree
duvetyn, duvetyne,
   duvetine
Dynelo
faille
felt
fine linen
flannel
flannelet, flannel-
   ette
fleece
foulard
frieze
fustian
gabardine
Georgette,
   Georgette crepe
gingham
gossamer
grenadine
grogram
grosgrain
gunny
haircloth
herringbone
homespun
hop sacking
horsehair
huckaback
Jacquard
jean
jersey
knitwear
lamé
Lastex
lawn
leatherette
linen
linene
linenette
linoleum
linsey-woolsey
lisle
list
longcloth
luster
mackinaw
mackintosh
madras
malines, maline
manta
mantua
marquisette
marseilles
mat
matting
melton
messaline

mohair
moiré, moire
moleskin
monk's cloth
mousseline [F.]
mousseline de
   soie [F.]
murrey
muslin
nainsook
nankeen, nankin
near-silk
net
netting
nylon
oilcloth
oil silk
organdy
organza
orlon
paisley
pepper-and-salt
percale
piqué
plaid
pongee
poplin
print
quilting
radium
rayon
rayon casheen
Revolite
rugging
russet
sacking
sailcloth
samite [middle
   ages]
Sarelon
sateen
satin
say
scrim
seersucker
serge
Shantung
sharkskin
sheers
sheeting
shirting
shoddy
silk
spun rayon
stamin
stammel
stockinet [esp.
   Eng.]
stuff
suède
swansdown
tabaret
tabby
taffeta, taffety
tapestry
tarpaulin
terry, terry cloth
thunder and light-
   ning
tick, ticking
toile [F.]

toweling
tricot
tricotine
tulle
tussah
tweed
twill
veiling
Velon
velours

velure
velvet
Vicara
Vinyon
voile
watered fabric
webbing
wool
worsted

16. laces

bobbinet
bobbin lace
bobbin net
Brussels point
Chantilly lace
duchesse lace
fillet, filet lace
Greek lace or
   point
guipure
Mechlin lace

Milan point
needle point
pillow lace
point, point lace
reticella
Roman lace or
   point
tatting
Valenciennes
Venetian point

17. papers

binder's board
blotting paper
bond paper
butcher paper
carbon, carbon
   paper
cardboard
cartridge paper
cellophane
cloth paper
copy or copying
   paper
crepe, crepe paper
curlpaper
drawing paper
face tissue
flimsy
flypaper
foolscap
glass paper
hand paper
hand tissue
ice paper
lace paper
letter paper
manila, Manila
   paper
millboard

music paper
newspaper
newsprint
note paper
onionskin
paperboard
papier-mâché
paraffin paper
parchment
pasteboard
plate paper
pulpboard
rice paper
roofing paper
sheathing paper
shop paper
strawboard
tarpaper
tissue, tissue paper
toilet tissue
tracing paper
vellum
wallpaper
wastepaper
wax paper
wrapping paper
writing paper

18. plastics

acetate
acetate nitrate
acrylic
alkyd
aminoplast
Bakelite
buna
casein
cellophane
celluloid
cellulose ether
coumarone idene
Formica
furane
lignin

Lucite
melamine
multiresin
neoprene
nitrate
nylon
phenolic
phenolic urea
Plexiglas
polymeric amide
resinoid
terpene
urea
vinyl
Vinylite

19. waxes

ader wax
beeswax
cerate
ceresin, ceresine
fossil wax

mineral wax
ozocerite
sealing wax
vegetable wax

378. CHEMICALS

NOUNS 1. **chemical,** organic chemical, inorganic chemical; fine chemicals, heavy chemicals; **element; radical;** compound; isomer, metamer; agent, reagent; **acid,** hydracid, oxyacid, sulphacid; **base, alkali,** nonacid; neutralizer, antacid; acidity, alkalinity.

2. trace element, microelement, micronutrient, minor element.

3. **valence,** positive valence, negative valence; monovalence, univalence; bivalence; trivalence; quadrivalence, tetravalence; multivalence, polyvalence; covalence; electrovalence.

4. **atomic weight,** atomic mass, atomic volume; **molecular weight,** molecular volume; atomic number, valence number.

5. chemicalization; alkalization, alkalinization; acidification, acidulation, acetification; carbonation, chlorination, hydration, hydrogenation, hydroxylation, nitration, mercerization, phosphatization; oxidation, oxidization; sulphation, sulphatization; fermentation, ferment, working; catalysis 53.2; electrolysis 341.22.

VERBS 6. chemicalize, chemical; alkalize, alkalinize, alkalify; acidify, acidulate, acetify; borate, carbonate, chlorinate, chromate, hydrate, hydrogenate, hydroxylate, nitrate, mercerize, oxidize, pepsinate, peroxidize, phosphatize; sulphate, sulphatize; ferment, work; catalyze 53.4; electrolyze 341.25.

ADJS. 7. chemical; biochemical, chemicobiologic; physicochemical, physiochemical, chemicophysical; chemicoastrological, chemicodynamic, chemicomechanical, chemicopharmaceutical, chemurgic(al), electrochemical, iatrochemical [hist.], macrochemical, microchemical, phytochemical, photochemical, radiochemical, thermochemical, zoochemical; elemental, elementary; alkaline, alkali, basic, nonacid; acid 431.7; isomeric, metameric.

8. valent; univalent, monovalent, monatomic; bivalent; trivalent; quadrivalent, tetravalent; multivalent, polyvalent; covalent.

9. chemistry

alchemy [hist.]
analytical
   chemistry

applied chemistry
atomic chemistry
biochemistry, bio-

chemy, bio-
chemics
bus ness chemistry
chemiatry [hist.]
chemical dynamics
chemical engineer-
  ing
chemicobiology
chemicoengineer-
  ing
chemicophysics
chemurgy
colloid chemistry
electrochemistry
engineering
  chemistry
geological
  chemistry
iatrochemistry
  [hist.]
industrial
  chemistry
inorganic
  chemistry
macrochemistry
metallurgical
  chemistry

microchemistry
mineralogical
  chemistry
nuclear chemistry
organic chemistry
pathological
  chemistry
petrochemistry
photochemistry
physical chemistry
physicochemistry
physiological
  chemistry
phytochemistry
psychobio-
  chemistry
pure chemistry
radiochemistry
theoretical
  chemistry
thermochemistry
ultramicrochem-
  istry
zoochemistry,
  zoochemy
zymurgy

10. chemists

alchemist [hist.]
biochemist
chemiatrist [hist.]
chemical engineer
electrochemist [hist.]
iatrochemist [hist.]
industrial chemist

metallurgical
  chemist
mineralogical
  chemist
photochemist
physicochemist
thermochemist

11. chemical elements

Actinium, Ac	Germanium, Ge
Aluminum, Al	Gold, Au
Americium, Am	Hafnium, Hf
Antimony, Sb	Helium, He
Argon, Ar	Holmium, Ho
Arsenic, As	Hydrogen, H
Astatine, At	Indium, In
Barium, Ba	Iodine, I
Berkelium, Bk	Iridium, Ir
Beryllium, Be	Iron, Fe
Bismuth, Bi	Krypton, Kr
Boron, B	Lanthanum, La
Bromine, Br	Lead, Pb
Cadmium, Cd	Lithium, Li
Calcium, Ca	Lutetium, Lu
Californium, Cf	Magnesium, Mg
Carbon, C	Manganese, Mn
Cerium, Ce	Mendelevium, Md
Cesium, Cs	Mercury, Hg
Chlorine, Cl	Molybdenum, Mo
Chromium, Cr	Neodymium, Nd
Cobalt, Co	Neon, Ne
Copper, Cu	Neptunium, Np
Curium, Cm	Nickel, Ni
Dysprosium, Dy	Niobium, Nb
Einsteinium, Es	Nitrogen, N
Erbium, Er	Nobelium, No
Europium, Eu	Osmium, Os
Fermium, Fm	Oxygen, O
Fluorine, F	Palladium, Pd
Francium, Fr	Phosphorus, P
Gadolinium, Gd	Platinum, Pt
Gallium, Ga	Plutonium, Pu

Polonium, Po
Potassium, K
Praseodymium, Pr
Promethium, Pm
Protactinium, Pa
Radium, Ra
Radon, Rn
Rhenium, Re
Rhodium, Rh
Rubidium, Rb
Ruthenium, Ru
Samarium, Sm
Scandium, Sc
Selenium, Se
Silicon, Si
Silver, Ag
Sodium, Na
Strontium, Sr
Sulfur, Sulphur, S

Tantalum, Ta
Technetium, Tc
Tellurium, Te
Terbium, Tb
Thallium, Tl
Thorium, Th
Thulium, Tm
Tin, Sn
Titanium, Ti
Tungsten (Wolf-
  ram), W
Uranium, U
Vanadium, V
Xenon, Xe
Ytterbium, Yb
Yttrium, Y
Zinc, Zn
Zirconium, Zr

12. principal chemicals

acetate
acetone
alcohol 304.17
aldehyde
amine
ammonia
anhydride
arsenate
arsenite
basic anhydride
benzoate
bicarbonate
bicarbonate of soda
bichloride of mer-
  cury
bisulfate
bisulfide
borate
borax
bromide
calcium carbide
carbide
carbohydrate
  307.24
carbonate
carbon dioxide
carbon monoxide
Chile saltpeter
chlorate
chloride
chlorite
chromate
citrate
copperas
cyanide
dichromate
dioxide
disulfate
disulfide
ester
ether

ethyl
fluoride
formaldehyde
fulminate
halide
halogen
hydrate
hydride
hydrocarbon
hydroxide
iodide
ketone
lactate
methyl
monoxide
niter
nitrate
nitride
nitrite
oxalate
oxide
permanganate
peroxide
petrochemical
phosphate
phosphide
phosphite
potash
sal ammoniac
salt
saltpeter
silicate
sodium bicar-
  bonate
sulphate, sulfate
sulphide, sulfide
sulphite, sulfite
tartrate
tetroxide
thiosulfate
trioxide

13. common acids

amino acid 307.26
ammono acid
aqua fortis
aqua regia
arsonic acid
butyric acid
carbolic acid

chloric acid
chlorous acid
chromic acid
citric acid
cyanic acid
formic acid
gallic acid

hydrochloric acid
hydrocyanic acid
hydrofluoric acid
hypochlorous acid
lactic acid
malic acid
muriatic acid
niacin
nicotinic acid
nitric acid
oil of vitriol

oxalic acid
perchloric acid
phenol
phosphoric acid
picric acid
prussic acid
salicylic acid
sulphuric acid
sulphurous acid
uric acid
vitriol

14. chemical instruments

alembic
aspirator
blowpipe
Büchner funnel
Bunsen burner
burette, buret
crucible
desiccator
distiller

etna
Kipp's apparatus
matrass
pestle and mortar
reagent bottle
receiver
retort
still
test tube

379. OILS, LUBRICANTS

NOUNS **1. oil,** *oleum* [L.]; **fat, grease;** ester; cerate; mineral ∼, vegetable *or* animal oil; fixed ∼, fatty ∼, volatile *or* essential oil; drying ∼, semidrying *or* nondrying oil.

2. lubricant, lubricator, **antifriction,** dope [slang]; graphite, plumbago, black lead; wax; mucilage, mucus, synovia [anat.].

3. ointment, balm, salve, lotion, cream, unguent, unguentum [pharm.], unction; lenitive, embrocation, demulcent, emolliont [all med.]; spikenard, nard; **pomade,** pomatum; brilliantine; cold cream, hand lotion, face cream.

4. petroleum, rock oil, fossil oil; **gasoline** *or* gasolene, gas [coll.], **petrol** [Eng:]; aviation gasoline, avgas; ethyl, ethyl gas; premium gas, high-octane gas; octane.

5. unctuousness, unctiousness, unctuosity; **oiliness, greasiness,** lubricity; **fattiness,** fatness, pinguidity; adiposis, adiposity; soapiness, saponacity [joc.]; smoothness, slickness, sleekness, slipperiness.

6. lubrication, oiling, greasing; anointment, unction.

7. lubritorium, lubritory; grease rack, grease pit.

VERBS **8. lubricate, oil, grease,** salve, pinguefy, liquor, dope [slang]; **anoint,** unguent, embrocate [med.], dress, pour oil upon; smear, daub; slick, slick on [both coll.]; lard; glycerolate, glycerinate, glycerinize; pomade; wax, beeswax; smooth the way, soap the ways [slang], grease the wheels [coll.].

ADJS. **9. unctuous,** unctious, unctional, unguinous; **oleaginous,** oleic [chem.]; un-

guentary, unguent, unguentous; **oily, greasy; fat, fatty,** adipose, sebaceous; pinguid, pinguedinous; blubbery, tallowy, suety; lardy, lardaceous; buttery, butyraceous; soapy, saponaceous; paraffinnic; smooth, slick, sleek, slippery.

10. lubricant, lubricating, **lubricative,** lubricatory, lubricational; lenitive, emollient [both med.].

11. mineral oils

anthracene oil
asphalt-base oil
Barbados tar
benzine
carbolic oil
coal oil
creosote
creosote oil
cresol
fuel oil
furnace oil
gasoline, gasolene
green oil
kerosene
light oil
middle oil

mineral seal oil
mineral sperm oil
mineral spirits
naphtha
naphthalene
naphthene-base oil
paraffin, paraffine
paraffin-base oil
petrolatum
petroleum
petroleum benzine
petroleum jelly
shale naphtha *or* spirit
shale oil

12. vegetable oils

absinthe
almond oil
anise *or* aniseed oil
avocado oil
bay *or* bayberry oil
beechnut oil
camphor
candlenut oil
carapa oil
castor *or* ricinus oil
citronella
clove oil
cocoa *or* cacao butter
coconut oil *or* butter
colza *or* rape oil
copaiba
copra oil
corn oil
cotton *or* cotton-seed oil
croton oil
eucalyptus oil
flaxseed oil
fusel, fusel oil
grain oil
gum spirit
kekuna oil
kokum butter

laurel butter *or* oil
lemon oil
linseed oil
Macassar oil
mace butter
maize oil
nut oil
oil of almonds
oil *or* spirits of turpentine
oleoresin
olive oil
palm butter
palm oil
peanut oil
pine-needle oil
pine oil
pine tar
pine-tar oil
resin oil
rosin grease
rosin oil
sesame oil
spikenard
sweet *or* edible oil
turpentine
walnut oil
wood oil
wood turpentine

13. animal oils

adipose tissue
blubber
bone oil
bottlenose oil
butter
butterfat
butterine

castor
cod-liver oil
cod oil
doegling oil
dripping, drippings
fat
fish oil

ghee [Ind.]
halibut-liver oil
Haliver Oil
lanolin
lard
lard oil
margarine
menhaden oil
mutton tallow
neat's-foot oil
oleo
oleomargarine
oleo oil
porpoise oil
salmon oil

sardine oil
seal oil
shark or shark-
    liver oil
shortening
spermaceti
sperm oil
suet
tallow
tallow oil
tuna oil
whale oil
wool fat or grease
wool oil

14. glyceryl esters

glycerin, glycerine
glycerin jelly
glycerite
glycerogel
glycerogelatin
glycerol
glycerole
margarin

olein, oleine
palmitin
stearin, stearine
trimargarin
triolein
tripalmitin
tristearine

380. RESINS

NOUNS 1. resin, resina; gums, gum resins; acaroid resins, gum acaroides; coumarone resins, fossil resins, lac resins, pine resins, vegetable resins; resinoid, synthetic resin; resene; resinate, colophonate; rosin, colophony colophonium.

VERBS 2. resin, resinize, resinate; rosin.

ADJS. 3. resinous, resinic, resiny; resinoid; rosiny; gummy, gummous, gummose, gumlike; asphaltic, bituminous, pitchy, tarry.

4. resins

amber
ambergris
ammoniac
amyrin
animé
asa dulcis
asphalt, asphaltum
balsam
Bengal kino
benjamin
benzoin
bitumen
brea
butea gum
butea kino
cachibou
camphor
coal tar
coal-tar pitch
colophony,
    colophonium
conima
copaiba
copal
copaline
copalite
copalm

C. pimela
dammar
elemi
elemin
euphorbium
fossil copal
frankincense
galbanum
garnet lac
guacin
guaiac, guaiacum
gum ammoniac
gum animé
gum archipin
gum benjamin or
    benzoin
gum butea
gum copal
gum dammar
gum elemi
gum euphorbium
gum galbanum
gum guaiac or
    guaiacum
gum juniper
gum kauri
gum kino

gum labdanum
gum-lac
gum myrrh
gum olibanum
gum opopanax
gum rosin
gum sagapenum
gum sandarac
gum shellac
gum storax
gutta-percha
herabol myrrh
incense resin
japan
kauri, kauri resin
    or gum
kino
labdanum
lac
lacquer
lignite tar
liquidamber,
    liquidambar
mastic
megilp, megilph

mineral pitch
myrrh
oleoresin
olibanum
opopanax
pitch
resin oil
resinol
resin opal
resin or rosin
    spirit
rosin
rosin oil
sagapenum
sandarac
seed-lac
shellac
Sonora lac
stick-lac
storax
storax benzoin
tar
varnish
wood rosin
wood tar

381. INORGANIC MATTER

NOUNS 1. inorganic matter, inanimate or lifeless matter, inorganized or unorganized matter, brute matter, mineral kingdom or world.

2. inanimateness, inanimation, lifelessness, inertness; insensibility, insentience, insensateness, senselessness, unconsciousness, unfeelingness.

3. inorganic chemistry; chemicals 378.

ADJS. 4. inorganic, unorganic, unorganized, inorganized, mineral, nonbiological.

ADJS. 5. inanimate, inanimated, unanimated, exanimate, azoic, nonliving, lifeless, soulless, inert, insentient, unconscious, nonconscious, insensible, insensate, senseless, unfeeling; dumb, mute.

382. MINERALS AND METALS

NOUNS 1. mineral; sulfur or sulphur, brimstone; mineral charcoal, mother of coal; mineral pitch, asphalt; mineralization.

2. ore, mineral [colloq.]; picture ore; muck.

3. metal, ore [poetic]; metallics; native metals, alkali metals, earth metals, alkaline-earth metals, noble metals, precious metals, rare metals, rare-earth metals or elements; metalloid, semimetal, nonmetal; copper, cuprum; mercury, quicksilver; bullion (gold or silver); gold dust; leaf, foil; Dowmetals [Dow Chemical Co.], Alcoa metals [Aluminum Corp. of Amer.]; metalwork, metalware; metallicity, metalleity.

4. alloy, alloyage, fusion, compound amalgam, metallide.

5. **cast, casting; ingot, bullion;** button, gate, regulus, pig, sow; sheet metal.

6. **mine,** pit; **quarry; diggings, workings;** open cut, opencast; bank; shaft; coal mine, colliery; gold mine, silver mine, etc.; **deposit,** pay dirt [U.S.]; **vein, lode,** dike, ore bed, pay streak [slang, U.S.]; shoot, ore shoot; chimney, stock; placer, placer deposit, placer gravel; country rock; lodestuff, gangue, matrix, veinstone.

7. **mining,** coal mining, gold mining, etc.; placer mining; hydraulic mining; prospecting; mining claim, lode claim, placer claim; gold fever; **gold rush;** lucky strike [coll., U.S.].

8. **miner,** mineworker; coal miner, collier [esp. Eng.]; gold miner, gold digger; gold panner; placer miner; quarry miner; **prospector,** desert rat [West., U.S.]. sour dough [U.S., Can. & Alaska]; **forty-niner** [U.S.], Argonaut [U.S., 1849]; hand miner, rockman, powderman, driller, draw man; butty.

9. **mineralogy,** mineralogical chemistry, crystallography; **petrology,** petrography, micropetrography; **geology** 384.4; mining geology, mining engineering.

10. **metallurgy,** metallography, metallurgical chemistry, metallurgical engineering, physical metallurgy, powder metallurgy, electrometallurgy, hydrometallurgy, pyrometallurgy.

11. **mineralogist; metallurgist,** electrometallurgist, metallurgical engineer; **petrologist,** petrographer; **geologist** 384.5; mining engineer.

VERBS 12. mineralize, mineralogize; petrify 355.7.

13. **mine;** quarry; pan, pan for gold; prospect; hit pay dirt, make a lucky strike [both U.S.].

ADJS. 14. **mineral;** asbestos, carbon, etc. 382.18; asbestine, carbonous, graphitic, micaceous, alabastrine, quartzose, silicic; sulphurous or sulfurous, sulphuric or sulfuric; ore-bearing, ore-forming.

15. **metal, metallic;** metalline, metalloid(al), metalliform; semimetallic; nonmetallic; metallorganic, organometallic; bimetallic, trimetallic; metalliferous, metalbearing; tempered, heat-treated, casehardened.

16. aluminum, chromium, platinum, chrome-nickel; brass, brassy, brazen; bronze, bronzy; copper, coppery, cuprous, cupreous; gold, golden, gilt; nickel, nickelic, nickelous, nickeline; silver, silvery; iron, ironlike, ferric, ferrous, ferruginous; steel, steely; tin,

tinny; lead, leaden; pewter, pewtery; mercurial, mercurous; phosphorous, phosphoric; gold-filled, gold-plated, silver-plated, etc.

17. **mineralogical, metallurgical,** petrological.

18. **minerals**

alabaster	maltha
amphibole	manganese
apatite	marcasite
aplite	marl
argonite	meerschaum
asbestos	mica
azurite	mineral charcoal
barite	mineral coal
bauxite	mineral naphtha
boron	mineral oil 379.11
brimstone	mineral pulp
brookite	mineral rubber
brucite	mineral salt
calcite	mineral tallow
carbon	mineral tar
celestite	mineral water
chalcedony	mineral wax
chameleon mineral	molybdenite
chlorite	monazite
chromite	obsidian
clay	olivine
coal 330.10	orthoclase
cobalt	ozocerite
coke	peat
corundum	perlite
cryolite	phosphate rock
crystal	pitchblende
diatomite	pumice
elaterite	pumicite
emery	pyrite
epidote	pyrites
epsomite	pyroxene
feldspar	quartz
fluorite	quicklime
fluorspar	realgar
fool's gold	rock crystal
garnet	rocks 383
glauconite	rhodonite
graphite	rutile
gypsum	salt
hatchettine,	selenite
hatchettite	siderite
holosiderite	silica
hornblende	silicate
ilmenite	spar
iolite	spinel
iron pyrites	spodumene
jet	sulfur, sulphur
kaolinite	talc, talcum
kyanite	tourmaline
lazurite	tripoli
lignite	vermiculite
lime	wollastonite
magnesite	wulfenite
malachite	

19. **ores**

argentite	galena
arsenopyrite	göthite
cassiterite	hematite
chalcocite	iron ore
chalcopyrite	ironstone
cinnabar	limonite

loadstone,	siderite
lodestone	stibnite
magnetite	tinstone
mispickel	turgite
pyrite	zincite

20. elementary metals

aluminum	niobium
americium	osmium
barium	palladium
beryllium	phosphorus
bismuth	platinum
cadmium	polonium
calcium	potassium
cerium	praseodymium
cesium	promethium
chromium	protactinium
cobalt	radium
copper	rhenium
dysprosium	rubidium
erbium	ruthenium
europium	samarium
gadolinium	scandium
gallium	silver
germanium	sodium
gold	strontium
hafnium	tantalum
holmium	technetium
indium	terbium
iridium	thallium
lanthanum	thorium
lead	thulium
lithium	tin
lutecium	titanium
magnesium,	tungsten
magnesia	uranium
manganese	vanadium
mercury	ytterbium
molybdenum	yttrium
neodymium	zinc
nickel	zirconium

21. alloys

admiralty metal	coin nickel
air-hardened steel	coin silver
albata	constantan
alloy iron	cupronickel
alloy steel	damask or
alnico	Damascus steel
aluminum bronze	decarbonized iron
babbitt, Babbitt	dental gold
metal	die steel
basic iron	drill steel
bearing steel	duralumin
bell metal	Duriron
beryllium bronze	electrum
brass	elinvar
britannia metal	fuse metal
bronze	galvanized iron
carboloy	gilding metal
carbon steel	German silver
cartridge brass	graphite steel
case-hardened	green gold
steel	grid metal
cast iron	gun metal
chisel steel	hard lead
chrome or	high brass
chromium steel	high-speed steel
chrome-nickel	hot-work steel
steel	hypernik
cinder pig	inconel

ingot iron	shot metal
invar	silicon bronze
leaded bronze	silicon steel
low brass	solder
manganese bronze	spiegeleisen
mine pig	stainless steel
monel metal	steel
Muntz metal	stellite
naval brass	sterling silver
nichrome	structural iron
nickel silver	structural steel
ni-hard iron	tin bronze
ni-resist iron	tombac
oil-hardened steel	tool steel
permalloy	type metal
perminvar	white gold
pewter	white metal
pig	Wood's metal
pig iron	wrought iron
pig lead	yellow brass
phosphor bronze	yellow gold
red brass	yellow metal
rose metal	

22. leaf metals

Dutch foil, leaf or	metal leaf
gold	silver foil
gold foil	silver leaf
gold leaf	tin foil
lead foil	

383. ROCK

NOUNS 1. **rock, stone;** igneous rock, sedimentary rock, metamorphic rock; volcanic rock, scoria; conglomerate, breccia; schist; rubble, rubblestone, brash; sarsen, sarsen stone, druid stone; monolith; crag, craig [Scot. & North. Eng.]; bedrock [U.S.].

2. **sand, grain of sand;** sands of the sea; sand pile, sand dune, sand hill; sand reef.

3. **gravel,** shingle [chiefly Eng.], chesil [dial., Eng.], grail [poetic], beach.

4. **pebble,** pebblestone, gravelstone, chuckie [Scot.]; jackstone, dibstone, checkstone [dial.]; fingerstone; slingstone; drakestone.

5. **boulder,** river boulder, shore boulder, glacial boulder.

6. **precious stone, gem,** gem stone, stone; semi-precious stone; oriental opal, ~ garnet, etc.; gem of the first water; birthstone.

ADJS. 7. **stone, rock;** marble, agate, etc. 383.9, 10; adamant, adamantine; flinty, flintlike; marbly, marblelike; granitic, granitelike; slaty, slatelike.

8. **stony, rocky;** stonelike, rocklike; lapideous, lithoid(al); sandy, gritty 360.12; gravelly, shingly; pebbly, pebbled; bouldery; craggy; monolithic.

9. native stones

anthraconite	aventurine
aplite	basalt

basanite
beetlestone
brimstone
brownstone
burr, buhr
burrstone,
  buhrstone
cairngorm
chalk
chalkstone
clinkstone
clint
crystal
dendrite
diabase
diorite
dolerite
dolomite
dripstone
eaglestone
fieldstone
flag, flagstone
flint
floatstone
freestone
gneiss
goldstone
granite
granulite
greenstone
grit
gritrock, gritstone
hairstone
inkstone
ironstone
lava

limestone
loadstone,
  lodestone
Lydian stone
marble
metal
milkstone
mudstone
obsidian
phonolite
pitchstone
porphyry
pumice
quarrystone
quartz
quartzite
rottenstone
sandstone
serpentine
shale
slabstone
slate
smokestone
snakestone
soapstone
stalactite
stalagmite
starstone
steatite
stinkstone
tinstone
touchstone
trap, traprock
tufa
wacke
whitestone

10. gem stones

adamant
adder stone
agate
alexandrite
amethyst
aquamarine
beryl
black opal
bloodstone
brilliant
carbuncle
carnelian
cat's-eye
chalcedony
chrysoberyl
chrysolite
chrysoprase
citrine
coral
demantoid
diamond
emerald
fire opal
garnet
girasol, girasole
harlequin opal

heliotrope
hyacinth
jacinth
jade, jadestone
jargon, jargoon
jasper
kunzite
lapis lazuli
moonstone
morganite
onyx
opal
peridot
plasma
rose quartz
ruby
sapphire
sard
sardonyx
spinel, spinel ruby
star sapphire
sunstone
topaz
tourmaline
turquoise
zircon

11. specialized stones

bakestone
bondstone
capstone
cobble,
  cobblestone

copestone, coping
  stone
cornerstone
crowstone
curbstone

dogstone
doorstone
edgestone
footstone
gravestone
grindstone
hagstone [Eng.]
hammerstone
headstone
kerbstone [Eng.]
keystone
kneestone
knockstone

lapstone
milestone
millstone
oilstone
pavestone
rubstone
stepstone,
  steppingstone
tilestone
tombstone
topstone
whetstone

384. LAND

NOUNS 1. land, earth, ground, soil, glebe [poetic], sod, clod, dirt, dust, clay, marl [poetic], mold [dial.]; terra [L.], terra firma; terrene, terrain [obs. exc. spec.]; dry land; arable land; marginal land; crust, lithosphere; topsoil, subsoil; alluvium, alluvion; adobe, dobe.

2. shore, coast, strand, playa [Sp.], beach, waterside, water front; shoreline; foreshore; bank, embankment; riverside; seashore, seacoast, seaside, seaboard, seabeach, seabank, sea margin, tidewater; coastland, littoral; rock-bound coast, ironbound coast; scar, scaur [Scot. & Ir.]; loom of the land.

3. landsman, landman, landlubber [naut.; derog.].

4. (science of land) geography, geographics; physiography, physical geography; geoscopy; geomorphology, geomorphogeny; geophysics; geodynamics; geology, geognosy, dynamic geology, physical geology, physiographic geology, stratigraphic geology, paleontological geology, cosmical geology, historical geology, structural or geotectonic geology, mining geology, geological chemistry, geological engineering; mineralogy 382.9.

5. (scientists) geographer, physiographer, geomorphogenist, geologist, geognost, geophysicist, geological engineer; mineralogist 382.11.

ADJS. 6. terrestrial, terrene; earthy, earthly, soily; telluric, tellurian; geophilous; terraqueous; fluvioterrestrial.

7. clayey, clayish; loamy, marly, gumbo, adobe.

8. alluvial, estaurine, fluviomarine.

9. coastal, lottoral, seaside; shoreward; riparian, riparial [zool.], riparious; riverain, riverine.

10. geographic(al), physiographic(al), geophysical, geologic(al), geognostic(al).

ADVS. 11. on land, on dry land, on terra

firma; onshore, ashore; alongshore; shoreward; by land, overland.

12. soils

adobe	kaolinite
argil	leaf mold
boulder clay	loam
china clay	marl
clay	mold
clunch	porcelain clay
dust	potter's clay
fuller's earth	residual clay
gumbo, gumbo	sand
soil	sedimentary clay
humus	silt
indurated clay	till
kaolin	

385. BODY OF LAND

NOUNS 1. **continent, mainland**; midcontinent; North America, South America, Africa, Europe, Asia, Eurasia, Australia, Greenland, Antarctica.

2. **island, isle** [chiefly poetic]; **islet**, holm, eyot or ait [Eng., chiefly dial.]; continental island; oceanic island; calf; **key**, cay, cayo [Sp.]; **reef**, coral reef, atoll; archipelago; South Sea Islands, Australasia; insularity.

3. **continental**, continentalist, mainlander.

4. **islander**, islandman, islesman, insular; islandry.

VERBS. 5. **insulate**, isolate, island, enisle.

ADJS. 6. **continental**, mainland.

7. **insular**, insulated, isolated; island, islandy, islandlike; seagirt; archipelagic.

386. PLAIN

Open Country.—NOUNS 1. **plain, plains**, flat, **flats**, level, **champaign country**, champaign, open country, **wide open spaces**; reach, stretch, expanse; **prairie**, lone prairie; **steppe** [Russ.], **pampas** [S. Amer.], pampa [Sp.], savanna [South. U.S.], tundra [Arctic], vega [S. Amer.], campo [S. Amer.], llano [Sp. Amer.], sebkha [N. Africa]; wold, weald; **veld or veldt**, grass veld, bushveld, tree veld [all S. Africa]; bush; **moor**, moorland, down, **downs, heath**, fell [Eng.]; lowland, lowlands; basin, playa [Sp.], salt pan; salt marsh; alkali flat; **desert** 165.2; plat, plot; **plateau**, tableland, table; **mesa**, mesilla [U.S.].

2. **plainsman**, plainswoman; moorman, moorlander; veldman, veldtsman [both S. Africa]; plainsfolk.

ADJS. 3. **champaign, plain, flat**, open; campestral, campestrian.

387. FLUIDITY

NOUNS 1. **fluidity**, liquidity, fluidness, liquidness, liquefaction; **fluency, flow**; wateriness; **juiciness**, sappiness, succulence; milkiness, lactescence; chylifaction, chylification [both physiol.]; serosity.

2. **fluid, liquid**, liquor; **juice, sap**, blood; latex [bot.], milk; whey; water 391.3; semiliquid 388.5.

3. (body fluids) **lymph**, humor, chyle, rheum; serous fluid, serum; peccant humor, **pus, matter**, corruption [dial.], ichor, sanies; leucorrhea, the whites; **mucus**, mucor [med.]; **phlegm**, pituite, snot [vulg.]; **saliva** 310.3; **urine** 309.5; **sweat** 309.7; **tear**, teardrop, lachryma; **milk**, mother's milk, colostrum, lactation.

4. **blood, gore**, claret [slang], ichor [Gr. myth.], cruor, humor; grume; **serum**, blood serum; **plasma**; synthetic plasma, dextran, Dextrone; **blood corpuscle or cell**; red corpuscles, erythrocytes; white corpuscles, leucocytes; **hemoglobin**; blood pressure; circulation; **blood group or type**, types O, A, B, AB; Rh-type, Rh-positive, Rh-negative; **Rh factor**, Rhesus factor; blood count; sanguinometer; bloodmobile; blood bank, blood donor center; blood donor.

5. flowmeter, fluidmeter, hydrometer.

ADJS. 6. **fluid**, fluidal; **fluent, flowing**; **liquid**, liquidy; watery 391.16; **juicy**, sappy, succulent.

7. (physiology) **lymphatic**, rheumy, ichorous, serous, sanious [med.]; chylific, chylifactive, chylifactory; **pussy**, purulent; tearlike, **lachrymal**, lachrymatory; bloody 367.8.

8. **milky**, lacteal, lacteous, **lactic**, galactic; lactescent, lactiferous; milk, milch.

388. SEMILIQUIDITY

NOUNS 1. **semiliquidity**, semifluidity; butteriness, creaminess, milkiness; pulpiness 389.

2. **viscidity, viscosity**, viscousness; thickness, spissitude, heaviness, stodginess; **stickiness, tackiness**, toughness; tenaciousness, tenacity; **gumminess**, gauminess, gumlikeness; **ropiness, stringiness**; mucilaginousness, sirupiness, gooeyness [slang, U.S.]; **glueyness**, gluelikeness; gelatinousness, gelatinity; **glutinousness**, glutinosity; doughiness, pastiness.

3. **mucosity, mucidness**, mucousness, pituitousness, snottiness [vulg.]; **clamminess**, sliminess.

4. muddiness, muckiness, **slushiness,** sloshiness, sludginess, **sloppiness,** slabbiness, squashiness, squelchiness, **ooziness,** softness, miriness; **turbidity,** turbidness, dirtiness.

5. semiliquid, semifluid; **goo, goop, gook,** gunk [all slang]; **paste,** pap, pudding, putty, **butter,** cream; **pulp** 389.2; **jelly,** gelatin, jell, gel, jam; **gluten,** mucilage; **dough,** batter; **sirup,** molasses, treacle [chiefly Eng.], rob; egg white, glair; starch, cornstarch; **curd,** clabber, bonnyclabber; gruel, porridge, loblolly; soup, gumbo, *purée.*

6. gum, chewing gum, bubble gum; chicle, chicle gum; mastic, mastic gum.

7. emulsion, emulsoid; emulsification; emulsifier.

8. mud, muck, dirt, clay, **slush, slosh,** sludge, sposh [dial., U.S.], squash, **slime,** slap [chiefly dial.], **slop, ooze, mire;** gumbo.

9. mud puddle, puddle, loblolly [dial., U.S.], slap [chiefly dial.], slop; **mudhole,** chuckhole [U.S.], chughole [dial., U.S.]; hog wallow [U.S.].

VERBS 10. emulsify, emulsionize; cream; churn, whip, beat up.

ADJS. 11. semiliquid, semifluid, semifluidic; buttery; creamy, milky, emulsive; **pulpy** 389.6; half-frozen, half-melted.

12. viscid, viscous, viscose; **thick,** heavy, stodgy; **sticky, tacky, tenacious,** tough; **ropy, stringy; gummy,** gaumy, gummous, gummose, gumlike; **mucilaginous, sirupy, gooey** [slang, U.S.]; **gluey,** gluelike; **gelatinous,** tremellose [bot.]; **glutinous,** glutenous, glutinose; slabby, slab [dial]; **doughy, pasty;** starchy, amylaceous; gumbo, gumbolike.

13. mucid, muculent, **mucous,** pituitous, snotty [vulg.]; **clammy,** sammy [chiefly dial.], **slimy,** slithery [chiefly dial.].

14. muddy, mucky, mucksy [dial.], **slushy, sloshy,** sozzly, sludgy, sposhy [dial., U.S.], **sloppy,** slabby, slab [dial.], splashy, plashy, **squashy, squelchy, oozy,** soft, **miry,** lutose; **turbid, dirty;** uliginous, uliginose.

389. PULPINESS

NOUNS **1. pulpiness,** pulpousness; softness, flabbiness; **mushiness,** mashiness, squashiness; **pastiness,** doughiness; **sponginess,** pithiness; fleshiness, succulence.

2. pulp, paste, **mash, mush,** smash, squash, crush; sauce, butter; paper pulp, wood pulp; pulpwood; pulp lead, white lead; dental pulp.

3. pulpification, **pulpefaction** [med.]; **maceration,** mastication.

4. pulper, pulpifier, **macerater** *or* macerator, pulp machine *or* engine; **masher,** smasher, potato masher, beetle.

VERBS 5. pulp, pulpify; **macerate,** masticate; **mash,** smash, squash, squish [dial.], crush.

ADJS. 6. pulpy, pulpous, pulplike; **pasty,** doughy; **mushy,** mashy; **squashy,** squelchy, squishy [dial.], squdgy [dial.]; soft, flabby; fleshy, succulent; **spongy,** pithy; baccate [bot.].

390. LIQUEFACTION

NOUNS **1. liquefaction, liquidization,** fluidification, fluidization; **liquescence,** deliquescence; dissolution, **solution,** dissolving, melting, running, fusion, solubilization; colliquation [med.].

2. solubility, solubleness; dissolvability, dissolvableness; dissolubility, dissolubleness; meltability, fusibility.

3. solution, dissolution, docoction, mixture; chemical solution; lixivium.

4. solvent, dissolvent, dissolver, dissolving agent, resolvent, resolutive, diluent, liquefier, liquefacient, menstruum; flux; universal solvent, alkahest.

VERBS 5. liquefy, liquidize, liquesce; fluidify, fluidize; **melt, run,** colliquate [med.]; fuse, flux; deliquesce; **dissolve,** solve, cut; solubilize, hold in solution.

ADJS. 6. liquefied, melted, molten; in solution, in suspension.

7. liquefying, liquefactive, liquescent, deliquescent, colliquative [med.], **melting; dissolving,** dissolutive, dissolutional.

8. solvent, dissolvent, resolvent, resolutive, diluent; alkahestic(al).

9. soluble, dissolvable, dissoluble, liquefiable, liquidable, **meltable,** fusible.

391. MOISTURE

NOUNS **1. moisture,** damp, wet; **dampness, moistness,** moistiness, **wetness,** wettishness, **wateriness;** soddenness, soppiness, sogginess; dewiness; mistiness, fogginess 403.4; exudation 302.6.

2. humidity, humidness, dankness, **mugginess,** stickiness [coll.]; absolute humidity, relative humidity; dew point; humidification.

3. water, *aqua* [L.], *agua* [Sp.], *eau* [F.], lymph [poetic], Adam's ale *or* wine [joc.], crystal [poetic], burn [Scot. & dial.], *aqua pura* [L.], H_2O; watery element, flood [poetic or rhetorical]; hydrol, dihydrol, trihydrol [all chem.]; hard water, soft water; heavy water; drinking water; rain water; ground water, spring water, well water; limewater; mineral water, waters; steam, water vapor; hydrosphere; head.

4. dew, dewdrops, "dew-beads" [G. Eliot], "the tears which stars weep" [P. J. Bailey], "tears of the sky for loss of the sun" [Chesterfield], "the gems of morning, but the tears of mournful eve" [Coleridge], "gems of earth and sky begotten" [G. Eliot]; night dew, evening damp, *serein* [F.]; fog drip; false dew.

5. sprinkle, spray, shower; **splash,** swash, slosh; **splatter,** spatter.

6. wetting, moistening, dampening, damping; **watering, irrigation; sprinkling, spraying,** sparging, aspersion, aspergation; splashing, swashing, splattering, spattering, affusion, baptism; **flooding,** inundation, deluge; submergence 318.2.

7. soaking, soakage, **drenching,** sousing; soak, drench, souse; **saturation,** permeation; **steeping,** seething, maceration; infusion, imbuement, imbruement, injection, impregnation; infiltration, percolation.

8. sprinkler, sparger, sparge, **sprayer,** spray, atomizer; aspergil, aspergillum [eccl.]; **shower,** shower bath, needle bath; syringe, fountain syringe, douche, enema; sprinkling *or* watering can, watering pot, watercart; sprinkler head.

9. (science of humidity) hygrology, hygrometry, psychrometry, hygrostatics.

10. (instruments) hygrometer, hygrograph, hygrodeik, hygroscope, hygrothermograph; psychrometer; humidor; hygrostat.

VERBS **11. be damp,** not have a dry thread; **reek, drip,** weep; **seep, ooze,** percolate; exude 302.15; sweat 309.14.

12. moisten, moist [dial.], **dampen,** damp, **wet;** humidify, humify; **water, irrigate;** dew, bedew; **sprinkle,** besprinkle, spray, sparge, asperge; **splash,** dash, swash, slosh, **splatter,** spatter, bespatter; dabble, paddle; slop, slobber; hose, hose down; syringe, douche; sponge.

13. soak, drench, drouk [chiefly Scot. & North Eng.], douche, **souse, sop,** sob [dial.], sodden; **saturate,** permeate; **bathe,** lave, wash, flush; water-soak, waterlog; **steep,** seethe, macerate, infuse, imbue, imbrue, impregnate, inject; infiltrate, percolate.

14. flood, float, **inundate, deluge;** submerge 318.7; pour on, flow on.

ADJS. **15. moist,** moisty; **damp,** dampish; **wet,** wettish; **humid, dank, muggy,** ticky [coll.]; dewy, roric, rorulent; rainy 393.10.

16. watery, waterish, **aqueous, aquatic,** hydrous; hydraulic; liquid 387.6; **splashy,** plashy, sloppy, swashy [Eng.].

17. soaked, drenched, soused, bathed, steeped; **saturated,** permeated; **watersoaked,** watter-sobbed [dial.], **waterlogged; soaking, sopping; wringing wet,** soaking wet, sopping wet, wet to the skin; **sodden,** soppy, **soggy,** sobby [dial.], soaky; reeking, dripping, dripping wet; flooded, inundated, deluged, awash.

18. wetting, dampening, moistening, watering; **drenching, soaking, sopping; irrigational,** irriguous.

19. hygric, hygrometric, hygroscopic, hygrophanous, hygrophilous, hygrothermal.

392. DRYNESS

NOUNS **1. dryness, aridness,** aridity, waterlessness; **drought** *or* drouth; juicelessness, saplessness; **thirst,** thirstiness; corkiness.

2. (comparisons) dust, bone, stick, mummy, biscuit, cracker.

3. drying, desiccation, siccation; **dehydration,** anhydration; anhydromyelia [med.]; evaporation, insolation, drainage, mummification.

4. drier, desiccator, desiccative, siccative, exsiccative, exsiccator; **dehydrator,** dehydrant; evaporator.

VERBS **5.** (be dry) thirst; drink up, soak up.

6. dry, dry up; **desiccate;** exsiccate; **dehydrate,** anhydrate; evaporate; air-dry; insolate, sun, sun-dry; smoke, smoke-dry; torrefy, burn, fire, kiln, **bake, parch,** scorch, sear; **wither, shrivel;** wizen, weazen, wizzen [dial.]; mummify; sponge, blot, soak up; **wipe,** swab, brush; drain 304.10.

ADJS. **7. dry, arid, waterless,** unwatered, undamped, anhydrous, **bone-dry,** dry as dust *or* a bone; droughty; juiceless, sapless; thirsty, thirsting, athirst; husky; high and dry.

8. rainless, fine, fair, bright and fair, pleasant.

9. dried, dried up, **dehydrated; desiccated,** desiccate, exsiccated; evaporated; **parched, baked,** burnt, scorched, **seared,** sear *or* sere, adust; **withered, shriveled;** wizened, weazened; corky; mummified.

10. drying, dehydrating; desiccative,

desiccant, exsiccative, exsiccant; siccative, siccant; evaporative.

11. watertight, drop-dry [naut.]; **waterproof,** moistureproof, dampproof, leakproof, dripproof, stormproof, storm-tight, rainproof, raintight, floodproof.

393. RAIN

NOUNS **1. rain, rainfall,** fall, **precipitation,** wet; **shower, sprinkle; drizzle,** mizzle [dial.], drisk [U.S.]; **mist,** misty rain; evening mist, *serein* [F.]; streams of rain, sheet of rain; "tremulous skeins of rain" [T. Aldrich], "the imprisoning rain — dear hermitage of nature" [Emerson], "the useful trouble of the rain" [Tennyson], "the raindrops' showery dance and rhythmic beat" [A. Coles]; rain water; raindrop.

2. rainstorm, brash [Scot. & dial.], scud [chiefly Scot. & dial., Eng.]; **cloudburst,** rainburst, burst of rain; waterspout, spout, rainspout; **downpour,** downflow, downfall, pour, pouring rain, spate, plash [chiefly dial.], **deluge, flood,** heavy rain, driving rain, drenching *or* soaking rain, drencher, soaker; goose drownder, fence lifter, gully washer, root searcher [all local, U.S.].

3. thunderstorm, thundersquall, thunder-gust, thunder-shower, thunderplump [Scot. & dial., Eng.].

4. wet weather, rainy weather, falling weather [coll.], dirty weather, dirt [coll., naut.], greasy weather [naut.], cat-and-dog weather [coll.], spell of rain, wet; rainy day; **rains,** rainy season, **monsoon;** predominance of Aquarius, reign of St. Swithin.

5. rain making, cloud seeding, nucleation; **rain maker,** rain doctor, cloud seeder; dry ice, carbon dioxide, CO_2.

6. Jupiter Pluvius [Rom, myth.], the Rain Giver.

7. rain gauge, pluviometer, pluvioscope, pluviograph; ombrometer; udometer, udomograph; hyetometer, hyetometrograph, hyetograph.

8. (science of precipitation) hyetology, hyetography; pluviography, pluviometry.

VERBS **9. rain, precipitate,** fall, wet [chiefly dial.]; weep [poetic]; **shower,** shower down; **sprinkle,** spit [coll.]; **drizzle,** mizzle [dial.]; **pour,** stream, pour with rain, come down in torrents, **rain cats and dogs** [coll.], "rain dogs and polecats" [Richard Brome], rain tadpoles *or* bullfrogs [slang, U.S.], rain pitchforks [coll.], "rain daggers with their points downward" [R. Burton], rain blue blazes [slang]; set in.

ADJS. **10. rainy, showery; pluvious,** pluvial; **drizzly,** drizzling, mizzly [now dial.], drippy; **misty,** misty-moisty [poetic]; pouring, streaming, cat-and-doggish [coll.].

394. STREAM

Running Water.—NOUNS **1. stream, watercourse,** wadi [Near East & N. Africa], kill [dial., U.S.], bourn *or* bourne, *arroyo* [Sp.]; **river,** "moving road" [Pascal]; **brook,** branch [U.S.]; **creek** [chiefly U.S.], crick [dial.]; **rivulet, streamlet,** brooklet, runlet, runnel, rundle [dial.], rindle [now chiefly dial.], beck [Eng.], gill, burn [chiefly Scot. & dial.], sike [chiefly Scot. & North. Eng.], lake [dial.]; run, race; **rill,** rillet; **freshet,** fresh; millstream; midstream, midchannel; King of Rivers, Amazon; Father of Waters, Mississippi.

2. headstream, headwaters, headwater, head, riverhead; source, fountainhead 152.5, 6.

3. tributary, feeder, **branch, fork,** prong [dial., U.S.], pup [slang, Alaska]; affluent, effluent; anabranch; billabong [Australia].

4. flow, flowing, **flux,** profluence, **stream, current,** tide [chiefly poetic], water flow; drift, driftage; **course,** onward course, **surge, gush, rush,** onrush, run, race, career; millrace, mill run; undercurrent, undertow; affluence, afflux, affluxion; confluence, concourse, conflux; backflow, reflux, refluence, regurgitation; backwash, backwater; downflow, **downpour,** defluxion; inflow 301.2; outflow 302.4.

5. torrent, river, flood, waterflood, **deluge,** cataract, niagara, sluice, spate, **pour;** freshet, fresh.

6. overflow, overflowing, overrunning, alluvion, **inundation, flood, deluge,** cataclysm; the Flood, the Deluge; washout.

7. trickle, tricklet, **dribble, drip,** dripping, drop, spurtle; percolation, distillation; **ripple, gurgle,** guggle, **burble,** bubble, babble, murmur, purl, trill; eavesdrop, eavedrop; stillicide, stillicidium.

8. lap, wash, swash, slosh, plash, splash.

9. jet, spout, spurt, spurtle, **squirt,** spray; rush, **gush,** flush; **fountain,** fount, font, *jet d'eau* [F., spurt of water]; geyser, spouter [coll.].

10. rapid, rapids, ripple [U.S.], **riffle** [U.S.], riff [local, U.S.], ripraps [local, U.S.]; chute, shoot.

11. waterfall, fall, **falls,** Niagara, niagara, **cataract, cascade,** force *or* foss

[Scot. & North. Eng.], linn [chiefly Scot.], sault [U.S. & Can.].

12. **eddy**, gurge, **surge, swirl**, twirl, whirl; **whirlpool**, vortex, gulf, **maelstrom;** Maelstrom, Charybdis, Galoforo; counter-current, counterflow, counterflux.

13. **tide**, tidal current or stream, tidal flow or flood, **tiderace; tidewater;** tideway, tide gate; **riptide**, rip; direct tide, opposite tide; spring tide; **high tide**, high water, full tide; **low tide**, low water; **neap tide**, neap; **flood tide, ebb tide;** rise of the tide, "the swelling tide" [Scott], flux, flow, flood; ebb, reflux, refluence; ebb and flow, flux and reflux.

14. **wave, billow**, surge, swell, heave, undulation; **sea**, heavy swell; ground swell; long sea, short sea; **roller**, roll; **comber**, comb, beachcomber [U.S.]; **surf, breakers;** wavelet, **ripple**, riffle [U.S.]; **tidal wave**, tide wave, bore, tidal bore, eagre; **white-caps**, white horses, ladies' fingers [naut. slang], skipper's daughters [naut. slang]; rough or heavy sea, rough water, dirty water or sea, pecky sea [coll.], choppy or chopping sea, chop, choppiness.

15. "the circling wave" [Vergil], "billows wild" [H.B. Stowe], "the furrow'd sea" [Shakespeare], "the lofty surge" [ibid.], "the billows' rage" [Byron], "the hell of waters" [ibid.], "roaring seas" [J. Gay], "the many-twinkling smile of ocean" [Keble]

16. **water gauge**, fluviograph, fluviometer, marigraph, Nilometer, hydrometrograph, hydrodynamometer.

VERBS 17. **flow, issue, stream, pour, surge, run, course, rush, gush, flush, flood;** flow in 301.10; flow out 302.13; flow back, surge back, ebb, regurgitate.

18. **overflow**, flow over, **run over, well over, brim over**, overbrim, overrun, pour out or over; **spill, slop, slosh**, spill out or over; **cataract, cascade;** inundate, engulf, overwhelm, **flood**, deluge.

19. **trickle, dribble**, dripple, **drip**, drop, spurtle; **filter**, percolate, distill or distil; **ripple, gurgle, guggle, burble, bubble**, babble, murmur, purl, trill.

20. **lap, plash, splash, wash, swash**, slosh.

21. **jet, spout, spurt**, spurtle, **squirt**, spray, **gush**, well, surge; vomit, vomit out or forth

22. **eddy**, gurge, **surge, swirl**, whirl, purl, reel, spin.

23. **billow, surge, swell**, heave, toss, roll, wave, **undulate;** comb; rise and fall, ebb and flow.

ADJS. 24. **streamy**, streamful; rivery, brooky, creeky; streamlike, riverine; fluvial, fluviatile.

25. **flowing, streaming, running, pouring**, gushing, rushing; surging, surgy; **fluent**, profluent, affluent; defluent, decurrent; diffluent, deliquescent; tidal; gulfy, vortical.

26. **flooded**, deluged, inundated, engulfed, overwhelmed, afloat.

395. CHANNEL

NOUNS 1. **channel, conduit, duct, way, passage, passageway**, adit, course; ditch, trench 262.2; culvert, culbert [dial.].

2. **watercourse, waterway, aqueduct**, water carrier; streamway, riverway; water gap, arroyo, flume [U.S.], wadi [Near East & N. Africa], donga [S. Africa], nullah [Anglo-India], caño [Sp.]; **gully**, gullyhole [chiefly dial.]; **canal**, Suez Canal, Panama Canal, Erie Canal; race, headrace, tailrace; spillway; irrigation ditch, water furrow, acequia [Sp. Amer.]; waterworks, waterwork.

3. **trough**, troughway, troughing, flume [U.S.], **gutter;** chute, shoot; pentrough, penstock [U.S.].

4. (founding) **gate**, ingate, runner, sprue, tedge.

5. **drain**, sough [Eng.], **sluice**, scupper; **sink**, sump; piscina or piscine [eccl.]; **gutter**, kennel; **sewer**, cloaca, headchute [naut.]; cloaca maxima.

6. **tube, pipe**, fistula; tubing, piping, tubulation; tubulure [chem.]; pipette, tubulet, tubule; **reed**, stem, straw; **hose;** pipe line; standpipe; water pipe, gas pipe, steam pipe; drainpipe, waste pipe; catheter [med.]; siphon, tap; efflux tube, adjutage; funnel; snorkel.

7. **main**, water main, gas main, fire main.

8. **spout**, beak, waterspout; gargoyle.

9. **nozzle**, nose, snout; rose, rosehead.

10. **valve**, gate; **faucet, spigot** [U.S.], tap [chiefly Eng.]; cock, **petcock**, stopcock; needle valve; valvule, valvula [anat.].

11. **floodgate**, flood-hatch, gate, **head gate**, penstock, water-gate; **sluice**, sluice gate; **lock**, lock gate, dock gate; tide gate, aboideau [Fr.-Can.]; **weir**, weir box, lock weir.

12. **hydrant, plug**, water plug, fireplug.

13. (anatomy) **duct, vessel, canal**, meatus; lymphatic; emunctory; pore; intes-

tines 224.6; urethra, ureter; vagina; oviduct, Fallopian tube; ostium.

14. blood vessel, artery, vein, capillary; aorta, pulmonary artery, carotid, jugular vein.

15. gullet, throat, esophagus or oesophagus, **gorge,** hals or halse [dial.], **weasand,** wizen [Scot. & dial., Eng.]; fauces, isthmus of the fauces; pharynx.

16. windpipe, trachea, weasand, wizen [Scot. & dial., Eng.]; bronchus *[pl.* bronchi], bronchia *[pl.]*, bronchial tube; epiglottis.

17. air passage, air duct, airway, air shaft, shaft; **air hole, blowhole,** breathing hole, spiracle, touchhole, spilehole; **vent, venthole,** ventage, ventiduct; transom, louver, louverwork.

18. chimney, flue, funnel, **stovepipe, smokestack,** smokeshaft.

VERBS **19. channel,** channelize, **conduct, convey,** put through, go through channels; pipe, funnel, siphon; trench 262.3

ADJS. **20. tubular,** tubate, tubiform, tubelike, pipelike; tubed, piped; cannular, fistular; bronchial, tracheal.

21. vascular, vesicular; arterial; venous, venose, veinous; capillary.

22. throated, throatlike, jugular.

23. valvular, valval, valvelike.

396. OCEAN

NOUNS **1. ocean, sea,** great sea, **main** or ocean main [poetic], the bounding main, mere [archaic or poetic], tide [chiefly poetic], salt water, **the brine,** the briny [slang], the briny deep, "the vasty deep" [Shakespeare], **the deep,** the deep sea, the deep blue sea, hyaline [poetic], drink or big drink [slang, U.S.], Davy Jones's locker [coll.]; pond, herring pond, fishpond, millpond [all joc.]; high sea, high seas; archipelago; the seven seas; ocean depths 208.3.

2. "great Neptune's ocean" [Shakespeare], "unpath'd waters" [ibid.], "the always wind-obeying deep" [ibid.], "Neptune's salt wash" [ibid.], "salt flood" [ibid.], "salt wave" [ibid.], "the whelming brine" [Cowper], "the great naked sea shouldering a loud of salt" [Sandburg], "the loud resounding sea" [Homer], "the farspooming Ocean" [Keats], "the treacherous sea" [Hood], "the desert of the sea" [Bible], "the wavy waste" [Hood], the watery waste, "old ocean's gray and melancholy waste" [Bryant], "the world of waters wild" [Thomson], "the rising world of

waters dark and deep" [Milton], "the bitter sea" [W. Morris], "the glad, indomitable sea" [B. Carman], "the clear hyaline, the glassy sea" [Milton], "the majestic main" [Thomson].

3. (oceans) Atlantic, Pacific, Arctic, Antarctic, Indian.

4. spirit of the sea, "the old man of the sea" [Homer], sea devil, Davy, **Davy Jones;** sea god, **Neptune,** Poseidon, Oceanus, Triton [all Gr. & Rom. myth]; Oceanid, Nereid, Thetis [all Gr. myth.]; Varuna [Hindu myth.]; **mermaid,** siren; merman, seaman.

5. oceanography, hydrography, bathymetry.

6. oceanographer, hydrographer.

ADJS. **7. oceanic, marine, maritime,** pelagic; nautical 274.60; oceanographic(al), hydrographic(al), bathymetric(al), bathyorographical; deep-sea 208.13.

ADVS. **8. at sea,** on the high seas; afloat 274.66, 67; by water, by sea.

9. oversea, overseas, transmarine, across the sea, over the drink [slang, U.S.]; abroad [U.S.].

10. oceanward, oceanwards, **seaward,** seawards; offshore, off.

397. LAKE, POOL

NOUNS **1. lake,** loch [Scot.], lough [Ir.], mere; tarn; lakelet, **pond,** pondlet, **pool,** linn [Scot.], dike [dial., Eng.], tank [U.S. & dial. Eng.]; standing water, still water, dead water; **water hole,** water pocket, *alberca* [Sp.]; fishpond; millpond, millpool; salt pond, salina; **puddle,** plash, sump [chiefly dial.], slab [chiefly dial.]; **wallow,** hog wallow, buffalo wallow; broad [local, Eng.], fen; lagoon, *laguna* [Sp. & It.]; **reservoir,** dam; **well, cistern,** tank.

2. lake dweller, laker, lacustrine, lacustrine dweller or inhabitant, **pile dweller** or builder.

3. lake dwelling, lacustrine dwelling, **pile house** or **dwelling,** crannog [prehistoric Celtic], palafitte, *Pfahlbauten* [Ger.; pl.].

ADJS. **4. lakish,** laky, lakelike; lacustrine, lacustral, lacustrian; pondy, pondlike, lacuscular.

398. INLET, GULF

NOUNS **1. inlet, estuary,** arm of the sea, arm, armlet, reach, loch [Scot.], mere [dial.]; **bay,** bight; **gulf; cove,** creek; **mouth,** firth or frith, kyle [Scot.], bayou

[U.S.]; **lagoon,** *laguna* [It. & Sp.]; **harbor,** natural harbor; road *or* roads, roadstead; **strait** *cr* straits, **narrow** *or* narrows, euripus, belt, gut, narrow seas; **sound; fiord** *or* fjord.

ADJS. **2.** gulfy, gulflike; gulfed, bayed.

399. MARSH

NOUNS **1. marsh,** marshland, **swamp,** swampland, fen, fenland, **morass,** moss [chiefly Scot. & North. Eng.], **bog, mire, quagmire,** slough, sump [chiefly dial.], swale [U.S.], wash, baygall [South. U.S.], *ciénaga* [Sp.], jheel [India], vlei [S. Africa]; bottom, **bottoms,** bottom land, holm [Eng.]; everglade, glade [both U.S.]; **moor,** moorland; peat bog; salt marsh; quicksand, cricksand [dial., U.S.]; mud **388.8, 9.**

VERBS **2. mire,** bemire, **sink,** sink in, **bog,** mire *or* bog down, stodge, stick in the mud.

ADJS. **3. marshy, swampy,** swampish, **moory,** moorish, fenny, paludal; **boggy,** boggish, **miry,** mirish, quaggy, quagmiry; **oozy,** plashy, splashy, spouty [coll.], poachy, squashy, squelchy, sloppy, sploshy [dial., U.S.], uliginose *or* uliginous, lutose, soft, spongy.

400. VAPOR

NOUNS **1. vapor, volatile, gas; fume, reek,** exhalation, breath, effluvium; **miasma,** miasm, mephitis, malaria, fetid air; **smoke,** smudge; wisp ∼, plume *or* puff of smoke; **damp,** chokedamp, blackdamp, firedamp, afterdamp [all mining]; flatus; **steam,** water vapor; cloud **403;** air **401;** rare ∼, noble *or* inert gas.

2. vaporousness, vaporiness, vaporosity; **airiness,** aeriness; **ethereality,** etherealism; **gaseousness,** gassiness, gaseity.

3. volatility, vaporability, vaporizability, evaporability.

4. vaporization, evaporation, volatilization, gasification, atomization, sublimation, distillation; **aeration,** aerification; etherealization, etherification; exhalation, exhaustion; fumigation; smoking; steaming.

5. vaporizer, evaporator; atomizer, spray; still, fine-still; retort.

6. vaporimeter, manometer; gas meter, gasometer; pneumatometer, spirometer; aerometer, airometer, air meter; eudiometer.

VERBS **7. vaporize, evaporate,** volatilize, gasify; sublimate, sublime; distill, fine-still; **etherize,** etherify; **aerate,** aerify;

carbonate; atomize, spray; **reek, fume,** exhale, exhaust, give off; **smoke; steam;** fumigate, perfume.

ADJS. **8. vaporous,** vaporish, vapory, vaporlike; **airy, aery, aerial, ethereal; gaseous, gassy,** gaslike, gasiform; vaporing; **reeking,** reeky; **fuming,** fumy; smoky, smoking; steamy, steaming; ozonic; oxygenous; oxyacetylene.

9. volatile, volatilizable; **vaporable,** vaporizable, vaporescent; **evaporative,** evaporable.

10. gases

acetylene	marsh gas
air gas	methane
ammonia	mustard gas
argon	natural gas
asphyxiating gas	neon
butane	nerve gas
carbon dioxide	nitrogen
carbon monoxide	oil gas
chlorine	oxygen
coal gas	ozone
ethane	phosgene
ether	poison gas
fluorine, fluorin	sewer gas
formaldehyde	sneeze gas
helium	tear gas
hydrogen	vesicatory gas
illuminating gas	war gas
krypton	water gas
laughing gas	xenon
lox (liquid oxygen)	

401. AIR

NOUNS **1. air, ether,** ozone [coll.].

2. atmosphere, aerosphere, sphere [poetic], lift [chiefly dial.]; hydrosphere.

3. (atmospheric layers) strata, layers; troposphere; substratosphere, tropopause; stratosphere, isothermal region; ionosphere, Heaviside layer *or* region; Appleton layer, F layer; photosphere, chromosphere.

4. weather, climate, clime; **the elements,** forces of nature; microclimate, macroclimate; stormy weather **161.4;** rainy weather **393.4;** windiness **402.16;** hot weather **327.6;** cold weather **332.3.**

5. (thermodynamics) isobar, isopiestic, isopiestic ∼, isobaric *or* isopiestic line; isotherm, isothermal line; isobase, isobath, isobathic line; isoplere, isometric, isometric line.

6. meteorology, climatology, weatherology [coll.], atmospherology, microclimatology; barometry, barometrography; pneumatics **346.5.**

7. weatherman [coll.], **weather prophet,** weather caster, weather sharp [slang], weathermaker [coll.]; **meteorologist,** cli-

matologist, weatherologist [coll.]; Old
Probabilities, Old Prob, Clerk of the
Weather [all joc., U.S.]; weather bureau,
U.S. Weather Bureau.

8. weather gauge, weather prophet;
barometer, baroscope, aneroid, weather-
glass, hygrometer, vacuometer; barograph,
barometrograph; weather balloon, radiosonde.

9. weather vane, weathercock, vane,
cock, wind vane, wind gauge or indicator;
wind cone, wind sleeve or cock.

10. ventilation, airing, aerage, **aeration,**
perflation, refreshment; **air conditioning,**
air cooling; oxygenation, oxygenization.

11. ventilator, aerator; air conditioner,
air filter, air cooler, ventilating or cooling
system; airway 395.17; fan 402.22.

VERBS. **12. air, aerate,** aerify, air out,
ventilate, wind, refresh, freshen; **air-condition,** air-cool; **fan,** winnow; oxygenate,
oxygenize.

ADJS. **13. airy,** aery, airish, **aerial,**
aeriform, airlike, **pneumatic, ethereal;**
exposed, lofty (as a room), roomy, light;
breezy 402.26; open-air, alfresco; **atmos-
pheric(al),** meteoric; stratospheric.

14. climatal, climatic(al), **elemental;**
meteorologic(al), climatologic(al); baro-
metric(al), barographic, baroscopic(al);
isobaric, isopiestic, isometric.

402. WIND

Air Flow.—NOUNS **1. wind, draft** or
draught, current, **air current,** breath, air,
movement of air, flatus, stream, flow; undercurrent; **inspiration, inhalation, indraft** or indraught, inflow, inrush, sufflation, insufflation, afflation, afflatus; **expiration, exhalation,** expulsion, efflation, exsufflation, emanation, aura [tech.].

2. "wind, that grand old harper" [Alex-
ander Smith], "scolding winds" [Shake-
speare], "the felon winds" [Milton], "the
wings of the wind" [Bible].

3. (wind god; the wind personified)
Aeolus [classical myth.], Vayu [Hindu
myth.]; Boreas (north wind), Eurus (east
wind); Zephyr or Zephyrus, Favonius (west
wind); Notus (south wind), Caurus
(northwest wind); Afer (southwest wind)
[Milton]; Wabun (east wind), Kabibonokka (north wind), Shawondasee (south
wind), Mudjekeewis (west wind) [all
Longfellow's *Hiawatha*].

4. puff, puff of air or wind, capful of
wind [naut.], whiff, whiffet.

5. breeze, light or gentle wind, soft-
blowing wind, **zephyr,** gale [poetic], air
[chiefly poetic], breath, breathing, breath
or stir of air; light or gentle breeze, moderate breeze, lady's wind [naut. slang]; fresh
breeze; cool breeze, doctor [coll.]; sea
breeze, ocean air; cat's-paw, catspaw.

6. gust, guest [naut. slang], **blast,** blow,
flaw, flurry, scud [chiefly Scot. & dial.,
Eng.].

7. hot wind, snow eater [coll., West.
U.S.], thawer [coll.]; chinook, **chinook
wind** [U.S.]; simoom or simoon [Arabia,
Syria & N. Africa], samiel [Turk.]; foehn,
khamsin [Egypt], harmattan [W. Africa],
sirocco [Mediterranean], solano [Sp. Medi-
terranean]; volcanic wind.

8. wintry wind, raw wind, sharp or
piercing wind, cold or icy wind, biting
wind, nipping or nippy wind, "a nipping
and eager air" [Shakespeare], icy blasts,
candelia [Sp. Amer.].

9. north wind, norther, mistral [Medi-
terranean], *bise* [F.], tramontane [Adriatic],
tramontanta [It.]; northeaster, **nor'easter,**
Euroclydon [Mediterranean], gregale
[Malta]; northwester, **nor'wester,** chocolate gale [naut. slang; W. Ind.]; south-
easter, **sou'easter,** Cape doctor [S. Africa];
southwester, **sou'wester; east wind,** easter, easterly, levant or levanter [Mediter-
ranean]; **west wind,** wester, westerly;
south wind, souther. *See also above* 402.3.

10. trade wind, trades [*pl.*], monsoon;
antitrades.

11. fall wind, gravity wind, katabatic
wind.

12. (nautical) **head wind,** dead wind,
muzzler, dead muzzler, noser or nose-ender
[slang]; **beam wind,** favorable wind, soldier's wind [coll.]; slant of wind.

13. windstorm, wind, big or great wind,
high wind, ill wind, storm, stormwind,
stormy winds, **tempest,** tempestuous wind,
"tempestuous rage" [Shakespeare]; **blow,**
blower [slang], violent or heavy blow, stiff
or strong wind; **squall,** thick squall, black
squall, white squall; **gale,** half a gale, whole
gale; **blizzard, tornado,** wuther [dial.];
hurricane, harrycane [dial.]; **thundersquall,** thunder-gust, *vendaval* [Mex.].

14. dust storm, sandstorm, devil [coll.,
India & S. Africa], dust devil [India & S.
Africa], black blizzard or roller [dial.],
shaitan [India], peesash [India], khamsin
[Egypt], sirocco [Mediterranean], simoom
or simoon [Arabia, Syria & N. Africa],

samiel [Turk.], harmattan [W. Africa],
Santa Anna [S. Calif.].

15. **whirlwind,** whirlblast, whirlicane,
wind eddy; **cyclone, tornado, twister**
[U.S.], rotary storm, willy-willy [Australia],
typhoon [tropics], *baguio* [Sp.; tropics];
sandspout, sand column, dust devil [India];
waterspout, rainspout.

16. **windiness,** airiness, **breeziness,** gustiness.

17. (science of wind) anemology, anemography, anemometry.

18. wind gauge, anemometer, anemoscope, anemograph, anemometrograph;
weather vane 401.8.

19. **breathing, respiration,** aspiration;
**inspiration, inhalation; expiration, ex-
halation; breath,** wind, breath of air;
pant, puff; wheeze; gasp, gulp; sniff, sniffle,
snuff, snuffle; sigh, suspiration; sneeze, sternutation; cough, hack; hiccough, hiccup.

20. **lungs,** bellows, lights [zool.]; ctenidia [zool.], branchiae [zool.]; gills.

21. **blower,** bellows; blowpipe, blowtube, blowgun.

22. **fan,** punkah [India], thermantidote
[India], flabellum [eccl.], electric fan.

VERBS 23. **blow, waft,** flow, stream,
move, issue; **puff,** huff [dial.]; whiff, whif-
fle; **breeze;** breeze up, freshen; **gather,
brew,** set in, blow up, **blow up a storm;**
bluster, wuther [dial.], squall; **storm,** rage,
blow great guns, blow a hurricane; blow
over.

24. **sough,** sigh, whisper, murmur, **sob,
moan,** groan, growl, snarl, **wail, howl,**
scream, **roar,** whistle, pipe, sing, sing in
the shrouds.

25. **breathe,** respire; **inhale, inspire,**
breathe in; **exhale, expire,** breathe out,
exhaust, expel; **puff,** huff [dial.], **pant,**
blow; **gasp,** gulp; wheeze; **sniff,** sniffle,
snuff, snuffle; **sigh,** suspire; sneeze; cough,
hack; hiccough, hiccup.

ADJS. 26. **windy, blowy; breezy, drafty**
or draughty, airy, airish [dial.]; **gusty,**
blasty, flawy, **squally;** blustery, blustering,
blusterous; brisk, fresh; windwayward
[poetic]; aeolian, favonian, boreal.

27. **stormy, tempestuous,** raging, storming, angry; turbulent 161.17; dirty, foul;
cyclonic, typhonic, typhoonish; rainy 393.10;
cloudy 403.8.

28. **wind-blown,** blown; **wind-swept,**
bleak, raw, exposed.

29. anemological, anemographic, anemo-
metric(al).

30. **respiratory,** breathing; inspiratory,
expiratory; nasal, rhinal; pulmonary.

31. sneezy, sternutative, errhine [med.].

403. CLOUD

NOUNS 1. **cloud, vapor, haze,** gauze,
film; mist, drisk [U.S.]; "the clouds—the
only birds that never sleep" [Victor Hugo];
fleecy cloud, billowy cloud; cloudling; storm
cloud, squall cloud; rain cloud, water carrier; thundercloud, thunderhead; cumulus,
cumulus cloud, woolpack; nimbus, cumulo-
nimbus; stratus, cirro-stratus, cumulo-cirro-
stratus, cirro-velum; strato-cumulus, cu-
mulo-stratus, snail cloud; alto-cumulus,
alto-stratus; cirrus, cirrus cloud, curl cloud;
cirro-cumulus, cumulo-cirrus, cirro-macula,
mackerel sky; cirro-nebula, cirrus haze;
cirro-fillum, cirrus stripe; mare's-tail, colt's-
tail, cat's-tail, cocktail; goat's-hair [coll.];
messengers [dial., Eng.]; scud, rack; cloudland.

2. cloud bank, "pillar of cloud" [Bible];
cloud cap, cap cloud.

3. **fog,** soup [slang]; pea soup, pea-soup
fog [both coll.]; London fog; **smog** [U.S.],
smaze [smoke-haze]; frost smoke; high fog.

4. **cloudiness, haziness, mistiness, fogginess,** nebulosity, nubilation, nimbosity,
"the low'ring element" [Milton]; **overcast,**
undercast [aviation]; heavy sky, dirty sky.

5. nephology, nephelognosy; nephologist.

6. nephelometer, nephelorometer, nephoscope.

VERBS 7. **cloud,** becloud, encloud, cloud
over, overcloud, **overcast,** overshadow,
shadow, shade, darken over, adumbrate,
nubilate, obscure; **smoke,** oversmoke; **fog,**
befog; **mist,** bemist, enmist; **haze.**

ADJS. 8. **cloudy,** vaporous, **hazy, misty,**
dirty, heavy; nebulous, nubilous, nimbose;
clouded, overclouded, **overcast; gloomy**
336.15; cloud-flecked; cirrous, cirrose; cumu-
lous, cumiliform, thunderheaded; stratous,
stratiform.

9. **cloud-covered,** cloud-laden, cloud-
curtained, cloud-hidden, cloud-wrapped,
cloud-enveloped, cloud-girt; **cloud-capped,**
cloud-topped.

10. **foggy,** soupy [slang]; pea-soup [coll.];
smoggy.

11. nephological.

404. BUBBLE

NOUNS 1. **bubble,** bleb, blob [chiefly
dial.], **globule,** vesicle, bulla [med.], blis-

ter, bladder; air bubble, soap bubble.

2. **foam, froth, spume,** fume, scud [coll.]; **spray, surf,** spoondrift *or* **spindrift,** "stinging, ringing spindrift" [Kipling]; **suds, lather,** soapsuds; **scum,** offscum; head, cream, collar [slang].

3. **effervescence** *or* effervescency, **bubbling,** frothing, foaming; **fizz** *or* fiz, fizzle; **ebullition,** ebullience *or* ebulliency; **fermentation,** ferment.

VERBS 4. **bubble,** bubble up, burble; **effervesce, fizz** *or* **fiz, fizzle,** sizzle, hiss, **sparkle,** snap, pop; **ferment,** work; **boil,** seethe, simmer; plop, wallop [Scot. & dial.], bleb [dial.], blob, blub, blubber [dial.]; guggle, gurgle; bubble over, boil over.

5. **foam, froth,** spume, cream; **lather,** suds, sud; scum, mantle; **aerate,** whip, beat, whisk.

ADJS. 6. **bubbly,** burbly; **bubbling,** burbling; **effervescent,** ebullient, fermentative, **fizzy, sparkling,** *mousseux* [F.].

7. **foamy, frothy,** spumy, creamy, yeasty; **sudsy,** suddy, **lathery,** soapy, soapsudsy, soapsuddy; heady, with a head on, with a collar on [slang], up [coll.].

405. ORGANIC MATTER

NOUNS 1. **organic matter,** animate *or* living matter, living nature, organized matter; **flora and fauna,** plant and animal life, animal and vegetable kingdom, biota [biol.]; plankton, nekton, benthos.

2. **organism,** organization, organic being, **living being** *or* thing, being, individual; bion, physiological individual; morphon, morphological individual; zoon, zooid.

3. **protoplasm,** plasma, plasm; cytoplasm, cytoplast; karyoplasm, nucleoplasm; germ plasm *or* plasma, idioplasm; bioplasm, ectoplasm, endoplasm, metaplasm, trophoplasm; protoplast, energid; centrosome; amoeba.

4. (hypothetical supramolecular vital unit) biophore *or* biophor, biogen, bioblast, pangen, plasome.

5. **cell,** cellule; plant cell, animal cell; plasma cell; somatic cell; corpuscle; erythroblast, megaloblast, mesoblast, microblast, normoblast; blastoderm, mesoderm; cellulose.

6. **gamete, germ cell,** reproductive cell; macrogamete, megagamete; microgamete.

7. **sperm, spermatozoa** (*pl.*), **seed, semen,** seminal *or* spermatic fluid, milt (of fishes); **sperm cell,** spermatozoon, male gamete; spermatozoid *or* spermatozooid,

antherozoid; spermatia [*pl.*; bot.]; spermatogonium; spermatocyte.

8. **ovum, egg, egg cell, female** gamete; ovicell, oœcium; oösphere; oösperm, zygote; oöcyte; oögonium; stirps.

9. **spore,** sporule; microspore; pollen; macrospore, megaspore; **swarm spore,** zoospore, planospore, planogamete; sporozoite; spore mother cell, sporocyte; oöspore, zygospore; sporocarp, cystocarp; spermogonium; sporangium, megasporangium, microsporangium; gonidangium; gametangium, antherid; gametophore; sporogonium, sporophyte; gametophyte; **sporophore,** spermatiophore; sporocyst.

10. **nucleus;** macronucleus, meganucleus; micronucleus; mesoplast; centriole, centrosome, centrosphere; **nucleolus;** karyosome, plasmosome, plastosome, germinal spot.

11. **chromosome,** idant, karyosome; sex chromosome, idiochromosome; W chromosome; X chromosome, accessory chromosome, monosome; Y chromosome; Z chromosome; genome; euchromosome, autosome; heterochromosome, allosome; univalent chromosome, chromatid; chromosome number, diploid number, haploid number.

12. **chromatin,** id; basichromatin, euchromatin, heterochromatin, oxychromatin.

13. **embryo, fetus,** blastula; germ; rudiment, anlage; **larva,** nymph; ovule.

14. **egg;** ovule; **roe,** spawn; yolk, yellow; white, egg white, glair, albumen; eggshell.

15. **mitosis,** cell division; amitosis, meiosis, diaster, karyomitosis, karyokinesis, cytokinesis.

16. (science of organisms) **biology,** aerobiology, agrobiology, electrobiology, ethnobiology, microbiology, radiobiology, bacteriology, biophysics, cytology, embryology, palynology, physiology, somatology; organic chemistry; biochemistry, biochemy, biochemics; biometry, biometrics; biotaxy, taxonomy; ecology, bioecology, bionomics; ontogeny, phylogeny; natural science (organic and inorganic sciences collectively); anatomy 244.7; zoology 414; botany 411; genetics 169.6.

17. **biologist,** bacteriologist, biochemist, biophysicist, biometrist, cytologist, ecologist, embryologist, geneticist, physiologist; morphologist, anatomist, histologist; naturalist, natural scientist; botanist 411.2; zoologist 414.2.

ADJS. **18. organic,** organized, **animate, living,** vital, zoetic; **biological,** biotic.

19. protoplasmic, plasmic, plasmatic; amoebic, amoeboid.

20. cellular, cellulous; unicellular, multicellular; corpuscular.

21. gametic; **spermatic,** spermic, **seminal,** spermatozoal, spermatozoan, spermatozoic; sporal, sporous, sporoid; sporogenous; chromosomal; chromatinic.

22. nuclear, nucleal, nucleary, nucleate; nucleolar, nucleolate, nucleolated.

23. embryonic, germinal, rudimentary; larval; fetal; in the bud.

24. egglike, ovicular, ovular, eggy; oviparous; ovarian; albuminous, albuminoid; yolked, yolky.

25. planktonic, nektonic, benthonic.

406. LIFE

NOUNS **1. life, living, vitality,** animation; spirit, soul; existence 1; viability.

2. "one dem'd horrid grind" [Dickens], "one long process of getting tired" [Butler], "a bridge of groans across a stream of tears" [P. J. Bailey], "a beauty chased by tragic laughter" [Masefield], "a tumble-about thing of ups and downs" [Disraeli], "a ladder infinite-stepped" [R. Burton], "a little gleam of Time between two eternities" [Carlyle], "a tale told by an idiot, full of sound and fury, signifying nothing" [Shakespeare], "a perpetual instruction in cause and effect" [Emerson], "a flame that is always burning itself out" [Shaw], "a long lesson in humility" [Barrie], "a document to be interpreted" [Amiel], "a fiction . . . made up of contradiction" [Blake], "a fatal complaint, and an eminently contagious one" [Holmes].

3. life force, force of life, living force, *vis vitae* or *vitalis* [L.], **vital force** or energy, *élan vital* [F.; Bergson], impulse of life, vital principle, **vital spark** or **flame,** Promethean spark, spark of life, divine spark, life principle, tuck [coll., U.S.], vital spirit, vital fluid, anima; **breath,** life breath, breath of life, breath of one's nostrils, divine breath, essence of life, pneuma, prana [Vedic & Hindu]; atman, jivatma, jiva [all Hindu]; blood, **lifeblood,** heartblood, heart's blood; growth force, bathmism [biol.].

4. the living, the quick; the quick and the dead.

5. vivification, vitalization, animation, quickening.

VERBS **6. live,** be alive, have life, **exist** 1.8, breathe, live and breathe, fetch or draw breath, draw the breath of life, walk the earth.

7. come to life, come into existence or being, come into the world, see the light, **be born;** quicken; **come to, revive,** show signs of life; **awake, awaken;** rise again, live again, rise from the grave, resurge, return, reappear.

8. vivify, vitalize, energize, animate, quicken, imbue or endow with life, give life to, put life or new life into, bring to life, bring or call into existence or being.

9. keep alive, keep body and soul together, be spared, have nine lives like a cat; support life.

ADJS. **10. living, alive,** live, very much alive, alive and kicking [coll.], conscious, breathing, quick, **animate,** animated, **vital,** zoetic [biol.], imbued or endowed with life, in the flesh, among the living, in the land of the living, on this side of the grave, aboveground; existent 1.13; viable.

11. life-giving, animating, animative, quickening, vivifying, energizing, Promethean.

407. DEATH

NOUNS **1. death, dying, decease, demise,** release, **passing away,** passing, departure, parting, ending, the end, end of life, cessation of life, loss of life, ebb of life, expiration, **dissolution, extinction,** annihilation, extinguishment, quietus, fall; summons of death, final summons; **sleep,** rest, eternal rest or sleep, the last sleep; last roundup [slang, West. U.S.], last rattler [tramp slang, U.S.]; the debt of nature, last debt; last muster, last curtain call [coll.], curtains [slang, U.S.]; jaws of death, hand or finger of death, shades of death; violent death 408; natural death; euthanasia; rigor mortis; megadeath.

2. "the latter end" [Bible], "the journey's end" [Shakespeare], "that dreamless sleep" [Byron], "a debt we all must pay" [Euripides], "the debt which cancels all others" [C. Colton], "the tribute due unto nature" [Sterne], "the sleeping partner of life" [Horace Smith], "a knell that summons thee to heaven or to hell" [Shakespeare], "that fell arrest without all bail" [ibid.], "kind Nature's signal of retreat" [Johnson], "a little sleep, a little slumber, a little folding of the hands to sleep" [Bible], "crossing of the bar" [Tennyson], "the downward path" [Horace], "the gate of life" [St. Bernard], "the crown of life" [Young], "an awfully big adventure" [J. M. Barrie].

3. (personification of death) **Death,** "Black Death" [Ovid], "Pale Death" [Horace], "the pale priest of the mute people" [Browning], "that grim ferryman" [Shakespeare], "Hell's grim Tyrant" [Pope], "the king of terrors" [Bible], **the Reaper,** the Grim Reaper, Old Floorer [slang], "the Pilot of the Galilean lake"; the angel of death, death's bright angel, Azrael; scythe or sickle of Death.

4. river of death, Styx, Stygian shore; Jordan, Jordan's bank; "valley of the shadow of death" [Bible].

5. sudden death, untimely end; stroke of death, death stroke; heart failure; suffocation 408.6; drowning, watery grave.

6. dying day, deathday, "the supreme day and the inevitable hour" [Vergil].

7. deathbed; deathwatch; death struggle, agony, death agonies; last breath or gasp, dying breath; **death rattle,** death groan.

8. swan song, death song, *chant du cygne* [F.].

9. bereavement, loss.

10. deathlikeness, deathliness, deadliness; **weirdness, eeriness, uncanniness,** unearthliness; ghostliness, ghostlikeness; **ghastliness, grisliness, gruesomeness;** paleness, haggardness, wanness, luridness, pallor; cadaverousness, corpselikeness.

11. mortality, mortalness; **death rate;** moribundity.

12. obituary, obit, necrology, register of deaths, roll of the dead, mortuary roll, bill of mortality.

13. corpse, dead body, **cadaver, carcass, body;** corpus delicti [law]; **stiff,** deader [both slang]; **the dead, the deceased,** the defunct, the departed, **decedent** [law], the late . . ., the late lamented; **remains,** mortal or organic remains, bones, relics [now poetic], reliquiae; dust, ashes, earth, clay, tenement of clay, "this mortal coil" [Shakespeare]; **carrion,** crowbait, food for worms; **mummy,** mummification; long pig.

14. death's-head, crossbones, skull and crossbones, *memento mori* [L.; literally, remember to die].

VERBS **15. die, decease, succumb, expire, perish,** cease to live, part, depart, quit this world, make one's exit, pass, pass on, pass away, meet one's death or end, end one's life or days, depart this life, **shuffle off this mortal coil,** put off mortality, **lose one's life,** lay down one's life, relinquish or surrender one's life, resign one's life or being, **give up the ghost,** yield the ghost, yield one's breath, breathe one's last, fall asleep, close one's eyes, take one's last sleep, turn one's face to the wall, pay the debt of nature, "put out to sea" [Tennyson], go out with the ebb, "go the way of all earth" [Bible], return to dust or the earth; die a natural death; die in harness, die with one's boots or shoes on; die lying down; die fighting, die in the last ditch; die a violent death 408.21.

16. (slang and colloquialisms) **croak, go west, kick the bucket,** kick in, slip one's breath or wind, go up, **pop off,** drop off, go off, step off, step off the deep end, knock off, pipe off, kick off, shove off, pass out, peg out, take the last count; check out, check in, cash in, hand or pass in one's checks or chips; kick up one's heels or toes, turn or cock up one's toes, turn up one's toes to the daisies; slip one's cable, coil up one's cable or rope [both naut. slang].

17. go to glory, go to kingdom come [slang], go to the happy hunting grounds, go home, go home feet first [slang], go to one's last home, go to one's long account, go over to or join the majority or great majority, **be gathered to one's fathers,** join one's ancestors, join the choir invisible; pass over, pass over Jordan, "walk through the valley of the shadow of death" [Bible], cross the Stygian ferry, give an obolus to Charon; awake to life immortal, "put on immortality" [Bible].

18. drop dead, fall down dead, bite the dust [coll.]; come to an untimely end, die all at once [joc.].

19. starve, starve to death; smother 408.19; catch one's death [chiefly coll.], catch one's death of cold.

20. drown, go to a watery grave, go to Davy Jones's locker [coll.], make a hole in the water [slang].

21. lay down one's life for one's country, make the supreme sacrifice, do one's bit; lose the number of one's mess [mil. slang].

22. bereave, leave, leave behind; orphan.

ADJS. **23. deathlike, deathly, deadly; weird, eerie, uncanny,** unearthly; ghostly, ghostlike; **ghastly, grisly, gruesome,** macabre; pale, wan, lurid, haggard; **ca-daverous,** corpselike; mortuary.

24. dead, lifeless, breathless, without life, **deceased, demised, defunct,** croaked [slang], departed, departed this life, **gone, passed on,** gone the way of all flesh, gone west [coll.], dead and gone, done for [coll.], dead and done for [coll.], no more, finished [coll.], taken off *or* away, released, fallen, bereft of life; **at rest,** resting easy [coll.], out of one's misery; **asleep,** sleeping, reposing; asleep in Jesus, dead in the Lord; **called home,** gone to a better land, out of the world, born into a better world, launched into eternity, gone to glory, gone to kingdom come [slang], "gathered to his fathers" [Bible], with the saints, numbered with the dead; carrion, food for worms; death-struck, death-stricken, smitten with death; stillborn; late, late-lamented.

25. stone-dead, dead as a doornail, dead as a herring, dead as mutton, cold [slang, U.S.], "as cold as any stone" [Shakespeare], stiff [slang].

26. drowned, asleep in the deep, in a watery grave, under hatches [naut. slang].

27. dying, expiring, going; **moribund,** near death, near one's end, at the end of one's rope [coll.], done for [coll.], at the point of death, **at death's door,** at the portals of death, in the jaws of death; **on one's last legs** [coll.], with one foot in the grave, tottering on the brink of the grave; booked [slang], under sailing orders [naut. slang]; on one's deathbed; at the last gasp.

28. bereaved, bereft; orphan, **orphaned,** parentless, fatherless, motherless.

29. post-mortem, postmortal, postmortuary, postmundane, post-obit, postobituary, posthumous.

ADVS. **30. deathly, deadly;** to the death, *à la mort* [F.].

PHRS. **31.** one's hour is come, one's days are numbered, one's race is run, one's doom is sealed, life hangs by a thread, Death knocks at the door, Death stares one in the face, the sands of life are running out.

408. KILLING

NOUNS **1. killing, slaying, slaughter, dispatch, extermination, destruction;** kill; **bloodshed,** blood, gore, flow of blood; mercy killing; stoning, lapidation; braining; shooting; poisoning; execution 1008.7; martyrdom.

2. homicide, manslaughter; murder, bloody murder [slang], foul play, the curse of Cain; **assassination,** removal, elimination; **liquidation, purge,** purging; thuggery, thuggism, thuggee.

3. butchery, butchering, **slaughter,** slaughtering; **carnage, massacre, decimation,** saturnalia of blood; **mass murder,** pogrom, genocide, race extermination.

4. (words in *-cide* referring to both doer or agent and deed) homicide, fratricide, matricide, parricide, regicide, infanticide, uxoricide, vaticide; aborticide, feticide.

5. suicide, self-murder, self-destruction, *felo-de-se* [Anglo-L.]; **disembowelment,** hara-kiri [Jap.], seppuku [Jap.], happy dispatch [joc.]; suttee, sutteeism [both India]; car of Jagannath *or* Juggernaut; race suicide.

6. suffocation, stuffocation [joc.], **smotheration, asphyxiation,** asphyxia; **strangulation,** strangling, garrote *or* garrotte; **choking,** choke; **drowning.**

7. fatality, fatal accident, violent **death, casualty,** disaster, calamity.

8. deadliness, lethality, fatality; malignance *or* malignancy, malignity, **virulence,** perniciousness.

9. deathblow, death stroke, mortal blow, lethal blow, quietus; *coup de grâce* [F., blow of mercy].

10. killer, slayer, slaughterer, butcher, croaker [slang], **bloodshedder;** massacrer; **manslayer, homicide, murderer,** Cain; **assassin,** assassinator; **cutthroat,** thug, bravo, gorilla [slang, U.S.], apache, gunman [chiefly U.S.]; **gun,** trigger man, torpedo [all crim. slang, U.S.]; **hatchet man,** highbinder [U.S.]; strangler, garroter; burker, burkite; cannibal, man-eater; headhunter; matador; mercy killer; thrill killer; homicidal maniac. *See also above* 408.4.

11. exterminator, eradicator, eradicant, **pesticide;** rodenticide, rat poison; vermicide; microbicide; fungicide; weed killer; **insecticide,** insect powder, bug bomb, aerosol bomb; Paris green, D.D.T., ompa (octa-methyl-pyrophosphoramide).

12. (place of slaughter) Aceldama *or* aceldama, field of blood *or* bloodshed; slaughterhouse, butchery, shambles, abattoir; stockyard.

VERBS **13. kill, slay, put to death,** deathify, deprive of life, **take life,** take one's life away, **do away with,** make away with, put out of the way, end, put an end to, dispatch, do to death, finish [chiefly coll.], finish off, take off, **dispose of, exterminate, destroy;** carry off *or* away, remove from life; launch into eternity, send to glory, send to kingdom come [slang], send to one's last account; cut off, nip in the bud; poison, chloroform, starve; execute 1008.19.

14. (slang and colloquialisms) **send west,** corpse, **croak, bump off** [U.S.], polish off, blot out, erase, wipe out, do for, **do in,** lay out, take care of, give the business *or* works, get [U.S.], fix, settle, put the kibosh on, kick into the beyond, put away, put one easy, put one out of his misery.

15. shed blood, spill blood, bloody one's hands with, dye *or* imbrue one's hands in blood, pour out blood like water, wade knee-deep in blood.

16. murder, commit murder, victimize; **assassinate,** remove; **purge, liquidate,** eliminate, get rid of, take for a ride [crim. slang, U.S.].

17. slaughter, butcher, massacre, decimate.

18. strike dead, fell, bring down, lay low; drop, drop *or* stop in one's tracks; **shoot,** shoot down, saw off [crim. slang, U.S.], shoot to death; cut down, **put to the sword;** jugulate, cut the throat; **deal a deathblow,** give the quietus, silence [slang], knock in *or* on the head; **brain,** blow ∼, knock *or* dash one's brains out; **stone,** lapidate, stone to death.

19. strangle, garrote *or* garrotte, **throttle, choke,** burke; **suffocate,** stuffocate [joc.], **stifle, smother, asphyxiate,** stop the breath; **drown.**

20. sign one's death warrant, strike the death knell of.

21. die a violent death, come to a violent end, meet with foul play, get one's everlasting [slang], welter in one's blood.

22. commit suicide, suicide [coll.], **take one's own life, kill oneself,** do away with oneself, put an end to oneself; blow one's brains out.

ADJS. **23. deadly, deathly,** deathful, **killing, destructive,** death-dealing, death-bringing, feral, internecine; **fatal, mortal, lethal; malignant,** malign, virulent, pernicious.

24. murderous, slaughterous; cutthroat; cruel 937.24; **bloodthirsty,** bloody-minded; **bloody,** gory, sanguine, sanguinary; red-handed; **homicidal;** suicidal.

409. INTERMENT

NOUNS **1. interment, burial,** burying, planting [coll.], inhumation, sepulture, en-

tombment; earth bath, ground sweat [both slang].

2. cremation, incineration, burning, reduction to ashes; pyre, funeral pile.

3. embalmment, embalming; mummification.

4. last offices, last honors, **last rites,** last duty *or* service, exequies, obsequies; Office of the Dead, Memento of the Dead, requiem, dirge, extreme unction, viaticum, [all Catholic Church]; funeral oration *or* sermon, funeral [dial.]; wake, deathwatch.

5. funeral, burial, burying [dial.]; funeral procession, dead march; dirge 873.5.

6. knell, passing bell, death bell, funeral ring, tolling, tolling of the knell.

7. mourner, griever, lamenter, keener [Ir.]; mute, professional mourner; **pallbearer,** bearer.

8. undertaker, mortician, funeral director; embalmer.

9. morgue, mortuary, deadhouse, lichhouse, **funeral home** *or* **parlor,** undertaker's establishment; **crematory,** crematorium, cinerarium, burning ghat [India].

10. hearse, dead wagon [slang].

11. coffin, casket [chiefly U.S.], box, shrine, kist [Scot.], pall [fig.]; crate, bone box *or* house, six-foot bungalow, wooden kimono *or* overcoat [all slang]; shell; **sarcophagus.**

12. urn, cinerary urn, funeral urn *or* vessel, bone pot, ossuary.

13. bier, litter.

14. graveclothes, shroud, winding sheet, cerecloth, cerements; pall.

15. graveyard, cemetery, burial ground, bone yard [slang, U.S.], burial yard, necropolis, polyandrium [Gr. antiq.], golgotha, **memorial park,** city *or* village of the dead, marble city [slang]; **churchyard,** God's acre; **potter's field;** Golgotha, Calvary; lich gate.

16. tomb, sepulcher; grave, pit, deep six [slang]; resting place, "the lone couch of his everlasting sleep" [Shelley]; last home, long home, narrow house, house of death, low house, low green tent; **crypt, vault,** burial chamber; ossuary, ossuarium; charnel house, bone house; **mausoleum; catacombs;** mastaba [archaeol.]; shaft grave tomb [archaeol.]; **shrine,** reliquary, memoria; tope, stupa [both Buddhist]; cenotaph; catafalque; dokhma [Persia]; tower of silence; pyramid; mound, tumulus, barrow.

17. monument, gravestone 568.11.

18. **epitaph**, inscription, *hic jacet* [L.].

19. **disinterment, exhumation,** disentombment, unearthing.

VERBS 20. **inter**, inhume, bury, plant [coll.], sepulture, inlearth, **lay to rest, consign to the grave,** put six feet under [slang], put to bed with a shovel [slang]; tomb, **entomb,** hearse; enshrine; inurn; coffin; hold *or* conduct a funeral, funeralize [South. U.S.], preach a funeral [dial.].

21. **cremate,** incremate, **incinerate, burn,** reduce to ashes.

22. **lay out; embalm;** mummify; lie in state.

23. count daisies, push up daisies, turn *or* cock up the toes to the daisies, become a landowner, take an earth bath *or* ground sweat [all joc.].

24. **disinter, exhume,** disentomb, unearth, unbury.

ADJS. 25. **funereal,** funeral, funerary, *funèbre* [F.], mortuary, exequial, obsequial, feral; sepulchral, tomblike; cinerary; necroscopic(al); **dismal** 870.25; **mournful** 870.27; dirgelike 873.18.

ADVS. 26. beneath the sod, underground, six feet under [slang], "in the dark union of insensate dust" [Byron]; at rest, resting in peace.

PHRS. 27. **R.I.P.,** *requiescat or requiescant in pace* [L., may he or she or they rest in peace], rest in peace; *hic jacet* [L.], *ci-gît* [F.], here lies.

410. PLANTS

NOUNS 1. **plants, vegetation; flora, plant life, vegetable kingdom;** herbage, flowerage; verdure, greenery, greens.

2. **growth,** stand, crop; plantation, planting clump, tuft, tussock, hassock.

3. **plant, vegetable,** wort; **herb;** seedling; cutting; seed plant, spermatophyte; exotic, hot-house plant; annual, biennial, triennial, perennial, evergreen; deciduous plant, ephemeral; cosmopolite; aquatic, hydrophyte; amphibian.

4. (varieties) **legume,** pulse, vetch, bean, pea; succulent; **weed; vine,** creeper, climber; **fern,** bracken; **moss,** liverwort; algae, fucus, conferva, confervoid; **seaweed,** kelp, sea moss, rockweed; gulfweed; sargasso, sargassum, sea lentil; wrack, sea wrack; **fungus,** lichen, mold *or* mould, rust, smut, puffball; mushroom, toadstool; plant families 411.4−8; fruits and vegetables 306a. 49−51.

5. **grass, pasture** *or* forage grass, lawn grass, ornamental grass; **cereal, grain,** corn [Eng.]; sedge; rush; reed, cane, bamboo; aftergrass, fog.

6. **turf, sod, sward,** greensward.

7. **green, lawn,** grassplot *or* grassplat, greenyard; **common, park, village green;** bowling green, putting green.

8. **grassland,** grass; **meadow,** meadow land, mead [poetic], swale, lea, haugh [Scot. & dial., Eng.], haughland [Scot.], vega [Sp. Amer. & Phil. I.]; **pasture,** pasturage, pasture land, field, park [Eng.], pen [Jamaica], *agostadero* [Sp.]; **range,** grazing; **prairie, savanna** [South. U.S.], **steppe,** steppeland, **pampas** [S. Amer.], pampa [Argentina], campo [esp. S. Amer.], llano [Sp. Amer.], tundra [Arctic]; **veld** *or* veldt, grass veld [both S. Africa].

9. **shrubbery; shrub, bush;** bramble, brier *or* briar, brier bush.

10. **tree,** timber [chiefly U.S.]; shade tree, fruit tree, timber tree; sapling, seedling; scrub; pollard; conifer, evergreen.

11. **woodland, wood, woods, timberland, timber, forest,** forest land, forestry; forest primeval; virgin forest; greenwood; **jungle,** jungles; wild, wildwood, wilderness; **bush,** bosch [Du.], scrub; boschveld [Du.], bushveld, tree veld [both S. Africa]; shrubland, scrubland; pine barrens, palmetto barrens; **park,** paradise, chase [Eng.]; park forest; hanger (wooded slope).

12. **grove, woodlet;** holt [arch. & dial.], hurst, spinney [Eng.], tope [India], shaw [arch. & dial.]; **orchard;** wood lot.

13. **thicket,** thick-set, clump; **copse, coppice,** copsewood, coppet, firth, frith [now dial. Eng.]; **bosk,** bosket *or* bosquet, boscage, *bocage* [F.]; covert; **brake,** canebrake [South, U.S.]; chaparral; chamisal [Calif.]; motte [local, U.S.]; ceja [Texas].

14. **brush, scrub, brushwood,** shrubwood, scrubwood, copsewood; deadwood.

15. **undergrowth, underwood, underbrush,** undershrubs, boscage, *bocage* [F.], firth, frith [now dial. Eng.]; heath.

16. **foliage, leafage,** ramage; foliation; praefoliation, vernation; spray.

17. **leaf, frond;** leaflet, foliole; lamina, blade, spear, spire, pile; **flag; needle,** pine needle; floral leaf, **petal,** sepal; bract, bractlet; bracteole; spathe; involucre, involucrum; glume, gluma; lemma; pile; cotyledon, seed leaf; stipule.

18. **branch,** fork, **limb, bough,** bush; **twig, sprig,** switch; **shoot,** offshoot, spear, frond; **sprout,** sprit, burgeon; **runner,**

flagellum, sarmentum, **tendril**, bine; sucker.

19. **stem, stalk, stock,** axis, caulis; **trunk,** bole; spear, spire; straw; reed; cane; cornstalk [U.S.]; culm, haulm; caudex; footstalk, pedicel, pedicellus or peliculus, pedicle, peduncle; leafstalk, petiole, petiolus, petiolule; seedstalk; caulicle; tigella, tigelle, tigellum, tigellus; funicule, funiculus; stipe, anthrophore, carpophore, gynophore.

20. **root,** radix, radical, radicle; rootlet; **taproot,** tap; **rhizome,** stock, rootstock; **tuber,** tubercle; **bulb,** corm, bulbil; earthnut.

21. **bud,** burgeon, gemma; gemmule, gemmula; plumule, acrospire; leaf bud, flower bud, rosebud.

22. **flower, posy, blossom, bloom;** blow; floweret, floret, floscule; wild flower; everlasting, amaranth [poetic]; "daisies pied and violets blue" [Shakespeare].

23. **bouquet, nosegay, posy,** boughpot, flower arrangement; **boutonniere,** buttonhole [coll.]; **corsage; spray; wreath,** festoon; **garland,** chaplet, lei.

24. **inflorescence,** florescence, efflorescence; flowerage, florification; **flowering, blossoming, blooming; blossom, bloom,** blow; unfolding, unfoldment; anthesis, full bloom.

25. (types of inflorescence) raceme, corymb, umbel, panicle, cyme, thyrsus, spadix, verticillaster; head, capitulum; spike, spikelet; ament, catkin, cattail; strobile, cone, pine cone.

26. (flower parts) petal; perianth, calyx, epicalyx, corolla, corona; androecium; stamen, microsporophyll; pistil, gynoecium; style, stigma; carpel.

27. **ear,** auricle, spike; ear of corn, mealie [S. Africa]; nubbin [U.S.]; **cob,** corncob [both U.S.].

28. **seed vessel, seedcase,** seedbox, pericarp; **capsule,** theca; **pod,** cod [chiefly dial.], seed pod; **hull, shell,** nutshell; legume, legumen; boll, bur or burr, follicle, silique, hip, peasecod.

29. **seed; stone, pit,** endocarp; **nut;** pip; **grain, kernel, berry;** wheat, oats, barley, rye, corn; legume, bean, pea; coffee, coffee bean; flaxseed, linseed; hayseed; bird seed.

30. (a vegetating) **vegetation, growth;** germination, pullulation; burgeoning, sprouting; budding, gemmation; luxuriation.

VERBS **31. vegetate, grow;** germinate, pullulate; root, take root, strike root; sprout up, shoot up, upsprout, upspear; flourish,

luxuriate, grow rank or lush; overgrow, overrun.

32. **burgeon,** put forth, burst forth; **sprout,** shoot; **bud, gemmate,** put forth buds; **leaf,** leave, leaf out, put forth leaves.

33. **flower, blossom, bloom,** blow, effloresce, floreate, burst into bloom.

ADJS. **34. vegetable,** vegetal, vegetative, vegetational, vegetarian; **plantlike; herbaceous,** herbal, herbous, herbose, herby; leguminous, leguminose, leguminiform; cereal; weedy; fruity, fruitlike; tuberous, bulbous; rootlike, rhizoid, radicular, radicated, radiciform; endogenous, exogenous.

35. algal, fucoid, confervoid; fungous, fungoid, fungiform.

36. **floral,** floreal; **flowery, florid;** flowered, florate, floriate, floriated; **flowering, blossoming, blooming,** florescent, inflorescent, efflorescent, in flower, in bloom, in blossom; uniflorous, multiflorous; radiciflorous, rhizanthous.

37. **arboreal,** arboral, arborean, arborary; **treelike,** arboriform, arborescent, dendroid, dendriform; bushy, shrubby, scrubby, scrubbly; bushlike, shrublike, scrublike; piny; coniferous; citrus.

38. **sylvan** or silvan, **woodland, forest; wooded,** timbered, forested, arboreous; **woody,** woodsy [coll., U.S.], bushy, shrubby, scrubby; bosky, copsy, braky.

39. **leafy,** leavy, bowery; foliated, foliate, foliose; foliaged, leaved.

40. **verdant, verdurous,** verdured; **mossy,** moss-covered, moss-grown; **grassy,** grasslike; turfy, swardy; turflike, cespitose; meadowy.

41. **luxuriant,** flourishing, **rank, lush;** dense, thick, heavy, gross; jungly, jungled; overgrown, overrun.

42. **perennial, evergreen;** hardy, half-hardy; **deciduous,** ephemeral.

43. **algae**

benthon	reindeer moss
conferva	rockweed
dulse	sargasso
fucoid	sargassum
fucus	scum
gulfweed	sea lettuce
Iceland moss	sea moss
Irish moss	seaweed
kelp	sea wrack
lichen	stonewort
plankton	wrack
pond scum	

44. **ferns**

adder's fern	basket fern
baby fern	beech fern

bladder fern
boulder fern
bracken
chair fern
cliff brake
climbing fern
curly grass
grape fern
hart's tongue
holly fern
lady fern
lip fern
maidenhair

marsh fern
moonwort
oak fern
Osmunda
ostrich fern
rattlesnake fern
rock brake
rock spleenworts
shield fern
snuffbox
walking fern
winter brake
wood fern

mock orange
monkshood
morning-glory
moss rose
motherwort
myrtle
narcissus
nasturtium
oleander
opium poppy
orchid
oxalis
pansy
passion flower
peony
periwinkle
petunia
phlox
pink
poinsettia
poppy
portulaca
primrose
Queen Anne's lace
ranunculus
resurrection plant
rhododendron
rose
rosemary
sage

shooting star
smilax
snapdragon
snowball
snowberry
snowdrop
spiraea
stock
strawflower
sunflower
sweet alyssum
sweet pea
sweet William
trillium
trumpet vine
tulip
umbrella plant
Venus' fly trap
verbena
vetch
viburnum
viola
violet
wallflower
water lily
wisteria
wolfbane
yarrow
yucca
zinnia

45. flowers

acacia
African violet
amaryllis
anemone
arbutus
arrowhead
asphodel
aster
azalea
baby-blue-eyes
baby's breath
bachelor button
begonia
bitterroot
black-eyed Susan
bleeding heart
blood-root
bluebell
bluet
bridal wreath
broom
butter ball
buttercup
cactus
calendula
camass, camas
camellia
camomile
campanula
candytuft
carnation
cat's-paw
cattail
century plant
Chinese lantern
Christmas rose
chrysanthemum
cineraria
clematis
clethra
cockscomb
columbine
cornel
cornflower
cosmos
cowslip
crocus
cyclamen
daffodil
dahlia
daisy
dandelion
delphinium
dogwood
duckweed
Dutchman's-

breeches
edelweiss
eglantine
fireweed
flax
fleur-de-lis
forget-me-not
forsythia
foxglove
foxtail
fuchsia
gardenia
gentian
geranium
gladiolus
goldenrod
groundsel
harebell
hawthorn
heather
hepatica
hibiscus
hollyhock
honeysuckle
horehound
hyacinth
hydrangea
Indian paintbrush
indigo
iris
jack-in-the-pulpit
japonica
jasmine
jonquil
knotweed
lady's-slipper
larkspur
laurel
lavender
lilac
lily
lily of the valley
lobelia
lotus
love-lies-bleeding
lupine
magnolia
mallow
marguerite
marigold
marsh mallow
marsh marigold
mayflower
mignonette
mimosa
moccasin flower

46. fungi

mold, mould
mushroom
puffball
rust
slime mold

smut
toadstool
truffle
yeast

47. grasses, grains

alfalfa
alfilaria
bamboo
barley
beach grass
beard grass
Bengal grass
bent, bent grass
Bermuda grass
black bent
bluegrass
bluejoint
bog grass
bristly foxtail
  grass
broomcorn
buckwheat
buffalo grass
bulrush
bunch grass
canary grass
cane
China grass
cocksfoot grass
corn
cotton grass
crab grass
durra
eelgrass
English rye
feather grass
finger-comb grass

finger grass
flyaway grass
four-leaved grass
gama or sesame
  grass
grama or mesquite
  grass
guinea grass
hairgrass
hassock grass
herd's grass
horsetail
Indian corn
Italian rye
Japanese lawn grass
kaffir corn
Kentucky bluegrass
little quaking grass
lovegrass
lyme
maize
meadow fescue
meadow foxtail
meadow grass
millet
myrtle grass
oats
orchard grass
paddy
palm-leaved grass
pampas grass
papyrus

peppergrass
pin grass
plume grass
pony grass
redtop
reed
ribbon grass
rice
rush
rye
scurvey
scutch
sedge
sesame
sheep's fescue
silk grass
sorghum
spear grass
squirrel tail grass

star grass
striped grass
sugar cane
switch grass
sword grass
tear grass
timothy
tufted hair grass
viper's grass
wheat
wild oats
wire grass
wood meadow
    grass
woolly beard grass
worm grass
yellow-eyed grass
zebra grass

48. herbs

angelica
anise
arrowroot
balm
basil
belladonna
borage
camomile
caraway
cardamom,
    cardamum
castor-oil plant
catnip, catmint
chervil
chickpea
chicory
clover
coriander
cowpea
deadly nightshade
death camass
dill
fennel
feverroot
figwort
ginseng
hemp
henbane
horehound

hyssop
licorice
liverwort
lucerne, lucern
mandrake
marjoram
mayapple
mint
monkshood
mullein
parsley
peppermint
purple medic
rosemary
rue
sage
savory
saxifrage
skunk cabbage
sorrel
soybean
spearmint
sweet cicely
tansy
tarragon
thyme
water cress
wintergreen

49. mosses

club moss
Florida moss
flowering moss
ground pine
hair cap moss
leafy liverwort
long moss
lycopodium

peat moss
red tipped moss
scale moss
Spanish moss
staghorn moss
tree moss
white moss

50. shrubs

alder
azalea
barberry
bayberry
blackberry
blackthorn
blueberry
box
broom

caper
chokeberry
clove tree
coca
coffee
cotton
cranberry
currant
daphne

elder
evergreen bitter-
    sweet
forsythia
frangipani
fuchsia
furze
gale
gardenia
genista
gooseberry
gorse
greasewood
guava
guayule
haw
heather
hemp tree
hibiscus
holly
hop tree
huckleberry
hydrangea
indigo
Juneberry
juniper
jute
kalmia
laurel
leatherleaf
lilac
locust
magnolia
maguey
manzanita
marijuana
mescal
mesquite
milkwort
mistletoe
mock orange

51. trees

acacia
ailanthus
alder
allspice
almond
apple
apricot
ash
aspen (cotton-
    wood)
avocado, alligator
    pear
bald cypress
balsa
balsam
banana
banyan
basswood (linden)
bayberry
beech
betelnut
birch
boxwood
Brazil-nut
breadfruit
buckeye
butternut
buttonwood

mountain lilac
myrica
myrtle
nandin
ninebark
oleander
Persian berry
photinia
pink ball
poison sumac
pomegranate
privet
pussy willow
queen of the
    meadow
rabbit berry
red bush
rhododendron
rosebay
rosemary
rose of Sharon
sage, sagebrush
sand myrtle
silk oak
sisal
snowberry
snow wreath
spiraea
sumac
symplocos
syringa
tamarisk
tobacco
turkeyberry
veronica
whin
wig tree
winter creeper
witch hazel
yellow root
zenobia

cacao
camphor tree (cin-
    namon)
candleberry
cashew
cassia
catalpa
cedar
cherry
chestnut (chinka-
    pin)
chinaberry tree,
    china tree
chincapin, chinka-
    pin, chinquapin
cinnamon (cam-
    phor-tree)
citron
clove
coco
coconut
cork
cottonwood
cypress
date palm
dogwood
ebony
elder

elm
eucalyptus
fig
fir
frankincense
ginkgo
golden wreath
grapefruit
guava
gum
hawthorn
hazel, hazelnut
hemlock
henna
hickory
holly
hornbeam
horse chestnut
ironwood
juniper (cedar)
kumquat
laburnum
lancewood
larch
laurel
lemon
lignum vitae
lime
linden (basswood)
litchi, litchi nut
locust
logwood
madroña
magnolia
mahogany
mango
mangrove
maple
medlar
mimosa
mountain ash
mulberry
nutmeg

nutwood
nux vomica
oak
olive
orange
palm
papaw, pawpaw
papaya
peach
pear
pecan
persimmon
pine
pistachio
plane
plum
pomegranate
poplar
quince
raffia palm
rain tree
redwood
rosewood
sandalwood
sassafras
satinwood
senna
sequoia
serviceberry
spruce
sycamore
tamarack
tamarind
tangerine
teak
thorn tree
tulip tree
upas
walnut
willow
witch hazel
yew

52. vines

bittersweet
clematis
dewberry
English ivy
grape
greenbrier
honeysuckle
hop
ivy

jasmine
liana
mistletoe
morning glory
poison ivy
trumpet creeper
Virginia creeper
wisteria

53. weeds

beggar ticks
bindweed
brake
bur
burdock
Canada thistle
cat's ear
chickweed
chicory
crab grass
crazyweed
creeping buttercup
dandelion
dock
fireweed

horsetail
Jimson weed
knawel
knotweed
lady's thumb
locoweed
mallow
may weed
milkweed
mustard
nettle
pigweed
plantain
poison ivy
poke, pokeweed

prickly lettuce
purslane
quackgrass
ragweed
sandbur
scarlet pimpernel
sheep's sorrel
shepherd's purse

smartweed
speedwell
spotted spurge
spurry
stinkweed
tarweed
thistle
tumbleweed

411. BOTANY

NOUNS **1. botany,** phytology; algology, bryology, dendrology, ecology, fungology, hydroponics, mycology, paleo-botany, physiological botany, phytobiology, phytochemistry, phytoecology, phytogeography, phytography, phytomorphology, phytopaleontology, phytopathology, phytotaxonomy, phytoteratology, phytotomy, phytotopography, pomology, structural botany, systematic botany, vegetable *or* plant anatomy, vegetable *or* plant pathology, vegetable *or* plant physiology.

2. botanist, phytologist; algologist, bryologist, dendrologist, ecologist, fungologist, herbalist, mycologist, phytobiologist, phytoecologist, phytogeographer, phytographer, phytopaleontologist, phytopathologist, phytoteratologist, pomologist.

3. phyton, phytomer.

4. Thallophyta (thallus plants), thallogens, thallophytes: algae; Cyanophyceae (blue-green algae); Chlorophyceae (green algae); Phaeophyceae (brown algae); Rhodophyceae (red algae); fungi, molds; Schizomycetes (fission fungi, bacteria); Myxomycetes (slime molds); Phycomycetes (algal fungi, water molds); Ascomycetes (sac fungi, lichen, lichen fungi); Penicillium (blue and green molds); Basidiomycetes (basidium fungi, rusts, smuts, puffballs, mushrooms, toadstools).

5. Bryophyta (moss plants), bryophytes: Hepaticae (liverworts); Musci (mosses); Iceland moss, Reindeer moss, rock moss.

6. Pteridophyta (fern plants), pteridophytes: Lycopodiales (ground pines, club mosses, quill worts); Lycopodiaceae (club mosses); Selaginallaceae; Sigillaria, Stigmaria; Equisetaceae, Equisetales (horsetails), equisetum; Calamites, calamite; Filicales, Filices (ferns), filicoids; Cycadofilicales, Cycadofilices (cycad ferns), cycadofilicales.

7. Lepidodendraceae (fossil trees): Lepidodendron, lepidodendroids, lepidodendrids.

8. Spermatophyta (seed plants), spermatophytes: Gymnospermae (naked-seeded plants), gymnosperms; Cycadales, cycads; Gnetales, gnetums; Ginkgoales, ginkgoes; Pinales or Coniferae (cone-bearing evergreens), conifers; Angiospermae (covered-seeded plants), angiosperms; Monocotyledones, Endogenae (cereals, palms, lilies, orchids, bananas, pineapples); monocotyledons, endogens; Dicotyledones (oaks, apples, sunflowers, peas), dicotyledons.

VERBS 9. botanize, herbalize.

ADJS. 10. botanic(al), phytologic(al); phytobiological, phytochemical, pomological, etc.

412. AGRICULTURE

NOUNS 1. agriculture, farming, husbandry; cultivation, culture; tillage, tilth; agrology, geoponics; agronomy, agronomics; agrogeology; dry farming, truck farming [U.S.], contour farming, sharecropping [U.S.].

2. horticulture, gardening, electro-horticulture; landscape gardening, landscape architecture; truck gardening, market gardening, olericulture; flower gardening, floriculture; viniculture, viticulture; aboriculture, silviculture.

3. forestry, woodcraft; lumbering [U.S. & Can.], logging; forestation; Forest Service [U.S.].

4. (gods of agriculture) vegetation spirit, corn god, Ceres, Dionysus or Dionysos, Gaea or Gaia, Triptolemus or Triptolemos; Demeter, Thesmophoros; Persephone, Prosperina, Prosperine, Persephassa, Kore or Cora; Flora; Pomona.

5. agriculturist, agriculturalist [U.S.], agriculturer; agrologist, agronomist; farmer, granger [U.S.], husbandman, yeoman, cultivator, tiller, tiller of the soil; peasant, rustic 917.8, 9; rancher, ranchman; grower, raiser; plowman, plowboy; crofter [Eng.]; dirt farmer [coll. U.S.]; dry farmer; truck farmer; sharecropper, cropper; peasant holder or proprietor; kulak [Russ.]; farm hand; planter, sower; reaper, harvester, harvestman; haymaker.

6. horticulturist, nurseryman, gardener; mali [India]; landscape gardener, landscapist, landscape architect; truck gardener, market gardener; florist, floriculturist; vinegrower, viniculturist, viticulturist; vintager, vigneron [F.]; aboriculturist, silviculturist.

7. forester, woodsman, woodman [Eng.], woodcraftsman; ranger, forest ranger; logger, lumberman [U.S. & Can.],

timberman, lumberjack [U.S. & Can.]; woodcutter, wood chopper.

8. farm, farmplace, farmstead, grange, location [Austral.], pen [Jamaica]; plantation, cotton plantation, etc.; ranch, rancho [Southwest. U.S.], rancheria [Southwest. U.S.]; dude ranch [U.S.]; croft, homecroft [Eng.]; homestead, steading; messuage, mains [Scot.], demesne farm, toft [Scot. & dial., Eng.], barton [Eng.], hacienda [Sp. Amer.]; dry farm; truck farm [U.S.]; dairy, dairy farm; chicken ranch, cattle ranch; farm land, arable land.

9. field, tract, plat, plot, patch, piece or parcel of land; cultivated land, arado [Southwest. U.S.]; clearing; hayfield, corn field, wheat field, etc.; paddy, rice paddy.

10. garden, jardin [F.]; paradise, garden spot; kitchen garden, market or truck garden, flower garden, rock garden, roof garden, sunken garden; botanic(al) garden, Jardin des Plantes [F.]; vineyard; bed, flower bed, border; herbarium, dry garden, hortus siccus.

11. nursery; conservatory, greenhouse, forcing house, summerhouse, glasshouse, lathhouse, hothouse, stovehouse [Eng.], coolhouse; force bed, forcing pit, hotbed, cold frame; arboretum, shrubbery; pinery, pinetum; vinery, grapery; orangery, peachery, etc.

12. growing, raising, rearing; green thumb.

13. cultivation, culture, tilling, dressing, working; harrowing; plowing, fallowing; contour plowing; weeding, hoeing, pruning, thinning.

14. planting, setting; sowing, seeding, semination, insemination; dissemination, broadcast, broadcasting; transplantation, resetting; retimbering, reforestation.

15. harvest, harvesting, reaping, gleaning, gathering, cutting; nutting; crop 809.4.

VERBS 16. farm, ranch; grow, raise, rear; crop; dryfarm; sharecrop [U.S.]; garden.

17. cultivate, culture, dress, work, till, till the soil; mulch; plow, list [U.S.], fallow, backset [U.S.]; harrow, rake; weed, weed out, hoe, cut, prune, thin; force.

18. plant, implant, set, put in; sow, seed, seed down, seminate, inseminate; disseminate, broadcast, sow broadcast; drill; bed; dibble; transplant, reset; timber, forest; retimber, reforest.

19. harvest, reap, crop, glean, gather, gather in, bring in, get in the harvest, reap

and carry; **pick**, pluck; dig, grabble; mow, cut; hay nut; crop herbs, herb [coll., U.S.], herbalize.

ADJS. `20. **agricultural**, **agrarian**, geoponic(al); agronomic(al); farm, **farming**; arable; rural 181.6.

21. **horticultural**; oleicultural; vinicultural, viticultural; arboricultural, silvicultural.

413. ANIMALS

NOUNS 1. **animal life**, **animal kingdom**, brute creation, **fauna**, Animalia [zool.], animality; birds, beasts and fish; fowls of the air, beasts of the field, fish of the sea, denizens of the day; domestic animals; livestock, stock, cattle; wild animals or beasts, wild life; game, big game, small game.

2. **animal**, **creature**, critter [dial.], creeter [dial.], living being or thing, creeping thing; **brute**, **beast**, varment or varmint [dial.], dumb animal or creature, dumb friend.

3. (varieties) **vertebrate**, **invertebrate**; **biped**, **quadruped**; **marsupial**, marsupian, marsupialian; **mammal**, mammalian; **canine**; **feline**; **rodent**, gnawer; **ungulate**; **ruminant**; insectivore, herbivore, carnivore; cannibal scavenger; amphibian; aquatic; cosmopolite; vermin, varment or varmint [dial.]; classifications 414.3–10.

4. (wild animals) fox, reynard; lion, Leo, king of beasts; bear, bar [dial.]; cougar, puma, panther, painter [U.S.], mountain lion, American lion, deer tiger; catamount [U.S.], catamountain; timber wolf, lobo [West., U.S.]; coyote, brush wolf, prairie wolf [U.S.], medicine wolf [West., U.S.]; guinea pig, cavy; hedgehog, porcupine, quill pig [slang]; woodchuck, groundhog, whistle-pig [local, U.S.]; raccoon, coon; opossum, possum; weasel, mousehound [local, Eng.]; wolverine, glutton; ferret, monk [coll. U.S. & Can.]; skunk, polecat [U.S.]; zoril, stink cat [S. Africa], Cape polecat; foumart, foulmart [Scot. & dial., Eng.]; monkey, monk [coll.].

5. (hoofed animals) **buffalo**, bison, American bison, cow of the plains; water buffalo, Indian buffalo; hartebeest, kaama [Africa]; gnu, wildebeest; camel, dromedary, oont [Anglo-India], ship of the desert; giraffe, camelopard.

6. **pachyderm**; elephant, Jumbo, hathi [India]; mammoth, wooly mammoth; mastodon; rhinoceros, rhino; hippopotamus, hippo, river horse.

7. **deer**; **stag**, **buck**, hart; roebuck; **doe**, hind, roe; deerlet; **fawn**.

8. **cattle**, **kine**; dairy cattle or cows, beef cattle; **bovine**, bovine animal; beef; **cow**, bossy [U.S.], cow-critter [dial., U.S.], cush or cusha [dial.], milch or milk cow, milcher, dairy cow; **bull**, bullock, top cow [dial.]; **steer**, stot [Scot. & dial. Eng.], gelding, castrate; **ox**, oxen (pl.); **calf**, heifer, yearling; dogie, leppy [both West. U.S.]; maverick [West. U.S.]; butthead, muley head, muley cow [dial.].

9. **sheep**, mutton [joc.]; **lamb**, lambkin, yeanling; teg, tag; **ewe**, ewe lamb; **ram**, tup, wether; bellwether.

10. **goat**; he-goat, buck, **billy goat**, billy [both coll.]; she-goat, **nanny goat**, nanny [both coll.]; **kid**, kiddy.

11. **swine**, **pig**, **hog**, porker; **shoat** or shote, piggy; **boar**, **sow**.

12. **horse**, hoss [dial.], **equine**, **steed**, nag [coll.], prancer [slang exc. spec.], dobbin; prad, quad [both slang, Eng.]; charger, courser [poetic]; **colt**, foal, filly (fem.); **mare**, girl [dial., U.S.]; brood mare, stock horse; **stallion**, studhorse, stud [U.S.], top horse [dial., U.S.], entire horse, entire; gelding, thoroughbred, blood horse; horseflesh [collective].

13. **pony**, nag, naggy; Shetland pony, Shetland, shelty; Indian pony, cayuse [West., U.S.]; tattoo [India], tat [Anglo-Indian]; cow pony; polo pony.

14. **bronco** or broncho, bronc [slang]; bucking bronco, buckjumper, sunfisher [slang]; range horse, mustang, broomtail.

15. (colored horses) bay, bayard; chestnut, gray, grizzle, roan, sorrel; pinto [West., U.S.], piebald, skewbald, calico pony [coll., U.S.], painted pony [coll., U.S.].

16. (inferior horse) **nag**, **plug** [coll.], hack, jade, crock, skate [slang], weed, screw [coll.], rip [coll.], crowbait [slang], scalawag or scallawag, Rosinante; goat, stiff, dog [all turf slang]; roarer, whistler; balky horse, balker, dweller; rogue, outlaw [West. U.S.], ladino [Southeast. U.S.].

17. (scrawny horse) rackabones [coll., U.S.], scrag, hatrack [slang], stack of bones.

18. (horses: uses) **hunter**, stalking-horse; road horse, roadster; **saddle horse**, saddler, **riding horse**, rider, **palfrey**, **mount**, remount; cavalry horse, cavalry [collective]; **driving horse**, carriage horse, coach horse, gigster; hack, hackney; **draft horse**, dray horse, cart horse; **work horse**, plow horse; shaft horse, thill horse, thiller; fill horse,

filler [both dial.]; wheel horse, wheeler; lead, leader; pack horse, sumpter, sumpter horse, bidet [mil.]; post horse.

19. race horse, racer, **gee-gee** [coll.], **bangtail,** pony [slang]; steeplechaser; entry, starter, nomination in the race; stake horse, staker; plate horse, plater; mudder, mud lark [both turf cant]; favorite, pot [Eng.]; stable, string.

20. gaited horse; ambler, galloper, trotter, single-footer; pacer, side-wheeler, sidewinder [both slang]; stepper, high-stepper, prancer; padnag, pad; racker, boneshaker [slang]; daisy cutter [slang].

21. (famous horses) Alborak (Mohammed's winged horse of ascension), Bayard (Rinaldo's bay steed), Black Bess (Dick Turpin's fleet mare), Black Saladin (Warwick's horse), Bucephalus (Alexander the Great's war horse), Copenhagen (Wellington's charger at Waterloo), Grani (Sigurd's magic steed), Houyhnhnm (ruling horse in *Gulliver's Travels*), Incitatus (the steed of Caligula, the Roman Emperor), Marengo (Napoleon's white horse), Pegasus (winged horse of Greek fable), Roan Barbary (favorite horse of Richard II), Rosinante (Don Quixote's bony steed), Sleipnir (Odin's eight-legged steed), Vegliantino or Veillantif (Orlando's steed), White Surrey (favorite horse of Richard III).

22. ass, donkey, jackass, jack, **burro,** dickey, neddy or Neddy, cuddy [Scot. & dial., Eng.], moke [slang], longear [coll.]; Jerusalem pony, Arcadian nightingale, Missouri hummingbird, mountain or Rocky Mountain canary [all joc.]; jenny, jenny ass, jennet.

23. mule, maud or Maud [slang]; hinny; sumpter mule, sumpter.

24. dog, canine, pooch [slang, U.S.], tyke or tike, tailwagger [slang], bowwow, snarleyyow [joc.]; **pup, puppy, whelp;** toy dog, lap dog; house dog, watchdog; sheep dog, shepherd or shepherd's dog; Seeing Eye dog; show dog, fancy dog; Dalmatian, coach dog; husky, Eskimo dog; Pomeranian, pom [coll.]; kennel, pack of dogs.

25. cur, cur-dog [dial.], **mongrel, mutt** [slang]; pariah dog, pye-dog [both India].

26. bitch, gyp [U.S.], slut, lady.

27. sporting dog, hunting dog, hunter, gun dog; hound, hound-dog [South. U.S.]; bird dog, water dog, setter, pointer, retriever.

28. cat, house cat, **feline, pussy, puss, pussy cat,** grimalkin, gib; **kitty, kitty-cat;** **kitten,** kit, kitling [dial.], catling; **tomcat,** tom; mouser; Cheshire cat, Chessycat [coll.].

29. hare, rabbit, bunny, lapin; jack rabbit; cottontail; Belgian hare, leporide; leveret (young hare); buck, doe.

30. reptile, reptilian; lizard, saurian; crocodile, croc [coll.], crocodilian; alligator, gator [slang, U.S.]; tortoise, turtle.

31. serpent, snake, viper, ophidian; pit viper.

32. frog, croaker, paddock [Scot. & dial., Eng.], pad [dial.]; **toad,** tree toad or frog; bullfrog; **tadpole, polliwog,** pollyfrog [dial., U.S.], pollywiggle [dial. or slang].

33. (marine animals) **fish,** Pisces [zool.]; game fish; crayfish [usu. Eng.], crawfish [usu. U.S. & Ir.], crawdad [local, U.S.], anklebone [coll.]; sea horse, hippocampus; porpoise, dolphin, sea pig; octopus, octopod, devilfish; crustaceans, mollusks 414.8, 9; shellfish 306.25.

34. bird, fowl; birdie; wild fowl or wildfowl; game bird; waterfowl, water bird; sea fowl; shore bird; oscine, passerine; migratory bird, migrant, bird of passage; songbird, warbler, feathered songster; bird of prey; eagle, bird of Jove; American eagle, bald eagle, bird of freedom, bird of Washington; owl, bird of Minerva, bird of night; peacock, bird of Juno; stormy petrel, Mother Carey's chicken; fulmar, Mother Carey's goose; woodpecker, peckerwood [dial., U.S.]; grouse, prairie chicken [U.S.].

35. poultry, fowl; domestic fowl, barnyard fowl, barn-door fowl, dunghill fowl; **chicken,** chick (esp. young), chicky, chickabiddy; **cock, rooster** [U.S.], chanticleer [poetic], cock-a-doodle or cock-a-doodle-doo [joc.]; cockerel, spring chicken, broiler, fryer; **hen,** biddy [coll.], Partlet; setting hen, brooder, skrock hen [dial., U.S.]; capon; poulard; Bantam, banty [coll.]; **goose,** gander; **duck,** drake; **turkey,** gobbler, turkey gobbler [coll.], tom, tom turkey.

ADJS. **36. animal,** animalian, animalistic; zoic, zooidal; zoologic(al); **brutish, brutal,** brute, brutelike; **bestial, beastly,** beastlike.

37. canine, doggish, doglike; vulpine, foxy, foxlike; wolfish, wolflike; tigerish, tigerlike.

38. feline, cattish, catty, catlike; kittenish; leonine, lionlike.

39. ursine, bearish, bearlike.

40. rodent, gnawing, verminous; mousy, mouselike; ratty, ratlike.

41. ungulate, hoofed; **equine,** equestrian, horsy, horselike; **asinine,** mulish; **ruminant; bovine,** vaccine, cowlike; cervine, deerlike; hircine, goatish, goatlike; sheepish, sheeplike; porcine, swinish, piggish, hoggish.

42. pachydermous, pachydermatous; elephantine, elephantoid; hippopotamic, hippopotamoid; rhinocerotic, rhinoceroid.

43. reptile, reptilian, **reptilelike,** reptiloid, reptiliform; reptant, repent, creeping, crawling, slithering; **lizardlike,** saurian, salamandrian, crocodilian.

44. serpentine, serpentile, serpentoid, serpentiform, **serpentlike; snakish,** snaky, **snakelike;** viperish, viperous, vipery, viperine, viperoid, viperiform, viperlike; anguine, colubrine, ophidian.

45. birdlike, birdy; avian, avicular; gallinaceous, rasorial; anserine, anserous, goosy.

46. fishlike, fishy; piscine, pisciform; piscatorial, piscatory; selachian.

47. vertebrate, vertebral; mammalian, marsupial, cetacean.

48. invertebrate, invertebral; protozoan, protozoal, protozoic; crustaceous, crustacean; molluscan, molluscoid.

49. animals

aardvark	black sheep	civet cat
addax	blue fox	coati
alpaca	bobcat	coon
American lion	brown bear	coon cat
Angora goat	brush deer	cotton mouse
ant bear	brush wolf	cotton rat
anteater	buffalo	cottontail
antelope	buffalo wolf	cougar
antelope chipmunk	burro	cow
or squirrel [U.S.]	burro deer	coyote
aoudad	cachalot	coypu
apar, apara	Caffre cat	deer
arctic fox	camel	deer mouse
arctic hare	camelopard	deer tiger
argali	Cape buffalo	dingo
armadillo	carabao	dog
ass	caracal	donkey
aurochs	carcajou	dormouse
babirusa	caribou	dromedary
Bactrian camel	Cashmere goat	duckbill, duck-
bandicoot	cat	billed platypus
bassarisk	catamount [U.S.],	dugong
bat	catamountain	echidna
bear	cat squirrel	eland
beaver	cattalo	elephant
Belgian hare	cavy	elk
bettong, bettonga	chamois	ermine
bezoar goat	cheetah	European polecat
bighorn	chevrotain	eyra
bison	chickaree	fallow deer
black bear	chigetai	ferret
black buck	chinchilla	field mouse
black cat	chipmunk	fisher
black fox	cinnamon bear	fitchew

flickertail	hog
flying fox	horse
flying lemur	hyena
flying marmot	ibex
flying phalanger	ice bear
flying squirrel	imperial mammoth
foumart	Indian buffalo
fox	jackal
fox squirrel	jackass
gaur	jack rabbit
gazelle	jaguar
gemsbok	jaguarundi
giant ground sloth	javeline
giraffe	jerboa
glutton	jerboa kangaroo
gnu	jumping mouse
gnu goat	*kaama* [Africa]
goat	Kadiak, Kodiak
goat antelope	bear
gopher	kalan
grasshopper mouse	kangaroo
gray fox	kangaroo mouse
gray wolf	kangaroo rat
grizzly bear	karakul
ground hog	kiang
ground squirrel	kinkajou
guib	kit fox
guinea pig	koala
hackee	kudu
hamster	lapin
hare	lemming
harnessed antelope	leopard
hartebeest	leopard cat
harvest mouse	leopardess
hedgehog	lion
herring hog	lioness
hippopotamus	llama
	lynx
	mammoth
	Marco Polo's sheep
	markhor
	marmot
	marten
	mastodon
	mazama
	meadow mouse
	mink
	mole
	mongoose
	moose
	mouflon
	mountain goat
	mountain lion
	mountain sheep
	mouse
	mouse deer
	mule
	mule deer
	musk deer
	musk hog
	musk ox
	muskrat
	musquash
	nilgai
	ocelot
	okapi
	onager
	oont [Anglo-India]
	opossum
	oryx
	otter

ounce
ox
pack rat
painter [U.S.]
panda
pangolin
panther
peba
peccary
peludo
phalanger
pig
pika
pine mouse
platypus
pocket gopher
pocket mouse
pocket rat
polar bear
polar fox
polecat
porcupine
possum
pouched rat
poyou
prairie dog
prairie fox
prairie wolf
pronghorn, prong-
  horn antelope
puma
rabbit
rabbit bandicoot
raccoon
rat
red deer
red fox
red squirrel
reindeer
rhinoceros
ring-tailed cat
rock squirrel
Rocky Mountain
  goat
roe, roe deer
roebuck
saber-toothed tiger
  or cat
sable
sable antelope
sambar
serval
sheep
shrew
shrew mole
silver fox
skunk
skunk bear

sloth
snowshoe rabbit
springbok, spring-
  buck
squirrel
stag
steinbok, steenbok
stoat
swamp rabbit
swift fox
swine
Syrian bear
takin
tamarin
tatou
tatouay
tatou peba
Thian Shan sheep
tiger
tiger cat
timber wolf
tree fox
tree squirrel
urial
urus
Virginia deer
vole
wallaby
wapiti
wart hog
waterbuck
water buffalo or
  ox
weasel
wharf rat
whistler
white fox
white-tail, white-
  tailed deer
white wolf
wild ass
wild boar
wildcat
wildebeest
wild goat
wild ox
wild sheep
wolf
wolverine
wombat
woodchuck
wood mouse
wood rat
woolly mammoth
yak
zebra
zebu
zoril

50. primates, monkeys

angwantibo
anthropoid ape
ape
baboon
Barbary ape
bonnet monkey
capuchin
chacma
chimpanzee
colobus
drill

entellus
flying lemur
gibbon
gorilla
grivet
guereza
hanuman
langur
lemur
lion-tailed monkey
macaque

mandrill
marmoset
mountain gorilla
orangutan, orang
proboscis monkey

rhesus
saki
siamang
spider monkey

51. reptiles

alligator
alligator lizard
beaded lizard
cayman
chameleon
congo snake or eel
crocodile
diamondback,
  diamondback
  turtle
dinosaurs 123.27
dragon
eft
flying dragon
gavial
gecko
Gila monster
glass snake
hawksbill turtle,
  hawk's-bill,
  hawksbill
hellbender [U.S.]

horned toad or
  lizard
iguana
leatherback
lizard
loggerhead, logger-
  head turtle
monitor
mud puppy [U.S.]
mugger [India]
newt
salamander
sea turtle
siren
skink
snapping turtle
terrapin
tortoise
tuatara
turtle
water dog

52. snakes

adder
anaconda
asp
black snake
boa
boa constrictor
bull snake
bushmaster
cobra
cobra de capello
constrictor
copperhead
coral snake
cottonmouth
diamondback
fer-de-lance
garter snake
gopher snake
harlequin snake
horned rattlesnake

horned viper or
  snake
king cobra
king snake
krait
mamba
milk snake
moccasin
pine snake
puff adder
python
racer
rattlesnake, rattler
rubber snake
sea snake
sidewinder
tree snake
water moccasin
water snake
worm snake

53. marine animals

crustaceans 414.8
dugong
elephant seal
fur seal
harbor seal
leatherback
manatee
mollusks 414.9

octopus
sea calf
sea cow
sea dog
sea elephant
seal
sea lion
walrus

54. cetaceans

baleen whale
beluga
blackfish
blue whale
cachalot
dolphin
finback

grampus
humpback
killer, killer whale
narwhal
porpoise
right whale
rorqual

sperm whale
sulphur-bottom
whale

55. fish

albacore
amber jack
anchovy
barbel
barn door skate
barracuda
basking shark
bass
black bass
blackfish
black sea bass
blue fish
bluegill
blue shark
bonefish
bonito
bowfin
bream
brook trout
brown trout
bullhead
burbot
butterfish
candlefish
capelin
carp
catfish
channel bass
char
chimaera
Chinook salmon
chub
cisco
cobia
cod, codfish
conger, conger eel
crappie
croaker
cut-throat trout
dace
darter
devilfish
dogfish
Dolly Varden
trout
drum
eel
eelpout
electric eel
filefish
flatfish
flounder
fluke
flying fish
flying gurnard
gar, garfish
giant sea bass
globefish
goatfish
goby
golden trout
goldfish
grayling
grilse
grouper
grunt

whalebone whale
zeuglodon,
zeuglodont

gudgeon
guitarfish
gunnel
guppy
haddock
hake
halibut
hammerhead
herring
hogfish
horse mackerel
jewfish
kingfish
kipper
lake trout
lamprey
lantern fish
ling
loach
mackerel
man-eater, man-
eater shark
marlin
menhaden
miller's-thumb
minnow
mudfish
muskellunge
oquassa
paddlefish
parr
perch
permit
pickerel
pike
pilchard
pilot fish
plaice
pollack
pompano
porbeagle
porgy
puffer
rabbit fish
rainbow trout
ray
redfin
redfish
roach
roosterfish
sailfish
salmon
salmon trout
sardine
sawfish
schnapper
scup
sea bass
sea bream
sea horse
sea perch
sea trout
sergeant fish
shark
shellfish 307.25
shiner

shovelhead
silver salmon
skate
smelt
snook
sole
speckled trout
sprat
steelhead
stickleback
sting ray
striped bass
sturgeon
sucker
Sunapee trout
sunfish
swordfish
tarpon

56. birds

aberdevine
albatross
Audubon's warbler
auk
auklet
bald eagle
baldpate
bank swallow
barn owl
barn swallow
bird of paradise
bittern
blackbird
Blackburnian
warbler
blackcap
black game
black grouse
bluebill
bluebird
blue jay
bobolink
bobwhite
booby
brant
brown thrasher
brush turkey
bullfinch
bunting
bush tit
bush wren
bustard
butcher bird
buzzard
Canada goose
canary
canvasback
capercaillie
caracara
cardinal, cardinal
bird
cassowary
catbird
cedarbird
cedar waxwing
chaffinch
chat
chewink
chickadee
chicken hawk
chimney swift

tautog
tench
thresher, thresher
shark
tiger shark
toadfish
torpedo
trout
tuna
tunny
turbot
wahoo
walleye
wall-eyed pike
weakfish
whitefish
whiting
yellowtail

chipping sparrow
cliff swallow
cockatoo
condor
coot
cormorant
cowbird
crane
creeper
crested jay
crossbill
crow
cuckoo
curlew
cushat
cygnet
darter
dickey, dickeybird
[coll.]
dipper
dodo
dove
duck
dunlin
eagle
eaglet
egret
eider, eider duck
emu
English sparrow
erne, ern
falcon
finch
fish hawk
flamingo
flicker
flycatcher
fly-catching
warbler
fool duck
frigate bird
fulmar
gallinule
gannet
gerfalcon,
gyrfalcon
gnatcatcher
goatsucker
godwit
golden eagle
goldfinch

goose
goshawk
grackle
graylag
grebe
grosbeak
grouse
guillemot
guinea cock
guinea fowl
guinea hen
gull
hangbird
harpy eagle
harrier
hawk
hawk owl
hermit thrush
heron
honker
hoopoe
hoot owl
horned owl
house finch
hummingbird
ibis
indigo bunting or
 bird
jackdaw
jay
junco
kea
kestrel
killdeer, killdee
kingbird
kingfisher
kinglet
kite
kittiwake
lapwing
lark
laughing jackass
linnet
loon
lovebird
lyrebird
macaw
magpie
mallard
man-o'-war bird
martin
mavis
meadow lark
merganser
merle, merl
mew
missel bird or
 thrush
moa
mockingbird
moor hen
mourning dove
mud hen
mute swan
myna, mina
nighthawk
nightingale
nutcracker
nuthatch
oriole
ortolan

osprey
ostrich
ouzel
owl
parakeet
parrot
partridge
passenger pigeon
peacock
peafowl
peahen
peewee
pelican
penguin
peregrine
petrel
pewee
pewit
phalarope
pheasant
phoebe
pigeon
pigeon hawk
pintail
pipit
plover
poorwill
ptarmigan
puffin
purple martin
quetzal
rail
raven
redbird
red grouse
redhead
red-headed
 woodpecker
redpoll
redstart
redwing
reedbird
rhea
ricebird
ringdove
ring ouzel
ringtail
road runner
robin
rook
ruddy duck
ruffed grouse
sage grouse [U.S.]
sage hen
sand martin
sandpiper
sapsucker
scarlet tanager
scaup duck
screech owl
sea duck
sea eagle
sea gull
sea mew
secretary bird
sheldrake
shrike
siskin
snipe
snowbird
snow bunting

snow goose
solan, solan
 goose
songbird
song sparrow
sparrow
sparrow hawk
spoonbill
sprig
squab
starling
stilt
stork
stormy petrel
swallow
swan
swift
tanager
teal, teal duck
tern
thrasher
thrush
tit
titlark
titmouse
towhee
tragopan
tree swallow
trumpeter

tumbler
turkey
turkey buzzard
turkey vulture
turnstone
turtledove
veery
vesper sparrow
vireo
vulture
waxwing
weaverbird,
 weaver
whistler
widgeon
wild duck
willet
wood duck
wood owl
woodpecker
wood pigeon
wren
wren-tit
yellowbird
yellowhammer
yellowlegs
yellowthroat
zebra finch

57. breeds of poultry

Ancona
Andalusian
Australorps
Bantam
Barred Plymouth
 Rock
Black Minorca
Black Orpington
Black Spanish
Black Sumatra
Blue Andalusian
Blue Orpington
Brahma
Buff Orpington
Campine
Cochin
Cornish
Dark Cornish
Dorking
Faverolle
Hamburg

Houdan
Jersey White
 Giant
Langshan
Leghorn
Minorca
New Hampshire
New Hampshire
 Red
Orpington
Plymouth Rock
Rhode Island Red
Speckled Sussex
Sumatra
Sussex
White Leghorn
White Orpington
White Plymouth
 Rock
White Wyandotte
Wyandotte

58. breeds of horses

Albino
American saddle
 horse
American
 Standardbred
Appaloosa
Arab, Arabian
Barb, barb
Belgian
bronco, broncho
cayuse [West.
 U.S.]
Cleveland Bay
Clydesdale
French Coach
 Horse
Galloway

German Coach
 Horse
Hackney
Hambletonian
Houyhnhnm
Indian pony
jennet
Lippizaner
Morgan
mustang
Narragansett
palomino
Percheron
Percheron
 Norman
Plantation walking
 horse

punch
quarter horse
saddle horse
She-land, Shetland
  pony
Shire, Shire
  horse
Spanish horse
Standardbred

Suffolk
Suffolk punch
tarpan
Tennessee walking
  horse
Thoroughbred
Turk
Waler
Welsh pony

59. breeds of cattle

Aberdeen Angus
Afrikander
Alderney
Angus
Ayrshire
Belted Galloway
Brahma, Brahman
Brahmany bull
Brown Swiss or
  Schwyz
Campagna di
  Roma
Charolais
Devon
Durham
Dutch Belted
Galloway
Guernsey
Hereford
Highland, West
  Highland

Holstein,
  Holstein-Friesian
Jersey
Lincolnshire Red
  Shorthorn
Longhorn,
  longhorn
Normande
Polled Durham or
  Shorthorn
Polled Hereford
Red Poll
Santa Gertrudis
Shorthorn,
  shorthorn
South Devon
Sussex
Welsh
zebu

60. breeds of sheep

Blackhead Persian
Cheviot
Columbia
Corriedale
Cotswold
Dorset
Down
English Leicester
Hampshire,
  Hampshire Down
Karakul
Kerry Hill
Le Contentin
Leicester
Lincoln
Merino
Oldenburg White
  Head

Oxford, Oxford
  Down
Panama
Rambouillet
Romanov
Romeldale
Romney
Ryeland
Scotch Blackface
  Highland
Shropshire
Southdown
Suffolk
Targhee
Welsh Mountain
Wensleydale

61. breeds of swine

Berkshire
Cheshire
Chester White
Duroc
Duroc-Jersey
Hampshire
Hereford
Landrace
Large Black

Mangalitza
Poland China
razorback
Spotted Poland
  China
Tamworth
Wessex
  Saddleback
Yorkshire

62. breeds of dogs

Aberdeen terrier
Afghan Hound
Airedale, Airedale
  terrier
badger dog

barbet
basset, basset
  hound
beagle
Bedlington terrier

Belgian griffon
Belgian sheep dog
  or shepherd
Blenheim spaniel
bloodhound
boarhound
Borden terrier
Borzoi
Boston bull or
  terrier
boxer
Briard
Brittany spaniel
Brussels griffon
bulldog, bull
  [U.S.]
bull terrier
butterfly dog
Cairn terrier
Cape hunting dog
Chihuahua
chow, chowchow
clumber spaniel
Clydesdale
coach dog
cocker spaniel
collie
dachshund,
  dachshound
Dalmation
Dandie Dinmont
  terrier
Deerhound,
  deerdog
dingo
Doberman
  pinscher
elkhound
English bulldog
English setter
English toy spaniel
Eskimo dog
field spaniel
foxhound
fox terrier
French bulldog
French poodle
gazelle hound
German police dog
German shepherd
  dog
German short-
  haired pointer
golden retriever
Gordon setter
Great Dane
Great Pyrenees
greyhound
griffon
harrier
hound
husky, Husky
Irish setter
Irish terrier
Irish water spaniel

Irish wolfhound
Japanese poodle
Japanese spaniel
keeshond
Kerry blue terrier
King Charles
  spaniel
Labrador retriever
lurcher
Maltese dog
Manchester terrier
mastiff
Mexican hairless
miniature poodle
Newfoundland
Norfolk spaniel
Old English sheep
  dog
otterhound
Pekingese, Pekinese
pointer
police dog
Pomeranian
poodle, poodle dog
pug
rat terrier
retriever
Russian wolfhound
saluki
Samoyed
schipperke
schnauzer
Scotch deerhound
Scotch terrier
Sealyham,
  Sealyham terrier
setter
sheep dog
shepherd
Shetland sheep dog
Siberian
  wolfhound
Skye terrier
spaniel
spitz, spitz dog
springer spaniel
St. Bernard
staghound
Sussex spaniel
terrier
toy poodle
toy spaniel
toy terrier
turnspit
water spaniel
Weimaraner
Welsh terrier
whippet
wire-haired fox
  terrier
wire-haired
  pinscher
wolfhound
Yorkshire terrier

63. breeds of cats

Abyssinian cat
Angora, Angora cat
Archangel cat
Burmese cat

Cheshire cat
Chinchilla cat
coon cat
Egyptian cat

Geoffroy's cat
Maltese cat
manul
Manx cat
margay
Pallas's cat

Persian cat
Russian cat
Siamese cat
tabby, tabby cat
tortoise-shell cat
Turkish cat

413a. INSECTS

NOUNS 1. insects, Insecta [zool.]; *classifications* 414.8.

2. insect, bug; beetle; arthropod; hexapod; myriapod; centipede, chilopod; millepede, diplopod.

3. ant, emmet [dial.], pismire, pissant [dial.], antymire [dial.]; red ant, black ant, house ant, agricultural ant, carpenter ant; slave ant, slave-making ant; termite, white ant; queen, worker, soldier.

4. bee, honeybee, bumblebee; queen, queen bee, worker, drone.

5. locust, acridian; cicada, cicala, dog-day cicada; grasshopper, hopper, hoppergrass [dial., U.S.]; cricket, cricket on the hearth.

6. vermin; louse, wood louse, plant louse; body louse, grayback or greyback; cootie, crumb [U.S.], seam squirrel, active citizen, bosom chum [all slang]; flea, sand flea, dog flea, cat flea; chigoe, chigger, jigger.

7. bloodsucker, parasite; leech; mosquito, skeeter [dial.], culex; bedbug, housebug [Eng.], chinch, B-flat [joc.]; tick, wood tick; gadfly, horsefly, deer fly; punkie, nosee-um [coll.]; gnat, midge, mite, nit.

8. worm; earthworm, angleworm, fishworm; nightwalker; measuring worm, inchworm.

ADJS. 9. insectile, insectlike, buggy; verminous; lepidopterous, lepidopteran.

10. wormlike, vermicular, vermiform.

11. insects

ant 413a.3
ant lion
aphid, aphis
assassin bug
bedbug
bee 413a.4
bee beetle
bee fly
billbug, billbeetle
black widow
blowfly
bluebottle
boll weevil
bookworm
borer, peach-tree
  borer, apple-tree
  borer, etc.
botfly
bristletail
buffalo bug

buffalo carpet
  beetle
buprestid beetle
butterfly
caddis fly
Cecropia moth
centipede
chigoe, chigger
chinch
chinch bug
cicada
cicala
cockchafer
cockroach
codling or codlin
  moth
Colorado beetle
crane fly
cricket
croton bug [U.S.]

cucumber flea
  beetle
curculio
daddy longlegs
deer fly
dobson
dragonfly
drosophila
dung beetle
earwig
elm-tree beetle
ephemerid
firebrat
firefly 335.5
flea 413a.5
flea beetle
flour weevil
fly
fruit fly
fruit-tree barb
  beetle
gadfly
gallfly
gnat
goldbug
grain beetle
grasshopper
harlequin cabbage
  bug
hawk moth
hellgrammite
horned bug
hornet
hornet fly
horn fly
horntail
horsefly
housefly
Japanese beetle
jigger, jigger flea
June bug or beetle
June fly
katydid
lacewing
ladybug, ladybird,
  lady beetle
Lepisma

locust
louse 413a.5
mantis, praying
  mantis
May fly
midge
millepede
miller
mite
mosquito
mosquito hawk
moth
nit
pill bug
podura
potato bug or
  beetle
punkie
roach
robber fly
rose beetle or bug
sawfly
scarab
scorpion
shad fly
silverfish
snout beetle
sow bug
spider
springtail
squash bug
stag beetle
stinkbug
syrphus fly
tarantula
termite
tick
tiger moth
tsetse fly
tumblebug
wasp
water bug
weevil, grain
  weevil, rice
  weevil, etc.
wood tick
yellow jacket

12. worms

angleworm
army worm
bollworm
cankerworm
caterpillar
cotton worm
cutworm
earthworm
ear or corn-ear
  worm
fireworm
galleyworm
glowworm
inchworm
leech

measuring worm
pinworm
roundworm
shipworm
silkworm
spileworm
tapeworm
tobacco worm
tomato worm
trematode
tussah
webworm
wireworm
woodworm

414. ZOOLOGY

NOUNS 1. zoology, anthropology 416.8, biology 405.16, anatomy 244.7, animal physiology, conchology, entomology, ethology, helminthology, herpetology, ichthyology, malaco.ogy, mammalogy, mastology, ophiology, ornithology, protozoology, taxidermy, vermeology, zoogeography, zoography, zoonomy.

2. zoologist, anthropologist, biologist 405.17, conchologist, entomologist, ethologist, helminthologist, herpetologist, ichthyologist, malacologist, mammalogist, mastologist, ophiologist, ornithologist, protozoologist, taxidermist, vermeologist, zoographer.

3. Protozoa (unicellular animals *as against* Metazoa, multicellular animals): Sarcodina; Actinopoda; Rhizopoda, rhizopods; Foraminifera, foraminifers; Radiolaria, radiolarians; Mastigophora, mastigophorans; Flagellata, Sporozoa, sporozoans; Gregarinida, Gregarinae, Gregarinaria, gregarines; Infusoria, infusorians.

4. Invertebrata, invertebrates: Zoophytes (plantlike animals); Porifera (sponges), poriferans; Spongiae, Spongiozoa; Calcarea; Hexactinellida; Demospongiae; Coelenterata *or* Coelentera (polyps, jellyfishes); Cnidaria; Hydrozoa (jellyfishes, medusae, polyps), hydrozoans; Scyphozoa; Anthozoa (corals, polyps), anthozoans; Ctenophora: Tentaculata; Nuda.

5. (Vermes, worms) Platyhelminthes (flatworms), platyhelminths: Turbellaria; Trematoda; Cestoda; Nemertinea; Nemathelminthes (roundworms), nemathelminths: Nematoda; Acanthocephala; Chaetognatha; Trochelminthes (wheel animalcules); Rotifera, rotifers; Gastrotricha; Annelida (segmented worms), annelids, annelidans, anneloids: Archiannelida; Chaetopoda; Hirudinea; Gephyrea, gephyreans.

6. Molluscoida (bryozoans, lamp shells): Bryozoa, Polyzoa (sea mosses); Phoronidea; Brachiopoda (lamp shells), brachiopods.

7. Echinodermata (starfishes, sea urchins): Pelmatozoa; Asterozoa; Ophiuroidea (brittle stars), ophiurids, ophiuroideans, ophiuroids, ophiurans; Asteroidea; Asteriidae, asteridians; Echinozoa; Echinoidea (sea urchins), echinoids; Holothurioidea (sea cucumbers), holothurians, holothures; Pelmatozoa; Crinoidea (stone lilies), crinoids, crinoideans; Cystoidea *or* Cystidea, cystideans, cystids; Blastoidea, blastoids; Edrioasteroida.

8. Arthropoda (crustaceans, insects): Myriapoda (centipedes, galleyworms, millepedes), myriapods; Branchiata; Tracheata; Crustacea, crustaceans, (shellfish 306a.25),

Trilobita, trilobites; Limuloidea; Xiphosura (king crabs); Entomostraca (barnacles), entomostracans; Malacostraca (lobsters, shrimps, crabs), malacostracans; Onychophora; Pauropoda; Diplopoda; Chilopoda; Symphyla; Insecta, insects; Arachnida *or* Arachnoidea (spiders, scorpions, mites, ticks), arachnids, arachnidans; Merostomata.

9. Mollusca, mollusks: Amphineura (chitons); Gastropoda (limpets, slugs, snails), gastropods, univalves; Scaphopoda (tooth shells, tusk shells), scaphopods; Lamellibranchia (oysters, clams, scallops, mussels), lamellibranches, bivalves; Pelecypoda; Cephalopoda (cuttlefish, squid, octopus, nautilus), cephalopods.

10. Chordata: Cephalochorda [lancelets]; Urochorda [tunicates]; Hemichorda; Craniata.

11. Vertebrata, vertebrates: Ostracodermi; Cyclostomata [lampreys], cyclostomes; Elasmobranchii; Pisces, fishes; Selachii [sharks, rays], selachians; Holocephali *or* Holocephala [chimeras, spooks], holocephalans *or* holocephalians; Teleostomi [ganoids, bony fishes], teleosts, teleosteans; Crossopterygii; Dipnoi [lungfishes], dipnoans; Amphibia, amphibians; Batrachia, batrachians; Reptilia, reptiles; Aves, birds.

12. Mammalia, mammals: Prototheria; Monotremata, monotremes; Theria; Metatheria; Marsupialia, marsupials; Eutheria; Placentalia, placentals; Primates, Lemuroidea, Anthropoidea; Edentata; Pholidota; Lagomorpha; Cetacea, cetaceans; Rodentia, rodents; Insectivora, insectivores; Herbivora, herbivores; Carnivora, carnivores; Canidae, canines; Felidae, Felinae, felines, cats; Ungulata, ungulates, hoofed animals; Ruminatea, ruminants.

ADJS. **13.** zoologic(al), entomologic(al), etc.; taxidermic, taxidermal.

415. ANIMAL HUSBANDRY

NOUNS **1.** **animal husbandry,** animal culture; breeding, stockbreeding; horsemanship, horsecraft, horse training, manège; pisciculture, fish culture; apiculture, bee culture, beekeeping; stock raising, cattle raising; sheepherding.

2. **stockman** [Austral. & U.S.], stock raiser, stockkeeper [Austral.]; breeder, stock breeder; sheepman; cattleman, cowman [U.S.]; **rancher,** ranchman; dairyman, dairy farmer; **stableman,** stableboy, **groom,** hostler *or* ostler, equerry; trainer, breaker;

broncobuster [slang, U.S.], buckaroo [Southwest. U.S.]; horseshoer, farrier.

3. **herder, drover, herdsman,** herdboy, grazier; **shepherd,** shepherdess, **sheepherder** [chiefly U.S.], sheepman; goatherd, goatherdess; swineherd, pigman; gooseherd, gooseboy, goosegirl; cowherd, oxherd, neatherd [Eng.], cowkeeper; **cowboy,** cowgirl, cow hand [U.S.], puncher *or* **cowpuncher** [coll., U.S.], cowman, cattleman [U.S.], ranchero [Sp. Amer. & Southwest. U.S.], *vaquero* [Sp. Amer.], Gaucho [So. Amer.]; horseherd, **wrangler** [West. U.S.].

4. **apiarist,** apiculturist, **beekeeper.**

5. (animal enclosures) **menagerie,** *Tiergarten* [G.]; zoological garden, **zoo** [coll.]; bear pit; vivarium; **aquarium,** fishery, fishpond; **apiary,** alvearium, alveary, **beehive,** hive; brooder; kennel, chicken house, aviary 190.18–20; pen 235.3, 11.

VERBS 6. (tend stock) **groom,** tend; rub down, brush, curry, currycomb; water, feed, fodder; bed, bed down, litter; milk.

7. **herd, drive,** drove, **shepherd,** ride herd on [West. U.S.]; spur, goad, prick, lash, whip; wrangle; punch cattle [U.S.]; round up; corral.

416. MANKIND

NOUNS 1. **mankind,** humankind, **man,** human species, **human race,** race of man, **humanity,** mortals, mortality, flesh, generation of man, *le genre humain* [F.], "the plumeless genus of bipeds" [Plato]; **homo sapiens,** homo, anthropos, Man.

2. **people, persons,** folk, folks, men, people in general; **public,** populace, general public, John Q. Public; **community, society,** world, world *or* community at large; **commonwealth, nation,** nationality, **state,** estate, polity, body politic.

3. **person, human, human being, man,** homo, anthropos, member of the human race; **mortal,** life, **soul,** living soul; **being,** creature, **individual,** personage, personality, **body,** somebody, one, some one *or* someone; **fellow** [chiefly coll.], beggar, wallah [coll., Anglo-India]; guy, joker, duck, party [all slang]; customer, member, scout [all coll.]; earthling, worldling; head, hand, nose.

4. **God's image,** lord of creation; "a god in ruins" [Emerson], "the aristocrat amongst the animals" [Heine], "a reasoning animal" [Seneca], "the most intelligent of animals—and the most silly" [Diogenes], "a tool-using animal" [Carlyle], "a tool-

making animal" [Franklin], "the only animal that blushes. Or needs to" [Mark Twain], "an intelligence served by organs" [Emerson], "an ingenious assembly of portable plumbing" [Christopher Morley], "Nature's sole mistake" [W. S. Gilbert], "that unfeather'd two-legged thing" [Dryden], "but breath and shadow, nothing more" [Sophocles], "political animal" [Aristotle].

5. (personality types) ectomorph, endomorph, mesomorph; phlegmatic; **introvert; extrovert,** syntone; ambivert; **highbrow, lowbrow,** middlebrow [all coll.].

6. **humanness, humanity,** mortality; **human nature,** the way you are; **frailty,** weakness, **human weakness,** weakness of the flesh, "thy nature's weakness" [Whittier], the weaknesses human flesh is heir to; human equation.

7. **humanization; anthropomorphism,** pathetic fallacy; animal soul, vegetable soul.

8. **anthropology,** anthropogeny, anthropography, anthropometry, anthropotomy, androtomy, ethnology, ethnography, sociology; anthroposophy, humanism; **anthropologist,** ethnologist, sociologist.

VERBS 9. **humanize,** humanify.

ADJS. 10. **human, mortal,** Christian [coll.]; **frail, weak,** fleshly, finite, **only human;** humanistic; anthropological.

11. **manlike, anthropoid,** humanoid; anthropomorphic.

12. **personal, individual.**

13. **public, general, common; communal, societal, social;** civic, civil; **national,** state; international, cosmopolitan; supernational, supranational.

ADVS. 14. **humanly,** mortally, after the manner of men.

417. PEOPLES

NOUNS 1. **peoples, races, cultures, nationalities,** ethnic groups.

2. (races) **Caucasian** *or* **white race;** Alpine race, Adriatic race, Teutonic race, Mediterranean race, Xanthochroi; **Mongolian** *or* **yellow race; Negro** *or* **black race; brown race;** Malayan race; prehistoric races 123.25.

3. **Caucasian, white man,** paleface; **Aryan,** Indo-Iranian; Nordic, Scandinavian; Norseman, Northman, Norman; Viking; Norse; Hindu, Indian; Semite, Semitic; Jew, Jewess, Hebrew, Israelite; Jewry; Arab, Arabian, Bedouin; Gypsy, Romany, Bohemian.

4. Mongolian, Mongol, Mongoloid, **yellow man;** yellow peril.

5. Indian, Injun [joc.], **American Indian,** Amerind, Red Indian, red man, **redskin;** buck; brave.

6. Eskimo, Innuit, Yuit, Aleut.

7. Negro, colored person, black, blackamoor, Jim Crow [slang, U.S.]; **darky,** Sambo, ebony [all coll.]; "the image of God . . . cut in ebony" [Fuller]; African, Ethiopian, Ethiop or Ethiope, "swarthy Ethiope" [Shakespeare]; colored man, man of color; buck, buck Negro [both coll., chiefly U.S.]; uncle [South. U.S.]; Negress, colored woman; mammy, auntie [both South. U.S.]; **pickaninny;** Negroid; mulatto 44.9; Afro-American, Afro-European, Afro-Asiatic.

8. Oriental, Easterner; **Asiatic,** Asian; Eurasian; East Indian; **Occidental,** Westerner; **European; American,** North American, South American; **African,** Afric; Afrikander.

9. (nationalities) **American,** Yankee, Yank [slang], Sammy [slang]; **Australian,** Aussie [slang], digger [slang]; **Canadian,** Canuck [slang]; French Canadian, Jean Baptiste [coll.]; **Chinaman,** Chinese, heathen Chinee [slang], Celestial, Sinaean; **Dutchman,** Hollander, butterbox [slang], Mynheer Closh [slang], Nic Frog; **Englishman,** Briton, Britisher, limey or lime-juicer [slang, U.S.], tommy [slang], Tommy Atkins; **Frenchman,** Frenchy [slang], Jean [coll.], Jean or Johnny Crapaud [coll.]; **German,** Dutchman [careless or slang], Fritz or Fritzie [slang], Heine [slang], Jerry [slang]; **Irishman,** Irisher, Hibernian, Paddy [coll.], Paddywhack [coll.], mick [slang], Teague [coll.], Greek or Grecian [slang, Eng.], Bogtrotter [slang]; **Japanese,** Jap [coll.], Nipponese, Nip [slang]; Nisei [native-born citizen of Japanese parentage, U.S.]; **Portuguese,** Portagee [coll. or dial.]; **Scot,** Scotchman, Scotsman, Caledonian, Jock [slang], Sandy [slang], Sawney [slang]; **Swiss,** Colin Tampon [coll.]; **Welshman,** Cambrian, Taffy [coll.].

ADJS. **10. Oriental,** Eastern; **Asiatic,** Asian; **Occidental,** Western; **European;** Balkan; **African.**

11. Jewish, Hebrew, Yiddish [slang], Israelite.

12. Negro, black, black-skinned, **colored,** nigrine; Negritic; Negroid.

13. Caucasian

Anglo-Norman	Arab, Arabian
Anglo-Saxon	Aryan
Aryo-Indian	Indo-German
Basque	Indo-Iranian
Bedouin	Israelite
Berber	Jew
Celt, Kelt	Latin
Celtic, Keltic	Nordic
Creole	Norman
Gypsy	Norse
Hamite	Romany
Hamitic	Semite
Hebrew	Semitic
Hindu	Teuton
Indian	Teutonic
Indo-Aryan	Turko-Iranian
Indo-European	Ural-Altaic

14. Mongolian, Mongoloid

Indo-Chinese	Mongolo-
Indonesian	Manchurian
Lapp	Mongolo-Tartar
Mongolo-	Mongolo-Turkic
Dravidian	Tartar

15. Slav

Croat, Croatian	Slavonian
Moravian	Slovak, Slovakian
Serb, Serbian,	Sorb, Sorbian
Servian	Wend

16. Indian

Ahtena	Hopi
Algonquian	Inca
Algonquin	Iroquois
Apache	Mahican
Araua	Mayan
Araucanian	Mohawk
Arawak	Mohican
Athabasca	Muskhogean
Athapascan	Ojibway
Aymara	Oneida
Aztec	Onondaga
Blackfoot	Paiute
Carib	Pueblo Indian
Cayuga	Quechua
Cherokee	Seminole
Chibcha	Seneca
Chickasaw	Shoshonean
Chipewyan	Sioux
Choctaw	Tapuya
Comanche	Tupi
Copper Indian	Ute
Creek	Uto-Aztecan
Dakota	Yellowknife

17. the brown race

Austronesian	Marquesan
Fiji	Melanesian
Fijian	Micronesian
Hawaiian	Polynesian
Malay, Malayan	Samoan
Malayo-	Tahitian
Polynesian	Tongan
Maori, Maorian	

18. Negro

Abongo	Bushman
Aëta	Geechee
Akka	Gullah
Bambute	Hottentot
Bantu	Mandingo
Bativa	Melanesian

Negrillo
Negrito
Papuan

Pygmy
Senegambian
Sudanese

19. aborigines

Ainu [Japan]
Australian
  [Austral.]
blackfellow
  [Austral.]
Dravidian [India]

Sakai
Toda [India &
  Ceylon]
Vedda, Veddah
  [Ceylon]

20. nationalities

Abyssinian
Afghan
American
Anglo-American
Anglo-Indian
Arab, Arabian
Arabic
Argentine,
  Argentinean
Australian
Austrian
Belgian
Bengalese
Bohemian
Bolivian
Brazilian
British
Briton
Bulgarian
Burmese
Cambodian
Cambrian
Canadian
Ceylonese
Chilean
Chinaman
Chinese
Colombian
Costa Rican
Cuban
Czech
Czechoslovakian
Dane
Danish
Dutch
Dutchman
Ecuadorian
Egyptian
English
Englishman
Estonian
Ethiopian
Filipino
Finn, Finlander
Finnish
French
Frenchman
Gallic
German
Germanic
Grecian
Greek
Guatemalan
Haitian
Hollander
Honduran
Hun
Hungarian
Icelander

Icelandic
Indian
Indonesian
Ionian
Ionic
Iranian
Iraqi
Irish
Irishman
Israeli
Israelite
Italian
Japanese
Latvian
Liberian
Libyan
Lithuanian
Maltese
Mexican
Moroccan
Muscovite
New Zealander
Nicaraguan
Nipponese
Norwegian
Panamanian
Paraguayan
Persian
Peruvian
Pole
Polish
Portuguese
Rhodesian
Rumanian
Russian
Scot
Scotch
Scotchman,
  Scotsman
Scottish
Slav
Slavonic
Slovak
Spanish
Spaniard
Sudanese
Swede
Swedish
Swiss
Syrian
Thailander
Turk
Turkish
Uruguayan
Venezuelan
Welsh
Welshman
Yugoslav
Yugoslavian

418. SEX

NOUNS 1. sex, kind, persuasion [joc.]; gender [coll. exc. gram.], genre [F.]; maleness, femaleness; "woman's secret" [James Stephens]; the facts of life, the birds and the bees.

2. sexuality, sexualism; carnality, sensuality, flesh, fleshliness; libido, sexual instinct or urge; potence 419.2; impotence; frigidity, coldness.

3. sex appeal [U.S.], S.A. [slang, U.S.], sexual attraction, charm, "that wondrous charm of sex" [B. W. Procter], It [slang, U.S.; 1922, 1920's], oomph [slang, U.S.; 1939, 1940's].

4. sexual desire, sensuous desire, bodily appetite, biological urge, venereal appetite or desire, lust, desire, itch, passion, carnal passion, fleshly lust, prurience or pruriency, concupiscence, hot blood, aphrodisia; lustfulness, libidinousness; lasciviousness 987.5; eroticism, erotism; nymphomania [med.]; satyrism, satyriasis [med.].

5. heat, rut, must; oestrus, oestrum, oestruation [all zool.].

6. love potion, aphrodisiac, philter; cantharis, blister beetle, Spanish fly.

7. procreation, coition 168; germ cell, sperm, ovum 405.6—8.

8. genitals, genitalia, sex organs; penis, phallus; gonads; testes, testicle, spermary; vulva; clitoris; ovaries; womb, venter [law].

9. sexlessness, asexuality, neutrality.

10. (sexual abnormality) homosexuality, homosexualism; intersexuality, intersexualism; bisexuality, bisexualism; epicenism, epicenity; hermaphroditism, androgynism, androgyny, gynandry, gynandrism; Lesbianism, Sapphism; mannishness 419.1; effeminacy 420.2; perversion, deviation, sexual perversion; sodomy, pederasty, pedophilia; bestiality; incest, incestuousness. See also psychology 688.32.

11. homosexual, homosexualist; intersex, sex-intergrade [biol.]; hermaphrodite, androgyne, gynandroid, bisexual, epicene; Lesbian, Sapphist; pervert, deviant, sex or sexual pervert; sodomist, sodomite, pederast.

12. (slang terms) homo, queer, fairy, pansy, queen, nance, Nancy or nancy, Molly or molly, Miss Molly, betty, painted Willie, fag.

13. sexology, sexologist.

VERBS 14. sex, sexualize.

15. lust, lust after, itch for, desire; be in heat or rut, rut, come in, oestruate.

16. breed 168.6–11.

ADJS. **17.** sexual, sex, sexlike, gamic, libidinal; erotic, venereal; carnal, sensual, fleshly; sexy, spicy [both slang]; erogenous, erogenic, erotogenic; sexed, oversexed, undersexed; intersexual; procreative 168.16; potent 419.12.

18. genital; phallic(al), penial; testicular, spermatic; vulvar, vulval; ovarian.

19. aphrodisiac, aphroditous [med.]; venereal.

20. lustful, prurient, concupiscent, lickerish, libidinous, salacious, passionate, hot-blooded, itching, horny [slang, U.S.], caigy [Scot. & dial., Eng.]; lascivious 987.29.

21. in heat, burning, hot; in rut, rutting, rutty, ruttish; in must, must, musty; oestrous, oestrual [both zool.].

22. unsexual, unsexed; sexless, asexual, neuter, neutral; cold, frigid; impotent.

23. homosexual, queer [slang]; bisexual, bisexed, epicene, monoclinous [bot.]; hermaphrodite, hermaphroditic; androgynous, androgynal, gynandrous, gynandrian; Lesbian, Sapphic; mannish 419.13; effeminate 420.15; perverted, deviant.

419. MASCULINITY

NOUNS **1.** masculinity, masculineness, maleness; manliness, manlihood, manhood, mannishness, manfulness, manlikeness; gentlemanliness, gentlemanlikeness.

2. virility, virileness, potence or potency, sexual power, manly vigor; ultramasculinity.

3. mankind, man, men, manhood, menfolk, menfolks, male sex, male variety [joc.].

4. male, male being, masculine; he, him.

5. man, male person, homo, hombre [Sp.], sire; fellow, feller [dial. & vulg.]; lad 125.5; chap, guy, buck, Jack, scout [all coll.]; bloke, bird, duck, cove, joker, jasper, bugger, John, Johnny [all slang]; mug [slang U.S.], swipe [slang, Eng.], horse [joc.], wallah [coll., Anglo-India]; gentleman, gent [vulg. or joc.], don, sahib [India].

6. he-man [coll.], two-fisted man [coll., U.S.], man with hair on his chest [joc.], cave man [joc.].

7. Mister, Mr., Master; Monsieur, M.; Messieurs, Messrs., MM.; signor or signore

[It.], signior or seignior, Sr., señor [Sp.], senhor [Pg.]; signorino [It.]; sir, sirrah [arch. & dial.]; baboo or babu [India], Don [Sp.], Herr [G.]; mein Herr [G.], Mynheer, meneer [S. Africa].

8. (male animals) tom, male brute [dial.]; cock, rooster [U.S.], chanticleer, cock-a-doodle or cock-a-doodle-doo [joc.]; cockerel; drake; gander; peacock; tom turkey, gobbler, turkey gobbler; dog; boar; stag, hart, buck; stallion, studhorse, stud [U.S.], top horse [dial., U.S.], entire horse, entire; tomcat, tom; he-goat, billy goat, billy [coll.]; ram, tup, wether; bull, bullock, top cow [dial.]; steer, stot [Scot. & dial., Eng.]; ox; gelding, castrate.

9. (masculine woman) Amazon, androgyne; Lesbian 418.11; tomboy, hoyden, romp.

VERBS **10.** masculinize, virilify, virify, mannify, dewomanize.

ADJS. **11.** masculine, male, bull, he-; manly, manlike, mannish, manful, andric; gentlemanly, gentlemanlike.

12. virile, potent, full-blooded; viripotent; ultramasculine, he-mannish [coll.], two-fisted [coll.], broadshouldered, hairychested [joc.].

13. mannish, mannified; unwomanly, unfeminine, uneffeminate; tomboyish, hoyden, rompish.

420. FEMININITY

NOUNS **1.** femininity, femineity, feminality, feminacy, feminism, feminineness, femaleness; womanliness, womanlikeness, womanishness, womanhood, womanity, muliebrity; ladylikeness, gentlewomanliness; matronliness, matronage, matronhood, matronship.

2. effeminacy, effeminateness, womanishness, unmanliness, androgyny, sissiness [coll.], prissiness [coll., U.S.], milksopism; homosexuality 418.10.

3. womankind, woman, women, femininity, womanhood, womenfolk, womenfolks, calico [joc., U.S.]; female sex, female variety [joc.]; the distaff; the sex, opposite sex, the fair, fair sex, softer sex, weaker sex, "the lesser man" [Tennyson]; the eternal feminine, das Ewig-Weibliche [G., Goethe; the ever-womanly].

4. female, female being, feminine [coll.]; she, her.

5. woman, womanbody [Scot. & North. Eng.], womanfolk [dial.], femme [F.], distaff, weaker vessel [joc.]; frow, Frau

[G.], *vrouw* [Du.]; **lady,** milady, gentle-woman; *donna* [It.], *doña* [Sp.], *dona* [Pg.], *domina* [L.]; bibi, Sahibah, *mem-sahib* [all India]; **matron,** dame, **dowager;** squaw; girl 125.6.

6. (slang and derogatory terms) **dame, hen,** biddy, petticoat, **skirt;** Jane, **broad,** calico, curve, fem, frail, moll [all U.S.].

7. "a rag and a bone and a hank of hair" [Kipling], "God's *second* mistake" [Nietzche], "one of Nature's agreeable blunders" [Hannah Cowley], "the last thing civilized by man" [Meredith], "sphinxes without secrets" [Oscar Wilde], "a necessary evil" [Latin proverb], "the female of the human species, and not a different kind of animal" [Shaw].

8. **Mistress, Mrs.,** missis *or* missus [illit.]; **madam, madame,** Mme., ma'am *or* mam [coll.], marm [dial.]; mesdames, Mmes.; *Frau* [G.], *vrouw* [Du.]; *signora* [It.], señora [Sp.], *senhora* [Pg.]; dame, *Donna* [It.], *Doña* [Sp.], *Dona* [Pg.]; *mem-sahib,* Sahibah, bibi [all India].

9. **Miss,** Missy [dial.]; *mademoiselle* [F.], Mlle.; *Fräulein* [G.]; *signorina* [It.], *señorita* [Sp.], *senhorita* [Pg.].

10. (female animals) hen, Partlet, biddy [coll.]; guinea hen; peahen; bitch, slut, gyp [U.S.]; sow; ewe, ewe lamb; she-goat, nanny goat *or* nanny [coll.]; doe, hind, roe; jenny; mare, girl [dial., U.S.]; brood mare, stock horse; filly; cow, bossy [U.S.], cush *or* cusha [dial.]; heifer; vixen; tigress; lioness; she-bear, she-lion, etc.

11. **mollycoddle, effeminate,** woman, old wife *or* woman, henhussy, **mother's darling, mamma's boy,** betty, Little Lord Fauntleroy; **milksop,** sop, tenderling, tame cat *or* pussy; sissy, prissy, molly, Molly, Miss Molly, Percy, muff, chicken, goody, goody-goody [all coll.]; **pantywaist,** cream puff, powder puff, ladyfinger, lily, weak sister [all slang]; soft, softy [both coll.].

12. feminization, womanization; effemination, effeminization, sissification [coll.].

VERBS 13. feminize, womanize, demasculinize; effeminize, effeminatize, effeminate, sissify [coll.].

ADJS. 14. **feminine,** female, muliebrile, distaff, she-; gynic, gynecic; **womanly, womanish, womanlike,** petticoat; **lady-like,** gentlewomanlike, gentlewomanly; **matronly,** matronal, matronlike; maidenly 124.11.

15. **effeminate, womanish,** old-woman-ish, **unmanly,** muliebrous, soft, chichi,

prissy [coll., U.S.]; **sissified,** sissy, **sissyish** [all coll.]; homosexual 418.23.

421. SENSATION

Physical Sensibility.—NOUNS 1. **sensation, sense, feeling,** impression, consciousness, awareness, perception; experience, sensory experience; response, response to stimuli.

2. **sensibility,** sensibleness, sentience *or* sentiency; receptiveness, receptivity; impressionability, impressibility, affectibility; **susceptibility,** susceptivity; perceptibility, perceptivity.

3. **sensitivity,** sensitiveness; responsiveness, sympathy; delicacy, tenderness, **thin skin; oversensitiveness,** oversensibility, hypersensitivity, supersensitivity, overtenderness; irritation, **irritability; touchiness,** techiness; ticklishness; allergy.

4. **sore spot,** sore point, soft spot, **quick,** raw, where the shoe pinches.

5. **senses, five senses,** touch, taste, smell, sight, hearing; sixth sense; sense organ, receptor.

6. **nerve,** neuron, protoneuron, **nervous system,** ganglion, spinal cord, solar plexus; neurology, neurologist.

VERBS 7. **sense, feel,** experience, taste, know; perceive, apprehend, be sensible of, be conscious *or* aware of; respond, respond to stimuli.

8. **sensitize,** sharpen, whet, quicken, stimulate, excite, stir, cultivate, refine.

9. **touch a sore spot,** touch a soft spot, touch on the raw, touch to the quick, touch a nerve, touch where it hurts, hit one where he lives [slang].

ADJS. 10. **sensory,** sensorial, sensitive, receptive [physiol. & psychol.]; sensuous; sensatory.

11. **neural, nervous,** nerval; neurological.

12. **sensible,** sentient; **susceptible,** susceptive; **receptive,** impressionable, impressive, impressible; **perceptive, conscious,** cognizant, **aware,** sensitive to, alive to.

13. **sensitive,** responsive, sympathetic; delicate, tender, **thin-skinned; oversensitive,** oversensible, hypersensitive, supersensitive, overtender; **irritable, touchy,** techy *or* tetchy; ticklish; allergic.

14. (keenly sensitive) **exquisite,** poignant, **acute,** sharp, keen, vivid, intense.

ADVS. 15. to be quick, on the raw.

422. INSENSIBILITY

Physical Unfeeling.—NOUNS 1. **insensibility,** insensibleness, **insensitivity,** insensitiveness, insentience; **unfeeling**, unfeelingness; callousness 854.3; **numbness**, dullness, deadness; pins and needles; anesthesia, analgesia [med.]; narcosis, electronarcosis, narcotization.

2.   **unconsciousness,   senselessness,** nothingness; oblivion, obliviousness [both coll.]; **faint, swoon, blackout,** syncope [med.], lipothymy or lipothemia; **coma, stupor,** sopor; sleep 710; twilight sleep, *Dämmerschlaf* [G.]; knockout, K.O. or kayo [slang, U.S.]; semiconsciousness, grayout [aero.].

VERBS 3. (render insensible) **deaden, numb,** benumb, blunt, dull, obtund, **desensitize;** paralyze, palsy; **anesthetize, put to sleep,** narcotize, drug, dope [slang], chloroform, etherize; freeze, refrigerate; **stupefy, stun,** bedaze, besot; knock unconscious, **knock out,** K.O. or kayo [slang, U.S.], lay out [slang], cold-cock [slang, U.S.], knock stiff.

4. **faint, swoon,** drop, succumb, keel over [coll., U.S.], fall in a faint, **pass out** [slang] **black out,** go out like a light; gray out (become semiconscious [aero.]).

ADJS. 5. **insensible, unfeeling, insensitive,** insentient, insensate; **dull,** obtuse, obdurate; **numb,** numbed, benumbed, dead, **deadened,** asleep, unfelt; callous 854.12.

6. **stupefied, stunned,** dazed, bedazed.

7. **unconscious, senseless, oblivious** [coll.], comatose, asleep, dead, **dead to the world,** cold, out, **out cold;** half-conscious, semiconscious.

8. **deadening,** numbing, dulling; **anesthetic,** analgesic, narcotic; stupefying, stunning.

423. PAIN

Physical Suffering.—NOUNS 1. **pain, suffering, hurt, hurting,** misery [dial.], malaise, **discomfort, distress;** aches and pains.

2. **pang,** wrench, throe; **twinge, twitch; nip,** pinch, tweak, bite, prick, **stab,** sharp ~, piercing, or stabbing pain; **shooting pain,** shooting, shoot; gnawing, gnawing or grinding pain; **crick,** kink, hitch; **stitch,** stitch in the side; cramp or cramps, Charley horse [coll., U.S.].

3. **smart,** smarting, **sting,** stinging; **tingle,** tingling; **burn,** burning, burning pain, fire.

4. **soreness, irritation,** inflammation; rankling, festering; sore 684.28; sore spot 421.4.

5. **ache,** aching, throbbing pain; **headache,** head, cephalagy or cephalalgia [med.], misery in the head [dial.]; splitting headache; **sick headache, migraine,** megrim, hemicrania [med.]; **backache; earache,** otalgia [med.]; **toothache,** odontalgia [med.]; **stomach-ache,** tummy-ache [slang], bellyache [vulg.], gut ache [vulg.]; colic, collywobbles [slang], fret [dial.]; gripes, gripe, tormina [med.]; gnawing, gnawing of the bowels.

6. **agony, anguish, torment, torture,** rack, cruciation, crucifixion, excruciating or agonizing pain, "pain with a thousand teeth" [W. Watson].

VERBS 7. **pain,** give or inflict pain, **hurt, wound, afflict, distress,** ail; burn; sting; nip, bite, tweak, pinch; pierce, prick, stab, cut; **irritate, inflame;** chafe, gall, fret, rasp, rub, grate; gnaw, grind; gripe; fester, rankle; **torture, torment,** rack, **agonize, harrow,** lacerate, lancinate, crucify, excruciate, wring, convulse; prolong the agony, kill by inches.

8. **suffer,** feel pain, **hurt, ache,** ail; smart, tingle; shoot; twinge, twitch; **wince,** blench, shrink, make a wry face; **agonize,** bleed [fig.], writhe.

ADJS. 9. **pained,** in pain, **hurt,** hurting, **suffering,** afflicted, wounded, distressed, in distress; **tortured, tormented,** racked, agonized, harrowed, lacerated, crucified, wrung, convulsed; on the rack, under the harrow.

10. **painful,** hurtful, **hurting,** distressing, afflictive; **acute, sharp,** piercing, stabbing, shooting, stinging, biting, gnawing; **poignant,** pungent, **severe,** cruel, harsh, grave, hard; **agonizing, excruciating,** torturous, tormenting, racking, **harrowing,** desolating, consuming.

11. **sore,** raw; smarting, tingling, burning; **irritated, inflamed,** fiery, angry, red; chafed, galled; **festering, rankling.**

12. **aching,** achy, **throbbing;** headachy, backachy, tooth-achy, stomach-achy [all coll.]; colicky, griping, torminal [med.]; migrainous.

13. **irritating,** irritative, irritant; **chafing, galling,** fretting, rasping, grating, grinding, stinging.

INTERJS. 14. ouch!, oh!

424. TOUCH

NOUNS 1. **touch,** tactus, taction; **contact** 199.5; feel, feeling; light touch, lambency, whisper, breath, kiss, caress; lick, lap; brush, graze, glance; stroke, rub.

2. **touching, feeling, fingering,** palpation; **handling,** manipulation; stroking, rubbing, kneading, massage.

3. touchableness, **tangibility, palpability,** tactility.

4. **feeler,** tactile organ; tactile process, antenna; tactile hair, vibrissa; barbel, barbule; cat whiskers; palp, palpus.

5. **finger, digit;** forefinger, index finger, index; ring finger, annulary; middle finger, medius; little finger, pinkie, minimus; thumb, pollex.

VERBS 6. **touch, feel,** feel of, palpate; **finger,** pass or run the fingers over, thumb; **handle,** palm, paw; **manipulate,** wield, ply; twiddle, tweedle [dial.]; come in contact 199.10.

7. **touch lightly,** touch upon; kiss, brush, sweep, graze, glance, scrape, skim.

8. **rub,** rub against, massage, knead; **stroke, caress; nuzzle,** nose, rub noses; mouth, lip.

9. lick, lap, tongue, mouth.

ADJS. 10. **tactile,** tactual.

11. touchable, **palpable, tangible,** tactile.

12. lambent, lightly touching, barely touching.

425. SENSATIONS OF TOUCH

NOUNS 1. tingle, tingling, thrill; **prickle,** prickles, prickling; **sting,** stinging; paresthesia [med.].

2. **tickle, tickling, titillation,** vellication; ticklishness, tickliness, touchiness.

3. **itch, itching,** itchiness; mange, scab, scabies; psora, pruritus, prurigo [all med.].

4. **creeps, cold creeps,** shivers, **cold shivers** [all coll.]; jimjams [slang], gringles [dial.], formication [med.].

VERBS 5. **tingle, thrill; itch;** scratch; **prickle,** prick, sting.

6. **tickle, titillate,** vellicate, kittle [Scot. & dial., Eng.]; goose [U.S.].

7. **feel creepy,** feel funny, creep, crawl, have the creeps or cold creeps [coll.].

ADJS. 8. **tingly,** tinglish, tingling, atingle; **prickly,** prickling.

9. **ticklish,** tickling, tickly, **titillative,** vellicative, **touchy,** kittle, kittlish [Scot. & dial., Eng.]; goosy [U.S.].

10. **itchy,** itching, scratchy [dial.], prurient; mangy, scabious, psoric [med.].

11. **creepy, crawly,** gringly [dial.], formicative [med.].

426. TASTE

Sense of Taste.—NOUNS 1. **taste, flavor, savor, relish; smack,** smatch [dial., Eng.]; **tang,** twang [dial., Eng.]; palate, tongue, tooth, stomach; taste in the mouth; aftertaste, farewell [dial.]; savoriness 427.

2. **sip, sup, lick, bite.**

3. tinge, trace 35.4.

4. **sample, specimen,** taster; example 25.2.

5. **tongue,** lingua, clapper [slang], clack [slang], red rag [slang, Eng.]; taste bud.

6. **tasting, savoring,** gustation, discussion [coll.].

VERBS 7. **taste,** taste of, **savor,** sip, sup, sample, discuss [coll.], roll on the tongue; smack, smatch [dial. Eng.].

ADJS. 8. **gustatory,** gustative; tastable, gustable.

9. **flavored,** flavorous, flavory; **sapid,** saporous; **savory,** flavorful 427.8, 9.

10. **lingual,** glossal; **tonguelike,** linguiform, lingulate.

427. SAVORINESS

NOUNS 1. **savoriness, palatableness,** palatability, **tastiness** [coll.], toothsomeness, goodness, **deliciousness,** scrumptiousness [slang], lusciousness, delectability; **flavorfulness,** flavorsomeness, flavorousness, flavoriness, sapidity.

2. **savor, relish, zest, gusto,** goût [F.]; gratification, enjoyment, delight.

3. **flavoring, flavor,** flavorer; **seasoning,** seasoner; **condiment, spice, relish;** condiments 306a.54.

VERBS 4. **taste good,** taste like more [joc.], tickle or flatter the palate, tempt the appetite.

5. **savor, relish,** like, enjoy, delight in, appreciate, smack the lips; taste 426.7.

6. **savor of, taste of,** smack of, taste like.

7. **flavor,** savor; **season, spice,** sauce; salt, pepper.

ADJS. 8. **savory,** savorous; **tasty** [coll.], good-tasting, to one's taste; **palatable, toothsome,** toothy [coll.], gusty [chiefly Scot.], sapid, good, good to eat, nice, agreeable, likable, pleasing; **delicious, luscious,** delightful, delectable, delicate, dainty, exquisite, ambrosial, nectareous, fit for a king; larruping, larruping-good, scrumptious, yummy [all slang].

9. **flavorful, flavorsome,** flavorous, flavory; full-flavored; nutty; **rich,** rich-flavored, fruity, too rich for one's blood.

10. appetizing, mouth-watering, tempting, tantalizing, provocative, piquant, moreish [coll.].

428. UNSAVORINESS

NOUNS 1. unsavoriness, unpalatableness, unpalatability, distastefulness, untastiness [coll.], undelectability.

2. bitterness, acridness, acridity, acrimony, acerbity; sourness 431; pungency 432; gall, gall and wormwood; bitters, astringent bitters; bitter pill.

3. nastiness, foulness, vileness, loathsomeness, repulsiveness, obnoxiousness, odiousness, offensiveness, disgustingness, nauseousness; repugnance 865.2; nauseant, sickener.

VERBS 4. repel, disgust, nauseate 864.13.

ADJS. 5. unsavory, unpalatable, unappetizing, untasty [coll.], untasteful, distasteful, dislikable, unlikable, undelicious, undelectable, uninviting, unpleasant, unpleasing, displeasing, disagreeable; ill-flavored, ill-tasted.

6. bitter, bitter as gall; acrid, acrimonious; acerb, acerbic, acerbate; hard, harsh, rough, austere; sour 431.6; pungent 432.6.

7. nasty, offensive, repulsive, repellent, repugnant, odious, abhorrent, disgusting, revolting, loathsome, fulsome, noisome, noxious, obnoxious, mawkish, brackish, foul, vile, bad; icky, ughy [both slang]; sickening, nauseating, nauseous, nauseant; rank, strong [coll.], high.

8. inedible, nonedible, uneatable, undrinkable.

429. INSIPIDNESS

NOUNS 1. insipidness, insipidity, tastelessness, flavorlessness, savorlessness, unsavoriness; weakness, thinness, mildness, wishy-washiness; flatness, staleness, deadness; vapidity, jejunity.

ADJS. 2. insipid, tasteless, flavorless, savorless; unsavory, unflavored; weak, thin, mild, wishy-washy, washy, watery, milk-and-water; flat, stale, dead, fade [F.]; vapid, jejune; indifferent, neither one thing nor the other.

430. SWEETNESS

NOUNS 1. sweetness, sweet, sweetishness, saccharinity; sugariness, sirupiness; oversweetness, richness, cloyingness; sugarcoating.

2. sweets 306a.36, 39.

3. sweetening, sweeting, sweetener;

short sweetening [dial., U.S.], sugar 307.5, 24; saccharin; long sweetening [dial., U.S.], molasses, treacle; sirup or syrup, maple sirup, cane sirup, corn sirup; sorghum, sorgo; grenadine.

4. nectar, ambrosia, honey, manna, honeydew; sugar-water, eau sucrée [F.].

VERBS 5. sweeten, edulcorate; sugar, honey; sugarcoat; candy; mull; sugar off [local U.S. & Can.].

ADJS. 6. sweet, sweetish, sweetened, saccharine; sugary, sugared, candied, honeyed or honied, sirupy; nectareous, ambrosial; mellifluous, mellifluent, sugarsweet, honeysweet, sweet as sugar or honey; sugarcoated; bitter-sweet; sour-sweet, sweet-sour.

7. oversweet, rich, cloying, luscious.

431. SOURNESS

NOUNS 1. sourness, sour, sourishness, tartness, tartishness, crabbedness, acerbity, verjuice; vinegarishness, vinegariness; unsweetness, dryness; bitterness 428.2; pungency 432; greenness, unripeness.

2. acidity, acidulousness, acetosity, acescency; acridness, acridity; causticity, astringency, mordancy; hyperacidity, subacidity.

3. sour; vinegar, souring [dial., Eng.]; pickle, sour pickle, sweet pickle, dill pickle, bread-and-butter pickle; acid 378.1, 13; verjuice; lemon, crab apple, chokecherry; sour grapes.

4. souring, acidification, acidulation, acetification, acescence; fermentation.

VERBS 5. sour, souren [Scot. & North. Eng.], turn sour; acidify, acidulate, acetify; ferment; set the teeth on edge.

ADJS. 6. sour, soured, sourish; tart, tartish; crab, crabbed; acerb, acerbic, acerbate; vinegarish, vinegary, sour as vinegar; bitter 428.6; pungent 432.6; unsweet, unsweetened, dry; green, unripe.

7. acid, acidulous, acidulent, acidulated; acetic, acetous, acetose, acescent; acrid, caustic, biting, astringent, mordant, vitriolic; citric, citrous, citrus; hyperacid; subacid, subacidulous.

432. PUNGENCY

NOUNS 1. pungency, piquancy, poignancy; sharpness, keenness, edge, causticity, astringency, mordancy, severity, austerity, harshness, roughness, acridity, acerbity; bitterness 428.2; sourness 431.

2. zest, zestfulness, briskness, liveliness, raciness; nippiness, snappiness [coll.], tanginess; spiciness, nuttiness [slang],

pepperiness, hotness; **tang**, twang [dial., Eng.]; **spice**, relish; **nip, bite**; punch, snap, zip, ginger [all coll.]; **kick**, guts [both slang].

3. **strength**, strongness; high flavor, *haut goût* [F.]; rankness, gaminess.

4. **saltiness, salinity**, brininess, brackishness; salt, brine; Lot's wife.

VERBS 5. **bite, nip**, bite the tongue, sting.

ADJS. 6. **pungent, piquant, poignant; sharp, keen**, piercing, stinging, **biting, acrid**, astringent, irritating, harsh, rough, severe, austere; **caustic**, mordant, escharotic [med.]; acerb, acerbic, acerbate; **bitter** 428.6; **sour** 431.6.

7. **zestful, brisk**, lively, racy, zippy [coll.], **nippy**, snappy [coll.], **tangy**, with a kick [slang]; spiced, seasoned, high-seasoned; **spicy**, nutty [slang]; **peppery**, hot, hot as pepper.

8. **strong**, strong-flavored, strong-tasting; **high**, high-flavored, high-tasted; **rank, gamy**.

9. **salty**, salt, salted, saltish, **saline**, briny, brackish.

433. TOBACCO

NOUNS 1. **tobacco**, *tabac* [F.]; terbacker, tobacker, baccer, backy [all dial.]; nicotia [poetic], nicotian, Lady Nicotine; **the weed** [coll.], fragrant weed, Indian weed or drug, filthy weed, "dirty weed" [G. Hemminger], "pernicious weed" [Cowper], "that tawney weed" [Jonson], "thou weed, who art so lovely fair and smell'st so sweet" [Shakespeare], "sublime tobacco" [Byron], "divine tobacco" [Spencer].

2. (tobaccos) Broadleaf, Burley [U.S.], Cuban, Havana, Havana seed, Latakia, Turkish, Virginia; bird's-eye [Eng.], canaster, leaf, lugs [So. U.S.]; seconds, shag, tabacum [pharm.]; funky tobacco.

3. **smoking tobacco**, smokings or smokin's [dial. or slang], smoke or smokes [slang], jack [slang, U.S.]; humidor.

4. **cigar**, weed [coll.]; segar, seegar [both dial.]; rope, woodbine, stinker [all slang]; **cheroot, stogie**, toby [slang, U.S.], corona, belvedere, Havana, colorado cigar; trichinopoly, trichi [coll.].

5. **cigarette**, gasper [slang, Eng.]; **cig, fag**, coffin nail or tack, **pill** [all slang]; cigarette papers.

6. **butt**, stub; old soldier, corpse, hobo's delight, dinch, dobe, scag, **snipe** [all slang].

7. **pipe**, tobacco pipe; corncob, corncob pipe; clay pipe, clay [coll.], TD [coll., U.S.];

meerschaum; hookah, narghile or nargileh; brier, *bruyère* [F.].

8. **chewing tobacco**, chewings or chewin's [dial. or slang], eating tobacco [dial.], spit-and-run [joc.]; navy, cavendish, niggerhead or negrohead; twist, pigtail; plug, cut plug; **quid**, cud [slang], fid [dial.], **chew**, chaw [dial.]; tobacco juice, ambeer [dial., U.S.].

9. **snuff**, snoose [coll., West. U.S.]; rappee; pinch of snuff, rear of snoose [slang, West. U.S.]; snuff bottle, snuffbox, snuff mill or mull [Scot.]; snuff stick or swab, snuff brush [So. U.S.], dip.

10. **nicotine**, nicotia; Nicotiana; nicotianin [chem.], tobacco camphor; tabacin.

11. **smoking, chewing**; smoke, puff, drag [slang]; tobaccoism, tabacosis, nicotinism.

12. **tobacco user**, tobaconalian [joc.], tobaccophile, tobaccoite, nicotian; smoker, chewer; snuffer, snuff dipper.

13. **tobacconist**; tobacco store, cigar store; snuffman.

14. **smoking room**, smoke room [chiefly Eng.], **smoker** [coll.], smokery, *tabagie* [F.].

VERBS 15. (use tobacco) **smoke**, funk [slang]; inhale, puff, draw, drag [coll.], pull; "smoke like a furnace" [Gilbert], "smoke like a chimney" [Barham]; **chew**, chaw [dial.], quid [dial.]; **take snuff**, dip or inhale snuff.

ADJS. 16. **tobacco**, tobaccoy, tobaccolike; **nicotinic**, nicotinian; smoking, chewing; snuffy; colorado.

434. ODOR

NOUNS 1. **odor, smell, scent**, flavor, savor, **essence**, redolence, effluvium, emanation, exhalation, breath, whiff, fume, trail; **fragrance** 435; **malodor** 436.

2. **odorousness, smelliness**, headlines; sharpness, keenness, pungency.

3. **smelling, olfaction**.

4. **sense of smell**, smell, smelling, scent, olfaction, olfactory.

5. **olfactories**, olfactory organs; **nose** 255.7; **nostrils**, noseholes [dial., Eng.], nares; olfactory nerves; olfactory pit.

VERBS 6. (have an odor) **smell**, smell of, be redolent of; emit ~, emanate or give out a smell, yield an odor, breathe, exhale; reek; stink 436.4.

7. **scent, perfume** 435.8.

8. **smell, scent, sniff**, snuff, nose, inhale, breathe, breathe in; smell of [coll.], get or take a whiff of [slang].

ADJS. 9. **odorous, odoriferous, smelling,** smellful, smellsome, **smelly,** whiffy [slang], nosy [coll.], scentful, redolent, effluvious; scented, odored, essenced; **fragrant** 435.9; **malodorous** 436.5.

10. **strong,** strong-smelling, strong-scented, **heady; pungent,** penetrating, piercing, sharp, keen; reeking, suffocating, unbearable.

11. **smellable,** olfactible or olfactable.

12. **olfactory,** olfactive.

13. keen-scented, quick-scented, **with a nose for.**

435. FRAGRANCE

NOUNS 1. **fragrance** or fragrancy, **perfume,** aroma, redolence, incense, bouquet, nosegay, sweet smell; **odor** 434; spice, spiciness; muskiness; fruitiness.

2. perfumery, *parfumerie* [F.]; **perfume,** *parfum* [F.], **scent, essence,** aromatic, ambrosia; attar, atar, otto, ottar; aromatic water, essential or volatile oil; floressence; balsam, balm; Balm of Gilead, balsam of Mecca; bay oil, oil of myrcia; champaca oil; rose oil, attar of roses, "the perfumed tincture of the roses" [Shakespeare]; *eau de jasmin* [F.]; lavender, heliotrope, jasmine; myrrh; bergamot; musk, civet.

3. **toilet water,** Florida Water; rose water, *eau de rose* [F.]; lavender water, *eau de lavande* [F.]; cologne, cologne water, Eau de Cologne; bay rum.

4. **incense;** joss stick; pastille; frankincense, olibanum; agalloch, calambac, aloes, lignaloes, linaloa.

5. **perfumer,** *parfumeur* [F.]; perfumeress, *parfumeuse* [F.]; thurifer, censer bearer.

6. (articles) perfumer, *parfumoir* [F.], perfumizer, fumigator, scenter, odorator, odorizer; atomizer, spray; censer, thurible, incensory, incense burner; vinaigrette, scent bottle, smelling bottle, scent box, scent ball; scent bag, sachet; pomander; potpourri.

VERBS 7. **be fragrant,** smell sweet, **smell good,** stink good [joc.]; "die of a rose in aromatic pain" [Pope].

8. **perfume, scent,** cense, incense, essence, thurify, aromatize, fumigate, embalm, rose-water; pastille.

ADJS. 9. **fragrant, aromatic,** odoriferous, redolent, perfumy, **perfumed, scented, sweet,** sweet-smelling, sweet-scented, savory, balmy, ambrosial; **odorous** 434.9; sweet as a rose, fragrant as new-mown hay; fruity; musky; spicy.

436. MALODOR

NOUNS 1. **malodor, fetor, stench, stink,** foul odor, bad smell, "the rankest compound of villainous smell that ever offended nostril" [Shakespeare]; reek, reeking; mephitis, miasm or miasma; body odor, **B.O.** [coll.]; **halitosis,** foul breath.

2. **fetidness,** malodorousness, **smelliness,** stinkingness, **odorousness,** noisomeness, **rankness, foulness,** putridness, vileness, offensiveness, repulsiveness; **mustiness,** fustiness, frowiness, frowziness, frowstiness [coll. & dial., Eng.]; must, fust [dial., Eng.], frowst; **rancidness,** rancidity; reastiness or reasiness [dial.]; rottenness 690.6.

3. **stinker,** stinkard; skunk, polecat, stink cat, zoril, fitchew, foumart; stinkbug; garlic, onion, leek; asafetida; stinkball, stinkpot, stink bomb; stinkstone; stinkwood.

VERBS 4. **stink,** smell, **smell bad,** offend the nostrils, stink in the nostrils, smell to heaven or high heaven; **reek,** funk [slang]; smell up [coll.], stink up; stink out.

ADJS. 5. **malodorous, fetid,** olid, **odorous, stinking,** smelling, bad-smelling, ill-smelling, **smelly,** smellsome, smellful, stenchy, whiffy [slang], nosy [coll.]; **foul,** vile, putrid, bad, fulsome, noisome, offensive, repulsive; rotten 690.38; **rank,** strong [coll.], high; **rancid,** reasty or reasy [dial.], reechy [dial., Eng.]; **musty,** fusty, frowy, frowzy, frowsty [coll. & dial., Eng.].

6. **reeking,** reeky; mephitic(al), miasmic, miasmal.

437. ODORLESSNESS

NOUNS 1. **odorlessness,** inodorousness, scentlessness, smell-lessness.

2. **deodorization,** fumigation, ventilation 401.10.

3. **deodorant,** deodorizer; fumigant, fumigator; lime, chlorine, chlorophyll.

VERBS 4. **deodorize,** fumigate; ventilate 401.12.

ADJS. 5. **odorless,** inodorous, nonodorous, smell-less, **scentless,** unscented.

6. **deodorant,** deodorizing.

438. VISION

NOUNS 1. **vision,** seeing; **sight, eyesight, eye,** light [poetic]; **perception,** discernment, ken; perspicacity, sharp or acute sight, quick sight; far-sight, farsightedness; clear sight, unobstructed vision.

2. **observation,** observance; looking,

watching, viewing, witnessing, espial; **notice**, note, **regard**; watch, lookout; spying, espionage.

3. look, sight, looksee [slang, U.S.], gander [slang, U.S.], eye, **view**, regard; sidelong look, glime [dial.]; leer, leering look; sly look; eyeful [coll., U.S.]; look-in; preview.

4. glance, glance of the eye, cast, slant [coll.]; **glimpse,** glint [Scot. & dial.], glim [Scot. & slang, U.S.], **peek, peep,** flash [slang]; wink, blink, flicker or twinkle of an eye; casual glance, **half an eye,** coup d'œil.

5. gaze, stare, gape, goggle; sharp ~, piercing or penetrating look; **ogle,** comehither look [coll.], bedroom eyes [slang, U.S.]; **glare, glower,** glaring or glowering look.

6. scrutiny, survey, contemplation, the eye [slang]; examination, **inspection** 484.3, 4; once-over, double-O [both slang, U.S.].

7. viewpoint, standpoint, point of view; outlook, attitude, position, posture, ground, venue; angle, slant [coll.]; light, respect, regard; mental outlook 523.2.

8. observatory, observation post; **lookout,** outlook; **watchtower,** tower; beacon, lighthouse, pharos; gazebo; belvedere; crow's-nest [naut.]; peephole, sighthole, loophole; ringside, **ringside seat; grandstand,** bleachers [U.S.]; **gallery,** top gallery; nigger heaven, paradise, peanut gallery [all slang].

9. eye, oculus, ocular [joc.], optic [now usu. joc.], **orb** [poetic], **peeper** [coll.], window [poetic], winker [coll.]; blinker, glim, lamp, ogle, goggle [all slang]; sights [dial. Eng. & slang], daylights [slang]; clear eyes, bright eyes, starry orbs; saucer eyes; naked eye, unassisted or unaided eye; tail [coll.], corner of the eye; eyeball, retina, lens, cornea, optic nerve; pupil, sight of the eye [dial.]; eyelid, lid; nictitating membrane.

10. sharp eye, piercing or penetrating eye, gimlet eye; **eagle eye; weather eye** [coll. or joc.], peeled eye [coll.], watchful eye.

11. (comparisons) eagle, hawk; cat, lynx, ferret, weasel; Argus.

VERBS **12. see, behold, observe, view,** witness, perceive, **discern,** spy, espy, descry, **sight,** have in sight, make out, spot [coll.], twig [coll.], discover, notice, distinguish, recognize, ken [dial.], **catch sight of,** get a load of [slang, U.S.], take in, look on or upon, cast the eyes on or upon, **set** or **lay eyes on, clap eyes on** [coll.]; pipe,

lamp, nail, peg [all slang]; **glimpse,** get or catch a glimpse of; see at a glance, see with half an eye; see with one's own eyes.

13. look, peer, direct the eyes, turn or bend the eyes, lift up the eyes; **peek, peep,** pry, take a peep or peek; play at peekaboo or bopeep; get an eyeful [coll., U.S.].

14. look at, take a look at, take a gander at [slang, U.S.], have a looksee [slang, U.S.], look on or upon, gaze at or upon; **watch, observe,** pipe [slang], **view,** regard; keep in sight or view, hold in view; look after, follow; spy upon.

15. scrutinize, survey, eye, **ogle,** contemplate, look over, give the eye [slang], give the once-over or double-O [slang, U.S.]; examine, **inspect** 484.31; size up [coll.], take one's measure [slang].

16. gaze, gloat, fix ~, fasten or rivet the eyes upon, keep the eyes upon; eye, ogle; **stare,** look [coll.], goggle, **gape,** gawk [coll.], gaup or gawp [dial.], gaze open-mouthed; crane, crane the neck; **rubber, rubberneck,** gander [all slang, U.S.]; look straight in the eye, look full in the face, hold one's eye or gaze, stare down; strain the eyes.

17. glare, glower, look daggers.

18. glance, glimpse, glint, cast a glance, glance at or upon, take a glance at, take a slant or squint at [slang].

19. look askance or **askant,** give a sidelong look, cut one's eye [slang], glime [dial.]; squint, look asquint; cock the eye; **look down one's nose** [coll.].

20. leer, leer the eye, look leeringly, give a leering look.

21. look away, avert the eyes, look another way, break one's eyes away, stop looking, turn away from, turn the back upon; drop one's eyes or gaze, cast one's eyes down; avoid one's gaze, cut eyes [coll.].

ADJS. **22. visual,** seeing; **ocular, optic**(al), ophthalmic; visible 443.6.

23. clear-sighted, clear-eyed; **farsighted,** farseeing, telescopic; **sharpsighted,** keen-sighted, sharp-eyed; **eagleeyed,** hawk-eyed, ferret-eyed, lynx-eyed, cat-eyed, Argus-eyed.

ADVS. **24. at sight,** as seen, at a glance; at first sight, **at the first blush;** prima facie [L.; law], upon presentation, on the spot.

439. DEFECTIVE VISION

NOUNS **1.** faulty eyesight, anopia, anopsia; **astigmatism,** astigmia; nystagmus; albinism; blindness 440.

2. **dim-sightedness**, dull-sightedness, **purblindness**, dim eyes, mote in the eye; blearedness, bleariness, lippitude.

3. **myopia**, **nearsightedness**, short-sightedness, near-sight, short sight.

4. presbyopia, **farsightedness**, long-sightedness, long sight.

5. **strabismus**, cast, cast in the eye; **squint** squinch [dial.], heterotropia; cross-eye, cross-eyedness, convergent strabismus, esotropia; upward strabismus, anoöpsia; walleye, exotropia.

6. (defective eyes) cross eyes, cockeyes, swiveleyes [slang], goggle eyes, walleyes, gooseberry eyes, saucer eyes; squint eyes, gimlet eyes [coll.]; klieg eyes [motion picture cant].

7. **winking**, **blinking**, nictitation; winker, blinkard.

VERBS 8. "see through a glass, darkly" [Bible], "see men as trees walking" [ibid.]; have a mote in the eye; see double.

9. **squint**, squinch [dial.], squint the eye, look asquint, screw up the eyes, skew, goggle, gime [dial.], look forty ways for Sunday [slang, U.S.].

10. **wink**, **blink**, nictitate, bat the eyes [coll.].

ADJS. 11. poor-sighted; **astigmatic(al)**; nystagmic; **nearsighted**, shortsighted, **myopic**, mope-eyed; **farsighted**, long-sighted, presbyopic; **squinting**, squinty, asquint, squint-eyed, squinch-eyed [dial.], boss-eyed [dial., Eng.], strabismal, strabismic; winking, **blinking**, blinky, blink-eyed.

12 **cross-eyed**, **cockeyed**, swiveleyed [slang], goggle-eyed, bug-eyed [slang], gooseberry-eyed, **walleyed**, saucer-eyed, moon-eyed, glare-eyed; one-eyed, monocular.

13. **dim-sighted**, dim, dull-sighted, dim-eyed, weak-eyed, feeble-eyed, mole-eyed; **purblind**, half-blind; bleary-eyed, blear-eyed filmy-eyed, film-eyed.

440. BLINDNESS

NOUNS 1. **blindness, sightlessless**, eyelessness, unseeingness, sightless eyes, anopsia, ablepsia; darkness, **benightedness**, "ever-during dark" [Milton], "total eclipse without all hope of day" [ibid.], "the precious treasure of his eyesight lost" [Shakespeare]; **blind side, blind spot**; dim-sightedness 439.2; snow blindness, niphablepsia; amaurosis, *gutta serena* [L.], drop serene; mental or psychic blindness; cataract.

2. **day blindness**, hemeralopia; **night blindness**, moon blindness, moon-blind, moonblink, day sight, nyctalopia.

3. **color blindness**; dichromatism; monochromatism, achromatopsia; red blindness, protanopia; green blindness, deuteranopia; red-green blindness, Daltonism; yellow blindness, xanthocyanopia; blue-yellow blindness, tritanopia.

4. **the blind**, the unseeing; blind man, benighted man; bat, mole; "blind leaders of the blind" [Bible].

5. (aids for the blind) **Braille**, New York point, Gall's serrated type, Boston type, Howe's American type, Moon or Moon's type, Alston's Glasgow type, Lucas's type, Frere's type; line letter, string alphabet, writing stamps; noctograph, writing frame; visagraph; seeing-eye dog.

VERBS 6. **blind**, blind the eyes, **strike blind**, darken, benight, dim, obscure, eclipse; **put one's eyes out**, gouge; **blindfold**, hoodwink, bandage; throw dust in one's eyes; **dazzle**, bedazzle, daze; glare; snow-blind.

7. **be blind**, not see, not see for looking [joc.], not see hair nor hide of [slang, U.S.]; walk in darkness, grope in the dark; lose sight of; be blind to, close or shut the eyes to, wink or blink at, look the other way.

ADJS. 8. **blind, sightless**, eyeless, visionless, **unseeing**, undiscerning, unobserving, unperceiving, blind in one eye and can't see out of the other [joc.], ableptical, **benighted**, dark [dial. & Ir.], in darkness, rayless, bereft of light, "O dark, dark, dark, amid the blaze of noon" [Milton]; **stoneblind**, stark-blind, **blind as a bat**, blind as a mole, blind as an owl; amaurotic; dim-sighted 439.13; hemeralopic, nyctalopic; color-blind.

9. **blinded**, darkened, obscured; **blindfolded**, blindfold, hoodwinked; **dazzled**, bedazzled, dazed; snow-blind, snow-blinded.

10. **blinding**, obscuring; **dazzling**, bedazzling.

441. SPECTATOR

NOUNS 1. **spectator, observer, looker, onlooker,** looker-on, **watcher,** gazer, viewer, seer, beholder, perceiver, percipient; **witness, eyewitness; bystander,** passerby; spectatress, spectatrix.

2. attender 185.5; theatergoer 609.42; audience 447.6.

3. **sight-seer**, excursionist, **rubberneck**

or **rubbernecker** [slang, U.S.]; slummer.

4. sight-seeing, rubbernecking [slang, U.S.]; excursion, **rubberneck tour** [slang, U.S.]; slumming.

VERBS **5.** spectate [slang], take in; watch 438.14; attend 185.8.

6. sight-see, see the sights, take in the sights, see the elephant [coll.]; rubber, **rubberneck** [both slang, U.S.]; lionize, see the lions; slum, go slumming.

ADJS. **7. spectatorial,** onlooking; sightseeing, rubberneck [slang, U.S.].

442. OPTICAL INSTRUMENTS

NOUNS **1. lens,** glass; eyepiece, eyeglass, ocular; hand lens; magnifying glass, magnifier; reading glass, reader [coll.]; condenser, bull's-eye; sunglass, burning glass; meniscus.

2. spectacles, specs [coll.], **glasses, eyeglasses,** pair of glasses *or* spectacles, barnacles [coll., Eng.], sights [dial., Eng. &. slang], glims [slang]; reading glasses, readers [coll.]; bifocals; pince-nez, nippers [slang]; horn-rimmed glasses; colored glasses, sunglasses, preserves; goggles, blinkers; eyeglass, monocle, *lorgnon* [F.], quizzing glass; lorgnette; contact lens.

3. telescope, glass, **spyglass, field glass; binoculars,** binocles; opera glass.

4. sight; sighthole; finder [camera]; bombsight; bead [U.S.], peep sight, open sight, leaf sight [all firearms].

5. mirror, glass, **looking glass,** seeing glass [dial.], reflector, speculum; hand mirror, magic mirror, window mirror, rear-view mirror, cheval glass, pier glass.

6. optics, optology, optometry; microscopy, microscopics; telescopy, stereoscopy, spectroscopy, spectrometry, abdominoscopy, gastroscopy; electron optics.

7. optician, oculist, ocularist, **optometrist, optologist;** microscopist, telescopist, etc.

ADJS. **8. optic(al),** optological, optometrical.

9. scopic, microscopic, telescopic, etc.; stereoscopic, three-dimensional, 3–D.

10. spectacled, bespectacled; oculate, oculated; goggled; monocled, monocular [joc.].

11. optical instruments

chromatrope	optometer
eriometer	photometer 334.42
image orthicon	prism
mass spectrograph	reflecting
microfilm viewer	goniometer
or reader	spectrograph

stigmatic grating	thaumatrope
spectrograph	viewer

12. scopes

abdominoscope	polemoscope
chromoscope	polyscope
gastroscope	pseudoscope
helioscope	sniperscope
kaleidoscope	snooperscope
periscope	stereoscope
polariscope	

13. microscopes

baby microscope	phase microscope
binocular	pinion focusing
microscope	microscope
compound	polarizing
microscope	microscope
dissecting	power microscope
microscope	projecting
electron	microscope
microscope	simple *or* single
gravure	microscope
microscope	stereomicroscope
laboratory	stereoscopic
microscope	microscope
metallurgical	surface microscope
microscope	ultramicroscope
phase contrast	X-ray microscope
microscope	

14. telescopes

astronomical	prism telescope
telescope	reflecting telescope
chromatoscope	refracting telescope
dumb telescope	radioscope
elbow telescope	radio telescope
finder telescope	teinoscope
inverting telescope	terrestrial telescope
mercurial telescope	vernier telescope
panoramic	water telescope
telescope	zenith telescope

15. spectroscopes and spectrometers

analytical	mass spectrometer
spectrometer	microspectroscope
diffraction	monochromator
spectroscope	prism spectroscope
direct-reading	spectrophotometer
spectrometer	spectroradiometer
direct-reading	star spectroscope
spectroscope	X-ray
Geiger counter	spectrometer
X-ray	
spectrometer	

443. VISIBILITY

NOUNS **1. visibility,** perceptibility, perceivability, discernibility, seeableness; exposure; outcrop, outcropping; the visible, the seen.

2. distinctness, plainness, evidence, obviousness; **clearness,** clarity, crystal-clearness; **definiteness,** definition; prominence, conspicuousness; high *or* low visibility, visibility zero [aeronaut.].

3. field of view, field of vision [psychol.], range *or* scope of vision, **sight,** line of sight, eyereach, **eyesight**, eyeshot, ken; **vista, view, horizon, prospect, perspective, outlook,** survey; range, scope; command domination, outlook over.

VERBS 4. **show,** show up, **appear, be visible,** be seen, be revealed, be evident, be noticeable, meet or strike the eye; **stand out,** stand forth, loom large, glare, **stare one in the face,** hit one in the eye, **stick out like a sore thumb.**

5. be exposed, stick out, crop out; live in a glass house.

ADJS. 6. **visible,** visual, **perceptible,** perceivable, **discernible, seeable,** beholdable, observable, noticeable, recognizable, to be seen; **in sight,** in view, in plain sight, in full view, à vue d'œil [F.], open, exposed, open or exposed to view; evident, in evidence, en évidence [F]; **manifest, apparent,** revealed, disclosed, unhidden, unconcealed.

7. **distinct, plain, clear, obvious,** evident, patent, unmistakable, not to be mistaken plain to be seen; **definite, defined, well-defined,** in focus; **clear-cut,** cleancut; crystal-clear, clear as crystal; as clear as day, as plain as a pikestaff [coll.], as plain as the nose on one's face, as plain as plain can be; **conspicuous,** glaring, staring, starkstaring, **prominent,** pronounced, wellmarked, well-pronounced, in bold ~, strong or high relief.

ADVS. 8. **visibly, perceptibly,** perceivably, discernibly, recognizably, noticeably; **manifestly, apparently,** evidently; **distinctly, clearly, plainly,** obviously, definitely, unmistakably; conspicuously, prominently, glaringly.

444. INVISIBILITY

NOUNS 1. **invisibility,** imperceptibility, unperceivability, indiscernibility, unseeableness, nonappearance; the invisible, the unseen.

2. **indistinctness, unclearness,** unplainness, **faintness,** paleness, feebleness, weakness, **dimness,** darkness, shadowiness, **vagueness,** indefiniteness, obscurity, uncertainty, indistinguishability; **blurriness, blearness; fuzziness, haziness,** mistiness, filminess, fogginess.

VERBS 3. **be invisible,** escape notice, lie hid, **blush unseen.**

ADJS. 4. **invisible, imperceptible,** unperceivable, **indiscernible,** undiscernible, **unseeable,** unbeholdable, unapparent, insensible, inappreciable, inconspicuous, sightless, **out of sight,** à perte de vue [F.];

unseen, unbeheld, unobserved, unnoticed, unperceived; behind the curtain or scenes.

5. **indistinct, unclear,** unplain, **indefinite,** undefined, ill-defined, ill-marked, faint, pale, feeble, weak, **dim,** dark, shadowy, **vague, obscure,** indistinguishable, unrecognizable, uncertain, confused, out of focus; **blurred, blurry,** bleared, bleary, blear; **fuzzy, hazy,** misty, filmy, foggy.

445. APPEARANCE

NOUNS 1. **appearance, appearing,** apparition, coming, forthcoming, rising, **materialization,** occurrence, manifestation, revelation, presentation, disclosure, exposure, opening, unfolding, unfoldment, rising of the curtain; **emergence,** issuance; showup [coll.], turnup.

2. **appearances,** exteriors, externals.

3. **aspect, look, view;** feature, favor, lineament, expression; **seeming, semblance,** image, likeness, effect, impression, ostent, **show, outward show,** display, front [coll.], outward or external appearance, apparent character; **air, mien,** demeanor, carriage, bearing, port, presence; **guise,** garb, complexion, color, cast, turn; **form, shape,** figure; **manner,** fashion, style; **respect, regard,** reference, light; **phase,** phasis, **facet, side,** angle, slant [coll.], twist [slang].

4. **looks, features, lineaments,** traits, lines; **countenance,** face, **visage,** feature, favor, brow, **physiognomy;** phiz, phizog [both slang]; cast of countenance, **cut of one's jib** [coll.], facial appearance or expression.

5. (thing appearing) **appearance, apparition,** phenomenon; **vision, image; shape, form,** figure, presence; phantom 1015.

6. **view, scene, sight; prospect, outlook,** lookout, **vista, perspective; scenery,** scenic view; scape, landscape, seascape, riverscape, waterscape, airscape, skyscape, cloudscape, cityscape, townscape; panorama, diorama, cosmorama, georama; bird's-eye view; phantasmagoria, shifting scene.

7. **spectacle, sight;** exhibit, **exhibition,** exposition, **show, display,** presentation, representation; **pageant,** pageantry; parade, pomp.

VERBS 8. **appear,** become visible, **make its appearance,** make or put in an appearance, appear to one's eyes, meet ~, catch *or* strike the eye, float before the eyes, **come in sight** *or* **view,** heave in sight [naut. *or* coll.], **show,** show itself, show its face, **show up** [coll.], **turn up,** come, **materialize,** present itself, present itself to the view, manifest itself, become manifest, reveal itself, discover itself, declare itself, expose *or* betray itself; **come to light,** see the light, see the light of day; **emerge, issue,** issue forth, come forth, come out, come forward, come to hand, come upon the stage; rise, arise, rear its head; look forth, peer *or* peep out; crop out, outcrop; loom, appear on the horizon; fade in.

9. burst forth, break forth, **pop up, bob up** [coll.], start up, spring up, burst upon the view; flare up, flash, gleam.

10. seem, appear, look, feel, sound, appear *or* seem to be, look to be, appear to one's eyes, have the appearance of, give the feeling of, strike one as; **appear like, seem like, look like, sound like; have every appearance of,** have all the earmarks of, have all the features of, have every sign *or* indication of.

ADJS. **11. apparent,** appearing, **seeming, ostensible;** outward, surface, superficial; visible 443.6.

ADVS. **12. apparently, seemingly, ostensibly, to all appearances,** *al parecer* [Span.], to all seeming, as it seems, to the eye; on the face of it, *prima facie* [L.]; on the surface, outwardly, superficially; at first sight *or* view, at the first blush.

446. DISAPPEARANCE

NOUNS **1. disappearance,** disappearing, **vanishing,** going, passing, departure; dissipation, dispersion; dissolution, dissolving, melting, evaporation, evanescence; fadeout, fading, fadeaway; vanishing point.

VERBS **2. disappear, vanish,** vanish from sight, do the vanishing act [slang, U.S.], depart, fly, flee, go, be gone, **go away,** pass, pass out *or* away, pass out of sight, pass out of the picture [coll.], retire from sight, become lost to sight, lose sight of; **perish, die,** die out *or* away, fade, **fade out** *or* **away,** do a fade-out [slang, U.S.], sink, sink away, dissolve, melt, melt away, evaporate, evanesce, **vanish into thin air,** go up in smoke; disperse, dispel, dissipate; cease, **cease to be;** leave no trace, "leave not a rack behind" [Shakespeare].

ADJS. **3. vanishing, disappearing,** passing, fleeting, flying, fading, dissolving, melting, evaporating, evanescent.

4. gone, away, gone away, missing, **no** more, lost, lost to sight *or* view, **out of sight.**

447. HEARING

NOUNS **1. hearing,** audition, sense of hearing, ear; listening, heeding, attention, auscultation; audibility; earful [slang].

2. a hearing, audition, tryout [coll., U.S.], **audience, interview,** conference; attention, favorable attention, ear.

3. good hearing, refined *or* acute sense of hearing, nice ~, quick ~, sharp *or* correct ear; **an ear for;** musical ear, ear for music.

4. earshot, earreach, **hearing,** range, reach, carry, carrying distance, **sound.**

5. listener, hearer, auditor, hearkener; eavesdropper, listener-in [coll.].

6. audience, auditory, **house, congregation;** theater, gallery; gods [coll.], gallery gods [coll.], celestials [slang]; orchestra; pit, pittites [Eng., theat.].

7. ear, "the hearing ear" [Bible], listener [slang], lug [chiefly Scot. & dial.]; concha, conch, shell; auricle, pinna, strium; lobe, lappet, lobule, ear lobe; labyrinth, vestibule, cochlea; auditory canal, acoustic *or* auditory meatus; Eustachian tube; tympanum, middle ear; eardrum, drumhead, tympanic membrane; malleus, hammer; incus, anvil; stapes, stirrup; cauliflower ear.

8. hearing aid, hard-of-hearing aid; ear trumpet, auriphone; auriscope, otoscope; amplifier, speaking trumpet, megaphone; stethoscope, stethophone, auscultator.

9. (science of hearing) otology, otoscopy, auriscopy, otopathy, otography, otoplasty, otorhinolaryngology.

10. otologist, autist; otorhinolaryngologist.

VERBS **11. listen,** hark, **hearken, heed, hear, attend,** give attention, **give ear,** give *or* lend an ear, bend an ear [coll.]; **listen to,** listen at [dial.], attend to, give a hearing to, give audience to, sit in on [coll.]; **listen in** [coll.]; **eavesdrop; keep one's ears open,** be all ear *or* ears [coll.], listen with both ears, strain one's ears; prick up the ears, cock the ears [coll.]; hang upon the lips of; hear out.

12. hear, catch, get [slang], take in; **overhear; hear of,** hear tell of [coll. & dial.], hear say [coll.], come to one's ear; get an earful [slang]; have an ear for.

13. be heard, fall upon the ear, catch *or* reach the ear, register [slang], make an impression, get across [coll.]; **have one's**

ear, reach, contact, get to; make oneself
heard, get through to, reach the ear of; ring
in the ear.

ADJS. **14. auditory,** audio, **hearing,**
aural, auricular, otic [tech.], acoustic(al),
phonic; audio-visual; microphonic; audible
449.15.

15. listening, attentive; open-eared, **all
ears** [coll.].

16. eared, auricled, auriculate; big-eared,
cauliflower-eared, close-eared, crop-eared,
dog-eared, droop-eared, flap-eared, flop-
eared, lop-eared, long-eared, mouse-eared,
prick-eared, sharp-eared.

INTERJS. **17. hark!,** hark ye!, hearken!,
hear! hear ye!, hear ye, hear ye!, list!,
listen!, oyez!, attend!, attention!

18. phones

audiophone	microphone
detectaphone	motophone
dictaphone	odophone
earphone	optophone
electrophone	osteophone
geophone	techniphone
headphone	telephone
hydrophone	558.5–8, 25
kinetophone	topophone
lithophone	tracheophone
magnetophone	

448. DEAFNESS

NOUNS **1. deafness, hardness of hearing,** deaf ears, "ears more deaf than ad-
ders" [Shakespeare].

2. deaf-and-dumbness, deaf-dumbness,
deaf-muteness, deaf-mutism, surdimutism.

3. the deaf, the hard-of-hearing; **deaf-
mute,** surdo-mute, deaf-and-dumb person;
lip reader.

4. dactylology, deaf-and-dumb alphabet,
manual alphabet; lip reading, oral method.

VERBS **5. be deaf,** have no ear; shut ~,
stop or close one's ears, **turn a deaf ear,**
fall on deaf ears.

6. deafen, deaf [dial.], **stun,** split the
ears.

ADJS. **7. deaf,** hard ~, dull or thick of
hearing, deaf-eared, dull-eared, earless, **unhearing,** surd; deafened, stunned; **stone-
deaf,** deaf as a stone, deaf as a door, ~ a
doorknob or doornail, deaf as a post, deaf as
an adder, "like the deaf adder that stoppeth
her ear" [Bible].

8. deaf and dumb, deaf-dumb, deaf-
mute.

449. SOUND

NOUNS **1. sound, noise,** report, sonant
[phonet.], sonance; sound waves.

2. tone, pitch, key, note, pervading
note, burden, strain, tenor, vein; **intonation,** tonation, **inflection,** modulation,
modification, **cadence, accent,** expression;
monotone, monotony; overtone, undertone;
demitone, semitone; fundamental tone,
fundamental; inherent or semantic tone.

3. timbre, tonality, **tone quality,** tone
color, color, coloring, clang, *Klang* [G.],
clang color or tint, *Klangfarbe* [G.].

4. voice, *voce* [It.], tongue, tone, **tone
of voice,** intonation or inflection of voice,
speech tune or melody.

5. (phonetics) **speech sound,** phone,
phoneme, voice, tone, sound, vocable, letter, articulation; ideophone; sonant, tonic,
vocal, vocal or voiced sound; nonsonant,
nonvocal, surd, voiceless sound, breath
sound; transition sound, glide; **vowel;** semi-
vowel, vowellike; **consonant;** monoph-
thong, diphthong, triphthong; digraph, trigraph; labial, bilabial; labiodental, denti-
labial; lingual; palatal, dental, alveolar;
dentilingual, linguadental; guttural, velar;
labioguttural, labiovelar; liquid; lateral;
cerebral; nasal; fricative, spirant; affricate;
continuant; stop, voiced or voiceless stop,
mute, check, occlusive; guna, vriddhi, svar-
abhakti [all Sanskrit].

6. sounding, sonation, sonification,
phonation; **articulation,** vocalization, voic-
ing; **pronunciation,** enunciation.

7. acoustics, phonics; diacoustics, diaphonics; catacoustics, cataphonics; polyphony; homophony; acoustician.

8. sonic; subsonics; **supersonics,** ultrasonics, black sound; speed of sound 268.3;
sound barrier, sonic barrier or wall.

9. phonetics, phonics; phonology,
phonography, orthoëpy, ideophonetics;
phonetism; sound or phonetic law; Grimm's
law, sound shifting or shift, *Lautverschie-
bung* [G.]; Verner's law.

10. phonetist, phoneticist, phonetician;
phonographer, orthoëpist.

11. (sound unit) decibel, phon.

VERBS **12. sound,** make a sound or noise,
give forth, noise; **utter,** articulate, vocalize,
voice, phonate; **pronounce,** enunciate,
sound out; **intone,** intonate; **inflect,** modulate.

ADJS. **13. sounded, voiced,** vocal, tonic,
phonic, sonant, sonantized, articulated, uttered, vocalized, pronounced, intoned, intonated; pretonic, posttonic; strong,
stressed, accented, heavy; weak, unaccented, unstressed, light.

14. **sounding,** sonant, sonantal, soniferous; tonal, tonic; monotone, monotonic.

15. **audible,** hearable; **distinct, clear,** plain, definite, articulate.

16. **acoustic(al), phonic;** diacoustic, polycoustic; polyphonic; homophonic; monaural; stereophonic.

17. **sonic;** subsonic, **supersonic,** ultrasonic, hypersonic, transonic or transsonic, faster than sound.

18. **phonetic, phonic;** lingual, glossal; dentilingual, liquid, etc. 449.5; vowel, vowellike, vocal, vocalic; consonantal; voiced 449.13; unvoiced 450.12; hard, soft; open, rounded; close, high; broad, low, long; short, flat; wide, lax; tense, narrow; palatal, palatalized, mouillé; dental, alveolar; lateral; glottal; mixed, central; stopped, muted, occlusive; nasal, nasalized, twangy; guttural, velar, throaty, thick.

ADVS. 19. **audibly, aloud,** out, **out loud;** distinctly, clearly, plainly.

450. SILENCE

NOUNS 1. **silence,** silentness, **soundlessness,** tonelessness, noiselessness, **stillness, quietness,** quietude, **quiet, still,** peace, whist [dial.], **hush,** shush, mum, lull, rest [music], inaudibility; golden silence; deathlike silence, deathlikeness, solemn or awful silence, silence of the grave or tomb; hush or dead of night, dead.

2. **muteness,** mutism, **dumbness, speechlessness,** voicelessness, wordlessness, tonguelessness, inarticulateness, aphonia [med.]; deaf-and-dumbness 448.2.

3. **mute,** dummy; deaf-mute 448.3.

4. **silencer, muffler,** muffle, **mute,** quietener, cushion; **damper,** damp, dampener; **soft pedal,** loud pedal [coll.], damper pedal; sordine, sourdine, *sordino* [It.]; hushcloth, silence cloth; baffle; **gag, muzzle,** bandage; antiknock.

VERBS 5. **be silent,** keep silence, **keep still** or **quiet; keep one's mouth shut,** shut up [coll.], **hold one's tongue,** keep one's tongue between one's teeth, bite the tongue, put a bridle on one's tongue, seal one's lips, shut or close one's mouth, save one's breath [coll.], hold one's breath, **not breathe a word,** not let out a peep [coll.], say nothing, not say boo, **keep mum,** hold one's peace, not let a word escape one, make no sign, keep to oneself, play dumb; not have a word to say, have not a word to throw at a dog; have a bone in the neck or throat, stick in one's throat.

6. (slang terms) keep one's trap shut, button up, button up one's lip, dummy up, clam up, close up like a clam.

7. (become silent) **hush,** shush, quiet, quieten [chiefly Eng.], **quiet down,** pipe down [coll.].

8. **silence, put to silence, hush,** hush-hush, **shush,** whist [dial.], **quiet,** quieten [chiefly Eng.], **still; soft-pedal,** put on the soft-pedal [both slang]; squash, squelch [coll.]; kibosh, put the kibosh on [both slang]; put the lid on, shut down on or upon [both coll.]; strike dumb, dumfound.

9. **muffle, mute, dull, soften, deaden,** kill, cushion, damp, **dampen,** drown, deafen, **smother,** stifle, choke, throttle, subdue, **suppress,** repress, stop, tone down; **soft-pedal,** put on the soft pedal.

10. **gag, muzzle,** muffle, throttle, choke off, stop, stop one's mouth, cut one short.

ADJS. 11. **silent, still,** stilly [poetic], **quiet,** quietsome [dial.], **hushed,** whist [dial.], **soundless,** toneless, noiseless, echoless; **inaudible,** unhearable, unheard; quiet as a mouse, mousy; silent as a post or stone, "noiseless as fear in a wide wilderness" [Keats], so quiet that one might hear a feather or pin drop; silent as the grave or tomb, still as death, "hush as death" [Shakespeare], deathlike, awful, solemn.

12. **unsounded, unvoiced,** unvocalized, unvocal, **voiceless,** toneless, nonsonant, nonintoned, **surd,** sharp, atonic, aphonic, aphonous, **mute,** quiescent [Semitic gram.], unpronounced, unuttered, unarticulated.

13. **tacit, wordless, unspoken,** unuttered, unexpressed, unsaid; **implicit** 544.7−9.

14. **mute, mum; dumb,** voiceless, tongueless, **speechless,** wordless, breathless; **tongue-tied,** inarticulate; aphonic, aphonous [both med.].

ADVS. 15. **silently,** in silence, **quietly, soundlessly,** noiselessly, inaudibly; quietlike, easy [both coll.].

INTERJS. 16. **silence!, hush!, shush!,** tush!, sh!, sh-sh!, hist!, whist! [chiefly dial.], whisht! [Ir. & dial.], chut!, tut!, pax!, *taistoi!* [F.], **be quiet!,** be silent!, be still!, **keep still!,** keep quiet!, quiet!, quiet please!, soft!, belay that! or there! [naut., coll.]; **hold your tongue!,** hold you jaw! or lip!, **shut up!** [coll.], **shut your mouth!** [coll.], save your breath!, not another word!, not another peep out of you!, mum!, mum's the word!

17. (slang terms) hush your mouth!, shut your trap!, button your lip!, pipe

down!, quee down! [U.S.], ring off!, lay off!, sound off!, dry up!, stow it!, chuck it!, can it!, cheese it!, nuff said!

451. FAINTNESS

Faint Sound.—NOUNS 1. **faintness, lowness, softness, gentleness, dimness, feebleness, weakness;** indistinctness, unclearness; pinfall.

2. muffled tone, veiled voice, *voce velata* [It.]; **mutedness, dullness, deadness,** flatness, tonelessness.

3. **thud,** dull thud; **thump,** flump, crump [coll., Eng.], **clop, clump, clunk,** plunk, plump, bump; pad, pat.

4. **murmur,** murmuring; **mutter,** muttering; soft voice, low voice, small or little voice, "still small voice" [Bible]; **undertone,** underbreath, bated breath; **whisper,** whispering, stage whisper; breath, sigh; susurration, susurrus.

5. **ripple,** etc. 451.11, ripple of laughter, ripple of applause.

6. **rustle,** etc. 451.12, rustling, frou-frou, "a little noiseless noise among the leaves, born of the very sigh that silence heaves" [Keats].

7. **hum,** etc. 451.13, **humming,** thrumming, booming, bombilation, bombination, **droning, buzzing,** whizzing, whirring, purring.

8. **sough,** etc. 451.14, **soughing, moaning, sighing,** sobbing, whining, wailing.

VERBS 9. steal or waft on the ear, melt in the air, float in the air.

10. **murmur, mutter,** lip, coo; **whisper,** susurrate, whisper in the ear; breathe, sigh, aspirate, "waft a sigh from Indus to the pole" [Pope].

11. **ripple,** rumble, **babble, burble,** bubble, **gurgle,** guggle, **purl, trill;** lap, plash, splash, swash, slosh, wash.

12. **rustle,** brustle [dial.], crinkle, whistle [dial.], stir; **swish,** whish, whisk, brush, sweep, flow.

13. **hum,** thrum, bum, boom, bombilate, bombinate, **drone, buzz,** whiz or whizz, whir, burr, birr, purr.

14. **sough, moan, sigh, sob, whine, wail.** "wail with a feeble moan" [Baillie].

15. **thud, thump,** etc. 451.3.

ADJS. 16. **faint, low, soft, gentle, dim, feeble, weak;** faint-sounding, low-sounding, soft-sounding; soft-voiced, low-voiced, faint-voiced, weak-voiced; murmured, whispered; indistinct, unclear.

17. **muffled, muted,** softened, damp-

ened, **smothered,** stifled, dulled, deadened, subdued, suppressed, repressed; dull, **dead, flat, toneless;** *sordo* [It.], sordine, sourdine.

18. **murmuring,** murmurous, murmurish; **whispering,** whisper, whispery; rustling; susurrous, susurrant.

19. **rippling, babbling, burbling,** bubbling, **gurgling,** guggling, **purling, trilling.**

20. **humming,** thrumming, **droning,** booming, **buzzing,** whizzing, whirring, purring.

ADVS. 21. **faintly, softly,** gently, dimly, feebly, weakly, faint, low; piano, pianissimo; *sordo* [It.], *sordamente* [It.], *à la sourdine* [F.].

22. *sotto voce* [It.], **under one's breath,** with bated breath, in a whisper, in an undertone, between the teeth; aside, in an aside, out of earshot.

452. LOUDNESS

NOUNS 1. **loudness,** loudishness; vehemence, powerfulness, fullness; sonorousness, sonority; surge of sound, surge, swell, swelling.

2. **noisiness,** noisefulness, **uproariousness,** tumultuousness, clamorousness, clangorousness, boisterousness, obstreperousness; vociferousness 458.5; boiler room or factory.

3. **noise,** loud noise, **racket, din, clamor,** clangor, clatter, jangle, rattle; **uproar, roar, tumult, hubbub,** hullabaloo, ballyhoo [coll.], bobbery, fracas, brawl, rumpus [coll.], ruckus [dial. & slang], ruction [chiefly dial.], rowdydow [coll.]; Dutch concert, cat's concert [both coll.]; pandemonium, Bedlam, hell or Bedlam let loose, hell broke loose [slang]; charivari, shivaree [dial., U.S.]; discord 460.

4. **blare, blast, peal; toot,** tootle, honk, trumpet, bugle, clarion [poetic]; **whistle,** tweedle; trumpet call, trumpet blast or blare, sound or flourish of trumpets, **fanfare,** tarantara, tantara, tantarara; tattoo [mil.]; taps [mil., U.S.].

5. **noisemaker,** razzle-dazzle, ticktack, bull-roarer, bull fiddle, horse-fiddle [coll., U.S.], catcall; whizzer, whizgig, whiz-bang; snapper, clapper, clack, clacker, cracker; rattle, rattlebox; horn, klaxon; whistle, steam whistle, siren; calliope, calliophone.

VERBS 6. **din, clamor;** boom, thunder 455.9; **resound,** ring, peal, ring or resound in the ears; **blast the ear,** pierce ∼, split or rend the ears, split one's head; deafen, stun; **rend the air** or skies, fill the air, make the welkin ring; shake or rattle the windows; awake or startle the echoes, awake the dead; surge, swell, rise.

7. **be noisy, make a noise** or **racket,** noise, racket, clamor, clangor, brawl, roar, **make an uproar;** kick up a dust or racket, kick up or raise a hullabaloo, raise the roof, raise Cain or Ned, raise the devil, raise hell or hell's delight, raise Hail Columbia, make or let hell pop, whoop it up [all slang]; not be able to hear oneself think.

8. **blare,** blast; **toot,** tootle, sound, peal, wind, blow; pipe, trumpet, bugle, clarion; **whistle,** tweedle, tweedledee; **honk, klaxon,** honk ~, sound or blow the horn; sound taps, sound a tattoo [both mil.].

ADJS. 9. **loud,** loudish, loud-sounding, high-sounding, big-sounding, stentorian, clarion, full, big, **powerful, vehement;** forte, fortissimo; **resounding,** ringing, pealing, sonorous; **deafening,** ear-deafening, **ear-splitting,** ear-rending, ear-piercing, piercing; booming 455.12; window-rattling, earth-shaking, enough to wake the dead.

10. **loud-voiced, loudmouthed,** full-mouthed, big-voiced, clarion-voiced, trumpet-voiced, trumpet-tongued.

11. **noisy,** noiseful, rackety, clattery, clangorous, **clamorous,** clamorsome [Scot. & North. Eng.], blatant, tonant, **uproarious, tumultuous,** turbulent, blustering, brawling, **boisterous,** obstreperous; vociferous 458.10.

ADVS. 12. **loudly, aloud,** loud, lustily; **noisily,** uproariously; ringingly, resoundingly; with a loud voice, at the top of one's voice, at the pitch of one's breath, in full cry, with one wild yell, with a whoop and a hurrah; forte, *fortemente* [It.], fortissimo.

453. RESONANCE

NOUNS 1. **resonance, sonorousness,** sonority, vibration, **vibrancy;** mellowness, richness, fullness; deepness, lowness, gravity; hollowness.

2. **reverberation, resounding,** reflection, repercussion, rebound, resound, echo, re-echo.

3. **ringing,** tintinnabulation, **pealing, chiming, tinkling,** tingling, **jingling,** dinging, dingling; **tolling,** knelling; **ring, peal, chime; toll,** knell; **tinkle,** tingle, **jingle,** dingle, ding, dingdong, ding-a-ling; clink, tink, ting, chink; clank, clang, clangor, clanking, clanging; jangle, jinglejangle.

4. **bell,** ringer, tintinnabulum; **gong,** triangle, **chimes,** dinner bell, ~ gong or chimes, doorbell, jingle bell, hand bell, cowbell; clapper, tongue.

5. **resonator, sounder,** resounder, reverberator; echo chamber.

VERBS 6. **resonate, vibrate,** pulse, throb.

7. **reverberate, resound,** sound, echo, re-echo, re-bound, reply, reflect, echo back, send back, return.

8. **ring,** tintinnabulate, **peal,** sound; **toll,** knell, sound a knell; **chime;** gong; **tinkle,** tingle, **jingle,** dingle, ding, dingdong, ding-a-ling; clink, tink, ting, chink; clank, clang, clangor; jangle, jinglejangle; ring in the ear, ring on the air.

ADJS. 9. **resonant, vibrant, sonorous;** mellow, rich, full; resonating, vibrating, pulsing, throbbing.

10. **deep,** deep-toned, deep-pitched, deep-set, deep-sounding, deepmouthed, deep-echoing; **hollow, sepulchral; low,** low-pitched, low-toned, grave, heavy; base, bass; baritone or barytone; contralto.

11. **reverberating,** reverberant, reverberatory; **resounding,** sounding, echoing, re-echoing, rebounding, repercussive.

12. **ringing, pealing, tolling,** sounding, chiming; **tinkling,** tingling, **jingling,** dinging; tintinnabular, tintinnabulary, tintinnabulant.

454. REPEATED SOUNDS

NOUNS 1. **drum, thrum, beat, pound, thump, throb;** drumming, beating, pounding, thumping, throbbing; pulsation 322.3; **palpitation,** pitapatation [joc.]; **patter, pitter-patter,** pitapat, pat-pat; rub-a-dub, rat-tattoo, rataplan, rantan or ran-tan [coll.], rat-a-tat, rat-tat, rat-tat-tat, rat-tattle, tat-tat, tat-tat-tat; **tattoo,** devil's tattoo; **drumbeat,** drum music; tom-tom; ruff, ruffle [both mil.]; *berloque* [F.; mil.].

2. **tick, ticktock,** ticktack, ticktick.

3. **rattle,** rattling, brattle [Scot. & North. Eng.], ruckle [Scot. & dial., Eng.], rattlety-bang; **clatter,** clutter, clitter [dial., Eng.], **clitterclatter,** chatter, clack, clacket [dial.]; racket 452.3.

VERBS 4. **drum, thrum, beat, pound, thump, throb, palpitate,** patter, pitter-patter, go pitapat or pitter-patter; pulsate 322.11; rub-a-dub, rat-a-tat, rat-tat, tat-tat, rataplan, rattattoo; beat or sound a tattoo, beat a devil's tattoo; ruffle, beat a ruffle [both mil.].

5. **tick, ticktock,** ticktack.

6. **rattle,** ruckle [Scot. & dial., Eng.], brattle [Scot. & North. Eng.]; **clatter,** clut-

ter, clatter [dial., Eng.], chatter, clack; rattle around, clatter about.

ADJS. 7. **drumming, thrumming, beating, pounding, thumping, throbbing,** palpitant; pitter-patter, pitapat.

8. **rattly,** rattling; **clattery,** clattering.

455. REPORT

Sudden and Violent Sounds.—NOUNS
1. **report,** sound; **crack, clap, bang,** slam, crash, clash, burst, bust [dial.], bounce; **knock, rap, tap,** smack, whack, thwack, whop or whap [dial.], swap [dial.], crump [coll., Eng.], bump; slap, flap, flop; chug (as of a motor).

2. **snap, crack;** flick, flip, fillip; click, clack; **crackle,** snapping, cracking, crackling, crepitation, decrepitation.

3. **detonation, fulmination,** explosion, discharge, burst, blast, **bang,** bingo, **pop, crack,** bark; **shot,** gunshot; percussion, repercussion, "the thunderlike percussion of thy sounds" [Shakespeare].

4. **boom,** booming, bombination, bombilation, cannonade, **peal,** reel [Scot.], **rumble,** grumble, **roll, roar,** bell.

5. **thunder,** thundering, **clap, crash,** clap ~, crash or peal of thunder, **thunderclap,** thunderpeal, thundercrack, thunderblast, thunderburst, thunderstroke; "heaven's artillery" [Shakespeare], "the thunder, that deep and dreadful organ-pipe" [ibid.], "the dread rattling thunder" [ibid.]; thunderstorm 393.3; Thor or Donar [Norse myth.], Jupiter Tonans [Rom. myth.], Indra [Hindu myth.].

VERBS 6. **crack, clap, crash,** slam, **bang,** clash, bounce; **knock, rap, tap,** smack, whack, thwack, whop or whap [dial.], swap [dial.], crump [coll., Eng.], bump; slap, flap; **slam-bang, slap-bang** [both coll.]; chug.

7. **snap, crack;** flick, flip, fillip; click, clack; **crackle,** crepitate, decrepitate.

8. **detonate, fulminate,** explode, go off, **bang, pop, crack,** bark, blast, burst on the ear.

9. **boom,** bombilate, bombinate, **thunder, peal, rumble, roll, roar,** bell.

ADJS. 10. **snapping, cracking; crackling,** crepitant.

11. **banging,** cracking, popping; knocking, rapping, tapping; slapping, flapping.

12. **thundering,** thunderous, thundery, thunderlike; **booming,** pealing, rumbling, rolling, roaring, crashing, **fulminating,** tonant.

ADVS. 13. bang, slap-bang, slam-bang [all coll.]; kerbang, kerbam, cachuck, cachunk [all slang].

INTERJS. 14. bang!, crash!; bam!, bingo!, bowie!, powie!, smacko!, socko! [all slang].

456. SIBILATION

Hissing Sounds.—NOUNS 1. **sibilation,** sibilance or sibilancy; **hiss, hissing,** siss [chiefly dial.], goose [theat. slang]; sizz, sizzle, sizzling; fizz, fizzle, fizzling; swish, whish; whiz or whizz, buzz, zip; wheeze, siffle [med.], *râle* [F.; med.], rhonchus [med.]; whistle, whistling; sneeze, sneezing, sternutation; snort, snork [dial.]; snore; sniff, sniffle, snuff, snuffle; spit (as of a cat), sputter; squash, squelch (as of wet boots); lisp.

VERBS 2. **sibilate, aspirate; hiss,** siss [chiefly dial.], goose [theat. slang]; sizzle, sizz [coll.]; fizzle, fizz; whiz or whizz, buzz, zip; swish, whish; whistle; wheeze; sneeze; snort, snork [dial.]; snore, saw logs [joc.]; sniff, sniffle, snuff, snuffle; spit (as a cat), sputter; squash, squelch; lisp.

ADJS. 3. **sibilant, hissing,** sissing [chiefly dial.]; sizzling, fizzling; wheezing, wheezy.

457. STRIDOR

Harsh and High Sounds.—NOUNS 1. **stridor,** stridence or stridency; stridulousness, stridulation; **shrillness,** highness, sharpness, acuteness; screechiness, squeakiness, creakiness, reediness.

2. **harshness, raucousness,** raucity; **coarseness,** rudeness, roughness, gruffness, grumness; **raspiness,** scratchiness, scrapiness; **hoarseness,** huskiness, dryness; roup, roupiness; gutturalness, thickness, throatiness; cracked voice.

3. (harsh sounds) **rasp, scratch, scrape, grate,** grind; crunch, craunch, scranch [chiefly dial.], scrunch, crump; burr; buzz, saw, snore; **jangle, clash, jar;** clank, clang, clangor; blare, bray; croak, caw; growl, snarl; grumble, groan; twang.

4. **screech, shriek, scream, squeal,** shrill, squeak, squawk, screak, creak; whistle, pipe; whine, wail; caterwaul.

5. (insect sounds) **stridulation,** cricking, creaking, chirking [Scot.]; crick, creak, chirk [Scot.].

VERBS 6. **stridulate,** crick, creak, chirk [Scot.].

7. **screech, shriek,** screak, creak, squeak, squawk, **scream, squeal,** shrill; whistle, pipe; whine, wail; caterwaul.

8. (sound harshly) **jangle, clash, jar;**
blare, bray; croak, caw; burr; buzz, saw,
snore; growl, snarl; grumble, groan; clank,
clang, clangor; twang, twank [chiefly dial.,
Eng.].

9. grate, rasp, scratch, scrape, grind;
crunch, craunch, scranch [chiefly dial.],
scrunch [coll. & dial.], crump.

10. grate on, jar on, grate upon the ear,
jar upon the ear, offend the ear, pierce ~,
split or rend the ears, *écorcher les oreilles*
[F., skin the ears], set the teeth on edge,
get on one's nerves, jangle the nerves.

ADJS. **11. strident,** stridulant, stridulous,
stridulating; strident-voiced.

12. high, high-pitched, high-toned, high-
sounding; treble, soprano, tenor, alto,
falsetto.

13. shrill, thin, sharp, acute, keen; **piercing,** penetrating, ear-piercing; **screechy,**
screeching, shrieky, shrieking, **squeaky,**
squeaking, screaky, creaky, creaking; whistling, piping; reedy.

14. harsh, raucous, harsh-sounding;
coarse, rude, rough, gruff, grum, ragged;
hoarse, **husky,** roupy, cracked, dry; **guttural,** thick, throaty; croaky, croaking;
squawky, squawking; brassy, brazen, metallic; stertorous.

15. grating, jarring, grinding; **jangling,**
jangly; **rasping,** raspy; scratching, scratchy;
scraping, scrapy.

458. CRY, CALL

NOUNS **1. cry, call, shout, yell,** hoot;
halloo, hollo, yo-ho; **whoop,** hoop; **howl,**
yowl, yawl [dial.]; bawl, bellow, roar;
scream, shriek, screech, squeal, squall;
yelp, yap, yawp, bark.

2. exclamation, ejaculation, expletive,
ecphonesis.

3. hunting cry, chevy, chivy or chivvy
[Eng.], tallyho, yoicks, view halloo.

4. outcry, vociferation, clamor, gaff;
hullabaloo, hubbub, uproar, brawl, **hue
and cry;** chorus.

5. vociferousness, vociferance, clamorousness, clamorsomeness [Scot. & North.
Eng.], blatancy; noisiness 452.2.

VERBS **6. cry, call, shout, yell,** hoot;
halloo, hollo, yo-ho; yoick; **whoop,** hoop;
howl, yowl, yawl [dial.]; bawl, bellow, roar,
roar or bellow like a bull; **scream, shriek,**
screech, squeal, squall; yelp, yap, yawp,
bark.

7. exclaim, give an exclamation, ejaculate, rap out.

8. vociferate, outcry, cry out, call out,
yell out, shout out, sing out; **clamor,** make
or raise a clamor; make an outcry, **raise a
hue and cry,** kick up a dust, raise a hullabaloo, raise Cain or Ned, raise the deuce
or devil, raise hell or hell's delight, raise
Hail Columbia, make an uproar.

9. cry aloud, raise or lift up the voice,
shout ~, cry or thunder at the top of one's
voice, split the throat or lungs, strain the
voice or throat, rend the air.

ADJS. **10. vociferous,** vociferant, vocifer-
ating; **clamorous,** clamorsome [Scot. &
North. Eng.]; **blatant,** obstreperous, brawling; **noisy** 452.11; crying, shouting, yelling,
bawling, screaming; yelping, yapping; loudmouthed, openmouthed.

11. exclamatory, ejaculatory.

459. ANIMAL SOUNDS

NOUNS **1. call, cry;** howl, bark, howling,
barking, etc. 459.2-5; ululation, ululu; birdcall, note, wood-note, clang; stridulation
457.5.

VERBS **2. cry, call; howl,** yowl, yawl
[dial.], ululate; wail, whine, pule; **squeal,**
squall, scream, screech, screak, squeak;
troat; **roar; bellow,** bell, blare, **bawl; moo,**
low; **bleat,** blate, blat [coll.]; **bray; whinny,**
neigh, nicker [chiefly dial.]; **bay,** bay at
the moon; **bark,** bowwow, latrate, give
tongue; **yelp,** yap, yip, yawp; **mew,** mewl,
meow, miaow, caterwaul.

3. grunt, gruntle; **snort,** snork [dial.].

4. growl, snarl, grumble, gnarl, yarr
[Scot. & dial., Eng.], snap, show one's
teeth.

5. (birds) **warble,** sing, carol; pipe,
whistle; **trill,** chirr, roll; **twitter,** tweet, twit
[Scot. & dial., Eng.]; chatter, chitter; **chirp,**
chirrup, cheep, peep, pip, yap [dial.];
quack, honk; cronk, crunk; **croak,** chirk
[Scot.], plunk, **caw; squawk; crow,** cock-
a-doodle, cock-a-doodle-doo; **cackle,** gaggle,
guggle; **cluck,** clack, chuck, chuckle; **gobble,** gabble; **hoot,** hoo; **coo; cuckoo.**

ADJS. **6. howling,** yowling, crying, wailing, whining, puling, bawling, ululant, blatant.

460. DISCORD

Dissonant Sounds.—NOUNS **1. discord,**
discordance or discordancy, **dissonance** or
dissonancy, diaphony [Gr. music], **cacophony; inharmoniousness,** unharmoniousness, disharmony, inharmony; **unmelodiousness,** unmusicalness, untunefulness,

tunelessness; atonality, atonalism; flatness, sharpness, sourness [coll.]; discordant note, **sour note** [coll.], off note.

2. **clash, jangle, jar;** harshness 457.2; noise 452.3.

VERBS **3.** discord, sound a sour note [coll.] **clash, jar, jangle,** conflict, jostle; grate 457.9, 10.

ADJS. **4. discordant, dissonant, cacophonous,** diaphonic(al) [Gr. music]; **inharmonious,** unharmonious, disharmonious, disharmonic, inharmonic(al); **unmelodious,** immelodious, nonmelodious; **unmusical,** untuneful, untunable, untuned, tuneless; atonal, absonant; **out of tune,** out of tone [dial.]; **off-key, off-tone, off-pitch,** off; flat, sharp, **sour** [coll.]; "above the pitch, out of tune, and off the hinges" [Rabelais], "like sweet bells jangled, out of tune and harsh" [Shakespeare].

5. clashing, jarring, jangling, jangly, ajar; **harsh, grating** 457.14, 15.

461. MUSIC

NOUNS **1. music,** "the speech of angels" [Carlyle], "the mosaic of the Air" [Marvell], "the harmonious voice of creation; an echo of the invisible world" [Mazzini], "the only universal tongue" [Sam. Rogers], "the universal language of mankind" [Longfellow], "the poor man's Parnassus" [Emerson], "the brandy of the damned" [Shaw], "nothing else but wild sounds civilized into time and tune" [Thomas Fuller].

2. melody, melodiousness, **tunefulness,** musicalness, musicality; **tune, tone,** musical sound; sweetness, dulcetness, mellifluence; siren strains, Lydian measures.

3. harmony, concord, concordance, concert, consonance or consonancy, accordance, **accord,** monochord, concentus, symphony, diapason; synchronism, synchronization; **attunement,** tune, attune; chime, chiming; unison, unisonance; euphony; light or heavy harmony; two-part ～, three-part harmony, etc.; harmony or music of the spheres; harmonics 462.

4. air, aria, tune, tone [dial.], **melody,** melodia, note, **song,** lay, descant, **strain,** measure [poetic]; canto, cantus.

5. piece, opus, **composition,** production, work; **arrangement,** adaptation, orchestration, harmonization; incidental music; chamber music; program music; étude, study, exercise; suite, set; pianologue; concerto, concertino, concerto grosso, concertante [all It.]; concertstück; variation,

descant, *air varié* [F.]; accompaniment, background; curtain raiser or lifter, curtain tune; recessional, chaser [slang]; swan song.

6. medley, potpourri, *divertissement* [F.]; fantasia, fantasie, *Fantasiestück.*

7. classical music, classic; concert music; symphonic music, symphony, symphonia; symphonic ode or poem, tone poem or poetry.

8. popular music, pop [slang], popular air or tune; hit, song hit, hit tune.

9. dance music, foot music [coll.], dance; syncopated music, **syncopation; ragtime,** rag [both coll.]; **jazz;** hot jazz, **swing,** jive [slang, U.S.]; bebop, bop [slang, U.S.]; boogie-woogie; rock-and-roll.

10. mensurable music, *musica mensurata* [L.]; measured music, *cantus mensurabilis* [ML.]; alteration, prolation, augmentation, diminution.

11. march, martial music; military march, quick or quickstep march; processional march, funeral or dead march; wedding march.

12. vocal music, song; **singing,** caroling [poetic], warbling, vocalism, **vocalization;** croon, crooning; yodel, yodeling; scat, scat singing; intonation; hum, humming; solmization, solfeggio, sol-fa, sol-fa exercise.

13. song, lay, lied, carol, **ditty,** canticle; **ballad,** ballade, *ballata* [It.]; *canzone* [It.]; canzonet, *canzonetta* [It.]; chant; recitative, *recitativo* [It.]; folk song or music, *Volkslied* [G.]; calypso; art song, *Kunstlied* [G.]; drinking song, *brindisi* [It.]; war song; love song, torch song [coll.]; serenade, serenata, *serena* [Pr.]; *aubade* [F.], *alba* [Pr.]; blues, blues song; croon, croon song; carol, Christmas carol, noël; anthem, national anthem; wedding song, bridal hymn, hymeneal, *Brautlied* [G.]; barcarole, boat song; chantey or chanty, shanty; minstrel songs, minstrelsy; theme song.

14. aria; arietta, ariette; *aria buffa, aria da capo, aria d'agilità, aria da chiesa, aria d'imitazione, aria fugata, aria parlante* [all It.]; bravura, *aria di bravura* [It.]; coloratura, colo: ature, *aria di coloratura* [It.]; cantabile, *aria cantabile* [It.].

15. lullaby, cradlesong, *berceuse* [F.], *Schlummerlied* [G.].

16. sacred music, hymn, hymn-tune, **psalm,** choral or chorale, anthem; motet; doxology, paean; recessional; **spiritual,** Negro spiritual; psalmody, hymnody, hymnology.

17. part music, part song, part singing;

solo, arioso; **duet,** duo, *duettino* [It.]; **trio,** terzet, terzetto; **quartet** or quartette; **quintet** or quintette; **sextet** or sextette, sestet; **septet** or septette, septuor; **octet** or octette.

18. chorus, unison; glee; cantata, lyric cantata; madrigal, madrigaletto.

19. round, rondo, rondeau, **roundelay,** catch, troll; rondino, rondoletto.

20. polyphony, polyphonism; **counterpoint,** contrapunto; **descant,** prick song, *cantus figuratus* [ML.]; plain song, *cantus planus* [ML.], *cantus firmus* [ML.], Gregorian chant or melody; *faux-bourdon* [F.].

21. monody, monophony, homophony.

22. part, melody or voice part, **voice, instrument;** descant, canto, cantus, soprano, tenor, treble; alto; contralto; baritone or barytone; base, bass, bassus.

23. response, responsory or responsary [Eccl.], report, answer; antiphon, antiphony, antiphonal chanting or singing; offertory, offertory sentence or hymn [Eccl.].

24. passage, phrase, strain, part, **movement;** division, roulade; period, musical sentence; section; **measure;** figure; *alla breve* [It.]; **verse, stanza;** burden, bourdon; **chorus, refrain,** response; falderal or folderol; cadenza, cadence, harmonic close; coda, tailpiece; ritornel or ritornelle, ritornello, symphony; intermezzo, interlude; bass passage, ground bass, *basso ostinato* [It.]; tutti, tutti passage; bridge, bridge passage.

25. (fast, slow, etc. passages) presto, prestissimo; allegro, allegretto; scherzo; adagio, adagietto; andante, andantino; largo, larghetto; crescendo; diminuendo; decrescendo; rallentando, ritardando; piano, pianissimo; forte, fortissimo; staccato; spiccato; legato.

26. overture, prelude, *Vorspiel* [G.], **introduction,** voluntary, descant, vamp; concert overture.

27. impromptu, extempore, improvisation, interpolation, vamp; lick, hot lick, riff [all slang, U.S.].

28. score, musical score or copy, **music,** copy, draft, transcript, text, arrangement; part; full or orchestral score, compressed or short score, piano score, vocal score, instrumental score; opera score, opera; **libretto;** sheet music; **songbook,** songster; hymnbook, hymnal; music paper, music demy; music roll.

29. staff, stave [chiefly Eng.]; line, ledger line; bar, bar line; space, degree; brace.

30. theme, motive, **motif;** leitmotiv, leitmotif.

31. (style) **execution, performance, rendering,** rendition; **touch, expression;** fingering; intonation; repercussion; pizzicato, staccato, spiccato, parlando, legato; demilegato, mezzo staccato, slur; glissando, gliss [slang], smear [slang].

32. musicianship; fiddlery; musicomania; musical ear, ear for music.

33. musicale, musical [coll.]; choral service, service of song, sing [coll.], singing [South. U.S.], community singing, singfest [slang], singsong [coll.], sing-sing [derog.]; music festival, *Sängerfest* [G.], eisteddfod [Welsh]; jam session [slang]; swan song, farewell performance.

34. concert, symphony concert, chamber concert; Philharmonic concert, philharmonic; popular concert, pop or pop concert [coll.], popular [coll.]; promenade concert, prom [coll.]; Dutch concert, cat's concert [both coll.]; **recital.**

35. (musical theatricals) **music drama,** lyric drama, *dramma per musica* [L.]; songplay, *Singspiel* [G.]; **opera,** grand opera, light opera, ballad opera; comic opera, *opéra bouffe* [F.], *opera buffa* [It.]; **operetta; musical comedy; ballet,** *opéra ballet* [F.], comedy ballet, *ballet d'action* [F.], *ballet divertissement* [F.]; **chorus show; song-and-dance act;** minstrel, **minstrel show; oratorio,** Passion music.

VERBS **36. harmonize,** be harmonious, chord, **accord,** consonate, symphonize, synchronize, **chime,** blend, tune, attune, atone, sound together, sound in tune; assonate; melodize, musicalize.

37. tune, tune up, attune, atone, chord [poetic], **put in tune;** voice, string; tone up, tone down.

38. strike up, strike up a tune, **strike up the band,** tune up [coll.], pipe up, pipe up a song, yerk out, **burst into song.**

39. sing, vocalize, carol [poetic], descant, lilt, troll; **warble,** trill, tremolo, quaver, shake; **chirp,** chirrup, twit [Scot. & dial., Eng.], **twitter;** pipe, whistle, tweedle, tweedledee; **chant; intone,** intonate; **croon; hum; yodel,** warble [U.S.]; roulade; chorus, choir, sing in chorus; minstrel; ballad; **serenade;** sol-fa, do-re-mi, solmizate.

40. play, perform, execute, render, tune [poetic]; concertize; **symphonize;** chord; accompany; play by ear.

41. strum, thrum, pluck, plunk, **pick,** twang, twank [dial., Eng.], sweep.

42. fiddle [coll.], violin, scrape [derog.], saw [coll. or derog.], bow.

43. blow a horn, sound or wind the horn, **sound**, blow, wind, **toot**, tootle, pipe, tweedle; bugle, carillon, clarion, fife, flute, trumpet, whistle; bagpipe, doodle [Scot & dial., Eng.]; lip.

44. syncopate, jazz or jazz up [slang], swing, jive [slang], rag [coll.].

45. beat time, keep time; pat, pat juba [South. U.S.]; beat the drum, **drum**, thrum, beat, thump, pound; tom-tom; ruffle beat or sound a tattoo.

46. conduct, direct, lead, wield the baton.

47. compose, write, arrange, score, set to music; musicalize, melodize, harmonize; **orchestrate**; instrument, instrumentate; **adapt**, make an adaptation; transcribe, transpose.

ADᶦS. **48. musical, musically inclined,** musicianly, with an ear for music; virtuosic; **music-loving**, music-mad, philharmonic.

49. melodious, melodic; **musical**, music-like; **tuneful**, tuny [coll.], tunable; fine-toned, **pleasant-sounding**, agreeable-sounding, pleasant, agreeable, euphonious; **lyric(al)**, melic; songful, songlike; **sweet, dulcet**, sweet-sounding, sweet-flowing; melifluent, mellifluous, mellisonant; music-flowing; rich, mellow; sonorous, canorous; golden, golden-toned; silvery, silver-toned; sweet-voiced, golden-voiced, silver-voiced, silver-tongued, golden-tongued, music-tongued; ariose, arioso.

50. harmonious, harmonic(al), *armonioso* [It.], symphonious; harmonizing, chiming, blending; **concordant**, consonant, accordant, according, **in accord**, in concord; synchronous, synchronized, in sync or sink [slang, U.S.]; **in tune**, in tone [dial.], tuned, attuned; in unison, in chorus; unisonous, unisonant; homophonic, monophonic, monodic; assonant, assonantal.

51. vocal, singing; **choral**, choric; operatic; hymnal; treble, soprano, tenor, alto, falsetto; coloratura; baritone or barytone; base, bass; lyric; dramatic.

52. instrumental, orchestral, symphonic, concert.

53. polyphonic, contrapuntal.

ADJS., ADVS. **54.** (directions, style) legato; staccato; spiccato; pizzicato; forte, fortissimo; piano, pianissimo; sordo; crescendo, accrescendo; decrescendo, diminuendo, morendo; dolce; amabile; affettuoso, con affetto; amoroso, con amore; lamentabile; agitato, con agitazione; leggiero; agil-

mente, con agilità; capriccioso, a capriccio; scherzando, scherzoso; appassionato, appassionatamente; abbandono; brillante; parlando; a cappella; trillando, tremolando, tremoloso.

55. (slowly) largo, larghetto, allargando; adagio, adagietto; andante, andantino, andante moderato; calando; a poco; lento; ritardando, rallentando.

56. (fast) presto, prestissimo; veloce; accelerando; vivace, vivacissimo; desto, con anima, con brio; allegro, allegretto; affrettando.

57. music forms

Abendmusik [G.]	humoresque
adagio	jig
allegro	juba [U.S.]
allemande [F.]	largo
andante	*malagueña* [Sp.]
arabesque	march
arioso	mazurka,
aubade [F.]	mazourka
bagatelle	minuet
ballad	monody
barcarole	*morceau* [F.]
bolero	*Nachtmusik* [G.]
bourrée [F.]	nocturne
boutade	one-step
branle	*passacaglia* [It.]
canon	*passamezzo* [It.,
cantabile	hist.]
capriccetto	pastoral, pastorale
caprice, capriccio	pibroch
carillon	polka
cavatina	polonaise
chaconne [F.],	reel
chaccon, *chacona*	requiem
[Sp.]	rhapsody
cinquepace	rigadoon
courante	saltarello
dirge 873.5	saraband
elegy	scherzo
epicedium	serenade
fandango	serenata
forlane [F.]	sonata
fox trot	sonatina
fugue	strathspey
furlana [It.]	tarantella
galliard	toccata
gallopade	*toccatina* [It.]
galop	two-step
gavotte, gavot	waltz, *valse* [F.]
habanera	ziganka
hornpipe	*Zigeunerlied* [G.]

462. HARMONICS

Musical Elements.—NOUNS **1. harmonics**, harmony; melodics; rhythmics; music, musicology.

2. harmonization; orchestration, instrumentation; arrangement, adaptation; phrasing, modulation, intonation, preparation, suspension, solution, resolution; tone painting.

3. tone, tonality 449.2, 3.

4. pitch, tune, **tone,** key, **note;** height, depth; relative pitch, absolute pitch; classic(al) pitch, concert or high pitch, diapason ~, normal ~, French ~, international or low pitch, Stuttgart or Scheibler's pitch, philharmonic pitch, philosophical pitch.

5. voice, voce [It.]; *voce di petto* [It.], chest voice; *voce di testa* [It.], head voice; base, bass, basso; basso profundo, deep bass; *basso cantante* [It.], lyric bass; drone, drone bass, bourdon, burden; baritone or barytone; tenor, lyric tenor; soprano, mezzosoprano, alto, contralto, coloratura, treble, falsetto.

6. scale, gamut, register, compass, range, diapason; diatonic scale, chromatic scale, enharmonic scale, major scale, minor scale, harmonic or melodic minor, whole-tone scale.

7. sol-fa, tonic sol-fa, do-re-mi; do, re, mi, fa, sol, la, ti, do.

8. (diatonic series) tetrachord, chromatic tetrachord, enharmonic tetrachord, Dorian tetrachord; hexachord, pentachord.

9. octave, *ottava* [It.], eighth; *ottava alta, ottava bassa* [both It.]; small octave, great octave; contraoctave, subcontraoctave, double contraoctave.

10. mode, octave species; major mode, minor mode; Greek modes, Dorian ~, Phrygian ~, Lydian ~, mixolydian ~, hypodorian ~, hypophrygian *and* hypolydian modes; ecclesiastical ~, Gregorian or medieval mode; authentic or plagal mode.

11. form, arrangement, pattern, design; song or lied form, primary form; sonata form, sonata allegro; fugue form, rondo form, etc.

12. notation, character, mark, symbol, signature, sign, *segno* [It.]; dot; custos, direct; cancel; measure or time signature, tempo mark, metronome or metronomic mark; pause; *presa* [It.], lead; slur, tie, ligature, vinculum, enharmonic tie; swell; accent, accent mark.

13. clef; C clef, soprano ~, alto or tenor clef; F or bass clef, G or treble clef.

14. note, musical note, notes of a scale; tone 449.2; **sharp, flat, natural;** incidental, incidental note; whole note, semibreve; double whole note, breve; half note, minim; quarter note, crotchet; eighth note, quaver; sixteenth note, semiquaver; thirty-second note, demisemiquaver; sixty-fourth note, hemidemisemiquaver; tercet, triplet; sustained note, drone; bourdon, burden; dominant, dominant note; enharmonic,

enharmonic note; staccato, spiccato; responding note, report; shaped note, patent note; consecutive fifths.

15. key; keynote; tonic, tonic key; major, minor, major or minor key, tonic major or minor; supertonic, mediant, submediant, dominant, subdominant, subtonic; pedal point, organ point.

16. harmonic, harmonic tone, overtone, upper partial tone; flageolet tone.

17. chord, major or minor chord, tonic chord, dominant chord; consonant chord, concord; enharmonic chord, enharmonic; broken chord, arpeggio; unbroken chord, *concento* [It.]; triad, common chord.

18. ornament, grace, arabesque, embellishment, *fioritura* [It.], *agrémens* [F.]; **flourish,** roulade, flight, **run,** passage; division, florid phrase or passage; coloratura; incidental, incidental note; grace note, birdy [slang], appoggiatura; *acciaccatura* [It.]; mordent, single mordent, double or long mordent; inverted mordent, pralltriller; turn, back or inverted turn; cadence, cadenza.

19. trill, trillo; trillet, *trilleto* [It.]; **tremolo,** tremolant, tremolando; quaver, quiver, tremble, tremor, flutter, falter, shake; **vibrato,** Bebung [G.].

20. interval, degree, **step,** note, tone; prime or unison interval, major or minor interval, harmonic or melodic interval, enharmonic interval, diatonic interval; whole step, major second; half step, half tone, semitone, minor second; diatonic semitone, chromatic semitone, less semitone, quarter semitone, tempered or mean semitone; quarter step, enharmonic diesis.

21. rest, pause, bar, measure; whole rest, semibreve; half rest, minim; quarter rest.

22. rhythm, meter, measure, number or numbers, movement, **cadence** or cadency, **lilt, swing;** authentic cadence, plagal cadence, mixed cadence, perfect or imperfect cadence, half cadence, deceptive or false cadence, interrupted or suspended cadence.

23. tempo, time, time pattern; simple time or measure, compound time or measure; two-part or duple time, three-part or triple time, four-part or quadruple time, five-part or quintuple time, six-part or sextuple time, seven-part or septuple time, nine-part or nontuple time; two-four ~, six-eight etc. time; mixed times; **syncopation,** syncope; **ragtime,** rag [coll.]; waltz time, andante tempo, etc. 461.57.

24. **accent**, accentuation, rhymical accent or accentuation, ictus, emphasis, stress; grammatical accent, rhetorical accent; musical ~, pitch or stress accent, intonation.

25. **beat**, throb, pulse, pulsation; downbeat, upbeat, offbeat; bar beat.

ADJS. 26. **tonal**, tonic; chromatic, enharmonic; semitonic.

27. **rhythmic(al)**, **cadent**, cadenced, **measured**, **metric(al)**; in rhythm, in numbers; beating, throbbing, pulsing, pulsating, pulsative, pulsatory.

28. **syncopated**; **ragtime**, ragtimey [coll.]; **jazz**; jazzy, jazzed, jazzed up [all slang]; hot, swingy [both slang].

ADVS. 29. **in time**, in tempo, *a tempo* [It.], **in the groove** [slang, U.S.].

463. MUSICIAN

NOUNS 1. **musician**, musico, **music maker**, musicianer [coll.], musiker [chiefly dial.], minstrel [poetic], **player**, performer, tunester, harmonist; artiste, **virtuoso**, virtuosa [fem.]; maestro; recitalist; soloist, duettist; musicologist; minstrelsy, tin-pan alley.

2. **syncopator**; ragtimer [coll.]; **jazz musician**, jazzer [slang]; **swing musician**, swingster [slang]; **hepcat**, cat [both slang].

3. **instrumentalist**, instrumentist; bandman, bandsman; symphonist; concertist; accompanist, accompanyist.

4. **wind musician**, wind-instrumentalist, wind ammer [slang], **horn player**, hornist, horner, piper, tooter; bassoonist, bugler, carillonneur, clarinetist, cornettist, fifer, oboist, piccoloist, saxophonist, trombonist; trumpeter, trumpet major [mil.]; flutist, flautist; lutist, lutanist; accordionist, concertinist.

5. **string musician**, strummer, thrummer, twanger; banjoist, citharist, guitarist, luter, lyrist, mandolinist, theorbist, zitherist; violinist, fiddle [Scot.], fiddler [coll. or derog.], tweedledee [derog.], catgut scraper [slang]; bass violinist, contrabassist; violoncellist, cellist or 'cellist [coll.], celloist [coll.]; violist, viola; harpist, harper.

6. **xylophonist**, marimbaist.

7. **pianist**, pianiste, pianofortist, piano player, ivory tickler or thumper [slang]; pianolist; harpsichordist, clavichordist, monochordist.

8. **organist**, organer, organ player.

9. **hurdy-gurdist**, hurdy-gurdyist, hurdy-gurdy man; organ-grinder.

10. **drummer**, drums [slang], *tambourgi* [Turk.], tympanist; kettledrummer, timpanist; taborer; tambourine, tambo [coll.]; drum corps.

11. **cymbalist**, cymbaler.

12. **orchestra**, **band**, **ensemble**, *Kapelle* [G.]; string orchestra; **symphony orchestra**, symphony; **brass band**, military band, German band, concert band, ragtime band, **jazz band**, swing band; street band, waits [hist.]; strings, woodwind or woodwinds, brass or brasses, string ~, woodwind or brass section.

13. **vocalist**, vocalizer, voice, **singer**, songster, songbird, warbler, caroler, melodist, cantor; songstress, singstress, *cantatrice* [F. & It.]; chanter, chantress; prima donna; improvisator, *improvvisatore* [It.], *improvvisatrice* [It., fem.]; blues singer, torch singer [coll.]; crooner; yodeler; psalm singer, hymner; Meistersinger, *Minnesänger* [G.], minnesinger; sol-faist.

14. (voices) tenor, lyric tenor, Irish tenor, bathtub tenor [joc.]; bassist, bass, base, basso; *buffo*, *basso buffo* [both It.]; basso profundo; coloratura, coloratura soprano, soprano, mezzo-soprano, alto, contralto, baritone.

15. **songbird**, singing bird, **songster**, feathered songster, warbler; nightingale, philomel [poetic]; bulbul, canary, cuckoo, lark, mavis, mockingbird, oriole, ringdove, song sparrow, thrush.

16. **minstrel**, **ballad singer**, **bard**, runer [Gothic], rhapsodist; wandering minstrel, **troubadour**, jongleur; street singer, wait [hist.]; serenader; **negro minstrel**, blackface; end man, bones; interlocutor; tambo, tambourine.

17. **chorist**, chorister, choirister, chorus singer, **choralist**; choirman, **choirboy**; chorus girl, chorine [slang], singsong girl [pidgin Eng.].

18. **choir**, **chorus**, *Kapelle* [G.], ensemble, voices; **glee club**, *Liedertafel*, *Liederkranz* [both G.], choral or singing club or society; *a cappella* choir; choral symphony, sing band [slang].

19. **conductor**, leader, **music director**, *Kapellmeister* [G.]; **orchestra leader**, **bandmaster**, band major, drum major [mil.].

20 **choirmaster**, chorister [U.S.], **song leader**, *maestro di cappella* [It.]; choir chaplain [eccl.], precentor, cantor.

21. **concertmeister**, concertmaster, *Konzertmeister* [G.], first violinist.

22. **composer, scorer, arranger;** melodist, melodizer; harmonist, harmonizer; **orchestrater** or orchestrator; symphonist; tone poet; ballad maker or writer, ballader, balladmonger; madrigalist; lyrist; hymnist, hymnographer, hymnologist; contrapuntist.

23. **music lover,** philharmonic, **music fan** [slang], musicofanatic; **jitterbug, hepcat,** cat [all slang]; musicmonger; concertgoer, operagoer; tonalist.

24. (patrons) the Muses, the Nine, sacred Nine, tuneful Nine, Pierides; Apollo, Apollo Musagetes; Orpheus, Erato, Euterpe, Polymnia or Polyhymnia, Terpsichore, Siren.

464. MUSICAL INSTRUMENTS

NOUNS 1. tweedledee, tweedledum; alto, tenor, baritone or barytone, bass; musical glasses, harmonica; jew's-harp or jews'-harp.
2. **string instruments,** strings; polychord, heptachord, hexachord; balalaika, crowd [Celtic], euphonon, harmonichord, mandore, melodicon, melodion, samisen, troubadour fiddle, vina [India].
3. **harp,** arpa [It.]; **lyre,** lira [It.]; aeolian harp or lyre; bell harp; **claviharp; cither,** cithara, **zither,** cittern, cithern, gittern; psaltery, psalter; dulcimer, symphonia; langspiel.
4. **lute,** luth [F.]; archlute, archilute; theorbo, téorbe [F.]; bandore, bandurria [Sp.], pandore, pandora, pandura; **banjo,** banjer [dial.]; banjo-zither; banjorine; **ukulele,** uke [coll.]; banjo-ukulele, banjo-uke, banjuke, banjulele; **guitar,** Spanish guitar, Hawaiian guitar; **mandolin,** mandola, mandore, mandolute, mando-bass, mandocello; tamboura or tambura, tanbur [Per.].
5. **viol,** vielle; **viola;** violette; treble viol, descant viol; alto or tenor viol, viol or viola da braccio; bass viol, viol or viola da gamba; violoncello, **cello** or 'cello [coll.]; violoncello piccolo; **contrabass,** double bass, violone, **bull fiddle** [coll.], doghouse [slang, U.S.]; basso da camera [It.], viola alta, viol or viola d'amore, viol or viola da spalla, viol or viola di bordone, viol or viola di fagotto; rebec or rebeck; trumpet marine, tromba marina.
6. **violin,** violino [It.], **fiddle** [coll.], crowd [dial., Eng.]; violinette, violino piccolo; kit, kit violin; tenor violin, violotta, Bratsche [G.]; Stradivarius, Stradivari, Strad [coll.]; Amati, Cremona, Guarnerius; bow, fiddlestick.

7. **wind instruments,** winds; **horn,** corno [It.], pipe [poetic], tooter; mouthpiece, lip.
8. **brass winds,** brass or brass-wind instruments, brasses, Blechinstrumente [G.]; **bugle,** bugle horn; **trumpet,** tromba; **clarion;** post horn; lituus; lure; **cornet,** cornet-à-pistons, cornopean; **trombone,** tromba da tirasi [It.]; slide trombone, sliphorn [slang], sackbut [arch.]; **saxophone,** sax [coll.]; **saxhorn,** saxtuba, saxcornet, Flügelhorn [G.]; **althorn** or alto horn, ballad horn; **tuba,** bass horn or saxhorn, basson russe [F.], tenor tuba, euphonium; sousaphone; ophicleide; **French horn,** horn, orchestral horn, corno di caccia [It.]; mellophone.
9. **wood winds,** wood or wood-wind instruments, woods; reed instruments, reeds; **flute,** flauto [It.]; recorder, fipple flute or pipe, flageolet; aulos; **fife,** Pfeife [G.]; pipe, tabor pipe; **piccolo,** flauto piccolo [It.]; **oboe,** hautboy; oboe d'amore [It.]; bass or basset oboe, heckelphone; tenoroon, oboe di caccia [It.]; musette; **bassoon;** double bassoon, contra bassoon, contrafagotto; bombardon, pommer; sonorophone; **clarinet** or clarionet; basset horn, corno di bassetto [It.]; **English horn,** cor anglais [F.], corno Inglese [It.]; ocarina, sweet potato [coll.]; hornpipe; serpent; whistle.
10. **bagpipe** or bagpipes, pipes, union pipes, doodlesack [Scot.], Dudelsack [G.], drone; musette; sordellina; chanter, drones.
11. **mouth organ,** mouth harp, harp, French harp [dial.], **harmonica,** harmonicon; Panpipe, Panpipes, Pandean pipes, syrinx.
12. **accordion,** dago's piano [joc.]; **concertina,** squiffer [slang, Eng.]; mellophone; bandonion.
13. **piano,** pianoforte; pianette, pianino; spinet; grand piano, grand; baby grand, parlor grand, concert grand; square piano, upright piano, upright; **clavier,** Klavier [G.]; **harpsichord,** clavicymbal, clavicembalo, cembalo; **clavichord,** clarichord, monochord, manichord or manichordon; clavicithern, clavicytherium; virginal, pair of virginals, couched harp; lyrichord; harmonichord; violin piano, piano-violin.
14. **player piano,** piano player, player, mechanical piano, Pianola; street piano; music roll, piano player roll.
15. **organ,** pipe organ, reed organ; electric organ, electro-pneumatic organ, tubular-pneumatic organ, tracker-action organ,

hydraulic organ; choralcelo, harmonium, melodeon, melodica, organophone, seraphine or seraphina, symphonion, vocalion; calliope, calliophone.

16. **hurdy-gurdy**, vielle, **barrel organ**, hand organ, grind organ, street organ.

17. **music box**, musical box; orchestrion, orchestrina.

18. **phonograph, graphophone, gramophone, record player**, talking machine, Victrola; **juke box** [slang, U.S.], **nickelodeon** [U.S.]; radio-phonograph combination; recorder, wire recorder, tape recorder; stylus, needle.

19. **record**, phonograph record, cylinder, disk, wax [cant]; transcription, electrical transcription; recording, tape recording, wire recording.

20. **percussion instruments**, percussions, percussives; battery [coll.]; **cymbals**, potlics [slang], *Becken* [G.]; **triangle; gong**, tonitruone; **bells**, tintinnabula; chime, **chimes; orchestral bells, glockenspiel**, carillon, lyra; **vibraphone**, vibes [slang]; **xylophone, marimba**, metallophone; celesta; **clappers**, snappers, **castanets**, bones, rattle, rattlebones.

21. **drum**, *caisse* [F.], tympan, tympanum, tympanon, tympany; **kettledrum**, kettle [coll.], timpani [pl.], timbal or tymbal, naker, nagara [India]; **snare drum**, side drum, *caisse roulante* [F.]; **bass drum**, *caisse grosse* [F.]; **tom-tom**, tam-tam; **timbrel**, tabor, **tambourine**, tambourin, *tambour de basque* [F.]; taboret, tabret; drumhead, drumskin; drumstick, jazz stick, tymp stick.

22. **keyboard**; console; **keys**, piano keys, ivories [slang].

23. **stop**, register; foundation stop, mutation stop; principal; melodia; diapason; cromorne, cromorna, cremona; dolcan, dulciana; bassoon, *fagotto* [It.]; celesta, flageolet, flute, gemshorn, serpent, trombone, tuba.

24. **string**, chord; fiddlestring, **catgut**; snare; music wire, piano wire.

25. **plectrum**, plectron, **pick**.

26. (aids) metronome, rhythmometer; tone measurer, monochord, sonometer; tuning fork, tuning bar, diapason; pitch pipe, tuning pipe.

465. INTELLECT

Mental Faculty.—NOUNS **1. intellect, mind, mentality, psyche**, nous, **reason**, *Vernunft* [G.], **intelligence, understand-**

ing, **brain, brains**, brain-stuff [coll.], gray matter [coll.], head.

2. **wits, senses**, mentals, **faculties**, parts, capacities, intellectual gifts or talents; consciousness.

3. **inmost mind**, inner recesses of the mind, heart, heart's core, cockles of the heart, heart of hearts, inmost heart or soul, secret or inner recesses of the heart, breast, bosom; inner man 5.4; subconscious mind 688.39.

4. **brain**, seat of thought, encephalon, head, headpiece; pate, sconce, noddle [all coll.]; noodle, noggin, bean, upper story [all slang]; sensory, sensorium.

5. (parts of brain) cerebellum, little brain; cerebrum; prosencephalon, forebrain; telencephalon, endbrain; diencephalon, betweenbrain, 'tweenbrain, 'twixtbrain; mesencephalon, midbrain; rhombencephalon, hindbrain; metencephalon; myelencephalon, afterbrain; medulla, medulla oblongata; pons; arbor vitae, tree of life; gray matter, white matter.

ADJS. 6. **mental, intellectual, rational, reasoning, thinking**; intelligent 466.12; psychic(al), psychologic(al), spiritual; cerebral; subjective, internal; endopsychic.

466. INTELLIGENCE, WISDOM

Mental Capacity.—NOUNS **1. intelligence, understanding**, *Verstand* [G.], **comprehension**, apprehension; sabe, savvy [both slang, U.S.]; **sense, wit**, mother wit, natural or native wit; intellect 465; **intellectuality**, intellectualism; **mentality**, rationality, intellectual power; capacity, mental capacity, caliber, reach or compass of mind; **I.Q.**, intelligence quotient, mental ratio, mental age; sanity 471; knowledge 474.

2. **smartness, braininess** [coll.], **brightness, brilliance, cleverness**, aptness, aptitude, native cleverness; sharpness, keenness, acuteness; quickness, nimbleness, adroitness, dexterity; sharp-wittedness, keen-wittedness, quick-wittedness, nimble-wittedness; nimble mind, quick parts, clear or quick thinking; ready wit, quick wit, sprightly wit, *esprit* [F.], nous [slang].

3. **shrewdness, artfulness, cunning**, cunningness, canniness [dial.]; slickness, slyness [dial.], foxiness [coll.]; subtility, subtilty, subtlety.

4. **sagacity**, sagaciousness, **astuteness, acumen**, gumption [coll. & dial.], flair; long head [coll.], longheadedness, hardheadedness; **foresight**; foresightedness; **farsight-**

edness, far-seeingness, long-sightedness; discernment, **insight**, penetration; perspicacity, perspicuity [erron.]; **perception**, percipience, apperception.

5. **wisdom**, wiseness, sageness, sapience, good or sound understanding; erudition 474.4, 5; **profundity**, profoundness, depth, abstruseness; "common sense in an uncommon degree" [Coleridge], "the right use of knowledge" [Spurgeon], "the pursuing of the best ends by the best means" [Francis Hutcheson], "the abstract of the past" [Holmes], "knowledge of things human and divine and of the causes by which those things are controlled" [Cicero].

6. **sensibleness**, reasonableness, reason, rationality, sanity, saneness, soundness; **sense**, good ~, common or plain sense, **horse sense** [coll., U.S.], due sense of; level head [coll.], **levelheadedness**, coolheadedness, coolness, soberness, sobriety, **sober-mindedness**, staidness, solidness, solidity.

7. **judiciousness**, **judgment**, good or sound judgment, sound reasoning, soundness of judgment; **prudence**, providence, policy, considerateness, consideration, circumspection, circumspectness, **thoughtfulness**; **discretion**, discreetness, **discrimination**.

8. **genius**, Geist [G.], spirit, soul; **inspiration**, afflatus, divine afflatus; fire of genius, lambent flame of intellect, coal from off the altar; talent 731.4; creative thought 533.2.

9. (intelligent being) **intelligence**, **intellect**, find, brain, mentality, consciousness.

VERBS 10. **have all one's wits about one**, have all one's marbles [slang], have a head on one's shoulders [slang], have something on one's head besides one's hat [slang], have one's head screwed on the right way, have it in one [slang]; know what's what 731.18; **be reasonable**, listen to reason.

11. **be brilliant**, **scintillate**, sparkle, coruscate, shine [chiefly coll.].

ADJS. 12. **intelligent**, **intellectual**, knowing, understanding, reasonable, rational, sensible, bright; sane 471.4; not so dumb [coll., U.S.], pas si bête [F.]; strongminded, strongheaded.

13. **clear-witted**, clearheaded, clear-sighted; awake, **wide-awake**, alive, alert, fly [slang].

14. **smart**, brainy [coll.], bright, brilliant, clever; apt, apprehensive; **sharp**, keen, cute [coll.], acute; **quick**, nimble, adroit, dexterous; **sharp-witted**, keen-witted, needle-witted; **quick-witted**, nimble-witted, quick on the trigger [slang]; smart as a whip, sharp as a tack [slang]; nobody's fool, no dumbbell, not born yesterday [all slang].

15. **shrewd**, **artful**, **cunning**, **knowing**, subtle, canny [dial.], slick, sly [dial.], pawky [Scot. & dial., Eng.], parlous [dial.]; foxy [coll.], crazy like a fox [slang].

16. **sagacious**, **astute**, argute; **understanding**, **discerning**, penetrating, piercing; **hardheaded**, longheaded; **foresighted**, foreseeing; forethoughted, forethoughtful; **farsighted**, farseeing, longsighted; perspicacious, perspicuous [erron.]; **perceptive**, percipient, apperceptive, appercipient.

17. **wise**, **sage**, sapient, savant [F.], **knowing**, gnostic [joc. or slang], owlish; **learned** 474.21; **profound**, deep, abstruse; authoritative, oracular; wise as an owl, wise as Solomon; wise beyond one's years, in advance of one's age, wise in one's generation.

18. **sensible**, **sound**, **sane**, **reasonable**, **rational**, **logical**; philosophical; **levelheaded**, heady [coll.], coolheaded, cool, sober, **sober-minded**, staid, solid, well-balanced.

19. **judicious**, judicial, judgmatic(al) [coll.]; **prudent**, prudential, politic, provident, **considerate**, circumspect, **thoughtful**, calculating, reflecting; **discreet**, discretionary, discriminative, discriminating; **well-advised**, well-judged, enlightened.

ADVS. 20. **intelligently**, **understandingly**, knowingly, discerningly; **reasonably**, rationally, sensibly; **smartly**, **cleverly**; shrewdly, artfully, cunningly; wisely, sagaciously, astutely; **judiciously**, **prudently**, discreetly, providently, considerately, circumspectly, thoughtfully.

467. WISE MAN

NOUNS 1. **wise man**, wiseman, sage, sapient, wisehead, man of wisdom; master; **mastermind**, master spirit of the age; adept, mahatma; **authority**, oracle, mentor; **intellect**, man of intellect; **thinker**, longhead; luminary, shining light; learned man 475.3, 4.

2. **Solomon**, Socrates, Plato, Mentor, Nestor, Confucius, Buddha, magnus Apollo.

3. **the wise**, the intelligent, the sensible,

the prudent, the knowing, the understanding.

4. the Wise Men, Seven Wise Masters, Seven Wise Men of Greece, Seven Sages, Philosophical Pleiad; Solon, Chilon, Pittacus, Bias, Periander, Epimenides, Cleobulus, Thales.

5. Magi, Three Wise Men, Wise Men of Egypt, Three Kings of Cologne; Gaspar, Melchior, Balthasar.

6. **wiseacre, wisenheimer** [slang, U.S.], wise guy [slang]; wiseling, **witling**; wise fool, Scottish Solomon; Gothamite, wise man of Gotham.

468. UNINTELLIGENCE

NOUNS 1. **unintelligence, unintellectuality, unwiseness, irrationality**; **senselessness, witlessness,** mindlessness, brainlessness, reasonlessness, lackwittedness; **ignorance** 476; **foolishness** 469; incapacity, ineptitude; low I.Q.

2. **unperceptiveness,** undiscerningness, inapprehensiveness, **incomprehension,** nonunderstanding; **blindness,** purblindness; **shortsightedness,** nearsightedness, dimsightedness.

3. **stupidity,** stupidness, **dumbness** [coll., U.S.], **doltishness,** oafishness, oafdom, dullardism, chumpishness [coll.], blockishness, lumpishness, sottishness, **asininity,** ninnyism, simpletonianism; **density,** denseness, opacity; grossness, crassness; **dullness, obtuseness,** sluggishness, slowness, stolidity, hebetude; **dull-wittedness,** slow-wittedness, dull-headedness, **thick-wittedness,** thick-headedness; numskulledness, numskullery, numskullism [all coll.]; unteachability, unlearnability.

4. **blockheadedness,** woodenheadedness [coll.], jolterheadedness, joltheadedness, chowderheadedness, chuckleheadedness [coll.], beetleheadedness, cabbageheadedness [coll.], sapheadedness [coll.], pigheadedness, muttonheadedness [coll.], fatheadedness [coll.], boneheadedness [slang], blunderheadedness.

5. **muddleheadedness,** addleheadedness, addlepatedness; dopeyness [slang], dizziness [coll.].

6. **empty-headedness,** empty-mindedness, absence of mind; **vacuity,** vacancy, emptiness, blankness; vacant attic, unfurnished garret, space to let, nobody home, nobody home in the upper story [all slang].

7. **shallowness, superficiality, unprofundity,** unprofoundness; shallow-wittedness, shallow-mindedness; **frivolousness,** lightness, frothiness, volatility.

8. **feeble-mindedness,** weak-mindedness; infirmity, weakness, feebleness, softness, **unsoundness.**

9. **mental deficiency,** amentia, subnormality, defectiveness; **arrested development,** retardment, backwardness; **simplemindedness,** simple-wittedness, simpleness, simplicity; **idiocy, imbecility, halfwittedness,** nitwittedness; moronity, moronism, morosis; insanity 472.

10. **senility,** senilism, senile weakness, senile dementia, caducity, decreptitude; **childishness,** second childishness, **second childhood;** old-womanishness, anility; **dotage, dotardism;** anecdotage [joc.], "talking age" [Goldsmith].

11. **puerility,** puerilism, **childishness,** childlikeness; **infantilism,** babyishness.

VERBS 12. have space to let [slang], have a block for a head, have a bone on one's neck; not see an inch beyond one's nose, not have enough sense to come in out of the rain, couldn't find one's way to first base; not set the Thames on fire.

ADJS. 13. **unintelligent, unintellectual, unthinking, unreasoning, irrational, unwise,** inept, inapt, **not bright; senseless,** insensate; **mindless, witless, reasonless, brainless,** headless; **lackwitted,** lackbrained, lean-minded, lean-witted, shortwitted; **foolish** 469.8; **ignorant** 476.13.

14. **undiscerning, unperceptive,** inapprehensive, **incomprehensive,** nonunderstanding; **shortsighted,** nearsighted, dimsighted; **blind,** purblind, blind as a bat; blinded, blindfold, blindfolded.

15. **stupid, dumb** [coll., U.S.], dullard, numskulled [coll.], **doltish,** blockish, chumpish [coll.], lumpish, **oafish,** sottish, **asinine,** Boeotian; **dense,** thick [coll.], opaque, gross, crass, fat; bovine, beefwitted, beef-brained, beefheaded; unteachable, unlearnable; dead from the neck up, dead above or between the ears, musclebound between the ears [all slang].

16. **dull,** obtuse, blunt, dim, stolid, wooden, heavy, sluggish, slow, **slowwitted,** hebetudinous; **dull-witted,** bluntwitted, dull-brained, dull-headed, dullpated; **thick-witted,** thick-headed, thickpated, thickskulled, thick-brained, fatwitted, gross-witted, gross-headed.

17. **blockheaded,** woodenheaded [coll.], stupidheaded, dumbheaded [slang, U.S.], blunderheaded, jolterheaded, joltheaded,

chowderheaded, chuckleheaded [coll.], beetleheaded, cabbageheaded [coll.], pumpkin-headed, sapheaded [coll.], lunkheaded [coll., U.S.], pigheaded, muttonheaded [coll.], fatheaded [coll.], boneheaded [slang], clodpated.

18. muddleheaded, fuddlebrained [coll.], scramblebrained [slang], addleheaded, **addlepated**, addlebrained, muddybrained, blear-witted; **dopey** [slang], **dizzy** [coll.], muzzy, foggy, foggy in the crumpet *or* upper story [slang].

19. empty-headed, empty-minded, empty-noddled, empty-pated, emptyskulled; **vacuous**, vacant, empty, blank, unoccupied; **rattlebrained,** rattleheaded; scatterbrained 530.16.

20. shallow, superficial, unprofound; shallow-witted, shallow-minded, shallowbrained, shallow-headed, shallow-pated; **frivolous,** light, volatile, frothy, barmy, barmy-brained, **featherbrained, birdwitted,** hen-headed [coll.].

21. feeble-minded, weak-minded, weak, feeble, infirm, **unsound,** soft, soft in the head, weak in the upper story [coll.].

22. mentally deficient, defective, retarded, **mentally retarded,** backward, arrested, subnormal, wanting [dial.], **not bright, not all there** [coll.]; **simpleminded,** simple-witted, simple, simpletonian; **half-witted,** half-baked [coll.]; **idiotic, moronic, imbecile, nitwitted** [slang]; crazy 472.24; babbling, driveling.

23. senile, decrepit; **childish,** childlike, in one's second childhood; old-womanish, anile, grannified [coll.]; **doting,** doited [chiefly Scot.]; dotard, dotardy; doddering, doddery.

24. puerile, childish, childlike; **infantile,** infantine; **babyish,** babish.

ADVS. **25. unintelligently, stupidly;** foolishly 469.11.

469. FOOLISHNESS

NOUNS **1. foolishness,** folly, foolery, foolheadedness [coll.], **stupidity, asininity,** *niaiserie* [F.], *bêtise* [F.]; **inanity,** fatuity, ineptitude; **silliness,** goosiness; **frivolousness,** frivolity; **senselessness, witlessness, thoughtlessness,** brainlessness; **idiocy, imbecility, craziness, madness,** lunacy, **insanity;** screwiness, nuttiness, wackiness, goofiness, daffiness, battiness, sappiness [all slang]; softness [coll.], spooniness [slang]; infatuation.

2. unwiseness, injudiciousness, im-prudence, indiscreetness, **indiscretion,** inconsideration, thoughtlessness, witlessness, unthoughtfulness; **unreasonableness, unsoundness, unsensibleness,** senselessness, reasonlessness, **irrationality,** inadvisability; inexpedience 669; unintelligence 468.

3. absurdity, absurdness, **ridiculousness;** ludicrousness 878.1; **nonsense,** nonsensicality, **stuff and nonsense; preposterousness,** fantasticalness, monstrousness, **outrageousness,** egregiousness.

4. (foolish act) folly, stupidity, act of folly, absurdity, *sottise* [F.], foolish *or* stupid thing, dumb thing to do [slang]; trick, fool's trick, dumb trick [coll.], boob stunt [slang]; **imprudence, indiscretion,** imprudent *or* unwise step; blunder 517.5.

5. stultification, nonsensification, infatuation.

VERBS **6. be foolish, act** *or* **play the fool;** get funny, put on the crazy act, play the giddy goat [all slang]; **fool,** tomfool [coll.], **trifle,** frivol [coll.]; **fool around** [coll.], horse around [slang, U.S.], clown, clown around; **make a fool of oneself,** make a monkey of oneself [slang], stultify oneself, put oneself out of court; **lose one's head, take leave of one's senses;** pass from the sublime to the ridiculous; reckon without one's host; strain at a gnat and swallow a camel.

7. stultify, nonsensify, infatuate, befool, **make a fool of,** make a monkey of [slang], play for a sucker [slang, U.S.].

ADJS. **8. foolish,** fool [coll.], foolheaded [coll.], **stupid, dumb** [slang], **asinine;** silly, dizzy [coll.], goosy, anserine; fatuous, fatuitous, inept, **inane; senseless, witless, thoughtless,** brainless; **idiotic,** imbecile, **crazy, mad,** daft, **insane;** cockeyed, screwy, nutty, wacky, goofy, daffy, loony, batty, sappy [all slang]; soft [coll.], spoony [slang], maudlin.

9. unwise, injudicious, imprudent, impolitic, indiscreet, inconsiderate, thoughtless, witless, unthoughtful, unthinking, unreflecting; **unreasonable, unsound, unsensible,** senseless, insensate, reasonless, **irrational,** inadvisable; inexpedient 669.5; **ill-advised, ill-considered,** ill-judged, ill-imagined, ill-contrived, ill-devised; unconsidered, unadvised; misadvised, misguided; penny-wise and pound-foolish; unintelligent 468.13.

10. absurd, nonsensical, ridiculous, poppycockish [coll.]; ludicrous 878.5; **foolish, crazy** 469.8; **preposterous,** fantastic(al), monstrous, **outrageous**, egregious, flagrant, gross, *cutré* [F.], extravagant, bizarre, high-flown.

ADVS. **11. foolishly, stupidly,** sillily, idiotically; **unwisely,** injudiciously, imprudently, indiscreetly, inconsiderately; senselessly, unreasonably, thoughtlessly, witlessly, unthinkingly; absurdly, ridiculously.

INTERJS. **12. nonsense!,** stuff!, stuff and nonsense!, fiddle-deedee!, fiddle-faddle! [coll.], **fiddlesticks!** [coll.]; applesauce!, fudge! baloney!, razzberries! [all slang, U.S.]; **pooh!,** poo!, phoo!, pooh-pooh!, **phooey!** [coll.], **poof!,** pish!, pish-pash!, pugh!, pshaw!, **bah!, bosh!** [coll.], balderdash!, hooey! [slang], humbug!, **poppycock!** [coll.], **rubbish!,** rats! [slang], twaddle!, in your hat! [slang]! **my eye!** [coll.]; come off!, come off of it! [both slang]; **tell it to the marines!** [coll.]; that's absurd!, that's ridiculous!, that's a laugh! [slang].

13. don't be absurd!, don't be ridiculous!, don't be silly!, don't be stupid!, don't be foolish!, don't be funny!, don't be like that!, don't talk rot!, don't make me laugh!, grow up!, be yourself!, be *or* act your age!, get hep! [slang, U.S.], get wise to yourself! [slang], blow wise to yourself! [slang, U.S.]; you kill me!, you slay me!

470. FOOL

NOUNS **1. fool,** tomfool, precious fool [coll.], **ninny,** ninnyhammer, **nincompoop** [coll.], looby, noddy, domnoddy, tommy noddy, nonny [dial.], noodle, foozle [coll.], gabby [coll.], dizzard [chiefly dial.], jobbernowl [coll., Eng.], *badaud* [F.], **zany,** gaby [coll.], doodle [U.S.], put, sop, sot [Scot.]; calf [coll.], mooncalf; soft [coll.], softy [coll.], softhead; shallowbrain, shallowpate; witling, wiseacre, Boeotian; no conjurer, no Solomon; ignoramus 476.9.

2. chump [coll.], **booby; boob, sap,** prize sap, **saphead, mutt, jerk,** flat, **goof,** goon, schlemiel [all slang].

3. dolt, dunce, dullard, dully [coll.], **numskull** [coll.], dummy *or* dumby, **dope** [slang, U.S.], duffer [coll.], block, stick [coll.], stock, *niais* [F.], donkey, ass, asshead, **thickwit,** stupid, stupidhead, dullhead, dumbhead, **dumbbell, dumb-bunny** [all slang, U.S.].

4. blockhead, woodenhead [coll.], squarehead [slang], **bonehead,** thickhead [coll.], thickskull, **lunkhead** [coll., U.S.],

chucklehead [coll.], **knucklehead** [slang], chowderhead, jolthead, jolterhead, muttonhead [coll.], loggerhead, beetlehead, noodlehead, cabbagehead [coll.], pumpkin head, **fathead** [coll.], blubberhead [slang], doughhead [slang, U.S.], bakehead [slang, U.S.], bullhead, blunderhead, dunderhead, dunderpate, clodpate, clodpole *or* clodpoll.

5. oaf, lout, loon, lown [dial. & Scot.], **lubber,** swab [dial. & slang], sawney [dial., Eng.], galoot [slang], gowk, **gawk,** gawky, **lummox** [slang], yokel, rube [slang], clod, clodhopper.

6. silly [coll.], sill [slang], **silly ass** [slang], spoony [slang], **goose.**

7. scatterbrain, scatterbrains, shatterbrain, shatterpate, **rattlebrain,** rattlehead, rattlepate, **harebrain,** featherbrain, giddybrain, giddyhead, giddypate, addlebrain, addlehead, **addlepate, flibbertigibbet;** dizzy, dizzy dame [both slang, U.S.].

8. simpleton, simp [slang], Simple Simon; **idiot,** driveling idiot; **imbecile, moron,** zombi [slang, U.S.], **nitwit** [slang], dimwit [slang], **half-wit,** lack-wit, lackbrain; **natural,** natural idiot, born fool, natural-born fool; ament, defective; cretin.

9. dotard, "the sickly dotard" [Prior]; driveler, babbler, *radoteur* [F.]; senile; fogy, **old fogy,** old wife *or* woman, grandmother, henhussy, betty [derog.].

10. (childish person) **child,** mere child, baby, infant, innocent.

471. SANITY

NOUNS **1. sanity, saneness,** sanemindedness, soundness, **soundness of mind,** soundmindedness, sound mind, right mind [coll.], senses, reason, **rationality,** lucidity, balance, wholesomeness; normalness, normality, normalcy; sobriety, sober senses; "a madness put to good uses" [Santayana]; a sound mind in a sound body; lucid interval [med.].

VERBS **2. come to one's senses,** sober down *or* up, cool down *or* off; get things into proportion, see in perspective.

3. bring to one's senses, bring to reason, bring round *or* around [coll.], restore, sober.

ADJS. **4. sane,** sane-minded, **rational,** reasonable, sensible, lucid, normal, wholesome, **sound,** mentally sound, soundminded, right, right-minded, **in one's right mind,** in possession of one's faculties *or* senses, all there [slang]; compos, compos mentis [both law]; sober, sober-minded, in one's sober senses.

472. INSANITY, MANIA

NOUNS 1. **insanity**, insaneness, unsaneness, **lunacy, madness, craziness, daftness**, queerness, dementedness, dementia, brainsickness, rabidness, **mania**, furor, *folie* [F.], bedlam, alienation, aberration, **derangement**, distraction, disorientation, mental disease, mental derangement *or* disorder, unbalance, unsoundness, **unsoundness of mind**, unbalanced mind, diseased *or* unsound mind, shattered mind, cracked brain, disordered mind *or* reason, senselessness, witlessness, reasonlessness; possession, pixilation [dial.]; mental deficiency 468.

2. (slang terms) **daffiness, nuttiness, battiness**, screwiness, goofiness, **wackiness**, whackiness, looniness *or* luniness, **balminess**; bats in the belfry, a screw loose, a tile *or* slate loose, lame brains, bubbles in the think tank.

3. **psychosis**, psychopathy, psychopathia, paralogy, psychopathic condition; **neurosis** 688.17; neuropsychosis, neuropsychopathy; pathopsychosis, pathoneurosis; Korsakoff's psychosis *or* disease, polyneuritic psychosis; amentia, fugue; dementia paralytica, general paralysis; senile dementia, senile psychosis, degenerative psychosis, senility; presenile dementia, Alzheimer's disease, Pick's disease; psychopathia sexualis, psychosexuality; pharmacopsychosis, drug addiction; arteriosclerotic psychosis, climacteric psychosis, dipsomania 994.3, exhaustive psychosis, gestational psychosis, hallucinosis, involuntary psychosis, hypomania, involutional psychosis, lycanthropy, metabolic psychosis, organic psychosis, paranomia, pathological lying, postinfectuous psychosis, psychasthenia, psycholepsy, psychokinesia, psychorhythmia, reactive *or* situational psychosis, toxic psychosis; moral insanity, pathomania, psychopathic personality.

4. **schizophrenia**, functional disintegration, mental dissociation, dissociation of personality, **split personality**, alternating personality, dual *or* double personality, multiple personality.

5. **dementia praecox, paranoia**, catatonia; hebephrenia, paraphrenia, schizophasia, schizothymia.

6. **melancholia**, "moping, melancholy and moonstruck madness" [Milton]; **hypochondria**, hyp *or* hyps [coll.]; **manic-de-**pressive insanity, affective psychosis, affective reaction psychosis; **cyclothymia**.

7. **rabies, hydrophobia**, canine madness; dumb rabies *or* madness, paralytic rabies; furious rabies.

8. **frenzy, furor**, fury, fever, **rage**; seizure, attack, **fit**, paroxysm; **amuck**, amok, murderous insanity *or* frenzy; corybantiasm.

9. **delirium**, deliriousness; phrenitis, paraphrenitis; brain fever, brain storm, calenture of the brain; incoherence, wandering, raving, ranting.

10. **delirium tremens**, *mania* or *dementia a potu* [L.], gallon distemper [slang]; **D.T.'s**, the horrors [both coll.]; **heebie-jeebies**, jim-jams, beezie-weezies, screaming meemies, blue Johnnies, blue devils, pink elephants, pink spiders, snakes, snakes in the boots, fantod [all slang].

11. **fanaticism**, fanaticalness, **rabidness, overzealousness**, overenthusiasm, ultrazealousness; zealotry, zealotism; extravagance, extremeness, excessiveness; overreligiousness 1026.3.

12. **mania, craze, infatuation**, enthusiasm, passion, fascination, crazy fancy, bug [slang], rage, furore, furor; Anglomania, erotomania, kleptomania, oniomania, poriomania.

13. **obsession, possession**, prepossession, preoccupation; **fixation** [psychol.], complex [coll.], fascination; **compulsion**, drive, morbid drive, obsessive compulsion, irresistible impulse; **monomania**, ruling passion, fixed idea, *idée fixe* [F.], one-tracked mind.

14. **insane asylum**, asylum, lunatic asylum, **madhouse**, bedlam, mental institution, institution, home, college; **bughouse**, nuthouse, bathouse, **loonybin**, booby **hatch** [all slang]; mental hospital, psychopathic hospital *or* ward; padded cell.

15. **lunatic, madman**, dement, **crackbrain**, cracked wit, phrenetic, frenetic, *aliéné* [F.], noncompos, bedlamite, Tom o' Bedlam; demoniac, energumen; **loon**, loony, **nut, crackpot, screwball**, bat, coot, goof [all slang]; **maniac**, raving lunatic; madcap; borderline case; idiot 470.8.

16. **psychotic**, psycho [slang], mental [coll.], **psychopath**, psychopathic case; psychopathic personality; paranoiac, paranoid; schizophrenic, schizo [slang], schizophrene, schizoid; schizothyme; megalomaniac; cyclothymiac, cyclothyme, cycloid; catatoniac; hebephreniac; hypochondriac, hypo [sl.]; manic-depressive; kleptomaniac,

klepto [slang]; dipsomaniac, dipso [slang], alcoholic.

17. **fanatic, infatuate,** bug [slang], **nut** [slang], **zealot, enthusiast,** energumen; **monomaniac,** crank [coll.]; lunatic fringe [coll., U.S.].

18. ɔsychiatry, alienism 688.3; psychiatrist, alienist 688.13.

VERBS 19. **be insane, be out of one's mind,** not be in one's right mind [coll.], **not be all there** [coll.], have a demon or devil; have bats in the belfry, have rats in the upper story, have a loose screw, have a tile or slate loose, have wheels in the head, have a hole in one's wig, have space to let, have a button missing, not have all one's buttons or marbles, have bubbles in the think tank [all slang]; have water topside [pidgin Eng.]; **wander, ramble; rave, rage,** rant, fume; dote, babble; drivel, drool, slaver; froth at the mouth.

20. **go mad, go crazy, take leave of one's senses,** lose one's senses or reason, **lose one's head,** crack up, go off one's head [coll.]; go off one's nut or chump, go off one's base or rocker, go off the track or trolley, blow one's top, lose one's taffy [all slang]; **run amuck, go berserk.**

21. **affect one's mind,** turn one's head, **go to one's head,** addle the wits.

22. **madden, dement, craze,** loco [coll., U.S.], **unbalance,** unhinge, **derange,** distract, frenzy, shatter, **drive insane,** ∼ mad or crazy, put out of one's mind; possess, pixilate [dial.].

23. ɔbsess, possess, beset, infatuate, preoccupy, be uppermost in one's thoughts; drive, compel, impel; grip, hold, get a hold on, not let go.

ADJS. 24. **insane,** unsane, **mad,** maddened, **crazy,** crazed, loco or locoed [coll., U.S.], **lunatic,** moon-struck, **daft,** queer, **non compos mentis** [law], non compos, unsound, manic, **demented, deranged,** disoriented, unhinged, **unbalanced,** unsettled, **distraught, cracked** [coll.], crackbrained, shatterbrained, shatterpated, madbrained, brainsick, not right, not right in one's head [coll.], not in one's right mind [coll.], **touched,** teched or tetched [dial.], touched in the head, off, off one's head [coll.], **out of one's mind,** out of one's head [coll.], out of one's senses or wits, **bereft** [coll.], bereft of reason, reasonless, senseless, witless, **not all there** [coll.]; mentally deficient 468.22.

25. (slang terms) **daffy, dotty, dippy,**

loony or **luny, goofy, wacky,** whacky, **balmy,** balmy in the crumpet, **potty, batty,** bats, nuts, **nutty, screwy,** screwball, screwballs, crackers [Eng.], loopy, beany, **buggy, bughouse,** bugs, **cuckoo,** slaphappy, ga-ga, haywire, off one's nut or chump, off in the upper story, off one's base or rocker, off the track or trolley, off the hinges, minus some buttons, nobody home, with bats in the belfry, just plain nuts.

26. **psychotic, psychopathic,** mental; **neurotic** 688.48; schizophrenic, schizoid, schizothymic; cyclothymic, cycloid; paranoiac, paranoid; catatonic, idiopathic, neuropsychopathic, lycanthropic, manic-depressive, kleptomaniac, hypochondriac.

27. **possessed,** all-possessed [coll., U.S.], possessed with a demon or devil, **pixilated** [dial.], bedeviled, demonized, devil-ridden.

28. **mad as a hatter,** mad as a March hare, mad as a weaver, "mad as Ajax" [Chapman], crazier than a bedbug, ∼ coot or loon, nutty as a fruitcake [slang]; **stark-mad, stark-staring mad.**

29. **rabid, maniac(al),** raving mad; **frenzied, frantic,** frenetic(al), phrenetic(al), **mad,** madding, **wild, furious, violent,** desperate; **distraught, distracted,** beside oneself; raving, raging, ranting; frothing at the mouth; **amuck, amok, berserk.**

30. **delirious,** phrenetic(al), **out of one's mind,** out of one's head [coll.], off one's head [coll.], **off; giddy, dizzy, lightheaded; wandering, rambling, raving, ranting,** babbling, doting, incoherent, flighty.

31. **fanatic(al),** phrenetic(al), **rabid; overzealous,** ultrazealous, **overenthusiastic,** zealotic(al); **extreme,** excessive, extravagant, inordinate, ultra; **unreasonable, irrational,** inconsistent; **wild-eyed,** wild-looking, haggard; overreligious 1026.11.

32. **obsessed, possessed,** prepossessed, **infatuated,** preoccupied, besotted, gripped, held; fixated [psychol.]; monomaniac(al).

33. **obsessive,** obsessional; **obsessing, possessing,** besetting, **preoccupying;** gripping, holding; driving, impelling; **compulsive,** compelling.

ADVS. 34. **madly, insanely, crazily;** deliriously; fanatically.

473. ECCENTRICITY

NOUNS 1. **eccentricity, idiosyncrasy,** idiocrasy, **erraticism,** erraticness, **queerness, oddity, peculiarity,** strangeness, freakishness, crochetiness, crankiness; abnormality, unnaturalness, irregularity, deviation, divergence, aberration; nonconformity, unconventionality 83.2, 3.

2. **quirk, twist,** kink, kink in one's horn [slang, U.S.], crank, quip, **crotchet,** conceit, maggot, maggot in the brain, bee in the bonnet or head [coll.].

3. **eccentric, erratic;** freak, character, **crank** [all coll.]; **crackpot, nut, screwball** [all slang]; queer potato 85.4; nonconformist 83.4.

ADJS. 4. **eccentric, erratic,** idiocratic(al), idiosyncratic(al), **queer,** queer in the head [coll.], **odd, peculiar,** strange, freakish, funny [coll.]; unnatural, abnormal, irregular, divergent, deviative; unconventional 83.8; **crotchety,** maggoty, buggy [slang], cranky, kinky [U.S.], twisted; **screwy, screwball, nutty, wacky,** whacky [all slang].

474. KNOWLEDGE

NOUNS 1. **knowledge,** knowing, know [coll.], ken, **acquaintance, familiarity,** privity; **information, intelligence;** practical knowledge, **experience, know-how;** self-knowledge.

2. **cognizance,** cognition; **recognition, realization; perception,** apperception; **consciousness, awareness,** mindfulness, sensibility; appreciation, appreciativeness.

3. **understanding, comprehension, apprehension,** conception; savvy, sabe [both slang, U.S.]; **grasp,** mental grasp, grip.

4. **learning,** lore, **enlightenment, education, instruction, edification;** acquirements, acquisitions, attainments, accomplishments; store of knowledge; liberal education; acquisition of knowledge 562.

5. **scholarship, erudition,** eruditeness, **learnedness,** reading, letters; **intellectuality,** intellectualism; **literacy; culture,** *Kultur* [G.]; book learning, booklore, bibliology; **bookishness,** bookiness; **pedantry,** pedantism, bluestockingism; bibliomania, book madness, biblioatry, bibliophilism; classicism, classical scholarship.

6. **profound knowledge,** deep knowledge, wide ~, vast or extensive knowledge; encyclopedic knowledge, pansophy; **omniscience,** all-knowingness.

7. slight knowledge 476.6.

8. tree of knowledge, tree of knowledge of good and evil; forbidden fruit.

9. **lore,** body of knowledge, store of knowledge, treasury of information; encyclopedia, circle of knowledge.

10. **science,** ology [chiefly joc.], **art,** study, branch of study, branch or department of knowledge; **technics, technology,** technicology; natural science, applied science, experimental science.

11. **scientist,** scientific [coll.], man of science; **technologist;** practical scientist, experimental scientist.

VERBS 12. **know,** ken [now chiefly Scot.], **perceive, apprehend, recognize, discern,** see, make out, conceive, **realize, appreciate, understand, comprehend,** fathom; savvy, sabe [both slang, U.S.]; have, possess; have knowledge of, be informed, be apprized of, have information about, be acquainted with, be conversant with, be cognizant of, be conscious or aware of.

13. **know well, know full well,** know damn well or darn well [slang], have a good or thorough knowledge of, be well-informed, **be up on** [coll.], be master of, **have down pat** [coll.], have down cold [slang, U.S.], have dead to rights [slang], have at one's fingers' ends or tips, have in one's head, **know by heart** or rote, **know like a book,** know like the back of one's hand, **know backwards, know inside out,** know down to the ground [coll.], *connaître le dessous des cartes* [F., know the undersides of the cards]; **know one's stuff, know one's onions** [both slang]; **know the ropes,** know all the ins and outs; know the score, know all the answers [both slang]; know what's what 731.18.

14. learn (acquire knowledge) 562.6; come to one's knowledge 555.14.

ADJS. 15. **knowing,** knowledgeable [coll.], gnostic [joc. or slang]; **cognizant, cognitive, conscious, aware, mindful, sensible,** intelligent; jerry, fly [both slang]; **understanding, comprehending,** comprehensive, apprehensive, apprehending, apprehensive; **perceptive,** apperceptive, percipient, appercipient [psychol.]; shrewd, sagacious, wise 466.15−17; **omniscient, all-knowing.**

16. **cognizant of, aware of, conscious of, mindful of, sensible to,** intelligent of, **appreciative of;** privy to, no stranger to; in the secret, let into, **in the know** [slang], behind the scenes or curtain; alive to, awake to; **wise to** [coll.], hep to [slang, U.S.], next to [slang, U.S.], on to [slang], up to [coll.]; apprized of, informed of; undeceived.

17. **hep,** hep to the jive, on the beam, in the groove [all slang, U.S.]; **knowing** [coll.], **wise** [slang], next [slang, U.S.].

18. **informed, enlightened, instructed,**

educated, taught; **posted,** posted up [both
coll.]; **up on,** up on one's stuff [slang]; up-
to-date *au courant* [F., in the current].

19. **versed in, informed in,** read *or* well-
read in, up in, forward in, strong in, at
home in, master of; **familiar with, conversant** with, **acquainted with,** *au fait* [F.].

20. **well-informed,** well-posted [coll.],
well-conned, well-educated, **well-grounded,
well-versed,** deep-versed; **well-read,** deep-
read, widely read.

21. **learned, erudite, educated,** cultured, lettered, literate; **scholarly,** scholastic, studious; wise 466.17; **profound,** deep,
abstruse.

22. **literary, book-learned,** book-read,
book-taught, book-fed, book-wise; **bookish,**
booky book-minded; book-loving, bibliophilic, bibliophagic; **pedantic,** inkhorn;
bluestocking, blue [coll.].

23. **intellectual,** intellectualistic; **highbrow,** highbrowed, highbrowish [all slang].

24. **self-educated,** self-taught, **self-made,**
autodidactic.

25. **knowable,** cognizable, recognizable,
understandable, comprehensible, discernible, perceptible, distinguishable, ascertainable, discoverable.

26. **known, recognized,** ascertained, received, perceived, discerned, **understood,**
comprehended, realized, appreciated; **pat,
down pat** [both coll.].

27. **well-known,** well-kenned, well-un-
derstood, well-recognized; **widely known,**
universally recognized, general, prevalent,
universal; **familiar,** familiar as household
words, household, **common, commonplace, popular, current, proverbial,** commonly known, known by every schoolboy;
talked-of, talked-about, in everyone's
mouth, on everyone's tongue.

28. **scientific; technical, technological,**
technicological; encyclopedic, pan-
sophic(al), pantologic(al).

ADVS. 29. **knowingly, consciously, wittingly,** understandingly, intelligently, studiously; as every schoolboy knows.

30. **to one's knowledge, to the best of
one's knowledge,** as far as one can see *or*
tell, as far as one knows, as well as can be
said.

475. INTELLECTUAL

NOUNS 1. **intellectual,** intellectualist,
Brahmin, egghead [slang]; **highbrow**
[coll.], "a person educated beyond his intelligence" [Brander Matthews].

2. **intelligentsia,** literati, illuminati.

3. **scholar,** scholastic, a gentleman and
a scholar; student 564; **learned man,** man
of learning, **savant,** pundit [India], illuminate; **literate;** literary man, littérateur *or*
litterateur, **man of letters;** bookman,
bibliosoph, biblionost; academician, schoolman; classicist, classicalist, Latinist.

4. **giant of learning,** colossus of knowledge; **mine of information,** encyclopedia,
walking encyclopedia; sage 467; genius
731.12.

5. **bookworm,** bookmonger, bibliophage;
grind, greasy grind, dig [all college slang,
U.S.]; **booklover,** bibliophile, bibliophilist;
bibliolater, bibliolatrist; bibliomaniac, bibliomane.

6. **pedant,** pedantess; **pedagogue; formalist, precisionist,** precisian; **bluestocking**
[coll.], blue [coll.], *bas bleu* [F.]; Gamaliel,
Dr. Pangloss.

7. **dilettante, half scholar,** sciolist, **dabbler,** trifler, smatterer.

476. IGNORANCE

NOUNS 1. **ignorance,** ignorantness, **unknowingness,** know-nothingness, nescience, empty-headedness; **unintelligence** 468;
unacquaintance, unfamiliarity; greenness,
greenhornism, verdancy, rawness, unripeness, green in the eye; **inexperience** 732.2;
simpleness, simplicity; crass ignorance,
"Oh, more than Gothic ignorance!"
[Fielding]; ignorantism, obscurantism.

2. "blind and naked Ignorance" [Ten-
nyson], "the mother of impudence" [C. H.
Spurgeon], "the mother of prejudice"
[John Bright], "the dominion of absurdity"
[J. A. Froude].

3. **incognizance, unawareness, unconsciousness, insensibility, unknowingness,
unmindfulness,** mindlessness, unwitting-
ness, blindness, deafness.

4. **unenlightenment, benightedness,** be-
nightment, dark, darkness.

5. **unlearnedness, inerudition,** ineducation, **unscholarliness,** unstudiousness, un-
letteredness; **illiteracy,** illiterateness; **unintellectuality,** unintellectualism.

6. **slight knowledge,** vague notion;
smattering, **smattering of knowledge,**
smattering of ignorance [joc.]; **half-learning,** sciolism; superficiality, shallowness;
dilettantism, dilettantship; Philistinism;
empiricism.

7. **the unknown,** the unknowable; **matter of ignorance,** sealed book; *terra in-*

cognita [L.], unexplored ground, virgin soil, Dark Continent; **unknown quantity**, x, y, z; dark horse.

8. Dark Ages, Middle Age *or* Ages; **medievalism**, Middle-Ageism; barbarism, Gothicism.

9. ignoramus, ignorant, ignatz [slang, U.S.], **know-nothing, greenhorn**, greeny [coll.], greener [slang], **lowbrow** [slang], no scholar; dunce, fool 470; illiterate; unintelligentsia, illiterati [joc.].

VERBS **10. be ignorant**, be green, have green in the eye; **know nothing**, know from nothing [slang, U.S.]; not know any better; **not know what's what**, not know what it is all about, not know the score [slang], not know any of the answers, not know the time of day *or* what o'clock it is, not know beans, **not know beans when the bag is open**, not know chalk from cheese, not know B from a bull's foot, ~ a battledore *or* a broomstick, **not know up from down**, not know which way is up, not know straight up.

11. be in the dark, be blind to, walk in darkness, grope in the dark, "see through a glass, darkly" [Bible].

12. not know, not rightly know [dial.], know not, know not what, know nothing of, have no idea, ~ notion *or* conception, **not have the first idea, not have the least** *or* **remotest idea**, not have the foggiest [slang], **not pretend to say**, not take upon oneself to say; not know the half of it; not know from Adam *or* Adam's off ox, not know from the man in the moon; wonder, wonder whether; pass [coll.], give up.

ADJS. **13. ignorant**, nescient, **unknowing**, uncomprehending, unhep [slang, U.S.], **know-nothing**, simple, **dumb** [coll., U.S.], empty, empty-headed; **unintelligent** 468.13; **uninformed, unenlightened**, unapprized, unposted [coll.]; **unacquainted, unconversant**, unversed, uninitiated, **unfamiliar**, a stranger to; **inexperienced** 732.17; **green**, green as grass *or* a gourd, verdant [coll.], unripe, raw.

14. unaware, unconscious, insensible, unknowing, incognizant, incognitive, uncognitive, **unmindful**, mindless, witless, unwitting, unsuspecting; unaware of, unconscious of, unmindful of, insensible to; **blind to, deaf to**, dead to; asleep, napping, **off one's guard**, caught napping, caught tripping.

15. unlearned, inerudite, unerudite, **uneducated**, unschooled, uninstructed, untutored, untaught, unedified, unguided; **illiterate**, unlettered, grammarless, unread; **unscholarly**, unscholastic, unstudious; **unliterary**, unbookish, unbooklearned, bookless, unbooked; **uncultured**, uncultivated, unrefined, rude, Philistine; **unintellectual; lowbrow**, lowbrowed, lowbrowish [all coll.].

16. half-learned, half-baked [coll.], sciolistic; shallow, superficial; immature, sophomoric(al); **dilettante**, dilettantish; empiric(al); **wise in one's own conceit**.

17. benighted, dark, in darkness, in the dark.

18. unknown, unbeknown [coll.], unheard, **unheard-of**, unapprehended, unapparent, unperceived, unsuspected, unexplained, unascertained, uninvestigated, unexplored, undisclosed, unrevealed, undivulged, undiscovered, unexposed, sealed.

ADVS. **19. ignorantly, unknowingly**, unconsciously, insensibly, unmindfully, unwittingly, witlessly, unsuspectingly, **unawares**; for anything *or* aught one knows, not that one knows.

INTERJS. **20. God knows!**, God only knows!, the Lord knows!, Heaven knows!, dear knows! [dial.], land knows! [coll.], nobody knows!, damned if I know! [vulg.], **it beats me!**, it has me guessing!, it's Greek to me!; **search me!**, you've got me!, ask me another! [all slang]; I give up!, I pass! [coll.]; **who knows?**, how should I know?; *je ne sais pas!* [F.], I don't know what!

477. THOUGHT

Exercise of the Intellect.—NOUNS **1. thought, thinking, cogitation**, cerebration, mentation, intellection, intellectualization, ratiocination; **reasoning** 481; **brainwork, headwork**, mental labor, workings of the mind; heavy thinking, tall headwork [slang]; straight thinking; idea 478.

2. consideration, contemplation, reflection, speculation, **meditation, musing, rumination, deliberation**, lucubration, study, pondering, weighing, revolving; advisement, counsel.

3. thoughtfulness, contemplativeness, reflectiveness; **pensiveness**, wistfulness, melancholy; **preoccupation, absorption, engrossment**, deep *or* profound thought; **concentration**, application.

4. thoughts, inmost thoughts, secret thoughts; **train of thought**, current *or* flow of thought *or* ideas, **stream of consciousness; association, association of ideas.

5. **mature thought**, ripe idea; **afterthought**, *arrière-pensée* [F.], second thought *or* thoughts; **reconsideration**, re-examination, review.

6. **self-communion**, self-counsel, self-consultation.

VERBS 7. **think, cogitate**, cerebrate, intellectualize; **reason** 481.15; **use one's head**, exercise the mind, set the brain *or* wits to work, bethink oneself, **put on one's thinking** *or* **considering cap** [coll.].

8. **think hard**, think one's head off [joc.], **rack** *or* **ransack the brains**, crack the brains [coll.], **beat** *or* **cudgel the brains**, work one's head to the bone [joc.], sweat over [coll.], stew over [slang], hammer *or* hammer away at, hammer out, do some heavy thinking, do some tall headwork [slang]; puzzle, **puzzle over**.

9. **concentrate**, concentrate the mind *or* thoughts, concentrate on *or* upon, **focus on** *or* **upon**, give the mind to, fix the thoughts upon, bring the mind to bear upon.

10. **think about, give** *or* **apply the mind to**, put one's mind to, apply oneself to, bend *or* turn the mind *or* thoughts to, direct the mind upon, **give thought to, trouble one's head about**, occupy the mind *or* thoughts with; think through, reason out.

11. **consider, contemplate, speculate, reflect, study, ponder, weigh, deliberate, debate, meditate, muse, brood, ruminate**, chew the cud [coll.], digest; **toy with**, play with, play around with, flirt *or* coquet with the idea.

12. **think over, ponder over, brood over, muse over**, mouse over [U.S.], **mull over** [coll., U.S.], **reflect over**, con over, **deliberate over**, run over, **meditate over, ruminate over**, chew over, turn over, **revolve**, revolve in the mind, turn over in the mind, put it through the meat grinder; **deliberate upon, meditate upon, muse on** *or* **upon**, bestow thought *or* consideration upon.

13. **take under consideration**, take counsel, take under advisement, take under active consideration, **think it over**, see about [coll.]; **sleep upon**, consult ~, advise with *or* take counsel of one's pillow.

14. **reconsider, re-examine**, review; revise one's thoughts, view in a new light, think better of.

15. **think of**, bethink oneself of, **entertain the idea**, entertain thoughts of; have

an idea of, have thoughts about; **have in mind, contemplate, consider, meditate**, take it into one's head; **bear in mind, keep in mind**, hold the thought; harbor an idea, keep *or* hold an idea, cherish ~, foster ~, nurse *or* nurture an idea.

16. (look upon mentally) **contemplate, look upon, view, regard**, see, view with the mind's eye, **envisage**, envision, feature [slang].

17. **occur to**, occur to one's mind, occur, **come to mind**, come into one's head, pass through one's head *or* mind, **enter one's mind**, pass in the mind *or* the thoughts, **cross one's mind**, flash on *or* across the mind; **strike**, hit, strike one, strike the mind; **suggest itself**, present itself, offer, present itself to the mind *or* thoughts.

18. **impress, make an impression, strike**, hit; catch the thoughts, arrest the thoughts, sink *or* penetrate into the mind, **sink in** [coll.].

19. **occupy the mind** *or* **thoughts**, engage the thoughts, monopolize the thoughts, fasten itself on the mind, take up one's thoughts; **preoccupy**, occupy, **absorb, engross**, absorb ~, enwrap *or* engross the thoughts; have in *or* on one's mind, **have on the brain** [coll.], have constantly in one's thoughts, run in the head; come uppermost, be uppermost in the mind.

ADJS. 20. **thoughtful**, cogitative, **contemplative, reflective, speculative, deliberative, meditative, ruminative**, ruminant, museful; **pensive**, wistful; thinking, reflecting, contemplating, pondering, deliberating, meditating, ruminating, musing; sober, serious, deep-thinking.

21. **absorbed, engrossed**, absorbed *or* engrossed in thought, rapt, **wrapped in thought, lost in thought**, immersed in thought, buried in thought, engaged in thought, occupied, **preoccupied**.

ADVS. 22. **thoughtfully**, contemplatively, reflectively, meditatively, ruminatively, musefully; **pensively**, wistfully.

PREPS. 23. **on one's mind, on the brain** [coll.], on one's chest [slang], in one's craw [slang], in the thoughts; in the heart, *in petto* [It.], in one's inmost thoughts.

INTERJS. 24. **think that over!**, put that in your pipe and smoke it! [slang].

478. IDEA

NOUNS 1. **idea**, idee [dial.], *Idee* [G.], **thought**, think [slang], **notion, fancy, concept, conception**, conceit, **percept**, perception, **impression**, mental impression; image; **mental image**, representation, eidolon, recept [psychol.]; **sentiment**, apprehension, reflection, observation, consideration; **opinion** 500.4; supposition, theory 478.

2. (philosophy) ideatum, ideate; noumenon; universal, universal concept *or* conception; idée-force.

3. (Platonic ideas) archetype, prototype, pattern, model, exemplar, ideal, form; transcendent idea *or* essence, universal essence, transcendent universal.

4. (Hegelian idea) the Absolute, the Absolute Idea, the Self-existent, the Self-determined, the realized ideal.

5. (Kantian idea) supreme principle of pure reason, regulative first principle, highest unitary principle of thought, transcendent nonimpirical concept.

6. **abstract idea, abstraction,** abstract, eternal object.

7. **main idea,** where the hen scratches [slang, U.S.], **big idea** [chiefly coll.].

8. **novel idea,** new *or* **latest wrinkle** [slang], new slant [coll.], new twist [slang].

9. **good idea,** not a bad idea; **bright thought,** bright *or* brilliant idea, **brain storm** [coll.], **inspiration.**

10. **absurd idea,** crazy idea, fool notion [coll.].

ADJS. 11. ideal, ideational, **conceptual, notional,** fanciful.

12. **ideaed, notioned,** thoughted.

479. ABSENCE OF THOUGHT

NOUNS 1. **thoughtlessness,** thoughtfreeness; vacuity, vacancy, **emptiness of mind, empty-headedness;** fatuity, inanity.

VERBS 2. **not think, make the mind a blank,** let the mind lie fallow; **not think of,** not consider, **not enter one's mind** *or* **head,** be far from one's thoughts.

3. **get it off one's mind, get it off one's chest** [slang], relieve one's mind; **put it out of one's thoughts,** dismiss from the mind *or* thoughts, push from one's thoughts, put away thought.

ADJS. 4. **thoughtless, thought-free,** incogitant, **unideaed, unthinking,** unreasoning; **vacuous,** vacant, blank, empty, **emptyheaded,** unoccupied; fatuous, inane.

5. **unthought-of, undreamt-of,** unconsidered.

480. INTUITION

NOUNS 1. **intuition, intuitiveness,** intuitivism; **second sight,** second-sightedness,

insight, inspiration; intuitive reason *or* knowledge, subconscious perception; anticipation, a priori knowledge; "a laconic apprehension of things seen and unseen" [P. K. Thomajan], "reason in a hurry" [Holbrook Jackson], "the strange instinct that tells a woman she is right whether she is or not" [anon.]; woman's intuition.

2. **instinct, sixth sense,** natural instinct, innate *or* inborn proclivity, native *or* natural tendency, blind *or* unreasoning impulse, vital impulse; **libido, id,** primitive self [all psychol.]; "the *not ourselves,* which is in us and all around us" [Matthew Arnold], "an unfathomable Somewhat, which is *Not we*" [Carlyle], "that which is imprinted upon the spirit of man by an inward instinct" [Bacon], "intelligence incapable of self-consciousness" [John Sterling], "untaught ability" [Bain].

3. **hunch** [coll., U.S.], **presentiment, premonition** [coll.], preapprehension, intimation, suspicion, **impression,** intuitive impression, **feeling,** forefeeling, vague feeling, funny feeling [slang].

VERBS 4. **sense, feel,** feel intuitively, **feel it in one's bones** [coll.], **have a feeling,** have a funny feeling [slang], **get** *or* **have the impression, have a hunch** [coll., U.S.], just know; a little bird told me, my little finger tells me.

ADJS. 5. **intuitive,** intuitional, **secondsighted,** sensing, feeling.

6. **instinctive,** natural, **inherent, innate,** inspirational, libidinal [psychol.]; **involuntary, automatic,** spontaneous, impulsive.

ADVS. 7. **intuitively,** by intuition; **instinctively,** automatically, spontaneously, on *or* by instinct.

481. REASONING

NOUNS 1. **reasoning, rationalizing, rationalization,** ratiocination; **rationalism, rationality;** specious reasoning 482; philosophy 499.

2. **logic,** logics; **dialectics,** dialectic, dialecticism; doctrine of terms, doctrine of the judgment, doctrine of inference; traditional *or* Aristotelian logic, modern *or* epistemological logic, pragmatic $\sim$, instrumental *or* experimental logic; psychological logic, psychologism; symbolic *or* mathematical logic, logistic.

3. (methods) a fortiori reasoning, a priori reasoning, a posteriori reasoning; discourse, discursive reasoning; **deduction, deductive reasoning,** syllogism; **induction,**

inductive reasoning, epagoge; philosophical induction, inductive *or* Baconian method; inference, inferentialism; generalization, particularization; synthesis, analysis; hypothesis and verification.

4. discussion, debate, debating, **deliberation,** agitation, canvassing, ventilation, review, **treatment, consideration,** investigation. **examination, study,** analysis; logical discussion, dialectic; buzz session [slang, U.S.]; panel discussion, open discussion, joint discussion; forum, open forum.

5. argumentation, argification [dial.], **argument,** argy-bargy [chiefly Scot. & dial., Eng.]; **controversy, dispute, disputation,** polemics, disceptation, litigation, pilpul, **contention, wrangling, bickering,** bicker, set-to [coll.], rhubarb [slang], hassel [slang], bowwow, passage of arms; war of words, verbal engagement *or* contest, passage of words, logomachy; paper war, *guerre de plume* [F.]; dingdong argument [coll.].

6. argument, *argumentum* [L., logic]; **case,** plea, *plaidoyer* [F.]; **reason,** consideration; pros, cons, **pros and cons.**

7. syllogism; prosyllogism; mode; figure; pseudosyllogism, paralogism; sorites, progressive *or* Aristotelian sorites, regressive *or* Goclenian sorites; enthymeme; dilemma, horns of a dilemma.

8. premise *or* premiss, prosyllogism, **proposition, position,** assumed position, sumption, **assumption,** supposal, presupposition, **hypothesis, thesis, theorem,** term, lemma **statement,** affirmation, assertion, basis, ground, foundation; **postulate,** postulation, postulatum; data; major premise, minor premise; a priori principle, apriorism; philosophical proposition, philosopheme; hypothesis ad hoc.

9. conclusion 493.4.

10. reasonableness, reasonability, **logicalness,** logicality, **rationality, sensibleness, soundness,** justness, justifiability, admissibility; **sense,** common sense, sound sense, **logic, reason;** plausibility 510.2.

11. good reasoning, right thinking, sound reasoning; cogent argument, cogency; strong argument, knockdown argument; good case, good reason, strong point.

12 reasoner, ratiocinator, **thinker;** rationalist, rationalizer; **logician,** logistician, logicalist, logicaster [derog.]; dialectic, dialectician; syllogist, syllogizer; sophist 482.6; philosopher 499.7.

13. controversialist, disputant, debater, **arguer,** argufier [coll.], wrangler, mooter, disceptator, pilpulist, eristic; polemic, polemist, polemicist; logomacher, logomachist; parliamentarian.

14. side, interest; **the affirmative,** pro, aye; **the negative,** con, no, nay.

VERBS **15. reason, rationalize,** logicalize, intellectualize; try conclusions; **theorize,** hypothesize; philosophize; syllogize; generalize, particularize.

16. discuss, debate, reason, deliberate, deliberate upon, talk, **talk over,** talk of *or* about, comment upon, reason about, discourse about, chew the rag [slang], **consider, treat,** handle, deal with, take up, **go into, examine,** investigate, analyze, sift, **study,** canvass, review, pass under review, controvert, ventilate, thresh out, reason the point, consider pro and con; **kick around,** knock around [both slang]; agitate, agitate *or* torture a question; think out loud [coll.].

17. argue, argy [dial.], argufy [coll. & dial.], argify [dial.], **dispute,** discept, moot, **bandy words, chop logic, plead,** join issue, **contend, contest,** spar [coll.], **bicker, wrangle,** hassle [slang], have it out; take one's stand upon, **put up an argument** [coll.]; take sides, take up a side; pettifog [coll.]; whistle down the wind [coll.], argue to no purpose.

18. be reasonable, be logical, make sense, stand to reason; hold good, hold water [coll.]; have a leg to stand on.

ADJS. **19. reasoning, rational,** ratiocinative; analytic(al).

20. argumentative, argumental, controversial, disputatious, contentious, eristic(al), polemic(al), logomachic(al), pilpulistic, dialectic(al); pro and con.

21. logical, reasonable, rational, sensible, sane, sound, legitimate, just, justifiable, admissible; credible 500.21; plausible 510.6; as it should be, as it ought to be; **well-founded, well-grounded.**

22. dialectic(al), syllogistic(al), soritical, epagogic, inductive, deductive, synthetic(al), enthymematic(al), categorical, hypothetical, conditional, discursive; a priori, a posteriori, a fortiori.

ADVS. **23. reasonably, logically, rationally, sensibly,** sanely, soundly; **in reason,** in all reason, within reason, within the bounds *or* limits of reason, within reasonable limitations, **within bounds,** within the bounds of possibility, as far as possible, in all conscience.

482. SOPHISTRY

Specious Reasoning.—NOUNS 1. **sophistry**, sophistication, sophism; philosophism, philosophastry, philosophastering; **casuistry**, Jesuitry, Jesuitism; paralogy, paralogism; **false** or **specious reasoning**, vicious reasoning, special pleading; **fallacy**, fallaciousness, **speciousness**, plausibleness, plausibility; ambiguity, ambiguousness; perversion, distortion, misapplication; vicious circle.

2. **illogicalness**, illogicality, **unreasonableness**, **irrationality**, **reasonlessness**, **senselessness**, **unsoundness**, unscientificness, invalidity, untenableness, inconclusiveness; **inconsistency**, incongruity, antilogy.

3. (specious argument) **sophism**, sophistry, philosophism, solecism, elench; paralogism, pseudosyllogism; claptrap, moonshine, empty words; bad case, weak point, flaw in an argument, "lame and impotent conclusion" [Shakespeare].

4. **quibble**, quiblet [U.S.], quiddity, *quodilibet* [L.], jesuitism, **cavil**, **bicker**, quip, quirk, boggle, shift, shuffle, dodge, **side step.**

5. **quibbling**, **caviling**, **bickering**, **equivocation**, tergiversation, prevarication, **hairsplitting**, subterfuge, **evasion**, **hedging**, **pussyfooting** [coll.], **side-stepping**, dodging, shifting, shuffling, fencing, parrying, boggling, paltering, begging of the question, "terminological inexactitude" [W. Churchill].

6. **sophist**, sophister; philosophist, philosoph or philosophe, philosophaster, philosophling; **casuist**, Jesuit; paralogist, paralogician.

7. **quibbler**, **caviler**, **equivocator**, prevaricator, palterer, shuffler, **hedger**; pussyfoot, **pussyfooter** [both coll.].

VERBS 8. **sophisticate**, paralogize, **reason ill**, reason in a circle; pervert, distort, misapply; prove that black is white and white black, put oneself out of court, travel out of the record, not have a leg to stand on.

9. **quibble**, **cavil**, **equivocate**, prevaricate, tergiversate, **bicker**, palter, boggle, fence, parry, shift, **shuffle**, **dodge**, shy, **evade**, **side-step**, **hedge**, **pussyfoot** [coll.], evade an issue; **beat about the bush**, beat the devil around the bush or stump; **beg the question**, *répondre en Normand* [F., reply in Norman]; **split hairs**; blow hot and cold; strain at a gnat and swallow a camel.

ADJS. 10. **illogical**, **unreasonable**, **irrational**, **reasonless**, **senseless**, without reason, **without rhyme or reason**, *sin ton ni son* [Span.]; **unscientific**, nonscientific, unphilosophical; **invalid**, unauthentic, faulty; inconclusive, inconsequent, inconsequential, not following; **inconsistent**, incongruous, absonant, loose, unconnected; **self-contradictory**, self-annulling.

11. **unsound**, **unsubstantial**, insubstantial, weak, feeble, poor, flimsy.

12. **baseless**, **groundless**, ungrounded, **unfounded**, ill-founded, unbased, **unsupported**, unsustained, **without foundation**, without basis or sound basis; **untenable**, **unsupportable**, unsustainable; **unwarranted**, idle, empty, vain.

13. **fallacious**, **fallible**, **specious**, **plausible**, hollow.

14. **sophistic(al)**, **philosophistic(al)**, casuistic(al), jesuitic(al), paralogical.

15. **quibbling**, **caviling**, **equivocatory**, captious, bickering, paltering, shuffling, hedging, pussyfooting [coll.], **evasive**; **hairsplitting**.

ADVS. 16. **illogically**, **unreasonably**, **irrationally**, **reasonlessly**, **senselessly**; baselessly, groundlessly; untenably, unsupportably, unsustainably; out of all reason, out of all bounds.

483. TOPIC

NOUNS 1. **topic**, **subject**, subject of thought, **subject matter**, what it is about, **theme**, **text**, motif, motive, consideration, business, affair, matter, matter in hand, **question**, **problem**, **issue**; **point**, point at issue, point in question, talking point; item on the agenda; head, heading, chapter; **thesis**, **proposition**, statement, theorem; food for thought, mental or intellectual pabulum; substance, meat; something to chew on, something to get one's teeth in; living issue, topic of the day.

2. **title**, **caption**, **heading**, **head**, superscription, rubric; **headline**, overline; banner, banner head or line, streamer; **scarehead** [U.S.], screamer [U.S.]; spread, spreadhead; drophead, hanger; masthead, flag [U.S.]; running head or title, jump head; **subhead**, **subheading**, **subtitle**; legend, motto, epigraph; letterpress; letterhead, billhead; imprint, title page.

VERBS 3. **title**, **caption**, **head**, head up [coll.]; **headline**; subtitle, subhead.

ADJS. 4. **topical, thematic**(al), **textual,**
subjective, nominal [gram.].
5. **local,** limited, restricted, particular.
6. **current, of current interest,** up-to-date, living, lively, alive.

484. INQUIRY

NOUNS 1. **inquiry,** enquiry, inquiring, inquiration [dial.], inquirendo, inquest, inquisition; inquiring mind.
2. **search,** searching, **quest, hunt,** hunting, hue and cry, looksee [slang, U.S.]; frisk, frisking, fan, fanning [all underworld slang, U.S.]; **rummage, ransacking; forage;** still hunt [U.S.]; perquisition, domiciliary visit [law]; lantern of Diogenes.
3. **examination,** examen, **exam** [coll.], ex [slang], **test, trial, quiz** [U.S.], go [Eng. Univ. cant]; oral examination, oral, **audition** [coll.], **hearing;** written examination, written [coll.]; midterms [U.S.], midyears [U.S.]; previous examination, little go [Cambridge Univ.], responsions, smalls [both Oxford Univ.]; first public examination, moderations or mods [Oxford Univ.]; final examination, final or **finals** [coll.], greats or great go [Oxford Univ.]; honors [Eng.], tripos [Cambridge Univ.].
4. **inspection, scrutiny, survey, review, perusal,** perlustration, **study, contemplation,** look-through, run-through, overhaul, overhauling.
5. **investigation,** indagation, **research, probe** [U.S.], inquiry into; searching investigation, close inquiry, exhaustive study; perquisition, perscrutation.
6. **exploration,** explore [coll.], **probe,** exploratory examination.
7. **check, checkup** [U.S.]; spot check; physical examination, **physical,** physical checkup [U.S.].
8. **analysis,** analyzation; **assay,** assaying; **diagnosis; breakdown,** breakup; **dissection,** anatomy; resolution, titration [chem. & physiol.], docimasy; **sifting,** winnowing; qualitative analysis, quantitative analysis, volumetric analysis, gravimetric analysis; ultimate analysis, proximate analysis.
9. **autopsy, post-mortem,** post-mortem examination, ex post facto examination; necropsy, necroscopy [both med.].
10. **re-examination,** reinquiry, **recheck, review,** revision, rebeholding.
11. **pre-examination,** presurvey, **preview,** presearch.
12. **reconnaissance,** reconnoissance;

recce, recco, recon [all mil. slang]; **reconnoitering,** reconnoiter, exploitation, scouting; **spying, espionage,** espial; counter-espionage.
13. **question, query, inquiry,** enquiry, **interrogation,** interrogatory; **demand;** interrogative [gram.]; **problem, issue,** contention, case or point in question, question or point at issue, **moot point** or case, question mark, *quodlibet* [L.]; vexed question, burning question, sixty-four dollar question; feeler, leading question; rhetorical question; catch question; catechism.
14. **questioning, interrogation, querying,** inquiring, **quiz** [U.S.], quizzing, **examination;** challenge, dispute; interpellation, bringing into question; catechizing, catechization; catechetical method, Socratic method or induction.
15. **grilling,** the grill [slang], roasting [coll.], sweating [slang]; **cross-examination,** cross-interrogation, **cross-questioning,** *question extraordinaire* [F.]; **third degree** [coll., U.S.].
16. **canvass** [U.S.], **survey, inquiry,** still hunt [coll., U.S. politics]; **questionnaire,** questionary; **poll, public-opinion poll;** Gallup poll, American Institute of Public Opinion.
17. **inquirer,** enquirer, **querier,** querist, **questioner,** questionist, **interrogator,** interrogatrix [*fem.*], **quizzer,** quiz, catechist; inquisitor, inquisitionist; **cross-questioner,** cross-interrogator, **cross-examiner;** interlocuter; **pollster,** poller.
18. **seeker, hunter, searcher,** perquisitor, zetetic; **researcher,** researchist, research worker.
19. **examiner,** examinant; **inspector,** inlooker, scrutinizer, perscrutator; **investigator,** indagator; **analyzer,** analyst.
20. **examinee,** questionee, quizzee.
VERBS 21. **inquire,** enquire, **ask, question, query; make inquiry,** take up ∼, institute ∼, pursue ∼, follow up ∼, conduct or carry on an inquiry, bring in question, ask about, ask questions, put queries; ask a question, put a question to, pose ∼, propose or propound a question, pop the question [coll.]; **demand, want to know;** inquisition, make inquisition.
22. **interrogate, question,** questionmark, **query, quiz** [U.S.], buzz [underworld slang, U.S.], **test, examine;** inquire of, put to the question, require an answer; catechize; **pump,** pump for information, worm out of; interpellate; interview.

23. grill, put on the grill [coll.], roast [coll.], sweat [slang], put the pressure on [coll.], put the screws to [slang, U.S.], go over [slang, U.S.]; **cross-examine, cross-question,** cross-interrogate; third-degree [slang, U.S.], put through the third degree [coll., U.S.].

24. seek, hunt, quest, pursue, go in pursuit of, follow, go in search of, prowl after, see after, try to find; **look up, hunt up; look for,** look out for, look around or about for, **search for,** seek for, **hunt for,** shop for [coll.], scout for [coll.]; **fish for,** angle for, bob for; dig for, delve for; **ask for,** inquire for; **gun for,** go gunning for; still-hunt [coll., U.S.].

25. search, hunt, look, explore; research; **hunt through, search through, look through, go through;** dig, delve, burrow, root, poke, pry; look round or around, poke around, nose around, smell around; mouse, mouse around; cast or beat about for, beat the bushes; range, forage; frisk, fan [both underworld slang, U.S.].

26. grope, grope for, **feel for, feel** or **pick one's way,** fumble, grabble, **feel around,** poke around, pry around, beat about, grope in the dark.

27. ransack, rummage, rake, scour, comb [U.S.]; rifle; **look everywhere,** look into every hole and corner, **look high and low,** look upstairs and downstairs, **look all over,** look all over hell [vulg.], turn upside down, turn inside out, **leave no stone unturned,** leave no avenue unexplored.

28. hunt out, search out, spy out, scout out [coll.], **ferret out,** fish out, pry out, dig out, root out, grub up.

29. trace, track, trail, run, **follow,** follow up, nose, nose out, **smell** or **sniff out,** follow the trail or scent of, follow one's nose; clue or clew, follow a clue or clew; **trace down, track down, run down, run to earth.**

30. investigate, indagate, **explore, look into,** peer into, **search into, go into, delve into,** dig into, poke into, pry into, dive into; **probe, sound, plumb, fathom;** go behind, go back of [coll., U.S.].

31. examine, inspect, scrutinize, survey, canvass, **look at,** peer at, **observe, scan,** peruse, **study, contemplate, consider; look over,** run the eye over, cast or pass the eyes over, go over, run over, pass over, pore over; overlook, overhaul; **review,** pass under review; **take stock of,** size or **size up** [coll.], take one's measure [slang];

check, **check over** or **through;** feel, feel of; autopsy, post-mortem.

32. analyze, make an analysis, assay, titrate [chem. & physiol.]; **dissect,** anatomize, **break down,** kick apart [slang], separate, reduce, resolve; **sift,** winnow, thrash out; parse [gram.], parse in all its moods and tenses.

33. make a close study of, examine thoroughly, **go deep into,** look closely at; examine point by point, go over step by step, view or try in all its phases; perscrutate, perlustrate, pervestigate.

34. examine cursorily, take a cursory view of, give a quick or cursory look, **scan** [coll.], **skim, skim over** or **through,** slur, slur over, slip or skip over or through, glance at, give the once-over [slang, U.S.], pass over lightly, **dip into, touch upon,** touch upon lightly or in passing, **hit the high spots** [coll.]; **thumb over,** flip through the pages, turn over the leaves.

35. re-examine, recheck, reinquire, **reconsider, review,** rebehold; retrace, retrace one's steps, go back over.

36. pre-examine, presurvey, **preview,** presearch.

37. reconnoiter, make a reconnaissance, case [underworld slang, U.S.], spy, **spy out** play the spy, peep out, scout, **scout out** [coll.], tout [slang].

38. canvass [U.S.], **survey,** make a survey; **poll, questionnaire** [coll.].

ADJS. **39. inquiring, questioning, querying, quizzical,** quizzing; **interrogatory,** interrogative, interrogational; **inquisitorial,** inquisitional; catechistic(al), catechetic(al).

40. searching, probing, prying, piercing, penetrating; in search or quest of, looking for, **out for,** on the lookout for, **in the market for,** loaded or out for bear [slang, U.S.]; all-searching.

41. examining, examinative, examinational; **inspectional,** inspectoral, inspectorial; **investigative,** indagative, investigatory; investigational; **exploratory,** explorative, explorational; analytic(al).

ADVS., *etc.* **42. in question, at issue,** in debate or dispute, **under consideration,** under active consideration, **under advisement,** *sub judice* [L.], in contemplation, under examination, *ad referendum* [L., for reference, for further consideration], up or open for discussion; **before the house, on the docket, on the agenda,** on foot, **on the table, on the floor, on the carpet,** on the tapis, *sur le tapis* [F.].

43. what?, huh?, hey?; what on earth?, what in the world?, what the hell? [slang]; what's the matter?; what's up?, what's afoot?, what's in the wind?; who?, which?

44. why?, wherefore?, why ever? *or* whyever? [coll.], why for? *or* whyfor? [dial.], for why? [dial.], *pourquoi?* [F.], *warum?* [G.], how?, **how come?** [coll.], how comes it?, how does it come to pass?, **how does it happen?, how is it?,** how so?, how ever? [coll.], on what account?, from what cause?, for what cause or reason?, what is the reason?, what is it all about?; why the deuce? *or* devil?, why the heck? *or* hell? [all coll.].

45. when?, at what time?, on what occasion?, how long ago?, how soon?, when ever? [coll.].

46. where?, whereabouts?, whence?, whither?, where away? [chiefly dial.], whereaway? [chiefly Scot.], whereto?, wheretill? [Scot.], to what *or* which place?

47. isn't it?, is it not?, ain't? [coll.], *n'est-ce pas?* [F.], *nicht wahr?* [G.], *¿verdad?* [Sp.].

48. really?, indeed?, is that so?, I wonder!, **you don't say!,** do tell! [coll., U.S.].

485. ANSWER

NOUNS **1. answer, reply, response,** respondence, replication, riposte *or* ripost, *riposte* [It.; mus.], **retort, rejoinder,** return, **comeback** [slang]; back answer, short answer; **repartee,** clever ~, ready *or* witty reply *or* retort, snappy comeback [slang]; yes-and-no answer, evasive reply; **acknowledgment,** receipt; rescript; echo, re-echo, reverberation.

2. rebuttal, counterstatement, counterreply, counterclaim, counterblast, countercharge, contraremonstrance; **rejoinder,** replication, rebutter, surrebutter, surrebuttal, surrejoinder [all law].

3. answerer, replier, responder, respondent, responser.

VERBS **4. answer,** make *or* give answer, **reply, respond,** say, **retort,** riposte *or* ripost, **rejoin,** return, return for answer, flash back; come back, come back at, come right back at [all slang]; answer back [coll.]; talk back [coll., U.S.]; **acknowledge,** make acknowledgment; **echo,** re-echo, reverberate.

5. rebut, make a rebuttal; **rejoin,** surrebut, surrejoin [all law]; **counterclaim,** countercharge.

6. answer to, respond to, react to, act in response.

ADJS. **7. answering, replying,** rejoining, returning; **responsive,** respondent, responding; antiphonal; echoing, re-echoing.

ADVS. **8. in answer,** in reply, in response, in return, in rebuttal.

486. SOLUTION

NOUNS **1. solution, resolution, answer, reason, explanation, finding,** determination, ascertainment; **outcome, denouement, result,** issue; **solving,** working, working out, finding out, resolving, clearing up, cracking; **unriddling,** unscrambling, unraveling, untangling, disentanglement; **decipherment, decoding.**

VERBS **2. solve, resolve,** find the solution *or* answer, **answer, explain, clear up,** set at rest, get, get right, do, work, **work out,** beat out, **make out, find out, figure out,** puzzle out; dope, **dope out** [both slang, U.S.]; **unriddle,** unscramble, undo, untangle, disentangle, unravel, ravel, ravel out; **decipher, decode, crack;** unlock, pick *or* open the lock; find the key of, find a clew *or* clue to; find, determine, ascertain; **get to the bottom of, fathom,** plumb, bottom; have it, hit it, hit upon a solution, hit the nail on the head, hit it on the nose [slang]; **guess,** divine, guess right.

ADJS. **3. solvable,** soluble, **resolvable,** workable, doable, answerable, explainable, determinable, ascertainable; **decipherable,** decodable.

487. DISCOVERY

NOUNS **1. discovery, finding,** determination; **detection,** catching, espial, recognition, distinguishment; **disclosure,** exposure, revelation, uncovering, unearthing; find, strike, lucky strike.

VERBS **2. discover, find, find out,** find up [dial., Eng.], get, determine; strike, hit; get ~, put *or* lay one's hands on, lay one's fingers on.

3. come across, run across; meet with, meet up with [coll.], fall in with, **encounter, run into,** bump into [coll.], come up against [coll.], run up against [coll.]; **come on** *or* **upon, hit upon,** light upon, alight upon, fall on *or* upon, fall across; **chance upon, happen upon, stumble on** *or* **upon,** stub one's toe upon, blunder upon.

4. uncover, unearth, disinter; **disclose, expose,** reveal, **bring to light; turn up,** dig up, root up; **hunt down,** trace down, track down, run down, run to earth.

5. detect, spot [coll.], **twig** [coll.], **spy, espy,** descry, notice, discern, see, **perceive, make out, recognize,** distinguish.

6. scent, sniff, smell, **get wind of;** sniff *or* smell out, nose out; smell a rat [coll.]; be on the right scent, be warm [coll.], burn [coll.].

7. catch, catch out [Eng.]; **catch up,** trip up, catch tripping; **catch napping, catch off-guard** *or* off one's guard, catch off-side, catch off base, catch asleep at the base; **catch at,** catch in the act, **catch red-handed,** catch *in flagrante delicto* [L.], **catch with one's pants down** [slang], catch flat-footed, have the goods on [slang].

8. (detect the hidden nature of) **see through, penetrate,** see down one's throat, see in its true colors, see the cloven hoof, open the eyes to; **be on to, be wise to,** be hep to, get *or* blow wise to, have one's measure, **have one's number,** be on to one's curves, have dead to rights [all slang]; be transparent.

9. turn up, show up, be found, discover itself, expose *or* betray itself, materialize, **come to light,** come to hand.

ADJS. **10.** on the right scent, **on the right track,** on the trail of; **hot, warm** [both coll.].

INTERJS. **11. eureka!,** I have it!, at last!, at long last!, finally!, *thalassa!* or *thalatta!* [Gr.].

488. EXPERIMENT

NOUNS **1. experiment, experimentation,** testing, trying, **trial; trial and error,** hit and miss; empiricism, **rule of thumb;** tentative, tentative method; control experiment, controlled experiment; blank determination [chem.]; docimasy; experimentalism; docimology; noble experiment.

2. test, trial, try; essay, assay; **proof,** verification; touchstone, criterion 489.2; crucial test; acid test; ordeal, crucible; probation; test case.

3. tryout [coll.], **workout** [slang]; **rehearsal,** practice; road test [fig.], dry run, shakedown cruise [coll., naut.], test hop [slang, aeronaut.]; audition [coll.], hearing.

4. feeler, probe, sound, **sounder; sounding board; trial balloon,** *ballon d'essai* [F.], pilot balloon, messenger balloon; kiteflying; barometer; weathervane, weathercock; straw to show the wind.

5. check, control; reagent, agent; lit-

mus paper, curcuma paper, turmeric paper.

6. experimenter, experimentist, experimentalist; **tester,** tryer-out; experimental engineer; assayer, essayer, essayist; analyst, analyzer.

7. experimentee, testee, **subject,** object, **guinea pig.**

VERBS **8. experiment,** make an experiment, **test, try,** cut and try [coll.], **test** *or* **try out** [coll.], put to the test, **put to the proof,** task, put to trial, bring to test, make a trial of, give a trial to, **give a try;** sample, taste; play around with [coll.], fool around with [slang]; essay, assay; **prove, verify;** give a tryout [coll.], give a workout [slang], **road-test** [fig.]; try one out, put one through his paces; experiment *or* practice upon, try it on, try it on the dog [theat. cant]; try on, try it for size [slang]; try one's strength, see what one can do.

9. feel out, sound out, sound, probe, feel, **feel the pulse; put** *or* **throw out a feeler,** send up a trial balloon, fly a kite; **see which way the wind blows,** see how the land lies.

10. stand the test, stand up, hold up, hold up in the wash, pass, **pass muster,** get by [slang], pass in the dark [coll.], meet *or* satisfy requirements.

ADJS. **11. experimental, test, trial;** testing, proving, trying; probative, probationary; docimastic(al); **speculative, tentative,** provisional; empirical; trial-and-error.

12. tried, tested, proved, tried and true.

ADVS. **13. experimentally,** by rule of thumb, by trial and error, by hit and miss.

14. on trial, under examination, **on** *or* **under probation,** under suspicion, **on approval.**

489. MEASUREMENT

NOUNS **1. measurement, measure; mensuration,** measuring, gauging; **estimation,** estimate; **assessment,** determination, rating; **appraisal,** appraisement; assizement, assize; **survey,** surveying; metage; metric system; calculation 87.3.

2. measure, gauge, gage, rule, yardstick [fig.], **standard,** norm, **pattern,** model, type, scale, canon, **criterion,** test, touchstone, check, barometer.

3. extent (quantity) 28, (degree) 29, (size) 194, (distance) 198, (length) 201.

4. (measuring device) **measure,** measurer, **gauge, gage,** gauger; **meter.**

5. (measures) liquid measure, dry measure, apothecaries' measure, linear measure, square measure, circular measure, cubic measure, volume measure, surface measure, area measure, surveyor's measure, land measure, board measure, feet board measure, chain measure, nautical measure.

6. co-ordinates, ordinate and abscissa, polar co-ordinates, latitude and longitude, altitude and azimuth, declination and right ascension.

7. **watermark, water line** or waterline; tidemark, floodmark, **high-water mark**; light water line, load water line, load-line mark, Plimsoll mark or line [all naut.].

8. **measurability,** mensurability, computability, determinability.

9. (science of measurement) **mensuration;** metrology; **geodesy,** geodetics, geodetic engineering; **surveying,** chorometry; topography, cartography, chorography; cadastration; planimetry; stereometry; hypsometry, hypsography, altimetry; craniometry; biometry.

10. **measurer,** meter, gauger; **geodesist,** geodete, geodetic engineer; **surveyor;** topographer, cartographer, chorographer.

VERBS 11. **measure, gauge,** mete, take the measure of, apply the yardstick to; **assess, estimate, rate, appraise;** appreciate, prize; **size, size up** [both coll.]; **weigh,** balance, poise; **survey;** plumb, probe, sound, fathom; span, pace, step, inch; calibrate, graduate; divide; caliper, dial; meter; calculate 87.11.

12. **measure off, mark off, lay off,** set off, rule off; **step off,** pace off; **measure out,** mark out, lay out.

ADJS. 13. **measuring, metric(al);** mensural, mensurative, mensurational; geodetic(al), geodesic(al); hypsographic(al), hypsometric(al); topographic(al), chorographic(al), cartographic(al).

14. **measured, metrical, rhythmical;** cadent, cadenced; ordered, balanced, stated; uniform 17.5; **deliberate, deliberated, calculated,** weighed, studied.

15. **measurable, mensurable,** mensural, gaugeable, fathomable, **estimable, determinable,** computable, assessable, appraisable; **appreciable, perceptible, noticeable.**

ADVS. 16. **measurably, appreciably, perceptibly,** noticeably.

17. linear measures

Angstrom, A.	centimeter, cm.
arpent [Can.]	chain, chn.
block	cubit, cub.
board foot, bd. ft.	decameter,
cable's length	dekameter, dkm.

decimeter, dcm.	mile, mi.
ell	millimeter, mm.
fathom, fthm.	millimicron
finger	minute, min.
foot, ft.	myriameter, mym.
footstep	nail
furlong, fur.	nautical mile,
hand	naut. mi.
handbreadth	pace
handsbreadth	palm
hectometer,	perch, p.
hectom.	point, pt.
inch, in.	pole, p.
kilometer, km.	quadrant, quad.
knot	rod, r.
land mile, l. mi.	second, sec.
league, lea.	statute mile, stat.
line	mi.
link, li.	step
meter, m.	stride
micron	yard, yd.
mil	

18. area measures

acre, a. or ac.	pole, p.
are, a.	rood, r.
arpent, arp.	section, sec.
centiare, ca.	square inch, foot
hectare, ha.	etc.
perch, p.	township

19. volume measures

barrel, bl.	gill, gi.
bushel, bu.	hectoliter, hl.
centiliter, cl.	hogshead, hhd.
cord, cd.	kiloliter, kl.
cubic foot, yard,	liquid pint, quart,
etc.	etc.
cup	liter, l.
decaliter, dekaliter,	magnum
dkl.	milliliter, ml.
decastere, ds.	minim, min.
deciliter, dl.	peck, pk.
dry pint, quart,	pint, pt.
etc.	quart, qt.
finger	stere, s.
fluid dram, fl. dr.	tablespoon, tbs.
fluid ounce, fl. oz.	teaspoon, ts.
gallon, gal.	

20. gauges

calipers	micrometer caliper
chain	plumb 208.17
compass	plumb rule
dial	protractor
dividers	quadrant
engineer's chain	rod
gradometer	rule
graduated scale	ruler
graduated tape	scale
Gunter's scale	sector
Gunter's or	set square
surveyor's chain	sextant
nonius	size stick
level	slide rule, sliding
line	scale
log	spirit level
log line	square
measuring machine	steel [coll.]
micrometer	straightedge

tape, tapeline, tape measure
theodolite
transit
transit theodolite

try square
T square
vernier
viagraph
yardstick

490. COMPARISON

NOUNS 1. comparison, compare; likening, comparing, assimilation, similitude, analogy; parallelization, parallelism; matching, measuring, weighing, balancing; opposing, opposition, contrast, confrontment, confrontation.

2. collation, verification, checking; check, cross-check.

3. comparability, comparableness, comparativeness; analogousness, relativity, commensurability; proportionateness, proportionability; ratio, proportion, balance; similarity 20.

VERBS 4. compare, liken, like [dial.], assimilate, similize; relate 9.4; liken to, compare with, make a comparison, bring into comparison; analogize, bring into analogy; draw a parallel, parallel, parallelize; match, put beside, put alongside, set side by side, place by the side of, place in juxtaposition, juxtapose, appose, confront, contrast, oppose, set in opposition, set off against, put or set over against, place against, set over against one another, set or pit against one another; measure, weigh, balance.

5. collate, verify, check, cross-check.

6. compare notes, exchange views or observations, match dope [slang, U.S.].

7. be comparable, compare, compare to or with, admit of comparison, be worthy of comparison, be fit to be compared; measure up to, come up to, match up with, stack up with [slang], hold a candle to [coll.]; match, parallel; vie, vie with; be like 20.7.

ADJS. 8. comparative, comparable; relative, not quite; proportionate, proportional, proportionable, commensurate, commensurable; analogous, analogical; comparing, matching; paralleling, parallel, parallelistic; much at one, much of a muchness [coll.]; similar 20.10.

ADVS. 9. comparatively, comparably, relatively, proportionately, in proportion.

PREPS., etc. 10. compared to, compared with, as compared with, by comparison with, in comparison, beside, aside of [dial.], over against, taken with, taken all in all; in proportion to, relative to,

according to, as to, in accordance with; than, then [dial.], as [dial.].

491. DISCRIMINATION

NOUNS 1. discrimination, discriminateness, discriminatingness, discriminativeness; discretion, discreetness; tact, tactfulness, grace, gracefulness, diplomacy, address, savoir-faire [F.]; finesse, refinement, delicacy, nicety, subtlety, refined discrimination, critical niceness; sensitivity, sensibility, sensitiveness, sympathetic perception; appreciation, appreciativeness; taste, discriminating taste, aesthetic or artistic judgment; particularness 894.

2. discernment, penetration, perception, perspicacity, flair; judgment, acumen 466.4–7.

3. distinction, contradistinction, distinguishment, differentiation, separation, division, segregation, demarcation; line of demarcation; nice or subtle distinction, hairsplitting.

4. (tactful person) diplomat, diplomatist [esp. Eng.].

VERBS 5. be discriminating, be discreet, exercise discretion or discrimination; be tactful, show tact, be diplomatic, take into account or consideration; pick and choose; use advisedly.

6. discriminate, distinguish, contradistinguish, separate, divide, segregate, sever, severalize, differentiate, demark, demarcate, set off, set apart, sift, screen; separate the sheep from the goats, separate the wheat from the tares, winnow the chaff from the wheat; draw the line, fix or set a limit; split hairs, make a nice or subtle distinction.

7. make a distinction, draw distinctions, distinguish between, see the difference; know which is which, know what's what [coll.], "know a hawk from a handsaw" [Shakespeare].

ADJS. 8. discriminating, discriminate, discriminative, selective; discretionary, discretional; discreet, tactful, graceful, diplomatic, politic; sensitive, appreciative; critical, diacritic(al); distinctive, distinguishing; differentiative, differential; nice, fine, delicate, subtle, refined; particular 894.9.

9. discerning, perceptive, perspicacious; astute, judicious 466.16–19.

ADVS. 10. discriminatingly, discriminatively, discriminately; discreetly, tactfully, gracefully, diplomatically, politicly, with finesse, with good grace.

492. INDISCRIMINATION

NOUNS **1. indiscrimination,** indiscriminateness, undiscriminatingness, undiscriminativeness; **uncriticalness, unparticularness,** unfastidiousness, **unscrupulousness, unconscientiousness,** unmeticulousness; casualness, promiscuousness, **promiscuity.**

2. indiscretion, indiscreetness; **imprudence** 469.2; **untactfulness,** tactlessness, ungracefulness.

3. indistinction, indistinctness, **indistinguishableness,** undistinguishableness; a distinction without a difference.

VERBS **4. confound, confuse,** mix, muddle, tumble, jumble, jumble together.

5. use loosely, use unadvisedly.

ADJS. **6. undiscriminating, indiscriminate,** indiscriminative, undiscriminative; indiscretionary, **uncritical,** uncriticizing; **unparticular,** unfastidious, **unscrupulous, unconscientious,** unmeticulous, unexacting; casual, **promiscuous.**

7. indiscreet, undiscreet; **imprudent** 469.9; **untactful,** tactless, **ungraceful, impolitic,** unpolitic, **undiplomatic.**

8. indistinguishable, undistinguishable, undistinguished, **indistinct,** indistinctive, **without distinction,** not to be distinguished, undiscriminated, **alike,** six of one and half a dozen of the other [coll.].

493. JUDGMENT

NOUNS **1. judgment,** adjudgment, adjudication, judicature; **arbitration** 803.2; good judgment 466.7.

2. criticism, criticalness; **censure** 967.3; critique, review, notice, report, comment; book review.

3. estimate, estimation; opinion 500.4; assessment, **appraisal,** appraisement, apprizement or apprisement, appreciation, valuation, **evaluation,** valorization, **rating.**

4. conclusion, result, consequence, consequent, corollary, logical result; **deduction, inference,** derivation, illation; induction; **non sequitur,** *fallacia consequentis* [L., it does not follow].

5. verdict, decision, determination, finding, diagnosis, reckoning, consideration [law]; **award, sentence,** report, **decree, ruling,** order, **pronouncement,** resolution, deliverance, action; precedent [law]; snap decision.

6. judge, judger, good judge; **connoisseur,** *cognoscente* [It.]; justice, arbiter 1000.

7. critic, criticizer; criticaster [derog.],

criticule, critikin; **censor,** censurer; **reviewer; commentator,** commenter; devil's advocate.

VERBS **8. judge,** exercise the judgment; adjudge, adjudicate; **consider, regard, deem, esteem, count, account,** make, call, think of, take for, set down as, allow [dial.], **suppose, presume, surmise, imagine, fancy;** opine, form an opinion, give or pass an opinion.

9. estimate, form an estimate, make an estimation; **reckon, calculate** [coll., U.S.], figure [coll.]; **assess, appraise,** apprize or apprise, **gauge, rate, rank,** class, mark, **value, evaluate,** valuate, valorize, place or set a value on, prize, appreciate; size up, take one's measure [both coll.].

10. conclude, draw a conclusion, **come to** or **arrive at a conclusion; deduce, derive,** extract, **gather,** collect, glean, fetch; **infer,** draw an inference; induce; **reason,** reason that; put two and two together.

11. decide, determine, find, hold, resolve, settle, fix, ascertain; make a decision, **make up one's mind,** settle one's mind.

12. sit in judgment, hold the scales; **hear,** give a hearing to; try 1002.17; arbitrate 803.6.

13. pass judgment, pronounce judgment, **bring in a verdict,** pronounce on, act on, **pronounce,** report, **award,** assign, **rule,** decree, order, ordain; **sentence,** pass sentence.

14. criticize, critique; **censure** 967.13, 14; review, comment upon, moralize upon.

15. rank, rate, be regarded, be thought of, be in one's estimation.

ADJS. **16. judicial, judiciary,** judgmatic(al) [coll.]; judicative, judicatory; juridic(al), juristic(al); **judicious** 466.19; critical 967.24.

ADVS. **17. all things considered,** on the **whole, taking one thing with another,** taking everything into consideration or account, everything being equal, other things being equal, taking into account, considering, after all, this being so; therefore, wherefore.

494. PREJUDGMENT

NOUNS **1. prejudgment,** forejudgment, **preconception, presumption, presupposition,** presupposal, presurmise, prenotion, prenotice, prevention, **prepossession, predilection,** predisposition, preapprehension, preconsideration, predecision, predetermination, preconclusion, foregone conclusion;

pre-estimate, pre-estimation; prejudice 525.3.

VERBS 2. **prejudge, forejudge, precon-ceive, presuppose, presume,** presurmise, **predetermine,** predecide, pre-estimate, preconsider, preconclude; **jump to a con-clusion,** go off half-cocked *or* at half cock [coll.], jump the gun [slang].

ADJS. 3. **preconceived, presumed, pre-supposed,** presurmised, **predetermined,** predecided.

4. predispositional, preconceptual, prede-cisive, prejudicial.

495. MISJUDGMENT

NOUNS 1. **misjudgment,** poor judgment, warped judgment; **miscalculation,** mis-computation, **misreckoning, misestima-tion,** misconjecture; misconstruction 551.1; error 517.

VERBS 2. **misjudge, miscalculate, mis-estimate, misreckon,** miscompute, mis-deem, misesteem, misthink, misconjecture; misconstrue 551.2; err 517.8; fly in the face of facts, reckon without one's host.

ADJS. 3. ill-judged 469.9.

496. OVERESTIMATION

NOUNS 1. **overestimation,** overestimate, overjudgment, **overreckoning,** overcalcula-tion, **overrating,** overassessment, overvalua-tion, overappraisal; **exaggeration** 615.

VERBS 2. **overestimate,** overjudge, **over-reckon,** outreckon, overcalculate, over-count, **overrate,** overassess, overappraise, overesteem, **overvalue,** overprize, over-measure, overstrain, strain, stretch, think *or* make too much of, attach too much im-portance to, make mountains out of mole-hills, catch at straws, make the most, ∼ best *or* worst of; **exaggerate** 615.3.

ADJS. 3. **overestimated, overrated,** over-valued; **exaggerated** 615.4.

497. UNDERESTIMATION

NOUNS 1. **underestimation,** underesti-mate, **underrating,** underreckoning, un-dervaluation; **depreciation, belittlement, minimization.**

VERBS 2. **underestimate, underrate,** underreckon, undervalue, underprize; mis-prize, disprize; **depreciate, minimize, be-little; make little of,** attach little impor-tance to, not do justice to, think little of, make *or* think nothing of, set little by, set light by, set no store by, set at nought, make light of, shrug off.

ADJS. 3. **underestimated, underrated,** undervalued; unvalued, unprized.

498. THEORY, SUPPOSITION

NOUNS 1. **theory, theorization;** theo-retics, theorics; **speculation,** contempla-tion; analysis, explanation; abstraction; Ein-stein theory, theory of relativity, continu-um theory, quantum theory, Einstein's photon theory, Einstein's field theory, uni-fied field theory, theory of exchanges, atomic theory, theory of evolution.

2. **supposition, supposal,** supposing, putation; **assumption, presumption,** con-jecture, **inference, surmise, guesswork; presupposition,** presupposal; **hypothesis,** working hypothesis; **postulate, postula-tion,** postulatum; **proposition, proposal,** position, thesis, theorem.

3. **guess, conjecture, inference, sur-mise;** shot, stab [both coll.]; **rough guess, wild guess,** blind guess, shot in the dark [coll.].

4. (vague supposition) **suggestion,** bare suggestion, **suspicion, inkling, hint,** inti-mation, **impression, idea, notion,** sneak-ing idea [coll.]; vague idea, hazy idea.

5. **suppositiousness, presumptiveness,** presumableness, theoreticalness, conjec-turableness, speculativeness.

6. **theorist, theorizer,** theoretic, theore-tician; **speculator,** notionalist; hypothesist, hypothesizer; doctrinaire.

7. **supposer,** assumer, surmiser, conjec-turer, **guesser,** guessworker.

VERBS 8. **theorize, hypothesize, specu-late;** think out loud, talk off the top of one's head [slang].

9. **suppose, assume, presume, surmise,** expect [chiefly coll.], **suspect,** suspicion [dial.], **infer, understand, gather, con-clude, deduce, judge, consider,** reckon [coll. or dial.], calculate [coll., U.S.], allow [dial.], **divine, imagine** [coll.], **fancy, dream, conceive, believe, deem,** repute, **feel, think,** be inclined to think, opine [chiefly joc.], say, dare say, be afraid [coll.]; take, take it, take it into one's head, take for, take to be, take for granted; let, let be.

10. **conjecture, guess,** give a guess, haz-ard a conjecture, venture a guess, risk as-suming *or* stating.

11. **presuppose, presurmise,** prefigure.

12. **postulate, predicate, posit** [logic], lay down, **enunciate,** state, stipulate, pose, moot, advance, submit; **propose, profound** 771.5, **6.**

ADJS. **13. theoretical, hypothetic(al),** speculative, **conjectural, academic(al),** abstract, ideal, impractical.

14. supposed, assumed, presumed, conjectured, **inferred,** accepted, understood, deemed, **reputed,** putative, accounted as; suppositional, supposititious; assumptive, **presumptive;** given, gratuitous, mooted; postulated, postulational.

15. supposable, presumable, assumable, conjecturable.

ADVS. **16. theoretically, hypothetically,** ideally; **in theory,** in idea, in the abstract, on paper; **in a sense,** in a certain sense, **in a way, in a manner, in a manner of speaking.**

17. supposedly, supposably, **presumably,** presumedly, assumably, assumedly, presumptively, assumptively, reputedly; suppositionally, supposititiously; **seemingly,** in seeming, in name only; quasi, as if, as though, as it were.

18. conjecturably, conjecturally; to guess, to make a guess, **as a guess,** as a rough guess.

CONJS. **19. supposing** [coll.], supposing that, **assuming that,** allowing that, on the assumption or supposition that, if by way hypothesis.

499. PHILOSOPHY

NOUNS **1. philosophy,** love of wisdom, handmaid of theology, **school of thought;** theory of knowledge, epistemology; sophistry 482; psychology [hist.], mental philosophy.

2. Platonic philosophy, Platonism, philosophy of the Academy; Aristotelian philosophy, Aristotelianism, philosophy of the Lyceum, Peripateticism, Peripatetic school; Stoic philosophy, Stoicism, philosophy of the Porch; Epicureanism, philosophy of the Garden.

3. idealism, critical idealism, epistemological idealism, metaphysical idealism, subjective idealism, objective idealism; absolute idealism, philosophy of the Absolute; transcendentalism, transcendental idealism; immaterialism; Berkeleianism; Platonism.

4. materialism 375.5.

5. monism, philosophical unitarianism, mind-stuff theory; pantheism, cosmotheism.

6. pluralism; dualism, mind-matter theory.

7. philosopher, philosophizer, philosoph,

philosophe; philosopheress, philosophess; sophist 482.6.

VERBS **8. philosophize,** reason 481.15.

ADJS. **9. philosophic(al),** philosophistic(al); sophistical 482.14; philosophicohistorical, philosophicolegal, philosophicojuristic, philosophicopsychological, philosophicoreligious, philosophicotheological.

10. acosmistic, animatistic, animist(ic), atomistic, cosmotheistic, eclectic(al), empirical, epicurean, eudaemonistic(al), existential; hedonist(ic), hedonic(al); humanist, humanistic(al); idealistic(al), materialistic 375.11, mechanistic, monistic(al), mystic(al), naturalistic, nominalist(ic); panlogical, panlogistical; pantheistic(al), positivist(ic), pragmatist(ic), rationalistic(al), realist(ic), sensationalistic, synchretistic(al), theistic, traditionalistic, transcendentalist(ic), utilitarian, vitalistic, voluntarist(ic).

11. Aristotelian, Peripatetic; Augustinian, Averroist(ic), Bergsonian, Berkeleian, Cartesian, Comtian, Eleatic, Gnostic(al), Hegelian, Neo-Hegelian, Heraclitean, Humean, Kantian, Leibnitzian, Megarian, Platonic, Neoplatonic; Pyrrhonic, Pyrrhonian; Pythagorean, Neo-Pythagorean, Schellingian, Scholastic, Neo-Scholastic, Schopenhauerian, Scotistic(al), Socratic, Spencerian, Stoic(al), Thomistic(al).

12. philosophies

acosmism	Elian or Elean
aestheticism	school
aesthetics	empiricism
African school	Epicureanism
agnosticism	Eretrian school
Alexandrian school	Eristic school
animalism	essentialism
animatism	ethicism
animism	ethics 955.1
Aristotelianism	eudaemonism
atomism	existentialism
Augustinianism	Fichteanism
Averroism	Gnosticism
Bergsonism	hedonism
Berkeleianism	Hegelianism
Cartesianism	Heracliteanism
casuistry	Herbartianism
Comtism	Hinduism
cosmology	humanism
cosmotheism	Humism
criticism	hylism, hylicism
Cynicism	hylotheism
Cyrenaic hedonism	hylozoism
Cyrenaicism	idealism
deism	ideology
dualism	immaterialism
eclecticism	individualism
egoism	intuitionism
egoistic hedonism	Ionic school
Eleaticism	Kantianism

Leibnitzianism
Manichaeism
materialism
mechanism
Megarianism
mental philosophy
metaphysics
Mimamsa
 [Hinduism]
monism
moralism
moral philosophy
mysticism
naturalism
natural philosophy
neocriticism
Neo-Hegelianism
Neoplatonism
Neo-Pythagorean-
 ism
Neo-Scholasticism
new ethical
 movement
nominalism
noumenalism
Nyaya [Hinduism]
ontologism
ontology
panlogism
panphenomenalism
panpneumatism
panpsychism
panteleogism
pantheism
panthelism
patristicism
patristic
 philosophy
Peripateticism
phenomenalism
philosophy of the
 ante-Nicene
 Fathers
philosophy of the
 post-Nicene
 Fathers
physicalism
physicism
Platonism

pluralism
political
 philosophy
positivism
pragmaticism
pragmatism
psychism
psychological
 hedonism
psychology [hist.]
Pyrrhonism
Pythagoreanism
rationalism
realism
Saiva Siddhanta
 [Hinduism]
Sankhya
 [Hinduism]
Schellingism
Scholasticism
Schopenhauerism
Scotism
sensationalism
sensism
skepticism
sociological school
Socratism
somatism
Sophism
Spencerianism
Spinozism
Stoicism
substantialism
Swedenborgianism
syncretism
theism
Thomism
traditionalism
transcendentalism
universalistic
 hedonism
utilitarianism
Uttara or Purva
 Mimamsa
 [Hinduism]
vitalism
voluntarism
zetetic philosophy

hylozoist
idealist
immaterialist
individualist
intuitionist
Kantian
Leibnitzian
Manichaean
materialist 375.6
mechanist
Megarian
metaphysician,
 metaphysicist
monist
moralist
mystic
naturalist
Neo-Hegelian
Neoplatonist
Neo-Pythagorean
nominalist
ontologist
panpsychist
pantheist
Peripatetic
phenomenalist
physicalist
physicist
Platonist
pluralist

positivist
pragmatist
psychist
Pyrrhonist
Pythagorean
rationalist
realist
scholastic
Scotist
sensationalist
sensist
skeptic
Socratist
somatist
Sophist
Spencerian
Spinozist
Stoic
substantialist
Swedenborgian
syncretist
theist
Thomist
traditionalist
transcendentalist
utilitarian
Vicoist
vitalist
voluntarist
zetetic

14. philosophers

Abelard
Albertus Magnus
Anaxagoras
Anaximander
Anaximenes
Anselm
Aristippus
Aristotle
Augustine
Averroes
Bacon, Francis
Bentham
Bergson
Berkeley
Boethius
Bonaventura
Cicero
Comte
Confucius
Croce
Democritus
Descartes
Dewey
Duns Scotus
Empedocles
Engels
Epictetus
Epicurus
Erigena
Fechner
Fichte
Frege
Gilson
Grotius
Hartmann
Hegel
Heidegger
Heraclitus
Herbart

Hobbes
Hume
Husserl
James
Jaspers
Kant
Kierkegaard
Leibniz
Leucippus
Locke
Lucretius
Mach
Maimonides
Malebranche
Manes
Marcus Aurelius
Maritain
Melissus
Mill
Nietzsche
Parmenides
Philo
Pierce
Plato
Plotinus
Protagoras
Pyrrho
Pythagoras
Rousseau
Russell
Santayana
Sartre
Schelling
Schopenhauer
Seneca
Spencer
Spinoza
Thales
Theophrastus

13. adherents

acosmist
agnostic
animalist
animatist
animist
Aristotelian
atomist
Averroist
Bergsonian
Berkeleian
Cartesian
casuist
Comtist
cosmologist
cosmotheist
Cynic
Cyrenaic
deist
dualist
eclectic

egoist
Eleatic
Elian
empiricist
epicurean
Eretrian
eristic
essentialist
eudaemonist
existentialist
Fichtean
Gnostic
hedonist
Hegelian
Heraclitean
Herbartian
humanist
Humist
hylicist
hylotheist

500

Thomas Aquinas
Whitehead
William of
  Ockham
Wittgenstein

Wundt
Xenophanes
Zeno of Elea
Zoroaster

500. BELIEF

NOUNS 1. belief, credence, credit, faith, trust, troth, hope, affiance; confidence, assurance; sureness, certainty 512; reliance, dependence; reliance on or in, dependence on; stock [slang], store [coll.]; credulity 501.

2. a belief, tenet, dogma, precept, principle, article, principle or article of faith, canon, maxim, rule; doctrine, teaching, system of belief; school, cult, ism; creed, credo, credenda; articles of religion, doctrinal statements; gospel, gospel truth; catechism.

3. conviction, persuasion, convincement; self-conviction, self-persuasion; firm belief, implicit belief, staunch belief, settled judgment, fixed opinion, unshaken confidence, steadfast faith, rooted or deep-rooted belief.

4. opinion, sentiment, feeling, impression, reaction, apprehension, notion, idea, thought, think [slang], thinking, way of thinking, attitude, position, view, eye, sight, light, observation, mind, conception, concept, conceit, estimation, estimate, consideration, theory, assumption, presumption, conclusion, judgment, personal judgment; point of view 523.2; public opinion, Mrs. Grundy, popular belief, vox populi [L., voice of the people]; climate of opinion.

5. profession, confession, declaration, profession ~, confession or declaration of faith.

6. believability, believableness, credibility, plausibility, tenability, conceivability; reliability 512.4.

7. believer, truster, accepter, receiver; religious believer 1026.4; true believer, orthodox; the faithful, the believing.

VERBS 8. believe, credit, accredit, trust, accept, receive, admit, buy [slang]; give credit or credence to, give faith to, take stock in [slang], set store by [coll.], attach some weight to; be led to believe; accept implicitly, take for granted, take or accept for gospel, take on faith, take on trust or credit; take one's word for, trust one's word, take at one's word, take one's dick [slang]; swallow 501.5.

9. think, opine, be of the opinion, be afraid [coll.], have the idea, have an idea,

suppose, assume, presume, judge, guess, surmise, suspect, expect [chiefly coll.], conceive, imagine, fancy, daresay or dare say; deem, esteem, hold, regard, consider, allow [dial.], reckon [coll.], calculate [coll., U.S.], estimate; hold as, account as, set down as or for, view as, look upon, have it, take, take it, take for.

10. hold the belief, have the opinion, entertain a belief or opinion adopt or embrace a belief, foster ~, nurture or cherish a belief, be wedded to.

11. be confident, have confidence, be satisfied, be convinced, feel sure, rest assured, rest in confidence; doubt not, have no doubt, have no misgivings, have no reservations.

12. believe in, have faith in, pin one's faith to, confide in, have confidence in, place or repose confidence in, place reliance in, trust in, put trust in, rest in, repose in, hope in, lay one's account for.

13. rely on or upon, depend on or upon, place reliance on, rest on or upon, repose on, lean on, stand on or upon, count on, calculate on, reckon on, lot on or upon [coll., U.S.], allot on or upon [dial., U.S. & Can.], bank on or upon [coll.], build upon; trust to or unto, tie to [slang, U.S.]; swear by, take one's oath upon; bet on, gamble on, stake on, lay money on, go bail on, bet one's bottom dollar on [all coll.].

14. trust, confide, rely, depend, rest, repose, place trust or confidence; trust in 500.12, deem trustworthy, think reliable or dependable, let out of one's sight.

15. convince, convict, convert, wean, win over, bring over, bring round, talk over, talk one around, bring to reason, bring to one's senses, persuade, satisfy, assure, lead to believe; sell, sell one on [both coll., U.S.]; sell a bill of goods [slang]; carry one's point, bring or drive home to; cram down the throat; have the ear of, gain the confidence of; be convincing, carry conviction.

16. convince oneself, persuade oneself, sell oneself [coll., U.S.], make oneself easy about, make oneself easy on that score, satisfy oneself on that point, make sure of, make up one's mind.

17. find credence, be believed, be accepted, be received, be swallowed [coll.], go down; pass current; possess the mind, take hold or possession of the mind.

ADJS. 18. believing, undoubting, unques-

tioning, unhesitating, **indubious, undoubt-**
ful, doubtless, questionless, without doubt
or question; under the impression, impressed with; **convinced, confident,** positive, **persuaded, satisfied, assured;** sure,
certain 512.13, 21.

19. trusting, trustful, trusty, **confiding,**
unsuspecting, unsuspicious, without suspicion; **credulous** 501.7; relying, depending,
reliant, dependent.

20. believed, credited, accredited,
trusted, accepted, admitted, received; **un-**
doubted, unsuspected, **unquestioned,** undisputed, uncontested.

21. believable, credible, tenable, conceivable, **plausible;** reliable 512.17; swal-
lowable, downable [both coll.]; **unques-**
tionable 512.15.

22. convincing, convictional, **persuasive,**
assuring, impressive, satisfying, satisfactory;
decisive, conclusive, determinative.

23. doctrinal, creedal, canonical, dog-
matic(al).

ADVS. **24. believingly, undoubtingly,**
undoubtfully, unquestioningly, unhesitatingly; **trustingly,** trustfully, unsuspectingly,
unsuspiciously; **with confidence,** on or
upon trust.

25. in one's opinion, to one's mind, in
one's thinking, **to one's way of thinking,**
the way one thinks, **in one's estimation,**
according to one's lights, as one sees it,
to the best of one's belief; in the opinion
of, in the eyes of.

PHRS. **26. I believe,** I do believe, **I think,**
methinks [poetic], I dare say, **it seems to**
me, in my opinion, in my judgment, to the
best of my belief, according to my belief,
to my eyes, according to my lights; **I have**
no doubt, I doubt not, **I am sure,** I am
convinced.

27. believe me, take my word for it,
you can take it from me [coll.], I'll answer
for it, **I assure you,** you may be sure, you
may rest assured, be assured, rest assured,
depend or rely upon it; I'll warrant you
521.10.

501. CREDULITY

NOUNS **1. credulity, credulousness; blind**
faith, unquestioning belief; **trustfulness,**
unsuspiciousness, unsuspectingness; **over-**
credulity, overcredulousness, overconfidence, overtrustfulness; gross credulity, infatuation; one's blind side.

2. gullibility, dupability, deceivability,
humbugability, exploitableness; easiness

[coll.], softness; **simpleness, simplicity,**
unsophistication, greenness, naïveness,
naïveté, naïvety.

3. superstition, superstitiousness, *Aber-*
glaube [G.]; popular belief, **old wives' tale;**
tradition, lore, folklore; black cat, broken
mirror.

4. trusting soul; dupe 618.

VERBS **5. be credulous,** accept unquestioningly; allow oneself to believe, kid oneself [slang]; **swallow,** down [both coll.];
swallow whole [coll.], **swallow hook, line**
and sinker [slang]; **eat up, lap up, de-**
vour, gulp down, gobble up or down [all
coll.]; bite, nibble, rise to the fly, take the
bait [all coll. or slang]; swing at [slang,
U.S.]; go for, **fall for,** tumble for [all
slang]; jump or rush to a conclusion, run
away with an idea; think the moon is made
of green cheese.

6. be superstitious, knock on wood, keep
one's fingers crossed.

ADJS. **7. credulous,** easy-believing, ready
or inclined to believe; **undoubting** 500.18;
trustful, trusting; unsuspicious, unsuspect-
ing; overcredulous, overconfident, over-
trustful, overtrusting.

8. gullible, dupable, pigeonable [slang];
deceivable, foolable, stuffable [slang], **de-**
ludable, exploitable, victimizable, humbugable, hoodwinkable; **easy** [coll.], easily imposed upon, easy to stuff [slang]; **simple,**
naïve or **naïf, unsophisticated,** green,
stupid, soft.

9. superstitious, fearful.

502. UNBELIEF

NOUNS **1. unbelief, disbelief; discredit,**
discredence; unbelievingness, unbelieffful-
ness; **incredulity** 503; misbelief, heresy
1023.2; infidelity, atheism, agnosticism
1029; minimifidianism.

2. doubt, doubtfulness, dubiousness,
dubiety; **question,** question in one's mind;
skepticism, skepticalness, Pyrrhonism; suspicion, suspiciousness; **distrust, mistrust,**
misdoubt, distrustfulness, mistrustfulness;
misgiving, self-doubt; **qualm,** qualmishness; apprehension 889.3; **uncertainty** 513;
shadow of doubt.

3. unbelievability, unbelievableness, incredibility, implausibility, inconceivability;
doubtfulness, questionableness, untenableness; unreliability 513.6.

4. unbeliever 1029.11, **12.**

VERBS **5. disbelieve, unbelieve,** misbelieve, **not believe,** not admit, not buy

[slang], take no stock in [slang], set no store by [coll.]; **discredit**, give no credit or credence to; **not swallow** 503.3.

6. **doubt, be doubtful, be dubious, be skeptical**, doubt the truth of, **have one's doubts**, have ~, harbor or entertain doubts or suspicions, **take with a grain of salt; distrust, mistrust**, misgive; **suspect**, suspicion [now dial.], smell a rat [coll.]; **question**, query, **challenge, dispute**, bring or call in question, raise a question, throw doubt upon, awake a doubt or suspicion; **doubt one's word**, give one the lie in his throat.

7. **be unbelievable**, be hard to believe, strain one's credulity, **stagger belief**; stagger, shake, shake one's faith; perplex, fill with doubt.

ADJS. 8. **unbelieving, disbelieving**, unbelieful; **faithless**, without faith; unconfident, unconvinced, unconverted; nullifidian, minimifidian; **incredulous** 503.4; **heretical** 1023.9; **irreligious** 1029.19.

9. **doubting, doubtful**, doubtsome [Scot. & dial., Eng.], **in doubt; dubious**, dubersome [dial.], duberous [dial.], juberous [South. U.S.]; **questioning; skeptic(al)**, Pyrrhonic, from Missouri [slang, U.S.]; **distrustful, mistrustful, untrustful**, mistrusting, untrusting; **suspicious, suspecting**, qualmish; uncertain 513.14.

10. **unbelievable, untenable, incredible**, unthinkable, **implausible**, inconceivable, not to be believed, **hard to believe**, hard of belief, beyond belief, tall [coll.]; **doubtful**, doubtable, dubitable, **questionable**, problematic(al), **unconvincing**, open to doubt or suspicion; **suspicious**, suspect; thin, a bit thin [both slang]; thick, a bit thick, a little too thick [all coll.]; **staggering**, **staggering belief; preposterous**, absurd, ridiculous.

11. unreliable 513.18.

12. **doubted, questioned**, disputed, contested; **moot**, mooted; **distrusted**, mistrusted; **suspect**, suspected; **under suspicion**, under a cloud.

ADVS. 13. **unbelievingly, doubtingly, doubtfully, dubiously**, questioningly, **skeptically**, suspiciously; **with a grain of salt**, with reservations, with some allowance, with caution.

INTERJS. 14. **I don't believe it!**, I doubt that!, **I'm from Missouri, you'll have to show me!, tell it to the marines!**, tell me another!, what are you talking about?, where do you get that stuff?, don't give me

that!, do tell!, let's hear another!, now I'll tell one!, that's what you say!, maybe I'm wrong!, yeah!, oh, yeah!, says who?, says you!, I'd like to know!, no thank you!, are you kidding?, don't kid yourself!, come!, come, now!, come, come!, come off of it!, now!, now-now!, aw, now!, go on!, my foot!, my eye!, all my eye!, in a pig's eye!, like fun!, you're crazy!; **nonsense!** 469.12, don't be ridiculous! 469.13.

503. INCREDULITY

NOUNS 1. **incredulity, incredulousness**, uncredulousness, refusal to believe; **inconvincibility**, unconvincibility; **suspiciousness**, suspicion; **skepticism** 502.2.

2. **ungullibility, undupability**, undeceivability; **sophistication**.

VERBS 3. **refuse to believe, not allow oneself to believe**, not kid oneself [slang]; **disbelieve** 502.5; **not swallow**, not be able to swallow or down [both coll.]; not go for, **not fall for** [both slang]; **not accept, reject**, ignore, shut one's eyes to, shut or stop one's ears to, turn a deaf ear to.

ADJS. 4. **incredulous**, uncredulous, **hard of belief**, shy of belief, disposed to doubt, indisposed to believe, unwilling to admit or accept; **inconvincible**, unconvincible; **suspicious, suspecting; skeptical** 502.9.

5. **ungullible, undupable, undeceivable, unfoolable, undeludable, unexploitable**, not easily imposed upon, not easy to stuff [slang], hoaxproof; **sophisticated, wise, hardheaded**; nobody's fool, not born yesterday [both slang].

504. EVIDENCE, PROOF

NOUNS 1. **evidence, proof**, medium of proof; **reason to believe**, grounds for belief; **grounds**, facts, data; **indication, manifestation, sign**, mark, token; **clue** 566.8; fingerprints; exhibit [law].

2. evidence in chief, primary or secondary evidence, external or extrinsic evidence, internal or instrinsic evidence, direct evidence, indirect evidence, circumstantial or presumptive evidence, documentary evidence, oral evidence, ex parte evidence, collateral evidence, cumulative evidence, incriminating evidence; hearsay evidence, hearsay [coll.]; corpus delicti [law], body of the crime.

3. **testimony**, testament [erron.], testification, attest, **attestation, witness**; testimonial, testimonium; **statement, declaration**, affirmation, avouchment, averment,

allegation, admission, profession, word; deposition, *procès-verbal* [F.]; compurgation; affidavit, affidavy [dial.]; instrument in proof, *pièce justificative* [F.].

4. (a proving) **proof, demonstration; determination, establishment, settlement;** conclusiveness, decisiveness; **conclusive evidence,** apodixis; burden of proof, *onus probandi* [L., law]; the proof of the pudding.

5. confirmation, substantiation, authentication, affirmation, attestation, **validation,** validification, **certification,** ratification; **verification, corroboration,** support, fortification, circumstantiation; documentation.

6. citation, reference, quotation; **exemplification,** illustration, demonstration; cross reference.

7. witness, eyewitness, earwitness; **bystander,** passerby; **deponent, testifier,** attestant, attester *or* attestor, attestator, voucher; cojuror, compurgator.

8. provability, demonstrability; confirmability, supportability, verifiability.

VERBS **9. evidence, evince, show,** shew [chiefly Eng.], **go to show,** tend to show; **demonstrate, illustrate,** exhibit, manifest, display, express, set forth; attest; approve; **indicate, signify,** mark, **denote, betoken, point to,** give indication of; **connote,** imply, involve; argue, breathe, tell, bespeak; **speak for itself,** speak volumes; have *or* carry weight, weigh.

10. testify, attest, give evidence, witness, **give** *or* **bear witness;** vouch, avouch, **depose,** depone, **warrant, swear,** acknowledge, certify, **give one's word,** deliver as one's act and deed.

11. prove, demonstrate, show, afford proof of, prove to be, prove true; **establish,** fix, **determine, ascertain,** make out; **settle,** settle the matter; **set at rest;** clinch, cinch [slang]; **prove one's point,** bring home to, bring off, make good, have *or* make out a case; hold good, hold water [coll.]; follow, follow from, follow as a matter of course.

12. confirm, affirm, attest, warrant, **substantiate, authenticate, validate, certify,** ratify; **verify,** circumstantiate; **corroborate, bear out,** support, uphold, sustain, fortify, strengthen; document; probate, prove [both law].

13. adduce, produce, **advance, present, offer,** assign, allege, plead; **bring forward,** bring on.

14. cite, name, call, call to mind; **instance,** produce an instance; **exemplify,** example, sample, **illustrate,** demonstrate; **quote,** quote chapter and verse, speak by the book.

15. refer to, appeal to, invoke; reference, make reference to; cross-reference, cross-refer, make a cross-reference.

16. have evidence *or* **proof,** possess incriminating evidence, **have something on** [coll.]; **have the goods on,** have the dope on, have the deadwood on, have dead to rights [all slang].

ADJS. **17. evidential, indicative, testatory,** probative; founded on, grounded on, based on; significant, telling, weighty; overwhelming, damning; **conclusive,** determinative, **decisive,** final; firsthand, authentic; hearsay, circumstantial, nuncupative; cumulative, presumptive, ex parte.

18. deducible, deductible, deductive, derivable, inducible, **inferable,** inferential, illative, consequential, sequential, following.

19. demonstrative, demonstrating, demonstrational; evincive, **explanatory, illustrative,** apodict(al); convincing, irresistible, categorical, explicit, crucial.

20. confirming, confirmatory, confirmative; **verifying,** verificative; **corroborating,** corroborative, collateral, supportive.

21. provable, demonstrable, demonstratable, evincible, attestable, **confirmable, substantiatable, establishable,** supportable, sustainable, **verifiable.**

22. proved, proven, demonstrated, shown; **established,** fixed, **settled, determined,** ascertained; **confirmed, substantiated,** attested, **authenticated, certified, validated,** valid; **verified,** circumstantiated; **corroborated,** borne out.

23. unrefuted, unconfuted, unanswered, undenied; **unrefutable** 512.15.

ADVS. **24. evidentially, according to,** as attested by; **in confirmation, in corroboration of, in support of;** under the hand of, under one's hand and seal; at first hand, at second hand.

25. to illustrate, to prove the point, as an example, by way of example, **for example, for instance,** to cite an instance, as the fellow said [slang]; e.g., *exempli gratia* [L.]; as, thus.

26. which see, q.v., *quod vide* [L.]; *loco citato* [L., in the place cited]; loc. cit., op. cit., o.c.; l.c.; *opere citato* [L., in the work cited],

PHRS. 27. it is proven, *probatum est* [L.], there is nothing more to be said, it must follow; Q.E.D., *quod erat demonstrandum* [L., which was to be demonstrated].

505. DISPROOF

NOUNS 1. disproof, disproval, invalidation, falsification, explosion, negation; exposure, exposition, exposé; *reductio ad absurdum* [L., a reduction to the absurd].

2. refutation, confutation, refutal, rebuttal, answer, complete answer; contradiction, opposition, controversion, contravention, traversal, denial, gainsaying; overthrowal, upset, subversion.

3. conclusive argument, knockdown argument, floorer, sockdolager [slang, U.S.], corker [slang]; clincher, crusher, settler, finisher, squelcher [all coll.].

VERBS 4. disprove, invalidate, discredit, falsify, belie, give the lie to; negate, negative; expose, show up; explode, blow up, blow sky-high, puncture, shoot full of holes; knock the bottom out of [coll.], knock the props out from under, take the ground from under, cut the ground from under one's feet, not leave a leg to stand on.

5. refute, confute, rebut, parry, answer, answer conclusively, dismiss, dispose of; contradict, controvert, contravene, traverse, oppose, dispute, deny, impugn, gainsay; overthrow, overturn, overwhelm, throw over, upset, subvert, defeat, confound, gravel [coll.], floor, finish [chiefly coll.]; settle, squash [chiefly coll.], squelch [chiefly coll.], crush, smash all opposition; silence, put or reduce to silence, shut up, stop the mouth of.

ADJS. 6. refuting, confuting, confutative, refutative, refutatory; contradictory, contrary, negatory.

7. disproved, invalidated, negated, discredited, falsified, belied; exposed, shown up; punctured, exploded; refuted, confuted; contradicted, disputed, denied, impugned; upset, overthrown, overturned; dismissed, discarded, rejected.

8. unproved, unproven, undemonstrated, unshown; untried, untested; unfounded 482.12; unestablished, unfixed, unsettled, undetermined, unascertained; unconfirmed, unsubstantiated, unattested, unauthenticated, unvalidated, uncertified, unverified, uncorroborated, unsustained, unsupported, unsupported by evidence;

inconclusive, indecisive; inconsequent, inconsequential, not following.

9. unprovable, undemonstrable, undemonstratable, unattestable, unconfirmable, unsubstantiatable, unsupportable, unsustainable, unverifiable.

10. refutable, confutable, disprovable, defeasible.

506. QUALIFICATION

NOUNS 1. qualification, limitation, restriction, modification, coloring, allowance, concession, cession, grant, consideration, grain of salt; reservation, exception, exemption; mental reservation, *arrière-pensée* [F.]; extenuating circumstances.

2. condition, provision, proviso, stipulation, specification, arrangement, situation, circumstance, case; string, a string to it [both coll.]; requisite, prerequisite, obligation; postulate, postulation; *sine qua non, conditio sine qua non* [both L.]; joker [U.S.]; clause; saving clause; escalator clause; terms, provisions, etc., grounds; ultimatum.

VERBS 3. qualify, modify, limit, restrict, restrain, narrow; affect, give a color to, take color from; adjust to, regulate by; temper, season, leaven, soften, modulate, moderate, assuage, mitigate, palliate, abate, reduce, diminish.

4. condition, make it a condition; stipulate, postulate, specify, define, fix, determine; insist upon, make a point of; bind, tie; have a string to it [coll.].

5. allow for, make allowance for, provide for, take account of, take into account or consideration, consider, reckon with, allow, grant, concede, acknowledge, admit, admit exceptions; disregard, leave out of account; discount, consider the source, take with a grain of salt.

6. depend, hang, rest, hinge; depend on or upon, hang on or upon, rest on or upon, rest with, repose upon, lie on, lie with, stand on or upon, be based on, be dependent on, be contingent on; hinge on or upon, turn on or upon, revolve on or upon, revolve around, hang around.

ADJS. 7. qualifying, qualificative, qualificatory; modifying, modificatory; limiting, restricting, limitative, restrictive; exceptional, exceptionable; extenuating, extenuatory; mitigating, mitigative, mitigatory, modulatory, palliative, assuasive, lenitive.

8. **conditional, provisional,** provisory, **iffy** [coll.]; specificative, stipulatory; **specified, stipulated,** fixed, stated, given.

9. **contingent, dependent, depending; contingent on, dependent on, depending on,** depending on circumstances; **subject to,** incidental to, incident to.

10. **qualified, modified, conditioned,** limited, restricted, guarded; **tempered, seasoned,** leavened, softened, **mitigated,** modulated.

ADVS. 11. **conditionally, provisionally,** admittedly, allowedly, by allowance, **with qualifications,** with a string to it [coll.]; with a reservation *or* exception, with a grain of salt; notwithstanding **33.8.**

CONJS. 12. **provided,** provided that, provided always, **providing,** with this proviso, it being provided; **on condition,** on condition that, **with the stipulation,** with the understanding, **in consideration of,** according as, subject to; **in case,** just in case, in any case, in either case, in case that, **in the event of,** in such a contingency or event; whether, whether or not *or* no.

13. **granting, admitting, allowing,** admitting that, allowing that, **supposing that,** on the supposition that.

14. **if,** gif [Scot. & dial., Eng.], gin [Scot.], namely if, if only, if so be, if it be so, if it be true that, if it so happens *or* turns out.

15. **so,** just so, so that, so as, **so long as, as long as;** even so, at that [coll.].

16. **unless,** less'n [dial.], unless that, **if not,** were it not, were it not that; **except, excepting,** except that, without [chiefly dial.]; **but, however.**

507. NO QUALIFICATIONS

NOUNS 1. **no qualifications,** no conditions, no reservations, no restrictions, etc. **506, no strings attached** [coll.]; **no ifs, ands or buts.**

ADJS. 2. **unqualified, unconditional,** unconditioned, **unrestricted, unlimited,** unmitigated, **unreserved,** without reserve; **implicit,** unquestioning, undoubting, unhesitating; **explicit, express,** clear, unmistakable; **peremptory, categorical, unequivocal,** indisputable, inappealable; **positive, absolute,** definite, definitive, determinate, decided, decisive, fixed, final; round, flat; **complete, entire, total, utter,** perfect, **downright,** outright, out-and-out, straight, straight-out [coll., U.S.], all-out.

508. POSSIBILITY

NOUNS 1. **possibility,** possibleness, conceivableness, **conceivability,** imaginability; **likelihood 510.1;** perhaps, what may be; **possible,** the possible, the attainable; potential, potentiality; contingency, eventuality; **chance, show** [coll.]; **outside chance** [coll.], off chance, remote possibility; good possibility, good chance, even chance **155.7, 8;** bare possibility **155.9.**

2. **practicability, practicality, feasibility; workability,** operability, actability, performability, negotiability [coll.]; **achievability, attainability;** surmountability, superability.

3. **accessibility,** access, **approachability,** reachableness, come-at-ableness [coll.], get-at-ableness; **penetrability,** perviousness, **passability,** navigability; obtainableness, **attainability, availability,** procurableness, securableness, gettableness, acquirability.

VERBS 4. **be possible, have** or **stand a chance** or **good chance,** have *or* stand a show [coll.], **bid** *or* **stand fair to;** have a leg to stand on; admit of, bear.

5. **make possible, put in the way of,** bring to effect, bring to bear.

ADJS. 6. **possible, within the bounds, ~** realm *or* range of possibility, humanly possible, earthly; **likely 510.5; conceivable,** conceivably possible, **imaginable, thinkable,** cogitable; plausible **510.6;** contingent, eventual; potential, in the cards.

7. **practicable, practical, feasible; workable,** performable, actable, operable, negotiable [coll.], doable; **achievable, attainable; surmountable,** superable, **overcomable.**

8. **accessible, approachable,** come-at-able [coll.], get-at-able, **reachable,** within reach, to be got at; **open,** open to; **penetrable,** pervious, passable, navigable; **obtainable, attainable, available,** procurable, securable, gettable, to be had.

ADVS. 9. **possibly, conceivably,** imaginably, feasibly; perhaps, perchance, haply; **maybe,** it may be, as it may be, as the case may be, for all *or* aught one knows; on the bare possibility, on the off chance, by merest chance.

10. **by any possibility, by any chance,** by any means, **by any manner of means; in any case, in any event,** in any way, in any possible way, **at any cost, at all,** if at all, ever.

11. **if possible,** if humanly possible, if

worst comes to worst, **God willing, wind and weather permitting;** as luck may have it, as it may chance, as it may turn up or out; all things considered, everything being equal.

509. IMPOSSIBILITY

NOUNS **1. impossibility, impossibleness, inconceivability,** absurdity; what cannot be, what can never be; no chance 155.10; impossible, the impossible, the unattainable; sour grapes.

2. impracticability, unpracticability, impracticality, unfeasibility; unworkability, inoperability, unperformability; **unachievability, unattainability;** insurmountability, insuperability.

3. inaccessibility, unaccessibility; **unapproachability,** un-come-at-ableness [coll.], unreachableness; **impenetrability,** imperviousness, **impassability,** unnavigability; unobtainableness, **unattainability, unavailability,** unprocurableness, unsecurableness, ungettableness, unacquirability.

VERBS **4. be impossible,** be an impossibility, **not have a chance,** be a waste of time.

5. attempt the impossible, look for a needle in a haystack or in a bottle of hay, try to be in two places at once, try to fetch water in a sieve, ~ catch the wind in a net, ~ weave a rope of sand, ~ get figs from thistles, ~ gather grapes from thorns, ~ make bricks from straw, ~ make cheese of chalk, ~ make a silk purse out of a sow's ear, ~ skin a flint, ~ change the leopard's spots, ~ wash a blackamoor white, ~ catch the weasel asleep.

ADJS. **6. impossible, not possible,** beyond the bounds of possibility or reason, contrary to reason, at variance with the facts; **inconceivable, unimaginable, unthinkable, not to be thought of, out of the question;** absurd, ridiculous, preposterous, outlandish, unheard-of.

7. impracticable, impractical, unfeasible; unworkable, unperformable, inoperable, undoable, unnegotiable [coll.]; **unachievable, unattainable;** insurmountable, unsurmountable, insuperable, unovercomable; **beyond one,** beyond one's power, beyond control, out of one's depth, too much for.

8. inaccessible, unaccessible; **unapproachable,** un-come-at-able [coll.]; **unreachable,** beyond reach, out of reach; **impenetrable,** impervious, **impassable,** un-

navigable; closed to, denied to, lost to; **unobtainable, unattainable, unavailable,** unprocurable, unsecurable, ungettable, unacquirable; not to be had, **not to be had for love or money.**

ADVS. **9. impossibly, inconceivably,** unimaginably, unthinkably, implausibly, incredibly.

510. PROBABILITY

NOUNS **1. probability, likelihood,** likeliness, **chance, liability, aptitude,** verisimilitude; **prospect,** outlook; favorable prospect, well-grounded hope; **good chance** 155.8; presumption, presumptive evidence; probable cause [law], reasonable ground or presumption; probabilism.

2. plausibility, ostensibility; **reasonability** 481.10; **credibility** 500.6.

VERBS **3. seem likely,** like to [coll.], admit of, offer a good prospect, have a good chance; **promise,** be promising, make fair promise, **bid** or **stand fair to,** lead one to expect.

4. think likely, flatter oneself, **dare say,** venture to say; **presume,** suppose 498.9; **gather, conclude,** deduce, take for granted.

ADJS. **5. probable, likely,** like [coll.], **liable, apt,** verisimilar, in the cards; **promising, hopeful,** fair, in a fair way; **presumable,** presumptive.

6. plausible, apparent, ostensible, specious, colorable; **reasonable** 481.21; **credible** 500.21; **conceivable** 508.6; **well-founded,** well-grounded; well-invented, *ben trovato* [It.].

ADVS. **7. probably, in all probability** or **likelihood,** likely, **most likely, very likely,** very like, like enough, as like as not [coll.]; **doubtlessly,** doubtless, **no doubt; presumably,** seemingly, apparently; all things considered, everything being equal; ten to one, a hundred to one, dollars to doughnuts [U.S.], all Lombard Street to a China orange.

PHRS. **8. there is reason to believe,** I am led to believe, it can be supposed, it might be thought, one can assume, appearances are in favor of, the chances or odds are, you can bet on it, you can just bet, you can't go wrong; I dare say or daresay, I venture to say.

511. IMPROBABILITY

NOUNS **1. improbability, unlikelihood,** unlikeliness; **doubtfulness, questionableness; implausibility,** incredibility; poor possibility, poor prospect, poor lookout [coll.]; small chance 155.9.

VERBS 2. be improbable, not be likely, be a stretch on the imagination, strain one's credulity, go beyond reason, go beyond the bounds of reason or probability.

ADJS. 3. improbable, unlikely, hardly possible; doubtful, questionable, doubtable, dubitable, more than doubtful; implausible, incredible, fishy [coll.].

PHRS. 4. not likely!, no fear!, I ask you!, you should live so long! [slang].

512. CERTAINTY

NOUNS 1. certainty, certitude, sureness, surety, assurance, assuredness; positiveness, absoluteness, definiteness, dead ~, moral or absolute certainty; unequivocalness, unmistakableness; infallibility, inerrability; inevitability 637.7.

2. (slang terms) sure thing, sure bet, sure card, cinch, lead-pipe cinch, open-and-shut case.

3. unquestionability, undeniability, indubitableness, indisputability, incontestability, incontrovertibility, irrefutability, unrefutability, unconfutability, incontrovertibility, irrefragability, unimpeachability; doubtlessness, questionlessness.

4. reliability, dependability, trustworthiness, faithworthiness; predictability, calculability; stability, substantiality, firmness, soundness, secureness, security, solidity, staunchness, stanchness, steadiness, steadfastness; authoritativeness, authenticity.

5. confidence, confidentness, sureness, assurance, assuredness, surety, security, certitude; trust 500.1; positiveness, cocksureness; self-confidence, self-assurance, self-reliance; poise 856.3; courage 891; overconfidence, oversureness, overweening, overweeningness.

6. dogmatism, dogmaticalness, positiveness, positivism, pragmatism, arbitrariness, peremptoriness, dictatorialness; opinionatedness, self-opinionatedness; infallibilism.

7. dogmatist, dogmatizer, opinionist, positivist, infallibilist, Sir Oracle.

8. ascertainment, certification, determination, establishment, assurance; reassurance, reassessment; verification, collation, check, checking; confirmation 504.5.

VERBS 9. be certain, be confident, feel sure, rest assured, have no doubt, doubt not; know, just know, know for certain; bet

on, gamble on, go bail on, bet one's bottom dollar on [all coll.]; stand to reason, admit of no doubt; go without saying, *aller sans dire* [F.].

10. dogmatize, lay down the law.

11. make sure, make certain, make sure of, make no doubt, remove or dismiss all doubt, assure, ensure, insure, certify, ascertain, find out, get at, see to it, see that, determine, decide, establish, settle, fix, clinch, cinch [slang], set at rest, find out exactly, find out once for all; assure or satisfy oneself, make oneself easy about or on that score; reassure.

12. verify, certify, audit, collate, check, check up [U.S.], check up on [coll.], check over or through, doublecheck, triple-check, cross-check, recheck, check and doublecheck, check up and down, check over and through, check in and out, "make assurance double sure" [Shakespeare]; confirm 504.12.

ADJS. 13. certain, sure, sure-enough [dial., U.S.]; positive, absolute, definite, perfectly sure; decided, decisive; clear, unmistakable; inevitable 637.15.

14. dead sure, sure as death, sure as death and taxes, sure as fate, sure as a gun or as a gun is iron [coll.], sure as eggs is eggs or X is X [coll.], sure as God made little green apples [slang], sure as hell or the devil [vulg.], as sure as I live and breathe [slang], sure as preaching [slang, U.S.].

15. unquestionable, undeniable, indubitable, indisputable, incontestable, irrefutable, unrefutable, unconfutable, incontrovertible, noncontroversial, irrefragable, unanswerable, inappealable, unimpeachable; unequivocal, univocal, unmistakable.

16. undoubted, indubious, unquestioned, undisputed, uncontested, uncontradicted, unchallenged, uncontroverted, doubtless, questionless, beyond a shade or shadow of doubt, past dispute, beyond question.

17. reliable, dependable, sure, sure-fire [slang, U.S.], trustworthy, trusty, faithworthy, to be depended or relied upon, to be counted or reckoned on; predictable, calculable; straight [slang]; secure, solid, sound, firm, fast, stable, substantial, established, staunch, stanch, steady, steadfast, faithful, unfailing; well-founded, well-grounded.

18. authoritative, authentic, official; cathedral, ex cathedra; standard, approved, accepted, received.

19. infallible, inerrable, inerrant, unerring.

20. assured, sure, made sure, bound, **determined, decided, ascertained, arranged, settled,** established, fixed, cinched [slang], set [coll.], stated, determinate, secure; **open-and-shut** [coll., U.S.], **in the bag** [slang], on ice [slang, U.S.].

21. confident, reliant, sure, secure, **assured,** reassured, decided, determined; **convinced,** positive, **cocksure; unhesitating,** unfaltering, unwavering; **undoubting** 500.18; **self-confident, self-assured, self-reliant,** sure of oneself; poised 856.13; unafraid 891.19; **overconfident, oversure,** overweening.

22. dogmatic(al), positive, positivistic, absolute, peremptory, arbitrary, dictatorial, magisterial, **pragmatic(al),** categoric(al); **opinionated,** opinioned, opinionative, conceited; **self-opinionated,** self-opinioned; doctrinary, doctrinaire.

ADVS. **23. certainly, surely, assuredly, positively, absolutely, definitely,** precisely, exactly, decidedly, decisively, distinctly, clearly, unequivocally, unmistakably; **for certain,** for sure [slang], for fair [slang], for a fact [coll.], and no mistake [coll.]; **of** or **for a certainty,** to a certainty, *à coup sûr* [F.]; **most certainly,** most assuredly; **indeed,** indeedy [coll., U.S.]; truly 515.16; **of course,** as a matter of course; **by all means,** by all manner of means; at any rate, at all events; nothing else but [slang], no two ways about it, no buts about it [coll.]; no ifs, ands or buts.

24. sure, to be sure, sure enough; sure thing, surest thing you know, sure Mike [all slang, U.S.].

25. unquestionably, undoubtedly, undoubtably [dial.], **indubitably, admittedly, undeniably,** indisputably, incontestably, incontrovertibly, irrefutably, irrefragably; **doubtlessly,** doubtless, **no doubt, without doubt,** beyond doubt or question, out of question.

26. without fail, whatever may happen, **come what may,** if worst comes to worst, come hell or high water [slang]; cost what it may, *coûte que coûte* [F.]; rain or shine, live or die, sink or swim.

PHRS. **27. it is certain,** there is no question, there is not a shadow of doubt, that's for sure [slang]; that goes without saying, *cela va sans dire* [F.]; that is evident, that leaps to the eye, *cela saute aux yeux* [F.].

513. UNCERTAINTY

NOUNS **1. uncertainty, incertitude, unsureness,** uncertainness; **unpredictability,** incalculability, unaccountability; **indetermination, indecision,** indecisiveness, undecidedness, undeterminedness; **hesitation,** hesitancy; suspense, state of suspense; **changeableness** 141; **irresolution** 625.

2. doubtfulness, dubiousness, doubt, dubiety, dubitation; **questionability, disputability,** contestability, controvertibility, refutability, confutability, deniability; disbelief 502.

3. bewilderment, disconcertion, embarrassment, confoundment; confusion 530.3; **perplexity, quandary; dilemma,** horns of a dilemma; **puzzle,** puzzlement; baffle, **bafflement; nonplus,** nonplusation; fix [coll.], hobble [coll.], pucker [coll.], stew [slang]; perturbation, disturbance, bother, pother.

4. vagueness, indefiniteness, indecisiveness, indeterminateness, indeterminableness, indefinableness, **unclearness, indistinctness,** haziness; **obscurity,** obscuration; **looseness, laxity,** inexactness; **broadness, generality.**

5. equivocalness, ambiguity 548.

6. unreliability, undependability, untrustworthiness, unfaithworthiness, **unsureness; insecurity, unsoundness, infirmity, instability,** insubstantiality, unsubstantiality, **unsteadfastness,** unsteadiness, shakiness; **precariousness,** ticklishness, slipperiness; speculativeness; **unauthoritativeness,** unauthenticity.

7. fallibility, errability, errancy.

8. (an uncertainty) **gamble** [coll.], chance [dial., U.S.], **tossup, touch and go;** contingency, double contingency, possibility upon a possibility; something or other; **question, open question;** blind bargain, pig in a poke; leap in the dark; needle in a haystack or bottle of hay.

VERBS **9. be uncertain, feel unsure; doubt,** have one's doubts, **question,** puzzle over; wonder, wonder whether; not know what to make of, not be able to make head or tail of; be at sea, float in a sea of doubt; **not know which way to turn,** not know where one stands, not know whether one stands on one's head or one's heels; flounder, beat about, go around in circles.

10. hang in doubt, stop to consider, think twice; **falter, hesitate, vacillate** 625.6–8.

11. **depend, pend,** all depend; **hang in the balance,** hang in suspense; hang by a thread, hang by the eyelids.

12. **bewilder, disconcert, dismay,** abash, embarrass, **put out,** disturb, perturb, pother, **bother,** moider [dial.], flummox [slang]; **confuse** 530.7.

13. **perplex, baffle, confound,** buffalo [slang, U.S.], bamboozle [coll.], **mystify, puzzle,** pose; **nonplus,** stick [coll.], tree [coll.], **stump** [coll., chiefly U.S.], put up a tree or stump [slang], **floor** [coll.], gravel [coll.], throw [slang], throw on one's beam ends, **get** [chiefly coll.], get one down [coll.], **beat** [coll.], lick [slang], put to it, put to one's wit's end; keep one guessing, keep in suspense.

ADJS. 14. **uncertain, unsure;** speculative, chancy [coll.], touch-and-go; **unpredictable, incalculable, unaccountable,** undivinable; equivocal, ambiguous 548.3; changeable 141.7.

15. **doubtful,** doubtsome [Scot. & dial., Eng.], iffy [coll.]; **in doubt,** in dubio [L.]; dubitable, doubtable, **dubious,** dubitative; **questionable, problematic(al),** debatable, disputable, contestable, controvertible, controversial, refutable, confutable, deniable; undemonstrable, unsustainable; suspicious; **suspect;** open, open to question or doubt; **in question,** in dispute, at issue; doubting 502.9.

16. **undecided, undetermined, unsettled,** unfixed; untold, uncounted; pendent, dependent, **pending,** depending; **in the balance, up in the air;** in suspense, in a state of suspense; **hesitant,** hesitating; **indecisive,** indeterminative; **irresolute** 625.9.

17. **vague, indefinite, indecisive, indeterminate,** indeterminable, indefinable, undefined, ill-defined, **unclear,** unplain, **indistinct, obscure, confused,** hazy, foggy, veiled, shadowy, shadowed forth; **loose, lax, inexact;** nonspecific, unspecified; **broad, general.**

18. **unreliable, undependable, untrustworthy,** unfaithworthy, **unsure,** not to be depended or relied on; **insecure, unsound, infirm, unstable,** unsubstantial, insubstantial, **unsteadfast,** unsteady, shaky; **precarious,** ticklish, slippery.

19. **unauthoritative, unauthentic,** unofficial, nonofficial, apocryphal.

20. **fallible, errable,** errant, mistakable.

21. **unconfident, unsure, unassured, insecure, unreliant,** unsure of oneself; unself-confident, unself-assured, unself-reliant.

22. **bewildered, dismayed, abashed, disconcerted,** embarrassed, **put-out,** disturbed, perturbed, **bothered,** all hot and bothered [slang, U.S.]; **confused** 530.12; mazed, in a maze; turned around, going around in circles, like a chicken with its head cut off [coll.]; in a pucker, in a hobble, in a fix [all coll.]; lost, astray, abroad, adrift, **at sea,** off the track, out of one's reckoning, out of one's bearings.

23. **in a dilemma,** on the horns of a dilemma; **perplexed, confounded, mystified, puzzled, baffled,** bushed, bamboozled [coll.], buffaloed [slang, U.S.]; **nonplused,** at a nonplus; **at a loss, at one's wit's end,** on one's beam ends, at the end of one's rope or tether; hard put, hard put to it, up against it [slang]; beat [coll.], licked [slang]; stuck, floored, graveled, stumped, treed, up a tree or stump [all coll.]; thrown, sunk [both slang]; **up in the air** [coll.], **on tenterhooks,** in suspense.

24. **bewildering, confusing, distracting, disconcerting, dismaying, embarrassing,** disturbing, perturbing, bothering; **perplexing, baffling, mystifying, puzzling,** confounding; intricate 46.4; enigmatical 547.15.

ADVS. 25. **uncertainly, unsurely; doubtfully, questionably,** dubitably, **dubiously;** things being as they are, the way things stand, in these uncertain times.

26. **vaguely, indefinitely,** indeterminably, indefinably, **indistinctly,** indecisively, obscurely; **broadly, generally,** in broad or general terms.

PHRS. 27. who knows?, who can tell?, who shall decide when doctors disagree?; you never can tell, don't be too sure.

514. GAMBLE

NOUNS 1. **gamble, chance, risk, hazard,** die; **speculation, venture;** flutter, flier or flyer [both slang]; plunge [slang]; **calculated risk; uncertainty** 513; **fortune, luck** 155.

2. **matter of chance,** gambling chance, chance at odds; hazard of the die, cast or throw of the dice, turn or roll of the wheel, turn of the table, turn of the cards, fall of the cards, flip of the coin; **tossup,** toss; heads or tails, touch and go; blind bargain, pig in a poke; leap in the dark, shot in the dark [slang]; potshot, random shot; potluck.

3. **wager, bet, stake, hazard, play,** shot [slang]; ante, blind [poker]; coppered bet [cant, U.S.], heeled bet [cant], open bet, sleeper [faro]; parlay [U.S.], paroli;

pyramid; flat play [cant]; sweepstakes, sweeps; pari-mutuel; book, handbook (record of bets).

4. pot, jack pot, pool, stakes, kitty [chiefly slang], *cave* [F.]; **bank**, tiger [faro].

5. odds, price; equivalent odds; **even** *or* **square odds**, even break [chiefly coll.], six-two-and-even [cant]; **short odds**, ten-to-one shot [slang]; **long odds**, long shot [slang], hundred-to-one shot [slang]; overlay [cant]; even chance, good chance, small chance, no chance 155.7–10.

6. gambling, gaming, sporting, **speculation**. play, playing; **betting, wagering**, staking; drawing *or* casting lots, sortition; cardsharping.

7. (games of chance) chuck-a-luck *or* chuckluck, chuck farthing, crack-loo *or* crackaloo [slang, U.S.], cup tossing, fantan, hazard, horse racing, keno, lotto, pinball, pitch *or* chuck and toss, roulette, sweepstake *or* sweepstakes; poker, faro, etc. (card games) 876.35.

8. dice, cubes, bones [coll.], **ivories**, devil's bones *or* teeth [all slang]; **craps**, crap shooting, elbow shaking [slang], crap game; indoor golf, African dominoes, Mississippi marbles, Memphis dominoes, animated dominoes *or* ivories [all joc.]; poker dice; loaded dice, false *or* crooked dice; flats, goads, tats [all slang]; dice box, devil's box [slang], bird cage.

9. (throw of dice) **throw, cast, roll, shot**, hazard of the die; dice throws (snake eyes, etc.) 90.3, 93.2, 96.1, 99.1–7; crap, craps, crabs (losing throw); natural, nick.

10. lottery, draw [slang, U.S.]; turkey draw [slang, U.S.]; **raffle**; lotto, Genoese *or* number lottery; tombola, interest lottery, Dutch *or* class lottery; sweepstakes; numbers pool; grab bag, ~ barrel *or* box [coll., U.S.].

11. (gambling device) gambling wheel, wheel, wheel of fortune, Fortune's wheel; roulette wheel; raffle wheel; pinball machine; slot machine, one-armed bandit [slang, U.S.]; gambling table, crap table.

12. pari-mutuel, pari-mutuel machine; totalizator, totalizer.

13. counter, check, chip, fish [slang], bone.

14. gambling house, gaming house, betting house, **gambling den, gambling hell**, hell, Domdaniel, *tripot* [F., slang]; joint, flat, crib [all slang]; casino; pool room; bucket shop.

15. bookmaker, bookie [coll.].

16. gambler, gamester, gamestress [fem.], **player, sportsman, sporting man**, sport [coll.], hazarder, **venturer**, adventurer; **better**, bettor, **wagerer**, punter; **speculator**, speculatist; plunger [slang]; petty gambler, piker [slang, U.S.]; tinhorn, tinhorn gambler [both slang]; sharpshooter [slang], **sharper**, sharp [slang]; **cardsharp**, cardsharper; crap shooter [coll.], dicer, elbow shaker [slang], knight of the elbow [joc.]; oraler [chiefly turf slang]; betting ring.

VERBS 17. gamble, game, sport, play, try one's luck *or* fortune; **speculate; draw lots**, lot, cut lots; **cast lots**, set on a cast; cut the cards *or* deck; match coins; toss up, flip the coin, call the coin, call heads *or* tails; shoot craps, play at dice; play the ponies [slang]; raffle off.

18. chance, risk, hazard, set at hazard; **venture**, adventure, venture upon; **gamble on**, take a gamble on; **take a chance**, take one's chance, take the chances of, try the chance, **chance it**, chance one's luck *or* hand [coll.], "stand the hazard of the die" [Shakespeare]; take *or* **run the risk**, run a chance, **take chances**, tempt fortune; **leave** *or* **trust to chance** *or* **luck**, rely on fortune, trust to the chapter of accidents; go it blind [slang], take a leap in the dark; buy a pig in a poke, *acheter chat en poche* [F.]; take potluck.

19. bet, wager, gamble, hazard, stake, post [slang], **punt, lay, lay down, make a bet, lay a wager**; take a flyer [slang]; plunge [slang]; pike [slang, U.S.]; **bet on** *or* **upon, back**; bet *or* play against, copper [cant, U.S.], buck *or* fight the tiger [faro]; parlay [U.S.], paroli; **ante, ante up**; double the blind, straddle [both poker]; **meet a bet, see, call, cover, fade** [dice], see one's blind [poker]; **pass; stand pat**.

ADJS. 20. speculative, uncertain 513.14; **hazardous, risky** 695.10.

PROVERBS 21. nothing ventured, nothing gained; nothing venture, nothing win; naught venture, naught have; nothing stake, nothing draw; nought lay down, nought take up; nought won by the one, nought won by the other.

515. TRUTH

Conformity to Fact or Reality.—NOUNS **1. truth, trueness, verity, veritability**, right; **unerroneousness, unfalseness**, unfallaciousness; the truth, the truth of the matter, the case, what is right, what's what [coll.]; **fact, reality** 1.2, 3; the true, ultimate truth; eternal verities; veracity 972.3.

2. the unvarnished truth, the naked truth, the plain truth, the unqualified truth, the honest truth, the sober truth, the exact truth; the straight truth, the straight of it [slang]; gospel, gospel truth, scripture, Bible, Bible truth; the truth, the whole truth and nothing but the truth.

3. accuracy, correctness, rightness; **exactness, exactitude; preciseness, precision;** mathematical precision, pinpoint precision, scientific exactness; faultlessness, perfection; definiteness, positiveness, absoluteness; faithfulness, fidelity; strictness, severity, rigidity, rigorousness, rigor; niceness, nicety, delicacy, subtlety, fineness, refinement; **meticulousness** 531.3.

4. validity, soundness, solidity, substantiality, goodness, **meritoriousness, justness,** sufficiency; authority, **authoritativeness; cogency,** weight, force, forcefulness, efficaciousness.

5. genuineness, authenticity, bona fideness, **legitimacy, realness, reality,** originality, naturality; **inartificiality,** unsyntheticness; **unspuriousness,** unspeciousness, unfictitiousness, unaffectedness; **honesty, sincerity;** unadulteration 45.1.

6. the real thing, the genuine article, the article [slang], the goods [slang, U.S.], the cheese or real cheese [slang], the McCoy or the real McCoy [slang, U.S.], the real Simon Pure, not an illusion.

VERBS **7. be true,** be the case; **carry conviction; ring true,** sound true, hold the ring of truth; **prove true,** prove to be, prove, turn out, come out, be in fact; **hold true, hold good, hold water** [coll.], hold together [coll.], **hold up, hold up in the wash** [slang], wash [coll.], stand up, stand the test, hold, remain valid.

8. be right, be correct, be O.K. or okay [coll.], **hit the nail on the head,** hit it on the nose [slang], score a bull's eye, have dead to rights [slang].

9. be accurate, dot the i's and cross the t's, draw or cut it fine [coll.], speak by the card.

10. come true, come about, come off, come out, turn out, come to pass, happen as expected.

ADJS. **11. true, unerroneous, unfalse, unfallacious, unmistaken; real, actual,** factual, **veritable,** sure-enough [dial. & slang, U.S.], true to the facts; **certain,** undoubted, unquestionable 512.13–16; unre-

futed, unconfuted, undenied; true as gospel, true as steel, true as touch or touchstone; substantially true, categorically true.

12. valid, sound, well-grounded, well-founded, solid, substantial, pucka [Anglo-India]; **good, meritorious, just,** sufficient; **cogent, weighty, forceful, authoritative;** effectual, efficacious; **legal, lawful, binding.**

13. genuine, authentic, real, natural, native, **legitimate, bona fide, good,** rightful, veridical, straight [slang], sure-enough [dial. & slang, U.S.], **sincere, honest,** honest-to-God [slang]; **inartificial, unsynthetic; unspurious, unspecious, unsimulated, unfaked, unfeigned, undisguised, uncounterfeited, unpretended, unaffected, unassumed; unassuming,** unpretending, unfeigning, undisguising; **unfictitious,** unfabricated, uninvented, unimagined, unideal; **original,** unimitated, uncopied; unexaggerated, undistorted, unflattering; unvarnished, uncolored, unqualified; **unadulterated** 45.6; **pure, simon-pure; sterling,** eighteen-carat, blown in the glass [slang, U.S.], all wool and a yard wide [coll.].

14. accurate, correct, right, proper, all right or alright [coll.], **O.K.** or okay [coll.], just right, dead right; dead to rights, bang to rights, right as rain [all slang]; straight, straight-up-and-down; **faultless, perfect;** letter-perfect; **meticulous** 531.12.

15. exact, precise, express, direct, just; even, square; **definite, positive, absolute,** absolutely ~, definitely or positively right; distinct, clear-cut, clean-cut, well-defined; **faithful,** servile; **unerring,** undeviating; **strict,** stern, severe, **rigorous,** rigid; mathematically exact, mathematical; scientifically exact, scientific; religiously exact, religious; **nice,** delicate, subtle, **fine,** refined; pinpoint.

ADVS. **16. truly, really,** really-truly [coll.], **verily,** veritably, forsooth, **in truth,** in good or very truth, **actually, in reality, in fact,** in point of fact, as a matter of fact, to tell the truth, to state the fact or truth, of a truth, with truth; **indeed,** indeedy [coll., U.S.]; **certainly,** undoubtedly 512.23–25; no buts about it [coll.], nothing else but.

17. genuinely, authentically, really, naturally, legitimately, rightfully, **honestly,** veridically; unaffectedly, unassumedly.

18. accurately, correctly, rightly, properly, straight [coll.]; **perfectly, faultlessly; just right,** just so [coll.], to-rights [coll. & dial.].

19. exactly, precisely, expressly; just, right [chiefly coll.], straight, even, square, dead, directly, squarely, point-blank; unerringly, undeviatingly; faithfully, servilely; strictly, rigidly; definitely, positively, absolutely; in every respect, in all respects, for all the world, neither more nor less.

20. to be exact, to be precise, strictly speaking, not to mince the matter.

21. to a nicety, to a T or tittle, to a turn, to a hair, to or within an inch.

PHRS. **22.** that's right, that is so, that's it, that's just it, it is that, *c'est ça* [F.]; you are right, right you are, that's a thought, you've got something there, I'll say, it is for a fact, amen, you speak truly, as you say, enough said, objection sustained; right, righto [coll.], quite, rather! [coll.]; you said it, you said a mouthful, now you're talking, you tell 'em, you can say that again, you're not kidding, that's for sure, ain't it the truth?, you're darn tootin [all slang]; don't I know it?, you're telling me?

516. MAXIM

NOUNS **1.** maxim, aphorism, apothegm, epigram, dictum, adage, proverb, gnome, saw, saying, sentence, phrase, word, byword, mot, motto, moral; proverbial saying; common or current saying; pithy saying, sententious expression or saying.

2. axiom, theorem, scholium; truism, truth, self-evident truth, general or universal truth, wise expression or saying, oracle; proposition, principle, principium, settled principle; formula, formulary; precept, prescript, prescription; recipe, receipt; rule, law, dictate, dictum; golden rule.

3. platitude, cliché, commonplace, banality, bromide or bromidium [slang], chestnut [coll.], corn [slang], triticism, trite saying, hackneyed or stereotyped saying, commonplace expression, cuckoo words, familiar tune, old song [coll.], old saw, old hat [slang], old story [coll.]; twice-told tale, retold story, warmed-over cabbage [coll.], *réchauffé* [F.]; reiteration 103.2; prosaicism, prosaism, prose; old joke 879.9.

4. motto, slogan, watchword; device [heraldry]; inscription, epigraph, epitaph.

VERBS **5.** aphorize, apothegmatize, epigrammatize.

ADJS. **6.** epigrammatic(al), aphoristic, proverbial, axiomatic(al); sententious,

pithy, piquant, succinct, terse, crisp, pointed; platitudinous 881.9.

ADVS. **7.** proverbially, as the saying is, as they say, as the fellow says [dial. or coll.], as it has been said, as it was said of old, to coin a phrase.

517. ERROR

NOUNS **1.** error, erroneousness; untrueness, untruth; wrongness, wrong; falseness, falsity; fallacy, fallaciousness; faultiness, defectiveness; errancy, aberrancy, aberration; perversion, distortion; misconstruction, misapplication; illusion 518; misjudgment 495; misinterpretation 551.

2. inaccuracy, inaccurateness, uncorrectness, inexactness, inexactitude, unpreciseness; approximation.

3. mistake, miss, miscarriage; error, erratum, corrigendum; fault, *faute* [F.]; misconception, misapprehension, misunderstanding; misstatement, misreport; misprint, typographical error; misidentification; miscalculation 495.1; misplay [U.S.]; misdeal; miscount.

4. slip, slip-up [coll.], miscue [slang]; lapse, *lapsus* [L.], oversight, omission, inadvertence or inadvertency, loose thread; misstep, trip, stumble, false or wrong step; slip of the tongue, *lapsus linguae* [L.]; slip of the pen, *lapsus calami* [L.].

5. blunder, faux pas, fox paw [joc.], *gaffe* [F.], solecism, bevue, balk; break, bad break [both coll.]; bloomer, blooper, boo-boo, bobble, misbobble, boner, bone, bonehead [all slang]; dumb trick [coll.], boob stunt [slang], fool mistake [coll.]; howler, scream, screamer [all slang]; stupidity, indiscretion 469.4; bungle 732.5.

6. grammatical error, solecism, misusage, missaying, mispronunciation; bull, Irish bull, Irishism, Hibernianism, Hibernicism; malapropism, malapropoism, malaprop, slipslop [coll.]; spoonerism; Partingtonism; Mrs. Malaprop [Sheridan], Mrs. Slipshop [Fielding], Mrs. Partington [B. P. Shillaber].

VERBS **7.** not hold water [coll.], not hold together [coll.], not stand up, not hold up, not hold up in the wash [coll.], not wash [coll.].

8. err, fall into error, go wrong, go amiss, go astray, go awry, stray, deviate, wander; lapse; slip, slip up, trip, stumble; miscalculate 495.2; misinterpret 551.2.

9. be wrong, be mistaken, be in the wrong, be in error, be at fault, miss the truth, have another guess coming [coll.]; receive a false impression, take the shadow for the substance; deceive oneself, be deceived; labor under a false impression.

10. bark up the wrong tree, back the wrong horse, take the wrong sow by the ear, ~ the wrong pig by the tail or the wrong bull by the horns, put the saddle on the wrong horse, count one's chickens before they are hatched, reckon without one's host, aim at a pigeon and kill a crow.

11. misdo, do amiss; misuse, misemploy, misapply; misconduct, mismanage; miscall, mis-cite, miscount, misdeal, misplay, misprint, misquote, misread, misreport, misspell.

12. mistake, make a mistake; miscue, make a miscue [both slang]; misidentify; misunderstand, misapprehend, misconceive.

13. blunder, make a blunder, make a faux pas, make or pull a boner, etc., 517.5, commit an absurdity, put one's foot in it [coll.], bull [slang, U.S.], goof, goof off [slang, U.S.], muff one's cue; misspeak, misspeak oneself [dial, or slang], put one's foot in one's mouth [slang]; blunder into, bonehead into [slang]; bungle 732.11.

ADJS. 14. erroneous, untrue, not true, not right; wrong, all wrong, peccant, perverse, corrupt; false, fallacious; faulty, faultful, defective, at fault; out, all out [coll.]; off, all off; wide, wide of the mark, beside the mark; out of line, out of keeping; amiss, awry, askew; erring, errant; aberrant, straying, astray, adrift; abroad, all abroad; perverted, distorted.

15. inaccurate, incorrect, inexact, unprecise; approximate, approximative; out of line, out of true, out of square.

16. mistaken, in error, under an error, at fault, wrong, in the wrong, all in the wrong, all wet [slang, U.S.]; off the track, off or out in one's reckoning; in the wrong box, in the right church but the wrong pew.

17. unauthentic, unauthoritative, unreliable 513.18, 19; unfounded 482.12; illusory 518.9; spurious 614.27.

ADVS. 18. erroneously, falsely, fallaciously; faultily, faultfully; untrue, untruely; wrong, wrongly; mistakenly; amiss, astray.

19. inaccurately, incorrectly, inexactly, unprecisely.

PHRS. 20. you are wrong, you are mistaken, you're all wet [slang], you have another guess coming [coll.], don't kid yourself [slang], you're crazy, it is like fun, it can't be, that isn't so.

518. ILLUSION

NOUNS 1. illusion, delusion; deception, trick; self-deception, self-deceit, self-delusion; misconception, misbelief, false belief, wrong impression, warped or distorted conception; bubble, chimera, vapor; ignis fatuus [L.], will-o'-the-wisp; dream, pipe dream [coll.]; fool's paradise.

2. illusoriness, illusiveness, delusiveness; falseness, fallaciousness; unreality, unactuality; unsubstantiality, immateriality; seeming, semblance, appearance, specious appearance, show, false show, false air, faux air [F.], false light.

3. fancy, imagining 533.5.

4. phantom, phantasm, phantasma, wraith, specter; shadow, shade; fantasy, phantasy; figment of the imagination, phantom of the mind; apparition, appearance; vision, image; shape, form, figure, presence; eidolon, idolum.

5. optical illusion, trick of eyesight.

6. mirage, fata morgana, looming; aftermirage, spectrum, ocular spectrum.

7. hallucination, fantastic vision, fantod [slang]; hallucinosis [psych.]; delirium tremens 472.10; nightmare, incubus [med.], bad dream.

VERBS 8. delude, deceive 616.13.

ADJS. 9. illusory, illusive, illusional, illusionary; delusory, delusive, delusional, deluding; imaginary 533.19; erroneous 517.14; deceptive 616.21; self-deceptive, self-deluding; phantasmal, fantastic, chimeric(al); unreal, unactual, unsubstantial; unfounded 482.12; false, fallacious, misleading; specious, seeming, apparent, ostensible, supposititious, all in the mind.

10. hallucinatory, hallucinative, hallucinational.

519. DISILLUSIONMENT

NOUNS 1. disillusionment, disillusion, disenchantment, disabusal, undeception, enlightenment, bursting of the bubble; awakening, rude awakening, the dawn of one's awakening; disappointment 539; debunkment [slang, U.S.].

VERBS 2. disillusion, dissillude, disenchant, disabuse, undeceive, unfool, correct, set right, put straight, tell the truth, enlighten, let into; free of, set free, clear the mind of; open one's eyes, awaken, wake up, unblindfold; disappoint 539.2; burst or prick the bubble, puncture one's balloon [coll.]; let the air out of, take the wind out of; knock the props out from under, take the ground from under; let down easy [coll.]; debunk [slang, U.S.]; expose, show up 554.1.

3. charge to experience.

ADJS. 4. disillusioning, disillusive, disenchanting, disabusing, undeceiving.

5. disillusioned, disenchanted, disabused, undeceived, enlightened, set right, put straight, free of, with one's eyes open; blasé; disappointed 539.5.

PHR. 6. came the dawn.

520. ASSENT

NOUNS 1. assent, acquiescence, compliance, agreement, acceptance, accession; consent 773.

2. affirmative; yes, yea, aye; nod, nod of assent; thumbs up.

3. acknowledgment, recognition, acceptance, admission, confession, concession, allowance, avowal.

4. ratification, endorsement, indorsement, acceptance, approval, sanction, O.K. or okay [slang], certification, confirmation, validation, authentication, authorization; affirmation, affirmance; stamp, stamp of approval; seal, signet, sigil; subscription, superscription, signature; countersignature; visa, visé; notarization.

5. unanimity, unanimousness; likemindedness, meeting of minds; understanding, mutual understanding; concurrence, consent, common assent or consent, consentience, consentaneity, accord, accordance, concord, concordance, agreement, general agreement; consensus, consensus of opinion; consensus omnium [L.], agreement of all; acclamation, general acclamation; unison, chorus, concert, one voice, one accord.

6. assenter, consenter, affirmant, accepter, acceptor, professor; covenantor.

7. endorser, indorser, subscriber, ratifier, certifier, confirmer; signer, signator, signatory; cosigner, cosignatory; underwriter, insurer.

VERBS 8. assent, give or yield assent, acquiesce, comply, accede, agree, agree to or with, take kindly to, hold with; accept, receive, buy [slang], take one up on [coll.]; subscribe to, lend oneself to; yes, say yes to; nod, give the nod, give a nod of assent; vote for, cast one's vote for, give one's voice for; consent 773.3.

9. concur, accord, consent, coincide, agree, gee [dial. & slang], agree with, agree in opinion, enter into one's view, enter into the ideas or feelings of, see eye to eye, be at one with, go with, go along with, fall ~, chime or strike in with, close with, meet, conform to; reciprocate, echo, ditto [coll.], say ditto to; join in the chorus, go ~, float or swim with the stream or current, get on the bandwagon [coll.], *hurler avec les loups* [F., howl with the wolves].

10. come to an agreement, agree, agree with, agree on or upon, arrive at an agreement, come to an understanding, come to terms, get together [coll.]; shake hands on, shake on it [coll.], strike hands; call it square [coll.], call it a go [coll.]; be a go [coll.], be a bargain, be on [slang].

11. acknowledge, accept, admit, own, confess, allow, avow, grant, warrant, concede, yield; recognize, respect, yield or submit to, defer to; come round to, abide by.

12. ratify, endorse, indorse, certify, confirm, affirm [law], validate, authenticate, accept, O.K. [slang], approve, sanction, authorize, accredit; pass, pass on or upon, give thumbs up [coll.]; amen, say amen to; visa, visé; underwrite, undersign, subscribe to; sign, autograph, sign on the dotted line, put one's John Hancock on [coll.], initial, put one's mark or cross on; cosign, countersign; seal, sign and seal, set one's seal, set one's hand and seal; rubberstamp [coll.]; notarize.

ADJS. 13. assenting, agreeing, acquiescing; acquiescent, compliant, submissive, agreed, content.

14. accepted, approved, received; acknowledged, admitted, allowed, granted, conceded, recognized, professed, confessed, avowed, warranted; unquestioned 512.16.

15. unanimous, solid [polit. cant, U.S.]; consentient, consentaneous, with one consent or voice; concurrent, concordant, of one accord; agreeing, in agreement, eye to eye; like-minded, of one mind, of the same mind, of a piece; at one, at one with, on all fours with; agreed on all hands, with on all counts, carried by acclamation.

ADVS. 16. affirmatively, in the affirmative.

17. unanimously, concurrently, consentaneously, by common consent, with one consent, with one accord, with one voice, in chorus, to a man, together, all

together, **as one,** as one man, one and all, on all hands; without contradiction, without a dissentient voice; by acclamation.

ADVS., *etc.* 18. yes, yea [chiefly coll.], aye *or* ay, *oui* [F.], *si* [Span.], ugh [Amer. Indian]; **yeah,** yep, **uh-huh,** un-hunh, um-hum, m-hum [all coll.]; yes sir, yes ma'am; yes sirree [coll., U.S.]; yes sirree Bob [slang, U.S.]; why yes, *mais si* [F.]; **indeed,** indeedy [coll., U.S.], **yes indeed,** yes indeedy [coll., U.S.]; **surely, certainly,** assuredly, most assuredly, exactly, precisely, absolutely, positively, really, truly, rather! [coll.], quite, to be sure; sure, sure Mike, sure thing, surest thing you know [all slang, U.S.]; **you bet,** you bet your life, you bet your boots [all slang]; **all right,** alright [coll.], right, righto [coll.], alrighty [slang]; O.K. *or* okay [coll.], Roger [slang]; fine [coll.], **good,** well and good, good enough, *c'est bien* [F., it is well]; **very well,** *très bien* [F.], *je veux bien* [F., I am very willing to do so]; naturally, *naturellement* [F.]; **of course,** even so, very much so, just so, as you say; that's right 515.22.

19. **be it so, so be it,** so mote it be, so shall it be, so it is, so is it; amen; **by all means,** by all manner of means.

PHRS. 20. **agreed, I agree with you,** I'll buy that [slang], I'm with you, I'm right in there with you, I go along with you there, I'm with you all the way; you are right 515.22; shake, shake pal [slang].

520a. DISSENT

NOUNS 1. **dissent,** dissentience; nonassent, nonconcurrence, nonagreement; **disagreement, difference, variance,** disparity, dissidence; dissension, disaccord 793; recusance *or* recusancy; nonconformity 83.2; apostasy 626.2.

2. **objection, protest, kick** [coll.], squawk [slang], howl [slang], protestation; **remonstrance, remonstration, expostulation; dispute, challenge; demur, scruple,** boggle; **exception,** rejection, **drawback;** protestantism; indignation meeting; grievance committee.

3. **dissenter, dissentient,** dissident, recusant; **objector,** objectioner, objectionist, demurrer; **protester, protestant; separatist,** come-outer [coll., U.S.]. schismatic; sectary, sectarian; nonconformist 83.4; apostate 626.5.

VERBS 4. **dissent,** dissent from, **disagree, differ,** not agree, disagree with, agree to disagree [joc.], divide on, be at variance;

take exception, take issue with, beg to differ, rise to a point of order.

5. **object, protest, kick** [coll.], put up a struggle *or* fight [coll.]; **squawk, howl,** holler, put up a squawk *or* howl, raise a howl [all slang]; cry out against, yell bloody murder; **remonstrate, expostulate;** raise objections, raise one's voice against, enter a protest; **dispute, challenge,** call in question; **demur, scruple,** boggle.

ADJS. 6. **dissentient, dissenting,** dissident, recusant; **disagreeing, differing;** at variance with, at odds with; schismatic(al), sectarian, sectary; nonconforming 83.6.

7. **protestant, protesting; objecting,** expostulative, expostulatory, remonstrative, remonstrant, deprecatory; under protest.

521. AFFIRMATION

NOUNS 1. **affirmation,** affirmance, **assertion, asseveration,** averment, **declaration,** allegation, position, profession, **statement,** word, say, saying, positive declaration *or* statement; **pronouncement,** announcement, annunciation, enunciation; predication, predicate [philos.]; protest, protestation; dictum, ipse dixit.

2. **deposition,** adjuration, **vouching, swearing, vouch, avouchment, avowal,** avowance, avow; **attestation,** attest; testimony 504.3; affidavit, affidavy [dial.].

3. **oath,** swear [coll.], **vow, word, assurance, guarantee, warrant,** solemn word *or* declaration; **pledge** 768.1; Bible oath; ironclad oath; judicial oath, extrajudicial oath; oath of office, official oath; oath of allegiance.

VERBS 4. **affirm, assert,** assever, asseverate, **aver, declare, say,** have one's say, **state,** allege, profess, protest, predicate, **pronounce,** lay down; announce, annunciate, enunciate; **maintain,** have, **contend,** maintain with one's last breath.

5. **depose,** depone; testify 504.10; **warrant, attest, guarantee, assure; vouch,** avouch, avow, **vow, swear,** swear the truth, assert under *or* on oath, make *or* take one's oath, take one's Bible oath; swear by bell, book and candle; call heaven to witness, declare *or* swear to God [coll.], swear to goodness [coll.], hope to die, cross one's heart (and hope to die), tell the world [slang], go bail on [coll.]; swear till one is black *or* blue in the face, swear till all's blue [both coll.].

6. **adjure,** administer an oath, put to one's oath, **put upon oath;** swear, **swear in.**

ADJS. **7. affirmative,** affirming, affirmant; **assertive,** assertative, assertional; **declarative,** declatory; predicative, predictory, predicational; pronunciative, pronunciatory; **positive,** absolute, emphatic, decided.

ADVS. **8. affirmatively, in the affirmative;** assertively, declaratively, predicatively; **positively,** absolutely, decidedly; emphatically, with emphasis; without fear of contradiction.

PHRS. **9. I must say,** give me leave to say, I can tell you, **I hope to tell you** [slang], let me tell you, I'd have you to know, **I'll say** [slang], **I'll venture to say,** I'll engage to say, I'll tell the world [slang]; mind you, mark my words; seriously, sadly, in sober sadness, in all soberness or seriousness, in all conscience, not to mince the matter, all joking aside or apart; no fooling, no kidding [slang]; indeed, in fact, i' faith; and how!, and I don't mean maybe! [both slang, U.S.]; not half! [coll., Eng.].

10. I'll warrant, I'll warrant you, **I assure you,** you may be sure, you may rest assured, I promise, you can take it from me [coll.], I'll answer for it, I'll be bound, I'll take my oath, upon oath, **upon my word,** upon my honor, **on my word of honor,** honor bright [coll.], by my troth, **believe me** [coll.], honest Injun [joc.], honest to God [coll.], so help me, so help me God, **I'll swear,** I'll swear or declare to God, I should hope to die, I'll eat my hat; I'll be−, I'll bet you.

522. NEGATION, DENIAL

NOUNS **1. negation,** abnegation; **negative, no,** nay, nix [slang].

2. denial, disavowal, **disaffirmation, disownment,** disallowance; **disclamation,** disclaimer; abjuration, abjurement, forswearing; **contradiction,** contravention, controversion, traversal, gainsaying.

VERBS **3. negate,** abnegate, negative; no, say no; shake the head, shrug the shoulders.

4. deny, not admit, not accept, not buy [coll.], refuse to admit or accept; **disclaim, disown, disaffirm, disavow, disallow,** abjure, forswear, renounce, repudiate; **contradict,** contravene, traverse, controvert, impugn, **dispute,** gainsay, oppose, contest, take issue with, join issue upon; belie, give the lie to, give one the lie in his throat.

ADJS. **5. negative,** negatory, abnegative; **denying, disclaiming,** disowning, disaffirming, disallowing, disavowing; **contradictory,**

contradicting, **opposing,** contrary, repugnant; abjuratory.

ADVS. **6. negatively, in the negative;** in denial, in contradiction.

7. no, nope [coll.], **nay,** non [F.], nix [slang], **unh-unh** [coll.]; certainly not, absolutely no, shucks no! [slang]; no sir, no sirree [coll., U.S.]; no ma'am, no mam [coll.]; **not,** not a bit, ~whit or jot; no such thing, nothing of the kind or sort, not so.

8. by no means, by no manner of means; on no account, in no respect, **in no case, under no circumstances, on no condition,** at no hand, no matter what; **not at all,** not in the least, never; no wise, noways, noway, nohow [dial.]; **not for the world,** not if one can help it, not if I know it, not at any price, not for love or money, not for the life of me, **not on your life** [coll.], not by a long chalk [coll.]; **not by a long shot** or **sight,** not by a darn sight, not a bit of it, not much, not a chance, fat chance, **nothing doing,** like fun, nuts to you!, I'll be hanged if [all slang]; to the contrary, tout au contraire [F.], quite the contrary, far from it; God forbid 967.27.

CONJS. **9. neither,** not either, **nor,** nor yet, or not, and not, also not.

PHRS. **10. isn't, aren't, ain't** [dial. or illit.].

523. MENTAL ATTITUDE

NOUNS **1. attitude,** mental attitude, psychology; **position, posture; way of thinking,** way of looking at things; **feeling, sentiment,** the way one feels; opinion 500.4.

2. outlook, mental outlook, partisan opinion; **point of view, viewpoint, standpoint;** position, posture, ground, from where I sit; **view,** sight, light, eye, respect, regard; angle, slant [coll.]; **frame of reference,** framework.

3. disposition, character, nature, temper, temperament, idiosyncrasy, individualism; **turn of mind, inclination, tendency,** set, **leaning,** animus, affection, propensity, proclivity, predilection, predisposition; **bent, turn, bias, slant,** cast, warp, twist.

4. mood, humor, temper, frame of mind, state of mind, **frame,** tone, vein, grain, streak, stripe, cue; **mind, heart, spirit,** mettle.

5. (pervading attitudes) **climate,** intellectual climate, moral climate, climate of opinion.

VERBS **6. take** the attitude, feel about it, look **at it, view,** look at in the light of; take that attitude, feel that way, want to be that way.

ADJS. **7. dispositional, temperamental, constitutional;** characteristic 80.13; innate 5.7.

8. disposed, dispositioned, **predisposed, prone, inclined,** given, bent, affected, tempered; **minded, of the mind,** of the feeling; **in the mood** or **humor,** in the vein.

524. BROAD-MINDEDNESS

NOUNS **1. broad-mindedness,** wide-mindedness, large-mindedness, noble-mindedness, "the result of flattening high-mindedness out" [George Saintsbury]; **unbigotedness,** unhideboundness, unprovincialism; broad mind.

2. liberalness, liberality, catholicity, **liberal-mindedness; breadth,** width, broadness, **latitude;** liberalism, latitudinarianism; **freethinking,** free thought.

3. open-mindedness, openness, accessibility, receptiveness, responsiveness, amenableness; persuadableness, persuasibility; open mind.

4. tolerance, toleration; **indulgence,** leniency **or** leniency, **condonation,** acceptance, **forbearance, patience,** long-suffering; **charitableness,** charity, **generousness, bigness,** bigheartedness, largeheartedness, greateheartedness, openheartedness; **sympathy, understanding,** sympathetic understanding.

5. unprejudice, unbias, unprejudicedness, unbiasedness; **impartiality, detachment, dispassionateness,** disinterestedness, disinterest; indifference, neutrality; unopinionatedness.

6. liberal, liberalist; **freethinker,** latitudinarian; broad man, big person.

VERBS **7. keep an open mind,** be big, judge not, suspend judgment, **view with indulgence,** listen to reason, open one's mind to, see both sides, **live and let live,** lean over backwards, tolerate 859.5; **accept, condone,** shut one's eyes to, look the other way, **wink at,** blink at, **overlook, disregard, ignore;** "swear allegiance to the words of no master" [Horace].

ADJS. **8. broad-minded,** wide-minded, large-minded, noble-minded; **broad,** broad-gauged [U.S.]; **unbigoted, unhidebound,** unprovincial.

9. liberal, liberal-minded, broad, wide, catholic, ecumenic(al), cosmopolitan, liberalistic, libertine [derog.]; **free-thinking,** latitudinarian; free-speaking, free-tongued.

10. open-minded, open, accessible, receptive, admissive, responsive, amenable; **persuadable,** persuasible.

11. tolerant, tolerating; **indulgent, lenient, condoning,** forbearing, **forbearant, patient, long-suffering; charitable,** generous, **big,** bighearted, largehearted, greathearted, broadhearted, widehearted, openhearted; **sympathetic, understanding.**

12. unprejudiced, unbiased, unprepossessed, unjaundiced; impartial, dispassionate, detached, disinterested, impersonal, respectless; indifferent, neutral; **unswayed, uninfluenced,** undazzled.

13. unopinionated, unopinioned, unwedded to an opinion; **unpositive, undogmatic,** unpragmatic(al); unsettled, unrooted; uninfatuated, unbesotted, unfanatical.

14. broadening, enlightening.

525. NARROW-MINDEDNESS

NOUNS **1. narrow-mindedness,** little-mindedness, small-mindedness; **smallness, littleness, meanness, pettiness; bigotry,** bigotedness; **illiberality,** uncatholicity; **narrowness, insularity,** insularism, provincialism; **hideboundness,** strait-lacedness, stuffiness [coll.]; **shortsightedness,** nearsightedness, purblindness; blind side, blind spot, mote in the eye; closed mind.

2. intolerance, intoleration; **uncharitableness,** ungenerousness; unforbearance.

3. prejudice, prejudgment, **predilection, prepossession,** preconception, predetermination; **bias, bent,** leaning, inclination, warp, twist; complex [coll.]; **jaundice,** jaundiced eye; **partiality,** onesidedness, undispassionateness, undetachment.

4. class consciousness, class prejudice, **discrimination,** social discrimination, minority prejudice; **racism,** racialism, race prejudice, race snobbery, racial discrimination; anti-Semitism, redbaiting; **social barrier,** class distinction; **color line,** color bar; Jim Crow law; **segregation,** apartheid [Afrikaan]; desegregation.

5. bigot, intolerant, illiberal, little person; opinionist 512.7; fanatic 472.17.

VERBS **6. close one's mind,** shut the eyes of one's mind; **view with a jaundiced eye,** not see beyond one's nose or an inch beyond one's nose, see but one side of the question, look only at one side of the shield.

7. **discriminate against,** draw the line, draw the color line, redbait.

8. **prejudice,** prejudice against, prepossess, predetermine, **jaundice, influence, sway, bias,** warp, twist.

9. (present with bias) **angle, slant.**

ADJS. 10. **narrow-minded,** little-minded, small-minded, narrowhearted, narrow-souled, narrow-spirited, mean-spirited; **small, little, mean, petty; bigoted,** bigotish; **illiberal,** unliberal, uncatholic; **narrow,** narrow-gauged [U.S.]; provincial, insular, parochial, confined; **hidebound,** creedbound, barkbound; **strait-laced,** stuffy [coll.]; shortsighted, nearsighted, purblind.

11. **intolerant,** untolerating; **unsympathetic,** nonunderstanding; **uncharitable, ungenerous; unindulgent,** uncondoning, unforbearing; deaf, deaf-minded, deaf to reason.

12. **prejudiced,** prepossessed, **biased, jaundiced,** colored, **partial,** one-sided, partisan, influenced, swayed, **interested, undetached,** undispassionate; class-conscious.

13. opinionated 512.22.

526. CURIOSITY

NOUNS 1. **curiosity,** curiousness; **inquisitiveness,** nosiness [coll.], snoopiness [coll., U.S.], prying; meddlesomeness 237.2; **interest,** interestedness, lively interest; thirst for knowledge, mental acquisitiveness, inquiring mind.

2. **inquisitive,** quidnunc, curiosity shop [slang]; **inquirer,** questioner, querier, querist, quiz, question box [slang], walking interrogation point or question mark [joc.]; **busybody,** busy [slang], **pry,** Paul Pry, snoop [U.S.], snooper [U.S.], nosy [coll.], nosy Parker [slang]; rubbernecker, rubberneck [both slang, U.S.]; eavesdropper; Peeping Tom; Lot's wife.

VERBS 3. **be curious, want to know, take an interest in,** take a lively interest, burn with curiosity; prick up the ears; stare, gape; rubber, rubberneck [both slang, U.S.].

4. **pry,** Paul-Pry, **snoop** [U.S.], nose, poke or stick one's nose in; peer, peep; meddle 237.7.

ADJS 5. **curious, inquisitive,** inquiring, quizzical; burning with curiosity, eaten up or consumed with curiosity, curious as a cat; **agape,** agog, all agog, open-mouthed, open-eyed; rubberneck, rubbernecked [both slang, U.S.]; overcurious, supercurious.

6. **prying,** snooping [U.S.], **nosy** [coll.], snoopy [coll., U.S.]; meddlesome 237.9.

527. INCURIOSITY

NOUNS 1. **incuriosity,** incuriousness, uninquisitiveness; **uninterestedness,** disinterest, distinterestedness, **unconcern,** indifference, indifferentness, **lack of interest;** carelessness, heedlessness, regardlessness, unmindfulness; intellectual inertia.

VERBS 2. **take no interest in, not** care; mind one's own business, pursue the even tenor of one's way, glance neither to the right nor to the left.

ADJS. 3. **incurious, uninquisitive,** uninquiring; **uninterested,** unconcerned, **indifferent;** careless, heedless, regardless, mindless, unmindful.

528. ATTENTION

NOUNS 1. **attention, attentiveness,** mindfulness, regardfulness, heedfulness; **heed,** ear; consideration, thought, mind [dial.]; **observation,** observance, advertence or advertency, **note, notice,** remark, regard, respect; care 531.

2. **interest,** concern, concernment, regard; **curiosity** 526; **enthusiasm,** passion; matter of interest, special interest.

3. **engrossment, absorption, intentness, concentration,** devotion, **application, occupation,** preoccupation, engagement, involvement, **immersion, submersion;** rapt attention, absorbed attention or interest; deep study, deep or profound thought.

4. **close attention,** close study, fixed regard, undivided attention, strict attention, special consideration.

VERBS 5. **attend to,** look to, **see to,** advert to; **pay attention to, pay regard to, give heed to;** give a thought to, trouble one's head about; give the mind to, direct the attention to, turn or bend the mind or attention to; **devote oneself to,** devote the mind or thoughts to, fix or rivet the mind or thoughts on, apply the mind or attention to, apply oneself to, **occupy oneself with,** concern oneself with, give oneself up to, be absorbed or engrossed in, **lose oneself in;** hang on, **hang on one's words; drink in,** drink in with rapt attention.

6. **heed, attend,** tend [dial.], **mind, watch, observe, regard,** look, **see,** view, mark, remark, animadvert, **note, notice,** take note or notice; note well, *nota bene* [L.].

7. hearken to, hark, **listen,** give ear to, lend an ear to, incline *or* bend an ear to, prick up the ears, **keep one's ears open,** have *or* keep an ear to the ground [U.S.], listen with both ears, **be all ears.**

8. pay attention *or* heed, **take heed,** give heed, **look out, watch out** [coll., U.S.], mind out [dial.]; **take care** 531.7; look lively *or* alive, look sharp, look slick *or* slippy, sit up and take notice, keep one's eye on the ball, not miss a trick, not overlook a bet [all coll.]; keep one's eyes open 531.8; attend to business, mind one's business; pay close *or* strict attention, give one's undivided attention.

9. take cognizance of, take note *or* **notice of,** take heed of, **take account of, take into consideration** *or* **account, bear in mind,** keep *or* hold in mind, reckon with, keep in sight *or* view, have in one's eye, have an eye to, have regard for.

10. call attention to, direct attention to, **bring under** *or* **to one's notice,** bring to attention, call *or* bring to notice, direct to the attention, **direct to,** address to; **point out,** point at *or* to, put *or* lay one's finger on.

11. meet with attention, fall under one's notice; **catch the attention,** catch ∼, meet *or* strike the eye, attract notice *or* attention, arrest *or* engage attention, fix *or* rivet one's attention, arrest the thoughts, awaken the mind *or* thoughts, **excite notice,** invite *or* solicit attention.

12. interest, concern, affect, touch, involve, affect the interest; **pique, titillate,** tantalize, **attract,** invite, **fascinate, excite, entertain,** pique one's interest, excite interest, excite *or* whet one's interest, arouse one's enthusiasm.

13. engross, absorb, immerse, **occupy, preoccupy, engage,** involve, monopolize, exercise, take up; **grip, hold,** arrest, **hold the interest, fascinate, enthrall, hold spellbound;** absorb the attention, claim one's thoughts, engross the mind *or* thoughts, engage the attention, involve the interest, occupy the attention, monopolize one's attention, engage the mind *or* thoughts.

14. come to attention, stand at attention [both mil.].

ADJS. **15. attentive, heedful, mindful, regardful,** advertent; **careful** 531.10; **observing,** observant; watchful, alert 531.13, 14; agog, openmouthed; open-eared, openeyed, **all eyes, all ears,** all eyes and ears; on the job [coll.], on the ball [slang], Jerry on the job [slang], Johnny on the spot [slang].

16. interested, concerned; **curious** 526.5; **piqued,** titillated, tantalized, **attracted,** fascinated, excited; keen on *or* about, **enthusiastic.**

17. engrossed, absorbed, occupied, preoccupied, engaged, devoted, devoted to, **intent,** intent on, monopolized, taken up with, involved, **caught up in,** wrapped in, **wrapped up in,** engrossed in, absorbed with *or* by, **lost in, immersed in,** submerged in, buried in; over head and ears in, head over heels in [coll.], up to the elbows in, up to the ears in.

18. gripped, held, fascinated, rapt, enthralled, spellbound, undistracted.

19. interesting, affecting, touching; **provocative,** provoking, thought-provoking, thought-challenging, thought-giving, thought-inspiring, thought-involving, thought-moving, thought-working; **titillating, tantalizing, inviting, exciting, entertaining; piquant,** lively, racy, juicy, succulent, spicy, rich.

20. engrossing, absorbing, consuming, **gripping,** holding, arresting, engaging, **fascinating, enthralling, spellbinding.**

ADVS. **21. attentively,** with attention; **heedfully,** mindfully, regardfully, advertently; observingly, observantly; **interestedly,** with interest; **raptly,** with rapt attention; engrossedly, absorbedly, preoccupiedly; devotedly, **intently,** without distraction, **with undivided attention.**

INTERJS. **22. attention!,** 'tention! [mil., coll.]; **look!,** see!, look you!, look here!, look to it!, witness!; lo!, behold!, lo and behold!; **hark!,** listen!, hark ye!, hear ye!, oyez!.

23. hail!, ahoy!, hello!, hollo!, hallo!, halloo!, halloa!, yo-ho!, hoo-hoo!, soho!, ho!, hey!, heigh!, hi!, hist!, *ecco!* [It.]; hello there!, ahoy there!, etc.

529. INATTENTION

NOUNS **1. inattention,** inattentiveness, **heedlessness, unheedfulness, unmindfulness, thoughtlessness,** *étourderie* [F.], inadvertence *or* inadvertency; **disregard,** disregardfulness, regardlessness; **inobservance,** unobservance; **unalertness,** unwariness, unwatchfulness; **obliviousness,** unconsciousness; negligence 532; distraction, absent-mindedness 530.

VERBS **2. wander from the subject,** let

one's attention wander, get off the track [coll.]

3. pay no attention, pay no mind [dial.], take no note or notice of, take no thought or account of, not heed, give no heed, pay no regard to; disregard, overlook, ignore, dissemble, pass over or by, pass up [slang, U.S.], let pass, think little of; slight, make light of; close or shut one's eyes to, not see for looking [joc.], be blind to, turn a blind eye, look the other way, blink at, wink at, connive at; stick one's head in the sand; play possum, possum [coll., U.S.]; turn a deaf ear to, let come in one ear and go out the other; have nothing to do with, have no truck with [coll. & dial.], let well enough alone; not trouble oneself with, not trouble one's head with or about.

4. dismiss, dismiss from one's thoughts, put out of mind, put out of one's head or thoughts, wean one's thoughts from, think no more of, forget, forget about it, let it go [coll.], drop the subject; turn one's back upon, turn away from, leave in or out in the cold [coll.]; put ~, set or lay aside, push or thrust aside or to one side; sink (as, to sink differences); turn up one's nose at, sneeze at, toss the head; shrug off, brush off or aside; laugh off or away, dismiss with a laugh.

5. escape notice, escape one, pass one by, not enter one's head, fall on deaf ears.

ADJS. 6. inattentive, unmindful, inadvertent; heedless, unheeding, unheedful; regardless, disregardful, disregardant; unobserving, inobservant, unobservant; undiscerning, unperceiving, unreflecting; distracted 530.10; negligent 532.10.

7. oblivious, unconscious, dead to the world; blind, deaf; preoccupied 530.11.

8. unalert, unwary, unwatchful, unvigilant; unprepared, unready; unguarded, off one's guard, asleep, sleeping, off-guard, off-side; napping, asleep at the base [slang, U.S.], asleep on the job [slang], not on the job [coll.], looking or gazing out of the window [slang].

530. DISTRACTION

Diversion of Attention; Mental Confusion.—NOUNS 1. distraction, diversion; distractedness.

2. abstraction, preoccupation, absorption, depth of thought; absentmindedness, absence of mind; bemusement, musing, musefulness; woolgathering, moonraking

[dial., Eng.], dreaming, daydreaming, pipe dreaming [coll.], castle-building; brown study, sombre rêverie [F.], study, reverie, muse, trance; dream, daydream, pipe dream [coll.]; stream of consciousness.

3. confusion, fluster, flustration [coll.], flutter, flurry, ruffle, rattle [slang], jingle [slang, U.S.]; muddle, muddlement, fuddle [coll.], fuddlement [coll.], befuddlement; daze, dazzle, razzle-dazzle [slang]; unsettlement, disorganization, demoralization, discomfiture, discomposure, disconcertion, bewilderment, embarrassment, disturbance, perturbation, pother, bother, botheration [coll.], stew [coll.], pucker [coll.]; haze, fog, maze; perplexity 513.3, 4.

4. dizziness, vertigo, vertiginousness, swimming, swimming of the head, giddiness, wooziness [slang], lightheadedness, scotomy or scotoma [med.]; dizzy round.

5. flightiness, giddiness, frothiness, volatility; thoughtlessness, witlessness, brainlessness.

VERBS 6. distract, divert, detract, distract the attention, divert or detract attention, divert the mind or thoughts, draw off the attention; put off the track, throw off the scent.

7. confuse, throw into confusion, fluster, flustrate [coll.], fuss or fuss up [slang], flutter, put into a flutter, flurry, rattle [coll.], jingle [slang, U.S.], ruffle, moider [dial., Eng.], mix up, ball up [slang, U.S.], entangle, muddle, fuddle [coll.], befuddle, fog, addle, addle the wits; daze, dazzle, bedazzle, razzle-dazzle [slang]; upset, unsettle, disorganize, demoralize, break up [coll.], shatter, disconcert, discomfit, discompose, bewilder, embarrass, put out, disturb, perturb, bother, pother; perplex 513.12, 13.

8. dizzy, giddy, make one's head swim, make one's head reel or whirl, go to one's head, turn one's head.

9. muse, moon [coll.], dream, daydream, pipe-dream [coll.], abstract oneself, let one's attention wander, let one's mind run on other things, dream of or muse on other things, go woolgathering, let one's wits go bird's nesting, be in a brown study, be absent, be somewhere else, forget oneself.

ADJS. 10. distracted, distraught, distrait; wandering, rambling; wild, frantic, beside oneself.

11. abstracted, bemused, preoccupied, absorbed; absent-minded, absent, faraway,

elsewhere, somewhere else, not all there; lost, lost in thought, wrapped in thought, dead to the world, unconscious, oblivious; museful, musing; dreaming, dreamy, moony [coll.], napping, daydreaming, daydreamy, pipe-dreaming [coll.]; woolgathering, a woolgathering, moonraking [dial., Eng.], castle-building, in the clouds, in a reverie.

12. confused, mixed-up, balled-up [slang]; flustered, flustery, ruffled, rattled [coll.], fussed up [slang]; upset, unsettled, disorganized, demoralized, shattered, disconcerted, discomposed, embarrassed, put out, disturbed, perturbed, bothered, all hot and bothered [slang]; in a stew [coll.], in a rattle [slang], in a razzle-dazzle [slang], in a pucker [coll.], in a pother; perplexed 513.22, 23.

13. muddled, in a muddle; fuddled [coll.], befuddled; muddleheaded, fuddlebrained [coll.]; puzzleheaded, puzzlepated; addled, addleheaded, addlepated, addlebrained; foggy, fogged, in a fog, hazy, muzzy [coll.], mazed.

14. dazed, dazzled, dazy, in a daze; silly, knocked silly; groggy [coll.], dopey [slang], woozy [slang]; punch-drunk [coll.], slaphappy [slang].

15. dizzy, giddy, vertiginous, swimming, turned around, going around in circles, like a chicken with its head cut off [coll.].

16. scatterbrained, shatterbrained, shatterpated, rattlebrained, rattleheaded, rattlepated, jinglebrained [slang], scramblebrained [slang], shuttle-witted [Scot.], cocklebrained, harebrain, harebrained, giddy, dizzy, ga-ga [slang, U.S.], hoitytoity, giddy-brained, giddy-headed, giddypated, giddy-witted, giddy as a goose; flighty, volatile, frothy, barmy, barmybrained, featherbrained; empty-headed 468.19; thoughtless, witless, brainless.

531. CARE

Close or Watchful Attention.—NOUNS 1. care, heed, concern, regard; attention 528; carefulness, heedfulness, regardfulness, mindfulness, thoughtfulness, consideration, solicitude, circumspection; caution 893.

2. painstaking, pains; diligence, assiduousness, assiduity; thoroughness, thoroughgoingness.

3. meticulousness, exactingness, scrupulousness, scrupulosity, conscientiousness, punctiliousness, particularness, particularity, fussiness, criticalness; finicalness, finickingness, finicality; exactness, exactitude, accuracy, preciseness, precision, correctness; strictness, rigidness, rigorousness; nicety, niceness, delicacy, subtlety, refinement; minuteness, circumstantiality.

4. vigilance, watchfulness, watching, observance; watch, surveillance, vigil, lookout, tout [slang], watch and ward; guard, guardedness; watchful eye, weather eye [coll.], peeled eye [coll.], sharp eye, eagle eye.

5. alertness, attentiveness; wakefulness, sleeplessness; readiness, promptness, promptitude; quickness, agility, nimbleness; smartness, brightness, keenness, sharpness.

VERBS 6. care, mind, heed, notice, think, consider, take heed or thought of; take an interest, be concerned.

7. be careful, take care or good care, take heed, have a care, exercise care; be cautious 893.5; take pains, take trouble, be painstaking, go to great pains, go to great lengths; mind, mind what one is doing or about, mind one's business, mind one's P's and Q's [coll.]; watch one's step [slang], pick one's steps, put the right foot forward; treat gently, handle with gloves or kid gloves.

8. be vigilant, be watchful, be on the watch or lookout, keep a good or sharp lookout, keep in sight or view; keep watch, keep watch and ward, keep vigil, keep tout [slang]; watch, look sharp, look about one, look with one's own eyes, be on one's guard, sleep with one eye open, have all one's eyes or wits about one, keep one's eyes open, keep a weather eye open [coll.], keep one's eyes peeled [slang], keep the ears on or to the ground, keep a nose to the wind; keep alert, be on the alert; look out, watch out [coll., U.S.], mind out [dial.], mind one's eye; look lively or alive, look slick or slippy [all coll.]; stop, look and listen.

9. look after, take care of 697.18.

ADJS. 10. careful, heedful, regardful, mindful, thoughtful, considerate, solicitous, circumspect; attentive 528.15; cautious 893.8.

11. painstaking, diligent, assiduous; thorough, thoroughgoing; elaborate, labored, studied, operose, fussy, highwrought.

12. meticulous, exacting, scrupulous, conscientious, religious, punctilious, punc-

tual, particular, fussy, curious, critical, attentive, scrutinizing; finical, finicking, finikin, finicky; exact, precise, accurate, correct; close, narrow; strict, rigid, rigorous; nice, delicate, subtle, fine, refined; minute, detailed.

13. vigilant, watchful, surveillant, observant; on the watch, on the lookout, aux aguets [F.]; on guard, on one's guard, guarded; with open eyes, with one's eyes open, with one's eyes peeled [coll.], with a weather eye open [coll.]; open-eyed, wide-eyed; all eyes, all ears, all eyes and ears; agog, all agog.

14. alert, on the alert, on the qui vive [F.], on one's toes, on the job [coll.], attentive; awake, wakeful, wide-awake, broad awake; sleepless, unsleeping; alive, live [chiefly U.S.]; ready, prompt, quick, agile, nimble, quick on the trigger [coll., U.S.]; smart, fly [slang], bright, keen, sharp; slick, slippy [both coll.]; there [slang], there with the goods [coll.], all there [coll.].

ADVS. 15. carefully, heedfully, regardfully, mindfully, thoughtfully, considerately, solicitously, circumspectly; cautiously 893.12; with care, with great care; painstakingly, diligently, assiduously; thoroughly, thoroughgoingly.

16. meticulously, exactingly, scrupulously, conscientiously, religiously, punctiliously, fussily; exactly, accurately, precisely, with exactitude, with precision; minutely, in detail.

17. vigilantly, watchfully, observantly; alertly, attentively; sleeplessly, unsleepingly.

18. be careful!, beware! 893.14.

532. NEGLECT

NOUNS 1. neglect, neglectfulness, negligence, inadvertence or inadvertency, dereliction, culpa [law]; remissness, laxity, laxness, slackness, looseness, laches; disregard, slight; inattention 529; oversight, overlooking, omission, default; procrastination 132.5.

2. carelessness, heedlessness, unheedfulness, disregardfulness, regardlessness, thoughtlessness, unthinkingness, inconsiderateness, inconsideration, unmindfulness, forgetfulness; recklessness 892.2; indifference 634; perfunctoriness; cursoriness, casualness; easiness; abandon, careless abandon.

3. slipshodness, slipshoddiness, sloven-

liness, slovenry, sloppiness [coll.], clumsiness; promiscuity, haphazardness; slapdash, a lick and a promise [both coll.]; bad job, sad work, slovenly performance; bungling 732.4.

4. unmeticulousness, unexactingness, unscrupulousness, unconscientiousness, unpunctiliousness, unparticularness, unfussiness, unfinicalness, uncriticalness; inexactness, inexactitude, inaccuracy, unpreciseness.

5. neglector or neglecter, negligent, ignorer, disregarder; procrastinator, waiter on Providence, Micawber; trifler 671.9; bungler 732.8.

VERBS 6. neglect, overlook, disregard, ignore; not care for, not take care of; pass over, gloss over; let slip, let slide [coll.], let go, let it ride [slang, U.S.], let take its course; let the grass grow under one's feet; not think or consider, not give a thought to, take no thought or account of, leave out of one's calculation; lose sight of, lose track of [U.S.]; forget oneself.

7. leave undone, leave, let go, leave go [illit. & dial.], pretermit, forbear, skip, jump, miss, omit, cut [coll.], let be or alone, let a-be [Scot. & dial., Eng.], pass over, pass up [slang U.S.], abandon; leave a loose thread, leave at loose ends, let dangle; procrastinate 132.10.

8. slight, overslight; scamp, skimp [coll.]; slur, slur over, pass over, slip or skip over, skim, skim over, skim the surface, touch upon, touch upon lightly or in passing, pass over lightly, hit the high spots [slang], give a lick and a promise [coll.]; cut corners, cut a corner.

9. do carelessly, do by halves, do in a slipshod fashion, do anyhow or all anyhow, do in any old way [coll.]; trifle with, mess around or about with [slang]; do offhand, dash off, knock off [coll.], throw off [coll.], toss off or out [coll.]; roughhew, rough-cast, slapdash [coll.], rough out; knock out [coll.], hammer or pound out, bat out [slang], slap out [coll.], shove out [coll.]; toss or throw together, knock together, piece together, patch together, patch, patch up, fudge, fudge up, fake up, slap up [coll.].

ADJS. 10. negligent, neglectful, neglecting, derelict, culpose [law], inadvertent, uncircumspect; inattentive 529.6; remiss, slack, lax, loose; slighting, slurring; scamping, skimping [coll.]; procrastinating 132.16.

11. careless, heedless, unheeding, un-

heedful, **disregardful,** disregardant, regardless, respectless, **thoughtless, unthinking, inconsiderate,** mindless, **unmindful,** forgetful; **reckless** 892.8; indifferent 634.5, 6; perfunctory; cursory, casual, offhand.

12. **slipshod,** slipshoddy, **slovenly,** sloppy [coll.]; **clumsy, bungling; haphazard, promiscuous, hit-or-miss,** hit-and-miss, hitty-missy [coll.].

13. **unmeticulous, unexacting, unpainstaking,** unscrupulous, **unconscientious,** unpunctilious, **unparticular, unfussy, unfinical, uncritical;** inexact, inaccurate, unprecise.

14. **neglected,** unattended to, uncaredfor; **disregarded, overlooked,** missed, passed over, passed up [slang, U.S.], **ignored, slighted;** undone, left undone, abandoned; in the cold, out in the cold [both coll.]; hid under a bushel, buried in a napkin.

15. **unheeded, unobserved, unnoticed, unnoted, unperceived, unseen,** unmarked, unremarked, unregarded, unminded, unconsidered, unthought-of.

16. **unexamined, unstudied,** unsearched, unscanned, unweighed, unsifted, unexplored.

ADVS. 17. **negligently, neglectfully,** inadvertently; **remissly,** laxly, slackly, loosely, lightly; **slightingly,** slurringly; scampingly, skimpingly [coll.].

18. **carelessly, heedlessly,** unheedingly, unheedfully, disregardfully, regardlessly, **thoughtlessly, unthinkingly, inconsiderately,** unmindfully, forgetfully; **recklessly** 892.11; perfunctorily; cursorily, casually, offhand; clumsily, bunglingly, sloppily [coll.]; haphazardly, promiscuously, hitty-missy [coll.], helter-skelter [coll.], ramble-scramble [slang], slapdash, anyhow, in any old way [coll.], any which way or anywhichway [slang].

19. **unmeticulously, unscrupulously, unconscientiously,** unfussily, **uncritically;** inexactly, inaccurately, unprecisely.

533. IMAGINATION

NOUNS 1. **imagination,** imagining, imaginativeness, imagery, **fancy, fantasy, phantasy,** conceit; mind's eye, "that inward eye which is the bliss of solitude" [Wordsworth]; flight of fancy, fumes of fancy; "We are such stuff as dreams are made on" [Shakespeare].

2. **creative thought,** conception; productive ~, constructive or creative imag-

ination, reproductive imagination, poetic imagination; inspiration, genius 466.8.

3. **invention, inventiveness, originality, creativity, ingenuity;** productivity, prolificacy, **fertility,** fecundity; fertile or pregnant imagination, fertile mind.

4. **lively imagination,** active fancy, **vivid imagination,** warm or ardent imagination, fiery or heated imagination, excited imagination, bold or daring imagination; verve, vivacity of imagination.

5. **figment of the imagination,** creature of the imagination, creation or coinage of the brain, fiction of the mind; **imagining, fancy,** idle fancy, "thick-coming fancies" [Shakespeare]; **fantasy, phantasy; phantasm** 518.4; **figment, invention; fiction,** myth, romance; **chimera, bubble,** vapor; **illusion** 518; man in the moon, Flying Dutchman, great sea serpent, pot of gold at the foot of the rainbow.

6. **visualization, envisioning,** envisaging, picturing, objectification; **picture, vision, image,** mental image, mental picture, visual image, percept, concept, **conception,** mental representation or presentation, *Vorstellung* [G.]; imagery, dreamery.

7. **idealism, idealization; ideal,** ideality; visionariness, fancifulness; **romanticism,** romance; utopianism; **quixotism,** quixotry; **impracticality,** unpracticalness, **unrealism,** unreality, unreasonableness, irrationality; **wishful thinking;** autistic thinking, dereistic thinking, autism, dereism [all psychol.].

8. **dreaminess,** dreamery, dreamfulness, musefulness; dreamlikeness; **dreaming, musing; daydreaming,** pipe dreaming [coll.], castle building.

9. **dream, reverie, muse, trance; daydream, pipe dream** [coll.], pipe [slang]; **brown study** 530.2; golden dream; **vision,** revelation; **nightmare,** incubus [med.], bad dream.

10. **air castle, castle in the air,** castle in the sky or skies, castle in Spain, *château en Espagne* [F.], pleasure dome of Kubla Khan.

11. **utopia, paradise, heaven, heaven on earth;** millennium, kingdom come; dreamland, wonderland, cloudland, fairyland; Eden, garden of Eden; Heavenly City, Celestial City, Land of Beulah, New Jerusalem; Promised Land, Land of Promise, land of plenty, land flowing with milk and honey, Canaan, Goshen; Shangri-la, Atlantis, Arcadia, Agapemone, Happy Valley

[Johnson], land of Prester John, Kingdom of Micomicon, Estotiland or Estotilandia [Milton], Laputa; Cockaigne, Lubberland; Dixie, Dixie Land.

12. imaginer, fancier, fancymonger; fantast, phantast; mythmaker; **inventor; creative artist.**

13. visionary, idealist, illusionist, seer, mopus [slang], **dreamer, daydreamer,** dreamer of dreams, castle-builder, lotuseater, **wishful thinker; romantic,** romanticist, romancer; Quixote, Don Quixote; utopian, utopianist, utopianizer, utopographer; enthusiast, rhapsodist, highflier.

VERBS **14. imagine, fancy, conceive,** conceit, figure to oneself; suppose 498.9; phantasize; give free rein to the imagination, let one's imagination run wild, allow one's imagination to run away with one.

15. visualize, vision, envision, envisage, picture, feature [slang], image, **objectify;** picture in one's mind, picture to oneself, view with the mind's eye, contemplate in the imagination, form a mental picture of, see, just see, have a picture of; **call up,** summon up, conjure up, **call to mind.**

16. idealize, utopianize, quixotize, rhapsodize; **romance,** romanticize; talk through one's hat [slang]; **build castles in the air.**

17. dream, muse; dream of, dream on; daydream, pipedream [coll.]; vision, conjure up a vision, "see visions and dream dreams" [Bible].

ADJS. **18. imaginative, inventive,** original, originative, **creative, ingenious;** productive, fertile, fecund, prolific; **inspired,** visioned.

19. imaginary, imaginational; **imagined, fancied; unreal,** unactual, nonexistent; supposititious, **all in the mind;** illusory 518.9.

20. fanciful, notional, flight; fancybred, fancy-born, fancy-built, fancy-framed, fancy-woven, fancy-wrought; dream-born, dream-built, dream-created; castle-built; **fantastic(al),** extravagant, preposterous, wild, high-flown.

21. fictitious, figmental, fictional, fictive; **fabulous,** mythic(al), mythological, legendary.

22. chimerical, airy, aerial, etherial, phantasmal; vaporous, vapory; air-built, airdrawn; cloud-built, cloud-born, cloudwoven.

23. ideal, idealized; Utopian or utopian, Arcadian, Edenic; millenial.

24. visionary, visional, viewy [coll.];

idealistic, **quixotic(al), romantic,** poetic(al), Platonic; **impractical, unpractical, unrealistic,** unscientific, unreasonable, irrational; starry-eyed, dewy-eyed; in the clouds, with one's head in the clouds.

25. dreamy, dreamful, museful; dreamy-eyed, dreamy-minded, dreamysouled; dreamlike; dreamlit; **dreaming, musing;** daydreamy, **daydreaming,** pipedreaming [coll.], castle-building; tranced, **entranced,** in a trance.

26. imaginable, imaginal, **fanciable, conceivable, thinkable,** cogitable; **supposable** 498.15.

INTERJS. **27. imagine!,** just imagine!, fancy!, **fancy that!,** can you feature that? [slang], well!, of all things!, did you ever!

534. UNIMAGINATIVENESS

NOUNS **1. unimaginativeness,** unfancifulness; **prosaicness,** prosaism, prosaicism, unpoeticalness; **staidness, stuffiness** [coll.]; **dullness, dryness;** aridness, aridity, barrenness; **unoriginality,** dearth of ideas.

2. (practical attitude) **realism,** realisticness, **practicalness, practicality, practical-mindedness, matter-of-factness,** pragmatism, unidealism, unromanticalness, unsentimentality; sensibleness, saneness, reasonableness, rationality.

3. realist, pragmatist, practical person.

VERBS **4. keep both feet on the ground,** keep one's feet on the ground and one's eyes on the stars; stick to the facts, call a spade a spade; **come down to earth,** come down out of the clouds, come down out of one's pink balloon.

ADJS. **5. unimaginative, unfanciful, unideal;** unidealized, unromanticized; **prosaic,** unpoetic(al); **staid, stuffy** [coll.]; **dull, dry;** arid, barren; **unoriginal, uninspired;** uninventive 165.5.

6. realistic, realist, **practical,** pragmatic(al), scientific, **unidealistic, unromantic, unsentimental, practical-minded,** straight-thinking, **matter-of-fact, down-to-earth, with both feet on the ground;** sensible, sane, reasonable, rational; sound, sound-thinking; literal, literal-minded.

535. MEMORY

NOUNS **1. memory, remembrance, recollection,** mind; **mind's eye,** eye of the mind, mirror of the mind; tablets of the memory, Memory's halls; corner or recess of the memory, inmost recesses of the memory; **artificial memory**; cryptamnesia (unrecognized memory [psychol.]).

2. "that inward eye" [Wordsworth], "the warder of the brain" [Shakespeare], "the treasury and guardian of all things" [Cicero], "the treasure house of the mind wherein the monuments thereof are kept and preserved" [Thomas Fuller], "storehouse of the mind, garner of facts and fancies" [Tupper], "the hearing of deaf actions, and the seeing of blind" [Plutarch], "the diary that we all carry around with us" [Wilde], "the thing I forget with" [child's definition].

3. **retention, retentiveness,** retentivity; good memory, retentive memory or mind; total memory, eidetic memory; camera eye.

4. **remembering, remembrance, recollection, recollecting, recall,** recalling; reflection, reconsideration; **retrospect,** retrospection, looking back; **reminiscence,** review, contemplation of the past, review of things past; **memorization,** memorizing, commitment to memory.

5. **recognition, identification, reidentification,** distinguishment, placement; realization 474.2.

6. **reminder,** remindal; **remembrance,** remembrancer; **suggestion, tip, hint, advice, admonition,** admonishment, **warning, word to the wise,** flea in the ear [coll.]; **prompt,** prompter, prompting; jogger [coll.], flapper; memorandum 568.3.

7. **memento, remembrance, token, trophy, souvenir, keepsake, relic,** favor, token of remembrance; memorial 568.11; love knot.

8. **memories, memorabilia,** memoranda, **memoirs,** memorials.

9. memorability, rememberability.

10. **mnemonics,** mnemotechny, mnemotechnics, mnemonization; Mnemosyne [Gr. myth.].

VERBS 11. **remember, recall, recollect,** member [dial.], recomember [dial., U.S.], mind, mind oneself [dial.]; **think of,** bethink oneself; **call to mind,** call up, summon up, conjure up, revive, renew, call back, bring back, "call back yesterday, bid time return" [Shakespeare]; **think back,** go back, **look back,** cast the eyes back, carry one's thoughts back, look back upon things past; retrospect, **see in retrospect,** go back over, retrace; review, pass in review, review in retrospect.

12. **reminisce,** cut up jack pots [slang, U.S.], rake up the past.

13. **recognize, know, tell, distinguish, make out,** make [slang]; **identify, place,** spot [coll.], nail [coll.], peg [slang], put one's hands on, put one's finger on; **reidentify,** know again, recover or recall knowledge of; realize 474.12.

14. **keep in memory, bear in mind,** keep or hold in mind, **keep in view,** have in mind, hold in the thoughts, carry in one's thoughts, retain in the thoughts; **retain, keep; treasure, cherish,** treasure up in the memory, enshrine in the memory, cherish the memory of; **keep up the memory of, keep the memory alive,** keep the wound green; brood over, dwell on or upon.

15. **be remembered,** sink in the mind, sink in [coll.], penetrate, make an impression; live or dwell in one's memory, remain in one's memory, remain indelibly impressed on the memory, **never be forgotten; haunt one's thoughts,** run in the head, be in one's thoughts, be on one's mind; not be able to forget, be unable to get out of one's head; **rankle,** rankle in the breast, get under one's skin [slang].

16. **recur,** recur to the mind, return to mind, **come to mind,** come back, come to one, come into one's head, **flash on the mind.**

17. **memorize, commit to memory,** con; **learn by heart,** get off by heart, **get by heart or rote,** learn word for word; know by heart, have by heart or rote, have at one's fingers' ends or tips; repeat by heart or rote, give word for word, repeat, repeat like a parrot, say one's lesson.

18. **fix in the mind** or memory, infix, impress, print, imprint, stamp, inscribe, etch, grave, engrave; **impress on the mind, get into one's head,** drive or hammer into one's head; **store in the mind,** bottle up, bury in one's mind, **burden the mind with,** load or stuff the mind with; inscribe in the memory, etch indelibly in the mind.

19. **refresh the memory, brush up, rub up,** polish up [coll.], get up on.

20. **remind,** mind [chiefly dial.], **put in mind,** remember, put in remembrance, bring back to the memory, bring to recollection, refresh the memory of; **remind one of, put one in mind of; take one back,** carry back, carry back in recollection; jog the memory, awaken or arouse the memory, flap the memory; **prompt,** give the cue; nudge, pull by the sleeve; **suggest to,** notify, mention to, call the attention to;

admcnish, advise, **warn**, give a word to the wise, put a flea in one's ear [coll.].

21. **try to recall**, think hard, tax or task the memory, **rack** or **ransack one's brains**, **cudgel one's brains**, crack one's brains [coll.]; have on the tip of one's tongue.

ADJS. 22. **recollective, memoried**; mnemonic; retentive; **retrospective**, in retrospect; **reminiscent, mindful, remindful, suggestive**, redolent.

23. **remembered, recollected, recalled; retained**, pent up in the memory, enduring, lasting, **unforgotten**; present to the mind, uppermost in one's thoughts; vivid, eidetic [psychol.], fresh, green, alive.

24. **memorable, rememberable, recollectable**; notable 670.18; *beatae memoriae* [L., of blessed memory].

25. **unforgettable, never to be forgotten**, never to be erased from the mind, indelible, indelibly impressed on the mind, fixed in the mind.

26. **memorial, commemorative**, kept in remembrance.

ADVS. 27. **by heart**, *par cœur* [F..], by rote, by or from memory, without book.

28. **in memory of**, to the memory of, in remembrance or commemoration, *in memoriam* [L.]; *memoria in aeterna* [L.], in perpetual remembrance.

536. FORGETFULNESS

NOUNS 1. **forgetfulness, unmindfulness, memorylessness**; short memory, mind or memory like a sieve; **obliviousness, oblivion**; nirvana; Lethe, waters of Lethe or oblivion, river of oblivion; **forgetting, forget** [coll.]; misremembrance; heedlessness 532.2.

2. **amnesia**, failure or loss of memory, **lapse of memory, memory gap**, blackout [coll.]; fugue [psychol.]; anterograde amnesia, retrograde amnesia, retroanterograde amnesia; infantile amnesia; lucunar amnesia, partial amnesia; agnosia, unrecognition; paramnesia, false memory; auditory or verbal amnesia, word deafness or blindness, amnesic aphrasia, alexia, lethologica; tactile amnesia, astereognosis; systematic amnesia.

3. (psychological memory obstruction) **block**, blocking, **mental block**.

VERBS 4. **be forgetful**, have a short memory, have no head.

5. **forget**, clean forget, **not remember**, disremember [dial. & coll.], disrecollect [dial.], fail to remember, forget to remember [jcc.], **have no remembrance** or recollection of, be unable to recollect or recall, draw a blank [slang]; **escape one**, slip or escape the memory; lose, lose sight of; misremember; have on the tip of the tongue; blow up, fluff [both theat. slang]; unlearn.

6. **efface** or **erase from the memory**, consign to oblivion, consign to the tomb of Capulets; **dismiss from one's thoughts** 529.4; forgive 945.3–5.

7. **be forgotten**, fade or die away from the memory, fall or sink into oblivion.

ADJS. 8. **forgotten, forgot**, clean forgotten, **unremembered, unrecollected, unretained, unrecalled**, past recollection or recall, bygone, out of the mind, lost, gone, gone out of one's head or recollection, consign to oblivion, buried or sunk in oblivion; out of sight out of mind.

9. **forgetful, forgetting, memoryless, unmemoried, unremembering, unmindful, oblivious**, Letheian, insensible to the past, with a mind or memory like a sieve; amnesic, amnestic; heedless 532.11.

10. **forgettable, unrememberable, unrecollectable**.

ADVS. 11. **forgetfully, forgettingly**, unmindfully, obliviously.

537. EXPECTATION

NOUNS 1. **expectation, expectance** or **expectancy; anticipation**, prospect; thought, contemplation; imminence 151; unastonishment 919.

2. **sanguine expectation**, hope 886.

3. **suspense**, state of suspense, abeyance [chiefly law]; **waiting, expectant waiting**; anxiety, apprehension 888.

VERBS 4. **expect**, be expectant, **anticipate**, have in prospect, have or keep in view, think, **contemplate**, have in contemplation, promise oneself; hope 886.7; presume 498.9; **take for granted**, accept; not be surprised or a bit surprised.

5. **look forward to**, look to, **look for**, watch for, look out for, watch out for [coll., U.S.], be on the watch or look out for, keep a good or sharp lookout for.

6. **await**, wait, **wait for, wait on** or upon [coll.], lie in wait for, stay or **tarry for**; watch, watch and wait or pray; **bide one's time**, bide, abide, **mark time**; hold one's breath; sweat it out, champ or chomp at the bit [both slang]; **wait up for**, stay up for, sit up for.

7. **expect to**, plan on 651.4–8.

8. **be expected**, be as one thought, turn out that way; expect it of, think that way

about, **not put it past** [coll., U.S.], **be just like one**, be one all over [slang]; be imminent 151.2; lead one to expect 542.10.

ADJS. **9. expectant,** expecting, in expectation *or* anticipation; **anticipative,** anticipant, anticipating, anticipatory; **waiting,** awaiting, waiting for; **looking forward to,** looking for, watching for, on the watch *or* lookout for; open-eyed, openmouthed; gaping, agape, agog, all agog; eager 633.9; hopeful 886.11; unsurprised, not surprised.

10. in suspense, on tenterhooks, on tiptoe, **on edge** [coll.], **with bated breath,** with muscles tense, biting one's nails; anxious, apprehensive 888.6.

11. expected, anticipated, awaited, foreseen; looked for, hoped for; **due, promised; coming, upcoming;** future, forward [com.]; **in prospect,** prospective; **in view,** in one's eye, on the horizon; imminent 151.3.

12. to be expected, as expected, **as one may have suspected,** as one might think *or* suppose; **expected of,** accepted, **taken for granted;** just like one, one all over [slang], in character.

ADVS. **13. expectantly,** expectingly, expectedly; anticipatively, **anticipatingly,** anticipatorily; hopefully 886.14; **with bated breath,** with breathless expectation; with ears pricked up, with eyes *or* ears strained.

PHRS. **14. what did you expect?,** that's the way it is, that's the way it goes, that's how things are; what did I tell you?, **I told you so;** see!, there!; what do you want me to do, cry?

538. INEXPECTATION

NOUNS **1. inexpectation,** nonexpectation, inexpectance *or* inexpectancy, **unexpectedness, unanticipation;** the unforeseen, the unlooked-for.

2. surprise, surprisal; **astonishment** 918; surpriser, startler, shocker; **blow,** staggerer [coll.]; **eye opener,** rouser [coll.]; **bolt out of** *or* **from the blue,** thunderbolt, thunderclap; **bombshell,** bomb; surprise package; surprise party [U.S.].

3. start, shock, jar [coll.], **jolt** [slang], turn [coll.], twitch [slang].

VERBS **4. not expect,** hardly expect, **not anticipate,** not look for, not bargain for, **not foresee,** not think to, have no thought of, have no expectation.

5. be startled, be taken by surprise, be given a start, be given a turn [coll.]; **start,** startle, **jump,** jump out of one's skin; **shy,** start aside.

6. be unexpected, come unawares, appear unexpectedly, turn up, pop up [chiefly coll.], bob up [coll.], drop from the clouds, appear like a bolt out of the blue, come *or* burst like a thunderclap *or* thunderbolt, burst *or* flash upon one, come *or* fall upon, steal *or* creep upon.

7. surprise, take by surprise, spring a surprise [coll.], **catch** *or* **take unawares,** catch *or* take short; **catch off-guard** 487.7; come upon expectedly *or* without warning, spring *or* pounce upon; spring a mine upon; drop in upon [coll.]; give a surprise party [U.S.]; **astonish** 918.5.

8. startle, start [Scot.], **shock, electrify,** jar [coll.], **jolt** [slang], **stagger, give a turn** [coll.], make one jump out of his skin, take aback [coll.], take away one's breath, throw on one's beam ends, throw off one's guard, **upset, unsettle,** bowl down *or* over [coll.], strike all of a heap [coll.]; **frighten** 889.14.

ADJS. **9. inexpectant,** unexpecting; **unanticipative,** unanticipating; **unsuspecting, unaware;** unwarned, unadvised, unadmonished; off one's guard 529.8.

10. unexpected, unanticipated, unlooked for, unhoped for, **unforeseen,** unforeseeable; beyond *or* past expectation, out of one's reckoning, more than expected, more than one bargained for; out of the blue, dropped from the clouds; sudden 113.5.

11. surprising, astonishing 918.11; **startling, shocking,** electrifying, staggering.

12. surprised, struck with surprise; **astonished** 918.8; **taken by surprise,** taken unawares, caught short.

13. startled, shocked, electrified, jarred [coll.], jolted [slang], **staggered, given a turn** [coll.], taken aback [coll.], **upset, unsettled,** bowled down *or* over [coll.], struck all of a heap [coll.].

14. unexpectedly, unanticipatedly, **unforeseeably,** *à l'improviste* [F.], **by surprise, unawares,** without notice *or* warning, in an unguarded moment, like a thief in the night; **out of a clear sky, out of the blue,** like a bolt from the blue; suddenly 113.9.

15. surprisingly, startlingly, to one's surprise, to one's great surprise; **astonishingly** 918.14.

PHRS. **16. little would one expect,** who would have thought?, can such things be?

539. DISAPPOINTMENT

Failure of Expectation.—NOUNS **1. disappointment,** sad *or* sore disappointment, bitter *or* cruel disappointment; **dashed hopes, blighted hope,** hope deferred, forlorn hope; **dash,** dash to one's hopes; **blow.** buffet; **frustration,** discomfiture, bafflement, defeat, balk, check, foil; **comedown, letdown** [coll.]; disillusionment 519; dissatisfaction 867; fallen countenance.

VERBS **2. disappoint,** defeat expectation *or* hope; **dash,** dash *or* blight one's hope; **balk, bilk, thwart, frustrate, baffle, defeat,** foil, cross; **put out,** put one's nose out of joint; **let down,** cast down; disillusion 519.2; dissatisfy 867.4.

3. be disappointing, not come up to expectation, not live *or* measure up to expectation, disappoint one's expectations, come *or* fall short.

4. be disappointed, get left [coll.]; look blank, look blue, look *or* stand aghast; laugh on the wrong side of one's mouth, laugh out of the other corner of the mouth [both coll.].

ADJS. **5. disappointed,** bitterly *or* sorely disappointed; **let down, put-out;** dashed, blighted; **balked,** bilked, **thwarted, frustrated,** baffled, defeated, foiled; out of one's reckoning; disillusioned 519.5; dissatisfied 867.5; regretful 871.8.

6. disappointing, not up to expectation; **unsatisfactory** 867.6.

7. due disappointment, headed for a fall.

540. FORESIGHT

NOUNS **1. foresight,** forseeing, **prevision;** prediction 541; divination, forecast; **foreglimpse,** foreglance, foregleam; **prospect,** prospection; **anticipation,** contemplation; **foresightedness; farsightedness,** longsightedness, farseeingness; sagacity, prudence 466.4–7; hindsight [coll., U.S.].

2. forethought, premeditation, predeliberation, preconsideration; **preconception,** preapprehension, prenotion, presumption, **presupposition,** presupposal, presurmise; caution 893.

3. foreknowledge, foreknowing, forewisdom, **precognition, preapprehension,** prescience, presage; presentiment, foreboding 542.

4. foretaste, antepast, prelibation.

5. foreseeability 541.8.

VERBS **6. foresee,** see beforehand, foreglimpse, foretaste, forecast, **divine, anticipate,** contemplate, **look forward to,** look ahead, look beyond, look ~, pry *or* peep into the future; see one's way; see how the land lies *or* the wind blows, see how the cat jumps [coll.]; **predict** 541.9.

7. foreknow, know beforehand, precognize; smell it in the wind, scent from afar; **have a presentiment, have a premonition** [coll.], forefeel, feel it in one's bones [coll.], just know.

ADJS. **8. foreseeing, foresighted; foreknowing, precognizant,** precognitive, prescient; divinatory 541.11; **forethoughted,** forethoughtful; **farseeing, farsighted,** longsighted; sagacious, prudent 466.16–19.

9. foreseeable 541.13; **foreseen** 541.14.

ADVS. **10. foreseeingly, foreknowingly,** with foresight; against the time when, for a rainy day.

541. PREDICTION

NOUNS **1. prediction, foretelling,** forecasting; **prognosis,** prognostication; **presage,** presagement, presaging; **prophecy,** prophesying, vaticination; **forecast, promise;** prenotice, prenotation; preannouncement, prepublication; foresight 540; foreboding 542; omen 542.2.

2. divination, divining, **augury,** pythonism; **soothsaying,** soothsay, hariolation; **fortunetelling,** crystalgazing; crystal ball; astrology 374.20; sorcery 1033; clairvoyance 1032.8.

3. divining rod *or* stick, wand, witch hazel, witch stick [slang], dowsing rod, doodlebug.

4. prophet, prophesier, predictor, forecaster, **foreteller, prognosticator, seer,** foreseer, foreknower, augur, presager, **diviner,** divinator, **soothsayer,** *vates* [L.]; psychic 1032.13; prophetess, seeress, divineress; python, pythoness; Cassandra; sphinx; druid; **fortuneteller,** crystal-gazer; palmist; geomancer; haruspice, haruspex, extispex; astrologer 374.23; weather prophet 401.7; Tiresias, the blind Theban; religious prophets 1020.

5. dopester, tipster [both slang]; **tout,** touter [both slang, U.S.].

6. sibyl; Pythia, Pythian, Delphic sibyl; Babylonian *or* Persian sibyl, Cimmerian sibyl, Cumaean sibyl, Erythraean sibyl, Hellespontine *or* Trojan sibyl, Libyan sibyl, Phrygian sibyl, Samian sibyl, Tiburtine sibyl.

7. oracle; Delphic *or* Delphian oracle,

Pythian oracle; Delphic tripod, tripod of the Pythia; Dodona, oracle or oak of Dodona; adytum; cave of the Cumaean sibyl; Sibylline Books or Oracles, Sibylline leaves.

8. predictability, divinability, foretellableness, **calculability,** accountability; **foreseeability,** foreknowableness.

VERBS **9. predict,** make a prediction, **foretell, forecast, prophesy, prognosticate,** vaticinate, **forebode, promise, divine, presage, augur;** see or tell the future, read the future, see in the crystal ball; **foresee** 540.6; dope, dope out [both slang, U.S.]; call the turn, call one's shot [both coll.]; **soothsay,** hariolate; **tell fortunes,** fortunetell, cast one's fortune; read one's hand, read tea leaves, cast a horoscope or nativity.

10. portend, foretoken 542.8−11.

ADJS. **11. predictive,** predictory, predictional; **foretelling,** forecasting; **prophetic(al),** divinatory, oracular, fateful, fatidic(al); **foreseeing** 540.8; **presageful,** presaging; **prognostic,** prognosticative, prognosticatory; auguring, augural; vaticinatory, vaticinal; sibyllic, sibylline; haruspical, extispicious; fortunetelling; weather-wise.

12. ominous, premonitory, foreboding 542.13, 14.

13. predictable, divinable, **foretellable, calculable,** accountable, antcipatable; **foreseeable, foreknowable,** precognizable.

14. predicted, prophesied, promised, presaged, **foretold, forecast, foreshown, foreseen,** foreglimpsed, **foreknown.**

15. forms of divination

aeromancy	cleromancy
alectoromancy,	coscinomancy
alectryomancy	crithomancy
aleuromancy	crystallomancy
alphitomancy	dactyliomancy
anthropomancy	extispicy
anthroposcopy	gastromancy
arithmancy	geloscopy
astrodiagnosis	genethlialogy,
astrognosy	genethliacs
astrology 374.20	geomancy
astromancy	gyromancy
austromancy	halomancy
axinomancy	haruspicy
belomancy	hieromancy
bibliomancy	hieroscopy
bletonism	horoscopy
botanomancy	hydromancy
capnomancy	ichthyomancy
ceromancy	lithomancy
chirognomy	meteoromancy
chirology	molybdomancy
chiromancy	myomancy
necromancy	pegomancy
nomancy	pessomancy,
numerology	psephomancy
oenomancy	psychomancy
omoplatoscopy	pyromancy
oneiromancy	rhabdomancy
onomancy	scapulimancy
onychomancy	sciomancy
ophiomancy	sideromancy
orniscopy	sortilege
ornithomancy	stichomancy
palmistry	theomancy

542. FOREBODING

NOUNS **1. foreboding,** forebodement, boding; **apprehension, misgiving; presentiment, premonition, preapprehension,** forefeeling, intimation, anticipation, augury, presage; prediction 541.

2. omen, portent, augury, auspice, divination, soothsay; **presage,** presager; prognostic, prognostication; premonitor, **premonitory sign; foretoken,** foretokening, **preindication,** presignification, prefiguration; **sign, token,** symptom, indicant, **indication; promise, intimation; foreshadow,** foreshadowing, foreshadower, shadow, adumbration; **warning, forewarning,** "warnings, and portents and evils imminent" [Shakespeare]; sign of the times.

3. harbinger, forerunner, precursor, messenger, herald.

4. (omens) birds of ill omen, storm petrels, Mother Carey's chickens; halcyon birds; gathering clouds, clouds on the horizon, storm clouds, messengers [dial., Eng.]; thundercloud, thunderhead; rainbow; shooting star; black cat; broken mirror.

5. ominousness, portentousness, portent, bodefulness, presagefulness, suggestiveness; fatefulness, doomfulness; darkness, blackness, gloominess, somberness, dreariness, sinisterness.

6. inauspiciousness, unpropitiousness, unfavorableness, unfortunateness, unluckiness, ill-fatedness.

7. auspiciousness, propitiousness, favorableness; luckiness, **fortunateness,** prosperousness; brightness, cheerfulness; good omen, good auspices, auspicium melioris aevi [L., omen of a better age].

VERBS **8. forebode, bode, portend, augur, presage,** divine, croak, prognosticate, auspicate, omen, be the omen of; **foreshow,** preshow; **foreshadow,** shadow, adumbrate, shadow forth, cast their shadows before; **threaten, menace, lower; warn, forewarn;** predict 541.9.

9. foretoken, preindicate, presignify, pretypify, prefigure, betoken, typify, **signify, indicate, point to, be a sign of.**

10 **promise, suggest, imply,** give ground for expecting, raise expectation, **lead one to expect,** hold out hope, make fair promise, **bid fair, stand fair to.**

11 **herald, harbinger, forerun;** announce, proclaim, preannounce.

ADS. 12. portended, foreboded, presaged, augured, foreshadowed, foreshown; indicated, signified; preindicated, foretokened, prefigured, pretypified, presignified; **promised, suggested, threatened;** predicted 541.14.

13. **ominous, portentous,** portending; **foreboding,** boding, **bodeful;** augural, presageful, monitory; **significant, indicative, suggestive;** fateful, doomful; **sinister,** dark, black, gloomy, somber, dreary; **threatening, menacing, lowering.**

14. **premonitory, forewarning,** presentimental; **foretokening, preindicative,** presignificant, prefigurative; **foreshowing, foreshadowing;** forerunning, precursory, precursive, precurrent; predictive 541.11.

15. **inauspicious, ill-omened,** ill-boding; unpropitious, unpromising, unfavorable, unfortunate, unlucky; bad, evil, poor, ill, untoward; dire, baleful, malific, malignant, malign; **ill-fated,** ill-starred, evil-starred; planet-stricken, planet-struck.

16. **auspicious,** of good omen, *de bon augure* [F.]; **propitious, favorable,** favoring, good; **promising,** of promise, full of promise; **fortunate, lucky,** prosperous; rosy, roseate, rose-colored, *couleur de rose* [F.]; bright, cheerful, happy, optimistic, sunny, golden, halcyon; encouraging, reassuring, cheering.

AVS. 17. **ominously, portentously, bodefully, forebodingly;** significantly, suggestively; darkly, gloomily, somberly, drearily, sinisterly; **threateningly, menacingly,** loweringly.

18. **inauspiciously, unpropitiously,** unpromisingly, unfavorably, unfortunately, unluckily, ill.

19. **auspiciously, propitiously,** promisingly, **favorably, well; fortunately, luckily;** brightly, cheerfully, happily; encouragingly, reassuringly.

543. MEANING

NOUNS 1. **meaning, significance,** signification, point, sense, idea, expression, **purport, import, implication, connotation,** denotation, construction; **drift,** tenor, bearing; **substance, gist,** pith, spirit, essence; **effect,** force, impact, value.

2. **intent, intention, purpose, aim, object, design,** plan, hang.

3. **explanation, definition, interpretation** 550.

4. **acceptation,** acception, accepted or received meaning.

5. **literalness,** literality, literalism, textualism, the letter; **literal meaning,** true or real meaning.

6. **meaningfulness, suggestiveness,** pregnancy; **significance,** significancy, significantness; **expressiveness,** mobility; eloquence, vividness, graphicness, picturesqueness; pithiness, meatiness.

7. **semantics, semiotics,** semantology, semasiology; orthology.

VERBS 8. **mean, signify, denote, connote, import,** purport, convey, spell, express, **imply, suggest,** argue, breathe, bespeak, betoken, **indicate.**

9. **intend,** have in mind 651.4.

ADJS. 10. **meaningful,** meaning; **significant,** significative; **suggestive, indicative; expressive,** mobile; **eloquent,** vivid, telling, graphic, picturesque; **pregnant, full of** meaning; **pithy, meaty** [U.S.], substantial, full of substance; pointed, full of point.

11. **meant,** implied 544.7, intended 651.9.

12. **literal, textual; verbatim,** verbal, **word-for-word;** following the letter, true to the letter; **faithful,** servile, religious, close, strict; **exact, precise; real, true, true to fact;** unfigurative, unmetaphorical.

13. **semantic,** semantological, semasiological; orthological.

ADVS. 14. **meaningfully, meaningly, significantly,** suggestively; **expressively, eloquently,** vividly, tellingly, graphicly, picturesquely.

15. **literally,** *literatim* [L.], to the letter, according to the letter, *au pied de la lettre* [F.]; **verbatim,** verbally, **word for word,** word by word, *mot à mot* [F.]; word for word and letter for letter, *verbatim et literatim* [L.]; in the same words, *ipsissimis verbis* [L.]; **faithfully,** servilely, religiously, closely, strictly; **exactly, precisely; really, truly.**

544. LATENCY

Underlying or **Implied Meaning.—**
NOUNS 1. **latency,** latentness, delitescence, undercurrent, more than meets the eye or

ear; **potentiality,** virtuality, possibility; dormancy 267.4.

2. **implication, connotation, import;** meaning 543; **suggestion,** allusion; **hint** 555.4; **inference, supposition,** presupposition, assumption, presumption.

VERBS 3. **be latent, underlie, lie under the surface, lurk,** smolder, make no sign, escape notice.

4. **imply, implicate, involve;** entail 76.4; **connote, import;** mean 543.8; **suggest,** bring to mind; **hint, intimate** 555.9; **allude to,** point to; **infer, suppose, presuppose,** assume, presume, understand, take for granted; mean to say, ~ imply *or* suggest.

ADJS. 5. **latent, lurking,** delitescent; **hidden** 613.12; **underlying, under the surface,** between the lines; dormant 267.12; **potential,** virtual, possible.

6. **suggestive, allusive, indicative, inferential,** referential; **insinuating,** insinuative, insinuatory; **implicative,** implicatory, implicational; constructive, constructional; **provocative,** provoking, **thought-provoking; stimulating,** stimulative.

7. **implied,** implicated, involved, **meant,** construed; **suggested, intimated, insinuated, hinted,** indicated; **inferred, supposed,** assumed, presumed, presupposed.

8. **tacit, implicit, understood,** taken for granted, fairly to be understood.

9. **unexpressed,** unpronounced, **unsaid, unspoken, unuttered,** unbreathed, unvoiced, wordless, silent; **unmentioned,** untalked-of, **untold,** unsung, unproclaimed, unpublished; unwritten, unrecorded.

ADVS. 10. **latently,** underlyingly; **potentially,** virtually.

11. **suggestively, allusively, inferentially,** insinuatingly; **provocatively,** provokingly; stimulatingly, stimulatively.

12. **tacitly, implicitly,** unspokenly, wordlessly, silently.

545. MEANINGLESSNESS

NOUNS 1. **meaninglessness,** unmeaningness, **senselessness,** nonsensicality; **insignificance,** unsignificancy; empty sound, "sounding brass and tinkling cymbal" [Bible], "a tale told by an idiot, full of sound and fury, signifying nothing" [Shakespeare]; dead letter.

2. **nonsense,** stuff, **stuff and nonsense,** pack of nonsense, **poppycock** [coll., U.S.], **falderal** *or* folderol, **bosh** [coll.], **buncombe** *or* bunkum [coll., orig. U.S.], bilge

[coll.], **balderdash, piffle** [coll.], *niaiserie* [F.], flummery, trumpery, **rubbish,** trash, truck [coll.], blatherskite [coll.], moonshine, fiddle-faddle [coll.], fiddledeedee, flumdiddle *or* flummadiddle [coll.], flapdoodle [coll.], fudge, **humbug,** hocuspocus; absurdity 469.3.

3. (slang terms) **tommyrot, rot, hogwash, malarkey,** tosh [chiefly Eng.], kibosh, **bunk,** hokum, **hooey,** bushwa *or* bushwah, blah [U.S.], huftymagufty, whoopla, hoopdedoodle, monkey-doodle, gook, **applesauce** [U.S.], **baloney** [U.S.], tripe, horsefeathers [U.S.].

4. (nonsensical talk) **twaddle,** twattle, **twiddle-twaddle, blather, babble,** babblement, bibble-babble, **gabble,** gibble-gabble, **blabber, gibber, jabber, patter,** prate, **prattle,** rattle, *bavardage* [F.], guff [slang], gash [Scot.], clack, **gas** [slang], **hot air** [slang], **bull** [slang, U.S.], blah [slang], blah-blah [slang], gammon [coll.], claptrap, skimble-scamble, slipslap [coll.], wish-wash; **drivel,** dribble, drool, slaver; **gibberish, jargon,** mumbo-jumbo, *baragouin* [F.]; **double talk, gobbledegook** [slang], bafflegab [slang, U.S.].

5. **unexpressiveness,** inexpressiveness, **expressionlessness;** deadpan [slang].

6. **inexpressibility, ineffability,** indescribability, indefinableness, **unutterability, unspeakability,** unmentionability, incommunicability.

VERBS 7. **be meaningless, mean nothing,** signify nothing, not mean a thing, not convey anything; not register, not ring any bells.

8. (talk nonsense) **twaddle,** twattle, **piffle** [slang], fudge, **blather, blabber, babble,** bibble-babble, **gabble,** gibble-gabble, **jabber, gibber, patter,** prate, **prattle,** fiddle-faddle [coll.], rattle, clack, gas [slang]; **talk through one's hat** [slang]; bull, **throw the bull,** feed the bull [all slang, U.S.]; **drivel,** drool, slaver, run off at the mouth [slang].

ADJS. 9. **meaningless, unmeaning, senseless,** purportless, importless; **insignificant,** unsignificant, unsignificative; **purposeless,** aimless, designless, **without rhyme or reason.**

10. **nonsensical, poppycockish** [coll.]; foolish, absurd 469.8, 10; gibberish; twaddling, twaddly; rubbishy, trashy; fiddle-faddle [coll.], skimble-scamble.

11. **inexpressive,** unexpressive; **expressionless, vacant, empty, blank, dull,** dead,

glassy, lusterless, **lackluster, stupid,** unintelligent, wooden, fishy, deadpan [slang].

12. unmeant, unsignified, unimplied, unsuggested, unintimated, unindicated, unintended; unintentional 155.17.

13. inexpressible, ineffable, indescribable, indefinable, undefinable, **unutterable, unspeakable,** unwhisperable, unmentionable, incommunicable.

ADVS. **14. meaninglessly,** unmeaningly, **senselessly,** nonsensically, insignificantly; **purposelessly,** aimlessly.

15. expressionlessly, vacantly, blankly, emptily, dully, stupidly, unintelligently, woodenly, glassily, fishily.

16. inexpressibly, ineffably, indescribably, indefinably, **unutterably, unspeakably,** unmentionably.

INTERJS. **17. nonsense!** 469.12.

546. INTELLIGIBILITY

NOUNS **1. intelligibility, comprehensibility, apprehensibility, understandability,** knowability, cognizability, explicability, conceivability, scrutability, penetrability, fathomableness; recognizability, distinguishability; articulateness, articulation.

2. clearness, clarity; plainness, distinctness, explicitness; definition, precision; **lucidity,** limpidity, perspicuity, transpicuity, transparency; unmistakableness, unequivocalness, unambiguousness.

3. legibility, decipherability, readability.

VERBS **4. be understandable, make sense;** be plain or clear, lie on the surface; **speak for itself,** tell its own tale, speak volumes.

5. (be understood) carry, **get over or across** [coll.], **register** [slang], **penetrate, sink in,** soak in; dawn on.

6. make clear, make it clear, **let it be understood,** make oneself understood, get or put over or across [coll.]; put in plain words or plain English, put in words of one syllable; clarify 550.11.

7. understand, comprehend, apprehend, conceive, realize, ken [chiefly Scot.], **savvy** [slang, U.S.], sense [coll., U.S.], read, **dig** [slang, U.S.], **fathom, follow,** get the idea, get the picture [slang], get into or through one's head or thick head [coll.]; **grasp, seize,** grasp or seize the meaning, get [slang], take, **take in,** catch, **catch on** [coll.], get the meaning of, get the hang of, catch or get the drift [slang]; **assimilate, absorb, digest.**

8. perceive, see, discern, make, **make out;** see the light, see daylight [coll.]; see

through, penetrate, see into, see into or through a millstone; see at a glance, see with half an eye.

ADJS. **9. intelligible, comprehensible, apprehensible,** discoverable, **knowable,** cognizable, explicable, accountable, conceivable, scrutable, **fathomable,** penetrable; **understandable,** easily understood, easy to understand; for the million, exoteric(al).

10. clear, crystal-clear, clear as crystal, clear as day; **recognizable,** distinguishable; **plain, distinct,** articulate; **definite,** defined, well-defined, **clear-cut,** clean-cut, crisp; **explicit, express,** precise; **unmistakable, unequivocal,** univocal, unambiguous, unconfused; **lucid,** pellucid, limpid, perspicuous, transpicuous, **transparent,** translucent, luminous.

11. legible, decipherable, readable, fair.

ADVS. **12. intelligibly, understandably, comprehensibly,** apprehensibly; **recognizably,** distinguishably; **clearly, lucidly,** limpidly, perspicuously, **plainly, distinctly,** definitely, articulately; **explicitly, expressly,** precisely; **unmistakably, unequivocally,** unambiguously; in plain terms or words, in plain English.

13. legibly, decipherably, readably, fairly.

547. UNINTELLIGIBILITY

NOUNS **1. unintelligibility, incomprehensibility,** inapprehensibility, **inunderstandability,** unununderstandability, unknowability, incognizability, unrecognizability; inscrutability, impenetrability, unfathomableness, unsearchableness; indiscernibility, indistinguishability, unascertainableness, undiscoverability; imperceptibility, impalpability, intangibility.

2. abstruseness, reconditeness; **profundity,** profoundness, deepness; **enigmaticalness,** mysteriousness.

3. obscurity, obscuration; **unclearness,** unclarity, unplainness, imperspicuity, opacity; **vagueness,** indistinctness, indeterminateness; dark, darkness.

4. illegibility, unreadability; undecipherability, indecipherability.

5. inexplicability, unexplainableness, undefinability, indescribability, unaccountableness, inconceivability; insolvability, inextricability.

6. (something **unintelligible**) Greek, Hebrew, Choctaw, **Dutch, double Dutch;** gibberish, jargon.

7. enigma, mystery, puzzle; Chinese

puzzle, **crossword puzzle, jigsaw puzzle; problem,** puzzling *or* baffling problem, why; **question,** question mark, vexed question, enigmatic question, sixty-four dollar question [slang]; **perplexity,** knot, knotty point, point to be solved; **puzzler, poser,** brain twister [slang], sticker [slang], grueler [slang, Eng.]; graveler, **floorer, stumper,** facer, staggerer [all coll.]; **nut to crack, hard nut to crack;** tough proposition [coll.], enough to puzzle a Philadelphia lawyer [coll., U.S.], "a perfect nonplus and baffle to all human understanding" [Southey].

8. riddle, conundrum, charade, rebus; logogriph, logogram; the Sphinx, riddle of the Sphinx.

VERBS **9. be incomprehensible, not make sense,** be Greek to, pass comprehension *or* understanding; riddle, speak in riddles.

10. not understand, be unable to comprehend, not have the first idea, be unable to get into *or* through one's head, not understand all one knows [joc.]; **not know what to make of,** make nothing of, not be able to account for, not be able to make head or tail of; be unable to see, not see for looking [joc.], not see the wood for the trees; **give up,** pass [coll.].

ADJS. **11. unintelligible, incomprehensible, inapprehensible, inunderstandable,** ununderstandable, unknowable, incognizable, **unrecognizable; unfathomable, inscrutable,** impenetrable, unsearchable; **indiscernible, indistinguishable,** unascertainable, undiscoverable; **imperceptible,** impalpable, intangible; **past comprehension,** beyond understanding; Greek to.

12. hard to understand, difficult, hard, tough [coll.], steep [coll.], heavy [coll.], cramp; knotty, knotted, crabbed; intricate, complicated 46.4.

13. obscure, vague, indistinct, indeterminate; equivocal 548.3; **unclear,** unplain, imperspicuous, opaque, muddy, **clear as mud** [joc.]; dark, dim, blind, shadowy, shadowed forth; cloudy, foggy, hazy, misty, nebulous; inarticulate, inarticulated.

14. recondite, abstruse; profound, deep; hidden 613.12; secret 612.12; **mysterious, mystic(al),** shrouded in mystery; arcane, arcanal; **esoteric, occult,** cabalistic(al), anagogic(al), acroamatic(al), abstract; **transcendent,** transcendental; metempiric(al).

15. enigmatic(al), problematic(al),

cryptic(al); **puzzling** 513.24, riddling; logogriphic, logogrammatic.

16. inexplicable, unexplainable, undefinable, indefinable, indescribable, **unaccountable,** inconceivable; **insolvable,** unsolvable, insoluble, inextricable.

17. illegible, unreadable, unclear; undecipherable, indecipherable.

ADVS. **18. unintelligibly, incomprehensibly,** inapprehensibly, inunderstandably, unrecognizably.

19. obscurely, vaguely, indistinctly, indeterminately; **unclearly,** unplainly, imperspicuously; illegibly.

20. reconditely, abstrusely; enigmatically, cryptically; **mysteriously,** mystically; esoterically, occultly.

21. inexplicably, unexplainably, undefinably, indescribably, **unaccountably,** inconceivably.

PREPS. **22. beyond one's comprehension, beyond,** past, above; **over one's head,** above one's bend [coll.]; beyond one's depth, **too deep for.**

PHRS. **23. I don't understand,** I can't feature [slang], **I can't see,** I don't see how *or* why, **it beats me** [coll.], you've got me [coll.], **it's beyond me,** it's too deep for me, it has me guessing, I don't have the first idea, it's Greek to me; **I give up,** I pass [coll.].

548. AMBIGUITY

NOUNS **1. ambiguity,** ambiguousness; **equivocalness,** equivocacy, equivocality; **double meaning,** duplexity in meaning; amphibology, amphilogy, amphilogism; ambilogy; uncertainty 513.

2. (ambiguous word or expression) **ambiguity, equivoque,** equivoke, equivocal, equivocality; *double-entendre, double entente, mot à double entente* [all F.]; **quibble,** verbal quibble; pun 879.8.

ADJS. **3. ambiguous,** double, duplex; **equivocal,** equivocatory; amphibolous, amphibological; uncertain 513.14; obscure, mysterious, enigmatic 547.13—15.

549. FIGURE OF SPEECH

NOUNS **1. figure of speech,** *façon de parler* [F.], **figure, image,** turn of expression, manner *or* way of speaking; imagery, figurativeness, figurative language.

2. (figures) **metaphor,** metaphorical expression; **simile,** similitude; allegory, allegorization; apologue, parable, fable; climax, anticlimax; euphemism, euphuism;

onomatopoeia, onomatopoësis; personification, prosopopoeia; satire, irony; antithesis, antonomasia, apostrophe, catachresis, enallage, exclamation, hyperbole, interrogation, litotes, metalepsis, metathesis, metonymy, synecdoche, tralatition, trope, vision.

VERBS 3. figure, figurize, **symbolize, typify;** similize, similitudinize; personify, personalize; allegorize, fable.

ADJS. 4. **figurative, symbolic(al), typical; metaphorical;** allusive, referential; allegoric(al), parabolic(al); euphemistic(al), euphuistic(al); ironic(al), satiric(al); antithetic(al), antonomastic(al), catachrestic(al), metonymic(al), tralatitious, tropical; **flowery** 599.12.

ADVS. 5. **figuratively, symbolically, typically; metaphorically; figuratively speaking,** so to say or speak, in a manner of speaking [coll.], **as it were.**

550. INTERPRETATION

NOUNS 1. **interpretation, construction,** light, way of putting; **diagnosis,** prognosis, prophasis [med.].

2. **rendering, rendition,** reddition; **version,** reading, lection.

3. **translation,** transcription; **paraphrase,** free translation, amplification, restatement, rewording; metaphrase, literal ~, verbal or word-for-word translation; gloss, interlinear, interlinear translation; key, clavis, Bohn; pony [U.S.], horse [Eng.], trot [U.S.], cab [Eng.], crib [all school slang]; Targum, Chaldee paraphrase.

4. **explanation, explication, elucidation, clarification, illumination,** enlightenment, *éclaircissement* [F.], enucleation, simplification; **exposition,** expounding, exegesis; **illustration, demonstration,** exemplification; **reason,** rationale; **solution** 486; "explanations explanatory of things explained" [Lincoln].

5. **definition, description,** delineation, determination, formulation; **meaning** 543.

6. **explanatory remark) comment,** commentary, commentation, **word of explanation; annotation,** notation, **note,** note of explanation; gloss, exegesis, scholium.

7. **interpretability,** construability; **explicability,** explainableness, accountableness; **definability,** determinability, describability; translatability.

8. **interpreter,** interpretress [fem.], dragoman [Near East & Persia], exegete; **explainer,** definer, explicator, exponent,

expositor, expounder, demonstrator; linguist [obs. exc. local], linguister or lingster [dial., U.S.]; **interlocutor,** interlocutress or interlocutrice or interlocutrix [fem.]; go-between 779.4; **translator,** translatress or translatrix [fem.]; metaphrast, paraphrast; oneirocritic (interpreter of dreams).

9. (science of interpretation) **exegetics,** hermeneutics; **diagnostics, prognostics,** symptomatology, pathognomy, semeiology, semeiotics [all med.]; **physiognomics,** physiognomy; metoposcopy; **oneirology,** oneirocriticism; epigraphy; glossology; paleography.

VERBS 10. **interpret, diagnose; construe,** put a construction on; infer, deduce, draw an inference; understand, **understand by,** be given to understand, **gather from, take to mean;** read, **read into;** read between the lines.

11. **explain, explicate, expound,** exposit, enucleate, **spell out,** unfold; **account for,** give reason for; **clarify, elucidate,** clear up, **make clear,** make plain, **simplify,** popularize; **illuminate,** enlighten, **shed** or **throw light upon,** shed new or fresh light upon; tell or show how, show the way; **demonstrate, show, illustrate,** exemplify; solve 486.2; explain oneself; explain away.

12. **define, describe,** delineate, determine, formulate, **give the meaning,** tell the meaning of.

13. **comment upon,** remark upon; **annotate, gloss.**

14. **translate, render, transcribe,** put or turn into, transfuse the sense of, make a new version of.

15. **paraphrase, rephrase, reword,** restate, rehash; give a free translation.

ADJS. 16. **interpretative, interpretive,** interpretational, hermeneutic(al); **constructive,** constructional; **diagnostic,** prognostic; symptomatological, semeiological.

17. **explanatory,** explaining, exegetic(al); **explicative,** explicatory; **expository,** expositive; **clarifying, elucidative; illuminating,** illuminative, enlightening; **demonstrative, illustrative,** exemplificative; **annotative,** scholiastic.

18. **definitional, definitive, descriptive,** delineative.

19. **translational,** translative; paraphrastic, metaphrastic.

20. **interpretable, construable;** deducible, inferential; **explainable,** explicable, accountable; **definable,** describable, determinable; translatable, **renderable.**

ADVS. **21.** in explanation, to explain; that is, that is to say, *id est* [L.], i.e., to wit, namely; *videlicet* [L.], viz.; *scilicet* [L.], scil., sc.; in other words, *en otros términos* [Span.], in words to that effect, to that effect; strictly speaking.

551. MISINTERPRETATION

NOUNS **1.** misinterpretation, misunderstanding, misapprehension, misconception; misrendering, mistranslation, eisegesis; misexplanation, misexplication; misconstruction, misapplication; false coloring, gloss; perversion, distortion, garbling; abuse of terms, misuse of words, catachresis; misreading, misquotation, mis-citation; "blunders round about a meaning" [Pope]; misjudgment 495.

VERBS **2.** misinterpret, misunderstand, misapprehend, misconceive, misdeem, misapply; misrender, misexplain, mistranslate; misread, misquote, mis-cite; misconstrue, put a false construction on, give a false coloring, give a false impression *or* idea, gloss; garble, pervert, distort, twist the meaning, stretch *or* strain the sense *or* meaning; misjudge 495.2.

ADJS. **3.** misinterpreted, misunderstood, misapprehended, misconceived, misconstrued; garbled, perverted, distorted; eisegetical, catachrestic(al).

4. misinterpretable, misunderstandable, mistakable.

552. COMMUNICATION

NOUNS **1.** communication, communion; intercourse, congress, commerce, converse, conversation, association, mutual intercourse; intercommunication, intercommunion, exchange, interchange; dealings, dealing, traffic, truck [coll.]; information 555; message 556.4; oral communication 595; correspondence 602; social intercourse 920.4.

2. impartation, impartment, imparting, conveyance, transfer, transference, transmission, transmittal, sharing.

3. (state of being in communication) contact, touch, connection.

4. communicativeness, talkativeness, conversableness; affability, conviviality; gregariousness 920.1; unreserve, unreservedness, unreticence, unrestraint, unconstraint, unrestriction; unrepression, unsuppression; unsecretiveness, untaciturnity; frankness 972.4; openness, freeness, outspokenness; accessibility, approachability; extroversion, outgoingness.

5. communicability, impartibility, conveyability, transmittability, transmissability, transferability; contagiousness 684.3.

VERBS **6.** communicate, have intercourse, hold communication; intercommunicate, interchange; commune with; deal with, traffic with, commerce with, have dealings with, have truck with [coll.]; converse 595.8.

7. impart, bestow, render, confer, convey, transmit, transfer, pass, pass on *or* along, hand on; share, share with; give 816.12; tell 555.7.

8. communicate with, get in touch *or* contact with, contact [coll.], reach, get to, make *or* establish connection; make advances, make overtures, approach [U.S.], make up to [coll.]; keep in touch *or* contact with, maintain connection; correspond 602.11.

ADJS. **9.** communicative, talkative, conversational, demonstrative, expansive, effusive; affable, convivial; gregarious 920.17; unreserved, unreticent, unshrinking, unrestrained, unconstrained, unhampered, unrestricted; unrepressed, unsuppressed; unsecretive, unsilent, untaciturn; frank 972.17; open, free, out-spoken, free-speaking, free-spoken, free-tongued; accessible, approachable; conversable, easy to speak to; extroverted, outgoing.

10. communicable, impartible, bestowable, conveyable, transmittable, transmissable, transferable; contagious 684.47.

553. MANIFESTATION

NOUNS **1.** manifestation, appearance, expression, evincement, evidence, indication; revelation, disclosure 554.

2. display, demonstration, show, showing, presentation, presentment, exhibition, exhibit, exposition, production, performance, representation; opening, unfolding, unfoldment.

3. manifestness, apparentness, obviousness, plainness, clearness, crystal-clearness, perspicuity, distinctness, patentness, palpability; evidence, evidentness, self-evidence; openness, overtness; visibility 443; unmistakableness, unquestionability 512.

4. conspicuousness, prominence, salience *or* saliency, boldness, noticeability, notability, pronouncedness, strikingness, outstandingness; flagrance *or* flagrancy, arrantness.

VERBS **5.** manifest, show, shew [chiefly

Eng.], exhibit, demonstrate, display, unfold, develop, **present**, represent, **evince**, **evidence**, indicate, **express**, show forth, set forth; produce, bring out, trot out [coll.], bring forth, bring forward or to the front, bring to or into view; **reveal, disclose** 554.4; **make plain, make it clear**, bring out in bold ~, strong or high relief.

6. (manifest oneself) **come out into the open**, show one's colors or true colors, wear one's heart upon one's sleeve; **speak up, speak out**, let one's voice be heard, stand up and be counted.

7. **be manifest, be apparent, be obvious**, be evident, be self-evident, lie on the surface, be seen with half an eye, stand to reason, need no explanation, **speak for itself**, tell its own story or tale; **go without saying**, aller sans dire [F.]; **leap to the eye**, cela saute aux yeux [F.]; **stare one in the face**, hit one in the eye, glare, stand out, stick out, stick out a mile.

ADJS. 8. **manifest, apparent, evident**, self-evident, **obvious, plain, clear**, perspicuous, definite, distinct, palpable, patent, ostensible; **express, explicit; visible**, perceptible, perceivable, discernible, seeable, observable, **noticeable; to be seen**, easy to be seen, plain to be seen; plain as day, plain as the nose on one's face, plain as a pikestaff, plain as the way to parish church; **crystal-clear**, clear as crystal; **unmistakable**, not to be mistaken, open-and-shut [coll., U.S.]; self-explanatory, self-explaining; indubitable 512.15.

9. **open**, overt, open as day; **revealed, disclosed, exposed**; bare, bald, naked.

10. **unhidden, unconcealed, uncovered**, unscreened, uncurtained, unveiled, uncloaked, undraped, unshrouded, unshaded; **unobscure, unobscured, unclouded; undisguised**, unmasked, uncamouflaged; **unsecretive**, aboveboard.

11. **conspicuous, noticeable, notable, prominent, bold, pronounced, salient, striking, outstanding**, in the foreground; **flagrant**, arrant; **glaring**, staring, starkstaring.

12. manifested, demonstrated, exhibited, shown.

13. **revealable, disclosable**, discoverable, manifestable, producible, presentable; **unconcealable**, unhidable.

ADVS. 14. **manifestly, apparently, evidently**, obviously, plainly, clearly, definitely, distinctly, **unmistakably**, palpably, patently, ostensibly; **expressly, explicitly; visibly**, perceptibly, perceivably, discernibly, observably, **noticeably.**

15. **openly**, before, before one, **before one's eyes** or very eyes, under one's nose [coll.], to one's face, face to face; **publicly**, in public; **in the open**, in open court, **in plain sight**, in broad daylight, in the face of day or heaven; in market overt, in the market place, at the crossroads; aboveboard, on the table; cards on the table, cartes sur table [F.].

16. **conspicuously, prominently, noticeably, notably, pronouncedly, saliently, strikingly, boldly, outstandingly**; arrantly, glaringly.

554. DISCLOSURE

NOUNS 1. **disclosure**, disclosing; **revelation**, revealment, revealing; apocalypse; **discovery**, discovering; manifestation 553; unfolding, unfoldment; **uncovering**, unveiling, **unmasking; exposure**, exposition, exposé; showup, showdown.

2. **divulgence**, divulgement, divulgation, evulgation; **betrayal**, betrayment, unwitting disclosure; **giveaway**, dead giveaway [both coll.]; **blabbing**, blabbering [slang], babbling, **tattling.**

3. **confession**, shrift, acknowledgment, **admission**, concession, avowal, avowance, owning, owning up [coll.], unbosoming; confessional, confessionary.

VERBS 4. **disclose, reveal, show**, discover, develop; manifest 553.5; unfold, unroll; **open**, open up, lay open, bare, lay bare, bring into the open; **expose, show up, bring to light**, hold up to view, hold up the mirror to; **unmask**, dismask; **uncover, unconceal**, unhide, unveil, unscreen, uncloak, undrape, uncurtain, unshroud, unkennel; show one's hand, put one's cards on the table.

5. **divulge**, divulgate, evulgate; **reveal, make known, tell**, breathe, whisper, utter, vent, give vent to, **give out**, let out, out with [coll.], come out with, come out with it [coll.], come it [slang]; break it to, **break the news**; let in on or to, let into the secret; publish 557.10, 11.

6. **betray**, peach [slang], beef [slang], split [slang], leak [slang], spill, **spill the beans** [slang]; **let the cat out of the bag** [coll.], **give away** [coll.], give away the racket [slang], give the show away [slang], betray a confidence, tell secrets, reveal a secret; **blab**, blabber [slang], babble, tat-

tle; tell tales, **tell tales out of school,** talk out of turn [crim. slang, U.S.], blow the gaff [naut. slang]; let slip, let fall or drop, let on [coll.], **let out;** blurt, **blurt out,** blat [coll.], blunder; inform on 555.11.

7. **confess,** break down and confess [slang], 'fess up [slang], **admit, acknowledge,** acknowledge the corn [coll., U.S.; circa 1840 +], allow, avow, concede, grant, **own, own up** [coll.], cough up [slang], "own the soft impeachment" [Sheridan]; **talk** [coll.], **sing** [slang, U.S.], squeak [slang], squawk [slang, U.S.]; come across [slang], come clean [slang, U.S.], spill one's guts [crim. slang, U.S.], turn inside out; **tell the truth,** throw off all disguise; **plead guilty,** own oneself in the wrong, humble oneself.

8. **unbosom oneself, make a clean breast,** get it off one's chest [slang], **get it out of one's system** [coll.], unburden one's mind, ~ conscience or heart, **take the load off one's mind,** out with it [coll.], spit it out [coll.], **open up** [coll.], lay bare one's mind.

9. **be revealed, become known, come to light,** come to one's ears, transpire, **leak out, get out, come out,** out, break forth, show its face; show its colors, be seen in its true colors.

ADJS. 10. **revealed, disclosed** 553.9, 10.

11. **revealing,** revelational, apocalyptic(al); **disclosing,** showing, exposing, betraying; eye-opening.

12. confessional, admissive.

555. INFORMATION

NOUNS 1. **information,** info [slang]; **enlightenment,** light; **acquaintance,** familiarization; **instruction** 560; **intelligence, knowledge;** the know, the dope, the goods, the scoop [all slang]; **communication, report, word,** account, statement, mention; **notice, notification;** intimation, monition; **news** 556; side light (indirect information),

2. **inside information,** private or confidential information; the low-down, inside, **inside dope,** inside wire, real know, wise chatter, hot tip [all slang].

3. **tip,** tip-off, point, pointer [all coll.]; steer, office [both slang]; **advice,** aviso; **whisper,** passing word, **word to the wise,** word in the ear, flea in the ear [coll.].

4. **hint,** intimation, indication, suggestion, suspicion, inkling, glimmer, glim-

mering; **cue, clue,** scent, telltale; **implication, allusion, insinuation, innuendo;** gentle hint, broad hint.

5. **informant, informer,** teller, apprizer, enlightener; **adviser,** monitor; **reporter,** notifier, **announcer,** annunciator; spokesman, mouthpiece; communicator, communicant; authority, witness; information; **tipster,** tipper [both coll.]; **tout,** touter [both slang]; insider [coll., U.S.].

6. **informer, snitch** [slang], snitcher [chiefly slang], **tattler, tattletale** [coll.], **telltale, talebearer, blab,** blabber, blabberer [slang], blabbermouth [slang], **betrayer,** delator, **squealer** [coll.], squeaker [slang], peacher [slang]; **stool pigeon** [coll.], stoolie [slang]; **fink** [slang], **nark** [slang], mouchard [F.]; **spy, undercover man,** spotter [cant, U.S.].

VERBS 7. **inform, tell, impart, communicate, apprize,** or apprise, **advise, give word,** mention to, **acquaint, enlighten,** familiarize, wise up [slang, U.S.], give the facts, give an account of, **make known,** give by way of information; **instruct** 560.10; present, give, hand it to [slang], set ~, lay or put before, put one in possession of; **let know, have one to know, give one to understand,** tell once and for all; **notify,** give notice or notification, serve notice; **report** 556.11; bring ~, send or leave word.

8. **post,** post up, **keep one posted** [all coll.]; fill one in, bring up to date.

9. **hint, intimate, suggest, insinuate, imply, indicate, signify;** give ~, drop or throw out a hint, give an inkling of; **hint at,** glance at, allude to, make an allusion to; **prompt,** give the cue; put in or into one's head, put the words in one's mouth.

10. **tip,** tip off, **give one a tip** [all coll.]; tip the wink, give the office [both slang]; **give a pointer to** [coll., U.S.], give points to [coll.]; put hep, **let in on,** let in on the know, let or **put next to,** put on to, put on to something hot [all slang]; give confidential information, mention privately or confidentially; whisper, breathe, whisper in the ear, **put a flea in one's ear** [coll.], earwig.

11. **inform on** or **against, tell on** [coll.], **blow upon** [coll.], **betray, tattle, blab; snitch, squeal, peach,** split, blow, blow the gaff [naut.], sell out, rat, stool, fink, nark, put the finger on, snitch on, squeal on, etc. [all slang]; turn informer; testify against, **bear witness against;** turn

state's evidence [U.S.], turn king's or queer's evidence [Eng.].

12. be informed 474.12, 13.

13. (become informed) get wise to [coll.], get hep to [slang, U.S.], get next to [slang, U.S.], get on to [slang]; become conscious or aware of, become alive or awake to, awaken to, open one's eyes to.

14. learn, come to one's knowledge, come to or reach one's ears, be told; hear, overhear; hear tell of, hear say [both coll.]; get scent of.

15. keep informed, keep posted, keep up on, keep up to date, keep abreast of the times; keep track of, keep count or account of, keep tab or tabs on [coll.], keep a check on, keep an eye on.

ADJS. 16. informed 474.18-20; informed of, in the know 474.16.

17. informative, informing, informational, instructive, enlightening; educational 560.18; advisory, monitory.

18. telltale, tattletale [coll.].

ADVS. 19. from information received, according to reports or rumor, from notice given, as a matter of general information, by common report, from what one can gather.

556. NEWS

NOUNS 1. news, tidings, intelligence, information, word; advice, aviso; newsiness [coll.]; newsworthiness; a nose for news.

2. good news, good world, glad tidings; gospel, evangel.

3. news item, piece or budget of news; article, story, copy [cant]; scoop, beat [both slang]; spot news [slang].

4. message, dispatch, word, communication, communiqué; intermessage; embassy, embassage; letter 602.2; express, special delivery; telegram 558.16; pneumatogram.

5. bulletin, newsletter, newsbill [Eng.]; news report, flash [U.S.].

6. report, rumor, flying rumor, hearsay, on-dit; talk, whisper, buzz, rumble [slang, U.S.], cry; idea afloat, news stirring; common talk, town talk, talk of the town, topic of the day; grapevine; scuttlebutt, latrine rumor [both sea slang]; canard, hoax, roorback [U.S. polit.].

7. gossip, gossiping, gossipry, newsmongery; talebearing, taletelling; tattle, tittle-tattle, babble, chat, chitchat, gup [Anglo-India], comment, talk, idle talk, "putting two and two together, and making it five" [Pascal]; piece of gossip, groundless rumor, tale, story.

8. scandal, dirt [slang], malicious gossip, "gossip made tedious by morality" [Oscar Wilde]; juicy morsel, choice bit of dirt [slang]; scandalmongery, scandalmongering, scandalmonging; slander 969.3; whispering campaign.

9. newsmonger, rumormonger, scandalmonger, gossip, gossiper, quidnunc, busybody, busy [slang], tabby [coll.], granny [derog.], talebearer, taleteller, telltale, tattletale [coll.], tattler, tittle-tattler, babbler, blab, blabber, blabberer [slang], chatterer, "a tale-bearing animal" [J. Harrington].

10. (secret news channel) grapevine, grapevine telegraph, bush telegraph [Africa], pipe line [U.S.], underground, underground route.

VERBS 11. report, give a report, give an account of, tell, relate; write up, make out or write up a report; bring word, tell the news, break the news, give tidings of; bring glad tidings, give the good word; announce 557.12; rumor 557.10.

12. gossip, tattle, tittle [chiefly dial.], tittle-tattle, prate, prattle, babble, chat, chatter, clatter, talk, retail gossip, dish the dirt [slang], tell idle tales.

ADJS. 13. newsy [coll.], newsful; newsworthy, with news value.

14. gossipy, gossiping; talebearing, taletelling.

15. reported, rumored, whispered; rumored about, whispered about, bruited about, bandied about; in circulation, in the air, going around, going about, current, rife, afloat, floating, in every one's mouth, all over the town.

ADVS. 16. as they say, as it is said, as the story goes or runs, as the fellow says [coll., U.S.], it is said.

557. PUBLICATION

NOUNS 1. publication, publishing, promulgation, evulgation, propagation, dissemination, diffusion, broadcast, broadcasting, spread, spreading, circulation, ventilation, airing, noising, bandying, bruiting about; issue, issuance; printing 601; book, periodical 603.

2. announcement, annunciation, enunciation; proclamation, pronouncement, pronunciamento, pronunciamiento [Sp.];

report, declaration, statement, mention, intimation; **notice, notification,** public notice; manifesto; edict 750.4.

3. **press release,** press, release, handout.

4. **publicity,** publicness, **notoriety, limelight** [coll.], **spotlight** [coll.], daylight, openness, **currency,** *réclame* [F.]; **ballyhoo,** hoopla [both slang]; report, public report; cry, hue and cry; **publicity story,** press notice; **write-up** [slang], **puff** [chiefly coll.], **plug** [slang, U.S.]; **blurb** [coll.], "a noise like a publisher" [Burgess].

5. **promotion** [U.S.], **build-up** [coll.], publicizing; **advertising,** "the mouthpiece of business" [J. R. Adams]; adcraft [coll.]; advertising campaign; skywriting.

6. **advertisement,** ad [coll.], **notice;** commercial [radio]; reader, reading notice; want ad [coll.], for-want advertisement, classified ad [U.S.]; teaser [slang, U.S.]; spread, double-page spread; agony column [coll.].

7. **poster, bill, placard, sign,** banner [cant], *affiché* [F.]; sheet, six sheet, twenty-four sheet, etc.; **signboard, billboard** [U.S.], bulletin board, hoarding [Eng.].

8. **advertising matter, literature** [coll.]; **leaflet,** leaf, **folder; handbill, bill, dodger** [U.S.], **flier, throwaway, handout; circular,** circular letter; encyclical, encyclical letter; broadside, broadsheet; program, programma.

9. **publicist,** publicizer; **publicity man** *or* **agent, press agent; advertiser, adman;** ad writer [coll.], adsmith [joc.], copy writer; **promoter, booster** [slang, U.S.], plugger [slang, U.S.]; blurbist [coll.]; **huckster,** hucksterer [both coll., U.S.]; **ballyhooer, ballyhoo man,** ballyhoo [all slang]; **barker,** spieler [slang]; skywriter; billposter, bannerman [cant]; sandwich boy *or* man.

VERBS 10. **publish, promulgate, propagate, circulate, diffuse, disseminate, broadcast, spread, spread word,** spread around *or* about, spread far and wide, publish abroad, **pass the word around,** hawk, hawk about, bruit, **bruit about, advertise,** put about, **bandy about, noise about,** cry about *or* abroad, noise *or* sound abroad, speak *or* talk of, voice, give tongue, set news afloat, **spread a report; rumor,** whisper, buzz, **rumor about,** whisper *or* buzz about.

11. **make public,** bring ∼, lay or drag before the public, **give out,** show forth, give to the world, **make known; divulge**

554.5; **ventilate, air,** give air to, bring into the open.

12. **announce,** annunciate, enunciate; **declare, state,** declare roundly; **notify,** intimate, give notice; **report,** make an announcement *or* report.

13. **proclaim,** cry, cry out, **promulgate,** celebrate, **herald,** herald abroad; **blazon,** blaze, blaze *or* blazon about *or* abroad; trumpet, trumpet *or* thunder forth, sound a trumpet, announce with flourish of trumpets *or* beat of drum; shout from the housetops, proclaim at the crossroads *or* market cross, proclaim at Charing Cross.

14. **issue, print, bring out, put out, get out,** get off [U.S.], **utter,** emit, vent, broach, put ∼, give *or* send forth, offer to the public.

15. **publicize,** give publicity; bring *or* drag into the limelight, throw the spotlight on [both coll.]; **advertise, promote** [U.S.], **boost** [slang], **plug** [slang, U.S.], **ballyhoo** [slang]; bark, spiel [both slang, U.S.]; **write up,** give a write-up [both coll.]; blurb [coll.]; press-agent [coll.]; **circularize;** bulletin; bill; **post bills,** post, post up, poster, placard; skywrite.

16. (be published) **come out,** break [newspaper], **issue,** go *or* come forth, find vent, take air, see the light, become public; **circulate, spread,** pass current, **get around** *or* **about,** get abroad, get afloat, go ∼, fly ∼, buzz *or* blow about, **go the rounds,** pass from mouth to mouth, go through the length and breadth of the land; spread like wildfire.

ADJS. 17. **public,** made public; **general, common,** common knowledge, common property; **open,** accessible, open to the public.

18. **promulgatory,** propagatory; proclamatory, annunciatory, enunciative; **declarative,** declaratory; heraldic.

ADVS. 19. **publicly, in public; openly** 553.15; in the limelight *or* spotlight [coll.].

558. COMMUNICATIONS

Telephone and Wireless.—NOUNS 1. **communications,** telecommunication; communication engineering, communications engineer.

2. **telephony,** telephonics, telephone mechanics, telephone engineering; high-frequency telephony.

3. **telegraphy,** telegraphics; railroad telegraphy, submarine telegraphy; simplex

telegraphy, multiplex telegraphy, duplex telegraphy, quadruplex telegraphy; single-current telegraphy, closed-circuit telegraphy; **teletype,** teletyping, teletypewriting, typotelegraphy; autotelegraphy, telautography; marconigraphy, Marconi wireless telegraphy; pantelegraphy; telepost; television; code 612.7.

4. wireless, wireless telephony, wireless telegraphy; radio; radiophony, **radiotelephony, radiotelegraphy,** hertzian telegraphy **telephotography,** telephoto, radiophotography, photoradio; line radio, wire or wired radio, wired wireless, wire wave communication, Squier system; SELCAL [Aircraft Selective Calling].

5. telephone, phone, set; subset, subscriber's subset; receiver, telephone receiver; mouthpiece, transmitter; telephone booth, call box; telemobile.

6. radiophone, radiotelephone, photophone, wireless telephone, **wireless.**

7. headphone, headset, earphones [coll.].

8. intercom [coll.], interphones, intercommunication system.

9. telephone exchange, telephone office, central office, **central;** automatic exchange, machine-switching office; automatic digit recognizer, Audrey [slang]; COZI [Communication Zone Indicator].

10. switchboard, call panel; **PBX,** private branch or business exchange; in or A board, out or B board.

11. telephone operator, telephone girl, **phone girl** [coll.], hello girl [slang], connection girl, **operator,** switchboard operator, exchange clerk, telephonist, **central;** long-distance; PBX operator.

12. telephone man, telephone mechanic, telephonic engineer; lineman 341.19.

13. telephoner, phoner, caller, **party,** calling party.

14. telephone number, phone number; telephone directory, phone book.

15. telephone call, phone call, call, ring [coll.], buzz [slang]; toll call, long-distance call, long distance, intercity service; dial tone, busy signal.

16. telegram, telegraph; wireless, wire [coll.], wireless telegram; **cablegram, cable; radiogram,** radiotelegram, radio [coll.], marconigram; **lettergram,** letter telegram, **day letter, night letter;** autotelegram, telautogram; heliogram; **flash,** news flash.

17. telephoto, wirephoto [coll.], telephotograph, radiophotograph, photoradiogram.

18. telegrapher, telegraphist, telegraph operator, telegraph clerk; **sparks,** brass pounder, dit-da artist [all slang]; amateur telegrapher, **ham** [slang]; radiotelegrapher; wireman, wire chief; telautographist.

19. interrupter, transmitter, sender, key, brass [slang], chopper [slang]; **receiver,** sounder, buzzer [slang].

20. line, wire line, telegraph line, telephone line; private line, party line [U.S.]; trunk, trunk line; cable, telegraph cable; coaxial cable, co-ax [coll.]; telephone network, balance network.

VERBS **21. telephone, phone, call,** call on the phone, put in or make a call, **call up, ring, ring up,** give a ring [coll.], give a buzz [slang], buzz [slang]; radiotelephone; dial; listen in; hold the phone or wire; hang up, ring off [coll.], buzz off [slang].

22. telegraph, telegram, flash; **wire,** wireless, send a wire [all coll.]; **cable; radio,** radiogram, radiograph, radiotelegraph, marconigraph; telephotograph, telephoto [coll.]; teletype; sign on, sign off.

ADJS. **23. telephonic,** magnetotelephonic, microtelephonic, monotelephonic, thermotelephonic, electrophonic; long-distance.

24. telegraphic, wireless; radiotelegraphic; autotelegraphic; phototelegraphic, telephotographic.

25. telephones

electrophone	mechanical or
extension phone	string telephone
French telephone	microtelephone
hand set	monotelephone
light-beam	pantelephone
telephone	thermophone,
magnetotelephone	thermotelephone
	wireless telephone

26. telegraphs

autotelegraph	multiplex
dial telegraph	needle telegraph
disk telegraph	pantelegraph
electric telegraph	phototelegraph
facsimile telegraph	quadruplex
field telegraph	radiotelegraph
heliograph	semaphore tele-
indicator telegraph	graph
inductophone	solar telegraph
magnetotelegraph	telautograph
marconigraph	telectrograph
Morse telegraph	telegraphoscope
multiple telegraph	writing telegraph

27. teletypes

printer	stock ticker
printing telegraph	telecon

teleprinter   typewriting tele-
teletypesetter   graph
teletypewriter   typotelegraph
ticker

28. telegraph recorders

photo transceiver   telegraphonograph
siphon recorder   telegraphophone
telegraphone   ticker tape

559. MESSENGER

NOUNS 1. **messenger, dispatch bearer,** commissionaire, **courier,** carrier, **runner,** express, post [chiefly hist.], poster, postboy, **postrider,** estafette, chiaus [Turkey]; dak, hircarra, peon, chuprassy [all India]; Mercury, Ariel, Hermes, Iris, Paul Revere.

2. **herald, harbinger;** evangel, bearer of glad tidings; herald angel, Gabriel.

3. **announcer,** annunciator, enunciator, nunciate; **proclaimer,** trumpeter; **crier, town crier,** bellman.

4. errand boy, chore boy; bellhop [slang, U.S.], bellboy.

5. **postman, mailman,** mail carrier [U.S.], letter carrier; postmaster, postmistress; postal clerk.

6. (mail carriers) carrier pigeon, carrier, homing pigeon; pigeon post, *Taubenpost* [G.]; post horse, poster; post coach, mail coach, postcart; post boat, packet boat, mail boat, mailer; mail train, mail car, post car, post-office car; mailplane.

560. TEACHING

NOUNS 1. **teaching, instruction, education, edification, enlightenment, schooling, tuition;** tutelage, tutorage, tutorship; tutoring, coaching; direction, guidance; **pedagogy,** pedagogics, didactics; catechization; information 555; re-education 145.3.

2. **inculcation, indocrination,** inoculation, **implantation,** infixion, **impression, instillment,** instillation, impregnation, **infusion,** imbuement; reindoctrination 145.3.

3. **training, preparation,** readying [coll.], **conditioning, grooming** [U.S.], qualification, cultivation, development, improvement; **discipline,** course of sprouts [coll., U.S.]; breaking, housebreaking; **upbringing, bringing-up,** fetching-up [dial.], **rearing, raising, breeding, nurture,** nurturing, fostering; **practice,** rehearsal; **exercise, drill,** drilling; apprenticeship, in-service training; military training, basic training; manual training, sloyd; vocational training.

4. **preinstruction,** pre-education; **initiation,** introduction; **priming,** cramming [coll.].

5. **instructions, directions, orders;** briefing, final instructions.

6. **lesson, teaching, instruction,** precept; **lecture,** harangue, **discourse,** disquisition, exposition, **talk,** prelection, homily; **sermon,** preachment; chalk talk [coll.]; **recitation,** recital; **assignment, exercise,** task, imposition; homework; **moral,** morality, moralization, moral lesson; object lesson.

7. **study,** branch of learning; **course,** course of study; **curriculum; subject;** major [U.S.], minor [U.S.], elective; refresher course; seminar; **three R's, A B C's;** reading, writing and arithmetic; liberal arts; humanities, humanism.

8. **physical education, physical culture,** gymnastics, calisthenics, eurythmics.

9. **primary education, secondary education, higher education; adult education;** liberal education; coeducation.

VERBS 10. **teach, instruct,** give instruction, give lessons in, **educate, school, edify, enlighten,** learn [illit.]; **direct, guide;** inform 555.7; **show,** show how; give an idea of, put up to [slang], put in the way of; put in the right, set right; improve one's mind, enlarge the mind; sharpen the wits, open the eyes; teach a lesson, give a lesson to; **ground,** teach the rudiments or elements; catechize; teach an old dog new tricks; reeducate 145.10.

11. **tutor, coach; prime, cram** [coll.], grind [coll.].

12. **inculcate, indoctrinate,** inoculate, **instill, infuse,** imbue, impregnate, **implant,** infix, impress; **impress upon the mind,** urge on the mind, beat into, beat or knock into one's head.

13. **train, drill, exercise; practice,** rehearse; **prepare, ready, condition,** qualify, **groom** [U.S.], fit, put in tune; form, lick into shape [coll.]; **rear, raise, bring up,** fetch up [dial.], upbring, bring up by hand; **breed, cultivate,** develop, improve; **nurture, foster,** dry-nurse [coll.]; **discipline,** take in hand; put through the mill [coll.], put through a course of sprouts [coll., U.S.]; **break,** bust [slang, U.S.], break in, housebreak.

14. **preinstruct, pre-educate; initiate,** introduce.

15. **give instructions,** give directions; **brief,** give a briefing.

16. **expound,** exposit; explain 550.11; set forth, state, present; **lecture, discourse,** harangue, hold forth, give or read a lesson; **preach,** sermonize; **moralize,** point a moral.

17. (teach the superfluous or impossible) teach a cock to crow, teach a dog to bark, teach a fish to bite, teach a hen to cluck, teach a serpent to hiss, teach iron to swim.

ADJS. **18. educational,** educative, **cultural,** educating, teaching; **instructive,** instructional; **tuitional,** tuitionary; **edifying, enlightening;** informative 555.17; didactic, preceptive; hortatory, homiletic(al); disciplinary; coeducational.

19. scholastic, academic, schoolish; scholarly 564.10; **pedagogical** 563.12; interscholastic, intercollegiate; intramural; nonscholastic, noncollegiate.

20. curricular, extracurricular.

561. MISTEACHING

NOUNS **1. misteaching,** misinstruction; misinformation, misknowledge, misintelligence; **misguidance,** misdirection, misleading; the blind leading the blind; college of Laputa.

2. propaganda, propagandism; **propagandist,** agitprop.

VERBS **3. misteach,** misinstruct, miseducate; **misinform,** misadvise; **misguide,** misdirect, **mislead.**

4. propagandize, propaganda, carry on a propaganda.

ADJS. **5. mistaught,** misinstructed; **misinformed,** misadvised; **misguided,** misdirected, **misled,** poor misguided.

6. misteaching, misinstructive, miseducative, unedifying; **misinforming, misleading,** misguiding, misdirecting.

562. LEARNING

Acquisition of Knowledge.—NOUNS **1. learning, edification,** mental cultivation, acquirement, attainment; **self-education;** self-instruction; **knowledge, erudition** 474; education 560; memorization 535.4.

2. absorption, ingestion, imbibing, assimilation.

3. study, studying, conning; **reading,** perusal; **contemplation** 477.2; **inspection** 484.4; **engrossment** 528.3; **brainwork, headwork, lucubration,** mental labor; grind [coll.], grinding [slang], boning [coll., U.S.]; **cramming,** cram [both coll.]; extensive study, wide reading; subject 560.7.

4. studiousness, scholarliness; bookishness 474.5, diligence 705.6.

5. teachability, educability, trainableness; **aptness,** quickness, readiness; **responsiveness, receptivity,** susceptibility; **willingness, docility; malleability,** moldability,

pliability, facility, plasticity, **impressionability,** formability.

VERBS **6. learn, get,** get off, get hold of [coll.], get into one's head; **gain knowledge,** pick up information, gather ~, collect or glean knowledge or learning; **find out,** discover, find, determine; **become informed,** gain knowledge or understanding of, acquire information or intelligence about, **learn about, find out about,** ascertain; acquaint oneself with, make oneself acquainted with, become acquainted with; come to one's knowledge 555.14.

7. absorb, get by osmosis; take in, ingest, imbibe, assimilate, **soak up,** drink in; soak in, seep in, percolate in.

8. memorize 535.17; fix in the mind 535.18.

9. master, make oneself master of, **gain command of, become adept in,** become familiar or conversant with, become versed or well-versed in, **get up in** or **on,** get up on one's stuff [slang, U.S.], get hep [slang, U.S.], gain a good or thorough knowledge of, **learn all about, get down pat** [coll.], get down cold [slang, U.S.]; **get the hang** or **knack of,** take to; **learn the ropes,** learn all the ins and outs; know well 474.13.

10. learn by experience, live and learn, go through the school of hard knocks; **learn a lesson,** be taught a lesson.

11. receive instruction, undergo schooling, go to or attend school, go into training; serve an apprenticeship, serve one's time.

12. study, regard studiously, con; **read,** peruse, go over; **contemplate** 477.11; **examine** 484.31; give the mind to 528.5; **pore over,** mouse over [U.S.]; bury oneself in, wade through, plunge into, mind one's book; dig [coll., U.S.], **grind** [slang], **bone** [coll., U.S.]; **lucubrate, burn the midnight oil,** burn the candle at both ends; make a study of.

13. browse, scan [coll.], **dip into,** thumb over, run over or through, glance or run the eye over or through, turn over the leaves.

14. study up, brush up, polish up [coll.], rub up; **study up on, read up on, get up on;** cram or cram up [coll.], **bone up** [slang, U.S.], coach up [coll.].

15. study to be, study for, read for, read law, etc.; **specialize in, go in for;** major in, minor in.

ADJS. **16. educated, learned** 474.18–24.

17. studious, scholarly, scholastic; bookish 474.22; diligent 705.21.

18. **teachable, instructable, educable,** educatable, schoolable, trainable; **apt,** quick, ready; **responsive, receptive,** susceptible; **willing, docile; malleable, moldable,** pliable, facile, plastic, **impressionable,** formable.

563. TEACHER

NOUNS 1. **teacher, instructor, educator,** preceptor, **mentor,** guide, docent, don [coll., Eng.], dominie [chiefly Scot.], pundit [India], guru [India], munshi [Anglo-India], mullah [Moham.], khoja [Moham.]; **master,** maestro; **pedagogue,** pedagogist; pedant, 475.6; **schoolteacher, schoolmaster,** schoolkeeper; guide 746.6; abecedarian; kindergartner or kindergartener; disciplinarian.

2. **instructress,** educatress, preceptress, **mistress,** pundity [India]; **schoolmistress, schoolma'am** or **schoolmarm** [U.S.], schooldame; tutoress; **governess,** duenna.

3. **schoolman, academician;** doctor; fellow.

4. (academic ranks from the highest down, chiefly U.S.) professor, prof [coll., U.S.]; associate professor, assistant professor, instructor, tutor, associate; assistant, adjunct.

5. **underteacher,** usher [Eng.]; precentor, coryphaeus [Oxford Univ.]; student or pupil teacher, monitor.

6. **tutor,** tutorer; **coach,** coacher; **private instructor,** *Privatdocent* or *Privatdozent* [G.], dry nurse [slang], bear leader [joc.]; crammer [coll.], grinder [college slang, Eng.].

7. **trainer, handler, groomer** [U.S.]; driller, drillmaster; **coach,** athletic coach, paedotribe [Gr. antiq.].

8. **lecturer,** lector [hist. & eccl.], **reader,** prelector, prolocutor, **preacher;** chalk talker [coll.].

9. **principal, headmaster,** headmistress; **dean,** dean of women, dean of men.

10. **faculty,** faculty members, **professorate,** teaching staff.

11. **instructorship, teachership,** preceptorship, schoolmastery; **tutorship,** tutorhood, tutorage, tutelage; **professorship,** professorhood, professorate; **chair,** chair of English, etc.; lectureship, readership; fellowship.

ADJS. 12. **pedagogic(al),** preceptoral, tutorial; tuitional, tuitionary; **teacherish,** teachery, teacherly, teacherlike; **schoolteacherish,** schoolteachery; **schoolmasterish,** schoolmastery, schoolmasterly, school-

mastering, schoolmasterlike; schoolmistressy, schoolma'amish; **professorial,** professorlike; pedantic 474.22.

564. STUDENT

NOUNS 1. **student, pupil, scholar,** scholastic, learner, studier, educatee, trainee, *élève* [F.], inquirer; schoolman, classman; auditor [U.S.]; monitor, prefect.

2. **discipline, follower, apostle,** chela [India]; proselyte 145.5.

3. **school child,** school kid [coll.]; **schoolboy,** school lad; **schoolgirl,** schoolmaid, schoolmiss, school lass; coed or co-ed [coll., U.S.]; kindergartner or kindergartener, grade schooler, high schooler.

4. **college student,** colleger, **collegian,** collegianer [Scot.], collegiate, **varsity student** [coll.], college boy or girl.

5. **undergraduate,** undergrad [coll.]; grader [U.S.]; underclassman [U.S.]; **freshman,** fresh [slang], freshie [slang], plebe or pleb [West Point & Annapolis]; **sophomore,** soph [coll.]; **upperclassman** [U.S.], **junior, senior;** sophister, junior or senior sophister [all Eng.]; commoner [Oxford Univ.], pensioner [Cambridge Univ.], sizar [Cambridge & Dublin], servitor [Oxford Univ.], exhibitioner, scholar, fellow commoner [Eng. Univ.]; demy [Magdalen Coll., Oxford]; questionist [Cambridge]; honor man, class man [Oxford Univ.]; wrangler, optime [both Cambridge Univ.]; passman.

6. **graduate,** grad [coll.]; **alumnus** [masc.], alumna [fem.], alumni; **postgraduate,** postgrad [coll.]; inceptor [Cambridge Univ.]; degrees 915.6.

7. **novice,** novitiate, **tyro, beginner,** entrant, **neophyte, tenderfoot,** freshman, **fledgling,** gosling [coll.], infant, catechumen, chela [India]; newcomer 78.4; ignoramus 476.9; **greenhorn,** greeny [coll.], greener [slang], *blancbec* [F., white-beak]; abecedarian, alphabetarian; **recruit, raw recruit, rooky** [slang]; initiate; debutant, debutante [fem.], deb [slang].

8. **probationer,** probationist, probe [slang]; **apprentice,** articled clerk.

9. **class, form,** school [Eng.], **grade,** room, division, remove [Eng.]; seminar, seminary.

ADJS. 10. **scholarly,** scholarlike, **scholastic;** studentlike, pupillike; schoolboyish, schoolgirlish; **collegiate,** college-bred; sophomoric(al); **studious** 562.17; **learned, bookish** 474.21, 22.

11. **probationary,** probational, on probation

565. SCHOOL

Institution of Learning.—NOUNS **1. school,** educational institution, school of education, **institute, academy,** seminary, *Schule* [Ger.], *école* [F.], *escuela* [Span.], phrontistery [rare or jocose].

2. (general) public school [U.S., Scot. & Brit. colonies], free school; private school; boarding school, *pensionnat* [F.]; night school, evening school; day school; summer school, vacation school; correspondence school, extension course, university extension; continuation school; finishing school; dame *cr* dame's school [chiefly Hist.]; platoon school, Gary school [both U.S.].

3. (endowed) provided school, council school [both Eng.]; board school [Brit. colonies]; voluntary school, nonprovided school both Eng.]; national school [Eng.]; charity school.

4. preschool, pre-elementary school; **infant school,** *salle d'asile* [F.]; **nursery,** nursery school; day nursery [U.S.], crèche; **kindergarten.**

5. elementary school, grammar school [U.S.], **grade school** [U.S.], the grades [U.S.]; **primary school,** primary; common school U.S.]; district school [U.S.].

6. secondary school, middle school [Eng.], Gymnasium [Europe, esp. Ger.]; *lycée* [F.], lyceum; **high school** [U.S.], high [coll.]; **junior high school** [U.S.], junior high [coll.], intermediate school [U.S.]; **senior high school** [U.S.], senior high [coll.]; **preparatory school,** prep school [coll., U.S.]; public school (in England, an exclusive endowed preparatory school, such as Eton and Harrow); seminary (a private secondary school); **grammar school** [Eng.], Latin school [U.S.], *Progymnasium* [Ger.]; *Realschule* [Ger.], real school; *Realgymnasium* [Ger.].

7. college, academy, Alma Mater; **university, varsity** [coll.], *université* [F.]; junior college; fresh-water college [coll., U.S.]; graduate school, post-graduate school; normal school, normal, teachers' training college; teachers' institute; law school, medical school, library school; coeducational school, dual school [chiefly Eng.].

8. vocational school, trade school, occupational school; business college *or* school, commercial school, secretarial school; industrial school; technical school, technological school *or* institute; polytechnic school, polytechnic; manual arts school, school of arts and crafts.

9. conservatory, conservatoire, *conservatorio* [It.]; **art school,** school of art; arts college; **music school,** college *or* academy of music; **dancing school,** *salle de danse* [F.].

10. religious school, denominational school, church school; **parochial school,** parish school; convent school; **seminary, divinity school, theological seminary; Bible school,** Bible institute; **Sunday school,** Sabbath school.

11. gymnasium, palaestra [antiq.]; wrestling school; fencing school, *salle d'armes* [F.].

12. riding school *or* academy, manage, manège *or* manege.

13. military school *or* academy; United States Military Academy, West Point; Royal Military Academy, Woolwich; Royal Military College, Sandhurst; naval school *or* academy; United States Naval Academy, Annapolis; Royal Naval College; ground school [aero.]; training ship, training plane, trainer.

14. chautauqua, lyceum [U.S.].

15. schoolhouse, school building; little red schoolhouse, "the schoolhouse by the road" [Whittier].

16. schoolroom, classroom; recitation room; lecture room *or* hall; theater, amphitheater.

17. directorate, board, syndicate; School Board, College Board, Board of Regents, Board of Education, Board *or* Prefect of Studies, Council of Education, Textbook Committee.

ADJS. **18. schoolish, scholastic, academic,** institutional, school; **collegiate;** preschool, pre-elementary.

566. INDICATION

NOUNS **1. indication,** signification, denotation, **designation,** denomination, specification, stipulation; **expression,** suggestion, **manifestation,** demonstration; show, showing.

2. sign, index, indicant, indicator; **symbol, emblem, token, symptom,** signal, **mark, earmark, badge,** stamp, signature, note, figure, cipher, type; image, picture, allegory; **representation,** representative; totem, totem pole *or* post; poster, signboard **557.7.**

3. pointer, index, lead; **direction, guide;** finger, hand, arrow; **signpost,** guidepost; finger post, handpost; signboard, guideboard; blaze.

4. mark, marking; scratch, scratching; **score,** scotch, cut, hack, gash, blaze; notch 261; **scar,** cicatrix; **brand, earmark; stigma,** stigmatism; **stain, discoloration** 677; **spot,** blotch, patch, splash; mottle, dapple; **dot,** point, tittle; polka dot; **jot,** jotting; **speck, speckle,** fleck, flick; tick; freckle, lentigo, mole; birthmark, nevus; caste mark, tilaka [Hindu].

5. line, stroke, dash, stripe, strip, streak, striation, striping, streaking, bar, band; hairline; lineation, delineation; sublineation, **underline,** underlining, **underscore,** underscoring; hatching; hachure.

6. print, imprint, impress, impression; dint, dent, indent, indentation, indention; **stamp,** seal; **fingerprint,** thumbprint, thumbmark; dactylogram, dactylograph; **footprint,** footmark, footstep, step, pad, pug [India], *piste* [F.]; ichnite, ichnolite.

7. track, trail, path, mark, line, wake; spoor, sign [U.S.], scent; **trace, vestige.**

8. clue, clew, **cue, key,** secret, scent, telltale; **evidence** 504.1; **hint, intimation, suggestion; lead** [coll.], hot lead [slang]; catchword, cue word.

9. marker, mark; bookmark; **landmark,** seamark; **milestone,** milepost; **cairn** or carn, menhir, catstone; Pillars of Hercules; lighthouse, watchtower, pharos.

10. identification, identification mark; **badge,** identification badge; identification tag [mil.], I.D. tag; **card,** calling card [U.S.], visiting card, *carte de visite* [F.]; press card; letter of introduction.

11. password, *mot de passe* [F.], pass, **watchword, countersign,** *mot d'ordre* [F.], **open-sesame,** tessera; grip [secret societies].

12. label, tag; stamp, sticker; **seal,** sigil, signet, cachet; **ticket,** docket, billet; stub, counterfoil; **token,** check, chop [Orient], tally; **brand, trade name,** trademark name; **trademark,** government mark; **hallmark,** countermark; price tag; plate; bookplate, book stamp, colophon, *ex libris* [L.].

13. gesture, gesticulation; motion, movement; beck, beckon; shrug; byplay, dumb show, **pantomime,** chironomy; sign language, dactylology, dactylography; deaf-and-dumb alphabet.

14. signal, sign; high sign, office, the wink, the nod [all slang]; wink, glance, leer; nod; nudge, touch; **alarm** 702; **beacon,** signal beacon; signal light, signal lamp or lantern; blinker; signal fire, beacon fire, watch fire, balefire; **flare,** flare-up; rocket, signal rocket, Roman candle; signal gun, signal shot; signal siren or whistle, signal bell or gong; police whistle, watchman's rattle; fog signal or alarm, fog bell, foghorn, fog whistle; bell signal, bell [naut.]; **traffic signal,** traffic lights, stop-and-go lights, red or stop light, green or go light; **semaphore,** semaphore signal; **wigwag;** heliograph, heliogram; signal post, signal mast; signal flag.

15. call, summons; moose call; **birdcall,** duck call, goose call, crow call, hawk call; **bugle call,** trumpet call; **reveille, taps,** last post [Eng.]; alarm, alarum; **battle cry,** rallying cry; Angelus, Angelus bell.

VERBS **16. indicate,** be indicative, be an indication of, be the sign of, give token, **betoken, signify,** note, **denote, denominate, mark;** evince, argue, bespeak, testify, attest; **show,** go to show; **manifest, express,** suggest, declare, reveal, disclose, display, set forth.

17. designate, signify, specify, stipulate, denominate, denote, mark; point at; **point to,** refer to, advert to, allude to, make an allusion to; **point out,** tick off [slang]; put or lay one's finger on.

18. mark, make a mark, put a mark on; pencil, chalk; **mark off, check off,** point off, tick off; **dot, spot, tick; speck, speckle,** fleck, freckle; mottle, dapple; **brand,** stigmatize; **stain, discolor** 677.6; **print, engrave** 576.12, 13; **score, scratch,** gash, scotch, scar; notch 261.4; **blaze,** blaze a trail; **line, seam,** trace, **stripe, streak, striate;** dash; hatch; **underline, underscore.**

19. label, tag; ticket, docket; **stamp,** seal; **brand, earmark;** hallmark.

20. gesture, gesticulate; motion, motion to; beckon, wiggle the finger at; wave the arms, saw the air; shrug, shrug the shoulders.

21. signal, signalize, **sign,** give a signal, make a sign; **give the high sign, tip the wink,** give the nod, give the office [all slang]; nod; nudge, touch; wink, glance, leer; hold up the hand; **wave,** wave the hand, wave a flag; **flag,** flag down; **unfurl a flag,** hoist a banner, break out a flag; **show one's colors,** exchange colors; speak, hail and speak [naut.]; **salute,** dip; jibber the kibber [naut. cant]; half-mast; flash; give or sound an alarm, raise a cry; beat the drum, sound the trumpet.

ADJS **22. indicative,** indicatory, indicant; indicating, signifying; **significant,** significative; **designative,** denotative, denominative, stipulatory, pointing out; **expressive, suggestive,** demonstrative, exhibitive; symptomatic, semeiotic, sematic, pathognomonic(al).

23. gestural, gesticulative, gesticulatory; pantomimic, **in pantomime,** in dumb show.

567. INSIGNIA

NOUNS **1. insignia, regalia, ensigns, emblems, badges, symbols;** badge, badge of office; livery, uniform, toga, mantle; cap and gown, mortarboard [coll.]; cockade; brassard; figurehead, eagle; cross, ankh, tau cross; swastika; hammer and sickle.

2. (heraldic insignia) heraldry, heraldic device or achievement; bearing, bearings; coat of arms, arms, armorial bearings, blazon; hatchment, achievement; escutcheon, scutcheon; crest, charge, field, shield; device, motto; pheon, broad arrow; cross; spread eagle; fleur-de-lis; garland, chaplet; ordinary, bar, bend, bend sinister, chevron, chief, cross, fesse, pale, pile, saltier; subordinary, billet, bordure, canton, flanche, fret, fusil, gyron, inescutcheon, label, lozenge, mascle, orle, quarter, rustre, tressure; supporters.

3. (royal insignia) regalia; scepter, rod, rod of empire; orb [Eng.]; purple, ermine, robe of state or royalty; purple pall; crown, royal crown, coronet, tiara, diadem; cap of maintenance, ~ dignity or estate, triple plume, Prince of Wales's feathers, uraeus [Egyptian]; seal, signet, privy seal or signet [Eng.].

4. (ecclesiastical insignia) tiara, triple crown; ring, keys; miter, crosier, crook, staff; cardinal's hat, bishop's lawn, ~ apron, ~ sleeves or gaiters; fillet.

5. (military insignia) chevron, stripe [slang]; star, bar, eagle [U.S.], spread eagle, crown [Eng.], oak leaf [U.S.], caduceus [U.S.]; aviation badge, wings [U.S.]; stripe, service stripe; epaulet or epaulette; Sam Browne belt [U.S.].

6. flag, pennant, pennon, **banner, streamer, bunting; ensign, standard, colors;** banneret, banderole, banderol; Old Glory [coll.], Stars and Stripes, Star-Spangled Banner; red, white and blue; tricolor, *drapeau tricolor* [F.]; white ~, blue or red ensign [Eng.]; whip, coachwhip; vexillum, labarum [both Rom. antiq.]; Jolly Roger,

blackjack; burgee, blue peter, gonfalon, guidon, jack, union jack, oriflamme, signal flag; flag at half mast, union down.

568. RECORD

NOUNS **1. record, recording; register, registry; chronicle, annals, account,** roll; list 88; **vestige, trace,** relic.

2. archives, public records, historical documents; chartulary, cartulary; **registry,** register office; chancery.

3. memorandum, memo [coll.], memoir, memorial [law], commonplace; reminder 535.6; **note, notation,** annotation, jotting; footnote; **entry,** register, **registry,** item; minute, **minutes.**

4. document, instrument, paper, parchment, scroll, roll, **writing;** scrip, script; holograph, chirograph; legal document, legal instrument; **papers,** ship's papers; dossier; **blank, form.**

5. certificate, certification; ticket, docket, token; **authority,** authorization; **credential, voucher, warrant,** note, diploma, testimonial; **affidavit,** affidavy [dial.]; deposition, witness, attestation, *procès-verbal* [F.]; visa, visé; **bill of health,** clean bill of health; navicert; **diploma** [educ.], sheepskin [coll., U.S.]; certificate of proficiency, testamur [Eng. univ.].

6. report, bulletin, brief, statement, account, accounting; account rendered, *compte rendu* [F.]; **minutes,** proceedings; **returns,** census report or returns, election returns.

7. (official documents) state paper, white paper; blue book [esp. Eng.], green book [esp. It.], red book [Austria], white book [esp. Ger., Pg. & Jap.]; yellow book [esp. F.], *livre jaune* [F.]; Statesman's Yearbook; Congressional Record [U.S.], Hansard [Eng.].

8. (registers) Lloyd's Register [Eng.]; genealogy, pedigree, studbook; social register, bluebook [coll., U.S.], studbook [joc.]; Who's Who; Almanach de Gotha [Ger. & F.]; Red Book, Royal Kalendar [both Eng. 1767–1893].

9. (recording media) bulletin board, scoreboard; tape, ticker tape; card, index card, filing card; microcard, microfilm; file 88.3.

10. (record books) **notebook, pocketbook,** blankbook; loose-leaf notebook; **memorandum book,** memo book [coll.], promptbook, engagement book, commonplace book, adversaria; address book; birthday book; workbook; blotter [U.S.]; **tablet,** table, writing tablet; diptych, triptych; pad, **scratch pad; scrapbook,** memory book [U.S.], **album; diary, journal; catalogue,** calendar; classified catalogue, *catalogue raisonné* [F.]; **yearbook,** annual; **log,** log book; **account book, ledger,** daybook; **cashbook,** petty cashbook; Domesday book.

11. monument, monumental *or* memorial record, **memorial,** memento, remembrance, testimonial; **marker; tablet,** stone, slab, hoarstone [Eng.]; **pillar,** shaft, column, memorial column; monolith, obelisk, **pyramid,** rostral column; **gravestone, tombstone;** headstone, footstone; cairn *or* carn; cenotaph; cromlech, dolmen, megalith, cyclolith [all archaeol.]; cross; arch; **shrine,** reliquary, memoria; tope, stupa [both Buddhist.].

12. recorder, registrar 569.1.

13. register, dictaphone 569.3.

14. registration, register, registry; recording, recordation; **enrollment,** matriculation; impanelment *or* empanelment; **listing, tabulation, cataloguing,** chronicling; **entry,** insertion; **booking, logging.**

VERBS **15. record,** put *or* place upon record; **inscribe,** inscroll; **register, enroll,** poll, matriculate, check in; impanel *or* empanel; **catalogue, chronicle,** calendar, **tabulate, list,** docket; **write,** commit *or* reduce to writing, put in writing, put in black and white, put on paper; **write out, make out,** fill out; **write up,** chalk, chalk up; **write down, mark down, jot down, put down, set down, take down; note, note down,** make a note; memorandize, make a memorandum; **post,** post up; **enter,** make an entry, insert, write in; **book, log.**

ADJS. **16. recording,** recordatory, registrational; autographic, self-recording.

17. recorded, registered, enrolled, inscribed, written down; **on record,** on file, on the books; in one's good *or* bad books.

18. documentary, documental.

569. RECORDER

NOUNS **1. recorder,** recordist; **registrar,** register, registerer; **clerk,** baboo [Ind.]; bookkeeper, accountant; **scribe,** scrivener; **secretary,** amanuensis; **stenographer** 600.17; notary, prothonotary, notary public; monitor, marker; scorekeeper, timekeeper.

2. annalist, chronicler 606.11.

3. recording instruments

anemograph	seismometer
autograph, auto-	seismometrograph
graphic recorder	seismoscope
barograph	self-registering
cash register	barometer, ther-
chronograph	mometer, etc.
dictagraph	siphon recorder
dictaphone	sound-on-film
differential	recorder
recorder	sound recorder
dynagraph	spectrograph
electrograph	sphygmograph
facsimile telegraph	stethograph
frequency recorder	tape recorder
gramophone	telautograph
graphophone	telechirograph
hydrograph	telecryptograph
hygrograph	telegraphone
log	telephonograph
oscillograph	telescriptor
pari-mutuel	telestereograph
perforated-tape	telethermograph
recorder	teletype, teletype-
phonograph	writer
pluviograph	telltale
pneumatograph	thermograph
radiograph	thermohumidi-
recording meter	graph
recording poten-	thermometrograph
tiometer, pyrom-	ticker, stock ticker
eter, etc.	time clock
register	totalizator
reproducer	turnstile
seismochronograph	votograph
seismograph	wire recorder

570. REPRESENTATION

NOUNS **1. representation, delineation, portrayal, portraiture, depiction,** depictment, picturization, design; **illustration,** exemplification, demonstration; imagery, iconography; art 572; drama 609.

2. impersonation, personation, personification; **characterization,** portrayal; **acting, playing, posing,** masquerade.

3. image, likeness, rememblance, semblance, similitude; **effigy,** icon; **copy** 24; **picture** 572.12; **portrait** 572.16; **photograph** 575.3; spitting image 20.6; miniature, model; **reflection,** shadow, mirroring.

4. figure, figurine; doll, dolly; **puppet, marionette;** fantocine, fantoccini; **mannequin** *or* manikin, model, dummy, lay figure; wax figure, wax, waxwork; jackstraw, man of straw; **sculpture; bust; statue, statuette,** statuary; **monument;** portrait bust *or* statue; carving, wood carving; figurehead.

5. representative, representation, **type, specimen,** embodiment; **cross section;** exponent; **example** 25.2.

6. symbol 566.2; **symbolism,** symbology;

symbolization, typification, figuration; prefiguration.

VERBS **7. represent, delineate, depict, portray, picture,** picturize, **illustrate;** draw, paint 572.20; register [slang], convey an impression of; take or catch a likeness, hit off.

8. stand for, go for, pass for, count for, answer for, stand in the place of, be taken as, be regarded as, be the equivalent of; pass as, serve as, go as, be accepted for.

9. typify, symbolize, symbol, emblematize, image, figure, **embody,** body forth; **personify,** personate, impersonate; **illustrate,** demonstrate, exemplify; **prefigure, pretypify,** shadow forth, adumbrate.

10. impersonate, personate; **pose as,** masquerade as, pass for, pretend to be, represent oneself to be; **characterize, portray;** act, enact, play, act as, act or play a part, act the part of, act out.

ADJS. **11. representative, illustrative, depictive, delineatory,** picaresque; **representational,** illustrational; **representing, portraying,** illlustrating; **typifying, symbolizing,** personifying, embodying; exemplary, sample.

12. typical, symbolic(al), symbolistic, **emblematic(al), figurative,** ideographic, ideal; **characteristic,** distinctive, distinguishing, peculiar, quintessential; **natural, normal,** usual, regular; **true to type,** true **to form,** the nature of the beast [slang].

571. MISREPRESENTATION

NOUNS **1. misrepresentation,** perversion, **distortion,** garbling, twisting; **coloring,** miscoloring, **false coloring; falsification** 614.9; misdrawing, mispainting; misstatement, misreport; overstatement, overdrawing; understatement, underdrawing.

2. bad likeness, daub, scratch; distortion, distorted image, anamorphosis.

VERBS **3. misrepresent, belie,** mispresent, give a wrong idea; **falsify** 614.16; **pervert, distort, garble, twist,** warp, wrench, twist the meaning of; **color,** miscolor, **give a false coloring,** put a false construction or appearance upon; **disguise,** camouflage; misstate, misreport; overstate, overdraw; understate, underdraw.

4. misdraw, mispaint; daub, scratch.

572. ART

NOUNS **1. art,** the arts; arts and crafts; **fine arts,** *beaux-arts* [F.]; **graphic arts,** arts of design; design, designing; representative art; art form; sculpture 573; ceramics

574; photography 575; engraving 576; decoration 899; artist 577.

2. "a treating of the commonplace with the feeling of the sublime" [Millet], "the conveyance of spirit by means of matter" [Salvador de Madariaga], "knowledge made efficient by skill" [Genung], "the expression of one soul talking to another" [Ruskin], "an instant arrested in eternity" [James Huneker], "a handicraft in flower" [George Iles], "science in the flesh" [Jean Cocteau], "life upon the larger scale" [E. B. Browning], "Nature made by Man to Man the interpreter of God" [Owen Meredith], "a shadow of the divine perfection" [Michelangelo], "life seen through a temperament" [Zola], "a form of catharsis" [Dorothy Parker].

3. craft, artcraft, **manual art, handicraft;** industrial arts; craftwork; woodcraft, metalcraft, stonecraft.

4. architecture, "frozen music" [Schelling], "the art of significant forms in space" [Claud Bragdon], "the printing press of all ages" [Lady Morgan]; landscape architecture, landscape gardening; civil architecture; functionalism, eclecticism.

5. (act or art of painting) **painting,** the brush; **portraiture** 570.1; illustration; water coloring, oil painting, finger painting; encaustic painting, encaustic, cerography; grisaille; portrait painting, landscape painting, marine painting, scene painting, poster painting, decorative painting, flower painting; genre painting, historical painting, magical painting, metaphysical painting.

6. (act or art of drawing) **drawing, sketching, delineation; black and white,** chiaroscuro or chiaro-oscuro; mechanical drawing; drafting; freehand.

7. scenography, ichnography, orthographic projection.

8. artistry, art, talent, artistic skill; pencil, brush; design, artistic invention; artiness [coll.], art-mindedness; artistic temperament; virtu, artistic quality.

9. style, lines, pencil; genre; **school,** movement; the grand style, high art.

10. composition, treatment, technique, design, arrangement; **values,** atmosphere, tone; shadow, shading; line; grouping; balance; perspective.

11. work of art, object of art, *objet d'art* [F.], art, piece, **work,** study, **design,** composition; creation, brain child; virtu, article or piece of virtu; artifact or artefact; **masterpiece,** masterwork; classic;

master, old master; museum piece; conversation piece; curio; grotesque; statue 570.4; mobile, stabile; *pasticcio* [It.], pastiche; artware; bric-a-brac.

12. **picture, picturization**, image, **likeness, representation, canvas**, study, icon, tableau, "a poem without words" [Horace]; photograph 575.3–10; **illustration**, illumination; **design, pattern**; copy, reproduction; print, color print; engraving, etching, block print 576.6–9; daub; abstraction, abstract, nonobjective; mural, cyclorama, montage, collage, pin-up, nude, pastoral, batik, tapestry, mosaic, stained glass window; decal, decalcomania.

13. **scene**, view, **scape; landscape**; waterscape, riverscape; seascape, seapiece; airscape, skyscape, cloudscape; cityscape, townscape; scenograph; panorama; diorama; exterior, interior.

14. **drawing, delineation**; sketch, **draft** *or* draught; **black-and-white**, chiaroscuro *or* chiaro-oscuro; **charcoal, crayon, pen-and-ink**; pencil drawing, charcoal drawing, water-color drawing, etc.; doodle [U.S.]; rough draft *or* copy, rough outline, design, *brouillon* [F.]; *ébauche* [F.]; diagram, graph; tracing.

15. **painting**, color; "a pretty mocking of the life" [Shakespeare], "silent poetry" [Simonides], "the intermediate somewhat between a thought and a thing" [Coleridge]; **oil painting**, oil; **water color**, water; finger painting; tempera; *gouache* [F.]; fresco; still life, study in still life, still [coll.].

16. **portrait, portraiture, portrayal**; head; profile; silhouette, shadow figure; miniature.

17. **cartoon, caricature, comic** [coll.]; comic strip, funny paper [slang], comics [U.S.], funnies [slang, U.S.]; comic book [U.S.]; comic supplement [U.S.]; animated cartoon.

18. **studio**, *atelier* [F.]; gallery 658.9.

19. (art materials) palette *or* pallet; easel; art paper, drawing paper, newsprint; sketchbook, sketchpad; palette knife, spatula; brush, paintbrush; air brush, spray gun; pencil, drawing pencil; crayon, charcoal, chalk, French chalk, pastel; stump; painter's cream; paint 361.7, 24.

VERBS **20. portray, picture**, picturize, **depict, limn**, draw *or* paint a picture; **paint** 361.14; **draw, sketch, delineate; draft** *or* draught, draw up; pencil, chalk, crayon, charcoal; dash off, scratch [coll.];

doodle; design; **diagram; cartoon**; copy, trace; stencil; hatch, crosshatch.

ADJS. **21. artistic(al), arty** [coll.]; **art-minded**, art-conscious; **aesthetic; tasteful; beautiful** 898.16; **ornamental** 899.9; **well-composed**, well-grouped, well-arranged, well-varied; of consummate art; in the grand style.

22. **pictorial**, pictury, **graphic(al)**, **picturesque**; photographic 575.19; scenographic; painty, pastose; monochrome, **polychrome**; freehand.

23. schools

American	Milanese
Barbizon	Modenese
Blue Rider group	Neapolitan
Bolognese	Paduan
British	plein-air
Dutch	Pre-Raphaelite
eclectic	Raphaelite
Flemish	Roman
Florentine	Scottish
French	Sienese
Honfleur	Tuscon
Italian	Umbrian
Lombard	Venetian

24. art styles

abstractionism	neotraditionalism
baroque	nonobjectivism
classicism, clas-sicalism	nonrepresenta-tionalism
cloisonnism	objectivism
constructivism	ornamentalism
conventionalism	pointillism
cubism	post-impressionism
Dadaism	pre-impressionism
divisionism	primitivism
existentialism	purism
expressionism	realism
Fauvism	representationism,
futurism	representation-alism
Gothicism	romanticism
idealism	suprematism
impressionism	surrealism
intimism	symbolism
modernism	synthesism
mysticism	traditionalism
naturalism	vorticism
neoclassicism	
neoimpressionism	

25. styles (adjs.)

abstract	neoclassic
classic(al)	neoimpression-ist(ic)
constructivist	
conventional	neotraditional
conventionalized	nonobjective
cubist	nonrepresenta-tional
existential	
expressionist(ic)	objective
Dadaist	objectivistic
futurist(ic)	pre-impression-ist(ic)
genre	
idealist(ic)	
impressionist(ic)	primitivistic
modernist(ic)	post-impression-ist(ic)
naturalistic	

puristic(al)
realistic
representational
representationist,
representationalist

romantic
romanticist(ic)
surrealist(ic)
symbolist(ic)
traditionalist(ic)

26. architectural styles

academic
baroque
Byzantine
early renaissance
Egyptian
English
French
German
Gothic
Greco-Roman
Greek

high renaissance
Italian
medieval
Mesopotamian
modern
Neo-Gothic
Persian
renaissance
Roman
Romanesque
Spanish

573. SCULPTURE

NOUNS 1. sculpture, sculpturing, modeling; statuary; monumental sculpture, architectural sculpture, decorative sculpture, garden sculpture, portrait sculpture; stone sculpture, clay sculpture, glass sculpture, metal sculpture, wire sculpture, paper sculpture; **wood carving**, xyloglyphy; wax modeling, ceroplastics; anaglyphy, anaglyptics, anaglyptography.

2. (sculptured piece) **sculpture; statue** 570.4; stone, marble, bronze, terra cotta; cast 24.6.

3. **relief,** relievo; **embossment,** boss; half relief, *mezzo-relievo* [It.]; high relief, *alto-relievo* [It.]; low relief, bas-relief, *basso-relievo* [It.]; *stiacciato* [It.]; hollow relief, *cavo-rilievo* [It.], coelanaglyphic sculpture; **intaglio,** *intaglio rilievo* or *rilevato* [It.]; repoussé; glyph, anaglyph; **mask; plaque; medallion; cameo;** cameo glass, sculptured glass.

4. **sculptor** 577.6.

5. (tools, materials) chisel, point, mallet, modeling tool, spatula; modeling clay, Plasticine, plastic.

VERBS 6. **sculpture,** sculp or sculpt [slang], insculpture; **carve,** chisel, cut, grave; **model, mold;** cast.

ADJS. 7. **sculptural,** sculpturesque; **statuary, statuesque,** statuelike; **monumental,** majestic; glyphic, glyptic(al); anaglyphic, anaglyptic(al); anastatic; ceroplast, ceroplastic.

8. **sculptured,** sculpt, scultile; **molded, modeled; carved, graven;** in relief, in high or low relief.

574. CERAMICS

NOUNS 1. ceramics, ceramic, pottery.
2. ceramic ware, ceramics; pottery,

crockery; pot, crock, vase, urn, jug, bowl; bisque, biscuit; mosaic; tile, tiling.

3. (materials) clay, potter's clay or earth, fire clay, adobe, terra cotta; porcelain clay, kaolin, china clay, china stone; flux.

4. **potter's wheel,** wheel; kick wheel, pedal wheel, power wheel.

5. **kiln, oven, stove, furnace;** acid kiln, brickkiln, cement kiln, enamel kiln, muffle kiln, limekiln, reverberatory kiln, stovehouse.

VERBS 6. pot, shape, **throw, turn,** throw or turn a pot; **fire,** bake.

ADJS. 7. **ceramic,** clay, enamel, china, porcelain, glass.

8. **ceramics**

Allervale pottery
basalt
Berlin ware
blackware
Castleford ware
champlevé,
  champlevé enamel
china, chinaware
clayware
cloisonné,
  cloisonné enamel
cottage china
crackle, crackle-
  ware
crouch ware
Crown Derby
delft, delftware
Dresden china
earthenware
eggshell porcelain
enamel, enamel-
  ware
faïence
glassware 338.2, 7
glazed ware
gombroon
ironstone ware or
  china

jasper ware
Leeds pottery
Limoges, Limoges
  ware
Lowestoft ware
lusterware, luster
  pottery
majolica
Meissen ware
Mexican pottery
old Worcester
Palissy ware
porcelain
queen's ware
Rockingham ware
salt-glazed ware
Satsuma ware
Sèvres, Sèvres ware
spode
Staffordshire ware
stoneware
terra cotta
Toft ware
Wedgwood ware
whiteware, white
  pottery
Worcester ware

575. PHOTOGRAPHY

NOUNS 1. **photography,** kodakry, picture-taking; **cinematography,** motion-picture photography; color photography, **technicolor,** photochromy, heliochromy; **3-D,** three-dimensional photography; photofinishing; photogravure 576.3.

2. **photographer** 577.5.

3. **photograph, photo** [coll.], heliograph, **picture,** shot [coll.]; **snapshot,** snap [coll.]; candid photograph; **still,** still photograph; photomural; montage, photomontage; aerial photograph, photomap; telephotograph, telephoto, wirephoto; photomicrograph, microphotograph; heliochrome, heliochromotype; sculptograph;

metallograph; photochronograph; cheese-cake [slang]; **mug**, mug shot [both slang, U.S.]; rogues' gallery [U.S.]; photobiography.

4. **tintype**, ferrotype; **daguerreotype**, calotype, collotype, talbotype.

5. **print**, photoprint, positive; **enlargement, blowup**; photocopy; microprint, microcopy; blueprint, cyanotype; **slide**, lantern slide; photogravure 576.8.

6. **photostat**, stat [coll.], photostatic copy.

7. shadowgraph, shadowgram, skiagraph, skiagram; photogram.

8. radiograph, radiogram, scotograph; **X ray**, X-ray photograph, roentgenograph, roentgenogram; fluorophotograph.

9. spectrograph, spectrogram; spectroheliogram, photospectroheliogram.

10. (motion pictures) **shot, take**; retake; close-up, long shot, medium shot, full shot, group shot, deuce shot, matte shot, process shot, boom shot, travel shot, trucking shot, follow-focus shot, pan shot, rap shot, reverse or reverse-angle shot, wild shot; motion picture 609.15.

11. **exposure**, time exposure.

12. **film, negative**; photographic paper; **plate**; motion-picture film, panchromatic film, microfilm, bibliofilm; sound-on-film, sound track; roll, cartridge; pack, bipack; frame.

13. **camera, kodak**; Kodak, Brownie, Rollieflex; motion-picture camera, cine-camera, cinematograph or kinematograph.

14. **projector**; motion-picture projector, cinematograph or kinematograph [chiefly Eng.], vitascope; **magic lantern**, stereopticon, megascope, slide projector.

15. **solution**; emulsion, dope; vehicle; developer, soup [slang]; hypo, sodium hyposulphite; wash; bath; stop bath, short-stop bath or solution.

VERBS 16. **photograph, photo** [coll.], kodak, take a photograph, **take a picture**, take one's picture, shoot [slang, U.S.]; **snap**, snapshot; **film**, filmize; **mug** [slang, U.S.]; daguerreotype, talbotype, calotype; photostat; microfilm; photomap; telephotograph; pan; X-ray, radiograph, roentgenograph.

17. **develop; print**; blueprint, **blow up**, enlarge.

18. **project, show, screen**.

ADJS. 19. **photographic**, photo; **photogenic**; photosensitive, panchromatic; photoactive; photomechanical; telephotograph-ic, telephoto; tintype; three-dimensional, 3–D.

20. fields of photography

aerophotography, aerial photography	phonophotography photogrammetry photomicography
astrophotography	photospectro-heliography
candid photography	phototopography
chromophotography	phototypography
chronophotography	phototypy pyrophotography
cinematography	radiography radiophotography
cinephotomicrography	sculptography skiagraphy
cystophotography	spectroheliography
heliophotography	spectrophotography
infrared photography	stroboscopic photography
macrophotography	telephotography
microphotography	uranophotography
miniature photography	X-ray photography

21. equipment, accessories

darkroom	periscopic lens
diaphragm	photoelectric meter
dryer	photoflash lamp
easel	photoflood lamp
enlarger	photographometer
exposure meter	photometer
filter	range finder
finder, view finder	reflector
flash gun	shutter
flashlight	telephoto lens
flash tube	timer
lens	tripod
light meter	viewer

22. cameras

aerial reconnaissance camera	photogrammeter
astrograph	photographic telescope
box camera	photomicrographic camera
camera lucida	
camera obscura	photomicroscope
candid camera	photopitometer
cinecamera	photospectroscope
cinematograph	photostat
data camera	Polaroid camera
electron-diffraction camera	precision camera press camera
flash camera	reflex camera
folding camera	spectrograph
hand camera	spectroheliograph
Iconoscope [TV]	spectrohelioscope
image orthicon	spectroscopic camera
laboratory camera	
microcamera	stereo camera
miniature camera, minicam	still camera telescopic camera
motion-picture camera	television camera tripod camera
photochronograph	X-ray machine

576. ENGRAVING

NOUNS 1. **engraving**, engravement, **graving, chasing**, enchasing, **tooling**, chiseling, incising, incision; **inscription,** inscript; **marking,** line, scratch; hatching, crosshatching; etch, **etching;** stipple, stippling; burr.

2. (processes) dry point, etching, intaglio, chalk engraving, half-tone engraving, process engraving, line engraving, steel engraving, stipple engraving, painter etching or graving; wood engraving, lignography, xylography; cerography, wax process, wax engraving or etching; pyrography; plate engraving, chalcography, glyphography, zincography; autotypy, autotypography; electrotypy, galvanography; helioengraving, heliogravure; heliotypy, heliotypography; aquatint, mezzotint; *criblé* [F.], *la manière criblée* [F.].

3. photoengraving, photogravure, rotogravure, gravure, photomechanical process; photoetching, photolithography, photochromography, photozincography.

4. lithography, lithogravure, chromolithography, lithotypy; photolithography, lithophotography; glyptography, glyptics.

5. printing, plate printing, copperplate printing, anastatic printing, lithographic printing, intaglio printing; **block printing,** xylography, xylotypography, linoleumblock printing, rubber-block printing; color printing, three-color process.

6. (an engraving) **engraving,** engravement; **print,** imprint, impression, impress; negative; color print; **etching; intaglio; lithograph,** chromolithograph, photolithograph; lithotype; glyptograph; wax engraving, cerograph, encaustic; chalk engraving, graphotype; **block, block print,** linoleum-block print, rubber-block print; wood engraving, **woodprint,** lignograph, xylograph; **cut, woodcut,** wood block; vignette; headpiece, tailpiece.

7. plate, steel plate, glyphograph; copperplate, chalcograph; zinc plate, zincograph; **stereotype,** autotype, lithotype; **electrotype,** galvanograph; photoelectrotype, photogalvanograph; fashion plate.

8. photoprint, photoengraving, photogravure, gravure, **rotogravure,** rotograph; helioengraving, heliograph, heliotype; photoetching, photointaglio, photoaquatint, photolithograph.

9. tint, aquatint, mezzotint, lithotint; half tone, half tint, demitint.

10. proof, artist's proof, proof before letter, open-letter proof, remarque proof.

11. graver, burin, style; point, etching point, dry point, needle, etcher, etching needle; etching ball; etching ground or varnish; die, punch, stamp, intaglio, last, mint, seal; engraver 577.8.

VERBS 12. engrave, grave, tool, chase, enchase, incise, sculpture, insculpture, **inscribe, character, mark,** line, crease, scratch, scrape, cut, carve, chisel; **stipple;** hatch, crosshatch.

13. imprint, print, impress, stamp, enstamp.

14. (processes) stereotype, electrotype; photoengrave, rotograph; lithograph, photolithograph, chromolithograph; mezzotint, demitint; intaglio; block-print.

15. etch, eat, eat out, corrode, bite, bite in.

ADJS. 16. engraved, graven, graved, chased, enchased, inscribed, incised, marked, lined, creased, cut, carved, glyphic; **sculptured,** insculptured, "insculp'd upon" [Shakespeare]; **printed, imprinted, impressed, stamped.**

17. glyptic(al), glyptographic; lapidary; lithographic, chromolithographic, photolithographic.

577. ARTIST

NOUNS 1. artist, *artiste* [F.], "a dreamer consenting to dream of the actual world" [Santayana]; master, **old master;** dauber, daubster; copyist; Royal Academician, R.A.

2. limner, delineator, depicter, picturer, portrayer; **illustrator,** illuminator.

3. drawer, sketcher, delineator; draftsman or draughtsman; crayonist, charcoalist, pastelist; **cartoonist, caricaturist.**

4. painter, paintress [fem.], brush, brother of the brush, **colorist,** painter stainer; **oil painter,** oil-colorist; **watercolorist;** finger painter; monochromist, polychromatist; enamelist, enameler; genre painter; historical painter; landscapist, miniaturist, portraitist, flower painter, marine painter, still-life painter, majolica painter, tile painter; scene painter, scenist; scenewright; scenographer.

5. photographer, photographist, kodaker; **cameraman, cinematographer;** snapshotter, snap shooter; daguerreotypist, calotypist, talbotypist; skiagrapher, shadowgraphist; radiographer, X-ray photographer.

6. sculptor, sculptress [fem.], sculpturer; statuary; figurer, *figuriste* [F.]; **modeler,** molder; graver, carver, chiseler; wood carver.

7. **ceramacist, potter;** glass blower.

8. **engraver,** graver; chaser, inscriber, carver; **etcher;** line engraver; painter etcher *or* engraver; **lithographer,** chromolithographer, photolithographer; cerographer, cerographist; chalcographer, glyphographer, glyptographer, lapidary, lignographer, photoengraver, xylographer, zincographer.

9. **designer,** costume designer, dress designer, color designer.

10. **architect,** architectress; landscape architect, landscape gardener; civil architect; functionalist.

11. **decorator,** ornamentist, ornamentalist; **dresser;** interior decorator, house decorator, floral decorator, table decorator, window decorator *or* dresser.

12. **stylists**

abstractionist	nonobjectivist
classicist	nonrepresenta-
constructivist	tionist
conventionalist	objectivist
cubist	plein-airist
Dadaist	pointillist
divisionist	post-impressionist
eclectic	pre-impressionist
existentialist	primitive, primi-
expressionist	tivist
Fauvist	purist
futurist	realist
idealist	representationist,
impressionist	representational-
intimist	ist
luminist	romanticist
modernist	suprematist
mystic	surrealist
naturalist	symbolist
neoclassicist	synthesist
neoimpressionist	traditionalist
neotraditionalist	vorticist

13. **painters**

Bellini	Degas
Bellows	Duchamp
Blake	Dufy
Boccioni	Dürer
Bonnard	Eakins
Botticelli	El Greco
Boucher	Ensor
Braque	Feininger
Bruegel	Filippo Lippi
Carra	Fra Angelico
Cézanne	Fragonard
Chagall	Francesca
Chardin	Franz Marc
Chirico	Friesz
Constable	Gainsborough
Copley	Gauguin
Corot	Gilbert Stuart
Correggio	Giotto
Courbet	Gleizes
Dali	Goya
Daumier	Grant Wood
David	Greuze
da Vinci	Gris

Guardi	Poussin
Hals	Raphael
Hans Arp	Redon
Hobbema	Rembrandt
Hodler	Renoir
Hogarth	Reynolds
Holbein	Rivera
Homer	Rockwell Kent
Ingres	Romney
Jongkind	Rossetti
Kandinsky	Rouault
Kirchner	Rousseau
Klee	Rubens
Kokoschka	Ryder
LeBrun	Schmidt-Rottluff
Léger	Sérusier
Le Havre	Seurat
Lorenzetti	Severini
Manet	Signac
Mantegna	Sisley
Marin	Soutine
Marquet	Stuart
Martini	Thomas Benton
Masaccio	Tintoretto
Masolino	Titian
Masson	Toulouse-Lautrec
Matisse	Turner
Max Ernst	Utrillo
Messina	Vallotton
Michelangelo	Van der Weyden
Millet	Vandyke
Modersohn-Becker	van Eyck
Modigliani	van Gogh
Mondrian	van Ruisdael
Monet	Velasquez
Munch	Veneziano
Murillo	Vermeer
Nolde	Veronese
Ozenfant	Vlaminck
Picabia	Vuillard
Picasso	Watteau
Pissarro	Whistler

14. **sculptors**

Brancusi	Michelangelo
Cellini	Phidias
della Robbia	Pisano
Donatello	Praxiteles
Epstein	Rodin
Ghiberti	Saint-Gaudens
Maillol	

578. LANGUAGE

NOUNS 1. **language, speech, tongue, talk, parlance, locution, idiom, lingua; lingo, patter** [both usu. joc. *or* derog.]; Basic English.

2. **classics; dead languages;** classicism, classicalism.

3. conventional *or* accepted speech; literary language; correct *or* good English, **Standard English, the king's** *or* **queen's English;** plain English, Anglo-Saxon.

4. **the vernacular,** vernacular language *or* tongue, spoken language, vulgate, **vulgar tongue; mother tongue, native language** *or* tongue, language of one's fathers;

langue du pays [F.]. *Landessprache* [G.]; American, American language, United States Yankee.

5. colloquialism, vernacularism, conversationalism; colloquial speech, substandard usage, unrefined speech; colloquial English, English as it is spoken.

6. jargon, lingo, lingua, **dialect** (class or regional speech), **cant, argot, patois, patter. talk, vernacular, vocabulary,** phraseology; **slang,** slanguage [joc.], slangism, jive [slang], hep talk [slang, U.S.]; **flash,** flash tongue; thieves' Latin, St. Giles's Greek peddler's French; back slang, rhyming slang; polyglot, pig Latin, dog Latin; **gibberish,** jabber, *baragouin* [F.]; Greek, double Dutch; **jabberwocky, double talk, gobbledegook** [slang], bafflegab [slang, U.S.].

7. class dialect, Academese, cinemese, collegese, economese, legalese, pedagese, societyese, stagese, telegraphese, Varietyese, Wall Streetese; journalese, newspaperese; officialese, federalese, Washingtonese; medical Greek, medicalese; businessese, commercialism, business English.

8. dialect, idiom, patois; **provincialism, localism, regionalism,** isogloss; **accent, brogue, twang;** baboo English, chee-chee [both Anglo-India]; Afrikaans, Cape Dutch; Low German, Plattdeutsch; *langue d'oc* [F.]; *langue d'oïl* [F.]; ogam [ancient Irish dialect]; French Canadian; Pennsylvania Dutch; Yankee [New England]; Brooklynese; Harlemese; cockney, cockneyese; Geechee [Georgia]; Gullah [S.E. U.S.]; Cajun [Louisiana], gumbo French; Finnglish.

9. (idioms) Anglicism, Briticism, Englishism; Americanism, Yankeeism; Gallicism, Frenchism; Irishism, Hibernicism; Canadianism, Scotticism, Germanism, Russianism, Latinism, etc.

10. lingua franca, jargon, koine; **pidgin** or **pigeon English,** talk-boy; talkeetalkee, talky-talky; *bêche-de-mer* [F., W. Pacific], beche-le-mar, beach-la-mar; kitchen Kaffir [Central & S. Africa]; bamboo English [Philippines]; Chinook [N.W. U.S. & S.W. Can.], Chinook or Oregon Jargon; Hausa [Central Africa], Hindustani [India], Kiswahili [E. Africa], Sabir [N. Africa], Swahili [Zanzibar].

11. linguistics, language, linguistic science, science of language, **philology,** speechcraft; glossology, glottology; lexicology 581.13; grammar 584; semantics 543.7;

syntactics, pragmatics, phonemics, **mor**phology, paleography.

12. linguist, linguister or lingster [dial.]; **philologist,** philologer, philologian, philologaster [derog.]; **grammarian,** grammatist, grammaticaster [derog.]; polyglot, polyglottonist; **etymologist,** etymologer; eponymist; **lexicologist, lexicographer,** lexiconist, glossologist; glossographer, glossarist, glossarian; glottologist; vocabulist, vocabularian; phonologist, orthoëpist; dialectician, dialectologist, dialector; semanticist, semasiologist; paleographer; Hebraist, Hellenist, Sanskritist, Sinologist.

13. colloquialist, colloquializer; **jargonist,** jargoner, jargonizer; **slangster,** jivester [slang].

VERBS **14. colloquialize,** vernacularize; jargon, jargonize, cant, sling the bat [slang, Anglo-India].

ADJS. **15. linguistic(al), philologic(al);** glossologic(al), glottologic(al); bilingual, diglot; polyglot; hexaglot.

16. colloquial, vernacular, conversational, unliterary, substandard, undignified, informal, unstudied, familiar, common, everyday.

17. jargonish, jargonal; **cant,** argotic, flash; **slang,** slangy, slangish, slangular [joc.].

18. idiomatic(al); dialect, dialectal, dialectic(al); provincial, regional.

19. language classifications

agglutinative	monosyllabic
analytic	polytonic
inflectional	synthetic
isolating	

20. linguistic families

Americanoid	Indian, American
Anatolic	Indian
Aryan	Indic
Assam-Burmese	Indo-Chinese
Austric	Indo-European
Austroasiatic	Indo-Germanic
Austronesian	Indo-Iranian
Baltic	Indonesian
Balto-Slavic	Iranian
Bantu	Italic
Bushman	Latinian
Carib	Mahori
Celtic	Malay
Chinese-Siamese	Malayo-Javanese
Dravidian	Malayo-Polynesian
Dravido-Munda	Manchu
Fijian	Melanesian
Finnic	Melano-Papuan
Finno-Tartar	Micronesian
Finno-Ugric	Mongolic
Germanic	Negrito
Hamitic	Osco-Umbrian
Hellenic	Paleo-Asiatic

Papuan
Phrygian
Polynesian
Romance,
  Romanic
Sabellian
Samoyed
Sawaiori
Scandinavian
Semitic
Sinitic
Sino-Tibetan
Slavic, Slavonic
Tagala
Tarapon
Teutonic
Thraco-Illyrian

Thraco-Phrygian
Tibeto-Burman
Tibeto-Chinese
Tibeto-Himalayan
Turanian
Turkic, Turko-
  Tartar
Ugrian
Ugro-Altaic
Ugro-Aryan
Ugro-Finnic
Ugro-Slavonic
Ugro-Tartarian
Ural-Altaic
Uralian
Zulu-Kaffir

Kavi
Kazan Tatar
Kharia
Khasi
Khmer
Khond
Khowar
Kiranti
Kirghiz
Kiriwina
Kodagu
Kohistani
Koibal
Kongoese
Korwa
Kuki
Kumyk
Kurdish
Kurukh
Lahnda
Lampong
Lamut
Lapp
Latin
Lettish
Limbu
Lithuanian
Livonian
Low German
Madurese
Magyar
Makassar
Malagasy
Malay
Malayalam
Maltese
Malto
Manchu
Mandarin
Mangar
Manobo
Manx
Maori
Marathi
Marquesan
Marshall
Maya
Meithei
Middle English
Mishmi
Misima
Mon
Mongolian
Montes
Mordvinian
Moro
Mru
Muong
Murmi
Muskogee
Naga
Newari
Niasese
Nicobarese
Niue
Nogai
Norwegian
Old English
Oraon
Oriya
Osmanli

Ossetic
Ostyak
Pahari
Palau
Palaung
Pali
Pampango
Pangasinan
Panjabi
Permian
Persian
Phrygian
Polish
Portuguese
Prakrit
Provençal
Quechuan
Rajasthani
Rejang
Rhaeto-Romanic
Romaic
Romany
Ronga
Rumanian
Russian
Sakai
Samoan
Sanskrit
Santali
Sassak
Savara
Scotch, Scottish
Selung
Semang
Serbo-Croatian
Shan
Shilha
Shina
Siamese
Sindhi
Singhalese
Slavic
Slovak
Slovenian
Sorbian
Soyot
Spanish
Sudanese
Swahili
Swedish
Syriac
Syryenian
Tagala
Tagalog
Tagula
Tahitian
Tamashek
Tamil
Tartar
Tavghi
Teleut
Telugu
Tibetan
Tigré
Tigriña
Tino
Tipura
Toda
Tokelau
Tongan
Tuamotuan

21. languages

Achinese
Afghan
Ainu
Aka
Albanian
Algonquin
Amharic
Anglo-French,
  Anglo-Norman
Anglo-Saxon
Annamese
Arabic
Aramaic
Araucan
Armenian
Assamese
Austral
Avestan
Aymara
Balinese
Baluchi
Bashkir
Basque
Batan
Battak
Bengali
Berber
Bihari
Bikol
Blackfoot
Brahui
Breton
British
Bugi
Bulgarian
Buriat
Burmese
Caroline
Castilian
Catalan
Cham
Chamorro
Cheremiss
Cherokee
Chibcha
Chin
Chinese
Chuvash
Coman
Coptic
Czechoslovak
Dafia

Danish
Dutch
Dyak
Egyptian
English
Eskimo
Estonian
Ethiopian
Fiji
Finnish
Flemish
Formosan
French
Frisian
Gadaba
Gaelic
Galcha
Garo
German
Gilbertese
Gold
Gondi
Gothic
Greek
Gujarati
Gypsy
Hawaiian
Hebrew
High German
Hindustani
Ho
Ibanag
Icelandic
Igorot
Ilokano
Irish
Italian
Jagatai
Jakun
Japanese
Javanese
Juang
Kabyle
Kachin
Kafiri
Kalmuck
Kamasin
Kanarese
Kara-Kalpak
Karen
Kashmiri
Kasubian

Tulu	Visayan
Tungus	Vote
Tupi	Wa
Turkoman	Welsh
Uigur	Yenisei
Ukrainian	Yiddish
Urcu	Yurak
Uzbek	Zenaga
Veps	Zulu

22. international languages

Antido	lingua internaciona
Arulo	Lingualumina
auxiliary language	Lingvo
Blaia Zimondal	Kosmopolita
Esperantido	Monario
Esperanto	Nov-Esperanto
Europan	Novial
Idiom Neutral	Nov-Latin
Ido	Occidental
Interlingua	Optez
international	Ro
auxiliary	Romanal
language	Solresol
Latinesce	Volapük
Latino, Latino sine	
flexione	

579. LETTER

Written Character.—NOUNS **1. letter,
character, sign, symbol,** alphabetic *or*
phonetic character; consonant, vowel 449.5;
cipher, device; monogram, monograph
[erron.].

2. (written characters) **script,** cursive;
print, printing; italic, **italics; roman; initial;** large letter, majuscule, uncial; **capital,**
cap [ccll.], upper case [print.]; small letter,
minuscule, lower case [print.].

3. (phonetic and ideographic symbols)
phonogram, phonograph; phonetic, phonetic symbol; **logogram,** logograph, gram-
malogue, word letter; **ideogram,** ideograph,
ideographic, ideoglyph; **pictograph,** picto-
gram; **hieroglyphic,** hieroglyph; hierogram,
hieratic symbol, demotic character; phonoglyph; **rune; cuneiform,** arrowhead; ogam,
ogham kana, Kanji, Iroha [all Jap.]; Rosetta stone; hieroglyphic writing, etc. 600.10.

4. alphabet, letters, letters of the alphabet, **A B C's,** abecedary; christcross *or*
crisscross, christcross-row *or* chriscross-row
[all arch. & dial. Eng.]; phonetic alphabet;
runic alphabet, futhorc *or* futharc; alphabetics, alphabetism.

5. (alphabets) Anglo-Saxon, Arabic,
Egyptian hieratic, Egyptian hieroglyphic,
English, German, Greek, Hebrew, Latin *or*
Roman, Phoenician, Russian *or* Cyrillic,
Sinaitic, Targu; Western Greek, Chalcid-
ian; Sanskrit, Devanagari, Nagari, Brah-
mi.

6. syllable, phone; monosyllable, dissyllable, polysyllable; affix, prefix, suffix;
syllabary.

7. spelling, orthography; phonetic spelling, phonetics, phonography; glossic, glossotype, palaeotype; spelling match *or* bee,
spelldown, spellingdown.

8. lettering, initialing, signature, inscription; alphabetization; transliteration.

VERBS **9. letter, initial,** inscribe, character, sign, mark, stamp; **capitalize; alphabetize,** alphabet; transliterate.

10. spell, orthographize; spell out, write
out, trace out; spell backward; outspell,
spell down [U.S.].

ADJS. **11. literal, lettered; alphabet-
ic(al),** abecedarian; large-lettered, majuscular, unicial, **capital,** capitalized, upper-case
[print.]; small-lettered, minuscular, lower-
case [print.].

12. syllabic, syllabized; monosyllabic,
dissyllabic, polysyllabic.

580. WORD

NOUNS **1. word, term, expression, locution, verbalism, vocable, utterance, articulation;** usage; ideophone; syllable,
monosyllable; semanteme, morpheme.

2. root, etymon, primitive; derivative.

3. formation, construction, word form;
back formation; clipped word; spoonerism;
acronym; homonym, metonym, heteronym;
analogue; synonym, poecilonym; antonym,
counterterm; acrostic.

4. technicalism, technical term, technicality; commercialism.

5. colloquialism, slang, localism 578.5–9.

**6. barbarism, corruption, vulgarism,
impropriety;** caconym; foreignism.

7. neologism, neology, neoterism, new
word *or* term, newfangled expression; **coinage;** nonce word; ghost word *or* name.

8. catchword, byword, counter word,
catch phrase, shibboleth, slogan, cry, **pet
expression;** vogue word, fad word, cuckoo
word.

9. hybrid, hybrid word; macaronicism,
macaronic; hybridism, contamination,
crossbreeding.

10. portmanteau word, portmanteau,
portmantologism; **blend-word,** blend, fusion, telescope word.

11. archaism, archaicism, antiquated
word *or* expression; obsoletism; obsolescence; monkish Latin; dead language.

**12. vocabulary, words, wordage, verbi-
age,** stock of words; lexicon 603.7.

13. lexicology, glossology; lexicography, lexigraphy, glossography; phonology, orthoëpy.

14. **etymology, derivation, origin,** genesis, glottogony, word history; eponymy, eponymism.

15. onomatopoeia, onomatopoesis; bow-wow theory, pooh-pooh theory; onomatopoeic word, onomatope, onomatoplasm.

16. **neologist, word-coiner,** neoterist; phraser, phrasemaker.

ADJS. 17. **verbal, literal;** vocabular, vocabulary.

18. lexical, lexicologic(al), glossologic(al); lexigraphic(al), lexicographic(al), glossographic(al).

19. **etymologic(al),** derivative, glottogonic; conjugate, paronymous.

20. neologic(al), neoteric(al).

581. NOMENCLATURE

NOUNS 1. **nomenclature, terminology, phraseology,** orismology, glossology, onomatology; toponymy; technology; antonomasia.

2. **naming, calling, denomination,** appellation, designation, characterization, definition, identification; **christening,** baptism.

3. **name, appellation,** appellative, **denomination, designation,** style, **cognomen,** moniker or monicker [slang], handle [slang]; title, handle to one's name [coll.]; empty title or name; **label, tag;** byname, epithet; middle name; eponym; namesake.

4. **proper name, first name, Christian name, given name,** baptismal name.

5. **surname, last name, family name,** patronymic, **cognomen,** byname; **maiden name.**

6. (Roman antiq.) praenomen, nomen, agnomen, cognomen.

7. **nickname, sobriquet** or soubriquet, byname, byword, cognomen; **pet name,** little name, babyism; John Doe, Richard Roe.

8. **alias, pseudonym,** anonym, **assumed name,** fictitious name, nom de guerre [F.]; **pen name,** nom de plume; stage name, nom de theatre [F.].

9. misnomer, wrong name.

10. **signature, sign manual, autograph, hand,** John Hancock [coll.]; mark, cross, ex, X; subscription, superscription, superscript; countersignature, countersign, countermark, counterstamp; visa, visé; monogram, cipher, device; seal, sigil, signet.

VERBS 11. **name, denominate, designate, call, term, style, dub, characterize,** define, describe, specify, identify; **title,** entitle or intitle; **label, tag; nickname; christen,** baptize.

12. **misname,** misnomer, **miscall,** misterm, call one out of one's name [coll.].

13. **be called, be known by** or **as,** go by, go as, go under, **go by the name of,** go or pass under the name of, bear the name of, rejoice in the name of; go under an assumed name, pass for, pass oneself off for.

ADJS. 14. **named, called,** y-clept [arch.], **termed, styled, titled,** denominated, denominate, **known as,** known by the name of; what one may well ∼, fairly ∼, properly or fitly call.

15. **nominal, titular, in name only; so-called,** quasi, would-be, soi-disant [F.]; **self-called, self-styled,** self-christened; cognominal; by whatever name, under any other name.

16. denominative, nominative, appellative; eponymous; by name.

17. **terminological,** phraseologic(al), glossological, orismological; technical, technologic(al).

582. ANONYMITY

NOUNS 1. **anonymity, anonymousness, namelessness;** anonym.

2. **what's-its-name, what's-his-name,** what's-her-name, **what-you-may-call-it,** what-you-may-call-'em, what-d'ye-call-'em, what-d'ye-call-it [all coll.]; you-know-who; je ne sais quoi [F.], I don't know what; **so-and-so,** such-and-such, Mr. or Mrs. So-and-So, "Sergeant What's-'is-name" [Kipling].

ADJS. 3. **anonymous, anon; nameless, unnamed,** undesignated, unspecified, unacknowledged, undefined, innominate, without a name, **unknown.**

583. PHRASE

NOUNS 1. **phrase, expression, locution, utterance,** verbalism; **clause; sentence,** period; **paragraph; idiom,** idiotism; turn of expression, peculiar expression; set phrase or term; phraseogram, phraseograph.

2. phrasing 586; syllabification, syllabication.

3. **phraser, phrasemaker, phrasemonger,** phraseman.

VERBS 4. **phrase, express, give expression** or **words to, word,** word it, verbalize, conceive, style, **put in words,** clothe in words, couch in terms, express by or in words, find words to express; **voice,** vocalize; **put,** present; **formulate,** formularize.

5. **syllable,** syllabify, syllabize, syllabicate; **paragraph; sentence.**

ADJS. 6. **phrased,** expressed, **worded,** formulated, styled, put, presented, couched; **phrasy** [coll.].

ADVS. 7. **in set phrases** or **terms, in good set terms, in round terms.**

584. GRAMMAR

NOUNS 1. **grammar,** rules of language, "the rule and pattern of speech" [Horace]; **inflection, syntax, accidence;** praxis, syllepsis, synopsis, paradigm, jussive; **conjugation, declension; parsing,** analysis.

2. **parts of speech;** modifier, qualifier; attributive, attribute; **adjective, adverb, preposition;** verbal adjective, gerundive; **participle,** present participle, past participle, perfect participle; partitive; intensive; **conjunction,** adversative, copulative, correlative, disjunctive; **interjection,** exclamatory noun or adjective; **particle; subject, predicate.**

3. **verb,** transitive, intransitive, active verb, passive verb, neuter verb, finite verb, deponent verb, link verb, copula; **verbal.**

4. **noun, pronoun,** substantive, common noun, proper noun, adherent noun, abstract noun, collective noun, quotation noun, adverbial noun; verbal noun, gerund; **infinitive,** split infinitive; **object,** direct object, indirect object.

5. **article,** definite article, indefinite article.

6. **person,** first person, second person, third person.

7. **case,** ablative, accusative, dative, genitive, instrumental, locative, nominative, possessive, vocative.

8. **gender,** masculine, feminine, neuter.

9. **mood,** mode; indicative, subjunctive, imperative; conditional, potential, obligative, permissive.

10. **tense,** point tenses, durative tenses; **present;** historical present; **past,** preterit; perfect; present perfect, future perfect; past perfect, **pluperfect;** progressive tense.

11. **punctuation,** punctuation marks; diacritical mark or sign; reference mark, reference; point, tittle; stop, end stop.

VERBS 12. **grammaticize; parse,** analyze; **inflect, conjugate, decline; punctuate,** mark, point; parenthesize.

ADJS. 13. **grammatic(al), correct,** accurate, proper; syntactic(al); inflective, inflectional; synoptic; substantive, nominal, pronominal; verbal, transitive, intransitive; attributive, adjectival, adverbial, prepositional, participial; conjunctive, copulative.

14. punctuation and reference marks

accent	grave accent, [`]
acute accent, [']	hyphen, [-]
ampersand, [&]	index, [☞]
apostrophe, [']	interrogation,
asterisk, [*]	interrogation mark
asterism, [*₊*]	or point, [?]
brace, [}]	leaders, [....] or
brackets, [ ]	[___]
breve, short accent,	macron, long
[˘]	accent, [¯]
caret, [∧]	obelisk, [†]
cedilla, [ç]	paragraph, [¶]
circumflex,	[℟]
[∧,ˆ, or ˜]	parallels, [‖]
colon, [:]	parenthesis, parens,
comma, [,]	[( )]
dagger, [†]	period, [.]
dash, [—]	point, [.]
decimal point,	prime, [']
[e.g., 1.2]	question mark, [?]
diaeresis, [¨]	quotation marks,
diesis, [‡]	quotes, [" "]
dot, [.]	section, [§]
double dagger, [‡]	semicolon, [;]
ellipsis, [...] or	star, [*]
[***]	tilde, [ñ]
exclamation,	umlaut, [¨]
exclamation mark	virgule, [/]
or point, [!]	

585. UNGRAMMATICALNESS

NOUNS 1. **ungrammaticalness,** bad or faulty grammar; abuse of terms, corruption of speech, talkee-talkee; cacology, cacography.

2. **solecism,** ungrammaticism, **misusage, missaying, misconstruction,** mispronunciation, **corruption,** impropriety; antiphrasis; malapropism 517.6.

VERBS 3. **murder the king's** or **queen's English,** break Priscian's head.

ADJS. 4. **ungrammatic(al),** solecistic(al), **incorrect,** inaccurate, inexact, faulty, improper, unseemly, incongruous; careless, slovenly, loose, lax, sloppy, slipshod, slipslop.

586. DICTION

NOUNS 1. **diction, phraseology, phrase, phrasing, wording, wordage, verbiage, vocabulary,** speech, talk [coll.], **language,** dialect, parlance, locution, expression, formulation, rhetoric, **grammar; idiom,** idiologism; composition.

2. **style, fashion, manner, mode,** strain, vein; **usage,** *usus loquendi* [L., usage in speaking]; **manner of speaking,** mode of expression, form of speech, use of words, choice of words, expression of ideas; "the dress of thoughts" [Dickens], "a certain absolute and unique manner of expressing a thing, in all its intensity and color" [Pater]; the grand style, *la morgue littéraire* [F.].

3. **stylist,** mannerist.

587. ELEGANCE

Of Language.—NOUNS 1. **elegance,** elegancy; **grace,** gracefulness; **taste,** tastefulness, good taste; **correctness,** seemliness, comeliness; **propriety, refinement,** discrimination, **restraint; polish, finish;** felicity, ease; clarity, distinction; **purity,** chastity, chasteness; **simplicity,** naturalness, unaffectedness; Atticism, Attic salt; classicism, classicalism; well-rounded *or* well-turned periods, flowing periods; the right word in the right place.

2. **harmony, proportion,** symmetry, **balance,** rhythm, concinnity; **euphony;** fluency, flow.

3. (affected elegance) **affectation,** affectedness, **pretentiousness, mannerism, artificiality,** unnaturalness; **euphuism, euphemism,** Gongorism; preciousness, preciosity; overniceness, overrefinement.

4. purist, classicist, Atticist.

5. euphuist, euphemist, Gongorist.

ADJS. 6. **elegant, tasteful, graceful,** neat, **refined, restrained; simple, unaffected, natural,** unlabored, easy; **pure,** chaste; classic(al), Attic, Ciceronian, academic(al); **polished, finished.**

7. **appropriate, proper, correct, seemly,** comely; **felicitous,** happy, neat, **apt,** well-chosen, **well-put,** well-expressed, inspired.

8. **harmonious, balanced,** symmetrical, concinnate; **euphonious,** euphonic(al); smooth, smooth-sounding; fluent, flowing, tripping.

9. (affectedly elegant) **euphuistic(al), affected, pretentious, mannered, artificial, unnatural;** precious, overnice, overrefined; gongoristic, Gongoresque.

588. INELEGANCE

Of Language.—NOUNS 1. **inelegance,** inelegancy; **gracelessness,** ungracefulness; **tastelessness,** bad taste; **impropriety,** indecorousness, unseemliness, incorrectness; impurity; **vulgarity,** vulgarism, Gothicism, barbarism, barbarousness, **coarseness, unrefinement,** grossness, rudeness, crudeness, uncouthness; cacology, poor diction; cacography, bad writing, loose *or* slipshod construction, ill-balanced sentences.

ADJS. 2. **inelegant, graceless,** ungraceful; **tasteless,** in bad taste, offensive to ears polite; **incorrect, improper; indecorous, unseemly,** uncourtly, undignified, **unpolished, unrefined;** impure, unclassical; **vulgar,** barbarous, **uncouth,** low, gross, **coarse,** harsh, rude, **crude,** outlandish; doggerel; mongrel; cacographic(al).

3. **stiff, stilted, formal,** *guindé* [F.], **labored,** ponderous, **forced,** cramped, awkward, halting.

589. PLAIN SPEECH

NOUNS 1. **plain speech,** plain speaking, **plain English,** plain words, household words; **plainness,** simpleness, **simplicity,** soberness, severity; naturalness, unaffectedness, matter-of-factness, unimaginativeness; prosaicness, prosiness, unpoeticalness.

VERBS 2. **speak plainly,** waste no words, **call a spade a spade, come to the point,** not beat about the bush.

ADJS. 3. **plain-speaking,** simple-speaking; **plain, simple,** unadorned, unvarnished, pure, neat, sober, severe; **natural, unaffected, matter-of-fact,** commonplace, homely, homespun; **prosaic,** prosing, prosy; unpoetical, unimaginative, dull, dry.

ADVS. 4. **plainly, simply,** naturally, unaffectedly, matter-of-factly; in plain words, **in plain English,** in words of one syllable; point-blank, to the point.

590. CONCISENESS

NOUNS 1. **conciseness,** briefness, brevity, "the soul of wit" [Shakespeare]; shortness, compactness; **curtness, crispness,** terseness, summariness; **pithiness, trenchancy,** piquancy, succinctness, neatness, pointedness, sententiousness.

2. laconics, laconism, laconicism, economy of language.

VERBS 3. **be brief, come to the point, make a long story short,** cut the matter short.

ADJS. 4. **concise, brief, short,** "short and sweet" [T. Lodge]; **condensed, compressed,** close, compact; compendious 202.8; **curt, crisp, terse,** summary; **pithy, trenchant,** piquant, **succinct,** neat, pregnant; **laconic,** sententious, epigrammatic(al); **pointed,** to the point.

ADVS. 5. concisely, briefly, shortly; curtly, crisply, tersely, summarily; pithily, trenchantly, piquantly, succinctly, pointedly; laconically, sententiously.

6. in brief, in short, in substance, in epitome, in outline, in a nutshell, in a capsule; in a word, in a few words; to be brief, to come to the point, to cut the matter short, to make a long story short.

591. DIFFUSENESS

NOUNS 1. diffuseness, profuseness, profusiveness, profusion; diffusiveness, diffusion; effusiveness, effusion; gush, gushing; flow of words, cloud of words; copiousness, exuberance, extravagance; redundancy, pleonasm.

2. wordiness, verbosity, verbiage, verbalism; prolixity, long-windedness, longiloquence.

3. discursiveness, desultoriness, aimlessness; rambling, maundering, wandering, roving.

4. digression, departure, deviation, discursion, excursion, excursus; episode.

5. circumlocution, roundaboutness, circuitousness, deviousness, obliqueness, indirection; periphrase, periphrasis.

6. expatiation, amplification, enlargement, expansion; development, explication.

VERBS 7. expatiate, amplify, dilate, expand, enlarge, enlarge upon, develop, evolve, explicate, descant, relate at large.

8. protract, extend, spin out, string out, draw out, stretch out, drag out, run out; pad, fill out; perorate, speak at length, spin a long yarn.

9. digress, get off the subject, wander from the subject, wander, ramble, maunder, stray, go astray, depart, deviate, turn aside, go off on a tangent.

10. circumlocute [joc.], go round about, beat about the bush, go round Robin Hood's barn; periphrase.

ADJS. 11. diffuse, diffusive; profuse, profusive; effusive, gushing, gushy; copious, exuberant, extravagant; redundant, pleonastic.

12. wordy, verbose; prolix, windy [coll.], longwinded, longiloquent; protracted, extended, lengthy, long, long-drawn-out, long-spun, spun-out; padded, filled out.

13. discursive, excursive, digressive, deviative; rambling, maundering, wandering, roving; desultory, loose, aimless, episodic, by the way.

14. circumlocutory, circumlocutional; roundabout, circuitous, devious, ambagious, oblique, indirect; periphrastic.

ADVS. 15. at length, at large, in full.

592. SPEECH

Utterance.—NOUNS 1. speech, language, talk, talking, speaking, discourse, comment, parole, palaver, prattle, gab [coll.]; chin music, chin, jaw, lip, yap, gaff [all slang]; words, accents; chatter 594.3; conversation 595; elocution 597.

2. "the mirror of the soul" [Publilius Syrus], "the image of life" [Democritus], "a faculty given to man to conceal his thoughts" [Talleyrand], "but broken light upon the depth of the unspoken" [G. Eliot].

3. utterance, articulation, vocalization, locution, phonation, breathing; voice, tongue; vocable, vocal; word, word of mouth, the spoken word.

4. remark, statement, crack [slang], word, say, saying, utterance, observation, reflection, expression; comment, note, mention; assertion; averment, allegation, pronouncement, position, dictum; declaration, dick [slang]; sentence, phrase; subjoinder, more last words.

5. articulateness, articulacy, articulation.

6. enunciation, pronunciation, articulation, utterance; manner of speaking, way of saying, mode of expression, tone of voice; delivery, attack; phonology, orthoëpy.

7. accent, accentuation; emphasis, stress; ictus, rhythmical stress; broad accent, strong accent, pure accent; native accent, foreign accent; brogue, twang, burr.

8. ventriloquism, ventriloquy; ventriloquist.

9. talker, speaker, sayer, utterer, patterer; chatterbox 594.5; conversationalist 595.7; public speaker 597.4.

10. vocal organs; tongue; vocal cords or bands, vocal lips, vocal processes, vocal folds; voice box, larynx, Adam's apple; syrinx; glottis, vocal chink.

VERBS 11. speak, talk, patter [chiefly slang], gab [coll.], wag the tongue [coll.], mouth, parley [chiefly joc.], hold forth; chatter 594.6; converse 595.8; declaim 597.8–10; chorus, chime.

12. (slang terms) yap, spiel [U.S.], chin, jaw, shoot one's face, shoot or bat the breeze, bump the gums [U.S.].

13. speak up, speak out, pipe up,

open one's lips or mouth, lift or raise one's voice, break silence; take the floor, rise to the occasion; put in a word, get in a word edgewise.

14. say, utter, breathe, sound, **voice,** vocalize, **articulate, enunciate, pronounce,** lip, give voice, give tongue, give utterance; **express,** give expression, verbalize, **word,** put in words, find words to express; **present,** deliver; **emit,** give, raise, **let out** [coll.], out with, come out with, put or set forth, pour forth; throw off, fling off; **tell, communicate, convey, impart;** have or say one's say, speak one's mind.

15. state, declare, assert, aver, allege; **relate, recite.**

16. remark, comment, observe, note; mention, let fall, make mention of; muse, reflect; opine [chiefly joc.], dare say.

17. (utter in a certain way) murmur, mutter, mumble, whisper, breathe, sigh; gasp, pant; exclaim, yell 458.6, 7; sing, warble, chant, coo, chirp; cackle, crow; bark, yelp, yap; growl, snap, snarl; hiss; grunt, snort; roar, bellow, bawl, thunder, boom; scream, shriek, screech, squeal, squawk; whine, wail.

18. address, speak to, talk to, bespeak [poetic]; **appeal to,** invoke; apostrophize; **approach,** make up to [coll.]; **buttonhole,** buttonhold, take by the button; take aside, talk to in private; **accost, call to, hail,** halloo, greet, salute.

19. pass one's lips, escape one's lips, fall from the lips or mouth.

ADJS. **20. spoken, uttered, said,** vocalized, **voiced, pronounced, sounded, articulated, enunciated; vocal,** voiceful [poetic]; **oral, verbal, unwritten,** nuncupative, parol, acroamatic(al); phonic, phonetic; outspoken.

21. speaking, talking; articulate; well-speaking, well-spoken, true-speaking, clean-speaking, clean-spoken, plain-speaking, plain-spoken, free-speaking, free-spoken, loud-speaking, loud-spoken, soft-speaking, soft-spoken; English-speaking, etc.

22. ventriloquial, ventriloquistic.

ADVS. **23. orally, vocally, verbally, by word of mouth,** viva voce [L.]; from the lips of, from his own mouth.

593. IMPERFECT SPEECH

NOUNS **1. speech defect,** impediment in one's speech, bone in the neck or throat; betacism, mytacism; **broken speech,**

cracked or broken voice, broken tones or accents, talkee-talkee; **nasalization,** nasal tone or accent, **twang,** nasal twang; **falsetto,** childish treble, false or artificial voice; **shake, quaver; drawl; lisp,** lisping; **croak,** crow; harshness, hoarseness 457.

2. inarticulateness, inarticulacy, inarticulation.

3. stammering, stuttering, hesitation, faltering; traulism, titubancy, titubation; stammer, stutter.

4. mumbling, muttering, maundering, mouthing; mumble, mutter; jabber, jibber, gabble.

5. mispronunciation, mispronouncement, misspeaking; cacology, cacoëpy.

VERBS **6. talk incoherently,** be unable to put two words together; have an impediment in one's speech, have a bone in one's neck or throat; **croak,** crow; **drawl,** drag; **lisp; shake, quaver;** mince, clip one's words.

7. stammer, stutter, hesitate, falter, halt; hammer [dial., Eng.], stumble; hem, haw, **hum or hem and haw.**

8. mumble, mutter, maunder, mouth; muffle, mump; jabber, gibber, gabble; splutter, sputter.

9. nasalize, nose, speak through one's nose, snuffle.

10. mispronounce, misspeak, missay, **murder the king's or queen's English.**

ADJS. **11.** (imperfectly spoken) **inarticulated,** inarticulate; **mispronounced,** cacoëpistic; **shaky,** shaking, **quavering,** tremulous, titubant; **drawling,** drawly, dragging; **lisping; throaty, guttural,** thick, velar; **nasal, twangy;** croaking, crowing; harsh, hoarse 457.11–15.

12. stammering, stuttering, halting, hesitating, faltering, stumbling.

594. TALKATIVENESS

NOUNS **1. talkativeness, loquacity,** loquaciousness, overtalkativeness, loose tongue; gabbiness, windiness, gassiness [all coll.]; **garrulousness,** garrulity; multiloquence, multiloquy; **volubility, fluency, glibness;** fluent tongue, **gift of gab** [coll.]; **effusiveness,** gushiness; effusion, gush, slush; flow of words, flux de bouche, ~ mots or paroles [F.].

2. logomania, logorrhea, cacoethes loquendi [L.], furor loquendi [L.].

3. chatter, chat, jabber, gibber, **babble,** babblement, prate, **prating, prattle,** palaver, gabble, gab [coll.], gaff [coll.], blab, blabber, blather, blether, clatter, clack, cackle, *caquet* [F.], *caqueterie* [F.], mag [coll.], *bavardage* [F.], twaddle, twattle, gibble-gabble, bibble-babble, chitter-chatter, prittle-prattle, tittle-tattle, mere talk, idle talk *or* chatter, "the hare-brained chatter of irresponsible frivolity" [Disraeli]; talky-talk, talky-talky, talkee-talkee [all coll.]; jaw, guff, gas, hot air, blah, blah-blah, yack, yackety-yack [all slang].

4. rigmarole, rigmarolery; amphigory, amphigouri.

5. chatterer, chatterbox, chatterbasket [dial.], chatterbag [dial.], babbler, jabberer, prater, prattler, gabbler, gibble-gabbler gabber [coll.], blabberer, blatherer, driveler, patterer, word-slinger [derog.], *moulin à paroles* [F., word mill]; blab, rattle, "agreeable rattle" [Goldsmith], blather, blatherskite [coll., U.S.]; mag [coll.], chattermag, magpie, jay; rattletrap, jaw-box, windbag, gasbag, windjammer, hot-air artist [all slang]; idle chatterer, talkative person, big *or* great talker [coll.], spendthrift of one's tongue.

VERBS 6. chatter, chat, prate, prattle, patter, palaver, babble, gabble, gibble-gabble, tittle-tattle, jabber, gibber, blab, blabber, blather, blether, blatter [chiefly dial.], clatter, twaddle, twattle, rattle, mag [coll.], clack, spout [coll.], spout off [coll.], pour forth, gush, talk to hear one's head rattle [coc.]; jaw, gas, yack, yackety-yack, run off at the mouth, shoot off one's mouth *or* face [all slang]; reel off; talk on, talk away, go on [coll.], run on, rattle on, ramble on, run on like a mill race; talk oneself hoarse, talk oneself out of breath; "varnish nonsense with the charms of sound" [C. Churchill].

7. talk one to death, talk one's head *or* ear off, talk one deaf and dumb, talk one into a fever, talk the hind leg off a mule.

8. outtalk, outspeak, talk down, outlast.

ADJS. 9. talkative, loquacious, talky, bablative, overtalkative, garrulous, chatty; gabby, windy, gassy [all coll.]; jawy [slang], gimbaljawed [slang, U.S.]; multiloquent, multiloquous; voluble, fluent; glib, flip [coll.]; effusive, expansive, gushy, slushy.

10. chattering, prattling, prating, gabbling, jabbering, gibbering, blabbing, blabbering, blathering.

ADVS. 11. talkatively, loquaciously, garrulously; volubly, fluently, glibly; effusively, gushingly.

595. CONVERSATION

NOUNS 1. conversation, *conversazione* [It.]; converse, conversing; interlocution, collocution, colloquy; communication, communion, commerce, intercourse, verbal intercourse, interchange of speech; discourse, colloquial discourse.

2. "a game of circles" [Emerson], "our account of ourselves" [ibid.]; "the sweeter banquet of the mind" [Pope], "the feast of reason and the flow of soul" [ibid.].

3. talk, palaver, speech, words, say [dial.]; confabulation, confab [coll.]; chinfest, talkfest, bull session [all slang]; dialogue, trialogue.

4. chat, friendly chat *or* talk, little talk, coze, causerie, collogue [dial.], visit [coll.]; tête-à-tête, heart-to-heart talk.

5. chitchat, chitter-chatter, tittle-tattle, bibble-babble, prittle-prattle, prattle, small talk.

6. conference, parley, palaver, confab [coll.], conclave, powwow [U.S.], huddle [slang], *pourparler* [F.], indaba [S. Africa], meeting, discussion 481.4, interchange of views; council, council of war; counsel, consultation, deliberation; interview, congress, audience, audition [coll.], hearing, reception; press conference; conference at the summit; council fire [North Am. Ind.].

7. conversationalist, converser, conversationist; talker, discourser, confabulator; collocutor, colloquist, colloquialist; interlocutor, interlocutress *or* interlocutrice *or* interlocutrix [fem.]; parleyer, palaverer; dialogist, dialoguer.

VERBS 8. converse, talk together, talk *or* speak with, converse with, visit with [coll., U.S.], discourse with, commune with, communicate with, commerce with, have a talk with, have a word with, bandy words, parley, palaver, chin [slang], chin-chin [pidgin Eng.], chew the rag [slang], shoot the breeze [slang], hold ~, carry on ~, join in *or* engage in a conversation; confabulate, confab [coll.]; colloque, colloquize; "inject a few raisins of conversation into the tasteless dough of existence" [O. Henry].

9. chat, visit [coll.], coze, have a friendly chat; have a little talk, have a heart-to-heart talk; talk with one in private, talk with tête-à-tête, be closeted with; make talk; prattle, prittle-prattle, tittle-tattle.

10. confer, hold conference, parley, palaver, counsel, powwow [U.S.], go into a

huddle [slang], **lay** or **put heads together;** collogue [coll.]; **confer with, consult with, advise with, discuss with, take up with,** reason with; discuss, talk over 481.16; **consult,** refer to, call in; **compare notes,** exchange observations or views.

ADJS. **11. conversational, colloquial,** confabulatory, interlocutory; **chatty,** chitchatty, cozy or cosy [Eng.]; tête-à-tête.

596. SOLILOQUY

NOUNS **1. soliloquy,** monology; **monologue;** apostrophe, aside.

2. soliloquist, soliloquizer; **monologist** or monologuist, monologian; Hamlet, Dr. Johnson.

VERBS **3. soliloquize,** monologize; **talk to oneself,** say to oneself, tell oneself, think out loud or aloud; address the four walls; apostrophize, say aside.

ADJS. **4. soliloquizing, monologic(al);** apostrophic.

597. ELOCUTION, PUBLIC SPEAKING

NOUNS **1. public speaking, declamation, speechmaking,** speaking, speeching, speechification [joc.]; **oratory, elocution, rhetoric;** eloquence 598; speechcraft, wordcraft; homiletics; demagogism, demagoguery; dramatics, **pyrotechnics,** sensationalism.

2. speech, speechification [joc.], speeching, **talk, discourse,** spiel [slang, U.S.], say; **oration,** elocution; **address,** public address; allocution, hortatory address; **recitation,** recital, reading; salutatory [U.S.], salutatory address; valediction, valedictory, valedictory address; inaugural address, inaugural [both U.S.]; smoke talk, chalk talk [both coll.]; pep talk [slang]; travelogue; talkathon; peroration.

3. lecture, prelection, **declamation, harangue, tirade,** screed, diatribe, exhortation; **sermon,** sermonet; preachment, preaching, preachification [coll.], preach [coll.], religious discourse.

4. speaker, talker, public speaker, speechmaker, speecher, speechifier [joc.], **spokesman,** spieler [slang, U.S.], jawsmith [slang, U.S.]; spokeswoman, speakeress [fem.]; **demagogue;** declaimer, ranter, haranguer, spouter [coll.]; panelist.

5. lecturer, prelector, discourser, reader; **preacher,** preacheress [fem.]; sermonizer, sermonist, sermoner; **expositor,** expounder; chalk talker [coll.].

6. orator, oratress or oratrix [fem.];

rhetorician, rhetor; silver-tongued orator, **spellbinder** [U.S.]; Demosthenes, Cicero, Winston Churchill, William Jennings Bryan; **soapbox orator,** soapboxer, stump orator.

7. elocutionist, elocutioner; **recitationist,** reciter, reader; improvisator, *improvisatore* [It.].

VERBS **8. make a speech, give a talk, deliver an address,** speechify [joc.], **speak, talk, discourse;** address; stump [coll., U.S.], go on or take the stump; platform, soapbox; take the floor.

9. declaim, hold forth, spout [coll.], spiel [slang, U.S.], mouth; **harangue, rant,** perorate, rodomontade; elocute [derog.], elocutionize; **recite,** read; **orate,** oration, oratorize [all coll.]; demagogue [coll., U.S.]; spellbind.

10. lecture, prelect, read or deliver a lecture; **preach,** preachify [coll.]; sermonize, read a sermon.

ADJS. **11. declamatory; elocutionary; oratorical, rhetorical;** eloquent 598.8; demagogic(al).

598. ELOQUENCE

NOUNS **1. eloquence, rhetoric, silver tongue, gift of gab** [coll.]; **oratory** 597.1; expression, **expressiveness,** vividness, graphicness; **meaningfulness** 543.6.

2. fluency, flow; smoothness, facility, ease; grace, gracefulness.

3. vigor, force, power, strength; vigorousness, forcefulness, effectiveness, impressiveness; strong language, "thoughts that breathe and words that burn" [Gray].

4. spirit, punch [slang], liveliness, raciness, sparkle; piquancy, poignancy, pungency.

5. vehemence, passion, verve, **ardor,** ardency, **fervor,** fervency, fire, glow, warmth.

6. loftiness, nobility, elevation, sublimity, grandeur, stateliness, majesty.

VERBS **7. have the gift of gab** [coll.], have a tongue in one's head; **scintillate,** shine, "pour the full tide of eloquence along" [Pope].

ADJS. **8. eloquent, silver-tongued,** silver; well-speaking, well-spoken; **rhetorical, oratorical;** Demosthenic, Demosthenian; Ciceronian, Tullian.

9. fluent, flowing, tripping; smooth, facile, easy, graceful.

10. expressive, graphic, vivid, suggestive, imaginative; **meaningful** 543.10.

11. vigorous, strong, powerful, force-ful, forcible, striking, telling, effective, impressive; sensational.

12. spirited, lively, racy, sparkling; nervous; picuant, poignant, pungent.

13. vehement, passionate, impassioned, ardent, fervent, burning, glowing, warm.

14. lofty, elevated, sublime, grand, majestic, stately; moving, inspiring.

ADVS. 15. eloquently, fluently, smoothly, trippingly on the tongue; expressively, vividly, graphicly; meaningfully 543.14; vigorously, powerfully, forcefully, spiritedly; tellingly, strikingly, effectively, impressively; vehemently, passionately, ardently, fervently, warmly, glowingly, in glowing terms.

599. GRANDILOQUENCE

NOUNS 1. grandiloquence, magniloquence, altiloquence; rhetoric, rhetorical-ness; high-flown diction, big or tall talk [coll.]; loftiness, grandiosity; pretentious-ness, pretension, affectation, ostentation; showiness, flashiness, Barnumism; infla-tion, turgidity, flatulence or flatulency, tumidness, tumidity; pompousness, pom-posity, stuffiness [coll.], orotundity; spread eagle, spread-eagleism [both coll., U.S.]; platitudinous ponderosity, polysyllabic pro-fundity, pompous prolixity; Johnsonese; prose run mad.

2. bombast, bombastry; fustian, high-falutin [coll.]; rant, rodomontade; bun-combe or bunkum [coll.], bunk [slang], hot air [slang], balderdash, gobbledegook [slang].

3. high-sounding words, lexiphanicism; sesquipedalianism, sesquipedalism; sesqui-pedalian word, sesquipedalism, big or long word, jawbreaker [slang], jawtwister, mouthful; antidisestablishmentarianism, honorificabilitudinitatibus [Shakespeare].

4. ornateness, floweriness, floridness, floridity; flowers of speech or rhetoric, pur-ple patches or passages, fine writing; orna-ment, ornamentation, adornment, embel-lishment, embroidery, frills; flourish, flour-ish of rhetoric.

5. phrasemonger, rhetorician.

VERBS 6. talk big [coll.], talk highfalutin [coll.], pontificate, bombast, bounce, blow [slang], vapor, inflate, Barnumize, lay or pile it on; buncomize, speak for Buncombe [U.S.].

7. smell of the lamp.

8. ornament, decorate, adorn, embel-lish, embroider, enrich; overcharge, over-load; flourish, flower; color, varnish, paint in glowing colors, tell in glowing terms; "to gild refined gold, to paint the lily, to throw a perfume on the violet" [Shake-speare].

ADJS. 9. grandiloquent, magniloquent, altiloquent; grandiose, grand, lofty, ele-vated, tall [coll.], stilted, imposing; osten-tatious, pretentious, affected; overdone, overwrought; showy, flashy, flaunting, garish; highflown, highfalutin or high-faluting [coll.], highflying, high-flowing, high-sounding, big-sounding, great-sound-ing, grandisonant, soncrous; rhetorical, pedantic, lexiphanic, sententious, Johnso-nian.

10. bombastic, pompous, stuffy [coll.], orotund, declamatory, fustian, mouthy, in-flated, swollen, swelling, turgid, tumid, flatulent; windy, gassy [both coll.].

11. sesquipedalian, sesquipedal; jawbreak-ing [slang], crackjaw.

12. ornate, elegant, rich, fancy, fan-ciful, figured; flowery, florid; figurative 549.4.

ADVS. 13. grandiloquently, grandiosely, grandly, loftily, imposingly; ostentatiously, pretentiously, affected, showily; bombasti-cally, pompously, stuffily [coll.], turgidly, tumidly, flatulently, windily [coll.].

14. ornately, elegantly, richly, fancily; flowerily, floridly.

600. WRITING

NOUNS 1. writing, script, scription; pen, pen and ink; quill driving [derog. or joc.]; inkslinging, ink spilling [slang], pen or pen-cil driving or pushing [all slang]; scriven-ing, scrivenery; typing [coll.], typewrit-ing; macrography, micrography; stroke or dash of the pen, coup de plume [F.].

2. authorship, writership, authorcraft, pencraft; literature; composition, prepara-tion, production, origination, inditement; artistry, literary power, ready pen; writer's itch, graphomania, scribblemania, ca-coëthes scribendi [L.].

3. inscription, inscript, engrossment, superscription, lettering; legend, motto, epigraph; dedication; epitaph.

4. handwriting, hand, fist [coll.]; chirography, calligraphy, autography; man-uscript, script, scrive [chiefly Scot.]; pen-manship, penscript, pencraft; graphology.

5. (style of handwriting) hand, fist

[coll.], pen; bold hand, round hand, slanting hand, perpendicular hand, letter hand, **longhand;** Spencerian writing, Italian writing; cursive, script; uncial, majuscule script.

6. (good writing) **calligraphy,** fine writing, elegant penmanship, **good hand,** good fist [coll.], copybook hand; calligraph, fine specimen.

7. (bad writing) **cacography, bad hand, poor fist** [coll.], cramped or crabbed hand; illegible handwriting, *griffonage* [F.].

8. **scribbling,** scribblement, scribblage; **scribble,** scrabble, scribble-scrabble, **scrawl, scratch, daub,** *barbouillage* [F.]; fly tracks, *pattes de mouche* [F., fly paws]; pothookery, pothooks, hangars, pothooks and hangers.

9. **stenography, speed writing,** brachygraphy, tachygraphy; **shorthand,** short writing; phonography, pasigraphy, polygraphy, logography, stenotypy; contraction.

10. (symbolic and ideographic writing) symbolography, symbolism, symbology; ideography, ideographics, ideoglyphics; acrophony; lexigraphy; **picture writing,** pictography; **hieroglyphics,** hieroglyphy, hieroglyphic writing; hieratic writing, demotic writing, hierography; **cuneiform;** ogam, ogham; **runes;** ideogram, pictograph, etc. 579.3.

11. (written matter) **writing, piece,** piece of writing, **copy, matter,** the written word; **composition, work, opus,** production, lucubration, brain child; **paper,** parchment, scroll; **document 568.4;** article **604.1; script,** scrip, scrive [chiefly Scot.]; **penscript, typescript; manuscript, MS., Ms., ms.;** flimsy; original, author's copy; potboiler.

12. (ancient manuscript) **codex;** palimpsest, *codex rescriptus* [L.]; papyrus; Rosetta stone.

13. **literature, letters, belles-lettres,** polite literature, republic of letters; **classics;** classicism, classicalism.

14. **writer, scribbler** [derog.], **penman,** pen, penner, pen or pencil driver or pusher [slang], **quill driver** [joc.], **inkslinger,** ink spiller [slang], knight of the plume, ~ pen or quill [joc.]; **scribe, scrivener, amanuensis, secretary,** recording secretary, **clerk,** baboo [India]; **copyist,** copier, transcriber; chirographer, calligrapher.

15. **author,** *littérateur* [F.], scribe [joc. or derog.], **composer,** inditer, adjective

jerker [slang], word painter, word-seller; **authoress,** writeress, penwoman; free lance [coll.]; ghostwriter, ghost; collaborator, coauthor; bookman, bookwright; magazinist; story writer, **short-story writer;** storyteller 606.10; **novelist,** novelettist; journalist 603.22; **annalist 606.11; poet 607.13; dramatist 609.41; essayist,** monographer, reviewer, pamphleteer; compiler, encyclopedist, bibliographer; best seller.

16. **hack writer,** hack, literary hack, grubstreet writer, **penny-a-liner,** creeper [slang], **scribbler, potboiler** [coll.].

17. **stenographer,** stenographist; **stenotypist; shorthander** [coll.]; brachygrapher, tachygrapher, phonographer, logographer.

18. **typist,** typer [coll.], typewriter.

VERBS 19. **write, pen, pencil,** drive or push the pen or pencil [slang]; stain or spoil paper, shed or spill ink [both joc.]; **scribe,** scrive [chiefly Scot.]; take pen in hand; **put in writing,** put in black and white; **write down, record 568.15;** shorthand, take down in shorthand; **typewrite, type** [coll.]; **transcribe,** copy, trace; manifold; **rewrite, revise.**

20. **scribble,** scrabble, scribble-scrabble, scratch, scrawl, daub; doodle.

21. **author, compose, indite,** formulate, produce, prepare, originate; dash off, knock off or out [coll.], throw on paper; free-lance; collaborate, coauthor; ghost, ghostwrite; novelize; scenarioize; pamphleteer; edit, editorialize.

22. **draw up, draft, write out, make out.**

23. **inscribe, engross,** inscroll, scribe; superscribe, scroll; enface; **dedicate,** address to.

ADJS. 24. **written, graphic,** penned, pencilled; inscribed, engrossed, inscrolled; **in writing, in black and white,** on paper; scriptural, scriptorial; manuscript, holograph, under one's hand; **longhand,** in longhand; italic, italicized; cursive, running, flowing; typewritten.

25. **scribbled,** scrabbled, **scratched,** scrawled; scribbly, scratchy, scrawly.

26. **literary, classical.**

27. ideographic(al), ideogrammic; runic; cuneiform; **hieroglyphic(al),** hieratic, demotic.

28. **stenographic(al),** tachygraphic(al); **shorthand,** in shorthand; phonographic(al), pasigraphic(al), polygraphic(al), logographic(al).

29. **clerical, secretarial.**

30. stationery, writing materials

ballpoint pen	pad
biblus, biblos	paper
blackboard	papyrus
China or Chinese	parchment
ink	pen
copying ink	pencil
copy or copying	plume
paper	printer's ink
demy	quill
flimsy	reed
foolscap	scratch pad
fountain pen	scroll
indelible ink	secret, invisible or
India or Indian	sympathetic ink
ink	slate
ink	snorkel pen
inkhorn	style
inkpot	stylograph,
inkstand	stylographic pen
inkwell	stylus
lambskin	table
(parchment)	tablet
lead pencil	vellum
letter paper	writing paper
note paper	

31. typewriters

addressing machine	stenograph
Addressograph	Stenotype
electric typewriter	teletype,
Flexowriter	teletypewriter
typewriter	ticker, stock ticker

601. PRINTING

NOUNS **1. printing, publishing,** publication; **typography,** type printing; autotypography, autotypy; chromotypography, chromotypy; chromoxylography; palaeotypography; phototypography, phototypy; stereotypography, stereotypy; xylotypography; engraving 576.6.

2. composing, composition, typesetting, presswork; sheetwork; imposition; justification.

3. print, imprint, stamp, impression, impress, letterpress; reprint, reissue; mackle, macule; offprint; offcut; offset, setoff.

4. copy, manuscript, typescript; **matter,** printed matter, type matter; live matter, dead matter, standing matter; reading matter, advertising matter; text, context; dummy.

5. proof, proof sheet, pull, slip, trial impression; galley, galley proof; page proof, foundry proof, plate proof, press proof, author's proof; revise, press revise; advance sheets.

6. type, print, stamp, letter; lowercase, minuscule; upper case, majuscule; capital, cap [coll.]; ligature, tie; bastard

type, bottle-assed type, fat-faced type; **pie** or **pi;** font, fount [Eng.].

7. space, patent space, justifying space; bar, slug; quadrat, quad; em quad, em; en quad, en; 3-em, thick space; 4-em, 5-em, thin space; 6-em, hair space.

8. press, printer, printing press or **machine; print shop, publishing house,** printery, printers, publishers.

9. pressroom, composing room, city room, local room, make-up room, proofroom; filing room, library, morgue [slang]; city desk, copy desk.

10. printer, pressman; compositor, typesetter; typographer; proofer; devil, **printer's devil;** stereotypist, stereotyper; linotypist, linotyper; electrotyper; job printer.

11. proofreader, reader; **copyreader,** copyholder.

VERBS **12. print, imprint, impress, stamp,** enstamp; engrave 576.12; run, run off, strike off; **publish, issue, bring out, put out, get out;** put to press, put to bed [cant], see through the press; prove, make a proof, pull; reprint, reissue.

13. autotype, electrotype, linotype, monotype, palaeotype, stereotype; mimeograph, multigraph, pantograph, hectograph.

14. compose, set, set in print, **set up,** stick [cant], **make up;** impose; justify, overrun; pie or pi, pie a form.

15. proofread, proof-correct, read, read or correct copy.

16. (be printed) go to press; come out, appear in print.

ADJS. **17. printed, in print;** typeset.

18. typographic(al), autotypic, stereotypic(al), palaeotypographic(al); chromotypic, chromotypographic; phototypic, phototypographic; **boldface, bold-faced,** blackface, black-faced, full-faced; **lightface,** light-faced; **upper-case, lower-case.**

19. types or printing processes

albertype	Monotype
electrotype	stenotype
Linotype	stereotype
lithotype	zincotype
logotype	

20. type sizes, point system

3-point, excelsior	6-point, nonpareil
3½-point, brilliant	7-point, minion
4-point, gem	8-point, brevier
4½-point,	9-point, bourgeois
diamond	10-point, elite or
5-point, pearl	long primer
5½-point, agate,	11-point, small
ruby	pica

12-point, pica
14-point, English
16-point,
  Columbian

18-point, great
  primer
48-point, cannon

21. type styles

antique	fullface
blackface	German text
black letter	Gothic
boldface, bold	Ionic
Caslon	italic
Caslon-old style	lightface
chapel text	modern
clarendon	normal
condensed	Old English
cursive	old style
Elzevir	roman
extended	sans serif
extraboldface,	script
extrabold	standard
extra-condensed	typescript
French	typewriter

22. presses

copying press	platen press
cylinder press	proof press
electrotype press	rotary press
letterpress	web press
perfecting press *or*	
machine	

23. copying machines

duplicator	Multigraph
hectograph	pantograph
mimeograph	

24. equipment

bank	gripper
bearer	guide
bed	gutter
bevel	letter foundry
blanket	matrix
boss	measure
boxes	overlay
brayer	platen
burr	quoin
case	ratchet
chase	reglet
composing frame	rounce
composing rule	slur
composing stand	stick, composing
footstick	stick
form	turtle
frame	tympan
frisket	type foundry
galley	type mold
gauge, page gauge	underlay

602. CORRESPONDENCE

NOUNS **1. correspondence, letter writing,** written communication, epistolary intercourse.

2. epistle, letter, message, communication, dispatch, missive, billet; note, line, chit *or* chitty [India]; **reply, answer, acknowledgment,** rescript, favor.

3. air letter; drop letter; fan letter; poison-pen letter; open letter; form letter [U.S.]; circular, circular letter, encyclical, encyclical letter, round robin; bulletin; bull, apostolic *or* papal brief; monitory, monitory letter; pastoral, pastoral epistle; letter of credence, letter credential; letter of credit, letter of delegation, letter of license, letter of indication [all com.]; dead letter.

4. card, post card, postal card, postal [coll., U.S.], letter card [Eng.]; picture post card.

5. mail, post, letters, correspondence, mailbag [fig.]; air mail; **parcel post,** parcels post, P.P.; letter post, printed paper *or* half-penny post, newspaper post, book post [all Eng.]; first-class $\sim$, second-class $\sim$, third-class *or* fourth-class mail; pigeon post, *Taubenpost* [G.]; rural free delivery [U.S.], R.F.D.; **special delivery,** express [Eng.]; registered mail; frank; fan mail; mailbag, letter bag; post day [Eng.].

6. postage; stamp, postage stamp; postmark.

7. mailbox, postbox, letter box; post-office box; drop, letter drop.

8. post office, P.O., post [Eng.].

9. correspondent, writer, **letter writer,** communicator; contributor; pen pal [slang]; addressee.

10. address, name and address, **direction, destination, inscription,** superscription; letterhead, billhead; **salutation, greeting.**

VERBS **11. correspond,** correspond with, **communicate with, write to,** write a letter, send a letter to; send a note, **drop a line** [coll.]; postcard; circularize; keep up a correspondence.

12. reply, answer, acknowledge; reply by return mail; please reply, R.S.V.P. (*répondez s'il vous plaît* [F.]).

13. mail, post, dispatch, send; airmail.

14. address, direct, assign, **inscribe,** superscribe; **greet, salute.**

ADJS. **15. epistolary,** epistolatory; **post, postal, mail.**

16. addresses, salutations

Dear —	Most Reverend Sir
Dear Dr. —	[church dignitary]
Dear Madam	My dear —
Dear Mr. —	My dear Madam
Dear Mrs. —	My dear Mr. —
Dear Sir	My dear Mrs. —
Gentlemen	My dear Reverend
Madam	— [clergyman]
May it please your	My Dear Sir
Majesty *or* Royal	My Lady
Highness [royalty]	[noblewoman]

My Lord
[nobleman]
Reverend —
[clergyman]
Reverend Sir
[clergyman]
Right Reverend
Sir [church
dignitary]
Sir
Venerable Sir
[church
dignitary]
Your Eminence
[dignitary]

Your Excellency
[nobleman]
Your Grace
[dignitary]
Your Ladyship
[noblewoman]
Your Lordship
[nobleman]
Your Majesty
[royalty]
Your Royal
Highness
[royalty]

17. conclusions, complimentary closes

affectionately
always
best wishes
cordially
cordially yours
ever
ever yours
faithfully
faithfully yours
lovingly
most sincerely
respectfully
respectfully yours
sincerely

sincerely yours
with all good
wishes
with all my love
with love
yours
yours affectionately
yours faithfully
yours in Christ
yours most
sincerely
yours respectfully
yours sincerely
yours truly

603. BOOK, PERIODICAL

NOUNS **1. book**, volume, tome, publication, writing, work, opus, production; opuscle opuscule; magnum opus, great work; folio; paperback, soft-cover, limpcover, hard-cover [all coll.]; playbook 609.25; songbook 461.28; notebook 568.10; storybook, novel; best seller [U.S.]; literature (printed matter of any kind [coll.]).

2. edition, issue, number, copy; printing, print, imprint, impression; library edition; back number.

3. rare book, early edition; first edition; Elzevir, Elzevir book or edition; Aldus, Aldine, Aldine book or edition; codex; incunabulum (book printed before 1500 A.D.), cradle book, Fifteener.

4. compilation, omnibus, ana, symposium; collection, collectanea, collectarium [eccl.]; miscellany, miscellanea, analecta; anthology, garland; delectus; quotation book; album, photograph album.

5. handbook, manual, enchiridion, vade mecum; copybook; cookbook; guidebook 746.9.

6. reference book, work of reference; encyclopedia, cyclopedia; concordance; catalogue, calendar, index; classified catalogue, catalogue raisonné [F.]; directory, city directory; telephone book, phone book [coll.]; bibliography.

7. dictionary, wordbook, lexicon, vocabulary; glossary, gloss; polyglot; onomasticon; dialect dictionary, idioticon; thesaurus, storehouse or treasury of words; gradus, rhyming dictionary; atlas; gazetteer, geographical dictionary.

8. textbook, text, schoolbook, manual, manual of instruction; primer, abecedarium; hornbook, battledore [both hist.]; grammar, reader; spelling book, speller [U.S.]; Lindley Murray, Cocker, McGuffey's Reader, New England Primer.

9. (manuals) algebra, anatomy, arithmetic, biology, geography, geology, geometry, history, logic, philosophy, psychology, physics, rhetoric, zoology.

10. booklet, pamphlet, brochure, chapbook, leaflet, folder, tract; circular 557.8; pocketbook; comic book [U.S.].

11. journal, gazette, periodical, serial, ephemeris; magazine; pulp, slick [both slang, U.S.]; pictorial; review; organ, house organ; bulletin; daily, weekly, biweekly, bimonthly, fortnightly, monthly, quarterly; annual, yearbook; daybook, diary 568.10.

12. newspaper, news, paper, sheet [slang], gazette; tabloid, tab [cant]; rotogravure [U.S.], rotograph; extra [U.S.], special.

13. make-up; page, leaf, folio; flyleaf; recto, verso or reverso; type page; title, title page, bastard title, binder's title, subtitle; imprint, printer's imprint; catchword, catch line; signature; dedication, inscription; text; index, contents, table of contents, table; errata.

14. part, section, division; book, volume, number; article; serial, livraison [F.]; fascicle, fasciculous; passage, phrase, clause, verse, paragraph, chapter, column.

15. (sizes) quarto, 4vo; octavo, 8vo; cap 8vo, crown 8vo, demy 8vo, foolscap 8vo, imperial 8vo, medium 8vo, post 8vo, pott 8vo, royal 8vo; duodecimo, twelvemo, 12mo; sextodecimo, sixteenmo, 16mo; octodecimo, eighteenmo, 18mo.

16. bookbinding, bibliopegy; binder, binding; cover, book cover; case, bookcase; slip case; jacket, book jacket, dust jacket [U.S.], slip cover; library binding; book cloth; bookboard, binder's board.

17. (bookbinding styles) Aldine, Arabesque, Byzantine, Etruscan, Fanfare, Grolier, Harleian, Jansenist, Maioli or Majoli, Roxburgh.

18. library, bookroom, bookery, bibliothèque [F.], bibliothec, bibliotheca, athenaeum; **public library, circulating library, lending library; rental library; book club; book wagon, bookmobile;** Bibliothèque Nationale, Bodleian Library, British Museum, Deutsche Bücherei, Library of Congress, Vatican Library; American Library Association, A.L.A.

19. **bookstore, bookshop,** *librairie* [F.], bookseller's; **bookstall,** bookstand.

20. **bookholder, bookrest,** book support, **book end; bookcase,** bookrack, bookstand, bookshelf; stack, bookstack; book table, book tray, book truck; folder; folio, **portfolio.**

21. **bookman,** bibliologist, bibliographer; **bookmaker,** bookwright; **publisher,** book publisher; **printer,** book printer; **bookbinder,** bibliopegist; bookstitcher; book-folder; **bookdealer, bookseller,** book agent; bibliopole, bibliopolist; book collector; **librarian,** bibliothec, bibliothecary, *bibliothécaire* [F.]; curator; bibliognost, bibliosoph.

22. **journalist, newspaperman, newsman, pressman** [cant, chiefly Eng.], news writer, **gazetteer,** gentleman *or* representative of the press; **reporter, leg man** [slang], interviewer; **cub reporter** [U.S.]; newspaperwoman, reporteress; **correspondent, foreign correspondent,** war correspondent, special correspondent, own correspondent; publicist; rewriter, **rewrite man** [U.S.]; reviser, diaskeuast; **editor,** subeditor, news editor; **copy editor** [U.S.], copyman, copy chief; reader, **copyreader;** editorial writer, leader writer [Eng.]; **columnist,** paragrapher, paragraphist.

23. **the press,** public press, **fourth estate;** Fleet Street [Eng.]; **journalism;** Associated Press, AP; United Press International, UPI.

24. **bibliology,** bibliography; bookcraft, bookmaking; bookselling, bibliopolism.

ADJS. 25. **bibliological,** bibliographic(al); bibliothecal, bibliothecary; bibliopolic; bibliopegic.

26. **journalistic,** journalese [coll.]; **periodical,** serial; magazinish, magaziny; newspaperish, newspapery; **editorial; reportorial.**

604. TREATISE

NOUNS 1. **treatise, article, paper,** piece, **essay,** treatment, tractate; **dissertation, discourse, discussion,** disquisition, descant, exposition, memoir, homily, screed; excursus; **study,** lucubration, étude; **thesis,** theme; sketch, monograph, *morceau* [F.],

paragraph, causerie; personal [coll., U.S.]; feature, special article.

2. **commentary, commentation; comment, remark; criticism,** critique; analysis; **review,** report, notice, **write-up** [coll.]; **editorial,** leading article, leader [chiefly Eng.]; gloss, running commentary.

3. **dissertator, discourser,** discurser, descanter, disquisitor, expositor; **essayist;** monographer.

4. **commentator,** commenter; expositor, expounder; annotator, scholiast; glossarist, glossographer; **critic,** art critic; **reviewer,** book reviewer; **editor,** leader writer; news analyst; publicist.

VERBS 5. **write upon,** touch upon, discuss, **treat of, deal with,** take up, handle, go into, canvass, ventilate; discourse, dissertate, descant; **comment upon,** remark upon; **criticize, review, write up.**

ADJS. 6. **dissertational, disquisitional;** discursive, discoursive; expository, expositorial; commentarial, commentatorial; critical.

605. COMPENDIUM

NOUNS 1. **compendium,** compend, **abridgment,** *abrégé* [F.], **condensation,** abbreviation, abbreviature, **brief, digest,** pandect, **abstract,** epitome, précis, **capsule, sketch, synopsis,** conspectus, syllabus, *aperçu* [F.]; survey, analysis; **outline,** skeleton, draft; topical outline; outlines, contents, heads.

2. **summary, résumé, review, capitulation, recapitulation;** rundown, runthrough; sum, substance, sum and substance.

3. **excerpt, extract, selection,** extraction, excerption; passage, selected passage.

4. **excerpts,** *excerpta* [L.], **extracts, gleanings,** cuttings, clippings, fragments, flowers, fugitive pieces *or* writings; ana, analects, analecta; **miscellany,** miscellanea; **collection,** collectanea.

VERBS 5. **abridge** 202.6; **summarize, brief, outline,** hit the high spots; capsule, capsulize; nutshell, **put it in a nutshell;** synopsize.

ADJS. 6. compendious, brief 202.8.

ADVS. 7. in brief, in a nutshell 590.6.

606. DESCRIPTION

NOUNS 1. **description, portrayal, portraiture, depiction, delineation, representation;** imagery, imagism; **word painting** *or* **picture, picture, portrait, image,** photograph, painting; **sketch,** pastel, vignette, monograph; **characterization,** character, character sketch; vivid description, graphic account.

2. narration, narrative, relation, recital, rehearsal, telling, retelling, recounting, recountal, review; **storytelling,** taletelling, yarn spinning.

3. account, statement, report, word; rendition, rendering.

4. chronicle, record; history, annals; ancient ~, medieval or modern history; **biography, memoir,** memorial, life, story, life story, adventures, fortunes, experiences; **autobiography, memoirs,** memorials, memorabilia; **journal, diary,** letters, confessions; **profile,** biograph, **biographical sketch;** obituary, necrology; photobiography; historiography, chronography; Clio (historic Muse).

5. (history) "a set of lies agreed upon" [Napoleon], "the unrolled scroll of prophesy" [James A. Garfield], "the chart and compass for national endeavor" [Sir Arthur Helps], "a voice forever sounding across the centuries the laws of right and wrong" [Froude], "a cyclic poem written by Time upon the memories of man" [Shelley], "the crystallisation of popular belief" [Don Piatt], "philosophy learned from examples" [Dionysius of Halicarnassus], "history is bunk" [Henry Ford], "history is merely gossip" [Oscar Wilde].

6. story, tale, yarn, account, narrative, narration, chronicle; **anecdote,** anecdotage; **epic, saga.**

7. fiction, work of fiction; **fairy tale,** *Märchen* [G.]; **legend, myth, fantasy,** folk tale or story; **fable,** *fabliau* [F.], **parable, allegory,** apologue; **romance,** gest, love story; bedtime story; nursery tale; Canterbury tale; adventure story, thriller [coll.], shocker [slang, Eng.]; detective story or yarn, "grue" [Stevenson]; ghost story; western story, western, westerner; science fiction, space fiction, space opera [radio & T.V.].

8. (fictional forms) **short story,** storiette; short-short; **novel;** novelette, novelet, *nouvelle* [F.], *novella* [It.], *novela* [Sp.]; **dime novel,** dreadful, penny dreadful, shilling shocker [slang, Eng.]; stream-of-consciousness novel.

9. (story elements) **plot,** subject, topic, plan, scheme, design, story line, continuity [motion pictures]; **action,** movement, incident; **complication;** device, contrivance,

gimmick [slang]; angle, slant, twist [all coll.]; **characterization; atmosphere,** mood, background; color, **local color.**

10. narrator, relator or relater, reciter, recounter, *raconteur* [F.]; **anecdotist; storyteller,** storier, taleteller, teller of tales, spinner of yarns, yarn spinner, word painter; story writer, short-story writer; **novelist,** novelettist; **fictionist,** fictioner; fabulist, fableist, fabler; storymaker, mythmaker; romancer, romancist; sagaman.

11. chronicler, chronographer, **annalist; historian,** historiographer; **biographer,** biographist, memorialist; Boswell; autobiographer, autobiographist.

VERBS **12. describe, portray, picture, depict, represent, delineate, paint,** draw, outline, set forth; **characterize,** character; analyze; **express,** give words to.

13. narrate, tell, relate, recount, render, report, **recite, rehearse,** review, retell, give an account of; tell a story, unfold a tale; storify, fictionize, romance; **novelize.**

14. chronicle, record; historify, historize; biographize.

ADJS. **15. descriptive, depictive,** expositive, **representative, delineative,** delineatory; **expressive, suggestive, vivid, graphic,** well-drawn; realistic, true to life, lifelike.

16. narrative, narrational; storytelling, story-writing; storied, storified; **anecdotal,** anecdotic(al); epic(al); Homeric.

17. fictional, fictionized; **mythical, legendary, fabulous;** parabolic(al), allegorical; **romantic, idealistic.**

18. historic(al), historiographic(al); **chronologic(al),** chronographic(al); **traditional, legendary;** biographic(al), autobiographic(al).

ADVS. **19. descriptively,** representatively; **expressively, suggestively, vividly, graphicly.**

607. POETRY

NOUNS **1. poetry, poesy,** poetics, **verse, song, rhyme** or rime; "musical thought" [Carlyle], "the harmonious unison of man with nature" [ibid.], "emotion recollected in tranquillity" [Wordsworth], "the rhythmical creation of beauty" [Poe], "the language of the gods" [S. Rogers], "painting with the gift of speech" [Simonides], "the exquisite expression of exquisite impressions" [Joseph Roux], "the poet's innermost feeling issuing in rhythmic language" [John Keble], "the record of the best and happiest moments of the happiest and best minds" [Shelley], "what Milton saw when he went blind" [Don Marquis], "the journal of a sea animal living on land, wanting to fly in the air" [Carl Sandburg], "the achievement of the synthesis of hyacinths and biscuits" [ibid.], "a product of the smaller intestines" [Dr. Cabanis].

2. (poetic forms) blank verse; free verse, vers libre; runic verse, runes; epic poetry or verse, epopee, epopoeia; elegiac poetry or verse, elegiac or elegiacs; satirical poetry, satire; heroic verse, mock-heroic verse; light verse, society verse, vers de societé [F.]; lyric poetry, ballad poetry, narrative poetry, alliterative poetry.

3. doggerel, crambo clink or jingle [Scot.], Hudibrastic verse; nonsense verse, amphigory, amphigouri; macaronics, macaronic verse; lame verses, limping meters, halting rhyme.

4. poem, verse, rhyme or rime, song, lay; verselet, versicle; jingle; amoebaeum, Anacreontic, ballad, ballade, eclogue, epode, cento, elegy, epigram, gazel, idyl or idyll, lyric, madrigal, metrical romance, monody, nursery rhyme, ode, palinode, limerick, narrative poem, rhapsody, satire, sestina, sonnet, triolet, virelay; epic, epos, epopee, epopoeia; pastoral, bucolic, georgic; rondeau, rondel, roundel, roundelay; dithyramb, dithyrambus.

5. (verse forms) monostich; couplet, distich; triplet, tercet, tristich; quatrain, tetrastich; pentastich, hexastich, heptastich, octastich; octave, ottava rima [It.]; sextet or sextette, sestet; dimeter, dipody; trimeter, tripody; tetrameter, tetrapody; pentameter, pentapody; hexameter, hexapody; heptameter, heptapody; Alexandrine; elegiac, elegiac couplet or distich, elegiac pentameter; heroic couplet; anapaest; iambic.

6. book of verse, anthology, garland; miscellany, "scattered remains of a poet" [Horace]; poetic works, poesy.

7. versification, poetization, prosody; poetics, poeticism; poetcraft, versecraft, versemaking; rhyming, rhymery or rimery [derog.]; versemongering, versemongery; poetastering, poetastery, poetastry, poetasterism; scansion, scanning; poetic license.

8. metrical pattern, verse form, meter, measure, verse, versification.

9. meter, measure, numbers; rhythm, cadence, movement, lilt, swing; accent, accentuation, metrical accent, stress, em-

phasis, ictus, beat; arsis, thesis; mora; measure, metrical unit; foot, metrical foot; iamb, iambus, iambic; trochee, spondee, anapaest, dactyl, triseme, tetraseme, antispast; caesura, diaeresis; catalexis.

10. rhyme or rime, jingle, clink, crambo [derog.]; alliteration, assonance; eye rhyme, masculine or feminine rhyme, perfect or imperfect rhyme, initial rhyme, end or tail rhyme, rhyme royal, bout-rimé [F.]; rhyme scheme; rhyming dictionary.

11. (poetic divisions) measure, strain; syllable; line; verse, monostich; stanza, stave, strophe; antistrophe; anacrusis; canto, book; refrain, chorus, burden, envoy, l'envoi [F.].

12. muse; tuneful Nine, the Nine, Pierides [all Gr. myth]; Apollo, Apollo Musagetes, Calliope, Helicon, Parnassus [all Gr. myth.]; Bragi [Norse myth.]; poetic genius, poesy [poetic], creative imagination 533.2, inspiration 466.8, fire of genius, coal from off the altar; Pierian spring.

13. poet, poetess [fem.], bard, minstrel [poetic], muse, Parnassian, scop [hist.], songsmith, composer, creator; "the painter of the soul" [D'Israeli], "a nightingale who sits in darkness and sings to cheer its own solitude with sweet sounds" [Shelley], "all who love, who feel great truths, and tell them" [P. J. Bailey]; rhymester or rimester, rhymer or rimer; versemaker, versesmith, versifier, verseman; versemonger, versifiaster; poetling, poetaster, poeticule, poetizer; ballad maker, ballader, balladmonger.

14. bard, minstrel, jongleur; troubadour, trovatore [It.], trouveur, trouvère, runer [Gothic], runesmith; Meistersinger, Minnesänger [both G.], minnesinger; improvisator, improvvisatore [It.], improvvisatrice [It., fem.].

15. (poets) minor poet, major poet; laureate, poet laureate; epic poet, epopoeist; pastoral poet, bucolic, bucoliast; rhapsodist, rhapsode [Gr. antiq.]; vers librist, vers libriste [F.]; dithyrambic, elegiast, idyllist, imagist, librettist, lyrist, odist, palinodist, satirist, scald, sonneteer.

16. poet-artist, poet-dramatist, poet-farmer, poet-historian, poet-humorist, poet-king, poet-musician, poet-novelist, poet-painter, poet-patriot, poet-pilgrim, poet-playwright, poet-priest, poet-saint, poet-satirist, poet-seer, poet-thinker, poet-warrior.

17. Bard of Avon, Shakespeare; Bard of Rydal Mount, Wordsworth; Bard of Ayrshire, Burns; Poets' Poet, Spenser.

18. poethood, poetship; poet-laureateship.

VERBS **19.** **poetize,** poeticize, poesy, **versify,** write or compose poetry, build the stately rime, sing deathless songs, make immortal verse, sing, "lisp in numbers" [Pope]; jingle; elegaize.

20. **rhyme** or rime, **assonate, alliterate,** go together; **scan,** cap verses or rhymes.

ADJS. **21.** **poetic(al), lyric(al), tuneful;** poetlike, poetwise; poetastric(al) [derog.]; dramatic, lyrico-dramatic; epic, epopoean, lyrico-epic; heroic; mock-heroic, Hudibrastic; pastoral, bucolic; amoebaeic, elegiac(al), dithyrambic, georgic, idyllic, rhapsodic(al), runic, scaldic; Alcaic, Anacreontic, Homeric, Ionic, Leonine, Melibean, Pierian, Pindaric, Sapphic; poetico-mythological, poetico-mystical, poetico-philosophic.

22. **metric(al), rhythmic(al), measured;** iambic, dactylic, spondaic, trochaic, anapaestic, antispastic.

23. **rhyming** or riming, rhymic or rimic; **assonant,** assonantal; **alliterative.**

ADVS. **24.** **poetically, lyrically, tunefully; metrically, rhythmically,** in measure.

608. PROSE

NOUNS **1.** **prose,** "words in their best order" [Coleridge]; **nonfiction;** poetic prose.

2. **prosaism, prosaicism; prosaicness, unpoeticalness; matter-of-factness,** unromanticism, unidealism, unsentimentality; **unimaginativeness** 534; **plainness,** commonness, commonplaceness, unembellishment; insipidness, flatness, vapidity; **dullness** 881.

VERBS **3.** **prose,** write prose or in prose.

ADJS. **4.** **prose,** in prose; **nonfiction,** nonfictional.

5. **prosaic,** prosy, prosing; **unpoetic(al),** nonpoetic, poetryless; rhymeless or rimeless, unrhymed or unrimed; **plain, common,** commonplace, **ordinary,** unembellished; **matter-of-fact,** unromantic, **unidealistic,** unsentimental, unimpassioned; **unimaginative** 534.5; insipid, vapid, flat; dull 881.6.

609. DRAMA

NOUNS **1.** **drama, the drama, the stage, the theater, the footlights, the boards;** "what literature does at night" [George Jean Nathan]; **show business;** stagedom, stageland, playland, land of make-believe; stardom; theatromania, theatrophobia.

2. **dramatics,** dramaturgy, dramaticism, dramatism; **theatrics,** theatricism, **theatricalism,** theatricals; **histrionics,** histrionicism, histrionism, dramatic ∼, histrionic or Thespian art; **melodramatics,** melodramatism, sensationalism.

3. **theatercraft, stagecraft,** stagery, scenecraft; **showmanship;** choreography.

4. **play,** stage play, piece, vehicle; **drama,** dramatic play; playlet; legitimate drama, legitimate stage, legit [slang, U.S.]; **melodrama,** mélodrame [F.], melodram, sensation drama, cliff hanger [slang]; sociodrama, psychodrama; **pageant,** spectacle, extravaganza, drama de tramoya; mystery; miracle play, miracle; morality play, morality; Passion play; pastoral; mask, masque; pantomime, dumb show; charade, proverb, proverbe [F.]; tableau, tableau vivant [F.]; dramalogue; monologue, monodrama, monodram; duologue, dialogue; triologue; **vaudeville;** review, revue, musical review; music drama, opera, ballet 461.35.

5. **tragedy,** tragédie [F.], tragic drama; tragedietta; buskin, cothurnus.

6. **comedy,** comédie [F.], comedia [Sp.]; comedy drama; tragicomedy, drame [F.]; sentimental comedy, comédie larmoyante [F.]; light comedy, comedietta; high comedy, genteel comedy, comedy of manners; comedy of character; low comedy, broad or raw comedy, comédie rosse [F.]; **slapstick,** slapstick comedy; **farce,** farce comedy, exode [Rom. antiq.]; **travesty,** travesti [F.]; **burlesque,** burletta; harlequinade, arlequinade [F.]; masked comedy; musical comedy; comedy ballet; comic opera, opera buffa [It.], comedie bouffe [F.]; comic relief.

7. (comedy: symbols) sock, coxcomb, cap and bells, motley.

8. **act, scene, number, turn,** stanza [slang]; coup de théâtre [F.]; **curtain raiser** or lifter, lever de rideau [F.]; introduction; expository, expository scene; **prologue,** epilogue; **entr'acte,** intermezzo, intermission, interlude, divertissement [F.]; **finale,** stet finale [cant]; afterpiece; exodus, exode, exodos; chaser [slang]; curtain call, curtain; hokum or hoke act [slang]; blackface act, black-and-tan [slang]; song and dance; strip tease [U.S.]; sketch, skit.

9. acting, playing, play-acting [coll.], performing, **performance,** playwork; **representation,** portrayal, **characterization; impersonation,** personation; mummery; ham or hammy acting [slang]; **business,** stage business, *jeu de théâtre* [F.], acting device, **bag of tricks; stunt, gag** [both coll.]; hokum, hoke [both slang]; buffoonery, slapstick; patter.

10. repertoire, repertory; stock [cant].

11. role, part, piece, cue, **lines, cast; character,** person, personage; lead, title role; bit, minor role; feeder, straight part [cant]; walking part, walk-on, walk-through; relief, comic relief; heavy [cant].

12. engagement, playing engagement; **stand,** one-night stand [cant]; **circuit,** borsch or borscht circuit.

13. theatrical performance, **performance, show,** pitch [slang, U.S.], **presentation,** presentment, **production, entertainment,** bill [U.S.], stage presentation or performance; **exhibit, exhibition;** variety performance, variety; benefit performance, benefit; personal appearance, flesh show [slang, U.S.]; rehearsal, dress rehearsal; première, premier performance; debut, bow; farewell performance, swan song, tenor's farewell [joc.].

14. (shows) **repertory show,** rep show [slang]; **floor show** [U.S.]; **chorus show,** leg show [slang]; hootchy-kootchy show, cooch or coochie show [slang]; **minstrel show,** minstrel; **rodeo** [U.S.]; **circus,** the big top, **carnival, side show; puppet show,** fantoccini, Punch-and-Judy show; peep show, raree show; galanty show, shadow show, *ombres chinoises* [F.].

15. motion picture, moving picture, movie [coll.], **picture, picture show** [U.S.], **motion-picture show, moving-picture show, movie show** [coll.], **film,** flicker [slang], flick [slang, Eng.], **cinema** [chiefly Eng.], **photoplay,** photodrama; **talkie** [coll.], talking picture, talk or talking film [coll.]; feature; preview, trailer; documentary film; educational film; newsreel; cinemelodrama; western, horse opera [slang]; horror picture, creepie [slang]; animated cartoon; 3–D, Cinemascope, Cinerama; Technicolor.

16. the cinema, the movies [coll.], **the films** [coll.], **the pictures** [coll.], **the screen,** the silver screen.

17. theater, theatre [chiefly Eng.], **playhouse,** house, theatron [Gr. antiq.], odeum; **opera house,** opera; **hall,** music hall, concert hall; **amphitheater, hippodrome, coliseum,** Colosseum, **stadium, bowl;** circle theater, arena theater, theater-in-the-round; legitimate theater, legit [slang, U.S.]; repertory theater; vaudeville theater; burlesque theater; **little theater,** community theater; Greek theater; **circus,** big top; showboat.

18. motion-picture theater, moving-picture theater, movie theater [coll.], movie show [coll.], picture show [U.S.], picture house [coll.], **cinema** [chiefly Eng.], cinema theater [Eng.], cinematograph or kinematograph [chiefly Eng.]; drive-in; nickelodeon [U.S.].

19. auditorium, house, front [cant]; bald-headed row [slang]; parquet, orchestra [U.S.]; **pit** [chiefly Eng.]; circle; **orchestra circle,** parquet circle, parterre; **dress circle,** horseshoe or diamond horseshoe [slang]; **stall** [chiefly Eng.], pit stall; **box,** box seat, **loge,** *baignoire* [F.]; stage boxes, proscenium boxes, parterre boxes; balcony, gallery; **peanut gallery,** nigger heaven, paradise [all slang].

20. stage, the boards; **platform 215.13;** proscenium; revolving stage; dead stage, live stage [both cant]; orchestra, orchestra pit; **bandstand,** bandwagon [U.S.]; right stage, R.; left stage, L.; down left, D.L.; down right, D.R.; up left, U.L.; up right, U.R.; wings, coulisse; dressing rooms, greenroom; flies, loft; gridiron; grid [coll.]; dock.

21. (stage requisites) **properties, props** [cant]; breakaway [cant]; practicable, practical, practical piece or prop [all cant]; costume **230.9;** make-up, grease paint, blackface, clown white.

22. lights; **footlights, foots** [slang], floats; **limelight, spotlight, spot** [slang]; marquee.

23. stage setting, stage-set, set, *mise en scène* [F.].

24. scenery, décor; **scene; screen, flat;** side scene, **wing,** coulisse, border; **tormentor,** tormentor wing; **teaser,** teaser curtain; **wingcut,** woodcut; **transformation,** transformation scene; flipper; **curtain,** cloth, rag [slang], hanging; **drop,** drop scene, drop curtain; **backdrop,** back cloth, back scene; **oleo** [cant], act drop or curtain; tab; fire curtain, asbestos.

25. playbook, promptbook, **script,** dialogue, text; **libretto, score,** opera; scenario, continuity; plot, scene plot; lines, actor's lines, side [slang].

26. **dramatist,** dramatizer; **playwright,** playwrightess [fem.], stagewright, **playwriter;** dramaturgist, dramaturge [F.]; **scriptwriter, scenario writer,** scenarist, scenarist, **screenwriter,** photoplaywright; **gagman; librettist;** tragedian, comedian; farcist, *farceur* [F.], *farceuse* [F., fem.], farcer; melodramatist; monodramatist; mimographer; **choreographer.**

27. **theaterman; showman,** exhibitor; producer, theatrician; **impresario,** *entrepreneur* [F.]; **director,** stage director, stage manager; set designer; costumier, costumière, costumer, costume designer; wigmaker; make-up man or artist; prompter, pit man; callboy; playreader; master of ceremonies, M.C. [slang]; ballyhoo man, spieler, barker [all slang]; ticket collector, gate man; usher, usherer, usher-in; usherette, usheress.

28. **stageman; stagehand,** flunky [derog.]; sceneman, **sceneshifter, grip** [cant, U.S.]; flyman; carpenter, chips [slang]; electrician, juicer [slang]; head electrician, gaffer [slang, U.S.]; machinist; scenist, scene painter, scenewright.

29. **agent, actor's agent,** playbroker, ten-percenter [slang, U.S.]; **booking agent,** advance agent; publicity man or agent; **manager,** actor-manager, acting manager.

30. **patron,** patroness; **backer, angel** [slang]. Thespis (reputed founder of Gr. drama), "the first professor of our art" [Dryden]; Dionysus [patron god of drama], Melpomene [Muse of tragedy], Thalia [Muse of comedy].

31. **playgoer, theatergoer;** attender 185.5, spectator 441, audience 447.6; moviegoer [coll.], **motion-picture fan** [slang]; first-nighter; standee [coll.]; **claquer,** *claqueur* [F.], clapper, hired applauder; pass holder, deadhead [coll.]; **waiting line, queue,** cue, tail.

VERBS 32. **dramatize,** theatricalize; melodramatize; movieize [coll.]; scenarioize; **present, stage, produce, put on** [coll.], put on the stage, **put on a show** [coll.], give a performance; premiere; open a show, open a show cold [cant]; try it on the dog [slang]; set the stage; ring up (the curtain), ring down (the curtain); **star, feature** [coll., U.S.], **headline;** paper the house [slang].

33. **act, perform, play, play-act** [coll.], tread the stage, strut the boards,

strut one's stuff [slang, U.S.]; appear, **appear on the stage;** act like a trouper; register (as emotion [slang]); emotionalize, emote [joc.]; pantomime; gag, patter [both slang]; slapstick; sketch; troupe, barnstorm [coll.]; make one's debut or bow, come out; act as foil or feeder, stooge [slang, U.S.], play straight for [cant]; **star,** have one's name in lights; double in brass [cant].

34. **enact, act out; represent, depict, portray, characterize;** act ~, play or perform a part, take a part, sustain a part, act or play the part of; **impersonate,** personate; **re-enact,** live over.

35. **overact,** chew up the scenery [joc.], act all over the stage; **ham, ham it up** [both slang]; **mug** [slang], grimace; spout, rant; milk a scene [cant].

36. **rehearse, practice, drill,** go through, go over, go through one's part, read one's lines.

ADJS. 37. **dramatic(al),** dramaturgic(al); **theatrical, histrionic, Thespian, make-believe, stagy,** scenic(al); theaterlike, stagelike; **spectacular, sensational,** vivid, striking, impressive; **melodramatic(al);** ham, hammy [both slang]; cinematic(al), cinematographic(al); monodramatic(al); vaudevillian; operatic; legitimate; protean [slang]; stellar, all-star [cant]; stage-struck; movie-minded [coll.]; stageworthy, theatricable.

38. **tragic(al),** tragicodramatic, heavy [cant]; buskined, cothurned.

39. **comic,** comicodramatic, tragicomic, farcical; slapstick, slapsticky.

ADVS. 40. **on the stage** or **boards,** before an audience, before the footlights, **in the limelight** or spotlight; on stage; upstage; backstage, off stage, behind the scenes.

610. ACTOR

NOUNS 1. **actor, player, performer,** stage player or performer, **play-actor** [coll.], **entertainer,** impersonator, Thespian, Roscius, artiste, mummer, theatrical [coll.], trouper, histrio; actress, play-actress [coll.]; pantomimist, pantomimic; dramatizer, dramatic actor; legitimate actor; old stager, old stage hand; strolling player, stroller, barnstormer [coll.]; character **actor,** character man or woman, character; **villain,** dirty heavy [slang], menace, Simon Legree; **juvenile, ingénue,** soubrette; **foil, feeder, stooge** [slang, U.S.], **straight man** [cant];

utility man, utility, general utility; protean [slang]; **vaudevillist,** vaudevillian; **chorus girl,** chorine [slang]; chorus boy or man; strip-teaser [U.S.]; matinee idol [slang].

2. (actors) "the only honest hypocrites" [Hazlitt], "bores to themselves, to others caviare" [Phaedrus]; "a sculptor who carves in snow" [Lawrence Barrett].

3. **motion-picture actor,** movie actor [coll.], photoplayer; **movie star** [coll.].

4. **ham,** ham actor, ham chewer, ham-fatter [all slang]; grimacer, grimacier.

5. **lead,** leading man or lady, **protagonist; star,** headliner, headline or feature attraction; **hero, heroine;** juvenile lead, *jeune premier* [F.]; first tragedian, heavy lead [cant]; **prima donna,** diva; *prima buffa* [It.]; première danseuse, coryphée.

6. **support,** supporting cast; **supernumerary,** super [cant], supe [cant]; **extra,** bit player [both motion pictures]; walking gentleman or lady, walk-on, mute [hist.]; figurant, figurante [fem.]; **understudy, stand-by,** substitute.

7. **tragedian,** *tragédien* [F.], tragedienne [fem.], **heavy** [cant].

8. **comedian,** *comédien* [F.], comedienne [fem.], **comic, funnyman;** farcist, farcer, *farceur* [F.], *farceuse* [F., fem.]; light comedian, genteel comedian, low comedian, slapstick comedian, hokum or hoke comic [slang].

9. **buffoon,** *buffo* [It.], mountebank; **clown, fool,** jester, zany, **merry-andrew,** jackpudding [hist.,], pickleherring, *Pickelhering* [G.], **motley fool,** wearer of the cap and bells; harlequin, harlequina [fem.]; pantaloon; Punch, Punchinello, Pulcinella, Polichinelle, Jack Pudding, Hanswurst, Columbine, Scaramouch, Punch and Judy.

10. **mummer,** mime, mimer, **mimic,** mimologist; guiser [Eng. & Scot.], guisard [Scot.].

11. **cast,** dramatis personae; **company, troupe;** repertory company, rep show [slang]; stock company, stock [cant]; chorus.

611. UNCOMMUNICATIVENESS

NOUNS 1. **uncommunicativeness,** closeness, unconversableness; **unsociability** 921; **secretiveness** 612.1.

2. **taciturnity, untalkativeness,** unloquaciousness; **silence, speechlessness,** wordlessness, **muteness,** dumbness; laconicalness, laconism, curtness, briefness,

brevity, conciseness, sententiousness, pauciloquy.

3. **reticence** or reticency, "the power of holding one's tongue" [Jowett]; **reserve,** reservation, **restraint, constraint;** suppression, repression; **backwardness,** retirement; **aloofness, standoffishness,** distance, remoteness, detachment; **coolness,** coldness, frigidity; **inaccessibility,** unapproachability; **undemonstrativeness,** unexpansiveness, unaffability; **introversion,** ingoingness.

4. **man of few words,** laconic, clam [coll., U.S.]; Spartan, Laconian.

VERBS 5. **keep to oneself,** keep one's own counsel; **hold one's tongue** 450.5; retire; **keep one's distance,** keep at a distance; **stand aloof,** hold oneself aloof.

ADJS. 6. **uncommunicative,** unconversable, unconversational; **unsociable** 921.5; secretive 612.17.

7. **taciturn, untalkative,** unloquacious, indisposed to talk; **silent, speechless,** wordless, **mute, mum,** dumb; close, **closemouthed,** close-tongued, close-lipped, **tight-lipped,** tongue-tied, word-bound; **laconic,** curt, brief, concise, sententious, pauciloquent, **sparing of words.**

8. **reticent, reserved, restrained,** constrained; **suppressed,** repressed; **backward, retiring,** shrinking, backward in going forward [joc.]; **aloof, standoffish,** offish [coll.], standoff, **distant,** remote, removed, detached; **cool,** cold, frigid; **inaccessible,** unapproachable; **undemonstrative,** unexpansive, unaffable; **introverted,** ingoing.

612. SECRECY

NOUNS 1. **secrecy,** secretness, dark; **concealment** 613; **secretiveness,** closeness; **uncommunicativeness** 611; **evasiveness,** evasion, subterfuge; huggermuggery.

2. **privacy,** retirement, seclusion; **confidentialness,** confidentiality; **intimacy.**

3. **veil of secrecy,** veil, curtain, pall; **iron curtain,** "curtains of fog and iron" [Churchill]; bamboo curtain; **suppression,** repression, stifling, smothering; **censorship,** blackout [coll.], **hush-up, seal of secrecy.**

4. **stealth,** stealthiness, **furtiveness, clandestineness, surreptitiousness, covertness,** slyness, shiftiness, sneakiness, slinkiness, underhand dealing; **prowl;** stalking, still hunt [U.S.].

5. **secret, confidence,** private or personal matter, confidential or **privileged**

communication [law]; deep, dark secret [coll.]; **top secret,** top-drawer secret [slang], guarded secret, classified information [mil.]; **mystery,** arcanum, deep *or* profound secret, sealed book, mystery of mysteries; skeleton in the closet, ~ cupboard *or* house.

6. cryptography, steganography, **secret writing;** cryptogram, cryptograph, steganogram; secret ~, invisible *or* sympathetic ink.

7. **code, cipher, signal, sign,** hieroglyphic; Morse code, cable code, telegraphic alphabet; dot, dash.

VERBS 8. **keep secret, keep mum,** keep dark; keep it a deep, dark secret [coll.]; secrete; conceal 613.7; **keep to oneself,** keep close *or* snug, keep back, keep from, **withhold,** hold out on [slang], not let it go further, **not tell,** hold one's tongue 450.5, not breathe a word, **not give away** [coll.], "tell it not in Gath" [Bible], **keep it under one's hat** [slang], keep under wraps [slang, U.S.], keep one's own counsel, play dumb, make no sign, not let the right hand know what the left is doing; keep in ignorance, keep *or* leave in the dark; classify [mil.].

9. **hush up, hush,** hush-hush, shush, huggermugger; **suppress,** repress, **stifle, smother, squash,** quash, kill, sit on *or* upon, put the lid on [slang]; **censor,** black out [coll.].

10. **tell confidentially,** tell a secret; mention privately, whisper, breathe, **whisper in the ear;** take aside, talk to in private, speak in privacy.

11. code, codify, cipher.

ADJS. 12. **secret,** close, dark; **hush-hush, top-secret,** classified [mil.], under wraps [slang, U.S.]; **unrevealable,** irrevealable, **undivulgable, undisclosable, untellable,** unwhisperable, unutterable; inviolable, inviolate.

13. **hidden** 613.12; recondite, mysterious 547.14.

14. **covert, clandestine,** unobtrusive, huggermugger; **surreptitious, undercover, underground,** under-the-counter, under-the-table, backdoor, hole-and-corner [coll.]; **underhand, underhanded;** furtive, stealthy, sly, shifty, sneaky, sneaking, skulking, slinking, slinky, feline, hangdog.

15. **private, privy; intimate, inmost,** innermost, inner, interior, inward; closet, cabinet; **secluded, sequestered,** withdrawn, retired.

16. **confidential,** auricular, inside

[slang], esoteric; **off the record,** not to be quoted, not for publication, unquotable, unpublishable.

17. **secretive,** secret; **close,** dark; **evasive,** shifty; **uncommunicative, close-mouthed** 611.6, 7.

18. cryptogrammic, cryptogrammatic(al), cryptographal, cryptographic(al), steganographic(al).

ADVS. 19. **secretly, secretively, in secret,** *in petto* [L.]; under one's hat [slang], in *or* up one's sleeve, nobody the wiser; **covertly, under cover,** *à couvert* [F.], under the cloak of; **behind the scenes,** in the background, in a corner, in the dark, behind the veil *or* curtain, behind the veil of secrecy; *sub rosa* [L.], under the rose, under the table, underboard, underground; *sotto voce* [It.], under the breath, with bated breath, in a whisper; in silence.

20. **surreptitiously, clandestinely,** unobtrusively, huggermugger; **furtively, stealthily, slyly,** shiftily, sneakily, sneakingly, skulkingly, slinkingly, slinkily; by stealth, **on the sly, on the quiet** *or* dead quiet [slang], on the q.t. [slang], *à la dérobée* [F.], *en tapinois* [F.], behind one's back, by a side door, by a side wind, **like a thief in the night;** underhand, underhandedly; in holes and corners, in a hole-and-corner way [both coll.].

21. **privately,** privily, **in private,** in privacy, in privy, alone together; apart, aside; **behind closed doors,** *januis clausis* [L.], *à huis clos* [F.], in camera, in chambers, in secret session.

22. **confidentially, in confidence,** in strict confidence, under the seal of secrecy, **off the record; between ourselves,** *entre nous* [F.], *inter nos* [L.], **between you and me,** *de vous à moi* [F.], between you and me and the bedpost [coll.].

613. CONCEALMENT

NOUNS 1. **concealment, hiding, secretion;** burial, burying; **covering,** screening 227.1; occultation, mystification; hiddenness, concealedness, covertness, reconditeness; secrecy 612; invisibility 444.

2. **cover, screen** 227.2; disguise 616.10.

3. **ambush, ambushment, ambuscade,** *guet-apens* [F.]; lurk, lurking hole *or* place; blind, stalking-horse; trap 616.11.

4. **hiding place, hideaway, hide-out** [coll.], hiding, hidlings *or* hidlins [Scot., Ir., & dial. Eng.], concealment, subterfuge,

cover, secret place, **retreat**, recess, corner, dark corner, **hole**, hidie-hole [Scot.], holes and corners; **refuge** 698; **covert**, coverture, undercovert; **cache**, stash [crim. slang, U.S.]; cubbyhole, cubby; closet; crypt, vault; fraid hole [slang, U.S.], funk hole [slang].

5. **covert way, secret passage, backway, back door,** sally port, **side door; back stairs,** *escalier dérobé* [F.]; **underground,** underground route, underground railroad [U.S.].

6. (something concealed) **nigger in the woodpile** [coll.], bug under the chip [coll., U.S.], **snake in the grass**; stowaway, blind baggage [slang]; **booby trap,** masked battery; sealed book.

VERBS 7. **conceal, hide; cover, cover up, screen, cloak, veil,** curtain, blanket, shroud, **enshroud, envelop, ensconce; mask,** bemask; **disguise, camouflage,** dissemble; **obscure,** cloud, becloud, befog, blind, **shade,** throw into the shade; **eclipse,** occult, **occultate;** put out of sight, keep under cover; cover up one's tracks, hide one's trail; hide one's light under a bushel, bury one's talent in a napkin.

8. **secrete, hide away,** keep hidden; **keep secret** 612.8; **cache,** stash [crim. slang, U.S.], deposit, plant [slang]; **bury,** sink; bosom, embosom.

9. (hide oneself) **hide, hide out** [coll.], hide away, **go into hiding,** stay in hiding; **lie hid** *or* **hidden, lie low** [coll.], lie perdu, lie snug *or* close, sit tight [slang], burrow, **hole up** [slang], **go underground,** hide in holes and corners, play at bopeep *or* hide and seek; keep out of sight, retire from sight, keep in the background, stay in the shade.

10. **lurk,** couch; **lie in wait,** lay wait; **sneak, skulk, slink, prowl, steal, creep,** pussyfoot [slang], gumshoe [slang, U.S.].

11. **ambush,** ambuscade; **lie in ambush,** lay wait for, **lie in wait for,** lay for [coll.], **waylay.**

ADJS. 12. **concealed, hidden, hid,** recondite, blind; **covered** 227.34; **covert, under cover; obscured,** clouded, clouded over, wrapped in clouds, in a cloud, ~ fog, ~ mist *or* haze; dark, in darkness, in the shade *or* dark; eclipsed, occultated, in eclipse, under an eclipse; buried; underground; close, secluded, sequestered.

13. **unrevealed, undisclosed,** undivulged, **unexposed,** unapparent, **invisible, unseen,** unperceived, unspied, unde-

tected, undiscovered, unexplored, untraced, untracked, unexplained, unsolved.

14. **obscure,** abstruse, mysterious 547.13, 14; **secret** 612.12; **unknown** 476.18; **latent** 544.5.

15. **disguised, camouflaged, in disguise; incognito,** incog [coll.].

16. **in hiding,** hidden out, **under cover,** in a dark corner, lying hid, perdue; in ambush.

17. **concealing, hiding,** obscuring; **covering** 227.37; unrevealing, nonrevealing, undisclosing.

614. FALSENESS

NOUNS 1. **falseness, falsehood,** falsity, unverity, untruth, **truthlessness, untrueness,** mendacity; **fallaciousness, fallacy; erroneousness** 517.

2. **spuriousness, phoniness** [slang], bogusness, **ungenuineness, unauthenticity,** unrealness, unreality, artificiality.

3. **sham, fakery** [coll.], feigning, pretending, feint, pretext, **pretense, pretension, false pretense** *or* **pretension; makebelieve,** acting, representation, **simulation;** dissembling, **dissemblance, dissimulation;** seeming, semblance, appearance, **show, false show,** outward show, false air, *faux air* [F.], "counterfeit presentment" [Shakespeare]; front [coll.], **false front** [slang], façade, face; color, coloring, false color; masquerade, disguise 616.10; posture, pose; affectation 901.

4. **falseheartedness,** doubleheartedness, doubleness of heart, **duplicity, two-facedness,** double-facedness, ambidexterity, **double-dealing,** Machiavellianism; **deceitfulness** 616.3; faithlessness, treachery 973.5, 6.

5. **insincerity, unsincereness, uncandidness,** uncandor, **unfrankness,** unseriousness, disingenuousness; shallowness, superficiality; emptiness, hollowness, hollowheartedness; mockery, hollow mockery.

6. **hypocrisy,** hypocriticalness, tartuffery, tartuffism, Pecksniffism, pharisaism; **mealymouthedness, unctuousness,** oiliness, blandness, glibness, smoothness; cant, mummery, snuffle, snivel; **lip service,** mouth honor; crocodile tears; sanctimony 1027.

7. **quackery,** quackishness, quackism, empiricism, **mountebankery,** mountebankism, **charlatanry,** charlatanism, **imposture;** humbug, humbuggery; **four-flushing** [coll.], **bluff.**

8. **untruthfulness,** untruth, **unveracity,**

inveracity, unveraciousness, truthlessness, mendaciousness, mendacity; **lying, fibbery,** pseudology; pathological lying, mythomania, pseudologia phantastica.

9. falsification, falsifying, confabulation [psychol.]; **perversion, distortion; misrepresentation,** misconstruction, misstatement; coloring, false coloring, miscoloring; **prevarication,** equivocation; **perjury,** false swearing.

10. fabrication, invention, concoction, forgery; fiction, figment, **myth,** fable, romance, extravaganza.

11. lie, falsehood, falsity, falsification, untruth, untruism, mendacity, **prevarication, fib,** tarradiddle [coll.], flam, *blague* [F.], twister [coll.], **story** [coll.], **trumped-up story, yarn** [coll.], **tale,** fairy tale [coll.], ghost story; farfetched story, **tall story** [coll.], **cock-and-bull story,** fish story [coll.]; exaggeration 615; half-truth, white lie; *suggestio falsi* [L., law]; canard; a pack of lies.

12. monstrous lie, consummate lie, **whopper** or whapper or wopper [coll.], rapper [dial. & slang], bounce, bouncer [coll.]; cram, crammer, banger, howler, stretcher, large or tall order [all slang]; gross ~, flagrant or shameless falsehood, **barefaced lie, dirty lie** [slang]; the big lie.

13. fake, fakement [both coll.]; **phony** [slang], cheat, falsificate; **sham, mock, imitation,** simulacrum, dummy, bam [slang], bastard, duffer [slang]; paste; tinsel, clinquant, pinchbeck, shoddy; **counterfeit, forgery; hoax, fraud** 616.7, 8; impostor 617.6.

14. humbug, humbuggery, humbugism; **bunk** [slang], **buncombe** or bunkum, **hokum** [slang], **bosh** [coll.], bull [slang], baloney [slang, U.S.], flimflam, claptrap, moonshine, gammon [coll.], *blague* [F.], jiggery-pokery [slang, Eng.].

VERBS **15.** ring false, **not ring true.**

16. falsify, belie, misrepresent, miscolor; misstate, misquote, misreport; **pervert, distort,** warp, garble, twist; put a false appearance upon, give a false coloring, give a color to, **color,** gild, gloss, varnish; dress up, embellish, embroider; **disguise, camouflage.**

17. tamper with, alter, **manipulate, juggle,** sophisticate, **doctor** [coll.], **cook** [coll.], deacon [coll.], duff [slang], hocus, hoke [slang]; adulterate 44.13; **load** (as dice) **salt,** plant [slang]; salt a mine.

18. fabricate, invent, manufacture, trump up, make up, get up, hatch, concoct, **cook up** [coll.], fudge up, fake up [coll.], hoke up [slang]; **counterfeit, forge;** fictionize, mythify.

19. lie, tell a lie, falsify, speak falsely, be untruthful, deviate from the truth, fib, story [coll.], fishify [slang], tarradiddle [coll.]; **stretch the truth,** draw the longbow; **exaggerate** 615.3; lie flatly, lie in one's throat, lie like a trooper or conjurer.

20. prevaricate, equivocate, weasel [coll.], palter, trifle with the truth, **mince the truth,** say one thing and mean another, play or play at fast and loose.

21. swear falsely, forswear, **perjure oneself,** bear false witness.

22. sham, fake [coll.], **feign, counterfeit, simulate,** gammon [coll.]; **pretend, make believe, make a show of,** make out like, make as if or as though, go through the motions [coll.]; let on, let on like; **affect,** profess, **assume,** put on; **dissimulate, dissemble; act, play,** play-act [coll.], **put on an act** [slang, U.S.], act or play a part; **put up a front** [slang], put on a front or false front [slang]; **four-flush** [slang], **bluff,** put up a bluff [coll.]; **play possum,** roll over and play dead; cry sour grapes.

23. pose as, act as, **masquerade as,** pass for, **pass off for,** set up for, act the part of, represent oneself to be, claim or pretend to be, **make false pretenses,** go under false pretenses, **sail under false colors.**

24. be hypocritical, act or **play the hypocrite;** cant, snuffle, snivel; give mouth honor, render lip service; clean the outside of the platter.

25. play a double game or **role, play both ends against the middle,** run with the hare and hold or hunt with the hounds.

ADJS. **26. false, untrue, truthless, not true,** void or devoid of truth, contrary to fact, in error, mendacious, **fallacious,** false as dicers' oaths; **erroneous** 517.14; unfounded 482.12.

27. spurious, ungenuine, unauthentic, apocryphal, **unreal, fake** [coll.], **phony** [slang], **sham, mock, counterfeit, bogus,** queer [slang], snide [slang], **dummy, make-believe,** so-called, factitious, supposititious, not what it is cracked up to be [slang]; **imitation** 22.9; **simulated, simulative, faked, feigned, counterfeited, pretended, affected, assumed,**

put-on; **artificial,** artful, **synthetic,** unnatural; bastard, illegitimate; **pseudo,** quasi, quasi-, near- (as *near-silk* [coll.]), ape- (as *ape-ware* [slang]); flash, pinchbeck, brummagem [slang, Eng.], tinsel, shoddy.

28. specious, seeming, apparent, colored, colorable, plausible, **ostensible.**

29. quack, quackish; charlatan, charlatanish; empirical.

30. fabricated, invented, hatched, concocted, trumped-up, made-up, cooked-up [coll.], **forged; fictitious,** fictive, fictional figmental, **mythical,** fabulous.

31. falsehearted, false-principled, falsedealing; double, ambidextrous, **doubledealing,** doublehearted, double-minded, doublehanded, double-tongued, double-faced, **two-faced,** Janus-faced; Machiavellian; **deceitful** 616.22; faithless, treacherous 973.19, 20.

32. insincere, unserious, uncandid, unfrank, disingenuous; **empty, hollow,** hollowhearted; **superficial, shallow;** left-handed.

33. hypocritic(al), canting, tartuffish, tartuffian, Pecksniffian, pharisaic(al); goody, **goody-goody** [both coll.]; **mealymouthed, unctuous, oily, bland, glib, smooth,** smooth-tongued, smooth-spoken; sanctimonious 1027.5.

34. untruthful, unveracious, unveridical, truthless, **lying,** mendacious; perjured, forsworn.

ADVS. **35. falsely, untruely,** truthlessly; **erroneously** 517.18; **untruthfully,** unveraciously; **spuriously,** ungenuinely; artificially, synthetically, unnaturally; speciously, seemingly, apparently, plausibly, ostensibly.

36. insincerely, unseriously, uncandidly; emptily, hollowly; superficially, shallowly; **hypocritically,** mealymouthedly, unctuously, blandly, glibly; over the left [slang].

615. EXAGGERATION

NOUNS **1. exaggeration,** exaggerating; **overstatement,** tall talk [coll.]; **hyperbole,** hyperbolism; **superlative,** extravagance; **magnification, enlargement,** amplification, aggrandizement, heightening, enhancement; **stretching, straining, overdrawing;** stretch, strain, stretch of the imagination; coloring, overcoloring; embellishment, embroidery, embroidering; over-estimation 496; **excess** 661; caricature; "a truth that has lost its temper" [Kahlil Gib-

ran]; spread eagle, spread-eagleism [both coll., U.S.].

2. much ado about nothing, storm *or* tempest in a teapot, much cry and little wool.

VERBS **3. exaggerate,** hyperbolize; **overstate,** overspeak, overtell; **overdraw,** overstress, overcharge, **overdo, carry too far;** overestimate 496.2; **stretch,** strain, stretch the truth, draw the long bow; **magnify, enlarge,** enlarge upon, amplify, aggrandize, extravagate, enhance, heighten, build up; pile up, heap up, pile on, pile *or* lay it on [coll.], **lay it on thick** [coll.], lay it on with a trowel [slang]; color, overcolor; embellish, embroider; talk big [coll.], talk in superlatives, deal in the marvelous, come it strong [slang], make much of, make the most of, maximize, run riot, out-Herod Herod; spread-eagle [coll., U.S.], make the eagle scream [U.S.]; make a mountain of a molehill.

ADJS. **4. exaggerated,** hyperbolic; **magnified, enlarged,** amplified, aggrandized, enhanced, heightened; colored, overcolored; embellished, embroidered; **overstated,** overtold; **overdrawn, overdone,** overwrought, overstressed; overestimated 496.3; overlarge, overgreat; **excessive** 661.17; **superlative,** extravagant, extreme; large, tall [both coll.]; **high-flown,** high-flying, highfalutin *or* high-faluten *or* highfaluting [coll.]; spread-eagle [coll., U.S.].

5. exaggerating, exaggerative, hyperbolic.

616. DECEPTION

NOUNS **1. deception, deceptiveness, trickiness, falseness;** fallaciousness, fallacy; **delusion,** delusiveness; deceiving, **victimization, dupery;** bamboozle, bamboozlement [both coll.]; flimflam, flimflammery [coll.]; spoof, spoofery [both slang]; circumvention, overreaching; ensnarement, insnarement, enmeshment, entanglement.

2. misleading, misguidance, misdirection, bum steer [slang, U.S.]; misinformation 561.1.

3. deceit, deceitfulness, guile, falseness, insidiousness, shadiness [coll.], **shiftiness, furtiveness, underhandedness,** surreptitiousness, indirection; **falseheartedness, duplicity** 614.4; **treacherousness** 973.6; craftiness 733.1; sneakiness 612.4; sneak attack.

4. chicanery, chicane, **skulduggery**

[coll., U.S.], trickery, knavery 973.2, dodgery, jobbery, pettifoggery, *espièglerie* [F.], *supercherie* [F.], jockeyism, artifice, corruption, cozenage; sharp practice, underhand dealing, foul play; shuffling, trimming; connivance, collusion.

5. juggling, jugglery, trickery, *escamotage* [F.], prestidigitation, conjuration, legerdemain, sleight of hand; hocus-pocus, hokeypokey [coll.], hanky-panky [coll.], jiggery-pokey [slang, Eng.].

6. trick, artifice, device, gimmick [slang, U.S.], wheeze [slang], *ficelle* [F.], subterfuge, blind, ruse, wile, shift, shuffle, dodge, sleight, pass, feint, fetch, catch [dial.], trepan, jape, *espieglèrie* [F.], chicanery [usu. pl.]; dirty trick, scurvy trick; sleight of hand, sleight-of-hand trick, legerdemain, hocus-pocus, *escamoterie* [F.]; juggle, juggler's trick; bag of tricks, tricks of the trade.

7. hoax, deception, deceit, sell [coll.], have [slang], spoof [slang], kid [slang], humbug, flam, flim-flam, chouse [coll.], bam [slang], barney [slang], cog, plant [slang]; fake, fakement [both coll.]; mare's-nest.

8. fraud, fraudulence *or* fraudulency, dishonesty; imposture, imposition; cheat, swindle, bucket shop, boiler room, gyp [slang], bilk, ramp [slang, Eng.], fishy transaction, piece of sharp practice; racket [coll., U.S.], job [slang]; graft [coll.]; bunko, cardsharping; gold brick [coll., U.S.]; straw bail, straw bond [both coll.]; straw bid [coll., U.S.]; ballot-box stuffing [U.S.].

9. confidence game, con game [slang], skin game [slang], bunko game, brace game, gum game [slang]; drop game [coll.]; panel game; shell game; thimblerig, thimblerigging.

10. disguise, camouflage, false colors, false front [slang], borrowed plumes; masquerade, mummery; incognito, incognita [fem.]; mask, masque, visor, vizard, false face; domino, domino mask.

11. trap, gin, springe, trepan; booby trap; pitfall, trapfall, deadfall, pit, *trou-de-loup* [F.]; flytrap, mousetrap, rattrap, bear trap, mantrap, deathtrap, firetrap; Venus's flytrap, Dionaea; trap door; spring-trap, spring net; spring gun, set gun; baited trap, tub to the whale.

12. snare, hook, sniggle; fishhook, fly, jig, silver hook; noose, lasso, lariate; net, dragnet, seine; cobweb; meshes, toils; bait, ground bait; birdlime.

VERBS 13. deceive, victimize, beguile, trick, hoax, dupe, gull, pigeon, bamboozle [coll.], jape, humbug, hum [slang *or* coll.]; take in, let in, put something over *or* across, slip one over on [coll.], put up a job on [slang], pull one's leg, come over [coll.], come it over [slang]; delude, deludher [Anglo-Ir.], mock; betray, play one false, double-cross [slang]; juggle, conjure; bluff.

14. fool, befool, make a fool of, practice on one's credulity; spoof, kid, cram, stuff, stuff up [all slang]; play a trick on, play upon; play a practical joke upon, send on a fool's errand.

15. mislead, misguide, misdirect, lead astray, give a bum steer [slang, U.S.]; throw off the scent, put on a false scent, drag *or* draw a red herring across the trail; misinform 561.3.

16. hoodwink, blindfold, blind, blind one's eyes, throw dust into the eyes, pull the wool over one's eyes.

17. (deceive, as by cheating *or* trickery) hornswoggle [slang, U.S.], bilk, flimflam [coll.], flam, bite [chiefly coll.], diddle [dial. & slang], daddle [coll.], jockey, chouse [coll.], hocus, hocus-pocus [coll.], gum [slang, U.S.], fob, fub, sell [slang], gudgeon, mump [chiefly dial.], do [coll.], do up brown [slang]; circumvent, get around; overreach, outreach.

18. cheat, fudge; swindle, defraud, practice fraud upon, sharp, con [slang, U.S.], finagle, fainaigue, pluck [slang], fleece, shave, mulct, beat [coll., U.S.], rook [coll.], gyp [U.S.], ramp [slang, Eng.], stick [coll.], sting [slang], pick [slang & dial.], gouge [coll., U.S.], chisel [slang, U.S.], cozen, cog, bucket [slang], trepan *or* trapan; do out of, flimflam out of [coll.], chouse out of [coll.], beguile of *or* out of; take for a sucker [slang, U.S.], sell one a bill of goods [slang], do in [slang], obtain under false pretenses; live by one's wits; bunko, play a bunko game; gold-brick, sell gold bricks [both coll., U.S.]; short-change [coll., U.S.]; stack the cards, pack the deal [slang], play with marked cards; cog a die, cog the dice; thimblerig; crib [slang].

19. impose upon 961.7, exploit 663.16.

20. trap, entrap, trepan, gin, catch in a trap; ensnare *or* insnare, snare, hook, hook in, sniggle, noose; inveigle 648.4; net, mesh, enmesh; tangle, entangle, involve; trip, trip up; set *or* lay a trap for, bait

the hook, spread the toils, throw a tub to a whale; lime, birdlime.

ADJS. **21. deceptive, deceiving, misleading, beguiling, false, fallacious; delusive,** delusory; illusory 518.9; **tricky,** trickish, tricksy; catch, catchy; flam, flimflam; **fishy** [coll.], questionable.

22. deceitful, fraudulent, false, guileful, insidious, shady [coll.], **shifty, tricky,** trickish, finagling, underhand, **underhanded, furtive, surreptitious,** indirect; **conniving,** collusive; **falsehearted, two-faced** 614.31; **treacherous** 973.20; sneaky 612.14; crafty 733.12; scheming 652.14.

ADVS. **23. deceptively, beguilingly,** falsely, fallaciously, delusively, **trickily, misleadingly;** under false colors, under cover of, under the garb of.

24. deceitfully, fraudulently, guilefully, insidiously, shadily [coll.], **shiftily, trickily, underhandedly,** furtively, surreptitiously, indirectly, like a thief in the night; treacherously 973.24.

617. DECEIVER

NOUNS **1. deceiver, hoaxer, deluder, beguiler, humbugger, bamboozler** [coll.], trepan; **dissembler,** dissimulator; **double-dealer,** Janus, Judas; Machiavelli, Machiavel, **Machiavelist;** dodger, Artful Dodger, Jeremy Diddler; serpent, snake, cockatrice, **snake in the grass;** jilt, jilter; gay deceiver; Indian giver [coll., U.S.].

2. trickster, tricker; **legerdemainist, juggler,** sleight-of-hand performer, **prestidigitator,** escamoteur [F.].

3. cheat, cheater; **swindler, defrauder; gypper,** gypster [both slang, U.S.]; **flimflammer** [coll.], **chiseler** [slang], bilker [coll.], diddler [coll. or slang], cozener, rook [slang], gull [slang], juggler, jockey, shuffler.

4. sharper, sharp [slang], **shark, slacker** [slang], spieler [coll., U.S. & Australasia], **bunkoman,** magsman [slang], gold-bricker [coll., U.S.], chevalier d'industrie [F.], skin [slang], Greek; **confidence man, con** man [slang], con [slang, U.S.]; **blackleg** [coll.], jackleg [slang, U.S.], leg [slang, Eng.]; carpetbagger [U.S., post-Civil War]; horse trader, horse coper [Eng.]; cardsharp, cardsharper; thimblerigger; ringer, coin ringer [both slang]; short-changer [coll., U.S.]; land shark, land pirate, mortgage shark.

5. bunko steerer, come-on man [slang, U.S.], **capper, decoy, decoy duck,** stool pigeon.

6. impostor, pretender, false pretender, **humbug,** precious humbug, **fraud** [coll.], **fake** [coll.], **faker** [coll.], **phony** [slang], **cheat,** gammoner [coll.], gull [slang]; **fourflusher** [slang], bluff, bluffer; **charlatan, quack,** quacksalver, **mountebank,** empiric, saltimbank, blagueur [F.]; **wolf in sheep's clothing,** ass in lion's skin, jackdaw in peacock's feathers.

7. masquerader, masker; **impersonator,** personator; **mummer, mime, mimer; disguiser,** guiser [Scot. & dial., Eng.], guisard [Scot.]; incognito, incognita [fem.].

8. hypocrite, fake [coll.], **phony** [slang], pharisee, tartufe, whited sepulcher, lip server, **canter,** snuffler, sniveler, "a saint abroad and a devil at home" [Bunyan]; Tartufe, Pecksniff, Mawworm, Joseph Surface.

9. liar, falsifier, untruther, **fibber,** fibster, **prevaricator,** equivocator, **fabricator,** romancer, fabulist, pseudologist [joc.], **story-teller** [coll.], storier [coll.], spinner of yarns; taradiddle, taradiddler [both coll.]; Ananias, Tom Pepper [naut. slang], Seapin; consummate liar, "liar of the first magnitude" [Congreve], menteur à triple étage [F., three-story liar], crammer [slang], bouncer [coll.], dirty liar [coll. or slang]; pathological liar, mythomaniac, pseudologue; **perjurer,** false witness.

10. traitor, treasonist, **betrayer, quisling, rat** [slang], **snake in the grass,** double-crosser [slang], double-dealer; turncoat 626.5; informer 555.6; archtraitor; Judas, Judas Iscariot, Benedict Arnold, Quisling, Brutus.

11. subversive, saboteur, fifth columnist; sympathizer, fellow traveller, security risk; **collaborationist,** collaborator, fraternizer; fifth column, underground; Trojan horse.

618. DUPE

Gullible Person.—NOUNS **1. dupe, gull,** cull [dial. & slang], **pigeon** [slang], **sucker,** fish [coll.], gudgeon, **victim,** hoaxee, come-on [slang, U.S.], **gobemouche** [F., fly swallower]; **easy mark** [coll., U.S.], **sitting duck,** trusting soul, **pushover** [slang, U.S.], cinch [slang]; game, fair game; **butt, goat** [slang]; toy, plaything; **cat's-paw** 656.3; mark, flat, mooch [all crim. slang, U.S.]; **fool,** April fool, monkey, chump [coll.], boob [slang], booby, sap [slang], jay [slang], put, Simple Simon; greenhorn, greeny [coll.], greener [slang]

2. gulliblity 501.2.

619. WILL

NOUNS **1. will, volition; inclination,** animus; desire, wish, mind, fancy, discretion, pleasure, will and pleasure; volitiency, velleity; conation [phychol.], conatus; resolution 622.

VERBS **2. will,** see or think fit, **wish, desire, choose to, have a mind to;** resolve 622.7.

3. have one's will, have one's way, write one's own ticket, do or go as one pleases, stand on one's rights, take the law into one's own hands, have the last word.

ADJS. **4. volitional,** volitionary, **willing, voluntary,** volitient; conative; willed [chiefly in composition, as strong-willed, self-willed, etc.].

ADVS. **5. at will,** at choice, at pleasure, al piacere [It.], **at one's pleasure,** a beneplacito [It.], at one's will and pleasure, at one's own sweet will, **at one's discretion,** à discrétion [F.], ad arbitrium [L.]; ad libitum [L.], ad lib; as one wishes, as it pleases or suits oneself, **in one's own way,** in one's own sweet way [coll.], **as one thinks best,** as it seems good or best, as far as one desires, according to one's purpose.

620. WILLINGNESS

NOUNS **1. willingness, compliance, unreluctance,** unloathness, ungrudgingness; agreeableness, **agreeability,** gameness [coll.], favorableness; **desirousness, eagerness; readiness,** promptness, forwardness, alacrity; good will or goodwill, cheerful consent; **willing heart, favorable disposition; willing ear.**

2. voluntariness, gratuitousness; spontaneity, spontaneousness; **self-determination,** self-activity; voluntaryism, voluntarism [chiefly philos.]; **volunteer.**

VERBS **3. be willing, be game** [coll.], **take kindly to,** dearly love to; be of favorable disposition, have a willing heart; be inclined, **be so inclined** or disposed, incline, lean to or towards; **have a mind to,** have half a mind to, have a good or great mind to, feel like [coll.]; would as lief, would as leave [dial.], would as lief as not, not care if one does [coll.]; **see** or **think fit,** think good or proper; **enter with a will,**

go into heart and soul, plunge into; lend ~, give or turn a willing ear.

4. volunteer, do of one's own accord, do on one's own hook [coll., U.S.], do on one's own account, do on one's own initiative, do on one's own volition, do of one's own free will, do upon one's own authority or responsibility, do on one's own sayso [coll.], take upon oneself, **take the responsibility,** take the bit between one's teeth, stand on one's own legs, paddle one's own canoe [coll.], take one's own course, use one's discretion.

ADJS. **5. willing, willinghearted;** disposed, inclined, minded, willed, prone; **well-disposed, well-inclined, favorably inclined** or disposed; **favorable, agreeable, compliant,** fain; **game** [coll.], **on** [slang]; **desirous, eager; ready,** prompt, forward, **ready and willing; in the mood,** ~ vein, ~ humor or mind, in a good mood; **glad, happy, cheerful, pleased, delighted; glad to,** etc.

6. ungrudging, ungrumbling, **unreluctant,** unloath, **nothing loath,** unaverse, unshrinking; **gracious, genial, cordial,** wholehearted.

7. voluntary, volunteer, gratuitous, spontaneous; free, freewill, willful; discretionary, discretional, arbitrary; **optional, elective; self-determined,** self-determining, self-active, self-acting; **unsought,** unbesought, **unasked,** unrequested, unsolicited, **uninvited,** unbidden, uncalled-for; **unforced,** unrequired, uncompelled.

ADVS. **8. willingly, with a will,** with good will, with right good will, de bonne volonté [F.]; **with pleasure,** avec plaisir [F.], **with delight,** de buena gana [Span.]; **gladly, happily,** delightedly, **cheerfully,** with good cheer, with a cheerful heart; heartily, **wholeheartedly,** with all one's heart, heart and soul, heart in hand, to one's heart's content; **eagerly,** with zest, with relish, with open arms; **readily,** promptly, at the drop of a hat [coll.].

9. agreeably, favorably, compliantly; nothing loath, lief, lieve, fain, as lief, as lief as not.

10. ungrudgingly, ungrumblingly, **unreluctantly,** without reluctance or demur; cordially, genially, graciously, **with good grace,** de bonne grâce [F.].

11. voluntarily, freely, gratuitously, spontaneously, willfully; optionally, by choice; **of one's own accord,** of one's own free will, on one's own [coll.], **on one's**

own hook [coll., U.S.], on one's own account *or* responsibility, on one's own say-so [coll.], on one's own initiative, of one's own volition, of one's own choice, at one's own discretion.

621. UNWILLINGNESS

NOUNS **1. unwillingness, disinclination, indisposition,** indisposedness, **reluctance,** renitence *or* renitency, averseness, aversion.

2. demur, scruple, qualm, diffidence, hesitation, hesitance *or* hesitancy, pause, boggle, falter; demurral, qualmishness, scrupulousness, scrupulosity; **stickling,** boggling, faltering; shrinking, recoil.

VERBS **3. be unwilling, would rather not, not care to,** not feel like [coll.], not find it in one's heart to, not have the heart *or* stomach to; mind, object to; balk, **balk at; beg off;** grudge, begrudge.

4. demur, scruple, stickle, stick at, boggle, falter, waver, **hesitate,** pause, **hang back, hang off,** hold off; **fight shy of,** shy at, shy, shrink, recoil, duck [slang], dodge, blink, blench, swerve, pull back; make bones about.

ADJS. **5. unwilling, disinclined, indisposed,** not in the mood; averse; **involuntary, forced.**

6. reluctant, renitent, **grudging, loath** *or* **loth;** backward, laggard, remiss, slack, slow to.

7. stickling, demurring, qualmish, scrupulous, diffident, hesitant, hesitating, faltering, boggling, shrinking, shy of, balky, balking, restive.

ADVS. **8. unwillingly, involuntarily, against one's will,** *a contre-cœur* [F.], against the grain, contrary to one's wishes; in spite of oneself, *malgré soi* [F.].

9. reluctantly, grudgingly, with a heavy heart, with a bad *or* an ill grace, *de mala gana* [Span.], **under protest.**

622. RESOLUTION

NOUNS **1. resolution, determination, decision, resolve, will, purpose; resoluteness, determinedness,** determinateness, **decisiveness,** decidedness, definiteness, **purposefulness; earnestness, seriousness;** "the dauntless spirit of resolution" [Shakespeare]; perseverance 623; obstinacy 624.

2. firmness, staunchness, stanchness, settledness, fixedness; unyieldingness 624.2.

3. pluck, spunk [coll.], **mettle, backbone** [coll.], game, **grit,** clear grit, sand [slang], **stamina, guts** [slang], pith, bottom; pluckiness, spunkiness [coll.], gameness, mettlesomeness.

4. will power, strong-mindedness, strength of mind, strength of purpose, strength, power, **moral fiber; iron will,** will of iron; a will *or* mind of one's own, the courage of one's convictions.

5. self-control, self-command, self-possession, self-mastery, self-government, self-direction, **self-restraint,** self-conquest, self-discipline, **self-denial, self-reliance;** control, restraint, discipline, possession, aplomb.

6. self-assertion, self-expression, self-assertiveness, self-expressiveness.

VERBS **7. resolve, determine, decide, will, purpose, make up one's mind,** make a resolution, make a point of; settle, fix, seal; conclude, come to a determination *or* conclusion, determine once for all.

8. be determined, have a mind *or* **will of one's own,** know one's own mind; **be in earnest, mean business** [coll.], mean what one says; have blood in one's eyes, be out for blood [both coll.]; **set one's mind** *or* **heart upon,** put one's heart into; devote oneself to, give oneself up to; buckle oneself, buckle to; steel oneself, brace oneself, grit one's teeth, set one's teeth *or* jaw; take the bit in one's teeth, put ∼, lay *or* set one's shoulder to the wheel, take the bull by the horns, nail one's colors to the mast; burn one's bridges, kick down the ladder, throw away the scabbard.

9. remain firm, stand fast, hold fast, **stand** *or* **hold one's ground,** keep one's footing, hold one's own; **stick to one's guns,** stick, stick fast, stick to one's colors, adhere to one's principles, not listen to the voice of the charmer; **take one's stand,** set one's back against the wall; **put one's foot down** [coll.], stand no nonsense.

10. not hesitate, think nothing of, think little of, **make no bones about** [coll.], have *or* make no scruple of, stick at nothing.

ADJS. **11. resolute, resolved, determined, bound** [coll., U.S.], **decided,** definite, decisive, determinate, **purposeful; earnest, serious;** perseverant 623.7; obstinate 624.8.

12. firm, staunch, stanch, solid, fixed, settled; set, sot [both dial.]; **unyielding** 624.9; unshaken, not to be shaken; undeflectable, not to be deflected.

13. unhesitating, unhesitant, unfaltering, unswerving, unflinching, unshrinking, dauntless, stick-at-nothing [coll.].

14. plucky, spunky [coll.], **gritty** [coll.], **mettlesome, game,** game to the backbone, game to the last *or* end.

15. strong-willed, strong-minded; self-controlled, controlled, self-disciplined; **self-possessed,** self-reliant; **self-assertive,** self-asserting, self-expressive.

16. determined upon, resolved upon, decided upon, intent upon, fixed upon, settled upon, **set on,** sot on [dial.], **bent on,** hell-bent on [slang].

ADVS. **17. resolutely, determinedly,** determinately, **decidedly,** decisively, **purposefully, with a will;** firmly, staunchly, stanchly; **seriously,** in all seriousness; **earnestly,** in earnest, in good earnest; dingdong [coll.], hammer and tongs, tooth and nail, *bec et ongles* [F.]; heart and soul, with all one s heart; perseveringly 623.8.

18. pluckily, spunkily [coll.], mettlesomely. **gamely,** manfully, like a man; on one's mettle.

19. unhesitatingly, unhesitantly, **unfalteringly, unswervingly,** unflinchingly, unshrinkingly.

20. come what may, *venga lo que venga* [Span.], *vogue la galère* [F., row the galley on, come what may], **cost what it may,** *coûte que coûte* [F.], whatever the cost, at any price, ~ cost *or* sacrifice, at all risks *or* hazards, **whatever may happen,** at all events, if worst comes to worst; in some way or other, *à bis ou à blanc* [F., in gray or white, in some way or other]; live or die, survive or perish, sink or swim, rain or shine, neck or nothing, once for all, in spite of hell and high water, as though life depended upon it.

623. PERSEVERANCE

NOUNS **1. perseverance, persistence** *or* persistency, insistence *or* insistency, singleness of purpose; resolution 622; **steadfastness, steadiness, constancy,** continuance; **endurance, stick-to-itiveness** [coll.], staying power, stay [chiefly coll.]; **pertinacity,** pertinaciousness, **tenacity,** tenaciousness, **doggedness,** relentlessness, dogged perseverance, bulldog tenacity; **diligence,** application, sedulousness, assiduousness, assiduity; **indefatigability,** tirelessness; **patience,** patience of Job.

VERBS **2. persevere, persist, endure, continue,** carry on, go on, **keep on,** keep up, keep at, **keep at it,** keep going; keep driving, **keep the ball rolling,** keep the pot boiling, keep up the good work [all coll.].

3. keep doggedly at, **plod, peg,** peg away *or* along, pound *or* hammer away at; **plug,** plug at it, plug away *or* along [all slang]; **keep one's nose to the grindstone.**

4. stay with it, stick with it [coll.], **hold on,** hold fast, **hang on,** hang on for dear life [coll.]; **stick to it** [coll.], stay [coll.], stick [slang], **stick to one's guns,** stick to one's last, ~ knitting *or* mutton [coll.]; not give up, **never say die,** not give up the ship [coll.]; **stay it out, stick it out** [slang], tough it out [slang], stick out, **hold out,** hold up, bear up, stand up; stay the distance [slang], stay the pace [slang], sit the bag [slang, U.S.].

5. prosecute to a conclusion, **go through with it, carry through, follow through,** see through [coll.], **see it through** [coll.], see out, follow out *or* up; go all the way, go to all lengths, go the whole length, go the limit [slang], **go the whole hog** [slang], go the whole figure [slang], go all out [slang]; **leave no stone unturned,** leave no avenue unexplored, move heaven and earth, go through fire and water, "ride with the whirlwind and direct the storm" [Addison].

6. be in at the death, die in the last ditch, die in harness, die in one's shoes, die at one's post, die game, **go down with flying colors.**

ADJS. **7. persevering, perseverant; persistent,** persisting, insistent; **enduring, continuing;** resolute 622.11; **diligent, assiduous, sedulous; dogged, pertinacious, tenacious, stick-to-itive** [coll.], stayable; **steadfast, steady, constant, unswerving,** unremitting, unintermitting, uninterrupted; **unfaltering, unwavering,** unflinching; relentless, **unrelenting; unrelaxing,** undrooping, unsleeping; **untiring,** unwearying, unflagging, never-tiring, **tireless,** weariless, **indefatigable,** unwearied; undiscouraged, undaunted, game to the end; **patient,** patient as Job.

ADVS. **8. perseveringly, persistently,** persistingly, insistently, **enduringly;** resolutely 622.17; **diligently,** assiduously, sedulously; **doggedly,** pertinaciously, tenaciously; **steadfastly,** steadily, constantly, unremittingly, unintermittingly, uninterruptedly; unswervingly, unwaveringly, unfalteringly, unflinchingly; relentlessly, unrelentingly; **indefatigably, tirelessly,** wearilessly, untiringly, unwearyingly, unflaggingly; **patiently.**

9. **through thick and thin,** through fire
and water, through evil report and good report, rain or shine, fair or foul, in sickness
and in health.

INTERJS. 10. carry on!, keep it up!, keep
at it!, stay with it!, stick with it! [coll.],
stand fast!, don't give up!, never say die!;
if at first you don't succeed, try, try again.

624. OBSTINACY

NOUNS 1. **obstinacy,** obstinateness,
**stubbornness, willfulness, headstrong-
ness;** self-will, mind or will of one's own;
doggedness, pertinacity, tenaciousness,
tenacity, "tough tenacity of purpose" [Sy-
monds], dogged resolution; **bullheadedness,** pigheadedness, mulishness; obduracy,
toughness, hardness, hardheadedness; stiff
neck, stiff-neckedness; bitter-enderism
[coll.]; opinionatedness 512.6.

2. **unyieldingness,** unbendingness, uncompromisingness, **inflexibility,** inexorability, **firmness,** adamantness, **rigidity;** unalterability, unchangeability, immutability,
immovability; irreconcilability, implaca-
bility; intransigence or intransigency, *intransigeance* [F.], intransigentism; **relentlessness,** unrelentingness; sternness, grimness.

3. **perversity,** *perversité* [F.], perverse-
ness, **contrariness, wrongheadedness,
waywardness, frowardness,** untowardness, troublesomeness, difficultness, cross-
grainedness, orneriness [coll. or dial.]; **cussedness,** pure cussedness [both coll., U.S.];
sullenness, sulkiness, stuffiness [coll.]; un-
cooperativeness.

4. **ungovernability, unmanageability, unruliness,** uncontrollability, indomitability,
intractability, incorrigibility, **unsubmissiveness, indocility,** irrepressibility, insuppres-
sibility; contumacy, contumaciousness; refractoriness, **recalcitrance** or recalcitrancy,
obstreperousness, restiveness, fractiousness;
balkiness; breachiness.

5. **impersuasibility,** unpersuadableness,
impersuadableness; deafness, blindness;
positiveness.

6. (obstinate person) **bullhead,** bullet-
head [coll., U.S.], pighead, mule [coll.],
donkey, ass, perverse fool; **uncompromiser,**
standpat or **standpatter** [coll.], stickler, irreconcilable; intransigent, *intransigeant*
[F.]; **opinionist,** positivist; **die-hard, bitter-ender** [coll.].

VERBS 7. **balk, stickle;** hold one's
ground, not budge, **not yield an inch;**
hold out, stand out, hang out; take no
denial, not take "no" for an answer; take
the bit in one's teeth, have the tail over the
lines [slang]; die hard.

ADJS. 8. **obstinate, stubborn; willful,**
self-willed, strong-willed; **headstrong,**
heady, *entêté* [F.]; **dogged,** bulldogged,
tenacious, pertinacious; bullheaded, bulletheaded [coll., U.S.], **pigheaded,** mulish,
stubborn as a mule; set, set in one's ways;
stiff-necked, stiff-backed, stiffhearted; opinionated 512.22.

9. **unyielding, unbending, inflexible,**
inexorable, **firm, stiff, rigid,** rigorous; **adamant,** adamantine; unmoved, unaffected;
immovable, not to be moved; **unalterable,** unchangeable, immutable; **uncompromising,** intransigent, irreconcilable, im-
placable, hard-shell [coll., U.S.]; **relentless,** unrelenting; stern, grim; iron, cast-
iron.

10. **obdurate,** tough, hard, casehardened, hardset, **hardheaded,** hardmouthed,
hard-bitted, hard-bitten.

11. **perverse, contrary, wrongheaded,**
snivy [dial.], **wayward, froward, untoward, difficult,** troublesome, cross-grained,
ornery [coll. or dial.]; sullen, sulky, stuffy
[coll.]; uncooperative, unhelpful.

12. **ungovernable, unmanageable, unruly, uncontrollable, indomitable, intractable, incorrigible, unsubmissive, indocile,**
irrepressible, insuppressible; **refractory,
recalcitrant,** contumacious, obstreperous,
wild, fractious; **restive,** resty [dial.]; balky,
balking; breachy; beyond control, out of
hand.

13. **unpersuadable,** impersuadable, impersuasible; deaf, blind; positive.

ADVS. 14. **obstinately, stubbornly,** willfully, headstrongly; **doggedly,** tenaciously,
pertinaciously; **bullheadedly,** pigheadedly,
mulishly; with set jaw, with sullen mouth,
with a stiff neck.

15. **unyieldingly, unbendingly, inflexibly,** inexorably, **adamantly,** obdurately,
firmly, stiffly, rigidly, rigorously; unalter-
ably, unchangeably, immutably, immov-
ably; uncompromisingly, intransigently,
irreconcilably, implacably; relentlessly, unrelentingly; sternly, grimly.

16. **perversely, contrarily,** contrariwise,
wrongheadedly, waywardly, frowardly,
cross-grainedly; sullenly, sulkily.

17. **ungovernably, unmanageably,**
unrulily, **uncontrollably,** indomitably, intractably, incorrigibly, unsubmissively, ir-

repressibly, insuppressibly; contumaciously, obstreperously, restively, fractiously.

625. IRRESOLUTION

NOUNS 1. irresolution, indetermination, indecision; irresoluteness, undeterminedness, indecisiveness, undecidedness; uncertainty 513; instability, inconstancy, unsettlement, infirmity of purpose; capriciousness, fickleness 627.2, 3; double-mindedness, yes-noism [slang]; halfheartedness, lukewarmness, Laodiceanism; half measures.

2. vacillation, fluctuation, oscillation, pendulation, alternation; wavering, shifting, shuffling, trimming, paltering; shilly-shally, shilly-shallying, dillydallying, seesawing.

3. hesitation, hesitance, hesitancy, hesitating; falter, faltering; suspense, state of suspense.

4. weak will, weak-mindedness, feeblemindedness; weakness, feebleness, faintness, frailty; infirmity, instability; spinelessness, invertebracy; pliability 356.2; abulia (loss of will power [psychol.]).

5. vacillator, shilly-shallyer, shilly-shally, dillydallier, waverer, shuffler, trimmer, palterer; doughface [coll.]; opportunist; Laodicean; weathercock, shuttlecock, butterfly, chameleon; ass between two bundles of hay.

VERBS 6. not know one's own mind, not know where one stands, not know whether one stands on one's head or one's heels, be uncertain 513.9; be of two minds, have two minds; flounder, stagger, stumble, boggle, beat about, go around in circles.

7. hesitate, pause, falter, hang back, hang in doubt, hang in suspense, hang fire, hover, wait to see how the cat jumps or the wind blows; think twice about, stop to consider, debate, balance, weigh one thing against another, consider both sides of the question; leave up in the air, leave ad referendum [L.].

8. vacillate, waver, fluctuate, alternate, pendulate, oscillate, wobble, wabble, palter, vary, trim, shift, shuffle, shuttle, swing from one thing to another; shilly-shally, dillydally, seesaw, teeter, totter, teeter-totter, back and fill, keep off and on, toss and turn, hum or hem and haw, will and will not, "let 'I dare not' wait upon 'I would'" [Shakespeare]; blow hot and cold 627.4.

ADJS. 9. irresolute, irresolved, unresolved; undecided, indecisive, undetermined, unsettled, infirm of purpose; uncertain 513.14; hesitant, hesitating; at loose ends, at a loose end; of two minds, double-minded; halfhearted, lukewarm, neither hot nor cold, Laodicean; capricious, fickle 627.5, 7.

10. vacillating, vacillatory, oscillatory; wobbly, wabbly; wavering, fluctuating, alternating, pendulating, oscillating, varying, shifting, shuffling, trimming, faltering, paltering; shilly-shallying, dilly-dallying, seesawing; willy-nilly, shilly-shally, "at war 'twixt will and will not" [Shakespeare]; going around in circles, like a chicken with its head cut off [coll.].

11. weak-willed, weak-minded, feebleminded, weak-kneed, weak, feeble, faint, frail; infirm, unstable, unsteady, unsound, shaky; spineless, invertebrate; without a will of one's own, unable to say "no"; dough-faced [coll.], pliable 356.9; abulic [psychol.].

ADVS. 12. irresolutely, irresolvedly, undecidedly, indecisively, undeterminedly; uncertainly 513.25; hesitantly, hesitatingly; waveringly, falteringly, vacillatingly; shilly-shally, shilly-shallyingly; halfheartedly, lukewarmly.

626. TERGIVERSATION

Change of Mind or Allegiance.—NOUNS 1. tergiversation, tergiversating; reverse, reversal; about-face, volte-face [F.], right-about-face, rightabout, a turn to the right-about.

2. apostasy, recreancy; reactionaryism, reactionism; perversion, diversion; desertion 631.2; backsliding 694.2.

3. recantation, withdrawal, disavowal, denial, forswearing, unsaying, repudiation, palinode; retraction, retractation; revokement, revocation; recall, recalling; disclaimer, disclamation; renunciation, renouncement; disownment, disowning; abjurement, abjuration; defection.

4. tergiversator, tergiversant; timeserver, timepleaser; double-dealer, ambidexter.

5. apostate, turncoat, turnback, recreant, renegade, runagate, crawfish [slang, U.S.], Vicar of Bray; deserter, turntail, runaway; rat, ratter [both slang]; traitor 617.10; bolter, mugwump [polit. cant, U.S.]; seceder, secessionist, secessioner; secesh, secesher [both coll., U.S.]; separatist, come-outer [coll., U.S.], schismatic; dissenter, dissentient, dissident, recusant;

heretic, pervert; **backslider,** recidivist; reversionist, reversioner; unrepatriate.

6. (trade-union cant) **rat, scab,** blackleg, knobstick [Eng.], snob [Eng.].

VERBS **7. tergiversate, change one's mind, change one's song,** ~ **tune** or **note,** sing a different tune, shift one's ground, go upon another tack, come round, swing from one thing to another.

8. apostatize, go over, change sides, fall off or away; **desert** 631.6; **turn one's coat,** turn cloak, *tourner casaque* [F.]; defect.

9. recant, retract, revoke, repudiate, renounce, abjure, forswear, disavow, disown, deny, disclaim, unsay, recall, call back, **take back, withdraw,** draw in one's horns; **eat one's words,** swallow, eat crow, eat humble pie; **back down** or **out,** climb down [both coll.]; crawfish [coll., U.S.], crawl [slang, U.S.]; back water, take water [slang, U.S.]; think better of it, be of another mind, have another guess coming.

ADJS. **10. tergiversating,** tergiversant; timeserving, trimming, ambidextrous, unreliable.

11. apostate, recreant, renegade, false, unfaithful; reactionary, reactionist; revulsive, revulsionary.

12. repudiative, repudiatory; **renunciative,** renunciatory; abjuratory, revocatory.

627. CAPRICE

NOUNS **1. caprice, whim, whimsey** or whimsy, whimwham, flimflam; **fancy,** fantasy, **conceit, notion,** fool notion [slang], **vagary,** *capriccio* [It.], boutade, freak, megrim; **fad, phase, passing fancy; quirk, crotchet,** quip, crank, kink, kink in one's horn [slang, U.S.]; maggot, maggot in the brain, bee in one's bonnet [coll.], flea in one's nose [slang]; **humor, mood,** fit; prank, escapade.

2. capriciousness, caprice; **whimsicalness,** whimsey or whimsy, whimsicality; **fancifulness,** fantasticality; **freakishness,** freakery; **erraticism, fitfulness; moodiness,** humorsomeness, temperamentalness.

3. fickleness, flightiness, frothiness, **giddiness,** dizziness, skittishness; **frivolousness,** frivolity; **lightness, levity,** *légèreté* [F.], lightheadedness, light-mindedness; shallowness, superficiality; **changeableness** 141; volatility, mercurialness; **uncertainty, unpredictability; irresponsibility, unreliability, undependability.**

VERBS **4. blow hot and cold,** play or play at fast and loose, keep off and on, turn and turn about, say one thing and do or mean another, have as many phases as the moon; **fluctuate** 141.5.

ADJS. **5. capricious, whimsical, fanciful, notional,** viewy [coll.], vagarious, fantasied, fantastic, freakish, maggoty, **crotchety,** kinky [U.S.]; **erratic, fitful;** wanton, wayward, vagrant; unrestrained, undisciplined, uncontrolled, fast and loose; arbitrary, unreasonable.

6. moody, moodish, **humorsome,** temperamental.

7. fickle, frivolous, flighty, frothy, yeasty, **giddy,** dizzy, skittish; **light,** lightsome, lightheaded, light-minded; shallow, superficial; **inconstant, changeable** 141.7; volatile, mercurial; **uncertain, unpredictable; irresponsible, unreliable, undependable,** not to be relied or depended upon.

ADVS. **8. capriciously, whimsically,** at one's own sweet will [coll.]; **erratically, fitfully,** by fits, by fits and starts; arbitrarily, unreasonably, without rhyme or reason, without counting the cost.

9. frivolously, flightily, lightly, shallowly, superficially.

628. IMPULSE

NOUNS **1. impulse,** natural impulse, blind impulse; **notion, fancy; sudden thought,** flash, inspiration.

2. impulsiveness, impetuousness, impetuosity; **hastiness,** overhastiness, quickness, suddenness; **precipitateness,** precipitance, precipitancy, precipitation.

3. thoughtlessness, unthoughtfulness, reasonlessness, **heedlessness, carelessness,** inconsideration.

4. unpremeditation, indeliberation, **undeliberateness,** uncalculatedness, undesignedness, unstudiedness; snap judgment, ~ decision, etc.

5. improvisation, extemporization, extempore, **impromptu, ad lib;** extemporaneousness, extemporariness.

6. improviser, improvisator, *improvvisatore* [It.], *improvvisatrice* [It.; fem.], extemporizer, impromptuist.

VERBS **7. act on the spur of the moment,** rise to the occasion; **blurt out,** say what comes uppermost, say the first thing that comes into one's head.

8. improvise, extemporize, ad-lib [coll.], do offhand, play it by ear [slang]; **dash off, strike off,** knock off, throw off, toss off or out; **make up, cook up.**

ADJS. **9. impulsive, impetuous, hasty,**

hurried, overhasty, quick, sudden, **precipitate, headlong**; uncontrolled, ungoverned.

10. unthinking, unreasoning, unreflecting, uncalculating, unthoughtful, **thoughtless,** reasonless, **heedless, carelessness,** inconsiderate.

11. unpremeditated, unmeditated, **uncalculated, undesigned, unstudied,** unprompted, unguided, unguarded; **indeliberate,** undeliberate, undeliberated; **unconsidered,** unadvised; **ill-considered,** ill-advised, ill-devised.

12. extemporaneous, extemporary, extempore, **impromptu,** unrehearsed; **improvised,** improvisional, improvisate, improvisatory, improvisatorial, improviso, *improvisé* [F.]; **ad-lib,** ad libitum; **offhand,** casual, snap.

ADVS. **13. impulsively, impetuously, hastily,** hurriedly, suddenly, quickly, **precipitately,** headlong.

14. on impulse, on a sudden impulse, **on the spur of the moment; without premeditation,** unpremeditatedly, uncalculatedly, undesignedly, indeliberately; unthinkingly, unreflectingly, unreasoningly, unthoughtfully, thoughtlessly, reasonlessly, heedlessly, carelessly, inconsiderately, unadvisedly.

15. extemporaneously, extemporarily, extempore, *à l'improviste* [F.], **impromptu, offhand,** out of hand, at or on sight, by ear, **ad-lib,** off the elbow [slang], at short notice.

629. AVOIDANCE

NOUNS **1. avoidance, shunning; evasion, elusion, circumvention, escape;** the lam; the slip, the shake [slang], the run-around [slang, U.S.], the go-by [slang]; **dodge, duck,** side step, shy; **subterfuge, shift,** shuffle, parry; **evasiveness, elusiveness.**

2. shirking, piking [slang], **malingering,** malingery, **goldbricking** [coll., U.S.].

3. shirker, shirk, slacker [coll.], **quitter** [U.S.], **piker** [slang], dodger; **malingerer,** eyeservant, eyeserver, soldier or old soldier [orig. naut. slang], sojer or soger [slang], sham Abram or Abraham [naut. cant]; **goldbricker, goldbrick** [both coll., U.S.]; funker [coll.], flunker [coll. U.S.]; **welsher** [slang]; truant; tax dodger.

4. flight, fleet, wing, bolt, scram [slang], **disappearing act** [slang]; **decampment,** absquatulation [joc., U.S.; circa 1830 +]; **elopement;** powder, runout powder, runout [all slang, U.S.]; leg bail, leg bail and land security [both slang]; hegira.

5. fugitive, fleer, runaway, renegade, runagate, bolter, levanter [Eng.], skedaddler [coll., U.S.]; **absconder, eloper; refugee, escapee, evacuee, émigré; displaced person,** D.P.

VERBS **6. avoid, shun, fight shy of,** keep from, **keep away from,** keep clear of, steer clear of [coll.], keep or get out of the way of, **give a wide berth;** give a miss [coll.], make way for, give place to; **keep one's distance,** keep at a respectful distance, keep ~, stand or hold aloof; have nothing to do with, **have no truck with** [coll.], be off of [slang]; have no hand in, take no part in; let alone, let well enough alone; turn away from, turn one's back upon, turn on one's heel, set one's face against, slam the door in one's face.

7. evade, elude, escape, miss, get out of, cheat, **circumvent,** double, **by-pass,** pass up [slang, U.S.], get around [coll.], **steal a march upon, give the slip,** give the go-by [slang], give the run-around [slang, U.S.], ditch [slang, U.S.], shake [slang], shuffle off, get away from, throw off the scent, play at hide and seek; lead one a chase or merry chase, lead one a dance or pretty dance; jump, skip [slang]; skip bail [slang].

8. dodge, duck [slang]; **shy,** swerve, sheer off; shrink, recoil 283.6, 7; **side-step, step aside;** parry, fence, ward off, shift or put off; **hedge,** pussyfoot [coll.], beat about the bush, beg the question.

9. shirk, slack, pike [slang], lay back [coll.]; lie or rest upon one's oars, not pull fair; lie down, lie down on, **lie down on the job,** dog on the job [all slang]; **malinger,** sham Abram or Abraham, soldier, soger or sojer [slang], act or come the old soldier [coll.], duck duty [slang], **goof off** [slang, U.S.], **goldbrick** [coll., U.S.], work one's ticket [slang], swing the lead [slang]; funk [coll.], flunk [coll., U.S.]; shirk out of [coll.], **get out of,** sneak or slip out of, slide out of [coll.]; welsh [slang].

10. flee, fly, take flight, take to flight, take wing, **run, cut and run** [coll.], leg it, **run off** or **away,** run away from, **take to one's heels, make off,** clear out [coll.], do the disappearing act; **beat a retreat, turn tail,** turn one's back upon, turn on one's heel, show the heels, show a clean or light pair of heels; **run for it,** "show it a fair pair of heels and run for it" [Shakespeare], make a break for it [coll.], **run for one's life; decamp,** absquatulate [joc.,

U.S.; circa 1830 +], **bolt**, skedaddle [coll., U.S.; circa 1861 +], clear out [coll.], **take French leave**, levant [Eng.], slip the cable; **skip**, skip out or up [both coll.]; **abscond, elope**, run away with.

11. (slang terms) **beat it, blow, scram, lam, take it on the lam**, take a powder or runout powder [all U.S.]; slope [U.S., circa 1830+], dust [U.S., circa 1860+], guy [Eng., circa 1874+], mizzle [Eng., circa 1781+], bunk [Eng., circa 1890+], skin out, duck out, duck and run, pull foot, cut stick, cut one's stick, walk one's chalks, make oneself scarce, take to the tall timber, fly the coop, give leg bail.

12. slip away, steal away, sneak off, slink off, mooch off [slang], shirk off or away [dial. & coll.], duck out [slang], slip out of.

ADJS. **13. avoidable, escapable**, eludible; evadable, evasible; preventable or preventible.

14. evasive, elusive, elusory; **shifty**, slippery, tricky, cagey [slang], shy; shirking, piking [slang], malingering.

15. fugitive, runaway, in flight, on the lam [slang, U.S.], hot [slang].

630. ESCAPE

NOUNS **1. escape**, 'scape, **getaway** [coll.], come-off [coll.]; **deliverance**, riddance, **release, liberation**; emergence, issuance, issue, vent; **leakage**, leak; **break**, jail-break; evasion 629.1; flight 629.4; escapism [psychol.].

2. narrow escape, hairbreadth escape, **close call** [coll.], **close shave** [coll.], near go [slang], near thing, near or narrow squeak [slang, Eng.], squeeze [slang], tight squeeze [slang].

3. (means of escape) outlet 302.9; leak; fire escape, life net, lifeboat, life line, drawbridge, sally port.

4. loophole, way out, way of escape, **alternative**, come-off [coll.], hole to creep out of; pretext 647.

5. escapee, escaper, escapist [psychol.]; refugee 629.5.

VERBS **6. escape**, 'scape, make or effect one's escape, make good one's escape, **get away**, make a getaway [coll.]; **free oneself**, deliver oneself, gain one's liberty, **get free, get clear of**, get out, bail out, **get out of**, get well out of, échapper belle [F., make a fortunate escape]; **break loose**, cut loose, break away, break one's bonds, slip the collar, shake off the yoke; **jump, skip** [both

coll.]; **break jail**, escape prison, fly the coop [slang]; evade 629.7; flee 629.10.

7. get off, come off, go free, go at liberty, stand from under [slang, U.S.]; **go scot free**, escape without penalty; **get away with** [slang, U.S.], get by, get away with murder, **get off cheap**; save one's bacon [coll.], escape with a whole skin; escape with or by the skin of one's teeth.

8. slip away, give one the slip, slip through one's hands or fingers; **slip out of**, slide out of, crawl or creep out of, sneak out of, wriggle or squirm out of, find a loophole.

9. find vent, issue forth, come forth, **emerge, issue**, come out, run out, **leak out**.

ADJS. **10. escaped, loose**, clear, disengaged, away, out of, well out of; free 760.19.

631. ABANDONMENT

NOUNS **1. abandonment, forsaking, leaving**, dereliction; **withdrawal**, evacuation; cessation 144.

2. desertion, defection, ratting [slang]; **secession**, bolt [U.S.]; apostasy 626.2; deserter 626.5, 6.

3. (giving up) **relinquishment, surrender, resignation, renouncement**, renunciation, abjurement, abjuration, **yielding**, forswearing.

4. derelict, castaway, castoff, cast-by, wastrel; **jettison**, jetsam, flotsam, flotsam and jetsam; waif, foundling, waifs and strays; orphan, dogie [West. U.S.].

VERBS **5. abandon**, forsake, **quit, leave**, leave behind, take leave of, depart from, turn one's back upon, bid a long farewell; **withdraw, back out**, azzle out of [dial. or slang], stand down [coll.], cry off; **vacate, evacuate; renege**, renig [coll.]; quit cold, leave flat [both coll.]; jilt, throw over, go back on [both coll.]; maroon; discard 666.7; defect.

6. desert, rat [slang], **leave in the lurch**, let down, **walk or run out on** [coll., U.S.], **go back on** [coll.], turn one's back upon; apostatize 626.8; **secede, bolt** [U.S.], pull out [coll.], withdraw one's support; sell out [slang].

7. give up, relinquish, surrender, yield, wave, forgo, resign, renounce, abjure, forswear, have done with, wash one's hands of, drop, drop all idea of, drop like a hot potato, **cease** 144.6, **desist from**, leave off, give over, lay down, hold or stay one's hand, throw up, throw over or overboard [coll.], throw up the cards, throw up the sponge.

ADJS. 8. abandoned, forsaken, deserted, left; derelict, castoff, castaway, cast-by.

632. DESIRE

NOUNS 1. desire, wish, want, wanting, hope, desideration; fancy, *béguin* [F.]; will, mind, pleasure, heart's desire; urge, libido [psychol.]; wish fulfillment; sexual desire 418.4; eagerness 633.

2. like, liking, love, fondness; relish, taste, gusto; passion, weakness [coll.], suppressed desire.

3. inclination, penchant, partiality, predilection, propensity, proclivity, leaning, bent, turn, bias, animus.

4. wistfulness, wishfulness, yearnfulness, nostalgia; wishful thinking; sheep's eyes, longing or wistful eye.

5. yearning, yen [coll., U.S.]; longing, hankering, pining, honing [dial.], aching, wearying; languishment, languishing; nostalgia, homesickness, *Heimweh* [Ger.], *mal* or *maladie du pays* [F.].

6. craving, coveting; hunger, thirst, appetite [all fig.]; itch, itching, itching palm; concupiscence, prurience or pruriency, cacoëthes.

7. appetite, appetence or appetency, stomach, tuck [slang], twist [slang, Eng.], tapeworm [joc.], wolf in the stomach; canine appetite; hunger, hungriness; empty stomach, emptiness [coll.], hollowness, hollow hunger, aching void [coll.]; thirst, thirstiness, polydipsia [med.], drought [chiefly dial.], torment of Tantalus; mouth-watering; sweet tooth [coll.].

8. greed, greediness, avarice, cupidity, avidity, voracity, rapacity, lust, avariciousness, avidness, voraciousness, ravenousness, rapaciousness, sordidness, exorbitance, covetousness, acquisitiveness, grasping; piggishness, hoggishness, swinishness; gluttony 992; inordinate desire, overgreediness; insatiable desire, insatiability.

9. aspiration, breathing, upward looking, "the desire of the moth for the star" [Shelley].

10. ambition, ambitiousness, go-ahead [coll.]; vaulting ambition; "the spur that makes man struggle with destiny" [Donald G. Mitchell], "the mind's immodesty" [D'Avenant], "the way in which a vulgar man aspires" [Henry Ward Beecher], "the evil shadow of aspiration" [George Macdonald], "the avarice of power" [C. C.

Colton], "avarice on stilts and masked" [Landor].

11. (object of desire) desire, desired; desideration, desideratum; idol, darling, apple of one's eye; something to be desired, "a consummation devoutly to be wish'd" [Shakespeare]; ambition, the height of one's ambition.

12. desirer, wisher, wanter, hankerer, coveter; aspirant, aspirer, seeker, solicitant, candidate.

13. desirability, likability, lovability; agreeability, acceptability, unobjectionability; attractiveness, seductiveness, provocativeness.

VERBS 14. desire, be desirous, wish, long, want, like, choose [coll.], do with [coll.], would fain do or have, would be glad of; fancy, take to, take a fancy to, have a fancy for; have a mind to, have an eye to, set one's eyes upon, take into one's head, have at heart, find in one's heart, lie at the heart; wish very much, wish to goodness.

15. want to, wish to, like to, love to, dearly love to; itch to, burn to; ache to [coll.], hurt to [dial.], die to.

16. wish for, hope for, yearn for, yen for [coll., U.S.], have a yen for [coll., U.S.], itch for, long for, pine for, hone for [dial.], ache for [coll.], hurt for [dial.], weary for, languish for, die for, sigh for, pant for, gape for, gasp for, cry for, clamor for, spoil for [coll.].

17. set one's heart or mind on, have one's heart set on, be set on or upon, be bent upon, want with all one's heart, want the worst way, give one's kingdom in hell for [slang].

18. crave, covet, raven for, starve, hunger after, thirst after, crave after, lust after, itch after, hanker after, aspire after, run mad after, be consumed with desire.

19. hunger, hunger for or after; feel hungry, starve [coll.]; have a good appetite, have a tapeworm, have a wolf in one's stomach, play a good knife and fork [coll.], lick one's chops [coll.]; thirst, thirst for or after.

20. aspire, be ambitious, aspire to, try to reach; keep one's eyes on the stars, "hitch one's wagon to a star" [Emerson], cry for the moon.

ADJS. 21. desirous, desiring, desireful, desiderative; wanting, wishing; appetitive, optative; eager 633.9.

22. **desirous of** or **to**, keen on, partial
to [coll.]; **itching for** or **to**, aching for or
to [coll.], hurting to [dial.], **dying to**, perishing to, spoiling for [coll.], wild to [coll.],
crazy to [coll.].

23. **wistful**, wishful, **longing, yearning**, yearnful, **hankering, languishing,
pining**, honing [dial.], **nostalgic, homesick.**

24. **itching**, with itching fingers; prurient, concupiscent; **lustful** 418.20.

25. **craving, ravening; hungering,**
hungry, thirsting, thirsty [all fig.]; **devoured by desire**, consumed with desire;
mad after, crazy for [coll.]; dying for, perishing for.

26. **hungry**, hungering, sharp-set, peck-
ish [coll.]; empty [coll.], hollow; **ravenous,**
dog-hungry [slang], hungry as a bear;
starved, famished, starving, famishing,
perishing with hunger; half-starved, half-
famished.

27. **thirsty**, thirsting, athirst; **dry**,
parched, droughty or drouthy [chiefly
dial.].

28. **greedy, avaricious, avid, voracious, rapacious, ravenous, ravening,
grasping, grabby** [slang], acquisitive,
openmouthed, devouring, lickerish or
liquorish, sordid, esurient, overgreedy;
covetous, coveting; **piggish, hoggish,**
swinish, a hog for, greedy as a hog; gluttonous 992.7; omnivorous, all-devouring; insatiable, insatiate; unquenchable, quenchless.

29. **aspiring, ambitious**, vaulting, sky-
aspiring, upward-looking, high-reaching;
bent or intent upon, set on or upon.

30. **desired, wanted**, coveted; **wished-
for**, hoped-for, longed-for; in demand,
popular.

31. **desirable**, to be desired, **much to
be desired**, after one's heart; **enviable**,
worth having; **likable**, lovable; **pleasing,
agreeable**, acceptable, unobjectionable;
attractive, taking, **seductive, provocative**,
tantalizing, exciting; appetizing, mouth-
watering.

ADVS. 32. **desirously**, desirefully; **wistfully**, wishfully, **longingly, yearningly**,
piningly, languishingly; cravingly, raven-
ingly, itchingly; hungrily, thirstily; aspir-
ingly, ambitiously.

33. **greedily, avariciously**, avidly,
ravenously, voraciously, rapaciously, **covet-
ously**, graspingly, devouringly; **piggishly,
hoggishly**, swinishly.

INTERJS. 34. would that!, would it were!,
O for!, if only!

633. EAGERNESS

NOUNS 1. **eagerness**, anxiousness, **anxiety, solicitude; avidity**, avidness, **keenness**, forwardness, readiness, **alacrity**, cheerful readiness, keen desire; **zest**, zestfulness,
gusto, verve, spirit; **impatience**, breathless
impatience.

2. **zeal, ardor, ardency, fervor, fervency, fervidness, fire, passion**, passionateness, impassionedness, vehemence, intentness, *empressement* [F.]; **devotion**, devoutness, devotedness; **heartiness**, cordiality; **earnestness, seriousness, sincerity.**

3. **enthusiasm**, enthusiasticalness; **infatuation**, fascination, keen interest; **craze**
472.12.

4. **overzealousness, overeagerness**, over-
anxiousness, overanxiety, **overenthusiasm,
overambitiousness; zealotry**, zealotism;
fanaticism 472.11.

5. **enthusiast, zealot, infatuate**, energumen, **eager beaver** [slang, U.S.], rhapsodist, highflier or highflyer, crank [coll.];
nut, bug [both slang]; **fanatic** 472.17; visionary 533.13; faddist, fadmonger; hobbyist.

6. **devotee, votary, fan** [slang], **fancier**, admirer, **follower**, pursuer, hound
[slang]; amateur, dilettante; rooter [slang,
U.S.].

VERBS 7. **jump at**, catch at, grab at,
grasp at, fall all over oneself.

8. **enthuse** [coll.], **rave** [coll.], **rhapsodize, carry on over** [coll.], make much
of, **make a fuss over**, make an ado or
much ado about, make a to-do over [coll.],
make over [coll.], take on over [coll.], go
on over or about [coll.], rave about [coll.],
whoop it up about [slang], get excited
about; effervesce, bubble over.

ADJS. 9. **eager, anxious**, solicitous; **desirous** 632.21; **avid, keen, zestful**, agog,
all agog, forward, ready, ready and willing,
bursting to; **impatient**, breathless, champing at the bit.

10. **zealous, ardent, fervent, fervid**,
vehement, **passionate, impassioned**, burning, on fire; **devout, devoted; hearty**,
cordial; **earnest, sincere, serious**, in earnest; intent, intent on.

11. **enthusiastic**, enthused [coll.], **infatuated**, glowing, full of enthusiasm; enthusiastic about, infatuated with, **keen on**
or **about; wild about**, crazy about, **mad
about**, gone on, all in a dither over [all

coll.]; all hopped up about, all worked up about, hepped up over, hot about, ~ for or or, steamed up about, hipped on, cracked on, bugs on, nuts on, ~ over or about [all slang].

12. overzealous, ultrazealous, overeager, overanxious, overdesirous, **overenthusiastic, overambitious;** fanatical 472.31.

ADVS. **13.** eagerly, anxiously, solicitously; **impatiently,** breathlessly; **avidly,** keenly, readily, zestfully; **enthusiastically,** with enthusiasm; **with alacrity,** with zest, with gusto, with relish, with open arms.

14. zealously, ardently, fervently, fervidly, vehemently, **passionately,** impassionedly, intently; **devoutly, devotedly;** heartily, cordially; earnestly, sincerely, seriously, in earnest.

634. INDIFFERENCE

NOUNS **1. indifference,** indifferentness; halfheartedness; **coolness,** coldness; **lukewarmness,** Laodiceanism; **neutrality,** neuterness; insipidity, vapidity.

2. unconcern, disinterest, **disregard,** dispassion, insouciance; **carelessness, heedlessness,** recklessness, regardlessness, mindlessness, **unmindfulness,** disregardfulness, negligence; **nonchalance,** lackadaisicalness, easygoingness; **listlessness, spiritlessness, heartlessness,** plucklessness, spunklessness; apathy 854.4.

3. undesirousness, unsolicitousness, inappetence or inappetency, uneagerness, **unambitiousness;** lack of appetite, anorexia [med.].

VERBS **4. not care, not mind, not give** or care a damn, not give a hoot [slang], not care whether school keeps or not, couldn't care less; care nothing for or about, not care a straw about, not care scat for [slang]; **take no interest in,** have no desire, have no taste or relish for.

ADJS. **5. indifferent, halfhearted; cool, cold;** lukewarm, Laodicean; neither hot nor cold, neither one thing nor the other; **neuter, neutral;** insipid, vapid, wishy-washy.

6. unconcerned, uninterested, disinterested, dispassionate, insouciant, all one to; **careless,** regardless, mindless, **unmindful,** heedless, reckless, negligent, perfunctory, disregardful; **nonchalant, blasé;** lackadaisical, easy, **easygoing,** devil-may-care, sans souci [F., without care]; pococurante, pococurantish; **listless, spiritless,**

heartless, pluckless, spunkless; apathetic 854.13.

7. undesirous, unsolicitous, inappetent, unattracted; **unenthusiastic,** uneager; **unambitious,** unaspiring.

ADVS. **8. indifferently, with indifference,** with utter indifference; cooly, coldly, lukewarmly, halfheartedly; for aught one cares.

9. unconcernedly, uninterestedly, disinterestedly, dispassionately; **carelessly,** regardlessly, mindlessly, **unmindfully, heedlessly,** recklessly, negligently, disregardfully; **nonchalantly,** lackadaisically; **listlessly, spiritlessly, heartlessly,** plucklessly, spunklessly; apathetically 854.15.

INTERJS. **10.** who cares!, never mind!, what does it matter!, what's the difference!, what are the odds!, what of it!, what boots it!, so what!, it's all one to me!

11. I should worry!, I should fret!, that's your lookout!, that's your pigeon! [slang], that's your tough luck!

635. CHOICE

NOUNS **1. choice, selection, election, pick,** choosing, choose [dial.]; **will,** volition; **decision, determination;** eclecticism; the pick 672.8.

2. option, optionality; **discretion,** discrimination; pleasure, will and pleasure; alternative, alternativity, alternate choice; dilemma, embarras de choix [F.]; choice of Hercules, Scylla and Charybdis.

3. adoption, embracement, acceptance, espousal; affiliation.

4. preference, preferability; **predilection,** prepossession, predisposition, prejudice, partiality; rather, drather, druther [all dial.]; preoption, first choice.

5. vote, voice, suffrage; poll; **ballot;** plebiscite, plebiscitum; **referendum;** yeas and nays, aye or ay, yes, nay, no; voice vote, viva-voce [L.]; hand vote, show of hands; absentee vote [U.S.], complimentary vote, casting vote, cumulative vote, fagot vote [Eng.], limited vote, popular vote [U.S.], protest vote, proxy, single vote, plural vote, transferable vote, nontransferable vote, straw vote, record vote, snap vote, plumper.

6. nomination, designation, naming, proposal.

7. election, appointment; political election 742.11–24.

8. selectivity, selectiveness, choicefulness, choosiness [U.S.]; discrimination 491.

9. **eligibility, qualification,** entitlement, **fitness,** fittedness, **suitability,** acceptability, worthiness, desirability; eligible, ineligible.

VERBS 10. **choose, elect, pick,** opt, make *or* take one's choice, make choice of, use *or* exercise one's option; pick and choose.

11. **select,** make a selection; **pick out, single out,** choose out; extract, excerpt; **decide between,** discriminate between, draw the line; **separate,** segregate, divide, set apart; **cull,** glean, winnow, sift; separate the wheat from the chaff *or* tares, separate the sheep from the goats.

12. **adopt, take up, go in for** [coll.], accept, **embrace,** espouse; mother, father, affiliate.

13. **decide upon, determine upon,** settle upon, fix upon, pitch upon; decide, determine, **make a decision,** make up one's mind; take a decisive step, **commit oneself,** cast the die, pass *or* cross the Rubicon; cast in one's lot with, take for better *or* for worse.

14. **prefer,** have preference; **favor, like better,** prefer to, set before *or* above, regard *or* honor before; **rather, had** *or* **have rather,** choose rather, have one's rathers, ~ drathers *or* druthers [dial.]; would as lief, would as leave [dial.]; think proper, see *or* think fit, think best, please, incline *or* lean towards.

15. **vote,** poll, ballot, **cast one's vote,** cast a ballot; hold up one's hand, stand up and be counted; plump; divide.

16. **nominate, name, designate;** put up, propose, name for office; run, run for office.

17. **elect, appoint, vote in,** place in office.

18. **put to choice,** offer, present, set before; put to vote, have a show of hands.

ADJS. 19. **elective,** electing, electoral; **optional, alternative,** disjunctive, discretional; **appointive** [U.S.], appointing, constituent; adoptive.

20. **selective,** elective, selecting, choosing, optant, eclectic(al); choiceful, **choicy** [coll., U.S.], **picky** [slang], **choosy** [U.S.]; discriminating 491.8; particular 894.9.

21. **eligible, qualified,** entitled, **fit,** fitted, **suitable,** acceptable, admissible, worthy, desirable.

22. **preferable,** preferential, **better,** preferred, **to be preferred,** more desirable.

23. **chosen, selected, picked;** select, elect; hand-picked; **adopted,** accepted, em-

braced, espoused; **elected,** appointed; **nominated,** designated, named.

ADVS. 24. **optionally,** at the option of, **at choice, at one's will,** electively, at one's discretion, at one's pleasure, on approval, if one wishes; alternatively, whether or not; either, or, and/or.

25. **preferably,** desirably, by choice *or* preference, in preference; **rather than,** sooner than, first, sooner, rather, before.

636. REJECTION

NOUNS 1. **rejection, repudiation, disownment, denial,** disclamation; **renouncement,** renunciation; abjurement, abjuration; exclusion, exception; repulsion, rebuff; spurning, scouting, scorning, disdaining.

VERBS 2. **reject, repudiate, renounce, disown, disclaim, deny,** abjure, forswear; exclude, except; **discard** 666.7; put away, shove away; brush aside, push aside; repulse, repel, rebuff; **spurn,** scout, **scorn, disdain,** turn one's back upon, **have nothing to do with,** set at nought.

ADJS. 3. **rejected, repudiated, renounced, disowned, denied,** forsworn; excluded, excepted; **discarded** 666.11; repulsed, rebuffed; **spurned,** scouted, **disdained, scorned;** out of the question, not to be thought of, declined with thanks.

4. **rejective, repudiative, renunciative,** abjuratory, declinatory.

INTERJS. 5. away with!, off with!, take away!

637. NECESSITY

NOUNS 1. **necessity,** necessariness, necessitude, necessitation; **obligation,** obligement; **compulsion,** compulsiveness; **must,** ought, a must item.

2. **requirement, requisite,** requisition, **necessary, necessity, need, want;** need for, **call for, demand,** demand for; desideratum, desideration; **prerequisite,** prerequirement; **essential,** indispensable; the necessary, the needful; the necessities, the necessaries, the decencies; the essentials, the bare necessities.

3. **needfulness,** requisiteness; **essentiality,** essentialness, vitalness; **indispensability,** irreplaceability.

4. **urgent need, dire necessity; exigency, urgency,** imperativeness, stress, pinch, "necessity's sharp pinch" [Shakespeare]; matter of necessity, case of need, **matter of life and death.**

5. involuntariness, instinctiveness, spontaneity, compulsiveness, reflex action, automatism, instinct, blind impulse.

6. choicelessness, no choice, no alternative, **Hobson's choice,** not a pin to choose, six of one and half a dozen of the other, distinction without a difference; any, anything; first come first served, that or nothing.

7. inevitability, inevitableness, **unavoidableness,** inescapableness, inevasibleness, unpreventability, uncontrollability, ineluctability, irrevocability, indefeasibility; **certainty.** sureness; the inevitable, the unavoidable, what must be; fate 638.2.

VERBS **8. necessitate, oblige,** compel 754.4, 5.

9. require, need, want, feel the want of, have occasion for, stand in need of, not be able to dispense with, not be able to do without; **call for,** cry for, clamor for; **demand,** ask, claim, exact; need *or* want doing, take doing; prerequire.

10. be necessary, lie under a necessity, be one's fate; **be obliged,** be under the necessity of, be in for; **must,** needs must, **should, ought,** ought to, **have to,** have got to [coll.], need, **need to,** have need to; cannot choose but, can't keep from, can't be avoided, not help, not be helped, **not help but,** cannot do otherwise; be forced *or* driven, be swept on, be pushed to the wall, be driven into a corner.

11. have no choice *or* **alternative, be no two ways about it;** take it or leave it [coll.], have that or nothing, "make a virtue of necessity" [Shakespeare].

ADJS. **12. necessary,** necessitous, necessitative; **obligatory, compulsory,** compulsive, compelling; **exigent, urgent, importunate,** imperative; irresistible, resistless; choiceless, without choice; must.

13. requisite, needful, required, needed, wanted, called for, in demand, in want of; **essential, indispensable,** irreplaceable, vital, integral; prerequisite.

14. involuntary, instinctive, automatic, mechanical, spontaneous, reflex, blind; **unconscious,** unthinking, **unwitting,** unintentional, unwilling; **compulsive,** compulsory, forced.

15. inevitable, unavoidable, avoidless, **inescapable,** inevasible, unpreventable, uncontrollable, ineluctable, irrevocable, indefeasible; **certain, sure,** sure as fate, sure as death, sure as death and taxes; fated 638.9.

ADVS. **16. necessarily,** needfully, requisitely; **of necessity,** from necessity, **of course,** perforce, as a matter of course, without choice, needs must, **willy-nilly,** willing or unwilling, *bon gré mal gré* [F.], whether one will or not, come what may; compulsively 754.11.

17. if necessary, if need be, if worst comes to worst; for lack of something better, *faute de mieux* [F.].

18. involuntarily, instinctively, automatically, mechanically, spontaneously, blindly; **unconsciously,** unthinkingly, **unwittingly,** unintentionally; **unwillingly** 621.8.

19. inevitably, unavoidably, inescapably, inevasibly, unpreventably, uncontrollably, ineluctably, irrevocably, indefeasibly; **certainly, surely.**

PHRS. **20. it is necessary, it must be,** it needs must be, it must needs be, it will be, it must have its way, it cannot be helped, there is no helping it *or* help for it, what will be shall be; it is written, it is in the cards *or* books; the die is cast.

638. PREDETERMINATION

NOUNS **1. predetermination, predestination,** foredestiny, **preordination,** foreordination; foregone conclusion.

2. fate, fatality, kismet, **fortune, lot,** cup [Biblical], **portion,** dispensation, necessity, appointed lot; **destiny,** destination, **end,** final lot; **doom,** foredoom, crack of doom; God's will, will of Heaven; **Providence,** Heaven, "a divinity that shapes our ends, rough-hew them how we will" [Shakespeare]; inevitability 637.7; handwriting on the wall; book of fate; Fortune's wheel, wheel of fortune *or* chance; astral influences, stars, planets; ides of March.

3. Fates, *Fata* [L.], Sisters three, Weird Sisters [*Macbeth*], Parcæ [Rom.], Moirai [Gr.], Norns [Teut.]; Clotho, Lachesis, Atropos [Gr. Fates]; Ananke, Nona, Decuma, Morta [Rom. Fates]; Urth, Verthandi, Skuld [Norse Fates].

4. determinism, fatalism; necessitarianism, necessarianism, necessism; predeterminism, predestinarianism, Calvinism.

5. determinist, fatalist; necessitarian, necessarian, necessist; automaton, robot, pawn; predestinationist, predestinarian, Calvinist.

VERBS **6. predetermine, predecide,** preresolve, pre-establish; **predestine,** predestinate; **preordain**, foreordain, foreordinate.

7. **destine**, destinate, **ordain**, devote, mark, appoint, have in store for; **doom**, foredoom.

ADJS. 8. **predetermined**, **predecided**, preresolved, pre-established, foregone; **predestined**, predestinate; **preordained**, foreordained.

9. **destined**, **fated**, ordained, written, devoted, marked, appointed, elect, set apart, in store; **doomed**, foredoomed; fateful, kismetic; inevitable 637.15.

10. **deterministic**, **fatalistic**; necessitarian, necessarian.

639. PREARRANGEMENT

NOUNS 1. **prearrangement**, preordering, **precontrivance**, preconcert; **put-up job** [coll.], **frame-up** [slang, U.S.], setup [slang], packed deal [slang]; open-and-shut case [coll., U.S.].

2. **schedule**, prospectus, **program** or programme, **line-up** [coll.], **bill**, card, **calendar**, docket [U.S.], book, slate [U.S.], blueprint, budget, program of operation, order of the day, things to be done; **agenda**, list of agenda; **register**, **roster**, panel, poll, muster, cadre; protocol; **bill of fare**, **menu**, carte; playbill.

VERBS 3. **prearrange**, **precontrive**, **predesign**, preorder, preconcert; **fix** [coll.], pack, set up [slang]; **stack the cards**, pack the deal [both slang]; put in the bag, put on ice, cinch, sew up [all slang]; frame, frame up, put up a job [all slang].

4. **schedule**, **line up** [coll.], **slate** [U.S.], book, bill, program, calendar, docket [U.S.], budget.

ADJS. 5. **prearranged**, **precontrived**, **predesigned**, preordered, preconcerted; **fixed** [coll.], packed, stacked [slang], **put-up** [coll.], set-up [slang], cut out; **in the bag**, on ice, cinched, sewed up [all slang]; open-and-shut [coll., U.S.], cut and dried or dry.

6. **scheduled**, slated [U.S.], booked, billed, to come.

640. CUSTOM, HABIT

NOUNS 1. **custom**, use, usage, wont, wonting, **way**, manner, **practice**, praxis, prescription, **observance**, consuetude, dastur [India]; institution, establishment; folkway; fashion 642; convention 643.

2. "a sort of second nature" [Cicero], "the universal sovereign" [Pindar], "that unwritten law, by which the people keep even kings in awe" [D'Avenant], "the law of one description of fools, and fashion of another" [C. C. Colton], "often only the antiquity of error" [Cyprian].

3. **habit**, habitude, settled disposition, one's old way, **second nature**, "the petrefaction of feelings" [L. E. Landon]; pattern, **habit pattern**; **trait**, trick, characteristic; force of habit.

4. **rule**, procedure, **common practice**, prescribed or set form, common or ordinary run of things, matter of course.

5. **routine**, run, **round**, beat, track, beaten path; **rut, groove**, well-worn groove, "a grave with the ends knocked out" [P. W. Wilson]; **treadmill**, squirrel cage; grind, daily grind [both coll.]; jog, trot; goose step; **red tape**, red-tapery, red-tapism.

6. **customariness**, accustomedness, wontedness, **habitualness**; prevalence, currency, run; **inveteracy**, inveterateness, confirmedness, settledness, fixedness.

7. **habituation**, **accustoming**, **conditioning**, seasoning, adaptation, adjustment, **familiarization**, naturalization; acclimation, acclimatization; **inurement**, hardening, casehardening.

8. **addiction**, addictedness, **confirmed** or **inveterate habit**, indulged inclination; **bad habit**, cacoëthes; drug addiction, morphinism, cocainism, barbiturism; alcoholism, chronic alcoholism, acute alcoholism, dipsomania; Circean cup.

9. **addict**, **fiend** [coll.], **habitual** [coll.], creature of habit; case, hard case [both slang]; drug addict, narcotic, dope fiend, dope [both slang]; alcoholic, drunkard, dipsomaniac.

VERBS 10. **accustom**, **habituate**, adapt, adjust, **condition**, season, **familiarize**, naturalize; acclimatize, acclimate [esp. U.S.]; **inure**, harden, caseharden; **confirm**, establish, set; addict.

11. **become a habit**, take root, **grow on one**.

12. **be wont**, wont, **make a practice of**, get into the way of; **take to**, accustom oneself to; contract or fall into a habit, addict oneself to, cling or adhere to; keep in practice, keep one's hand in; run to pattern, run true to form.

13. **get in a rut**, move or travel in a groove or rut, run on in a groove, follow the beaten path, go round like a horse in a mill, go on in the old jog-trot way; get wound up in red tape.

ADˑS. **14. customary, wonted,** consuetu**d**inary; **usual** 84.8; accepted, set, prescriptive; standard, regulation; prevalent, popular, current; conventional 643.7.

15. habitual, regular, frequent, besetting, persistent, repetitive, recurring, recurrent; **routine,** well-trodden.

16. accustomed, wont, wonted, used; adapted, adjusted, **conditioned, familiarized,** naturalized, seasoned; acclimated, acclimatized.

17. used to, attuned to, **familiar with,** conversant with, **at home in,** no stranger to.

18. habituated, *habitué* [F.]; **in the habit of, given to, addicted to,** wedded to, d**e**voted to, permeated with, imbued with, soaked in, wrapped up in, bound up in or with, never free from; **in a rut.**

19. confirmed, inveterate, chronic(al), estab**l**ished, long-established, **fixed, settled,** rooted; **deep-rooted,** deep-set, deep-settle**d, deep-seated,** deep-fixed; **infixed, ingrained,** implanted, ingrafted; **inured,** hardened, casehardened; set, **set in one's ways,** settled in habit.

ADˑVS. **20. customarily,** accustomedly, wontedly; **usually** 84.9; **as is the custom,** *como de costumbre* [Span.], *comme d'habitud*e [F.]; as is usual, as things go, as the world goes, as the sparks fly upwards.

21. habitually, regularly, frequently, persistently, repetitively, recurringly; **inveterately, chronically;** from habit, **by** or **from force of habit,** as is one's wont.

641. UNACCUSTOMEDNESS

NOU**N**S **1. unaccustomedness,** unwontedness, unusedness; **unfamiliarity,** unacquaintance, unconversance, newness to.

VE**R**BS **2. break of, cure, stop, wean,** turn away, alienate, detach, unaccustom; wear off.

3. break the habit, cure oneself of, wean oneself from, break the pattern, break one's chains or fetters; **give up,** leave off, abandon, drop, stop, discontinue, shake [slang, U.S.], throw off, rid oneself of; swear off 990.8; give a new dress to old ideas, do old things in a new way.

ADJS. **4. unaccustomed, unused, unwonted;** uninured, unseasoned; unhabituated, **not in the habit of,** ungiven to, unwedded to, undevoted to; **unused to, unfamiliar with,** unacquainted with, unconversant with, new to, a stranger to.

642. FASHION

NOUNS **1. fashion, style, mode, vogue,** *ton* [F.], **bon ton,** prevailing taste; custom 640; convention 643; **swim** [coll.], **current of fashion;** height of fashion; star of fashion, glass of fashion, "the glass of fashion and the mould of form" [Shakespeare]; the new look.

2. fashionableness, fashionability; **stylishness, modishness; popularity,** prevalence, currency.

3. smartness, chic; spruceness, nattiness, neatness, trimness, sleekness; **dapperness,** jauntiness; sharpness, spiffiness, classiness, niftiness [all slang]; dressiness [coll.], spruciness [slang], sportiness [coll.]; swankness, swankiness [both coll.].

4. the rage, the go [coll.], **the thing, the last word** [slang], *dernier cri* [F., the latest cry], **the latest thing,** the latest wrinkle [slang], the latest scream [slang].

5. fad, craze, rage, wrinkle [slang]; faddishness, faddiness [coll.], faddism, fadmongery; **faddist,** fadmonger.

6. society, *société* [F.], fashion, fashionable society, **polite society,** *bon ton* [F.], **high society,** high life, *beau monde* [F.]; *monde* [F.], world, world of fashion; Vanity Fair, Mayfair; **social circle, smart set** [coll.], the four hundred [U.S.], upper ten [coll.], **upper ten thousand, upper crust** [coll.], upper cut [coll.]; **cream of society,** elite; café society; court, drawing room; social register [U.S.].

7. person of fashion, fashionable, man or woman of the world, leader of fashion; **socialite** [coll.]; **clubwoman,** clubman; **debutante, deb** [coll., U.S.], subdeb [coll., U.S.].

VERBS **8. catch on,** become popular, become the rage.

9. be fashionable, be the style, be the rage, be the thing, be all the go [coll.]; have a run, pass current; cut a figure in society [coll.], give a tone to society; set the fashion or style.

10. follow the fashion, get in the swim [coll.], get on the band wagon [slang], join the parade, follow the crowd, go with the stream ∼, tide or current, keep in step, do as others do; keep up, **keep up appearances,** keep up with the Joneses.

ADJS. **11. fashionable, in fashion, in style, in vogue,** being done; **all the rage,** all the go [coll.]; **popular,** prevalent, current; **up-to-date,** up-to-datish, up-to-the-minute, up-to-dick [slang], up [coll.], abreast of the times; **in the swim**, on the boat [slang]; new-fashioned, new-fashion [dial.].

12. stylish, modish, vogueish; **alamode,** in the mode; *à la française, à la parisienne, à l'anglaise, à l'americaine* [all F.].

13. smart, chic; well-dressed, well-groomed, dressed to advantage; **spruce, natty,** neat, trim, sleek, smug, trig, tricksy; **dapper,** dashing, jaunty, braw [Scot.]; sharp, spiffy, classy, nifty [all slang]; **dressy** [coll.], **sprucy** [slang], **sporty** [coll.]; **swank, swanky** [both coll.]; swell [slang], nobby [slang, esp. Eng.]; chichi, *recherché* [F.].

14. ultrafashionable, ultrastylish, ultra-smart.

15. faddish, faddy [coll.], fadmongering. ing.

ADVS. **16. fashionably, stylishly,** mod-ishly, up-to-dately; **alamode,** *à la mode* [F.], in the latest style *or* mode.

17. smartly, chicly, **sprucely, nattily,** neatly, trimly, sleekly; **dapperly,** jauntily, dashingly; dressily [coll.], sprucily [slang], sportily [coll.]; swankly, swankily [both coll.].

643. CONVENTION

Conventional Usage.—NOUNS **1. con-vention, conventionalism, conventional-ity,** *convenance* [F.]; **social usage, form, formality,** order of the day; **custom 640;** conformity 82; **propriety, decorum,** cor-rectness, *bienséance* [F.], good form; **Grundyism,** Mrs. Grundy, Babbittry [U.S.], Main Street.

2. the conventions, the conventionals [coll.], **the proprieties, mores, dictates of society,** dictates of Mrs. Grundy.

3. conventionalist, conformist 82.2.

4. conventionalization, stylization.

VERBS **5. conventionalize, stylize.**

6. conform, follow the rule 82.3, 4.

ADJS. **7. conventional, customary,** popu-lar, **traditional, formal, prescriptive,** stipu-lated, established, fixed; **accepted,** recog-nized, acknowledged, received, admitted, approved, being done; **correct, right, proper, orthodox, decorous,** *de rigueur* [F.]; according to use *or* custom, accord-ing to the dictates of society *or* Mrs. Grundy; conformable 82.5.

8. conventionalized, styled.

ADVS. **9. conventionally,** acceptedly; **cus-tomarily, popularly, traditionally;** correctly,

properly, decorously, orthodoxly, as is proper, as it should be, *comme il faut* [F.].

644. FORMALITY

NOUNS **1. formality, form, formalness; ceremony, ceremonial, ceremoniousness; ritual,** rituality; **outward form,** show, mere show; outwardness, externality, superficial-ity; **stiffness, stiltedness,** primness, rigid-ness, starchiness, buckram; **solemnity,** gravity.

2. formalism, ceremonialism, ritualism; pedantry, pedantism, pedanticism; preci-sianism, preciseness, scrupulousness, punc-tiliousness, punctilio.

3. etiquette, social code, rules of con-duct; **formalities,** social procedures, social conduct; **manners, amenities,** civilities, elegancies, **social graces, mores, propri-eties, decorum,** good form; **protocol,** dip-lomatic code; punctilio, point of etiquette.

4. (ceremonial function) **ceremony,** ceremonial; **rite, ritual; formality, solem-nity; service, function,** duty, office, prac-tice, observance, performance; **exercise,** exercises [both U.S.]; celebration, solemni-zation; religious ceremony 1038; commence-ment, commencement exercises; gradua-tion, graduation exercises; baccalaureate service; inaugural; initiation; formal; empty ceremony, mummery [derog.].

VERBS **5. formalize,** ceremonialize, ritual-ize, solemnize, dignify.

6. stand on ceremony, observe the formalities.

ADJS. **7. formal,** formular, formulary; formalist, formalistic; **outward, external,** modal, superficial, surface; **affected,** man-nered; pedantic(al), academic.

8. ceremonious, ceremonial; ritualistic, ritual; functional, functionary; **solemn,** sober; **pompous, stately,** lofty, majestic, courtly, dignified, imposing, august.

9. stiff, stilted, studied, prim, rigid, set, fixed, starch, starched, buckram, in buck-ram.

10. punctilious, scrupulous, precise, precisian, exact; **orderly, methodical,** sys-tematic, regular.

ADVS. **11. formally,** in due form, in set form; **ceremoniously, ritually,** ritualisti-cally; **outwardly, externally,** superficially, on the surface; for form's sake, *pro forma* [L.], **as a matter of form,** for the sake of appearances, to keep *or* save face.

12. stiffly, stiltedly, starchly, primly, rigidly, fixedly, studiedly.

645. INFORMALITY

NOUNS 1. **informality, informalness,** unceremoniousness; **casualness,** offhandedness, ease, easiness, easygoingness; Bohemianism; unconventionality 83.3; **familiarity; naturalness,** simplicity, plainness, homeliness, **unaffectedness,** unassumingness, unconstraint; irregularity.

VERBS 2. **not stand on ceremony,** let one's hair down [slang], be oneself, come as you are.

ADJS. 3. **informal, unceremonious; casual, offhand,** offhanded, easy, easygoing, free and easy, on the free and easy [slang]; Bohemian; unconventional 83.8; **familiar; natural,** simple, plain, homely, **unaffected, unassuming,** unstudied, undignified, unconstrained; irregular; unofficial.

ADVS. 4. **informally, unceremoniously,** without ceremony, *sans cérémonie* [F.], *sans façon* [F.]; **casually,** offhand, offhandedly; familiarly; **naturally,** simply, plainly, **unaffectedly, unassumingly,** undignifiedly; *en famille* [F., with the family].

646. MOTIVATION, INDUCEMENT

NOUNS 1. **motive, reason, cause, ground,** grounds, basis, occasion, call, matter, score, account, consideration, interest, sake; intention 651; ulterior motive.

2. **motivation,** moving, **actuation, prompting,** animation; influence 171.

3. **inducement,** determination; enlistment, engagement; **persuasion,** suasion, persuasive, persuasiveness; exhortation, hortation; coaxing, wheedling, cajolery, cajolement, blandishment.

4. **incitement,** incitation, **instigation,** stimulation, excitement, fomentation, agitation, **inflammation,** firing, rabble-rousing; **provocation,** irritation, exasperation, exacerbation, infuriation.

5. urging, pressing, plying; **encouragement,** abetment; **insistence,** instance; goading, prodding, spurring, pricking, needling.

6. **urge,** urgency; **impulse,** impulsion; press, pressure, drive, push, compulsion, constraint, high pressure.

7. incentive, **interest, inducement, encouragement, invitation, provocative, incitement; stimulus,** stimulative, fillip, whet.

8. **goad, spur, prod,** prick, sting, thorn; gad, gadfly; oxgoad; ankus [India]; rowel; whip, lash.

9. **inspiration, elevation, exaltation,** lift, uplift; **infusion, infection;** fire, firing; **animation, exhilaration,** enlivenment; afflatus, divine afflatus; genius, animus, moving *or* animating spirit.

10. **prompter, mover,** impeller, inducer, actuator, **animator,** moving spirit; **encourager,** abettor, **inspirer,** firer, sparker, spark plug [coll.]; **stimulator,** gadfly; coaxer, coax [coll.], wheedler, cajoler.

11. **instigator, inciter,** incentor, exciter, urger; **provoker,** provocator, *provocateur* [F.], *agent provocateur* [F.]; **agitator,** fomenter, inflamer; agitprop; **rabble rouser,** rouser, **ringleader,** demagogue; **firebrand,** incendiary; seditionist, seditionary; **troublemaker,** mischief-maker.

VERBS 12. **motivate, move, impel,** force, compel, propel, **stimulate, animate, actuate,** move to action; promote, foster; advance, forward, further.

13. **prompt, provoke, evoke, elicit, call up,** summon up, muster up, call forth.

14. **urge, press, ply, push,** crowd [coll., U.S.], **constrain,** bear upon, work on [coll.], twist one's arm [slang]; **pressure, high-pressure,** bring pressure to bear upon, throw one's weight into, throw one's weight into the scale; **coax,** wheedle, cajole, blandish, plead with; **exhort,** call on *or* upon, advocate, recommend; insist, persist, **insist upon.**

15. **goad, prod,** poke, **spur,** prick, needle; whip, lash, flog.

16. **urge on, egg on** [coll.], hound on, hie on, hasten on, hurry on; **goad on, spur on,** drive on, whip on; cheer on, root on [slang].

17. **incite, instigate, put up to** [slang]; set on, sick on; **foment,** ferment, **agitate, excite, stir up,** work up, whip up; **inflame, fire; provoke,** pique, nettle, irritate, exasperate, exacerbate; **infuriate,** madden, frenzy, lash into a fury; pour oil on the fire, feed the fire, add fuel to the flame, fan, fan the flame, blow the coals, stir the embers, apply the torch.

18. **kindle,** enkindle, light up, **fire, spark, trigger,** touch off, set off, start.

19. **rouse, arouse, raise,** raise up, waken, awaken, wake up; **stir, stir up,** set astir.

20. **inspire,** inspirit, spirit, spirit up; **lift, uplift,** elevate, exalt, boost, give one a lift; **fire,** fire one's imagination; **animate, exhilarate,** enliven; **infuse, infect,** inform.

21. **encourage,** give encouragement, pat *or* clap on the back; **invite,** ask for; **abet,** aid and abet, **back up,** support, counte-

nance, keep in countenance; **foster, nurture,** nourish, feed.

22. induce, prompt, move, move one to; **influence, sway,** incline, carry, bring, lead, **lead one to;** turn, turn one's head; **determine, dispose,** decide; enlist, procure, engage, interest in, get to do.

23. persuade, prevail on or **upon,** prevail with; **bring round,** bring to reason, bring to one's senses; **win over,** bring over, draw over, gain over; **talk over, talk into,** argue into, out-talk [coll.]; wangle into, hook or hook in [slang], land [coll.]; sell [coll.], sell one on [coll.], sell a bill of goods [slang]; wear down, soften up, overcome, overcome one's resistance, twist one's arm [joc.].

24. persuade oneself, make oneself easy about, make sure of, make up one's mind; be persuaded, rest easy.

ADJS. **25. motivating, moving, animating, actuating, impelling,** impulsive; urgent, insistent, pressing, driving, compelling.

26. inspiring, inspirational, inspiriting; uplifting, lifting, elevating; animating, exhilarating, enlivening.

27. provocative, provoking; exciting, excitive; prompting, **rousing, stirring; stimulating,** stimulative; **encouraging,** inviting.

28. incitive, inciting, incentive; **instigative,** instigating; **agitative,** agitational; **inflammatory, incendiary,** fomenting, rabble-rousing.

29. persuasive, suasive, persuading; hortative, hortatory; exhortative, exhortatory.

30. moved, prompted, impelled, constrained, stimulated, **actuated,** animated; minded, inclined, of a mind to, with half a mind to.

31. inspired, exalted, elevated, uplifted; fired, afire, on fire.

647. PRETEXT

Ostensible Motive.—NOUNS **1. pretext, pretense, pretension, show;** false pretense 614.3; **excuse, apology;** poor excuse, lame excuse; **shift, makeshift;** handle, peg to hang on; **subterfuge,** refuge, feint, gesture, put-off, dust thrown in the eye; **blind,** guise, mask, **cover,** cloak, veil; gloss, varnish, color.

2. assumption, claim, profession, allegation.

VERBS **3. pretext,** make a pretext of; **pre-**tend, make a pretense of; **allege, claim,** profess, purport, avow, assume.

ADJS. **4. pretexted, pretended, alleged, claimed, professed, purported,** avowed, **assumed, ostensible, specious,** so-called, in name only.

ADVS. **5. ostensibly, allegedly,** purportedly, professedly, avowedly; under the pretext of, **as a pretext,** as an excuse, as a makeshift.

648. ALLUREMENT

Attractive Inducement.—NOUNS **1. allurement, enticement, inveiglement,** invitation, *agacerie* [F.]; inducement 646.7; **temptation,** tantalization; **seduction,** seducement; **fascination, captivation, enchantment,** enthrallment or inthrallment; witchery, bewitchery, bewitchment; **attraction, interest, charm, glamour** or glamor, appeal; sex appeal, S.A. [slang]; attractiveness, charmingness, seductiveness, winsomeness, winning ways; song of the Sirens, voice of the tempter; forbidden fruit.

2. lure, charm, **come-on** [slang], drawing card; **decoy,** decoy duck, stool pigeon; **bait,** ground bait, baited trap; **snare,** hook, silver hook.

3. tempter, seducer, seductor, **enticer,** inveigler, charmer, fascinator, tantalizer; **temptress, enchantress,** seductress, **siren;** Siren, Circe, Lorelei or Lurlei, Parthenope; **vampire,** vamp [slang], femme fatale.

VERBS **4. lure,** allure, **entice, seduce; inveigle, decoy,** draw, **draw on, lead on,** angle on [slang], give the come-on [slang]; ensnare 616.20; draw in, suck in [slang], rope in [slang, U.S.]; bait, offer bait to, bait the hook, angle with a silver hook; gild the pill.

5. attract, interest, appeal, engage, fetch [coll.], attract one's interest, be attractive, take one's fancy; **invite,** court, beckon; **tempt, tantalize, titillate, pique;** whet the appetite, make one's mouth water, *faire venir l'eau à la bouche* [F.].

6. fascinate, captivate, charm, becharm, **beguile, intrigue, enthrall** or inthrall, **enrapture, enravish, entrance, enchant, witch, bewitch,** vamp [slang], carry away; hypnotize, mesmerize.

ADJS. **7. alluring, fascinating, captivating, charming,** glamorous, **enchanting, entrancing,** ravishing, **enravishing, intriguing, enthralling** or inthralling, witching, **bewitching; attractive, interesting,** appealing, engaging, taking, fetching [coll.], catching, winning, winsome, prepossessing, exciting, killing [coll.], heart-robbing; **seductive**, seducing, **enticing**, **inviting**, come-hither [slang]; **tempting**, **tantalizing**, titillating, titillative; **provocative**, *provoquant* [F.]; appetizing, mouthwatering; siren, sirenic.

ADVS. **8. alluringly, fascinatingly**, captivatingly, charmingly, enchantingly, entrancingly, enravishingly, intriguingly, bewitchingly; attractively, appealingly, engagingly, winsomely; **enticingly, seductively; temptingly**, provocatively, tantalizingly.

649. BRIBERY

Corrupt Inducement.—NOUNS **1. bribery**, bribing, **purchase**, subornation, **corruption**, graft [coll.], bribery and corruption.

2. bribe, sop, sop to Cerberus, sop in the pan; **palm oil,** oil of palms [both joc.]; **grease** [slang], soap [slang, U.S.]; gratuity, *douceur* [F.], bonus [coll.], baksheesh [near East], boodle [coll.]; hush money.

VERBS **3. bribe,** throw a sop to, put a sop into the pan; **grease,** oil, anount, **grease** *or* **oil the palm** *or* **hand, tickle the palm, fix** [all coll.]; square, palm, sugar [all slang]; **purchase,** buy, **buy off,** subsidize, hire; suborn, corrupt, tamper with, approach, angle with a silver hook; reach [slang], get at [coll.], get to [slang, U.S.].

650. DISSUASION

NOUNS **1. dissuasion, determent,** deterrence; remonstrance, expostulation, admonition, monition.

2. deterrent, determent; **discouragement,** disincentive [coll.]; damp, damper, **wet blanket,** cold water, chill.

VERBS **3. dissuade, talk out of** [coll.], kid out of [slang]; remonstrate, expostulate, admonish, cry out against.

4. disincline, indispose, disaffect, disinterest; **deter,** divert, repel, turn from, wean from; **discourage,** disencourage [dial.]; **throw cold water on,** throw *or* lay a wet blanket on, damp, dampen, cool, chill, quench, blunt.

ADJS. **5. dissuasive,** dissuading, disinclining, **discouraging;** expostulatory, admonitory, monitory.

651. INTENTION

NOUNS **1. intention, intent, purpose,** function, **design, plan,** project, proposal, counsel, **contemplation,** consideration, meaning, expectation, notion, mind, will, eye, view, purview [law], prospect, lookout, inclination, animus, sake; motive 646.1; determination (fixed intention) 622.1.

2. objective, object, aim, end, goal, destination, mark, point, pursuit, object in mind, end in view; **target,** butt, bull's eye, quintain; final cause, ultimatum, *raison d'être* [F.], "the be-all and the end-all" [Shakespeare]; by-purpose, by-end.

3. premeditation, predeliberation, preconsideration, **predetermination,** preresolution, forethought, aforethought.

VERBS **4. intend, purpose, plan** [coll.], **design, mean,** mind [dial.], **propose,** expect, think, **aim,** aim at, drive at, endeavor, destine, aspire to *or* after, bid for, go for, labor for, be at *or* after, set before oneself, purpose to oneself, harbor a design, determine upon, take into one's head.

5. intend to, mean to, aim to, propose to, expect to, hope to, anticipate, look forward to; fix to, go to, allow to [all dial.].

6. plan on, figure on, count on, calculate on [all coll.]; reckon on, allot on *or* upon [both dial.]; lot on *or* upon [coll., U.S.]; bank on *or* upon [coll.], bargain for, lay one's account for.

7. contemplate, meditate, consider, study to, think of, dream of, talk of; **have in mind,** have *in petto* [It.], **have in view** *or* **contemplation,** have in one's eye, have an eye to, **have a mind to,** have half a mind to, have a good *or* great mind to.

8. premeditate, preresolve, predetermine, predeliberate, preconsider, forethink.

ADJS. **9. intentional, intended,** purposed, **designed,** aimed, **meant,** meaning, **purposeful, willful, voluntary, conscious,** knowing, witting, **deliberate,** deliberated, **calculated,** contemplated, meditated, considered, studied, planned, advised, weighed, express; teleological.

10. premeditated, predeliberated, preconsidered, predetermined, preresolved, prepense, **aforethought.**

ADVS. **11. intentionally, purposely,** purposefully, **on purpose,** a-purpose [dial.], **deliberately, designedly,** expressly, pointedly, **willfully, voluntarily, wittingly, consciously, knowingly,** advisedly, studiously, **calculatedly,** contemplatedly, meditatedly, premeditatedly, **with premeditation,** with intent, by design, with one's eyes open; with malice aforethought, in cold blood.

PREPS., ETC. **12. for, to; in order to** *or*

that, for to [dial.], so, **so that, so as to; for the purpose of,** to the end that, with the intent that, with the view of, with a view to, with an eye to; in contemplation of, in consideration of; in pursuance of, pursuant to; **on account of, for the sake of;** for that, therefor; for this, *ad hoc* [L.]; for each, per.

652. PLAN

NOUNS 1. **plan, scheme, design,** device, contrivance, conception; the sketch, the picture [both coll.]; **method,** way, **arrangement,** system, disposition, layout, setup, lineup; schema, schematism, scheme of arrangement; blueprint, program of action, working plan, ground plan, master plan; intention 651.

2. **project,** projection; **proposal,** proposition, presentation, submission, suggestion.

3. **diagram, plot, chart, blueprint,** graph; **design, pattern,** copy, cartoon; **sketch, draft** or draught, drawing; rough, *brouillon* [F.], *ébauche* [F.]; **outline, delineation,** skeleton, figure, profile; house plan, ground plan; elevation, projection.

4. **map, chart,** *carte du pays* [F., map of the country]; outline map, relief map, contour map, road map, photomap; globe; atlas; hachure; cartography, chorography, ichnography, topography; cartographer, chorographer, ichnographer, topographer.

5. **policy,** polity, principles; **program, procedure,** course, line, plan of action; **platform.**

6. **intrigue,** intriguery; **plot, scheme,** game, little game; underplot, counterplot; **conspiracy,** confederacy, **complicity, collusion, connivance,** complot, cabal; **artifice** 733.3; **contrivance,** contriving; **scheming,** schemery, plotting, finagling [coll.]; **machination,** manipulation, **maneuvering,** engineering; wirepulling [coll.], pipelaying [slang, U.S.].

7. **planner, designer,** deviser, contriver, framer, projector, enterpriser; organizer, promoter; architect, builder.

8. **schemer, plotter,** finagler [coll.], fainaguer [dial., Eng.], Machiavellian; **intriguer,** intrigant; **conspirer,** conspirator, **conniver;** maneuverer, machinator; wirepuller [coll.], pipelayer [slang, U.S.].

VERBS 9. **plan, devise, contrive, design,** frame, cast, concert, lay plans, take steps or measures; work out, strike out; **arrange,** make arrangements; **line up,** set up, ready up [coll.], work up; lay down a plan, shape or mark out a course; **project,** forecast, plan ahead; intend 651.4.

10. **plot, scheme, intrigue,** figure for [coll.]; **conspire, connive,** collude, complot, cabal, clique [coll.]; hatch, **hatch up,** cook up [coll.], brew, concoct, hatch a plot, put up a job [slang]; **maneuver,** machinate, engineer, wangle [coll.], angle, finagle [coll.], fainague [dial., Eng.]; counterplot, countermine.

11. (make a plan of) **plot, map, chart, blueprint; diagram,** graph; **sketch, draw up, make out,** draw up a plan; map out, plot out; **lay out,** set out, mark out, chalk out, cut out; lay off, mark off.

12. **outline,** line, **delineate,** describe, define, brief; **sketch, draft** or draught, trace; block, block in or out; rough in.

ADJS. 13. **planned, devised, contrived, plotted,** arranged; **projected, in prospect, in view,** *in petto* [It.]; **under consideration,** under active consideration, under advisement; on the docket, on the table, on the anvil, on the carpet or tapis, *sur le tapis* [F.].

14. **scheming,** schemy [coll.], **schemeful; calculating, designing, contriving, plotting, intriguing; conniving,** connivant, conspiring, collusive; up to.

15. schematic, diagrammatic.

653. PURSUIT

NOUNS 1. **pursuit,** pursuing, pursuance, prosecution; **following,** follow, follow-up; **chase,** shag [slang]; scramble, struggle.

2. **hunting,** gunning, shooting, venery; sport, sporting; **hunt, chase,** *battue* [F.], chevy or chivy [Eng.], shikar [India], hue and cry; coursing; fox hunting; hawking; falconry; still hunt [U.S.], search 484.2.

3. **fishing,** fishery, **angling;** rod and reel; whaling; fly fishing; trolling, trawling; piscatology, halieutics.

4. **pursuer,** pursuant, **chaser, follower.**

5. **hunter, huntsman,** sportsman, **Nimrod,** shikari or shikaree [India]; huntress, sportswoman; stalker; courser; trapper; big-game hunter; white hunter.

6. **fisher, fisherman, angler,** wormer [coll.]; piscator, piscatorian, piscatorialist; Waltonian, "the compleat angler" [I. Walton]; dibber, dibbler; troller, trawler; jacker [U.S.]; drifter; whaler.

7. **quarry, game, prey,** chase, victim, the hunted; kill; big game.

VERBS 8. **pursue,** prosecute, **follow,**

follow up; **go after, run after,** make after, prowl after, go in pursuit of; **chase, give chase;** shag [slang], shack [coll., U.S.]; run, run in pursuit of; pursue a course, hold a course, steer or shape one's course, direct or bend one's steps; practice, carry on 703.7.

9. hunt, go hunting, **chase,** run, chevy, shikar [India], sport; course; ride to hounds, follow the hounds; hound, dog; hawk, falcon; fowl; still-hunt [U.S.], stalk; flush, start; seek, search 484.24, 25.

10. fish, go fishing, **angle,** bob for, cast one's hook or net; bait the hook; shrimp, whale, clam [U.S.]; fly-fish; trawl, troll; bob, dap, dib, dibble, drive, gig, grig, guddle [chiefly Scot.], seine, spin, spoon, torch, whiff.

ADJS. **11. pursuing, following,** pursuant; **in pursuit,** in hot pursuit, in full cry.

PREPS. **12. after, in pursuit** or **pursuance of,** in search of, out for, on the lookout for, in the market for, loaded or out for bear [slang, U.S.]; on the track or trail, on the scent.

INTERJS. **13.** (hunting cries) halloo!, yoicks!, soho!; tallyho!, tallyho over!, tallyho back!

654. BUSINESS, OCCUPATION

NOUNS **1. business, occupation, employment, work, activity;** affair, matter, concern, concernment, **interest,** lookout [coll]; what one is doing or about; commerce 825.

2. task, work, stint, job, job of work, piece of work; **chore** [U.S.], char or chare [esp. Eng.], odd job; **assignment, charge,** errand, mission, commission, imposition, **duty,** care, exercise; things to do, agenda, matters in hand, irons in the fire, fish to fry; homework; fatigue duty [mil.].

3. function, office, duty, job, place; **role,** part, cue; **capacity,** character, position, condition, relation.

4. (sphere of work or activity) **field, sphere,** province, department, orb, orbit, realm, domain, demesne; walk, **walk of life;** beat, round.

5. position, situation, job [coll.], employment, service, **office, post,** place, station, berth, billet, appointment, engagement, chargeship, incumbency; opening, vacancy.

6. vocation, occupation, business, work, line, line of business or work, **calling,** mission, **profession, practice,** pursuit, **way** [coll.]; specialty, métier or

metier; racket, game, lay [all slang]; **career,** life, lifework, life's work; **trade,** industry; **craft,** art, handicraft.

7. avocation, hobby, hobbyhorse, side line.

8. vocationalism, professionalism; unprofessionalism, **amateurism.**

VERBS **9. busy, occupy, engage,** devote, spend, **employ,** busy oneself, pass ~, employ or spend the time; occupy one's time, take up one's time; attend to business, attend to one's work.

10. busy oneself with, occupy or engage oneself with, employ oneself in or upon, pass ~, employ or spend one's time in; **engage in,** devote oneself to, apply oneself to, address oneself to; concern oneself with, make it one's business; **be about, be doing,** be occupied with, be engaged or employed in, be at work on; have one's hands in, have in hand.

11. practice, follow as an occupation 703.7.

12. ply one's trade, labor in one's vocation, carry on a business or trade, **drive a trade, do** or **transact business,** keep shop; set up in business, hang out one's shingle [coll., U.S.].

13. officiate, function, serve, perform, act, act or play one's part, **do duty,** discharge or perform the office, ~ duties or functions of, serve in the office or capacity of.

14. hold office, fill an office, occupy **a** post, hold down a job [slang].

ADJS. **15. businesslike, practical, efficient,** thorough, prompt; workaday, workday, prosaic.

16. occupational, vocational, career [U.S.]; **professional, pro** [coll.]; technical, industrial; official, functional.

17. nonoccupational, nonvocational; **unprofessional, amateurish,** unbusinesslike; **avocational,** hobbyhorsical [joc.].

ADVS. **18. professionally,** vocationally; as a profession or vocation; in the course of business, all in the day's work.

19. unprofessionally, amateurishly.

655. WAY

NOUNS **1. way, wise, manner, means, mode,** form, **fashion, style,** cut, tone, guise; **method,** system, usage; **procedure, process,** proceeding, course, practice, order, lines, line, line of action; *modus operandi* [L.], mode of procedure; the way of, the how.

2. route, itinerary, trajectory, circuit,

orbit, walk, beat, round, **course**, run, march, tack, line.

3. path, track, trail, road, line, line of way *or* road; **pathway,** footpath, footway; **walk,** walkway [U.S.]; **sidewalk,** *trottoir* [F.], foot pavement [Eng.], boardwalk; public walk, promenade, esplanade, alameda [Southwest. U.S.], parade, *prado* [Sp.], mall; towpath; bridle path; berm *or* berme; run, runway; beaten track *or* path, rut, groove.

4. passageway, pass, passage, defile; corridor, aisle, alley, lane, avenue, channel, artery; opening, aperture; inlet 301.5; outlet 302.9; connection, communication; covered way, gallery, arcade, colonnade, cloister, ambulatory; underpass, overpass.

5. byway, bypath, byroad, by-lane, by-street, side road, side street; **by-pass,** by-passage, by-route, **detour,** roundabout way; bypaths and crooked ways; backway, back stairs, back door, side door; back street; highways and byways.

6. road, roadway, thoroughfare, concourse, drag [slang, U.S.]; **street, avenue; highway,** highroad, **boulevard, turnpike,** pike, coach road; main road, main drag [slang, U.S.], state highway [U.S.], King's *or* Queen's highway [Eng.], royal road, broad highway; **arterial,** artery, arterial highway [all U.S.]; **expressway,** express highway, **thruway, freeway,** speedway, **superhighway,** *autobahn* [Ger.], *autostrada* [It.]; post road; parkway; **driveway,** drive; place, row, court; **lane,** vennel [Scot. & dial., Eng.]; **alley,** alleyway; causeway, causey, dike, embankment.

7. pavement, pave [chiefly U.S.], *pavé* [F.], paving; macadam, asphalt, tar; cement, concrete; bricks, tile; stone, pavestones, tilestones; flags, flagstones, flagging; cobblestones, cobbles; curbstone, kerbstone [Eng.], edgestone; curb, kerb [Eng.], curbing.

8. railway, railroad, rail, line; tram [Eng.], tramline [Eng.], tramway, tramroad; trolley track, streetcar line, street railway; interurban; elevated railway, elevated [coll.], el *or* L [coll.]; subway [U.S.], underground [Eng.], tube; electric railway, cable railway, horse railway; monorail; light railroad; main line, trunk, trunk line; branch, feeder, by-line; siding, sidetrack, turnout; switchback; junction; terminus, terminal [U.S.], the end of the line.

9. cableway, ropeway, wireway, wire road, cable *or* rope railway; telpher, telpherway, telpher ropeway, telpher line *or* railway.

10. bridge, span, viaduct; overbridge, overpass; drawbridge, bascule bridge; floating bridge, bateau bridge, pontoon; footbridge; toll bridge; suspension bridge; cantilever bridge; gangplank, gangboard, gangway; steppingstone, stepstone; pass, ford, ferry; Bifrost [myth.].

ADVS. **11. how,** in what **way** *or* **manner,** by what mode *or* means, to what extent, in what condition, for what reason, by what name, to what effect, at what price; after this fashion, in this way, in such wise, on the lines of, along these lines; **thus, so,** as, thus and so.

12. anyhow, anyway, anywise, in any way, by any means, by any manner of means, in any event, at any rate, in any case, **nevertheless, nonetheless, however, regardless,** at all, nohow [dial.].

13. somehow, someway [coll.], somegate [Scot. & North. Eng.], **in some way,** in some way or other, by some means, in some such way, **somehow or other** *or* another, in one way or another, after a fashion, no matter how; **by hook or by crook,** by fair means or foul.

656. MEANS

NOUNS **1. means,** ways, **ways and means,** means to an end; **wherewithal,** wherewith; **resources,** disposable resources; expedients, devices; measures, steps; method 655.1; expedient 668.2.

2. instrumentality, agency; machinery, mechanism; mediation, intermediation, intermediacy; subservience *or* subserviency.

3. instrument, tool, implement, vehicle, organ, hand; **agent, medium;** intermedium, intermediary, intermediate, interagent; servant, slave, handmaid; **cat's-paw, puppet, pawn,** creature, stooge [slang], jackal; toy, plaything; dupe 618.

VERBS **4. find means,** find a way, provide the wherewithal; get by hook or by crook, obtain by fair means or foul; beg, borrow, or steal.

5. be instrumental, serve, subserve, promote, minister, officiate; serve as, act as *or* for.

ADJS. **6. instrumental, implemental; useful, serviceable, helpful,** conducive; subservient, ministerial; mediatorial, intermedial, intermediary, intermediate, intervening.

7. by hand, manual, hand.

PREPS. 8. by means of, by the agency of, through the instrumentality of, by the aid of, by use of, by way of, by dint of, by the act of, through the medium of, by or in virtue of, at the hand of; with, herewith, therewith, wherewith, wherewithal, along with; whereby, thereby, hereby; through, by, per; on, upon.

ADVS. 9. by hand, manually.

657. PROVISION, EQUIPMENT

NOUNS 1. provision, providing; equipment, accouterment; supply, supplying; furnishing, furnishment; investment, endowment, arrayal; provisioning, purveyance; armament; replenishment, reinforcement; preparation 718.

2. provisions, supplies 658.1; provender 3062.5.

3. accommodations, accommodation; lodgings 187.3; bed, board; board and room, bed and board; subsistence, keep.

4. equipage, equipment; furniture, furnishings, furnishment; fixtures, fittings, appointments, accouterments, appurtenances, appliances, conveniences; upholstery; plumbing; outfit, apparatus, gear, plant, paraphernalia, things; traps [coll.], trappings; rig, rigging; tackle, tack [dial.]; matériel, impedimenta, armament, munitions; kit, duffel [U.S.].

5. harness, caparison, tack [U.S.], tackle; headgear, bridle, halter, freno [West. U.S.], headstall, cavesson, hackamore [West. U.S.], jaquima [Southwest. U.S.]; bit, snaffle; breeching, britchen [dial.]; crupper; bellyband, girth, cinch [U.S.], surcingle; yoke, poke [local U.S.]; tug, trace; reins, lines, ribbons [coll.]; jerk line [West. U.S.]; checkrein, bearing rein, martingale.

6. provider, supplier, furnisher; purveyor, purveyancer, provisioner, caterer, victualer, sutler [mil.]; commissary, commissariat; quartermaster, steward, maniple, purser, batman.

VERBS 7. provide, supply, furnish, invest, clothe, endow, give, afford, accommodate, present, contribute, yield; stock, store; fund; provide for, make provision or due provision for; prepare 718.6; find; fill, fill up; replenish, reinforce, recruit.

8. equip, furnish, outfit, gear, prepare, fit, fit up or out, rig, rig up or out, turn out, appoint, accouter, array, dress, deck,

fettle [dial., Eng.]; arm, heel [slang, U.S.]; man, staff; munition; mechanize [mil.].

9. provision, provender, purvey, cater, feed, victual, forage.

10. accommodate, furnish accommodations; lodge 187.11; put up, board, bed and board, board and room.

11. make a living, earn a living or livelihood, make or earn one's keep, make or work one's way, support oneself, make both ends meet, support existence, keep body and soul together, keep the wolf from the door, keep or hold one's head above water, keep afloat; eke out, make out, scrape along, manage, get by.

ADJS. 12. provided, supplied, furnished, invested, clothed, endowed; equipped, fitted, outfitted, rigged, accoutered, arrayed; armed, heeled [slang, U.S.]; prepared 718.16.

13. well-provided, well-supplied, well-furnished, well-stocked, well-found, well-prepared; well-equipped, well-fitted, well-appointed; well-armed, well-heeled [slang, U.S.].

658. STORE, SUPPLY

NOUNS 1. store, treasure, hoard, collection, accumulation, cumulation, amassment, budget, repertory; stores, supplies, provisions; munitions; larder, commissariat.

2. supply, fund, stock; staple, supply on hand, stock in trade; resource, resources; assets, capital, available means; grist, grist to the mill.

3. reserve, reserves, reservoir, stockpile, reserve supply, something in reserve; reserve fund, nest egg, savings, backlog [coll.], a shot in the locker [coll.]; ace in the hole [slang], a card up one's sleeve; relay.

4. source of supply, source, staple; well, fountain, fount, font, spring, wellspring; quarry; mine, gold mine, bonanza [U.S.]; lode, vein.

5. storage, stowage; cold storage, dry storage.

6. storehouse, storeroom, store, storage, depository, repository, conservatory, reservoir, repertory, depot, magazine, magasin [F.], staple, lumber room, stock room; closet, cupboard; treasury, treasure house; bank, vault 834.13, 14; warehouse, wareroom, entrepôt [F.], godown [Oriental]; armory, arsenal, dump; dock; lumberyard [U.S. & Can.].

7. garner, granary, elevator [U.S.],

silo; mow, rick, haymow, hayloft, hayrick.

8. **larder, pantry,** buttery, spence [chiefly Scot.], stillroom [Eng.]; dairy, dairy house *or* room.

9. **museum; gallery,** art gallery, picture gallery; **salon,** saloon [esp. Eng.]; pinakotheke *or* pinacotheca, glyptotheca; Metropolitan Museum, National Museum, British Museum, Louvre, Madame Tussaud's.

VERBS 10. **store, stow,** lay in store; lay in, lay in a supply, ~ stock *or* store; store away, stow away, **put away, lay away,** pack away; lay down, stow down, salt down *or* away [coll.]; **deposit,** reposit, lodge; **cache,** stash [criminal slang, U.S.]; **bank,** coffer, hutch; warehouse, reservoir; file, file away.

11. **store up, lay up, put up, save up,** hoard up, treasure up, garner up, heap up, pile up, **accumulate,** cumulate, **collect, amass, stockpile;** garner, gather into barns; **hoard, treasure,** stock, fund.

12. **reserve, preserve, save, keep,** retain, withhold, keep *or* hold back; **keep in reserve,** keep on hand, keep by one; set *or* put aside, set apart, put ~, lay *or* set by; save up, save to fall back upon, keep as a nest egg, **provide for** *or* **against a rainy day, feather one's nest,** look after the main chance [coll.]; husband, husband one's resources.

13. **have in store** *or* **reserve,** have to fall back upon, have something to draw on, have something laid by, have something laid by for a rainy day.

ADJS. 14. **stored, accumulated,** amassed, laid up; **hoarded,** treasured.

15. **reserved, preserved, saved, kept,** retained, withheld, kept in reserve; **spare, to spare.**

ADVS. 16. **in store,** in stock, in supply, **on hand,** in ordinary.

17. **in reserve,** back, behind, away, aside, by.

659. SUFFICIENCY

NOUNS 1. **sufficiency,** sufficientness, **enough, adequacy,** adequateness, competence *or* competency, satisfactoriness, satisfaction, satisfactory amount; slight sufficiency [joc.], "an elegant sufficiency" [Thomson]; no less, no more and no less.

2. **plenty,** plenitude, **plentifulness,** plenteousness; **amplitude,** ampleness; **abundance,** copiousness, exuberance, galore [coll.]; **bountifulness,** liberalness, liberality, generousness, **generosity,** lavishness, lavishment, **extravagance, prodigality; wealth,** opulence *or* opulency, richness, affluence; **fullness,** full measure, repleteness, overflow; **prevalence,** profuseness, **profusion; superabundance** 661.2; great abundance, great plenty, ample sufficiency, enough and to spare; fat of the land, "a land flowing with milk and honey" [Bible]; Abundantia (goddess of plenty).

3. **cornucopia,** horn of plenty, horn of Amalthea.

VERBS 4. **suffice, do,** just do, serve, avail, **answer, satisfy,** qualify, meet, fulfill, answer *or* serve the purpose, meet requirements; **pass muster, fill the bill** [coll.], get by [slang], do in a pinch, pass in the dark [coll.]; reach, go around.

5. **abound,** exuberate, **teem, teem with,** creep with, crawl with, swarm with, bristle with; flow, stream, rain, pour, shower; overflow, overrun.

ADJS. 6. **sufficient,** sufficing; **enough, ample, plenty, satisfactory,** comfortable [coll.]; **adequate,** commensurate, proportionate, correspondent, equal, competent, suitable, decent, valid, due; good, **good enough,** plenty good enough [coll.]; sufficient for, ~ to *or* unto, equal to.

7. **plentiful, plenty, plenteous,** plenitudinous, "plenty as blackberries" [Shakespeare]; **ample, abundant,** abounding, copious, exuberant; **bountiful,** bounteous, **lavish, generous,** liberal, **extravagant, prodigal,** free; **luxuriant, rich,** fat, **wealthy, opulent, affluent;** full, flush, replete, overflowing; **profuse,** profusive, effuse, diffuse, diffusive; **prevalent,** prevailing, rife, rampant, epidemic, besetting; teeming 101.10; **superabundant** 661.20; enough and to spare; wantless, without want; cheap, a dime a dozen.

ADVS. 8. **sufficiently, amply,** satisfactorily, **enough; adequately,** commensurately, proportionately, correspondently, competently, suitably, to the good; fully, in full measure, to the full.

9. **plentifully,** plenteously, plenty [coll.], aplenty [coll.], in plenty; **abundantly,** in abundance, copiously, galore [coll.], no end [coll., U.S.]; **superabundantly** 661.25; **bountifully,** bounteously, **lavishly, generously, liberally, extravagantly,** prodigally, freely, without stint; **luxuriantly,** richly, opulently, exuberantly, affluently; **profusely,** diffusely, effusely; prevalently, prevailingly.

660. INSUFFICIENCY

NOUNS 1. insufficiency, inadequacy, insufficientness, inadequateness, short supply, none to spare.

2. meagerness, slightness, smallness, spareness, puniness; thinness, leanness, slimness, slenderness, narrowness; exiguousness, exiguity.

3. scarcity, scarceness; sparsity, sparseness; scantiness, scantness, scantity, scant sufficiency [coll.]; dearth, paucity, poverty; rarity, rareness, uncommonness.

4. want, lack, need, deficiency, shortcoming, short [coll.], shortage, wantage; absence, omission; destitution, deprivation, starvation, famine.

5. pittance, dole, scrimption [dial.], drop in the bucket; mite, bit 35.2; short allowance, short-commons, half rations, pinchgut money or pay [sea slang]; cheeseparings and candle ends.

VERBS 6. want, lack, need, require; miss, feel the want of; be found wanting, kick the beam; fall short, come short, run short; fail, fail of or in.

ADJS. 7. insufficient, unsufficing, inadequate, too little, not enough, unequal to; slack at a low ebb, at low-water mark.

8. meager, slight, small, spare, puny, exiguous; poor, stinted, frugal, sparing, impoverished; thin, lean, slim, slender, narrow, straitened, limited.

9. scarce, sparse, close; scant, scanty; scrimp, scrimpy [coll.]; skimp, skimpy [coll.], skimping [chiefly coll.]; in short supply, at a premium; rare, uncommon; scarcer than hen's teeth, scarce as ice water in hell [both coll.]; not to be had, not to be had for love or money, not to be had at any price.

10. ill-provided, ill-furnished, ill off; unprovided, unsupplied, unreplenished, unfed; unstored, untreasured; empty-handed, barehanded, shorthanded.

ADJS., PREPS. 11. wanting, lacking, needing, missing, failing, in want of; for want of, in default of, in the absence of; deficient, defective, faulty, found wanting; short, short of, scant of; shy, shy of or on [both slang]; without, minus [coll.], less, sans; out of, destitute of, bare of, void of, devoid of, empty of, forlorn of, bereft of, deprived of, denuded of, unpossessed of, unblest with, bankrupt in, out of pocket, at the end of one's rope or tether.

ADVS. 12. insufficiently; inadequately.

13. meagerly, slightly, sparely, punily, poorly, frugally, sparingly.

14. scarcely, sparsely, scantily, skimpily [coll.], scrimpily [coll.]; rarely, uncommonly.

661. EXCESS

NOUNS 1. excess, excessiveness, inordinacy, inordinateness, immoderateness, immoderacy, immoderation, extravagance or extravagancy, intemperance, intemperateness; extreme, extremity, extremes; overlargeness, overgreatness; overmuch, overmuchness, too much; exorbitance or exorbitancy, undueness; outrageousness, unreasonableness, preposterousness, monstrousness, fabulousness, egregiousness; extremism, radicalism; exaggeration 615; overindulgence 991.

2. superabundance, overabundance, overplentifulness, overplenteousness, overplenty, oversufficiency, overmuchness, overcopiousness, overlavishness, overluxuriance, overbounteousness, overnumerousness; lavishness, prodigality; plenty 659.2; more than enough, enough and to spare, enough in all conscience, much of a muchness [coll.]; overdose, overmeasure, "enough, with over-measure" [Shakespeare]; too much of a good thing, egg in one's beer [slang, U.S.], toujours perdrix [F., always partridge]; drug, drug on the market; embarras de richesses [F., embarrassment of riches], money to burn [coll.]; overpopulation.

3. overfullness, plethora, surfeit, glut, engorgement, repletion, congestion; saturation, supersaturation; overload, overburden, overcharge, surcharge, overweight; overflow, deluge, flood.

4. superfluity, superfluousness; redundancy, redundance; unnecessariness, needlessness; luxury, extravagance; frill, frills, frillery [all coll.]; frippery, embellishment, embroidery, gingerbread; expletive, padding, filling.

5. surplus, surplusage, overplus, overage, overset, overrun, overmeasure, oversupply; remainder, balance, leftover, extra, spare, plus.

6. overdoing, overgoing, overcarrying, overreaching, supererogation; overuse; overwork, overexertion, overexercise, overexpenditure, overtaxing, overstrain, tax, strain; overstudy; too many irons in the fire.

7. overextension, overdrawing, over-

stretching, overstrain, overstraining, stretching, straining, stretch, strain; **overexpansion**, overdistention, inflation [econ.]; overgrowth, overdevelopment, hypertrophy [med. & biol.].

8. **extremist, radical,** irreconcilable, diehard, bitter-ender [U.S.].

VERBS 9. **superabound,** overabound, **know no bounds;** overflow, flood; overrun, overspread, overswarm, overgrow, overwhelm, fill, run through, run riot, meet one at every turn; remain on one's hands, hang heavy on hand; "my cup runneth over" [Bible], it never rains but it pours.

10. **exceed, surpass, pass, transcend, go beyond;** overgo, overpass, overstep, overrun, overreach, overcarry, overshoot, overshoot the mark.

11. **overdo, go too far, carry too far,** go to an extreme, **go to extremes, go overboard; run into the ground;** supererogate; overplay, overplay one's hand [coll.], overreach oneself; **overtax, overtask, overexert, overexercise, overstrain,** overspend, overexpend, overdrive; overtrain; **overwork,** overlabor, overelaborate, overdevelop; overstudy, burn the candle at both ends; have too many irons in the fire; overuse; exaggerate 615.3; overindulge 991.5.

12. **pile it on,** lay it on, **lay it on thick,** lay it on with a trowel [slang]; pile Ossa upon Pelion.

13. **carry coals to Newcastle,** carry salt to Dysart, bring owls to Athens, carry timber to a wood, teach fishes to swim, kill the slain, butter one's bread on both sides, put butter on bacon, paint the lily, "to gild refined gold, to paint the lily, to throw a perfume on a violet" [Shakespeare].

14. **overextend, overdraw, overstretch, overstrain,** stretch, strain; **overexpand,** overdistend, overdevelop, inflate [econ.].

15. **oversupply, overprovide,** overfurnish, overequip; **overstock,** overstore; overprovision, overprovender; overdose; drug, drug the market; **flood, deluge,** inundate, engulf, swamp, whelm, overwhelm.

16. **overload,** overlade, **overburden,** overweight, overweigh, **overcharge,** surcharge; **overfill,** stuff, crowd, cram, pack, congest, choke; overstuff, overfeed; **surfeit, glut, gorge; saturate,** soak, drench; supersaturate, supercharge.

ADJS. 17. **excessive, inordinate, immoderate, intemperate, extravagant, extreme,** superlative, overweening, overboard, *outré* [F.]; **overlarge, overgreat,** overbig;

overmuch, too much; **exorbitant, undue,** unwarranted, fancy, high; large, tall, stiff, steep, unchristian [all coll.]; **out of bounds** *or* **all bounds,** out of sight [coll.]; **unreasonable,** unconscionable; **outrageous, preposterous,** monstrous, fabulous, egregious, desperate.

18. **superfluous, redundant; excess, in excess; unnecessary, unessential,** nonessential, **needless,** unneeded, uncalledfor; expletive, *de trop* [F.], supererogatory; spare, to spare; on one's hands, heavy on hand.

19. **surplus,** overplus; **remaining,** unused, **leftover, over, over and above, in addition, to boot, extra, spare,** supernumerary.

20. **superabundant,** overabundant, **plentiful** 659.7, **overplentiful,** overplenteous, overplenty, **oversufficient, overmuch,** overmany, **lavish, prodigal,** overlavish, overcopious, overluxuriant, overexuberant, overbounteous, **overgenerous,** overliberal, overprolific, overnumerous; overpopulated, overpopulous.

21. **overfull, overloaded, overladen, overburdened,** overweighted, **overcharged,** surcharged, plethoric; **saturated,** drenched, soaked; supersaturated, supercharged; **surfeited, glutted, gorged; stuffed,** overstuffed, overfed; **congested,** stuffed up; **overstocked, oversupplied; overflowing,** overwhelmed, running over, filled to overflowing; **bursting,** ready to burst, bursting at the seams.

22. **overdone, overwrought;** overdrawn, overstretched, overstrained; exaggerated 615.4.

ADVS. 23. **excessively, inordinately, immoderately, intemperately, extremely,** superlatively; **overly,** overweeningly, over, **overmuch,** too much; **too,** too-too [coll.]; **exorbitantly, unduly,** unwarrantedly; **unreasonably,** unconscionably; **outrageously, preposterously,** monstrously, fabulously, egregiously, grossly, desperately.

24. **in** *or* **to excess, to extremes,** to the extreme, too far, to a fault, out of all proportion, out of sight [coll.].

25. **superabundantly,** overabundantly, lavishly, prodigally, extravagantly, more than enough; plentifully 659.9; without measure, out of measure, beyond measure.

26. **superfluously, redundantly;** unnecessarily, needlessly, beyond need.

27. **in excess of,** over, beyond, past, above, **over and above, extra,** overplus.

662. SATIETY

NOUNS 1. **satiety, satiation, satisfaction, surfeit, glut,** plethora, repletion, engorgement; **fill, full** [coll.], **bellyful** [vulg.], skinful [coll.]; more than enough, enough in all conscience, too much of a good thing, all one can stand or take.

2. **satedness,** surfeitedness, cloyedness, jadedness, fullness, overfullness; fed-upness, fed-uppedness [both slang].

3. cloyer, surfeiter, sickener, nauseant; **overdose;** a diet of cake; warmed-over cabbage, "cabbage repeatedly" [Juvenal].

VERBS 4. **satiate, sate, satisfy, surfeit, glut,** gorge, cloy, jade, pall; **fill,** fill up; stuff, overstuff; **overfill,** overgorge, overdose, overfeed.

5. **have enough,** have about enough of, have quite enough, **have one's fill,** have too much, have too much of a good thing, **have a bellyful** [vulg.], have a skinful [coll.], have an overdose of, **be fed up** [slang], have all one can take or stand, not have or take any more of.

ADJS. 6. **satiated, sated, satisfied, surfeited, gorged,** surfeit-gorged, **glutted, cloyed,** jaded; **full,** full of, with one's fill of, **overfull,** stuffed, overstuffed, overgorged, overfed; **fed-up,** fed to the gills or neck [all slang]; **with a bellyful** [vulg.], with a skinful [coll.], with enough of; disgusted, **sick of,** tired of, sick and tired of.

7. **satiating,** sating, satisfying, surfeiting, **filling,** overfilling, glutting, gorging, jading; **cloying,** cloysome.

663. USE

NOUNS 1. **use, employment,** employ; **exercise,** exercitation, **exertion,** active use; application, appliance, **administration,** adhibition; disposition, disposal; recourse, resort; consumption, usance [both econ.]; wear.

2. **usage, practice, conduct, procedure;** custom 640; **treatment, handling,** management.

3. **utility, usefulness, usability,** utilizability, **serviceability,** helpfulness, profitability, **applicability,** availability; **practicability,** practicality; efficacy, efficiency, adequacy.

4. **benefit, service, avail, profit, advantage,** convenience, interest, behalf, behoof, **stead; value, worth,** money's worth.

5. **function, purpose, design,** end use.

6. **functionalism, utilitarianism;** functional design, functional furniture, ~ housing, etc.

7. (in law) usufruct, right of use, user, enjoyment of property.

8. **utilization,** using; employment, management, handling, manipulation, operation; exploitation.

9. **user,** employer; consumer, absorber, enjoyer.

VERBS 10. **use, utilize, make use of,** do with; **employ,** ply, work, manage, handle, manipulate, operate, wield; **practice,** play; exercise, exert, put out.

11. **apply, put to use,** carry out, **put in practice** or **operation,** put in force, enforce; **administer,** adhibit, bring to bear upon; **devote, bestow,** spend, put, give, tender, dispense, deal, dispose of.

12. **treat, handle, deal with,** do with, have to do with, have business with.

13. **spend** (as time), expend, **pass, lead,** employ, **put in,** devote, bestow, give to; while, wile, beguile.

14. **avail oneself of, resort to,** have recourse to, **turn to,** look to, recur to, fall back upon, take to [coll.], betake oneself to, take up with, lay one's hand to; convert or turn to use, put into requisition, press or enlist into service, call or bring into play, call or draw forth.

15. **take advantage of, make the most of,** make good use of, **turn to account** or **good account,** turn to one's advantage, use to advantage, put to advantage, **find one's account** or **advantage in,** reap the benefit of; improve the occasion 129.9; **profit by,** exploit, capitalize on [U.S.], make capital of, make a good thing of [coll.], **trade on,** cash in on [coll., U.S.]; make the best or most of, make a shift with.

16. (take unfair advantage of) **exploit, take advantage of, use,** make use of, **use for one's own ends,** make a cat's-paw of, make a handle of, work [coll.], work for a good thing [slang], play for a sucker [slang, U.S.]; practice upon, work upon, play on or upon; **impose upon,** presume upon; milk, bleed [coll.].

17. **avail,** be of use, **serve, suffice, do,** answer, **answer** or **serve the purpose,** inure, serve one's turn, fill the bill [coll.], bestead, **stand one in stead** or **good stead,** stand one in hand; advantage, be of advantage or service to; **profit, benefit,** remunerate, gain, reap the benefit of.

ADJS. **18. useful,** of use, of service, **serviceable, helpful,** instrumental, implemental, commodious; good for; beneficial 672.21; **practical,** practicable; **functional, utilitarian,** of general utility.

19. handy, convenient, advantageous; available, accessible, **ready, at hand,** to hand, **on hand,** on tap, on tab, on deck [coll.], on call, at one's call *or* beck and call, at one's disposal; all-round [coll.], of all work.

20. effectual, effective, active, **efficient,** efficacious; capable, competent, adequate.

21. valuable, of value; **profitable,** gainful, remunerative, well-spent, **worthwhile,** worth one's salt; invaluable, inestimable, priceless, beyond price.

22. usable, utilizable; applicable, appliable; **expendable,** spendable, disposable, dispensable, replaceable; exploitable.

23. used, employed, practiced, exercised, applied; secondhand 123.18.

24. in use, in practice, in force, **in** service, in operation, in commission.

ADVS. **25. usefully,** to good use; **profitably,** gainfully; **advantageously, to advantage,** to the good, to profit, to good effect; effectually, effectively, efficiently, capably, competently, adequately; serviceably, functionally, practically.

26. handily, conveniently, readily, availably, accessibly.

664. CONSUMPTION

A Using Up.—NOUNS **1. consumption,** absorption; **expenditure,** spending; **waste,** wastage; **depletion, exhaustion,** impoverishment, dissipation, decrement, drain.

VERBS **2. consume, spend, expend; use, use up,** dispose of; absorb, eat, eat up, swallow, swallow up; finish, finish off; **exhaust, deplete,** impoverish, drain, drain of resources; run out of.

3. waste 852.4.

4. run out, give out; run dry, dry up.

5. go to waste, run to waste, go to pot [coll.], go down the drain [coll.]; waste away, wear out *or* away; run *or* go to seed, fall "into the sere, the yellow leaf" [Shakespeare]; **dissipate,** scatter to the winds, "waste its sweetness on the desert air" [Gray].

ADJS. **6. used up, consumed,** finished; gone; **spent,** exhausted, effete, dissipated, depleted, impoverished, drained, worn out; wasted 852.9.

665. MISUSE

NOUNS **1. misuse, misusage; misemployment, misapplication, mishandling,** mismanagement, misdirection, misappropriation; perversion, prostitution; profanation, desecration; malpractice.

2. mistreatment, ill-treatment, mal-treatment, ill-use, ill-usage, **abuse,** molestation; outrage, atrocity.

3. persecution, oppression, harassment; **witch-hunting,** witch-hunt, McCarthyism.

VERBS **4. misuse, misemploy, misapply, mishandle,** mismanage, misdirect, misappropriate; pervert, prostitute; profane, desecrate.

5. mistreat, maltreat, ill-treat, ill-use, abuse, molest; do wrong, do wrong by; outrage, do violence, do one's worst; mishandle, manhandle; buffet, batter, bruise, maul, knock about; rough, rough up.

6. persecute, oppress, **torment, harass,** harry, beset; pursue, hunt down.

666. DISUSE

NOUNS **1. disuse, disusage, desuetude;** nonuse, nonemployment; nonprevalence; unprevalence; **obsolescence,** obsoleteness, obsoletism.

2. discontinuance, abandonment, forbearance, desistance, abstinence.

3. discard, discardment, **rejection,** riddance, removal, elimination, relegation; **scrapping,** junking [slang]; **reject, throwaway, castaway,** castoff; jettison, jetsam; rejectamenta.

VERBS **4. disuse,** cease to use, **abandon, discontinue,** quit, stop, drop, **give up,** leave off, cut out, desist, have done with.

5. not use, do without, dispense with, **let alone,** not touch; **abstain, refrain,** forgo, forbear, spare, waive; keep back, reserve.

6. put away, lay away, lay up, lay up in a napkin; **put aside,** lay ~, set *or* push aside, side [coll.], lay *or* set by, lay off, shunt; **pigeonhole, shelve,** put on the shelf; **table,** lay on the table; table the motion, pass to the order of the day, nol-pros [law].

7. discard, reject, throw away, throw out, cast behind, **get rid of,** get quit of, get shut *or* shet of [dial.], rid oneself of, **dispose of,** do away with, part with, give away, **cast off,** jettison, relegate, remove, eliminate, slough, bilge [sea slang], dump, throw over, **throw** *or* **heave overboard,**

throw out the window, throw or cast to the dogs, wash one's hands of.

8. scrap, trash, **junk** [slang], scrap-heap, consign to the scrap heap; wastebasket, put in file thirteen [joc.].

9. obsolesce, fall into disuse, go out, pass away; supersede.

ADJS. **10. disused, abandoned, discontinued,** done with; out, **out of use; old, stale, outworn,** worn-out, past use, not worth saving; **obsolete,** obsolescent; on the shelf.

11. discarded, rejected, **castoff,** castaway scrap, junk [coll.].

12. unused, unemployed, unapplied, unexercised, unessayed; **unspent,** undisposed of; untouched, unhandled; untrodden, unbeaten; **new, firsthand,** original.

667. USELESSNESS

NOUNS **1. uselessness, inutility; needlessness,** unnecessity; **bootlessness,** purposelessness; **fruitlessness,** unprofitableness, profitlessness, unprofitability; **worthlessness,** valuelessness; inefficacy 157.3; unserviceability, unusability, inoperativeness, unhelpfulness; functionlessness.

2. futility, vanity, inanity, nugacity, otiosity; **vicious circle, rat race** [coll.].

3. labor in vain, labor lost, labor of Sisyphus; work of Penelope, Penelope's web; **wild-goose chase,** goose chase, bootless errand.

4. refuse, waste, wastage, wastements, waste matter, **offal,** draff, shoddy; **leavings,** sweepings, **scraps,** orts, oddments, odds and ends; **garbage,** swill, hogwash [coll.]; **offscourings,** outscourings, scourings, rinsings; parings, raspings, filings, shavings; **dregs** 43.2; **scum,** offscum; **riffraff,** raff [dial.]; chaff, stubble; weeds, tares; deadwood; rags, bones; wastepaper; scrap iron.

5. rubbish, rubble, **trash, junk** [coll.], **scrap,** dust [Eng.], **debris** or **débris, litter,** clutter, lumber, clamjamfry [chiefly Scot.], rummage [chiefly dial.], truck [coll.], **stuff,** tripe [slang], crap [slang].

6. trash pile, rubbish heap; dust hole [Eng.], glory hole [coll.]; wasteyard, junk yard [coll.], dump.

7. wastepaper basket, wastebasket, waste bin [Eng.].

VERBS **8. labor in vain, go on a wild-goose chase, beat the air,** lash the waves, tilt at windmills, sow the sand, bay at the moon, preach or speak to the winds, whistle jigs to a milestone, roll the stone of Sisyphus, milk the ram, milk a he-goat into a sieve, pour water into a sieve, hold a farthing candle to the sun, look for a needle in a haystack or bottle of hay, lock the stable door after the horse is stolen.

ADJS. **9. useless,** of no use, no go [coll.]; **purposeless,** of no purpose; **bootless,** sleeveless [dial.], feckless; **unavailing,** of no avail; ineffectual 157.15.

10. needless, unnecessary, unessential, nonessential, unneeded, **uncalled-for,** unrequired.

11. worthless, valueless, good-for-nothing or ~ **naught,** no good [coll.], N.G. [coll., U.S.], no-account [dial., U.S.], dear at any price, not worth-while, not worth having, not worth mentioning or speaking of, not worth a thought, not worth a rap, ~ a continental, ~ a damn, etc., not worth the powder and shot, not worth the pains, not worth one's salt, of no earthly use, fit for the dust hole.

12. fruitless, gainless, profitless, **unprofitable,** unremunerative, nonremunerative, **unrewarding,** rewardless.

13. vain, futile, empty, idle, inane, fatuous, fatuitous, nugatory, nugacious, effete, barren, sterile, otiose.

14. unserviceable, unusable, inoperative; **unhelpful,** unconducive; functionless, nonfunctional, nonutilitarian.

ADVS. **15. uselessly, needlessly,** unnecessarily, bootlessly, fruitlessly, **futilely, vainly,** purposelessly, to little purpose, **to no purpose.**

INTERJS. **16. what's the use!,** of what use!, what's the good!, *cui bono!* [L.], for what good!, no use!, it's no use!, I give up!

668. EXPEDIENCE

NOUNS **1. expedience, expediency; desirability, advisability, commendableness,** recommendability; **fitness, fittingness, appropriateness, seemliness, suitability,** worthiness, acceptability, feasibility, seasonableness, opportuneness, dueness, rightness, decorousness, propriety, decency; **advantage,** advantageousness, convenience; profitability, worth-whileness; wisdom, prudence 466.5–7.

2. expedient, expediency, measure, step, means, means to an end, **resort,** resource, avail, **device,** contrivance, artifice, subterfuge, **shift,** dodge [coll.], kink, ruffle, working proposition; **temporary expedient, makeshift,** *pis aller* [F.], stopgap; last resort *or* resource, *dernier ressort* [F.], last shift, last expedient, a shot in the locker [coll.], a card up one's sleeve.

VERBS 3. **make shift, make do,** make out [coll., U.S.], **manage,** manage with, manage to get along, do with, do as well as one can; eat one's cake and have it too.

ADJS. 4. **expedient, desirable,** to be desired, much to be desired; **advisable,** advisory, commendable, recommendable; **appropriate, meet, fit,** fitten [dial.], **fitting,** befitting, **becoming, seemly,** likely, congruous, **suitable,** sortable, acceptable, feasible, seasonable, opportune, due, right, proper, decorous, nice, decent, good, worthy; **advantageous, convenient,** favorable; profitable, worthwhile, worth one's while; **wise, politic** 466.17–19.

5. **practical,** practicable; **efficient,** effective.

6. **makeshift,** makeshifty, shifty, **temporary, provisional,** tentative.

ADVS. 7. **expediently, fittingly,** fitly, **appropriately,** becomingly, **suitably,** sortably, congruously, acceptably, feasibly, conveniently, seasonably, opportunely, rightly, properly, nicely, decorously, decently; desirably, advisably, commendably; advantageously, to advantage, all to the good.

669. INEXPEDIENCE

NOUNS 1. **inexpedience, inexpediency, undesirability, inadvisability;** unwiseness 469.2; **unfitness, unfittingness,** unbecomingness, **inappropriateness, unsuitability,** incongruity, **unmeetness,** untowardness, **unseemliness,** inaptitude, unseasonableness, inopportuneness, unfortunateness, infelicity; **impropriety,** indecorousness, indecency, undueness, wrongness, objectionability; inadmissibility, ineligibility, unqualification.

2. **disadvantage, drawback, detriment, liability,** disinterest, prejudice, damage, hurt, harm, injury; handicap 728.6.

3. **inconvenience,** discommodity, incommodity, disaccommodation, **trouble, bother;** inconvenientness, **unhandiness,** awkwardness, clumsiness, troublesomeness.

VERBS 4. **inconvenience,** put to inconvenience, **put out, discommode,** incommode, disaccommodate, disoblige, disadvantage, **trouble, bother,** put to trouble, **impose upon,** put on *or* upon.

ADJS. 5. **inexpedient, undesirable, inadvisable,** uncommendable; **unwise,** impolitic 469.9; **unfit, unfitting,** unbefitting,

unbecoming, misbecoming, **inappropriate, unsuitable, unmeet,** untoward, inept, inapt, **unseemly,** unhandsome, incongruous, ill-suited, malapropos, *mal à propos* [F.], inopportune, unseasonable, infelicitous, unfortunate, unhappy; **improper, indecorous,** indecent, undue, wrong, bad, objectionable; inadmissible, ineligible, unqualified; out of place, out of character *or* keeping, in the wrong place; unworthy, unworthy of; beneath one, undignified, *infra dignitatem* [L.], infra dig [coll.].

6. **disadvantageous,** unadvantageous, **unfavorable,** unsatisfactory; **detrimental,** deleterious, injurious, harmful, prejudicial, disserviceable.

7. **inconvenient, incommodious,** discommodious, **unhandy, awkward,** clumsy, troublesome.

ADVS. 8. **inexpediently, undesirably,** inadvisably; **unfittingly,** unbecomingly, **inappropriately, unsuitably,** ineptly, inaptly, incongruously, inopportunely, unseasonably, infelicitously, unfortunately, unhappily.

9. **disadvantageously,** unadvantageously; **inconveniently,** unhandily, with difficulty, ill.

PHRS. 10. it will never do, I wouldn't do it if I were you, it doesn't pay, it's not worth the trouble, the game is not worth the candle.

670. IMPORTANCE

NOUNS 1. **importance, significance, consequence,** salience, concern, concernment, consideration, import, note, mark, **moment, weight,** interest, matter, materiality; value, worth.

2. **notability, noteworthiness,** remarkableness, memorability; **prominence, eminence, greatness,** distinction, prestige.

3. **gravity, seriousness,** solemnity; no joke, no laughing matter.

4. **urgency, insistence,** imperativeness, importunateness, exigency, **press,** pressure, stress, pinch, matter of life and death.

5. **matter of importance,** thing of interest, matter of concern, object of note, one for the book [slang], something to write home about; notabilia, memorabilia, great doings.

6. **salient point, the point,** cardinal point, great point, **main point,** main thing, precise thing, essential matter, *sine qua non* [L.]; **essential,** fundamental, gravemen, material point; **gist, nub** [coll., U.S.],

pith, jet, chat [coll.]; **crux, crucial** or **critical point**; key, keystone, cornerstone; landmark, milestone.

7. feature, highlight, high spot [U.S.], outstanding feature.

8. personage, person of importance or consequence, **great man,** big man [coll.], man of mark, **somebody,** something, **notable,** notability, figure, name, big name, **bigwig,** great gun [coll.], nabob, **mogul,** big ~, great or grand mogul, panjandrum, "the Grand Panjandrum himself" [S. Foote], mugwump [coll.], pasha or bashaw [Turk.], sachem, great card, heavyweight [coll.], a person to be reckoned with; very important person, **VIP** [slang]; **worthy,** pillar of society; **dignitary,** dignity; **magnate,** power; tycoon [coll., U.S.], baron [U.S.]; the great, "the choice and master spirits of the age" [Shakespeare].

9. (slang terms) **big shot** [U.S.], big gun, **wheel** [U.S.], **big wheel** [U.S.], **big bug,** big cheese, **high-muck-a-muck** [U.S.], nob, **big it** or **It,** gilded rooster; his nabs or nibs, his importance [all joc.].

10. chief, principal, paramount, top sawyer [coll.], first fiddle, biggest frog in the pond [slang, U.S.]; king, railroad king, etc.; prima donna, star.

VERBS **11. matter,** import, signify, **count, tell, weigh, carry weight,** draw water [slang, U.S.], cut some ice [coll.]; be something be somebody, amount to some shucks [slang, U.S.].

12. value, esteem, treasure, prize, appreciate, care for, **rate highly,** think highly of, **think well of, think much of,** set much by, set store by, give ~, attach or ascribe importance to; make much of, make over [coll.], make a fuss or stir about, make an ado or much ado about.

13. emphasize, stress, lay emphasis or stress upon, place emphasis on, give emphasis to, **accent, accentuate, punctuate, mark, point up,** spearhead; **highlight,** spotlight; **star,** asterisk; **underline,** underscore; overemphasize, overstress, overaccentuate.

14. feature [coll., U.S.], headline [coll.], star.

15. dramatize, play up [coll.], extravagate, color, make a production of.

ADJS. **16. important, consequential, momentous, considerable,** substantial, **great, grand,** big, noble, august, **eminent, prominent,** conspicuous, **outstanding, distinguished,** egregious [joc.], quite a shucks [slang, U.S.]; big-time [slang], big-league,

major-league, heavyweight [coll.]; high-powered [coll.], double-barreled [slang]; bigwig, bigwigged; name, big-name [both coll.]; front-page.

17. of importance, of significance, of consequence, of note, of concern, of moment, of weight; not to be overlooked or despised, not to be sneezed at [coll.].

18. notable, noteworthy, remarkable, marked, of mark; **memorable,** rememberable, unforgettable, never to be forgotten; monumental; **extraordinary, exceptional,** special, rare.

19. significant, striking, telling, trenchant, pregnant.

20. salient, signal, material, to the point.

21. weighty, heavy, ponderous; **grave,** sober, somber, **solemn, serious,** earnest; fateful, fatal.

22. emphatic, decided, positive, energetic, forceful, **forcible;** emphasized, stressed, accented, accentuated, punctuated, pointed, marked, underlined.

23. urgent, imperative, imperious, **compelling, pressing,** crying, clamorous, **insistent,** instant, importunate, **exigent; crucial,** critical, acute.

24. vital, of vital importance, **essential,** fundamental, radical.

25. paramount, principal, leading, foremost, main, chief, prime, **primary,** capital, cardinal, **dominant,** predominant, master, controlling, commanding, ruling, **overruling,** all-absorbing.

ADVS. **26. importantly, significantly,** consequentially, momentously, greatly, grandly, eminently, prominently, conspicuously, outstandingly; notably, markedly, remarkably; saliently, signally, materially.

671. UNIMPORTANCE

NOUNS **1. unimportance, insignificance,** irrelevance or irrelevancy, **immateriality,** ineffectuality, **inconsequence,** inconsequentiality, unnoteworthiness, indifference; **smallness,** littleness, slightness, inconsiderableness, negligibility; **pettiness,** puniness, pokiness, picayunishness [U.S.].

2. paltriness, poorness, **baseness, meanness,** sorriness, sadness, pitifulness, despicableness, miserableness, wretchedness, vileness, shabbiness, cheapness, worthlessness, unworthiness.

3. trivialty, trivialness; **superficiality,** shallowness; **frivolity,** frivolousness, lightness, levity; **foolishness,** silliness, inanity; idleness, futility; **much ado about nothing,** tempest or storm in a teacup or teapot, *tempête dans un verre d'eau* [F., tempest in a glass of water], much cry and little wool.

4. **trivia,** trifles; **trumpery,** frippery, gimcrackery, claptrap, **rubbish,** trash, chaff, truck [coll.], stuff; froth, foam, smoke, "trifles light as air" [Shakespeare]; minutiae, details, minor details.

5. **trifle, triviality, bagatelle,** fribble, **gimcrack, gewgaw, trinket, bauble,** toy, **knickknack,** kickshaw, whimwham, fiddle-stick, fidfad [coll.], fiddle-faddle [coll.], falderal or folderol; pin, button, hair, straw, rush, feather, bubble, fig, prune, peanut, peppercorn, bean, hill of beans [coll.], molehill, row of pins [coll.], pinch of snuff; curse, continental [U.S.], hoot [slang], shucks [slang], damn, tinker's dam or damn; picayune [coll.], pistareen; rap, sou, halfpenny, farthing, brass farthing, cent, red cent [coll., U.S.], two cents; song, old song; drop in the ocean, dust in the balance, feather in the scale, snap of the fingers; fleabite, pinprick; joke, jest, farce, child's play.

6. **insignificancy,** trivial or paltry affair, small or trifling matter, **no great matter,** matter of indifference, a little thing, *peu de chose* [F.], hardly or scarcely anything, matter of no importance or consequence, no object, **nothing, naught,** mere nothing, nothing in particular, nothing to signify, nothing to speak or worth speaking of, nothing to boast of, nothing to write home about; thing of naught, nullity, nihility, obscurity.

7. **a nobody,** insignificancy, mediocrity, **little fellow, man in the street; nonentity,** obscurity, a nothing, cipher, "an O without a figure" [Shakespeare], nobody one knows, no one knows who; lightweight [coll.], whippersnapper, whiffet [coll.], scrub, runt, tinhorn [slang], no great shakes [coll.]; man of straw, jackstraw; **small beer, small fry;** Mr. and Mrs. Nobody, John Doe and Richard or Mary Roe; Tom, Dick, and Harry; Brown, Jones, and Robinson.

8. **trifling,** dallying, **dalliance,** flirtation, coquetry, toying, fiddling, playing, fooling, monkeying [coll., U.S.]; **puttering,** pottering [esp. Eng.], piddling, peddling, dabbling.

9. **trifler, dallier, putterer,** potterer [esp. Eng.], piddler, dabbler; boondoggler [slang, U.S.]; **flirt, coquet.**

VERBS 10. **be unimportant,** be of no importance, **not matter,** not count [coll.], cut no ice [coll.], signify nothing, go for nothing, little matter, make no matter, **not make any difference; not amount to anything,** not amount to a hill of beans [coll.], not amount to a damn [slang], not amount to shucks [slang]; feel like two cents [coll.].

11. **attach little importance to,** make little of, **make light of,** think little of, think small beer of [coll.], **make** or **think nothing of,** take no account of, set little by, set no store by, set at naught, snap one's fingers at; not care a straw about, not care shucks for [slang], not give a hoot or two hoots for [slang], not give a damn about, not give a dime a dozen for.

12. **make much ado about nothing,** make mountains out of molehills, have a storm or tempest in a teacup or teapot.

13. **trifle, dally, flirt, coquet, toy, fiddle,** faddle [dial., Eng.], fiddle-faddle [coll.], fribble, frivol [coll.], **play, fool, monkey** [coll., U.S.]; **putter, potter** [esp. Eng.], **piddle,** peddle, **dabble;** boondoggle [slang, U.S.]; play around, fool around, monkey around [coll., U.S.], mess around [coll.]; **toy with,** etc., finger with, fidget with, twiddle, tweedle [dial.].

ADJS. 14. **unimportant, of no importance,** of little or small importance, of no great importance, **of no account,** of no significance, of no concern, of no matter, of little or no consequence, no great shakes [coll., U.S.]; no skin off one's nose or elbow [coll.].

15. **insignificant, inconsequential,** unnoteworthy; **immaterial,** irrelevant, unessential, **not vital,** neither here nor there; **inconsiderable,** inappreciable, negligible; **small, little,** minute.

16. **trivial, trifling;** fribble, fribbling; fidfad, fiddle-faddle [both coll.]; **slight,** slender, flimsy, meager; **superficial, shallow; frivolous, light;** idle, futile; nugatory, nugacious; **foolish, silly, inane,** unworthy of serious consideration.

17. **petty,** petit [law], minor, inferior; puny, measly [slang], **poky** or **pokey, piddling,** peddling, pindling [coll., U.S.], niggling, pettifogging; picayune, picayunish [U.S.]; **small-time** [slang], tinhorn [slang], **one-horse** [coll.], **two-by-four** [coll.], jerkwater [coll., U.S.]; small-fry.

18. **paltry, poor, base,** common, **mean,** sorry, sad, **pitiful, despicable, contemptible,** beneath contempt, **miserable, wretched, vile, shabby,** scrubby, **shoddy, scurvy,** scummy, cheesy [slang, U.S.]; beggarly, niggardly; trashy, rubbishy, riffraff; trumpery, claptrap, gimcracky [coll.]; tinpot, tin-potty [both slang]; **cheap,** catchpenny, twopenny-halfpenny, two-for-a-cent or -penny, dime-a-dozen.

19. **unworthy, worthless,** unworthy of regard or consideration, beneath notice.

ADVS. 20. **unimportantly, insignificantly, inconsequentially,** immaterially, irrelevantly, unessentially; **pettily, paltrily; trivially,** triflingly, superficially, shallowly, frivolously, lightly, idly.

PHRS. 21. **it does not matter,** it matters not, it does not signify, **it is of no consequence** or importance, n'importe [F.], **it makes no difference,** it cannot be helped, it is all the same; it will all come out in the wash [coll.], it will be all the same a hundred years hence.

22. **no matter, never mind,** think no more of it, do not give it another thought, let it pass, let it go [coll.], ignore it, forget it [coll.], skip it [slang], drop it [slang].

23. **what does it matter?,** what matter?, **what's the difference?,** what's the diff? [slang], what do I care?, what of it?, what boots it?, what's the odds?; for aught one cares.

672. GOODNESS

Good Quality or Effect.—NOUNS 1. **goodness, excellence, quality,** class [slang]; **virtue,** grace; **merit,** desert; **value, worth;** fineness, goodliness, niceness; **superiority,** first-rateness; virtuousness 978.

2. **superexcellence, supereminence,** superfineness, **superbness,** exquisiteness, **magnificence,** marvelousness.

3. **tolerableness,** tolerability, goodishness, fairishness, **adequateness, satisfactoriness,** acceptability, admissibility.

4. **good, welfare,** well-being; **interest, advantage; behalf, behoof; benefit,** benefaction, blessing, boon; **profit,** avail, gain; world of good.

5. **good thing,** a thing to be desired, "a consummation devoutly to be wished" [Shakespeare]; **treasure,** gem, jewel, diamond, pearl; boast, pride, **pride and joy;** prize, plum, catch, find [coll.].

6. **first-rater,** top-notcher [both coll.];

wonder, prodigy, caution [coll.], one in a thousand, one in a way.

7. (slang terms) **dandy, jim-dandy,** dilly, **humdinger, pip,** pippin, **peach, brick, lulu,** nifty, **daisy,** darb, honey, sweetheart, dream, lollapaloosa, **corker, crackajack,** knockout, beat, trump, hummer, rip-hummer, dazzler, oner, winner, the cheese, the nuts.

8. **best,** very best, best ever, the tops [slang]; **quintessence,** prime, optimum, superlative; **choice, pick, select, elect,** elite; **cream, flower,** fat; cream of the crop, flower of the flock, pick of the bunch, pièce de resistance, crème de la crème [F.], salt of the earth; **prize,** champion, queen; nonesuch, nonpareil [F.]; gem of the first water.

9. **beneficialness, helpfulness,** salutariness, **advantageousness,** favorableness, profitableness; usefulness 663.

10. **harmlessness,** hurtlessness, uninjuriousness, **innocuousness,** unobnoxiousness, inoffensiveness, innocence.

VERBS 11. **benefit, do good, help, serve,** contribute, advantage, favor, **profit,** avail, do a world of good; be the making of, make a man of; do no harm, break no bones, break no squares.

12. **vie,** outvie, challenge comparison, emulate, rival.

ADJS. 13. **good, excellent,** bueno [Sp.], bon [F.], bonzer [slang, Austral.], bonny [Scot.], **fine, nice,** goodly, **splendid, capital,** elegant [coll.], clever [chiefly dial.], braw [Scot.], famous [coll.], royal, noble, gallows [slang & dial.]; very good, très bon [F.]; estimable 966.19; virtuous 978.7.

14. (slang terms) **great, grand,** rum, bully, ripping [esp. Eng.], **dandy, swell, keen,** hot, **nifty,** nobby [esp. Eng.], peachy, **hunkydory,** jake [U.S.], crackajack, solid [U.S.], bang-up, jam-up, slap-up, ace-high, **fine and dandy,** just dandy, but good, O.K., okay, A-Okay, kayo, a bit of all right [Eng.].

15. **superior,** crack, above par; **highgrade, high-class,** high-quality, high-caliber, high-test; sterling, golden; pure gold, all wool; gilt-edged, gilt-edge [both coll.].

16. **first-rate, first-chop** [Anglo-Ind. & coll.], **tiptop** [coll.], **top-notch** [coll.], tophole [slang, chiefly Eng.], topflight, tops [slang]; **first-class,** classic, in a class by itself; **A1,** A one, A number 1 [all coll.].

17. **up to par,** up to standard, up to sample, **up to snuff** [slang]; **up to the**

mark, up to the notch, **up to scratch,** up to the handle or knocker [all coll.].

18. superb, super [slang], **superexcellent,** superfine, **exquisite; magnificent,** tremendous, colossal, immense, **marvelous, wonderful,** glorious, divine, terrific, sensational [all coll.]; as good as good can be, as good as they make 'em, out of this world [slang].

19. best, very best, **prime,** optimum, optimal, quintessential, of the first water; **choice, select, elect, picked,** hand-picked; **prize, champion;** matchless, peerless **36.17.**

20. tolerable, goodish, fair, fairish, moderate, tidy [coll.], **decent,** respectable, presentable, good enough, well enough, **pretty good,** pretty well, **not bad,** not amiss, not half bad, not so bad, **adequate, satisfactory, all right,** alright [coll.], better than nothing; **acceptable,** admissible, **passable,** unobjectionable, unexceptionable.

21. beneficial, good for, helpful, aidful, **salutary, advantageous,** favorable, **profitable,** edifying; useful **663.18.**

22. harmless, hurtless, **uninjurious, innocuous,** innoxious, innocent, unobnoxious, inoffensive; nonmalignant, nonpoisonous, nontoxic, nonvirulent, nonvenomous.

ADVS. **23. excellently, nicely,** finely, **capitally, splendidly, famously,** royally, nobly, rippingly [slang]; first-rately, first-rate [coll.]; **well,** very well, **fine** [coll.], aright, not amiss, all for the best, in great shape [slang].

24. superbly, exquisitely; **magnificently,** tremendously, immensely, terifically, **marvelously, wonderfully,** gloriously, divinely [all coll.].

25. tolerably, fairly, fairishly, **moderately, rather, pretty;** fairly well, pretty well; **adequately, satisfactorily,** passably, acceptably, presentably, decently.

26. beneficially, helpfully, salutarily, advantageously, favorably, profitably; for one's benefit, for one's good, to one's advantage, to or in one's interest, in one's favor.

673. BADNESS

Bad Quality or Effect.—NOUNS **1. badness, evilness,** peccancy, damnability; wickedness **979.5.**

2. terribleness, dreadfulness, awfulness [coll.], **horribleness, atrociousness** [coll.], outrageousness, egregiousness, scandalousness, shamefulness, infamousness, heinousness, nefariousness, direness, **baseness,** grossness, wretchedness, odiousness, obnoxiousness, abominableness, detestableness, despicableness, contemptibleness, hatefulness, **vileness,** rankness, foulness, fulsomeness.

3. evil, bad, wrong, ill; harm, hurt, injury, damage, detriment; mischief, havoc, hob [coll.]; outrage, atrocity; abomination, grievance, vexation, woe, crying evil; **bane 674;** fly in the ointment, worm in the apple or rose, skeleton in the closet, snake in the grass, "something rotten in the state of Denmark" [Shakespeare]; ills that flesh is heir to, "all ills that men endure" [Cowley]; the worst.

4. bad influence, evil star, **ill wind,** frowns of fortune; evil genius, **hoodoo** [coll.], **jinx** [slang], **Jonah,** jadu [Hind.].

5. harmfulness, hurtfulness, injuriousness, banefulness, balefulness, detrimentalness, deleteriousness, perniciousness, mischievousness, noxiousness, noisomeness, malignance or malignancy, malignity; insalubrity **682.**

VERBS **6. harm, hurt, injure,** wound, **damage,** prejudice, disadvantage, disserve; **wrong,** do wrong, do wrong by, do evil, do a mischief, do an ill office to; **molest,** lay a hand on, get into trouble; abuse, outrage; play mischief or havoc with, play hob with [coll.].

ADJS. **7. bad, evil, ill, wrong,** arrant, peccant, untoward; black, sinister; wicked, sinful **979.17.**

8. (slang terms) **punk, bum, lousy,** cheesy, crumby, snide, grim, rotten, putrid, stinking, Godawful, goshawful.

9. terrible, dreadful, awful [coll.], **horrible,** horrid, **atrocious** [coll.], enormous, impossible [coll.], **deplorable,** lamentable, regrettable, pitiful, pitiable, woeful, grievous, sad, dismal, grave, gross, flagrant, **outrageous,** heinous, villainous, **scandalous,** shameful, shocking, infamous, nefarious, egregious, **dire, vile, wretched,** base, **odious, obnoxious, abominable, detestable, despicable, contemptible,** hateful, rank, foul, fulsome, noisome, ghastly; too bad; as bad as they make 'em [coll.], as bad as bad can be; worst.

10. execrable, damnable; cursed **970.9, 10;** infernal [coll.], hellish, devilish, diabolic(al), beastly [coll.], ungodly [coll.], ruddy.

11. evil-fashioned, evil-shaped, evil-qualitied, evil-looking, evil-favored, evil-hued, evil-faced, evil-headed, evil-eyed, evil-savored, evil-affected, evil-gotten.

12. harmful, hurtful, scatheful *or* scathful [dial.], **baneful,** baleful, **injurious, damaging, detrimental,** deleterious, pernicious, mischievous, noxious, noisome; **malignant,** malign, malefic(al); prejudicial, disadvantageous, disserviceable; corrosive, corroding; insalubrious 682.4.

ADVS. **13. badly,** bad [coll.], **ill,** wrong, evil, evilly, wrongly, amiss, to one's cost.

14. terribly, dreadfully, horribly, horridly, **awfully** [coll.], **atrociously** [coll.], **deplorably,** lamentably, regrettably, pitifully, woefully, grievously, sadly, grossly, flagrantly, **outrageously,** scandalously, shamefully, shockingly, infamously, egregiously, execrably, **vilely, wretchedly, basely,** odiously, obnoxiously, abominably, detestably, despicably, contemptibly, foully; awful, dreadful [both dial. & coll.]; something fierce *or* terrible [slang].

674. BANE

NOUNS **1. bane,** curse, **affliction,** infliction, visitation, **plague,** pestilence, pest, scourge, **torment,** grievance, woe; evil, harm 673.3; vexation 864.2; thorn, thorn in the flesh *or* side, pea in the shoe.

2. blight, blast; canker, cancer; mold, fungus, mildew, smut, must, rust; rot, dry rot; worm, worm in the apple *or* rose; moth, "moth and rust" [Bible].

3. poison, venom, venin, **virus, toxic,** toxin, toxicant, leaven; deliriant, delirifacient; pesticide 408.11; toxicology.

4. miasma, miasm, **mephitis,** effluvium, malaria; coal gas, chokedamp, blackdamp.

5. sting, stinger, dart; **fang,** tang [dial.]; bee sting, snake bite.

6. poisons

aconite	cyanide of
antimony	potassium
arsenic	D.D.T.
arsenious acid	hemlock
arsenious oxide	hydrocyanic acid
bichloride of	hydrocyanide
mercury	nicotine
carbolic acid	nitrogen
carbon dioxide	Paris green
carbon monoxide	poison gas
carbonic acid	prussic acid
carbonic gas	ptomaine
chlorine	rat poison
chlorine dioxide *or*	strychnine
peroxide	tannic acid
	tannin
corrosive sublimate	tartar emetic

7. poisonous plants

banewort	nightshade
belladonna	nux vomica
black nightshade	opium poppy
castor-oil plant	poison bean
Congo tobacco	poisonberry
deadly nightshade	poisonbush
death camass	poison grass
death cup	poison hemlock
foxglove	poison ivy
Gastrolobium	poison laurel
greyana	poison oak
hellebore	poison rhubarb
hemp	poison sumac
henbane	poison tobacco
Indian hemp	poisonweed
Jimson weed	pokeweed
locoweed	sheep laurel
May apple	Swainsona
mescal	upas
monkshood	water hemlock
mushroom	

675. PERFECTION

NOUNS **1. perfection,** finish; **faultlessness, flawlessness,** defectlessness, indefectibility; spotlessness, stainlessness, taintlessness; immaculateness, impeccability.

2. soundness, intactness, wholeness, entireness, completeness, **integrity.**

3. acme of perfection, pink, pink of perfection, height, acme, ultimate, summit, culmination, consummation, quintessence, *ne plus ultra* [L., no more beyond].

4. ideal 25.4; paragon 983.4.

VERBS **5. perfect,** develop, improve 689.10; complete 720.6.

ADJS. **6. perfect,** pure, ideal; **faultless, flawless,** defectless; spotless, stainless, taintless, unblemished, untainted, unspotted; immaculate, impeccable; indefective, indefectible; beyond all praise, irreproachable, *sans peur et sans reproche* [F., without fear and without reproach].

7. sound, intact, whole, entire, complete; sound as a roach, right as a trivet.

8. undamaged, unharmed, unhurt, uninjured, unscathed, **unspoiled,** unimpaired; harmless, scatheless; **unmarred,** unmarked, unscarred, unscratched, undefaced, unbruised; **unbroken,** unshattered, untorn; undemolished, undestroyed; undeformed, unmaimed; unfaded, unworn, unwithered, bright, fresh.

9. perfected, finished, polished, refined; elaborate, high-wrought.

ADVS. **10. perfectly,** purely, ideally; **faultlessly, flawlessly,** spotlessly; immaculately, impeccably; **wholly, entirely, completely;** clean, clean as a whistle.

11. to perfection, to a turn, to a T, to

a fare-thee-well *or* fare-ye-well [coll.], to a finish, to a nicety, to the limit, with a finish, just right.

676. IMPERFECTION

NOUNS 1. imperfection, imperfectness; faultiness, defectiveness; shortcoming, deficiency, inadequacy, inadequateness; unsoundness, incompleteness; impairment 690; immaturity, undevelopment 719.4.

2. fault, *faute* [F.], defect, flaw, weak point, bug [slang, U.S.], screw loose; catch [coll.], snag, drawback; demerit; weakness, frailty, infirmity, failure, failing, foible, shortcoming, defection; blemish, taint 677; hole, hole in one's coat.

VERBS 3. fall short, come short, fall down [slang], not measure up, not come up to par, not come up to the mark, not come up to scratch [coll.], not pass muster, miss the mark.

ADJS. 4. imperfect, not perfect; defective, faulty, at fault, in default; inadequate, deficient, short of, lacking, wanting, found wanting, weighed in the balance and found wanting; off; unsound, incomplete, unfinished, partial; impaired 690.27; blemished 677.8; immature, undeveloped 719.11, 12.

ADVS. 5. imperfectly, inadequately, deficiently; incompletely, partially; faultily, defectively.

677. BLEMISH

NOUNS 1. blemish, disfigurement, disfiguration, defacement; scar, cicatrix; scratch; scab; blister, vesicle [med.]; pock, pockmark; nevus [med.], birthmark, mole; freckle, lentigo; blackhead; wart, verruca [med.]; fault 676.2.

2. discoloration, discolorization, discolorment, discolor; bruise 690.8.

3. stain, taint, tarnish, mark; stigma, stigmatism; maculation, macule, macula; spot, blot, blotch, patch, speck, speckle, fleck, flick; daub, dab; smirch, smudge, smutch, smut, smot [Scot.], smear, blur; splotch, splash, spatter; bloodstain; touch of the tar brush [coll.].

VERBS 4. blemish, disfigure, deface, mar, scar.

5. spot, bespot, blot, blotch, speck, speckle, bespeckle; freckle; flyspeck; spatter, splatter, splash, splotch.

6. stain, bestain, discolor, taint, attaint, tarnish, mark, stigmatize, maculate, fox, slubber [chiefly dial.]; smirch, soil 680.18;

smear, besmear, daub, bedaub; blur, slur [chiefly dial.], slurry [dial. Eng.]; darken, blacken; smoke, besmoke; scorch, singe.

7. bloodstain, bloody, ensanguine, imbrue.

ADJS. 8. blemished, disfigured, defaced, marred.

9. stained, discolored, tainted, tarnished, stigmatic(al), foxy; maculate, maculated, macular; spotted 373.13; smirched, soiled 680.23; darkened, blackened, murky; smoky; inky.

10. bloodstained, bloody, gory, ensanguined.

678. MEDIOCRITY

NOUNS 1. mediocrity, mediocreness, fairishness, moderateness, neutrality, indifference, matter of indifference; tolerableness 672.3.

2. ordinariness, averageness, normality, commonness, commonplaceness, common or garden variety [coll.]; unexceptionality, unremarkableness, unnoteworthiness.

3. inferiority, inferiorness, poorness, baseness, meanness, commonness, coarseness; second-rateness, third-rateness, fourth-rateness; inadequacy, deficiency, unsatisfactoriness.

4. low grade, low class, low quality; second best.

5. second-rater, third-rater, fourth-rater, tinhorn [slang].

VERBS 6. get by, pass in the dark; make shift, make do.

ADJS. 7. mediocre, middling, fair, fairish, fair to middling [coll.], moderate, medium, neutral, neuter, betwixt and between [coll.]; tolerable 672.20; so-so, so-soish [chiefly coll.], *couci-couci* [F.], *comme ci comme ça* [F.]; of a kind, of a sort, of sorts [coll.]; nothing to brag about, not much to boast of, nothing to write home about.

8. indifferent, neither hot nor cold, neither one thing nor the other, "not below mediocrity, nor above it" [Johnson]; insipid, wishy-washy [coll.], namby-pamby, milk-and-water.

9. ordinary, average, common, commonplace, common or garden [coll.]; unexceptional, unremarkable, unnoteworthy, no great shakes [coll.].

10. inferior, poor, punk [slang], base, mean, common, coarse, cheesy [slang, U.S.]; inadequate, deficient, unsatisfactory; secondary, second-best; second-rate,

third-rate, fourth-rate; **second-class,** third-class, fourth-class; **low-grade, low-class,** low-quality, low-test.

11. **below par,** below standard, **below the mark** [coll.], **not up to scratch** [coll.], not up to snuff [slang], not up to sample *or* specification, off.

ADVS. 12. **mediocrely, middlingly,** fairly, fairishly, middling [coll.], fair to middling [coll.], moderately, mediumly, **indifferently, so-so;** tolerably 672.25.

13. **inferiorly, poorly,** basely, meanly, commonly, inadequately.

679. CLEANNESS

NOUNS 1. **cleanness,** cleanliness; **purity,** pureness, clarity; **immaculateness,** immaculacy; **spotlessness,** stainlessness, taintlessness; asepsis, sterility; tidiness 59.3.

2. **cleansing, cleaning;** detersion, abstersion, **purification,** defecation, lustration [eccl.], edulcoration [chem.]; clarification; **purge,** purging, purgation, expurgation, catharsis; dry cleaning, steam cleaning.

3. **sanitation,** hygienization; **disinfection, decontamination, sterilization;** pasteurization, flash-pasteurization; fumigation.

4. **washing, ablution,** lustration [joc.]; lavation, laving, lavage; lavatory, lavabo [both eccl.]; **wash, wash-up;** rinse, rinsing; douche; sponge, sponging; shampoo; washout, elution [chem.], elutriation; scrub, scrubbing, swabbing, mopping, scouring.

5. **laundering, laundry,** tubbing; **wash,** washing, washwork; washday.

6. **bathing,** balneation, natation.

7. **bath,** bathe [chiefly Eng.], tub [coll.]; **shower,** shower bath, needle bath, hot *or* cold shower; sponge bath, sponge; hip bath, sitz bath; sweat bath, steam bath, vapor bath, hot-air bath, Turkish bath, Russian bath, Finnish bath; electric bath, radium bath, sulphur bath, acid bath.

8. **lavatory, washroom; bathroom, bath** [coll.], balneum [Rom. hist.]; **toilet** [U.S.], toilet room; water closet 680.13; **bathhouse,** cabaña, bagnio; sweat room, *sauna* [Finn.], sudatorium, sudarium, caldarium [Rom. hist.], tepidarium, vaporarium.

9. **laundry,** washery; washhouse, washshed; **laundromat.**

10. **bathing place,** balneary, balnearium [Rom. hist.]; **baths,** public baths, balneae [Rom. hist.].

11. **swimming pool,** pool, plunge, natatorium; swimming hole.

12. **washbasin, washbowl,** washdish, basin, bowl; **lavatory, washstand;** tub, washtub; bathtub, bath; sink, kitchen sink; piscina, lavabo [both eccl.]; washpot, washing pot; wash boiler, wash barrel, wash pitcher, washing maid, dishpan, finger bowl.

13. **cleaner,** cleaner-up, cleaner-off, cleaner-out; **janitor,** janitress; cleaning woman *or* man, mehtar [Bengal]; dry cleaner; vacuum cleaner, vacuum [U.S.].

14. **washer,** launderer; **laundress,** laundrywoman, **washerwoman,** washwoman, washerwife [Scot.], washmaid, washing maid, *lavandera* [Sp.]; **laundryman,** washerman, washman, *lavandero* [Sp.], dhobi [India]; **dishwasher,** pot-walloper [slang], scullion; dishwiper.

15. **sweep,** sweeper; **street sweeper,** crossing sweeper, white wings [local, U.S.], dustman [Eng.], scavenger; **chimney sweep** *or* sweeper, flue cleaner.

16. **cleanser, cleaner;** wash, lotion; **soap; detergent,** abstergent; **solvent,** cleaning solvent; lixiviator, lixivium; purifier, purificator, mundatory [eccl.]; dentifrice, tooth paste *or* powder.

VERBS 17. **clean, cleanse; purify, purge,** expurgate, deterge, depurate, defecate, lustrate [eccl.], elutriate; **clarify, clear;** clear out, rout out, sweep out, clean house, make a clean sweep; tidy 60.11; scavenge; wipe, wipe off; dust, dust off; steam-clean, dry-clean *or* -cleanse; delouse.

18. **wash, bathe,** lave; **launder,** tub, buck [dial.]; wash out, elute; **rinse,** flush; sponge; **scrub, swab,** swob, **mop, scour,** full, holystone; soap, lather; shampoo; syringe, douche; gargle.

19. **groom, tidy,** fettle [dial.], **brush up; preen,** plume; manicure.

20. **comb,** curry, card, rake, heckle, hackle, hatchel.

21. **sweep, brush,** wipe, whisk, broom; vacuum [coll.], vacuum-clean; crumb [coll.].

22. **sanitize,** hygienize; **disinfect, decontaminate, sterilize;** pasteurize, flash-pasteurize; fumigate; chlorinate; boil; whitewash.

ADJS. 23. **clean,** cleanly; **pure,** clear, white, fair, kosher; **immaculate, spotless,** taintless, stainless; **unsoiled, unsullied,** unsmudged, unstained, untarnished, **unspotted,** unblemished; **unpolluted,** untainted, **undefiled;** clean as a whistle, clean as a new penny.

24. cleaned, cleansed; purified, purged, refined; tidy 59.8; "empty, swept and garnished" [Bible].

25. **sanitary, hygienic, prophylactic, setrile, uninfected;** disinfected, decontaminated, sterilized; pasteurized.

26. **cleansing, cleaning;** detergent, abstergent; **purifying,** purificatory, expurgatory, depurative; purgative, purging, cathartic.

ADVS. 27. **cleanly,** clean; **purely, immaculately, spotlessly.**

28. cleansers

benzene	chloride of lime
benzine	detergent
benzol	lye
benzolin	sal soda
bluing	soda
borax	sodium carbonate
carbon	washing crystals
tetrachloride,	washing powder
carbon tet [coll.]	washing soda

29. soaps

amole	liquid soap
bath soap	marine soap
brown soap	powdered soap,
Castile soap	soap powder
glycerin soap	saddle soap
granulated soap	soap flakes
green soap	soft soap
laundry soap	tar soap
lead or metallic	toilet soap
soap	wash ball

30. cleaning devices

bath towel	rake
besom	scraper
broom	scrubber
brush	scrubbing board
carpet cleaner or	serviette
sweeper	sponge
comb	sudarium
dishcloth	swab, swob
dish mop	toilet paper
dish towel	toothbrush
dishwasher	toothpick
door mat	towel
dustcloth	turkish towel
duster	vacuum cleaner
dustpan	washboard
facecloth	wash brush
face towel	washcloth
feather duster	washer
hackle	washing engine
handkerchief	washing machine
hand towel	washrag
hose	whisk broom,
mop	whisk
napkin	wisp

680. UNCLEANNESS

NOUNS 1. **uncleanness,** uncleanliness, immundity; **impurity,** unpureness; **dirti-**ness, griminess, grubbiness, dinginess; untidiness 62.6; muddiness 388.4.

2. **filthiness, foulness,** vileness, rankness, nastiness, fulsomeness, noisomeness; fetidness 436.2; odiousness, repulsiveness 862.2; hoggishness, piggishness, swinishness.

3. **squalor,** squalidness, **sordidness,** meanness.

4. **defilement, befoulment,** abomination; **pollution, contamination, infection.**

5. **soil,** soilure, soilage; **smirch, smudge,** smutch, smear, **spot,** blot, blotch; **stain** 677.3.

6. **dirt, grime;** dust; soot, smut; mud 388.8.

7. **filth, muck, corruption,** ordure, sordes, foul matter; excrement 309.3, 4; rot 690.6.

8. **slime, slop,** sossle [dial.], slubber [chiefly dial.], sludge, slush, slosh, sposh [U.S.], slab [now chiefly dial.], **muck, mire.**

9. **offal,** slough, draff; refuse 667.4, **offscourings,** offscum, scum, riffraff, scum of the earth; **carrion; garbage, swill,** slop, slops, hogwash [coll.]; dishwater; bilge water, bilge; **sewage,** sewerage; scurf, furfur, dandruff.

10. **dunghill, manure pile, midden** [chiefly dial.], mixen [dial., Eng.], colluvies.

11. **sty, pigsty,** pigpen; **stable,** Augean stable; dump, hole [both slang]; **slum,** rookery; the slums.

12. (receptacle of filth) **sink,** sink of corruption, sump, sough [dial., Eng.]; **cesspool,** septic tank; **sewer, drain,** cloaca, cloaca maxima.

13. **water closet, w.c., closet, toilet, latrine,** cloaca, cabinet d'aisance [F.], convenience, necessary [dial.]; lavatory 679.8; **jakes, john,** johnny, can, Mrs. Jones, locus [all slang]; sanctum sanctorum, holy of holies [both joc.]; **privy, outhouse,** backhouse, backy [dial.], biffy, Chic Sale [slang, U.S.]; head, roundhouse [both naut.]; **rest room, comfort station;** ladies', girls' room, powder room; men's, gents', boys' room.

14. **chamber, bedchamber,** pot, potty [child's], chamber pot, **thunder mug** [slang], jerry [Eng.], jordan [Scot. & dial., Eng.]; urinal; **bedpan,** duck [slang], submarine [slang]; toilet chair, chair-chair [slang].

15. **pig, swine,** hog [all coll.]; slattern 62.7.

VERBS 16. wallow in the mire.

17. dirty, bedirty, dirt, **sully,** slubber [chiefly dial.], grime, **begrime;** muck, muck up [coll.]; **muddy,** bemuddy; mire, bemire; slime, beslime; dust, bedust; soot, bescot; roil, rile [coll., chiefly U.S.].

18. soil, besoil; **spot, stain** 677.5, 6; black, **blacken;** smirch, besmirch, smutch, besmutch, smut, besmut, **smudge,** besmudge, **smear,** besmear, daub, bedaub.

19. defile, foul, befoul; filthify, filthy [dial.], nasty [dial.], benasty [dial., U.S.], mess [coll.]; **pollute, corrupt,** contaminate, infect; taint, tarnish.

20. spatter, splatter, splash, **bespatter,** besplatter, besplash.

21. draggle, bedraggle, **drabble,** bedrabble, dabble, bedabble, daggle, drabble in the mud.

ADJS. **22. unclean, uncleanly;** not kosher; **unwashed,** unbathed, unscrubbed, unscoured, unswept, unwiped; **impure,** unpure; **polluted, contaminated, infected, corrupted;** not to be handled without gloves.

23. soiled, sullied, dirtied, smirched, besmirched, smudged, spotted, **tarnished,** tainted, **stained; defiled,** fouled, **befouled;** draggled, drabbled, bedraggled.

24. dirty, grimy, grubby, smirchy, dingy; messy [coll.], mussy [coll., U.S.]; **untidy** 62.14; **muddy** 388.14; **dusty;** smutty, smutchy, smudgy; sooty, smoky, snuffy.

25. filthy, foul, black, **vile,** rank, **nasty,** fulsome, noisome; **fetid** 436.5; **putrid,** rotten 690.38; **odious, repulsive** 862.9; slimy, miry; scurfy, lentiginous; maggoty, flyblown.

26. hoggish, piggish, swinish.

27. squalid, sordid, mean, wretched, shabby; slumlike, slummy.

ADVS. **28. uncleanly,** uncleanlily; **impurely,** unpurely; **dirtily,** grimily; **filthily, foully,** nastily, vilely, rankly, fulsomely, noisomely.

681. SALUBRITY

NOUNS **1. salubrity,** salubriousness, salutariness, **wholesomeness, healthfulness,** healthiness, beneficialness, goodness for.

2. hygiene, hygienics, hygiology; sanitation 679.3.

3. hygienist, hygieist or hygeist, hygiologist; sanitarian.

VERBS **4.** make for health, conduce to health, **be good for,** agree with.

ADJS. **5. salubrious, salutary, wholesome, healthful, healthy, beneficial,** benign, good, **good for;** hygienic, sanitary; constitutional, for one's health.

682. INSALUBRITY

NOUNS **1. insalubrity,** insalubriousness, unsalutariness, **unwholesomeness, unhealthfulness,** unhealthiness, noxiousness, noisomeness; harmfulness 673.5.

2. poisonousness, toxicity, venomousness; virulence or virulency, noxiousness, destructiveness, deadliness; "death in the pot" [Bible].

VERBS **3.** disagree with, not be good for.

ADJS. **4. insalubrious, unsalutary, unwholesome, unhealthful, unhealthy,** noxious, noisome, peccant, bad, **bad for;** harmful 673.12; unhygienic, unsanitary, insanitary; morbific(al), morbiferous [med.]; pathogenic.

5. poisonous, toxic, toxicant, toxiferous; **venomous,** envenomed; **virulent, noxious, malignant,** malign, **destructive, deadly;** mephitic(al), miasmal, miasmic, miasmatic.

683. HEALTH

NOUNS **1. health,** heal [Scot.], **wellbeing,** physical condition; bloom, flush; Hygeia [Gr.], Aesculapius [Rom.].

2. healthiness, healthfulness, soundness, wholesomeness, healthy body; **good health,** good state of health, "good estate of body" [Bible], a sound mind in a sound body; **robust health,** rugged health, rude health, glowing health, "health that snuffs the morning air" [Grainger]; **fine fettle,** fine whack [slang], fine or high feather [coll.], fine shape, top shape [slang], mint condition; clean bill of health.

3. haleness, heartiness, robustness, vigorousness, ruggedness, lustiness, hardiness, strength, vigor.

VERBS **4. enjoy good health,** have a clean bill of health; **feel good,** feel fine, feel like a million [coll.], never feel better; feel one's oats, be full of pep [both slang]; burst with health, bloom, flourish; keep body and soul together.

5. get well; recuperate 692.19; recover 692.20.

ADJS. **6. healthy, healthful,** enjoying health, in health, in shape, in condition; **fit,** fine [coll.], fit and fine [coll.]; **in good health,** in good case, **in the pink** [coll.], in the pink of condition, in mint condition, in good or fine shape, **in fine fettle,** in fine whack [slang], in fine or high feather [coll.], **chipper** [coll., U.S.], bobbish [slang], fit as a fiddle [coll.], bursting with health, full of life and vigor, full of beans [slang], feeling one's oats [slang].

7. **well, unailing, unsick, unsickly;** all right, doing nicely, up and about, on one's legs, alive and kicking [coll.], sitting up and taking nourishment; tolerable [dial.], fair, as well as can be expected, can't complain.

8. **sound,** whole, wholesome; unimpaired 675.8; sound of mind and body, sound of wind and limb, sound as a whistle, sound as a bell, sound as a roach, hard as nails [coll.].

9. **hale, hearty,** hale and hearty, **robust,** robustious]joc.], **vigorous, strong, rugged,** rude, hardy, lusty, bouncing.

10. **fresh,** green, **blooming,** flush; fresh as a daisy or rose, fresh as April.

684. DISEASE

NOUNS 1. **disease, illness, sickness, malady, ailment,** ail, ailing, **indisposition, disorder, complaint,** morbidity, **affliction,** affection, **infirmity,** disability, defect, distemper; lesion; **sickishness,** alloverishness [dial.], seediness [coll.], rockiness [slang, U.S.], the pip [coll.]; complication; contagious or infectious disease, febrile disease, sporadic disease; endemic disease, endemic; "all ills that men endure" [Cowley].

2. **unhealthiness,** healthlessness; **ill health,** poor health; **sickliness,** peakedness [coll.], languishment; **feebleness,** frailty 159; **infirmity, unsoundness,** unwholesomeness, debility, debilitation, decrepitude; delicacy, delicate health; valetudinarianism; invalidism, invalidity; morbidity, morbidness; pathology, pathological condition.

3. **infection, contagion,** corruption, contamination, pollution, taint, virus; miasma, miasm; **contagiousness, infectiousness, communicability,** impartibility, inoculability.

4. **epidemic, plague, pestilence,** pest, pandemia, murrain [veterinary]; bubonic plague, white plague, Black Death; pesthole, plague spot; Pandora's box.

5. **seizure,** grip, **attack,** assault, access, visitation; **stroke; fit,** ictus; **spasm, throe, paroxysm, convulsion,** epitasis, eclampsia, frenzy; epilepsy, falling sickness, grand mal, petit mal, psychic epilepsy, Jacksonian epilepsy; apoplexy, bloodstroke; tonic spasm, entasia, tetanus; holotony, laryngismus; clonic spasm, clonus; cramp, Charley

horse [coll., U.S.]; caisson disease, the bends.

6. **fever, feverishness,** calenture, febrility, febricity, pyrexia; **heat, fire, fever heat;** flush, hectic flush; hectic fever, hectic; intermittent fever, intermittent; remittent fever, remittent; pernicious fever; congestive fever; delirium 472.9.

7. **collapse, breakdown, crack-up** [coll.], **prostration;** nervous prostration or breakdown.

8. (diseases) anemia, pernicious anemia; ankylosis; anthrax, woolsorter's disease; appendicitis; arthritis, lumbago; arteriosclerosis, hardening of the arteries; asphyxia, apnea; ataxia, tabes, locomotor ataxia; athlete's foot; beriberi; Bright's disease, nephritis, nephrosis; bursitis; chlorosis, greensickness; cirrhosis; colitis; cretinism; cyanosia, cyanopathy; diabetes; dropsy, edema; dysentery, bloody flux; elephantiasis; encephalitis; gallstones, biliary calculus; gastritis; goiter, struma, bronchocele, tracheocele; gout, podagra; hypertension, high blood pressure; hemophilia; jaundice, yellow jaundice, icterus; leukemia, leucocythemia; lockjaw, trismus, tetanus; malnutrition, dystrophy, cachexia; mastoiditis; meningitis, spinal meningitis; milk leg; neuritis; paresis, softening of the brain; pellagra; peritonitis; phlebitis; pyorrhea, Riggs' disease; rheumatism, rheumatiz [dial.], rheumatics [dial.]; rhinitis; rickets, rachitis; rupture; hernia, bubonocele; sclerosis; scurvy; stiff neck, torticollis; sinusitis; thrombosis, coronary thrombosis; trichinosis; varicosis, varicose veins; vitamin deficiency, ariboflavinosis; xerophthalmia.

9. (febrile and infectious diseases) ague, aguer [dial.]; dengue, dandy, dandy fever, breakbone fever; malaria, malarial fever; pox; chicken pox, varicella; cow pox, vaccinia; smallpox, variola; cholera, Asiatic cholera, cholera morbus; diphtheria, diphtheritis; leprosy, lepra; measles, rubeola, German measles; mumps, parotitis; rabbit fever, tularemia; rheumatic fever; scarlet fever, scarlatina; sleeping or sleepy sickness, African lethargy, encephalitis lethargica; trench fever, trench mouth; typhoid fever, typhoid, enteric fever; typhus, jail fever, famine fever, spotted fever; yaws, frambesia; yellow fever, yellow jack.

10. (veterinary) anthrax, splenic fever, charbon, milzbrand, malignant pustule; bighead; blackleg, black quarter, quarter evil or ill; cattle plague, rinderpest, steppe

murrain, glanders, milk sickness; foot-and-mouth disease, aphthous fever; distemper; gapes; heaves; hog cholera; loco; mange, scabies; pip; parrot fever, psittacosis; rot, sheep rot; staggers, megrims, blind staggers, mad staggers, stomach staggers; stringhalt, springhalt; Texas fever, blackwater.

11. (eye diseases) conjunctivitis, glaucoma, pinkeye, trachoma; cataract, caligo, pin and web, amaurosis, gutta serena.

12. (respiratory diseases) angina, angina pectoris; bronchitis, bronchiolitis; catarrh, rheum; cold, common cold, coryza, the sniffles, the snuffles; croup; grippe, grip [U.S.], la grippe [F.]; influenza, flu [coll.]; laryngitis; pharyngitis; pleurisy, pleuritis; pneumonia, bronchopneumonia, lobar pneumonia, phthisi-pneumonia; thrush; tonsillitis, amygdalitis, cynanche, quinsy; whooping cough, pertussis.

13. tuberculosis, t.b. [coll.], breast complaint, white plague, phthisis; consumption, pulmonary phthisis or tuberculosis; galloping consumption; scrofula, scrofulotuberculosis, tuberculous lymphadenitis, king's evil; fibrotuberculosis, nephrotuberculosis, paratuberculosis, pseudotuberculosis, miliary tuberculosis.

14. wasting disease, consumption, marasmus, emaciation, atrophy.

15. venereal disease, V.D., cupid's itch, Venus's curse, French disease, Gallic disease, morbus gallicus [L.]; clap or claps, dose of claps, dose [all slang]; syphilis, blood disease, pox, great pox, French pox, Spanish pox; gonorrhea, blennorrhea, blennorrhagia, blueballs [slang].

16. heart disease, heart condition; carditis, endocarditis, myocarditis, pericarditis, pyopericarditis; angina pectoris, palpitation of the heart, palpitation; heart attack; heart failure.

17. nervous disorder, neuropathy; neuritis; neuralgia; sciatica, ischialgia; face ague, trigeminal neuralgia, tic, tic douloureux; fidgets, floccillation, tilmus; epilepsy, falling sickness; chorea, the jerks, St. Vitus's dance; subsultus; paresthesia; neurosis 688.17.

18. shock, mental shock, trauma, nociassociation; shellshock, combat or battle fatigue.

19. paralysis, paralyzation, palsy; stroke, shock [coll.]; paresis; motor paralysis, sensory paralysis; hemiplegia, paraplegia, diplegia; shaking palsy, Parkinson's disease,

paralysis agitans; infantile paralysis, poliomyelitis, polio; neuroparalysis.

20. heatstroke, heat prostration; sunstroke, sun [coll.], coup de soleil [F.], siriasis, insolation; calenture, thermic fever.

21. indigestion, dyspepsia, stomach condition; acidosis; heartburn, cardialgia, pyrosis, water qualm; colic, gripe, gripes, tormina; constipation.

22. nausea, nauseation, queasiness, squeamishness, qualmishness, qualm, weewows [dial.], pukes [coll.], heaves [slang]; seasickness, mal de mer [F.]; airsickness; carsickness; vomiting 308.8.

23. poisoning, intoxication, intoxation, venenation; septic poisoning, septicity; blood poisoning, sepsis, septicemia, toxemia, pyemia; autointoxication; botulism.

24. radiation sickness, radiodermatitis, radionecrosis; X-ray cancer, roentgen cancer.

25. allergy; hay fever, rose cold; asthma, bronchial asthma, cardiac asthma.

26. skin disease, dermatosis; dermatitis; dermatomycosis.

27. rash, brash, eruption, efflorescence, breaking-out; eczema, tetter; itch, scabies, psora, psoriasis; acne; canker rash; dartre, exanthema; erysipelas, St. Anthony's fire; erythema; herpes; shingles, herpes zoster; ringworm, herpes circinatus; hives, urticaria, nettle rash, uredo; impetigo; lichen, papular rash; miliaria, pemphigus, rupia; prickly heat, lichen tropicus.

28. sore, inflammation, fire, pet [coll., South. U.S.]; wound 690.7; swelling, rising; pustule, papule, papula, fester, pock; ulcer, ulceration; blister, bleb, blob [chiefly dial.], bulla, blain; whelk, wheal; welt [coll.], whelp [dial., U.S.], wale; pimple; boil, furuncle; gumboil; carbuncle; canker, canker sore, noma, water canker; cold sore, fever blister; sty; abscess, gathering, aposteme; whitlow, felon, paronychia; bubo, chancre; hemorrhoids, piles; bunion; chilblain, kibe; fistula; polyp; stigma; scab, eschar; suppuration, festering.

29. growth, morbid or malignant growth, excrescence, neoplasm; proud flesh; exostosis; tumor, tumefaction, tumescence, intumescence; sarcoma; cancer, carcinoma; tubercle, tuber; cyst, wen; fungus, fungosity; callus, callosity; corn, clavus; wart, verruca; mole, nevus.

30. gangrene, mortification, necrosis, sphacelus, sphacelation; caries, cariosity; slough.

31. sickling, sufferer; valetudinarian, *valétudinaire* [F.], valetudinarist; **invalid; shut-in;** incurable; **patient, case,** victim; inpatient, outpatient; apoplectic, consumptive, dyspeptic, epileptic, rheumatic, spastic; carrier; **the sick, the infirm,** "the halt, the lame, and the blind" [Bible].

32. cripple, defective, handicapped person, impotent, incapable; amputee; the crippled, the handicapped, the halt, the lame.

VERBS **33. ail, suffer,** labor under, be affected with, complain of; **feel ill,** feel awful, feel something terrible, not feel like anything [coll.], feel like the walking dead; look green about the gills [slang].

34. take sick *or* **ill, sicken,** take down [coll.]; **catch, contract, get, take,** acquire, incur, sicken of, **come down with** [coll.], be stricken by, fall a victim to; catch cold; take one's death [dial.]; **break out,** break out in a rash, erupt; run a temperature, fever; be laid by the heels, drop in one's tracks.

35. fail, weaken, sink, decline, run down, lose strength, lose one's grip, **waste away,** dwindle, droop, flag, wilt, wither, fade, languish, pine, peak, "dwindle, peak and pine" [Shakespeare].

36. go lame, founder.

37. afflict, disorder, derange; sicken, indispose; weaken, enfeeble, reduce, debilitate, extenuate, devitalize; **invalid,** invalidate, incapacitate, disable; lay up, confine, hospitalize.

38. infect, communicate, disease, contaminate, taint.

39. poison, empoison, envenom.

ADJS. **40. unhealthy, unwholesome, morbid,** pathologic(al); healthless, in poor health; **infirm, unsound,** invalid, debilitated; **sickly, cranky** [dial.], peaked [coll.]; **weakly, feeble, frail** 159.12–21; **poor,** poorish, poorly [chiefly coll.], porely [dial.], poorlyish [chiefly coll.]; valetudinary, valetudinarian; reduced, reduced in health; **languishing, failing** 159.21; **rundown,** used up [coll.], dragged out; haggard 204.19; pale 362.9.

41. ill, ailing, sick, unwell, indisposed, taken ill, down, bad, on the sick list; **sickish,** all-overish [dial.], **seedy** [coll.], rocky [slang, U.S.], **under the weather** [U.S.], **out of sorts** [coll.], below par [coll.], off, off-color, off one's form, off one's feed [coll.], down in the mouth; faint, faintish, feeling faint; feeling awful, feeling

something terrible; dog-sick [slang], sick as a dog; laid low, in a bad way, at a low ebb; critically ill, in danger, on the critical list.

42. nauseated, queasy, squeamish, qualmish, qualmy, qualm-sick, weewowy [dial.]; disgusted 864.23; sick [coll.], **sick at the stomach,** sick to the stomach [dial.]; pukish, puky [both vulg.]; seasick, carsick, airsick.

43. feverish, fevered, feverous, in a fever, **hectic,** febrile, **flushed, hot,** burning, fiery, pyretic, inflamed; delirious 472.30.

44. laid up, confined, invalided, in hospital; **bedridden, bedfast, sick abed;** prostrate, on one's back, flattened out [coll.].

45. diseased, morbid, infected, contaminated, tainted, vitiated, peccant, corrupt; **poisoned,** septic(al); cankerous, ulcerous, gangrenous, carious, cankered, ulcerated, gangrened, mortified, sphacelate.

46. anemic, chlorotic; bilious, dyspeptic; dropsical, hydropic(al); gouty, podagric; neuritic, neuralgic, neurasthenic; pneumonic, pulmonic; phthisic(al), consumptive; palsied, paralytic; rheumatic, rheumaticky [dial. & coll.]; rickety, rachitic; syphilitic, luetic; tabid, tabetic; tubercular, tuberculous; allergic, apoplectic, arthritic, choleric, colicky, diabetic, edematous, encephalitic, epileptic, hypertensive, influenzal, laryngitic, leprous, malarial, measly, nephritic, pleuritic, scabietic, scorbutic(al), scrofulous, syntectic(al), traumatic, tumorous, variolar.

47. contagious, infectious, infective, **catching, taking,** spreading, **communicable,** impartible, inoculable; zymotic; pestiferous, pestilential; **epidemic,** epizootic, pandemic; endemic(al); sporadic.

685. REMEDY

NOUNS **1. remedy, cure, corrective,** reparation; **relief, help, aid, assistance;** restorative, analeptic; specific, specific remedy; alterant, alterative; prescription, recipe, receipt.

2. nostrum, sovereign remedy; patent medicine, quack remedy.

3. panacea, cure-all, heal-all, universal remedy, catholicon, polychrest; elixir, elixir of life, *elixir vitae* [ML.]; philosophers' stone.

4. medicine, medicament, medicinal, therapeutic; **drug, physic,** pharmacon; herbs, "the physic of the field" [Pope]; elixir, balsam, balm, cordial; tisane, ptisan;

drops; inhalant; electuary, confection, conserve; lincture, linctus; simple; officinal.

5. dose, draft or draught, potion, portion, pharmacoposia; broken dose; booster, booster dose.

6. pill, bolus, tablet, capsule, lozenge, troche.

7. tonic, stimulant, bracer, arouser, reviver [slang], roborant, pick-me-up [coll.], pickup [slang]; cardiac; peptic.

8. palliative, alleviative, lenitive, assuasive, assuager.

9. balm, lotion, liniment, salve, ointment, unguent, unguentum, unction, oil, embrocation, emollient, demulcent, abirritant; fomentation; traumatic, harquebusade, vulnerary; collyrium, eyesalve, eyewater, eyewash.

10. narcotic, opiate, drug, dope [slang]; opium, hop or hops [U.S.], gow or ghow [slang, U.S.]; snow (cocaine or heroin [slang]); lotus [Gr. legend]; knockout drops, mickey finn [both slang, U.S.].

11. sedative, depressant, calmative, tranquilizer, soother, quietener, pacifier; analgesic, anodyne, paregoric, painkiller [coll.]; hypnotic, soporific, somnifacient, sleep-inducer, sleeping pills, sleeping draught; barbiturate, goofballs [slang]; antispasmodic; soothing sirup.

12. antipyretic, antifebrile, febrifuge, fever-reducer.

13. anesthetic, anesthesiant; local or general anesthetic; refrigeration, freezing.

14. cough medicine, cough sirup, cough drops, horehound.

15. laxative, cathartic, physic, purge, purgative, aperient, deobstruent; carminative; diuretic.

16. emetic, vomitive, vomit, nauseant.

17. enema, clyster, glyster, lavage, lavement.

18. prophylactic, preventive, preventative, protective; antiseptic, antisepsis, disinfectant, germicide, bactericide, bacteriocidin, microbicide; dentifrice, toothpaste or powder; mouthwash, gargle; fumigant, fumigator.

19. vermifuge, vermicide, anthelmintic, helminthic, helminthagogue.

20. counteractant, counteractive; irritant, counterirritant; antiperiodic; antacid, gastric antacid, alkalizer, neutralizer; antihistamine.

21. antidote, antipoison, counterpoison, countervenom, alexipharmic, alexiteric, theriaca or theriac.

22. antitoxin, immunotoxin; antivenin, antivenene; serum, antiserum; antibody, antiantibody; antigen.

23. vaccine, stock vaccine, bovine, vaccine, humanized vaccine; homologous or autogenous vaccine, heterogenous vaccine, multivalent or polyvalent vaccine; bacterin, tetanobacterin, typhobacterin, etc.; T.A.B. vaccine, typhoid-paratyphoid A and B vaccine, triple vaccine; BCG vaccine (Bacillus Calmette-Guérin), Calmette's vaccine.

24. miracle drugs, wonder drugs, magic bullets; antibiotic; sulfa drug, sulfa, sulfonamide.

25. diaphoretic, sudorific.

26. vesicant, vesicatory, epispastic.

27. suppurative, suppurant; maturative, maturant.

28. dressing, bandaging, application; plaster, emplastrum; court plaster; mustard plaster; poultice, cataplasm, epithem, sinapism; compress, pledget, stupe; dossil, tent; fingerstall; tampon, tampion; bandage, band, binder, cravat, roller, fillet, tourniquet; sling, splint; brace; cast, plaster cast; tape, adhesive tape; Band-Aid; lint, cotton, gauze, sponge.

29. pharmacology, pharmacy, pharmaceutics, posology, dosology.

30. pharmacist, pharmacologist, pharmaceutist, pharmacopolist, posologist, druggist, chemist [Eng.], chemist and druggist [Eng.], pharmaceutical chemist, apothecary, dispenser, gallipot [coll.].

31. drugstore, pharmacy, druggery, chemist's shop [Eng.], apothecary's shop, dispensary, dispensatory.

32. pharmacopoeia, pharmacopedia, dispensatory.

VERBS **33.** remedy, cure 692.13–15; treat 687.33.

ADJS. **34.** remedial, curative, therapeutic, healing, corrective, emendatory, alterative, restorative, analeptic(al); sanative, sanatory; medicinal, medicative; therial, theriacal.

35. palliative, lenitive, alleviative, assuasive, balmy, balsamic, demulcent, emollient, abirritative.

36. antidotal, alexiteric, alexipharmic(al); antitoxic; antibiotic; antiluetic, antisyphilitic; antiscorbutic; antiperiodic; antipyretic, antifebrile, febrifugal; antacid.

37. prophylactic, preventive, protective; antiseptic, aseptic, disinfectant, germicidal, bactericidal; vermifugal, anthelmintic, helminthic.

38. tonic, stimulating, bracing, invigorating, roborant, corroborant.

39. sedative, calmative, calmant, depressant, soothing, tranquilizing, quietening, neurotic; narcotic, opiatic; analgesic, anodyne, paregoric(al); hypnotic, soporific, somniferous, somnifacient, sleep-inducing.

40. anesthetic, anesthesiant, deadening, numbing.

41. cathartic, laxative, purgative, aperient, deobstruent, purifying, cleansing, depurative; carminative; diuretic.

42. emetic, vomitive, vomitory.

43. pharmaceutic(al), pharmacological.

44. medicines

antiscorbutic	hormones 310.2,
Atabrine	10
atebrin	insulin
bismuth	mepacrine
cortisone	pepsin
ephedrine	sassafras
ergot	Vichy water
expectorant	vitamins 307.23
histamine	

45. balms

antiphlogistine	glycerole
arnica	gum arabic
balm of Gilead	lanolin
camphor	menthol
camphorated	Mentholatum
menthol	mercurial ointment
cerate	olive oil
glycerin, glycerine	petrolatum
glycerite	petroleum jelly
glycerogel	vaseline
glycerogelatin	Vicks
glycerol	zinc ointment

46. stimulants

adrenalin,	digitalis
adrenaline	epinephrine
alcohol	kola
amphetamine	nikethamide
amphetamine	nux vomica
sulphate	picrotoxin
aromatic spirits of	quassia
ammonia	quinine
Benzedrine	sal-ammoniac
benzoin	salts
caffeine	smelling salts
coffee	strychnine
Dexedrine	tea
digitalin	

47. narcotics

bhang [India]	Indian hemp
cannabis	laudanum
cocaine	marijuana,
codein, codeine	marihuana
ganja [India]	morphine
hashish	nepenthe,
hemp	nepenthes
heroin	opium
hyoscyamus	stramonium

48. sedatives and hypnotics

aconite	nembutal
allonal	pentobarbital
amytal	phenacetin
atropine	phenobarbital
barbital	pyramidon
barbitone	reserpine
barbituric acid	scopolamine
belladonna	seconal
bromide	Serpusil
chloral hydrate	sodium amytal
dial	sodium bromide
dilantin, dilantin	sodium pentothal
sodium	trional
diphenylhydantoin	valerian
ipral	veronal

49. analgesics

acetanilid	headache powder
acetysalicylic acid	methyl salicylate
Anacin	phenacetin
aspirin	quinine
Bufferin	sodium salicylate

50. anesthetics

A.C.E. mixture	ether
(alcohol,	ethylene
chloroform and	exhilarating gas
ether)	gas
anesthetic ether	laughing gas
anesthyl	nitrous oxide
butadiene	novocain
C.E. mixture	nupercaine
(chloroform and	procaine
ether)	protoxide of
chloral	nitrogen
chloroform	

51. antiseptics

A.B.C. powder	hydrogen peroxide
(boric acid,	hypochlorous
bismuth	acid
subnitrate and	iodine
calomel)	iodoform
alcohol	Listerine
benzoic acid	Lysol
bichloride of	mercurochrome
mercury	merthiolate
bismuth	peroxide
borax	resorcinol
boric acid	sulphur
cresol	thymol
formaldehyde	tincture of iodine
gentian violet	turpentine

52. antibodies

agglutinin	hemagglutinin
allergen	hemolysin
anaphylactin	heterolysin
atopen	isolysin
bactericidin	lysin
bacteriolysin	precipitin
bacteriophage	reagin
hapten	

53. antibiotics

actinomycin	chlortetracycline
aureomycin	dihydrostrepto-
bacitracin	mycin
chloramphenicol	gramicidin
chloromycetin	mycomycin

reomycin
penicillin
polymyxin
streptomycin
streptothricin

subtilin
terramycin
tryothricin
viomycin

54. sulfa drugs

sulfadiazine
sulfaguanidine
sulfamerazine
sulfamethazine
sulfamethylthia-
zole

sulfanilamide
sulfapyrazine
sulfapyridine
sulfasuxidine
sulfathalidine
sulfathiazole

55. laxatives

agar
bran
calomel
cascara
castor oil
compound
 cathartic pills,
 C.C. pills
cream of tartar
Epsom salts
ipecac,
 ipecacuanha

magnesia
milk of magnesia
mineral oil
mineral water
phenolphthalein
psyllium seed
salts
Seidlitz powder
senna
sodium phosphate
sodium sulphate
sulphur

56 antacids

Alka-Seltzer
aluminum
 hydroxide
bicarbonate of soda
Bromo Seltzer
calcium carbonate
magnesium
 carbonate

milk of magnesia
seltzer
seltzer water
sodium
 bicarbonate

686. HEALING ARTS

NOUNS 1. **medicine, materia medica,**
physic, leechcraft [hist.]; therapy 687; anatomic medicine, comparative medicine,
clinical medicine, constitutional medicine,
experimental medicine, group medicine, industrial medicine, internal medicine, physical medicine, preventive medicine, psychosomatic medicine 688.4, tropical medi-
cine, veterinary medicine; eclectic medi-
cine, eclecticism; socialized medicine, state
medicine, federal medicine; forensic or legal
medicine, medical jurisprudence, medicolegal medicine; military medicine, naval
medicine, aviation medicine, space medicine.

2. (systems) **osteopathy; chiropractics,**
chiropraxis; **chiropody,** chiropodistry,
podiatry; **pediatrics; orthopedics,** orthopedia, orthopraxy, orthopraxis; **obstetrics,**
tocology, tocogony, midwifery; **naturopathy;** allopathy, homeopathy, heteropathy; faith healing 1018.12.

3. **surgery,** operative surgery, clinical
surgery, general surgery; major surgery,
minor surgery; aseptic surgery, antiseptic

surgery; dental surgery, orthopedic surgery,
veterinary surgery; plastic surgery, reparative surgery; chiroplasty; electrosurgery, galvanosurgery; radiosurgery; operation 687.23–
28.

4. **dentistry,** aesthetic dentistry, operative dentistry, prosthenic dentistry, surgical
dentistry; orthodontics, orthodontia.

5. **doctor,** doc [coll.], **physician,** physi-
cianer, physicker [coll.], Doctor of Medicine, **M.D., medical practitioner, medical
man, medic,** medical [coll.], **medico**
[coll.], med [slang], croaker [slang, U.S.],
Galen [joc.]; **therapist,** therapeutist; bonesetter; general practitioner, G.P. or g.p.
[coll., Eng.]; family doctor; country doctor;
intern, resident, house physician, resident
physician; physician in ordinary; locum
tenens, locum [coll.]; medical attendant,
attending physician; consultant; **medical
examiner, coroner.**

6. **quack,** quacksalver, **medicaster,**
medicine man, medicine monger, *médecin
tant pis* [F., makeshift doctor], horse doctor [derog.]; abortionist.

7. **specialist; osteopath,** osteopathist;
chiropractor, chiropractic; **orthopedist;
pediatrician,** pediatrist; **chiropodist,
podiatrist,** foot doctor, corn doctor [joc.];
dermatologist, skin man [slang]; internist;
neurologist; psychiatrist 688.13; gynecologist; gerontologist, geriatrician; eye-ear-
nose-throat specialist; **oculist,** optometrist,
ophthalmologist, eye doctor; aurist, otologist; pathologist; hydropathist; allopath,
allopathist; homeopath, homeopathist;
immunologist; serologist; anesthesiologist;
radiologist, radiotherapist; health physicist.

8. **surgeon,** sawbones [slang, U.S.]; operator, operative surgeon; plastic surgeon;
phlebotomist.

9. **dentist,** tooth doctor, toothdrawer,
jawsmith [slang]; **dental surgeon,** operative dentist; D.D.S., Doctor of Dental Surgery; D.D.Sc., Doctor of Dental Science;
D.M.D., Doctor of Dental Medicine; **orthodontist;** radiodontist.

10. **obstetrician,** *accoucheur* [F.]; **midwife,** *accoucheuse* [F.], gamp [coll.];
granny, granny doctor, granny woman [all
South. U.S.].

11. **veterinary, veterinarian, vet** [coll.],
horse doctor.

12. **mind-healer,** mental healer; **faith
healer,** faith curer, faith-curist; **Christian
Science practitioner,** D.C.S., Doctor of
Christian Science.

13. **nurse, sister,** nursing sister, granny [South. U.S.]; trained nurse; registered nurse, R.N.; practical nurse; dirty nurse; scrub nurse; night float; probe [slang], **probationer,** probationist.

14. (staff) orderly; dresser; anesthetist; radiographer, X-ray technician.

15. Hippocrates; Aesculapius [Rom. myth.], Asclepius [Gr. myth.].

16. practice of medicine, medical practice; internship; Hippocratic oath.

VERBS 17. **practice medicine,** doctor [coll.]; treat 687.33; intern.

ADJS. 18. **medical,** surgical, osteopathic, chiropractic, chiropodic, pediatric, orthopedic, obstetric(al), dental, orthodontic, neurological, naturopathic, hydropathic, allopathic, homeopathic, heteropathic; clinical.

19. medical sciences

acology	medical sociology
anatomy	mental hygiene
anesthesiology	mycology
antibiotics	neurology
antiseptics	nosogeny
audiology	nosology
bacteriology	ophthalmology
biology	optometry
cardiography	otology
dermatology	parasitology
diagnostics	pathology
electropathology	physiology
embryology	physiopathology
endocrinology	protozoology
epidemiology	psychology 688
etiology	radiopathology
fluoroscopy	semeiology
geriatrics	serology
gerontology	symptomatology
gynecology	surgical anatomy
gyniatrics	teratology
health physics	therapeutics 687
hematology	tocology
hygiene	toxicology
immunochemistry	traumatology
immunology	

687. THERAPY

NOUNS 1. **therapy, therapeutics,** therapeusis; healing arts 686; psychotherapy 688.5–7; medicines 685.

2. (systems) aerosol therapy, biologic therapy, cold therapy, collapse therapy, constitutional therapy, contact therapy, fever therapy, glandular therapy, gold therapy, intravenous therapy, maggot therapy, malarial therapy, musical therapy, nonspecific therapy, occupational therapy, vocational therapy, oxygen therapy, physical therapy, replacement therapy, shock therapy 688.7, specific therapy, substitutional therapy, suggestion therapy 688.6, faith healing 1018.12.

3. **actinotherapy,** aerotherapy, arsenotherapy, bacteriotherapy, bibliotherapy, cardiotherapy, chemotherapy, climatotherapy, dermatotherapy, dietotherapy 307.14, dosimetry, endocrinotherapy, frigotherapy, galactotherapy, hemotherapy, iodotherapy, naturopathy, organotherapy, pharmacotherapy, phototherapy, physiotherapy, pneumatotherapy, ultrasonic therapy.

4. **hydrotherapy,** hydrotherapeutics, **hydropathy, water cure;** cold-water cure.

5. **heat therapy, thermotherapy,** pyrotherapy; heliotherapy, solar therapy; fangotherapy; hot bath, sweat bath, sunbath.

6. **diathermy,** medical diathermy, surgical diathermy; electrodiathermy; **radiothermy,** high-frequency treatment; short-wave diathermy, ultra-short-wave diathermy, microwave diathermy; ultrasonic diathermy.

7. **electrotherapy,** electrotherapeutics, galvanotherapy, electropathy; magnetotherapy; telectrotherapeutics, electrophototherapy; electroanesthesia, electrobiology, electrobioscopy, electrocardiography, electrocardiophonography, electrochemistry, electrocystoscopy, electroencephalography, electrohemostasis, electromassage, electromyography, electron optics, electrophysiology; electrosurgery, galvanosurgery; electrocautery, galvanocautery; intragastric electrization.

8. **radiotherapy,** radiotherapeutics, radiopraxis, ray therapy, radiation therapy, irradiation therapy, irradiation, therapeutic radiology, deep therapy; interstitial irradiation therapy, intercavitary irradiation therapy; radiant light therapy, ionic medication, infrared therapy, ultraviolet therapy; X-ray therapy, roentgenotherapy, roentgen ray therapy, roentgenization, roentgenism; X-ray dosimetry, roentgenometry; isotope therapy; radium therapy, curietherapy, teleradium therapy, radiumization; radium bath; radiosurgery.

9. **radiology,** radiography, radioscopy, fluoroscopy, etc. 326.7.

10. (radiotherapeutic substances) radium; radioisotope, tracer; radioiodine; radiode; implant; atomic cocktail.

11. (radiotherapeutic and diagnostic aids) X-ray machine, fluoroscope, Somascope, orthodiagraph; radium cannon.

12. (diagnostic grams) X ray, radio-

graph, **radiogram**; fluorophotograph; orthodiagram; encephalograph, encephalogram; electroencephalograph, electronencephalogram, EEG; electrocorticogram; electrocardiogram, ECG; telectrocardiogram, TECG; electromyogram, EMG; vagogram, electrovagogram, EVG.

13. case history, anamnesis [psychol.].

14. **diagnostics**, prognostics, pathognomy; symptomatology, semeiology, semeiotics.

15. **diagnosis**, analysis, interpretation; deductive diagnosis, differential diagnosis, pathological diagnosis, topographic diagnosis, post-mortem diagnosis; microscopical diagnosis, radiodiagnosis, electrodiagnosis, electroanalysis; clinical diagnosis, laboratory diagnosis; physical diagnosis, anatomic diagnosis; examination, physical examination, digital examination, oral examination, etc.; urinalysis, uroscopy; biopsy.

16. **prognosis**, prophasis, prognostication; prognostic, **symptom**, sign.

17. **treatment**, medical treatment; **cure**, curative measures; **medication**, medicamentation; regimen, regime; first aid, domestic medicine; hospitalization.

18. (methods) prophylaxis, preventative treatment; active treatment, after treatment, causal treatment, conservative treatment, empiric treatment, expectant treatment, palliative treatment, perennial treatment, preseasonal treatment, rational treatment, specific treatment; crossfire treatment, diathermic treatment, dietetic treatment, drip treatment, drug treatment, electrotherapeutic treatment, fever treatment, heat treatment, hot-air treatment, light treatment, radiotherapeutic treatment, shock treatment, starvation treatment, surgical treatment, tonic treatment, vibration treatment.

19. **immunization**, antisepsis; immunization therapy, immunotherapy; vaccine therapy, vaccinotherapy; serum therapy, serotherapy, serotherapeutics; scratch test, patch test; **immunology**, immunochemistry; immunity theory, side-chain theory; immunity.

20. **inoculation**, **vaccination**; **injection**, **hypodermic**, hypodermic injection, **shot** [slang]; shot in the arm [slang]; booster, booster shot [slang]; antitoxin, vaccine 685.22, 23.

21. (methods) percutaneous, subcutaneous, intracutaneous, intramuscular, intravenous, intramedullary, intracardiac,

intrathecal, intranasal, inhalation, oral, sublingual, rectal, vaginal.

22. **transfusion**, blood transfusion; serum 387.4; blood bank; blood donor center; bloodmobile; blood donor.

23. **surgery** 686.3; cautery, cauterization; electrolysis, electrolyzation; electrocautery, electroscission, electroresection.

24. **operation**, surgical operation, the knife [coll.]; major operation, minor operation; capital operation, serious operation; ablative operation, anastomotic operation, bloodless operation, compensating operation, crescent operation, elective operation, emergency operation, exploratory operation, fenestration operation, high operation, interval operation, palliative operation, radical operation, shelf operation; **section, resection**; **excision**, removal; **amputation**.

25. (surgical removal) appendectomy, arteriectomy, craniectomy, cystectomy, enterectomy, gastrectomy, hyperdermatomy, hysterectomy, mammectomy, nephrectomy, omphalectomy, oophorectomy, oophorocystectomy, orchidectomy, pancreatectomy, pericardiectomy, pneumonectomy, prostatectomy, salpingectomy, tonsillectomy, ureterectomy, urethectomy, venectomy; castration.

26. (surgical incision) amygdalotomy, ankylotomy, arteriotomy, blepharotomy, caecotomy, cardiotomy, celiotomy, cholecystotomy, cirsotomy, coccygotomy, colpotomy, craniotomy, cystotomy, dichotomy, duodenotomy, elytrotomy, embryotomy, enterotomy, fallotomy, gastroenterotomy, gastrotomy, glossotomy, hebetomy, herniotomy, hysterotomy, laparotomy, lithotomy, lobotomy, mastotomy, nephrotomy, neurotomy, ornithotomy, ovariotomy, pancreatotomy, phrenicotomy, pneumonotomy, prostatotomy, salpingotomy, sclerotomy, thoracotomy, thyrotomy, tonsillotomy, trichotomy, ureterotomy, urethrotomy, varicotomy, venotomy; frontal lobotomy, psychosurgery; orchidotomy; caesarian, caesarian section *or* operation.

27. **plastic surgery**, reparative surgery, plastic operation, reconstructive operation; cosmetic operation, **face lifting**; arterioplasty, balanoplasty, batrachoplasty, blepharoplasty, bronchoplasty, canthoplasty, cardioplasty, colpoplasty, cystoplasty, dermoplasty, enteroplasty, gastroplasty, genyoplasty, heteroplasty, labioplasty, mammilloplasty, neuroplasty, otoplasty, pharyngoplasty, rhinoplasty, zooplasty.

28. **bloodletting, bleeding,** cupping, venesection, phlebotomy; leeching.

29. **hospital,** *hôpital* [F.], **infirmary,** valetudinarium [Rom. antiq.]; sick berth *or* bay [naut.]; **clinic,** *clinique* [F.], polyclinic; general hospital, *hôtel-Dieu* [F.]; surgical hospital, osteopathic hospital, convalescent hospital, children's hospital, maternity *or* lying-in hospital, mental hospital 472.14; base hospital, field hospital, station hospital, hospital station, evacuation hospital [all mil.]; **sanitarium, sanatorium,** *maison de santé* [F.], health station, *hôtel des invalides* [F.]; hospice, asylum, home; Red Cross; **ward,** maternity ward, fever ward, etc.; sickroom; sickbed.

30. **pesthouse,** lazar house, lazaret, lazaretto, lock hospital [Eng.], isolation ward.

31. **health resort, spa, watering place,** waters [dial.], baths, springs, mineral springs; warm *or* hot springs, thermae; pump room.

VERBS 32. **diagnose,** analyze, interpret; prognose.

33. **treat, doctor,** minister to, attend; nurse; **cure, remedy, heal;** dress the wounds, bandage, poultice, plaster, strap, splint; bathe, lick, lick one's wounds; massage, rub; operate on; physic, purge, flux.

34. **medicate,** medicine, physic, drug, dope [slang], dose; salve, oil, anoint, embrocate.

35. **irradiate,** radiumize, **X-ray,** roentgen, roentgenize.

36. **bleed, cup, let blood;** leech; transfuse, give a transfusion.

37. **immunize,** immune; **inoculate, vaccinate,** shoot [slang].

38. **undergo treatment,** take one's medicine, take the cure; doctor, take medicine; go under the knife [coll.].

39. **medical and surgical instruments**

aspirator	electroneurotone
bedpan	electrostethophone
bistoury	electrotherm
cardiograph	fluoroscope
catheter	forceps
cystoscope	germicidal lamp
cytoanalyzer	heat lamp
diaphanoscope	hemostat
diathermy	hypodermic, hypo
drain	[coll.]
drain tube	kidney basin
electrocardiograph	lance
electrocystoscope	lancet
electrodiaphone	laparotomy pack,
electroencephalo-	lap pack
graph	microscope

microstethophone	speculum
microstethoscope	sphygmograph
microwave	sphygmomanom-
diathermy	eter
machine	sphygmometer
nebulizer	spirograph
needle	spirometer
ophthalmoscope	splint
orthodiagraph	stethograph
orthoscope	stethometer
otoscope	stethophone
percussion hammer	stethoscope
pneumatograph	stiletto
pneumatometer	stomach pump
pneumatoscope	stomach tube
pneumeter	stylet
probe	surgeon's saw
pus basin	surgical knife
radiometer	suture
resectoscope	suture needle
respirometer	swab
roentgenoscope	syringe
rubber gloves	telecardiophone
sanguinometer	tongue depressor
scalpel	trepan
short-wave	trephine
diathermy	trocar
machine	urinalysis kit
specimen bottle	X-ray machine

40. **respirators**

inhalator	oxygen mask
inspirator	oxygen tank
iron lung	oxygen tent
lungmotor	resuscitator
pulmotor	

688. PSYCHOLOGY AND PSYCHOTHERAPY

NOUNS 1. **psychology,** psychics, mental science, science of the mind, science of human behavior, reactology; psychonomics, psychonomy; abnormal psychology, morbid psychology; academic psychology, analytic(al) psychology, applied psychology, animal psychology, child psychology, clinical psychology, comparative psychology, differential psychology, dynamic psychology, experimental psychology, existential psychology, faculty psychology, functional psychology, genetic psychology, individual psychology, industrial psychology, neuropsychology, parapsychology, popular psychology, rational psychology, self psychology, structural psychology; physiological psychology, psychophysiology; psychobiochemistry, psychobiology, psychophysics, psychomathematics; psycho-asthenics, psychodynamics, psychostatics, psychogenetics, psychological hedonism; psychotechnics, psychotechnology; holistic theory.

2. (systems) Freudian psychology, Freudianism; Gestalt psychology, configurationism; behavior psychology, behaviorism,

Watson's psychology, motor psychology; association psychology, associationism, mental chemistry; apperceptionism; dianetics.

3. psychiatry, psychiatrics, **alienism;** neuropsychiatry; prophylactic psychiatry, mental hygiene; psychopathology; psychodometry.

4. psychosomatic medicine, medicopsychology, psychic medicine; psychosocial medicine.

5. psychotherapy, psychotherapeutics, **mental healing,** mind cure; group therapy; occupational therapy, vocational therapy; recreational therapy, play therapy; sector therapy, associative anamnesis; narcotherapy, narcoanalysis, narcosynthesis, amytal or pentothal interview; sodium amytal or pentothal, truth serum, "talk-out drug"; hypnotherapy, hypnoanalysis, hypnotism, hypnosis, narcohypnosis; psychosurgery; total push.

6. suggestion therapy, suggestionism; hypnotic suggestion, posthypnotic suggestion; **autosuggestion,** self-suggestion; sleep treatment, prolonged narcosis; suggestibility, power of suggestion.

7. shock therapy, shock treatment; electroshock therapy, protein shock therapy, metrazol shock therapy, hypoglycemic shock therapy, insulin shock therapy; insulin coma therapy, ICT; convulsive shock therapy, CST.

8. psychoanalysis, psychanalysis, depth interview; psychoanalytic therapy, depth psychology, psychology of depths; psychognosis, psychognosy; dream analysis, interpretation of dreams, dream symbolism.

9. psychodiagnostics, psychodiagnosis, psychological or psychiatric evaluation; Rorschach method.

10. psychometry, psychometrics, **intelligence testing;** psychological screening; psychography; psychogram, psychograph, profile; psychometer, I.Q. meter [slang]; psychodometer; lie detector, psychogalvanometer.

11. psychological test, mental test; **aptitude test,** Oseretsky test, Stanford scientific aptitude test; **personality test,** Bernreuter personality inventory, Brown personality inventory, Minnesota multiplastic personality inventory; **association test,** controlled association test, free association test; **apperception test,** thematic apperception test, card test; **Rorschach** test, ink-blot test; **intelligence test,** I.Q. test; alpha test, beta test, Babcock-Levy test, Binet or Binet-Simon test, Goldstein-Sheerer test, Kent mental test, aussage test; Wechsler-Bellevue intelligence scale, Gesell's development schedule, Minnesota preschool scale, Cattell's infant intelligence scale; intelligence quotient, I.Q.

12. psychologist, psychologue; clinical psychologist; psychotechnician, psychotechnologist; psychobiologist, psychobiochemist, psychophysiologist, psychophysicist; psychographer, psychographist; Freud, Adler, Jung, Watson, Pavlov.

13. psychiatrist, psychiater, **alienist,** nut doctor [slang], deficiency expert [jocose]; **psychopathist,** psychopath, psychopathologist; **psychotherapist,** psychotherapeutist, mind-curist; narcotherapist; hypnotherapist; **psychoanalyst,** psychoanalyzer, analyst; psychometrician; neuropsychiatrist; somatist.

14. (pathological personality types) neurotic personality, **neurotic, psychoneurotic,** neuropath, neuro [slang]; weak personality, maladjusted personality, inadequate personality, inferior personality, immature personality, emotionally unstable personality, perverse personality, hostile personality; antisocial personality, sociopath; escapist; psychotic personality, psychotic 472.16; mentally defective personality, ament 470.8; hypochondriac, hypochondriast, hypo [coll.], imaginary invalid, *malade imaginaire* [F.]; alcoholic 994.10; exhibitionist, narcissist, masochist, sadist, voyeur. •

15. (personality defects) inferiority, inadequacy, emotional immaturity; emotional instability, lability; moral deficiency, pathological mendacity.

16. (social adjustment defects) antisocialism, hostility, perversity; destructive reaction, assaultive reaction; maladjustment, social maladjustment, situational maladjustment.

17. neurosis, psychoneurosis, neuroticism, neurotic or psychoneurotic disorder, functional nervous disorder; parapathy, parapathia; acroneurosis, aeroneurosis, pathoneurosis, thermoneurosis; actual neurosis, anxiety neurosis, blast neurosis, fright neurosis, traumatic neurosis, transference neurosis; compulsion neurosis, obsessional neurosis, obsessive-compulsion neurosis; occupational neurosis, copodyskinesia, professional neurasthenia; combat or war neurosis, combat or battle fatigue, shell-shock; nervous breakdown or prostration, crack-up [slang.].

18. **psychosis** 472.3–6.

19. (causes) primary cause, predisposing cause, precipitating cause; stress, stress tolerance; frustration, external frustration, internal frustration; ambivalence, ambivalence of impulse; psychological need, social approval; trauma, mental or emotional shock.

20. (neurotic reactions) anxiety reaction, asthenic reaction, compensatory reaction, conversion reaction, dissociation reaction, emotional instability reaction, flight reaction, immaturity reaction, neurotic-depressive reaction, obsessive-compulsive reaction, passive-aggressive reaction, passive-dependence reaction, phobic reaction, psychasthenic reaction, somatization reaction, shock reaction, stress reaction; chain reaction, vicious circle.

21. (psychosomatic disorders) anesthesia, analgesia; abulia, bulimia, cyclothymia, neurasthenia, paresthesia, parorexia, psychalgia, psychastemia, psychentonia, psychesthesia, psychoepilepsy, stereotypy.

22. (emotional disturbances) emotionalism; anxiety, precordial anxiety, free-floating anxiety; hysteria, hysterics, anxiety hysteria, conversion hysteria; melancholia, hypochondria, depression, dejection; detachment, abstraction, preoccupation; apathy, lethargy, indifference, unresponsiveness, insensibility; stupor, catatonic stupor; euphoria, elation.

23. (thought disturbances) blocking, block, mental block; psychotaxia; paralogia, mental confusion; flight of ideas; delusion, delusion of persecution, delusion of grandeur, nihilistic delusion; hallucinosis 518.7; delirium 472.9, 10.

24. (psychomotor disturbances) convulsions, jerks, tremors, twitching; chorea, tic, etc. 684.17.

25. (speech abnormalities) dysarthria, stammering, stuttering, lisping; incoherence; echolalia, verbigeration; aphasia, jargon aphasia, paraphasia; mutism; aphonia, hysterical aphonia.

26. (amnesic states) amnesia 536.2; fugue; disorientation, amnesic dissociation; word deafness or blindness, auditory or verbal amnesia, alexia; aphrasia, amnesic aphrasia; apraxia, amnesic apraxia; agnosia; agraphia; amnesic amimia; paranomia; confabulation; catalepsy, catalepsis, cataplexy;

trance, dream state; somnambulism, sleep-walking; electroshock, electronarcosis.

27. **dissociation**, mental or emotional dissociation, disconnection; dissociation of personality, personality disorganization or disintegration; **split personality**, double or dual personality; multiple personality; schizoidism, **schizophrenia**, schizothymia; depersonalization.

28. **mania, obsession, compulsion** 472.12, 13; *folie de toucher* [F.].

29. **fixation**, libido fixation or arrest, **arrested development**; infantile fixation, pregenital fixation; **regression**, relapse, retreat to immaturity.

30. **complex**, inferiority complex, superiority complex, Oedipus or nuclear complex, Electra complex, persecution complex; castration complex, etc.; ideas of reference.

31. **introversion**, ingoingness, subjectivity; introspection, introspectiveness, introspectionism, subjective thinking; **extroversion**, outgoingness, extrospection, objectivity, syntony; **ambiversion**; **introvert**; **extrovert**, syntone; **ambivert**.

32. **perversion**; coprophilia, necrophilia, paraphilia; psychosexuality, psychopathia sexualis; sexual abnormality 418.10; erotomania, eromania, eroticomania; aphrodisia, bestiality, exhibitionism, fetishism, narcissism, nympholepsy, nymphomania, pedophilia, psycholagny, scotophilia, voyeurism; satyrism, satyriasis; sadism, masochism; bloodthirst, cannibalism.

33. **hypochondria**, hypochondry, hypochondriasis, *la maladie sans maladie* [F.].

34. **defense mechanism**, defense reaction, dynamism; biological ∼, psychological or sociological adjustive reactions; **negativism**; **escapism**, escape mechanism; escape, flight, withdrawal, flight into idleness, etc.; **isolation**, emotional insulation; **fantasy**, escape into fantasy, dreamlike thinking, autistic or dereistic thinking, autism, dereism; **compensation**, overcompensation, decompensation; substitution; **sublimation**; projection, blame-shifting; displacement; **rationalization**; psychotaxis.

35. **suppression, repression, inhibition**, resistance, restraint, censorship; block, blockage; reaction formation; rigid control; **suppressed desire**.

36. **catharsis**, purgation, abreaction, **emotional release**, outlet; acting-out, psychodrama.

37. **conditioning**; psychagogy, reeduca-

tion, reorientation; **conditioned reflex,** conditioned response; simple *or* unconditioned reflex.

38. adjustment, adjustive reaction; re**adjustment, rehabilitation;** psychosynthesis, integration of personality.

39. psyche, psychic apparatus; mind 465; preconscious, foreconscious, coconscious; **subconscious, unconscious, subconscious** *or* **unconscious mind,** submerged mind, subliminal, subliminal self; **libido,** psychic *or* libidinal energy, motive force, vital impulse, urge, desire; ego-libido, object-libido; **id,** primitive self, instinct; **ego,** conscious self; **superego,** ethical self, conscience, censor; ego-ideal; ego-id conflict.

40. engram, trace, traumatic trace *or* memory, unconscious memory, memory pattern.

41. pattern, figure, configuration, Gestalt; **behavior pattern,** behavior, explicit behavior, implicit behavior; psychic disposition, predisposition, tendency; social attitudes *or* behavior, social pathology.

42. association, association of ideas, mental linking; controlled association, free association, association by contiguity, association by similarity; stream of consciousness.

43. transference, emotional attachment, identification, introjection, projection; positive transference, negative transference; **empathy,** rapport.

44. cathexis, desire concentration; charge, energy charge, cathectic energy; anticathexis, countercharge; hypercathexis, overcharge.

VERBS **45. psychologize, psychiatrize, psychoanalyze.**

ADJS. **46. psychological,** psychic(al); **psychopathic,** psychopathological; **psychosomatic,** psychoorganic, psychophysical, psychophysiological, psychobiologic(al); psychogenic, psychogenetic, functional; psychodynamic, psychofugal, psychoneurologic(al), psychosexual, psychosocial, psychotechnical.

47. psychiatric, neuropsychiatric; **psychotherapeutic; psychoanalytic(al);** psychoeducational.

48. neurotic, psychoneurotic, parapathic; neurasthenic, psychasthenic; pathoneurotic; masochistic, sadistic; hypochondriac.

49. psychotic 471.26.

50. introverted, introvert, introversive,

subjective, ingoing, introspective, inlooking; undemonstrative 611.8.

51. extroverted, extrovert, extroversive, **outgoing, objective,** extrospective, **demonstrative, open,** syntonic; **unreserved** 552.10.

52. subconscious, unconscious, subliminal, extramarginal; superconscious, supraliminal; coconscious.

689. IMPROVEMENT

NOUNS **1. improvement, betterment,** bettering; melioration, **amelioration; mend,** mending, **amendment,** emendation; **progress,** progression, headway; **advance,** advancement; **promotion, furtherance,** preferment; **rise, lift, uplift,** upswing, up [coll.], pickup [slang]; **enhancement,** enrichment; restoration, recovery 692.

2. development, refinement, elaboration, **perfection,** maturation.

3. cultivation, culture, *Kultur* [G.], refinement, **polish;** menticulture, mind culture, cultivation of the mind; race culture, **civilization,** acculturation; euthenics, eugenics; culture zone.

4. revision, revise, revisal; revised edition; **emendation, amendment, correction, rectification;** redaction, revampment; **rewrite,** rewriting, rescript.

5. reform, reformation; regeneration 145.2; reformism; progressivism, progressism; radicalism, radical reform; reformandum.

6. reformer, reformist, reformado; book burner; **progressive,** progressivist, progressionist; radical, red.

VERBS **7.** (get better) **improve, grow better,** show improvement; **mend,** amend; meliorate, ameliorate; **look up** [coll.], **pick up** [coll.], perk up; **develop,** shape up; **advance, progress, make progress,** make headway, gain, gain ground, go forward, get *or* go ahead, come on, come along [coll.], get along, make strides *or* rapid strides, make up for lost time.

8. rally, come about *or* round, **take a favorable turn,** take a turn for the better, turn the corner, raise one's head, gain strength; **recuperate, recover** 692.19, 20.

9. (make better) **improve, better,** make an improvement; improve upon, refine upon; **mend, amend, emend,** emendate; meliorate, **ameliorate; advance, promote,** forward, bring forward, bring on; **lift, uplift;** upgrade; **enhance, enrich,** fatten, lard; better oneself; be the making of.

10. **develop**, elaborate, **cultivate**, **refine**, polish, finish, **perfect**, mature.

11. **touch up**, **brush up**, **furbish**, furbish up, vamp up, rub up, brighten up, polish, polish up, shine [coll.].

12. **revise**, redact, **revamp**, **rewrite**, **rework**, work over; **emend**, **amend**, emendate; **rectify**, **correct**; edit, blue-pencil.

ADJS. 13. **improved**, **bettered**, advanced, ameliorated, enhanced, enriched; developed, perfected.

14. **better**, better off, better for, all the better for.

15. **improving**, **bettering**; meliorative, **ameliorative**; **progressive**, progressing, advancing, ongoing; mending, **on the mend**, on the lift [dial., U.S.], on the upgrade, looking up [coll.].

16. **emendatory**, **corrective**; revisory, revisional; **reformatory**, reformative, reformational.

17. **improvable**, ameliorable; **emendable** 692.25.

690. IMPAIRMENT

NOUNS 1. **impairment**, **damage**, **injury**, **harm**, **hurt**, hurting, detriment, loss; **disrepair**, **dilapidation**; frazzle, fray; **breakage**; breakdown, collapse; sabotage; mayhem [law].

2. **corruption**, **pollution**, **contamination**, **defilement**, **poisoning**, vitiation; **perversion**, prostitution; denaturalization, sophistication.

3. **deterioration**, decadence or decadency, **degradation**, **debasement**, derogation, deformation; **degeneration**, degeneracy, degenerateness; **depravation**, depravedness; **retrogression**, retrogradation, retrocession; backwardation, backwardization; devolution, involution; **decline**, declination, declension, come-down, **descent**, **drop**, **fall**, falling off, slump, lapse, wane, ebb.

4. **waste**, wastage, **consumption**; withering, wilting, marcescence; emaciation 204.6.

5. **decay**, **decomposition**, **disintegration**, **dissolution**, resolution, breakup, disorganization, **corruption**, spoilage, dilapidation, ravages of time; **wear**, **wear and tear**; **erosion**, **corrosion**; oxidation, oxidization; rust, "moth and rust" [Bible]; mildew, mold 674.2.

6. **rot**, rottenness, foulness, putridness, putridity; **putrefaction**, putrescence; **mortification**, necrosis, gangrene, sphacelation, sphacelus; caries, cariosity; dry rot.

7. (hurt or damage sustained) **injury**, **hurt**, **lesion**; **wound**, **trauma**; sore 684.28; cut, incision, scratch, gash; puncture, stab; laceration, mutilation; abrasion, scuff, scrape, gall; burn, first ~, second or third degree burn; scuff-burn, mat-burn, floor-burn, flash burn; break, fracture, rupture; strain, sprain; wrench, wrick; concussion; mortal wound, "wounds immedicable" [Milton].

8. **bruise**, **contusion**, **discoloration**, **black-and-blue mark**; **black eye**, eye in mourning [joc.]; shiner, shanty, goog, mouse [all slang].

9. **wreck**, **ruins**, **ruin**; mere wreck, wreck of one's former self; nervous wreck; rattletrap; rackabones [U.S.], jade, skate [U.S.], tacky [South. U.S.], plug [slang or coll., U.S.].

VERBS 10. **impair**, **damage**, endamage, **injure**, **harm**, **hurt**; **worsen**, make worse, deteriorate, put back; **dilapidate**; break 49.11, 12.

11. **spoil**, **mar**, **ruin**, queer [coll.], blight, blast, dash; **upset**, disrupt, disorganize; **foul up**, louse up, snafu, bugger, bugger up, gum up, gee up, jim up, gum up the works [all slang]; **mess up**, **hash up**, make a hash or mess of [all coll.]; **play havoc with**, play hob with [coll.], play the mischief with, play the deuce or devil with [coll.], play hell or merry hell with [slang]; cook [slang], dish [slang], cook one's goose [coll.], settle one's hash [coll.].

12. **corrupt**, **debase**, **degrade**, **degenerate**, **deprave**, **debauch**, **defile**, **contaminate**, **pollute**, **vitiate**, **poison**, **infect**, **taint**, canker, ulcerate; **pervert**, warp, prostitute; denaturalize, leaven, alloy, sophisticate.

13. (inflict an injury) **injure**, **hurt**; **wound**, scotch; stab, stick, pierce; cut, gash, scratch; scuff, scrape, chafe, fret, gall, bark, skin; lacerate, tear, rend; mutilate, mangle, maim, make mincemeat of; disfigure, deface; scar; sprain, strain; wrench, wrick; bloody.

14. **bruise**, **contuse**, dinge [chiefly Eng.]; bung, bung up [both slang]; **buffet**, **batter**, maul, pound, beat, beat black and blue; give a black eye, hang a shanty on [slang, U.S.].

15. **cripple**, becripple; **lame**; hamstring, hock, hough [chiefly Scot.]; wing; disable 157.9.

16. **undermine**, sap, mine, sap the foundatiors of; sabotage.

17. **deteriorate, worsen, get** or **grow worse**. get no better fast [coll.]; **degenerate**, derogate, **retrogress**, retrograde; go to the bad 691.23; let oneself go, let down; be the worse for, be the worse for wear, have seen better days.

18. **decline, sink, fail, fall**, wane, ebb, subside, lapse, **run down**, go down, **go downhill, fall away, fall off**, go off [coll.], slip, slide, slump, hit a slump; hit the skids, go on the toboggan [both slang, U.S.]; reach the depths, touch bottom, hit rockbottom.

19. **languish, pine, droop, flag, wilt; fade**, fade away; **wither, shrivel, dry up**, sear, fall "into the sere, the yellow leaf" [Shakespeare]; wizen, wizzen [dial.]; die on the vine.

20. **waste, waste away, consume away**, pine away; atrophy, emaciate; run to waste, run to seed.

21. **wear, wear away, wear down, wear off**; abrade, fret, rub off; fray, frazzle, tatter, **wear ragged; wear out**; weather.

22. **corrode, erode**, eat, gnaw, eat into, eat away, gnaw at the root of; canker, cankereat; **oxidize, rust**.

23. **decay, decompose, disintegrate**; go or fall into decay, go or fall to pieces, break up, crumble, crumble into dust; **spoil**, spile [dial.], **corrupt**, canker, **go bad; rot, putrefy**, putresce; fester, rankle; **mortify**, gangrene, sphacelate; mold, molder, mildew.

24. **break** 49.11, 12; **come apart, come** or **fall to pieces**; break open, give way or away, start, spring a leak, come apart at the seams.

25. **break down, founder**; collapse, cave in, topple, totter, topple down or over, tremble or nod to its fall.

26. **get out of order, get out of whack** [slang], get out of kilter or kelter [coll.], get out of commission [coll.], get out of gear, get out of joint, go wrong, go kaput [slang], **go on the blink** or **fritz** [slang], **go haywire** [slang, U.S.], give out, conk out [slang].

ADJS. 27. **impaired, damaged, hurt, injured, harmed**; deteriorated, worsened; **worse**, worse off, the worse for, all the worse for; imperfect 676.4; **broken** 49.23; sprung.

28. **spoiled, marred, ruined**, queered [coll.]; messed up, hashed up [both coll.];

fouled up, loused up, buggered up, gummed up, jimmed up [all slang].

29. **crippled**, game [coll.]; **lame, halt**, halting; spavined.

30. **worn, well-worn, deep-worn**, the worse for wear; timeworn; shopworn, shelfworn; worn to the stump, worn to the bone; **worn ragged**, worn to rags, worn to threads; **threadbare**, bare.

31. **shabby, shoddy, seedy** [coll.], **tacky** [coll., U.S.], poky, ratty [slang]; **ragged, tattered**, rent, frayed, frazzled; in rags, in tatters; **out at the elbows**, out at the heels, **down at the heel** or **heels**, on one's uppers.

32. **dilapidated, ramshackle, tumbledown, broken-down, run-down**, gone to rack and ruin; **battered**, beaten up, beatup [slang].

33. **weatherworn, weather-beaten, weathered**, weather-battered, weather-wasted, weather-eaten, weather-bitten, weatherscarred; faded, washed-out.

34. **wasted, withered**, shriveled, wilted, wizened, dried up; **emaciated** 204.19; worn to a shadow, reduced to a skeleton, "worn to the bones" [Shakespeare].

35. **worn out, used up** [coll.], fit for the dust hole or wastepaper basket; **exhausted, spent**, effete; done, done up, done for [all coll.]; **run-down**, laid low, at a low ebb, in a bad way, far-gone, on one's last legs.

36. **in disrepair, out of order**, out of working order, out of condition, out of repair, out of fix [coll.], **out of whack** [slang], **out of kilter** or **kelter** [coll.], **out of commission** [coll.], **out of sorts** [coll.], out of tune, out of joint, out of gear, **on the fritz** [slang], **on the blink** [slang], haywire [slang, U.S.]; **broken** 49.23.

37. **putrefactive, putrescent**, putrefacient, septic, carious; saprogenic, saprogenous; saprophilous, saprophytic.

38. **decayed, decomposed; spoiled, corrupt**, peccant, bad, gone bad; **rotten, putrid, putrified**, foul, carrion; **mortified**, sphacelate; gangrened, gangrenous; cankered, ulcerated; rotten at or to the core.

39. **tainted, touched, off**; stale, rancid, reasy or reasty [dial.], reechy [dial., Eng.]; sour, soured, blinky [dial.]; **rank, strong** [coll.], high.

40. **blighted, blasted, blown**; flyblown, maggoty; **moth-eaten, worm-eaten; moldy** or **mouldy**, moldering, mildewed, mossgrown; **musty, fusty**, frowy, frowzy, frowsty [coll. & dial., Eng.].

41. corroded, eroded; rusty, rust-eaten, rust-worn, rust-cankered.

42. damaging, injurious 673.12; corrupting, corruptive; corrosive, corroding; erosive, eroding.

43. deteriorating, worsening; decadent, degenerate; retrogressive, retrograde, backward, from better to worse; **declining, sinking, failing,** falling, waning, subsiding, slipping, sliding, slumping; **languishing, pining,** drooping, flagging, wilting; **wasting,** fading, **withering,** shriveling; tabetic, marcescent.

44. on the wane, on the decline, on the downgrade, on the downward track; tottering, nodding to its fall.

691. DESTRUCTION

NOUNS **1. destruction, ruin, ruination,** blue ruin [slang], perdition; wreck, wrack, rack, **wrack** or **rack and ruin;** ballyhack, ballywack, ballywrack [all slang.]; **devastation, ravage, havoc, desolation, waste, consumption;** decimation; **dissolution,** breakup, disruption, disorganization, undoing; vandalism; the road to ruin.

2. end, fate, doom.

3. fall, downfall, prostration; **overthrow, overturn, upset,** *bouleversement* [F.], **subversion,** suppression.

4. debacle, *débâcle* [F.]; **cataclysm, catastrophe; breakup,** breaking up; **breakdown, collapse; crash, smash, smashup,** crack-up [coll.]; **wreck,** shipwreck [fig.]; cave-in, cave [both coll.]; washout.

5. demolition, demolishment; wrecking, wreckage; **dismantlement,** disassembly; **mutilation,** mangling.

6. extinction, extermination, elimination, eradication, extirpation, **annihilation,** extinguishment; **abolition,** abolishment; liquidation, purge.

7. obliteration, erasure, effacement, expunction, blot, blotting; cancellation, cancel; deletion.

8. destroyer, ruiner, wrecker, demolisher, mutilator; **vandal,** Hun; exterminator, annihilator; **iconoclast,** idoloclast, idol breaker; biblioclast; nihilist; dynamiter, dynamitard.

9. eradicator, expunger, **eraser,** rubber, India rubber, sponge.

VERBS **10. destroy,** deal destruction; **ruin,** ruinate, bring to ruin, lay in ruins; **wreck,** shipwreck [fig.]; damn, seal the doom of; **devastate, desolate,** waste, **lay waste, ravage, havoc;** decimate; devour,

swallow up; gut, gut with fire, ravage with fire and sword.

11. do for, fix [coll.], **settle,** kibosh [slang], put the kibosh on [slang], give the quietus, do in, knock in or on the head, deal a deathblow to, knock out, K.O. [slang], deal a knock-out blow; nip, nip in the bud or head; cut short, make short work of.

12. put an end to, make an end of, **end, finish,** finish off [chiefly coll.], **dispose of, get rid of, do away with,** make away with, **kill,** put out of the way, put out of existence.

13. annihilate, abolish, nullify, undo, bring to naught or nought, napoo [slang].

14. exterminate, eliminate, eradicate, extirpate; wipe out [coll.], wipe up [slang], cut out, pull out; root up or out, uproot, pull or pluck up by the roots, cut up root and branch, strike at the root of, lay the ax to the root of; **remove, cut off,** take off; **liquidate, purge;** sweep away, make a clean sweep.

15. extinguish, quench, snuff out, put out, stamp or trample out; **smother,** choke, stifle; **suppress, quash,** squash [chiefly coll.], squelch [coll.], **quell,** put down.

16. obliterate, expunge, efface, erase, raze, blot, sponge, **wipe out,** rub out, **blot out,** sponge out; cancel, strike out, scratch out, rule out; delete, dele.

17. demolish, wreck, undo, unbuild, unmake, **dismantle, dissassemble; take apart, tear apart,** take ∼, **pull** ∼, **pick** or **tear to pieces,** pull in pieces, tear to rags or tatters; break to pieces, smash, shatter 49.12; mutilate, mangle, maim, make mincemeat of.

18. blow up, blast; mine, spring a mine.

19. raze or **rase, fell, level,** prostrate, raze to the ground or dust; **pull down, tear down, take down,** bring down, break down, throw down, cast down, beat down, knock down or over; cut down, chop down, mow down; blow down; burn down.

20. overthrow, overturn, overwhelm, upset, subvert, throw down or over.

21. (be destroyed) **fall,** fall to the ground, tumble, topple, tremble or nod to its fall; **break up,** crumble, crumble to dust, go or fall to pieces; go by the board, go out the window, go up the spout [coll.].

22. perish, expire, succumb, die, cease, end, come to an end, go, pass, **pass away, vanish, disappear,** fade away, run

out, peg out [slang], conk out [slang], come
to nothing or naught, be no more; be done
for, be all over with, be all up with [coll.],
be all U.P. [slang].

23. **go to ruin,** go to wreck, **go to
wrack** or **rack and ruin, go to the bad,**
go wrong, **go to the dogs, go to pot** [coll.],
go to the deuce or devil [coll.], go to hell
[slang], go to perdition, go to glory [coll.];
go to smash, go to shivers, go to smithers
or smithereens [chiefly coll.], go to sticks
or sticks and staves [slang]; go up [coll.],
go under.

24. **drive to the dogs,** drive to ruin,
drive to the bad.

ADJS. 25. **destructive,** destroying; **ruinous,** ruining; demolishing, demolitionary;
disastrous, calamitous, cataclysmic, cataclysmal, **catastrophic(al);** fatal, fateful;
deadly 408.23; **devastating, desolating,**
ravaging, wasting, wasteful, consumptive,
withering, wide-wasting; vandal, vandalish;
subversive, subversionary.

26. **exterminative,** exterminatory, **annihilative, eradicative,** extirpative, extirpatory, all-destroying, all-devouring.

27. **ruined, destroyed, wrecked,
blasted, undone, done for** [coll.], done
up [coll.], finished, kaput [slang]; spoiled
690.28; irremediable 887.15; fallen, overthrown; **devastated, desolated,** ravaged,
wasted; ruinous, in ruins; gone to wrack
and ruin, gone to pot [coll.], gone to the
dogs.

692. RESTORATION

NOUNS 1. **restoration, restitution, re-
establishment, reinstatement,** reinvest-
ment, reconstitution, replacement, reorganization, rehabilitation, readjustment,
redintegration, reconversion, reactivation;
improvement 689.

2. **reclamation, recovery, retrieval,**
redemption, salvation, salvage.

3. **revival,** revivification, **renewal,** resurrection, resuscitation, reanimation, resurgence, reversion; **resumption,** résump-
tion [F.]; **renaissance,** renascence; **rebirth,** new birth; **rejuvenation,** rejuvenes-
cence, second youth; **regeneration,** regen-
eracy, regenerateness, regenesis, palingenesis.

4. **renovation, renewal;** refreshment,
reconditioning; furbishment, refurbish-
ment.

5. **reconstruction, recreation,** remak-

ing, rebuilding, refashioning; re-formation,
reformation; remodeling, remodelment; recast.

6. **reparation, repair,** repairing, **fixing,
mending;** overhaul, overhauling; **rectification, correction,** redress, making right, satisfaction, compensation; trouble shooting
[coll.].

7. **cure, curing, healing;** disinfection;
instauration; cicatrization.

8. **recovery, rally, pickup** [slang, U.S.],
comeback [coll.], return; **recuperation,
convalescence;** recruital, recruiting, recruitment.

9. **restorability, reparability,** improvability, curability, recoverability, retrievabil-
ity, redeemability, corrigibility.

10. **mender, fixer,** doctor [coll.], re-
pairer, **repairman;** trouble man, **trouble
shooter** [coll.]; **mechanic,** mechanician;
tinker; cobbler; renovator.

VERBS 11. **restore, put back, replace,**
place in statu quo [L.]; **re-establish, re-
instate,** re-estate, **reinstall,** reinvest, revest, reconstitute, reorganize, rehabilitate,
reintegrate, readjust, refit; convert, reconvert; reactivate; recruit, reinforce, fill up, fill
up the ranks; return, give back 821.4.

12. **redeem, reclaim, recover,** retrieve, ransom; salvage, salve.

13. **remedy, rectify, correct, right,**
amend, emend, emendate, adjust, regulate,
redress, make good or right, **put right,** set
right, put or set to rights, put or set straight,
set up, make all square.

14. **repair, mend, fix, fix up** [coll.], do
up, doctor [coll.], put in repair, put in
shape, put in order or condition; **condition,**
commission, ready; **service, overhaul;** touch
up, retouch; vamp, vamp up; botch, botch
up; patch, **patch up;** tinker, tinker up;
cobble; bushel [U.S.]; sew up, darn; recap,
retread.

15. **cure,** recure, work a cure, **remedy,
heal,** recuperate, **restore to health,** bring
round or around, set on one's feet or legs;
break up (as a cold); relieve, stay; snatch
from the jaws of death.

16. **revive, revivify, renew; reanimate,
regenerate, rejuvenate,** put new life into;
resuscitate, bring to; **resurrect,** bring back,
call back, recall to life, raise from the dead;
rewarm, warm up or over; **rekindle,** relight,
reheat the ashes, stir the embers.

17. **renovate,** renovize, **renew;** refresh,
recondition; furbish, refurbish.

18. **make over, redo, remake,** recon-

struct, recreate, rebuild, reform, refashion, revamp, recast, remodel, new-model.

19. **recuperate, recruit, gain strength,** recruit *or* renew one's strength, **get better;** improve 689.7; **rally, pick up,** perk up, brace up [coll.], raise one's head, take a new *or* fresh lease on life, feel like a giant refreshed; **take a favorable turn,** turn the corner, take a turn for the better; **convalesce,** sleep it off.

20. **recover, rally, revive,** return, **get well,** over [dial. & slang], **get over,** get the better of, **pull through,** pull round *or* around, come round *or* around [coll.], get round *or* around [coll.], come back [coll.], make a comeback [coll.], get up, get about, get back in shape [coll.], be oneself again; **survive,** weather the storm, live to light again; **come to,** come to oneself, show signs of life; come up, come up smiling [both coll.]; come out of it, pull *or* snap out of it, bounce back up [all slang].

21. **heal, heal over,** close up, skin over, cicatrize, heal *or* right itself; **knit, set.**

ADJS. 22. **restorative, restitutive,** restitutory, analeptic(al) [med.]; reparative, reparatory; curative 685.34.

23. **recuperative,** recuperatory; revivatory, reviviscent; **convalescent;** buoyant, resilient, elastic.

24. **renascent,** redivivus, renewed, revived, resurgent, reappearing.

25. **remediable, curable,** medicable; **emendable,** amendable, **correctable,** rectifiable, corrigible; **improvable,** ameliorable; **reparable,** repairable, **mendable, fixable;** restorable, recoverable, retrievable, reclaimable, redeemable.

693. REFRESHMENT

NOUNS 1. **refreshment,** refection, refreshing, **bracing, exhilaration, stimulation,** enlivenment, vivification, **invigoration,** reinvigoration, revivification; regalement, regale; ventilation.

VERBS 2. **refresh, freshen,** freshen up, fresh up [chiefly dial.]; **revive,** revivify, **reinvigorate,** reanimate, re-enliven; **exhilarate, stimulate, invigorate,** fortify, animate, vivify, quicken, brisk, brisken; brace, **brace up,** buck up [coll.], perk up, chirk up [coll.], set up, set on one's legs *or* feet [coll.]; renew one's strength, put *or* breathe new life into; **regale, cheer,** refresh the inner man.

3. **ventilate,** cool, air, fan.

ADJS. 4. **refreshing,** refreshful; **bracing, exhilarating, stimulating, invigorating;** regaling, cheering.

5. **fresh, brisk, cool,** lively, vigorous, energetic; **pure,** sweet, clear.

6. **refreshed,** like a giant refreshed; **invigorated, exhilarated,** stimulated, animated.

7. **unwearied, untired, unfatigued,** unexhausted.

694. RELAPSE

NOUN: 1. **relapse, lapse,** declension, falling back; **reversion,** regression 146; **reverse, reversal; setback,** backset; **return,** revival, renewal, recrudescence.

2. **backsliding, backslide; fall, fall from grace;** recidivism, recidivation [criminol.]; apostasy 626.2.

3. **backslider,** recidivist, reversionist; apostate 626.5.

VERBS 4. **relapse, lapse, backslide,** slide back, **slip back,** sink back, **fall back,** fall off *or* away, have a relapse, be overcome, be overtaken, **return to, revert to,** yield again to, fall again into, recidive; revert, **regress** 146.4; **fall, fall from grace.**

ADJS. 5. **relapsing, lapsing, backsliding,** recidivous, recrudescent; **regressive** 146.7; apostate 626.11.

695. DANGER

NOUNS 1. **danger, peril, jeopardy, hazard, risk; endangerment, imperilment;** cause for alarm, rocks *or* breakers ahead, gathering clouds; dangerous ground, thin ice.

2. **dangerousness, hazardousness, riskiness, perilousness; unsafeness,** unhealthiness [coll.]; **precariousness, ticklishness,** touchiness, criticalness, delicacy, ticklish business [coll.]; **insecurity, unsoundness,** infirmity, instability, unsteadiness, shakiness; **unreliability,** undependability, untrustworthiness; **unsureness,** uncertainty, doubtfulness, dubiousness.

3. **exposure, openness,** liability, susceptibility; **unprotection, defenselessness,** helplessness.

4. **vulnerability, pregnability,** penetrability, assailability, vincibility; vulnerable point, **weak point, soft spot,** heel of Achilles, "the soft underbelly of Europe" [Churchill].

5. (hidden danger) snags, rocks, reefs; shallows, shoals; sands, quicksands; sandbank, sand bar, Goodwin sands; rock-

bound or ironbound coast, lee shore; undertow, undercurrent; pitfall 617.11; snake in the grass, snake in one's bosom.

VERBS 6. **endanger, imperil,** peril; **risk, hazard;** jeopardize, jeopard, jeopardy, compromise; **expose,** lay open; **put in danger, put in jeopardy,** put on the spot [slang]; incur danger, run into or encounter danger.

7. **take chances, take a chance, risk, run the chance,** ~ risk or hazard; **expose oneself, lay oneself open to,** open the door to; **tempt Providence, defy danger,** skate on thin ice, stand or sleep on a volcano, sit on a barrel of gunpowder, live in a glass house, put one's head in the lion's mouth, beard the lion in his den, march up to the cannon's mouth, play with fire, go through fire and water, go out of one's depth, go to sea in a sieve, carry too much sail, sail too near the wind; risk one's life, take one's life in one's hand.

8. **be in danger,** have one's name on the danger list, have the chances or odds against one; be despaired of, be overdue [naut]; hang by a thread; tremble on the verge, totter on the brink; feel the ground sliding from under one; have to run for it.

ADJS. 9. **dangerous,** dangersome [dial.], **perilous,** parlous [arch.], jeopardous, bad, attended ~, beset or fraught with danger.

10. **hazardous, risky, chancy** [coll.], riskish, riskful, full of risk; **adventurous,** venturous, venturesome; **speculative,** unsound, wildcat.

11. **unsafe,** unhealthy [coll.]; **unreliable, undependable, untrustworthy; unsure,** uncertain, doubtful, dubious; **insecure, unsound,** infirm, unstable, unsteady, shaky, tottery.

12. **precarious, ticklish, touchy, critical, delicate;** slippery, slippy; on thin ice, on slippery ground; hanging by a thread, trembling in the balance.

13. **in danger, in jeopardy, in peril,** on the spot [slang], in a bad way; **endangered, imperiled, jeopardized;** at the last extremity, between the hammer and the anvil, between Scylla and Charybdis, between two fires, between the devil and the deep blue sea.

14. **unprotected, unshielded, unsheltered,** uncovered, unscreened, **unguarded, undefended,** unfortified, unarmored, unarmed, weaponless, guardless, **defenseless,** helpless.

15. **exposed, open,** naked; liable, susceptible.

16. **vulnerable, pregnable,** penetrable, expugnable; assailable, attackable, surmountable; conquerable, beatable, vincible.

ADVS. 17. **dangerously, perilously, hazardously, riskily,** unsafely; **precariously,** ticklishly, critically.

696. SAFETY

NOUNS 1. **safety,** safeness, **security,** surety; danger past, storm blown over, clear coast; **protection, safeguard** 697; collective security.

VERBS 2. **be safe, be on the safe side;** weather, ride out, weather the storm; keep one's head above water, tide over; light upon one's feet; save one's bacon [coll.], save one's neck; bear a charmed life, possess nine lives.

3. **play safe** [coll.], **keep on the safe side,** take precautions 893.6, make sure, look before one leaps.

ADJS. 4. **safe, secure, safe and sound; protected** 697.20; on the safe side; unthreatened, unmolested.

5. **unhazardous, undangerous, unperilous, unrisky, unprecarious;** dependable, reliable, trustworthy, sound, stable, steady, firm, "founded upon a rock" [Bible]; as safe as houses.

6. **in safety, out of danger,** out of the meshes, **in the clear, out of harm's reach** or way; under cover, under lock and key; in shelter, in harbor or port, at anchor, in the shadow of a rock; on sure ground, on terra firma, high and dry, above water.

7. **snug, cozy;** airworthy; seaworthy, seakindly.

ADVS. 8. **safely, securely,** reliably, dependably; with safety, **with impunity.**

INTERJS. 9. **all's well!,** all clear!, all serene!

697. PROTECTION

NOUNS 1. **protection, guard, safekeeping;** safety 696; **shelter, cover,** shade, shadow, lee, the shadow of a rock; refuge 698; preservation 699; defense 797.

2. **protectorship, guardianship;** care, charge, keeping, custody, auspices, patronage, tutelage, guidance, wing; ward, wardship, wardenship, watch and ward; oversight, jurisdiction, management, government.

3. **safeguard,** palladium; **guard, shield, screen,** aegis; **bulwark;** backstop; **fender, bumper, buffer;** cowcatcher [U.S.], pilot;

dashboard, mudguard; windshield [U.S.], windscreen [Eng.]; safety rail, guardrail, handrail; safety valve, blow valve, snifting valve; insulator, insulation; lightning rod, lightning conductor; contraceptive.

4. protector, protectress, **safekeeper;** tower, pillar, tower of strength; **defender** 797.7; "our help and our shield" [Bible], "a very present help in time of trouble" [ibid.].

5. guardian, governor [slang], **patron, warden,** warder, **custodian, keeper, caretaker, curator;** janitor [U.S.]; castellan; game warden, gamekeeper; ranger, rangeman, range rider [chiefly West. U.S.]; guardian angel 1012.19.

6. chaperon, gooseberry [slang], third person; **governess,** duenna.

7. nurse, nursemaid, nurserymaid, nursegirl, *bonne* [F.], amah [Oriental], ayah [India], mammy [U.S.], granny [South. U.S.], nanny [Africa]; dry nurse, wet nurse; **baby sitter,** sitter.

8. guard, guarder, **warden,** warder, Cerberus; **outguard, outpost,** Cossack post; **advanced guard, vanguard,** van; **rear guard;** coast guard; guardsman, gendarme; yeoman, yeoman of the guard, beefeater [all Eng.]; jailer 759.10; railway *or* train guard, flagman; lifeguard, lifesaver [coll.]; goalkeeper, goalie; garrison; cordon.

9. watchman, **watch,** watcher, watchkeeper; **lookout,** lookout man; **sentinel, sentry,** vedette; **patrol, patrolman,** patroller; night watchman, Charley [Eng.]; fire watcher, fire guard; airplane spotter.

10. watchdog, bandog, house dog; Cerberus.

11. doorkeeper, doorman, gatekeeper, porter, janitor, concierge, durwaun [Anglo-India], chokidar [Anglo-India], ostiary, usher, tiler *or* tyler.

12. picket, picketeer, picketer; picket guard, outlying picket, inlying picket [all mil.]; goon squad, flying squadron [both labor union].

13. bodyguard, retainer, burkundaz [India]; **convoy, escort,** safe-conduct, safeguard.

14. policeman, police, constable, police constable, officer [coll.], police officer, sheriff, shrieve, marshal, gendarme, bluecoat [coll.], beagle [coll.], peace officer, law enforcement agent, arm of the law; bobby, peeler [both coll., Eng.]; cop, copper, bull, harness bull, flatfoot, gumshoe, gumshoe man [all slang]; detective

779.10; policewoman, sheriffess, police matron; **patrolman** [esp. U.S.], roundsman [U.S.]; **bailiff,** bumbailiff [derog., Eng.], bound bailiff [Eng.], tipstaff, catchpole *or* catchpoll; deputy sheriff, deputy; sergeant at arms; sergeant, lieutenant, captain, inspector, superintendent, commissioner; government man [U.S.], **G-man** [coll.].

15. police, police force, law enforcement agency; **constabulary,** constablery; **posse; vigilantes,** vigilance committee; Gestapo [Ger.]; F.B.I., Federal Bureau of Investigation [U.S.]; Mounted Police [Can.], Mounties [coll.]; military police, M.P.; shore patrol, S.P.; polizia, carabinieri [It.]; sûreté, gendarmes [F.]; Scotland Yard [Eng.]; CHEKA, N.K.V.D., M.V.D., O.G.P.U. [Russ.]; INTERPOL, International Criminal Police Commission [U.N.].

16. constableship, sheriffship, sheriffhood; shrievalty, sheriffalty, sheriffry; constablewick, sheriffwick; policedom, sheriffdom.

VERBS **17.** protect, guard, safeguard, ensure, insure, bless, make safe, bear one harmless; **defend** 797.8; **shelter, shield, screen, cover,** cloak, shroud, panoply, ensconce; **harbor, haven,** house, nestle; compass about, fence round; arm, armor.

18. care for, take care of, provide for, support; take charge of, take under one's **wing; look after,** see after, **attend to, minister to,** look *or* see to, take about [Scot.], look *or* watch out for [coll.], keep an eye on *or* upon, keep a sharp eye on *or* upon, **watch over,** keep watch over, stand over, watch, **mind, tend,** attend; keep tab *or* tabs on [coll.], keep cases; **shepherd,** ride herd on [slang, West. U.S.]; **chaperon,** matronize, play gooseberry; baby-sit [coll.]; **foster, nurture, cherish, nurse;** mother, father, be a mother *or* father to.

19. watch, keep watch, keep guard, keep vigil, keep watch and ward; stand guard, stand sentinel; tout, keep tout [both slang]; be on the lookout 531.8; mount guard; police, patrol, go on one's beat.

ADJS. **20.** protected, guarded, safeguarded, defended, ensured; safe 696.4–7; **sheltered, shielded,** screened, covered, cloaked, shrouded, panoplied, ensconced, undercover; armed 797.14; invulnerable 158.17, 18.

21. under the protection of, under the shield of, under the aegis of, under the wing *or* wings of, under the shadow of one's wing.

22. protective, prophylactic; protecting, guarding, safeguarding, sheltering, shielding, screening, covering; **guardian, tutelary;** defensive 797.11; contraceptive.

698. REFUGE

NOUNS **1. refuge, sanctuary,** safehold, ark; stronghold 717.4; **asylum, haven, port, harbor** [all generally]; harbor of refuge, port in a storm; "a refuge for the oppressed, a refuge in time of trouble" [Bible]; rock, "the rock of my refuge" [Bible], "my strong rock" [ibid.].

2. recourse, resource, resort, subterfuge; last resort *or* resource, *dernier ressort* [F.].

3. shelter, cover, covert, coverture; *abri* [F.], dugout, cave; funk hole [slang, chiefly Eng.] fraid hole [slang, U.S.]; storm cellar, cyclone cellar; air-raid shelter, bomb shelter, bombproof, fallout shelter; safety zone, safety isle *or* island.

4. asylum, home; poorhouse, almshouse, townhouse [U.S.], farm [coll.]; **orphanage; hospice,** hospital [hist.], hospitium [Rom. hist.], xenodochium [medieval].

5. retreat, seclusion, recess; hiding place, hideaway, hide-out [coll.]; **sanctum, sanctum sanctorum,** adytum; privacy, secret place; **den,** lair, mew; **cloister,** hermitage, anchorage; **ivory tower,** "ivory tower of aloofness from life" [Dorothy Canfield Fisher].

6. harbor, haven; port, seaport; harborage, **anchorage,** moorings; **roadstead,** road, roads; bund, bunder [both Oriental]; berth; **dock,** dockage, marina, basin; dry dock, slip; shipyard, dockyard; **wharf, pier;** landing, landing place *or* stage; quay, key; jetty, jutty; breakwater, mole, embankment; water wing; boathouse.

VERBS **7. take refuge, take shelter,** seek refuge, **claim sanctuary,** fly to, run into port, throw oneself into the arms of; bar the gate, lock *or* bolt the door, raise the drawbridge, let the portcullis down.

8. find refuge, make port, reach home, reach in time.

699. PRESERVATION

NOUNS **1. preservation,** preserval, **conservation, saving, salvation, keeping, safekeeping,** maintenance, support; protection 697.

2. (means of preservation) curing, seasoning, salting, brining, pickling, corning, kippering, jerking, marination; **drying,** dry-curing; dehydration, anhydration, evapora-

tion, desiccation; **smoking,** fuming, smoke-curing; **refrigeration,** freezing, quick-freezing; **embalming,** mummification; **canning,** tinning [chiefly Eng.]; bottling, potting.

3. preservative, conservative; salt, brine, vinegar, formaldehyde, embalming fluid.

4. preserver, saver, keeper, safekeeper; lifesaver.

5. life preserver, life jacket, life belt, safety belt, swimming belt, cork jacket, Mae West [slang]; life buoy, safety buoy, buoy, breeches buoy; water wings; lifeboat, life raft; life net; life line.

6. (place set apart for conservation) preserve, reserve, reservation, conservation; **park,** paradise; national park; forest preserve *or* reserve; Indian reservation; **sanctuary** 698.1, game reserve, bird sanctuary, etc.; soil conservation, soil bank.

VERBS **7. preserve, conserve, save,** spare; **keep,** keep safe, secure; **guard, protect** 697.17; **maintain, sustain,** uphold, support, **keep up,** keep alive, not willingly let die.

8. (preserve from decay) preservatize; **cure,** season, salt, brine, marinate *or* marinade, pickle, corn, kipper, jerk; **dry, dry-cure,** dry-salt; dehydrate, anhydrate, evaporate, desiccate; **smoke,** fume, **smoke-cure,** smoke-dry; **refrigerate,** freeze, quick-freeze; **embalm,** mummify.

9. put up, do up; **can,** tin [chiefly Eng.]; bottle, jar, pot.

ADJS. **10. preservative,** preservatory; **conservative,** conservatory; **preserving,** conserving, saving, keeping; protective 697.22.

11. preserved, conserved, **kept,** saved, spared; **untainted, unspoiled;** intact, undamaged 675.7, 8; **well-preserved,** well-conserved, **well-kept,** in a good state of preservation.

700. RESCUE

NOUNS **1. rescue, deliverance,** delivery; **extrication, release, freeing, liberation,** emancipation; **salvation,** salvage, **redemption,** ransom; **recovery, retrieval;** savior 940.2.

VERBS **2. rescue,** come to the rescue; **save, redeem,** ransom, **salvage; recover, retrieve; deliver, free,** set free, **release, extricate, liberate,** emancipate, *tirer d'affaire* [F., rescue from a difficulty]; snatch from the jaws of death.

ADJS. **3. rescuable, savable,** redeemable, deliverable, extricable.

INTERJS. **4. help!**; save us!, **to the rescue!,** *au secours!* [F.]; man overboard!

701. WARNING

NOUNS **1. warning, caution, caveat; advice,** aviso; **admonition,** monition, admonishment, **exhortation;** notice, notification; **word to the wise,** *verbum sapienti* [L.], word in the ear, flea in the ear [coll.]; **lesson, example,** deterrent example, warning piece; warning voice; **alarm** 702; threat 971.

2. forewarning, prewarning, **premonition, precaution;** prenotification, prenotice; **foreboding** 542; **portent,** "warnings, and portents and evils imminent" [Shakespeare].

3. warning sign, monitor; **premonitory sign,** premonitor; **symptom,** premonitory symptom, prodrome [med.]; **omen** 542.2, omens 542.4; **handwriting on the wall,** *mene, mene, tekel, upharsin* [Heb.]; gathering clouds, clouds on the horizon, messengers [dial., Eng.]; thundercloud, thunderhead; red light, red flag; quarantine flag, yellow flag, yellow jack; danger sign, death's head, skull and crossbones; warning signal 702.3.

4. high sign, office, hard word [all slang]; tip, tip-off.

5. warner, jiggerman *or* jiggers man [slang, U.S.]; **lookout, lookout man; sentinel,** sentry; **signalman,** signaler, signalist; flagman, flags [slang]; lighthouseman.

VERBS **6. warn, caution, advise, admonish, exhort; give warning,** address a warning to, notify, give notice, tell once and for all; threaten 971.2; **alert,** warn against, put on one's guard; sound the alarm 702.6.

7. tip off, put a flea in one's ear [both coll.]; **give the high sign,** tip the wink, give the office [all slang].

8. forewarn, prewarn, precaution, prenotify, tell in advance; **forebode** 542.8.

ADJS. **9. warning,** cautioning, **cautionary; monitory,** monitorial; exemplary; **admonitory,** admonishing.

10. forewarning, premonitory, foreboding 542.13, 14; **precautionary,** precautional.

INTERJS. **11. beware!,** 893.14; jiggers!, cheese it! [both slang].

702. ALARM

NOUNS **1. alarm, apprehension, consternation,** dismay; **agitation,** disturbance, disquiet, **perturbation, trepidation,** disconcertion; **fright** 889.

2. note of alarm, hue and cry, sound of trumpet, beat of drum; war cry, war whoop.

3. (alarm signal) **alert,** *alerte* [F.]; air-raid alarm; all-clear; tocsin, alarm bell; signal of distress, SOS, flag at half-mast *or* half-staff; fiery cross; fog signal *or* alarm, foghorn, fog bell; burglar alarm; fire alarm, fire bell, fire flag, still alarm; siren, whistle; horn, klaxon; hooter, buzzer; police whistle, watchman's rattle; alarm clock.

4. false alarm, hoax, cry of wolf; bugbear, bugaboo, bogy; flash in the pan, dud.

VERBS **5. alarm, agitate, disturb,** perturb, disquiet, disconcert, dismay, put the wind up, give cause for alarm; **frighten** 889.14; startle 538.8.

6. alert, arouse, put on the alert; **warn** 701.6; **sound the alarm,** give ∼, raise ∼, beat *or* turn in an alarm, ring the tocsin; cry wolf.

ADJS. **7. alarmed, aroused; agitated, disturbed,** perturbed, **apprehensive,** disquieted, disconcerted, dismayed; **frightened** 889.24; **startled** 538.13.

8. alarming, startling, disturbing, disquieting, disconcerting, dismaying; **frightening** 889.27.

703. ACTION

Voluntary Action.—NOUNS **1. action,** acting, doing; **practice,** praxis; **exercise,** exercitation; **operation,** movement; working, workings; employment, work; swing, play; activity 705.

2. performance, execution, transaction, discharge, dispatch *or* despatch, production, **achievement, effectuation; commission, perpetration;** completion 720; plus performance.

3. act, action, deed, do [coll.], **doing,** thing, thing done, **feat, stunt** [coll.], **exploit,** adventure, **enterprise,** achievement, accomplishment, **performance, transaction,** proceeding, job, gest *or* geste, step, measure, maneuver, bout, turn, passage, effort, move, coup, stroke, blow, touch, go [coll.]; overt act [law]; acta, doings, dealings.

VERBS **4. act, serve, function, operate, work, play;** move, proceed, go it [coll.].

5. take action, take steps *or* **measures,** take steps and measures; do something, **do something about; act on** *or* **upon,** go upon; lift a finger, stretch forth one's hand, strike a blow.

6. **do, bring about,** bring to pass, pro-duce, effect, effectuate, **achieve; make,** render, pay; **inflict, wreak,** do to; com-mit, perpetrate; pull [slang], pull off [coll.]; go and do, up and do, take and do [all dial. or coll.].

7. **practice, exercise, employ,** use; carry on, conduct, prosecute, wage; fol-low, **pursue; engage in,** work at, devote oneself to, apply oneself to, employ oneself in; **take up,** take to, undertake, take in hand, turn one's hand to, **go in** or **out for** [coll.], make it one's business, follow as an occupation; specialize in 81.4.

8. **perform, execute, transact,** dis-**charge, dispatch** or **despatch,** administer; dispose of, take care of [coll.], deal with; **put on,** stage [U.S.]; **enact,** go through; accomplish, complete 720.4–6.

9. **carry out,** carry through, work out, **bring off,** carry off, **put through,** get through; **put into effect, put in** or **into practice,** carry into effect, carry into execu-tion, **translate into action,** put in action or motion.

10. **do one's do** [coll.]; do one's stuff, do the needful, speak one's piece, come through [all slang].

ADJS. 11. **acting,** performing, practicing, serving, functioning, operating, working; in action 163.12.

INTERROGS. 12. what's doing?, what's cooking?, what's buzzin', cousin?, what's up?, what gives?, what's the deal?, what's with it? [all slang.].

704. INACTION

Voluntary Inaction.—NOUNS 1. **inac-tion,** passiveness, **passivity,** passivism; stand**stillism,** standpattism [coll.]; **do-nothingism,** do-nothingness, do-nothing policy, Fabian policy, let-alone principle, ~ doctrine or policy, laissez-faire policy, **laissez-faireism;** *laissez faire, laisser faire, laisser aller, laissez aller* [all F.]; watching and waiting, watchful waiting; inactivity 706; quiescence 267.

VERBS 2. **do nothing,** not stir, **not lift a finger** or **hand,** not move a foot, **sit back, sit on one's hands,** fold one's arms, twiddle one's thumbs; pass the time, fill up the time, beguile the time, while away the time, while away the tedious hours, bide one's time, take time, mark time, kick or cool one's heels [coll.], watch and wait, hang fire, rest and be thankful; lie or rest upon one's oars, repose on one's laurels; idle 706.10.

3. **refrain, abstain, hold, spare,** for-**bear, forgo,** keep from.

4. **let alone,** leave alone, **leave** or **let well enough alone,** let be, let things take their course, let it have its way, leave things as they are, *laisser faire,* ~ *passer* or *aller* [F.], live and let live; **take no part in, have nothing to do with,** have no hand in, stand or hold aloof.

5. **let go,** leave go [illit. & dial.], let pass, **let slip, let slide** [coll.], let it ride [slang, U.S.].

ADJS. 6. **do-nothing,** doless [dial.]; let-alone; **laissez-faire,** *laisser-faire, laissez-aller, laisser-aller* [all F.]; inactive, idle 706.15, 16.

ADVS. 7. **at a stand** or **standstill,** at a halt.

705. ACTIVITY

NOUNS 1. **activity, action,** activeness; **movement,** motion, stir; **proceedings, do-ings, goings-on;** business 654.

2. **liveliness, animation, vivacity,** vi-vaciousness, **sprightliness, spiritedness, briskness,** breeziness, peppiness [slang]; **life, spirit, verve;** energy, pep [slang], vim 160.

3. **quickness, swiftness, alacrity;** readi-ness, smartness, sharpness; **promptness,** promptitude; dispatch or despatch, expedi-tion; **agility, nimbleness, spryness.**

4. **bustle, fuss, flurry, flutter,** fluster, sputter, splutter, ferment, stew [coll.], stir, hubbub, ado, bother, pother; **restlessness,** unquiet, flutteriness, fussiness, fidgetiness.

5. **busyness, press of business,** no sine-cure, plenty to do, many irons in the fire, great doings, busy hum of men, the mad-ding crowd, the thick of things, the battle of life.

6. **industry,** industriousness, assiduous-ness, **assiduity, diligence, application,** sedulousness, zealousness; energeticalness, strenuousness, laboriousness, indefatigabil-ity.

7. **enterprise,** enterprisingness, initia-tive, aggression, **aggressiveness, pushful-ness,** pushingness; **push, drive, hustle,** get, **getup, get-up-and-get** or ~ **go, go-ahead,** go-to-itiveness, **up-and-comingness,** up-and-doingness [all coll.]; go-getterism, the get-there [both slang]; adventurousness, ven-turousness, venturesomeness, adventure-someness; gumption, spunk [both coll.]; **ambitiousness** 632.10.

8. **man of action**, busy bee, **hustler** [coll.], rustler [slang, U.S.], **go-getter** [slang], go-ahead [coll.], live man [U.S.], **live wire** [coll.], powerhouse [coll.], **human dynamo** [coll.], hummer [slang], humdinger [slang, U.S.], **eager beaver** [slang]; enthusiast 633.5; new broom.

VERBS 9. **be busy, have one's hands full,** have many irons in the fire; not have a moment to spare, not have a moment that one can call one's own; have other things to do, have other fish to fry; busy oneself 654.9, 10.

10. **stir,** stir about, **bestir oneself,** stir one's stumps [coll.], make a stir.

11. **bustle, fuss,** make a fuss, **flutter,** sputter, **fidget;** rush around, tear around, hurry about, buzz about, dart to and fro, go around like a chicken with its head cut off.

12. **hustle** [coll.], **rustle** [slang, U.S.], **push, scramble, go it,** go it strong, lay about one, step lively [coll.], break one's neck, hum [coll.], **make things hum,** make the sparks fly, make up for lost time; press on, drive on; go ahead, forge ahead, shoot ahead, go full steam ahead.

13. (slang terms) **hop** or **jump on it,** bear down on it, **hit the ball,** pour it on, go all out, lay oneself out, go at bald-headed, go to town on.

14. **keep going, keep on, carry on,** peg away, **keep at it,** keep moving, keep driving [coll.], **keep the pot boiling** [coll.], keep the ball rolling; **keep busy, keep one's nose to the grindstone.**

15. make the most of one's time, improve the shining hour, make hay while the sun shines, not let the grass grow under one's feet, get up early, catch a weasel asleep.

ADJS. 16. **active, lively, animated, spirited, vivacious, sprightly, spry, breezy, brisk, energetic,** smacking, spanking; **alive, live** [chiefly U.S.], full of life, full of pep [slang], full of go [coll.]; **peppy** [slang]; **snappy** [coll.]; chirk, chipper [both coll., U.S.]; pert, peart [dial.]; mercurial, quicksilver.

17. **quick, swift, expeditious, prompt,** instant, ready, smart, sharp, quick on the trigger [coll., U.S.]; **agile, nimble, fleet, spry,** fly [slang].

18. **astir, stirring,** agoing, afoot, **on foot;** in full swing.

19. **bustling,** fussing, fluttering; **fluttery, fussy, fidgety;** restless, unquiet.

20. **busy,** full of business; **occupied, engaged, employed, working; at work,** at it, on duty, on the job [slang]; in collar [coll.], in harness; hard at work, **hard at it; on the move, on the go,** on the run, **on the hop** or **jump** [coll.]; busy as a bee, busy as a hen with one chicken [coll.], busier than a one-armed paper hanger (with the itch) [coll.]; up to one's ears or elbows in; tied up.

21. **industrious, assiduous, diligent, sedulous,** zealous; **energetic,** strenuous, hard, laborious, **hardworking,** never idle; sleepless, unsleeping; indefatigable 623.7.

22. **enterprising, aggressive, pushing,** pushful, not backward in going forward [joc.]; **up-and-coming,** up-and-doing, **go-ahead,** go-to-itive, hustling, gumptious [all coll.]; **ambitious** 632.29; adventurous, venturous, venturesome, adventuresome.

ADVS. 23. **actively, busily; lively,** sprightly, **briskly, breezily, energetically,** animatedly, vivaciously, spiritedly, with life and spirit; allegro, allegretto [both music]; full tilt, in full swing.

24. **quickly, swiftly, expeditiously,** readily, promptly, sharply, instantly; agilely, nimbly, spryly.

25. **industriously, assiduously, diligently, sedulously,** zealously; **energetically,** strenuously, laboriously.

706. INACTIVITY

NOUNS 1. **inactivity, inaction,** inactiveness, suspended animation; motionlessness, quiescence 267.

2. **idleness,** idlehood; **unemployment, inoccupation;** idle hands, idle hours, time hanging on one's hands; otiosity, "a life of dignified otiosity" [Thackeray]; technological unemployment.

3. **idling, loafing,** lazing; loaf, laze [both coll.]; **dallying,** dillydallying; **dawdling,** loitering, lingering; lounging, lolling.

4. **indolence, laziness,** laze [coll.], **sloth,** slothfulness, laggardness, lackadaisicalness, dilatoriness, remissness, do-nothingness, faineance or faineancy, inexertion, inertia; **shiftlessness,** hobism, vagrancy; spring fever; ergophobia.

5. **languor,** languidness, languorousness, languishment; **listlessness,** lifelessness, **dullness, sluggishness,** heaviness, dopiness [coll.]; supineness; **lassitude, lethargy,** oscitance or oscitancy, kef, phlegm; lentitude, hebetude; torpidness, torpor, torpidity, torpescence; stupor, stupefaction;

drowsiness 710.1; fatigue 715; "the sad fatigue of idleness" [M. Green].

6. lazybones, lazybone, lazyboots [coll.], lazylegs, indolent, Weary Willie [coll.], sleepyhead, lie-abed.

7. idler, his idleship [joc.]; loafer, lounger, loller, bench warmer [slang]; do-nothing, do-little, fainéant, sluggard, slug, mope, moper, lubber, stick-in-the-mud [coll.]; time waster, time killer; dallier, dillydallier; dawdler, dawdle, laggard, loiterer, lingerer, waiter on Providence; putterer, potterer; doodler, diddler [coll.]; clock watcher; eyeservant, eyeserver; after-noon farmer.

8. bum, bummer, stiff, moocher, dead one or 'un [all slang]; good-for-nothing, good-for-naught, ne'er-do-well, wastrel, lazzarone; hobo, tramp 273.3; beggar 772.8.

9. nonworker, drone; the unemployed, the forgotten man.

VERBS 10. idle, do nothing, laze, lazy [coll.]. loaf, lounge; lie around, lounge around, loll around, lollop around [coll., Eng.], sit around, stand around, stall around [slang], loiter about or around, cooter around [dial., U.S.]; bum [U.S.]; bum around [U.S.], haze, haze around, mooch, mooch around [all slang]; swing the lead, swing the bat, whip the cat [all slang]; goof off, lie down on the job, dog on the job [all slang]; loaf on [coll.], lay or lie down on [slang], idle at one's ex-pense; sleep at one's post.

11. waste time, consume time, kill time, idle ~, trifle ~, fritter or fool away time, while away the time, pass the time, lose time, waste the precious hours, burn daylight; let the grass grow under one's feet; twiddle one's thumbs, fold one's arms, whistle for want of thought.

12. dally, dillydally; putter, potter [esp. Eng.], piddle, peddle, diddle [coll.], doodle, dawdle, loiter, linger, lag, poke, take one's time.

13. take it easy, take things as they come, drift, drift with the current, swim with the stream, lead an easy life, live a life of ease, eat the bread of idleness; lie or rest upon one's oars, rest or repose on one's laurels, lie back on one's record.

14. lie idle, lie fallow; lie or lay off; lie up, lie on the shelf; ride at anchor, lay or lie by, lay or lie to [all naut.]; have noth-ing to do, have nothing on [slang].

ADJS. 15. inactive, unactive; quiescent, motionless 267.10—12; sedentary.

16. idle, fallow, otiose; unemployed, un-occupied, disengaged, désœuvré [F.], job-less, out of work, out of employ, out of a job, out of harness, out of collar [coll.], free, at liberty, at leisure; leisure, leisured; off duty, off work, off.

17. indolent, lazy, do-nothing, fainé-ant, slothful, laggard; lackadaisical, dila-tory, remiss, slack, lax, easy; shiftless, un-enterprising, nonaggressive, good-for-noth-ing, ne'er-do-well; drony, dronish; bone-idle, born tired [joc.]; lazy as Ludlam's dog.

18. languid, languorous, listless, lifeless, pepless [slang], lethargic(al), hebetudi-nous, lentitudinous, supine, phlegmatic, lymphatic, sluggish, dopey [slang], droopy, dull, heavy, leaden, lumpish, torpid, in-ert, dead, exanimate; sleepy 710.19; weary 715.6.

707. HASTE

NOUNS 1. haste, hurry, scurry, rush, dash, drive, scuttle, scamper, scramble, hustle [coll.], bustle, flutter, flurry, helter-skelter; switch of a hurry [dial.], no time to be lost.

2. hastiness, hurriedness, quickness, ex-peditiousness; swiftness, speed 268; furious-ness, feverishness; precipitousness, precipi-tance or precipitancy, precipitation; sud-denness, abruptness; impetuousness, im-petuosity, impulsiveness, rashness.

3. hastening, hurrying, speeding, for-warding, quickening, acceleration, dis-patch or despatch, expedition.

VERBS 4. hasten, haste [literary & dial.], hurry, expedite, dispatch, accelerate, speed, speed up, hurry up [coll.], rush, quicken, hustle [coll.], bustle, precipitate, forward; urge 646.14—16; push, press, crowd; hurry on, hasten on, drive on, hie on, push on; hurry along, rush along, speed along, speed on its way; push through, railroad through [coll., U.S.].

5. make haste, hasten, hurry, hurry up [coll.]; rush, chase, tear, scurry, scam-per, scramble, scuttle, hustle [coll.], bustle; bestir oneself, get going [slang]; move quickly 268.9—14; hurry on, dash on, bundle on, press or push on; break one's neck [coll.], fall all over oneself [slang]; lose no time, not lose a moment; make short work of, make the best of one's time or way, make up for lost time.

6. (slang terms) step on it, snap into it, hop to it, bear down on it, hump, hump it, hump oneself, get a hump, ~ hustle,

~ **move** *or* **wiggle on,** stir one's stumps, not spare the horses.

7. rush into, plunge into, dive into, plunge, plunge headlong; **not stop to think,** go off half-cocked *or* at half cock [coll., U.S.], leap before one looks.

8. be in a hurry, have no time to lose *or* spare, not have a moment to spare, work against time.

ADJS. **9. hasty, hurried, quick,** flying, **expeditious; swift, speedy** 268.19; **furious,** feverish; slap-bang, slapdash; **cursory,** passing, snap, superficial.

10. precipitate, precipitant, precipitous; **sudden,** abrupt; **impetuous, impulsive,** rash; headlong, breakneck.

11. hurried, rushed, pushed, pressed, crowded, **pressed for time,** hard pushed *or* pressed, hard run.

ADVS. **12. hastily, hurriedly, quickly, expeditiously,** apace, amain, hand over hand *or* fist; **swiftly, speedily** 268.21; with haste, with great *or* all haste, with a rush; furiously, feverishly; **helter-skelter, hurry-scurry,** holus-bolus, hotfoot [coll.], pell-mell; slapdash, slap-bang [coll.]; cursorily, superficially.

13. posthaste, in posthaste; post, express; by post, by express, by air mail, by return mail; by cable, by telegraph, by wireless [coll.]; by forced marches.

14. in a hurry, in haste, in hot haste, in all haste; in short order 268.23; against time, against the clock.

15. precipitately, precipitantly, precipitously; **suddenly,** abruptly; **impetuously, impulsively, rashly;** headlong, headfirst, headforemost, head over heels, heels over head, *à corps perdu* [F.].

INTERJS. **16. make haste!, hurry up!** [coll.]; rush!, immediate!, urgent!; **step lively!,** look lively *or* alive! [coll.], look slick *or* slippy! [slang], look sharp!; chop-chop!, wicky-wicky!, mooey pronto! [all pidgin Eng.]; quickmarch!, double!, on the double! [all mil.].

17. (slang terms) **step on it!,** snap into it!, **make it snappy!, get a move on!,** get a hump on!, get a wiggle on!, **shake a leg!,** stir your stumps!, wiggle your boots!, get the lead out!, don't spare the horses!

708. LEISURE

NOUNS **1. leisure, ease, convenience,** freedom; **free time, spare time,** odd moments, idle hours, dodge times [slang], time to spare, time to burn [slang, U.S.], time on one's hands, time at one's disposal *or* command; time, one's own sweet time [coll.].

2. leisureliness, unhurriedness, unhastiness, hastelessness; **slowness** 269; **deliberateness,** deliberation.

VERBS **3. have time,** have time to spare, have plenty of time, be in no hurry.

4. take one's leisure, take one's ease, **take one's time,** take one's own sweet time [coll.], do at one's leisure *or* convenience; go slow 269.6–9.

ADJS. **5. leisure, leisured,** at leisure; idle, unoccupied, free, open, spare.

6. leisurely, unhurried, unhasty, hasteless, easy, **deliberate; slow** 269.10.

7. at one's leisure, at one's convenience, at one's own sweet time [coll.], when it is handy, when you have the time, when you have a minute to spare, when you have a moment to call your own, when the time is ripe.

709. REST, REPOSE

NOUNS **1. rest, repose, ease, relaxation,** "sweet repose and rest" [Shakespeare]; quiet, **tranquility** 267; inactivity 706; sleep 710.

2. respite, recess, rest, pause, halt, stay, lull, **break,** interlude, **intermission,** spell, letup [coll.], layoff, **time out** [coll.]; **breathing spell,** breathing time, breathing place, breathing space, breath, **breather,** breathing; coffee break, cigarette break; the pause that refreshes.

3. vacation, holidays; leave, leave of absence, furlough, ticket of leave [Eng.]; **liberty,** shore leave; **sabbatical,** sabbatical leave; weekend; busman's *or* postman's holiday.

4. holiday, red-letter day, gala day, fete day, festival day, day of festivities, feria; legal holiday [U.S. & Can.], bank holiday [Eng.]; high holiday, high day [Biblical], high days and holidays; Christmas, May-day, etc. 137.13.

5. day of rest, *dies non* [L.]; Sabbath, Sunday, Lord's Day, First day.

VERBS **6. rest, repose, take rest, take one's ease, take it easy** [coll.], take life easy, rest and be thankful; go to rest, settle to rest; lie down, snug down, recline, lounge, couch, sprawl, loll.

7. relax, unlax [slang], unbend, slack, slacken, ease; **ease up, let up,** slack up, slack off, **ease off, let down, slow down,**

let up on; rest one's face and hands [joc.].

8. **take a rest, take a break, take time out** [coll.], pause, lay off, **knock off** [coll.], recess, **take a recess**, take five [slang, U.S.]; stop for breath, catch one's breath, breathe.

9. **vacation, holiday**, take a holiday, make holiday; **take a leave of absence**, take leave, go on leave, go on furlough, take one's sabbatical; weekend; Sunday, Christmas, etc. [coll.].

ADJS. 10. **vacational, holiday**, ferial, festal; sabbatic(al).

ADVS. 11. **at rest, at ease**, at one's ease; abed, in bed.

12. **on vacation**, on leave, on furlough.

INTERJS. 13. **at ease!**, stand at ease!, stand easy!, at rest!, **as you were!**; relax!, **take it easy!**

710. SLEEP

NOUNS 1. **sleepiness, drowsiness**, somnolence *or* somnolency, oscitance *or* oscitancy; lethargy; languor 706.5; sand in the eyes, heavy eyelids.

2. **sleep**, sleepry [Scot.], **slumber, repose**, silken repose, somnus, the arms of Morpheus; the balmy, doss [Eng.], shut-eye [all slang]; unconsciousness 422.2; **land of Nod**, slumberland, sleepland, dreamland; hibernation, estivation.

3. **nap, doze, drowse, snooze** [coll.], snoozle [chiefly dial.], **cat nap**, calk [naut. slang], wink, **forty winks** [coll.], wink of sleep, spot of sleep [slang, Eng.], noddins and bobbins [coll.]; siesta, blanket drill [mil. slang], beauty sleep [coll.].

4. **sweet sleep, balmy sleep, downy sleep**, soft sleep, gentle sleep, smiling sleep, golden slumbers; "folded sleep" [Tennyson], "dewy-feathered sleep" [Milton], "the honey-heavy dew of slumber" [Shakespeare], peaceful sleep, sleep of the just; restful sleep, good night's sleep, "sleep that knits up the ravell'd sleave of care" [Shakespeare].

5. **deep sleep, profound sleep, heavy sleep, sound sleep**, unbroken sleep, wakeless sleep, the sleep of the dead, "sleep such as makes the darkness brief" [Martial].

6. **stupor, sopor, daze, coma, trance, swoon** [poetic]; **lethargy**, lethargic sleep.

7. **hypnosis**, mesmeric *or* hypnotic sleep, somnolism, somnipathy, hypnotic somnolence; lethargic hypnosis; somnambulistic hypnosis; cataplexy, catalepsy,

thanatosis, cataleptic hypnosis, animal hypnosis; autohypnosis, self-hypnosis.

8. **hypnotism, mesmerism**; hypnology; hypnotization, mesmerization; **animal magnetism**; od, odyl *or* odyle, odylic force, biod, elod, magnetod, pantod; hypnotic suggestion, posthypnotic suggestion, autosuggestion.

9. **hypnotist, mesmerist**, hypnotizer, mesmerizer.

10. **sleep-inducer, sleep-producer, sleep-provoker, sleep-bringer, sleep-stuff**; **hypnotic, soporific, somnifacient**; sleeping draught 685.11, 48; lullaby 461.15.

11. **Morpheus, Somnus, Hypnos** [all Gr. myth.]; **sandman**, dustman; "sweet father of soft rest" [Wm. Drummond].

12. **sleeper, slumberer**; sleeping beauty; **sleepyhead**, sleepy [coll.]; somnivolent, lie-abed.

VERBS 13. **sleep, slumber**, get some shut-eye [slang], pound the ear [slang, U.S.], rest in the arms of Morpheus; **doze, drowse, snooze** [coll.], snoozle [chiefly dial.]; **nap**, take a nap, catch a wink, take forty winks [coll.]; sleep soundly, **sleep like a top** *or* **log**, sleep like the dead; snore, saw logs [slang], drive pigs to market [coll.]; oversleep.

14. **hibernate**, estivate, **hole up**, winter.

15. **go to sleep**, settle to sleep, go off to sleep, **fall asleep**, drop asleep, **drop off**, calk off [naut. slang], drift "gently down the tides of sleep" [Longfellow]; **doze off**, drowse off, nod off; close the eyes, "let fall the shadow of mine eyes" [Shakespeare].

16. **go to bed, retire, turn in** [coll.], roll in [coll.], crawl in [slang], **hit the hay** [slang], flop [slang, U.S.], lay me down to sleep; bed, bed down, sack up [mil. slang]; go night-night, go bye-lo, go beddie-bye.

17. **put to bed**, bed; cradle; **tuck in.**

18. **put to sleep, lull to sleep**, rock to sleep; **hypnotize, mesmerize**, magnetize, psychologize; **entrance**, trance, put in a trance.

ADJS. 19. **sleepy, drowsy**, dozy, snoozy [coll.], **slumberous**, slumbery, nappy, dreamy, **half asleep**; sleepful, sleep-filled, yawny, stretchy [coll.], oscitant; **heavy, heavy-eyed, heavy with sleep**, sleep-swollen, sleep-drowned, sleep-drunk, drugged with sleep; **somnolent**, somniferous, soporific; **lethargic(al)**, comatose; languid 706.18.

20. **asleep, sleeping, slumbering**, in the

arms or lap of Morpheus, in the land of Nod; **sound asleep, fast asleep, dead asleep**, deep asleep, in a sound sleep, sound as a top, **unconscious, oblivious**, comatose, dormant, dead, **dead to the world;** wakeless, unwakened, unawakened.

21. **sleep-inducing**, sleep-producing, sleep-bringing, sleep-causing, sleep-compelling, sleep-inviting, sleep-provoking, sleep-tempting; **soporific, somniferous**, somnifacient; sedative 685.39.

22. **hypnotic**, hypnoidal, **mesmeric(al)**; odylic.

711. WAKEFULNESS

NOUNS 1. **wakefulness, sleeplessness**, restlessness; **insomnia**, pervigilium, "the wakey nights" [Sir Thomas Wyatt]; insomniac [coll.]; alertness 531.5.

2. **awakening, wakening**, rousing, arousal; rude awakening.

VERBS 3. **keep awake**, keep one's eyes open; keep alert, be vigilant 531.8; stay awake, **toss and turn**, not sleep a wink.

4. **awake, awaken, wake, wake up**, rouse, arouse; call, knock up [Eng.]; open one's eyes; stir [coll.].

5. **get up, get out of bed**, arise, rise, rise up, **rise and shine** [slang], **turn out** [coll.], roll out [slang], pile out [slang]; **show a leg, hit the deck**, lash and carry [all sea slang].

ADJS. 6. **wakeful, sleepless**, slumberless, unsleeping; restless.

7. **awake**, wake [dial.], conscious; **wide awake**, broad awake; alert 531.14.

ADVS. 8. **sleeplessly, unsleepingly**; wakefully, with one's eyes open; alertly 531.17.

712. ENDEAVOR

NOUNS 1. **endeavor, effort, exertion**; striving, struggle, strain.

2. **attempt, trial, effort, essay, undertaking**; move, stroke; **try, go, fist, fling**, shot [all coll.]; **crack, whack, slap, dab, stab, lick, jab, stagger**, whirl, shy [all slang]; offer, bid, strong bid.

3. **one's best, one's level best** [coll.], **one's utmost**, one's damndest or darndest [slang], one's best endeavor, the best one can, the best one knows how, all one can do, all one's got [coll.], **the top of one's bent**, as much as in one lies.

VERBS 4. **endeavor, strive, struggle**, strain, labor, **exert oneself**; seek, study, aim.

5. **attempt, try, essay, offer**; undertake,

venture, venture on or upon; **make an attempt or effort**, lift a finger, lift the hand; **make a try**, give it a try, give it a fling, **take a fling at, have a go at**, have at it, go to market [all coll.]; **give it a whirl**, take a shy at, take a crack or whack at, **make a stab or jab at**, make a stagger at, make a pass at [all slang]; try anything once.

6. **try to**, try and [coll.], **attempt to, endeavor to**, strive to, seek to, study to, aim to, venture to, pretend to.

7. **try for, strive for**, strain for, struggle for, pull for, bid for, make a bid or strong bid for, make a play for [coll.].

8. **see what one can do**, see what can be done, see if one can do, do what one can, use one's endeavor, **try one's hand**, try one's luck.

9. **make a special effort**, go out of the way, go out of one's way, **put oneself out**, put oneself out of the way, lay oneself out [coll.], trouble oneself, **go to the trouble**, take trouble, **take pains**, redouble one's efforts.

10. **try hard**, push, make a bold push, **file a strong bid** [coll.], bunch the hits [slang, U.S.], **put one's back to or into**, put one's heart into, hump it [slang, U.S.], try until one is black in the face, **lay oneself out** [coll.], knock oneself out [slang], break one's neck [coll.], break an arm or blood vessel, break a hamestring [slang, West. U.S.]; do or break a leg, do or bust a gut [slang]; **try and try**; try, try, try again.

11. **do one's best**, do one's level best [coll.], **do one's utmost**, try one's best or utmost, do or try one's damndest or darndest [slang], **do all one can**, do the best one can, **do the best one knows how**, do all in one's power, do as much as in one lies, do what lies in one's power; put all one's strength into, put one's whole soul in, strain every nerve; go all out [coll.], go the limit, shoot the works [slang], give it all one's got [coll.]; do oneself justice, do oneself proud [coll.]; be on one's mettle.

12. **make every effort, spare no efforts or pains, go all lengths**, go the whole length, go through fire and water, move heaven and earth, leave no stone unturned, leave no avenue unexplored.

ADVS. 13. **out for**, out to, trying for, **on the make** [coll., U.S.].

14. **one's best**, etc. 712.3; **at the top of**

one's bent, to one's utmost, as far as possible.

713. UNDERTAKING

NOUNS 1. undertaking, enterprise, venture, adventure, engagement, project, proposition [coll., U.S.]; business, task 654; attempt 712.2.

2. big undertaking, large or tall order [slang].

VERBS 3. undertake, assume, accept, take on, take upon oneself, take upon one's shoulders; take in hand, put in hand, put or turn one's hand to, put or set the hand to; engage in, devote oneself to, apply oneself to, address oneself to, give oneself up to; take up, betake oneself to, go into, go in or out for [coll.]; enter on or upon, embark in or upon, venture upon, go upon, launch forth, set forward; set about, go about, go to do; set to, turn to, buckle to, fall to; tackle [coll.], pitch into [coll.], plunge into, fall into, launch into or upon, go at, set at, have at it [coll.]; put one's hand to the plow, put or lay one's shoulder to the wheel, take the bull by the horns; attempt 712.5.

4. have in hand, have one's hands in, have on one's hands or shoulders; be in the hands of, pass through one's hands; be on the anvil or stocks, be in the fire.

5. bite off more than one can chew [coll.], have too many irons in the fire.

ADJS. 6. undertaken, assumed, accepted; in hand, on the anvil, on the stocks, in the fire.

714. EXERTION

NOUNS 1. exertion, effort; endeavor 712; trouble, pains; great effort, dead lift, hard ∼, strong or long pull, "a long pull, a strong pull, and a pull all together" [Dickens].

2. strain, stress, stress and strain, tension, stretch, rack; tug, pull, haul, heft [dial.]; overexertion, overstrain.

3. struggle, fight, battle, tussle, scuffle, wrestle.

4. work, labor, employment, industry, toil, moil, travail, toil and trouble, sweat of one's brow; fatigue, fag [coll., Eng.], faggery; drudgery, slavery, grind [coll.]; manual labor, handwork, handiwork, elbow grease [joc.]; hand's turn, stroke of work, stroke; lick, lick of work, stitch of work [all coll.]; task 654.2.

5. hard work or labor, hard [cant],

warm work, hard or tough grind [coll.]; hard job 729.2; laboriousness, toilsomeness, effortfulness, strenuousness, arduousness, onerousness, operoseness, burdensomeness, troublesomeness.

6. exercise, exercising; practice, drill, workout; athletics, gymnastics, calisthenics, eurythmics, setting-up exercises, daily dozen; constitutional [coll.], stretch; violent exercise, breather [coll.].

7. exerciser, horizontal bar, trapeze, weight, dumbbell, bar bell.

VERBS 8. exert, exercise, ply, employ, use, put forth, put out, lay out.

9. exert oneself, put forth one's strength, tax one's energies, lay oneself out [coll.]; endeavor 712.4; apply oneself, hump oneself [slang, U.S.], buckle down, knuckle down [coll., U.S.], bear down on it [slang], lay to; lay to the oars, ply the oar, take the laboring oar.

10. strain, tense, stress, stretch, rack; pull, tug; strain the muscles, strain every nerve; overexert, overstrain.

11. struggle, strive, contend, fight, battle, buffet, scuffle, tussle, wrestle, lay about one, work or fight one's way, agonize, huff and puff.

12. work, labor, toil, moil, toil and moil, travail; busy oneself 654.9, 10; turn a hand, do a hand's turn; chore, do the chores [both U.S.]; char, do chars [both Eng.].

13. work hard, scratch, dig [coll., U.S.], hustle [coll.], fag, sweat [coll.], slave, sweat and slave [coll.]; hit the ball, bear down on it, pour it on, not spare the horses [all slang]; work one's head off [coll.], work one's fingers to the bone; work like a horse or cart horse, work like a dog, work like a slave or galley slave, work like a coal heaver, work like a Briton, work like a nigger [coll.], sweat like a nigger at election [slang, U.S.]; work overtime, do double duty, work double hours or double tides; work day and night, work late, sit up, lucubrate, burn the midnight oil, burn the candle at both ends; overwork 661.11.

14. drudge, grind [coll.], dig [coll.], grub, plod, peg, plug [slang], hammer, peg away or along, plug away or along [slang], hammer away, pound away, work away; keep one's nose to the grindstone; wade through.

15. set to work, get busy, fall to work, fall to, buckle to or down to [coll.], turn to, set to or about, set at, put or set one's

hand to, start in, enter on or upon, launch into or upon; **get on the job,** get going [both coll.]; **go to it,** get with it, get cracking, have at it, hop or jump to it [all slang]; **attack, tackle** [coll.], tackle down or to [coll.]; **plunge into,** dive into; **pitch in** or **into,** light into, wade into, tear into, sail into [all coll.]; put or lay one's shoulder to the wheel, put one's hand to the plow.

16. **task, tax, burden,** oppress; **work, busy,** keep busy, fag, sweat [coll.], **drive;** overtask, overtax, overburden, overwork, overdrive.

ADJS. 17. **work;** workaday, workday, prosaic.

18. **laboring, working, toiling; struggling, striving,** straining; **drudging,** grubbing, **plodding,** pegging, plugging [slang]; hard-working 705.21.

19. **laborious, toilsome, arduous, strenuous,** effortful, operose, onerous, burdensome, troublesome; wearisome 715.11; heavy [coll.], hefty [coll., U.S.], tough [coll.]; uphill; Herculean; labored, forced, strained; hard-fought, hard-earned.

ADVS. 20. **laboriously, arduously, toilsomely, strenuously,** operosely, onerously, burdensomely, troublesomely; effortfully, with effort, **hard,** by the sweat of one's brow; with all one's might, **with might and main,** with much ado, with a strong hand; **hammer and tongs, tooth and nail,** *bec et ongles* [F.], heart and soul.

715. FATIGUE

NOUNS 1. **fatigue, tiredness, weariness,** wearifulness; tire [chiefly dial.], tucker [coll., U.S.]; weakness, enfeeblement; faintness, faintishness, goneness; languor 706.5; tension fatigue, tenigue; strain, eyestrain.

2. **exhaustion,** exhaustedness; **collapse, prostration.**

3. **breathlessness, shortness of breath,** short-windedness; panting, gasping; dyspnea, labored breathing.

VERBS 4. **fatigue, tire, weary, exhaust, gruel,** fag, tucker [coll., U.S.], wilt, flag, jade, harass, frazzle [chiefly U.S.]; wear, wear on or upon, wear down; **tire out, wear out, fag out, tucker out** [coll., U.S.], poop out [slang]; **use up** [coll.], do up [coll.], knock up [coll., Eng.], tuck up [coll., Eng.], take the tuck out of; do in, beat, **poop, bush** [all slang]; wind, breathe, put out of breath; overtire, overweary, overfatigue; weary or tire to death; prostrate.

5. **get tired, grow weary, tire, weary,** fatigue, jade; **flag, droop,** faint, sink, wilt; **play out, poop out** [slang], peter out [coll.], peg out [slang], run out, burn out; gasp, pant, puff, blow, puff and blow; collapse, drop, succumb.

ADJS. 6. **fatigued, fagged, tired, weary,** wearied, weariful, jaded, frazzled [chiefly U.S.], run ragged, run-down, good and tired; unrefreshed, unrestored; weak, enfeebled; **faint,** faintish, feeling faint; drooping, droopy; languid 706.18; worn, worn-down, worn to a frazzle or shadow, toilworn, weary-worn; wayworn, wayweary; foot-weary, weary-footed, footsore; tired-armed; tired-winged, weary-winged; weary-laden, "tired and weary-laden" [Bible].

7. tired-looking, weary-looking, tired-eyed, tired-faced, haggard, seedy [coll.].

8. **exhausted, spent; tired out, worn-out, fagged out, tuckered out** [coll., U.S.], **played out,** pooped out [slang], pegged out [slang], run-out; **used up** [coll.], done up [coll.], knocked up [coll., Eng.], tucked up [coll., Eng.], washed-up [coll.]; **all in, bushed, pooped, beat,** beat-up [all slang]; beaten, **dead-beat;** done [coll.], **done in** [slang]; **dog-tired,** dog-weary; dead [coll.], **dead-tired, tired to death,** weary unto death, dead-alive, more dead than alive, dead in one's shoes, **out on one's feet,** ready to drop, on one's last legs; prostrate, *hors de combat* [F.].

9. **overtired, overweary,** overwearied, overfatigued, overspent.

10. **breathless, winded,** pumped [slang], blown; **out of breath,** short of breath or wind; short-winded, short-breathed, broken-winded, touched in the wind, dyspneal.

11. **fatiguing, wearying,** wearing, tiring, exhausting, grueling [coll.], killing; tiresome, fatiguesome, **wearisome,** weariful, mortal [coll.]; toilsome 714.19.

716. WORKER, DOER

NOUNS 1. **doer,** actor, performer, **worker, practitioner,** perpetrator; **producer, maker,** author, mover; **agent,** medium; **executor,** executant, executrix; **operator,** operative, operant.

2. (working person) **worker, laborer, toiler,** moiler; **workman, workingman; workwoman, workingwoman,** workgirl; jobholder, wageworker, **wage earner, breadwinner;** employee, servant 748; **hand, work-**

hand; laboring man, common laborer, navvy [Eng.]; day laborer; casual, casual laborer; menial, flunky [derog.]; roustabout [U.S.], lumper; pieceworker, jobber; white-collar worker.

3. **drudge, grub, hack, fag,** fagger, **plodder, slave,** galley slave, **work horse,** beast of burden; hewers of wood and drawers of water; dig, grind, greasy grind [all school slang, U.S.].

4. **professional,** professionist; gownsman; the profession.

5. **amateur, ham** [slang], **nonprofessional;** apprentice, prentice [coll.].

6. **craftsman, handicraftsman,** craftworker; **artisan,** artificer, mechanic, wright; **technician;** artist, artiste; journeyman, skilled laborer; master, master craftsman, master workman, master carpenter, etc.

7. **smith,** smither [Eng.], forger, forgeman, metalworker; Vulcan [Rom. myth.], Hephaestus [Gr. myth.].

8. craftsmen, workers

architect	mason
armorer	miller
barber	paper hanger
beautician	plumber
bricklayer	potter
builder	puddler
cabinetmaker	puttier
carpenter	spinner
chandler	steam fitter
contractor	steeplejack
cooper	stonecutter
farm hand	stonemason
forger	tanner
founder	tinker
fuller	tinner
gas fitter	upholsterer
glass blower	warehouseman
glazer	weaver
glazier	welder
hairdresser	woodcraftsman
lather	wrecker
manicurist	

9. engineers

aeronautical engineer	electrical engineer
agricultural engineer	electronics engineer
architectural engineer	experimental engineer
army engineer	geodetic engineer
automatic control systems engineer	geological engineer
automotive engineer	highway engineer
bridge engineer	hydraulic engineer
chemical engineer	industrial engineer
civil engineer	marine engineer
communications engineer	mechanical engineer
construction engineer	metallurgical engineer
	military engineer
	mill engineer

mining engineer	rocket engineer
municipal engineer	sanitary engineer
naval engineer	structural engineer
ordnance engineer	
radar engineer	telephone engineer
radio engineer	textile engineer
railroad engineer	transportation engineer
research engineer	

10. smiths

anvilsmith	ironsmith
axlesmith	knifesmith
blacksmith	locksmith
bladesmith	picksmith
boilersmith	platinumsmith
boltsmith	sawsmith
brass-smith	scissors-smith
bronzesmith	scythesmith
carriagesmith	silversmith
clocksmith	stonesmith
coachsmith	swordsmith
coppersmith	tinsmith
goldsmith	tiresmith
gunsmith	toolsmith
hammersmith	wiresmith
hedgesmith	

11. wrights

boatwright	pitwright
bookwright	plowwright
butterwright	shipwright
candlewright	tilewright
cartwright	timberwright
coachwright	wagonwright
gatewright	wainwright
housewright	wheelwright
millwright	

12. makers

anvil maker	bulletmaker
arrow maker	bushmaker
axmaker or axemaker	buttermaker
	button maker
bagmaker	cabinetmaker
balance maker	cakemaker
barrelmaker	candlemaker
basketmaker	candymaker
bedmaker	canvas maker
beermaker	capmaker
bellmaker	carpetmaker
bellowsmaker	cartmaker
beltmaker	casemaker
blanketmaker	cementmaker
blockmaker	chainmaker
board maker	chairmaker
bobbin maker	cheese maker
bodymaker	cider maker
boilermaker	cigarette maker
boltmaker	cigar maker
bookmaker	cloakmaker
bootmaker	clockmaker
bottlemaker	clogmaker
bowmaker	clothmaker
boxmaker	coachmaker
brakemaker	coffinmaker
breadmaker	collar maker
brickmaker	colormaker
bridgemaker	combmaker
broommaker	coremaker
brushmaker	couchmaker
bucketmaker	cradlemaker

cratemaker
cupmaker
diemaker
dishmaker
dollmaker
doormaker
dressmaker
fanmaker
feather maker
feltmaker
fiddle maker
glassmaker
glovemaker
gluemaker
gunmaker
harness maker
hatmaker
hookmaker
ice maker
inkmaker
ironmaker
kettlemaker
lacemaker
lampmaker
leathermaker
lens maker
lockmaker
map maker
modelmaker
nail maker
needlemaker

netmaker
papermaker
patternmaker
penmaker
pie maker
porcelain maker
potmaker
road maker
ropemaker
rugmaker
sackmaker
saddle maker
safemaker
sailmaker
saltmaker
sausage maker
sawmaker
scale maker
scarf maker
screw maker
scythe maker
shoemaker
soapmaker
steelmaker
sugar maker
tentmaker
tilemaker
watchmaker
wigmaker
wine maker

13. workers

brassworker
butterworker
chalkworker
clothworker
fieldworker
flintworker
garmentworker
glassworker
goldworker
ironworker

metalworker
needleworker
saltworker
sawworker
shellworker
steelworker
waxworker
wireworker
woodworker

717. WORKPLACE

NOUNS 1. **workplace, workshop, shop;** establishment, institution, house, firm, concern; workhouse; workroom; studio; parlor [U.S.], beauty parlor, etc.; barbershop; butcher shop, butchery.

2. **hive,** hive of industry, **beehive,** alveary; sweatshop.

3. **plant; factory,** manufactory, manufacturing plant, *usine* [F.]; push-button plant, automatic *or* robot factory; assembly line; pilot plant, defense plant; munition plant, armory, arsenal; power plant 341.18; atomic energy plant; machine shop; mill, sawmill, flour mill, etc. 347.20; mint; refinery, oil refinery; bindery, bookbindery; packing house; cannery; creamery; mailery; pottery; tannery.

4. **works,** bleachworks, boilerworks, brassworks, copperworks, gasworks, glassworks, ironworks, printworks, saltworks, scrapworks, steelworks, tryworks, waterworks, wireworks.

5. **forge, furnace, bloomery; foundry,** smelter; **smithy,** smithery, **blacksmith shop.**

6. **repair shop,** fix-it shop [slang]; garage; roundhouse; shipyard, dockyard.

7. **laboratory, lab** [coll.]; research laboratory; servo laboratory, servolab.

8. **office,** shop [slang]; chambers; closet, cabinet, bureau; embassy, consulate, legation, chancery, chancellery; box office; branch, local office.

718. PREPARATION

NOUNS 1. **preparation,** preparing, fixing [coll., U.S.], **readying,** ready [coll.], making ready; **provision, arrangement,** preparatory act *or* measure; note of preparation; concoction, compounding; processing, treatment; equipment 657; training 560.3; manufacture 166.3; groundwork, foundation 215.6.

2. **fitting,** fit [coll.]; **conditioning; adaptation, adjustment; qualification,** capacitation, enablement; **equipment, furnishing,** furnishment.

3. (a preparation) preparative, preparatory; **concoction, confection, composition, mixture.**

4. **preparedness, readiness; fitness,** fittedness, suitedness, suitableness, **suitability; qualification,** qualifiedness, **competence, ability, capability;** ripeness, maturity.

5. **preparer,** preparator, *préparateur* [F.]; preparationist; **trail blazer, pathfinder; forerunner** 66; paver, pavior, **paver of the way.**

VERBS 6. **prepare, make** *or* **get ready, ready, fix** [coll., U.S.]; **provide, arrange; make preparations** *or* **arrangements,** sound the note of preparation, settle preliminaries; fix up [coll.], ready up [slang], put in *or* into shape; dress; treat, process.

7. **make up, get up, fix up** [coll.], **concoct, compound, compose, put together;** make 166.12.

8. **fit, condition, adapt, adjust,** set, suit, tune, attune, put in tune, ~ trim, ~ train, ~ gear *or* working order; **qualify,** capacitate, **equip, furnish,** enable.

9. **prime, load,** charge; wind, wind up; screw up; steam up, get up steam.

10. **prepare to, get ready to,** fix to [South. U.S.], be about to, hold oneself in readiness.

11. **prepare for, provide for,** fix for

[dial.] look out for, **make provision** or **due provision for;** provide against, make sure against, forearm; **provide for** or **against a rainy day,** prepare for the evil day, **feather one's nest,** lay in provisions, keep as a nest egg, save to fall back upon, have a rod in pickle, lay by, husband one's resources; set one's house in order; clear the decks, clear for action, close one's ranks.

12. prepare the way, pave the way, break the ice, smooth the path or road, **clear the way,** open the way, open the door to; go in advance, **blaze the trail; prepare the ground,** cultivate the soil, sow the seed; lay the groundwork or foundation, lay the first stone; lead up to.

13. prepare oneself, get ready, get set [coll.]; gird up one's loins, buckle on one's armor, get into harness, shoulder arms; trim one's tackle or foils, sharpen one's tools, whet the knife or sword.

14. be prepared, be ready, hold oneself in readiness, watch and pray or wait; keep one's powder dry, "put your trust in God; but mind to keep your powder dry" [ascribed to Cromwell].

15. (be fitted) **qualify, measure up** [U.S.], have the qualifications.

ADJS. **16. prepared, ready,** in readiness, all ready, good and ready, prepared and ready; **ripe, mature; set, all set,** on the mark [all coll.]; **primed, loaded for bear** [slang, U.S.]; rough-and-ready; ready for anything, "prepared for either course" [Vergil]; in harness, in the saddle, booted and spurred; **armed,** well-armed; in arms, up in arms, in battle array, sword-in-hand.

17. provided, equipped 657.12; **well-prepared** 657.13.

18. fitted, adapted, adjusted, suited; qualified, fit, competent, able, capable; well-qualified, well-fitted, well-suited.

19. prepared for, ready for, fixed for [coll.], set or all set for [coll.]; go [space slang]; loaded for, primed for; equal to, up to.

20. ready-prepared, ready-made, ready-formed, ready-shapen, ready-mixed, ready-furnished, ready-dressed, ready-cooked; ready-built, prefabricated; ready-to-wear, ready-for-wear; ready-cut, cut and dried or dry.

21. preparatory, preparative; provident, provisional.

ADVS. **22. in readiness, in store, in reserve;** in anticipation.

23. in preparation, in course of preparation, in agitation, **in progress** or **process, going on,** in embryo, **in production,** under construction, **in the works, in the making, in hand,** in train, on the stocks, on the anvil, **in the fire;** under revision.

ADJS., ADVS. **24. afoot, on foot, afloat, astir,** abroach, abroad, **brewing, brooding,** forthcoming.

PREPS. **25.** in preparation for, against, for, in order to.

PHRS. **26. ready!, get set!,** on your mark!, one for the money, two for the show, three to get ready, and four to go!

719. UNPREPAREDNESS

NOUNS **1. unpreparedness, unreadiness; unfitness,** unfittedness, unsuitedness, **unsuitableness; unsuitability; unqualifiedness,** unqualification, **disqualification,** unendowment, incompetence, incapability.

2. improvidence, unprovision; **thriftlessness, unthriftiness; shiftlessness,** fecklessness, thoughtlessness, heedlessness; negligence 532; laxity, laxness, slackness, looseness, remissness; lackadaisicalness, happy-go-luckiness.

3. (raw or original condition) **naturalness,** artlessness, inartificiality; **natural state,** nature, **state of nature,** nature in the raw.

4. undevelopment, nondevelopment; **immaturity,** immatureness, **rawness, unripeness,** greenness; **unfinish,** unfinishedness, unpolishedness, **unrefinement, uncultivation; crudity,** crudeness, **rudeness, coarseness,** roughness, the rough.

5. raw material; rough diamond, diamond in the rough; **unlicked cub;** virgin soil; fallow ground, fallow, balk.

VERBS **6. be unprepared,** not be ready; lie fallow; go off half-cocked or at half cock [coll.]; be taken unawares, be caught napping.

7. make no provision, take no thought of, take no thought of tomorrow, let tomorrow take care of itself, live for the day, live from hand to mouth.

ADJS. **8. unprepared, unready, unprimed; unarranged,** unorganized; **unmade, unmanufactured,** unconcocted, **unhatched,** uncontrived, undevised; **unbegun.**

9. unfitted, unfit, unsuited, unadapted; unqualified, disqualified, incompetent, **incapable; unequipped, unfurnished, unprovided, unsupplied,** unarmed; **unendowed,** uninvested, unclothed.

10. raw, crude; uncooked, unbaked, unboiled.

11. immature, unripe, raw, green, unseasoned, unmellowed, kutcha [coll., Anglo-Ind.]; undigested, ill-digested; half-baked [coll.]; half-cocked [coll., U.S.], at half cock [coll.].

12. undeveloped, unfinished, unlicked, unformed, unfashioned, unwrought, unlabored, unworked, unprocessed; unblown; uncut, unhewn; crude, rude, coarse, unpolished, unrefined; uncultivated, uncultured; rough, roughcast, roughhewn, in the rough; rudimentary, rudimental; embryonic, in embryo, in ovo [L.].

13. (in the raw or original state) natural, native, in a state of nature; artless, inartificial; virginal, untouched, unsullied.

14. fallow, untilled, uncultivated, unsown.

15. improvident, unproviding; thriftless, unthrifty, uneconomical; hand-to-mouth; shiftless, feckless, thoughtless, heedless; negligent 532.10, 11; slack, lax, loose, remiss; lackadaisical, happy-go-lucky.

720. ACCOMPLISHMENT

Act of Accomplishing; Entire Performance.—NOUNS 1. accomplishment, achievement, fulfillment or fulfilment, performance, execution, effectuation, implementation, discharge, dispatch or despatch, consummation, realization, attainment, production, fruition; fait accompli [F.], accomplished fact.

2. completion, completing, finish, finishing, conclusion, end, ending, termination, close, windup [coll.], work done; perfection; ripeness, maturity, maturation, full development.

3. finishing touch, finisher [coll.], copestone, cap, crown, crowning of the edifice.

VERBS 4. accomplish, achieve, effect, effectuate, compass, consummate, do, execute, produce, make, enact, perform, discharge, fulfill or fulfil, realize, attain, fetch [dial. & coll.]; work, work out; dispatch or despatch, dispose of, knock off [coll.], polish off [slang], take care of [coll.], deal with, put away, set at rest, make short work of; succeed, manage 722.6–12; do the job [coll.], do or turn the trick [slang].

5. bring about, bring to pass, bring to effect, bring to a happy issue; implement, carry out, turn out, carry through, carry into execution; bring off, carry off, pull off [coll.], turn off; put through, get through, bring through, put over or across [slang]; come it, come through with [both coll.].

6. complete, perfect, finish, finish off, conclude, terminate, end, carry to completion, prosecute to a conclusion; get through, get done, get through with, get it over, get it over with; finish up, clean up [coll.], wind up [coll.], close up [U.S.], button up [coll.], put the lid on it [slang], call it a day [slang]; round out; top off, crown, cap; give the finishing touches, put the finishing touches on, finalize; break the back or neck of.

7. do up brown [slang], do to a turn, do to a frazzle [slang], do down to the ground [coll.], not do by halves, do oneself proud [coll.]; go all lengths, go to all lengths, go the whole length or way; go the limit, go the whole figure, go the whole hog, go all out, shoot the works [all slang].

8. ripen, ripe, mature, maturate, mellow; reach maturity, come or draw to a head; bring to maturity, bring to a head.

ADJS. 9. accomplished, achieved, effected, effectuated, consummated, executed, discharged, fulfilled, realized, compassed, attained; dispatched or despatched, disposed of, set at rest; wrought, wrought out; mission accomplished.

10. completed, done, finished, concluded, terminated, ended, finished up, washed-up [coll.], through, done with, out of hand, all said and done; all over but the shouting.

11. complete, perfect, consummate, exhaustive, fully realized.

12. ripe, mature, mellow, full-grown, fully developed.

ADVS. 13. to completion, to the end, to the full, to the limit, to a finish, to a frazzle [slang], à outrance [F.], to crown all.

721. NONACCOMPLISHMENT

NOUNS 1. nonaccomplishment, nonachievement, nonperformance, nonexecution, noncompletion, nonfulfillment, unfulfillment; work of Penelope, Sisyphean labor, ∼ toil or task.

VERBS 2. neglect, leave undone 532.6, 7.

ADJS. 3. unaccomplished, unachieved, unperformed, unexecuted, unfulfilled, unconsummated, unrealized, unattained; unfinished, uncompleted, undone; re infecta [L., the matter being unfinished].

722. SUCCESS

NOUNS 1. success, successfulness; go; fortunate outcome, prosperous issue; prosperity 726; accomplishment 720; victory 724.

2. sure success, natural [coll.]; sure thing, sure bet, sure card, cinch [all slang].

3. great success, howling or roaring success slang]; éclat, brilliant success; killing [coll.]; hit, big hit, smash [slang], smash hit [slang], striking success, ten-strike [coll.]; scream, riot, panic, howl, wow, sensation [all slang].

4. score, hit, bull's-eye, bell ringer [slang]; goal, touchdown [U.S.]; slam, grand slam; strike, ten-strike; hole, hole in one; home run, homer [coll.], three-bagger [slang].

5. successful person) made man; comer [slang, U.S.].

VERBS 6. succeed, prevail, be successful, meet with success; go, come off, go off; prosper 726.7; fare well, work well, do or work wonders, go great guns [coll.]; make a hit, click [slang], connect [slang], catch on [coll.], take [coll.], take on [coll., Eng.], go over [coll.], go over big [slang]; pass, graduate.

7. achieve one's purpose, gain one's end or ends; make one's point, make one's hand, make a good fist [coll.].

8. score a success, score, hit it, hit the mark, ring the bell, turn up trumps, strike twelve; make a killing [coll.].

9. make good, achieve success, make a success, make one's mark; give a good account of oneself, bear oneself with credit, do all right by oneself [coll.], do oneself proud [coll.], get on, come on [coll.], get ahead [coll., U.S.]; go places, go far, go to town [coll.]; rise, rise in the world; arrive, get there [slang]; come out on top, come out on top of the heap [slang]; be a success, be made; make a noise in the world [coll.], cut a swath, set the world, ~ river or Thames on fire.

10. succeed with, crown with success; make a go of it, make an out of it [slang]; accomplish, achieve 720.4; bring off, carry off, pull off [coll.]; put through, bring through; put over or across [both slang]; get away with it, get by [both slang].

11. manage, contrive, succeed in; make out, get on or along, come on or along [coll.], go on; scrape along, worry along [U.S.], muddle through [Eng.], get by, manage somehow; come it, make it [both

coll.]; make the grade, cut the mustard, do or turn the trick [all slang]; clear, clear the hurdle; negotiate [coll.], engineer; swing [coll., U.S.], put over [slang], put through, swing the deal.

12. win through, win out [coll.], come through [slang], beat the game; triumph 724.3; make head against, stem the torrent, ~ tide or current; weather out, weather the storm, live through, keep one's head above water, tide over.

ADJS. 13. successful, succeeding, crowned with success; prosperous, fortunate 726.12–14; triumphant 724.8; ahead of the game, out in front, on top, on top of the heap [slang]; made; coming [coll.].

ADVS. 14. successfully, swimmingly, well, to one's heart's content; to some purpose, to good purpose; beyond all expectation, beyond one's fondest dreams.

723. FAILURE

NOUNS 1. failure, unsuccessfulness, successlessness, nonsuccess, no go [coll.]; ill success, poor fist [coll.]; defeat 725; losing game; "lame and impotent conclusion" [Shakespeare]; bankruptcy 840.3.

2. flop, bust, frost, flivver, fizzle, lemon, washout [all slang]; turkey [theat. slang]; flat failure, dull thud [slang].

3. collapse, crash, smash, comedown, breakdown, fall, downfall, cropper [coll.]; nose dive, tailspin [both slang]; explosion, bursting of the bubble.

4. miss, near miss; slip, slip-up [coll.], slip 'twixt cup and lip.

5. abortion, miscarriage, miscarrying, abortive attempt; misfire, flash in the pan, dud [slang], brutum fulmen [L., insensible thunderbolt].

6. fiasco, botch, hash, mess, muddle, mull [coll., Eng.].

7. flunk [coll., U.S.], washout [slang]; plow, pluck [both slang, Eng.].

8. (unsuccessful person) failure, flop [slang, U.S.], washout [slang]; false alarm [slang], flash in the pan, dud [slang]; flunker [coll., U.S.], flunky [slang, U.S.]; bankrupt 840.4.

VERBS 9. fail, be unsuccessful, fail of success, come to grief, lose, lose out [coll.]; get left, not get to first base [both slang, U.S.]; flop, flummox, lay an egg, draw a blank [all slang]; go up [coll.], go to the wall, go on the rocks; fold, fold up [both slang]; go bankrupt 840.7; take the count, take it on the chin [both slang]; crap out [slang], throw sixes [slang, U.S.]; strike out, fan, fan out, go down swinging [slang, U.S.].

10. **sink, founder,** go down, go under [coll.].

11. **fall, fall down** [slang], fall down on the job [coll.]; **fall through, fall to the ground,** fall between two stools; **fall dead,** fall stillborn; **fall flat,** fall flat on one's face, flat out [coll.]; **collapse,** fall in; **crash,** go to smash.

12. **come to nothing,** be all over or up with; fail miserably, fail ignominiously; **peter out,** peg out, poop out [all slang]; **fizzle, fizzle out** [both coll.]; **misfire,** miss fire, flash in the pan; **blow up, explode, end or go up in smoke,** go up like a rocket and come down like the stick.

13. **miss, miss the mark,** miss one's aim, miss stays [naut.]; slip, slip up [coll.].

14. **miscarry,** abort; **go amiss,** go astray, go wrong, go on a wrong tack, take a wrong turn, take an ugly turn.

15. **stall,** stick, die, go dead, **conk out** [slang].

16. **flunk,** flunk out [both coll., U.S.]; **fair** [coll.], pluck [coll., Eng.], plough [slang, Eng.], bust [slang, U.S.], wash out [slang].

ADJS. 17. **unsuccessful,** successless, failing, stickit [Scot.]; **unfortunate** 727.14; **abortive,** abortional; miscarrying, miscarried; stillborn; **fruitless,** bootless, sterile, addle, lame, ineffectual, ineffective, inefficacious, of no effect.

ADVS. 18. **unsuccessfully,** successlessly, **without success;** fruitlessly, bootlessly, ineffectually, ineffectively, inefficaciously, to little or no purpose, **in vain.**

724. VICTORY

NOUNS 1. **victory, triumph, conquest,** a feather in one's cap [coll.]; **winning,** win [coll.]; knockout, K.O. [slang]; walkover, walkaway [both coll.]; Pyrrhic victory; moral victory; winning streak [coll., U.S.]; success 722.

2. **victor,** victress [fem.], **winner,** triumpher; **conqueror,** defeater, **vanquisher,** subduer, subjugator; conquistador; master, master of the situation; hero, conquering hero; champion, champ [slang]; pancratiast [Gr. antiq.]; runner-up.

VERBS 3. **triumph, prevail, be victorious,** beat the Dutch [coll.], **come off with flying colors,** chain victory to one's car;

succeed 722.6; break the record, reach a new high [coll.].

4. **win, gain, capture, carry;** win out [coll.], win through, come through [slang], carry it, carry off or away; **win ~, carry or gain the day,** win the battle, beat the game, come out first, finish in front, get under the wire, **make a killing** [coll.], remain in possession of the field; **win the prize,** win the palm or laurels, bear the palm, bear away the bell, **bring home the bacon** [coll., U.S.], take the cake [slang, U.S.], win one's spurs; fluke, win by a fluke [both slang].

5. **win hands down** [coll.], win in a canter or walk [slang], **walk off or away with,** walk off with the game, **walk over** [coll.], walk over the course; have the game in one's own hands, have the ball at one's feet; **take or carry by storm,** carry all before one, make short work of.

6. **triumph over, prevail over; get the better or best of,** get the start of; **surmount, overcome,** get over, rise above, se tirer d'affaire [F., get out of a difficulty]; defeat 725.6.

7. **gain the ascendancy, get the advantage, gain the upper or whip hand,** get a pull over [slang], get the edge on, ~ bulge on, ~ deadwood on, ~ jump on or drop on [all slang], get a strangle hold on.

ADJS. 8. **victorious, triumphant,** triumphal, **winning, prevailing;** conquering, vanquishing, defeating, overcoming; ascendant, in the ascendant, in ascendancy; successful 722.13; set up [coll.], flushed with success.

9. **undefeated, unbeaten,** unlicked [coll.], **unvanquished, unconquered,** unsubdued, unquelled, unbowed.

ADVS. 10. **triumphantly,** victoriously, **in triumph, with flying colors.**

725. DEFEAT

NOUNS 1. **defeat, beating, drubbing, licking** [coll.]; **vanquishment,** conquerment, **conquering,** mastery, subjugation, subdual; **overthrow,** overturn, overcoming; **fall, downfall,** collapse, smash, crash; **undoing,** ruin; deathblow, quietus; Waterloo; failure 723.

2. **discomfiture, rout,** repulse, rebuff; **frustration,** bafflement; **checkmate,** check, balk, foil; **reverse,** reversal, setback.

3. **utter defeat,** total defeat, overwhelming defeat, crushing defeat, smashing de-

feat, decisive defeat; **smear, smearing, clobbering, shellacking** [all slang]; **white-wash. whitewashing** [both coll.]; **shutout** [U.S.].

4. ignominious defeat, abject defeat, inglorious defeat, disastrous defeat, bitter defeat, stinging defeat.

5. loser, defeatee, underdog [U.S.], **also-ran;** victim, prey; booby.

VERBS **6. defeat, worst, best, get the better** or **best of, outdo; triumph over** 724.6; **beat,** drub; **lick, whip, thrash, trim** [all coll.]; **skin,** euchre, **put the kibosh on** [all slang]; **fix, settle, settle one's hash,** cook one's goose, **put one's nose out of joint** [all coll.]; **do for** [coll.], do in [slang], silence, **kill, knock on the head,** deal a deathblow, puts *hors de combat* [F.]; **undo, ruin;** lick to a frazzle [coll., U.S.], beat hollow or all hollow [coll.]; nose out; whip-saw (worst in two ways [U.S.]).

7. overcome, surmount; **overpower,** overmaster, overmatch; **overthrow, over-turn,** overset; **upset,** trip up, lay by the heels; floor, gravel [coll.], make bite the dust.

8. overwhelm, snow under [coll., U.S.]; defeat utterly, deal a crushing or smashing defeat; **smear, clobber, shellac** [all slang]; **whitewash** [coll.], **shut out.**

9. discomfit, rout, put to rout, put to flight, put out of court.

10. conquer, vanquish; subdue, sub-jugate. master; **reduce, crush, humble,** bend, **bring one to his knees;** roll or trample in the dust, tread or trample underfoot, trample down, ride down, override.

11. thwart, frustrate, checkmate 728.15, 16.

12. lose, lose out [coll.], lose the day, come off second best, **get** or **have the worst of it, meet one's Waterloo;** fall, succumb, go down, go under, **bite** or **lick the dust,** take the count [slang].

ADJS **13. lost,** unwon.

14. defeated, worsted, bested, out-done; beaten, beat; **licked,** whipped, trimmed, settled, fixed [all coll.]; **skinned,** euchred, thrown for a loss [all slang]; **dis-comfited,** put to rout; **overcome, over-thrown,** upset, overturned, overmatched; **overpowered, overwhelmed,** overmas-tered, overborne overridden; **fallen,** down; floored, graveled [coll.]; silenced, killed, done in [slang]; **undone, done for** [coll.], ruined, all up with [coll.], *hors de combat* [F., out of the battle].

15. shut out, whitewashed [coll.], un-scoring.

16. conquered, vanquished; subdued, subjugated, mastered; **reduced, crushed,** broken, **humbled,** brought to one's knees.

17. overpowering, overcoming, over-whelming, overmastering.

726. PROSPERITY

NOUNS **1. prosperity,** prosperousness, thriving condition; **success** 722; **welfare, well-being;** comfortable or easy circum-stances, **comfort, ease, life of ease,** the life of Riley, the good life; **clover, velvet** [slang], **bed of roses, luxury,** lap of lux-ury, Easy Street [coll.]; **fat of the land;** fleshpots, fleshpots of Egypt; milk and honey, loaves and fishes; purple and fine linen; high standard of living.

2. good fortune or **luck, fortune, luck,** fortunateness, luckiness, nigger luck [slang], the breaks [slang]; felicity, blessing, smiles of fortune.

3. stroke of luck, piece of good luck, **lucky strike** [slang, U.S.], hit, ten-strike [coll.]; **fluke** [slang], scratch hit [slang]; **break** [slang], good or lucky break [slang]; **run of luck, streak of luck** [coll.].

4. good times, piping times, bright ~, palmy or halcyon days; fair weather, sun-shine, bright clouds; **golden age, golden time,** Saturnian age, *Saturnis regne* [L.], millennium.

5. roaring trade, land-office business [coll., U.S.]; boom.

6. fortunate or **lucky dog** [coll.]; man of substance.

VERBS **7. prosper, fare well, get on well,** get on swimmingly; **turn out well,** take a favorable turn; **succeed** 722.6; **come on, come along** [coll.], **get on, get along** [U.S.]; progress, make progress, make head-way.

8. thrive, flourish, boom; blossom, bloom, flower; fructify, bear fruit; batten, fatten, grow fat.

9. be prosperous, make good, make one's mark, rise or get on in the world, **make a noise in the world** [coll.], do all right by oneself [coll.]; make one's fortune, make one's pile [slang], feather one's nest; drive a roaring trade, do a land-office busi-ness [coll., U.S.].

10. live in clover, live on velvet [slang], **live a life of ease,** live the life of Riley, **live high,** live high on the hog [coll.], live on the fat of the land, roll in the lap of

luxury, bask in the sunshine, have a good or
fine time of it.

11. be fortunate, be lucky, be in luck,
have all the luck, have one's moments,
bear a charmed life; get a break, get
the breaks, break good for [all slang]; hold
aces [slang], turn up trumps [coll.]; have
a run of luck, hit a streak of luck [coll.];
have a stroke of luck, **make a lucky strike**
[slang, U.S.], strike oil [slang, U.S.], **strike
it rich,** come into money, drop into a good
thing.

ADJS. **12. prosperous,** in a fair way, in
good case; **successful** 722.13; **well off, well-
to-do, well-fixed** [coll., U.S.], **well situated,** set up [coll.]; **comfortable,** comfortably situated, easy, at one's ease, on
Easy Street [coll.], **in clover, on velvet**
[slang], on a bed of roses, in luxury; up in
the world, on top of the heap [slang].

**13. thriving, flourishing, prospering,
booming;** vigorous, exuberant; in full
swing, going strong [coll.].

**14. fortunate, lucky, providential; in
luck,** in a good way [slang]; blest, blest
with luck; born under a lucky star, born
with a silver spoon in one's mouth, born
on the sunny side of the hedge; auspicious
542.16.

ADVS. **15. prosperously, thrivingly,**
flourishingly, boomingly, swimmingly.

16. fortunately, luckily, providentially,
as luck would have it.

INTERJS. **17. good luck!, best wishes!,**
the best of luck!, the very best!, Godspeed!,
God bless you!, all good go with you!, peace
be with you!, *pax vobiscum!* [L., peace be
with you!], may your shadow never be less!

727. ADVERSITY

NOUNS **1. adversity,** adverse circumstances; **hardship, trouble,** hard lines, hard
knocks [coll.], hard case, hard life, hard
or unhappy lot, ups and downs of life;
affliction 864.8.

**2. misfortune, mishap, misadventure,
mischance,** *contretemps* [F.], grief; **disaster, calamity, catastrophe, cataclysm,
tragedy;** shock, blow, hard or nasty blow;
accident, casualty; collision, crash; wreck,
shipwreck, smash [coll.], smash-up, crack-
up [coll.], pile-up [coll.].

3. reverse, reversal, reverse of fortune,
setback, backset, throwback [coll.]; **comedown,** descent, down.

4. unfortunateness, unluckiness, luck-

lessness; unprosperousness; inauspiciousness 542.6.

**5. bad luck, ill luck, hard luck, tough
luck** [coll.], bad or tough break [slang],
rum go [slang], pretty come-off [coll.],
devil's own luck; evil fortune, evil dispensation; frowns of fortune, ill wind; broken
fortunes.

6. hard times, bad times, sad times,
time out of joint; evil day, rainy day; depression, recession.

7. unfortunate, poor unfortunate, the
sport of fortune; the underprivileged, depressed class.

VERBS **8. go hard with,** go ill with, run
one hard; **oppress, weigh on** or **upon,**
weigh heavy on, weigh down, bear hard
upon, lie on, lie hard or heavy upon, bear
the brunt.

**9. have trouble, have a hard time of
it,** be up against it [coll.]; try one, put one
out; be put to one's shifts or wit's end, dash
one's head against a stone wall, not know
which way to turn.

10. come to grief, have mishap; run
aground, stick in the mud, go on the rocks,
split upon a rock; sink, drown, founder.

**11. fall on evil days, go down in the
world,** go downhill, come down, have a
comedown, fall from one's high estate;
deteriorate, degenerate, sink, decline; **go
to pot** [coll.], go to the dogs; reach the
depths, touch bottom, hit rock-bottom;
have seen better days.

12. bring bad luck, hoodoo [coll., U.S.];
jinx, Jonah, put the jinx on [all slang].

ADJS. **13. adverse, untoward, unfavorable,** sinister; contrary, conflicting, opposing, opposed, opposite, in opposition.

**14. unfortunate, unlucky, unprovi-
dential,** unblest, **unprosperous,** sad, unhappy, hapless, fortuneless, luckless, donsie
[Scot.], **out of luck, S.O.L.** [slang], short
of luck; **down on one's luck** [coll.], badly
or ill off, behindhand, down in the world,
in adverse circumstances; underprivileged,
depressed; ill-starred, evil-starred, born under an evil star; inauspicious 542.15.

**15. disastrous, calamitous, catastrophic-
(al), cataclysmic,** cataclysmal, **tragical,**
ruinous, dire, black, grievous, deplorable.

ADVS. **16. adversely, untowardly, unfavorably;** contrarily, conflictingly, opposingly, oppositely.

17. unfortunately, unluckily, unprov-
identially, sadly, unhappily, **as ill luck
would have it;** if worst comes to worst.

18. disastrously, calamitously, catastrophically, cataclysmically, tragically.

INTERJS. 19. worse luck!, too bad!, better luck next time!

728. HINDRANCE

NOUNS 1. hindrance, hindering, hampering; check, and impediment, holdback; obstruction, stoppage; interruption, interception, interference; retardation, retardment; detention, detainment, delay, setback; restraint 758; inhibition, cramp, strangle hold; obstructionism.

2. prevention, stop, stoppage, estoppel [law], stay, halt, forestalling; prohibition, forbiddance; determent, deterrence, discouragement; preclusion, obviation; foreclosure.

3. frustration, thwarting, balking, foiling; discomfiture, disconcertion, bafflement, confounding; defeat, upset; check, checkmate, balk, foil.

4. obstacle, obstruction, obstructive, obstructant; block, blockade; difficulty, hurdle; deterrent, determent; drawback, objection; stumbling block, stumbling stone; hitch, catch, rub; snag, planter [local, U.S.], sawyer [U.S.], snags and sawyers [U.S.].

5. barrier, bar; gate, portcullis; fence; wall, stone wall; bulwark, rampart, buffer, bulkhead, parapet; bank, embankment, mound, mole, dike; dam, weir, barrage, boom [logging], milldam, beaver dam, roadblock; backstop.

6. impediment, imposition, embarrassment, hamper; handicap, disadvantage, penalty; encumbrance, burden, burthen, onus, cross, weight, dead weight, millstone round one's neck; load, pack; impedimenta, lumber.

7. curb, check, countercheck, arrest, stay, stop, holdback; brake, clog, drag, remora, scotch, skid; spoke, spoke in one's wheel; checkrein, bearing rein, martingale; bit, snaffle, curb bit; sea anchor, drift anchor, drift sail, drag sail or sheet.

8. hinderer, impeder; obstructionist, obstructer; frustrater, thwarter; filibuster, filibusterer [both U.S.].

9. marplot, addleplot; spoilsport, damper, wet blanket, kill-joy, crapehanger [slang], dog in the manger [coll.].

VERBS 10. hinder, impede, inhibit, arrest, check, countercheck, curb, snub; interrupt, intercept, interfere; retard, slacken, delay, detain; restrain 758.7; hold back, keep back, set back, hold up [coll.], keep or hold in check.

11. hamper, impede, cramp, embarrass; trammel, entrammel; encumber or incumber, cumber, burden, lumber, saddle with, weigh down, hang like a millstone round one's neck; handicap, put at a disadvantage.

12. obstruct, clog, stand in the way; block, blockade, block up; bar, barricade, bolt, lock; debar, shut out; shut off, close off; choke, choke off; stop up 265.7.

13. stop, estop, stay, halt, bring to a stop, put a stop or end to; block, stall, stymie, stump [coll., chiefly U.S.], deadlock; nip in the bud.

14. prevent, prohibit, forbid; save, help, keep from; deter, discourage; avert, keep off, ward off, stave off, fend off, fend, repel, deflect, turn aside; forestall, foreclose; preclude, exclude, debar, obviate, anticipate, remove, dispose of, rule out.

15. thwart, frustrate, foil, cross, balk, scotch, spike, checkmate; traverse, contravene, counteract, counterwork; defeat, discomfit, upset, disrupt; confound, flummox [slang], discountenance, disconcert, baffle, nonplus, throw on one's beam ends; circumvent, elude; spoil, ruin, dish [coll.], dash, blast; throw a wrench in the machinery, throw a monkey wrench into the works [coll.]; put a spoke in one's wheel, scotch the wheel, spike one's guns, put one's nose out of joint [coll.], upset one's applecart; take the wind out of one's sails, steal one's thunder, cut the ground from under one, knock the bottom out of [coll.]; tie one's hands, clip the wings of.

16. (slang terms) queer, crab, foul up, louse up, snafu, gum, gum up, gum up the works; crimp [U.S.], put a crimp in; queer the act, crab one's act, crab the deal; cramp one's style.

ADJS. 17. hindering, hindersome [dial.]; inhibitive, inhibiting; obstructive, obstructing, obstruent; interruptive, interrupting; interceptive, intercepting, intrusive, obtrusive, in the way.

18. hampering, impeding, impedimental, impedimentary, onerous, burdensome, cumbersome, cumbrous, encumbering.

19. preventive, preventative, prophylactic [med.]; prohibitive, forbidding; deterrent, deterring, discouraging; preclusive, forestalling.

20. frustrating, confounding, disconcerting, baffling, defeating.

ADVS. **21. under handicap,** at a disadvantage, on the hip, with everything against one.

729. DIFFICULTY

NOUNS **1. difficulty,** difficultness; **hardness,** toughness [coll.], ruggedness, crabbedness; **arduousness,** laboriousness, strenuousness, toilsomeness; **troublesomeness,** bothersomeness, irksomeness; onerousness, burdensomeness; formidability.

2. tough proposition [coll.], large *or* tall order [slang]; **hard job, tough job** [coll.], **chore,** man-sized job; Herculean task, Augean task, task of Sisyphus, Sisyphean labor; **uphill work** *or* **going, heavy sledding,** hard pull [coll.], dead lift; tough lineup to buck [slang], hard road to travel; hard row to hoe, hard row of stumps [both coll., U.S.]; **handful** [coll.], all one can manage.

3. trouble, matter, headache [slang]; **bother,** pother; botherment, botheration [both coll.]; **inconvenience, disadvantage;** ado, great ado; peck of troubles, "sea of troubles" [Shakespeare]; hornet's nest.

4. predicament, plight, pickle [chiefly coll.], hobble [coll.], **strait, pinch, pass,** pretty pass, pretty pickle [coll.], nice *or* pretty predicament, **sorry plight, pretty kettle of fish** [coll.], pretty *or* nice go [coll.]; how-do-you-do, how-d'ye-do, how-de-do, nice *or* pretty how-do-you-do [all coll.]; **spot, tight spot,** tight squeeze [all coll.]; **scrape, jam** [coll., U.S.], rattle [slang], **box, hole** [coll.], plunge [dial.], **hot water** [coll.]; slough, quagmire; **embarrassment,** embarrassing position *or* situation; **complication,** imbroglio, **mess,** holy mess [coll.], **muddle, mix** [coll.], scramble, **stew** [coll.]; the devil to pay, hell to pay [slang].

5. impasse, corner, hole [coll.]; **cul-de-sac,** blind alley, dead end, dead-end street; **extremity, end of one's rope** *or* **tether,** wit's end, **nonplus;** stalemate, deadlock, dead set, stand, standstill, halt, stop.

6. dilemma, horns of a dilemma, **quandary,** perplexity; **vexed question,** hard nut to crack; knotty point, knot, node, nodus, Gordian knot; paradox; asses' bridge, *pons asinorum* [L.].

7. crux, hitch, brunt, stress, **pinch, rub,** squeeze [coll.], where the shoe pinches.

8. unwieldiness, unmanageability; un-handiness, inconvenience; **awkwardness, clumsiness; cumbersomeness,** ponderousness, bulkiness, hulkiness.

VERBS **9. be difficult, take some doing.**

10. have difficulty, have trouble, have a hard time of it, run one hard, put one out, have much ado with; labor under difficulties, labor under a disadvantage; struggle, flounder, boggle, beat about; swim against the current, buffet the waves; walk on eggshells *or* hot coals, dance on a hot griddle; fish in troubled waters.

11. get into trouble, plunge into difficulties, go off *or* in at the deep end [coll.]; **let oneself in for, put one's foot in it** [coll.]; **get in a jam** [coll., U.S.], **get into a scrape,** get in a mess, get in a hole [coll.], put oneself in a spot [slang], get in hot water [coll.]; burn one's fingers; get all tangled, ∼ snarled *or* wound up, get all balled up [slang].

12. trouble, bother, pother, **disturb, perturb, put out,** put out of the way, put to it, give one trouble, make it tough for [coll.]; ail, be the matter.

13. cause trouble, bring trouble, bring down upon one, bring down upon one's head, bring down around one's ears; **stir up a hornet's nest,** bring a hornet's nest about one's ears; **raise hob,** raise hell, raise merry hell, play hob, play hell, play the mischief, play the deuce *or* devil [all coll.].

14. put in a hole [coll.], put in a spot [slang]; **involve,** enmesh, embarrass, entangle.

15. corner, run *or* drive into a corner, **tree** [coll.], chase up a tree [coll.] *or* stump [slang, U.S.], drive to the wall, **put one's back to the wall,** have on the ropes.

ADJS. **16. difficult,** difficile; **not easy,** no picnic; **hard, tough** [coll.], **rough, rugged,** crabbed, wicked [slang], mean [slang], formidable; **arduous, strenuous, toilsome, laborious,** Herculean; steep [coll.], uphill, tough going [coll.]; hard-fought; hard-earned; knotty, knotted; thorny, spiny, set with thorns; easier said than done.

17. troublesome, bothersome, irksome, painful, plaguy [coll.]; **burdensome,** onerous, operose, heavy [coll.], hefty [coll., U.S.]; **trying,** grueling [coll.].

18. unwieldy, unmanageable; un-handy, inconvenient; **awkward, clumsy; cumbersome,** ponderous, bulky, hulky.

19. in trouble, in Dutch [slang, U.S.], in chancery, **behind the eightball** [coll.,

U.S.], out on a limb [coll., U.S.]; in deep water, out of one's depth.

20. in a predicament, in a sorry plight, in a pretty pass, **in a mess** or **muddle, in a scrape, in a jam** [coll., U.S.], in a spot [slang], in the soup [slang], in a cleft stick **in a fix,** in a tight spot, **in a hole,** in a box, in hot water, in the suds, in a hobble, **in a pickle,** in a nice or pretty pickle [all coll.].

21. in a dilemma, on the horns of a dilemma, **in a quandary,** at cross-purposes; between Scylla and Charybdis, between two stools, between the devil and the deep blue sea.

22. at an impasse, at an extremity, **at one's wit's end, at a loss,** at a stand or standstill; **nonplused,** at a nonplus; floored, graveled [both coll.].

23. cornered, in a corner, with one's back to the wall, **treed** [coll.], **up a tree** [coll.], up a stump [slang, U.S.]; **at bay,** aux abois [F.].

24. straitened, reduced to straits, in desperate straits, **pinched,** sorely pressed, **hard pressed,** hard-set, **hard run,** run hard, **hard up** [slang], **up against it** [slang], put to it, hard put [coll.], hard put to it [coll.], put to one's shifts, driven from pillar to post; **in extremities,** in extremis [L.], **at the end of one's rope** or **tether.**

25. stranded, grounded, aground, **on the rocks,** high and dry; **stuck,** stuck or set fast; foundered, swamped; castaway, wrecked, shipwrecked.

ADVS. **26.** difficultly, **with difficulty,** with much ado; hardly, **arduously, strenuously, laboriously,** toilsomely; **troublesomely,** bothersomely, irksomely; **burdensomely,** onerously, operosely; formidably.

27. unwieldily, unmanageably; unhandily, inconveniently; **awkwardly, clumsily; cumbersomely,** ponderously.

INTERROGS. **28.** what's the matter?, what's the trouble?, what's wrong?, what's eating you? [slang], what's crackin' your pod? [dial.].

730. FACILITY

NOUNS **1. facility, ease, easiness,** facileness, **effortlessness;** freedom, free play; clear coast, clear course, clear stage; smooth road, royal road, highroad; plane or plain sailing, smooth or straight sailing.

2. wieldiness, wieldableness, **manageability;** handiness, convenience, untroublesomeness.

3. easy thing, mere child's play, simple twist of the wrist; **cinch, snap,** soft snap, pipe, **pushover, setup,** breeze, duck soup, picnic, pie, gravy [all slang]; sinecure.

4. facilitation, easing, smoothing; **speeding,** expedition, quickening, hastening.

5. disembarrassment, disentanglement, disencumbrance, disburdening, unhampering; **extrication,** disengagement, **freeing,** clearing.

VERBS **6. facilitate, ease; grease the wheels** [coll.]; smooth, **smooth** or **pave the way,** grease or soap the way [slang], prepare the way, **clear the way,** make all clear for, make way for, open the way, open the door to; **speed, expedite,** quicken, hasten; **help along,** help on its way; aid 783.11.

7. disembarrass, disencumber, disburden, unhamper; **disentangle,** disembroil; **extricate,** disengage, **free, clear.**

8. go easily, run smoothly, work well, work like a machine, go like clockwork, flow, roll, glide, slide, coast, sweep, sail.

9. have it easy, have it soft [coll.], have it all one's own way, have the game in one's hands; walk over the course, win in a walk or canter, win hands down [coll.].

10. take it easy, go easy [both coll.]; swim with the stream, drift with the current, go with the tide; take it in one's stride, make little or light of, think nothing of.

ADJS. **11. easy, facile, effortless,** soft [coll.], cushy [slang], plain, **simple,** simple as ABC [coll.], easy as pie [slang], easy as falling off a log [coll.], nothing to it [coll.], like shooting fish in a barrel, like taking candy from a baby; smooth, glib; **light,** unburdensome; **easygoing,** easyflowing, easy-running, easy-osey [Scot.].

12. wieldy, wieldable, manageable; handy, convenient, untroublesome.

ADVS. **13. easily,** easy [illit. or coll.], facilely, **effortlessly, readily, simply,** lightly, swimmingly, without difficulty, like nothing [slang], slick as a whistle [slang]; hands down [coll.], with one hand tied behind one's back, singlehanded; **smoothly,** on wheels, like clockwork; on easy terms.

731. SKILL

NOUNS **1. skill, skillfulness, expertness, cleverness; dexterity,** dexterousness or dextrousness; **adroitness, adeptness, deftness,** handiness, quickness, readiness; **competence, proficiency,** efficiency; **facility,**

prowess, address, finesse, craft; **know-how** [coll., U.S.], savvy [slang, U.S.]; smartness 466.2; cunning 733; **ingenuity,** ingeniousness; resource, resourcefulness; **mastery,** mastership, **command;** marksmanship, seamanship, airmanship, horsemanship, etc.

2. **agility, nimbleness, spryness.**

3. **versatility, ambidexterity,** many-sidedness, all-roundedness [coll.]; **adaptability,** adjustability.

4. **talent, gift, endowment,** dowry, dower, natural gift, **genius,** instinct, **faculty, power, ability, capability, capacity;** caliber, bore [coll.]; **forte,** speciality, long suit, strong point; **equipment, qualification,** habilitation; talents, parts; the goods, the stuff, what it takes [all slang].

5. **aptitude,** aptness, felicity; **bent, turn,** propensity, **leaning,** inclination, tendency; turn for, capacity for, gift for, genius for; an eye for, an ear for.

6. **knack, art, hang, trick,** sleight.

7. **art, science, craft; technique,** technic, **technics,** technology, technical knowledge or skill, technical know-how [coll.]; mechanics, mechanism; method 655.1.

8. **accomplishment, acquirement, attainment;** finish.

9. **experience, practice,** practical knowledge; background, past experience; **worldly wisdom,** knowledge of the world, **sophistication,** blaséness; *savoir-faire* [F.], wit, address.

10. **masterpiece, masterwork,** *chef d'œuvre* [F.]; **master stroke,** *coup* [F.], *coup de maître* [F.]; *coup d'état* [F.]; *tour de force* [F.]; trump, trump card.

11. **proficient, expert, adept,** dab [coll.], dabster [coll. or dial.], darb [slang], likely lad, **man of parts,** ace [chiefly coll.], crack [coll.], crackajack [slang], crackerjack [coll., U.S.], shark [slang], sharp [slang], bear [slang, U.S.], caution [coll.], whiz or whizz [slang, U.S.], graduate, topnotcher [coll.], no slouch [slang, U.S.]; natural [coll.]; **professional; Jack-of-all-trades,** Jack-of-all-works, handy man; **authority;** connoisseur, *connaisseur* [F.]; marksman, crack shot; efficiency expert.

12. **master, past master;** master hand, **good hand,** skilled or practiced hand; **mastermind,** master head, mahatma; sage 467; **prodigy, wizard** [chiefly coll.]; **genius,** man of genius; mental genius, intellectual prodigy, mental giant; infant prodigy, boy wonder; Einstein, Goethe, Admirable Crichton.

13. picked man, medalist or medallist, prizeman; **champion,** champ [slang].

14. **veteran,** vet [coll.]; **old hand, oldtimer** [coll.], old file, **old stager, old soldier,** old campaigner, war horse [coll.], longhorn [coll., West. U.S.]; salt or old salt [coll.], old sea dog [coll.], shellback [slang], barnacle-back [slang].

15. **sophisticate,** man of experience, **man of the world;** man about town; **cosmopolitan,** cosmopolite, citizen of the world.

VERBS 16. **excel in, shine in** or **at** [chiefly coll.], be master of, be there at [slang], be up to [coll.], have it in one [coll.], be at home in, **have a bent** or **turn for, have a good head for,** have an ear for, have an eye for; have something or stuff on the ball, have plenty on the ball [all slang, U.S.].

17. **know one's stuff** [slang], **know one's onions** [slang, U.S.], **know the ropes, know all the ins and outs,** know all the tricks, know all the tricks of the trade, know all the moves of the game.

18. **know what's what, know a thing or two, know the time of day,** know what's o'clock, know what o'clock it is [all coll.]; **know what it's all about, know the score** [slang], know all the answers [slang, U.S.], "know a hawk from a handsaw" [Shakespeare], have all one's wits about one, see into or through a millstone; **know one's way about,** know the ways of the world, have been around [slang], have been through the mill [coll.], have seen the lions, have cut one's wisdom teeth or eyeteeth [coll.], **not be born yesterday;** know on which side one's bread is buttered.

19. **exercise skill,** demonstrate one's ability, **strut one's stuff** [slang, U.S.]; exercise one's discretion, look after the main chance, make a virtue of necessity, cut one's coat according to one's cloth, play one's cards well.

ADJS. 20. **skillful, expert, proficient; dexterous** or **dextrous, adroit, deft, adept, apt, handy,** quick, ready; **clever,** cute [coll.], peart [dial.], slick, neat, clean, fancy, likely, excellent; **masterly, masterful;** crack [coll.], crackajack [slang], crackerjack [coll., U.S.]; smart 466.14; cunning 733.12; **ingenious,** resourceful, Daedalian; artistic; workmanlike, **well-done.**

21. **agile, nimble, spry,** fleet, fly [slang]; **nimble-footed,** light-footed, sure-footed; **nimble-fingered,** neat-fingered, neathanded.

22. **competent, capable, able, efficient, qualified, fit, fitted, suited, worthy,** capable of; fit or fitted for, cut out for [coll.]; **equal to, up to;** up to snuff [slang], up to the mark [coll.], *au fait* [F.]; well-qualified, well-fitted, well-suited; there, there with the goods [both slang].

23. **versatile, ambidextrous,** two-handed, **all-round** [coll.], all-around [coll., U.S.], **many-sided,** generally capable; **adaptable,** adjustable; amphibious.

24. **skilled, accomplished, practiced,** trained, prepared, primed, finished; initiated, initiate; technical; **talented, gifted,** endowed; conversant 474.19.

25. **skilled in,** proficient in, adept in, **good at,** expert at, there at [slang], it at [slang], **handy at, a hand** or **good hand at,** master of, strong in, at home in; **up in,** well up in, up on one's stuff [slang, U.S.]; well-versed 474.19, 20; with an eye for, with an ear for.

26. **experienced, practiced,** seasoned, veteran, old, an old dog at [coll.]; **worldly-wise,** world-wise, wise in the ways of the world; **sophisticated,** hard-boiled [coll.], blasé, dry behind the ears [jocose], not born yesterday.

27. **well-laid, well-devised,** well-designed, well-planned, well-worked-out; **well-invented,** *ben trovato* [It.]; **well-weighed, well-reasoned,** well-considered, well-thought-out; **cunning, clever.**

ADVS. 28. **skillfully, expertly, proficiently,** excellently, well; **cleverly,** neatly, ingeniously; cunningly 733.15; **dexterously, adroitly, deftly, adeptly,** aptly, handily; agilely, nimbly, spryly; **competently, capably, ably,** efficiently; **masterly, masterfully;** workmanlike; artistically; with skill, with consummate skill, with finesse.

732. UNSKILLFULNESS

NOUNS 1. **unskillfulness,** skill-lessness, **inexpertness, uncleverness; inadeptness, undexterousness** or undextrousness, **undeftness; unproficiency,** inefficiency; **incompetence** or incompetency, **inability, incapability,** incapacity, inadequacy; **inaptitude,** inaptness, unaptness, ineptness; unfitness, unfittedness; unqualification, disqualification; maladjustment.

2. **inexperience,** unexperience, unexperiencedness; **rawness, greenness,** unripeness; ignorance 476; **unfamiliarity,** unacquaintance, unaccustomedness; **amateurishness,** amateurism.

3. **clumsiness, awkwardness, maladroitness, unhandiness,** left-handedness, heavy-handedness; butterfingers [coll.], handful of thumbs [joc.]; **ungainliness,** uncouthness, **ungracefulness,** gracelessness, inelegance; **gawkiness,** gawkishness; **lubberliness, oafishness,** lumpishness, blockishness, clownishness; **cumbersomeness,** cumbrousness, **ponderousness,** bulkiness, hulkiness, unwieldiness.

4. **bungling, blundering,** boggling, **fumbling,** muffing, **botchery,** blunderheadedness; carelessness 532.2; too many cooks.

5. **bungle, blunder, botch,** boggle-de-botch or boggle-dy-botch [coll.], **boggle,** bobble [slang], foozle [coll.], barney [slang, Eng.], bevue; **fumble, muff,** fluff [theat. slang], miscue [slang]; slip, trip, stumble; *gaucherie, étourderie, balourdise* [all F.]; hash, mess [both coll.]; bad job, poor fist [coll.], sad work, clumsy performance.

6. **mismanagement, mishandling, misconduct,** misdirection, misguidance, **misgovernment, misrule;** misadministration, maladministration; malfeasance, misfeasance; bad policy, impolicy; inexpedience or inexpediency.

7. **incompetent, incapable,** poor stick [coll.]; **no conjuror,** one who will not set the Thames on fire; greenhorn 476.9.

8. **bungler, blunderer,** blunderbuss, blunderhead, bullhead, boggler, foozler [coll.], slubberer; clumsy [coll.], clumse [dial., South. U.S.]; **fumbler,** fumble-fist [coll.], butterfingers [coll.]; muff, **muffer** [both coll.]; **botcher,** bosher [coll.], hash [chiefly Scot.]; bull in a china shop.

9. **lubber,** looby, **lout, oaf, gawk,** gowk, gawky, gawkhammer [dial., Eng.], **clown,** swab [slang], duffer [coll.], loon, lown [Scot. & dial.], lobster [slang], donkey, **lummox** [slang], galoot [slang], bohunk [slang, U.S.], chucklehead [coll.], lunkhead [coll., U.S.], doit [Scot. & North. Eng.], **slouch, slob** [derog.], lump [coll.], hulk, dub [slang], stick [coll.], **clod; clodhopper,** clodpoll or clodpole, yokel, rube [slang]; colt, calf [both coll.]; awkward squad [mil.].

VERBS 10. **not have the knack,** not be up to [coll.], not have it in one [coll.].

11. **bungle, blunder, boggle, bobble** [coll.], bull [slang, U.S.], slubber, foozle [coll.], **muff, fudge, fumble,** have a handful of thumbs [joc.]; flounder, lumber, hobble, stumble, slip, trip, stub one's toe, miss one's footing, miscue [slang]; **put one's**

foot in it [coll.]; cobble; blunder on or upon; blunder into, barge in or into [coll.], bonehead into [slang]; blunder away.

12. botch, bitch [vulg.], bosh [coll.], mar, spoil, butcher, murder, make sad work of, make a poor fist at or of [coll.]; hash, hash up, mess up, make a mess or hash of [all coll.]; foul up, louse up, goof up, gum up, gum up the works, mess up the contract [all slang]; bugger, bugger up [both slang, U.S.]; play havoc with; play the mischief with, play the deuce or devil with [all coll.]; play hell or merry hell with, play whaley with, play horse with [all slang].

13. mismanage, mishandle, misconduct, misdirect, misguide, misgovern, misrule; misadminister, maladminister.

14. not know what one is about, not know one's interest, not see an inch beyond one's nose, stand in one's own light, not know on which side one's bread is buttered, quarrel with one's bread and butter, kill the goose that lays the golden egg, pay dearly for one's whistle, reckon without one's host, throw a stone in one's own garden, cut one's own throat, play with fire, burn one's fingers, jump out of the frying pan into the fire, bring the house about one's ears, put oneself out of court, sow the wind and reap the whirlwind, lock the stable door after the horse is stolen, count one's chickens before they are hatched, buy a pig in a poke, aim at a pigeon and kill a crow, strain at a gnat and swallow a camel, put the cart before the horse, bark up the wrong tree, back the wrong horse, get the wrong bull by the horns, get the wrong pig by the tail or sow by the ear [coll.], put the saddle on the wrong horse, put a square peg into a round hole, run before one can walk, go further and fare worse.

ADJS. 15. unskillful, skill-less, artless, inexpert, unproficient, inefficient, unclever; undexterous or undextrous, undeft, inadept, unfacile; unapt, inapt, inept, poor.

16. unskilled, unaccomplished, unpracticed, untrained, untutored, uninitiated, unprepared, unprimed, unfinished; untalented, ungifted, unendowed; amateurish.

17. inexperienced, unexperienced, unpracticed, untried, unseasoned, uninitiated; raw, green, green as grass or a gourd, verdant [coll.], unripe, half-baked [coll.], fresh, not dry behind the ears [joc.]; unskilled in, unpracticed in, unconversant with, unaccustomed or unused to, unfamil-

iar or unacquainted with, new to, a stranger to; ignorant 476.13.

18. out of practice, soft [coll.], rusty, gone or run to seed [coll.], not what one used to be [coll.].

19. incompetent, incapable, unable, inadequate, unequipped, unqualified, ill-qualified, unfit, unfitted, unadapted, not equal or up to, not cut out for [coll.]; unadjusted, maladjusted.

20. clumsy, awkward, fudgy [U.S.]; bungling, blundering, blunderheaded; maladroit, unhandy, left-handed, backhanded, heavy-handed, clumsy-fisted, butterfingered [coll.], all thumbs, fingers all thumbs, with a handful of thumbs; stiff; ungainly, uncouth, ungraceful, graceless, inelegant, gauche [F]; gawky, gawkish; lubberly, oafish, clownish, lumpish, blockish; ponderous, cumbersome, cumbrous, lumbering, hulking, hulky, bulky, unwieldy.

21. ill-managed, ill-conducted; ill-devised, ill-contrived; mismanaged, misconducted; misdirected, misguided, misadvised; ill-advised 469.9.

ADVS. 22. unskillfully, inexpertly, unproficiently, inefficiently, uncleverly; incompetently, incapably, inadequately, unfitly; undexterously, undeftly, inadeptly, unfacilely; unaptly, inaptly, ineptly, poorly.

23. clumsily, awkwardly; bunglingly, blunderingly; maladroitly, unhandily; ungracefully, gracelessly, inelegantly, uncouthly; ungainly, lubberly; ponderously, cumbersomely, cumbrously, lumberingly, hulkingly, hulkily, bulkily.

733. CUNNING

NOUNS 1. cunning, cunningness, craft, craftiness, artfulness, wiliness, slyness, insidiousness, shiftiness, cageyness [slang], leeriness [slang], foxiness, slipperiness, trickiness; canniness, shrewdness, sharpness, acuteness, astuteness; cleverness 731.1; subtlety, subtilty, subtleness, finesse; "the dark sanctuary of incapacity" [Chesterfield], "the ape of wisdom" [Locke]; satanic cunning, the cunning of the serpent.

2. Machiavellianism, Machiavellism; politics, diplomacy, diplomatics; jobbery, graft [coll.].

3. artifice, art, craft, wile, device, wily device, contrivance, expedient, design, scheme, trick, fetch, fakement [coll.], gimmick [slang, U.S.], ruse, red herring, shift, shuffle, dodge, artful dodge, game, little

game; sleight, feint; **subterfuge**, blind; deceit, trickery 616.3, 4.

4. stratagem, machination, manipulation, wirepulling [coll.]; **intrigue** 652.6; **maneuver,** maneuvers, **maneuvering,** tactical maneuvers; **strategy,** strategics; **tactics,** devices, expedients; coup, stroke, bold stroke; *coup d'état, coup de main* [both F.]; *ruse de guerre* [F., stratagem of war].

5. circumvention, evasion, elusion, frustration, foiling; the go-by [coll.], the runaround [slang, U.S.]; **outwitting,** outsmarting [coll., U.S.], outguessing, **outmaneuvering,** outdoing.

6. slyboots [joc.], sly dog [coll.], sly old fish [coll.], **fox,** coon [coll., chiefly U.S.], **dodger,** Artful Dodger, file [slang], crafty rascal, smooth *or* slick citizen [coll.], **slicker** [slang], **trickster,** keener [West. U.S.], Philadelphia lawyer [coll., U.S.].

7. strategist, tactician; maneuverer, machinator, manipulator, wirepuller [coll.]; schemer, **intriguer** 652.8.

8. Machiavellian, Machiavel; **diplomat,** diplomatist, **politician;** jobber, grafter [coll.].

VERBS **9. live by one's wits,** play a deep game; finesse; Machiavellize.

10. maneuver, manipulate, machinate, jockey, engineer; intrigue 652.10; **finagle,** fainague [dial., Eng.], **wangle,** angle; gerrymander [polit., U.S.]; bore from within.

11. outwit, outsmart [coll., U.S.], outguess, **outmaneuver,** out-poker [slang], outgeneral, outflank, outdo, get the better *or* best of; **overreach,** outreach; **circumvent,** get *or* come round, **evade, elude, frustrate, foil,** give the go-by [coll.], give the run-around [slang, U.S.], steal a march upon, leave in the lurch; be too much for, be too deep for.

ADJS. **12. cunning, crafty, artful, wily, sly,** insidious, **shifty, cagey** [slang], leery [slang], pawky [Scot. & dial., Eng.], arch, **smooth, slick** [slang], slim [S. Africa], **slippery, foxy,** feline, vulpine, Machiavellian; **canny, shrewd,** knowing, sharp, acute, astute; **clever** 731.20; subtle, subtile; **tricky,** trickish, tricksy; politic, diplomatic; deep, deep-laid; cunning as a fox *or* serpent, crazy like a fox [slang], slippery as an eel, not to be caught with chaff, too clever by half.

13. scheming, designing 652.14.

14. strategic(al), tactical, maneuvering.

ADVS. **15. cunningly, craftily, artfully,** wilily, insidiously, shiftily, cageyly [slang], foxily, trickily, smoothly, slick [slang];

slyly, on the sly [coll.]; **cannily, shrewdly,** knowingly, astutely; **cleverly** 731.28; subtly, subtilely.

734. ARTLESSNESS

NOUNS **1. artlessness, ingenuousness, guilelessness; simplicity,** simpleness, plainness; simpleheartedness, simplemindedness; **unsophistication,** unsophisticatedness; **naïveté,** naïvety, naïveness, childlikeness; trustfulness, unsuspiciousness; openness, open-heartedness; **candor** 972.4; singleheartedness, single-mindedness, singleness of heart.

2. naturalness, naturalism, nature; **unaffectedness, unassumingness,** unpretendingness, unpretentiousness, undisguise; **inartificiality,** unartificialness, genuineness.

3. unsophisticate, square [slang], simple soul, naïve, naïf, **ingénue, innocent,** child, mere child, infant, babe, lamb, dove, gosling [coll.].

VERBS **4. wear one's heart on one's** sleeve, look one in the face.

ADJS. **5. artless, simple,** plain, **natural,** native, **guileless;** simplehearted, simpleminded; **ingenuous,** *ingénu* [F.]; **unsophisticated, naïve,** naïf, childlike; trustful, trusting, confiding, unsuspicious; open, open-hearted; **frank** 972.17; singlehearted, single-minded.

6. unaffected, unassuming, unpretending, unpretentious, unfeigning, undisguising, undissimulating, undissembling, undesigning; **genuine, inartificial,** unartificial.

ADVS. **7. artlessly, ingenuously, guilelessly;** simply, plainly, naturally; naïvely, naïfly; openly, open-heartedly.

735. BEHAVIOR

NOUNS **1. behavior, conduct, deportment, comportment, manner, manners, demeanor,** mien, *maintien* [F.], **carriage, bearing,** port, guise, air, address, presence, *prestance* [F.], observance; **way,** ways; practice, praxis; procedure, proceeding; action, **actions,** acts, goings on; pattern, behavior pattern.

2. good behavior, good manners, correct deportment.

3. behaviorism, behavior psychology; permissive behavior [child psychol.].

VERBS **4. behave, act, do,** go on; behave oneself, conduct oneself, manage oneself, comport oneself, deport oneself, demean oneself, bear oneself, carry oneself; acquit oneself.

5. **be good,** be nice, **behave oneself,** act well, **do right,** do what is right, do the right thing, keep out of mischief, mind one's P's and Q's [coll.], be on one's good *or* best behavior.

6. **treat, use, do by, deal by, act** *or* **behave toward,** conduct oneself toward, act with regard to.

ADJS. 7. **behavioral,** behaviorist, behavioristic; **behaved,** behaviored, **mannered,** demeanored.

736. MISBEHAVIOR

NOUNS 1. **misbehavior, misconduct, misdemeanor,** misdoing; **naughtiness,** badness, impropriety; **disorderly conduct,** disorder, disorderliness; **rowdiness,** rowdyism [U.S.], **ruffianism;** roughhouse, horseplay.

2. **mischief, mischievousness; devilment,** deviltry, devilry; **roguishness,** roguery; **waggery,** waggishness; **impishness,** puckishness, elfishness; **prankishness,** pranksomeness; sportiveness, playfulness, *espièglerie* [F.].

3. **mischief-maker,** mischief, **rogue, devil;** wag; **rowdy, cutup** [slang], ruffian; **imp, elf, pixy, puck, minx,** little devil, little rascal, little monkey, *enfant terrible* [F., naughty child].

VERBS 4. **misbehave, misdemean,** misdo, **misbehave oneself, misconduct oneself, misdemean oneself,** behave ill; **act up, carry on** [coll.], carry on something scandalous [coll.]; **cut up** [slang], horse around [coll.]; roughhouse [slang, U.S.], cut up rough [slang]; get into mischief.

ADJS. 5. misbehaving, unbehaving; **naughty, bad,** improper; **disorderly, rowdy,** rowdyish, **ruffianly.**

6. **mischievous,** mischief-loving, full of mischief; **roguish, waggish, devilish,** arch; **impish, puckish, elfish,** elvish; **prankish,** pranky, pranksome; **tricky,** trickish, tricksy; **playful,** sportive, *espiègle* [F.].

ADVS. 7. **mischievously, roguishly,** waggishly, devilishly; impishly, puckishly, elfishly; prankishly, trickily, playfully, sportively, in fun.

737. AUTHORITY

Legal or Rightful Power.—NOUNS 1. **authority, prerogative, right, power,** faculty, competency; **the say, the say-so** [coll.]; divine right, *jus divinum* [L.]; authoritarianism.

2. **authoritativeness,** powerfulness, potence *or* potency, puissance, might, mightiness; **masterfulness,** lordliness, imperious-ness, magisterialness, **arbitrariness;** peremptoriness, autocraticalness, highhandedness, dictatorialness, bossiness [coll., U.S.].

3. **prestige, influence, pressure, weight,** weightiness, **moment, consequence,** eminence.

4. **jurisdiction, command, control, power, rule;** obedience [esp. eccl.].

5. **dominion, dominance** *or* **dominancy, domination; sovereignty, supremacy,** primacy; **predominance** *or* predominancy, predomination, preponderance, prepotence *or* prepotency, prepollence *or* prepollency; ascendance *or* **ascendancy, upper** *or* **whip hand;** balance of power; eminent domain.

6. **mastership,** masterhood, masterdom, **mastery; leadership, headship, lordship,** hegemony; directorship 745.4; chieftainship, chieftaincy, chieftainry, chiefery; presidentship, presidency; premiership; princeship, princedom; suzerainty; regency, regentship; prefectship, prefecture; protectorship, protectorate; seneschalship, seneschalsy, seneschalty; pashaship, pashadom, pashalik; magistrateship, magistrature, magistracy; consulship, consulate; chancellorship, chancellery; seigniory *or* seigneury, seignoralty; deanship, deanery; patriarchship, patriarchy, patriarchate; popeship, popehood, papacy; dictatorship, dictature.

7. **sovereignty, royalty,** regnancy, **regality, majesty, imperiality;** empire, empery; **emperorship,** emperorhood; **kingship,** kinghood; queenship, queenhood; kaisership, kaiserdom; sultanship, sultanate; caliphship, caliphate; the throne, the crown, the purple; regalia 567.3.

8. **scepter,** staff *or* rod of office, rod of empire; **rod, staff,** wand, baton, mace, truncheon, fasces [Roman]; caduceus; gavel; portfolio.

9. (seat of authority) **saddle** [coll.], **helm, driver's seat;** seat, chair, bench; divan, leewan; woolsack [British]; seat of state.

10. **throne,** royal seat, Peacock throne [Chinese], musnud [Oriental]; gaddi, rajgaddi [both India].

11. (acquisition of authority) **accession; usurpation,** arrogation, assumption, seizure.

VERBS 12. **possess authority, have power,** have the power, have the right, have the say, hold the prerogative, have the portfolio; **carry authority,** go (as, what he says *goes* [coll.]); show one's authority, throw one's weight around [coll.].

13. **take command, take charge, take**

over, take the helm, take the reins of government, take the reins into one's hand, ascend or mount the throne; assume command, usurp, assume, arrogate, seize, wrest; usurp or seize the throne, usurp the prerogatives of the crown.

ADJS. 14. authoritative, clothed with authority; commanding, imperative; ruling 739.17; powerful, potent, puissant, mighty; influential, weighty, momentous, consequential, substantial, considerable; official, ex officio; authoritarian.

15. imperious, imperial, masterful, lordly, magisterial; arrogant 910.9; arbitrary, peremptory, absolute, positive; autocratic(al), highhanded; dictatorial, bossy [coll., U.S.]; domineering, overbearing, overruling; despotic, tyrannical, tyrannous, grinding, oppressive.

16. sovereign, suzerain; regal, royal, majestic, purple; kinglike, kingly, "every inch a king" [Shakespeare]; imperial, imperious, imperatorial; monarchic(al), monarchal, monarchial; tetrarchic(al); princely, princelike; queenly, queenlike; dynastic(al).

17. royalist, royalistic, imperialistic, monarchistic.

ADVS. 18. authoritatively, with authority; commandingly, imperatively; powerfully, potently, puissantly, mightily; influentially, weightily, momentously, consequentially; officially, ex cathedra [L., from the chair, with authority].

19. imperiously, masterfully, magisterially; arbitrarily, peremptorily; autocratically, highhandedly; domineeringly, overbearingly; despotically, tyrannically.

20. by authority of, in the name of, in or by virtue of; by order of the king, de par le Roi [F.].

21. in authority, in power, in charge, in control, in command, at the head, at the helm, at the wheel, in the saddle [coll.], on the throne; "drest in a little brief authority" [Shakespeare].

738. LAWLESSNESS

Absence of Authority.—NOUNS 1. lawlessness, licentiousness, license, uncontrol, unrestraint; irresponsibility, unaccountability; interregnum.

2. anarchy, anarchism; disorderliness, unruliness, misrule, disorder, disorganization, confusion, chaos; nihilism, terrorism, reign of terror; club law, lynch law; mob rule or law, mobocracy, ochlocracy.

3. anarchist, anarch; nihilist, terrorist; revolutionist 147.3.

VERBS 4. take the law in one's own hands, act on one's own responsibility, do or go as one pleases, answer to no man, "swear allegiance to the words of no master" [Horace]; when the cat's away the mice will play.

ADJS. 5. lawless, licentious, licensed; ungoverned, undisciplined, unrestrained, uncontrolled, uncurbed, unbridled, unreined, reinless; irresponsible, unaccountable, unanswerable.

6. anarchic(al), anarchistic(al); unruly, disorderly, disorganized, chaotic; nihilistic, terroristic.

ADVS. 7. lawlessly, licentiously; anarchically, chaotically.

739. GOVERNMENT

NOUNS 1. government, governance, discipline, regulation; direction, management, supervision 745; administration, dispensation; regime, régime [F.], regimen; rule, sway; reign, regnancy; empire, empery; civil government, political government.

2. control, controlment, mastery, mastership, command, power, jurisdiction, dominion, domination; hold, grasp, grip, gripe; hand, clutches; helm, reins of government.

3. the government, the authorities, the powers that be, "them above" [Eliot]; sircar [India], Sublime Porte [Turk.]; Uncle Sam [U.S.], John Bull [Eng.].

4. (governments) federal government, federation, confederation; republic, commonwealth; democracy, representative government, constitutional or parliamentary government, "government of the people, by the people, for the people" [Lincoln]; social democracy; welfare state; dictatorship, police state, garrison state; aristocracy, aristarchy; oligarchy; monarchy, absolute monarchy, limited monarchy; autocracy, autarchy, monocracy; diarchy, duarchy, duumvirate; triarchy, triumvirate; regency; papacy; theocracy, thearchy; patriarchy, patriarchate; gerontocracy; heteronomy; autonomy, self-government, home rule, self-determination; dominion rule, colonial government, colonialism; pantisocracy; stratocracy, military government, militarism, martial law, rule of the sword; technocracy; bureaucracy; provisional government; coalition government.

5. matriarchy, matriarchate, metrocracy, petticoat government; gynarchy, gynocracy, gynecocracy.

6. (class rule; slang terms) moneyocracy, landocracy, cottonocracy, beerocracy, oiligarchy.

7. supra-national government, supergovernment, community of nations; **world government,** Federal World Government, World Federation, World Federalism; Atlantic Union; European Union; United Nations 741.

8. (principles of government) **democratism,** republicanism, federalism, constitutionalism, parliamentarianism; **monarchism,** imperialism, czarism; **Fascism,** Neo-Fascism; **Naziism** or **Nazism,** national socialism; **centralism,** statism; **communism, socialism** 743.4, 5; **capitalism,** state capitalism; free enterprise; **feudalism,** feudality, feodality, feudal system; paternalism.

9. absolutism, autocracy; totalitarianism, dictatorship.

10. despotism, tyranny, domineering, domination, oppression; heavy hand, high hand, iron hand, iron heel or boot; club law, big stick, *argumentum baculinum* [L., argument of the cudgel]; terrorism, reign of terror.

VERBS **11. govern, regulate; command,** officer, captain, **head, lead,** be master, be at the head of, **preside over; direct, manage, supervise** 745.8–10; **administer,** administrate; discipline; stand over.

12. control, hold in hand, have in one's power, gain a hold upon; have control of, **have under control, have in hand** or **well in hand;** be master of the situation, hold one's own, have the ball at one's feet, have it all one's own way, have the game in one's own hands; pull the strings or wires.

13. rule, sway, reign, wield the scepter, wear the crown, sit on the throne; rule over, overrule.

14. dominate, predominate, preponderate, prevail; **have the ascendancy, have the upper** or **whip hand,** have on the hip; **master,** have the mastery of; **rule the roost** [coll., U.S.], wear the breeches [coll.]; take the lead, play first fiddle; **lead by the nose, turn around one's little finger, keep under one's thumb,** bend to one's will.

15. domineer, domineer over, **lord it over,** carry with a high hand; browbeat, henpeck; **tyrannize, grind, oppress,** aggrieve, keep under, keep down, beat down; **overbear,** overawe; override, ride over, trample or tread upon, trample or tread down, **trample** or **tread under foot,** crush under an iron heel, **ride roughshod over;** hold or keep a tight hand upon, rule with a rod of iron.

ADJS. **16. governmental, gubernatorial;** democratic(al), republican, fascist, oligarchic(al), aristocratic(al), theocratic(al); federal, federalist(ic); constitutional, parliamentarian; monarchic(al), monarchial; autocratic(al), monocratic, absolute, totalitarian, despotic, dictatorial; patriarchal, patriarchic(al); matriarchal, matriarchic(al); heteronomous; autonomous, self-governing, self-determinated.

17. governing, controlling, regulating, commanding; ruling, reigning, sovereign, regnant; **master, chief,** general, **boss** [coll., U.S.], **head; dominant, predominant,** preponderant, prepotent, prepollent, prevalent, **leading, paramount, supreme,** hegemonic(al); ascendant, in the ascendant, in ascendancy; at the head, in chief; in charge 737.21.

18. executive, administrative, ministerial; **directing, managing** 745.12.

ADVS. **19. under control, in hand,** well in hand; **in one's power,** under one's control.

740. LEGISLATURE

NOUNS **1. legislature,** legislative body; **parliament, congress, diet, soviet** [Russia]; Washington Monkey House, cave of the winds [both jocose, U.S.]; rubber-stamp congress [U.S.]; lame-duck congress or session [U.S.; abolished 1933].

2. Parliament [Eng., Can., Germany, Greece, Hungary, Irish Free State, Italy, Poland, Rumania, U. of So. Africa, Yugoslavia], **Congress** [U.S., Brazil, Cuba, Mexico], Bundesversammlung [Austria, Switzerland], The Chambers [Belgium], Cortes [Spain], Cortes Geraes [Portugal], Federal Parliament [Australia], General Assembly [New Zealand], Imperial Diet [Japan], National Assembly [Czechoslovakia, France], National Congress [Argentina, Brazil, Chile], Oireachtas [Irish Free State], Rigsdag [Denmark], Riksdag [Sweden], States-General [Netherlands], Storting [Norway], Supreme Soviet [U.S.S.R.], Knesset [Israel].

3. upper house, upper chamber; **Senate** [U.S., Australia, Brazil, Can., Cuba, Czechoslovakia, France, Greece, Italy, Poland, Rumania, U. of So. Africa, Yugoslavia], **House of Lords** [Eng.], Bundesrat [Austria], Cámara de Senadores [Chile, Mexico], Cortes [Spain], Eduskunta [Finland], Felsöház [Hungary], First Chamber [Netherlands], Första Kammaren [Sweden], House of Peers [Japan], Lagting [Norway], Landsting [Denmark], Legislative Council [New Zealand], National Assembly [Portugal], Seanad Eireann [Irish Free State], Ständerat [Switzerland], Union Council [Russia].

4. lower house, lower chamber; **House of Representatives** [U.S., Australia, New Zealand, Japan], the House [U.S.]; **House of Commons** [Eng., Can.], Andra Kammaren [Sweden], Boule [Greece], Chamber of Deputies [Brazil, Chile, Czechoslovakia, France, Italy, Mexico, Rumania, Yugoslavia], Chamber of Representatives [Belgium, Cuba], Council of Nationalities [Russia], Dail Eireann [Irish Free State], Diet [Poland], Folketing [Denmark], House of Assembly [U. of So. Africa], House of Deputies [Argentina], Képviselöház [Hungary], Nationalrat [Austria, Switzerland], Odelsting [Norway], Second Chamber [Netherlands].

5. (U.S. legislative committees) committee of the whole House, committee on committees, committee on rules, finance committee, joint committee, recess committee, special committee, standing committee, steering committee, sifting committee, ways and means committee, subcommittee; judiciary committee, the Morgue [slang]; investigating committee, smelling committee; House Committee on Un-American Activities, Un-American Committee [joc.].

6. (U.S. executive departments) Department of State [foreign office], Department of the Treasury, Department of Justice, Department of Defense, Department of the Interior, Department of Agriculture, Department of Commerce, Department of Labor, Department of Health, Education and Welfare, Post Office Department.

7. Cabinet, Ministry [France].

8. (U.S. Cabinet) Secretary of State, Secretary of the Treasury, Secretary of Defense, Secretary of the Interior, Secretary of Agriculture, Secretary of Commerce, Secretary of Labor, Secretary of Health, Education and Welfare, Postmaster General, Attorney General.

9. (English Cabinet) Lord of the Treasury, Lord Chancellor, Lord President of the Council, Lord Privy Seal, Chancellor of the Exchequer, Secretaries of State, First Lord of the Admiralty, President of the Board of Trade, Minister of Health, Secretary of Scotland, President of the Board of Education, Ministers of Agriculture and Fisheries, Minister of Labor.

10. (U.S. governmental advisers) **brain trust,** intellectual awkward squad [jocose].

11. (U.S. administrative agencies) Bureau of Reclamation, BuRec; Civil Aeronautics Board, CAB; Export-Import Bank of Washington, EIB; Farm Credit Administration, FCA; Farm Security Administration, FSA; Federal Aviation Agency, FAA; Federal Communications Commission, FCC; Federal Deposit Insurance Corporation, FDIC; Federal Housing Administration, FHA; Federal Public Housing Authority, FPHA; Federal Power Commission, FPC; Federal Security Agency, FSA; Federal Trade Commission, FTC; Federal Works Agency, FWA; Field Service Branch, FSB (formerly Agricultural Adjustment Agency, AAA); Food and Drug Administration, FDA; Interstate Commerce Commission, ICC; National Housing Agency, NHA; National Labor Relations Board, NLRB; Reconstruction Finance Corporation, RFC; Securities and Exchange Commission, SEC; Tennessee Valley Authority, TVA; U.S. Maritime Commission, USMC; Veterans' Administration, VA; War Shipping Administration, WSA.

12. service, civil service, air service, diplomatic service, etc.; Secret Service [U.S.], S.S.; Federal Bureau of Investigation [U.S.], F.B.I.

13. (Washington institutions) White House, Executive Mansion, the Mansion; Office of Government Reports, "the Madhouse"; Library of Congress, "the Morgue"; Patent Office, "the Nuthouse"; U.S. Treasury, the public crib; Pentagon.

14. Capitol, Statehouse [of a state], **courthouse** [of a county].

15. legislation, legislature, lawmaking; direct legislation, reciprocal legislation, retroactive legislation, social legislation; **enactment,** enaction, constitution, passage, passing; **resolution,** concurrent resolution, joint resolution; motion; question, privileged question, previous question; point of order; act 996.3.

16. (legislative procedure) **closure,** closure by compartment, kangaroo closure, guillotine; **filibustering,** speaking for Bun-

combe [both U.S.]; filibuster [U.S.], talkathon [slang]; **logrolling** [U.S.]; steam-roll-
er methods.

17. veto, executive veto, absolute veto,
qualified *or* limited veto, suspensive *or* suspensory veto, item veto, pocket veto; sena-
torial courtesy.

18. referendum, constitutional referendum, statutory referendum, optional *or*
facultative referendum, compulsory *or* mandatory referendum; **mandate; plebiscite.**

19. bill, omnibus bill, hold-up bill, rip-
per bill [slang, U.S.], companion bills;
strike bill, sandbagger [slang], bell ringer
[slang, U.S.]; **clause, proviso;** enacting
clause, dragnet clause, escalator clause, saving clause; **rider,** joker [slang]; **calendar,**
Calendar of Bills and Resolutions, Calendar
of the Committee of the Whole House
[U.S.].

VERBS **20. legislate,** make *or* enact laws,
enact, pass, constitute, ordain, put in
force; **put through,** jam through, **railroad
through** [coll.], lobby through [U.S.];
table, pigeonhole, smother; pocket; take the
floor, get the floor, have the floor; yield the
floor; **filibuster,** speak for Buncombe [both
U.S.]; **logroll,** roll logs [both U.S.].

ADJS. **21. legislative,** legislatorial, lawmaking; **parliamentary, congressional;** sen-
atorial; bicameral.

741. UNITED NATIONS

NOUNS **1. United Nations, U.N.**

2. (organs) Secretariat, General Assem-
bly, Security Council, Trusteeship Council;
Economic and Social Council, ECOSOC;
International Court.

3. (agencies) Food and Agricultural Or-
ganization, FAO; Intergovernmental Maritime Consultative Organization, IMCO;
International Bank for Reconstruction and
Development, World Bank; International
Civil Aviation Organization, ICAO; Inter-
national Labor Organization, ILO; Interna-
tional Monetary Fund, the Fund; Interna-
tional Refugee Organization, IRO; Inter-
national Telecommunications Union, ITU;
International Trade Organization, ITO;
United Nations Educational, Scientific and
Cultural Organization, UNESCO; United
Nations Relief and Rehabilitation Admin-
istration, UNRRA; Universal Postal Union,
UPU; World Health Organization, WHO;
World Meteorological Organization,
WMO.

4. (Security Council commissions)

Atomic Development Authority (pro-
posed), Atomic Energy Commission, Conventional Armaments Commission, Military Staff Committee.

5. (ECOSOC commissions) Commission on Narcotic Drugs, Commission on
the Status of Women, Economic and Employment Commission, Fiscal Commission,
Human Rights Commission, Population
Commission, Social Commission, Statistical Commission, Transport and Communications Commission.

6. (economic commissions) Economic
Commission for Europe, ECE; Economic
Commission for Asia and the Far East,
ECAFE; Economic Commission for Latin
America, ECLA; International Children's
Emergency Fund, UNICEF.

7. Interim Committee, the Little Assembly.

8. Secretary General.

742. POLITICS

NOUNS **1. politics,** "economics in action"
[Robert La Follette], "the science of exi-
gencies" [Theodore Parker]; practical politics, *Realpolitik* [Ger.]; party *or* partisan
politics, partisanism; power politics, *Macht-
politik* [Ger.]; career politics; petty politics,
peanut politics [slang]; kid-glove politics,
silk-stocking politics [both slang]; ward
politics; bossism [slang, U.S.].

2. political science, poly-sci [school
slang]; political economy, pol-econ [school
slang], "dismal science" [Carlyle]; civil government, civics [U.S.]; geopolitics, *Geo-
politik* [Ger.].

3. statesmanship, statecraft, "the wise
employment of individual meanness for the
public good" [Lincoln]; kingcraft, queen-
craft; senatorship.

4. policy, polity; line, **party line;** peanut policy [slang, U.S.]; bipartisan policy;
noninterference, nonintervention, *laissez
faire* [F.], laissez-faireism, let-alone doctrine
or policy; go-slow policy; government control, managed currency, price supports,
planned economy; free enterprise; autarky,
economic self-sufficiency; bimetallism;
opportunism; localism, sectionalism;
McCarthyism.

**5. foreign policy, foreign affairs; di-
plomacy, diplomatics,** diplomatism; total
diplomacy; shirt-sleeve diplomacy; dollar
diplomacy, dollar imperialism; nationalism,
internationalism; expansionism; contain-
ment; militarism, preparedness; tough

policy, the big stick, twisting the lion's tail; nonresistance, isolationism, neutralism, coexistence; compromise, appeasement; peace offensive; good-neighbor policy; open-door policy, open door; Monroe Doctrine [U.S.].

6. program; Square Deal [Theodore Roosevelt], New Deal [Franklin D. Roosevelt], Fair Deal [Truman]; austerity program [Eng.]; Five-Year Plan [Russia]; Point Four [U.S.].

7. platform, program, declaration of policy; **plank; issue;** keynote, keynote speech [both U.S.].

8. convention, powwow; preliminary convention, nominating convention, constitutional convention.

9. caucus, legislative or congressional caucus, mixed or mongrel caucus, packed caucus, parlor caucus; secret caucus, dark-lantern caucus.

10. candidacy, candidature [Eng.]; candidatis [slang], office hunger, the presidential bee [U.S.].

11. nomination, caucus nomination, direct nomination, petition nomination; acceptance speech.

12. electioneering, politicking [slang], **stumping** [U.S.], **whistle-stopping** [slang, U.S.], prop-stopping (by plane: [slang, U.S.]); rabble-rousing; **rally,** pep meet [slang].

13. campaign, drive, crusade; all-out campaign, hard-hitting campaign, hoopla or hurrah campaign [slang], boodle campaign [coll.]; **canvass, solicitation,** front-porch campaign; still hunt, gumshoe campaign [slang]; **stump excursion** [U.S.], stumping tour [U.S.], **whistle-stop campaign** [slang, U.S.], swing round the circle; campaign commitments; campaign button.

14. smear campaign, mudslinging campaign; **whispering campaign; muckraking, mudslinging, dirty politics** [slang]; roorback, political canard; last-minute lie; fishing expedition [slang]; boring from within.

15. election, general election, by-election; partisan election, nonpartisan election; **primary,** primary election; direct primary, open primary, closed primary, mandatory primary, optional primary, preference primary, presidential primary [U.S.], white primary [U.S.]; runoff primary [U.S.]; disputed or contested election.

16. election district, precinct, ward, borough [N.Y.C.]; gerrymander, gerrymandered district [both U.S.]; shoestring district [U.S.]; silk-stocking district or ward.

17. suffrage, franchise, right to vote; universal suffrage, adult suffrage, manhood suffrage, woman or female suffrage; **suffragism, suffragettism; suffragist;** woman-suffragist, **suffragette.**

18. voting, preferential voting, machine voting, proxy voting, absentee voting, writing in; proportional representation, cumulative system or voting, single system or voting, plural system or voting, Hare system, list system; pipelaying [slang, U.S.], colonization of voters; **plebiscite,** plebiscitum, **referendum.**

19. vote 635.5.

20. ballot, slate [U.S.], **ticket** [U.S.], vote, voting paper [Eng.]; straight ticket, split ticket, party ticket, machine ticket, reform ticket [all U.S.]; Australian ballot, Massachusetts ballot [U.S.], Indiana ballot [U.S.]; absentee ballot, advisory ballot, blanket ballot, envelope ballot, joint ballot, nonpartisan ballot, office-bloc ballot, presidential short ballot [U.S.], proportional representation ballot, sample ballot, who's who ballot.

21. polls, poll, polling place; ballot box, voting booth, voting machine, pollbook.

22. returns, election returns, **poll,** count; landslide [U.S.], tidal wave.

23. electorate, electors; **constituency,** constituents; electoral college [U.S.].

24. voter, elector, balloter; straw voter, fagot voter [Eng.], floater [U.S.], repeater, proxy; instructed voter, manageable voter; ballot-box stuffer; nonvoter, stay-at-home voter.

25. party, major party, minor party, third party; Republican Party, G.O.P., Grand Old Party [all U.S.]; Democratic Party [U.S.], Farmer-Labor Party [U.S.], Socialist Party, Socialist-Labor Party [U.S.], Communist Party, Labor Party, Prohibition Party [U.S.]; Conservative Party, Liberal Party, Labour Party [all Eng.]; **faction, camp; machine,** political or party machine; Tammany Hall [U.S.].

26. partisanism; Republicanism, Democratism [both U.S.]; Conservatism, Toryism [both Eng.]; Liberalism, Whiggism [both Eng.]; Fascism; Naziism or Nazism, National Socialism [both Ger.].

27. nonpartisanism, independence, neutralism; anythingarianism, nothingarianism; **mugwumpery,** mugwumpism [both U.S.].

28. partisan, party member, party man; regular, stalwart, party-liner; Republican [U.S.], Democrat [U.S.], Dixiecrat [U.S. Southern Democrat], Socialist, Communist, Prohibitionist [U.S.], Labourite [Eng.]; Conservative, Tory [both Eng.]; Liberal, Whig [both Eng.]; Fascist, Black Shirt [It.]; Nazi, National Socialist [both Ger.].

29. nonpartisan, independent, neutral, mugwump [U.S.], anythingarian, nothingarian.

30. political influence, wirepulling [coll.]; backstairs influence; social pressure, public opinion; special-interest pressure, group pressure; influence peddling [U.S.]; lobbying, lobbyism; petition, petition jobbing; logrolling [U.S.].

31. wirepuller [coll.]; logroller [U.S.]; influence peddler, four-percenter [both U.S.].

32. pressure group, interest group, special-interest group, special interests; financial interests, farm interests, labor interests, etc.; minority interests, minority groups; grievance committee.

33. lobby, legislative lobby, third house [jocose, U.S.]; people's lobby; special-interests lobby; lobbyist, lobbyer, lobby member [jocose]; parliamentary agent.

34. front, movement, coalition; political front; popular front, people's front; communist front, etc.; grass-roots movement, grass roots.

35. (political corruption) graft, boodleism [coll.], jobbery; pork-barrel legislation [slang, U.S.]; political intrigue, pipelaying [slang]; fat frying, frying of fat [both U.S.]; plunderbund [coll.].

36. spoils of office, boodle [coll.], graft; spoils system.

37. political patronage, favors of office, pap [coll.], pork [slang, U.S.], plum, melon [slang, U.S.].

38. (political fund, U.S.), pork barrel, barrel, jack pot [all slang]; campaign fund; slush fund, yellow-dog fund, soap [all slang]; public crib, public teat, public trough [all slang].

39. officialism, bureaucracy; beadledom, Bumbledom; red-tapism, red-tapery; red tape, pink ribbons [slang].

40. officialese, federalese, Washingtonese; political doubletalk, gobbledegook [slang], bafflegab [slang]; buncombe [coll.]; pussyfooting; weasel words.

VERBS **41.** politick [slang], politicize; look after one's fences, mend one's fences; caucus; gerrymander [U.S.].

42. run for office, run [U.S.]; throw or toss one's hat in the ring [coll.], enter the lists, stand for [Eng.], stand to run [jocose], "choose to run" [Coolidge].

43. electioneer, campaign; stump, take the stump, take to the stump, stump the country [all U.S.]; swing round the circle; whistle-stop [slang, U.S.], prop-stop (by plane: [slang, U.S.]); canvass, solicit votes.

44. support, go with the party, follow the party line; get on the bandwagon [coll.].

45. nominate, elect, vote 635.15–17.

46. hold office, hold or occupy a post, fill an office, be in office.

ADJS. **47.** political, politic; geopolitical; diplomatic(al); suffragist(ic).

48. partisan, party; bipartisan, biparty.

49. nonpartisan, neutral, mugwumpian [U.S.], on the fence.

743. POLITICAL PRINCIPLES

NOUNS **1.** conservatism 140.3.

2. middle of the road, fence [coll.], center.

3. liberalism, progressivism; leftism [coll.], left-wingism; left, left wing; third force.

4. radicalism, extremism, ultraism; communism, communalism, Marxism, bolshevism, sovietism; revolutionism, revolutionary socialism; anarchism, nihilism; Communist International, Comintern; Communist Information Bureau, Cominform; Politburo; iron curtain, bamboo curtain; red-baiting; red scare; loyalty investigation, witch hunt.

5. socialism, "the degenerate capitalism of bankrupt capitalists" [H. L. Mencken]; collectivism, collective ownership; nationalism; state socialism; Fourierism, phalansterism, phalansterianism; Saint-Simonianism.

6. welfarism, Benthamism, "the greatest happiness of the greatest number" [Bentham]; social security, social insurance; retirement benefits, old-age insurance, old-age pension; Townsend plan, revolving pension plan; unemployment insurance; health insurance, socialized medicine; welfare state.

7. capitalism, bourgeoisie [F.], capitalistic system; free enterprise; state capitalism; the interests, vested interests; moneyed interests, moneyocracy [jocose]; landed interests, landocracy [jocose].

8. **individualism;** individualist, rugged individualist.

9. **conservative** 140.4.

10. **liberal,** liberalist, **progressive, left-ist,** left-winger, soft-shell [coll., U.S.].

11. **radical, extremist,** ultraist; **red,** rouge [coll.]; **communist,** communalist, commie [slang], Marxist; **bolshevist,** bolshevik, bolshie [coll.]; **revolutionary,** revolutionist; **anarchist,** nihilist; first-string communist, second-string communist; mild radical, parlor bolshevik; pink, pinkie, pinko [all slang]; **fellow traveler,** sympathizer, security risk; Fifth Amendment Communist [U.S.]; **lunatic fringe.**

12. **socialist, collectivist, nationalist;** state socialist; Fourierist, phalansterian; Saint-Simonian, Saint-Simonist.

13. **capitalist, bourgeois, plutocrat,** bloated plutocrat.

14. (advocate) democratist, federalist, monarchist.

VERBS 15. **democratize,** republicanize.

16. **communize** 813.7.

ADJS. 17. **conservative** 140.8.

18. **liberal,** liberalistic, **progressive,** soft-shell [coll., U.S.]; **leftist** [coll.], left, **left-wing,** on the left, left of center.

19. **radical, red, extreme,** ultra, extremistic, ultraist(ic); pink; **communistic,** communalistic, bolshevistic; **revolutionary,** revolutionist; **anarchist(ic),** nihilist(ic).

20. **socialist, socialistic, collectivist(ic), nationalistic;** Fourieristic, phalansterian; Saint-Simonian.

21. **individualist(ic),** nonsocialist(ic).

22. **capitalist(ic), plutocratic(al), bourgeois.**

744. POLITICIAN

NOUNS 1. **politician,** politico, "one that would circumvent God" [Shakespeare], "one whose greatest asset is his lie-ability" [anon.]; geopolitician; machine politician, Tammany man [U.S.]; old campaigner, war horse; wheel horse; reformer, trust buster [slang, U.S.]; opportunist, trimmer; carpetbagger [slang, U.S.]; dollar-a-year man [U.S.].

2. **statesman,** stateswoman, Solon; "a politician who is held upright by equal pressure from all directions" [Eric Johnston], "a successful politician who is dead" [Thomas B. Reed]; elder statesman.

3. **legislator, lawmaker,** lawgiver; legislatress, legislatrix; **congressman,** congresswoman, congressist, congressionist, Member of Congress, M.C.; **senator,** senatress, senatrix; **representative,** representative in Congress; ranking member, ranking minority member [both U.S.]; Speaker of the House [U.S.]; floor leader [U.S.]; whip, party whip; watch dog of the treasury [U.S.]; bloc, farm bloc, etc.

4. (petty politician) **peanut politician** [slang, U.S.], **politicaster,** statemonger, political dabbler.

5. (corrupt politician) **dirty politician** [slang], jackleg politician [slang, U.S.]; **grafter,** boodler [coll.]; spoilsman, spoilsmonger.

6. (political intriguer) strategist, machinator, **wirepuller** [coll.], pipelayer [slang, U.S.]; **logroller** [U.S.].

7. (political leader) **boss** [slang, U.S.], dictator, cacique; sachem, Grand Sachem [both U.S.]; **man higher up, power behind the throne;** kingmaker; keynoter [coll.], policy maker; standardbearer; ringleader 646.11.

8. **henchman,** hanger-on; heeler, **ward heeler** [both coll., U.S.]; hatchetman.

9. **candidate, aspirant,** office seeker or hunter, job seeker, handshaker [slang], baby kisser [slang], promising politician [jocose]; running mate [U.S.]; **dark horse;** stalking-horse; favorite son [U.S.]; presidential timber [U.S.]; also-ran, has-been; lame duck [U.S.].

10. **campaigner, electioneerer,** electioneer [esp. Eng.], **stumper** [U.S.], stumpster [coll., U.S.], whistle-stopper [slang, U.S.]; stump orator [U.S.], soapbox orator [slang]; muckraker.

11. **officeholder,** job holder, officebearer, Jack-in-office; **incumbent,** incumbent of office; holdover; new broom; barnacle; president-elect; ins, the powers that be.

ADJS. 12. **statesmanlike,** statesmanly.

745. DIRECTION, MANAGEMENT

NOUNS 1. **direction, management,** conduct; **government** 739; **regulation,** ordering; **guidance, lead, leading;** steerage, pilotage.

2. **supervision, superintendence, surveillance, oversight,** eye of the master; **charge, care, auspices, jurisdiction;** bossism [slang, U.S.].

3. **administration,** ministration, **ministry; disposition,** disposal, **dispensation;** officiation.

4. **directorship, directorate, manager-**

ship, leadership, headship, governorship, administratorship, executiveship, generalship, captainship; mastership 737.6; superintendence *or* superintendency, intendancy, foremanship, supervisorship; stewardship, proctorship.

5. helm, rudder, reins, reins of government.

6. husbandry, ménage *or* menage, domestic management, housekeeping, homemaking, housewifery; domestic economy, home economics [U.S.].

7. efficiency engineering, scientific management; efficiency engineer, efficiency expert [U.S.].

VERBS 8. direct, manage, regulate, engineer [U.S.], conduct, carry on, handle, run [coll., U.S.]; govern 739.11; mastermind [slang]; quarterback, call the signals; order, prescribe, cut out work for; head, head up, officer; lead, shepherd, take the lead, lead on; take command 737.13.

9. guide, steer; drive, run [coll., U.S.]; tool, wheel [both slang, U.S.]; chauffeur; pilot, take the helm, be at the helm; rein, handle *or* hold the reins, take the reins, be in the driver's seat, crack the whip; herd, ride herd on [slang & West. U.S.].

10. supervise, superintend, boss [coll.], oversee, overlook, look after, see to, watch over, stand over, keep an eye on *or* upon, keep in order; straw-boss [coll.].

11. administer, administrate; officiate; preside, preside over, preside at the board; chairman, occupy the chair.

ADJS. 12. directing, directive, directory; managing, managerial; governing 739.17; regulating, regulative; head, chief, leading, guiding.

13. supervising, supervisory, overseeing, surveillant, superintendent, boss [coll.].

14. administrative, administrating, ministerial; executive, officiating, presiding.

ADVS. 15. in charge 737.21; in the charge of, in the hands of, in the care of; under the auspices of, under the aegis of; in one's charge, on one's hands, under one's care, under one's jurisdiction.

746. DIRECTOR

NOUNS 1. director, *directeur* [F.], rector, manager, conductor; governor, head 747; comptroller, auditor; monitor; floorwalker, floorman [both U.S.], husband, ship's husband, supercargo; impresario.

2. superintendent, super [slang], intendant; supervisor, foreman, overman, boss [coll.], *caporal* [Sp. Amer.], gaffer [Eng.]; ganger; taskmaster; overseer, overlooker; inspector, surveyor, visitor; subforeman, straw boss [coll.]; slave driver (overseer of slaves [U.S.]).

3. steward, factor, bailiff, seneschal; major-domo, maître d'hôtel; proctor, procurator; curator, librarian; clerk of works; landreeve; croupier.

4. chairman, chairwoman, chair, speaker, presiding officer.

5. leader, conductor, header; precentor, coryphaeus; file leader; pacemaker, pacesetter; bellwether, bell mare, forehorse; standardbearer; leader of men; forerunner 66.1; ringleader 646.11.

6. guide, guider; shepherd, cicerone, mercury; courier, dragoman [Near East], *valet de place* [F.]; pilot, helmsman; steersman, steerer; pointer, guidepost 566.3.

7. guiding star, cynosure, polestar, polar star, lodestar, Polaris, North Star, *l'Etoile du Nord* [F.].

8. compass, gyrocompass, gyroscopic compass, gyrosyn, magnetic compass, mariner's compass, radio compass, surveyor's compass; needle, magnetic needle.

9. directory, guidebook, handbook, manual; city directory, business directory, etc.; telephone directory, telephone book, phone book [coll.]; itinerary, road map, roadbook; Baedeker, Bradshaw, Murray.

10. directorate, directory, direction, management, administration; the administration, the executive, executive arm *or* branch; board, board of directors; interlocking directorate; cadre.

747. MASTER

Person in Authority.—NOUNS 1. master, lord, lord and master, *padrone* [It.], *patron* [F.], seigneur, seignior, boss [coll.], baas [Du., esp. So. Africa], inkos *or* inkosi [So. Africa], bwana [Central & E. Africa]; employer; paterfamilias, patriarch.

2. mistress, governess, dame, madam; matron, housewife, goodwife [hist.], housemistress, housekeeper, homemaker; rectoress *or* rectress; mother superior; first lady [U.S.].

3. head, headman, chief, sachem, principal, paramount; superior, senior; dean, doyen; leader, duce [It.], Führer *or* Fuehrer [Ger.]; big chief [slang, U.S.], Grand Sachem [U.S. politics], chief itch

and rub [joc.], big cheese [slang], **big wheel** [slang], **kingpin** [coll., U.S.], **kingfish** [coll.], top sawyer [coll.], first fiddle, lord of the ascendant, cock of the walk, ~ loft or roost.

4. figurehead, nominal head, dummy, front [coll., U.S.]; puppet.

5. executive, executive officer, **administrator,** *entrepreneur* [F.], provost, prefect, warden, *alcalde* [Sp.], archon, dewan [India]; **president,** prexy [slang], **chancellor** [college]; **vice-president.**

6. governor, ruler, captain, **commander,** commandant, **overman,** overlord; **director, manager** 746; controller, comptroller; **dictator;** oligarch.

7. head of state, chief of state, chief executive; premier, prime minister, chancellor, Führer or Fuehrer [Ger.], grand vizier [Turk.], eparch [Gr.], doge [hist. Venice & Genoa]; **president,** the man in the White House [U.S.]; **vice-president,** V.P., the Veep [slang, U.S.], His Superfluous Excellency [jocose, U.S.].

8. potentate, sovereign, suzerain, **monarch, ruler,** dynast, **crowned head, emperor,** imperator, **king,** anointed king, the anointed, majesty, royalty, royal, royal person, royal highness; **prince** 916.8; kinglet; paramount, lord paramount, overlord, overking; liege, liege lord; **chief, chieftain.**

9. (rulers) **Caesar** [Rom.], **Kaiser** [Ger.], czar or tsar [Russ.], Dalai Lama [Tibet]; **Pharaoh** [ancient Egypt]; pendragon [ancient Brit.]; **mikado,** Tenno [both Jap.]; shogun [Jap.], tycoon (so called by foreigners); **Mogul,** Great or Grand Mogul [both Mongol]; shah, padishah [both Eastern, esp. Persia], Sophy [hist. Persia]; Negus [Abyssinia, Ethiopia]; bey [Tunis], dey [hist. Tunis & Tripoli]; hospodar [hist. Polish & Lithuanian]; **sheik** or sheikh, sherif [both Arab]; sachem, sagamore, werowance [all Amer. Indian]; Inca [Incan]; cacique [West Indies, Peru, Mexico, Philippines]; kaid [No. Africa], induna [So. Africa].

10. (Indian rulers [India]) **raja** or rajah, **maharaja** or maharajah, rana, maharana, maharao, rawal, rawat, rao, rain, raikwar, raikbar, raikat, raja bahadur, maharaja bahadur, rai or rao bahadur, Gaekwar, thakur, Nizam, nawab, Jam, mirza, dewan, sirdar.

11. (Mohammedan rulers) **Sultan,** Grand Turk, Grand Seignior; caliph, Imam, sayid, hakim, khan, Nizam, nawab, wali or vali, amir, emir, mir, mirza, mian, dewan.

12. empress, queen, czarina or tsarina [Russ.], sultana [Moham.]; rani, maharani, begum [all India]; princess 916.9; queen mother, queen dowager.

13. regent, protector, vice-king; prince regent.

14. (regional governors) **governor,** governor general, lieutenant governor; **viceroy,** exarch, stadholder or stadtholder [Netherlands], nabob [India], subahdar [India], khedive [Turk.]; palatine; tetrarch [Rom.]; burgrave [hist. Ger.]; collector, deputy commissioner [both India]; hospodar, voivode [both Moldavia & Walachia]; dey [hist. Algiers], bey or beg [Turk.], beglerbeg or beylerbey [Ottoman], satrap [Persia], mandarin [China], woon [Burmese].

15. tyrant, despot; autocrat, autarch; **dictator,** Caesar, czar; usurper, arrogator; **oppressor, hard master; taskmaster,** driver, **slave driver,** Simon Legree; **martinet, disciplinarian,** stickler.

16. officialdom, bureaucracy; the authorities; the powers that be, "them above" [Eliot]; directorate 745.4; ministry.

17. official, officer, officiant; **functionary,** *fonctionnaire* [F.]; **officeholder,** office-bearer, placeman; **bureaucrat,** mandarin, red-tapist; blimp, stuffed shirt [both slang]; Jack-in-office, the Grand Panjandrum himself.

18. public official, public servant, public functionary; **magistrate,** syndic, corregidor [Sp.], kuan [China]; pasha, bashaw [both Turk.].

19. (public officials) **congressman** 744.3; **minister,** vizier [Turk.]; chancellor; lord lieutenant [Brit.]; **commissioner,** commissionaire; commissar [Russia]; city manager; **mayor,** *maire* [F.], Lord Mayor [Eng.], mayoress [U.S.]; burgomaster, burghmaster, warden [Conn.]; archon [Gr. antiq.]; **councilman,** councilwoman, councilor, city councilman; elder, city father; alderman, bailie [Scot.]; selectman.

20. bailiff, constable, tipstaff [Eng.]; reeve, portreeve [both hist. Eng.]; lictor [Rom. antiq.]; mace-bearer, sergeant-at-arms [Eng.].

21. (military officials) **officer,** rating [slang], rated man; **brass hat** [slang]; the brass [slang, U.S.].

22. commissioned officer; commanding officer, C.O.; **commander,** commandant, the Old Man [slang], aga [Moham.];

commander in chief, generalissimo, captain general, hetman [Russ.], seraskier [Turk.], sirdar [Turkey, Egypt, etc.]; General of the Army [U.S.]; marshal, *maréchal* [F.]; field marshal; chief of staff; general, lieutenant general, major general, adjutant general; brigadier general, brigadier [U.S.]; colonel, lieutenant colonel; major; captain, cap [slang]; brigadier [Eng.]; centurion; subahdar [India]; ressaldar, ressaidar [both India]; subaltern, sub [coll.]; lieutenant, luff [colloq., Eng.], jemadar [India]; first lieutenant; second lieutenant, shavetail [slang, U.S.], one-star wonder [jocose, U.S.]; sublieutenant [Eng.]; provost marshal; quartermaster [U.S.], Q.M.; adjutant, brigade major [Eng.]; aide-de-camp, A.D.C.; officer of the day, orderly officer, O.D.; staff officer; petty officer.

23. noncommissioned officer, noncom [coll.], N.C.O.; warrant officer; sergeant, sarge [slang], kick [slang, U.S.], havildar [India]; first sergeant [U.S.], top sergeant [coll., U.S.], top kick [slang, U.S.]; master sergeant, sergeant major, sergeant first class, technical sergeant, staff sergeant, provost sergeant, line sergeant, quartermaster sergeant, mess sergeant; acting sergeant, lance sergeant [Eng.]; corporal, naik [India]; acting corporal, lance corporal [Eng.], lance Jack [slang, Eng.]; drum major; color sergeant, ensign, cornet, standardbearer; cadet.

24. (naval officers) admiral, vice-admiral, rear admiral, commodore, captain, commander, navarch [Gr. antiq.], lieutenant commander, lieutenant, lieutenant junior grade, ensign, mate, quartermaster; warrant officer, chief warrant officer; skipper, master.

25. (military ranks) generalcy, generalate, generalship; colonelcy, colonelship; majorship, majority; captaincy, captainry, captainship; lieutenancy, lieutenantship; sergeantcy, sergeancy, sergeantship; corporalship; brevet rank.

748. SERVANT, EMPLOYEE

NOUNS **1.** servant, servitor, retainer, dependent, follower, assistant 785.6, help [U.S.], menial, slavey [coll.], gillie; underling, subordinate; minion, myrmidon, man Friday; slave 762.7.

2. employee, employé or employe; hireling, mercenary, pensionary [derog.]; hired man, hired hand [coll.], hired help [U.S.]; wage earner, wageworker.

3. man, manservant; boy, *garçon* [F.].

4. attendant, tender, servant in attendance, waiter, usher, squire, yeoman [hist.]; bearer, khidmatgar, hamal, chokra [all India]; office boy; page, buttons [coll.], footboy; bellboy, bellhop [slang, U.S.]; caddie; bootblack, boots; trainbearer; cupbearer; attaché; orderly [mil.].

5. lackey, flunky, stooge [slang]; valet, *valet de chambre* [F.]; gentleman, gentleman's gentleman; footman, *valet de pied* [F.].

6. waiter, waitress; carhop; headwaiter, maître d'hôtel.

7. domestic, domestic servant, house servant; kitchenman; scullion; dishwasher, potwalloper [slang].

8. maid, maidservant, servitrix, servantess, girl, servant girl, hired girl [U.S.], lady help [Brit.], biddy [coll., U.S.], amah [Oriental]; handmaid, handmaiden; lady's maid, lady's waiting maid, waiting maid or woman, lady in waiting, abigail, soubrette, *bonne* [F.], ayah [India]; housemaid; parlormaid; kitchenmaid, scullery maid, Cinderella; chambermaid, *femme* or *fille de chambre* [F.], bedmaker; milkmaid; charwoman.

9. (college servant) cad [Eng.], gyp [Cambridge Univ.], scout [Oxford Univ.], skip [Trinity College, Dublin].

10. factotum, do-all [coll.], general servant [Eng.], general [coll.], man of all work; maid of all work, *bonne pour tout faire* [F.], general housework maid [U.S.], slavey [coll.].

11. major-domo, steward, house steward, butler, chamberlain, maître d'hôtel, seneschal, khansamah or khansaman [India].

12. staff, personnel, employees, the help [esp. U.S.], force, crew, gang, associates; retinue 73.6; servantry; office force, office, clerical staff.

13. service, servitude, servitorship; employment, employ; ministry, ministration; attendance, tendance.

VERBS **14.** serve, work for; minister or administer to, pander to, do service to; help 783.11; care for, do for [coll.], look after, take care of; wait on or upon, attend, tend, attend on or upon, dance attendance upon, wait on hand and foot; lackey, valet, fag, maid.

ADJS. **15.** serving, ministering, ministerial, waiting, attending, attendant, in the train of, in one's pay or employ; helping 783.20.

16 menial, ignoble, low, lowly, abject, base, mean; servile 905.12.

749. PRECEPT

NOUNS 1. precept, prescript, prescription, instruction, direction, stage direction, charge, injunction, dictate, dictum.

2. rule, law, canon, code, maxim, convention; regulation, *règlement* [F.]; principle, principia, settled principle; standard, model; working rule; golden rule.

3. formula, formulary, form; recipe, receipt; prescription; instructions, directions.

4. technicality, punctilio, nice or fine point, nicety, delicacy, subtlety; detail, item, particular.

ADJS. 5. preceptive, didactic, instructive; prescriptive, prescript, prescribed, dictated; formulary, standard, regulation.

750. COMMAND

An Order Given.—NOUNS 1. command, commandment, order, bidding, behest, hest, will, do [coll.], say-so [coll.], word, word of command, *mot d'ordre* [F.].

2. injunction, charge; mandate, rescript, imperative; dictate, dictation.

3. direction, directive, instruction; precept, prescript, prescription; general orders, order of the day [both mil.].

4. decree, decreement, decretum, decretal [eccl.]; edict, *edictum* [L.]; law 996.3; rule, ruling; ordinance, ordonnance, appointment; proclamation, pronouncement, pronunciamento [Sp.], *pronunciamiento* [Sp.], declaration, manifesto; fiat, firman [Orient.], ukase, bull, brevet; *hattisherif, hatti-humayun* [both Turk., hist.]; decree law, *decret loi* [F.]; *senatus consultum* [L., decree of the senate], senatus-consult.

5. summons, bidding, beck, call, calling, nod, beck and call; convocation; evocation, calling forth.

6. (legal order) writ, process, precept, notice, notification; warrant, bench warrant, search warrant, death warrant, warrant of arrest; mittimus, mandamus, caveat, capias, nisi prius [Eng.], fieri facias.

7. summons [law], writ of summons, subpoena, citation, monition; venire, venire facias, venire facias juratores, venire facias de novo; habeas corpus, writ of habeas corpus; garnishment.

8. process server, summoner.

VERBS 9. command, order, dictate, direct, instruct, bid, enjoin, charge, call on or upon; decree, rule, ordain; give an order, issue a command, give the word or word of command; call the tune [coll.], call the signals or play [slang]; order about or around; call to order.

10. prescribe, lay down, set, appoint, mark out.

11. lay down the law, give the law to, put one's foot down [coll.], read the riot act.

12. summon, call, muster, demand; call for, send for or after, bid come; cite, summons [coll.], subpoena, serve, call in question; page; convoke, call together; call away; summon up, muster up, call up, bring up; evoke, call forth, summon forth, call out; recall, call back, call in.

ADJS. 13. mandatory, imperative, commanding, compulsory, peremptory, obligatory, must; decisive, final, conclusive, binding, irrevocable, without appeal.

14. directive, instructive; prescriptive, prescript, preceptive; jussive; decretory, decretive, decretal.

ADVS. 15. commandingly, mandatorily, imperatively, peremptorily, compulsorily, obligatorily.

16. by order or command, at the word of command, as ordered or required, to order.

751. DEMAND

NOUNS 1. demand, claim, call, exaction, requisition, requirement; call for, demand for; heavy demand, draft, drain; insistent demand, rush; ultimatum.

2. stipulation, postulation.

3. insistence, importunity, contention, maintaining; emphasis, stress.

VERBS 4. demand, ask, make a demand; call for, call on or upon one for, come upon one for, appeal to for; cry for, clamor for; require, exact, require at the hands of; requisition, make or put in requisition, lay under contribution.

5. claim, pretend; challenge, lay claim to; make out a case; assert, vindicate a claim, ~ right or title to.

6. stipulate, postulate, lay down, make a point of.

7. insist, maintain, contend, assert roundly or positively; insist on or upon, stickle for, make a point of, set one's heart or mind upon; emphasize, stress, press, lay emphasis or stress upon; assert oneself, raise one's voice, take one's stand upon,

stand on *or* upon, stand upon one's rights, **put one's foot down** [coll.], lay down the law; take no denial, stand no nonsense, not take "no" for an answer, maintain with one's last breath, have the last word.

ADJS. 8. **demanding, exacting,** exigent; **insistent,** instant, **importunate, urgent,** pressing, crying, clamorous.

9. requisitionary, requisitory.

ADVS. 10. **demandingly, exactingly,** exigently; **insistently, importunately, urgently,** pressingly, clamorously, at the top of one's voice.

11. **on demand,** at demand, **on call,** upon presentation, when due.

752. ADVICE

NOUNS 1. **advice, counsel,** opinion, **recommendation, suggestion,** advocacy; **direction, instruction,** guidance; **charge, injunction; exhortation,** hortation, **admonition,** expostulation, remonstrance.

2. piece of advice, **word of advice, word to the wise,** *verbum sapienti* [L.], word in the ear, **flea in the ear** [coll.], **tip** [coll.].

3. **consultation,** parley 595.6; council 753.

4. **adviser** *or* advisor, **counsel, counselor,** consultant, recommender, instructor, coach, guide, **mentor,** Nestor; admonisher, admonitor, monitor; kibitzer [coll., U.S.].

5. **advisee,** counselee.

VERBS 6. **advise, counsel, recommend, suggest, advocate; instruct,** coach, guide, direct; prescribe, dictate; give a piece of advice, put a flea in one's ear [coll.]; kibitz [slang, U.S.].

7. **enjoin, charge,** call upon; **urge,** prompt, move; **admonish, exhort,** expostulate, remonstrate, preach.

8. **confer,** consult with 595.10.

9. **take advice, follow advice,** follow, follow implicitly; be advised by, have at one's elbow, take one's cue from.

ADJS. 10. **advisory, commendatory,** recommendatory; consultative, consultatory; **admonitory,** monitory, monitorial; **expostulative,** expostulatory; **remonstrative,** remonstratory, remonstrant; **exhortative,** exhortatory, hortative, hortatory, preachy [coll.].

11. **advised, considered, calculated,** meditated, contemplated, deliberated, studied, weighed, thought out.

ADVS. 12. **advisedly, consideredly, calculatedly,** meditatedly, contemplatedly;

on reconsideration, on second thought, on better advice.

753. COUNCIL

NOUNS 1. **council,** deliberative *or* advisory body; **congress, diet, synod, soviet,** indaba [So. Africa]; junta, divan, musnud, camarilla, durbar [India], Sanhedrin [Jewish antiq.]; syndicate; privy council, common council, county council, parish council, city council; brain trust [U.S.]; indignation meeting; council of war; council fire [N. Amer. Ind.].

2. **conference** 595.6; assembly 74.2; parliament 740; tribunal 999.

3. **committee,** subcommittee, court, chamber, cabinet, bench, staff, board.

4. **forum,** discussion group, **round table, panel;** open forum.

5. (ecclesiastical) chapter, church, classis, conclave, conference, congregation, consistory, conventicle, convention, convocation, directory, presbytery, session, synod, vestry; parochial council *or* court, parochial church council; diocesan ~, provincial ~, national ~, plenary ~, general ~, universal *or* ecumenical council.

ADJS. 6. council, curule; synodal, synodic(al).

ADVS. 7. **in conference, in consultation, in a huddle** [slang], in conclave, **in session,** sitting.

754. COMPULSION

NOUNS 1. **compulsion, obligation,** obligement; **necessity,** requirement 637; **forcing,** enforcement; **constraint, duress,** coaction; **pressure,** press, **high pressure** [coll.].

2. **force,** *ultima ratio* [L., the final argument]; **brute force,** main force, physical force; the force of might *or* right, the right of the strong, *le droit du plus fort* [F.]; steam roller [coll.], sledgehammer.

3. **coercion, violence,** high-pressure methods; **the strong arm** [coll.], the sword, the big stick, the club, *argumentum baculinum* [L., argument of the cudgel]; club ~, lynch ~, mob *or* martial law.

VERBS 4. **compel, force, make,** have, cause, cause to; **constrain, enforce, drive,** impel; use force upon, force one's hand.

5. **oblige, necessitate, require,** exact, demand, call for, say it must be done, take no denial.

6. **press, pressure** [coll.], **high-pressure** [coll., U.S.], squeeze [coll.], twist one's arm

[slang]; **bring pressure to bear upon, put pressure on,** bear upon, bear down, bear down upon, bear against, bear hard upon; put the screw or screws on, put the screw or screws to [slang], put under the screw or screws, put or turn on the screw, screw.

7. **coerce,** use violence, **strong-arm** [slang], blackjack, hijack, dragoon, "carry a big stick" [T. Roosevelt].

8. have to 637.10.

ADJS. 9. **compulsory, compulsive, compelling; pressing, driving;** constraining, coactive; **necessary** 637.12; **obligatory, imperative,** imperious, importunate, peremptory, binding.

10. **forcible, forceful,** high-pressure; **coercive,** strong-arm [coll.], violent.

ADVS. 11. **compulsorily, compulsively, compellingly; of necessity** 637.16; obligatorily, imperatively, imperiously, importunately, peremptorily; by stress of, under press of.

12. **forcibly, forcefully, by force,** by a strong arm; by force of arms, vi et armis [L.]; at the point of a gun, at the point of the sword or bayonet; under the lash.

755. STRICTNESS

NOUNS 1. **strictness, severity, harshness; stringency,** astringency; **austerity, sternness,** grimness, ruggedness, forbiddingness; toughness [coll.], hard-boiledness [coll.], hardheadedness.

2. **firmness, rigor, rigorousness,** rigidness, rigidity, stiffness, hardness, obdurateness, **inflexibility,** inexorability, unyieldingness, unbendingness, unrelentingness, **relentlessness.**

3. **firm hand, iron hand,** heavy hand, strong hand, tight hand, tight rein.

VERBS 4. **hold or keep a tight hand upon,** keep a firm hand on, keep a tight rein on, rule with an iron hand, rule with a rod of iron; keep in line.

5. **deal hardly or harshly with,** deal hard measure to, lay a heavy hand on, bear hard upon, come down on or upon [coll.], ride roughshod over, give short shrift to, not hold one's punches [slang].

ADJS. 6. **strict, exacting,** exigent, not to be trifled with; **stringent,** astringent; **severe, harsh,** dour [Scot.], unsparing; **stern, grim, austere,** rugged, forbidding; **tough** [coll.], **hard-boiled** [coll.], hard-headed, Spartan; Procrustean.

7. **firm, rigid, rigorous,** stiff, hard, obdurate, **inflexible, inexorable, unyielding,** unbending, **uncompromising, relentless,** unrelenting; iron; ironbound, ironclad [coll.]; ironhanded.

ADVS. 8. **strictly, severely, stringently, harshly; sternly,** grimly, **austerely,** ruggedly, forbiddingly; toughly [coll.], hardheadedly.

9. **firmly, rigidly, rigorously,** stiffly, hardly, obdurately, **inflexibly,** inexorably, unyieldingly, unbendingly, uncompromisingly, **relentlessly,** unrelentingly; ironhandedly, with a firm, ~ strong, ~ heavy, ~ tight or iron hand.

756. LAXNESS

NOUNS 1. **laxness, laxity, slackness, looseness;** remissness 532; leniency 757; unrestraint 760.2.

2. **unstrictness, unsevereness, unharshness;** unsternness, unaustereness; **flexibility,** pliancy.

VERBS 3. **hold a loose rein, give free rein to,** give the reins to, **give one his head,** give a free course to, give rope enough.

ADJS. 4. **lax, slack, loose,** relaxed, licensed, weak; remiss 532.10; lenient 757.8; unrestrained 760.22.

5. **unstrict, unexacting; unsevere, unharsh; unstern,** unaustere, unforbidding; **flexible, pliant, yielding.**

757. LENIENCY

NOUNS 1. **leniency, lenience,** lenientness, lenity; **clemency,** clementness; **mildness, gentleness,** softness, moderateness; easiness, easygoingness; laxness 756; mercy 942.1.

2. **forbearance,** forbearing; **tolerance** 524.4.

3. **compliance, complaisance,** obligingness, accommodatingness, **agreeableness,** kindness, kindliness, graciousness, generousness, decency, amiability.

4. **indulgence, humoring,** favoring, obliging, gratification, pleasing; **pampering, coddling,** mollycoddling, spoiling; permissive behavior [psychol.].

5. **spoiled child,** enfant gâté [F.], pampered darling, mama's boy, mollycoddle; enfant terrible [F.], naughty child.

VERBS 6. **be easy on,** handle with gloves, spare the rod; **tolerate,** bear with 859.5.

7. **indulge, humor, favor, oblige,** please, gratify, satisfy, **cater to; give way to,** yield to, let one have his own way; **pamper,**

coddle, mollycoddle, spoil; spare the rod and spoil the child.

ADJS. **8. lenient, mild, gentle, clement,** soft, moderate, **easy,** easygoing; lax 756.4; merciful 942.7.

9. forbearing, forbearant; tolerant 524.11.

10. indulgent, compliant, complaisant; obliging, accommodating, agreeable, amiable, gracious, generous, kind, kindly, decent.

11. indulged, pampered, coddled, spoiled.

758. RESTRAINT

NOUNS **1. restraint, constraint;** inhibition, cohibition; **control, curb,** check, rein, arrest; hindrance 728; thought control.

2. suppression, repression; subdual, quelling, crushing; quashing, squashing, squelching [coll.]; smothering, stifling, strangling, throttling; extinguishment, quenching; crackdown [coll., U.S.].

3. restriction, limitation, confinement, stint, cramp, hamper, trammel, strangle hold.

4. shackle, fetter, hamper, trammel, manacle, gyve, bond, **bonds,** irons, chains; handcuffs, cuffs, darbies or derbies [slang]; stocks, bilboes; hobbles, hopples; strait jacket, strait-waistcoat; yoke, collar; bridle, halter; muzzle, gag; tether, picket; leash, leading strings; reins.

5. lock, bolt, bar, padlock.

6. restrictionist, repressionist, monopolist, protectionist.

VERBS **7. restrain, constrain, control, govern,** guard, contain, keep under control, put or lay under restraint; **inhibit,** cohibit; **curb, check, arrest, bridle, rein,** snub; hold, keep, withhold, hold up [coll.], **keep from;** hinder 728.10; **hold back, keep back,** set back; **hold in, keep in,** pull in, rein in; **hold** or **keep in check,** hold in leash, keep under wraps [slang, U.S.]; hold fast, keep a tight hand on.

8. suppress, repress; keep down, hold down, keep under; **subdue, quell, put down,** crush; **quash, squash, squelch** [coll.]; **extinguish,** quench, kill; **smother, stifle,** strangle, throttle, choke off; sit on or upon, sit down on [both slang]; crack down on [coll., U.S.], clamp down on [coll.], shut down on or upon [coll.], put the lid on [slang]; bottle up, cork; kibosh, put the kibosh on [both slang].

9. restrict, limit, confine, cramp, hamper, trammel, impede, stint, keep in or within bounds.

10. bind, tie, tie up, lash, leash, pinion, fasten, secure, make fast; **hamper, trammel,** entrammel; rope, string, strap; **chain,** enchain; **shackle, fetter, manacle,** gyve, put in irons, forge fetters; **handcuff, tie one's hands; tie hand and foot,** hog-tie [coll., U.S.]; forefoot [slang, West. U.S.]; hobble, hopple; tether, picket, moor, peg or stake out; tie down, pin down, peg down; get a strangle hold on, put a half nelson on [coll.]; **bridle, muzzle, gag.**

ADJS. **11. restraining, constraining;** inhibiting, inhibitive, cohibitive; **suppressive, repressive.**

12. restrictive, limitative, restricting, limiting, confining, cramping, hampering.

13. restrained, constrained, inhibited, guarded; controlled, curbed, bridled; **under restraint,** under control, in check, under wraps [slang, U.S.]; in or on leash, in leading strings.

14. suppressed, repressed, subdued, smothered, stifled.

15 restricted, limited, confined, cramped, hampered, trammeled, impeded, stinted.

16. bound, tied, hampered, trammeled; **in bonds,** in irons or chains, ironbound; rock-bound; landlocked; weatherbound, wind-bound, icebound; hidebound, barkbound; musclebound.

759. CONFINEMENT

NOUNS **1. confinement, constraint, restraint;** restriction 758.3.

2. quarantine, sanitary cordon, *cordon sanitaire* [F.], cordon; **isolation,** segregation, separation, seclusion; quarantine flag, yellow flag, yellow jack.

3. imprisonment, incarceration, internment, impoundment; immurement, immuration; **detention, captivity, duress, durance;** term of imprisonment 107.4.

4. commitment, committal, consignment; recommitment, remand; transportation.

5. custody, keep, keeping, care, charge, ward, hold, protective or preventive custody.

6. arrest, arrestment, pinch [slang]; **capture, apprehension, seizure.**

7. prison, jail [U.S.], **gaol** [Eng.], prisonhouse, jailhouse [U.S.], penal institution or settlement, lockup, keep, **bastille** or bastile, **calaboose** [local, U.S.], bagnio,

clink [coll.], choky [slang, Eng.], chauki [India], *oubliette* [F.], hole, tolbooth [Scot.], bridewell [Eng.]; limbo, hell; cage, coop: pound, pinfold or penfold.

8. (slang terms) jug, **can** [U.S.], **coop, cooler, booby hatch, hoosegow** [U.S.], stir [U.S.], quod, rattle [naut.], college.

9. (prisons) **police station,** station house, station [coll.], watchhouse, thana [India]; **penitentiary,** pen [slang], state prison, the big house [U.S.]; **guardhouse,** guardroom [both mil.]; **brig** [naut.]; **dungeon,** donjon, black hole; **house of detention; reformatory,** reform school, house of correction, bridewell [Eng.]; workhouse [U.S.]; debtor's prison, sponging house; detention camp, **concentration camp;** cell, hole; bull pen [coll., U.S.]; death house [U.S.].

10. jailer, gaoler [Eng.], **keeper, warder,** custodian, **turnkey,** screw [slang]; guard 697.8; **warden,** principal keeper.

11. prisoner, captive, *détenu* [F.], cageling; **convict,** con [slang]; **jailbird** [coll., U.S.], gaolbird [coll., Eng.], stir bird [slang, U.S.], collegian [slang, Eng.]; lag, lagger [both slang]; **internee; prisoner of war, POW;** political prisoner; lifer [U.S.]; trusty [U.S.]; parolee, parolist, ticket-of-leave man or ticket-of-leaver [Eng.]; ex-convict; chain gang [U.S.].

VERBS **12. confine, keep in, shut in,** coop in, hem in, fence in, wall in, rail in; **shut up, coop up,** box up, mew up, bottle up, cork up, seal up, button up; pen, coop, pound, mew, cloister, cage, encage; close the door upon.

13. constrain, restrain, hold in constraint or restraint; restrict 758.9; shackle 758.10.

14. quarantine, isolate, segregate, separate, seclude.

15. imprison, incarcerate, intern, impound, immure; **jail** [U.S.], gaol [Eng.], jug [slang]; throw or cast in prison, clap or lay under hatches, clap up; **lock up,** lock in, bolt in, put or keep under lock and key; hold captive, hold in captivity.

16. arrest, make an arrest, put under arrest, **take captive, take prisoner,** take up, **pick up** [coll.], **apprehend, capture,** seize, collar [coll.], lay by the heels, **take into custody; pinch,** make a pinch, nab, lag, pull, pull in, **run in** [all slang].

17. commit, consign, commit to prison, send to jail, **send up** [slang, U.S.]; commit to an institution, institutionalize; recom-

mit, remit, remand; transport, lag [slang].

18. stand committed, do or serve time [coll.].

ADJS. **19. confined,** in confinement, **shut-in** [U.S.], **pent-up,** under constraint or restraint; restricted 758.15.

20. imprisoned, incarcerated, interned, impounded, immured; **in prison,** in stir [slang, U.S.], in captivity, **behind bars,** locked up, under lock and key, under hatches, in durance vile.

21. under arrest; in custody, in charge, in hold.

760. FREEDOM

NOUNS **1. freedom, liberty, license, loose;** run, the run of [both coll.]; "the right to live as we wish" [Epictetus], "the right to act without interference within the limits of the law" [J. Oerter], "the right to kick about the lack of it" [Will Rogers], "political power divided into small fragments" [Thomas Hobbes], "the choice of working or starving" [Samuel Johnson].

2. unrestraint, unconstraint; unreserve, uninhibitedness; **uncontrol,** unruliness; **abandon,** abandonment; **licentiousness,** incontinence, wantonness, riotousness, wildness, irrepressibility; laxness 756.

3. latitude, scope, room, range, way; **margin,** elbowroom, leeway [coll.], wide berth; **free scope, free hand,** free play, free course, free field and no favor; swing, play, full swing; rope, rope enough to hang oneself.

4. independence, self-determination, self-reliance, self-containment, self-sufficiency, self-subsistence; **self-government,** self-direction; **autonomy,** home rule; individualism, rugged individualism, innerdirection; Declaration of Independence [U.S.].

5. free will, discretion, option, choice, say-so [coll.], free decision, **full consent.**

6. own free will, own account, own accord, own hook [coll., U.S.], own sayso [coll.], own discretion, own choice, **own initiative,** own responsibility, own volition, own authority, own power; own way, own sweet way [coll.].

7. exemption, exception, **immunity;** release, discharge; **franchise, license, liberty;** privilege 956.4.

8. noninterference, nonintervention, nonresistance; **isolationism; laissez-faireism,** let-alone principle, ~ **doctrine** or policy; *laissez faire, laisser faire, laissez aller,* *laisser aller* [all F.]; Monroe Doctrine [U.S.]; free enterprise, free trade.

9. **civil liberty, civil rights;** four freedoms [U.S.], freedom of speech, freedom of religion, freedom from want, freedom from fear; free speech; free press [U.S.], freedom *or* liberty of the press; academic freedom [U.S.].

10. **freeman,** freewoman; liveryman [Eng.]; burgess, burgher; freedman, freedwoman, deditician [Rom.].

11. **independent, free lance; individualist,** rugged individualist; freethinker; freetrader; **nonpartisan,** neutral, mugwump [polit., U.S.]; isolationist.

VERBS 12. **free,** liberate 761.4; liberalize.

13. **exempt, free, release,** discharge, **let off** [coll.], pass over, **excuse,** spare, except, dispense from; dispense with, save the necessity; remit, remise [law]; absolve 1005.4.

14. **give a free hand, give the run of** [coll.], give the freedom of, give one leeway [coll.], give full play; **give rein** *or* **free rein to,** give the reins to, give bridle to, give one line, give one rope, give a loose to; **let one have his head,** give one the head, give one his head, give head; let go one's own way, let one go at will; open the door to, leave the door open.

15. **not interfere, leave** *or* **let alone,** leave well enough alone, **keep hands off,** let it take its course, *laisser faire* [F.], *laisser aller* [F.], live and let live, leave to oneself, mind one's own business, let sleeping dogs lie.

16. **be free,** feel free, feel at liberty; **go at large,** breathe free air; **have free scope,** have a free hand, have the run of [coll.].

17. **let oneself go,** let go, let loose [coll.], **give way to,** open up, go all-out, pull out all stops; go unrestrained, run wild, have one's fling.

18. (be independent *or* self-sufficient) **shift for oneself, fend for oneself,** strike out for oneself, **look out for number one** [slang]; **go it alone,** be one's own man, pull a lone oar, play a lone hand [coll.], **paddle one's own canoe** [coll.]; **stand on one's own legs** *or* **two feet,** stand on one's own [coll.]; **go on one's own,** go one's own way, take one's own course; do on one's own, do on one's own hook *or* say-so [coll.], do in one's own sweet way [coll.]; **have a will of one's own,** have one's own way, do what one likes, ~ wishes *or* chooses, **do as one pleases,** go as one

pleases, please oneself [coll.], **suit oneself;** freelance.

ADJS. 19. **free, at liberty, at large, loose,** unengaged, disengaged, **clear,** in the clear, on the loose [coll.], go-as-you-please; footloose, foot-loose and fancy-free; scot-free; free as air, free as a bird.

20. **independent,** one's own man; freespirited; **self-determined,** inner-directed, **self-reliant,** self-sufficient, self-subsistent, self-contained; self-governed, **self-governing,** self-directing; **autonomous,** sovereign; nonpartisan, neutral.

21. **free-acting,** free-going, free-moving, free-working, free-wheeling; freehanded.

22. **unrestrained, unconstrained, unforced,** uncompelled, uncoerced; **uninhibited, unsuppressed, unrepressed,** unreserved; **uncurbed, unchecked, unbridled,** unmuzzled; **unreined,** reinless; **uncontrolled,** ungoverned, **unruly;** out of control, out of hand, out of one's power; **abandoned, incontinent, licentious,** wanton, rampant, riotous, wild, irrepressible; lax 756.4.

23. **unhampered, untrammeled, unhandicapped, unimpeded,** unhindered, unprevented, unobstructed; unencumbered, unburdened, unladen, unembarrassed, disembarrassed.

24. **unrestricted, unconfined, unbound,** unbounded; **unlimited,** limitless, illimitable; unqualified, unconditioned, **unconditional;** absolute, **arbitrary,** full, plenary; open, **wide-open.**

25. **unbound,** untied, **unfettered,** unshackled, unchained.

26. **unsubject,** ungoverned, unenslaved, **unenthralled;** unvanquished, unsubdued, unquelled; freeborn, free-bred.

27. **exempt, immune, clear;** exempted, **released, excused,** excepted, let off [coll.], spared; **privileged, licensed,** favored; **unliable,** unsubject, irresponsible, unaccountable, unanswerable.

28. **quit, clear, free, rid; free of, clear of, quit of, rid of,** red of [dial.], **shut of** [dial. & coll.], shet of [dial.].

ADVS. 29. **freely, free; without restraint,** without stint; unreservedly, with abandon; outright, openly.

30. **independently, alone, by oneself,** all by one's lonesome [coll.], under one's own power, out of one's own head, on one's own [coll.], **on one's own hook** [coll., U.S.], on one's own initiative; **on one's own account** *or* **responsibility,** on one's

own say-so [coll.], **of one's own free will, of one's own accord,** of one's own volition, at one's own discretion.

761. LIBERATION

NOUNS **1. liberation, freeing; deliverance,** delivery; rescue 700; **emancipation,** disenthrallment, manumission; enfranchisement, affranchisement; Emancipation Proclamation [U.S.].

2. **release,** unhanding, **loosing,** unloosing; **discharge, dismissal;** parole.

3. **extrication, freeing, clearing; disengagement,** disentanglement, disembarrassment, disembroilment; dislodgement.

VERBS **4. liberate, free, deliver, set free,** set at liberty, set at large; **emancipate,** manumit, disenthrall or disinthrall; enfranchise, affranchise; rescue 700.2.

5. **release, unhand, let go, let loose, turn loose,** cast loose, let out, let off, let go free; **discharge, dismiss;** parole [U.S.], put on parole.

6. **loose,** loosen, unloose, unloosen; **unbind, untie,** unstrap, unlash, untruss, unpinion **unfetter, unshackle, unmanacle,** unchain, unhandcuff, untie one's hands; unleash, untether, unhobble; unharness, unyoke, uncollar, unbridle; unmuzzle, ungag; unlock unlatch, unbolt, unbar; uncoop, uncage.

7. **extricate, free, release, clear, get out;** disengage, disentangle, disembarrass, disembroil; dislodge, displant; cut loose, tear loose.

8. **free oneself from,** deliver oneself from, get free of, get quit of, **get rid of,** get clear of, **get out of,** get well out of; **throw off, shake off.**

9. **go free,** go scot free, go at liberty, get off, get out of.

ADJS. **10. liberated, freed, emancipated;** free 760.19; on parole.

INTERJS. **11. unhand me!,** unhand me, villain!, let go!, let me go!

762. SUBJECTION

NOUNS **1. subjection, subjugation; bondage, captivity; thrall,** thralldom, enthrallment, inthrallment; **slavery, enslavement; servitude,** bond service; **serfdom,** serfhood; vassalage, vassalism; helotry, helotism; villenage, villeinhood; peonage, peonism; feudalism; badge of slavery.

2. **subservience** or subserviency, subordinancy, **subordination, inferiority.**

3. **dependence** or dependency, slavish dependence; chargeship, wardship; clientship, clientage, cliency.

4. **subdual, quelling,** crushing, reduction, humbling, humiliation; breaking, taming; conquering 725.1; suppression 758.2.

5. **subject, vassal;** liege, liege man, liege subject; people.

6. **dependent, charge, ward,** trust, client, protégé, encumbrance; pensioner, pensionary; public charge.

7. **serf, vassal,** helot; **captive, thrall,** âme damnée [F., damned soul]; **slave,** servant; **bondman,** bondsman, bondslave; bondwoman, bondswoman, bondmaid, odalisque or odalisk; galley slave; villein or villain, churl or ceorl, theow [all hist.]; peon.

VERBS **8. subjugate, subject; enslave; enthrall,** inthrall, bethrall; **take captive,** lead captive or into captivity; **hold in subjection,** hold in bondage, **hold captive,** hold in captivity; **hold down,** keep down, keep under; **keep under one's thumb,** have at one's apron strings, hold in leash, hold in leading strings, hold in swaddling clothes, hold or keep at one's beck and call.

9. **subdue, master, quell, crush, reduce,** beat down, break down; suppress 758.8; conquer 725.10; bring under, **bring to terms; humble,** bend, **bring one to his knees; bend to one's will,** twist ∼, turn or wind around one's little finger, make lie down and roll over, **lead by the nose,** make a puppet of, make a sport or plaything of, use as a doormat, treat like dirt under one's feet; tread or trample under foot, roll or trample in the dust, drag at one's chariot wheel.

10. **break, bust** [slang, U.S.]; **tame,** gentle [coll. & dial.], break in, break to harness; housebreak.

11. **depend on, lean on,** be at the mercy of, not dare to say one's soul is his own.

ADJS. **12. subject, dependent; subservient, subordinate, inferior;** liege, vassal; feudal, feudatory.

13. **subjugated,** subjected, **enslaved, enthralled, captive, bond, unfree; in subjection, in bondage, in captivity,** in slavery, in bonds; **in one's power,** in one's control, in one's hands or clutches, in one's pocket, **under one's thumb,** at one's mercy, under one's command or orders, at one's beck and call, at one's feet, a slave to; in leading strings, tied to one's apron strings, led by the nose.

14. **subdued, quelled,** crushed, broken, reduced, humbled, brought to one's knees.

15. **downtrodden,** downtrod; **oppressed; abused,** misused; **henpecked, browbeaten;** treated like dirt under one's feet.

PREPS. 16. **under, below, beneath,** underneath, subordinate to; at the feet of; under the heel of.

763. SUBMISSION

NOUNS 1. **submission,** submittal, **yielding, compliance,** complaisance, **acquiescence; obedience** 764; subjection; **resignation,** resignedness; **deference,** subservience; **passivity,** passiveness, nonresistance.

2. **surrender,** cession, capitulation, renunciation, abandonment, relinquishment, backdown [coll.]; recession, recedence.

3. **submissiveness, docility,** tractability, yieldingness, compliableness, pliancy, pliability, flexibility, plasticity, facility.

4. **manageability, governability, controllability,** handleableness, corrigibility, towardness, towardliness, untroublesomeness.

5. **meekness, gentleness,** tameness, mildness, quietness, lamblikeness; humility 904.

VERBS 6. **submit, comply, acquiesce,** accede, relent, succumb, resign, resign oneself; **knuckle down** or **under,** knock under; **obey** 764.2; eat out of one's hand.

7. **yield, give way, give ground, back down,** give up, **give in,** cave in [coll.].

8. **surrender,** cede, capitulate, acknowledge defeat, **cry quits,** cry pax, **say uncle** [slang], **throw in the towel, toss** or **throw up the sponge** [coll.], show or wave the white flag, lower ∼, haul down or strike one's flag or colors, lay down or deliver up one's arms, hand over one's sword, deliver up the keys, yield the palm, draw in one's horns [coll.], come to terms.

9. **submit to, yield to, defer to,** bow to, give way to.

10. **bow down,** bow, bend, stoop, **bow one's head,** bend the neck, **bow submission; bow to,** bend to, **knuckle to** [coll.], bend or bow to one's will, bend to one's yoke; kneel to, **bend the knee to, fall on one's knees before,** crouch before, **fall at one's feet,** throw oneself at the feet of, prostrate oneself before, lie down to [slang]; **truckle to,** cringe to, kowtow, bow and scrape.

11. **eat dirt, eat crow, eat humble pie, lick the dust,** kiss the rod.

ADJS. 12. **submissive, compliant,** complaisant, complying, **acquiescent;** obedient 764.3; subject; **resigned,** uncomplaining; unassertive; **passive, unresisting,** nonresisting, unresistant, nonresistant.

13. **docile, tractable, yielding,** compliable, pliant, pliable, flexible, plastic, facile, like putty in one's hands.

14. **manageable, governable, controllable,** handleable, corrigible, restrainable, toward, towardly, untroublesome; domitable, tameable.

15. **meek, gentle, mild,** quiet, subdued, chastened; **tame,** tamed, broken; lamblike, gentle as a lamb; humble 904.9.

16. **deferential, obeisant, subserviant;** crouching, prostrate, on one's knees, on one's marrowbones [joc. or slang], on bended knee.

ADVS. 17. **submissively, compliantly,** complaisantly, **acquiescently;** obediently 764.6; **resignedly,** uncomplainingly, with resignation; **passively,** unresistingly, unresistantly.

18. **docilely, tractably, yieldingly,** compliably, pliantly, pliably, flexibly, plastically, facilely.

19. **meekly, gently, tamely, mildly,** quietly.

PHRS. 20. as you please, if you please, as you wish, as my lord wills, don't mind me.

764. OBEDIENCE

NOUNS 1. **obedience** or obediency, **compliance, acquiescence; submission** 763; **dutifulness,** duteousness; **observance,** attentiveness; law-abidingness.

VERBS 2. **obey, mind, heed, keep,** observe, regard, listen to; **comply,** yield obedience; **do what one is told,** do as one says, do the will of, do one's bidding, come at one's call, lie down and roll over [slang]; take orders, attend to orders, do suit and service, follow the lead of; answer the helm; **submit** 763.6.

ADJS. 3. **obedient, compliant,** complying, **acquiescent; submissive** 763.12; **dutiful,** duteous; loyal, faithful, devoted; lawabiding.

4. **at one's command,** at one's pleasure, at one's disposal, at one's nod, at one's call, **at one's beck and call.**

5. **henpecked, tied to one's apron strings,** on a string, on a leash, in leading strings.

ADVS. 6. **obediently, compliantly, acquiescently; submissively** 763.17; **dutifully,** duteously; loyally, faithfully, devotedly; in obedience to, in compliance with.

7. obediently yours, at your service, ∼ command *or* orders, as you please.

765. DISOBEDIENCE

NOUNS 1. disobedience, nonobedience; undutifulness, unduteousness; insubordination, unsubmissiveness, indocility, noncompliance, unresignedness; lawlessness, waywardness, frowardness; intractability 624.4.

2. refractoriness, recalcitrance, contumacy, contumaciousness, obstreperousness, unruliness, restiveness, fractiousness, orneriness [coll. *or* dial.]; breachiness.

3. rebelliousness, mutinousness, riotousness; insurrectionism, insurgentism; seditiousness.

4. revolt, rebellion; mutiny, mutineering; insurrection, insurgence, riot, *Putsch* [Ger.] *émeute* [F.]; uprising, rising, outbreak; general uprising, *levée en masse* [F.]; *Jacquerie* [F., peasant revolt]; sedition; revolution 147; strike 787.7.

5. rebel, revolter; insurgent, insurrectionist; mutineer; rioter, brawler; malcontent, *frondeur* [F.]; agitator 646.11; revolutionist 147.3; insubordinate.

VERBS 6. disobey, not mind, not heed, not keep *or* observe, not listen to, pay no attention to, ignore, disregard, defy, fly in the face of, go counter to, set at naught.

7. violate, transgress 767.4.

8. revolt, rebel, kick over the traces; rise up, rise, arise, rise up in arms; mutiny, mutineer; insurrect [coll.]; riot, run riot; revolutionize 147.4; strike 787.9.

ADJS. 9. disobedient, transgressive, violative, lawless, wayward, froward; undutiful, unduteous.

10. insubordinate, unsubmissive, indocile, incompliant, uncomplying, unresigned; intractable 624.12.

11. refractory, recalcitrant, contumacious, obstreperous, unruly, restive, resty [dial.], fractious, ornery [coll. *or* dial.]; breachy.

12. rebellious, rebel, rebelly [coll.]; mutinous, mutineering; insurgent, insurrectionary, insurrectional, riotous; seditious, seditionary; revolutionary 147.5.

ADVS. 13. disobediently, insubordinately, unsubmissively, indocilely, uncompliantly, unresignedly; intractably 624.17; obstreperously, contumaciously, restively, fractiously; rebelliously, mutinously.

766. OBSERVANCE

NOUNS 1. observance, observation; keeping, heeding; performance, practice, execution, discharge; acquittal, acquittance; fulfillment *or* fulfilment, satisfaction.

VERBS 2. observe, keep, heed, follow, regard, respect, comply with, conform to, abide by, adhere to; live up to, act up to; be faithful to, keep faith with, do justice to, do the right thing with; fulfill *or* fulfil, fill, meet, satisfy, fill the bill; make good, keep *or* make good one's word *or* promise, be as good as one's word, acquit oneself, redeem one's pledge, stand to one's engagement.

3. perform, practice, do, execute, discharge, carry out, carry into execution, do one's office.

ADJS. 4. observant, faithful, true, loyal, constant, as good as one's word; punctual, punctilious, scrupulous, meticulous.

767. NONOBSERVANCE

NOUNS 1. nonobservance, inobservance, unobservance; disregard 529.1; neglect 532; nonfulfillment *or* nonfulfilment, nonperformance; failure, dereliction, delinquency, omission, default, slight, oversight; dead letter.

2. violation, infraction, breach, break; infringement, transgression, trespass, contravention; offense 997.4; breach of promise, breach of trust *or* faith, breach of privilege; breach of the peace.

VERBS 3. disregard, pay no regard to 529.3; neglect 532.6.

4. violate, break; infringe, transgress, trespass, contravene, trench on, trample on *or* upon, trample under foot, drive a coach and four *or* six through, set at naught, take the law into one's own hands.

ADJS. 5. nonobservant, inobservant, unobservant; disregardful 529.6; negligent 532.10; unfaithful, untrue, unloyal, inconstant.

768. PROMISE

NOUNS 1. promise, pledge, troth, plight, parole, word, word of honor, solemn declaration *or* word; oath, vow 521.3; avowal, avowance, avouchment, avow; assurance, insurance, guarantee, warrant, warranty.

2. engagement, undertaking, commitment, agreement, obligation; contract 769; pre-engagement.

3. betrothal, betrothment, engagement,

affiance, troth, marriage contract *or* vow, plighted faith *or* love; banns.

VERBS 4. promise, give *or* make a promise, hold out an expectation; pledge, plight, give *or* pass one's word, give one's parole, give one's word of honor, plight one's troth, pledge *or* plight one's honor; swear 521.5; vow, avow, vouch, avouch; warrant, guarantee, assure.

5. engage, undertake, commit, agree, answer for, be answerable for, be bound to; contract 769.6.

6. affiance, affy, betroth, troth, plight one's troth, plight faith, pledge one's faith to, take the vows *or* marriage vows, engage *or* promise in marriage, contract marriage, become engaged; publish the banns.

ADJS. 7. promissory, votive; under *or* upon oath, on one's word, on one's word of honor, upon the Book, under hand and seal.

8. promised, pledged, bound, committed, compromised, in for it [coll.]; contracted 769.12; engaged, plighted, affianced, betrothed, intended [coll.].

PHRS. 9. I promise, I'll warrant 521.10.

769. COMPACT

NOUNS 1. compact, pact, contract, covenant, convention, agreement, stipulation, understanding, arrangement, entente, mise; bargain, dicker [chiefly coll., U.S.], deal [coll.], go [coll.], whiz *or* whizz [slang, U.S.]; cartel; protocol; bond, binding agreement, ironclad agreement; gentleman's agreement, *entente cordiale* [F.]; collective agreement; promise 768.

2. treaty, concord, concordat; alliance, league; capitulation; charter, charta, carta; Magna Charta *or* Carta, Atlantic Charter; NATO, North Atlantic Treaty Organization; SEATO, Southeast Asia Treaty Organization.

3. (contracts) indenture, indent; contract by deed, specialty; deed *or* covenant of indemnity, recognizance; policy [insurance].

4. arrangement, settlement, adjustment, conclusion, disposal, disposition, bundobust [India].

5. execution (as of a deed or contract), rendering, completion; discharge, fulfillment *or* fulfilment; transaction, prosecution; effectuation, enforcement.

VERBS 6. contract, covenant, bargain, agree, engage, stipulate, agree to, bargain for; promise 768.4; indent.

7. treat with, negotiate, bargain, make terms.

8. come to an agreement 520.10; strike a bargain 825.15.

9. arrange, settle, adjust, compose, fix, make up, straighten out; conclude, close, close with, settle with; dispose of, set at rest.

10. execute (as a deed or contract), complete; make, render; discharge, fulfill *or* fulfil, administer; carry out, carry through, put through; transact, prosecute; effect, effectuate; enforce, put in force; make out, fill out; sign, seal; sign, seal and deliver.

ADJS. 11. contractual, covenantal, conventional.

12. contracted, covenanted, agreed, bargained, engaged, stipulated; promised 768.8; arranged, settled; under hand and seal, signed, sealed; signed, sealed and delivered.

ADVS. 13. as agreed upon, as promised, as contracted for, according to the contract, ~ bargain *or* agreement.

770. SECURITY

Thing Given as a Pledge.—NOUNS 1. security, surety, indemnity; guaranty, guarantee; warranty, warrant; insurance, assurance; bond, tie; stocks and bonds 832.

2. pledge, gage, pignus [law], vadium [law]; earnest, handsel; pawn, hock [slang, U.S.]; bail, replevin, replevy; mainprise [hist.]; hostage.

3. deposit, stake, forfeit; caution money, caution; collateral, collateral security *or* warranty; margin.

4. deed, deed poll, deed of arrangement, deed of assumption; escrow; muniments, title deeds and papers.

5. mortgage, monkey [slang, Eng.]; vadium mortuum, dead pledge [both law]; vadium vivum, living pledge [both law]; antichresis; hypothec [law], hypothecation; bottomry, bottomry bond; blanket mortgage, closed mortgage, participating mortgage, leasehold mortgage, trust mortgage.

6. lien, real security; pignus legale, pignus judiciale [both law].

7. debenture, debenture bond, naked debenture, floating debenture, mortgage debenture.

8. guarantor, guaranty, guarantee, surety; insurer, underwriter; sponsor; godparent, godfather, godmother, bondsman, bailsman; mainpernor [hist.].

9. warrantee, guarantee; insuree,

policyholder; sponsoree; godchild, godson, goddaughter.

10. guarantorship, guaranteeship; **sponsorship**, sponsion.

VERBS 11. **guarantee, guaranty, warrant, assure, insure,** ensure, **certify,** secure; **sponsor,** be sponsor for, **back, stand behind,** stand for [coll.], stand up for; **endorse,** indorse; **underwrite,** undersign, subscribe to.

12. **pledge,** impignorate, handsel; **deposit, stake,** post, put up; **pawn,** put in pawn; **hock,** spout, put up the spout [all slang]; **mortgage,** hypothecate, bottomry; bond [U.S.]; **go bail.**

13. **patent, copyright.**

ADJS. 14. **guaranteed, warranted, certified, insured,** ensured, **assured, certain, sure.**

15. **pledged,** staked, posted, put up, on deposit, at stake, as earnest; **pawned,** in pawn, **in hock** [slang], up the spout [slang].

16. **in trust,** held in trust, held in pledge, fiduciary; **in escrow.**

771. OFFER

NOUNS 1. **offer, proffer, presentation, tender, bid, submission; advance,** advancement; **overture,** approach; **asking price.**

2. **proposal, proposition,** position, **suggestion,** instance, statement; **motion,** resolution.

3. **ultimatum,** last word, final offer.

VERBS 4. **offer, proffer present, tender, submit, extend,** prefer, **hold out,** hold forth, put forth, place in one's way, lay at one's feet, put or place at one's disposal; put up.

5. **propose,** proposition [slang], **submit, advance,** put forward, bring forward, put or set forth, hold forth, set up, put ~, set or lay before; **bring up, broach,** introduce, start; **move, make a motion.**

6. **propound, state, pose, moot, put it to,** put it up to [coll.]; postulate 498.12.

7. **bid,** bid for, make a bid.

8. **make advances,** approach, overture, make an overture.

9. **urge upon, press upon,** ply upon, push upon, force upon, thrust upon; **press, ply;** insist 751.7.

10. **volunteer, come forward, offer** or **present oneself,** be at one's service; **bid for, stand for.**

772. REQUEST

NOUNS 1. **request,** asking; **desire, wish,** expressed desire; **petition, suit, address; requisition,** application; **demand** 751; **touch** [slang]; round robin (a begging letter).

2. **entreaty, appeal, plea, call,** cry; **supplication, prayer, rogation** [eccl.], **beseechment, imploration,** impetration, obsecration, obtestation, adjuration, imprecation; **invocation,** solemn entreaty, invocatory plea or prayer.

3. **importunity, urging, pressing, plying,** taxing, dunning; **teasing,** pestering, plaguing; **coaxing,** wheedling, cajolery, cajolement, blandishment.

4. **invitation, invite** [coll.], **bid** [coll., U.S.], bidding, biddance, **call, calling, summons.**

5. **solicitation, canvass; suit, addresses; courting, wooing.**

6. **beggary, mendicity,** mendicancy; **begging,** mooching [slang], cadging [coll.], bumming [slang, U.S.], **panhandling** [slang].

7. **petitioner, supplicant, suppliant, suitor; solicitor** 828.7; **applicant, solicitant, claimant, aspirant, seeker; candidate,** postulant; **bidder.**

8. **beggar, mendicant, moocher** [slang], cadger [coll.], mumper, **panhandler** [slang], schnorrer [Yiddish], fakir [India], sannyasi [India]; **bum,** bummer [both slang, U.S.]; hobo, tramp 273.3; loafer 706.7, 8.

VERBS 9. **request, ask,** make a request, beg leave, make bold to ask; **desire, wish,** express a wish for; **ask for,** bespeak, **call for,** trouble one for, whistle for [coll.]; **requisition,** make a requisition, make application, **apply for,** file for, **put in for; demand** 751.4.

10. **petition,** prefer a petition, **pray, sue; apply to, put to, call on** or **upon;** memorialize.

11. **entreat, implore, beseech, beg, crave, plead, appeal; pray, supplicate,** impetrate; **adjure, conjure; invoke,** imprecate; **call on** or **upon, cry on** or **upon, appeal to, cry to;** kneel to, fall on one's knees, throw oneself at the feet of, get or come down on one's marrowbones [slang]; plead for, clamor for, cry for; raise or lift up one's voice, cry aloud; call for help.

12. **importune, urge, press, push, ply,** tax, dun, **beset, besiege,** set upon, work on [coll.], run hard; **tease, pester, plague; coax, wheedle, cajole, blandish.**

13. **invite, ask, call,** bid [chiefly dial.], **summon, call in, bid come,** issue an invitation, request the presence of, request the pleasure of one's company.

14. **solicit, canvass,** tout [coll.]; **court, woo, sue,** make interest; **seek, bid for,** put up for [slang]; fish for, angle for.

15. go a-begging, **beg, mooch** [slang], mump, **cadge** [coll.], **bum** [slang, U.S.], **panhandle** [slang]; **hit up, touch,** make a touch [all slang]; pass the hat [coll.].

ADJS. 16. **solicitous,** cap in hand; **supplicatory, suppliant,** supplicant, supplicating; **prayerful;** invocative, invocatory; **petitionary; begging,** mendicant; on one's knees or bended knees, on one's marrowbones [slang].

17. **imploring, entreating, beseeching, pleading, appealing,** imploratory, imprecatory, precatory.

18. **importunate, urgent** 751.8; **teasing,** pestering, plaguing; **coaxing,** wheedling, cajoling.

19. **invitational,** inviting, invitatory.

INTERJS. ETC. 20. **please,** pretty please, prithee [arch.], pray, do, **pray do,** be so good as, be good enough, have the goodness, will you, may it please you; **if you please,** *s'il vous plaît* [F.]; I beg you, *je vous prie* [F.]; for God's ∼, goodness ∼, heaven's or mercy's sake!

773. CONSENT

NOUNS 1. **consent, assent, agreement, acceptance, approval; permission** 775; **willingness,** unreluctance, unloathness, ungrudgingness.

2. **acquiescence, compliance, concession,** accession, accedence.

VERBS 3. **consent, assent,** give consent, yield assent, say yes; **accept, agree to,** hear to [coll.]; approve, **approve of,** hold with, be in favor of, take kindly to; **be willing,** turn a willing ear; have no objection, not refuse; permit 775.10.

4. **acquiesce, comply with,** fall in with, **concede, accede, yield, give in,** back down, come round or around, come over, come to; **deign, vouchsafe,** deign to, condescend to.

ADJS. 5. **consenting, assenting,** approving, agreeing, accordant; consentient, consentant, consentive; **acquiescent, compliant,** compliable; **willing, agreeable,** content; unreluctant, unloath, nothing loath, ungrudging, unrefusing; permissive 775.15.

ADVS. 6. **consentingly, assentingly,** approvingly, agreeably, accordingly; acquiescently, compliantly, compliably; willingly 620.8.

7. **yes** 520.18.

774. REFUSAL

NOUNS 1. **refusal, rejection;** nonconsent, nonacceptance, noncompliance; **declination,** declension, declinature; **denial,** disclamation, disclaimer, disallowance; negation, abnegation; unwillingness 621.

2. **repulse, rebuff,** peremptory ∼, flat or point-blank refusal.

VERBS 3. **refuse, decline,** not consent, refuse consent; **reject, turn down** [slang], decline to accept, not buy [slang]; not think of, not hear of or to [coll.]; **say no,** negative, negate, abnegate; be unwilling 621.3; **turn thumbs down on,** thumb down [both slang]; turn one's back upon, turn a deaf ear to, set oneself against, set one's face against, stand aloof, have nothing to do with, wash one's hands of; hold out [against]; put or set one's foot down [coll.], refuse point blank; decline with thanks.

4. **deny, disclaim, disallow, withhold,** hold back, put back; grudge, begrudge; close the hand or purse.

5. **repulse, rebuff, repel,** shut or slam the door in one's face, turn away, send to the rightabout [coll.], send away with a flea in the ear [coll.]; deny oneself to, refuse to receive, not be at home to.

ADJS. 6. **unconsenting,** nonconsenting; **unwilling** 621.5; **uncompliant,** uncomplying, uncomplaisant, inacquiescent; rejective, declinatory; deaf to, not willing to hear of.

7. **out of the question,** not to be thought of, impossible.

ADVS. 8. **no,** by no means 522.7, 8.

PHRS. 9. I refuse, I won't, I will not, I will no such thing, far be it from me, not if I can help it, not if I know it, not on your life, count me out, I'm not taking any, it's no go, like fun I will, I'll be hanged if I will, catch me, try and make me, you have another guess coming, you should live so long, I'll see you in hell first; nothing doing, nuts to you [both slang].

775. PERMISSION

NOUNS 1. **permission, leave, allowance,** admission, accordance, vouchsafement;

consent 773; **license, liberty;** the go-ahead, the green light [both coll.].

2. **sufferance, tolerance,** toleration, **indulgence,** countenance, connivance.

3. **authorization, authority, sanction, warrant,** warranty; empowerment or **impowerment,** entitlement or intitlement, enfranchisement, certification; ratification 520.4.

4. **carte blanche, full authority,** full power, free hand.

5. **grant, concession;** charter, charta, carta; royal grant, purwannah [Anglo-Ind.], firman [Orient.].

6. **permit, license, warrant;** brevet; fiat; imprimatur.

7. **pass, passport, safe-conduct,** *passepartout* [F.], safeguard, protection, warrant of security; clearance, clearance papers.

8. **patent, copyright,** letters patent, certificate of invention, *brevet d'invention* [F.].

9. **permissibility, allowableness, admissibility;** warrantableness, sanctionableness; legitimacy, lawfulness, licitness, legality.

VERBS 10. **permit, allow, let,** leave [dial.], give permission, give leave; **consent** 773.3; **grant, admit,** accord, vouchsafe; give the go-ahead, give the green light [both coll.].

11. **suffer, countenance,** have, **tolerate,** bear with, put up with, stand for [coll.], hear to [coll.]; shut one's eyes to, wink at, blink at, connive at.

12. **authorize, sanction, warrant,** entitle or intitle; **empower** or impower, give power, **enable; license, privilege;** charter; enfranchise, franchise; certificate; ratify 520.12.

13. **give carte blanche,** give full power or authority, give a free hand, leave alone, leave it to one, leave the door open.

14. **may, can** (loosely), have permission, be permitted or allowed.

ADJS. 15. **permissive,** admissive, permitting, allowing; consenting 773.5; **unprohibitive,** nonprohibitive; **tolerative,** tolerating, suffering, **tolerant, indulgent.**

16. **permissible, allowable, admissible;** warrantable, sanctionable; licit, lawful, legitimate, legal.

17. **permitted,** permissioned, **allowed,** admitted; tolerated, on sufferance; unprohibited, unforbidden; unconditional.

18. **authorized,** empowered or impow-

ered, entitled or intitled; **warranted, sanctioned; licensed, privileged;** chartered; franchised, enfranchised; patented, patent; copyrighted, copyright.

ADVS. 19. **permissively,** admissively; **tolerantly, indulgently,** nothing loath.

20. **permissibly, allowably,** admissibly; with permission, *avec permission* [F.], by one's leave; licitly, lawfully, legitimately, legally.

PHRS. 21. **by your leave,** with your permission, if you please, may I?

776. PROHIBITION

NOUNS 1. **prohibition, forbiddance,** forbiddal; **disallowance,** denial; **ban, embargo, injunction, proscription,** inhibition; **interdict,** interdiction; **taboo** or tabu, no-no [child's word]; forbidden fruit; Eighteenth Amendment, Volstead Act [both U.S.].

2. **veto, negative;** absolute veto, qualified or limited negative or veto, suspensive or suspensory veto, item veto, pocket veto [U.S.].

VERBS 3. **prohibit, inhibit, forbid, disallow,** deny, withhold, say no to; **bar,** debar, preclude, exclude, exclude from, shut out, shut the door; **ban,** put under the ban; **enjoin,** put under an injunction; **proscribe, interdict,** put under an interdiction; embargo, **lay** or **put an embargo on; taboo** or tabu; warn off; forbid the banns.

4. **not permit** or **allow, not have, not suffer** or **tolerate,** not countenance, not put up with; not stand for, not hear of, put or set one's foot down on [all coll.].

5. **veto,** put one's veto upon, **negative,** kill.

ADJS. 6. **prohibitive, prohibitory,** prohibiting, **forbidding;** inhibitive, inhibitory; proscriptive, interdictive, interdictory; preclusive, exclusive.

7. **prohibited, forbidden,** forbade, forbad, forbid, *verboten* [Ger.]; **unpermissible,** nonpermissible, not permitted or allowed, **unallowed,** disallowed, out of the question, not to be thought of; unauthorized, unsanctioned, unlicensed; banned, under the ban, contraband; taboo or tabu, untouchable.

INTERJS. 8. **don't!,** enough!, stop!, desist!, forbear!, leave off!, hands off!, no more of that!, that will never do!; cut it out!, lay off!, cheese it!, can it!, nix!, ixnay!, nix on that! [all slang].

777. REPEAL

NOUNS 1. repeal, revocation, revokement, rescindment, rescission, recall, retraction, abrogation, withdrawal, reversal; countermand, counterorder; renege, renig [coll.]; annulment, nullification, invalidation, vacation, vacatur [law], defeasance [law]; cancellation, cancel, write-off; abolition, abolishment.

VERBS 2. repeal, revoke, rescind, reverse, abrogate, retract, recall, call back, take back, withdraw; renege, renig [coll.]; countermand, counterorder; abolish, do away with; cancel, write off; annul, nullify, disannul, invalidate, vacate, avoid [law], make void, declare null and void; overrule, override, set aside.

ADJS. 3. invalid, void, null and void.

778. COMMISSION

Vicarious Authority.—NOUNS 1. commission, delegation, deputation; assignment, consignment; errand, task, office; mission, legation, embassy; authority, authorization; warrant, license, mandate, charge, trust, brevet, diploma, exequatur; agency, agentship; proxy, procuration, power of attorney.

2. appointment, constitution, assignment, designation, nomination, naming, selection; ordainment, ordination.

3. installation, installment, instatement, induction, inauguration, investiture, placement; accession, accedence, attainment; coronation, enthronement.

4. engagement, employment; retainment, briefing [Eng., law]; pre-engagement, bespeaking; reservation (as of seats); booking; featherbedding (labor union requirement to employ unneeded workmen).

5. hiring, hire; rental, rent; lease, let [coll., Eng.], demise; lend-lease.

6. enlistment, enrollment; conscription, draft, induction, impressment, press, detachment, call, call-up, summons, call to the colors, letter from Uncle Sam [U.S.]; recruitment, recruital, recruiting; mobilization, muster, levy; Selective Service [U.S.], compulsory military service; separation center.

7. indenture, binding over; apprenticeship.

8. assignee, consignee, committee; appointee, selectee, nominee, candidate; licensee, licentiate; garnishee; assignee in fact [law].

VERBS 9. commission, authorize, empower or impower, accredit; delegate, depute, deputize; assign, consign; commit, convey, charge, entrust or intrust, give in charge; detail, detach [mil.], send out, mission, send on a mission.

10. appoint, constitute, assign, designate, nominate, name, select; ordain, ordinate.

11. install, instate, induct, inaugurate, invest, place, put in, place in office; chair, enchair; crown, throne, enthrone; accede, attain to.

12. engage, contract for; bespeak, preengage, secure or bespeak the services of; employ, give a job, put on, take on, hire on [coll.], sign up or on [coll.]; retain, brief [Eng., law]; reserve (as seats); book.

13. hire, hire out; lease, let, let out, demise; rent, rent out; charter; subrent, sublease, sublet, underlet; farm, job; lend-lease, lease-lend.

14. enlist, list, enroll, sign up or on [coll.]; conscript, draft, induct, press, impress, commandeer, detach, detach for service, summon, select, call up, call to active duty, call to the colors; recruit, mobilize, muster, levy, raise, muster in [U.S.]; beat up for recruits.

15. indenture, indent, article, bind, bind over; apprentice.

ADJS. 16. commissioned, authorized, accredited; delegated, deputized, appointed; noncommissioned.

17. hired, hireling, paid, mercenary, venal; let, leased; chartered.

18. indentured, articled, bound over; apprenticed, prentice or 'prentice.

ADVS. 19. for hire, for rent, to let, to lease.

779. DEPUTY, AGENT

NOUNS 1. deputy, proxy, representative, substitute, alternate, alter ego, surrogate, secondary, dummy, stand-in, pinch hitter [coll.]; exponent, advocate, champion; lieutenant, vicar; locum tenens, locum [coll.]; friend at or in court, amicus curiae [law]; next friend, prochein ami [both law].

2. delegate, legate; commissioner, commissary, commissionaire, commissar [Russia], dubash [India]; messenger, emissary, envoy; walking delegate.

3. agent, instrument, tool; steward, factor, proctor, procurator, functionary, gomashta [India], institor, one's man of

business; clerk, secretary; underagent; general agent, special agent; actor's agent, claim agent, commission agent, freight agent, land agent, loan agent, passenger agent, purchasing agent, sales agent, station agent, ticket agent, traveling agent.

4. go-between, middleman, intermediary, medium, intermedium, intermediate, interagent, internuncio, broker; connection [U.S.], front, front man [all crim. slang, U.S.]; negotiator, negotiant, negotiatress or negotiatrix [fem.]; interpleader [law]; mediator 803.3.

5. spokesman, spokeswoman, spokester, speaker, mouthpiece; prolocutor, prolocutress or prolocutrice or prolocutrix [fem.]; interlocutor, interlocutress or interlocutrice or interlocutrix [fem.].

6. diplomat, diplomatist, diplomatic agent, diplomatic; emissary, envoy, legate, minister; ambassador, ambassadress; plenipotentiary, minister plenipotentiary, ambassador extraordinary; ambassador-at-large; nuncio, internuncio; vice-legate; resident, minister resident; chargé d'affaires; consul, consul general, vice-consul, proconsul [Rom. antiq.], consular agent; Foreign Service officer [U.S.], executive agent, colonial agent; attaché, chancellor, councilor of embassy; career man or diplomat, careerist.

7. foreign office, Foreign Service [U.S.]; diplomatic staff or corps, corps diplomatique [F.]; embassy, legation.

8. vice-agent, vice [coll.]; vice-president, vice-chairman, vice-governor, vice-director, vice-master, vice-dean, vice-dictator; vice-warden, vice-provost; vice-general, vice-admiral; regent, vice-regent, viceroy, vicegerent, vicar, vice-emperor, vice-king, vice-sultan, vice-caliph; vice-queen, vicereine; vice-priest, vice-pope, vice-bishop, vice-abbot, vice-prefect, vice-prior, vice-rector.

9. secret agent, emissary, undercover man, inside man [slang]; spy, espier; spotter [U.S.]; scout, tout [slang], reconnoiterer; intelligence agent or officer.

10. detective, operative [U.S.], investigator, sleuth [U.S.], man hunter, Sherlock Holmes; hawkshaw, sleuthhound, beagle [all coll.]; dick, tec, gumshoe, gumshoe man, flatfoot, busy, nose [all slang]; police detective, plain-clothes man [coll.], mouchard [F.], bull or fly bull [slang, U.S.]; private detective, private eye [coll.], private-inquiry agent; hotel detective, house dick [slang, U.S.]; arson investigator; federal agent, G-man [coll., U.S.]; Federal Bureau of Investigation, F.B.I. [U.S.].

11. secret service, S.S.; intelligence bureau or department; intelligence, military intelligence, counterintelligence.

12. (group of delegates) delegation, deputation, commission, mission; committee, subcommittee.

VERBS 13. represent, act for, substitute for, stand for, appear for, answer for, hold a brief for, act in the place of, fill one's shoes, stand in the stead of, serve in one's stead; front for, go to the front for [both slang].

ADJS. 14. deputy, deputative; acting, representative; vice, vicegerent.

15. diplomatic(al), consular, ambassadorial, ministerial.

PREPS. 16. by proxy, in behalf of 148.12.

780. PROMOTION, DEMOTION

NOUNS 1. promotion, preferment, advancement, advance, boost [coll.], raise, elevation, upgrading [U.S.]; exaltation, aggrandizement; ennoblement; graduation, passing.

2. demotion, degrading, downgrading [U.S.], debasement, abasement, reduction, Irish promotion [joc.]; bump, bust [both slang].

VERBS 3. promote, prefer, advance, boost [coll.], raise, elevate, upgrade [U.S.]; kick upstairs [joc.]; exalt, aggrandize; ennoble, knight, esquire; pass, graduate.

4. demote, degrade, downgrade [U.S.], debase, abase, reduce, lower, give an Irish promotion [joc.]; bump, bust [both slang].

781. DEPOSAL

Removal from Office.—NOUNS 1. deposal, deposition, removal, suspension, retirement, displacement, deprivation, ousting, cashiering, unseating; dismissal 308.5, purge, liquidation; overthrow, overthrowal; dethronement, disenthronement, discrownment; disbarment, disbarring, disbenching; discanonization; unfrocking, unchurching, secularization.

VERBS 2. depose, remove from office, divest or deprive of office, remove, suspend, retire, displace, oust, cashier, break, bust [slang]; dismiss 308.18; purge, liquidate; overthrow; unseat, unsaddle; dethrone, disenthrone, unthrone, uncrown, discrown, disbar, disbench; discanonize; unfrock, unchurch, secularize; address out of office, read out of.

782. RESIGNATION

Retirement from Office.—NOUNS **1. resignation,** demission, **retirement,** retiral, **withdrawal; abdication;** relinquishment 631.3.

VERBS **2. resign, retire,** demit, **quit,** leave, **vacate,** withdraw from; relinquish, give up 631.7; retire from office, give up one's post, hang up one's ax [coll.]; **tender** or **hand in one's resignation,** send in one's papers; **abdicate,** renounce the throne, give up the crown.

ADJS. **3. retired,** disengaged, in retirement.

783. AID

NOUNS **1. aid, help, assistance, succor, relief, service, benefit,** accommodation; ministry, ministration; yeoman's service.

2. assist, helping hand, hand, lift, boost [slang, U.S.], leg up; help in time of need, help at a dead lift.

3. support, maintenance, sustainment, sustentation, **sustenance,** subsistence, provision; **keep,** upkeep; **livelihood,** living, meat, bread, daily bread; **nurture, nourishment;** manna, manna in the wilderness.

4. patronage, fosterage, tutelage, sponsorship, auspices, aegis, **care, guidance, championship, countenance, favor, interest,** advocacy, **encouragement, backing, abetment.**

5. furtherance, advancement, advance, **promotion, forwarding,** facilitation, speeding, expedition.

6. self-help, self-helpfulness, **self-support,** self-sustainment, self-improvement.

7. helper, assistant 785.6; **benefactor** 940.

8. reinforcements, support, relief, auxiliaries, succors, contingents, recruits.

9. facility, accommodation, appliance, convenience, advantage.

10. helpfulness; favorableness, beneficialness; **usefulness,** serviceability; **advantageousness,** profitability.

VERBS **11. aid, help, assist, succor, relieve; benefit, avail,** be of some help, do good, do a world of good; **favor, befriend; give help,** come to the aid of, lend one's aid, give ~, **lend** or **bear a hand** or **helping hand,** turn a hand, stretch forth a helping hand; **give an assist, give a leg up,** give a shoulder, give a lift, boost [slang], help a lame dog over a stile; **set up,** put on one's feet, give new life to, be the making of; see one through.

12. support, lend support, give ~, furnish or afford support, **sustain, maintain, keep,** upkeep, **uphold,** hold up, bear, upbear, **bear up,** bear out, bolster, **bolster up,** buttress, prop, prop up, crutch.

13. back, back up, stand behind, stand back of, get behind, get in behind, get in back of; **stand by,** stick by, stick up for [coll.]; **second, take the part of,** take up ~, adopt or espouse the cause of, make interest for, **go to bat for** [slang], take up the cudgels for, run interference for [coll.]; side with, take sides with.

14. abet, aid and abet, encourage, advocate, hold a brief for [coll.], **countenance,** keep in countenance, **endorse, lend oneself to,** lend one's countenance to, lend one's favor or support to, lend one's name to, give one's support or countenance to, give moral support to; **subscribe to,** contribute to, **favor,** go for [coll.], smile upon, shine upon.

15. patronize, sponsor, promote, take up.

16. foster, nurture, nourish, feed, sustain, cultivate, **cherish,** fondle; **nurse,** suckle, cradle; dry-nurse, wet-nurse.

17. further, forward, advance, promote, favor advantage, **facilitate,** set ~, put or push forward, give an impulse to, speed, expedite, quicken, hasten, lend wings to.

18. serve, render service, do service for, **work for, labor in behalf of; minister to,** pander to, cater to; wait on or upon, attend.

19. oblige, accommodate, favor, do a favor, do a service.

ADJS. **20. helping,** assisting, serving; **assistant, auxiliary,** adjuvant, **subservient,** subsidiary, ancillary; **accessory, accessary; ministerial,** ministering, ministrant.

21. helpful, aidful, helpsome [dial.]; **beneficial, profitable, salutary,** good for; **useful, serviceable;** contributory, conducive, furthersome [chiefly Scot.]; **at one's service,** at one's command, at one's beck and call.

22. favorable, advantageous, propitious; well-disposed, well-affected, **well-intentioned, well-meant, well-meaning.**

23. self-helpful, self-helping, self-improving; **self-supporting, self-sustaining;** self-supported, self-sustained.

ADVS. **24. helpfully,** helpingly; **usefully,** serviceably; **beneficially,** favorably, profitably, advantageously, to advantage, to the good.

PREPS. 25. helped by, with the help or assistance of, by the aid of; by means of 656.8.

26. for, on or in behalf of, in the name of, on account of, on the part of, for the sake of, in the service of, in furtherance of, in favor of.

27. behind, back of [coll., U.S.], supporting, in support of.

784. CO-OPERATION

NOUNS 1. co-operation, co-operancy, collaboration, co-working, coaction, concurrence, concert, teamwork; joint effort, common effort, mutual assistance, collective action, union in action; coadjument, coadjuvancy; coefficiency, coefficacy; co-agency, coadministration; synergy, synergism [both physiol.]; co-operativeness, collaborativeness.

2. collusion, complicity 652.6.

3. affiliation, alliance, alignment, association, combination, union, unification, coalition, fusion, league, federation, confederation, confederacy, consolidation, incorporation; hookup, tie-up, tie-in [all coll.]; partnership, copartnership, cahoots [slang]; fraternity, confraternity, fraternization, fraternalism; fellowship, sodality, comradeship, colleagueship, freemasonry.

VERBS 4. co-operate, collaborate, co-work, coact, concur, concert, coadjuvate; work together, act together, pull together, hold or hang together, keep together, stand together, stand shoulder to shoulder, lay one's heads together, league ~, band or club together, be in league with, unite one's efforts, act in concert, join in, play ball [coll.], work to one end.

5. conspire, collude 652.10.

6. side with, take sides with, join, join with, join up with [slang], unite with, strike in with, throw in with [slang], swing in with [coll.], go along with, line up with [coll.], align with, range with, stand up with, stand in with [slang], join hands with, go hand in hand with, act with, take part with, go in with, cast in one's lot with, join one's fortunes with, make common cause with, pool one's interests; go in partnership with, go or go in cahoots with [slang]; enlist under the banner of, rally round, flock to.

ADJS. 7. co-operative, co-operating, co-operant; collaborative, coactive, coacting,

co-working, coefficient; concurrent, concurring, concerted; combined 52.5; coadjuvant, coadjutant, coadjutive; synergetic, synergistic; uncompetitive, noncompetitive.

8. conniving, collusive 652.14.

ADVS. 9. co-operatively, co-operatingly, coactively, concurrently, jointly, conjointly, concertedly, in concert with, together, with, as one, as one man; side by side, hand in hand, hand in glove, shoulder to shoulder, back to back, "all for one, one for all" [Dumas].

10. in co-operation, in collaboration, in partnership, in cahoots [slang], in collusion.

785. CONFEDERATE

NOUNS 1. confederate, associate, consociate, colleague, companion, fellow, attendant, consort, confrere, ally, auxiliary, adjunct; comrade 926.4.

2. partner, pardner [slang, chiefly U.S.], pard [slang, U.S.], mate, teammate, comate, copartner, side partner, side-kick or sidekicker [slang, U.S.]; nominal ~, holding-out or quasi partner, general partner, special partner, ostensible partner, silent partner; secret partner, dormant or sleeping partner, dummy.

3. accomplice, fellow conspirator, abettor, partner or accomplice in crime; particeps criminis, socius criminis [both L., law]; accessory, accessory before the fact, accessory after the fact.

4. collaborator, co-operator, coactor; co-author; collaborationist.

5. co-worker, cohelper, coaid, workfellow, fellow worker, butty [dial., Eng.]; teammate, yokefellow, yokemate; benchfellow, shopmate.

6. assistant, helper, aider, aid, help, helpmate, helpmeet, helping hand, arm of flesh; attendant, second, acolyte, dry nurse [slang]; servant 748; adjutant, adjuvant; coadjutant, coadjutor, coadjuvant; coadjutress, coadjutrix; aide-de-camp.

7. right-hand man, right hand, man Friday; henchman, flunky, stooge [slang], lackey, gillie, jackal, minion, myrmidon.

8. supporter, upholder, maintainer, sustainer, support; mainstay, stand-by [coll.], reliance, dependence; abettor, seconder, second; candleholder, bottleholder [coll.]; backer, promoter, angel [slang], patron, Maecenas, friend at or in court; champion, advocate, exponent,

protagonist; **well-wisher,** favorer, encourager, sympathizer; **partisan,** sectary, votary.

786. ASSOCIATION

Body of Associates.—NOUNS **1. association, society; alliance, coalition, league, union,** bloc, axis; **federation, confederation,** confederacy; **combination,** combine [coll., U.S.]; *Bund, Verein* [both Ger.]; **gang, ring,** tong [Chin.], bund [slang, U.S.]; plunderbund [coll., U.S.]; machine; Sonderbund [Swiss hist.]; customs union, Zollverein [Ger.].

2. group, band 74.3.

3. community, society, commonwealth, family, body; colony, settlement; familistery, *familistère* [F.].

4. fellowship, sodality; **society, guild,** order; **brotherhood, fraternity,** confraternity, fraternal order; **sisterhood, sorority; club,** country club [U.S.].

5. party (body of partisans), **interest, side; faction,** division, **sect,** wing, splinter group; the interests.

6. school, college; **sect,** class, order; **denomination, communion,** church; **persuasion, ism;** disciples, followers, adherents, imitators.

7. clique, coterie, set, knot, **circle, ring,** junto, junta, cabal, camarilla, camp, **clan, club,** group, push [slang], mob [slang]; **crowd, bunch,** outfit [all coll.]; cell, inner circle.

8. organization, establishment, foundation, institution, institute.

9. company, firm, concern, house; business, **industry, enterprise,** business establishment, commercial enterprise; **partnership,** copartnership; **corporation,** corporate body, body corporate; joint-stock company; **merger,** consolidating company; **trust, syndicate, cartel,** pool, consortium; **monopoly,** combination in restraint of trade; stock company 831.15; holding company; operating company; utility, public utility.

10. branch, organ, division, wing, arm, offshoot; **affiliate, associate;** chapter [U.S.], lodge (of a secret society), post (of a veterans' organization [U.S.]); **local;** branch office.

11. member, belonger, insider, cardholder; **enrollee,** enlistee; **associate,** socius; **fellow;** brother, sister; honorary member; member in good standing; charter member; clubman, clubwoman, clubber, clubbist; fraternity man, sorority woman;

guildsman; committeeman; conventionist, conventioner; joiner [coll.]; pledge.

12. membership, members, associates, **personnel,** constituency; belonging.

13. partisanism, partisanship, **partiality; factionalism, sectionalism,** faction; sectarianism, denominationalism; **cliquism,** cliquishness, cliquyness; **clannishness,** clanship; party spirit, *esprit de corps* [F.]; the old college spirit.

VERBS **14. join,** join up [slang], **enter, go into,** come into; **enlist, enroll, sign up** *or* **on** [coll.], take up membership; associate oneself with, affiliate with [U.S.], league with.

15. belong, hold membership, be a member.

ADJS. **16. associational, social, society, communal;** organizational; coalitional; clubbable [coll.].

17. cliquish, cliquy, **clannish.**

18. partisan, party; **partial,** interested; **factional, sectional;** sectarian, sectary, denominational.

787. LABOR UNION

NOUNS **1. labor union,** trade union, trades union [esp. Eng.], trade guild [Eng.]; organized labor; craft union, horizontal union; industrial union, vertical union; independent union, wildcat union [U.S.]; local, local union; company union.

2. union shop, preferential shop, closed shop [U.S.], open shop [U.S.].

3. labor unionist, trade unionist, trades unionist [esp. Eng.], unionist, cardholder, brass man [slang, U.S.].

4. striker, walkouter [slang, U.S.]; sit-down striker; holdout, holdouter (one who "holds out" for higher pay [both slang]).

5. (strike enforcer) **picket; goon** [slang, U.S.], strong-arm man; goon squad [slang, U.S.].

6. strikebreaker, scab [slang], **rat** [slang], **fink** [slang, U.S.], **blackleg** [Eng.], scissorbill [slang, West. U.S.].

7. strike, walkout [coll., U.S.], turnout [coll., esp. Eng.], tie-up [U.S.], hartal [India]; revolt 765.4; sit-down strike, sitdown, slowdown; wildcat strike, outlaw strike; quickie [slang, U.S.]; sympathy strike; **boycott,** boycottage; buyer's strike.

8. lockout, shutout.

VERBS **9. strike, go on strike, go out, walk out,** turn out; revolt 765.8; sit down; **boycott;** picket; hold out for [coll.].

10. lock out, bar, bar out, shut out.

11. scab [slang], rat [slang], fink [slang, U.S.], blackleg [Eng.], break strike.

788. OPPOSITION

NOUNS 1. opposition, opposing, opposure; resistance 790; counteraction, counterworking; contradiction, contravention; impugnation, impugnment; crosscurrent, undercurrent, head wind.

2. hostility, antagonism, repugnance, oppugnance or oppugnancy, antipathy, inimicality; contrariness, contrariety; conflict, clashing, collision.

VERBS 3. oppose, counter, counteract, counterwork, cross, antagonize, go or act in opposition to, go against, run against, run counter to, fly in the face of; set oneself against, set one's face against, turn one's back upon; take issue with, take one's stand against; make a stand against, make a dead set against.

4. resist, withstand 790.3.

5. contend against, militate against, contest, combat, battle, fight against, strive against, struggle against, labor against, put up a fight or struggle [coll.], grapple with, fight, buck [coll.], buffet, beat against, beat up against; breast, stem, breast or stem the tide, ~ current or flood, breast the wave, buffet the waves.

6 confront, affront, encounter, meet, face.

7. contradict, contravene, oppugn, belie, gainsay; be contrary to, come in conflict with, be or play at cross-purposes.

8. be against, be agin [dial.]; discountenance 967.10, 11; not hold with, not have anything to do with.

ADJS. 9. oppositional, opponent, opposing, opposed; anti [coll.], adverse; contrary, counter, opposite, oppositive, overthwart, cross, antithetic(al); contradictory, oppugnant; unfavorable, unpropitious; hostile, antagonistic(al), repugnant, unfriendly, inimical, alien, antipathetic(al); conflicting, clashing.

10. in opposition, at variance, at cross-purposes, at odds, at issue, at war with, up in arms, with crossed bayonets, at daggers drawn, in hostile array.

ADVS., PREPS. 11. opposed to, adverse to, counter to, in opposition to, in conflict with, at cross-purposes; against, agin [dial.], dead against; versus, vs.; con, contra; contrariwise, counter, cross, athwart.

789. OPPONENT

NOUNS 1. opponent, adversary, antagonist, assailant, foe, enemy, adverse party; combatant 798; the opposition.

2. competitor, contestant, contender, player, entrant; rival, corrival, emulator; the field.

3. oppositionist, opposer; obstructionist, obstructive; disputant, litigant; wrangler, brawler.

790. RESISTANCE

NOUNS 1. resistance, withstanding; opposition 788; stand, front; repulsion, repellence or repellency, repulse, rebuff; reaction, countertendency, repugnance or repugnancy, renitence or renitency; recalcitrance or recalcitrancy, recalcitration.

VERBS 2. resist, withstand, stand, stand up, bear up, hold up, hold out; be proof against, bear up against; repel, repulse.

3. offer resistance, withstand, stand, take one's stand, make a stand, make a stand against, take one's stand against, stand up to, stand up against, stand at bay, set one's face against, fly in the face of, put up a front; face up to, face down, face out; reluct, make a determined resistance; kick against, recalcitrate, kick against the pricks; put up a fight or struggle [coll.], not take lying down.

4. oppose 788.3; strive against 788.5.

5. stand fast, stand or hold one's ground, make a resolute stand, hold one's own, remain firm, stick, stick fast, stick to one's guns, stay it out, stick it out [coll.], hold out, not give up, not submit, never say die; fight to the last ditch, die hard, sell one's life dearly, go down with flying colors.

ADJS. 6. resistant, resisting, withstanding; unyielding, unsubmissive 624.9–12; proof against 158.18; repellent, repulsive, repugnant; recalcitrant, renitent, up in arms.

791. DEFIANCE

NOUNS 1. defiance, defial, defying; daring, daringness; audacity, boldness, bravado, insolence; contempt, contemptuousness; disregard, despite.

2. challenge, stump [coll., U.S.], cartel; dare, double-dare; defy or defi [slang], defial; gage, gauntlet, glove, slap of the glove.

VERBS 3. defy, bid defiance to, hurl defiance at; **dare**, double-dare; **challenge**, call out, stump [coll., U.S.], throw *or* fling down the gauntlet, ~ glove *or* gage, throw *or* toss one's hat in the ring [coll.]; knock the chip off of one's shoulder; affront, pluck by the beard, slap one's face, double *or* shake the fist at; show fight, show one's teeth; dance the war dance.

4. flout, scout, disregard, slight, scorn, spurn, despise, contemn, treat with contempt, set at defiance, set at naught, **snap the fingers at; thumb one's nose at**, bite the thumb at; laugh at, laugh to scorn, laugh out of court.

5. brave 891.11.

6. show *or* **put up a bold front**, bluster, look big, stand with arms akimbo.

7. take a dare, accept a challenge, **call one's bluff** [coll.].

ADJS. **8. defiant, defying, daring**, challenging; **bold, audacious**, insolent, **contemptuous, disregardful**, greatly daring, regardless of consequences.

ADVS. **9. in defiance of**, in the teeth of, in the face of, under one's very nose.

INTERJS. **10. I defy you!**, I dare *or* double-dare you!, come on!, come if you dare!, do your worst!, hoity-toity!

792. ACCORD

Harmonious Relationship.—NOUNS **1. accord**, accordance, **concord**, concordance, **harmony**, symphony; **rapport**, **affinity**, response, *rapprochement* [F.]; **sympathy**, empathy, fellow feeling; **agreement**, correspondence, **understanding**, **likemindedness**; congeniality, compatibility; unity, unison, union; communion, community of interests; bonds of harmony, cement of friendship; happy family.

VERBS **2. accord, agree**, correspond, gee [slang & dial.], cotton [coll.], **get along with**, get on with, hit it off with [coll.], harmonize with, **be in harmony with**, fall *or* chime in with, blend in with, go hand in hand with, **be at one with**, sing in chorus; **sympathize**, empathize, reciprocate, respond, understand one another, enter into one's views, enter into the ideas *or* feelings of.

ADJS. **3. accordant, concordant, harmonious**; in accord, in harmony, in concert, in rapport, *en rapport* [F.]; **sympathetic**, empathic, **understanding**; **likeminded**, of the same mind, of one mind, at one; agreeing, corresponding; agreeable, congenial, compatible, reconcilable.

793. DISACCORD

Unharmonious Relationship.—NOUNS **1. disaccord**, disaccordance, **discord**, discordance *or* discordancy, **unharmoniousness**, inharmoniousness, disharmony, inharmony; **conflict, friction**; clash, clashing, jar; strained relations, tension; contention 794; enmity 927.

2. disagreement, difficulty, misunderstanding, difference, variance, disparity, odds, cross-purposes, difference of opinion.

3. dissension, dissent, dissidence, faction, *brouillerie* [F.].

4. falling-out, breach of friendship, parting of the ways; **alienation, estrangement, disaffection**, disfavor, outs; **breach, break, rupture, schism, split, rift**, disruption, separation, division; division in the camp, house divided against itself, "rift within the lute" [Tennyson]; open rupture, breaking off of negotiations, recall of ambassadors.

5. quarrel, dispute, controversy, altercation, fight, squabble, contention, strife, set-to [coll.], run-in [slang, U.S.], **bicker, wrangle**, snarl, cample [dial., Eng.], jangle, jar, tow-row [Scot. & dial., Eng.], *démêlé* [F.]; **scrap**, hassel, **rhubarb**, beef, barney [all slang]; **tiff**, miff [dial. & slang]; **spat, words, high words**, cuss-fight [slang]; **feud**, blood feud, vendetta; family jars.

6. row [coll.], **fracas**, fraction [dial.], **rumpus** [coll.], **ruckus** [dial. & slang], ruction [chiefly dial.], stramash [chiefly Scot.], breeze [coll.], squall [coll.], shindy [slang], fuss, touse [chiefly dial.].

7. brawl, broil, embroilment, embranglement, imbroglio; riot.

8. bone of contention, apple *or* brand of discord; **bone to pick**, crow to pluck; *casus belli* [L.], grounds for war, battleground.

VERBS **9. disaccord, disagree, differ**, differ in opinion, hold opposite views, **be at variance**, pull different ways, have no measures with, misunderstand one another; **conflict, clash**, collide, jostle, jangle, jar; live like cat and dog, live a cat-and-dog life.

10. have a bone to pick with, have a crow to pluck with.

11. fall out, have a falling-out, **break with**, split, separate, divide, **part company with**, break squares with, come to *or* reach a parting of the ways.

12. quarrel, disagree, differ; dispute,

altercate, **fight, squabble, scrap** [slang], **tiff, spat** [U.S.], **bicker, row** [coll.], **wrangle,** brabble, brangle, jangle, cample [dial., Eng.], cangle [Scot.], hassel [slang], fratch [dial.], spar [coll.], **have words with,** set to, join issue, fall foul of, lock horns, make the fur fly.

13. brawl, broil, turn the house out of window; **make** *or* **kick up a row,** kick up *or* raise a dust, raise a breeze *or* squall [all slang].

14. pick a quarrel, fasten a quarrel on; pick a bone with, pluck a crow with.

15. sow dissension; alienate, estrange, separate, divide, disunite, disaffect, come between; **set at odds,** set at variance; **set against,** pit against, **sick on** *or* **at, set on,** set by the ears, set at one's throat.

ADJS. **16. disaccordant, unharmonious,** inharmonious, disharmonious, **discordant,** dissident, inaccordant, out of accord; **disagreeing, differing; conflicting, clashing,** colliding; like cats and dogs.

17. at odds, at variance, at loggerheads, at cross-purposes, at sixes and sevens; at war, at strife, at feud, at daggers drawn, up in arms.

794. CONTENTION

NOUNS **1. contention, contest,** contestation; **conflict, strife, struggle; altercation, controversy, disputation,** litigation; **fighting, scrapping** [slang]; **quarreling, bickering, wrangling, squabbling; contentiousness,** quarrelsomeness 949.7; cat-and-dog life; Kilkenny cats.

2. competition, rivalry, corrivalry, emulation, *concours* [F.]; run for one's money.

3. a contest, engagement, encounter, rencounter, *rencontre* [F.]; **fight, battle, combat, war, scrap** [slang], **set-to** [coll.], run-in [slang, U.S.], barney [slang, Eng.], **fray,** affray; **conflict, collision, clash, brush,** skirmish, **tussle, scuffle, struggle,** scramble, mix-up [coll.], embroilment, **melee,** *mêlée* [F.], scrimmage, brabble; affair, action; bout, match, go [coll.]; joust, tilt; tournament, tourney; *passage d'armes* [F.], passage at *or* of arms, clash of arms; game 876.9.

4. (fights) pitched battle, battle royal, hand-to-hand fight, stand-up fight [coll.], running fight *or* engagement, tug of war; bullfight, tauromachy; dogfight; cockfight; warfare 795.

5. free-for-all, free fight, knock-down-drag-out [coll.]; derby.

6. death struggle, struggle for life or death, **fight to the death,** war to the death *or* knife, *guerre à mort* or *à outrance* [F.], fight to the last ditch.

7. duel, single combat, monomachy, satisfaction, **affair of honor;** triangular duel.

8. fencing, swordplay; sparring.

9. boxing, fisticuffs, pugilism, prize fighting, the fights [coll.], the ring; **boxing match,** box fight [slang], **prize fight,** spar, bout, mill [cant]; shadowboxing.

10. wrestling, rassling *or* rastling [dial., U.S.], *sumo* [Jap.]; jujitsu, judo; catch-as-catch-can; Greco-Roman, Cornish, Westmorland, Cumberland [all styles of wrestling].

11. racing; horse racing, the turf, the sport of kings.

12. race, run, heat; dash, hundred-yard dash etc.; foot race, automobile race, motorcycle race, dog race; boat race, yacht race, Torpids [Oxford Univ.], regatta; torch race, lampadedromy, lampadephoria [both Gr. antiq.]; marathon, marathon race; relay, relay race; sprint, sprint race; match race, obstacle race, hurdle race, cross-country race, point-to-point race, three-legged race, sack race, potato race, go-as-you-please [coll.].

13. horse race, harness race, invitational race, claiming race, plate race, stake race, purse race, derby; handicap race, handicap; chase, steeplechase; sweepstake *or* sweepstakes, sweep *or* sweeps [coll.].

VERBS **14. contend, contest; fight, scrap** [slang], **battle, combat, war,** put up a fight [coll.]; wage war 795.19; **strive, stuggle,** scramble, **tussle, scuffle; wrestle,** rassle *or* rastle [dial., U.S.], go to the mat with; **come to blows,** exchange blows *or* fisticuffs, **box,** mill [slang], spar; **fence,** thrust and parry; **joust, jostle, tilt, tourney,** run a tilt *or* a tilt at, couch one's lance, break a lance with; **duel,** fight a duel, give satisfaction; skirmish; fight one's way; fight the good fight.

15. lift one's hand against, draw the sword against, take up the cudgels; square up *or* off [coll.], come to the scratch; **pitch into** [coll.], **sail into** [coll.], light into [slang, U.S.], lay into [slang]; attack 796.15.

16. encounter, clash, collide, come up against, fall *or* run foul *or* afoul of; close with, come to close quarters, bring to bay, meet *or* fight hand to hand.

17. engage, take on [slang], **join issue,**

try conclusions, join battle, do or give battle, engage in battle.

18. **contend with, engage with, fight with,** strive with, struggle with, wrestle with, grapple with, bandy with; measure swords with, tilt with, **cross swords;** exchange shots, shout it out with [coll.]; **lock horns,** fall or go to loggerheads; tangle with [slang], mix it up with [slang], have a brush with; have it out, fight or battle it out; fight tooth and nail, fight like devils.

19. **compete, compete with, vie with,** cope with, enter into competition; **rival, emulate,** outvie.

20. **race,** race with, run a race; horse-race, boat-race.

21. **contend for,** strive for, struggle for, fight for, vie for; stickle for, stipulate for, make a point of.

22. **dispute, contest,** take issue with; **fight over, quarrel over,** wrangle over, squabble over, bicker over, strive or contend about.

ADJS. 23. **contending,** contesting; **contestant,** disputant; striving; struggling; fighting, battling, warring; contentious 949.26.

24. **competitive,** competing, **vying,** rivaling, **rival,** emulous, in competition or rivalry; **cutthroat.**

795. WARFARE

NOUNS 1. **warfare, war, combat, fighting,** armed conflict, military operations, the war game, the sword, arbitrament of the sword, appeal to arms or the sword, force or might of arms; **state of war, hostilities,** belligerence or belligerency, open war; **hot war, shooting war;** total war.

2. "an epidemic insanity" [Emerson], "a brain-spattering, windpipe-slitting art" [Byron], "the feast of vultures, and the waste of life" [ibid.], "the business of barbarians" [Napoleon], "the trade of kings" [Dryden]; "a by-product of the arts of peace" [Ambrose Bierce], "a conflict which does not determine who is right — but who is left" [anon.].

3. civil war, revolutionary war, religious war, war of attrition; preventive war, war to end war; world war; Armageddon.

4. aerial warfare, naval warfare, amphibious warfare, land warfare, three-dimensional war (air, land, sea), trench warfare, siege warfare, underground warfare; offensive warfare, defensive warfare; mobile warfare, war of movement; position warfare,

war of position; irregular warfare, guerrilla warfare, bushfighting; biological warfare, bacteriological warfare, virus warfare, germ war; chemical warfare; atomic war, atom war, A-war, H-war; push-button war.

5. **cold war,** inactive war, twilight war, armed neutrality; **psychological warfare, war of nerves;** technological war, slide-rule war; economic warfare.

6. **battle** 794.3; **attack** 796.

7. **battle array,** order of battle; open order; close formation; echelon [navy].

8. **campaign,** war, **drive, expedition,** hostile expedition; **crusade,** jihad [Moham.].

9. **operation,** action; **maneuver,** movement, evolution; **mission;** combined operations, joint operations, co-ordinated operations; active operations, amphibious operations, flying operations, fluid operations, major or minor operations, night operations, overseas operations; war game, dry run.

10. **strategy, tactics,** maneuvering, military evolutions; applied tactics; offensive strategy, defensive strategy; aerial tactics, infantry tactics, cavalry tactics, mobile tactics, columnar tactics, mob tactics, fire tactics, barrier tactics, shock tactics, blitzkrieg tactics, linear tactics, grand tactics, maneuver tactics; kriegspiel, *Kriegspiel* [Ger.]; diversion, feint, diversionary movement; encirclement, encircling movement; defense in depth; demonstration; peace offensive.

11. **warcraft,** war, arms, military science, art or rules of war; siegecraft; generalship, soldiership; chivalry, knighthood, errantry, knight-errantry, knightly skill; logistics.

12. **declaration of war, challenge.**

13. **call to arms, rally,** service call; **mobilization, muster,** levy; recruitment 778.6; **rallying cry,** slogan, watchword; **battle cry,** war cry, war whoop; drum call to arms, *rappel* [F.], tom-tom.

14. **service,** duty; active service or duty.

15. **militarization,** activation; remilitarization, reactivation; arms race.

16. **warlikeness,** unpeacefulness; **combativeness, contentiousness;** hostility, **antagonism; aggression, aggressiveness; belligerence** or belligerency, **pugnacity,** bellicosity, fight, chip on one's shoulder; martiality, militancy; **militarism,** militaryism; **chauvinism, jingoism,** bellicism, **warmongering,** waving of the bloody shirt; warpath.

17. (militaristic devices) battle flag, bloody shirt, fiery cross [Scot. hist.]; hatchet, tomahawk; martial music, war song, battle hymn, national anthem.

18. war-god, Mars [Rom.], Ares [Gr.], Odin or Woden [Norse], Tyr [Hindu]; war-goddess, Bellona, Juno Curitis or Quiritis [both Rom.].

VERBS 19. war, wage war, make war, carry on war or hostilities, engage in hostilities wield the sword; battle, fight 794.14; smell powder; spill blood, imbrue the hands in blood; give one's life for one's country.

20. make war on, levy war on, "let slip the dogs of war" [Shakespeare]; declare war, challenge, throw or fling down the gauntlet, dig up the tomahawk, take up the hatchet, open hostilities.

21. go to war, go on the warpath, raise up in arms, take to arms, take arms, take up arms, take up the cudgels or sword, fly to the sword, appeal to the sword; take the field.

22. campaign, make an expedition, go on a crusade.

23. serve, do duty; see or do active duty; bear arms, carry arms, shoulder arms, shoulder a gun.

24. call to arms, rally; mobilize, muster, levy, beat up for; recruit 778.14; give the battle cry, cry havoc; wave the bloody shirt.

25. militarize, activate; reactivate, remilitarize, take out of mothballs [slang].

ADJS. 26. warlike, militant, fighting, warring, battling; martial, military; warriorlike, soldiery, soldierlike; combative, contentious, gladiatorial; belligerent, pugnacious, bellicose, armigerous, aggressive, offensive, scrappy [slang], fighty [dial.], full of fight; fierce, savage; unpeaceful, unpacific; hostile, antagonistic, inimical.

27. militaristic, warmongering; chauvinistic, chauvinist, chauvin; jingoistic, jingoist, jingoish, jingo.

28. in arms, under arms, sword-in-hand; embattled, battled, in battle array.

ADVS. 29. at war, up in arms; in the midst of battle, in the thick of the fray; in the cannon's mouth, at the point of the gun; at swords' points, at the point of the bayonet or sword.

INTERJS. 30. to arms!, aux armes! [F.], to your tents, O Israel!

31. wars

American Revolution	Austrian Succession Balkan Wars
Boer War	Korean War
Civil War (American)	Macedonian-Persian War
Civil War (English)	Mexican War
Civil War (Spanish)	Napoleonic Wars
Civil Wars (Roman)	Peloponnesian War
Crimean War	Punic Wars
Crusades	Russian Revolution
Franco-Prussian War	Russo-Japanese War
French and Indian War	Samnite War
French Revolution	Seven Weeks' War
Gallic Wars	Sino-Japanese War
Greco-Persian Wars	Spanish-American War
Hundred Years' War	Spanish Succession War
Italian War	Thirty Years' War
	War of 1812
	Wars of the Roses
	World War I
	World War II

32. battles

Actium	Granicus
Adrianople	Hampton Roads
Aegates Isles	Hastings
Agincourt	Hohenlinden
Antietam	Inchon
Anzio	Ipsus
Arbela	Issus
Austerlitz	Ivry
Ayacucho	Jena
Balaklava	Jutland
Bannockburn	Königgrätz
Bataan	Lake Erie
Battle of Britain	Lake Trasimenus
Battle of the Bulge	Langside
Belleau Wood	Leipzig
Bismarck Sea	Lepanto
Blenheim	Leuctra
Borodino	Lexington-Concord
Bosworth Field	Leyte Gulf
Bouvines	Lucknow
Boyne	Lüle-Burgas
Buena Vista	Lützen
Bull Run	Manila Bay
Bunker Hill	Mantinea
Cannae	Marathon
Caporetto	Marengo
Caudine Forks	Marne
Chaeronea	Marston Moor
Châlons	Metaurus
Chancellorsville	Meuse-Argonne
Château-Thierry	Midway Island
Chattanooga	Milvian Bridge
Chickamauga	Mukden
Constantinople	Naseby
Coral Sea	Nashville
Crécy	Navarino
Cunaxa	New Orleans
Cuzco	Nile
Dardanelles	Normandy
Drogheda	Okinawa
Dunkirk	Orléans
El Alamein	Panipat
Flodden	Pearl Harbor
Fontenay	Pharsalus
Fontenoy	Philippi
Fredericksburg	Plassey
Gettysburg	Plataea

Plevna	Spotsylvania
Poitiers	Stalingrad
Port Arthur	Syracuse
Pultowa	Tannenberg
Pydna	Testri
Quebec	Teutoburgerwald
Ravenna	Thermopylae
Rossbach	Tours
Saint-Mihiel	Trafalgar
Salamis	Valmy
Santiago de Cuba	Verdun
Saratoga	Vicksburg
Sea of Japan	Vienna
Sedan	Wagram
Sempach	Waterloo
Sevastopol	Xeres
Singapore	Yalu River
Soissons	Yorktown
Solferino	Ypres
Somme	Zama
Spanish Armada	

796. ATTACK

NOUNS 1. attack, assault; offense, offensive, aggression; onset, onslaught; strike, descent; charge, rush, dead set at, run an or against; drive, push [slang]; sally, sortie; *coup de main* [F., bold stroke, sudden attack]; banzai attack or charge; breakthrough; counterattack, counteroffensive; amphibious attack; gas attack; assault and battery.

2. surprise attack, surprise, surprisal, *ruade* [F.]; sneak attack, Pearl Harbor.

3. thrust, pass, lunge, swing, cut, stab, jab [coll.]; feint; carte or quarte and tierce; home thrust.

4. raid, foray, razzia; invasion, incursion, inroad, irruption; dragonnade or dragoonade; air raid; shuttle raid [aero.]; escalade, boarding.

5. siege, besiegement, beleaguerment; encompassment, investment, encirclement, envelopment; vertical envelopment; pincer movement.

6. storm, storming, taking by storm.

7. bombardment, cannonade, hate [slang]; strafe, strafing; blitzkrieg, blitz; robot blitz.

8. bombing, dive-bombing, glide-bombing, skip-bombing, shuttle bombing, area bombing, pattern bombing, carpet bombing, precision bombing, saturation bombing, tactical bombing, strategic bombing.

9. gunfire, fire, fireworks, shooting, gunplay [slang], trigger talk [slang]; shellfire; rocket fire; antiaircraft fire, flak; cross fire, direct fire, dry fire, file fire, ground fire, horizontal fire, vertical fire, percussion fire, platoon fire, plunging fire, raking fire,

ricochet fire, rolling fire, time fire, fire of demolition; firepower.

10. volley, salvo, burst, spray, fusillade, drumfire; cannonade, cannonry; broadside, enfilade; barrage, anti-aircraft barrage, box barrage, emergency barrage, normal barrage, standing barrage, rolling or creeping barrage.

11. stabbing, piercing; knifing; the sword; impalement, transfixion, transfixation.

12. stoning, lapidation.

13. assailant, assailer, attacker, assaulter, aggressor; invader, raider.

14. zero hour, H-hour; D-day, target day.

VERBS 15. attack, assault, assail, assume or take the offensive; go at, come at, have at, make at, set at, put at, lay at, go for [coll.], launch out against, make a set or dead set at; pitch into [coll.], light into [slang, U.S.], sail into [coll.], head into [slang], wade into [coll.], lay into [slang]; fall on or upon, set on or upon, put upon, descend on, pounce upon, crack down on [slang]; lift a hand against, draw the sword against, take up the cudgels; lay hands on, lay a hand on, bloody one's hands with; gang up on [U.S.].

17. let out at, let drive at, let fly at; lash out at, strike out at; strike at, hit at, poke at, thrust at, swing at, take a swing at, take a poke at, make a thrust or pass at, aim or deal a blow at, take a fling or shy at; cut and thrust; feint.

18. launch an attack, mount an attack; advance against or upon, march upon or against, bear down upon; strike; flank; press the attack, follow up the attack; counterattack; sneak-attack; gas.

19. charge, rush, rush at, fly at, run at, dash at, make a dash or rush at; tilt at, make a tilt at, run a tilt at, ride full tilt against; jump off, go over the top [coll.].

20. besiege, lay siege to, encompass, surround, encircle, envelope, invest, set upon on all sides; beset, beleaguer, harry, lay about one, drive or press one hard, attack tooth and nail; storm, take by storm; soften up; coventrize.

21. raid, foray, make a raid; invade, inroad, make an inroad, make an irruption into; escalade, scale the walls, board.

22. pull a gun on, draw a gun on, draw iron [slang, U.S.]; get the drop on, beat to the draw [both slang, U.S.].

23. fire upon, fire at, shoot at, pop at,

take a shot at, fire a shot at, let off a gun at, "let slip the dogs of war" [Shakespeare]; open fire, open up on [slang]; draw a bead on [U.S.], level at; snipe, snipe at; **bombard, strafe, shell**, cannonade, barrage, blitz; pepper, fusillade, fire a volley; rake, enfilade; pour a broadside into; cannon; **torpedo**, submarine [coll.].

24. **shoot** 284.13.

25. **bomb**, drop a bomb, lay an egg [slang]; dive-bomb, glide-bomb, skip-bomb, pattern-bomb.

26. **mine**, sap, plant a battery; spring a mine.

27. **stab, stick, pierce**, plunge in, run through; **impale**, spit, **transfix**, transpierce; **spear**, lance, poniard, bayonet, saber, sword put to the sword; **knife**, dirk, dagger, stiletto; spike.

28. **gore**, horn, tusk.

29. **pelt; stone**, rock [coll., U.S.], lapidate; pellet; brickbat [coll.]; egg [coll.].

30. **hurl at, throw at, cast at**, heave at, fling at, sling at, toss at, shy at, fire at [coll.], let fly at; hurl against, hurl at the head of.

ADJS. 31. **attacking**, assailing, assaulting; **invading**, invasive, incursive, irruptive.

32. **aggressive, offensive, combative**, on the offensive.

ADVS. 33. **under attack, under fire**.

INTERJS. 34. **attack!**, advance!, **charge!**, "charge, Chester, charge! On, Stanley, on!" [Scott], over the top!, up and at them!, give 'em hell! [coll.]; fire!, open fire!

797. DEFENSE

NOUNS 1. **defense**, defence [Eng.], **guard**, ward; **protection** 697; self-defense, self-protection, self-preservation; the defensive.

2. **civil defense**; Civil Defense Administration, Air Defense Command; conelrad (control of electromagnetic radiation for civil defense).

3. **armor**, armature, **defensive arms**; caparison, panoply, harness; **mail, coat of mail; protective covering**, cortex, **thick skin**; shell [zool.] 227.16; spines, needles [both zool.].

4. **fortification**, muniment; **bulwark, rampart, parapet**; vallation, vallum [Rom. antiq.], contravallation or countervallation; circumvallation; **earthwork, embankment**; bank, dike, mole, mound; fence wall; **stockade, palisade**, laager [S. Africa], sangar [India]; **barrier, barricade**; abatis;

entanglement, barbed-wire entanglement; fieldwork, lunette; **battlement**, merlon; casemate; battery; buttress, abutment; breastwork, banquette, mantelet or mantlet, tenaille or tenail, ravelin, curtain; demilune, half-moon; bastion, demibastion, redan; faussebraie or faussebraye, advanced work, hornwork, outwork, barbican, redoubt, sconce, fortalice, glacis; scarp, escarp, escarpment, counterscarp; machicolation, bartizan, loophole, balistraria; portcullis, chevaux de frise [pl.]; postern gate, sally port.

5. **entrenchment** or intrenchment, trench, ditch, fosse; vanfoss; **moat; dugout**, abri; **bunker; foxhole**, slit trench; approach trench, communication trench, fire trench, deliberate trenches, gallery, parallel, coupure; sap, single or double sap, flying sap; mine, countermine.

6. **stronghold**, hold, safehold, fasthold, **fastness**, keep, ward, **bastion**, donjon, propugnaculum, **citadel**, castle, tower, tower of strength; **fort, fortress**, fortification, kila [India], pa [New Zealand]; acropolis; garrison, post; peel, peel tower, peelhouse; rath [Ir. antiq.]; martello tower, martello; blockhouse, wooden walls; pillbox; bolt position, *Riegelstellung* [Ger.]; **bridgehead, beachhead**.

7. **defender, champion, advocate**, upholder; vindicator, apologist; **protector** 697.4; **guard** 697.8; paladin, knight-errant.

VERBS 8. **defend, guard, shield**, screen, secure, guard against; **protect** 697.17; flank.

9. **fortify**, embattle, battle; **arm; man**; garrison, engarrison, man the garrison; **barricade, blockade**; bulwark, wall, fence; embank, bank; entrench or intrench, intreat, dig in; mine, countermine.

10. **fend off, ward off, stave off, hold off**, keep off, beat off, parry; **hold** or **keep at bay**, keep at arm's length; **repel, repulse, rebuff, drive back**, put back, push back; **rout, put to flight**.

ADJS. 11. **defensive**, defending, **guarding**, shielding, screening; **protective** 697.22; self-defensive, self-protective, self-preservative.

12. **fortified**, embattled, battled; castellated, casemated, machicolated.

13. **armored**, panoplied; armor-plated, "in complete steel" [Shakespeare]; mailed, mailclad; ironclad, ironbound; encuirassed, loricate, loricated [all zool.]; panzer [mil.].

14. **armed, heeled** [slang, U.S.]; accoutered, in arms, under arms, sword-in-

hand; **well-armed,** well-heeled [slang, U.S.], heavy-armed, full-armed, bristling with arms, **armed to the teeth,** armed cap-a-pie; light-armed.

15. defensible, defendable, fencible, **tenable.**

ADVS. **16. defensively, in defense,** in self-defense; **on the defensive,** on guard; **at bay,** *aux abois* [F.], with one's back to the wall.

17. armor

aegis	habergeon
armet	hauberk
backplate	headpiece
bard, barde	heaume
basinet	helm
beaver	helmet
breastplate	jamb
brigandine	lorica
buckler	morion
cabasset	nose guard
camail	nosepiece
casque	*pédieux* [F.]
casquetel	*Pickelhaube* [Ger.]
chamfron	plate
coif	rerebrace
corselet, corslet	sallet, salade
cubitiere	scutum [Rom.
cuirass	antiq.]
cuisse	shield
face guard	siege cap
gauntlet	sollerets
gas mask	vambrace
gorget	visor
greaves	

798. COMBATANT

NOUNS **1. combatant, fighter, battler,** scrapper [slang], **contestant, contender, competitor,** disputant, wrangler, struggler, tussler, scuffler; **belligerent,** militant; gladiator; jouster; swordsman, blade, *sabreur* [F.], *beau sabreur* [F.]; fencer, swordplayer; duelist; gamecock, fighting cock.

2. pugilist, pug [slang], **boxer, fighter, prize fighter,** fisticuffer, bruiser, miller, [slang or cant], sparrer; flyweight, bantamweight, featherweight, lightweight, welterweight, middleweight, light heavyweight, heavyweight.

3. wrestler, rassler or rastler [dial., U.S.], grappler, scuffler, matman [coll.].

4. bullfighter, toreador, *torero* [Sp.]; picador; matador.

5. militarist, warmonger, war dog or hound; **chauvinist,** chauvin; **jingo,** jingoist; Rajput [India].

6. serviceman, military man, uniform; navy man 275.4; air serviceman 278.3; militiaman; commando, commandoman, Ranger

[U.S.]; storm trooper; *légionnaire* [F.], legionary.

7. soldier, warrior, wayfarer, **brave,** fighting man, **man-at-arms,** rifle, gun; **cannon fodder,** *Kanonenfutter* [Ger.], food for powder; warrioress, Amazon; spearman, pikeman, halberdier.

8. (nationalities) **doughboy, G.I.,** G.I. Joe, Sammy, **Yank** [U.S.]; Tommy Atkins, **tommy,** Johnny [English]; redcoat [Eng. hist.]; bing boy [Canadian]; poilu [French]; Aussie, digger [Australian]; Jock, lady of or from hell [Scottish]; Fritz, Jerry, Heinie, Hun, Boche [German]; Janizary or Janissary [Turkish]; sepoy [India]; askari[Africa].

9. enlisted man, noncommissioned officer; common soldier, peon; **private,** buck private [slang, U.S.]; private first class, Pfc.

10. infantryman, foot soldier, footslogger [slang], dogface [slang, U.S.]; light infantryman, chasseur, Zouave.

11. artilleryman, artillerist, cosmoline [slang, U.S.]; **gunner,** guns [slang], gun, cannoneer; machine gunner, *mitrailleur* [F.]; **rifleman,** musketeer, jäger [Ger. & Austria], *tirailleur* [F.]; carabineer, *carabinier* [F.], *carabiniere* [It.], *carabinero* [Sp.]; fusilier, fusileer; **sharpshooter,** *bersagliere* [It.]; **sniper,** body snatcher [slang]; **torpedoer,** torpedoist; **bomber,** bomb thrower, **bombardier;** grenadier.

12. cavalryman, mounted infantryman, **trooper;** dragoon, light or heavy dragoon; lancer, lance, uhlan; hussar, Cossack [Russ. hist.], cuirassier, spahi [Turk. & Algerian], sowar [India].

13. engineer; seabee [U.S.]; sapper, sapper and miner.

14. guardsman, gendarme; **yeoman,** yeoman of the guard, **beefeater** [Eng.].

15. irregular, casual, Croat [hist.], bashibazouk [Turk.]; **guerrilla,** partisan or partizan; **bushfighter,** bushwhacker [U.S.]; underground, resistance.

16. mercenary, hireling, *condottiere* [It.], *franctireur* [F.], free lance, free companion [hist.], **soldier of fortune,** adventurer, Hessian [U.S.].

17. recruit, rookie [slang, U.S.], **conscript,** drafted man, **draftee, inductee, selectee, enlistee,** enrollee, trainee, boot [slang, U.S.]; **raw recruit,** tenderfoot; awkward squad; recruits, draft, levy, Landsturm.

18. veteran, vet [coll.], campaigner, old campaigner, old soldier, war horse [coll.].

19. (military units) **unit,** tactical unit, **outfit** [slang]; division, subdivision, section, wing, regiment, battalion, garrison, company, troop, brigade, legion, phalanx, cohort, platoon, battery, maniple [Rom. hist.], combat team; squad, squadron; detachment, detail, posse; kitchen police, K.P.; column, flying column; rank, file; train, combat train, field train; cadre.

20. corps; army corps, *corps d'armée* [F.]; corps troops; New Zealand Army Corps, Anzacs [coll.]; drum corps, bugle corps; Engineer Corps, Corps of Engineers; Tank Corps, panzer division; Army Service Corps, Quartermaster Corps, Service of Supplies, service company, ~ battery *or* troop; Signal Corps, Medical Corps, Chemical Warfare Corps, Officers' Reserve Corps; JANSCO, Joint Army-Navy Signal Corps [U.S.].

21. arm, branch, service.

22. army, this man's army [slang], **armed force,** fighting machine, **military, soldiery, forces, troops, host,** array, Sabaoth; ranks, rank and file; regular *or* active army, regulars; the line, troops of the line; line of defense, first ~, second etc. line of defense; ground forces, ground troops, commandos, shock troops; storm troops, ski troops; task force; occupation force.

23. standing army; militia, organized militia, national militia, mobile militia, territorial militia, reserve militia; **National Guard,** *garde nationale* [F.], state guard [U.S.]; minutemen [U.S. hist.], trainband [Eng. hist.].

24. reserves, auxiliaries, *corps de réserve* [F.], **second line of defense,** Landwehr; army reserves, home reserves, territorial reserves, territorial *or* home defense army, supplementary reserves, organized reserves; USAR, U.S. Army Reserve.

25. volunteers, volunteer militia, volunteer navy.

26. horse and foot; cavalry, horse, mounted infantry *or* rifles; **infantry,** foot, rifles; artillery, gunners, field artillery, light artillery, heavy artillery, horse artillery.

27. navy, naval forces, **first line of defense; fleet,** flotilla, argosy, armada, squadron, escadrille [F.], division, task force; mosquito fleet; U.S.N., United States Navy; R.N., Royal Navy; marine, mercantile *or* merchant marine; naval militia; naval reserve, Royal Naval Reserve; coast guard; Seabees, Naval Construction Battalion; yeomanry.

28. marines, Marine Corps, the first to fight, **leathernecks** [slang], jollies [slang, Eng.], **devil dogs** [slang, U.S.], **gyrenes** [slang, U.S.]; horse marines.

29. air service, air force, air arm, flying corps, fourth arm [coll.], "airy navies grappling in the central blue" [Tennyson]; strategic air force, tactical air force; squadron, flight [U.S.], wing.

30. Air Force; U.S.A.F., U.S. Air Force; U.S.A.A.F., U.S. Army Air Force; R.A.F., Royal Air Force; R.C.A.F., Royal Canadian Air Force; R.A.A.F., Royal Australian Air Force; USNAS, U.S. National Air Service; NAD, Naval Air Division [U.S.], Navy Air, Fleet Air Arm [Eng.]; ANAC, Army-Navy Air Corps [U.S.]; FEAF, Far East Air Force; Air Command, Bomber Command, Coastal Command; SAC, Strategic Air Command; ATC, Air Transport Command [U.S.]; ATS, Air Transport Service [U.S.]; MATS, Military Air Transport Service [U.S.]; NATS, Naval Air Transport Service [U.S.]; CASU, Carrier Aircraft Service Unit [U.S.]; ARF, Airborne Reconnaissance Force [U.S.]; Paratroops.

31. (women's services) WAVE, Waves, Women Accepted for Volunteer Emergency Service [U.S.]; WAC, Wacs, Women's Army Corps [U.S.]; WRAC, Wracs, Women's Royal Army Corps; WAAC, Waacs, Women's Army Auxiliary Corps [Eng.]; WREN, Wrens, Women's Royal Naval Corps; WAF, Wafs, Women's Air Force [U.S.]; WRAF, Wrafs, Women's Royal Air Force; WAAF, Waafs, Women's Auxiliary Air Force [Eng.]; WASP, Wasps, Women's Air Force Service Pilots [U.S.]; WAM, Wams, Women's Reserve of the Marine Corps [U.S.]; Spars, Women's Auxiliary of the U.S. Coast Guard (from their motto, *semper paratus*, "always ready").

32. guards, household troops; **yeomen of the guard, beefeaters,** Life Guards, Horse Guards, Foot Guards, Grenadier Guards, Coldstream Guards, Scots Guards, Irish Guards [all Eng.]; Swiss Guards.

33. war horse, charger, courser, trooper.

799. ARMS

NOUNS **1. arms, weapons,** deadly weapons; **armament, munitions, ordnance,** munitions of war, *apparatus belli* [L., apparatus of war]; gunnery, musketry; small arms; side arms, *armes blanches* [F.]; panoply, stand of arms.

2. armory, arsenal, magazine, dump;

ammunition depot, ammo dump [slang]; park, gun park, artillery park, park of artillery.

3. ballistics, gunnery, artillery; archery.

4. sword, blade, good or trusty sword; steel, cold steel.

5. firearm, gun, shooter [coll.], shooting iron [slang, U.S.], piece; gat, rod, iron [all crim. slang, U.S.]; **rifle, musket; pistol,** barker [slang], oscar [crim. slang, U.S.]; automatic, repeater, **revolver;** six-shooter, six gun [both coll.]; flame thrower or projector, *Flammenwerfer* [Ger.], *lanceflamme* [F.].

6. artillery, cannon, cannonry, ordnance, engines of war, dogs of war [coll.]; field artillery; heavy artillery, heavy field artillery; siege artillery, bombardment weapons, breakthrough weapons, battering or siege train; mountain artillery, coast artillery, trench artillery, antiaircraft artillery; battery; **cannon,** big gun; field gun, field-piece.

7. antiaircraft gun, A.A. gun, Ack-Ack [slang], Archie [slang], aerogun, *Fliegerabwehrkanone* [G.]; skysweeper.

8. ammunition, munition, ammo [coll.], **powder and shot,** iron rations [army slang].

9. explosive, high explosive; **powder,** nitro powder, smokeless powder; **gunpowder,** "villanous saltpetre" [Shakespeare]; **guncotton,** nitrocotton; **nitroglycerin,** cellulose nitrate, pyroxylin, melinite, cordite, gelignite, lyddite, Ballistite; **TNT** or **T.N.T.,** trinitrotoluene, trinitrotoluol; **dynamite,** giant powder; fulgurite, thunder tube [coll.]; petard; carcass.

10. charge, load; blast; war head.

11. cartridge, cartouche or cartouch, shell; ball cartridge; blank cartridge, dry ammunition.

12. missile, projectile, trajectile, bolt; brickbat, stone, rock; countermissile; **rockets and flying missiles 280.**

13. (types of military missiles) ATA, air-to-air; ATG, air-to-ground; ATS, air-to-ship; GTA, ground-to-air; GTG, ground-to-ground; STS, ship-to-shore.

14. shot, bar shot, buckshot, canister shot, cannon shot, chain shot, langrage or langrel shot, round shot, swan shot; grapeshot, grape, *mitraille* [F.]; **ball,** cannon ball, rifle ball; **bullet,** slug, pellet; dumdum bullet, expanding bullet, explosive bullet, man-stopping bullet; **shell,** high-explosive shell; **shrapnel; torpedo,** fish [slang]; homing torpedo, Chase-me-Charlie [slang]; dud [coll.].

15. bomb, bombshell, pineapple [slang, U.S.], **infernal machine; grenade,** hand grenade, rifle grenade, concussion grenade; depth bomb, ash can [slang]; trench mortar bomb, oilcan [slang], Minnehaha [slang, World War I]; aerial bomb, egg [slang].

16. atomic bomb, atom bomb, A-bomb, fission bomb, nuclear explosive; **hydrogen bomb, H-bomb,** fusion bomb, thermonuclear bomb, one megaton bomb, super bomb, superatomic bomb, hell bomb; **plutonium bomb.**

17. arrow, shaft, dart, bolt; reed, quarrel [hist.], vire; chested arrow, footed arrow, bobtailed arrow, self arrow, cloth-yard shaft; arrowhead, barb; flight, volley.

18. bow, crossbow, longbow, self bow, carriage bow.

19. sling, slingshot, beany [slang]; throwing or throw stick, spear thrower, womera; **catapult,** arbalest, ballista, trebuchet or trebucket.

20. launcher, projector; rocket launcher **280.11.**

21. brass knuckles, knucks [coll.], brass knucks [coll.], knuckles, knuckle-dusters.

22. weapons

arrow	halberd, halbert
assagai	hanger
ax, axe	hatchet
baselard	javelin
battle-ax	jereed, jerrid
bayonet	katar [India]
belduque [Southwest. U.S.]	knife
	kukri [India]
bilbo	lance
bill	Lochaber ax
black bill	machete
blade	missile
blowgun, blowpipe	partisan
bola, bolas	pike
bolo [P.I.]	poleax, poleaxe
boomerang	poniard
bow and arrow	rapier
bowie knife	saber
brickbat	scimitar
broadax	shaft
broadsword	skean
brown bill	skean dhu [Scot.]
claymore	slung shot
creese, kris	smallsword
cutlass	spear
dagger	spontoon
dart	stiletto
dirk	sword
dudgeon [hist.]	sword bayonet
falchion	swordstick
Ferrara	throwing knife or
foil	iron
gisarme	Toledo
glaive [hist.]	

tomahawk	tuck [hist.]
trench knife	yataghan

23. clubs

bastinado	mace
bat	quarterstaff
billy	ram, battering ram
blackjack	sandbag
bludgeon	shillelagh
cane	staff
cudgel	stick
knobkerrie [S.	truncheon
Africa]	waddy [Australia]
life preserver	war club
loaded cane	

24. guns

aerogun	Long Tom
air rifle or gun	machine gun
antiaircraft gun,	magazine gun
AA gun	matchlock
antisubmarine	Maxim gun
mortar	*Minenwerfer*
antitank gun	[Ger.], minnie
atomic cannon	[slang]
atomic gun, atom	mine thrower
gun	M-1 [U.S.
automatic	Army]
auto-rifle	mortar
bazooka	mountain gun
Big Bertha [slang,	musket
World War I]	musketoon
blunderbuss	muzzle-loader
breechloader	needle gun
Brown Bess	nuclear or thermo-
Browning	nuclear weapon
automatic rifle,	pedrero
BAR	petronel [hist.]
bulldog	pistol
burp gun	pom-pom
caliver	popgun
cannon	repeater
carbine	revolver
carronade	rifle
chassepot	rifled cannon
culverin	rocket gun
deringer [U.S.]	shotgun
Dreyse rifle	siege gun
escopette, escopet	six-shooter [coll.]
falconet	skysweeper
field gun, fieldpiece	small-bore
firelock	smoothbore
flame thrower or	submachine gun
projector	superbazooka
flintlock	swivel, swivel gun
forty-five	ten-pounder
fowling piece	thirty-thirty
fusil [hist.]	thirty-two
Garand rifle	Tommy gun [coll.,
Gatling gun	U.S.], Thompson
hackbut, hagbut	submachine gun
harquebus	trench gun or
horse pistol	mortar
howitzer	twenty-two
jingal	wind gun
Lewis gun	Y-gun

25. gun makes

Armstrong	Colt
Benet-Mercie	Enfield
Browning	Flobert
Garling	Mossberg
Gatling	Paixhans
Krupp	Parrott
Lancaster	Remington
Lee-Enfield	Savage
Lee-Metford	Snider
Lewis	Springfield
Luger	Stevens
Mannlicher	Vickers
Marlin	Vickers-Maxim
Martini-Henry	Westley Richards
Mauser	Whitworth
Maxim	Winchester
Minié	

26. gun parts

barrel	gunflint
bolt	gunlock
breech	gunstock
butt	hair trigger
chamber	hammer
cock	lock
cylinder	magazine
flintlock	sight
gun carriage	trigger

27. torpedoes

aerial torpedo	rocket torpedo
bangalore torpedo	spar torpedo
homing torpedo	submarine torpedo

28. bombs

aerial bomb	fire bomb
antipersonnel	fragmentation
bomb	bomb
antisubmarine	gas bomb
bomb	hedgehog
atomic bomb, A-	hydrobomb
bomb	hydrogen bomb,
azon bomb	H-bomb
bat	incendiary, in-
blockbuster [coll.]	cendiary bomb
citybuster [coll.]	plutonium bomb
concussion bomb	pyrotechnic bomb
concussion mortar	razon bomb
bomb	roc
delayed-action	rocket bomb 280.3
bomb	smoke bomb
demolition bomb	stink bomb
depth bomb	tear-gas bomb
dynamite bomb	time bomb
electron bomb	trench mortar
fireball	bomb

29. mines

aerial mine	masked battery
antenna mine	oyster mine
antipersonnel mine	pressure mine
booby trap	set gun
buoyant mine	sonic or acoustic
ground mine	mine
land mine	spring gun
Leon mine	submarine mine
magnetic mine	

800. ARENA

NOUNS 1. **arena, scene of action,** scene, **field,** ground, walk, course, sphere; theater, stage, platform; **amphitheater,** circus, **hippodrome**, **coliseum**, Colosseum, **stadium**, **bowl**; gymnasium, gym [coll.], palaestra; lists, campus [Rom. antiq.]; tiltyard, tilting ground; **pit**, cockpit; bear garden; **ring**, prize ring, bull ring; Field of Mars, *Campus Martius* [L.], *Champ de Mars* [F.]; athletic field 876.13.

2. **battlefield**, **battleground**, field, combat area, **field of battle**, field of slaughter, field of blood *or* bloodshed, aceldama *or* akeldama; **the front**, front line, battle line, line of battle; theater, **theater of operations**, theater *or* seat of war; ETO, European theater of operations; over there [U.S.], out there [Eng.]; no man's land; jump area; campground, camp, encampment, tented field.

801. PEACE

NOUNS 1. **peace**, *pax* [L.]; **peacetime**, piping time of peace, the storm blown over; freedom from war, exemption from hostilities, public tranquillity, "on earth peace, good will toward men" [Bible]; **harmony**, accord 792.

2. **peacefulness**, **tranquillity**, **serenity**, **calmness**, **quiet**, quietude, quietness, quiet life; order, orderliness, law and order.

3. **peace of mind**, peace of heart, peace of soul, peace of God [theol.], "peace . . . which passeth all understanding" [Bible].

4. **peaceableness**, **unpugnaciousness**, uncontentiousness, nonaggression; **pacifism**, pacificism.

5. **noncombatant**, nonbelligerent, nonresistant; **civilian**, citizen.

6. **pacifist**, pacificist, peace man, **peace lover**, peacemonger [derog.]; **conscientious objector**, conchie [slang].

VERBS 7. **keep the peace**, remain at peace, wage the peace.

8. (Biblical) "be at peace among yourselves," "follow after the things which make for peace," "follow peace with all men," "as much as lieth in you, live peaceably with all men," "seek peace, and pursue it," "have peace one with another," "be of one mind, live in peace."

ADJS. 9. **pacific**, pacificatory; **peaceful**, **peaceable**, peacelike; **tranquil**, **serene**, halcyon, **calm**, **quiet**, untroubled, orderly, **at peace**; concordant 792.3; bloodless; peacetime.

10. **unbelligerent**, unhostile, unbellicose, **unpugnacious**, uncontentious, unmilitant, unmilitary, **nonaggressive**, non-

combative, nonmilitant; noncombatant, civilian; **pacifistic**.

INTERJS. 11. **peace be with you!**, peace be to you!, *pax vobiscum!* [L.]; "peace be to this house!" [Bible], "peace be within thy walls, and prosperity within thy palaces" [ibid.], "let the peace of God rule in your hearts" [ibid.]; go in peace!, *"vade in pace!"* [Vulgate].

802. PACIFICATION

NOUNS 1. **pacification**, **conciliation**, **propitiation**, **placation**, **appeasement**, **mollification**, dulcification; **calming**, **soothing**, **tranquilization** 162.2; **mediation** 803; placability.

2. **peace offering**, pacifics [pl.]; **overture**, advances; placation, propitiatory gift; **olive branch**; **white flag**, truce flag, flag of truce; calumet, peace pipe, **pipe of peace**.

3. **reconciliation**, reconcilement, *rapprochement* [F.], **reunion**, shaking of hands.

4. **adjustment**, accommodation, arrangement, settlement, terms.

5. **truce**, **armistice**, **peace**, **pacification**, treaty of peace, suspension of hostilities; breathing spell, cooling-off period; truce *or* peace of God, Pax Dei; temporary arrangement, *modus vivendi* [L.]; hollow truce, *pax in bello* [L., peace in war]; cartel; cartel ship.

6. **disarmament**; **demilitarization**, deactivation, reconversion.

VERBS 7. **pacify**, pacificate; **conciliate**, **placate**, **propitiate**, **appease**, **mollify**, dulcify; **calm**, **soothe**, tranquilize 162.7; smooth, smooth over, smooth down, smooth one's feathers; allay, lay, lay the dust; pour oil on the troubled waters, pour balm into.

8. **reconcile**, **bring to terms**, **bring together**, reunite, heal the breach; **harmonize**, restore harmony, put in tune; adjust, settle, compose, accommodate, arrange matters, settle differences, set straight; **mend**, patch, **patch up**, fix up [coll.], patch up a friendship *or* quarrel.

9. **make peace**, cease hostilities, raise a siege; **bury the hatchet**, **smoke the pipe of peace**; negotiate a peace, dictate peace; mediate 803.6; make a peace offering, hold out the olive branch, hoist ∼, show *or* wave the white flag.

10. **make up**, kiss and make up [coll.], make it up, make matters up, **shake hands**,

come round, come together, come to an understanding, come to terms, let the wound heal; settle one's differences, mend one's fences [polit. slang, U.S.].

11. disarm, lay down one's arms, sheathe the sword, turn swords into plowshares; demilitarize, deactivate, reconvert.

ADJS. 12. pacificatory, pacific; conciliatory, reconciliatory; propitiatory, propitiative; placative, placatory; mollifying, appeasing.

13. pacifying, soothing 162.15.

14. pacifiable, placable, appeasable.

803. MEDIATION

NOUNS 1. mediation, intermediation, intercession; intervention, interposition, interference; interagency; good offices.

2. arbitration, arbitrament; negotiation, bargaining; umpirage, mediatorship; diplomacy, diplomatics, diplomatism; peace conference, parley.

3. mediator, intermediator, intermediate agent, intermediate, intermedium, intermediary, interagent, internuncio; intercessor, interceder; intervener, interventor, interventionist; go-between, middleman, medium; connection, front, front man [all crim. slang, U.S.]; deputy, agent 779; spokesman, spokeswoman, mouthpiece; interlocutor, interlocutress or interlocutrice or interlocutrix [fem.]; negotiator, negotiant, negotiatress or negotiatrix [fem.]; parlementaire [F.], parliamentary, parliamentary agent; ad hoc arbitrator.

4. arbitrator, arbiter, moderator; umpire, referee, judge.

5. peacemaker, make-peace, pacifier, pacificator, reconciler; conciliator, propitiator, appeaser.

VERBS 6. mediate, intermediate, intercede, go between; intervene, interpose, interfere, step in; negotiate, bargain, treat with, make terms, meet halfway; arbitrate, moderate; umpire, referee, judge.

7. settle, arrange, adjust, straighten out, bring to terms or an understanding; make peace 802.9.

ADJS. 8. mediatory, mediatorial, mediative, mediating; intermediatory, intermediary, intermedial, interventional; intercessory, intercessional; interlocutory; diplomatic(al).

804. NEUTRALITY

NOUNS 1. neutrality, neutralism; impartiality; independence, nonpartisanism; anythingarianism, nothingarianism; mugwumpery, mugwumpism [both polit., U.S.].

2. indifference, indifferentness; indefiniteness, indeterminateness.

3. mid-course, middle course or way, midway; middle ground, middle of the road, fence [coll.]; medium, happy medium; mean, golden mean; compromise [coll.]; half measures, half-and-half measures.

4. neutral, neuter; independent, nonpartisan; anythingarian, nothingarian.

VERBS 5. remain neutral, stand neuter, keep in the middle of the road, sit on the fence [coll.], straddle [coll.], go halfway, strike or preserve a balance, trim.

6. steer a middle course, hold ~, keep or preserve a middle course, keep a happy medium, keep the golden mean, avoid both Scylla and Charybdis.

ADJS. 7. neutral, neuter, negative; indefinite, indeterminate; indifferent, impartial; neither one thing nor the other, neither hot nor cold; even, half-and-half, fifty-fifty [slang, U.S.]; on the fence [coll.], in the middle of the road; independent, nonpartisan.

805. COMPROMISE

Mutual Concession.—NOUNS 1. compromise, composition, concession, adjustment, abatement of differences; mid-course 804.3.

VERBS 2. compromise, make or reach a compromise, make concessions, compound, adjust, make an adjustment; strike a balance, take the mean, meet halfway, split the difference, go fifty-fifty [slang, U.S.], give and take; steer a middle course 804.6; make the best or most of, make a virtue of necessity.

806. POSSESSION

NOUNS 1. possession, possessing, seizin or seisin, nine points of the law; occupancy, occupation; hold, holding; tenancy, tenantry, tenure; apronstring tenure [coll.]; gavelkind; villenage, villeinhold; socage; chivalry, knight service; dependency; métayage [F.], métayer system; prepossession, preoccupancy; chose in possession, bird in hand; property 808.

2. ownership, possessorship, dominium; proprietorship, proprietary, lordship; seigniory, seignioralty; landownership, landowning, landholding.

3. **own,** one's own, one's very own.

4. **monopoly,** monopolization; **corner,** a corner on; engrossment, absorption; forestallment; appropriation, impropriation; usucapion or usucaption [Rom. law], prescription.

VERBS 5. **possess, have, hold, maintain, occupy, fill, enjoy,** boast; be possessed of, have in hand, have in one's possession; command, have at one's command or disposal.

6. **own,** have for one's own or very own, have to one's name, call one's own.

7. **monopolize,** hog [slang], take it all, have all to oneself; engross, absorb; forestall, regrate [hist.]; appropriate, impropriate; **corner,** get a corner on, corner the market; usucapt [Rom. law].

8. **belong to,** pertain to, appertain to; vest in.

ADJS. 9. **possessed, owned; own,** of one's own; **in one's possession, in hand,** on hand, by one, at one's command or disposal; in stock, in store.

10. **possessing, holding, occupying, owning; in possession of, possessed of,** seized of, master of; endowed with, blest with, instinct with, fraught with, laden with, charged with; worth; landowning, landholding.

11. **possessive,** possessory; selfish 976.5.

12. **monopolistic,** monopolitical; monopolizing, engrossing, absorbing.

PRONS. 13. my, mine; your, yours, thine [archaic or poetic]; our, ours; their, theirs; his, hers, its.

PREPS. 14. **with,** having, to one's name.

807. POSSESSOR

NOUNS 1. **possessor, holder, keeper,** haver, enjoyer; haves [coll.].

2. **proprietor,** proprietary, **owner;** proprietress, proprietrix; impropriator, impropriatrix; **master, mistress; lord,** laird [Scot.]; **landlord, landlady;** lord of the manor, lord of the paramount; mesne lord, mesne; **host, hostess,** mine host; innholder, innkeeper, restaurateur, hotelkeeper, *hôtelier* [F.], maître d'hôtel; householder 189.7.

3. **landowner,** landholder, **landlord,** property owner, zamindar [India]; freeholder; landed interest, landed gentry.

4. **tenant, occupant,** occupier, **resident; lodger,** roomer [U.S.], paying guest; **renter,** rentee, **lessee;** subtenant, sublessee, underlessee; tenant on sufferance, tenant at will;

tenant from year to year, tenant for years, tenant for life.

5. **trustee,** fiduciary, holder of the legal estate, cestui que trust or qui trust [law]; depository, depositary, depositee.

808. PROPERTY

NOUNS 1. **property, properties, possessions, holdings,** havings, goods, chattels, **effects,** estate and effects.

2. **belongings, appurtenances,** appointments, accessories, perquisites, appendages, appanages; **things,** duds [slang], traps [coll.], trappings, rattletraps, paraphernalia; personal effects, chattels personal, movables [law]; one's all.

3. **impedimenta,** luggage, dunnage, baggage, bag and baggage.

4. **estate, interest, equity, stake, right, title, claim,** holding; use, trust, benefit; absolute interest, vested interest, contingent interest, beneficial interest, equitable interest; easement, right of common, right of user; term, limitation; settlement, strict settlement.

5. **(estates)** particular estate, legal estate, equitable estate, paramount estate, estate at sufferance, estate at will, estate for years; estate for life, estate pur autre vie [law]; feudal estate, feudatory; fee, feud or feod, fief, estate in fee; fee simple; fee tail, estate tail or in tail; copyhold; lease, leasehold; remainder; reversion; expectancy, estate in expectancy.

6. **freehold,** estate of freehold; alodium, alod; frankalmoign, tenure in or by free alms [both Eng. law]; mortmain, dead hand.

7. **real estate, realty,** real property, chattels real, tenements; landed property or estate, land, lands, ground, acres; hereditaments, corporeal or incorporeal hereditament; acquest; domain, demesne; messuage, manor, honor [feudal law, Eng.], toft [Scot. & dial., Eng.], zamindari [India].

8. **assets, means, resources,** circumstances; stock, stock in trade; what one is worth, what one will cut up for [coll.]; funds 833.14; wealth 835; **material assets,** tangible assets, tangibles; intangible assets, intangibles; current assets, deferred assets, fixed assets, frozen assets, liquid assets, quick assets.

ADJS. 9. **propertied,** proprietary; **landed,** praedial.

10. **real;** manorial, seignioral, seigneurial; feudal, feudatory, feodal.

11. freehold, leasehold, copyhold; alodial.

809. ACQUISITION

NOUNS **1. acquisition,** gaining, **acquirement. obtainment,** obtention, **attainment,** securement; **procurement,** procuration; money-making, moneygrubbing.

2. collection, gathering, gleaning, **accumulation,** cumulation, **amassment.**

3. gain, profit, get, make, **take,** take-in [coll.], rake-off [slang, U.S.]; **gains, profits, earnings, winnings, returns,** avails, **receipts,** gettings, makings; pickings, gleanings; pelf, lucre, filthy lucre; perquisite; cleanup [slang]; net or neat profit, net; gross profit, gross; paper profits; capital gains.

4. yield, output; proceeds, produce, product; **crop, harvest,** fruit, vintage, bearing; second crop, aftermath; bumper crop.

5. find, finding, **discovery; trove,** trover. *trouvaille* [F.]; treasure-trove, buried treasure; foundling.

6. godsend, boon, blessing; windfall, windfall profits; loaves and fishes.

VERBS **7. acquire, get, gain, obtain, secure,** procure; **win,** score; **earn,** make; reap, harvest; contract, take, catch (as a disease); net, bag, sack; come or enter into possession, **come into, come by,** come in for; draw, derive.

8. take possession, take up, take over, get hold of [coll.], get at, **lay hands on,** get one's fingers or hands on.

9. collect, gather, glean, take up, pick up, get or gather in, get together, scrape together; accumulate 658.11; **scrape up,** rake up, dig up, round up, scare up [slang].

10. profit, make or **draw profit, make money,** coin money, **capitalize on,** commercialize, **cash in on,** make capital out of, make a good thing of [coll.], turn to profit or account, **realize on,** make money by, obtain a return, turn a penny or an honest penny; make the pot boil, bring grist to the mill; realize, clear.

11. be profitable, pay, answer.

ADJS. **12. obtainable, attainable, available,** to be had.

13. acquisitive, acquiring; grasping, grabby [slang].

14. gainful, productive; **profitable, remunerative, lucrative,** fat, **paying,** well-paying; advantageous, worthwhile.

ADVS. **15. profitably, gainfully,** remuneratively, lucratively, **at a profit,** for money; advantageously, to advantage, to profit, to the good.

810. LOSS

NOUNS **1. loss, privation, deprivation, bereavement;** forfeit, **forfeiture;** sacrifice, expense, cost; detriment, injury, damage; destruction, ruin, perdition, total loss; losing streak [coll., U.S.].

2. waste, wastage, **exhaustion, depletion,** dissipation, consumption, expenditure, impoverishment, decrement, drain, shrinkage, leakage.

3. losses, losings.

4. loser; good loser, sport [slang], **good sport** [slang].

VERBS **5. lose,** incur loss, **suffer loss,** meet with a loss, burn one's fingers; drop, kiss good-by [both slang]; let slip, let slip through the fingers; **forfeit, sacrifice;** go behind, fall behind; **miss,** wander from, go astray from; **mislay,** misplace; lose out; come out at the little or small end of the horn [both coll.].

6. waste, squander 852.3, 4.

ADJS. **7. lost, gone;** forfeited, forfeit; by the board, out the window; long-lost; lost to; irretrievable 887.15.

8. bereft, bereaved, divested, denuded, **deprived of,** shorn of, parted from, off one's hands; **out of,** minus [coll.], wanting, lacking; out of pocket; cut off, cut off without a cent.

ADVS. **9. at a loss, unprofitably,** to the bad [coll.]; in the red [slang, U.S.]; out (as, *out* a dollar).

811. RETENTION

NOUNS **1. retention,** retainment, prehension [chiefly zool.], **keeping, holding, maintenance, preservation;** retentiveness, retentivity; prehensility; tenacity 50.2.

2. hold, purchase, grasp, grip, gripe, **clutch, clinch, clench;** seizure 820.2; bite, nip; **cling,** clinging; **clasp, hug, embrace;** grapple; firm hold, tight grip, iron grip.

3. (wrestling holds) half nelson, strangle hold, toe hold, lock, hammer lock, headlock, scissors.

4. (prehensile organs) **clutches, claws, talons,** pounces, ungues, ungulae; **nails,** fingernails, toenail, thumbnail; **pincers,** nippers, manus, chelae; **tentacles,** tentacula; **fingers,** digits, hooks [slang]; **hands,** paws; **fists,** dukes [slang]; palm.

VERBS **5. retain, keep, maintain, pre-**

serve, persist in; hold one's own, hold one's ground.

6. **hold**, secure; **hold on,** hang on, hold on to; **grip,** gripe, **grasp, clutch, clinch, clench**; bite, nip; grapple; **clasp, hug, embrace;** cling, **cling to,** stick to, adhere to; hold fast or tight, keep a firm hold upon, hold on like a bulldog, hang on for dear life [coll.], keep hold of, never let go.

7. (hold or cherish, as a thought or feeling) **hold, keep, harbor,** bear, support; have, have and hold; **cherish,** fondle, indulge, entertain, treasure; **foster, nurture, nurse**; embrace, hug, cling to; bosom, embosom, take to the bosom.

ADJS. 8. **retentive,** keeping, holding, gripping, grasping; **tenacious,** clinging, stick-to-itive [coll.]; viselike.

9. **prehensile,** raptorial; clawed, taloned; fingered, digitate or digitated, digital.

10. **incommunicable,** noncommunicable, **unimpartible**; inalienable, indefeasible; noninfectious, noncontagious, not catching.

ADVS. 11. **for keeps** [coll.], to keep, **for good,** for good and all, for always.

12. **gripping instruments**

chuck	grip
clamp	holdfast
clasp	jaws (as of a vise)
clinch	nippers
cramp	nutcracker
dog	pincers, pinchers
forceps	*pincette* [F.]
grab	pliers
grapnel	tongs
grapple	tweezers
grappler	vise
grappling iron or	wrench 347.17
hook	

812. RELINQUISHMENT

NOUNS 1. **relinquishment, release,** dispensation; disposal, disposition, riddance; **abandonment, renunciation,** resignation; **surrender,** cession, **yielding,** forgoing, forswearing; sacrifice.

2. **waiver, quitclaim,** deed of release.

VERBS 3. **relinquish, give up,** render up, **surrender, yield,** cede, spare, drop, resign, **waive, forgo,** forswear, **renounce, abandon,** disgorge, throw up, dismiss, have done with, wash one's hands of; **part with,** give away, dispose of, kiss good-by [slang]; **sacrifice,** make a sacrifice; quitclaim.

4. **release, let go,** leave go [illit. & dial.], **let loose of,** unhand, unclutch, unclasp, relax one's hold.

ADJS. 5. **sacrificing, sacrificial.**

813. PARTICIPATION

NOUNS 1. **participation, partaking,** contribution; **sharing,** snacks, whacks [slang]; cahoots, cahoot [both slang]; partnership, copartnership; cotenancy.

2. **communion,** community; **communism,** socialism 743.4, 5; profit sharing.

3. **communization,** communalization, **socialization, nationalization, collectivization,** bolshevization.

4. **participator, participant, partaker,** sharer; party, **a party to,** accessory; partner, copartner; cotenant; shareholder.

VERBS 5. **participate, partake, contribute,** lend oneself to; **have a hand in,** have a finger in, have a finger in the pie, have to do with, be a party to; participate in, partake of or in, **take part in,** take an active part in, play or perform a part in, get in the act [slang]; **enter into,** go into; **join in,** sit in [coll.], chip in [coll.]; bear a hand, pull an oar.

6. **share, share in,** come in for a share, go shares, go snacks, go cahoots [slang]; **divide with, divvy up** [slang], halve, go halves, go halvers [coll.], **go fifty-fifty** [slang, U.S.], split the difference, **share and share alike**; do one's share or part, pull one's weight; co-operate 784.4; apportion 814.7.

7. **communize,** communalize, **socialize, collectivize, nationalize,** bolshevize.

ADJS. 8. **participating, participative,** participant, participatory; **partaking, sharing**; companionate.

9. **communal, common,** general, public, **mutual,** commutual, **joint,** conjoint, **in common,** share and share alike; co-operative 784.7; profit-sharing.

10. **communistic,** socialistic 743.19, 20.

814. APPORTIONMENT

NOUNS 1. **apportionment, portioning, division, partition,** repartition, partitionment, partitioning, parcelling, **dividing, sharing,** splitting.

2. **distribution,** dispersion; dole, doling; **dispensation,** administration, **disposal,** disposition, issuance.

3. **allotment, assignment, consignment, appointment**; appropriation; **allocation,** billeting; ordainment, ordinance, ordination.

4. (assignment to a use) **dedication, devotion, consecration,** hollowing.

5. **portion, share, interest, part,** piece, divvy [slang], **cut** [slang, U.S.], whack

[slang], snack, lot, allotment, end [coll.], contingent, proportion, percentage, measure, quantum, quota, deal, dole, meed, pittance, modicum, mess; dividend; commission, rake-off [slang, U.S.]; equal share, half, halver [coll.]; lion's share, Benjamin's mess, big end [slang].

6. allowance, ration, budget, stipend; pin money, pittance; budgeting, rationing.

VERBS 7. apportion, portion, parcel, partition, part, divide, share, share with, divide with, divide into shares, divide up, divvy up [slang], split, split up, carve, cut up, whack up [coll.]; cut a melon [slang, U.S.].

8. proportion, proportionate; prorate [U.S.].

9. parcel out, portion out, deal out, dole out, mete out; mete, dole, deal; distribute, disperse; dispense, dispose, issue, administer, give out.

10. allot, lot, assign, consign, appoint, detail, allocate, billet; set apart, set out, set off, mark off, portion off; assign to, appropriate to or for; reserve, set aside, set apart for, mark out for; ordain, destine.

11. budget, ration; allowance, put on an allowance.

12. (assign to a use) dedicate, devote, consecrate, hollow, set apart.

ADJS. 13. apportionable, divisible, distributable, dispensable, severable.

14. proportionate, proportional; distributive, distributional; respective, particular, separate, several.

ADVS. 15. proportionately, in proportion, pro rata; distributively; respectively, particularly, severally, each to each; by lot; share and share alike, in equal shares.

815. TRANSFER OF PROPERTY OR RIGHT

NOUNS 1. transfer, transference; conveyance, conveyancing; delivery, deliverance; assignment, assignation; consignment, consignation; conferment, conferral; cession; transmission, transmittal; demise; alienation, abalienation; amortization, amortizement; enfeoffment; deeding [U.S.]; lease and release.

2. devolution, succession, reversion; shifting use, shifting trust.

VERBS 3. transfer, convey, deliver, hand, pass, negotiate; hand over, turn over, pass over; assign, consign, confer, cede; make over, set over; sign over, sign away; transmit, hand down, hand

on, pass on, devolve upon; demise; alienate, alien, abalienate, amortize; enfeoff; deed [U.S.].

4. change hands, change ownership; devolve, pass on, succeed.

ADJS. 5. transferable, conveyable, negotiable, alienable; assignable, consignable; devisable, bequeathable; heritable, inheritable.

816. GIVING

NOUNS 1. giving, donation; bestowal, bestowment; presentation, presentment; conferment, conferral; delivery, deliverance, surrender; communication, impartation, impartment; disposal, disposition, dispensation; vouchsafement, accordance; contribution, subscription; accommodation, provision, supplying, furnishment; liberality 851.

2. commitment, consignment, assignment, delegation, relegation, commendation, remanding, entrustment.

3. charity, almsgiving; philanthropy 936.4; bread line [U.S.].

4. gift, present, presentation, cadeau [F.], offering, fairing, award, grant, vouchsafement, liberality; oblation 1030.7; handsel, hansel; box; Christmas gift; peace offering; Indian gift [coll., U.S.]; white elephant [coll.].

5. gratuity, largess, bounty, sportula, pourboire [F.], cumshaw, baksheesh [Near East], dash or dashee [Africa]; perquisite, perks [pl., slang]; fee, consideration, compensation; tip, douceur [F.], Trinkgeld [Ger.]; grease, salve, oil of palms [all slang]; premium, bonus, boot [now dial.], lagniappe [Louisiana], pilon [Southwest, U.S.]; honorarium; bribe 649.2.

6. donation, donative; contribution, subscription, tribute; alms, charity, dole, handout [slang, U.S.]; alms fee, pittance, widow's mite; Peter or Peter's pence or penny; offertory, collection.

7. benefit, benefaction, benevolence, blessing, favor, boon.

8. subsidy, subvention; subsidization; grant, bounty; allowance, stipend, allotment; aid, assistance, help, pecuniary aid; grant-in-aid; alimony; annuity, tontine; pension, old-age insurance, retirement benefits.

9. endowment, investment, settlement, foundation; dower; dowry, dot, portion, marriage portion; thirds; appanage.

10. bequest, bequeathal, legacy, de-

vise; inheritance 817.2; **will, testament,** last will and testament; probate, attested copy; codicil.

11. giver, donor, donator, presenter, bestower, conferrer, grantor, vouchsafer; fairy godmother; cheerful giver; **contributor, subscriber;** almsgiver, almoner; **philanthropist** 936.8; assignor, consignor; settler [law]; testate, testator, testatrix; feoffor; Indian giver [coll., U.S.].

VERBS **12. give, present, donate** [chiefly U.S.], tip [slang, except as a gratuity], slip [slang], let have; **bestow, confer, award, allot, render,** bestow on, impart, communicate; **grant,** accord, **allow,** vouchsafe, yield, afford; **tender,** extend, issue, dispense, administer; serve, help to; deal, dole, mete; **give out, deal out, dole out, mete out, hand out** [coll.], dish out [coll.], fork out [slang], shell out [slang]; make a present of, gift, give as a gift.

13. deliver, hand, pass, reach, forward, put into the hands of; transfer 270.9; **hand over,** give over, deliver over, fork over [slang], **pass over, turn over,** come across with [slang]; hand in, give in; **surrender,** resign.

14. contribute, subscribe, chip in [coll.], kick in [slang, U.S.]; contribute to, **give to, donate to** [chiefly U.S.]; put something in the pot, sweeten the kitty [poker].

15. furnish, supply, provide, afford, provide for; **accommodate with,** favor with, indulge with; **heap upon,** pour on, shower down upon, lavish upon.

16. commit, consign, assign, delegate, relegate, confide, commend, remit, remand, give in charge; **entrust** or intrust, trust, give in trust.

17. endow, invest, vest in; endow with, bless with; **settle on** or **upon; dower; bequeath, bequest, leave, devise, will to,** hand down, hand on, pass on, transmit; entail.

18. subsidize, finance; aid, assist, help; pension, pension off.

19. thrust upon, force upon, press upon, push upon, obtrude on, ram or cram down one's throat.

20. give away, dispose of, **part with,** sacrifice, spare.

ADJS. **21. charitable** 936.16; generous 851.4.

22. giveable, presentable, bestowable, impartible, communicable; allowable, concessional.

23. given, allowed, accorded, granted, vouchsafed; gratuitous 848.5; God-given, providential.

24. donative, contributory, tributary.

25. endowed, dowered, invested; subsidiary, stipendiary, pensionary; testate, testamentary; intestate.

ADVS. **26.** to his heirs, to one and his heirs forever, to the heirs of his body, to his heirs and assigns, to his executors, ~ administrators and assigns.

INTERJS. **27. you are welcome!, don't mention it!,** think no more of it!, forget it! [coll.], not another word!, glad to do it!

817. RECEIVING

NOUNS **1. receiving,** receival, **reception, recipience** or recipiency, **receipt;** securement, derivation, assumption, acceptance; admission, admittance.

2. inheritance, heritance, **heritage, patrimony, birthright,** descent; bequest 816.10; reversion; entail; heirship, heirdom; primogeniture, ultimogeniture; coheirship, coparcenary or coparceny, jointure; gavelkind; hereditament, corporeal or incorporeal hereditament; **heritable,** movable, heirship movable [Scot.]; **heirloom.**

3. recipient, receiver; payee, endorsee, drawee; holder [law].

4. beneficiary, *bénéficiare* [F.]; **donee, grantee; assignee, assign; devisee, legatee;** feoffee; almsman, almswoman; stipendiary; pensioner, pensionary; annuitant.

5. heir, heritor, inheritor; **heiress,** inheritress, inheritrix; coheir, coparcener; heir portioner [Scot.]; heir expectant; **heir apparent,** apparent heir; **heir presumptive,** presumptive heir; legal heir, heir at law, heir general, heir whatsoever [Scot.]; heir of inventory [Scot.], beneficiary heir; heir of provision, heir by destination; heir of the body; reversioner; remainderman.

VERBS **6. receive, get, obtain, gain,** secure, have, come by, be in receipt of; **admit, accept,** take, **take in,** take off one's hands; pocket, put into one's pocket; **derive, draw,** draw or derive from; drag down, pull down [both slang]; have coming in, have in prospect, come in for, have an income of.

7. inherit, heir, come into, come in for, come by, step into a fortune, step into the shoes of, succeed to.

8. be received, come in, come to hand, pass or fall into one's hands, go into one's pocket, come or fall to one, fall to one's share or lot; accrue.

ADJS. **9. receiving, receptive, recipient,** on the receiving end.

10. received, accepted, admitted, recognized, approved.

818. LENDING

NOUNS **1. lending, loaning;** advance, advancing, advancement; lend-lease.

2. loan, lend [coll. & dial.], **advance,** accommodation; call loan, call money, time money; package loan; foreign loan, external loan.

3. lender, loaner; moneylender, moneymonger, money broker; banker 834.10; **usurer,** Shylock, loan shark [coll.]; **pawnbroker,** pawn [coll.], lumberer [slang]; my uncle [slang]; mortgagor, mortgage holder.

4. pawnshop, pawnbrokery, pawn [coll.], **hock shop** [slang], spout [slang], *mont de piété* [F.], my uncle's [slang], sign of the three balls.

VERBS **5. lend, loan, advance,** accommodate with, come across or down with the needful [slang]; lend-lease, lease-lend.

ADJS. **6. loaned, lent.**

ADVS. **7. on loan,** on security; in advance.

819. BORROWING

NOUNS **1. borrowing,** money-raising; pawning, pledging, hocking [slang]; downstream borrowing [finance]; debt, debtor 838.

2. adoption, appropriation, assumption; imitation, simulation, copying, mocking; borrowed plumes.

VERBS **3. borrow,** borrow the loan of [joc.], take up [coll.], get the needful [slang], get on credit or trust; **raise money,** raise the wind [slang], fly a kite [slang]; **touch, hit up,** hit one for [all slang]; run into debt 838.6; pawn 770.12; borrow of Peter to pay Paul.

4. adopt, appropriate, take, take on, **assume,** make use of; **imitate, simulate,** copy, mock, steal one's stuff [slang, U.S.].

820. TAKING

NOUNS **1. taking,** possession, taking possession; acquisition 809; reception 817.

2. seizure, grab, snatch; hold 811.2; **catch,** catching; **capture,** caption; **apprehension,** prehension [chiefly zool.]; dragnet, stakeout.

3. appropriation, impropriation [Eng. eccl. law], **adoption, assumption,** usurpa-

tion, arrogation; annexation, commandeering [both coll.]; preoccupation, prepossession, pre-emption.

4. (seizure and appropriation) **attachment,** annexation; **confiscation,** sequestration; impoundage, impoundment; **commandeering, impressment;** levy; distraint, distress [both law]; garnishment [law]; execution [law]; androlepsia or androlepsy [law].

5. deprivation, deprivement, **privation, divestment, bereavement;** curtailment, abridgement; disentitlement.

6. dispossession, disseizin or disseisin [law], expropriation; eviction 308.2; disendowment; **disinheritance,** disherison, disownment; foreclosure.

7. rapacity, rapaciousness, wolfishness, ravenousness, predacity; **extortion,** bloodsucking, vampirism.

8. take, catch, capture, seizure, **haul.**

9. taker; partaker; catcher, captor, capturer.

10. extortionist, extortioner; **bloodsucker, vampire,** harpy, vulture, bird of prey; profiteer.

VERBS **11. take, possess,** take possession; **get,** get into one's hold or possession; contract, catch (as a disease); partake; **accept,** pocket; acquire 809.7; receive 817.6.

12. seize, take or get hold of, lay **hold of,** catch or grab hold of, **lay hands on,** clap hands on [coll.], get one's fingers or hands on, get between one's finger and thumb; **grab, grasp, grip,** gripe, **grapple, snatch, clutch,** claw, clinch, clench; **clasp, hug, embrace;** snap up, nip up, whip up, catch up; take by assault or storm, ravish, rape, lay violent hands on; take by the throat, throttle.

13. seize on or **upon,** fasten upon; **spring** or **pounce upon,** swoop down upon; **catch at, snatch at,** snap at, jump at, make a grab for, scramble for.

14. catch, snatch, nip; land, nail [both coll.]; hook, snag, snare, sniggle, spear, harpoon; **ensnare** or **insnare,** enmesh or inmesh, **entangle,** tangle, foul, tangle up with; net, mesh; bag, sack; **trap, entrap;** lasso, rope [U.S.], noose; lodge, stick.

15. capture, apprehend, collar [coll.], **nab** [slang], grab [coll.], lay by the heels, take prisoner.

16. appropriate, impropriate [Eng. eccl. law], **adopt,** apply, **assume, usurp,** arrogate, accroach, convert [law]; **annex, commandeer** [both coll.]; take possession of, possess oneself of, take for oneself, arrogate to oneself, take up, **take over, help oneself to,** make use of, make free with, dip one's hands into, lay under contribution; preoccupy, prepossess, pre-empt; jump a claim.

17. (seize and appropriate) **attach,** annex; **confiscate,** sequester, sequestrate, impound; **commandeer,** press, **impress;** levy, distrain, replevy [all law]; garnishee, garnish [both law].

18. **take from,** take away from, **deprive of,** relieve one of, ease one of; **deprive, bereave, divest;** curtail, abridge, cut off; disentitle.

19. **wrest,** wring, wrench, rend; **extort,** exact, squeeze; **force from, wrest from, wrench from, wring from, tear from, rend from,** snatch from, pry loose from.

20. **dispossess,** disseize *or* disseise [law], expropriate; **evict** 308.14; disendow; **disinherit, disown,** cut out of one's will, **cut off,** cut off with a shilling, cut off without a cent; foreclose.

21. **strip, fleece, shear,** skin [slang], flay, pluck [slang], **despoil, divest,** displume; **milk; bleed,** bleed white; absorb, swallow up; exhaust, drain, dry, suck dry; **impoverish,** eat out of house and home.

ADJS. 22. **taking, catching;** contagious 684.47; privative, deprivative; confiscatory.

23. **rapacious, ravenous,** ravening, **vulturous, wolfish,** lupine; vampirish, **bloodsucking,** parasitic(al); **grasping,** grabby [slang]; all-devouring, all-engulfing.

821. RESTITUTION

NOUNS 1. **restitution, restoration, return;** rendition, reddition; recommitment, remandment, remand; remitter.

2. **reparation, recompense, compensation, indemnification, retribution,** redress, **atonement, amends, requital.**

3. **recovery,** regainment; **retrieval,** retrieve; **recuperation,** recoup, recoupment; **retake,** retaking, recapture; **repossession,** resumption, reoccupation; **reclamation,** revindication; **redemption,** ransom; salvage, trover; replevin, replevy [both law].

VERBS 4. **restore, return, give back,** take back, bring back, put back; remit, send back; recommit, remand.

5. **make restitution,** make reparation, make **amends, recompense, compensate,** requite, indemnify.

6. **recover, regain, retrieve,** recuperate, **recoup, get back,** come by one's own;

redeem, ransom; **reclaim,** revindicate; **repossess,** resume, reoccupy; **retake,** recapture, take back; replevin, replevy [both law].

ADJS. 7. **restitutive,** restitutory, **restorative;** compensatory, indemnificatory, redemptive, retributive, reparative; reversionary, revertible.

ADVS. 8. **in restitution,** in reparation, in recompense, in compensation, in retribution, in requital, in amends, in atonement, to atone for.

822. THEFT

NOUNS 1. **theft, thievery,** stealage, **stealing,** thieving, **purloining,** swiping [slang, U.S.], lifting [coll.], snatching, snitching [slang], pinching [slang], conveyance; **appropriation,** annexation [coll.]; **pilfering,** pilferage, pilfer, **filching,** scrounging [slang]; abstraction; sneak thievery; shoplifting; poaching; embezzlement, peculation.

2. **larceny,** petit *or* petty larceny, grand larceny, simple larceny, mixed ∼, compound *or* aggravated larceny.

3. **robbery,** robbing; **burglary,** burglarizing, burgle [coll.]; housebreaking, second-story work; **safecracking,** safebreaking, safeblowing; bank robbery; **highway robbery, holdup** [slang, U.S.], stick-up [slang], holdup *or* stick-up job [slang]; **pocket picking,** pickpocketing, pickpocketry, pickpocketism.

4. **cattle stealing,** cattle lifting [coll.], **cattle rustling** [coll., U.S.], abaction [law].

5. **plundering, pillaging, looting, sacking,** ransacking, rifling, spoiling, despoiling; **pillage, plunder,** sack, rapine, spoliation, spoilation, depredation, direption [hist.], ravage, ravaging, ravagement, rape, ravishment; maraud, marauding, foraging; raid, foray, razzia.

6. **piracy, buccaneering, privateering; freebooting,** freebootery; filibustering, filibusterism; letter of marque.

7. **plagiarism,** plagiarizing, **piracy,** literary piracy, conveyance, appropriation, borrowing [joc.]; autoplagiarism.

8. **abduction, kidnaping; shanghaiing,** crimping, impressment.

9. **extortion,** shakedown [slang]; **blackmail, badger game;** Black Hand [U.S.]; Camorra [It.].

10. **a theft, steal,** grab, filch, pinch [slang], lift [slang]; **job,** caper [both slang, U.S.]; robbery, burglary, etc.

11. **booty**, spoil, **spoils**, **loot**, **swag** [slang], **plunder**, pillage, prize, haul, take, grab, seizure, pickings, lift [slang], **filch**, steal, stealings, stealage, stolen goods; **boodle** [polit., cant], **graft** [coll.], perquisite, pork barrel [polit. cant, U.S.], spoils of office; blackmail.

12. **thievishness**, larcenousness, priggism [cant]; light fingers, sticky fingers [joc.]; banditry, banditism; brigandage, latrocinium [Rom. hist.]; kleptomania.

VERBS 13. **steal**, **thieve**, **purloin**, **swipe** [slang, U.S.], **appropriate**, borrow [joc.], **take**, snatch, snaffle [chiefly dial., Eng.], manavel or manarvel [naut. slang], palm, bag, cabbage, prig [cant], ramp [slang, Eng.]. **make off with**, walk off with, run off or away with, take away, disregard the distinction between *meum* and *tuum*; lift, hook, crib, annex [all coll.]; **cop**, **pinch**, nip, snitch, nick, mooch, snare [all slang]; abstract; **pilfer**, **filch**, scrounge [slang]; poach; rustle (as cattle [coll., U.S.]); embezzle, peculate.

14. **rob**, commit robbery; **burglarize** [coll.] burgle [coll.], commit burglary; pickpocket, **pick one's pockets**; **hold up** [coll.], **stick up** [slang], bail up [slang, Australia]; **highjack** or hijack [coll., U.S.]; rob Peter to pay Paul.

15. **plunder**, **pillage**, **loot**, **sack**, **ransack**, rifle, spoil, spoliate, despoil, depredate, prey on or upon, ravage, ravish, raven, sweep, gut; fleece 820.21; maraud, forage, raid.

16. **pirate**, buccaneer, privateer, freeboot, filibuster.

17. **plagiarize**, **pirate**, convey, borrow [joc.], appropriate, **pick one's brains**.

18. **abduct**, abduce, **carry off** or **away**, run off or away with, spirit away; **kidnap**, snatch [slang, U.S.]; **shanghai**, crimp, impress.

19. **extort**, shake down [slang], squeeze, screw, sponge, wring from; **blackmail**, levy blackmail; badger, play the badger game.

ADJS. 20. **thievish**, **thieving**, **larcenous**, priggish [cant], stealy, **light-fingered**, **sticky-fingered** [joc.]; burglarious; brigandish; piratic(al), piraty, piratelike; pickpocket.

21. **plunderous**, **plundering**, **looting**, pillaging, ravaging, marauding, spoliative; predatory, predaceous.

823. THIEF

NOUNS 1. **thief**, **robber**, stealer, purloiner, lifter [slang], **crook** [coll., U.S.], gun [slang], *chor* [Gypsy]; prig, prigger [both slang]; larcenist, larcener; **pilferer**, **filcher**, scrounger [slang]; sneak thief, prowler; shoplifter; poacher; land pirate, land rat; chicken thief; grave robber, ghoul; embezzler, peculator.

2. **pickpocket**, cutpurse; fingersmith, dip, ganef, file, wire [all slang]; **purse snatcher**; swell mob, swell-mobsmen [both slang]; light-fingered gentry.

3. **burglar**, **yegg** or **yeggman** [slang], cracksman [slang]; **housebreaker**, second-story thief or worker; **safecracker**, safebreaker, safeblower, peteman or peterman [slang, U.S.]; bank robber.

4. **bandit**, **brigand**, rover, dacoit [India], picaroon; **gangster** [coll., U.S.], mobsman, racketeer; **thug**, desperado 941.4; sandbagger; Mau Mau [E. Africa]; banditti.

5. **highwayman**, **highway robber**, hightoby [slang, Eng.], **footpad**, road agent [West. U.S.], bushranger [Australia]; holdup, **holdup man**, stick-up man [all slang, U.S.]; **highjacker** or hijacker [slang, U.S.].

6. **plunderer**, **pillager**, **looter**, **marauder**, rifler, sacker, spoiler, despoiler, spoliator, depredator, ravisher, ravager; **wrecker**; harpy, falcon, hawk.

7. **freebooter**, **filibusterer**, mosstrooper [hist.], rapparee.

8. **pirate**, **corsair**, **buccaneer**, **privateer**, rover, picaroon; viking, sea king; Paul Jones, Captain Kidd, Long John Silver.

9. **cattle thief**, duffer [slang, Australia], abactor, abigeus; **rustler**, **cattle rustler** [both coll., U.S.].

10. **plagiarist**, plagiarizer, **pirate**, literary pirate.

11. **abductor**, **kidnaper**; **shanghaier**; crimp, crimper.

12. (famous thieves) Robin Hood, Jesse James, Claude Duval, Bill Sikes, Jack Sheppard, Robert Macaire, Dick Turpin, Jonathan Wild, Autolycus, Macheath, Nevison, Thief of Bagdad.

13. **den of thieves**, den of Cacus; Alsatia, Whitefriars.

824. ILLICIT BUSINESS

NOUNS 1. **illicit business**, **racket** [coll., U.S.]; **black market**, gray market; liquor traffic, narcotics traffic; **bootlegging** [U.S.], **moonshining** [coll., U.S.], moonlighting [slang]; booklegging [slang, U.S.].

2. **smuggling**, fair trade [18th-century euphemism], contrabandage, contraband-

ism, contrabandery; gunrunning, rumrunning [U.S.].

3. contraband, run goods; bootleg 994.21.

4. racketeer; black marketeer, gray marketeer; **bootlegger** [U.S.], **moonshiner** [coll., U.S.], moonlighter [slang, U.S.]; booklegger [slang, U.S.].

5. smuggler, contrabandist, runner; gunrunner, rumrunner [U.S.].

6. fence, receiver, **receiver of stolen goods;** swagman or swagsman, smasher, lock [all slang].

VERBS **7.** (deal in illicit goods) push, shove [both slang, U.S.]; **sell under the counter; black-market; bootleg** [U.S.], **moonshine** [coll., U.S.], moonlight [slang, U.S.]; bookleg [slang, U.S.]; fence.

8. smuggle, run, sneak.

825. COMMERCE

Business Dealings.—NOUNS **1. commerce, trade, traffic, truck, intercourse, dealing, dealings; business, business intercourse;** merchantry, mercantile business; industry; market; big business, small business; free enterprise, private enterprise; fair trade, free trade, reciprocal trade, unilateral trade, multilateral trade; balance of trade; restraint of trade; slave trade.

2. barter, bartering, **trade, trading, trafficking; exchange,** interchange, swapping [coll.], give-and-take; **buying and selling,** bargain and sale; jobbing; truck system.

3. negotiation, bargaining, haggling, higgling, **dickering** [U.S.], **chaffering;** dicker [U.S.], chaffer, haggle; collective bargaining, package bargaining; pattern bargaining.

4. transaction, business transaction, **deal,** business deal, **negotiation,** operation, turn; package deal.

5. bargain, deal [coll.], engagement, dicker [U.S.]; **trade, swap** [coll.]; horse trade; trade-in [U.S.]; blind bargain, pig in a poke; hard bargain.

6. custom, good will.

7. business cycle, prosperity, crisis, recession, depression, liquidation, recovery.

8. commercialism, mercantilism; industrialism; Mercury (god of commerce).

9. commercialization; industrialization.

VERBS **10. trade, deal, traffic, truck; barter; exchange,** change, interchange, give in exchange, give and take; **swap** [coll.], switch, swap horses [coll.]; trade off; trade in [U.S.]; **trade out of,** swap out of [coll.]; **trade sight-unseen** or **unsight-unseen,** make a blind bargain, sell a pig in a poke.

11. buy and sell, market, merchandise; **carry on business,** carry on or ply a trade, drive a trade, be in business, be in the city, keep a shop; job; scalp [U.S.].

12. deal in, trade in, traffic in, handle [U.S.].

13. trade with, deal with, traffic with, have dealings with, have truck with, do or transact business with, frequent as a customer, **patronize** [coll.]; open an account with, have an account with.

14. bargain, drive a bargain, negotiate, dicker [U.S.], bid for; **haggle,** higgle, chaffer, huckster, stickle, cheapen, beat down; underbid, outbid; drive a hard bargain.

15. strike a bargain, make a bargain, make a dicker [U.S.], put through a deal; bargain for, agree to; **come to terms** 520.10; be a bargain, be a go [coll.], be on [slang].

16. commercialize; industrialize.

ADJS. **17. commercial,** trading, **mercantile,** merchant; industrial; wholesale, retail.

826. PURCHASE

NOUNS **1. purchase, buy; buying,** purchasing; **shopping, marketing;** windowshopping; shopping spree; repurchase, rebuying.

2. (commercial) emption, *emptio* [L., law], right of emption or sole emption; pre-emption, refusal, right of pre-emption, prior right of purchase; coemption; purchasing power.

3. clientele, clientry, clientage, **patronage** [coll.], **custom; market,** public, purchasing public.

4. customer, client; patron, patronizer [both coll.]; contact [slang, U.S.], business contact; **prospect,** sucker [slang]; customer agent [coll.].

5. buyer, purchaser, emptor [law.], **consumer,** vendee; **shopper,** marketer; window-shopper; coemptor, coemptionator.

6. by-bidder, capper [slang], **straw bidder** [coll., U.S.], decoy, stool pigeon, come-on man [slang, U.S.], Peter Funk [U.S.].

VERBS **7. purchase, buy,** procure, make or complete a purchase, make a buy, blow oneself to [slang]; buy up, take up [coll.]; buy out; buy off; buy in, buy into; repurchase, rebuy, buy back.

8. shop, market, go shopping or a-shopping, go marketing; window-shop.

9. bid, make a bid, offer; **by-bid,** cap [slang]; bid up; bid in [U.S.].

ADᵈS. **10. purchasing, buying,** emptional; coemptional; cliental.

11. bought, boughten [dial.], purchased.

827. SALE

NOUNS **1. sale,** disposal; wholesale, retail; **market, demand,** outlet; buyer's market, seller's market; mass market; conditional sale; tie-in sale, tie-in; turnover; bill of sale.

2. selling, marketing; vending, peddling, hawking, huckstering; sales campaign; salesmanship, high-pressure salesmanship.

3. (a sale) closing-out sale, sellout [slang]; fire sale; bazaar or bazar.

4. auction, auction sale, roup [Scot. & North. Eng.], vendue, cant [chiefly Ir.], outcry, sale by outcry, sale at or by auction, sale to the highest bidder; Dutch auction; bid, bidding; straw bid [coll., U.S.]; bybid, cap [slang]; by-bidding, capping [slang]; auction stand, block, sale block.

5. sales talk, pitch [slang], spiel [slang, U.S.], ballyhoo [slang].

6. sales resistance, consumer or buyer resistance.

7. salability, salableness, **marketability,** vendibility, venality.

VERBS **8. sell, market,** dispose of, move, sell off, make or effect a sale, convert into cash, turn into money; **sell out,** close out [U.S.]; sell up; **retail,** regrate, sell retail, sell over the counter; **wholesale,** sell wholesale; dump, unload; sacrifice, sell at a sacrifice or loss; resell, sell over; undersell, undercut, cut under; sell forward (for future delivery); realize, sell for.

9. vend, dispense, **peddle, hawk, huckster,** higgle; high-pressure [coll., U.S.].

10. put up for sale, put up, offer for sale.

11. auction, auction off, auctioneer, sell at auction [esp. U.S.], sell by auction [esp. Eng.], put up to or at auction, put on the block, sell at the spear, bring to or under the hammer, roup [Scot. & North. Eng.], cant [chiefly Ir.], outcry; knock down, sell to the highest bidder.

ADJS **12. salable, marketable,** merchantable, vendible, venal; in demand.

13. unsalable, nonsalable, **unmarketable,** etc.; on one's hands, on the shelves, unbought, unsold.

ADVS. **14. for sale,** to sell, in or on the market, in the marts of trade; at a bargain, marked down.

15. at auction [esp. U.S.], by auction [esp. Eng.], on the block, under the hammer, at the spear.

828. BUSINESSMAN, MERCHANT

NOUNS **1. businessman,** businesswoman; small businessman, little fellow; big businessman, tycoon [coll., U.S.], baron [U.S.], big butter-and-egg man [slang, U.S.]; **industrialist,** captain of industry; king, railroad king, etc.

2. merchant, merchandiser, **trader,** trafficker, **dealer,** monger, chandler; **tradesman,** tradeswoman; **storekeeper, shopkeeper,** shopman; tallyman, tallywoman, roupingwife [Scot.]; retailer, regrater; wholesaler; importer, exporter; distributor or distributer.

3. (merchants) grocer, groceryman; greengrocer; fruiterer; butcher, meatman; poulterer; fishmonger, fishwife; ironmonger [esp. Eng.], hardwareman; perfumer, parfumeur [F.]; bookdealer, chandler, confectioner, florist, furrier, jeweler, newsdealer, saddler, stationer, tobacconist.

4. salesman, seller, salesperson, salesclerk; **saleswoman,** saleslady, salesgirl; **clerk,** counterjumper [coll.]; soda jerk or jerker [slang]; **agent, sales agent,** selling agent; scalper, ticket scalper; sales engineer; sales manager; salespeople, sales force.

5. traveling salesman, traveler, commercial traveler, traveling agent, traveling man or woman, commis-voyageur [F.], knight of the road, bagman, **drummer** [U.S.], runner [coll.]; solicitor 828.6; book agent, bookseller.

6. vendor or vender, **peddler** or pedlar, huckster, hawker, higgler, cadger, monger, colporteur, chapman [Eng.]; cheapJack, cheap-John [both coll.]; faker [slang], camelot [F.]; sutler, vivandier [F.]; costerman, costermonger [both chiefly Eng.]; newsboy, newsy [coll., U.S.]; milkman, iceman [U.S.].

7. solicitor or soliciter, **canvasser, petitioner,** runner [U.S.]; **tout** [slang], touter [coll.]; **pitchman** [U.S.]; **barker** [coll.], spieler [slang, U.S.]; ballyhooer, **ballyhoo man** [both slang].

8. auctioneer, rouper [Scot. & North. Eng.], Peter Duff [slang, U.S.].

9. broker, bill broker, cotton broker, hotel broker, insurance broker, mortgage broker; stockbroker 831.10; pawnbroker 818.3; money broker, money changer, cambist; real-estate broker, realtor [U.S.].

10. ragman, old-clothesman; **junkman** [U.S.], junk dealer.

11. tradesmen, tradespeople, tradesfolk, merchantry.

829. MERCHANDISE

NOUNS 1. **merchandise, commodities, wares, goods,** effects, vendibles, **consumer goods,** goods for sale; stock, staples, stock in trade; line, line of goods; side line [U.S.]; job lot.

2. **commodity, ware,** vendible, **product,** article, item, article of merchandise; staple; best seller [U.S.]; special, feature, leader, lead item; loss leader; seconds; drug, drug on the market.

3. **dry goods, soft goods;** textiles 377.5, 15; yard goods, white goods, linens, napery; men's wear, ladies' wear, children's wear, infants' wear; sportswear, sporting goods; leatherware, leather goods.

4. **hardware, ironmongery** [esp. Eng.], **hard goods,** durable goods; fixtures, appliances 657.4; tools and machinery 347; tableware, dinnerware; silverware, flatware, hollow ware; metalware, brassware, copperware, ironware, tinware; woodenware; glassware; chinaware, earthenware, clayware; stoneware, graniteware; enamelware; ovenware.

5. **housewares;** kitchenware; furniture, furnishings.

6. **notions** [U.S.], sundries, novelties, knicknacks; toilet goods, toiletries; cosmetics; giftware.

7. **groceries,** grocery; green goods, produce, truck.

830. MARKET

Place of Trade.—NOUNS 1. **market, mart, store, shop,** boutique [F.], gunge [India]; house, establishment; wareroom, warehouse [chiefly Eng.], magasin [F.]; **retail store; wholesale house,** discount house, mail-order house; **general store, department store, variety store; co-op** [coll.], co-operative; **dime store** [U.S.], **ten-cent store,** five-and-ten [coll., U.S.]; dollar store [U.S.]; chain store; drive-in; concession [U.S.]; **trading post,** post [U.S.]; counting-house; supermarket [U.S.].

2. **market place, mart; open market,** market overt; **emporium,** rialto, staple; bazaar or bazar, fair, exposition.

3. **booth, stall, stand;** newsstand [U.S.].

4. **market hall,** tolbooth or tollbooth [chiefly Scot.], tollhouse [local, Eng.].

5. (stores) hardware store, ironmongery [Eng.]; stationery store, stationers; confectionery, candy store, sweet shop; drugstore, chemist's shop [Eng.]; tobacco store, cigar store, tobacconists; second-hand store, antique shop; finding store [U.S.], grindery warehouse [Eng.]; horse market, Tattersall's; bookstore 603.19, clothing store, dry goods store, florists, fur store, furniture store, haberdashery, jewelry store, leather goods store, liquor store, saddlery, shoe store, sporting goods store.

6. **grocery,** grocery store [both U.S.]; greengrocery, vegetable store or market; groceteria; butcher shop, meat market; delicatessen; bakery, bakeshop; dairy, creamery.

7. **commissary** [U.S.], **canteen,** sutlery; Post Exchange [U.S.], P.X.

8. **gas station, filling station** [U.S.], service station [U.S.].

9. **vender,** vending machine; **slot machine,** one-arm bandit [slang, U.S.]; automat.

10. **salesroom,** wareroom; showroom.

11. **counter,** shopboard; notion counter; showcase.

831. STOCK MARKET

NOUNS 1. **stock market, the market,** ticker market; open market, competitive market; steady market, strong market, hard or stiff market; unsteady market, spotted market; technical market; long market; topheavy market.

2. **active market,** brisk market, lively market, swimming market; easy market.

3. **inactive market,** slow market, stagnant market, flat market, tired market, sick market, drugged market, sleeping market, dead market; tight market.

4. **rising market,** booming market, buoyant market, bulging market; **bull market,** bullish market.

5. **declining market,** sagging market, retreating market, off market, soft market, hungry market; **bear market,** bearish market; **slump,** sag; break, break in the market; **crash,** smash.

6. **rigged market,** manipulated market, pegged market, put-up market.

7. **stock exchange, exchange, change,** 'change, stock market, bourse, **board;** the Exchange, New York Stock Exchange, the Big Board; brokers' board; **curb, curb**

market, outside market; board room; exchange floor, arena of the bears and bulls; pit, corn pit, wheat pit, etc.; quotation board, board.

8. the street, financial district, financial front: Wall Street [U.S.], the Street; Lombard Street [Eng.]; the Bourse [Paris, Berlin].

9. stockbrokerage, brokerage, brokerage office; **bucket shop;** private wire house; sell-and-switch house.

10. stockbroker, sharebroker [Eng.], **broker, jobber, stockjobber,** dealer, stock dealer; stock-exchange broker, *agent de bourse* [F.]; floor broker, floor trader, floorman, room man, boardman, pit man; curb broker; outsider, stag [Eng.]; odd-lot dealer; two-dollar broker; broker's agent, customers' man; bond crowd.

11. speculator, adventurer, operator; big operator, smart operator; **plunger;** scalper; lame duck (one unable to fulfill his engagements).

12. bear, short, short seller; shorts, short interest, short side, short account, bear account.

13. bull, long, long seller, margin purchaser: longs, long interest, long side, long account, bull account.

14. stockholder, stockowner, **shareholder,** coupon clipper [slang]; bondholder: stockholder of record.

15. stock company, share company; joint-stock company; holding company; issuing company; stock insurance company; bonding company, guarantee association; banking syndicate; parent company.

16. trust, investment trust; corporate trust; rigid *or* fixed trust, flexible *or* manageable trust; open-end trust, closed-end trust; horizontal trust.

17. pool, gross-money pool, net-money-receipts pool, bear pool, bull pool, blind pool, bobtail pool.

18. stockbroking, brokerage, stockbrokerage, **jobbing, stockjobbing,** stockjobbery, stock dealing; bucketing, legal bucketing; scaling.

19. speculation, agiotage; **venture,** flutter; flier, plunge; scalping; liquidation, profit taking; arbitrage; buying in, covering shorts; washing, washed *or* wash sale; short sale; spot sale; round trade *or* transaction, turn; risk *or* venture capital, equity capital.

20. manipulation, rigging, higgling; **raid,** bear raid, bull raid; **corner,** corner in, corner on the market, monopoly.

21. option, put, call, put and call, right of put and call; spread; discretionary order.

22. panic, bear panic, bull panic, rich man's panic.

VERBS **23. speculate, venture,** operate, **play the market,** buy ∼, sell *or* deal in futures; **plunge,** take a flier; scalp; bucket, bucketshop; stag, stag the market [Eng.]; trade on margin; pyramid; be long, be long of the market, be on the long side of the market; be short, be short of the market, be on the short side of the market, be caught short; margin up, apply *or* deposit margin; wait out the market, hold on; salt down; miss the market, overstay the market; scoop the market, make a scoop *or* killing.

24. sell, convert, liquidate; throw on the market, dump, unload; **sell long,** go long; **sell short,** go short, make a short sale; cover one's sale *or* delivery, cover one's short, fulfill a short sale; make delivery, clear the trade; close out, sell out, terminate the account; average, average out.

25. manipulate the market, rig the market, higgle the market; bear, **bear the market;** bull, **bull the market;** raid the market; hold *or* peg the market, milk the market; water; wash sales.

26. corner, get a corner on, **corner the market;** monopolize, engross; buy up, absorb, assimilate.

832. SECURITIES

NOUNS **1. securities, stocks and bonds;** gilt-edged securities, personal securities, assented securities, specific securities, trustee securities, corporation securities, international securities, cats and dogs (of doubtful value); negotiables, negotiable securities; listed securities, unlisted securities; digested securities, undigested securities; junior securities, senior securities; futures; shorts; shifting *or* floating securities, bearer securities; convertible securities, converts; government securities, governments; industrials, utilities, cottons, grains, etc.; threes, three per cents, sixes, six per cents, etc.; portfolio.

2. stock, stocks, shares [Eng.]; bank stock, bonus stock, capital stock, certificated stock, corporate stock, convertible stock, cumulative stock, ex-dividend stock, fancy stock, joint stock, guaranteed stock, no-par stock, preferred stock, trustee stock, watered stock; common stock, ordinary shares [Eng.]; full stocks, half stocks, quarter stocks; steels, coppers, etc.; Big Steels,

Little Steels; rails, American rails; rolling stock, rollers; stock note; stock list; stock ledger, share ledger [Eng.].

3. share, lot; preference share; dummy share; holding, shareholding, stockholding; block; full lot, round lot, board lot, foot lot; odd lot.

4. bond, adjustment bond, baby bond, bond to bearer, bonus bond, callable bond, convertible bond, coupon bond, equipment bond, guaranteed bond, income bond, insular bond, internal bond, legal bond, participating bond, open-end bond, registered bond, serial bond, sinking-fund bond, tax-exempt bond, underlying bond; debenture, debenture bond; government bond, Federal reserve bank note; war bond, defense bond, Liberty bond [World War I]; municipal bond, corporation stock [Eng.]; mortgage bond, general mortgage bond, trustee mortgage bond, etc.; bottomry bond; firsts, first-mortgage bonds; seconds, second-mortgage bonds; consolidated bonds, consolidated annuities, consols; joint bonds, J.B.'s.

5. stock certificate, certificate of stock; street certificate; interim certificate; **coupon.**

6. issue, issuance; **flotation,** floatation [Eng.]; stock issue, bond issue; outstanding issue; blue chip (issue of high value).

7. dividend, stock dividend; **plum, melon** [slang, U.S.]; cumulative dividend, accrued dividends; interim dividend; dividend off, ex dividend; dividend on, cum dividend [Eng.]; Irish dividend [joc.], assessment.

8. price, quotation; basing point; bid and asked prices, delivery or settling price, exhaust price, future price, market price, off price, price current, spot price, technical price; offered price, bid; put price, call price; opening price, closing price; fixed price, rock-bottom price; cable rate, check rate, demand draft rate, stock rate; parity; **par,** issue par; par value, nominal or face par or value; no-par value; cost and freight, C. and F.; bearish prices, bullish prices; swings, fluctuations; flurry, flutter; rally.

9. margin; collateral; spread; thin margin, shoestring margin.

10. (commodities) spots, spot grain, etc., cash grain; futures, future grain, etc.

11. ticker, stock ticker; ticker tape.

VERBS **12. issue, float,** put on the market; float a bond issue.

13. declare a dividend, cut a melon [slang, U.S.].

PREPS. **14.** at the market price, at the market; at the opening price, at the opening; at a discount, out of favor, below par; above par; at par, at par or face value.

833. MONEY

NOUNS **1. money, currency, legal tender, medium of exchange,** circulating medium, *dinero* [Sp.]; **cash,** coinage, mintage, coin of the realm, **silver,** sterling [Eng.], dollars, almighty dollars; **gold,** gelt [joc.], gilt [chiefly slang], ochre [slang, Eng.]; **the wherewithal,** the wherewith; lucre, **filthy lucre** [coll.], pelf, muck [derog.], root of all evil, mammon; "the sinews of war" [Libanius], "the sinews of affairs" [Laertius], "the ruling spirit of all things" [Publilius Syrus]; dollar currency, hard currency; fractional currency, postal currency; managed currency.

2. (slang terms) **the actual, the needful, dough, jack, kale, mazuma,** mopus, rhino, spondulics or spondulix, oof, ooftish, wampum, possibles, ballast, boodle, blunt, bunce, moss, gingerbread, corn, corn in Egypt, dust, sugar, salt, brass, tin, chink, rocks, dibs, simoleons, shekels, berries, chips, bones, bucks, iron men, plunks, clinkers, beans, bullets, remedy, salve, grease, ointment, oil of palms, cabbage.

3. wampum, wampumpeag, peag, sewan, roanoke, cowrie, amole.

4. specie, hard money, hard cash; **coin,** piece, piece of money, piece of silver or gold; chip, chinker, clinker, jingler, banger, shiner, brad, button, holy stone, mint drop, nail, rock [all slang]; rouleau (roll of coins).

5. gold piece, yellow boy [slang, Eng.], slug [hist.]; ten-dollar gold piece, ned [slang], eagle [all U.S.]; five-dollar gold piece, half ned [slang], half eagle [all U.S.]; twenty-dollar gold piece, double eagle [both U.S.]; guinea, sovereign, pound sovereign, crown, half crown [all Eng.]; doubloon [old Span.]; ducat [European]; napoleon, louis d'or [both F.]; moidore [Portugal & Brazil]; mohur [Calcutta; former India & Persia].

6. paper money; folding money, the long green, mint leaves, lettuce, rags [all slang]; fiat money [U.S.]; **bill,** dollar bill, etc.; **note,** negotiable note, legal-tender note; **bank note,** Federal reserve note, national-bank note; government note, currency note [Eng.], treasury note; **greenback** [U.S.], frogskin [slang, U.S.]; blueback [U.S. Confederacy, Civil War]; silver certificate; gold certificate, yellow boy [slang]; scrip [U.S.], shinplaster [slang, U.S. hist.]; *assignat* [F.].

7. (U.S. denominations) mill; cent, penny [coll.], copper, red cent [coll.]; five cents, nickel [coll.], jitney [slang]; picayune, fipperny bit [both hist.]; ten cents, dime; bit, short bit, long bit [all coll.]; twenty-five cents, quarter, two bits [coll.]; fifty cents, half dollar, four bits [coll.]; dollar, $; buck, smacker, bean, berry, bone, boffo [all slang]; silver dollar, cart wheel, iron man [both slang]; fiver ($5), five spot [both slang]; tenner ($10), ten spot, sawbuck [all slang]; century ($100 [slang]); grand ($1000 [slang]).

8. (Eng. denominations) mite; farthing; halfpenny, ha'penny, bawbee [coll.], mag *or* meg [slang]; penny, d.; pence [pl.]; twopence. tuppence; threepence, thrippence, threepenny bit *or* piece; fourpence, fourpenny. groat; sixpence, tanner [slang], teston; shilling, s., bob [slang]; florin; half crown; crown, dollar [slang]; pound, £, quid [slang]; guinea; fiver (£5), tenner (£10), pony (£25), monkey (£500), plum (£100 000), marigold (£1,000,000) [all slang].

9. (foreign denominations) anna, rupee, pie *or* pai [India]; azteca [Mexico]; belga [Belgium]; cent [China, Netherlands, etc.]; centavo [Portugal, Argentina, Mexico, etc.]; centesimo [Italy, Uruguay]; centime [Belgium, France, Switzerland]; centimo [Spain, Venezuela, etc.]; conto [Brazil, Portugal]; dinar [Iraq, Iran, Yugoslavia]; doit, cuit [Dutch]; dollar [China, Mexico, etc.]; drachma [Greece]; escudo [Portugal]; florin, guilder, gulden, stiver [Netherlands]; franc [France, Belgium, Switzerland]; groschen [Austria]; kopeck, ruble [Russia]; krona [Sweden]; krone [Denmark, Norway, Austria]; lira [Italy, Turkey]; mark, reichsmark, pfennig [Germany]; piaster *or* piastre [Near East]; milreis, reis [Brazil]; peseta [Spain]; peso [Argentina, Mexico, etc.]; pistareen, piece of eight [Span. hist.]; rial [Iran]; sen, yen [Japan]; schilling [Austria]; shekel [ancient Near East]; soldo [Italy] sou [France].

10. counterfeit, false *or* bad money, bogus, queer [slang], snide [slang], base coin, flash note; green goods [slang, U.S.]; forgery, bad check, rubber check [slang]; kite [slang].

11. negotiable instrument *or* paper, commercial paper, paper; bill of exchange,

bill, note, certificate, hundi [India]; check, cheque [Eng.]; blank check; traveler's check; money order, M.O.; postal order [U.S.], post-office order [Eng.]; order, draft *or* draught, warrant, voucher, debenture; promissory note, I O U; note of hand; acceptance, acceptance bill, bank acceptance, trade acceptance; due bill; demand *or* sight bill, sight draft [U.S.]; time bill; exchequer bill, treasury bill [both Eng.]; checkbook.

12. token, counter, slug, chip, dib, scrip, coupon; check, ticket, tag; hat check, baggage check.

13. sum, amount of money; round *or* lump sum.

14. funds, finances, moneys, exchequer, purse, budget, pocket, treasure, substance, assets, resources, pecuniary resources, means, commands, command of money; bank account; bottom dollar [coll.].

15. capital, stock, fund; principal, corpus; circulating capital, floating capital; fixed capital, working capital, equity capital, risk *or* venture capital.

16. bank roll; roll, wad [both slang, U.S.].

17. ready money, the ready [coll.], *argent comptant* [F.], cash, money in hand.

18. petty cash, pocket money, pin money, spending money, change, small change.

19. precious metals; gold, ochre [slang, Eng.], gilt [chiefly slang]; nugget, gold nugget, slug; silver, copper, nickel, coin gold *or* silver; bullion, ingot, bar.

20. standard of value, gold standard, silver standard; monometallism, bimetallism; money of account.

21. (science of coins) numismatics, numismatology; chrysology; numismatist, numismatologist.

22. monetization, issuance, utterance, circulation; remonetization; demonitization.

23. coining, coinage, mintage; counterfeiting, forgery.

24. coiner, minter, mintman, moneyer; counterfeiter, forger, smasher [slang], duffer [slang, Eng.].

VERBS 25. monetize, issue, utter, circulate; remonetize, reissue; demonetize.

26. coin, mint; counterfeit, forge, shove the queer [slang].

27. cash, cash in [coll., U.S.], convert into cash.

ADJS. 28. monetary, pecuniary, financial; capital; fiscal; sumptuary; nummary; numismatic(al); sterling.

29. convertible, liquid.

834. FINANCE AND INVESTMENT

NOUNS 1. finance, finances, money matters; economics 849.4.

2. financing, backing, financial backing, sponsorship, patronization, promotion, support; stake [coll.], grubstake [coll.], meal ticket [slang, U.S.]; subsidy 816.8.

3. investment, risk, venture; prime investment; sinking fund; annuity.

4. banking, money dealing, money changing; investment banking.

5. financial condition, state of the exchequer.

6. solvency, soundness, solidity, responsibility, reliability; unindebtedness.

7. crisis, financial crisis; dollar crisis, dollar gap.

8. financier, financist, financialist [coll.], capitalist, investor; tycoon [coll., U.S.], baron [U.S.].

9. financer, backer, sponsor, patron, promoter, supporter, angel [slang]; staker [coll.], grubstaker [coll.], meal ticket [slang, U.S.].

10. banker, money dealer, moneymonger; money-changer, money broker; moneylender 818.3; cambist; investment banker; bank clerk, cashier, teller.

11. treasurer, bursar, purser, purse bearer, cashier, cashkeeper; chamberlain, curator, steward, trustee; depositary, depository; receiver, liquidator; paymaster; Secretary of the Treasury [U.S.], Chancellor of the Exchequer [Eng.].

12. treasury, treasure house; storehouse 658.6; depository, repository; hold, stronghold, strong room; strongbox, safe, coffer, locker, chest; vault, crypt; safe-deposit or safety-deposit box or vault; moneybox, cash box; till, tiller; cash register; bursary [of a college or monastery]; exchequer, fisc; public treasury, public crib [coll., U.S.].

13. bank, savings bank, investment bank, commercial bank, bank of issue or circulation, bank of deposit, bank of discount, joint-stock bank [Eng. & Australia]; central bank, branch bank, member bank, regional bank, chain banks; national bank, state bank; reserve bank, Federal reserve bank [U.S.]; federal land bank, federal intermediate credit bank, federal home loan bank, farm loan association; Bank of Eng-land, Old Lady of Threadneedle Street; Bank of France; World Bank; clearing house; pet bank; piggy bank.

14. purse, wallet, pocketbook, portemonnaie, poke [dial. and thieves' slang], pocket; bag, handbag, moneybag; billfold [U.S.]; purse strings.

VERBS 15. finance, financier; back, sponsor, patronize, promote, support, provide for; capitalize, provide capital or money for, pay for, bank-roll [slang], put up the money; stake, grubstake [both coll.]; subsidize 816.18; set up, set up in business; refinance.

16. invest, place, put, sink; risk, venture; make an investment, lay out money, salt down or away [coll.], place or put out to interest; invest in, put money in, sink money in, pour money into, tie up one's money in, buy in or into.

ADJS. 17. solvent, sound, substantial, solid, good, reliable, responsible, sound as a dollar; able to pay, good for, unindebted 839.23.

835. WEALTH

NOUNS 1. wealth, riches, opulence or opulency, affluence; abundance 659.2; richness, wealthiness; prosperity, prosperousness, comfortable or easy circumstances, independence; money, lucre, pelf, mammon; substance, property, possessions, material wealth; assets 833.14; fortune, treasure, handsome fortune; long purse, full purse, heavy purse, well-lined purse, moneybags [coll.], purse of Fortunatus; embarras de richesses [F., embarrassment of riches], money to burn [coll.]; fleshpots of Egypt.

2. large sum, good sum, tidy sum [coll.], pretty penny [coll.], king's ransom, mint, pot [coll. & slang]; power ~, mint ~, barrel or raft of money [all coll.]; pile, wad [both slang]; thousands, millions, cool million, etc.

3. (rich source) mine, mine of wealth, gold mine, bonanza [U.S.], El Dorado, Golconda.

4. the golden touch, Midas touch; philosophers' stone; Pactolus.

5. the rich, the wealthy, the well to do, the haves [coll.]; plutocracy, timocracy.

6. rich man, wealthy man, moneyed man, man of wealth, man of means or substance, have [coll.], richling, moneybags [coll.], jack-full-of-money [slang]; nabob, tippybob [slang]; capitalist, pluto-

crat, bloated plutocrat; millionaire, multi-millionaire, billionaire; parvenu 917.10.

7. Croesus, Midas, Plutus, Dives, Timon of Athens, Danaë, Rockefeller, Vanderbilt, Whitney, DuPont, Ford.

VERBS 8. enrich, richen.

9. grow rich, get rich, fill or line one's pockets, feather one's nest, make or coin money, have the golden touch; make a fortune, make one's pile [slang]; strike it rich, come into money; make good, get on in the world, do all right by oneself [coll.].

10. have money, command money, have the wherewithal; afford, well afford.

11. live well, live high, live in clover, roll or wallow in wealth, roll in the lap of luxury, have money to burn [coll.].

12. worship mammon, worship the golden calf.

ADJS. 13. wealthy, rich, affluent, opulent, pecunious, moneyed, in the money [coll. or slang], in funds or cash, well-to-do, well to do in the world, well off, well-situated, well-fixed [coll., U.S.], prosperous, comfortable, able [now dial.], set up [coll.], provided for, well provided for, fat, flush, flush with or of money, abounding in riches, made of money, rolling or wallowing in wealth, worth a great deal, frightfully rich, disgustingly rich, big-rich [dial.], rich as Croesus; well-heeled, oofy, tinny, lousy rich, filthy rich [all slang]; independent, independently rich.

836. POVERTY

NOUNS 1. poverty, poorness, unprosperousness; impecuniousness, impecuniosity; straits, difficulties, distress, embarrassment, embarrassed ~, reduced or straitened circumstances, slender or narrow means, low water [slang, U.S.], light purse; broken fortune; Queer Street; "mother of miseries" [Southey], "not the possession of little, but the nonpossession of much" [Antipater].

2. indigence, penury, pennilessness, moneylessness; pauperism, impoverishment; beggary, beggarliness; homelessness; destitution, privation; neediness, want, need, lack, necessity; hand-to-mouth existence, bare subsistence, wolf at the door; empty purse or pocket, "a beggarly account of empty boxes" [Shakespeare].

3. the poor, the needy, the have-nots [coll.], the down-and-out; the forgotten man, "the forgotten man at the bottom of the economic pyramid" [F. D. Roosevelt]; poor whites, poor white trash [both So. U.S.].

4. poor man, poorling, have-not [coll.]; poor devil, *pauvre diable* [F.]; down-and-out, down-and-outer; pauper, starveling; beggar 772.8; almsman, almswoman, charity case, casual; bankrupt 840.4.

VERBS 5. be poor, be hard up [coll.], live on Queer Street, find it hard going, have seen better days, walk on one's uppers; be in want, want, need, lack; starve, live from hand to mouth; not have a penny or sou, not have a penny to bless oneself with, not have a shot in the locker; go on the parish; make a poor mouth.

6. impoverish, reduce, pauperize, beggar, bring on the parish; eat out of house and home; bankrupt 840.8.

ADJS. 7. poor, ill off, badly or poorly off, hard up [coll.], impecunious, unmoneyed, unprosperous; reduced, in reduced circumstances; straitened, in straitened circumstances, narrow, in narrow circumstances, embarrassed, distressed, pinched, put to one's shifts or last shifts, at the end of one's rope, on the edge or ragged edge [coll.], under hatches, down to bedrock, on Queer Street; short of money, out of pocket; unable to make both ends meet, unable to keep the wolf from the door; poor as a church mouse, poor as a coot [coll.], poor as Job, poor as Job's turkey [coll.], not worth a rap.

8. indigent, poverty-stricken; needy, necessitous, in want; beggared, beggarly; impoverished, pauperized, bereft, bereaved, stripped, fleeced; down at heels, down at the heel, on or down on one's uppers, out at the heels, out at elbows, in rags.

9. destitute, down-and-out, penniless, moneyless, fortuneless, out of funds, without a sou, *qui n'a pas le sou* [F.], without a penny to bless oneself with, without a shot in the locker; bankrupt 840.11; homeless; propertyless, landless.

10. (slang terms) broke, busted, flat, flat broke, stone-broke, stony, strapped, beat, oofless, beanless.

837. CREDIT

NOUNS 1. credit, trust, tick [coll.], strap [slang, Eng.]; commercial credit; movable credit, *crédit mobilier* [F.]; line of credit;

installment plan [U.S.]; **rating, credit rating.**

2. account, credit account, charge account; bank account, checking account [U.S.]; **bank balance;** expense account.

3. credit instrument; paper credit; letter of credit, *lettre de créance* [F.], circular note; credit slip [Eng.], deposit slip, certificate of deposit; negotiable instruments 833.11.

4. creditor, creditress; debtee; credit man; bill collector, collection agent; dunner, dun.

VERBS **5. credit, accredit; charge, charge to one's account,** credit to, place to one's credit *or* account.

6. give *or* **extend credit,** sell on credit, trust, entrust *or* intrust; tick, give tick [both coll.]; carry [U.S.], carry on one's books.

7. receive credit, take credit, **charge,** charge to one's account, keep an account with, go on tick [coll.]; have one's credit good for.

ADJS. **8. accredited,** credited, of good credit, **well-rated.**

ADVS. **9. to one's credit** *or* **account,** to the credit *or* account of, to the good.

10. on credit, on account, *à compte* [F.], **on trust, on tick** [coll.]; on terms, on good terms, on easy terms, on budget terms.

838. DEBT

NOUNS **1. debt, indebtedness,** indebtment, **obligation, liability,** due, **dues,** score, amount due, outstanding debt; floating debt; funded debt; borrowing 819; maturity.

2. arrears, arrear, arrearage; **deficit,** default, deferred payment; dollar gap.

3. interest, premium, price, rate; interest rate, rate of interest; discount rate; **usury,** excessive *or* exorbitant interest; simple interest, compound interest; net interest, gross interest; compensatory interest; lucrative interest; penal interest.

4. debtor, borrower; mortgagee.

VERBS **5. owe, be indebted,** be obliged for, lie under an obligation, be bound to pay.

6. go in debt, run into debt, get into debt, plunge into debt, incur *or* contract a debt, **run up a bill,** ~ a score *or* an account; borrow 819.3; outrun *or* overrun the constable [coll.].

7. mature, accrue, fall due.

ADJS. **8. indebted, in debt,** plunged in debt, in difficulties, embarrassed, in embarrassed circumstances, encumbered *or* incumbered, tied up, involved; deep in debt, involved *or* deeply involved in debt, over head and ears in debt, up to one's ears in debt.

9. chargeable, liable, answerable for.

10. due, owed, owing, payable, redeemable, mature, **outstanding, unpaid,** in arrear *or* arrears.

839. PAYMENT

NOUNS **1. payment,** paying, pay-off; defrayment, defrayal; **discharge, settlement, clearance, liquidation, amortization,** amortizement, **retirement,** satisfaction; quittance, **acquittance,** acquitment, acquittal; remittance; installment; down payment; cash, spot cash; prepayment.

2. repayment, reimbursement, recoupment, return, restitution; **refund,** refundment, kickback [coll.].

3. recompense, remuneration, compensation, reward; requital, requitement, quittance, **retribution, reparation, redress,** satisfaction, **atonement, amends,** return, restitution; **indemnity,** indemnification; price, consideration; meed, guerdon; solatium, damages, smart money; salvage.

4. pay, payment, remuneration, compensation [U.S.], financial remuneration; **salary, wage, wages,** income, earnings, hire; real wages; living wage; minimum wage, base pay; take-home pay; portal-to-portal pay; severance pay; discontinuance *or* dismissal wage; escalator wages, escalator clause; wage scale, sliding scale; pay roll; wage-freeze.

5. fee, stipend, allowance, emolument, tribute, dastur *or* dasturi [India]; **reckoning, footing,** shot, scot; retainer, retaining fee; hush money, blackmail; blood money; mileage.

6. (extra pay *or* allowance) **bonus, premium,** boot [now dial.], batta [India], **bounty,** cumshaw, solatium; honorarium; overtime pay; bonus system.

7. dividend; royalty; commission, rake-off [slang, U.S.].

8. (the bearing of another's expense) **treat,** shout [slang]; Dutch treat [coll.].

9. payer, remunerator, compensator, recompenser; defrayer; liquidator; taxpayer, ratepayer [Eng.].

VERBS **10. pay, render, tender; recompense, remunerate, compensate, reward,** guerdon, indemnity, satisfy; salary, fee; remit; prepay.

11. repay, return; **reimburse,** recoup; **requite,** quit, **atone, make amends,** make restitution, make reparation; pay in kind, pay one in his own coin, give tit for tat; **refund,** kick back [coll.].

12. settle with, reckon with, account with, **settle** or **square accounts with,** get **even** or **quits with,** even up the score [slang], wipe or clear off old scores, pay old debts.

13. pay off, pay up, pay out [coll.], pay in full, **discharge, settle,** satisfy, **clear, liquidate, amortize,** retire, take up, lift [U.S.], take up and pay off, acquit oneself of; settle or square accounts, make accounts square, strike a balance.

14. pay out, hand out, **fork** or **shell out** [slang]; expend 841.5.

15. pay over, hand over; ante, **ante up,** stump up [coll., Eng.], put up; put down, lay down, lay one's money down.

16. (slang terms) **kick in, fork over, pony up** [U.S.], cough up, come across, come through with, come down with, come down with the needful, plank down, post, decorate the palm or counter, tickle or grease the palm; pay to the tune of; come again.

17. pay cash, make a cash payment, cash, **pay spot cash, pay cash down,** pay down on the nail [slang], put one's money on the line [slang], pay at sight, pay in advance, pay as you go; pay cash on delivery, pay C.O.D.

18. pay for, pay the costs, **bear the expense** or **cost,** pay the piper; **defray,** defray expenses; pay the bill, **foot the bill** [coll.], pick up the tab [slang]; honor a bill, acknowledge, redeem; pay one's way, pay one's shot, pay one's footing; pay one's share, chip in [coll.], go Dutch [slang].

19. treat, treat to, **stand treat,** go treat, stand to [coll.], stand the shot [coll.], pay sauce for all [coll.]; **set up,** stand up, blow to, shout [all slang]; stand drinks, buy one's thirst [slang].

20. draw wages; pull down, drag down [both slang].

ADJS. **21. paying, remunerative;** compensating, compensative, compensatory; rewarding, rewardful; repaying, satisfying, reparative; retributive, retributory.

22. paid, discharged, settled, liquidated, acquitted, paid in full; **spent, expended;** salaried, waged; prepaid, postpaid.

23. unindebted, unowed; **out of debt,**

above water, clear, all clear, all straight; solvent 834.17.

ADVS. **24. in compensation,** as compensation, in recompense, **in reward,** in requital, in reparation, in retribution, in restitution, **in amends,** in atonement, to atone for.

25. cash down, money down, down, on the nail [slang], **collect** [U.S.]; cash on delivery, **C.O.D.;** on demand, on call [U.S.]; pay-as-you-go.

840. NONPAYMENT

NOUNS **1. nonpayment, default,** delinquence or delinquency; protest, repudiation; dishonor, dishonoring; bad debt, dishonored or protested bill.

2. moratorium, write-off, cancellation, sponging; whitewash, whitewashing [both coll., Eng.].

3. insolvency, bankruptcy, failure; crash, collapse, bust [slang, U.S.]; run upon a bank; insufficient funds, overdrawn account.

4. insolvent, insolvent debtor, lame duck [stock exchange]; **bankrupt,** failure.

5. defaulter, defaultant, defalcator, delinquent, nonpayer; **welsher** [slang], absconder, lavanter, eloper, skedaddler [coll., U.S.]; tax dodger.

VERBS **6. not pay, dishonor,** repudiate, protest, stop payment; **default,** defalcate; **welsh** [slang], shirk out of [coll.]; button up one's pockets, draw the purse strings; pay under protest.

7. go bankrupt, go broke [slang], become insolvent or bankrupt, **fail,** break, bust [slang, U.S.], **crash,** collapse, fold, **fold up,** go up [coll.], **go under** [coll.], **be ruined,** go to ruin, go on the rocks, go to the wall, go to pot [coll.], go to the dogs; be gazetted.

8. bankrupt, ruin, break, bust [slang]; impoverish 836.6.

9. declare a moratorium, write off, whitewash [coll., Eng.], absolve, clear, cancel, nullify, sponge, wipe out, wipe the slate clean.

ADJS. **10. defaulting,** defaultant, nonpaying; **delinquent,** behindhand, in arrear or arrears.

11. insolvent, bankrupt, broken, **broke** [slang], busted [slang, U.S.], **ruined,** failed, on the rocks; destitute 836.9; gazetted, in the gazette.

12. unpaid, unremunerated, uncompensated, unrecompensed, **unrewarded**, unrequited.

13. unpayable, irredeemable, inconvertible.

841. EXPENDITURE

NOUNS **1. expenditure, spending, disbursement;** payment 839; deficit spending.

2. spendings, outgoings, outgo, **outlay**, money going out.

3. expenses, expense, costs, charges, burden of expenditure; **overhead**, operating expense, general expenses, nut [slang]; direct costs, indirect costs; distributed costs, undistributed costs; prime cost; cost of living, cost-of-living index, cost-of-living allowance.

4. spender, expender, expenditor, disburser.

VERBS **5. spend, expend, disburse, pay out**, put out, fork or shell out [slang], lay out, outlay; pay 839.10; put one's hands in one's pockets, open the purse, loose or untie the purse strings; burn in one's pocket, burn a hole in one's pocket; go or run through.

6. afford, well afford, spare, **spare the price**, bear, stand, support, endure, undergo, meet the expense of.

842. RECEIPTS

NOUNS **1. receipts, receipt, income, revenue, profits, earnings, returns, proceeds,** produce, avails, take, takings, intake, takein [coll.], get, gettings, make, makings; gains 809.3; gate receipts, gate, box office; net receipts, net; gross receipts, gross; net income, gross income; earned income, unearned income; disposable income.

2. (written acknowledgment) **receipt, acknowledgment, voucher, bill,** warrant [Eng.]; **receipt in full**, receipt in full of all demands, release, acquittance, quittance, discharge.

VERBS **3. yield, bring in, afford, pay, return.**

843. ACCOUNTS

NOUNS **1. accounts; outstanding accounts,** uncollected or unpaid accounts; **accounts receivable,** receipts, assets; **accounts payable,** expenditures, liabilities.

2. account, reckoning, tally, terrier [law], **score;** profit and loss account; debtor and creditor account; open or running account, cash account; account current; account rendered, *compte rendu* [F.]; account stated; balance.

3. statement, bill, bill of accounts or costs, **account, reckoning, score** [slang], damage [slang]; **check** [U.S.], tab [slang]; **dun;** invoice, manifest, bill of lading; budget.

4. account book, ledger, journal, daybook, register, registry, record book, books; **log,** logbook or log book; **cashbook,** petty cashbook; purchase ledger, accounts payable ledger; sales ledger, accounts receivable ledger; bankbook, passbook; balance sheet.

5. entry, item, minute, note, notation; single entry, double entry; **credit, debit.**

6. accounting, accountancy, bookkeeping; business ~, commercial or monetary arithmetic; cost accounting; audit, auditing.

7. accountant, bookkeeper, clerk, actuary, registrar, recorder, calculator, reckoner; cost accountant; certified public accountant, C.P.A. [U.S.]; chartered accountant, C.A. [Eng.]; **auditor,** bank examiner; accountant general.

VERBS **8. keep accounts, keep books,** make up or cast up accounts; make an entry, enter, post, post up, book, docket [U.S.], log, note, minute; credit, debit; charge off; capitalize; carry [U.S.], carry on one's books; carry over; balance, balance accounts, balance the books, strike a balance; close the books, close out.

9. take account of, take stock, overhaul; **inventory; audit,** examine the books.

10. falsify accounts, garble accounts, cook or doctor accounts [coll.], salt; surcharge.

11. bill, send a statement; invoice; **dun,** press, call, demand payment.

ADJS. **12.** accounting, bookkeeping.

844. PRICE

NOUNS **1. price, cost, expense,** expenditure, **charge, rate, figure, amount,** damage [slang], score [slang], tab [slang].

2. quotation, quoted price; asking price, offered price, bid; current price, market price, price current, current quotation; list price; net or neat price, net; fixed price, *prix fixe* [F.]; flat rate; package price; stock market quotations 832.8.

3. worth, value, account, rate; face value, face; par value; net worth; conversion factor or value, labor content; money's worth, pennyworth, value received.

4. valuation, evaluation, valorization, pricing, **assessment, appraisal,** appraisement, apprizement *or* apprisement, estimation, rating.

5. price index, business index; price level; price ceiling, ceiling price, ceiling, top price; floor price, floor, bottom price; demand curve.

6. price controls, price fixing; price supports, rigid supports, flexible supports; price-freeze; escalator clause.

7. fee, due, dues, toll, charge, charges, demand, exaction, exactment; scot, shot, scot and lot; hire; fare, carfare; entrance *or* admission fee, admission; cover charge [U.S.], *couvert* charge; portage, towage; wharfage, anchorage, dockage; pilotage; storage, cellarage; brokerage; salvage.

8. freightage, freight, haulage, carriage, cartage, drayage, expressage [U.S.], lighterage; poundage, tonnage.

9. rent, rental, rent-roll; rent charge, rentcharge; rack rent, rackrent; quitrent.

10. tax, taxation, duty, tariff, tribute, contribution, assessment, cess, levy, toll, impost, imposition, revenue, avania [Turkey]; tithe, tenths [hist.]; surtax, supertax; direct tax, indirect tax; progressive tax *or* taxation, graduated taxation; single tax, *impôt unique* [F.]; doomage [U.S.], assessment on default; tax return, joint return; tax dodging; conscience money; tax exemption.

11. taxes, internal revenue; excise, excise tax; custom, customs, customs duty; import tax, export tax; poll tax, poll, head tax, capitation tax, capitation; salt tax, gabelle; state tax, provincial tax, likin [China]; property tax, personal property tax; death duty, estate duty; liquor tax, abkari [India]; *ad valorem* tax, capital gains tax, corporation tax, excess profits tax, gift tax, income tax, inheritance tax, license tax, occupation tax, octroi, nuisance tax, processing tax, production tax, sales tax, school tax, severance tax, use tax, war profits tax, withholding tax.

12. taxer, taxman; tax collector, taxgatherer, tax receiver, tax taker, collector of internal revenue; assessor, tax assessor; exciseman [Eng.]; customs, Bureau of Customs and Excise [Eng.], Bureau of Internal Revenue [U.S.]; custom house.

VERBS 13. price, set a price on, fix the price of, place a value on, value, evaluate, valuate, valorize, appraise, apprize *or* apprise, assess, rate, prize; quote a price.

14. charge, demand, ask, require, exact, assess, levy, impose; tax, assess a tax upon, lay *or* put a duty on; doom [U.S.];

tithe (put *or* pay a tithe on); prorate, assess pro rata; charge for, stick for [coll.].

15. cost, sell for, fetch, bring, bring in, yield, afford; put *or* set one back [slang], stand one in [coll.]; come to, run to *or* into, amount to, mount up to, come up to.

ADJS. 16. priced, valued, evaluated, assessed, appraised, rated, prized; worth, valued at, good for; ad valorem (according to value), pro rata (according to rate).

17. chargeable, taxable, assessable, dutiable, leviable; tithable.

18. tax-free, tax-exempt.

ADVS. 19. at a price, for a consideration; to the amount of, to the tune of [coll.].

845. DISCOUNT

NOUNS 1. discount, cut, deduction, abatement; rebate, rebatement; write-off, charge-off; depreciation, reduction; allowance, concession, qualification, setoff, drawback; percentage; breakage; poundage; agio; contango [Eng.]; salvage; tare, tare and tret.

VERBS 2. discount, cut, deduct, bate, abate; rebate; take off, strike off, write off, charge off; depreciate, reduce; allow, make allowance.

ADVS. 3. at a discount, at a reduction, below par.

846. DEARNESS

NOUNS 1. preciousness, dearness, valuableness; pricelessness, invaluableness.

2. expensiveness, dearness, costliness, highness; stiffness, steepness [both coll.]; richness, sumptuousness, luxuriousness.

3. high price, great price, fancy price, good price, steep *or* stiff price [coll.], famine price, pretty penny [coll.]; inflationary prices; inflation, expansion; inflationary spiral; inflationary gap.

4. exorbitance *or* exorbitancy, extravagance, excess, excessiveness, inordinateness, immoderateness, immoderation, undueness, unreasonableness, outrageousness, preposterousness.

5. overcharge, surcharge, overassessment, overpayment; usury; extortion, exploitation, holdup [slang]; profiteering.

VERBS 6. cost much, cost money [coll.], cost a pretty penny [coll.], run into money.

7. overcharge, surcharge, overtax, hold up [coll.], soak [slang], stick [slang], lay it on, lay it on thick [coll.], make pay through the nose; extort, exploit, skin [slang], fleece, bleed, bleed white; profiteer.

8. **overpay**, overspend, pay too much, pay big [slang], pay size, **pay dearly**, pay dearly or too dear for one's whistle, **pay through the nose**, pay the devil.

9. **inflate**, expand.

ADJS. 10. **precious**, **dear**, **valuable**, worthy, rich, golden, **of great price**, worth a pretty penny [coll.], worth a king's ransom, worth its weight in gold, good as gold, precious as the apple of the eye; **priceless**, **invaluable**, inestimable, **beyond price**, too precious for words.

11. **expensive**, **dear**, **costly**, **high**, **high-priced**, fancy; stiff, steep [both coll.]; rich, sumptuous, luxurious.

12. **exorbitant**, **excessive**, **extravagant**, inordinate, **immoderate**, undue, unwarranted, unreasonable, unconscionable, outrageous, preposterous, out of bounds, out of sight [coll.]; **extortionate**, **cutthroat**, usurious, exacting, inflationary; dearbought.

ADVS. 13. **dear**, **dearly**; at a high price, at great cost, at a great rate, at heavy cost, at great expense, *à grands frais* [F.], at a premium.

14. **preciously**, **valuably**, worthily; pricelessly, invaluably.

15. **expensively**, richly, sumptuously, luxuriously.

16. **exorbitantly**, extortionately, **excessively**, **extravagantly**, **inordinately**, immoderately, unduely, unreasonably, unconscionably, outrageously, preposterously.

847. CHEAPNESS

NOUNS 1. **cheapness**, **inexpensiveness**, reasonableness, moderateness, nominalness; drug on or in the market.

2. **low price**, **nominal price**, reasonable price, moderate price; bargain prices, budget prices.

3. **bargain**, advantageous purchase, buy [coll.], **good buy**, *bon marché* [F.]; **steal**, snap, pickup [all slang]; money's worth, pennyworth, good pennyworth.

4. **cheapening**, **depreciation**, **devaluation**, reduction, lowering; deflation; decline, slump, sag [slang]; price fall, break [U.S.]; price cut, cut, slash, markdown.

VERBS 5. **be cheap**, cost little, not cost anything; buy dirt-cheap, buy for a song or old song, buy at a bargain, buy for a mere nothing; get one's money's worth, get a good pennyworth.

6. **cheapen**, **depreciate**, **devaluate**, lower, reduce, **mark down**, beat down; cut prices, cut, slash, shave, trim, pare; come down or fall in price, decline, sag, slump, run off; deflate; break, give way; reach a new low [coll.].

ADJS. 7. **cheap**, **inexpensive**, unexpensive, **low**, **low-priced**, frugal, reasonable, moderate, nominal; worth the money, well worth the money, worth the whistle; cheap or good at the price, cheap at half the price [joc.].

8. **dirt-cheap**, cheap as dirt, dog-cheap [coll.], cheap and nasty [coll.], **a dime-a-dozen**, two-for-a-penny, twopenny-halfpenny, sixpenny, bargain-basement, five-and-ten, dime-store.

9. **reduced**, cut, slashed, **marked down**; cut-rate; half-price.

ADVS. 10. **cheaply**, **cheap**, on or upon the cheap [coll., Eng.]; **inexpensively**, reasonably, moderately, nominally; **at a bargain**, *à bon marché* [F.], for a song or mere song, at small cost, at a low price, at budget prices, at piggy-bank prices; at cost or cost price, at prime cost.

848. GRATUITOUSNESS

Absence of Charge.—NOUNS 1. **gratuitousness**, gratuity, **freeness**, costlessness, expenselessness, complimentariness, no charge, labor of love; gift 816.4–6.

2. **complimentary ticket**, pass, free pass, free admission, Annie Oakley [slang, U.S.].

3. pass holder, **deadhead** [coll.].

VERBS 4. **give**, present 816.12.

ADJS. 5. **gratuitous**, gratis, free, for free [slang], **for nothing**, free for nothing [joc.], for love, scot-free, shot-free, free as air; costless, expenseless, untaxed, without charge, free of cost or expense; unbought, unpaid-for; **complimentary**, **on the house**; given 816.23; giftlike, gifty [coll.]; eleemosynary.

ADVS. 6. **gratuitously**, gratis, free, freely, for nothing, without charge.

849. ECONOMY

NOUNS 1. **economy**, **thrift**, **thriftiness**, economicalness, savingness, unwastefulness; **frugality**, frugalness; parsimony (excessive frugality) 850; carefulness, care, chariness, canniness [Scot.]; **prudence**, **providence**, forehandedness; **husbandry**, management, good management; austerity, austerity program [Eng.]; planned economy.

2. **economizing**, **economization**, Hoover-

ism [coll., U.S.]; **saving, scrimping,** skimping [coll.], scraping.

3. retrenchment, curtailment, reduction of expenses; cutback, rollback [coll.].

4. economics, econ [school slang], economic science; political economy, public economy; social economy or economics; collective economy; home economics [U.S.], domestic economy; dynamic economics; theoretical economics, plutology.

5. standard of living or life, standard of comfort.

6. economist, frugalist; economizer, saver, save-all.

VERBS **7. economize, save,** Hooverize [coll., U.S.]; scrimp, skimp [coll.], **scrape,** scrape and save; **husband,** husband one's resources, keep within compass, keep within one's means or budget, cut one's coat according to one's cloth, look after the main chance [coll.].

8. retrench, cut down, cut down expenses, **curtail expenses;** cut corners; cut back, roll back [coll.]; take in a reef, take a reef.

ADJS. **9. economical, thrifty, frugal,** unwasteful; **prudent, provident,** forehanded; careful, chary, canny [Scot.]; **saving,** economizing; spare, **sparing;** scrimping, skimping [coll.]; parsimonious 850.9; labor-saving.

10. economic, economical; socio-economic, politico-economical.

ADVS. **11. economically, thriftily, frugally,** husbandly; prudently, providently; carefully, charily, cannily [Scot.]; sparingly, with a sparing hand.

850. PARSIMONY

Excessive Frugality.—NOUNS **1. parsimony,** parsimoniousness; frugality 849.1; **stinting, pinching, scrimping,** skimping [coll.]; scamping, cheeseparing.

2. niggardliness, penuriousness, meanness, shabbiness, churlishness, **smallness, littleness,** pettiness, **cheapness; sordidness,** mercenariness, venality.

3. stinginess, ungenerosity, illiberality, tightness [coll.], nearness, closeness, closefistedness, closehandedness, tightfistedness, hardfistedness.

4. miserliness, miserism, **moneygrubbing,** pennypinching [slang], hoarding; avarice 632.8.

5. niggard, tightwad [slang, U.S.], **skinflint,** skin [slang], screw, pinchfist,

pinchgut [vulg.], Scotchman [joc.], churl, curmudgeon.

6. miser, moneygrubber, moneygrub, muckworm, lickpenny, save-all, scrimp [coll.], hunks [coll.], codger [dial., Eng.]; Harpagon, Euclio, Silas Marner, Daniel Dancer.

VERBS **7. stint, scrimp, skimp** [coll.], **scamp, scant, screw, pinch,** pinch pennies; starve, famish, live upon nothing; grudge, begrudge.

8. withhold, hold back, hold out on [slang], not give the time of day [joc.].

ADJS. **9. parsimonious, sparing,** cheeseparing, **stinting, scamping, scrimping,** skimping [coll.], skimp [coll.], skimpy [coll.], chary; frugal 849.9; penny-wise, penny-wise and pound foolish.

10. niggardly, niggard, penurious, grudging, mean, shabby, **small, little,** petty, **cheap,** churlish, curmudgeonly; **sordid,** mercenary, venal.

11. stingy, illiberal, ungenerous, Scotch [joc.], **tight** [coll.], **near, close, closefisted,** closehanded, tightfisted, hardfisted, hard; near as the bark on a tree, "as close as a vise" [Hawthorne].

12. miserly, save-all, **moneygrubbing,** pinching, **penny-pinching** [slang]; avaricious 632.28.

ADVS. **13. parsimoniously, sparingly,** stintingly, scrimpingly, skimpingly [coll.].

14. niggardly, stingily, illiberally, ungenerously, closefistedly, closehandedly, tightfistedly; meanly, shabbily, sordidly.

851. LIBERALITY

Generous Giving.—NOUNS **1. liberality,** liberalness, freeness; **generosity,** generousness, **unselfishness, munificence,** largess; bountifulness, bounteousness, **bounty;** openhandedness, freehandedness, open or free hand; openheartedness, bigheartedness, largeheartedness, greatheartedness, freeheartedness; open heart, big ~, large or great heart; **magnanimity** 977.2.

2. cheerful giver, free giver.

VERBS **3. give freely,** give cheerfully, give with an open hand, give with both hands, put one's hands in one's pockets, open the purse, loose or untie the purse strings, **spare no expense, heap upon,** lavish upon, shower down upon, give the coat off one's back, give **until it hurts;** keep the change!

ADJS. **4. liberal, free,** free with one's money; **generous, munificent, princely,**

handsome; **unselfish,** ungrudging; **unsparing,** unstinting; stintless, unstinted, without stint; **bountiful,** bounteous, **lavish,**
profuse; **openhanded,** freehanded, open;
openhearted, **bighearted,** largehearted,
greathearted, freehearted; **magnanimous**
977.6.

ADVS. **5.** liberally, freely; **generously,
munificently,** handsomely; **unselfishly,** ungrudgingly; **unsparingly,** unstintingly;
bountifully, bounteously, **lavishly,** profusely; openhandedly, freehandedly; open-
heartedly, bigheartedly, largeheartedly,
greatheartedly, freeheartedly; with open
hands, with both hands, with an unsparing
hand, without stint.

852. PRODIGALITY

NOUNS **1. prodigality, extravagance,** over-
liberality; profligacy, incontinence; intemperance 991; lavishness, profuseness,
profusion; **wastefulness,** waste; **dissipation,
squandering;** pound-foolishness, pound-
folly, penny wisdom; conspicuous consumption.

2. prodigal, wastrel, waster, **squan-
derer; spendthrift,** wastethrift, spender,
spend-all, high roller [slang, U.S.]; prodigal
son.

VERBS **3. squander, lavish,** play ducks
and drakes with; **dissipate,** scatter, sow
broadcast, scatter to the winds; **run
through,** go through; **throw away,** throw
one's money away, **spend money like
water,** hang the expense; gamble away;
blow, blow in [both slang]; squander one's
substance in riotous living, burn the candle
at both ends.

**4. waste, consume, spend, expend, use
up, exhaust;** lose; spill; pour down the
drain, pour water into a sieve; cast pearls
before swine, kill the goose that lays the
golden egg, *manger son blé en herbe* [F.,
eat one's wheat before it is ripe], waste
powder and shot.

5. waste away, consume away; **fool
away, fritter away,** fribble away, drivel
away, **trifle away,** dally away, potter away,
muddle away, diddle away [coll.]; idle away,
while away.

**6. misspend, throw good money after
bad,** throw the helve after the hatchet.

7. overspend, spend more than one has,
outrun *or* overrun the constable [coll.];
shoot one's bolt, shoot one's wad [slang];
overdraw, overdraw one's account, overdraw
the badger [coll., Eng.].

ADJS. **8. prodigal, extravagant, lavish,**
profuse, **overliberal,** overlavish, **spendthrift, wasteful,** profligate, incontinent,
dissipative; intemperate 991.7; pound-foolish, penny-wise and pound-foolish; easy
come, easy go.

9. wasted, squandered, dissipated,
consumed, spent, used, lost; **gone to waste,**
run to seed, gone to pot [coll.], down the
drain [coll.]; misspent.

853. FEELINGS

NOUNS **1. feelings, emotions, affections,
sentiments, passions, sensibilities,** suscep-
tibilities, **sympathies,** tender susceptibili-
ties.

2. (seat of affections; hence, affections,
deepest feelings) **heart, soul, breast,
bosom,** inmost heart *or* soul, heart's core,
heartstrings, cockles of the heart, bottom
of the heart.

**3. feeling, emotion, affection, senti-
ment, passion,** deep sense; sensation, impression, experience.

4. (capacity of emotion) **sensibility,
sensitivity;** susceptibility, susceptivity; affectibility, impressibility, impressionability.

**5. sympathetic response, sympathy,
fellow feeling,** response, reaction, echo,
chord, sympathetic chord.

6. tender feeling, tenderness, softness,
gentleness, delicacy; **tenderheartedness,**
softheartedness, warmheartedness, tender ~, sensitive *or* warm heart, soft place
in one's heart.

**7. sentimentality, sentiment, sentimen-
talism,** bathos, nostalgia, sweetness and
light, hearts and flowers; mawkishness,
inanity; namby-pamby, namby-pambyism;
mushiness, sloppiness [both coll.]; **mush,**
slush, slop, goo, schmaltz, sob stuff [all
slang]; sob story [slang].

8. emotionalism, emotionality, emo-
tionalization, demonstrativeness; **sensationalism, melodrama,** melodramatics,
blood and thunder, yellow journalism; emotional appeal, heart interest [slang].

9. fervor, fervency, fervidness, **passion,**
passionateness, impassionedness, **ardor,**
ardency, *empressement* [F.], warmth of
feeling, **warmth, heat, fire,** verve, furor,
gusto, vehemence, heartiness, cordiality,
unction; zeal 633.2; spirit, heart, soul.

VERBS **10. feel,** get *or* receive an impression, entertain ~, harbor *or* cherish a feeling; experience 150.8.

11. respond, react, echo, catch the flame or infection, enter into the spirit of.

12. take to heart, lay to heart, treasure up in the heart, find in one's heart; lie at the heart.

13. have a tender heart; be all heart, have a soft place in one's heart, wear one's heart on one's sleeve.

14. emotionalize, emote [U.S.], give free play to the emotions; sentimentalize, gush [coll.], slop over [slang, U.S.].

15. affect, touch, move, stir; melt, soften, melt the heart; penetrate, pierce, go through one; touch a chord, touch a sympathetic chord, touch one's heart, tug at the heart or heartstrings, go to one's heart, come home to; touch to the quick, touch on the raw, flick one on the raw.

16. impress, affect, strike, hit, smite; make an impression, make a dent in, make an impact upon, come in upon, be borne in upon, sink in [coll.], strike home, come home to, hit the mark [coll.]; tell, have a strong effect, strike hard, impress forcibly.

17. impress upon, bring home to, make it felt; stamp, etch, engrave.

ADJS. 18. emotional, emotive, affectional, affective, feeling; soulful; demonstrative.

19 sensible, sensitive; emotionable, impassionable; susceptible, susceptive; impressionable, impressible, affectible, receptive; responsive, sympathetic.

20. tender, soft, gentle, delicate, thin-skinned; tenderhearted, softhearted, warm-hearted.

21. sentimental, soft, mawkish, maudlin, sticky [slang]; mushy, sloppy, gushing [all coll.]; namby-pamby, insipid, inane; romantic; nostalgic; oversentimental.

22. fervent, fervid, passionate, impassioned, ardent, hearty, cordial, keen, breathless; zealous 633.10; warm, burning, heated, hot, red-hot, fiery, flaming, glowing, ablaze, afire, on fire, boiling over; delirious, feverish, febrile, flushed; intoxicated, drunk.

23. affecting, touching, moving, pathetic.

24. affected, moved, touch, impressed; impressed with or by, penetrated with, seized with, imbued with, devoured by.

25. deep-felt, heartfelt, homefelt; deep, profound, indelible; pervading, absorbing; penetrating, piercing; poignant, keen, sharp, acute.

ADVS. 26. feelingly, emotionally, touchingly, movingly, with feeling.

27. fervently, fervidly, passionately, impassionedly, ardently, keenly, breathlessly; warmly, heatedly, glowingly; heartily, cordially, kindly, heart and soul, with all one's heart, from the bottom of one's heart.

28. sentimentally, mawkishly, maudlinly; mushily, sloppily, gushingly [all coll.].

854. LACK OF FEELINGS

Emotional Unfeeling.—NOUNS 1. unfeeling, unfeelingness; emotionlessness, unemotionalism; dispassion, dispassionateness, unpassionateness; passionlessness, spiritlessness, heartlessness, soullessness; coldness, coolness, frigidity; cold-heartedness, cold-bloodedness; cold heart, cold blood; unresponsiveness, unsympatheticalness; unimpressionableness, unimpressibility; insusceptibility, unsusceptibility; impassiveness, impassibility, impassivity; immovability, untouchability; dullness, obtuseness, obtundity.

2. insensibility, insensibleness, unconsciousness, obliviousness, oblivion.

3. callousness, callosity, callus; insensitivity, insensitiveness; hardness, hardenedness, hardheartedness, hardness of heart, hard heart, heart of stone; obduracy, induration, inuredness, imperviousness; thick skin, rhinocerous hide.

4. apathy, indifference, unconcern, disinterest, dispassion, inappetence or inappetency, insouciance; listlessness, spiritlessness, heartlessness, plucklessness, spunklessness; lethargy, phlegm, lethargicalness, phlegmaticalness, phlegmaticness, dullness, sluggishness, languidness, supineness, comatoseness, torpidness, torpor, torpidity; stupor, stupefaction; numbness, benumbedness.

VERBS 5. not to be affected by, remain unmoved; have a thick skin, have a heart of stone.

6. callous, sear, harden, caseharden, harden the heart, ossify, steel, brazen, indurate, inure; brutalize, brutify.

7. dull, blunt, obtund, hebetate.

8. numb, benumb, paralyze, deaden, stun, stupefy.

ADJS. 9. unfeeling, unemotional, nonemotional, emotionless; unpassionate, dispassionate, unimpassioned; passionless, spiritless, heartless, soulless; cold, cool, frigid, frozen, coldhearted, cold-blooded, cold as charity; **unresponsive,** unresponding, **unsympathetic(al);** unimpressionable, unimpressible; insusceptible, unsusceptible; **impassive,** impassible; immovable, untouchable; dull, obtuse.

10. **insensible, unconscious, oblivious,** blind to, deaf to, dead to, lost to.

11. **unaffected, unmoved, untouched,** unimpressed, unstruck, unstirred, unruffled, unanimated, uninspired; unfelt.

12. **callous, calloused, seared, insensitive, thick-skinned,** pachydermatous, **hard, hardhearted, hardened,** casehardened, indurated, impervious, inured, steeled against, proof against, as hard as nails.

13. **apathetic(al), indifferent, unconcerned, disinterested, uninterested,** insouciant; **listless, spiritless,** heartless, pluckless, spunkless; **lethargic(al), phlegmatic(al),** dull, sluggish, torpid, languid, supine, comatose; **stupefied,** in a stupor; **numb,** numbed, benumbed.

ADVS. 14. **unfeelingly,** insensibly; **unemotionally,** emotionlessly; **dispassionately,** unpassionately; **spiritlessly, heartlessly,** coldly, coldheartedly, **cold-bloodedly, in cold blood;** with dry eyes.

15. **apathetically, indifferently, unconcernedly,** disinterestedly, uninterestedly, impassively; **listlessly, spiritlessly,** heartlessly, plucklessly, spunklessly; **lethargically, phlegmatically,** dully, numbly.

855. EXCITEMENT

NOUNS 1. **excitement,** emotion, excitedness; **stimulation, exhilaration.**

2. **thrill, sensation,** titillation; **tingle,** tingling; quiver, tremor, **tremor of excitement;** flush, rush of emotion; kick, boot, bang, lift [all slang].

3. **agitation, perturbation; turbulence, turmoil,** tumult; **commotion,** disturbance, ado, to-do [coll.]; flurry, ruffle, bustle, stir, whirl, hurry, hurry-scurry, hurly-burly; ferment, fermentation, effervescence, ebullition, fume, blood boiling.

4. **trepidation,** trepidity; **disquiet,** disquietude, inquietude; **unrest, restlessness; fidgets,** fidgetiness; **shakes,** shivers [coll.]; dithers [coll.]; **quivering, quavering, quaking, shaking;** quiver, quaver, shiver, didder, twitter, tremor, tremble, flutter; palpitation, pitapatation [joc.], pitapat, pitterpatter; throb, throbbing; panting, heaving.

5. **dither** [coll.], **tizzy** [slang], dodaw

[slang], **pucker** [coll.], **twitter,** twitteration [coll.], **flutter, fluster,** flusteration *or* flustration [coll.], fuss, pother, bother, **stew** [coll.], flap [Eng.], **taking** [coll.].

6. **fever of excitement,** fever, heat, fever heat, fire.

7. **fury, furor,** furore, fire and fury; **passion,** rage, raging *or* tearing passion, towering rage *or* passion, **frenzy,** madness, **delirium.**

8. **outburst,** outbreak, burst, **flare-up,** blaze, **explosion,** eruption, upheaval, convulsion; storm, tempest, gust, whiff.

9. **excitability,** excitableness, emotional instability; mettlesomeness, edginess, skittishness, startlishness; nervousness 857.

10. **excitation, excitement; agitation, perturbation; stimulation, exhilaration,** animation; electrification, galvanization; **provocation, irritation,** aggravation [coll.], exasperation, exacerbation, fomentation, inflammation, infuriation.

VERBS 11. **excite, impassion, move, affect,** infect; **stir, stir up,** set astir, stir the feelings, stir the blood, play on the feelings; **work up,** work into; **provoke, pique;** incite 646.17; **arouse,** rouse, raise, raise up; **awaken,** awake, wake, waken, wake up; call up, summon up, call forth; **kindle,** enkindle, light up; **fire, inflame,** heat, warm, foment, set on fire, fire *or* warm the blood; fan, blow up; fan the fire *or* flame, blow the coals, stir the embers, feed the fire, add fuel to the fire, raise to a fever heat; overexcite.

12. **stimulate, whet, sharpen, quicken,** enliven, animate, **exhilarate,** invigorate; fillip, give a fillip; infuse life into, give new life to.

13. **irritate, exasperate,** aggravate [coll.], **provoke, pique,** chafe, sting, cut, wound, cut to the heart *or* quick; **infuriate, madden,** try one's temper, stir the blood, make one's blood boil, lash into a fury.

14. **agitate, perturb,** perturbate, **disturb, trouble, disquiet, discompose,** stir, **ruffle,** shake, shake up, upset, jolt, jar, stagger, electrify, galvanize, put about, turn one's head, give one a turn [coll.], strike all of a heap [coll.].

15. **fluster,** flusterate [coll.], **flutter,** flurry, fuss *or* fuss up [slang], dither [coll.], put in a taking [coll.].

16. **thrill, tickle, titillate,** intoxicate, fascinate, flush, give a thrill, **give one a kick** *or* boot [slang], take one's breath away.

17. **get excited,** catch the infection,

work oneself up, work oneself into a sweat *or* lather [coll.], get hot under the collar, run a temperature [slang], race one's motor [slang]; turn a hair; **explode, blow up** [coll., U.S.], **flare up,** flash up, flame up, fire up, take fire; **fly into a passion,** fly off, **fly off the handle** [slang], go *or* fly off at a tangent, **hit the ceiling** [slang], go into hysterics, go hog-wild [slang, U.S.]; **rage, rave, rant, storm, tear.**

18. (be excited) **thrill,** tingle, **tingle with excitement;** glow; swell, swell with emotion, be full of emotion; draw a deep breath, heave, pant; throb, palpitate, go pit-apat; **tremble, shiver, quiver, quaver, quake,** flutter, twitter, **shake,** shake like an aspen leaf; **fidget,** have the fidgets; toss and turn, toss, tumble; twist and turn, wriggle, wiggle, writhe, squirm; twitch, jerk.

19. **seethe, fume,** foam, simmer, burn, stew [coll.], be in a stew [coll.], boil, boil over.

20. **change color,** turn color, mantle; **pale,** whiten, turn pale; darken, turn black in the face, look black *or* blue; **flush, blush,** crimson, color, turn red.

ADJS. 21. **excited,** impassioned, *éperdu* [F.], on the *qui vive;* **thrilled,** atingle; **stimulated, exhilarated; moved, stirred,** aroused, fired, inflamed, **wrought up, worked up,** keyed up, hopped up [slang], fussed up [slang]; carried away; bursting, ready to burst.

22. **in a dither** [coll.], **in a tizzy** [slang], in a codaw [slang], **in a pucker** [coll.], **in a twitter, in a taking** [coll.], in a flutter, in a fluster, in a flurry, in a pother, in a bother, in a turmoil, in a stew [coll.], in a sweat *or* muck of sweat [coll.].

23. **heated, passionate, warm, hot,** red-hot, flaming, **burning, fiery, glowing, fervent, fervid; feverish,** febrile, hectic [coll.], flushed; burning with excitement, het up [dial.], hot under the collar [coll.]; seething, ebullient, boiling over.

24. **agitated, perturbed, disturbed, troubled,** disquieted, discomposed, flustered, ruffled, shaken; tremulous, tremulant; in a quiver, all of a flutter *or* twitter.

25. **turbulent,** tumultuous, tempestuous, boisterous, clamorous, uproarious.

26. **frenzied, frantic;** raging, raving, ranting, fuming, foaming at the mouth; **wild,** hog-wild [slang, U.S.]; **violent, fierce, furious; mad, rabid,** demoniac(al), **distracted, delirious, beside oneself,** out of one's wits; **hysteric(al),** in hysterics; wild-

eyed, wild-looking, haggard, harrowed; black *or* blue in the face.

27. **overwrought, overexcited; overcome,** overwhelmed, overpowered, overmastered; **upset,** *bouleversé* [F.], struck all of a heap [coll.].

28. **restless,** restive, **uneasy,** unquiet, unsettled, unrestful; **fidgety,** fussy, fluttery.

29. **excitable,** edgy; **skittish,** startlish; **high-strung,** high-spirited, **mettlesome,** high-mettled; nervous 857.11.

30. **passionate, fiery, vehement,** violent, furious, fierce, wild; demonstrative; hotheaded, madcap; simmering, volcanic, ready to burst forth.

31. **exciting, thrilling, stirring, moving, breathtaking,** killing [coll.]; heart-stirring, heart-thrilling, heart-swelling, heart-expanding, soul-stirring, spirit-stirring, deepthrilling; impressive, striking, telling; **provocative,** provoking, *provoquant* [F.]; tantalizing 648.7; **stimulating,** stimulative, exhilarating; electric, galvanic; **overwhelming,** overpowering, overcoming, overmastering, more than flesh and blood can bear.

32. **penetrating, piercing,** stabbing, cutting, stinging, biting, keen, brisk, sharp, caustic, astringent.

33. **sensational, lurid,** yellow, melodramatic, Barnumesque; thrilly [coll.], spine-chilling; blood-and-thunder, cloak-and-dagger.

ADVS. 34. **excitedly, agitatedly;** with beating *or* leaping heart, with heart beating high, with heart going pitapat *or* pitter-patter, with heart in mouth; with glistening eyes.

35. **heatedly, passionately,** warmly, hotly, glowingly, fervently, fervidly, feverishly.

36. **frenziedly, frantically,** wildly, furiously, violently, fiercely, madly, rabidly, distractedly, deliriously, till one is black *or* blue in the face.

37. **excitingly, thrillingly,** stirringly, movingly; provocatively, provokingly; stimulatingly, exhilaratingly.

856. INEXCITABILITY

NOUNS 1. **inexcitability,** inexcitableness; **imperturbability,** imperturbableness; inirritability, unirritableness; **dispassion,** dispassionateness, unpassionateness, cold-bloodedness; steadiness; **even temper;** unnervousness 858; **impassiveness,** impassivity; stolidity, bovinity.

2. composure, countenance; calmness, placidity, serenity, tranquillity, peacefulness; quiet, quietude; imperturbation, indisturbance; coolness, coolheadedness, sang-froid [F.].

3. equanimity, poise, aplomb, equilibrium, balance, ballast; levelheadedness, level head [coll.], well-balanced or well-regulated mind; self-possession, self-control, self-command, self-restraint, restraint, possession, presence of mind; confidence, assurance, self-confidence, self-assurance; philosophicalness, philosophy.

4. sedateness, staidness, soberness, sobriety, sober-mindedness.

5. nonchalance, casualness, offhandedness; easygoingness, lackadaisicalness; indifference, unconcern 634.

VERBS 6. compose, calm 162.7; set one's mind at ease or rest, make one easy.

7. compose oneself, control oneself, restrain oneself, collect oneself, get hold of oneself, get organized [slang], master one's feelings; calm down, cool off, sober down, simmer down [coll.].

8. (control one's feelings) suppress, repress, keep under, smother.

9. keep cool, keep calm, keep one's head, keep one's shirt on [slang], take it easy, not turn a hair.

ADJS. 10. inexcitable, imperturbable, undisturbable; unirritable, inirritable; dispassionate, unpassionate, cold-blooded; steady, even-tempered; impassive, stolid, bovine; unnervous 858.2.

11. unexcited, unperturbed, undisturbed, untroubled, unagitated, unruffled, unflustered, unstirred, unimpassioned.

12. calm, placid, quiet, tranquil, serene, peaceful; cool, coolheaded, cool as a cucumber [coll.], cool as custard [coll.]; philosophic(al).

13. composed, collected, recollected, levelheaded; poised, balanced, well-balanced; self-possessed, self-controlled, self-restrained; confident, assured, self-confident, self-assured.

14. sedate, staid, sober, sober-minded.

15. nonchalant, blasé; indifferent, unconcerned 634.5, 6; casual, offhand; easygoing, easy, free and easy, devil-may-care, lackadaisical, dégagé [F.].

ADVS. 16. calmly, placidly, quietly, tranquilly, serenely; coolly, composedly, levelheadedly.

17. nonchalantly, casually, offhandedly, easygoingly, lackadaisically.

857. NERVOUSNESS

NOUNS 1. nervousness, nerves, state of nerves, case of nerves, attack of nerves; agitation, trepidation 855.3, 4; butterflies [slang]; fidgets, fidgetiness; twitching, vellication [med.]; stage fright; buck fever [coll.]; nervous stomach.

2. jitters, willies, heebie jeebies, jimjams, jimmies, jingles [all slang]; jumps, shakes, trembles, dithers, all-overs [all coll.]; shivers, cold shivers [both coll.]; sweat, cold sweat.

3. tension, tenseness, strain, stress, stress and strain, mental strain, nervous tension or strain.

4. frayed nerves, frazzled nerves, jangled nerves, raw nerves.

5. nervous disorders 684.17, 18; neurosis 688.17; nervous breakdown 684.7.

6. nervous wreck, wreck, a bundle of nerves.

VERBS 7. fidget, have the fidgets; jitter, have the jitters, etc. [both slang]; tremble 855.18.

8. lose one's nerve, lose one's head, lose self-control; lose courage 890.8; break down, crack up [coll.], blow up [coll., U.S.], blow one's top [slang], go haywire [slang, U.S.], go to pieces, have a nervous breakdown.

9. get on one's nerves, jangle the nerves, grate on, jar on, put on edge, set the teeth on edge, go against the grain; irritate 864.18; fidget.

10. unnerve, unman, undo, unstring, unbrace, demoralize, shake, upset, dash, knock down, crush, overcome, prostrate.

ADJS. 11. nervous, nervy [coll., Eng.]; high-strung, overstrung, a bundle of nerves, all nerves; excitable 855.29; edgy, on edge, nerves on edge, on the ragged edge [coll.].

12. jittery [slang], jumpy, skittery [dial.], twittery, twitterly [coll.], all-overish [coll.]; shaky, shivery, quivery, in a quiver; tremulous, tremulant, trembly; fidgety, fidgeting; fluttery, all of a flutter or twitter; twitchy, twitchety [both coll.]; agitated 855.24; shaking, trembling, quivering, shivering; all shook up [coll.].

13. tense, strained, taut, unrelaxed, under a strain.

14. unnerved, unmanned, unstrung, undone, demoralized, shaken, upset, dashed, stricken, crushed; shot, shot to

pieces, nerves all shot; prostrate, prostrated, overcome.

15. nerve-racking *or* ~ wracking, nerve-rending, nerve-shaking, nerve-trying, nerve-stretching; jarring, grating.

ADVS. 16. nervously, shakily, shakingly, tremulously, tremblingly, quiveringly; fidgetily, fidgetingly.

858. UNNERVOUSNESS

NOUNS 1. unnervousness, nervelessness; calmness, inexcitability 856; unshakiness, untremulousness; **steadiness**, steady-handedness, steady nerves; strong nerves, nerves of steel; nerve-deafness.

ADJS. 2. unnervous, nerveless, without a nerve in one's body; strong-nerved, iron-nerved, steel-nerved; **calm, inexcitable** 856.10-12; steady, steady-nerved, steady-handed; unshaky, unshaken, unquivering, untremulous; unflinching, unshrinking, unblenching, unblinking; relaxed, unstrained; nerve-deaf.

859. PATIENCE

NOUNS 1. patience, patientness; **tolerance**, toleration; **indulgence**, lenience; **forbearance**, forbearing; **sufferance**, endurance; **long-suffering**, longanimity; **stoicism**, fortitude, self-control; patience of Job, ' patience on a monument" [Shakespeare], "patience sovereign o'er transmuted ill" [Johnson]; "the art of hoping" [Vauvenargues]; perseverance 623.

2. **resignation, meekness, submissiveness**, submission, acquiescence, compliance, incomplainingness; **passiveness**, passivity; passive resistance, nonresistance; quietism, Quakerism.

3. **stoic**, Spartan, Indian, man of iron.

VERBS 4. be patient, forbear, bear with composure, wait, keep one's shirt on [slang]; carry on, carry through; "have patience and endure" [Ovid].

5. endure, bear, stand, support, sustain, suffer, tolerate, abide, bide, aby, go [coll., U.S.], stick [coll.]; bear with, put up with, take up with, abide with, stand for [coll.], brook, brave; lump, like it or lump it [both coll., U.S.].

6. accept, condone, countenance; reconcile oneself to, resign oneself to, yield *or* submit to; accustom oneself to, accommodate oneself to, adjust oneself to; accept one's fate, lay in the lap of the gods; **make the best of it**, make the most of it, make the best of a bad bargain, make a virtue of

necessity; submit with a good grace, **grin and bear it**, grin and abide; take in good part, take in one's stride; rise above it.

7. take, pocket, swallow, down, stomach, eat, digest, disregard; swallow an insult, pocket the affront, turn the other cheek; take it lying down.

8. **bear up under, bear the brunt, stand the gaff** *or* **racket** [slang], take it [coll.], take it on the chin [slang], take it like a man, not let it get one down [slang].

9. be borne, **go down**, go down with [coll.].

ADJS. 10. **patient**, armed with patience, patient as Job; **tolerant**, tolerative, tolerating; **indulgent**, lenient; **forbearant**, forbearing; **long-suffering**, longanimous; **enduring**, endurant; stoic(al), Spartan, self-controlled; persevering 623.7.

11. **resigned, meek, submissive**, acquiescent, compliant, **uncomplaining; passive**, unresisting.

ADVS. 12. **patiently**, enduringly, stoically; **tolerantly**, **indulgently**, leniently, forbearantly, forbearingly, more in sorrow than in anger; "like patience on a monument smiling at grief" [Shakespeare]; perseveringly 623.8.

13. **resignedly, meekly, submissively**, passively, acquiescently, compliantly, uncomplainingly.

860. IMPATIENCE

NOUNS 1. **impatience**, impatientness, unpatientness [chiefly dial.], breathless impatience; **anxiety, eagerness** 633; **restlessness**, restiveness, disquietude, uneasiness; sweat, lather, stew [all coll.]; **fretfulness**, fretting, chafing; impetuousness 628.2.

2. **intolerance**, intoleration, **unforbearance**, nonendurance.

3. **the last straw**, the straw that breaks the camel's back, the limit, the limit of one's patience, all one can bear.

VERBS 4. be impatient, hardly wait; itch to, burn to; **champ at the bit, pull at the leash; chafe, fret, fuss; stew**, sweat, sweat and stew, get *or* work oneself into a lather, ~ sweat *or* stew [all coll.]; wait impatiently, sweat it out [slang].

5. **have no patience with**, be out of all patience; **lose patience**, run out of patience.

ADJS. 6. **impatient**, unpatient [chiefly dial.]; breathless; champing at the bit, rarin' to go [slang, U.S.]; **anxious, eager** 633.9; all anxioused up [dial.], all hopped up

[slang], all in a lather, ~ sweat *or* stew
[coll.]; edgy, **on edge; restless,** restive, uneasy; **fretful,** fretting, chafing; impetuous
628.9.

7. intolerant, unforbearing, unindulgent.

ADVS. **8. impatiently,** breathlessly; **anxiously** 633.13; fretfully; restlessly, restively,
uneasily; intolerantly.

861. PLEASANTNESS

NOUNS **1. pleasantness,** pleasingness,
pleasurefulness, **pleasurableness, enjoyableness; agreeableness,** agreeability; geniality,
cordiality, amiability, amenity; goodness,
goodliness, niceness.

2. delightfulness, delectability, exquisiteness, loveliness; **charm,** winsomeness,
attractiveness, fascination, captivation,
enchantment, entrancement, bewitchment,
enravishment.

3. cheerfulness 868; brightness, sunniness; sunny side, bright side; fair weather.

VERBS **4.** make things pleasant, sweeten,
gild, gild the lily *or* pill.

ADJS. **5. pleasant, pleasing, pleasureful,
pleasurable, enjoyable,** pleasure-giving;
likable, desirable, to one's liking, to one's
taste, to *or* after one's fancy, after one's
own heart; **agreeable,** not hard to take
[slang]; **gratifying,** satisfying, grateful; welcome, welcome as the roses in May; genial,
cordial, amiable, good, goodly, nice, fine;
cheerful 868.10.

6. delightful, exquisite, lovely; thrilling,
titillative; **charming, engaging, appealing,**
prepossessing, **enchanting,** bewitching, entrancing, enthralling *or* inthralling, intriguing, fascinating, captivating, ravishing,
enravishing, winning, winsome, taking,
fetching [coll.], killing [coll.], heart-robbing; beatific(al); divine, sublime; **heavenly,** paradisiac(al), empyrean, Elysian, out
of this world [slang].

7. delectable, delicious, savory; sweet,
dulcet.

8. palmy, bright, sunny, halcyon,
Saturnian.

ADVS. **9. pleasantly, pleasingly,** pleasurefully, **pleasurably, enjoyably; gratifyingly,** satisfyingly; agreeably, genially, cordially, amiably, kindly; cheerfully 868.17.

10. delightfully, delectably, deliciously,
exquisitely; **charmingly, engagingly, appealingly, enchantingly,** bewitchingly, entrancingly, intriguingly, fascinatingly, ravishingly, enravishingly; winningly, winsomely.

862. UNPLEASANTNESS

NOUNS **1. unpleasantness,** unpleasingness; **disagreeableness,** disagreeability, *désagrément* [F.]; **undesirability,** unattractiveness; **distastefulness,** unsavoriness, unpalatability, **undelectability.**

2. offensiveness, odiousness, repulsiveness, disgustingness, nauseousness, mawkishness, **loathsomeness, vileness, foulness,**
nastiness, fulsomeness, noisomeness, noxiousness, **obnoxiousness, hatefulness,**
abominability, contemptibility, despicability, detestability.

3. horribleness, horridness, **dreadfulness,
terribleness,** awfulness [coll.], hideousness.

4. distressfulness, grievousness, painfulness; lamentability, deplorability, pitiability.

5. vexatiousness, irksomeness, tiresomeness, wearisomeness; **troublesomeness,
bothersomeness,** worrisomeness, plaguesomeness, peskiness [coll., U.S.], pestiferousness [coll.]; provocativeness.

6. oppressiveness, burdensomeness,
onerousness, weightiness, heaviness.

7. intolerability, unbearableness, insupportableness, insufferableness, **unendurability.**

ADJS. **8. unpleasant, unpleasing, unenjoyable; displeasing, disagreeable; unlikable,** dislikable; **undesirable,** unattractive,
uninviting, unalluring; **distasteful,** untasteful, unpalatable, unsavory, unappetizing,
undelicious, **undelectable;** sour, bitter.

9. offensive, odious, repulsive, repellent, **repugnant, revolting,** forbidding, **disgusting, sickening,** mawkish, **loathsome,
vile, foul,** nasty, fulsome, noisome, noxious,
obnoxious, abhorrent, hateful, abominable, contemptible, despicable, detestable,
execrable, beneath *or* below contempt;
nauseating, nauseous, nauseant.

10. horrid, horrible, horrific, **horrifying;
dreadful, terrible,** awful [coll.], hideous,
beastly [coll.]; dire, grim; appalling, shocking.

11. distressing, distressful; afflicting, afflictive; **painful,** sore; **grievous,** dolorous;
lamentable, deplorable, pitiable, piteous,
rueful, woeful, **sad,** mournful; **pathetic,**
affecting, touching, moving; comfortless,
uncomfortable.

12. mortifying, embarrassing, crushing,
disconcerting, awkward, disturbing.

13. annoying, irritating, galling, **provoking,** provocative, **aggravating** [coll.], exasperating; **vexatious**, vexing, irking, **irk-some**, tiresome, wearisome; **troublesome, bothersome, worrisome,** bothering, troubling, disturbing; plaguing, plaguesome, plaguy [coll.], beastly [coll., U.S.]; **pesky** [coll., U.S.], pestilent, pestiferous [coll.]; tormenting, harassing, worrying; pestering, teasing; importunate, importune.

14. **agonizing, excruciating, harrowing,** racking, rending, **desolating,** consuming; **tormenting,** torturous; **heartbreaking,** heart-rending, **heartsickening,** heartwounding, heart-corroding.

15. **oppressive, burdensome,** onerous, weighty, heavy, overburdensome.

16. **insufferable, intolerable, insupportable, unendurable, unbearable,** past bearing, not to be borne or endured, more than flesh and blood can bear, enough to drive one mad, enough to provoke a saint, enough to make a preacher swear [coll.], enough to try the patience of Job.

ADVS. **17.** unpleasantly, unpleasingly; displeasingly, offensively.

18. **distressingly,** distressfully; **painfully,** sorely, **grievously,** lamentably, deplorably, pitiably, ruefully, woefully, sadly, pathetically; agonizingly, excruciatingly, harrowingly, heartbreakingly.

19. annoyingly, irritatingly, provokingly, **aggravatingly** [coll.], exasperatingly; vexatiously, irksomely, tiresomely, wearisomely; **troublesomely, bothersomely, worrisomely.**

20. insufferably, intolerably, unbearably, unendurably, insupportably.

863. PLEASURE

NOUNS **1.** **pleasure, enjoyment; gratification, satisfaction,** great satisfaction; **relish, zest, gusto,** joie de vivre [F.]; titillation; fruition; amusement 876.

2. **happiness, gladness, delight,** delectation; **joy, joyfulness,** joyance; **cheer, glee,** sunshine; cheerfulness, gaiety 868; overjoyfulness, overhappiness; intoxication; **rapture,** ravishment, **enchantment,** transport, unalloyed happiness; euphoria; **elation,** exaltation; **ecstasy,** ecstatics; **bliss,** blissfulness; beatitude, beatification, blessedness; felicity, paradise, heaven, third or seventh heaven.

3. **treat, delight;** regalement, regale, feast, banquet, feast or banquet of the soul.

4. pleasure-loving, hedonism, hedonics.

VERBS **5.** **please, give pleasure,** be to one's liking, meet one's wishes, take one's

fancy, strike one right, hit the right spot [slang]; make a hit [coll.], go over big [slang].

6. **gratify, satisfy;** slake, appease, allay, assuage, quench; regale, feed, feast; do one's heart good, warm the cockles of the heart.

7. **gladden,** happify, make happy; bless, beatify; cheer 868.6.

8. **delight,** delectate; **tickle, titillate, thrill,** tickle to death [coll.], tickle pink [slang]; wow, slay, knock dead [all slang]; **enrapture, enthrall, enchant,** entrance, fascinate, captivate, bewitch, **charm,** becharm; enravish, ravish, imparadise; transport, carry away, send [slang].

9. **be pleased, feel happy; delight,** joy, take great satisfaction; walk or tread on air, be in heaven, fall or go into raptures.

10. **enjoy,** be pleased with, receive or derive pleasure from, take delight or pleasure in, get a kick out of [slang]; **like, love,** adore [coll.]; **delight in, rejoice in,** indulge in, luxuriate in, revel in, riot in, bask in, wallow in, swim in; feast on, gloat over or on; **relish, appreciate,** roll under the tongue, smack the lips; devour, eat up.

11. **enjoy oneself,** appreciate oneself [dial.], have a good time.

ADJS. **12.** **pleased, delighted,** proud [chiefly dial.]; **glad, gladsome; charmed,** intrigued [coll.]; **thrilled; tickled,** tickled to death [coll.], tickled pink [slang]; **gratified, satisfied;** pleased with, taken with, favorably impressed with, sold on [slang]; pleased as Punch, pleased as a child with a new toy.

13. **happy, joyful, joyous;** cheerful 868.10; **blissful,** "throned on highest bliss" [Milton]; blest, blessed; beatified, beatific(al); thrice happy, "thrice and four times blessed" [Vergil]; happy as a lark, happy as a king, happy as the day is long, happy as a clam at high water [U.S.].

14. **overjoyed,** overjoyful, overhappy; **rapturous,** raptured, **enraptured, enchanted,** entranced, enravished, ravished, rapt, **in raptures,** transported, in a transport of delight, **carried away,** beside oneself, beside oneself with joy, all over oneself [slang]; **ecstatic,** in ecstasies, rhapsodic(al); imparadised, **in paradise,** in heaven; **elated,** elate, exalted, jubilant, exultant, flushed.

15. **pleasure-loving,** gay; hedonic(al), hedonistic.

ADVS. **16.** **happily, gladly, joyfully,** joyously, **delightedly,** with pleasure, to one's delight; blissfully, blessedly; **ecstatically,** rhapsodically, **rapturously; elatedly,** jubilantly, exultantly.

INTERJS. 17. goody!, goody, goody!; whee!, wow!; u-mm!, mmmm!, oooo!, ou-la-la!; oh boy!, boy!, man!, hot dog!, hot ziggety! [all slang].

864. DISPLEASURE

NOUNS 1. **displeasure, dissatisfaction,** disaffection; **discomfort,** uncomfortableness, malaise; **disquiet,** inquietude, **uneasiness,** discomposure, vexation of spirit; unhappiness 870.2; disgust 865.2.

2. **annoyance, vexation, aggravation** [coll.]; **nuisance, pest, bother,** botheration [coll.], **trouble; bore,** crashing bore [slang]; **worry,** worriment [coll.]; **headache, pain in the neck** [both slang]; harrassment, molestation; devilment, bedevilment; vexatiousness 862.5.

3. **irritation, provocation;** fret, gall, chafe; irritant; pea in the shoe.

4. **mortification, chagrin, distress; embarrassment, abashment, discomfiture,** disconcertion, discomposure, disturbance, confusion; skeleton in the closet.

5. **pain, distress,** suffering, passion, dolor [poetic]; ache, aching; pang, wrench, throe; wound, injury, hurt; cut, stroke; shock, blow, hard or nasty blow.

6. **wretchedness,** bitterness, infelicity, **misery, anguish, agony, woe,** bale; sadness, grief 870; **heartache,** aching heart, heavy heart, bleeding heart, broken heart; **desolation,** prostration; extremity, depth of misery.

7. **torment, torture,** cruciation, crucifixion, passion, rack, laceration, lancination; persecution; martyrdom; purgatory, hell, hell upon earth; nightmare, horror.

8. **affliction,** infliction; **curse, woe,** distress, grievance, sorrow; **trouble,** peck of troubles, "sea of troubles" [Shakespeare]; **care,** canker worm of care; **burden, oppression, cross, load,** encumbrance, weight, millstone around one's neck; thorn, thorn in the side, crown of thorns; bitter pill, bitter draft or draught, bitter cup, cup or waters of bitterness; gall, gall and wormwood; "the thousand natural shocks that flesh is heir to" [Shakespeare], "all the ills that men endure" [Cowley].

9. **trial, tribulation,** trials and tribulations; **ordeal,** fiery ordeal, the iron entering the soul.

10. **tormentor,** torment; **pest, pesterer;**

tease, teaser; annoyer, harasser, harrier, badgerer, heckler, plaguer, persecutor; **bully,** big bully.

11. **sufferer,** victim, prey; **wretch,** poor devil, object of compassion; martyr.

VERBS 12. **displease,** displeasure [dial.], **dissatisfy,** disaffect, disoblige, not sit right with [coll.].

13. **offend,** give offense; **repel, revolt;** disgust, nauseate, sicken, make one sick, turn the stomach, stink in the nostrils, stick in one's throat, stick in one's crop, ~ craw or gizzard [coll.]; **horrify, appall,** shock; make the flesh creep, make one shudder.

14. **pain, grieve,** aggrieve, anguish; **hurt, wound,** bruise, **hurt the feelings;** pierce, prick, stab, cut, sting; **cut up** [coll.], **cut to the heart,** wound ~, sting or cut to the quick; touch a soft spot, touch where it hurts, hit one where he lives [slang]; step on one's corns; barb the dart.

15. **distress, afflict, trouble, bother, disturb, perturb, disquiet, discomfort,** agitate, upset, put to it.

16. **mortify, chagrin; embarrass, abash, discomfit, disconcert,** discompose, confuse, confound, **put out,** put out of face or countenance, put to the blush.

17. **annoy, irk, vex, nettle, provoke, pique,** miff [dial. & slang], peeve [coll.], distemper, **ruffle, disturb,** discompose, **roil,** rile [coll. & dial.], aggravate [coll.], exasperate, exercise, try the patience; **put one's back up,** bristle; **gripe,** give one a pain [coll.]; **get, get one's goat,** get under one's skin, get in one's hair, burn up, brown off [all slang].

18. **irritate, gall, chafe, fret,** grate, grit [coll.], rasp; **get on one's nerves, grate on,** set on edge, set the teeth on edge, go against the grain; **rub the wrong way.**

19. **torment, molest, bother,** pother, **trouble; harass, harry, heckle, hector, badger,** bait, bullyrag, **worry,** chevy, chivy or chivvy [Eng.], fash [chiefly Scot. & North. Eng.]; **pester, tease,** tantalize, devil [coll.], bedevil, needle, ride [slang], **pick on** [coll.], tweak the nose, give a bad time [slang]; **plague,** beset, infest; **persecute.**

20. **torture, torment, agonize, harrow,** rack, scarify, crucify, excruciate, lacerate, lancinate, macerate, convulse, wring; prolong the agony, kill by inches; martyr, martyrize; punish 1008.10.

21. **prey on the mind,** prey on or upon, weigh on, weigh on the heart; **haunt,** haunt the memory; torment, harass, plague, ob-

sess, beset, besiege; **fester, rankle,** gnaw, corrode.

22. **suffer, hurt, ache, bleed;** anguish, **suffer anguish; agonize,** writhe; moan, groan cry out; go hard with, have a bad time of it; quaff the bitter cup, drain the cup of misery to the dregs.

ADJS. 23. **displeased, dissatisfied;** sorry, unhappy about; **offended; repelled,** revolted; **disgusted, sickened,** sick of; nauseated 684.42; **horrified,** horror-stricken, horror-struck; **appalled,** shocked.

24. **annoyed, irritated,** galled, chafed; bothered, **troubled, disturbed, ruffled,** roiled riled [coll. & dial.]; **irked, vexed, piqued, nettled, provoked,** peeved [coll.], miffed [dial. & slang], **griped, aggravated** [coll.], **exasperated;** burnt up, browned off [both slang].

25. **distressed, afflicted; troubled,** bothered, **disturbed, perturbed, disquieted,** discomforted, discomposed, agitated, upset; **uncomfortable,** uneasy, ill at ease; **mortified, chagrined; embarrassed,** abashed.

26. **pained, grieved,** aggrieved; **hurt, wounded,** injured; anguished, aching, bleeding.

27. **tormented,** plagued, harassed, harried.

28. **tortured, harrowed, agonized,** convulsed, wrung, racked, crucified, lacerated, lancinated; on the rack, under the harrow.

29. **wretched, miserable;** woeful, woebegone; crushed, stricken, cut up [coll.], cut to the heart; heart-stricken, heart-struck; deep-troubled, steeped to the lips in misery; unhappy, sorrowful 870.20–30.

ADVS. 30. to one's displeasure, to one's disgust.

INTERJS. 31. **bother!, botheration!,** rats!, the devil!, fine business!, how do you like that!, well, I like that!, isn't it the limit!, of all the . . .!, it shouldn't happen to a dog!

865. DISLIKE

NOUNS 1. **dislike, distaste, disrelish;** disaffection, **disfavor, disinclination;** displeasure 864; **hate** 928.

2. **aversion, repugnance, repulsion,** antipathy, allergy [coll.], **abomination, abhorrence, horror,** mortal horror; **disgust, loathing;** nausea 684.22; shuddering, cold sweat.

3. **sickener, nauseant.**

VERBS 4. **dislike, mislike,** disaffect, disfavor, not like, have no liking for, **have no**

use for [coll., U.S.], **not care for,** entertain ~, conceive or take a dislike to, not be able to bear, ~ endure or abide; **disrelish,** have no taste for, not have the stomach for; **hate, loathe** 928.4.

5. **feel disgust,** be nauseated, **sicken at,** have a bellyful [vulg.]; **gag, retch,** keck, heave.

6. shudder at, shrug the shoulders at; turn up the nose at, look askant or askance at; shrink from, recoil, revolt at; grimace, make a wry face or wry mouth.

7. **repel, disgust** 864.13.

ADJS. 8. **abhorrent, averse to,** adverse to, allergic to [coll.], loath, shy of, sick of, out of conceit with; **disgusted** 864.23.

9. **unlikable** or **unlikeable, dislikable, unlovable;** odious 862.9; intolerable 862.16.

10. **uncared-for, unvalued;** unpopular, out of favor; **unappreciated,** misunderstood; thankless; unwept, unlamented, unmourned, undeplored.

11. **unloved, unbeloved, unendeared,** loveless; **lovelorn,** forsaken, rejected, jilted, crossed in love.

12. **unwanted,** unwished, undesired; **unwelcome,** unasked, unbidden, uninvited, uncalled-for, unasked-for.

INTERJS. 13. **fough!, foh!, pah!;** ugh!, phew!, pew!

866. CONTENT

NOUNS 1. **content, contentment,** contentedness, satisfiedness; **satisfaction,** entire satisfaction; ease, peace of mind; happiness 863.2.

2. **complacence** or complacency, bovinity; **self-complacence** or ~ complacency, **self-satisfaction, self-content,** self-contentedness.

3. **satisfactoriness, sufficiency, adequacy; acceptability,** admissibility, **tolerability,** agreeability, unobjectionability, unexceptionability.

VERBS 4. **content, satisfy;** gratify 863.6; put or set at ease, set one's mind at ease or rest.

5. **be content, rest satisfied,** rest and be thankful, be reconciled to, take the good the gods provide, let well enough alone; have no kick coming [slang], can't complain; content oneself with, settle for.

6. be satisfactory, **suffice** 659.4.

ADJS. 7. **content, contented, satisfied; pleased** 863.12; happy 863.13; **at ease,** at one's ease, easygoing; **comfortable,** of good comfort; without care, *sans souci* [F.].

8. **untroubled, unbothered, undisturbed,** unworried, unvexed, unplagued, untormented.

9. **well-content,** well-contented, **well-pleased, well-satisfied,** highly satisfied.

10. **complacent,** bovine; **self-complacent, self-satisfied,** self-content, **self-contented.**

11. **satisfactory, satisfying; sufficient,** sufficing, **adequate,** commensurate, ample, equal to.

12. **acceptable,** admissible, **agreeable,** unobjectionable, unexceptionable; **O.K.,** okay, all right [all coll.]; **passable,** good enough.

13. **tolerable, bearable, endurable, supportable, sufferable.**

ADVS. 14. **contentedly,** to one's heart's content; **satisfiedly,** with satisfaction; **complacently,** self-complacently, self-satisfiedly, self-contentedly.

15. **satisfactorily,** satisfyingly; **acceptably, agreeably,** admissibly; **sufficiently,** adequately, commensurately, amply, enough; **tolerably, passably.**

16. **to one's satisfaction,** to one's delight, to one's great glee; to one's taste, to the king's or queen's taste.

INTERJS. 17. **very well!, good!,** well and good!, good for you!, that will do!, all the better!, so much the better!

867. DISCONTENT

NOUNS 1. **discontent,** discontentment, discontentedness; **dissatisfaction,** unsatisfaction, dissatisfiedness; **disappointment** 539; **displeasure** 864; unhappiness 870.2; ill-humor 949; **disgruntlement,** vexation of spirit; heartburn, heartburning; cold comfort.

2. **unsatisfactoriness,** dissatisfactoriness; **inadequacy, insufficiency; unacceptability,** inadmissibility, unsuitability, undesirability, objectionability; **intolerability** 862.7.

3. **malcontent,** *frondeur* [F.]; **complainer,** complainant, **faultfinder, grumbler,** growler, **murmurer,** mutterer, griper, croaker; kicker, **grouch, crank** [all coll.]; **crab,** grouser, **bellyacher** [all slang]; reactionary, reactionist; rebel 765.5.

VERBS 4. **dissatisfy, discontent, disgruntle, displease,** disappoint, dishearten, put out [coll.].

ADJS. 5. **discontented, dissatisfied, disgruntled, displeased,** disappointed; **unsatisfied, ungratified;** malcontent, malcontented; unhappy 870.21; out of humor 949.17.

6. **unsatisfactory,** dissatisfactory; **unsatisfying, ungratifying; displeasing,** disappointing, disheartening, not up to expectation; **inadequate,** incommensurate, **insufficient.**

7. **unacceptable,** inadmissible, unsuitable, undesirable, **objectionable,** exceptionable, impossible; **intolerable** 862.16.

ADVS. 8. **discontentedly, dissatisfiedly.**

9. **unsatisfactorily,** dissatisfactorily; **unsatisfyingly, ungratifyingly; inadequately, insufficiently; unacceptably,** inadmissibly, unsuitably, undesirably, objectionably; intolerably 862.20.

868. CHEERFULNESS

NOUNS 1. **cheerfulness,** cheeringness, **cheer;** blitheness, blithesomeness; **gladness,** gladsomeness; **happiness** 863.2; **pleasantness,** winsomeness, geniality; brightness, radiance, sunniness.

2. **good humor, good spirits,** good cheer; **high spirits,** altitudes [coll.], exhilaration, rare good humor.

3. **lightheartedness,** lightness, levity; **buoyancy,** resilience, bounce [coll.]; **jauntiness,** debonairness, carefreeness; **breeziness,** airiness; light heart.

4. **gaiety or** gayety, gayness, *allégresse* [F.]; **liveliness,** vivacity, life, **animation, spiritedness,** sprightliness, zestfulness, **exuberance; spirits,** animal spirits; **friskiness,** skittishness, coltishness, rompishness, rollicksomeness, capersomeness; **sportiveness, playfulness, frolicsomeness,** gamesomeness.

5. **merriment,** merriness; **hilarity,** hilariousness; **joy,** joyfulness, joyousness; **glee,** gleefulness, high glee; **jollity,** jolliness, **joviality,** jocularity, jocundity; **levity; mirth,** mirthfulness, **amusement;** laughter 874.4.

VERBS 6. **cheer, gladden,** brighten, put in good humor; **encourage, hearten;** inspire, inspirit, **raise the spirits,** buoy up, boost, give a lift [slang]; **exhilarate,** animate, invigorate, liven, enliven; **rejoice,** rejoice the heart, do the heart good.

7. **elate, exalt,** elevate, lift, uplift, flush.

8. **cheer up,** take heart, drive dull care away; **brighten up,** light up, **perk up; buck up,** brace up, chirk up [all coll.]; come out of it, snap out of it [slang].

9. **be of good cheer,** bear up, **keep one's spirits up,** keep one's chin up [coll.], keep a stiff upper lip [slang]; smile, laugh 874.8, 9.

ADJS. 10. **cheerful, cheery,** cheerfulsome [dial.], of good cheer, in good spirits;

blithe, blithesome; **glad, gladsome; happy**
863.13; **pleasant, genial,** winsome; **bright,**
sunny, bright and sunny, **radiant,** riant,
sparkling, beaming; smiling, laughing.

11. **lighthearted,** light, lightsome; **buoyant,** corky [coll.], resilient; **jaunty, debonair**
or debonaire, **carefree,** free and easy;
breezy, airy.

12. **in high spirits,** in high feather, in
one's altitudes [coll.].

13. **pert,** peart [dial.], chirk [coll., U.S.],
chirrupy [coll.], chirpy, **chipper** [coll.,
U.S.], canty [Scot. & dial., Eng.], "crouse
an' canty" [Burns].

14. **gay,** gay as a lark; **spirited,** sprightly,
lively, animated, vivacious, zestful, zippy
[coll.], exuberant, *folâtre* [F.]; **frisky,** antic
[dial., U.S.], skittish, coltish, rompish,
capersome; **full of beans, feeling one's
oats** [both slang]; **sportive, playful,** frolicsome, gamesome; rollicking, rollicky [coll.],
rollicksome.

15. **merry, mirthful, hilarious; joyful,
joyous, gleeful,** gleesome; **jolly,** buxom,
bully [slang], boon; **jovial,** jocund, jocular;
laughter-loving, mirth-loving, risible; merry
as a cricket or grig, "as merry as the day is
long" [Shakespeare].

16. **cheering,** gladdening; **encouraging,
heartening; inspiring,** inspiriting; **exhilarating,** animating, enlivening, invigorating;
cheerful, cheery, glad, joyful.

ADVS. 17. **cheerfully,** cheerily, with good
cheer, with a cheerful heart; **lightheartedly,**
lightly; **pleasantly,** genially, blithely;
gladly, happily, joyfully, smilingly.

18. **gayly, exuberantly, spiritedly,** animatedly, **vivaciously,** zestfully, with zest.

19. **merrily, gleefully, hilariously;** jovially, jocundly, jocularly; **mirthfully,**
laughingly.

INTERJS. 20. **cheer up!,** chin up!, never
say die!, "hence, loathed Melancholy!"
[Milton], cheer up, the worst is yet to
come!

869. SOLEMNITY

Solemn Feeling.—NOUNS 1. **solemnity,**
solemnness, soberness, sobriety, gravity,
somberness, grimness; sedateness, staidness, demureness, decorousness; seriousness, earnestness, **thoughtfulness,** sober-
mindedness; **long face,** straight face.

VERBS 2. **keep a straight face,** keep one's
countenance, repress a smile, wipe the
smile off one's face, keep from laughing.

ADJS. 3. **solemn, sober, grave, somber,**

grim; **sedate, staid,** demure, decorous;
serious, earnest, thoughtful, sober-minded;
long-faced, grim-faced, grim-visaged; sober
as a judge, grave as an undertaker.

ADVS. 4. **solemnly, soberly,** gravely,
somberly, grimly; **sedately, staidly,** demurely, decorously; **seriously, earnestly,**
thoughtfully, sober-mindedly.

870. SADNESS

NOUNS 1. **sadness,** sadheartedness; **heavy-
heartedness,** heavy heart, **heaviness of
heart;** pathos, bathos (excessive or insincere pathos).

2. **unhappiness,** infelicity; displeasure
864; discontent 867; **uncheerfulness,** cheerlessness; **joylessness,** unjoyfulness; mirthlessness, unmirthfulness, infestivity;
wretchedness, misery.

3. **dejection, depression, oppression,** dejectedness, **downheartedness,** downcastness;
discouragement, disheartenment; lowness,
lowness or depression of spirits, **low spirits,**
drooping spirits, sinking heart; **despondence** or **despondency,** despondentness,
spiritlessness, heartlessness; black despondency, "Slough of Despond" [Bunyan].

4. **hypochondria,** hypochondry, hyp or
hyps [coll.].

5. **melancholy, melancholia,** melancholiness; **pensiveness, wistfulness,** tristfulness.

6. **blues** [coll.], blue devils [coll.], mulligrubs [slang], mumps, **dumps** [coll.], **doldrums,** dismals, dolefuls [coll.], mopes,
megrims, lachrymals.

7. **gloom, gloominess, dismalness,** somberness, **gravity, solemnity; dreariness,**
drearisomeness; wearifulness, wearisomeness.

8. **glumness,** grumness, **moroseness,** sullenness, **moodiness,** mumpishness, dumpishness; mopishness, mopiness [coll.].

9. **heartache, aching heart,** bleeding
heart; heartsickness, heartsoreness; **heart-
break, broken heart,** brokenheartedness,
heartbrokenness.

10. **sorrow, grief, woe;** heartgrief, heartfelt grief; languishment, pining; **anguish,
misery, agony;** prostration; lamentation 873.

11. **sorrowfulness, mournfulness,** ruefulness, **woefulness, dolefulness,** dolorousness, **plaintiveness,** grievousness, lugubriousness; tearfulness 873.2.

12. **disconsolateness,** disconsolation, **in-
consolability,** comfortlessness; **desolation,**
desolateness; forlornness; despair 887.2.

13. **sourpuss** [slang], sourbelly [joc.]; mope, brooder.

14. **kill-joy, spoilsport, crapehanger** [slang]; damp, damper, **wet blanket;** skeleton at the feast.

VERBS 15. (be sad) hang the head, pull *or* make a long face, laugh on the wrong side of the mouth, grin a ghastly smile, look blue, sing the blues [coll.].

16. **despond, lose heart,** give way; despair 887.10; droop, sink, languish; reach the depths, touch bottom, hit rock-bottom.

17. **grieve, sorrow; mourn** 873.8–14; pine, pine away; **brood over, mope, fret,** take on [coll.]; **eat one's heart out,** break one's heart over; **agonize,** ache, bleed.

18. **sadden,** hyp [coll.], cast a gloom upon; **deject, depress, cast down,** lower, lower the spirits; **discourage, dishearten, dispirit;** damp, dampen, damp *or* dampen the spirits; dash, knock down, beat down; sink, sink one's soul.

19. (cause sorrow to) **grieve, sorrow,** plunge into sorrow; draw tears, bring to tears; **anguish, cut up** [coll.], wring ∼, pierce ∼, lacerate *or* rend the heart, pull at the heartstrings; **break one's heart, make one's heart bleed;** desolate, leave an aching void; prostrate.

ADJS. 20. **sad,** saddened; sadhearted, **sad of heart; heavyhearted,** heavy; sad-faced, long-faced; sad-eyed; sad-voiced.

21. **unhappy, uncheerful,** uncheery, **cheerless, joyless, unjoyful,** unsmiling; mirthless, unmirthful, infestive; **out of humor,** out of sorts, in bad humor *or* spirits; **sorry,** sorryish; displeased 864.23; discontented 867.5; **wretched, miserable.**

22. **dejected, depressed, downhearted, downcast,** cast down, bowed-down; **discouraged, disheartened, dispirited,** dashed; low, **feeling low,** low-spirited, **in low spirits,** sunk [slang]; **down in the mouth** [coll.], **in the doldrums, in the dumps** *or* doleful dumps, in the depths; **despondent,** desponding; spiritless, heartless, **woebegone;** crestfallen, chapfallen *or* chopfallen; drooping, droopy, languishing, pining.

23. **melancholy,** melancholic, **blue;** atrabilious, atrabiliar; **pensive,** *penseroso* [It.], **wistful,** tristful.

24. **hypochondriac(al),** hypochondrial, hypped [coll.].

25. **gloomy, dismal, somber, sombrous, solemn, grave,** *triste* [F.], **funereal,** saturnine; dark, black, gray; **dreary,** drear, drearisome; weary, weariful, wearisome.

26. **glum,** grum, **morose, sullen,** mumpish, dumpish; **moody,** moodish; mopish, mopy [coll.], **moping.**

27. **sorrowful, mournful, rueful, woeful, doleful, dolorous,** *doloroso* [It.], **plaintive, grievous, lamentable,** lugubrious; tearful 873.17; **grieved,** aggrieved, in grief, plunged in grief.

28. **sorrow-stricken,** sorrow-struck, sorrow-wounded, sorrow-torn, sorrow-worn, sorrow-wasted, sorrow-beaten, sorrow-blinded, sorrow-clouded, sorrow-shot, sorrow-burdened, sorrow-laden, sorrow-sighing, sorrow-sobbing, sorrow-sick.

29. **disconsolate, inconsolable,** comfortless, **forlorn;** desolate, *désolé* [F.]; **sick, sick at heart, heartsick,** soul-sick, heartsore; despairing 887.12.

30. **overcome,** crushed, stricken, **cut up** [coll.], **desolated,** prostrated, undone; **heart-stricken,** heart-struck; **heartbroken,** brokenhearted.

31. **depressing,** depressive, **oppressive; discouraging, disheartening, dispiriting; sad, melancholy, gloomy, dismal, dreary,** joyless, cheerless, chill, cold.

ADVS. 32. **sadly, gloomily, dismally, drearily,** somberly, sombrously, solemnly, gravely, with a long face.

33. **unhappily, uncheerfully,** cheerlessly, joylessly, unjoyfully.

34. **dejectedly, downheartedly;** discouragedly, **disheartenedly, dispiritedly; despondently,** spiritlessly, heartlessly; **disconsolately,** inconsolably, forlornly.

35. **melancholily, pensively,** wistfully, tristfully.

36. **glumly,** grumly, **morosely, sullenly; moodily,** moodishly; mopishly, mopily [coll.], mopingly.

37. **sorrowfully, mournfully, ruefully, woefully, dolefully, dolorously, plaintively, grievously,** lugubriously; **heartbrokenly,** brokenheartedly; **tearfully,** with tears in eyes.

871. REGRET

NOUNS 1. **regret,** regretfulness; **remorse,** remorsefulness; **sorrow, grief, sorriness,** repining; **contrition,** contriteness, attrition [theol.]; bitterness, heartburning.

2. **compunction, qualms,** pangs, **pangs of conscience,** sting ∼, pricking ∼, twinge *or* twitch of conscience, touch of conscience, **voice of conscience,** pricking of heart.

3. **self-reproach,** self-reproachfulness,

self-accusation, self-condemnation, self-conviction, self-humiliation.

4. penitence, repentance, change of heart; reformation 145.2; deathbed repentance; penance 1010.3.

5. penitent, confessor, "a sadder and a wiser man" [Coleridge]; prodigal son, prodigal returned; Magdalen.

VERBS 6. regret, deplore, repine, be sorry for; rue, rue the day; bemoan, bewail; reproach oneself, kick oneself [slang], bite one's tongue, take shame; cry over spilled milk.

7. repent, think better of, change one's mind, plead guilty, own oneself in the wrong, humble oneself; do penance 1010.6; reform 145.9.

ADJS. 8. regretful, remorseful, sorry, rueful, repining, unhappy about; conscience-stricken, conscience-smitten; self-reproachful, self-reproaching, self-accusing, self-condemning, self-convicting, self-humiliating; "wild with all regret" [Tennyson].

9. penitent, repentant; penitential, penitentiary; contrite, abject, humble; touched, softened, melted.

10. regrettable, much to be regretted; deplorable 673.9.

ADVS. 11. regretfully, remorsefully, sorrily, ruefully, unhappily.

12. penitently, repentantly; contritely, abjectly, humbly.

INTERJS. 13. what a pity!, too bad!, that's too bad!

872. UNREGRETFULNESS

NOUNS 1. unregretfulness, unremorsefulness, unsorriness, unruefulness; remorselessness, regretlessness, sorrowlessness.

2. impenitence, impenitentness; nonrepentance, irrepentance; uncontriteness, unabjectness; seared conscience, heart of stone; hardness of heart, hardness, induration, obduracy.

VERBS 3. harden the heart, steel oneself.

ADJS. 4. unregretful, unregretting, unremorseful, unsorry, unsorrowful, unrueful; remorseless, regretless, sorrowless, griefless; unsorrowing, ungrieving, unrepining.

5. impenitent, unrepentant, unrepenting; uncontrite, unabject; untouched, unsoftened, unmelted; hard, hardened, obdurate.

6. unregretted, unrepented.

ADVS. 7. unregretfully, unremorsefully, unruefully; remorselessly, sorrowlessly, impenitently; without regret, without remorse, without compunction, without any qualms.

873. LAMENTATION

NOUNS 1. lamentation, lamenting, mourning, grieving, sorrowing, wailing, bewailing, bemoaning, "weeping and gnashing of teeth" [Bible]; sorrow 870.10.

2. weeping, sobbing, crying, bawling; blubbering, snivelling; tears, lachrymals, flood of tears, fit of crying; cry, good cry [both coll.]; tearfulness, melting mood; tearful eyes, swimming ~, brimming or overflowing eyes; tear, teardrop, lachryma; lachrymatory, tear bottle.

3. lament, plaint; murmur, mutter; moan, groan; whine, whimper; wail, wail of woe; sob; cry, outcry, scream, howl, yowl, bawl; ululu, ululation; jeremiad.

4. complaint, grievance, beef [slang, U.S.]; kick, gripe [both coll.]; howl, holler, squawk, grouse [all slang]; complaining, grumbling, murmuring; bellyaching, squawking, grousing, bitching [all slang]; indignation meeting; grievance committee.

5. dirge, funeral or death song, coronach [Scot. & Ir.], keen [Ir.], elegy, epicedium, requiem, monody, threnody, funeral or dead march.

6. (mourning garments) mourning, weepers, weeds, widow's weeds, crape, black; deep mourning; sackcloth and ashes; cypress, cypress lawn; mourning band, weed [coll.]; mourning ring.

7. mourner 409.7.

VERBS 8. lament, mourn, grieve, sorrow, keen [Ir.], weep over, bewail, bemoan, deplore, repine, give sorrow words; elegize.

9. wring one's hands, tear one's hair, gnash one's teeth, beat one's breast, roll on the ground.

10. weep, sob, cry, greet [dial.], bawl, boohoo; blubber, snivel; shed tears, drop a tear; pipe, pipe the eye [both slang]; burst into tears, give way to tears, melt or dissolve in tears, break down, break down and cry; cry one's eyes out, cry oneself blind.

11. wail, ululate; moan, groan; howl, yowl, yawl [dial.]; cry, squall, bawl, yell, scream; cry out, make an outcry; bay at the moon.

12. whine, whimper, yammer [dial.], pule.

13. complain, kick [coll.], **grumble, murmur, mutter, grouch** [coll.], growl, clamor, croak, grunt, yelp, howl [coll.], raise a howl [coll.], put up a squawk or howl [slang]; **squawk, holler, gripe, crab, bellyache, beef, grouse,** bitch [all slang]; **take on** [coll.], **fret,** fuss, make a fuss about, fret and fume; air a grievance, register a complaint; quarrel with one's bread and butter.

14. go into mourning; put on mourning, wear mourning, wear the willow.

ADJS. **15. mourning, lamenting, grieving, sorrowing;** wailing, bewailing, bemoaning; **in mourning,** in sackcloth and ashes.

16. plaintive, mournful, wailful, lamentive, ululant; **sorrowful** 870.27; **complaining, querulous, fretful;** whining, whiny, whimpering, puling.

17. tearful, teary, weepy; lachrymal, lachrymose, lachrymatory; in the melting mood, on the edge of tears, ready to cry; **weeping, sobbing, crying;** blubbering, snivelling; **in tears,** with tears in one's eyes, with tearful or watery eyes, with swimming ~, brimming or overflowing eyes, with eyes suffused, bathed or dissolved in tears, "like Niobe, all tears" [Shakespeare].

18. dirgelike, elegiac(al), epicedial, threnetic(al), threnodial.

ADVS. **19. plaintively, mournfully,** lamentingly, wailfully; **sorrowfully** 870.37; complainingly, querulously, fretfully.

INTERJS. **20. alas!,** alack!, oh!, ah!, O dear!, ah me!, woe's me!, alas the day!, alackaday!, lackaday! lackadaisy!, welladay!, wellaway!, heigh-ho!, that I had ever been born!

874. REJOICING

NOUNS **1. rejoicing, jubilation,** jubilance, jubilee; **exultation,** elation, triumph; merriment 868.5; celebration 875.

2. cheer, huzza, hurrah, hurray, hooray, rah; **cry, shout, yell** [U.S. & Can.], tiger [coll.]; hosanna, hallelujah or halleluiah, alleluia or alleluiah or alleluja; applause 966.2.

3. smile, smiling; bright smile, gleaming smile, beam; **grin,** grinning; broad grin, toothful grin; sardonic grin, **smirk, simper.**

4. laughter, laughing, laugh, boff [theat. slang]; **titter; giggle; chuckle, chortle;** cackle, crow; **snicker, snigger,**

snort; haw-haw, hee-hee, tee-hee; **guffaw, horselaugh; hearty laugh, belly laugh** [slang], Homeric laughter, cachinnation; **shout, shriek,** shout of laughter; burst or outburst of laughter, peal or roar of laughter, gales of laughter; fit of laughter, convulsion, "laughter holding both his sides" [Milton].

5. mirth 868.5.

VERBS **6. rejoice, jubilate, exult, glory, joy, delight,** bless or thank one's stars, congratulate oneself, hug oneself, rub one's hands, clap hands, throw up one's cap; dance or skip for joy, dance, skip, frisk, rollick, revel; sing, carol, chirp, chirrup, lilt.

7. cheer, give a cheer, **cry, shout, yell,** cry for joy, yell oneself hoarse; huzza, hurrah, hurray, hooray; applaud 966.10.

8. smile, crack a smile [slang], break into a smile; **beam,** smile brightly; **grin,** grin like a Cheshire cat [coll.]; **smirk, simper.**

9. laugh, burst out laughing, burst into laughter, burst out, laugh outright; **titter; giggle; chuckle, chortle;** cackle, crow; **snicker,** snigger, snort; haw-haw, hee-hee, tee-hee; **guffaw,** horselaugh; **shout, shriek,** give a shout or shriek of laughter; **roar,** cachinnate, roar with laughter; shake with laughter, shake like jelly; be convulsed with laughter, go into convulsions; burst or split with laughter, split [coll.], **split one's sides,** laugh fit to burst or bust [slang], **be in stitches** [coll.], hold one's sides; laugh oneself sick, ~ silly or limp, die or nearly die laughing; laugh in one's sleeve, laugh in one's beard.

ADJS. **10. rejoicing,** delighting, exulting; **jubilant, exultant, elated,** elate, flushed.

ADVS. **11. rejoicingly,** delightingly, exultingly; **jubilantly, exultantly, elatedly.**

INTERJS. **12. hurrah!, hurray!,** hooray!, rah!, r-r-rah!, ray!, huzza!, hip, hip, hurrah!, *hoch!* [Ger.], cheerio!, three cheers!, one cheer more!, whoops!, whoopee!, hoopee!, yippee!, wow!, wowee!, hail!, all hail!, aha!, tra-la-la!; glory be!, praise be!, praise the Lord!, Heaven be praised!; **hallelujah!** 1030.16.

875. CELEBRATION

NOUNS **1. celebration,** celebrating; **observance, solemnization; commemoration,** memorialization, remembrance, memory; jubilee; **festivity** 876.3; revel 876.6; rejoicing 874; ovation, triumph [Rom. antiq.]; *feu de joie* [F., bonfire of celebration]; salute, salvo; flourish of trumpets, fanfare, fanfaronade.

2. serenade; charivari, shivaree [dial., U.S.].

VERBS 3. celebrate, observe, keep, honor; commemorate, memorialize; solemnize, signalize, hallow, mark with a red letter hold jubilee, jubilize, jubilate, maffick [coll., Eng.]; make merry 876.26; kill the fatted calf; sound a fanfare, blow the trumpet, beat the drum, fire a salute.

4. serenade; shivaree [dial., U.S.].

ADJS. 5. celebrative, celebrating; commemorative, commemorating, memorial; solemn.

ADVS. 6. in honor of, in commemoration of, in memory or remembrance of, to the memory of.

876. AMUSEMENT

Pleasurable Diversion.—NOUNS 1. amusement, entertainment, pleasure, enjoyment, diversion, divertisement, divertissement [F.], recreation, relaxation, regalement; pastime, passe-temps [F.]; mirth 868.5.

2. fun, play, sport, game; good time, pleasant time, big time [coll.], high time or high old time [coll.], picnic [slang], great fun, time of one's life; a short life and a merry one.

3. festivity, merrymaking, merriment, gaiety or gayety, jollity, jollification [coll.], joviality, conviviality, whoopee [slang, U.S.]; skylarking, racketing, holiday-making; revelry, revelment, reveling, revels.

4. festival, festivity, festive occasion, fiesta [Sp.], fete or fête, gala, gala affair, blowout [slang], jamboree [slang], high jinks [coll.], do [coll.], great doings [coll.]; Holi, Dewali [both Hind.]; Bariram, Muharram [both Moham.]; fête champêtre F., rural festival]; feast, banquet, junket [U.S.]; picnic, squantum [local, U.S.]; clambake, bake [U.S.], fish fry, barbecue U.S.]; wayzgoose; beanfeast [Eng.], kettledrum [coll.]; fair, feria [Sp.], carnival; kermis or kermess; Mardi gras; Saturnalia; field day, gala day, feria.

5. frolic, play, romp, rollick, frisk, gambol, caper, dido [coll., U.S.], rig, fredaine [F.].

6. revel, lark [coll.], escapade, échappée [F.], high-go; celebration 875; spree, bout, fling, randy [Scot. & dial., Eng.], randan [dial. & slang]; rantan or ran-tan, bust, tear, beano [all slang]; bender, hellbender, shindy, toot, bat, bum [all slang,

U.S.]; carouse, carousal; orgy, debauch; drinking bout 994.5.

7. round of pleasure, whirl, merry-go-round, the rounds, the dizzy rounds.

8. sports; athletics, agonistics; gymnastics, palaestra; acrobatics; track, track and field; soccer, association football; Rugby, Rugger [coll.].

9. game, sport, play; contest 794.3; event, meet; bout, match, go [coll.]; singles, doubles; twosome, threesome, foursome; double-header [U.S.]; decathlon; play-off, run-off.

10. tournament, tourney, Turnerfest [Ger.], gymkhana, field day [U.S.]; regatta; carrousel; track meet; Olympic games, the Olympics; Olympiad.

11. (place of amusement) cabaret, tavern, roadhouse; café dansant, café chantant; night club, night spot [coll., U.S.]; juke joint [slang, U.S.]; casino; amusement park.

12. playroom, rumpus room [coll., U.S.]; gymnasium, gym [coll.]; pool room or hall, billiard room; bowling alley.

13. playground; field, athletic field, playing field; football field, gridiron [U.S.]; baseball field, diamond [U.S.]; infield, outfield; archery ground, cricket ground, croquet ground or lawn, bowling green, polo ground; links, golf links, golf course; fairway, putting green; court, badminton court, basketball court, tennis court, racket court, squash court; racecourse, track, course, turf, oval; stretch; rink, glaciarium, ice rink, skating rink.

14. pleasance, pleasure garden or ground, park, paradise, common, commons.

15. (amusement devices) merry-go-round, carrousel, roundabout, whirligig, flying horses; Ferris wheel; seesaw, teeter-totter; swing; roller coaster; chutes, chute-the-chutes [coll.].

16. plaything, sport, toy, bauble, knickknack or nicknack, gimcrack, gewgaw, kickshaw, whimwham, trinket; doll, paper doll, rag doll, puppet, marionette; dollhouse, doll carriage; toy soldiers; hobbyhorse, cockhorse, rocking horse; top, teetotum; pinwheel; jack-in-the-box; jack, jackstone; jackstraw; blocks; checkerboard, chessboard; marble, mig; balls 254.13; football, pigskin [coll., U.S.]; racket, battledore; bat, baseball bat, cricket bat; cue.

17. playing cards, cards; picture cards, face cards, court cards; ace, king, queen,

joker; jack, knave; bower, right *or* left bower, best bower; diamonds, hearts, clubs, spades; hand; dummy; royal flush, flush, full house, straight, three of a kind, pair; singleton; trump, ruff; trick; rubber; round; pack, deck.

18. **chessman,** man, piece; bishop, knight, king, queen, pawn; rook, castle.

19. **player, frolicker,** frisker, gamboler; **pleasure seeker,** pleasurer, pleasurist, **playboy** [slang, U.S.]; **reveler, merry-maker,** skylarker, **carouser,** cutup [slang]; contestant 789.2.

20. **sportsman,** sport, gamester; sports-woman, gamestress; ballplayer, baseballer, cricketer; batter, catcher, baseman, in-fielder, outfielder, shortstop, outfield, bat-tery; footballer, lineman, halfback, quarter-back, fullback, tackle; center; guard; golfer; poloist; pugilist, wrestler 798.2, 3; racer 268.6; jumper 317.4; skater; archer, bowman, tox-ophilite.

21. **athlete, gymnast,** palaestrian; pan-cratiast; **acrobat,** tumbler, contortion-ist; funambulist, ropewalker, ropedancer.

22. **master of ceremonies, M.C.,** mar-shal; **toastmaster;** master of the revels, revel master; Lord of Misrule, Abbot of Unreason [Scot.].

VERBS 23. **amuse, entertain, divert,** regale, beguile, recreate, enliven, exhilarate, put in good humor; **delight, tickle, titil-late,** tickle the fancy; raise a smile *or* laugh, convulse, set the table in a roar, be the death of one; wow, slay, knock dead [all slang].

24. **amuse oneself,** take one's pleasure, give oneself over to pleasure, be on pleasure bent; **have fun, have a good time,** live it up [slang]; drown care, drive dull care away; beguile the time, kill time, while away the time.

25. **play, sport, disport;** frolic, rollick, **gambol, frisk, romp, caper,** cut capers [coll.], antic, curvet, cavort [U.S.], flounce, trip, skip, dance; **cut up** [slang], cut a dido [coll., U.S.], horse around [slang], carry on [coll.].

26. **make merry, revel, roister,** jolly, lark [coll.], skylark, **make whoopee** [slang, U.S.], go it [coll.], let oneself go, **blow** *or* **let off steam;** cut loose, let loose, let go, whoop it up, kick up one's heels, hell around, raise hell, blow off the lid [all slang]; step out [coll., U.S.], go places and do things, see life, **paint the town red** [slang]; go the dizzy rounds, go on the

merry-go-round [slang]; **celebrate** 875.3; spree, **go on a spree,** go on a bust, ~ toot *or* bender [slang]; **carouse,** wanton, de-bauch, run a rig, **sow one's wild oats, have one's fling.**

27. "eat, drink, and be merry" [Bible], feast, banquet, junket.

ADJS. 28. **amused, diverted, entertained; delighted, tickled, titillated;** "pleased with a rattle, tickled with a straw" [Pope].

29. **amusing, entertaining, diverting,** beguiling; recreative, recreational; **delight-ful,** titillative, titillating; humorous 878.5; killing, slaying [both slang].

30. **festive, festal; merry, gay, jolly, jovial, joyous, joyful,** gladsome, convivial, gala, hilarious; merrymaking, on the loose [coll.].

31. **playful, sportive, sportful; frolic-some,** gamesome, rompish, larkish, caper-some; waggish 736.6.

32. **sporting,** sports; **athletic,** agonistic; **gymnastic,** palaestral; **acrobatic.**

ADVS. 33. **for fun,** for the fun of it; for the ducks of it, for kicks, for laughs, for the heck *or* hell of it, for the devil of it [all slang]; just to be doing.

34. sports and games

acey-deucy	football
archery	fox and geese
association foot-	French and
ball	English
backgammon	games of chance
badminton	514.7
bagatelle	gobang
ball	golf
balloon ball	halma
bandy	hammer throwing
baseball	handball
basketball	hide-and-seek
battledore and	hockey
shuttlecock	hopscotch
billiards	horseshoes
blindman's buff	hurdling
boccie [It.]	ice hockey
boloball	ice skating
bowling, bowls	jacks, jackstones
boxing 794.9	jackstraws
captain ball	*jai alai* [Sp.]
cat	lacrosse
catch	lawn tennis
checkers, chequers	leapfrog
chess	mah-jongg
Chinese checkers	marbles
crambo	merels
cricket	mumble-the-peg,
croquet	mumblety-peg
curling	ninepins
deck tennis	pall-mall
discus	pallone
dominoes	parcheesi
draughts	Ping-pong
fencing	polo
fives	pool

pushball
putting the weight
　or shot
pyramids
quintain
quoits
racing 794.11–13
rackets
roller skating
rounders
Rugby
sharpshooting
shinny
shogi
shooting
shot-put
shuffleboard,
　shovelboard
skating
skittles
sledding

snooker
soccer
softball
squash
table tennis
tennis
tenpins
tent pegging
tetherball
tiddlywinks
tilting
tipcat
tivoli
tobogganing
trap bat and ball
trapshooting
tug of war
volleyball
water polo
wrestling 794.10

35. card games

all fours
auction bridge
baccarat
banker
beggar-my-neighbor
bezique
blackjack
blind poker
bluff
boston
brag
bridge
canasta
cassino
commerce
commit
connections
contract bridge,
　contract
cribbage
draw poker
Earl of Coventry
écarté [F.]
euchre
faro
five hundred
flinch
fright
frog
gin
gin rummy
goat
gobang
hearts
keno
lansquenet

loo
lottery
lotto
matrimony
monte
napoleon
old maid
omber, ombre
pairs
patience
penny ante
picquet
pinochle
Pit
poker
Polish bank
put
quadrille
quinze
reverse
rouge et noir [F.]
rum
rummy
Russian bank
seven-up
skat
snipsnapsnorum
solitaire
speculation
squeezers
straight poker
stud poker
thirty-one
twenty-one
vingt-et-un [F.]
whist

877. DANCING

NOUNS 1. dancing, terpsichore, the
dance, the light fantastic; choreography,
choregraphy [esp. Eng.]; ballet; hoofing
[coll.], tap-dancing, soft-shoe dancing; jit-
ter-bugging [coll.].

2. dance, hop [coll.], fandango [coll.],
cantico [local, U.S.]; shindig, shindy [both

slang, U.S.]; ball, bal [F.]; masked ball,
masque, mask, masquerade ball, masquerade, bal masqué [F.], bal costumé [F.];
cornwallis [U.S. hist.]; promenade, prom
[coll., U.S.]; country dance, square dance,
barn dance; stag dance; ballet, concert
dance; nautch [India].

3. dancer, danseur [F.], terpsichore,
terpsichorean [coll.]; jitterbug [coll.], hepcat [slang]; hoofer [coll.], step dancer, tap
dancer, clog dancer, heel-and-toe dancer;
figure dancer, figurant, figurante; skirt
dancer; ballet dancer, ballet girl, ballerina,
danseuse, coryphée; première danseuse
[F.]; chorus girl, chorus boy or man;
geisha, geisha girl [both Japan]; nautch
girl, bayadere [both India]; hula girl; taxi
dancer; wallflower [coll.].

4. ballroom, dance hall; dance palace;
casino.

VERBS 5. dance, trip the light fantastic,
trip, skip, hop, foot, prance [coll.]; jitterbug [coll.], jive [slang], cut a rug [slang];
hoof [coll.], clog, tap-dance; truck, shuffle;
waltz, valse; one-step, two-step, fox-trot,
turkey-trot, tango, polka, rumba or rhumba,
samba, Charleston, jig, shimmy.

ADJS. 6. dancing, terpsichorean; choreographic, choregraphic [esp. Eng.].

7. dances

allemande [F.]
apache dance [F.]
barn dance
beguine
bolero
bourrée [F.]
boutade
branle
breakdown
bubble dance
cakewalk
can-can
cantico, kanticoy
cha-cha-cha
Charleston
chonchina [Jap.]
clog
conga
cotillion
country dance
courante [F.]
danse du ventre
　[F.]
fan dance
fandango
fling
folk dance
fox trot
furlana [It.]
galliard
gallopade
galop
gavotte, gavot

German
gopak, hopak
　[Russ.]
habañera
Highland fling
hootchy-kootchy
hornpipe
hula, hula-hula
interpretative
　dance
jig
jota
juba [U.S.]
lancers
lindy
longways dance
malagueña [Sp.]
mambo
marengue
mazurka
minuet
morris dance
one-step
pachanga
passamezzo [It.]
pas seul [F.]
polka
polonaise
Portland fancy
quadrille
reel
rigadoon
round dance

rumba, rhumba
saltarello
samba
saraband
schottische
Scotch reel
shimmy
Sir Roger de
  Coverley
skirt dance
snake dance
square dance
strathspey

sword dance
tango
tap dance
tarantella,
  tarantelle [F.]
trepak [Russ.]
turkey trot
twist, the
two-step
Virginia reel
waltz, valse
ziganka

8. dance steps

arabesque
buck and wing
chassé
coupé
double shuffle
gambado, *gambade*
[F.]

grapevine
heel-and-toe
pas [F.]
pigeonwing
quickstep
shuffle

878. HUMOROUSNESS

Humorous Quality.—NOUNS 1. humorousness, funniness, amusingness, laughableness; wittiness 879; drollness, drollery; whimsicalness, quizzicalness; ludicrousness, ridiculousness, absurdity, absurdness; richness, pricelessness [slang].

2. comicalness, comicality; farcicalness, farcicality; farce, mere farce.

3. the humorous, the comic; the ridiculous, the ludicrous; the funny side.

4. bathos, anticlimax, comedown.

ADJS. 5. humorous, funny, amusing; witty 879.15; droll, whimsical, quizzical; laughable, risible, good for a laugh; ludicrous, ridiculous, absurd; rich, priceless [slang], killing [coll.], slaying [slang], screaming, too funny or killing for words [coll.], too funny for anything or any use [coll.].

6. comic(al), farcical; burlesque 965.14; tragicomic(al), seriocomic(al), mockheroic.

ADVS. 7. humorously, amusingly, funnily, laughably; wittily 879.18; drolly, whimsically, quizzically; comically, farcically; ludicrously, ridiculously, absurdly.

879. WIT AND HUMOR

NOUNS 1. wit, humor, pleasantry, *esprit* [F.], salt; Attic wit, Attic salt, Atticism; ready wit, quick wit, nimble wit; comedy 609.6.

2. wittiness, humorousness, funniness; facetiousness; jocularity, jocoseness, jocosity; smartness, cleverness, brilliance; pungency, saltiness; keenness, sharpness; keen-wittedness, quick-wittedness, nimble-wittedness.

3. drollery, drollness; whimsicality, whimsicalness.

4. waggishness, waggery; roguishness 736.2; playfulness, sportiveness; prankishness, pranksomeness; trickery, trickiness, trickishness, *espièglerie* [F.].

5. buffoonery, buffoonism, clownery, harlequinade; clownishness, buffoonishness; foolery, fooling, tomfoolery; horseplay; shenanigans, monkeyshines [both slang, U.S.].

6. joke, jest, gag [slang], wheeze, jape; fun, sport, play; story, yarn, funny story, good story; dirty story, *double-entendre* [F.]; shaggy-dog or hairy-dog story; capital joke, good one; point, cream of the jest; jestbook.

7. witticism, pleasantry, *plaisanterie* [F.]; play of wit, *jeu d'esprit* [F.]; crack [slang, U.S.], wisecrack [slang]; quip, quirk, quiz, crank, conceit, bright or happy thought, bright or brilliant idea; mot, bon mot, smart saying; flash of wit, scintillation; sally, flight of wit; repartee, retort, riposte or ripost, snappy comeback [slang]; facetiae, quips and cranks; persiflage 880.1.

8. wordplay, play upon words, *jeu de mots* [F.], missaying, corruption, paronomasia, *calembour* [F.], abuse of terms; pun, punning; equivoque, equivoke, equivocality; *double-entendre*, double entente, *mot à double entente* [all F.]; anagram, logogram, logograph, metagram; acrostic, double acrostic; amphiboly, amphibologism; palindrome.

9. old joke, old wheeze, trite joke, hoary-headed joke, joke with whiskers [joc.]; chestnut, corn, corny joke, oldie [all slang]; Joe Miller, Joe Millerism; twice-told tale, retold story, warmed-over cabbage [coll.], *réchauffé* [F.].

10. prank, trick, practical joke, waggish trick, quiz, *boutade* [F.], antic, caper, frolic; monkeyshine, shine, shenanigan [all slang, U.S.].

11. sense of humor, risibility, risibilities, risibles.

12. humorist, wit, funnyman, spark, *bel-esprit* [F.], "agreeable rattle" [Goldsmith], life of the party; joker, jester, quipster, wisecracker [slang]; wag, wagwit; zany, madcap, cutup [slang, U.S.]; prankster; comedian, clown 609.38, 39; punster, punner; epigrammatist; burlesquer, caricaturist, parodist; reparteeist; witling; Joe Miller; gagman.

VERBS 13. joke, jest, wisecrack [slang],

quip, jape, fun [coll.], make fun, Joe-Mil-
lerize; crack a joke, cut jokes, get off a
joke, tell a good story; pun; scintillate,
sparkle.

14. perpetrate a joke, play tricks or
pranks, play a practical joke, trick, play
a joke or trick on, make merry with; pull
one's leg.

ADJS. 15. witty, humorous, funny; jocular, joky [coll.], joking, jesting, jocose;
facetious; whimsical, droll; smart, clever,
brilliant, scintillating, sparkling, sprightly;
keen, sharp, pungent; salty, salt, Attic;
keen-witted, quick-witted, nimble-witted.

16. clownish, buffoonish.

17. waggish; roguish 736.6; playful,
sportive; prankish, pranky, pranksome;
tricky, trickish, tricksy.

ADVS. 18. wittily, humorously; jocularly, jocosely; facetiously; whimsically,
drolly.

19. in fun, in sport, in play, in jest,
in joke, as a joke, jokingly, jestingly, with
tongue in cheek.

880. BANTER

NOUNS 1. banter, badinage, persiflage, pleasantry, raillery, sport, good-
natured banter; ridicule 965; chaff, twit,
quiz; jest, joke, jape, josh [slang, U.S.];
jolly, rag, jive [all slang]; exchange, give-
and-take.

2. bantering, twitting, chaffing, joking, jesting, japing, teasing, hazing
[U.S.], quizzing, joshing [slang, U.S.];
jollying, guying, deviling [all coll.];
kidding, ribbing, ragging, razzing, roasting [all slang].

3. banterer, persifleur [F.], chaffer,
twitter, jollyer [coll.], kidder [slang],
guyer [coll.], ribber [slang], josher [slang,
U.S.], ragger [slang].

VERBS 4. banter, twit, chaff, rally, joke,
jest, jape, tease, haze [U.S.], quiz, josh
[slang, U.S.]; jolly, guy, devil, ride [all
coll.]; kid, rib, rag, razz, roast, jive [all
slang]; poke fun at, make fun of, make
merry with; ridicule 965.8.

ADJS. 5. bantering, chaffing, twitting,
jollying [coll.], kidding [slang], joshing
[slang, U.S.], teasing, quizzical.

881. DULLNESS

Lack of Wit or Interest.—NOUNS 1. dullness, dryness, uninterestingness; stuffiness, stodginess; barrenness, baldness,
aridity, jejunity; insipidness, insipidity,
vapidness, vapidity, flatness, tastelessness;
characterlessness, colorlessness, pointless-
ness; deadness, lifelessness, spiritlessness;
slowness, pokiness, unliveliness; tediousness 882.2; dreariness, drearisomeness;
heaviness, ponderousness.

2. prosaicness, prosiness; prosaism,
prosaicism, prose; matter-of-factness, unimaginativeness; matter of fact.

3. triteness, corniness [slang], banality, banalness, hackneyedness, commonplaceness, commonness, familiarness, plat-
itudinousness; staleness, mustiness, fustiness; cliché 516.3.

VERBS 4. fall flat, fall flat as a pancake;
leave one cold; wear thin.

5. prose, platitudinize, sing a familiar
tune.

ADJS. 6. dull, dry, dry-as-dust; stuffy,
stodgy; arid, barren, blank, bald, jejune;
insipid, vapid, flat, tasteless; characterless,
colorless, pointless; dead, lifeless, spiritless, cold; slow, poky or pokey, pedestrian,
plodding, unlively; tedious 882.8; dreary,
drearisome; heavy, ponderous, elephantine; dull as dish water, "weary, stale, flat
and unprofitable" [Shakespeare].

7. uninteresting, unexciting; unenter-
taining, unenjoyable, unamusing, unfunny,
unwitty.

8. prosaic, prose, prosy, prosing; matter-of-fact, unimaginative, unimpassioned.

9. trite, corny [slang], banal, platitudinous, stereotyped, stock, set, commonplace, common, familiar, bromidic [slang],
old hat [coll.], back-number, bewhiskered,
warmed-over, cut and dried; hackneyed,
hackney; well-known 474.27; stale, musty,
fusty; worn, timeworn, well-worn, moth-
eaten, threadbare, worn thin.

ADVS. 10. dully, dryly, uninterestingly;
stuffily, stodgily; lifelessly, spiritlessly;
slowly, ploddingly; tediously 882.12; drearily,
drearisomely; heavily, ponderously.

11. tritely, cornily [slang], banally,
commonplacely, commonly, familiarly,
hackneyedly, stalely.

882. TEDIUM

NOUNS 1. tedium, monotony, humdrum, irk; sameness, sameliness, samesomeness [dial.], wearisome sameness, the
same old thing; undeviation, unvariation,
invariability; time on one's hands, time
hanging heavily on one's hands.

2. tediousness, monotonousness; hum-

drumness, humdrumminess; **dullness** 881; wearisomeness, wearifulness; **tiresomeness, irksomeness,** drearisomeness; **boresomeness,** boringness; prolixity, longwindedness.

3. **weariness, tiredness,** wearifulness; **boredom,** boredness; **ennui;** life-weariness, world-weariness.

4. **bore,** crashing bore [slang], frightful bore; **pest, nuisance; headache, pain in the neck** [both slang]; dryasdust, humdrum; proser, twaddler; **drip,** droop, **pill, flat tire** [all slang]; **wet blanket;** buttonholer.

VERBS 5. **weary, tire, irk,** wear, wear on or upon, **make one tired,** weary or tire to death; jade, give one a bellyful [slang].

6. **bore,** leave one cold, set or send to sleep; **bore stiff** [slang], bore to tears, bore to death or extinction, bore to distraction, bore out of one's life, bore out of all patience; buttonhole.

7. **harp upon, dwell on** or **upon,** harp upon one or the same string, sing the same old song or tune, mount or ride a hobby [coll.].

ADJS. 8. **tedious, monotonous, humdrum,** singsong, dingdong [coll.], jogtrot, harping, everlasting, too much with us [coll.]; **dreary,** drearisome; **dull** 881.6; prolix, long-winded.

9. **wearying,** wearing, **tiring; wearisome,** wearful; **tiresome, irksome,** mortal [coll.]; **boring, boresome,** yawny [coll.].

10. **weary,** wearful; **tired,** wearied, irked; good and tired, tired to death, weary unto death; sick, **sick of, tired of, sick and tired of;** jaded; fed up, with a bellyful [both slang]; blasé, life-weary, world-weary, tired of living.

11. **bored, uninterested;** bored stiff [slang], bored to death or extinction, bored to tears.

ADVS. 12. **tediously, monotonously,** harpingly, everlastingly; **boringly,** boresomely; **wearisomely, tiresomely, irksomely,** drearisomely; dully 881.10.

INTERJS. 13. ho, hum!, heigh ho!, what a life!

883. AGGRAVATION

NOUNS 1. **aggravation, worsening; intensification, heightening,** deepening, increase, enhancement, amplification, enlargement, magnification; **exasperation,** exacerbation; **annoyance, irritation** 864.2, 3.

VERBS 2. **aggravate, worsen,** make worse; **intensify, heighten,** deepen, increase, en-

hance, amplify, enlarge, magnify, build up; **exasperate,** exacerbate; **annoy, irritate** 864.71, 18.

3. **worsen,** get or grow worse; **go from bad to worse, jump out of the frying pan into the fire,** avoid Scylla and fall into Charybdis, sow the wind and reap the whirlwind.

ADJS. 4. **aggravated, worse, worsened; intensified, heightened,** increased, enhanced, amplified, magnified, enlarged; **exasperated,** exacerbated; **irritated, annoyed** 864.24.

5. **aggravating,** aggravative; **exasperating,** exasperative; **annoying, irritating** 862.13.

ADVS. 6. **aggravatingly, exasperatingly; annoyingly** 862.19.

7. **worse and worse, from bad to worse,** out of the frying pan into the fire.

884. RELIEF

NOUNS 1. **relief, easement,** easing, ease; **reduction, diminishment, lessening; alleviation, mitigation, palliation,** softening, assuagement, allayment, appeasement, mollification, subduement; soothing, salving; dulling, deadening.

2. **release, deliverance, freeing,** removal; reprieve; catharsis, emotional release.

3. **lightening, disburdening,** disencumbrance, disembarrassment; a load off one's mind.

4. **sense** or **feeling of relief,** sigh of relief.

VERBS 5. **relieve, give relief; ease, ease matters; reduce, diminish, lessen; alleviate, mitigate, palliate,** soften, assuage, allay, lay, appease, mollify, subdue, soothe; salve, pour balm into, pour oil on; poultice, foment, stupe; slake, slacken; **dull, deaden,** dull or deaden the pain; temper the wind to the shorn lamb, lay the flattering unction to one's soul.

6. **release, free, deliver,** reprieve, remove, free from.

7. **lighten, disburden,** disencumber, disembarrass; **set one's mind at ease** or **rest,** set at ease, take the load off one's mind, smooth the ruffled brow of care.

8. **be relieved, feel relief,** feel better about it; **breathe easy** or **easier,** breathe more freely, breathe again; **heave a sigh of relief,** draw a long or deep breath.

ADJS. 9. **relieving, easing, alleviative,** alleviating, **mitigative,** mitigating, **palliative,** lenitive, assuasive, softening, subduing, soothing, demulcent, emollient, balmy, balsamic; dulling, deadening.

885. COMFORT

NOUNS 1. **comfort, ease, well-being;** clover, velvet [slang], bed of roses; life of ease 726.1; solid comfort.

2. comfortableness, easiness; restfulness, peace, peacefulness; coziness, snugness; friendliness, warmness; **homelikeness,** homeyness [coll.], homeliness; commodiousness, roominess, convenience; luxuriousness.

3. creature comforts, comforts, conveniences, good things of life, cakes and ale, all the comforts of home, all the heart can desire.

4. consolation, solace, solacement, **en-couragement, assurance, reassurance, comfort,** crumb of comfort, "kind words and comfortable" [Cowper]; relief 884.

5. **comforter,** consoler, solacer, encourager.

VERBS 6. **comfort, console, solace,** give comfort, bear up; ease, **put or set at ease;** relieve 884.5; **assure, reassure; encourage, hearten,** pat on the back; **cheer** 868.6; wipe away the tears, "rejoice with them that do rejoice, and weep with them that weep" [Bible].

7. take comfort, **take heart,** pull oneself together.

8. be at ease, stand easy [Eng.]; **make oneself comfortable,** make oneself at home, feel at home; live a life of ease 726.10.

9. (make snug or comfortable) **snug,** snug down or up; tuck in.

10. **snuggle, nestle, cuddle,** snug [chiefly dial.], cuddle up, curl up; snuggle up to, snug up or together [chiefly dial.].

ADJS. 11. **comfortable,** comfy [slang]; **easy,** easeful; **restful,** peaceful, **relaxing;** soft, cushioned; cozy or cosy, **snug,** snug as a bug in a rug; friendly, warm; **homelike,** homey [coll.], homely, lived-in; commodious, roomy, convenient; luxurious.

12. at ease, at one's ease, easy, relaxed, at rest; at home, in one's element.

13. comforting, consoling, consolatory, of good comfort; assuring, reassuring; en-couraging, **heartening; cheering** 868.16; re-lieving 384.9.

ADVS. 14. **comfortably,** easily, with ease; restfully, peacefully; cozily, snugly; commodiously, roomily, conveniently; luxuriously, voluptuously.

15. **in comfort,** in ease, **in clover, on velvet** [slang], on a bed of roses.

886. HOPE

NOUNS 1. **hope, hopefulness, hopes,** fond or fervent hope; **desire** 632; **expecta-tion** 537; sanguine expectation, happy or cheerful expectation; **trust, confidence,** faith, reliance, affiance, conviction, assur-ance, security, well-grounded hope; assump-tion, presumption; **promise,** good or bright prospect; great expectations, high hopes.

2. "desire and expectation rolled into one" [Ambrose Bierce], "the parent of faith" [C. A. Bartol], "the second soul of the unhappy" [Goethe], "the dream of those that wake" [Prior], "the thing with feathers that perches in the soul" [Emily Dickinson].

3. **optimism,** optimisticalness, Pollyan-naism [U.S.], cheerful ~, bright or rosy outlook; **cheerfulness** 868; bright side, sil-ver lining; "the noble temptation to see too much in everything" [G. K. Chesterton], "a mania for declaring when things are going badly that all is well" [Voltaire], "a kind of heart stimulant — the digitalis of failure" [Elbert Hubbard].

4. **ray of hope,** gleam or glimmer of hope, star of hope.

5. **airy hopes,** dream, golden dream, pipe dream [coll.], bubble, chimera, fool's paradise.

6. **optimist,** hoper, Pollyanna [U.S.], ray of sunshine [slang]; "a proponent of the doctrine that black is white" [Ambrose Bierce], "one who makes the best of it when he gets the worst of it" [anon.], "one who makes the most of all that comes and the least of all that goes" [Sara Teasdale], "one who doesn't care what happens as long as it happens to somebody else" [anon.].

VERBS 7. **hope,** be or live in hopes, en-tertain or harbor the hope, cling to the hope, cherish ~, foster or nurture the hope; **expect** 537.4; **trust,** confide, presume, feel confident, rest assured; pin one's hope upon, put one's trust in, hope in, rely on, lean upon; hope for, desire 632.14–16; **hope against hope,** hope to God [coll.].

8. be hopeful, **get one's hopes up,** keep one's spirits up, take heart, be of good cheer; **hope for the best,** knock on wood, keep one's fingers crossed; catch at a straw.

9. be optimistic, **look on the bright side, look through rose-colored glasses,**

voir en couleur de rose [F., see in rose color]; think the best of, **make the best of it,** say that all is for the best, put a good or bold face upon, put the best face upon; count one's chickens before they are hatched, count one's bridges before they are crossed.

10. **give hope,** hold out hope, inspire hope, **raise one's hopes,** raise expectations, **lead one to expect; cheer** 868.6; **assure, reassure; promise,** bid fair, make fair promise.

ADJS. 11. **hopeful,** hoping, **in hopes,** full of hope, in good heart; **expectant** 537.9; **sanguine,** fond; **confident,** assured; undespairing.

12. **optimistic(al),** bright, sunny; **cheerful** 868.10; **rosy,** roseate, rose-colored, *couleur de rose* [F.].

13. **promising,** of promise, full of promise, **favorable,** looking up; **propitious** 542.16; **encouraging,** cheering, reassuring.

ADVS. 14. **hopefully,** hopingly; **expectantly** 537.13; **optimistically;** sanguinely, fondly; confidently.

887. HOPELESSNESS

NOUNS 1. **hopelessness,** no hope; **inexpectation** 538; **futility** 667.2; **impossibility** 509.

2. **despair, desperation,** desperateness; **despondency** 870.3; **disconsolateness** 870.12; forlornness; cave of despair, cave of Trophonius.

3. **irreclaimability, irretrievability,** irredeemability, irrecoverableness; incorrigibility, irreformability; irrevocability, irreversibility; **irreparability, incurability,** irremediableness, curelessness, remedilessness, immedicableness.

4. **forlorn hope,** vain expectation; *verlornen hoop* [Du.], *verlorner Posten* [Ger.], *enfants perdus* [F.].

5. dashed hopes, blighted hope, hope deferred; **disappointment** 539.

6. **pessimism, cynicism,** malism; **uncheerfulness** 870.2; **gloominess,** dismalness, **gloomy outlook;** defeatism; retreatism; "fancying clouds where no clouds be" [Thomas Hood]; "the name that men of weak nerve give to wisdom" [Bernard De Voto].

7. **pessimist, cynic,** malist, **calamity howler** [coll.], **worrywart** [slang], seek-sorrow, Job's comforter; defeatist; retreatist; "one who is not happy except when he is miserable" [anon.], "a man who feels bad when he feels good for fear he'll feel worse when he feels better" [George Burns], "one who is always building dungeons in the air" [Galsworthy], "a man who thinks everybody as nasty as himself, and hates them for it" [George Bernard Shaw], "one who has been intimately acquainted with an optimist" [Elbert Hubbard].

8. **hopeless case; goner,** gone goose or gosling, gone coon, dead duck [all slang].

VERBS 9. **be pessimistic, look on the dark side,** think or make the worst of, put the worst face upon.

10. **despair,** despair of, **despond,** falter, lose hope, **lose heart, abandon hope,** give up hope, **give up,** give up all hope or expectation, give way, yield to despair, turn one's face to the wall.

11. **shatter one's hopes,** dash ∼, crush or blight one's hope, dash the cup from one's lips, drive to despair or desperation.

ADJS. 12. **hopeless,** without hope; **desperate, despairing, in despair,** *au desespoir* [F.]; **despondent** 870.22; **disconsolate** 870.29; **forlorn.**

13. **futile, vain** 667.13.

14. **impossible,** out of the question, not to be thought of, no go [coll.].

15. **past hope, beyond recall,** past praying for; **irretrievable, irrecoverable, irreclaimable,** irredeemable; **incorrigible,** irreformable; **irrevocable, irreversible; irremediable, irreparable, incurable,** cureless, remediless, immedicable, beyond remedy; **ruined,** undone; lost, gone.

16. **pessimistic,** pessimist, **cynical;** uncheerful 870.21; **gloomy,** dismal; defeatist.

ADVS. 17. **hopelessly, desperately,** forlornly; impossibly.

18. **irreclaimably, irretrievably, irrecoverably,** irredeemably; **irrevocably,** irreversibly; **irremediably, incurably, irreparably.**

888. ANXIETY

Troubled Thought.—NOUNS 1. **anxiety,** anxiousness, anxietude, angst; **solicitude, apprehension,** apprehensiveness, diffidence, misgiving, foreboding, suspense; **fear** 889; **concern,** concernment, anxious concern; **care,** cankerworm of care; **distress,** trouble, vexation; **uneasiness, perturbation, disturbance, agitation, disquiet,** disquietude, inquietude; **pucker, all-overs** [both coll.]; overanxiety; anxious seat or bench.

2. **worry,** worriment [coll.], worriedness; worrying, fretting; harassment, torment.

VERBS 3. **concern, trouble, bother, disturb, disquiet, agitate.**

4. (make anxious) **worry, vex, fret, harass, harry, torment,** plague, beset.

5. (feel anxious) **worry,** worry oneself, worry one's head about, worry oneself sick; **fret, fuss, chafe,** stew [coll.], take on [coll.], fret and fume; bite one's nails.

ADJS. 6. **anxious, concerned, apprehensive, solicitous,** diffident, misgiving; **fearful** 889.22, 23; **troubled, bothered; uneasy, perturbed, disturbed, disquieted, agitated; on pins and needles,** on tenterhooks, on the anxious seat or bench; anxioused up [dial.], all hot and bothered [slang]; alloverish, in a pucker, in a stew [all coll.]; overanxious, overapprehensive.

7. **worried, vexed, fretted; harassed,** harried, tormented, plagued; worried sick, worried stiff [slang].

8. **careworn,** heavy-laden.

9. **worrisome, worrying;** fretting, chafing; **harassing, tormenting, plaguing; annoying** 862.13.

ADVS. 10. **anxiously, concernedly, apprehensively,** solicitously, diffidently, misgivingly, **uneasily;** worriedly.

889. FEAR

NOUNS 1. **fear, fright; scare,** boof [local, U.S.]; **alarm,** feeze [coll., U.S.], **consternation, dismay; dread, awe; terror, horror,** abject fear; **phobia;** funk, blue funk [both coll.]; **panic,** panic fear or terror; **stampede,** chute [West. U.S.]; **cowardice** 890.

2. **fearfulness,** afraidness; **timidity, timorousness, shyness;** skittishness, startlishness, jumpiness.

3. **apprehension,** apprehensiveness, **diffidence, misgiving, qualm,** qualmishness, all-overs [coll.]; **anxiety** 888; **doubt** 502.2; **foreboding** 542.

4. **trepidation,** trepidity, **perturbation, fear and trembling; agitation** 855.3, 4; **uneasiness, disquiet,** disquietude, inquietude; **nervousness** 857; **stage fright,** mike fright [radio slang]; palpitation, heartquake; shivers or cold shivers [coll.], creeps or cold creeps [coll.], jimjams [slang]; sweat, cold sweat.

5. **intimidation, bullying, browbeating; cowing, bulldozing** [coll., U.S.], **buffaloing** [slang, U.S.]; demoralization.

6. **terrorization, scaremongering;** terrorism, reign of terror.

7. **alarmist, terrorist, scaremonger;** sheep in wolf's clothing.

8. **frightener, scarer;** scarebabe, scaresinner; scarecrow, scare-bird; **horror, terror,** holy terror; **bugbear** 1014.10; **ogre,** ogress; bête noire, fee-faw-fum; incubus, nightmare; Gorgon, Hurlothrumbo.

VERBS 9. **fear, be afraid; apprehend, have qualms,** eye askance; **dread, stand in dread** or awe of, stand aghast; be on pins and needles, sit upon thorns; have one's heart in one's mouth.

10. **take fright, take alarm;** funk, go into a funk [both coll.]; **lose courage** 890.8; **pale,** grow or turn pale, change or turn color; **freeze.**

11. **start, startle, jump,** jump out of one's skin; **shy,** fight shy, start aside, booger [dial.], **boggle.**

12. **flinch, shrink, quail, cringe, wince, blench, blink.**

13. **tremble, shake, quake, shiver, quiver, quaver;** tremble in one's boots or shoes, tremble like an aspen leaf, shake all over.

14. **frighten, fright, affright,** funk [coll.]; **scare,** skeer [dial.], scarify [dial.]; give a scare, give a turn; **alarm, disquiet,** raise apprehensions; **shake, stagger; startle** 538.8; **unnerve, unman, demoralize;** make one's hair stand on end, make one's blood run cold, freeze or curdle the blood, make one's teeth chatter, make one tremble, take one's breath away.

15. **put in fear,** put the fear of God into, **throw a scare into** [slang], scare the life out of, scare the pants off of, scare hell out of [slang]; **panic, stampede.**

16. **terrify, awe,** strike terror into; **horrify, appall, shock,** make one's flesh creep; **frighten out of one's wits** or **senses,** frighten from one's propriety, **scare stiff** [slang], scare spitless [coll.], scare to death; **strike dumb,** strike all of a heap [coll.]; **stun, stupefy, paralyze, petrify, freeze.**

17. **daunt, deter, shake, stop; discourage, dishearten;** faze [coll. or dial.], feeze or feaze [dial., Eng.; coll., U.S.]; **awe, overawe.**

18. **dismay, disconcert, appall, astound, confound, abash, discomfit, put out, take aback** [coll.].

19. **intimidate, cow, browbeat, bulldoze** [coll., U.S.], **buffalo** [slang, U.S.], **bludgeon, dragoon; bully, hector, harass,** huff; **bluster,** bluster out of or into; **terrorize,** put in bodily fear; **threaten** 971.2.

20. **frighten off, scare away,** bluff off, put to flight.

ADJS. 21. **afraid, scared; feared,** afeared,

ascared, askeered, skeered, skeert, scairt [all dial.]; fear-stricken, fear-struck; haunted with fear.

22. fearful, fearing, fearsome, **in fear; cowardly** 890.10; **timorous, timid, shy, shrinking;** scary, eerie or eery; **skittish,** skittery [dial.], startlish, jumpy; **tremulous,** trembling, shaky, shivery; nervous 857.11.

23. apprehensive, diffident, misgiving, qualmish, qualmy, all-overish [coll.]; anxious 888.6.

24. frightened, in a fright, in a funk or blue funk [coll.]; **alarmed,** disquieted; **startled** 538.13; more frightened than hurt.

25. terrified, terror-stricken, terror-struck, terror-smitten, terror-shaken, terror-troubled, terror-riven, terror-ridden, terror-driven, terror-crazed, terror-haunted; **awed,** awe-stricken, awe-struck; **horrified,** horror-stricken, horror-struck; **appalled, astounded,** dismayed, aghast; frightened out of one's wits, **scared to death,** scared spitless [coll.]; unmanned, undone; **stunned, petrified, stupefied, paralyzed,** frozen, **scared stiff** [slang]; white as a sheet, pale as death or a ghost.

26. panicky, panicked, in a panic, panic-stricken, panic-struck.

27. frightening, frightful, frightsome [Scot.]; **fearful,** fearsome, fear-inspiring; **scary** [coll.], skeery [dial.], scaring, scareful [dial.], scaresome [dial.]; **alarming, startling,** disquieting, dismaying, disconcerting.

28. terrifying, terrorful, terrorsome, terrorific, terror-striking, terror-inspiring, terror-bringing, terror-giving, terror-breeding, terror-breathing, terror-bearing, terror-fraught; **bloodcurdling, hair-raising** [coll.]; petrifying, stunning, stupefying.

29. terrible, terrific, tremendous; horrid, horrible, horrifying, horrific, horrendous; **dreadful,** dread, dreaded; **awful,** awesome, awe-inspiring; **shocking, appalling,** astounding; dire, direful, fell; formidable, redoubtable; ghastly, morbid; Gorgonian, Gorgonlike.

30. creepy, eerie or eery, **weird,** uncanny.

ADVS. **31. fearfully, apprehensively, diffidently,** for fear of; **timorously, timidly,** shyly; **tremulously, tremblingly, with fear and trembling;** with heart in mouth, with bated breath.

32. in fear, in terror, in awe, in alarm, in consternation; in mortal fear, in fear of one's life.

33. frightfully, fearfully; alarmingly, startlingly, disquietingly, dismayingly, disconcertingly; **shockingly, appallingly,** astoundingly; **terribly, terrifically, tremendously; dreadfully, awfully; horridly, horribly,** horrifyingly, horrifically, horrendously.

34. phobias

acrophobia	heresyphobia
aelurophobia	herpetophobia
aerophobia	hydrophobia
agoraphobia	hypnophobia
airphobia	hypsophobia
algophobia	lyssophobia
androphobia	monophobia
Anglophobia	necrophobia
anthropophobia	negrophobia
astraphobia	neophobia
bacteriophobia	nosophobia
batophobia	nyctophobia
batrachophobia	ochlophobia
bibliophobia	pantophobia
brontephobia	pharmacophobia
brontophobia	phobophobia
cardiophobia	phonophobia
cibophobia	photophobia
claustrophobia	psychophobia
cremnophobia	pyrophobia
cynophobia	Russophobia
demonophobia	scotophobia
dermatophobia	sitiophobia,
doraphobia	sitophobia
dromophobia	stasiphobia
dysmorphophobia	syphilophobia
ergophobia	teleophobia
felinophobia	thalassophobia
feminophobia	thanatophobia
Francophobia	theophobia
Gallophobia	topophobia
gamophobia	toxicophobia
Germanophobia	xenophobia
hagiophobia	zoophobia
hemophobia	

890. COWARDICE

NOUNS **1. cowardice, cowardliness; fear** 889; **faintheartedness,** faintheart, weakheartedness, **chickenheartedness,** henheartedness, pigeonheartedness; **yellowness** [coll.], white-liveredness, weak-kneedness; weakness, softness; unmanliness, unmanfulness; milksoppiness, milksoppishness, milksopism.

2. uncourageousness, unvaliantness, unvalorousness, unheroicness, ungallantness, unintrepidness; **plucklessness, spunklessness** [coll.], **gritlessness,** spiritlessness, heartlessness.

3. dastardliness, pusillanimousness, pusillanimity, poltroonishness, **poltroonery,** poltroonism, baseness, cravenness.

4. cold feet [slang, U.S.], weak knees,

faint heart, chicken heart, **yellow streak** [slang], white feather.

5. coward, jellyfish, invertebrate, **weakling,** weak sister [coll.], milksop, softy [slang, U.S.], baby, **big baby, chicken** [slang, white liver [coll.], white feather; fraid-cat, **fraidy-cat,** scaredy-cat [all slang]; funk, funker, flunker [all coll.]; "one who in a perilous emergency thinks with his legs" [Ambrose Bierce].

6. poltroon, **dastard,** craven, recreant, caitiff, arrant coward; **sneak,** slink [dial. & coll.], Jerry sneak.

VERBS **7. dare not,** dassn't [dial.]; **have a yellow streak** [slang], **have cold feet** [slang, U.S.], be unable to say "bo" to a goose.

8. lose one's nerve, lose courage, **get cold feet** [slang, U.S.], **show the white feather:** falter, boggle; **funk** [coll.], **flunk** [coll., U.S.]; **back out, funk out** coll.], **flunk** out [coll., U.S.], **chicken out** [slang].

9. cower, quail, cringe, crouch, skulk, sneak, slink.

ADJS. **10. cowardly,** cowardy [dial.], **coward; afraid, fearful** 889.21, 22; **overtimorous,** overtimid; **fainthearted,** weakhearted, **chickenhearted,** henhearted, pigeonhearted; **white-livered,** lily-livered, milk-livered; **yellow, with a yellow streak** [both coll.]; **weak-kneed, chicken** [slang], afraid of one's shadow; weak, soft; unmanly, unmanful; milksoppy, milksoppish; **funking, funky** [both coll.].

11. uncourageous, unvaliant, unvalorous, **unheroic,** ungallant, **unintrepid, undaring,** unable to say "bo" to a goose; unwarlike, unsoldierlike; **pluckless, spunkless** [coll.], **gritless,** spiritless, heartless.

12. dastardly, dastard; **poltroonish,** poltroon **pusillanimous,** base, craven, recreant, caitiff; dunghill, dunghilly.

13. cowering, quailing, cringing; skulking, sneaking, **slinking,** sneaky, slinky.

ADVS. **14. uncourageously, unvaliantly,** unvalorously, **unheroically,** ungallantly, unintrepidly, undaringly; plucklessly, spunklessly [coll.], gritlessly, spiritlessly, heartlessly; faintheartedly, weakheartedly, chickenheartedly, weak-kneedly.

891. COURAGE

NOUNS **1. courage, courageousness; bravery,** braveness, **boldness, valor,** valorousness. **valiancy, gallantry,** gallantness, **intrepidity,** intrepidness, **prowess,** virtue;

doughtiness, stalwartness, stoutness, stoutheartedness, lionheartedness, greatheartedness; **heroism,** heroicalness; chivalry, chivalrousness, knightliness; manliness, manfulness, manhood; Dutch courage [coll.].

2. "fear that has said its prayers" [Dorothy Bernard], "fear holding on a minute longer" [Gen. Patton], "taking hard knocks like a man when occasion calls" [Plautus], "doing without witness everything that one is capable of doing before all the world" [La Rochefoucauld].

3. fearlessness, dauntlessness, unfearfulness, unafraidness, **unapprehensiveness; confidence** 512.5; untimidness, untimorousness, unshyness, unbashfulness.

4. fortitude, hardihood, hardiness; **pluckiness, spunkiness** [coll.], grittiness [coll.], nerviness [coll.], mettlesomeness; **gameness,** gaminess; **resolution,** resoluteness, bulldog courage.

5. nerve, spunk [coll.], **pluck, grit,** clear grit, sand [slang], **stamina, backbone** [coll.], pith, **mettle,** bottom, game, **guts** [slang], **intestinal fortitude** [joc.]; heart, spirit; stout heart, heart of oak.

6. daring, derring-do; bravado, bravura; **audacity,** audaciousness, overboldness; **adventurousness,** venturousness, **venturesomeness,** adventuresomeness, **enterprise;** foolhardiness 892.3.

7. exploit, feat, deed, enterprise, achievement, adventure, bold stroke, heroic act or deed.

8. (brave person) **brave, stalwart, gallant, valiant,** man of courage or mettle, a man; **hero,** demigod, paladin; **heroine,** demigoddess; the brave.

9. encouragement, heartening, inspiration, emboldening, **assurance,** reassurance, pat or clap on the back.

VERBS **10. dare, venture, make bold to,** make so bold as to, **have the nerve,** have the courage of one's convictions, "dare do all that may become a man" [Shakespeare], "be strong, and quit yourselves like men" [Bible]; **defy** 791.3.

11. brave, face, confront, affront, front, meet, meet boldly; **set at defiance** 791.4; **face up to, stand up to,** look full in the face, put a bold face upon, show or present a bold front, **meet head on,** face up, face the music [coll.]; **brazen,** brazen out or through; **beard,** "beard the lion in his den" [Scott]; put one's head in the lion's mouth, take the bull by the horns, march up to the cannon's mouth, bell the cat, go through fire and water, run the gantlet, take one's life in one's hands.

12. **outbrave, outdare; outface,** face down, face out; **outbrazen,** brazen out; **outlook, outstare,** stare down, stare out of countenance.

13. **nerve oneself, steel oneself, get up nerve,** muster ~, summon up or gather courage, pluck up heart, screw up one's nerve or courage, "screw your courage to the sticking place" [Shakespeare].

14. **take courage, take heart,** take heart of grace; **brace up, buck up,** spunk up [all coll.].

15. keep up one's courage, bear up, **keep one's chin up** [coll.], **keep a stiff upper lip** [slang], hold up one's head.

16. **encourage, hearten, embolden, nerve,** pat or clap on the back, **assure, reassure; inspire,** inspirit; buck up, brace up, spunk up [all coll.]; put upon one's mettle, make a man of; cheer 868.6.

ADJS. 17. **courageous, brave, bold, valiant, valorous, gallant, intrepid,** doughty, hardy, stalwart, stout, stouthearted, ironhearted, lionhearted, greathearted, boldspirited, bold as a lion; **heroic,** herolike; **chivalrous,** chivalric, knightly; manly, manful.

18. **plucky, spunky** [coll.], **gritty** [coll.], **nervy** [coll.], **resolute, game,** gamy; **spirited,** spiritful, **mettlesome.**

19. **unafraid, unfearing, unfearful;** unapprehensive, undiffident; **confident** 512.21; **fearless, dauntless,** awless or aweless, dreadless; **unfrightened,** unscared, unalarmed, unterrified; **untimid,** untimorous, unshy, unbashful.

20. **undaunted, undismayed,** unappalled, unabashed, unawed; **unflinching, unshrinking,** unquailing, uncringing, unwincing, unblenching, unblinking.

21. **daring, audacious,** overbold; **adventurous, venturous, venturesome,** adventuresome, enterprising; foolhardy 892.9.

ADVS. 22. **courageously, bravely, boldly, heroically, valiantly,** valorously, **gallantly, intrepidly,** doughtily, stoutly, hardily, stalwartly; **pluckily, spunkily** [coll.], **resolutely, gamely; fearlessly,** unfearingly, unfearfully; **daringly,** audaciously; chivalrously, knightly, yeomanly.

892. RASHNESS

NOUNS 1. **rashness, brashness, incautiousness, imprudence, indiscretion,**

injudiciousness, improvidence; **unwariness,** unchariness; overcarelessness; overconfidence, oversureness; temerity.

2. **recklessness,** devil-may-careness; **carelessness** 532.2; **impetuousness,** impetuosity, hotheadedness; **hastiness, hurriedness; furiousness,** desperateness, wantonness, wildness; **precipitateness,** precipitousness, precipitance, precipitancy, precipitation.

3. **foolhardiness,** harebrainedness; **audacity,** audaciousness; **presumption,** presumptuousness; **daring,** daredeviltry, daredevilry, fire-eating; adventurousness 891.6.

4. **daredevil,** devil, **madcap, madbrain,** hotspur, hellcat, rantipole, harum-scarum [coll.], fire-eater [coll.]; **adventurer,** adventuress.

VERBS 5. (be rash) carry too much sail, sail too near the wind, go out of one's depth, go to sea in a sieve, take a leap in the dark, buy a pig in a poke, count one's chickens before they are hatched, reckon without one's host, catch at straws, lean on a broken reed, put all one's eggs in one basket, live in a glass house.

6. **court danger,** mock or defy danger, tempt Providence, play a desperate game, ride for a fall; play with fire, march up to the cannon's mouth, put one's head in a lion's mouth, beard the lion in his den, sit on a barrel of gunpowder, sleep on a volcano.

ADJS. 7. **rash, brash, incautious, imprudent, indiscreet,** injudicious, improvident; **unwary, unchary;** overcareless; overconfident, oversure, overweening; temeritous.

8. **reckless,** devil-may-care; **careless** 532.11; **impetuous,** hotheaded; **hasty,** hurried; **furious,** desperate, mad, wild, wanton, harum-scarum [coll.]; **precipitate, precipitous, precipitant; headlong, breakneck;** slapdash, slapbang; accident-prone.

9. **foolhardy, harebrained,** madcap, madbrain, madbrained; **audacious, presumptuous; daring,** daredevil, fire-eating, death-defying; adventurous 891.21.

ADVS. 10. **rashly, brashly, incautiously, imprudently, indiscreetly,** injudiciously, improvidently; **unwarily,** uncharily.

11. **recklessly,** happen what may; **carelessly** 532.18; **impetuously,** hotheadedly; **hastily,** hurriedly; **furiously,** desperately, wildly, wantonly, **madly,** like mad [coll.], like crazy [slang]; **precipitately,** precipitously, precipitantly; **headlong,** headfirst, headforemost, **head over heels,** heels over head, à corps perdu [F.]; slapdash, slapbang

[coll.], slam-bang [coll.]; helter-skelter, ramble-scramble [coll.], hurry-scurry, holus-bolus.

12. **foolhardily, daringly, audaciously,** presumptuously, harebrainedly.

893. CAUTION

Provident Care.—NOUNS 1. **caution,** cautiousness; **care, heed, solicitude;** carefulness, heedfulness, mindfulness, regardfulness; **gingerliness,** guardedness; **prudence, circumspection, discretion,** canniness [Scot.], judiciousness; calculation, deliberation; safeness, safety first; Fabianism, Fabian policy.

2. **wariness, chariness, caginess** [slang], leeriness [slang]; **suspicion,** suspiciousness; **distrust,** distrustfulness.

3. **precaution,** precautiousness; **forethought, foresight,** forethoughtfulness; **providence,** provision, forearming; precautions, steps, measures, steps and measures; **safeguard,** preventive measure.

4. **overcautiousness,** overcaution, **overcarefulness,** overwariness.

VERBS 5. **be cautious, be careful;** think twice, give it a second thought; make haste slowly, take it easy [coll.]; put the right foot forward, pick one's steps, feel one's ground or way, pussyfoot, tiptoe, go on tiptoe.

6. **take precautions, take steps** or **measures,** take steps and measures; **prepare** or **provide for** or **against,** forearm; **guard against, make sure against,** make sure, "make assurance double sure" [Shakespeare], **play safe** [coll.], keep on the safe side; **look before one leaps;** see how the land lies or the wind blows, see how the cat jumps [coll.]; clear the decks, batten down the hatches, take in a reef, have an anchor to windward.

7. **beware, take care, have a care,** take heed, take heed at one's peril; keep at a respectful distance, keep out of harm's way; mind, mind one's business, mind one's eye [coll.]; **be on one's guard,** be on the watch or lookout; **look out, watch out** [coll., U.S.], mind out [dial.]; **look sharp,** look slick or slippy [coll.], look lively or alive [coll.], keep one's eyes open, keep a weather eye open [coll.], keep one's eye peeled [slang], **watch one's step** [slang], look about one; stop, look and listen.

ADJS. 8. **cautious, careful,** heedful, mindful, regardful; **prudent, circumspect,** canny [Scot.], **discreet, politic, judicious,** noncommittal; unadventurous, unenterprising, undaring; **gingerly; guarded,** on guard, on one's guard; Fabian; safe, on the safe side.

9. **wary, chary, cagey** [slang], **leery** [slang], **suspicious,** suspecting, **distrustful,** shy of.

10. **precautious,** precautionary, precautional; **forethoughtful,** forethoughted, **foresighted,** foreseeing, forehanded [U.S.]; **provident,** provisional.

11. **overcautious,** overcareful, overwary.

ADVS. 12. **cautiously, carefully,** heedfully, mindfully regardfully; **prudently, circumspectly,** cannily [Scot.], **discreetly,** judiciously; **gingerly,** guardedly, easy [coll.]; with caution, with care.

13. **warily, charily,** cagily [slang], leerily [slang], suspiciously, distrustfully.

INTERJS. 14. **beware!,** caution!, careful!, be careful!, **take care!,** have a care!, **look out!, watch out!** [coll., U.S.], mind out! [dial.], mind your eye! [coll.], **watch your step!,** look sharp!, look slick or slippy! [coll.], look lively or alive! [coll.], easy!, take it easy! [coll.], go easy! [coll.], go slow!, danger!, below there!, **jiggers!** [slang].

894. FASTIDIOUSNESS

NOUNS 1. **fastidiousness, particularity,** particularness; **scrupulousness,** scrupulosity; punctiliousness, punctilio; preciseness, precision; **meticulousness, conscientiousness,** criticalness; discrimination, discriminatingness, discriminativeness; selectiveness, pickiness [slang], choosiness [U.S.]; perfectionism, precisianism.

2. **finicalness,** finickiness, finickingness, finicality; **fussiness,** persniketiness [coll.]; **squeamishness,** queasiness.

3. **nicety, niceness, delicacy,** delicateness, daintiness, fineness, refinement.

4. **overfastidiousness, overparticularity, overscrupulousness, overconscientiousness,** overmeticulousness, **overnicety;** overcriticalness, hypercriticism, hairsplitting.

5. **exclusiveness,** selectness, selectiveness; **cliquishness,** clannishness; **snobbishness,** snobbery, snobbism.

6. **perfectionist, precisian,** precisianist, stickler.

7. **fuss-budget** [coll.], fuss, fusser, **fuddyduddy** [slang], granny, old woman, old maid.

VERBS 8. **be hard to please,** fuss, pick and choose; **turn up one's nose at,** disdain, scorn, spurn.

ADJS. 9. **fastidious, particular, scrupu-**

lous, meticulous, conscientious, exacting, precise, punctilious; **discriminating**, discriminative; **selective**, picky [slang], choosy [U.S.], choicy [coll., U.S.]; **critical**, "nothing if not critical" [Shakespeare]; perfectionist(ic).

10. **finical, finicky,** finicking, finikin; **fussy,** fuss-budgety [coll.]; **squeamish,** queasy, persnickety [coll.], difficult, hard to please.

11. **nice, dainty, delicate,** *délicat* [F.], fine, refined, exquisite.

12. overfastidious, **overparticular,** overscrupulous, **overconscientious,** overmeticulous, **overnice,** overprecise, oversqueamish; **overcritical,** hypercritical, ultracritical, hairsplitting.

13. **exclusive,** selective, **select,** elect; **cliquish,** clannish; **snobbish,** snobby.

ADVS. 14. **fastidiously, particularly, scrupulously, meticulously, conscientiously,** critically, punctiliously; discriminatingly, discriminatively, selectively; **finically,** finickily, finickingly; **fussily; squeamishly,** queasily.

895. TASTE

Good Taste.—NOUNS 1. **taste, tastefulness; elegance,** grace, gracefulness; **refinement,** finesse, **polish, culture, cultivation,** refined or cultivated taste; niceness, nicety, **delicacy,** daintiness; **discrimination** 491; acquired taste, "caviare to the general" [Shakespeare].

2. "love of beauty" [Emerson], "good sense delicately put in force" [Chévier], "the microscope of the judgment" [Rousseau], "a fine judgment in discerning art" [Horace], "the literary conscience of the soul" [Joubert].

3. **decorousness,** gentility, decency, properness, propriety, **seemliness,** becomingness.

4. **restraint,** unobtrusiveness, quietness, subduedness, quiet taste; simplicity 900.

5. (aesthetic or artistic taste) **virtuosity,** virtu; **connoisseurship,** dilettantism, fine art of living; epicurism, epicureanism; gastronomy, *friandise* [F.]; aesthetics.

6. **aesthete,** esthete, man of taste, lover of beauty.

7. **connoisseur,** *connaisseur* [F.], *cognoscente* [It.]; **judge,** good judge, **critic, expert,** authority; **epicure,** epicurean; **gourmet, gourmand, bon** *vivant* [F.]; **virtuoso;** dilettante, amateur.

ADJS. 8. **tasteful,** tasty [coll.], **in good** taste; **aesthetic,** artistic; **pure, chaste;** classic(al), Attic; **simple,** unaffected 900.6, 7; **quiet, restrained,** subdued, unobtrusive.

9. **elegant,** graceful; **refined, polished, cultivated, cultured;** nice, fine, delicate, dainty.

10. **decorous,** genteel, decent, proper, **seemly, becoming.**

ADVS. 11. **tastefully, with taste;** aesthetically, artistically; elegantly, gracefully; decorously, genteelly, decently, properly, seemly, becomingly; quietly, unobtrusively; simply 900.10.

896. VULGARITY

NOUNS 1. **vulgarity,** vulgarness, vulgarism; **inelegance** or inelegancy, **indelicacy, impropriety, indecency, indecorum,** indecorousness, unseemliness, ungentility; **untastefulness,** tastelessness; bad or poor taste, *mauvais goût* [F.].

2. **coarseness, grossness,** *grossièreté* [F.], **rudeness, crudeness,** crudity, **crassness,** rawness, roughness, earthiness; ribaldness, ribaldry; **obscenity** 988.

3. **unrefinement, uncouthness, uncultivation,** uncultivatedness, unculturedness; uncivilizedness, wildness; **barbarism,** barbarousness, barbarity, Gothicism; **savagery,** savagism; **brutality,** brutishness, bestiality.

4. **boorishness, churlishness,** carlishness, loutishness, lubberliness, lumpishness, cloddishness, clownishness; **ruffianism,** rowdyism; parvenuism.

5. **commonness, commonplaceness,** ordinariness, homeliness; **lowness, baseness, meanness; ignobility,** plebeianism.

6. **vulgarian,** low or vulgar **fellow,** mucker [slang, U.S.], guttersnipe [coll.], *épicier* [F.]; **bounder** [coll.], **cad; boor,** churl, clown, lout, looby; rough, **ruffian,** roughneck [slang], **rowdy;** vulgarist, ribald, smuthound [slang], Jack Nasty, human spittoon.

7. **barbarian, savage,** Goth.

8. **vulgarization,** coarsening; popularization.

VERBS 9. **vulgarize,** coarsen; popularize.

ADJS. 10. **vulgar, inelegant, indelicate, indecorous, indecent, improper, unseemly,** unbeseeming; **ungenteel,** undignified; **untasteful,** tasteless, in bad or poor taste; **offensive,** offensive to ears polite.

11. **coarse, gross, rude, crude, crass,** raw, rough, earthy; ribald; **obscene** 988.5-9.

12. **unrefined, unpolished, uncouth,** unkempt, uncombed, unlicked; **unculti-**

vated, uncultured; **uncivilized**, noncivilized, uncivil; wild, untamed; **barbarous,** barbaric, barbarian; outlandish, Gothic or gothic; primitive; **savage, brutal,** brutish, bestial; wild-and-wooly, rough-and-ready.

13. **boorish, churlish,** carlish, **loutish,** lubberly, lumpish, cloddish, clownish, boobyish, bohunkish [slang, U.S.]; yokelish 181.7; rowdy, **rowdyish, ruffianly,** roughneck [slang], raffish, raised in a barn.

14. **common, commonplace, ordinary;** plebeian 917.11; homely, homespun; **general, public, popular;** vernacular.

15. **low, base, mean, ignoble,** vile, scurvy, sorry, scrubby, beggarly; low-minded, base-minded.

ADVS. 16. **vulgarly, uncouthly, inelegantly,** indelicately, indecorously, indecently improperly, unseemly, untastefully, offensively; **coarsely, grossly, rudely, crudely,** crassly, roughly; ribaldly.

897. UGLINESS

NOUNS 1. **ugliness, uncomeliness, unsightliness, unattractiveness,** unhandsomeness, unbeautifulness, unprettiness, unloveliness, unprepossessingness, inelegance; **homeliness,** plainness; unshapeliness, shapelessness; ungracefulness, gracelessness; ungainliness 732.3.

2. **hideousness,** horridness, horribleness, frightfulness, dreadfulness, terribleness, awfulness [coll.]; **repulsiveness,** repugnantness, offensiveness, forbiddingness, loathsomeness; ghastliness, gruesomeness, grisliness.

3. forbidding countenance, vinegar aspect, wry face, face that would stop a clock.

4. **eyesore, sight** [coll.], **fright,** mess, object, figure; ugly duckling; baboon; monster; witch, bag, harridan.

VERBS 5. **look bad;** look something terrible, look like hell, look like the deuce or devil, look a sight or fright, look a mess, look like something the cat brought in [all coll.].

ADJS. 6. **ugly, uncomely, unsightly, unattractive, unhandsome, unpretty, unlovely, inelegant; unbeautiful,** unbeauteous, beautiless; **homely, plain;** not much to look at, not much for looks, short on looks [coll.], hard on the eyes [slang], pretty for the shape she's in [joc.]; ugly as sin, ugly as the wrath of God, homely as a mud fence, homely enough to sour milk, homely enough to stop a clock, not fit to be seen.

7. **unprepossessing, ill-favored,** hard-favored, evil-favored; ill-looking, evil-looking; hard-featured, hard-visaged; grim, grim-faced, grim-visaged.

8. **unshapely,** shapeless, **ill-shaped,** ill-made, ill-proportioned; misshapen, misproportioned; grotesque, monstrous.

9. **ungraceful,** graceless; **ungainly** 732.20.

10. **inartistic,** unartistic, **unaesthetic;** unornamental, undecorative.

11. **hideous, horrid, horrible, frightful,** dreadful, terrible, awful [coll.]; **repulsive,** repelling, **repugnant,** offensive, forbidding, loathsome, revolting; **ghastly,** gruesome, grisly.

ADVS. 12. uglily, homelily, uncomelily, **unattractively, unhandsomely, unbeautifully, unprettily.**

13. **hideously, horridly, horribly, frightfully,** dreadfully, terribly, awfully [coll.]; **repulsively, repugnantly,** offensively, forbiddingly, loathsomely, revoltingly; gruesomely, ghastly.

898. BEAUTY

NOUNS 1. **beauty, beautifulness, beauteousness, prettiness, handsomeness, attractiveness, loveliness, pulchritude, charm,** grace, elegance, exquisiteness; bloom, glow; the beautiful; beauty unadorned.

2. "the soul shining through its crystalline covering" [Jane Porter], "eternity gazing at itself in a mirror" [Kahlil Gibran], "the sensible image of the Infinite" [Bancroft], "God's handwriting" [Emerson], "a perfume without a name" [A. D. Ficke], "a form of genius" [Oscar Wilde].

3. **comeliness, fairness,** sightliness, personableness, becomingness, pleasingness, goodliness, agreeability.

4. **good looks,** good appearance, good effect; **shapeliness,** good figure, good shape, belle tournure [F.].

5. **daintiness, delicacy,** delicateness; cuteness [coll., U.S.], cunningness [coll.].

6. **gorgeousness,** ravishingness; **gloriousness,** heavenliness, sublimity; **splendor,** splendidness, splendorousness, splendrousness; **brilliance,** brightness, radiance, luster.

7. **thing of beauty,** vision, picture [coll.], poem, eyeful [coll., U.S.], **sight or treat for sore eyes** [slang].

8. **a beauty, charmer,** charmeuse [F.]; **beaut,** dream, looker, good looker, **stunner, dazzler,** fetcher, peach, knockout, **raving beauty** [all slang]; belle, reigning beauty; beau ideal, paragon, phoenix; "the

face that launch'd a thousand ships" [Marlowe].

9. (famous beauties) Venus [Rom. myth.], Venus of Milo; Aphrodite, Hebe [both Gr. myth.]; Adonis, Apollo, Apollo Belvedere, Hyperion, Antinoüs, Narcissus [all Gr. & Rom. myth.]; Astarte [Phoenician myth.]; Balder, Freya [both Norse myth.]; Helen of Troy, Cleopatra; the Graces, houri, peri.

10. beautification, prettification, **adornment;** decoration 899; beauty treatment, *traitement de beauté* [F.]; facial [coll.]; manicure; hairdressing.

11. make-up, cosmetics; war paint, drugstore complexion [both joc.]; powder, talcum, talcum powder; rouge, paint, lip rouge; nail polish; grease paint, clown white; mascara, eye shadow; cold cream, hand cream *or* lotion, vanishing cream, foundation cream; foundation, base; mudpack; lipstick, *crayon pour les lèvres* [F.]; eyebrow pencil; puff, powder puff; compact, vanity case.

12. beautician, beautifier; hairdresser, *coiffeur* [F.], *coiffeuse* [fem.; F.]; barber; manicurist, *manucure* [F.].

13. beauty parlor *or* salon, *salon de beauté* [F.]; barbershop [U.S.].

VERBS **14. beautify, prettify,** pretty up [dial.], grace, **adorn;** decorate 899.7; set off, set off to advantage *or* good advantage, become one; glamorize.

15. look good; look like a million, look fit to kill, knock dead, knock one's eyes out [all slang]; take the breath away, beggar all description; shine, beam, bloom.

ADJS. **16. beautiful, beauteous,** endowed with beauty; **pretty, handsome, attractive,** pulchritudinous, **lovely,** graceful, elegant, fine, exquisite, flowerlike; aesthetic; eye-filling, easy on the eyes, good for sore eyes, not hard to look at, long on looks, looking fit to kill, pretty as a speckled pup [all slang]; pretty as a picture, "lovely as the day" [Longfellow], "fair as is the rose in May" [Chaucer]; tall, dark and handsome.

17. comely, fair, good-looking, well-favored, personable, presentable, agreeable, becoming, pleasing, goodly, bonny, likely [chiefly dial.], **sightly,** braw [Scot.]; pleasing to the eye, lovely to behold; shapely 247.6.

18. dainty, delicate, minion; **cute** [coll., U.S.], cunning [coll.], cute as a bug's ear *or* as a bug in a rug, just too cute for words.

19. gorgeous, ravishing; raving, devastating, **stunning,** killing [all slang]; glorious, heavenly, divine, sublime; resplendent, splendorous, splendrous, splendid, resplendently beautiful; **brilliant,** bright, radiant, shining, beaming, glowing, blooming, sparkling, **dazzling.**

20. beautifying, cosmetic; decorative 899.9.

ADVS. **21. beautifully,** beauteously, **prettily, handsomely, attractively, becomingly,** comelily; elegantly, exquisitely.

22. daintily, delicately; cutely [coll., U.S.], cunningly [coll.].

23. gorgeously, ravishingly; ravingly, devastatingly, stunningly [all slang]; **gloriously,** divinely, sublimely; **resplendently,** splendidly, splendorously, splendrously; **brilliantly,** brightly, radiantly, glowingly, **dazzlingly.**

899. ORNAMENTATION

NOUNS **1. ornamentation, ornament; decoration,** décor; **adornment, embellishment,** embroidery, elaboration; garnish, garnishment, garniture; trimming, trim; flourish; emblazonment, emblazonry; illumination; window dressing.

2. ornateness, elegance, fanciness, fineness, **elaborateness;** richness, luxuriousness, luxuriance; **floweriness,** floridness, floridity; flamboyance; **overelegance,** overelaborateness, overornamentation; baroqueness, baroque.

3. frippery, finery, gaudery, gaiety *or* gayety, bravery, **trumpery,** flashery [slang], trickery, chiffon, trappings, superfluity; **frills, frillery,** frilling, frilliness; foofarow [orig. dial.], fuss [coll.], froufrou; gingerbread; tinsel, clinquant, pinchbeck, paste; gilt, gilding.

4. trinket, gewgaw, knickknack, nicknack, knack, **gimcrack,** kickshaw, whimwham, **bauble,** fribble, bibelot, toy, gaud; bric-a-brac.

5. jewelry, bijouterie, ice [slang]; costume jewelry, junk jewelry [coll.], scatter pins.

6. jewel, bijou; **gem,** stone, precious stone; rhinestone; pin, brooch, stickpin, breastpin, chatelaine; ring, circle, earring, nose ring; bracelet, wristlet, wristband, armlet, anklet; chain, necklace, torque; locket; beads, chaplet, wampum; bangle; charm; fob; crown, coronet, diadem, tiara.

VERBS **7. ornament, decorate, adorn, dress, trim, garnish,** array, **deck, bedeck,**

dizen, bedizen; **beautify 898.14; embellish,
furbish,** embroider, enrich, grace, set off
or out, paint, color, blazon, emblazon, paint
in glowing colors; **dress up, spruce up**
[coll.], doll up [slang, U.S.], fix up [coll.,
U.S.], **primp up,** prink up, prank up, trick
up *or* out, deck out, fig out; primp, prink,
prank, preen; smarten, **smarten up,** dandify,
titivate *or* tittivate.

8. figure, filigree; spangle, bespangle;
bead; tinsel; jewel, bejewel, gem, diamond;
ribbon, beribbon; flounce; flower, garland,
wreathe; feather, plume; flag; illuminate;
paint 361.14; engrave 576.12.

ADJS. 9. **ornamental, decorative,** adorn-
ing, embellishing.

10. **ornamented, adorned, decorated,
embellished,** garnished, trimmed, bediz-
ened; figured; flowered; festooned,
wreathed; spangled, bespangled, spangly;
jewelled, bejewelled; beaded; plumed,
feathered; beribboned.

11. **ornate, elegant, fancy, fine, chichi;
elaborate,** labored, high-wrought; rich,
luxurious, luxuriant; flowery, florid; flamboyant; fussy, frilly; **overelegant,** overelaborate, overlabored, overworked, overwrought; baroque, arabesque.

12. ornamentations

aglet	fretwork
aigrette	fringe
appliqué	frog
arabesque	frostwork
arras	garland
batik	graffito
beading	guilloche
beaten work	hanging
bouquet	helix
boutonniere	imbrication
bow	inlay
bugle	lacework
chaplet	metalwork
corsage	motif
cul-de-lampe [F.]	niello
cuspidation	openwork
cutwork	panache
damascene,	panelwork
damask	parquetry
diaper, diapering	plume
drapery	pompom
drawn work	quilting
egret	reeding
embroidery	rosette
epaulet, epaulette	ruffle
fancywork	scroll
feather	sequin
festoon	snood
figure work	spangle
filigree	spiral
fillet	stenciling
fleuron [F.]	strapwork
foliage	striping
foliation	tapestry

tassel	vermiculation
tooling	vignette
tracery	wreath

13. architectural ornamentations

acanthus	fret
apophyge	frieze
astragal	listel
beading	molding, moulding
beak	ogee
billet	ovolo
boss	patera
cartouche	pendant
cavetto	quatrefoil
cinquefoil	reed
congé [F.]	scotia
cornice	scrollhead
cusp	splay
cyma	terminal
fascia	torus
fillet	trefoil
finial	volute
foil	

900. SIMPLICITY

Plainness; Unaffectedness.—NOUNS **1.
simplicity, simpleness, plainness,** ordinariness, **commonness, commonplaceness,**
homeliness, prosaicness, prosiness, matter-
of-factness; common *or* garden variety.

2. **naturalness,** inartificiality; **unaffectedness,** unassumingness, **unpretentiousness.**

3. **unadornment, unembellishment,**
unornamentation; bareness, baldness,
nakedness, nudity, undress, beauty unadorned.

4. **inornateness, unelaborateness,** un-
fanciness, unfussiness; austerity, severity.

VERBS 5. **simplify,** chasten, restrain.

ADJS. 6. **simple, plain, ordinary, common, commonplace, prosaic, prosy,** matter-of-fact, homely, homespun, everyday,
workday, workaday, household, garden,
common *or* garden; pure, **pure and simple.**

7. **natural,** native; **inartificial,** unartificial; **unaffected, unpretentious,** unpretending, unassuming, unfeigning.

8. **unadorned, undecorated, unornamented, unembellished,** ungarnished, unfurbished, unvarnished, untrimmed; **undressed,** undecked, unarrayed; bare, bald,
blank, naked, nude.

9. **inornate,** unornate, **unelaborate,** unfancy, unfussy; austere, severe.

ADVS. 10. **simply, plainly,** ordinarily,
commonly, commonplacely, prosaically,
matter-of-factly.

11. **naturally, unaffectedly,** unpretentiously, unassumingly.

901. AFFECTATION

NOUNS 1. affectation, affectedness; pretension, pretense, airs, put-on [dial. & slang]; show, false show, mere show; front, false front [both coll.]; sham 614.3; artificiality, unnaturalness, insincerity; prunes and prisms.

2. mannerism, *minauderie* [F.], trick of behavior, trick, quirk, habit, peculiarity, idiosyncrasy.

3. posing, pose, posturing, attitudinizing, attitudinarianism; peacockery, peacockishness.

4. foppery, foppishness, dandyism, coxcombry, puppyism, conceit.

5. (affected niceness) overniceness, overpreciseness, overrefinement, elegance, preciosity; goody-goodyism, goody-goodness [both coll.]; purism; euphuism; euphemism.

6. prudery, prudishness, priggishness, primness, smugness, stuffiness [coll.], old-maidishness, strait-lacedness, stiffneckedness, hideboundness, narrowness, puritanicalness, Quakerishness; false modesty, overmodesty, demurity, *mauvaise honte* [F.].

7. affecter, lump of affectation; mannerist; pretender, actor, play-actor [coll.], performer; purist; euphuist, euphemist.

8. poser, poseur, posturer, posturist, posture maker, attitudinarian, attitudinizer.

9. dandy, fop, coxcomb, macaroni [hist.], gallant, dude [coll.], sport [slang, U.S.], swell [coll.], exquisite, blood, fine gentleman, carpet knight, popinjay, puppy [derog.], jackanapes, jack-a-dandy, bantam cock [coll.], fribble; beau, spark, blade, ladies' man, lady-killer [slang], masher; man about town, boulevardier.

10. fine lady, *grande dame* [F.]; *precieuse* [F.]; belle, toast.

11. prude, prig, puritan, bluenose [U.S.], goody-goody [coll.], old maid; Victorian, mid-Victorian.

VERBS 12. affect, assume, put on, pretend, simulate, counterfeit, sham, fake [coll.], feign, make out like [coll.], make a show of, act, play, play-act [coll.], act or play a part, put up a front [slang]; strike (assume, as an attitude).

13. pose, posture, attitudinize, peacock, strike an attitude, pose for effect.

14. mince, mince it, prink [dial., Eng.]; simper, smirk, bridle.

ADJS. 15. affected, pretentious; man-

nered, *maniéré* [F.]; artificial, unnatural, insincere; theatrical, stagy, histrionic; overdone, overacted.

16. assumed, put-on, pretended, simulated, faked [coll.], feigned, counterfeited; spurious, sham 614.27.

17. foppish, dandified, dandy, coxcomical, conceited.

18. (affectedly nice) overnice, overprecise, precious, *précieuse* [F.], overrefined, elegant, mincing, simpering, namby-pamby; goody-goody, goody, good-good [all coll.]; euphuistic(al), euphemistic(al).

19. prudish, priggish, prim, smug, stuffy [coll.], old-maidish, overmodest, demure, strait-laced, stiff-necked, hidebound, barkbound, narrow, puritanical, Quakerish, Victorian, mid-Victorian.

ADVS. 20. affectedly, pretentiously; elegantly, mincingly; for effect, for show.

21. prudishly, priggishly, primly, smugly, stuffily [coll.], strait-lacedly, stiffneckedly, puritanically.

902. OSTENTATION

Pretentious Show.—NOUNS 1. ostentation, ostentatiousness, ostent; pretentiousness, pretension, pretense; airiness [coll.], loftiness.

2. pretensions, vain pretensions; airs, lugs [coll., U.S.], dog [coll.], side [slang], swank [coll.].

3. showiness, flashiness, jazziness [slang], jauntiness, sportiness [coll.], gaiety or gayety, glitter, glare; gaudiness, gaudery, tawdriness; gorgeousness, colorfulness; garishness, loudness [coll.], blatancy, obtrusiveness, vulgarness, crudeness.

4. display, show, exhibition, parade, *étalage* [F.]; pageantry, pageant, "insubstantial pageant" [Shakespeare]; fanfaronade, blazon, flourish, flaunt; shine, dash, splash, splurge [all coll.]; figure; exhibitionism, showing-off.

5. grandeur, grandness, grandiosity, magnificence, splendor, glory; nobility, proudness, stateliness, majesty; impressiveness, imposingness; sumptuousness, elegance, elaborateness, luxuriousness, plushness [slang]; swankness, swankiness [both coll.]; luxury, barbaric splendor.

6. pomp, circumstance, pride, state, solemnity; pomp and circumstance, "pride, pomp, and circumstance" [Shakespeare]; heraldry [poetic], "trump and solemn heraldry" [Coleridge].

7. pompousness, pomposity, pontifica-

tion, stuffiness [coll.], inflation; orotundity
599.1.

8. swagger, strut, swank [coll.], bounce;
swaggering, strutting; **swashbucklery,** swash-
buckling, swashbucklering; peacockishness,
peacockery.

9. (pompous person) **stuffed shirt**
[slang, U.S.], blimp [slang], Colonel Blimp;
bloated aristocrat.

10. swaggerer, strutter, swanker [coll.],
swashbuckler, peacock, bantam cock
[coll.].

11. **show-off** [coll.], **exhibitionist,**
flaunter; grandstander, grandstand player
[both slang, U.S.].

VERBS **12. put oneself forward,** come
forward, attract attention, make oneself
conspicuous.

13. cut a dash, make a show, **cut** or
make **a figure;** cut a shine, cut a feather,
make a splash, make a splurge [all coll.];
splurge [coll.], splash [slang].

14. give oneself airs, put on airs, put
on [slang], put on side [slang], put on lugs
[coll., U.S.], put on dog or the dog [coll.],
put up a front [slang], ritz it [slang], look
big, put on big looks, **swank** [slang], swell,
swell it, act the grand seigneur; pontificate,
play the pontiff.

15. strut, swagger, swank [slang],
prance, stalk, peacock, swashbuckle.

16. show off [coll.], **grandstand** [slang,
U.S.], play to the gallery or galleries [coll.];
exhibit or parade one's wares [slang, U.S.],
strut one's stuff [slang, U.S.], go through
one's paces, take it big [slang], come or do
the heavy [slang], act up, chuck one's
weight about [slang].

17. flaunt, parade, display, exhibit,
air, put forward, put forth, hold up, flash
[coll.], sport [coll.]; **flourish,** brandish,
wave; dangle, dangle before the eyes; emblazon, blazon forth.

ADJS. **18. ostentatious, pretentious,**
ambitious, airy [coll.], lofty, tall [coll.],
highfalutin or highfaluting [coll.], **high-**
flown, highflying, fandangle [coll.]; **high-**
toned [coll., U.S.], **fancy,** classy [slang],
flossy slang, U.S.], ritzy [slang]; **swank,**
swanky, swanking [all coll.].

19. showy, flaunting, flashy, flashing,
glittering, **jazzy** [slang], splashy [slang],
splurgy [coll.]; **gay,** jaunty, dashing; gallant, brave, braw [Scot.], daring; **sporty**
[coll.], dressy [coll.], doggy [coll., U.S.];
frilly [coll.], frothy, chichi; rory-tory, rory-
cum-tory [both dial.].

20. gaudy, tawdry; gorgeous, colorful;
garish, loud [coll.], **blatant,** glaring, flaring, screaming [coll.], obtrusive, vulgar,
crude; meretricious.

21. grandiose, grand, magnificent,
splendid, splendacious [slang], **glorious,**
superb, fine, swell [slang]; **imposing, im-**
pressive, awful, awe-inspiring; **noble,**
proud, stately, majestic, princely; **sump-**
tuous, elegant, elaborate, luxurious, extravagant, de luxe or deluxe, plush [slang],
Corinthian; palatial; Olympic, Olympian.

22. pompous, inflated, swollen, bloated,
tumid, turgid, flatulent, gassy [coll.],
stuffy [coll.], stilted; **bombastic** 599.10.

23. swaggering, strutting; swashbuck-
ling, swashbucklering; peacockish, pea-
cocky.

24. theatrical, stagy, dramatic, histrionic; spectacular.

ADVS. **25. ostentatiously, pretentiously,**
airily, loftily; with flourish of trumpet, with
beat of drum, with flying colors.

26. showily, flauntingly, flashily, glit-
teringly; gayly, jauntily, dashingly; gallantly, bravely, daringly.

27. gaudily, tawdrily; gorgeously, col-
orfully; **garishly, blatantly,** glaringly, flar-
ingly, obtrusively.

28. grandiosely, grandly, magnifi-
cently, splendidly, gloriously, superbly;
nobly, proudly, majestically; imposingly,
impressively; **sumptuously, elegantly,**
elaborately, luxuriously, extravagantly; pala-
tially.

29. pompously, stuffily [coll.], stiltedly;
bombastically 599.13.

903. PRIDE

NOUNS **1. pride, proudness, pridefulness;**
self-esteem, self-respect, self-consequence,
face; vanity, conceit **907;** arrogance **910;**
boastfulness **908.**

2. dignity, dignifiedness, **stateliness,**
portliness, courtliness, grandeur, loftiness;
nobility, lordliness, princeliness; **majesty,**
kingliness, queenliness; augustness, venerability; **sedateness, solemnity, gravity,** sobriety.

3. proudling [derog.], proud-belly [slang];
highflier or highflyer, beggar on horseback;
egoist **907.5;** boaster **908.5;** the proud.

VERBS **4. be proud,** hold up one's head,
hold one's head high, **hold one's nose in**
the air, bridle; look one in the face or eye.

5. pride oneself, preen oneself, plume
oneself on, pique oneself, **congratulate**

oneself, hug oneself; **be proud of, take
pride in,** glory in, exult in.

6. **make proud,** do proud [coll.], **gratify, elate,** flush, turn one's head.

7. **save face,** save one's face, preserve
one's dignity.

ADJS. 8. **proud, prideful,** proudful
[dial.]; **self-esteeming, self-respecting;**
proudhearted, proud-minded, proud-
spirited, proud-blooded; proud-looking; as
proud as Punch, proud as Lucifer, proud as
a peacock; purse-proud.

9. **vain,** conceited 907.8–12; **arrogant** 910.9;
boastful 908.9.

10. **puffed up,** swollen, bloated, swollen
or bloated with pride; **elated,** flushed,
flushed with pride.

11. **lofty, elevated,** high, high-flown,
highfalutin or highfaluting [coll.], high-
toned [coll., U.S.]; high-minded, lofty-
minded; high-headed, high-nosed [coll.].

12. **dignified, stately, imposing,
grand, courtly, portly,** magisterial, aristo-
cratic(al); **noble,** lordly, princely; **majestic,** regal, royal, kingly, queenly; **august,
venerable;** sedate, solemn, sober, grave.

ADVS. 13. **proudly,** pridefully, **with
pride;** with head erect, with head held
high, with nose in air; like a lord, *en grand
seigneur* [F.].

14. **dignifiedly,** with dignity; nobly,
stately, imposingly, loftily, grandly, portlily,
magisterially; majestically, regally, royally;
augustly, venerably; sedately, solemnly,
soberly, gravely.

904. HUMILITY

NOUNS 1. **humility, humbleness, meekness; lowliness,** lowlihood, poorness,
meanness, smallness, ingloriousness, undis-
tinguishedness; **modesty,** unpretentiousness 906; plainness, simpleness, homeliness.

2. **humiliation, mortification;** embarrassment 864.4; **abasement,** debasement,
letdown, setdown, **comedown,** descent,
deflation, humbled pride; **shame, disgrace;** shamefacedness, hangdog look.

3. **condescension,** condescendence; patronage, patronization.

VERBS 4. **humiliate, humble; mortify,**
crush, abash; embarrass 864.16; put out, put
out of face or countenance; **shame, disgrace,** put to shame, put to the blush; **deflate,** let down; take it out of, take the
shine out of [coll.], take the starch out of
[slang], take the rise out of [slang]; put
one's nose out of joint [coll.], put a tuck in

one's tail [coll.], cut one's comb [coll.],
make one sing small [coll.].

5. **abase, debase, degrade, reduce,**
diminish, **demean,** lower, **bring low,**
bring down, take down, set down; take a
fall out of [slang], knock one off his perch;
take down a peg, take down a peg or two
[both coll.].

6. **humble oneself, demean oneself,**
climb down [coll.], get down from one's
high horse [coll.]; **put one's pride in one's
pocket; eat humble pie,** eat crow, eat dirt,
lick the dust; draw in one's horns [coll.],
sing small [coll.], lower one's note or
tone.

7. **condescend, deign, vouchsafe;
stoop, descend, unbend,** lower oneself; be
so good as to, so forget oneself; patronize.

8. **be humiliated,** be put out of countenance; **feel small, feel cheap,** look foolish
or silly, could sink through the floor; **take
shame, be ashamed, feel ashamed of
oneself,** be put to the blush; hang one's
head, hide one's diminished head, hide
one's face, not dare to show one's face, not
have a word to say for oneself; drink the
cup of humiliation to the dregs.

ADJS. 9. **humble, lowly,** low, **poor,
mean,** small, inglorious, undistinguished;
modest, unpretentious 906.9; **plain,** simple, homely; humble-looking, humble-
visaged.

10. **humblehearted, humble-minded,**
humble-spirited, poor in spirit; **meek,**
meekhearted, meek-minded, meek-spirited;
abject.

11. **humbled,** reduced, diminished,
bowed-down, in the dust; on one's knees,
on one's marrowbones [coll.].

12. **humiliated, mortified, embarrassed, chagrined, abashed,** crushed,
out of countenance; **ashamed,** shamed,
shamefaced; crestfallen, chapfallen or chopfallen, hangdog.

13. **humiliating,** humiliative, **mortifying, embarrassing,** crushing.

ADVS. 14. **humbly, meekly;** modestly
906.14; with due deference, with bated
breath, "with bated breath and whispering
humbleness" [Shakespeare]; **abjectly,** on
bended knee, **on one's knees,** on one's
marrowbones [slang], on all fours, with
one's tail between one's legs.

905. SERVILITY

NOUNS 1. **servility, slavishness,** subservience or subserviency, **meniality,** abject-

ness, baseness, meanness; submissiveness 763.3.

2. **obsequiousness, sycophancy,** fawnery, **toadyism,** flunkyism, parasitism; ingratiation, insinuation; **truckling, fawning, toadying,** toadeating, groveling, footlicking **bootlicking** [slang, U.S.], backscratching, tufthunting; **apple-polishing, handshaking** [both slang, U.S.]; timeserving; obeisance, prostration.

3. **sycophant, toady,** toad, toadeater, footlicker, bootlick or **bootlicker** [slang, U.S.], lickspit, lickspittle, **truckler, fawner,** courtier, kowtower, groveler, reptile; **backslapper,** back-scratcher, clawback [dial., Eng.]; **handshaker, apple-polisher, yes man** all slang, U.S.]; flunky, lackey, stooge [slang], spaniel, jackal; snob, tufthunter, timeserver; Sir Pertinax MacSycophant.

4. **parasite,** sucker [slang], barnacle, leech; **sponger,** sponge [coll.], free-loader [slang, U.S.], smell-feast; beat, dead beat [both slang].

5. **hanger-on,** dangler, adherent, appendage, **dependent, satellite, follower,** shadow, tagtail, led captain; **henchman,** heeler [coll., U.S.], ward heeler [polit., U.S.].

VERBS 6. **fawn, truckle; toady,** toadeat; **bootlick** [slang, U.S.], lickspittle, lick one's shoes, lick the feet of; **grovel,** crawl, creep, cower, cringe, crouch, stoop, kneel, bend the knee, fall on one's knees, prostrate oneself, throw oneself at the feet of, fall at one's feet, kiss one's feet, kiss the hem of one's garment, lick the dust, make a doormat of oneself; **kowtow, bow, bow and scrape.**

7. **toady to, truckle to, pander to, cater to; wait on** or **upon,** do service, fetch and carry, do the dirty work of.

8. **curry favor, court, pay court to,** make court to, run after [coll.], dance attendance on; **shine up to,** make up to [coll.]; **suck up to, play up to,** act up to [all slang]; fawn upon, fall over or all over [slang] **handshake** [slang, U.S.], **polish the apple** [slang].

9. **ingratiate oneself,** insinuate oneself, worm oneself in, creep into the good graces of, get next to [coll.], **get on the good or right side of.**

10. **attach oneself to,** pin or fasten oneself upon, hang about, dangle, hang on the skirts of, hang on the sleeve of, **follow,** follow at heel; follow the crowd, get on the band wagon, go with the stream, hold with the hare and run with the hounds.

11. sponge, **sponge on** [both coll.]; feed on, fatten on, batten on, live off of.

ADJS. 12. **servile, slavish,** subservient, menial, base, mean; submissive 763.12.

13. **obsequious,** courtly, **sycophantic(al), toadyish, fawning, truckling, ingratiating, toadying,** toadeating, **bootlicking** [slang, U.S.], footlicking, backscratching; **groveling,** sniveling, cringing, cowering, crouching, crawling, reptilian; **parasitic(al),** leechlike, sponging [coll.]; timeserving; **abject,** beggarly, hangdog; obeisant, prostrate, on one's knees, on one's marrowbones [slang], on bended knee.

ADVS. 14. **servilely, slavishly,** subserviently, menially, "in a bondman's key" [Shakespeare]; submissively 763.17.

15. **obsequiously, sycophantically, ingratiatingly, fawningly, truckingly;** hat-in-hand, cap-in-hand; **abjectly,** grovelingly, on one's knees.

906. MODESTY

NOUNS 1. **modesty, meekness;** humbleness 904; **unpretentiousness,** unassumingness, unpresumptuousness, **unostentatiousness,** unambitiousness, unobtrusiveness, unboastfulness.

2. **self-effacement, self-depreciation,** self-detraction.

3. **reserve, restraint, constraint,** backwardness, retiring disposition.

4. **shyness, timidity,** timidness, timorousness, **bashfulness, coyness, demureness,** demurity, diffidence, skittishness, mousiness; self-consciousness.

5. **blushing, flushing,** coloring, mantling, reddening, crimsoning; **blush, flush,** suffusion.

6. shrinking violet, modest violet, mouse.

VERBS 7. **efface oneself,** reserve oneself, retire, **retire into one's shell, keep in the background,** keep one's distance, remain in the shade, take a back seat [coll.], hide one's face, hide one's light under a bushel, pursue the noiseless tenor of one's way, blush unseen, "do good by stealth and blush to find it fame" [Pope].

8. **blush, flush,** mantle, **color,** change color, color up, redden, crimson, turn red, get red in the face, blush up to the eyes.

ADJS. 9. **modest, meek;** humble 904.9; **unpretentious,** unpretending, **unassuming,** unpresuming, unpresumptuous, un-

ostentatious, unobtrusive, unboastful; unambitious, unaspiring.

10.   self-effacing,   self-depreciative;
deprecatory, deprecative.

11. reserved, restrained, constrained;
quiet; backward, retiring, shrinking.

12. shy, timid, timorous, bashful, coy,
demure, diffident, skittish, mousy; self-conscious, conscious.

13. blushing, blushful; flushed, red,
ruddy, red in the face; shamefaced,
sheepish.

ADVS. 14. modestly, meekly; humbly
904.14; unpretentiously, unpretendingly,
unassumingly, unpresumptuously, unos-
tentatiously, unobtrusively; quietly, without
ceremony, sans façon [F.].

15. shyly, timidly, timorously, bashfully,
coyly, demurely, diffidently; shamefacedly,
sheepishly, blushingly, with downcast eyes.

907. VANITY

NOUNS 1. vanity, vainness; overproud-
ness, overweening pride; self-importance,
self-esteem, self-respect, self-assumption;
self-admiration, self-worship, self-endearment, self-love, amour-propre [F.]; self-
satisfaction, self-content, self-complacency,
self-sufficiency; vainglory, vaingloriousness;
"the sixth insatiable sense" [Carlyle], "an
itch for the praise of fools" [Browning].

2. pride 903; arrogance 910; boastfulness
908.

3. egotism, egoism, egoisticalness, ego-
tisticalness, ego [coll.], self-interest, individualism, "the tongue of vanity" [Chamfort];
egocentricity, self-centeredness, self-cen-
terment; selfishness 976.

4. conceit, conceitedness, self-conceit,
self-conceitedness;   stuck-upness   [coll.],
chestiness [slang, U.S.], swelled-headed-
ness, swelled head; cockiness [coll.], pertness, perkiness; "vanity driven from all
other shifts, and forced to appeal to itself
for admiration" [Hazlitt], "a case of mistaken nonentity" [Barbara Stanwyck].

5. egotist, egoist, egocentric, individualist;   swellhead   [slang],   stuck-upper
[coll.], it or It [coll.], big It [slang], braggart 908.5, know-it-all, no modest violet, the
only pebble on the beach [U.S.]; "a person
of low taste, more interested in himself
than in me" [Ambrose Bierce].

VERBS 6. be stuck on oneself [slang],
think no small beer of oneself, think one is
it [slang], grow too big for one's shoes or
breeches, know it all, have no false modesty,

be blinded by one's own glory, lay the
flattering unction to one's soul; fish for
compliments; boast 908.6; give oneself airs
902.14.

7. puff up, inflate, swell; go to one's
head, turn one's head.

ADJS. 8. vain, vainglorious, overproud,
overweening; self-important, self-esteeming, self-respecting, self-assuming, consequential;   self-admiring,   self-worshiping,
self-loving, self-endeared; self-satisfied, self-
content, self-contented, self-complacent,
self-sufficient.

9. proud 903.8; arrogant 910.9; boastful
908.9.

10. egotistic(al), egoistic(al), self-interested; egocentric, self-centered; selfish
976.5.

11. conceited, self-conceited, self-opinionated; stuck-up [coll.], set up [coll.],
puffed up, chesty [slang, U.S.], swelled-
headed, too big for one's shoes or breeches;
biggoty or biggity, brigetty [all dial.]; cocky
[coll.], pert, perk, perky; peacockish, pea-
cocky; know-it-all, overwise, wise in one's
own conceit.

12. stuck on oneself [slang], impressed
with oneself, pleased with oneself, full of
oneself, all wrapped up in oneself.

ADVS. 13. vainly, self-importantly; egotistically, egoistically; conceitedly, self-con-
ceitedly; cockily [coll.], pertly, perkily.

908. BOASTING

NOUNS 1. boasting, bragging; boastfulness, braggadocio, braggartism, braggardism, braggartry; boast, brag; vaunt, bounce,
bombast, bravado, fanfaronade, gasconade,
rodomontade; bluster, swagger 909; vanity,
conceit 907; jactation, jactitation; heroics.

2. tall talk [coll.], big talk [slang], fine
talk, highfalutin or highfaluting [coll.]; hot
air, gas, bunk [all coll.]; tall story [coll.],
fish story [joc.].

3. self-approbation, self-praise, self-laud-
ation, self-gratulation, self-applause, self-
puffery, self-glorification; vainglory, vaingloriousness.

4. exultation, elation, triumph, jubilation; gloating.

5. braggart, boaster, brag, braggadocio, bouncer [coll.], fanfaron; blowhard,
blower, hot-air artist, gasbag, windbag, big
bag of wind, windjammer, windy [all
slang]; blusterer 909.2; Fourth-of-July orator; Braggadocio, Rodomont, Thraso, Gascon.

VERBS 6. **boast, brag,** make a boast of, vaunt, flourish, gasconade, vapor, puff, blow [slang], **blow off** [slang], **talk big** [coll.], draw the longbow, bunch the hits [slang, U.S.], spread oneself [coll.], advertise [slang], brag oneself up [slang], **blow one's own trumpet, toot one's own horn,** *faire claquer son fouet* [F., make one's whip crack]; bluster, swagger 909.3; speak for Buncombe [U.S.]; spread-eagle [coll., U.S.], make the eagle scream [U.S.].

7. **flatter oneself,** conceit oneself, **congratulate oneself,** hug oneself, shake hands with oneself, **pat oneself on the back,** take merit to oneself.

8. **exult,** triumph, glory, delight, joy, jubilate; **crow,** crow over [both coll.]; **gloat,** gloat over.

ADJS. 9. **boastful, braggart, boasting, bragging,** vaunting, vaporing, gasconading, fanfaronading, fanfaron; vain, conceited 907.8–11; **vainglorious,** self-glorious, self-lauding, self-applauding, self-praising, self-flattering.

10. **inflated, swollen, windy** [coll.], gassy [coll.], **bombastic,** high-swelling, **high-flown, highfalutin** or highfaluting [coll.], **pretentious,** extravagant, big, tall [coll.].

11. **exultant,** exulting, **elated,** elate, **jubilant, triumphant, flushed,** cock-a-hoop, in high feather.

ADVS. 12. **boastfully,** boastingly, braggingly, vauntingly, vaingloriously.

13. **exultantly,** exultingly, elatedly, jubilantly, triumphantly, in triumph.

909. BLUSTER

NOUNS 1. **bluster,** blustering, blusteration [coll.]; **swagger,** swashbucklery; **bravado,** bounce, rant, rodomontade, fanfaronade; sputter, splutter; fuss, bustle, fluster, flurry; bluff, bluster and bluff; boastfulness 908.

2. **blusterer, swaggerer,** swashbuckler, fanfaron, bravo, roisterer, vaporer, blatherskite [coll.]; ranter, raver; slang-whanger [slang]; bluff, bluffer; braggart 908.5.

VERBS 3. **bluster, swagger,** swashbuckle; bounce, vapor, roister, rollick, gasconade, kick up a dust [coll.]; sputter, splutter; rant, rage, rave, storm; slang-whang [slang]; bluff, bluster and bluff, put up a bluff [coll.]; brag 908.6.

ADJS. 4. **blustering,** blustery, blusterous; **boisterous,** roisterous, roistering, rollicking; ranting, raging, raving, storming; tumul-

tuous 161.17; noisy, "full of sound and fury" [Shakespeare].

910. ARROGANCE

NOUNS 1. **arrogance,** arrogantness; **pride,** proudness; **haughtiness, hauteur; loftiness, toploftiness** [coll.]; stuck-upness [coll.], uppishness [coll.], uppitiness [coll., U.S.]; hoighty-toitiness, hoity-toity; haughty airs, cornstarchy airs [coll.]; high horse, high or tight ropes, altitudes [all coll.].

2. **presumptuousness,** presumption, assumption; **insolence** 911.

3. **lordliness, imperiousness,** masterfulness, magisterialness, **high-and-mightiness;** domineeringness, overbearance.

4. **aloofness, standoffishness,** offishness [coll.], distantness, remoteness.

5. **disdainfulness,** disdain, **contemptuousness, superciliousness,** contumeliousness, cavalierness, you-be-damnedness [slang].

6. **snobbery, snobbishness,** snobbiness, snobbism; **priggishness, priggery,** priggism; snootiness, snottiness, sniffiness [all slang]; high-hattedness, high-hattiness [both slang]; "the pride of those who are not sure of their social position" [Berton Braley].

7. **snob, prig,** stuck-upper [coll.], high-hatter [slang]; **highbrow** [slang], Brahmin; name dropper; "he who meanly admires a mean thing" [Thackeray].

VERBS 8. **give oneself airs** 902.14; hold one's nose in the air, look down one's nose, toss the head, bridle; climb or get on the high ropes, mount or get on one's high horse, ride the high horse [all coll.].

ADJS. 9. **arrogant, proud, haughty; lofty, toplofty** [coll.]; high-flown, high-falutin or highfaluting [coll.]; high-headed, high-nosed [coll.]; **stuck-up** [coll.], uppity [coll., U.S.], **upstage** [coll.], **hoity-toity,** big, big as you please, six feet above contradiction; on one's high horse, on one's tight or high ropes, in one's altitudes [all coll.].

10. **presumptuous,** presuming, assuming, overweening, would-be; **insolent** 911.8.

11. **lordly, imperious, masterful,** magisterial, **high and mighty;** domineering, overbearing; dictatorial 737.15.

12. **aloof, standoffish,** standoff, offish [coll.], distant, remote.

13. **disdainful, contemptuous, supercilious,** contumelious, cavalier, you-be-damned [slang].

14. **snobbish,** snobby, **priggish,** snippy [coll.]; **snooty,** snotty, sniffy [all slang]; **high-hat,** high-hatted, high-hatty [all slang]; patronizing, condescending.

ADVS. 15. arrogantly, proudly, haughtily, aloofly; loftily, toploftily [coll.]; imperiously, magisterially; **disdainfully, contemptuously,** superciliously, contumeliously; with nose in air, with nose turned up, with head held high, with arms akimbo.

16. presumptuously, overweeningly; **insolently** 911.11.

17. **snobbishly,** snobbily, **priggishly,** snootily, snottily [both slang].

911. INSOLENCE

NOUNS 1. **insolence,** procacity, contumely; **audacity, effrontery,** boldness, assurance, hardihood; **presumption,** presumptuousness; **arrogance** 910.

2. **impudence, impertinence,** flippancy, cockiness [coll.], freshness [slang, U.S.], cheekiness [coll.]; **brazenness,** brassiness [coll.], face of brass; **rudeness,** brashness, disrespectfulness.

3. **cheek,** face, brass [all coll.], **nerve, gall,** crust [all slang].

4. **sauciness,** sassiness [dial., U.S.]; **sauce** [coll.], sass [dial., U.S.], lip [slang], **back talk** [coll., U.S.].

5. (impudent person) malapert, cheeker [slang], saucebox [coll.]; minx, hussy [joc.]; smarty [slang, U.S.], **smart aleck** [coll., U.S.], wise guy [slang, U.S.]; boldface, brazenface.

VERBS 6. **have the audacity, have the cheek; have the gall,** have a nerve, have one's nerve [all slang]; **get fresh** [slang, U.S.], get smart [coll.]; teach one's grandmother to suck eggs [coll.].

7. **sauce** [coll.], sass [dial., U.S.], **talk back,** answer back [coll.], give one any of one's lip [slang].

ADJS. 8. **insolent,** insulting, **audacious,** procacious, bodacious [dial.], bumptious, contumelious; **arrogant** 910.9; **presumptuous,** presuming, overpresumptuous; forward, obtrusive, familiar; cool, cold; **disdainful** 910.13.

9. **impudent, impertinent, pert,** malapert, flip [coll.], flippant, cocky [coll.], **fresh** [slang, U.S.], **cheeky** [coll.], facy [dial.], crusty [slang], gally [slang, U.S.], nervy [slang], uncalled-for; **rude, disrespectful,** brash, bluff; **saucy,** sassy [dial., U.S.]; smart [coll.], smarty [coll.], smartalecky [coll., U.S.].

10. **brazen,** brazenfaced, boldfaced, barefaced, brassy [coll.], **bold,** bold as brass [coll.], unblushing, unabashed, awless or aweless, **shameless,** dead or lost to shame.

ADVS. 11. insolently, audaciously, procaciously, bumptiously, contumeliously; **arrogantly** 910.15; presumptuously, obtrusively.

12. **impudently, impertinently,** pertly, flippantly, cockily [coll.], cheekily [coll.], saucily; **rudely,** brashly, disrespectfully.

13. **brazenly,** brazenfacedly, **boldly,** boldfacedly, **shamelessly,** unblushingly.

912. REPUTE

NOUNS 1. **repute, reputation,** "the bubble reputation" [Shakespeare]; **name,** character, figure; **fame, famousness, renown, kudos** [coll.], report, **glory,** éclat, **celebrity, popularity,** recognition, a place in the sun; **notoriety,** notoriousness, talk of the town.

2. **reputability,** reputableness; **good** or **high repute,** good report, good odor, good or fair name, name to conjure with.

3. **esteem, honor, regard, respect,** account, favor, consideration, credit, worth.

4. **prestige, dignity; rank, standing,** position, station, status.

5. **distinction, mark, note; importance, consequence,** significance; **notability, prominence, eminence, greatness;** elevation, exaltation, loftiness, high mightiness; nobility, grandeur, sublimity.

6. **illustriousness,** luster, **brilliance** or brilliancy, radiance, splendor or splendour, resplendence or resplendency, glory, blaze of glory.

7. posthumous fame, **memory, remembrance; immortality,** lasting fame, niche in the hall of fame; immortal name, "ghost of a great name" [Lucan].

8. **glorification, ennoblement, dignification, exaltation,** elevation, magnification, aggrandizement; enthronement; immortalization, enshrinement; deification, apotheosis; lionization.

9. **celebrity,** man of mark or note, **notable, notability, luminary, great man,** worthy, name, **big name,** figure, **somebody,** rara avis [L., rare bird]; personage 670.8; cynosure, "the observed of all observers" [Shakespeare]; lion, social lion; hero, heroine; immortal; luminaries, galaxy, constellation.

VERBS 10. **be somebody,** be something; figure, make or cut a figure, cut a dash [coll.], make a splash [coll.], **make a noise in the world,** leave one's mark; live, flourish; shine, glitter, gleam, glow.

11. **gain recognition,** be recognized, come into one's own, come to the front, come into vogue.

12. **honor,** confer or bestow honor upon; **dignify,** adorn, grace; **distinguish,** signalize, confer distinction on.

13. **glorify,** glamorize; **exalt,** elevate, raise, uplift, set up, **ennoble,** aggrandize, magnify, exalt to the skies; crown; throne, enthrone; immortalize, enshrine, hand one's name down to posterity; deify, apotheosize

14. **lionize,** run after.

15. **reflect honor on,** shed a luster on, redound to one's honor.

ADJS. 16. **reputable, estimable, honorable,** noble, worthy, creditable; **respectable,** highly respectable; **well-thought-of,** held in esteem, in good odor, in favor, in high favor.

17. **distinguished,** distingué; **noted, notable,** marked, of note, of mark; **famous, famed,** honored, **renowned, celebrated, popular, notorious, well-known,** in everyone's mouth, on everyone's tongue or lips, talked-of, talked-about; far-famed, far-heard.

18. **prominent, conspicuous, outstanding,** to the front, in the limelight [coll.]; **important,** consequential, significant.

19. **eminent, high, exalted,** elevated, lofty, sublime; **great, big** [coll.], **grand;** mighty, high and mighty.

20. **illustrious,** lustrous, **glorious,** brilliant, radiant, splendid, splendorous, splendrous, splendent, resplendent, bright, shining.

ADVS. 21. **reputably, estimably, honorably,** nobly, respectably, worthily, creditably.

22. **famously, notably, notedly, notoriously,** popularly, celebratedly; **prominently, eminently,** conspicuously, outstandingly; **illustriously,** gloriously.

913. DISREPUTE

NOUNS 1. **disrepute, ill-repute,** bad repute, bad name, bad odor, bad report; **disesteem, dishonor, discredit; disfavor,** ill-favor.

2. **disreputability,** disreputableness, discreditableness, dishonorableness, **unrespectability;** disgracefulness, shamefulness.

3. **baseness, lowness, meanness,** poorness, pettiness, paltriness, smallness, littleness, pokiness, beggarliness, shabbiness, shoddiness, scrubbiness, scumminess, scabbiness, scurviness, abjectness, wretchedness, miserableness, despicableness, contemptibility, abominableness, execrableness, obnoxiousness, odiousness, vileness, foulness, rankness, fulsomeness, grossness, nefariousness, heinousness, atrociousness, monstrousness.

4. **infamy,** infamousness; **ignominy,** ignominiousness; ingloriousness, **ignobility,** odium, obloquy, opprobrium, "a long farewell to all my greatness" [Shakespeare].

5. **disgrace, scandal, humiliation; shame,** dirty shame [slang], crying or burning shame; **reproach,** byword, byword of reproach, a disgrace to one's name.

6. **stigma,** stigmatism; **brand,** badge of infamy; **slur,** reproach, imputation, stigmatization; **black eye** [coll.], black mark; **stain, taint,** attaint, tarnish, blur, **smirch,** smutch, smudge, spot, blot, **blot on** or **in one's escutcheon;** bend or bar sinister, baton, champain, point champain [all her.]; mark of Cain; broad arrow [Eng.].

VERBS 7. **incur disgrace,** earn a bad name, forfeit one's good opinion, fall into disrepute, seal one's infamy; **lose face, lose caste; disgrace oneself,** lower oneself, demean oneself, act beneath oneself, derogate, stoop, descend, fall from one's high estate.

8. **disgrace, dishonor, discredit,** reflect discredit upon, bring into discredit, reproach, cast reproach upon, be a reproach to; **shame, put to shame,** impute shame to, hold up to shame, bring shame upon; **humiliate** 904.4; **degrade, debase,** bring low.

9. **stigmatize, brand; stain,** tarnish, taint, attaint, blot, **blacken, smear,** bespatter, **sully,** soil, defile, vilify; **slur,** cast a slur upon, blow upon; **defame** 969.9, 10; **give a black eye** [coll.], give a black mark, put in one's bad or black books; give a bad name, give a dog a bad name; expose, expose to infamy; pillory, gibbet; burn or hang in effigy.

ADJS. 10. **disreputable, discreditable, dishonorable, unrespectable, ignoble, ignominious, infamous,** inglorious; **notorious.**

11. **disgraceful, shameful,** pitiful, deplorable, opprobrious, sad, sorry, too bad; **humiliating,** humiliative; **scandalous,** shocking, outrageous.

12. **base, low**, low-down [coll.], **mean**, poor, petty, paltry, small, little, **shabby**, **shoddy**, scrubby, scummy, scabby, **scurvy**, snide [slang], mangy [coll.], measly [slang], cheesy [slang, U.S.], poky or pokey, beggarly, **wretched, miserable**, abject, **despicable, contemptible**, abominable, execrable, **obnoxious**, odious, vile, foul, dirty, rank, fulsome, gross, flagrant, grave, arrant, nefarious, heinous, reptilian, atrocious, monstrous, enormous, unmentionable.

13. **in disrepute**, in bad odor; **in disfavor, in bad** [coll.], in one's bad or black books, **out of favor**, out of countenance, at a discount; **in disgrace, in Dutch** [slang, U.S.], **in the doghouse** [slang], under a cloud; disgraced, shamed, loaded with shame, unable to show one's face.

14. **unrenowned**, renownless, nameless, inglorious, **unnotable, unnoted**, unnoticed, **undistinguished, unfamed**, uncelebrated, unhonored, unglorified, unpopular; **unknown**, obscure, unheard-of.

ADVS. 15. **disreputably, discreditably, dishonorably, unrespectably, ignobly, ignominiously, infamously**, ingloriously.

16. **disgracefully**, deplorably, **scandalously**, shockingly, outrageously; **shamefully**, to one's shame, to one's shame be it spoken.

17. **basely, meanly**, poorly, pettily, **shabbily, shoddily**, scurvily, **wretchedly, miserably**, abjectly, **despicably, contemptibly**, abominably, execrably, obnoxiously, odiously, vilely, foully, grossly, flagrantly, arrantly, **nefariously**, heinously, atrociously, monstrously.

INTERJS. 18. **shame!, for shame!**, shame on you!, **fie!**, fie upon!, tck-tck!, tsh-tsh!, tst-tst!

914. AN HONOR

Token of Esteem.—NOUNS 1. **honor**, great honor, distinction, glory, credit, ornament; "blushing honors" [Shakespeare].

2. **award, reward, prize**; booby prize, consolation prize; Nobel Prize, Pulitzer Prize; sweepstakes; jack pot; Oscar, Motion Picture Academy Award.

3. **trophy**, palm, laurel, **laurels**, bays, crown, chaplet, wreath, garland, **feather in one's cap** [coll.]; civic crown, ~ garland or wreath [Rom. antiq.]; cup, loving cup, pot [slang].

4. **citation**, eulogy, mention, honorable mention.

5. **decoration**, decoration of honor, ornament; ribbon, riband; blue ribbon, cordon bleu [F.]; red ribbon, red ribbon of the Legion of Honor; cordon, grand cordon; garter; star, gold star.

6. **medal**, medallion; military medal, service medal, war medal, soldier's medal; Medal of Honor, Distinguished Service Medal, Distinguished Service Cross, Navy Cross, Distinguished Flying Cross, Silver Star Medal, Order of the Purple Heart, Congressional medal [all U.S.]; Distinguished Conduct Medal, Military Cross, Victoria Cross, Distinguished Service Order, Distinguished Flying Cross [all British]; Croix de guerre, Médaille Militaire [both French]; Iron Cross, Pour le mérite [both German]; Medal for Valor, Cross of Merit [both Italian]; Carnegie medal.

7. **scholarship**, fellowship.

VERBS 8. **honor, do honor**, pay regard to, give ~, pay or render honor to; **cite** [mil.]; **decorate**, pin a medal on; crown, crown with laurel.

9. **win the prize**, win the palm or laurels, bear the palm, bear away the bell, **take the cake** [slang, U.S.], **bring home the bacon** [coll., U.S.], **win one's spurs**.

ADJS. 10. **honored, distinguished**; laureate, crowned with laurel.

11. **honorary, honorable, honorific(al)**.

ADVS. 12. **with honor**, with distinction; cum laude, magna cum laude, summa cum laude, insigne cum laude, honoris causa [all L. scholastic].

915. TITLE

Appellation of Dignity or Distinction.—NOUNS 1. **title, honorific, honor**, title of honor; **handle**, handle to one's name [both slang].

2. (honorifics) **Excellency, Eminence, Grace, Honor, Reverence, Worship**, Your ~, His or Her Excellency, etc.; **Lord, My Lord**, milord, **Lordship**, Your or His Lordship; **Lady, My Lady**, milady, mem-sahib [India], **Ladyship**, Your or Her Ladyship; **Highness, Royal Highness, Imperial Highness, Serene Highness**, Your ~, His or Her Highness, etc.; **Majesty, Royal Majesty, Imperial Majesty, Serene Majesty**, Your ~, His or Her Majesty, etc.

3. **Sir, sire**, sirrah [arch. & dial.]; **Esquire**; Master, **Mister** 419.7; mirza [Per.], effendi [Turk.], sirdar [Orient], emir [Moham.], mian [India], malik [Hind.], huzoor

[India], khan [Orient], Mir [India], sahib [India], burra or burra sahib [India], nawab [India], bahadur [Hind.].

4. Mistress, madame 420.8, 9.

5. (ecclesiastical titles) Reverend, his Reverence [chiefly joc.]; Monsignor; Holiness, His Holiness; Dom, Brother, Sister, Father. Mother.

6. degree, academic degree; **bachelor,** baccalaureate, *baccalaureus* [L.]; **master,** masterate; **doctor,** doctorate.

ADJS. **7.** titular, titulary; honorific(al).

8. the Noble, the Most Noble, the Most Excellent, the Most Worthy, the Most Worshipful; the Honorable, the Most Honorable, the Right Honorable; the Reverend, the Very Reverend, the Right Reverend, the Most Reverend.

9. academic degrees

A.A., Associate of Arts	LL. D., Doctor of Laws
A.B., Bachelor of Arts (Artium Baccalaureus)	M.A., Master of Arts
Adj. A., Adjunct in Arts	M.D., Doctor of Medicine
A.M., Master of Arts (Artium Magister)	M.S., Master of Science
	Mus. D., Doctor of Music
B.A., Bachelor of Arts	Ph. D., Doctor of Philosophy
B.S., Bachelor of Science	S. B., Bachelor of Science
D.D., Doctor of Divinity	Sc. D., Doctor of Science
D.D.S., Doctor of Dental Surgery	S. M., Master of Science
D. Ed., Doctor of Education	S.T.D., Doctor of Sacred Theology
Jur. D., Doctor of Jurisprudence	Th.D., Doctor of Theology
Litt. D., Doctor of Letters	

916. NOBILITY

Noble Rank or Birth.—NOUNS **1.** nobility, nobleness; **aristocracy,** aristocraticalness; **gentility,** genteelness, *gentilhommerie* [F.]; quality, rank, distinction; birth, high or noble birth, ancestry, high or honorable descent; blood, **blue blood,** blue blood of Castile, "all the blood of all the Howards" [Pope]; royalty 737.7.

2. the nobility, noblesse, aristocracy, the elite, the elect, the classes, upper classes or circles, upper cut [coll.], upper crust [coll.], upper ten [coll.], upper ten thousand, the four hundred [U.S.], high life, *haut monde* [F.]; the old nobility, *ancienne noblesse* [F.]; First Families of Virginia, F.F.V.s [U.S.]; **peerage,** baronage, kwazoku [Jap.], lords temporal and spiritual; knightage, chivalry; royalty.

3. gentry, gentlefolk, gentlefolks, gentlepeople, better sort, "caste of Vere de Vere" [Tennyson]; lesser nobility, *petite noblesse* [F.]; samurai, shizoku [both Jap.]; landed gentry, squirearchy.

4. noble, nobleman, nob [slang]; **gentleman,** *gentilhomme* [F.]; **peer;** aristocrat, **patrician,** Brahman or Brahmin [India], **blue blood,** thoroughbred, silkstocking, swell [coll.], upper-cruster [slang, U.S.]; **grandee,** magnifico, magnate, optimate; **lord,** laird [Scot.], lordling; seignior, seigneur, signior, *signor* [It.], *señor* [Sp.], *senhor* [Pg.], don [Sp.]; pasha or bashaw, one-tailed ∼, two-tailed or three-tailed pasha or bashaw [all Turk.]; hidalgo [Sp.], fidalgo [Pg.].

5. (noblemen) duke, grand duke, archduke, marquis, earl, count, viscount, baron, daimio [Jap.], baronet; squire, squireen [joc., Eng.]; esquire, armiger; palsgrave, waldgrave, margrave, landgrave.

6. knight, cavalier, chevalier, *caballero* [Sp.], *Ritter* [Ger.], "a very parfit gentil knight" [Chaucer]; **knight-errant,** knight-adventurer; companion; bachelor, knight bachelor; baronet, knight baronet; banneret, knight banneret; Bayard, Gawain, Lancelot, Sidney, Sir Galahad, Don Quixote.

7. noblewoman, gentlewoman, peeress; lady, dame [hist.], *doña* [Sp.], *dona* [Pg.], khanum [Orient]; duchess, grand duchess, archduchess, marchioness, viscountess, countess, baroness, margravine.

8. prince, *Prinz* [Ger.], *Fürst* [Ger.], knez [Russ.], atheling [hist.], sheik or sheikh [Moham.], sherif [Moham.], mirza [Per.], khan [Orient], emir [Turk. & Moham.], shahzada [Ind.]; princeling, princelet; crown prince, heir apparent; heir presumptive; prince consort; prince regent; **king** 747.8; Indian ruling princes 747.10; Mohammedan ruling princes 747.11.

9. princess, *princesse* [F.], infanta [Sp. & Pg.], czarevna or tsarevna [Russ.]; rani, maharani, begum, shahzadi, kumari or kunwari, raj-kumari, malikzadi [all Ind.]; crown princess; **queen** 747.12.

10. (rank or office) lordship, ladyship; dukedom, marquisate, earldom, barony, baronetcy; viscountship, viscountcy, viscounty; knighthood, knight-errantship; seigniory, seigneury, seignioralty; pashaship, pashadom; princeship, princedom; kingship, queenship 737.7.

ADJS. **11. noble,** of rank, high, exalted; **aristocratic(al), patrician; gentle, genteel,** of gentle blood; gentlemanly, gentlemanlike; ladylike, quite the lady; knightly, chivalrous; ducal, archducal; princely, princelike; kingly, kinglike, "every inch a king" [Shakespeare]; queenly, queenlike; titled.

12. wellborn, well-bred, blooded [U.S.], **blue-blooded,** fancy-bred, fancy, breedy [coll.], of good breed; **thoroughbred,** purebred, pure-blooded, *pur sang* [F.], fullblooded [U.S.], hot-blooded [turf cant]; **highborn,** highbred; born to the purple.

917. COMMONALTY

NOUNS **1. commonalty,** commonality, commonage, commons; **the common people,** the common run [coll.], the rank and file, the third estate, the salt of the earth; **proletariat,** *bourgeoisie* [F.]; **the lower classes,** the lower cut [coll.], the other half; the peasantry.

2. the people, the populace, the public, John Q. Public; demos, democracy; Tom, Dick, and Harry; Brown, Jones, and Robinson.

3. the masses, the hoi polloi, the many, **the multitude,** the crowd, **the mob,** the mobility [joc.], the horde, the million, "the four million" [O. Henry], the majority, the herd, **the vulgar** or **common herd,** *profanum* or *ignobile vulgus* [L.], **the great unwashed** or unnumbered, "the multitude of the gross people" [Erasmus], "manyheaded multitude" [Sidney], "the beast with many heads" [Shakespeare], "the blunt monster with uncounted heads, the still-discordant wavering multitude" [Shakespeare].

4. rabble, the rout, the ruck, common ruck, canaille, roughscuff [coll., U.S.], ragabash or ragabrash [Scot. & dial., Eng.], ragtag [coll.], "the tag-rag people" [Shakespeare], **rag-tag and bobtail;** rag, tag and bobtail.

5. riffraff, raff, chaff, **trash, rubbish,** dregs, sordes, offscourings, offscum, scum, scum of the earth, dregs ∼, scum ∼, offscum or offscourings of society, swinish multitude, vermin, cattle.

6. the underprivileged, the forgotten man, the submerged tenth.

7. commoner, common man, little man, little fellow, average man, man in the street, one of the people; **plebeian,** pleb [slang]; **proletarian, bourgeois,** *roturier* [F.]; democrat, republican; pariah [India]; cockney; Joe Doakes, John Smith, Mr. Snooks, Mr. or Mrs. Brown or Smith.

8. peasant, countryman, countrywoman, **provincial,** son of the soil, tiller of the soil; **peon,** hind [Eng.], fellah [Arab.], ryot [India], tyke or tike [Scot. & dial.], muzhik, moujik [both Russ.]; sons of Martha, hewers of wood and drawers of water.

9. rustic, bucolic [joc], **yokel, hick** [slang], **rube** or reub [slang, U.S.], **hoosier** [coll., U.S.], **hayseed** [slang], **bumpkin,** country bumpkin, lumpkin, Tony Lumpkin [Goldsmith], clod, **clodhopper** [coll.], hobnail, joskin, **jake** [coll., U.S.], chawbacon [slang], hodge [coll.], swain, churl, carl [dial.], **boor,** clown, lout, looby, put, chuff; farmer 412.5.

10. upstart, parvenu, bounder [coll.], would-be, adventurer, sprout [slang], mushroom, skipjack, "an upstart crow decked in our feathers" [Peele]; *bourgeois gentilhomme* [F.], would-be gentleman; *nouveau riche* [F.], **newly-rich,** pig in clover [slang], codfish aristocrat [U.S.]; codfish aristocracy [U.S.]; social climber; status seeker.

ADJS. **11. plebeian, ignoble, common,** commonplace, plain, ordinary, **lowly,** low, mean, **humble,** homely; **lowborn,** lowbred, baseborn, earthborn; ungenteel, shabbygenteel; vulgar, rude 896.10–15; below the salt; cockney, born within sound of Bow bells.

12. middle-class, *bourgeois* [F.], **proletarian.**

13. parvenu, upstart, mushroom, risen from the ranks; **newly-rich.**

918. WONDER

NOUNS **1. wonder,** wonderment, **astonishment, amazement,** amaze [poetic], **astoundment,** confoundment, **bewilderment,** flabbergastation [coll.], **surprise, awe,** admiration.

2. marvel, wonder, prodigy, miracle, phenomenon, astonishment, amazement, wonderment, wonderful thing, amazing or astonishing thing, quite a thing, really something, sensation, stunner [slang], wonder-for-hogs [slang, U.S.]; one for the book, something to brag or shout about, something to write home about [all slang]; rarity, nonesuch, exception, one in a thousand, one in a way; curiosity, gazingstock, sight, spectacle; wonders of the world.

3. wonderfulness, wondrousness, marvelousness, miraculousness, phenomenalness, prodigiousness, stupendousness, remarkableness, extraordinariness.

VERBS 4. wonder, marvel, be astonished, ~ amazed or astounded; gape, look or stand aghast or agog, stare, stare openmouthed, open one's eyes, rub one's eyes, hold one's breath; not be able to account for, not know what to make of, not believe one's eyes, ~ ears or senses.

5. astonish, amaze, astound, surprise, startle, stagger, bewilder, flabbergast [coll.], confound, overwhelm; awe, awestrike, strike with wonder or awe; dumfound, dumfounder, strike dumb, strike dead; strike all of a heap, throw on one's beam ends, bowl down or over [all coll.]; dazzle, bedazzle, daze, bedaze; stun, stupefy, petrify, paralyze.

6. take one's breath away, turn one's head, make one's head swim, make one's hair stand on end, make one's tongue cleave to the roof of one's mouth, make one stare, make one sit up and take notice, carry one off his feet.

7. beggar or baffle description, stagger belief.

ADJS 8. astonished, amazed, surprised, astounded, flabbergasted [coll.], bewildered, confounded, dumfounded, staggered, overwhelmed, unable to believe one's senses or eyes; aghast, agape, agog, all agog, wide-eyed, openmouthed, breathless; thunderstruck, wonder-struck, wonder-stricken, awe-struck, struck all of a heap [coll.]; awed, awful, awesome; spellbound, lost in wonder or amazement.

9. wonderful, wondrous, marvelous, miraculous, phenomenal, prodigious, stupendous, extraordinary, exceptional, remarkable, striking; passing strange, "wondrous strange" [Shakespeare]; incredible, inconceivable, unimaginable, incomprehensible.

10. awesome, awful, awing, awe-inspiring.

11. astonishing, amazing, surprising, startling, astounding, bewildering, confounding, staggering, stunning [slang], overwhelming.

12. indescribable, ineffable, inexpressible, unutterable, unspeakable.

ADVS. 13. wonderfully, wondrously, marvelously, miraculously, phenomenally, prodigiously, stupendously, extraordinarily, exceptionally, remarkably, strikingly; incredibly, inconceivably, unimaginably, incomprehensibly.

14. astonishingly, amazingly, astoundingly, bewilderingly, staggeringly, confoundingly; surprisingly, startlingly, to one's surprise or great surprise, to one's astonishment or amazement; for a wonder, strange to say.

15. indescribably, ineffably, inexpressibly, unutterably, unspeakably.

16. in wonder, in astonishment, in amazement, in bewilderment, in awe, in admiration, with gaping mouth.

INTERJS. 17. (of astonishment or surprise) my word!, I declare!, well I never!, of all things!, as I live and breathe!, what!, indeed!, really!, surely!, how now!, what on earth!, what in the world!, I'll be jiggered!, hush or shut my mouth!, dog my cats!, blow me down!, strike me dead!, shiver my timbers! [all coll.].

18. oh!, O!, ah!, la!, lo!, lo and behold!, hello!, halloo!, heyday!, whew!, phew!, wow!, yipes!, yike!

19. my!, oh, my!, dear!, dear me!, goodness!, gracious!, goodness gracious!, my goodness!, my stars!, good gracious!, good heavens!, good lack!, lackadaisy!, welladay!, hoity-toity!, zounds!, 'sdeath!, adzooks!, gad so!, bless my heart!, God bless me!, heavens and earth!, for crying out loud! [slang].

20. imagine!, fancy!, fancy that!, just imagine!, only think!, of all things!, well!, I never!, can you feature that!, can you beat that!, it beats the Dutch!, do tell!, you don't say!, the devil or deuce you say!, I'll be!, what do you know!, what do you know about that!, who would have thought it!, did you ever!, can it be!, can such things be?, will wonders never cease!

919. UNASTONISHMENT

NOUNS 1. unastonishment, unamazement, awlessness, wonderlessness; expectation 537.

VERBS 2. accept, take for granted; not blink an eye, not turn a hair.

ADJS. 3. unastonished, unsurprised, unamazed, unastounded, undumfounded, unbewildered; undazzled, undazed; unawed, awless or aweless, wonderless; expecting, expected 537.9–12.

INTERJS. **4. no wonder!,** of course!, why not?, what would you think?, what would you expect?

920. SOCIABILITY

NOUNS **1. sociability,** sociality, sociableness, social-mindedness, **gregariousness, affability,** companionability; clubbability or clubability [coll.], clubbishness, clubbism; intimacy, familiarity; **friendliness** 925; **communicativeness** 552.4.

2. camaraderie, comradery, **good-fellowship.**

3. conviviality, joviality, jollity, gaiety or gayety, heartiness, cheer, good cheer.

4. social intercourse, intercourse, communication, communion, intercommunion, intercommunication, community, commerce, congress, converse, conversation, social relations.

5. association, consociation, **fellowship, companionship, company, society;** fraternization.

6. visit, call, **social call;** visiting, visitation; round of visits.

7. appointment, engagement, date [coll., U.S.], arrangement, interview; engagement book.

8. rendezvous, tryst, assignation, meeting, meet; trysting place, meeting place, place of assignation; assignation house; love nest [coll.].

9. social gathering, social, sociable [U.S.], social affair, affair, gathering, gettogether [coll.]; **reception,** at home or athome, salon, levee; soiree or soirée; matinee; conversazione [It.], conversation [18th cent.]; reunion, family reunion; wake.

10. party, entertainment, blowout [slang]; **festivity** 876.4; shindy, shindig [both slang, U.S.]; **ball** 877.2; stag, stag party [both coll.]; hen party [slang]; house party; housewarming, house-raising, infare [chiefly dial.], hanging of the crane; shower, donation party [U.S.]; surprise party; garden party, lawn party, fête champêtre [F.]; masquerade, masque, mask; coffee party, Kaffeeklatsch [Ger.]; cocktail party; smoker [coll.]; kettledrum [coll.].

11. tea, afternoon tea, five-o'clock tea, high tea; **tea party,** tea fight [slang], drum.

12. bee [U.S.], quilting bee, raising bee, spelling bee; husking bee, cornhusking, corn shucking, husking.

13. debut, coming out [coll.], presentation, coming-out party [coll.].

14. (sociable person) mixer, **good mixer** [both coll., U.S.].

VERBS **15. associate with,** assort with, sort with, consort with, **mingle with, mix with, touch elbows** or **shoulders with,** eat off the same trencher; **fraternize,** fellowship, join in fellowship; **keep company with,** bear one company, walk hand in hand with; join, take up with [coll.], tie up with [slang]; **flock together,** herd together, club together, clique or clique with [coll.], gang or mob up with [slang], hang around with [coll.], hunt or run in couples; chum, **chum with,** chum together [all coll.]; pal, pal with, pal up or around with [all slang].

16. visit, make or pay a visit, **call on** or **upon, drop in,** run in, look in, look one up, see, stop off or over [coll.], beat up one's quarters [coll.]; leave one's card.

ADJS. **17. sociable, social,** social-minded, **gregarious, affable; companionable,** companionate; clubbable or clubable [coll.], clubbish; **communicative** 552.9; **friendly** 925.14.

18. convivial, boon, free and easy, hailfellow-well-met; **jovial, jolly,** hearty, festive, gay.

19. intimate, familiar, cozy or cosy, chatty, tête-à-tête.

ADVS. **20. sociably,** socially, gregariously, affably; companionably, arm in arm, hand in hand.

921. UNSOCIABILITY

NOUNS **1. unsociability,** insociability, unsociableness, dissociability; **ungregariousness,** uncompanionability; **unfriendliness** 927; **uncommunicativeness** 611; self-sufficiency, self-containment.

2. aloofness, standoffishness, remoteness, distance; **coolness,** coldness, frigidity; inaccessibility, unapproachability.

3. seclusiveness, exclusiveness; seclusion 922.

VERBS **4. keep to oneself, stand aloof,** hold oneself aloof, keep one's distance, keep at a distance, keep in the background, retire, retire into the shade, creep into a corner.

ADJS. **5. unsociable,** insociable, dissociable, unsocial; **ungregarious,** nongregarious; **uncompanionable,** unclubbable or unclubable [coll.]; **unfriendly** 927.10; **uncommunicative** 611.6; close, snug; self-sufficient, self-contained.

6. aloof, standoffish, standoff, **distant,**

remote, removed; **cool**, cold, frigid; seclusive, exclusive; inaccessible, unapproachable.

922. SECLUSION

NOUNS 1. **seclusion**, reclusion, **retirement**, **withdrawal**, **retreat**, recess; sequestration, separation, detachment, apartness; **isolation**, "splendid isolation" [Sir William Goschen]; **privacy**, **secrecy**; rustication; isolationism [polit.].

2. **hermitism**, hermitry, eremitism, anchoritism.

3. **solitude**, solitariness, **aloneness**, loneness; **loneliness**, **lonesomeness**.

4. **forlornness**, **abandonment**, **desertion**, desolation; friendlessness, kithlessness, fatherlessness, motherlessness, homelessness; helplessness, defenselessness.

5. **recluse**, solitaire, solitary, solitudinarian; **shut-in** [U.S.]; **hermit**, eremite, anchorite, anchoret; santon, Marabout [both Moham.]; hermitess, anchoress, anchoretess; ascetic; closet cynic; stylite, pillarist, pillar saint; Hieronymite, Hieronymian; Diogenes, Timon of Athens, St. Simeon Stylites.

6. **stay-at-home**, **homebody**.

7. **isolationist** [polit.], seclusionist.

VERBS 8. **seclude oneself**, **go into seclusion**, **retire**, **go into retirement**, retire from the world, abandon or forsake the world, live in retirement, lead a retired life, lead a cloistered life, shut oneself up, live alone, live apart; stay at home; rusticate; take the veil.

ADJS. 9. **secluded**, **retired**, **withdrawn**; **isolated**, insular, **separate**, separated, **apart**, detached, removed; **remote**, **out-of-the-way**, in a backwater, out-of-the-world; **unfrequented**, unvisited.

10. **private**, privy, **secret**, **hidden**.

11. **recluse**, sequestered, cloistered, shut up or in; **hermitic(al)**, eremitic(al), hermitish; anchoritic(al); **stay-at-home**, domestic.

12. **solitary**, **alone**; **in solitude**, by oneself, all alone; **lonely**, **lonesome**, **lone**.

13. **forlorn**, lorn; **abandoned**, **forsaken**, **deserted**, **desolate**, Godforsaken [coll.]; friendless, unfriended, kithless, fatherless, motherless, homeless; helpless, defenseless.

ADVS. 14. **in seclusion**, **in retirement**, in retreat, in solitude; in privacy, in secrecy; "far from the madding crowd's ignoble strife" [Gray], "the world forgetting by the world forgot" [Pope].

923. HOSPITALITY, WELCOME

NOUNS 1. **hospitality**, hospitableness, receptiveness; **cordiality**, amiability, graciousness, **friendliness**, neighborliness; **generosity**, liberality, openheartedness; open door.

2. **welcome**, **reception**, *accueil* [F.]; hearty welcome, cordial ∼, hearty or warm reception, the glad hand [slang], open arms; embrace, hug.

3. **greetings**, **salutations**, salaams; **regards**, best wishes 934.8.

4. **greeting**, **salutation**, salute; **hail**, **hello**, how-do-you-do; accost, address; nod, bow, bob; curtsy 962.2; wave; handshake, hand-clasp; embrace, hug, kiss; smile, smile of recognition.

5. **host**, mine host; **hostess**, receptionist; landlord 807.2.

6. **guest**, visitor, visitant, **caller**, company (sing. or pl. [coll.]); frequenter, habitué; uninvited guest, gate crasher [coll.]; moocher, free loader [both slang].

VERBS 7. **receive**, **admit**, accept, take in, let in, open the door to; **be at home to**, have the latchstring out [U.S.], keep a light in the window, put out the welcome mat, keep the door open, keep an open house.

8. **entertain**, entertain guests; preside, do the honors [coll.]; give a party, throw a party [slang]; spread oneself [coll.].

9. **welcome**, make welcome, **bid one welcome**, hold out the hand, extend the right hand of friendship; **embrace**, **hug**, receive with open arms; give a warm reception to, kill the fatted calf.

10. **greet**, **hail**, **accost**, address; salute, make one's salutations; **bid or say hello**, bid good day, ∼ good morning, etc.; exchange greetings, **pass the time of day**; **give one's regards** 934.13; shake hands, shake [slang], press or squeeze one's hand; nod to, bow to, move to [dial., Eng.]; curtsy 962.6; tip the hat to, lift the hat, touch the hat or cap; take one's hat off to, uncover; pull the forelock; kiss, greet with a kiss, kiss hands or cheeks.

ADJS. 11. **hospitable**, **receptive**, welcoming; **cordial**, amiable, gracious, **friendly**, neighborly; **open**, openhearted; **generous**, liberal.

12. **welcome**, welcome as the roses in May; **agreeable**, desirable, acceptable; **grateful**, gratifying, pleasing.

ADVS. 13. **hospitably**, with open arms.

INTERJS. 14. **welcome!**, *bienvenu!* [F.]; glad to see you!, proud to see you! [dial.,

U.S.]; come in!, make yourself at home!, light and rest your saddle! [South. U.S.]; you are welcome!, don't mention it!

15. greetings!, salutations!, cheerio! [esp. Eng.], aloha! [Hawaiian], banzai! [Jap.]; hello!, hullo!; hail!, heigh!, hi!; how do you do!, how are you!, comment allez-vous! [F.]; good day!, good morning!, bon jour! [Fr.]; good afternoon!, good evening!, bon soir! [Fr.].

16. (colloquialisms) howdy!, howdy-do!, how-de-do!, how-do-ye-do!, how-d'ye-do!, hi ya!; how's things?, how's tricks?, how goes it?, how's every little thing?, how's the world treating you?

924. INHOSPITALITY

NOUNS 1. inhospitality, inhospitableness, unhospitableness, unreceptiveness; uncordialness, ungraciousness, unfriendliness, unneighborliness.

2. ostracism, ostracization; banishment 308.4; proscription, ban; boycott, boycottage; blackball, black list.

3. outcast, social outcast, outcast of society, castaway, derelict, Ishmael, Cagot [F.]; pariah, untouchable [India], leper; outcaste [India], déclassé [F.]; outlaw, proscrit [F.]; expelee, evict [coll., Eng.], evictee, evacuee, évacué [F.]; displaced person, D.P.; exile, expatriate, man without a country.

VERBS 4. have nothing to do with, have no truck with [coll. & dial.], refuse to associate with, steer clear of [coll.], spurn, turn one's back upon; deny oneself to, refuse to receive, not be at home to; shut the door upon, sport one's oak [Univ. slang, Eng.].

5. ostracize, disfellowship; banish 308.16; proscribe, ban, outlaw, put under the ban; boycott, blackball, black-list, draw up or sign a round robin.

ADJS. 6. inhospitable, unhospitable; unreceptive, closed; uncordial, ungracious, unfriendly, unneighborly.

7. unwelcome, unwanted; unagreeable, undesirable, unacceptable; uninvited, unasked, unbidden.

8. outcast, castoff, castaway, derelict; outside the pale, outside the gates; rejected, disowned; abandoned, forsaken 922.13.

925. FRIENDSHIP

NOUNS 1. friendship, friendliness; amicability, amicableness, amity, peaceableness, unhostility; amiability, amiableness,

congeniality, well-affectedness; neighborliness, neighborlikeness; sociability 920; love 929.

2. fellowship, companionship, comradeship, colleagueship, chumship [coll.], palship [slang], consortship; brotherhood, fraternity, fraternalism, sodality, confraternity; sisterhood, sorority; brotherliness, sisterliness; community of interest, esprit de corps [F., common spirit].

3. good terms, good understanding, good footing, friendly relations; harmony, rapport 792; favor, good will, good graces, favorable regard, the good or right side of [coll.]; stand-in, in [both slang].

4. acquaintance, acquaintedness; introduction, presentation, knockdown [slang].

5. familiarity, intimacy, closeness, nearness, thickness [coll.]; chumminess [coll.], palliness [slang].

6. cordiality, geniality, heartiness, ardency, warmness, warmheartedness.

7. devotion, devotedness; fastness, firmness, stanchness, staunchness; triedness, trueness, tried-and-trueness.

8. cordial friendship, warm or ardent friendship, devoted friendship, bosom friendship, intimate or familiar friendship, sincere friendship, beautiful friendship, fast or firm friendship, stanch or staunch friendship, loyal friendship, lasting friendship.

VERBS 9. be friends, have the friendship of, have the ear of; know, be acquainted with; associate with 920.15; cotton to, hit it off [both coll.]; be on good terms, stand in or in with [coll.]; keep on good terms, keep or hold in with [coll.].

10. make friends with, gain the friendship of, strike up a friendship, strike up with [coll.], take up with [coll.], shake or strike hands with, put one's horses together; get acquainted, make or scrape acquaintance with, pick up an acquaintance with; get chummy with [coll.], buddy up [slang]; win friends, win friends and influence people.

11. cultivate, cultivate the friendship of, court, pay court to, pay addresses to, seek the company of, run after [coll.], shine up to, make up to [coll.], play up to [slang], hold out or extend the right of friendship or fellowship; make advances, approach, break the ice.

12. get on good terms with, get into favor, get in the good graces of, get in good with, get in with [coll.], get on the in

with [slang], get next to [coll.], **get on the good** or **right side of** [coll.].

13. **introduce, present, acquaint,** make acquainted, give an introduction, give a knockdown [slang], do the honors [coll.].

ADJS. 14. **friendly,** friendlike; **amicable, peaceable,** unhostile; **harmonious** 792.3; **amiable, congenial,** pleasant, agreeable, favorable, **well-affected,** well-disposed, well-intentioned, well-meaning, well-meant; brotherly, fraternal; sisterly; neighborly, neighborlike; sociable 920.17.

15. **cordial, genial,** hearty, ardent, warm, warmhearted.

16. **friends with,** friendly with, at home with; acquainted.

17. **on good terms,** on a good footing, on friendly or amicable terms, **on speaking terms,** in visiting terms, on borrowing terms [joc.]; **in good with,** in with [coll.], on the in with [slang], in [slang, U.S.], **in favor, in one's good graces,** in one's good books, on the good or right side of [coll.].

18. **familiar, intimate,** close, near, on familiar or intimate terms; hand-in-hand, hand and glove; thick, **thick as thieves** [both coll.].

19. **chummy** [coll.]; pally, palsy, palsy-walsy, buddy-buddy [all slang].

20. **devoted, fast,** firm, stanch, staunch; tried, true, **tried and true.**

ADVS. 21. **amicably,** friendly, friendliwise; **amiably, congenially,** pleasantly, agreeably, favorably; **cordially, genially,** heartily, ardently, warmly, with open arms; familiarly, intimately; arm in arm, hand in hand.

926. FRIEND

NOUNS 1. **friend, acquaintance,** sympathizer, amigo [S. West. U.S.]; **confident,** confidant [masc.], confidante [fem.], repository; **intimate,** familiar, **close friend,** intimate or familiar friend; **bosom friend,** friend of one's bosom; best friend; alter ego [L.], other self; brother; neighbor; casual acquaintance, pickup [coll.].

2. "another I" [Zeno], "a second self" [Cicero], "a single soul dwelling in two bodies" [Aristotle], "a person with whom I may be sincere" [Emerson], "a person with whom you dare to be yourself" [Frank Crane], "one who knows your faults, yet loves you in spite of your virtues" [anon.].

3. **good friend, devoted friend,** warm or ardent friend, **faithful friend,** trusted or trusty friend, fidus Achates [L., faithful

Achates], constant friend, stanch or staunch friend, fast friend, "a friend that sticketh closer than brother" [Bible]; **friend in need,** friend indeed, jack-at-a-pinch.

4. **companion, fellow,** fellow companion, **comrade,** camarade [F.], **mate,** comate, company, **associate,** consociate, compeer, confrere, consort, **colleague, partner,** pardner [slang, chiefly U.S.], pard [slang, U.S.], copartner, side-partner, **sidekick** or sidekicker [slang, U.S.], **crony,** old crony, **chum** [coll.], **buddy** [coll.], **pal** [slang], billy [chiefly dial.]; **roommate,** chamberfellow, bedfellow, bedmate, bunkie [coll., U.S.]; **schoolmate,** schoolfellow, classmate, classfellow, school companion, school chum, fellow student or pupil; **playmate,** playfellow; **teammate,** yokefellow, yokemate; workfellow 785.5; shipmate; messmate.

5. **boon companion,** boonfellow; **good fellow,** jolly fellow, hearty, bon vivant [F.]; pot companion.

6. **fellow man, fellow creature,** fellow being, fellow mortal, fellow sufferer.

7. **friends,** two of a kind, birds of a feather, "two bodies with one soul inspired" [Homer]; inseparable friends, inseparables.

8. (famous friendships) Achilles and Patroclus, Castor and Pollux, Damon and Pythias, David and Jonathan, Diomedes and Sthenelus, Epaminondas and Pelopidas, Hercules and Iolaus, Nisus and Euryalus, Pylades and Orestes, Theseus and Pirithoüs, Christ and the beloved disciple; The Three Musketeers, Soldiers Three.

PHRS. 9. a friend in need is a friend indeed, "thank God for a trusty chum!" [Kipling].

927. ENMITY

NOUNS 1. **enmity, unfriendliness,** inimicality; **uncordiality,** unamiability, ungeniality; coolness, coldness, chilliness, chill, frost; hatred 928.

2. **disaccord** 793; alienation, estrangement 793.4.

3. **hostility, antagonism, repugnance,** antipathy; conflict, collision, clash, clashing.

4. **animosity,** animus, ambition [dial.]; ill will, ill feeling, **hard feelings; bad blood,** ill blood, feud; **bitterness, rancor,** acrimony, virulence, venom, vitriol.

5. **grudge,** crow to pick, ~ pluck or pull, bone to pick; peeve, pet peeve [both coll.].

6. **enemy, foe,** foeman, **adversary,** an-

tagonist, Philistine; bitter enemy; sworn
enemy; open enemy; public enemy; archenemy, devil; "my nearest and dearest
enemy" [Middleton].

VERBS 7. antagonize, set against, set at
odds; provoke, envenom, embitter, infuriate, madden; alienate, estrange 793.15.

8. disagree, fall out, quarrel 793.9–14.

9. bear ill will, bear malice, have it in
for [coll.], hold it against, be down on
[coll.]; bear a grudge, owe a grudge, have
a bone to pick with; have a crow to pick,
~ pluck or pull with, have a rod in pickle.

ADJS. 10. unfriendly, inimical, unamicable; uncordial, unamiable, ungenial; cool,
cold, chill, chilly, frosty; unsociable 921.5.

11. hostile, antagonistic, repugnant, an-
tipathetic(al), set against; virulent, bitter.

12. alienated, estranged, disaffected,
separated, divided, disunited, torn; irreconcilable.

13. at outs, on the outs [coll.], at enmity, at variance, at odds, at loggerheads,
at daggers drawn.

14. on bad terms, not on speaking
terms; in bad with [coll.], in bad odor with,
in one's bad or black books.

ADVS. 15. unamicably, inimically; uncordially, unamiably, ungenially; coolly,
coldly, chillily, frostily; hostilely, antagonistically.

928. HATE

NOUNS 1. hate, hatred; dislike 865; detestation, abhorrence, aversion, antipathy,
loathing, execration, abomination, odium;
vials of hate or wrath.

2. enmity 927; bitterness, animosity 927.4.

3. (detested thing) anathema, abomination, detestation, aversion, abhorrence,
antipathy, execration.

VERBS 4. hate, detest, loathe, abhor,
execrate, abominate, hold in abomination,
take an aversion to, shudder at, utterly detest.

5. dislike, disrelish 865.4.

ADJS. 6. abhorrent, loathing; averse to
865.8; disgusted 864.23.

7. hateful, detestable 862.9; unlikable
865.9.

929. LOVE

NOUNS 1. love, amor, affection, attachment, devotion; fondness, like, liking,
fancy, shine [slang, U.S.]; passion, tender
feeling or passion, ardor, ardency, fervor,
heart, flame; adoration, worship; regard,
admiration; idolatry, idolization, idolism;
popular regard, popularity; faithful love,
truelove; free love, free-lovism; love-making
930.

2. "an insatiate thirst of enjoying a
greedily desired object" [Montaigne], "the
heart's immortal thirst to be completely
known and all forgiven" [Henry Van
Dyke], "the fulfilling of the law" [Bible],
"the reflection of a man's own worthiness
from other men" [Emerson], "a spiritual
coupling of two souls" [Ben Jonson], "two
souls with but a single thought, two hearts
that beat as one" [Bellinghausen], "what
makes the world go round, with that worried expression" [Fred Allen].

3. amorousness, lovingness; affection,
affectionateness, demonstrativeness; romanticism, sentimentality; lovesickness,
lovelornness.

4. infatuation, infatuatedness, passing
fancy; crush, mash, pash, case [all slang];
puppy love, calf love [both coll.].

5. parental love, natural affection,
storge [Gr.], mother or maternal love,
father or paternal love.

6. love affair, affair, amour, romance,
liaison, entanglement, intrigue; flirtation;
triangle, eternal triangle.

7. lovability, likability, adorability,
sweetness, loveliness, lovesomeness; charm,
appeal; winsomeness, winning ways.

8. Love, Cupid [Rom.], Amor [Rom.],
Eros [Gr.], Kama [Hindu]; Venus [Rom.],
Aphrodite [Gr.], Astarte [Phoenician],
Freya [Norse].

9. cupid, cupidon, amor, amourette,
amoretto, amorino [It.].

10. sweetheart, sweetie [coll.], sweet
patootie [slang, U.S.]; honey, etc. (terms
of endearment) 930.5; date [coll., U.S.];
steady [slang, U.S.]; conquest, catch, captive.

11. lover, admirer, adorer, amorist, infatuate, paramour; suitor, wooer, courter,
sparker [dial. & slang, U.S.], pursuer, follower; inamorato, beau, swain, man, gallant, cavalier, squire, esquire, caballero
[Span.]; amoroso, cavalier servente [both
It.]; boy friend, fellow, young man, flame,
spark [all coll.]; love-maker; spooner, petter, necker [all slang]; Lothario, Casanova,
Romeo, Don Juan.

12. loved one, love, beloved, darling,
dear, dear one, dearly beloved, well-beloved, truelove, beloved object, object of
one's affections, light of one's eye or life;

crush; inamorata, *amorosa* [It.], ladylove, lady, mistress, girl [coll.], girl friend [coll.], best girl [coll.], lass, lassie, jo [Scot.], gill, jil, Jill, Dulcinea.

13. favorite, preference; darling, idol, jewel, apple of one's eye, man after one's own heart; pet, fondling, cosset; spoiled child or darling, *enfant gâté* [F.]; teacher's pet; matinée idol.

14. soulmate, affinity, spiritual affinity.

15. fiancé [*masc.*], fiancée [*fem.*], affianced, betrothed, future, intended [coll.].

16. loving couple, lovebirds, turtledoves, bill-and-cooers; Romeo and Juliet, Antony and Cleopatra, Pelléas and Mélisande, Abélard and Héloïse, Daphnis and Chloë, Aucassin and Nicolette.

VERBS 17. love, be fond of, be in love with, care for, like, fancy, have a fancy for, have eyes for [coll.], go for [slang], take an interest in, dote on *or* upon, be sweet upon [coll.]; have a crush ~, mash *or* case on [all slang]; be desperately in love, have it bad [slang].

18. hold dear, cherish, prize, treasure; admire, regard, esteem, revere; adore, idolize, worship, dearly love, think worlds *or* the world of, love to distraction.

19. fall in love, fall for [slang], lose one's heart, become enamored, be smitten [coll.]; take to, take a liking *or* fancy to, take a shine to [slang, U.S.], cotton to [coll.], become attached to; fall head and ears *or* head over heels in love, be swept off one's feet.

20. enamor, endear; win one's heart, win the love *or* affections of, take the fancy of, make a hit with [slang]; charm, becharm, infatuate, fascinate, attract, allure, captivate, bewitch, enrapture, carry away, turn one's head, inflame with love; seduce, vamp [slang], draw on, tempt, tantalize.

ADJS. 21. beloved, loved, dear, darling, precious; pet, favorite; adored, admired, esteemed, revered; cherished, prized, treasured, held dear; well-liked, popular; well-beloved, dearly beloved, dear to one's heart, after one's heart *or* own heart, dear as the apple of one's eye.

22. lovable, likable *or* likeable, adorable, admirable, lovely, lovesome, sweet, winning, winsome; charming 648.7; angelic, seraphic(al); caressable, kissable; cuddlesome, cuddly.

23. amorous, amatory, erotic; loverly, loverlike; passionate, ardent, impassioned.

24. loving, lovesome; fond, adoring, devoted, affectionate, demonstrative, romantic, sentimental, tender, soft [coll.], spoony [slang]; lovelorn, lovesick, languishing.

25. enamored, charmed, becharmed, fascinated, captivated, bewitched, enraptured; infatuated, infatuate; smitten, badly smitten [both coll.]; heartsmitten, bitten [coll.]; hard hit [slang], far-gone [coll.].

26. in love, head over heels in love, over head and ears in love.

27. fond of, enamored of, partial to, sweet on *or* upon [coll.], mashed on [slang]; stuck on [slang], in love with, attached to, wedded to, devoted to, wrapped up in; taken with, smitten with [coll.], struck with; gone on *or* upon, far gone on *or* upon, hipped on, keen about *or* over, wild about, mad about, crazy over *or* about [all coll.]; nuts about [slang].

ADVS. 28. lovingly, fondly, affectionately, tenderly, dearly, adoringly, devotedly; amorously, ardently, passionately; with love, with affection, with all one's love.

930. LOVE-MAKING, ENDEARMENT

NOUNS 1. love-making, dalliance, billing and cooing; spooning [slang], petting [coll.], necking [slang]; fondling, caressing, hugging, kissing; cuddling, snuggling, nestling, nuzzling; bundling; coition 168.3.

2. hug, embrace, squeeze, clasp, fold, enfoldment, infoldment, accolade; bear hug [coll.].

3. kiss, buss, smack, smooch [slang], osculation.

4. endearment; caress, pat; sweet talk, soft words, honeyed words, sweet nothings; blandishments, artful endearments.

5. (endearments) darling, dear, deary, sweetheart, sweetie, sweet, sweets, sweetkins, honey, honey bunch, honey child, sugar, love, lover, precious, precious heart, pet, petkins, babe, baby, cherub, angel, chick, chickabiddy, buttercup, duck, duckling, lamb, lambkin, snookums.

6. courtship, courting, wooing; court, suit, addresses; gallantry; serenade.

7. proposal, marriage proposal, offer of marriage; engagement 768.3.

8. flirtation, coquetry, dalliance; flirtatiousness, coquettishness, coyness; sheep's eyes, goo-goo eyes [slang, U.S.], amorous

looks, coquettish glances, come-hither look; ogle, side glance.

9. **philandering**, philander, lady-killing [slang].

10. **flirt, coquette,** gold digger [slang, U.S.], vamp [slang].

11. **philanderer**, philander, woman chaser, **ladies' man,** heartbreaker; **masher, lady-killer, wolf,** skirt chaser, man on the make, big-time operator [all slang].

12. **love letter,** billet-doux, mash note [slang]; valentine.

VERBS 13. **make love,** bill and coo; **spoon** [slang], **pet** [coll.], **neck** [slang], smooch [slang]; dally, toy, trifle, wanton; sweet-talk [dial., U.S.], whisper sweet nothings; copulate 168.3.

14. **caress, pet,** pat; **fondle,** dandle, coddle, cocker, cosset; pat on the head or cheek, chuck under the chin.

15. **cuddle, snuggle, nestle,** nuzzle; lap; bundle.

16. **hug, embrace, clasp, press, squeeze** [coll.], fold, **enfold,** infold, bosom, embosom, put or throw one's arms around, take to one's arms, fold to the heart, press to the bosom.

17. **kiss, osculate,** buss, smack, smooch [slang]; blow a kiss.

18. **flirt, coquet; philander,** gallivant; **make eyes at, ogle,** eye, cast coquettish glances, **cast sheep's eyes at,** make googoo eyes at [slang, U.S.], faire les yeux doux [F., make sweet eyes], look sweet upon [coll.].

19. **court, woo,** caterwaul [derog.], sue, press one's suit, **pay court** or **suit to,** make suit to, pay one's court to, address, pay one's addresses to, pay attentions to, set up to [dial.], lay siege to; **pursue,** follow; chase, hustle [both slang, U.S.]; set one's cap at or for [coll.]; serenade.

20. **spark** [coll.], squire, esquire, beau, sweetheart [coll.], swain.

21. **go with,** go together, **keep company;** take out, date [coll., U.S.].

22. **propose, pop the question** [coll.], ask for one's hand; become engaged 768.6.

ADJS. 23. **flirtatious, flirty; coquettish,** coy.

931. MARRIAGE

NOUNS 1. **marriage, matrimony, wedlock,** holy wedlock, match, union, matrimonial union, "a world-without-end bargain" [Shakespeare]; bond of matrimony, wedding knot, nuptial tie or knot; married

state or status, coverture, cohabitation; bed, marriage bed, bridebed; intermarriage, miscegenation; misalliance, mésalliance [F.], ill-assorted marriage.

2. (kinds of marriage) **monogamy,** monogyny, monandry; **bigamy,** digamy, deuterogamy; trigamy; **polygamy,** polygyny, polyandry; morganatic marriage, left-handed marriage; marriage of convenience, mariage de convenance [F.]; love match; levirate, leviration; companionate marriage, trial marriage; common-law marriage; concubinage.

3. **marriageability,** nubility, concubitancy.

4. **wedding, marriage,** espousement, bridal, hymen; **nuptials,** spousals, espousals, hymeneal rites; wedding song, marriage song, nuptial song, epithalamy, epithalamium, hymen, hymeneal; wedding veil, saffron veil or robe; bridechamber, bridal suite, nuptial apartment; **honeymoon.**

5. wedding attendant, usher; **best man,** bridesman, groomsman; **bridesmaid,** bridemaiden, maid or matron of honor.

6. **newlywed; bridegroom, groom; bride,** plighted bride, blushing bride; war bride, G.I. bride [slang, U.S.]; honeymooner.

7. **spouse, mate,** yokemate, partner, consort, **better half** [joc.], "bone of my bones, and flesh of my flesh" [Bible].

8. **husband, married man,** man, benedict, goodman [arch. or dial.], old man [joc.]; cuckold.

9. **wife, married woman,** wedded wife, goodwife [arch. or dial.], squaw [Indian], woman, lady [obs. or uncultivated], matron, old woman [joc.], feme, feme covert [law], gray mare [slang], **better half, helpmate,** helpmeet, rib [dial. & joc.], wife of one's bosom; concubine, common-law wife; bachelor's wife, Coeleb's wife.

10. **married couple,** wedded pair, **man and wife,** husband and wife, man and woman, vir et uxor [L.]; newlyweds, **bride and groom.**

11. **harem, seraglio,** serai, gynaeceum; zenana, purdah [both India].

12. **miscegenator,** miscegenist; **monogamist,** monogynist; **bigamist,** digamist, deuterogamist; trigamist; **polygamist,** polygynist, polyandrist; Mormon, Turk, Bluebeard.

13. **matchmaker, marriage broker,** matrimonial agent, schatchen [Yiddish]; matrimonial agency or bureau.

14. (god of marriage) Hymen, Hera,

Teleia [all Gr.]; Juno, Pronuba [Rom.], Frigg [Norse].

VERBS 15. (join in marriage) **marry, wed,** nuptial, **join, unite, hitch** [slang], **splice** [coll.], couple, match, join together, **unite in marriage,** join or unite in holy wedlock, tie the nuptial or wedding knot, make one; give away, give in marriage; publish ∼, proclaim or bid the banns.

16. (get married) **marry, wed,** contract matrimony, espouse, wive, **take to wife,** take to oneself a wife, **get hitched** [slang], be spliced [coll.], become one, be made one, pair off, go off [coll.], give one's hand to, bestow one's hand upon, lead to the hymeneal altar, be asked in church, take for better or for worse; remarry, rewed; intermarry, interwed, miscegenate.

17. **honeymoon,** go on a honeymoon.

18. **cohabit,** live together, live as man and wife, share one's bed and board.

ADJS 19. **matrimonial, marital, conjugal, connubial, nuptial,** wedded, married, hymeneal; epithalamic; spousal, husbandly, wifely; bridal.

20. **monogamous,** monogynous, monandrous; **bigamous,** digamous; **polygamous,** polygynous, polyandrous; morganatic; miscegenetic.

21. **marriageable,** nubile, concubitous.

22. **married, wedded,** one, one bone and one flesh.

932. CELIBACY

NOUNS 1. **celibacy,** singleness, single blessedness; **bachelorhood,** bachelorship; **spinsterhood,** maidenhood, maidenhead, virginity; **monasticism,** monachism; misogamy, misogyny.

2. **celibate,** célibataire [F.]; monk, monastic; misogamist, misogynist.

3. **bachelor,** bach [slang], single man, lone wolf [coll.].

4. **spinster,** spinstress, **old maid,** maid, maiden, bachelor girl, single woman, lone woman, feme sole [law]; **virgin,** vestal, vestal virgin.

VERBS 5. **live alone,** enjoy single blessedness, bach or bach it [slang], keep bachelor quarters.

ADJS. 6. **celibate; monastic,** monachal, monkish; misogamic, misogynous.

7. **unmarried, unwedded,** unwed, **single,** sole [law], spouseless, wifeless, husbandless; **bachelorly,** bachelorlike; **spinsterly,** spinsterish, spinsterlike; **old-maidish,** old-

maidenish, maiden, maidenly; virgin, virginal.

933. DIVORCE, WIDOWHOOD

NOUNS 1. **divorce,** divorcement, **separation,** judicial separation, separate maintenance.

2. **divorcee,** divorcé [masc.], divorcée [fem.].

3. **widowhood,** viduage, viduation; **widowerhood,** widowership; grasswidowhood; weeds, widow's weeds.

4. **widow,** widow woman [chiefly dial.], relict; dowager, queen dowager, etc.; **widower,** widowman [dial.]; grass widow, grass widower.

VERBS 5. **divorce, separate,** part, split up [coll.], unmarry, put away, obtain a divorce, come to a parting of the ways.

6. **widow,** bereave.

ADJS. 7. widowly, widowish, widowlike; widowed, widowered.

934. COURTESY

NOUNS 1. **courtesy,** courteousness, **politeness, civility,** amenity, urbanity, comity, affability; **graciousness,** gracefulness; complaisance, complacency; respect, respectfulness, deference.

2. **gallantry,** gallantness, **chivalry,** chivalrousness, knightliness, courtliness, courtly politeness, noblesse oblige [F.].

3. **mannerliness, manners, good manners,** good or polite deportment, bienséance [F.]; savoir-faire [F.], savoir-vivre [F.].

4. **breeding, good breeding; refinement,** polish, culture, cultivation; **gentility,** gentleness, genteelness, elegance; gentlemanliness, gentlemanlikeness, ladylikeness.

5. **suavity, suaveness, smoothness, smugness, blandness, unctuousness,** oiliness, **glibness,** mealymouthedness, fulsomeness, prévenance [F.]; fair words, soft words, sweet or honeyed words, incense; soft sawder, soft soap, butter [all coll.].

6. **a courtesy, civility,** amenity, urbanity, attention, polite act, act of courtesy or politeness; favor 936.7.

7. **amenities, civilities,** gentilities, elegancies.

8. **regards, compliments, respects,** égards [F.], devoirs [F.]; **best wishes, good** wishes, best regards, kind regards; love, best love; greetings 923.3; remembrances, kind remembrances; compliments of the season.

9. **gallant, cavalier,** chevalier, knight, "a verray parfit gentil knight" [Chaucer].

10. "the very pink of courtesy" [Shakespeare], "the very pine-apple of politeness" [Sheridan], "the mirror of all courtesy" [Shakespeare].

VERBS 11. mind one's manners, mind one's P's and Q's [coll.]; keep a civil tongue in one's mouth; mend one's manners.

12. pay one's respects to, make one's compliments to, present oneself, pay attentions to, do service, wait on or upon.

13. give one's regards, give one's compliments, give one's love, give one's best regards, give one's best, send one's regards, ~ compliments, etc.; wish one joy, wish one luck, bid Godspeed; send compliments of the season, wish many happy returns of the day, wish a merry Christmas and a happy New Year.

ADJS. 14. courteous, polite, civil, urbane, gracious, graceful, affable, fair; complaisant, complacent; obliging, accommodating; respectful, deferential, attentive, ceremonious.

15. gallant, courtly, chivalrous, chivalric, knightly.

16. mannerly, well-mannered, good-mannered, well-behaved, well-spoken.

17. well-bred, highbred, well-brought-up; cultivated, cultured, polished, refined, genteel, gentle; gentlemanly, gentlemanlike, ladylike.

18. suave, smooth, smug, bland, glib, unctuous, oily, soapy [coll.], buttery [coll.], fulsome, ingratiating; suave-spoken, fine-spoken, fair-spoken, soft-spoken, smooth-spoken, smooth-tongued, oily-tongued, honey-tongued, honey-mouthed, mealy-mouthed.

ADVS. 19. courteously, politely, civilly, urbanely, mannerly; gallantly, chivalrously, courtly, knightly; graciously, gracefully, with a good grace; complaisantly, complacently; obligingly, accommodatingly; respectfully, attentively, deferentially.

935. DISCOURTESY

NOUNS 1. discourtesy, discourteousness; impoliteness, unpoliteness; rudeness, incivility, inurbanity, ungraciousness, ungallantness, uncourtliness, ungentlemanliness, unmannerliness, ill breeding, bad or ill manners, conduct unbecoming a gentleman.

2. disrespectfulness 963; insolence 911.

3. gruffness, brusqueness, brusquerie [F.], curtness, shortness, sharpness, abrupt-

ness, bluntness, brashness; harshness, roughness, severity; surliness, crustiness, bearishness, churlishness.

ADJS. 4. discourteous, uncourteous; impolite, unpolite; rude, "rude and scant of courtesy" [Scott]; uncivil, ungracious, ungallant, uncourtly, inaffable, uncomplaisant, unaccommodating; disrespectful 963.5; insolent 911.8.

5. unmannerly, unmannered, mannerless, ill-mannered, ill-behaved, ill-conditioned.

6. ill-bred, ungenteel, ungentle, caddish; ungentlemanly, ungentlemanlike; unladylike, unfeminine; vulgar, boorish, unrefined 896.10−13.

7. gruff, brusque, curt, short, sharp, snippy [coll.], abrupt, blunt, bluff, brash, cavalier; harsh, rough, severe; surly, crusty, bearish, churlish.

ADVS. 8. discourteously, impolitely, rudely, uncivilly, ungraciously, ungallantly, ungenteelly.

936. KINDNESS, BENEVOLENCE

NOUNS 1. kindness, kindliness; benignity, benignancy; goodness, niceness; graciousness; kindheartedness, warmheartedness, softheartedness, tenderheartedness, goodness or warmth of heart, loving-kindness, milk of human kindness.

2. good nature, good humor, good disposition, good temper, sweet temper, good-naturedness, good-humoredness, good-temperedness, bonhomie or bonhommie; amiability, affability, geniality, cordiality; gentleness, mildness.

3. considerateness, consideration, thoughtfulness, mindfulness, heedfulness, regardfulness, attentiveness, solicitousness, solicitude, thought, regard, concern, delicacy; indulgence, toleration; complaisance, complacency; accommodatingness, obligingness, agreeableness.

4. benevolence, benevolentness, beneficence, charity, charitableness, philanthropy; altruism, philanthropism, humanitarianism, welfarism, do-goodism, "the luxury of doing good" [Goldsmith]; good will, grace, brotherly love, Christian charity or love, good will to or toward man; bigheartedness, largeheartedness, great-heartedness; generosity 851; giving 816.

5. welfare; welfare work, social service, social work; child welfare, etc.; commonweal or common weal, public welfare.

6. benevolences, philanthropies, charities; works, good works.

7. favor, kindness, benefit, benefaction, benevolence, benignity, blessing, service, turn, good turn, good or kind deed, office, good or kind offices, obligation, grace, act of grace, courtesy, *beau geste* [Fr., graceful gesture], act of kindness, kindly act, labor of love.

8. philanthropist, altruist, benevolist, humanitarian, do-gooder, well-doer, power for good; welfare worker, social worker; almsgiver, almoner; Robin Hood.

9. a friend of or to man, "the friend of man, to vice alone a foe" [Burns], "little friend of all the world" [Kipling], "friend to the friendless, to the sick man health" [Coleridge], "one who loves his fellowmen" [Hunt].

VERBS 10. be kind, be good or nice to, show kindness to; treat well, do right by; favor, oblige, accommodate.

11. be considerate, consider, respect, regard, think of, be thoughtful of, have consideration or regard for.

12. be benevolent, bear good will, wish well, have one's heart in the right place; practice the Golden Rule, do as you would be done by, do unto others as you would have them do unto you.

13. do good, do a favor, do a kindness, do a good turn, do a good or kind deed, render a service, confer a benefit; benefit, help ⁻83.11.

ADJS. 14. kind, kindly; benign, benignant; good, nice, boon [poetic]; gracious; kindhearted, warmhearted, softhearted, tenderhearted, tender; sympathetic, sympathizing; brotherly, fraternal; humane, human; Christian, Christly, Christlike.

15. good-natured, well-natured, good-humored, good-tempered, sweet-tempered; amiable, affable, genial, cordial, clever [coll., U.S.]; gentle, mild; easy to get along with.

16. benevolent, beneficent, charitable, philanthropic(al), altruistic, humanitarian; bighearted, largehearted, greathearted, freehearted; generous 851.4; almsgiving, eleemosynary.

17. considerate, thoughtful, mindful, heedful, regardful, solicitous, attentive, delicate, mindful of others; complaisant, complacent; accommodating, accommodative, obliging, indulgent, agreeable.

18. well-meaning, well-meant, well-affected, well-disposed, well-intentioned.

ADVS. 19. kindly, benignly, benignantly; good, nicely, well; kindheartedly, warmheartedly, softheartedly, tenderheartedly; humanely, humanly.

20. good-naturedly, good-humoredly; amiably, affably, genially, cordially; graciously, in good part.

21. benevolently, beneficently, charitably, philanthropically, altruistically, bigheartedly, with good will.

22. considerately, thoughtfully, mindfully, heedfully, regardfully, solicitously, attentively.

937. UNKINDNESS, MALEVOLENCE

NOUNS 1. unkindness, unkindliness; unbenignity, unbenignness; unamiability, uncordiality, ungraciousness, ungeniality; unsympatheticness, uncompassionateness.

2. unbenevolentness, uncharitableness, ungenerousness.

3. inconsiderateness, inconsideration, unthoughtfulness, unmindfulness, unheedfulness, thoughtlessness, heedlessness, respectlessness, disregardfulness, forgetfulness.

4. malevolence, ill will, ill nature, ill-disposedness; evil eye, blighting glance.

5. malice, maliciousness, maleficence; malignance or malignancy, malignity; meanness [coll.], orneriness [coll. or dial.], hatefulness, invidiousness; deviltry, devilry, devilment; malice prepense or aforethought, evil intent.

6. spite, despite; spitefulness, cattiness.

7. virulence, rancor, venomousness, venom, vitriol, gall.

8. causticity, mordancy, mordacity; acrimony, asperity, acridity, acerbity, bitterness, tartness; sharpness, keenness, incisiveness, trenchancy; "sharp-toothed unkindness" [Shakespeare].

9. harshness, roughness; severity, austerity, hardness, sternness, grimness, inclemency; stringency, astringency.

10. heartlessness, unfeeling, unnaturalness; coldness, coldheartedness, coldbloodedness; hardheartedness, hardness, hardness of heart, heart of stone; callousness, callosity; obduracy; unmercifulness 943.

11. cruelty, cruelness, ruthlessness 943.1; inhumanity; brutality, brutalness, brutishness, bestiality; barbarity, barbarousness; savagery, viciousness, violence, fiendishness, truculence; fierceness, ferociousness,

ferocity; bloodthirst, bloodthirstiness, cannibalism.

12. (brutal act) cruelty, brutality, barbarity, inhumanity.

13. disservice, ill service, ill turn, bad turn.

ADJS. 14. unkind, unkindly, ill; unbenign, unbenignant; unamiable, uncordial, ungracious, ungenial; unsympathetic, unsympathizing; uncompassionate, uncompassioned.

15. unbenevolent, unbeneficent, uncharitable, unphilanthropic(al), unaltruistic, ungenerous.

16. inconsiderate, unthoughtful, unmindful, unheedful, disregardful, thoughtless, heedless, respectless, mindless, unthinking, forgetful; uncomplaisant, uncomplacent; unaccommodating, unobliging, disobliging.

17. malevolent, ill-disposed, evil-disposed, ill-natured, ill-affected, ill-conditioned, ill-intentioned.

18. malicious, maleficent, malefic; malignant, malign; mean [coll.], ornery [coll. or dial.], hateful, invidious.

19. spiteful, despiteful; catty, cattish.

20. virulent, rancorous, vitriolic; venomous, envenomed.

21. caustic, mordant, mordacious, corrosive; acrimonious, acrid, acid, acerbic, bitter, tart; sharp, keen, incisive, trenchant, cutting, penetrating, piercing, biting, stinging, stabbing, scathing, scorching, withering.

22. harsh, rough, rugged; severe, austere, stringent, astringent, hard, stern, dour [Scot.], grim, inclement, unsparing.

23. heartless, unfeeling, unnatural; cold, cold of heart, coldhearted, coldblooded; hard, hardened, hard of heart, hardhearted, stonyhearted, marblehearted, flinthearted; callous, calloused; obdurate; unmerciful 943.3.

24. cruel, cruel-hearted; ruthless 943.3; brutal, brutish, brute, bestial; barbarous, barbaric; savage, ferocious, vicious, fierce, atrocious, truculent, fell; inhumane, inhuman, unhuman; fiendish, fiendlike; demoniac(al), diabolic(al), devilish, satanic, hellish, infernal; bloodthirsty, bloody-minded; murderous 408.24; Draconian, Tartarean.

ADVS. 25. unkindly, ill; unbenignly, unbenignantly; unamiably, uncordially, ungraciously, ungenially; unsympathetically, uncompassionately.

26. unbenevolently, unbeneficently, uncharitably, unphilanthropically, unaltruistically, ungenerously.

27. inconsiderately, unthoughtfully, thoughtlessly, heedlessly, unthinkingly.

28. maliciously, malevolently, maleficently, malignantly, meanly [coll.], ornerily [coll. or dial.], hatefully; spitefully, in spite; with bad intent, with malice prepense or aforethought.

29. harshly, roughly; severely, austerely, stringently, sternly, grimly, inclemently, unsparingly.

30. heartlessly, callously, unfeelingly, coldheartedly; cold-bloodedly, in cold blood.

31. cruelly, brutally, brutishly, bestially; barbarously, savagely, ferociously, viciously, fiercely, atrociously, truculently; ruthlessly 943.4; inhumanely, inhumanly, unhumanly; fiendishly, diabolically, devilishly.

938. MISANTHROPY

NOUNS 1. misanthropy, misanthropism, cynicism, antisociality.

2. misanthrope, misanthropist; antisocialist, man-hater, cynic; misogynist, woman-hater.

ADJS. 3. misanthropic(al), antisocial, man-hating, cynical; misogynous, woman-hating; unpatriotic.

939. PUBLIC SPIRIT

NOUNS 1. public spirit, social consciousness; civism, citizenism.

2. patriotism, love of country; nationalism, nationality; Americanism, Anglicism, Briticism, etc.; chauvinism, jingoism, overpatriotism; patriotics, flag waving, flaggery [joc.]; spread eagle, spread-eagleism [both U.S.].

3. patriot, patriotess [fem.]; chauvin, jingo, chauvinist, jingoist; patrioteer [coll.], flag waver, spread-eagleist [coll., U.S.]; hundred-percenter, hundred-percent American; pay-roll patriot.

VERBS 4. patrioteer [coll.], spread-eagle, make the eagle scream [both coll., U.S.].

ADJS. 5. patriotic, nationalistic; overpatriotic, flag-waving, spread-eagle [coll., U.S.]; chauvinist(ic), chauvin; jingoist(ic), jingo.

940. BENEFACTOR

NOUNS 1. benefactor, benefactress, benefiter, succorer, befriender; ministrant, ministering angel; Samaritan, **good Samaritan; helper,** aider, assister, help, aid, helping hand. "a very present help in time of trouble" [Bible]; friend in need, friend indeed, jack-at-a-pinch; patron, backer 785.8.

2. savior, saviour [esp. Eng.], **redeemer,** deliverer, **liberator,** rescuer, freer, **emancipator,** manumitter.

941. EVILDOER

NOUNS **1. evildoer, malefactor,** malfeasant, malfeasor, malevolent; wrongdoer 984.8.

2. troublemaker, mischief-maker; agitator 646.11.

3. hellion [coll.], **devil, hellcat, terror** [coll.], holy terror [slang], roarer or hell-roarer [slang], ring-tailed roarer [slang, U.S.].

4. ruffian, rough, roughneck [slang], **tough** [coll., U.S.], **bravo,** bruiser [coll.], mug [slang], ugly customer [slang]; **rowdy,** roisterer; **thug, hoodlum** [coll.], hood [slang, U.S.], **hooligan** [slang], larrikin [Austral. & Eng.], gorilla [slang, U.S.], plug-ugly [slang, U.S.], **desperado, cutthroat,** apache; strongarm man [coll.], muscle man [crim. slang, U.S.], goon [slang, U.S.]; bludgeoner, bludgeon man; gunman; gun, trigger man, rodman, torpedo [all crim. slang, U.S.]; hatchet man, highbinder [U.S.].

5. bully, bucko, bouncer [coll.], hector, **bulldozer** [coll., U.S.], browbeater.

6. savage, barbarian, brute, beast, animal, tiger, hyena; Indian, wild Indian, redskin; cannibal, man-eater, anthropophagite.

7. monster, fiend, demon, devil, devil incarnate; hellhound, shaitan [coll.]; vampire, lamia, harpy, ghoul; ogre, ogress; Frankenstein's monster.

8. vixen, witch, hag, hellhag, hellcat, virago, termagant, grimalkin, Jezebel, beldam or beldame, she-wolf, tigress, ogress, siren, fury.

942. PITY

NOUNS **1. pity, sympathy,** feeling, **commiseration; compassion, mercy,** ruth, humanity; **clemency,** quarter, favor, grace; tender mercies; charity 936.4; leniency, forbearance 757; self-pity.

2. compassionateness, mercifulness, ruthfulness, softheartedness, tenderness, gentleness; bowels of mercy; bleeding heart.

VERBS **3. pity, be sorry for;** commiser-

ate, compassionate; sympathize, **sympathize with,** feel for, weep for, have one's heart bleed for.

4. have pity, have mercy upon, take pity on or **upon;** melt, thaw; relent, forbear, relax, give quarter; put out of one's misery; be cruel to be kind.

5. (excite pity) **move, touch, soften,** melt, melt the heart, appeal to one's better feelings.

6. beg for mercy, ask for pity, cry for quarter, beg for one's life; fall on one's knees, throw oneself at the feet of.

ADJS. **7. pitiful, pitying; sympathetic,** sympathizing; **compassionate, merciful,** ruthful, **clement,** gentle, soft, tender, **tenderhearted,** softhearted, warmhearted; **humane,** human; lenient, forbearant 757.8–10; charitable 936.16.

8. self-pitying, self-pitiful, sorry for oneself.

ADVS. **9. pitifully,** sympathetically; **compassionately, mercifully,** ruthfully, clemently, humanely.

INTERJS. **10. mercy!,** for pity's sake!, for mercy's sake!; have mercy!, cry you mercy!; woe betide!

11. poor thing!, poor dear!, poor fellow!; God help you!

943. PITILESSNESS

NOUNS **1. pitilessness, unmercifulness, uncompassionateness,** mercilessness, **ruthlessness,** inclemency, relentlessness; **heartlessness, cruelty** 937.10, 11; remorselessness, unremorsefulness; short shrift; tender mercies [iron.].

VERBS **2. show no mercy,** give no quarter, turn a deaf ear to, claim one's "pound of flesh" [Shakespeare].

ADJS. **3. pitiless, unpitying, unpitiful; unsympathetic,** unsympathizing; **uncompassionate,** uncompassioned; **merciless, unmerciful, ruthless,** bowelless, inclement, relentless; **heartless, cruel** 937.23, 24; remorseless, unremorseful.

ADVS. **4. pitilessly,** unsympathetically; mercilessly, **unmercifully, ruthlessly,** uncompassionately, inclemently, relentlessly; cruelly 937.31; remorselessly, unremorsefully.

944. CONDOLENCE

NOUNS **1. condolence,** condolement, consolation, commiseration, sympathy.

VERBS **2. condole with, commiserate, sympathize with,** express sympathy for, send one's condolences; **console,** wipe away one's tears; sorrow with, grieve with, weep with, share one's sorrow, "weep with them that weep" [Bible].

ADJS. **3. condolent,** consolatory, commiserative, **sympathetic.**

945. FORGIVENESS

NOUNS **1. forgiveness,** forgivingness; unresentfulness, unrevengefulness; **condonation,** overlooking, disregard; **indulgence, forbearance,** longanimity, long-suffering; **magnanimity** 977.2.

2. pardon, excuse; **amnesty,** indemnity, grace, oblivion; **absolution,** remission, remission of sin; **exoneration, exculpation** 1005.

VERBS **3. forgive, pardon,** excuse, give or grant forgiveness; amnesty, grant amnesty to; **absolve,** remit, give absolution, grant remission; **exonerate, exculpate** 1005.4; blot out one's sins, wipe the slate clean.

4. condone, overlook, disregard, ignore, pass over, close or shut one's eyes to, **blink** or **wink at,** connive at; allow for, make allowances for; bear with, endure, regard with indulgence; pocket the affront.

5. forget, forgive and forget, dismiss from one's thoughts, think no more of, not give it another or a second thought, let it go [coll.], let pass, **let bygones be bygones;** write off, charge off, charge to experience.

ADJS. **6. forgiving,** placable, conciliatory; **magnanimous, generous** 977.6; **forbearing,** forbearant; longanimous, long-suffering; unresentful, unrevengeful; more in sorrow than in anger.

7. forgiven, pardoned, excused, condoned; unresented; unavenged, unrevenged; uncondemned.

INTERJS. **8. pardon me!,** excuse me!, forgive me!, **I beg your pardon!**

946. CONGRATULATION

NOUNS **1. congratulation,** gratulation, **felicitation,** blessing, **compliment;** good wishes, best wishes.

VERBS **2. congratulate,** gratulate, **felicitate,** bless, **compliment,** tender or offer one's congratulations, ~ felicitations or compliments; shake one's hand, pat on the back; **rejoice with,** wish one joy.

ADJS. **3. congratulatory,** congratulant, congratulational; gratulatory, gratulant; complimentary.

INTERJS. **4. congratulations!,** bless you!,

take a bow!; nice going!, fine business!, bully for you!, shake! [all slang].

947. GRATITUDE

NOUNS **1. gratitude, gratefulness, thankfulness, appreciation, appreciativeness.**

2. thanks, thanksgiving, praise, benediction; grace, prayer of thanks; thank-you; acknowledgment; thank offering.

VERBS **3. be grateful, be much obliged,** feel ~, be or lie under an obligation; **be thankful,** thank God, thank or bless one's stars; **appreciate,** be appreciative of; never forget; overflow with gratitude.

4. thank, bless; give one's thanks, **express one's appreciation; offer thanks,** give ~, tender or render thanks, return thanks; acknowledge, make acknowledgments of; fall on one's knees, get down on one's marrowbones [joc.].

ADJS. **5. grateful, thankful; appreciative,** sensible; **obliged, much obliged,** beholden, indebted to, under obligation.

INTERJS. **6. thanks!, thank you!,** I thank you!, *merci!* [F.], *gracias!* [Span.], gramercy!, **much obliged!,** many thanks!, thank you kindly!; I thank you very much!, *merci beaucoup!* [F.], *je vous remercie beaucoup!* [F.].

7. thank God!, thank Heaven!, thanks be to God!, glory be to God!, Heaven be praised!

948. INGRATITUDE

NOUNS **1. ingratitude, ungratefulness, unthankfulness, unappreciativeness;** "benefits forgot" [Shakespeare].

2. ingrate, ungrateful wretch.

VERBS **3. be ungrateful,** feel no obligation, not appreciate, owe one no thanks; look a gift horse in the mouth.

ADJS. **4. ungrateful, unthankful,** thankless, **unappreciative,** unmindful.

5. unthanked, unacknowledged, unrequited, unrewarded, forgotten; ill-requited, ill-rewarded.

INTERJS. **6. thank you for nothing!**

949. ILL-HUMOR

NOUNS **1. ill-humor,** bad humor, **bad temper,** ill temper, **ill nature,** filthy or rotten humor; sourness, biliousness; choler, bile, gall, spleen; anger 950.5; discontent 867.

2. irascibility, irritability, iracundity, **crossness, crankiness, testiness,** crustiness, huffiness, **cantankerousness** [coll.], **crabbedness,** churlishness, bearishness, snappishness, waspishness; **meanness** [coll.], **orneriness** [coll. & dial.], disagreeability, ugliness [coll., U.S.]; **perversity,** cross-grainedness, fractiousness.

3. **hot temper, temper,** quick *or* short temper, irritable temper, warm temper, fiery temper, **hotheadedness,** hot blood.

4. **touchiness, techiness** *or* tetchiness; **sensitiveness,** oversensitiveness, temperamentalness.

5. **petulance** *or* petulancy, **peevishness,** pettishness, **querulousness, fretfulness;** shrewishness, vixenishness.

6. **grouchiness** [coll.], **crabbiness, grumpiness;** grouch [coll.].

7. **contentiousness, quarrelsomeness; disputatiousness, argumentativeness,** litigiousness; **belligerence** 795.16.

8. **sullenness, sulkiness, surliness, moroseness, glumness,** grumness, grimness, stuffiness [coll.], mumpishness, *bouderie* [F.]; **moodiness,** moodishness; mopishness, mopiness [coll.].

9. **sullen looks,** black looks, long face; **scowl, frown,** lower *or* lour, **glower,** glout [dial.], **gloom** [chiefly Scot.], glooming; pout.

10. **sulks,** sullens, **mopes,** mumps, grumps [coll.], frumps [dial.], mulligrubs [slang], dorts [dial.], dods [coll.], glooming; **pouts,** pout.

11. (ill-humored person) **sorehead, grouch,** crank, **crosspatch,** crooked stick [all coll.]; **bear,** grizzly bear; fury, tartar, dragon, ugly customer [slang]; **hothead,** hotspur; **spitfire,** fire-eater [coll.].

12. **shrew, vixen,** virago, **termagant,** fury, witch, beldam *or* beldame, frump [coll.], cat, tigress, she-wolf; **scold,** common scold.

VERBS 13. **have a temper,** have a devil in one, be possessed of the devil.

14. **sulk, mope, grump** [coll.], frump; **grouch** [slang], grout [coll., U.S.], fret; get oneself in a sulk, take the dods [coll.].

15. **look sullen,** look black, look black as thunder, gloom, pull *or* make a long face; **frown, scowl,** knit the brow, lower *or* lour, **glower,** glout [dial.]; **pout,** make a lip, hang one's lip.

16. **sour,** acerbate, exacerbate; **embitter,** bitter, envenom.

ADJS. 17. **out of humor,** out of temper, out of sorts, **in a bad humor,** in a shocking humor, on one's ear [slang]; **angry** 950.26.

18. **ill-humored, bad-tempered,** ill-tempered, **ill-natured,** ill-affected, ill-disposed, ill-conditioned.

19. **irascible, irritable, cross,** cranky, testy, crusty, huffy, patchy [dial.], **cantankerous** [coll.], cankered, **crabbed,** spleeny, splenetic, iracund, churlish, bearish, snappish, waspish; **mean** [coll.], ornery [coll. & dial.], disagreeable, ugly [coll., U.S.]; **perverse,** fractious, cross-grained.

20. **touchy, techy** *or* tetchy, miffy [dial. & slang]; **sensitive,** oversensitive, temperamental, **thin-skinned.**

21. **peevish, petulant,** pettish, **querulous,** fretful; shrewish, vixenish, vixenly; nagging, naggy [coll.].

22. **grouchy** [coll.], grouty [coll., U.S.], **crabby, grumpy,** grumbly [coll.], grumbling, growling.

23. **sour,** soured, **sour-tempered,** vinegarish; **choleric, dyspeptic, bilious,** jaundiced; **bitter,** embittered.

24. **sullen, sulky, surly, morose,** stuffy [coll.], rusty [dial., Eng.], mumpish, dumpish, **glum,** grum, grim; **moody,** moodish; **mopish,** mopy [coll.], moping; **glowering,** lowering *or* louring, **scowling, frowning;** dark, black; black-browed, beetle-browed.

25. **hot-tempered, hotheaded, passionate,** hot, fiery, peppery, spunky [coll.]; **quick-tempered, short-tempered;** hasty, quick, "sudden and quick in quarrel" [Shakespeare]; volcanic, combustible.

26. **contentious, quarrelsome; disputatious,** controversial, litigious, polemic(al); **argumentative,** argumental; scrappy [slang], fighty [dial.]; cat-and-doggish, cat-and-dog; **belligerent** 795.26.

ADVS. 27. **ill-humoredly, ill-naturedly; irascibly, irritably, crossly, crankily,** testily, huffily, cantankerously [coll.], crabbedly, sourly, churlishly, crustily, bearishly, snappily; perversely, fractiously, cross-grainedly.

28. **peevishly, petulantly,** pettishly, **querulously, fretfully.**

29. **grouchily** [coll.], **crabbily, grumpily,** grumblingly.

30. **sullenly, sulkily, surlily, morosely,** mumpishly, **glumly,** grumly, grimly; **moodily,** mopingly; gloweringly, loweringly *or* louringly, scowlingly, frowningly.

950. RESENTMENT

NOUNS 1. **resentment,** resentfulness; **displeasure; vexation, irritation, annoyance,** aggravation [coll.], exasperation.

2. **offense, umbrage, pique.**

3. **bitterness,** bitter resentment, bitter-

ness of spirit; **rancor**, virulence, acrimony, asperity; **choler**, gall, bile, spleen; animosity 927.4; soreness, rankling; gnashing of teeth.

4. indignation, indignant displeasure, righteous indignation.

5. anger, wrath, ire, mad [dial. & coll.]; angriness, irateness, wrathfulness, soreness [coll.], madness [coll.], "a transient madness" [Horace]; infuriation, enragement; vials of wrath, grapes of wrath.

6. temper, dander [coll.], Irish [coll. & dial.], monkey [coll. or slang, Eng.], spunk [coll.]; bad temper 949.

7. dudgeon, high dudgeon; **huff, pique, pet, tiff**, miff [coll.], sniff [slang], tizzy [slang], pucker [coll.], taking [coll.]; **fume**, ferment, stew [coll.].

8. fit of anger, fit, tantrum [coll.], **duck fit** [slang], cat fit [slang], **conniption** [coll., U.S.], paroxysm, convulsion.

9. outburst of anger, **outburst**, burst, **explosion**, eruption, flare-up [coll.], access, blaze of temper; **storm, scene**, high words.

10. rage, passion; fury, furor; towering rage or passion, raging or tearing passion, furious rage; vehemence, violence.

11. (cause of umbrage) **provocation, affront, offense**, "head and front of one's offending" [Shakespeare]; *casus belli* [L., grounds for war], red rag, slap in the face.

VERBS **12. resent**, be resentful, feel resentment, feel hurt.

13. take amiss, take ill, **take in bad part**, take to heart, not take it as a joke; **take offense, take umbrage**, take huff, take pet, take it in snuff, miff [coll.], be offended.

14. (show resentment) redden, color, flush, mantle; growl, snarl, gnarl, snap, show one's teeth; gnash or grind one's teeth, champ the bit; bite one's thumb; give a dirty look [slang], look daggers.

15. (be angry) **burn, seethe, simmer**, sizzle, smoke, smolder; **fume**, stew [coll.], boil, fret, chafe; foam at the mouth; breathe fire and fury; **rage, storm, rave, rant**, bluster; take on, go on, carry on [all coll.]; kick up a row, ~ dust or shindy, raise Cain, ~ the devil, ~ Ned, ~ the mischief or the roof [all slang], tear up the earth; throw a fit, have a conniption [coll., U.S.], have a duck fit or cat fit [slang], go into a tantrum; stamp the foot.

16. vent one's anger, vent one's rancor, ~ choler or spleen, pour out the vials of one's wrath; **snap at, bite** or snap one's

nose off, bite or take one's head off, jump down one's throat; expend one's anger on, take it out on [coll.].

17. (become angry) **anger, lose one's temper**, forget oneself, let one's angry passions rise; **get mad, get sore** [both coll.]; **get one's gorge up**, get one's blood up, **get one's dander up** [coll.], get one's monkey up [coll. or slang Eng.], get one's Irish up [coll. & dial.], get the wind up [coll.]; **bridle**, bridle up, **bristle**, bristle up, get one's quills or hair up, stand on one's hind legs; take the dods [coll.], get in a sniff or tizzy [slang]; **see red** [coll.]; **get hot under the collar** [slang], work oneself into a lather, ~ sweat or stew [coll.]; reach boiling point, boil over.

18. flare up, blaze up, fire up, flame up, spunk up, ignite, kindle, take fire.

19. fly into a rage or **passion**, fly out, fly off at a tangent; **fly off the handle, go up in the air, hit the ceiling**, go off on one's ear, go into a tailspin, have a hemorrhage [all slang]; **explode, blow up** [coll.]; blow one's top or stack, blow a fuse [all slang].

20. offend, give offense, give umbrage, affront, outrage; grieve, aggrieve; wound, hurt, sting, hurt the feelings; step or tread on one's toes.

21. anger, make one angry, make one mad or **sore** [coll.], distemper, set by the ears; **raise one's gorge** or **choler**, raise one's dander [coll.], **put** or **get one's dander up** [coll.], put or get one's monkey up [coll. or slang, Eng.], put or get one's Irish up [coll. and dial.], put or get one's wind up [coll.], get one's mad up [dial. & coll.]; make one hot under the collar, burn up [both slang].

22. provoke, incense, arouse, inflame, embitter; **vex, irritate, annoy, aggravate** [coll.], **exasperate**, exacerbate, **nettle**, fret, chafe; **pique, peeve** [coll.], miff [coll.], huff; **ruffle, roil, rile** [coll., chiefly U.S.], ruffle one's feathers; bristle, put or get one's back up, set up, put one's hair, ~ fur, ~ bristles or quills up; stir up, work up, stir one's bile, stir the blood.

23. enrage, infuriate, madden, drive one mad, frenzy, lash into fury, work one into a passion, **make one's blood boil**.

ADJS. **24. resentful**, resenting; **bitter**, embittered, rancorous, acrimonious.

25. provoked, incensed, vexed, piqued, peeved [coll.], miffed [dial. & slang], **nettled, irritated**, annoyed, aggravated [coll.], exasperated, put out.

26. angry, angered, **indignant, irate,** ireful, **wroth, wrathful,** wrathy [chiefly coll.], **mad** [coll.], **sore** [coll.], stuffy [coll.], waxy [slang, Eng.]; wrought-up, worked up, riled up [coll.].

27. hot [slang], het up [dial.], **hot under the collar** [slang]; burning, seething, simmering, smoldering, sizzling, boiling; flushed with anger.

28. in a temper, in a huff, in a pet, in a sniff [slang], in a tizzy [slang], in a pucker [coll.], in a taking [coll.], in a stew [coll.], in a wax [slang], **in high dudgeon.**

29. infuriated, infuriate, in a rage, ~ passion or fury; **furious,** fierce, wild, savage; raving mad [coll.], **rabid,** foaming at the mouth; **fuming,** in a fume; **raging, raving ranting, storming;** mad as a hornet; mad as a wet hen; fighting mad, roaring mad, good and mad [all coll.]; hopping mad, mad as hops, fit to be tied [all slang].

ADVS. **30. angrily, indignantly,** irately, wrathfully, infuriatedly, infuriately, furiously, heatedly; **in anger,** in hot blood, in the heat of passion.

951. JEALOUSY

NOUNS **1. jealousy,** jalousie [F.], jealousness, heartburn, **jaundice,** jaundiced eye, green in the eye [coll.], "the jaundice of the soul" [Dryden]; "green-eyed jealousy," "green-eyed monster," "a monster begot upon itself, born on itself" [all Shakespeare]; envy 952.

2. suspiciousness, suspicion, doubt, misdoubt, mistrust, distrust, distrustfulness.

VERBS **3. have green in the eye** [coll.], view with a jaundiced eye; **suspect,** distrust, mistrust, doubt, misdoubt.

ADJS. **4. jealous, jaundiced,** jaundice-eyed, yellow-eyed, green-eyed, yellow, green, green with jealousy; **envious** 952.4; **suspicious,** distrustful.

952. ENVY

NOUNS **1. envy,** enviousness, **covetousness;** grudging, grudgingness; **jealousy** 951; rivalry.

2. "the green sickness" [Shakespeare], "a pain of mind that successful men cause their neighbors" [Onasander], "emulation adapted to the meanest capacity" [Ambrose Bierce], "the sincerest form of flattery" [Churton Collins].

VERBS **3. envy,** be envious of, **covet,** cast envious eyes; **grudge, begrudge.**

ADJS. **4. envious,** envying, green with envy; **jealous** 951.4; **covetous,** desirous of; **grudging, begrudging.**

953. RETALIATION

NOUNS **1. retaliation, reciprocation,** exchange, interchange, give-and-take; **retort, reply,** return, comeback [coll.]; **counter,** counterblow, counterstroke, counterblast.

2. requital, reprisal, retribution, recompense, repayment, reward, comeuppance or comeuppings [coll., U.S.]; **reparation, redress, amends, satisfaction,** quittance, return of evil for evil; **revenge** 954.

3. tit for tat, measure for measure, like for like, blow for blow, a Roland for an Oliver, **an eye for an eye,** a tooth for a tooth, "eye for eye, tooth for tooth, hand for hand, foot for foot" [Bible].

VERBS **4. retaliate, retort,** counter, strike back, hit back at [coll.], give in return; **reciprocate,** give in exchange, give and take; **get back at** [slang], come back at [coll.], turn the tables upon.

5. requite, make requital, ~ reprisal or retribution, get satisfaction; **repay,** pay, **pay back,** pay off, pay out [coll.], pay home; **give one his comeuppance** or comeuppings [coll., U.S.], give one his deserts, give one what is coming to him.

6. give in kind, cap, match, give as good as was sent; repay in kind, **pay one in his own coin, give one a dose of his own medicine** [coll.]; return the like, return the compliment; return like for like, **return evil for evil;** return blow for blow, **give one tit for tat,** give measure for measure, give an eye for an eye and a tooth for a tooth.

7. get even with [coll.], even the score, **settle with, settle** or **square accounts,** settle the score [coll.], fix [coll.], serve one out [coll.], pay off old scores, pay back in full measure, be or make quits; **take revenge** 954.4.

ADJS. **8. retaliatory,** retaliative; **retributive,** retributory; reparative, reciprocal.

ADVS. **9. in retaliation, in exchange,** in reciprocation; **in return,** in reply; **in requital, in reprisal,** in retribution, in reparation, in amends; **in revenge,** en revanche [F.].

954. REVENGE

NOUNS **1. revenge, vengeance, avengement,** sweet revenge; **retaliation, reprisal** 953.

2. revengefulness, vengefulness, **vindictiveness**, rancor, grudgefulness.

3. **avenger,** vindicator; Nemesis, Eumenides.

VERBS 4. **revenge, avenge, take revenge,** have one's revenge, wreak one's vengeance; **retaliate, get even with** 953.4–7.

5. **harbor revenge,** breathe vengeance; have accounts to settle, have a crow to pick, ~ pluck or pull with, have a rod in pickle; nurse one's revenge, brood over, dwell on or upon, keep the wound open.

ADJS. 6. **revengeful, vengeful,** avenging; **vindictive,** vindicatory; **punitive,** punitory; rancorous, grudgeful; retaliatory 953.8.

ADVS. 7. in revenge, in retaliation 953.9.

955. ETHICS

NOUNS 1. **ethics, principles,** standards, moral principles; **code, code of morals** or **ethics;** Ten Commandments, decalogue; social ethics, professional ethics.

2. **ethical** or moral philosophy, ethology, ethnomics, aretaics, casuistry, deontology, eudaemonism, empiricism, evolutionism, hedonism, intuitionism, perfectionism, Stoicism, utilitarianism; egoistic ethics, altruistic ethics, Christian ethics; comparative ethics.

3. **morality, morals,** morale; virtue 978; ethicality, ethicalness; moral climate.

4. **amorality,** unmorality; amoralism.

5. **conscience,** grace, **sense of right and wrong;** inward monitor, censor, ethical self, superego [psychol.]; **voice of conscience,** still small voice within; tender conscience; conscientiousness 972.2; twinge of conscience 871.2.

ADJS. 6. **ethical,** ethologic(al); **moral,** moralistic.

7. **amoral,** unmoral, nonmoral.

956. RIGHT

NOUNS 1. **right,** rightfulness; what is right or proper, what should be, what ought to be, the seemly, the thing, the proper thing, the right or proper thing to do.

2. **propriety, decorum, decency;** correctness, properness, decorousness, goodness, niceness, seemliness; fitness, suitability 668; proprieties, decencies.

3. (a right or privilege) **right, due,** droit [law]; **prerogative,** power, authority; faculty, appurtenance; **claim,** demand, **interest, title,** pretension, pretense, prescription [law]; birthright; inalienable right; vested right or interest.

4. **privilege, license, liberty, freedom, immunity;** franchise, patent, grant; favor, indulgence, **special favor.**

5. **human rights,** rights of man; civil rights 760.9.

6. **woman's rights,** rights of women; feminism, womanism; **woman** or **female suffrage,** suffragettism.

7. **feminist,** womanist; **suffragist,** womansuffragist, suffragette.

ADJS. 8. **right,** rightful; **fit,** suitable 668.4; **proper, correct, decorous,** good, nice, decent, seemly, due, **right and proper,** as it should be, as it ought to be, according to Hoyle [coll.]; in the right.

ADVS. 9. **rightly, rightfully, right; by rights,** by right, with good right, **as is right** or **only right; properly,** correctly, as is proper or fitting; **in justice,** in equity; in reason, in all conscience.

957. WRONG

NOUNS 1. **wrong,** wrongfulness; **impropriety, indecorum;** incorrectness, improperness, indecorousness, unseemliness; unfitness, unsuitability 669.

2. **abomination,** terrible thing; **scandal, disgrace, shame, pity,** infamy, ignominy.

ADJS. 3. **wrong, wrongful; improper, incorrect, indecorous,** undue, unseemly; unfit, unsuitable 669.5; not the thing, hardly the thing.

ADVS. 4. **wrongly, wrongfully, wrong; improperly,** incorrectly, indecorously.

958. DUENESS

NOUNS 1. **dueness, entitlement,** deservedness.

2. **due, one's due,** what is coming to one; **right** 956.3.

3. **deserts, just deserts, merits, dues,** due reward or punishment, **comeuppance** or comeuppings [coll., U.S.], comings [slang, U.S.], one's [slang], all that is coming to one.

VERBS 4. **be due to,** be the due of, **be entitled to,** have a right or title to, have a claim upon, **have it coming.**

5. **deserve, merit,** rate [slang], earn, be in line for [coll.], **be worthy of,** be deserving, richly deserve.

6. **get one's deserts,** get one's dues, get one's comeuppance or comeuppings [coll., U.S.], get one's comings [slang, U.S.], get one's [slang, U.S.], get what is coming to one; serve one right, be rightly served; get

for one's pains, reap the fruits *or* benefit of, reap where one has sown.

ADJS. 7. **due, owed, owing,** coming, coming to.

8. **rightful,** proper 956.8; **fit,** becoming 668.4.

9. **warranted, justified, entitled,** qualified; **deserved, merited,** richly deserved.

10. **due to, entitled to,** with a right to; **deserving,** meriting, worthy of; attributable, ascribable.

ADVS. 11. **duly,** rightfully, as is one's due *or* right.

959. UNDUENESS

NOUNS 1. **undueness,** undeservedness.

2. **presumption, assumption, imposition; liberty, license, freedom, undue liberty, familiarity, presumptuousness,** freedom abused.

3. (taking to oneself unduly) **usurpation, arrogation, appropriation,** assumption, adoption.

4. **usurper,** arrogator, pretender.

VERBS 5. **not be entitled to,** have no right *or* title to, have no claim upon.

6. **presume, assume, venture, hazard, dare,** pretend, attempt, **make bold,** make free, **take the liberty,** take upon oneself.

7. **presume on** *or* **upon, impose on** *or* **upon,** encroach upon, obtrude upon; **take liberties,** take a liberty, make free with *or* of, abuse one's rights, abuse a privilege, give an inch and take an ell.

8. (take to oneself unduly) **usurp, arrogate, appropriate,** assume, adopt, take over, arrogate *or* accroach to oneself, pretend to.

ADJS. 9. **undue, unowed, unowing; undeserved, unmerited,** unearned; **unwarranted, unjustified,** unentitled; preposterous, outrageous.

10. **unmeet** 669.5; **improper** 957.3.

11. **presumptuous, presuming.**

960. DUTY

Moral Obligation.—NOUNS 1. **duty, obligation,** charge, onus, devoir, must, ought, **bounden duty,** what ought to be done, "stern daughter of the voice of God" [Wordsworth]; **business, place** 654.3; **line of duty; call of duty.**

2. **responsibility,** incumbency; **liability,** accountability, amenability; blame.

VERBS 3. **should, ought to,** had best, had better, be expedient, will be wise to.

4. **behoove,** become, befit, beseem; **owe it to,** owe it to oneself.

5. **be the duty of, be incumbent on** *or* **upon,** stand on *or* upon, be bound to, be ~, stand *or* lie under an obligation.

6. **be responsible for,** stand responsible for, **be liable for,** be answerable *or* accountable for, have to answer for; **be one's responsibility, rest with,** lie upon, devolve on, rest on the shoulders of, lie on one's head, lie at one's door, fall to one's lot.

7. **incur a responsibility,** become bound to, become sponsor for.

8. **take** *or* **accept the responsibility, take upon oneself, answer for;** sponsor, be *or* stand sponsor for; do at one's own risk *or* peril; **take the blame,** take the rap for [crim. slang, U.S.]; shift the blame *or* responsibility, pass the buck [coll.].

9. **do one's duty,** perform ~, fulfill *or* discharge one's duty, do what one has to do, do what is expected of one, do the expected, do the needful, do justice to, do *or* act one's part; answer the call of duty.

10. **meet an obligation,** satisfy one's obligations, stand to one's engagement, stand up to, **acquit oneself, make good,** redeem one's pledge.

11. **obligate, oblige, require,** bind, pledge, saddle with, put under an obligation.

ADJS. 12. **dutiful,** duteous; **obedient** 764.3.

13. **incumbent on** *or* **upon,** chargeable to, up to [coll.], behooving.

14. **obligatory, binding, imperative,** imperious, peremptory, mandatory, must, *de rigueur* [F.]; **necessary, required** 637.12, 13.

15. **obliged, obligated,** obligate, **under obligation; bound, duty-bound,** in duty bound; **beholden, bounden; obliged to,** beholden to, bound *or* bounden to, **indebted to.**

16. **responsible, answerable; liable, accountable,** amenable, unexempt from; responsible for, at the bottom of; to blame.

ADVS. 17. **dutifully,** duteously, in the line of duty, as in duty bound; beyond the call of duty.

961. IMPOSITION

A Putting or Inflicting Upon.—NOUNS 1. **imposition, infliction,** laying on; laying on of hands, imposition of hands.

2. **administration,** giving, bestowal; application, appliance, adhibition.

3. **charge, duty, tax,** task; **burden,** weight, load, onus.

VERBS 4. **impose, put on** *or* **upon, lay on** *or* **upon,** enjoin; **put, place, set, lay;** levy, exact; **tax,** task, charge, burden with; **affix, fasten upon,** saddle with; subject to; lay hands on, lay on hands.

5. **inflict, wreak, do to,** bring, bring upon, bring down upon.

6. **administer, give, bestow; apply, put on** *or* **upon,** lay on *or* upon, place upon, put to, address, devote, adhibit.

7. **impose on** *or* **upon,** inflict upon, etc. (*above*); **play on** *or* **upon, practice upon,** work upon, put on *or* upon, put over *or* across on [slang]; **palm upon, pass off on, work of on, fob off on,** foist off on, **foist upon;** palm off, pass off, fob off, play off, foist off.

8. **take advantage of** 663.16; **presume upon** 959.7; **deceive** 616.13.

962. RESPECT

NOUNS 1. **respect, regard,** consideration, appreciation; **esteem,** estimation; **reverence, veneration,** awe; **deference,** deferential *or* reverential regard; **honor, homage,** duty; great respect, high regard, admiration, adoration, **idolization,** hero worship; courtesy 934.

2. **obeisance,** reverence, homage; **bow, nod, bob,** bend, inclination, inclination of the head, **curtsy, salaam, kowtow,** scrape, bowing and scraping; **genuflection** *or* genuflexion, kneeling, bending the knee; prostration; salute, salutation, presenting arms.

3. **respects, regards,** *égards* [F.], duties, *devoirs* [F.].

VERBS 4. **respect, regard, esteem,** hold in esteem, **admire,** think much of, think well of, think highly of, have *or* hold a high opinion of; **appreciate, value, prize; revere, reverence,** hold in reverence, **venerate, honor, look up to,** defer to, put on a pedestal, **idolize, adore,** worship the ground one walks on.

5. **do** *or* **pay homage to,** pay respect to, pay tribute to, **do** *or* **render honor to;** salute, present arms.

6. **make obeisance, salaam, kowtow, bow,** make one's bow, bow down, **nod,** incline ∼, bend *or* bow the head, bend the neck, move to [dial., Eng.], **bob,** bob down, **curtsy** *or* curtsey, bob a curtsy, bend, make a leg [archaic], scrape, **bow and scrape; genuflect, kneel,** bend the knee, get down

on one's knees, get down on one's marrowbones [joc.], throw oneself on one's knees, fall on one's knees, fall down before, fall at the feet of, prostrate oneself, kiss the hem of one's garment.

7. **command respect,** inspire respect; awe 918.5.

ADJS. 8. **respectful, regardful,** attentive; **deferential,** dutiful, honorific, ceremonious, cap in hand; **courteous** 934.14.

9. **reverent,** reverential; **venerative,** venerational; awful, awesome; solemn.

10. **obeisant,** prostrate, on one's knees, on one's marrowbones [slang], on bended knee.

11. **respected, esteemed, revered,** reverenced, **venerated,** honored, well-thought-of, appreciated, valued, prized, in high esteem *or* estimation.

12. **venerable, reverend, estimable, honorable,** worshipful, august; awful, dreadful; time-honored.

PREPS. 13. **in deference to,** with due respect, with all respect, **with all due respect to** *or* **for,** saving, excusing the liberty.

963. DISRESPECT

NOUNS 1. **disrespect, disrespectfulness,** lack of respect, **disesteem,** dishonor, irreverence; **discourtesy** 935; insolence 911.

2. **indignity, affront, offense, injury;** scurrility, contumely, despite, flout, brickbat [coll.]; **insult, aspersion,** uncomplimentary remark, left-handed *or* backhanded compliment, slap in the face; cut, "unkindest cut of all" [Shakespeare]; **outrage, atrocity,** enormity.

VERBS 3. **disrespect,** not respect, disesteem, hold a low opinion of; **show disrespect for,** show a lack of respect for, **be disrespectful,** treat with disrespect; trifle with, make bold *or* free with, take a liberty.

4. **affront, offend,** give offense to, disoblige, **outrage;** dishonor, humiliate, treat with indignity; **insult,** call names, hurl a brickbat [coll.], slap in the face, take *or* pluck by the beard; **add insult to injury.**

ADJS. 5. **disrespectful, irreverent,** awless *or* aweless; **discourteous** 935.4; insolent, impudent 911.8, 9.

6. **insulting, insolent, abusive,** offensive, derisive, contumelious, calumnious; scurrilous, scurrile; backhand, backhanded, left-handed.

7. **unrespected, unregarded, unrevered,** unvenerated, unhonored, unenvied.

964. CONTEMPT

NOUNS 1. **contempt, disdain, scorn,** contemptuousness, disdainfulness, scornfulness, despite, contumely, sovereign contempt; arrogance 910; ridicule 965.

2. **snub, rebuff, repulse; slight, spurn,** disregard, the go-by [slang]; **cut, cut direct, the cold shoulder** [all coll.].

VERBS 3. **disdain, scorn, despise,** contemn, disprize, misprize, be contemptuous of, feel contempt for, **hold in contempt,** hold cheap, look down upon, look with scorn upon, view with a scornful eye; sneer at 965.9; sniff at, sneeze at, snap one's fingers at, shrug one's shoulders at; care nothing for, think nothing of, set at naught.

4. **spurn,** scout, **turn up one's nose at,** scorn to receive or accept, not want any part of; spit upon.

5. **snub, rebuff, repulse; high-hat,** highbrow, upstage [all slang]; **look down one's nose at,** look cool or coldly upon; **coldshoulder,** turn a cold shoulder upon, **give a or the cold shoulder,** give or turn the shoulder [all coll.]; turn one's back upon, turn away from, turn on one's heel, set one's face against, slam the door in one's face, send away with a flea in the ear [coll.], show one his place, teach one his distance.

6. **slight, ignore,** disregard, overlook, neglect, pass by, pass up [slang, U.S.], give the go-by [slang], leave in or out in the cold [coll.], take no note or notice of, pay no attention or regard to, refuse to acknowledge or recognize; **cut** [coll.], **cut dead** [slang].

7. **avoid, shun,** dodge, steer clear of [coll.], have no truck with [coll. & dial.]; **keep one's distance,** keep at a respectful distance, **keep ~, stand or hold aloof;** keep at a distance, keep at arm's length.

ADJS. 8. **contemptuous, disdainful,** scornful, sneering, withering, contumelious; arrogant 910.9.

ADVS. 9. **contemptuously, disdainfully,** scornfully; in or with contempt, in disdain, in scorn; sneeringly, with a sneer, with curling lip.

INTERJS. 10. **bah!, pah!, phoo!**

965. RIDICULE

NOUNS 1. **ridicule, derision, mockery,** raillery; scoffing, jeering, twitting, taunting; banter 880.

2. **gibe** or **jibe, scoff, jeer,** fleer, flout, mock, **taunt, twit,** quip, jest, jape; scurrility, caustic remark; **cut,** cutting remark, verbal thrust; **fling, crack** [slang], **slap, rap** [slang, U.S.], **slam** [coll.], wipe [dial. & slang], jab [slang], **dig** [coll.], dirty dig [slang]; gibing retort, rude reproach, short answer, back answer, comeback [slang]; parting shot, Parthian shot.

3. **boo, hoot, catcall;** pooh, pooh-pooh; Bronx cheer, raspberry, razz [all slang, U.S.]; hissing, hiss, bird [slang], goose [theat. slang].

4. scornful laugh or smile, snicker or snigger, smirk, sardonic grin, leer, fleer, sneer, snort.

5. **sarcasm, irony, cynicism, satire,** asteism [rhet.]; causticity 937.8.

6. **burlesque, parody, satire,** farce, mockery, imitation, take-off [coll.]; **travesty,** travestie [F.]; caricature, caricatura [It.].

7. **laughingstock,** jestingstock, gazingstock, **derision, mockery, figure of fun** [coll.], byword, byword of reproach, jest, joke, quiz, **butt,** target, stock, goat [slang], toy, game, fair game, victim, monkey.

VERBS 8. **ridicule, deride,** ride [coll.], **pan** [slang], **razz** [slang, U.S.]; **make fun** or **game of, poke fun at,** make merry with, pull one's leg [coll.]; **laugh at,** grin at, smile at, snicker or snigger at; laugh in one's sleeve, laugh in one's beard; **laugh to scorn,** laugh out of court; **point at, point the finger of scorn.**

9. **scoff, jeer,** gibe or jibe, barrack [dial., Eng. & Austral.], **mock,** mob [dial., Eng.], revile, **rail at, rally, twit, taunt,** jape, quizz, niggle, flout, scout, gird, have a fling at, cast in one's teeth; **pooh, pooh-pooh;** sneer, **sneer at,** fleer, curl up one's lip.

10. **boo, hiss, hoot,** catcall, give the raspberry or Bronx cheer [slang, U.S.], whistle at.

11. **burlesque, satirize, parody, caricature,** travesty, hit or take off on.

ADJS. 12. **derisive, derisory; mocking, ridiculing, scoffing,** jeering, sneering, twitting, taunting.

13. **sarcastic(al), ironic(al), sardonic(al), cynical, satiric(al),** Rabelaisian, dry; caustic 937.21.

14. **burlesque, satiric(al),** farcical, parodic(al), caricatural, macaronic(al), doggerel.

ADVS. 15. **derisively, mockingly,** scoffingly, jeeringly, sneeringly, "with scoffs, and scorns and contumelious taunts" [Shakespeare].

INTERJS. 16. pooh!, poo!, pugh!, pooh-pooh!, poof!, phooey!, pfooey!, pish!, pish-pash!, pshaw!, tut!, tut-tut!, fiddlesticks!, [coll.], fiddledeedee!, a fig for!; nuts!, in your hat!, come off of it! [all slang].

966. APPROBATION

NOUNS 1. approbation, approval; sanction, acceptance, countenance, favor; endorsement, O.K. 520.4.

2. applause, plaudit, *éclat*; acclaim, acclamation; clap, handclap, **clapping**, hand clapping, clapping of hands; cheer 874.2; burst of applause, peal or thunder of applause; round of applause, hand, big hand; ovation, standing ovation; encore.

3. commendation, good word; boost, build-up [both slang]; puff, blurb [slang], plug [slang, U.S.]; honorable mention.

4. recommendation, recommend [coll.]; advocation, advocacy; reference, credential, voucher, testimonial, chit [Anglo-Indian]; character reference, character, certificate of character; letter of introduction.

5. praise, bepraisement; laudation, laud; glorification, glory, honor; eulogy, *éloge* [F.], eulogium; encomium, accolade, panegyric; paean; tribute, meed of praise.

6. compliment, polite commendation, complimentary or flattering remark; bouquet, posy [both coll.]; tradelast, T.L. [both coll.]; flattery 968.

7. praiseworthiness, laudability, commendableness, estimableness, meritoriousness, exemplariness, admirability.

8. commender, eulogist, eulogizer; praiser, lauder, extoller, encomiast, panegyrist, booster [coll., U.S.], puffer, *prôneur* [F.]; applauder, claquer, *claquer* [F.]; claque.

VERBS 9. approve, approve of, think well of; sanction, accept; endorse, O.K. 520.12; countenance, keep in countenance; hold with, uphold; favor, be in favor of, view with favor, take kindly to.

10. applaud, acclaim, hail; clap, clap the hands, give a hand or big hand; cheer 874.7; root for [slang, U.S.], cheer on; encore; cheer or applaud to the very echo.

11. commend, speak well or highly of, speak in high terms of, have or say a good word for; boost [coll., U.S.], plug [slang, U.S.]; recommend, advocate, put in a word or good word for; clap or pat on the back.

12. praise, bepraise; laud, belaud; eulogize, panegyrize, pay tribute; extol, glor-ify, magnify, exalt, bless; cry up, crack up [coll.], brag up [slang], blow up, puff, puff up; boast of, brag on [coll.], make much of; celebrate, emblazon, sound or resound the praises of, ring one's praises, sing the praises of, beat the drum for; praise to the skies, *porter aux nues* [F.].

13. compliment, pay a compliment, make one a compliment, give a bouquet or posy [coll.], say something nice about; flatter 968.5; hand it to, have to hand it to [both slang].

14. meet with approval, find favor with, pass muster, recommend itself, do credit to; redound to the honor of; ring with the praises of.

ADJS. 15. approbatory, commendatory, complimentary, laudatory, acclamatory, eulogistic(al), panegyric(al), encomiastic-(al), appreciative; flattering 968.9.

16. approving, favorable, favoring, in favor of, well-disposed.

17. uncritical, uncriticizing, uncensorious, unreproachful.

18. approved, favored; accepted, received, admitted; recommended, highly touted [coll.].

19. praiseworthy, worthy, commendable, laudable, estimable, admirable, meritorious, creditable; exemplary, model; deserving, well-deserving; beyond all praise, *sans peur et sans reproche* [F., without fear and without reproach].

ADVS., PREPS. 20. in favor of, for, pro, all for.

INTERJS. 21. bravo!, *bravissimo!* [It.], well done!, hear, hear!, aha!; hurrah! 874.12; good!, fine!, excellent!, great!, swell! [slang], bully!, bully for you!, good for you!, good enough!, attaboy! [slang]; encore!, *bis!* [F.], take a bow!, one cheer more!

22. hail!, all hail! *ave!* [L.], *vive!* [F.], *viva!* [It.], *evviva!* [It.], long life to!, glory be to!, honor be to!

967. DISAPPROBATION

NOUNS 1. disapprobation, disapproval; disfavor, disesteem, dim view [slang]; opposition, opposure; rejection, thumbs down; objection 520a.2.

2. deprecation, discommendation, dispraise, disvaluation; disparagement 969.

3. censure, reprehension, reprobation, blame, denunciation, denouncement, decrial, condemnation, damnation; castigation, excoriation.

4. criticism, judgment, adverse criticism, animadversion, imputation, reflection, aspersion, stricture, obloquy; **knock** [slang, U.S.], **slam** [coll.], **rap** [slang], **hit** [coll.], home thrust; **faultfinding,** carping, caviling; nagging; hypercriticism, overcriticalness, hairsplitting.

5. reproof, reproval; **rebuke, reprimand, reproach,** reprehension, **scolding, chiding, upbraiding,** objurgation, exprobration, hearing [Scot.]; **admonishment, admonition; correction,** castigation, rap on the knuckles; lecture, lesson, sermon, curtain lecture.

6. (reproof; colloquialisms) piece or bit of one's mind, **talking-to,** speaking-to, jobation, wigging, roasting, **raking-down,** dressing, dressing-down, setdown.

7. (reproof; slang terms) **bawling-out,** cussing-out, **calling-down, jacking-up,** going-over, grooming, ragging, lick with the rough side of the tongue, what-for.

8. berating, rating, jawing [slang], **tongue-lashing; revilement, abuse,** vituperation, invective, contumely, hard ~, cutting or bitter words; **tirade, diatribe,** jeremiad, screed, philippic.

9. reproving look, dirty or nasty look [slang], black look, frown, scowl.

9a. faultfinder, frondeur [F.], momus; **critic,** criticizer; censor, censurer; carper, caviler; **scold,** common scold.

VERBS **10. disapprove, disapprove of,** not approve; **disfavor, view with disfavor, frown at** or **upon,** look black upon, look askance or askant at, make a wry face at, **turn up the nose at,** shrug the shoulders at; **take a dim view of** [slang], not take kindly to, not hold with, hold no brief for [coll.], not go for [slang], not want or have any part of; **object to,** take exception to; **oppose,** set oneself against, set one's face against; **reject,** disallow, not hear of; **turn thumbs down on,** thumb down [both coll.]; frown down; say no to, shake the head at.

11. discountenance, not countenance, **not tolerate,** not suffer, not abide, not endure, not bear with, not put up with, **not stand for** [coll.], not stick [coll.], not go [coll., U.S.].

12. deprecate, discommend, dispraise, disvalue, not be able to say much for; **disparage** 969.8.

13. censure, reprehend; **blame,** lay or cast blame upon; **reproach,** impugn; **condemn,** damn, "damn with faint praise" [Pope]; **denounce,** denunciate; **decry,** cry down, exclaim ~, declaim or inveigh against, cry out against, cry out on or upon, cry shame upon, raise one's voice against, raise a hue and cry against; **reprobate,** hold up to reprobation; animadvert on or upon, reflect upon, cast reflection upon, cast a reproach or slur upon; throw a stone at, cast or throw the first stone.

14. criticize, judge, pan [coll., U.S.], **knock** [coll., U.S.], **slam** [coll.], hit, rap [slang], take a rap at; criticize severely 967.21.

15. find fault, faultfind, pick holes, pick a hole in one's coat, cut up, pick ~, pull or tear apart, pick ~, pull or **tear to pieces;** carp, cavil; "hint a fault and hesitate dislike" [Pope].

16. nag, carp at, fuss at, fret at, yap at [coll.], **pick at** [coll.], peck at, nibble at, **pester, henpeck, pick on** or **upon** [coll.].

17. reprove, rebuke, reprimand, reprehend, **scold, chide, admonish, upbraid,** exprobrate, objurgate, have words with; **lecture,** read a lesson or lecture to; **correct,** rap on the knuckles; **take to task,** call to account, bring to book, call on the carpet, read the riot act; take up, take down, set down.

18. (reprove; colloquialisms) **call down, dress down,** speak or talk to, **tell off,** tell a thing or two, **give a piece** or **bit of one's mind, rake** or **haul over the coals,** give it to, trim, come down on or upon, jump on or upon, jump down one's throat.

19. (reprove; slang terms) **bawl out, give a bawling out** [both U.S.]; **chew out,** cuss out, **jack up** [U.S.], sit on or upon, lambaste, give a going-over, tell where to get off; **give what-for,** give jesse or jessie, give the deuce or devil, give hell or hail Columbia.

20. berate, rate, betongue, jaw [slang], clapper-claw [dial.], tongue-lash, give a lick with the rough side of the tongue; **rail at,** rag, thunder or fulminate against, blow up, rave against, yell at, bark or yelp at; **revile, abuse,** vituperate, load with reproaches.

21. (criticize or reprove severely) **attack, assail** 796.15; **castigate, flay,** lash, slash, excoriate, scarify, scathe, **roast** [coll.], scorch, blister, trounce.

ADJS. **22. disapprobatory, disapproving,** unapproving; **unfavorable,** poor, low; **uncomplimentary;** unappreciative.

23. censorious, condemnatory, damnatory, denunciatory, reproachful, blameful,

reprobative, objurgatory; deprecative, deprecatory; **disparaging** 969.13; invective, inveighing; reviling, abusive, vituperative.

24. critical, judicial, "nothing if not critical" [Shakespeare]; **faultfinding,** carping, caviling, captious, cynical; nagging; hypercritical, ultracritical, overcritical, hairsplitting.

25. unpraiseworthy, illaudable; uncommendable, discommendable; **objectionable,** exceptionable, unacceptable, not to be thought of.

26. blameworthy, blameable, to blame; **reprehensible,** censurable, reproachable, reprovable; **culpable,** chargeable, impeachable, accusable, indictable, imputable.

INTERJS. **27. God forbid!,** Heaven forbid!, Heaven forfend!, forbid it Heaven!; by no means!, not for the world!, not on your life! [coll.], not if I know it!, nothing doing! [coll.], perish the thought!, I'll be hanged if . . . ! [coll.].

968. FLATTERY

NOUNS **1. flattery, adulation;** praise 966.5; **blandishment,** palaver, **cajolery,** cajolement, wheedling; **blarney,** buncombe or bunkum, taffy [all coll.]; **soft soap, soft sawder,** sawder, soap, butter, salve [all coll.]; oil, grease, eyewash [all slang]; fair ∼, sweet or honeyed words, soft or honeyed phrases, incense, pretty lies; compliment 966.6; sycophancy 905.2.

2. unction, "that flattering unction" [Shakespeare]; **unctuousness,** oiliness, **mealymouthedness;** flattering tongue; insincerity 614.5.

3. overpraise, overcommendation, overlaudation, overestimation.

4. flatterer, flatteur [F.], adulator, courtier, slaverer; **cajoler, wheedler; backslapper,** back-scratcher; blarneyer, softsoaper, soft-sawderer [all coll.]; sycophant 905.3.

VERBS **5. flatter,** adulate, conceit; **cajole, wheedle, blandish,** palaver, glaver [dial.]; slaver, beslaver, beslubber, beplaster; oil the tongue, lay the flattering unction to one's soul, make fair weather; **praise, compliment** 966.12, 13; fawn upon 905.6–9.

6. (colloquialisms) **soft-soap,** soft-sawder, sawder, butter, honey; **blarney,** jolly, pull one's leg; lay it on, lay it on thick.

7. (slang terms) honeyfogle [U.S.], **butter up,** soap, oil; string along, kid along; lay it on with a trowel.

8. overpraise, overcommend, overlaud; overesteem, overestimate.

ADJS. **9. flattering, adulatory; complimentary** 966.15; **blandishing, cajoling, wheedling;** fair-spoken, fine-spoken, smooth-spoken, smooth-tongued, **mealymouthed,** honey-mouthed, honey-tongued, honeyed, oily-tongued; oily, buttery [coll.], soapy [slang], **unctuous,** smooth, bland; insincere 614.32; courtly, courtierly; obsequious 905.13.

969. DISPARAGEMENT

NOUNS **1. disparagement, depreciation, detraction,** derogation, **belittling,** discrediting, decrial; disapprobation 967.

2. defamation, defamation of character; **vilification,** defilement, blackening, denigration; **smear,** smear word, smear campaign; **muckraking, mudslinging.**

3. slander, scandal, libel, traducement; calumny, calumniation; backbiting.

4. aspersion, slur, reflection, imputation, insinuation, innuendo; disparaging or uncomplimentary remark; personality, personal remark.

5. lampoon, pasquinade, pasquil, squib, satire, chronique scandaleuse [F.]; roorback [polit., U.S.].

6. disparager, depreciator, detractor, derogator, knocker [coll., U.S.]; **slanderer,** libeler, backbiter; calumniator, traducer; **muckraker, mudslinger.**

7. lampooner, lampoonist, satirist, pasquinader.

VERBS **8. disparage, depreciate, belittle,** degrade, debase, **run down** [coll.], **knock** [coll., U.S.], backcap [U.S.]; **discredit,** blow upon, bring into discredit, reflect discredit upon; detract from, derogate from, cut one down to size [slang]; **decry,** cry down; speak ill of, speak slightingly of, not speak well of; disapprove of 967.10.

9. defame, malign; asperse, cast aspersions on, cast reflections on; **slur,** cast a slur on; give a bad name, give a dog a bad name.

10. vilify, vilipend, **defile, sully, soil, smear,** smirch, besmirch, bespatter, tarnish, **blacken,** denigrate, blacken one's good name, give a black eye [coll.]; stigmatize 913.9; **muckrake, throw mud at,** heap dirt upon, drag through the mud; call names, engage in personalities.

11. slander, libel; calumniate, traduce; stab in the back, backbite, speak ill of behind one's back.

12. **lampoon, satirize, pasquinade,** dip the pen in gall.

ADJS. 13. **disparaging, derogatory, depreciatory,** depreciative, deprecatory, detractory, pejorative, contumelious; censorious 967.23; **defamatory,** vilifying; **slanderous, scandalous, libelous;** calumnious, calumniatory; scurrilous, scurrile.

970. MALEDICTION

NOUNS 1. **malediction,** malison, **curse,** damnation, denunciation, commination, imprecation, execration; blasphemy; anathema, anathema maranatha [erron.]; ban, proscription, thunders of the Vatican.

2. **abuse, vilification,** revilement, **vituperation, invective,** opprobrium, obloquy, contumely, calumny, scurrility, blackguardism; more bark than bite.

3. **swearing, cursing,** cussing [coll., esp. U.S.], **profanity,** profane swearing, foul ~, bad ~, strong or unparliamentary language, language [coll.], billingsgate, ribaldry, evil speaking.

4. **oath,** profane oath, **curse,** cuss [coll., esp. U.S.], cuss word [coll., U.S.], **swearword** [coll.], swear [coll.], foul invective, rapper [dial.], **expletive, epithet,** dirty name [slang], sailor's blessing [joc.].

VERBS 5. **curse,** accurse, **damn,** darn [coll.], **confound,** blast, blame [coll.], anathematize, execrate, imprecate; call down evil upon, call down curses on the head of; put a curse on; curse up hill and down dale; curse with bell, book, and candle blaspheme.

6. **swear, curse, cuss** [coll., esp. U.S.], curse and swear, execrate, rap out an oath, rip out an oath [coll.], fall a cursing, use language [coll.], let out religion [joc.]; swear like a trooper, make the air blue, swear till one is black or blue in the face.

7. **abuse, vilify, revile,** vituperate, blackguard, call names; **swear at,** damn, cuss out [slang].

ADJS. 8. **maledictory,** imprecatory, **damnatory,** epithetic(al); **abusive,** vituperative, contumelious; calumnious, calumniatory; scurrilous, scurrile; blasphemous, profane.

9. **cursed,** accursed, **damned, damnable,** execrable.

10. (euphemisms) **darned,** danged, **confounded,** deuced, blessed, **blasted,** dashed, blamed, doggoned, dadblasted, dadblamed, dadburned, goldarned, goldanged, infernal,

hell-fired, all-fired; bloody, ruddy [both Eng.].

INTERJS. 11. **damn!,** confound it!, hang it!, devil take!, a plague upon!

12. (euphemistic oaths) darn!, dern!, dang!, dash!, drat!, consarn!, blast!, blame!, goldarn!, goldang!, golding!, gosh-darn!, plague-gone!, doggone!, dingbust!, dagnab!, dadrot!, daddrat!, dadburn!, dadblast!, dadblame!

13. gosh!, gee!, gad!, by Jove!, *parbleu!* [F.].

971. THREAT

NOUNS 1. **threat, menace;** denunciation, commination; imminence 151; foreboding 542; warning 701; intimidation 889.5.

VERBS 2. **threaten, menace,** bludgeon, utter threats against, shake ~, double or clench the fist at; denounce, comminate; **lower** or lour, look threatening; **be imminent** 151.2; forebode 542.8; warn 701.6; intimidate 889.19.

ADJS. 3. **threatening, menacing,** minatory; **lowering** or louring; **imminent** 151.3; **ominous,** foreboding 542.13; denunciatory, comminatory, abusive.

972. PROBITY

NOUNS 1. **probity, rectitude, uprightness,** upstandingness; **integrity, honesty, honor;** honorableness, worthiness, estimableness, reputability, nobility; respectability; principles, high principles, high-mindedness; character, good character, moral strength.

2. **conscientiousness, scrupulousness,** scrupulosity, **scruples;** scruple, point of honor, punctilio; qualm 621.2; twinge of conscience 871.2; overconscientiousness, overscrupulousness; fastidiousness 894.

3. **veracity,** veraciousness, **truthfulness,** truth, veridicality, truthtelling, truth-speaking, truth-loving.

4. **candor, candidness, frankness, sincerity,** plain dealing; ingenuity, ingenuousness; artlessness 734; openness, openheartedness; freedom, freeness; **unreserve,** unrestraint, unconstraint; **forthrightness, directness, straightforwardness; outspokenness,** plain-spokenness, plain speaking; **bluntness,** bluffness, brusqueness.

5. **undeceptiveness, undeceitfulness,** guilelessness.

6. **trustworthiness,** faithworthiness, trustiness, trustability, **reliability, dependability,** responsibility, sureness; unfalse-

ness, unperfidiousness, untreacherousness; incorruptibility, inviolability.

7. fidelity, faithfulness, loyalty, faith; **constancy, steadfastness,** stanchness, firmness; trueness, troth, true blue; good faith, *bona fides* [L.], *bonne foi* [F.]; **allegiance, fealty, homage;** bond, tie; attachment, adherence, adhesion; devotion, devotedness.

8. man of honor, man of his word, gentleman, *gentilhomme* [F.], *galantuomo* [It.]; **honest man,** white man [slang, U.S.], square or straight shooter [coll.]; true-blue, truepenny, true Briton; trusty, faithful.

VERBS **9. keep faith with,** not fail, **keep one's word** or **promise,** be as good as one's word, redeem one's pledge, acquit oneself, make good.

10. shoot straight [coll.], draw a straight furrow, **put one's cards on the table,** level with [slang].

11. speak or **tell the truth,** speak or tell true, paint in its true colors, tell the truth and shame the devil; tell the truth, the whole truth and nothing but the truth.

12. be frank, speak plainly, speak out, speak one's mind, say what one thinks, **call a spade a spade.**

ADJS. **13. upright,** uprighteous, **upstanding,** right; **honorable, reputable,** estimable, creditable, worthy, noble, sterling, manly, yeomanly, Christian [coll.], white [slang]; **respectable,** highly respectable; **ethical, moral; principled, high-principled,** high-minded, right-minded; uncorrupt, uncorrupted; truehearted, true-souled, true-spirited; true-dealing, true-disposing, true-devoted; **law-abiding,** law-loving, law-revering.

14. honest, straight, square, four-square, **fair and square; square-dealing,** square-shooting, **straight-shooting,** up-and-up, **on the up-and-up, on the level,** on the square, straight-up-and-down [coll.]; open, **aboveboard, open and aboveboard;** genuine 515.13; singlehearted; honest as the day is long.

15. conscientious, tender-conscienced; **scrupulous,** punctilious, punctual, religious, strict, nice; fastidious 894.9; overconscientious, overscrupulous.

16. veracious, truthful, true, veridical; truth-telling, truth-speaking, truth-declaring, truth-passing, truth-bearing, truth-loving, truth-seeking, truth-desiring, truth-guarding, truth-filled; true-speaking, true-meaning, true-tongued.

17. candid, frank, sincere, ingenuous, frankhearted; **open,** openhearted, transparent; artless 734.5; **straightforward, direct,** straight [coll.], **forthright,** downright, straight-out [coll.], whole-footed [coll.], flat-footed [slang, U.S.]; plain, broad; **unreserved,** unrestrained, unconstrained; free; **outspoken, plain-spoken,** free-spoken, free-speaking, free-tongued; explicit, unequivocal; **blunt,** bluff, brusque; heart-to-heart.

18. undeceptive, undeceitful, undissembling, undissimulating, undeceiving, undesigning; **guileless,** unbeguiling, unbeguileful; unassuming, unpretending, unfeigning, undisguising, unflattering; undissimulated, undissembled; unassumed, unaffected, unpretended, unfeigned, undisguised, unvarnished, untrimmed.

19. trustworthy, trusty, trustable, faithworthy, **reliable, dependable,** responsible, straight [slang], sure, to be trusted, **to be depended** or **relied upon,** to be counted or reckoned on, as good as one's word; tried, true, **tried and true;** unfalse, unperfidious, untreacherous; incorruptible, inviolable.

20. faithful, loyal, devoted; **true, true-blue,** true to one's colors; **constant, steadfast,** steady, unfailing, stanch, firm, "marble-constant" [Shakespeare].

ADVS. **21. honorably, honestly,** uprightly, upstandingly; **conscientiously, scrupulously.**

22. truthfully, truly, veraciously; to tell the truth, to speak truthfully; in truth, in sooth [archaic], of a truth, with truth, in good or very truth.

23. frankly, candidly, sincerely, in all seriousness or soberness, in all conscience; in plain words or English, straight from the shoulder, not to mince the matter, without equivocation, with no nonsense, all joking aside or apart.

24. faithfully, loyally, devotedly; **constantly, steadfastly,** steadily, stanchly, firmly; in or with good faith, *bona fide* [L.].

973. IMPROBITY

NOUNS **1. improbity, dishonesty,** dishonor; **unscrupulousness,** unconscientiousness; **corruption,** corruptness; **crookedness,** criminality, **fraudulence** or fraudulency, underhandedness, indirection.

2. knavery, roguery, rascality, rascalry, **villainy,** reprobacy, scoundrelism; chicanery 616.4; knavishness, roguishness, scampishness, villainousness, feloniousness.

3. deceitfulness 616.3; falseheartedness

614.4; untruthfulness 614.8; sharp practice 616.4; fraud 616.8; craftiness 733.1; intrigue 652.6.

4. **untrustworthiness,** unfaithworthiness, untrustiness, **unreliability, undependability,** irresponsibility.

5. **infidelity, unfaithfulness,** faithlessness; **inconstancy, unsteadfastness,** fickleness; **disloyalty,** unloyalty; **falsity,** falseness, untrueness; disaffection, recreancy, dereliction; bad faith, *mala fides* [L.], Punic faith; breach of promise, breach of trust *or* faith, barratry [law].

6. **treachery,** treacherousness; **perfidy,** perfidiousness, falseheartedness; **duplicity, double-dealing; foul play,** dirty work at the crossroads [slang].

7. **treason,** petty treason, misprision of treason; high treason, *lèse-majesté* [F.], lese majesty; sedition; collaboration, fraternization.

8. **betrayal,** betrayment, **double cross** [slang], sellout [slang], Judas kiss.

9. **corruptibility, venality,** bribability, purchasability.

VERBS 10. (be dishonest) live by one's wits; deceive 616.13; cheat 616.18; falsify 614.16; lie 614.19.

11. be **unfaithful,** not keep faith with, **go back on** [coll.], **fail, let down;** break one's word *or* promise, go back on one's word [coll.]; forsake, desert 631.5, 6.

12. **play one false,** prove false; **stab in the back,** knife [slang, U.S.]; bite the hand that is feeding you.

13. **betray, double-cross** [slang], cross up [slang, U.S.], two-time [slang], sell out [slang]; inform on 555.11.

14. **act the traitor,** quisle, turn against, go over to the enemy, sell oneself; collaborate, fraternize.

ADJS. 15. **dishonest, dishonorable; unconscientious,** unconscienced, unconscionable, **unscrupulous, unprincipled,** unethical; **corrupt,** rotten; **crooked, criminal, fraudulent;** underhand, underhanded; shady [coll.], dark, sinister, insidious, indirect; fishy [coll.], questionable; ill-gotten, ill-got.

16. **knavish, roguish, scampish, rascally, scoundrelly,** blackguardly, villainous, felonious, reprobate, recreant.

17. **deceitful** 616.22; falsehearted 614.31; untruthful 614.34; crafty 733.12; scheming 652.14.

18. **untrustworthy,** unfaithworthy, untrusty, trustless, **unreliable, undependable,**

irresponsible, unsure, not to be trusted, not to be depended *or* relied upon.

19. **unfaithful,** faithless, of bad faith; **inconstant, unsteadfast,** fickle; **disloyal,** unloyal; **false, untrue,** not true to; disaffected, recreant, derelict, barratrous [law].

20. **treacherous, perfidious,** falsehearted; **shifty,** slippery, tricky; **double-dealing,** double, ambidextrous; two-faced 614.31.

21. **traitorous,** double-crossing [coll.], betraying, Iscariotic(al); **treasonable,** treasonous.

22. **corruptible, venal,** bribable, purchasable, mercenary, hireling.

ADVS. 23. **dishonestly, dishonorably;** unscrupulously, unconscientiously; **crookedly, fraudulently,** underhandedly, like a thief in the night, by fair means or foul; **deceitfully** 616.24.

24. **perfidiously,** falseheartedly; **unfaithfully,** faithlessly; **treacherously;** traitorously, treasonably.

974. JUSTICE

NOUNS 1. **justice, justness; equity,** equitableness, evenhandedness, measure for measure, give-and-take; **right,** rightfulness, what is right; poetic justice; retributive justice, nemesis; scales of Justice.

2. "truth in action" [Disraeli], "right reason applied to command and prohibition" [Cicero], "the firm and continuous desire to render to everyone that which is his due" [Justinian].

3. **fairness,** fair-mindedness, candor; the fair thing, the right *or* proper thing, the handsome thing [coll.]; **square deal** [coll.], fair shake [slang]; **fair play,** cricket [coll.]; sportsmanship, good sportsmanship, sportsmanliness, sportsmanlikeness.

4. **impartiality,** detachment, **dispassionateness, disinterestedness,** disinterest, **unbias,** unbiasedness, a fair field and no favor.

5. Justice, Justitia, blind *or* blindfolded Justice; Jupiter Fidius, Deus Fidius, Fides, Fides publica *or* Fides populi Romani [all Rom.]; Nemesis, Rhadamanthus [both Gr.]; Astraea [Gr. & Rom.].

VERBS 6. **be fair,** do the fair thing, do the handsome thing [coll.], do the right thing by; **do justice to,** see justice done, see one righted, serve one right, shoot straight with [coll.]; **give a square deal** [coll.], give a fair shake [slang]; give the Devil his due; give and take; lean over backwards.

7. **play fair,** tote fair [dial., U.S.], **play**

the game [coll.], play cricket [coll.], be a good sport, show a proper spirit.

ADJS. 8. just, fair, square, fair and square; equitable, balanced, level [coll.], even, evenhanded; right, rightful; due, deserved, merited; meet, fit, proper, good, as it should or ought to be.

9. fair-minded; sporting, sportsmanly, sportsmanlike; square-dealing, square-shooting [both coll.].

10. impartial, impersonal, candid, dispassionate, disinterested, detached; unbiased, uninfluenced, unswayed.

ADVS. 11. justly, fairly, fair, in a fair manner; rightfully, deservedly; equitably, equally, evenly, upon even terms; impartially, impersonally, dispassionately, disinterestedly, without distinction, without regard or respect to persons, without fear or favor.

12. in justice, in equity, in reason, in all conscience, in all fairness, to be fair, as is only fair or right, as is right, ~ just or fitting.

975. INJUSTICE

NOUNS 1. injustice, unjustness; inequity, iniquity, inequitableness, iniquitousness.

2. unfairness; unsportsmanliness, unsportsmanlikeness; foul play, foul, a hit below the belt.

3. partiality, one-sidedness; bias, leaning, inclination; undispassionateness, undetachment; partisanism, partisanship; favoritism, preference, nepotism.

4. (an injustice) wrong, injury, grievance, disservice, raw deal [slang]; imposition; great wrong, grave or gross injustice.

5. unjustifiability, unwarrantability, indefensibility; inexcusability, unpardonability, unforgivableness, inexpiableness, irremissibility.

VERBS 6. not play fair, hit below the belt, give a raw deal [slang].

7. do one an injustice, wrong, do wrong, do wrong by, do one a wrong, do a disservice; do a great wrong, do a grave or gross injustice.

8. favor, prefer, show preference, play favorites.

ADJS. 9. unjust, inequitable, unequitable, iniquitous, unbalanced, uneven; wrong, wrongful, unrightful; undue, unmeet, undeserved, unmerited.

10. unfair, not fair; unsporting, unsportsmanly, unsportsmanlike, not cricket [coll.]; foul, below the belt.

11. partial, interested, partisan, one-sided, undetached, undispassionate, biased, warped, influenced, swayed.

12. unjustifiable, unwarrantable, unallowable, unreasonable, indefensible; inexcusable, unpardonable, unforgivable, inexpiable, irremissible.

ADVS. 13. unjustly, unfairly; wrongfully, wrongly, undeservedly; inequitably, iniquitously, unequally, unevenly; partially, interestedly, one-sidedly, undispassionately.

976. SELFISHNESS

NOUNS 1. selfishness, selfism, self-seeking, self-pleasing, self-indulgence, self-advancement, self-devotion, self-jealousy, self-sufficiency, self-consideration, self-solicitude, self-absorption, self-occupation; self-interest, self-interestedness, interest; egotism 907.3; possessiveness.

2. ungenerousness, unmagnanimousness, illiberality, meanness, smallness, littleness, pettiness; niggardliness, stinginess 850.2, 3.

3. self-seeker, self-pleaser, self-advancer; egotist 907.5; timepleaser, timeserver, temporizer; fortune hunter, tuft-hunter; monopolist, hog, road hog, endseat hog [coll.]; dog in the manger.

VERBS 4. please oneself, gratify oneself, indulge ~, pamper or coddle oneself, consult one's own wishes, look after one's own interests, take care of or look out for number one [coll.].

ADJS. 5. selfish, self-seeking, self-pleasing, self-advancing, self-indulgent, self-jealous, self-sufficient, self-interested, self-considerative, self-besot, self-devoted, self-occupied, self-absorbed, wrapped up in oneself; self-centered, egotistical 907.10; possessive.

6. ungenerous, illiberal, unchivalrous, mean, small, little, petty; niggardly, stingy 850.10, 11.

ADVS. 7. selfishly, for oneself, in one's own interest, from selfish or interested motives, to gain some private ends.

977. UNSELFISHNESS

NOUNS 1. unselfishness, selflessness, self-forgetfulness; self-subjection, self-subordination, self-abasement; self-neglect, self-neglectfulness; self-renunciation, self-renouncement; self-denial, self-abnegation; self-sacrifice, sacrifice, self-immolation, self-devotion; disinterest, distinterestedness.

2. magnanimity, magnanimousness, generosity, generousness, liberality, lib-

eralness; **bigness, bigheartedness,** great-heartedness, largeheartedness, big ~, large *or* great heart; noble-mindedness, high-mindedness; **nobleness,** princeliness, great-ness, loftiness, elevation, exaltation, sub-limity; chivalry, chivalrousness, knightli-ness, errantry, knight-errantry; heroism.

VERBS 3. not have a selfish bone in one's body; put oneself out, go out of the way, lean over backwards; sacrifice, make a sacri-fice.

4. observe the Golden Rule, do as one would be done by, do unto others as you would that they should do unto you, put oneself in the place of others.

ADJS. 5. **unselfish, selfless,** self-uncon-scious, self-forgetful, self-abasing; self-neglectful, self-neglecting; **self-denying,** self-renouncing, self-abnegatory; **self-sacri-ficing,** sacrificing, self-devotional; disinter-ested.

6. **magnanimous, generous, liberal; big, bighearted,** greathearted, largehearted; no-ble-minded, high-minded; **noble,** princely, handsome, great, high, elevated, lofty, exalted, sublime; chivalrous, knightly; heroic.

ADVS. 7. **unselfishly,** for others, forget-ful of self.

8. **magnanimously, generously, liberally; bigheartedly,** greatheartedly, largeheart-edly; **nobly,** handsomely; chivalrously, knightly.

978. VIRTUE

Moral Goodness.—NOUNS 1. **virtue, vir-tuousness,** goodness, **righteousness; moral-ity,** moral rectitude; **saintliness,** saintlike-ness, angelicalness; **godliness** 1026.2.

2. "the health of the soul" [Joubert], "the fount whence honour springs" [Mar-lowe], 'the adherence in action to the na-ture of things" [Emerson], "victorious resistance to one's vital desire to do this, that or the other" [James Branch Cabell], "to do unwitnessed what we should be capable of doing before all the world" [La Rochefoucauld].

3. **purity, chastity** 986; **innocence** 982.

4. **uncorruptness,** uncorruptedness; **un-sinfulness,** sinlessness; **unwickedness,** un-iniquitousness; undegenerateness, unde-pravedness, undissoluteness, undebauched-ness.

5. **cardinal virtues,** prudence, justice, temperance, fortitude, faith, hope, charity.

VERBS 6. **be good,** do no evil; keep in

the right path, walk the straight path, fol-low the straight and narrow, keep on the straight and narrow way; fight the good fight.

ADJS. 7. **virtuous, good, moral; right-eous,** just, right-minded; **angelic(al),** seraphic; **saintly,** saintlike; **godly** 1026.9.

8. **chaste, pure** 986.4; **innocent** 982.6.

9. **uncorrupt,** uncorrupted; **unsinful,** sinless; **unwicked,** uniniquitous, unerring, unfallen; undegenerate, undepraved, unde-moralized, undissolute, undebauched.

979. VICE

Moral Badness.—NOUNS 1. **vice,** "a fail-ure of desire" [Gerald S. Lee]; **bad habit,** besetting sin; **fault, failing** 676.2; **wrong-doing** 980.

2. **immorality,** unmorality; **amorality,** nonmorality.

3. **unvirtuousness,** ungoodness; **unright-eousness, ungodliness,** unsaintliness, un-angelicalness; unchastity 987; waywardness, wantonness, prodigality; delinquency, moral delinquency; peccability.

4. **iniquity, evil,** bad, wrong, error, ob-liquity, reprobacy, peccancy; **sin** 980.2.

5. **wickedness, badness, naughtiness,** evilness, viciousness, sinfulness, iniqui-tousness; baseness, vileness, foulness, ar-rantness, nefariousness, heinousness, villain-ousness; fiendishness, hellishness; devilish-ness, devilry, deviltry.

6. **turpitude, moral turpitude; corrup-tion,** corruptness, rottenness; **decadence** *or* decadency, debasement, degradation, de-moralization, abjection; **degeneracy,** degen-erateness, degeneration; **depravity,** pravity, depravedness, depravation; **dissoluteness, profligacy;** abandonment, abandon.

7. **obduracy, hardness, hardheartedness, callousness,** heartlessness, hardness of heart, heart of stone.

8. **evil nature,** the Devil within one, Adam, old Adam, offending Adam; cloven foot *or* hoof, horns.

9. **weakness,** weakness of the flesh, **frailty,** infirmity; **failing,** failure; weak point *or* side, foible.

10. **sink, sink of corruption; den of in-iquity,** den, Alsatian den, Domdaniel, hell, hellhole; hole, joint [both slang].

11. Sodom, Gomorrah, Babylon.

VERBS 12. **sin,** do wrong 980.3.

13. **go wrong,** go astray, err, deviate from the path of virtue, leave the straight and narrow; **fall,** lapse, slip, trip; **degener-**

ate 690.17; **go to the bad** 691.23; backslide 694.4.

14. **demoralize, vitiate,** drive to the dogs; **corrupt** 690.12; **sully, soil, defile.**

ADJS. 15. **immoral,** unmoral; **amoral,** nonmoral.

16. **unvirtuous,** virtueless, ungood; **unrighteous, ungodly, unsaintly, unangelic(al);** unchaste 987.23; wayward, wanton, prodigal; erring, fallen; frail, weak, infirm; peccable; of easy virtue 987.26.

17. **wicked, vicious, evil, bad, naughty, wrong, sinful, iniquitous,** peccant, reprobate; dark, black; **base, low, vile,** foul, rank, flagrant, arrant, nefarious, heinous, villainous, abominable, atrocious, enormous, monstrous, execrable, damnable; shameful, disgraceful, scandalous, infamous.

18. **diabolic(al), devilish,** demoniac(al), satanic, Mephistophelean or Mephistophelian; **fiendish,** fiendlike; **hellish,** hellborn, **infernal.**

19. **corrupt,** corrupted, vice-corrupted; **rotten,** tainted, contaminated, vitiated; warped, perverted; **decadent,** debased, degraded, demoralized, **depraved, debauched, dissolute, degenerate,** profligate, abandoned, gone to the bad or dogs, sunk or steeped in iniquity, rotten at or to the core.

20. **evil-minded, evilhearted,** blackhearted; **base-minded,** low-minded, low-thoughted.

21. **hardened, hard, tough,** hard-boiled [coll.]; **casehardened, obdurate,** inured, indurated; **callous,** calloused, **seared; hardhearted,** heartless; shameless, lost to shame, lost to all sense of honor.

22. **irreclaimable, irredeemable, irreformable,** incorrigible, past praying for; shriftless, graceless; **lost.**

ADVS. 23. **wickedly, evilly, sinfully, iniquitously,** peccantly, viciously; basely, vilely, foully, rankly, arrantly, flagrantly.

980. WRONGDOING

NOUNS 1. **wrongdoing, evildoing,** misdoing, **misconduct, misdemeanor,** misfeasance, malfeasance, malversation, **malpractice,** evil courses, machinations of the devil; **sin,** "thou scarlet sin" [Shakespeare], "the transgression of the law" [Bible]; **crime, criminality; vice** 979; misprision, negative or positive misprision, misprision of treason or felony [law].

2. **misdeed, misdemeanor,** misfeasance,

malfeasance, malefaction, **offense** or offence, **wrong, iniquity, evil,** peccancy, *malum* [L., law]; tort [law]; **error, fault,** indiscretion, peccadillo, trip, slip, lapse; **transgression,** trespass; **sin,** "deed without a name" [Shakespeare]; unpardonable ~, deadly or mortal sin; sin of commission; sin of omission, nonfeasance, omission, failure, dereliction, delinquency; **crime, felony;** capital crime; **outrage, atrocity,** enormity.

VERBS 3. **do wrong,** do amiss, **misdemean oneself,** err, offend; **sin,** sinner it [joc.], commit sin; transgress, trespass.

ADJS. 4. **wrongdoing, evildoing,** malefactory, malfeasant; **sinful** 979.17; **criminal, felonious.**

981. GUILT

NOUNS 1. **guilt, guiltiness; criminality,** peccancy; **culpability,** reprehensibility, blamability, chargeability, impeachability; dirty hands, red or bloody hands; guilty conscience.

VERBS 2. **catch red-handed** 487.7; look like the cat that swallowed the canary.

ADJS. 3. **guilty,** peccant, **criminal, to blame, at fault,** faulty, on one's head; **culpable** 967.26.

4. **red-handed,** red-hand, **in the act** or **very act,** *in flagrante delicto* [L.].

ADVS. 5. **guiltily,** shamefacedly, sheepishly, with a guilty conscience.

982. INNOCENCE

Freedom from Guilt.—NOUNS 1. **innocence,** innocency, innocentness; **unguiltiness, guiltlessness, faultlessness, blamelessness, sinlessness,** offenselessness; **spotlessness,** stainlessness, taintlessness; **purity,** cleanness, immaculacy, impeccability; clean hands, clean slate, clear conscience.

2. **childlikeness,** lamblikeness, dovelikeness.

3. **inculpability,** unblamability, **unblameworthiness,** irreproachability, irreprehensibility, uncensurability, unimpeachability.

4. **innocent,** babe, newborn babe, child, mere child, lamb, dove.

VERBS 5. **know no wrong,** have clean hands, have a clear conscience, look as if butter would not melt in one's mouth.

ADJS. 6. **innocent, unguilty, not guilty, guiltless, faultless, blameless, sinless,** offenseless, with clean hands, "blameless in life and pure of crime" [Horace]; clear, in the clear; without reproach, *sans reproche* [F.]; innocent as a lamb, lamblike, dovelike, childlike.

7. **spotless**, stainless, taintless, unspotted, **untainted, unsoiled, unsullied, undefiled; pure, clean, immaculate,** impeccable, white, "without unspotted, innocent within'" [Dryden].

8. **inculpable, unblamable, unblameworthy, irreproachable, irreprehensible,** uncensurable, **unimpeachable, unobjectionable, unexceptionable,** above suspicion.

ADVS. 9. **innocently,** guiltlessly, **unguiltily,** with a clear conscience; **unknowingly,** unconsciously, unawares.

983. REPUTABLE PERSONS

NOUNS 1. **worthy,** prince, nature's nobleman, man after one's own heart; *persona grata* [L.], acceptable person; **good fellow,** capital fellow, **good sort,** right sort, a decent sort of fellow, no end of a fellow; **gem,** jewel, pearl, diamond; rough diamond, diamond in the rough; honest man **972.8**.

2. (slang terms) **brick, trump, good egg,** stout fellow, stout fellah [Eng.], nice guy, good Joe [U.S.], likely lad, no slouch.

3. **good citizen, respectable citizen, pillar of society,** pillar of the church, **the salt of the earth;** Christian, white man [both coll.].

4. **paragon, ideal,** beau ideal, *beau idéal* [F.], *chevalier sans peur et sans reproche* F., fearless and irreproachable gentleman]: **good example,** shining example; examplar, **model, pattern, standard,** mirror, "the observed of all observers" [Shakespeare]; one in a thousand *or* ten thousand, man of men, a man among men.

5. **hero, god, demigod,** phoenix; **heroine,** goddess, demigoddess.

6. **saint, angel,** cherub, seraph; the good, the righteous.

7. **good woman,** heaven's noblest gift, "a perfect woman, nobly planned" [Wordsworth]; **virgin,** vestal, vestal virgin, Madonna.

984. DISREPUTABLE PERSONS

NOUNS 1. **unworthy,** disreputable; *persona non grata* [L.], unacceptable person; bad example.

2. **wretch,** mean wretch, **beggarly fellow, beggar, blighter** [slang, chiefly Eng.], bum [slang], **lowlifer** [slang], **mucker** [slang, U.S.], *âme-de-boue* [F., soul of mud], caitiff, bezonian, budmash [India],

pilgarlic; devil, **poor devil,** *pauvre diable* [F.], poor creature, *mauvais sujet* [F., poor subject]; **sad case,** sad sack [slang], sad dog [coll.]; **good-for-nothing, good-for-naught, no-good** [coll.], **ne'er-do-well,** wastrel, losel [arch. exc. dial.], *vaurien* [F.], worthless fellow; derelict, human wreck.

3. **rascal,** precious rascal, **rogue, knave, scoundrel, villain, blackguard, scamp, scalawag** [coll.], skeesicks [coll., U.S.], rascalion *or* rascallion, rapscallion, rap [slang], **devil,** *drôle* [F.], **limb** [coll.], **loon, lown** [dial. & Scot.]; *enfant terrible* [F., terrible child]; **shyster** [U.S.]; sneak, Jerry Sneak.

4. "a rascally yeaforsooth knave," "a foulmouthed and calumnious knave," "poor cuckoldy knave," "a poor, decayed, ingenious, foolish, rascally knave," "an arrant, rascally, beggarly, lousy knave," "a slipper and subtle knave, a finder of occasions," "a whoreson, beetle-headed, flapear'd knave," "filthy, worsted-stocking knave; a lily-livered, action-taking knave," "a knave; a rascal; an eater of broken meats; a base, proud, shallow, beggarly, three-suited, hundred-pound, filthy, worsted-stocking knave" [all Shakespeare].

5. **reprobate, rep, rip** [coll.], recreant, miscreant, *polisson* [F.]; **bad** *or* **sorry lot** [coll.], **bad egg** [slang], bad hat [slang], **wrong'un** [slang]; **scapegrace, black sheep; lost soul,** lost sheep, *âme damnée* [F.], fallen angel; degenerate, pervert.

6. **louse, heel, rat, stinker,** stinkard, bugger, cuss, bastard, son of a bitch, S.O.B. [all slang]; **cur,** dog, hound, whelp, mongrel; **reptile, viper, serpent, snake;** varmint [dial.], hyena [coll.], **swine; skunk,** polecat; insect, worm.

7. **cad, bounder** [coll.], **rotter**]slang].

8. **wrongdoer, malefactor, sinner,** transgressor, delinquent; malfeasor, misfeasor, nonfeasor [all law]; misdemeanant, misdemeanist; **culprit,** offender; evildoer **941**.

9. **criminal, felon, crook** [coll.], **public enemy, lawbreaker,** scofflaw; **gangster** [coll., U.S.], **racketeer;** swindler **617.3, 4;** thief **823;** thug **941.4; desperado,** desperate criminal; **outlaw,** fugitive, *proscrit* [F.]; **convict,** jailbird [U.S.], gaolbird [Eng.]; gallows bird [coll.].

10. **the underworld,** gangland, gangdom, the rackets, **the mob,** the syndicate [all slang, U.S.]; **the Mafia;** Black Hand.

11. **the wicked,** the bad, the evil, the unrighteous, the reprobate; sons of men, sons of Belial, sons *or* children of the devil,

children of darkness; **scum of the earth,** dregs of society.

985. SENSUALITY

NOUNS **1. sensuality,** sensualism, **sensuousness; voluptuousness,** luxuriousness, luxury; sybaritism; epicurism, epicureanism.

2. carnality, carnal-mindedness; **fleshliness,** flesh; animal or carnal nature, the flesh, the beast, Adam, the Old Adam, the offending Adam; animality, animalism, **bestiality,** brutishness, **brutality;** coarseness, grossness; swinishness.

3. sensualist, sensuist; **voluptuary,** sybarite, Heliogabalus, **hedonist,** bon vivant [F.], carpet knight; epicure, epicurean; gourmet, gourmand.

VERBS **4. sensualize,** carnalize, coarsen, brutify.

ADJS. **5. sensual, sensuous; voluptuous,** luxurious; epicurean, sybaritic(al).

6. carnal, carnal-minded, fleshly; animal, animalistic, theroid; **brutish, brutal,** brute; **bestial,** beastly, beastlike; coarse, gross; swinish.

986. CHASTITY

NOUNS **1. chastity, virtue,** virtuousness, honor; **purity,** cleanness; **immaculacy,** spotlessness, stainlessness, taintlessness; uncorruptness 978.4.

2. decency, seemliness, **propriety, decorum,** decorousness, elegance, delicacy; **modesty,** shame, pudicity.

3. continence or continency; abstinence 990.2; celibacy; virginity; Platonic love, Platonism.

ADJS. **4. chaste, virtuous; pure,** purehearted, pure in heart; **clean,** cleanly; **immaculate, spotless,** stainless, taintless, white; **unsoiled, unsullied, undefiled,** untarnished, unstained, unspotted, untainted; uncorrupt 978.9; "as chaste as Diana" [Shakespeare], "as chaste as unsunn'd snow" [ibid.], "chaste as morning dew" [Young].

5. decent, modest, decorous, delicate, elegant, proper, becoming, seemly.

6. continent; abstinent 990.10; celibate; virginal, virgin; Platonic.

7. undebauched, undissipated, undissolute, unwanton, unlicentious.

987. UNCHASTITY

NOUNS **1. unchastity,** unchasteness; **unvirtuousness; impurity,** uncleanness; **indecency** 988.

2. incontinence, uncontinence; intemperance 991; unrestraint 760.2.

3. profligacy, dissoluteness, licentiousness; wildness, fastness, rakishness; libertinism, libertinage; **dissipation, debauchery,** debauchment; **venery,** wenching, whoring.

4. wantonness, waywardness; looseness, laxity, lightness, loose morals, easy virtue.

5. lasciviousness, lechery, lecherousness, lewdness, bawdiness, salacity, salaciousness, **lust, lustfulness,** prurience or pruriency, concupiscence, lickerishness, libidinousness, lubricity, **sensuality,** eroticism, goatishness; satyrism, satyriasis [med.].

6. seduction, seducement, **betrayal; violation,** abuse; **debauchment, defloration,** deflowering, **defilement,** ravishment, ravage, despoilment; **rape,** stupration.

7. (illicit intercourse) **adultery,** criminal conversation [law]; **fornication;** free love, free-lovism; **incest;** concubinage; cuckoldry.

8. prostitution, harlotry, whoredom, bordel, social evil, **streetwalking,** meretricious traffic, Mrs. Warren's profession; whoremonging, whoremastery.

9. brothel, house of prostitution, house of joy or ill fame, **bawdyhouse,** whorehouse [vulg.], **bordello,** bagnio, Shinjuku [Jap.], stew, dive, den of vice, sink of iniquity; cat house, crib, joint [all slang]; panel house or den; red-light district, tenderloin, stews, street of fallen women.

10. libertine, profligate, rake, rip [coll.], **roué,** wanton, paillard [F.], loose fish [coll.], debauchee, rounder [slang], **wolf** [slang], woman chaser, skirt chaser [slang], gay dog, gay deceiver, chartered libertine.

11. lecher, satyr, goat, old goat, whoremonger, whoremaster, whorehound [slang].

12. seducer, betrayer, deceiver; **debaucher, ravisher,** ravager, violator, despoiler, defiler; raper, rapist.

13. adulterer, fornicator; adulteress, fornicatress, fornicatrix.

14. strumpet, trollop, wench, hussy, slut, jade, baggage, bag [slang], piece [slang], cocotte [F.], grisette, lorette [F.], **tart** [slang], **chippy** [slang, U.S.], **floozy** [slang], broad [slang, U.S.], bitch [vulg.], drab, trull, quean, harridan, Jezebel, mopsy [dial., Eng.], wanton, bad woman, **loose woman,** easy woman [coll.], woman of easy virtue, frail [slang, U.S.], frail sister; pickup.

15. demimonde, demimondaine, demirep [slang]; **courtesan** or courtezan, adventuress. hetaera [ancient Greece]; Jezebel, Messalina, Delilah, Thais, Phryne, Aspasia, Lais.

16. **prostitute, harlot, whore,** *fille de joie* [**F.**], daughter of joy, **scarlet woman,** unfortunate woman, painted woman, fallen woman, erring sister, **streetwalker,** woman of the town, *poule* [F.], cat [slang], bat [slang], stew, meretrix, Cyprian, Paphian; white slave; Sadie Thompson, Mrs. Warren.

17. **mistress,** woman, **kept woman,** kept mistress, **paramour,** concubine, doxy, spiritual wife.

18. **procurer, pimp,** pander, *maquereau* [F.], **bawd,** runner [slang, U.S.]; **gigolo,** fancy man; procuress, *conciliatrix* [L.], madam [coll.]; white slaver.

VERBS 19. **debauch, wanton,** rake, chase women, whore, sow one's wild oats; **dissipate** 991.6; fornicate, commit adultery; grovel, wallow, wallow in the mire.

20. **seduce, betray, deceive,** mislead, lead astray; **debauch, deflower, ravish,** ravage, despoil, ruin; **defile,** soil, sully; **violate, abuse; rape,** force.

21. **prostitute;** pimp, procure, pander.

22. **cuckold,** father upon; wear horns, wear the horn.

ADJS. 23. **unchaste, unvirtuous,** unvirginal; **impure, unclean; indecent** 988.5; soiled, sullied, smirched, besmirched, defiled.

24. **incontinent,** uncontinent; intemperate 991.7; unrestrained 760.22.

25. **profligate, licentious,** free; **dissolute, dissipated, debauched,** abandoned; **wild, fast,** gay, rakish; rakehell, rakehellish, rakehelly.

26. **wanton, wayward,** Paphian; **loose,** lax, slack, loose-moraled, of loose morals, of easy virtue, easy [coll.], **light,** no better than she should be.

27. **freeloving; adulterous,** illicit; incestuous.

28. **prostitute, prostituted, whorish,** harlot, scarlet, fallen, meretricious, streetwalking, on the town *or* streets, on the *pavé* [F.].

29. **lascivious, lecherous, salacious, lustful,** prurient, concupiscent, lickerish, libidinous, lubricous, **lewd, bawdy,** erotic, **sensual,** fleshly; goatish, satyric(al).

988. INDECENCY

NOUNS 1. **indecency, indelicacy,** inelegance *or* inelegancy, **indecorousness,** in-

decorum, **impropriety,** unseemliness; unchastity 987.

2. **immodesty,** unmodestness, impudicity; **shamelessness,** unembarrassedness; **brazenness,** forwardness, boldness.

3. **vulgarity, uncouthness, coarseness,** grossness, rankness, rawness; raciness, saltiness, spiciness.

4. **obscenity,** bawdry, **ribaldry, pornography,** salacity, **smut, dirt, filth; lewdness,** bawdiness, salaciousness, dirtiness, smuttiness, **foulness, filthiness,** nastiness, vileness, offensiveness; scurrility, fescenninity.

ADJS. 5. **indecent, indelicate, inelegant, indecorous, improper, unseemly,** unbecoming.

6. **immodest,** unmodest; **shameless,** unashamed, unembarrassed, unabashed, unblushing; **brazen,** brazenfaced; **forward,** bold.

7. **risqué, risky, racy,** salty, **spicy, off-color** [U.S.], suggestive [U.S.], scabrous.

8. **vulgar, uncouth, coarse, gross,** rank, raw, broad, low.

9. **obscene, lewd, bawdy, ribald, pornographic, salacious,** sultry [slang], lurid, **dirty, smutty,** impure, unchaste, unclean, **foul, filthy, nasty,** vile, fulsome, offensive, unprintable, not to be mentioned to ears polite; scurrilous, scurrile, Fescennine; foul-mouthed, foul-tongued, foul-spoken.

989. ASCETICISM

NOUNS 1. **asceticism, austerity;** puritanism, anchorism, Sabbatarianism, cynicism; Yoga; **mortification,** maceration, flagellation; **abstinence** 990.2; austerity program [Eng.].

2. **ascetic, puritan,** Sabbatarian, cynic; abstainer 990.4; hermit 922.5; yogi, yogin; sannyasi, bhikshu [both India]; dervish, fakir [both Moham.]; flagellant.

ADJS. 3. **ascetic, austere, puritanical,** anchoritic(al), Sabbatarian; **abstinent** 990.10.

990. TEMPERANCE

NOUNS 1. **temperance,** temperateness, **moderation,** sobriety, frugality, forbearance, abnegation; **renunciation,** renouncement; denial, **self-denial;** restraint, **self-restraint; self-control,** self-discipline.

2. **abstinence,** abstention, abstainment, **abstemiousness;** avoidance, eschewal; total

abstinence, **teetotalism**; nephalism, Rechabitism; Encratism; Pythagorism, Pythagoreanism; gymnosophy; Stoicism; vegetarianism, fruitarianism; **continence** 986.3; **asceticism** 989.

3. **prohibition**, prohibitionism; Eighteenth Amendment [U.S.].

4. **abstainer**, abstinent; **teetotaler**, teetotalist; nephalist, Rechabite, hydropot, water-drinker; vegetarian, fruitarian; banian, banya [both Hindu]; gymnosophist; Pythagorean, Pythagorist; Encratite, Apostolic; **ascetic** 989.2.

5. **prohibitionist, dry** [slang]; Good Templar; Anti-Saloon League [U.S.], Band of Hope [Eng.]; Women's Christian Temperance Union, W.C.T.U.

VERBS 6. **restrain oneself**, constrain oneself, curb oneself, hold back; **limit oneself**, **restrict oneself**; **control oneself**, contain oneself, discipline oneself, exercise self-control or self-restraint, keep oneself under control, keep in or within bounds, keep within compass, know when one has had enough; mortify oneself, mortify the flesh, control the fleshly lusts, control the carnal man or the old Adam, "let the passions be amenable to reason" [Cicero].

7. **abstain**, abstain from, refrain, **refrain from**, forbear, **forgo**, spare, withhold, hold back, **avoid, shun,** eschew, **keep from**, keep ~, stand or hold aloof from, have nothing to do with, take no part in, have no hand in, **let alone**, let well enough alone, **deny oneself**, do without, not touch; "look not upon the wine when it is red" [Bible].

8. **swear off, renounce,** forswear, **give up**, abandon, stop, discontinue; take the pledge, get on the wagon or water wagon [slang].

ADJS. 9. **temperate, moderate,** sober, frugal, restrained, **sparing,** stinting, measured.

10. **abstinent,** abstentious, **abstemious**; teetotal; sworn off, on the wagon or water wagon [slang]; vegetarian, fruitarian; **continent** 986.6; **ascetic** 989.3.

11. antisaloon [U.S.], dry [coll., U.S.].

ADVS. 12. **temperately, moderately,** sparingly, stintingly, frugally, in moderation, within compass or bounds.

991. INTEMPERANCE

NOUNS 1. **intemperance,** intemperateness, **inabstinence; indulgence, self-indulgence; overindulgence,** overdoing; un-

restraint, uncontrol; **immoderation,** immoderacy, immoderateness; inordinacy, inordinateness; excess, excessiveness; prodigality, extravagance; crapulence or crapulency, crapulousness; **incontinence** 987.2; **gluttony** 992; **drunkenness** 994.

2. **dissipation, licentiousness; riotous living,** free living, high living [coll.]; **debauchery,** debauchment; **carousal,** carouse; **debauch, orgy,** saturnalia.

3. **dissipater** or dissipator, rounder [coll.], free liver, high liver [coll.], high roller [slang, U.S.]; nighthawk, night owl [both coll.].

VERBS 4. **indulge,** indulge oneself, indulge one's appetites, "indulge in easy vices" [Johnson]; **give oneself up to,** give free course to, give free rein to; live well or high, live on the fat of the land; indulge in, luxuriate in, wallow in; "look upon the wine when it is red" [Bible].

5. **overindulge, overdo, carry to excess,** carry too far; dine not wisely but too well.

6. **dissipate,** plunge into dissipation, **debauch, wanton, carouse,** run riot, live hard or fast, squander one's money in riotous living, burn the candle at both ends, sow one's wild oats, have one's fling, "eat, drink, and be merry" [Bible].

ADJS. 7. **intemperate, inabstinent; indulgent, self-indulgent; overindulgent,** overindulging; **immoderate,** inordinate, **excessive,** prodigal, extravagant; crapulous, crapulent; **unrestrained** 760.22; **incontinent** 987.24; **gluttonous** 992.7; bibulous 994.44.

8. **dissipated, licentious, riotous,** dissolute, debauched; free-living, high-living [coll.].

9. **orgiastic,** saturnalian, Corybantic.

ADVS. 10. **intemperately,** prodigally, **immoderately,** inordinately, excessively, **in** or **to excess,** without restraint.

992. GLUTTONY

NOUNS 1. **gluttony,** gluttonousness, **greed,** greediness, voraciousness, voracity, ravenousness, edacity, crapulence or crapulency, gulosity; **piggishness, hoggishness,** swinishness, "swinish gluttony" [Milton]; overindulgence, overeating; intemperance 991.

2. **epicurism,** epicureanism, **gourmanderie,** gastronomy, gastrology [joc.].

3. **glutton,** greedy eater, hefty or husky eater [coll.], belly-god, greedygut or greedyguts [vulg.], gorger, gormandizer, guttler,

cormorant; **hog, pig** [both coll.], trencherman.

4. **gourmand, gourmet;** epicure, epicurean; gastronome, gastronomist; Apicius.

VERBS 5. gluttonize, gormandize, **indulge one's appetite; gorge,** engorge, glut, cram, **stuff,** batten, guttle, guzzle, **devour,** raven, bolt, gobble, gulp, **wolf,** gobble ~, gulp ~, bolt or wolf down, whale down [coll.], play a good knife and fork [coll.], eat like a horse, eat one's head off [coll.], eat out of house and home.

6. **overeat,** overgorge, **overindulge,** make a pig or hog of oneself.

ADJS 7. **gluttonous, greedy,** voracious, ravenous, edacious, Apician; **piggish, hoggish, swinish;** crapulous, crapulent; intemperate 991.7; omnivorous, all-devouring.

8. overfed, overgorged, overindulged.

ADVS 9. **gluttonously, greedily,** voraciously ravenously, edaciously; piggishly, hoggishly, swinishly.

993. FASTING

NOUNS 1. **fasting,** punishment of Tantalus.

2. **fast,** spare or meager diet, lenten diet, "lenten entertainment" [Shakespeare]; short-commons, short rations; xerophagy, xerophagia; Barmecide feast.

3. **fast day,** jour maigre [F.], fish day, banyan day; **Lent,** Quadragesima, Quadragesima Sunday; Ramadan [Moham.].

VERBS 4. **fast,** not eat, go hungry, dine with Duke Humphrey.

ADJS 5. **fasting,** uneating, unfed; **lenten,** quadragesimal.

994. INTOXICATION

NOUNS 1. **intoxication, inebriation, inebriety,** insobriety, **drunkenness, tipsiness,** befuddlement; fuddle, fuddlement, tipsification, obfuscation [all coll.]; Dutch courage, pot-valiance or pot-valiancy, pot-valor; hang-over [slang, U.S.].

2. **bibulousness,** bibacity, bibaciousness, bibulosity; crapulence, crapulousness; **intemperance** 991; bacchanalianism; Bacchus [Rom. myth.], Dionysus [Gr. myth.].

3. **alcoholism, dipsomania,** oenomania or oinomania, alcoholic psychosis, pathological drunkenness; delirium tremens 472.10; grog blossom, bottle nose [both coll.]; gin drinker's liver.

4. **drinking, tippling,** guzzling, bibbing; winebibbing, winebibbery; **toping,** boozing, swilling [all coll.]; potation, compotation, symposium [hist.].

5. **spree, drinking bout,** bout, **celebration,** potation, wassail, guzzle [vulg.], randy [Scot. & dial., Eng.], randan [dial. & slang]; **carouse, carousal,** drunken carousal or revelry; booze, fuddle [both coll.]; **binge, drunk,** soak, bust, tear, skate, rantan or ran-tan, bout with John Barleycorn [all slang]; **bender,** hellbender, **toot, bat,** bum, jag, souse [all slang, U.S.]; bacchanal, bacchanalia, bacchanalian; **debauch, orgy.**

6. **dram, drink, potation,** potion, libation [joc.], **nip,** nipper, draught or draft, drop, sip, sup, suck, drench, guzzle [vulg.], jigger [slang, U.S.]; peg, swig, swill, pull, toothful, tickler [all coll.]; snort, jolt, shot, snifter, smile, wet, facer, calker or caulker, coffin nail, nail in the coffin, drop in the eye [all slang].

7. **bracer, refresher, pick-me-up** [all coll.]; pickup, reviver [both slang]; hair of the dog, hair of the dog that bit you [both coll.].

8. (specific drinks) **eye opener** [slang, U.S.], morning's morning [slang], antifogmatic [joc., U.S.]; **nightcap** [coll.], sundowner [slang]; **chaser** [coll., U.S.], poussecafé [F.], apéritif [F.]; parting cup, stirrup cup, doch-an-dorrach [Scot.]; cheerer [Scot. & N. of Eng.], cheering drink or cup; mickey finn [slang, U.S.], hocus, knockout drops [slang, U.S.].

9. **toast, pledge;** Dutch bargain, wet bargain.

10. **drunkard, inebriate,** sot, **tippler, toper,** bibber, guzzler, swiller, soaker, lovepot, tosspot, **barfly,** thirsty soul, devotee of Bacchus, slave of the beast; **boozer,** bouser, fuddler, swigger, tun [all coll.]; winebibber, wino [slang, U.S.], oenophilist; hard drinker, big drunk [slang]; **alcoholic, dipsomaniac;** carouser, reveler, wassailer; bacchanal, bacchanalian; pot companion.

11. (slang terms) **drunk, lush,** lusher, **soak,** sponge, hooch hound, **boozehound,** ginhound, elbow bender or crooker, bottle sucker, swillbelly, swillpot, swillbowl, tank, Admiral of the Red; **souse, stew,** bum, rummy, rum hound, booze fighter [all U.S.].

12. **liquor,** intoxicating liquor, "the luscious liquor" [Milton], **hard liquor** [U.S.], **spirits, ardent spirits, intoxicant,** toxicant, inebriant, **potable,** potation, **beverage, drink, strong drink,** alcoholic drink

or beverage, **alcohol,** aqua vitae, brew, the creature [dial. & joc.], firewater, **grog,** tipple, fuddle [coll.], budge [local, U.S.], guzzle [vulg.], pot, social lubricant, Bacchus, nectar of the gods; **booze,** bouse [both coll.]; **rum,** the Demon Rum [both U.S.]; the bottle, the cup, the cup that cheers, "the ruddy cup" [Scott], little brown jug; punch bowl, the flowing bowl.

13. (slang terms) **likker, hooch,** lush, alky, fogram *or* fogrum [naut.], lap, gullet wash, tangle-legs, diddle, tape, ammunition, eyewater, neck oil, oil of joy, joy water, whoopee water [U.S.], crazy water, conversation water, tiger milk, nose paint, sorrow drowner, bosom friend, courage, Dutch courage, liquid courage, tonic, medicine, snake medicine, corpse reviver.

14. (strong liquor; slang and joc.] busthead [U.S.], popskull, cutthroat, stingo, bottled dynamite, liquid fire, boilermaker's delight.

15. (bad liquor; slang and joc.) **rotgut,** craw rot, poison, rat poison, formaldehyde, embalming fluid, shellac, coffin varnish.

16. (liquors) applejack, Jersey lightning [slang, U.S.]; gin, ruin [slang, Eng.], blue ruin [slang]; corn whisky, corn [coll., U.S.]; **cordial, liqueur.**

17. **beer,** "barmy beer" [Dryden]; malt, swipes [Eng.], hops, suds [all slang]; small beer, belch [vulg.].

18. **wine,** *vin* [F.], *vino* [Sp.], "the wine that is red" [Bible]; vintage wine, dry *or* sweet wine, heavy *or* light wine, full *or* thin wine, rough *or* smooth wine, still wine, sparkling wine; new wine, must.

19. **mixed drink, cocktail, highball** [U.S.], **punch.**

20. **home-brew,** bathtub gin [slang, U.S.], bottled-in-barn [joc.]; kaffir beer [Africa].

21. **bootleg** [U.S.], **hooch, moonshine** [coll.]; shine [U.S.], moonlight, mountain dew [all slang].

22. **bootlegging** [U.S.], **moonshining** [coll.], moonlighting [slang]; **rumrunning** [U.S.].

23. **liquor dealer,** rummy [slang, U.S.]; **bartender, barkeeper,** barkeep [U.S.], barman [Eng.], tapster, publican [Eng.]; barmaid, tapstress, **vintner,** wine merchant; **distiller, brewer, brewmaster.**

24. **bootlegger** [U.S.], **moonshiner** [coll.], moonlighter [slang, U.S.]; blind-pigger [slang, U.S.]; **rumrunner** [U.S.].

25. **barroom, bar, taproom,** tap [coll.],

tavern, pothouse, mughouse, alehouse, rumshop [U.S.], grogshop, dramshop, groggery [U.S.], gin mill [slang], exchange [slang, U.S.], boozer [slang, Eng.]; **saloon** [U.S.], drinking saloon, saloon bar [Eng.]; **public house,** public [coll., Eng.], **pub** [slang, Eng.]; **beer parlor,** beerhouse, jerry shop [slang, Eng.], beer garden; **cocktail lounge;** cabaret; wine shop, *bistro* [coll., F.]; rathskeller [U.S.]; barrel house [slang, U.S.], honky-tonk [U.S.], dive [chiefly U.S.].

26. **speakeasy** [slang, U.S.], blind tiger [slang], blind pig [slang, U.S.], shebeen [Ir. & Scot.].

27. **distillery, still,** distiller; **brewery,** brewhouse; **winery,** wine press; bottling works.

VERBS 28. **intoxicate, inebriate, addle, befuddle,** bemuse, besot, go to one's head, make one see double; **tipsify, fuddle,** overtake [all coll.]; **swack, plaster, pickle,** crock, stew, souse, boozify, pollute, illuminate, disguise [all slang].

29. **tipple, drink,** dram [esp. Eng.], **nip,** grog, **guzzle,** swizzle, soak, bib, tun, quaff, sip, sup, lap, lap up, take a drop, take a whet, slake one's thirst, cheer *or* refresh the inner man, drown one's sorrows, commune with the spirits [joc.]; toss off *or* down, toss one's drink; drink off *or* up, drain the cup, drink bottoms-up, leave no heeltaps; drink deep; drink hard, drink like a fish; take to drink *or* drinking, "follow strong drink" [Bible].

30. (colloquialisms) **tope, booze,** bouse, swig, swill, fuddle, moisten *or* wet one's clay, wet one's whistle *or* swallow; take a hair of the dog *or* of the dog that bit you.

31. (slang terms) **liquor, liquor up,** lush, souse, bum [U.S.], tank up, fire up, prime up, hit the booze *or* bottle, exercise ~, bend ~, crook *or* raise the elbow, dip the beak, take a drop in the eye, splice the main brace, drown the shamrock.

32. **get drunk,** drunken, take a drop too much; **get plastered,** ~ **pickled,** etc., tie one on, get a bun on [all slang].

33. (be drunk) **show one's drinks** [coll.], have a drop too much, have one over the eight [coll.], have more than one can hold, have a jag on [slang], see double; **stagger, reel; pass out** [slang, U.S.].

34. **go on a spree, go on a binge** [slang], **go on a drunk** [slang], **go on a toot,** ~ **bat** *or* **bender** [slang, U.S.], carouse, spree, revel, wassail, debauch, "eat,

drink, and be merry" [Bible], paint the town red [slang].

35. drink to, toast, pledge, drink a toast to, drink *or* pledge the health of, look toward [coll.]; hobnob, hob-and-nob, drink hob-and-nob *or* hob-a-nob; wet [slang], wet a bargain *or* deal [slang], make a Dutch bargain *or* wet bargain.

36. distill *or* distil, **brew.**

37. bootleg [U.S.], **moonshine** [coll.], moonlight [slang].

ADJS **38. intoxicated, inebriated,** inebriate, inebrious, **drunk, drunken, tipsy,** in liquor, **in one's cups, under the influence,** the worse for liquor; nappy, beery; **giddy, dizzy,** muddled, addled, flustered, bemused, reeling, seeing double; **mellow, merry,** jolly, happy, gay, glorious; **full, fou** [Scot.] **besotted,** sodden, drenched, far-gone; drunk as a lord, drunk as a fiddler *or* piper, drunk as an owl, drunk as David's sow; crapulent, crapulous; **maudlin.**

39. (colloquialisms) **fuddled,** groggy, muzzy, flush, flushed, obfuscated, boozy, bousy, ginny, overtaken, with one over the eight.

40. (slang terms) **swacked, plastered, pickled,** soused, soaked, boiled, fried, canned, tanked, potted, corned, **crocked, crocko,** shellacked, **tight,** heeled, lush, lushy, jingled, squiffy, balmy, hiccius-doccius [Eng.], afflicted, fresh, jug-bitten, oiled, lubricated, polluted, screwed, raddled, sprung, cut, sewed up, organized, disguised, gilded, **high,** elevated, high as a kite, in one's airs *or* altitudes, out of altitudes, **lit up,** illuminated, glowing, fired up, charged up, hopped up, jagged up, loaded, primed, **stinko,** pie-eyed, cockeyed, cock-eyed drunk, roaring *or* rip-roaring drunk.

41. (nautical figures) **half-seas over,** bearing *or* flying the ensign, listing to starboard, decks-awash, **three sheets in the wind,** carrying *or* with too much sail, in the wind *or* wind's eye, with the top gallant sails out.

42. full of Dutch courage, pot-valiant, pot-valorous.

43. dead-drunk, blind drunk, blind [coll.], overcome, out [coll.], **out cold** [slang], passed out [slang, U.S.], **blotto** [slang], **stiff** [slang], helpless, under the table.

44. bibulous, bibacious, drunken, sottish, liquorish, given *or* addicted to drink, **liquor-loving,** liquor-drinking, drinking, toping [coll.], tippling, winebibbing.

45. intoxicating, intoxicative, **inebriating,** inebriative, inebriant, heady.

46. alcoholic, spirituous, ardent, strong, hard [U.S.], with a kick [slang]; winy, vinous.

INTERJS. **47.** (toasts) **skoal!, prosit!,** cheerio!, down the hatch!, here's how!, here's to you!, here's looking at you!, here's mud in your eye!, here's good luck!, here's to absent friends!

48. alcoholic beverages

ale	lager, lager beer
applejack	[U.S.]
armagnac	malt extract
arrack	mead
Bacardi	metheglin
beer	Munich beer
bitters [Eng.]	near-beer
bock beer, bock	Pilsener beer
[U.S.]	pombe [Africa]
bourbon	porter
brandy	pulque
clean rum	rum
cognac	rye, rye whisky
corn whisky	sake, saki
Danzig brandy	schenk beer
Dubonnet	schnapps
gin	Scotch whiskey,
goldwater	Scotch
Hollands, Holland	sloe gin
gin	stout
Irish whiskey	tequila
Jamaica gin	vodka
Jamaica rum	weiss beer
kirsch, kirsch-	whisky, whiskey
wasser	

49. wines

amontillado	mulled wine
Bordeaux	muscatel
Burgundy	port
canary	red wine
Catawba	Rhine wine
Chablis	Riesling
champagne	ruby port
Chianti	sack
claret	sauterne
dago red [slang,	sherry
U.S.]	sparkling
hock	Burgundy
Madeira	tawny port
Malaga	Tokay
malmsey	vermouth
manzanilla	*vin du pays* [F.]
May wine	*vin ordinaire* [F.]
Medoc	*vin rosé* [F.]
Moselle	white wine

50. liqueurs and cordials

absinthe, absinth	*crème de moka*
anisette	[F.]
Benedictine	*crème de noyau*
cassis	[F.]
Chartreuse	curaçao
Cointreau	Drambuie
crème de cacao	kümmel
[F.]	maraschino
crème de menthe	Pernod

51. mixed drinks

bishop	lamb's wool
Bloody Mary	Manhattan
brandy Alexander	martini
brandy and soda,	mint julep
B.S.	Moscow mule
brandy smash	negus
Bronx cocktail	old-fashioned
buttered rum	pink lady
cobbler	planter's punch
coffee royale	posset
collins	purl
cooler	rickey
Cuba Libre	side car
daiquiri	sling
eggnogg	smash
fizz	sour
flip	stinger
gin fizz	swizzle
gin rickey	toddy
gin sling	Tom and Jerry
grasshopper	Tom Collins
highball	wassail
hot toddy	whisky smash
Irish coffee	whisky sour
julep	

995. SOBRIETY

Unintoxicated State.—NOUNS 1. **sobriety, soberness;** unintoxicatedness, uninebriatedness, undrunkenness; temperance 990.

VERBS 2. **sober up,** sober off; sleep it off.

ADJS. 3. **sober,** in one's sober senses, in one's right mind, in possession of one's faculties; **unintoxicated, uninebriated,** uninebriate, uninebrious, undrunk, undrunken, untipsy; cold sober [coll.], **sober as a judge;** able to walk the chalk, able to walk the chalk mark or line [both coll.]; temperate 990.9.

4. **unintoxicating,** nonintoxicating, uninebriating; **nonalcoholic, soft** [U.S.].

996. LEGALITY

NOUNS 1. **legality, legitimacy, lawfulness, legitimateness, licitness,** rightfulness; constitutionality; legalism, constitutionalism.

2. **legalization, legitimatization;** authorization, sanction; legislation, enactment 740.15.

3. **law,** *lex* [L.], *jus* [L.], statute, rubric, canon, institution; **ordinance,** ordonnance; **act, enactment, measure,** legislation; **rule, ruling;** prescript, prescription; **regulation,** *règlement* [F.]; **dictate,** dictation; form, formula, formulary, formality; standing order; bylaw or byelaw; **decree** 750.4; **bill** 740.19.

4. (laws) common law, *jus commune*

[L.]; unwritten law, *lex non scripta* [L.]; written or statute law, *lex scripta* [L.], *jus scriptum* [L.]; constitutional law; civil law, *jus civile* [L.]; criminal law, crown law [Eng.]; penal law; public law, *jus publicum* [L.]; international law, law of nations, *jus inter gentes* [L.], *droit des gens* [F.]; local law, law of the place, *lex loci* or *situs* [L.]; law of the land, *lex terrae* [L.]; law of the domicile, *lex domicilii* [L.]; law of general application, *lex generalis* [L.]; law of the forum, *lex fori* [L.]; mercantile law, *lex mercatorum* or *mercatoria* [L.]; commercial law, law merchant; canon or ecclesiastical law, *jus ecclesiasticum* [L.], Corpus Juris Canonici; Roman law, Corpus Juris Civilis; blue law; dry law; gag law.

5. **code, digest,** pandect, capitulary [chiefly pl.], **body of law,** corpus juris, code of laws, digest of law; equity; codification.

6. **constitution,** written constitution, unwritten constitution; constitutional amendment; Eighteenth Amendment, the Noble Experiment, the Lost Cause; Twentieth Amendment, lame-duck act; Bill of Rights.

7. **jurisprudence, law,** legal science; nomology, nomography; forensic or legal medicine, medical jurisprudence, medicolegal medicine; forensic psychiatry; forensic or legal chemistry; criminology.

VERBS 8. **legalize, legitimatize,** legitimize, legitimate, make legal, declare lawful; **authorize, sanction;** constitute, ordain, establish, put in force; prescribe, formulate; regulate, make a regulation; decree 750.9; legislate, enact 740.20.

9. **codify,** digest.

ADJS. 10. **legal, legitimate,** legit [slang], **licit, lawful,** rightful, according to law, within the law; **judicial,** juridic(al); **authorized, sanctioned,** valid; **constitutional;** statutory, statutable; lawlike.

11. **jurisprudent,** jurisprudential; legalistic; forensic; nomistic, nomothetic(al); criminologic(al).

ADVS. 12. **legally, legitimately, licitly, lawfully,** by law, *de jure* [L.], in the eyes of the law.

997. ILLEGALITY

NOUNS 1. **illegality, unlawfulness, illicitness,** lawlessness, wrongfulness; unauthorization; unconstitutionality; **criminality,** criminalism; outlawry; illicit business 824.

2. **illegitimacy, illegitimateness,** illegit-

imaticn; **bastardy,** bastardism; bend or bar sinister, baton [both her.].

3. lawbreaking, violation of law; transgression, trespass, trespassing.

4. offense or offence, **wrong,** illegality; violation 767.2; **crime, felony; misdemeanor;** tort [law]; delict, delictum [both law].

VERBS **5. break the law, violate the law,** violate 767.4, **transgress,** trespass, disobey the law, offend against the law, fly in the face of the law, set the law at defiance, set the law at naught, disregard the law, take the law into one's own hands; commit a crime.

ADJS. **6. illegal, unlawful, illegitimate, illicit,** nonlicit, nonlegal, lawless, wrongful, **against the law; unauthorized,** unallowed, unwarranted, unwarrantable, unofficial; **unconstitutional,** nonconstitutional; actionable; **criminal, felonious; outlaw, outlawed; contraband,** bootleg [U.S.], black-market; under-the-table, under-the-counter.

7. illegitimate, spurious, false; **bastard,** misbegot, **misbegotten,** miscreated, baseborn, born out of wedlock, **without benefit of clergy.**

ADVS. **8. illegally, unlawfully, illegitimately,** illicitly; criminally, feloniously; contrary to law, in violation of law.

998. JURISDICTION

Administration of Justice.—NOUNS **1. jurisdiction,** legal authority, ∼ power or right; original or appellate jurisdiction, exclusive or concurrent jurisdiction, civil or criminal jurisdiction, common-law or equitable jurisdiction, in rem or in personam jurisdiction.

2. judicature, judicatory; **justice,** the wheels of justice; judgment 493.

3. magistracy, magistrature, magistrateship; **judgeship,** justiceship; mayoralty, mayorship.

4. bureau, office, department, cutcherry [India]; secretariat, ministry, commissariat [Russ.]; municipality, bailiwick; constabulary, constablery, sheriffry, sheriffalty, shrievalty; constablewick, sheriffwick.

VERBS **5. administer justice,** administer, administrate; preside, preside at the board; sit in judgment 1002.17.

ADJS. **6. judicatory,** judicatorial, judicative, **juridic**(al); **judicial, judiciary,** judgmatic(al) [coll.]; magisterial.

999. TRIBUNAL

NOUNS **1. tribunal, forum, board,** curia, Areopagus; judicature, judicatory, judiciary; council 753; inquisition, the Inquisition.

2. court, law court, court of law, ∼ **justice** or **arbitration;** durbar [India], divan [Orient.], **bar,** bar of justice.

3. (courts) circuit court, common-law court, county court, criminal court, district court, divorce court, juvenile court, police court, prize court, superior court, court of claims, court of domestic relations, court of errors, court of first instance, court of record, court of requests, court of wards; appellate court, court of review; assizes, court of assize; chancery, chancery court, court of chancery, court of conscience; court of inquiry [mil.], court of honor; equity court, court of equity; hustings, hustings court; probate court, court of probate; sessions, court of sessions, petty ∼, quarter ∼, special or general sessions; kangaroo court [coll., U.S.], mock court, moot court.

4. (U.S. courts) Supreme Court, United States Supreme Court; United States District Court, United States Circuit Court of Appeals, Federal Court of Claims, Court of Private Land Claims.

5. (British courts) court of admiralty, Court of Appeal, Court of Criminal Appeal, Court of Common Pleas, Court of Common Bank, Court of Common Council, Court of Divorce and Matrimonial Causes, Court of Exchequer, Court of Exchequer Chamber, Court of Queen's or King's Bench, Court of St. James's or James, Court of the Duchy of Lancaster, High Court, High Court of Appeal, High Court of Justice, High or Supreme Court of Judicature, Judicial Committee of the Privy Council, Lords Justices' Court, Palatine Court, Rolls Court, Stannary Court, superior courts of Westminster, Vice Chancellor's Court; court of attachments, woodmote; wardmote, wardmote court; Green Cloth or Greencloth, Board of Green Cloth.

6. (ecclesiastical courts) Papal Court, Curia, Rota, Sacra Romana Rota, Court of Arches [Eng.], Court of Peculiars [Eng.].

7. court-martial, general ∼, special or summary court-martial, drumhead court-martial.

8. seat of justice, judgment seat, mercy seat, **bench,** woolsack [Eng.].

9. courthouse, court; town hall, townhouse; courtroom; jury box; witness stand *or* box, dock.

ADJS. **10. tribunal, judicial,** judiciary, curial; appellate.

1000. JUDGE

NOUNS **1. judge, magistrate, justice,** judicator, alcalde [Spain], beak [slang, Eng.], mittimus [joc.]; **justice of the peace,** J.P.; **arbiter, arbitrator, moderator; umpire,** referee; his honor, his worship, his lordship, his nibs [slang]; Mr. Justice; critic 493.6, 7.

2. (historical) tribune, praetor, ephor, archon, syndic, podesta [It.]; justiciar, justiciary [both Eng. & Scot.].

3. (Mohammedan) mollah, ulema, hakim, mufti, cadi.

4. (special judges) judge advocate, J.A., presiding judge, probate judge, police judge, ~ justice *or* magistrate, P.J.; circuit judge; ordinary, judge ordinary; judge *or* justice of assize; puisne judge *or* justice; lay judge, wooden judge [U.S., coll.]; assessor, legal assessor; barmaster [Eng.], chancellor [U.S.], vice-chancellor, squire [U.S.], jurat, recorder, master, amicus curiae.

5. Chief Justice, Justice of the Supreme Court [U.S.], Lord Chief Justice [Eng.]; Lord Justice, Lord Chancellor, Master of the Rolls, Baron of the Exchequer [all Eng.]; Judge Advocate General [mil., U.S.].

6. Pontius Pilate, Solomon, Minos, Rhadamanthus.

7. jury, panel, sessions [Scot.], country, twelve men in a box; inquest, jury of inquest; grand jury, petty *or* petit jury, coroner's jury, trial jury, jury of the vicinage, jury of matrons *or* women, blue-ribbon jury *or* panel.

8. juror, juryman, jurywoman; talesman; foreman of the jury, jury chancellor [Scot.]; grand-juror, grand-juryman; petty-juror, petty-juryman; recognitor [Eng. hist.].

1001. LAWYER

NOUNS **1. lawyer, attorney, attorney-at-law, barrister,** barrister-at-law, **counselor** *or* counsellor, counselor-at-law, **counsel,** legal adviser, **solicitor, advocate, pleader, mouthpiece** (esp. criminal [slang]), vakil *or* vakeel [Anglo-India], green bag [coll.]; proctor, procurator; friend at *or* in court, amicus curiae; deputy, agent 779; intercessor 803.3.

2. (one who professes or is versed in law) legist, jurist, jurisprudent, jurisconsult, **Philadelphia lawyer** [U.S.].

3. shyster, ambulance chaser, pettifogger [all coll.].

4. (special lawyers) district **attorney,** D.A.; prosecuting attorney, prosecutor; public prosecutor; public pleader *or* defender; special pleader; private attorney, attorney in fact; criminal lawyer, mouthpiece [slang]; law agent, writer to the signet [both Scot.]; sergeant-at-law [Eng.]; civilian; publicist; conveyancer; leader [Eng.]; attorney general, A.G.; solicitor general, S.G.; Solicitor Supreme Court, S.S.C.; King's *or* Queen's counsel, K.C., Q.C., silk, silk gown, silk-gownsman [all Eng.]; junior barrister *or* counsel, stuff gown, stuff-gownsman [all Eng.].

5. bar, legal profession, members of the bar.

VERBS **6. practice law,** practice at the bar; take silk, be admitted to the bar.

ADJS. **7. lawyerly,** lawyerlike, **barristerial.**

1002. LAWSUIT

NOUNS **1. lawsuit, suit,** suit in *or* at law; **litigation, prosecution,** action, **legal action,** proceedings; legal remedy; case, cause, cause in court; *cause célèbre* [F.].

2. summons, subpoena 750.7.

3. arraignment, indictment, impeachment; charge 1003; presentment; information; bill of indictment, true bill.

4. empanelment, impanelment.

5. trial, hearing, inquiry, inquisition, inquest, assize; court-martial; examination, cross-examination 484.14, 15; mistrial; change of venue.

6. pleadings, arguments at the bar; plea, pleading, argument; **defense,** statement of defense; demurrer, general *or* special demurrer; refutation 505.2; rebuttal 485.2.

7. declaration, statement, allegation, allegation *or* statement of facts, procèsverbal; **deposition,** affidavit; claim; complaint; bill, bill of complaint; libel, narratio; nolle prosequi, nol. pros.; nonsuit.

8. testimony 504.3; **evidence** 504.

9. verdict, sentence 493.5; acquittal 1005; condemnation 1006, penalty 1007.

10. appeal, appeal motion, application for retrial, appeal to a higher court; writ of error; certiorari, writ of certiorari.

11. litigant, litigator, litigationist; suitor, party to a suit; **plaintiff** 1003.5; **defendant** 1003.6; witness 504.7; accessory, accessory before *or* after the fact; panel, parties litigant.

VERBS **12. sue, prosecute, litigate,** go into litigation, **bring suit,** put in suit, sue *or* prosecute at law, **go to law,** seek in law, appeal to the law, seek justice *or* legal redress, implead, **bring action against,** prosecute a suit against, take *or* institute legal proceedings against, **take** *or* **have the law of** or **on** [coll.], law [coll. & dial.], take to court, bring into court, hale ~, haul *or* drag into court, bring a case before the court *or* bar, bring to justice, bring to trial, **put on trial,** bring to the bar, take before the judge; set down for hearing.

13. **summons,** subpoena 750.12.

14. **arraign, indict, impeach,** find an indictment against, prefer *or* file a claim, have *or* pull up [coll.], bring up for investigation; prefer charges 1003.7; non-pros.

15. **impanel a jury,** impanel, empanel, panel.

16. **call to witness,** bring forward, put on the witness stand; swear in 521.6; take oath 521.5; testify 504.10.

17. **try,** try a case, conduct a trial, **hear,** give a hearing to; **judge, sit in judgment;** court-martial.

18. **plead,** implead, conduct pleadings, argue at the bar; **plead one's case,** make a plea, tell it to the judge [joc.]; hang the jury [coll.]; rest, rest one's case.

19. **bring in a verdict, pass sentence** 493.13; acquit 1005.4; convict 1006.3; penalize 1007.4.

ADJS. 20. **litigious,** litigant, litigatory; causidical; litigable, actionable.

PHRS. 21. **in litigation,** in court, in chancery, in jeopardy, **at law,** at bar, at the bar, **on trial,** up for investigation *or* hearing, before the court, ~ bar *or* judge.

1003. ACCUSATION

NOUNS 1. **accusation,** accusal, **charge,** complaint, blame, imputation, delation, reproach, taxing; **denunciation,** denouncement; **impeachment, arraignment, indictment,** "the soft impeachment" [Sheridan]; information, information against; gravamen of a charge.

2. **incrimination,** crimination, **inculpation,** implication, involvement; attack, assault.

3. **recrimination,** retort, countercharge.

4. **trumped-up charge,** false witness; put-up job, frame-up, frame [all slang].

5. **accuser,** accusant, accusatrix [fem.]; incriminator, delator; informer 555.6; impeacher, indicter *or* indictor; **plaintiff, prosecutor, complainant,** claimant, appel-

lant, libelant, suitor, party to a suit; the prosecution.

6. **accused, defendant,** respondent, correspondent, libelee, suspect, prisoner.

VERBS 7. **accuse,** bring accusation; **charge, prefer** *or* **bring charges;** complain, **lodge a complaint; impeach, arraign, indict,** article; **denounce,** denunciate; point the finger at, put the finger on [crim. slang, U.S.]; impute, fasten on *or* upon, pin on [coll.], hang something on [slang]; tax, task, take to task *or* account; reproach, twit, taunt with; report, put on report.

8. **blame,** blame on *or* upon [coll.], **lay the blame on,** lay *or* cast blame upon, place *or* fix the blame *or* responsibility for.

9. **accuse of, charge with,** saddle with, lay to one's charge, place to one's account, lay to one's door, bring home to, cast *or* throw in one's teeth, throw *or* thrust in the face of.

10. **incriminate,** criminate, **inculpate,** implicate, involve; cry out against, cry out on *or* upon, cry shame upon, raise one's voice against; attack, assail; throw a stone at, cast *or* throw the first stone.

11. **recriminate,** countercharge, retort an accusation.

12. **trump up a charge, bear false witness; frame,** frame up, put up a job [all slang].

ADJS. 13. **accusing,** accusatory, accusative; imputative, denunciatory; recriminatory.

14. **incriminating,** incriminatory, criminatory; inculpative, inculpatory.

15. **accused,** charged, blamed; under attack, under fire.

1004. JUSTIFICATION

NOUNS 1. **justification, vindication;** exculpation 1005; rationalization.

2. **defense** *or* defence, **plea, pleading;** argument, statement of defense; answer, reply, counterstatement; refutation 505.2, rebuttal 485.2; demurrer, general *or* special demurrer [all law]; denial, objection, exception; special pleading [law].

3. **apology,** apologia, apologetic.

4. **excuse,** alibi [coll.], **out** [coll., U.S.]; lame excuse, poor excuse.

5. **extenuation, mitigation, palliation,** softening; extenuative, palliative; whitewash, whitewashing; gloss, varnish, color; qualification, allowance; extenuating circumstances.

6. **warrant, reason,** good reason, **cause,** call, **right, basis,** ground, foundation.

7. **justifiability, vindicability, defensibility; excusability,** pardonableness, forgivableness, remissibility, veniality; warrantableness, allowableness, admissibility, reasonableness, legitimacy.

8. **justifier,** vindicator; defender, pleader; advocate, proponent; **apologist,** apologizer, apologete.

VERBS 9. **justify, vindicate,** do justice to; **warrant,** account for, show sufficient grounds for, give good reasons for; **rationalize,** pragmatize; **exculpate** 1005.4.

10. **defend,** offer or say in defense, allege in support or vindication, **support, uphold, sustain, maintain,** assert; **plead for,** make a plea, offer as a plea, plead one's case or cause; **advocate,** champion, espouse, stand up for, speak up for, contend for, speak for, argue for, urge reasons for, put in a good word for.

11. **excuse,** alibi [coll.], offer excuse for, give as an excuse, cover with excuses; plead ignorance; **apologize for,** make apology for; alibi out of [coll.], crawl out of, lie out of.

12. **extenuate, mitigate, palliate,** soften, mince; **gloss over,** put a gloss upon, put a good face upon, varnish, whitewash, color, lend a color to; **allow for,** make allowance for; give the Devil his due.

ADJS. 13. **justifying,** justificatory; **vindicative,** vindicatory; **excusing,** excusatory; **apologetic(al),** deprecatory; **extenuating,** extenuative, palliative.

14. **justifiable, vindicable, defensible; excusable, pardonable, forgivable,** expiable, remissible, exemptible, venial; **condonable,** dispensable; **warrantable,** allowable, admissible, reasonable, legitimate; unobjectionable, inoffensive.

1005. ACQUITTAL

NOUNS 1. **acquittal,** acquittance, quittance; **exculpation,** disculpation; **exoneration,** absolution, vindication, remission, compurgation, clearance, quietus; **pardon, excuse, forgiveness; discharge, release, dismissal.**

2. **exemption, immunity,** impunity; **amnesty,** indemnity.

3. **reprieve,** respite, grace.

VERBS 4. **acquit, exculpate, exonerate, absolve,** give absolution; **vindicate, justify; pardon, excuse, forgive;** remit, grant remission, remit the penalty of; **amnesty,**

grant amnesty to; **discharge, release, dismiss, free,** set free, let off [coll.], let go; **exempt,** exempt from, dispense from; clear, clear the skirts of; shrive, purge; blot out one's sins, wipe the slate clean; whitewash.

5. **reprieve,** respite, give or grant a reprieve.

1006. CONDEMNATION

NOUNS 1. **condemnation, damnation, doom;** proscription; **denunciation,** denouncement; **censure** 967.3; **conviction; sentence,** judgment, rap [slang]; death sentence, death warrant.

2. **attainder,** attainture, attaintment; bill of attainder.

VERBS 3. **condemn, damn, doom; denounce,** denunciate; **censure** 967.13; **convict,** find guilty, bring home to; proscribe; pronounce judgment 493.13; **sentence,** pronounce sentence, pass sentence on; penalize 1007.4; attaint; sign one's death warrant.

4. **stand condemned,** be convicted, be found guilty.

ADJS. 5. **condemnatory, damnatory,** denunciatory, proscriptive; **censorious** 967.23.

1007. PENALTY

NOUNS 1. **penalty, penalization,** penance [loosely], penal retribution; **punishment** 1008; compensation, price; the devil to pay.

2. **handicap, disadvantage** 728.6.

3. **fine,** mulct, amercement, sconce, damages; distress, distraint; forfeit, forfeiture; escheat, escheatment; doomage [local, U.S.].

VERBS 4. **penalize,** put ∼, impose or inflict a penalty on; **punish** 1008.10; handicap, put at a disadvantage.

5. **fine,** mulct, amerce, sconce, estreat; distrain, levy a distress.

ADVS. 6. **on pain of,** on or under penalty of.

1008. PUNISHMENT

NOUNS 1. **punishment, chastisement, chastening, correction, discipline, castigation,** infliction, scourge, ferule, what-for [slang]; pay, payment; **retribution,** retributive justice, nemesis; **penalty,** penal retribution; judgment (providential punishment); deserts 958.3.

2. (forms of punishment) penal servitude, hard labor, rock pile, galleys; torture, torment, martyrdom; the gantlet, keelhauling, tar-and-feathering, railriding, picket-

ing, the rack, impalement, dismemberment; strappado, estrapade; auto-da-fé, *auto de fe* [Sp.].

3. **slap**, smack; **cuff**, **box**, buffet; blow 282.4; **rap on the knuckles**, box on the ear, slap in the face.

4. **whipping**, **beating**, **thrashing**, **spanking**, **flogging**, flagellation, scourging, flailing, swingeing, trouncing, basting, **drubbing**, buffeting, belaboring; **lashing**, **lacing**, stripes; horsewhipping; strapping, belting, leathering [coll.], rawhiding [U.S.], cowhiding; **switching**; **clubbing**, cudgeling, caning, truncheoning, fustigation, bastinado; battery.

5. (colloquialisms) **licking**, larruping, walloping, whaling, lathering, **hiding**, **tanning**, jacketing, grooming, dressing, **dressing-down**; **paddling**, shingling [both U.S.].

6. (slang terms) strap oil, hazel oil, hickory oil, birch oil, dose of strap oil, etc.

7. **capital punishment**, **execution**, judicial murder; **hanging**, floorless jig [slang], the gallows, the rope *or* noose; **lynching**, necktie party *or* sociable [slang, U.S.]; **crucifixion**; **electrocution**, the chair [coll.], the hot seat [slang]; **decapitation**, decollation, beheading, the guillotine; **strangling**, strangulation, garrote; **shooting**, fusillade; **burning**, burning at the stake; **poisoning**, hemlock.

8. **executioner**, executionist, Jack Ketch [Eng.]; **hangman**, topsman [slang], topping cove [slang, Eng.]; **lyncher**; **electrocutioner**; headsman, **beheader**, **decapitator**; **strangler**, garroter.

9. **penology**, penologist.

VERBS 10. **punish**, **chastise**, **chasten**, **discipline**, **correct**, **castigate**, **penalize**; take to task, bring to book, bring *or* call to account; deal with, settle with, settle *or* square accounts, **give one his deserts**, serve one right; inflict upon, visit upon; give a lesson to, make an example of; pillory; masthead [naut.].

11. (colloquialisms) **attend to**, do for, take care of, serve one out, **give it to**, give it one, give one Jesse, take *or* have it out of; pay, pay out, **fix**, **settle**, settle one's hash, settle the score, give one his gruel, **give one his comeuppance** [U.S.]; come down on *or* upon; dirty one's hands with.

12. (slang terms) **give what-for**, give a going-over, climb one's frame [U.S.], clean one's plow, cure, do in, let have it, light into [U.S.], land on, mop *or* wipe up the earth with.

13. **slap**, smack; **cuff**, **box**, buffet; strike 282.14; slap the face, box the ears, give a rap on the knuckles.

14. **whip**, give a whipping, ~ beating *or* thrashing, **beat**, **thrash**, **spank**, **flog**, scourge, flagellate, flail, frail [dial.], whale, whop [dial.], wallop [dial.], smite, swinge, thump, trounce, baste, wipe [dial. or slang], cob [dial., Eng.], mill [cant], **pummel**, pommel, **drub**, **buffet**, **belabor**, lay on; **lash**, **lace**, cut, stripe; horsewhip; knout; **strap**, belt, leather [coll.], rawhide [U.S.], cowhide; **switch**, birch, give the stick; **club**, **cudgel**, cane, truncheon, fustigate, bastinado.

15. (colloquialisms) **lick**, **larrup**, **wallop**, whale, welt, trim, flax [U.S.], lather, hide, tan, **tan one's hide**, groom, comb, dress, dress down, give a dressing *or* dressing-down, jacket, lace one's jacket, warm, warm one's jacket; **paddle**, shingle [both U.S.].

16. (slang terms) **lambaste**, lam, rib-roast, clobber, fan, anoint, towel [Eng.], dust one's jacket *or* doublet, give a dose of birch oil, ~ strap oil, ~ hickory oil *or* hazel oil, take it out of one's hide *or* skin.

17. **thrash soundly**, blister, **batter**, **beat up** [slang], beat to a mummy *or* jelly, bruise, **beat black and blue**, beat the sap *or* tar out of [slang].

18. **torture**, put to the question; rack, put on *or* to the rack; dismember, tear limb from limb; draw and quarter, break on the wheel, tar and feather, ride on a rail, picket [hist.], keelhaul, impale, grill.

19. **execute**, **put to death**, inflict capital punishment; **electrocute**, burn [slang]; **behead**, **decapitate**, decollate, guillotine, bring to the block; **crucify**; **shoot**; burn, **burn at the stake**; **strangle**, garrote, bowstring.

20. **hang**, hang by the neck, **string up** [coll.], gibbet, noose, neck, scrag [coll.], bring to the gallows; **lynch**; **stretch**, crap, tuck up, turn off [all slang].

21. (be hanged; slang) **swing**, dance upon nothing, kick the air, ~ wind *or* clouds.

22. (be punished) **suffer**, suffer for, suffer the consequences *or* penalty, take ~, have *or* get one's gruel [coll.], **get** *or* **catch it** [coll.], get *or* catch it in the neck [slang]; **get one's deserts** 958.6; be doubly punished, get it coming and going [slang], sow the wind and reap the whirlwind.

23. **take one's punishment**, take the

consequences, take one's medicine, pay the piper, face the music [coll.], make one's bed and lie on it; stand the racket, take the rap [both slang, U.S.].

24. (deserve punishment; colloquialisms) have it coming, be for it or in for it, be heading for a fall.

ADJS. 25. punishing, chastening, grueling [coll.]; penal, punitive, punitory, inflictive, castigatory.

1009. INSTRUMENTS OF PUNISHMENT

NOUNS 1. whip, lash, scourge, flagellum, azote [Sp.]; strap, thong, rawhide, cowhide, black snake or blacksnake, kurbash, sjambok [S. Africa], belt, razor strap; knout; bullwhip, bullwhack [both U.S.]; horsewhip; crop; quirt; chabouk [Orient.]; rope's end; cat, cat-o'-nine-tails; whiplash.

2. rod, stick, switch; paddle, ruler, ferule; birch, rattan; cane; club 799.23; rod in pickle.

3. (devices) pillory, stocks, finger pillory; cucking stool, ducking stool, trebuchet; whipping post, branks, triangle or triangles, wooden horse, treadmill, crank, galleys.

4. (instruments of torture) rack, wheel, Iron Maiden of Nuremberg; screw, thumbscrew; boot, Oregon boot [U.S.], iron heel, scarpines; Procrustean bed, bed of Procrustes.

5. (instruments of execution) scaffold; block, guillotine, ax, maiden [Scot. hist.]; stake; cross; gallows, gibbet, tree, drop; hangman's rope, noose, rope, mecate [Sp.], halter, hemp, hempen collar, ~ necktie or bridle [slang]; electric chair, death chair, chair, hot seat [slang]; death chamber, lethal chamber, gas chamber.

1010. ATONEMENT

NOUNS 1. atonement, reparation, amends, restitution, propitiation, expiation, redress, recompense, compensation, redemption, reclamation, satisfaction, quittance; indemnity, indemnification; compromise, composition.

2. apology, excuse, regrets; acknowledgment, confession 554.3; abject apology; amende honorable [F.].

3. penance, mortification, maceration, flagellation, lustration; purgation, purgatory; sackcloth and ashes; hair shirt; cutty stool [Scot.].

VERBS 4. atone, atone for, propitiate, expiate, compensate, recompense, redress, redeem, repair, satisfy, give satisfaction, make amends, make reparation, ~ compensation or expiation, make good, make right, make up for, make matters up, pay the forfeit or penalty, wipe off old scores, set one's house in order; live down.

5. apologize, beg pardon, ask forgiveness, beg indulgence, express regret; take back 626.9; get or fall down on one's knees, get down on one's marrowbones [joc.].

6. do penance, shrive oneself, stand in a white sheet, repent in sackcloth and ashes.

ADJS. 7. propitiatory, expiatory, piacular, satisfactional; apologetic(al).

1011. DEITY

NOUNS 1. deity, divinity, divineness; godliness, godlikeness; godhood, godhead, godship, Fatherhood.

2. God, Lord, Jehovah, Providence, Heaven, the Deity, the Divinity, the Supreme Being, the Almighty, the All-powerful, the Infinite, the Infinite Being, the Everlasting, the Eternal, the Eternal Being, the Absolute, the Absolute Being, the Omnipotent, the Omniscient, Omnipotence, Omniscience, the All-wise, the All-knowing, the All-merciful, the All-holy, the Infinite Spirit, the Supreme Soul, the King of Kings, the Lord of Lords, Demiurge, I Am, the Preserver, the Maker, the Creator, the First Cause, Author or Creator of all things.

3. Deus [L.], Theos [Gr.], Dieu or dieu [F.], Allah [Moham.], Khuda [Hind.], kami [Jap.], the Great Spirit [N. Amer. Indian].

4. (Brahmanism) Brahma, the Supreme Soul, the Essence of the Universe; Atman, the Universal Ego or Self; Vishnu, the Preserver; Siva or Shiva, the Destroyer, the Regenerator.

5. (Buddhism) Buddha, the Blessed One, the Teacher, the Lord Buddha.

6. (Zoroastrianism) Mazda, Ormazd, Ahura-Mazda, the Lord of Wisdom, the Wise Lord, the Wise One, the King of Light, the Guardian of Mankind.

7. (Christian Science) Mind, Divine Mind, Spirit, Soul Principle, Life, Truth, Love.

8. world spirit or soul, anima mundi [L.], universal life force, world principle, world-self, universal ego or self, infinite spirit, supreme soul or principle, oversoul, nous, archeus, logos or Logos, mahat [Theosophy], World Reason.

9. **Nature, Mother Nature,** Dame Nature, "Beldame Nature" [Milton].

10. **the Trinity,** the Holy Trinity, the Triune, the Triunity, the Triune God, the Trinity in Unity, **Godhead,** Threefold Unity, Three in One and One in Three; **Father, Son and Holy Ghost;** Trimurti, Hindu trinity or triad.

11. **God the Father,** the Father, the All-father, the Holy Father, Our Father, Our Father which art in Heaven.

12. **God the Son, Christ,** the Christ, Jesus, Jesu [poetic], **Jesus Christ,** Jesus of Nazareth, the Nazarene, the Galilean, the Man of Sorrows, **the Messiah,** the Anointed, **the Saviour, the Redeemer,** the Mediator, the Intercessor, the Advocate, the Judge, **the Son of God, the Son of Man,** the Son of David, the Son of Mary, the Only-Begotten, the Lamb, **the Lamb of God, Immanuel,** Emmanuel, **the Master, the King of Kings,** the Lord of Lords, the King of Kings and Lord of Lords, the King of Heaven, the King of Glory, the King of the Jews, the Lord our Righteousness, the Sun of Righteousness, **the Prince of Peace,** the Good Shepherd, the Risen, the Way, the Door, the Truth, the Life, the Bread of Life, the Light of the World, the Vine, the True Vine; the Christ Child, the Infant Jesus.

13. **Logos, the Word,** the Word Made Flesh, **the Incarnation,** the Hypostatic Union.

14. **God the Holy Ghost, the Holy Ghost, the Holy Spirit,** the Spirit of God, the Spirit of Truth, Paraclete, the Comforter, the Consoler, the Intercessor, the Dove.

15. (divine attributes) infinity, eternity; infinite goodness, infinite justice, infinite truth, infinite love, infinite mercy; omniscience or omnisciency, infinite wisdom; omnipotence or omnipotency, infinite power; omnipresence, ubiquity; unity, immutability; holiness, glory, light; majesty, sovereignty.

16. (divine functions) creation, preservation, dispensation; providence, dealings ~, dispensations or visitations of providence.

17. (Christly functions) salvation, redemption, atonement, propitiation; mediation, intercession; judgment.

18. (functions of the Holy Ghost) inspiration, unction, regeneration, sanctification, consolation, grace.

ADJS. 19. **divine,** heavenly, celestial; **godly, godlike; Christly, Christlike.**

20. **almighty, omnipotent,** all-powerful; **omniscient,** all-wise, all-knowing, all-seeing; **infinite,** omnipresent, ubiquitous; sovereign, supreme.

PHRS. 21. under God; God willing, *Deo volente* [L.], D.V.; *jure divino* [L.], by divine right; in Jesus' name, in His name, in His fear, to His glory.

1012. MYTHICAL AND PAGAN GODS AND SPIRITS

NOUNS 1. **the gods,** the immortals, "whatever gods may be" [W. E. Henley]; the major deities, the greater gods, *di majores* [L.]; the minor deities, the lesser gods, *di minores* [L.]; pantheon; theogony.

2. **god,** *deus* [L.], **deity, divinity,** immortal, heathen god, pagan deity or divinity; **goddess,** *dea* [L.]; deva [Hind., Buddhism], devi [fem.], the shining ones; **idol** [Biblical], false god, devil-god.

3. **godling,** godlet, godkin, **demigod,** half-god, hero; demigoddess, heroine.

4. (gods and goddesses) gods of fertility 164.5; gods of the hearth 190.26; earth gods 374.7; moon goddesses 374.9; sun gods 374.11; sea gods 396.4; rain gods 393.6; wind gods 402.3; thunder gods 455.5; god of lightning 334.17; agricultural gods 412.4; war gods 795.18; gods of love 929.8; muse 607.12; Fates 638.3; gods of the nether world 1017.5.

5. (Greek and Roman gods) Olympic gods, Olympians; Zeus, Jupiter, Jove; Jupiter Fulgur or Fulminator, Jupiter Tonans, Jupiter Pluvius, Jupiter Optimus Maximus, Jupiter Fidius; Helios, Hyperion, Phaëthon; Apollo, Apollon, Phoebus, Phoebus Apollo; Mars, Ares; Mercury, Hermes; Neptune, Poseidon; Vulcan, Hephaestus; Bacchus, Dionysus; Pluto, Hades, Dis, Orcus; Saturn, Kronos or Cronus; Cupid, Eros; Hymen; Momus; the Sphinx.

(goddesses) Juno, Hera or Here; Demeter, Ceres; Persephone, Proserpina, Proserpine, Persephassa, Kore or Cora, Despoina; Diana, Artemis; Athena, Minerva; Nike; Venus, Aphrodite; Hestia, Vesta; Rhea, Cybele; Gaea or Gaia, Tellus; Ate.

6. (Norse gods) Aesir, Vanir; Balder, Bor, Bori, Bragi, Forseti, Frey or Freyr, Heimdall, Höder or Hödr, Hoenir, Loki, Njorth or Njord, Odin or Woden, Reimthursen, Thor or Donar, Tyr or Tiu, Ull or Ullr, Vali, Vitharr or Vidar, Ymir.

(goddesses) Freya or Freyja, Frigg or Frigga, Hel, Nanna, Ithunn or Idun, Sif, Sigyn.

7. (Hindu and Brahmanic gods) Agni, Dyaus, Ganesa, Ganpati; Hanuman, Indra, Marut, Savitar, Soma, Surya, Varuna, Vayu, Yama.

(goddesses) Chandi, Devi, Durga, Gauri, Kali, Lakshmi, Parvati, Sarasvati, Uma, Ushas.

8. avatars of Vishnu: Buddha, Kalki, Karma, Krishna, Matsya, Narsinh, Parshuram, Rama, Vaman, Varah; Juggernaut, Jagannath.

9. (Egyptian gods) Anubis, Bast, Horus, Isis, Khem, Min, Neph, Nephthys, Nut, Osiris, Ptah, Ra or Amen-Ra, Set, Thoth.

10. (aboriginal gods) manito [Algonquian], huaca [ancient Peruvian], mana [Polynesian], nagual [Mex. and Cent. Amer. Indian], pokunt [Shoshonean], tamanoas [Chinook], wakan [Amer. Indian], Zemi [Taino].

11. (various) Baal, Moloch, Shamash [Semitic]; Dagon [Philistine]; Astarte or Ashtoreth [Phoenician]; Anu, Bel, Ea [Babylonian]; Mumbo Jumbo [African].

12. spirit, intelligence, supernatural being; specter 1015; evil spirits 1014.

13. elemental, elemental spirit; sylph, gnome, salamander, undine.

14. fairyfolk, elfenfolk, shee or sidhe [Ir. & Scot.], **the little people** or **men,** the good folk or people [coll.], denizens of the air; **fairyland,** faërie or faëry [arch.].

15. fairy, sprite, fay, fairy man or woman; **elf, brownie, pixy, gremlin,** ouphe, hob, cluricaune [Ir.], kobold, nisse [Scandinavian], peri; **imp, goblin** 1014.8, 9; **gnome,** dwarf; **sylph,** sylphid; **banshee** or banshie [Ir. & Scot.]; **leprechaun** [Ir.]; fairy queen; Ariel, Mab, Oberon, Titania.

16. nymph; nymphet, nymphlin [both poetic]; **dryad,** hamadryad, wood nymph; tree nymph; **oread,** mountain nymph; limoniad, meadow or flower nymph; Napaea, glen nymph; Hyades or Hyads; Pleiades, Atlantides.

17. water spirit, ~ sprite or nymph; undine, nix, nixie [fem.], kelpie or kelpy; naiad, limniad, fresh-water nymph; Oceanid, Nereid, sea nymph, ocean nymph, **mermaid,** sea-maid, sea-maiden, siren; Thetis; **merman,** man fish; **Neptune** [Rom.], "the old man of the sea" [Homer]; Oceanus, Poseidon, Triton [all Gr.]; Davy Jones, Davy.

18. sylvan deity, faun, satyr, silenus, panisc or panisk, paniscus [fem. panisca]; **Pan** [Gr.], **Faunus** [Rom.], Vitharr or Vidar [Norse], the goat god.

19. familiar spirit, familiar; **genius, good genius,** daimon, daemon, demon, numen [L.], totem [Algonquian]; **guardian, guardian spirit, guardian angel,** angel, good angel, ministering angel, **fairy godmother, guide, control,** attendant godling or spirit, invisible helper, special providence; **tutelary** or **tutelar god,** ~ **genius** or **spirit,** tutelary; genius tutelae, genius loci, genius domus, genius familiae [all L.]; lares, lar familiaris [L.], lares praestites, lares compitales, lares viales, lares permarini [all L.]; penates, lares and penates [both Rom.]; evil genius.

20. Santa Claus or Klaus, Santa, Saint Nicholas, Kriss Kringle [U.S.], Father Christmas.

21. mythology, mythicism; **legend, lore, folklore,** mythical lore; fairy lore, fairyism.

ADJS. **22. mythic(al), mythological; fabulous, legendary.**

23. fairy, faery, **fairylike;** sylphine, sylphish, sylphy, sylphidine, sylphlike; elfin, elfish, elflike; gnomish, gnomelike.

24. nymphic(al), nymphal, nymphean, nymphlike.

1013. ANGEL

NOUNS **1. angel, celestial,** celestial or heavenly being; messenger of God; **saint; seraph,** angel of love; **cherub, cherubim,** cherubin, angel of light; principality, archangel; recording angel.

2. heavenly host, host of heaven, choir invisible, Sons of God, ministering spirits.

3. (celestial hierarchy of Pseudo-Dionysius) seraphim, cherubim, thrones; dominations or dominions, virtues, powers; principalities, archangels, angels.

4. Azrael, angel of death, death's bright angel; Abdiel, Chamuel, Gabriel, Jophiel, Michael, Raphael, Uriel, Zadkiel.

5. Madonna, Holy Mary; Our Lady, Notre Dame [F.]; **Mother of God,** Dei Mater [L.], Deipara, Theotokos; mater dolorosa [L.], the Sorrowful Mother; Queen of Heaven, Regina Caeli [L.]; Queen of Angels, Regina Angelorum [L.]; Star of the Sea, Stella Maris [L.]; **the Virgin,** the Blessed Virgin, **the Virgin Mary,** the Virgin Mother; Sancta Virgo Virginum [L.], Holy Virgin of Virgins; Virgo Sponsa Dei

[L.], Virgin Bride of the Lord; *Virgo Clemens* [L.], Virgin Most Merciful; *Virgo Gloriosa* [L.], Virgin Most Glorious; *Virgo Potens* [L.], Virgin Most Powerful; *Virgo Praedicanda* [L.], Virgin Most Renowned; *Virgo Sapientissima* [L.], Virgin Most Wise; *Virgo Veneranda* [L.], Virgin Most Venerable; Immaculate Conception.

ADJS. **6. angelic, seraphic, cherubic; heavenly, celestial;** archangelic.

1014. EVIL SPIRITS

NOUNS **1. evil spirits, demonkind, powers of darkness;** host of hell, denizens of hell, inhabitants of Pandemonium, souls in hell, lost souls, the lost, the damned.

2. devil, *diable* [F.], *diablo* [Sp.], *diabolus* [L.], *deil* [Scot.], *Teufel* [G.].

3. Satan, Satanas, **the Devil,** the Demon, the Fiend, the Foul Fiend, the Wicked One, **the Evil One,** the Evil Spirit, **the Tempter,** the Adversary, the archfiend, the archenemy, the Common Enemy, the Devil Incarnate, the Author or Father of Evil, the Father of Lies, the serpent, the Old Serpent, the Prince of the Devils, the Prince of Darkness, the Prince of this world, the Prince of the power of the air, His Satanic Majesty, the angel of the bottomless pit.

4. (slang terms) **the Deuce, the Dickens, Old Harry,** Old Nick, Old Ned, Old Horny, Old Scratch, Old Gooseberry, Old Bendy, Old or Auld Clootie, Old Poker, the Old Gentleman.

5. Lucifer, Beelzebub, Belial, Ehlis, Azazel, Ahriman [Zoroastrianism], Mephistopheles, Mephisto, Shaitan, Sammael, Asmodeus, Abaddon, Apollyon.

6. (god of evil) Set [Egyptian], Typhon [Gr.], Loki [Norse]; gods of the nether world 1017.5.

7. demon, fiend, devil, satan, deva [Zoroastrianism], shedu [Biblical], gyre [Scot.], bad or evil spirit, unclean spirit; **hellion** [coll.]; cacodemon, incubus, succubus; **jinni** or jinnee, genie, genius, jinniyeh [fem.]; evil genius; afreet, barghest, flibbertigibbet, troll; **ogre, ogress; ghoul,** lamia, vampire, Harpy.

8. imp. pixy, sprite, elf, puck, kobold, *diablotin* [F.], tokoloshe [S. Africa], **gremlin, bad fairy,** bad peri; little or young devil, devilkin, deviling; erlking; Puck, Robin Goodfellow, Hob, Hobgoblin.

9. goblin, hobgoblin, hob, ouphe.

10. bugbear, bugaboo, bogy or **bogey,** bogle, boggle, boggart or boggard; **boogy, booger, bugger,** bug [all dial.]; **boogerman,** boogyman [both dial., U.S.]; bête noire, fee-faw-fum, Mumbo Jumbo or mumbo jumbo.

11. Fury, avenging spirit; the Furies, the Erinyes, the Eumenides, the Dirae; Alecto, Erinys, Megaera, Tisiphone.

12. changeling, elf child, oaf, auf [dial.].

13. werefolk, were-animals; werewolf, lycanthrope, *loup-garou* [F.]; werejaguar, uturuncu [S. Amer. Indian]; wereass, werebear, werecalf, werefox, werehyena, wereleopard, weretiger.

14. devilishness, demonishness, fiendishness; devilship, devildom; horns, the cloven hoof, the Devil's pitchfork.

15. diabolism, demonism, Satanism, devilry, diablerie, demonry; demonomy, demonianism; sorcery 1033; demonolatry, demon ~, devil or chthonian worship; demonomancy; demonology, diabolology or diabology, demonography, devil lore.

16. diabolist, demonist; demonomist, demoniast; demonologist, demonologer; demonolater, chthonian, devil worshiper; sorcerer 1033.5.

VERBS **17. demonize,** devilize, diabolize; **possess, obsess; bewitch,** bedevil 1034.10.

ADJS. **18. demoniac(al), demonic(al),** demonish, demonlike; **devilish, devillike; satanic, diabolic(al); hellish** 1017.6; **fiendish,** fiendlike; ghoulish, ogreish; inhuman.

19. impish, puckish, elfish, elvish; mischievous 736.6.

1015. SPECTER

NOUNS **1. specter, ghost,** *Geist* [G.], **spirit,** sprite, **spook** [coll.], **phantom,** phantasm, phantasma, **wraith, shade,** shadow, **apparition,** appearance, presence, shape, form, eidolon, idolum, revenant, larva [Rom. rel.], disembodied spirit, soul of the dead; astral spirit, astral; unsubstantiality, immateriality, incorporeal, incorporeity, incorporeal being or entity; duppy, duffy [both W. Ind. & U.S. Negro]; vision, theophany; materialization; haunt or hant [dial.]; banshee; poltergeist; control, guide [Spiritualism]; lemures [Rom. rel.].

2. White Lady, the White Lady of Avenel [Scot.], the White Ladies of Normandy; Brocken specter.

3. double, etheric double or self, cowalker, *Doppelgänger* [G.], doubleganger, fetch, wraith.

4. **spookiness** [coll.], **eeriness, weirdness, uncanniness.**

5. **possession, obsession,** spirit control.
VERBS 6. **haunt,** hant [dial.], **spook** [coll.]; **possess, obsess.**

ADJS. 7. **spectral,** specterlike; **ghostly,** ghostish, ghosty, ghostlike; **spiritual,** psychic(al); **phantomlike,** phantom, phantomic(al); **wraithlike,** wraithy, shadowy; ethereal 4.5; incorporeal 376.7; supernatural 85.14.

8. **disembodied,** discarnate, decarnate, decarnated.

9. **spooky,** spookish; **weird, eerie** or eery, **uncanny,** unearthly.

10. **haunted,** hanted [dial.], **spooked** [coll.], spooky, spirit-haunted, ghost-haunted, specter-haunted; **possessed, obsessed,** ghost-ridden.

1016. HEAVEN

Abode of the Deity and Blessed Dead.—
NOUNS 1. **heaven, paradise, glory, eternity, kingdom come** [slang], happy hunting grounds [N. Amer. Indian], Land of the Leal [Scot.], the happy land, the Promised Land, the world above, eternal home, abode of the blessed, inheritance of the saints in light; Beulah, Beulah Land, Land of Beulah; **kingdom of heaven,** God's kingdom, heavenly kingdom, kingdom of God, kingdom of glory; God's presence, presence of God; Abraham's bosom.

2. "my Father's house" [Bible], "God's residence" [E. Dickinson], "mansions in the sky" [I. Watts], "the bosom of our rest" [Newman], "the treasury of everlasting joy" [Shakespeare], "that radiant shore" [F. D. Hemens], "the great world of light, that lies behind all human destinies" [Longfellow].

3. **the hereafter,** afterworld, afterlife 121.2.

4. **Zion, Holy City,** New Jerusalem, Heavenly or Celestial City, City Celestial, Heavenly City of God, "heaven's high city" [F. Quarles].

5. **heaven of heavens, seventh heaven,** empyrean [Dante and Milton], throne of God, God's throne, the great white throne.

6. (Christian Science) bliss, harmony, spirituality, the reign of Spirit, the atmosphere of Soul.

7. (Mormon) celestial glory, terrestrial glory, telestial glory.

8. (Mohammedan) Alfardaws, Assama; Falak al aflak [the highest heaven].

9. (Hindu, Buddhist and theosophy) **nirvana;** devaloka, land of the gods; kamavachara, kamaloka; devachan.

10. (mythological) Olympus, Mount Olympus; Elysium, Elysian fields; Islands or Isles of the Blessed, Happy Isles, Fortunate Isles or Islands; garden of the Hesperides, Bower of Bliss.

11. (Norse) Valhalla, Asgard, Glathsheim, Vingolf, Valaskjalf, Hlithskjalf, Thruthvang or Thruthheim, Bilskirnir, Ydalir, Sökkvabekk, Breithablik, Folkvang, Sessrymnir, Noatum, Thrymheim, Glitnir, Himinbjorg, Vithi.

12. (removal to heaven) **resurrection, translation,** apotheosis; **ascension,** the Ascension; **assumption,** the Assumption.

ADJS. 13. **heavenly,** heavenish; **paradisaic(al),** paradisiac(al); **celestial,** supernal, ethereal; **unearthly,** unworldly; **otherworldly,** extraterrestrial, extramundane, transmundane, transcendental; Elysian, Olympian; blessed, beatific(al); from on high.

1017. HELL

NOUNS 1. **hell, Hades, Sheol, Gehenna,** Tophet, Abaddon, Naraka, jahannan [Hind.], avichi or avici, **perdition,** pandemonium, **inferno,** the pit, **the bottomless pit,** the abyss, "a vast, unbottom'd, boundless pit" [Burns], **nether world,** lower world, **underworld,** infernal regions, abode or world of the dead, abode of the damned, place of torment, the grave, shades below; **purgatory, limbo;** Pandemonium [hell's capital].

2. **hell-fire,** fire and brimstone, lake of fire and brimstone, everlasting fire or torment, "the fire that never shall be quenched" [Bible].

3. (mythological) **Hades,** Orcus, Tartarus, Avernus, Acheron, pit of Acheron [all classical myth.]; Amenti [Egyptian], Aralu [Babylonian]; Hel, Niflhel, Niflheim or Nifelheim, Naströnd [all Norse].

4. (rivers of Hades) Styx, Stygian creek; Acheron, River of Woe; Cocytus, River of Wailing; Phlegethon, River of Fire; Lethe, River of Forgetfulness.

5. (gods of the nether world) Pluto [Gr. & Rom.], Orcus [Rom.], Hades [Gr.], Dis [Rom.]; Rhadamanthus, Erebus, Charon, Cerberus, Minos; Osiris; Persephone, Proserpine, Proserpina, Persephassa, Despoina,

Kore *cr* Cora [all Gr. & Rom.]; Hel, Loki, Frigg [all Norse]; Satan 1014.3.

ADJS. 6. **hellish, infernal,** sulfurous, chthorian; pandemonic, pandemoniac; devilish 1014.18; Plutonic, Plutonian; Tartarean, Tartareous; Stygian, Styxian; Lethean, Acherontic(al); hellborn.

7. in hell, below.

1018. RELIGIONS, CULTS, SECTS

NOUNS 1. **religion,** religious belief *or* faith, **belief, faith,** teaching.

2. **cult, ism;** cultism.

3. **sect,** sectarism, religious order, **denomination, persuasion, faction, church,** communion, community, group, fellowship, affiliation, order, school, party, society, body, organization; **schism,** division.

4. **sectarianism,** sectarism, **denominationalism,** partisanism, the clash of creeds; schismatism; syncretism, eclecticism.

5. **theism; monotheism,** unipersonalism; **polytheism,** multitheism; **ditheism,** dyotheism, dualism; **tritheism; pantheism,** cosmotheism, theopantism, acosmism; physitheism; physicomorphism; hylotheism; hecastotheism; anthropotheism, anthropomorphism, anthropolatry; allotheism; henotheism; autotheism; sciotheism; zootheism, theriotheism; **deism.**

6. **Christianity,** Christianism.

7. **Catholicism,** Catholicity; Roman Catholicism, Romanism, Rome; popery, popeism, papism, papistry [all derog.]; ultramontanism; Mariology, Mariolatry; Catholic Church, Roman Catholic Church, Church of Rome, Scarlet Woman [derog.]; Greek Church, Greek Orthodox Church.

8. **Protestantism;** dissent 520a; apostasy 626.2; new theology.

9. **Anglicanism;** High-Churchism, Low-Churchism; Church of England, Established Church; High Church, Low Church; Broad Church, Free Church.

10. **Judaism,** Hebraism, Hebrewism, Jewish, Israelitism; rabbinism, Talmudism, Pharisaism, Karaism *or* Karaitism.

11. **Mohammedanism, Moslemism,** Islam, Islamism; Sufism, Wahabiism.

12. **faith-curism, faith healing,** mental healing; divine healing, theotherapy; Christian Science; New Thought, Higher Thought, Practical Christianity, Mental Science, Divine Science Church.

13. **religionist,** religioner; believer 1026.4; **cultist,** ist.

14. **theist; monotheist,** unipersonalist;

polytheist; ditheist, dualist; tritheist; **pantheist,** cosmotheist; hylotheist; henotheist; zootheist; **deist.**

15. **Christian,** Nazarene, Nazarite.

16. **sectarian,** sectary, **denominationalist,** factionist, schismatic.

17. **Catholic,** Roman Catholic, Romanist, papist *or* Papist [derog.]; ultramontane.

18. **Protestant,** non-Catholic; dissenter 520a.3; apostate 626.5.

19. **Judaist,** Hebraist, **Hebrew, Jew,** Israelite; rabbinist, Talmudist, Sadducee, Pharisee, Karaite.

20. **Mormon,** Latter-day Saint, Josephite [coll.].

21. **Mohammedan,** Mussulman, **Moslem,** Islamite; Shiite, Shiah, Sectary; Motazilite, Sunnite, Wahabi, Sufi; dervish; abdal.

22. **faith-curist,** faith curer, mental healer; New Thoughter *or* Thoughtist, Mental Scientist; Christian Scientist, Christian Science Practitioner.

ADJS. 23. **theistic; monotheistic; polytheistic,** ditheistic, tritheistic; **pantheistic,** cosmotheistic; physicomorphic; anthropomorphic, anthropotheistic; **deistic.**

24. **sectarian,** sectary, **denominational,** schismatic(al); Episcopal, Episcopalian; Baptist, Methodist, etc. 1018.34.

25. **nonsectarian, undenominational;** interdenominational.

26. **Protestant,** non-Catholic; dissentient 520a.6; apostate 626.11.

27. **Catholic(al);** Roman Catholic, Roman, Romish [chiefly derog.]; popish, papish, papist *or* Papist, papistic(al) [all derog.]; ultramontane.

28. **Judaical, Jewish, Hebrew,** Hebraic(al), Hebraistic(al), Israelite, Israelitic, Israelitish.

29. **Mohammedan,** Moslem, Islamic, Islamitic, Islamistic.

30. (Oriental) Buddhist, Buddhistic(al); Brahmanic(al), Brahminic(al); Vedic, Vedantic; Confucian, Confucianist; Taoist(ic); Shintoist(ic); Zoroastrian.

31. religions

anthroposophy	Gnosticism
Babism, Babiism, Babi	gymnosophy
	Hinduism
Bahaism	Jainism
Brahmanism	Judaism
Brahmoism	Lamaism
Buddhism	Magianism
Christianity	Mandaeism
Confucianism	Mohammedanism
Ethical Culture	Moslemism

reincarnationism
Sabaeanism
Saivism
Shinto, Shintoism
Sikhism
Sufism
Taoism
Theosophy

Vedanta,
Vedantism
Wahabiism
yoga, yogism
Zen, Zen
  Buddhism
Zoroastrianism,
Zoroastrism

32. Christian systems

Adventism, Second
  Adventism
Anabaptism
Anglicanism
Anglo-Catholicism
Antinomianism
Arianism
Athanasianism
Boehmenism
Calvinism
Catholicism
Christian Science
Congregationalism
Episcopalianism
Erastianism
Homoiousianism
Homoousianism
Jansenism
latitudinarianism
Laudism,
  Laudianism
Liberal
  Catholicism
Lutheranism
Methodism
Moral
  Rearmament

Mormonism
New Thought
Origenism
Oxford Movement
Practical
  Christianity
Presbyterianism
Protestantism
Puritanism
Puseyism
Quakerism
quietism
Roman
  Catholicism
Rosicrucianism
Sabellianism
Salvation Army
Socinianism
Stundism
Swedenborgianism
Tractarianism
Trinitarianism
Ubiquitarianism
Unitarianism
Universalism
Wesleyanism,
  Wesleyism

33. religionists

Anthroposophist
Babist
Brahman,
  Brahmin,
  Brahminist
Buddhist
Christian
Confucianist
Gentoo
Gheber
Gnostic
gymnosophist
Hindu
Jain, Jaina
Judaist

Lamaist, Lamaite
Magian, Magus
Mandaean
Mohammedan
Moslem
Parsi
reincarnationist
Sabaean
Shintoist
Sikh
Taoist
Theosophist
Vedantist
yogi, yogin, yogist
Zoroastrian

34. Christian sectaries

Adventist, Second
  Adventist
Amish, Amish
  Mennonite
Anabaptist
Anglican
Anglo-Catholic
Antinomian
Arian
Athanasian
Baptist
Bible Christian
Boehmenist
Bryanite
Calvinist
Campbellite

Catholic
Christadelphian
Christian Scientist
Churchman
Congregationalist
Davidist
Disciple of Christ
Dunker
Ebionite
Episcopalian
Erastian
Eusebian
Evangelical
  Congregationalist
Familist
Friend

German Baptist
Gideon
Glassite
High-Churchman
Homoiousian
Homoousian
Huguenot
Independent
Irvingite
Jansenist
Jehovah's Witness
Jovinianist
latitudinarian
Latter-day Saint
Laudist, Laudian
Liberal Catholic
Low-Churchman
Lutheran
Mennonite
Methodist
Mormon
Presbyterian

Protestant
Protestant
Episcopal
Puritan
Puseyite
Quaker
quietist
Restitutionist
Roman Catholic
Rosicrucian
Sandemanian
Seventh-Day
  Adventist
Shaker
Stundist
Swendenborgian
Tractarian
Trinitarian
Ubiquitarian
Unitarian
Universalist
Wesleyan

1019. SCRIPTURE

NOUNS 1. **scripture, scriptures, sacred writings, Bible.**

2. **the Bible, Scripture, the Scriptures,** Holy Scriptures, Holy Writ, the Book, the Good Book, the Book of Books, the Word, the Word of God; Vulgate, Septuagint, Douay Bible, Authorized *or* King James Version, Revised Version, American Revised Version; Testament; canon.

3. **Old Testament,** the Law; Hexateuch, Octateuch; Pentateuch, Torah, the Law, the Jewish *or* Mosaic Law, Law of Moses; the Prophets, Nebiim, Major *or* Minor Prophets; Hagiographa, Ketubim; Apocrypha.

4. **New Testament;** Gospels, Evangels, the Gospel, Good *or* Glad Tidings; Synoptic Gospels; Epistles, Pauline Epistles, Catholic Epistles, Johannine Epistles; Acts, Acts of the Apostles; Apocalypse, Revelation.

5. **Talmud,** Mishnah *or* Mishna, Gemara; Masora *or* Masorah.

6. (non-Biblical) **Koran,** Alcoran [Mohammedan]; Avesta, Zend-Avesta [Zoroastrian]; Granth, Adigranth [Sikh]; Tripitaka [Buddhist], agama [Hindu], Tao Tê Ching [Chinese], the Eddas [Scandinavian], Arcana Caelestia [Swedenborgian], **Book of Mormon** [Mormon], Science and Health with Key to the Scriptures [Christian Science].

7. (Brahmanic) **Veda,** Rig-Veda, Yajur-Veda, Sama-Veda, Atharva-Veda; Brahmana, Upanishad, Aranyaka; shastra, sruti, smriti, purana, tantra; Bhagavad-Gita.

8. **revelation,** torah [Jewish]; inspira-

tion, afflutus, divine inspiration; theopneusty, theopneustia; theophany, theophania.

ADJS. 9. **scriptural, Biblic(al)**; revealed, revelational, apocalyptic(al); inspired, theopneustic; evangelic(al), evangelistic, gospel; apostolic(al); textual, textuary; canonical.

10. Talmudic(al), Mishnaic, Gemaric.

1020. PROPHETS AND RELIGIOUS FOUNDERS

NOUNS 1. **prophet**, *vates sacer* [L., sacred prophet]; Amos, Daniel, Ezekiel, Habakkuk, Haggai, Hosea, Isaiah, Jeremiah, Joel, Jonah, Joseph, Joshua, Malachi, Micah, Nahum, Obadiah, Samuel, Zechariah, Zephaniah.

2. (Christian founders) **evangelist, apostle, disciple,** saint; **the Fathers,** Apostolic Fathers, Anti-Nicene Fathers, Nicene Fathers, Post-Nicene Fathers.

3. (non-Biblical) Buddha, Gautama Buddha [Buddhism]; Mahavira, Vardhamana Jnatiputra [Jainism]; Mirza Ali Mohammed of Shiraz, the Bab [Babism]; Mohammed [Mohammedanism], Confucius [Confucianism], Laotzu [Taoism], Zoroaster *or* Zarathustra [Zoroastrianism], Nanak [Sikhism], Ram Mohan Roy [Brahmo-Samaj], Swedenborg [Swedenborgianism], Joseph Smith [Mormonism], Mary Baker Eddy [Christian Science].

1021. THEOLOGY

NOUNS 1. **theology, religion, divinity;** theologism; doctrinism, doctrinalism, doctrinal theology; canonics; dogmatics, dogmatic theology; physicotheology; natural *or* rational theology; hierology, hagiology; hierography, hagiography; soteriology; apologetics; secularism; rationalism.

2. **doctrine** 500.2; **creed,** credo; credenda, articles of religion *or* faith; Apostles' Creed, Nicene Creed, Athanasian Creed; Catechism.

3. **theologian,** theologist, theologizer; theologer, theologician; **divine;** scholastic, schoolman; theological *or* divinity student, theological, theologue [coll.]; canonist.

ADJS. 4. **theologic(al), religious, divine;** doctrinal, doctrinary; canonic(al); physicotheological.

1022. ORTHODOXY

True Belief.—NOUNS 1. **orthodoxy,** orthodoxism; orthodoxness, orthodoxicalness;

soundness, soundness of doctrine; catholicism, catholicity; **authoritativeness,** authenticity; canonicalness, canonicity; the truth, religious truth, gospel truth.

2. **the faith,** the Faith, true faith, apostolic faith, "the faith once delivered unto the saints" [Bible].

3. **Christianity,** Christianism; Christendom.

4. **the Church,** Holy Church, Church of Christ, the Bride of the Lamb, body of Christ, temple of the Holy Ghost, body of Christians, members in Christ, disciples *or* followers of Christ; apostolic church; universal church, the church universal; church visible, church invisible; church militant, church triumphant.

5. **true believer,** orthodox Christian; orthodox, orthodoxist; textualist, textuary; canonist; fundamentalist; the orthodox.

6. **hyperorthodoxy;** puritanism, puritanicalness; strait-lacedness, stiff-neckedness, hideboundness; **bigotry** 525; **dogmatism** 512.6; fundamentalism, precisianism; bibliolatry; Sabbatarianism, sabbatism.

7. **bigot** 525.5; **dogmatist** 512.7.

ADJS. 8. **orthodox,** orthodoxical; of the faith, of the true faith; **sound,** sound on the goose [slang], firm, faithful, true, true-blue; catholic; Christian; evangelical; **scriptural,** canonical; literal, textual; standard, customary, conventional; **authoritative,** authentic, accepted, received, approved; correct, right, proper.

9. **hyperorthodox,** puritanical, straitlaced; hidebound, creed-bound; **bigoted** 525.10; **dogmatic** 512.22.

1023. UNORTHODOXY

False Belief.—NOUNS 1. **unorthodoxy, heterodoxy;** unorthodoxness, **unsoundness,** un-Scripturality; uncatholicism, uncatholicity; **unauthoritativeness,** unauthenticity; nonconformity 83.2.

2. **heresy,** false doctrine, **misbelief; fallacy, error** 517.

3. **infidelity,** infidelism; unchristianity; gentilism; **unbelief** 1029.5.

4. **paganism, heathenism;** paganry, heathenry; pagandom, heathendom; pagano-Christianism; allotheism; animism, animatism; idolatry 1031.

5. **misbeliever, heretic,** pervert; nonconformist 83.4.

6. **infidel; unbeliever** 1029.11; **non-Christian; gentile,** Gentile; **non-Jew,** goy *or* goi, goyim [pl.]; **non-Mohammedan,**

Moslem, *giaour* [Turk.], Kaffir; zendik, zendician, zendikite [all Moham.]; **non-Mormon.**

7. **pagan, heathen;** allotheist; animist; idolater 1031.4.

VERBS 8. **misbelieve, err,** stray, deviate, wander, go astray, go wrong, fall into error; be wrong, be mistaken, be in error; serve Mammon.

ADJS. 9. **unorthodox,** nonorthodox, **heterodox, heretical; unsound,** uncatholic; **unscriptural,** uncanonical, apocryphal; **unauthoritative,** unauthentic, unaccepted, unreceived, unapproved; **fallacious,** erroneous 517.14.

10. **infidel,** infidelic(al), misbelieving; unbelieving 1029.19; **unchristian, non-Christian; gentile,** Gentile, ethnic(al); **non-Jewish,** uncircumcised; **non-Mohammedan,** non-Moslem, non-Islamic; **non-Mormon.**

11. **pagan, paganish,** paganic(al), paganist(ic); **heathen, heathenish;** pagano-Christian; allotheistic; animist, animistic; idolatrous 1031.7.

1024. SANCTITY

Sacred Quality.—NOUNS 1. **sanctity,** sanctitude; **sacredness, holiness,** hallowedness; sacrosanctness, sacrosanctity; heavenliness, divineness; venerableness, **venerability;** awesomeness, awfulness; inviolableness, **inviolability;** ineffability, unutterability, unspeakability, inexpressibility; godliness 1026.2.

2. **the sacred, the holy;** the ineffable, the unutterable, the unspeakable, the inexpressible.

3. **sanctification,** hallowing; **purification;** beatification, beatitude, blessing; **glorification,** exaltation; **consecration,** dedication, devotion, setting apart; sainting, canonization, enshrinement; grace; justification, justification by faith; psychiasis.

4. **redemption, salvation,** conversion, regeneration, reformation, adoption; rebirth, new birth.

VERBS 5. **sanctify, hallow; purify,** cleanse, wash one's sins away; **bless,** beatify; **glorify,** exalt; **consecrate,** dedicate, devote, set apart; saint, canonize, enshrine.

6. **redeem,** regenerate, reform, convert, **save,** give salvation.

ADJS. 7. **sacred, holy, sacrosanct;** religious, spiritual, heavenly, divine; vener-

able, awesome, awful; **inviolable,** inviolate; **ineffable,** unutterable, unspeakable, inexpressible.

8. **sanctified, hallowed;** blessed, blest, beatified; consecrated, devoted, dedicated, set apart; sainted.

1025. UNSANCTITY

NOUNS 1. **unsanctity,** unsanctitude; **unsacredness, unholiness,** unhallowedness; **profanity,** profaneness.

2. **the profane,** the unholy; the temporal, the mundane.

ADJS. 3. **unsacred,** nonsacred, **unholy,** unhallowed, unsanctified; **profane,** secular, temporal, mundane.

1026. PIETY

NOUNS 1. **piety, piousness,** pietism; religion, faith; **religiousness,** religionism, religious-mindedness; **devoutness,** devotion, devotedness; faithfulness, dutifulness; **reverence,** veneration; **zeal,** zealousness, zealotry, zealotism.

2. **godliness,** godlikeness; **sanctity,** sanctitude; odor of sanctity, beauty of holiness; **righteousness, holiness,** goodness; **spirituality,** spiritual-mindedness, holy-mindedness, godly-mindedness, heavenly-mindedness; **purity,** pureness, pure-heartedness, pureness of heart; **saintliness,** saintlikeness; saintship, sainthood; **Christianity, Christliness,** Christlikeness; angelicalness, seraphicalness; heavenliness; **unworldliness,** unearthliness, otherworldliness.

3. **overreligiousness,** overpiousness, overrighteousness, **overzealousness,** overdevoutness; **fanaticism** 472.11; sanctimony 1027.

4. **believer,** truster, accepter, receiver; pietist, religionist, saint; **devotee,** devotionalist, **zealot; Christian,** good Christian; **churchgoer,** churchman, churchite; pillar of the church; **convert,** proselyte, neophyte, catechumen; **disciple,** follower; fanatic 472.17.

5. **the believing,** the faithful, the righteous, the good; the elect, the saved; the children of God, the children of light; Christendom.

VERBS 6. **have faith,** trust in God; **believe** 500.8; keep the faith, fight the good fight, let one's light shine.

7. **be converted,** get religion [coll., U.S.], receive *or* accept Christ, stand up for Jesus.

ADJS. 8. **pious,** pietistic(al); **religious,** religious-minded; **devout,** devoted; zealous, zealotic(al); **reverent,** reverential, venerat.ve, venerational, solemn; faithful, dutiful; believing 500.18; Christian, Christianly, Christianlike.

9. godly, godlike; **righteous, holy,** good; **spiritua.,** spiritual-minded, holy-minded, godly-minded, heavenly-minded; **pure,** purehearted, pure in heart; **saintly,** saintlike; **Christly, Christlike; angelic**(al), seraphic(al); heavenly; **unworldly,** unearthly, otherworldly, not of the earth, not of this world.

10. regenerate, regenerated, **converted,** saved, reborn.

11. overreligious, ultrareligious, overpious, overrighteous, **overzealous,** overdevout; **fanatical** 472.31; sanctimonious 1027.5.

1027. SANCTIMONY

NOUNS **1. sanctimony, sanctimoniousness; pietism,** piety, **piousness,** pietisticalness, false piety; **religionism, religiosity; self-righteousness;** goodiness, goody-goodiness [both coll.]; pharisaism, pharisaicalness; tartuffery, tartuffism; **falseness, insincerity, hypocrisy** 614; affectation 901; **cant,** mummery, snivel, snuffle; unctuousness, mealymouthedness.

2. lip service, mouth honor, lip homage, lip worship, lip devotion, lip praise, lip reverence; formalism, solemn mockery.

3. pietist, religionist, **hypocrite,** religious hypocrite, canting hypocrite, pious fraud, whited sepulcher, **pharisee,** tartufe, Holy Willie [Burns], "a saint abroad and a devil at home" [Bunyan]; **canter,** ranter, snuffler, sniveler; dissembler, dissimulator; affecter, poser 901.7, 8; **lip server,** lip worshiper, formalist; **Pharisee,** scribes and **Pharisees;** Tartufe, Pecksniff, Mawworm, Joseph Surface.

VERBS **4. cant,** snuffle, snivel; give mouth honor, render lip service.

ADJS. **5. sanctimonious,** sanctified, **pious, pietistic**(al), **self-righteous,** pharisaic(al), holier-than-thou; goody, goody-goody [both coll.]; **false, insincere, hypocritical** 614.26–33; affected 901.15; tartuffish, tartuffian canting, snivelling, unctuous, mealymouthed.

1028. IMPIETY

NOUNS **1. impiety, impiousness; irreverence,** undutifulness; **irreligion** 1029.

2. sacrilege, blasphemy; profanity, profaneness; sacrilegiousness, blasphemousness; **desecration, profanation.**

3. sacrilegist, blasphemer, Sabbath-breaker.

VERBS **4. desecrate, profane,** dishonor, unhallow, commit sacrilege.

5. blaspheme; vilify, abuse 970.7; curse, swear 970.6; take in vain.

ADJS. **6. impious, irreverent,** undutiful; **profane,** profanatory; **sacrilegious,** blasphemous; **irreligious** 1029.15.

1029. IRRELIGION

NOUNS **1. irreligion, unreligiousness; undevoutness;** indevoutness, indevotion, undutifulness; **impiety** 1028; indifference 634.

2. worldliness, earthliness, earthiness, mundaneness; **unspirituality,** carnality; worldly-mindedness, earthly-mindedness, carnal-mindedness; materialism.

3. ungodliness, unrighteousness, unholiness, unsaintliness, unangelicalness; unchristianliness, un-Christlikeness, un-Christliness; **wickedness, sinfulness** 979.5.

4. unregeneracy, godlessness, **reprobacy,** gracelessness, shriftlessness.

5. unbelief, disbelief; infidelity, infidelism, faithlessness; **atheism; agnosticism;** nullifidianism, minimifidianism; secularism.

6. skepticism, doubt, incredulity, Pyrrhonism, Humism; scoffing 965.1.

7. freethinking, free thought, **latitudinarianism.**

8. antireligion; anti-Christianism, anti-Christianity; anti-Scripturism.

9. iconoclasm, iconoclasticism, image breaking.

10. irreligionist; worldling, earthling; **materialist** 375.6; **iconoclast,** idoloclast; antichristian, anti-Christian, antichrist.

11. unbeliever, disbeliever, nonbeliever; **atheist, infidel, pagan, heathen; agnostic;** nullifidian, minimifidian; secularist.

12. skeptic, doubter, dubitant, doubting Thomas, scoffer, Pyrrhonist, Humist.

13. freethinker, latitudinarian, *esprit fort* [F.].

VERBS **14. disbelieve,** doubt 502.5, 6; scoff 965.9.

ADJS. **15. irreligious, unreligious; undevout,** indevout, indevotional, undutiful; **impious** 1028.6; indifferent 634.5.

16. worldly, earthly, earthy, terrestrial, **mundane,** temporal; **unspiritual, profane,** carnal, secular; worldly-minded, earthly-minded, carnal-minded; **materialistic,** material.

17. **ungodly, unrighteous, unholy,** un-saintly, unangelic(al); **unchristian,** un-christianly; **un-Christlike,** un-Christly; **wicked, sinful** 979.17.

18. **unregenerate, unconverted,** god-less, reprobate, graceless, shriftless, **lost, damned.**

19. **unbelieving, disbelieving, faithless; infidel,** infidelic(al); **pagan, heathen; atheistic(al),** atheist; **agnostic(al);** nul-lifidian, minimifidian; unchristian.

20. **skeptic(al), doubtful, dubious, in-credulous,** Humean, Pyrrhonic.

21. **freethinking, latitudinarian.**

22. **antireligious;** antichristian, anti-Christian; anti-Scriptural; **iconoclastic.**

1030. WORSHIP

NOUNS **1. worship, adoration, devotion, homage, veneration, reverence,** "tran-scendent wonder" [Carlyle]; latria, dulia, hyperdulia [all R.C.Ch.]; idolatry 1031.

2. **glorification,** glory, **praise,** laudation, laud, exaltation, magnification.

3. **paean,** laud; hosanna, hallelujah or halleluiah, alleluia or alleluiah or alleluja; **hymn,** hymn of praise, **doxology, psalm, anthem,** motet, canticle, choral or chorale; chant, versicle; Introit, Miserere; Gloria, Gloria in Excelsis, Gloria Patri; *Te Deum,* Agnus Dei, Benedicite, Magnificat, Nunc Dimittis; response, responsory or respon-sary, report, answer; Trisagion; antiphon, antiphony; offertory, offertory sentence or hymn.

4. **prayer,** holy breathing, **supplication, invocation,** imprecation, importunity, im-ploration, impetration, entreaty, beseech-ment, appeal, petition, suit, orison, obsecra-tion, obtestation, rogation; intercession; **grace, thanks, thanksgiving;** litany; breviary, canonical prayers; collect, collect of the Mass, collect of the Communion; Angelus; paternoster or Pater Noster, the Lord's Prayer; Hail Mary, Ave, Ave Maria; Kyrie eleison; chaplet; rosary, beads, bead-roll; prayer wheel or machine.

5. **benediction, blessing,** benison, invo-cation, benedicite; sign of the cross; laying on of hands.

6. **propitiation,** appeasement 802; atone-ment 1010.

7. **oblation, offering, sacrifice, immo-lation,** incense; libation, drink offering; burnt offering, holocaust; thank offering, votive offering, heave offering, peace offer-ing, sacramental offering, sin or piacular offering, whole offering; human sacrifice, mactation, infanticide, hecatomb; idolo-thyte; self-sacrifice, self-immolation; suttee-ism; scapegoat, suttee; offertory, collection.

8. **divine service, service, office, duty, exercises, devotions;** meetings; church service, church; revival, revival meeting, protracted meeting, camp meeting [U.S.], big meeting [dial.], anxious meeting; praise meeting [local, U.S.]; watch meeting, watch night; prayer meeting, prayers, prayer; morning devotions, ∼ services or prayers, matins, lauds; prime, prime song; tierce, undersong; sext; none, nones; novena; eve-ning devotions, ∼ services or prayers, ves-per, vespers, vigils, evensong; complin or compline, night song or prayer; Mass 1038.9.

9. **worshiper,** adorer, communicant, celebrant, churchgoer; congregation; idol-ater 1031.4.

VERBS **10. worship, adore, reverence, venerate, revere, honor,** do or pay hom-age to, pay divine honors to, do service, lift up the heart, bow down and worship, hum-ble oneself before; **idolize** 1031.5, 6.

11. **glorify, praise, laud, exalt, extol,** magnify, bless, celebrate; praise God, praise or glorify the Lord, bless the Lord, praise God from whom all blessings flow; praise Father, Son and Holy Ghost; sing praises, sing the praises of, sound or resound the praises of; doxologize, hymn.

12. **pray, supplicate,** invoke, petition, make supplication; **beseech** 772.11; offer a prayer, send up a prayer, commune with God; say one's prayers; tell one's beads, recite the rosary; **say grace, give** or **re-turn thanks;** pray over.

13. **bless, give one's blessing,** give benediction, confer a blessing upon, invoke benefits upon; cross, make the sign of the cross over or upon; lay hands on.

14. **propitiate,** make propitiation; ap-pease 802.7; **offer sacrifice,** sacrifice, make sacrifice to, immolate before, offer up an oblation.

ADJS. **15. worshipful,** worshiping; **ador-ing,** adorant; **devout,** devotional; **rever-ent,** reverential; **venerative,** venerational; solemn; at the feet of; on one's knees, on bended knee; prone or prostrate before, in the dust.

INTERJS. **16. hallelujah** or halleluiah!, alleluia or alleluiah!, **hosanna!, praise God!,** praise the Lord!, praise ye the Lord!, "praise ye Him . . . all His hosts!" [Bible]; Heaven be praised!, glory to God!, glory be to God!, glory be to God in the highest!, bless the Lord!, "bless the Lord, O my soul: and all that is within me, bless His holy name!" [Bible], "hallowed be Thy Name!" [ibid.]; thanks be to God!, *Deo gratias!* [L.].

17. O Lord!, our Father Who art in heaven!; God grant!, pray God that!; God bless!, God save!, God forbid!

1031. IDOLATRY

NOUNS 1. idolatry, idolatrousness, idolism, idololatry, idolodulia, idol worship; iconolatry, iconoduly; fetishism; demonism, demonolatry, demon *or* devil worship; animal worship, zoolatry; fire worship, pyrolatry, Parsiism, Zoroastrianism; sun worship, heliolatry; star worship, Sabaism; hero worship; hagiolatry; ecclesiolatry; bibliolatry; idolomancy.

2. idolization, fetishization; deification, apotheosis.

3. idol, fetish, joss [Chin.], *thakur* [Hind.] graven image, golden calf, "the yellow god" [J. Milton Hayes]; devil-god, "the god of my idolatry" [Shakespeare]; Baal, Juggernaut.

4. idolater, idolatress, idolizer, idolatrizer, idolist, idol worshiper; fetishist; demon *or* devil worshiper, demonolater, chthonian; animal worshiper, zoolater; fire worshiper, pyrolater, Parsi, Zoroastrian; sun worshiper, heliolater; star worshiper, Sabaist; bibliolater, bibliolatrist; ecclesiolater.

VERBS 5. idolize, idolatrize, idolify, idol; fetishize, fetish; make an idol of, deify, apotheosize.

6. worship idols, "When all fathers worshipt stocks and stones" [Milton]; worship the golden calf, *adorer le veau d'or* [F.].

ADJS. 7. idolatrous, idolatric(al), idololatric(al), idol-worshiping; idolistic, fetishistic; demonolatrous, chthonian; heliolatrous; bibliolatrous; zoolatrous; idolothytic, idolothyte.

1032. OCCULTISM

NOUNS 1. occultism, mysticism; esoterics, esotericism, esoterism, esotery; cabalism, cabala; yoga, yogism, yogeeism; theosophy, anthroposophy, Esoteric Buddhism; Rosicrucianism; Masonry, Freemasonry, Freemasonism; symbolics, symbolism; anagogics; anagoge; mystery.

2. supernaturalism, supranaturalism, preternaturalism, transcendentalism; the supernatural, the supersensible.

3. metaphysics, hyperphysics, transphysical science, the first philosophy *or* theology.

4. psychics, psychism, psychicism; parapsychology, psychical research; metapsychics, metapsychism; psychosophy; panpsychism; psychic monism.

5. spiritualism, spiritism; mediumism; séance, sitting; spirit 1015.

6. psychical phenomena, spirit manifestation; materialization; spirit rapping, table tipping *or* turning; poltergeistism, poltergeist; telekinesis, psychokinesis, power of mind over matter; levitation; trance speaking; psychorrhagy; automatism, psychography, automatic ~, trance *or* spirit writing; ouija board, ouija; planchette.

7. ectoplasm, exteriorized protoplasm; aura, emanation, effluvium; ectoplasy.

8. extrasensory perception, ESP; clairvoyance, lucidity, second sight, insight, sixth sense; intuition 480; foresight 540; premonition 542; clairsentience, clairaudience, crystal vision, psychometry, metapsychosis.

9. telepathy, mental telepathy, mind reading, thought transference, telepathic transmission; telepathic dreams, telepathic hallucinations.

10. divination 541.2, 15; sorcery 1032.

11. occultist, esoteric, mystic, cabalist, supernaturalist, transcendentalist; adept, mahatma [both Theos.]; yogi, yogin, yogist; theosophist, anthroposophist; Rosicrucian; Mason, Freemason.

12. psychist, psychicist; parapsychologist; metapsychist; panpsychist; metaphysician, metaphysicist.

13. psychic, spiritualist, spiritist, medium, witch of Endor; ecstatic, spirit rapper; automatist, psychographist.

14. clairvoyant; clairaudient; psychometer, psychometrist.

15. telepathist, mental telepathist, mind reader, thought reader.

16. diviner 541.4; sorcerer 1033.5–9.

17. psyche, spirit, spiritus, *Geist* [G.], soul, heart, mind, anima, anima humana, nephesh [Hebrew]; shade, shadow, manes [Rom. rel.]; breath, pneuma, breath of life, divine breath; atman, purusha, buddhi, jiva, jivatma [all Hinduism], ba, khu [both Egyptian relig.]; ruach [Kabbalism]; spiritual being, inner man, "the Divinity that stirs within us" [Addison]; ego, the self, the I.

18. life principle, vital principle, vital

spirit *or* soul, **vital force**, prana [Hinduism]; essence *or* substance of life, individual essence, *ousia* [Gr.]; divine spark, vital spark *or* flame.

19. astral body, astral, linga sharira, design body, subtle body, vital body, etheric body, bliss body, Buddhic body, spiritual body, soul body; kamarupa, desire *or* kamic body; causal body; mental *or* mind body.

20. (seven principles of man, theosophy) spirit, atman; mind, manas; soul, buddhi; life principle, vital force, prana; astral body, linga sharira; physical ∼, dense *or* gross body, sthula sharira; principle of desire, kama.

21. spiritualization, etherealization, idealization; **dematerialization,** immaterialization, unsubstantialization; **disembodiment,** disincarnation.

VERBS **22. spiritualize,** spiritize; etherealize; idealize; **dematerialize,** immaterialize, unsubstantialize; **disembody,** disincarnate.

23. hold a séance *or* sitting; call up spirits 1033.11.

ADJS. **24. occult, esoteric(al), mystic(al), mysterious,** anagogic(al); metapsychic(al), metaphysic(al); cabalic, cabalistic(al); **supernatural** 85.14; theosophic(al), theosophist; Rosicrucian; Masonic(al), Freemasonic(al).

25. psychic(al), spiritual; spiritualistic, spiritistic; mediumistic; **clairvoyant,** second-sighted, clairaudient, clairsentient, **telepathic; extrasensory,** psychosensory; supersensible, supersensual, pretersensual; telekinetic, psychokinetic; automatist; psychometric(al).

1033. SORCERY

NOUNS **1. sorcery, necromancy, magic,** sortilege, **wizardry,** theurgy, gramarye [chiefly hist.], rune, glamour; **witchcraft,** spellcraft; **witchery,** witchwork, bewitchery, enchantment; **voodooism, voodoo,** hoodoo, wanga [W. Ind. & South. U.S.]; juju, jujuism [both W. Africa]; obeah, obeahism; shamanism; magism, magianism; fetishism; vampirism; thaumaturgy, thaumaturgia, thaumaturgics, thaumaturgism; alchemy; white *or* natural magic; sympathetic magic; **divination** 541.2, 15; spell, charm 1034.

2. black magic, the black art; **diabolism, demonism,** Satanism, demonry, devilry, diablerie; demonomancy; Black Mass.

3. (practices) magic circle; ghost dance; sabbat, witches' meeting *or* Sabbath; ordeal, ordeal by battle, ∼ fire, ∼ water *or* lots.

4. conjuration, conjurement, evocation, invocation; **exorcism,** exorcisation; exsufflation [eccl. hist.]; **incantation** 1034.4.

5. sorcerer, necromancer, wizard, miracle-worker, wonder-worker, warlock, theurgist; thaumaturge, thaumaturgist; **conjuror,** exorciser, exorcist; **diviner** 541.4; dowser, water witch, witch-wiggler [dial.]; diabolist 1014.16; Faust, Comus.

6. magician, mage, magus, magian; Houdini, Merlin.

7. witchman, witch master; **shaman,** shamanist; **voodoo,** voodooist, wangateur [South. U.S.]; **witch doctor,** obeah doctor, **medicine man,** mundunugu [E. Africa], isangoma [S. Africa]; witch-hunter, witchfinder.

8. sorceress, shamaness; **witch,** witchwoman [dial.], witchwife [Scot., Ir. & North. Eng.], hex [local U.S.], **hag,** lamia; witch of Endor; Weird Sisters [Shakespeare].

9. charmer, enchanter, bewitcher, spellbinder; **enchantress, siren,** vampire; Circe; Medusa, Gorgon, Stheno, Eurale.

VERBS **10.** sorcerer, shamanize; wave a wand, rub the ring *or* lamp; ride a broomstick.

11. conjure, conjure up, exorcise, evoke, invoke, raise, summon, call up; **call up spirits,** conjure *or* conjure up spirits, summon spirits, raise ghosts, evoke from the dead, "call spirits from the vasty deep" [Shakespeare].

12. exorcise, lay; **lay ghosts,** cast out devils.

13. cast a spell, bewitch 1034.8–11.

ADJS. **14. sorcerous, necromantic, magic(al),** magian, thaumaturgic(al), cantrip, weird; wizardlike, wizardly; shaman, shamanic, shamanist(ic); witchlike, witchy, witch; voodoo, hoodoo [coll.], voodooistic; incantatory, incantational; talismanic(al); phylacteric(al).

1034. SPELL, CHARM

NOUNS **1. spell,** magic spell, **charm,** glamour, weird [Scot.], cantrip [chiefly Scot.], wanga [W. Ind. & South. U.S.]; demonifuge; hand of glory; evil eye.

2. bewitchment, witchery, bewitchery; enchantment, entrancement, fascination, captivation; bedevilment; **possession, obsession.**

3. **trance, ecstasy,** ecstasis, **rapture;**
yoga trance, dharana, dhyana, samadhi;
hypnosis 710.7.

4. **incantation, conjuration, exorcism,**
magic words or formula; hocus-pocus, abracadabra, mumbo jumbo; open-sesame; bell,
book and candle.

5. **talisman, charm, amulet, fetish,**
antinganting [P.I.], periapt, phylactery;
voodoo, hoodoo, juju [W. Africa], obeah
[coll.], Mumbo Jumbo or mumbo jumbo;
good-luck charm, lucky piece, rabbit-
foot, lucky bean; mascot, *mascotte* [F.];
madstone [U.S.]; love charm, philter;
scarab, scarabaeus, scarabee; veronica,
sudarium; swastika, fylfot, gammadion.

6. **wand,** rod, magic wand; Aaron's rod.

7. **wish-bringer,** wish-giver; Aladdin's
lamp, magic ring, magic belt, magic spectacles, magic carpet, seven-league boots;
wishing well, wishing stone; wishing cap,
Fortunatus's cap; cap of darkness, Tarnkappe, Tarnhelm; fern seed; wishbone,
wishing bone, merrythought.

VERBS 8. **cast a spell,** spell, **spellbind;**
entrance, trance, put in a trance; **hypnotize, mesmerize.**

9. **charm,** becharm, **enchant, fascinate,**
captivate, glamour.

10. **bewitch,** witch, hex [local U.S.];
voodoo, hoodoo [coll.]; **possess, obsess;**
bedevil, diabolize, demonize; hagride; overlook, look on with the evil eye, cast the evil
eye.

11. **put a curse on,** put a hex on [local
U.S.], put a juju on [W. Africa], put obeah
on [coll.].

ADJS. 12. **bewitching, witching;** charming, **enchanting, entrancing, spellbinding,**
fascinating, glamorous, Circean.

13. **enchanted, charmed,** becharmed,
charm-struck, charm-bound; **spellbound,**
spell-struck, spell-caught; **fascinated,** captivated; **hypnotized, mesmerized;** under
a spell, in a trance.

14. **bewitched,** witched, witch-charmed,
witch-held, witch-struck; hag-ridden; **possessed, obsessed.**

1035. THE MINISTRY

The Ecclesiastical Profession.—NOUNS 1.
the ministry, the church, the cloth, the
pulpit, the desk; **priesthood,** priestship;
apostleship.

2. **ecclesiology,** churchcraft, priestcraft.

3. **clericalism,** sacerdotalism; priesthood,
priestism [derog.]; episcopalianism; ultramontanism.

4. **monasticism,** monachism, monkery,
monkhood, friarhood; celibacy 932.

5. (ecclesiastical offices and dignities)
cardinalate, cardinalship; primacy, primateship; archbishopric, archiepiscopate, archi-
episcopacy; prelacy, prelature, prelateship,
prelatehood; bishopric, bishopdom; episcopate, episcopacy; deanery, deanship; can-
onry, canonicate; curacy, cure; rectorate,
rectorship; vicariate, vicarship; pastorate,
pastorship; deaconry, deaconship; arch-
deaconry; chaplaincy, chaplainship; abbacy;
presbytery, presbyterate.

6. **papacy,** papality, pontificate, popedom, the Vatican, Apostolic See, See of
Rome.

7. **hierarchy,** hierocracy; theocracy.

8. **diocese, see,** stall, **parish,** province;
prebend, prebendaryship, prebendal stall.

9. **benefice,** living, **incumbency,** glebe,
advowson; curacy, cure, charge, cure or care
of souls; prelacy, rectory, vicarage.

10. **orders, holy orders;** calling, election,
nomination, appointment, preferment, induction, institution, installation, investiture; conferment, presentation; **ordination,**
ordainment, consecration, canonization,
reading in [Eng.].

VERBS 11. **take holy orders,** take orders,
take vows, read oneself in [Eng.]; **take the
veil.**

12. **ordain,** frock, **canonize,** consecrate;
saint.

ADJS. 13. **ecclesiastic(al), churchly;**
ministerial, **cleric(al),** sacerdotal, **pastoral;** priestly, priestish; prelatic(al), prelatial; episcopal, episcopalian; archiepiscopal;
canonical; capitular, capitulary; abbatical,
abbatial; Anglican; Aaronic(al), Levit-
ic(al); ultramontane; evangelistic(al); rab-
binic(al); priest-ridden.

14. **monastic,** monachal, **monasterial,
monkish;** conventual.

15. **papal, pontifical,** apostolic(al);
popish, papish, papist or Papist, papis-
tic(al) [all derog.].

16. hierarchic(al), hierarchal; theo-
cratic(al), theocratist.

17. ordained; in orders, in holy orders.

1036. CLERGY

NOUNS 1. **clergy, ministry,** the cloth;
clerical order, clericals; **priesthood,** priestery [derog.]; presbytery; prelacy; Sacred College.

2. clergyman, **divine,** ecclesiastic, churchman, cleric, clerical, **clerk, clerk in holy orders, minister, minister of the Gospel, parson, pastor,** *abbá* [F.], curate, angel, servant of God, shepherd, pilot [slang], sky pilot [slang], Holy Joe [naut. slang], devil-dodger [coll.], blackcoat [coll.], reverend [coll.]; **chaplain;** the Reverend, the very *or* right Reverend, his Reverence [chiefly joc.]; Doctor of Divinity, D.D.

3. preacher, sermoner, sermonizer, sermonist; pulpiter, pulpiteer [derog.]; circuit rider [U.S.].

4. priest, father, father in Christ, padre, abuna, cassock, hierophant, presbyter; curé, parish priest; confessor, father confessor, spiritual father *or* director, penitentiary.

5. clergywoman, priestess, ministress, pastoress, parsoness, preacheress.

6. evangelist, revivalist; **missionary,** missioner; missionary apostolic, missionary rector [both Cath.]; propagandist, colporteur.

7. beneficiary, incumbent; resident, residentiary.

8. (church dignitaries) ecclesiarch, hierarch, patriarch, high priest; pope, pontiff, papa, Holy Father, servant of the servants of God; antipope; cardinal, cardinal bishop, cardinal priest, **cardinal deacon,** primate, exarch, metropolitan, archpriest, archbishop, bishop, angel, prelate, diocesan, suffragan, coadjutor, bishop coadjutor, dean, subdean, archdeacon, prebendary, canon, rural dean, rector, vicar, chaplain, curate; penitentiary, Grand Penitentiary; devil's advocate, promoter of the faith.

9. (minor and lay officers) clerk, parish clerk, Bible clerk; reader, Bible reader, lay reader, lecturer, lector, anagnost; capitular, capitulary; elder, elderman, teaching elder, lay elder, ruling elder; deacon, deaconess; churchwarden, churchmaster [dial., Eng.]; sidesman; almoner; verger, vergeress; beadle, bedral *or* bederal [Scot.], *suisse* [F.]; sexton; sacristan, sacrist; acolyte, thurifer, choir chaplain, precentor, succentor.

10. (Mormon) priest, elder, deacon, teacher; Aaronic priesthood, Melchizedek priesthood.

11. (Jewish) rabbi, rabbin; prophet, priest, high priest, Levite, scribe.

12. (Mohammedan) imam, kahin, kasis, sheik, mullah, murshid, mufti, hadji, muezzin, dervish, abdal, fakir, santon.

13. (Hindu) Brahman, pujari, purohit, pundit, guru, bashara, vairagi *or* bairagi, Ramwat, Ramanandi; sannyasi; yogi, yogin; bhikshu, bhikhari.

14. (Buddhist) bonze, bhikku, poonghie [Burma], talapoin [Indo-China]; lama [Tibet]; Grand Lama, Dalai Lama, Panchen Lama.

15. (pagan) druid, druidess; flamen [Rom.]; hierophant, hierodule, hieros, daduchus, mystes, epopt [all Gr.].

16. religious, *religieux* [F.]; **monk,** monastic; brother, lay brother; cenobite, conventual; caloyer, hieromonach; **mendicant, friar;** pilgrim, palmer; stylite, pillarist, pillar saint; beadsman *or* bedesman; prior, claustral *or* conventual prior, grand prior, general prior; abbot; lay abbot, abbacomes; hermit 922.5; ascetic 989.2; celibate 932.2.

17. (religious orders) Franciscan, Gray Friar, Friar Minor, Minorite, Observant, Recollect *or* Recollet, Conventual, Capuchin; Dominican, Black Friar, Friar Preacher, preaching friar *or* brother; Carmelite, White Friar; Augustinian, Augustinian hermit, Austin friar, begging hermit; Benedictine, Black Monk; Jesuit, Loyolite; Crutched Friar, Crossed Friar [hist.]; Templar, Hospitaler; Bernardine, Bonhomme, Carthusian, Cistercian, Cluniac, Gilbertine, Lorettine, Maturine, Premonstratensian, Trappist.

18. nun, sister, *religieuse* [F.], clergywoman, conventual; abbess, prioress; **mother superior,** lady superior, superioress, the reverend mother; canoness, regular *or* secular canoness; novice, postulant.

1037. LAITY

NOUNS **1. laity, laymen;** brethren, people; flock, fold, sheep; **congregation,** assembly; **parish,** society [U.S.]; class [Methodist Ch.].

2. layman, laic, secular, **churchman, parishioner;** brother, sister, lay brother, lay sister; laywoman, churchwoman; catechumen.

ADJS. **3. lay,** laic(al); **nonecclesiastical,** nonclerical, nonministerial, nonpastoral, nonreligious; **secular,** secularist, secularistic; temporal, popular, civil; congregational.

1038. RELIGIOUS RITES

NOUNS **1. ritualism,** rituality, ceremonialism, **formalism,** liturgism; symbolism,

symbolics; sacramentalism, sacramentarian-
ism; sabbatism, Sabbatarianism; Anglicanism, High-churchism; liturgics, liturgiol-
ogy.

2. ritualist, ceremonialist, liturgist, formalist, formulist, formularist; sacramentalist, sacramentarian; sabbatist, Sabbatarian;
Anglican, High-churchman, High-church-
ist.

3. rite, ritual, rituality, liturgy, holy
rite; ceremony, ceremonial; formality,
solemnity; form, formula, formulary; service, function, duty, office, practice, observance; sacrament, sacramental, mystery;
ordinance; institution.

4. (rites) celebration, high celebration;
processional; litany, greater or lesser litany;
invocation, invocation of saints; transfiguration; confirmation, imposition or laying on
of hands; confession, auricular confession,
the confessional, the confessionary; sign of
the cross; pax, kiss of peace; love feast,
agape; reciting the rosary, telling of beads;
thurification, incense; aspersion, Asperges;
lustration; circumcision.

5. seven sacraments, mysteries; baptism, confirmation, the Eucharist, penance,
extreme unction, holy orders, matrimony.

6. unction, sacred unction, sacramental
anointment, chrism, chrisom, chrismation,
chrismatory; extreme unction, last rites,
viaticum; ointment; chrismal or chrismale.

7. baptism, baptizement; christening;
immersion; sprinkling, aspersion, aspergation; affusion, infusion; baptism for the
dead; baptismal regeneration; chrisomloosing; baptistery, font.

8. Eucharist, Lord's Supper, Last Supper, Communion, Holy Communion, the
Sacrament, the Holy Sacrament; Postcommunion; intinction; consubstantiation,
impanation, subpanation, transubstantiation; real presence; elements, consecrated
elements, bread and wine, body and blood
of Christ; host, wafer, loaf, bread, altar
bread, consecrated bread; Sacrament Sunday.

9. Mass, Mess [Scot. & dial.], Missa
[L.], Eucharistic rites; the Liturgy, the
Divine Liturgy; High Mass, Missa solemnis
[L.]; Low Mass, Missa bassa [L.]; Rosary
Mass, Rosary, Rosary of the Seven Dolors
of Mary; Dry Mass, Missa sicca [L.];
Liturgy of the Presanctified, Missa prae-
sanctificatorum [L.]; Missa publica, Missa
privata, Missa cantata or media, Missa ad-
ventitia or manualis, Missa capitularis,
Missa legata [all L.]; requiem, dirge,
Memento of the Dead.

10. (parts of the Mass) Prayers at Foot
of the Altar, Introit, Kyrie eleison, Gloria,
Collect, Epistle, Gradual and Alleluia or
Tract, Gospel, Credo, Offertory, Lavabo,
Secreta, Preface, Sanctus, Tersanctus;
Canon, Memento of the Living, Consecra-
tion, Elevation of the Host, Anamnesis,
Memento of the Dead; Pater Noster or
paternoster, Fraction, Agnus Dei, Pax,
Communion, Postcommunion, Dismissal,
Blessing, Last Gospel.

11. (sacred and ritualistic articles)
relics, sacred relics; monstrance; Host;
eucharistial, pyx, ciborium; tabernacle; ark
[Biblical]; crucifix, cross, rood, holy cross or
rood; osculatory, pax; Agnus Dei; icon,
bambino [It.], veronica, Pietà [It.]; sacramental; holy water; holy-water sprinkler,
aspergillum, asperges, asperger; thurible,
censer, incensory; cruet, urceole; rosary,
beads, beadroll; chaplet; prayer wheel or
machine; candle, votive candle, paschal
candle; Sanctus bell, sacring bell; Sangraal
or Sangreal, Holy Grail.

12. (ritualistic manual) ritual, rituale
[L.], manual, formulary, church book,
service book; rubric, canon, ordinal, breviary; missal, Mass book; farse; lectionary;
pontifical; Virginal; prayer book, Book of
Common Prayer, euchologion or euchology,
litany.

13. psalter, psalmbook; Psalm Book,
Book of Common Order; the Psalms, Book
of Psalms, the Psalter, the Psaltery.

14. holyday, holy day, hallowday [dial.,
Eng.]; holytide; feast, fast; Sabbath, Sunday, Lord's day; saint's day.

15. (holy days) Advent; Christmas 137.5;
Candlemas, Candlemas Day; Epiphany,
Twelfthtide, Twelfth-night, Twelfth-day;
Lent, Lententide; Quadragesima, Quadra-
gesima Sunday; Holy Week, Passion Week;
Ash Wednesday, Maundy Thursday, Good
Friday; Easter, Easter Saturday, ~ Sunday
or Monday; Eastertide, Easter Time; Ascen-
sion Day, Holy Thursday; Pentecost, Whit-
suntide, Whitsun, Whitweek, Pinkster
[U.S.]; Whitsunday, Whitmonday, Whit-
Tuesday, White Sunday, etc.; Trinity Sun-
day, Corpus Christi; Hallowmas, Allhallow-
mas, Allhallowtide, Allhallows, All Saints'
Day; All Souls' Day; Lammas, Lammas
Day, Lammastide; Michaelmas, Michaelmas Day, Michaelmastide; Martinmas; An-

nunciation, Annunciation Day, Lady Day; Ember days.

16. (Jewish) Tishah b'ab or bov, fast day; Passover, Pesach; Pentecost, Shabuoth, Feast of Weeks; Yom Kippur, Day of Atonement; Sukkoth, Feast of Tabernacles; Simhath Torah, Rejoicing over the Law; Rosh Hashana, New Year; Hanukkah, Feast of the Dedication; Purim, Feast of Lots.

VERBS 17. celebrate, observe, keep, solemnize; communicate, attend Communion, receive the Sacrament, partake of the Lord's Supper; attend or celebrate Mass.

18. minister, officiate, do duty, perform a rite, perform service or divine service; administer a sacrament, administer the Eucharist, etc.; anoint, chrism; confirm, impose, lay hands on; make the sign of the cross.

19. baptize, christen; dip, immerse; sprinkle, asperge.

20. confess, make confession; shrive, hear confession; absolve, administer absolution, administer extreme unction.

ADJS. 21. ritualistic, ritual; ceremonial, ceremonious; formal, formular, formulary; liturgic(al), liturgistic(al); Anglican, High-Church; sacramental, sacramentarian; eucharistic(al); baptismal; paschal.

1039. ECCLESIASTICAL ATTIRE

NOUNS 1. canonicals, clericals [coll.], robes, cloth; vestments, vesture; liturgical garments, ceremonial attire; pontificals, pontificalia, episcopal vestments.

2. robe, frock, mantle, gown, cloak.

3. staff, pastoral staff, crosier or crozier, cross, cross-staff, crook, paterissa.

ADJS. 4. vestmental, vestmentary.

5. canonicals

alb, alba	cotta
almuce	cowl
amice	crucifix
apron	cuculla
bands	dalmatic
biretta, berretta	episcopal ring
bishop's ring	fanon, fano, fannel
black gown	Geneva bands
buskins	Geneva cloak or
calotte	gown
cap	hood
capuche, capuchin	lawn sleeves
cardinal's hat	maniple
cassock	mantelletta
chasuble	mantellone
chimer, chimere	miter
cincture	mozzetta
cingulum	pallium
cope	rochet

Salvation Army	succinctorium
bonnet	surplice
sandals	tiara
scapular, scapulary	tippet
scarf	tonsure
shovel hat	triple crown
simar	tunic
skullcap	tunicle
soutane	vakass, vagas
stole	zucchetto
subcingulum	

1040. RELIGIOUS INSTITUTIONS

NOUNS 1. church, kirk [Scot. & dial., Eng.], bethel, meetinghouse, church house [South. U.S.], house of God, place of worship, house of worship or prayer; conventicle, ebenezer [Eng.]; mission; basilica, major or patriarchal basilica, minor basilica.

2. temple, fane [hist.]; cathedral, cathedral church, duomo [It.]; tabernacle; synagogue; mosque, masjid [Moham.]; dewal, girja [both Hindu]; pagoda; kiack [Buddhist]; joss house [Pidgin Eng.]; pantheon.

3. chapel, chapel of ease, chapel royal; oratory, oratorium; chantry; sacellum, sacrarium.

4. shrine, holy place, dagoba [India], naos [Gr. antiq.]; sacrarium, delubrum [both Rom. antiq.]; tope, stupa [both Buddhist]; reliquary, reliquaire [F.].

5. sanctuary, holy of holies, sanctum, sanctum sanctorum, sacrarium [Rom. antiq.].

6. cloister, monastery, abbey, friary; priory, priorate; lamasery [Tibet]; convent, nunnery.

7. parsonage, pastorage, pastorate, pastorium [South. U.S.], manse, church house, clergy house; presbytery, rectory, vicarage, deanery; glebe.

8. bishop's palace; Vatican; Lambeth, Lambeth palace.

9. (church interior) vestry, sacristy, sacrarium [Mid. Ages], diaconicon or diaconicum; baptistery, font; ambry, apse, blindstory, chancel, choir, cloisters, confessional, crypt, Easter sepulcher, nave, porch, presbytery, rood loft, rood stair, rood tower, ~ spire or steeple, transept, triforium.

10. (church furnishings) piscina; stoup, holy-water stoup or basin; paten; reredos; jube, rood screen, chancel screen; altar cloth, cerecloth, chrismal; communion or sacrament cloth, oblation cloth, fanon or fannel, corporal or corporale; pyx cloth or veil; rood cloth; baldachin, baldacchino

[It.]; kneeling stool, *prie-dieu* [F.]; prayer rug, ~ carpet *or* mat.

11. altar, scrobis [Rom. antiq.]; bomos, eschara, hestia [all Gr. antiq.]; **Lord's table**, holy table, **Communion table**, chancel table, table of the Lord, God's board; rood altar; altar desk, missal stand; credence, prothesis, table *or* altar of prothesis; predella, superaltar, retable, gradin; altarpiece, altar stole, altar side, altar rail, altar stead, altar mound, altar carpet, altar stair; altar facing *or* front, frontal; altar slab, altar stone, mensal.

12. pulpit, rostrum, ambo; **lectern**, desk, reading desk.

13. (seats) **pew; stall;** mourners' bench [U.S.], anxious bench *or* seat, penitent form; amen corner [U.S.]; sedilia.

ADJS. **14. churchly, churchish, ecclesiastical;** churchlike, templelike; cathedrallike, catedralesque; tabernacular; synagogical, synagogal; pantheonic.

15. claustral, cloistered; **monastic,** monachal, **monasterial; conventual,** conventical.

INDEX GUIDE

[See also the suggestions on How to Use, p. viii.]

The expanded array of synonyms in this new revision of Roget's International Thesaurus has been made easily accessible by an improved and simplified index.

The numbers after the index entries refer to specific paragraphs in the various categories of ideas into which the text is divided, and not to pages.

Thus the number 1035.13 after the entry Aaronic(al) refers to the thirteenth paragraph of category 1035, entitled The Ministry.

The first and last category numbers on each page appear at the top of that page of text so that the reader can flip quickly to the precise location of the desired synonyms. The index is provided with similar alphabetical headings.

When an index entry has more than one connotation, each usage and its location in the text are clearly specified by the indented words and phrases in lighter type.

Synonyms and related words for the noun abandon, for example, will be found in three places in the text: as "carelessness" in the second paragraph of category 532; as "unrestraint" in the second paragraph of category 760; and as "turpitude" in the sixth paragraph of category 979.

These identifications are not always definitions or synonyms of the main index entry. Under the entry accord on page 662, the identification "music" is given as the designation of the subject matter in paragraph 461.3; "harmony" was not used as the identification because it has nonmusical meanings which correspond to other identifications of accord — "concord" and "agreement."

Grammatical labels (nouns, verbs, adjs., etc.) have been used in the index only when it is necessary to prevent confusion about the part of speech. Thus the noun abandon is distinguished from the verb, but the adjectival form abandoned is not labeled.

So that the index would not be unwieldy, a considerable number of words and phrases in the text were not included. These omissions, which do not impair the efficiency of the index, are of three basic kinds:

Very few of the Word List entries have been indexed because they are, for the most part, common nouns which do not have synonyms. Access to these lists has been made easy by indexing the general terms under which they are classed. Thus, the specific items contained in the fourteen Word Lists appended to category 192, Receptacle, are found through the index entries for receptacle, basin, pot, pan, cup, etc.

Many words and phrases have been left out of the index because they could not reasonably be expected to serve as a starting place in the search for synonyms. The verbal phrase do an about-face, for instance, was left out in favor of the simpler verb form about-face, which appears in the same paragraph of text.

Finally, when the entries for several different forms of the same word repeat references to the same categories, the less familiar form is sometimes omitted. The noun abashment, for example, was excluded because it repeated the category references for the verb abash and the adjective abashed. The reader who needs synonyms for the noun abashment can find them through either the verb or the adjective entries and by looking among the nouns in the category to which he is referred. Each category in the text is uniformly arranged by part of speech: nouns, verbs, adjectives, adverbs, prepositions, conjunctions, interjections, and phrases, in that order.

INDEX

abnegative 522.5
abnormal
  unnatural 85.9
  eccentric 473.4
abnormality
  irregularity 85
  oddity 85.5
  sexual ~ 418.10
  eccentricity 473.1
abnormally 85.16
abnormity 85.1
aboard 183.24
  ALL ABOARD
    navigation 274.79
    embarkation 300.23
aboard ship 274.66
abode habitation 187.1
  dwelling place 190
  ABODE OF THE
    BLESSED 1016.1
  ABODE OF THE
    DAMNED 1017.1
  ABODE OF THE DEAD
    the hereafter 121.2
    hell 1017.1
abolish destroy 691.13
  repeal 777.2
abolition, abolishment
  destruction 691.6
  repeal 777.1
abomasum 192.3
A-bomb 799.16
A-bomb shelter 325.15
abominability 862.2
abominable
  terrible 673.9
  odious 862.9
  disreputable 913.12
  wicked 979.17
abominableness
  terribleness 673.2
  disreputability 913.3
abominably
  exceedingly 34.25
  terribly 673.14
  disreputably 913.17
abominate 928.4
abomination evil 673.3
  defilement 680.4
  repugnance 865.2
  hatred 928.1,3
  wrong 957.2
à bon marché 847.10
aboriculture 412.2
aboriculturist 412.6
aboriginal
  nouns ancient 123.7
  native 189.3
  adjs. beginning 68.13
  primitive 123.11
  original 152.16
  native 188.7
aboriginality 123.1
aborigine
  ancient 123.7
  native 189.3
  types of ~ 417.19
ab origine 68.16
abort have an abortion
  166.19
  fail 723.14

aborticide 408.4
abortion
  monstrosity 85.6
  miscarriage 166.9
  failure 723.5
abortional 723.17
abortionist 686.6
abortive 723.17
abortive attempt 723.5
abound 659.5
  ABOUND WITH 101.5
abounding 659.7
about
  advs. nearly 35.13
  approximately
    199.26
  around 232.13
  preps. concerning
    9.12
  near 199.20
  ABOUT TO 121.13
  BE ABOUT 654.10
  BE ABOUT TO 718.10
about-face
  nouns reversal 294.3
  tergiversation 626.1
  verbs 294.10
about-ship 274.32
above
  adjs. superior 36.13
  higher 206.24
  advs. additionally
    40.10
  aloft 206.27
  in excess of 661.27
  preps. over 227.40
  inunderstandable
    547.22
above all 36.19
aboveboard
  unhidden 553.10
  honest 972.14
aboveground 406.10
above-mentioned 64.5
abovestairs 206.27
ab ovo 68.16
abracadabra 1034.4
abradant
  nouns 259.4
  adjs. 349.10
abrade scrape off 42.10
  rub 349.7
  wear 690.21
Abraham's bosom
  1016.1
abrase 349.7
abrasion
  rubbing 349.2
  injury 690.7
abrasive
  nouns 259.4,14
  adjs. 349.10
abreaction 688.36
abreast
  adjs. 217.6
  preps. 241.11
abreast of 238.6
abreast of the times
  modern 122.14
  fashionable 642.11
abrégé 605.1

abri burrow 256.5
  shelter 698.3
  dugout 797.5
abridge shorten 202.6
  deprive of 820.18
abridged 202.9
abridger 202.4
abridgment,
  abridgement
  reduction 39.1
  shortening 202.3
  compendium 605.1
  deprivation 820.5
abroach 718.24
abroad
  adjs. absent 186.10
  bewildered 513.22
  erroneous 517.14
  advs. in foreign parts
    78.6
  broadly 178.10;
    198.17
  wide of 198.19
  outside 223.10
  oversea 396.9
  in preparation
    718.24
abrogate 777.2
abrogation 777.1
abrupt sudden 113.5
  steep 218.18
  sharp-cornered 250.6
  bluff 258.3
  hasty 707.10
  brusque 935.7
abruption 49.2
abruptly
  suddenly 113.9
  short 202.13
  hastily 707.15
abruptness
  suddenness 113.2
  steepness 218.6
  bluffness 258.1
  haste 707.2
  brusqueness 935.3
abscess 684.28
abscission
  excision 42.3
  severance 49.2
abscond 629.10
absconder fleer 629.5
  defaulter 840.5
absence
  nonexistence 2
  nonpresence 186
  want 660.4
absence without leave
  186.4
absent nonexistent 2.7
  not present 186.9
  abstracted 530.11
absentation 186.4
absentee 186.5
absentee ballot 742.20
absenteeism 186.4
absentee vote 635.5
absently 186.15
absent-minded 530.11
absent-mindedness
  530.2

absent oneself 186.7
absolute actual 1.15
  downright 34.14
  unmixed 45.6
  utter 56.11
  omnipotent 156.12
  unqualified 507.2
  certain 512.13
  dogmatic 512.22
  exact 515.15
  assertive 521.7
  arbitrary 737.15
  autocratic 739.16
  unlimited 760.24
  THE ABSOLUTE
    idea 478.4
    God 1011.2
absolutely really 1.16
  positively 34.21
  completely 56.16
  certainly 512.23
  exactly 515.19
  yes 520.18
  affirmatively 521.8
absoluteness
  certainty 512.1
  exactness 515.3
absolute zero 327.2
absolution
  forgiveness 945.2
  acquittal 1005.1
absolutism 739.9
absolve
  ~ of debt 840.9
  pardon 945.3
  acquit 1005.4
  shrive 1038.20
absonant
  discordant 460.4
  illogical 482.10
absorb
  ~ the shock 162.8
  take in 305.13
  digest 307.16
  ~ the thoughts
    477.19
  understand 546.7
  ~ the interest
    528.13
  learn 562.7
  consume 664.2
  monopolize 806.7
  take all 820.21
  corner 831.26
absorbed
  ~ in thought 477.21
  interested 528.17
  abstracted 530.11
absorbedly 528.21
absorbency 305.6
absorbent
  nouns 305.6
  adjs. 305.17
absorber 663.9
absorbing
  engrossing 528.20
  monopolistic 806.12
  deep-felt 853.25
absorption
  taking in 305.6
  digestion 307.1

thoughtfulness 477.3
engrossment 528.3
abstraction 530.2
learning 562.2
consumption 664.1
monopolization
806.4
absquatulate
scram 300.10
decamp 629.10
absquatulation 629.4
abstain not use 666.5
not do 704.3
be abstinent 990.7
abstainer ascetic 989.2
abstinent 990.4
abstainment 990.2
abstemious 990.10
abstemiousness 990.2
abstention 990.2
abstentious 990.10
abstergent
nouns 679.16
adjs. 679.26
abstersion 679.2
abstinence
disuse 666.2
continence 986.3
asceticism 989
abstention 990.2
abstinent
nouns 990.4
adjs. continent 986.6
ascetic 989.3
abstemious 990.10
abstract
nouns idea 478.6
picture 572.12
compendium 605.1
IN THE ABSTRACT
separately 49.26
in theory 498.16
verbs deduct 42.7
eliminate 77.5
shorten 202.6
~ oneself 530.9
steal 822.13
adjs. ur concrete 4.8
theoretical 498.13
recondite 547.14
abstracted 530.11
abstract idea 478.6
abstraction
deduction 42.1
disjunction 49.1
abstract idea 478.6
theory 498.1
absent-mindedness
530.2
picture 572.12
neurosis 688.22
theft 822.1
abstriction 49.2
abstruse wise 466.17
learned 474.21
unintelligible 547.14
hidden 613.12
absurd
nonsensical 469.10
unbelievable 502.10
impossible 509.6

ludicrous 878.5
absurdity
foolishness 469.3,4
impossibility 509.1
ludicrousness 878.1
abulia, abuleia
weak will 625.4
neurosis 688.21
abulic 625.11
abuna 1036.4
abundance
large amount 34.3
plenty 659.2
abundant
plentiful 101.9;
659.7
fertile 164.9
Abundantia 659.2
abundantly
greatly 34.17
plentifully 659.9
abuse
nouns mistreatment
665.2
revilement 967.8
malediction 970.2
debauchment 987.6
ABUSE OF TERMS
misinterpretation
551.1
ungrammaticalness
585.1
wordplay 879.8
verbs mistreat 665.5
harm 673.6
revile 967.20
curse 970.7
debauch 987.20
ABUSE ONE'S RIGHTS
959.7
abused 762.15
abusive insulting 963.6
reviling 967.23
maledictory 970.8
threatening 971.3
abut 199.9,13
ABUT ON
adjoin 199.9
rest on 215.23
abutment
juxtaposition 199.3
buttress 215.4
fortification 797.4
abuttal 199.3
abutter 199.6
abutting 199.16
aby 859.5
abysm gorge 200.3
pit 208.2; 256.4
abysmal 208.10
abyss cleft 200.3
pit 208.2; 256.4
ocean depths 208.3
THE ABYSS 1017.1
abyssal 208.10,13
A.C. 341.2
Academese 578.7
academic
theoretical 498.13
educational 560.19
schoolish 565.18

elegant 587.6
formal 644.7
academic degrees
915.9
academic freedom
760.9
academician
scholar 475.3
teacher 563.3
academy 565.1,7
acanaceous 257.13
Acanthocephala 414.5
a cappella 461.54
a capriccio 461.54
acarpous 165.4
accede assent 520.8
submit 763.6
consent 773.4
be instated 778.11
accedence
consent 773.2
instatement 778.3
accelerando 461.56
accelerate
speed up 268.15
atomize 325.16
hasten 707.4
acceleration
pickup 268.5
hastening 707.3
accelerator
quickening 268.5
atomic ~ 325.11,26
accelerometer 268.8
accendible 328.27
accent
nouns inflection
449.2
musical ~ 462.12,
24
dialect 578.8
speech 592.7
cadence 607.9
verbs 670.13
accents 592.1
accentuate 670.13
accentuation
musical ~ 462.24
accent 592.7
cadence 607.9
accept believe 500.8
~ unquestioningly
501.5
assent 520.8,11
ratify 520.12
be open-minded
524.7
expect 537.4
adopt 635.12
undertake 713.3
consent 773.3
~ a challenge 791.7
receive 817.6
take 820.11
tolerate 859.6
be unastonished
919.2
be hospitable 923.7
~ responsibility
960.8

approve of 966.9
NOT ACCEPT
be incredulous 503.3
deny 522.4
acceptable
desirable 632.31
eligible 635.21
expedient 668.4
tolerable 672.20
satisfactory 866.12
welcome 923.12
acceptance
assent 520.1,3,4
tolerance 524.4
adoption 635.3
consent 773.1
receiving 817.1
bill 833.11
approbation 966.1
acceptance speech
742.11
acceptation 543.4
accepted
~ fact 1.3
assumed 498.14
believed 500.20
unquestioned
512.16
authoritative 512.18
admitted 520.14
expected of 537.12
~ meaning 543.4
chosen 635.23
customary 640.14
conventional 643.7
undertaken 713.6
received 817.10
approved 966.18
orthodox 1022.8
accepter believer 500.7
assenter 520.6
religionist 1026.4
acception 543.4
access increase 38.1
approach 295.1
accessibility 295.2
entranceway 301.5
admission 305.3
reachableness 508.3
~ of illness 684.5
outburst of anger
950.9
accessary 783.20
accessibility
persuadability 171.5
perviousness 264.9
approachability
295.2
attainability 508.3
open-mindedness
524.3
communicativeness
552.4
accessible
persuasible 171.15
pervious 264.21
approachable 295.5
open to 508.8
open-minded 524.10
communicative
552.9

public 557.17
handy 663.19
accession increase 38.1
addition 40.1
adjunct 41.1
assent 520.1
~ to power 737.11
consent 773.2
instatement 778.3
accessories 808.2
accessory
nouns nonessential
6.2
addition 41.1
accompaniment 73.3
accomplice 785.3
participator 813.4
litigant 1002.11
adjs. extrinsic 6.4
additional 40.9
accompanying 73.9
assistant 783.20
**accessory before the
fact, accessory
after the fact**
accomplice 785.3
litigant 1002.11
acciaccatura 462.18
accidence 584.1
accident
nonessential 6.2
chance event 155.6
disaster 727.2
accidental
nouns 6.2
adjs. unessential 6.4
incidental 8.6
occasional 129.12
chance 155.15
accidentally 155.18
accident-prone 892.8
acclaim
nouns 966.2
verbs 966.10
acclamation
unanimity 520.5
applause 966.2
acclamatory 966.15
acclimate, acclimatize
640.10
**acclimated,
acclimatized**
640.16
acclinate 218.17
acclivity 218.6
**acclivous,
acclivitous** 218.17
accolade
embrace 930.2
praise 966.5
accommodate
suit 26.12
adjust 30.7
conform 82.3
lodge 187.11
orient 289.12
furnish 657.7,10
help 783.19
reconcile 802.8
~ oneself to 859.6
favor 936.10

ACCOMMODATE WITH
conform 82.3
furnish 816.15
lend 818.5
accommodating
indulgent 757.10
courteous 934.14
considerate 936.17
accommodation
adjustment 26.4
co-ordination 30.3
conformity 82.1
capacity 194.2
orientation 289.5
subsistence 657.3
aid 783.1,9
reconciliation 802.4
giving 816.1
loan 818.2
accommodations
lodgings 187.3
subsistence 657.3
accommodative 936.17
accompanier 73.4
accompaniment
attendant 73
concurrence 176.1
music 461.5
**accompanist,
accompanyist**
accompanier 73.4
musician 463.3
accompany
keep company 73.7
synchronize 118.3
~ musically 461.40
accompanying
attending 73.9
concurrent 176.4
accomplice 785.3
accomplish
achieve 720.4
succeed 722.6-12
accomplished
achieved 720.9
skilled 731.24
accomplished fact
fact 1.3
accomplishment
720.1
accomplishment
deed 703.3
completion 720
skill 731.8
accomplishments
474.4
accord
nouns agreement 26.1
conformity 82.1
music 461.3
unanimity 520.5
concord 792
OF ONE ACCORD
520.15
OF ONE'S OWN ACCORD
voluntarily 620.11
independently
760.30
OUT OF ACCORD
disagreeing 27.6
disaccordant 793.16

OWN ACCORD 760.6
WITH ONE ACCORD
concurrently 176.5
unanimously 520.17
verbs agree 26.7,11
conform 82.3
concur 176.2
harmonize 461.36
comply 520.9
permit 775.10
get along 792.2
give 816.12
accordance
uniformity 17.1
similarity 20.1
agreement 26.1
conformity 82.1
concurrence 176.1
music 461.3
unanimity 520.5
permission 775.1
accord 792.1
giving 816.1
IN ACCORDANCE WITH
in agreement 26.14
in conformity 82.7
compared with
490.10
accordant
consistent 17.5
agreeing 26.14
conformable to 82.6
concurrent 176.4
harmonious 461.50
consenting 773.5
in accord 792.3
according 461.50
ACCORDING AS 506.12
ACCORDING TO
conformable to
82.6,8
proportionately
490.10
ACCORDING TO
RUMOR 555.19
accordingly thus 8.9
consequently 153.9
therefore 154.6
according to Hoyle
956.8
GO ACCORDING TO
HOYLE 82.4
accordion 464.12
accordionist 463.4
accordion pleat 263.2
accost
nouns 923.4
verbs address 592.18
greet 923.10
accouchement 166.9
account
nouns sum 86.3
numeration 87.5,6
list 88.4
information 555.1
record 568.1,6
description 606.3,6
motive 646.1
credit ~ 837.2
accounting 843.2

reckoning 843.3
value 844.3
repute 912.3
BRING TO ACCOUNT
1008.10
GIVE A GOOD ACCOUNT
OF ONESELF 722.9
GIVE AN ACCOUNT OF
inform 555.7
report 556.11
narrate 606.13
HAVE ACCOUNTS TO
SETTLE 954.5
HAVE AN ACCOUNT
WITH 825.13
KEEP ACCOUNT OF
keep track 87.13
keep informed
555.15
OF NO ACCOUNT
671.14
ON ACCOUNT 837.10
ON ACCOUNT OF
because of 154.9
for 651.12; 783.26
ON NO ACCOUNT
nowise 35.14
by no means 522.8
ON ONE'S OWN
ACCOUNT
voluntarily 620.11
independently
760.30
PLACE TO ONE'S
ACCOUNT
attribute to 154.3
accuse of 1003.9
TO GOOD ACCOUNT
156.14
verbs 493.8
ACCOUNT FOR
attribute to 154.3
explain 550.11
justify 1004.9
ACCOUNT WITH
839.12
accountability
predictability 541.8
liability 960.2
accountable
attributable 154.5
predictable 541.13
intelligible 546.9
explainable 550.20
liable 960.16
accountancy 843.6
accountant
recorder 569.1
bookkeeper 843.7
account book
record 568.10
ledger 843.4
accounted as 498.14
accounting
nouns automatic ~
348.7
report 568.6
accountancy 843.6
adjs. 843.12
accounts 843
KEEP ACCOUNTS 843.8

accouple 47.5
accouplement 47.1
accouter, accoutre
  cost ume 230.40
  equip 657.8
accoutered
  equipped 657.12
  armed 797.14
accouterment, accou-
  trement 657.1
accouterments,
  accoutrements
  dress 230.2
  equipment 657.4
accredit believe 500.8
  sanction 520.12
  commission 778.9
  extend credit 837.5
accredited
  believed 500.20
  commissioned
  778.16
  well-rated 837.8
accretion increase 38.1
  coherence 50.1
accroach
  appropriate 820.16
  ~ to oneself 959.8
accrual 38.1
accrue accumulate 38.6
  be received 817.8
  fall due 838.7
ACCRUE FROM 153.6
accrued dividends
  832 7
accruement 38.1
accubation 213.2
acculturation 689.3
accumbency 213.2
accumbent 213.9
accumulate
  increase 38.6
  collect 74.17
  store up 658.11
accumulation
  increase 38.1
  assemblage 74.8
  store 658.1
  acquisition 809.2
accumulative
  additive 40.7
  cumulative 74.23
accumulator 74.14
accuracy
  correctness 515.3
  meticulousness
  531.3,12
accurate correct 515.14
  meticulous 531.12
  grammatical 584.13
accurse 970.5
accursed 970.9
accusable 967.26
accusal 1003.1
accusant 1003.5
accusation 1003
accusative case 584.7
  accusing 1003.13
accusatory 1003.13
accusatrix 1003.5
accuse 1003.7

accused
  nouns 1003.6
  adjs. 1003.15
accuser 1003.5
accustom 640.10
ACCUSTOM ONESELF
  TO
  be wont 640.12
  reconcile oneself
  859.6
accustomed usual 84.8
  used to 640.16
ace small amount 35.2
  superior 36.4
  one 89.3
  short distance 199.2
  aviator 278.3
  proficient 731.11
  playing card 876.17
ACE IN THE HOLE
  advantage 36.2
  reserve 658.3
WITHIN AN ACE OF
  199.20
ace-high 672.14
Aceldama, Akeldama,
  aceldama, akel-
  dama
  butchery 408.12
  battlefield 800.2
acerb bitter 428.6
  sour 431.6
  pungent 432.6
acerbate
  verbs 949.16
  adjs. bitter 428.6
  sour 431.6
  pungent 432.6
acerbic bitter 428.6
  sour 431.6
  pungent 432.6
  caustic 937.21
acerbity
  acrimony 160.4
  bitterness 428.2
  sourness 431.1
  pungency 432.1
  causticity 937.8
acervatim 101.13
acervation 74.8
acescence 431.4
acescency 431.2
acetic, acescent 431.7
acetification
  chemicalization
  378.5
  souring 431.4
acetify
  chemicalize 378.6
  sour 431.5
acetose, acetous 431.7
acetosity 431.2
acetylene torch,
  acetylene welder
  328.13
ache
  nouns coldness 332.2
  pain 423.5
  mental pain 864.5
ACHES AND PAINS
  423.1

verbs feel pain 423.8
  be distressed 864.22
  grieve 870.17
ACHE FOR 632.16
ACHE TO 632.15
Acheron 1017.3,4
Acherontic(al)
  1017.6
achievable 508.7
achieve arrive 299.6
  do 703.6
  accomplish 720.4
  succeed 722.6–12
achievement
  arrival 299.1
  insignia 567.2
  performance 703.2
  deed 703.3
  accomplishing 720.1
  exploit 891.7
Achilles and
  Patroclus 926.8
Achilles' heel 695.4
aching
  nouns coldness 332.2
  pain 423.5
  longing 632.5
  mental pain 864.5
  adjs. hurting 423.12
  anguished 864.26
ACHING FOR, ACHING
  TO 632.22
aching heart
  anguish 864.6
  grief 870.9
aching void 632.7
achroma, achromasia
  362.6
achromaticity, achro-
  mation color 361.5
  colorlessness 362.1
achromatization 362.3
achromatize 362.5
achromatopsia 440.3
achromic, achromatic
  362.7
achy 423.12
acicular 257.12
acid
  nouns amino ~
  307.26
  extinguisher 331.3
  chemical 378.1,13
  adjs. acrimonious
  160.12
  sour 431.7
  caustic 937.21
acidification,
  acidulation
  chemicalization
  378.5
  souring 431.4
acidify, acidulate
  chemicalize 378.6
  sour 431.5
acidity acrimony 160.4
  chemistry 378.1
  sourness 431.2
acidosis 684.21
acid test 488.2
acidulated, acidulent,

acidulous 431.7
Ack-Ack 799.7
Ack Emma 133.1
acknowledge
  answer 485.4
  testify 504.10
  allow for 506.5
  recognize 520.11
  confess 554.7
  ~ by mail 602.12
  ~ defeat 763.8
  pay 839.18
  thank 947.4
acknowledged
  traditional 123.12
  admitted 520.14
  conventional 643.7
acknowledgment
  answer 485.1
  recognition 520.3
  confession 554.3
  epistle 602.2
  receipt 842.2
  thanksgiving 947.2
acmatic, acmic 210.9
acme
  consummation 56.4
  summit 210.2
  ~ of perfection
  675.3
acne 684.27
acolyte assistant 785.6
  churchman 1036.9
acomia 231.4
acomous 231.17
acosmism 1018.5
acosmistic 499.10
acoustic(al)
  auditory 447.14
  phonic 449.16
acoustician 449.7
acoustics 449.7
à couvert 612.19
acquaint inform 555.7
  introduce 925.13
ACQUAINT ONESELF
  WITH 562.6
acquaintance
  knowledge 474.1
  information 555.1
  friendship 925.4
  friend 926.1
MAKE ACQUAINTANCE
  WITH 925.10
acquainted 925.16
ACQUAINTED WITH
  474.19
acquest 808.7
acquiesce assent 520.8
  submit 763.6
  consent 773.4
acquiescence
  conformity 82.1
  assent 520.1
  submission 763.1
  obedience 764.1
  consent 773.2
  patience 859.2
acquiescent
  conformable 82.5
  assenting 520.13

submissive 763.12
obedient 764.3
consenting 773.5
patient 859.11
acquirability 508.3
acquire incur 174.4
sicken of 684.34
get 809.7
acquired taste 895.1
acquirement
learning 562.1
skill 731.8
acquisition 809.1
acquirements 474.4
acquiring 809.13
acquisition 809
acquisitions 474.4
acquisitive
greedy 632.28
acquiring 809.13
acquit 1005.4
ACQUIT ONESELF
conduct oneself 735.4
fulfill 766.2
do one's duty 960.10
keep faith with 972.9
ACQUIT ONESELF OF 839.13
acquitment 839.1
acquittal
observance 766.1
payment 839.1
exculpation 1005
acquittance
observance 766.1
payment 839.1
receipt 842.2
acquittal 1005.1
acquitted 839.22
acreage 178.1
acres 808.7
acrid
acrimonious 160.12
bitter 428.6
acid 431.7
pungent 432.6
caustic 937.21
acridian 413a.5
acridity
acrimony 160.4
bitterness 428.2
acidity 431.2
pungency 432.1
causticity 937.8
acrimonious
acrid 160.12
bitter 428.6
caustic 937.21
resentful 950.24
acrimony
acridity 160.4
bitterness 428.2
animosity 927.4
causticity 937.8
resentment 950.3
acroamatic(al)
recondite 547.14
oral 592.20
acrobat 876.21

acrobatic 876.32
acrobatics
aerobatics 277.10
gymnastics 876.8
acroneurosis 688.17
acronym 580.3
acrophony 600.10
acropolis 797.6
acrospire 410.21
across
adjs. 220.9
advs. 220.13
preps. 198.21
across-the-board 76.6
across the grain 220.13
acrostic word 580.3
wordplay 879.8
act
nouns process 163.2
~ of God 166.9
theatrical ~ 609.8
action 703.3
~ of grace 936.7
law 996.3
IN THE ACT 981.4
IN THE ACT OF
about to 121.13
operating 163.12
PUT ON AN ACT 614.22
verbs operate 163.6
function 163.8
impersonate 570.10
~ on the stage 609.33
pretend 614.22
officiate 654.13
do 703.4
behave 735.4
affect 901.12
ACT A PART
impersonate 570.10
enact 609.34
pretend 614.22
affect 901.12
ACT FOR
substitute for 148.5
serve as 656.5
be deputy 779.13
ACT ON
operate 163.7
influence 171.9
pass judgment 493.13
act 703.5
ACT ONE'S PART
officiate 654.13
do one's duty 960.9
ACT OUT
impersonate 570.10
enact 609.34
ACT THE PART OF
function as 163.9
impersonate 570.10
enact 609.34
pose as 614.23
ACT UP
misbehave 736.4
show off 902.16
ACT UP TO

fulfill 766.2
curry favor 905.8
ACT WITH 784.6
ACT YOUR AGE! 469.13
acta 703.3
actable
workable 163.11
practicable 508.7
acting
nouns impersonation 570.2
dramatics 609.9
pretense 614.3
action 703.1
adjs. operating 163.12
performing 703.11
deputy 779.14
acting-out 688.36
actinic 334.40
actinic ray
radioray 326.3
ray 334.5
actinism 334.5
actinology, actinometry 334.22
Actinopoda 414.3
actinotherapy 687.3
action operation 163.1
mechanism 347.5
automation 348.3
verdict 493.5
story incident 606.9
doing 703
act 703.3
activity 705.1
collective ~ 784.1
contest 794.3
military ~ 795.9
legal ~ 1002.1
IN ACTION 163.12
MOVE TO ACTION 646.12
OUT OF ACTION 157.17
PUT IN ACTION 703.9
TAKE ACTION 703.5
actionable illegal 997.6
litigable 1002.20
action and reaction
aviation 277.30
reaction 283.1
actions 735.1
activate
energize 160.10
atomize 325.16
radioactivate 326.9
militarize 795.25
activation
animation 160.8
militarization 795.15
activation energy 325.14
activator 160.5
active
energetic 160.11
operating 163.12
effective 663.20
lively 705.16

active list 88.1
active service 795.14
activity
movement 152.10
energy 160
radioactivity 326.1
business 654.1
activeness 705.1
actor
stage player 610.1
doer 716.1
pretender 901.7
actor-manager 609.29
actress 610.1
Acts, Acts of the Apostles 1019.4
acts 735.1
actual real 1.15
present 120.2
true 515.11
actuality 1.2
actualize 223.5
actually really 1.16
positively 34.21
truly 515.16
actual thing 14.3
actuary
mathematician 87.9
accountant 843.7
actuate
set in motion 266.5
impel 282.11
prompt 646.12
actuating
impelling 282.22
motivating 646.25
actuator 646.10
acuity 257.1
aculeate 257.12
acumen 466.4
acuminate
verbs 257.9,10
adjs. 257.12
acumination 257.1,4
acupuncture, acupunctuation 264.3
acute energetic 160.11
violent 161.15
sharp 257.11
keenly sensitive 421.14
painful 423.10
shrill 457.13
smart 466.14
critical 670.23
crafty 733.12
deep-felt 853.25
acute alcoholism 640.8
acutely 34.20
acuteness
violence 161.1
sharpness 257.1
shrillness 457.1
smartness 466.2
craftiness 733.1
A.D. 105.13
ad 557.16
adage 516.1
adagio, adagietto
nouns 461.25

advs. 461.55
Adam, offending
 Adam
 evil nature 979.8
 carnal nature 985.2
 SINCE ADAM 119.15
adamant
 nouns 355.6
 adjs. immovable
  142.16
 inflexible 355.12
 stone 383.7
 obstinate 624.9
adamantine
 inflexible 355.12
 stone 383.7
 obstinate 624.9
Adam's apple 592.10
Adam's-needle 257.8
adapt
 accommodate 26.12
 conform 82.3
 modify 139.6
 orient 289.12
 ~ music 461.47
 accustom 640.10
 fit 718.8
adaptability
 elasticity 357.1
 versatility 731.3
adaptable
 conformable 82.5
 elastic 357.7
 versatile 731.23
adaptation
 adjustment 26.4
 conformity 82.1
 orientation 289.5
 evolution 321.4
 musical ~ 461.5
 orchestration 462.2
 habituation 640.7
 fitting 718.2
adapted suitable 26.19
 accustomed 640.16
 fitted 718.18
 ADAPTED TO 82.6
A-day 129.6
adcraft 557.5
add put with 40.3
 calculate 87.11
 ADD TO
 increase 38.4
 add 40.4
 ADD UP 87.12
 ADD UP TO 54.7
added 40.8
addendum
 addition 41.1
 sequel 67.1
add fuel to the fire
  855.11
add fuel to the flame
 intensify 38.5
 ignite 328.21
 fuel 330.8
 incite 546.17
addict
 nouns 640.9
 verbs 640.10
addicted

~ to 640.18
~ to drink 994.44
addiction 640.8
adding 87.3
add insult to injury
  963.4
addition increase 38
 accession 40
 adjunct 41.1,3
 computation 87.3,4
 IN ADDITION
 additionally 40.10
 surplus 661.19
additional extrinsic 6.4
 more 40.9
 new 122.8
additive 40.7
additory
 nouns 41.1
 adjs. 40.7
additum, additament
  41.1
addle
 verbs confuse 530.7
 inebriate 994.28
 ADDLE THE WITS
 derange 472.21
 confuse 530.7,8
 adjs. 723.17
addlebrain, addlehead,
  addlepate 470.7
addlebrained, addle-
  headed, addle-
  pated
 stupid 468.18
 muddled 530.13
addleplot 728.9
address
 nouns abode 190.1
 tact 491.1
 speech 597.2
 direction 602.10
 types of ~ 602.16
 skill 731.1
 sophistication 731.9
 behavior 735.1
 request 772.1
 greeting 923.4
 verbs speak to 592.18
 declaim 597.8
 inscribe 602.14
 greet 923.10
 court 930.19
 put on 961.6
 ADDRESS ONESELF TO
 busy oneself 654.10
 undertake 713.3
 ADDRESS TO
 direct to 528.10
 dedicate 600.23
addressee
 inhabitant 189.2
 correspondent 602.9
addresses
 solicitation 772.5
 courtship 930.6
 PAY ONE'S ADDRESSES
  TO 930.19
adduce 504.13
adducent 287.5
adduct 287.4

adduction 287.1
adductive 287.5
adelomorphic 85.9
à demain 300.25
adept
 nouns wise man 467.1
 proficient 731.11
 occultist 1032.11
 adjs. 731.20
 BECOME ADEPT IN
  562.9
adequacy ability 156.2
 sufficiency 659.1
 utility 663.3
 satisfactoriness 866.3
adequate able 156.13
 sufficient 659.6
 effectual 663.20
 tolerable 672.20
 satisfactory 866.11
adhere 50.5
 ADHERE TO
 be wont 640.12
 observe 766.2
 hold 811.6
adherence
 coherence 50.1
 fidelity 972.7
adherent
 nouns adhesive 50.3
 follower 292.2
 ~ of a philosophy
  499.13
 hanger-on 905.5
 adjs. 50.9
adherents 786.6
adherer 50.3
adhesion
 coherence 50.1
 fidelity 972.7
adhesive
 nouns types of ~
  48.6,9
 adherent 50.3
 adjs. 50.9
adhesiveness 50.2
adhesive plaster 50.3
adhesives 377.7
adhesive tape 685.28
adhibit apply 663.11
 administer 961.6
adhibition
 application 663.1
 administration
  961.2
ad hoc 651.12
ad hoc arbitrator
  803.3
adiaphanous 340.3
adiathermal(ic)
  327.31
adiathermancy 327.17
adieu 300.4,25
Adigranth 1019.6
ad infinitum 104.4
ad interim 109.5
adios 300.25
adipose 379.9
adipose tissue 194.8
adiposis, adiposity
 fatness 194.8

unctuousness 379.5
adit entranceway 301.5
 channel 395.1
adjacency 199.3
adjacent 199.16
adjective
 accessory 41.1
 part of speech 584.2
adjoin 199.9,13
adjoining 199.16
adjourn 132.9
adjournment,
  adjournal 132.4
adjudge,
  adjudicate 439.8
adjudgment,
  adjudication 493.1
adjunct
 nonessential 6.2
 addition 41
 component 58.2
 teacher 563.4
 confederate 785.1
adjuration
 deposition 521.2
 entreaty 772.2
adjure swear in 521.6
 entreat 772.11
adjust adapt 26.13
 co-ordinate 30.7
 organize 60.9
 conform 82.3
 size 194.15
 orient 289.12
 habituate 640.10
 remedy 692.13
 fit 718.8
 settle 769.9
 reconcile 802.8
 mediate 803.7
 compromise 805.2
 ADJUST ONESELF TO
  859.6
 ADJUST TO
 conform 82.3
 qualify 506.3
adjustable
 conformable 82.5
 versatile 731.23
adjusted personality
  688.38
adjustive reaction
  688.38
adjustment
 working order 7.3
 adaptation 26.4
 co-ordination 30.3
 organization 60.2
 conformity 82.1
 orientation 289.5
 habituation 640.7
 psychological ~
  688.38
 fitting 718.2
 settlement 769.4
 reconciliation 802.4
 compromise 805.1
 IN ADJUSTMENT 59.7
 MAKE AN ADJUST-
  MENT 805.2
adjutage 395.6

adjutant officer 747.22
   assistant 785.6
adjuvant
   nouns 785.6
   adjs. 783.20
Adler 688.12
ad lib, ad libitum
   nouns 628.5
   verbs 628.8
   adjs. 628.12
   advs. at pleasure
      619.5
   extemporaneously
      628.15
adman 557.9
administer
   ~ an oath 521.6
   put to use 663.11
   perform 703.8
   govern 739.11
   manage 745.11
   execute 769.10
   dispense 814.9
   give 816.12
   apply 961.6
   ~ justice 998.5
ADMINISTER TO
   748.14
administrate
   govern 739.11
   manage 745.11
   administer justice
      998.5
administration
   use 663.1
   government 739.1
   management 745.3
   directorate 746.10
   apportionment
      814.2
   application 961.2
administrative
   governing 739.18
   directing 745.14
administrator 747.5
admirable
   adorable 929.22
   praiseworthy 966.19
Admirable Crichton
   731.12
admiral 747.24
admiration
   wonder 918.1
   love 929.1
   respect 962.1
IN ADMIRATION
   918.16
admire adore 929.18
   respect 962.4
admirer fan 633.6
   lover 929.11
admissibility
   fitness 26.5
   receptivity 305.9
   reasonableness
      481.10
   tolerableness 672.3
   permissibility 775.9
   satisfactoriness
      866.3
   justifiability 1004.7

admissible relevant 9.8
   receptive 305.16
   logical 481.21
   eligible 635.21
   tolerable 672.20
   permissible 775.16
   satisfactory 866.12
   justifiable 1004.14
admission
   inclusion 76.1
   naturalization 188.4
   letting in 305.2
   testimony 504.3
   acknowledgment
      520.3
   confession 554.3
   permission 775.1
   receiving 817.1
   ~ fee 844.7
Admission Day 137.12
admissive
   receptive 305.16
   open-minded 524.10
   confessional 554.12
   permissive 775.15
admissory 305.16
admit include 76.3
   naturalize 188.5
   let in 305.10
   believe 500.8
   allow for 506.5
   acknowledge 520.11
   confess 554.7
   permit 775.1
   receive 817.6
   ~ hospitably 923.7
ADMIT OF
   have a chance
      155.13
   be liable 174.3
   ~ comparison
      490.7
   be possible 508.4
   seem likely 510.3
   ~ no doubt 512.9
NOT ADMIT
   disbelieve 502.5
   deny 522.4
admittance
   letting in 305.2
   receiving 817.1
admitted
   traditional 123.12
   believed 500.20
   acknowledged
      520.14
   conventional 643.7
   permitted 775.17
   received 817.10
   approved 966.18
   ~ to the bar 1001.6
admittedly
   conditionally 506.11
   certainly 512.25
admix 44.11
admixture 44.1,5
admonish
   remind 535.20
   dissuade 650.3
   warn 701.6
   advise 752.7

reprove 967.17
admonisher,
   admonitor 752.4
admonishment
   reminder 535.6
   warning 701.1
   reproof 967.5
admonition
   reminder 535.6
   dissuasion 650.1
   warning 701.1
   advice 752.1
   reproof 967.5
admonitory
   dissuasive 650.5
   warning 701.9
   advisory 752.10
ado commotion 62.4
   bustle 705.4
   trouble 729.3
   excitement 855.3
MAKE AN ADO
   create a disturbance
      62.8
   enthuse 633.8
MAKE AN ADO ABOUT
   670.12
WITH MUCH ADO
   laboriously 714.20
   with difficulty
      729.26
adobe
   nouns sod house
      190.5
   brick 377.2
   clay 384.1
   ceramics 574.3
   adjs. 384.7
adolescence 124.6
adolescent
   nouns 125.1
   adjs. 124.13
Adonis 898.9
adopt naturalize 188.5
   choose 635.12
   ~ the cause of
      783.13
   borrow 819.4
   appropriate 820.16
   usurp 959.8
adoption
   naturalization 188.4
   choice 635.3
   borrowing 819.2
   appropriation 820.3
   usurpation 959.3
   conversion 1024.4
adoptive 635.19
adorable 929.22
adorant 1030.15
adoration love 929.1
   veneration 962.1
   worship 1030.1
adore enjoy 863.10
   love 929.18
   revere 962.4
   worship 1030.10
adored 929.21
adorer lover 929.11
   worshiper 1030.9
adoring loving 929.24

worshipful 1030.15
adorn
   ~ speech 599.8
   beautify 898.14
   decorate 899.7
   dignify 912.12
adornment
   ornate speech 599.4
   beautification
      898.10
   decoration 899.1
adown 314.13
ad referendum 484.42
ad rem relevant 9.8
   apt 26.18
adrenal 310.9
Adriatic race 417.2
adrift
   adjs. irrelevant 10.6
   unfastened 49.21
   unfixed 141.7
   unanchored 274.65
   bewildered 513.22
   erroneous 517.14
   advs. 49.26
adroit smart 466.14
   skillful 731.20
adroitness
   smartness 466.2
   skill 731.1
adscititious
   extrinsic 6.4
   completing 56.14
adsmith 557.9
adsorb 305.13
adsorbent
   nouns 305.6
   adjs. 305.17
adulate 968.5
adulation 968.1
adulator 968.4
adulatory 968.9
adult
   nouns 127
   adjs. 126.12
adulterant,
   adulteration 44.3
adulterate 44.13
adulterer 987.13
adulteress 987.13
adulterous 987.27
adultery 987.7
adulthood 126.2
adumbrate
   darken 336.10
   cloud 403.7
   foreshadow 542.8
   typify 570.9
adumbration
   image 24.7
   darkening 336.7
   foreshadowing 542.2
aduncity 251.1
aduncous 251.8
adust burnt 328.29
   dried 392.9
ad valorem 844.16
advance
   nouns increase 38.1
   progression 293.1
   approach 295.1

development 321.2
improvement 689.1
offer 771.1
promotion 780.1
furtherance 783.5
loan 818.1,2
GO IN ADVANCE
antecede 64.2
precede 291.2
prepare the way
  718.12
IN ADVANCE
early 131.11
before 239.13
on loan 818.7
IN ADVANCE OF 36.20
MAKE ADVANCES
influence 171.9
communicate with
  552.8
offer 771.8
make friends 925.11
verbs increase 38.6
elapse 105.5
contribute 152.13
progress 293.2
approach 295.3
develop 321.6
postulate 498.12
adduce 504.13
actuate 646.12
improve 689.7,9
offer 771.5
promote 780.3
further 783.17
lend 818.5
ADVANCE UPON
overstep 311.9
attack 796.18
interjs. approach!
  295.6
attack 796.34
advance agent 609.29
advanced
modern 122.14
aged 126.15
precocious 131.8
improved 689.13
advanced work 797.4
advance guard 239.2
advancement
progression 293.1
overstepping 311.3
development 321.2
improvement 689.1
offer 771.1
promotion 780.1
furtherance 783.5
lending 818.1
advances 802.2
advantage
nouns superiority 36.2
purchase 286.2
use 665.4
expedience 668.1
good 672.4
facility 783.9
BE OF ADVANTAGE
  663.17
GET THE ADVANTAGE
  724.7

GIVE AN ADVANTAGE
  36.12
HAVE THE ADVANTAGE
  36.11
PUT TO ADVANTAGE
improve the
  occasion 129.9
utilize 663.15
TAKE ADVANTAGE OF
improve the
  occasion 129.9
use 663.15,16
TO ADVANTAGE
usefully 663.25
expediently 668.7
helpfully 783.24
profitably 809.15
TO ONE'S ADVANTAGE
  672.26
verbs be of use 663.17
benefit 672.11
further 783.17
advantageous
handy 663.19
expedient 668.4
beneficial 672.21
helpful 783.22
profitable 809.14
advene 40.6
Advent 1038.15
advent
approach of time
  121.5
approach 295.1
arrival 299.1
adventitious
extrinsic 6.4
incidental 8.6
completing 56.14
chance 155.6
adventitiousness 155.1
adventure
nouns occurrence
  150.2
chance event 155.6
deed 703.3
undertaking 713.1
exploit 891.7
verbs 514.18
adventurer
traveler 273.1
gambler 514.16
soldier 798.16
speculator 831.11
daring man 892.4
upstart 917.10
adventures 606.4
adventuress
daring woman 892.4
courtesan 987.15
adventure story 606.7
adventurous
risky 695.10
enterprising 705.22
daring 891.21
adverb 584.2
adverbial 584.13
adversaria 568.10
adversary
opponent 789.1
enemy 927.6

THE Adversary
  1014.3
adversative 584.2
adverse contrary 15.5
unwilling 621.5
untoward 727.13
opposed 788.9
ADVERSE TO
opposed to 788.11
disliking 865.8
IN ADVERSE CIRCUM-
  STANCES 727.14
adversely 727.16
adverseness 621.1
adversity hardship 727
affliction 864.8
advertence,
advertency 528.1
advertent 528.15
advertise
bruit about 557.10
publicize 557.15
boast 908.6
advertisement 557.6
advertiser 557.9
advertising 557.5
advert to
attend to 528.5
point to 566.17
advice
reminder 535.6
information 555.3
news 556.1
consultation 595.6
warning 701.1
counsel 752
TAKE ADVICE 752.9
advisability 668.1
advisable 668.4
advise remind 535.20
inform 555.7
warn 701.6
counsel 752.6
ADVISE WITH
~ one's pillow
  477.13
confer 595.10
advised
intentional 651.9
considered 752.11
advisedly
intentionally 651.11
consideredly 752.12
advisement 477.2
UNDER ADVISEMENT
in question 484.42
planned 652.13
adviser, advisor
informant 555.5
counsel 752.4
advisory
informative 555.17
expedient 668.4
admonitory 752.10
advocacy advice 752.1
patronage 783.4
recommendation
  966.4
advocate
nouns deputy 779.1
supporter 785.8

defender 797.7
lawyer 1001.1
justifier 1004.8
THE Advocate
  1011.12
verbs espouse a cause
  152.14
urge 646.14
advise 752.6
support 783.14
recommend 966.11
plead for 1004.10
advocation 966.4
advowson 1035.9
adynamia 159.1
adynamic 159.12
adytum den 191.8
oracle 541.7
retreat 698.5
adzooks 918.19
Aegir 194.13
aegis protection 697.3
patronage 783.4
UNDER THE AEGIS OF
protection 697.21
auspices 745.15
aeolian 402.26
aeolian harp, aeolian
  lyre 464.3
Aeolus 402.3
aeon, eon age 107.5
long time 110.4
aerage 401.10
aerate vaporize 400.7
air 401.12
froth 404.5
aeration
vaporization 400.4
ventilation 401.10
aerator 401.11
aerial
nouns 343.35
adjs. lofty 206.19
aeronautical 277.55
vaporous 400.8
airy 401.13
fanciful 533.22
aerie 190.21
aerification 400.4
aeriform 401.13
aerify vaporize 400.7
air 401.12
aeriness 400.2
aero
nouns 279.1
verbs 277.42
aerobatic 277.55
aerobatics 277.10
aerobiology 405.16
aeroboat 279.8
aerocartography 277.2
aerocraft 279.1
aerocurve 277.22
aerodone 279.12
aerodonetic 277.55
aerodonetics 277.2
aerodrome 277.19
aerodromics 277.1
aerodynamic
aeronautical 277.55
pneumatic 346.13

aerodynamics
  aviation 277.2
  pneumatics 346.5
aerodyne 279.1
aerographic 346.13
aerography
  aviation 277.2
  pneumatics 346.5
aerogun 799.7
aerohydroplane 279.8
aerolite 374.15
aerologic 346.13
aerology aviation 277.2
  pneumatics 346.5
aeromarine 277.55
aeromechanic
  aircraftsman 278.6
  mechanic 346.7
aeromechanical
  aeronautical 277.55
  mechanical 346.11
  pneumatic 346.13
aeromechanics
  aviation 277.2
  mechanics 346.1,5
aerometer
  densimeter 353.8
  meter 400.6
aerometry
  aviation 277.2
  pneumatics 346.5
aeromotors 279.17
aeronat 279.11
aeronaut flyer 278
  astronaut 281.8
aeronautical 277.55
aeronautics
  aviation 277
  astronautics 281
  air service 798.29,30
aeronautism 277.1
aeronef 279.1
aeroneurosis 688.17
aeropathy 277.3
aerophobia 277.3
aerophotography
  277.2
aerophysical
  aeronautical 277.55
  physical 324.3
  pneumatic 346.13
aerophysicist 324.2
aerophysics
  aviation 277.2
  physics 324.1
  pneumatics 346.5
aeroplane
  nouns 279.1
  verbs 277.42
aeroplaner,
  aeroplanist 278.1
aeropleustic 277.55
aeroscopic 346.13
aeroscopy
  aviation 277.2
  pneumatics 346.5
aerosol bomb 408.11
aerosphere 401.2
aerostat 279.11
aerostatic
  aeronautical 277.55

pneumatic 346.13
aerostatics
  aviation 277.2
  pneumatics 346.5
aerostation
  aviation 277.2
  pneumatics 346.5
aerostat parts 279.19
aerotechnical
  aeronautical 277.55
  pneumatic 346.13
aerotechnics
  aviation 277.2
  pneumatics 346.5
aerotherapy 687.3
aery vaporous 400.8
  airy 401.13
Aesculapius
  healthiness 683.1
  medicine 686.15
Aesir 1012.6
aesthete 895.6
aesthetic artistic
  572.21
  tasteful 895.8
  beautiful 898.16
aesthetics 895.5
afar 198.16
afeared 889.21
Afer 402.3
affability
  communicativeness
  552.4
  sociability 920.1
  courtesy 934.1
  amiability 936.2
affable
  communicative
  552.9
  sociable 920.17
  courteous 934.14
  amiable 936.15
affair concern 150.3
  thing 375.4
  topic 483.1
  business 654.1
  fight 794.3
  ~ of honor 794.7
  social ~ 920.9
  amour 929.6
affairs 150.4
affect relate 9.3
  involve 76.4
  influence 171.7
  frequent 185.10
  qualify 506.3
  interest 528.12
  feign 614.22
  ~ emotionally
  853.15,16
  excite 855.11
  assume 901.12
AFFECT ONE'S MIND
  472.21
affectation
  elegance 587.3
  grandiloquence
  599.1
  sham 614.3
  mannerism 901
affected disposed 523.8

elegant 587.9
  grandiloquent 599.9
  sham 614.27
  formal 644.7
  impressed 853.24
  mannered 901.15
BE AFFECTED WITH
  684.33
NOT BE AFFECTED BY
  854.5
affecter 901.7
affectibility
  sensibility 421.2
  emotional ~ 853.4
affecting
  interesting 528.19
  touching 853.23
  pathetic 862.11
affection
  disposition 523.3
  illness 684.1
  emotion 853.3
  love 929.1,3
affectional 853.18
affectionate 929.24
affections 853.1
affective 853.18
affettuoso 461.54
affiance
  nouns belief 500.1
  betrothal 768.3
  hope 886.1
  verbs 768.6
affianced
  nouns 929.15
  adjs. 768.8
affidavit
  testimony 504.3
  affirmation 521.2
  certificate 568.5
  deposition 1002.7
affiliate
  nouns 786.10
  verbs league 52.4
  fix the paternity
  154.4
  naturalize 188.5
  adopt 635.12
AFFILIATE WITH
  786.14
  adjs. related 9.6
  associated 52.6
affiliated related 9.6
  consanguineous
  11.7
  leagued 52.6
affiliation relation 9.1
  consanguinity 11.1
  alliance 52.1
  lineage 169.4
  naturalization 188.4
  adoption 635.3
  co-operation 784.3
  sect 1018.3
affinal, affined 12.4
affinitive related 9.6
  similar 20.13
affinity relation 9.1
  marital ~ 12
  similarity 20.2
  agreement 26.1

accord 792.1
  soulmate 929.14
affirm confirm 504.12
  ratify 520.12
  assert 521.4
affirmance
  ratification 520.4
  assertion 521.1
affirmant
  nouns 520.6
  adjs. 521.7
affirmation
  premise 481.8
  testimony 504.3,5
  ratification 520.4
  assertion 521
affirmative
  nouns 520.2
  IN THE AFFIRMATIVE
  assent 520.16
  affirmatively 521.8
  THE AFFIRMATIVE
  481.14
  adjs. 521.7
affix
  nouns addition 41.1
  syllable 579.6
  verbs add 40.3
  fasten 47.7
  impose 961.4
affixation
  addition 40.1
  attachment 47.3
affixed 40.8
afflation 402.1
afflatus wind 402.1
  genius 466.8
  inspiration 646.9
  revelation 1019.8
afflict pain 423.7
  sicken 684.37
  distress 864.15
afflicted in pain 423.9
  distressed 864.25
  drunk 994.40
afflicting, afflictive
  862.11
affliction bane 674.1
  illness 684.1
  distress 864.8
affluence flow 394.4
  abundance 659.2
  wealth 835.1
affluent
  nouns 394.3
  adjs. flowing 394.25
  abundant 659.7
  wealthy 835.13
afflux, affluxion 394.4
afford provide 657.7
  give 816.12,15
  have money 835.10
  ~ to pay 841.6
  bring in 842.3
  cost 844.15
affranchise free 761.4
  license 775.12
affranchisement 761.1
affray 794.3
affrettando 461.56
affricate rub 349.6

speech sound 449.5
affrication 349.1
affright 889.14
affront
  nouns offense 950.11
    indignity 963.2
  verbs confront 239.8
    oppose 788.6
    defy 791.3
    brave 891.11
    offend 950.20
    dishonor 963.4
affusion wetting 391.6
    baptism 1038.7
affy 768.6
afield 198.19
afire burning 327.27
    inspired 646.31
    fervent 853.22
aflame 327.27
aflicker burning 327.27
    flickery 334.36
afloat
  adjs. existent 1.13
    adrift 49.21
    unfixed 141.7
    happening 150.9
    floating 274.64,65
    flooded 394.26
    rumored 556.15
  advs. on board 274.66
    in preparation
    718.24
  KEEP AFLOAT 657.11
afluking 274.63
afoot
  adjs. 705.18
  advs. on foot 272.42
    in preparation
    718.24
afore 116.6
afore-going
    preceding 64.5
    former 119.8
aforehand 131.11
aforementioned 64.5
aforenamed 64.5
aforesaid 64.5
aforethought
  nouns 651.3
  adjs. former 64.5
    premeditated 651.10
aforetime 119.10
a fortiori
  adjs. 481.22
  advs. 36.19
a fortiori reasoning
    481.3
afoul 274.76
afraid scared 889.21
    cowardly 890.10
  BE AFRAID
    suppose 498.9
    think 500.9
    fear 889.9
afreet 1014.7
afresh once more 91.6
    freshly 103.17
    newly 122.16
Afric 417.8
Africa 385.1

African
  nouns Negro 417.7
    Occidental 417.8
  adjs. 417.10
African dominoes
    514.8
Afrikaans 578.8
Afrikander 417.8
Afro-American 417.7
Afro-Asiatic 417.7
Afro-European 417.7
aft
  nouns 134.1
  adjs. 240.8
  advs. after 240.13
    astern 274.73
after
  nouns 134.1
  adjs. subsequent
    117.3
    rear 240.8
    following 292.6
  advs. subsequently
    117.5
    behind 240.13
  preps. concerning
    9.12
    in imitation 22.12
    in spite of 33.9
    according to 82.8
    subsequent to 117.7
    because of 154.9
    in pursuit 653.12
  AFTER ALL
    nevertheless 33.8
    considering 493.17
  AFTER A WHILE
    in the future 121.9
    soon 131.16
  BE AFTER 651.4
after- 117.4
afterage 123.13
afterbirth 67.3
afterbrain 465.5
aftercome
    afterpart 67.2
    aftereffect 153.4
afterdamp 400.1
after-death 117.4
after-dinner 117.4
aftereffect 153.4
afterglow
    aftermath 67.3
    glow 334.2
aftergrass
    aftermath 67.3
    grass 410.5
aftergrowth, aftercrop,
    afterclap
    aftermath 67.3
    aftereffect 153.4
afterguard 275.6
afterlife 121.2
aftermath
    afterglow 67.3
    aftereffect 153.4
    crop 809.4
aftermirage 518.6
aftermost 240.8
afternoon
  nouns 134.1

adjs. 134.7
afterpain 67.3
afterpart sequel 67.2
    rear 240.1
afterpiece
    afterpart 67.2
    latter part 240.1
    act 609.8
aftertaste
    aftermath 67.3
    aftereffect 153.4
    taste 426.1
afterthought
    sequel 67.1
    reflection 477.5
aftertime 121.1
afterwards
    subsequently 117.5
    in the future 121.9
afterworld 121.2
aga 747.22
again
  advs. on the other
    hand 33.8
    moreover 40.10
    anew 91.6
    repeatedly 103.17
    then 105.11
    newly 122.16
  AGAIN AND AGAIN
    103.16
  AGAIN AND YET AGAIN
    94.6
  interjs. 103.18
against
    in contact with
    199.23
    opposite to 238.6
    toward 289.28
    in preparation for
    718.25
    opposed to 788.11
  AGAINST THE CLOCK
    707.14
  AGAINST THE GRAIN
    contrarily 15.7
    cross-grained 260.12
    backwards 294.13
    unwillingly 621.8
  AGAINST THE LAW
    997.6
agalloch 435.4
agama 1019.6
agape
    love feast 1038.4
agape
    gaping 264.18
    curious 526.5
    expectant 537.9
    astonished 918.8
Agapemone 533.11
age
  nouns century
    107.2,5,6
    geological ∼ 107.10
    historical ∼ 107.11
    long time 110.4
    lifetime 110.5
    remote ∼ 119.3
    ancientness 123.1
    time of life 126

∼ of discretion
    126.2
    advanced ∼ 126.5
    old ∼ 468.10
  COME OF AGE 126.9
  IN ALL AGES 112.12
  OF AGE 126.12
  verbs antiquate 123.9
    grow old 126.10
aged elderly 126.15
    senile 468.23
agee, ajee 218.14
agee-jawed 218.14
ageless eternal 112.7
    ancient 123.10
agency operation 163.1
    instrumentality
    656.2
    commission 778.1
  BY THE AGENCY OF
    656.8
agenda schedule 639.2
    business 654.2
  ON THE AGENDA
    484.42
agent
    collection ∼ 74.14;
    837.4
    cause 152.4
    chemical ∼ 378.1
    test 488.5
    theatrical ∼ 609.29
    instrument 656.3
    doer 716.1
    deputy 779.3
    colonial ∼ 779.6
    salesman 828.4
    matrimonial ∼
    931.13
agent provocateur
    646.11
agentship 778.1
agglomerate
  nouns cohesion 50.4
    accumulation 74.8
  verbs 74.17
  adjs. 74.21
agglomeration
    coherence 50.1,4
    accumulation 74.8
agglutinate
  verbs 50.7
  adjs. 50.8
agglutination 50.1
aggrandize
    increase 38.4
    enlarge 196.4
    exaggerate 615.3
    promote 780.3
    glorify 912.13
aggrandizement
    increase 38.1
    expansion 196.1
    exaggeration 615.1
    promotion 780.1
    glorification 912.8
aggravate
    intensify 38.5
    irritate 855.13
    annoy 864.17
    worsen 883.2

anger 950.22

aggravating
  annoying 862.13
  exasperative 883.5
aggravation
  intensification 38.2
  excitement 855.10
  annoyance 864.2
  worsening 883
  resentment 950.1
aggregate
  nouns all 54.3
  accumulation 74.8
  sum 86.3
  IN THE AGGREGATE
   54.12
  verbs total 54.7
  accumulate 74.17
  adjs. whole 54.8
  massed 74.21
aggregation
  coherence 50.1
  combination 52.1
  accumulation 74.8
aggression
  enterprise 705.7
  aggressiveness
   795.16
  attack 796.1
aggressive
  enterprising 705.22
  belligerent 795.26
  offensive 796.32
aggressor 796.13
aggrieve
  oppress 739.15
  displease 864.14
  offend 950.20
aggrieved
  displeased 864.26
  sorrowful 870.27
aggroup 74.17
aghast appalled 889.25
  astonished 918.8
  LOOK AGHAST
  be disappointed
   539.14
  wonder 918.4
  STAND AGHAST 889.9
agile fast 268.19
  alert 531.14
  quick 705.17
  nimble 731.21
agility alertness 531.5
  quickness 705.3
  nimbleness 731.2
agilmente 461.54
agin 788.11
aging
  nouns 126.6
  adjs. 126.16
agio 845.1
agiotage 831.19
agitate
  discompose 63.4
  shake 323.10
  discuss 481.16
  incite 646.17
  alarm 702.5
  excite 855.14
  distress 864.15

concern 888.3

agitated
  turbulent 161.17
  disturbed 323.17
  alarming 702.8
  excited 855.24
  distressed 864.25
  anxious 888.6
agitatedly
  troublously 323.23
  excitedly 855.34
agitation
  turbulence 161.2
  shaking 323.1
  discussion 481.4
  incitement 646.4
  alarm 702.1
  excitement 855.3,
   10
  anxiety 888.1
  IN AGITATION 718.23
agitato 461.54
agitator mixer 44.10
  vibrator 323.9
  instigator 646.11
agitprop
  propagandist 561.2
  agitator 646.11
aglow burning 327.27
  glowing 334.30,38
agnate
  nouns 11.2
  adjs. related 9.6
  consanguineous 11.7
  connatural 20.13
agnation relation 9.1
  consanguinity 11.1
Agni 1012.7
agnomen 581.6
agnosia amnesia 536.2
  neurosis 688.26
agnostic
  nouns 1029.11
  adjs. 1029.19
agnosticism 1029.5
Agnus Dei
  anthem 1030.3
  the Mass 1038.10
  religious article
   1038.11
ago, agone
  adjs. 119.5
  advs. 119.12
agog curious 526.5
  attentive 528.15
  vigilant 531.13
  expectant 537.9
  eager 633.9
  astonished 918.8
agoing 705.18
agonistic 876.32
agonistics 876.8
agonize pain 423.7,8
  struggle 714.11
  torture 864.20
  be distressed 864.22
  grieve 870.17
agonizing
  painful 423.10
  excruciating 862.14
agony

death struggle 407.7
  pain 423.6
  distress 864.6
  grief 870.10
agony column 557.6
agora 182.7
agraphia 688.26
agrarian rural 181.6
  agricultural 412.20
agrarianism 181.3
agree coincide 14.4
  correspond 26.7
  make ~ 26.11
  assent 520.8,9,10
  promise 768.5
  contract 769.6
  get along 792.2
  AGREE TO
  assent 520.8
  contract 769.6
  consent 773.3
  bargain for 825.15
  AGREE TO DISAGREE
   520a.4
  AGREE WITH
  conform 82.3
  assent 520.8,9,10
  be healthful 681.4
  NOT AGREE 520a.4
agreeable
  in agreement 26.14
  savory 427.8
  musical 461.49
  willing 620.5
  desirable 632.31
  indulgent 757.10
  consenting 773.5
  accordant 792.3
  pleasant 861.5
  satisfactory 866.12
  comely 898.17
  welcome 923.12
  friendly 925.14
  considerate 936.17
  AGREEABLE TO 82.6
agreeableness
  willingness 620.1
  indulgence 757.3
  pleasantness 861.1
  considerateness
   936.3
agreeable-sounding
  461.49
agreed acquiescent
  520.13,20
  contracted 769.12
agreeing
  in agreement 26.14
  assenting 520.13,15
  consenting 773.5
  accordant 792.3
agreement
  identity 14.1
  similarity 20.1
  correspondence 26
  conformity 82.1
  assent 520.1,5
  promise 768.2
  compact 769.1
  consent 773.1
  accord 792.1

COME TO AN AGREE-
  MENT 520.10
agrestic 181.6
agricultural rural 181.6
  farming 412.20
agriculture 412
agriculturist, agricul-
  turalist 412.5
agrobiology 405.16
agrogeology,
  agrology 412.1
agrologist 412.5
agronomic 412.20
agronomist 412.5
agronomy, agronomics
  412.1
aground stuck 142.17
  navigation 274.77
  stranded 729.25
agua 391.3
ague shaking 323.2
  disease 684.9
aguer 684.9
aguey, aguish 332.16
ah! alas! 873.20
  oh! 918.18
aha! hurrah! 874.12
  bravo! 966.21
Ahasuerus 273.2
ahead early 131.11
  before 239.13
  forward 293.7
  AHEAD OF 36.14
  AHEAD OF THE GAME
  surpassing 36.14
  successful 722.13
ahind 240.12
ah me! 873.20
ahoy!
  navigation 274.79
  attention! 528.23
  SHIP AHOY! 274.79
Ahriman 1014.5
Ahura-Mazda 1011.6
aid
  nouns remedy 685.1
  help 783
  assistant 785.6
  subsidy 816.8
  benefactor 940.1
  BY THE AID OF
  by means of 656.8
  helped by 783.25
  COME TO THE AID OF
   783.11
  verbs help 783.11
  subsidize 816.18
  AID AND ABET
  incite 646.21
  support 783.14
aide-de-camp
  officer 747.22
  assistant 785.6
aider assistant 785.6
  benefactor 940.1
aidful beneficial 672.21
  helpful 783.21
aidless 157.18
ail
  nouns 684.1
  verbs pain 423.7,8

be ill 684.33
trouble 729.12
aileron roll 277.11
ailing
  nouns 684.1
  adjs. 684.41
ailment 684.1
aim
  nouns direction 289.1
  meaning 543.2
  objective 651.2
  verbs direct 289.6,8
  intend 651.4
  endeavor 712.4
  ~ a blow at 796.17
aimless orderless 62.11
  purposeless 155.16
  meaningless 545.9
  desultory 591.13
ain't 484.47; 522.10
AIN'T IT THE TRUTH?
  515.22
air
  nouns
  unsubstantiality 4.3
  posture 183.4
  aura 232.3
  aviation 277.38
  liquid ~ 333.7
  lightness 352.3
  sky 374.2
  atmosphere 401
  wind 402.1,5
  appearance 445.3
  melody 461.4
  behavior 735.1
  GIVE THE AIR 308.17
  GO ON THE AIR 343.28
  GO UP IN THE AIR
    950.19
  IN THE AIR
  aloft 206.27
  reported 556.15
  LEAVE UP IN THE AIR
    625.7
  verbs aerate 401.12
  publish 557.11
  refresh 693.3
  display 902.17
  ~ a grievance
    873.13
air arm 798.29
air base 277.19
air-borne 277.56
air braking 281.14
air brush 572.19
air bubble 404.1
air-built
  unsubstantial 4.5
  fanciful 533.22
air bump 277.38
airburst 280.10
aircast 343.21,28
aircaster 343.26
air castle 533.10
air-condition 401.12
air conditioner 401.11
air conditioning
  401.10
air-conscious 277.55
air-cool cool 333.10

ventilate 401.12
air-cooled 333.13
air cooler cooler 333.3
  ventilator 401.11
air cooling
  cooling 333.1
  ventilation 401.10
air cover 277.8
aircraft airplane 279
  rocket 280.1
  rocket ship 281.2
aircraft carrier 276.8
aircraftsman
  aviation 278.6
  rocket engineer
    280.6
aircrew 278.4
air current 402.1
air-drawn 533.22
airdrome 277.19
airdrop 277.7
air-dry 392.6
air duct 395.17
airfield 277.19
air force 798.29
airfreight 270.3
airhead 239.2
air hole holes 264.4
  aviation 277.38
  duct 395.17
airily 902.25
airiness
  unsubstantiality 4.1
  lightness 352.1
  rarity 354.1
  vaporousness 400.2
  windiness 402.16
  lightheartedness
    868.3
  ostentation 902.1
airing walk 272.12
  ventilation 401.10
  publication 557.1
  GO FOR AN AIRING
    272.23
airish airy 401.13
  breezy 402.26
air lane 277.39
airless 267.14
airlift
  nouns 277.7
  verbs 277.42
airlike 401.13
air line
  short cut 202.5
  straight line 249.2
  aeronautics 277.1
  airway 277.39
air mail
  nouns 602.5
  BY AIR MAIL 707.13
  verbs send 270.14
  mail 602.13
airman 278.1
airmanship
  aviation 277.3
  skill 731.1
air meter, airometer
  400.6
air-minded 277.55
airpark 277.19

air passage 395.17
airplane
  nouns 279.1,15
  verbs 277.42
airplaner, airplanist
  278.1
airplaning 277.1
air pocket 277.38
airport 277.19
airproof 158.18
air raid aviation 277.8
  ~ shelter 698.3
  raid 796.4
air route 277.39
airs affectation 901.1
  pretensions 902.2
  PUT ON AIRS 902.14
airscape view 445.6
  picture 572.13
airship 279.11
airsick aviation 277.55
  nauseated 684.42
airspace 277.38
air speed
  velocity 268.1
  aviation 277.37
airstrip 277.20
airtight proof 158.18
  tight 265.12
air umbrella 277.8
air volume 277.22
airward 206.27
airway air route 277.39
  air duct 395.17
air-wise 277.55
airworthy
  aeronautical 277.55
  safe 696.7
airy unsubstantial 4.5
  any 28.6
  lofty 206.19
  light 352.10
  rare 354.7
  vaporous 400.8
  aery 401.13
  breezy 402.26
  fanciful 533.22
  lighthearted 868.11
  ostentatious 902.18
aisle 655.4
ait See eyot
ajar open 264.18
  discordant 460.5
ajee See agee
akimbo
  adis. 250.6
  advs. 218.22
akin related 9.6
  consanguineous 11.7
  similar 20.13
à la 20.18
alabaster
  nouns 259.3
  adjs. 363.9
alabastrine
  whitish 363.9
  alabaster 382.14
à la carte 306.11
alack! 873.20
alacrity
  promptness 131.3

willingness 620.1
  eagerness 633.1
  quickness 705.3
Aladdin's lamp 1034.7
à la king 306a.56
alameda 655.3
à la mode, alamode
  642.12,16
à la mort 407.30
alarm
  nouns call 566.15
  apprehension 702
  fright 889.1
  verbs startle 538.8
  arouse 702.5
  frighten 889.14
alarm clock 702.3
alarmed
  startled 538.13
  aroused 702.8
  frightened 889.24
alarming
  disturbing 702.7
  frightening 889.27
alarmist 889.7
alarum 566.15
alas! 873.20
Alaska 332.5
alate, alated 41.5
alba 461.13
albeit 33.8
Alberich 195.6
albescence 363.1
albescent 363.9
albication,
  albification 363.4
albinism
  whiteness 363.1
  faulty vision 439.1
albinistic 363.11
albino 363.1
Albion 180.4
Alborak 413.21
album
  scrapbook 568.10
  book 603.4
albumen 405.14
albuminoid,
  albuminous 405.24
Alcaic 607.21
alcalde official 747.5
  judge 1000.1
alchemy
  conversion 145.1
  sorcery 1033.1
alcohol
  types of ~ 304.17
  liquor 994.12
alcoholic
  nouns psychotic
    472.16
  addict 640.9
  drunkard 994.10
  adjs. 994.46
alcoholic beverage
  994.12,48–50
alcoholism
  delirium tremens
    472.10
  addiction 640.8
  dipsomania 994.3

Alcoran 1019.6
alcove arbor 190.11
 room 191.3
 recess 256.7
Aldebaran 374.5
alderman 747.19
Aldine
 ~ book 603.3
 ~ binding 603.17
Aldus 603.3
Alecto 1014.11
alee 241.9
alehouse 994.25
alembic
 transformer 139.4
 conversion 145.7
alert
 nouns 702.3
 ON THE ALERT 531.14
 verbs warn 701.6
 alarm 702.6
 adjs. prompt 131.9
 clear-witted 466.13
 vigilant 531.14
alertness 531.5
Aleut 417.6
Alexandrine 607.5
alexia amnesia 536.2
 neurosis 688.26
alexipharmic,
 alexiteric
 nouns 685.21
 adjs. 685.36
Alfardaws 1016.8
alfresco
 adjs. open-air 223.7
 airy 401.13
 advs. 223.10
algae plants 410.4,43
 botany 411.4
algal 410.35
algebra
 mathematics 87.18
 manual 603.9
algebraic 87.17
algebraist 87.9
algebraize 87.11
algid 332.15
algidity 332.1
algific 333.12
algologist 411.2
algology 411.1
alias
 nouns 581.8
 advs. 16.10
alibi
 nouns 1004.4
 verbs 1004.11
alien
 nouns 78.3
 verbs 815.3
 adjs. unrelated 10.5
 extraneous 78.5
 opposed 788.9
alienable 815.5
alienage 78.1
alienate wean 641.2
 estrange 793.15
 convey 815.3
alienated 927.12
alienation

insanity 472.1
 falling-out 793.4
 conveyance 815.1
alienism
 extraneousness 78.1
 psychiatry 688.3
alienist 688.13
alight
 verbs land 277.49
 descend 314.7
 adjs. burning 327.27
 lighted 334.38
align, aline
 arrange 60.8
 line up 71.6
 level 213.6
 parallelize 217.5
 ALIGN WITH 784.6
alignment 784.3
alike
 adjs. identical 14.6
 uniform 17.5
 similar 20.10
 indistinguishable
 492.8
 advs. 14.8
alikeness 20.1
aliment food 306a.3
 nutrition 307.3
alimentary 307.19
alimentation 307.1
alimony 816.8
aline See align
aliquot
 adjs. 86.8
 advs. 55.6
alive
 adjs. living 406.10
 clear-witted 466.13
 topical 483.6
 alert 531.14
 unforgotten 535.23
 lively 705.16
 ALIVE TO
 sensible 421.12
 aware of 474.16
 ALIVE WITH 101.10
 BE ALIVE 406.6
 BECOME ALIVE TO
 555.13
 KEEP ALIVE
 maintain 143.4
 live 406.9
 preserve 699.7
 LOOK ALIVE
 pay attention 528.8
 be vigilant 531.8
 hurry! 707.16
 beware 893.7,14
 advs. 268.21
alive and kicking
 living 406.10
 well 683.7
alkahest 390.4
alkahestic 390.8
alkali
 nouns 378.1
 adjs. 378.7
alkaline antacid 177.9
 nonacid 378.7
alkalinity 378.1

alkalize 378.6
alkalizer antacid 177.3
 medicine 685.20
alky 994.13
all
 nouns 54.3
 AT ALL
 of any kind 61.9
 possibly 508.10
 anyhow 655.12
 IN ALL 54.12
 NOT AT ALL
 no 2.11
 nowise 35.14
 never 106.4
 by no means 522.8
 ONE'S ALL 808.2
 adjs. entire 54.8
 every 79.14
 advs. 54.12
alla breve 461.24
all-absorbing 670.25
all agog curious 526.5
 vigilant 531.13
 expectant 537.9
 eager 633.9
 astonished 918.8
Allah 1011.3
all along 112.11
all-American
 nouns 189.4
 adjs. 188.7
all and sundry 79.14
allargando 461.55
all-around
 surrounding 232.10
 versatile 731.23
allay moderate 162.6
 pacify 802.7
 satisfy 863.6
 relieve 884.5
allayment
 moderation 162.2
 relief 884.1
all but 199.25
all clear
 all's well! 696.9
 unindebted 839.23
all-clear 702.3
all-comprehensive
 79.13
all-comprehensiveness
 104.1
all-destroying 691.26
all-devouring
 greedy 632.28
 all-destroying 691.26
 rapacious 820.23
 gluttonous 992.7
allegation
 testimony 504.3
 affirmation 521.1
 remark 592.4
 pretext 647.2
 legal pleading
 1002.7
allege adduce 504.13
 affirm 521.4
 state 592.15
 pretend 647.3

ALLEGE IN SUPPORT
 1004.10
alleged 647.4
allegiance 972.7
allegorical
 figurative 549.4
 fictional 606.17
allegorize 549.3
allegory
 figure of speech
 549.2
 emblem 566.2
 story 606.7
allegretto
 nouns 461.25
 advs. music 461.56
 lively 705.23
allegro
 nouns 461.25
 advs. music 461.56
 lively 705.23
alleluia, alleluiah
 nouns cheer 874.2
 paean 1030.3
 interjs. 1030.16
all-embracing 79.13
all-engulfing 820.23
allergic
 sensitive 421.13
 diseased 684.46
 ALLERGIC TO 865.8
allergy
 sensitivity 421.3
 disease 684.25
 antipathy 865.2
alleviate reduce 39.8
 moderate 162.6
 lighten 352.6
 relieve 884.5
alleviation
 decrease 39.1
 moderation 162.2
 lightening 352.4
 relief 884.1
alleviative
 nouns mitigator 162.3
 medicine 685.8
 adjs. palliative 162.16
 lightening 352.15
 remedial 685.35
 relieving 884.9
alleviator 162.3
alley 655.4,6
alley cat 62.7
alley-oop! 313.17
alleyway 655.6
All-father 1011.11
all-filling 79.13
all-fired
 adjs. 970.10
 advs. 34.26
all for 966.20
all fours 272.9
all get out 56.4
all gone 2.10
all hail! hurrah! 874.12
 bravo! 966.22
all hands 79.4
All-holy 1011.2
alliance relation 9.1
 family tie 11.1

alone
  adjs. solitary 89.8
    unique 89.9
    in solitude 922.12
  advs. simply 45.9
    singly 89.13
    privately 612.21
    independently
      760.30
  LEAVE ALONE
    be conservative
      140.6
    do nothing 704.4
    not interfere 760.15
    permit 775.13
along with 73.10
    lengthwise 201.15
    forward 293.7
  ALONG WITH
    as well as 40.11,12
    with 73.10
    by means of 656.8
alongshore 384.11
alongside
    parallel 217.6
    beside 241.11
    ~ ship 274.74
  GO ALONGSIDE
    parallel 217.4
    sail 274.37
  PUT ALONGSIDE 490.4
aloof
  adjs. reserved 611.8
    haughty 910.12
    unsociable 921.6
  advs. at a distance
    198.15
    aloft 206.27
  HOLD ALOOF
    avoid 629.6
    let alone 704.4
    snub 964.7
  HOLD ALOOF FROM
    990.7
  HOLD ONESELF ALOOF
    be uncommunicative
      611.5
    be unsociable 921.4
  KEEP ALOOF
    keep one's distance
      198.7
    avoid 629.6
    snub 964.7
  KEEP ALOOF FROM
    990.7
aloofness reserve 611.3
    haughtiness 910.4
    unsociability 921.2
alopecia 231.4
aloud audibly 449.19
    loudly 452.12
alow 207.11
alp 206.7
alpen 206.23
alpenstock 216.2
alpestrine 206.23
alpha 68.2
alpha and omega 54.3
alphabet
  nouns rudiments 68.5
    letters 579.4

    verbs 579.9
alphabetarian 564.7
alphabetic(al) 579.11
alphabetics 579.4
alphabetize
    classify 61.6
    letter 579.9
alpha ray 326.3
alpha test 688.11
alpine, alpigene
    /206.23
already prior to 116.6
    until now 120.4
alright See all right
alrighty 520.18
Alsatia 823.13
also 40.10,12
also-ran loser 725.5
    candidate 744.9
altar 1040.11
altarpiece 1040.11
alter
  nouns 80.5
  verbs castrate 42.11
    change 139.5,6
    ~ one's course
      290.3
    falsify 614.17
alterability 141.1
alterable 141.6
alterant alterer 139.4
    remedy 685.1
alteration
    castration 42.5
    change 139.1
    music 461.10
alterative
  nouns alterant 139.4
    remedy 685.1
  adjs. changeable
      141.6
    remedial 685.34
altercate 793.12
altercation
    quarrel 793.5
    contention 794.1
altered 139.9
alter ego
    counterpart 20.5
    self 80.5
    deputy 779.1
    friend 926.1
alterer 139.4
alternate
  nouns substitute
      148.2
    deputy 779.1
  verbs take turns 108.4
    intermit 137.6
    fluctuate 141.5
    interchange 149.4
    oscillate 322.12
    vacillate 625.8
  adjs. periodic 137.8
    substitute 148.8
    back-and-forth
      322.18
alternately 137.12
alternating
    changeable 141.7
    vacillating 625.10

alternation
    mathematics 86.4
    periodicity 137.2
    changeableness
      141.3
    interchange 149.1
    oscillation 322.4
    vacillation 625.2
alternative
  nouns substitute
      148.2
    loophole 630.4
    option 635.2
  HAVE NO ALTERNA-
    TIVE 637.11
  adjs. substitute 148.8
    optional 635.19
alternator 148.2
althorn, alto horn
      464.8
although 33.8
altiloquence 599.1
altiloquent 599.9
altimeter height 206.14
    measure 250.4
    instrument 277.59
altimetric(al) 206.26
altimetry
    height 206.14
    measurement 489.9
altitude height 206.1
    aviation 277.41
altitudes
    high spirits 868.2
    haughty airs 910.1
  IN ONE'S ALTITUDES
    in high spirits
      868.12
    arrogant 910.9
    drunk 994.40
alto
  nouns height 206.2
    voice part 461.22
    voice 462.5
    singer 463.14
    instrument 464.1
  adjs. high-pitched
      457.12
    vocal 461.51
alto-cumulus 403.1
altogether
  nouns 54.3
  IN THE ALTOGETHER
    231.14
  advs. wholly 54.12
    completely 56.15
    generally 79.15
  preps. 40.11
alto horn See althorn
alto-stratus 403.1
altruism 936.4
altruist 936.8
altruistic 936.16
alum 197.6
aluminum 382.16
alumna, alumni,
    alumnus 564.6
alveary apiary 415.5
    workshop 717.2
alveola 256.2
alveolar

    nouns 449.5
  adjs. pitted 256.17
    phonetics 449.18
alveolate 256.17
alveolus, alveolation
      256.2,6
Alviss 195.6
always
    universally 79.16
    forever 112.11
  FOR ALWAYS 811.11
A.M., a.m. 133.1
amabile 461.54
amadou 330.6
amah nursemaid 697.7
    maidservant 748.8
amain by force 156.16
    swiftly 268.21
    hastily 707.12
amalgam mixture 44.5
    alloy 382.4
amalgamate mix 44.11
    combine 52.3
amalgamation
    mixture 44.1
    combination 52.1
amanuensis
    recorder 569.1
    scribe 600.14
amaranth 410.22
amaranthine 112.9
amass
    form a whole 54.6
    accumulate 74.17
    store up 658.11
amassment
    accumulation 74.8
    store 658.1
    acquisition 809.2
amateur
    radio ~ 343.27
    devotee 633.6
    nonprofessional
      716.5
    dilettante 895.7
amateurish
    unprofessional
      654.17
    unskilled 732.16
Amati 464.6
amatory 929.23
amaurosis
    blindness 440.1
    disease 684.11
amaurotic 440.8
amaze
  nouns 918.1
  verbs 918.5
amazement 918.1,2
amazing
  adjs. 918.11
  advs. 34.23
amazing thing 918.2
Amazon stream 394.1
    masculine 419.9
    warrioress 798.7
ambages
    convolution 253.1
    circuit 319.3
ambagious
    circuitous 319.7

airplane 279.8
plant 410.3
animal 413.3;
414.11
amphibious
mixed 44.15
adaptable 731.23
amphibology 548.1
amphibolous 548.3
amphiboly 879.8
amphigory,
amphigouri
rigmarole 594.4
poetry 607.3
amphilogy,
amphilogism 548.1
Amphineura 414.9
amphitheater
schoolroom 565.16
theater 609.17
arena 800.1
ample full 56.12
spacious 178.9
large 194.17
broad 203.6
plenty 659.6,7
satisfactory 866.11
ampliation 196.1
amplification
increase 38.1
expansion 196.1
development 321.2
radio 343.18
paraphrase 550.3
expatiation 591.6
exaggeration 615.1
aggravation 883.1
amplifier
loud-speaker 343.4
megaphone 447.8
amplify increase 38.4
enlarge 196.4
develop 321.6
electricity 341.23
expatiate 591.7
exaggerate 615.3
aggravate 883.2
amplitude
amount 28.1
greatness 34.1
fullness 56.2
spaciousness 178.5
size 194.1
breadth 203.1
aviation 277.22
plenitude 659.2
amply
sufficiently 659.8
satisfactorily 866.15
amps 341.11
amputate 42.10
amputation
excision 42.3
surgical ~ 687.24
amputee 684.32
amtrac 271.16
amuck, amok
nouns 472.8
adjs. 472.29
RUN AMUCK

create a disturbance
62.8
become violent
161.14
go mad 472.20
amulet 1034.5
amuse 876.23
AMUSE ONESELF
876.24
amused 876.28
amusement
mirth 868.5
entertainment 876
amusement park
876.11
amusing
entertaining 876.29
humorous 878.5
amygdalitis 684.12
amygdalotomy 687.26
amylaceous 388.12
ana collection 74.10
book 603.4
excerpts 605.4
anabolism 307.9
anabranch 394.3
anachronism 115
anachronous 115.3
Anacreontic 607.21
anacrusis 607.11
anaglyph 573.3
anaglyphic(al) 573.7
anaglyphy 573.1
anaglyptic(al) 573.7
anagnost 1036.9
anagoge 1032.1
anagogic(al)
mystical 547.14
esoteric 1032.24
anagram 879.8
anal 224.12
analecta book 603.4
excerpts 605.4
analects 605.4
analeptic 685.1
analeptic(al)
remedial 685.34
restorative 692.22
analgesia
insensibility 422.1
neurosis 688.21
analgesic
nouns 685.11,49
adjs. deadening 422.8
anodyne 685.39
analogical normal 84.7
comparative 490.8
analogize 490.4
analogon 20.4
analogous
corresponding 13.12
similar 20.11
comparable 490.8
analogue correlate 13.4
similar 20.4
word 580.3
analogy similarity 20.1
comparison 490.1
analysis dissection 49.4
classification 61.1
automatic ~ 348.7

logic 481.3
discussion 481.4
examination 484.8
theory 498.1
parsing 584.1
commentary 604.2
compendium 605.1
diagnosis 687.15
analyst
examiner 484.19
experimenter 488.6
psychoanalyst
688.13
analytic(al)
mathematical 87.17
reasoning 481.19
examinational 484.41
analytic(al) psychol-
ogy 688.1
analyzation 484.8
analyze dissect 49.17
discuss 481.16
examine 484.32
parse 584.12
describe 606.12
diagnose 687.32
analyzer
types of ~ 348.36
examiner 484.19
experimenter 488.6
analyzing 348.20
Anamnesis 1038.10
anamnesis 687.13
anamorphism 248.1
anamorphosis
distortion 248.1
misrepresentation
571.2
Ananias 617.9
Ananke 638.3
anapaest verse 607.5
meter 607.9
anapaestic 607.22
anaphrodisiac 162.17
anarch, anarchist
revolutionist 147.3
nihilist 738.3
radical 743.11
anarchic(al)
revolutionist 147.6
lawless 738.6
anarchism
revolutionism 147.2
lawlessness 738.2
politics 743.4
anarchistic
lawless 738.6
radical 743.19
anarchy confusion 62.2
lawlessness 738.2
anastatic 573.7
anastomose 52.3
anastomosis 52.1
anastrophe 219.3
anat 49.4
anathema
abomination 928.3
malediction 970.1
anathematize 970.5
anatomic(al) 244.9
anatomist 405.17

anatomize
dissect 49.17
analyze 484.32
anatomy
dissection 49.4
structure 244.1
skeleton 244.5
morphology 244.7
the body 375.3
analysis 484.8
manual 603.9
anatripsis 349.3
anatriptic 349.9
ancestor 66.1
ancestorial 169.13
ancestors 169.7
ancestral
primitive 123.11
parental 169.13
THE ANCESTRAL
HALLS 190.3
ancestress 169.7
ancestry
progenitorship 169
high descent 916.1
anchor
nouns 276.16,32
AT ANCHOR
motionless 267.11
ships 274.75
safe 696.6
HAVE AN ANCHOR TO
WINDWARD 893.6
verbs fasten 47.7
secure 142.9
settle 183.18
cast ~ 274.16
anchorage
anchors 276.16
haven 698.5,6
charge 844.7
anchoretic(al) 922.11
anchor ice 332.6
anchorite, anchoritess,
anchoret, anchor-
ess 922.5
anchoritic(al)
recluse 922.11
ascetic 989.3
anchoritism
seclusion 922.2
asceticism 989.1
anchors aweigh!
274.79
anchor watch 108.3
ancienne noblesse
916.2
ancient
nouns 123.7
adjs. old 123.10
elderly 126.15
ancient history 606.4
anciently 119.13
Ancient Mariner
wanderer 273.2
mariner 275.1
ancientness 123.1
ancient times 119.3
ancillary
additional 40.9
helpful 783.20

and
  nouns 41.1
  conjs. 40.12
  AND ALL
    additionally 40.10
    et cetera 40.13
  AND OTHERS 40.13
  AND SO ON, AND SO
    FORTH 40.13
andante
  nouns 461.25
  advs. 461.55
andante moderato
  461.55
andantino
  nouns 461.25
  advs. 461.55
and how! 521.9
andiron 328.15
and/or 635.24
Andra Kammaren
  740.4
andric 419.11
androecium 410.26
androgynal 418.23
androgyne
  hermaphrodite
    413.11
  masculine 419.9
androgynous 418.23
androgyny
  hermaphroditism
    413.10
  effeminacy 420.2
androlepsia 820.4
androtomy 416.8
Andvari 195.6
anear 199.20
aneath 207.11
anecdotage
  dotage 468.10
  anecdotes 606.6
anecdotal 606.16
anecdote 606.6
anecdotist 606.10
anemia
  paleness 362.2
  ailment 684.8
anemic pale 362.9
  sickly 684.46
anemograph 402.18
anemographic 402.29
anemography 402.17
anemological 402.29
anemology 402.17
anemometer 402.18
anemometric(al)
  402.29
anemometrograph
  402.18
anemometry 402.17
anemoscope 402.18
anent 9.12
aneroid 401.8
anesthesia
  insensibility 422.1
  neurosis 688.21
anesthesiologist 686.7
anesthetic
  nouns 685.13,50
  adjs. deadening 422.8

anodyne 685.40
anesthetist 686.14
anesthetize 422.3
anew again 91.6
  repetition 103.17
  newly 122.16
anfractuous
  sinuous 253.6
  spiral 253.8
angel
  ~ of death 407.3
  theatrical patron
    609.30
  backer 785.8
  financer 834.9
  endearment 930.5
  good person 983.6
  guardian spirit
    1012.19
  celestial being 1013
  pastor 1036.2
  clergyman 1036.8
angel cake, angel food
  cake 306a.41
angelic(al)
  lovable 929.22
  virtuous 978.7
  seraphic 1013.6
  godly 1026.9
Angelus call 566.15
  prayer 1030.4
anger
  nouns 950.5
  verbs become angry
    950.17
  make angry 950.21
angered 950.26
angina 684.12
angina pectoris 684.16
angiography 244.7
angiology 244.7
Angiospermae,
  angiosperms 411.8
angle
  nouns crook 250.2
  types of ~ 250.13
  ~ of attack 277.23
  fork 298.4
  viewpoint 438.7
  aspect 445.3
  attitude 523.2
  story 606.9
  AT AN ANGLE 218.22
  verbs oblique 218.9
  crook 250.5
  fork 298.7
  bias 525.9
  intrigue 652.10
  fish 653.10
  maneuver 733.10
  ANGLE AWAY 250.5
  ANGLE FOR
    seek 484.24
    solicit 772.14
  ANGLE OFF
    oblique 218.9
    angle 250.5
  ANGLE ON 648.4
angler 653.6
angleworm 413a.8
Anglican

nouns 1038.2
  adjs. ecclesiastical
    1035.13
  ritualistic 1038.21
Anglicanism
  religion 1018.9
  ritualism 1038.1
Anglicism
  nationalism 180.6
  idiom 578.9
  patriotism 939.2
Anglicize 188.5
angling 653.3
Anglomania 472.12
Anglo-Saxon 578.3
angrily
  turbulently 161.25
  irately 950.30
angry turbulent 161.17
  stormy 402.27
  sore 423.11
  indignant 950.26
angst 888.1
anguiform 253.7
anguille 306a.24
anguilliform 253.7
anguine sinuous 253.7
  serpentine 413.44
anguish
  nouns pain 423.6
  distress 864.6
  grief 870.10
  verbs pain 864.14
  suffer 864.22
  grieve 870.19
angular crooked 250.6
  forked 298.10
angularity 250
angustifoliate, angusti-
  rostrate, angusti-
  sellate, angusti-
  septal 204.13
anhydrate dry 392.6
  preserve 699.8
anhydration
  drying 392.3
  preservation 699.2
anhydromyelia 392.3
anhydrous 392.7
anigh 199.20
anile 468.23
anility 468.10
anima life force 406.3
  soul 1032.17
animadversion 967.4
animadvert 528.6
anima humana
  1032.17
animal
  nouns prehistoric ~
    123.26
  creature 413.2
  types of ~ 413.49–
    63
  savage 941.6
  adjs. animalistic
    413.36
  carnal 985.6
animal and vegetable
  kingdom 405.1
animal cell 405.5

animalcular 195.14
animalcule 195.7
animal culture 415.1
Animalia 413.1
animalism
  materialism 375.5
  carnality 985.2
animalistic
  animal 413.36
  carnal 985.6
animality
  animal life 413.1
  carnality 985.2
animal kingdom
  class 61.4
  animals 413.1
animal life 413.1
animal nature 985.2
animal soul 416.7
animal spirits 868.4
animal worship 1031.1
anima mundi 1011.8
animate
  verbs energize 160.9
  impel 282.11
  vivify 406.8
  prompt 646.12
  inspire 646.20
  refresh 693.2
  stimulate 855.12
  cheer 868.6
  adjs. organic 405.18
  living 406.10
animated
  energetic 160.11
  alive 406.10
  prompted 646.30
  refreshed 693.6
  lively 705.16
  gay 868.14
animated cartoon
  cartoon 572.17
  motion picture
    609.15
animated dominoes,
  animated ivories
  514.8
animater 160.5
animation
  energy 160.3
  invigoration 160.7
  life 406.1
  vivification 406.5
  motivation 646.2
  inspiration 646.9
  liveliness 705.2
  excitement 855.10
  gaiety 868.4
animatism
  immaterialism 376.3
  religion 1023.4
animatistic
  animistic 376.8
  philosophical 499.10
animative
  energizing 160.13
  animistic 376.8
  life-giving 406.11
animator 646.10
animism
  immaterialism 376.3

religion 1023.4
animist
nouns immaterialist
376.4
religionist 1023.7
animist(ic)
animative 376.8
philosophical 499.10
pagan 1023.11
animosity 927.4
animus
disposition 523.3
will 619.1
desire 632.3
moving spirit 646.9
intention 651.1
enmity 927.4
anion 341.22
anionic 341.29
ankh 567.1
ankle
nouns joint 47.4
legs 272.16
verbs 272.26
anklebone 413.33
ankle-deep deep 208.9
shallow 209.5
anklet band 252.3
ornament 899.6
ankus 646.8
ankylosis 684.8
ankylotomy 687.26
anlage rudiment 152.7
foundation 215.6
embryo 405.13
anna 833.9
annalist
chronologist 114.10
recorder 569.2
historian 606.11
annals chronicle 114.9
record 568.1
history 606.4
anneal 355.7
**Annelida, annelidans,
annelids, anneloids**
414.5
annex
nouns 41.1,3
verbs add 40.3
appropriate 820.16,
17
steal 822.13
annexation
addition 40.1
adjunct 41.1
appropriation 820.3,
4
theft 822.1
Annie Oakley 848.2
annihilate
extinguish 331.7
destroy 691.13
annihilated 2.10
annihilation
extinguishment
331.2
death 407.1
destruction 691.6
annihilative 691.26
annihilator 691.8

anniversary
commemoration
137.4,12
holy days 1038.15
anniversary days
137.13
anno Domini 105.13
annotate 550.13
annotation
comment 550.6
note 568.3
annotative 550.17
annotator 604.4
announce
forerun 116.3
affirm 521.4
presage 542.11
proclaim 557.12
announcement
radio ~ 343.23
affirmation 521.1
proclamation 557.2
announcer
radio ~ 343.26
informant 555.5
proclaimer 559.3
annoy irritate 864.17
anger 950.22
annoyance
vexation 864.2
resentment 950.1
annoyed
irritated 864.24
provoked 950.25
annoyer 864.10
annoying 862.13
annual
nouns plant 410.3
record book 568.10
book 603.11
adjs. 137.9
annual epact 114.5
annual period 128.1
annuitant 817.4
annuity subsidy 816.8
investment 834.3
annul neutralize 177.7
repeal 777.2
annular 252.10
annular eclipse 336.9
annularity 252.1
annulary 424.5
annulet 252.5
annulling 177.9
annulment
neutralization 177.2
repeal 777.1
annulus 252.2
annum 107.2
annunciate
affirm 521.4
announce 557.12
annunciation
affirmation 521.1
announcement
557.2
Annunciation Day
1038.15
annunciator
informant 555.5
messenger 559.3

annunciator system
348.5
annunciatory 557.18
anodic 342.15
anodyne
nouns 685.11
adjs. palliative 162.16
analgesic 685.39
anoint lubricate 379.8
bribe 649.3
medicate 687.34
whip 1008.16
chrism 1038.18
Anointed, the 1011.12
anointed king 747.8
anointment 379.6
**anomalistic,
anomalous** 85.9
anomaly, anomalism
85.1,5
anon
adjs. 582.3
advs. then 105.11
in the future 121.9
soon 131.16
anonym
pseudonym 581.8
anonymity 582.1
**anonymity, anony-
mousness** 582.1
anonymous 582.3
anoöpsia, anopia
439.1,5
anopsia
faulty vision 439.1
blindness 440.1
anorexia 634.3
another
nouns different thing
16.3
extra 41.4
adjs. other 16.8
additional 40.9
new 122.8
anoxia 277.18
anserine goosy 413.45
silly 469.8
anserous 413.45
answer
nouns reaction 283.1
music 461.23
reply 485
solution 486.1
refutation 505.2
epistle 602.2
defense 1004.2
responsory 1030.3
IN ANSWER 485.8
verbs correspond 13.8
suit 26.8
react 283.5
reply 485.4
solve 486.2
refute 505.5
~ by mail 602.12
suffice 659.4
avail 663.17
be profitable 809.11
ANSWER BACK
retort 485.4
sauce 911.7

**ANSWER CON-
CLUSIVELY** 505.5
ANSWER FOR
typify 570.8
promise 768.5
be deputy 779.13
take responsibility
960.8
ANSWER THE PURPOSE
suit 26.8
suffice 659.4
avail 663.17
ANSWER TO
pertain to 9.3
correspond 26.7
respond to 485.6
ANSWER TO NO MAN
738.4
I'LL ANSWER FOR IT
believe me 500.27
I'll warrant 521.10
answerable
commensurate 26.14
solvable 486.3
responsible 960.16
ANSWERABLE FOR
838.9
ANSWERABLE TO 82.6
BE ANSWERABLE FOR
promise 768.5
be responsible 960.6
answering
corresponding 13.12
responsive 485.7
ant 413a.3
antacid
nouns neutralizer
177.3
chemical 378.1
medicine 685.20,56
adjs. neutralizing
177.9
neutral 378.7
remedial 685.36
Antaeus
strong man 158.6
giant 194.13
antagonism
contrariety 15.1
disagreement 27.1
counteraction 177.1
opposition 788.2
warlikeness 795.16
hostility 927.3
antagonist
opponent 789.1
enemy 927.6
antagonistic
contrary 15.5
disagreeing 27.6
counteractive 177.8
hostile 788.9
belligerent 795.26
hostile 927.11
antagonize
counteract 177.6
oppose 788.3
alienate 793.15
provoke 927.7
Antarctic 396.3

antarctic
　nouns 332.5
　adjs. 289.15
Antarctica 385.1
ante
　nouns 514.3
　verbs bet 514.19
　pay 339.15
ante-bellum 116.5
antecede precede 64.2
　be prior 116.3
antecedence,
　antecedency
　precedence 64.1
　previousness 116.1
antecedent
　nouns forerunner 66.1
　precedence 116.2
　adjs. preliminary 64.4
　prior 116.4
antecedents 169.7
antechamber 191.20
ante Christum 105.13
antedate
　nouns date 114.4
　previousness 116.1
　verbs date 114.13
　be prior 116.3
antediluvian
　nouns 123.7,8
　adjs. 123.13
antelope 268.7
ante meridiem 133.1,6
antenatal 68.14
antenna
　types of ~ 343.35;
　345.23
　feeler 424.4
antepast
　serving 306.10
　appetizer 306a.9
　foretaste 540.4
anteparriarchal 123.11
anteposition
　precedence 64.1
　contraposition 238.1
　precession 291.1
anterior
　precedent 64.4
　prior 116.4
　front 239.11
anteroom 191.20
anthelion 334.14
anthelmintic
　nouns 685.19
　adjs. 685.37
anthem song 461.13
　music 461.16
　hymn 1030.3
antherid 405.9
antherozoid 405.7
anthesis 410.24
anthill heap 74.9
　mound 206.5
anthology
　compilation 603.4
　poetry book 607.6
Anthozoa 414.4
anthracite 330.9
anthrax 684.8,10
anthrophore 410.19

anthropogeny, anthro-
　pography 416.8
anthropoid 416.11
Anthropoidea 414.12
anthropolatry 1018.5
anthropological 416.10
anthropologist
　zoologist 414.2
　anthropology 416.8
anthropology 416.8
anthropometry 416.8
anthropomorphic
　manlike 416.11
　theistic 1018.23
anthropomorphism
　humanization 416.7
　religion 1018.5
anthropophagite 941.6
anthropos 416.1,3
anthroposophist
　1032.11
anthroposophy
　anthropology 416.8
　occultism 1032.1,11
anthropotheism
　1018.5
anthropotheistic
　1018.23
anthropotomy
　anatomy 244.7
　anthropology 416.8
anti
　contrary 15.5
　opposed 788.9
anti- 177.10
antiaircraft artillery
　799.6,7
antiantibody 685.22
antibiotic
　nouns 685.24,53
　adjs. remedial 685.36
antibody 685.22,52
antic
　nouns caper 317.2
　prank 879.10
　verbs caper 317.6
　frolic 876.25
　adjs. 868.14
anticathexis 688.44
antichresis 770.5
antichrist 1029.10
antichristian 1029.22
anti-Christian 1029.10
anti-Christianism, anti-
　Christianity 1029.8
anticipant 537.9
anticipatable 541.13
anticipate
　be beforehand 131.6
　expect 537.4
　foresee 540.6
　intend to 651.5
　preclude 728.14
　NOT ANTICIPATE
　538.4
anticipated 537.11
anticipating
　pregnant 168.18
　expectant 537.9
anticipation
　prolepsis 115.1

earliness 131.1
intuition 480.1
expectation 537.1
foresight 540.1
foreboding 542.1
IN ANTICIPATION
　beforehand 131.11
　expectant 537.9
　in readiness 718.22
anticipatory,
　anticipative
　early 131.7
　expectant 537.9
anticlimax
　figure of speech
　549.2
　bathos 878.4
anticlinal 218.16
anticyclone 267.5
antidotal 685.36
antidote
　counteractant 177.3
　medicine 685.21
antifebrile
　nouns 685.12
　adjs. 685.36
antifogmatic 994.8
antifreeze 333.8
antifriction 379.2
antigen 685.22
antigodlin, antigoglin
　218.20
antihistamine 685.20
antiknock 450.4
antilogy 482.2
antiluetic 685.36
antimissile 280.2
antinganting 1034.5
Antinoüs 898.9
antiorgastic 162.17
antipasto 306a.9
antipathetic(al)
　contrary 15.5
　opposed 788.9
　hostile 927.11
antipathy
　contrariety 15.1
　counteraction 177.1
　opposition 788.2
　repugnance 865.2
　hostility 927.3
　hatred 928.1,3
antiperiodic
　nouns 685.20
　adjs. 685.36
antiphon, antiphony
　music 461.23
　responsory 1030.3
antiphonal 485.7
antiphrasis 585.2
antipodal
　opposite 15.6
　contrapositive 238.5
antipode 15.2
antipodes
　opposite 15.2
　region 179.6
　poles 238.2
antipoints 238.2
antipoison 685.21
antipole 15.2

antipoles 238.2
antipope 1036.8
antipyretic
　nouns 685.12
　adjs. 685.36
antiquarian
　nouns 123.5
　adjs. 123.20
antiquarianism 123.4
antiquary 123.5
antiquate 123.9
antiquated 123.13
antiquated expression
　580.11
antiquation 123.3
antique
　nouns old thing 123.6
　antiquated person
　123.8
　adjs. old 123.10
　antiquated 123.13
antique dealer 123.5
antiquities
　archaisms 123.6
　ancient manuscripts
　600.12
antiquity
　the past 119.3
　oldness 123.1
antireligious 1029.22
antisaloon 990.11
antiscorbutic 685.36
anti-Scriptural 1029.22
anti-Semitism 525.4
antisepsis
　antiseptic 685.18
　immunization
　687.19
antiseptic
　nouns 685.18,51
　adjs. 685.37
antiserum 685.22
antisocial 938.3
antisocialism 688.16
antisocialist 938.2
antisocial personality
　688.14
antispasmodic 685.11
antispast 607.9
antispastic 607.22
antistrophe 607.11
antisun 334.14
antisyphilitic 685.36
antithesis
　contrariety 15.1
　opposite 15.2
　contraposition 238.1
　figure of speech
　549.2
antithesize 15.3
antithetic(al)
　contrary 15.5
　opposite 238.5
　figurative 549.4
　opposed 788.9
antitoxic 685.36
antitoxin 685.22
antitrades 402.10
antitype 25.1
antivenene,
　antivenin 685.22

antlia 255.7
antonomasia
  figure of speech
    549.2
  nomenclature 581.1
antonomastic(al)
    549.4
Antony and Cleopatra
    929.16
antonym opposite 15.2
  word 580.3
antonymous 15.5
antrum 256.2
antymire 413a.3
Anu 1012.11
Anubis 1012.9
A number 1 672.16
anus 224.6
anvil instrument 145.7
  incus 447.7
  ON THE ANVIL
  planned 652.13
  undertaken 713.6
  in preparation
    718.23
anxiety eagerness 633.1
  neurosis 688.22
  concern 888.1
  fear 889
anxious eager 633.9
  concerned 888.6
  fearful 889.22,23
anxious seat 1040.13
  ON THE ANXIOUS SEAT
    888.6
any
  nouns some 28.3
    aught 79.5
    no choice 637.6
  adjs. some 28.6
    every 79.14
    one 89.7
anybody 79.5
anyhow
  adjs. 62.15
  advs. carelessly 532.18
    anyway 655.12
anyone anybody 79.5
  whoever 79.7
  one 89.7
anyplace 183.23
anything some 28.3
  any 79.5
  no choice 637.6
anythingarian
  nonpartisan 742.29
  neutral 804.4
any time, any time
  now 151.4
anyway 655.12
anywhere 183.23
Anzacs 798.20
A-Okay 672.14
A one, A 1
  seaworthy 276.18
  first-rate 672.16
aorist(ic) 119.6
aorta 395.14
à outrance
  extremely 34.22
  utterly 56.17

to the end 70.12
  to completion
    720.13
apace promptly 131.15
  swiftly 268.21
  hastily 707.12
apache assassin 408.10
  thug 941.4
apart
  adjs. unrelated 10.5
    unjoined 49.20
    alone 89.8
    distant 198.8
    secluded 922.9
  advs. separately 49.26
    singly 89.13
    away 198.18
    in private 612.21
apartheid
  segregation 77.3
  prejudice 525.4
apartment 191.4
à pas de geant 268.21
apathetic(al) 854.13
apathetically 854.15
apathy neurosis 688.22
  unfeeling 854.4
ape
  nouns imitator 22.4
    types of ~ 413.50
  verbs 22.6
ape-man 123.6
aperçu 605.1
aperient 685.15,41
apéritif
  appetizer 306a.9
  drink 994.8
à perte de vue
  out of sight 198.22
  invisible 444.4
aperture opening 264.1
  entranceway 301.5
  passageway 655.4
apery 22.2
aphasia 688.25
aphonia
  muteness 450.2
  neurosis 688.25
aphonic 450.12,14
aphorism 516.1
aphoristic 516.6
aphorize 516.5
aphrasia 688.26
aphrodisia
  upheaval 161.5
  coition 168.3
  pruriency 418.4
  psychosexuality
    688.32
aphrodisiac
  nouns 418.6
  adjs. 418.19
Aphrodite
  beauty 898.9
  love 929.8
  goddess 1012.5
aphthous fever 684.10
apiarian 415.4
apiary 415.5
apical 210.9
Apician 992.7

Apicius 992.4
apiculture 415.1
apiece 80.19
apish 22.10
apishamore 227.12
aplenty 659.9
à plomb
  nouns 142.1
  advs. 212.13
aplomb
  nouns stability 142.1
  perpendicularity
    212.1
  equanimity 856.3
  adjs. 622.5
apnea 684.8
Apocalypse 1019.4
apocalypse 554.1
apocalyptic(al)
  revelational 554.11
  scriptural 1019.9
a poco 461.55
apocope 202.3
Apocrypha 1019.3
apocryphal
  unauthoritative
    513.19
  false 614.27
  unorthodox 1023.9
apodict(al) 504.19
apodixis 504.4
apodosis 70.1
apogee climax 56.4
  highest point 210.2
  astronomy 374.16
apograph 24.4
apoise
  equiponderant 30.10
  on even keel 276.19
Apollo, Apollon
  sun 374.11
  music 463.24
  poetic muse 607.12
  beauty 898.9
  god 1012.5
Apollyon 1014.5
apologete 1004.8
apologetic 1004.3
apologetic(al)
  justifying 1004.13
  propitiatory 1010.7
apologetics 1021.1
apologia 1004.3
apologist
  defender 797.7
  justifier 1004.8
apologize 1010.5
  APOLOGIZE FOR
    1004.11
apologizer 1004.8
apologue
  figure of speech
    549.2
  story 606.7
apology pretext 647.1
  justification 1004.3
  excuse 1010.2
  MAKE APOLOGY FOR
    1004.11
apoplectic
  nouns 684.31

adjs. 684.46
apoplexy 684.5
aport leftward 243.7
  larboard 274.72
apostasy
  recreancy 626.2
  desertion 631.2
  backsliding 694.2
apostate
  nouns 626.5
  adjs. 626.11
apostatize
  change sides 626.8
  desert 631.6
aposteme 684.28
a posteriori 481.22
apostle disciple 564.2
  evangelist 1020.2
Apostles' Creed
    1021.2
apostleship 1035.1
Apostolic 990.4
apostolic(al)
  scriptural 1019.9
  papal 1035.15
apostolic brief 602.3
apostolic church
    1022.4
apostrophe
  figure of speech
    549.2
  soliloquy 596.1
apostrophic 596.4
apostrophize
  address 592.18
  say aside 596.3
apothecaries' measure
    489.5
apothecary 685.30
apothegm 516.1
apothegmatize 516.5
apotheosis ideal 25.4
  glorification 912.8
  resurrection 1016.12
  idolization 1031.2
apotheosize
  glorify 912.13
  idolize 1031.5
appall horrify 864.13
  shock 889.16
  dismay 889.18
appalled
  displeased 864.23
  horrified 889.25
appalling
  remarkable 34.10
  horrible 862.10
  frightful 889.29
appanage adjunct 41.1
  property 808.2
  endowment 816.9
apparatus tool 347.1
  equipment 657.4
apparatus belli 799.1
apparel
  nouns 230.1
  verbs 230.38
apparent visible 443.6
  seeming 445.11
  plausible 510.6
  illusory 518.9

manifest 553.8
specious 614.28
apparently
visibly 443.8
seemingly 445.12
presumably 510.7
manifestly 553.14
speciously 614.35
apparition
appearance 445.1,5
illusion 518.4
specter 1015.1
**appassionatamente,
appassionato**
46.54
appeal
nouns attraction
648.1
entreaty 772.2
lovability 929.7
legal ~ 1002.10
prayer 1030.4
WITHOUT APPEAL
750.13
verbs attract 648.5
entreat 772.11
APPEAL TO
cite 504.15
address 592.18
implore 772.11
appealing
attractive 648.7
entreating 772.17
delightful 861.6
appear occur 150.6
attend 185.8
be seen 443.4
become visible 445.8
seem 445.10
~ unexpectedly
538.6
~ in print 601.16
act 609.33
appearance
appearing 445
illusion 518.2,4
manifestation 553.1
false show 614.3
specter 1015.1
HAVE EVERY
APPEARANCE OF
seem like 20.7
seem 445.10
KEEP UP APPEAR-
ANCES 642.10
MAKE AN APPEARANCE
attend 185.8
arrive 299.6
appear 445.8
PUT A FALSE AP-
PEARANCE UPON
misrepresent 571.3
falsify 614.16
appease
tranquilize 162.7
pacify 802.7
satisfy 863.6
relieve 884.5
appeasement
pacification 802.1
political ~ 742.5

relief 884.1
appellant 1003.5
appellate 999.10
appellate court 999.3
appellation 581.2,3
appellative 581.16
append add 40.3
place after 65.4
appendage
nonessential 6.2
addition 41.1
accompaniment 73.3
tail 240.5
follower 292.2
hanger-on 905.5
appendages 808.2
appendant
nouns 41.1
adjs. added 40.8
sequential 65.5
appendectomy 687.25
appendicitis 684.8
appendix addition 41.1
sequel 67.1
vermiform ~ 224.6
apperception
sagacity 466.4
cognizance 474.2
apperceptionism 688.2
apperception test
688.11
**apperceptive,
appercipient**
sagacious 466.16
knowing 474.15
appertain to relate 9.3
belong to 806.8
appetence, appetency
632.7
appetite 632.6,7
appetitive 632.21
appetizer 306a.9
appetizing
savory 427.10
desirable 632.31
tempting 648.7
applaud cheer 874.7
acclaim 966.10
applause cheer 874.2
approbation 966.2
apple 215.19
APPLE OF ONE'S EYE
desired one 632.11
favorite 929.13
applejack 994.16
apple-pie order 59.3
apple-polisher 905.3
applesauce
nouns 545.3
interjs. 469.12
Appleton layer 401.3
appliance tool 347.1
use 663.1
facility 783.9
application 961.2
appliances 657.4
applicability
relevance 9.2
aptness 26.5
utility 663.3
applicable relevant 9.8

apt 26.18
usable 663.22
applicant 772.7
application
relevance 9.2
addition 41.1
attribution 154.1
mental ~ 477.3
engrossment 528.3
perseverance 623.1
use 663.1
medical ~ 685.28
assiduity 705.6
requisition 772.1
administration 961.2
MAKE APPLICATION
772.9
apply relate to 9.4
attribute 154.2
put to use 663.11
appropriate 820.16
administer 961.6
APPLY ONESELF TO
think about 477.10
attend to 528.5
do 703.7
undertake 713.3
exert oneself 714.9
appoggiatura 462.18
appoint elect 635.17
destine 638.7
equip 657.8
prescribe 750.10
assign 778.10
allot 814.10
appointed
chosen 635.23
destined 638.9
commissioned
778.16
appointedly 34.21
appointment
election 635.7
office 654.5
ordinance 750.4
assignment 778.2
allotment 814.3
engagement 920.7
holy orders 1035.10
appointments
equipment 657.4
belongings 808.2
apportion dispose 60.8
allot 814.7
apportionment
arrangement 60.1
allotment 814
appose
juxtapose 199.13
compare 490.4
apposite relevant 9.8
apt 26.18
apposition
relevance 9.2
fitness 26.5
juxtaposition 199.3
appraisable 489.15
appraisal
measurement 489.1
assessment 493.3
pricing 844.4

appraise
measure 489.11
assess 493.9
price 844.13
appraisement
measurement 489.1
assessment 493.3
pricing 844.4
appreciable
tangible 3.4
ponderable 351.19
measurable 489.15
appreciate
increase 38.6
savor 427.5
know 474.12
measure 489.11
assess 493.9
rate highly 670.12
enjoy 863.10
be grateful 947.3
respect 962.4
NOT APPRECIATE
948.3
appreciation
increase 38.1
awareness 474.2
discrimination 491.1
estimation 493.3
gratitude 947.1
respect 962.1
appreciative
discriminating 491.8
grateful 947.5
approbatory 966.15
apprehend sense 421.7
know 474.12
understand 546.7
arrest 759.16
capture 820.15
dread 889.9
apprehensible 546.9
apprehension
intelligence 466.1
understanding 474.3
idea 478.1
opinion 500.4
doubt 502.2
foreboding 542.1
alarm 702.1
arrest 759.6
seizure 820.2
anxiety 888.1
fearfulness 889.3
apprehensive
smart 466.14
knowing 474.15
alarming 702.8
anxious 888.6
fearful 889.23
apprentice
nouns novice 564.8
worker 716.5
verbs 778.15
apprenticeship
training 560.3
indenture 778.7
apprize, apprise
appraise 493.9
inform 555.7
price 844.13

arraign indict 1002.14
  accuse 1003.7
arraignment
  indictment 1002.3
  accusation 1003.1
arrange
  ~ itself 59.4
  order 60.7
  ~ music 461.47
  plan 652.9
  prepare 718.6
  contract 769.9
  ~ matters 802.8
  mediate 803.7
arranged orderly 59.6
  organized 60.13
  settled 512.20
  planned 652.13
  contracted 769.12
arrangement
  order 59.1
  distribution 60
  structure 244.1
  musical ~ 461.5,28;
    462.2,11
  condition 506.2
  art 572.10
  plan 652.1
  preparation 718.1
  compact 769.1,4
  conciliation 802.4
  engagement 920.7
  MAKE ARRANGEMENTS
  plan 652.9
  prepare 718.6
arranger 463.22
arrant downright 34.14
  obvious 553.11
  bad 673.7
  disreputable 913.12
  wicked 979.17
array
  nouns order 59.1
  arrangement 60.1
  series 71.2
  throng 74.4
  clothing 230.1
  army 798.22
  verbs arrange 60.8
  clothe 230.38
  equip 657.8
  adorn 899.7
arrayal 657.1
arrayed
  clothed 230.44
  furnished 657.12
arrears, arrearage
  shortcoming 312.1
  debt 838.2
  IN ARREARS
  deficient 57.4
  behindhand 312.6
  due 838.10
  defaulting 840.10
arrest
  nouns stop 144.2
  retardation 269.4
  hindrance 728.1,7
  restraint 758.1
  custody 759.6
  UNDER ARREST 759.21

verbs delay 132.7
  stop 144.11
  retard 269.9
  ~ the interest
    528.13
  hinder 728.10
  restrain 758.7
  take prisoner 759.16
  ARREST THE
    THOUGHTS
  thought 477.18
  catch attention
    528.11
arrested
  retarded 269.12
  unintelligent 468.22
arrested development
  unintelligence 468.9
  fixation 688.29
arresting 528.20
arrière-pensée
  sequel 67.1
  afterthought 477.5
  qualification 506.1
arrish 67.3
arrival
  airplane landing
    277.15
  coming 299
  comer 301.4
  welcome, greetings
    923.2–4
arrive come to 299.6
  be successful 722.9
  ARRIVE AT
  ~ a conclusion
    493.10
  ~ an agreement
    520.10
arriving 299.10
arrogance
  haughtiness 910
  insolence 911
arrogant haughty
    910.9
  insolent 911.8
arrogate
  assume command
    737.13
  appropriate 820.16
  usurp 959.8
arrogation
  attribution 154.1
  ~ of power 737.11
  appropriation 820.3
  usurpation 959.3
arrogator tyrant 747.15
  usurper 959.4
arrosive 349.10
arrow speed 268.7
  pointer 566.3
  missile 799.17
arrowhead
  cuneiform 579.3
  missile 799.17
arrowheaded, arrow-
    like, arrowy
    257.14
arroyo ravine 200.3
  stream 394.1
  watercourse 395.2

arse 240.4
arsenal
  storehouse 658.6
  factory 717.3
  armory 799.2
arsenotherapy 687.3
arsis 607.9
arson 328.7
arsonist, arsonite
    328.8
art science 474.10
  artistry 572.8
  work of ~ 572.11
  schools of ~ 572.23
  sculpture 573
  ceramics 574
  photography 575
  engraving 576
  vocation 654.6
  skill 731.6,7
  artifice 733.3
  decoration 899
  THE ARTS 572.1
art-conscious 572.21
artcraft 572.3
Artemis moon 374.9
  goddess 1012.5
arterial
  nouns 655.6
  adjs. 395.21
arteriectomy 687.25
arterioplasty 687.27
arteriosclerosis 684.8
arteriotomy 687.26
artery vessel 395.14
  passageway 655.4,6
artful shrewd 466.15
  artificial 614.27
  cunning 733.12
Artful Dodger
  deceiver 617.1
  crafty person 733.6
artfully
  shrewdly 466.20
  cunningly 733.15
artfulness
  shrewdness 466.3
  cunning 733.1
arthritic 684.46
arthritis 684.8
arthropod 413a.2
Arthropoda 414.8
article
  nouns particular 8.2
  section 55.2
  integer 89.4
  object 375.4
  belief 500.2
  news ~ 556.3
  ~ of virtue 572.11
  grammar 584.5
  clause 603.14
  treatise 604.1
  ~ of merchandise
    829.2
  ~ of faith 1021.2
  THE ARTICLE
  the thing 26.6
  the real thing 515.6
  verbs indenture
    778.15

bring charges
    1003.7
articled 778.18
articled clerk 564.8
articulate
  verbs fasten 47.8
  sound 449.12
  say 592.14
  adjs. jointed 47.17
  audible 449.15
  intelligible 546.10
  speaking 592.21
articulated
  sounded 449.13
  spoken 592.20
articulation joint 47.4
  speech sound 449.5
  sounding 449.6
  articulateness 546.1
  word 580.1
  speech 592.3,5,6
artifact relic 123.6
  work of art 572.11
artifice
  deception 616.4,6
  expedient 668.2
  cunning 733.3
artificer
  builder 166.10
  mechanic 346.7
  artisan 716.6
artificial elegant 587.9
  false 614.27
  affected 901.15
artificiality
  elegance 587.3
  falseness 614.2
  affectation 901.1
artillery army 798.26
  ballistics 799.3,6
artilleryman, artillerist
    798.11
artiness 572.8
artisan
  mechanic 346.7
  craftsman 716.6
artist painter 577
  artisan 716.6
artiste musician 463.1
  artist 577.1
  actor 610.1
  artisan 716.6
artistic
  art-minded 572.21
  skillful 731.20
  tasteful 895.8
  beautiful 898.16
  ornamental 899.9
artistry art 572.8
  authorship 600.2
artless natural 719.13
  unskilled 732.15
  ingenuous 734.5
  frank 972.17
artlessness
  naturalness 719.3
  ingenuousness 734
  candor 972.4
art styles 572.24
art stylists 577.12
artware 572.11

arty, art-minded
572.21
ary 28.6
Aryan 417.3
as
advs. similarly 20.18
equally 30.12
for example 504.25
thus 555.11
conjs. since 154.8
than 490.10
AS AGREED UPON
769.13
AS A MATTER OF
COURSE
generally 79.15
usually 84.9
consequently 153.9
certainly 512.23
necessarily 637.16
AS A MATTER OF FACT
actually 1.16
truly 515.16
AS A MATTER OF
FORM 644.11
AS A RESULT OF
154.9
AS A RULE
generally 79.15
usual y 84.9
AS A WHOLE
wholly 54.12
generally 79.15
AS EVERY SCHOOLBOY
KNOWS 474.29
AS FAR AS
until 105.10
to 193.20
AS FOR 9.10
AS IF
as though 20.19
seemingly 498.17
AS IS
ditto 14.8
in statu quo 140.10
AS IT MAY BE
eventually 150.12
by chance 155.18
possibly 508.9
AS IT OUGHT TO BE
logical 481.21
right 956.8
just 974.8
AS IT SEEMS 445.12
AS IT WERE
as though 20.19
seemingly 498.17
figuratively 549.5
AS LIEF 620.9
AS LIKE AS NOT 510.7
AS LONG AS
while 105.9
provided 506.15
AS LUCK WOULD
HAVE IT
by chance 155.18
if possible 508.11
luckily 726.16
AS MAY BE EXPECTED
usually 84.9
imminently 151.4

AS ONE MAN
simultaneously
118.6
concurrently 176.5
unanimously 520.17
co-operatively 784.9
AS REGARDS 9.10
AS THE CASE MAY BE
accordingly 8.9
by chance 155.18
possibly 508.9
AS THE CROW FLIES
289.25
AS THE DAY IS LONG
110.14
AS THE SAYING IS
516.7
AS THE STORY GOES
556.16
AS THE WORLD GOES
eventually 150.12
customarily 640.20
AS THEY SAY
proverbially 516.7
rumored 556.16
AS THINGS GO
accordingly 8.9
eventually 150.12
since 154.8
customarily 640.20
AS THOUGH
as if 20.19
seemingly 498.17
AS TO
apropos 9.10
compared to 490.10
AS WELL 40.10
AS WELL AS
equally with 30.12
including 40.11
and 40.12
AS WELL AS CAN BE
EXPECTED 683.7
asafetida 436.3
asbestic 331.9
asbestine
incombustible
331.9
mineral 382.14
asbestos
fireproofing 331.5
theater drop 609.24
ascared 889.21
ascend be high 206.15
slope 218.10
fly 277.45
rise 313.8
ascendance 737.5
ascendancy
superiority 36.1
influence 171.1
dominion 737.5
IN ASCENDANCY
superior 36.13
influential 171.14
victorious 724.8
governing 739.17
ascendant
superior 36.13
influential 171.14
ascending 313.14

victorious 724.8
governing 739.17
ascendants 169.7
ascending
sloping 218.17
rising 313.14
ascension ascent 313.1
translation 1016.12
THE ASCENSION
1016.12
ascensional 313.14
Ascension Day
1038.15
ascent acclivity 218.6
rise 313
elevation 315
ascertain
find out 486.2
decide 493.11
prove 504.11
make sure 512.11
learn 562.6
ascertainable
knowable 474.25
solvable 486.3
ascertainment
solution 486.1
certification 512.8
ascetic
nouns recluse 922.5
puritan 989.2
abstainer 990.4
adjs. austere 989.3
abstinent 990.10
asceticism
austerity 989
abstinence 990.2
ascititious extrinsic 6.4
completing 56.14
Asclepius 686.15
Ascomycetes 411.4
ascribable
attributable 154.5
due to 958.10
ascribe 154.2
ASCRIBE IMPOR-
TANCE TO 670.12
ascription 154.1
aseity 1.5
asepsis 679.1
aseptic 685.37
asexual 418.22
asexuality 418.9
Asgard 1016.11
ash residue 43.2
ashes 328.16
ashamed 904.12
BE ASHAMED 904.8
ash-blond 363.10
ashcake 306a.27
ashen, ashy
burnt 328.29
pale 362.9
gray 365.3
ashes ash 328.16
corpse 407.13
ash-gray 365.3
ashiness 362.2
ashore 384.11
ashtray 192.8

Ash Wednesday
1038.15
Asia region 179.6
continent 385.1
Asian, Asiatic 417.8,
10
aside
nouns interjection
236.2
apostrophe 596.1
IN AN ASIDE 451.22
advs. away 198.18
sidewise 241.8
to the side 241.10
sotto voce 451.22
in private 612.21
in reserve 658.17
preps. 241.11
ASIDE FROM
apart from 49.26
besides 77.9
ASIDE OF 490.10
asinine mulish 413.41
stupid 468.15
foolish 469.8
asininity
stupidity 468.3
foolishness 469.1
ask inquire 484.21
require 637.9
demand 751.4
request 772.9
invite 772.13
assess 844.14
ASK FOR
seek 484.24
encourage 646.21
request 772.9
ASK ME ANOTHER!
476.20
I ASK YOU! 511.4
askance, askant
adjs. 218.14
advs. obliquely
218.23
sideways 241.8
LOOK ASKANCE
438.19
LOOK ASKANCE AT
show dislike 865.6
disapprove of
967.10
askari 798.8
askeered 889.21
askew
adjs. disorderly 62.12
awry 218.14
crooked 248.11
faulty 517.14
advs. 218.23
asking 772.1
aslant
adjs. 218.15
advs. 218.24
asleep dead 407.24
numb 422.5
unconscious 422.7
unaware 476.14
inattentive 529.8
half ~ 710.19
sleeping 710.20

ASLEEP IN THE DEEP
407.26
ASLEEP ON THE JOB
529.8
FALL ASLEEP
die 407.15
go to sleep 710.15
aslope
adjs. 218.15
advs. 218.24
Asmodeus 1014.5
asomatous 376.7
Aspasia 987.15
aspect
component 58.2
posture 183.4
astrology 374.20
appearance 445.3
aspen 323.18
aspergation
wetting 391.6
baptism 1038.7
asperge
sprinkle 391.12
baptize 1038.19
asperger, asperges
1038.11
Asperges 1038.4
aspergil 391.8
aspergillum
sprinkler 391.8
religion 1038.11
asperity
roughness 260.1
causticity 937.8
resentment 950.3
asperous 226.7
asperse 969.9
aspersion
wetting 391.6
insult 963.2
criticism 967.4
disparagement
969.4
rite 1038.4
baptism 1038.7
asphalt
nouns mineral 382.1
pavement 655.7
verbs 227.24
asphaltic 380.3
asphyxia
suffocation 408.6
disease 684.8
asphyxiate 408.19
asphyxiation 408.6
aspic 306a.12
aspirant
solicitant 632.12
political ~ 744.9
candidate 772.7
aspirate
sound softly 451.10
sibilate 456.2
aspiration
suction 304.2
breathing 402.19
ambition 632.9
aspire ascend 313.10
be ambitious 632.20
ASPIRE TO

aspire 632.20
intend 651.4
aspirer 632.12
aspiring lofty 206.19
ambitious 632.29
asportation 270.3
asquint
adjs. awry 218.14
squinting 439.11
advs. obliquely
218.23
sideways 241.8
ass rump 240.4
donkey 413.22
dolt 470.3
obstinate person
624.6
ASS IN LION'S SKIN
misfit 27.4
impostor 617.6
assail attack 796.15
incriminate 1003.10
assailability 695.4
assailable 695.16
assailant
opponent 789.1
attacker 796.13
assailer 796.13
Assama 1016.8
assassin 408.10
assassinate 408.16
assassination 408.2
assault
nouns ~ of illness
684.6
attack 796.1
incrimination
1003.2
ASSAULT AND
BATTERY 796.1
TAKE BY ASSAULT
820.12
verbs 796.15
assaulter 796.13
assay
nouns analysis 484.8
test 488.2
verbs analyze 484.32
test 488.8
assayer 488.6
assaying 484.8
assemblage all 54.3
gathering 74
putting together
74.13
assemble
come together
74.15
bring together
74.17
assembled 74.21
assembly
meeting 74.1,2
putting together
74.13
~ hall 190.15
religious ~ 1037.1
assembly line
assembly 74.13
production 166.2
factory 717.3

assent
nouns acquiescence
520
consent 773.1
verbs acquiesce 520.8
consent 773.3
assenter 520.6
assenting
acquiescent 520.13
consenting 773.5
assert affirm 521.4
state 592.15
claim 751.5
vindicate 1004.10
ASSERT ONESELF
751.7
assertion
premise 481.8
affirmation 521.1
remark 592.4
assertive, assertative
521.7
asses' bridge 729.6
assess measure 489.11
estimate 493.9
price 844.13
charge 844.14
assessable
measurable 489.15
chargeable 844.17
assessment
measurement 489.1
estimate 493.3
stock ~ 832.7
value 844.4
tax 844.10
assessor tax ~ 844.12
judge 1000.4
assets resources 658.2
property 808.8
funds 833.14
wealth 835
accounts 843.1
assever, asseverate
521.4
asseveration 521.1
asshead 470.3
assiduity
painstaking 531.2
perseverance 623.1
industry 705.6
assiduous
painstaking 531.11
persevering 623.7
industrious 705.21
assign
nouns 817.4
verbs specify 80.9
attribute 154.2
pass judgment
493.13
allege 504.13
address 602.14
commission 778.9,
10
allot 814.10
transfer 815.3
commit 816.16
assignable
attributable 154.5
transferable 815.5

assignation
attribution 154.1
transfer 815.1
rendezvous 920.8
assignation house
920.8
assignee
consignee 778.8
beneficiary 817.4
assignment
specification 80.6
attribution 154.1
lesson 560.6
task 654.2
commission 778.1,2
allotment 814.3
transfer 815.1
commitment 816.2
assignor 816.11
assimilate
make alike 20.8
adapt 26.11
domesticate 188.5
absorb 305.13
digest 307.16
liken 490.4
understand 546.7
learn 562.7
corner 831.26
ASSIMILATE TO
conform 82.3
convert 145.8
assimilation
adaptation 26.4
conversion 145.1
naturalization 188.4
absorption 305.6
digestion 307.1
anabolism 307.9
comparison 490.1
learning 562.2
assimilative 307.21
assist
nouns 783.2
verbs help 783.11
subsidize 816.18
assistance
remedy 685.1
aid 783.1
subsidy 816.8
assistant
nouns teacher 563.4
servant 748.1
helper 785.6
adjs. 783.20
assister 940.1
assize
measurement 489.1
trial 1002.5
assizement 489.1
assizes 993.3
associate
nouns similar 20.4
teacher 563.4
confederate 785.1
organization 786.10
member 786.11
comrade 926.4
verbs relate 9.4
join 47.5
league 52.4

ASSOCIATE ONESELF
    WITH 786.14
ASSOCIATE WITH
    accompany 73.7
    fraternize 920.15
adjs. allied 9.6
    leagued 52.6
    concurrent 176.4
associated related 9.6
    joined 47.13
    leagued 52.6
    concurrent 176.4
associates staff 748.12
    membership 786.12
association
    relation 9.1
    combination 52.1
    company 73.2
    concurrence 176.1
    thoughts 477.4
    communication
        552.1
    ~ of ideas 688.42
    affiliation 784.3
    society 786.1
    fellowship 920.5
associational 786.16
associationism 688.2
associative relative 9.5
    combining 52.7
assonance
    resemblance 20.3
    agreement 26.1
    alliteration 607.10
assonant similar 20.17
    harmonious 461.50
    poetic 607.23
assonate
    sound alike 20.9
    harmonize 461.36
    rhyme 607.20
assort sort 60.10
    classify 61.6
ASSORT WITH
    agree 26.9
    accompany 73.7
    fraternize 920.15
assorted various 19.4
    arranged 60.13
    classified 61.8
assortment
    mixture 44.6
    sorting 60.3
    miscellany 74.12
assuage
    moderate 162.6
    soften 356.6
    qualify 506.3
    satisfy 863.6
    relieve 884.5
assuagement
    moderation 162.2
    softening 356.5
    relief 384.1
assuager
    mitigator 162.3
    medicine 685.8
assuasive
    nouns 685.8
    adjs. palliative 162.16
    softening 356.16

qualifying 506.7
    remedial 685.35
    relieving 884.9
assume don 230.42
    suppose 498.9
    think 500.9
    imply 544.4
    feign 614.22
    allege 647.3
    undertake 713.3
    take charge 737.13
    borrow 819.4
    appropriate 820.16
    affect 901.12
    make bold 959.6
    usurp 959.8
ONE CAN ASSUME
    510.11
assumed
    supposed 498.14
    implied 544.7
    sham 614.27
    alleged 647.4
    undertaken 713.6
    affected 901.16
assumed name 581.8
assumer 498.7
assuming 910.10
ASSUMING THAT
    498.19
assumption
    conversion 145.1
    premise 481.8
    supposition 498.2
    opinion 500.4
    implication 544.2
    pretext 647.2
    ~ of power 737.11
    receiving 817.1
    borrowing 819.2
    appropriation 820.3
    hope 886.1
    arrogance 910.2
    undue liberty 959.2
    usurpation 959.3
    translation 1016.12
THE ASSUMPTION
    1016.12
assurance belief 500.1
    sureness 512.1,5,8
    oath 521.3
    promise 768.1
    security 770.1
    poise 856.3
    comfort 885.4
    hope 886.1
    emboldening 891.9
    audacity 911.1
assure
    convince 500.15
    make sure 512.11
    depose 521.5
    promise 768.4
    guarantee 770.11
    comfort 885.6
    give hope 886.10
    embolden 891.16
I ASSURE YOU
    believe me 500.27
    I'll warrant 521.10
assured

convinced 500.18
    sure 512.20,21
    guaranteed 770.14
    poised 856.13
    hopeful 886.11
BE ASSURED 500.27
assuredly
    positively 34.21
    certainly 512.23
    yes 520.18
Assyrian 123.6
Astarte fertility 164.5
    moon 374.9
    beauty 898.9
    Love 929.8
    god 1012.11
asteism 965.5
astereognosis 536.2
asteridians,
    Asteriidae 414.7
asterisk 670.13
asterism 374.12
astern
    advs. abaft 240.13
    aft 274.73
    rearward 294.13
    interjs. 274.81
asteroid 374.6
asteroidal 374.25
Asteroidea,
    Asterozoa 414.7
asthenia 159.1
asthenic 159.12
asthma 684.25
astigmatic 439.11
astigmatism 439.1
astir
    adjs. 705.18
    advs. 718.24
astonish 918.5
astonished 918.8
astonishing
    remarkable 34.10
    amazing 918.11
astonishment 918.1,2
astound appall 889.18
    astonish 918.5
astounded
    horrified 889.25
    astonished 918.8
astounding
    frightful 889.29
    astonishing 918.11
astoundment 918.1
astraddle 215.26
Astraea 974.5
astral
    nouns 1015.1
    adjs. 374.25
astral body 1032.19,20
astral influences 638.2
astral plane 376.1
astral spirit 1015.1
astray
    adjs. bewildered
        513.22
    erroneous 517.14
    advs. abroad 198.19
    amiss 312.7
    wrong 517.18
GO ASTRAY

stray 290.4
    fall short 312.4
    err 517.8
    digress 591.9
    miscarry 723.14
    be wicked 979.13
    misbelieve 1023.8
GO ASTRAY FROM
    810.5
LEAD ASTRAY
    mislead 616.15
    seduce 987.20
astriction
    fastening 47.3
    contraction 197.1
astride 215.26
astringency
    acrimony 160.4
    contraction 197.1
    acidity 431.2
    pungency 432.1
    sternness 755.1
    harshness 937.9
astringent
    nouns 197.6
    adjs. acrimonious
        160.12
    styptic 197.11
    acid 431.7
    pungent 432.6
    stern 755.5
    penetrating 855.32
    harsh 937.22
astringent bitters
    astringent 197.6
    bitterness 428.2
astroalchemist 374.23
astrochemist 374.22
astrochemistry 374.19
astrodiagnosis 374.20
astrography, astrogeny,
    astrogony 374.19
astrolabe 250.4
astrologer,
    astrologian 374.23
astrological,
    astrologous 374.25
astrology 374.20
astromancer 374.23
astromancy 374.20
astronaut 281.8
astronautical 281.16
astronautics 281
astronavigate 281.15
astronavigation 281.1
astronomer 374.22
astronomical
    tremendous 34.11
    large 194.16
    celestial 374.25
astronomical figure
    86.1
astronomy 374.19
astrophotographer
    374.22
astrophotography,
    astrophotometry
    374.19
astrophysical 324.3
astrophysicist
    physicist 324.2

attaintment, attainture
  1006.2
attar, attar of roses
  435.2
attemper 162.6
attempt
  nouns 712.2
  verbs ~ the
    impossible 509.5
  endeavor 712.5
  presume 959.6
attend
  verbs accompany
    73.7
  escort 73.8
  ensue 117.2
  result 153.5
  be present at 185.8
  listen 447.11
  heed 528.6
  ~ school 562.11
  doctor 687.33
  look after 697.18
  serve 748.14
  help 783.18
ATTEND TO
  listen 447.11
  pay attention 528.5
  ~ business 528.8;
    65~.9
  look after 697.18
  ~ orders 764.2
  punish 1008.11
  interj. 447.17
attendance
  accompaniment
    73.5
  presence 185.4
  service 748.13
attendant
  nouns
  accompaniment
    73.3
  accompanier 73.4
  attender 185.5
  follower 292.2
  medical ~ 686.5
  servant 748.4
  confederate 785.1,6
  adjs. accompanying
    73.9
  subsequent 117.3
  present 185.12
  serving 748.15
attender
  frequenter 185.5
  spectator 441
  audience 447.6
  theatergoer 609.42
attending
  accompanying 73.9
  serving 748.15
attention
  nouns hearing 447.1,2
  heed 528
  care 531
  courtesy 934.6
COME TO ATTENTION
  528.14
PAY ATTENTION
  attend to 528.5

heed 528.8
take care 531.7
keep one's eyes
  open 531.8
PAY ATTENTIONS TO
  court 930.19
  pay respects 934.12
PAY NO ATTENTION
  529.3
PAY NO ATTENTION TO
  disobey 765.6
  snub 964.6
  interjs. listen! 447.17
  hark! 528.22
attentive
  listening 447.15
  heedful 528.15
  careful 531.10
  meticulous 531.12
  watchful 531.13
  alert 531.14
  courteous 934.14
  considerate 936.17
  respectful 962.8
attentiveness
  attention 528.1
  alertness 531.5
  obedience 764.1
  considerateness
    936.3
attenuate
  verbs reduce 39.8
  weaken 159.10
  dilute 159.11
  thin 204.11
  rarefy 354.5
  adjs. thin 204.15
  fine 350.8
  rare 354.7
attenuated
  diluted 159.19
  thin 204.15
  emaciated 204.19
  fine 350.8
  rare 354.7
attenuation
  decrease 39.1
  weakening 159.5
  thinness 204.4
  emaciation 204.6
  rarification 354.2
attest
  nouns testimony
    504.3
  deposition 521.2
  verbs evidence 504.9
  testify 504.10
  authenticate 504.12
  depose 521.5
  indicate 566.16
attestable 504.21
attestation
  proof 504.3,5
  deposition 521.2
  certificate 568.5
attestator, attester,
  attestor 504.7
attested 504.22
Attic simple 45.5
  elegant 587.6
  witty 879.15

tasteful 895.8
attic garret 191.16
  head 210.5
Atticism, Attic salt
  elegant style 587.1
  wit 879.1
Atticist 587.4
Attic wit 879.1
attire
  nouns 230.1
  verbs 230.38
attired 230.44
attitude posture 183.4
  viewpoint 438.7
  opinion 500.4
  mental ~ 523.1
TAKE THE ATTITUDE
  523.6
attitudinal 183.20
attitudinarian 901.8
attitudinize 901.13
attorney 1001.1
attract pull 287.4
  interest 528.12
  lure 648.5
  enamor 929.20
ATTRACT ATTENTION
  catch attention
    528.11
  be ostentatious
    902.12
attractant 287.2
attracted 528.16
attracting 287.5
attraction
  pulling power 287.1
  magnetism 341.7
  electric ~ 341.9
  headline ~ 610.5
  allurement 648.1
attractive
  attracting 287.5
  desirable 632.31
  alluring 648.7
  beautiful 898.16
attractiveness
  attraction 287.1
  desirability 632.13
  allurement 648.1
  delightfulness 861.2
  beauty 898.1
attractor
  attractant 287.2
  lure 648.2
attrahent
  nouns 287.2
  adjs. 287.5
attributable
  ascribable 154.5
  due to 958.10
attribute
  nouns characteristic
    80.3
  part of speech 584.2
  verbs 154.2
attribution 154
attributive
  nouns 584.2
  adjs. 584.13
attrition
  abrasion 349.2

contrition 871.1
attritus 360.5
attune
  nouns 461.3
  verbs adjust 26.13
  tune 461.36,37
  fit 718.8
attuned 461.50
ATTUNED TO 640.17
attunement
  adjustment 26.4
  harmony 461.3
aubade 461.13
auburn
  reddish-brown
    366.4
  red-haired 367.11
Aucassin and
  Nicolette 929.16
auchenium 48.5
au courant 474.18
auction
  nouns 827.4
  verbs 827.11
auctioneer
  nouns 828.8
  verbs 827.11
aud 190.15
audacious
  defiant 791.8
  daring 891.21
  foolhardy 892.9
  insolent 911.8
audacity
  defiance 791.1
  daring 891.6
  foolhardiness 892.3
  insolence 911.1
audible 449.15
audience
  hearing 447.2
  listeners 447.6
  interview 595.6
audio 447.14
audioemission 344.4
audio-frequency
  343.31
audiophile 343.25
audio-visual 447.14
audit
  nouns 843.6
  verbs check 87.14
  verify 512.12
  ~ accounts 843.9
audition
  hearing 447.1,2
  examination 484.3
  tryout 488.3
  interview 595.6
auditor listener 447.5
  student 564.1
  comptroller 746.1
  accountant 843.7
auditorium
  hall 190.15
  theater 609.19
auditory
  nouns 447.6
  adjs. hearing 447.14
  audible 449.15
auditory canal 447.7

nouns 484.9
verbs 484.31
autorotation 277.12
autosome 405.11
autostrada 655.6
autosuggestion
  psychology 688.6
  hypnotism 710.8
autotelegram 558.16
autotelegraphy 558.3
autotheism 1018.5
autotype
  nouns 576.7
  verbs 501.13
autotypy
  engraving 576.2
  printing 601.1
autumn
  nouns old age 126.5
  season 128.4
  adjs. 128.8
autumnal 128.8
autumnal equinox
  season 128.7
  astronomy 374.16
auxiliaries
  reinforcements
    787.8
  army 798.24
auxiliary
  nouns nonessential
    6.2
  confederate 785.1
  adjs. extrinsic 6.4
  additional 40.9
  assistant 783.20
avail
  nouns use 663.4
  expedient 668.2
  good 672.4
  OF NO AVAIL 667.9
  verbs suffice 659.4
  be of use 663.17
  benefit 672.11
  help 783.11
AVAIL ONESELF OF
  improve the
    occasion 129.9
  make use of 663.14
availability
  accessibility 508.3
  utility 663.3
available
  vacant 186.14
  attainable 508.8
  handy 663.19
  obtainable 809.12
avails gains 809.3
  receipts 842.1
avalanche
  nouns 314.4
  verbs 314.9
avania 344.10
avant-courier 66.1
avant-garde 239.2
avarice 632.8
avaricious 632.28
avast! cease 144.13
  navigation 274.79
avatar 139.2

avatars of Vishnu
  1012.8
avaunt! 308.28
Ave, Ave Maria
  1030.4
ave! 966.22
avenge 954.4
avengement 954.1
avenger 954.3
avenging 954.6
avenging spirit
  1014.11
avenue outlet 302.9
  passageway 655.4
  road 655.6
aver affirm 521.4
  state 592.15
average
  nouns mean 32.1
  generality 79.3
  ON AN AVERAGE
  all in all 32.5
  generally 79.15
  verbs strike a balance
    32.2
  sell stock 831.24
  adjs. mean 32.3
  mediocre 678.9
averment
  testimony 504.3
  affirmation 521.1
  remark 592.4
Avernus 1017.3
averroist(ic) 499.11
averse 621.5
AVERSE TO 865.8
aversion
  unwillingness 621.1
  repugnance 865.2
  hatred 928.1,3
avert turn aside 290.6
  prevent 728.14
AVERT THE EYES
  438.21
Aves 414.11
Avesta 1019.6
avgas 379.4
avian 413.45
aviary 190.20
aviate 277.42
aviation
  aeronautics 277.1
  air service 798.29,30
aviator
  astronaut 278.1
  air force 798.29
aviatorial 277.55
aviatrix, aviatress,
    aviatrice 278.2
avichi, avici 1017.1
avicular 413.45
avid greedy 632.28
  eager 633.9
avidity greed 632.8
  eagerness 633.1
aviette 279.12
avigate 277.42
avigation 277.4
avigator 278.4
avion 279.1
avionics aviation 277.2

electronics 342.1
aviso
  information 555.3
  news 556.1
  warning 701.1
avocation 654.7
avocational 654.17
avoid shun 629.6
  repeal 777.2
  snub 964.7
  abstain 990.7
AVOID ONE'S GAZE
  438.21
avoidable 629.13
avoidance evasion 629
  abstinence 990.2
avoidless 637.15
avoirdupois 351.1
avouch
  bear witness 504.10
  vouch 521.5
  promise 768.4
avouchment
  testimony 504.3
  deposition 521.2
  promise 768.1
avow
  nouns deposition
    521.2
  promise 768.1
  verbs acknowledge
    520.11
  vouch 521.5
  confess 554.7
  allege 647.3
  promise 768.4
avowal
  acknowledgment
    520.3
  deposition 521.2
  confession 554.3
  promise 768.1
avowed
  acknowledged
    520.14
  alleged 647.4
avulse 304.9
avulsion
  severance 49.2
  extraction 304.1
avuncular 11.7
await come 121.6
  be imminent 151.2
  wait for 537.6
awake
  verbs come to 406.7
  wake up 711.4
  excite 855.11
AWAKE THE DEAD
  452.6
  adjs. clear-witted
    466.13
  alert 531.14
  unsleeping 711.7
AWAKE TO 474.16
BECOME AWAKE TO
  555.13
awaken come to 406.7
  disillusion 519.2
  provoke 646.19
  wake up 711.4

excite 855.11
AWAKEN TO 555.13
awakening
  disillusionment
    519.1
  waking 711.2
award
  nouns verdict 493.5
  gift 816.4
  trophy 914.2
  verbs pass judgment
    493.13
  give 816.12
aware sensible 421.12
  cognizant 474.15
BE AWARE OF
  sense 421.7
  know 474.12
BECOME AWARE OF
  555.13
awareness
  sensation 421.1
  consciousness 474.2
awash floating 274.64
  flooded 391.17
away
  adjs. absent 186.9
  distant 198.8
  vanished 446.4
  escaped 630.10
  advs. elsewhere
    186.17
  at a distance 198.15
  apart 198.18
  aside 241.10
  hence 300.21
  in reserve 658.17
KEEP AWAY FROM
  keep one's distance
    198.7
  avoid 629.6
  preps. deducted 42.13
  back 294.13
  interjs. 308.28
awe
  nouns dread 889.1
  wonder 918.1
  reverence 962.1
IN AWE
  fearfully 889.32
  in wonder 918.16
  verbs frighten 889.16
  daunt 889.17
  astonish 918.5
aweather 241.9
aweigh 274.65
awe-inspiring
  awful 889.29
  magnificent 902.21
  wonderful 918.10
aweless See awless
awesome
  awe-inspiring
    889.29
  awed 918.8
  wonderful 918.10
  reverential 962.9
  sacred 1024.7
awe-struck
  fear-struck 889.25
  astonished 918.8

awful
 adjs. great 34.12
  silent 450.11
  terrible 673.9
  unpleasant 862.10
  fearful 889.29
  hideous 897.11
  impressive 902.21
  awed 918.8
  wonderful 918.10
  reverent 962.9
  venerable 962.12
  sacred 1024.7
 advs. exceedingly
  34.25
  terribly 673.14
awhile 111.9
awkward
  pregnant 168.18
  bulky 194.19
  inelegant 588.3
  inconvenient 669.7
  unwieldy 729.18
  clumsy 732.20
  embarrassing
   862.12
awkward age 124.7
awkwardness
  pregnancy 168.6
  bulkiness 194.9
  inconvenience 669.3
  unwieldiness 729.8
  clumsiness 732.3
awkward squad
  clumsiness 732.9
  recruits 798.17
awless, aweless
  fearless 891.19
  brazen 911.10
  unastonished 919.3
  irreverent 963.5
awn 229.9
awned 229.25
awning 227.2
awny 229.25
A.W.O.L. 186.4,11
awry
 adjs. disorderly 62.12
  askew 218.14
  faulty 517.14
 advs. 218.23
ax 1009.5
axe, the 308.5
axial 225.12
axiom 516.2
axiomatic 516.6
axis center 225.2
  fulcrum 286.3
  axle 320.5
  stem 410.19
  alliance 786.1
axle 320.5
axle box 320.6
axletree 320.5
ayah nursemaid 697.7
  maidservant 748.8
aye
 nouns pro 481.14
  assent 520.2
  vote 635.5
 advs. forever 112.12

yes 520.18
aye, aye! 274.79
Azazel 1014.5
azimuth horizon 213.4
  direction 289.3
azimuth circle 212.2
azoic 381.5
azote 1009.1
Azrael death 407.3
  angel 1013.4
azteca 833.9
azure
 nouns blue 371.1
  sky 374.2
 verbs 371.2
 adjs. 371.3
azurean, azure-blue
  371.3
azygous 89.9
azzle out of 631.5

B

ba 1032.17
Baal fertility 164.5
  god 1012.11
  idol 1031.3
baas 747.1
Bab 1020.3
Babbitt 82.2
Babbittry 643.1
babble
 nouns trickle 394.7
  nonsense 545.4
  gossip 556.7
  chatter 594.3
 verbs trickle 394.19
  burble 451.11
  be insane 472.19
  twaddle 545.8
  blab 554.6
  gossip 556.12
  chatter 594.6
babbler dotard 470.9
  gossip 556.9
  chatterer 594.5
babbling
 nouns 554.2
 adjs. rippling 451.19
  feeble-minded
   468.22
  delirious 472.30
babe girl 125.6
  infant 125.7
  unsophisticate
   734.3
  endearment 930.5
  innocent 982.4
Babel 62.5
bablative 594.9
baboo mister 419.7
  recorder 569.1
  scribe 600.14
baboo English 578.8
baboon 897.4
baby
 nouns youngling
  125.1
  girl 125.6
  infant 125.7
  weakling 159.6

miniature 195.5
  childish person
   470.10
  coward 890.5
  endearment 930.5
 verbs 166.19
 adjs. babyish 124.12
  diminutive 195.11
baby bond 832.4
baby bunting 125.7
baby carriage 271.6
baby grand 464.13
babyhood 124.5
babyish, babish
  infant 124.12
  puerile 468.24
babyism 581.7
baby kisser 744.9
baby linen 230.30
Babylon 979.11
Babylonian 123.6
Babylonian sibyl
  541.6
baby-sit 697.18
baby sitter 697.7
baby-sized 195.11
baccalaureate, bac-
  calaureus 915.6
baccalaureate service
  644.4
baccate 389.6
baccer 433.1
bacchanal,
  bacchanalian
  drinking bout 994.5
  tippler 994.10
bacchanalia 994.5
Bacchus
  drinking 994.2
  liquor 994.12
  god 1012.5
bach
 nouns 932.3
 verbs 932.5
bachelor degree 915.6
  knight 916.6
  celibate 932.3
bachelor girl 932.4
bachelorhood 932.1
bachelorlike 932.7
bachelor's wife 931.9
back
 nouns support 215.2
  background 232.2
  rear 240.1
  anatomy 240.3
 BACK TO BACK
  behind 240.12
  side by side 241.12
  co-operatively 784.9
 ON ONE'S BACK
  helpless 157.18
  recumbent 213.9
 ON THE BACK OF
  215.26
 THE BACK OF BEYOND
  198.4,9
 WITH ONE'S BACK TO
  THE WALL
  cornered 729.23
  at bay 797.16

 verbs support 215.22
  carry 270.11
  reverse 294.7
  mount 313.12
  bet on 514.19
  sponsor 770.11
  second 783.13
  finance 834.15
 BACK AND FILL
  fluctuate 141.5
  sail 274.32
  alternate 322.12
  vacillate 625.8
 BACK AWAY 294.7
 BACK DOWN
  withdraw 294.6
  recant 626.9
  yield 763.7
  consent 773.4
 BACK OFF 294.7
 BACK OUT
  retreat 294.6
  recant 626.9
  withdraw 631.5
  lose courage 890.8
 BACK THE WRONG
  HORSE
  err 517.10
  mismanage 732.14
 BACK UP
  support 215.22
  reverse 294.7
  encourage 646.21
  second 783.13
 BACK WATER
  retard 269.9
  go astern 274.36
  reverse 294.7
  recant 626.9
 adjs. in past 119.9
  late 132.15
  back-country 181.8
  rear 240.8
  reversed 294.12
 advs. in return 33.7
  ago 119.12
  backward 294.13
  in reserve 658.17
 BACK AND FORTH
  reciprocally 13.14
  variably 141.8
  interchangeably
   149.7
  to and fro 322.20
 BACK OF 783.27
 GET IN BACK OF
  783.13
 interjs. 274.81
backache 423.5
back answer
  retort 485.1
  gibe 965.2
backbite 969.11
backbiter 969.6
backbiting 969.3
backbone
  mainstay 215.2
  pluck 622.3
  courage 891.5
 TO THE BACKBONE
  56.17

bad time 130.2
bad times 727.6
bad turn 937.13
Baedeker 746.9
baffle
  nouns muffler 450.4
  quandary 513.3
  verbs perplex 513.13
  disappoint 539.2
  thwart 728.15
baffled
  perplexed 513.23
  disappointed 539.5
bafflegab
  doubletalk 545.4
  jargon 578.6
  officialese 742.40
bafflement
  perplexity 513.3
  disappointment 539.1
  defeat 725.2
  frustration 728.3
baffling
  perplexing 513.24
  frustrating 728.20
baft abaft 240.13
  astern 274.73
bag
  nouns sack 192.2
  belly 192.3
  droop 214.2
  purse 834.14
  strumpet 987.14
  IN THE BAG
  assured 512.20
  prearranged 639.5
  verbs load 183.16
  sag 214.6
  sack 235.9
  bulge 255.10
  secure 809.7
  catch 820.14
  steal 822.13
bag and baggage
  808.3
bagatelle 671.5
baggage
  types of ~ 192.22
  freight 270.7
  belongings 808.3
  strumpet 987.14
baggage car 271.13
baggage check 833.12
baggage man 273.13
baggage train 271.12
baggy, bagging
  loose 51.5
  sagging 214.10
  bulging 255.14
bagman 828.5
bagnio
  bathhouse 679.8
  prison 759.7
  brothel 987.9
bag of bones 204.8
bag of tricks
  acting device 609.9
  deception 616.6
bagpipe
  nouns 464.10

verbs 461.43
BAGPIPE A SAIL
  274.22
bags
  large amount 34.3
  types of ~ 192.20
baguio 402.15
bah! nonsense! 469.12
  contempt 964.10
bahadur 915.3
baignoire 609.19
bail
  nouns ladle 192.7
  security 770.2
  GO BAIL 770.12
  GO BAIL ON
  rely on 500.13
  be certain 512.9
  vouch 521.5
  verbs 270.16
  BAIL OUT
  parachute 277.53
  escape 630.6
bailie 747.19
bailiff
  constable 697.14
  steward 746.3
  official 747.20
bailiwick
  district 179.5
  bureau 998.4
bailsman 770.8
bairagi See vairagi
Bairam 137.12
bairn 125.3
bait
  nouns fulcrum 286.3
  lunch 306.7
  snare 616.12
  lure 648.2
  verbs inveigle 648.4
  harass 864.19
  BAIT THE HOOK
  trap 616.20
  lure 648.4
  fish 653.10
bake
  nouns 876.4
  verbs be hot 327.21
  cook 329.4
  dry 392.6
  fire 574.6
baked cooked 329.6
  dried 392.9
bakehead
  trainman 273.13
  seaman 275.6
  dolt 470.4
bakehouse 329.3
baker's dozen 99.7
baker's legs 272.16
bakery kitchen 329.3
  store 830.6
bakeshop 830.6
baking
  nouns 329.1
  verbs 327.25
baksheesh bribe 649.2
  gratuity 816.5
bal 877.2
balalaika 464.2

balance
  nouns equality 30.1
  average 32.1
  offset 33.2
  remainder 43.1
  stability 142.1
  symmetry 247.1
  sanity 471.1
  comparison 490.3
  painting 572.10
  euphony 587.2
  surplus 661.5
  ~ of accounts 843.2
  equanimity 856.3
  IN THE BALANCE
  513.16
  OFF BALANCE 31.5
  verbs even 17.4
  equal 30.6
  equalize 30.7
  counterbalance 33.5
  check accounts
  87.14
  stabilize 142.8
  symmetrize 247.4
  weigh 351.10
  measure 489.11
  compare 490.4
  debate 625.7
  BALANCE ACCOUNTS
  843.8
  BALANCE THE BOOKS
  check 87.14
  accounting 843.8
balanced equable 17.5
  equiponderant
  30.10
  symmetrical 247.5
  measured 489.14
  euphonious 587.8
  self-possessed
  856.13
  just 974.8
balance of power
  737.5
balance of trade 825.1
balance sheet 843.4
balancing
  nouns offsetting 33.1
  symmetrization
  247.3
  weighing 351.9
  comparison 490.1
  adjs. 33.6
balanoplasty 687.27
balcony gallery 191.22
  platform 215.13
  theater ~ 609.19
bal costumé 877.2
bald bare 231.14
  hairless 231.17
  open 264.17
  unconcealed 553.9
  dull 881.6
  unadorned 900.8
baldachin 1040.10
bald eagle 413.34
Balder beauty 898.9
  god 1012.6
balderdash
  nonsense 545.2

bombast 599.2
bald fact 1.3
bald-headed 231.17
bald-headed row
  609.19
baldly 231.19
baldness
  hairlessness 231.4
  dullness 881.1
  unadornment 900.3
baldpate 231.4
baldric belt 252.3
  zodiac 252.3
baldy 231.4
bale
  nouns bundle 74.7
  load 193.2
  burden 351.7
  woe 864.6
  verbs 74.19
baleen 357.3
balefire 327.12
  signal 566.14
baleful
  inauspicious 542.15
  harmful 673.12
balefully 34.25
balefulness 673.5
balistraria 797.4
balk
  nouns blunder 517.5
  disappointment
  539.1
  fallow land 719.5
  defeat 725.2
  hindrance 728.3
  verbs disappoint
  539.2
  be unwilling 621.3
  be obstinate 624.7
  thwart 728.15
Balkan 417.10
balked 539.5
balker 413.16
balkiness 624.4
balking
  nouns 728.3
  adjs. stickling 621.7
  obstinate 624.12
balky stickling 621.7
  obstinate 624.12
ball
  nouns sphere 254.2
  types of ~ 254.13
  missile 799.14
  dance 877.2
  HIT THE BALL
  begin 68.6
  be active 705.13
  work hard 714.13
  KEEP THE BALL
  ROLLING
  persevere 623.2
  be industrious
  705.14
  ON THE BALL 528.15
  verbs 254.7
  BALL THE JACK
  268.9
  BALL UP
  complicate 46.3

confuse 63.3
fluster 530.7
ballad
nouns song 461.13
poem 607.4
verbs 461.39
ballad born 464.8
ballad maker, ballader
composer 463.22
poet 507.13
ballad opera 461.35
ballad poetry 607.2
ballad singer 463.14
ballad writer 463.22
ball-and-socket joint
47.4
ballast
nouns counterbalance
33.2
weight 351.4
money 833.2
equanimity 856.3
verbs stabilize 142.8
weight 351.12
ballata 461.13
ball bearing 320.7
balled up
complex 46.4
disordered 62.15
confused 530.12
ballerina 877.3
ballet music 461.35
dance 877.1,2
ballet d'action 461.35
ballet dancer 877.3
ballet divertissement
461.35
ballet girl 877.3
ballista 799.19
ballistic 284.16
ballistic missile 280.2
ballistics 799.3
Ballistite 799.9
ballon 279.11
ballonet ceiling
277.38
balloon
nouns tire 252.4
aircraft 279.11
types of ~ 279.18
verbs expand 196.5
aviate 277.42
BALLOON IN 277.49
ballooner 278.7
ballooning 277.1
ballooning in 277.15
balloonist 278.7
ballot
nouns vote 635.5
political ~ 742.20
verbs 635.15
ballot box 742.21
ballot-box stuffer
742.24
ballot-box stuffing
616.8
balloter 742.24
ballplayer 876.20
ballproof 158.18
ballroom 877.4
bally 34.26

ballyhack 691.1
ballyhoo
nouns noise 452.3
publicity 557.4
publicist 557.9
sales talk 827.5
verbs 557.15
ballyhooer
publicist 557.9
solicitor 828.7
ballyhoo man
publicist 557.9
theaterman 609.27
solicitor 828.7
ballywack, ballywrack
691.1
balm mitigator 162.3
ointment 379.3
perfume 435.2
medicine 685.4
lotion 685.9
types of ~ 685.45
POUR BALM INTO
calm 162.7
pacify 802.7
relieve 884.5
balminess 472.2
Balm of Gilead 435.2
balmy
nouns 710.2
adjs. fragrant 435.9
insane 472.25
healing 685.35
relieving 884.9
drunk 994.40
**balneae, balnearium,
balneary** 679.10
balneation
swimming 274.11
bathing 679.6
balneum 679.8
baloney
nouns nonsense
545.3
humbug 614.14
interjs. 469.12
balourdise 732.5
balsa 276.11
balsam perfume 435.2
medicine 685.4
balsamic
remedial 685.35
relieving 884.9
Balthasar 467.5
baluster 216.4
balustrade
balusters 216.4
fence 235.4
balustrading
balusters 216.4
fence 235.4
bam sham 614.13
deception 616.7
bambino infant 125.7
icon 1038.11
bamboo cane 377.4
plant 410.5
bamboo curtain
frontier 234.5
secrecy 612.3
communism 743.4

bamboo English
578.10
bamboozle
nouns 616.1
verbs baffle 513.13
deceive 616.13
bamboozled 513.23
bamboozlement 616.1
bamboozler 617.1
ban
nouns
prohibition 776.1
ostracism 924.2
malediction 970.1
PUT UNDER THE BAN
prohibit 776.3
ostracize 924.5
verbs outlaw 308.16
prohibit 776.3
ostracize 924.5
banal 881.9
banality cliché 516.3
triteness 881.3
banally 881.11
band
nouns company 74.3
strip 205.4
cincture 252.3
frequency ~ 343.16
striation 373.5
orchestra 463.12
line 566.5
bandage 685.28
verbs join 47.5
bind 47.9
~ together 52.4
encircle 232.7
striate 373.7
bandage
nouns wrapper
227.19
gag 450.4
dressing 685.28
verbs bind 47.9
blindfold 440.6
~ wounds 687.33
bandaging
wrapping 227.19
dressing 685.28
bandeau 230.24
banded 373.15
banded together
47.13
banderol, banderole
567.6
bandied about 556.15
bandit thief 823.4
thug 941.4
banditry 822.12
bandmaster 463.19
Band of Hope 990.5
bandog 697.10
bandonion 464.12
bandore 464.4
bandsman 463.3
bandstand 609.20
bandurria 464.4
bandwagon 609.20
GET ON THE BAND-
WAGON
concur 520.9

be fashionable
642.10
politics 742.44
attach oneself
905.10
bandy
verbs 149.4
adjs. bandy-legged
248.12
bowed 251.10
bandying 557.1
bandy-legged 248.12
BANDY ABOUT 557.10
BANDY WITH 794.18
bandy words
argue 481.17
converse 595.8
bane evil 673.3
curse 674.1
vexation 864.2
baneful 673.12
bang
nouns energy 160.2
blow 282.4
report 455.1,3
thrill 855.2
IN A BANG 113.9
verbs coiffure 229.22
shut 265.6
collide 282.13
strike 282.14,15
crack 455.6,8
BANG INTO 282.13
advs. suddenly 113.9
slam-bang 455.13
interjs. 455.14
banger
big thing 194.11
falsehood 614.12
coin 833.4
banging great 34.13
huge 194.21
cracking 455.11
bangle 899.6
bang-off 113.8
bangtail 413.19
bang-up 672.14
banian 990.4
banish 308.16
banishment 308.4
banister 216.4
banjo, banjer 464.4
banjoist 463.5
banjorine 464.4
**banjo-ukelele,
banjo-uke** 464.4
bank
nouns series 71.2
heap 74.9
shoal 209.2
buttress 215.4
incline 218.4
quarry 382.6
shore 384.2
stakes 514.4
barrier 728.5
fortification 797.4
treasury 834.13
verbs row 71.6
heap 74.18
slope 218.10

aviate 277.46
~ a fire 328.21
store 658.10
embank 797.9
BANK ON
rely on 500.13
plan on 651.6
BANK UP 74.18
bank acceptance
833.11
bank account
funds 833.14
account 837.2
bank balance 837.2
bankbook 843.4
bank clerk 834.10
banker
moneylender 818.3
financier 834.10
bank examiner 843.7
bank holiday 709.4
banking
aviation 277.10
finance 834.4
banking syndicate
831.15
bank note 833.6
bank robber 823.3
bank robbery 822.3
bank roll
money 833.16
finance 834.15
bankrupt
nouns 840.4
verbs ruin 840.8
impoverish 836.6
adjs. destitute 836.9
insolvent 840.11
BANKRUPT IN 660.11
bankruptcy 840.3
bank stock 832.2
banlieues, banlieus
232.1
banned 776.7
banner
nouns headline 483.2
poster 557.7
flag 567.6
adjs. 36.16
banneret flag 567.6
knight 916.6
banner line 483.2
bannerman 557.9
banns 768.3
banquet
nouns feast 306.9
treat 863.3
festival 876.4
verbs feast 306.22
revel 876.27
banquette 797.4
banshee, banshie
fairy 1012.15
spirit 1015.1
bant 204.12
Bantam 413.35
bantam
nouns 195.4
adjs. 195.11
bantam cock
dandy 901.9

swaggerer 902.10
bantamweight
nouns weight 351.3
pugilist 798.2
adjs. 352.12
banter
nouns pleasantry 880
ridicule 965
verbs tease 880.4
ridicule 965.8
banterer 880.3
bantering
nouns 880.2
adjs. 880.5
Bantingism 204.9
bantingize 204.12
bantling child 125.3
bastard 170.5
banty
nouns diminutive
195.4
Bantam 413.35
adjs. 195.11
banya 990.4
banyan day 993.3
banzai! 923.15
banzai attack, banzai
charge 796.1
baptism
initiation 68.4
immersion 318.2
wetting 391.6
naming 581.2
sacrament 1038.5,7
baptismal
initiative 68.13
sacramental 1038.21
baptismal name 581.4
baptistery font 1038.7
church ~ 1040.9
baptize dilute 159.11
immerse 318.7
name 581.11
administer rite
1038.19
bar
nouns shoal 209.2
counter 215.15
shaft 216.1
obstruction 265.3
pry 286.4
striation 373.5
bear 413.4
music staff 461.29
musical rest 462.21
line 566.5
insignia 567.2,5
type ~ 601.7
barrier 728.5
lock 758.5
bullion 833.19
barroom 994.25
court 999.2
legal profession
1001.5
AT THE BAR, AT BAR
1002.21
BEHIND BARS 759.20
verbs exclude 77.4
fence in 235.7
lock 265.6

close 265.7
striate 373.7
obstruct 728.12
prohibit 776.3
lock out 787.10
BAR THE GATE 698.7
preps. 77.9
baragouin
nonsense 545.4
jargon 578.6
barb
nouns feather 229.17
bristle 260.3
speed 268.7
arrowhead 799.17
verbs 257.10
BARB THE DART
864.14
barbarian
nouns alien 78.3
vulgarian 896.7
savage 941.6
adjs. extraneous 78.5
uncivilized 896.12
barbaric
extraneous 78.5
savage 161.20
uncivilized 896.12
cruel 937.24
barbaric splendor
902.5
barbarism
ignorance 476.8
word 580.6
inelegant style
588.1
vulgarity 896.3
barbarity
vulgarity 896.3
cruelty 937.11,12
barbarous
extraneous 78.5
savage 161.20
inelegant 588.2
uncivilized 896.12
cruel 937.24
barbarously
savagely 161.26
cruelly 937.31
barbarousness
inelegant style
588.1
vulgarity 896.3
cruelty 937.11
barbate 229.25
barbecue
nouns meat 306a.12
picnic 876.4
verbs 329.4
barbecued 329.6
barbecuing 329.1
barbed 257.12
barbed-wire entangle-
ment 797.4
barbel 424.4
bar bell 714.7
barbellate 260.9
barber 898.12
barbershop
shop 717.1
haircutting 898.13

barbican tower 206.11
battlement 797.4
barbicel 229.17
barbigerous
hairy 229.24
bearded 229.25
barbiturate 685.11
barbiturism 640.8
barbouillage 600.8
barbule
filamentule 229.17
feeler 424.4
barcarole 461.13
bard minstrel 463.16
poet 607.13,14
barde 306a.16
Bard of Avon, Bard of
Ayrshire 607.17
bare
verbs divest 231.5
open 264.12
disclose 554.4
adjs. mere 35.9
simple 45.5
vacant 186.12
naked 231.14
open 264.17
exposed 553.9
threadbare 690.30
unadorned 900.8
barebacked 231.16
barebone 204.8
bare-chested 231.16
barefaced bare 231.16
impudent 911.10
barefaced lie 614.12
barefoot 231.15
barehanded
bare 231.16
empty-handed
660.10
bareheaded 231.16
bare-kneed 231.16
barelegged 231.16
barely scarcely 35.12
simply 45.9
narrowly 204.21
nakedly 231.19
bareness
vacancy 186.2
nudity 231.3
unadornment 900.3
bare possibility 155.9
bare-throated 231.16
barfly 994.10
bargain
nouns compact 769.1
transaction 825.5
cheapness 847.3
AT A BARGAIN
for sale 827.14
cheaply 847.10
BE A BARGAIN 825.15
INTO THE BARGAIN
40.10
MAKE A BARGAIN
825.15
STRIKE A BARGAIN
520.10
verbs contract
769.6,7

vulgarity 896.5
servility 905.1
infamy 913.3
wickedness 979.5
base pay 839.4
baser 37.6
bash
nouns 282.4
verbs 282.14
bashara 1036.13
bashaw official 747.18
bashaw See pasha
bashful 906.12
bashfully 906.15
bashfulness 906.4
bashi-bazouk 798.15
basic fundamental 5.8
original 152.16
underlying 211.8
alkaline 378.7
basically 5.10
Basic English 578.1
basic facts 1.4
basichromatin 405.12
basic load 277.27
basic trainer 279.10
basic training 560.3
basilar 211.8
basilica 1040.1
basin
types of ∼ 192.12
bed 211.4
cavity 256.2
plain 386.1
washbasin 679.12
dock 698.6
basing point 832.8
basis cause 152.1
foundation 215.6
starting point 300.5
premise 481.8
motive 646.1
justification 1004.6
WITHOUT BASIS
482.12
bask 328.18
BASK IN 863.10
BASK IN THE
SUNSHINE 726.10
basket
nouns 192.4,19
verbs 235.9
basketball court
876.13
basketry, basketwork
220.3
bas-relief 573.3
bass
nouns voice part
461.22
voice 462.5
singer 463.14
instrument 464.1
adjs. low-toned 453.10
vocal 461.51
Bassalia 208.3
Bassalian 208.13
bass clef 462.13
bass drum 464.21
basset horn 464.9
basset oboe 464.9

bass horn 464.8
bassist 463.14
basso voice 462.5
singer 463.14
bass oboe 464.9
basso buffo 463.14
bassoon 464.9,23
bassoonist 463.4
basso profundo
463.14
bass passage 461.24
bass saxhorn 464.8
bassus 461.22
bass viol 464.5
bass violinist 463.5
Bast 1012.9
bastard
nouns illegitimate
child 170.5
sham 614.13
scoundrel 984.6
adjs. odd 85.11
false 614.27
illegitimate 997.7
bastardism 997.2
bastard type 601.6
bastardy 997.2
baste hit 282.15
cook 329.4
whip 1008.14
bastille, bastile 759.7
bastinado
nouns 1008.4
verbs 1008.14
basting cooking 329.1
whipping 1008.4
bastion
fortification 797.4
stronghold 797.6
bastos 215.19
bat
nouns velocity 268.2
blow 282.4
blindness 440.4
lunatic 472.15
revel 876.6
baseball ∼ 876.16
prostitute 987.16
spree 994.5
BAT OF AN EYE 113.3
BAT OUT OF HELL
268.7
verbs 282.14
BAT AROUND 272.22
BAT OUT 532.9
BAT THE BREEZE
592.12
BAT THE EYES 439.10
GO TO BAT FOR
783.13
batch
nouns quantity 28.2
large amount 34.4
bunch 74.6
accumulation 74.8
amount made 167.4
lump 194.10
verbs 74.17
bate decrease 39.6
reduce 39.8
relax 162.9

discount 845.2
bateau 276.2
bateau bridge 655.10
bated breath 451.4
bath
photography 575.15
bathe 679.7
lavatory 679.8
bathtub 679.12
Bath chair 271.7
bathe
nouns swim 274.11
bath 679.7
verbs swim 274.59
drench 391.13
wash 679.18
medicate 687.33
bathed 391.17
BATHED IN SWEAT
309.20
BATHED IN TEARS
873.17
bather 274.12
bathhouse 679.8
bathing
aquatics 274.11
washing 679.6
bathing beauty 274.12
bathing suit 230.29
bathmism 406.3
bathometry 208.4
bathos
sentimentality 853.7
sadness 870.1
ludicrousness 878.4
bathouse 472.14
bathroom 679.8
baths
meeting place
190.23
bathing place
679.10
health resort 687.31
bathtub radome 345.2
washbasin 679.12
bathtub gin 994.20
bathyal 208.13
bathyal zone 208.3
bathybic 208.13
bathycolpian,
bathycolpic 208.14
bathymetric(al)
deep-sea 208.13
oceanic 396.7
bathymetry
sounding 208.4
ocean 396.5
bathyorographic(al)
deep-sea 208.13
oceanic 396.7
bathypelagic 208.13
bathysmal 208.13
bathysphere 318.5
batik 572.12
batman 657.6
baton scepter 737.8
stigma 913.6
illegitimacy 997.2
Batrachia 414.11
batrachians 414.11
batrachoplasty 687.27

bats 472.25
BATS IN THE BELFRY
472.2
batta 839.6
battalion
company 74.3
military unit 798.19
batten fasten 47.8
secure 142.9
close 265.6
prosper 726.8
eat greedily 992.5
BATTEN DOWN THE
HATCHES
navigation 274.50
take precautions
893.6
BATTEN ON 905.11
BATTEN UPON 306.25
batter
nouns
semiliquid 388.5
ballplayer 876.20
verbs pound 282.15
abuse 665.5
bruise 690.14
thrash 1008.17
battered 690.32
battery
set 74.11
types of ∼ 341.39
percussives 464.20
fortification 797.4
military unit 798.19
artillery 799.6
ballplayers 876.20
beating 1008.4
battiness
foolishness 469.1
insanity 472.2
battle
nouns
struggle 714.3
fight 794.3
list of battles 795.32
BATTLE OF LIFE
705.5
verbs struggle 714.11
oppose 788.5
fight 794.14
wage war 795.19
fortify 797.9
battle cry 566.15
battled
embattled 795.28
fortified 797.12
battledore
elastic 357.3
textbook 603.8
racket 876.16
battledore and
shuttlecock 149.1
battle fatigue 688.17
battlefield 800.2
battleground
casus belli 793.8
battlefield 800.2
battle line 800.2
battlement
serration 261.3
fortification 797.4

battleplane 279.9
battler 798.1
battle royal 794.4
battleship 276.7
battlewagon 276.7
battling
  contending 794.23
  militant 795.26
battological 103.14
battologize 103.8
battology 103.3
battue 653.2
batty foolish 469.8
  insane 472.25
bauble trifle 671.5
  toy 876.16
  trinket 899.4
Baucis and Philemon
  127.4
Baumé gravity 351.5
bavardage
  nonsense 545.4
  chatter 594.3
bavin 330.3
bawbee 833.8
bawd 987.18
bawdiness
  unchastity 987.5
  obscenity 988.4
bawdry
  nouns 988.4
  adjs. unchaste 987.29
  obscene 988.9
bawdyhouse 987.9
bawl
  nouns shout 458.1
  plaint 873.3
  verb shout 458.6
  bellow 459.2
  say 592.17
  wail 873.10,11
BAWL OUT 967.19
bawling
  nouns 873.2
  adjs. vociferous
  458.10
  howling 459.6
bawling-out 967.7
bay
  nouns recess 256.7
  window 264.7
  inlet 398.1
  horse 413.15
  AT BAY
  cornered 729.23
  on the defensive
  797.16
  KEEP AT BAY 797.10
  verbs 459.2
  BAY AT THE MOON
  howl 459.2
  do in vain 667.8
  wail 873.11
  adjs. 366.4
bayadere 877.3
Bayard 413.21
bayard
  nouns horse 413.15
  knight 916.6
  adjs. 366.4
bay-colored 366.4

bayed 398.2
baygall 399.1
bay oil 435.2
bayonet 796.27
AT THE POINT OF THE
  BAYONET 795.29
bayonet legs 272.16
bayou 398.1
bay rum 435.3
bays 914.3
bay window
  belly 192.3
  window 264.7
bazaar, bazar
  sale 827.3
  market 830.2
bazoo 264.5
bazooka 280.11
B.C. 105.13
be 1.8
BE IT SO 520.19
beach
  nouns pebbles 383.3
  shore 384.2
  verbs 274.44
beachcomber
  vagabond 273.3
  wave 394.14
beachhead
  bridgehead 239.2
  stronghold 797.6
beacon
  nouns aviation
  277.16
  fire 327.12
  types of ~ 335.9,10
  radio ~ 343.5
  radar ~ 345.7
  watchtower 438.8
  signal 566.14
  verbs go before 291.2
  shine brightly
  334.23
  give light 334.28
beacon fire fire 327.12
  signal 566.14
beacon station 345.6
bead
  nouns drop 254.3
  sight 442.4
  verbs ball 254.7
  ornament 899.8
beading 234.7
beadle 1036.9
beadledom 742.39
beadlike 254.10
beadroll roll 88.5
  prayers 1030.4
  rosary 1038.11
beads jewelry 899.6
  prayers 1030.4
  rosary 1038.11
bead-shaped 254.10
beadsman 1036.16
beads of sweat 309.7
beady 254.10
beagle
  policeman 697.14
  detective 779.10
beak
  nouns prow 239.3

nose 255.7
spout 395.8
judge 1000.1
verbs 282.17
beaked, beaklike 251.9
be-all 54.3
beam
  nouns breadth 203.1
  shaft 216.3
  types of ~ 216.8
  side 241.1
  ship part 276.26
  aviation 277.16
  ~ of light 334.5
  radio ~ 343.13
  television ~ 344.4
  radar ~ 345.11
  smile 874.3
  ON THE BEAM
  broadside 241.8
  straight 249.7
  hep 474.17
  verbs shine 334.23
  radiobroadcast
  343.28
  radar 345.15
  smile 874.8
  be beautiful 898.15
beam direction 277.22
beaming
  shining 334.30
  cheerful 868.10
  gorgeous 898.19
beam wind 402.12
beamy 334.30
bean head 210.5
  plant 410.4
  seed 410.29
  brain 465.4
  trifle 671.5
  dollar 833.7
beanery 306.14
beanfeast 876.4
beanless 836.10
beano 876.6
bean pole
  skinny person 204.8
  tall person 206.12
beans
  vegetable 306a.35
  money 833.2
  FULL OF BEANS
  healthy 683.6
  gay 868.14
beanstalk 204.8
beany
  nouns 799.19
  adjs. 472.25
bear
  nouns animal 413.4
  proficient 731.11
  speculator 831.12
  surly person 949.11
  verbs produce 166.17
  be situated 183.10
  support 215.22
  wear 230.43
  carry 270.11
  thrust 282.12
  head 289.8
  admit of 508.4

lend support 783.12
cherish 811.7
~ the market
  831.25
afford 841.6
endure 859.5
BEAR A CHARMED
  LIFE
be safe 696.2
be lucky 726.11
BEAR A CHILD 166.19
BEAR AGAINST 754.6
BEAR A GRUDGE 927.9
BEAR A HAND
  help 783.11
  participate 813.5
BEAR AWAY 274.25,32
BEAR DOWN
  depress 316.4
  compel 754.6
BEAR DOWN ON
  sail for 274.37
  approach 295.3
BEAR DOWN ON IT
  be active 705.13
  hurry 707.6
  exert oneself 714.9
  work hard 714.13
BEAR DOWN UPON
  approach 295.3
  compel 754.6
  attack 796.18
BEAR FALSE WITNESS
  falsify 614.21
  accuse falsely
  1003.12
BEAR FOR 289.10
BEAR FRUIT
  bear 166.17
  prosper 726.8
BEAR HARD UPON
  burden 351.13
  oppress 727.8
  compel 754.6
  be severe 755.5
BEAR IN MIND
  think of 477.15
  take cognizance
  528.9
  remember 535.14
BEAR IN WITH THE
  LAND 274.37
BEAR NO RESEM-
  BLANCE 21.2
BEAR OFF
  oblique 218.9
  sail 274.25,31,32
  sail from 274.38
  deviate 290.3
  turn aside 290.6
BEAR OFF THE LAND
  274.39
BEAR ON
  concern 9.3
  rest on 215.23
  weigh on 351.11
BEAR ONE COMPANY
  accompany 73.7
  associate with
  920.15

becharmed 1034.13
bêche-de-mer, beche-
le-mar 578.10
beck stream 394.1
gesture 566.13
call 750.5
AT ONE'S BECK AND
CALL
ready 663.19
subjugated 762.13
at command 764.4
helpful 783.21
Becken 464.20
beckon
nouns 566.13
verbs gesture 566.20
invite 648.5
becloud
darken 336.10
opaque 340.2
cloud 403.7
conceal 613.7
become
come to be 1.12
suit 26.8
originate 68.12
be converted 145.12
behoove 960.4
BECOME OF 153.5
BECOME ONE
beautify 898.14
marry 931.16
becoming fit 26.19
expedient 668.4
tasteful 895.10
comely 898.17
decent 986.5
becripple
disable 157.9
impair 690.15
bed
nouns ocean bottom
208.3
bottom 211.4
foundation 215.6
couch 215.20
types of ~ 215.34
stratum 226.1
flower ~ 412.10
accommodations
657.3
marriage 931.1
BED OF PROCRUSTES
1009.4
BED OF ROSES
prosperity 726.1
comfort 885.1
MAKE ONE'S BED AND
LIE ON IT 1008.23
verbs establish
142.10
lodge 187.11
inset 303.4
plant 412.18
~ down 415.6
go to bed 710.16
put to bed 710.17
bedarken
darken 336.10
blacken 364.7
bedaub smear 227.26

paint 361.14
stain 677.6
soil 680.18
bedaze stupefy 422.3
astonish 918.5
bedazzle
be bright 334.23
blind 440.6
confuse 530.7
astonish 918.5
bedbug 413a.7
bedchamber
bedroom 191.7
toilet 680.14
bedclothes, bedcover
227.11
bedding
foundation 215.6
underbedding
215.21
underlayer 226.1
bedclothes 227.11
bedeck clothe 230.38
adorn 899.7
bedesman 1036.16
bedevil
complicate 46.3
torment 864.19
bewitch 1034.10
bedew 391.12
bedfellow 926.4
bedgown 230.21
bedim 336.11
bedirty 680.17
bedizen
dress up 230.41
adorn 899.7
Bedlam 452.3
bedlam insanity 472.1
madhouse 472.14
bedlamite 472.15
bed linen 227.11
bedmaker 748.8
bedmate 926.4
bedog 292.3
Bedouin nomad 273.4
Arabian 417.3
bedpan 680.14
bedrabble 680.21
bedraggle 680.21
bedraggled 62.14
bedral, bederal 1036.9
bedrape 230.38
bedridden 684.44
bedrock bottom 211.1
foundation 215.6
stone 383.1
DOWN TO BEDROCK
836.7
bedroom 191.7
bedroom eyes 438.5
bedspread 227.11
bed springs 215.21
bedstead 215.20
bedstraw 215.21
bedtime 134.5
bedtime story 606.7
bedust 680.17
bedwarf 39.9
bee insect 413a.4
sociable 920.12

BEE IN THE BONNET
473.2
bee culture 415.1
beef
nouns muscularity
158.2
meat 306a.13
weight 351.1
bovine 413.8
quarrel 793.5
complaint 873.4
verbs blab 554.6
complain 873.13
beef-brained, beef-
headed 468.15
beef cattle 413.8
beefeater guard 697.8
yeoman 798.14
beefiness
muscularity 158.2
corpulence 194.8
beefsteak 306a.18
beef tea 306a.13
beefy muscular 158.14
fleshy 194.18
beehive apiary 415.5
workshop 717.2
beekeeper 415.4
beeline
short cut 202.5
straight line 249.2
Beelzebub 1014.5
beer 994.17
beer garden, beer
parlor 994.25
beerocracy 739.6
beery 994.38
bee sting 674.5
beeswax 379.8
beetle
nouns masher 389.4
bug 413a.2
verbs 214.7
adjs. 214.11
beetle-browed
overhanging 214.11
sullen 949.24
beetle-crusher 211.5
beetlehead 470.4
beetling 214.3
beezer 255.7
beezie-weezies 472.10
befall occur 150.5
chance 155.11
befit suit 26.8
behoove 960.4
befitting fit 26.19
timely 129.10
expedient 668.4
befog dim 336.11
cloud 403.7
conceal 613.7
befool infatuate 469.7
deceive 616.14
before prior to 116.6
formerly 119.10
early 131.11
in the presence of
185.16
in front 239.13
openly 553.15

rather than 635.25
before Christ 105.13
beforehand 131.11
before-mentioned
64.5
beforetime
adjs. 131.7
advs. 119.10
befoul
complicate 46.3
defile 680.19
befoulment 680.4
befriend 783.11
befriender 940.1
befringe 234.10
befuddle
confuse 530.7
inebriate 994.28
befuddlement
confusion 530.3
drunkenness 994.1
beg 772.11,15
BEG FOR MERCY
942.6
BEG LEAVE 772.9
BEG OFF 621.3
BEG PARDON 1010.5
BEG THE QUESTION
quibble 482.9
hedge 629.8
BEG TO DIFFER
520a.4
beg, borrow, or steal
656.4
beget generate 166.15
procreate 168.9
begetter
creator 166.10
parent 169.8
beggar
nouns hobo 273.3
person 416.3
mendicant 772.8
~ on horseback
903.3
wretch 984.2
verbs 836.6
BEGGAR ALL DESCRIP-
TION 898.15
BEGGAR DESCRIPTION
918.7
beggarly paltry 671.18
indigent 836.8
vulgar 896.15
obsequious 905.13
infamous 913.12
beggarly fellow 984.2
beggar's-lice 257.8
beggary
mendicity 772.6
indigence 836.2
begging
nouns 772.6
adjs. 772.16
begging hermit
1036.17
begging of the
question 482.5
begild paint 361.14
yellow 369.3
begin 68.6

beginner
  inaugurator 166.10
  novice 564.7
beginning
  commencement 68
  source 152.5
BEGINNING AND END
  54.3
BEGINNING OF THE
  END 70.3
IN THE BEGINNING
  68.16
MAKE A NEW
  BEGINNING 143.6
begird 232.7
begirt 232.12
beglerbeg, beylerbey
  747.14
begone
  verbs 300.9
  interjs. 308.28
begrime 680.17
begrudge
  be unwilling 621.3
  refuse 774.4
  stint 850.7
  envy 952.3
beguile deceive 616.13
  fascinate 648.6
  spend 663.13
  amuse 876.23
BEGUILE OF, BEGUILE
  OUT OF 616.18
BEGUILE THE TIME
  do nothing 704.2
  amuse oneself
  876.24
beguiler 617.1
béguin 632.1
begum empress 747.12
  princess 916.9
behalf interest 663.4
  good 672.4
IN BEHALF OF
  instead of 148.12
  in support of 783.26
behave 735.4
BEHAVE ILL 736.4
BEHAVE ONESELF
  735.4,5
behavior
  psychological ~
  688.41
  conduct 735
BE ON ONE'S BEST
  BEHAVIOR 735.5
behaviorism
  psychology 688.2
  behavior 735.2
behaviorist 735.7
behavior psychology
  psychology 688.2
  behaviorism 735.2
behead 1008.19
beheader 1008.8
beheading 1008.7
behemoth 194.14
behest 750.1
behind
  nouns rear 240.1
  rump 240.4

adjs. retarded 269.12
  after 292.6
advs. late 132.18
  in back of 240.12
  in arrears 312.6
  in reserve 658.17
BEHIND ONE'S BACK
  behind 240.12
  surreptitiously
  612.20
preps. later than 117.7
  supporting 783.27
behindhand
  adjs. mistimed 115.3
  late 132.15
  unfortunate 727.14
  defaulting 840.10
  advs. late 132.18
  in arrears 312.6
behold
  verbs 438.12
  interjs. 528.22
beholden
  grateful 947.5
  obliged 960.15
beholder 441.1
behoof interest 663.4
  good 672.4
behoove 960.4
beige 369.4
beignet 306a.43
being
  nouns existence 1.1
  thing 3.3
  organism 405.2
  person 416.3
GIVE BEING TO
  166.15
  adjs. existent 1.13
  present 120.2
BEING AS HOW 154.8
BEING DONE
  fashionable 642.11
  conventional 643.7
NOT BEING DONE 83.8
bejewel 899.8
Bel 1012.11
belabor 1008.14
belated 132.15
belaud 966.12
belay fasten 47.9
  cease 144.6
BELAY THAT!, BELAY
  THERE!
  cease 144.13
  navigation 274.79
  silence! 450.16
belch
  nouns
  eructation 308.9
  small beer 994.17
  verbs erupt 161.12
  eructate 308.25
beldam, beldame
  crone 127.3
  violent person 161.9
  vixen 941.8
  shrew 949.12
beleaguer
  hem in 232.6
  besiege 796.20

beleaguerment 796.5
bel-esprit 879.12
belfry tower 206.11
  head 210.5
belga 833.9
Belgian hare 413.29
Belial 1014.5
belie disprove 505.4
  deny 522.4
  misrepresent 571.3
  falsify 614.16
  oppose 788.7
belief credence 500.2
  certainty 512
  religion 1018.1
BEYOND BELIEF
  502.10
HARD OF BELIEF
  unbelievable 502.10
  incredulous 503.4
NURTURE A BELIEF
  500.10
believable
  credible 500.21
  unquestionable
  512.15
  reliable 512.17
believe suppose 498.9
  credit 500.8
  swallow 501.5
BELIEVE ME 500.27
HARD TO BELIEVE
  502.10
NOT BELIEVE 502.5
REFUSE TO BELIEVE
  503.3
believer truster 500.7
  religious ~ 1026.4
believing
  undoubting 500.18
  sure 512.13,21
belittle minimize 39.9
  underestimate 497.2
  disparage 969.8
bell
  nouns the time 114.2
  ringer 453.4
  roar 455.4
  signal 566.14
  verbs roar 455.9
  bellow 459.2
BELL THE CAT 891.11
bell, book and candle
  1034.4
bellboy, bellhop
  messenger 559.4
  attendant 748.4
belle beauty 898.8
  fine lady 901.10
belles-lettres 600.13
bell harp 464.3
bellicose 795.26
bellicosity 795.16
bellied 255.15
belligerence, belliger-
  ency war 795.1
  pugnacity 795.16
belligerent
  nouns 798.1
  adjs. 795.26
bellman 559.3

bell mare 746.5
Bellona 795.18
bellow
  nouns 458.1
  verbs shout 458.6
  bawl 459.2
  say 592.17
bellows lungs 402.20
  blower 402.21
bell ringer
  success 722.4
  bill 740.19
bells 464.20
bell-shaped 251.16
bell signal 566.14
bell tower 206.11
bellwether
  sheep 413.9
  leader 746.5
belly
  nouns stomach 192.3
  bottom 211.1
  verbs 255.10
bellyache
  nouns 423.5
  verbs 873.13
bellyacher 867.3
bellyband
  saddle ~ 215.19
  band 252.3
  harness 657.5
belly-buster 318.1
bellyful fill 56.3
  satiety 662.1
GIVE ONE A BELLY-
  FUL 882.5
HAVE A BELLYFUL
  be satiated 662.5
  feel disgust 865.5
belly-god 992.3
belly gunner 278.4
bellying 255.14
bellyland 277.49
belly laugh 874.4
belly-whop 272.34
belly-whopper 318.1
belong go 183.9
  be a member
  786.15
BELONG TO
  inhere 5.5
  pertain to 9.3
  be possessed by
  806.8
belongings
  kinsmen 11.2,6
  property 808.2
beloved
  nouns 929.12
  adjs. 929.21
below
  advs.
  on earth 374.29
  in hell 1017.7
  preps. less than 37.9
  under 207.11
  in subjection 762.16
HIT BELOW THE BELT
  975.6
belowstairs 207.11

belt
  nouns region 179.1
  stratum 226.1
  waistband 230.65
  band 252.3
  blow 282.4
  stripe 373.5
  strait 398.1
  whip 1009.1
  verbs fasten 47.9
  encircle 232.7
  strike 282.14
  whip 1008.14
belted 232.12
belting 1008.4
belvedere cigar 433.4
  observatory 438.8
bemask 613.7
bemingle 44.11
bemire
  bog down 399.2
  dirty 630.17
bemist dim 336.11
  opaque 340.2
  cloud 403.7
bemoan regret 871.6
  lament 873.8
bemuddy 680.17
bemuse 994.28
bemused
  abstracted 530.11
  drunk 994.38
ben 224.14
benasty 630.19
bench plateau 206.4
  table 215.15
  seat 215.18
  official seat 737.9
  committee 753.3
  judgment seat 999.8
benchfellow 785.5
bench warmer 706.7
bench warrant 750.6
bend
  nouns knot 48.3
  obliquity 218.3
  angle 250.2
  bending 251.3
  deviation 290.1
  crouch 316.3
  insignia 567.2
  obeisance 962.2
  verbs tie 47.9
  influence 171.7
  oblique 218.9
  angle 250.5
  curve 251.6
  direct 289.6
  deviate 290.3
  deflect 290.5
  crouch 316.8
  be pliant 356.7
  conquer 725.10
  subdue 762.9
  submit 753.10
  bow 962.6
BEND AN EAR
  listen 447.11
  heed 528.7
BEND ONE'S STEPS
  653.8

BEND THE ELBOW
  994.31
BEND THE KNEE
  truckle 905.6
  make obeisance
    962.6
BEND THE MIND TO
  think about 477.10
  attend to 528.5
BEND THE NECK
  submit 763.10
  make obeisance
    962.6
BEND THE THOUGHTS
  TO 477.10
BEND TO
  tend 173.3
  submit 763.10
BEND TO ONE'S WILL
  influence 171.7
  dominate 739.14
  subdue 762.9
  submit 763.10
bendable 356.9
bender revel 876.6
  spree 994.5
bendified
  crooked 248.11
  curved 251.7
bending 356.9
BENDING THE KNEE
  962.2
bends
  astronautics 281.11
  illness 684.5
bend sinister
  insignia 567.2
  stigma 913.6
  illegitimacy 997.2
bendsome 356.9
bendwise 218.20
beneath below 207.11
  in subjection 762.16
BENEATH CONTEMPT
  paltry 671.18
  odious 862.9
BENEATH NOTICE
  671.19
BENEATH ONE 669.5
BENEATH THE SKY
  374.29
BENEATH THE SOD
  409.26
Benedicite
  canticle 1030.3
  benediction 1030.5
benedict 931.8
Benedict Arnold
  617.10
Benedictine 1036.17
benediction
  thanksgiving 947.2
  prayer 1030.5
GIVE BENEDICTION
  1030.13
benefaction
  good 672.4
  gift 816.7
  kindness 936.7
benefactor
  patron 785.8

benefiter 940
benefactress 940.1
benefice 1035.9
beneficence 936.4
beneficial
  good for 672.21
  salubrious 681.5
  helpful 783.21
beneficiary
  donee 817.4
  clergyman 1036.7
benefit
  nouns ~ performance
    609.13
  use 663.4
  good 672.4
  aid 783.1
  estate 808.4
  gift 816.7
  kindness 936.7
  verbs profit 663.17
  do good 672.11
  help 783.11
benefiter 940.1
benevolence
  giving 816
  gift 816.7
  generosity 851
  altruism 936.4
  kindness 936.7
benevolent
  generous 851.4
  kind 936.16
benevolently 936.21
benevolist 936.8
Bengal heat 327.4
benight 440.6
benighted
  night-overtaken
    134.10
  blind 440.8
  ignorant 476.17
benightedness
  blindness 440.1
  ignorance 476.4
benign
  salubrious 681.5
  kind 936.14
benignancy 936.1
benignant 936.14
benignity
  goodness 936.1
  kindness 936.7
benignly 936.19
benison 1030.5
benjamin 230.13
Benjamin's mess
  main part 54.5
  majority 100.2
  lion's share 814.5
benjy 230.14
benny overcoat 230.13
  hat 230.25
bent
  nouns tendency
    173.1
  obliquity 218.3
  direction 289.1
  disposition 523.3
  prejudice 525.3
  desire 632.3

  aptitude 731.5
HAVE A BENT FOR
  731.16
  adjs. crooked 248.11
  angular 250.6
  curved 251.7
  minded 523.8
BENT ON 622.16
BENT UPON 632.29
benthal 208.13
Benthamism 743.6
benthon 208.3
benthonic
  deep-sea 208.13
  organic 405.25
benthopelagic 208.13
benthos
  ocean bottom 208.3
  organisms 405.1
benthoscope 318.5
benumb freeze 332.11
  numb 422.3
  ~ emotionally
    854.8
benumbed
  numb 422.5
  apathetic 854.13
benzene ring 325.7
benzine 334.20
beplaster 968.5
bepraise 966.12
bequeath 816.17
bequeathable 815.5
bequeathal 816.10
bequest
  nouns legacy 816.10
  inheritance 817.2
  verbs 816.17
berate 967.20
berating 967.8
berceuse 461.15
bereave die 407.22
  deprive 820.18
  widow 933.6
bereaved
  ~ by death 407.28
  deprived of 810.8
  impoverished 836.8
bereavement
  death 407.9
  loss 810.1
  divestment 820.5
bereft
  ~ by death 407.28
  insane 472.24
  deprived of 810.8
  impoverished 836.8
BEREFT OF 660.11
BEREFT OF LIFE
  407.24
BEREFT OF LIGHT
  440.8
berg 332.6
bergamot 435.2
Bergsonian 499.11
beribbon 899.8
beriberi 684.8
Berkelian
  immaterialist 376.4
  philosophical
    499.11

between 236.14
betweenbrain 465.5
betwixt 236.14
BETWIXT AND
    BETWEEN
  between 236.14
  mediocre 678.7
Beulah 1016.1
bevel obliquity 218.1
  ~ square 250.4
beveled 218.15
bever 306.7
beverage
  nonalcoholic ~
    306a.47
  intoxicant 994.12
beverages
  types of ~ 306a.48
  types of alcoholic ~
    994.48–50
bevue b under 517.5
  bungle 732.5
bevy company 74.3
  throng 74.4
  flock 74.5
  multitude 101.3
bewail regret 871.6
  lament 873.8
beware
  verbs 893.7
  interjs. 893.14
bewhisker 229.20
bewhiskered
  bearded 229.25
  trite 831.9
bewilder
  perplex 513.12
  fluster 530.7
  astonish 918.5
bewildered
  perplexed 513.22
  astonished 918.8
bewildering
  perplexing 513.24
  astonishing 918.11
bewilderment
  perplexity 513.3
  confusion 530.3
  wonder 918.1
bewitch
  fascinate 648.6
  delight 863.8
  enamor 929.20
  witch 1034.10
bewitched
  enamored 929.25
  witch-charmed
    1034.14
bewitcher 1033.9
bewitchery
  allurement 648.1
  sorcery 1033.1
  spell 1034.2
bewitching
  alluring 648.7
  delightful 861.6
  spellbinding
    1034.12
bewitchment

allurement 648.1
delightfulness 861.2
spell 1034.2
bey 747.9
beyond
  advs. additionally
    40.10
  in excess of 661.27
  preps. exceeding
    36.20
  later than 117.7
  ~ the ability 157.20
  past 198.21
  inunderstandable
    547.22
bezel 218.1
bezonian 984.2
B-flat 413a.7
Bhagavad-Gita 1019.7
bheesty 270.5
bhikhari 1036.13
bhikku 1036.14
bhikshu ascetic 989.2
  religious 1036.13
biannual 137.9
bias
  nouns tendency
    173.1
  obliquity 218.3
  diagonal 218.7
  sage 467.4
  disposition 523.3
  prejudice 525.3
  desire 632.3
  partiality 975.3
  verbs influence 171.7
  oblique 218.9
  deflect 290.5
  prejudice 525.8
  adjs. slanting 218.15
  diagonal 218.20
  advs. 218.26
biased slanting 218.15
  diagonal 218.20
  prejudiced 525.12
  partial 975.11
biaxial 92.5
bib
  nouns 230.17
  verbs drink 306.27
  tipple 994.29
bibacious 994.44
bibaciousness 994.2
bibacity 994.2
bib and tucker 230.6
bibber 994.10
bibbing 944.4
bibble-babble
  nouns nonsense 545.4
  chatter 594.3
  chitchat 595.5
  verbs 545.8
bibelot 899.4
bibi lady 420.5
  mistress 420.8
Bible truth 515.2
  scripture 1019.1,2
Bible clerk 1036.9
Bible institute 565.10
Bible oath 521.3
Bible reader 1036.9

Bible school 565.10
Bible truth 515.2
Biblic(al) 1019.9
biblioclast 691.8
bibliofilm 575.12
bibliognost
  scholar 475.3
  bookman 603.21
bibliographer
  writer 600.15
  bookman 603.21
bibliographic(al)
    603.25
bibliography
  book 603.6
  bibliology 603.24
bibliolater, bibliolatrist
  scholar 475.5
  idolater 1031.4
bibliolatrous 1031.7
bibliolatry
  scholarship 474.5
  hyperorthodoxy
    1022.6
  worship 1031.1
bibliological 603.25
bibliologist 603.21
bibliology
  booklore 474.5
  bibliography 603.24
bibliomane, biblio-
    maniac 475.5
bibliomania 474.5
bibliopegic 603.25
bibliopegist 603.21
bibliopegy 603.16
bibliophage 475.5
bibliophagic 474.22
bibliophile,
    bibliophilist 475.5
bibliophilic 474.22
bibliophilism 474.5
bibliopole,
    bibliopolist 603.21
bibliopolic 603.25
bibliopolism 603.24
bibliosoph
  scholar 475.3
  bookman 603.21
bibliothec
  library 603.18
  librarian 603.21
bibliotheca 603.18
bibliothécaire 603.21
bibliothecal 603.25
bibliothecary
  nouns 603.21
  adjs. 603.25
bibliothèque,
    Bibliothèque
    Nationale 603.18
bibliotherapy 687.3
bibulosity 994.2
bibulous
  absorbent 305.17
  intemperate 991.7
  tippling 994.44
bibulousness 994.2
bicameral
  bipartite 92.5
  legislature 740.21

bicentenary,
    bicentennial
  number 99.8
  anniversary 137.4
biceps 158.2
bicker
  nouns argument
    481.5
  cavil 482.4
  quarrel 793.5
  verbs flutter 323.12
  flicker 334.25
  argue 481.17
  quibble 482.9
  quarrel 793.12
  BICKER OVER 794.22
bickering
  nouns argument
    481.5
  caviling 482.5
  contention 794.1
  adjs. flickering
    334.36
  quibbling 482.15
bicolor, bicolored
    373.9
biconjugate 90.8
bicorn 251.11
bicuspid
  nouns 257.7
  adjs. bipartite 92.5
  dental 257.17
bicycle
  nouns 271.8,27
  verbs 272.32
bicycler, bicyclist
    273.11
bicycling 272.6
bid
  nouns attempt 712.2
  offer 771.1
  invitation 772.4
  ~ at auction 827.4
  offered price 832.8;
    844.2
  verbs command
    750.9
  offer 771.7
  invite 772.13
  ~ at auction 826.9
  summon 750.12
  invite 772.13
  have a chance
    155.13
  be liable 174.3
  be possible 508.4
  seem likely 510.3
  promise 542.10
  give hope 886.10
  intend 651.4
  try for 712.7
  offer 771.7

volunteer 771.10
solicit 772.14
bargain 825.14
BID GODSPEED
  take leave 300.18
  give regards 934.13
BID GOOD-BY 300.18
BID GOOD DAY, BID
  HELLO 923.10
BID IN 826.9
biddance 772.4
bidder 772.7
bidding
  command 750.1
  summons 750.5
  invitation 772.4
  ~ at auction 827.4
DO ONE'S BIDDING
  764.2
biddy hen 413.35
  dame 420.6
  female 420.10
  maidservant 748.8
bide endure 110.6
  wait 132.11
  continue 143.3
  await 537.6
  tolerate 859.5
BIDE ONE'S TIME
  wait 132.11
  tarry 537.6
  do nothing 704.2
bidet 413.18
bien cuit 329.7
biennial
  nouns anniversary
    137.4
  plant 410.3
  adjs. 137.9
bienséance
  convention 643.1
  mannerliness 934.3
bientôt 131.16
bienvenu! 923.14
bier 409.13
bifacial double 91.3
  two-sided 241.7
biff
  nouns 282.4
  verbs 282.14
bifid 92.5
bifidity 92.1
bifocals 442.2
bifold 91.3
biforked 298.10
biforking 298.3
biform 91.3
biformity 90.1
Bifrost 655.10
bifteck 306a.18
bifurcate
  verbs 298.7
  adjs. 298.10
bifurcated 298.10
bifurcation 298.3
big
  verbs 168.11
  adjs. grown-up
    126.12
  pregnant 168.18
  large 194.16

loud 452.9
tolerant 524.11
important 670.16
boastful 908.10
arrogant 910.9
famous 912.19
magnanimous 977.6
BIG AS YOU PLEASE
  910.9
IN A BIG WAY 194.24
LOOK BIG
  be defiant 791.6
  be ostentatious
    902.14
TOO BIG FOR ONE'S
  BREECHES 907.11
bigamist 931.12
bigamous 931.20
bigamy 931.2
big baby
  weakling 159.6
  coward 890.5
big beef 158.6
big-bellied 196.13
Big Board 831.7
big bruiser 158.6
big bug 670.9
big bully 864.10
big business 825.1
big businessman 828.1
big cheese
  personage 670.9
  chief 747.3
big chief 747.3
big-eared 447.16
bigeminate 90.8
big end 814.5
big feed 306.9
big game
  animals 413.1
  game 653.7
big-game hunter 653.5
biggen increase 38.4
  enlarge 196.4
bigger 38.7
biggish 194.16
biggoty, biggity
  907.11
big gun
  personage 670.9
  cannon 799.6
big hand 966.2
bighead 684.10
big heart
  generosity 851.1
  magnanimity 977.2
bighearted
  tolerant 524.11
  generous 851.4
  benevolent 936.16
  magnanimous 977.6
bigheartedly
  generously 851.5
  benevolently 936.21
  magnanimously
    977.8
big hit 722.3
big house 759.9
bight angle 250.2
  bay 398.1
big idea 478.7

big it, big It
  personage 670.9
  egotist 907.5
big-league 670.16
big lie, the 614.12
big man 670.8
big meeting 1030.8
big mogul 670.8
big name
  personage 670.8
  celebrity 912.9
big-name 670.16
bigness
  pregnancy 168.6
  size 194.1,6
  tolerance 524.4
  magnanimity 977.2
big operator 831.11
bigot fanatic 472.17
  opinionist 512.7
  intolerant 525.5
bigoted 525.10
big person 524.6
big-rich 835.13
big season 128.1
big shot 670.9
big-sounding
  loud 452.9
  grandiloquent 599.9
Big Steels 832.2
big stick
  tough policy 742.5
  coercion 754.3
  despotism 739.10
big talk
  grandiloquence
    599.1
  brag 908.2
big talker 594.5
big time 876.2
big-time 670.16
big-time operator
  930.11
big top tent 227.8
  show 609.14
  circus 609.17
big undertaking 713.2
big-voiced 452.10
big wheel
  personage 670.9
  master 747.3
bigwig
  nouns 670.8
  adjs. 670.16
big wind 402.13
big word 599.3
bijou 899.6
bijouterie 899.5
bijugate 90.8
bike nest 190.21
  bicycle 271.8
bikini 230.29
bilabial 449.5
bilateral double 91.3
  two-sided 241.7
bilboes 758.4
bile digester 307.7
  secretion 310.2
  ill humor 949.1
  resentment 950.3
bilge

nouns bulge 255.3
  nonsense 545.2
  offal 680.9
verbs eliminate 77.5
  bulge 255.10
  discard 666.7
bilingual 578.15
bilious ill 684.46
  sour-tempered
    949.23
bilk
  nouns 616.8
  verbs disappoint
    539.2
  deceive 616.17
bilked 539.5
bilker 617.3
bill
  nouns list 88.4
  beak 255.7
  point of land 255.8
  advertisement
    557.7,8
  drama 609.13
  schedule 639.2
  legislative ~ 740.19
  money 833.6,11
  receipt 842.2
  statement 843.3
  legal declaration
    1002.7
  verbs publicize 557.15
  schedule 639.4
  dun 843.11
billabong 394.3
bill and coo 930.13
bill-and-cooers 929.16
billboard 557.7
bill broker 828.9
bill collector
  collector 74.14
  creditor 837.4
billed beaked 251.9
  scheduled 639.6
billet
  nouns stick 377.3
  ticket 566.12
  insignia 567.2
  epistle 602.2
  office 654.5
  verbs house 187.11
  assign 814.10
billet-doux 930.12
billeting
  housing 187.3
  assignment 814.3
billfold 834.14
billhead
  heading 483.2
  address 602.10
billiard room
  room 191.12
  playroom 876.12
billiard table 213.3
billing and cooing
  930.1
billingsgate 970.3
billion
  nouns 99.12
  adjs. 101.7
billionaire 835.6

billionth 99.32
bill-like 251.9
bill of accounts, bill of
   costs 843.3
bill of attainder
   1006.2
bill of complaint
   1002.7
bill of exchange
   833.11
bill of fare list 88.4
   menu 306.12
   schedule 639.2
bill of health 568.5
bill of indictment
   1002.3
bill of lading 843.3
bill of mortality
   407.12
Bill of Rights 996.6
bill of sale 827.1
billow
   nouns 394.14
   verbs bulge 255.10
   surge 394.23
billowing 255.14
billowy wavy 253.10
   swelling 255.14
billposter 557.9
bill-shaped 251.9
Bill Sikes 823.12
billy goat 413.10
   male animal 419.8
   comrade 926.4
Bilskirnir 1016.11
bimetallic 382.15
bimetalism
   policy 742.4
   money 833.20
bimonthly
   nouns 503.11
   adjs. 137.9
binary 91.3
binary digit
   number 86.2
   computer data
   348.19
binary scale 348.19
binary system 348.19
binate 91.3
bind fasten 47.9
   stick together 50.7
   border 234.10
   constipate 265.7
   stipulate 506.4
   shackle 758.10
   indenture 778.15
   obligate 960.11
BIND OVER 778.15
BIND UP
   fasten 47.9
   wrap 74.19
binder adhesive 48.6
   wrapper 227.19
   book ~ 603.16
   bandage 685.28
binder's board 603.16
binder's title 603.13
bindery 717.3
binding
   nouns fastening 47.3

wrapping 227.19
   edging 234.7
   book ~ 603.16
   adjs. joining 47.16
   valid 515.12
   imperative 750.13
   compulsory 754.9
   obligatory 960.14
binding agreement
   769.1
binding energy 325.14
binding over 778.7
bindle 74.7
bindle stiff 273.3
bine 410.18
bing 74.9
bing boy 798.8
binge 994.5
GO ON A BINGE
   994.34
binghi
   aboriginal 123.7
   aborigine 189.3
bingo
   nouns 455.3
   interjs. 455.14
binocles 442.3
binocular 92.5
binoculars 442.3
binomial 92.5
bioblast 405.4
biochemical 378.7
biochemics, biochem-
   istry, biochemy
   dietetics 307.14
   biology 405.16
biochemist
   nutritionist 307.13
   biologist 405.17
biod 710.8
bioecology 405.16
biogen 405.4
biogenesis 166.6
biogenetic 166.24
biograph 606.4
biographer
   chronicler 569.2
   memorialist 606.11
biographic(al) 606.18
biographical sketch
   606.4
biographist
   chronicler 569.2
   biographer 606.11
biographize 606.14
biography 606.4
biological 405.18
biological species 11.4
biological urge 418.4
biological warfare
   795.4
biologic therapy 687.2
biologist
   naturalist 405.17
   botanist 411.2
   zoologist 414.2
biology genetics 169.6
   natural science
   405.16
   botany 411
   zoology 414

manual 603.9
bioluminescence
   334.13
biometrics 405.16
biometrist 405.17
biometry
   biology 405.16
   measurement 489.9
bion 405.2
bionomics 405.16
biophore, biophor
   405.4
biophysical 324.3
biophysicist
   physicist 324.2
   biologist 405.17
biophysics
   physics 324.1
   biology 405.16
bioplasm 405.3
biopsy 687.15
biostatics 346.2
biota 405.1
biotaxy
   classification 61.1
   biology 405.16
biotic 405.18
bipack 575.12
biparous 91.3
bipartisan 742.48
bipartisan policy
   742.4
bipartite
   unjoined 49.20
   in two parts 92.5
bipartition 92.1
biparty 742.48
biped 92.5
bipeds 413.3
bipetalous 92.5
bipinnate 92.5
biquadrate
   nouns 96.1
   verbs 97.2
biquadratic
   quarternary 96.4
   quadruplicate 97.3
birch
   nouns 1009.2
   verbs 1008.14
birch oil 1008.6
bird oddity 85.4
   aviator 278.1
   guided missile 280.2
   fowl 413.34,56
   zoology 414.11
   man 419.5
   ~ in hand 806.1
   hissing 965.3
A LITTLE BIRD TOLD
   ME 480.4
BIRDS OF A FEATHER
   counterparts 20.5
   friends 926.7
BIRDS OF ILL OMEN
   542.4
bird cage
   aviary 190.20
   dice box 514.8
birdcall
   wood-note 459.1

signal 566.15
bird dog 413.27
birdhouse 190.20
birdie 413.34
birdies 343.24
birdlike 413.45
birdlime
   nouns 616.12
   verbs 616.20
birdling 125.8
birdman 278.1
bird of freedom, bird
   of Jove, bird of
   Juno, bird of night
   413.34
bird of passage
   wanderer 273.2
   bird 413.34
bird of prey
   bird 413.34
   extortionist 820.10
bird sanctuary 699.6
birds, beasts and fish
   413.1
bird's-eye
   nouns 433.2
   adjs. 76.6
bird's-eye view 445.6
bird-witted 468.20
birdwoman 278.2
birdy
   nouns grace note
   462.18
   birdlike 413.45
birr 451.13
birth beginning 68.3
   childbirth 166.9
   lineage 169.4
   heredity 169.6
   nobility 916.1
BY BIRTH 5.9
GIVE BIRTH 166.19
GIVE BIRTH TO
   152.11
birth control 166.9
birthday 137.4
birthday book 568.10
birthday suit 231.3
IN ONE'S BIRTHDAY
   SUIT 231.14
birthmark mark 566.4
   blemish 677.1
birthplace 152.8
birth rate 166.9
birthright
   inheritance 817.2
   right 956.3
birthstone 383.6
birth throe 166.9
bis
   nouns 103.5
   interjs. encore!
   103.18
   bravo! 966.21
biscuit
   pommel 215.19
   bread 306a.29
   cooky 306a.42
   dryness 392.2
   bisque 574.2
bise 402.9

bisect middle 69.3
 halve 92.3
bisected 92.4
bisection middle 69.2
 halving 92
bisexual
 nouns 418.11
 adjs. 418.23
bishop
 chessman 876.18
 churchman 1036.8
bishopdom, bishopric
 1035.5
bishop's apron,
 bishop's garters,
 etc. 567.4
bismarck 306a.43
bison 413.5
bisque soup 306a.10
 ceramic 574.2
bissextile day 137.4
bistro
 restaurant 306.14
 barroom 994.25
bit small amount 35.2
 piece 55.3
 binary digit 86.2;
 348.19
 enlistment 107.3
 short time 111.3
 short distance 199.2
 role 609.11
 harness 657.5
 curb 728.7
 coin 833.7
A BIT OF 34.20
A BIT OF ALL RIGHT
 672.14
A BIT ON THE OFF
 SIDE 21.4
A BIT THICK 502.10
BIT BY BIT
 gradually 29.6
 piecemeal 55.8
BIT OF ONE'S MIND
 967.6
NOT A BIT 2.3
NOT A BIT OF IT
 nowise 35.14
 by no means 522.8
TO BITS 49.27
bitch
 nouns slattern 62.7
 dog 413.26
 female animal
 420.10
 strumpet 987.14
 verbs botch 732.12
 complain 873.13
bite
 nouns acrimony
 160.4
 morsel 306.2
 lunch 306.7
 pang 423.2
 taste 426.2
 pungency 432.2
 hold 811.2
 verbs pierce 264.15
 chill 332.11
 pain 423.7

be pungent 432.5
be credulous 501.5
etch 576.15
deceive 616.17
grip 811.6
BITE IN 576.15
BITE OFF MORE THAN
 ONE CAN CHEW
 713.5
BITE ONE'S HEAD OFF
 950.16
BITE ONE'S THUMB
 950.14
BITE ONE'S TONGUE
 871.6
BITE THE DUST
 die 407.18
 be defeated 725.12
BITE THE HAND THAT
 IS FEEDING YOU
 973.12
BITE THE TONGUE
 be pungent 432.5
 be silent 450.5
biting
 acrimonious 160.12
 cold 332.15
 painful 423.10
 acid 431.7
 pungent 432.6
 penetrating 855.32
 caustic 937.21
bitten 929.25
bitter
 verbs 949.16
 adjs. acrimonious
 160.12
 cold 332.15
 acrid 428.6
 sour 431.6
 pungent 432.6
 unpleasant 862.8
 hostile 927.11
 caustic 937.21
 sour-tempered
 949.23
 resentful 950.24
bitter almond 306a.38
bitter cup 864.8
bitter defeat 725.4
bitter disappointment
 539.1
bitter draft, bitter
 draught 864.8
bitter end 70.2
bitter-end 140.8
bitter-ender
 conservative 140.4
 obstinate person
 624.6
 extremist 661.8
bitter enemy 927.6
bitter fact 1.3
bitterly 34.25
bitterness
 acrimony 160.4
 cold 332.1
 acridness 428.2
 remorse 871.1
 animosity 927.4
 causticity 937.8

resentment 950.3
bitter pill
 bitterness 428.2
 affliction 864.8
bitter resentment
 950.3
bitters 428.2
bittersweet 430.6
bitter words 967.8
bituminous
 coaly 330.9
 resinous 380.3
bivalent bipartite 92.5
 valent 378.8
bivalves 414.9
bivouac
 nouns camping 187.4
 camp 190.25
 verbs 187.12
biweekly
 nouns 603.11
 adjs. 137.9
bizarre odd 85.12
 absurd 469.10
blab
 nouns informer 555.6
 gossip 556.9
 chatter 594.3
 chatterer 594.5
 verbs tattle 554.6
 inform on 555.11
 chatter 594.6
blabber
 nouns nonsense
 545.4
 informer 555.6
 gossip 556.9
 chatter 594.3
 verbs twaddle 545.8
 tattle 554.6
 chatter 594.6
black
 nouns blackness
 364.1
 colors, pigments
 364.13
 Negro 417.7
 mourning 873.6
 verbs blacken 364.7
 soil 680.18
 adjs. lightless 336.14
 dark 336.15
 black-colored 364.8
 Negro 417.12
 ominous 542.13
 evil 673.7
 filthy 680.25
 disastrous 727.15
 sad 870.25
 sullen 949.24
 wicked 979.17
LOOK BLACK
 turn color 855.20
 look sullen 949.15
blackamoor 417.7
black and blue 364.12
black-and-blue mark
 690.8
black-and-tan 609.8
black and white
 572.6,14

IN BLACK AND WHITE
 600.24
PUT IN BLACK AND
 WHITE
 record 568.15
 write 600.19
black ant 413a.3
black art 1033.2
blackball 924.2
Black Bess 413.21
black blizzard 402.14
black-browed 949.24
black cat
 superstition 501.3
 omen 542.4
blackcoat 1036.2
blackdamp
 vapor 400.1
 poison 674.4
Black Death 684.4
blacken black 364.7
 stain 677.6
 soil 680.18
 stigmatize 913.9
 defame 969.10
blackening
 blacking 364.5,6
 vilification 969.2
black eye bruise 690.8
 stigma 913.6
GIVE A BLACK EYE
 bruise 690.14
 vilify 696.10
 stigmatize 913.9
blackface
 nouns blacking 364.6
 minstrel 463.16
 grease paint 609.21
 adjs. 601.18
black-faced 601.18
black frost 332.8
black gang 275.6
blackguard
 nouns 984.3
 verbs 970.7
blackguardism 970.2
blackguardly 973.16
Black Hand
 extortion 822.9
 gangland 984.10
blackhead 677.1
black-hearted 979.20
black hole 759.9
blackish 364.9
blackjack
 nouns 567.6
 verbs hit 282.19
 coerce 754.7
blackleg
 nouns sharper 617.4
 scab 626.6
 disease 684.10
 strikebreaker 787.6
 verbs 787.11
black-letter 123.16
black list 924.2
black look 967.9
black magic 1033.2
blackmail
 nouns extortion
 822.9,11

payment 839.5
verbs 822.19
Black Maria 271.10
black mark 913.6
black market 824.1
black-market 997.6
Black Mass 1033.2
blackness color 364
ominousness 542.5
blackout
aviation 277.18
astronautics 281.11
darkening 336.8
unconsciousness
422.2
amnesia 536.2
secrecy 612.3
black out
aviation 277.52
darker 336.10
faint 422.4
suppress 612.9
black quarter 684.10
black race 417.2
black roller 403.14
Black Saladin 413.21
black sheep 984.5
Black Shirt 742.28
black-skinned
dark 364.10
Negro 417.12
blacksmith shop 715.5
blacksnake, black
snake 1009.1
black sound 449.8
black spot 344.5
black squall 402.13
blacktop 227.24
blackwash 364.7
blackwater 684.10
bladder sack 192.2
bubble 404.1
blade runner 271.18
knife 347.2
leaf 410.17
swordsman 798.1
sword 799.4
dandy 901.9
blade angle 277.23
blague
falsehood 614.11
humbug 614.14
blagueur 617.6
blah nonsense 545.3,4
chatter 594.3
blain 684.28
blamability 981.1
blamable 967.26
blame
nouns attribution
154.1
responsibility 960.2
censure 967.3
accusation 1003.1
verbs attribute to
154.3
censure 967.13
curse 970.5
accuse 1003.8
blamed cursed 970.10
accused 1003.15

blameful 967.23
blameless 982.6
blame-shifting 688.34
blameworthy 967.26
blanc-bec 564.7
blanch pale 362.5,6
whiten 363.6
blanching 362.3
blancmange 306a.39
bland
temperate 162.10
hypocritical 614.33
suave 934.18
flattering 968.9
bland diet 307.10
blandish coax 646.14
importune 772.12
flatter 968.5
blandishment
coaxing 646.3
importunity 772.3
flattery 968.1
blandishments 930.4
blandly 614.36
blandness
hypocrisy 614.6
suaveness 934.5
blank
nouns void 186.3
document 568.4
adjs. absolute 34.14
vacant 186.12
closed 265.9
empty-headed
468.19
thoughtless 479.4
expressionless
545.11
dull 881.6
unadorned 900.8
LOOK BLANK 539.4
blankbook 568.10
blank cartridge
impotent 157.6
cartridge 799.11
blank check 833.11
blank determination
488.1
blanket
nouns 227.2,10
verbs cover 227.21
conceal 613.7
adjs. 76.6
blanket ballot 742.20
blanket drill 710.3
blanketed 227.34
blanketing 227.1
blankly
vacantly 186.15
expressionlessly
545.15
blankness 468.6
blank verse 607.2
blare
nouns glare 334.4
toot 452.4
harsh sound 457.3
verbs toot 452.8
sound harshly 457.8
bellow 459.2

blaring 343.24
blarney
nouns 968.1
verbs 968.6
blasé
disillusioned 519.5
unconcerned 634.6
worldly-wise 731.26
nonchalant 856.15
life-weary 882.10
blaspheme curse 970.5
be sacrilegious
1028.5
blasphemer 1028.3
blasphemous
maledictory 970.8
impious 1028.6
blasphemy
malediction 970.1
sacrilege 1028.2
blast
nouns explosion
161.7
jet ~ 280.9
gust 402.6
blare 452.4
bang 455.3
blight 674.2
explosive 799.10
AT FULL BLAST
268.24
verbs explode 161.13
freeze 333.11
blare 452.8
detonate 455.8
spoil 690.11
blow up 691.18
frustrate 728.15
curse 970.5
BLAST THE EAR 452.6
blasted
blighted 690.40
ruined 691.27
cursed 970.10
blasting 343.24
blasting cap 330.7
blast lamp 328.13
blastogenesis 166.6
blastoids 414.7
blastula 405.13
blast wave 325.15
blasty 402.26
blat bleat 459.2
blurt out 554.6
blatancy
vociferousness 458.5
garishness 902.3
blatant noisy 452.11
vociferous 458.10
howling 459.6
garish 902.20
blate 459.2
blather
nouns nonsense 545.4
chatter 594.3
verbs twaddle 545.8
chatter 594.6
blathering 594.10
blatherskite
nonsense 545.2
chatterer 594.5

blusterer 909.2
blatter 594.6
blaze
nouns notch 261.1
fire 327.12,13
light 334.4
flash 334.6
sign 566.3
mark 566.4
outburst of passion
855.8
~ of glory 912.6
IN A BLAZE
burning 327.27
illuminated 334.38
LIKE BLAZES 161.24
verbs notch 261.4
burn 327.21
catch fire 328.22
flash 334.23
proclaim 557.13
mark 566.18
BLAZE A TRAIL
mark 566.18
prepare the way
718.12
BLAZE UP
catch fire 328.22
become angry
950.18
blazed 261.5
blazing
nouns 328.5
adjs. burning 327.27
flashing 334.34
blazon
nouns coat of arms
567.2
display 902.4
verbs proclaim
557.13
embellish 899.7
blazon abroad, blazon
about 557.13
blazon forth 902.17
bleach
nouns decoloration
362.3
decolorant 362.4
types of ~ 362.11
verbs 362.5,6
bleachers 438.8
bleaching 362.3
bleachworks 717.4
bleak bare 186.12
cold 332.15
dismal 336.15
wind-swept 402.28
bleak weather 332.3
blear
nouns 336.5
verbs 336.11
adjs. dim 336.18
indistinct 444.5
bleared, bleary
dim 336.18
indistinct 444.5
blear-eyed 439.13
blear-witted 468.18
bleat 459.2
bleb bulge 255.3

bubble 404.1
pustule 684.28
Blechinstrumente
464.8
bleed
exude 302.15
let out 304.10
feel pain 423.8
exploit 663.16
let blood 687.36
despoil 820.21
overcharge 846.7
be distressed 864.22
grieve 870.17
BLEED WHITE
despoil 820.21
overcharge 846.7
bleeding
nouns hemorrhage
309.8
bloodletting 687.28
adjs. 864.26
bleeding heart
anguish 864.6
grief 870.9
pity 942.2
blemish
nouns 677
verbs disfigure 248.7
mar 677.4
blemished
deformed 248.12
disfigured 677.8
blench recoil 283.7
wince 423.8
fight shy 621.4
flinch 889.12
blend
nouns mixture 44.5
combination 52.1
word 580.10
verbs mix 44.11
combine 52.3
be converted 145.12
harmonize 461.36
BLEND IN WITH 792.2
blender 44.10
blend-word 580.10
**blennorrhagia, blen-
norrhea** 684.15
blepharoplasty 687.27
blepharotomy 687.26
bless
make happy 863.7
felicitate 946.2
thank 947.4
praise 966.12
protect 697.17
sanctify 1024.5
glorify 1030.11
give benediction
1030.13
BLESS MY HEART!
918.19
BLESS ONE'S STARS
rejoice 874.6
be thankful 947.3
BLESS THE LORD
glorify 1030.11
hallelujah! 1030.16
BLESS YOU! 946.4

blessed happy 863.13
cursed 970.10
heavenly 1016.13
sanctified 1024.8
blessed event 166.9
Blessed One, the
1011.5
blessing good 672.4
good fortune 726.2
godsend 809.6
gift 816.7
favor 936.7
felicitation 946.1
beatification 1024.3
benediction 1030.5
rite 1038.10
GIVE ONE'S BLESSING
1030.13
blest, blest with luck
fortunate 726.14
happy 863.13
sanctified 1024.8
blether
nouns 594.3
verbs 594.6
blight
nouns 674.2
verbs freeze 333.11
spoil 690.11
BLIGHT ONE'S HOPE
disappoint 539.2
destroy hope 887.11
blighted
disappointed 539.5
spoiled 690.40
blighted hope
disappointment
539.1
hopelessness 887.5
blighter 984.2
blighting glance 937.4
Blighty 180.2,4
blimp fat man 194.12
dirigible 279.11
bureaucrat 747.17
pompous person
902.9
blind
nouns ante 514.3
ambush 613.3
trick 616.6
pretext 647.1
artifice 733.3
BLIND LEADING THE
BLIND 561.1
verbs make blind
440.6
conceal 613.7
hoodwink 616.16
adjs. closed 265.9
dim-sighted 439.13
sightless 440.8
undiscerning 468.14
inattentive 529.7
obscure 547.13
concealed 613.12
obstinate 624.13
involuntary 637.14
dead-drunk 994.43
BE BLIND TO
be blind 440.7

be ignorant 476.11
disregard 529.3
BLIND AS A BAT
blind 440.8
undiscerning 468.14
blind alley 729.5
blind-alley 265.9
blind baggage 613.6
blind bargain
uncertainty 513.8
gamble 514.2
bargain 825.5
blinded blind 440.9
undiscerning 468.14
blinders 337.2
blind faith 501.1
blind flying 277.1
blindfold
nouns 337.2
verbs blind 440.6
hoodwink 616.16
adjs. blinded 440.9
undiscerning 468.14
blind gut 224.6
blind impulse
impulse 628.1
instinct 480.2
involuntariness
637.5
blind Justice 974.5
blindly 637.18
blind man 440.4
blindness
dim-sightedness
439.2
sightlessness 440
unperceptiveness
468.2
incognizance 476.3
impersuasibility
624.5
blind pig 994.26
blind-pigger 994.24
blind pool 831.17
blinds 337.2
blind side, blind spot
blindness 440.1
narrow-mindedness
525.1
blind staggers 684.10
blindstory 1040.9
blink
nouns twinkle 334.7
light 334.9
glimpse 438.4
ON THE BLINK 690.36
verbs recoil 283.7
glitter 334.24
wink 439.10
fight shy 621.4
flinch 889.12
BLINK AT
be blind to 440.7
be open-minded
524.7
disregard 529.3
suffer 775.11
condone 945.4
NOT BLINK AN EYE
919.2
blinkard 439.7

blinker
light shield 337.3
eye 438.9
signal 566.14
blinkers
eyelashes 229.12
eyeshade 337.2
goggles 442.2
blink-eyed 439.11
blinking
nouns twinkling 334.7
winking 439.7
adjs. glittering
334.35
winking 439.11
blinky glittery 334.35
blinking 439.11
tainted 690.39
blintz 306a.44
bliss happiness 863.2
heaven 1016.6
bliss body 1032.19
blister
nouns bulge 255.3
bubble 404.1
blemish 677.1
pustule 684.28
verbs burn 328.23
criticize 967.21
thrash 1008.17
blister beetle 418.6
blistered 328.29
blistering
nouns 328.5
adjs. 327.25
blithe 868.10
blitz
nouns 796.7
verbs 796.23
blitzkrieg 796.7
blitzkrieg tactics
795.10
blizzard
snowstorm 332.9
windstorm 402.13
bloat 196.4
bloated
distended 196.12
pompous 902.22
proud 903.10
bloated aristocrat
902.9
bloated plutocrat
capitalist 743.13
rich man 835.6
blob
nouns globule 254.2
bulge 255.3
bubble 404.1
pustule 684.28
verbs 404.4
bloc
legislative ~ 744.3
alliance 786.1
block
nouns set 74.11
plot 179.4
city ~ 182.6
lump 194.10
obstruction 265.3
solid 353.6

dolt 470.3
forgetfulness 536.3
engraving 576.6
mental ~ 688.23
inhibition 688.35
obstacle 728.4
auction stand 827.4
shares 832.3
executioner's ~
1009.5
HAVE A BLOCK FOR A
HEAD 468.12
ON THE BLOCK
827.15
PUT ON THE BLOCK
827.11
verbs clog 265.7
outline 652.12
obstruct 728.12
hinder 728.13
BLOCK OUT
form 245.6
outline 652.12
BLOCK UP
clog 265.7
obstruct 728.12
blockade
nouns exclusion 77.1
closure 265.1
obstruction 265.3
obstacle 728.4
verbs exclude 77.4
hem in 232.6
shut in 235.5
obstruct 265.7
bar 728.12
fortify 797.9
blockage
obstruction 265.3
inhibition 688.35
hindrance 728.1
blockhead 470.4
blockheaded 468.17
blockhouse
house 190.8
stronghold 797.6
blockiness 202.2
blocking
forgetfulness 536.3
mental ~ 688.23
blockish stupid 468.15
clumsy 732.20
block print 576.6
block-print 576.14
blocks 876.16
blocky 203.10
bloke 419.5
blond, blonde
nouns 361.8
adjs. 363.10
blondness 363.1
blood
~ relation 11.1
kinsmen 11.2
lineage 169.4
sap 387.2
gore 387.4
life force 406.3
bloodshed 408.1
dandy 901.9
nobility 916.1

BE OUT FOR BLOOD
622.8
MAKE ONE'S BLOOD
BOIL
irritate 855.13
enrage 950.23
OF GENTLE BLOOD
916.11
RUNNING IN THE
BLOOD 5.7
blood and thunder
853.8
blood bank
blood 387.4
transfusion 687.22
blood boiling 855.3
blood brother, blood
sister 11.3
blood cell 387.4
blood-colored 367.8
bloodcurdling 889.28
blood disease 684.15
blood donor
blood 387.4
transfusion 687.22
blooded 916.12
blood feud 793.5
blood heat 327.1
blood horse 413.12
blood-hot 327.24
bloodless pale 362.9
peaceful 801.9
bloodletting 687.28
bloodline 169.4
blood money 839.5
blood poisoning
684.23
blood pressure 387.4
blood pudding
306a.21
blood-red 367.8
blood relationship 11
blood serum 387.4
bloodshed 408.1
bloodstain
nouns 677.3
verbs 677.7
bloodstroke 684.5
bloodsucker
insect 413a.7
extortionist 820.10
bloodsucking 820.7
bloodthirst
perversion 688.32
cruelty 937.11
bloodthirsty 408.24
blood transfusion
687.22
blood type 387.4
blood vessel 395.14
blood-warm 327.24
bloody
verbs bleed 309.15
bloodstain 677.7
wound 690.13
BLOODY ONE'S HANDS
WITH
kill 408.15
attack 796.15
adjs. deucedly 34.26
blood-red 367.8

murderous 408.24
gory 677.10
cursed 970.10
bloody flux
defecation 309.2
disease 684.8
bloody hands 981.1
bloody-minded
murderous 408.24
cruel 937.24
bloody murder 408.2
bloody-red 367.8
bloody shirt 795.17
bloom
nouns heat glow
327.11
television 344.5
reddening 367.3
blossom 410.22,24
healthiness 683.1
beauty 898.1
verbs glow 327.21
flower 410.32
be healthy 683.4
thrive 726.8
be beautiful 898.15
bloomer 517.5
bloomery 717.5
blooming
nouns 410.24
adjs. red 367.10
flowering 410.36
healthy 683.10
beautiful 898.19
blooper 517.5
blooping radio 343.24
television 344.5
blossom
nouns flower 410.22
flowering 410.24
verbs develop 321.6
flower 410.32
thrive 726.8
blossoming
nouns development
321.2
flowering 410.24
adjs. 410.36
blot
nouns blemish 677.3
soil 680.5
obliteration 691.7
stigma 913.6
verbs absorb 305.13
blacken 364.7
dry 392.6
spot 677.5
obliterate 691.16
stigmatize 913.9
BLOT OUT
excise 42.8
absorb 305.13
obscure 336.10
kill 408.14
obliterate 691.16
BLOT OUT ONE'S SINS
amnesty 945.3
absolve 1005.4
blotch
nouns spot 373.3
mark 566.4

blemish 677.3
soil 680.5
verbs blacken 364.7
color 373.7
spot 677.5
blotched 373.13
blotchiness 364.3
blotchy dingy 364.11
spotted 373.13
blotter
absorbent 305.6
notebook 568.10
blotting
nouns absorption
305.6
obliteration 691.7
adjs. 305.17
blotto 994.43
blou, blouse
waist 230.15
types of ~ 230.54
blow
nouns hit 282.4
gust 402.6
wind 402.13
bloom 410.22,24
surprise 538.2
disappointment
539.1
act 703.3
calamity 727.2
distress 864.5
beating 1008.4
AT A BLOW 113.8
EXCHANGE BLOWS
794.14
RETURN BLOW FOR
BLOW 953.6
verbs leave 300.10
puff 402.23,25
flower 410.32
toot 468.8
inform on 555.11
talk big 599.6
flee 629.11
get tired 715.5
squander 852.3
boast 908.6
BLOW A FUSE 950.19
BLOW A HORN 461.43
BLOW A HURRICANE
402.23
BLOW A KISS 930.17
BLOW DOWN
fell 316.5
raze 691.19
BLOW HOT AND COLD
fluctuate 141.5
quibble 482.9
be capricious 627.4
BLOW IN
arrive 299.6
squander 852.3
BLOW ME DOWN!
918.17
BLOW OFF
disperse 75.6
boast 908.6
BLOW OFF STEAM
876.26
BLOW ONE'S BRAINS

OUT 408.18,22
BLOW ONE'S OWN
TRUMPET 908.6
BLOW ONE'S TOP
go mad 472.20
be unnerved 857.8
become angry
950.19
BLOW OUT
erupt 161.12
explode 161.13
eject 308.23
extinguish 331.7
BLOW OVER
end 70.6
fell 316.5
stop blowing 402.23
BLOW THE CHANCE
130.6
BLOW THE COALS
incite 646.17
excite 855.11
BLOW THE GAFF
betray 554.6
inform on 555.11
BLOW UP
explode 161.13
expand 196.4
brew 402.23
disprove 505.4
forget 536.5
~ a photograph
575.17
demolish 691.18
fail 723.12
excite 855.11
get excited 855.17
be unnerved 857.8
become angry
950.19
praise 966.12
berate 967.20
BLOW UPON
inform on 555.11
stigmatize 913.9
discredit 969.8
blower wind 402.13
bellows 402.21
braggart 908.5
blowgun 402.21
blowhard 908.5
blowhole holes 264.4
air hole 395.17
blown
wind-blown 402.28
flyblown 690.40
winded 715.10
blowoff 70.1
blowout
explosion 161.7
feast 306.9
ejection 308.7
festival 876.4
party 920.10
blowpipe
conversion 145.7
heater 328.13
blower 402.21
blowtorch
blast lamp 328.13
welder 347.21

blowtube 402.21
blowup
explosion 161.7
photograph 575.5
blow valve 697.3
blowy 402.26
blowzy slovenly 62.14
ruddy-faced 367.10
blubber bubble 404.4
weep 873.10
blubberhead 470.4
blubbering
nouns 873.2
adjs. 873.17
blubbery 379.9
bludgeon bully 889.19
threaten 971.2
bludgeoner 941.4
blue
nouns color 371.1,4
heavens 374.2
bluestocking 475.6
OUT OF THE BLUE
538.10
verbs 371.2
adjs. utter 56.11
blue-colored 371.3
bluestocking 474.22
melancholy 870.23
BLUE IN THE FACE
855.26
LOOK BLUE
be disappointed
539.4
turn color 855.20
be sad 870.15
blueback 833.6
blueballs 684.15
Bluebeard 931.12
blue blood 916.1
blue-blooded 916.12
bluebook 568.8
blue book 568.7
blue chip 832.6
bluecoat 697.14
blue devils
delirium tremens
472.10
blues 870.6
blue ensign 567.6
blue funk 889.1
blue-green 370.4
bluejacket 275.4
blue Johnnies 472.10
blue law 996.4
blue moon
indefinite time
106.2
long time 110.4
blueness 371.1
bluenose 901.11
blue-pencil edit 42.8
revise 689.12
blue peter 567.6
blue point 306a.25
blueprint
nouns photograph
575.5
plan 652.1
diagram 652.3
schedule 639.2

verbs print 575.17
plot 652.11
blue ribbon 914.5
blue-ribbon jury
1000.7
blue ruin
destruction 691.1
gin 994.16
blues song 461.13
sadness 870.6
blue sky 374.2
blues singer 463.13
bluestocking
nouns 475.6
adjs. 474.22
blue streak 268.7
blue-water sailor
275.1
bluff
nouns precipice
212.3
falseness 614.7
charlatan 617.6
bluster 909.1
blusterer 909.2
verbs four-flush
614.22
deceive 616.13
bluster 909.3
BLUFF OFF 889.20
adjs. steep 218.18
blunt 258.3
impudent 911.9
gruff 935.7
candid 972.17
bluffer charlatan 617.6
blusterer 909.2
bluffness
bluntness 258.1
candor 972.4
bluing 371.1
bluish 371.3
bluish-green 370.4
bluishness 371.1
blunder
nouns stupidity
469.4
faux pas 517.5
bungle 732.5
verbs stumble 323.15
err 517.13
blurt out 554.6
bungle 732.11
blunderer 732.8
blunderhead
dolt 470.4
bungler 732.8
blunderheaded
stupid 468.17
clumsy 732.20
blundering
nouns 732.4
adjs. 732.20
blunt
nouns 833.2
verbs weaken 159.10
moderate 162.6
dull 258.2
deaden 422.3
discourage 650.4
~ the feelings 854.7

adjs. dull 258.3
stupid 468.16
gruff 935.7
candid 972.17
blunt-edged 258.3
blunting
nouns
weakening 159.5
moderation 162.2
adjs. 162.14
blunt-pointed 258.3
blunt-witted 468.16
blur
nouns dimness 336.5
blotch 677.3
stigma 913.6
verbs dim 336.11
stain 677.6
blurb
nouns publicity 557.4
commendation
966.3
verbs 557.15
blurbist 557.9
blurred, blurry
dim 336.18
indistinct 444.5
blurt 554.6
BLURT OUT
blab 554.6
be impulsive 628.7
blush
nouns heat glow
327.11
color 361.2
reddening 367.3
modesty 906.5
PUT TO THE BLUSH
embarrass 864.16
humiliate 904.4
verbs redden 367.5
turn color 855.20
~ modestly 906.8
blushing
reddening 367.12
modest 906.13
blushing bride 931.6
bluster
nouns commotion
62.4
turbulence 161.2
agitation 323.1
boastfulness 908
swagger 909
verbs blow 402.23
be defiant 791.6
bully 889.19
brag 908.6
swagger 909.3
rage angrily 950.15
BLUSTER OUT OF,
BLUSTER INTO
889.19
bluster and bluff
bluster 909.1
swagger 909.3
blusteration 909.1
blusterer
braggart 908.5
swaggerer 909.2

blustering
  nouns 909.1
  adjs. turbulent 161.17
    windy 402.26
    noisy 452.11
    boisterous 909.4
blusterous, blustery
  turbulent 161.17
  windy 402.26
  blustering 909.4
bo 273.3
boar hog 413.11
  male animal 419.8
board
  nouns table 215.15
    border 234.4
    meal 306.5
    food 306a.1
    wood 377.3
    school ~ 565.17
    accommodations
      657.3
    directorate 746.10
    committee 753.3
    stock exchange
      831.7
    tribunal 999.1
  GO BY THE BOARD
    go overboard 274.47
    be destroyed 691.21
  GO ON BOARD
    embark 300.17
    mount 313.12
  ON BOARD
    here 183.24
    present 185.12
    ~ ship 274.66
  ON THE BOARDS
    609.40
  verbs copulate
    168.10
    cover 227.25
    navigation 274.50
    go aboard 300.17
    feed 306.15
    get meals 306.19
    mount 313.12
    accommodate
      657.10
    invade 796.21
'board! 300.23
board and board
  274.74
board and room
  nouns 657.3
  verbs 657.10
boarder lodger 189.8
  eater 306.13
boarding wood 377.3
  invasion 796.4
boardinghouse 190.13
boarding school 565.2
board lot 832.3
boardman 831.10
board measure 489.5
board of directors
  746.10
board room 831.7
boards, the stage 609.1
  drama 609.20
board walk 655.3

boar's nest 190.9
boast
  nouns good thing
    672.5
    brag 908.1
  verbs have 806.5
    brag 908.6
    bluster 909.3
  BOAST OF 966.12
boaster 908.5
boastful vain 907.8
  bragging 908.9
boasting
  nouns 908.1
  adjs. 908.9
boat
  nouns automobile
    271.9
    watercraft 276.2
    ship 276.3
    types of ~ 276.21–
      25
    airplane 279.1
  verbs transport
    270.12
    navigate 274.13
boatable 274.62
boater 275.5
boathouse
  shelter 190.17
  anchorage 698.6
boating 274.1
boatlike 251.12
boatload 193.2
boatman 275.5
boat race
  nouns 794.12
  verbs 794.20
boat-shaped 251.12
boatsman 275.5
boat song 461.13
boat steerer 275.8
boatswain 275.7
bob
  nouns refrain 103.5
    plumb 212.6
    hairdo 229.15
    float 276.11
    tap 282.6
    jerk 285.3
    shake 323.3
    weight 351.6
    shilling 833.8
    greeting 923.4
    obeisance 962.2
  verbs cut off 42.10
    coiffure 229.22
    tap 282.16
    jerk 285.5
    jump 317.6
    oscillate 322.9
    shake 323.11
    fish 653.10
    curtsy 962.6
  BOB FOR
    seek 484.24
    fish 653.10
  BOB UP
    arrive 299.6
    rise 313.9
    appear 445.9

be unexpected
  538.6
bob and wheel 103.5
bobbery 452.3
bobbish 683.6
bobble
  nouns shake 323.3
    blunder 517.5
    bungle 732.5
  verbs oscillate 322.9
    shake 323.11
    bungle 732.11
bobby 697.14
bobbysocker,
  bobbysoxer 125.6
bob skates 271.19
bobtail 308.5
bobtailed arrow
  799.17
bobtail pool 831.17
bob wheel 103.5
bo camp 190.25
bodacious 911.8
bode 542.8
bodeful 542.13
bodice 230.15
bodied 375.10
bodiless
  unsubstantial 4.4
  incorporeal 376.7
bodily
  adjs. 375.9
  advs. wholly 54.12
    in person 185.15
bodily size 203.2
boding
  nouns 542.1
  adjs. 542.13
body
  nouns substantiality
    3.1
    entity 3.3
    main part 54.5
    company 74.3
    throng 74.4
    collection 74.10
    bulk 194.1
    thickness 203.2
    bodice 230.15
    solid 353.6
    figure 375.3
    corpse 407.13
    person 416.3
    community 786.3
    sect 1018.3
  IN A BODY
    wholly 54.12
    together 73.11
  verbs 375.8
  BODY FORTH 570.9
body and breeches
  56.18
body clothes 230.22
body corporate 786.9
bodyguard escort 73.5
  guard 697.13
body heat 327.1
body louse 413a.6
body odor sweat 309.7
  malodor 436.1
body politic

state 180.1
  community 416.2
body snatcher 798.11
Boeotian
  stupid 468.15
  fool 470.1
boff 874.4
boffo 833.7
bog
  nouns 399.1
  verbs 399.2
bog apple 306a.35
bogey 279.9
boggart, boggard
  1014.10
boggish 399.3
boggle
  nouns quibble 482.4
    objection 520a.2
    demur 621.2
    bungle 732.5
    bogy 1014.10
  verbs quibble 482.9
    object 520a.5
    demur 621.4
    be irresolute 625.6
    have difficulty
      729.10
    bungle 732.11
    shy 889.11
    lose courage 890.8
boggle-de-botch, bog-
  gle-dy-botch 732.5
boggler 732.8
boggling
  nouns quibbling
    482.5
    stickling 621.2
    bungling 732.4
  adjs. 621.7
boggy 399.3
bogle 1014.10
Bogtrotter 417.9
bogus
  nouns 833.10
  adjs. 614.27
bogy, bogey
  false alarm 702.4
  bugbear 1014.10
Bohemian
  nouns nonconformist
    83.4
    race 417.3
  adjs. unconventional
    83.8
    informal 645.3
Bohemianism
  unconventionality
    83.3
    informality 645.1
Bohn 550.3
bohunk 732.9
bohunkish 896.13
boil
  nouns food 306a.7
    boiling 328.2
    pimple 684.28
  verbs be violent
    161.11
    be hot 327.21
    seethe 328.19

cook 329.4
bubble 404.4
clean 679.22
fume 855.19
be angry 950.15
BOIL DOWN 202.6
BOIL OVER
bubble over 404.4
fume 855.19
become angry
950.17
boiled cooked 329.6
drunk 994.40
boiled eggs 306a.26
boiled meat 306a.12
boiler factory 452.2
boiler head 273.12
boilermaker's delight
994.14
boiler room
noisiness 452.2
swindle 616.8
boilerworks 717.4
boiling
nouns quantity 28.2
bunch 74.6
seething 328.2
cooking 329.1
adjs. hot 327.25
angry 950.27
BOILING OVER
fervent 853.22
excited 855.23
boiling point 327.2
boiling water 327.9
boisterous
violent 161.19
noisy 452.11
excited 855.25
blustering 909.4
boisterousness 452.2
bold steep 218.18
protruding 255.13
in relief 255.17
seaworthy 276.18
obvious 553.11
defiant 791.8
courageous 891.17
impudent 911.10
immodest 988.6
boldface
nouns 911.5
adjs. 601.18
bold hand 600.5
boldly
obviously 553.16
courageously 891.22
impudently 911.13
boldness
protuberance 255.2
obviousness 553.4
defiance 791.1
courage 891.1
impudence 911.1
immodesty 988.2
bold-spirited 891.17
bold stroke
strategy 733.4
exploit 891.7
bole 410.19
bolide 374.15

boll 410.28
boloney, bologna
306a.21
bolo punch 282.5
Bolshevik, Bolshevist
revolutionist 147.3
radical 743.11
Bolshevism,
Bolshevikism
revolutionism 147.2
communism 743.4
Bolshevist(ic)
revolutionist 147.6
communistic 743.19
Bolshevization
naturalization 188.4
communization
813.3
Bolshie
revolutionist 147.3
bolshevist 743.11
bolster
nouns 215.21
verbs 215.22
bolstered 215.25
bolstering 215.24
bolt
nouns bundle 74.7
thunderbolt 334.17
flight 629.4
secession 631.2
lock 758.5
missile 799.12
shaft 799.17
BOLT FROM THE
BLUE
lightning 334.17
surprise 538.2
verbs fasten 47.8
sort 60.10
segregate 77.6
lock 265.6
speed 268.10
devour 306.21
sift 354.6
flee 629.10
secede 631.6
barricade 728.12
eat greedily 992.5
BOLT IN 759.15
bolter sorter 60.4
apostate 626.5
fleer 629.5
bolting 354.3
bolt of lightning
334.17
bolus bite 306.2
pill 685.6
bomb
nouns surprise 538.2
missile 799.15
types of ~ 799.28
verbs 796.25
bombard
atomize 325.16
fire upon 796.23
bombardier
aviation 278.4
serviceman 798.11
bombardment
atomic ~ 325.8

attack 796.7
bombardment
weapons 799.6
bombardon 464.9
bombast
nouns grandiloquence
599.2
brag 908.1
verbs 599.6
bombastic
grandiloquent
599.10
pompous 902.22
boastful 908.10
bomber 798.11
bomber pilot 278.3
bombilate, bombinate
hum 451.13
boom 455.9
bombilation
hum 451.7
boom 455.4
bombing 796.8
bombing locator
345.2
bombing mission
277.8
bombproof
nouns 698.3
adjs. 158.18
bombshell
surprise 538.2
bomb 799.15
bomb shelter 698.3
bombsight 442.4
bomb thrower 798.11
bomos 1040.11
bon 672.13
bona fide
genuine 515.13
faithfully 972.24
bona fideness 515.5
bona fides 972.7
bonanza
source of supply
658.4
rich source 835.3
bond
nouns connection 48
shackle 758.4
covenant 769.1
security 770.1
stocks and bonds
832.4
allegiance 972.7
verbs 770.12
adjs. 762.13
bondage 762.1
bond crowd 831.10
bondholder 831.14
bonding company
831.15
bond issue 832.6
bondman 762.7
bond of matrimony
931.1
bond of union 48.1
bonds 758.4
IN BONDS
bound 758.16
subjugated 762.13

bond service 762.1
bondslave 762.7
bondsman serf 762.7
guarantor 770.8
bonds of harmony
792.1
bone
nouns skeleton 244.6
types of ~ 244.12
hardness 355.6
dryness 392.2
counter 514.13
blunder 517.5
dollar 833.7
HAVE A BONE TO PICK
WITH
disagree 793.10
bear ill will 927.9
MAKE BONES ABOUT
621.4
verbs 562.12
BONE UP 562.14
adjs. 244.11
bone box 409.11
bone-dry 392.7
bonehead dolt 470.4
blunder 517.5
boneheaded 468.17
bone house
coffin 409.11
tomb 409.16
bone-idle 706.17
bone of contention
793.8
bone pot 409.12
boner 517.5
bones skeleton 244.5
the body 375.3
corpse 407.13
end man 463.16
rattlebones 464.20
dice 514.8
refuse 667.4
money 833.2
bonesetter 686.5
boneshaker
bicycle 271.8
horse 413.20
bone yard 409.15
bonfire 327.12
bonhomie,
bonhommie 936.2
Bonhomme 1036.17
boniness 204.5
boning 562.3
bon jour! 923.15
bon mot 879.7
bonne
nursemaid 697.7
maidservant 748.8
bonne foi 972.7
bonne nuit! 300.26
bonner 327.12
bonnet hood 227.23
coif 230.39
bonny good 672.13
comely 898.17
bonnyclabber
curd 353.7
semiliquid 388.5
bon soir! 923.15

bon ton fashion 642.1
    society 642.6
bonus
    extra amount 41.4
    bribe 549.2
    gratuity 816.5
    extra pay 839.6
bonus bond 832.4
bonus stock 832.2
bonus system 839.6
bon vivant
    epicure 895.7
    boonfellow 926.5
    voluptuary 985.3
bon voyage! 300.25
bony thin 204.16
    osseous 244.11
    hard 355.10
bonze 1036.14
bonzer 672.13
boo
    nouns 965.3
    verbs 955.10
boob fool 470.2
    dupe 518.1
boo-boo 517.5
boob stunt
    stupidity 469.4
    blunder 517.5
booby breast 255.6
    fool 470.2
    dupe 518.1
    loser 725.5
booby hatch
    madhouse 472.14
    prison 759.8
boobyish 896.13
booby prize 914.2
booby trap
    hidden thing 613.6
    trap 616.11
boodle bunch 74.6
    bribe 549.2
    political spoils
        742.36
    booty 822.11
    money 833.2
boodle campaign
    742.13
boodleism 742.35
boodler 744.5
boof 889.1
booger
    nouns 1014.10
    verbs 839.11
boogerman 1014.10
boogie-woogie 461.9
boogy 1014.10
boogyman 1014.10
boohoo 373.10
book
    nouns section 55.2
    bet record 514.3
    volume 603
    ~ part 603.14
    canto 607.11
    playbook 609.25
    schedule 639.2
    verbs list 88.7
    register 568.15
    schedule 639.4

engage 778.12
enter accounts
    843.8
Book, the 1019.2
book agent
    bookman 603.21
    salesman 828.5
bookbinder 603.21
bookbindery 717.3
bookbinding 603.16
book burner 689.6
bookcase
    book binder 603.16
    bookholder 603.20
book club 603.18
bookcraft 603.24
book collector 603.21
book cover 603.16
bookdealer
    bookman 603.21
    merchant 828.3
booked dying 407.27
    scheduled 639.6
book end 603.20
bookery 603.18
book-fed 474.22
book-folder 603.21
bookholder 603.20
bookie 514.15
bookiness 474.5
booking
    registration 568.14
    engagement 778.4
booking agent 609.29
bookish 474.22
book jacket 603.16
bookkeeper
    recorder 569.1
    accountant 843.7
bookkeeping 843.6
book-learned 474.22
book learning 474.5
bookleg 824.7
booklegger 824.4
bookless 476.15
booklet 603.10
booklore 474.5
booklover 475.5
book-loving 474.22
bookmaker
    gambler 514.15
    bookman 603.21
bookmaking 603.24
bookman
    scholar 475.3
    author 600.15
    bibliologist 603.21
bookmark 566.9
book-minded 474.22
bookmobile 603.18
bookmonger 475.5
Book of Books, the
    1019.2
Book of Mormon
    1019.6
book of verse 607.6
bookplate 566.12
book post 602.5
book publisher 603.21
bookrack 603.20
book-read 474.22

bookrest 603.20
book review 493.2
book reviewer 604.4
bookroom 603.18
books 843.4
bookseller
    bookman 603.21
    salesman 828.5
bookselling 603.24
bookshelf 603.20
bookshop 603.19
book stamp 566.12
bookstand
    bookstall 603.19
    bookcase 603.20
bookstitcher 603.21
bookstore 603.19
book table 603.20
book-taught 474.22
book truck 603.20
book wagon 603.18
book-wise 474.22
bookworm 475.5
bookwright
    author 600.15
    bookmaker 603.21
booky 474.22
boom
    nouns increase 38.1
    raft 276.11
    lever 286.4
    thunder 455.4
    prosperity 726.5
    obstruction 728.5
    verbs increase 38.6
    speed 268.9
    navigation 274.50
    push 284.10
    hum 451.13
    thunder 455.9
    say 592.17
    thrive 726.8
boomerang
    nouns 283.2
    verbs 283.6
booming
    nouns hum 451.7
    boom 455.4
    adjs. humming
        451.20
    thundering 455.12
    thriving 726.13
boom shot 575.10
boon
    nouns good 672.4
    godsend 809.6
    gift 816.7
    adjs. jolly 868.15
    convivial 920.18
    kindly 936.14
boon companion
    926.5
boondock, boondocks
    181.2
boondoggle
    nouns 205.2
    verbs 671.13
boondoggler 571.9
boonfellow 926.5
boor vulgarian 896.6
    rustic 917.9

boorish
    countrified 181.7
    uncouth 896.13
boost
    nouns increase 38.1
    push 282.2
    lift 315.2
    promotion 780.1
    assist 783.2
    commendation
        966.3
    GIVE A BOOST 315.7
    verbs increase 38.4
    push 282.12
    lift 315.5
    publicize 557.15
    inspire 646.20
    promote 780.3
    help 783.11
    hearten 868.6
    commend 966.11
booster
    rocket ~ 280.4
    television ~ 344.9
    publicist 557.9
    dose 685.5
    vaccination 687.20
    commender 966.8
boot
    nouns bonus 41.4
    types of ~ 230.60
    marine 275.4
    kick 282.9
    discharge 308.1
    dismissal 308.5
    recruit 798.17
    gratuity 816.5
    extra pay 839.6
    thrill 855.2
    scarpines 1009.4
    TO BOOT
    additionally 40.10
    surplus 661.19
    verbs shoe 230.39
    kick 282.20
    to horse! 300.24
    discharge 308.18
    BOOT OUT 308.12
bootblack 748.4
booted 230.44
booted and spurred
    718.16
boot-giver 308.10
booth hut 190.9
    compartment 191.2
    store 830.3
boothy See **bothy**
bootleg
    nouns 994.21
    verbs deal illicitly
        824.7
    moonshine 994.37
    adjs. 997.6
bootlegger
    illicit dealer 824.4
    moonshiner 994.24
bootless
    ineffectual 157.15
    useless 667.9
    unsuccessful 723.17
bootless errand 667.3

marsh 399.1
pluck 622.3
courage 891.5
AT BOTTOM 5.10
AT THE BOTTOM OF
causal 152.15
resulting from 153.8
responsible for
960.16
BOTTOM OF THE
HEART
inmost heart 5.4
affections 853.2
BOTTOM OF THE SEA
208.3
GO TO THE BOTTOM
capsize 274.46
sink 318.8
verbs 486.2
BOTTOM ON 211.6
adjs. 211.7
bottom dollar
end 70.2
money 833.14
bottom glade 256.9
bottom land 399.1
bottomless 208.10
bottomless pit
pit 208.2
hell 1017.1
bottommost 211.7
bottomry bond
mortgage 770.5
bond 832.4
bottoms dregs 43.2
valley 256.9
marsh 399.1
bottom sawyer 37.3
bottom side 211.1
bottom side up,
bottom up 219.8
bottom waters 208.3
bouche mouth 264.6
food 306a.1
bouderie 949.8
boudoir 191.7
bouge 255.10
bough member 55.4
branch 410.18
boughpot 410.23
bought, boughten
826.11
bougie 335.2
bougie decimale
334.21
bouillabaisse 306a.11
bouilli 306a.12
bouillon 306a.10
boulder 383.5
Boule 740.4
boulevard 655.6
boulevardier 901.9
bouleversé 855.27
bouleversement
revolution 147.1
destruction 691.3
bounce
nouns outburst 161.6
recoil 283.2
bound 317.1
shake 323.3

radio reflection
343.13
springiness 357.1
bang 455.1
falsehood 614.12
lightheartedness
868.3
ostentation 902.8
brag 908.1
bluster 909.1
THE BOUNCE 308.1,5
verbs recoil 283.6
discharge 308.12,18
leap 317.5,6
shake 323.11
bang 455.6
talk big 599.6
bluster 909.3
BOUNCE BACK
recoil 283.6
radar 345.16
BOUNCE BACK UP
692.20
BOUNCE UPON 199.11
bounce drill 277.15
bouncer ouster 308.10
falsehood 614.12
liar 617.9
braggart 908.5
bully 941.5
bounces 345.11
bouncing
nouns 317.3
adjs. lusty 158.13
corpulent 194.18
recoiling 283.10
jumping 317.7
healthy 683.9
bouncy 323.21
bound
nouns boundary
234.3
bounce 283.2
leap 317.1
verbs speed 268.11
circumscribe 233.4
limit 233.5
border 234.10
enclose 235.5
bounce 283.6
leap 317.5
BOUND BACK 283.6
adjs. limited 233.8
enclosed 235.10
constipated 265.11
certain 512.20
determined 622.11
restrained 758.16
promised 768.8
obliged 960.15
BE BOUND TO
promise 768.5
be one's duty 960.5
BE BOUND TO PAY
838.5
BECOME BOUND TO
960.7
BOUND OVER 778.18
BOUND UP IN
joined 47.15
habituated 640.18

boundary bound 234.3
fence 235.4
bound bailiff 697.14
bounded 233.8
bounden 960.15
bounden duty 960.1
bounder
vulgarian 896.6
upstart 917.10
scoundrel 984.7
bounding
nouns circumscription
233.1
jumping 317.3
adjs. 283.10
bounding main, the
396.1
boundless 104.3
bounds 234
BEYOND ALL BOUNDS
34.22
BEYOND THE BOUNDS
198.22
BEYOND THE BOUNDS
OF POSSIBILITY
509.6
GO OUT OF BOUNDS
83.5
HAVE NO BOUNDS
be infinite 104.2
be eternal 112.6
KEEP IN BOUNDS,
KEEP WITHIN
BOUNDS
moderate 162.6
restrict 758.9
be temperate 990.6
OUT OF BOUNDS
restricted 233.9
unreasonable 482.16
excessive 661.17
exorbitant 846.12
WITHIN BOUNDS
palliative 162.16
in reason 481.23
temperately 990.12
bounteous
plentiful 659.7
generous 851.4
bountiful fertile 164.9
plentiful 659.7
generous 851.4
bountifulness
fertility 164.1
abundance 659.2
generosity 851.1
bounty gift 816.5,8
premium 839.6
generosity 851.1
bouquet
nosegay 410.23
fragrance 435.1
compliment 966.6
GIVE A BOUQUET
966.13
Bourbon 140.4
bourdon staff 216.2
music 461.24
voice 462.5
note 462.14
bourg 182.1

bourgade 182.2
bourgeois
nouns capitalist
743.13
commoner 917.7
adjs. capitalistic
743.22
middle-class 917.12
bourgeois gentil-
homme 917.10
bourgeoisie
capitalism 743.7
commonalty 917.1
bourn, bourne
destination 299.5
stream 394.1
bourse 831.7
bouse
nouns 994.12
verbs navigation
274.50
tipple 994.30
bouser 994.10
bousy 994.39
bout turn 108.2
round 137.3
act 703.3
contest 794.3
fight 794.9
revel 876.6
game 876.9
spree 994.5
boutade caprice 627.1
prank 879.10
boutique 830.1
boutonniere 410.23
bovine
nouns 413.8
adjs. cowlike 413.41
stupid 468.15
impassive 856.10
complacent 866.10
bovinity
inexcitability 856.1
complacence 866.2
bow
nouns fiddlestick
464.6
weapon 799.18
verbs 461.42
bow
nouns encore 103.6
curve 251.2
bend 251.3
bulge 255.3
ship part 276.26
stage debut 609.13
greeting 923.4
obeisance 962.2
verbs bend 251.6
submit 763.10
kowtow 905.6
make obeisance
962.6
BOW AND SCRAPE
be submissive
763.10
truckle 905.6
kowtow 962.6
BOW DOWN AND
WORSHIP 1030.10

BOW OUT
depart 300.8
exit 302.11
dismiss 308.17
BOW TO
concede superiority
37.5
submit to 763.9
greet 923.10
bowdlerize 42.9
bowed 251.10
bowed-down
dejected 870.22
humbled 904.11
bowelless 943.3
bowel movement
309.2
bowels pit 208.2
insides 224.4
intestines 224.6
BOWELS OF MERCY
942.2
BOWELS OF THE
EARTH 208.2
bower cottage 190.8
arbor 190.11
playing card 876.17
Bower of Bliss
1016.10
bowery 410.39
bowing 251.3
bowing and scraping
962.2
bowl
nouns cavity 256.2
throw 284.4
ceramic 574.2
amphitheater
609.17
washbowl 679.12
arena 800.1
verbs be concave
256.12
hollow 256.13
propel 284.10
throw 284.12
roll 320.10
BOWL ALONG
speed 268.9
walk 272.27
BOWL DOWN, BOWL
OVER
fell 316.5
startle 538.8
astonish 918.5
bowlegs
deformity 248.3
legs 272.16
bowling 320.1
bowling alley 876.12
bowling green
plane 213.3
green 410.7
playground 876.13
bowman shooter 284.9
archer 876.20
bow-shaped 251.10
bowshot
short distance 199.2
shot 284.5
bowsprit 239.3

bowstring 1008.19
bow window 264.7
bowwow
nouns dog 413.24
argument 481.5
verbs 459.2
bow-wow theory
580.15
box
nouns cottage 190.8
compartment 191.2
blow 282.8
coffin 409.11
theater ~ 609.19
predicament 729.4
present 816.4
chastisement 1008.3
verbs stow 183.16
enclose 235.9
hit 282.18
fight 794.14
chastise 1008.13
BOX IN
shut in 235.5
confine 235.6
BOX OFF 274.32
BOX THE EARS
1008.13
BOX UP
cramp 235.6
enclose 235.9
confine 759.12
box barrage 796.10
boxcar 271.13
boxcar number 86.1
boxcars 99.7
boxer 798.2
box fight 794.9
boxing crating 235.2
pugilism 794.9
boxing match 794.9
box kite 279.14
box office office 717.8
receipts 842.1
box pleat 263.2
box score 86.3
box seat 609.19
box springs 215.21
box-top mission 277.8
box waggon 271.13
boy
nouns lad 125.5
porter 270.5
fellow 419.5
servant 748.3
interjs. 863.17
boycott
nouns strike 787.7
ostracism 924.2
verbs strike 787.9
ostracize 924.5
boycottage
strike 787.7
ostracism 924.2
boy friend 929.11
boyhood youth 124.2
boys 125.2
boyish 124.11
boys' room 680.13
bra 230.24
brabble quarrel 793.12

contest 794.3
brace
nouns two 90.2
support 215.2
rigging 276.31
music 461.29
bandage 685.28
verbs tie 47.9
strengthen 158.11
support 215.22
tighten 355.9
refresh 693.2
BRACE ONESELF 622.8
BRACE UP
strengthen 158.11
recuperate 692.19
refresh 693.2
cheer up 868.8
take courage 891.14
encourage 891.16
braced 215.25
brace game 616.9
bracelet band 252.3
ornament 899.6
brace of shakes 111.3
bracer support 215.2
stimulant 685.7
pick-me-up 994.7
braces 214.5
brachygraphy 600.9
bracing
nouns 693.1
adjs. supporting
215.24
cool 332.13
tonic 685.38
refreshing 693.4
bracken 410.4
bracket
nouns class 61.2
types of ~ 215.29
verbs relate 9.4
join 47.5
couple 90.5
enclose 235.8
bracket capital 210.4
bracketed
joined 47.13
coupled 90.8
bracketing 47.1
brackish
distasteful 428.7
salty 432.9
bract, bractlet,
bracteole 410.17
brad 833.4
Bradshaw 746.9
brae 206.5
brag
nouns boast 908.1
braggart 908.5
verbs boast 908.6
bluster 909.3
BRAG ON, BRAG UP
966.12
braggadocio 908.1
braggardism 908.1
braggart
nouns boaster 908.5
blusterer 909.2
adjs. 908.9

braggartism 908.1
bragging
nouns 908.1
adjs. 908.9
Bragi
poetic muse 607.12
god 1012.6
Brahma 1011.4
Brahman, Brahmin
nobleman 916.4
religious 1036.13
Brahmana 1019.7
Brahmanic(al)
1018.30
Brahmi 579.5
Brahmin
intellectual 475.1
snob 910.7
Brahminic(al)
1018.30
braid
nouns cord 205.2
plait 221.3
hair 229.7
verbs 221.7
brail 205.2
Braille 440.5
brain
nouns vitals 224.5
intellect 465.1,4
intelligence 466.9
ON THE BRAIN 477.23
verbs 408.18
brain box 210.6
brain child
creation 167.1
work of art 572.11
writing 600.11
brain fever 472.9
braininess 466.2
braining 408.1
brainless
unintelligent 468.13
foolish 469.8
giddy 530.16
brainpan 210.6
brains 465.1
brainsickness 472.1
brain storm
delirium 472.9
bright idea 478.9
brain-stuff 465.1
brain trust
advisors 740.10
council 753.1
brain twister 547.7
brainwashing 145.3
brainwork
thought 477.1
study 562.3
brainy 466.14
braise 329.4
brake
nouns thicket 410.13
curb 728.7
verbs 269.9
brakeman 273.13
braky 410.38
bramble
adherent 50.3
thorn 257.8

shrub 410.9
brambly 257.13
bran chaff 227.17
  food 306a.4
  mea. 360.5
branch
  nouns member 55.4
    class 61.2
    lineage 169.4
    descendant 170.4
    fork 298.4
    stream 394.1
    headstream 394.3
    bough 410.18
    railway 655.8
    local office 717.8
    affiliate 786.10
    military ~ 798.21
  verbs spread 196.6
    fork 298.7
branch bank 834.13
branched 298.10
branchiae 402.20
Branchiata 414.8
branching
  nouns 298.3
  adjs. 298.10
branchlike 298.10
branch office 786.10
branch of knowledge
  474.10
branch of learning
  560.7
branch of study
  474.10
brand
  nouns kind 61.3
    earmark 80.3
    burn 328.6
    branding iron
      328.14
    burned wood
      328.16
    lighter 330.4
    torch 335.3
    mark 566.4
    label 566.12
    stigma 913.6
  verbs burn 328.23
    mark 566.18,19
    stigmatize 913.9
branding 328.5
branding iron 328.14
brandish
  nouns 322.2
  verbs wave 322.10
    flaunt 902.17
brand-new 122.10
brangle 793.12
branks 1009.3
branniness 360.1
branny 360.11
brash
  nouns dash 268.4
    stone 383.1
    rain 393.2
    rash 684.27
  adjs. brittle 359.4
    rash 892.7
    impudent 911.9
    gruff 935.7

brashness
  rashness 892.1
  impudence 911.2
  gruffness 935.3
brass
  nouns plate 227.28
    telegraph sender
      558.19
    officers 747.21
    money 833.2
    impudence 911.3
  adjs. 382.16
brassard 567.1
brass band 463.12
brasses
  musicians 463.12
  brass winds 464.8
brass farthing 671.5
brass hat 747.21
brassiere 230.24
brassiness 911.2
brass knuckles 799.21
brass man 787.3
brass pounder 558.18
brass section 463.12
brass tacks 1.4
GET DOWN TO BRASS
  TACKS 80.10
brassware 829.4
brass-wind
  instruments 464.8
brassworks 717.4
brassy brass 382.16
  harsh-sounding
    457.14
  impudent 911.10
brat 125.4
bratling elf 125.4
brattice, brattish
  236.5
brattle 454.3
bravado
  defiance 791.1
  daring 891.6
  braggadocio 908.1
  bluster 909.1
brave
  nouns Indian 417.5
    warrior 798.7
    ~ man 891.8
  verbs set at defiance
    791.4
    endure 859.5
    face bravely 891.11
  adjs. courageous
    891.17
    showy 902.19
braveness 891.1
bravery 899.3
bravissimo! 966.21
bravo
  nouns assassin 408.10
    blusterer 909.2
    ruffian 941.4
  interjs. 966.21
bravura music 461.14
  daring 891.6
braw
  well-dressed 642.13
  excellent 672.13
  handsome 898.17

showy 902.19
brawl
  nouns turmoil 62.4
    turbulence 161.2
    uproar 452.3
    clamor 458.4
    quarrel 793.7
  verbs clamor 452.7
    quarrel 793.13
brawler rioter 765.5
  disputant 789.3
brawling noisy 452.11
  vociferous 458.10
brawn 158.2
brawny
  muscular 158.14
  corpulent 194.18
bray
  nouns 457.3
  verbs pulverize 360.9
    sound harshly 457.8
    animal sound 459.2
braze solder 50.7
  plate 227.28
brazen
  verbs callous 854.6
    brave 891.11
  adjs. bronze-colored
    366.4
    brass 382.16
    harsh-sounding
      457.14
    impudent 911.10
    immodest 988.6
brazenface 911.5
brazenfaced
  impudent 911.10
  immodest 988.6
brazier, brasier 716.8
Brazil nut 306a.38
breach
  nouns break 49.3
    interruption 72.2
    cleft 200.2
    infraction 767.2
    falling-out 793.4
  verbs 264.14
breachiness
  refractoriness 624.4
  disobedience 765.2
breach of faith
  violation 767.2
  infidelity 973.5
breach of friendship
  793.4
breach of privilege
  767.2
breach of promise,
  breach of trust
  violation 767.2
  bad faith 973.5
bread
  nouns food 306a.1
    breadstuff 306a.27
    livelihood 783.3
    Eucharist 1038.8
  verbs crumb 75.7
    feed 306.15
bread-and-butter
  pickle 431.3

bread and wine
  1038.8
breadbasket 192.3
bread line 816.3
Bread of Life, the
  1011.12
breadstuff 306a.27
breadth extent 178.1
  size 194.1
  width 203
  broad-mindedness
    524.2
breadth and depth
  203.2
breadthways,
  breadthwise 203.9
breadwinner 716.2
break
  nouns breakage 49.3
    interruption 72.2
    respite 109.1
    pause 144.3
    a chance 155.1
    cleft 200.2
    broken circuit 341.4
    blunder 517.5
    escape 630.1
    injury 690.7
    recess 709.2
    stroke of luck 726.3
    violation 767.2
    falling-out 793.4
    market decline
      831.5
    price fall 847.4
  MAKE A BREAK FOR
    run for 289.10
    flee 629.10
  WITHOUT A BREAK
    71.11
  verbs fracture 49.11
    change 139.5
    interrupt 144.10
    weaken 159.9
    domesticate 188.5
    tack 274.32
    cashier 308.18
    dawn 334.27
    be published 557.16
    train 560.13
    subdue 762.10
    violate 767.4
    depose 781.2
    bankrupt 840.8
    depreciate 847.6
  BREAK A BLOOD
    VESSEL 712.10
  BREAK A LANCE WITH
    794.14
  BREAK AN ARM
    712.10
  BREAK AWAY 630.6
  BREAK BACK 146.5
  BREAK BOUNDS 83.5
  BREAK BREAD 306.17
  BREAK BULK
    trim ship 274.51
    unload 308.21
  BREAK CAMP 300.16
  BREAK COVER 302.12
  BREAK DOWN

dissect 49.17
classify 61.6
analyze 484.32
break 690.25
raze 691.19
subdue 762.9
be unnerved 857.8
weep 873.10
BREAK DOWN AND
CONFESS 554.7
BREAK EVEN 30.6
BREAK FORTH
emerge 302.12
appear 445.9
be revealed 554.9
BREAK FREE 281.15
BREAK GOOD FOR
726.11
BREAK GROUND
initiate 68.9
weigh anchor
274.19
BREAK IN
tame 188.5
intrude 237.5
interrupt 237.6
open 264.14
enter 301.7
train 560.13
subdue 762.10
BREAK INTO 264.14
BREAK INTO A SMILE
874.8
BREAK IN UPON 237.5
BREAK IT TO 554.5
BREAK IT UP 49.19
BREAK LOOSE 630.6
BREAK NO BONES
672.11
BREAK OF 641.2
BREAK OFF 144.10
BREAK ONE'S BONDS
630.6
BREAK ONE'S CHAINS
641.3
BREAK ONESELF
AWAY 300.6
BREAK ONE'S EYES
AWAY 438.21
BREAK ONE'S HEART
870.19
BREAK ONE'S NECK
be active 705.12
hasten 707.5
strive 712.10
BREAK ONE'S WORD
973.11
BREAK ON THE
WHEEL 1008.18
BREAK OPEN
open 264.14
break 690.24
BREAK OUT
originate 68.12
erupt 161.12
~ in a rash 684.34
BREAK OUT A FLAG
274.55; 566.21
BREAK OUT BALLAST
274.51
BREAK OUT IN A

SWEAT 309.14
BREAK PRISCIAN'S
HEAD 585.3
BREAK SILENCE
592.13
BREAK SQUARES WITH
793.11
BREAK STRIKE 787.11
BREAK THE HABIT
641.3
BREAK THE ICE
initiate 68.9
prepare the way
718.12
make friends 925.11
BREAK THE LAW
997.5
BREAK THE NECK OF
render powerless
157.11
accomplish 720.6
BREAK THE NEWS
tell 554.5
report 556.11
BREAK THE PATTERN
641.3
BREAK THE RECORD
724.3
BREAK THE SOUND
BARRIER
speed 268.9
fly 277.42
BREAK THE THREAD
144.10
BREAK THROUGH
264.14
BREAK TO PIECES
49.12
BREAK TO SMITHERS,
BREAK TO SMITH-
EREENS 49.12
BREAK UP
shatter 49.12
separate 49.19
disintegrate 53.3
disband 75.9
adjourn 132.9
crumble 360.10
unsettle 530.7
decay 690.23
be destroyed 691.21
cure 692.15
BREAK WATER 274.49
BREAK WITH 793.11
breakable
fragile 159.14
brittle 359.4
breakage break 49.3
impairment 690.1
discount 845.1
breakaway 609.21
breakbone fever 684.9
breakdown
dissection 49.4
revolution 147.1
bed 215.20
analysis 484.8
physical ~ 684.7
impairment 690.1
debacle 691.4
failure 723.3

breaker 415.2
breakers 394.14
breakfast
nouns 306.6
verbs feed 306.15
dine 306.19
breakfast food 306a.34
breaking
domestication 188.4
training 560.3
subdual 762.4
breaking-out 684.27
breaking up 691.4
breaking water 274.8
breakneck
steep 218.18
hasty 707.10
reckless 892.8
break of day 133.3
breakthrough 796.1
breakthrough weapons
799.6
breakup
dissection 49.4
disintegration 53.1
dispersion 75.3
revolution 147.1
analysis 484.8
decay 690.5
destruction 691.1
debacle 691.4
breakwater
buttress 215.4
jetty 698.6
breast
nouns inner nature
5.4
bosom 255.6
~ of fowl 306a.23
gland 310.9
inmost mind 465.3
feelings 853.2
AT THE BREAST
124.12
verbs 788.5
BREAST THE TIDE
788.5
breast complaint
684.13
breasted 255.18
breast feathers 229.18
breast-feed 306.16
breastpin 899.6
breast stroke 274.11
breastwork 797.4
breath instant 113.3
vapor 400.1
wind 402.1
breeze 402.5
respiration 402.19
life 406.3
touch 424.1
odor 434.1
soft sound 451.4
respite 709.2
spirit 1032.17
HOLD ONE'S BREATH
wait 132.11
be quiescent 267.7
be silent 450.5
await 537.6

wonder 918.4
IN THE SAME BREATH
at once 113.8
simultaneously
118.6
OUT OF BREATH
715.10
PUT OUT OF BREATH
715.4
UNDER THE BREATH
612.19
WITH BATED BREATH
sotto voce 451.22
expectantly 537.13
secretly 612.19
humbly 904.14
breathe imbue 44.12
respire 402.25
live 406.6
smell 434.6
scent 434.8
sound softly 451.10
evince 504.9
mean 543.8
divulge 554.5
tip 555.10
say 592.14,17
whisper to 612.10
rest 709.8
exhaust 715.4
BREATHE EASY 884.8
BREATHE FIRE AND
FURY 950.15
BREATHE IN
inhale 305.12
smell 434.8
BREATHE NEW LIFE
INTO 693.2
BREATHE ONE'S LAST
407.15
BREATHE OUT 308.22
BREATHE VENGEANCE
954.5
NOT BREATHE A WORD
be silent 450.5
keep secret 612.8
breather respite 709.2
exercise 714.6
breathing
nouns breeze 402.5
respiration 402.19
utterance 592.3
aspiration 632.9
respite 709.2
adjs. respiratory
402.30
living 406.10
breathing hole 395.17
breathing spell
respite 709.2
truce 802.5
breathless
airless 267.14
dead 407.24
speechless 450.14
eager 633.9
winded 715.10
fervent 853.22
impatient 860.6
astonished 918.8
breathless impatience

alertness 531.5
auspiciousness
  542.7
pleasantness 861.3
cheerfulness 868.1
gorgeousness 898.6
bright outlook 886.3
bright prospect 886.1
Bright's disease 684.8
bright side
pleasantness 861.3
optimism 886.6
bright smile 874.3
brillante 461.54
brilliance, brilliancy
brightness 334.4
smartness 466.2
wittiness 879.2
gorgeousness 898.6
illustriousness 912.6
brilliant bright 334.32
smart 466.14
witty 879.15
gorgeous 898.19
illustrious 912.20
brilliantine 379.3
brilliantly 898.23
brilliant success 722.3
brim
nouns 234.4
UP TO THE BRIM
  56.18
verbs 56.7
BRIM OVER 394.18
brimful 56.12
brimmer 56.3
brimming 56.12
brimming eyes 873.2
brimstone 382.1
brinded 373.15
brindle
nouns 373.5
adjs. 373.15
brine
nouns ocean 396.1
salt 432.4
preservative 699.3
verbs 699.8
bring entail 76.4
lead 152.12
fetch 270.15
sail 274.30
induce 646.22
sell for 844.15
inflict 961.5
BRING ABOUT
cause 152.11
operate 163.6
produce 166.11
tack 274.32
do 703.6
accomplish 720.5
BRING AROUND
convert 145.11
make sane 471.3
cure 692.15
BRING BACK
fetch 270.15
remember 535.11
resurrect 692.16
return 821.4

BRING BEFORE 239.9
BRING DOWN
incur 174.4
fell 316.5
kill 408.18
raze 691.19
humble 904.5
BRING DOWN UPON
incur 174.4
inflict 961.5
BRING FORTH
generate 166.15
bear 166.17
elicit 304.12
manifest 553.5
BRING FORWARD
confront with 239.9
adduce 504.13
manifest 553.5
improve 689.9
propose 771.5
call to witness
  1002.16
BRING HOME THE
  BACON
beat 36.6
win 724.4
gain honor 914.9
BRING HOME TO
attribute to 154.3
convince 500.15
prove 504.11
impress upon
  853.17
accuse of 1003.9
convict 1006.3
BRING IN
introduce 305.14
harvest 412.19
yield 842.3
cost 844.15
BRING IN QUESTION
inquire 484.21
doubt 502.6
BRING INTO BEING
generate 166.15
vivify 406.8
BRING INTO DISCREDIT
disgrace 913.8
disparage 969.8
BRING INTO THE OPEN
disclose 554.4
publish 557.11
BRING LOW
lower 316.4
humble 904.5
disgrace 913.8
BRING NEAR
similarize 20.8
juxtapose 199.13
BRING OFF
prove 504.11
do 703.9
accomplish 720.5
succeed with 722.10
BRING ON
induce 152.12
incur 174.4
adduce 504.13
improve 689.9
BRING OUT

elicit 304.12
exhibit 553.5
publish 557.14
print 601.12
BRING OVER
convert 145.11
convince 500.15
persuade 646.23
BRING PRESSURE TO
  BEAR UPON
influence 171.9
urge 646.14
compel 754.6
BRING ROUND
tack 274.32
make sane 471.3
convince 500.15
persuade 646.23
cure 692.15
BRING THROUGH
accomplish 720.5
succeed with 722.10
BRING TO
stop 144.11
convert 145.8
sail 274.26
revive 692.16
BRING TO BEAR UPON
relate to 9.4
operate on 163.7
apply 663.11
BRING TO BOOK
reprove 967.17
punish 1008.10
BRING TO EFFECT
cause 152.11
make possible 508.5
bring about 720.5
BRING TOGETHER
assemble 74.17
reconcile 802.8
BRING TO LIGHT
elicit 304.12
find 487.4
disclose 554.4
BRING TO MIND
resemble 20.7
imply 544.4
BRING TO ONE'S
  SENSES
make sane 471.3
convince 500.15
persuade 646.23
BRING TO PASS
cause 152.11
do 703.6
accomplish 720.5
BRING TO REASON
make sane 471.3
convince 500.15
persuade 646.23
BRING TO TERMS
subdue 762.9
reconcile 802.8
BRING UP
stop 144.8
confront with 239.9
vomit 308.24
train 560.13
summon up 750.12
propose 771.5

BRING UPON
incur 174.4
inflict 961.5
BRING UP THE REAR
be behind 240.7
follow 292.3
BRING UP TO DATE
update 114.13
modernize 122.6
post 555.8
bringing-up 560.3
brininess 432.4
brining 699.2
brink 234.4
ON THE BRINK OF
about to 121.13
near 199.22
on the verge 234.15
briny
nouns 396.1
adjs. 432.9
briquette 330.1
brisk
verbs 693.2
adjs. transient 111.8
energetic 160.11
cold 332.15
breezy 402.26
pungent 432.7
fresh 693.5
lively 705.16
stimulating 855.32
brisken 693.2
brisket breast 255.6
meat cut 306a.17
briskly
energetically 160.14
actively 705.23
briskness cold 332.1
pungency 432.2
liveliness 705.2
bristle
nouns 260.3
verbs stand up 212.7
rumple 260.5
ruffle 864.17
become angry
  950.17
anger 950.22
BRISTLE UP
stick up 255.9
become angry
  950.17
BRISTLE WITH
be numerous 101.5
abound 659.5
bristles 229.8
bristling
thickly set 74.22
thick with 101.10
bristly 260.9
bristly 229.24
Bristol fashion 276.20
Britain 180.4
Britannia 180.4
britchen 657.5
britches 230.18
Briticism
nationalism 180.6
idiom 578.9
patriotism 939.2

Britisher 417.9
Briton 417.9
brittle fragile 359.4
  friable 360.13
brittleness
  fragility 359
  friability 360.3
broach
  nouns 264.3
  verbs inaugurate
    68.13
  open 264.11
  perforate 264.15
  draft off 304.10
  publish 557.14
  propose 771.5
  BROACH TO 274.34
broaching 304.2
broad
  nouns girl 125.6
  pool 397.1
  woman 420.6
  strumpet 987.14
  adjs. general 79.10
  extensive 79.12
  spacious 178.9
  large 194.17
  wide 203.6
  phonetics 449.18
  indefinite 513.17
  broad-minded 524.8
  liberal 524.9
  candid 972.17
  indecent 988.8
broad arrow
  insignia 567.2
  stigma 913.6
broad awake
  alert 531.14
  awake 711.7
broad-beamed 203.7
broad-bodied 203.8
broadcast
  nouns dispersion 75.1
  radio ~ 343.21
  sowing 412.14
  publication 557.1
  verbs disperse 75.5
  radiocast 343.28
  sow 412.18
  publish 557.10
  adjs. 75.10
broadcaster
  distributor 75.4
  radio ~ 343.5,26
broadcasting
  dispersion 75.1
  radio ~ 343.19
  sowing 412.14
  publication 557.1
Broad Church 1018.9
broad comedy 609.6
broad daylight 334.10
broaden increase 38.4
  generalize 79.8
  enlarge 196.4
  expand 196.5
  widen 203.4
broadening
  nouns 196.1
  adjs. 524.14

broad-gauge 203.6
broad-gauged 524.8
broad grin 874.3
broadhearted 524.11
broad hint 555.4
broad jump 317.1
Broadleaf 433.2
broadly
  extensively 178.10
  far 198.17
  indefinitely 513.26
broad man 524.6
broad-mindedness
  524.1
broadness
  largeness 194.6
  breadth 203.1
  generality 513.4
  broad-mindedness
    524.2
broad-ribbed 203.7
broadsheet 557.8
broadshouldered
  strong 158.14
  he-mannish 419.12
broadside
  nouns side 241.1
  advertisement 557.8
  gunfire 796.10
  advs. breadthwise
    203.9
  sideways 241.8
  BROADSIDE ON
  sideways 241.8
  ships 274.76
broad-sterned 203.7
broadways, broadwise
  203.9
Brobdingnagian
  nouns strong man
    158.6
  giant 194.13
  adjs. strong 158.15
  gigantic 194.20
brochure 603.10
Brocken specter
  1015.2
brogue dialect 578.8
  accent 592.7
broil
  nouns embroilment
    62.4
  turbulence 161.2
  food 306a.7
  broiling 329.1
  brawl 793.7
  verbs be hot 327.21
  cook 329.4
  brawl 793.13
broiler food 306a.22
  hot day 327.7
  fowl 413.35
broiling
  nouns 329.1
  adjs. 327.25
broke penniless 836.10
  bankrupt 840.11
broken severed 49.23
  incoherent 51.4
  discontinuous 72.4
  irregular 138.3

domesticated 188.9
  rough 260.6
  conquered 725.16
  subdued 762.14
  tame 763.15
  bankrupt 840.11
broken chord 462.17
broken color 361.6
broken dose 685.5
broken-down 690.32
broken fortune 836.1
broken ground 260.2
broken heart
  anguish 864.6
  grief 870.9
brokenly
  discontinuously 72.5
  irregularly 138.4
  roughly 260.11
broken mirror
  superstition 501.3
  omen 542.4
broken off 72.4
broken speech 593.1
broken thread 72.1
broken-winded 715.10
broker
  intermediary 779.4
  pawnbroker 818.3
  dealer 828.9
  stockbroker 831.10
  marriage ~ 931.13
brokerage office 831.9
  stockbrokerage
    831.18
  charge 844.7
broker's agent 831.10
brokers' board 831.7
brolly umbrella 227.7
  parachute 279.13
  MAKE A BROLLY-HOP
    277.53
bromide
  conformist 82.2
  cliché 516.3
bromidic 881.9
bromidite 82.2
bromidium 516.3
bronchia, bronchial
  tube 395.16
bronchial 395.20
bronchial asthma
  684.25
bronchitis 684.12
bronchocele 684.8
bronchoplasty 687.27
bronchopneumonia
  684.12
bronco, broncho
  413.14
broncobuster
  horseman 273.8
  trainer 415.2
Bronx cheer 965.3
  GIVE THE BRONX
    CHEER 965.10
bronze
  nouns 573.2
  verbs 366.2
  adjs. reddish-brown
    366.4

  metallic 382.16
Bronze Age 107.6
bronze-colored 366.4
brooch 899.6
brood
  nouns people 11.4
  family 11.6
  posterity 170.1
  young 170.2
  verbs incubate
    116.16
  meditate 477.11
  BROOD OVER
  ponder 477.12
  remember 535.14
  grieve 870.17
  harbor revenge
    954.5
brooder
  breeding place 152.8
  hen 413.35
  enclosure 415.5
  sad person 870.13
brooding
  nouns 166.7
  adjs. 718.24
brood mare
  horse 413.12
  female animal
    420.10
brook
  nouns 394.1
  verbs 859.5
Brooklynese 578.8
broom 679.21
broomstick 204.8
broomtail 413.14
broth 306a.10
brothel 987.9
brother relative 11.3
  counterpart 20.5
  member 786.11
  ecclesiastical title
    915.5
  friend 926.1
  religious 1036.16
  layman 1037.2
brother-german 11.3
brotherhood
  kinship 11.1
  society 786.4
  fellowship 925.2
brother-in-law 12.2
brotherliness 925.2
brotherly
  friendly 925.14
  kind 936.14
brotherly love 936.4
brothership 11.1
brow summit 210.2
  border 234.4
  forehead 239.5
  countenance 445.4
browbeat
  domineer 739.15
  bulldoze 889.19
browbeaten 762.15
browbeater 941.5
browbeating 889.5
brown
  nouns color 366.1

colors, pigments
366.5,6
verbs 329.4
adjs. 366.3
brown Betty 306a.45
browned 329.6
Brownie 575.13
brownie dwarf 195.6
cake 306a.42
elf 1012.15
brownish 366.3
brownishness 366.1
brownout 336.8
brown race race 417.2
types of ~ 417.17
brown study 530.2
brows 229.12
browse graze 306.25
read 562.13
bruise
nouns 690.8
verbs crush 360.9
abuse 665.5
wound 690.14
grieve 864.14
beat 1008.17
bruiser pugilist 798.2
ruffian 941.4
bruit, bruit about
557.10
bruited about 556.15
bruiting about 557.1
brumal winter 128.8
cold 332.15
brummagem 614.27
brunch 306.6
brunet, brunette
nouns 361.8
adjs. 366.3
brunt shock 282.3
crux 729.7
brush
nouns wilderness
165.2
hinterland 181.2
tuft 229.9
tail 240.5
firewood 330.3
brushwood 410.14
touch 424.1
art 572.8
paintbrush 572.19
artist 577.4
conflict 794.3
HAVE A BRUSH WITH
794.18
THE BRUSH 572.5
verbs graze 199.10
speed 268.9
wipe 392.6
groom 415.6
touch 424.7
swish 451.12
sweep 679.21
BRUSH ASIDE
disregard 529.4
reject 636.2
BRUSH UP
refresh the memory
535.19
study up 562.14

touch up 689.11
brush ape 189.10
brush wolf 413.4
brushwood
firewood 330.3
thicket 410.14
brusque gruff 935.7
candid 972.17
brusqueness
gruffness 935.3
candor 972.4
Brussels biscuit
306a.29
brustle 451.12
brutal savage 161.20
animal 413.36
barbarous 896.12
cruel 937.24
carnal 985.6
brutality
barbarism 896.3
ruthlessness 937.11
cruelty 937.12
carnality 985.2
brutalize 854.6
brutalness 937.11
brute
nouns animal 413.2
savage 941.6
adjs. animal 413.36
cruel 937.24
carnal 985.6
brute creation 413.1
brute fact 1.3
brute force
power 156.1
compulsion 754.2
BY BRUTE FORCE
156.16
brute matter
matter 375.2
inorganic matter
381.1
brutify callous 854.6
sensualize 985.4
brutish savage 161.20
animal 413.36
barbarous 896.12
cruel 937.24
carnal 985.6
brutishness
barbarism 896.3
cruelty 937.11
carnality 985.2
Brutus wig 229.14
traitor 617.10
bryologist 411.2
bryology 411.1
bryophyta,
bryophytes 411.5
Bryozoa, bryozoan
414.6
bub brother 11.3
boy 125.5
bubble
nouns
unsubstantiality 4.3
ephemeron 111.5
bulge 255.3
lightness 352.3
trickle 394.7

air globule 404
illusion 518.1
fancy 533.5
trifle 671.5
airy hopes 886.5
verbs trickle 394.19
foam 404.4
burble 451.11
BUBBLE OVER
bubble 404.4
enthuse 633.8
bubble gum 388.6
bubbling
nouns 404.3
adjs. bubbly 404.6
burbling 451.19
bubby boy 125.5
breast 255.6
bubo 684.28
bubonic plague 684.4
bubonocele 684.8
buccaneer
nouns 823.8
verbs 822.16
buccaneering 822.6
Bucephalus 413.21
buck
nouns sawhorse
215.11
jump 317.1
animal 413.7,10,29
Indian 417.5
Negro 417.7
man 419.5
male animal 419.8
dollar 833.7
verbs carry 270.11
butt 282.12
jump 317.5
launder 679.18
oppose 788.5
BUCK OFF 184.6
BUCK THE TIGER
514.19
BUCK UP
dress up 230.41
refresh 693.2
cheer up 868.8
take courage 891.14
encourage 891.16
buckaroo
horseman 273.8
horse trainer 415.2
bucket
nouns pail 192.6
ship 276.3
LIKE BUCKETS IN A
WELL 322.20
verbs bail 270.16
cheat 616.18
bucketshop 831.23
bucketing 831.18
bucket shop
nouns gambling
514.14
swindle 616.8
stockbrokerage
831.9
verbs 831.23
buck fever 857.1
bucking bronco,

buckjumper
jumper 317.4
horse 413.14
buckjump
nouns 317.1
verbs 317.5
buckle
nouns 248.1
verbs fasten 47.8
distort 248.5
BUCKLE DOWN 714.9
BUCKLE TO
be determined
622.8
undertake 713.3
set to work 714.15
buckling 47.3
bucko 941.5
buck private 798.9
buckra 363.3
buckram
nouns 644.1
adjs. 644.9
bucks 833.2
buckshot 799.14
bucktooth 257.7
bucoliast 607.15
bucolic
nouns poem 607.4
poet 607.15
rustic 917.9
adjs. rural 181.6
poetic 607.21
bud
nouns brother 11.3
boy 125.5
rudiment 152.7
plant ~ 410.21
IN THE BUD
beginning 68.13
embryonic 405.23
verbs grow 196.7
graft 303.5
sprout 410.31
BUD FROM 153.6
Buddha sage 467.2
Blessed one 1011.5
deity 1012.8
religious 1020.3
buddhi
psyche 1032.17
soul 1032.20
Buddhic body
1032.19
Buddhist, Buddhis-
tic(al) 1018.30
budding
nouns growth 196.3
vegetation 410.30
adjs. 124.10
buddy brother 11.3
boy 125.5
comrade 926.4
buddy up 925.10
budge
nouns 994.12
verbs 266.4
NOT BUDGE 624.7
budget
nouns quantity 28.2
bundle 74.7

accumulation 74.8
bag 192.2
program 639.2
store 658.1
allowance 814.6
funds 833.14
statement 843.3
verbs schedule 639.4
ration 814.11
budgeting 814.6
budmash 984.2
buff
nouns 231.3
IN NATIVE BUFF
231.14
verbs polish 259.7
rub 349.6
adjs. leather 228.7
yellow 369.4
buffalo
nouns 413.5
verbs baffle 513.13
bully 889.19
buffaloing 889.5
buffalo robe 227.10
buffalo wallow 397.1
buff-colored 369.4
buffer guard 697.3
barrier 728.5
buffet counter 215.15
restaurant 306.14
buffet
nouns blow 282.8
disappointment
539.1
chastisement 1008.3
verbs hit 282.15,18
abuse 665.5
bruise 690.14
struggle 714.11
oppose 788.5
whip 1008.13
chastise 1008.14
BUFFET THE WAVES
pitch 274.58
have difficulty
729 10
oppose 788.5
buffeting 1008.4
buffo singer 463.14
buffoon 610.9
buffoon 610.9
buffoonery
drama 609.9
wit 879.5
bug
nouns insect 413a.2
craze 472.12
fanatic 472.17
enthusiast 633.5
fault 676.2
bugbear 1014.10
SNUG AS A BUG IN A
RUG 885.11
verbs 255.10
bugaboo, bugbear
false alarm 702.4
bogy 1014.10
bug bomb 408.11
bug-eyed
pop-eyed 255.15

poor-sighted 439.12
bugger
nouns chap 419.5
wretch 984.6
booger 1014.10
verbs disable 157.9
spoil 690.11
botch 732.12
buggy
nouns automobile
271.9
caboose 271.13
adjs. insectile 413a.9
insane 472.25
eccentric 473.4
bughouse
nouns 472.14
adjs. 472.25
bugle
nouns nose 255.7
toot 452.4
instrument 464.8
verbs toot 454.19
play a ~ 461.43
bugle call 566.15
bugle corps 798.20
bugler 463.4
bugs 472.25
bugs on 633.11
build
nouns structure 244.1
form 245.1
physique 245.4
verbs increase 38.4
construct 166.12
establish 183.17
BUILD CASTLES IN
THE AIR 533.16
BUILD ON 211.6
BUILD UP
increase 38.4
exaggerate 615.3
aggravate 883.2
BUILD UPON 500.13
builder
producer 166.10
planner 652.7
building making 166.3
house 190.5
structure 244.2
build-up
promotion 557.5
commendation
966.3
built 166.27
BUILT ON 211.9
BUILT ON SAND 4.7
bulb, bulbil, bulblet
globule 254.2
root 410.20
bulbose, bulbous
bulging 255.14
tuberous 410.34
bulbul 463.15
bulge
nouns advantage 36.2
protuberance 255.3
GET THE BULGE ON
724.7
verbs 255.10
bulged swollen 196.12

protuberant 255.15
bulging 255.14
bulgy 255.15
bulimia 688.21
bulk
nouns quantity 28.1
main part 54.5
accumulation 74.8
majority 100.2
size 194.1
mass 194.10
thickness 203.2
verbs loom 34.7
assemble 74.17
expand 196.4
enlarge 196.5
bulkhead
partition 236.5
door 301.6
barrier 728.5
bulkiness
massiveness 194.9
unwieldiness 729.8
clumsiness 732.3
bulky
substantial 3.5
massive 194.19
thick 203.8
unwieldy 729.18
clumsy 732.20
bull
nouns bullock 413.8
male animal 419.8
error 517.6
nonsense 545.4
epistle 602.3
humbug 614.14
policeman 697.14
decree 750.4
speculator 831.13
BULL IN A CHINA SHOP
pandemonium 62.5
bungler 732.8
verbs blunder 517.13
talk nonsense 545.8
bungle 732.11
~ the market
831.25
adjs. large 194.16
male 419.11
bulla knob 255.3
bubble 404.1
pustule 684.28
bull account 831.13
bulldog
nouns 50.3
verbs 316.5
bulldog courage 891.4
bulldogged 624.8
bulldog tenacity 623.1
bulldoze level 213.6
browbeat 889.19
bulldozer
tractor 271.16
bully 941.5
bullet proton ~ 325.8
missile 799.14
bulletheaded 624.8
bulletin
nouns newsletter
556.5

record 568.6
message 602.3
periodical 603.11
verbs 557.15
bulletin board
poster 557.7
record 568.9
bulletproof 158.18
bullets 833.2
bull fiddle
noisemaker 452.5
instrument 464.5
bullfight 794.4
bullfrog 413.32
bullhead dolt 470.4
obstinate person
624.6
bungler 732.8
bullheadedness 624.1
bullhorn 343.4
bullion metal 382.3
money 833.19
bullnecked 203.8
bullock bull 413.8
male animal 419.8
bull panic 831.22
bull pen 759.9
bull pool 831.17
bull raid 831.20
bull ring 800.1
bull-roarer 452.5
bull session 595.3
bull's-eye center 225.2
window 264.7
shot 284.5
star 374.5
lens 442.1
target 651.2
success 722.4
bullwhack 1009.1
bullwhacker 273.9
bullwhip 1009.1
bully
nouns beef 306a.13
tormentor 864.10
ruffian 941.5
verbs 889.19
adjs. good 672.14
jovial 868.15
interjs. 966.21
BULLY FOR YOU!
946.4
bully beef 306a.13
bullying 889.5
bullyrag 864.19
bulwark
nouns buttress 215.4
protection 697.3
barrier 728.5
fortification 797.4
verbs 797.9
bum
nouns rump 240.4
vagabond 273.3
idler 706.8
beggar 772.8
revel 876.6
wretch 984.2
spree 994.5
drunkard 994.11
verbs hum 451.13

idle 706.10
beg 772.15
tipple 994.31
BUM A RIDE 272.30
BUM AROUND 706.10
adjs. 673.8
bumbailiff 697.14
bumbershoot 227.7
bumblebee 413a.4
bumblebomb 280.3
Bumbledom 742.39
bummer
vagabond 273.3
idler 706.8
beggar 772.8
bump
nouns bulge 255.3
swelling 255.4
air pocket 277.38
push 282.2
collision 282.3
shake 323.3
thud 451.3
bang 455.1
demotion 780.2
verbs push 282.12
collide 282.13
discharge 308.18
shake 323.11
bang 455.6
demote 780.4
BUMP INTO
meet 199.11
collide 282.13
find 487.3
BUMP OFF 408.14
bumped 255.14
bumper
nouns fill 56.3
big thing 194.11
guard 697.3
adjs. 194.16
bumper crop 809.4
bumping
nouns 308.5
adjs. 194.21
bumpkin 917.9
bumptious 911.8
bumptiously 911.11
bumpy bulging 255.14
rough 260.6
jolting 323.21
bum steer 616.2
GIVE A BUM STEER
616.15
bun head 210.5
hair 229.7
food 306a.30
bunce 833.2
bunch
nouns quantity 28.2
company 74.3
flock 74.5
group 74.6
multitude 101.3
set 786.7
verbs league 52.4
congregate 74.15
assemble 74.17
BUNCH THE HITS
try hard 712.10

brag 908.6
bunch-backed 248.13
buncombe, bunkum
nonsense 545.2
bombast 599.2
humbug 614.14
brag 908.2
flattery 968.1
bund band 74.3
harbor 698.6
association 786.1
bunder 698.6
Bundesrat 740.3
Bundesversammlung
740.2
bundle
nouns 74.7
BUNDLE OF NERVES
857.11
verbs parcel 74.19
speed 268.9
walk 272.27
send 284.14
send off 308.17
cuddle 930.15
BUNDLE OFF
send off 284.14
send away 308.17
BUNDLE ON 707.5
BUNDLE UP
bundle 74.19
clothe 230.38
bundling 930.1
bundobust 769.4
bundu 181.2
bung
nouns 265.4
verbs stop up 265.7
throw 284.12
bruise 690.14
bungalow 190.8
bunghole 264.4
bungle
nouns 732.5
verbs 732.11
bungler 732.8
bungling
nouns 732.4
adjs. careless 532.12
clumsy 732.20
bunion 684.28
bunk
nouns bed 215.20
nonsense 545.3
bombast 599.2
humbug 614.14
brag 908.2
verbs reside 187.8
flee 629.11
bunker 797.5
bunkhouse 190.9
bunkie 926.4
bunko
nouns 616.8
verbs 616.18
bunko steerer 617.5
bunkum
See buncombe
bunny 413.29
bunt
nouns tail 240.5

butt 282.2
blow 282.6
propulsion 284.1
verbs butt 282.12
knock 282.16
push 284.10
bunting 567.6
buoy
nouns float 276.11
life ~ 699.5
verbs 352.8
buoyance, buoyancy
lightness 352.1
resilience 357.1
lightheartedness
868.3
buoyant light 352.13
resilient 357.7
recuperative 692.23
cheerful 868.11
bur, burr
adherent 50.3
thorn 257.8
seed vessel 410.28
burble
nouns 394.7
verbs trickle 394.19
bubble 404.4
ripple 451.11
burbling
bubbling 404.6
rippling 451.19
burden
nouns ~ of a song
103.5
load 193.2
capacity 194.2
weight 351.7
tone 449.2
music 461.24
voice 462.5
note 462.14
~ of proof 504.4
poetic refrain
607.11
impediment 728.6
~ of expenditure
841.3
care 864.8
imposition 961.3
verbs saddle on 40.3
weigh down 351.13
overburden 661.16
task 714.16
hamper 728.11
BURDEN WITH 961.4
burdensome
ponderous 351.17
laborious 714.19
impedimental
728.18
difficult 729.17
oppressive 862.15
bureau office 717.8
department 998.4
bureaucracy
government 739.4
officialism 742.39
officialdom 747.16
bureaucrat 747.17

burg 182.1
burgee 567.6
burgeon
nouns sprout 410.18
bud 410.21
verbs grow 196.7
sprout 410.31
burgeoning
growth 196.3
vegetation 410.30
burgess, burgher
townsman 189.6
freeman 760.10
burgh 182.1
burghal 182.9
burghmaster 747.19
burglar 823.3
burglar alarm 702.3
burglarize 822.14
burglarizing 822.3
burglarproof 158.18
burglary robbery 822.3
theft 822.10
burgle
nouns 822.3
verbs 822.14
burgomaster 747.19
burgrave 747.14
burial
submergence 318.2
interment 409.1
funeral 409.5
concealment 613.1
burial ground 409.15
buried
underground 208.11
underwater 208.12
concealed 613.12
BURIED IN 528.17
buried treasure 809.5
burin 576.11
burke 408.19
burker 408.10
burkite 408.10
burkundaz escort 73.5
bodyguard 697.13
burl 255.3
burlesque
nouns drama 609.6
parody 965.6
verbs 965.11
adjs. 965.14
burlesquer 879.12
burletta 609.6
Burley 433.2
burly 194.18
burn
nouns burning 328.6
water 391.3
brook 394.1
hurt 423.3
injury 690.7
verbs be near 199.8
be hot 327.21
ignite 328.21
catch fire 328.22
torrefy 328.23
give light 334.23
tan 366.2
dry 392.6

cremate 409.21
pain 423.7
detect 487.6
~ with excitement
  855.19
be angry 950.15
execute 1008.19
BURN DAYLIGHT
  706.11
BURN ONE'S BRIDGES
  622.8
BURN ONE'S FINGERS
have trouble 729.11
mismanage 732.14
suffer loss 810.5
BURN THE CANDLE AT
  BOTH ENDS
study hard 562.12
overdo 661.11
work hard 714.13
squander 852.3
dissipate 991.6
BURN THE MIDNIGHT
  OIL
study 562.12
work hard 714.13
BURN UP
incinerate 328.24
annoy 864.17
anger 950.21
burnable 328.27
burned 329.29
burner jet 328.10
incinerator 328.12
blowtorch 328.13
types of ~ 335.12
burning
  nouns combustion
    328.5
cremation 409.2
pain 423.3
execution 1008.7
  adjs. near 199.14
hot 327.25
blazing 327.27
shining 334.30
in heat 418.21
sore 423.11
eloquent 598.13
zealous 633.10
feverish 684.43
fervent 853.22
excited 855.23
angry 950.27
burning ghat
crematory 328.12
morgue 409.9
burning glass 442.1
burning mountain
  161.6
burnish
  nouns gloss 259.2
polish 259.4
  verbs shine 259.7
rub 349.6
burnished
polished 259.10
shiny 334.33
burnishing 349.1
burnout 280.10
burnsides 229.8

burnt burned 328.29
red 367.10
dried 392.9
BURNT UP 864.24
burnt almond 306a.38
burnt cork 364.6
burnt offering 1030.7
burp
  nouns 308.9
  verbs 308.25
burr
  nouns adherent 50.3
thorn 257.8
seed vessel 410.28
harsh sound 457.3
engraving 576.1
accent 592.7
  verbs whir 451.13
sound harshly 457.8
burro 413.22
burrow
  nouns lair 190.22
tunnel 256.5
  verbs settle 183.18
tunnel 256.15
search 484.25
hide 613.9
bursar 834.11
bursary 834.12
bursitis 684.8
burst
  nouns break 49.3
outburst 161.6
explosion 161.7
spurt 268.4
flare 327.13
~ of rain 393.2
bang 455.1
detonation 455.3
gunfire 796.10
~ of passion 855.8
~ of laughter 874.4
~ of anger 950.9
~ of applause 966.2
PUT ON A BURST OF
  SPEED 268.17
  verbs fracture 49.11
explode 161.13
BURST FORTH
erupt 161.12
grow 196.7
emerge 302.12
sprout 410.31
appear 445.9
BURST IN
open 264.14
enter 301.7
BURST INTO FLAME
  328.22
BURST INTO
  LAUGHTER 874.9
BURST INTO SONG
  461.38
BURST INTO TEARS
  873.10
BURST LIKE A BUBBLE
  111.6
BURST OUT 874.9
BURST THE BUBBLE
  519.2
BURST UPON 199.11

BURST WITH HEALTH
  683.4
  adjs. 49.23
bursting full 56.12
explosive 161.23
overfull 661.21
excited 855.21
burthen 728.6
bury submerge 318.7
inter 409.20
conceal 613.8
BURY ONESELF IN
  562.12
BURY THE HATCHET
  802.9
burying
interment 409.1
funeral 409.5
concealment 613.1
bus vehicle 271.1
automobile 271.9
bus boy 270.5
bus driver 273.10
bush
  nouns wilderness
    165.2
hinterland 181.2
lining 227.20
plain 386.1
shrub 410.9
woodland 410.11
branch 410.18
  verbs spread 196.6
tire 715.4
bushed
perplexed 513.23
tired out 715.8
bushel
  nouns 34.3
  verbs 692.14
busheler 230.34
bushelman 230.34
bushfighter 798.15
bushfighting 795.4
bushing lining 227.20
bearing 320.7
bushman 189.10
bush pilot 278.1
bushranger 823.5
bush telegraph 556.10
bush veld
hinterland 181.2
plain 386.1
woodland 410.11
bushwa, bushwah
  545.3
bushwhacker
forerunner 66.1
bushfighter 798.15
bushy hairy 229.24
shrubby 410.37,38
busily 705.23
business affair 150.3
topic 483.1
acting device 609.9
occupation 654.6
firm 786.9
commerce 825.1
HAVE NO BUSINESS
  THERE
be unrelated 10.3

not conform 83.5
MAKE IT ONE'S
  BUSINESS
specialize 81.4
engage in 703.7
NONE OF YOUR
  BUSINESS 237.10
business contact 826.4
business cycle 825.7
business deal 825.4
business district 182.5
businessese 578.7
business establishment
  786.9
business index 844.5
business intercourse
  825.1
businesslike
orderly 59.6
practical 654.15
businessman 828.1
business school 565.8
business transaction
  825.4
businesswoman 828.1
busk 274.32
buskin costume 230.9
tragic drama 609.5
busload 193.2
busman 273.10
busman's holiday
  709.3
buss
  nouns 930.3
  verbs 930.17
bust
  nouns breast 255.6
bang 455.1
figure 570.4
failure 723.2
demotion 780.2
bankruptcy 840.3
revel 876.6
spree 994.5
  verbs fracture 49.11
explode 161.13
tame 188.5
cashier 308.18
train 560.13
flunk 723.16
subdue 762.10
demote 780.4
depose 781.2
bankrupt 840.8
BUST A GUT 712.10
BUST IN
intrude 237.5
open 264.14
enter 301.7
busted severed 49.23
penniless 836.10
bankrupt 840.11
bustee 182.2
busthead 994.14
bustle
  nouns agitation 323.1
activity 705.4
haste 707.1
excitement 855.3
bluster 909.1

night club 876.11
barroom 994.25
cabbage
nouns 833.2
verbs 822.13
cabbagehead 470.4
cabbageheaded
468.17
cabby, cabdriver 273.9
caber 216.3
cabin
nouns house 190.8
room 191.9
verbs reside 187.8
confine 235.6
cabin boy 275.6
cabined
housed 187.15
confined 235.10
cabinet
nouns private room
191.8
radio ~ 343.3
office 717.8
political ~ 740.7
committee 753.3
adjs. 612.15
cable
nouns cord 205.2
cablegram 558.16
telegraph ~ 558.20
verbs fasten 47.9
telegraph 558.22
cable car 271.13
cable code 612.7
cablegram 558.16
cable railway 655.8,9
cabman 273.9
caboodle all 54.4
bunch 74.6
whole ~ 79.4
caboose
railway car 271.13
kitchen 329.3
cache
nouns 613.4
verbs hide 613.8
store 658.10
cachet 566.12
cachexia
debility 159.1
disease 684.8
cachinnate 874.9
cachination 874.4
cacique
politician 744.7
chief 747.9
cack 215.19
cackle
nouns chatter 594.3
laughter 874.4
verbs crow 459.5
say 592.17
laugh 874.9
cacodemon 1014.7
cacoëpistic 593.11
cacoëpy 593.5
cacoëthes desire 632.6
bad habit 640.8
cacoëthes loquendi
594.2

cacoëthes scribendi
600.2
cacographic(al) 588.2
cacography
ungrammaticalness
585.1
inelegant style
588.1
writing 600.7
cacology
ungrammaticalness
585.1
inelegant style
588.1
mispronunciation
593.5
caconym 580.6
cacophonous 460.4
cacophony 460.1
cactus 257.8
cad servant 748.9
vulgarian 896.6
scoundrel 984.7
cadastral 88.8
cadastration 489.9
cadastre, cadaster 88.1
cadaver 407.13
cadaverous
emaciated 204.19
ghastly 362.9
corpselike 407.23
caddie 748.4
caddish 935.6
cadeau 816.4
cadence
lowering 314.2
inflection 449.2
cadenza 461.24
ornament 462.18
rhythm 462.22
meter 607.9
cadenced, cadent
rhythmical 462.27
measured 489.14
cadenza music 461.24
ornament 462.18
cadet 747.23
cadge 772.15
cadger beggar 772.8
vendor 828.6
cadging 772.6
cadi 1000.3
cadre list 88.1
framework 244.4
schedule 639.2
officers 746.10
military unit 798.19
caduceus
insignia 567.5
scepter 737.9
caducity 468.10
caecal
intestinal 224.12
closed 265.9
caecotomy 687.26
caecum 224.6
caelum 374.2
Caelus 374.2
Caesar 747.9,15
caesarian, caesarian
section 687.26

caesura
interruption 72.2
pause 144.3,4
interval 200.1
poetry 607.9
café 306.14
café chantant 876.11
café society 642.6
cafeteria 306.14
cafuso 44.9
cage
nouns 759.7
verbs pen in 235.5
confine 759.12
cageling 759.11
cagey evasive 629.14
cunning 733.12
wary 893.9
cagily
cunningly 733.15
warily 893.13
caginess
cunning 733.1
wariness 893.2
Cagot 924.3
cahoots, cahoot
partnership 784.3
participation 813.1
GO IN CAHOOTS
league 52.4
co-operate 784.6
cahot bump 255.3
cavity 256.3
caigy 418.20
caille 306a.22
Cain 408.10
cairn, carn
landmark 566.9
monument 568.11
caisse 464.21
caisson 192.19
caisson disease 684.5
caitiff
nouns coward 890.6
wretch 984.2
adjs. 890.12
cajole coax 646.14
importune 772.12
flatter 968.5
cajoler coaxer 646.10
flatterer 968.4
cajolery, cajolement
coaxing 646.3
importunity 772.3
flattery 968.1
Cajun 578.8
cake
nouns food 306a.41
solid 353.6
verbs coagulate
353.10
solidify 355.8
caked, caky 353.14
cakes and ale 885.3
calaboose 759.7
calambac 435.4
Calamites, calamite
411.6
calamitous
destructive 691.25
disastrous 727.15

calamity fatality 408.7
misfortune 727.2
calamity howler 887.7
calamus 229.17
calando 461.55
calathiform 256.16
Calcarea 414.4
calcification 355.5
calcify 355.7
calcimine 361.14
calcination 328.5
calcinatory
nouns 328.12
adjs. 328.25
calcine 328.23
calcitrate 282.20
calcitration 282.9
calculable
computable 87.16
reliable 512.17
predictable 541.13
calculate
compute 87.11
judge 493.9
suppose 498.9
think 500.9
CALCULATE ON
rely on 500.13
plan on 651.6
calculated
measured 489.14
intentional 651.9
advised 752.11
CALCULATED TO
173.6
calculated risk 514.1
calculating
numerative 87.15
judicious 466.19
scheming 652.14
calculation
computation 87.3
caution 893.1
calculator
computer 87.8
types of ~ 87.19
electronic
computer 348.16
accountant 843.7
calculus
mathematics 87.18
concretion 355.5
caldarium 679.8
caldron 145.7
Caledonian 417.9
calefacient,
calefactory 328.25
calefaction 328.1
calembour 879.8
calendar
nouns catalogue 88.3
chronology 114.8
record book 568.10
book 603.6
schedule 639.2
legislative ~
740.19
verbs list 88.7
chronicle 114.14
press 259.6
record 568.15

schedule 639.4
calender
 nouns 259.13
 verbs 259.6
calendric(al) 114.15
calends, kalends
 catalogue 88.3
 calendar 114.8
calenture
 ~ of the brain 472.9
 fever 684.6,20
calf youngling 125.8
 legs 272.16
 iceberg 332.6
 island 385.2
 bovine 413.8
 fool 470.1
 clumsy fellow 732.9
calf days 124.1
calf love 929.4
caliber degree 29.1
 capability 156.2
 diameter 203.3
 intelligence 466.1
 ability 731.4
calibrate 489.11
calibrating circuit
 348.6
calico
 nouns 420.3,6
 adjs. 373.12
calico pony 413.15
calid 327.24
caliginous 336.14
caligo 684.11
caliper 489.11
caliph 747.11
caliphate, caliphship
 737.7
calisthenics
 study 560.8
 exercise 714.6
calk
 nouns 710.3
 verbs 265.7
calker end-all 70.4
 dram 994.6
call
 nouns cause 152.1
 shout 458.1
 animal ~ 459.1
 telephone ~ 558.15
 signal 566.15
 motive 646.1
 bidding 750.5
 demand 751.1
 appeal 772.2
 invitation 772.4
 recruitment 778.6
 ~ to arms 795.13
 option 831.21
 visit 920.6
 ~ of duty 960.1
 justification 1004.6
 ON CALL
 ready 663.19
 on demand 751.11
 collect 839.25
 WITHIN CALL
 present 185.12
 near 199.20

verbs shout 458.6
 animal sound 459.2
 consider 493.8
 cite 504.14
 meet a bet 514.19
 telephone 558.21
 name 581.11
 waken 711.4
 summon 750.12
 invite 772.13
 dun 843.11
CALL A SPADE A SPADE
 be practical 534.4
 speak plainly 589.2
 be frank 972.12
CALL ATTENTION TO
 direct to 528.10
 remind 535.20
CALL BACK
 remember 535.11
 recant 626.9
 revive 692.16
 recall 750.12
 repeal 777.2
CALL DOWN 967.18
CALL DOWN CURSES
 ON THE HEAD OF
 970.5
CALL FOR
 entail 76.4
 fetch 270.15
 require 637.9
 summon 750.12
 demand 751.4
 oblige 754.5
 request 772.9
CALL FORTH
 induce 152.12
 elicit 304.12
 prompt 646.13
 avail oneself of
 663.14
 summon 750.12
 excite 855.11
CALL IN
 consult 595.10
 recall 750.12
 invite 772.13
CALL IN QUESTION
 doubt 502.6
 protest 520a.5
 summons 750.12
CALL INTO BEING
 generate 166.15
 vivify 406.8
CALL INTO PLAY
 663.14
CALL IT A DAY
 stop 144.8
 complete 720.6
CALL IT A GO 520.10
CALL NAMES
 insult 963.4
 vilify 969.10
 curse 970.7
CALL OFF
 end 70.7
 enumerate 87.10
CALL ON, CALL UPON
 urge 646.14
 command 750.9

petition 772.10
 beseech 772.11
 visit 920.16
CALL ONE'S BLUFF
 791.7
CALL ONE'S SHOT
 541.9
CALL OUT
 elicit 304.12
 cry out 458.8
 summon forth
 750.12
 challenge 791.3
CALL THE ROLL 87.10
CALL THE SIGNALS
 direct 745.8
 command 750.9
CALL TO 592.18
CALL TO ACCOUNT
 reprove 967.17
 punish 1008.10
CALL TO ARMS
 795.24
CALL TO MIND
 cite 504.14
 visualize 533.15
 remember 535.11
CALL TO ORDER
 750.9
CALL TO THE COLORS
 778.14
CALL TO WITNESS
 1002.16
CALL UP
 evoke 304.12
 visualize 533.15
 remember 535.11
 telephone 558.21
 prompt 646.13
 summon up 750.12
 recruit 778.14
 excite 855.11
 conjure 1033.11
callant, callan 125.5
call box 558.5
callboy 609.27
called for 637.13
caller
 telephoner 558.13
 visitor 923.6
calligrapher 600.14
calligraphy 600.4,6
calling naming 581.2
 vocation 654.6
 bidding 750.5
 invitation 772.4
 holy orders 1035.10
calling card 566.10
calling-down 967.7
Calliope 607.12
calliope rocket
 launcher 280.11
 noisemaker 452.5
 organ 464.15
callithump 62.4
call letters 343.22
callous
 verbs harden 355.7
 make unfeeling
 854.6
 adjs. hardened 355.13

unfeeling 854.12
 heartless 937.23
 wicked 979.21
callousness
 callosity 355.1
 unfeeling 854.3
 heartlessness 937.10
 wickedness 979.7
callow 124.10
callowness 124.3
callus, callosity
 hardening 355.5
 growth 684.29
calm
 nouns 267.5
 verbs 162.7
CALM DOWN 856.7
 adjs. quiescent
 267.10
 peaceful 801.9
 composed 856.12
calmant, calmative
 nouns 162.3
 adjs. palliative 162.16
 sedative 685.39
calmness
 quiescence 267.1
 peace 801.2
 mental ~ 856.2
calorie 327.18
calorie counter 307.10
calorific 328.25
calorimetry 327.20
calotype
 nouns 575.4
 verbs 575.16
calotypist 577.5
caloyer 1036.16
calumet 802.2
calumniate 969.11
calumniator 969.6
calumnious
 insulting 963.6
 slanderous 969.13
 maledictory 970.8
calumny slander 969.3
 malediction 970.2
Calvary 409.15
calve 166.19
Calvinism 638.4
calx 328.16
calypso 461.13
calyx 410.26
camarade 926.4
camaraderie 920.2
Cámara de Senadores
 740.3
camarilla
 council 753.1
 clique 786.7
camber arch 251.4
 convexity 255.1
 aviation 277.22
cambist broker 828.9
 financier 834.10
camboose See **caboose**
Cambrian 417.9
cambric tea 159.7
camel beast of burden
 270.6
 animal 413.5

verbs tilt 218.10
  tack 274.32
  careen 274.45
  talk ~ 578.14
  be hypocritical
    614.24
  auction 827.11
  be sanctimonious
    1027.4
  adjs. 578.17
cantabile 461.14
cantankerous 949.19
cantankerously 949.27
cantata 461.18
cantatrice 463.13
canteen
  restaurant 306.14
  store 830.7
canter
  nouns run 268.4
  hypocrite 617.8
  pietist 1027.3
  verbs run 268.11
  ride 272.33
cantharis 418.6
canthoplasty 687.27
canticle song 461.13
  hymn 1030.3
cantico 877.2
cantilever 215.29
canting 218.15
cantle
  small amount 35.2
  part 55.1
  saddle 215.9
cantlet
  small amount 35.2
  part 55.1
canto melody 461.4,22
  poetry 607.11
canton
  nouns district 179.5
  insignia 567.2
  verbs partition 49.18
  quarter 187.11
cantonment 190.1,25
cantor 463.13,20
cantorial side 243.1
cantrip
  nouns 1034.1
  adjs. 1033.14
**cantus figuratus, can-
  tus firmus** 461.20
cantus mensurabilis
  461.10
canty 868.13
Canuck 417.9
canvas tent 227.8
  sail 276.14
  picture 572.12
  UNDER CANVAS
  covered 227.34
  sailing 274.67
canvass
  nouns survey 484.16
  political ~ 742.13
  solicitation 772.5
  verbs discuss 481.16
  examine 484.31,38
  write upon 604.5
  ~ for votes 742.43

solicit 772.14
canvasser 828.7
canvassing 481.4
canyon, cañon 200.3
canzone, canzonet
  461.13
cap
  nouns summit
    210.2,3
  capital 210.4
  lid 227.5
  headdress 230.25
  types of ~ 230.59
  detonator 330.7
  capital letter 579.2
  type 601.6
  finisher 720.3
  captain 747.22
  by-bid 827.4
  PUT ON ONE'S THINK-
    ING CAP 477.7
  verbs excel 36.5
  top 210.8
  cover 227.23
  coif 230.39
  complete 720.6
  by-bid 826.9
  give in kind 953.6
capability
  ability 156.2
  qualification 718.4
  skill 731.4
capable able 156.13
  effectual 663.20
  qualified 718.18
  competent 731.22
  CAPABLE OF 174.5
capacious
  spacious 178.9
  large 194.17
capacitance 341.15
capacitate fill 56.7
  qualify 718.8
capacity character 7.5
  ability 156.2
  size 194.2
  electric ~ 341.15
  intelligence 466.1
  function 654.3
  skill 731.4
cap and bells
  costume 230.9
  comedy 609.7
cap and gown 567.1
cap-a-pie 56.19
caparison
  nouns horsecloth
    227.12
  dress 230.2
  harness 657.5
  armor 797.3
  verbs 230.40
cape
  nouns types of ~
    230.50
  point of land 255.8
  verbs 274.29
caper
  nouns leap 317.2
  theft 822.10
  frolic 876.5

prank 879.10
  verbs leap 317.6
  frolic 876.25
**capercorner, caper-
  cornered** 218.20,
  26
capersome
  frisky 868.14
  playful 876.31
capias 750.6
capillament
  filament 205.1
  hair 229.2
capillarity 287.1
capillary
  nouns 395.14
  adjs. threadlike 205.7
  hairlike 229.23
  vascular 395.21
capital
  nouns city 182.4
  crown 210.4
  letter 579.2
  type 601.6
  supply 658.2
  funds 833.15
  adjs. chief 36.16
  top 210.9
  capitalized 579.11
  important 670.25
  excellent 672.13
  financial 833.28
capital cities 180.9
capital gains 809.3
capitalism
  government 739.8
  politics 743.7
capitalist
  politics 743.13
  financier 834.8
  rich man 835.6
capitalist(ic) 743.22
capitalize letter 579.9
  finance 834.15
  credit 843.8
  CAPITALIZE ON
  utilize 663.15
  profit 809.10
capital parts 210.17
capital punishment
  1008.7
capital styles 210.16
capitation 844.11
Capitol 740.14
capitular, capitulary
  nouns 1036.9
  adjs. 1035.13
capitulate 763.8
capitulation
  summation 87.5
  compendium 605.2
  surrender 763.2
  treaty 769.2
capitulum 410.25
caplump 289.26
cap of maintenance
  567.3
capon
  nouns food 306a.22
  fowl 413.35
  verbs 42.11

caponize 42.11
caporal 746.2
capper end-all 70.4
  bunko steerer 617.5
  by-bidder 826.6
capriccioso 461.54
caprice 627.1
capricious
  irregular 138.3
  whimsical 627.5
capriciously
  irregularly 138.4
  changeably 141.8
  whimsically 627.8
capriciousness
  irregularity 138.1
  whimsicalness 627.2
**Capricorn,
  Capricornus** 128.7
capriole
  nouns 317.1,2
  verbs 317.5,6
capsheaf 210.3
capsize
  nouns 219.2
  verbs overturn 219.6
  ~ a boat 274.46
capstan 286.7
capsular 192.9
capsule
  nouns seedcase
    410.28
  compendium 605.1
  pill 685.6
  IN A CAPSULE 590.6
  verbs enclose 235.9
  summarize 605.5
  adjs. 202.9
capsulize
  condense 202.6
  summarize 605.5
captain
  nouns shipmaster
    275.7
  police ~ 697.14
  chief 747.6,22,24
  verbs 739.11
Captain Kidd 823.8
captainship
  directorship 745.4
  rank 747.25
caption
  nouns title 483.2
  seizure 820.2
  verbs 483.3
captious
  caviling 482.15
  faultfinding 967.24
captivate
  fascinate 648.6
  delight 863.8
  enamor 929.20
  bewitch 1034.9
captivated
  enamored 929.25
  spellbound 1034.13
captivating
  alluring 648.7
  delightful 861.6
captivation
  allurement 648.1

delightfulness 861.2
spell 1034.2
captive
nouns prisoner
755.11
serf 762.7
sweetheart 929.10
adjs. 762.13
HOLD CAPTIVE
imprison 759.15
subjugate 762.8
captive nations 180.1
captivity
imprisonment 759.3
bondage 762.1
IN CAPTIVITY
imprisoned 759.20
subjugated 762.13
captor 320.9
capture
nouns arrest 759.6
seizure 820.2,8
verbs win 724.4
arrest 759.16
catch 820.15
Capuchin 1036.17
caput 210.3
caquet 594.3
car
automobile 271.9
railway ~ 271.13
types of ~ 271.22
carabineer, carabinier
798.11
carabinieri 697.15
caracole, caracol
nouns 317.2
verbs ride 272.33
caper 317.6
carapace 227.16
caravan
procession 71.4
wagon 271.2
railway 271.13
caravansary 190.13
carbarn 190.17
carbineer 284.9
carbohydrate
nutrient 307.5
types of ~ 307.24
carbon copy 24.4
residue 43.2
burnt residue
328.16
fuel 330.1
carbonaceous, carbon-
iferous 330.9
Carbonaro 147.3
carbonate
chemicalize 378.6
aerate 400.7
carbonated water
306a.47
carbonation 378.5
carbon black 364.6
carbon dioxide
refrigerant 333.7
cloud seeding 393.5
carbonization 328.5
carbonize 328.23
carbonous 382.14

carbon tetrachloride
331.3
carbuncle 684.28
carcass skeleton 244.5
body 375.3
corpse 407.13
explosive 799.9
carcinoma 684.29
card
nouns oddity 85.4
calling ~ 566.10
record 568.9
post ~ 602.4
schedule 639.2
CARD UP ONE'S
SLEEVE
advantage 36.2
reserve 658.3
last resort 668.2
HAVE A CARD UP
ONE'S SLEEVE
36.11
THE CARD 26.6
verbs disinvolve 45.4
comb 679.20
cardboard 377.10
card catalogue 88.3
card games 876.35
cardholder
member 786.11
labor unionist 787.3
cardiac
nouns 685.7
adjs. 224.12
cardialgia 684.21
cardinal
nouns number 86.2
churchman 1036.8
adjs. chief 36.16
red 367.7
most important
670.25
cardinalate 1035.5
cardinal point 670.6
cardinal points 289.3
cardioid 251.18
cardioplasty 687.27
cardiotherapy 687.3
carditis 684.16
cards 876.17
IN THE CARDS
imminent 151.3
liable 174.6
possible 508.6
probable 510.5
inevitable 637.20
PLAY ONE'S CARDS
WELL 731.19
PUT ONE'S CARDS ON
THE TABLE
disclose 554.4
be honest 972.10
cardsharp
gambler 514.16
cheat 617.4
cardsharping
gambling 514.6
fraud 616.8
care
nouns attention 528
carefulness 531.1

task 654.2
protection 697.2
supervision 745.2
custody 759.5
patronage 783.4
thriftiness 849.1
affliction 864.8
anxiety 888.1
caution 893.1
~ of souls 1035.9
HAVE A CARE
be careful 531.7
beware 893.7
IN THE CARE OF
745.15
WITH CARE
carefully 531.15
cautiously 893.12
WITHOUT CARE 866.7
verbs 531.6
CARE FOR
rate highly 670.12
look after 697.18
serve 748.14
love 929.17
CARE NOTHING FOR
964.3
NOT CARE
be incurious 527.2
be indifferent 634.4
NOT CARE FOR
neglect 532.6
dislike 865.4
NOT CARE TO 621.3
careen tilt 218.10
~ a ship 274.45
careening 218.15
career
nouns course 266.2
speed 268.2
flow 394.4
vocation 654.6
verbs 268.10
adjs. 654.16
career man, careerist
779.6
carefree 868.11
careful
attentive 528.15
heedful 531.10
thrifty 849.9
cautious 893.8
BE CAREFUL
take care 531.7
be cautious 893.5
carefully
with care 531.15
thriftily 849.11
cautiously 893.12
careless slovenly 62.14
incurious 527.3
negligent 532.11
ungrammatical
585.4
impulsive 628.10
unconcerned 634.6
reckless 892.8
carelessly
negligently 532.18
impulsively 628.14

unconcernedly
634.9
recklessly 892.11
carelessness
slovenry 62.6
incuriosity 527.1
negligence 532.2
impulsiveness 628.3
unconcern 634.2
bungling 732.4
recklessness 892.2
caress
nouns touch 424.1
endearment 930.4
verbs stroke 424.8
fondle 930.14
caressable 929.22
caressing 930.1
caretaker 697.5
careworn 888.8
carfare 844.7
cargador 270.5
cargo load 193.2
freight 270.7
carhop
nouns 748.6
verbs 277.48
carhopping 277.14
caricatural 965.14
caricature
nouns picture 572.17
exaggeration 615.1
burlesque 965.6
verbs 965.11
caricaturist artist 577.3
humorist 879.12
carillon
nouns 464.20
verbs 461.43
carillonneur 463.4
cariosity, caries
gangrene 684.30
decay 690.6
carious
diseased 684.45
putrefactive 690.37
carl 917.9
carlish
countrified 181.7
boorish 896.13
carload 193.2
carman 273.9
Carmelite 1036.17
carminative
nouns 685.15
adjs. 685.41
carmine
verbs 367.4
adjs. 367.7
carn See **cairn**
carriage 408.3
carnal
nouns 418.17
adjs. sensual 985.6
unspiritual 1029.16
carnality
sexuality 418.2
sensuality 985.2
unspirituality
1029.2
carnalize 985.4

carnal knowledge
  168.3
carnal passion 418.4
carnation 367.7
carnival show 609.14
  fair 876.4
Carnivora 414.12
carnivore eater 306.13
  animal 413.3
carnivorous 306.29
carnivorousness 306.1
car of Jagannath,
  car of Juggernaut
  408.5
carol
  nouns 461.13
  verbs warble 459.5
  sing 461.39
  rejoice 874.6
caroler 463.13
caroling 461.12
carom
  nouns 282.3
  verbs 282.13
carotid 395.14
carousal revel 876.6
  dissipation 991.2
  spree 994.5
carouse
  nouns revel 876.6
  dissipation 991.2
  spree 994.5
  verbs make merry
  876.26
  dissipate 991.6
  spree 994.34
carouser
  reveler 876.19
  tippler 994.10
carp 967.15
carpel 410.26
carpenter 609.27
carpenter's square
  212.6
carper 967.9a
carpet
  nouns flooring 211.3
  rug 227.9
  types of ~ 227.44
  ON THE CARPET
  in question 484.42
  planned 652.13
  verbs 227.24
carpetbagger
  swindler 617.4
  politician 744.1
carpet knight
  fop 901.9
  voluptuary 985.3
carping
  nouns 967.4
  adjs. 967.24
carpophore 410.19
carport 190.17
carrefour 220.2
carriage posture 183.4
  transportation 270.3
  vehicle 271.1,4
  railway 271.13
  types of ~ 271.21
  mien 445.3

behavior 735.1
  charge 844.8
carriage bow 799.18
carriage horse 413.18
carried away
  excited 855.21
  overjoyed 863.14
carrier conveyor 270.5
  ship 276.8
  radio wave 343.14
  messenger 559.1
  mail ~ 559.5,6
  diseased person
  648.31
carrier pigeon
  carrier 270.5
  mail carrier 559.6
carrion
  nouns corpse 407.13
  offal 680.9
  adjs. dead 407.24
  rotten 690.38
carrottop 361.8
carroty
  red-headed 367.11
  orangeish 368.2
carrousel
  whirligig 320.4
  tournament 876.10
  merry-go-round
  876.15
carry
  nouns range 178.2
  transportation 270.3
  earshot 447.4
  verbs escort 73.8
  be pregnant 168.13
  extend 178.7
  support 215.22
  wear 230.43
  transport 270.11
  be understood 546.5
  sway 646.22
  capture 724.4
  extend credit 837.6
  ~ an account 843.8
  CARRY ALL BEFORE
  ONE 724.5
  CARRY AUTHORITY
  737.12
  CARRY AWAY
  remove 270.10
  kill 408.13
  fascinate 648.6
  win 724.4
  abduct 822.18
  delight 863.8
  enamor 929.20
  CARRY BACK 535.20
  CARRY COALS TO
  NEWCASTLE
  661.13
  CARRY CONVICTION
  convince 500.15
  sound true 515.7
  CARRY IN ONE'S
  THOUGHTS 535.14
  CARRY INTO
  EXECUTION
  carry out 703.9
  accomplish 720.5

observe 766.3
CARRY OFF
  remove 270.10
  kill 408.13
  do 703.9
  accomplish 720.5
  succeed with 722.10
  win 724.4
  abduct 822.18
CARRY ON
  endure 110.6
  continue 143.3
  be violent 161.10
  operate 163.5
  persevere 623.2
  practice 703.7
  keep going 705.14
  misbehave 736.4
  manage 745.8
  be patient 859.4
  frolic 876.25
  rage angrily 950.15
CARRY ON A BUSINESS
  do business 654.12
  trade 825.11
CARRY ONE OFF HIS
  FEET 918.6
CARRY ONE'S
  THOUGHTS BACK
  535.11
CARRY ON OVER 633.8
CARRY ON WAR
  795.19
CARRY OUT
  operate 163.6
  apply 663.11
  do 703.9
  accomplish 720.5
  observe 766.3
  execute 769.10
CARRY OUT THE
  ANCHOR 274.16
CARRY OVER
  transfer 270.9
  ~ an account 843.8
CARRY THE DAY 724.4
CARRY THROUGH
  operate 163.6
  persevere 623.5
  do 703.9
  accomplish 720.5
  execute 769.10
  be patient 859.4
CARRY TO 198.6
CARRY TO COM-
  PLETION 720.6
CARRY TOO FAR
  exaggerate 615.3
  overdo 661.11
  overindulge 991.5
CARRY TOO MUCH
  SAIL
  risk 695.7
  be rash 892.5
CARRY WEIGHT
  have influence
  171.10
  weigh 351.10
  be proof 504.9
  be important
  670.11

carryall 271.10
carrying 270.3
CARRYING TOO MUCH
  SAIL 994.41
carrying distance
  447.4
car-sick 684.42
carsickness 684.22
cart
  nouns 271.3
  PUT THE CART BE-
  FORE THE HORSE
  invert 219.5
  mismanage 732.14
  verbs 270.12
  CART AWAY 270.10
carta treaty 769.2
  charter 775.5
cartage
  transportation 270.3
  charge 844.8
carte list 88.4
  menu 306.12
  bill of fare 639.2
carte blanche 775.4
  GIVE CARTE BLANCHE
  775.13
cartel compact 769.1
  syndicate 786.9
  challenge 791.2
  truce 802.5
carter 273.9
Cartesian 499.11
cart horse 413.18
Carthusian 1036.17
cartilage
  hardness 355.6
  toughness 358.2
cartilaginification
  355.5
cartilaginous
  hard 355.10
  tough 358.4
cartload 193.2
cartman 273.9
cartographer
  surveyor 489.10
  map maker 652.4
cartographic(al)
  489.13
cartography
  surveying 489.9
  mapping 652.4
carton
  nouns 284.5
  verbs 235.9
cartoon
  nouns picture 572.17
  design 652.3
  verbs 572.20
cartoonist 577.3
cartouche, cartouch
  799.11
cartridge film 575.12
  gun ~ 799.11
cartulary 568.2
cart wheel
  somersault 219.2
  dollar 833.7
carve sever 49.10
  make 166.12

form 245.6
furrow 262.3
sculpture 573.6
engrave 576.12
apportion 814.7
CARVE ONE'S WAY
293 4
carved
sculptured 573.8
engraved 576.16
carver sculptor 577.6
engraver 577.8
carving 570.4
caryatid 216.5
casa 190.5
Casanova 929.11
cascade
nouns 394.11
verbs fall 314.5
cataract 394.18
cascade control 348.3
case
nouns condition 7.1
circumstance 8.2
example 25.2
oddity 85.4
types of receptacle
192.19
pillowcase 227.11
cover 227.18
frame 244.4
argument 481.6
condition 506.2
grammar 584.7
book cover 603.16
addict 640.9
patient 684.31
infatuation 929.4
suit in law 1002.1
HAVE A CASE 504.11
IN ANY CASE
notwithstanding
33.8
provided 506.12
possibly 508.10
anyhow 655.12
IN CASE
in the event of
150.13
provided 506.12
IN GOOD CASE
healthy 683.6
prosperous 726.12
IN NO CASE
nowise 35.14
by no means 522.8
IN THAT CASE
accordingly 8.9
then 105.11
THE CASE
fact 1.3
truth 515.1
verbs box 235.9
reconnoiter 484.37
caseation 353.4
caseharden
strengthen 158.11
harden 355.7
habituate 640.10
callous 854.6
casehardened

hardened 355.13
metallic 382.15
obstinate 624.10
inveterate 640.19
callous 854.12
wicked 979.21
case history 687.13
casein 353.7
casemate 797.4
casemated 797.12
casement frame 244.4
window 264.7
caseous 353.14
casern 190.25
Casey Jones 273.12
cash
nouns money
833.1,17
payment 839.1
CASH ON DELIVERY
839.25
verbs convert 833.27
pay ~ 839.17
CASH IN
die 407.16
cash 833.27
CASH IN ON
utilize 663.15
profit 809.10
cashbook
record 568.10
account book 843.4
cash box 834.12
cash down 839.25
cashier
nouns 834.10,11
verbs discharge
308.18
depose 781.2
cashiering 308.5
cashkeeper 834.11
cash register 834.12
casing cover 227.18
frame 244.4
tire 252.4
casino
gambling ~ 514.14
tavern 876.11
ballroom 877.4
cask
nouns 192.18
verbs 235.9
casket
nouns 409.11
verbs 235.6
Cassandra 541.4
casserole 306a.7
cassideous 251.23
cassock 1036.4
cast
nouns nature 5.3
reproduction 24.6
mold 25.6
small amount 35.4
kind 61.3
characteristic 80.3
count 86.3
tendency 173.1
~ skin 228.5
form 245.1
throw 284.4

color 361.1
metal ~ 382.5
glance 438.4
squint 439.5
appearance 445.3
~ of dice 514.9
disposition 523.3
role 609.11
theatrical ~ 610.11
bandage 685.28
verbs calculate 87.11
give birth 166.19
put 183.13
shed 231.10
form 245.6
veer 274.32
throw 284.12
eject 308.12
vomit 308.24
plan 652.9
CAST A BALLOT
635.15
CAST ABOUT FOR
484.25
CAST A GLOOM UPON
870.18
CAST A HOROSCOPE
541.9
CAST ANCHOR 274.16
CAST A SHADOW
336.10
CAST A SLUR ON 969.9
CAST A SLUR UPON
stigmatize 913.9
censure 967.13
CAST A SPELL 1034.8
CAST AT 796.30
CAST A TRAVERSE
274.53
CAST AWAY
unmoor 274.19
shipwreck 274.44
CAST BLAME UPON
censure 967.13
accuse 1003.8
CAST DOWN
disappoint 539.2
demolish 691.19
deject 870.18
CAST FORTH
disperse 75.6
eject 308.23
CAST IN ONE'S LOT
WITH
decide upon 635.13
side with 784.6
CAST IN ONE'S TEETH
decide upon 635.13
confront with 239.9
ridicule 965.9
accuse of 1003.9
CAST LIGHT UPON
334.28
CAST LOOSE
unmoor 274.19
navigation 274.50
free 761.5
CAST LOTS 514.17
CAST OFF
eliminate 77.5
doff 231.6

unmoor 274.19
get rid of 308.19
discard 666.7
CAST ONE'S EYES
DOWN 438.21
CAST ONE'S NET
653.10
CAST OUT 308.12,16
CAST OUT DEVILS
1033.12
CAST SHEEP'S EYES AT
930.18
CAST THE DIE 635.13
CAST THE EYES ON
438.12
CAST THE EYES OVER
484.31
CAST THE FIRST
STONE
censure 967.13
incriminate 1003.10
CAST THE LEAD 208.8
CAST UP
sum up 87.12
occur 150.6
raise 212.8
elevate 315.5
castaneous 366.4
castanets 464.20
castaway
nouns derelict 631.4
discard 666.3
outcast 924.3
adjs. abandoned
631.8
discarded 666.11
stranded 729.25
outcast 924.8
cast-by
nouns 631.4
adjs. 631.8
caste rank 29.2
class 61.2
castellan 697.5
castellated 797.12
castellation 261.3
caste mark 566.4
castigate
criticize 967.21
punish 1008.10
castigation
censure 967.3,5
punishment 1008.1
castigatory 1008.25
casting
reproduction 24.6
calculation 87.3
throwing 284.3
metal ~ 382.5
casting weight
counterbalance 33.2
weight 351.4
cast-iron 624.9
castle house 190.7
~ in Spain 533.10
stronghold 797.6
chessman 876.18
castle-builder 533.13
castle-building
nouns bemusement
530.2

dreaming 533.8
adjs. bemused 530.11
dreaming 533.25
castle-built 533.20
castoff
nouns derelict 631.4
discard 666.3
adjs. abandoned
631.8
discarded 666.11
outcast 924.8
Castor and Pollux
couple 90.4
corposant 334.13
friends 926.8
castrametation 187.4
castrate
nouns steer 413.8
male animal 419.8
verbs expurgate 42.9
geld 42.11
castration
expurgation 42.4
gelding 42.5
operation 687.25
casual
nouns laborer 716.2
soldier 798.15
almsman 836.4
adjs. nonessential 6.4
incidental 8.6
orderless 62.11
incidental 129.12
occasional 136.3
chance 155.15
haphazard 155.16
indiscriminate 492.6
careless 532.11
extemporaneous
628.12
informal 645.3
nonchalant 856.15
casually
by chance 155.18
haphazardly 155.19
carelessly 532.18
informally 645.4
nonchalantly
856.17
casualness
chance 155.1
indiscrimination
492.1
carelessness 532.2
informality 645.1
nonchalance 856.5
casualty
fatality 408.7
accident 727.2
chance event 155.6
casuist 482.6
casuistic(al) 482.14
casuistry
sophistry 482.1
ethics 955.2
casus belli
grounds 793.8
provocation 950.11
cat tractor 271.16
feline 413.28
breeds of ~ 413.62

sharp eyes 438.11
hepcat 463.2,23
shrew 949.12
prostitute 987.16
whip 1009.1
catabasis 39.2
catabiased 218.20
catabolism 307.9
catacaustic 251.2
catachresis
figure of speech
549.2
misinterpretation
551.1
catachrestic(al)
figurative 549.4
misinterpreted
551.3
cataclasm 49.2
cataclysm
revolution 147.1
upheaval 161.5
deluge 394.6
ruin 691.4
disaster 727.2
cataclysmic
revolutionary 147.5
ruinous 691.25
disastrous 727.15
catacombs 409.16
catacoustics 449.7
catafalque
platform 215.13
shrine 409.16
catalepsy
neurosis 688.26
hypnosis 710.7
catalexis 607.9
catalogue
nouns list 88.3
record book 568.10
book 603.6
verbs classify 61.6
list 88.7
record 568.15
catalyst 53.2
catalytic 53.6
catalyze 53.4
catamenia 309.9
catamenial
monthly 137.9
menstrual 309.21
catamount, cata-
mountain 413.4
cat-and-dog 949.26
CAT-AND-DOG LIFE
794.1
CAT-AND-DOG
WEATHER 393.4
cat-and-doggish
rainy 393.10
contentious 949.26
cat and mouse 345.6
cataphonics 449.7
cataplasm 685.28
cataplexy
neurosis 688.26
hypnosis 710.7
catapult
nouns aviation 277.6
weapon 799.19

verbs 284.12
cataract
nouns torrent 394.5
waterfall 394.11
blindness 440.1
disease 684.11
verbs fall 314.5
cascade 394.18
catarrh 684.12
catastrophe end 70.1
revolution 147.1
result 153.2
ruin 691.4
disaster 727.2
catastrophic(al)
radical 147.5
ruinous 691.25
disastrous 727.15
catatonia 472.5
catatoniac 472.16
catatonic 472.26
catatonic stupor
688.22
catawampous, cata-
wamptious 218.14
catcall
nouns noisemaker
452.5
hoot 965.3
verbs 965.10
catch
nouns rondo 461.19
trick 616.6
good thing 672.5
fault 676.2
obstacle 728.4
seizure 820.2,8
sweetheart 929.10
verbs stick 142.11
conceive 168.12
overtake 299.9
ignite 328.22
hear 447.12
discover 487.7
understand 546.7
~ a disease 684.34
get 809.7
take 820.11
seize 820.14
CATCH A LIKENESS
570.7
CATCH A RIDE
hitchhike 272.30
ride 272.32
CATCH AT
discover 487.7
be eager 633.7
snatch at 820.13
CATCH AT A STRAW
886.8
CATCH AT STRAWS
overestimate 496.2
be rash 892.5
CATCH A WINK
710.13
CATCH HOLD OF
820.12
CATCH IT 1008.22
CATCH OFF-GUARD
487.7
CATCH ON

understand 546.7
become fashionable
642.8
succeed 722.6
CATCH ONE'S DEATH
407.19
CATCH SIGHT OF
438.12
CATCH THE EYE
appear 445.8
catch attention
528.11
CATCH THE FLAME
853.11
CATCH THE
INFECTION
respond 853.11
get excited 855.17
CATCH UNAWARES
538.7
CATCH UP
overtake 299.9
detect 487.7
CATCH UP IN 175.2
adjs. 616.21
catch-as-catch-can
794.10
catcher seizer 820.9
ballplayer 876.20
catching
nouns discovery
487.1
seizure 820.2
adjs. captivating
648.7
contagious 684.47
taking 820.22
NOT CATCHING
811.10
catchpenny 671.18
catchpole, catchpoll
697.14
catch question 484.13
catchweed 257.8
catchweight 351.3
catchword cue 566.8
byword 580.8
book ~ 603.13
catchy irregular 138.3
deceptive 616.21
catechetic(al) 484.39
catechetical method
484.14
Catechism 1021.2
catechism
questions 484.13
belief 500.2
catechist 484.17
catechistic(al) 484.39
catechize
interrogate 484.22
teach 560.10
catechumen
convert 145.5
novice 564.7
religionist 1026.4
layman 1037.2
categoric(al)
classificational 61.7
dogmatic 512.22
categorical

logic 81.22
demonstrative
504.19
unqualified 507.2
categorically true
515.11
categorization 61.1
categorize 61.6
category 61.2
IN THE SAME
CATEGORY 9.6
catena 71.3
catenary 251.2
catenation 71.3
cater
catercorner 218.11
provision 657.9
CATER TO
indulge 757.7
minister to 783.18
toady to 905.7
caterer 657.6
caterpillar larva 125.9
tractor 271.16
caterwaul
nouns 457.4
verbs screech 457.7
miaow 459.2
court 930.19
cat-eyed 38.23
catgut 464.24
catharsis
defecation 309.2
purgation 679.2
psychological ~
688.36
relief 884.2
cathartic
nouns 685.15
adjs. cleansing 679.26
laxative 685.41
cathedral
nouns 1040.2
adjs. 512.18
catheter 395.6
cathexis 638.44
cathodic 342.15
cathodofluorescence,
cathocolumines-
cence 342.5
Catholic 1018.17
catholic
universal 79.13
liberal 524.9
orthodox 1022.8
Catholic(al) 1018.27
Catholic Epistles
1019.4
Catholicism 1018.7
catholicism
universality 79.1
orthodoxy 1022.1
Catholicity 1018.7
catholicity
universality 79.1
broad-mindedness
524.2
orthodoxy 1022.1
Catholicization 145.4
Catholocize 145.11
catholicize 79.8

catholicon 685.3
cat house 987.9
cation 341.22
catkin 410.25
catlike 413.38
catling
youngling 125.8
kitten 413.28
cat nap 710.3
cat-o'-nine-tails
1009.1
catoptric(al) 334.40
catoptrics 334.22
cats 414.12
cats and dogs 832.1
LIKE CATS AND DOGS
793.16
cat's-paw breeze 402.5
dupe 618
instrument 656.3
MAKE A CAT'S-PAW OF
663.16
cat's-tail 403.1
catstone 566.9
cattail 410.25
cattalo 44.8
cattiness 937.6
cattle livestock 413.1
kine 413.8
breeds of ~ 413.59
rabble 917.5
cattleman 415.2,3
catty catlike 413.38
spiteful 937.19
cattycorner
adjs. 218.20
advs. 218.26
Caucasian
white man 363.3
race 417.3
Caucasian race
race 417.2
types of ~ 417.13
caucus
nouns assembly 74.2
political ~ 742.9
verbs 742.41
caucus nomination
742.11
cauda 240.5
caudal last 70.10
of a tail 240.10
caudate 240.10
caudation 240.5
caudex 410.19
caudle 307.10
caught 142.17
BE CAUGHT NAPPING
719.6
BE CAUGHT SHORT
831.23
CAUGHT NAPPING
476.14
CAUGHT SHORT 538.12
CAUGHT UP IN
involved 175.4
absorbed 528.17
caulicle 410.19
cauliflower ear 447.7
caulk 265.7
caulker 994.6

Caurus 402.3
causable 166.29
causal 152.15
causal body 1032.19
causal treatment
687.18
causation 152.1
causative
causal 152.15
creative 166.23
cause
nouns source 152.1
principle 152.10
motive 646.1
suit in law 1002.1
justification 1004.6
CAUSE FOR ALARM
695.1
GIVE CAUSE FOR
ALARM 702.5
THE FIRST CAUSE
1011.2
verbs bring about
152.11
compel 754.4
caused 166.25
CAUSED BY 153.8
causeless
chance 155.15
purposeless 155.16
causerie chat 595.4
treatise 604.1
causeway
nouns 655.6
verbs 227.24
causidical 1002.20
caustic
nouns curve 251.2
corrosive 328.14
acid 378.12
adjs. acrimonious
160.12
acid 431.7
pungent 432.6
penetrating 855.32
virulent 937.21
causticity
acrimony 160.4
acidity 431.2
pungency 432.1
asperity 937.8
cauter 328.14
cauterant
nouns 328.14
adjs. 328.25
cauterization
burning 328.5
surgery 687.23
cauterize 328.23
cautery burning 328.5
cauterant 328.14
surgery 687.23
caution
nouns oddity 85.4
first-rater 672.6
warning 701.1
proficient 731.11
care 893
WITH CAUTION
unbelievingly
502.13

cautiously 893.12
verbs 701.6
cautionary 701.9
caution money 770.3
cautious 893.8
BE CAUTIOUS 893.5
cautiously 893.12
cavalcade 71.4
cavalier
nouns escort 73.5
horseman 273.8
knight 916.6
lover 929.11
gallant 934.9
adjs. haughty 910.13
gruff 935.7
cavalier servente
follower 292.2
lover 929.11
cavalry horses 413.18
army 798.26
cavalryman 798.12
cave
nouns lair 190.22
cavern 256.5
stakes 514.4
debacle 691.4
shelter 698.3
verbs 256.13
CAVE IN
weaken 159.9
collapse 197.10
hollow out 256.13
open 264.14
break down 690.25
yield 763.7
caveat warning 701.1
writ 750.6
cave dweller 123.7
cave-in collapse 197.4
debacle 691.4
cave man
ancient 123.7
he-man 419.6
cavendish 433.8
cave of Trophonius
887.2
cavern 256.5
cavernous 256.16
cavesson 657.5
caviar, caviare 306a.24
cavil
nouns 482.4
verbs quibble 482.9
find fault 967.15
caviler quibbler 482.7
faultfinder 967.9a
caviling
nouns quibbling
482.5
faultfinding 967.4
adjs. quibbling
482.15
faultfinding 967.24
cavity
compartment 191.2
pit 208.2
hollow 256.2
cavorite 281.11
cavort
nouns 317.2

verbs curvet 317.6
  frolic 876.25
cavy 413.4
caw
  nouns 457.3
  verbs sound harshly
    457.8
  croak 459.5
cay 385.2
cease
  nouns 144.1
  WITHOUT CEASE
    71.11
  verbs come to an end
    70.6
  discontinue 144.6
  disappear 446.2
  perish 691.22
  CEASE TO BE
  cease 2.5
  disappear 446.2
  NEVER CEASE
  be infinite 104.2
  be eternal 112.6
  continue 143.3
ceaseless
  continuous 71.9
  perpetual 112.7
  constant 135.5
ceaselessness
  continuity 71.1
  perpetuity 112.1
  constancy 135.2
cede surrender 763.8
  relinquish 812.3
  assign 815.3
ceil cover 227.23
  line 227.30
ceiling
  consummation 56.4
  roof 227.6
  aviation 277.38
  rocket ~ 280.10
  price 844.5
celebrant 1030.9
celebrate
  proclaim 557.13
  commemorate
    875.3
  make merry 876.26
  praise 966.12
  glorify 1030.11
  ~ a sacrament
    1038.17
celebrated 912.17
celebrating
  nouns 875.1
  adjs. 875.5
celebration
  ceremony 644.4
  rejoicing 874
  celebrating 875
  festivity 876.3
  revel 876.6
  spree 994.5
  rite 1038.4
celebrity fame 912.1
  famous person
    912.9
celerity 268.1

celesta
  instrument 464.20
  stop 464.23
Celestial 417.9
celestial
  nouns 1013.1
  adjs. astral 374.25
  divine 1011.19
  angelic 1013.6
  paradisaical 1016.13
celestial body 374.5
Celestial City
  utopia 533.11
  heaven 1016.4
celestial equator,
    celestial longitude
    374.16
celestial glory 1016.7
celestial navigation
  navigation 274.2
  aviation 277.4
celestial spaces 374.3
celibacy
  unmarried state 932
  continence 986.3
celibate
  nouns 932.2
  adjs. unmarried 932.6
  continent 986.6
celiotomy 687.26
cell
  compartment 191.2
  biology 405.5
  prison ~ 759.9
  coterie 786.7
cellar 191.17
cellarage 844.7
cellarway 301.6
cell division 405.15
cellist 463.5
cello 337.4
cello, 'cello 464.5
cellular vascular 192.9
  cellulous 405.20
cellule
  compartment 191.2
  biology 405.5
cellulose 405.5
cellulose nitrate 799.9
cellulous 405.20
cembalo 464.13
cement
  nouns adhesive 48.6
  hardness 355.6
  concrete 377.2
  pavement 655.7
  verbs fasten 47.7
  stick together 50.7
  pave 227.24
  plaster 227.27
  solidify 355.8
  adjs. 355.10
cementation 50.1
cementwork 227.1
cemetery 409.15
cenobite 1036.16
cenotaph tomb 409.16
  monument 568.11
cense 435.8
censer scenter 435.6
  thurible 1038.11

censer bearer
  thurifer 435.5
  churchman 1036.9
censor
  nouns critic 493.7
  superego 688.39
  conscience 955.5
  faultfinder 967.9a
  verbs expurgate 42.9
  suppress 612.9
censorious
  condemnatory
    967.23
  disparaging 969.13
censorship
  expurgation 42.4
  suppression 612.3
  inhibition 688.35
censurable 967.26
censure
  nouns 967.3
  verbs expurgate 42.9
  condemn 967.13
censurer critic 493.7
  faultfinder 967.9a
census
  nouns 88.5
  verbs 87.10
cent
  trifle 671.5
  coin 833.7,9
cental 99.8
centavo 833.9
centenarian 127.2
centenary, centennial
  nouns hundred 99.8
  anniversary 137.4
  adjs. hundredth
    99.29
  periodic 137.9
center
  nouns nucleus 5.2
  middle 225.2
  political ~ 743.2
  player 876.20
  IN THE CENTER OF
    225.17
  OFF CENTER 225.16
  verbs centralize
    225.10
  converge 297.2
centermost 225.12
center of attention
  225.4
center of gravity
  center 225.2
  aviation 277.24
center of life 5.4
centesimal 99.29
centigrade
  centuple 99.29
  thermal 327.30
centigrade scale
  327.18
centigram, centiliter,
    centimeter 99.8
centime 833.9
centipede
  hundred 99.8
  insect 413a.2
centistere 99.8

cento 607.4
central
  nouns telephone
    office 558.9
  phone girl 558.11
  adjs. chief 36.16
  middle 225.12
  phonetics 449.18
centralism
  centralization 225.9
  government 739.8
centrality 225
  centralization 225.9
centralize
  center 225.10
  converge 297.2
centrally 225.17
centric(al) 225.12
centricality 225.1
centrifugal 298.8
centrifuge 49.6
centriole center 225.3
  nucleus 405.10
centripetal
  centric 225.14
  converging 297.3
centroid 225.2
centroidal 225.12
centrolineal
  centric 225.14
  converging 297.3
centrosome
  center 225.3
  protoplasm 405.3
  nucleus 405.10
centrum, centry 225.2
centumvir,
    centumvirate 99.8
centuple, centuplicate
  verbs 99.16
  adjs. 99.29
centuple calorie
  327.18
centurion
  hundred 99.8
  officer 747.22
century hundred 99.8
  age 107.2
  long time 110.4
  money 833.7
cephalalgy,
    cephalalgia 423.5
cephalic 210.13
cephalopods 414.9
ceramacist 577.7
ceramic
  nouns 574.1
  adjs. 574.7
ceramics
  pottery 574.1,2
  types of ~ 574.18
cerate 379.1
Cerberus
  guard 697.8,10
  god 1017.5
cereal
  nouns food 306a.34
  plant 410.5
  adjs. 410.34
cerebellum 465.5

cerebral
nouns 449.5
adjs. 465.6
cerebrate 477.7
cerebration 477.1
cerebrum 465.5
cerecloth
gravec othes 409.14
chrismal 1040.10
cerements 409.14
ceremonial
nouns ceremony
644.1,4
religious ~ 1038.3
adjs. formal 644.8
ritualistic 1038.21
ceremonialism
formalism 644.2
religious ~ 1038.1
ceremonialist 1038.2
ceremonialize 644.5
ceremonious
formal 644.8
polite 934.14
deferential 962.8
ritualistic 1038.21
ceremony
formality 644.1
function 644.4
religious ~ 1038.3
WITHOUT CEREMONY
informally 645.4
modest y 906.14
Ceres fertility 164.5
agriculture 412.4
goddess 1012.5
cerise 367.7
cernuous 214.9
cerograph 576.6
cerographer, cerogra-
phist 577.8
cerography
painting 572.5
engraving 576.2
ceroplast 573.7
ceroplastics 573.1
certain sor te 28.6
special 80.12
plural 100.7
sure 512.13
inevitab e 637.15
guaranteed 770.14
BE CERTAIN 512.9
MAKE CERTAIN
512.11
certainly
positively 34.21
surely 512.23
truly 515.16
yes 520.28
inevitably 637.19
CERTAINLY NOT
522.7
certainty sureness 512
inevitability 637.7
certificate
nouns voucher 568.5
money 833.11
verbs 775.12
certification
confirmation 504.5

ascertainment 512.8
ratification 520.4
certificate 568.5
authorization 775.3
certified
proved 504.22
guaranteed 770.14
certify
attest 504.10,12
make sure of
512.11,12
ratify 520.12
guarantee 770.11
certiorari 1002.10
certitude 512.1,5
cerulean
nouns 374.2
adjs. 371.3
cervine 413.41
cervix 48.5
cespitose 410.40
cess 844.10
cessation 144.1
cession
qualification 506.1
surrender 763.2
relinquishment
812.1
assignment 815.1
cesspool 680.12
Cestoda 414.5
cestus 252.3
Cetacea, cetaceans
types of ~ 413.54
animals 414.12
cetacean 413.47
chabouk 1009.1
Chaetopoda 414.5
chafe
nouns 864.3
verbs warm 328.17
grate 349.7
make sore 423.7
injure 690.13
excite 855.13
be impatient 860.4
annoy 864.18
fret 888.5
fume 950.15
anger 950.22
chafed galled 423.11
irritated 864.24
chaff
nouns remains 43.1
husk 227.17
radar 345.13
lightness 352.3
refuse 667.4
trumpery 671.4
banter 880.1
riffraff 917.5
verbs 880.4
chaffer
nouns bargaining
825.3
banterer 880.3
verbs 825.14
chagrin
nouns 864.4
verbs 864.16

chagrined
mortified 864.25
humiliated 904.12
chain
nouns series 71.3
mountain range
206.9
atomic ~ 325.7
pothook 328.15
ornament 899.6
verbs fasten 47.9
shackle 758.10
chain gang 759.11
chain reaction
series 71.3
vicissitudes 155.5
atomics 325.8
psychology 688.20
chain reactor 325.12
chains 758.4
IN CHAINS 758.16
chain shot 799.14
chain store 830.1
chair
nouns seat 215.18
types of ~ 215.31
professorship
563.11
official seat 737.9
chairman 746.4
electric ~ 1009.5
THE CHAIR 1008.7
verbs convey 270.12
instate 778.11
chairman
nouns 746.4
verbs 745.11
chaise 271.4
Chalcidian 579.5
chalcograph 576.7
chalcographer 577.8
chalcography 576.2
Chaldean 374.23
chalet 190.8
chalk
nouns white 363.2
drawing 572.19
verbs whiten 363.6
mark 566.18
record 568.15
draw 572.20
CHALK OUT 652.11
chalkiness
powderiness 360.1
whiteness 363.1
chalk talk lesson 560.6
address 597.2
chalky
powdery 360.11
crumbly 360.13
white 363.8
challenge
nouns questioning
484.14
protest 520a.2
defial 791.2
declaration of war
795.12
verbs confront with
239.9
doubt 502.6

protest 520a.5
claim 751.5
defy 791.3
declare war 795.20
chalone 310.2
chamber
nouns room 191.1
compartment 191.2
bedroom 191.7
bedchamber 680.14
committee 753.3
verbs 235.5
chamberfellow 926.4
chamberlain
major-domo 748.11
treasurer 834.11
chambermaid 748.8
chamber music 461.5
Chamber of Deputies
740.4
chambers
apartment 191.4
office 717.8
IN CHAMBERS 612.21
chameleon
changeability 141.4
variegation 373.6
vacillator 625.5
chameleonic, chame-
leonlike 373.11
chamfer 262.3
chamisal 410.13
champ
nouns bite 306.2
victor 724.2
champion 731.13
verbs 306.25
CHAMP AT THE BIT
wait 132.12
be expectant 537.6
be impatient 860.4
CHAMP THE BIT
950.14
champaca oil 435.2
champaign
nouns 386.1
adjs. 386.3
champain 913.6
champion
nouns the best 672.8
victor 724.2
expert 731.13
deputy 779.1
supporter 785.8
defender 797.7
verbs 1004.10
adjs. leading 36.16
best 672.19
championship
supremacy 36.3
patronage 783.4
chance
nouns quantity 28.2
large amount 34.6
turn 108.2
opportunity 129.2
fortuity 155
liability 174.1
distance 198.1
possibility 508.1
probability 510.1

uncertainty 513.8
gamble 514.1
BY ANY CHANCE
508.10
BY CHANCE
at random 62.17
by accident 155.18
HAVE A CHANCE
admit of 155.13
be possible 508.4
HAVE A GOOD CHANCE
be possible 508.4
seem likely 510.3
MISS THE CHANCE
130.6
NOT A CHANCE 522.8
NOT HAVE A CHANCE
have no chance
155.14
be impossible 509.4
OUTSIDE CHANCE
small chance 155.9
possibility 508.1
RUN THE CHANCE
be liable 174.3
risk 695.7
TAKE A CHANCE
chance 514.18
risk 695.7
verbs happen 155.11
gamble 514.18
CHANCE UPON 487.3
adjs. 155.15
chancel 1040.9
chancellery
office 717.8
authority 737.6
chancellor
executive 747.5
head of state 747.7
official 747.19
diplomat 779.6
judge 1000.4
Chancellor of the
Exchequer
official 740.9
treasurer 834.11
chance-medley 155.4
chancery
archives 568.2
office 717.8
court 999.3
IN CHANCERY
in trouble 729.19
in litigation
1002.21
chancre 684.28
chancy chance 155.15
uncertain 513.14
risky 695.10
chandelier 335.6
chandelle
nouns 277.10
verbs 277.45
Chandi 1012.7
chandler 828.2,3
change
nouns alteration 139
substitution 148.1,2
stock exchange
831.7

money 833.18
verbs be changed
139.5
alter 139.6
substitute 148.4
interchange 149.4
~ clothes 230.42
move 266.4
remove 270.10
trade 825.10
CHANGE BACK 146.5
CHANGE COLOR
pale 362.6
get excited 855.20
be frightened
889.10
blush 906.8
CHANGE HANDS 815.4
CHANGE INTO 145.8
CHANGE ONE'S MIND
tergiversate 626.7
repent 871.7
CHANGE ONE'S WAYS
145.9
changeability
changeableness
141.1
interchangeability
149.3
changeable
ununiform 18.2
irregular 138.3
alterable 141.6
inconstant 141.7
interchangeable
149.5
capricious 627.5
fickle 627.7
changeableness
alterability 141
capriciousness 627.2
fickleness 627.3
changeably 141.8
changeless 140.7
changelessness 140.1
changeling
substitute 148.2
elf child 1014.12
change of life 126.7
change of venue
1002.5
change-over 145.1
channel
nouns strait 204.3
bed 211.4
trench 262.2
outlet 302.9
radio ~ 343.16
conduit 395
passageway 655.4
verbs furrow 262.3
convey 270.13
channelize 395.19
chant
nouns song 461.13
religious ~ 1030.3
verbs sing 461.39
say 592.17
chanter singer 463.13
bagpipe 464.10

chantey, chanty
461.13
chanticleer
cock 413.35
male animal 419.8
chantry 1040.3
chaos confusion 62.2
formlessness 246.1
cosmic space 374.3
anarchy 738.2
chaotic
confused 62.15
formless 246.4
disorganized 738.6
chap
nouns split 49.3
cleft 200.2
man 419.5
verbs 49.11
chaparral 410.13
chapatty 306a.44
chapbook 603.10
chapeau 230.25
chapel 1040.3
chaperon
nouns attendant 73.5
guardian 697.6
verbs escort 73.8
care for 697.18
chapfallen, chopfallen
dejected 870.22
humiliated 904.12
chaplain 1036.2,8
chaplaincy 1035.5
chaplet band 252.3
garland 410.23
insignia 567.2
jewelry 899.6
trophy 914.3
prayers 1030.4
beadroll 1038.11
chapman 828.6
chaps 264.5
chapter
nouns section 55.2
topic 483.1
book ~ 603.14
council 753.5
organization 786.10
verbs 49.18
chapter and verse 8.11
QUOTE CHAPTER AND
VERSE
circumstantiate 8.5
cite 504.14
char
nouns 654.2
verbs burn 328.23
chore 714.12
character
nouns nature 5.3
capacity 7.5
kind 61.3
characteristic 80.3
oddity 85.4
number 86.1
musical ~ 462.12
eccentric 473.3
temperament 523.3
letter 579.1
description 606.1

role 609.11
actor 610.1
function 654.3
reputation 912.1
reference 966.4
moral strength
972.1
IN CHARACTER
characteristic 80.13
to be expected
537.12
OUT OF CHARACTER
inapt 27.7
inexpedient 669.5
verbs engrave 576.12
letter 579.9
describe 606.12
characteristic
nouns peculiarity
80.3
habit 640.3
adjs. differentiative
16.9
peculiar 80.13
typical 570.12
characterization
distinction 80.8
impersonation
570.2
naming 581.2
description 606.1,9
drama 609.9
characterize
distinguish 80.11
represent 570.10
name 581.11
describe 606.12
enact 609.34
characterless 881.6
charade riddle 547.8
drama 609.4
charbon 684.10
charcoal
nouns residue 43.2
burned wood
328.16
fuel 330.1
black 364.6
drawing 572.14,19
verbs blacken 364.7
draw 572.20
charge
nouns fill 56.3
attribution 154.1
load 193.2
rocket ~ 280.9
electric ~ 341.5
burden 351.7
insignia 567.2
task 654.2
cathexis 688.44
protection 697.2
supervision 745.2
precept 749.1
injunction 750.2
advice 752.1
custody 759.5
dependent 762.6
commission 778.1
attack 796.1

~ of explosive
799 10
price 844.1
fee 844.7
duty 960.1
imposition 961.3
accusation 1003.1
curacy 1035.9
GIVE IN CHARGE
commission 778.9
commit 816.16
IN CHARGE
in control 737.21
in custody 759.21
IN THE CHARGE OF
745.15
TAKE CHARGE 737.13
WITHOUT CHARGE
848.5,6
verbs fill 56.7
~ a gun 284.13
radioactivate 326.9
electrify 341.23
burden 351.13
prepare 718.9
command 750.9
advise 752.7
commission 778.9
attack 796.19
credit 837.5,7
assess 844.14
impose 961.4
accuse 1003.7
CHARGE OFF
debit 343.8
discount 845.2
forgive 945.5
CHARGE TO 154.3
CHARGE TO
EXPERIENCE
be disillusioned
519.3
forgive 945.5
chargeability 981.1
chargeable
liable 338.9
taxable 844.17
culpable 967.26
CHARGEABLE TO
960.13
charge account 837.2
chargé d'affaires 779.6
charge-off 845.1
charger horse 413.12
war horse 798.33
chargesh p
office 654.5
dependence 762.3
charily thriftily 849.11
warily 893.13
chariness
thriftiness 849.1
wariness 893.2
chariot 271.1
charioteer 273.9
charitable
tolerant 524.11
benevolent 936.16
charitably 936.21
charities 936.6
charity tolerance 524.4

almsgiving 816.3
alms 816.6
benevolence 936.4
virtue 978.5
charivari uproar 452.3
serenade 875.2
charlatan
quack 614.29
impostor 617.6
charlatanism,
charlatanry 614.7
Charleston 877.5
Charley horse
pain 423.2
illness 684.5
charlotte, charlotte
russe 306a.45
charm
nouns sex appeal
418.3
allurement 648.1,2
delightfulness 861.2
beauty 898.1
ornament 899.6
lovability 929.7
spell 1034.1
talisman 1034.5
verbs fascinate 648.6
delight 863.8
enamor 929.20
bewitch 1034.9
charmed
delighted 863.12
enamored 929.25
bewitched 1034.13
charmer enticer 648.3
beauty 898.8
bewitcher 1033.9
charming
alluring 648.7
delightful 861.6
bewitching 1034.12
charnel house 409.16
Charon 1017.5
charqui 306a.13
charred 328.29
chart
nouns list 88.2
diagram 652.3
map 652.4
verbs ~ a course
274.14
map 652.11
charta treaty 769.2
charter 775.5
charter
nouns treaty 769.2
grant 775.5
verbs license 775.12
hire 778.13
chartered
licensed 775.18
hired 778.17
chartreuse 370.4
chartulary 568.2
charwoman 748.8
chary thrifty 849.9
parsimonious 850.9
wary 893.9
Charybdis 394.12

chase
nouns furrow 262.1
park 410.11
pursuit 653.1,2
quarry 653.7
race 794.13
verbs escort 73.8
emboss 255.11
speed 268.10
repulse 288.2
engrave 576.12
pursue 653.8,9
hasten 707.5
court 930.19
CHASE AFTER 270.15
CHASE ALONG 300.14
CHASE OUT 308.13
CHASE UP A TREE
729.15
chased
embossed 255.17
engraved 576.16
chaser music 461.5
engraver 577.8
act 609.8
pursuer 653.4
drink 994.8
chasing 576.1
chasm cleft 200.2,3
pit 208.2
gulf 256.4
opening 264.1
chasseur 798.10
chaste elegant 587.6
tasteful 895.8
uncorrupt 978.9
pure 986.4
chasten
moderate 162.6
restrain 900.5
punish 1008.10
chastened
tempered 162.11
meek 763.15
chasteness 587.1
chastening
nouns 1008.1
adjs. mitigating
162.14
punishing 1008.25
chastise 1008.10
chastisement 1008.1
chastity
elegant style 587.1
uncorruptness 978.4
purity 986
chat
nouns jist 5.2
gossip 556.7
chatter 594.3
conversation 595.4
main point 670.6
verbs gossip 556.12
chatter 594.6
converse 595.9
chateau 190.7
chatelaine 899.6
chatoyant 373.10
chatta 227.7
chattels 808.1

chatter
nouns clatter 454.3
prattle 594.3
verbs shiver 332.10
clatter 454.6
twitter 459.5
gossip 556.12
prattle 594.6
chatterbox, chatter-
bag 594.5
chatterer gossip 556.9
chatterbox 594.5
chattering
cold 332.16
prattling 594.10
chatty talkative 594.9
conversational
595.11
sociable 920.19
chauffeur
nouns 273.10
verbs drive 272.32
guide 745.9
chaussure 230.27
chautauqua 565.14
chauvin
nouns militarist
798.5
patriot 939.3
adjs. militaristic
795.27
overpatriotic
939.5
chauvinism
militarism 795.16
overpatriotism
939.2
chauvinist
nouns militarist 798.5
patriot 939.3
adjs. militaristic
795.27
overpatriotic 939.5
chaw
nouns chew 306.2
quid 433.8
verbs chew 306.25
chew tobacco
433.15
chawbacon 917.9
chay 271.4
cheap
adjs. plentiful 659.7
paltry 671.18
inexpensive 847.7
niggardly 850.10
BE CHEAP 847.5
HOLD CHEAP 964.3
advs. 847.10
GET OFF CHEAP 630.7
cheapen
haggle 825.14
depreciate 847.6
cheapening 847.4
cheaply 847.10
cheapness
paltriness 671.2
inexpensiveness
847
niggardliness
850.2

cheat
  nouns sham 614.13
    swindle 616.8
    cheater 617.3
    impostor 617.6
  verbs deceive 616.18
    elude 629.7
check
  nouns craze 49.3
    count 87.6
    stop 144.2
    retardation 269.4
    plaid 373.4
    speech sound 449.5
    examination 484.7
    test 488.5
    measure 489.2
    collation 490.2
    verification 512.8
    counter 514.13
    disappointment
      539.1
    label 566.12
    defeat 725.2
    hindrance 728.1,3
    curb 728.7
    restraint 758.1
    money order 833.11
    money 833.12
    bill 843.3
  IN CHECK 758.13
  KEEP A CHECK ON
    keep account of
      87.13
    keep informed
      555.15
  verbs agree 26.7
    break 49.11
    delay 132.7
    stop 144.11
    retard 269.9
    monitor 343.29
    variegate 373.7
    examine 484.31
    collate 490.5
    verify 512.12
    hinder 728.10
    restrain 758.7
  CHECK IN
    arrive 299.6
    die 407.16
    register 568.15
  CHECK OFF 566.18
  CHECK OUT
    leave 300.15
    die 407.16
  CHECK THE GROWTH
    OF 202.6
  CHECK WITH 30.6
  adjs. 373.14
checked varied 19.4
    retarded 269.12
    checkered 373.14
checker
  nouns 373.4
  verbs change 139.5
    variegate 373.7
checkerboard
    checker 373.4
    game 876.16
checkered varied 19.4

changeable 141.6
    checked 373.14
checkerwork 373.4
checkmate
  nouns defeat 725.2
    hindrance 728.3
  verbs 728.15
check rate 832.8
checkrein
    harness 657.5
    curb 728.7
checkstone 383.4
checkup 484.7
Chedreux 229.14
chee-chee 578.8
cheek jowl 241.1
    impudence 911.3
  CHEEK BY JOWL
    with 73.10
    side by side 241.12
  HAVE THE CHEEK
    911.6
cheeker 911.5
cheeks 264.6
cheeky 911.9
cheep 459.5
cheer
  nouns food 306a.1
    pleasure 863.2
    cheerfulness 868.1
    huzza 874.2
    conviviality 920.3
    applause 966.2
  BE OF GOOD CHEER
    be cheerful 868.9
    be hopeful 886.8
  verbs bid Godspeed
      300.18
    regale 693.2
    gladden 868.6
    rejoice 874.7
    applaud 966.10
  CHEER ON
    urge 646.16
    applaud 966.10
  CHEER THE INNER
    MAN 994.29
  CHEER UP 868.8
cheerful
    homelike 190.28
    auspicious 542.16
    ungrudging 620.5
    happy 863.13
    gay 868.10
    cheering 868.16
cheerful giver
    giver 816.11
    generosity 851.2
cheerfully
    auspiciously 542.19
    willingly 620.8
    gayly 868.17
cheerfulness
    auspiciousness
      542.7
    happiness 863.2
    good cheer 868
cheering
    auspicious 542.16
    regaling 693.4
    gladdening 868.16

hopeful 886.13
**cheering cup, cheer-
    ing drink** 994.8
cheerio!
    farewell! 300.25
    hurrah! 874.12
    greetings! 923.15
    toast 994.47
cheerless
    unhappy 870.21
    depressing 870.31
cheer ship 274.55
cheery 868.10,16
cheese 306a.52
  THE REAL CHEESE
    515.6
cheese blintz 306a.44
cheesecake
    food 306a.41
    photograph 575.3
cheese it!
    stop it! 144.14
    beat it! 308.29
    shut up! 450.17
    jiggers! 701.11
    don't! 776.8
cheeseparing
  nouns 850.1
  adjs. 850.9
**cheeseparings and
    candle ends** 660.5
cheesy paltry 671.18
    bad 673.8
    inferior 678.10
    disreputable 913.12
cheetah 373.6
chef 329.2
chef d'oeuvre 731.10
  CHEKA 697.15
chela disciple 564.2
    novice 564.7
chelae 811.4
chemical
  nouns substance
      378.1
    types of ~ 378.12
  verbs 378.6
  adjs. of chemicals
      378.7
    acid 431.7
chemical elements
    378.11
chemicalization 378.5
chemicalize 378.6
chemical warfare
    795.4
chemicoelectric
    341.27
chemicophysics 324.1
**chemiluminescence,
    chemicolumines-
    cence** 334.13
chemisorb 305.13
chemist
    types of ~ 378.10
    druggist 685.30
chemistry 378.9
chemist's shop
    pharmacy 685.31
    store 830.5
chemotherapy 687.3

cheque 833.11
cherish
    remember 535.14
    care for 697.18
    foster 783.16
    hold 811.7
    hold dear 929.18
  CHERISH A BELIEF
    500.10
  CHERISH AN IDEA
    477.15
cherished 929.21
cheroot 433.4
cherry 367.7
chersonese 255.8
cherub child 125.3
    endearment 930.5
    good person 983.6
    angel 1013.1
cherubic 1013.6
cherubim, cherubin
    1013.1,3
Cheshire cat 413.28
chesil 383.3
chessboard
    checker 373.4
    game 876.16
chessman 876.18
chest breast 255.6
    coffer 834.12
  ON ONE'S CHEST
    477.23
chestnut
  nouns horse 413.15
    old story 516.3
    old joke 879.9
  adjs. reddish-brown
      366.4
    red-haired 367.11
chest voice 462.5
chesty 907.11
cheval glass 442.5
chevalier knight 916.6
    gallant 934.9
chevaux de frise 797.4
chevron zigzag 218.8
    insignia 567.2,5
**chevronwise,
    chevrony** 218.21
chevy
  nouns
    hunting cry 458.3
    hunt 653.2
  verbs speed 268.10
    hunt 653.9
    harass 864.19
chew
  nouns bite 306.2
    ~ of tobacco 433.8
  verbs masticate
      306.25
    ~ tobacco 433.15
  CHEW OUT 967.19
  CHEW THE CUD
    ruminate 306.25
    ponder 477.11
  CHEW THE RAG
    discuss 481.16
    converse 595.8
chewer 433.12

chewing
nouns mastication
306.1
tobacco ~ 433.11
adjs. masticatory
306.30
tobacco 433.16
chewy 358.4
chiaroscuro 572.6,14
chiasma 220.1
chiasmal, chiasmic
220.8
chiasmus 219.3
chiaus 559.1
chic
nouns 642.3
adjs. 642.13
chicane 616.4
chicanery
trickery 616.4
trick 616.6
knavery 973.2
chichi
effeminate 420.15
stylish 642.13
elegant 899.11
showy 902.19
chick child 125.3
youngling 125.8
chicken 413.35
endearment 930.5
chicken
nouns youngling
125 1
girl 125.6
weakling 159.6
food 306a.22
fowl 413.35
mollycoddle 420.11
coward 890.5
LIKE A CHICKEN WITH
ITS HEAD CUT OFF
bewildered 513.22
giddy 530.15
vacillating 625.10
adjs. 890.10
chickenhearted 890.10
chicken pox 684.9
chickling 125.8
chicky
youngling 125.8
chicken 413.35
chicle 388.6
chide 967.17
chiding 967.5
chief
nouns insignia 567.2
principal 670.10
ruler 747.3,8
adjs. supreme 36.16
first 68.15
top 210.9
front 239.11
most important
670.25
governing 739.17
directing 745.12
chiefery 737.6
chiefly mainly 36.19
mostly 54.13
first 68.16

chieftain 747.8
**chieftaincy,
chieftainry**
country 180.1
authority 737.6
chiffon 899.3
chigger, chigoe
413a.6
chignon 229.7
chilblain 684.28
chilblains 333.2
child urchin 125.3
product 167.1
offspring 170.3
childish person
470.10
unsophisticate
734.3
innocent 982.4
WITH CHILD 168.18
**childbearing, child-
bed, childbirth**
166.9
childhood 124.2
childish young 124.11
senile 468.23
puerile 468.24
childishness
youth 124.4
senility 468.10
puerility 468.11
childkind 125.2
childless 165.4
childlike young 124.11
senile 468.23
puerile 468.24
artless 734.5
innocent 982.6
children youth 125.2
posterity 170.1
THE CHILDREN OF
GOD 1026.5
CHILDREN OF THE
DEVIL 984.11
child's play 671.5
chiliad, chiliarch
99.10
chill
nouns cold 332.1,2
deterrent 650.2
unfriendliness 927.1
verbs be cold
332.10,11
refrigerate 333.10
discourage 650.4
adjs. cool 332.13
depressing 870.31
unfriendly 927.10
chiller 333.3
chilling
nouns coldness 332.2
cooling 333.1
adjs. 333.12
chilly cool 332.13,16
unfriendly 927.10
chilopod 413a.2
Chilopoda 414.8
chime
nouns ringing 453.3
harmony 461.3
orchestral ~ 464.20

verbs agree 26.7
ring 453.8
harmonize 461.36
speak 592.11
CHIME IN 237.6
CHIME IN WITH
agree 26.7
conform 82.3
concur 520.9
accord 792.2
chimera illusion 518.1
fancy 533.5
airy hopes 886.5
chimeric(al)
unsubstantial 4.5
illusory 518.9
fanciful 533.22
chiming
nouns ringing 453.3
harmony 461.3
adjs. ringing 453.12
harmonious 461.50
chimney cleft 200.3
ore shoot 382.6
flue 395.18
chimney corner
home 190.3
fireside 328.11
chimney sweep 679.15
chin
nouns anatomy 239.6
talk 592.1
KEEP ONE'S CHIN UP
bear up 868.9
be courageous
891.15
verbs yap 592.12
converse 595.8
China 180.9
china 574.7
Chinatown 182.5
chinaware 829.4
chinch 413a.7
chine ridge 206.6
bulge 255.3
Chinese 417.9
chink
nouns cleft 200.2
furrow 262.1
ringing 453.3
money 833.2
verbs open 264.11
stop up 265.7
ring 453.8
chinker 833.4
chinky 200.7
chinook 402.7
chintzy 377.9
chinwhisker 181.6
chin whiskers 229.8
chip
nouns small amount
35.3
break 49.3
piece 55.3
flake 226.3
betting ~ 514.13
coin 833.4
token 833.12
CHIP OFF THE OLD
BLOCK

counterpart 20.5
duplicate 24.3
offspring 170.3
CHIP ON ONE'S
SHOULDER 795.16
verbs 49.11
CHIP IN
interrupt 237.6
participate 813.5
contribute 816.14
pay 839.18
chipper healthy 683.6
lively 705.16
cheerful 868.13
chippy 987.14
chips
ship's carpenter
275.6
stageman 609.28
money 833.2
chirk
nouns 457.5
verbs stridulate 457.6
croak 459.5
adjs. lively 705.16
cheerful 868.13
chirograph 568.4
chirography 600.4
chironomy 566.13
chiroplasty 686.3
chiropodic 686.18
chiropodist 686.7
**chiropodistry, chirop-
ody** 686.2
chiropractic
nouns 686.7
adjs. 686.18
**chiropractics, chiro-
praxis** 686.2
chiropractor 686.7
chirp, chirrup
cheep 459.5
sing 461.39
say 592.17
rejoice 874.6
chirpy, chirrupy
868.13
chirr 459.5
chisel
nouns 573.5
verbs make 166.12
form 245.6
furrow 262.3
sculpture 573.6
engrave 576.12
swindle 616.18
CHISEL IN 237.5
chiseler
sculptor 577.6
cheat 617.3
chiseling 576.1
chit child 125.3
diminutive 195.4
epistle 602.2
recommendation
966.4
chitchat gossip 556.7
chat 595.5
chitchatty 595.11
chitin 227.16
chiton 414.9

chitter 459.5
chitter-chatter
  chatter 594.3
  chitchat 595.5
chitterlings
  intestines 224.6
  pork 306a.16
chitty 602.2
chivalric brave 891.17
  courteous 934.15
chivalrous
  brave 891.17
  knightly 916.11
  courteous 934.15
  magnanimous 977.6
chivalry
  knightly skill 795.11
  tenure 806.1
  courage 891.1
  knightage 916.2
  courtesy 934.2
  magnanimity 977.2
chivy 653.2
chlorinate
  chemicalize 378.6
  disinfect 679.22
chlorination 378.5
chlorine
  nouns 437.3
  adjs. 370.4
chloroform kill 408.13
  anesthetize 422.3
Chlorophyceae 411.4
chlorophyll
  green 370.1
  deodorant 437.3
chlorosis 684.8
chlorotic
  anemic 362.9
  sickly 684.46
chock
  verbs 56.7
  adjs. 56.12
chock-full, chuck
  56.12
chocolate 366.3
Choctaw 547.6
choice
  nouns selection 635
  the best 672.8
  free will 760.5
  AT CHOICE
  at will 619.5
  optionally 635.24
  BY CHOICE
  voluntarily 620.11
  preferably 635.25
  OWN CHOICE 760.6
  WITHOUT CHOICE
  necessary 637.12
  necessarily 637.16
  adjs. 672.19
choiceful 635.20
choiceless 637.12
choicelessness 637.6
choicy selective 635.20
  particular 894.9
choir
  nouns chorus 463.18
  church part 1040.9
  verbs 461.39

choirboy 463.17
choir chaplain
  choirmaster 463.20
  churchman 1036.9
choir invisible 1013.2
choirister, choirman
  463.17
choirmaster 463.20
choke
  nouns 408.6
  verbs clog 265.7
  stifle 327.21
  extinguish 331.7
  strangle 408.19
  muffle 450.9
  overfill 661.16
  exterminate 691.15
  hinder 728.12
  CHOKE OFF
  silence 450.10
  hinder 728.12
  suppress 758.8
chokecherry 431.3
chokedamp
  vapor 400.1
  poison 674.4
chokidar 697.11
chokra 748.4
choky 759.7
cholecystotomy
  687.26
choler ill humor 949.1
  resentment 950.3
cholera 684.9
choleric
  diseased 684.46
  sour-tempered
  949.23
cholesterol 307.9
chomp
  nouns 306.2
  verbs 306.25
chondric 355.10
chondrification
  355.5
chonk 306.25
choose
  nouns 635.1
  verbs desire 632.14
  select 635.10
  CHOOSE TO 619.2
choosing
  nouns 635.1
  adjs. 635.20
choosy
  selective 635.20
  particular 894.9
chop
  nouns cheek 241.1
  blow 282.4
  feed 306a.4
  meat 306a.19
  wave 394.14
  label 566.12
  verbs sever 49.10
  change 139.5
  jerk 285.5
  CHOP DOWN
  fell 316.5
  raze 691.19

chopfallen
  See chapfallen
chophouse 306.14
chopped-off 72.4
chopper 558.19
choppiness
  irregularity 138.1
  roughness 260.1
  waves 394.14
chopping 194.18
choppy
  discontinuous 72.4
  irregular 138.3
  rough 260.6
  jolting 323.21
chops 264.5
chopsticks 347.3
chor 823.1
choral
  nouns music 461.16
  hymn 1030.3
  adjs. 461.51
choralcelo 464.15
choral society, choral
  symphony 463.18
chorale music 461.16
  hymn 1030.3
choralist 463.17
chord
  nouns radius 203.3
  right line 249.2
  musical ~ 462.17
  music string 464.24
  sympathetic ~
  853.5
  verbs harmonize
  461.36
  tune 461.37
  ~ music 461.40
Chordata 414.10
chore
  nouns task 654.2
  hard job 729.2
  verbs 714.12
chorea 684.17
chore boy 559.4
choreographer 609.26
choreographic, chore-
  graphic 877.6
choreography, cho-
  regraphy
  drama 609.3
  dancing 877.1
choric 461.51
chorine chorist 463.17
  performer 610.1
chorister 463.17,20
chorographer
  surveyor 489.10
  map maker 652.4
chorographic(al)
  489.13
chorography
  topography 183.8
  surveying 489.9
  mapping 652.4
chorometry 489.9
chortle
  nouns 874.4
  verbs 874.9

chorus
  nouns refrain 103.5
  outcry 458.4
  music 461.18,24
  choir 463.18
  unanimity 520.5
  poetic refrain
  607.11
  theatrical ~ 610.11
  IN CHORUS
  simultaneously
  118.6
  harmonious 461.50
  unanimously 520.17
  verbs echo 22.5
  sing 461.39
  speak 592.11
chorus girl
  chorist 463.17
  performer 610.1
  dancer 877.3
chorus show
  music 461.35
  show 609.14
chosen 635.23
chouse
  nouns 616.7
  verbs 616.17
chow 306a.2
chowchow
  nouns 44.6
  adjs. 44.15
chowder 306a.11
chowderhead 470.4
chowderheaded
  468.17
chrestomathy 74.10
chrism, chrisom
  nouns 1038.6
  verbs 1038.18
chrismal, chrismale
  chrismal cloth
  1038.6
  cerecloth 1040.10
chrisomloosing 1038.7
Christ 1011.12
christcross, crisscross
  cross 220.4
  alphabet 579.4
christen
  inaugurate 68.10
  name 581.11
  baptize 1038.19
Christendom
  Christianity 1022.3
  Christians 1026.5
christening
  naming 581.2
  baptism 1038.7
Christian
  nouns worthy 983.3
  religionist 1018.15
  believer 1026.4
  adjs. human 416.10
  benign 936.14
  respectable 972.13
  orthodox 1022.8
  pious 1026.8
Christian Era 107.11
Christianity
  religion 1018.6

clash
nouns collision 282.3
  bang 455.1
  harsh sound 457.3
  dissonance 460.2
  disaccord 793.1
  contest 794.3
  hostility 927.3
verbs go counter to
  15.3
  disagree 27.5
  counteract 177.6
  collide 282.13
  of colors 361.15
  bang 455.6
  sound harshly 457.8
  be discordant 460.3
  disaccord 793.9
  contend with
  794.16
CLASH WITH 16.5
clashing
nouns contrariety
  15.1
  disagreement 27.1
  counteraction 177.1
  opposition 788.2
  disaccord 793.1
  hostility 927.3
adjs. contrary 15.5
  disagreeing 27.6
  counteractive 177.8
  off-color 361.21
  dissonant 460.5
  opposing 788.9
  disaccordant 793.16
clasp
nouns fastener 48.7
  grip 811.2
  embrace 930.2
verbs fasten 47.8
  adhere 50.5
  stay near 199.12
  hold 811.6
  seize 820.12
  hug 930.16
clasping 47.3
class
nouns rank 29.2
  category 61.2
  classification 61.5
  school ~ 564.9
  excellence 672.1
  sect 786.6
  religious ~ 1037.1
verbs classify 61.6
  rate 493.9
class consciousness
  525.4
classic
nouns music 461.7
  work of art 572.11
adjs. 672.16
classic(al)
  elegant 587.6
  literary 600.26
  tasteful 895.8
classicalism
  language 578.2
  elegant style 587.1
  literature 600.13

classicism
  scholarship 474.5
  language 578.2
  elegant style 587.1
  literature 600.13
classicist scholar 475.3
  purist 587.4
classics
  languages 578.2
  literature 600.13
classification
  organization 60.2
  categorization 61
classificational, classi-
  ficatory 61.7
classified
  catalogued 61.8
  secret 612.12
classify organize 60.9
  categorize 61.6
  ~ information
  612.8
classifying 348.20
classis 753.5
classman 564.1
classmate 926.4
classroom 565.16
classy stylish 642.13
  ostentatious 902.18
clatter
nouns noise 452.3
  rattle 454.3
  chatter 594.3
verbs rattle 454.6
  gossip 556.12
  chatter 594.6
clattering 454.8
clattery noisy 452.11
  rattly 454.8
clause section 55.2
  proviso 506.2
  phrase 583.1
  passage 603.14
  legislative ~ 740.19
claustral 1040.15
clavichord, clavier
  464.13
clavichordist 463.7
claviharp 464.3
clavis key 264.10
  translation 550.3
clavus 684.29
claw 820.12
clawback 905.3
clawed 811.9
clawlike 251.8
claws 811.4
clay
nouns softness 356.4
  the body 375.3
  soil 384.1
  mud 388.8
  corpse 407.13
  pipe 433.7
  potter's ~ 574.3
adjs. 574.7
clayey soft 356.12
  earthy 384.7
clayware 829.4
clean
verbs tidy 60.11

  cleanse 679.17
CLEAN OUT 308.20
CLEAN UP
  tidy 60.11
  complete 720.6
adjs. complete 56.11
  tidy 59.8
  well-shaped 247.6
  unsoiled 679.23
  clever 731.20
  innocent 982.7
  chaste 986.4
advs. quite 56.16
  perfectly 675.10
  cleanly 679.27
clean bill of health
  certificate 568.5
  healthiness 683.2
clean-cut
  well-shaped 247.6
  distinct 443.7
  precise 515.15
  clear 546.10
cleaned 679.24
cleaner
  cleaner-up 679.13
  cleanser 679.16
clean hands 982.1
cleaning
nouns 679.2
adjs. 679.26
cleaning devices
  679.30
cleanliness 679.1
cleanly
adjs. clean 679.23
  chaste 986.4
advs. 679.27
cleanness tidiness 59.3
  cleanliness 679.1
  innocence 982.1
  chastity 986.1
cleanse refine 354.6
  clean 679.17
  sanctify 1024.5
cleansed 679.24
cleanser
  cleaner 679.16
  types of ~ 679.28,
  29
clean-shaven 231.17
cleansing
nouns refinement
  354.3
  cleaning 679.2
adjs. cleaning 679.26
  cathartic 685.41
clean slate void 186.3
  innocence 982.1
clean-speaking, clean-
  spoken 592.21
clean sweep 147.1
MAKE A CLEAN SWEEP
  revolutionize 147.4
  evacuate 308.20
  clean 679.17
  exterminate 691.14
cleanup tidying 60.5
  gain 809.3
clear
verbs eliminate 77.5

  hurdle 317.5
  refine 354.6
  cleanse 679.17
  negotiate 722.11
  disembarrass 730.7
  free 761.7
  ~ a profit 809.10
  pay off 839.13
  ~ of indebtedness
  840.9
  acquit 1005.4
CLEAR AWAY
  disperse 75.6
  eliminate 77.5
  evacuate 308.20
CLEAR FOR ACTION
  trim ship 274.51
  prepare 718.11
CLEAR OFF OLD
  SCORES 839.12
CLEAR OUT
  eliminate 77.5
  depart 300.9
  evacuate 308.20
  flee 629.10
  clean 679.17
CLEAR THE DECKS
  tidy 60.11
  eliminate 77.5
  trim ship 274.51
  evacuate 308.20
  prepare 718.11
  take precautions
  893.6
CLEAR THE LAND
  274.39
CLEAR THE THROAT
  310.6
CLEAR THE WAY
  prepare the way
  718.12
  facilitate 730.6
CLEAR UP
  tidy 60.11
  solve 486.2
  explain 550.11
adjs. unfastened
  49.21
  complete 56.11
  blank 186.12
  open 264.17
  light 334.31
  transparent 338.4
  clearly seen 443.7
  audible 449.15
  unqualified 507.2
  certain 512.13
  intelligible 546.10
  manifest 553.8
  escaped 630.10
  clean 679.23
  fresh 693.5
  free 760.19
  exempt 760.27
  rid 760.28
  unindebted 839.23
  innocent 982.6
CLEAR AS MUD
  547.13
CLEAR OF
  wide of 198.19

free of 760.28
GET CLEAR OF
  escape 630.6
  free oneself 761.8
MAKE ALL CLEAR FOR
  730.6
MAKE IT CLEAR
  make understood
    546.6
  manifest 553.5
clearage 308.6
clearance
  riddance 77.2
  open space 178.4
  aviation 277.41
  evacuation 308.6
  permit 775.7
  payment 839.1
  acquittal 1005.1
clear coast
  safety 696.1
  facility 730.1
clear conscience
  982.1
clear-cut
  distinct 443.7
  precise 515.15
  explicit 546.10
clear-eyed 438.23
clearheaded 466.13
clearing
  open space 178.4
  cleared land 412.9
  disembarrassment
    730.5
  freeing 761.3
clearing house 834.13
clearly distinctly 443.8
  audibly 449.19
  certainly 512.23
  intelligibly 546.12
  manifestly 553.14
clearness
  transparency 338.1
  distinctness 443.2
  intelligibility 546.2
  manifestness 553.3
clear-sighted
  clear-eyed 438.23
  discerning 466.13
clear stage
  opportunity 129.2
  facility 730.1
clearway 277.20
clear-witted 466.13
cleat 47.8
cleavable 49.25
cleavage severance 49.2
  atomic ~ 325.8
cleave sever 49.10
  adhere 50.5
  bisect 92.3
  open 264.11
  ~ the atom 325.16
cleavers 257.8
cleaving 50.8
clef 462.13
cleft
  nouns crack 200.2
  notch 261.1
  adjs. severed 49.22

divided 92.4
  rift 200.7
clemency
  leniency 757.1
  mercy 942.1
clement lenient 757.8
  merciful 942.7
clench
  nouns 811.2
  verbs hold 811.6
  seize 820.12
Cleopatra 898.9
clerestory, clearstory
  floor 191.23
  top 210.1
clergy 1036
clergy house 1040.7
clergyman 1036.2
clergywoman 1036.5,
  18
cleric 1036.2
cleric(al)
  secretarial 600.29
  ecclesiastical
    1035.13
clericalism 1035.3
clericals clergy 1036.1
  canonicals 1039.1
clerk recorder 569.1
  scribe 600.14
  agent 779.3
  salesman 828.4
  accountant 843.7
  clergyman 1036.2,9
cletch brood 170.2
  nest 190.21
cleuch, cleugh 200.3
clever smart 466.14
  excellent 672.13
  skillful 731.20
  well-devised 731.27
  cunning 733.12
  witty 879.15
  good-natured
    936.15
cleverness
  smartness 466.2
  skill 731.1
  cunning 733
  wittiness 879.2
clew See clue
cliché platitude 516.3
  old joke 879.9
click
  nouns 455.2
  verbs snap 455.7
  succeed 722.6
client
  dependent 762.6
  customer 826.4
clientage
  dependence 762.3
  clientele 826.3
cliental 826.10
clientele, clientry
  826.3
cliff 212.3
cliff hanger 609.4
climacteric
  menopause 126.7
  crisis 129.4

climacteric(al)
  129.11
climatal 401.14
climate latitude 179.3
  atmosphere 232.3
  weather 401.4
  attitudes 523.5
climatic(al) top 210.9
  climatal 401.14
climatologic(al)
  401.14
climatologist 401.7
climatology
  aviation 277.2
  meteorology 401.6
climatotherapy 687.3
climax
  nouns consummation
    56.4
  result 153.2
  summit 210.2
  figure of speech
    549.2
  verbs 210.8
climb
  nouns acclivity 218.6
  ascent 313.1
  verbs slope up 218.10
  fly 277.45
  ascend 313.11
CLIMB ON 313.12
climber
  mountaineer 313.6
  vine 410.4
clime zone 179.3
  climate 401.4
clinch
  nouns 811.2
  verbs fasten 47.7
  prove 504.11
  make sure 512.11
  hold 811.6
  seize 820.12
clincher end-all 70.4
  settler 505.3
cling
  nouns coherence 50.1
  hold 811.2
  verbs adhere 50.5
  hold 811.6
CLING TO
  adhere 50.5
  stay near 199.12
  be wont 640.12
  hold 811.6,7
clinging
  nouns 811.2
  adjs. coherent 50.8
  retentive 811.8
clingy 50.9
clinic 687.29
clinical 686.18
clink
  nouns assonance 20.3
  ringing 453.3
  rhyme 607.10
  prison 759.7
  verbs 453.8
clinker residue 43.2
  cinder 328.16

brick 377.2
  coin 833.4
clinometer 250.4
clinquant sham 614.13
  frippery 899.3
Clio 606.4
clip
  nouns piece 55.3
  velocity 268.2
  blow 282.4
AT A CLIP 118.6
  verbs cut off 42.10
  fasten 47.8
  shorten 202.6
  speed 268.9
  strike 282.14
CLIP ONE'S WORDS
  593.6
CLIP THE WINGS
  disable 157.9
  slow down 269.9
  thwart 728.15
clipper 268.6
clipping 55.3
clippings 605.4
clique
  nouns 786.7
  verbs plot 652.10
  associate with
    920.15
cliquish
  clannish 786.17
  exclusive 894.13
cliquishness
  partisanism 786.13
  exclusiveness 894.5
cliquy 786.17
clitoris 418.8
clitter
  nouns 454.3
  verbs 454.6
cloaca drain 395.5
  sewer 680.12
  toilet 680.13
cloak
  nouns cover 227.2
  garment 230.12
  types of ~ 230.50
  pretext 647.1
  clerical ~ 1039.2
UNDER THE CLOAK OF
  612.19
  verbs cover 227.21
  mantle 230.39
  conceal 613.7
  protect 697.17
cloak-and-dagger
  855.33
cloaked
  covered 227.34
  protected 697.20
cloaking
  nouns 227.1
  adjs. 227.37
cloakroom 191.15
clobber
  nouns 230.1
  verbs strike 282.14
  defeat 725.8
  beat 1008.16

clock

nouns timepiece
114.6
types of ~ 114.17
verbs 114.11
clock watcher 706.7
clockwise
adjs. 242.4
advs. 320.16
clockworks
complication 46.2
timepiece 114.6
mechanism 347.5
LIKE CLOCKWORK
steadily 17.8
methodically 59.9
regularly 137.10
smoothly 259.12
clod neck 48.5
lump 194.10
roast 306a.17
the body 375.3
soil 384.1
dolt 470.5
clumsy fellow 732.9
rustic 917.9
cloddish
countrified 181.7
boorish 896.13
clodhopper oaf 470.5
clumsy fellow 732.9
rustic 917.9
clodhoppers 230.27
clodhopping 181.7
clodpate 470.4
clodpated 468.17
clodpolish 181.7
clodpoll, clodpole
dolt 470.4
clumsy fellow 732.9
clog
nouns obstruction
265.3
log 377.3
curb 728.7
verbs stop up 265.7
obstruct 728.12
dance 877.5
clogged 265.11
cloison 236.5
cloister
nouns corridor
191.18
passageway 655.4
retreat 698.5
monastery 1040.6
verbs immure 235.6
confine 759.12
cloistered
enclosed 235.10
recluse 922.11
monastic 1040.15
cloisters 1040.9
clonus, clonic spasm
684.5
clop
nouns hoofbeat
272.1
stamp 282.10
thud 451.3
verbs 282.2

close

nouns end 70.3
cessation 144.1
tract 179.4
enclosure 235.3
~ of letters 602.17
completion 720.2
verbs end 70.5
stop 144.12
surround 232.6
enclose 235.5
shut 265.6
come together
297.2
settle with 769.9
CLOSE OFF 728.12
CLOSE ONE'S EYES TO
be blind to 440.7
disregard 529.3
condone 945.4
CLOSE ONE'S MIND
525.6
CLOSE ONE'S RANKS
718.11
CLOSE OUT
sell out 827.8
sell stock 831.24
close the books
843.8
CLOSE UP
close 265.6,8
come together
297.2
heal 692.21
complete 720.6
CLOSE WITH
adhere 50.5
sail for 274.37
converge 297.2
concur 520.9
settle with 769.9
fight 794.16
close
adjs. related 9.7
approximative 20.14
faithful 24.8
fast 47.14
crowded 74.22
imminent 151.3
near 199.14
narrow 204.13
closed 265.12
airless 267.14
sultry 327.28
dense 353.12
phonetics 449.18
meticulous 531.12
literal 543.12
concise 590.4
close-mouthed
611.7
secret 612.12
secretive 612.17
concealed 613.12
scarce 660.9
stingy 850.11
unsociable 921.5
intimate 925.18
advs. securely 47.18
closely 199.24
densely 353.15

CLOSE ABOUT

near 199.20
around 232.13
CLOSE UPON
about 35.13
about to 121.13
near 199.20
approximately
199.26
close call 630.2
closed
enclosed 235.10
shut 265.9
unreceptive 924.6
CLOSED TO
uninfluenceable
172.4
denied to 509.8
closed shop 787.2
**closefisted, close-
handed** 850.11
close-haul 274.27
**close-lipped, close-
mouthed** 611.7
closely close 199.24
narrowly 204.21
densely 353.15
literally 543.15
closeness likeness 20.1
nearness 199.1
narrowness 204.1
airlessness 267.6
sultriness 327.5
density 353.1
uncommunicative-
ness 611.1
secretive 612.1
stinginess 850.3
intimacy 925.5
**close quarters, close
range** 199.2
close shave 630.2
close study 528.4
closet
nouns private room
191.8
cloakroom 191.15
hiding place 613.4
storeroom 658.6
water ~ 680.13
office 717.8
BE CLOSETED WITH
595.9
verbs 235.6
adjs. 612.15
close-tongued 611.7
close-up 575.10
closing
nouns end 70.3
cessation 144.1
closure 265.1
adjs. 70.9
closure joint 47.4
stop 144.5
enclosure 235.1
closing 265
legislative ~ 740.16
clot
nouns 353.7
verbs 353.10
clotbur 50.3

cloth

nouns sail 276.14
fabric 377.5
stage curtain 609.24
canonicals 1039.1
THE CLOTH
ministry 1035.1
clergy 1036.1
adjs. 377.9
clothe empower 156.9
cover 227.21
dress 230.38
provide 657.7
clothed clad 230.44
provided 657.12
clothes
bedclothes 227.11
apparel 230.1
old ~ 230.5
clotheshorse 215.17
clothes pole 204.8
clothier 230.32
clothing 230.1
Clotho 638.3
clotted 353.14
cloture 144.5
cloud
nouns throng 74.4
multitude 101.3
haze 403
IN THE CLOUDS
aloft 206.27
bemused 530.11
visionary 533.24
UNDER A CLOUD
under suspicion
502.12
in disgrace 913.13
verbs darken
336.10,11
opaque 340.2
becloud 403.7
conceal 613.7
cloud-built
unsubstantial 4.5
fanciful 533.22
cloudburst 393.2
cloud-capped
lofty 206.20
clouded 403.9
clouded
dark 336.15,18
mottled 373.12
cloudy 403.8
concealed 613.12
cloudiness
dimness 336.5
opaqueness 340.1
haziness 403.4
cloudland
clouds 403.1
utopia 533.11
cloudless 334.31
cloud seeder
aviation 278.1
rain maker 393.5
cloudy dark 336.15,18
opaque 340.3
hazy 403.8
obscure 547.13
clough 200.3

clout
  nouns 282.4
  verbs 282.14
cloven divided 92.4
  cleft 200.7
cloven hoof
  evil nature 979.8
  devilishness 1014.14
clover three 93.1
  prosperity 726.1
  comfort 885.1
  IN CLOVER
  prosperous 726.12
  in comfort 885.15
cloverleaf 220.2
clown
  nouns buffoon 610.9
  clumsy fellow 732.9
  vulgarian 896.6
  rustic 917.9
  verbs 469.6
clownery 879.5
clownish
  countrified 181.7
  clumsy 732.20
  buffoonish 879.16
  boorish 896.13
clownishness
  clumsiness 732.3
  buffoonery 879.5
  boorishness 896.4
cloy 662.4
cloyed 662.6
cloyer 662.3
cloying
  oversweet 430.7
  satiating 662.7
club
  nouns ball 190.15
  society 786.4,7
  weapons 799.23
  verbs league 52.4
  hit 282.19
  beat 1008.14
clubbable 786.16
clubbish 920.17
clubbishness,
    clubbism 920.1
clubfoot foot 211.5
  deformity 248.3
clubfooted 248.12
clubhouse 190.15
club law
  anarchy 738.2
  despotism 739.10
  force 754.3
clubman, clubwoman
  socialite 642.7
  member 786.11
cluck 459.5
clue
  nouns evidence 504.1
  hint 555.4
  clew 566.8
  verbs 484.29
clump
  nouns bunch 74.6
  chunk 194.10
  lump 255.3
  stamp 282.10
  growth 410.2

thicket 410.13
thud 451.3
  verbs assemble 74.17
  trudge 272.27
  stamp 282.2
clumpish 194.19
clumsiness
  bulkiness 194.9
  carelessness 532.3
  inconvenience 669.3
  unwieldiness 729.8
  awkwardness 732.3
clumsy
  nouns 732.8
  adjs. bulky 194.19
  slipshod 532.12
  awkward 669.7
  unwieldy 729.18
  blundering 732.20
Cluniac 1036.17
clunk lump 194.10
  thud 451.3
cluricaune 1012.15
cluster
  nouns 74.6
  verbs 74.15,17
clutch
  nouns crisis 129.4
  brood 170.2
  nest 190.21
  hold 811.2
  verbs hold 811.6
  seize 820.12
clutches control 739.2
  talons 811.4
  IN ONE'S CLUTCHES
    762.13
clutter
  nouns jumble 62.3
  radar 345.12
  clatter 454.3
  litter 667.5
  verbs disarrange 63.2
  clatter 454.6
clypeate, clypeiform
    251.22
cluster 685.17
Cnidaria 414.4
coach
  nouns railway car
    271.13
  teacher 563.6,7
  adviser 752.4
  verbs haul 270.12
  teach 560.11
  advise 752.6
coach-and-four 271.5
coach house 190.17
coaching 560.1
coachman 273.9
coach road 655.6
coachwhip 567.6
coact concur 176.2
  co-operate 784.4
coaction
  concurrence 176.1
  compulsion 754.1
  co-operation 784.1
coactive
  concurrent 176.4
  compulsory 754.9

co-operative 784.7
coactor 785.4
coadjument 784.1
coadjutant, coadjuvant
  nouns 785.6
  adjs. 784.7
coadjutor
  assistant 785.6
  churchman 1036.8
coadjuvate 784.4
coadministration
    784.1
coadunate
  verbs combine 52.3
  concur 176.2
  adjs. united 52.5
  concurrent 176.4
coadunation 52.1
coagency 784.1
coagulate 353.10
coagulated 353.14
coagulation
  coherence 50.1
  thickening 353.4
coagulum 353.7
coaid 785.5
coal
  nouns residue 43.2
  ember 327.15
  cinder 328.16
  fuel 330.1
  types of ~ 330.10
  black 364.4
  verbs char 328.23
  fuel 330.8
coal car 271.13
coal dust 330.2
coalesce
  identify 14.5
  mingle 44.11
  combine 52.3
coalescence
  identification 14.2
  amalgamation 44.1
  combination 52.1
coalescent, coalescing
    89.12
coal gas 674.4
coalition
  combination 52.1
  front 742.34
  affiliation 784.3
  alliance 786.1
coalitional 786.16
coalition government
    739.4
coal mine 382.6
coal oil 334.20
Coalsack 374.14
coal scuttle 192.6
coal tongs 328.15
coaly
  carbonaceous 330.9
  black 364.8
coaptation 26.4
coarctation 204.2
coarse thick 203.8
  rough 260.6
  granular 350.6
  harsh-sounding
    457.14

inelegant 588.2
inferior 678.10
unfinished 719.12
vulgar 896.11
carnal 985.6
indecent 988.8
coarse-grained
  rough 260.6
  coarse 350.6
coarsen
  roughen 260.4
  give texture 350.4
  vulgarize 896.9
  sensualize 985.4
coarseness
  raucousness 457.2
  inelegant style 588.1
  inferiority 678.3
  unfinish 719.4
  vulgarity 896.2
coast
  nouns slide 314.4
  shore 384.2
  verbs glide 272.34
  sail 274.41
  slide 314.9
  go easily 730.8
coastal
  bordering 234.11
  seaside 384.9
coaster 192.8
coast guard
  guard 697.8
  military 798.27
coastguardsman
    275.4
coasting
  gliding 272.8
  astronautics 281.14
coastland 384.2
coastward, coastways,
    coastwise 274.71
coat
  nouns lamina 226.2
  cover 227.2
  coating 227.13
  pelt 228.1
  hair 229.2
  garment 230.13
  types of ~ 230.51
  ~ of paint 361.12
  ~ of arms 567.2
  verbs cover 227.26
  cloak 230.39
  paint 361.14
coated 227.34
coating lamina 226.2
  covering 227.1
  painting 361.11
  ~ of paint 361.12
coauthor
  nouns writer 600.15
  collaborator 785.4
  verbs 600.21
coax
  nouns 646.10
  verbs urge 646.14
  importune 772.12
co-ax 558.20
coaxer 646.10
coaxial, coaxal 225.15

cohesiveness 50.2
cohibit 758.7
cohibition 758.1
cohibitive 758.11
cohort
  company 74.3
  military unit 798.19
cohue 74.4
coif cover 227.23
  clothe 230.39
coifed 230.44
coiffeur, coiffeuse
  898.12
coiffure
  nouns 229.15
  verbs 229.22
coign of vantage 36.2
coil
  nouns piece 201.3
  hair 229.7
  curl 253.2
  verbs 253.5
coin
  nouns corner 250.2
  money 833.4
  verbs invent 166.14
  mint 833.26
  COIN A PHRASE 516.7
  COIN MONEY 835.9
coinage
  invention 166.5
  product 167.1
  word 580.7
  money 833.1
coincide
  be identical 14.4
  correspond 26.7
  synchronize 118.3
  concur 176.2
  agree 520.9
coincidence
  identity 14.1
  correspondence 26.1
  simultaneousness
   118.1
  concurrence 176.1
coincident
  coinciding 14.7
  correspondent
   26.14
  joint 47.12
  concurrent 176.4
coincidental 14.7
coinciding
  identical 14.7
  equivalent 30.9
coined 166.28
coiner 833.24
coining 833.23
coinstantaneous
  118.4
coition, coitus 168.3
cojuror 504.7
coke slag 328.16
  fuel 330.1
col 200.3
colander sorter 60.4
  strainer 354.4
colatorium 354.4
cold
  nouns coldness 332

disease 684.12
IN THE COLD, OUT-IN
  THE COLD 532.14
adjs. frigid 332.15
  feeling ∼ 332.16
  lackluster 336.19
  cool-colored 361.16
  dead 407.25
  unsexual 418.22
  unconscious 422.7
  reserved 611.8
  indifferent 634.5
  unfeeling 854.9
  depressing 870.31
  dull 881.6
  insolent 911.8
  unsociable 921.6
  unfriendly 927.10
  heartless 937.23
  BE COLD 332.10
  GET DOWN COLD
   562.9
  OUT COLD
  unconscious 422.7
  dead-drunk 994.43
cold blood 854.1
IN COLD BLOOD
  intentionally 651.11
  unfeelingly 854.14
  cruelly 937.30
cold-blooded
  heterothermic
   332.20
  unfeeling 854.9
  inexcitable 856.10
  heartless 937.23
cold-cock 422.3
cold cream
  lotion 379.3
  cosmetic 898.11
cold creeps
  chilliness 332.2
  sensation 425.4
  apprehension 889.4
cold fact 1.3
cold feet 890.4
cold frame 412.11
cold front 332.4
coldhearted
  unfeeling 854.9
  heartless 937.23
coldness cold 332.1
  lackluster 336.6
  sex 418.2
  reserve 611.3
  indifference 634.1
  unfeeling 854.1
  unsociability 921.2
  unfriendliness 927.1
  heartlessness 937.10
cold pack 333.3
cold shivers
  shaking 323.2
  chilliness 332.2
  creeps 425.4
  nervousness 857.2
  horror 889.4
cold-short 359.5
cold shoulder
  nouns 964.2
  verbs 964.5

cold sore 684.28
cold steel knife 347.2
  sword 799.4
cold storage
  refrigeration 333.6
  storage 658.5
cold sweat
  sweat 309.7
  nervousness 857.2
  repugnance 865.2
  trepidation 889.4
cold war 795.5
cold water 650.2
cold-water flat 191.4
cold wave
  hairdo 229.15
  coldness 332.3
coleslaw 306a.36
colic
  nouns stomach-ache
   423.5
  illness 684.21
  adjs. 224.12
Colin Tampon 417.9
Coliseum See
  Colosseum
coliseum
  amphitheater 609.17
  arena 800.1
colitis 684.8
collaborate
  coauthor 600.21
  co-operate 784.4
  be traitorous 973.14
collaboration
  co-operation 784.1
  treason 973.7
collaborative 784.7
collaborator
  coauthor 600.15
  traitor 617.11
  confederate 785.4
collage 572.12
collapse
  nouns cave-in 197.4
  physical ∼ 684.7
  impairment 690.1
  debacle 691.4
  exhaustion 715.2
  failure 723.3
  defeat 725.1
  bankruptcy 840.3
  verbs fall in 197.10
  fall through 312.3
  break down 690.25
  get tired 715.5
  fail 723.11
  go bankrupt 840.7
collapsible 197.11
collar
  nouns band 252.3
  foam 404.2
  shackle 758.4
  IN COLLAR 705.20
  verbs arrest 759.16
  capture 820.15
collate compare 490.5
  check 512.12
collateral
  nouns nonessential
   6.2

relative 11.2
  security 770.3
  margin 832.9
  adjs. extrinsic 6.4
  related 9.6
  consanguineous
   11.7
  additional 40.9
  accompanying 73.9
  simultaneous 118.4
  contingent 150.11
  parallel 217.6
  corroborative
   504.20
collaterality 217.1
collating 348.20
collation meal 306.7
  comparison 490.2
  verification 512.8
colleague
  confederate 785.1
  comrade 926.4
colleagueship
  affiliation 784.3
  comradeship 925.2
Collect 1038.10
collect
  nouns 1030.4
  verbs assemble
   74.15,17
  deduce 493.10
  store up 658.11
  procure 809.9
  ∼ oneself 856.7
  advs. 839.25
collectanea
  collection 74.10
  book 603.4
  excerpts 605.4
collectarium 603.4
collected
  assembled 74.21
  composed 856.13
collection
  assemblage 74.1,10
  book 603.4
  excerpts 605.4
  store 658.1
  acquisition 809.2
  donation 816.6
  offering 1030.7
collective 79.10
collective bargaining
  825.3
collectively
  wholly 54.12
  together 73.11
collectivism 743.5
collectivist 743.12
collectivity 54.1
collectivization 813.3
collectivize 813.7
collector art ∼ 74.14
  governor 747.14
colleen 125.6
college
  madhouse 472.14
  school 565.7
  prison 759.8
  society 786.6
collegese 578.7

collegiate
nouns 564.4
adjs. scholarly 564.10
  college 565.18
collibert 189.7
collide disagree 27.5
  sail into 274.43
  strike 282.13
  clash in color 361.15
  disaccord 793.9
  contend with
    794.16
colliding
  off-color 361.21
  disaccordant 793.16
collier 382.8
colliery 382.6
collimate, collineate
  217.5
collimation, collinea-
  tion 217.1
colliquate melt 328.20
  liquefy 390.5
colliquation 390.1
colliquative 390.7
collision
  contrariety 15.1
  counteraction 177.1
  clash 282.3
  accident 727.2
  opposition 788.2
  contest 794.3
  hostility 927.3
collocate arrange 60.8
  locate 183.11
collocation
  arrangement 60.1
  placement 183.6
collocution 595.1
collocutor 595.7
collogue
nouns 595.4
verbs 595.10
collop piece 55.3
  rasher 226.2
colloque 595.8
colloquial
  vernacular 578.16
  conversational
    595.11
colloquialism 578.5
colloquialist
  colloquializer 578.13
  converser 595.7
colloquialize 578.14
colloquist 595.7
colloquize 595.8
colloquy 595.1
collotype 575.4
collude 652.10
collusion
  chicanery 616.4
  conspiracy 652.6
  in ~784.10
collusive
  deceitful 616.22
  conniving 652.14
colluvies 680.10
collyrium 685.9
collywobbles 423.5

cologne 435.3
colon stop 144.4
  intestine 224.6
colonel 747.22
colonelship, colonelcy
  747.25
colonial 189.9
colonialism 739.4
colonic 224.12
colonist 189.9
colonization 187.2
colonize 187.10
colonnade
  corridor 191.18
  columns 216.5
  passageway 655.4
colonnette 216.5
colony swarm 74.5
  settlement 180.1
  community 786.3
colophon sequel 67.1
  bookplate 566.12
colophonate 380.1
color
nouns kind 61.3
  variable 348.9
  hue 361
  vividness 361.3
  colorant 361.7
  whites 363.12
  blacks 364.13
  grays 365.5
  browns 366.5,6
  ruddiness 367.1
  reds, pinks
    367.13,14
  oranges 368.3
  yellows 369.7
  greens 370.6
  blues 371.4
  purples 372.4
  appearance 445.3
  tone ~ 449.3
  painting 572.15
  literary ~ 606.9
  false show 614.3
  pretext 647.1
  extenuation 1004.5
  GIVE A COLOR TO
  change 139.6
  qualify 506.3
  falsify 614.16
verbs imbue 44.12
  distort 248.6
  apply ~ 361.13
  redden 367.5
  misrepresent 571.3
  euphonize 599.8
  falsify 614.16
  exaggerate 615.3
  dramatize 670.15
  turn ~ 855.20
  embellish 899.7
  blush 906.8
  anger 950.14
  extenuate 1004.12
colorable
  tingible 361.16
  plausible 510.6
  specious 614.28
colorado 433.16

colorama 361.1
colorant 361.7
coloration 361.1,10
coloratura
nouns aria 461.14
  voice 462.5
  music 462.18
  singer 463.14
adjs. 461.51
colorature 461.14
color bar
  segregation 77.3
  prejudice 525.4
color-blind 440.8
color blindness 440.3
colorcast
nouns 344.2
verbs 344.14
color circle, color
  cycle 361.6
colored hued 361.17
  dark 364.10
  Negro 417.12
  prejudiced 525.12
  specious 614.28
  exaggerated 615.4
colored person 417.7
colorful
  colored 361.19
  many-colored 373.9
  gaudy 902.20
colorific 361.16
colorifics 361.9
coloring
nouns coloration
    361.1,10
  color 361.7
  reddening 367.3
  tone color 449.3
  qualification 506.1
  misrepresentation
    571.1
  false show 614.3
  falsification 614.9
  exaggeration 615.1
  blushing 906.5
adjs. 367.12
color instruments
  361.25
colorist 577.4
colorless
  dreary 336.19
  hueless 362.7
  dull 881.6
color line 525.4
color print
  picture 572.12
  engraving 576.6
colors 567.6
  WITH FLYING COLORS
  in triumph 724.10
  ostentatiously
    902.25
color sergeant 747.23
color spectrum 361.6
colory
  colorful 361.19
  many-colored 373.9
colossal great 34.11
  mammoth 194.20
  high 206.19

  superb 672.18
Colosseum, Coliseum
  theater 609.17
  arena 800.1
colossus
  strong man 158.6
  giant 194.13
  tower 206.11
colostrum 387.3
colpoplasty 687.27
colporteur
  vendor 828.6
  evangelist 1036.6
colpotomy 687.26
colt boy 125.5,7
  horse 413.12
  clumsy fellow 732.9
coltish 868.14
colt's-tail 403.1
colubrine 413.44
columbarium, colum-
  bary 190.20
Columbia 180.3
Columbine 610.9
columella 216.5
columelliform 254.11
column
  procession 71.4
  tower 206.11
  pillar 216.5
  cylinder 254.4
  monument 568.11
  book ~ 603.14
  military unit 798.19
columnar, columnal,
  columned 254.11
columnist 603.22
colures 374.16
coma
  unconsciousness
    422.2
  sleep 710.6
comate
  accompanier 73.4
  confederate 785.2
  comrade 926.4
comatose
  unconscious 422.7
  drowsy 710.19,20
  apathetic 854.13
comb
nouns ridge 206.6
  teeth 257.5
  wave 394.14
verbs disinvolve 45.4
  billow 394.23
  search 484.27
  groom 679.20
  whip 1008.15
combat
nouns fight 794.3
  war 795.1
verbs oppose 788.5
  fight 794.14
combatant 798.1
combat area 800.2
combat fatigue
  illness 684.18
  neurosis 688.17
combat flight 277.8
combative

COME UP TO
 equal 30.6
 overtake 299.9
 compare with 490.7
 cost 844.15
COME WHAT MAY
 without fail 512.26
 resolutely 622.20
 necessarily 637.16
TO COME
 future 121.8
 imminent 151.3
 approaching 295.4
 scheduled 639.6
interjs. approach!
  295.6
 disbelief 502.14
come-at-able
 approachable 295.5
 accessible 508.8
comeback retort 485.1
 recovery 692.8
 witticism 879.7
 retaliation 953.1
 gibe 965.2
**comedia, comedietta,
 comédie** 609.6
**comedian,
  comedienne**
 dramatist 609.26
 actor 610.8
comedown
 descent 314.1
 disappointment
  539.1
 degradation 690.3
 failure 723.3
 misfortune 727.3
 bathos 878.4
 humiliation 904.2
comedy 609.6
come-hither 648.7
comeliness
 elegant style 587.1
 beautifulness 898.3
comely shapely 247.6
 elegant 587.7
 beautiful 898.17
come-off
 occurrence 150.2
 escape 630.1,4
come-on dupe 618.1
 lure 648.2
come-outer
 dissenter 520a.3
 apostate 626.5
comer incomer 301.4
 success 722.5
comestible 306.31
comestibles 306a.1
comet 374.5
cometary 111.8
**comeuppance,
  comeuppings**
 requital 953.2
 deserts 958.3
**GIVE ONE HIS
  COMEUPPANCE**
 retaliate 953.5
 punish 1008.11
comfit 306a.39

comfort
nouns quilt 227.11
 prosperity 726.1
 relief 884
 ease 885
 consolation 885.4
**ALL THE COMFORTS
  OF HOME** 885.3
IN COMFORT 885.15
verbs cheer 868.6
 relieve 884.5
 console 885.6
comfortable
nouns 227.11
adjs. homelike 190.28
 adequate 659.6
 prosperous 726.12
 wealthy 835.13
 contented 866.7
 easy 885.11
**comfortable circum-
  stances** 726.1
comforter quilt 227.11
 consoler 885.5
THE COMFORTER
 1011.14
comforting
 cheering 868.16
 relieving 884.9
 consoling 885.13
comfortless
 distressing 862.11
 disconsolate 870.29
comfort station
 680.13
comfy 885.11
comic
nouns cartoon 572.17
 comedian 610.8
THE COMIC 878.3
adjs. 609.39
comic(al) odd 85.11
 humorous 878.6
comic book
 cartoons 572.17
 book 603.10
comicodramatic
 609.39
comic opera
 music 461.35
 drama 609.6
comic relief
 drama 609.6
 role 609.11
comics, comic strip
 572.17
**Cominform, Com-
  mintern** 743.4
coming
nouns advent 121.5
 imminence 151.1
 approach 295.1
 arrival 299.1
 appearance 445.1
adjs. future 121.8
 eventual 150.11
 imminent 151.3
 approaching 295.4
 arriving 299.10
 emerging 302.18
 expected 537.11

 successful 722.13
 due 958.7
HAVE IT COMING
 be due to 958.4
 deserve 1008.24
coming after
 sequence 65.1
 posteriority 117.1
coming and going
 322.4
coming out debut 68.4
 presentation 920.13
comings 958.3
comity 934.1
comma 144.4
command
nouns scope of vision
 443.3
 proficiency 731.1
 authority 737.4
 control 739.2
 commandment 750
AT ONE'S COMMAND
 obedient 764.4
 helpful 783.21
 in possession 806.9
BY COMMAND 750.16
IN COMMAND 737.21
verbs rise above
 206.16
 govern 739.11
 order 750.9
 have 806.5
commandant 747.6,22
commandeer
 conscript 778.14
 appropriate 820.16,
 17
commandeering
 820.3,4
commander
 shipmaster 275.7
 chief 747.6,22,24
commanding most
 important 670.25
 authoritative 737.14
 governing 739.17
 imperative 750.13
commandment 750.1
commando 798.6
commandos 798.22
commands computer
 data 348.19
 funds 833.14
comme ci comme ça
 678.7
comme il faut 643.9
commemorate 875.3
commemoration
 anniversary 137.4
 celebration 875.1
IN COMMEMORATION
 535.28
**IN COMMEMORATION
  OF** 875.6
commemorative
 memorial 535.26
 celebrative 875.5
commence 68.6
commencement
 beginning 68.1

 source 152.5
 ceremony 644.4
commend
 commit 816.16
 praise 966.11
commendable
 expedient 668.4
 praiseworthy 966.19
commendation
 commitment 816.2
 approbation 966.3
commendatory
 advisory 752.10
 approbatory 966.15
commender 966.8
commensurable
 calculable 87.16
 proportionable
  490.8
commensurate
 corresponding 26.14
 equal 30.8
 calculable 87.16
 proportionate 490.8
 adequate 659.6
 satisfactory 866.11
comment
nouns critique 493.2
 annotation 550.6
 gossip 556.7
 discourse 592.1
 remark 592.4
 commentary 604.2
verbs 592.16
COMMENT UPON
 discuss 481.16
 criticize 493.14
 explain 550.13
 write upon 604.5
commentarial 604.6
**commentary,
  commentation**
 explanation 550.6
 treatise 604.2
commentator
 radio ~ 343.26
 critic 493.7
 dissertator 604.4
commenter
 critic 493.7
 commentator 604.4
commerce
 copulation 168.3
 communication
  552.1
 conversation 595.1
 trade 825
 social intercourse
  920.4
commercial
nouns radio 343.21,
 23
 advertisement 557.6
adjs. 825.17
commercialism
 jargon 578.7
 term 580.4
 mercantilism 825.8
commercialize
 capitalize on 809.10

make commercial
825.16
commercial law 996.4
commercial paper
833.11
commercial traveler
828.5
commie 743.11
comminate 971.2
commination
malediction 970.1
threat 971.1
comminatory 971.3
commingle 44.11
comminute
verbs 360.9
adjs. 350.11
comminution 360.4
comminutor 360.7
commiserate
sympathize 942.3
condole with 944.2
commiseration
pity 942.1
condolence 944.1
commiserative 944.3
commissar
official 747.19
delegate 779.2
commissariat
provider 657.6
stores 658.1
bureau 998.4
commissariate 306a.5
commissary
provider 657.6
delegate 779.2
store 830.7
commission
nouns fettle 7.3
task 654.2
performance 703.2
commissioning 778
delegation 779.12
share 314.5
payment 839.7
IN COMMISSION
in order 59.7
in use 663.24
OUT OF COMMISSION
disabled 157.17
in disrepair 690.36
verbs fix 692.14
delegate 778.9
commissionaire
messenger 559.1
official 747.19
delegate 779.2
commissioned 778.16
commissioner
police ~ 697.14
official 747.19
delegate 779.2
commissure 47.4
commit
~ to memory
535.17
do 703.6
~ to prison 759.17
promise 768.5
commission 778.9

consign 816.16
~ a crime 997.5
commitment
imprisonment 759.4
promise 768.2
consignment 816.2
committal 759.4
committed 768.8
committee
council 753.3
assignee 778.8
commission 779.12
committeeman 786.11
commix 44.11
commixture
mixture 44.1
compound 44.5
commodious
spacious 178.9
serviceable 663.18
comfortable 885.11
commodiousness
spaciousness 178.5
comfortableness
885.2
commodity
appliance 347.1
ware 829.2
commodore 747.24
common
nouns green 410.7
pleasance 876.14
IN COMMON
~ with 9.5
communal 813.9
THE COMMON 84.3
adjs. mutual 13.13
prevalent 79.11
usual 84.8
frequent 135.4
public 416.13
well-known 474.27
made public 557.17
colloquial 578.16
prosaic 608.5
paltry 671.18
mediocre 678.9,10
communal 813.9
trite 881.9
vulgar 896.14
plain 900.6
plebeian 917.11
**commonage, common-
ality, commonalty**
917.1
**common consent,
common assent**
520.5
commoner
student 564.5
common man 917.7
common knowledge
557.17
common law
tradition 123.2
law 996.4
common-law marriage
931.2
common man 917.7
commonness
prevalence 79.2

usualness 84.2
frequency 135.1
prosaicness 608.2
ordinariness 678.2
inferiority 678.3
triteness 881.3
vulgarity 896.5
plainness 900.1
commonplace
nouns
cliché 516.3
memorandum 568.3
THE COMMONPLACE
84.3
adjs. usual 84.8
well-known 474.27
plain-speaking 589.3
prosaic 608.5
mediocre 678.9
trite 881.9
vulgar 896.14
plain 900.6
plebeian 917.11
commonplaceness
usualness 84.2
prosaicness 608.2
mediocrity 678.2
triteness 881.3
vulgarity 896.5
plainness 900.1
common practice
640.4
common run
generality 79.3
the ~ 917.1
~ of things 640.4
commons
dining room 191.11
rations 306a.6
pleasance 876.14
commonalty 917.1
common sense
sense 466.6
reasonableness
481.10
common stock 832.2
common variety
mediocrity 678.2
plainness 900.1
**commonweal, com-
mon weal** 936.5
commonwealth
country 180.1
population 189.1
community 416.2
republic 739.4
society 786.3
commorant
nouns 189.2
adjs. 187.14
commotion
rumpus 62.4
turbulence 161.2
agitation 323.1
excitement 855.3
communal
public 416.13
communistic
743.19,20
co-operative 784.7
social 786.16

common 813.9
communalism 743.4
communalist 743.11
communalize 813.7
commune
nouns 179.5
verbs ~ with 552.6
converse 595.8
~ with the spirits
994.29
~ with God
1030.12
communicable
transferable 270.17
impartable 552.10
contagious 684.47
giveable 816.22
communicant
informant 555.5
worshiper 1030.9
communicate
be joined 47.11
transfer 270.9
have intercourse
552.6
inform 555.7
say 592.14
converse 595.8
infect 684.38
give 816.12
attend Communion
1038.17
COMMUNICATE WITH
get in touch 552.8
correspond 602.11
communicating 47.16
communication
joining 47.1
transfer 270.1
intercourse 552.1
information 555.1
message 556.4
oral ~ 595
conversation 595.1
epistle 602.2
passageway 655.4
giving 816.1
social intercourse
920.4
**communication
engineering**
radio 343.2
telephone 558.1
communications 558
communicative
unreserved 552.9
gregarious 920.17
communicator
informant 555.5
correspondent 602.9
Communion
sacrament 1038.8
Eucharist 1038.10
communion
communication
552.1
conversation 595.1
communism 743.4,5
denomination 786.6
concord 792.1
participation 813.2

complainant
  complainer 867.3
  plaintiff 1003.5
complainer 867.3
complaining
  nouns 373.4
  adjs. 873.16
complaint
  illness 684.1
  plaint 873.4
  legal declaration
    1002.7
  accusation 1003.1
complaisance
  indulgence 757.3
  submission 763.1
  courtesy 934.1
  considerateness
    936.3
complaisant
  indulgent 757.10
  submissive 763.12
  courteous 934.14
  considerate 936.17
complement
  nouns counterpart
    20.5
  addition 41.1
  supplement 56.5
  verbs correspond 13.8
  complete 56.6
complemental,
  complementary
  correlative 13.12
  completing 56.14
complete
  verbs complement
    56.6
  perfect 675.5
  finish 720.6
  execute 769.10
  adjs. entire 56.9
  unqualified 507.2
  intact 575.7
  completed 720.11
completed 720.10
completeness
  wholeness 56
  intactness 675.2
completing
  nouns 720.2
  adjs. 56.14
completion
  result 153.2
  completing 720.2
  execution 769.5
  TO COMPLETION
    720.13
completive,
  completory 56.14
complex
  nouns complication
    46.2
  whole 54.1
  prepossession
    472.13
  prejudice 525.3
  psychological ~
    688.30
  adjs. mixed 44.15
  complicated 46.4

complexion mode 7.4
  color 361.1
  tinge 361.13
  appearance 445.3
complexioned,
  complected 361.17
complexity 46
complexus
  complication 46.2
  whole 54.1
compliable
  submissive 763.13
  acquiescent 773.5
compliance
  conformity 82.1
  assent 520.1
  willingness 620.1
  indulgence 757.3
  submission 763.1
  obedience 764.1
  consent 773.2
  patience 859.2
  IN COMPLIANCE WITH
  in conformity 82.7
  obediently 764.6
compliant
  conformable 82.5
  acquiescent 520.13
  willing 620.5
  indulgent 757.10
  submissive 763.12
  obedient 764.3
  consenting 773.5
  patient 859.11
complicate 46.3
complicated 46.4
complication
  complexity 46.1
  disease 684.1
  predicament 729.4
complicity 652.6
compliment
  nouns congratulation
    946.1
  praise 966.6
  flattery 968
  RETURN THE
    COMPLIMENT
  interchange 149.4
  retaliate 953.6
  verbs congratulate
    946.2
  praise 966.13
  flatter 968.5
complimentariness
  848.1
complimentary
  gratuitous 848.5
  congratulatory
    946.3
  approbatory 966.15
  flattering 968.9
complimentary
  closes 602.17
complimentary ticket
  848.2
compliments 934.8
  MAKE ONE'S COMPLI-
    MENTS TO 934.12
  OFFER ONE'S COM-
    PLIMENTS 946.2

compline, complin
  1030.8
complot
  nouns 652.6
  verbs 652.10
comply conform 82.3
  assent 520.8
  submit 763.6
  obey 764.2
  COMPLY WITH
  observe 766.2
  consent 773.4
complying
  submissive 763.12
  obedient 764.3
compo 44.5
component part 55
  constituent 58.2,5
comport
  ~ with 26.9
  ~ oneself 735.4
comportment 735.1
compos, compos
  mentis 471.4
compose
  constitute 58.3
  arrange 60.8
  conform 82.3
  calm 162.7
  make up 166.12
  ~ music 461.47
  write 600.21
  print 601.14
  prepare 718.7
  settle 769.9
  reconcile 802.8
  ~ oneself 856.7
composed
  arranged 60.13
  collected 856.13
  COMPOSED OF 58.4
composer
  music ~ 463.22
  writer 600.15
  poet 607.13
composing 601.2
composing room
  601.9
composite
  nouns 44.5
  adjs. mixed 44.15
  unitary 89.10
composition
  mixture 44.5
  constitution 58
  making 166.3
  product 167.1
  structure 244.1
  musical ~ 461.5
  art 572.10,11
  diction 586.1
  authorship 600.2
  piece of writing
    600.11
  typesetting 601.2
  preparation 718.3
  compromise 805.1
  atonement 1010.1
compositor 601.10
compost 164.4

composure
  quiescence 267.1
  inexcitability 856.2
compotation
  drinking 306.3
  tippling 994.4
compote 306a.39
compound
  nouns mixture 44.5
  chemical 378.1
  alloy 382.4
  verbs mix 44.11
  combine 52.3
  ~ for 148.4
  make 166.12
  prepare 718.7
  compromise 805.2
  adjs. 44.15
compounding 718.1
compound time, com-
  pound measure
  462.23
comprehend
  include 76.3
  know 474.12
  understand 546.7
comprehended 474.26
comprehensibility
  546.1
comprehensible
  knowable 474.25
  intelligible 546.9
comprehension
  inclusion 76.1
  intelligence 466.1
  understanding 474.3
  BEYOND ONE'S
    COMPREHENSION
    547.22
  PAST COMPREHEN-
    SION 547.11
comprehensive
  thorough 56.10
  inclusive 76.6
  universal 79.13
  large 194.17
  knowing 474.15
compress
  nouns 685.28
  verbs decrease 39.7
  contract 197.7
  squeeze 197.8
  shorten 202.6
  densify 353.9
compressed
  contracted 197.12
  shortened 202.9
  dense 353.12
  concise 590.4
compressibility 197.5
compression
  contraction 197.1
  squeezing 197.2
  shortening 202.3
  densification 353.3
compressor 197.6
comprisal 76.1
comprise number 54.7
  include 76.3
  involve 76.4

BE COMPRISED IN
1.11
comprising 76.5
compromise
nouns political ~
742.5
mid-course 804.3
composition 805
atonement 1010.1
verbs jeopardize
695.6
make concessions
805.2
compromised 768.8
compte rendu
report 568.6
account 843.2
comptroller
director 746.1
governor 747.6
compulsion
obsession 472.13
necessity 637.1
urging 646.6
compelling 754
compulsive
obsessive 472.33
necessary 637.12
involuntary 637.14
compelling 754.9
compulsiveness
necessity 637.1
involuntariness
637.5
compulsory
necessary 637.12
involuntary 637.14
mandatory 750.13
compelling 754.9
compunction 871.2
compurgation
testimony 504.3
absolution 1005.1
compurgator 504.7
computability 489.8
computable
calculable 87.16
measurable 489.15
computation
calculation 87.3
automatic ~ 348.7
compute 87.11
computer
calculator 87.8
electronic ~
348.16,31
computer engineer
348.22
computer units 348.32
computing
nouns 348.20
adjs. 87.15
compuctive 87.15
comrade 926.4
comradery 920.2
comradeship
affiliation 784.3
fellowship 925.2
Comtian 499.11
Comus 1033.5

con
nouns the negative
481.14
confidence man
617.4
convict 759.11
verbs memorize
535.17
study 562.12
swindle 616.18
advs. 788.11
conation 619.1
conative 619.4
conatus
tendency 173.1
volition 619.1
concameration
curvature 251.1
arch 251.4
concatenation
joining 47.1
series 71.3
~ of events 155.5
concave
nouns 256.2
verbs 256.13
adjs. 256.16
concavity
incurvature 256
cavity 256.2
conceal 613.7
concealed
covered 227.34
unknown 476.18
latent 544.5
obscure 547.13
abstruse 547.14
secret 612.12
hidden 613.12
concealment
screen 227.2
invisibility 444
secrecy 612
hiding 613.4
disguise 616.10
concede
allow for 506.5
acknowledge 520.11
confess 554.7
consent 773.4
conceded 520.14
conceit
nouns eccentricity
473.2
idea 478.1
opinion 500.4
fancy 533.1
caprice 627.1
witticism 879.7
foppery 901.4
vanity 907.4
boastfulness 908
verbs imagine 533.14
~ oneself 908.7
flatter 968.5
conceited
opinionated 512.22
foppish 901.17
proud 903.8
vain 907.11
boastful 908.9

conceivability
believability 500.6
possibility 508.1
intelligibility 546.1
conceivable
believable 500.21
possible 508.6
imaginable 533.26
intelligible 546.9
conceive
originate 152.11
become pregnant
168.12
know 474.12
suppose 498.9
think 500.9
imagine 533.14
understand 546.7
express 583.4
concenter,
concentralize
focus 225.11
converge 297.2
concento 462.17
concentralization
focalization 225.9
convergence 297.1
concentrate
nouns 304.7
verbs intensify 38.5
contract 197.7
focus 225.11
converge 297.2
extract 304.14
densify 353.9
think about 477.9
concentrated
contracted 197.12
dense 353.12
concentration
intensification 38.2
contraction 197.1
focalization 225.9
convergence 297.1
extraction 304.6,7
densification 353.3
mental ~ 477.3
engrossment 528.3
concentration camp
camp 190.25
prison 759.9
concentric(al) 225.15
concentricity 225.1
concentus 461.3
concept idea 478.1
opinion 500.4
imagining 533.6
conception
pregnancy 168.5
comprehension
474.3
idea 478.1
opinion 500.4
imagining 533.2,6
plan 652.1
HAVE NO CONCEPTION
476.12
conceptual 478.11
concern
nouns relevance 9.2
affair 150.3

interest 528.2
care 531.1
business 654.1
importance 670.1
workplace 717.1
firm 786.9
anxiety 888.1
consideration 936.3
OF CONCERN 670.17
verbs relate 9.3
implicate 175.2
interest 528.12
trouble 888.3
CONCERN ONESELF
WITH
attend to 528.5
busy 654.10
concerned
implicated 175.3
interested 528.16
anxious 888.6
BE CONCERNED
531.6
concerning 9.11
concernment
relevance 9.2
affair 150.3
interest 528.2
business 654.1
importance 670.1
anxiety 888.1
concerns 150.4
concert
nouns agreement
26.1
concurrence 176.1
music 461.3
musical ~ 461.34
unanimity 520.5
co-operation 784.1
IN CONCERT 792.3
IN CONCERT WITH
simultaneously
118.6
co-operatively 784.9
verbs plan 652.9
co-operate 784.4
adjs. 461.52
concertante 461.5
concert band 463.12
concerted
concurrent 176.4
co-operative 784.7
concert hall
hall 190.15
theater 609.17
concertina 464.12
concertinist 463.4
concertist 463.3
concertmaster, con-
certmeister 463.21
concerto 461.5
concession
qualification 506.1
acknowledgment
520.3
confession 554.3
consent 773.2
grant 775.5
compromise 805.1
market 830.1

channel 395.19
~ music 461.46
carry on 703.7
~ oneself 735.4
direct 745.8
CONDUCT TO 289.7
conductance
electric ~ 341.13
electronics 342.9
conduction
transfer 270.1
conveyance 270.3
electric ~ 341.13
**conductional, con-
ductive** 270.17
conduction current
341.2
conductivity 341.13
conductor
escort 73.5
operator 163.4
trainman 273.13
electric ~ 341.13
music ~ 463.19
director 746.1,5
conduit 395.1
conduplicate 91.3
conduplication 91.1
cone
nouns roundness
254.5
loud-speaker ~
343.4
pine ~ 410.25
verbs 254.6
conelrad radio 343.2
defense 797.2
**cone-shaped, coned,
conelike** 254.12
Conestoga wagon
271.2
confab
nouns 595.3,6
verbs 595.8
confabulation
conversation 595.3
falsification 614.9
neurosis 688.26
confabulator 595.7
confabulatory 595.11
confection
sweet 306a.39
medicine 685.4
preparation 718.3
**confectionary, con-
fectionery** sweet
306a.39
store 850.5
confectioner 828.3
confections 230.4
confederacy
conspiracy 652.6
affiliation 784.3
alliance 786.1
confederate
nouns partner 785
comrade 926.4
verbs 52.4
adjs. 52.6
confederation
combination 52.1

government 739.4
affiliation 784.3
alliance 786.1
confer
talk over 481.16
communicate 552.7
consult with 595.10
consign 815.3
give 816.12
~ distinction on
912.12
~ a benefit 936.13
conference
audition 447.2
discussion 481.4
parley 595.6
council 753.5
IN CONFERENCE
753.7
conferment
consignment 815.1
giving 816.1
holy orders 1035.10
conferral
consignment 815.1
giving 816.1
conferrer 816.11
conferva 410.4
confervoid
nouns 410.4
adjs. 410.35
confess
acknowledge 520.11
own up 554.7
shrive 1038.20
confession
~ of faith 500.5
avowal 520.3
owning up 554.3
religious ~ 1038.4
confessional
nouns confession
554.3
church ~ 1040.9
THE CONFESSIONAL
1038.4
adjs. 554.12
confessions 606.4
confessor
penitent 871.5
priest 1036.4
confetti
sweets 306a.39
color 373.6
confidant, confidante
926.1
confide trust 500.14
commit 816.16
hope 886.7
CONFIDE IN 500.12
confidence
belief 500.1
sureness 512.5
secret 612.5
poise 856.3
hope 886.1
courage 891
WITH CONFIDENCE
500.24
confidence game
616.9

confidence man
617.4
confident
nouns 926.1
adjs. convinced
500.18
sure 512.21
poised 856.13
hopeful 886.11
unafraid 891.19
confidential 612.16
**confidentiality, con-
fidentialness** 612.2
confidentially
612.22
confidently 886.14
confiding
trusting 500.19
artless 734.5
configuration
contour 234.2
form 245.1
constellation 374.12
psychological ~
688.41
configurationism
688.2
confine
nouns boundary
234.3
enclosure 235.3
verbs specialize 81.4
delay 132.7
limit 233.5
enclose 235.6
~ with illness
684.37
restrain 758.9
imprison 759.12
confined
specialized 81.5
local 179.9
narrow 204.13
limited 233.8
enclosed 235.10
narrow-minded
525.10
sick abed 684.44
restrained 758.15
shut-in 759.19
confinement
childbed 166.9
narrowness 204.1
circumscription
233.2
enclosure 235.1
restraint 758.3
imprisonment 759
confines region 179.1
bounds 234.1
ON THE CONFINES OF
199.22
confining
limited 233.8
limiting 233.10
restraining 758.12
confirm
fix firmly 142.10
strengthen 158.11
substantiate 504.12
ratify 520.12

habituate 640.10
impose 1038.18
confirmability 504.8
confirmable 504.21
confirmation
establishment 142.2
substantiation
504.5
ratification 520.4
sacrament 1038.4,5
IN CONFIRMATION
504.24
**confirmative, con-
firmatory** 504.20
confirmed
established 142.14
proved 504.22
habitual 640.19
confirmer 520.7
confirming 504.20
confiscate 820.17
confiscation 820.4
confiscatory 820.22
confiture 306a.39
conflagrant 327.27
conflagrate 328.21
conflagration 327.12
conflagrative 327.26
conflict
nouns contrariety
15.1
counteraction 177.1
opposition 788.2
disaccord 793.1
contention 794.1
contest 794.3
hostility 927.3
COME IN CONFLICT
WITH
go counter to 15.3
counteract 177.6
oppose 788.7
verbs go counter to
15.3
disagree 27.5
counteract 177.6
jangle 460.3
disaccord 793.9
CONFLICT WITH
go counter to 15.3
differ 16.5
counteract 177.6
conflicting
contrary 15.5
counteractive 177.8
adverse 727.13
opposing 788.9
disaccordant 793.16
confluence
meeting 47.1
assemblage 74.1
concurrence 176.1
convergence 297.1
flow 394.4
confluent 297.3
conflux
assemblage 74.1
convergence 297.1
flow 394.4
confocal focal 225.14
converging 297.3

conform 82.3
CONFORM TO
conc.ir 520.9
observe 766.2
CONFORM WITH 26.9
NOT CONFORM
not comply 83.5
dissent 520a.4
conformable
agreeable 26.14
adaptable 82.5
conventional 643.7
conformance
agreement 26.1
conformity 82.1
conformation
agreement 26.1
conformity 82.1
structure 244.1
form 245.1
forming 245.5
conformer, conformist
82.2
conformity
agreement 26.1
compliance 82
symmetry 247.1
conventionality 643
confound
complicate 46.3
be indiscriminate
492.4
refute 505.5
perplex 513.13
thwart 728.15
embarrass 864.16
dismay 889.18
astonish 918.5
curse 970.5
confounded
complex 46.4
perplexed 513.23
astonished 918.8
cursed 970.10
confounding
perplexing 513.24
thwarting 728.3
frustrating 728.20
astonishing 918.11
confoundment
bewilderment 513.3
wonder 918.1
confraternity
affiliation 784.3
society 786.4
fellowship 925.2
confrere
confederate 785.1
comrade 926.4
confrication 349.1
confront oppose 238.4
face 239.8
compare 490.4
oppose 788.6
brave 891.11
CONFRONT WITH
239.9
confrontation,
confrontment
contraposition
238.1

comparison 490.1
confronting 238.6
Confucius sage 467.2
religious 1020.3
confuse
complicate 46.3
muddle 63.3
be indiscriminate
492.4
perplex 513.12,13
fluster 530.7
embarrass 864.16
confused
complex 46.4
jumbled 62.15
indistinct 444.5
uncertain 513.17
perplexed 513.22,23
flustered 530.12
Confusian,
Confusianist
1018.30
confusion muddle 62.2
perplexity 513.3,4
fluster 530.3
anarchy 738.2
embarrassment
864.4
IN CONFUSION
62.15,16
confutability 513.2
confutable
refutable 505.10
questionable 513.15
confutation 505.2
confutative 505.6
confute 505.5
confuted 505.7
confuting 505.6
con game 616.9
congé 308.5
congeal freeze 333.11
thicken 353.10
congealed
frozen 333.14
thickened 353.14
congealment
freezing 333.1
thickening 353.4
congelation
coherence 50.1
freezing 333.1
thickening 353.4
congener 20.4
congeneracy 20.2
congeneric, con-
generical 20.13
congenerous
related 9.6
similar 20.13
congenial
affinitive 20.13
compatible 26.14
accordant 792.3
friendly 925.14
congeniality
affinity 20.2
compatibility 26.1
accord 792.1
friendliness 925.1

congenially 925.21
congenital 5.7
congeries 74.8
congest fill 56.7
block up 265.7
overfill 661.16
congested full 56.12
clogged 265.11
overfull 661.21
congestion
fullness 56.2
obstruction 265.3
overfullness 661.3
congestive fever 684.6
conglobation 74.8
conglomerate
nouns cohesion 50.4
accumulation 74.8
miscellany 74.12
solid 353.6
stone 383.1
verbs mix 44.11
accumulate 74.17
adjs. mixed 44.15
gathered 74.21
conglomeration
miscellany 44.6
coherence 50.1
cohesion 50.4
accumulation 74.8
solid 353.6
conglutinate 50.7
conglutination 50.1
congratulant 946.3
congratulate 946.2
CONGRATULATE
ONESELF
rejoice 874.6
pride oneself 903.5
boast 908.7
congratulation 946
congratulational, con-
gratulatory 946.3
congregate
verbs 74.15
adjs. 74.21
congregation
assemblage 74.1,2
audience 447.6
council 753.5
churchgoers 1030.9
laity 1037.1
congregational
1037.3
Congress 740.2
congress assembly 74.2
copulation 168.3
convergence 297.1
communication
552.1
interview 595.6
parliament 740.1
council 753.1
social intercourse
920.4
congressional 740.21
congressional caucus
742.9
Congressional medal
914.6

congressman, congres-
sionist, congres-
sist 744.3
Congreve 330.5
congruence, con-
gruency 26.1
congruent 26.14
CONGRUENT WITH
82.6
congruity
agreement 26.1
conformity 82.1
symmetry 247.1
congruous
agreeing 26.14
fitting 668.4
conic, conical 254.12
conifer 410.10
coniferous 410.37
conifers 411.8
conjecturable 498.15
conjectural 498.13
conjecture
nouns 498.2,3
verbs 498.10
conjectured 498.14
conjecturer 498.7
conjoin join 47.5
concur 176.2
adjoin 199.9
conjoint mutual 13.13
joint 47.12
combined 52.5
accompanying 73.9
concurrent 176.4
mutual 813.9
conjugal 931.19
conjugate
verbs join 47.5
couple 90.5
~ a verb 584.12
adjs. related 9.6
combined 52.5
coupled 90.8
etymological 580.19
conjugated 90.8
conjugation
joining 47.1
combination 52.1
duality 90.1
juxtaposition 199.3
grammar 584.1
conjunct 47.12
conjunction
joining 47.1
combination 52.1
concurrence 176.1
juxtaposition 199.3
part of speech
584.2
IN CONJUNCTION
WITH
with 40.11
together with 73.10
conjunctiva 228.3
conjunctival 89.12
conjunctive
joining 47.16
combined 52.5
unifying 89.12
grammar 584.13

conjunctivitis 684.11
conjuncture
  circumstance 8.1
  crisis 129.4
conjuration
  trickery 616.5
  exorcism 1033.4
  incantation 1034.4
conjure juggle 616.13
  entreat 772.11
  invoke 1033.11
  CONJURE UP
  visualize 533.15
  remember 535.11
  ~ spirits 1033.11
conjurement 1033.4
conjuror 1033.5
conk
  nouns head 210.5
  nose 255.7
  verbs 282.14
  CONK OUT
  weaken 159.9
  stall a plane 277.51
  go wrong 690.26
  perish 691.22
  stall 723.15
con man 617.4
conn, cond 274.14
connatal 5.7
connate
  congenital 5.7
  related 9.6
  similar 20.13
connateness 20.2
connatural
  innate 5.7
  related 9.6
  similar 20.13
connaturalize 20.8
connaturalness,
  connature 20.2
connect
  relate to 9.3,4
  join 47.5
  be joined 47.11
  adjoin 199.9
  succeed 722.6
  CONNECT UP 71.5
  CONNECT WITH 154.3
connected related 9.6
  similar 20.13
  joined 47.13
  continuous 71.9
connecting
  joining 47.16
  unifying 89.12
connecting link
  bond 48.1
  intermediary 236.4
connection
  relation 9.1,2
  family tie 11.1
  family ~ 12.1
  junction 47.1,4
  bond 48.1
  series 71.2
  ~ with 154.1
  coition 168.3
  juxtaposition 199.3
  intermediary 236.4

communication
  552.3
  passage 655.4
  go-between 779.4
  mediator 803.3
  IN CONNECTION WITH
  apropos 9.10
  adjacent 199.16
  WITHOUT CONNEC-
  TION 10.6
connectional
  joining 47.16
  unifying 89.12
connections 11.2
connective
  nouns 48.1
  adjs. associative 9.5
  joining 47.16
  unifying 89.12
connective tissue
  228.4
conner 275.8
conning 562.3
conniption 950.8
connivance
  chicanery 616.4
  conspiracy 652.6
  permission 775.2
connivant 652.14
connive 652.10
  CONNIVE AT
  disregard 529.3
  suffer 775.11
  condone 945.4
connivent 297.3
conniver 652.8
conniving
  deceitful 616.22
  scheming 652.14
connoisseur
  judge 493.6
  expert 731.11
  epicure 895.7
connotation
  meaning 543.1
  implication 544.2
connote
  evidence 504.9
  mean 543.8
  imply 544.4
connubial 931.19
conoid
  nouns 254.5
  adjs. 254.12
conquer 725.10
conquerable 695.16
conquered 725.16
conquering
  nouns 725.1
  adjs. 724.8
conquering hero
  724.2
conqueror 724.2
conquest victory 724.1
  sweetheart 929.10
conquistador 724.2
cons 481.6
consanguine 11.7
consanguinean
  nouns 11.2
  adjs. 11.7

consanguinity 11.1
conscience
  superego 688.39
  sense of right 955.5
  conscientiousness
  972.2
  HAVE A CLEAR
  CONSCIENCE 982.5
  IN ALL CONSCIENCE
  certainly 34.21
  in reason 481.23
  affirmation 521.9
  rightfully 956.9
  sincerely 972.23
  in justice 974.12
  TWINGE OF CON-
  SCIENCE 871.2
conscience money
  844.10
conscience-smitten,
  conscience-
  stricken 871.8
conscientious
  faithful 24.8
  meticulous 531.12
  fastidious 894.9
  scrupulous 972.15
conscientiousness
  meticulousness
  531.3
  fastidiousness 894.1
  scrupulousness
  972.2
conscientious objector
  801.6
conscious alive 406.10
  sensible 421.12
  cognizant 474.15
  intentional 651.9
  awake 711.7
  shy 906.12
  CONSCIOUS OF 474.16
consciousness
  sensation 421.1
  mind 465.2
  intelligence 466.9
  awareness 474.2
conscious self 688.39
conscript
  nouns 798.17
  verbs 778.14
conscription 778.6
consecrate
  devote 814.12
  sanctify 1024.5
  ordain 1035.12
consecrated 1024.8
consecrated bread,
  consecrated
  elements 1038.8
Consecration 1038.10
consecration
  dedication 814.4
  sanctification
  1024.3
  ordination 1035.10
consecution
  sequence 65.1
  series 71.2
consecutive
  continuous 71.10

subsequent 117.3
consecutiveness
  sequence 65.1
  continuity 71.1
consensus
  agreement 26.3
  unanimity 520.5
consent
  nouns concurrence
  520.5
  acquiescence 773
  permission 775
  verbs agree 520.9
  give ~ 773.3
  permit 775.10
  WITH ONE CONSENT
  520.15
consentaneity
  agreement 26.3
  unanimity 520.5
consentaneous
  agreeing 26.16
  unanimous 520.15
consentant 773.5
consenter 520.6
consentience 520.5
consentient
  agreeing 26.16
  unanimous 520.15
  consenting 773.5
consenting
  acquiescent 773.5
  permissive 775.15
consentive 773.5
consequence
  greatness 34.2
  effect 153.1
  influence 171.1
  deduction 493.4
  importance 670.1
  authority 737.3
  distinction 912.5
consequent
  nouns effect 153.1
  deduction 493.4
  adjs. consistent 26.15
  succeeding 65.5
  resultant 153.7
consequential
  great 34.8
  resultant 153.7
  influential 171.13
  deducible 504.18
  important 670.16
  authoritative 737.14
  self-important 907.8
  famous 912.18
consequently
  accordingly 8.9
  as a result 153.9
  therefore 154.6
conservation
  maintenance 140.2
  preservation 699.1,6
Conservatism 742.26
conservatism
  unprogressivism
  140.8
  moderation 162.1
  laissez-faireism 704
conservatist 140.4

Conservative 742.28
conservative
nouns unprogressive
140.4,8
moderate 162.4
preservative 699.3
adjs. moderate 161.12
preservative 699.10
conservatively 162.16
Conservative Party
742.25
conservatoire, con-
servatorio 565.9
conservatory
nursery 412.11
school 565.9
storehouse 658.6
preservatory 699.10
conserve
nouns sweet 306a.39
medicine 685.4
verbs 699.7
conserved 699.11
conserving 699.10
consider
think about 477.11
think of 477.15
discuss 481.16
examine 484.31
judge 493.8
suppose 498.9
think 500.9
allow for 506.5
care 531.6
intend 651.7
be considerate
936.11
considerable
nouns 34.4
adjs. great 34.8
numerous 101.7
large 194.16
important 670.16
authoritative 737.14
advs. 34.17
considerate
judicious 466.19
careful 531.10
kind 936.17
considerateness
judiciousness 466.7
kindness 936.3
consideration
judiciousness 466.7
contemplation
477.2
idea 478.1
reasoning 481.4,6
topic 483.1
verdict 493.5
opinion 500.4
qualification 506.1
attention 528.1
care 531.2
motive 646.1
intention 651.1
importance 670.1
gratuity 816.5
compensation 839.3
repute 912.3

considerateness
936.3
respect 962.1
FOR A
CONSIDERATION
in compensation
33.7
at a price 844.19
IN CONSIDERATION OF
since 154.8
provided 506.12
for 651.12
UNDER CONSIDERA-
TION
in question 484.42
planned 652.13
considered
intentional 651.9
advised 752.11
considering
advs. 493.17
preps. 154.8
consign
~ to prison 759.17
commission 778.9
allot 814.10
transfer 815.3
commit 816.16
CONSIGN TO A PLACE
183.11
consignable 815.5
consignation 815.1
consignee 778.8
consignment
shipment 270.7
~ to prison 759.4
commission 778.1
allotment 814.3
transfer 815.1
commitment 816.2
consignor 816.11
consilience 176.1
consilient 176.4
consimilarity 20.1
consist 58.1
CONSIST IN 1.11
CONSIST WITH 26.10
consistency
uniformity 17.1
consonance 26.1
coherence 50.1
conformity 82.1
symmetry 247.1
stiffness 355.2
consistent
uniform 17.5
consonant 26.15
coherent 50.8
CONSISTENT WITH
82.6
consistory 753.5
consociate
nouns confederate
785.1
comrade 926.4
verbs 52.4
consociation
company 73.2
fellowship 920.5
consolation
comfort 885.4

condolence 944.1
religious ~ 1011.18
consolation prize
914.2
consolatory
comforting 885.13
condolent 944.3
console
nouns radio cabinet
343.3
control desk 343.10
control panel
348.15
organ ~ 464.22
verbs comfort 885.6
condole with 944.2
consoler 885.5
consolidate
intensify 38.5
combine 52.3
densify 353.9
consolidated
combined 52.5
dense 353.12
consolidation
intensification 38.2
coherence 50.1
combination 52.1
densification 353.3
affiliation 784.3
consoling 885.13
consols 832.4
consommé 306a.10
consonance
uniformity 17.1
agreement 26.1
music 461.3
consonant
nouns 449.5
adjs. uniform 17.5
consistent 26.15
harmonious 461.50
consonantal 449.18
consonate 461.36
consort
accompanier 73.4
confederate 785.1
companion 926.4
spouse 931.7
consort with agree 26.9
accompany 73.7
fraternize 920.15
consortium 786.9
consortship
company 73.2
fellowship 925.2
conspecific 20.13
conspectus 605.1
conspicuous
remarkable 34.10
distinct 443.7
obvious 553.11
important 670.16
distinguished
912.18
MAKE ONESELF CON-
SPICUOUS 902.12
conspicuousness
distinctness 443.2
obviousness 553.4
conspiracy 652.6

conspirator 652.8
conspire
concur 176.2
plot 652.10
conspirer 652.8
conspiring 652.14
constable
policeman 697.14
bailiff 747.20
constablery, constabu-
lary police 697.15
bureau 998.4
constableship 697.16
constancy
uniformity 17.2
continuousness
71.1
durability 110.1
perpetuity 112.1
continualness 135.2
permanence 140.1
stability 142.1
perseverance 623.1
fidelity 972.7
constant
nouns 142.6
adjs. uniform 17.5
continuous 71.9
durable 110.10
perpetual 112.7
continual 135.5
permanent 140.7
unchangeable
142.18
persevering 623.7
observant 766.4
faithful 972.20
constellation
stars 374.12
names of ~ 374.30
celebrities 912.9
consternation
alarm 702.1
dismay 889.1
IN CONSTERNATION
889.32
constipate 265.7
constipated 265.11
constipation
obstruction 265.3
illness 684.21
constituency
electorate 742.23
membership 786.12
constituent
nouns 58.2
adjs. component 58.5
elective 635.19
constituents
matter 375.2
electorate 742.23
constitute
compose 58.3
create 166.13
enact 740.20
appoint 778.10
legalize 996.8

BE CONSTITUTED BY
1.11
constitution
character 5.3
composition 58.1
creation 166.4
structure 244.1
enactment 740.15
appointment 778.2
laws 996.6
constitutional
nouns walk 272.12
exercise 714.6
adjs. innate 5.7
dispositional 523.7
healthful 681.5
governmental
739.16
legal 996.10
constitutionalism
government 739.8
legalism 996.1
constitutionality 996.1
constitutive 152.15
constrain
moderate 162.6
urge 646.14
compel 754.4
restrain 758.7
confine 759.13
~ oneself 990.6
constrained
moderate 162.11
reserved 611.8
prompted 646.30
restrained 758.13
modest 906.11
constraining
compulsory 754.9
restraining 758.11
constraint
moderation 162.1
reserve 611.3
urge 646.6
compulsion 754.1
restraint 758.1
confinement 759.1
modesty 906.3
constrict 197.7
constricted 204.13
constriction
contraction 197.1
narrowing 204.2
constrictor 197.6
constringe 197.7
constringency 197.1
constringent 197.11
construability 550.7
construable 550.20
construct
nouns 244.2
verbs 166.12
constructed 166.27
construction
composition 58.1
making 166.3
structure 244.1,2
meaning 543.1
interpretation 550.1
word form 580.3

PUT A FALSE CON-
STRUCTION ON
distort 248.6
misinterpret 551.2
misrepresent 571.3
UNDER CONSTRUC-
TION
in production
166.30
in preparation
718.23
constructional
structural 166.22
suggestive 544.6
interpretational
550.16
constructive
creative 166.23
suggestive 544.6
interpretive
550.16
constructive imagina-
tion 533.2
constructor 166.10
construe 550.10
construed 544.7
consubstantiation
transformation
139.2
Eucharist 1038.8
consuetude 640.1
consuetudinary 640.14
consul 779.6
consular 779.15
consulate office 717.8
authority 737.6
consult 595.10
consultant
doctor 686.5
adviser 752.4
consultation 595.6
IN CONSULTATION
753.7
consultative, con-
sultatory 752.10
consume decline 39.6
disintegrate 53.3
eat 306.20
burn 328.24
use up 664.2
waste 852.4
CONSUME TIME
spend time 105.6
idle 706.11
consumed
burnt up 328.29
used up 664.6
wasted 852.9
consumer eater 306.13
user 663.9
buyer 826.5
consuming
agonizing 423.10
engrossing 528.20
harrowing 862.14
consummate
verbs top 210.8
accomplish 720.4
adjs. downright
34.14
thorough 56.10

perfect 720.11
consummated 720.9
consummating 210.10
consummation
entirety 56.4
end 70.1
result 153.2
perfection 675.3
accomplishment
720.1
consumption
decrement 39.3
shrinking 197.3
eating 306.1
use 663.1
using up 664
disease 684.13,14
deterioration 690.4
destruction 691.1
loss 810.2
consumptive
nouns 684.31
adjs. diseased 684.46
destructive 691.25
contact
nouns contiguity
199.5
communication
552.3
customer 826.4
IN CONTACT 199.17
IN CONTACT WITH
199.23
verbs come in ~
199.10
be heard 447.13
communicate with
552.8
interjs. 277.58
contact lens 442.2
contagion 684.3
contagious 684.47
contagious disease
684.1
contagiousness 684.3
contain number 54.7
include 76.3
involve 76.4
enclose 235.5
restrain 758.7
~ oneself 990.6
BE CONTAINED IN
1.11
CONTAINED IN 58.4
container 192.1
containing 76.5
contaminate
adulterate 44.13
radioactivate 326.9
defile 680.19
infect 684.38
corrupt 690.12
contaminated
radioactive 326.10
impure 680.22
diseased 684.45
vice-corrupted
979.19
contamination
adulteration 44.3
radioactive ~ 326.1

word 580.9
defilement 680.4
infection 684.3
corruption 690.2
contango 845.1
contemn defy 791.4
disdain 964.3
contemplate
look at 438.15
consider
477.11,15,16
examine 484.31
expect 537.4
foresee 540.6
intend 651.7
contemplated
intentional 651.9
advised 752.11
contemplation
scrutiny 438.6
thought 477.2
examination 484.4
theory 498.1
~ of the past 535.4
expectation 537.1
foresight 540.1
intention 651.1
IN CONTEMPLATION
484.42
IN CONTEMPLATION
OF 651.12
contemplative 477.20
contemporaneity,
contemporaneous-
ness 118.1
contemporaneous
simultaneous 118.4
present 120.2
contemporary
nouns 118.2
adjs. simultaneous
118.4
present 120.2
modern 122.14
contemporize 118.3
contempt
defiance 791.1
arrogance 910
disdain 964
ridicule 965
IN CONTEMPT OF
27.10
contemptibility
odiousness 862.2
disreputability
913.3
contemptible
paltry 671.18
terrible 673.9
odious 862.9
disreputable 913.12
contemptibleness
673.2
contemptuous
defiant 791.8
haughty 910.13
disdainful 964.8
contemptuousness
defiance 791.1
haughtiness 910.5
contempt 964.1

contralto
nouns voice part
461.22
voice 462.5
singer 463.14
adjs. 453.10
contraoctave 462.9
contrapose,
contraposit 238.4
contraposita 238.2
contraposition
contrariety 15.1
opposition 238
contrapositive
contrary 15.5
opposite 238.5
contrapositives 238.2
contraption
a novelty 122.2
apparatus 347.1
contrapuntal 461.53
contrapuntist 463.22
contrapunto 461.20
contraremonstrance
485.2
contrariety
oppositeness 15
opposition 788.2
contrarily
oppositely 15.7
otherwise 16.11
perversely 624.16
adversely 727.16
contrariness
perversity 624.3
opposition 788.2
contrariwise
advs. contrarily 15.7
crosswise 220.13
perversely 624.16
preps. 788.11
contrary
nouns 15.2
TO THE CONTRARY
contrarily 15.7
by no means 522.8
adjs. opposite 15.5
refutive 505.6
denying 522.5
perverse 624.11
adverse 727.13
opposed 788.9
GO CONTRARY TO
15.3
ON THE CONTRARY
15.7
contrast
nouns contrariety
15.1
contraposition
238.1
comparison 490.1
verbs oppose 238.4
compare 490.4
CONTRAST WITH 15.3
contrasted 15.5
contravallation, coun-
tervallation 797.4
contravene
go counter to 15.3
counteract 177.6

refute 505.5
deny 522.4
thwart 728.15
violate 767.4
oppose 788.7
contravention
refutation 505.2
denial 522.2
violation 767.2
opposition 788.1
contrawise 220.13
contrecoup 283.2
contretemps 727.2
contribute
tend 173.3
provide 657.7
benefit 672.11
participate 813.5
give 816.14
CONTRIBUTE TO
conduce to 152.13
aid 783.14
give to 816.14
contributary 40.9
contribution
participation 813.1
donation 816.1,6
impost 844.10
contributor
correspondent
602.9
donor 816.11
contributory
helpful 783.21
donative 816.24
contrite 871.9
contritely 871.12
contriteness,
contrition 871.1
contriturate 360.9
contrivance
invention 166.5
tool 347.1
story ~ 606.9
plan 652.1
intrigue 652.6
expedient 668.2
artifice 733.3
contrive fare 7.6
induce 152.12
invent 166.14
plan 652.9
manage 722.11
contrived 652.13
contriver 652.7
contriving
nouns invention
166.5
intrigue 652.6
adjs. 652.14
control
nouns moderation
162.1
influence 171.1
automatic ~
280.10
regulator 348.14
test 488.5
self-control 622.5
dominion 737.4
government 739.2

restraint 758.1
guardian spirit
1012.19
spirit 1015.1
BEYOND CONTROL
unachievable 509.7
unmanageable
624.12
IN CONTROL 737.21
UNDER CONTROL
in hand 739.19
restrained 758.13
verbs moderate 162.6
influence 171.8
pilot a plane 277.43
govern 739.12
curb 758.7
CONTROL ONESELF
compose oneself
856.7
be temperate 990.6
controllability 763.4
controllable 763.14
controlled
moderate 162.11
self-controlled
622.15
restrained 758.13
controller
regulator 348.14
governor 747.6
controlling
most important
670.25
governing 739.17
control mechanisms
348.34
control system 348.5
controversial
argumentative
481.20
questionable 513.15
contentious 949.26
controversialist
481.13
controversion
refutation 505.2
denial 522.2
controversy
argument 481.5
quarrel 793.5
contention 794.1
controvert
discuss 481.16
refute 505.5
deny 522.4
controvertibility 513.2
controvertible 513.15
contumacious
ungovernable
624.12
disobedient 765.11
contumacy
ungovernability
624.4
disobedience 765.2
contumelious
haughty 910.13
insolent 911.8
insulting 963.6

contemptuous
964.8
derogatory 969.13
maledictory 970.8
contumeliousness
910.5
contumely
insolence 911.1
indignity 963.2
contempt 964.1
revilement 967.8
malediction 970.2
contuse 690.14
contusion 690.8
conundrum 547.8
convalesce 692.19
convalescence 692.8
convalescent 692.23
convection
transfer 270.1,3
conveyance 270.3
convection current
341.2
convenance 643.1
convene 74.16
convenience
timeliness 129.1
appliance 347.1
advantage 663.4
suitability 668.1
toilet 680.13
leisure 708.1
untroublesomeness
730.2
facility 783.9
comfort 885.2
AT ONE'S CON-
VENIENCE 708.7
conveniences
appliances 657.4
comforts 885.3
convenient
opportune 129.10
nearby 199.15
available 663.19
expedient 668.4
untroublesome
730.12
comfortable 885.11
convent 1040.6
conventical 1040.15
conventicle
assembly 74.2
council 753.5
church 1040.1
convention
assembly 74.2
conformity 82
custom 640
conventionalism
643
political ~ 742.8
rule 749.2
council 753.5
compact 769.1
conventional
nouns 82.2
adjs. conformable
82.5
usual 84.8
traditional 123.12

coolhouse
  cooler 333.6
  nursery 412.11
coolie 270.5
cooling
  nouns 333.1
  adjs. 333.12
cooling-off period
  802.5
cooling system 401.11
coolly 634.8
coolness cold 332.1
  levelheadedness
    466.6
  reserve 611.3
  indifference 634.1
  unfeeling 854.1
  inexcitability 856.2
  unsociability 921.2
  unfriendliness 927.1
coolth 332.1
coom, comb 330.2
coomb hollow 256.8
  valley 256.9
coon
  nouns racoon 413.4
  crafty person 733.6
  verbs 313.11
coon's age 110.4
coop
  nouns enclosure
    235.3
  coupé 271.9
  prison 759.7,8
  verbs pen in 235.5
  confine 759.12
co-op 830.1
cooped 235.10
co-operancy 784.1
co-operant
  concurrent 176.4
  co-operative 784.7
co-operate
  verbs 784.4
  adjs. 652.10
co-operating 784.7
co-operatingly, coop-
  eratively 784.9
co-operation
  collusion 652.6
  collaboration 784
co-operative
  nouns 830.1
  adjs. combined 52.5
  collusive 652.14
  co-operating 784.7
co-operator 785.4
co-ordinate
  nouns 20.5
  verbs harmonize
    26.11
  equalize 30.7
  organize 60.9
  integrate 247.4
  adjs. equal 30.9
  concurrent 176.4
  symmetrical 247.5
co-ordinates 489.6
co-ordination
  adjustment 26.4
  equalization 30.3

organization 60.2
  integration 247.3
  automatic ~ 348.7
coot oddity 85.4
  lunatic 472.15
cootie 413a.6
cop
  nouns cone 254.5
  policeman 697.14
  verbs 822.13
coparcenary,
  coparceny 817.2
coparcener 817.5
copartner
  confederate 785.2
  participator 813.4
  comrade 926.4
copartnership
  affiliation 784.3
  company 786.9
  participation 813.1
cope
  nouns cover 227.2
  sky 374.2
  verbs 227.21
  COPE WITH 794.19
coped 227.34
Copenhagen 413.21
copestone 720.3
copiable 22.11
copier imitator 22.4
  scribe 600.14
copilot
  nouns 278.1
  verbs 277.43
co-pilot 273.10
copious
  abundant 101.9
  fertile 164.9
  diffuse 591.11
  abundant 659.7
copiousness
  productiveness
    164.1
  diffuseness 591.1
  abundance 659.2
copper
  nouns metal 382.3
  policeman 697.14
  cent 833.7
  coin 833.19
  verbs plate 227.28
  bet against 514.19
  adjs. reddish-brown
    366.4
  metallic 382.16
copperplate 576.7
copper plate 227.14
copper-plate 227.28
coppers 832.2
copperware 829.4
copperworks 717.4
coppet 410.13
coprolite, coprolith
  309.4
coprophilia 688.32
copsewood 410.13,14
copsy 410.38
copter 279.5
copula bond 48.1
  copulation 168.3

verb 584.3
copulate
  verbs join 47.5
  procreate 168.10
  adjs. 47.13
copulation
  joining 47.1
  coition 168.3
copulative
  nouns 584.2
  adjs. joining 47.16
  conjunctive 584.13
copy
  nouns replica 24
  pattern 25.1
  musical ~ 461.28
  news 556.3
  picture 572.12
  writing 600.11
  printing 601.4
  edition 603.2
  counterfeit 614.13
  pattern 652.3
  verbs imitate 22.5,8
  draw 572.20
  transcribe 600.19
  borrow 819.4
copybook 603.5
copycat
  nouns 22.4
  verbs 22.6
copyhold
  nouns 808.5
  adjs. 808.11
copyholder 601.11
copying
  imitation 22.1
  borrowing 819.2
copying machines
  601.23
copyist imitator 22.4
  artist 577.1
  scribe 600.14
copyman 603.22
copyreader
  proofreader 601.11
  newspaperman
    603.22
copyright
  nouns 775.8
  verbs 770.13
  adjs. 775.18
copy writer 557.9
coquet
  nouns 671.9
  verbs trifle 671.13
  flirt 930.18
coquetry trifling 671.8
  flirtation 930.8
coquette 930.10
coquettish 930.23
coquillage 306a.25
Cora See Kore
coral
  nouns 414.4
  adjs. 367.9
coralline, coral-
  colored 367.9
coral reef shoal 209.2
  point of land 255.8
  island 385.2

cord
  nouns string 205.2
  types of ~ 205.9
  wood 377.3
  verbs 47.9
cordage
  capacity 194.2
  ropework 205.3
cordate, cordiform
  251.18
cordial
  nouns medicine
    685.4
  liquor 994.16
  types of ~ 994.50
  adjs. ungrudging
    620.6
  zealous 633.10
  fervent 853.22
  pleasant 861.5
  hospitable 923.11
  friendly 925.15
  kind 936.15
cordiality zeal 633.2
  fervor 853.9
  pleasantness 861.1
  hospitality 923.1
  friendliness 925.6
  kindness 936.2
cordillera 206.9
cording 205.3
cordite 799.9
cordon circle 252.3
  guards 697.8
  sanitary ~ 759.2
  decoration 914.5
corduroy
  nouns 260.2
  adjs. 262.4
cordwood 377.3
core gist 5.2
  center 225.2
corelate 13.5
corelated, corelative
  13.9
corelation 13.1
coriaceous 358.4
Corinthian 902.21
corium 228.4
cork
  nouns bark 228.2
  stopper 265.4
  float 276.11
  lightness 352.3
  verbs stop up 265.7
  blacken 364.7
  suppress 758.8
  ~ up 759.12
corker end-all 70.4
  settler 505.3
  good thing 672.7
corkiness 392.1
cork jacket 699.5
corkscrew
  nouns coil 253.2
  opener 264.10
  extractor 304.8
  verbs 253.4
  adjs. 253.8
corky withered 197.13
  buoyant 352.13

corrival 789.2
corrivalry 794.2
corroborant 685.38
corroborate 504.12
corroborated 504.22
corroborating, cor-
  roborative 504.20
corroboration 504.5
  IN CORROBORATION
  OF 504.24
corrode
  disintegrate 53.3
  etch 576.15
  deteriorate 690.22
  rankle 864.21
corroded 690.41
corroding
  harmful 673.12
  corrosive 690.42
corrosion
  disintegration 53.1
  decay 690.5
corrosive
  nouns 328.14
  adjs. disintegrative
    53.5
  harmful 673.12
  corroding 690.42
  caustic 937.21
corrugate
  verbs furrow 262.3
  wrinkle 263.6
  adjs. furrowed 262.4
  wrinkled 263.8
corrugated
  furrowed 262.4
  wrinkled 263.8
corrugation
  roughness 260.3
  furrow 262.1
  wrinkle 263.3
corrupt
  verbs adulterate
    44.13
  bribe 649.3
  defile 680.19
  debase 690.12
  spoil 690.23
  adjs. wrong 517.14
  diseased 684.45
  spoiled 690.38
  dishonest 973.15
  wicked 979.19
corrupted
  impure 680.22
  wicked 979.19
corruptibility
  perishability 111.1
  venality 973.9
corruptible
  perishable 111.7
  venal 973.22
corrupting 690.42
corruption
  adulteration 44.3
  distortion 248.2
  pus 309.6
  fluid 387.3
  word 580.6
  solecism 585.2
  chicanery 616.4

bribery 649.1
defilement 680.4
filth 680.7
infection 684.3
deterioration 690.2
decay 690.5
political ～ 742.35
wordplay 879.8
dishonesty 973.1
vice 979.6
corruptive 690.42
corruptness
  dishonesty 973.1
  turpitude 979.6
corsage bodice 230.15
  flowers 410.23
corsair 823.8
corselet, corset, corset
  cover 230.23
cortege
  procession 71.4
  attendance 73.6
Cortes 740.2,3
cortex
  protective covering
    227.16
  skin 228.2
  armor 797.3
cortical 228.6
coruscate
  glitter 334.24
  be smart 466.11
coruscation 334.6
corybantiasm 472.8
Corybantic 991.9
corymb 410.25
coryphaeus
  teacher 563.5
  leader 746.5
coryphée
  star performer
    610.5
  dancer 877.3
coryza 684.12
cosign 520.12
cosignatory, cosigner
  520.7
cosmetic 898.20
cosmetics
  merchandise 829.6
  make-up 898.11
cosmic great 34.11
  universal 374.24
cosmic dust 374.15
cosmic evolution
  374.18
cosmic ray 326.3
cosmism 374.18
cosmogonal, cos-
  mogonic 374.24
cosmogony 374.18
cosmographer,
  cosmogoner 374.21
cosmographic(al)
  374.24
cosmography 374.18
cosmologist 374.21
cosmology
  existence 1.7
  science 374.18
cosmonaut 281.8

cosmonautical 281.16
cosmonautics 281.1
cosmopolitan
  nouns citizen 189.4
  sophisticate 731.15
  adjs. universal 79.13
  international
    416.13
  liberal 524.9
cosmopolite
  citizen 189.4
  plant 410.3
  animal 413.3
  sophisticate 731.15
cosmorama 445.6
cosmos, kosmos 374.1
cosmotheism
  philosophy 499.5
  religion 1018.5
cosmotheist 1018.14
cosmotheistic
  philosophical
    499.10
  theistic 1018.23
Cossack 798.12
Cossack post
  outpost 239.2
  outguard 697.8
cosset
  nouns 929.13
  verbs 930.14
cost
  nouns loss 810.1
  price 844.1
  AT ANY COST
  regardless 33.9
  possibly 508.10
  come what may
    622.20
  AT COST 874.10
  AT GREAT COST 846.3
  AT PRIME COST
    847.10
  WITHOUT COUNTING
    THE COST 627.8
  verbs 844.15
costate 262.4
costerman, coster-
  monger 828.6
costive 265.11
costiveness 265.3
costless 848.5
costlessness 848.1
costliness 846.2
costly 846.11
cost of living 841.3
costs 841.3
costume
  nouns clothing 230.1
  suit 230.6
  character dress
    230.9
  verbs 230.40
costumé 230.44
costume jewelry 899.5
costumer, costumier
  clothier 230.32
  theaterman 609.27
cosy See cozy
cot 190.8

cote 190.6,8
cotenancy 813.1
cotenant 813.4
coterie 786.7
coterminous 118.4
cothurned 609.38
cothurnus 609.5
cottage 190.8
cottager, cotter,
  cottier 189.7
cotton
  nouns 685.28
  verbs agree 26.7
  get along 792.2
  COTTON TO
  be friends 925.9
  be enamored 929.19
cotton belt 181.1
cottonocracy 739.6
cottons 832.1
cottontail 413.29
cottony soft 356.15
  cloth 377.9
cotyledon 410.17
couch
  nouns lair 190.22
  bed 215.20
  types of ～ 215.33
  verbs squat 207.4
  recline 213.5
  lower 316.4
  crouch 316.8
  lurk 613.10
  repose 709.6
couchant, couché
  213.9
couched 583.6
couched harp 464.13
cougar 413.4
cough
  nouns 402.19
  verbs 402.25
  COUGH UP
  confess 554.7
  pay 839.16
cough drops, cough
  sirup 685.14
coulee canyon 200.3
  bed 211.4
couleur de rose
  pink 367.2
  auspicious 542.16
  optimistic 886.12
coulisse 609.20,24
couloir 200.3
council
  nouns assembly 74.2
  conference 595.6
  parliament 740
  advisory body 753
  tribunal 999
  adjs. 753.6
councilman,
  councilor 747.19
counsel
  nouns deliberation
    477.2
  consultation 595.6
  intention 651.1
  advice 752.1

book ~ 603.16
hiding place 613.4
pretext 647.1
protection 697.1
refuge 698.3
UNDER COVER
covered 227.34
secretly 612.19
concealed 613.12,16
safe 696.6
protected 697.20
verbs compensate
  33.4
include 76.3
brood 166.16
copulate 168.10
extend 178.7
put on 227.21
stop up 265.7
traverse 272.19
aim at 239.6
paint 361.14
meet a bet 514.19
conceal 613.7
protect 697.17
COVER GROUND
speed 263.13
travel 272.17
progress 293.2
COVER UP FOR 148.7
coverage 227.1,2
cover charge
eating 306.11
charge 844.7
coverchief 230.25
covered covert 227.34
protected 697.20
COVERED WITH 79.13
covered wagon
wagon 271.2
railway car 271.13
covering
nouns incubator
  166.7
cover 227.1,2
painting 361.11
adjs. inclusive 76.5
overlying 227.37
protecting 697.22
covering materials
  227.46
coverlet, coverlid
  227.10
overt
nouns lair 190.22
cover 227.2
plumage 229.18
thicket 410.13
hiding place 613.4
refuge 698.3
adjs. covered 227.34
secret 612.14
concealed 613.12
overtness
clandestineness
  612.4
concealment 613.1
overture cover 227.2
hiding place 613.4
refuge 698.3
marriage 931.1

covet desire 632.18
envy 952.3
coveted 632.30
coveter 632.12
coveting
nouns 632.6
adjs. 632.28
covetous
greedy 632.28
envious 952.4
covetousness
greed 632.8
envy 952.1
covey company 74.3
throng 74.4
flock 74.5
multitude 101.3
cow
nouns bovine 413.8
breeds of ~ 413.59
female animal
  420.10
verbs 889.19
cowalker 1015.3
coward
nouns 890.5
adjs. 890.10
cowardice fear 889
uncourageousness
  890
cowardliness 890.1
cowardly
afraid 889.21
uncourageous
  890.10
cowbarn, cow byre
  190.16
cowbell 453.4
cowboy, cowgirl
horseman 273.8
cowkeeper 415.3
cower crouch 316.8
quail 890.9
grovel 905.6
cowering
cowardly 890.13
obsequious 905.13
cow hand 415.3
cowhide
nouns 1009.1
verbs 1008.14
cowhiding 1008.4
cowing 889.5
cowl 227.21
cowled 227.34
cowlick 229.6
cowlike 413.41
cowman 415.2,3
cow of the plains
  413.5
cowork 176.2
co-work 784.4
co-worker 785.5
coworking
nouns 176.1
adjs. 176.4
co-working
nouns 784.1
adjs. 784.7
cow pony 413.13
cow pox 684.9

cowpuncher
horseman 273.8
cowkeeper 415.3
cowrie 833.3
cowshed 190.16
cox 275.8
coxcomb
comedy 609.7
fop 901.9
coxcombry 901.4
coxcomical 901.17
coxswain
nouns 275.8
verbs 274.14
coy bashful 906.12
coquettish 930.23
coyness
bashfulness 906.4
coquettishness
  930.8
coyote 413.4
coze
nouns 595.4
verbs 595.9
cozen 616.18
cozenage 616.4
cozener 617.3
coziness 885.2
cozy, cosy
homelike 190.28
chatty 595.11
snug 696.7
comfortable 885.11
sociable 920.19
crab
nouns winch 286.7
lifter 315.3
food 306a.25
malcontent 867.3
verbs ~ a plane
  277.46
thwart 728.16
complain 873.13
adjs. 431.6
crab apple 431.3
crabbed complex 46.4
sour 431.6
abstruse 547.12
difficult 729.16
irascible 949.19
crabbedness
complexity 46.1
sourness 431.1
difficulty 729.1
ill humor 949.2
crabbing 277.10
crabby 949.22
crabs two 90.3
dice 514.9
crabsidle 241.5
crack
nouns break 49.3
instant 113.3
short distance 199.2
cleft 200.2
furrow 262.1
blow 282.4
report 455.1
snap 455.2
bang 455.3
remark 592.4

attempt 712.2
proficient 731.11
joke 879.7
gibe 965.2
verbs break 49.11
furrow 262.3
open 264.11
strike 282.14
bang 455.6
snap 455.7
detonate 455.8
solve 486.2
CRACK DOWN ON
suppress 758.8
attack 796.15
CRACE ON
accelerate 268.15
~ sail 274.22
CRACK THE WHIP
  745.9
CRACK UP
~ a plane 277.50
collide 282.13
go mad 472.20
be unnerved 857.8
praise 966.12
adjs. superior 672.15
expert 731.20
crackable 359.4
crackajack
nouns superior 36.4
good thing 672.7
proficient 731.11
adjs. good 672.14
expert 731.20
crackbrain 472.15
crackbrained 472.24
crackdown 758.2
cracked severed 49.22
cleft 200.7
harsh-sounding
  457.14
insane 472.24
CRACKED ON 633.11
cracker
backsettler 189.10
food 306a.29
dryness 392.2
noisemaker 452.5
cracking
nouns snapping 455.2
solution 486.1
adjs. snapping 455.10
banging 455.11
GET CRACKING 714.15
crackjaw 599.11
crackle
nouns craze 49.3
snap 455.2
verbs break 49.11
crisp 359.2
snap 455.7
crackling
nouns 455.2
adjs. 455.10
cracklings 306a.16
crack-loo, crackaloo
  514.7
crack of doom
doomsday 121.3
fate 638.2

stridulation 457.5
verbs stridulate 457.6
screech 457.7
creaky 457.13
cream
nouns lotion 379.3
semiliquid 388.5
foam 404.2
the best 672.8
verbs emulsify 388.10
foam 404.5
adjs. 369.4
creamer 49.6
creamery
manufactory 717.3
store 830.6
creaminess
whiteness 363.1
semiliquidity 388.1
cream puff
weakling 159.6
pastry 306a.40
mollycoddle 420.11
creamy yellow 369.4
emulsive 388.11
foamy 404.7
crease
nouns fold 263.1
wrinkle 263.3
verbs fold 263.5
wrinkle 263.6
engrave 576.12
create cause 152.11
make 166.12
creation making 166.3
product 167.1
universe 374.1
work of art 572.11
divine function
1011.16
ALL CREATION
consummation 56.4
universe 374.1
IN ALL CREATION
178.11
creational 166.21
creative
productive 164.9
originative 166.23
inventive 533.18
creativity 533.3
creator cause 152.4
producer 166.10
poet 607.13
THE CREATOR 1011.2
creature being 3.3
product 167.1
food 306a.1
animal 413.2
person 415.3
cat's-paw 656.3
creature comfort
food 306a.1
comforts 885.3
creature of habit 640.9
crèche 565.4
credence belief 500.1
prothesis 1040.11
GIVE CREDENCE TO
500.8

GIVE NO CREDENCE TO
502.5
credenda belief 500.2
religious ~ 1021.2
credential
voucher 568.5
recommendation
966.4
credibility 500.6
credible 500.21
credit
nouns belief 500.1
financial ~ 837
account entry 843.5
repute 912.3
honor 914.1
DO CREDIT TO 966.14
GET ON CREDIT 819.3
GIVE NO CREDIT TO
502.5
ON CREDIT 837.10
verbs believe 500.8
extend ~ 837.5
~ to account 843.8
creditable
reputable 912.16
praiseworthy 966.19
honorable 972.13
credited
believed 500.20
well-rated 837.8
creditor 837.4
Credo 1038.10
credulity 501
credulous
undoubting 500.18
gullible 501.7
BE CREDULOUS 501.5
creed, credo
belief 500.2
religious ~ 1021.2
creek crack 200.2
stream 394.1
cove 398.1
creep
nouns slow motion
269.2
crawl 272.9
verbs linger on 110.7
go slow 269.6
crawl 272.25
feel creepy 425.7
sneak 613.10
grovel 905.6
CREEP UPON 538.6
CREEP WITH
be numerous 101.5
pervade 185.7
infest 311.6
abound 659.5
creeper plant 410.4
hack writer 600.16
creepers 230.30
creeping
nouns crawling 272.9
radio 343.24
adjs. slow 269.10
crawling 272.38
reptile 413.43
creeps chilliness 332.2
sensation 425.4

apprehension 889.4
creepy crawly 425.11
scary 889.30
cremate burn 328.24
~ the dead 409.21
cremation
burning 328.5
~ of the dead 409.2
crematorium,
crematory
incinerator 328.12
morgue 409.9
crème de la crème
672.8
Cremona 464.6
cremona 464.23
crena 261.1
crenate, crenated
261.5
crenation, crenelation,
crenulation 261.2
crêpé 253.6
crepitant 455.10
crepitate 455.7
crepitation 455.2
crepuscle, crepuscule
foredawn 133.4
dusk 134.3
crepuscular 134.8
crescendo
nouns 461.25
adjs. increasing 38.8
music 461.54
advs. increasingly
38.9
music 461.54
crescent
nouns city ~ 182.8
curve 251.5
moon 374.8
adjs. increasing 38.8
crescent-shaped
251.11
crest
nouns mountaintop
206.8
summit 210.2,3
feathers 229.16
cockscomb 261.2
insignia 567.2
verbs 210.8
crested topped 210.11
tufted 229.29
crestfallen
dejected 870.22
humiliated 904.12
cretaceous 363.8
cretin 470.8
cretinism 684.8
crevasse
nouns cleft 200.3
pit 208.2
verbs 264.11
crevice 200.2
crew company 74.3
air ~ 278.4
staff 748.12
crib
nouns hut 190.9
room 191.2
bed 215.34

gambling den
514.14
translation 550.3
brothel 987.9
verbs confine 235.6
cheat 616.18
steal 822.13
cribbed 235.10
cribble 354.4
criblé 576.2
cribriform 264.20
crick
nouns creek 394.1
pain 423.2
stridulation 457.5
verbs 457.6
cricket footstool 215.5
insect 413a.5
fair play 974.3
NOT CRICKET 975.10
cricketer 876.20
crier 559.3
crime
wrongdoing 980.1,2
illegality 997.4
criminal
nouns swindler
617.3,4
thief 823
thug 941.4
felon 984.9
adjs. dishonest
973.15
felonious 980.4
guilty 981.3
illegal 997.6
criminality
improbity 973.1
wrongdoing 980.1
guilt 981.1
illegality 997.1
criminate 1003.10
crimination 1003.2
criminatory 1003.14
criminology 996.7
crimp
nouns curl 229.5
fold 263.1
wrinkle 263.3
shanghaier 823.11
verbs curl 253.5
gash 261.4
fold 263.5
wrinkle 263.6
thwart 728.16
shanghai 822.18
adjs. 360.13
crimper 823.11
crimson
verbs redden 367.4,5
turn color 855.20
blush 906.8
adjs. 367.7
crine 229.2,4
cringe
nouns 283.3
verbs shrink 283.7
flinch 389.12
cower 390.9
grovel 905.6
CRINGE TO 763.10

cringing
  cowering 890.13
  obsequious 905.13
crinite 229.24
crinkle
  nouns 253.1
  verbs wind 253.4
  wrinkle 263.3,6
  rustle 451.12
crinkled, crinkly 263.8
crinkling 253.1
Crinoidea, crinoideans,
  crinoids 414.7
crinose 229.24
cripple
  nouns 684.32
  verbs disable 157.9
  impair 690.15
crippled
  disabled 157.16
  injured 690.29
crisis
  critical point 129.4
  business ∼ 825.7
  financial ∼ 834.7
crisp
  verbs curl 253.5
  fold 263.5
  crinkle 263.6
  make ∼ 359.2
  adjs. curly 253.9
  cold 332.15
  brittle 359.4
  friable 360.13
  epigrammatic 516.6
  clear-cut 546.10
  concise 590.4
Crispin 230.37
crispness cold 332.1
  brittleness 359.1
  friability 360.3
  conciseness 590.1
crisscross
  nouns 220.4
  verbs 220.6
  adjs. 220.8
  advs. 220.13
criterion standard 25.1
  rule 84.4
  measure 489.2
critic judge 493.7
  commentator 604.4
  connoisseur 895.7
  faultfinder 967.9a
critical crucial 129.11
  discriminating 491.8
  exacting 531.12
  dissertational 604.6
  urgent 670.23
  precarious 695.12
  particular 894.9
  censorious 967.24
critical point
  crisis 129.4
  crux 670.6
criticism
  judgment 493.2
  commentary 604.2
  censure 967.4
criticize judge 493.14

comment upon
  604.5
  censure 967.14
criticizer judge 493.7
  faultfinder 967.9a
critique
  nouns criticism 493.2
  commentary 604.2
  verbs 493.14
croak
  nouns harsh sound
  457.3
  speech defect 593.1
  verbs die 407.16
  kill 408.14
  sound harshly 457.8
  caw 459.5
  forebode 542.8
  speech defect 593.6
  complain 873.13
croaker killer 408.10
  frog 413.32
  doctor 686.5
  complainer 867.3
croaking
  harsh-sounding
  457.14
  ∼ voice 593.11
Croat 798.15
crock
  nouns horse 413.16
  ceramic 574.2
  verbs 994.28
crocked 994.40
crockery 574.2
crocodile 413.30
crocodile tears 614.6
crocodilian
  nouns 413.30
  adjs. 413.43
Croesus 835.7
croft field 179.4
  farm 412.8
Cro-Magnon man
  123.25
cromlech 568.11
cromorna, cromorne
  464.23
crone 127.3
cronk 459.5
Cronus See Kronos
crony 926.4
crook
  nouns staff 216.2
  bend 218.3
  angle 250.2
  curve 251.2
  pothook 328.15
  insignia 567.4
  thief 823.1
  criminal 984.9
  pastoral staff 1039.3
  verbs angle off 218.9
  distort 248.5
  angle 250.5
  curve 251.6
  deflect 290.5
crookbacked 248.13
crookbilled 251.8
crooked askew 218.14
  bent 248.11

  angular 250.6
  hooked 251.8
  circuitous 319.7
  dishonest 973.15
crookedness
  distortion 248.1
  dishonesty 973.1
crooken
  angle off 218.9
  distort 248.5
crooknosed 251.8
croon
  nouns 461.12,13
  verbs 461.39
crooner 463.13
crop
  nouns bunch 74.6
  produce 167.2
  belly 192.3
  hair 229.4
  breast 255.6
  growth 410.2
  yield 809.4
  whip 1009.1
  verbs cut off 42.10
  graze 306.26
  farm 412.16
  harvest 412.19
CROP OUT
  be exposed 443.5
  appear 445.8
CROP UP
  originate 68.12
  occur 150.6
crop-eared 447.16
cropper fall 314.3
  farmer 412.5
  failure 723.3
croquettes 306a.12
crore 99.11
crosier staff 216.2
  insignia 567.4
cross
  nouns crossbreed 44.8
  staff 216.2
  cruciform 220.4
  insignia 567.1,2
  monument 568.11
  signature 581.10
  impediment 728.6
  care 864.8
  crucifixion 1009.5
  holy ∼ 1038.11
  crosier 1039.3
  verbs crossbreed 44.14
  counteract 177.6
  intersect 220.6
  navigate 274.13
  go across 311.8
  disappoint 539.2
  thwart 728.15
  oppose 788.3
  give blessing
  1030.13
CROSS OFF 42.8
CROSS ONE'S HEART
  521.5
CROSS ONE'S MIND
  477.17
CROSS SWORDS 794.18

CROSS THE PATH OF
  199.11
CROSS THE RUBICON
  635.13
CROSS UP 973.13
  adjs. hybrid 44.16
  crossing 220.8
  transverse 220.9
  cruciform 220.10
  opposed 788.9
  ill-humored 949.19
  advs. 220.13
  preps. 788.11
crossbar
  nouns 220.5
  verbs 220.6
crossbarred 220.11
crossbones
  cross 220.4
  death 407.14
crossbow 799.18
crossbred 44.16
crossbreed
  nouns 44.8
  verbs 44.14
crossbreeding
  interbreeding 44.4
  word 580.9
cross-check
  nouns 490.2
  verbs collate 490.5
  verify 512.12
crosscurrent
  counterforce 177.4
  opposition 788.1
crosscut
  nouns 202.5
  verbs cut across 202.7
  intersect 220.6
  adjs. 220.8
crossed hybrid 44.16
  intersected 220.8
  crucial 220.10
cross-examination
  484.15
cross-examine 484.23
cross-examiner 484.17
cross-eye 439.5
cross-eyed 439.12
cross-fertilization
  168.4
cross fire
  interchange 149.1
  gunfire 796.9
cross-grained
  adjs. rough 260.6
  coarse 350.6
  perverse 624.11
  irascible 949.19
  advs. crosswise 220.13
  against the grain
  260.12
crosshatch
  draw 572.20
  engrave 576.12
crosshatching 576.1
crossing
  nouns crossbreeding
  44.4
  intersection 220

compress 197.8
pulverize 360.9
mash 389.5
refute 505.5
conquer 725.10
suppress 758.8
subdue 762.9
unman 857.10
humiliate 904.4
crushable 359.4
crushed
conquered 725.16
subdued 762.14
unnerved 857.14
wretched 864.29
~ with grief 870.30
humiliated 904.12
crusher 505.3
crushing
nouns pulverization
360.4
suppression 758.2
subdual 762.4
adjs. mortifying
862.12
humiliating 904.13
crust
nouns incrustation
227.15
~ of bread 306a.27
lithosphere 384.1
impudence 911.3
verbs 227.29
Crustacea, crustaceans
shellfish 306a.25
animals 414.8
crustacean,
crustaceous 413.48
crusty hard 355.13
impudent 911.9
gruff 935.7
ill-humored 949.19
crutch
nouns support 215.2
staff 216.2
crotch 298.4
verbs support 215.22
lend support 783.12
Crutched Friar
1036.17
crux cross 220.4
crucial point 670.6
difficulty 729.7
cry
nouns call 458
animal ~ 459.1
rumor 556.6
publicity 557.4
catchword 580.8
entreaty 772.2
weeping 873.2
plaint 873.3
cheer 874.2
verbs call 458.6
animal sound 459.2
proclaim 557.13
wail 873.10,11
cheer 874.7
CRY BACK 146.5
CRY DOWN
decry 967.13

disparage 969.8
CRY FOR
wish for 632.16
need 637.9
demand 751.4
entreat 772.11
CRY HAVOC 795.24
CRY OUT
vociferate 458.8
proclaim 557.13
suffer 864.22
wail 873.11
CRY OUT AGAINST
object 520a.5
dissuade 650.3
decry 967.13
accuse 1003.10
CRY OVER SPILLED
MILK 871.6
CRY QUITS 763.8
CRY UP 966.12
CRY WOLF 702.6
crying
nouns 873.2
adjs. vociferous
458.10
howling 459.6
urgent 670.23
insistent 751.8
weeping 873.17
crypt
compartment 191.2
follicle 256.2
tomb 409.16
hiding place 613.4
coffer 834.12
church ~ 1040.9
cryptamnesia 535.1
cryptic(al) 547.15
cryptogram 612.6
cryptogrammatic(al),
cryptographic(al)
612.18
cryptograph 612.6
crystal
nouns snowflake
332.9
water 391.3
adjs. 338.4
crystal ball 541.2
crystal-clear
transparent 338.4
distinct 443.7
intelligible 546.10
obvious 553.8
crystal-gazer 541.4
crystal-gazing 541.2
crystalline 338.4
crystallinity 338.1
crystallization 355.5
crystallize form 59.4
solidify 355.8
crystallized 355.13
crystallography 382.9
ctenidia 402.20
Ctenophora 414.4
cub
nouns boy 125.5
youngling 125.8
verbs 166.19
cubby, cubbyhole

nook 191.3
small place 195.3
hiding place 613.4
cube
nouns 250.2
verbs triple 94.2
dice 96.3
cubed, cubiform
250.10
cubes 514.8
cubicle room 191.1
bedroom 191.7
cubic measure 489.5
cubiculum 191.7
cuckold
nouns 931.8
verbs 987.22
cuckoldry 987.7
cuckoo
nouns imitator 22.4
songbird 463.15
verbs 459.5
adjs. 472.25
cud bite 306.2
quid 433.8
cuddle snuggle 885.10
fondle 930.15
cuddlesome, cuddly
929.22
cuddling 930.1
cuddy 413.22
cudgel hit 282.19
beat 1008.14
CUDGEL THE BRAINS
think hard 477.8
remember 535.21
cudgeling 1008.4
cue humor 5.3
part 7.5
hair 229.7
tail 240.5
mood 523.4
hint 555.4
clue 566.8
role 609.11
waiting line 609.31
function 654.3
billiard ~ 876.16
GIVE THE CUE
remind 535.20
hint 555.9
cuff
nouns garment part
230.66
blow 282.8
chastisement
1008.3
verbs hit 282.18
chastise 1008.13
cuffs 758.4
cui bono? 667.16
cuirassier 798.12
cuisine food 306a.1
cooking 329.1
kitchen 329.3
cul-de-sac 729.5
culex 413a.7
culinary 329.5
cull
nouns 618.1
verbs 635.11

culm soot 328.16
coal dust 330.2
stem 410.19
culmen 210.2
culminate 210.8
culminating 210.10
culmination end 70.1
result 153.2
summit 210.2
perfection 675.3
culpa 532.1
culpability 981.1
culpable
blameworthy 967.26
guilty 981.3
culpose 532.10
culprit 984.8
cult belief 500.2
religion 1018.2
cultist 1018.13
cultivate till 412.17
sensitize 421.8
train 560.13
improve 689.10
~ the soil 718.12
foster 783.16
~ friendship 925.11
cultivated
refined 895.9
well-bred 934.17
cultivation
agriculture 412.1
farming 412.13
training 560.3
improvement 689.3
refinement 895.1
good breeding 934.4
cultivator 412.5
cultural 560.18
culture
nouns people 11.4
Stone Age ~ 123.24
agriculture 412.1
cultivation 412.13
learning 474.5
refinement 689.3
taste 895.1
good breeding
934.4
verbs 412.17
cultured
learned 474.21
refined 895.9
well-bred 934.17
cultures 417.1
culvert 395.1
cumber
nouns 351.7
verbs burden 351.13
hamper 728.11
cumbersome
bulky 194.19
burdensome 351.17
impedimental
728.18
unwieldy 729.18
clumsy 732.20
cumbrance 351.7
cumbrous
bulky 194.19
ponderous 351.17

gambol 317.2
verbs leap 317.5
  caper 317.6
  frolic 876.25
curvilineal 251.7
curving
  nouns 251.1
  adjs. 251.7
curvy 251.7
cush, cusha cow 413.8
  female animal
    420.10
cushion
  nouns shock absorber
    162.3
  pillow 215.21
  softness 356.5
  muffler 450.4
  verbs soften 162.8
  support 215.22
  mute 450.9
cushioned 885.11
cushioning 162.14
cushy 730.11
cusp 257.4
cusped 257.12
cuspid 257.7
cuspidate
  verbs 257.10
  adjs. 257.12
cuss
  nouns oath 970.4
  scoundrel 984.6
  verbs 970.6
  CUSS OUT
    scold 967.19
    curse 970.7
cussedness 624.3
custard 306a.45
custodian
  guardian 697.5
  jailer 759.10
custody
  protection 697.2
  imprisonment 759.5
  IN CUSTODY 759.21
custom
  nouns tradition 123.2
  habit 640
  fashion 642
  convention 643
  business ~ 825.6
  clientele 826.3
  tax 844.11
  adjs. 166.27
customary usual 84.8
  traditional 123.12
  habitual 640.14
  conventional 643.7
  orthodox 1022.8
customer person 416.3
  client 826.4
custom-made 166.27
customs 844.11,12
custos 462.12
cut
  nouns grade 29.1
  reduction 39.4
  split 49.3
  piece 55.3
  truancy 186.4

cleft 200.2,3
short ~ 202.5
slice 226.2
form 245.1
notch 261.1
furrow 262.1
trench 262.2
blow 282.4
lash 282.8
mark 566.4
engraving 576.6
style 655.1
injury 690.7
thrust 796.3
share 814.5
discount 845.1
price ~ 847.4
mental pain 864.5
offense 963.2
snub 964.2
gibe 965.2
A CUT ABOVE 36.14
CUT OF ONE'S JIB
  445.4
verbs reduce 39.7
excise 42.8
castrate 42.11
adulterate 44.13
sever 49.10
dilute 159.11
play truant 186.8
form 245.6
notch 261.4
furrow 262.3
open 264.11
strike 282.14
hasten off 300.14
chill 332.11
color 361.15
dissolve 390.5
weed 412.17
harvest 412.19
pain 423.7
leave undone 532.7
sculpture 573.6
engrave 576.12
injure 690.13
discount 845.2
~ prices 847.6
irritate 855.13
distress 864.14
snub 964.6
whip 1008.14
CUT ACROSS
  short-cut 202.7
  intersect 220.6
CUT A FIGURE
  be ostentatious
    902.13
  be famous 912.10
CUT ALONG 268.9
CUT AND RUN
  hasten off 300.14
  flee 629.10
CUT A RUG 877.5
CUT A SWATH 722.9
CUT CAPERS
  caper 317.6
  frolic 876.25
CUT DOWN
  reduce 39.7

fell 316.5
kill 408.18
raze 691.19
economize 849.8
CUT IN
  intrude 237.5
  interrupt 237.6
CUT LOOSE
  create a disturbance
    62.8
  become violent
    161.14
  navigation 274.50
  escape 630.6
  free 761.7
  make merry 876.26
CUT NO ICE 671.10
CUT OFF
  remove 42.10
  disjoin 49.8
  exclude 77.4
  interrupt 144.10
  kill 408.21
  exterminate 691.14
  deprive of 820.18
  disinherit 820.20
CUT ONE DOWN TO
  SIZE 969.8
CUT ONE'S EYETEETH
  126.9
CUT ONE'S OWN
  THROAT 732.14
CUT OUT
  excel 36.6
  excise 42.8
  eliminate 77.5
  cease 144.6
  replace 148.6
  plot 652.11
  disuse 666.4
  exterminate 691.14
CUT SHORT
  stop 144.11
  shorten 202.6
  destroy 691.11
CUT THE CARDS
  514.17
CUT THE GROUND
  FROM UNDER
  render powerless
    157.11
  disprove 505.4
  thwart 728.15
CUT THE MATTER
  SHORT 590.3
CUT THE MUSTARD
  be able 156.10
  succeed 722.11
CUT UP
  partition 49.18
  be disorderly 62.9
  misbehave 736.4
  apportion 814.7
  pain 864.14
  grieve 870.19
  frolic 876.25
  find fault 967.15
  adjs. severed 49.22
  diluted 159.19
  cleft 200.7
  furrowed 262.4

engraved 576.16
cheapened 847.9
drunk 994.40
CUT AND DRIED
  prearranged 639.5
  ready-prepared
    718.20
  trite 881.9
CUT OFF 810.8
CUT OUT 639.5
CUT OUT FOR 731.22
CUT UP
  wretched 864.29
  heartbroken 870.30
cutaneous 228.6
cutback
  reduction 39.4
  retrenchment 849.3
cutcherry 998.4
cute dainty 35.8
  smart 466.14
  clever 731.20
  pretty 898.18
cuticle 228.1
cuticular 228.6
cutie 125.6
cutis 228.4
cutlery 347.2,3
cutlet 306a.19
cutoff 202.5
cutpurse 823.2
cut-rate 847.9
cutter tooth 257.7
  knife 347.2
cutthroat
  nouns assassin 408.10
  thug 941.4
  liquor 994.14
  adjs. murderous
    408.24
  competitive 794.24
  exorbitant 846.12
cutting
  nouns castration 42.5
  adulteration 44.3
  severance 49.2
  piece 55.3
  plant 410.3
  harvesting 412.15
  adjs. separating
    49.24
  acrimonious 160.12
  violent 161.15
  sharp 257.11
  cold 332.15
  penetrating 855.32
  caustic 937.21
cuttings 605.4
cutting words 967.8
cutty stool 1010.3
cutup mischief-
  maker 736.3
  reveler 876.19
  wag 879.12
cyanean, cyaneous,
  cyanic 371.3
cyanopathy 684.8
Cyanophyceae 411.4
cyanosis 684.8
cyanotype 575.5
Cybele 1012.5

blindness 440.1
indistinctness 444.2
ignorance 476.4
ominousness 542.5
obscurity 547.3
IN DARKNESS
darkling 336.21
blind 440.8
ignorant 476.17
concealed 613.12
darksome dark 336.14
murky 336.16
dark-colored 364.9
darky night 134.4
Negro 417.7
darling
nouns child 125.3
desired one 632.11
sweetheart 929.12,
13
endearment 930.5
adjs. 929.21
darn
verbs mend 692.14
curse 970.5
interjs. 970.12
darned
adjs. 970.10
advs. 34.26
dart
nouns speed 268.7
stinger 674.5
weapon 799.17
verbs speed 268.10
throw 284.12
DART AHEAD 268.17
DART TO AND FRO
705.11
dartre 684.27
Darwinism 321.4
darzee 230.34
dash
nouns small amount
35.4
tinge 44.7
bond 48.1
energy 160.2
rush 268.4
blow 282.4
disappointment
539.1
line 566.5
code 612.7
haste 707.1
race 794.12
splurge 902.4
MAKE A DASH FOR
289.10
verbs adulterate
44.13
speed 268.10
strike 282.14
throw 284.12
splash 391.12
disappoint 539.2
mark 556.18
ruin 690.11
frustrate 728.15
unnerve 857.10
deject 870.18
DASH AHEAD 268.17

DASH AT 796.19
DASH DOWN 316.5
DASH INTO 282.13
DASH OFF
hasten off 300.12
do offhand 532.9
draw 572.20
write 600.21
improvise 628.8
DASH ON 707.5
DASH ONE'S HOPE
disappoint 539.2
destroy hope 887.11
interjs. 970.12
dashboard 697.3
dashed
disappointed 539.5
unnerved 857.14
dejected 870.22
cursed 970.10
dashedly 34.26
dashee 816.5
dashing fast 268.19
dapper 642.13
showy 902.19
dassn't 890.7
dastard
nouns 890.6
adjs. 890.12
dastardliness 890.3
dastardly 890.12
dastur custom 640.1
fee 839.5
data
computer ~ 348.19
logic 481.8
evidence 504.1
data transmission
345.8
date
nouns age 107.5
time 114.4
appointment 920.7
sweetheart 929.10
MAKE A DATE 114.13
TO DATE 120.4
verbs time 114.13
court 930.26
dated
chronological
114.15
out-of-date 123.16
dateless timeless 106.3
eternal 112.7
ancient 123.10
date line 114.4
datemark
nouns 114.4
verbs 114.13
dative 584.7
daub
nouns bad likeness
571.2
picture 572.12
scribble 600.8
stain 677.3
verbs smear 227.26
paint 361.14
lubricate 379.8
misdraw 571.4
scribble 600.20

stain 677.6
soil 680.18
dauber, daubster
577.1
daughter 170.3
daughter element
325.10
daughterhood 170.6
daughterly, daughter-
like 170.7
daughter of joy 987.16
daunt 889.17
dauntless
resolute 622.13
fearless 891.19
dauntlessness 891.3
David and Jonathan
926.8
Davy, Davy Jones
396.4; 1012.17
Davy Jones's locker
208.3; 396.1
dawdle
nouns slow goer
269.5
idler 706.7
verbs procrastinate
132.10
linger 132.11
go slow 269.8
idle 706.12
dawdler
slow goer 269.5
idler 706.7
dawdling
nouns delay 132.3
lingering 269.3
idling 706.3
adjs. 269.11
dawn
nouns beginning 68.1
daybreak 133.3
CAME THE DAWN
519.6
verbs 334.27
DAWN ON 546.5
dawning 133.3
dawn rocket 281.2
day
point of time 107.1
period 107.2
age 107.5
date 114.4
daylight 334.10
DAY AFTER DAY
repeatedly 103.16
long 110.14
constantly 135.7
DAY AND NIGHT 135.7
DAY BY DAY
repeatedly 103.16
periodically 137.11
DAYS GONE BY 119.1
DAYS OF OLD, DAYS OF
YORE, GOOD OLD
DAYS 119.2
HAVE HAD ITS DAY
119.4
ONE FINE DAY 121.12
THE OTHER DAY
122.17

THIS DAY, THESE
DAYS 120.1
day blindness 440.2
daybook record 568.10
account book 843.4
daybreak 133.3
day coach 271.13
daydream
nouns bemusement
530.2
dream 533.9
verbs muse 530.9
dream 533.17
daydreamer 533.13
daydreaming
nouns bemusement
530.2
dreaming 533.8
adjs. bemused 530.11
dreaming 533.25
day laborer 716.2
day letter 558.16
daylight dawn 133.3
light 334.10
publicity 557.4
daylights 438.9
daylight-saving time
114.3
daylong 110.12
day nursery 565.4
Day of Atonement
1038.16
Day of Judgment
121.3
day of rest 709.5
day-peep 133.3
day school 565.2
day shift 108.3
dayshine 334.10
day sight 440.2
dayspring 133.3
daystar star 374.5
sun 374.10
daytime 334.10
daze
nouns confusion
530.3
stupor 710.6
IN A DAZE 530.14
verbs be bright
334.23
blind 440.6
confuse 530.7
astonish 918.5
dazed stupefied 422.6
blinded 440.9
confused 530.14
dazy 530.14
dazzle
nouns 530.3
verbs be bright
334.23
blind 440.6
confuse 530.7
astonish 918.5
dazzled blinded 440.9
confused 530.14
dazzler
good thing 672.7
beauty 898.8
dazzling bright 334.32

blinding 440.10
beautiful 898.19
D-day zero hour 129.6
attack 796.14
D.D.T. 408.11
dea 1012.2
deacon
nouns 1036.9,10
verbs 614.17
deaconess 1036.9
deaconry 1035.5
deaconship 1035.5
deactivate
demobilize 75.9
demilitarize 802.11
deactivation
demobilization 75.3
demilitarization
802.6
dead
nouns 450.1
THE DEAD 407.13
adjs. nonexistent 2.10
utter 56.11
passé 123.15
dead-end 265.9
inert 267.12
lackluster 336.19
lifeless 407.24
numb 422.5
unconscious 422.7
insipid 429.2
muffled 451.17
expressionless
545.11
listless 706.18
asleep 710.20
tired out 715.8
dull 881.6
DEAD TO
unaware 476.14
insensible to 854.10
DEAD TO SHAME
911.10
DEAD TO THE WORLD
unconscious 422.7
inattentive 529.7
abstracted 530.11
asleep 710.20
GO DEAD 723.15
HAVE DEAD TO RIGHTS
know 474.13
see through 487.8
have evidence
504.16
be right 515.8
advs. absolutely 34.21
directly 289.25
exactly 515.19
dead-alive 715.8
dead band 348.10
dead beat 905.4
dead-beat 715.8
dead-color
nouns 361.12
verbs 361.14
dead duck 887.8
deaden weaken 159.10
moderate 162.6
cushion 162.8
numb 422.3

muffle 450.9
~ emotionally
854.8
relieve 884.5
dead end 729.5
dead-end 265.9
deadened
lackluster 336.19
numb 422.5
muffled 451.17
deadening
nouns weakening
159.5
moderation 162.2
relief 884.1
adjs. mitigating
162.14
numbing 422.8
anesthetic 685.40
relieving 884.9
deader 407.13
deadfall 616.11
dead giveaway 554.2
dead hand 808.6
deadhead 609.31;
848.3
dead heat 30.4
deadhouse 409.9
dead letter
meaningless 545.1
letter 602.3
nonobservance
767.1
dead lift
exertion 714.1
difficulty 729.2
deadline limit 233.3
boundary 234.3
deadliness
deathlikeness 407.10
fatality 408.8
virulence 682.2
dead loads 34.5
deadlock
nouns standstill 267.3
impasse 729.5
verbs 728.13
deadly
adjs. great 34.12
deathlike 407.23
fatal 408.23
virulent 682.5
advs. extremely 34.25
deathly 407.30
deadly sin 780.2
deadly weapons 799.1
dead march
slow motion 269.2
funeral 409.5
music 461.11
dirge 873.5
dead market 831.3
dead matter 601.4
dead muzzler 402.12
deadness
lackluster 336.6
numbness 422.1
insipidness 429.1
muffled sound 451.2
dullness 881.1

dead one, dead 'un
706.8
deadpan 545.5
dead pledge 770.5
dead rap 20.6
dead reckoning 87.3
dead set
standstill 267.3
impasse 729.5
dead shot 284.9
dead stage 609.20
dead stand 267.3
dead-stick landing
277.15
dead-still 267.11
dead stop stop 144.2
standstill 267.3
dead time 348.11
dead-tired 715.8
dead wagon 409.10
dead water 397.1
dead weight 728.6
dead wind
counterforce 177.4
wind 402.12
deadwood
advantage 36.2
brush 410.14
uselessness 667.4
dead zone 348.10
deaf
verbs 448.6
adjs. deaf-eared 448.7
intolerant 525.11
inattentive 529.7
obstinate 624.13
DEAF AND DUMB,
DEAF-DUMB 448.8
DEAF TO
unaware 476.14
unconsenting 774.6
insensible to 854.10
deaf-and-dumb
alphabet
deafness 448.4
gesture 566.13
deaf ears 448.1
FALL ON DEAF EARS
be deaf 448.5
escape notice 529.5
deafen
make deaf 448.6
muffle 450.9
be loud 452.6
deafened 448.7
deafening 452.9
deaf-minded 525.11
deaf-mute 448.3,8
deafness
unhearing 448
incongnizance 476.3
impersuasibility
624.5
deal
nouns quantity 28.2
large amount 34.4
board 377.3
compact 769.1
share 814.5
business ~ 825.4,5
verbs dispose 60.8

~ a blow 282.14
administer 663.11
apportion 814.9
give 816.12
trade 825.10
DEAL BY 735.6
DEAL HARSHLY WITH
755.5
DEAL IN 825.12
831.23
DEAL OUT
dispose 60.8
disperse 75.5
apportion 814.9
give 816.12
DEAL WITH
concern 9.3
manipulate 163.5
discuss 481.16
communicate 552.6
write upon 604.5
treat 663.12
do 703.8
dispose of 720.4
trade with 825.13
punish 1008.10
dealbation
bleaching 362.3
whitening 363.4
dealer merchant 828.2
stockbroker 831.10
dealings affairs 150.4
intercourse 552.1
acts 703.3
commerce 825.1
dean
senior 127.5
principal 563.9
master 747.3
churchman 1036.8
deanery home 190.3
authority 737.6
ministry 1035.5
parsonage 1040.7
deanship
seniority 126.3
authority 737.6
ministry 1035.5
dear
nouns sweetheart
929.12
endearment 930.5
adjs. precious 846.10
expensive 846.11
beloved 929.21
HOLD DEAR 929.18
dear-bought 846.12
dearly
expensively 846.13
lovingly 929.28
dearly beloved
sweetheart 929.12
beloved 929.21
dearness
preciousness 846.1
expensiveness 846.2
dearth
~ of ideas 534.1
scarcity 660.3
deary 930.5
death decease 407

violent ~ 408
AT DEATH'S DOOR
　407.27
BE THE DEATH OF
　ONE 376.23
MEET ONE'S DEATH
　407.15
PUT TO DEATH
　kill 408.13
　execute 1008.19
deathbed 407.7
death bell 409.6
deathblow end-all 70.4
　death stroke 408.9
　defeat 725.1
death-bringing 408.23
death chamber,
　death chair 1009.5
deathday 407.6
death-dealing 408.23
death-defying 892.9
death duty 844.11
death fire 327.12
deathful 408.23
death house 759.9
deathify 408.13
deathless
　immortal 112.9
　indestructible
　　142.19
death light 335.2
deathlike
　deathly 407.23
　silent 450.11
deathly
　deathlike 407.23
　deadly 408.23
death rate 407.11
death rattle 407.7
death sentence 1006.1
death's-head
　death 407.14
　danger sign 701.3
death song
　swan song 407.8
　dirge 873.5
death stroke
　end-all 70.4
　death 407.5
　deathblow 408.9
death-struck 407.24
death struggle
　death 407.7
　fight 794.6
deathtrap 516.11
death warrant
　warrant 750.6
　sentence 1006.1
SIGN ONE'S DEATH
　WARRANT
　kill 408.20
　sentence 1006.3
deathwatch
　death 407.7
　wake 409.4
deb initiate 564.7
　debutante 642.7
debacle
　revolution 147.1
　destruction 691.4
debar exclude 77.4

obstruct 728.12
forbid 728.14
prohibit 776.3
debark 299.8
debarkation 299.2
debarment 77.1
debarred 77.7
debase
　adulterate 44.13
　lower 316.4
　corrupt 690.12
　demote 780.4
　abase 904.5
　disgrace 913.8
　depreciate 969.8
debased low 207.6
　lowered 316.10
　wicked 979.19
debasement
　lowness 207.1
　lowering 316.1
　deterioration 690.3
　demotion 780.2
　abasement 904.2
　turpitude 979.6
debatable 513.15
debate
　nouns 481.4
　IN DEBATE 484.42
　verbs deliberate
　　477.11
　discuss 481.16
　be irresolute 625.7
debater 481.13
debating 481.4
debauch
　nouns revel 876.6
　orgy 991.2
　spree 994.5
　verbs corrupt 690.12
　make merry 876.26
　wanton 987.19
　seduce 987.20
　dissipate 991.6
　spree 994.34
debauched
　wicked 979.19
　profligate 987.25
　dissolute 991.8
debauchee 987.10
debaucher 987.12
debauchery
　profligacy 987.3
　dissipation 991.2
debauchment
　profligacy 987.3
　rape 987.6
　dissipation 991.2
debenture
　pledge 770.7
　bond 832.4
　money order 833.11
debilitate
　weaken 159.10
　sicken 684.37
debilitated
　weak 159.12
　sickly 684.40
debilitating 159.20
debilitation
　weakness 159.1

weakening 159.5
sickliness 684.2
debility
　weakness 159.1
　sickliness 684.2
debit
　nouns 843.5
　verbs 843.8
debonair, debonaire
　868.11
de bon augure 542.16
de bonne grâce 620.10
de bonne volonté
　620.8
debouch
　nouns 302.9
　verbs emerge 302.12
　eject 308.23
débouché 302.9
debris, débris
　remains 43.1
　deposit 270.8
　disintegration 360.5
　rubbish 667.5
debt borrowing 819
　indebtment 838
　IN DEBT 838.8
　OUT OF DEBT 839.23
debtee 837.4
debtor 838.4
debtor's prison 759.9
debunk 519.2
debunkment 519.1
debus 299.8
debut
　introduction 68.4
　theatrical ~ 609.13
　coming out 920.13
debutant, debutante
　initiate 564.7
　socialite 642.7
decade ten 99.6
　period 107.2
decadence, decadency
　deterioration 690.3
　turpitude 979.6
decadent
　deteriorating 690.43
　wicked 979.19
decagon, decahedron
　99.6
decagonal
　tenfold 99.22
　angular 250.11
decahedral 99.22
decal, decalcomania
　572.12
décalage 277.22
decaliter 99.6
Decalogue 99.6
decalogue 955.1
decameter 99.6
decamp
　depart 300.11,16
　flee 629.10
decampment
　departure 300.1
　flight 629.4
decanal side 242.1
decant 304.10
decapitate 1008.19

decapitation 1008.7
decare 99.6
decarnate, decarnated
　bodiless 376.7
　spectral 1015.8
decastyle 99.6
decasyllabic 99.22
decasyllable 99.6
decathlon 876.9
decay
　nouns 690.5
　verbs 690.23
decayed 690.38
decease
　nouns 407.1
　verbs 407.15
deceased 407.24
　THE DECEASED 407.13
decedent 407.13
deceit
　sneakiness 612.4
　falseheartedness
　　614.4
　deceitfulness 616.3
　deception 616.7
　craftiness 733.1
　treacherousness
　　973.6
deceitful
　sneaky 612.14
　falsehearted 614.31
　deceptive 616.22
　scheming 652.14
　crafty 733.12
　treacherous 973.20
deceivability 501.2
deceivable 501.8
deceive
　take in 616.13
　seduce 987.20
　DECEIVE ONESELF
　　517.9
deceiver hoaxer 617
　seducer 987.12
deceiving
　nouns 616.1
　adjs. 616.21
decelerate 269.9
deceleration 269.4
decemvir, decemvirate
　99.6
decencies 956.2
　THE DECENCIES 637.2
decency
　seemliness 668.1
　indulgence 757.3
　tastefulness 895.3
　propriety 956.2
　chastity 986.2
decennary ten 99.6
　decade 107.2
decennial 137.4
decent clothed 230.44
　adequate 659.6
　suitable 668.4
　tolerable 672.20
　lenient 757.10
　tasteful 895.10
　proper 956.8
　chaste 986.5
　NOT DECENT 231.13

decrement
decrease 39.3
deduction 42.6
consumption 664.1
loss 810.2
decrepit aged 126.17
weak 159.15
senile 468.23
decrepitate 455.7
decrepitation 455.2
decrepitude
old age 126.5
weakness 159.3
senility 468.10
sickliness 684.2
decrescence 39.1
decrescendo
nouns decline 39.2
diminuendo 461.25
adjs. 39.11; 461.54
decrescent
nouns 374.8
adjs. 39.11
decretal
nouns 750.4
adjs. 750.14
decrial
denunciation 967.3
disparagement 969.2
decry denounce 967.13
disparage 969.8
Decuma 638.3
decumbency 213.2
decumbent 213.9
decuple 99.22
decurrence, decurrency 314.2
decurrent 394.25
decurtate 202.8
decurvation, decurvature 251.1
decurve 251.6
decussate
verbs 220.6
adjs. 220.8
decussated 220.8
decussation 220.1
dedicate
inscribe 600.23
devote 814.12
consecrate 1024.5
dedicated 1024.8
dedication
inscription 600.3
title 603.13
devotion 814.4
consecration 1024.3
deditician 760.10
deduce deduct 42.7
elicit 304.12
infer 493.10
suppose 498.9
think likely 510.4
construe 550.10
deducible
derivable 504.18
construable 550.20
deduct
subtract 42.7
discount 845.2

deductible 504.18
deduction
subtraction 42
thing deducted 42.6
logic 481.3
inference 493.4
discount 845.1
deductive
subtractive 42.12
logic 481.22
deducible 504.18
deductive reasoning 481.3
deed
nouns act 703.3
~ of indemnity 769.3
pledge 770.4
~ of release 812.2
exploit 891.7
verbs 815.3
deeding 815.1
deed poll 770.4
deem judge 493.8
suppose 498.9
think 500.9
deemed 498.14
deep
nouns pit 208.2
ocean depths 208.3
THE DEEP 396.1
adjs. great 34.8
wide 203.6
deep-down 208.9
deep-colored 361.17
deep-toned 453.10
wise 466.17
learned 474.21
abstruse 547.14
cunning 733.12
deep-felt 853.25
DEEP IN 132.18
GO DEEP INTO 484.33
TOO DEEP FOR 547.22
deep-bosomed 208.14
deep-dye
establish 142.10
dye 361.13
deep-dyed
thorough 56.10
established 142.14
dyed 361.18
deep-echoing 453.10
deepen
intensify 38.5
broaden 203.4
lower 208.7
aggravate 883.2
deep-engraven
established 142.14
deep 208.9
deepening
intensification 38.2
lowering 208.6
aggravation 883.1
deepest 208.15
deep-felt 853.25
deepfreeze, deep-freezer 333.5
deep-freeze 333.11
deep freezing 333.1

deep-freezing 333.12
deep-grounded 142.14
deep-laid
established 142.14
deep 208.9
cunning 733.12
deepmost 208.15
deep mourning 873.6
deepmouthed 453.10
deepness depth 208.1
~ of tone 453.1
abstruseness 547.2
deep-pitched 453.10
deep-read 474.20
deep-rooted
established 142.14
deep 208.9
habitual 640.19
deep-rooted belief 500.3
deep sea 208.3
THE DEEP SEA, THE DEEPS 396.1
deep-sea 208.13
deep-sea diver 318.4
deep-sea diving 318.3
deep-sea man 275.1
deep-seated
intrinsic 5.6
established 142.14
deep 208.9
habitual 640.19
deep-set
established 142.14
deep 208.9
deep-toned 453.10
habitual 640.19
deep six 409.16
deepsome 208.9
deep-toned 453.10
deer 413.7
deer fly 413a.7
deerlike 413.41
deer tiger 413.4
deface disfigure 248.7
blemish 677.4
injure 690.13
defaced
deformed 248.12
blemished 677.8
defacement
deformity 248.3
blemish 677.1
de facto 1.16
defalcate 840.6
defalcation
deficiency 57.2
shortcoming 312.1
defalcator 840.5
defamation 969.2
defamatory 969.13
defame 969.9
default
nouns shortcoming 312.1
neglect 532.1
nonobservance 767.1
deficit 838.2
nonpayment 840.1

IN DEFAULT
deficient 57.4
defective 676.4
IN DEFAULT OF 660.11
verbs 840.6
defaultant
nouns 840.5
adjs. 840.10
defaulter 840.5
defaulting 840.10
defeasance 777.1
defeasible 505.10
defeat
nouns
disappointment 539.1
failure 723
vanquishment 725
frustration 728.3
verbs refute 505.5
disappoint 539.2
triumph over 724.6
beat 725.6
frustrate 728.15
defeated
disappointed 539.5
vanquished 725.14
defeatee 725.5
defeater 724.2
defeating
victorious 724.8
frustrating 728.20
defeatism 887.6
defeatist
nouns 887.7
adjs. 887.16
defecate
excrete 309.11
refine 354.6
purify 679.17
defecation
excretion 309.2
excrement 309.4
refinement 354.3
purification 679.2
defecator 354.4
defect
nouns deficiency 57.2
fault 676.2
illness 684.1
verbs apostatize 626.6
forsake 631.5
defection radar 345.12
abjurement 626.3
desertion 631.2
fault 676.2
defective
nouns idiot 470.8
cripple 684.32
adjs. deficient 57.4
mentally deficient 468.22
erroneous 517.14
lacking 660.11
imperfect 676.4
defectlessness 675.1
defend protect 697.17
guard 797.8

justify 1004.10
defendable 797.15
defendant 1003.6
defended 697.20
defender
protector 697.4
guard 697.8
champion 797.7
justifier 1004.8
defending 797.11
defense, defence
protection 697
guard 797
legal plea 1002.6
justification 1004.2
defenseless
helpless 157.18
unprotected 695.14
forlorn 922.13
defense mechanism
688.34
defense plant 717.3
defensibility 1004.7
defensible
defendable 797.15
justifiable 1004.14
defensive
protective 697.22
defending 797.11
ON THE DEFENSIVE
797.16
THE DEFENSIVE 797.1
defensive warfare
795.4
defer 132.8
DEFER TO
acknowledge 520.11
submit to 763.9
respect 962.4
deference
submission 763.1
politeness 934.1
respect 962.1
IN DEFERENCE TO
962.13
deferential
submissive 763.16
courteous 934.14
respectful 962.8
deferment 132.4
deferral 132.4
defial 791.1
defiance 791
HURL DEFIANCE AT
791.3
IN DEFIANCE OF
at variance 27.10
defiantly 791.9
defiant 791.8
deficiency
inferiority 37.1
incompleteness
57.1
lack 57.2
want 660.4
imperfection 676.1
inadequacy 678.3
deficient
incomplete 57.4
short of 312.5
lacking 660.11

imperfect 676.4
inferior 678.10
deficit deficiency 57.2
debt 838.2
defile
nouns ravine 200.3
strait 204.3
passageway 655.4
verbs file 71.8
march 272.29
dirty 680.19
corrupt 690.12;
979.14
stigmatize 913.9
vilify 969.10
debauch 987.20
defiled soiled 680.23
unchaste 987.23
defilement
befoulment 680.4
corruption 690.2
vilification 969.2
debauchment 987.6
defiler 987.12
definability 550.7
definable 550.20
define
characterize 80.11
fix 142.10
circumscribe 233.4
limit 233.5
stipulate 506.4
explain 550.12
name 581.11
outline 652.12
defined limited 233.8
distinct 443.7
explicit 546.10
definer 550.8
definite special 80.12
limited 233.8
distinct 443.7
audible 449.15
unqualified 507.2
certain 512.13
exact 515.15
explicit 546.10
manifest 553.8
resolute 622.11
definition
characterization
80.8
circumscription
233.1
television 344.5
distinctness 443.2
explanation 550.5
meaning 543.3
intelligibility 546.2
naming 581.2
definitional 550.18
definitive final 70.10
limiting 233.10
unqualified 507.2
definitional 550.18
deflagrate 328.23
deflagration 328.5
deflate reduce 39.7
collapse 197.10
depreciate 847.6
humiliate 904.4

deflated 197.14
deflation
reduction 39.1
collapse 197.4
depreciation 847.4
humiliation 904.2
deflationary 197.11
deflect oblique 218.9
bend 251.6
turn aside 290.5
avert 728.14
deflection
obliquity 218.1
bend 251.3
deviation 290.2
deflective 290.8
deflexure
obliquity 218.1
deflection 290.2
defloration 987.6
deflower 987.20
defluent 394.25
defluxion
outflow 302.4
descent 314.1
downflow 394.4
deform
transform 139.7
misshape 248.7
deformation
deformity 248.3
degradation 690.3
deformed 248.12
deformity 248.3
defraud 616.18
defrauder 617.3
defray 839.18
defrayal 839.1
defrayer 839.9
defrayment 839.1
defrost 328.20
deft 731.20
deftness 731.1
defunct
nonexistent 2.10
dead 407.24
defy
nouns 791.2
verbs confront with
239.9
disobey 765.6
challenge 791.3
brave 791.5; 891.11
DEFY DANGER
risk 695.7
court danger 892.6
defying
nouns 791.1
adjs. 791.8
dégagé 856.15
degauss 341.24
degeneracy
deterioration 690.3
turpitude 979.6
degenerate
nouns 984.5
verbs corrupt 690.12
deteriorate 690.17
be unfortunate
727.11
adjs. decadent 690.43

wicked 979.19
degeneration
reversed feedback
348.6
deterioration 690.3
turpitude 979.6
deglutition 306.1
degradation
deterioration 690.3
turpitude 979.6
degrade corrupt 690.12
demote 780.4
abase 904.5
disgrace 913.8
depreciate 969.8
degraded 979.19
degrading 780.2
degree grade 29
music 461.29
musical ~ 462.20
academic ~ 915.6
types of academic ~
915.9
BY DEGREES
gradually 29.6
piecemeal 55.8
TO A DEGREE 29.7
TO THE NTH DEGREE
56.17
degreewise 29.6
dehisce 264.16
dehiscence 264.2
dehiscent split 200.7
gaping 264.18
dehydrant 392.4
dehydrate dry 392.6
preserve 699.8
dehydrated 392.9
dehydrating 392.10
dehydration
drying 392.3
preservation 699.2
dehydrator 392.4
dehydrofreezing
333.1
deice 328.20
deification
glorification 912.8
idolization 1031.2
deify glorify 912.13
idolize 1031.5
deign consent 773.4
condescend 904.7
deil 1014.2
Dei Mater 1013.5
Deipara 1013.5
deism 1018.5
deist 1018.14
deistic 1018.23
deity divinity 1011
god 1012.2
THE DEITY 1011.2
deject 870.18
dejecta 309.3
dejected 870.22
dejection
defecation 309.2
excrement 309.3
neurosis 688.2
downheartedness
870.3

dejecture 309.3
dejeuré, déjeuner
  305.6
dejob 308.18
de jure 996.12
delaminate 226.5
delamination 226.4
delation 1003.1
delator informer 555.6
  accuser 1003.5
delay
  nouns lateness 132.2
    retardation 269.4
    hindrance 728.1
  WITHOUT DELAY
    instantly 113.8
    promptly 131.15
  verbs detain 132.7
    postpone 132.8
    wait 132.11
    go slow 269.8
    retard 269.9
    hinder 728.10
delayage 132.2
delayed late 132.15
    retarded 269.12
delayed-action 132.15
delaying 132.16
delectability
    savoriness 427.1
    delightfulness 861.2
delectable
    delicious 427.8
    delightful 861.7
delectate 863.8
delectation 863.2
delectus 603.4
delegate
  nouns 779.2
  verbs commission
    778.9
    commit 816.16
delegated 778.16
delegation
    commission 778.1
    delegates 779.12
    commitment 816.2
delete, dele excise 42.8
    obliterate 691.16
deleterious
    disadvantageous
      669.5
    harmful 673.12
deletion excision 42.3
    obliteration 691.7
deliberate
  verbs ponder 477.11
    discuss 481.16
  adjs. slow 269.10
    measured 489.14
    intentional 651.9
    leisurely 708.6
deliberated
    measured 489.14
    intentional 651.9
    advised 752.11
deliberately
    tardily 132.19
    slowly 269.13
    intentionally 651.11

deliberateness
    slowness 269.1
    leisureliness 708.2
deliberating 477.20
deliberation
    slowness 269.1
    thought 477.2
    discussion 481.4
    consultation 595.6
    leisureliness 708.2
    caution 893.1
deliberative 477.20
deliberative body
    753.1
delicacy
    nice distinction 16.2
    daintiness 35.1
    frailty 159.2
    thinness 204.4
    food 306a.8
    fineness 350.3
    lightness 352.1
    softness 356.1
    fragility 359.1
    sensitivity 421.3
    finesse 491.1
    preciseness 515.3
    meticulousness
      531.3
    sickliness 684.2
    precariousness 695.2
    punctilio 749.4
    tender feeling 853.6
    fastidiousness 894.3
    taste 895.1
    prettiness 898.5
    considerateness
      936.3
    decency 986.2
délicat 894.11
delicate dainty 35.8
    frail 159.14
    thin 204.15
    fine 350.8
    light 352.11
    soft 356.8
    fragile 359.4
    soft-colored 361.22
    sensitive 421.13
    delicious 427.8
    discriminative 491.8
    precise 515.15
    meticulous 531.12
    precarious 695.12
    tender 853.20
    fastidious 894.11
    tasteful 895.9
    pretty 898.18
    considerate 936.17
    decent 986.5
delicateness
    fastidiousness 894.3
    prettiness 898.5
delicatessen 830.6
delicious tasty 427.8
    delightful 861.7
deliciousness 427.1
delictum, delict 997.4
delight
  nouns relish 427.2
    pleasure 863.2

    treat 863.3
  TO ONE'S DELIGHT
    happily 863.16
    satisfactorily 866.16
  WITH DELIGHT 620.8
  verbs please 863.8
    be pleased 863.9
    rejoice 874.6
    amuse 876.23
    exult 908.8
  DELIGHT IN
    savor 427.5
    enjoy 863.10
delighted willing 620.5
    pleased 863.12
    amused 876.28
delightful
    delicious 427.8
    pleasant 861.6
    amusing 876.29
Delilah 987.15
delimit, delimitate
    233.4
delimitation 233.1
delineate
    define 550.12
    represent 570.7
    draw 572.20
    describe 606.12
    outline 652.12
delineation
    bounding 234.2
    definition 550.5
    line 566.5
    representation 570.1
    drawing 572.6
    sketch 572.14
    description 606.1
    diagram 652.3
delineative
    definitional 550.18
    descriptive 606.15
delineator 577.2,3
delineatory
    outlinear 234.14
    representative
      570.11
    descriptive 606.15
delinquence 840.1
delinquency
    shortcoming 312.1
    nonobservance
      767.1
    nonpayment 840.1
    moral ~ 979.3
    nonfeasance 980.2
delinquent
  nouns defaulter
    840.5
    wrongdoer 984.8
  adjs. 840.10
deliquesce
    diminish 39.6
    liquefy 390.5
deliquescence 390.1
deliquescent
    decreasing 39.11
    liquefactive 390.7
    diffluent 394.25
deliriant, delirifacient
    674.3

delirious
    unsane 472.30
    fervent 853.22
    overwrought 855.26
delirium
    unsaneness 472.9
    excitement 855.7
delirium tremens
    472.10
delitescence 544.1
delitescent 544.5
deliver transfer 270.9
    utter 592.14
    rescue 700.2
    free 761.4
    consign 815.3
    give 816.13
    relieve 884.6
  DELIVER ONESELF
    630.6
  DELIVER ONESELF
    FROM 761.8
deliverable 700.3
deliverance
    verdict 493.5
    escape 630.1
    rescue 700.1
    liberation 761.1
    conveyancing 815.1
    giving 816.1
    relief 884.2
deliverer 940.2
delivery birth 166.9
    enunciation 592.6
    rescue 700.1
    liberation 761.1
    conveyancing 815.1
    giving 816.1
dell ravine 200.3
    valley 256.9
delocalization 270.2
delocalize 270.10
delouse 679.17
Delphic, Delphian
    oracle 541.7
delta 255.8
deltaic 255.19
deltal 255.19
deltoid
    three-parted 95.4
    triangular 250.8
delubrum 1040.4
deludable 501.8
delude 616.13
deluder 617.1
deludher 616.13
deluding 518.9
deluge
  nouns flooding 391.6
    rain 393.2
    torrent 394.5
    flood 394.6
    superabundance
      661.3
  verbs submerge 318.7
    flood 391.14
    overflow 394.18
    oversupply 661.15
deluged
    drenched 391.17
    flooded 394.26

delusion illusion 518.1
  deception 616.1
  neurosis 688.23
delusional 518.9
delusive illusory 518.9
  deceptive 616.21
de luxe, deluxe 902.21
delve dig 256.15
  search 484.25
  DELVE FOR 484.24
  DELVE INTO 484.30
demagnetize 341.24
demagogic, demagogal
  597.11
demagogism 597.1
demagogue
  nouns speaker 597.4
  instigator 646.11
  verbs 597.9
demagoguery 597.1
demand
  nouns exaction 304.5
  question 484.13
  requirement 637.2
  claim 751
  market 827.1
  fee 844.7
  right 956.3
  IN DEMAND
  desired 632.30
  requisite 637.13
  salable 812.12
  ON DEMAND
  on call 751.11
  C.O.D. 839.25
  verbs exact 304.13
  ask 484.21
  require 637.9
  summon 750.12
  call for 751.4
  oblige 754.5
  assess 844.14
  DEMAND PAYMENT
  843.11
demanding 751.8
demarcate
  circumscribe 233.4
  discriminate 491.6
demarcation
  distinction 16.4
  circumscription
  233.1
  discrimination
  491.3
demark 491.6
demasculinization
  157.5
demasculinize
  castrate 42.11
  unman 157.12
  feminize 420.13
dematerialization
  immaterialization
  376.5
  spiritualization
  1032.21
dematerialize
  immaterialize 376.6
  spiritualize 1032.22
demean 904.5

DEMEAN ONESELF
  behave 735.4
  humble oneself
  904.6
  disgrace oneself
  913.7
demeanor
  posture 183.4
  mien 445.3
  behavior 735.1
demeanored 735.7
dement
  nouns 472.15
  verbs 472.22
demented 472.24
dementia 472.1
dementia praecox
  472.5
demerit 676.2
demesne sphere 179.2
  sphere of work
  654.4
  property 808.7
Demeter
  fertility 164.5
  agriculture 412.4
  goddess 1012.5
demibastion 797.4
demigod,
  demigoddess
  brave person 891.8
  hero 983.5
  godling 1012.3
demi-jour 336.4
demilegato 461.31
demilitarization 802.6
demilitarize 802.11
demilune
  half moon 374.8
  fortification 797.4
demimondaine, demi-
  monde 987.15
demirep 987.15
demise
  nouns death 407.1
  lease 778.5
  conveyance 815.1
  verbs lease 778.13
  convey 815.3
demised 407.24
demisemiquaver
  462.14
demission 782.1
demit 782.2
demitint
  nouns color 361.6
  engraving 576.9
  verbs 576.14
demitone 449.2
Demiurge 1011.2
demiurgic 166.23
demivolt 317.1
demob 75.9
demobilization 75.3
demobilize 75.9
democracy
  government 739.4
  the people 917.2
Democrat 742.28
democrat 917.7

democratic, demo-
  cratical 739.16
Democratic Party
  742.25
Democratism 742.26
democratism 739.8
democratist 743.14
democratize 743.15
demoiselle 125.6
demolish shatter 44.12
  destroy 691.17
demolisher 691.8
demolishing 691.25
demolishment 691.5
demolition 691.5
demolitionary 691.25
demon
  violent person 161.9
  fiend 941.7
  familiar spirit
  1012.19
  evil spirit 1014.7
  HAVE A DEMON
  472.19
  THE DEMON 1014.3
demonetization 833.22
demonetize 833.25
demoniac 472.15
demoniac, demoniacal
  overwrought 855.26
  cruel 937.24
  wicked 979.18
  devilish 1014.18
demoniast 1014.16
demonic, demonical
  1014.18
demonifuge 1034.1
demonism
  diabolism 1014.15
  demonolatry 1031.1
  black magic 1033.2
demonist 1014.16
demonize
  diabolize 1014.17
  bewitch 1034.10
demonized 472.27
demonkind 1014.1
demonlike 1014.18
demonography
  1014.15
demonolater
  diabolist 1014.16
  idolater 1031.4
demonolatrous 1031.7
demonolatry
  diabolism 1014.15
  worship 1031.1
demonologist 1014.16
demonology 1014.15
demonomancy
  diabolism 1014.15
  necromancy 1033.2
demonry
  diabolism 1014.15
  black magic 1033.2
demonstrability 504.8
demonstrable, demon-
  stratable 504.21
demonstrate
  check 87.14

  show 504.9
  prove 504.11
  exemplify 504.14
  explain 550.11
  manifest 553.5
  typify 570.9
demonstrated
  proved 504.22
  manifested 553.12
demonstrating 504.19
demonstration
  exemplification 25.2
  proof 504.4
  citation 504.6
  explanation 550.4
  display 553.2
  indication 566.1
  representation 570.1
  military ~ 795.10
demonstrational
  504.19
demonstrative
  evidential 504.19
  explanatory 550.17
  communicative
  552.9
  indicative 566.22
  extroverted 688.51
  emotional 853.18
  passionate 855.30
  affectionate 929.24
demonstrator 550.8
demon worship
  diabolism 1014.15
  demonolatry 1031.1
demoralization
  mental confusion
  530.3
  intimidation 889.5
  turpitude 979.6
demoralize
  confuse 530.7
  unnerve 857.10
  frighten 889.14
  vitiate 979.14
demoralized
  confused 530.12
  unnerved 857.14
  wicked 979.19
demos 917.2
Demosthenes 597.6
Demosthenic 598.8
demote 780.4
demotic 600.27
demotic character
  579.3
demotic writing
  600.10
demotion 780.2
demulcent
  nouns ointment
  379.3
  balm 685.9
  adjs. palliative 162.16
  softening 356.16
  remedial 685.35
  relieving 884.9
demulsion
  soothing 162.2
  softening 356.5

demur
nouns objection
52Ca.2
unwillingness 621.2
WITHOUT DEMUR
62C.10
verbs object 520a.5
be unwilling 621.4
demure solemn 869.3
prim 901.19
coy 906.12
demurely
solemnly 869.4
coyly 906.15
demureness
staidness 869.1
coyness 906.4
demurity
primness 901.6
coyness 906.4
demurral 621.2
demurrer
objector 520a.3
legal pleading
1002.6
legal plea 1004.2
demurring 621.7
demy 554.5
den lair 190.22
haunt 190.23
dive 190.24
private room 191.8
retreat 698.5
~ of thieves 823.13
~ of iniquity
979 10
~ of vice 987.9
denary 99.22
denaturalization
adulteration 44.3
corruption 690.2
denaturalize
adulterate 44.13
corrupt 690.12
denature 139.7
dendriform
branching 298.10
treelike 410.37
dendroid 410.37
dendrologist 411.2
dendrology 411.1
dengue 684.9
deniability 513.2
deniable 513.15
denial
refutation 505.2
disclamation 522.2
recantation 626.3
rejection 636.1
refusal 774.1
prohibition 776.1
temperance 990.1
demurrer 1004.2
TAKE NO DENIAL
be obstinate 624.7
insist 751.7
oblige 754.5
denied refuted 505.7
rejected 636.3
DENIED TO 509.8
denier 205.1

denigrate
blacken 364.7
defame 969.10
denigration
blackening 364.5
defamation 969.2
denization 188.4
denizen
nouns inhabitant
189.2
citizen 189.4
verbs people 187.10
domesticate 188.5
denizens
~ of the day 413.1
~ of the air
1012.14
~ of hell 1014.1
denominate
verbs specify 80.9
indicate 566.16
designate 566.17
name 581.11
adjs. 581.14
denomination
kind 61.3
specification 80.6
indication 566.1
naming 581.2
name 581.3
school 786.6
religious ~ 1018.3
denominational
classificational 61.7
partisan 786.18
sectarian 1018.24
denominationalism
partisanship 786.13
sectarianism 1018.4
denominationalist
1018.16
denominative
classificational 61.7
indicative 566.22
nominative 581.16
denotation
meaning 543.1
indication 566.1
denotative 566.22
denote evidence 504.9
mean 543.8
indicate 566.16
signify 566.17
denouement end 70.1
result 153.2
solution 486.1
denounce
censure 967.13
threaten 971.2
accuse 1003.7
condemn 1006.3
denouncement
censure 967.3
accusation 1003.1
condemnation
1006.1
de novo again 103.17
newly 122.16
dense crowded 74.22
opaque 340.3
compact 353.12

luxuriant 410.41
stupid 468.15
densely 353.15
denseness
compactness 353.1
stupidity 468.3
densification
condensation 353.3
solidification 355.5
densify
condense 353.9
solidify 355.8
densimeter,
densitometer 353.8
density
opaqueness 340.1
compactness 353
stupidity 468.3
dent
nouns indentation
256.6
tooth 257.5
imprint 566.6
MAKE A DENT IN
853.16
verbs 256.14
dental
nouns tooth 257.7
consonant 449.5
adjs. of teeth 257.17
phonetics 449.18
surgical 686.18
dental surgery 686.3
dentate, dentated
261.5
dented 256.17
denticle 257.5
denticulation
teeth 257.5
serration 261.2
dentiform 257.17
dentifrice
cleanser 679.16
prophylactic 685.18
dentil tooth 257.5
serration 261.2
dentilingual 449.5
dentist 686.9
dentistry 686.4
dentoid 257.17
denture 257.6
denudation 231.1
denude 231.5
denuded
divested 231.12
bereft 810.8
DENUDED OF 660.11
denunciate
censure 967.13
accuse 1003.7
condemn 1006.3
denunciation
censure 967.3
malediction 970.1
threat 971.1
accusation 1003.1
condemnation
1006.1
denunciatory
censorious 967.23
threatening 971.3

accusing 1003.13
condemnatory
1006.5
deny refute 505.5
disclaim 522.4
recant 626.9
reject 636.2
refuse 774.4
prohibit 776.3
DENY ONESELF 990.7
DENY ONESELF TO
refuse 774.5
be inhospitable
924.4
denying 522.5
deobstruct 264.12
deobstruent
nouns 685.15
adjs. 685.41
deodorant
nouns 437.3
adjs. 437.6
deodorization
ventilation 401.10
deodorizing 437.2
deodorize
ventilate 401.12
stop odor 437.4
deodorizer 437.3
deodorizing 437.6
deontology 955.2
deorganization 63.1
depart leave 300.6
exit 302.11
die 407.15
disappear 446.2
digress 591.9
DEPART FROM
differ 16.5
deviate 290.3
abandon 631.5
departed past 119.5
gone 300.20
dead 407.24
THE DEPARTED
407.13
departer 302.10
departing
differing 16.7
deviating 290.7
leaving 300.19
department
region 179.1
sphere 179.2
sphere of work
654.4
bureau 998.4
**Department of Agri-
culture, Depart-
ment of State,**
etc. 740.6
department store
830.1
departure
difference 16.1
deviation 290.1
leaving 300
egress 302
death 407.1
disappearance 446.1
digression 591.4

flight 629.4
depend hang 214.6
  rely 500.14
  be contingent 506.6
  be uncertain 513.11
DEPEND ON, DEPEND
UPON
  rely on 500.13
  be contingent 506.6
  be subject 762.11
dependability
  sureness 512.4
  trustworthiness
    972.6
dependable
  sure 512.17
  safe 696.5
  trustworthy 972.19
dependence
  suspension 214.1
  support 215.2
  belief 500.1
  subjection 762.3
  mainstay 785.8
dependency
  suspension 214.1
  subjection 762.3
  possession 806.1
dependent
  nouns follower 292.2
  retainer 748.1
  subject 762.6
  hanger-on 905.5
  adjs. liable 174.6
  pendent 214.9
  reliant 500.19
  conditional 506.9
  uncertain 513.16
  subject 762.12
BE DEPENDENT ON
  506.6
depending
  pendent 214.9
  relying 500.19
  conditional 506.9
  uncertain 513.16
depersonalization
  688.27
depict represent 570.7
  portray 572.20
  describe 606.12
  enact 609.34
depiction
  representation 570.1
  description 606.1
depictive
  representative
    570.11
  descriptive 606.15
depictment 570.1
depilation 231.4
depilatory 231.4
depilous 231.17
deplete
  evacuate 308.20
  consume 664.2
depleted 664.6
depletion
  vacancy 186.2
  evacuation 308.6
  consumption 664.1

loss 810.2
deplorability 862.4
deplorable
  terrible 673.9
  disastrous 727.15
  grievous 862.11
  disgraceful 913.11
deplore regret 871.6
  lament 873.8
deploy 196.6
deployment 196.1
depone testify 504.10
  depose 521.5
deponent 504.7
depopulate 308.15
depopulation 308.3
deport 308.16
DEPORT ONESELF
  735.4
deportation 308.4
deportment 735.1
deposal
  dismissal 308.5
  ~ from office 781
depose
  dismiss 308.18
  testify 504.10
  affirm 521.5
  ~ from office 781.2
deposit
  nouns sediment 43.2
  deposition 183.6
  silt 270.8
  precipitation 353.5
  ore 382.6
  pledge 770.3
ON DEPOSIT 770.15
  verbs lay eggs 166.18
  put down 183.15
  precipitate 353.11
  store 658.10
  pledge 770.12
depositary
  trustee 807.5
  treasurer 834.11
deposite 613.8
depositee 807.5
deposition
  sediment 43.2
  placement 183.6
  testimony 504.3
  affirmation 521.2
  affidavit 568.5
  ~ from office 781.1
  legal declaration
    1002.7
depository
  storehouse 658.6
  trustee 807.5
  treasurer 834.11
  treasury 834.12
depot
  railroad station
    183.3
  storehouse 658.6
deprave 690.12
depraved 979.19
depravedness,
depravation
  deterioration 690.3
  turpitude 979.6

depravity 979.6
deprecate 967.12
deprecation 967.2
deprecative
  modest 906.10
  censorious 967.23
deprecatory
  protesting 520a.7
  modest 906.10
  censorious 967.23
  derogatory 969.13
  apologetic 1004.13
depreciate reduce 39.7
  undervalue 497.2
  discount 845.2
  cheapen 847.6
  disparage 969.8
depreciation
  decrease 39.1
  undervaluation
    497.1
  discount 845.1
  cheapening 847.4
  disparagement
    969.1
depreciative 969.13
depreciator 969.6
depreciatory 969.13
depredate 822.15
depredation 822.5
depredator 823.6
depress reduce 39.7
  deepen 208.7
  indent 256.14
  lower 316.4
  deject 870.18
depressant 685.11,39
depressed low 207.6
  indented 256.17
  lowered 316.10
  underprivileged
    727.14
  dejected 870.22
depressing 870.31
depression
  lowness 207.1
  deepening 208.6
  cavity 256.2
  notch 261.1
  lowering 316.1
  neurosis 688.22
  hard times 727.6
  business ~ 825.7
  dejection 870.3
depressive 870.31
deprivation
  want 660.4
  deposal 781.1
  loss 810.1
  divestment 820.5
deprivative 820.22
deprive
  ~ of life 408.13
  take from 820.18
DEPRIVED OF
  lacking 660.11
  bereft 810.8
deprivement 820.5
depth breadth 203.1
  deepness 208
  pit 208.2

pitch 462.4
  wisdom 466.5
BEYOND ONE'S DEPTH
  beyond one 157.20
  too deep 208.16
  inunderstandable
    547.22
GO OUT OF ONE'S
DEPTH
  risk 695.7
  be rash 892.5
OUT OF ONE'S DEPTH
  too deep 208.16
  impracticable 509.7
  in trouble 729.19
depthless slight 35.7
  shallow 209.5
depths 208.3
IN THE DEPTHS
  870.22
REACH THE DEPTHS
  degenerate 690.18
  be unfortunate
    727.11
  despond 870.16
depurate refine 354.6
  cleanse 679.17
depuration 354.3
depurative
  cleansing 679.26
  cathartic 685.41
deputation
  commission 778.1
  delegation 779.12
deputative 779.14
depute 778.9
deputize 778.9
deputized 778.16
deputy
  nouns
  ~ sheriff 697.14
  agent 779
  adjs. 779.14
deputy commissioner
  747.14
deracinate 304.9
deracination 304.1
derange
  disarrange 63.2
  madden 472.22
  sicken 684.37
deranged
  disorderly 62.12
  insane 472.24
derangement
  disorder 62.1
  disarranging 63.1
  insanity 472.1
derbies See **darbies**
derby hat 238.59
  contest 794.5
  horse race 794.13
dereism fantasy 533.7
  autism 688.34
derelict
  nouns castaway 631.4
  outcast 924.3
  wretch 984.2
  adjs. negligent 532.10
  abandoned 631.8
  outcast 924.8

unfaithful 973.19
dereliction
　negligence 532.1
　abandonment 631.1
　nonobservance
　　767.1
　infidelity 973.5
　nonfeasance 980.2
deride 955.8
de rigueur
　conventional 643.7
　obligatory 960.14
derision ridicule 965.1
　laughingstock 965.7
derisive
　insulting 963.6
　ridiculing 965.12
derisory 965.12
derivable 504.18
DERIVABLE FROM
　154.5
derivation
　source 152.5
　effect 153.1
　lineage 169.4
　deduction 493.4
　etymology 580.14
　receiving 817.1
DERIVATION FROM
　154.1
derivational
　resultant 153.7
　attributable 154.5
derivative
　nouns effect 153.1
　word 530.2
　adjs. resultant 153.7
　attributable 154.5
　etymological 580.19
derive elicit 304.12
　deduce 493.10
　acquire 809.7
　receive 817.6
DERIVE FROM
　result from 153.6
　trace to 154.4
　receive 817.6
DERIVE PLEASURE
　FROM 863.10
derma 228.4
dermal 228.6
dermatitis 684.26
dermatogen 228.2
dermatologist 686.7
dermatomycosis,
　dermatosis 684.26
dermatotherapy 687.3
dermic 228.6
dermis 228.4
dermoplasty 687.27
dernier cri
　a novelty 122.2
　the rage 642.4
dernier ressort
　last resort 668.2
　refuge 698.2
derogate
　deteriorate 690.17
　disgrace 913.7
DEROGATE FROM
　969.8

derogation
　deterioration 690.3
　disparagement
　　969.1
derogator 969.6
derogatory 969.13
derrick tower 206.11
　lifter 315.3
derring-do 891.6
dervish ascetic 989.2
　religionist 1018.21
　clergyman 1036.12
descant
　nouns prelude 66.2
　music 461
　dissertation 604.1
　verbs sing 461.39
　expatiate 591.7
　dissertate 604.5
descanter 604.3
descend slope 218.10
　fly down 277.49
　go down 314.5
　gravitate 351.15
　condescend 904.7
　demean oneself
　　913.7
DESCEND ON 796.15
DESCEND TO
　PARTICULARS
　circumstantiate 8.5
　particularize 80.10
DESCEND UPON
　314.10
descendant 170.3
descendants 170.1
descendent 314.11
descending
　sloping 218.16
　downgoing 314.11
descent lineage 169.4
　posterity 170.1
　declivity 218.5
　rocket ~ 280.10
　motion down 314
　degradation 690.3
　misfortune 727.3
　attack 796.1
　inheritance 817.2
　humiliation 904.2
describability 550.7
describable 550.20
describe
　characterize 80.11
　~ a circle 319.4
　define 550.12
　designate 581.11
　portray 606.12
　outline 652.12
description
　characterization
　　80.8
　definition 550.5
　portrayal 606
OF EVERY DESCRIP-
　TION 19.4
descriptive
　definitional 550.18
　depictive 606.15
descriptively 606.19
descry see 438.12

detect 487.5
desecrate misuse 665.4
　profane 1028.4
desecration
　misuse 665.1
　profanation 1028.2
desegregation 525.4
desensitize 422.3
desert
　nouns 165.2
　adjs. unproductive
　　165.4
　barren 186.12
desert
　nouns 672.1
　verbs apostatize 626.8
　walk out on 631.6
deserted
　vacant 186.13
　abandoned 631.8
　forlorn 922.13
deserter 626.5
desertion
　apostasy 626.2
　abandonment 631.2
　forlornness 922.4
desert rat
　backsettler 189.10
　prospector 382.8
deserts 958.3
GET ONE'S DESERTS
　958.6
GIVE ONE HIS DESERTS
　retaliate 953.5
　punish 1008.10
deserve 958.5
deserved
　warranted 958.9
　just 974.8
deserving
　entitled to 958.10
　praiseworthy 966.19
déshabillé 230.20
desiccant 392.10
desiccate
　verbs dry 392.6
　preserve 699.8
　adjs. 392.9
desiccated 392.9
desiccation
　drying 392.3
　preservation 699.2
desiccative
　nouns 392.4
　adjs. 392.10
desiccator 392.4
desideration
　desire 632.1
　idol 632.11
　requirement 637.2
desiderative 632.21
desideratum
　desire 632.11
　requirement 637.2
design
　nouns musical ~
　　462.11
　meaning 543.2
　representation 570.1
　art 572.1
　artistry 572.8

composition 572.10
　work of art 572.11
　pattern 572.12
　drawing 572.14
　story plot 606.9
　intention 651.1
　plan 652.1,3
　function 663.5
　artifice 733.3
BY DESIGN 651.11
WITHOUT DESIGN
　155.20
　verbs draw 572.20
　intend 651.4
　plan 652.9
designate specify 80.9
　indicate 566.17
　name 581.11
　nominate 635.16
　appoint 778.10
designated 635.23
designation kind 61.3
　specification 80.6
　indication 566.1
　name 581.2,3
　nomination 635.6
　appointment 778.2
designative 566.22
designed 651.9
designer artist 577.9
　planner 652.7
designing
　nouns 572.1
　adjs. 652.14
designless
　purposeless 155.16
　meaningless 545.9
desinence 144.1
desirability
　likability 632.13
　eligibility 635.9
　expedience 668.1
desirable
　to be desired 632.31
　eligible 635.21
　expedient 668.4
　pleasant 861.5
　welcome 923.12
desirably
　preferably 635.25
　expediently 668.7
desire
　nouns sexual ~ 418.4
　will 619.1
　wish 632
　eagerness 633
　libido 688.39
　request 772.1
HAVE NO DESIRE
　634.4
　verbs lust 418.15
　will 619.2
　wish 632.14
　request 772.9
desired
　nouns 632.11
　adjs. 632.30
TO BE DESIRED
　desirable 632.31
　expedient 668.4
desireful 632.21

desiring 632.21
desirous lustful 418.20
 willing 620.5
 wanting 632.21
 eager 633.9
 envious 952.4
 BE DESIROUS 632.14
 DESIROUS OF 632.22
desist
 verbs cease 144.6
 disuse 666.4
 DESIST FROM 631.7
 interjs. cease! 144.13
 don't! 776.8
desistance
 cessation 144.1
 disuse 666.2
desk table 215.16
 lectern 1040.12
 THE DESK 1035.1
desolate
 verbs depopulate
  308.15
 devastate 691.10
 grieve 870.19
 adjs. barren 186.12
 dismal 336.15
 disconsolate 870.29
 forlorn 922.13
desolated
 ruined 691.27
 heartbroken 870.30
desolateness
 vacancy 186.2
 sadness 870.12
desolating
 painful 423.10
 destructive 691.25
 agonizing 862.14
desolation waste 165.2
 depopulation 308.3
 dismalness 336.2
 devastation 691.1
 wretchedness 864.6
 sadness 870.12
 forlornness 922.4
despair
 nouns
 despondency 870.3
 disconsolateness
  870.12
 hopelessness 887.2
 verbs 887.10
despairing 887.12
despatch, despatched
 See dispatch, etc.
despecificate 16.6
despecification 16.4
desperado
 ruffian 941.4
 criminal 984.9
desperate
 frantic 472.29
 extreme 661.17
 hopeless 887.12
 reckless 892.8
desperately
 exceedingly 34.24
 excessively 661.23
 hopelessly 887.17
 recklessly 892.11

desperateness
 despair 887.2
 recklessness 892.2
desperation 887.2
despicability 862.2
despicable
 paltry 671.18
 terrible 673.9
 odious 862.9
 disreputable 913.12
despicableness
 paltriness 671.2
 terribleness 673.2
 disreputability
  913.3
despise defy 791.4
 disdain 964.3
despite
 nouns defiance 791.1
 spite 937.6
 indignity 963.2
 contempt 964.1
 IN DESPITE OF 33.9
 preps. 33.9
despiteful 937.19
despoil fleece 820.21
 plunder 822.15
 debauch 987.20
despoiler
 plunderer 823.6
 debaucher 987.12
despoiling 822.5
despoilment 987.6
Despoina 1012.5;
  1017.5
despond
 lose heart 870.16
 despair 887.10
despondence, de-
 spondency 870.3
despondent 870.22
despot 747.15
despotic
 tyrannical 737.15
 governmental
  739.16
despotism 739.10
desquamate
 delaminate 226.5
 scale 231.11
desquamation
 delamination 226.4
 cast skin 228.5
 divestment 231.1
desquamative 231.18
dess 226.1
dessert 306.10
destinate 638.7
destination end 70.1
 journey's end 299.5
 address 602.10
 destiny 638.2
 objective 651.2
destine
 predetermine 638.7
 intend 651.4
 allot 814.10
destined 638.9
destiny end 70.1
 fate 638.2

destitute
 penniless 836.9
 bankrupt 840.11
 DESTITUTE OF 660.11
destitution want 660.4
 poverty 836.2
desto 461.56
destroy kill 408.13
 ruin 691.10
destroyed 691.27
destroyer ship 276.7
 ruiner 691.8
 THE DESTROYER
  1011.4
destroying 691.25
destructibility 159.2
destructible 159.14
destruction
 killing 408.1
 ruin 691
 loss 810.1
destructive
 deadly 408.23
 poisonous 682.5
 ruinous 691.25
destructiveness 682.2
desuetude 666.1
desultory
 orderless 62.11
 irregular 138.3
 changeable 141.7
 deviative 290.7
 wavering 323.19
 discursive 591.13
desynonymization
  16.4
desynonymize 16.6
detach disjoin 49.8
 demobilize 75.9
 wean 641.2
 commission 778.9
 draft 778.14
detached
 unrelated 10.5
 unjoined 49.20
 incoherent 51.4
 alone 89.8
 unprejudiced
  524.12
 reserved 611.8
 secluded 922.9
 impartial 974.10
detachment
 disjunction 49.1
 part 55.1
 company 74.3
 demobilization 75.3
 aloneness 89.2
 unprejudice 524.5
 aloofness 611.3
 neurosis 688.22
 draft 778.6
 military unit 798.19
 seclusion 922.1
 impartiality 974.4
detail
 nouns circumstance
  8.2
 part 55.1
 detachment 74.3
 technicality 749.4

military unit 798.19
 GO INTO DETAIL
 circumstantiate 8.5
 develop 321.6
 IN DETAIL
 in full 8.11
 piecemeal 55.8
 meticulously 531.16
 verbs circumstantiate
  8.5
 sum up 87.12
 elaborate 321.7
 commission 778.9
 assign 814.10
detailed
 circumstantial 8.7
 meticulous 531.12
details 671.4
detain delay 132.7
 retard 269.9
 hinder 728.10
detained late 132.15
 retarded 269.12
detainment 728.1
detect 487.5
detection
 radar ~ 345.9
 discovery 487.1
detective 779.10
detective story 606.7
detectors 348.35
detention delay 132.2
 retardation 269.4
 hindrance 728.1
 imprisonment 759.3
detention camp
 camp 190.25
 prison 759.9
deter disincline 650.4
 prevent 728.14
 daunt 889.17
deterge 679.17
detergent
 nouns 679.16
 adjs. 679.26
deteriorate
 worsen 690.10,17
 go to the bad
  691.23
 be unfortunate
  727.11
deteriorated 690.27
deteriorating 690.43
deterioration 690.3
determent
 dissuasion 650.1,2
 prevention 728.2
 hindrance 728.4
determinability
 measurability 489.8
 definability 550.7
determinable
 directable 289.14
 solvable 486.3
 measurable 489.15
 definable 550.20
determinant
 cause 152.1
 gene 169.6
determinate
 special 80.12

limited 233.8
unqualified 507.2
certain 512.20
resolute 622.11
determination
specification 80.6
circumscription
233.1
solution 486.1
finding 487.1
measurement 489.1
verdict 493.5
proof 504.4
ascertainment 512.8
definition 550.5
resolution 622.1
choice 635.1
inducement 646.3
determinative
nouns 152.1
adjs. final 70.10
convincing 500.22
evidential 504.17
determine end 70.5
specify 80.9
induce 152.12
influence 171.8
circumscribe 233.4
limit 233.5
direct 289.6
find out 486.2
discover 487.2
decide 493.11
prove 504.11
stipulate 506.4
ascertain 512.11
define 550.12
learn 562.6
resolve 522.7
choose 635.13
prompt 646.22
determined
limited 233.8
proved 504.22
assured 512.20
sure 512.21
resolute 622.11
determiner 169.6
determinism 638.4
determinist 638.5
deterministic 638.10
deterrence
dissuasion 650.1
prevention 728.2
deterrent
determent 650.2
obstacle 728.4
preventive 728.19
deterring 728.19
detersion 679.2
detest 928.4
detestability 862.2
detestable
terrible 673.9
obnoxious 862.9
detestation 928.1,3
dethrone 731.2
dethronement 781.1
detonate
explode 161.13
bang 455.8

detonating 161.23
detonation
explosion 161.7
bang 455.3
detonator 330.7
detorsion 248.1
detour
nouns circuit 319.3
by-pass 655.5
verbs deviate 290.3
go around 319.6
detract deduct 42.7
distract 530.6
DETRACT FROM 969.8
detraction 969.1
detractor 969.6
detractory 969.13
detrain 299.8
detriment
disadvantage 669.2
harm 673.3
impairment 690.1
loss 810.1
detrimental
disadvantageous
669.6
harmful 673.12
detrital, detrited
360.11
detrition 349.2
detritus remains 43.1
deposit 270.8
disintegration 360.5
detrude 316.4
detruncate 42.10
detruncation 42.3
detrusion 316.1
deuce 90.3
GIVE THE DEUCE
967.19
GO TO THE DEUCE
691.23
LOOK LIKE THE
DEUCE 897.5
PLAY THE DEUCE
WITH
play havoc 690.11
cause trouble
729.13
botch 732.12
THE DEUCE 1014.4
THE DEUCE YOU SAY!
918.20
deuce-ace 93.2
deuced 970.10
deucedly 34.26
deuce shot 575.10
Deus 1011.3
deus 1012.2
Deus Fidius 974.5
deuteranopia 440.3
deuterium 325.5
deuterogamist 931.12
deuterogamy 931.2
deuterons 325.6
deva god 1012.2
devachan 1016.9
devaloka 1016.9
devaluate 847.6
devaluation 847.4

Devanagari 579.5
devastate
depopulate 308.15
destroy 691.10
devastated 691.27
devastating
destructive 691.25
beautiful 898.19
devastation
depopulation 308.3
destruction 691.1
develop mature 126.9
generate 166.15
enlarge 196.4,5
grow 196.7
evolve 321.6
display 553.5
disclose 554.4
train 560.13
~ a photograph
575.17
expatiate 591.7
perfect 675.5
improve 689.7,10
developed
mature 126.12
improved 689.13
developer 575.15
developing 321.7,
development
maturation 126.6
effect 153.1
generation 166.6
growth 196.3
evolution 321.2
training 560.3
expatiation 591.6
improvement 689.2
Devi 1012.7
devi 1012.2
deviability 141.2
deviable 141.7
deviant
nouns 418.11
adjs. 418.23
deviate change 139.5
veer 218.9
turn aside 290.3
deflect 290.5
err 517.8
digress 591.9
misbelieve 1023.8
DEVIATE FROM 16.5
deviating
differing 16.7
deviative 290.7
circuitous 319.7
deviation
difference 16.1
ununiformity 18.1
abnormality 85.1
change 139.1
obliquity 218.1
distortion 248.1
indirect course 290
circuit 319.3
homosexuality
418.10
eccentricity 473.1
digression 591.4

deviative differing 16.7
ununiform 18.2
abnormal 85.9
irregular 138.3
oblique 218.13
distorted 248.10
deviating 290.7
eccentric 473.4
discursive 591.13
deviatory
ununiform 18.2
deviative 290.7
device tool 347.1
motto 516.4
insignia 567.2
cipher 579.1
signature 581.10
story ~ 606.9
trick 616.6
plan 652.1
expedient 668.2
artifice 733.3
devices means 656.1
tactics 733.4
devil
nouns dust storm
402.14
printer's ~ 601.10
mischief-maker
736.3
daredevil 892.4
archenemy 927.6
hellion 941.3
fiend 941.7
wretch 984.2,3
evil spirit 1014.2,7
GIVE THE DEVIL
967.19
GIVE THE DEVIL
HIS DUE
be fair 974.6
extenuate 1004.12
GO TO THE DEVIL
691.23
HAVE A DEVIL 472.19
LOOK LIKE THE DEVIL
897.5
PAY THE DEVIL 846.8
PLAY THE DEVIL
play havoc 690.11
cause trouble 729.13
botch 732.12
RAISE THE DEVIL
create a disturbance
62.9
be noisy 452.7
vociferate 458.8
be angry 950.15
THE DEVIL 1014.3
THE DEVIL AND ALL
all 54.3
everyone 79.4
THE DEVIL TO PAY
predicament 729.4
penalty 1007.1
THE DEVIL WITHIN
ONE 979.8
verbs cook 329.4
torment 864.19
banter 880.4
devil-dodger 1036.2

devil dog, devil dogs
275.4; 798.28
devildom 1014.14
deviled 329.6
devilfish 413.33
devil-god god 1012.2
idol 1031.3
deviling banter 880.2
imp 1014.8
devilish
execrable 673.10
mischievous 736.6
cruel 937.24
wicked 979.18
demoniacal 1014.18
hellish 1017.6
devilishly
exceedingly 34.26
mischievously 736.7
cruelly 937.31
devilize 1014.17
devilkin 1014.8
devil lore 1014.15
devil-may-care
unconcerned 634.6
nonchalant 856.15
reckless 892.8
devilment
mischief 736.2
annoyance 864.2
malice 937.5
devil-ridden 472.27
devilry mischief 736.2
malice 937.5
wickedness 979.5
diabolism 1014.15
black magic 1033.2
devil's advocate
critic 493.7
churchman 1036.8
devil's bones 514.8
devil's box 514.8
devil's dozen 99.7
devilship 1014.14
devil's tattoo 454.1
devil's teeth 514.8
deviltry mischief 736.2
malice 937.5
wickedness 979.5
devil worship
diabolism 1014.15
demonolatry 1031.1
devil worshiper
diabolist 1014.16
idolater 1031.4
devious oblique 218.13
deviative 290.7
circuitous 319.7
circumlocutory
591.14
devisable 815.5
devise
nouns 816.10
verbs create 166.12
invent 166.14
plan 652.9
bequeath 816.17
devised 652.13
devisee 817.4
deviser
inventor 166.10

planner 652.7
devising 166.5
devitalization 159.5
devitalize
unman 157.12
weaken 159.10
sicken 684.37
devitalized
unmanned 157.19
weakened 159.18
devitalizing 159.20
devoid
nonexistent 2.7
vacant 186.12
DEVOID OF 660.11
devoir 960.1
devoirs regards 934.8
respects 962.3
devolution
degradation 690.3
transfer 815.2
devolve 815.3,4
DEVOLVE ON 960.6
Devonshire cream
353.7
devote destine 638.7
employ 654.9
use 663.11,13
dedicate 814.12
apply 961.6
consecrate 1024.5
DEVOTE ONESELF TO
attend to 528.5
be determined
622.8
busy oneself 654.10
do 703.7
undertake 713.3
devoted
engrossed 528.17
zealous 633.10
destined 638.9
obedient 764.3
friendly 925.20
loving 929.24
faithful 972.20
consecrated 1024.8
pious 1026.8
DEVOTED TO
habituated 640.18
fond of 929.27
devotee votary 633.6
religious ∼ 1026.4
devotion
engrossment 528.3
zeal 633.2
dedication 814.4
friendship 925.7
love 929.1
fidelity 972.7
consecration 1024.3
piety 1026.1
worship 1030.1
devotional 1030.15
devotionalist 1026.4
devotions 1030.8
devour take in 305.11
eat 306.20
be credulous 501.5
destroy 691.10
delight in 863.10

gorge 992.5
DEVOURED BY 853.24
devourer 306.13
devouring 632.28
devourment 306.1
devout zealous 633.10
pious 1026.8
worshipful 1030.15
dew
nouns 391.4
verbs 391.12
dewal 1040.2
Dewali 876.4
dewan official 747.5
ruler 747.10,11
dew-beater 211.5
dewdrop drop 254.3
dew 391.4
dewiness 391.1
dewomanize 419.10
dew point 391.2
dews 99.6
dewy 391.15
dewy-eyed 533.24
dexter right 242.1
right-hand 242.4
dexterity
right-handedness
242.2
smartness 466.2
skill 731.1
dexterous, dextrous
right-handed 242.5
smart 466.14
skillful 731.20
dextrad 242.7
dextral 242.4
dextrality 242.2
dextrally 242.7
dextran 387.4
dextrocardial 242.4
dextrocularity, dextro-
duction 242.2
dextromanual 242.5
Dextrone 387.4
dextrorotation 242.2
dextrorotatory, dex-
trorse 242.4
dextrosinistral
ambidextrous 242.6
left-handed 243.6
dextroversion 242.2
dey 747.9,14
dharana, dhyana
1034.3
dhobi 679.14
dhoti 230.19
dhu 364.8
diabetes 684.8
diabetic 684.46
diable 1014.2
diablerie, diabolism
demonism 1014.15
black magic 1033.2
diablo 1014.2
diabolic, diabolical
execrable 673.10
cruel 937.24
wicked 979.18
devilish 1014.18

diabolist
demonist 1014.16
sorcerer 1033.5
diabolize
demonize 1014.17
bewitch 1034.10
diabology, diabolology
1014.15
diabolus 1014.2
diacaustic 251.2
diaconicon, dia-
conicum 1040.9
diacoustic 449.16
diacritical
differentiative 16.9
distinguishing 491.8
diacritical mark 584.11
diadem circle 252.2
insignia 567.3
ornament 899.6
diaeresis
dissection 49.4
poetry 607.9
diagnose
interpret 550.10
∼ a disease
687.32
diagnosis
analysis 484.8
decision 493.5
interpretation 550.1
medical ∼ 687.15
diagnostic
differentiative 16.9
interpretative
550.16
diagnostics
interpretation 550.9
medicine 687.14
diagonal
nouns 218.7
adjs. 218.20
diagonality 218.1
diagonalize 218.11
diagonally 218.26
diagram
nouns drawing
572.14
plan 652.3
verbs draw 572.20
plot 652.11
diagrammatic 652.15
dial measure 489.11
telephone 558.21
dialect
nouns language
578.6,8
diction 586.1
adjs. 578.18
dialectal 578.18
dialectic logic 481.2,4
reasoner 481.12
dialectical
logic 481.20,22
dialect 578.18
dialectical
materialism 375.5
dialectician
reasoner 481.12
philologist 578.12
dialecticism 481.2

dialectologist 578.12
dialogist 595.7
dialogue
  conversation 595.3
  drama 609.4
  playbook 609.25
dialoguer 595.7
dial tone 558.15
dialysis 53.2
dialytic 53.6
dialyze 53.4
diamagnetic
  repelling 288.3
  magnetic 341.28
diamagnetism
  repulsion 288.1
  magnetism 341.7
diameter middle 69.1
  thickness 203.3
diametric, diametrical
  15.6
diamond
  nouns angle 250.2
  hardness 355.6
  gem stone 383.10
  good thing 672.5
  baseball field 876.13
  admirable person
    983.1
  DIAMOND IN THE
    ROUGH
  inexperienced person
    246.2
  unpreparedness
    719.5
  good person 983.1
  verbs 899.8
diamond horseshoe
  609.19
diamonds 876.17
Diana moon 374.9
  goddess 1012.5
dianetics 688.2
diapason gamut 178.2
  harmony 461.3
  scale 462.6
  stop 464.23
  tuning fork 464.26
diaper 230.19
diaphane, diaphanous
  338.4
diaphonic, dia-
  phonical 460.4
diaphonics 449.7
diaphony 460.1
diaphoresis 309.7
diaphoretic
  sweating 309.20
  medicine 685.25
diaphragm
  middle 69.1
  midriff 236.5
  loud-speaker ~
    343.4
diarchy 739.4
diarrhea 309.2
diarthrosis 47.4
diary chronicle 114.9
  record book 568.10
  autobiography
    606.4

diaskeuast 603.22
diastatic 352.16
diaster 405.15
diastole 196.2
diastrophism 161.5
diathermal 327.31
diathermic 327.31
diathermy 687.6
diathesis 173.1
diatomic 325.17
diatonic scale 462.6
diatribe lecture 597.3
  berating 967.8
dib
  nouns 833.12
  verbs 653.10
dibasic 325.17
dibber 653.6
dibble plant 412.18
  fish 653.10
dibbler 653.6
dibs 833.2
dibstone 383.4
dice
  nouns cube 250.2
  craps 514.8
  PLAY AT DICE 514.17
  verbs 96.3
diced 250.10
dicer hat 230.25
  gambler 514.16
dichotomize 92.3
dichotomy
  bisection 92.1
  operation 687.26
dichroism 373.1
dichromatic
  chromatic 361.16
  variegated 373.9
dichromatism 440.3
dichromic 373.9
dick
  declaration 592.4
  detective 779.10
Dickens 1014.4
dicker
  nouns ten 99.6
  compact 769.1
  bargaining 825.3
  bargain 825.5
  verbs 825.14
dickering 825.3
dickey bosom 230.15
  donkey 413.22
Dicotyledones,
  dicotyledons 411.8
dictate
  nouns axiom 516.2
  precept 749.1
  command 750.2
  law 996.3
  verbs order 750.9
  advise 752.6
  DICTATE PEACE 802.9
dictated 749.5
dictates of society
  643.2
dictation
  command 750.2
  law 996.3

dictator
  political ~ 744.7
  ruler 747.6,15
dictatorial
  dogmatic 512.22
  bossy 737.15
  autocratic 739.16
  arrogant 910.9
dictatorship
  authority 737.6
  government 739.4,9
dictature 737.6
diction 586
dictionary 603.7
dictum maxim 516.1,2
  declaration 521.1
  remark 592.4
  precept 749.1
didactic
  instructive 560.18
  preceptive 749.5
didactics 560.1
didder
  nouns quiver 323.3
  trepidation 855.4
  verbs quiver 323.11
  shiver 332.10
didders 332.3
diddle
  nouns 994.13
  verbs deceive 616.17
  waste time 706.12
  DIDDLE AWAY 852.5
diddler cheat 617.3
  time waster 706.7
dido caper 317.2
  frolic 876.5
die
  nouns mold 25.6
  dado 215.8
  cube 250.2
  hazard 514.1
  graver 576.11
  THE DIE IS CAST
    637.20
  verbs cease to be 2.5
  be extinguished
    331.8
  decease 407.15
  disappear 446.2
  perish 691.22
  stall 723.15
  DIE AWAY
  decrease 39.6
  end 70.6
  recede 296.2
  be extinguished
    331.8
  disappear 446.2
  DIE FOR 632.16
  DIE GAME 623.6
  DIE HARD
  be obstinate 624.7
  resist 790.5
  DIE LAUGHING 874.9
  DIE ON THE VINE
  weaken 159.9
  deteriorate 690.19
  DIE TO 632.15
die-hard, diehard

  nouns conservative
    140.4
  obstinate person
    624.6
  extremist 661.8
  adjs. 140.8
dielectric
  nouns 341.13
  adjs. 341.33
dielectric heat 327.1
dielectric heating
  328.1
diencephalon 465.5
diesel-propelled
  284.17
diesel propulsion
  284.2
dies non, dies non
  juridicus
  timelessness 106.1
  holiday 709.5
diet
  nouns assembly 74.2
  nutrition 307.10
  parliament 740.1
  council 753.1
  verbs 307.17
dietal 307.22
dietary
  nouns 307.10
  adjs. 307.22
die temper 355.4
dietetic 307.22
dietetics 307.14
dietetic treatment
  687.18
dietician 307.13
dietotherapeutics,
  dietotherapy
  307.14
Dieu, dieu 1011.3
diff 16.1
differ vary 16.5
  not resemble 21.2
  disagree 27.5
  dissent 520.a.4
  ~ in opinion
    793.9,12
difference
  nouns contrariety 15
  variance 16
  dissimilarity 21
  disagreement 27.1
  inequality 31
  sum 86.3
  change 139.1
  dissent 520a.1
  disaccord 793.2
  IT MAKES NO DIF-
    FERENCE 671.21
  NO DIFFERENCE 14.1
  WITH A DIFFERENCE
    16.10
  WITHOUT DIF-
    FERENCE 14.6
  verbs 16.6
different
  contrary 15.5
  other 16.7
  diversified 19.4
  dissimilar 21.4

dilogy 703.3
diluent 390.4,8
dilute adulterate 44.13
  weaken 159.11
diluted 159.19
dilution
  adulteration 44.3
  weakening 159.5
diluvium residue 43.2
  deposit 270.8
dim
  nouns 336.5
  verbs darken
    336.11,13
  fade 362.5
  blind 440.6
  adjs. darkish 336.18
  pale 362.9
  dim-sighted 439.13
  indistinct 444.5
  faint-sounding
    451.16
  stupid 468.16
  obscure 547.13
dime 833.7
dime-a-dozen
  plentiful 659.7
  paltry 671.18
  cheap 847.8
dime novel 606.8
dimension
  extent 178.1
  size 194.1
dimensional 178.8
dimension control
  348.8
dimensions 194.1
dime store 830.1
dime-store 847.8
dimeter 607.5
dim-eyed 439.13
dim eyes 439.2
dimidiate
  verbs 92.3
  adjs. 92.4
diminish decrease 39.6
  reduce 39.7
  moderate 162.6
  taper 204.10
  recede 296.2
  qualify 506.3
  relieve 884.5
  abase 904.5
diminished
  reduced 39.10
  humbled 904.11
diminishing
  decreasing 39.11
  mitigating 162.14
  receding 296.5
diminishment
  decrease 39.1
  relief 884.1
diminuendo
  nouns decrease 39.2
  music 461.25,54
  adjs. 39.11,12
diminution
  decrease 39.1
  moderation 162.2
  lowering 316.1

music 461.10
diminutive
  nouns 195.4
  adjs. 195.11
dimly 451.21
dimmed 362.8
dimmer 336.5
dimming 336.7
dimness
  darkishness 336.5
  paleness 362.2
  indistinctness 444.2
  faint sound 451.1
dimout 336.8
dimple
  nouns 256.6
  verbs 256.14
dimpled 256.17
dimpsy
  nouns 134.3
  adjs. 336.18
dim-sighted
  weak-eyed 439.13
  undiscerning 468.14
dim view 967.1
dimwit 470.8
din
  nouns 452.3
  verbs repeat 103.10
  be loud 452.6
dinamode 160.6
dinar 833.9
dinch 433.6
dine feed 306.15
  eat 306.19
  DINE OUT 306.19
diner
  dining car 271.13
  eater 306.13
  restaurant 306.14
diner, diné 306.6
dinero 833.1
dinette room 191.11
  luncheon 306.6
ding
  nouns 453.3
  verbs repeat 103.10
  ring 453.8
dingdong
  nouns repetitiousness
    103.4
  ringing 453.3
  verbs 453.8
  adjs. samely 17.6
  repetitious 103.15
  tedious 882.8
  advs. 622.17
dinge blacken 364.7
  bruise 690.14
dinghy 271.13
dinginess
  darkness 364.3
  dirtiness 680.1
dinging
  nouns 453.3
  adjs. 453.12
dingle
  nouns valley 256.9
  storm door 301.6
  ringing 453.3
  verbs 453.8

dingling 453.3
dingus 375.4
dingy dark 364.11
  gray 365.3
  dirty 680.24
dining 306.1
dining car
  railway car 271.13
  restaurant 306.14
dining hall
  room 191.11
  restaurant 306.14
dinkiness 195.1
dinky
  inconsiderable 35.7
  little 195.9
dinner
  nouns 306.6
  verbs feed 306.15
  dine 306.19
dinner bell 453.4
dinner clothes 230.11
dinnerware 829.4
dinosaurian 194.20
dinosaurs 123.26
dinotherian 194.20
dint
  nouns power 156.1
  dent 256.6
  blow 282.4
  imprint 566.6
  BY DINT OF
  by virtue of 156.17
  by means of 656.8
  verbs 256.14
diocesan 1036.8
diocese district 179.5
  ecclesiastical ~
    1035.8
Diogenes 922.5
Dionaea 616.11
Dionysus, Dionysos
  agriculture 412.4
  drama 609.30
  drinking 994.2
  god 1012.5
dioptrics 334.22
diorama view 445.6
  picture 572.13
dip
  nouns declivity 218.5
  cavity 256.2
  plunge 318.2
  candle 335.2
  snuff stick 433.9
  pickpocket 823.2
  verbs slope 218.10
  ladle 270.16
  signal ship 274.55
  aviate 277.46
  plunge 318.7
  signal 566.21
  baptize 1038.19
  DIP INTO
  skim over 484.34
  browse 562.13
  DIP ONE'S HANDS
    INTO 820.16
  DIP SNUFF 433.15
diphtheria, diph-
  theritis 684.9

dingling 453.3
diphthong 449.5
diphyletic dual 90.6
  lineal 169.14
diplegia 684.19
diploma
  certificate 568.5
  commission 778.1
diplomacy tact 491.1
  cunning 733.2
  politics 742.5
  arbitration 803.2
diplomat, diplomatist
  tactful person 491.4
  crafty person 733.8
  envoy 779.6
diplomatic
  nouns 779.6
  adjs. tactful 491.8
  cunning 733.12
  political 742.47
  consular 779.15
  mediatorial 803.8
  BE DIPLOMATIC 491.5
diplomatic code 644.3
diplomatic corps
  779.7
diplomatics
  cunning 733.2
  politics 742.5
  arbitration 803.2
diplomatic service
  740.12
diplomatism
  politics 742.5
  arbitration 803.2
diplopod 413a.2
Diplopoda 414.8
dipnoans 414.11
dipody 607.5
dipper 192.7
dipping sloping 218.16
  submergence 318.2
dippy 472.25
dipsey 208.13
dipso 472.16
dipsomania
  addiction 640.8
  alcoholism 994.3
dipsomaniac
  psychotic 472.16
  addict 640.9
  drunkard 994.10
diptych 568.10
Dirae 1014.11
dire
  inauspicious 542.15
  very bad 673.9
  disastrous 727.15
  horrible 862.10
  fearful 889.29
direct
  nouns 462.12
  verbs influence 171.8
  pilot 274.14
  point 289.6
  ~ music 461.46
  teach 560.10
  address 602.14
  govern 739.11
  manage 745.8
  command 750.9

advise 752.6
DIRECT ATTENTION TO
  528.5,10
DIRECT ONE'S COURSE
  272.17
DIRECT ONE'S COURSE
  FOR 289.10
DIRECT ONE'S STEPS
  653.8
DIRECT THE EYES
  438.13
DIRECT THE MIND
  UPON 477.10
DIRECT TO 289.7;
  528.10
adjs. continuous 71.9
  lineal 169.14
  straight 249.5
  straightforward
    289.13
  exact 515.15
  candid 972.17
advs. 289.25
directable 289.14
direct current 341.2
direct fire 796.9
directing 745.12
direction trend 173.2
  bearing 289
  instruction 560.1
  pointer 566.3
  address 602.10
  government 739
  management 745
  directorate 746.10
  precept 749.1
  directive 750.3
  advice 752.1
IN EVERY DIRECTION
  289.27
IN THE DIRECTION OF
  289.28
directional 289.15
directions
  instructions 560.5
  formula 749.3
GIVE DIRECTIONS
  560.15
directive
  nouns 750.3
  adjs. directable
    289.14
  directional 289.15
  directing 745.12
  commanding 750.14
direct line
  lineage 169.4
  straight line 249.2
IN A DIRECT LINE
  lineal 169.14
  directly 289.25
directly
  promptly 131.15
  soon 131.16
  straight 289.25
  exactly 515.19
directness
  straightness 249.1
  candor 972.4
direct object 584.4

director
  electronic brain
    348.16
  theaterman 609.26
  manager 746
  governor 747
directorate
  school ~ 565.17
  directorship 745.4
  directors 746.10
directorship 745.4
directory
  nouns book 603.6
  guide 746.9
  directorate 746.10
  council 753.5
  adjs. 745.12
direct primary 742.15
direct signal 343.13
direful 889.29
dire necessity 637.4
direness 673.2
direption 822.5
dirge last rites 409.4
  lament 873.5
  Mass 1038.9
dirgelike 873.18
dirigible
  nouns 279.11
  adjs. 289.14
dirk
  nouns 799.22
  verbs 796.27
dirt
  nouns dirty weather
    161.4
  soil 384.1
  mud 388.8
  wet weather 393.4
  scandal 556.8
  grime 680.6
  obscenity 988.4
HEAP DIRT UPON
  969.10
  verbs 680.17
dirt-cheap 847.8
dirtied 680.23
dirtiness
  opaqueness 340.1
  dinginess 364.3
  muddiness 388.4
  uncleanness 680.1
  obscenity 988.4
dirty
  verbs 680.17
DIRTY ONE'S HANDS
  WITH 1008.11
  adjs. untidy 62.14
  opaque 340.3
  dingy 364.11
  muddy 388.14
  stormy 402.27
  cloudy 403.8
  unclean 680.24
  mean 913.12
  obscene 988.9
GIVE A DIRTY LOOK
  950.14; 967.9
dirty hands 981.1
dirty work 905.7
Dis 1012.5;1017.5

disability
  inability 157.2
  illness 684.1
disable
  incapacitate 157.9
  invalid 684.37
disabled 157.16
disablement 157.2
disabusal 519.1
disabuse 519.2
disabused 519.5
disabusing 519.4
disaccommodate
  669.4
disaccommodation
  669.3
disaccord
  nouns difference 16.1
  disagreement 27.1
  unconformity 83.1
  unharmoniousness
    793
  contention 794
  enmity 927
  verbs disagree 27.5
  be unharmonious
    793.9
DISACCORD WITH 16.5
disaccordance
  difference 16.1
  disagreement 27.1
  unconformity 83.1
  disharmony 793.1
disaccordant
  differing 16.7
  disagreeing 27.6
  unharmonious
    793.16
disadvantage
  nouns inexpedience
    669.2
  handicap 728.6
  trouble 729.3
AT A DISADVANTAGE
  728.71
PUT AT A DISAD-
  VANTAGE
  handicap 728.11
  penalize 1007.4
  verbs inconvenience
    669.4
  harm 673.6
disadvantageous
  inexpedient 669.6
  detrimental 673.12
disaffect
  disincline 650.4
  alienate 793.15
  displease 864.12
  dislike 865.4
disaffected
  alienated 927.12
  unfaithful 973.19
disaffection
  alienation 793.4
  displeasure 864.1
  dislike 865.1
  disloyalty 973.5
disaffirm 522.4
disaffirmation 522.2
disaffirming 522.5

disagree
  be incongruous 27.5
  dissent 520a.4
  differ in opinion
    793.9
  quarrel 793.12
DISAGREE WITH
  differ 16.5
  dissent 520a.4
  be insalubrious
    682.3
disagreeability
  unpleasantness
    862.1
  ill humor 949.2
disagreeable
  unsavory 428.5
  unpleasant 862.8
  ill-humored 949.19
disagreeing
  differing 16.7
  incongruous 27.6
  dissentient 520a.6
  unharmonious
    793.16
disagreement
  difference 16.1
  incongruity 27
  nonconformity 83.2
  dissent 520a.1
  difference of
    opinion 793.2
IN DISAGREEMENT
  16.7
IN DISAGREEMENT
  WITH 27.10
disallow deny 522.4
  refuse 774.4
  prohibit 776.3
  disapprove of
    967.10
disallowance
  denial 522.2
  refusal 774.1
  prohibition 776.1
disallowed 776.7
disallowing 522.5
disannul 777.2
disappear
  cease to be 2.5
  vanish 446.2
  perish 691.22
disappearance 446
disappearing
  nouns 446.1
  adjs. 446.3
disappearing act
  629.4
disappoint
  disillusion 519.2
  defeat expectation
    539.2
  dissatisfy 867.4
disappointed
  disillusioned 519.5
  let down 539.5
  discontented 867.5
  regretful 871.8
disappointing below
  expectation 539.6
  unsatisfactory 867.6

disappointment
  disillusionment 519
  dashed hopes 539
  dissatisfaction 867
disapprobation
  disapproval 967
  disparagement 969
disapprobatory 967.22
disapproval
  objection 520a.2
  disapprobation
    967.1
disapprove 967.10
DISAPPROVE OF
  disfavor 967.10
  disparage 969.8
disapproving 967.22
disarm render
  powerless 157.11
  demilitarize 802.11
disarmament 802.6
disarmed 157.16
disarrange 63.2
disarranged 62.12
disarrangement
  disorder 62.1
  misarrangement 63
disarray
  nouns 62.1
  verbs disarrange 63.2
  undress 231.7
disassemble
  take apart 49.14
  demolish 691.17
disassembly
  dismantlement 49.5
  demolition 691.5
disassimilation 307.9
disassociation
  unrelatedness 10.1
  disjunction 49.1
disaster fatality 408.7
  misfortune 727.2
disastrous
  destructive 691.25
  calamitous 727.15
disavow deny 522.4
  recant 626.9
disavowal
  denial 522.2
  recantation 626.3
disavowing 522.5
disbalance 31.3
disband 75.9
disbandment 75.3
disbar 781.2
disbarment 781.1
disbelief
  unbelief 502.1
  irreligion 1029.5
disbelieve
  not believe 502.5
  not swallow 503.3
disbeliever 1029.11
disbelieving
  unbelieving 502.8
  irreligious 1029.19
disbench 781.2
disbranch 49.15
disburden
  unload 308.21

  lighten 352.6
disembarrass 730.7
  relieve 884.7
disburdening
  lightening 352.4
  disembarrassment
    730.5
  relief 884.3
disburse 841.5
disbursement 841.1
disburser 841.4
discalceate 231.15
discanonization 781.1
discanonize 781.2
discard
  nouns
  elimination 77.2
  disuse 666.3
  verbs 666.7
discarded
  disproved 505.7
  disused 666.11
discardment 666.3
discarnate
  bodiless 376.7
  spectral 1015.8
discept 481.17
disceptation 481.5
disceptator 481.13
discern see 438.12
  know 474.12
  detect 487.5
  understand 546.8
discerned 474.26
discernibility 443.1
discernible
  visible 443.6
  knowable 474.25
  manifest 553.8
discerning
  sagacious 466.16
  discriminative 491.9
discernment
  seeing 438.1
  sagacity 466.4
  discrimination
    491.2
discerp 49.10
discerption 49.2
discharge
  nouns explosion
    161.7
  shot 284.5
  emission 302.2
  ejection 308.1,7
  dismissal 308.5
  excretion 309.1
  excrement 309.3
  electric ~ 341.6
  report 455.3
  performance 703.2
  accomplishment
    720.1
  exemption 760.7
  release 761.2
  observance 766.1
  execution 769.5
  payment 839.1
  receipt 842.2
  acquittal 1005.1
  verbs erupt 161.12

  fire 161.13
  shoot 284.13
  emit 302.15
  eject 308.12,23
  dismiss 308.18
  unload 308.21
  excrete 309.10
  do 703.8
  accomplish 720.4
  exempt 760.13
  release 761.5
  observe 766.3
  execute 769.10
  pay off 839.13
  acquit 1005.4
DISCHARGE ONE'S
  DUTY 960.9
DISCHARGE THE
  DUTIES OF 654.13
discharged
  accomplished 720.9
  paid 839.22
dischargee 308.11
disciple
  nouns convert 145.5
  student 564.2
  evangelist 1020.2
  believer 1026.4
  verbs 145.11
disciples 786.6
disciplinarian
  teacher 563.1
  tyrant 747.15
disciplinary 560.18
discipline
  nouns training 560.3
  self-control 622.5
  government 739.1
  punishment 1008.1
  verbs train 560.13
  govern 739.11
  punish 1008.10
DISCIPLINE ONESELF
  990.6
disclaim deny 522.4
  recant 626.9
  reject 636.2
  refuse 774.4
disclaimer
  denial 522.2
  recantation 626.3
  refusal 774.1
disclaiming 522.5
disclamation
  denial 522.2
  recantation 626.3
  rejection 636.1
  refusal 774.1
disclosable 553.13
disclose open 264.12
  discover 487.4
  manifest 553.5
  reveal 554.4
  indicate 566.16
disclosed visible 443.6
  unhidden 553.9
disclosing 554.1,11
disclosure
  appearance 445.1
  discovery 487.1
  manifestation 553

  revelation 554
discobolus 284.8
discoid 252.10
discolor
  nouns 677.2
  verbs decolor 362.5
  stain 677.6
discoloration
  decoloration 362.3
  stain 677.2
  bruise 690.8
discolored faded 362.8
  stained 677.9
discomfit
  confuse 530.7
  defeat 725.9
  frustrate 728.15
  embarrass 864.16
  dismay 889.18
discomfited 725.14
discomfiture
  confusion 530.3
  frustration 539.1;
    728.3
  defeat 725.2
  embarrassment
    864.4
discomfort
  nouns pain 423.1
  displeasure 864.1
  verbs 864.15
discomforted 864.25
discommend 967.12
discommendable
  967.25
discommendation
  967.2
discommode 669.4
discommodious 669.7
discommodity 669.3
discompose
  disarrange 63.4
  agitate 323.10
  fluster 530.7
  excite 855.14
  embarrass 864.16
  ruffle 864.17
discomposed
  disorderly 62.12
  agitated 323.17
  confused 530.12
  excited 855.24
  distressed 864.25
discomposure
  disorder 62.1
  disarranging 63.1
  fluster 530.3
  displeasure 864.1
  embarrassment
    864.4
disconcert
  bewilder 513.12
  fluster 530.7
  alarm 702.5
  thwart 728.15
  embarrass 864.16
  dismay 889.18
disconcerted
  bewildered 513.22
  confused 530.12
  alarmed 702.7

disembarrass
　unhamper 730.7
　extricate 761.7
　relieve 884.7
disembarrassed 760.23
disembarrassment
　unhampering 730.5
　extrication 761.3
　relief 884.3
disembodied
　bodiless 376.7
　spectral 1015.8
disembodiment
　disincarnation 376.5
　spiritualization
　　1032.21
disembody
　disincarnate 376.6
　spiritualize 1032.22
disembogue
　emerge 302.12
　eject 308.23
disemboguement
　308.7
disembowel 304.11
disembowelment
　evisceration 304.3
　suicide 408.5
disembroil
　disinvolve 45.4
　disembarrass 730.7
　extricate 761.7
disembroilment 761.3
disemplane 299.8
disemploy 308.18
disemployment 308.5
disenable 157.9
disenchant 519.2
disenchantment 519.1
disencourage 650.4
disencumber
　lighten 352.6
　disembarrass 730.7
　relieve 884.7
disencumberment
　352.4
disencumbrance
　disembarrassment
　　730.5
　relief 884.3
disendow 820.20
disendowment 820.6
disengage
　unfasten 49.9
　disembarrass 730.7
　extricate 761.7
disengaged
　unjoined 49.20
　escaped 630.10
　unemployed 706.16
　free 760.19
　retired 782.3
disengagement
　disjunction 49.1
　disembarrassment
　　730.5
　extrication 761.3
disentangle
　disinvolve 45.4
　solve 486.2
　disembarrass 730.7

extricate 761.7
disentanglement
　simplification 45.2
　solution 486.1
　disembarrassment
　　730.5
　extrication 761.3
disenthrall 761.4
disenthrallment 761.1
disenthrone 781.2
disentitle 820.18
disentitlement 820.5
disentomb 409.24
disequalization 16.4
disequalize
　differentiate 16.6
　disproportion 31.2
disesteem
　nouns disrepute
　　913.1
　disrespect 963.1
　disapproval 967.1
　verbs be 963.3
disfavor
　nouns alienation
　　793.4
　dislike 865.1
　disrepute 913.1
　disapproval 967.1
　IN DISFAVOR 913.13
　verbs dislike 865.4
　disapprove 967.10
disfellowship
　nouns 308.4
　verbs banish 308.16
　ostracize 924.5
disfigure deform 248.7
　blemish 677.4
　injure 690.13
disfigured
　deformed 248.12
　blemished 677.8
disfigurement
　deformity 248.3
　blemish 677.1
disgorge erupt 161.12
　eject 308.23
　vomit 308.24
　relinquish 812.3
disgorgement 308.7,8
disgrace
　nouns humiliation
　　904.2
　disrepute 913.5
　abomination 957.2
　verbs humiliate 904.4
　shame 913.8
disgraced 913.13
disgraceful
　shameful 913.11
　wicked 979.17
disgruntle 867.4
disgruntled 867.5
disguise
　nouns costume 230.9
　masquerade 616.10
　verbs misrepresent
　　571.3
　conceal 613.7
　falsify 614.16
　inebriate 994.28

disguised
　in disguise 613.15
　drunk 994.40
disguiser 617.7
disgust
　nouns 865.2
　TO ONE'S DISGUST
　　864.30
　verbs 864.13
disgusted
　satiated 662.6
　nauseated 684.42
　offended 864.23
disgusting nasty 428.7
　odious 862.9
dish
　nouns receptacle
　　192.1
　serving 306.10
　food 306a.7
　types of food
　　306a.55
　verbs be concave
　　256.12
　hollow 256.13
　ladle 270.16
　spoil 690.11
　frustrate 728.15
　give 816.12
　DISH THE DIRT 556.12
dishabille
　undress 230.20
　types of ～ 230.57
　IN DISHABILLE
　　230.46
disharmonious
　disagreeing 27.6
　unharmonious
　　460.4
　disaccordant 793.16
disharmony
　disagreement 27.1
　disorder 62.1
　unmelodiousness
　　460.1
　disaccord 793.1
dishearten
　dissatisfy 867.4
　deject 870.18
　daunt 889.17
disheartened 870.22
disheartening
　unsatisfactory 867.6
　discouraging 870.31
disheartenment 870.3
dished 256.16
disherison 820.6
dishevel 63.2
disheveled 62.13
dishevelment 62.1
dishing 256.16
dishonest
　untruthful 614.34
　deceitful 616.22
　scheming 652.14
　crafty 733.12
　dishonorable 973.15
dishonesty
　falseheartedness
　　614.4

untruthfulness
　614.8
　deceit 616.3
　sharp practice 616.4
　fraud 616.8
　improbity 973.1
dishonor
　nouns nonpayment
　　840.1
　disrepute 913.1
　disrespect 963.1
　improbity 973.1
　verbs not pay 840.6
　disgrace 913.8
　disrespect 963.4
　desecrate 1028.4
dishonorable
　disreputable 913.10
　dishonest 973.15
dishonorable
　　discharge 308.5
dishonoring 840.1
dishpan 679.12
dishwasher
　cleaner 679.14
　scullion 748.7
dishwater 680.9
dishwiper 679.14
disillude 519.2
disillusion
　nouns 519.1
　verbs disenchant
　　519.2
　disappoint 539.2
　expose 554.4
disillusioned
　disenchanted 519.5
　disappointed 539.5
disillusioning 519.4
disillusionment
　disenchantment
　　519
　disappointment
　　539
disincarnate
　disembody 376.6
　spiritualize 1032.22
disincarnation
　disembodiment
　　376.5
　spiritualization
　　1032.21
disincentive 650.2
disinclination
　unwillingness 621.1
　dislike 865.1
disincline 650.4
disinclined 621.5
disinclining 650.5
disinfect 679.22
disinfectant 685.18,
　37
disinfected 679.25
disinfection
　decontamination
　　679.3
　cure 692.7
disingenuous 614.32
disinherit 820.20
disinheritance 820.6

disintegrate
  decompose 53.3
  disband 75.9
  crumble 360.9,10
  decay 690.23
disintegrated 360.11
disintegrating 53.5
disintegration
  dissolution 53
  disbandment 75.3
  pulverization 360.4
  decay 690.5
disintegrative 53.5
disintegrator 281.13
disinter
  exhume 409.24
  find 487.4
disinterest
  nouns unprejudice
    524.5
  incuriosity 527.1
  unconcern 634.2
  disadvantage 669.2
  apathy 854.4
  impartiality 974.4
  unselfishness 977.1
  verbs 650.4
disinterested
  unprejudiced 524.12
  unconcerned 634.6
  apathetic 854.13
  impartial 974.10
  unselfish 977.5
disinterment 409.19
disinthrall See
  disenthrall
disinvolve 45.4
disjoin 49.8
disjoined 49.20
disjoint
  unjoint 49.16
  dislocate 184.4
disjointed
  unjoined 49.20
  dislocated 184.8
disjointing 184.1
disjointure 49.1
disjunct 49.20
disjunction 49
disjunctive
  nouns 584.2
  adjs. separating 49.24
  discontinuous 72.4
  alternative 635.19
disk surface 223.2
  lamina 226.2
  circle 252.2
  wheel 320.4
  record 464.19
disk jockey 343.26
dislikable
  unsavory 428.5
  unpleasant 862.8
  unlikable 865.9
dislike
  nouns displeasure
    864
  disaffection 865
  hate 928
  verbs not like 865.4
  hate 928.4

dislimb 49.15
dislocate
  disjoint 49.16
  displace 184.4
dislocated
  disjointed 49.20
  disorderly 62.12
  displaced 184.8
dislocation
  disjunction 49.1
  displacement 184
dislocatory 184.7
dislodge
  unplace 184.5
  remove 270.10
  evict 308.14
  extricate 761.7
dislodgment,
  dislodgement
  unplacement 184.2
  eviction 308.2
  extrication 761.3
disloyal 973.19
disloyalty 973.5
dismal dark 336.15
  terrible 673.9
  sad 870.25
  depressing 870.31
  pessimistic 887.16
dismals 870.6
dismantle
  disassemble 49.14
  disrobe 231.7
  demolish 691.17
dismantlement
  disassembly 49.5
  demolition 691.5
dismask 554.4
dismast 49.14
dismay
  nouns alarm 702.1
  consternation 889.1
  verbs bewilder 513.12
  alarm 702.5
  disconcert 889.18
dismayed
  bewildered 513.22
  alarming 702.8
  horrified 889.25
dismaying
  bewildering 513.24
  alarmed 702.7
  frightening 889.27
dismember
  take apart 49.15
  torture 1008.18
dismemberment
  disassembly 49.5
  punishment 1008.2
dismiss
  send away 308.17
  discharge 308.18
  refute 505.5
  disregard 529.4
  release 761.5
  depose 781.2
  relinquish 812.3
  acquit 1005.4
  DISMISS FROM THE
    MIND
  not think of 479.3

disregard 529.4
  forgive 945.5
Dismissal 1038.10
dismissal
  discharge 308.5
  release 761.2
  deposal 781
  acquittal 1005.1
dismissed 505.7
dismount
  disassemble 49.14
  unhorse 184.5
  get down 314.7
dismounting 49.5
disobedience
  intractability 624.4
  insubordination 765
disobedient
  intractable 624.12
  insubordinate 765.9
disobey
  not mind 765.6
  violate 767.4
  ~ the law 997.5
disoblige
  inconvenience 669.4
  displease 864.12
  give offense 963.4
disobliging 937.16
disomatous 91.3
disorder
  nouns disorderliness
    62
  illness 684.1
  misbehavior 736.1
  anarchy 738.2
  IN DISORDER
  disorderly 62.12
  in disarray 62.16
  verbs disarrange 63.2
  sicken 684.37
disordered 62.12
disorderly
  in disorder 62.12
  violent 161.18
  rowdy 736.5
  unruly 738.6
disorganization
  disintegration 53.1
  disorder 62.1
  disarranging 63.1
  disbandment 75.3
  fluster 530.3
  decay 690.5
  destruction 691.1
  anarchy 738.2
disorganize
  disintegrate 53.3
  disarrange 63.2
  disband 75.9
  fluster 530.7
  upset 690.11
disorganized
  disorderly 62.12
  confused 530.12
  chaotic 738.6
disorientation
  orientation 289.5
  psychosis 472.1
  neurosis 688.26
disoriented 472.24

disown deny 522.4
  recant 626.9
  reject 636.2
  disinherit 820.20
disowned
  rejected 636.3
  outcast 924.8
disowning
  denying 522.5
  recantation 626.3
disownment
  denial 522.2
  recantation 626.3
  rejection 636.1
  disinheritance 820.6
disparage disapprove
  of 967.10
  depreciate 969.8
disparagement
  disapprobation 967
  depreciation 969
disparager 969.6
  censorious 967.23
  derogatory 969.13
disparate 31.4
disparity
  disagreement 27.1
  inequality 31.1
  dissent 520a.1
  disaccord 793.2
dispart disjoin 49.8
  interspace 200.4
  open 264.11
dispassion
  indifference 634.2
  apathy 854.1,4
  inexcitability 856.1
dispassionate
  unprejudiced
    524.12
  unconcerned 634.6
  unemotional 854.9
  inexcitable 856.10
  impartial 974.10
dispatch, despatch
  nouns promptness
    131.3
  speed 268.1
  ejection 308.1
  killing 408.1
  message 556.4
  epistle 602.2
  performance 703.2
  quickness 705.3
  hastening 707.3
  accomplishment
    720.1
  verbs send 270.14
  eat 306.20
  kill 408.13
  mail 602.13
  do 703.8
  hasten 707.4
  accomplish 720.4
dispatched,
  despatched 720.9
dispatcher 273.13
dispel disperse 75.6
  get rid of 308.19
  disappear 446.2

dispensable
applicable 663.22
apportionable
814.13
condonable 1004.14
dispensary 685.31
dispensation
dispersion 75.1
fate 638.2
rule 739.1
management 745.3
relinquishment
812.1
apportionment
814.2
giving 816.1
divine function
1011.16
dispensatory 685.31,
· 32
dispense disperse 75.5
administer 663.11
apportion 814.9
give 816.12
vend 827.9
absolve 1005.4
DISPENSE WITH
not use 666.5
exempt 760.13
dispenser 685.30
dispeople 308.15
disperse scatter 75.5,9
refract 290.5
radiate 298.6
disappear 446.2
apportion 814.9
dispersed 75.10
dispersion
scattering 75
refraction 290.2
radiation 298.2
disappearance 446.1
apportionment
814.2
dispersive 75.12
dispirit 870.18
dispirited 870.22
dispiriting 870.31
displace
substitute 148.4
supplant 148.6
dislocate 184.4
remove 270.10
discharge 308.18
depose 781.2
displaced 184.8
displaced person
refugee 529.5
outcast 924.3
displacement
transformation
139.2
supersedence 148.1
dislocation 184.1
draft 203.5
removal 270.2
psychological ~
688.34
deposal 781.1
displant 761.7

display
nouns radar ~
345.11
appearance 445.3,7
manifestation 553.2
ostentation 902.4
verbs demonstrate
504.9
manifest 553.5
indicate 566.16
flaunt 902.17
displease
not please 864.12
dissatisfy 867.4
displeased
not pleased 864.23
discontented 867.5
displeasing
unsavory 428.5
unpleasant 862.8
unsatisfactory 867.6
displeasure
nouns dissatisfaction
864
disgust 865.2
unhappiness 870.2
resentment 950.1
verbs 864.12
displume divest 231.5
fleece 820.21
disport 876.25
disposable 663.22
disposal order 59.1
arranging 60.1
elimination 77.2
use 663.1
administration
745.3
settlement 769.4
relinquishment
812.1
apportionment
814.2
giving 816.1
sale 827.1
AT ONE'S DISPOSAL
available 663.19
at command 764.4
in possession 806.9
dispose arrange 60.8
influence 171.7,8
tend 173.3
put 183.11
bear for 289.8
induce 646.22
apportion 814.9
DISPOSE OF
end 70.7
eliminate 77.5
eat 306.20
get rid of 308.19
kill 408.13
refute 505.5
use 663.11
use up 664.2
discard 666.7
destroy 691.12
do 703.8
accomplish 720.4
obviate 728.14
settle 769.9

relinquish 812.3
give away 816.20
sell 827.8
disposed
arranged 60.13
minded 523.8
willing 620.5
DISPOSED OF 720.9
DISPOSED TO 173.6
disposition nature 5.3
order 59.1
arranging 60.1
elimination 77.2
tendency 173.1
placement 183.6
temperament 523.3
plan 652.1
use 663.1
administration
745.3
settlement 769.4
relinquishment
812.1
apportionment
814.2
giving 816.1
dispositional
temperamental
523.7
minded 523.8
dispossess evict 308.14
take from 820.20
dispossession
eviction 308.2
deprivation 820.6
disposure 60.1
dispraise
nouns 967.2
verbs 967.12
dispread
verbs 75.5
adjs. 75.10
disprize
underestimate 497.2
disdain 964.3
disproof 505
disproportion
nouns incongruity
27.2
inequality 31.1
verbs 31.2
disproportionate
incongruous 27.9
unequal 31.4
disprovable 505.10
disproval 505.1
disprove 505.4
disputability 513.2
disputable 513.15
disputant
arguer 481.13
oppositionist 789.3
contestant 794.23
combatant 798.1
disputation
argument 481.5
contention 794.1
disputatious
argumentative
481.20
contentious 949.26

dispute
nouns argument
481.5
questioning 484.14
protest 520a.2
quarrel 793.5
IN DISPUTE
in question 484.42
questionable 513.15
PAST DISPUTE 512.16
verbs argue 481.17
doubt 502.6
refute 505.5
protest 520a.5
deny 522.4
quarrel 793.12
fight over 794.22
disputed
doubted 502.12
refuted 505.7
disqualification
inability 157.2
unfitness 719.1
unskillfulness 732.1
disqualified
disabled 157.16
unqualified 719.9
disqualify 157.10
disquiet
nouns agitation 323.1
alarm 702.1
excitement 855.4
displeasure 864.1
anxiety 888.1
apprehension 889.4
verbs agitate 323.10
alarm 702.5
excite 855.14
distress 864.15
concern 888.3
frighten 889.14
disquieted
agitated 323.17
alarmed 702.7
excited 855.24
distressed 864.25
anxious 888.6
frightened 889.24
disquieting
alarming 702.8
frightening 889.27
disquietude
agitation 323.1
excitement 855.4
impatience 860.1
anxiety 888.1
apprehension 889.4
disquiparant 31.4
disquisition
lesson 560.6
dissertation 604.1
disquisitional 604.6
disquisitor 604.3
disrecollect 536.5
disregard
nouns inattention
529.1
neglect 532.1
unconcern 634.2
defiance 791.1
condonation 945.1

slight 964.2
verbs discount 506.5
be open-minded
524.7
pay no attention
529.3
neglect 532.6
disobey 765.6
defy 791.4
tolerate 859.7
condone 945.4
snub 964.6
disregardant
inattentive 529.6
careless 532.11
disregarded 532.14
disregardful
inattentive 529.6
careless 532.11
unconcerned 634.6
defiant 791.8
inconsiderate
937.16
disrelated 10.5
disrelish
nouns 865.1
verbs 865.4
disremember 536.5
disrepair 690.1
IN DISREPAIR 690.36
disreputability 913.2
disreputable
nouns 984.1
adjs. 913.10
disreputably 913.15
disrepute 913
IN DISREPUTE 913.13
disrespect
nouns insolence 911
discourtesy 935
disesteem 963
verbs 963.3
disrespectful
insolent 911.8
impudent 911.9
discourteous 935.4
irreverent 963.5
BE DISRESPECTFUL
963.3
disrobe 231.7
disrupt upset 690.11
thwart 728.15
disruption
severance 49.2
destruction 691.1
alienation 793.4
dissatisfaction
displeasure 864.1
discontent 867.1
dissatisfactory 867.6
dissatisfied
displeased 864.23
discontented 867.5
dissatisfy
displease 864.12
discontent 867.4
dissect divide 49.17
analyze 484.32
dissection
separation 49.4
analysis 484.8

disseize, disseise
820.20
disseizin, disseisin
820.6
disselboom 216.1
dissemblance
dissimilitude 21.1
dissimulation 614.3
dissemble
disregard 529.3
disguise 613.7
feign 614.22
dissembler
deceiver 617.1
hypocrite 1027.3
dissembling 614.3
disseminate
disperse 75.5
sow 412.18
publish 557.10
disseminated 75.10
dissemination
dispersion 75.1
sowing 412.14
publication 557.1
dissension 793.3
dissent
nouns nonconformity
83.2
nonagreement 520a
apostasy 626.2
dissension 793.3
verbs 520a.4
dissenter
nonconformist 83.4
protestant 520a.3
apostate 626.5
dissentience 520a.1
dissentient
nouns protestant
520a.3
apostate 626.5
adjs. nonconforming
83.6
protestant 520a.6
dissenting 520a.6
dissepiment 236.5
dissertate 604.5
dissertation 604.1
dissertational 604.6
dissertator 604.3
disserve 673.6
disservice
unkindness 937.13
wrong 975.4
disserviceable
disadvantageous
669.6
detrimental 673.12
dissever 49.10
disseverance 49.2
dissidence
disagreement 27.1
dissent 520a.1
dissension 793.3
dissident
nouns dissenter
520a.3
apostate 626.5
adjs. disagreeing 27.6
dissentient 520a.6

disaccordant 793.16
dissiliency 161.6
dissimilar
different 16.7
unlike 21.4
dissimilarity
difference 16
unlikeness 21
dissimilate
make unlike 21.3
vary 139.6
dissimilation 21.1
dissimilitude 21.1
dissimulate 614.22
dissimulation 614.3
dissimulator
deceiver 617.1
hypocrite 1027.3
dissipate disperse 75.6
disappear 446.2
go to waste 664.5
squander 852.3
be intemperate
991.6
dissipated
dispersed 75.10
spent 664.6
wasted 852.9
profligate 987.25
intemperate 991.8
dissipater, dissipator
991.3
dissipation
decrement 39.3
dispersion 75.1
disappearance 446.1
consumption 664.1
loss 810.2
prodigality 852.1
profligacy 987.3
intemperance 991.2
dissipative
dispersive 75.12
prodigal 852.8
dissociability 921.1
dissociable 921.5
dissociate disjoin 49.8
decompose 53.4
dissociated 10.5
dissociation
unrelatedness 10.1
decomposition 53.2
atomics 325.8
psychological ~
688.27
dissociative 53.6
dissogeny 168.2
dissolubility 390.2
dissoluble
separable 49.25
soluble 390.9
dissolute
wicked 979.19
profligate 987.25
dissipated 991.8
dissolution
disintegration 53.1
dispersion 75.3
liquefaction 390.1
solution 390.3
death 407.1

disappearance 446.1
decay 690.5
destruction 691.1
dissolutional 390.7
dissolutive 390.7
dissolvability 390.2
dissolvable
separable 49.25
soluble 390.9
dissolve cease to be 2.5
disintegrate 53.3
disperse 75.6,9
adjourn 132.9
liquefy 390.5
disappear 446.2
dissolvent 390.4,8
dissolver 390.4
dissolving
nouns liquefaction
390.1
disappearance 446.1
adjs. liquefactive
390.7
vanishing 446.3
dissolving agent 390.4
dissonance
difference 16.1
disagreement 27.1
unmelodiousness
460.1
dissonant
differing 16.7
disagreeing 27.6
unmelodious 460.4
dissuade 650.3
dissuading 650.5
dissuasion 650
dissuasive 650.5
dissyllabic 579.12
dissyllable 579.6
distaff
nouns spindle 320.5
woman 420.5
adjs. 420.14
distaff side kin 11.2
lineage 169.4
distal 198.8
distance
nouns remoteness 198
background 232.2
reserve 611.3
unsociability 921.2
AT A DISTANCE
distant 198.8
far 198.15
DISTANCE OF TIME
durability 110.3
antiquity 119.3
IN THE DISTANCE
198.14
KEEP AT A RESPECT-
FUL DISTANCE
keep one's distance
198.7
avoid 629.6
beware 893.7
KEEP ONE'S DISTANCE
keep away from
198.7
be uncommunicative
611.5

avoid 629.6
be modest 906.7
be unsociable 921.4
snub 964.7
verbs 36.9
distant farfetched 10.7
remote 198.8
reserved 611.8
haughty 910.12
unsociable 921.6
distant future 121.1
distant past 119.3
distaste 865.1
distasteful
unsavory 428.5
unpleasant 862.8
distemper
nouns color 361.7
disease 684.1,10
verbs paint 361.14
vex 864.17
anger 950.21
distend
expand 196.4,5
bulge 255.10
distended 196.12
distensive 196.9
distention
expansion 196.2
swell 255.4
distich couplet 90.2
verse 607.5
distill, distil
leak 302.14
extract 304.14
trickle 394.19
vaporize 400.7
~ liquor 994.36
distillate 304.7
distillation
leakage 302.5
extraction 304.6,7
trickle 394.7
vaporization 400.4
distiller
liquor maker 994.23
distillery 994.27
distillery 994.27
distinct different 16.7
separate 49.20
clearly seen 443.7
audible 449.15
precise 515.15
explicit 546.10
manifest 553.8
distinction
difference 16.1
differentiation 16.4
greatness 34.2
characterization
80.8
discrimination
491.3
elegant style 587.1
importance 670.2
repute 912.5
honor 914.1
nobility 916.1
DISTINCTION WITH-
OUT A DIFFERENCE
equivalence 30.2

indiscrimination
492.3
choicelessness 637.6
MAKE A DISTINCTION
differentiate 16.6
distinguish 491.7
WITHOUT
DISTINCTION
identical 14.7
equally 30.12
indistinguishable
492.8
impartially 974.11
distinctive
differentiative 16.9
characteristic 80.13
discriminative 491.8
typical 570.12
distinctly clearly 443.8
audibly 449.19
unmistakably
512.23
intelligibly 546.12
manifestly 553.14
distinctness
difference 16.1
visibility 443.2
explicitness 546.2
manifestness 553.3
distingué 912.17
distinguish
differentiate 16.6
characterize 80.11
see 438.12
detect 487.5
discriminate 491.6
recognize 535.13
honor 912.12
distinguishable
knowable 474.25
intelligible 546.10
distinguished
great 34.9
superior 36.13
different 16.7
characteristic 80.13
special 80.12
important 670.16
famous 912.17
honored 914.10
BE DISTINGUISHED
FROM 16.5
**Distinguished Con-
duct Medal, Dis-
tinguished Flying
Cross,** etc. 914.6
distinguishing
differentiative 16.9
discriminating 491.8
typical 570.12
distinguishment
differentiation 16.4
detection 487.1
discrimination 491.3
recognition 535.5
distort contort 248.5
reason ill 482.8
misinterpret 551.2
misrepresent 571.3
falsify 614.16

distorted
twisted 248.10
erroneous 517.14
misinterpreted 551.3
distortion
contortion 248
sophistry 482.1
error 517.1
misinterpretation
551.1
misrepresentation
571.1,2
falsification 614.9
distortive 248.9
distract
madden 472.22
~ the attention
530.6
distracted mad 472.29
distraught 530.10
overwrought 855.26
distracting 513.24
distraction
insanity 472.1
distractedness 530
distrain seize 820.17
fine 1007.5
distraint seizure 820.4
fine 1007.3
distrait 530.10
distraught
mad 472.24,29
distracted 530.10
distress
nouns pain 423.1
seizure 820.4
poverty 836.1
displeasure
864.4,5,8
anxiety 888.1
fine 1007.3
verbs pain 423.7
displease 864.15
distressed
pained 423.9
poor 836.7
troubled 864.25
distressful 862.11
distressing
painful 423.10
grievous 862.11
distributable 814.13
distribute
arrange 60.8
disperse 75.5
apportion 814.9
distributed 75.10
distribution
arrangement 60.1
dispersion 75.1
apportionment
814.2
distributional 814.14
distributive
dispersive 75.12
respective 814.14
distributor
broadcaster 75.4
merchant 828.2
district
nouns 179.1,5

verbs 49.18
district attorney
1001.4
distrust
nouns doubt 502.2
wariness 893.2
jealousy 951.2
verbs doubt 502.6
be jealous 951.3
distrusted 502.12
distrustful
doubtful 502.9
wary 893.9
jealous 951.4
disturb
discompose 63.4
agitate 323.10
bewilder 513.12
fluster 530.7
alarm 702.5
trouble 729.12
excite 855.14
distress 864.15
annoy 864.17
concern 888.3
disturbance
commotion 62.4
disarrangement 63.1
turbulence 161.2
agitation 323.1
distraction 530.3
perplexity 513.3
alarm 702.1
excitement 855.3
embarrassment
864.4
anxiety 888.1
disturbed
agitated 323.17
bewildered 513.22
confused 530.12
alarmed 702.7
excited 855.24
annoyed 864.24
distressed 864.25
anxious 888.6
disturbing
bewildering 513.24
alarming 702.8
embarrassing 862.12
annoying 862.13
disunion
disagreement 27.1
disjunction 49.1
disunite disjoin 49.8
alienate 793.15
disunited
unjoined 49.20
alienated 927.12
disunity 27.1
disusage 666.1
disuse
nouns antiquation
123.3
disusage 666
verbs 666.4
disused passé 123.15
out of use 666.10
disvaluation 967.2
disvalue 967.12

ditch
  nouns trench 262.2
  entrenchment 797.5
  verbs play truant
    186.8
  furrow 262.3
  ∼ a plane 277.49
  evade 629.7
ditheism 1018.5
ditheist 1018.14
ditheistic 1018.23
dither
  nouns tremble 323.3
  excitement 855.5
  IN A DITHER 855.22
  verbs shiver 332.10
  excite 855.15
dithers
  chilliness 332.2
  trepidation 855.4
  jitters 857.2
dithery 332.16
dithyramb 607.4,15
dithyrambic 607.21
ditto
  nouns duplicate 24.3
  equal 30.5
  repetition 103.5
  verbs coincide 14.4
  copy 22.5
  equal 30.6
  duplicate 91.2
  repeat 103.7
  concur 520.9
  advs. likewise 14.8
  again 103.17
ditty 461.13
diuretic
  nouns 685.15
  adjs. 685.41
diurnal 137.9
diva 610.5
divagate digress 290.3
  stray 290.4
divagation 290.1
divan
  official seat 737.9
  council 753.1
  court 999.2
divaricate
  verbs open 264.11
  deviate 290.3
  diverge 298.5,7
  DIVARICATE FROM
    16.5
  adjs. 298.8
divarication
  ununiformity 18.1
  deviation 290.1
  divergence 298.1,3
dive
  nouns low resort
    190.24
  navigation 274.8
  aviation 277.10
  plunge 318.1
  brothel 987.9
  saloon 994.25
  verbs ∼ a submarine
    274.49
  swim 274.59

∼ a plane 277.47
  plunge 318.6
DIVE IN 68.6
DIVE INTO
  explore 484.30
  be precipitate 707.7
  set to work 714.15
dive-bomb 796.25
dive-bombing 796.8
diver 318.4
diverge oblique 218.9
  deviate 290.3,5
  divaricate 298.5
DIVERGE FROM 16.5
divergence
  difference 16.1
  ununiformity 18.1
  disagreement 27.1
  abnormality 85.1
  obliquity 218.1
  deviation 290.1
  divarication 298
  eccentricity 473.1
divergent
  differing 16.7
  ununiform 18.2
  disagreeing 27.6
  abnormal 85.9
  diverging 298.8
  eccentric 473.4
divers different 16.7
  various 19.4
  several 101.8
ON DIVERS OCCA-
  SIONS 136.5
diverse
  different 16.7
  multiform 19.4
diversification
  differentiation 16.4
  diversity 19.1
  change 139.1
diversified 19.4
diversiform 19.3
diversify
  differentiate 16.6
  vary 19.2
  change 139.5,6
diversion change 139.1
  deviation 290.1
  distraction 530.1
  apostasy 626.2
  military ∼ 795.10
  amusement 876.1
diversity
  difference 16.1
  multiformity 19.1
  disagreement 27.1
  change 139.1
divert deflect 290.5
  distract 530.6
  disincline 650.4
  amuse 876.23
diverted 876.28
diverting 876.29
**divertisement,
    divertissement**
  music 461.6
  entr'acte 609.8
  amusement 876.1
Dives 835.7

divest strip 231.5
  take from 820.18,21
divested
  stripped 231.12
  bereft 810.8
divestment
  stripping 231
  deprivation 820.5
divesture 231.1
divide
  nouns 206.10
  verbs differentiate
    16.6
  disjoin 49.8
  partition 49.18
  sort 60.10
  classify 61.6
  segregate 77.6
  calculate 87.11
  bisect 92.3
  partition off 236.9
  open 264.11
  diverge 298.5
  measure 489.11
  distinguish 491.6
  select 635.11
  vote 635.15
  quarrel 793.11
  alienate 793.15
  apportion 814.7
  DIVIDE ON 520a.4
  DIVIDE WITH 813.6
divided
  unjoined 49.20
  halved 92.4
  alienated 927.12
dividend
  mathematical
    element 86.9
  share 814.5
  stock ∼ 832.7
  payment 839.7
dividing
  nouns 814.1
  adjs. 49.24
dividing line 236.5
divinability 541.8
divinable 541.13
divination
  astrology 374.20
  foresight 540.1
  prediction 541.2
  forms of ∼ 541.5
  omen 542.2
  clairvoyance 1032.8
  sorcery 1033
divinator 541.4
divinatory
  foreseeing 540.8
  predictive 541.11
divine
  nouns theologian
    1021.3
  clergyman 1036.2
  verbs guess 486.2
  suppose 498.9
  foresee 540.6
  predict 541.9
  forebode 542.8
  adjs. superb 672.18
  delightful 861.6

beautiful 898.19
  godlike 1011.19
  theological 1021.4
  sacred 1024.7
divine afflatus
  genius 466.8
  inspiration 646.9
divine breath
  life force 406.3
  soul 1032.17
divine healing 1018.12
divine inspiration
    1019.8
Divine Liturgy 1038.9
Divine Mind 1011.7
diviner 541.4
divine right 737.1
divine service 1030.8
divine spark
  life force 406.3
  spirit 1032.18
diving aviation 277.10
  plunging 318.3
diving bell 318.5
divining 541.2
divining rod 541.3
Divinity, the 1011.2
divinity deity 1011.1
  god 1012.2
  theology 1021.1
divisible
  separable 49.25
  apportionable
    814.13
division
  differentiation 16.4
  disjunction 49.1
  part 55.1
  classification 61.1
  class 61.2,5
  segregation 77.3
  mathematics 87.4
  bisection 92.1
  region 179.1
  partition 236.5
  divergence 298.1
  musical ∼ 461.24
  music 462.18
  discrimination
    491.3
  school ∼ 564.9
  book ∼ 603.14
  faction 786.5,10
  alienation 793.4
  military ∼ 798.19
  naval ∼ 798.27
  apportionment
    814.1
  sect 1018.3
divisional 61.7
divorce
  nouns disjunction
    49.1
  matrimonial ∼
    933.1
  verbs disjoin 49.8
  unmarry 933.5
**divorcé, divorcee,
    divorcée** 933.2
divorcement
  disjunction 49.1

divorce 933.1
divulgate 554.5
divulgation 554.2
divulge reveal 554.5
  publish 557.10,11
divulgence 554.2
divulsion 49.2
divvy
  nouns 814.5
  verbs partition 49.18
  apportion 814.7
DIVVY UP
  partition 49.18
  apportion 814.7
Dixie, Dixieland
  region 179.7
  utopia 533.11
Dixiecrat 742.28
dizen dress up 230.41
  adorn 899.7
dizzard 470.1
dizziness
  stupidity 468.5
  vertigo 530.4
  fickleness 627.3
dizzy
  nouns 470.7
  verbs 530.8
  adjs. stupid 468.18
  foolish 469.8
  delirious 472.30
  giddy 530.15,16
  fickle 627.7
  tipsy 994.38
dizzy round
  whirl 320.2
  dizziness 530.4
THE DIZZY ROUNDS
  876 7
do
  nouns occurrence
    150 2
  sol-fa 462.7
  act 703.3
  command 750.1
  festival 876.4
  verbs fare 7.6
  suit 25.8
  cause 152.11
  produce 166.11
  attend 185.8
  travel 272.18
  traverse 272.19
  cook 329.4
  solve 486.2
  deceive 616.17
  suffice 659.4
  avail 663.17
  act 703.6
  accomplish 720.4
  behave 735.4
  observe 766.3
DO AGAIN 103.7,11
DO ALL IN ONE'S
  POWER 712.11
DO ALL RIGHT BY
  ONESELF
  succeed 722.9
  prosper 726.9
  grow rich 835.9

DO AS ONE PLEASES
  have one's way
    619.3
  be lawless 738.4
  be independent
    760.18
DO AS ONE SAYS 764.2
DO AS OTHERS DO
  conform 82.4
  be fashionable
    642.10
DO AS WELL AS ONE
  CAN 668.3
DO AWAY WITH
  get rid of 308.19
  kill 408.13
  discard 666.7
  destroy 691.12
  abolish 777.2
DO AWAY WITH
  ONESELF 408.22
DO BY 735.6
DO FOR
  kill 408.14
  ruin 691.11
  defeat 725.6
  care for 748.14
  punish 1008.11
DO IN
  kill 408.14
  cheat 616.18
  ruin 691.11
  fatigue 715.4
  defeat 725.6
  punish 1008.12
DO LIKE 22.5
DO ONESELF PROUD
  eat heartily 306.22
  do one's best 712.11
  do thoroughly 720.7
  succeed 722.9
DO ONE'S STUFF
  703.10
DO OUT OF 616.18
DO SOMETHING 703.5
DO TELL!
  is that so? 484.48
  disbelief 502.14
  astonishment
    918.20
DO TO
  do 703.6
  inflict 961.5
DO UNTO OTHERS, etc.
  be benevolent
    936.12
  be unselfish 977.4
DO UP
  tie up 47.9
  tidy 60.11
  wrap up 74.19
  repair 692.14
  preserve 699.9
  fatigue 715.4
DO UP BROWN
  deceive 616.17
  thoroughly 720.7
DO WHAT IS
  EXPECTED OF ONE
  960.9

DO WHAT ONE CAN
  712.8
DO WHAT ONE IS TOLD
  764.2
DO WITH
  desire 632.14
  make use of 663.10
  deal with 663.12
  make shift 668.3
DO WITHOUT
  not use 666.5
  abstain 990.7
DO WONDERS 722.6
HAVE TO DO WITH
  concern 9.3
  treat 663.12
  participate 813.5
JUST DO 659.4
NOT HAVE ANYTHING
  TO DO WITH 788.8
interjs. 772.20
doable
  workable 163.11
  solvable 486.3
  practicable 508.7
do-all 748.10
dobbin 413.12
dobe sod house 190.5
  adobe 384.1
  cigarette butt 433.6
doc 686.5
docent 563.1
doch-an-dorrach 944.8
docile
  teachable 562.18
  compliant 763.13
docility
  teachability 562.5
  compliance 763.3
docimastic(al) 488.11
docimasy
  analysis 484.8
  experiment 488.1
docimology 488.1
dock
  nouns tail 240.5
  hangar 277.21
  theater ~ 609.20
  storage 658.6
  anchorage 698.6
  witness stand 999.9
  verbs cut off 42.10
  ~ a ship 274.16
dockage
  anchorage 698.6
  charge 844.7
docked 57.5
docker 275.10
docket
  nouns ticket 566.12
  certificate 568.5
  schedule 639.2
ON THE DOCKET
  in question 484.42
  planned 652.13
  verbs ticket 566.19
  record 568.15
  schedule 639.4
  enter accounts 843.8
dock gate 395.11
dock hand 275.10

dockyard
  anchorage 698.6
  repair shop 717.6
doctor
  nouns breeze 402.5
  teacher 563.3
  physician 686.5
  psychiatrist 688.13
  mender 692.10
  degree 915.6
  verbs adulterate 44.13
  falsify 614.17
  practice medicine
    686.17
  treat 687.33
  take medicine
    687.38
  repair 692.14
doctorate 915.6
doctoring 44.3
doctrinaire
  nouns 498.6
  adjs. 512.22
doctrinal
  creedal 500.23
  theological 1021.4
doctrinalism 1021.1
doctrinary
  dogmatic 512.22
  theological 1021.4
doctrine 500.2
doctrine of inference,
  doctrine of terms,
  doctrine of the
  judgment 481.2
doctrinism 1021.1
document
  nouns 568.4
  verbs circumstantiate
    8.5
  corroborate 504.12
documental 568.18
documentary 568.18
documentary evidence
  504.2
documentary film
  609.15
documentation 504.5
dodaw 855.5
IN A DODAW 855.22
dodder 159.8
doddering aged 126.17
  unsteady 159.16
  senile 468.23
dodecagonal, dodeca-
  hedral 250.11
dodge
  nouns recoil 283.3
  quibble 482.4
  trick 616.6
  avoidance 629.1
  expedient 668.2
  artifice 733.3
  verbs recoil 283.7
  quibble 482.9
  fight shy 621.4
  avoid 629.8
  snub 964.7
dodger bread 306a.28
  handbill 557.8
  deceiver 617.1

shirker 629.3
crafty person 733.6
dodgery 616.4
dodge times 708.1
dodging 482.5
dodo
  antiquated person
    123.8
  nonflier 278.5
Dodona 541.7
dods 949.10
doe deer 413.7
  animal 413.29
  female animal
    420.10
doer 716.1
doff 231.6
dofunny 375.4
dog
  nouns foot 211.5
  jalopy 271.9
  horse 413.16
  canine 413.24
  breeds of ~ 413.62
  male animal 419.8
  airs 902.2
  scoundrel 984.6
  DOG IN THE MANGER
  marplot 728.9
  self-seeker 976.3
  GONE TO THE DOGS
  ruined 691.27
  wicked 979.19
  GO TO THE DOGS
  go to the bad 691.23
  be unfortunate
    727.11
  go bankrupt 840.7
  PUT ON THE DOG
  dress up 230.41
  be ostentatious
    902.14
  verbs follow 292.3
  hunt 653.9
  DOG ON THE JOB
  shirk 629.9
  loaf 706.10
dog-cheap 847.8
dog days
  summer 128.3
  hot weather 327.6
doge 747.7
dog-ear
  nouns 263.1
  verbs 263.5
dog-eared
  folded 263.7
  eared 447.16
dogface 798.10
dogfight 794.4
dog flea 413a.6
dogged
  persevering 623.7
  obstinate 624.8
doggedness
  perseverance 623.1
  obstinacy 624.1
doggerel
  nouns 607.3
  adjs. inelegant 588.2
  burlesque 965.14

dogging 292.1
doggish 413.37
doggy 902.19
doghole 190.18
doghouse
  kennel 190.18
  small place 195.3
  bull fiddle 464.5
  IN THE DOGHOUSE
    913.13
dogie youngling 125.8
  calf 413.8
  orphan 631.4
dog Latin 578.6
doglike 413.37
dogma 500.2
dogmatic
  doctrinal 500.23
  certain 512.22
dogmatics 1021.1
dogmatism 512.6
dogmatist 512.7
dogmatize 512.10
do-gooder 936.8
do-goodism 936.4
dog pound 190.18
dog race 794.12
dogs 230.27
dog's age 110.4
dog-sick 684.41
dogs of war 799.6
Dog Star 374.5
dog-tired 715.8
dogtooth 257.7
dogtrot dash 268.4
  slow motion 269.2
dog trot 269.6
dogwam 190.18
dogwatch 108.3
dog-weary 715.8
dohickey 375.4
doing
  nouns affair 150.3
  action 703.1,3
  adjs. 150.9
doings affairs 150.4
  acts 703.3
  activity 705.1
doit
  clumsy fellow 732.9
  coin 833.9
doited 468.23
dojigger, dojiggy
    375.4
dokhma 409.16
dolcan 464.23
dolce 461.54
doldrums calm 267.5
  blues 870.6
  IN THE DOLDRUMS
    70.22
dole
  nouns small amount
    35.2
  part 55.1
  pittance 660.5
  share 814.2,5
  alms 816.6
  verbs apportion 814.9
  give 816.12
doleful 870.27

dolefuls 870.6
doless 704.6
doling 814.2
do-little 706.7
doll girl 125.6
  miniature 195.5
  figure 570.4
  plaything 876.16
doll up dress 230.41
  adorn 899.7
dollar 833.7–9
dollar crisis 834.7
dollar currency 833.1
dollar diplomacy
    742.5
dollar gap
  crisis 834.7
  deficit 888.2
dollars to doughnuts
    510.7
dollar store 830.1
doll carriage 876.16
dollhouse
  small place 195.3
  plaything 876.16
dollish 124.12
dolly 570.4
dolmen 568.11
dolor 864.5
dolorous
  grievous 862.11
  sad 870.27
dolorously
  exceedingly 34.25
  sadly 870.37
dolphin 413.33
dolt 470.3
doltish 468.15
Dom 915.5
domain sphere 179.2
  country 180.1
  sphere of work 654.4
  property 808.7
domal 190.27
Domdaniel
  gambling den
    514.14
  den of iniquity
    979.10
dome
  nouns house 190.5
  mansion 190.7
  tower 206.11
  head 210.5
  ceiling 227.6
  arch 251.4
  verbs roof 227.23
  arch 251.6
Domesday book
    568.10
domestic
  nouns 748.7
  adjs. household 188.8
  stay-at-home 922.11
domesticality 188.3
domestic animals
    413.1
domesticate
  settle down 183.18
  naturalize 188.5
domesticated 188.9

domestication 188.4
domestic economy
  husbandry 745.6
  economics 849.4
domesticity 188.3
domesticize 188.5
domicile
  nouns 190.1
  verbs reside 187.8
  house 187.11
domiciled 187.15
domiciliary 190.27
domiciliate
  domicile 187.8
  house 187.11
  domesticate 188.5
domiciliated
  housed 187.5
  domesticated 188.9
domiciliation
  housing 187.3
  domestication 188.4
domina 420.5
dominance
  influence 171.1
  dominion 737.5
dominant
  nouns note 462.14
  music 462.15
  adjs. chief 36.16
  influential 171.14
  most important
    670.25
  ruling 739.17
dominate
  rise above 206.16
  govern 739.14
domination
  influence 171.1
  scope of vision 443.3
  dominion 737.5
  control 739.2
  domineering 739.10
dominations 1013.3
domineer 739.15
domineering
  nouns 739.10
  adjs. masterful 737.15
  arrogant 910.11
Dominican 1036.17
dominie 563.1
dominion sphere 179.2
  country 180.1
  authority 737.5
  control 739.2
dominions 1013.3
dominium 806.2
domino 616.10
domitable 763.14
domus 190.1
Don 419.7
don
  nouns man 419.5
  teacher 563.1
  nobleman 916.4
  verbs 230.42
Dona, Doña 420.8
dona, doña
  woman 420.5
  noblewoman 916.7
Donar See Thor

double Dutch
  unintelligibility 547.6
  jargon 578.6
double-dye 361.13
double eagle 833.5
double-edged
  acrimonious 160.12
  sharp 257.11
double-entendre
  ambiguity 548.2
  joke 879.6
  witticism 879.8
double entente
  ambiguity 548.2
  witticism 879.8
double entry 843.5
double-faced
  double 91.3
  falsehearted 614.31
double fin 99.6
doubleganger 1015.3
double-header 876.9
doublehearted 614.31
double image 344.5
double march 272.15
double meaning 548.1
double-minded
  falsehearted 614.31
  irresolute 625.9
double-O 438.6
double-page spread
  557.6
double personality
  psychosis 472.4
  dissociation 688.27
double-prop 279.2
double-quick
  nouns 272.15
  GO ON THE DOUBLE-
    QUICK 300.12
  adjs. 268.19
  IN DOUBLE-QUICK
    TIME 268.21
double-reef 274.52
doubles 876.9
double sap 797.5
double sawbuck 99.7
doublet 90.2
double talk
  gibberish 545.4
  jargon 578.6
double time 272.15
  IN DOUBLE TIME
    268.21
double-tongued
  614.31
doubletree 220.5
doubling
  duplication 91.1
  lining 227.20
  fold 263.1
doubloon 833.5
doublure 227.20
doubly 91.4
doubt
  nouns skepticism
    502.2
  uncertainty 513.2
  apprehension 889.3
  jealousy 951.2
  irreligion 1029.6

BEYOND A SHADOW
  OF DOUBT 512.16
BEYOND DOUBT
  512.25
HAVE NO DOUBT
  believe 500.11
  be certain 512.9
HAVE ONE'S DOUBTS
  doubt 502.6
  be uncertain 513.9
IN DOUBT
  doubting 502.9
  uncertain 513.15
NO DOUBT
  probably 510.7
  certainly 512.25
THROW DOUBT UPON
  502.6
WITHOUT DOUBT
  undoubting 500.18
  certainly 512.25
verbs be doubtful
  502.6
  be uncertain 513.9
  be jealous 951.3
DOUBT NOT
  believe 500.11
  be certain 512.9
DOUBT ONE'S WORD
  502.6
I DOUBT NOT 500.26
I DOUBT THAT! 502.14
doubtable
  unbelievable 502.10
  improbable 511.3
  questionable 513.15
doubted 502.12
doubter 1029.12
doubtful
  skeptical 502.9
  unbelievable 502.10
  improbable 511.3
  uncertain 513.15
  precarious 695.11
  infidel 1029.20
  BE DOUBTFUL 502.6
doubting 502.9
doubting Thomas
  1029.12
doubtless
  adjs. believing 500.18
  certain 512.16
  advs. probably 510.7
  unquestionably
    512.25
doubtsome
  doubting 502.9
  uncertain 513.15
douche
  nouns syringe 391.8
  washing 679.4
  verbs sprinkle 391.12
  drench 391.13
  syringe 679.18
dough pliancy 356.4
  semiliquid 388.5
  money 833.2
doughboy
  dumpling 306a.33
  soldier 798.8
doughface 625.5

dough-faced
  influenceable 171.15
  pliant 356.9
doughhead 470.4
doughiness 388.2
doughnut 306a.43
doughtiness 891.1
doughty strong 158.13
  courageous 891.17
doughy soft 356.12
  viscid 388.12
  pulpy 389.6
dour severe 755.6
  harsh 937.22
douse
  nouns 282.4
  verbs doff 231.6
  strike 282.14
  dip 318.7
  extinguish 331.7
dousing
  submergence 318.2
  extinguishment
    331.2
dout 331.7
Dove, the 1011.14
dove
  unsophisticate 734.3
  innocent 982.4
dove-colored 365.3
dovecot, dovecote
  190.20
dovelike 982.6
dovetail
  nouns 47.4
  verbs interlock 13.7
  fit 26.9,12
  fasten 47.8
dovetailed 250.6
dowager matron 420.5
  widow 933.4
dowdiness 62.6
dowdy
  nouns slattern 62.7
  pastry 306a.40
  adjs. 62.14
dower
  nouns talent 731.4
  endowment 816.9
  verbs 816.17
dowered 816.25
dowhacky 375.4
down
  nouns hill 206.5
  hair 229.8
  feather 229.16
  fluffy 229.19
  descent 314.1
  lightness 352.3
  softness 356.4
  plain 386.1
  misfortune 727.3
  verbs swallow 306.20
  descend 314.5
  fell 316.5
  be credulous 501.5
  endure 859.7
  NOT BE ABLE TO
    DOWN 503.3
  adjs. lower 207.8
  descending 314.11

ill 684.41
  defeated 725.14
DOWN AT THE HEELS
  slovenly 62.14
  shabby 690.31
  poor 836.8
DOWN IN THE
  MOUTH
  ill 684.41
  dejected 870.22
DOWN ON ONE'S LUCK
  727.14
DOWN PAT 474.26
DOWN THE DRAIN
  852.9
  advs. downward
    314.13
  cash ∼ 839.25
BE DOWN ON 927.9
DOWN THE ALLEY
  249.7
DOWN THE HATCH
  994.47
DOWN THE WIND
  274.68
DOWN TO 105.10
DOWN TO THE
  GROUND 56.18
GO DOWN SWINGING
  723.9
GO DOWN WITH
  859.9
GO DOWN WITH
  FLYING COLORS
  persevere 623.6
  resist 790.5
downable 500.21
down-and-out
  nouns 836.4
  adjs. 836.9
downbear 316.4
downbeat 462.25
downcast
  nouns 316.2
  adjs. downturned
    314.12
  lowered 316.10
  dejected 870.22
  WITH DOWNCAST
    EYES 906.15
downcome 314.1
downcoming 314.11
downcurve 284.4
down East 179.7
down-Easter 189.11
downfall
  descent 314.1
  rain 393.2
  ruin 691.3
  failure 723.3
  defeat 725.1
downfalling 314.11
downflow
  descent 314.1
  rain 393.2
  flow 394.4
downgate 218.5
downgoing 314.11
downgrade
  nouns 218.5

ON THE DOWNGRADE
690.44
verbs reduce 39.7
demote 780.4
adjs. 218.16
advs. slantingly
218.24
down 314.13
downgrading 780.2
downhanging 314.12
downhearted 870.22
downhill
nouns 218.5
adjs. 218.16
advs. slantingly
218.24
down 314.13
GO DOWNHILL
weaken 159.9
slope 218.10
deteriorate 690.18
be unfortunate
727.11
downiness 356.1
down left, down
right, etc. 609.20
downline 314.13
down payment 839.1
downpour
descent 314.1
rain 393.2
flow 394.4
down-reaching 314.11
downright
adjs. utter 34.14
thorough 56.10
vertical 212.10
unqualified 507.2
candid 972.17
advs. absolutely 34.21
down 314.13
downrush 314.1
downs 386.1
downside 211.1
downsinking 314.11
downstairs
below 207.11
down 314.13
downstream 314.3
downstreet 314.13
downthrow
overthrow 219.2
precipitation 316.2
downthrown 316.10
down-to-earth 534.6
downtown
nouns 182.5
adjs. 182.9
advs. 314.13
downtrend, downturn
decline 39.2
downturn 314.1
downtrod 762.15
downtrodden 762.15
downturned 314.12
down under 179.6
downward
adjs. 314.11
advs. 314.13
down-wash 277.36
down-wind 277.49

downwith 314.13
downy
nouns 215.20
adjs. feathery 229.27
nappy 350.7
soft 356.14
dowry talent 731.4
dower 816.9
dowser 1033.5
dowse sail 274.52
dowsing rod 541.3
doxologize 1030.11
doxology
music 461.16
paean 1030.3
doxy 987.17
doyen senior 127.5
dean 747.3
doze
nouns 710.3
verbs 710.13
DOZE OFF 710.15
dozen 99.7
dozer 271.16
dozy 710.19
drab
nouns small amount
35.2
slattern 62.7
strumpet 987.14
adjs. dull 336.19
brown 366.3
drabble draggle 214.6
befoul 680.21
drabbled 680.23
drabbletail 62.7
drabbletailed 62.14
drabness 336.6
drachma 833.9
Draconian 937.24
draff dregs 43.2
refuse 667.4
offal 680.9
draft, draught
nouns depth 208.5
pull 285.2
drink 306.4
air current 402.1
music score 461.28
drawing 572.14
compendium 605.1
diagram 652.3
dose 685.5
big demand 751.1
conscription 778.6
recruits 798.17
money order 833.11
dram 994.6
verbs draw off 304.10
draw 572.20
draw up 600.22
outline 652.12
conscript 778.14
draftee 798.17
draft horse 413.18
drafting, draughting
drawing off 304.2
drawing 572.6
draftsman,
draughtsman 577.3

drafty, draughty
402.26
drag
nouns influence
171.2
retardation 269.4
aviation 277.33
smoke 433.11
road 655.6
curb 728.7
PUT ON THE DRAG
269.9
verbs escort 73.8
linger on 110.7
trail 214.6
smooth 259.5
go slow 269.6
lag 269.8
pull 285.4
lag behind 292.4
smoke 433.15
drawl 593.6
DRAG BEFORE THE
PUBLIC 557.11
DRAG DOWN
receive 817.6
draw wages 839.20
DRAG IN
foist in 10.4
interpose 236.7
DRAG INTO 175.2
DRAG INTO COURT
1002.12
DRAG ON
linger on 110.7
continue 143.3
DRAG ONE'S FEET
269.6
DRAG OUT
protract 110.9
lengthen 201.9
go slow 269.6
elicit 304.12
expatiate 591.8
DRAG THROUGH THE
MUD 969.10
DRAG UP 315.8
dragged-out
protracted 110.11
lengthened 210.12
run-down 684.40
dragging slow 269.11
drawling 593.11
draggle trail 214.6
drag 285.4
befoul 680.21
draggled
bedraggled 62.14
fouled 680.23
draggletail 62.7
draggletailed 62.14
dragnet snare 616.12
catching 820.2
dragnet clause 740.19
dragoman
interpreter 550.8
guide 746.6
dragon monster 85.20
violent person 161.9
sorehead 949.11

dragonnade,
dragoonade 796.4
dragoon
nouns 798.12
verbs coerce 754.7
intimidate 889.19
drag sail, drag sheet
728.7
drain
nouns outflow 302.4
channel 395.5
consumption 664.1
sewer 680.12
big demand 751.1
loss 810.2
verbs run out 302.13
draft off 304.10
evacuate 308.20
filter 354.6
consume 664.2
take all 820.21
DRAIN OF RESOURCES
664.2
DRAIN THE CUP
drink 306.27
tipple 994.29
drainage outflow 302.4
draining 304.2
emptying 308.6
drying 392.3
drained empty 186.12
used up 664.6
draining
drafting 304.2
emptying 308.6
filtering 354.3
drainpipe 395.6
drake duck 413.35
male animal 419.8
drakestone 383.4
dram
nouns small amount
35.2
drink 306.4
~ of liquor 994.6
verbs 994.29
drama
music ~ 461.35
the stage 609
play 609.4
dramalogue 609.4
dramatic vocal 461.51
poetic 607.21
pretentious 902.24
dramatic(al) 609.37
dramaticism 609.2
dramatics
oratory 597.1
theatrics 609.2
dramatis personae
610.11
dramatist 609.26
dramatize
theatricalize 609.32
play up 670.15
dramatizer
dramatist 609.26
actor 610.1
dramaturge 609.26
dramaturgic 609.37
dramaturgist 609.26

~ the wounds
687.33
prepare 718.6
decorate 899.7
whip 1008.15
DRESS DOWN
scold 967.18
whip 1008.15
DRESS IN 230.42
DRESS UP
dress 230.41
falsify 614.16
decorate 899.7
dress circle 609.19
dressed 230.44
DRESSED UP 230.45
dresser
decorator 577.11
therapist 686.14
dressing
fertilizer 164.4
clothing 230.1
food 306a.37
cultivation 412.13
medical ~ 685.28
reproof 967.6
whipping 1008.5
dressing rooms 609.20
dressmaker
seamstress 222.2
garmentmaker
230.35
dressmaking 230.31
dress rehearsal 609.13
dress suit 230.11
dress-ups 230.10
dressy stylish 642.13
showy 902.19
dribble
nouns drip 302.5
slobber 310.3
trickle 394.7
nonsense 545.4
verbs leak 302.14
slobber 310.6
trickle 394.19
driblet 35.5
IN DRIBLETS 55.8
dribs-like
piecemeal 55.8
sparsely 102.8
dried 392.9
DRIED UP
withered 197.13
dried 392.9
wasted 690.34
drier paint ~ 361.7
desiccator 392.4
drift
nouns flock 74.5
heap 74.9
trend 173.2
course 266.2
deposit 270.8
aviation 277.34
direction 289.1
deviation 290.1
radio 343.24
stream 394.4
meaning 543.1
GET THE DRIFT 546.7

ON THE DRIFT 272.41
verbs heap 74.18
wander 272.22
sail 274.31
float 274.57
soar 277.42
stray 290.4
idle 706.13
DRIFT ALONG 293.3
DRIFT AWAY 296.2
driftage course 266.2
stream 394.4
drift anchor, drift
sail 728.7
drifter wanderer 273.2
fisherman 653.6
drifting
nouns 290.1
adjs. 272.36
driftless 155.16
driftway 274.9
driftwood 377.3
drill
nouns types of tools
347.15
training 560.3
exercise 714.6
verbs excavate 256.15
bore 264.15
plant 412.18
train 560.13
rehearse 609.36
driller
excavator 256.10
miner 382.8
trainer 563.7
drilling 560.3
drillmaster 563.7
drink
nouns draft 306.4
beverage 306a.47
ocean 396.1
~ of liquor 994.6
intoxicant 994.12
types of mixed ~
994.51
~ offering 1030.7
GIVEN TO DRINK
994.44
verbs absorb 305.13
quaff 306.27
tipple 994.29
DRINK IN
absorb 305.13
drink 306.27
pay attention 528.5
learn 562.7
DRINK TO 994.35
DRINK UP
absorb 305.13
drink 306.27
be dry 392.5
tipple 994.29
drinkable
nouns 306a.47
adjs. 306.32
drinking
nouns imbibing 306.3
tippling 994.4
adjs. 994.44
drinking bout 994.5

drinking song 461.13
drinking water 391.3
drip
nouns leak 302.5
trickle 394.7
bore 882.4
verbs leak 302.14
be damp 391.11
trickle 394.19
dripping
nouns leakage 302.5
trickle 394.7
adjs. 391.17
dripple 394.19
dripproof 392.11
drippy 393.10
drisk drizzle 393.1
mist 403.1
drive
nouns herd 74.5
crusade 152.10
energy 160.2
ride 272.7
obsession 472.13
urge 646.6
driveway 655.6
enterprise 705.7
haste 707.1
campaign 742.13
military ~ 795.8
attack 796.1
GO FOR A DRIVE
272.32
verbs operate 163.5
excavate 256.15
ride 272.32
make leeway 274.31
pilot 277.43
impel 282.11
thrust 282.12
propel 284.10
herd 415.7
obsess 472.23
fish 653.10
work 714.16
guide 745.9
compel 754.4
DRIVE A BARGAIN
825.14
DRIVE AHEAD 293.4
DRIVE AT 651.4
DRIVE AWAY
disperse 75.6
repulse 288.2
DRIVE BACK
repulse 288.2
fend off 797.10
DRIVE CRAZY 472.22
DRIVE HOME TO
500.15
DRIVE IN 303.6
DRIVE INTO ONE'S
HEAD 535.18
DRIVE ON
forge ahead 293.4
urge on 646.16
be industrious
705.12
hasten 707.4
DRIVE OUT 308.13
DRIVE STAKES

settle 183.18
camp 187.12
DRIVE THE PEN
600.19
DRIVE TO DESPERA-
TION 887.11
DRIVE TOGETHER
74.17
DRIVE TO RUIN
691.24
DRIVE TO THE WALL
729.15
drive-in
restaurant 306.14
theater 609.18
market 830.1
drivel
nouns slobber 310.3
nonsense 545.4
verbs slobber 310.6
be insane 472.19
talk nonsense 545.8
DRIVEL AWAY 852.5
driveler dotard 470.9
chatterer 594.5
driveling 468.22
driver operator 163.4
reinsman 273.9
propeller 284.7
taskmaster 747.15
driver's seat 737.9
BE IN THE DRIVER'S
SEAT 745.9
driveway 655.6
driving
nouns operation
163.1
travel 272.6
adjs. impelling
282.22
propulsive 284.15
obsessing 472.33
motivating 646.25
compulsory 754.9
KEEP DRIVING
persevere 623.2
be industrious
705.14
drizzle
nouns 393.1
verbs 393.9
drizzling, drizzly
393.10
droich 195.6
droit 956.3
droll amusing 878.5
witty 879.15
drollery, drollness
humorousness
878.1
wit 879.3
drome 277.19
dromedary
beast of burden
270.6
animal 413.5
dromomania 472.12
drone
nouns slow goer
269.5
bee 413a.4

voice 462.5
note 462.14
bagpipe 464.10
nonworker 706.9
verbs 451.13
droning
nouns 451.7
adjs. 451.20
dronish, drony 706.17
drool
nouns slobber 310.3
nonsense 545.4
verbs slobber 310.6
be insane 472.19
talk nonsense
545.8
droop
nouns weakling 159.6
hang 214.2
gait 272.14
sinkage 314.2
bore 882.4
verbs weaken 159.9
hang 214.6
decline 314.6
sicken 684.35
wilt 690.19
tire 715.5
despond 870.16
drooping loose 51.5
weak 159.12
languishing 159.21
hanging 214.10
descending 314.11
deteriorating 690.43
fatigued 715.6
dejected 870.22
drop
nouns small amount
35.5
advantage 36.2
pause 144.3
declivity 218.5
sphere 254.3
drip 302.5
descent 314.1
plunge 318.1
trickle 394.7
letter ~ 602.7
stage ~ 609.24
degradation 690.3
dram 994.6
gallows 1009.5
AT THE DROP OF THE
HAT
first 68.16
willingly 620.8
DROP BY DROP
gradually 29.6
piecemeal 55.8
DROP IN THE BUCKET
small amount 35.6
pittance 660.5
trifle 671.5
DROP IN THE EYE
994.6
GET THE DROP ON
aim at 289.6
have advantage
36.11
draw a gun 796.22

HAVE A DROP TOO
MUCH 994.33
verbs outdistance
36.9
weaken 159.9
lay eggs 166.18
give birth 166.19
slope 218.10
shoot down 284.13
leak 302.14
descend 314.5
fell 316.5
let ~ 316.7
plunge 318.6
gravitate 351.15
trickle 394.19
kill 408.18
faint 422.4
give up 631.7
break a habit 641.3
disuse 666.4
get tired 715.5
lose 810.5
relinquish 812.3
DROP A BOMB 796.25
DROP ANCHOR 183.18
DROP DEAD 407.18
DROP EVERYTHING
144.6
DROP FROM THE
CLOUDS 538.6
DROP IN
enter 301.7
visit 920.16
DROP IN ONE'S TRACKS
kill 408.18
sicken 684.34
DROP IN UPON 538.7
DROP IT
cease 144.6
stop it! 144.14
no matter 671.22
DROP OFF
decrease 39.6
fall off 314.5
die 407.16
fall asleep 710.15
DROP ON 314.10
DROP ONE'S EYES
438.21
DROP THE CURTAIN
70.7
DROP THE SUBJECT
529.4
LET DROP
drop 316.7
divulge 554.6
drop curtain 609.24
drop-dry proof 158.18
seaworthy 276.15
watertight 392.11
drop-forge 245.6
drop game 616.9
drophead 483.2
drop kick 282.9
drop-kick 282.20
droplet drop 35.5
sphere 254.3
dropped 39.10
dropping
nouns 314.1

adjs. sloping 218.16
descending 314.11
droppings 309.4
drops 685.4
dropsical
swollen 196.12
diseased 684.46
dropsy swelling 196.2
disease 684.8
dross dregs 43.2
slag 328.16
drought, drouth
dryness 392.1
thirst 632.7
droughty, drouthy
dry 392.7
thirsty 632.27
drouk 391.13
drove
nouns 74.5
verbs 415.7
drover 415.3
drown submerge 318.7
die 407.20
kill 408.19
muffle 450.9
come to grief 727.10
DROWN CARE 876.24
DROWN ONE'S
SORROWS 994.29
DROWN THE
SHAMROCK 994.31
drowned 407.26
drowning death 407.5
killing 408.6
drowse
nouns 710.3
verbs 710.13
DROWSE OFF 710.15
drowsiness
languor 706.5
sleepiness 710.1
drowsy
soothing 162.15
sleepy 710.19
drub
nouns blow 282.4
stamp 282.10
verbs stamp 282.2
pound 282.15
defeat 725.6
beat 1008.14
drubbing defeat 725.1
beating 1008.4
drudge
nouns cabin boy
275.6
toiler 716.3
verbs 714.14
drudgery 714.4
drudging 714.18
drug
nouns
superabundance
661.2
medicine 685.4
narcotic 685.10
types of ~ 685.44–
56
commodity 829.2

verbs adulterate
44.13
anesthetize 422.3
oversupply 661.15
medicate 687.34
drug addict 640.9
drug addiction
psychosis 472.3
addiction 640.8
druggery 685.31
drugging 44.3
druggist 685.30
drugstore
pharmacy 685.31
store 830.5
druid prophet 541.4
priest 1036.15
druid stone 383.1
drum
nouns dive 190.24
cylinder 254.4
beat 454.1
tympan 464.21
tea party 920.11
verbs repeat 103.10
pulsate 322.11
beat 454.4
beat time 461.45
DRUM OUT 308.13
drumbeat 454.1
drum corps
drummer 463.10
military 798.20
drumfire 796.10
drumhead
eardrum 447.7
music 464.21
drumhead courtmartial
999.7
drumlin 206.5
drum major
conductor 463.19
officer 747.23
drummer
musician 463.10
salesman 828.5
drumming
nouns pulsation
322.3
beating 454.1
adjs. 454.7
drums 463.10
drumskin 464.21
drumstick
thigh 272.16
food 306a.23
music 464.21
drunk
nouns spree 994.5
drunkard 994.11
GO ON A DRUNK
994.34
adjs. fervent 853.22
inebriated 994.38
GET DRUNK 994.32
drunkard addict 640.9
tippler 994.10
drunken
verbs 994.32
adjs. inebriated
994.38

bibulous 994.44
drunkenness
  intemperance 991
  intoxication 994.1
druther 635.4
dry
  nouns 990.5
  verbs drain 304.10
  dehydrate 392.6
  preserve 699.8
  exhaust 820.21
  DRY UP
  sear 197.9
  dry 392.6
  shut up! 450.17
  be used up 664.4
  deteriorate 690.19
  adjs. unfertile 165.4
  barren 186.12
  arid 392.7
  unsweet 431.6
  hoarse 457.14
  unimaginative 534.5
  plain-speaking 589.3
  thirsty 632.27
  sarcastic 965.13
  dull 881.6
  antisaloon 990.11
  DRY BEHIND THE
    EARS 731.26
  NOT DRY BEHIND
    THE EARS
  immature 124.10
  inexperienced
    732.17
dryad 1012.16
dryasdust
  antiquarian 123.5
  bore 882.4
dry-as-dust 881.6
dry-clean 679.17
dry cleaner 679.13
dry cleaning 679.2
dry-cure 699.8
dry-curing 699.2
dry dock 698.6
dry-farm 412.16
dry goods
  fabrics 377.5
  merchandise 829.3
dry ice ice 332.6
  refrigerant 333.7
  cloud seeding 393.5
drying
  nouns desiccation
    392.3
  preservation 699.2
  adjs. 392.10
dry land 384.1
  ON DRY LAND 384.11
dry measure 489.5
dry nurse
  tutor 563.6
  nurse 697.7
  assistant 785.6
dry-nurse
  feed 306.16
  train 550.13
  nurture 783.16
dry point
  engraving 576.2

graver 576.11
dry rot blight 674.2
  decay 690.6
dry run aviation 277.8
  rehearsal 488.3
  war 795.9
dry-salt 699.8
dry storage 658.5
duad 90.2
duadic 90.6
dual two 90.6
  double 91.3
dual-control trainer
  279.10
dualism duality 90.1
  philosophy 499.6
  ditheism 1018.5
dualist 1018.14
dualistic 90.6
duality 90
dually 91.4
dual personality
  psychosis 472.4
  dissociation 688.27
duarchy 739.4
dub
  nouns double 20.5
  duplicate 24.3
  substitute 148.2
  clumsy fellow 732.9
  verbs copy 22.8
  double 91.2
  smooth 259.5
  name 581.11
  DUB IN 148.4
dubash 779.2
duberous, dubersome
  502.9
dubiety
  skepticism 502.2
  uncertainty 513.2
dubious
  skeptical 502.9
  uncertain 513.15
  precarious 695.11
  infidel 1029.20
  BE DUBIOUS 502.6
dubitable
  unbelievable 502.10
  improbable 511.3
  uncertain 513.15
dubitant 1029.12
dubitation 513.2
dubitative 513.15
ducal 916.11
ducat 833.5
duce 747.3
duchess 916.7
duchy 180.1
duck
  nouns naught 2.2
  oddity 85.4
  seaplane 279.8
  dodge 283.3
  food 306a.22
  plunge 318.2
  fowl 413.35
  person 416.3
  man 419.5
  evasion 629.1
  bedpan 680.14

endearment 930.5
  verbs absent oneself
    186.8
  draw back 283.7
  dip 318.7
  fight shy 621.4
  dodge 629.8
  DUCK AND RUN 629.11
  DUCK DUTY 629.9
  DUCK OUT
  flee 629.11
  slip away 629.12
duck fit 950.8
ducking 318.2
ducking stool 1009.3
duckling child 125.3
  youngling 125.8
  duck 306a.22
  endearment 930.5
duck soup 730.3
duct channel 395.1
  anatomy 395.13
ductibility 356.2
ductile pliant 356.9
  elastic 357.7
ductility
  pliancy 356.2
  elasticity 357.1
dud
  nouns nullity 4.2
  impotent 157.6
  garment 230.3
  false alarm 702.4
  failure 723.5,8
  shell 799.14
  verbs 230.38
dude tourist 273.1
  dandy 901.9
Dudelsack 464.10
dude ranch 412.8
dudgeon 950.7
duds clothing 230.1,
  2,5
  belongings 808.2
due
  nouns debt 838.1
  charge 844.7
  right 956.3
  one's ∼ 958.2
  adjs. expected 537.11
  adequate 659.6
  expedient 668.4
  owing 838.10
  right 956.8
  coming to 958.7
  just 974.8
  BE DUE TO
  result from 153.6
  be entitled 958.4
  DUE TO
  resulting from 153.8
  attributable 154.5
  because of 154.9
  entitled to 958.10
  advs. 289.25
  IN DUE COURSE
  in time 121.11
  opportunity 129.13
  after a while 131.16
  IN DUE FORM 644.11

IN DUE TIME
  in time 121.11
  opportunely 129.13
  early enough 131.12
  soon 131.16
due bill 833.11
duel
  nouns 794.7
  verbs 794.14
duelist 798.1
dueness
  expedience 668.1
  entitlement 958
duenna chaperon 73.5
  instructress 563.2
  guardian 697.6
dues debt 838.1
  charge 844.7
  deserts 958.3
  GET ONE'S DUES
    958.6
due season 129.3
duet, duettino 461.17
duettist 463.1
duff
  nouns 306a.45
  verbs 614.17
duffel 657.4
duffer oddity 85.4
  dolt 470.3
  sham 614.13
  clumsy fellow 732.9
  thief 823.9
  counterfeiter 833.24
duffy 1015.1
dug 255.6
dugout cave 256.5
  shelter 698.3
  military ∼ 797.5
duit 833.9
duke 916.5
dukedom
  country 180.1
  nobility 916.10
dukes 811.4
dulcet musical 461.49
  pleasant 861.7
dulciana 464.23
dulcification
  mollification 162.2
  softening 356.5
dulcify mollify 162.7
  soften 356.6
  calm 802.7
dulcimer 464.3
Dulcinea 929.12
dulia 1030.1
dull
  verbs weaken 159.10
  moderate 162.6
  blunt 258.2
  dim 336.11
  decolor 362.5
  deaden 422.3
  muffle 450.9
  ∼ the feelings 854.7
  relieve 884.5
  adjs. weak 159.12
  blunt 258.3
  inert 267.12
  lackluster 336.19

gray 365.3
insensitive 422.5
muffled 451.17
stupid 468.16
unimaginative 534.5
expressionless 545.11
plain-speaking 589.3
listless 706.18
unfeeling 854.9,13
uninteresting 881.6
tedious 882.8
dullard
 nouns 470.3
 adjs. 468.15
dull-brained 468.16
dulled blunted 258.3
 muffled 451.17
dull-edged 258.3
dullhead 470.3
dull-headed 468.16
dullification 258.1
dullify 258.2
dulling
 nouns weakening 159.5
 moderation 162.2
 relief 884.1
 adjs. mitigating 162.14
 deadening 422.8
 relieving 884.9
dullish 258.3
dullness
 weakness 159.1
 bluntness 258.1
 lackluster 336.6
 grayness 365.1
 numbness 422.1
 muffled sound 451.2
 stupidity 468.3
 unimaginativeness 534.1
 languor 706.5
 apathy 854.1,4
 uninterestingness 881
 tediousness 882.2
dull-sighted 439.13
dull thud thud 451.3
 failure 723.2
dull-witted 468.16
dully 470.3
duly 958.11
dumb
 inanimate 381.5
 mute 450.14
 stupid 468.15
 foolish 469.8
 ignorant 476.13
 taciturn 611.7
 NOT SO DUMB 466.12
dumb animal 413.2
dumbbell dolt 470.3
 exerciser 714.7
 NO DUMBBELL 466.14
dumb-bunny 470.3
dumbness
 muteness 450.2

stupidity 468.3
tacitumity 611.2
dumb show
 gesture 566.13
 drama 609.4
 IN DUMB SHOW 566.23
dumb trick folly 469.4
 blunder 517.5
dumbwaiter 315.5
dumdum bullet 799.14
dumfound
 strike dumb 450.8
 astonish 918.5
dumfounded 918.8
dummy
 nouns nonentity 4.2
 model 25.5
 substitute 148.2
 mute 450.3
 dolt 470.3
 figure 570.4
 printing 601.4
 sham 614.13
 figurehead 747.4
 deputy 779.1
 sleeping partner 785.2
 playing card 876.17
 adjs. substitute 148.8
 sham 614.27
dummy up 450.6
dump
 nouns hovel 190.10
 dive 190.24
 storehouse 658.6
 wasteyard 667.6
 filthy place 680.11
 armory 799.2
 verbs unload 308.21
 discard 666.7
 sell 827.8
 sell stock 831.24
dumpcart 271.3
dumpiness 202.2
dumpish glum 870.26
 sullen 949.24
dumpling
 fat man 194.12
 food 306a.33
dumps 870.6
 IN THE DUMPS 870.22
dumpy 202.10
dun
 nouns dunner 837.4
 bill 843.3
 verbs importune 772.12
 bill 843.11
 adjs. dull 336.19
 brown 366.3
dunce 470.3
dunderhead 470.4
dun-drab 366.3
dune 206.5
dung
 nouns 309.4
 verbs 309.11
dungeon 759.9

dunghill
 nouns 680.10
 adjs. 890.12
dunghill fowl 413.35
dungy 309.18
dunk 318.7
dunnage 808.3
dunner 837.4
dunning 772.3
duo 461.17
duodecillion 99.13
duodecimal 99.24
duodecimo
 nouns miniature 195.5
 book size 603.15
 adjs. 195.11
duodenal
 twelfth 99.24
 intestinal 224.12
duodenotomy 687.26
duodenum 224.6
duologue 609.4
duomo 1040.2
dupability 501.2
dupable 501.8
dupe
 nouns duplicate 24.3
 gullible person 618.1
 cat's-paw 656.3
 verbs duplicate 22.8
 copy 91.2
 repeat 103.7
 deceive 616.13
dupery 616.1
duple 91.3
duple time 462.23
duplex
 nouns 190.12
 adjs. double 91.3
 ambiguous 548.3
duplexity 90.1
duplicate
 nouns counterpart 20.5
 copy 24.3
 IN DUPLICATE 22.12
 verbs copy 22.8
 double 91.2
 repeat 103.7
 adjs. identical 14.6
 analogous 20.11
 double 91.3
duplicated 103.12
duplication
 reproduction 22.3
 copy 24.3
 doubling 91
 repetition 103.1
duplicative 103.14
duplicature 263.1
duplicity duality 90.1
 falseheartedness 614.4
 deceitfulness 616.3
 treachery 973.6
duppy 1015.1
durability
 substantiality 3.1
 endurance 110

everlastingness 112
durable
 substantial 3.5
 enduring 110.10
 everlasting 112.7
durableness 110.1
durance 759.3
duration time 105.1
 term 107.3
 durability 110.1
 permanence 140.1
durbar hall 190.15
 council 753.1
 court 999.2
duress
 compulsion 754.1
 imprisonment 759.3
Durga 1012.7
during 105.8
durity 355.1
durwaun 697.11
dusk
 nouns 134.3
 verbs 336.13
 adjs. twilight 134.8
 dark 336.16
 dark-colored 364.9
duskiness
 darkness 336.4
 dark color 364.2
dusky twilighty 134.8
 dark 336.15,16
 dark-colored 364.9
dust
 nouns commotion 62.4
 lightness 352.3
 powder 360.5
 soil 384.1
 dryness 392.2
 corpse 407.13
 rubbish 667.5
 dirt 680.6
 money 833.2
 IN THE DUST
 humbled 904.11
 worshipful 1030.15
 RETURN TO DUST 407.15
 verbs powder 75.7
 decamp 300.11
 flee 629.11
 clean 679.17
 dirty 680.17
 DUST ONE'S DOUBLET 1008.16
dust bowl 181.1
dust devil 402.14,15
dustee 44.9
dust hole 667.6
dust jacket
 wrapper 227.19
 book cover 603.16
dustman street sweeper 679.15
 sandman 710.11
dust storm 402.14
dust-tight 265.12
dusty old 123.14
 powdery 360.11
 gray 365.3

shrill 457.13

earreach
short distance 199.2
earshot 447.4

earring band 252.3
ornament 899.6

earshot
short distance 199.2
earreach 447.4
OUT OF EARSHOT
out of range 198.22
sotto voce 451.22

ear-splitting 452.9

Earth 374.6

earth burrow 190.22
base 211.3
plane 213.3
world 374.7
land 384.1
corpse 407.13
ON EARTH 374.29

earthborn 917.11

earthenware 829.4

earth flax 331.5

earthling person 416.3
irreligionist 1029.10

earthly worldly 374.27
materialistic 375.11
terrestrial 384.6
possible 508.6
unspiritual 1029.16

earth metals 382.3

earthnut 410.20

earthquake 161.5

earth-shaking 452.9

earthwork 797.4

earthworm 413a.8

earthy earthly 374.27
terrestrial 384.6
coarse 896.11
unspiritual 1029.16

ear trumpet 447.8

earwig 555.10

earwitness 504.7

ease
nouns elegant style
587.1
eloquence 598.2
informality 645.1
leisure 708.1
rest 709.1
prosperity 726.1
facility 730.1
content 866.1
relief 884.1
comfort 885.1
AT EASE
at rest 709.11
contented 866.7
comfortable 885.12
WITH EASE 885.14
verbs abate 39.8
slacken 51.3
relax 162.9
lighten 352.6
soften 356.6
rest 709.7
facilitate 730.6
relieve 884.5
comfort 885.6

EASE OFF
slacken 51.3
relax 162.9
slow down 269.9
turn aside 290.6
rest 709.7
EASE THE RUDDER
274.33
EASE UP TO 295.3

easeful 885.11

easel 572.19

easement
lightening 352.4
estate 808.4
relief 884.1

ease-off, ease-up 269.4

easier said than done
729.16

easily slowly 269.13
softly 356.17
effortlessly 730.13
comfortably 885.14

easing
nouns relaxation
162.2
lightening 352.4
softening 356.5
facilitation 730.4
relief 884.1
adjs. mitigating
162.14
lightening 352.15
softening 356.16
relieving 884.9

East 179.6,7

east
nouns 289.3
verbs 289.9

eastbound 289.16

East End, East Side
182.5

Easter, Easter Sunday
1038.15

easter
nouns 402.9
verbs 289.9
adjs. 289.19

eastern 289.15

Easterner 417.8

Eastern time 114.3

Easter sepulcher
1040.9

East Indian 417.8

eastland 179.6,7

eastward 289.3,19

easy
adjs. loose 51.5
slow 269.10
light 352.11
soft 356.8
quietly 450.15
gullible 501.8
elegant 587.6
eloquent 598.9
unconcerned 634.6
informal 645.3
indolent 706.17
leisurely 708.6
prosperous 726.12
not hard 730.11
lenient 757.8

nonchalant 856.15
comfortable 885.11
at rest 885.12
loose-moraled
987.26
EASY COME, EASY GO
852.8
MAKE ONESELF EASY
ABOUT
convince oneself
500.16
make sure 512.11
persuade oneself
646.24
NOT EASY 729.16
advs. easily 730.13
cautiously 893.12

easygoing
dilatory 132.16
unconcerned 634.6
informal 645.3
easy 730.11
lenient 757.8
nonchalant 856.15
contented 866.7

easy mark 618.1

easy market 831.2

easy-paced 269.10

Easy Street 726.1

easy virtue 987.4

eat feed 306.17
etch 576.15
consume 664.2
corrode 690.22
tolerate 859.7
EAT CROW, EAT
HUMBLE PIE
recant 626.9
be submissive
763.11
humble oneself
904.6
EAT LIKE A BIRD
306.24
EAT LIKE A HORSE
feast 306.22
be greedy 992.5
EAT ONE'S CAKE AND
HAVE IT TOO 668.3
EAT ONE'S HEART OUT
870.17
EAT ONE'S WORDS
626.9
EAT OUT OF HOUSE
AND HOME
eat much 306.22
exhaust 820.21
impoverish 836.6
be gluttonous 992.5
EAT OUT OF ONE'S
HAND 763.6
EAT THE WIND OUT
OF 274.28
EAT UP
devour 306.20
be credulous 501.5
consume 664.2
delight in 863.10
NOT EAT 993.4

eatable 306.31

eatables 306a.1

eater diner 306.13
glutton 992.3
gourmand 992.4

eatery 306.14

eating feeding 306
gluttony 992

eats 306a.2

eau 391.3

Eau de Cologne 435.3

eau sucrée 430.4

eaves 227.6

eavesdrop
nouns 394.7
verbs 447.11

eavesdropper
listener 447.5
inquisitive 526.2

ébauche
drawing 572.14
draught 652.3

ebb
nouns decline 39.2
deterioration 690.3
AT A LOW EBB
under par 37.9
low 207.10
lowered 316.10
insufficient 660.7
ill 684.41
impaired 690.35
verbs decrease 39.6
recede 296.2
flow back 394.17
deteriorate 690.18
adjs. 209.5

ebb and flow
nouns alternation
322.4
tides 394.13
verbs alternate
322.12
surge 394.23

ebbing 296.5

ebb tide
low water 207.2
tide 394.13

ebenezer 1040.1

Eblis 1014.5

E-boat 276.7

ebon 364.4

ebony
nouns black 364.1
Negro 417.7
adjs. 364.8

ebullience, ebulliency
boiling 328.2
effervescence 404.3

ebullient
boiling 327.25
effervescent 404.6
excited 855.23

**ebulliometer, ebul-
lioscope** 328.2

ebullition
turbulence 161.2
agitation 323.1
boiling 328.2
effervescence 404.3
excitement 855.3

education
re-education 145.3
learning 474.4
instruction 560.1
educational
informative 555.17
instructive 560.18
pedagogical 563.12
scholarly 564.10
educational film
609.15
educational
institution 565.1
educative 560.18
educator 563.1
educatress 563.2
educe 304.12
eduction
deduction 42.6
elicitation 304.4
eductive 304.15
edulcorate 430.5
edulcoration 679.2
Eduskunta 740.3
eel coil 253.2
food 306a.24
eellike 253.7
eerie, eery
deathlike 407.23
scary 889.22
fearful 889.30
spooky 1015.9
efface 691.16
EFFACE FROM THE
MEMORY 536.6
EFFACE ONESELF
906.7
effacement 691.7
effect
nouns result 153
force 156.1
influence 171.1
appearance 445.3
meaning 543.1
HAVE EFFECT 163.8
IN EFFECT
actually 1.16
essentially 5.10
OF NO EFFECT 723.17
PUT INTO EFFECT
703.9
TO GOOD EFFECT
663.25
WITH TELLING
EFFECT 156.14
verbs cause 152.11
induce 152.12
do 703.6
accomplish 720.4
execute 769.10
effected 720.9
effective
cogent 156.11
able 156.13
operative 163.10
influential 171.13
eloquent 598.11
effectual 663.20
expedient 668.5
effectiveness
force 156.1

eloquence 598.3
effective pitch 277.31
effects property 808.1
wares 829.1
effectual able 156.13
operative 163.10
influential 171.13
valid 515.12
useful 663.20
effectuate
produce 166.11
bring about 703.6
accomplish 720.4
execute 769.10
effectuation
production 166.1
performance 703.2
accomplishment
720.1
execution 769.5
effeminacy
homosexuality
418.10
womanishness
420.2
effeminate
nouns 420.11
verbs 420.13
adjs. homosexual
418.23
womanish 420.15
effeminize
castrate 42.11
unman 157.12
feminize 420.13
effendi 915.3
effervesce
bubble 404.4
enthuse 633.8
effervescence,
effervescency
bubbling 404.3
excitement 855.3
effervescence 404.6
effete aged 126.17
ineffectual 157.15
exhausted 664.6
vain 667.13
worn out 690.35
efficacious able 156.13
operative 163.10
influential 171.13
valid 515.12
effectual 663.20
efficacy ability 156.2
utility 663.3
efficiency ability 156.2
utility 663.3
proficiency 731.1
efficiency expert
expert 731.11
manager 745.7
efficient able 156.13
operative 163.10
businesslike 654.15
effectual 663.20
expedient 668.5
competent 731.22
effigy 570.3
efflation 402.1
effleurer 274.57

effloresce
incrust 227.29
powder 360.10
bloom 410.33
efflorescence
powderiness 360.1,5
flowering 410.24
rash 684.27
efflorescent
powdered 360.11
blossoming 410.36
effluence 302.4
effluent
nouns 394.3
adjs. 302.19
effluvious 434.9
effluvium fume 400.1
odor 434.1
poison 674.4
ectoplasm 1032.7
efflux 302.4
effluxion 302.4
effort act 703.3
endeavor 712.1
attempt 712.2
exertion 714.1
MAKE EVERY EFFORT
712.12
WITH EFFORT 714.20
effortful 714.19
effortless 730.11
effortlessness 730.1
effrontery 911.1
effulgence 334.4
effulgent 334.32
effuse
verbs issue 302.12
filter 302.15
excrete 309.10
adjs. 659.7
effusion outflow 302.4
exudation 302.6
excretion 309.1
diffuseness 591.1
talkativeness 594.1
effusive
flowing out 302.19
expansive 552.9
diffuse 591.11
talkative 594.9
égards regards 934.8
respects 962.3
egest 309.10
egesta 309.3
egestion 309.1
egestive 309.17
egg
nouns origin 152.7
ovum 405.8
embryo 405.14
aerial bomb 799.15
EGG IN ONE'S BEER
661.2
verbs 796.29
EGG ON 646.16.20
eggbeater 323.9
egg beater 44.10
egghead 475.1
egglike 405.24
eggplant 306a.35
eggs 306a.26

egg-shaped 252.11
eggshell
nouns 405.14
adjs. 363.9
egg white
semiliquid 388.5
egg 405.14
eggy 405.24
ego self 80.5
psyche 688.39
conceit 907.3
spirit 1032.17
egocentric 907.5,10
egocentricity 907.3
egohood 80.4
ego-ideal 688.39
egoism 907.3
egoist 907.5
egoistic ethics 955.2
ego-libido 688.39
egotism vanity 907.3
selfishness 976
egotist egoist 907.5
boaster 908.5
egotistic(al)
vain 907.10
selfish 976.5
egotistically 907.13
egregious
remarkable 34.10
flagrant 34.14
absurd 469.10
excessive 661.17
important 670.16
terrible 673.9
egregiously
eminently 36.18
excessively 661.23
terribly 673.14
egress
nouns departure 300
emergence 302
outlet 302.9
verbs 302.11
egression 302.1
Egyptian 123.6
Egyptian darkness
336.1
Egyptologist 123.23
Egyptology 123.22
eider 229.19
eiderdown
bedcover 227.11
down 229.19
softness 356.4
eidetic 535.23
eidolon idea 478.1
illusion 518.4
phantom 1015.1
eidouranion 374.17
eight 99.4
Eighteenth
Amendment
prohibition 776.1;
990.3
law 996.6
eighter 99.4
eightfold 99.20
eighth
nouns 462.9
adjs. 99.20

eighth note 462.14
eighty 99.7
Einstein 731.12
Einstein theory
  fourth dimension
    178.5
  theory 498.1
eisegesis 551.1
eisegetical 551.3
eisteddfod
  assembly 74.2
  musicale 461.33
either 635.24
IN EITHER CASE
  506.12
ejaculate eject 308.23
  excrete 309.10
  exclaim 458.7
ejaculation
  ejection 308.7
  excretion 309.1
  exclamation 458.2
ejaculative 308.26
ejaculatory 458.11
eject eliminate 77.5
  erupt 161.12
  expel 308.12
ejecta, ejectamenta
  309.3
ejection
  elimination 77.2
  expulsion 308
  excrement 309.3
ejective 308.26
ejectment 308.1
eke out
  supplement 56.6
  protract 110.9
  ~ a living 657.11
el, ell 250.2
el, L 655.8
elaborate
  verbs dwell on 103.9
  make 166.12
  develop 321.6
  improve 689.10
  adjs. complicated
    46.4
  painstaking 531.11
  perfected 675.9
  ornate 399.11
  sumptuous 902.21
elaboration
  reiteration 103.2
  making 166.3
  development 321.2
  refinement 689.2
  decoration 899.1
élan vital 406.3
elapse 105.5
elapsed 119.5
Elasmobranchii 414.11
elastic
  nouns 357.3
  adjs. expansive 196.9
  pliant 356.9
  resilient 357.7
  recuperative 692.23
elastic axis 277.25
elastic center 277.24

elasticity
  rebound 283.2
  pliancy 356.2
  resilience 357.1
elasticize 357.6
elate
  verbs cheer 868.7
  make proud 903.6
  adjs. overjoyed
    863.14
  jubilant 874.10
  exultant 908.11
elated
  overjoyed 863.14
  jubilant 874.10
  puffed up 903.10
  exultant 908.11
elation
  euphoria 688.22
  delight 863.2
  rejoicing 874.1
  exultation 908.4
elbow
  nouns joint 47.4
  angle 250.2
  arm 286.5
AT ONE'S ELBOW
  199.15
HAVE AT ONE'S
  ELBOW 752.9
OFF THE ELBOW
  628.15
RAISE THE ELBOW
  994.31
  verbs angle 250.5
  thrust 282.12
ELBOW ONE'S WAY
  293.4
elbow bender, elbow
  crooker 994.11
elbow grease
  rubbing 349.1
  manual labor 714.4
elbowroom
  room 178.3
  free scope 760.3
elbow shaker 514.16
eld the past 119.2
  oldness 123.1
elder
  nouns oldster 127.2
  senior 127.5
  grandfather 169.11
  grandmother 169.12
  official 747.19
  churchman
    1036.9,10
  adjs. older 123.19
  senior 126.18
elderliness 126.5
elderly 126.15
elderman 1036.9
eldermost, eldest
  oldest 123.19
  senior 126.18
elders 169.7
elder statesman 744.2
El Dorado 835.3
Eleatic 499.11
elect
  nouns 672.8

THE ELECT
  elite 916.2
  Christians 1026.5
  verbs choose 635.10
  vote in 635.17
  adjs. chosen 635.23
  destined 638.9
  choice 672.19
  exclusive 894.13
elected 635.23
electing 635.19
election
  mathematics 86.4
  choice 635.1,7
  political ~ 742.15
  holy orders 1035.10
election district
  742.16
electioneer
  nouns 744.10
  verbs 742.43
electioneering 742.12
election returns
  returns 568.6
  voting 742.22
elective
  nouns 560.7
  adjs. voluntary 620.7
  optional 635.19,20
elective operation
  687.24
elector 742.24
electoral 635.19
electoral college
  742.23
electors 742.23
Electra complex
  688.30
electragist 341.19
electric
  nouns electromobile
    271.9
  train 271.12
  streetcar 271.14
  adjs.
  of electricity 341.27
  exciting 855.31
electrical devices
  341.38
electrical engineer
  341.20
electrical parts 341.38
electrical transcription
  transcription 24.4
  radio 343.21
  record 464.19
electric bath 679.7
electric brain 348.16
electric car 271.14
electric chair 1009.5
electric charge 341.5
electric conduction
  341.13
electric current 341.2
electric detonator
  330.7
electric discharge
  341.6
electric eye 342.12
electric fan 402.22
electric field 341.3

electric fluid 341.2
electric heat 327.1
electric-heat 328.17
electric horsepower
  341.17
electrician
  electricity 341.19
  radiotrician 343.27
  stageman 609.28
electricity speed 268.7
  illuminant 334.20
  electrics 341
  sciences of ~
    341.34
electricize 341.23
electric light 334.18
electric meters 341.40
electric organ 464.15
electric power
  power 156.4
  electricity 341.17
electric railway 655.8
electric refrigeration
  333.1
electric shock 341.6
electric train 271.12
electric units 341.35
electrification
  electrization 341.21
  excitement 855.10
electrify
  electrize 341.23
  startle 538.8
  excite 855.14
electrifying
  electrical 341.27
  startling 538.11
electrize 341.23
electroaffinity 341.9
electroanalysis 687.15
electroanesthesia
  687.7
electroballistic 341.30
electrobiological
  341.30
electrobiologist
  341.20
electrobiology
  biology 405.16
  therapy 687.7
electrobioscopy 687.7
electrocardiogram
  687.12
electrocautery
  therapy 687.7
  surgery 687.23
electrochemical
  electric 341.27,30
  chemical 378.7
electrochemist 341.20
electrochemistry
  687.7
electrocoating
  coating 227.14
  electrolysis 341.22
electrocomputer
  348.16
electrocute 1008.19
electrocution 1008.7
electrocutioner 1008.8

electrodiagnosis
687.15
electrodiathermy
687.6
electrodynamic 341.27
electroencephalograph
687.12
electroencephalog-
raphy 687.7
electroetching 341.22
electrogalvanize
341.25
electrogild 341.25
electrograving 341.22
electrohemostasis
687.7
electro-horticulture
412.2
electrokinetic 341.27
electrolier 335.6
electroluminescence
334.13
electroluminescent
334.37
electrolysis
electricity 341.22
surgery 687.23
electrolyte 341.22
electrolytic 341.29
electrolyzation 687.23
electrolyze 341.25
electromagnet 287.3
electromagnetic
341.28
electromagnetic
induction 341.14
electromagnetic wave
343.14
electromagnetism
341.7
electromagnetize
341.24
electromassage 687.7
electromechanical
341.27
electrometallurgical
341.30
electrometallurgist
electrotechnologist
341.20
mineralogist 382.11
electrometallurgy
382.10
electrometric 341.27
electromobile 271.9
electromotive 341.27
electromotive force
341.10
electromyogram
687.12
electromyography
687.7
electron
minute thing 195.7
electronics 342.3
electron affinity 342.3
electronarcosis
unconsciousness
422.1
coma 688.26
electron current 342.6

electron diffraction
342.5
electron dynamics
342.1
electronegative 341.32
electron emission
342.5
electron flow
342.6
electronic 342.15
electronic brain
348.16
electronic calculator
348.16
electronic circuit
342.8
electronic control
348.3
electronic cop 345.5
electronic devices
342.20
electronic effect 342.4
electronic engineer
342.14
electronic engineering
342.1
electronic heating
388.1
electronic-mechanical
control 348.3
electronic meters
342.21
electronic navigation
277.4
electronic physicist
physicist 324.2
electronics 342.14
electronic refrigeration
333.1
electronics
radionics 342
radio ~ 343.2
television ~ 344
radar ~ 345
automation ~ 348
electron layers 342.3
electron microscopy
342.1
electron optics
electronics 342.1
optics 442.6
therapy 687.7
electron pair 342.3
electron physics
physics 324.1
electronics 342.1
electron ray 342.5
electron-ray tube
342.12
electron shower 326.3
electron spin 342.3
electron theory 342.2
electron tube
342.11,16–18
electron volt
electricity 341.11
electronics 342.7
electroosmosis 305.6
electrophonic 558.23
electrophototherapy
687.7

electrophysical 324.3
electrophysicist 341.20
electrophysics
physics 324
electronics 342.1
electrophysiological
341.30
electrophysiologist
341.20
electrophysiology
687.7
electroplate
plate 227.28
electrolyze 341.25
electroplated 227.35
electropneumatic
341.27
electro-pneumatic
organ 464.15
electropolar 341.28
electropositive 341.32
electropower
power 156.4
electricity 341.17
electropult 277.6
electroreceptive
341.27
electroscission 687.23
electroscopic 341.27
electroshock 688.26
electroshock therapy
688.7
electrostatic(al)
341.27
electrostatic field
341.3
electrostatic induction
341.14
electrostatics 346.2
electrostatic spraying
system 348.5
electrosurgery
surgery 686.3
therapy 687.7
electrotechnical
341.30
electrotechnician
341.19
electrotherapy 687.7
electrothermal 341.27
electrotype
nouns 576.7
verbs engrave 576.14
print 601.13
electrotyper 601.10
electrotypy 576.2
electrovagogram
687.12
electrovalence 378.3
electuary 685.4
eleemosynary
gratuitous 848.5
charitable 936.16
elegance
linguistic ~ 587
taste 895.1
beauty 898.1
ornateness 899.2
overniceness 901.5
sumptuousness
902.5

politeness 934.4
decency 986.2
elegancies
etiquette 644.3
amenities 934.7
elegancy 587.1
elegant speech 587.6
grandiloquent
599.12
excellent 672.13
tasteful 895.9
beautiful 898.16
ornate 899.11
overnice 901.18
sumptuous 902.21
chaste 986.5
elegantly
grandiloquently
599.14
tastefully 895.11
beautifully 898.21
affectedly 901.20
sumptuously
902.28
elegiac, elegiacs
poetry 607.2
verse 607.5
elegiac(al)
poetic 607.21
dirgelike 873.18
elegiast 607.15
elegize versify 607.19
lament 873.8
elegy poem 607.4
dirge 873.5
element
component 58.2
cause 152.1
environment 232.4
chemical ~ 378.1
IN ONE'S ELEMENT
at home 187.18
at one's ease 885.12
OUT OF ITS ELEMENT
out of place 27.7
misplaced 184.10
OUT OF ONE'S
ELEMENT 83.7
elemental
nouns 1012.13
adjs. elementary 5.8
simple 45.5
beginning 68.13
original 152.16
basic 211.8
chemical 378.7
climatal 401.14
elemental spirit
1012.13
elementary
fundamental 5.8
simple 45.5
beginning 68.13
original 152.16
basic 211.8
chemical 378.7
elementary mathe-
matics 87.2
elementary particles
325.6

embarkation 300.3
embarkment
  inauguration 68.4
  departure 300.3
embarras de choix
  635.2
embarras de richesses
  superabundance
    661.2
  wealth 835.1
embarrass
  involve 175.2
  bewilder 513.12
  fluster 530.7
  impede 728.11
  give trouble 729.14
  mortify 864.16
embarrassed
  bewildered 513.22
  confused 530.12
  poor 836.7
  in debt 838.8
  mortified 864.25
  humiliated 904.12
embarrassed circum-
  stances 836.1
embarrassing
  bewildering 513.24
  mortifying 862.12
  humiliating 904.13
embarrassment
  involvement 175.1
  bewilderment 513.3
  confusion 530.3
  impediment 728.6
  predicament 729.4
  poverty 836.1
  mortification 864.4
embassage 556.4
embassy home 190.3
  message 556.4
  office 717.8
  commission 778.1
  diplomats 779.7
embattle 797.9
embattled
  in arms 795.28
  fortified 797.12
embay 232.6
embed infix 142.10
  inset 303.4
embedment
  fixity 142.2
  insertion 303.1
embellish
  ~ speech 599.8
  falsify 614.16
  exaggerate 615.3
  ornament 899.7
embellished
  exaggerated 615.4
  ornamented 899.10
embellishing 899.9
embellishment
  musical ~ 462.18
  ornate speech 599.4
  exaggeration 615.1
  superfluity 661.4
  decoration 899.1
ember residue 43.2
  live coal 327.15

Ember days 1038.15
embezzle 822.13
embezzlement 822.1
embezzler 823.1
embitter
  antagonize 927.7
  sour 949.16
  anger 950.22
embittered
  sour-tempered
    949.23
  resentful 950.24
emblazon color 361.13
  embellish 899.7
  display 902.17
  praise 966.12
emblazonment 899.1
emblazonry
  coloring 361.10
  decoration 899.1
emblem
  prototype 25.2
  symbol 566.2
emblematic(al)
  570.12
emblematize 570.9
emblems 567.1
embodied 375.10
EMBODIED IN 58.4
embodiment
  combination 52.1
  whole 54.1
  composition 58.1
  inclusion 76.1
  incorporation 375.7
  representative 570.5
embody combine 52.3
  form a whole 54.6
  compose 58.3
  include 76.3
  incorporate 375.8
  typify 570.9
embodying 570.11
embolden 891.16
emboldening 891.9
embolism, embolus
  265.3
embonpoint 194.8
embosom
  surround 232.6
  conceal 613.8
  cherish 811.7
  embrace 930.16
embosomed 183.19
emboss 255.11
embossed 255.17
embossment 573.3
embouchement, em-
  bouchure 264.6
embow 251.6
embowed 251.10
embrace
  nouns clasp 811.2
  welcome 923.2
  greeting 923.4
  hug 930.2
  verbs include 76.3
  wrap 227.22
  surround 232.6
  adopt 635.12
  hold 811.6,7

seize 820.12
welcome 923.9
hug 930.16
embraced 635.23
embracement
  inclusion 76.1
  surrounding 232.5
  adoption 635.3
embracing
  inclusive 76.5
  surrounding 232.9
embrangle 46.3
embrangled 46.4
embranglement 793.7
embrasure 261.3
embrocate
  anoint 379.8
  medicate 687.34
embrocation
  ointment 379.3
  balm 685.9
embroider
  ~ speech 599.8
  falsify 614.16
  exaggerate 615.3
  embellish 899.7
embroidered 615.4
embroiderer 222.2
embroidery
  ornate speech 599.4
  exaggeration 615.1
  superfluity 661.4
  decoration 899.1
embroil 63.4
embroilment
  commotion 62.4
  turbulence 161.2
  agitation 323.1
  brawl 793.7
  contest 794.3
embrown 366.2
embryo
  rudiment 152.7
  biology 405.13
IN EMBRYO
  beginning 68.13
  original 152.16
  in preparation
    718.23
  undeveloped 719.12
embryologist 405.17
embryology 405.16
embryonic
  beginning 68.13
  original 152.16
  germinal 195.14;
    405.23
  undeveloped 719.12
embryotomy 687.26
embus 300.17
emcee 343.26
emend, emendate
  improve 689.9
  revise 689.12
  remedy 692.13
emendable 692.25
emendation 689.1,4
emendatory
  remedial 685.34
  corrective 689.16

emerald, emerald-
  green 370.4
emerge
  come out 302.12
  appear 445.8
  escape 630.9
emergence
  egress 302.2
  appearance 445.1
  escape 630.1
emergency 129.4
emergency barrage
  796.10
emergency operation
  687.24
emergency rations
  306a.6
emergent, emerging
  302.18
emersion 302.2
emery 259.8
emesis 308.8
emetic
  nouns 685.16
  adjs. 685.42
émeute 765.4
emigrant
  migrant 273.5
  outgoer 302.10
emigrate
  migrate 272.21
  go out 302.16
emigration
  migration 272.4
  exodus 302.7
émigré migrant 273.5
  outgoer 302.10
  refugee 629.5
emigree 273.5
Eminence 915.2
eminence
  greatness 34.2
  influence 171.1
  height 206.1,2
  importance 670.2
  authority 737.3
  famousness 912.5
eminent great 34.9
  superior 36.13
  high 206.19
  protruding 255.13
  important 670.16
  famous 912.19
eminent domain 737.5
eminently
  superlatively 36.18
  importantly 670.26
  famously 912.22
emir ruler 747.11
  title 915.3
  prince 916.8
emissary
  delegate 779.2
  diplomat 779.6
  agent 779.9
emission
  issuance 302.2
  discharge 308.7
  excretion 309.1
emissive 308.26
emit exude 302.15

let out 308.22
excrete 309.10
publish 557.14
utter 592.14
emitter current 342.6
emitter resistance
342.10
emitter signal voltage
342.7
Emmanuel 1011.12
emmet 413a.3
emollient
nouns ointment
379.3
balm 685.9
adjs. softening 356.16
lubricant 379.10
remedial 685.35
relieving 884.9
emolument 839.5
emote act 609.33
emotionalize 853.14
emotion feeling 853.3
excitement 855.1
BE FULL OF EMOTION
855.18
emotionable 853.19
emotional 853.18
emotional appeal
853.8
emotional attachment
688.43
emotional dissociation
688.27
emotional instability
psychology 688.15
excitability 855.9
emotional insulation
688.34
emotionalism 688.22
emotionalize
act 609.33
emote 853.14
emotionally 853.26
emotionally unstable
personality 688.14
emotional release
catharsis 688.36
relief 884.2
emotional shock
688.19
emotionless 854.9
emotionlessly 854.14
emotionlessness
854.1
emotions 353.1
emotive 853.18
empanel list 88.7
enroll 558.15
~ a jury 1002.15
empanelment
enrollment 568.14
~ of jurors 1002.4
empathic 792.3
empathize 792.2
empathy
psychology 688.43
sympathy 792.1
empennage 240.5
emperor 747.8

emperorhood, em-
perorship 737.7
empery
country 180.1
sovereignty 737.7
government 739.1
emphasis
musical ~ 462.24
accent 592.7
cadence 607.9
insistence 751.3
GIVE EMPHASIS TO
670.13
WITH EMPHASIS
521.8
emphasize
stress 670.13
insist 751.7
emphasized 670.22
emphatic
insistent 521.7
significant 670.22
emphatically
remarkably 34.23
insistently 521.8
empire country 180.1
sovereignty 737.7
government 739.1
empiric 617.6
empiric(al)
half-learned 476.16
experimental 488.11
philosophical 499.10
quack 614.29
empiricism
half-learning 476.6
experiment 488.1
quackery 614.7
ethics 955.2
empiric treatment
687.18
emplace 183.11
emplacement
location 183.1
placement 183.6
platform 215.13
emplane 300.17
emplastrum 685.28
employ
nouns rise 663.1
service 748.13
IN ONE'S EMPLOY
748.15
OUT OF EMPLOY
706.16
verbs spend time
105.6
occupy 654.9
use 663.10,13
practice 703.7
exert 714.8
hire 778.12
EMPLOY ONESELF IN
703.7
EMPLOY ONE'S TIME
IN 654.10
employed used 663.23
busy 705.20
employee, employé
716.2; 748.2
employees 748.12

employer user 663.9
master 747.1
employment
occupation 654.1,5
use 663.1,8
action 703.1
work 714.4
service 748.13
hiring 778.4
empoison 684.39
emporium 830.2
empower, impower
enable 156.9
authorize 775.12
commission 778.9
empowered,
impowered 775.18
empowerment,
impowerment
enablement 156.8
authorization 775.3
empress 747.12
empressement
zeal 633.2
fervor 853.9
emptily
vacantly 186.15
expressionlessly
545.15
insincerely 614.36
emptiness
vacancy 186.2
empty-headedness
468.6
insincerity 614.5
hunger 632.7
EMPTINESS OF MIND
479.1
emptio 826.2
emption 826.2
emptional 826.10
emptor 826.5
empty
verbs flow out 302.13
draft off 304.10
evacuate 308.20
adjs. ineffectual
157.15
vacant 186.12
empty-headed
468.19
ignorant 476.13
thoughtless 479.4
unwarranted 482.12
expressionless 545.11
insincere 614.32
hungry 632.26
vain 667.13
EMPTY OF 660.11
empty-handed 660.10
empty-headed
stupid 468.19
ignorant 476.13
thoughtless 479.4
scatterbrained
530.16
empty-headedness
unintelligence 468.6
ignorance 476.1
thoughtlessness
479.1

emptying
drafting off 304.2
evacuation 308.6
empty purse, empty
pocket 836.2
empty sound 545.1
empty space
aviation 277.38
cosmic space 374.3
empty stomach 632.7
empty title 581.3
empty words 482.3
empurple 372.2
empyreal 374.25
empyrean
nouns 374.2; 1016.5
adjs. celestial 374.25
delightful 861.6
emulate
imitate 22.7
rival 672.12
compete with
794.19
emulation
imitation 22.1
competition 794.2
emulative 22.10
emulator 789.2
emulous 794.24
emulsification, emulsi-
fier 388.7
emulsify 388.10
emulsion
semiliquid 388.7
photographic ~
575.15
emulsionize 388.10
emulsive 388.11
emulsoid 388.7
emunctory
outlet 302.9
duct 395.13
en, en quad 601.7
enable
empower 156.9
qualify 718.8
authorize 775.12
enablement
empowerment 156.8
qualification 718.2
enact
impersonate 570.10
act out 609.34
perform 703.8
accomplish 720.4
legislate 740.20
enactment
legislation 740.15
law 996.3
enallage 549.2
enamel
verbs coat 227.26
paint 361.14
adjs. 574.7
enameler, enamelist
577.4
enameling 361.11
enamel kiln 574.5
enamelware 829.4
enamor 929.20

enamored 929.25
BECOME ENAMORED 929.19
ENAMORED OF 929.27
en attendant 109.5
en avant 293.8
en bloc 54.12
encage 759.12
encamp 187.12
encampment
  camping 187.4
  camp 190.25
  military ~ 800.2
encase, encasement, etc. See incase, etc.
encaustic
  painting 572.5
  engraving 576.6
enceinte
  nouns 179.4
  adjs. 168.18
encephalic 210.13
encephalitis lethargica 684.9
encephalon 465.4
enchain 758.10
enchair 778.11
enchant
  fascinate 648.6
  delight 863.8
  bewitch 1034.9
enchanted
  overjoyed 863.14
  bewitched 1034.13
enchanter 1033.9
enchanting
  alluring 648.7
  delightful 861.6
  bewitching 1034.12
enchantment
  allurement 648.1
  delightfulness 861.2
  delight 863.2
  sorcery 1033.1
  bewitchment 1034.2
enchantress
  temptress 648.3
  bewitcher 1033.9
enchase 576.12
enchased 576.16
enchasing 576.1
enchiridion 603.5
enchymatous 196.12
encincture
  nouns 232.5
  verbs 232.7
encircle include 76.3
  circle 232.7
  circumscribe 233.4
  circuit 319.4
  besiege 796.20
encirclement
  surrounding 232.5
  military ~ 795.10
  siege 796.5
enclasp 232.6
enclave 179.4
enclose, inclose
  include 76.3
  surround 232.6
  circumscribe 233.4

shut in 235.5
enclosed, inclosed
  surrounded 232.11
  confined 235.10
enclosed, the 193.5
enclosing, inclosing
  inclusive 76.5
  surrounding 232.9
enclosure, inclosure
  contents 193.5
  surrounding 232.5
  pen 235.3
  types of ~ 235.11,12
enclothe 230.38
encloud
  darken 336.10
  cloud 403.7
encomiast 966.8
encomiastic(al) 966.15
encomium 966.5
encompass
  include 76.3
  surround 232.6
  circumscribe 233.4
  enclose 235.5
  circuit 319.4
  besiege 796.20
encompassment
  surrounding 232.5
  siege 796.5
encore
  nouns curtain call 103.6
  applause 966.2
  verbs 966.10
  interjs. again! 103.18
  bravo! 966.21
encounter
  nouns meeting 199.4
  collision 282.3
  contest 794.3
  verbs experience 150.8
  meet 199.11
  confront 239.8
  collide 282.13
  find 487.3
  oppose 788.6
  contend with 794.16
encourage
  incite 646.21
  abet 783.14
  cheer 868.6
  comfort 885.6
  embolden 891.16
encouragement
  inducement 646.5,7
  aid 783.4
  comfort 885.4
  emboldening 891.9
GIVE ENCOURAGE-MENT 646.21
encouraging
  auspicious 542.16
  provocative 646.27
  cheering 868.16
  comforting 885.13
  hopeful 886.13
Encratism 990.2

Encratite 990.4
encrimson 367.4
encroach
  intrude 237.5
  overstep 311.9
ENCROACH UPON 959.7
encroachment
  intrusion 237.1
  overstepping 311.3
encrust 227.29
encuirassed 797.13
encumber, incumber
  saddle on 40.3
  burden 351.13
  hamper 728.11
encumbered, incumbered
  burdened 351.18
  in debt 838.8
encumbrance, incumbrance
  burden 351.7
  impediment 728.6
  dependent 762.6
  care 864.8
encyclical, encyclical letter
  advertisement 557.8
  letter 602.3
encyclopedia
  knowledge 474.9
  learned man 475.4
  book 603.6
encyclopedic
  comprehensive 76.6
  scientific 474.28
encyclopedist 600.15
encyst 235.9
end
  nouns remnant 43.1
  piece 55.3
  termination 70
  ~ of the book 70.1
  cessation 144.1
  result 153.2
  limit 233.3
  ~ of burning 280.10
  death 407.1
  fate 638.2
  objective 651.2
  ruin 691.2
  completion 720.2
  share 814.5
AT LOOSE ENDS 625.9
AT THE END OF ONE'S ROPE
  dying 407.27
  perplexed 513.23
  lacking 660.11
  straitened 729.24
  poor 836.7
COME TO A VIOLENT END 408.21
END OF ONE'S ROPE 729.5
END OF THE LINE
  end 70.1
  R.R. terminal 655.8
END ON 239.15
END TO END 199.16

MAKE BOTH ENDS MEET 657.11
NO END
  exceedingly 34.17
  numerously 101.13
  abundantly 659.9
NO END OF, NO END TO
  innumerable 101.11
  infinite 104.3
  long 201.11
ON END
  continuously 71.11
  upright 212.12
PUT AN END TO
  end 70.7
  kill 408.13
  destroy 691.12
  prevent 728.13
TO THAT END 154.6
TO THE END
  throughout 56.18
  to a finish 70.12
  completion 720.13
WITHOUT END
  infinite 104.3
  infinitely 104.4
  perpetual 112.7
  perpetually 112.10
  long 201.11
  verbs terminate 70.5
  stop 144.6,11
  result 153.5
  kill 408.13
  destroy 691.12
  perish 691.22
  complete 720.6
END ONE'S DAYS 407.15
END UP IN SMOKE
  fall through 312.3
  fail 723.12
NEVER END
  be infinite 104.2
  be eternal 112.6
end-all 70.4
endamage 690.10
endanger 695.6
endangered 695.13
endangerment 695.1
endbrain 465.5
endear 929.20
endearment 930.4
endeavor
  nouns 712
  verbs purpose 651.4
  strive 712.4
ended concluded 70.8
  completed 720.10
endemic
  nouns 684.1
  adjs. characteristic 80.13
  native 188.7
  vs. epidemic 684.47
endenizen 188.5
ender 70.4
endermatic, endermic 228.6
enderon 228.4
en déshabillé 230.46

PUT IN PLAIN
ENGLISH 546.6
English horn 464.9
Englishism
nationality 180.6
idiom 578.9
Englishize 188.5
Englishman 417.9
English-speaking, etc.
592.21
engorge
swallow 305.11
eat 306.23
overeat 992.5
engorgement
taking in 305.4
overfullness 661.3
satiety 662.1
engraft, engrafted
See ingraft, etc.
engram 688.40
en grande tenue,
en grande toilette
230.45
en grand seigneur
903.13
engrave infix 142.10
fix in the mind
535.18
enchase 576.12
impress upon 853.17
engraved
infixed 142.14
graven 576.16
engravement 576.1,6
engraver 577.8
engraving
chasing 576
print 576.6
engross
absorb 305.13
~ the thoughts
477.19
~ the interest
528.13
inscribe 600.23
monopolize 806.7
corner 831.26
engrossed
~ in thought
477.21
interested 528.17
inscribed 600.24
BE ENGROSSED IN
528.5
engrossment
absorption 305.6
thoughtfulness
477.3
attention 528.3
inscription 600.3
monopolization
806.4
engulf swallow 305.11
submerge 318.7
inundate 394.18
oversupply 661.15
engulfed
submerged 208.12
flooded 394.26
engulfment

taking in 305.4
submergence 318.2
enhance
intensify 38.5
exaggerate 615.3
improve 689.9
aggravate 883.2
enhancement
intensification 38.2
exaggeration 615.1
improvement 689.1
aggravation 883.1
enharmonic
nouns scale 462.6
note 462.14
chord 462.17
adjs. 462.26
enharmonic diesis,
enharmonic
interval 462.20
enigma 547.7
enigmatic(al)
puzzling 513.24
inexplicable 547.15
enigmatically 547.20
enigmaticalness 547.2
enisle 385.5
enjoin command 750.9
advise 752.7
prohibit 776.3
impose 961.4
enjoy savor 427.5
have 806.5
delight in 863.10
ENJOY GOOD HEALTH
683.4
ENJOY ONESELF
863.11
enjoyable 861.5
enjoyableness 861.1
enjoyably 861.9
enjoyer user 663.9
possessor 807.1
enjoyment
relish 427.2
pleasure 863.1
amusement 876.1
enkindle
ignite 328.21
incite 646.18
excite 855.11
enkindling 328.26
enlace 221.7
enlarge increase 38.4
expand 196.4,5
develop 321.6
~ a photograph
575.17
expatiate 591.7
exaggerate 615.3
aggravate 883.2
enlarged
increased 38.7
expanded 196.10
exaggerated 615.4
aggravated 883.4
enlargement
increase 38.1
expansion 196.1
development 321.2
photograph 575.5

expatiation 591.6
exaggeration 615.1
aggravation 883.1
enleagued 52.6
en l'ensemble 231.14
enlighten
illuminate 334.28
disillusion 519.2
explain 550.11
inform 555.7
teach 560.10
enlightened
illuminated 334.38
wise 466.19
informed 474.18
disillusioned 519.5
enlightener 555.5
enlightening
illuminating 334.39
broadening 524.14
explanatory 550.17
informative 555.17
instructive 560.18
enlightenment
lighting 334.19
learning 474.4
disillusionment
519.1
explanation 550.4
information 555.1
instruction 560.1
enlist induce 646.22
engage 778.14
join 786.14
ENLIST INTO SERVICE
663.14
ENLIST UNDER THE
BANNER OF 784.6
enlisted man 798.9
enlistee
member 786.11
recruit 798.17
enlistment term 107.3
inducement 646.3
engagement 778.6
enliven energize 160.9
inspire 646.20
stimulate 855.12
cheer 868.6
amuse 876.23
enlivenment
animation 160.7
inspiration 646.9
refreshment 693.1
en masse wholly 54.12
together 73.11
enmesh involve 175.2
ensnare 616.20
embarrass 729.14
catch 820.14
enmist dim 336.11
cloud 403.7
enmity discord 793
unfriendliness 927
hatred 928
AT ENMITY 927.13
ennead 99.5
enneahedral 99.21
enneastyle
nouns 99.5
adjs. 99.21

ennoble
promote 780.3
glorify 912.13
ennui 882.3
enormity
greatness 34.1
hugeness 194.7
indignity 963.2
misdeed 980.2
enormous great 34.11
mammoth 194.20
atrocious 673.9
infamous 913.12
wicked 979.17
en otros términos
550.21
enough
nouns 659.1
ENOUGH AND TO SPARE
plenty 659.2
plentiful 659.7
superabundance
661.2
ENOUGH SAID
that's final 70.13
that's right 515.22
ENOUGH TO DRIVE
ONE MAD 862.16
ENOUGH TO WAKE
THE DEAD 452.9
HAVE ENOUGH 662.5
JUST ENOUGH TO
SWEAR BY 35.5
NOT ENOUGH 660.7
WITH ENOUGH OF
662.6
adjs. 659.6
GOOD ENOUGH
yes 520.18
ample 659.6
tolerable 672.20
satisfactory 866.12
bravo! 966.21
advs. sufficiently
659.8
satisfactorily
866.15
LIKE ENOUGH 510.7
OFTEN ENOUGH 135.6
interjs. cease 144.13
don't! 776.8
en passant
incidentally 129.14
in passing 270.20
enquire 484.21
enquirer 484.17
enquiry 484.1,13
enrage 950.23
enragement 950.5
en rapport
in agreement 26.14
in accord 792.3
enrapture
fascinate 648.6
delight 863.8
enamor 929.20
enraptured
overjoyed 863.14
in love 929.25
enravish
fascinate 648.6

delight 863.8
enravished 863.14
enravishing
    alluring 648.7
    delightful 861.6
enravishment 861.2
en règle orderly 59.6
    conformably 82.9
en revanche 953.9
enrich fertilize 164.8
    vitaminize 307.18
    ~ speech 599.8
    improve 689.9
    richen 835.8
    embellish 899.7
enrichment
    fertilization 164.3
    vitaminization
        307.12
    improvement 689.1
enrobe 230.38
enroll list 88.7
    record 568.15
    enlist 778.14
    join 786.14
enrollee
    member 786.11
    recruit 798.17
enrollment
    listing 88.6
    registration 568.14
    enlistment 778.6
en route 270.20
EN ROUTE FOR 293.7
ensanguine 677.7
ensanguined 677.10
ensate 257.16
ensconce
    establish 183.17
    conceal 613.7
    protect 697.17
ensconced
    located 183.19
    protected 697.20
ensemble
    nouns all 54.3
    musicians 463.12,18
    advs. 73.10
enshrine
    enclose 235.5
    entomb 409.20
    glorify 912.13
    saint 1024.5
ENSHRINE IN THE
    MEMORY 535.14
enshrinement
    glorification 912.8
    sainting 1024.3
enshroud wrap 227.22
    clothe 230.38
    conceal 613.7
ensiform 257.16
ensign flag 567.6
    officer 747.23,24
ensigns 567.1
ensilage 306a.4
enslave 762.8
enslaved 762.13
enslavement 762.1
ensnare, insnare
    trap 616.20

inveigle 648.4
    catch 820.14
ensnarement 616.1
ensphere 232.7
enstamp
    engrave 576.13
    print 601.12
ensue come next 65.3
    be subsequent 117.2
    result 153.5
ensuing
    succeeding 65.5
    subsequent 117.3
    resultant 153.7
ensure
    make sure 512.11
    protect 697.17
    guarantee 770.11
ensured
    protected 697.20
    guaranteed 770.14
entail
    nouns 817.2
    verbs involve 76.4
    endow 816.17
entailment 76.2
entangle
    complicate 46.3
    involve 175.2
    confuse 530.7
    ensnare 616.20
    embarrass 729.14
    enmesh 820.14
entanglement
    complexity 46.1
    involvement 175.1
    ensnarement 616.1
    barricade 797.4
    love affair 929.6
en tapinois 612.20
entasia 684.5
entente cordiale
    agreement 26.2
    compact 769.1
enter begin 68.8
    list 88.7
    go in 301.7
    insert 303.3
    register 568.15
    join 786.14
    ~ accounts 843.8
ENTER INTO
    compose 58.3
    participate 813.5
ENTER ON, ENTER
    UPON
    begin 68.8
    undertake 713.3
    set to work 714.15
ENTER ONE'S MIND
    477.17
enteric 224.12
enteric fever 684.9
entering
    arriving 299.10
    incoming 301.13
enterography,
    enterology 224.7
enterotomy 687.26
enterprise

ambitiousness
    632.10
act 703.3
initiative 705.7
undertaking 713.1
firm 786.9
daring 891.6
exploit 891.7
enterpriser 652.7
enterprising
    up-and-coming
        705.22
    daring 891.21
entertain
    interest 528.12
    cherish 811.7
    amuse 876.23
    ~ guests 923.8
ENTERTAIN A BELIEF
    500.10
ENTERTAIN DOUBTS
    502.6
ENTERTAIN THE HOPE
    886.7
ENTERTAIN THE IDEA
    477.15
ENTERTAIN THE
    INNER MAN 306.17
entertainer 610.1
entertaining
    interesting 528.19
    amusing 876.29
entertainment
    repast 306.5
    theatrical ~ 609.13
    amusement 876.1
    party 920.10
entêté 624.8
enthrall, inthrall
    engross 528.13
    fascinate 648.6
    subjugate 762.8
    delight 863.8
enthralling,
    inthralling
    interesting 528.20
    alluring 648.7
    delightful 861.6
enthrallment,
    inthrallment
    allurement 648.1
    bondage 762.1
enthrone
    instate 778.11
    exalt 912.13
enthronement
    instatement 778.3
    exaltation 912.8
enthuse 633.8
enthusiasm
    craze 472.12
    interest 528.2
    eagerness 633.3
WITH ENTHUSIASM
    633.13
enthusiast
    fanatic 472.17
    visionary 533.13
    zealot 633.5
enthusiastic
    interested 528.16

eager 633.11
enthymematic(al)
    481.22
enthymeme 481.7
entice 648.4
enticement 648.1
enticer 648.3
enticing 648.7
entincture 44.12
entire
    nouns horse 413.12
    stallion 419.8
    adjs. whole 54.8
    complete 56.9
    unqualified 507.2
    intact 675.7
entirely wholly 54.12
    completely 56.15
    solely 89.14
    perfectly 675.10
entirety whole 54.1
    all 54.3
    completeness 56.1
IN ITS ENTIRETY
    54.12
entitle, intitle
    name 581.11
    authorize 775.12
entitled, intitled
    eligible 635.21
    authorized 775.18
    warranted 958.9
entitlement
    qualification 635.9
    authorization 775.3
    dueness 958.1
entity existence 1.1
    thing 3.3
    integer 89.4
entoderm 228.4
entomb confine 235.6
    inter 409.20
entombment 409.1
entomologic(al)
    414.13
entomologist 414.2
entomology 414.1
Entomostraca, ento-
    mostracans 414.8
entourage
    attendance 73.6
    envious 232.1
en-tout-cas 227.7
entr'acte
    interim 109.1
    act 609.8
entrails insides 224.4
    intestines 224.6
entrain 300.17
entrainment 300.3
entrammel
    hamper 728.11
    restrain 758.10
entrance
    nouns vestibule
        191.19
    ingress 301.1
    entranceway 301.5
    insertion 303.1
    admission 305.3

MAKE AN ENTRANCE
301.9
verbs fascinate 648.6
hypnotize 710.18
delight 863.8
spellbind 1034.8
entranced
dreaming 533.25
overjoyed 863.14
entrance fee 844.7
entrancement
ingress 301.1
delightfulness 861.2
bewitchment
1034.2
entrancing
alluring 648.7
delightful 861.6
bewitching 1034.12
entrant incomer 301.4
beginner 564.7
competitor 789.2
entrap ensnare 616.20
catch 820.14
entreat 772.11
entreating 772.17
entreaty appeal 772.2
prayer 1030.4
entre deux âges 126.13
entrée, entree
ingress 301.1
admission 305.3
food 306.10
entremets 306.10
entrench, intrench
establish 142.10
intrude 237.5
fortify 797.9
ENTRENCH ON 311.9
entrenchment,
intrenchment
establishment 142.2
intrusion 237.1
overstepping 311.3
fortification 797.5
entre nous 612.22
entrepôt 658.6
entrepreneur
theaterman 609.27
administrator 747.5
entresol 191.23
entrust, intrust
commission 778.9
consign 816.16
extend credit 837.6
entrustment 816.2
entry vestibule 191.19
ingress 301.1
entranceway 301.5
admission 305.3
race horse 413.19
memorandum 568.3
registration 568.14
account ∼ 843.5
MAKE AN ENTRY
register 568.15
enter accounts 843.8
entryway 301.5
entwine 221.7
entwined 221.8
entwinement 221.1

entwining
nouns 221.1
adjs. 221.9
enucleate 550.11
enucleation 550.4
enumerate
number 87.10
list 88.7
enumeration
numeration 87.1
list 88.1
enumerative 87.15
enunciate
sound 449.12
postulate 498.12
affirm 521.4
announce 557.12
say 592.14
enunciated 592.20
enunciation
sounding 449.6
affirmation 521.1
announcement
557.2
pronunciation 592.6
enunciative 557.18
envelop wrap 227.22
clothe 230.38
surround 232.6
conceal 613.7
envelope
nouns 227.19
verbs 796.20
enveloped
covered 227.34
surrounded 232.11
enveloping
covering 227.37
surrounding 232.9
envelopment
covering 227.1
wrapping 227.19
surrounding 232.5
siege 796.5
envenom
poison 684.39
antagonize 927.7
embitter 949.16
envenomed
venomous 682.5
virulent 937.20
enviable 632.31
envious jealous 951.4
covetous 952.4
environ 232.6
environment
surroundings 232
encompassment
232.5
environmental 232.8
environs 232.1
envisage
confront 239.8
contemplate 477.16
visualize 533.15
envisaging 533.6
envision
contemplate 477.16
visualize 533.15
envisioning 533.6

envoy
poetic refrain
607.11
delegate 779.2
diplomat 779.6
envy
nouns jealousy 951
covetousness 952
verbs 952.3
enwrap, inwrap
wrap 227.22
clothe 230.38
surround 232.6
enzymes 307.8,27
enzymic 352.16
enzymologist 307.13
enzymology 307.14
eolith 123.6
eolithic 123.20
eon See aeon
Eos 133.2
epact 114.5
epagoge 481.3
epagogic 481.22
Epaminondas and
Pelopidas 926.8
eparch 747.7
epaulet, epaulette
567.5
éperdu 855.21
ephemeral
nouns ephemeron
111.5
plant 410.3
adjs. short-lived 111.7
deciduous 410.42
ephemerality 111.1
ephemeris
calendar 114.8
periodical 603.11
ephemeron 111.5
ephor 1000.2
epiblast 228.4
epic saga 606.6
poem 607.4
epic(al)
narrative 606.16
poetic 607.21
epicalyx 410.26
epicarp 228.2
epicarpal 228.6
epicedial 873.18
epicedium 873.5
epicene
nouns 418.11
adjs. 418.23
epicenism, epicenity
418.10
epicenter 225.2
épicier 896.6
epic poet 607.15
epic poetry 607.2
epicranium 210.6
epicure
connoisseur 895.7
voluptuary 985.3
gourmand 992.4
epicurean
nouns epicure 895.7
voluptuary 985.3
gourmand 992.4

adjs. philosophical
499.10
voluptuous 985.5
Epicureanism 499.2
epicureanism,
epicurism
aesthetic taste 895.5
voluptuousness
985.1
gourmanderie 992.2
epicycle 252.7
epidemic
nouns 684.4
adjs. prevalent 79.11
abundant 659.7
contagious 684.47
epidermal, epidermic
228.6
epidermis 228.4
epigenesis 166.6
epigenetic 166.24
epiglottis 395.16
epigram maxim 516.1
poem 607.4
epigrammatic(al)
axiomatic 516.6
laconic 590.4
platitudinous 881.9
epigrammatist 879.12
epigrammatize 516.5
epigraph title 483.2
motto 516.4
inscription 600.3
epigraphy 550.9
epilepsy illness 684.5
disease 684.17
epileptic
nouns 684.31
adjs. 684.46
epilogue sequel 67.1
act 609.8
Epimenides 467.4
Epiphany 1038.15
episcopacy 1035.5
Episcopal 1018.24
episcopal 1035.13
Episcopalian 1018.24
episcopalian 1035.13
episcopalianism
1035.3
episcopal vestments
1039.1
episcopate 1035.5
episode
discontinuity 72.1
occurrence 150.2
interjection 236.2
digression 591.4
episodic
interjectional
236.10
desultory 591.13
epispastic 685.26
episperm 227.16
epistemological
idealism 499.3
epistemological
logic 481.2
epistemology 499.1
Epistle 1038.10
epistle 602.2

eremite 922.5
eremitic(al) 922.11
eremitism 922.2
erenow prior 116.6
  formerly 119.10
erg 160.6
ergal 160.1
ergo 154.6
ergophobia 706.4
Erie Canal 395.2
Erinyes, the 1014.11
eristic 481.13
eristic(al) 481.20
erlking 1014.8
ermine 567.3
erode decline 39.6
  disintegrate 53.3
  deteriorate 690.22
erogenic, erogenous
  418.17
eromania 688.32
Eros Love 929.8
  god 1012.5
erose irregular 18.2
  notched 261.5
erosion
  decrement 39.3
  disintegration 53.1
  wear 690.5
erosive
  disintegrative 53.5
  eroding 690.42
erotic sexual 418.17
  amatory 929.23
  lascivious 987.29
eroticism
  sexual desire 418.4
  lasciviousness 987.5
eroticomania 688.32
erotism 418.4
erotogenic 418.17
erotomania
  craze 472.12
  psychosexuality
   688.32
err miscalculate 495.2
  go wrong 517.8
  misinterpret 551.2
  be sinful 979.13
  do wrong 980.3
  misbelieve 1023.8
errability 513.7
errable 513.20
errancy fallibility 513.7
  error 517.1
errand task 654.2
  commission 778.1
errand boy 559.4
errant
  wandering 272.36
  deviating 290.7
  circuitous 319.7
  fallible 513.20
  erroneous 517.14
errantry
  knightly skill 795.11
  magnanimity 977.2
errata 603.13
erratic
  nouns 473.3
  adjs. abnormal 85.9

irregular 138.3
  changeable 141.7
  wandering 290.7
  eccentric 473.4
  capricious 627.5
erraticism
  abnormality 85.1
  changeableness
   141.2
  eccentricity 473.1
  capriciousness 627.2
erratum 517.3
errhine 402.31
erring sister 987.16
erroneous
  not true 517.14
  illusory 518.9
error
  computer ∼ 348.19
  misjudgment 495
  miscalculation 495.1
  erroneousness 517.3
  illusion 518
  misinterpretation
   551
  iniquity 979.4
  misdeed 980.2
  BE IN ERROR
  err 517.9
  misbelieve 1023.8
  IN ERROR
  mistaken 517.16
  false 614.26
  UNDER AN ERROR
  517.16
ersatz
  nouns 148.2
  adjs. 148.8
erstwhile 119.7
erubescence 367.1,3
erubescent 367.12
eruct, eructate
  erupt 161.12
  eject 308.23
  belch 308.25
eructation
  eruption 161.6
  ejection 308.7,9
erudite 474.21
erudition 474.5
erupt
  burst forth 161.12
  eject 308.23
  break out in a rash
   684.34
eruption
  outburst 161.6
  ejection 308.7
  rash 684.27
  outburst of passion
   855.8
  outburst of anger
   950.9
eruptive 161.23
erysipelas, erythema
  684.27
Erythraean sibyl 541.6
erythroblast 405.5
erythrocytes 387.4
escadrille 798.27

escalade
  nouns climb 313.1
  invasion 796.4
  verbs climb 313.11
  invade 796.21
escalator 315.5
escalator clause
  provision 506.2
  clause 740.19
  wages 839.4
  prices 844.6
escalier dérobé
  back stairs 313.3
  covert way 613.5
escallop, escalop
  nouns 261.2
  verbs convolve 253.4
  notch 261.4
  cook 329.4
escalloped, escaloped
  notched 261.5
  cooked 329.6
escamotage 616.5
escamoterie 616.6
escamoteur 617.2
escapable 629.13
escapade caprice 627.1
  revel 876.6
escape
  nouns evasion 629.1
  escaping 630
  escapism 688.34
  verbs evade 629.7
  get away 630.6
  ESCAPE EARTH 281.15
  ESCAPE NOTICE
  be invisible 444.3
  inattention 529.5
  be latent 544.3
  ESCAPE ONE
  escape notice 529.5
  forget 536.5
  ESCAPE ONE'S LIPS
  592.19
escaped loose 630.10
  free 760.19
escapee refugee 629.5
  escaper 630.5
escape mechanism
  688.34
escaper 630.5
escape velocity
  aviation 277.37
  astronautics 281.14
escapism escape 630.1
  psychology 688.34
escapist escaper 630.5
  neurotic 688.14
escarp 797.4
escarpment
  precipice 212.3
  fortification 797.4
eschar scab 227.15
  sore 684.28
eschara 1040.11
escharotic
  nouns 328.14
  adjs. caustic 160.12
  stinging 432.6
eschatology 121.3

escheat
  nouns reversion 146.1
  forfeiture 1007.3
  verbs 146.4
escheatment 1007.3
eschew 990.7
eschewal 990.2
escort
  nouns attendant 73.5
  guard 697.13
  verbs 73.8
escritoire 215.16
escrow 770.4
  IN ESCROW 770.16
escudo 833.9
escuela 565.1
esculent 306.31
escutcheon 567.2
esker 206.6
Eskimo 417.6
Eskimo dog 413.24
esophagus, oesophagus
  395.15
esoteric
  nouns 1032.11
  adjs. personal 80.12
  recondite 547.14
  secret 612.16
  occult 1032.24
esotericism, esoterics,
  esoterism, esotery
  1032.1
esoteric reality 5.4
esotropia 439.5
especial 80.12
especially chiefly 36.19
  particularly 80.16
espial
  observation 438.2
  espionage 484.12
  detection 487.1
espiègle 736.6
espièglerie
  trickery 616.4
  deception 616.6
  mischievousness
   736.2
  prankishness 879.4
espier 779.9
espionage
  observation 438.2
  reconnaissance
   484.12
esplanade level 213.3
  walkway 655.3
espousal 635.3
espousals 931.4
espouse
  ∼ a cause 152.14
  adopt 635.12
  marry 931.16
  plead for 1004.10
  ESPOUSE THE CAUSE
  OF 783.13
espoused 635.23
espousement 931.4
esprit smartness 466.2
  wit 879.1
esprit de corps
  partisanism 786.13
  fellowship 925.2

cultivation 689.3
eulogist 966.8
eulogistic(al) 966.15
eulogium 966.5
eulogize 966.12
eulogy citation 914.4
praise 966.5
Eumenides 954.3
THE EUMENIDES
1014.11
eumerogenesis 166.6
eunuch 157.6
eunuchize 42.11
euphemism, euphuism
figure of speech
549.2
elegance 587.3
affectation 901.5
euphemist, euphuist
euphuist 587.5
affecter 901.7
euphemistic(al)
figurative 549.4
affected 901.18
euphonic(al) 587.8
euphonious
pleasant-sounding
461.49
speech 587.8
euphonium,
euphonon 464.8
euphony
harmony 461.3
speech 587.2
euphoria
neurosis 688.22
happiness 863.2
euphuism, euphuist
See **euphemism,**
etc.
euphuistic(al)
figurative 549.4
elegant 587.9
affected 901.18
Eurale 1033.9
Eurasia region 179.6
continent 385.1
Eurasian
crossbreed 44.8
Asian 417.8
eureka! 487.11
euripus 398.1
Euroclydon 402.9
Europe 385.1
European 417.8,10
Europeanization
188.4
Europeanize 188.5
European plan 306.11
European theater of
operations 800.2
European Union
739.7
Eurus 402.3
eurythmics
symmetry 247.1
study 560.8
exercise 714.6
eurythmy 247.1
Eustachian tube 447.7
Euterpe 463.24

euthanasia 407.1
euthenics 689.3
Eutheria 414.12
eutrophy 307.1
evacuate depart 300.8
void 308.20
exhaust 308.22
defecate 309.11
withdraw 631.5
evacuation
departure 300.1
voidance 308.6
defecation 309.2
withdrawal 631.1
évacué emigrant 273.5
outcast 924.3
evacuee
emigrant 273.5
refugee 629.5
outcast 924.3
evadable 629.13
evade quibble 482.9
avoid 629.7
circumvent 733.11
evaluate assess 493.9
price 844.13
evanesce 446.2
evanescence
transience 111.1
infinitesimalness
195.2
disappearance 446.1
evanescent
ephemeral 111.7
infinitesimal 195.13
vanishing 446.3
evangel
glad tidings 556.2
messenger 559.2
evangelic(al)
scriptural 1019.9
orthodox 1022.8
evangelist
apostle 1020.2
clergyman 1036.6
evangelistic(al)
scriptural 1019.9
ministerial 1035.13
Evangels 1019.4
evaporability 400.3
evaporable 400.9
evaporate
cease to be 2.5
be transient 111.6
dry 392.6
vaporize 400.7
disappear 446.2
preserve 699.8
evaporated 392.9
evaporation
drying 392.3
vaporization 400.4
disappearance 446.1
preservation 699.2
evaporative
drying 392.10
volatile 400.9
evaporator drier 392.4
vaporizer 400.5
evasible 629.13

evasion
quibbling 482.5
secretiveness 612.1
avoidance 629.1
circumvention
733.5
evasive
quibbling 482.15
secretive 612.17
elusive 629.14
eve 134.2
ON THE EVE OF
121.13
even
nouns 134.2
verbs make uniform
17.4
equal 30.6
equalize 30.7
level 213.6
symmetrize 247.4
smooth 259.5
EVEN OFF 30.6
EVEN THE SCORE
953.7
EVEN UP THE SCORE
839.12
adjs. uniform 17.5
equal 30.8
moderate 162.13
level 213.8
parallel 217.6
symmetrical 247.5
straight 249.5
smooth 259.9
exact 515.15
neutral 804.7
just 974.8
GET EVEN WITH
pay 839.12
retaliate 953.7
take revenge 954.4
PUT ON AN EVEN
KEEL 274.51
advs. still 33.8
especially 36.19
exactly 515.19
EVEN SO
nevertheless 33.8
yes 520.18
so 506.15
even break tie 30.4
even chance 155.7
even odds 514.5
evenhanded 974.8
evening
nouns afternoon
134.1
close of day 134.2
symmetrization
247.3
adjs. 134.8
evening devotions
1030.8
evening dress, evening
gown 230.11
evening mist 393.1
evening school 565.2
evening star 374.5
evenness
uniformity 17.1

equality 30.1
horizontalness 213.1
symmetry 247.1
smoothness 259.1
even odds
even chance 155.7
odds 514.5
evensong 1030.8
even Stephen
nouns 30.4
adjs. 30.8
event circumstance 8.1
occurrence 150.2
effect 153.1
game 876.9
AT ALL EVENTS
notwithstanding
33.8
certainly 512.23
come what may
622.20
IN ANY EVENT
notwithstanding
33.8
possibly 508.10
anyhow 655.12
IN THAT EVENT 8.9
IN THE EVENT OF
in case 150.13
provided 506.12
even temper 856.1
even-tempered 856.10
even tenor
uniformity 17.2
order 59.1
eventful 150.10
eventide 134.2
eventual final 70.10
future 121.8
ultimate 150.11
liable 174.6
possible 508.6
eventuality
circumstance 8.1
futurity 121.4
contingency 150.1
effect 153.1
accident 155.6
liability 174.1
possibility 508.1
eventually
finally 70.11
in time 121.11
ultimately 150.12
eventuate occur 150.5
result 153.5
eventuation
eventuality 150.1
effect 153.1
ever forever 112.12
constantly 135.7
at all 508.10
EVER AND AGAIN
112.12
EVER MORE 38.9
EVER SO
considerably 34.17
especially 36.19
HARDLY EVER
unusually 85.16

infrequently 136.4
NOT EVER 106.4
ever-abiding 112.7
everbearing 112.8
ever-being 112.7
everblooming 112.8
ever-changing 141.6
everduring 112.7
everglade 399.1
evergreen
 nouns 410.3,10
 adjs. perennial 112.8;
  410.42
 ever-new 122.7
everlasting
 nouns eternity 112.2
 flower 410.22
 THE EVERLASTING
  1011.2
 adjs. perpetual 112.7
 tedious 882.8
everlasting fire, ever-
 lasting torment
 1017.2
everlastingness 112.1
everliving
 everlasting 112.7
 immortal 112.9
evermore 112.12
ever-new
 perennia 112.8
 new 122.7
ever-recurring 103.13
eversion 219.1
evert 219.5
every 79.14
 EVERY BIT 56.18
 EVERY NOW AND
  THEN, EVERY ONCE
  IN A WHILE
  haphazardly 62.17
  repeatedly 103.16
  occasionally 136.5
  irregularly 138.4
everybody 79.4
everyday usual 84.8
 frequent 135.4
 colloquial 578.16
 plain 900.6
every man Jack 79.4
everyone 79.4
 IN EVERYONE'S
  MOUTH
  well-known 474.27
  rumored 556.15
  famous 912.17
very one 79.14
very other
 periodic 137.8
 by turns 137.12
verything 54.3
 EVERYTHING BEING
  EQUAL
  considering 493.17
  if possible 508.11
  probably 510.7
 WITH EVERYTHING
  THAT IS IN ONE
  156.15
very-way 289.27

everywhere
 universally 79.16
 all over 178.11
 everywhither 289.27
every which way
 in disorder 62.16
 everywhither 289.27
every whit 56.18
everywhither
 everywhere 178.12
 in every direction
  289.27
evict
 nouns evictee 308.11
 outcast 924.3
 verbs 308.14
eviction 308.2
evictor 308.10
evidence
 nouns distinctness
  443.2
 proof 504
 manifestation
  553.1,3
 clue 556.8
 GIVE EVIDENCE
  504.10
 IN EVIDENCE 443.6
 verbs evince 504.9
 manifest 553.5
evident visible 443.6,7
 manifest 553.8
evidential 504.17
evidentially 504.24
evidently
 perceptibly 443.8
 manifestly 553.14
evil
 nouns bad 673.3
 bane 674
 iniquity 979.4
 misdeed 980.2
 DO EVIL 673.6
 RETURN OF EVIL FOR
  EVIL 953.2
 THE EVIL 984.11
 adjs. inauspicious
  542.15
 bad 673.7
 wicked 979.17
 advs. 673.13
evil-affected 673.11
evil dispensation 727.5
evil-disposed 937.17
evildoer
 malefactor 941
 wrongdoer 984.8
evildoing
 nouns 980.1
 adjs. 980.4
evil eye
 malevolence 937.4
 charm 1034.1
evil-eyed 673.11
evil genius evil 673.4
 familiar spirit
  1012.19
 demon 1014.7
evil-gotten 673.11
evil-headed 673.11
evilhearted 979.20

evil hour 130.2
evil-hued 673.11
evil-looking
 evil 673.11
 unprepossessing
  897.7
evil-minded 979.20
Evil One, the 1014.3
evil-qualitied 673.11
evil-savored 673.11
evil speaking 970.3
evil spirits 1014
evil star 673.4
evil-starred
 inauspicious 542.15
 unfortunate 727.14
evince evidence 504.9
 manifest 553.5
 indicate 566.16
evincement 553.1
evincible 504.21
evincive 504.19
eviscerate
 weaken 159.10
 disembowel 304.11
eviscerated 159.18
evisceration
 devitalization 159.5
 disembowelment
  304.3
evocation
 elicitation 304.4
 summons 750.5
 conjuration 1033.4
evocative 304.15
evoke induce 152.12
 elicit 304.12
 prompt 646.13
 summon 750.12
 conjure 1033.11
evolute 321.5
evolution
 mathematics 87.4
 evolvement 321
 maneuver 795.9
evolutional,
 evolutionary 321.7
evolutionism
 evolution 321.4
 ethics 955.2
evolve create 166.12
 extricate 304.9
 develop 321.5
 expatiate 591.7
evolvement
 extraction 304.1
 evolution 321.1
evulgate 554.5
evulgation
 disclosure 554.2
 publication 557.1
evulse 304.9
evulsion 304.1
evviva 966.22
ewe, ewe lamb
 sheep 413.9
 female animal
  420.10
ex
 nouns X 220.4
 examination 484.3

signature 581.10
preps. barring 77.9
 out of 302.21
exacerbate
 incite 646.17
 aggravate 883.2
 embitter 949.16
 anger 950.22
exacerbation
 incitement 646.4
 excitement 855.10
 aggravation 883.1
exact
 verbs extract 304.13
 require 637.9
 demand 751.4
 oblige 754.5
 wrest from 820.19
 assess 844.14
 levy 961.4
 adjs. detailed 8.7
 faithful 24.8
 limited 233.8
 precise 515.15
 meticulous 531.12
 literal 543.12
 formal 644.10
exacting
 elicitory 304.15
 meticulous 531.12
 demanding 751.8
 strict 755.6
 extortionate 846.12
 fastidious 894.9
exaction
 extraction 304.5
 demand 751.1
 charge 844.7
exactitude
 accuracy 515.3
 meticulousness
  531.3
exactly
 punctually 131.14
 squarely 289.26
 certainly 512.23
 precisely 515.19
 yes 520.18
 meticulously 531.16
 literally 543.15
exactment 844.7
exactness
 accuracy 515.3
 meticulousness
  531.3
exaggerate
 intensify 38.5
 overestimate 496.2
 overstate 615.3
exaggerated
 overestimated 496.3
 overstated 615.4
 excessive 661.17
exaggeration
 intensification 38.2
 overestimation 496
 overstatement 615
 excess 661
exalt increase 38.4
 elevate 315.6
 inspire 646.20

excommunicate
308.15
excommunication
308.4
ex-convict 759.11
excoriate peel 231.8
criticize 967.21
excoriation
divestment 231.1
censure 967.3
excrement 309.3
**excremental, excre-
mentary** 309.18
excrescence
outgrowth 196.3
protrusion 255.2
growth 684.29
**excrescent, excrescen-
tial** 255.13
excrete
discharge 309.10
secrete 310.5
excretion
bodily discharge
309
secretion 310
excretionary, excretive
309.17
excretory
egestive 309.17
secretory 310.7
excruciate
pain 423.7
torture 864.20
excruciating
painful 423.10
agonizing 862.14
exculpate 1005.4
exculpation 1005.1
excursion
obliquity 218.1
journey 272.5
deviation 290.1
circuity 319.1
circuit 319.3
sight-seeing 441.4
digression 591.4
excursionist
traveler 273.1
sight-seer 441.3
excursive
digressive 290.7
circuitous 319.7
discursive 591.13
excursus
digression 290.1
circuity 319.1
digression 591.4
dissertation 604.1
excurvate 255.12
**excurvation,
excurvature**
curvature 251.1
convexity 255.1
excurved 255.12
excusable 1004.14
excuse
nouns pretext 647.1
pardon 945.2
justification 1004.4
acquittal 1005.1

apology 1010.2
verbs exempt 760.13
forgive 945.3
justify 1004.11
acquit 1005.4
EXCUSE ME 945.8
excused
exempted 760.27
forgiven 945.7
excusing 1004.13
ex dividend 832.7
execrable
terrible 673.10
odious 862.9
infamous 913.12
cursed 970.9
wicked 979.17
execrate hate 928.4
curse 970.5,6
execration
aversion 928.1,3
malediction 970.1
executant 716.1
execute
produce 166.11
~ music 461.40
do 703.8
accomplish 720.4
observe 766.3
transact 769.10
put to death
1008.19
EXECUTE A MANEUVER
274.48
executed
produced 166.25
accomplished 720.9
execution
production 166.1
musical ~ 461.31
performance 703.2
accomplishment
720.1
observance 766.1
transaction 769.5
attachment 820.4
capital punishment
1008.7
**executioner, execu-
tionist** 1008.8
executive
nouns 747.5
THE EXECUTIVE
746.10
adjs. governing
739.18
directing 745.14
**executive branch, ex-
ecutive arm** 746.10
Executive Mansion
740.13
executor, executrix
producer 166.10
performer 716.1
exegentic(al) 550.17
exegesis 550.4,6
exegete 550.8
exegetics 550.9
exemplar
example 25.2
idea 478.3

paragon 983.4
exemplary
model 25.8
representative
570.11
monitory 701.9
commendable
966.19
exemplification
example 25.2
verification 504.6
explanation 550.4
representation 570.1
exemplificative 550.17
exemplify
cite 504.14
explain 550.11
typify 570.9
exempli gratia 504.25
exempt
verbs free 760.13
absolve 1005.4
adjs. 760.27
exemption
qualification 506.1
immunity 760.7
~ from hostilities
801.1
impunity 1005.1
exequatur 778.1
exequial 409.25
exequies 409.4
exercise
nouns operation
163.1
etude 461.5
training 560.3
lesson 560.6
ceremony 644.4
task 654.2
use 663.1
action 703.1
exercising 714.6
IN EXERCISE 163.12
verbs engross 528.13
train 560.13
use 663.10
practice 703.7
exert 714.8
annoy 864.17
EXERCISE THE ELBOW
994.31
exerciser 714.7
exercises
ceremony 644.4
divine service
1030.8
exercising 714.6
exercitation use 663.1
action 703.1
exert use 663.10
put forth 714.8
EXERT ONESELF
endeavor 712.4
exert 714.9
exertion use 663.1
endeavor 712.1
effort 714
exfiltrate 302.15
exfiltration 302.6
exfoliate

delaminate 226.5
scale 231.11
exfoliation
delamination 226.4
divestment 231.1
exfoliatory 231.18
exhalation fume 400.1
vaporization 400.4
expiration 402.1
respiration 402.19
odor 434.1
exhale exhaust 308.22
reek 400.7
breathe 402.25
smell 434.6
exhaust
nouns 280.9
verbs weaken 159.10
drain 304.10
evacuate 308.20
let out 308.22,23
reek 400.7
exhale 402.25
consume 664.2
fatigue 715.4
take all 820.21
waste 852.4
exhausted
used up 664.6
worn out 690.35
tired out 715.8
exhausting
weakening 159.20
fatiguing 715.11
exhaustion
vacancy 186.2
evacuation 308.6
vaporization 400.4
consumption 664.1
fatigue 715.2
loss 810.2
exhaustive
thorough 56.10
complete 720.11
exhaustive psychosis
472.3
exhaustive study 484.5
exhaustless 104.3
exhaust price 832.8
exhaust velocity
281.14
exhibit
nouns spectacle 445.7
evidence 504.1
display 553.2
theatrical ~ 609.13
verbs demonstrate
504.9
manifest 553.5
flaunt 902.17
exhibition
spectacle 445.7
manifestation 553.2
theatrical ~ 609.13
ostentation 902.4
exhibitioner 564.5
exhibitionism
psychosexuality
688.32
showing-off 902.4

appearance 445.3
tone 449.2
musical ~ 461.31
meaning 543.1
manifestation 553.1
indication 566.1
word 580.1
phrase 583.1
diction 586.1
remark 592.4
eloquence 598.1
expressionless 545.11
expression of ideas 586.2
expressive
meaningful 543.10
indicative 566.22
eloquent 598.1
descriptive 606.15
expressman 270.5
express train
speed 268.7
train 271.12
expressway 655.6
exprobrate 967.17
exprobration 967.5
expropriate 820.20
expropriation 820.6
expugnable 695.16
expulsion
elimination 77.2
ejection 308.1,7
expiration 402.1
expunction 691.7
expunge excise 42.8
obliterate 691.16
expunger 691.9
expurgate excise 42.9
cleanse 679.17
expurgation
excision 42.4
cleansing 679.2
expurgatory 679.26
exquisite
nouns 901.9
adjs. keenly sensitive 421.14
delicious 427.8
superb 672.18
delightful 861.6
fastidious 894.11
beautiful 898.16
exquisitely very 34.20
superbly 672.24
delightfully 861.10
beautifully 898.21
exsiccant 392.10
exsiccate 392.6
exsiccated 392.9
exsiccative
nouns 392.4
adjs. 392.10
exsiccator 392.4
exsufflation
expiration 402.1
exorcism 1033.4
extant existent 1.13
present 120.2
extemporaneous 628.12

extemporaneously 628.15
extemporary 628.12
extempore
nouns musical ~ 461.27
improvisation 628.5
adjs. 628.12
advs. 628.15
extemporization 628.5
extemporize 628.8
extemporizer 628.6
extend increase 38.4
generalize 79.8
endure 110.6
protract 110.9
postpone 132.8
continue 143.4
stretch 178.7
expand 196.4,5
spread 196.6
lengthen 201.9
widen 203.4
straighten 249.4
expatiate 591.8
proffer 771.4
give 816.12
EXTEND CREDIT 837.6
EXTEND OUT
be distant 198.5
be long 201.8
EXTEND THE RIGHT HAND OF FRIEND-SHIP 923.9
EXTEND THE RIGHT OF FELLOWSHIP 925.11
EXTEND TO 198.6
extended
increased 38.7
protracted 110.11
spacious 178.9
expanded 196.10
lengthened 201.12
diffuse 591.12
extensibility
pliancy 356.2
elasticity 357.1
extensible pliant 356.9
elastic 357.7
extensile
expansile 196.9
pliant 356.9
elastic 357.7
extension increase 38.1
addition 41.1,3
sequence 65.1
protraction 110.2
~ of time 132.4
continuance 143.1
extent 178.1
expansion 196.1
lengthening 201.5
extension course 565.2
extensive
widespread 79.12
spacious 178.9
large 194.17
expansive 196.9
long 201.11
broad 203.6

extensively
widely 178.10
lengthily 201.14
extent amount 28.1
degree 29.1
space 178.1
size 194.1
distance 198.1
length 201.1
breadth 203.1
TO A CERTAIN EXTENT 35.11
TO A GREAT EXTENT 34.17
TO A SMALL EXTENT 35.10
TO NO EXTENT 2.11
TO SOME EXTENT 29.7
extenuate reduce 39.8
weaken 159.10
thin 204.11
sicken 684.37
justify 1004.12
extenuated 204.15
extenuating
qualifying 506.7
justifying 1004.13
extenuating circum-stances
qualification 506.1
extenuation 1004.5
extenuation
decrease 39.1
weakening 159.5
thinness 204.4
justification 1004.5
extenuative
nouns 1004.5
adjs. 1004.13
exterior
nouns outside 223.2
picture 572.13
adjs. extraneous 78.5
external 223.6
exteriority 223
exteriorize 223.5
exteriors 445.2
exterminate
get rid of 308.19
kill 408.13
annihilate 691.14
extermination
killing 408.1
destruction 691.6
exterminator
pesticide 408.11
destroyer 691.8
external
nouns 223.2
adjs. extrinsic 6.3
extraneous 78.5
exterior 223.6
formal 644.7
external appearance 445.3
external evidence 504.2
external frustration 688.19

externality
extrinsicality 6.1
exteriority 223.1
formality 644.1
externalization 223.4
externalize 223.5
external loan 818.2
externally
outwardly 223.9
formally 644.11
externals 445.2
external secretion 310.1
exterrestrial
external 223.8
extraterrestrial 374.26
exterritorial 223.8
extinct
nonexistent 2.10
past 119.5
passé 123.15
extincteur 331.3
extinction
extinguishment 331.2
death 407.1
destruction 691.6
extinguish excel 36.7
~ fire 331.7
destroy 691.15
suppress 758.8
extinguished 331.11
extinguisher 331.3
extinguishment
quenching 331.2
death 407.1
destruction 691.6
suppression 758.2
extirpate excise 42.8
exterminate 691.14
extirpation
excision 42.3
destruction 691.6
extirpatory 691.26
extispex 541.4
extispicious 541.11
extol praise 966.12
glorify 1030.11
extort extract 304.13
wrest from 820.19
steal 822.19
overcharge 846.7
extortion
extraction 304.5
seizure 820.7
robbery 822.9
overcharge 846.5
extortionary 304.15
extortionate
extractive 304.15
exorbitant 846.12
extortionist 820.10
extra
nouns nonessential 6.2
additional amount 41.4
newspaper 603.12
actor 610.6

surplus 661.5
adjs. extrinsic 6.4
  additional 40.9
  odd 136.3
  surplus 661.19
advs. additionally
  40.10
  in excess of 661.27
extract
  nouns essence 304.7
    excerpt 605.3
  verbs take out 304.9
    deduce 493.10
    select 635.11
  EXTRACT ROOTS 87.11
extraction
  lineage 169.4
  withdrawal 304
  extract 304.7
  excerpt 605.3
extractive 304.15
extractor 304.8
extracts 605.4
extracurricular 560.20
extradite 308.16
extradition 308.4
extrados 223.2
extrajudicial oath
  521.3
extralateral 223.8
extrality 223.1
extramarginal 688.52
extramundane
  supernatural 85.14
  external 223.8
  extraterrestrial
    374.26
  immaterial 376.7
  heavenly 1016.13
extramural 223.8
extraneous
  extrinsic 6.3
  unrelated 10.5
  foreign 78.5
extraneousness
  extrinsicality 6.1
  foreignness 78
extranuclear 325.18
extraordinarily
  remarkably 34.23
  unusually 85.17
  wonderfully 918.13
extraordinary
  unusual 85.13
  notable 670.18
  wonderful 918.9
extrapolar, extra-
  provincial 223.8
extrasensory 1032.25
extrasensory
  perception 1032.8
extrasolar
  external 223.8
  astronomy 374.26
extraterrestrial
  external 223.8
  extramundane
    374.26
  heavenly 1016.13
extraterritorial 223.8
extratribal 223.8

extravagance
  fanaticism 472.11
  diffuseness 591.1
  exaggeration 615.1
  abundance 659.2
  excess 661.1,4
  exorbitance 846.4
  prodigality 852.1
  intemperance 991.1
extravagant
  drastic 161.15
  absurd 469.10
  fanatical 472.31
  fanciful 533.20
  diffuse 591.11
  exaggerated 615.4
  plentiful 659.7
  excessive 661.17
  exorbitant 846.12
  prodigal 852.8
  luxurious 902.21
  boastful 908.10
  intemperate 991.7
extravagantly
  plentifully 659.9
  superabundantly
    661.25
  exorbitantly 846.16
  luxuriously 902.28
extravaganza
  drama 609.4
  falsehood 614.10
extravagate
  exaggerate 615.3
  dramatize 670.15
extravasate
  nouns 309.3
  verbs filter 302.15
    erupt 308.23
    excrete 309.10
extravasation
  ejection 308.7
  effusion 309.1
  excretion 309.3
extravasion 302.6
extreme
  nouns
  consummation 56.4
  end 70.2
  excess 661.1
  GO TO EXTREMES
    661.11
  IN THE EXTREME
    34.22
  THE OTHER EXTREME
    15.2
  TO THE EXTREME
    661.24
  adjs. greatest 34.15
  final 70.10
  drastic 161.15
  farthest 198.12
  fanatical 472.31
  excessive 661.17
  exaggerated 615.4
  radical 743.19
  NOT EXTREME 140.8
extremely most 34.22
  excessively 661.23
extreme unction
  last rites 409.4

  sacrament 1038.5,6
extremist
  irreconcilable 661.8
  radical 743.11
extremity
  consummation 56.4
  end 70.2
  crisis 129.4
  summit 210.2
  foot 211.5
  excess 661.1
  impasse 729.5
  wretchedness 864.6
  AT THE LAST
    EXTREMITY 695.13
  TO THE LAST
    EXTREMITY 70.12
extricable 700.3
extricate extract 304.9
  rescue 700.2
  disembarrass 730.7
  free 761.7
extrication
  extraction 304.1
  rescue 700.1
  disembarrassment
    730.5
  freeing 761.3
extrinsic 6.3
extrinsicality 6
extrinsic evidence
  504.2
extrospection 688.31
extrospective 688.51
extroversion
  communicativeness
    552.4
  psychological ~
    688.31
extroversive 688.51
extrovert
  nouns personality
    416.5
  psychology 688.31
  adjs. 688.51
extrude
  protrude 255.9
  expel 308.12
extruding 255.13
extrusion
  protrusion 255.2
  expulsion 308.1
extrusive 308.26
exuberance
  diffuseness 591.1
  abundance 659.2
  friskiness 868.4
exuberant fertile 164.9
  diffuse 591.11
  abundant 659.7
  thriving 726.13
  frisky 868.14
exuberate 659.5
exudate
  nouns 309.3,7
  verbs emit 302.15
    excrete 309.10
exudation
  emission 302.6
  excretion 309.1,3,7

exudative
  exuding 302.20
  excretory 309.17
exude emit 302.15
  excrete 309.10,14
exult rejoice 874.6
  boast 908.8
  EXULT IN 903.5
exultant
  overjoyed 863.14
  jubilant 874.10
  boastful 908.11
exultantly
  happily 863.16
  jubilantly 874.11
  boastfully 908.13
exultation
  rejoicing 874.1
  boasting 908.4
exulting
  rejoicing 874.10
  boastful 908.11
exurb, exurbia 182.1
exurbanite 189.6
exuviae 228.5
exuvial 231.18
exuviate 231.10
exuviation 231.1
eye
  nouns circle 252.5
  holes 264.4
  sight 438.1,3
  visual organ 438.9
  opinion 500.4
  point of view 523.2
  intention 651.1
  ALL EYES
    attentive 528.15
    vigilant 531.13
  AN EYE FOR AN EYE
    interchange 149.1
    reprisal 953.3
  EYE TO EYE 520.15
  HAVE AN EYE FOR
    731.16
  HAVE AN EYE TO
    heed 528.9
    desire 632.14
    intend 651.7
  HAVE EYES FOR
    929.17
  IN ONE'S EYE
    imminent 151.3
    expected 537.11
  KEEP AN EYE ON
    keep informed
    555.15
    care for 697.18
    supervise 745.10
  KEEP ONE'S EYES
    OPEN
    be vigilant 531.8
    keep awake 711.3
    beware 893.7
  MEET THE EYE
    be seen 443.4
    appear 445.8
    catch attention
    528.11
  RUN THE EYE OVER
    examine 484.31

recede 296.2
dim 336.13
pale 362.5
lose color 362.6
disappear 446.2
meet a bet 514.19
sicken 684.35
deteriorate 690.19
FADE AWAY
cease to be 2.5
recede 296.2
disappear 446.2
deteriorate 690.19
perish 691.22
fade insipid 429.2
fadeaway 446.1
faded pale 362.8
impaired 690.33
fadeless
immortal 112.9
deep-dyed 361.18
fadeout 543.19,24
fade-out 446.1
fadge 26.12
fading
nouns radio 343.24
decoloration 362.3
disappearance 446.1
adjs. aging 126.16
languishing 159.21
receding 296.5
vanishing 446.3
deteriorating 690.43
fadmonger
enthusiast 633.5
fad 642.5
fadmongering 642.15
fad word 580.8
faeces 309.4
faërie, faëry 1012.14
faery 1012.23
Fafnir 194.13
fag
nouns homosexual
418.12
cigarette 433.5
work 714.4
drudge 716.3
verbs work hard
714.13
work 714.16
fatigue 715.4
wait on 748.14
fag end remnant 43.1
end 70.2
fagged 715.6
fagger 716.3
faggery 714.4
fagot bundle 74.7
firewood 330.3
fagotto 464.23
fagot vote 635.5
fagot voter 742.24
fail weaken 159.9
fall short 660.6
~ in health 684.35
deteriorate 690.18
be unsuccessful
723.9
flunk 723.16
go bankrupt 840.7

be unfaithful
973.11
NOT FAIL 972.9
failed 840.11
failing
nouns fault 676.2
vice 979.9
adjs. deficient 57.4
languishing 159.21
deteriorating 690.43
unsuccessful 723.17
preps. 660.11
failure fault 676.2
nonsuccess 723.1,8
defeat 725
nonobservance
767.1
bankruptcy 840.3
bankrupt 840.4
vice 979.9
nonfeasance 980.2
failure of memory
536.2
fain
adjs. 620.5
advs. 620.9
fainague
intrigue 652.10
maneuver 733.10
fainaguer 652.8
fainaigue 616.18
faineance, faineancy
706.4
fainéant
nouns 706.7
adjs. 706.17
faint
nouns 422.2
verbs swoon 422.4
get tired 715.5
adjs. weak 159.12
dim 336.18
pale 362.9
indistinct 444.5
faint-sounding
451.16
weak-willed 625.11
ill 684.41
fatigued 715.6
advs. 451.21
faintheart 890.1
fainthearted 890.10
faintish weak 159.12
ill 684.41
fatigued 715.6
faintly slightly 35.10
weakly 159.22
faint-sounding
451.21
faintness
weakness 159.1
dimness 336.5
paleness 362.2
indistinctness 444.2
faint sound 451
weak will 625.4
fatigue 715.1
fair
nouns bazaar 830.2
festival 876.4
THE FAIR 420.3

adjs. light 362.10
whitish 363.9
rainless 392.8
probable 510.5
legible 546.11
tolerable 672.20
mediocre 678.7
clean 679.23
tolerably well 683.7
comely 898.17
courteous 934.14
just 974.8
BE FAIR 974.6
BY FAIR MEANS OR
FOUL
somehow 655.13
dishonestly 973.23
FAIR AND SQUARE
honest 972.14
just 974.8
FAIR OR FOUL 623.9
FOR FAIR
decidedly 34.21
utterly 56.17
for certain 512.23
IN A FAIR WAY
probable 510.5
prosperous 726.12
IN A FAIR WAY TO
173.6
NOT FAIR 975.10
advs. quite 56.16
justly 974.11
Fair Deal 742.6
faire claquer son fouet
908.6
faire les yeux doux
930.18
faire venir l'eau à
la bouche 648.5
fair field 129.2
A FAIR FIELD AND NO
FAVOR 974.4
fair game dupe 618.1
laughingstock 965.7
fairing 816.4
fairly rather 29.7
positively 34.21
legibly 546.13
tolerably 672.25
mediocrely 678.12
justly 974.11
fair name 912.2
fairness
lightness 362.2
whitishness 363.1
comeliness 898.3
justice 974.3
fair play 974.3
fair sex 420.3
fair-spoken
suave 934.18
flattering 968.9
fairway seaway 274.10
airstrip 277.20
golf ~ 876.13
fair weather
good times 726.4
pleasantness 861.3
fair-weather sailor
275.1

fair winds 230.11
fair words
suaveness 934.5
flattery 968.1
fairy
nouns homosexual
418.12
sprite 1012.15
adjs. 1012.23
fairyfolk 1012.14
fairy godmother
giver 816.11
guardian spirit
1012.19
fairyism 1012.21
fairyland
utopia 533.11
fairies 1012.14
fairylike 1012.23
fairy lore 1012.21
fairy tale story 606.7
falsehood 614.11
faisan 306a.22
fait accompli fact 1.3
accomplishment
720.1
faith belief 500.1
hope 886.1
fidelity 972.7
virtue 978.5
religion 1018.1
piety 1026.1
GIVE FAITH TO 500.8
HAVE FAITH 1026.6
HAVE FAITH IN
500.12
IN GOOD FAITH
972.24
OF BAD FAITH 973.19
OF THE FAITH, OF
THE TRUE FAITH
1022.8
PLEDGE ONE'S FAITH
TO 768.6
THE FAITH, THE
FAITH 1022.2
WITHOUT FAITH
502.8
faith curer, faith curist
therapist 686.12
religionist 1018.22
faith-curism 1018.12
faithful
nouns 972.8
THE FAITHFUL
believers 500.7
religionists 1026.5
adjs. lifelike 20.16
copy 24.8
reliable 512.17
exact 515.15
literal 543.12
obedient 764.3
observant 766.4
constant 972.20
orthodox 1022.8
devout 1026.8
BE FAITHFUL TO
766.2
faithfully
exactly 515.19

literally 543.15
obediently 764.6
loyally 972.24
faithfulness
exactness 515.3
fidelity 972.7
piety 1026.1
faith healer 686.12
faith healing 1018.12
faithless
unbelieving 502.8
falsehearted 614.31
unfaithful 973.19
irreligious 1029.19
faithlessness
infidelity 973.5
irreligion 1029.5
faithworthy
dependable 512.17
trustworthy 972.19
fake
nouns sham 614.13
deception 616.7
impostor 617.6
hypocrite 617.8
verbs sham 614.22
affect 901.12
FAKE UP
do carelessly 532.9
trump up 614.18
adjs. 614.27
fakement sham 614.13
deception 616.7
artifice 733.3
faker impostor 617.6
peddler 828.6
fakir beggar 772.8
ascetic 989.2
religious 1036.12
Falak al aflak 1016.8
falcade 317.2
falcate, falciform
251.13
falcon
nouns 823.6
verbs 653.9
falderal, folderol
refrain 461.24
nonsense 545.2
trifle 671.5
fall
nouns decrease 39.2
autumn 128.4
hang 214.2
declivity 218.5
veil 230.26
descent 314.1
tumble 314.3
plunge 318.1
rainfall 393.1
waterfall 394.11
death 407.1
~ of the cards
514.2
degradation 690.3
ruin 691.3
relapse 694.2
failure 723.3
defeat 725.1
BE HEADING FOR A
FALL 1008.24

TAKE A FALL OUT OF
904.5
verbs decrease 39.6
occur 150.5
hang down 214.6
slope 218.10
descend 314.5
tumble 314.8
plunge 318.6
rain 393.9
deteriorate 690.18
be destroyed 691.21
backslide 694.4
fail 723.11
be defeated 725.12
~ in price 847.6
be sinful 979.13
FALL ACROSS
encounter 199.11
find 487.3
FALL A CURSING
970.6
**FALL ALL OVER
ONESELF**
be eager 633.7
hasten 707.5
FALL A VICTIM TO
684.34
FALL AWAY
decrease 39.6
fall short 312.2
apostatize 626.8
deteriorate 690.18
relapse 694.4
FALL BACK
be behind 240.7
recoil 283.7
retreat 294.6
relapse 694.4
FALL BACK UPON
663.14
FALL BEHIND
be behind 240.7
lag 292.4
regress 294.5
lose 810.5
FALL DOWN
drift 274.31
fall through 312.3
descend 314.5
fall 314.8
be imperfect 676.3
fail 723.11
**FALL DOWN ON ONE'S
KNEES** 1010.5
FALL DUE 838.7
FALL FLAT
fall through 312.3
fall 314.8
fail 723.11
be dull 881.4
FALL FOR
be credulous 501.5
be enamored 929.19
FALL FOUL OF
encounter 199.11
collide 282.13
quarrel 793.12
contend with
794.16

FALL FROM GRACE
relapse 694.2
backslide 694.4
**FALL FROM ONE'S
HIGH ESTATE**
be unfortunate
727.11
be disgraced 913.7
FALL IN
form 59.4
line up 71.7
collapse 197.10
fail 723.11
FALL INTO
be converted 145.12
incur 174.4
undertake 713.3
FALL INTO A HABIT
640.12
FALL INTO DECAY
690.23
FALL INTO DISREPUTE
913.7
FALL INTO DISUSE
666.9
**FALL INTO ONE'S
HANDS** 817.8
FALL INTO PLACE
59.4
FALL IN WITH
agree 26.7
conform 82.3,4
incur 174.4
converge 297.2
find 487.3
concur 520.9
consent 773.4
accord 792.2
FALL OFF
decrease 39.6
come apart 49.7
drop off 314.5
apostatize 626.8
deteriorate 690.18
relapse 694.4
FALL ON
light on 314.10
find 487.3
attack 796.15
FALL ON EVIL DAYS
727.11
FALL ON ONE'S KNEES
submit 763.10
entreat 772.11
truckle 905.6
beg mercy 942.6
thank 947.4
make obeisance
962.6
FALL OUT
result 153.5
quarrel 793.11
FALL SHORT
be inferior 37.4
not reach 312.2
disappoint 539.3
want 660.6
be imperfect 676.3
FALL THROUGH
fall short 312.3
fail 723.11

FALL TO
begin 68.6
eat 306.17
undertake 713.3
set to work 714.15
FALL TO DUST 360.10
FALL TO ONE 817.8
FALL TO ONE'S LOT
chance 155.11
be one's duty 960.6
FALL TO PIECES
come apart 49.7
disintegrate 53.3
crumble 360.10
decay 690.23,24
be destroyed 691.21
FALL TO THE GROUND
fall through 312.3
be destroyed 691.21
fail 723.11
FALL UPON
encounter 199.11
arrive at 299.7
find 487.3
be unexpected 538.6
attack 796.15
LET FALL
drop 316.7
divulge 554.6
say 592.16
NOT FALL FOR 503.3
fallacia consequentis
493.4
fallacious
illogical 482.13
erroneous 517.14
illusory 518.9
false 614.26
deceptive 616.21
fallacy sophistry 482.1
error 517.1
falseness 614.1
deception 616.1
fallback recoil 283.3
retrogression 294.2
fallen reduced 39.10
downthrown 316.10
undercooked 329.8
dead 407.24
ruined 691.27
defeated 725.14
unvirtuous 979.16
prostitute 987.28
fallen angel 984.5
fallen countenance
539.1
fallen woman 987.16
fall guy 148.3
fallibility 513.7
fallible
fallacious 482.13
errable 513.20
falling
nouns 314.1
adjs. sloping 218.16
descending 314.11
deteriorating 690.43
falling leaf 277.12
falling off
moderation 162.2
deterioration 690.3

radio 343.5
fanned 196.11
fannel 1040.10
fanning
nouns 484.2
adjs. 196.11
fanny 240.4
fanon 1040.10
fan-shaped 196.11
fantail 240.5
fan-tan 514.7
fantasia, fantasie 461.6
fantasied 627.5
Fantasiestück 461.6
fantast 533.12
fantastic(al)
unusual 85.12
absurd 469.10
illusory 518.9
fanciful 533.20
capricious 627.5
fantasticality 627.2
fantasy illusion 518.4
fancy 533.1,5
story 606.7
caprice 627.1
escapism 688.34
fantoccini figure 570.4
puppet show 609.14
fantod
delirium tremens
472.10
hallucination 518.7
far
adjs. 198.8
advs. very much
34.19
distantly 198.16
A FAR CRY 16.1
AS FAR AS POSSIBLE
utterly 56.17
reasonably 481.23
one's best 712.14
BY FAR 34.19
FAR AFIELD 198.19
FAR AHEAD 131.8
FAR AND WIDE
by far 34.19
extensively 178.10
far 198.17
FARAWAY
distant 198.8
abstracted 530.11
FAR BE IT FROM ME
774.9
FAR BETWEEN 49.20
FAR FROM IT
unlike 21.5
amiss 312.7
by no means 522.8
FAR OFF 198.8,16
FAR ON 132.18
GO FAR
endure 110.6
achieve success
722.9
GO TOO FAR 661.11
SPREAD FAR AND WIDE
557.10
faradic electricity
341.1

farce
forcemeat 306a.37
drama 609.6
trifle 671.5
farcicalness 878.2
burlesque 965.6
farcer, farceur,
farceuse, farcist
dramatist 609.26
comedian 610.8
farcical
comicodramatic
609.39
humorous 878.6
burlesque 965.14
farcicality 878.2
far cry 198.2
fardel 74.7
fare
nouns passenger
273.1
food 306a.1
charge 844.7
verbs contrive 7.6
turn out 153.5
travel 272.17
journey 272.20
eat 306.17
FARE WELL
succeed 722.6
prosper 726.7
FARE YOU (YE)
WELL 300.25
far-embracing 79.12
farewell
nouns leave-taking
300.4
aftertaste 426.1
verbs 300.18
adjs. 300.19
interjs. 300.25
farewell performance
musicale 461.33
drama 609.13
far-extending 79.12
far-famed 912.17
farfetched 10.7
farfetched story
614.11
far-flung
extensive 79.12
long 201.11
far-flying 79.12
fargoing
extensive 79.12
long 201.11
far-gone
nouns 175.4
adjs. impaired
690.35
enamored 929.25
drunk 994.38
far-heard 912.17
farina cereal 306a.34
meal 360.5
farinaceous 360.11
farm
nouns farmhouse
190.5
grange 412.8
poorhouse 698.4

verbs ranch 412.16
let out 778.13
adjs. 412.20
farmer
agriculturist 412.5
peasant 917.8,9
farmerish 181.7
farm hand 412.5
farmhouse 190.5
farming
nouns 412.1
adjs. 412.20
farm interests 742.32
farm land, farmplace,
farmstead 412.8
farm machinery
347.19
farness 198.1
far piece 198.2
farrago 62.3
far-ranging 79.12
far-reaching
extensive 79.12
long 201.11
farrier 415.2
farrow 170.2
farse 1038.12
farseeing
clear-sighted 438.23
sagacious 466.16
foreseeing 540.8
farseeingness
sagacity 466.4
foresight 540.1
far-sight 438.1
farsighted
clear-sighted 438.23
presbyopic 439.11
sagacious 466.16
foreseeing 540.8
farsightedness
vision 438.1
presbyopia 439.4
sagacity 466.4
foresight 540.1
far-spread, far-spread-
ing 79.12
farther
adjs. additional 40.9
thither 198.10
advs. 40.10
preps. 198.21
farthermost 198.12
farthest
adjs. final 70.10
most distant 198.12
advs. 198.12
farthing fourth 98.2
trifle 671.5
coin 833.8
farthing dip 335.2
fasces 737.8
fascia ribbon 205.4
band 252.3
fascicle section 55.2
bunch 74.6
book 603.14
fascicled, fasciculated
74.21
fascinate
interest 528.12,13

captivate 648.6
thrill 855.16
delight 863.8
enamor 929.20
bewitch 1034.9
fascinated
interested 528.16,18
enamored 929.25
spellbound 1034.13
fascinating
interesting 528.20
alluring 648.7
delightful 861.6
bewitching 1034.12
fascination
craze 472.12
obsession 472.13
enthusiasm 633.3
allurement 648.1
delightfulness 861.2
spell 1034.2
fascinator 648.3
fascine 74.7
Fascism
government 739.8
partisanism 742.26
Fascist 742.28
fascist 739.16
fash 864.19
fashion
nouns mode 7.4
form 245.1
appearance 445.3
diction 586.2
custom 640
style 642
society 642.6
convention 643
way 655.1
AFTER A FASHION
to a degree 35.11
somehow 655.13
AFTER THIS FASHION
655.11
IN FASHION 642.11
OUT OF FASHION
123.16
verbs create 166.12
form 245.6
fashionability 642.2
fashionable
nouns 642.7
adjs. 642.11
BE FASHIONABLE
642.9
fashionable society
642.6
fashionably 642.16
fashioned 166.27
fashion plate 576.7
fasnacht 306a.43
fast
nouns fastening 48.2
spare diet 993.2
holyday 1038.14
verbs 993.4
adjs. fastened 47.14
stable 142.13
stuck 142.17
close 265.12
speedy 268.19

fast-dyed 361.18
  sure 512.17
  devoted 925.20
  profligate 987.25
MAKE FAST
  fasten 47.7
  secure 142.9
  bind 758.10
PLAY AT FAST AND
    LOOSE
  fluctuate 141.5
  falsify 614.20
  be capricious 627.4
advs. securely 47.18
  swiftly 268.21
GO FAST 268.9
FAST BY 199.20
fast day fast 993.3
  holyday 1038.16
fast-dye 361.13
fast-dyed 361.18
fasten attach 47.7
  secure 142.9
  close 255.6
  bind 758.10
FASTEN ITSELF ON
  THE MIND 477.19
FASTEN ON 1003.7
FASTEN ONESELF
  UPON 905.10
FASTEN THE EYES
  UPON 438.16
FASTEN UP 214.8
FASTEN UPON
  attribute to 154.3
  seize 820.13
  impose 961.4
  accuse 1003.7
fastened fast 47.14
  fixed 142.15
  stuck 142.17
fastener fastening 48.2
  types of ~ 48.7–9
fastening
  attachment 47.3
  fastener 48.2
faster than sound
  fast 268.20
  supersonic 449.17
fasthold 797.6
fasti 114.8
fastidious 894.9
fastidiously 894.14
fastidiousness 894
fastigium 210.2
fasting
  nouns 993
  adjs. 993.5
fastness stability 142.1
  velocity 268.1
  stronghold 797.6
  devotedness 925.7
  profligacy 987.3
fat
  nouns fatness 194.8
  oil 379.1
  best part 672.8
  verbs 196.8
  adjs. fertile 164.9
  corpulent 194.18
  paunchy 196.13

thick 203.8
fatty 379.9
stupid 468.15
plentiful 659.7
profitable 809.14
wealthy 835.13
GROW FAT 726.8
Fata 638.3
fatal deadly 408.23
  important 670.21
  destructive 691.25
fatalism 638.4
fatalist 638.5
fatalistic 638.10
fatality death 408.7
  deadliness 408.8
  fate 638.2
fata morgana
  luminescence
    334.13
  mirage 518.6
fat chance 522.8
fate end 70.1
  luck 155.1
  inevitability 637.7
  destiny 638.2
  ruin 691.2
BE ONE'S FATE
  chance 155.11
  be necessary 637.10
fated
  inevitable 637.15
  destined 638.9
fateful
  prophetic 541.11
  portentous 542.13
  fated 638.9
  important 670.21
  destructive 691.25
fatefulness 542.5
Fates 638.3
fat-faced type 601.6
fat frying 742.35
fathead 470.4
fatheaded 468.17
Father 915.5
Father, Son and Holy
  Ghost 1011.10
father
  nouns senior 127.5
  cause 152.4
  creator 166.10
  sire 169.9
  priest 1036.4
BE A FATHER TO
  697.18
THE FATHER 1011.11
THE FATHERS 1020.2
verbs originate 152.11
  affiliate 154.4
  procreate 168.9
  adopt 635.12
  care for 697.18
FATHER UPON
  attribute to 154.3
  cuckold 987.22
Fatherhood 1011.1
fatherhood 169.2
father-in-law 12.2
fatherland 180.2

fatherless
  helpless 157.18
  orphan 407.28
  forlorn 922.13
fatherlike 169.13
father love 929.5
fatherly 169.13
Father of Evil, Father
  of Lies 1014.3
Father of Waters
  394.1
fathers 169.7
fathership 169.2
Father Time
  time 105.2
  elder 127.2
fathom
  take soundings
    208.8
  know 474.12
  probe 484.30
  solve 486.2
  measure 489.11
  understand 546.7
fathomable
  measurable 489.15
  intelligible 546.9
fathomage 208.4
fathomless 208.10
fatidic(al) 541.11
fatigue
  nouns weakening
    159.5
  languor 706.5
  work 714.4
  tiredness 715.1
  verbs 715.4,5
fatigued 715.6
fatigue duty 654.2
fatigues 230.1
fatiguing 715.11
fat lot 34.5
fatness
  corpulence 194.8
  thickness 203.2
  oiliness 379.5
fat of the land
  plenty 659.2
  prosperity 726.1
fatten enrich 164.8
  enlarge 196.8
  improve 689.9
  prosper 726.8
FATTEN ON 905.11
FATTEN UPON 306.25
fattish 194.18
fatty
  nouns 194.12
  adjs. 379.9
fatuitous
  unsubstantial 4.5
  ineffectual 157.15
  foolish 469.8
  vain 667.13
fatuity
  unsubstantiality 4.1
  ineffectualness
    157.3
  foolishness 469.1
  thoughtlessness
    479.1

fatuous
  unsubstantial 4.5
  ineffectual 157.15
  foolish 469.8
  thoughtless 479.4
  vain 667.13
fat-witted 468.16
faubourgs 232.1
fauces 395.15
faucet 395.10
fault cleft 200.2
  error 517.3
  defect 676.2
  blemish 677
  misdeed 980.2
AT FAULT
  erroneous
    517.14, 16
  defective 676.4
  guilty 981.3
BE AT FAULT 517.9
FIND FAULT 967.15
TO A FAULT 661.24
faultfind 967.15
faultfinder
  complainer 867.3
  criticizer 967.9a
faultfinding
  nouns 967.4
  adjs. 967.24
faultful 517.14
faultiness error 517.1
  imperfection 676.1
faultless
  correct 515.14
  perfect 675.6
  innocent 982.6
faultlessness
  accuracy 515.3
  perfection 675.1
  innocence 982.1
faultsman 341.19
faulty
  illogical 482.10
  erroneous 517.14
  ungrammatical
    585.4
  deficient 660.11
  defective 676.4
  guilty 981.3
faun 1012.18
fauna 413.1
Faunus 1012.18
faussebraie, fausse-
  braye 797.4
Faust 1033.5
faute error 517.3
  fault 676.2
faute de mieux
  instead 148.11
  if necessary 637.17
faux air
  illusion 518.2
  sham 614.3
faux-bourdon 461.20
faux pas 517.5
MAKE A FAUX PAS
  517.13
faveolate 256.17
favonian 402.26
Favonius 402.3

favor
nouns influence 171.2
face 239.4
appearance 445.3,4
token 535.7
epistle 602.2
aid 783.4
gift 816.7
esteem 912.3
friendship 925.3
kindness 936.7
quarter 942.1
privilege 956.4
approbation 966.1
BE IN FAVOR OF
consent 773.3
approve of 966.9
DO A FAVOR
help 783.19
do good 936.13
GET INTO FAVOR
925.12
IN FAVOR
reputable 912.16
friendly with 925.17
IN FAVOR OF
for 783.26
approving 966.16
for 966.20
IN HIGH FAVOR
912.16
IN ONE'S FAVOR
672.26
OUT OF FAVOR
of securities 832.14
uncared-for 865.10
in disrepute 913.13
verbs resemble 20.7
prefer 635.14
benefit 672.11
indulge 757.7
help 783.11,14,17,
19
show kindness
936.10
approve of 966.9
play favorites 975.8
FAVOR WITH 816.15
favorable
timely 129.10
auspicious 542.16
willing 620.5
advantageous 668.4
beneficial 672.21
helpful 783.22
hopeful 886.13
friendly 925.14
approving 966.16
favorably
auspiciously 542.19
willingly 620.9
beneficially 672.26
helpfully 783.24
amicably 925.21
favorably inclined,
favorably disposed
620.5
favored
privileged 760.27
approved 966.18
favorer 785.8

favoring
nouns 757.4
adjs. resembling
20.10
auspicious 542.16
approving 966.16
favorite
nouns race horse
413.19
darling 929.13
PLAY FAVORITES
975.8
adjs. 929.21
favoritism 975.3
favors of office 742.37
fawn
nouns 413.7
verbs give birth
166.19
truckle 905.6
fawner 905.3
fawnery 905.2
fawning
nouns 905.2
adjs. 905.13
fay white man 363.3
fairy 1012.15
faze 889.17
F.B.I. police 697.15
service 740.12
detectives 779.10
fealty 972.7
fear
nouns nervousness
857
anxiety 888
fright 889.1
types of phobias
889.34
cowardice 890
IN FEAR
fearful 889.22
fearfully 889.32
FOR FEAR OF 889.31
PUT IN BODILY FEAR
889.19
PUT IN FEAR 889.15
WITH FEAR AND
TREMBLING 889.31
verbs 889.9
fearful great 34.12
superstitious 501.9
nervous 857.11
anxious 888.6
afraid 889.22
frightening 889.27
cowardly 890.10
fearfulness 889.2
fearing 889.22
fear-inspiring 889.27
fearless 891.19
fearlessness 891.3
fearsome
fearful 889.22
frightening 889.27
fear-struck 889.21
feasibility
practicability 508.2
expedience 668.1
feasible
practicable 508.7

expedient 668.4
feast
nouns banquet 306.9
treat 863.3
festival 876.4
holyday 1038.14
verbs eat 306.22
gratify 863.6
revel 876.27
FEAST ON 863.10
FEAST UPON 306.25
feasting 306.1
feat deed 703.3
exploit 891.7
feather
nouns kind 61.3
plume 229.16
plumage 229.18
lightness 352.3
trifle 671.5
A FEATHER IN ONE'S
CAP
victory 724.1
trophy 914.3
IN FINE FEATHER
strong 158.16
dressed up 230.45
healthy 683.6
verbs grow 126.9
cover 227.30
fledge
229.21
~ an oar 274.56
aviate 277.46
decorate 899.8
FEATHER ONE'S NEST
be saving 658.12
prepare for 718.11
prosper 726.9
grow rich 835.9
featherbedding 778.4
featherbrain 470.7
featherbrained
shallow-witted
468.20
scatterbrained
530.16
feathered
plumaged 229.28
ornamented 899.10
featheredge
edge 234.4
sharp edge 257.2
featheredged 257.11
feathered songster
bird 413.34
songbird 463.15
feathering 229.18
feathers
plumage 229.18
clothing 230.1
THE FEATHERS
215.20
featherweight
nouns diminutive
195.4
weight 351.3
pugilist 798.2
adjs. 352.12
feathery
plumy 229.27

light 352.10
soft 356.14
feature
nouns component
58.2
characteristic 80.3
special 81.2
appearance 445.3,4
special article 604.1
motion picture
609.15
salient point 670.7
commodity 829.2
verbs resemble 20.7
specialize 81.4
envisage 477.16
imagine 533.15
headline 609.32
give prominence
670.14
adjs. 81.5
feature attraction
610.5
featured 81.5
featureless 246.4
features
outline 234.2
face 239.4
looks 445.4
feaze 45.4
febricity 684.6
febrifugal 685.36
febrifuge 685.12
febrile
feverish 684.43
fervent 853.22
excited 855.23
febrility 684.6
fecal 309.18
feces, faeces
sediment 43.2
excrement 309.4
feck 28.1
feckless
ineffective 157.15
useless 667.9
improvident 719.15
feculence 309.4
feculent 309.18
fecund
productive 164.9
inventive 533.18
fecundate
make fruitful 164.8
fertilize 168.11
fecundation
enrichment 164.3
fertilization 168.4
fecundative
fertilizing 164.11
procreative 168.16
fecundity
productiveness
164.1
inventiveness 533.3
federal
federative 52.7
governmental
739.16
federal agent 779.10

feudalism
  government 739.8
  serfdom 762.1
feudality 739.8
feudal system 739.8
feudatory
  nouns 808.5
  adjs. subject 762.12
    feodal 808.10
feu de joie 875.1
fever
  nouns frenzy 472.8
    delirium 472.9
    sickness 684.6
    excitement 855.6
  verbs 684.34
fever heat
  heat 327.1
  fever 684.6
  excitement 855.6
feverish
  delirious 472.30
  fevered 684.43
  hasty 707.9
  fervent 853.22
  excited 855.23
feverous 684.43
fever ward, etc.
  687.29
few
  nouns a number
    101.2
    small number 102.2
  THE FEW 102.3
  adjs. 102.4
  FEW AND FAR
    BETWEEN 102.5
  IN A FEW WORDS
    590.6
  NO FEW, NOT A FEW
    101.7
fewer 102.6
fewness 102
fiancé, fiancée
  929.15
fiasco 723.6
fiat decree 750.4
  sanction 775.6
fiat money 833.6
fib
  nouns 614.11
  verbs 614.19
fibber 617.9
fibbery 614.8
fiber nature 5.3
  filament 205.1
  types of ~ 205.8
  texture 350.1
fibril, fibrilla 205.1
fibriliform, fibroid,
  fibry 205.7
fibrous
  threadlike 205.7
  tough 358.4
fibster 617.9
ficelle 616.6
fickle
  changeable 141.7
  capricious 627.7
  unfaithful 973.19

fickleness
  changeableness 141
  capriciousness 627.3
  infidelity 973.5
fictile 356.9
fictility 356.2
fiction fancy 533.5
  story 606.7
  falsehood 614.10
fictional
  imaginary 533.21
  narrative 606.17
  fictitious 614.30
fictitious, fictive
  imaginary 533.21
  false 614.30
fictitious name 581.8
fid 433.8
fidalgo 916.4
fiddle
  nouns violinist 463.5
  violin 464.6
  PLAY FIRST FIDDLE
    take precedence
    36.10
    dominate 739.14
  PLAY SECOND FIDDLE
    37.4
  verbs violin 461.42
  trifle 671.13
fiddledeedee
  nouns 545.2
  interjs. nonsense!
    469.12
    pooh! 965.16
fiddle-faddle
  nouns nonsense
    545.2
    trifle 671.5
  verbs procrastinate
    132.10
    twaddle 545.8
    trifle 671.13
  adjs. nonsensical
    545.10
    trivial 671.16
  interjs. 469.12
fiddler 463.5
fiddlery 461.32
fiddlestick
  bow 464.6
  trifle 671.5
fiddlesticks!
  nonsense! 469.12
  pooh! 965.16
fiddlestring 464.24
fidelity
  exactness 515.3
  faithfulness 972.7
Fides, Fides publica
  Romani 974.5
fidfad
  nouns 671.5
  adjs. 671.16
fidget twitch 323.13
  bustle 705.11
  be agitated 855.18
  be nervous 857.7
  make nervous 857.9
  FIDGET WITH 671.13

fidgetiness
  twitching 323.5
  bustle 705.4
  trepidation 855.4
  nervousness 857.1
fidgets
  twitching 323.5
  disease 684.17
  trepidation 855.4
  nervousness 857.1
fidgety jerky 323.30
  bustling 705.19
  excitable 855.28
  nervous 857.12
fiducial 142.13
fiduciary
  nouns 807.5
  adjs. 770.16
fidus Achates 926.3
fie! 913.18
fief 808.5
field extent 178.1
  sphere 179.2
  tract 179.4
  airport 277.19
  magnetic ~ 341.3
  pasture 410.8
  farm 412.9
  insignia 567.2
  sphere of work
    654.4
  arena 800.1
  battlefield 800.2
  athletic ~ 876.13
  OFF THE FIELD
    157.17
  TAKE THE FIELD
    795.21
  THE FIELD 789.2
field artillery
  army 798.26
  guns 799.6
field day 876.4,10
field emission 342.5
field glass 443.2
field hospital 687.29
field marshal 747.22
field of blood
  shambles 408.12
  battlefield 800.2
Field of Mars 800.1
field of vision 443.3
fieldpiece 799.6
fieldwork 797.4
fiend
  violent person 161.9
  addict 640.9
  monster 941.7
  evil spirit 1014.7
  THE FIEND 1014.3
fiendish cruel 937.24
  wicked 979.18
  demoniacal 1014.18
fierce violent 161.15
  savage 161.20
  something ~
    673.14
  belligerent 795.26
  overwrought 855.26
  passionate 855.30
  cruel 937.24

  furious 950.29
fierceness
  violence 161.1
  cruelty 937.11
fieri facias 750.6
fiery violent 161.21
  hot 327.26
  inflammable 328.27
  red 367.6
  sore 423.11
  feverish 684.43
  fervent 853.22
  excited 855.23
  passionate 855.30
  hot-tempered
    949.25
fiery cross fire 327.12
  alarm 702.3
  call to arms 795.17
fiery ordeal 864.9
fiery temper 949.3
fiesta feast 306.9
  festival 876.4
fife
  nouns 464.9
  verbs 461.43
fifer 463.4
fifteen 99.7
Fifteener 603.3
fifth number 99.14
  quinary 99.17
fifth column 617.11
fifty 99.7
fifty cents 833.7
fifty-fifty equal 30.9
  mixed 44.15
  half 92.2
  halved 92.4
  neutral 804.7
  GO FIFTY-FIFTY
    compromise 805.2
    share 813.6
fifty percent 92.2
fig fettle 7.3
  clothing 230.1
  trifle 671.5
  A FIG FOR! 965.16
  TRY TO GET FIGS
    FROM THISTLES
    509.5
fight
  nouns struggle 714.3
  quarrel 793.5
  battle 794.3
  pugnacity 795.16
  PUT UP A FIGHT
    object 520a.5
    oppose 788.5
    resist 790.3
    fight 794.14
  THE FIGHTS 794.9
  verbs struggle 714.11
    oppose 788.5
    quarrel 793.12
    battle 794.14
    wage war 795.19
    attack 796.15
  FIGHT ONE'S BATTLES
    OVER AGAIN 103.8
  FIGHT ONE'S WAY
    forge ahead 293.4

struggle 714.11
fight 794.14
FIGHT SHY 889.11
FIGHT SHY OF
demur 621.4
avoid 629.6
FIGHT THE GOOD
FIGHT
espouse a cause
152.14
fight 794.14
be good 978.6
be religious 1026.6
FIGHT THE TIGER
514.19
FIGHT TO THE LAST
DITCH
resist 790.5
fight 794.6
fighter
combatant 798.1
pugilist 798.2
fighter pilot 278.3
fighting
nouns contention
794.1
war 795.1
adjs. contending
794.23
militant 795.26
fighting chance 155.9
fighting cock 798.1
fighting machine
798.22
fighting man 798.7
fighty
pugnacious 795.26
contentious 949.26
fig leaf 230.3
figment fancy 533.5
falsehood 614.10
figmental
imaginary 533.21
fictitious 614.30
figment of the imagi-
nation
illusion 518.4
fancy 533.5
fig out
dress up 230.41
adorn 899.7
figural 86.8
figurant, figurante
actor 610.6
dancer 877.3
figurate 86.8
figuration
outline 234.2
form 245.1
forming 245.5
representation
570.6
figurative
numerical 86.8
metaphorical 549.4
typical 570.12
flowery 599.12
figure
nouns number 86.1
outline 234.2
form 245.1

human form 245.4
body 375.3
appearance 445.3,5
musical ~ 461.24
logic 481.7
phantasm 518.4
~ of speech
549.1
symbol 566.2
image 570.4
diagram 652.3
personage 670.8
psychological ~
688.41
price 844.1
eyesore 897.4
dash 902.4
reputation 912.1
celebrity 912.9
~ of fun 965.7
MAKE A FIGURE
be ostentatious
902.13
be famous 912.10
verbs calculate 87.11
shape 245.6
judge 493.9
personify 549.3
symbolize 570.9
ornament 899.8
be distinguished
912.10
FIGURE FOR 652.10
FIGURE ON 651.6
FIGURE OUT
calculate 87.11
solve 486.2
FIGURE TO ONESELF
533.14
FIGURE UP 87.12
figured
grandiloquent
599.12
ornamented 899.10
figure dancer 877.3
figurehead
insignia 567.1
figure 570.4
nominal head 747.4
figurer 577.6
figures 87.2
figurine 570.4
figuriste 577.6
filament
nouns fiber 205
barb 229.17
verbs 205.6
filamentary
threadlike 205.7
hairlike 229.23
filamentule
threadlet 205.1
barbule 229.17
filch
nouns theft 822.10
booty 822.11
verbs 822.13
filcher 823.1
filching 822.1
file
nouns series 71.2

catalogue 88.3
crafty person 733.6
military unit 798.19
pickpocket 823.2
IN FILE 71.12
ON FILE
classified 61.8
on record 568.17
verbs classify 61.6
defile 71.8
list 88.7
sharpen 257.10
smooth 259.8
march 272.29
abrade 349.7
store 658.10
FILE A CLAIM
1002.14
FILE A STRONG BID
712.10
FILE FOR 772.9
FILE OFF
remove 42.10
file 71.8
march 272.29
filed 61.8
file fire 796.9
filer à l'anglaise 186.8
filet de sole 306a.24
filial 170.7
filiate 154.4
filiation kinship 11.1
lineage 169.4
descendant 170.4
filibuster
nouns obstructionist
728.8
legislation 740.16
verbs temporize
132.10
legislate 740.20
pirate 822.16
filibusterer
obstructionist 728.8
freebooter 823.7
filibustering
legislation 740.16
piracy 822.6
Filicales, Filices
plants 411.6
filicoids 411.6
filiform
threadlike 205.7
hairlike 229.23
filigree
nouns 220.3
verbs 899.8
filing listing 88.6
grinding 349.2
filing card 568.9
filings remains 43.1
raspings 360.5
refuse 667.4
filing system 88.3
fill
nouns full measure
56.3
satiety 662.1
verbs render complete
56.7
occupy 76.3

pervade 185.7
stop up 265.7
provide 657.7
superabound 661.9
overfill 661.16
satiate 662.4
fulfill 766.2
possess 806.5
FILL AN OFFICE
654.14; 742.46
FILL IN
complete 56.6
shallow 209.3
FILL IN FOR
spell off 108.4
substitute for 148.5
FILL ONE IN 555.8
FILL ONE'S POCKETS
835.9
FILL ONE'S SHOES
supplant 148.6
be deputy 779.13
FILL OUT
supplement 56.6
expand 196.5
round out 254.6
write out 568.15
protract 591.8
execute 769.10
FILL THE AIR 452.6
FILL THE BILL
suffice 659.4
avail 663.17
fulfill 766.2
FILL UP
compensate 33.4
fill 56.7
stop up 265.7
provide 657.7
satiate 662.4
recruit 692.11
filled 56.12
fille de chambre 748.8
fille de joie 987.16
filler filling 193.1
fill horse 413.18
fillet band 205.4
ring 252.3
insignia 567.4
bandage 685.28
fillet of sole 306a.24
fill-in 148.2
filling
nouns contents 193.1
weft 221.4
superfluity 661.4
adjs. completing
56.14
satiating 662.7
filling station 830.8
fillip
nouns blow 282.6
throw 284.4
snap 455.2
stimulus 646.7
verbs toss 284.12
snap 455.7
stimulate 855.12
filly girl 125.6
horse 413.12

FLARE UP
blaze 327.21
burst forth 445.9
get excited 855.17
become angry
950.18
flared 96.11
flare-up
outburst 161.6
blaze 327.13
signal 566.14
~ of passion 855.8
outburst of anger
950.9
flaring spread 196.11
burning 327.27
flashing 334.34
gaudy 902.20
flash
nouns instant 113.3
explosion 161.7
clothes 230.10
blaze 327.13
~ of light 334.6
glance 438.4
news report 556.5
telegram 558.16
argot 578.6
sudden thought
628.1
IN A FLASH
instantly 113.7
quickly 268.23
verbs shine 334.23
burst forth 445.9
signal 566.21
telegraph 558.22
flaunt 902.17
FLASH BACK 485.4
FLASH ON THE MIND
occur to 477.17
be remembered
535.16
FLASH UP 855.17
FLASH UPON ONE
538.6
adjs. cant 578.17
false 614.27
flash burn
atomics 325.15
injury 690.7
flashery clothes 230.10
ornament 899.3
flashily 902.26
flashing
transient 111.8
flashy 334.34
showy 902.19
flash in the pan
nouns
unsubstantiality 4.2
impotent 157.6
false alarm 702.4
failure 723.5,8
verbs
be unproductive
165.3
fail 723.12
flashlight 334.6
flash note 833.10

flash of lightning
instant 113.3
lightning 334.17
flash of wit 879.7
flash tongue 578.6
flashy flashing 334.34
grandiloquent 599.9
showy 902.19
flat
nouns apartment
191.4
shoal 209.2
plane 213.3
~ tire 252.4
smoothness 259.3
flatcar 271.13
plain 386.1
note 462.14
fool 470.2
gambling den
514.14
stage ~ 609.24
dupe 618.1
verbs 361.14
FLAT OUT
fall through 312.3
fail 723.11
adjs. uniform 17.5
deflated 197.14
level 213.8
prostrate 213.9
smooth 259.9
inert 267.12
lackluster 336.19
champaign 386.3
insipid 429.2
phonetics 449.18
toneless 451.17
off-key 460.4
unqualified 507.2
prosaic 608.5
penniless 836.10
dull 881.6
LEAVE FLAT 631.5
advs. 213.10
flatcar 271.13
flat coat 361.12
flatfoot
deformity 248.3
policeman 697.14
detective 779.10
flatfooted 248.12
flat-footed 972.17
flatform 215.13
flathat 277.48
flathatting 277.14
flatly 213.10
flatness
horizontalness 213.1
smoothness 259.1
lackluster 336.6
insipidness 429.1
dead sound 451.2
dissonance 460.1
prosaicness 608.2
dullness 881.1
flat play 704.9
flat rate 844.2
flats plain 386.1
dice 514.8
flat-sided 204.16

flat silver 347.3
flat spin 277.12
flatten even 17.4
level 213.6
smooth 259.5
FLATTEN OUT 277.49
flattened out 684.44
flattener 70.4
flatter
fawn upon 905.6–9
praise 966.12
compliment 966.13
cajole 968.5
FLATTER ONESELF
think likely 510.4
boast 908.7
FLATTER THE PALATE
427.4
flatterer
sycophant 905.3
adulator 968.4
flattering
insincere 614.32
obsequious 905.13
complimentary
966.15
adulatory 968.9
flattery
insincerity 614.5
sycophancy 905.2
praise 966.5
compliment 966.6
adulation 968
flatteur 968.4
flat tire tire 252.4
bore 882.4
flattop 276.8
flatulence, flatulency
distension 196.2
grandiloquence
599.1
flatulent
inflated 196.12
bombastic 599.10
pompous 902.22
flatus distension 196.2
gas 400.1
air current 402.1
flatware
tableware 347.3
merchandise 829.4
flat wash 361.12
flatways, flatwise
213.10
flaunt
nouns brandish 322.2
ostentation 902.4
verbs brandish 322.10
display 902.17
flaunter 902.11
flaunting
nouns 322.2
adjs. grandiloquent
599.9
ostentatious 902.19
flautist 463.4
flauto 464.9
flavor
nouns characteristic
80.3
taste 426.1

flavoring 427.3
odor 434.1
verbs imbue 44.12
savor 427.7
flavor control 348.8
flavored 426.9
flavorful 427.9
flavoring 427.3
flavorless 429.2
flavorous, flavory
flavored 426.9
savory 427.9
flavorsome 427.9
flaw cleft 200.2
gust 402.6
sophism 482.3
fault 676.2
flawless 675.6
flawy 402.26
flax 1008.15
flaxen, flax-colored
369.4
flaxen-haired 369.5
flaxseed 410.29
flay peel 231.8
fleece 820.21
criticize 967.21
F layer 401.3
flea 413a.6
PUT A FLEA IN ONE'S
EAR
remind 535.20
tip 555.10
warn 701.7
advise 752.6
fleabite 671.5
flea-bitten 373.13
flea in one's nose
627.1
flea in the ear
reminder 535.6
tip 555.3
warning 701.1
advice 752.2
flèche 206.11
flèche de lard 306a.16
fleck
nouns small amount
35.2
minute thing 195.7
flake 226.3
hair 229.6
speckle 373.3
mark 566.4
blotch 677.3
verbs variegate 373.7
mark 566.18
flecked, fleckered
373.13
flection bending 251.3
fold 263.1
fledge
grow feathers 126.9
feather 229.21
fledgling
youngling 125.1,8
novice 564.7
flee hasten off 300.14
disappear 446.2
take to flight 629.10

fleece
  nouns hair 229.2
    softness 356.4
  verbs divest 231.5
    swindle 616.18
    strip 820.21
    overcharge 846.7
fleeced 836.8
fleecy woolly 229.24
  soft 356.14
fleer
  nouns runaway 629.5
    derision 965.2,4
  verbs 965.9
fleet
  nouns company 74.3
    ships 276.1
    ~ of planes 279.9
    flight 629.4
    navy 798.27
  verbs be transient
    111.6
    speed 268.9
  adjs. transient 111.8
    shallow 209.5
    fast 268.19
    quick 705.17
    nimble 731.21
fleeting
  transient 111.7
  evanescent 446.3
Fleet Street 603.23
flesh kinsmen 11.2
  meat 306a.12
  physicality 375.1
  the body 375.3
  mankind 416.1
  sexuality 418.2
  carnality 985.2
  IN THE FLESH
    personally 80.17
    in person 185.15
    living 406.10
  MAKE THE FLESH
    CREEP 864.13
  THE FLESH 985.2
flesh and blood 375.1
  MORE THAN FLESH
    AND BLOOD CAN
    BEAR
    exciting 855.31
    insufferable 862.16
  ONE'S OWN FLESH
    AND BLOOD 11.2
flesh-color 367.9
flesh eater 306.13
flesh-eating 306.29
fleshiness
  corpulence 194.8
  pulpiness 389.1
fleshless 204.16
fleshly physical 375.9
  human 416.10
  sexual 418.17
  sensual 985.6
  lascivious 987.29
fleshpots 726.1
fleshpots of Egypt
  prosperity 726.1
  wealth 835.1

flesh show
  television 344.2
  drama 609.13
fleshy fat 194.18
  pulpy 389.6
fleur-de-lis 567.2
flex
  nouns 251.3
  verbs 251.6
flexibility
  pliancy 356.2
  elasticity 357.1
  unstrictness 756.2
  compliance 763.3
flexible pliant 356.9
  elastic 357.7
  unstrict 756.5
  compliant 763.13
flexible supports 844.6
flexile pliant 356.9
  elastic 357.7
flexion 251.3
flexor 158.2
flexuosity zigzag 218.8
  convolution 253.1
flexuous zigzag 218.21
  convolutional 253.6
  circuitous 319.7
  pliant 356.9
flexure bending 251.3
  fold 263.1
flibbertigibbet
  scatterbrain 470.7
  fiend 1014.7
flick
  nouns blow 282.6
    jerk 285.3
    snap 455.2
    mark 566.4
    motion picture
    609.15
    blotch 677.3
  verbs strike 282.16
    jerk 285.5
    flutter 323.12
    snap 455.7
  FLICK ONE ON THE
    RAW 853.15
flicker
  nouns flutter 323.4
    flame 327.12
    ~ of light 334.8
    ~ of an eye 438.4
    motion picture
    609.15
  verbs flutter 323.12
    burn 327.21
    shine waveringly
    334.25
flickering
  nouns 334.8
  adjs. irregular 138.3
    fluttering 323.19
    burning 327.27
    flickery 334.36
flickery, flicky
  fluttery 323.19
  flickering 334.36
flier, flyer
  speeder 268.6
  train 271.12

aviator 278.1
  gamble 514.1
  handbill 557.8
  speculation 831.19
flies 609.20
flight
  nouns throng 74.4
    flock 74.5
    multitude 101.3
    husk 227.17
    course 266.2
    speed 268.1
    migration 272.4
    flying 277.1
    aeronautics 277.7
    rocket ~ 280.10
    musical ~ 462.18
    running away 629.4
    escapism 688.34
    air force 798.29
    ~ of arrows 799.17
  IN FLIGHT
    flying 277.57
    fugitive 629.15
  PUT TO FLIGHT
    defeat 725.9
    repulse 797.10
    scare away 889.20
  TAKE A FLIGHT
    277.42
  verbs 284.13
flight deck
  carrier 276.8
  airstrip 277.20
flight path 277.22
flight plan 277.8
flight reaction 688.20
flighty delirious 472.30
  frivolous 530.16
  fanciful 533.20
  fickle 627.7
flimflam
  nouns humbug
    614.14
    deception 616.1,7
    caprice 627.1
  verbs 616.17
  adjs. 616.21
flimflammer 617.3
flimflammery 616.1
flimsiness frailty 159.2
  thinness 204.4
  rarity 354.1
  flaccidity 356.3
flimsy
  nouns 600.11
  adjs. frail 159.14
    thin 204.15
    rare 354.7
    flaccid 356.10
    illogical 482.11
    trivial 671.16
flinch
  nouns 283.3
  verbs recoil 283.7
    cringe 889.12
flinder 55.3
flinderate 49.12
fling
  nouns throw 284.4
    attempt 712.2

revel 876.6
  gibe 965.2
HAVE A FLING AT
  have a chance
    155.13
  ridicule 965.9
HAVE ONE'S FLING
  go unrestrained
    760.17
  make merry 876.26
  dissipate 991.6
  verbs put 183.13
    rush 268.10
    throw 284.12
FLING AT 796.30
FLING DOWN 316.5
FLING DOWN THE
  GAUNTLET
    challenge 791.3
    declare war 795.20
FLING OFF
  depart 300.13
  get rid of 308.19
  say 592.14
flinger 284.8
flinging 284.3
flint lighter 330.4
  hardness 355.6
flinthearted 937.23
flip
  nouns tap 282.6
    throw 284.4
    jerk 285.3
    snap 455.2
  verbs flick 282.16
    toss 284.12
    jerk 285.5
    flap 323.12
    snap 455.7
FLIP THE COIN
  514.17
FLIP THROUGH THE
  PAGES 484.34
  adjs. glib 594.9
    impertinent 911.9
flippancy 911.2
flippant 911.9
flipper
  swimming 274.11
  arm 286.5
  stage panel 609.24
flirt
  nouns flip 282.6
    throw 284.4
    jerk 285.3
    trifler 671.9
    coquette 930.10
  verbs flip 282.16
    toss 284.12
    jerk 285.5
    trifle 671.13
    coquet 930.18
FLIRT WITH THE IDEA
  477.11
flirtation trifling 671.8
  love affair 929.6
  coquetry 930.8
flirtatious 930.23
flit
  nouns speed 268.1

sound softly 451.12
abound 659.5
go easily 730.8
FLOW FROM 153.6
FLOW IN 301.10
FLOW ON 391.14
FLOW OVER 394.18
flow control 348.8
flower
 nouns essence 5.2
 blossom 410.22
 the best 672.8
 IN FLOWER 410.36
 verbs develop 321.6
 blossom 410.33
 ~ speech 599.8
 thrive 726.8
 embellish 899.8
flowerage
 flowers 410.1
 flowering 410.24
flower bed 412.10
flower bud 410.21
flowered
 floral 410.36
 ornamented 899.10
floweret 410.22
flowering
 nouns development
 321.2
 blossoming 410.24
 adjs. 410.36
flowerlike 898.16
flower of age 126.2
flower of life 124.1
flowers
 types of ~ 410.45
 excerpts 605.4
flowery
 floral 410.36
 figurative 549.4
 grandiloquent
 599.12
 ornate 899.11
flowing
 nouns gliding 272.8
 flow 394.4
 adjs. pendent 214.9
 fluid 387.6
 streaming 394.25
 elegant 587.8
 eloquent 598.9
 cursive 600.24
flowing periods 587.1
flowmeter 387.5
flowoff 302.4
flu 684.12
fluctuate
 intermit 138.2
 be changeable 141.5
 oscillate 322.9
 vacillate 625.8
fluctuating
 irregular 138.3
 changeable 141.7
 oscillating 322.14
 vacillating 625.10
fluctuation
 irregularity 138.1
 changeableness
 141.3

oscillation 322.1
vacillation 625.2
fluctuations 832.8
flue
 nouns fluff 229.19
 lightness 352.3
 softness 356.4
 chimney 395.18
 verbs 196.6
 adjs. 196.11
flue cleaner 679.15
flued 196.11
fluency
 fluidity 387.1
 elegance 587.2
 loquacity 594.1
 eloquence 598.2
fluent fluid 387.6
 flowing 394.25
 elegant 587.8
 loquacious 594.9
 eloquent 598.9
fluently
 talkatively 594.11
 eloquently 598.15
fluff
 nouns girl 125.6
 down 229.19
 lightness 352.3
 softness 356.4
 bungle 732.5
 verbs 536.5
fluffy downy 229.27
 nappy 350.7
 soft 356.14
Flügelhorn 464.8
flugelman See fugle-
 man
fluid
 nouns electric ~
 341.2
 liquid 387.2
 semiliquid 388.5
 water 391.3
 adjs. changeable
 141.6
 liquid 387.6
 watery 391.16
fluidal 387.6
fluid drive 347.6
fluidification 390.1
fluidify 390.5
fluidimeter 387.5
fluidity
 changeableness
 141.1
 liquidity 387
fluidization 390.1
fluidize 390.5
fluid operations 795.9
fluing 196.11
fluke
 nouns accident 155.6
 stroke of luck 726.3
 BY A FLUKE 155.18
 verbs 724.4
flukiness 155.1
fluking 274.63
fluky 155.15
flumadiddle
 thing 375.4

nonsense 545.2
flume
 nouns ravine 200.3
 conduit 395.2,3
 verbs 270.13
flummery
 cereal 306a.34
 nonsense 545.2
flummox
 bewilder 513.12
 fail 723.9
 thwart 728.15
flump
 nouns 451.3
 verbs 314.6
flunk
 nouns 723.7
 verbs shirk 629.9
 fail 723.16
 lose courage 890.8
flunker
 shirker 629.3
 failure 723.8
 coward 890.5
flunky
 stagehand 609.28
 menial 716.2
 flunker 723.8
 lackey 748.5
 henchman 785.7
 toady 905.3
flunkyism 905.2
fluoresce 334.26
fluorescence 334.13
fluorescent 334.37
fluorescent light
 334.18
fluorescent paint
 326.5
fluorophotograph
 photograph 575.8
 medicine 687.12
fluoroscope 687.11
fluoroscopy 326.7
flurried 323.17
flurry
 nouns agitation 323.1
 snowstorm 332.9
 gust 402.6
 confusion 530.3
 bustle 705.4
 haste 707.1
 stock market ~
 832.8
 excitement 855.3
 bluster 909.1
 verbs agitate 323.10
 fluster 530.7
 excite 855.15
flush
 nouns heat glow
 327.11
 color 361.2
 reddening 367.3
 jet 394.9
 healthiness 683.1
 fever 684.6
 thrill 855.2
 cards 876.17
 blush 906.5
 verbs level 213.6

be hot 327.21
redden 367.5
drench 391.13
gush 394.17
start game 653.9
rinse 679.18
excite 855.16
turn color 855.20
elate 868.7
make proud 903.6
blush 906.8
anger 950.14
adjs. full 56.12
 even 213.8
 ruddy 367.10
 abundant 659.7
 healthy 683.10
 wealthy 835.13
 drunk 994.39
advs. evenly 213.10
 squarely 289.26
flushed hot 327.25
 reddened 367.10
 feverish 684.43
 fervent 853.22
 excited 855.23
 elated 863.14
 jubilant 874.10
 puffed up 903.10
 blushing 906.13
 exultant 908.11
 drunk 994.39
flushness 213.1
fluster
 nouns agitation 323.1
 distraction 530.3
 bustle 705.4
 excitement 855.5
 bluster 909.1
 verbs distract 530.7
 excite 855.15
flusterate 855.15
flustered
 confused 530.12
 excited 855.24
 drunk 994.38
flustery 530.12
flustrate 530.7
flustration
 confusion 530.3
 dither 855.5
flute
 nouns furrow 262.1
 instrument 464.9,23
 verbs furrow 262.3
 twill 263.5
 play a ~ 461.43
fluted
 furrowed 262.4
 twilled 263.7
fluting 262.1
flutist 463.4
flutter
 nouns spurt 268.4
 flicker 323.4
 sparkle 334.8
 tremolo 462.19
 gamble 514.1
 confusion 530.3
 bustle 705.4
 haste 707.1

fold
nouns lamina 226.2
  enclosure 235.3
  doubling 263
  embrace 930.2
  laity 1037.1
verbs middle 69.3
  collapse 197.10
  double over 263.5
  close 265.6
  fail 723.9
  go bankrupt 840.7
  hug 930.16
FOLD ONE'S ARMS
  do nothing 704.2
  idle 706.11
FOLD UP
  end 70.7
  collapse 197.10
  close up 265.6
  fail 723.9
  go bankrupt 840.7
foldable 197.11
folded 263.7
folder
  advertisement 557.8
  booklet 603.10
  bookholder 603.20
folderal, folderol See
  falderol
folding 263.4
foliaceous 226.6
foliage 410.16
foliate
  verbs 87.10
  adjs. 410.39
foliated
  laminated 226.6
  leafy 410.39
foliation
  pagination 87.1
  lamination 226.4
  foliage 410.16
folie 472.1
folie de toucher
  688.28
folio book 603.1
  page 603.13
  bookholder 603.20
foliole 410.17
foliose 410.39
folk race 11.4
  population 189.1
  people 416.2
Folketing 740.4
folklore
  tradition 123.2
  superstition 501.3
  mythology 1012.21
folk music, folk song
  461.13
folks kinsmen 11.2
  family 11.6
  people 416.2
folk story, folk tale
  606.7
Folkvang 1016.11
folkway 640.1
follicle cavity 256.2
  seedcase 410.28

follow
nouns 653.1
verbs resemble 20.7
  emulate 22.7
  come next 65.3
  specialize 81.4
  conform 82.3
  be subsequent 117.2
  result 153.5
  parallelize 217.5
  be behind 240.7
  go behind 292.3
  look after 438.14
  seek 484.24,29
  prove true 504.11
  understand 546.7
  pursue 653.8
  practice 703.7
  take advice 752.9
  observe 766.2
  be a hanger-on
    905.10
  court 930.19
FOLLOW A COURSE
  289.11
FOLLOW CLOSE UPON
  stay near 199.12
  approach 295.3
FOLLOW OUT
  be thorough 56.8
  persevere 623.5
FOLLOW THE BEAM
  277.43
FOLLOW THE BEATEN
  PATH
  conform 82.4
  routine 640.13
FOLLOW THE CROWD
  conform 82.4
  be fashionable
    642.10
  be obsequious
    905.10
FOLLOW THE LEAD
  OF 764.2
FOLLOW THROUGH
  623.5
FOLLOW UP
  be thorough 56.8
  trace 484.29
  persevere 623.5
  pursue 653.8
follower
  accompanier 73.4
  attendant 292.2
  disciple 564.2
  devotee 633.6
  pursuer 653.4
  servant 748.1
  hanger-on 905.5
  lover 929.11
  believer 1026.4
followers 786.6
followers of Christ
  1022.4
following
nouns emulation 22.1
  sequence 65.1
  accompaniment
    73.6
  posteriority 117.1

going after 292.1
  pursuit 653.1
adjs. resembling
    20.10
  succeeding 65.5
  subsequent 117.3
  resultant 153.7
  trailing 292.5
  deducible 504.18
  pursuing 653.11
NOT FOLLOWING
  illogical 482.10
  unproved 505.8
follow-me-lads 229.5
follow-up sequel 67.1
  pursuit 653.1
folly
  foolishness 469.1,4
  blunder 517.5
foment
nouns 323.1
verbs heat 328.17
  incite 646.17
  excite 855.11
  relieve 884.5
fomentation
  turbulence 161.2
  incitement 646.4
  lotion 685.9
  excitement 855.10
fonctionnaire 747.17
fond
nouns 215.6
adjs. sanguine 886.11
  loving 929.24
fondle foster 783.16
  cherish 811.7
  caress 930.14
fondling pet 929.13
  love-making 930.1
fondness liking 632.2
  love 929.1
fons et origo 152.6
font source 152.6
  jet 394.9
  type 601.6
  source of supply
    658.4
  baptistry 1038.7;
    1040.9
fontanel 264.1
food nutriment 306a.1
  types of ~
    306a.48–56
  health ~ 307.28
food for thought
  483.1
food for worms
nouns 407.13
adjs. 407.24
foodstuff 306a.1
food value 307.1
foofaraw
  commotion 62.4
  frills 899.3
foo fighter 281.3
fool
nouns ninny 470
  ignoramus 476.9
  clown 610.9
  dupe 618.1

MAKE A FOOL OF
  stultify 469.7
  fool 616.14
verbs act the ~
    469.6
  deceive 616.14
  trifle 671.13
FOOL AROUND WITH
  tamper 237.7
  experiment 488.8
FOOL AWAY 852.5
FOOL WITH 237.7
adjs. 469.8
foolable 501.8
foolery
  foolishness 469.1
  buffoonery 879.5
foolhardy
  adventurous 891.21
  rash 892.9
fooling trifling 671.8
  buffoonery 879.5
NO FOOLING 521.9
foolish stupid 469.8
  trifling 671.16
DON'T BE FOOLISH!
  469.13
foolishness folly 469
  triviality 671.3
foolproof 158.18
fool's paradise
  illusion 518.1
  airy hopes 886.5
foot
nouns base 211.2
  anatomy 211.5
  metrical unit 607.9
  infantry 798.26
AT ONE'S FEET
  nearly 199.15
  subjugated 762.13
AT THE FEET OF
  in subjection 762.16
  worshipful 1030.15
AT THE FOOT OF
  207.11
FOOT BY FOOT 55.8
HAVE ONE FOOT IN
  THE GRAVE 159.8
KEEP ON FOOT 143.4
ON FOOT
  existent 1.13
  happening 150.9
  operating 163.12
  afoot 272.42
  under consideration
    484.42
  astir 705.18
  in preparation
    718.24
PUT ON ONE'S FEET
  DOWN
  stand fast 142.12
  be determined
    622.9
  order 750.11
  insist 751.7
PUT ONE'S FOOT IN
  ONE'S MOUTH
  be inopportune
    130.5

blunder 517.13
PUT ON ONE'S FEET
  785.11
PUT THE RIGHT FOOT
  FORWARD
  be careful 531.7
  be cautious 893.5
WITH ONE FOOT IN
  THE GRAVE
  aged 126.17
  dying 407.27
  verbs walk 272.26,27
  dance 877.5
FOOT THE BILL
  839.18
FOOT UP 87.12
footage 201.1
foot-and-mouth
  disease 684.10
football ball 254.2
  game 876.16
football field 876.13
footboy 748.4
footbridge 655.10
foot-candle 334.21
footfall 272.13
footgear 230.27
Foot Guards 798.32
foothills 206.5
foothold footing 215.5
  purchase 286.2
footing state 7.1
  rank 29.2
  calculation 87.3
  position 183.3
  support 215.5
  purchase 286.2
  fee 839.5
ON A FOOTING WITH
  30.3
ON A GOOD FOOTING
  925.17
footlicker 905.3
footlicking
  nouns 905.2
  adjs. 905.13
footlights light 334.18
  theater 609.22
THE FOOTLIGHTS
  609.1
foot-loose
  wandering 272.36
  free 760.19
footman 748.5
footmark 566.6
footpad 823.5
footpath 655.3
footprint 566.6
foot race 794.12
footrest support 215.5
  stair 313.5
foots 609.22
footslog 272.29
footslogger 798.10
foot soldier 798.10
footsore 715.6
footstep length 201.7
  footfall 272.13
  stair 313.5
  footprint 566.6

footstone foundation
  stone 215.7
  monument 568.11
footstool 215.5
footwear 230.27
foot-weary 715.6
footwork 272.10
foozle
  nouns fool 470.1
  bungle 732.5
  verbs 732.11
fop 901.9
foppery 901.4
foppish 901.17
for instead of 148.12
  because of 154.9
  to 651.12
  in preparation for
  718.25
  in behalf of 783.26
  in favor of 966.20
FOR AGES 110.14
FOR ALL ME 80.17
FOR ALL THAT 33.8
FOR AS MUCH AS,
  FORASMUCH AS
  154.8
FOR EACH
  per 80.20
  for 651.12
FOR EVER AND A DAY
  110.14
FOR THE MOST PART
  chiefly 36.19
  mostly 54.13
  generally 79.15
  usually 84.9
forage
  nouns search 484.2
  fodder 306a.4
  verbs feed 306.15
  search 484.25
  provision 657.9
  plunder 822.15
foraging 822.5
foramen 264.1
Foraminifera,
  foraminifers 414.3
foray
  nouns raid 796.4
  pillage 822.5
  verbs 796.21
forbad, forbade 776.7
forbear
  verbs leave undone
  532.7
  not use 666.5
  refrain 704.3
  be patient 859.4
  have pity 942.4
  abstain 990.7
  interjs. 776.8
forbearance
  tolerance 524.4
  disuse 666.2
  leniency 757.2
  patience 859.1
  forgiveness 945.1
  temperance 990.1
forbearant
  tolerant 524.11

  lenient 757.9
  patient 859.10
  forgiving 945.6
forbid
  verbs prevent 728.14
  prohibit 776.3
  adjs. 776.7
forbiddal 776.1
forbiddance
  prevention 728.2
  prohibition 776.1
forbidden fruit
  knowledge 474.8
  temptation 648.1
  taboo 776.1
forbidding
  preventive 728.19
  stern 755.6
  prohibitive 776.6
  revolting 862.9
  ugly 897.11
force
  nouns quantity 28.1
  throng 74.4
  effect 153.3
  power 156.1
  energy 160.1
  violence 161.1
  influence 171.1
  magnetic ~ 341.10
  waterfall 394.11
  validity 515.4
  meaning 543.1
  eloquence 598.3
  staff 748.12
  compulsion 754.2
BY FORCE
  with force 156.16
  compulsorily 754.12
IN FORCE
  operating 163.12
  in use 663.24
PUT IN FORCE
  apply 663.11
  enact 740.20
  execute 769.10
  legalize 996.8
  verbs thrust 282.12
  strain 311.9
  hasten growth
  412.17
  motivate 646.12
  compel 754.4
  rape 987.20
FORCE FROM 820.19
FORCE IN 303.6
FORCE OPEN 264.14
FORCE OUT 308.13
FORCE UPON
  urge upon 771.9
  thrust upon 816.19
force bed 412.11
forced farfetched 10.7
  inelegant 588.3
  unwilling 621.5
  involuntary 637.14
  labored 714.19
forced landing 314.3
forced march 272.12
BY FORCED MARCHES
  707.13

forceful potent 156.11
  energetic 160.11
  valid 515.12
  eloquent 598.11
  emphatic 670.22
  compulsory 754.10
forceless
  impotent 157.13
  uninfluential 172.3
forcemeat
  food 306a.12
  stuffing 306a.37
force of friction 349.5
force of inertia 156.5
force of life
  force 156.5
  life force 406.3
forceps 304.8
forces
  ~ of nature 401.4
  armed ~ 798.22
forcible potent 156.11
  energetic 160.11
  eloquent 598.11
  emphatic 670.22
  compulsory 754.10
forcibly
  powerfully 156.14
  by force 156.16
  energetically 160.14
  compulsorily 754.12
forcing house, forcing
  pit 412.11
Ford 835.7
ford
  nouns shallow 209.2
  pass 655.10
  verbs 311.8
fore
  nouns 239.1
TO THE FORE 239.13
  adjs. prior 116.4
  former 119.7
  front 239.11
fore and aft
  throughout 56.19
  ships 274.73
forearm
  nouns 286.5
  verbs provide against
  718.11
  take precautions
  893.6
forebears 169.7
forebode predict 541.9
  portend 542.8
foreboding
  nouns prediction 541
  presentiment 542.1
  anxiety 888.1
  adjs. 542.13
forebrain 465.5
forecast
  nouns foresight 540.1
  prediction 541.1
  verbs foresee 540.6
  predict 541.9
  plan ahead 652.9
  adjs. 541.14
forecaster 541.4
forecasts 348.7

foreclose
  preclude 728.14
  dispossess 820.20
foreclosure
  prevention 728.2
  dispossession 820.6
foreconscious 688.39
foredawn 133.4
foreday 133.1
foredestiny 638.1
foredoom
  nouns 638.2
  verbs 638.7
foredoomed 638.9
forefathers 169.7
forefeel 540.7
forefeeling
  hunch 480.3
  premonition 542.1
forefinger 424.5
forefoot
  nouns 211.5
  verbs 758.10
forefront 239.1
foreglimpse
  nouns 540.1
  verbs anticipate 131.6
  foresee 540.6
foregoer 66.1
foregoing
  nouns 291.1
  adjs. preceding 64.5
  former 119.8
  adjs. former 64.5
  leading 291.3
foregone 638.8
foregone conclusion
  preconception 494.1
  predetermination
    638.1
foreground 239.1
  IN THE FOREGROUND
  before 239.13
  manifest 553.11
fore-gut 224.6
forehand
  nouns advantage 36.2
  front 239.1
  adjs. early 131.7
  front 239.11
forehanded early 131.7
  thrifty 849.9
  precautious 893.10
forehead 239.5
forehorse 746.5
foreign extrinsic 6.3
  unrelated 10.5
  extraneous 78.5
  IN FOREIGN PARTS
    78.6
foreign accent 592.7
foreign affairs 742.5
foreign body 78.2
foreign-born 78.5
foreign correspondent
    603.22
foreigner 78.3
foreign influx 301.3
foreignism 580.6
foreign office 740.6,
    779.7

Foreign Service 779.7
forejudge 494.2
forejudgment 494.1
foreknow 540.7
foreknowable 541.13
foreknowledge
  foresight 540.3
  presentiment 542
foreknown 541.14
foreland front 239.1
  headland 255.8
foreleg 272.16
forelock 229.6
forelooper 66.1
foreman 746.2
foreman of the jury
    1000.8
foremanship 745.4
forementioned 64.5
foremost
  adjs. chief 36.16
  first 68.15
  front 239.11
  preceding 291.3
  most important
    670.25
  advs. 239.13
forenamed 64.5
forenoon 133.1
forensic 996.11
forensic medicine
  medicine 686.1
  jurisprudence 996.7
foreordain 638.6
foreordained 638.8
foreordination 638.1
foreparents 169.7
fore part, forepart
    239.1
forepaw 211.5
forepost 239.2
forequarter 239.1
forerun be prior 116.3
  anticipate 131.6
  precede 291.2
  presage 542.11
forerunner
  precursor 66.1
  harbinger 542.3
foresee
  anticipate 131.6
  foreknow 540.6
  predict 541.9
foreseeable 541.13
foreseeing
  nouns 540.1
  adjs. sagacious 466.16
  foreknowing 540.8
  divinatory 541.11
  precautious 893.10
foreseen
  expected 537.11
  predicted 541.14
foreseer 541.4
foreshadow
  nouns 542.2
  verbs 542.8
foreshadowed 542.12
foreshadowing 542.14
foreshore 384.2
foreshorten 202.6

foreshow 542.8
foreshowing 542.14
foreshown
  predicted 541.14
  portended 542.12
foreside 239.1
foresight
  sagacity 466.4
  prevision 540
  prediction 541
  precaution 893.3
foresighted
  sagacious 466.16
  foreseeing 540.8
  precautious 893.10
forest
  nouns 410.11
  verbs 412.18
  adjs. 410.38
forestall
  anticipate 131.6
  prevent 728.14
  monopolize 806.7
forestallment 806.4
forestation 412.3
forester
  woodlander 189.10
  agriculturist 412.7
forest fire fighter
    331.4
forest preserve, forest
  reserve 699.6
forest primeval 410.11
forest ranger 412.7
forestry forest 410.11
  agriculture 412.3
forests 181.2
foretaste
  nouns appetizer
    306a.9
  foreknowledge
    540.4
  verbs anticipate 131.6
  foresee 540.6
foretell 541.9
foretelling
  nouns 541.1
  adjs. 541.11
forethought
  foresight 540.2
  premeditation 651.3
  precaution 893.3
forethoughtful
  sagacious 466.16
  foreseeing 540.8
  precautious 893.10
foretoken
  nouns 542.2
  verbs 542.9
foretokening 542.14
foretold 541.14
fore tooth 257.7
forever
  nouns 112.2
  advs. 112.12
forewarn
  forebode 542.8
  warn 701.8
forewarning
  nouns foreboding
    542

warning 701.2
  adjs. 542.14
forewisdom 540.3
foreword 66.2
forfeit
  nouns pledge 770.3
  loss 810.1
  fine 1007.3
  PAY THE FORFEIT
    1010.4
  verbs 810.5
  adjs. 810.7
forfeiture loss 810.1
  fine 1007.3
forgather 74.15
forgathering 74.2
forge
  nouns 717.5
  verbs create 166.12
  form 245.6
  counterfeit 614.18
  coin 833.26
  FORGE AHEAD
  progress 293.4
  be industrious
    705.12
  FORGE FETTERS
    758.10
forged 614.30
forger smith 716.7
  counterfeiter 833.24
forgery
  falsehood 614.10,13
  counterfeit 833.10,
    23
forget
  nouns 536.1
  verbs disregard 529.4
  not remember 536.5
  forgive 945.5
  FORGET IT
  no matter 671.22
  you are welcome
    816.27
  FORGET ONESELF
  be engrossed 530.9
  neglect 532.6
  become angry
    950.17
  NEVER FORGET 947.3
forgetful
  careless 532.11
  memoryless 536.9
  inconsiderate
    937.16
  BE FORGETFUL 536.4
  FORGETFUL OF SELF
    977.7
forgetfulness
  carelessness 532.2
  obliviousness 536
  inconsiderateness
    937.3
forgettable 536.10
forgivable 1004.14
forgive pardon 945.3
  acquit 1005.4
  FORGIVE AND FORGET
    945.5
  FORGIVE ME! 945.8
forgiven 945.7

forgiveness pardon 945
  magnanimity 977.2
  exoneration 1005.1
  ASK FORGIVENESS
    1010.5
forgiving
  placable 945.6
  magnanimous 977.6
forgo give up 631.7
  do without 666.5
  refrain 704.3
  relinquish 812.3
  abstain 990.7
forgotten past 119.5
  unremembered
    536.8
  unthanked 948.5
forgotten man, the
  the unemployed
    706.9
  the poor 836.3
  the underprivileged
    917.6
fork
  nouns divergence
    298.4
  headstream 394.3
  bough 410.18
  verbs ladle 270.16
  pitch 284.12
  diverge 298.7
  FORK OUT
  give 816.12
  pay out 839.14
  expend 841.5
  FORK OVER
  hand over 816.13
  pay 839.16
forked 298.10
forking
  nouns 298.3
  adjs. 298.10
forks 347.3
forlorn
  disconsolate 870.29
  hopeless 887.12
  forsaken 922.13
forlorn hope
  disappointment
    539.1
  hope 887.4
forlornness
  despair 887.2
  aloneness 922.4
form
  nouns fettle 7.3
  mode 7.4
  mold 25.6
  arrangement 60.1
  kind 61.3
  rule 84.4
  lair 190.22
  bench 215.18
  outline 234.2
  structure 244
  shape 245
  human ~ 245.4
  body 375.3
  appearance 445.3,5
  musical ~ 462.11
  idea 478.3

phantasm 518.4
class 564.9
document 568.4
convention 643.1
formality 644.1
way 655.1
formula 749.3
law 996.3
specter 1015.1
ritual 1038.3
IN GOOD FORM 59.7
OUTWARD FORM
  appearance 445.2,4
  formality 644.1
verbs compose 58.3
take form 59.4
create 166.12
establish 166.13
shape 245.6
take shape 245.7
train 560.13
FORM A WHOLE
  54.6
FORM THE FOUNDA-
  TION OF 215.23
formable pliant 356.9
  teachable 562.18
formal
  nouns dress clothes
    230.11
  ceremony 644.4
  adjs. conditional 7.7
  orderly 59.6
  structural 244.9
  formative 245.8
  stilted 588.3
  conventional 643.7
  ceremonious 644.7
  ritualistic 1038.21
formaldehyde
  preservative 699.3
  liquor 994.15
formalism
  ceremonialism 644.2
  lip worship 1027.2
  ritualism 1038.1
formalist
  nouns conformist
    82.2
  pedant 475.6
  lip server 1027.3
  ritualist 1038.2
  adjs. 644.7
formalistic 644.7
formalities 644.3
formality rule 84.4
  convention 643.1
  ceremony 644
  law 996.3
  religious ~ 1038.3
formalize form 245.6
  ceremonialize 644.5
format 244.1
formation
  composition 58.1
  order 59.1
  arrangement 60.1
  making 166.3
  establishment 166.4
  structure 244.1
  form 245.1

forming 245.5
word form 580.3
GET IN FORMATION
  71.7
KEEP IN FORMATION
  274.48
formation cruising
  274.7
formation flying
  277.9
formative
  creative 166.23
  formational 245.8
  pliant 356.9
formature 245.5
formed 166.27
FORMED OF 58.4
former foregoing 64.5
  prior 116.4
  past 119.7
formerly
  prior to 116.6
  previously 119.10
formication 425.4
formicative 425.11
formidable
  difficult 729.16
  redoubtable 889.29
forming making 166.3
  shaping 245.5
formless 246.4
form letter 602.3
formula rule 84.4
  axiom 516.2
  prescription 749.3
  law 996.3
  ritual 1038.3
formular formal 644.7
  ritualistic 1038.21
formularize 583.4
formulary
  nouns rule 84.4
  axiom 516.2
  formula 749.3
  law 996.3
  ritual 1038.3,12
  adjs. formal 644.7
  prescriptive 749.5
  ritualistic 1038.21
formulate
  create 166.12
  define 550.12
  express 583.4
  write 600.21
  ~ laws 996.8
formulated 583.6
formulation
  making 166.3
  definition 550.5
  diction 586.1
formulist 1038.2
formenst, forment
  in juxtaposition
    199.21
  beside 241.11
fornicate
  copulate 168.10
  debauch 987.19
fornication
  copulation 168.3
  adultery 987.7

fornicator 987.13
fornix 251.4
forsake 631.5
FORSAKE THE WORLD
  922.8
forsaken
  vacant 186.13
  abandoned 631.8
  lovelorn 865.11
  forlorn 922.13
Forseti 1012.6
forsooth 515.16
forswear deny 522.4
  falsify 614.21
  recant 626.9
  abandon 631.7
  reject 636.2
  relinquish 812.3
  abstain 990.8
forswearing
  denial 522.2
  recantation 626.3
  abandonment 631.3
  relinquishment
    812.1
forsworn
  untruthful 614.34
  rejected 636.3
fort 797.6
fortalice 797.4
forte specialty 81.1
  talent 731.4
forte, fortissimo
  nouns 461.25
  adjs. 452.9
  advs. loudly 452.12
  music 461.54
forth forward 293.7
  away 300.21
  out 302.21
forthcoming
  nouns imminence
    151.1
  approach 295.1
  issuance 302.1
  appearance 445.1
  adjs. future 121.8
  imminent 151.3
  approaching 295.4
  emerging 302.18
  in preparation
    718.24
forthright
  adjs. 972.17
  advs. promptly
    131.15
  directly 289.25
forthwith 131.15
fortification
  adulteration 44.3
  strengthening 158.5
  vitaminization
    307.12
  corroboration 504.5
  stronghold 797.4,6
fortified 797.12
fortify add to 40.4
  adulterate 44.13
  strengthen 158.11
  vitaminize 307.18
  corroborate 504.12

fourth
　nouns 98.2
　adjs. 57.4
fourth arm 798.29
fourth-class 678.10
fourth estate 603.23
fourthly 97.5
Fourth-of-July orator
　908.5
fourth-rate 678.10
fourth stomach 192.3
four-up 271.5
four-up driver 273.9
four-wheeler 271.4
fowl
　nouns food 306a.22
　bird 413.34,35
　verbs 553.9
fowls of the air 413.1
fox
　nouns animal 413.4
　crafty person 733.6
　verbs 577.6
fox fire 334.13
foxhole 797.5
fox hunting 653.2
foxiness
　shrewdness 466.3
　cunning 733.1
fox paw 517.5
fox trot
　nouns 268.4
　verbs run 268.11
　dance 877.5
foxy
　reddish-brown 366.4
　foxlike 413.37
　smart 466.15
　stained 677.9
　cunning 733.12
foyer 191.19
fracas commotion 62.4
　uproar 452.3
　row 793.6
fractile 359.4
Fraction 1038.10
fraction part 55.1
　commotion 62.4
　mathematical
　　element 86.9
　row 793.6
fractional partial 55.6
　mathematics 86.8
fractious
　unruly 624.12
　disobedient 765.11
　ill-humored 949.19
fracturable 359.4
fracture
　nouns break 49.3
　crack 200.2
　injury 690.7
　verbs 49.11
frae 300.21
fragile frail 159.14
　brittle 359.4
fragility frailty 159.2
　brittleness 359.1
fragment
　nouns 55.1
　verbs 49.12

fragmentary 55.6
fragments 605.4
fragrance, fragrancy
　odor 434
　perfume 435
fragrance control
　348.8
fragrant odorous 434.9
　sweet-smelling 435.9
fragrant weed 433.1
fraid hole
　cellar 191.17
　hiding place 613.4
　shelter 698.3
fraidy-cat 890.5
frail
　nouns girl 125.6
　woman 420.6
　strumpet 987.14
　verbs pound 282.15
　whip 1008.14
　adjs. weak 159.14
　thin 204.15
　fragile 359.4
　human 416.10
　weak-willed 625.11
　morally ~ 979.16
frailty weakness 159.2
　thinness 204.4
　fragility 359.1
　humanness 416.6
　weak will 625.4
　fault 676.2
　moral ~ 979.9
frame
　nouns nature 5.3
　setting 215.10
　border 234.4
　structure 244.1
　framework 244.4
　skeleton 244.5
　form 245.1
　human form 245.4
　body 375.3
　mood 523.4
　film 575.12
　false charge 1003.4
　verbs make 166.12
　invent 166.14
　border 234.10
　form 245.6
　prearrange 639.3
　plan 652.9
　accuse falsely
　　1003.12
frame of mind 523.4
frame of reference
　523.2
frame-up
　prearrangement
　　639.1
　false charge 1003.4
framework
　outline 234.2
　frame 244.4
　viewpoint 523.2
framing making 166.3
　frame 244.4
franc 833.9
franchise
　nouns suffrage 742.17

　exemption 760.7
　right 956.4
　verbs 775.12
franchised 775.18
Franciscan 1036.17
franc-tireur 798.16
frangibility
　frailty 159.2
　brittleness 359.1
frangible
　fragile 159.14
　brittle 359.4
frank
　nouns frankfurter
　　306a.21
　mail 602.5
　adjs. artless 734.5
　candid 972.17
　BE FRANK 972.12
frankalmoign 808.6
Frank Chance 155.2
Frankenstein's
　monster 941.7
frankfurter 306a.21
frankhearted 972.17
frankincense 435.4
franklinic electricity
　341.1
frankly 972.23
frankness
　artlessness 734
　candor 972.4
frantic
　turbulent 161.17
　rabid 472.29
　distracted 530.10
　overwrought 855.26
frappé 306a.46
fratch 793.12
frater 11.3
fraternal
　friendly 925.14
　kind 936.14
fraternalism
　affiliation 784.3
　fellowship 925.2
fraternal order 786.4
fraternity kinship 11.1
　affiliation 784.3
　society 786.4
　fellowship 925.2
fraternity man 786.11
fraternization
　affiliation 784.3
　association 920.5
　treason 973.7
fraternize associate
　with 920.15
　be traitorous 973.14
fraternizer 617.11
fratricide 408.4
Frau woman 420.5
　mistress 420.8
fraud
　fraudulence 616.8
　impostor 617.6
　PRACTICE FRAUD
　　UPON 616.18
fraudulence, fraudu-
　lency fraud 616.8

　improbity 973.1
fraudulent
　deceitful 616.22
　dishonest 973.15
fraught 56.13
　FRAUGHT WITH
　　806.10
　FRAUGHT WITH
　　DANGER 695.9
Fräulein 420.9
fray
　nouns frazzle 690.1
　contest 794.3
　IN THE THICK OF THE
　　FRAY 795.29
　verbs fret 349.7
　wear 690.21
frayed 690.31
frayed nerves 857.4
frazil 332.6
frazzle
　nouns 690.1
　TO A FRAZZLE 720.13
　WORN TO A FRAZZLE
　　715.6
　verbs fray 349.7
　wear 690.21
　fatigue 715.4
frazzled frayed 690.31
　fatigued 715.6
freak
　nouns monstrosity
　　85.6
　eccentric 473.3
　caprice 627.1
　adjs. 85.12
freakery
　changeableness
　　141.2
　capriciousness 627.2
freakish
　fantastic 85.12
　changeable 141.7
　eccentric 473.4
　capricious 627.5
freckle
　nouns speckle 373.3
　mark 566.4
　blemish 677.1
　verbs speckle 373.7
　mark 566.18
　spot 677.5
freckled, freckly
　373.13
fredaine 876.5
free
　verbs rescue 700.2
　disembarrass 730.7
　exempt 760.13
　liberate 761.4,7
　relieve 884.6
　acquit 1005.4
　FREE OF 519.2
　FREE ONESELF 630.6
　FREE ONESELF FROM
　　761.8
　adjs. unfastened
　　49.21
　vacant 186.14
　open 264.17

communicative
  552.9
voluntary 620.7
abundant 659.7
not busy 706.16
leisure 708.5
at liberty 760.19
clear 760.28
gratuitous 848.5
generous 851.4
candid 972.17
licentious 987.25
FREE OF 760.28
GIVE FREE REIN TO
be lax 756.3
be intemperate
  991.4
MAKE FREE WITH
presume on 959.7
appropriate 820.16
show disrespect
  963.3
NEVER FREE FROM
640.18
advs. freely 760.29
gratuitously 848.6
free-acting 760.21
free admission 848.2
free and easy
unconventional 83.8
informal 645.3
nonchalant 856.15
lighthearted 868.11
convivial 920.18
free association
  688.42
free association test
  688.11
freeboot 822.16
freebooter 823.7
freebooting 822.6
freeborn, free-bred
  760.26
Free Church 1018.9
free city 180.1
free companion
  798.16
free course 760.3
freed 761.10
freedman 760.10
freedom leisure 708.1
facility 730.1
liberty 760
privilege 956.4
presumption 959.2
candor 972.4
FOUR FREEDOMS
  760.9
freedom from war
  801.1
free electron 342.3
free enterprise
government 739.8
policy 742.4
capitalism 743.7
noninterference
  760.8
commerce 825.1
free-for-all 794.5
free giver 851.2
free-going 760.21

freehand
  nouns 572.6
  adjs. 572.22
free hand
free scope 760.3
carte blanche 775.4
generosity 851.1
freehanded
free 760.21
generous 851.4
freehearted
generous 851.4
benevolent 936.16
freehold
  nouns 808.6
  adjs. 808.11
freeholder 807.3
freeing rescue 700.1
disembarrassment
  730.5
liberation 761.1,3
relief 884.2
free lance
writer 600.15
independent 760.11
soldier 798.16
free-lance
write 600.21
be independent
  760.18
free living
  nouns 991.2
  adjs. 991.8
free-loader
sponger 905.4
guest 923.6
free love love 929.1
illicit love 987.7
freeloving 987.27
freely
voluntarily 620.11
abundantly 659.9
without restraint
  760.29
gratuitously 848.6
generously 851.5
freeman 760.10
Freemason 1032.11
Freemasonic(al)
  1032.24
Freemasonry 1032.1
freemasonry 784.3
free-moving 760.21
free nations 180.1
freeness
communicativeness
  552.4
gratuitousness 848.1
generosity 851.1
candor 972.4
free orbit 281.14
free pass 848.2
free play
facility 730.1
free scope 760.3
HAVE FREE PLAY
163.8
free press 760.9
freer 940.2
free-speaking
liberal 524.9

communicative
  552.9
speaking 592.21
candid 972.17
free speech 760.9
free-spirited 760.20
free-spoken
communicative
  552.9
spoken 592.21
candid 972.17
freethinker
liberal 524.6
independent 760.11
latitudinarian
  1029.13
freethinking
  nouns liberalism
  524.2
latitudinarianism
  1029.7
  adjs. liberal 524.9
latitudinarian
  1029.21
free thought
liberalism 524.2
latitudinarianism
  1029.7
free time 708.1
free-tongued
liberal 524.9
communicative
  552.9
candid 972.17
free trade
noninterference
  760.8
commerce 825.1
freetrader 760.11
free translation 550.3
free verse 607.2
freeway 655.6
freewheeling
  nouns 347.6
  adjs. 760.21
freewill 620.7
free will 760.5
OF ONE'S OWN FREE
WILL
voluntarily 620.11
independently
  760.30
free-working 760.21
freezable 333.12
freeze
  nouns 332.3
  verbs stabilize 142.8
remain motionless
  267.7
be cold 332.10,11
refrigerate 333.11
anesthetize 422.3
preserve 699.8
~ with fear
  889.10,16
FREEZE OUT 308.13
FREEZE THE BLOOD
889.14
FREEZE TO 50.5
freezer 333.5

freezing
  nouns refrigeration
  333.1
anesthetic 685.13
preservation 699.2
  adjs. cold 332.15
refrigerative 333.12
freezing mixture 333.7
freezing point 332.1
freezing weather 332.3
freight
  nouns load 193.2
transportation 270.3
shipment 270.7
train 271.12
burden 351.7
charge 844.8
BY FREIGHT 270.19
  verbs fill 56.7
load 183.16
ship 270.14
burden 351.13
freightage
transportation 270.3
cargo 270.7
charge 844.8
freight agent 779.3
freight car 271.13
freighted 351.18
freighter carrier 270.5
train 271.12
freight train 271.12
French Canadian
nationality 417.9
dialect 578.8
French chalk 572.19
French disease 684.15
French doughnut
  306a.43
French dressing
  306a.37
French harp 464.11
French horn 464.8
Frenchification 188.4
Frenchify 188.5
Frenchism 578.9
French leave 186.4
Frenchman 417.9
French toast 306a.27
Frenchy 417.9
frenetic 472.15
frenetic(al) 472.29
freno 657.5
frenzied
turbulent 161.17
rabid 472.29
overwrought 855.26
frenzy
  nouns turbulence
  161.2
insanity 472.8
illness 684.5
excitement 855.7
  verbs madden 472.22
incite 646.17
enrage 950.23
frequence
oftenness 135.1
attendance 185.4
frequency
oftenness 135

radio ~ 343.15
frequency band
  343 16
frequency modulation
  343 17
frequency spectrum
  343 15
frequent
  verbs 185.10
  adjs. recurrent 103.13
  many times 135.4
  habitual 640.15
  FREQUENT AS A
    CUSTOMER 825.13
frequenter
  attender 185.5
  visitor 923.6
frequently
  repeatedly 103.16
  often 135.6
  habitually 640.21
Frere's type 440.5
fresco
  nouns paint 361.11
  painting 572.15
  verbs 361.14
frescoing 361.11
fresh
  nouns stream 394.1
  flood 394.5
  freshman 564.5
  adjs. original 23.3
  additional 40.9
  new 122.7,8
  cool 332.13
  breezy 402.26
  unforgotten 535.23
  unfaded 675.8
  healthy 683.10
  refreshing 693.5
  inexperienced
    732 17
  impudent 911.9
  drunk 994.40
  GET FRESH 911.6
freshen cool 333.10
  air 401.12
  breeze up 402.23
  refresh 693.2
  FRESHEN THE WAY
    274 23
freshet stream 394.1
  flood 394.5
freshie 564.5
freshly again 91.6
  newly 122.16
freshman
  student 564.5
  novice 564.7
freshness
  originality 23.1
  newness 122.1
  impudence 911.2
fresh start
  beginning 68.1
  resumption 143.2
fret
  nouns network 220.3
  colic 423.5
  insignia 567.2

  irritation 864.3
  verbs agitate 323.10
  grate 349.7
  make sore 423.7
  injure 690.13
  wear 690.21
  be impatient 860.4
  annoy 864.18
  grieve 870.17
  complain 873.13
  worry 888.4,5
  be peevish 949.14
  fume 950.15
  anger 950.22
  FRET AT 967.16
fretful
  impatient 860.6
  plaintive 873.16
  peevish 949.21
fretted
  interlaced 221.8
  worried 888.7
fretting
  nouns abrasion 349.2
  impatience 860.1
  worrying 888.2
  adjs. abrasive 349.10
  irritating 423.13
  impatient 860.6
  worrying 888.9
fretwork 220.3
Freud 688.12
Freudianism 688.2
Frey, Freyr
  fertility 164.5
  god 1012.6
Freya, Freyja
  beauty 898.9
  Love 929.8
  goddess 1012.6
friability
  brittleness 359
  pulverableness
    360.3
friable 360.13
friandise 895.5
friar 1036.16
friarhood 1035.4
Friar Minor, Friar
  Preacher 1036.17
friar's lantern 334.13
friary 1040.6
fribble
  nouns trifle 671.5
  trinket 899.4
  fop 901.9
  verbs 671.13
  FRIBBLE AWAY 852.5
  adjs. 671.16
fribbling 671.16
fricandeau, fricandel,
  fricandelle,
  fricando 306a.12
fricassee
  nouns 306a.11
  verbs 329.4
fricasseed 329.6
fricative
  nouns 449.5
  adjs. 349.9

friction
  nouns counteraction
    177.1
  rubbing 349
  disaccord 793.1
  adjs. 349.9
frictional 349.9
frictionize 349.6
fried cooked 329.6
  drunk 994.40
friedcake 306a.43
fried eggs 306a.26
fried sole 306a.24
friend 926
  A FRIEND OF MAN
    936.9
friend at court
  influence 171.6
  deputy 779.1
  supporter 785.8
  lawyer 1001.1
friend indeed, friend
  in need
  friend 926.3
  benefactor 940.1
friendless alone 89.8
  helpless 157.18
  forlorn 922.13
friendlessness 922.4
friendliness
  comfortableness
    885.2
  sociability 920
  hospitality 923.1
  amicability 925.1
friendly
  adjs. homelike 190.28
  harmonious 792.3
  comfortable 885.11
  sociable 920.17
  hospitable 923.11
  amicable 925.14
  advs. 925.21
friendly relations
  925.3
friends 926.7
friendship
  harmony 792
  amicability 925
  love 929
  HAVE THE FRIEND-
    SHIP OF 925.9
frier See fryer
Frigg, Frigga
  marriage 931.14
  goddess 1012.6
  god 1017.5
fright
  nouns fear 889.1
  eyesore 897.4
  IN A FRIGHT 889.24
  LOOK A FRIGHT 897.5
  TAKE FRIGHT 890.8
  verbs 889.14
frighten startle 538.8
  scare 889.14
  FRIGHTEN OFF 889.20
  FRIGHTEN OUT OF
    ONE'S WITS 889.16
frightened 889.24
frightener scarer 889.8

  bugbear 1014.10
frightening 889.27
frightful great 34.12
  frightening 889.27
  hideous 897.11
frightfully
  exceedingly 34.25
  fearfully 889.33
  hideously 897.13
fright neurosis 688.17
frigid cold 332.15
  unsexual 418.22
  reserved 611.8
  unfeeling 854.9
  unsociable 921.6
Frigidaire, frigidaire
  333.4
frigidarium 333.6
frigidity cold 332.1
  sex 418.2
  reserve 611.3
  unfeeling 854.1
  unsociability 921.2
Frigid Zones
  latitude 179.3
  cold place 332.5
frigorific(al) 333.12
frigotherapy 687.3
frijoles 306a.35
frill edging 234.7
  ruffle 263.1,5
  superfluity 661.4
frillery
  superfluity 661.4
  frippery 899.3
frilling edging 234.7
  frippery 899.3
frills
  ornate speech 599.4
  superfluity 661.4
  frippery 899.3
frilly ornate 899.11
  showy 902.19
fringe
  nouns border 234.4
  edging 234.7
  verbs 234.10
fringe area 344.5
fringed 234.12
fringes 234.1
frippery
  clothes 230.10
  superfluity 661.4
  trumpery 671.4
  frillery 899.3
frisk
  nouns caper 317.2
  search 484.2
  frolic 876.5
  verbs ride 272.33
  caper 317.6
  search 484.25
  rejoice 874.6
  frolic 876.25
frisker 876.19
friskiness 868.4
frisky 868.14
frith See firth
fritter
  nouns small amount
    35.3

fructify make
  productive 164.8
  bear 166.17
  fertilize 168.11
  prosper 726.8
frugal meager 660.8
  inexpensive 847.7
  economical 849.9
  parsimonious 850.9
  temperate 990.9
frugalist 849.6
frugality
  economy 849.1
  parsimony 850
  temperance 990.1
frugally
  meagerly 660.13
  economically 849.11
  temperately 990.12
fruit
  nouns effect 153.1
  product 167.1
  posterity 170.1
  types of ~ 306a.50
  yield 809.4
  verbs 166.17
fruitarian
  nouns 990.4
  adjs. 990.10
fruitarianism 990.2
fruitful 164.9
fruitfulness 164.1
fruitiness 435.1
fruition bearing 166.8
  attainment 720.1
  pleasure 863.1
fruitless
  ineffectual 157.15
  barren 165.4
  useless 667.12
  unsuccessful 723.17
fruity
  rich-flavored 427.9
  fragrant 435.9
frumenty 306a.34
frump
  nouns slattern 62.7
  crone 127.3
  shrew 949.12
  verbs 949.14
frumpish 62.14
frumps 949.10
frustrate
  neutralize 177.7
  disappoint 539.2
  thwart 728.15
  circumvent 733.11
frustrated 539.5
frustrater 728.8
frustrating 728.20
frustration
  neutralization 177.2
  disappointment 539.1
  psychological ~ 688.19
  defeat 725.2
  thwarting 728.3
  circumvention 733.5
fry
  nouns young 170.2

food 306a.7
  verbs be hot 327.21
  cook 329.4
fryer, frier
  youngling 125.8
  fowl 306a.22
  poultry 413.35
frying 329.1
frying of fat 742.35
frying pan 192.14
JUMP OUT OF THE
  FRYING PAN INTO
  THE FIRE
  mismanage 732.14
  worsen 883.3
fub 616.17
fucoid 410.35
fucus 410.4
fud rump 240.4
  tail 240.5
fuddle
  nouns confusion
  530.3
  drunkenness 994.1
  spree 994.5
  liquor 994.12
  verbs confuse 530.7
  inebriate 994.28
  tipple 994.30
fuddlebrained
  stupid 468.18
  muddled 530.13
fuddled
  muddled 530.13
  drunk 994.39
fuddy-duddy
  nouns fogy 123.8
  fuss-budget 894.7
  adjs. 123.17
fudge
  nouns 545.2
  verbs do carelessly
  532.9
  twaddle 545.8
  cheat 616.18
  bungle 732.11
  FUDGE IN 236.7
  FUDGE TOGETHER
  166.12
  FUDGE UP
  do carelessly 532.9
  trump up 614.18
  interjs. 469.12
fudgy 732.20
Fuehrer See Führer
fuel
  nouns nuclear ~
  325.10
  combustible 330.1
  oils 379
  gas 400.10
  verbs 330.8
fuel ship 281.2
fugacious 111.7
fugacity 111.1
fugitive
  nouns runaway 629.5
  outlaw 984.9
  adjs. transient 111.7
  roving 272.36
  runaway 629.15

fugitive pieces, fugi-
  tive writings 605.4
fugleman, flugelman,
  fugler 25.1
fugue psychosis 472.3
  amnesia 536.2
  neurosis 688.26
fugue form 462.11
Führer, Fuehrer
  747.3,7
-ful 28.8
fulcrum 286.3
fulcrumage 286.1
fulcum 215.2
fulfill, fulfil
  complete 56.6
  satisfy 659.4
  accomplish 720.4
  observe 766.2
  execute 769.10
fulfilled 720.9
fulfilling 56.14
fulfillment, fulfilment
  accomplishment
  720.1
  observance 766.1
  execution 769.5
fulgent, fulgid 334.32
fulgor, fulgour 334.4
fulgurant 334.34
fulgurate 334.23
fulgurating 334.34
fulguration 161.7
fulgurite 799.9
fuliginosity 364.3
fuliginous
  opaque 340.3
  dingy 364.11
full
  nouns fullness 56.2
  fill 56.3
  satiety 662.1
  IN FULL
  in detail 8.11
  completely 56.15
  diffusely 591.15
  TO THE FULL
  utterly 56.17
  amply 659.8
  to completion
  720.13
  verbs 679.18
  adjs. detailed 8.7
  great 34.8
  complete 56.12
  fat 194.18
  broad 203.6
  thick 203.8
  clogged 265.11
  full-colored 361.17
  loud 452.9
  resonant 453.9
  abundant 659.7
  overfull 661.21
  satiated 662.6
  unlimited 760.24
  drunk 994.38
  IN FULL CRY
  loudly 452.12
  in pursuit 653.11

UNDER FULL STEAM
  268.24
  advs. 289.26
full age 126.2
full-armed 797.14
full authority 775.4
fullback 876.20
full blast 156.1
full-blooded
  strong 158.13
  rubicund 367.10
  virile 419.12
  thoroughbred
  916.12
full bloom
  maturity 126.2
  blossoming 410.24
  IN FULL BLOOM
  126.12
full-blown
  mature 126.12
  full-sized 194.22
full-charged 56.13
full dress 230.11
  IN FULL DRESS 230.45
full-faced 601.18
full feather 230.10
full fidelity 343.1
full-flavored 427.9
full-fledged
  mature 126.12
  full-grown 194.22
full-fraught 56.13
full-grown
  enlarged 38.7
  mature 126.12
  full-sized 194.22
  ripe 720.12
full house 876.17
full-laden 56.13
full meal 306.8
full measure fill 56.3
  plenty 659.2
full-mouthed 452.10
fullness, fulness
  greatness 34.1
  completeness 56.2
  loudness 452.1
  resonance 453.1
  abundance 659.2
  overfullness 661.3
  satiety 662.2
  IN THE FULLNESS OF
  TIME
  in time 121.11
  opportunely 129.13
full particulars 8.2
full size 194.3,22
full speed ahead
  swiftly 268.24
  navigation 274.81
full stop stop 144.2
  standstill 267.3
full tilt 705.23
  FULL TILT AT 289.25
fully in full 8.11
  completely 56.15
  amply 659.8
fully developed
  mature 126.12
  ripe 720.12

fulmar 413.34
fulminate
  explode 161.13
  detonate 455.8
  FULMINATE AGAINST
  967.20
fulminating
  explosive 161.23
  thundering 455.12
fulmination
  explosion 161.7
  lightning 334.17
  detonation 455.3
fulsome nasty 428.7
  malodorous 436.5
  bad 673.9
  foul 680.25
  odious 862.9
  base 913.12
  suave 934.18
  obscene 988.9
fumble
  nouns 732.5
  verbs confuse 63.3
  grope 484.26
  bungle 732.11
fumble-fist, fumbler
  732.8
fume
  nouns turbulence
    161.2
  agitation 323.1
  smoke 328.16
  vapor 400.1
  foam 404.2
  odor 434.1
  excitement 855.3
  anger 950.7
  verbs be violent
    161.11
  smoke 327.22
  bleach 362.5
  vaporize 400.7
  be insane 472.19
  preserve 699.8
  ~ with excitement
    855.19
  be angry 950.15
fumes of fancy 533.1
fumigant
  deodorant 437.3
  disinfectant 685.18
fumigate fume 400.7
  perfume 435.8
  deodorize 437.4
  disinfect 679.22
fumigation
  vaporization 400.4
  deodorization 437.2
  disinfection 679.3
fumigator
  perfumer 435.6
  deodorant 437.3
  disinfectant 685.18
fuming
  nouns 699.2
  adjs. smoking 327.27
  fumy 400.8
  overwrought 855.26
  infuriated 950.29

fun
  nouns amusement
    876.2
  jest 879.6
  FOR THE FUN OF IT
  876.33
  IN FUN
  mischievously 736.7
  in jest 879.19
  LIKE FUN
  disbelief 502.14
  by no means 522.8
  MAKE FUN OF
  banter 880.4
  ridicule 965.8
  verbs 879.13
funambulist 876.21
function
  nouns operation
    163.1
  ceremony 644.4
  purpose 651.1
  role 654.3
  use 663.5
  rite 1038.3
  verbs operate 163.8
  officiate 654.13
  act 703.4
functional
  operative 163.10
  ceremonious 644.8
  official 654.16
  utilitarian 663.18
  psychogenic 688.46
functional design
  663.6
functional disintegra-
  tion 472.4
functional housing
  187.3
functionalism
  architecture 572.4
  utilitarianism 663.6
functionalist 577.10
functional psychology
  688.1
functionary
  nouns official 747.17
  agent 779.3
  adjs. 644.8
functioning
  nouns 163.1
  adjs. operating
    163.12
  acting 703.11
fund
  nouns supply 658.2
  political ~ 742.38
  capital 833.15
  THE FUND 741.3
  verbs provide 657.7
  store up 658.11
fundament
  foundation 215.6
  rump 240.4
fundamental
  nouns principle 5.2
  foundation 215.6
  tone 449.2
  salient point 670.6
  adjs. essential 5.8

  original 152.16
  basic 211.8
  vital 670.24
fundamental colors
  361.6
fundamentalism
  1022.6
fundamentalist
  1022.5
fundamentality 5.1
fundamentally
  essentially 5.10
  quite 34.21
fundamental tone
  449.2
funds moneys 833.14
  IN FUNDS 835.13
  OUT OF FUNDS 836.9
funèbre 409.25
funeral
  nouns procession 71.4
  burial 409.4,5
  dirge 873.5
  adjs. 409.25
funeral director 409.8
funeral home, funeral
  parlor 409.9
funeralize 409.20
funeral march
  slow motion 269.2
  music 461.11
  dirge 873.5
funeral oration 409.4
funeral pile
  death fire 327.12
  cremation 409.2
funeral ring 409.6
funeral song 873.5
funeral urn, funeral
  vessel 409.12
funerary 409.25
funereal dark 336.15
  mortuary 409.25
  sad 870.25
  mournful 870.27
  dirgelike 873.18
fungi
  types of ~ 410.46
  plants 411.4
fungible 149.5
fungicide 408.11
fungiform, fungoid
  410.35
fungologist 411.2
fungology 411.1
fungosity 684.29
fungous 410.35
fungus plant 410.4
  plants 411.4
  blight 674.2
  growth 684.29
funicular, funiculate
  205.7
funicule, funiculus
  410.19
funk
  nouns fright 889.1
  coward 890.5
  IN A FUNK, IN A BLUE
  FUNK 889.24
  verbs smoke 327.22

  smoke tobacco
    433.15
  smell bad 436.4
  shirk 629.9
  take fright 889.10
  frighten 889.14
  lose courage 890.8
funker shirker 629.3
  coward 890.5
funk hole
  cellar 191.17
  hiding place 613.4
  shelter 698.3
funking, funky 890.10
funky tobacco 433.2
funnel
  nouns cone 254.5
  tube 395.6
  flue 395.18
  verbs pipe 270.13
  converge 297.2
  channel 395.19
funnellike, funnel-
  shaped 254.12
funnies 572.17
funnily 878.7
funniness
  humorousness 878.1
  wittiness 879.2
funny odd 85.11
  eccentric 473.4
  humorous 878.5
  witty 879.15
funny feeling 480.3
funnyman
  comedian 610.8
  humorist 879.12
funny paper 572.17
fur
  nouns coating 227.13
  pelt 228.1
  furs 228.8
  hair 229.2
  fuzz 229.19
  MAKE THE FUR FLY
  793.12
  PUT ONE'S FUR UP
  950.22
  verbs 227.30
furbelow 234.7
furbish polish 259.7
  touch up 689.11
  renovate 692.17
  embellish 899.7
furcate
  verbs 298.7
  adjs. 298.10
furcation 298.3
furcula, furculum
  298.4
furfur 680.9
furfuraceous
  scurfy 226.7
  branny 360.11
furfuration 226.4
Furies, the 1014.11
furious violent 161.15
  turbulent 161.17
  frenzied 472.29
  hasty 707.9
  overwrought 855.26

gage measure 489.2,4
  pledge 770.2
  challenge 791.2
gaggle 459.5
gagman writer 609.26
  humorist 879.12
gagtooth 257.7
Gaia See Gaea
gaiety, gayety
  colorfulness 361.3
  cheerfulness 868.4
  festivity 876.3
  ornament 899.3
  showiness 902.3
  conviviality 920.3
gain
  nouns increase 38.1
  electricity 341.16
  time lead 348.11
  benefit 672.4
  profit 809.3
  verbs increase 38.6
  incur 174.4
  arrive 299.6
  profit 663.17
  improve 689.7
  win 724.4
  acquire 809.7
  receive 817.6
GAIN A HOLD UPON
  gain influence
    171.12
  govern 739.12
GAIN COMMAND OF
  562.9
GAIN ENTREE 301.9
GAIN GROUND
  accelerate 268.15
  progress 293.2
  improve 689.7
GAIN ONE'S END 722.7
GAIN ONE'S LIBERTY
  630.6
GAIN OVER 646.23
GAIN RECOGNITION
  912.11
GAIN STRENGTH
  increase 38.6
  improve 689.8
  recuperate 692.19
GAIN THE CONFI-
  DENCE OF 500.15
GAIN THE FRIENDSHIP
  OF 925.10
GAIN TIME
  be early 131.5
  temporize 132.10
GAIN UPON
  approach 295.3
  overtake 299.9
GAIN WEIGHT 196.8
gainer 318.1
gainful
  profitable 663.21
  productive 809.14
gaining 809.1
gainless 667.12
gains 809.3
gainsay refute 505.5
  deny 522.4
  oppose 788.7

gainsaying
  refutation 505.2
  denial 522.2
gait velocity 268
  slowness 269
  journey 272.5
  pace 272.14
gaiters 230.62
gal 125.6
gala
  nouns 876.4
  adjs. 876.30
galactic 387.8
galactic longitude
  374.16
galactotherapy 687.3
gala day
  vacation 709.4
  festivity 876.4
galanty show 609.14
galaxy throng 74.4
  Milky Way 374.13
  celebrities 912.9
galbe outline 234.2
  form 245.2
gale 402.5,13
galeiform 251.23
Galen 686.5
galigaskins 230.18
galilee 191.19
galiongee 275.4
gall
  nouns secretion 310.2
  bitterness 428.2
  abrasion 690.7
  irritation 864.3
  affliction 864.8
  impudence 911.3
  virulence 937.7
  ill humor 949.1
  resentment 950.3
  verbs grate 349.7
  make sore 423.7
  injure 690.7
  annoy 864.18
gallant
  nouns brave man
    891.8
  dandy 901.9
  lover 929.11
  cavalier 934.9
  adjs. courageous
    891.17
  showy 902.19
  courteous 934.15
gallantry
  courage 891.1
  courtship 930.6
  courtesy 934.2
galled chafed 423.11
  irritated 864.24
galleon 276.6
gallery corridor 191.18
  porch 191.21
  balcony 191.22
  platform 215.13
  observatory 438.8
  audience 447.6
  theater ～ 609.19
  passageway 655.4
  museum 658.9

entrenchment 797.5
PLAY TO THE
  GALLERY 902.16
gallery gods 447.6
galley kitchen 329.3
  proof 601.5
galleys
  types of ～ 276.25
  punishment 1008.2;
    1009.3
galley slave
  drudge 716.3
  slave 762.7
galley-west 248.11
Gallic disease 684.15
Gallicism 578.9
Gallicize 188.5
gallimaufry 44.6
gallinaceous 413.45
galling
  nouns 349.2
  adjs. abrasive 349.10
  chafing 423.13
  annoying 862.13
gallipot 685.30
gallivant gad 272.22
  philander 930.18
galloon 234.7
gallop
  nouns 268.4
  verbs run 268.11
  ride 272.33
galloper 413.20
gallows
  nouns suspender
    214.5
  hanging 1008.7
  execution 1009.5
  adjs. 672.13
  advs. 34.20
gallows bird 984.9
gallstones 684.8
galluses 214.5
gally 911.9
galoot oddity 85.4
  dolt 470.5
  clumsy fellow 732.9
galore
  nouns large amount
    34.4
  abundance 659.2
  advs. 659.9
Galtonian theory
  169.6
galvanic
  electric 341.27
  exciting 855.31
galvanic current 341.2
galvanic shock 341.6
galvanism 341.1
galvanist 341.20
galvanization
  electrolysis 341.22
  excitement 855.10
galvanize plate 227.28
  electrify 341.23
  electrogalvanize
    341.25
  excite 855.14
galvanocautery 687.7
galvanography 576.2

galvanometric, gal-
  vanoscopic 341.27
galvanosurgery
  surgery 686.3
  therapy 687.7
Galways 229.8
Gamaliel 475.6
gamb, gambe 272.16
gambado
  nouns 317.2
  verbs 317.6
gamble
  nouns luck 155
  uncertainty 513.8
  risk 514
  verbs 514.17,19
GAMBLE AWAY 852.3
GAMBLE ON
  rely on 500.13
  be certain 512.9
  chance 514.18
gambler 514.16
gambling 514.6
gambling house
  514.14
gambling table 514.11
gambol
  nouns caper 317.2
  frolic 876.5
  verbs caper 317.6
  frolic 876.25
gambrel 272.16
game
  nouns teeth 257.6
  meat 306a.12
  animals 413.1
  dupe 618.1
  pluck 622.3
  scheme 652.6
  quarry 653.7
  profession 654.6
  artifice 733.3
  contest 794.3
  amusement 876.2,9
  types of ～ 876.34,
    35
  courage 891.5
  laughingstock 965.7
PLAY THE GAME
  conform 82.4
  play fair 974.7
  verbs 514.17
  adjs. willing 620.5
  plucky 622.14
  crippled 690.29
  courageous 891.18
GAME TO THE END
  plucky 622.14
  persevering 623.7
gamecock 798.1
gamekeeper 697.5
game reserve 699.6
gamesome gay 868.14
  playful 876.31
gamester
  gambler 514.16
  sportsman 876.20
gamete 405.6
gametic
  generative 166.24
  cellular 405.21

gametophore, gameto-
  phyte 405.9
game warden 697.5
gamic -18.17
gamin 273.3
gaminess
  strong flavor 432.3
  courage 891.4
gaming 514.6
gammadion 1034.5
gamma radiation,
  gamma ray 326.3
gammer
  old woman 127.3
  grandmother 169.12
gammon
  nouns ham 306a.16
  nonsense 545.4
  humbug 614.14
  verbs 514.22
gammoner 617.6
gammy 169.12
gamp umbrella 227.7
  midwife 686.10
gams 272.16
gamut series 71.2
  range 178.2
  scale 462.6
gamy
  strong-flavored
    432.8
  courageous 891.18
gander
  nouns goose 413.35
  male animal 419.8
  look 438.3
  verbs 438.16
ganef 823.2
Ganesa 1012.7
gang
  nouns company 74.3
  staff 748.12
  ring 786.1
  verbs league 52.4
  go 272.17
GANG ALONG 300.6
GANG AROUND 74.15
GANG UP ON 796.15
GANG UP WITH 920.15
gangboard 655.10
ganger 746.2
gangland, gangdom
  98-.10
gangling, gangly
  thin 204.16
  rangy 206.21
ganglion
  nerve center 225.5
  nerve 421.6
gangplank 655.10
gangrene
  nouns disease 684.30
  decay 690.6
  verbs 690.23
gangrened, gangrenous
  diseased 684.45
  decayed 690.38
gangster thief 823.4
  criminal 984.9
gangue 382.6

gangway
  nouns 655.10
  interjs. 264.23
Ganpati 1012.7
gantlet 1008.2
RUN THE GANTLET
  navigate 274.13
  brave 891.11
gaol, gaoler, etc. See
  jail, etc.
gap
  nouns cleft 200.2,3
  opening 264.1
  verbs 264.16
gape
  nouns gap 200.2
  opening 264.1
  yawn 264.2
  stare 438.5
  verbs yawn 264.16
  stare 438.16
  be curious 526.3
  wonder 918.4
gapes yawning 264.2
  disease 684.10
gaping
  nouns 264.2
  adjs. cleft 200.7
  yawning 264.18
  expectant 537.9
garage
  for vehicles 190.17
  repair shop 717.6
garb
  nouns clothing 230.1
  appearance 445.3
UNDER THE GARB OF
  616.23
  verbs 230.38
garbage refuse 667.4
  offal 680.9
garble distort 248.6
  misinterpret 551.2
  misrepresent 571.3
  falsify 614.16
garbled
  mutilated 57.5
  distorted 248.10
  misinterpreted 551.3
garçon boy 125.5
  servant 748.3
garden
  nouns 412.10
  verbs 412.16
  adjs. mediocre 678.9
  plain 900.6
gardener 412.6
gardening 412.2
garden of the Hes-
  perides 1016.10
garden party 920.10
garden variety
  mediocrity 678.2
  plainness 900.1
gare 183.3
Gargantua 194.13
Gargantuan 194.20
gargle
  nouns 685.18
  verbs 679.18
gargoyle 395.8

garish glaring 334.32
  grandiloquent 599.9
  gaudy 902.20
garishly 902.27
garishness 902.3
garland
  nouns circle 252.2
  flowers 410.23
  insignia 567.2
  compilation 603.4
  anthology 607.6
  trophy 914.3
  verbs 899.8
garlic 436.3
garment
  nouns 230.3
  verbs 230.38
garmentmaker
  seamstress 222.2
  clothier 230.33
garment parts 230.66
garments, garmenture
  230.1
garner
  nouns 658.7
  verbs 658.11
garnish
  nouns 899.1
  verbs attach 820.17
  adorn 899.7
garnishee
  nouns 778.8
  verbs 820.17
garnishment
  summons 750.7
  attachment 820.4
  decoration 899.1
garret attic 191.16
  head 210.5
garrison
  nouns guards 697.8
  fort 797.6
  military unit
    798.19
  verbs 797.9
garrison state 739.4
garrote
  nouns strangulation
    408.6
  execution 1008.7
  verbs strangle 408.19
  execute 1008.19
garroter killer 408.10
  executioner 1008.8
garrulity 594.1
garrulous 594.9
garter
  nouns 914.5
  verbs 47.9
gas
  nouns illuminant
    334.20
  gasoline 379.4
  vapor 400.1
  types of ~ 400.10
  nonsense 545.4
  chatter 594.3
  brag 908.2
GIVE HER THE GAS
  268.15
  verbs twaddle 545.8

  chatter 594.6
  attack 796.18
gasbag chatterer 594.5
  braggart 908.5
gas chamber 1009.5
Gascon 908.5
gasconade
  nouns 908.1
  verbs boast 908.6
  bluster 909.3
gasconading 908.9
gaseity 400.2
gaselier 335.6
gaseous
  unsubstantial 4.5
  rare 354.7
  vaporous 400.8
gash
  nouns cleft 200.2
  notch 261.1
  furrow 262.1
  nonsense 545.4
  mark 566.4
  injury 690.7
  verbs sever 49.10
  notch 261.4
  furrow 262.3
  mark 566.18
  injure 690.13
gasification 400.4
gasiform 400.8
gasify 400.7
gas jet 328.10
gasket 265.5
gaslight 334.18
gaslit 334.38
gas main 395.7
gasoline, gasolene
  illuminant 334.20
  petrol 379.4
gasometer 400.6
gasp
  nouns 402.19
  verbs be hot 327.21
  breathe 402.25
  say 592.17
  get tired 715.5
GASP FOR 632.16
Gaspar 467.5
gasper 433.5
gasping 715.3
gas pipe 395.6
gas station 830.8
gassy
  flatulent 196.12
  vaporous 400.8
  talkative 594.9
  bombastic 599.10
  pompous 902.22
  boastful 908.10
gastrectomy 687.25
gastric 192.10
gastric juice
  digester 307.7
  secretion 310.2
gastritis 684.8
gastronome, gas-
  tronomist 992.4
gastronomic(al)
  306.29

gastronomy
artistic taste 895.5
gourmanderie 992.2
gastroplasty 687.27
Gastropoda,
gastropods 414.9
gastroscopy 442.6
gastrotomy 687.26
Gastrotricha 414.5
gasworks 717.4
gat 799.5
gate portal 301.6
metal 382.5
trough 395.4
valve 395.10
floodgate 395.11
barrier 728.5
receipts 842.1
GIVE THE GATE
send away 308.17
discharge 308.18
THE GATE 308.5
gate crasher
intruder 237.3
guest 923.6
gatekeeper 697.11
gate man 609.27
gatepost 216.4
gateway 301.6
gather
nouns 263.1
verbs assemble
74.15,17
be imminent 151.2
grow 196.7
fold 263.5
brew 402.23
harvest 412.19
deduce 493.10
suppose 498.9
think likely 510.4
procure 809.9
GATHER AROUND
form 59.4
assemble 74.15
GATHER COURAGE
891.13
GATHER FROM 550.10
GATHER UP 315.8
GATHER WAY
sail 274.23
make headway 293.2
gatherer 74.14
gathering
nouns assemblage
74.1
assembly 74.2
harvesting 412.15
abscess 684.28
acquisition 809.2
social ∼ 920.9
adjs. 151.3
gathering clouds
omen 542.4
danger 695.1
warning 701.3
gathering place 190.23
gator 413.30
gauche 732.20
gaucherie 732.5

Gaucho
horseman 273.8
cowkeeper 415.3
gaud 899.4
gaudery clothes 230.10
ornament 899.3
gaudiness 902.3
gaudy 902.20
gauge
nouns size 194.1
measure 489.2,4
types of ∼ 489.20
verbs size 194.15
measure 489.11
assess 493.9
gaugeable 489.15
gauger
exciseman 74.14
measurer 489.4,10
gauging 489.1
gaumy 388.12
gaunt desolate 186.12
thin 204.16
gauntlet 791.2
gaunty 204.16
gaup, gawp 438.16
Gauri 1012.7
Gautama Buddha
1020.3
gauze light filter 337.4
haze 403.1
dressing 685.28
gauzy
gossamery 338.4
fine 350.8
cloth 377.9
gavel 737.8
gavelkind
possession 806.1
coheirship 817.2
gavelock 286.4
Gawain 916.6
gawk
nouns dolt 470.5
clumsy fellow 732.9
verbs 438.16
gawkhammer 732.9
gawky
nouns dolt 470.5
clumsy fellow 732.9
adjs. thin 204.16
clumsy 732.20
gawp See gaup
gay colorful 361.19
pleasure-loving
863.15
cheerful 868.14
festive 876.30
showy 902.19
convivial 920.18
profligate 987.25
drunk 994.38
gay dog 987.10
gayety See gaiety
Gay Nineties 107.7
gaze
nouns 438.5
verbs 438.16
gazebo 438.8
gazel 607.4
gazelle 268.7

gazer 441.1
gazette journal 603.11
newspaper 603.12
gazetted 840.11
gazetteer
dictionary 603.7
newspaperman
603.22
gazingstock
wonder 918.2
laughingstock 965.7
geanticlinal 251.7
geanticline 251.3
gear
nouns condition 7.3
cordage 205.3
clothing 230.1
rigging 276.12
mechanism 347.5,6
equipment 657.4
IN GEAR 13.11
IN HIGH GEAR
268.21
IN LOW GEAR 269.13
OUT OF GEAR
out of order 62.12
disabled 157.17
dislocated 184.8
in disrepair 690.36
PUT IN GEAR 718.8
verbs intermesh 13.7
equip 657.8
GEAR TO
adjust to 26.13
conform 82.3
GEAR UP 268.15
gearbox 347.6
gearing, gearshift
347.6
gee
verbs agree 26.7
turn right 290.6
concur 520.9
harmonize 792.2
interjs. 970.13
gee box 345.2
Geechee 578.8
gee-gee 413.19
geezer oddity 85.4
elder 127.2
Gegenschein 334.15
Gehenna 1017.1
Geiger counter 326.13
Geigers 326.4
geisha 877.3
Geist genius 466.8
ghost 1015.1
psyche 1032.17
geke 85.4
gel
nouns 388.5
verbs 353.10
gelatin food 306a.39
semiliquid 388.5
gelatinate 353.10
gelatination 353.4
gelatin filter 337.4
gelatinity 388.2
gelatinous 388.12
geld 42.11
gelding castration 42.5

steer 413.8
horse 413.12
male animal 419.8
gelid cold 332.15
frozen 333.14
gelidity 332.1
gelignite 799.9
gelling 353.4
gelt 833.1
gem
nouns muffin 306a.30
precious stone 383.6
types of ∼ 383.10
good thing 672.5
jewel 899.6
admirable person
983.1
verbs 899.8
Gemara 1019.5
Gemaric 1019.10
geminate
verbs 91.2
adjs. 91.3
gemination 91.1
Gemini 90.4
gemma, gemmule
410.21
gemmate grow 196.7
bud 410.32
gemmation
growth 196.3
budding 410.30
gemshorn 464.23
gendarme guard 697.8
policeman 697.14,15
guardsman 798.14
gender sex 418.1
grammar 584.8
gene 169.6
genealogical 169.14
genealogy
lineage 169.5
register 568.8
general
nouns officer 747.22
factotum 748.10
adjs. common 79.10
public 416.13
well-known 474.27
indefinite 513.17
made public 557.17
in chief 739.17
communal 813.9
vulgar 896.14
IN GENERAL 79.15
General Assembly
parliament 740.2
U.N. 741.2
generalate, generalcy
747.25
generality
average 32.1
main part 54.5
universality 79
indefiniteness 513.4
generalization
generality 79.1
logic 481.3
generalize
universalize 79.8
reason 481.15

generally
in general 79.15
usually 84.9
approximately 199.26
indefinitely 513.26
general orders 750.3
general practitioner 686.5
general sessions 999.3
generalship
directorship 745.4
rank 747.25
warcraft 795.11
general store 830.1
generate cause 152.11
originate 166.15
procreate 168.9
~ electricity 341.23
generation age 107.5
lifetime 110.5
origination 166.6
procreation 168.2
~ of man 416.1
generative
creative 166.24
procreative 168.16
generator cause 152.4
producer 166.10
generic 79.10
generosity
abundance 659.2
liberality 851.1
hospitality 923.1
magnanimity 977.2
generous fertile 164.9
large 194.17
tolerant 524.11
plentiful 659.7
indulgent 757.10
liberal 851.4
hospitable 923.11
magnanimous 977.6
genesiology 169.6
genesis beginning 68.3
generation 166.6
birth 166.9
evolution 321.3
etymology 580.14
genethliacs, genethlialogy 374.20
genetic congenital 5.7
generative 166.24
hereditary 169.15
geneticist 405.17
genetic psychology 683.1
genetics 169.6
genetous 5.7
genetrix 169.10
genial
generative 166.24
warm 327.24
ungrudging 620.6
pleasant 861.5
cheerful 868.10
friendly 925.15
amiable 936.15
geniality
pleasantness 861.1
cheerfulness 868.1

friendliness 925.6
amiability 936.2
genic 169.15
geniculate, geniculated 250.6
genie 1014.7
genital
generative 166.24
sex 418.18
genitalia, genitals 418.8
genitive
nouns 584.7
adjs. 166.24
genius
inherent nature 5.3
intelligence 466.8
creative thought 533.2
inspiration 646.9
talent 731.4
prodigy 731.12
familiar spirit 1012.19
jinni 1014.7
genocide 408.3
genome 405.11
genre kind 61.3
gender 418.1
art 572.9
genre painting 572.5
gent 419.5
genteel refined 895.10
well-born 916.11
well-bred 934.17
gentile
nouns 1023.6
adjs. racial 11.8
infidel 1023.10
gentilhomme
nobleman 916.4
man of honor 972.8
gentilism 1023.3
gentilities 934.7
gentility
nationality 11.4
refinement 895.3
nobility 916.1
good breeding 934.4
gentle
verbs domesticate 188.5
tame 762.10
adjs. temperate 162.10
slow 269.10
light 352.11
soft 356.8
faint-sounding 451.16
lenient 757.8
meek 763.15
tender 853.20
well-born 916.11
well-bred 934.17
kindly 936.15
humane 942.7
gentlefolk, gentlefolks 916.3
gentleman man 419.5
valet 748.5

nobleman 916.4
man of honor 972.8
gentlemanly
manly 419.11
noble 916.11
well-bred 934.17
gentleman's agreement 769.1
gentleness
moderation 162.1
lightness 352.1
softness 356.1
soft sound 451.1
leniency 757.1
meekness 763.5
tender feeling 853.6
good breeding 934.4
kindliness 936.2
mercifulness 942.2
gentlewoman
woman 420.5
noblewoman 916.7
gentry 916.3
genuflect 962.6
genuflection, genuflexion 962.2
genuine
unadulterated 45.6
authentic 515.13
unaffected 734.6
genuineness
unadulteration 45.1
authenticity 515.5
artlessness 734.2
genus kind 61.3
class 61.5
genyoplasty 687.27
geocentric(al) 225.12
geodesic(al) 489.13
geodesist
mathematician 87.9
measurer 489.10
geodesy, geodetics 489.9
geodynamics 384.4
geognost 384.5
geognostic(al) 384.10
geognosy 384.4
geographer 384.5
geographic(al) 384.10
geographics 384.4
geography
topography 183.8
land 384.4
manual 603.9
geoid 254.2
geologic(al) 384.10
geological ages 107.10
geologist
mineralogist 382.11
geognost 384.5
geology
mineralogy 382.9
land 384.4
manual 603.9
geomancer 541.4
geometer, geometrician 87.9
geometric(al) 87.17
geometric figures 250.14

geometry
mathematics 87.18
manual 603.9
geomorphogenist 384.5
geomorphogeny 384.4
geomorphology
morphology 244.7
land 384.4
geophilous 384.6
geophysical
physical 324.3
terrestrial 384.10
geophysicist
physicist 324.2
geologist 384.5
geophysics
physics 324.1
land 384.4
geopolitical 742.47
geopolitician 744.1
geopolitics 742.2
geoponic(al) 412.20
geoponics 412.1
georama 445.6
georgic
nouns 607.4
adjs. 607.21
geoscopy 384.4
geostatics 346.2
geosynclinal 251.7
geosyncline 251.3
geotropism 351.5
Gephyrea, gephyreans 414.5
geriatrician 686.7
germ origin 152.7
microorganism 195.17
biology 405.13
German
nationality 417.9
~ alphabet 579.5
german
nouns 11.2
adjs. 11.7
germane
nouns 11.2
adjs. relevant 9.8
kindred 11.7
germanium triode 342.13
germ cell 405.6
germicidal 685.37
germicide 685.18
germinal
original 152.16
embryonic 195.14
rudimentary 405.23
germinate grow 196.7
vegetate 410.31
GERMINATE FROM 153.6
germination
growth 196.3
vegetation 410.30
germ plasm, germ plasma 405.3
germ war 795.4
gerocomy 126.8
gerontic 126.17

gerontocracy 739.4
gerontologist 686.7
gerontology 126.8
gerrymander
  nouns 742.16
  verbs maneuver
    733.10
  politics 742.41
Gerth 194.13
gerund 584.4
gerundive 584.2
gest, geste
  romance 606.7
  act 703.3
Gestalt 688.41
Gestalt psychology
    688.2
Gestapo 697.15
gestate
  originate 152.11
  be pregnant 168.13
gestation
  incubation 166.7
  pregnancy 168.6
gesticulate 566.20
gesticulation 566.13
gesture
  nouns sign 566.13
  pretext 647.1
  verbs 566.20
get
  nouns energy 160.2
  young 170.2
  enterprise 705.7
  gain 809.3
  receipts 842.1
  verbs be converted
    145.12
  induce 152.12
  beget 168.9
  incur 174.4
  speed 268.11
  fetch 270.15
  arrive 299.6
  depart 300.9
  kill 408.14
  hear 447.12
  solve 486.2
  discover 487.2
  baffle 513.13
  understand 546.7
  learn 562.6
  sicken of 684.34
  acquire 809.7
  receive 817.6
  take 820.11
  annoy 864.17
GET ABOUT
  be published 557.16
  recover 692.20
GET ACQUAINTED
    925.10
GET ACROSS
  be heard 447.13
  be understood 546.5
  make clear 546.6
  succeed with 721.10
GET A FOOTING 183.18
GET AHEAD
  increase 38.6
  progress 293.2

improve 689.7
succeed 722.9
GET AHEAD OF
  outdistance 36.9
  anticipate 131.6
  precede 291.2
  pass 311.8
GET A LOAD OF
    438.12
GET ALONG
  fare 7.6
  age 126.10
  advance 293.2
  depart 300.6
  improve 689.7
  manage 722.11
  prosper 726.7
GET ALONG WITH
    792.2
GET AROUND
  be published 557.16
  deceive 616.17
  evade 629.7
GET AT
  influence 171.9
  arrive at 299.7
  ascertain 512.11
  bribe 649.3
  acquire 809.8
GET AWAY
  depart 300.6
  escape 630.6
GET AWAY WITH
  eat 306.20
  escape 630.7
GET AWAY WITH IT
    722.10
GET BACK 821.6
GET BACK AT 953.4
GET BEHIND
  lag 292.4
  back 783.13
GET BY
  contrive 7.6
  stand the test 488.10
  escape 630.7
  eke out 657.11
  pass muster 659.4
  be tolerable 678.6
  succeed 722.10,11
GET DOWN
  swallow 306.20
  alight 314.7
  crouch 316.8
GET FROM 304.12
GET IN
  collect 74.17
  arrive 299.6
  enter 301.7
  board 313.12
  procure 809.9
GET IN THE ACT 813.5
GET IT 1008.22
GET NO PLACE FAST
    269.6
GET OFF
  begin 68.7
  depart 300.6,7
  dismount 314.7
  publish 557.14
  learn 562.6

escape 630.7
go free 761.9
GET ON
  fare 7.6
  age 126.10
  don 230.42
  depart 300.6
  mount 313.12
  succeed 722.9
  manage 722.11
  prosper 726.7
GET ONE's 958.6
GET ON TO 555.13
GET OUT
  depart 300.9
  exit 302.11
  extract 304.9
  be revealed 554.9
  publish 557.14
  print 601.12
  escape 630.6
  extricate 761.7
GET OVER
  move over 266.4
  be understood 546.5
  make clear 546.6
  recover 692.20
  succeed with 721.10
  surmount 724.6
GET TO
  begin 68.6
  extend to 198.6
  arrive 299.6
  be heard 447.13
  communicate with
    552.8
  bribe 649.3
GET UP
  make 166.12
  rise 212.7
  dress up 230.41
  trump up 614.18
  recover 692.20
  ~ from bed 711.5
  prepare 718.7
GET UP ON
  refresh the memory
    535.19
  study up 562.14
get-at-able
  approachable 295.5
  accessible 508.8
getaway 630.1
gettings gains 809.3
  receipts 842.1
get-together
  assembly 74.2
  sociable 920.9
getup
  composition 58.1
  structure 244.1
  enterprise 705.7
get-up 230.2
gewgaw trifle 671.5
  toy 876.16
  trinket 899.4
geyser
  hot springs 327.9
  jet 394.9
gharry 271.4
gharry-wallah 273.9

ghastly
  adjs. pale 362.9
  deathlike 407.23
  terrible 673.9
  frightful 889.29
  hideous 897.11
  advs. 897.13
ghat 204.3
ghetto 182.5
ghost
  nouns substitute
    148.2
  TV image 344.5
  ghostwriter 600.15
  specter 1015.1
GIVE UP THE GHOST
    407.15
  verbs substitute for
    148.5
  ghostwrite 600.21
ghostlike, ghostly
  deathlike 407.23
  specterlike 1015.7
ghost story
  story 606.7
  falsehood 614.11
ghost town 182.1
ghost word 580.7
ghostwrite
  substitute for 148.5
  write 600.21
ghost writer
  substitute 148.2
  writer 600.15
ghoul
  grave robber 823.1
  fiend 941.7
  demon 1014.7
ghoulish 1014.18
ghow 685.10
ghurry period 107.1
  timepiece 114.6
ghyll 256.9
G.I. 798.8
giant
  nouns strong man
    158.6
  colossus 194.13
  adjs. 194.20
giaour 1023.6
gib 413.28
gibber
  nouns nonsense 545.4
  chatter 594.3
  verbs twaddle 545.8
  mumble 593.8
  chatter 594.6
gibberish
  nouns nonsense 545.4
  unintelligibility
    547.6
  jargon 578.6
  adjs. 545.10
gibbet
  nouns 1009.5
  verbs stigmatize
    913.9
  hang 1008.20
gibbosity 255.2
gibbous
  humpbacked 248.13

humped 251.10
convex 255.12
gibe, jibe
nouns 965.2
verbs 965.9
giblets vitals 224.5
food 306a.23
Gibraltar 158.7
giddiness
dizziness 530.4
flightiness 530.5
fickleness 627.3
giddy
verbs 530.8
adjs. delirious 472.30
dizzy 530.15
scatterbrained
530 16
fickle 627.7
tipsy 994.38
**giddybrain, giddyhead,
giddypate** 470.7
gift
nouns talent 731.4
present 816.4
verbs 816.12
gifted 731.24
giftlike 348.5
gift of gab
talkativeness 594.1
eloquence 598.1
gig 653.10
giganteen, gigantic
194.20
giggle
nouns 374.4
verbs 874.9
gigolo 937.18
gigot legs 272.16
meat 306a.15
gigster 413.18
Gilbertine 1036.17
gild coat 227.26
paint 361.14
yellow 369.3
falsify 614.16
make pleasant 861.4
GILD THE PILL
lure 648.4
make pleasant 861.4
gilded yellow 369.4
drunk 994.40
Gilded Age 107.7
gilding
painting 361.11
ornament 899.3
gill valley 256.9
brook 394.1
sweetheart 929.12
gillie
townsman 189.6
servant 748.1
henchman 785.7
gills 402.20
gilt
nouns ornament
899.3
money 833.1,19
adjs. yellow 369.4
gold 382.16

gilt-edge, gilt-edged
672.15
gimbal
fulcrum 286.3
axle 320.5
gimbaljawed 594.9
gimcrack
nouns mechanical
device 347.1
trifle 671.5
toy 876.16
trinket 899.4
adjs. flimsy 159.14
paltry 671.18
gimcrackery 671.4
gimcrackiness 159.2
gimlet eye 438.10
gimlet eyes 439.6
gimmal 286.3
gimmick
apparatus 347.1
thing 375.4
story 606.9
trick 616.6
artifice 733.3
gin
nouns trap 616.11
liquor 994.16
verbs thresh 77.6
trap 616.20
conjs. 506.14
ginger energy 160.2
pungency 432.2
gingerbread
nouns superfluity
661.4
money 833.2
frills 899.3
adjs. 159.14
gingerly
adjs. 893.8
advs. 893.12
gingham 227.7
ginhound 994.11
gink 85.4
Ginkgoales, ginkgoes
411.8
gin mill 994.25
ginny 994.39
giraffe 413.5
gird bind 47.9
strengthen 158.11
encircle 232.7
ridicule 965.9
GIRD UP ONE'S LOINS
strengthen 158.11
prepare oneself
718.13
girders 216.8
girding fastening 47.3
surrounding 232.5
girdle
nouns corset 230.23
band 252.3
verbs bind 47.9
encircle 232.7
girdled 232.12
girdled 232.12
girl maid 125.6
mare 413.12
female animal
420.10

maidservant 748.8
sweetheart 929.12
girlhood youth 124.2
girls 125.2
girlish, girllike 124.11
girt
nouns saddle ~
215.19
band 252.3
verbs 47.9
adjs. 232.12
girth
nouns size 194.1
saddle ~ 215.19
band 252.3
harness 657.5
verbs 47.9
gismo 375.4
gist essence 5.2
content 193.4
meaning 543.1
main point 670.6
gîte 190.2
gittern 464.3
give
nouns pliancy 356.2
elasticity 357.1
verbs attribute 154.2
be pliant 356.7
inform 555.7
utter 592.14
provide 657.7
bestow 663.11
present 816.12
administer 961.6
GIVE AND TAKE
compensate 33.4
interchange 149.4
compromise 805.2
trade 825.10
retaliate 953.4
be fair 974.6
GIVE AWAY
divulge 554.6
discard 666.7
break 690.24
relinquish 812.3
give 816.20
marry 931.15
GIVE BACK 821.4
GIVE FORTH
sound 449.12
publish 557.14
GIVE FREELY 851.3
GIVE IN
yield 763.7
consent 773.4
deliver 816.13
GIVE IT TO
reprove 967.18
punish 1008.11
GIVE OFF
exude 302.15
let out 308.22
excrete 309.10
reek 400.7
GIVE ONESELF UP TO
attend to 528.5
be determined 622.8
undertake 713.3
indulge 991.4

GIVE OUT
weaken 159.9
let out 308.22
divulge 554.5
publish 557.11
be used up 664.4
go wrong 690.26
apportion 814.9
give 816.12
GIVE OVER
cease 144.6
give up 631.7
deliver 816.13
GIVE UP
not know 476.12
not understand
547.10
abandon 631.7
break a habit 641.3
disuse 666.4
yield 763.7
relinquish 812.3
despair 887.10
swear off 990.8
GIVE UPON 239.10
NOT GIVE AWAY 612.8
NOT GIVE UP
not weaken 158.9
persevere 623.4
resist 790.5
giveable 816.22
give-and-take
nouns interchange
149.1
barter 825.2
banter 880.1
retaliation 953.1
justice 974.1
adjs. 149.5
giveaway 554.2
given assumed 498.14
conditional 506.8
minded 523.8
accorded 816.23
gratuitous 848.5
GIVEN TO
disposed to 173.6
habituated 640.18
given name 581.4
giver 816.11
giving
nouns presentation
816
liberality 851
philanthropy 936.4
administration 961.2
adjs. 356.9
gizzard belly 192.3
vitals 224.5
intestines 224.6
food 306a.23
glabrate 259.9
glabrous
hairless 231.17
smooth 259.9
glace 306a.46
glacé glazed 259.10
shiny 334.33
glaciable 333.12
glacial icy 332.15
frozen 333.14

glaciarium 876.13
glaciate 333.11
glaciation glacier 332.6
  freezing 333.1
  hardening 355.5
glacier, glacieret 332.6
glacification 333.1
glacify freeze 333.11
  harden 355.7
glacis incline 218.4
  fortification 797.4
glad willing 620.5
  pleased 863.12
  cheerful 868.10,16
gladden
  make happy 863.7
  cheer 868.6
gladdening 868.16
glade open space 178.4
  patch of light 334.5
  everglade 399.1
gladiate 257.16
gladiator 798.1
gladiatorial 795.26
gladness
  happiness 863.2
  cheerfulness 868.1
glad rags 230.10
gladsome
  pleased 863.12
  cheerful 868.10
  festive 876.30
Glad Tidings 1019.4
glad tidings 556.2
glair semiliquid 388.5
  egg white 405.14
glamorize
  beautify 898.14
  glorify 912.13
glamorous
  charming 648.7
  bewitching 1034.12
glamour
  nouns charm 648.1
  magic 1033.1
  spell 1034.1
  verbs 1034.9
glance
  nouns glint 334.6
  touch 424.1
  glimpse 438.4
  signal 566.14
  AT A GLANCE 438.24
  verbs glaze 259.7
  be deflected 290.6
  glint 334.23
  touch 424.7
  look 438.18
  signal 566.21
  GLANCE AT
  look 438.18
  skim over 484.34
  hint at 555.9
  GLANCE OVER
  skim over 484.34
  browse 562.13
gland 310.9
glanders 684.10
glandular, glandulous 310.8

glare
  nouns brightness 334.4
  glower 438.5
  showiness 902.3
  verbs shine 334.23
  glower 438.17
  dazzle 440.6
  stand out 443.4
  be obvious 553.7
glaring
  downright 34.14
  bright 334.32
  distinct 443.7
  obvious 553.11
  garish 902.20
glass
  nouns drinking vessel 192.15
  smoothness 259.3
  temperature 327.19
  transparent 338.2
  types of ~ 338.7
  lens 442.1
  telescope 442.3
  mirror 442.5
  verbs reflect 22.5
  cover 227.25
  adjs. glassy 338.5
  ceramic 574.7
glass blower 577.7
glasses 442.2
glasshouse 412.11
glassiness
  lackluster 336.6
  transparency 338.1
glassware glass 338.2
  merchandise 829.4
glasswork 338.2
glassworks 717.4
glassy smooth 259.10
  shiny 334.33
  lackluster 336.19
  transparent 338.5
  expressionless 545.11
Glathsheim 1016.11
glaucoma 684.11
glaucous 370.4
glaver 968.5
glaze
  nouns polish 259.2
  ice 332.6
  verbs cover 227.25
  polish 259.7
  enamel 361.14
glazed polished 259.10
  dull 336.19
glazing 361.11
gleam
  nouns small amount 35.4
  light 334.2,5,6
  verbs shine 334.23
  burst forth 445.9
  be illustrious 912.10
gleaming, gleamy 334.30
glean harvest 412.19
  deduce 493.10
  select 635.11

  procure 809.9
gleaning
  harvesting 412.15
  acquisition 809.2
gleanings
  excerpts 605.4
  gains 809.3
glebe soil 384.1
  benefice 1035.9
  pastorate 1040.7
glee music 461.18
  pleasure 863.2
  merriment 868.5
glee club 463.18
gleeful 868.15
glen 256.9
glib loquacious 594.9
  hypocritical 614.33
  facile 730.11
  suave 934.18
glibness
  loquacity 594.1
  hypocrisy 614.6
  suaveness 934.5
glide
  nouns sweep 272.8
  aviation 277.10
  slide 314.4
  speech sound 449.5
  verbs elapse 105.5
  be converted 145.12
  sweep 272.34
  fly 277.42
  slide 314.9
  go easily 730.8
glide-bomb 796.25
glider boat 276.10
  aircraft 279.12
glim
  small amount 35.4
  light 335.1
  glance 438.4
  eye 438.9
glime
  nouns 438.3
  verbs look askance 438.19
  squint 439.9
glimmer
  nouns glitter 334.7
  hint 555.4
  verbs 334.24
glimmering
  nouns glimmer 334.7
  hint 555.4
  adjs. 334.35
glimpse
  nouns 438.4
  verbs 438.12,18
glims 442.2
glint
  nouns light 334.2,6
  glimpse 438.4
  verbs gleam 334.23
  glimpse 438.18
glinting 334.30
glisk 334.24
glissade
  nouns 314.4
  verbs glide 272.34
  slide 314.9

glissando slide 314.4
  music 461.31
glisten, glister
  nouns 334.7
  verbs 334.24
glitter
  nouns glimmer 334.7
  showiness 902.3
  verbs glimmer 334.24
  be illustrious 912.10
glittering
  nouns 334.7
  adjs. glimmering 334.35
  showy 902.19
glittery 334.34
gloam
  nouns 134.3
  verbs 336.13
gloaming 134.3
gloat gaze 438.16
  exult 908.8
  GLOAT OVER
  delight in 863.10
  exult 908.8
gloating 908.4
global universal 79.13
  spherical 254.9
globate 254.9
globe
  nouns sphere 254.2
  light ~ 337.3
  earth 374.7
  map 652.4
  verbs 254.7
globelike, globe-shaped 254.9
globe-trotter 273.1
globe-trotting 272.1
globoid
  nouns 254.2
  adjs. 254.9
globosity, globularity 254.1
globous, globular 254.9
globule drop 35.5
  sphere 254.2
  bubble 404.1
glochidiate 260.9
glockenspiel 464.20
glomerate 74.21
glomeration 74.8
gloom
  nouns darkness 336.2,3
  sadness 870.7
  sullen look 949.9
  verbs darken 336.10,13
  look sullen 949.15
gloominess
  darkness 336.2
  ominousness 542.5
  sadness 870.7
  pessimism 887.6
glooming dusk 134.3
  sullenness 949.9,10
gloomy dark 336.15
  foreboding 542.13
  sad 870.25

depressing 870.31
pessimistic 887.16
Gloria
  doxology 1030.3
  rite 1038.10
glorification
  honoring 912.8
  praise 966.5
  sanctification
    1024.3
  worship 1030.2
glorify honor 912.13
  praise 966.12
  sanctify 1024.5
  worship 1030.11
glorious superb 672.18
  beautiful 898.19
  magnificent 902.21
  illustrious 912.20
  drunk 994.38
glory
  nouns halo 334.14
  grandeur 902.5
  fame 912.1,6
  honor 914.1
  praise 966.5
  divine attribute
    1011.15
  heaven 1016.1
  glorification 1030.2
  GO TO GLORY
  die 407.17
  go to ruin 691.23
  verbs rejoice 874.6
  exult 908.8
  GLORY IN 903.5
Glory be to God!
  gratitude 947.7
  hallelujah! 1030.16
glory hole nook 191.3
  dust hole 667.6
gloss
  nouns shallowness
    209.1
  polish 259.2
  shine 334.2
  interpretation
    550.3,6
  misinterpretation
    551.1
  dictionary 603.7
  commentary 604.2
  pretext 647.1
  extenuation 1004.5
  verbs coat 227.26
  polish 259.7
  enamel 361.14
  whitewash 363.7
  explain 550.13
  misinterpret 551.2
  falsify 614.16
  GLOSS OVER
  whitewash 363.7
  neglect 532.6
  extenuate 1004.12
glossa lingual 426.10
  phonetic 449.18
glossarian 578.12
glossarist
  philologist 578.12
  annotator 604.4

glossary 603.7
glossic 579.7
glossiness 259.1
glossing 361.11
glossographer
  philologist 578.12
  annotator 604.4
glossographic(al)
  580.18
glossography 580.13
glossologic(al)
  linguistic 578.15
  lexical 580.18
  terminological
    581.17
glossologist 578.12
glossology
  interpretation 550.9
  linguistics 578.11
  lexicology 580.13
  nomenclature 581.1
glossotomy 687.26
glossotype 579.7
glossy sleek 259.10
  shiny 334.33
glottal 449.18
glottis 592.10
glottogonic 580.19
glottogony 580.14
glottologic(al) 578.15
glottologist 578.12
glottology 578.11
glout
  nouns 949.9
  verbs 949.15
glove
  types of ~ 230.63
  challenge 791.2
glover 230.32
glow
  nouns heat ~ 327.11
  shine 334.2
  warm color 361.2
  reddening 367.3
  eloquence 598.5
  beauty 898.1
  verbs be hot 327.21
  shine 334.23
  redden 367.5
  ~ with emotion
    855.18
  be illustrious 912.10
glower
  nouns glare 438.5
  sullen look 949.9
  verbs glare 438.17
  look sullen 949.15
glowering 949.24
glowfly 335.5
glowing
  burning 327.27
  luminous 334.30
  red 367.6,10
  eloquent 598.13
  enthusiastic 633.11
  fervent 853.22
  excited 855.23
  beautiful 898.19
  drunk 994.40
glowworm 335.5
gloze glow 334.23

  whitewash 363.7
glue
  nouns adhesive 48.6
  fastener 48.9
  verbs 50.7
gluey adhesive 50.9
  viscid 388.12
glum sad 870.26
  sullen 949.24
gluma, glume 410.17
glut
  nouns overfullness
    661.3
  satiety 662.1
  verbs stuff 306.23
  overfill 661.16
  satiate 662.4
  gorge 992.5
gluteal 240.9
gluten adhesive 48.6
  semiliquid 388.5
glutenous, glutinose
  388.12
glutinosity
  tenacity 50.2
  viscidity 388.2
glutinous
  adhesive 50.9
  viscid 388.12
glutted overfull 661.21
  satiated 662.6
glutton
  wolverine 413.4
  greedy eater 992.3
gluttonize 992.5
gluttonous
  intemperate 991.7
  greedy 992.7
gluttony
  intemperance 991
  greed 992
glycerinate, glycerin-
  ize, glycerolate
  379.8
glyceryl esters 379.14
glyph 573.3
glyphic
  sculptural 573.7
  engraved 576.16
glyphograph 576.7
glyphographer 577.8
glyphography 576.2
glyptic(al)
  sculptural 573.7
  engraving 576.17
glyptics 576.4
glyptograph 576.6
glyptographer 577.8
glyptography 576.4
glyptotheca 658.9
glyster 685.17
G-man police 697.14
  detective 779.10
gnarl
  nouns complication
    46.2
  contortion 248.1
  knot 255.3
  verbs distort 248.5
  roughen 260.4
  snarl 459.4

  be angry 950.14
gnarled complex 46.4
  knotted 255.16
  rough 260.8
gnash
  nouns 306.2
  verbs 349.8
  GNASH ONE'S TEETH
  grieve 873.9
  be angry 950.14
gnat
  minute thing 195.7
  insect 413a.7
gnaw chew 306.25
  grind 349.8
  pain 423.7
  corrode 690.22
  rankle 864.21
gnawer 413.3
gnawing
  nouns 423.2,5
  adjs. grinding 349.10
  rodent 413.40
  painful 423.10
Gnetales, gnetums
  411.8
gnome dwarf 195.6
  maxim 516.1
  sprite 1012.13
  elf 1012.15
gnomelike, gnomish
  1012.23
gnomic(al) 516.6
gnostic wise 466.17
  knowing 474.15
Gnostic(al) 499.11
gnu 413.5
go
  nouns dose 55.5
  spell 108.1
  turn 108.2
  occurrence 150.2
  energy 160.2
  examination 484.3
  act 703.3
  attempt 712.2
  success 722.1
  compact 769.1
  contest 794.3
  game 876.9
  ALL THE GO 642.11
  BE A GO
  agree 520.10
  be a bargain 825.15
  HAVE A GO AT 712.5
  MAKE A GO OF IT
    722.10
  NO GO
  useless 667.9
  failure 723.1
  hopeless 887.14
  ON THE GO
  traveling 272.41
  busy 705.20
  verbs cease to be 2.5
  fare 7.6
  be converted 145.12
  be operative 163.8
  tend 173.3
  extend 178.7
  belong 183.9

move 272.17
travel 272.18
sail 274.30
bear for 289.8
progress 293.2
recede 296.2
depart 300.6
fade 362.6
disappear 446.2
perish 691.22
succeed 722.6
carry authority
    737.12
tolerate 859.5
GO ABOUT
prevail 79.9
wander 272.22
tack 274.32
turn round 294.9
circuit 319.4
be published 557.16
undertake 713.3
GO AFTER
come next 65.3
be subsequent 117.2
fetch 270.15
follow 292.3
pursue 653.8
GO AGAINST
counteract 177.6
oppose 788.3
GO AGROUND 274.44
GO AHEAD
begin 68.6
go before 291.2
proceed 293.2
improve 689.7
be industrious
    705.12
GO AHEAD OF 64.2
GO ALL OUT
be thorough 56.8
speed 268.14
persevere 623.5
be active 705.13
do one's best 712.11
do up brown 720.7
go unrestrained
    760.17
GO ALOFT 277.44
GO ALONG
continue 143.3
travel 272.17
proceed 293.2
depart 300.6
GO ALONG WITH
accompany 73.7
concur 176.3
agree 520.9
co-operate 784.6
GO AROUND
surround 232.6
circuit 319.4
round 319.5
detour 319.6
be enough 659.4
GO AROUND IN
    CIRCLES
be uncertain 513.9
be irresolute 625.6

GO AS
represent 570.8
be called 581.13
GO AS ONE PLEASES
have one's way
    619.3
be lawless 738.4
be independent
    760.18
GO AWAY
separate 49.19
recede 296.2
diverge 298.5
depart 300.6
disappear 446.2
GO BACK
recur 103.11
revert 146.5
retreat 294.6
remember 535.11
GO BACK ON
desert 631.5,6
be unfaithful 973.11
GO BACK OVER
re-examine 484.35
remember 535.11
GO BACK TO
resume 143.6
revert 146.6
revisit 185.9
GO BEFORE
antecede 64.2
be prior 116.3
anticipate 131.6
precede 291.2
GO BEHIND
regress 294.5
investigate 484.30
lose 810.5
GO BEYOND 661.10
GO BY
conform 82.3
elapse 105.5
pass 311.8
be called 581.13
GO DOWN
capsize 274.46
descend 314.5
sink 314.6
founder 318.8
find credence
    500.17
deteriorate 690.18
fail 723.10
be defeated 725.12
be borne 859.9
GO FOR
fetch 270.15
head for 289.10
be credulous 501.5
represent 570.8
intend 651.4
abet 783.14
attack 796.15
love 929.17
GO IN
narrow 204.10
enter 301.7
GO IN FOR
specialize 81.4

study for 562.15
take up 635.12
do 703.7
undertake 713.3
GO INTO
compose 58.3
begin 68.8
enter 301.7
develop 321.6
discuss 481.16
investigate 484.30
write upon 604.5
undertake 713.3
join 786.14
participate 813.5
GO IT
speed 268.9
act 703.4
be active 705.12
make merry 876.26
GO IT ALONE 760.18
GO OFF
occur 150.5
explode 161.13
turn aside 290.6
diverge 298.5
depart 300.6
~ the air 343.24
die 407.16
detonate 455.8
deteriorate 690.18
succeed 722.6
marry 931.16
GO ON
be disorderly 62.9
endure 110.6
linger 110.7
continue 143.3
resume 143.6
be violent 161.10
proceed 293.2
depart 300.6
chatter 594.6
persevere 623.2
manage 722.11
behave 735.4
rage angrily 950.15
GO OUT
end 70.6
exit 302.11
be extinguished
    331.8
obsolesce 666.9
strike 787.9
GO OVER
reiterate 103.8
traverse 272.19
grill 484.23
examine 484.31
read 562.12
rehearse 609.36
apostatize 626.8
succeed 722.6
GO THROUGH
undergo 150.8
penetrate 301.9
chill 332.11
search 484.25
rehearse 609.36
perform 703.8
squander 852.3

GO THROUGH
    CHANNELS 395.19
GO TO
attend 185.8
extend to 198.6
travel 272.24
intend to 651.5
GO TO IT 714.15
GO UNDER
be called 581.13
go to ruin 691.23
fail 723.10
be defeated 725.12
go bankrupt 840.7
GO UP
increase 38.6
ascend 313.8
die 407.16
go to ruin 691.23
fail 723.9
go bankrupt 840.7
GO WITH
agree 26.9
accompany 73.7
concur 176.3
border on 199.9
accord 520.9
court 930.26
GO WITHOUT SAYING
be certain 512.9
be manifest 553.7
NOT GO FOR
be incredulous
    503.3
disapprove 967.10
adjs. 718.9
go-about 273.2
goad
nouns 646.8
verbs prod 282.12
herd 415.7
urge 646.15
go-ahead
nouns progress 293.1
ambition 632.10
enterprise 705.7
go-getter 705.8
THE GO-AHEAD 775.1
adjs. progressive
    293.5
enterprising 705.22
goal end 70.1
destination 299.5
objective 651.2
score 722.4
goalie, goalkeeper
    697.8
go-as-you-please
nouns 794.12
adjs. 760.19
goat scapegoat 148.3
animal 413.10
horse 413.16
dupe 618.1
laughingstock 965.7
lecher 987.11
GET ONE'S GOAT
    864.17
goatee 229.8
goatherd 415.3

goatish
goatlike 413.41
lascivous 987.29
gob quantity 28.2
large amount 34.5
piece 55.3
accumulation 74.8
lump 194.10
mouth 264.5
sailor 275.4
mouthful 306.2
gobbet 55.2
gobble devour 306.21
gabble 459.5
eat greedily 992.5
GOBBLE UP 501.5
gobbledegook
doubletalk 545.4
jargon 578.6
bombast 599.2
officialese 742.40
gobbler turkey 413.35
male animal 419.8
gobe-mouche 618.1
go-between
intermediary 236.4
interagent 779.4
mediator 803.3
goblin 1014.9
gobo 337.3
go-by, the
evasion 629.1
circumvention 733.5
snub 964.2
gocart 271.6
God 1011.2
GOD BLESS YOU!
farewell! 300.25
best wishes! 726.17
GOD FORBID! 967.27
GOD HELP YOU!
942.11
GOD KNOWS! 476.20
GOD WILLING
if possible 508.11
Deo volente
1011.21
god
wind ~ 402.3
hero 983.5
deity 1012.2
THE GODS 1012.1
godchild 770.9
go-devil 271.15
Godforsaken
vacant 186.13
forlorn 922.13
God-forsaken 198.9
God-given 816.23
godhead 1011.10
godhood 1011.1
godkin, godlet 1012.3
godless 1029.18
godlike divine 1011.19
godly 1026.9
godliness
divinity 1011.1
godlikeness 1026.2
godling 1012.3
godly divine 1011.19
pious 1026.9

godown 658.6
godparent 770.8
God's acre 409.15
God's board 1040.11
God's country 180.2
godsend 809.6
godship 1011.1
God's image 416.4
God's kingdom
1016.1
Godspeed
nouns 300.4
interjs. farewell!
300.25
best wishes! 726.17
God's will 638.2
God the Father
1011.11
God the Holy Ghost
1011.14
God the Son 1011.12
goer attender 185.5
speeder 268.6
traveler 273.1
outgoer 302.10
Gog and Magog
194.13
go-getter 705.8
goggle
nouns stare 438.5
eye 438.9
verbs bulge 255.10
roll 320.10
stare 438.16
squint 439.9
adjs. 255.15
goggled
protruding 255.15
spectacled 442.10
goggle-eyed 439.12
goggles eyeshade 337.2
spectacles 442.2
going
nouns travel 272.1
departure 300.1
disappearance 446.1
adjs. operating
163.12
traveling 272.35
dying 407.27
GET GOING
begin 68.7
bestir oneself 707.5
set to work 714.15
GOING AROUND
556.15
GOING AROUND IN
CIRCLES 513.22
GOING ON
happening 150.9
operating 163.12
in progress 293.6
in preparation
718.23
KEEP GOING
continue 143.3,4
persevere 623.2
be industrious
705.14
going-over 967.7

GIVE A GOING-OVER
reprove 967.19
punish 1008.12
goings on affairs 150.4
behavior 735.1
goings-on 705.1
goiter 684.8
Golconda 835.3
gold
nouns 833.1,19
adjs. yellow 369.4
metallic 382.16
goldanged, goldarned
970.10
goldbrick
nouns fraud 616.8
malingerer 629.3
verbs 629.9
gold-brick 616.18
gold-bricker 617.4
gold digger
miner 382.8
coquette 930.10
gold dust 382.3
golden yellow 369.4
metallic 382.16
musical 461.49
auspicious 542.16
very good 672.15
valuable 846.10
Golden Age 107.7
golden age 726.4
golden calf 1031.3
golden-haired 369.5
golden hours 108.3
golden mean
mean 32.1
moderation 162.1
mid-course 804.3
golden opportunity
129.3
golden rule
axiom 516.2
rule 749.2
PRACTICE THE
GOLDEN RULE
936.12
gold fever 382.7
goldilocks 361.8
gold mine mine 382.6
source of supply
658.4
rich source 835.3
gold piece 833.5
gold-plated
plated 227.35
metallic 382.16
gold standard 833.20
gold star 914.5
golfer 876.20
Golgotha, golgotha
409.15
Goliath
strong man 158.6
giant 194.13
gomashta 773.3
Gomorrah 979.11
gonad 310.9
gonads 418.8
gondola 271.13

gondolier, gondoliere
275.5
gone nonexistent 2.10
past 119.5
weak 159.12
absent 186.9
departed 300.20
dead 407.24
vanished 446.4
forgotten 536.8
used up 664.6
lost 810.7
past hope 887.15
GONE ON
enthusiastic 633.11
enamored 929.27
GONE OUT 123.15
gone-by past 119.5
obsolete 123.15
goneness 715.1
goner 887.8
gonfalon 567.6
gong
nouns bell 453.4
orchestral ~ 464.20
verbs 453.8
Gongorism 587.3
Gongorist 587.5
gongoristic 587.9
gonidangium 405.9
goniometer 250.4
goniometry 250.3
gonorrhea 684.15
goo semiliquid 388.5
sentimentality 853.7
goober, goober pea
306a.38
good
nouns 672.4
ALL TO THE GOOD
668.7
THE GOOD
good persons 983.6
the righteous 1026.5
TO THE GOOD
sufficiently 659.8
advantageously
663.25
helpfully 783.24
profitably 809.15
to one's credit 837.9
adjs. full 56.12
savory 427.8
valid 515.12
genuine 515.13
auspicious 542.16
ample 659.6
expedient 668.4
excellent 672.13
salubrious 681.5
solvent 834.17
pleasant 861.5
kind 936.14
proper 956.8
estimable 966.19
just 974.8
virtuous 978.7
godly 1026.9
AS GOOD AS
equivalent 30.9
almost 199.25

BE GOOD
  behave 735.5
  be virtuous 978.6
DO GOOD
  benefit 672.11
  help 783.11
  be benevolent
    936.13
FOR GOOD
  forever 112.12
  for keeps 811.11
GOOD AS GOLD 846.10
GOOD AT 731.25
GOOD FOR
  useful 663.18
  beneficial 672.21
  salubrious 681.5
  helpful 783.21
  able to pay 834.17
  worth 844.16
LOOK GOOD 898.15
MAKE GOOD
  compensate 33.4
  complete 56.6
  prove 504.11
  remedy 692.13
  succeed 722.9
  prosper 726.9
  fulfill 766.2
  grow rich 835.9
  do one's duty
    960.10
  keep faith with
    972.9
  atone for 1010.4
NOT BE GOOD FOR
    682.3
advs. yes 520.18
  kindly 936.19
interjs. very well!
    866.17
  bravo! 966.21
Good Book, the
    1019.2
good-by, good-bye
nouns 300.4
interjs. 300.25
good cheer
  cheerfulness 868.2
  conviviality 920.3
WITH GOOD CHEER
  willingly 620.8
  cheerfully 868.17
good-day!
  farewell! 300.25
  greetings! 923.15
good faith 972.7
good fellow
  boonfellow 926.5
  worthy 983.1
good-fellowship 920.2
good folk, the 1012.14
good footing 925.3
good form
  convention 643.1
  etiquette 644.3
good-for-nothing
nouns idler 706.8
  wretch 984.2
adjs. worthless 667.11
  indolent 706.17

Good Friday 1038.15
good humor
  cheerfulness 868.2
  good nature 936.2
PUT IN GOOD HUMOR
  cheer 868.6
  amuse 876.23
good-humored 936.15
goodish 672.20
goodliness
  goodness 672.1
  pleasantness 861.1
  comeliness 898.3
good looker 898.8
good-looking 898.17
good luck
nouns 726.2
interjs. farewell!
    300.25
  best wishes 726.17
goodly great 34.8
  large 194.16
  excellent 672.13
  pleasant 861.5
  comely 898.17
goodman 931.8
good-natured 936.15
good-neighbor policy
    742.5
goodness
nouns savoriness
    427.1
  validity 515.4
  excellence 672
  pleasantness 861.1
  kindness 936.1
  propriety 956.2
  virtue 978.1
  godliness 1026.2
interjs. 918.19
good news 556.2
good night! 300.26
good offices
  mediation 803.1
  kindness 936.7
goods freight 270.7
  fabrics 377.5
  property 808.1
  merchandise 829.1
HAVE THE GOODS ON
  catch 487.7
  have evidence
    504.16
THE GOODS
  ability 156.2
  the real thing 515.6
  information 555.1
  talent 731.4
good Samaritan 940.1
Good Shepherd, the
    1011.12
goods waggon 271.13
good-tempered 936.15
Good Templar 990.5
Good Tidings 1019.4
goodwife
  mistress 747.2
  wife 931.9
good will
  willingness 620.1
  custom 825.6

favor 925.3
  benevolence 936.4
good word
  good news 556.2
  commendation
    966.3
goody
nouns delicacy 306a.8
  mollycoddle 420.11
adjs. hypocritical
    614.33
  overnice 901.18
  sanctimonious
    1027.5
interjs. 863.17
goody-goody
nouns mollycoddle
    420.11
  prude 901.11
adjs. hypocritical
    614.33
  overnice 901.18
  sanctimonious
    1027.5
gooey 388.12
goof
nouns oddity 85.5
  fool 470.2
  lunatic 472.15
verbs 517.13
GOOF OFF
  blunder 517.13
  shirk 629.9
  loaf 706.10
GOOF UP 732.12
goofballs 685.11
go-off beginning 68.1
  occurrence 150.2
  departure 300.2
goofy foolish 469.8
  insane 472.25
goo-goo eyes 930.8
gook native 189.3
  goo 388.5
goon fool 470.2
  strike enforcer 787.5
  thug 941.4
goon squad
  pickets 697.12
  strike enforcers
    787.5
goop oddity 85.4
  goo 388.5
goose
nouns food 306a.22
  fowl 413.35
  hiss 456.1
  fool 470.6
  boo 965.3
verbs tickle 425.6
  hiss 456.2
gooseberry escort 73.5
  chaperon 697.6
gooseboy 415.3
goose bumps 332.2
goose chase 667.3
goose egg 2.2
goose flesh 332.2
goose grass 257.8
gooseherd 415.3

goose step gait 272.15
  routine 640.5
goose-step 272.29
goosy anserine 413.45
  ticklish 425.9
  silly 469.8
G.O.P. 742.25
gopura 206.11
Gordian knot
  complication 46.2
  knot 48.3
  dilemma 729.6
gore
nouns blood 387.4
  bloodshed 408.1
verbs 796.28
gorge
nouns belly 192.3
  ravine 200.3
  obstruction 265.3
  throat 395.15
verbs eat 306.23
  overfill 661.16
  satiate 662.4
  overeat 992.5
gorged overfull 661.21
  satiated 662.6
gorgeous
  colorful 361.19
  beautiful 898.19
  showy 902.20
gorger 992.3
Gorgon monster 85.20
  ogre 889.8
  charmer 1033.9
Gorgonian,
  Gorgonlike 889.29
gorilla
  assassin 408.10
  monkey 413.50
  thug 941.4
gormandize 992.5
gormandizer 992.3
gory blood-red 367.8
  murderous 408.24
  bloody 677.10
Goshen 533.11
gosling novice 564.7
  unsophisticate 734.3
Gospel 1038.10
THE GOSPEL 1019.4
gospel
nouns belief 500.2
  truth 515.2
  glad tidings 556.2
adjs. 1019.9
Gospel side 243.1
gospel truth
  belief 500.2
  truth 515.2
  orthodoxy 1022.1
gossamer
nouns filament 205.1
  lightness 352.3
adjs. transparent
    338.4
  fine 350.8
gossamery
  unsubstantial 4.5
  flimsy 159.14
  silky 205.7

transparent 338.4
fine 350.8
light 352.10
cloth 377.9
gossip
 nouns tattle 556.7
 newsmonger 556.9
 verbs 556.12
gossipy, gossipy
 556.14
Goth 896.7
Gothamite 467.6
Gothic
 antiquated 123.13
 barbarous 896.12
gothic 896.12
Gothicism
 ignorance 476.8
 inelegant style 588.1
 vulgarism 896.3
go-to-itiveness 705.7
gouache color 361.7
 painting 572.15
gouge
 nouns 262.1
 verbs excavate 256.15
 groove 262.3
 perforate 264.15
 blind 440.6
 swindle 616.18
goulash 306a.11
gourmand, gourmet
 connoisseur 895.7
 voluptuary 985.3
 glutton 992.4
gourmanderie 992.2
gout 684.8
goût 427.2
gouty 684.46
govern influence 171.8
 regulate 739.11
 manage 745.8
 supervise 745.10
 curb 758.7
governable 763.14
governess
 instructress 563.2
 guard an 697.6
 mistress 747.2
governing
 ruling 739.17
 managing 745.12
government
 guardianship 697.2
 rule 739
 management 745
governmental 739.16
government control
 742.4
governor father 169.9
 mechanism 348.14
 guardian 697.5
 director 746
 chief 747.6,14
governorship 745.4
gow, ghow speed 268.1
 narcotic 685.10
gowk dolt 470.5
 clumsy fellow 732.9
gown
 nouns garment 230.3

dress 230.16
 clerical ~ 1039.2
 verbs 230.39
gownsman 716.4
goy, goi 1023.6
grab
 nouns seizure 820.2
 theft 822.10
 booty 822.11
 verbs 820.12,15
 GRAB AT 633.7
grab bag 514.10
grabble harvest 412.19
 grope 484.26
grabby greedy 632.28
 acquisitive 809.13
 rapacious 820.23
Grace 915.2
grace
 nouns music 462.18
 tact 491.1
 elegant style 587.1
 eloquence 598.2
 excellence 672.1
 taste 895.1
 beauty 898.1
 kindness 936.4,7
 clemency 942.1
 forgiveness 945.2
 thanksgiving 947.2
 conscience 955.5
 reprieve 1005.3
 divine function
 1011.18
 sanctification
 1024.3
 prayer 1030.4
 IN ONE'S GOOD
 GRACES 925.17
 THE GRACES 898.9
 WITH A BAD GRACE
 621.9
 verbs beautify 898.14
 adorn 899.7
 dignify 912.12
graceful tactful 491.8
 elegant 587.6
 eloquent 598.9
 tasteful 895.9
 beautiful 898.16
 courteous 934.14
gracefulness
 tactfulness 491.1
 elegant style 587.1
 eloquence 598.2
 taste 895.1
 politeness 934.1
graceless
 inelegant 588.2
 clumsy 730.20
 unbeautiful 897.9
 shiftless 979.22
 unregenerate
 1029.18
gracelessness
 inelegant style 588.1
 clumsiness 732.3
 unbeautifulness
 897.1
 unregeneracy 1029.4
grace note 462.18

gracias! 947.6
gracile 204.15
gracious
 adjs. ungrudging
 620.6
 indulgent 757.10
 hospitable 923.11
 courteous 934.14
 kind 936.14
 interjs. 918.19
graciousness
 indulgence 757.3
 hospitality 923.1
 politeness 934.1
 kindness 936.1
grad 564.6
gradatim 29.6
gradation
 graduation 29.3
 series 71.2
gradational 29.5
grade
 nouns degree 29.1
 class 61.2
 incline 218.4
 school ~ 564.9
 GRADE BY GRADE 29.6
 MAKE THE GRADE
 be able 156.10
 succeed 722.11
 THE GRADES 565.5
 verbs graduate 29.4
 classify 61.6
 size 194.15
 level 213.6
 smooth 259.5
graded arranged 60.13
 classified 61.8
grader 564.5
grade school 565.5
gradient
 nouns 218.4
 adjs. 272.35
gradin shelf 215.14
 predella 1040.11
grading 61.1
gradino 215.14
gradual
 gradational 29.5
 slow 269.10
gradually
 by degrees 29.6
 slowly 269.13
graduate
 nouns student 564.6
 proficient 731.11
 verbs grade 29.4
 size 194.15
 measure 489.11
 pass 722.6
 promote 780.3
graduate school 565.7
graduation
 gradation 29.3
 ceremony 644.4
 promotion 780.1
graduation exercises
 644.4
gradus 603.7
graff 262.2

graft
 nouns fraud 616.8
 bribery 649.1
 Machiavellianism
 733.2
 political ~ 742.35,
 36
 boodle 822.11
 verbs fasten 47.7
 ingraft 303.5
grafter intriguer 733.8
 politician 744.5
graham cracker
 306a.29
grail 383.3
grain
 nouns nature 5.3
 small amount 35.2
 kind 61.3
 minute thing 195.7
 minuteness 195.8
 food 306a.4
 texture 350.1
 granule 360.6
 plant 410.5
 seed 410.29
 types of ~ 410.47
 mood 523.4
 GO AGAINST THE
 GRAIN
 ruffle 260.5
 make nervous 857.9
 irritate 864.18
 IN THE GRAIN 5.6
 WITH A GRAIN OF
 SALT
 unbelievingly
 502.13
 conditionally 506.11
 verbs give texture
 350.4
 granulate 360.9,10
 dye 361.13
grain-eater 306.13
grain-eating 306.29
grained 350.6
grain-fed 194.18
graininess
 coarseness 350.2
 granularity 360.2
grainy coarse 350.6
 granular 360.12
grallatorial 274.61
gramarye 1033.1
graminivore 306.13
graminivorous 306.29
gramalogue 579.3
grammar
 rudiments 68.5
 language 584
 bad ~ 585.1
 diction 586.1
 textbook 603.8
grammarian 578.12
grammarless 476.15
grammar school
 565.5,6
grammatic(al) 584.13
grammatical accent
 462.24
grammaticaster 578.12

grammaticize 584.12
grammatist 578.12
gramophone 464.18
grampus 194.12
granary 658.7
grand
nouns thousand
99.10
~ piano 464.13
money 833.7
adjs. great 34.8
large 194.16
eloquent 598.14
grandiloquent 599.9
important 670.16
good 672.14
grandiose 902.21
dignified 903.12
eminent 912.19
grandam, grandame
old woman 127.3
grandmother 169.12
grandaunt 11.3
grandchild, grand-
children 170.1,3
grand dame 901.10
grand duchy 180.1
grand duke, grand
duchess 916.5,7
grandee 916.4
grandeur
greatness 34.1
eloquence 598.6
ostentation 902.5
dignity 903.2
distinction 912.5
grandfather
old man 127.2
grandparent 169.11
grandfatherly 169.13
grandiloquence 599
grandiloquent 599.9
grandiose
grandiloquent 599.9
ostentatious 902.21
grandiosity
grandiloquence
599.1
splendor 902.5
grandisonant 599.9
grand jury 1000.7
grand larceny 822.2
grand mal 684.5
grandmaternal 169.13
Grand Mogul 747.9
grand mogul 670.8
grandmother
old woman 127.3
grandparent 169.12
dotard 470.9
grandmotherly 169.13
grandness
greatness 34.1
largeness 194.6
grandeur 902.5
grand opera 461.35
grandparent 169.8
grandparentage 169.1
grandparental, grand-
paternal 169.13

Grand Penitentiary
1036.8
grand piano 464.13
Grand Sachem
politician 744.7
chief 747.3
Grand Seignior 747.11
grandsire 169.11
grand slam 722.4
grandstand
nouns 438.8
verbs 902.16
grandstander, grand-
stand player
902.11
grand style, the
art 572.9
diction 586.2
grand tactics 795.10
grand tour 272.5
Grand Turk 747.11
granduncle 11.3
grand vizier 747.7
grange abode 190.6
farm 412.8
granger 412.5
Grani 413.21
granite 355.6
granitelike
hard 355.10
stone 383.7
graniteware 829.4
granitic hard 355.10
stone 383.7
granivore 306.13
granivorous 306.29
grannified 468.23
granny fogy 123.8
old woman 127.3
grandmother 169.12
gossip 556.9
midwife 685.10
nurse 686.13
nursemaid 697.7
fuss-budget 894.7
grant
nouns qualification
506.1
sanction 775.5
gift 816.4
subsidy 816.8
right 956.4
verbs allow for 506.5
acknowledge 520.11
confess 554.7
permit 775.10
give 816.12
GRANT AMNESTY TO
pardon 945.3
acquit 1005.4
granted acknowledged
520.14
given 816.23
grantee 817.4
Granth 1019.6
granther 169.11
grant-in-aid 816.8
granting 506.13
grantor 816.11
granular coarse 350.6
granulated 360.12

granularity
coarseness 350.2
graininess 360.2
granular snow 332.6
granulate
verbs roughen 260.4
grain 350.4
harden 355.8
pulverize 360.9
crumble 360.10
adjs. 360.12
granulated
rough 260.6
coarse 350.6
hardened 355.13
granular 360.12
granulater 360.7
granulation
roughness 260.1
TV interference
344.5
coarseness 350.2
solidification 355.5
granularity 360.2
pulverization 360.4
granule
small amount 35.2
grain 360.6
granulet 360.6
granulization 360.4
granulize 360.9
grape 799.14
grapery 412.11
grapeshot 799.14
grapes of wrath 950.5
grapevine 556.6,10
graph drawing 572.14
diagram 652.3,11
graphic
meaningful 543.10
pictorial 572.22
eloquent 598.10
written 600.24
descriptive 606.15
graphic arts 572.1
graphicness
meaningfulness
543.6
eloquence 598.1
graphite 379.2
graphitic 382.14
graphology 600.4
graphomania 600.2
graphometer 250.4
graphophone 464.18
graphostatics 346.2
graphotype 576.6
grapple
nouns 811.2
verbs fasten 47.7
hold 811.6
seize 820.12
GRAPPLE WITH
oppose 788.5
contend with
794.18
grappler 798.3
grasp
nouns handle 215.11
understanding 474.3
control 739.2

hold 811.2
verbs adhere 50.5
understand 546.7
hold 811.6
seize 820.12
GRASP AT 633.7
grasping
nouns 632.8
adjs. greedy 632.28
acquisitive 809.13
holding 811.8
rapacious 820.23
grass
nouns spring 128.2
plants 410.5
grassland 410.8
types of ~ 410.47
LET THE GRASS GROW
UNDER ONE'S FEET
neglect 532.6
waste time 706.11
verbs graze 306.15
fell 316.5
grass-eater 306.13
grass-eating 306.29
grass-green 370.4
grasshopper 413a.5
grassland 410.8
grassplot, grassplat
410.7
grass roots
source 152.5
the country 181.1
movement 742.34
grass widow, grass
widower 933.4
grassy 410.40
grate
nouns sorter 60.4
network 220.3
fire iron 328.15
harsh sound 457.3
verbs crisscross 220.7
grind 349.7
pulverize 360.9
chafe 423.7
sound harshly 457.9
annoy 864.18
GRATE ON
sound harshly
457.10
make nervous 857.9
annoy 864.18
grated 220.11
grateful
welcome 923.12
thankful 947.5
pleasant 861.5
gratefulness 947.1
grater 360.7
gratification
relish 427.2
indulgence 757.4
pleasure 863.1
gratified 863.12
gratify feed 306.15
indulge 757.7
please 863.6
make proud 903.6
~ oneself 976.4

gratifying
  pleasing 861.5
  welcome 923.12
grating
  nouns sorter 60.4
  network 220.3
  fire iron 328.15
  adjs. irritating 423.13
  harsh-sounding
    457.15
  nerve-racking
    857.15
gratis
  adjs. 848.5
  advs. 348.6
gratitude 947
gratuitous
  assumed 498.14
  voluntary 620.7
  given 816.23
  gratis 848.5
gratuitousness
  voluntariness 620.2
  gift 816.4–6
  no charge 848
gratuity bribe 649.2
  gift 816.5
  gratuitousness 848.1
gratulant 946.3
gratulate 946.2
gratulation 946.1
gratulatory 946.3
graupel 332.7
gravamen 670.6
grave
  nouns excavation
    256.4
  trench 262.2
  sepulcher 409.16
  THE GRAVE
  the hereafter 121.2
  hell 1017.1
  verbs excavate 256.15
  fix in the mind
    535.18
  sculpture 573.6
  engrave 576.12
  adjs. great 34.8
  dark 364.9
  painful 423.10
  low-pitched 453.10
  important 670.21
  dire 673.9
  solemn 869.3
  sad 870.25
  dignified 903.12
  infamous 913.12
graveclothes 409.14
graved 576.16
gravel
  nouns grain 360.6
  stone 383.3
  verbs fell 316.5
  refute 505.5
  baffle 513.13
  defeat 725.7
graveled
  baffled 513.13
  defeated 725.14
  at an impasse
    729.22

graveler end-all 70.4
  puzzle 547.7
gravelstone 383.4
graven infixed 142.14
  sculptured 573.8
  engraved 576.16
graveness 364.2
graven image 1031.3
graver tool 576.11
  sculptor 577.6
  artisan 577.8
grave robber 823.1
gravestone 568.11
graveyard 409.15
graveyard shift 108.3
gravid 168.18
gravidity, gravidness
  168.6
graving 576.1
gravitate
  descend 314.5
  tend 351.15
GRAVITATE TOWARDS
  173.3
gravitation
  attraction 287.1
  descent 314.1
  gravity 351.5
gravitational, gravi-
  tative 351.20
gravity
  attraction 287.1
  weight 351.1,5
  low pitch 453.1
  formality 644.1
  importance 670.3
  grimness 869.1
  sadness 870.7
  dignity 903.2
gravure 576.3,8
gravy food 306a.37
  easy thing 730.3
gray, grey
  nouns color 365.1
  colors, pigments
    365.5
  horse 413.15
  verbs 365.2
  adjs. aged 126.15
  dark 336.15
  gray-colored 365.3
  sad 870.25
grayback, greyback
  413a.6
graybeard, greybeard
  127.2
gray-bearded, grey-
  bearded 126.15
gray-haired, grey-
  headed aged
  126.15
  gray 365.4
gray hairs, grey hairs
  126.15
grayish, greyish 365.3
gray mare, grey mare
  931.9
gray matter, grey
  matter 465.1,5
graze
  nouns 424.1

  verbs touch 199.10
  sideswipe 282.13
  feed 306.15
  browse 306.26
  abrade 349.7
  touch 424.7
grazier 415.3
grazing abrasion 349.2
  pasture 410.8
grease
  nouns oil 379.1
  bribe 649.2
  tip 816.5
  money 833.2
  flattery 968.1
  verbs lubricate 379.8
  bribe 649.3
GREASE THE PALM
  649.3
GREASE THE WHEELS
  lubricate 379.8
  facilitate 730.6
greased lightning
  268.7
grease paint
  theater 609.21
  cosmetics 898.11
grease pit, grease rack
  379.7
greasiness 379.5
greasing 379.6
greasy 379.9
greasy grind
  bookworm 475.5
  drudge 716.3
greasy weather 393.4
great grand 34.8
  chief 36.16
  drastic 161.15
  pregnant 168.18
  large 194.16
  important 670.16
  good 672.14
  famous 912.19
  magnanimous 977.6
IN GREAT MEASURE
  34.17
great, the 670.8
great-aunt 11.3
great beyond, the
  121.2
Great Britain 180.4
great calorie 327.18
great circle 374.16
great-circle track 249.2
greatcoat 230.13
great deal
  nouns 34.4
  advs. 34.17
Great Divide 206.10
greater superior 36.13
  higher 206.24
great expectations
  886.1
great go 484.3
great-grandchildren
  170.1
great-grandfather
  169.11
great-grandmother
  169.12

great gun 670.8
GO GREAT GUNS 722.6
great heart
  generosity 851.1
  magnanimity 977.2
greathearted
  tolerant 524.11
  generous 851.4
  brave 891.17
  benevolent 936.16
  magnanimous 977.6
great hereafter, the
  121.2
great man
  personage 670.8
  celebrity 912.9
greatness
  ~ in degree 34
  pregnancy 168.6
  largeness 194.6
  importance 670.2
  famousness 912.5
  magnanimity 977.2
great octave 462.9
great out-of-doors, the
  223.3
great pox 684.15
greats 484.3
great-sounding 599.9
Great Spirit, the
  1011.3
great-uncle 11.3
great unknown, the
  121.2
great unwashed, the
  917.3
great white throne, the
  1016.5
Grecian 417.9
greed, greediness
  avarice 632.8
  gluttony 992.1
greedy
  avaricious 632.28
  gluttonous 992.7
greedygut, greedyguts
  992.3
Greek
  Irishman 417.9
  unintelligibility
    547.6
  jargon 578.6
  ~ alphabet 579.5
  sharper 617.4
  BE GREEK TO 547.9
Greek calends 106.2
Greek Church, Greek
  Orthodox Church
  1018.7
Greek modes 462.10
green
  nouns color 370.1
  colors, pigments
    370.6
  grassplot 410.7
  verbs 370.3
  adjs. new 122.7
  immature 124.10
  greenish 370.4
  sour 431.6

illness 684.5
gripp 684.12
control 739.2
hold 311.2
verbs obsess 472.23
interest 528.13
hold 311.6
seize 320.12
gripe
nouns colic 423.5
illness 684.21
control 739.2
hold 311.2
complaint 873.4
verbs pain 423.7
hold 311.6
seize 320.12
annoy 864.17
complain 873.13
griped 864.24
griper 857.3
griping 423.12
grippe 684.12
gripped
obsessed 472.32
interested 528.18
gripping
obsessing 472.33
interesting 528.20
holding 811.8
griqua 44.9
grisaille 572.5
grisette 987.14
grisliness
deathlikeness 407.10
hideousness 897.2
grisly deathlike 407.23
hideous 897.11
grist quantity 28.2
supply 658.2
gristle 358.2
gristly 358.4
grit
nouns texture 350.1
grain 360.6
pluck 622.3
courage 891.5
verbs 864.18
GRIT ONE'S TEETH
622.8
gritless 890.11
gritlessness 890.2
grits 360.5
grittiness
coarseness 350.2
granularity 360.2
courage 891.4
gritty coarse 350.6
granular 360.12
plucky 622.14
courageous 891.18
grizzle
nouns gray hair 229.3
wig 229.14
horse 413.15
verbs whiten 363.6
gray 365.2
grizzled **grizzly**
white 363.8
gray 365.3
grizzliness 363.1

grizzling 363.4
grizzly bear 949.11
groan
nouns harsh sound
457.3
plaint 873.3
verbs blow 402.24
sound harshly 457.8
suffer 864.22
moan 873.11
groat 833.8
groats 360.5
grocer 828.3
grocery food 306a.5
merchandise 829.7
store 830.6
grog
nouns 994.12
verbs 994.29
grog blossom 994.3
groggery 994.25
grogginess 159.3
groggy
unsteady 159.16
dazed 530.14
drunk 994.39
grogshop 994.25
groin jetty 215.4
crotch 298.4
Grolier 603.17
grommet 252.5
groom
nouns stableman
415.2
bridegroom 931.6
verbs tidy 60.11
tend stock 415.6
train 560.13
preen 679.19
whip 1008.15
groomer 563.7
grooming
training 560.3
reproof 967.7
whipping 1008.5
groomsman 931.5
groove
nouns excavation
256.4
furrow 262.1
routine 640.5
track 655.3
IN A GROOVE 17.7
IN THE GROOVE
straight 249.7
in tempo 462.29
hep 474.17
verbs 262.3
grooved 262.4
grope 484.26
GROPE IN THE DARK
be blind 440.7
be ignorant 476.11
grope 484.26
Groschen 833.9
gross
nouns main part 54.5
twelve dozen 99.8
profit 809.3
receipts 842.1
IN THE GROSS 54.12

adjs. downright **34.14**
whole 54.8
fat 194.18
thick 203.8
coarse 350.6
luxuriant 410.41
stupid 468.15
absurd 469.10
inelegant 588.2
very bad 673.9
vulgar 896.11
infamous 913.12
carnal 985.6
indecent 988.8
gross-headed 468.16
grossièreté 896.2
grossness fatness 194.8
thickness 203.2
coarseness 350.2
stupidity 468.3
inelegant style 588.1
terribleness 673.2
vulgarity 896.2
baseness 913.3
carnality 985.2
indecency 988.3
gross profit 809.3
gross receipts 842.1
grotesque
nouns 572.11
adjs. fantastic 85.12
deformed 248.12
ugly 897.8
grotesqueness 85.3
grotto 256.5
grouch
nouns complainer
867.3
ill humor 949.6
sorehead 949.11
verbs complain
873.13
be grouchy 949.14
grouchy 949.22
ground
nouns cause 152.1
region 179.1
position 183.3
ocean bottom 208.3
base 211.3
bed 211.4
plane 213.3
foundation 215.6
background 232.2
paint 361.12
land 384.1
viewpoint 438.7
premise 481.8
attitude 523.2
motive 646.1
arena 800.1
justification 1004.6
GIVE GROUND
retreat 294.6
yield 763.7
GO OVER THE SAME
GROUND 103.8
KEEP BOTH FEET ON
THE GROUND 534.4
ON THAT GROUND
154.6

TAKE THE GROUND
FROM UNDER
disprove 505.4
disillusion 519.2
verbs establish 142.10
found 183.17
go aground 274.44
fell 316.5
~ electricity 341.26
instruct 560.10
GROUND ON 211.6
adjs. 211.7
ground bait
snare 616.12
lure 648.2
ground crew 278.5
grounded stuck 142.17
stranded 729.25
GROUNDED ON
based on 211.9
evidential 504.17
ground fire 796.9
ground floor 191.23
GET IN ON THE
GROUND FLOOR
68.7
ground forces 798.22
groundhog
nonflier 278.5
animal 413.4
ground hog 256.10
groundhog day 137.12
groundless
unsubstantial 4.7
unfounded 482.12
ground log 268.8
groundman 341.19
ground plan 652.1,3
ground rules 84.4
grounds dregs 43.2
cause 152.1
foundation 215.6
evidence 504.1
condition 506.2
motive 646.1
~ for war 793.8
real estate 808.7
SHOW SUFFICIENT
GROUNDS FOR
1004.9
ground school
aeronautics 277.1
school 565.13
groundsel, groundsill
215.9
ground sweat 409.1
ground swell 394.14
ground troops 798.22
groundwork 215.6
LAY THE GROUND-
WORK 718.12
group
nouns class 61.2
company 74.3
bunch 74.6
set 786.7
sect 1018.3
verbs arrange 60.8
classify 61.6
assemble 74.17
size 194.15

groupage 60.2
grouped
  arranged 60.13
  classified 61.8
grouping
  organization 60.2
  classification 61.1
  class 61.2
  painting 572.10
group medicine 686.1
group pressure 742.30
group therapy 688.5
grouse
  nouns fowl 306a.22
  bird 413.34
  complaint 873.4
  verbs 873.13
grouser 867.3
grousing 873.4
grout 949.14
grouty 949.22
grove clump 74.6
  valley 256.9
  woodlet 410.12
grovel crawl 272.25
  crouch 316.8
  wallow 320.13
  truckle 905.6
  debauch 987.19
groveler 905.3
groveling
  nouns 905.2
  adjs. 905.13
grow increase 38.6
  mature 126.9
  be converted 145.12
  raise 166.11
  become larger 196.7
  become higher
    206.17
  develop 321.6
  vegetate 410.31
  raise 412.16
GROW ON ONE 640.11
GROW OUT OF 153.6
GROW OVER 311.5
GROW TO 50.5
GROW TOGETHER
  be joined 47.11
  adhere 50.5
GROW UP
  grow 196.7
  become higher
    206.17
  uprise 313.8
grower
  producer 166.10
  farmer 412.5
growing
  nouns 412.12
  adjs. 38.8
growl
  nouns 457.3
  verbs blow 402.24
  sound harshly 457.8
  snarl 459.4
  say 592.17
  complain 873.13
  be angry 950.14
growler 867.3
growling 949.22

grown enlarged 38.7
  grown-up 126.12
  adult 126.12; 127.1
  produced 166.25
growth increase 38.1
  conversion 145.1
  enlargement 196.3
  development 321.2
  vegetation 410.2,30
  neoplasm 684.29
grub
  nouns larva 125.9
  food 306a.2
  drudge 716.3
  verbs dig 256.15
  eat 306.18
  drudge 714.14
GRUB OUT 304.9
GRUB UP
  extract 304.9
  eat 306.18
  seek 484.28
grubbery 306a.2
grubbiness
  slovenry 62.6
  dirtiness 680.1
grubbing 714.18
grubby slovenly 62.14
  infested 311.11
  dirty 680.24
grubstake
  nouns 834.2
  verbs 834.15
grubstaker 834.9
grubstreet writer
  600.16
grudge
  nouns 927.5
  verbs be unwilling
    621.3
  refuse 774.4
  stint 850.7
  envy 952.3
grudgeful 954.6
grudgefulness 954.2
grudging
  nouns 952.1
  adjs. reluctant 621.6
  niggardly 850.10
  envious 952.4
gruel
  nouns weakness 159.7
  cereal 306a.34
  diet 307.10
  semiliquid 388.5
GET ONE'S GRUEL
  1008.22
  verbs weaken 159.10
  tire 715.4
grueler 547.7
grueling
  weakening 159.20
  exhausting 715.11
  trying 729.17
  punishing 1008.25
gruesome
  deathlike 407.23
  hideous 897.11
gruesomeness
  deathlikeness 407.10
  hideousness 897.2

gruff
  harsh-sounding
    457.14
  brusque 935.7
gruffness
  raucousness 457.2
  brusqueness 935.3
grum
  harsh-sounding
    457.14
  glum 870.26
  sullen 949.24
grumble
  nouns rumble 455.4
  harsh sound 457.3
  verbs sound harshly
    457.8
  growl 459.4
  complain 873.13
grumbler 867.3
grumbling
  nouns 873.4
  adjs. 949.22
grumbly 949.22
grume clot 353.7
  blood 387.4
grumness
  raucousness 457.2
  glumness 870.8
  sullenness 949.8
grumous 353.14
grump 949.14
grumpiness 949.6
grumps 949.10
grumpy 949.22
Grundyism 643.1
grunt
  nouns 341.19
  verbs snort 459.3
  say 592.17
  complain 873.13
grunter 341.19
gruntle 459.3
G string 230.19
G suit
  space suit 281.12
  gravity 351.5
guano 164.4
guarantee
  nouns oath 521.3
  promise 768.1
  security 770.1,8,9
  verbs depose 521.5
  promise 768.4
  guaranty 770.11
guaranteed 770.14
guaranteeship 770.10
guarantor 770.8
guaranty
  nouns 770.1,8
  verbs 770.11
guard
  nouns trainman
    273.13
  vigilance 531.4
  protection 697.1
  safeguard 697.3
  warden 697.8
  jailer 759.10
  defense 797.1
  player 876.20

OFF ONE'S GUARD
  unaware 476.14
  unalert 529.8
ON GUARD
  vigilant 531.13
  on the defensive
    797.16
  cautious 893.8
  verbs protect 697.17
  restrain 758.7
  defend 797.8
GUARD AGAINST
  defend 797.8
  take precautions
    893.6
guarded
  qualified 506.10
  vigilant 531.13
  protected 697.20
  restrained 758.13
  cautious 893.8
guarder 697.8
guardhouse 759.9
guardian
  nouns protector 697.5
  ~ spirit 1012.19
  adjs. 697.22
guardian angel
  1012.19
guardianship 697.2
guarding
  protecting 697.22
  defensive 797.11
guardless 695.14
guardrail 697.3
guardroom 759.9
guards 798.32
guardsman
  guard 697.8
  soldier 798.14
Guarnerius 464.6
gubernatorial 739.16
guddle 653.10
gudgeon
  nouns axle 320.5
  dupe 618.1
  verbs 616.17
guerdon
  nouns 839.3
  verbs 839.10
guerre de plume
  481.5
guerrilla 798.15
guerrilla warfare 795.4
guess
  nouns 498.3
HAVE ANOTHER
  GUESS COMING
  be mistaken 517.9
  recant 626.9
  verbs divine 486.2
  conjecture 498.10
  think 500.9
KEEP ONE GUESSING
  513.13
TO GUESS 498.18
guesser 498.7
guesswork 498.2
guest visitor 923.6
  gust 402.6
guet-apens 613.3

guff nonsense 545.4
chatter 594.3
guffaw
nouns 374.4
verbs 874.9
guggle
nouns 394.7
verbs trickle 394.19
bubble 404.4
burble 451.11
cackle 459.5
guggling 451.19
gugu 189.3
guidable 289.14
guidance
instruction 560.1
protection 697.2
direction 745.1
advice 752.1
patronage 783.4
guide
nouns teacher 563.1
sign 566.3
director 746.6
adviser 752.4
guardian spirit
1012.19
spirit 1015.1
verbs escort 73.8
influence 171.8
pilot 274.14
go before 291.2
teach 560.10
direct 745.9
advise 752.6
BE GUIDED 82.3
guidebook 746.9
guided missile 280.2
guideless 157.18
guidepost 566.3
guider 746.6
guiding 745.12
guiding star 746.7
guidon 567.6
guild 786.4
guilder 833.9
guildhall 190.15
guildsman 786.11
guile 616.3
guileful 616.22
guileless 734.5
guilelessness
artlessness 734.1
undeceitfulness
972.5
guillotine
nouns closure 740.16
executioner's ~
1009.5
THE GUILLOTINE
1003.7
verbs 1008.19
guilt 981
guiltiness 981.1
guiltless 982.6
guiltlessness 982.1
guilty culpable 967.26
to blame 981.3
FIND GUILTY 1006.3
NOT GUILTY 982.6

PLEAD GUILTY
confess 554.7
repent 871.7
guilty conscience
981.1
guindé 588.3
guinea 833.5,8
guinea hen 420.10
guinea pig
animal 413.4
experimentee 488.7
guisard, guiser
mummer 610.10
disguiser 617.7
guise mode 7.4
cover 227.2
clothing 230.1
appearance 445.3
pretext 647.1
way 655.1
behavior 735.1
guitar 464.4
guitarist 463.5
gula 48.5
gulch 200.3
gulden 833.9
gules 367.1
gulf cleft 200.2,3
pit 208.2
chasm 256.4
opening 264.1
whirlpool 394.12
inlet 398.1
gulfed, gulflike 398.2
gulfweed 410.4
gulfy rotary 320.15
vortical 394.25
gulflike 398.2
gull
nouns cheat 617.3
impostor 617.6
dupe 618.1
verbs 616.13
gullah 578.8
gullet 395.15
gullet wash 994.13
gullibility
credulity 501.2
dupe 618
gullible 501.8
gully
nouns ravine 200.3
watercourse 395.2
verbs 262.3
gully washer 393.2
gulosity 992.1
gulp
nouns swallow 305.4
drink 306.4
gasp 402.19
verbs swallow 305.11
devour 306.21
gasp 402.25
eat greedily 992.5
GULP DOWN
swallow 305.11
devour 306.21
be credulous 501.5
eat greedily 992.5
gulping 305.4

gum
nouns elastic 357.3
chewing ~ 388.6
verbs stick together
50.7
chew 306.25
deceive 616.17
thwart 728.16
GUM UP, GUM UP THE
WORKS
disable 157.9
spoil 690.11
thwart 728.16
botch 732.12
gumbo
nouns soup 306a.10
semiliquid 388.5
mud 388.8
adjs. earthy 384.7
viscid 388.12
gumbo French 578.8
gumboil 684.28
gumbolike 388.12
gumlike
resinous 380.3
viscid 388.12
gumminess 388.2
gummose, gummous
resinous 380.3
viscid 388.12
gummy
adhesive 50.9
resinous 380.3
viscid 388.12
gummyness 50.2
gumption
sagacity 466.4
enterprise 705.7
gumptious 705.22
gums anatomy 257.6
resins 380.1
gumshoe
nouns policeman
697.14
detective 779.10
verbs creep 272.25
sneak 613.10
gun
nouns shooter 284.9
assassin 408.10
soldier 798.7,11
firearm 799.5
types of ~ 799.24
makes of ~ 799.25
thief 823.1
hoodlum 941.4
PULL A GUN ON
796.22
verbs 284.13
GUN FOR, GO GUN-
NING FOR 484.24
GUN THE MOTOR
268.15
guna 449.5
guncotton 799.9
gunfire 796.9
gunge 830.1
gunk 388.5
gun loader 275.6
gunman
shooter 284.9

assassin 408.10
hoodlum 941.4
gunner seaman 275.6
aerial ~ 278.4
shooter 284.9
soldier 798.11
gunners 798.26
gunnery
shooting 284.3
guns 799.1
ballistics 799.3
gunning 653.2
gun parts 799.26
gunplay 796.9
gunpowder 799.9
SIT ON A BARREL OF
GUNPOWER
risk 695.7
court danger 892.6
gunrunner 824.5
gunrunning 824.2
gunshot
short distance 199.2
shot 284.5
detonation 455.3
gup 556.7
gurge
nouns whirl 320.2
eddy 394.12
verbs whirl 320.11
eddy 394.22
gurgle
nouns 394.7
verbs trickle 394.19
bubble 404.4
burble 451.11
gurgling 451.19
guru teacher 563.1
religious 1036.13
gush
nouns flow 394.4
jet 394.9
diffuseness 591.1
talkativeness 594.1
verbs flow out 302.13
flow 394.17,21
chatter 594.6
sentimentalize
853.14
gushiness 594.1
gushing
nouns 591.1
adjs. flowing 394.25
diffuse 591.11
sentimental 853.21
gushy diffuse 591.11
effusive 594.9
gust outburst 161.6
wind 402.6
excitement 855.8
gustable edible 306.31
tastable 426.8
gustation 426.6
gustative, gustatory
426.8
gustiness 402.16
gusto savor 427.2
liking 632.2
eagerness 633.1
fervor 853.9
pleasure 863.1

WITH GUSTO 633.13
gusty windy 402.26
  palatable 427.8
gut
  nouns 398.1
  verbs eviscerate
    304.11
    destroy 691.10
    plunder 822.15
gute Nacht! 300.26
guts stamina 158.1
  insides 193.1
  vitals 224.4
  intestines 224.6
  pungency 432.2
  pluck 622.3
  courage 891.5
gutta serena
  blindness 440.1
  disease 684.11
gutter trench 262.2
  conduit 395.3,5
guttersnipe
  gamin 273.3
  vulgarian 896.6
gutting 304.3
guttle gorge 306.23
  eat greedily 992.5
guttler 992.3
guttural
  nouns 449.5
  adjs. phonetics 449.18
  hoarse 457.14
gutturalness 457.2
guttural voice 593.11
guy
  nouns oddity 85.4
  person 416.3
  man 419.5
  verbs decamp 300.11
  flee 629.11
  banter 880.4
guyer 880.3
guying 880.2
guys 276.31
guzzle
  nouns drink 306.4
  spree 994.5
  dram 994.6
  liquor 994.12
  verbs drink 306.27
  eat greedily 992.5
  tipple 994.29
guzzler 994.10
guzzling 994.4
gym, gymnasium
  hall 190.15
  arena 800.1
  playroom 876.12
Gymir 194.13
gymkhana 876.10
Gymnasium 565.6
gymnast 876.21
gymnastic 876.32
gymnastics study 560.8
  exercise 714.6
  athletics 876.8
gymnosophist 990.4
gymnosophy 990.2

Gymnospermae,
  gymnosperms
  411.8
gynaeceum 931.11
gynandrian 418.23
gynandrism 418.10
gynandroid 418.11
gynandrous 418.23
gynandry 418.10
gynarchy, gynecocracy,
  gynocracy 739.5
gynecic, gynic 420.14
gynecologist 686.7
gynoecium 410.26
gynophore 410.19
gyp
  nouns bitch 413.26
  female animal
    420.10
  swindle 616.8
  servant 748.9
  verbs 616.18
gypper, gypster 617.3
Gypsy 417.3
gypsy 273.4
gyral 320.15
gyrate 320.9
gyrating 320.14
gyration 320.1
gyrational, gyratory
  320.15
gyre
  nouns whirl 320.2
  demon 1014.7
  verbs 320.9
gyrene 275.4
gyrenes 798.28
gyro 279.5
gyrocompass 746.8
gyrodine 279.5
gyron 567.2
gyropilot 277.59
gyroplane 279.5
gyroscope 142.21
gyroscopic, gyrostatic
  320.15
gyrostatics
  rotation 320.8
  mechanics 346.2
gyrosyn 746.8
gyve
  nouns 758.4
  verbs 758.10

H

Habakkuk 1020.1
habeas corpus 750.7
haberdasher 230.36
haberdashery
  headdress 230.25
  garment making
    230.31
  store 830.5
habiliment 230.1
habilitation 731.4
habit
  nouns nature 5.3
  clothing 230.1
  suit 230.6
  custom 640.3

  mannerism 901.2
  BY FORCE OF HABIT
    640.21
  IN THE HABIT OF
    640.18
  NOT IN THE HABIT OF
    641.4
  verbs 230.40
habitability 187.6
habitable 187.16
habitancy
  habitation 187.1
  population 189.1
habitant
  inhabitant 189.2
  settler 189.9
habitat 190.4
habitation
  inhabiting 187
  abode 190.1
habit maker 230.34
habit pattern 640.3
habitual
  nouns 640.9
  adjs. orderly 59.6
  customary 640.15
habitually 640.21
habitualness 640.6
habituate 640.10
habituated 640.18
habituation 640.7
habitude 640.3
habitué
  nouns attender 185.5
  visitor 923.6
  adjs. 640.18
hachis 306a.12
hachure line 566.5
  map drawing 652.4
hacienda abode 190.6
  farm 412.8
hack
  nouns gash 261.1
  cough 402.19
  horse 413.16,18
  mark 566.4
  writer 600.16
  drudge 716.3
  verbs sever 49.10
  ride 272.33
  cough 402.25
hackamore 657.5
hackle
  nouns feather 229.16
  plumage 229.18
  verbs sever 49.10
  comb 679.20
hackman 273.9
hackney
  nouns 413.18
  adjs. 881.9
hackneyed 881.9
hackneyed saying
  516.3
hacky 273.9
Hades
  god 1012.5; 1017.5
  hell 1017.1,3
hadj 272.5
hadji pilgrim 273.1
  priest 1036.12

Haeckelism 321.4
haft 215.11
hag crone 127.3
  ugly person 897.4
  vixen 941.8
  witch 1033.8
Haggai 1020.1
haggard thin 204.19
  pale 362.9
  deathlike 407.23
  wild-eyed 472.31
  tired-looking 715.7
  overwrought 855.26
haggardness
  thinness 204.5
  paleness 362.2
  deathlikeness
    407.10
haggle
  nouns 825.3
  verbs sever 49.10
  bargain 825.14
haggling 825.3
Hagiographa 1019.3
hagiography 1021.1
hagiolatry 1031.1
hagiology 1021.1
hagridden 1034.14
hagride 1034.10
ha-ha 262.2
hail
  nouns ice 332.7
  greeting 923.4
  verbs storm 332.12
  accost 592.18
  greet 923.10
  acclaim 966.10
  interjs. attention!
    528.23
  hurrah! 874.12
  greetings! 923.15
  bravo! 966.22
hail-fellow-well-met
  920.18
Hail Mary 1030.4
hailstone, hailstorm
  332.7
hair
  nouns small amount
    35.2
  weakness 159.7
  short distance 199.2
  narrowness 204.1
  fur, tresses 229.2
  bristle 260.3
  trifle 671.5
  GET IN ONE'S HAIR
    864.17
  GET ONE'S HAIR UP
    950.17
  MAKE ONE'S HAIR
    STAND ON END
    918.6
  NOT SEE HAIR NOR
    HIDE OF 440.7
  TO A HAIR 515.21
  verbs 229.30
hairbreadth, hairs-
  breadth short
  distance 199.2
  narrowness 204.1

hairbreadth escape
　630.2
haircut 229.15
haircuts 229.31
hairdo coiffure 229.15
　types of ~ 229.30,
　31
hairdresser 898.12
hairdressing 898.10
hairiness 229.1
hairless 231.17
hairlet 229.2
hairlike
　trichoid 229.23
　bristlelike 260.10
hairline slight
　difference 16.2
　line 556.5
hair of the dog 994.7
hairpiece 229.13
hair-raising 889.28
hair remover 231.4
hair space 601.7
hairsplitting
　nouns quibbling
　　482.5,15
　distinction 491.3
　overparticularity
　　894.4
　hypercriticism 967.4
　adjs. overparticular
　　894.12
　hypercritical 967.24
hairy hirsute 229.24
　bristly 260.9
hairy-chested 419.12
hairy-dog story 879.6
hakim ruler 747.11
　judge 1000.3
halberdier 798.7
halcyon
　tranquil 267.10
　auspicious 542.16
　peaceful 801.9
　pleasant 861.8
halcyon birds 542.4
halcyon days 726.4
hale
　verbs 235.4
　adjs. strong 158.13
　healthy 683.9
haleness 683.3
half
　nouns division 92.2
　share 814.5
　advs. 114.16
half-and-half
　nouns 92.2
　adjs. equal 30.9
　mixed 44.15
　deficient 57.4
　halved 92.4
　neutral 804.7
half an eye 438.4
half a second 113.3
halfback 876.20
half-baked
　premature 131.8
　half-witted 468.22
　half-learned 476.16
　unprepared 719.11

inexperienced
　732.17
half-blind 439.13
half blood 44.8
half-blooded 44.16
half-breed, half-caste
　nouns 44.8
　adjs. 44.16
half brother 11.3
half century 99.7
half-cocked
　premature 131.8
　unprepared 719.11
　GO OFF HALF-COCKED
　be inopportune
　　130.5
　preconclude 494.2
　be precipitate 707.7
　be unprepared 719.6
half-conscious 422.7
half crown 833.5,8
half dollar 833.7
half eagle 833.5
half-famished 632.26
half-frozen
　cold 332.16
　semiliquid 388.11
half-god 1012.3
half-hardy 410.42
halfhearted
　irresolute 625.9
　indifferent 634.5
half-learned 476.16
half-learning 476.6
half-life 326.14
half-light 336.4
half-mast 566.21
half measures
　irresolution 625.1
　mid-course 804.3
　BY HALF MEASURES
　　57.6
half-moon
　crescent 251.5
　moon 374.8
　fortification 797.4
half nelson 811.3
half past 114.16
halfpenny trifle 671.5
　coin 833.8
halfpint 195.9
half-price 847.9
half sawbuck 99.1
half-starved 632.26
half step gait 272.15
　music 462.20
half tone color 361.6
　music 462.20
　engraving 576.9
half-truth 614.11
halfway 69.5
　GO HALFWAY 804.5
half-way 233.8
halfway house 69.2
halfway station 281.5
half-wit 470.8
half-witted 468.22
halieutics 653.3
halitosis 436.1
hall
　manor house 190.5

building 190.15
　corridor 191.18
　theater 609.17
hallelujah, halleluiah
　nouns cheer 874.2
　paean 1030.3
　interjs. 1030.16
hallmark
　nouns 566.12
　verbs 566.19
halloo
　nouns 458.1
　verbs call 458.6
　accost 592.18
　interjs. attention!
　　528.23
　hunting cry 653.13
　oh! 918.18
hallow celebrate 875.3
　sanctify 1024.5
hallowday 1038.14
hallowed 1024.8
hallowing 1024.3
Hallowmas 1038.15
hallucination 518.7
hallucinatory, halluci-
　national 518.10
hallucinosis
　psychosis 472.3
　hallucination 518.7
hallway 191.18
halo circle 252.2
　nimbus 334.14
hals, halse neck 48.5
　gullet 395.15
halt
　nouns delay 132.2
　stop 144.2
　standstill 267.3
　respite 709.2
　prevention 728.2
　impasse 729.5
　AT A HALT 704.7
　THE HALT 684.32
　verbs cease 144.6,8,
　　11
　be weak 159.8
　lag 269.8
　limp 272.27
　stammer 593.7
　prevent 728.13
　adjs. 690.29
　interjs. 144.13
halter
　nouns harness 657.5
　shackle 758.4
　hangman's rope
　　1009.5
　verbs 47.10
halting
　inelegant 588.3
　stammering 593.12
　lame 690.29
halve bisect 92.3
　share 813.6
　BY HALVES 57.6
　DO BY HALVES 532.9
　GO HALVES 813.6
　IN HALVES 92.4
halved 92.4

halver half 92.2
　share 814.5
　GO HALVERS 813.6
halving 92.1
halyards 276.31
ham
　nouns village 182.2
　thigh 272.16
　meat 306a.16
　radioman 343.27
　telegrapher 558.18
　~ actor 610.4
　amateur 716.5
　verbs 609.35
　adjs. 609.37
hamadryad 1012.16
hamal 748.4
hamate 251.8
hamburg 306a.18
hamburger
　beef 306a.13
　steak 306a.18
　sandwich 306a.31
hamfatter 610.4
hamiform 251.8
Hamlet 596.2
hamlet 182.2
hammer
　nouns 447.7
　UNDER THE HAMMER
　　827.15
　verbs repeat 103.10
　pound 282.15
　stammer 593.7
　drudge 714.14
　HAMMER AWAY AT
　　think hard 477.8
　　persevere 623.3
　HAMMER INTO ONE'S
　　HEAD 535.18
　HAMMER OUT
　　forge 245.6
　　think hard 477.8
　　do carelessly 532.9
hammer and sickle
　567.1
hammer and tongs
　resolutely 622.17
　laboriously 714.20
hammer lock 811.3
hammers 347.16
hammy 609.37
ham operator 343.27
hamper
　nouns basket 192.4
　impediment 728.6
　restraint 758.3,4
　verbs basket 235.9
　burden 351.13
　hinder 728.11
　restrain 758.9,10
hampered
　burdened 351.18
　restrained 758.15,16
hampering
　nouns 728.1
　adjs. impeding
　　728.18
　restraining 758.12
ham shack 343.9

IN THE HANDS OF
745.15
OFF ONE'S HANDS
810.3
ON ALL HANDS
on every side 232.14
unanimously 520.17
ON HANDS AND KNEES
272.38
ON ONE'S HANDS
superfluous 661.18
in one's charge
745.15
unsold 827.13
PUT INTO THE HANDS
OF 816.13
PUT ONE'S HANDS ON
discover 487.2
remember 535.13
WITH OPEN HANDS
851.5
handsel
nouns pledge
770.2,12
gift 816.4
verbs 63.9
handshake
nouns 923.4
verbs 905.8
handshaker
candidate 744.9
toady 905.3
handshaking 905.2
handsome
generous 851.4
beautiful 898.16
magnanimous 977.6
THE HANDSOME
THING 974.3
handsomely
generously 851.5
beautifully 898.21
magnanimously
977.3
handsomeness 898.1
handspike 286.4
handspring 317.1
handstaff 216.2
hand-to-mouth 719.15
handwear 230.63
handwork 714.4
handwriting 600.4
handwriting on the
wall
fate 638.2
warning 701.3
handy nearby 199.15
convenient 663.19
wield 730.12
skillful 731.20
handy man 731.11
hang
nouns droop 214.2
declivity 218.5
meaning 543.2
knack 731.6
GET THE HANG OF
understand 546.7
master 562.9
verbs procrastinate
132.10

droop 214.6
suspend 214.8
hover 313.10
depend on 506.6
~ the head 870.15
~ one's head 904.8
~ the jury 1002.18
execute 1008.20
HANG ABOUT
wait 132.11
stay near 199.12
toady 905.10
HANG AROUND
wait 132.11
frequent 185.10
depend on 506.6
HANG AROUND WITH
accompany 73.7
associate with
920.15
HANG A SHANTY ON
690.14
HANG BACK
procrastinate 132.10
recoil 283.7
lag 292.4
demur 621.4
be irresolute 625.7
HANG BY A THREAD
be uncertain 513.11
be in danger 695.8
HANG FIRE
procrastinate 132.10
stick 144.7
be unproductive
165.3
be inert 267.8
be irresolute 625.7
do nothing 704.2
HANG HEAVY ON HAND
661.9
HANG IN EFFIGY
913.9
HANG IN THE
BALANCE 513.11
HANG OFF 621.4
HANG ON
adhere 50.5
attribute to 154.3
depend on 506.6
be absorbed 528.5
persevere 623.4
hold on 811.6
HANG OPEN 264.16
HANG OUT
reside 187.8
overhang 214.7
be unyielding 624.7
HANG OUT AT 185.10
HANG OUT ONE'S
SHINGLE 654.12
HANG OUT THE
WASHING 274.21
HANG OVER
be imminent 151.2
overhang 214.7
HANG SOMETHING ON
1003.7
HANG THE EXPENSE
852.3

HANG TOGETHER
be consistent 26.10
join 47.5
be joined 47.11
cohere 50.5
co-operate 784.4
HANG UP
postpone 132.8
suspend 214.8
~ the phone 558.21
HANG UPON 506.6
HANG UP ONE'S HAT
183.18
HANG UP ONE'S
SHINGLE 183.18
HANG UP THE FIDDLE
144.7
hangar
for vehicles 190.17
aviation 277.21
hangdog
furtive 612.14
ashamed 904.12
fawning 905.13
hangdog look 904.2
hanger pendant 214.4
suspender 214.5
woodland 410.11
drophead 483.2
hanger-on
follower 292.2
political ~ 744.8
sycophant 905.5
hangers
types of ~ 214.14
scribbling 600.8
hanging
nouns pendency
214.1
pendant 214.4
declivity 218.5
stage curtain 609.24
execution 1008.7
adjs. loose 51.5
pendent 214.9
sloping 218.16
downcast 314.12
hanging gardens 218.4
hangman 1008.8
hangman's rope
1009.5
hangout 190.23
hangover 117.1
hang-over 994.1
hank piece 55.3
lump 194.10
hank and hank 30.8
hanker after 632.18
hankerer 632.12
hankering
nouns 632.5
adjs. 632.23
hanky-panky 616.5
Hansard 568.7
hansel 816.4
Hanswurst 610.9
Hanukkah 1038.16
Hanuman 1012.7
hap
nouns occurrence
150.2

chance 155.1
chance event 155.6
verbs occur 150.5
chance 155.11
haphazard
nouns 155.4
adjs. orderless 62.11
random 155.16
careless 532.12
haphazardness
disorder 62.1
carelessness 532.3
hapless 727.14
haploid number
405.11
haply 508.9
happen occur 150.5
turn out 153.5
chance 155.11
HAPPEN UPON 487.3
HAPPEN WHAT MAY
892.11
happening
nouns occurrence
150.2
chance event 155.6
adjs. 150.9
happenstance
occurrence 150.2
chance event 155.6
happify 863.7
happily
auspiciously 542.19
willingly 620.8
gladly 863.16
cheerfully 868.17
happiness
gladness 863.2
cheerfulness 868
happy apt 26.18
timely 129.10
auspicious 542.16
elegant 587.7
willing 620.5
joyful 863.13
cheerful 868.10
drunk 994.38
MAKE HAPPY 863.7
happy-go-lucky 719.15
happy hunting
grounds 1016.1
Happy Isles 1016.10
happy land 1016.1
happy landing! 300.25
happy medium
mean 32.1
moderation 162.1
mid-course 804.3
Happy Valley 533.11
hara-kiri 408.5
harangue
nouns lesson 560.6
lecture 597.3
verbs expound 560.16
declaim 597.9
haranguer 597.4
harass
persecute 665.6
fatigue 715.4
torment 864.19,21
worry 888.4

bully 889.19

harassed
  tormented 864.27
  worried 888.7
harasser 864.10
harassing
  tormenting 862.13
  worrying 888.9
harassment
  persecution 665.3
  annoyance 864.2
  worry 888.2
harbinger
  nouns forerunner
    66.1
  omen 542.3
  messenger 559.2
  verbs 542.11
harbor
  nouns inlet 398.1
  haven 698.1,6
  IN HARBOR 696.6
  verbs house 187.11
  ∼ an idea 477.15
  ∼ a design 651.4
  protect 697.17
  cherish 811.7
  ∼ revenge 954.5
harborage 698.6
hard
  nouns 714.5
  adjs. strong 158.13
  rigid 355.10
  painful 423.10
  bitter 428.6
  ∼ of hearing 448.7
  phonetics 449.18
  abstruse 547.12
  obstinate 624.10
  industrious 705.21
  difficult 729.16
  strict 755.7
  stingy 850.11
  callous 854.12
  impenitent 872.5
  harsh 937.22
  heartless 937.23
  hardened 979.21
  alcoholic 994.46
  GO HARD WITH
    suffer hardship
    727.8
  suffer 864.22
  HARD AS NAILS
    strong 158.13
  healthy 683.8
  HARD AT IT 705.20
  HARD UP
    straitened 729.24
    poor 836.7
  NOT HARD TO TAKE
    861.5
  advs. near 199.20
  laboriously 714.20
  HARD ALEE, HARD
    AWEATHER 274.80
  HARD BY 199.20
hard and fast
  ∼ rule 84.4
  aground 274.77
hard bargain 825.5

hard-bitten 624.10
hard blow
  calamity 727.2
  distress 864.5
hard-boiled
  hard 355.10
  sophisticated 731.26
  strict 755.6
  hardened 979.21
hard case addict 640.9
  hardship 727.1
hard cash 833.4
hard-cover 603.1
hard currency 833.1
hard-earned
  laborious 714.19
  difficult 729.16
harden
  strengthen 158.11
  indurate 355.7
  toughen 358.3
  habituate 640.10
  callous 854.6
  HARDEN THE HEART
    inure 854.6
  be impenitent 872.3
hardened
  indurate 355.13
  inveterate 640.19
  callous 854.12
  impenitent 872.5
  heartless 937.23
  wicked 979.21
hardening
  nouns strengthening
    158.5
  induration 355.5
  habituation 640.7
  ∼ of the arteries
    684.8
  adjs. 355.14
hard fact 1.3
hard-featured 897.7
hardfisted 850.11
hard-fought
  laborious 714.19
  difficult 729.16
hard grind 714.5
hardheaded
  sagacious 466.16
  ungullible 503.5
  obstinate 624.10
  strict 755.6
hardheadedness
  sagacity 466.4
  obstinacy 624.1
  strictness 755.1
hardhearted
  unfeeling 854.12
  heartless 937.23
  wicked 979.21
hard hit 929.25
hardihood
  courage 891.4
  audacity 911.1
hardily 891.22
hardiness
  strength 158.1
  healthiness 683.3
  courage 891.4

hard knocks 727.1
hard labor labor 714.5
  punishment 1008.2
hard lines 727.1
hardly scarcely 35.12
  unusually 85.16
  infrequently 136.4
  narrowly 204.21
  with difficulty
    729.26
  strictly 755.9
hard money 833.4
hardmouthed 624.10
hardness rigidity 355
  obstinacy 624.1
  difficulty 729.1
  strictness 755.2
  callousness 854.3
  impenitence 872.2
  harshness 937.9
  heartlessness 937.10
  wickedness 979.7
hard-of-hearing, the
    448.3
hardpan 211.1
hard pressed, hard
  run
  hurried 707.11
  straitened 729.24
hard pull
  exertion 714.1
  difficulty 729.2
hard put
  baffled 513.23
  straitened 729.24
hard-set
  obstinate 624.10
  straitened 729.24
Hardshell 140.4
hard-shell
  conservative 140.8
  uncompromising
    624.9
hardship 727.1
hardtack 306a.29
hard times 727.6
HAVE A HARD TIME
  OF IT
  have trouble 727.9
  have difficulty
    729.10
hard tommy 306a.29
hard-visaged 897.7
hardware 829.4
hardwareman 828.3
hard water 391.3
hardwood 377.3
hard words 967.8
hard work labor 714.5
  hard job 729.2
hard-working 705.21
hardy strong 158.13
  perennial 410.42
  healthy 683.9
  courageous 891.17
hare speed 268.7
  animal 413.29
harebrain
  nouns 470.7
  adjs. 530.16

harebrained
  scatterbrained
    530.16
  foolhardy 892.9
harefoot 211.5
harelip 248.3
harem 931.11
Hare system 742.18
Hargrave kite 279.14
haricots 306a.35
hariolate 541.9
hariolation 541.2
hark
  verbs listen 447.11
  heed 528.7
  HARK BACK TO 146.6
  interjs. listen! 447.17
  attention! 528.22
Harleian 603.17
Harlemese 578.8
harlequin
  multicolor 373.1
  buffoon 610.9
harlequina 610.9
harlequinade
  drama 609.6
  buffoonery 879.5
harlot
  nouns 987.16
  adjs. 987.28
harlotry 987.8
harm
  nouns disadvantage
    669.2
  evil 673.3
  impairment 690.1
  DO NO HARM 672.11
  OUT OF HARM'S
    REACH 696.6
  verbs hurt 673.6
  impair 690.10
harmattan 402.7,14
harmed 690.27
harmful
  disadvantageous
    669.6
  detrimental 673.12
  insalubrious 682.4
harmfulness
  badness 673.5
  insalubrity 682
harmless
  uninjurious 672.22
  undamaged 675.8
harmlessness 672.10
harmonic 462.16
harmonica 464.1,11
harmonic(al) 461.50
harmonical
  progression 86.7
harmonichord
  instrument 464.2
  piano 464.13
harmonic interval
    462.20
harmonic minor 462.6
harmonicon 464.11
harmonic proportion
    86.6
harmonics 462
harmonic tone 462.16

harmonious
  agreeing 26.14
  orderly 59.6
  conformable to 82.6
  musical 461.50
  euphonious 587.8
  in accord 792.3
harmoniously 59.9
harmonist 463.1,22
harmonium 464.15
harmonization
  attunement 26.4
  organization 60.2
  symmetrization
    247.3
  music 461.5
  orchestration 462.2
harmonize even 17.4
  agree 26.7,11
  organize 60.9
  conform 82.3
  symmetrize 247.4
  ~ tones 461.36,47
  reconcile 802.8
HARMONIZE WITH
  792.2
harmonizer 463.22
harmonizing 461.50
harmony
  agreement 26.1
  order 59.1
  conformity 82.1
  symmetry 247.1
  music 461.3
  harmonics 462.1
  euphony 587.2
  accord 792.1
  heaven 1016.6
IN HARMONY 792.3
IN HARMONY WITH
  in agreement 26.14
  in conformity 82.7
harmony of the
  spheres stars 374.4
  harmony 461.3
harness
  nouns dress 230.2
  uniform 230.7
  parachute ~ 279.13
  caparison 657.5
  armor 797.3
IN HARNESS
  employed 705.20
  prepared 718.16
OUT OF HARNESS
  706.16
  verbs 47.10
harness bull 697.14
harness race 794.13
harp 454.3,11
harp upon
  dwell on 103.9
  be boresome 882.7
Harpagon 850.6
harper 463.5
harping
  nouns 103.4
  adjs. repetitious
    103.15
  tedious 882.8
harpingly 882.12

harpist 463.5
harpoon 820.14
harpoon log 268.8
harpsichord 464.13
harpsichordist 463.7
Harpy 1014.7
harpy
  extortionist 820.10
  plunderer 823.6
  fiend 941.7
harquebusade 685.9
harridan
  ugly person 897.4
  strumpet 987.14
harried
  harassed 864.27
  worried 888.7
harrier 864.10
harrow
  nouns 257.5
UNDER THE HARROW
  in pain 423.9
  tortured 864.28
  verbs smooth 259.5
  cultivate 412.17
  pain 423.7
  torture 864.20
harrowed
  in pain 423.9
  overwrought 855.26
  tortured 864.28
harrowing
  nouns 412.13
  adjs. painful 423.10
  agonizing 862.14
harry persecute 665.6
  besiege 796.20
  harass 864.19
  worry 888.4
HARRY OUT 308.13
harrycane 402.13
harsh
  acrimonious 160.12
  off-color 361.21
  painful 423.10
  bitter 428.6
  pungent 432.6
  harsh-sounding
    457.14
  inelegant 588.2
  severe 755.6
  gruff 935.7
  unkind 937.22
harshness
  acrimony 160.4
  pungency 432.1
  raucousness 457.2
  severity 755.1
  gruffness 935.3
  unkindness 937.9
harsh-sounding 457.14
hart deer 413.7
  male animal 419.8
hartal 787.7
hartebeest 413.5
harum-scarum
  nouns 892.4
  adjs. boisterous
    161.19
  reckless 892.8
  advs. 62.16

haruspex 541.4
haruspical 541.11
haruspice 541.4
harvest
  nouns autumn 128.4
  effect 153.1
  produce 167.2
  harvesting 412.15
  crop 809.4
  verbs reap 412.19
  acquire 809.7
harvester 412.5
harvest moon 374.8
harvest time 128.4
has-been
  nouns 744.9
  adjs. 123.16
hash
  nouns mixture 44.6
  jumble 62.3
  food 306.12
  failure 723.6
  bungle 732.5
  botcher 732.8
MAKE A HASH OF
  shatter 49.12
  spoil 690.11
  botch 732.12
MAKE A HASH OF IT
  63.3
  verbs shatter 49.12
  botch 732.12
hashed 57.5
HASHED UP 690.28
hashery 306.14
hash house 306.14
hasp 47.8
hassel
  nouns argument
    481.5
  quarrel 793.5
  verbs 793.12
hassle
  nouns 62.2
  verbs 481.17
hassock tuft 74.6
  growth 410.2
hastate 257.15
haste
  nouns speed 268.1
  hurry 707
IN HASTE 707.14
MAKE HASTE
  speed 268.10
  hasten 707.5
MAKE HASTE SLOWLY
  893.5
WITH GREAT HASTE
  swiftly 268.21
  hastily 707.12
  verbs speed 268.10
  hasten 707.4
hasteless 708.6
hasten speed 268.10
  urge 646.14–16
  hurry 707.4,5
  facilitate 730.6
  further 783.17
HASTEN OFF 300.12
hastening
  hurrying 707.3

facilitation 730.4
hastily
  prematurely 131.13
  swiftly 268.21
  impulsively 628.13
  hurriedly 707.12
  recklessly 892.11
hastiness
  prematurity 131.2
  impulsiveness 628.2
  hurriedness 707.2
  recklessness 892.2
hasty sudden 113.5
  premature 131.8
  speedy 268.19
  impulsive 628.9
  hurried 707.9
  reckless 892.8
  hot-tempered
    949.25
hasty pudding
  cereal 306a.34
  food 306a.45
hat
  nouns headdress
    230.25
  types of ~ 230.59
KEEP IT UNDER ONE'S
  HAT 612.8
  verbs hood 227.23
  coif 230.39
hatch
  nouns 301.6
  verbs invent 166.14
  generate 166.15
  incubate 166.16
  be born 166.20
  line 566.18
  draw 572.20
  engrave 576.12
  trump up 614.18
  plot 652.10
hatched
  born 166.26
  trumped-up 614.30
hatchel 679.20
hatchery 152.8
hatchet 795.17
hatchet face 204.5
hatchet-faced 204.18
hatchetman 744.8
hatchet man
  assassin 408.10
  thug 941.4
hatching
  invention 166.5
  incubation 166.7
  birth 166.9
  brood 170.2
  lines 566.5
  engraving 576.1
hatchment 567.2
hatchway 301.6
hate
  nouns bombardment
    796.7
  hatred 928
  verbs dislike 865.4
  detest 928.4
hateful terrible 673.9
  odious 862.9

trial 1002.5

HEAVE THE LEAD
208.8
HEAVE TO 274.26
heave hɔ! 274.79
heave-hɔ 308.12
Heaven fate 638.2
God 1011.2
HEAVEN BE PRAISED!
hurrah! 874.12
gratitude 947.7
hallelujah! 1030.16
HEAVEN FORBID!
967.27
HEAVEN KNOWS!
476.20
heaven sky 374.2
utopia 533.11
bliss 863.2
paradise 1016
IN HEAVEN 863.14
heaven-kissing 206.20
heavenliness
beautifulness 898.6
sacredness 1024.1
godliness 1026.2
heavenly
celestial 374.25
delightful 861.6
beautiful 898.19
divine 1011.19
angel c 1013.6
paradisaical 1016.13
sacred 1024.7
godly 1026.9
heavenly being 1013.1
heavenly body 374.5
Heavenly City
utopia 533.11
heaven 1016.4
heavenly host 1013.2
heavenly kingdom
1016.1
heavenly-minded
1026.9
heaven on earth
533 11
heaven-reaching
206 20
heavenward
toward 289.28
upward 313.16
heaven-wide 79.13
heave offering 1030.7
heaves vomiting 308.8
disease 684.10
nausea 684.22
heavily inertly 267.18
weightily 351.21
densely 353.15
dully 881.10
heaviness
pregnancy 168.6
weight 351.1
viscidity 388.2
languor 706.5
oppressiveness 862.6
dullness 881.1
heaving
throwing 284.3
retching 308.8
trepidation 855.4

Heaviside layer 401.3
heavy
nouns big person
194.12
role 609.11
tragedian 610.7
adjs. substantial 3.5
great 34.8
pregnant 168.18
thick 203.8
steep 218.18
inert 267.12
weighty 351.16
dense 353.12
viscid 388.12
cloudy 403.8
luxuriant 410.41
stressed 449.13
low-toned 453.10
stupid 468.16
abstruse 547.12
tragical 609.38
important 670.21
listless 706.18
sleepy 710.19
laborious 714.19
difficult 729.17
oppressive 862.15
sad 870.20
dull 881.6
advs. 351.21
heavy-armed 797.14
heavy chemicals 378.1
heavy electron 342.3
heavy-eyed 710.19
heavy hand
despotism 739.10
strictness 755.3
heavy-handed 732.20
heavyhearted 870.20
heavy hydrogen 325.5
heavy-laden
loaded 56.13
careworn 888.8
heavy purse 835.1
heavy-set
corpulent 194.18
thick 203.8
heavy sky 403.4
heavy sledding 729.2
heavy water
isotope 325.5
water 391.3
heavyweight
nouns superior 36.4
big person 194.12
weight 351.3
personage 670.8
boxer 798.2
adjs. heavy 351.16
important 670.16
hebdomadal,
hebdomadary
137.9
Hebe 898.9
hebephrenia 472.5
hebephreniac 472.16
hebetate 854.7
hebetic 124.13
hebetomy 687.26

hebetude
stupidity 468.3
languor 706.5
hebetudinous
stupid 468.16
listless 706.18
Hebraic(al) 1018.28
Hebraism 1018.10
Hebraist
philologist 578.12
religionist 1018.19
Hebraistical 1018.28
Hebrew
nouns Jew 417.3
unintelligibility
547.6
~ alphabet 579.5
Judaist 1018.19
adjs. Jewish 417.11
Judaical 1018.28
Hebrewism 1018.10
hecastotheism 1018.5
Hecate, Hekate 374.9
hecatomb
hundred 99.8
sacrifice 1030.7
heckelphone 464.9
heckle comb 679.20
harass 864.19
heckler 864.10
hectic
nouns heat flush
327.11
reddening 367.3
fever 684.6
adjs. reddened 367.10
feverish 684.43
excited 855.23
hectograph 601.13
hector
nouns 941.5
verbs harass 864.19
bully 889.19
hedge
nouns 234.3
verbs offset 33.5
surround 232.6
pen 235.7
quibble 482.9
side-step 629.8
hedged 235.10
HEDGED IN 233.7
hedgehog
rocket launcher
280.11
animal 413.4
hedgehop 277.48
hedgehopping 277.14
hedger 482.7
hedging
nouns 482.5
adjs. 482.15
hedonics 863.4
hedonism
pleasure-loving
863.4
ethics 955.2
hedonist sensualist
985.3
philosopher 499.13

hedonistic,
hedonic(al)
philosophical 499.10
pleasure-loving
863.15
heebie-jeebies
delirium tremens
472.10
jitters 857.2
heed
nouns attention
528.1
care 531.1
caution 893.1
GIVE HEED 528.8
verbs listen 447.11
be attentive 528.6
care 531.6
obey 764.2
observe 766.2
NOT HEED
disregard 529.3
disobey 765.6
heedful
attentive 528.15
careful 531.10
cautious 893.8
considerate 936.17
heedfulness
attention 528.1
care 531.1
caution 893.1
considerateness
936.3
heeding
listening 447.1
observance 766.1
heedless
incurious 527.3
inattentive 529.6
careless 532.11
impulsive 628.10
unconcerned 634.6
improvident 719.15
inconsiderate 937.16
heedlessness
incuriosity 527.1
inattention 529.1
carelessness 532.2
impulsiveness 628.3
unconcern 634.2
improvidence 719.2
inconsiderateness
937.3
heel
nouns foot 211.5
latter part 240.1
stern 240.6
scoundrel 984.6
SHOW THE HEELS
629.10
UNDER THE HEEL OF
762.16
verbs careen 274.45
deviate 290.3
follow 292.3
turn around 294.9
equip 657.8
HEEL OVER 274.46
heeled
equipped 657.12

armed 797.14
drunk 994.40
heeler follower 292.2
ward ~ 744.8
hanger-on 905.5
heeling 292.1
heel of Achilles
weakness 159.4
vulnerability 695.4
heelpiece 240.1
heeltap, heeltaps 43.2
hefner candle 334.21
heft
nouns main part 54.5
weight 351.1
effort 714.2
verbs lift 315.5
weigh 351.10
heftiness 351.1
hefting 351.9
hefty strong 158.13
heavy 351.16
laborious 714.19
difficult 729.17
Hegelian 499.11
hegemonic(al)
chief 36.16
ruling 739.17
hegemony 737.6
hegira 629.4
he-goat goat 413.10
male animal 419.8
heifer girl 125.6
bovine 413.8
female animal
420.10
heigh!
attention! 528.23
hello! 923.15
height
nouns degree 29.1
highness 206
summit 210.2
pitch 462.4
perfection 675.3
AT ITS HEIGHT
extreme 34.15
exceeding 36.20
verbs heighten
206.18
raise 315.5
heighten
intensify 38.5
make higher 206.18
raise 315.5
exaggerate 615.3
aggravate 883.2
heightened
increased 38.7
exaggerated 615.4
aggravated 883.4
heightening
intensification 38.2
exaggeration 615.1
aggravation 883.1
height finder 345.4
heighth 206.1
height pressure 277.28
heights 206.2
Heimdall 1012.6
Heimweh 632.5

Heine 417.9
Heinie 798.8
heinous terrible 673.9
infamous 913.12
wicked 979.17
heinously 913.17
heinousness
terribleness 673.2
infamousness 913.3
wickedness 979.5
heir
nouns 817.5
verbs 817.7
heir apparent,
heir presumptive
heir 817.5
prince 916.8
heirdom 817.2
heiress 817.5
heirloom 817.2
heirs 170.1
TO HIS HEIRS 816.26
heirship, heirship
movable 817.2
heist
nouns increase 38.1
lift 315.2
verbs increase 38.4
hoist 315.5
Hekate See Hecate
Hel goddess 1012.6
Hades 1017.3
god 1017.5
held stuck 142.17
supported 215.25
obsessed 472.32
interested 528.18
HELD UP 132.15
Helen of Troy 898.9
helical spiral 253.8
solar 374.25
helicline 218.4
helicoid, helicoidal
253.8
Helicon 607.12
helicopter 279.5
helidrome 277.19
heliochrome, helio-
chromotype 575.3
heliochromy 575.1
helioengraving 576.2,8
Heliogabalus 985.3
heliogram
telegram 558.16
signal 566.14
heliograph
signal 566.14
photograph 575.3
engraving 576.8
heliographic 334.40
heliography 334.22
heliogravure 576.2
heliolater 1031.4
heliolatrous 1031.7
heliolatry 1031.1
heliological 334.40
heliology, heliometry
334.22
Helios sun 374.11
god 1012.5
heliotherapy 687.5

heliotrope 435.2
heliotype 576.8
heliotypography,
heliotypy 576.2
heliport 277.19
helix 253.2
helix angle 277.23
hell pit 208.2
hot place 327.10
gambling den
514.14
prison 759.7
torment 864.7
den of iniquity
979.10
Hades 1017
COME HELL OR HIGH
WATER 512.26
FOR THE HELL OF IT
876.33
GET THE HELL OUT
300.10
GO TO HELL 691.23
HELL BROKE LOOSE
pandemonium 62.5
uproar 452.3
HELL FOR LEATHER
268.21
HELL TO PAY 729.4
HELL UPON EARTH
864.7
LOOK LIKE HELL
897.5
PLAY HELL WITH
play havoc 690.11
botch 732.12
RAISE HELL
create a disturbance
62.9
be noisy 452.7
vociferate 458.8
cause trouble 729.13
make merry 876.26
TO HELL AND BACK
178.12
hell around
create a disturbance
62.9
make merry 876.26
hellbender revel 876.6
spree 994.5
hell-bent 268.21
HELL-BENT ON 622.16
hell bomb 799.16
hellborn
wicked 979.18
hellish 1017.6
hellcat
violent person 161.9
daredevil 892.4
hellion 941.3,8
Hellenist 578.12
Hellespontine sibyl
541.6
hell-fire 1017.2
hell-fired
adjs. 970.10
advs. 34.26
hellhag 941.8
hellhole 979.10

hellhound
violent person 161.9
fiend 941.7
hellion
violent person 161.9
mischief-maker
941.3
demon 1014.7
hellish
execrable 673.10
cruel 937.24
wicked 979.18
devilish 1014.18
infernal 1017.6
hellishly 34.26
hellishness 979.5
hello
nouns 923.4
interjs. attention!
528.23
oh! 918.18
greetings! 923.15
hell-roarer
violent person 161.9
hellion 941.3
helm
nouns steering gear
276.33
place of power 737.9
control 739.2
management 745.5
AT THE HELM 737.21
BE AT THE HELM
745.9
verbs 274.14
HELM ALEE, HELM
AWEATHER 274.80
helmetlike, helmet-
shaped 251.23
helminthagogue
685.19
helminthic
nouns 685.19
adjs. 685.37
helminthologist 414.2
helminthology 414.1
helmsman
coxswain 275.8
guider 746.6
helot 762.7
helotism 762.1
helotry 762.1
help
nouns serving 306.10
remedy 685.1
servant 748.1
aid 783.1
assistant 785.6
subsidy 816.8
benefactor 940.1
BE OF SOME HELP
783.11
THE HELP 748.12
WITH THE HELP OF
783.25
verbs benefit 672.11
prevent 728.14
aid 783.11
subsidize 816.18
HELP ALONG 730.6

HELP ONESELF TO
820.16
HELP UP 315.7
NOT HELP 637.10
interjs. 700.4
helper assistant 785.6
benefactor 940.1
helpful
instrumental 656.6
useful 663.18
beneficial 672.21
helping 783.21
helpfully
beneficially 672.26
helpingly 783.24
helpfulness
usefulness 663.3
beneficialness 672.9
help 783.10
helping
nouns 306.10
adjs. 733.20
helpless
impotent 157.18
unprotected 695.14
forlorn 922.13
dead-drunk 994.43
helplessness
impotence 157.4
defenselessness
695.3
forlornness 922.4
helpmate, helpmeet
assistant 785.6
wife 931.9
helpsome 783.21
helter-skelter
nouns confusion 62.4
haste 707.1
adjs. 62.15
advs. in disorder
62.16
carelessly 532.18
hastily 707.12
recklessly 892.11
helve 215.11
hem
nouns 234.4,7
verbs surround 232.6
border 234.10
pen 235.7
stammer 593.7
HEM AND HAW
stammer 593.7
vacillate 625.8
HEM IN
surround 232.6
enclose 235.5
confine 759.12
he-man 419.6
he-mannish 419.12
hemeralopia 440.2
hemeralopic 440.8
Hemichorda 414.10
hemicrania 423.5
hemicycle 252.8
hemiplegia 684.19
hemisphere half 92.2
realm 179.2
hemispheric(al)
252.9

hemlock 1008.7
hemmed 235.10
HEMMED IN 233.7
hemoglobin 387.4
hemophilia 684.8
hemorrhage 309.8
HAVE A HEMORRHAGE
950.19
hemorrhea 309.8
hemorrhoids 684.28
hemotherapy 687.3
hemp 1009.5
hempen bridle
rigging 276.12
hangman's rope
1009.5
hen fowl 413.35
female 420.6,10
hence therefore 154.6
away 186.17
away from 300.21
henceforth, hence-
forwards 121.10
henchman
follower 292.2
political ~ 744.8
right-hand man
785.7
hanger-on 905.5
hen cote 190.19
hen-headed 468.20
henhearted 890.10
henheartedness 890.1
henhouse 190.19
henhussy
mollycoddle 420.11
dotard 470.9
henna
verbs 367.4
adjs. 366.4
hennery 190.19
henotheism 1018.5
henotheist 1018.14
hen party 920.10
henpeck domineer
over 739.15
nag 967.16
henpecked
downtrodden
762.15
obedient 764.5
hep 474.17
BE HEP TO 487.8
GET HEP
nonsense 469.13
master 562.9
GET HEP TO 555.13
HEP TO 474.16
Hepaticae 411.5
hepcat
musician 463.2
jitterbug 463.23
dancer 877.3
Hephaestus
smith 716.7
god 1012.5
heptachord 464.2
heptad 99.3
heptagon 99.3
heptagonal
sevenfold 99.19

angular 250.11
heptahedral 99.19
heptahedron 99.3
hep talk 578.6
heptamerous 99.19
heptameter seven 99.3
verse 607.5
heptangular 99.19
heptapody 607.5
heptarchy 99.3
heptastich seven 99.3
verse 607.5
Heptateuch 99.3
heptatomic 325.17
her self 80.5
female 420.4
Hera marriage 931.14
goddess 1012.5
Heraclitean 499.11
herald
nouns forerunner
66.1
harbinger 542.3
messenger 559.2
verbs forerun 116.3
presage 542.11
proclaim 557.13
heraldic 557.18
heraldic device 567.2
heraldry insignia 567.2
pomp 902.6
herb
nouns 410.3
verbs 412.19
herbaceous, herbose,
herbous, herby
410.34
herbage 410.1
herbal 410.34
herbalist 411.2
herbalize
botanize 411.9
gather herbs 412.19
herbarium 412.10
Herbivora 414.12
herbivore eater 306.13
animal 413.3
herbivores 414.12
herbivorous 306.29
herbs
types of ~ 410.48
medicine 685.4
Herculean
strong 158.15
gigantic 194.20
laborious 714.19
difficult 729.16
Herculean task 729.2
Hercules
strong man 158.6
giant 194.13
support 215.3
Hercules and Iolaus
926.8
herd
nouns 74.5
THE HERD 917.3
verbs fly 277.43
shepherd 415.7
drive 745.9

accompany 73.7
assemble 74.15
associate with
920.15
herdboy, herder,
herdsman 415.3
Here 1012.5
here
nouns 183.2
advs. now 120.3
in this place 183.24
present 185.14
HERE AND NOW 120.3
HERE AND THERE
intermittently 72.5
scatteringly 75.13
sparsely 102.8
in places 183.26
HERE LIES 409.27
HERE, THERE AND
EVERYWHERE
178.11
HERE TODAY AND
GONE TOMORROW
111.7
NOT HERE 186.17
interjs. 295.6
HERE'S TO YOU!
994.47
hereabout, hereabouts
here 183.24
approximately
199.26
hereadays 120.3
hereafter
nouns 121.1
THE HEREAFTER
121.2
adjs. 121.8
advs. 121.10
hereat now 120.3
hence 154.6
here 183.24
hereby 656.8
hereditability 169.6
hereditable 169.16
hereditament 817.2
hereditaments 808.7
hereditary innate 5.7
ancestral 169.15
heredity 169.6
herein 224.14
hereinabove 64.6
hereinafter 117.6
hereinbefore 64.6
hereinto hereof 9.11
hereto 183.24
hereness 185.1
hereon 9.11
heresy 1023.2
heretic
nonconformist 83.4
apostate 626.5
religious ~ 1023.5
heretical 1023.9
hereto 183.24
heretofore
nouns 119.1
advs. prior to 116.6
formerly 119.10

hereunto hereof 9.11
  until now 120.4
  hereto 183.24
hereupon 9.11
herewith
  advs. 73.10
  preps. 656.8
Her Highness, Her
  Majesty, etc. 915.2
heritability 169.6
heritable
  nouns 817.2
  adjs. inheritable
    169.16
  assignable 815.5
heritage
  heredity 169.6
  inheritance 817.2
heritance 817.2
heritor 817.5
hermaphrodite
  nouns 418.11
  adjs. 418.23
hermaphroditic
  418.23
hermaphroditism
  418.10
hermeneutic(al)
  550.16
hermeneutics 550.9
Hermes
  messenger 559.1
  god 1012.5
hermetic(al) 265.12
hermit 922.5
hermitage 698.5
hermitic, hermitish
  922.11
hermitism 922.2
hermitry 922.2
hernia 684.8
herniotomy 687.26
hero actor 610.5
  victor 724.5
  brave man 891.8
  celebrity 912.9
  admired person
    983.5
  demigod 1012.3
heroic huge 194.20
  poetic 607.21
  courageous 891.17
  magnanimous 977.6
heroically 891.22
heroicalness 891.1
heroic couplet 607.5
heroics 908.1
heroic verse 607.2
heroine actor 610.5
  brave woman 891.8
  celebrity 912.9
  admired person
    983.5
  demigoddess 1012.3
heroism courage 891.1
  magnanimity 977.6
herolike 891.17
hero worship
  idolization 962.1
  idolatry 1031.1
herpes 684.27

herpetologist 414.2
herpetology 414.1
Herr 419.7
herring-gutted 204.16
herring pond 396.1
hers 806.13
herself 80.5
hertzian telegraphy
  558.4
hertzian wave 343.14
hesitance demur 621.2
  irresolution 625.3
hesitancy
  uncertainty 513.1
  irresolution 625.3
hesitant
  uncertain 513.16
  unwilling 621.7
  irresolute 625.9
hesitantly, hesi-
  tatingly 625.12
hesitate
  procrastinate 132.10
  pause 144.9
  stammer 593.7
  demur 621.4
  be irresolute 625.7
NOT HESITATE 622.10
hesitating
  nouns 625.3
  adjs. uncertain
    513.16
  stammering 593.12
  unwilling 621.7
  irresolute 625.9
hesitation
  procrastination
    132.5
  pause 144.3
  uncertainty 513.1
  stammering 593.3
  demur 621.2
  irresolution 625.3
Hesper, Hesperus
  374.5
Hessian 798.16
hest 750.1
Hestia gods of the
  household 190.26
  goddess 1012.5
hestia 1040.11
het 328.28
HET UP
  excited 855.23
  angry 950.27
hetaera 987.15
heteratomic, hetero-
  atomic 325.17
heterochromatin
  405.12
heterochromosome
  405.11
heteroclite
  abnormal 85.9
  irregular 138.3
heterocycle 325.7
heterocyclic 325.17
heterodox 1023.9
heterodoxy 1023.1
heterodyne 343.31
heterogamy 168.4

heterogeneity
  difference 16.1
  variety 19.1
heterogeneous
  different 16.7
  diversified 19.4
  mixed 44.15
heterogenesis 166.6
heterogenetic 166.24
heteromorphic
  multiform 19.3
  abnormal 85.9
heteromorphism
  multiformity 19.1
  abnormality 85.1
heteromorphous 19.3
heteronomous 739.16
heteronomy 739.4
heteronuclear 325.18
heteronym 580.3
heteropathic 686.18
heteropathy 686.2
heteroplasty 687.27
heteroproteide 307.6
heterothermic 332.20
heterotopia
  transformation
    139.2
  displacement 184.1
heterotopic 184.7
heterotropia 439.5
hetman 747.22
hew sever 49.10
  form 245.6
HEW DOWN 316.5
hex
  nouns 1033.8
PUT A HEX ON
    1034.11
  verbs 1034.10
Hexabiblos, hexa-
  bromide 99.2
hexachord six 99.2
  music 462.8
  instrument 464.2
hexacosihedroid 99.2
Hexactinellida 414.4
hexad
  nouns 99.2
  adjs. 99.18
hexaglot 578.15
hexagon 99.2
hexagonal
  sixfold 99.18
  angular 250.11
hexagram 99.2
hexahedral
  sixfold 99.18
  angular 250.11
hexahedron 99.2
hexamerous 99.18
hexameter six 99.2
  verse 607.5
hexangular 99.18
hexapod six 99.2
  insect 413a.2
hexapody six 99.2
  verse 607.5
hexarchy 99.2
hexastich six 99.2

verse 607.5
hexastyle
  nouns 99.2
  adjs. 99.18
Hexateuch six 99.2
  Bible 1019.3
hexatomic
  sixfold 99.18
  atomic 325.17
hexavalent 99.2
hey! 528.23
heyday of youth
  124.1
HF pulse 345.10
H-hour
  zero hour 129.6
  attack 796.14
hiatus interval 200.1
  opening 264.1
hibernal wintry 128.8
  cold 332.15
hibernate 710.14
hibernation 710.2
Hibernian 417.9
Hibernianism,
  Hibernicism
  error 517.6
  idiom 578.9
hiccius-doccius 994.40
hiccup, hiccough
  nouns 402.19
  verbs 402.25
hic jacet
  epitaph 409.18
  here lies 409.27
hick
  nouns 917.9
  adjs. 181.6
hickdom 181.1
hickey 375.4
hickish 181.7
hickory oil 1008.6
hick town 182.3
hid 613.12
HID UNDER A BUSHEL
  532.14
LIE HID
  be invisible 444.3
  hide 613.9
hidalgo 916.4
hidden
  unknown 476.18
  latent 544.5
  obscure 547.13
  abstruse 547.14
  secret 612.12
  concealed 613.12
  secluded 922.10
hide
  nouns pelt 228.1
  types of ∼ 228.8
HIDE AND HAIR 56.18
PLAY AT HIDE AND
  SEEK 629.7
  verbs conceal 613.7
  hide oneself 613.9
  whip 1008.15
HIDE ONE'S FACE
  be humiliated 904.8
  be modest 906.7

HIDE ONE'S LIGHT
UNDER A BUSHEL
906.7
hideaway
  hiding place 613.4
  retreat 698.5
hidebound
  narrow-minded
    525.10
  bound 758.16
  strait-laced 901.19
  hyperorthodox
    1022.9
hideous odious 862.10
  ugly 867.11
hide-out, hiding place
  hiding 613.4
  retreat 698.5
hiding
  nouns concealment
    613.1.4
  whipping 1008.5
  GO INTO HIDING 613.9
  adjs. 613.17
hidlings, hidlins 613.4
hie hasten 268.10
  go 272.17
  HIE ON
    urge on 646.16
    hasten 707.4
  HIE TO 272.24
hiemal wintry 128.8
  cold 352.15
hierarch 1036.8
hierarchal, hierarchic
  1035.16
hierarchy 1035.7
hieratic 600.27
hieratic symbol 579.3
hierocracy 1035.7
hierodule 1036.15
hieroglyph 579.3
hieroglyphic
  nouns character
    579.3
  secret symbol 612.7
  adjs. 600.27
hieroglyphics 600.10
hierogram 579.3
hierography
  writing 600.10
  theology 1021.1
hierology 1021.1
hieromonach 1036.16
Hieronymian,
  Hieronymite 922.5
hierophant 1036.4,15
hieros 1036.15
hi-fi
  nouns 343.1
  adjs. 343.31
higgle haggle 825.14
  vend 827.9
  HIGGLE THE MARKET
    831.25
higgledy-piggledy
  nouns 62.3
  adjs. 62.15
  advs. 62.16
higgler 828.6

higgling
  bargaining 825.3
  market rigging
    831.20
high
  nouns ~ gear
    347.6
  school 565.6
  IN HIGH 268.21
  ON HIGH 206.27
  REACH A NEW HIGH
    724.3
  adjs. great 34.9
  lofty 206.19
  unsavory 428.7
  high-flavored 432.8
  fetid 436.5
  phonetics 449.18
  high-pitched 457.12
  excessive 661.17
  tainted 690.39
  expensive 846.11
  proud 903.11
  exalted 912.19
  noble 916.11
  magnanimous 977.6
  drunk 994.40
  advs. 206.27
  HIGH AND DRY
    stuck 142.17
    dry 392.7
    safe 696.6
    stranded 729.25
  HIGH AND LOW
    178.11
  HIGH AND MIGHTY
    arrogant 910.11
    eminent 912.19
high art 572.9
highball
  nouns 994.19
  verbs 268.9
highbinder
  assassin 408.10
  thug 941.4
high birth 916.1
high blood pressure
  684.8
highborn 916.12
highbred
  highborn 916.12
  well-bred 934.17
highbrow
  nouns personality
    416.5
  intellectual 475.1
  snob 910.7
  adjs. 474.23
high-brow 964.5
high-caliber 672.15
high celebration
  1038.4
High Church 1018.9
High-Church 1038.21
High-Churchism
  Anglicanism 1018.9
  ritualism 1038.1
High-churchman
  1038.2
high-class 672.15
high-colored 361.19

high comedy 609.6
High Court 999.5
high day 709.4
high descent 916.1
high diver 318.4
high dudgeon 950.7
higher superior 36.13
  above 206.24
higher education
  560.9
higher mathematics
  87.2
Higher Thought
  1018.12
higher-up 36.4
highest supreme 36.15
  top 210.9
highest degree 56.4
high explosive 799.9
highfalutin,
  highfaluting
  nouns bombast 599.2
  brag 908.2
  adjs. grandiloquent
    599.9
  exaggerated 615.4
  ostentatious 902.18
  proud 903.11
  boastful 908.10
  arrogant 910.9
high feather 683.2
high-fi See hi-fi
high fidelity 343.1
high-fidelity 343.31
highflier, highflyer
  visionary 533.13
  enthusiast 633.5
  proud person 903.3
high-flowing 599.9
high-flown
  absurd 469.10
  fanciful 533.20
  grandiloquent 599.9
  exaggerated 615.4
  ostentatious 902.18
  proud 903.11
  boastful 908.10
  arrogant 910.9
highflying
  grandiloquent 599.9
  exaggerated 615.4
  ostentatious 902.18
high frequency 343.15
high-frequency 343.31
high-geared 156.11
high-go 876.6
high-grade 672.15
high hand 739.10
  WITH A HIGH HAND
    156.16
highhanded 737.15
highhandedness 737.2
high-hat
  verbs 964.5
  adjs. 910.14
high-hatted 910.14
high-hatter 910.7
high-hatty 910.14
high-headed
  proud 903.11
  arrogant 910.9

high holiday 709.4
high hopes 886.1
high horse 910.1
  GET DOWN FROM
  ONE'S HIGH HORSE
    904.6
  GET ON ONE'S HIGH
  HORSE 910.8
highjack, hijack
  822.14
highjacker, hijacker
  823.5
high jinks 876.4
high jump 317.1
highland
  nouns 206.3
  adjs. 206.22
highlands
  the country 181.1
  uplands 206.3
high life society 642.6
  aristocracy 916.2
highlight
  nouns light 334.1
  feature 670.7
  verbs illuminate
    334.28
  emphasize 670.13
high liver 991.3
high-living 991.8
high lope 268.4
highly 34.17
High Mass 1038.9
high-mettled 855.29
high mightiness 912.5
high-minded
  proud 903.11
  honorable 972.13
  magnanimous 977.6
high-mindedness
  probity 972.1
  magnanimity 977.2
high-muck-a-muck
  670.9
Highness 915.2
highness height 206.1
  shrillness 457.1
  expensiveness 846.2
high-nosed
  proud 903.11
  arrogant 910.9
high old time 876.2
high-pitched
  high 206.19
  high-sounding
    457.12
high-pockets 206.12
high-potency 156.11
high-powered
  potent 156.11
  important 670.16
high pressure
  urge 646.6
  compulsion 754.1
high-pressure
  verbs urge 646.14
  compel 754.6
  sell 827.9
  adjs. potent 156.11
  compulsory 754.10

high-pressure area
277.38
high-priced 846.11
high priest 1036.8,11
high-principled 972.13
high-protein diet
307.10
high-quality 672.15
high-reaching
lofty 206.19
aspiring 632.29
highroad road 655.6
facility 730.1
high roller
spendthrift 852.2
dissipater 991.3
high school 565.6
high seas 396.1
ON THE HIGH SEAS
sailing 274.67
at sea 396.8
high-seasoned 432.7
high-set 206.19
high sign signal 566.14
warning 701.4
high society 642.6
high-sounding
loud 452.9
high-toned 457.12
grandiloquent 599.9
high-spirited 855.29
high spirits 868.2
high spot 670.7
high-stepper 413.20
high-strung
excitable 855.29
nervous 857.11
high-swelling 908.10
high-tail 268.11
high-tasted 432.8
high tea 920.11
high-tension 341.31
high-test 672.15
high tide fullness 56.2
high water 206.13
tide 394.13
high time
opportunity 129.3
fun 876.2
hightoby 823.5
high-toned
high-pitched 457.12
ostentatious 902.18
proud 903.11
high treason 973.7
high visibility 443.2
high water
fullness 56.2
high tide 394.13
high-water mark 489.7
highway 655.6
highwayman 823.5
highway robbery 822.3
highways and byways
655.5
high wind 402.13
high words
quarrel 793.5
anger 950.9
high-wrought
painstaking 531.11

perfected 675.9
elaborate 899.11
high yellow 44.9
hijack 754.7
hike
nouns increase 38.1
walk 272.12
verbs increase 38.4
walk 272.29
hasten off 300.14
hiker 273.6
hiking 272.10
hilarious merry 868.15
festive 876.30
hilarity 868.5
hill
nouns heap 74.9
elevation 206.5
verbs 74.18
hillbilly 189.10
hill-dwelling 206.22
hillock 206.5
hillside 218.4
hilltop 206.8
hilly 206.23
him self 80.5
male 419.4
Himinbjorg 1016.11
hind
nouns deer 413.7
female animal
420.10
peasant 917.8
adjs. 240.8
hindbrain 465.5
hind end rear 240.1
rump 240.4
hinder
verbs obstruct 728.10
restrain 758.7
adjs. 240.8
hinderer 728.8
hindering
nouns 728.1
adjs. 728.17
hindermost 240.8
hindersome 728.17
hind-gut 224.6
hindhand 240.8
hindhead 240.1
hind leg 272.16
hindmost 240.8
hindquarter 240.3
hindrance
obstruction 728
restraint 758
hindsight 540.1
Hindu 417.3
Hindustani 578.10
Hindu triad 1011.10
hindward, hindwards
rearward 240.14
backwards 294.13
hinge
nouns joint 47.4
crisis 129.4
axle 320.5
verbs fasten 47.8
depend 506.6
hinging post 216.4
hingle 320.5

hinny 413.23
hint
nouns trace 35.4
tinge 44.7
supposition 498.4
reminder 535.6
intimation 555.4
clue 566.8
verbs 555.9
hinted 544.7
hinterland
nouns back country
181.2
background 232.2
adjs. 181.8
hinterlander 189.10
hip haunch 241.1
pod 410.28
ON THE HIP 728.21
hipped on
enthusiastic 633.11
fond of 929.27
hippety-hop
nouns step 272.13
hop 317.1
verbs skip 272.27
hop 317.5
hippiness 194.8
hipping, hippen
230.19
hippo
behemoth 194.14
hippopotamus 413.6
hippocampus 413.33
Hippocrates 686.15
Hippocratic oath
686.16
hippodrome
amphitheater
609.17
arena 800.1
hippopotamic
ponderous 194.19
pachydermous
413.42
hippopotamus
behemoth 194.14
animal 413.6
hippy 194.18
hips 240.4
hircarra 559.1
hircine 413.41
hire
nouns hiring 778.5
salary 839.4
charge 844.7
FOR HIRE 778.19
verbs bribe 649.3
engage 778.13
hired 778.17
hireling
nouns employee
748.2
mercenary 798.16
adjs. hired 778.17
corruptible 973.22
hiring 778.5
hirsute hairy 229.24
feathery 229.27
bristly 260.9

hirsuteness, hirsutism
229.1
Hirudinea 414.5
his 806.13
His Highness, His
Majesty, etc. 915.2
His Holiness 915.5
his honor, his worship,
etc. 1000.1
his nibs
personage 670.9
judge 1000.1
hispid hairy 229.24
bristly 260.9
hispidity
hairiness 229.1
roughness 260.1
hispidulous 229.24
his Reverence
ecclesiastical title
915.5
clergyman 1036.2
hiss
nouns sibilation
456.1
derision 965.3
verbs effervesce 404.4
sibilate 456.2
say 592.17
boo 965.10
hissing
nouns radio noise
343.24
sibilation 456.1
derision 965.3
adjs. 456.3
histogenesis 166.6
histogenetic 166.24
histologist 405.17
histology 244.7
historian 569.2;
606.11
historic(al) 606.18
historic eras, historic
periods 107.11
historify 606.14
historiographer
chronicler 569.2
historian 606.11
historiographic(al)
606.18
historiography 606.4
historize 606.14
history manual 603.9
chronicle 606.4
histrio 609.32
histrionic
dramatic 609.37
affected 901.15
pretentious 902.24
histrionics 609.2
hit
nouns blow 282.4
song ~ 461.8
success 722.3,4
stroke of luck 726.3
criticism 967.4
MAKE A HIT
succeed 722.6
please 863.5

support 215.22
obsess 472.23
~ the thought
477.15
decide 493.11
think 500.9
be true 515.7
interest 528.13
refrain 704.3
~ the prerogative
737.12
restrain 758.7
possess 806.5
retain 811.6,7
HOLD A BRIEF FOR
be deputy 779.13
support 783.14
HOLD ACES
have advantage
36.11
be lucky 726.11
HOLD A CLOSE WIND
274.27
HOLD A HIGH OPINION
OF 962.4
HOLD A LOOSE REIN
756.3
HOLD BACK
delay 132.7
slow down 269.9
reserve 658.12
hinder 728.10
restrain 758.7
refuse 774.4
stint 850.8
restrain oneself
990.6
abstain 990.7
HOLD DOWN
~ a job 654.14
suppress 758.8
subjugate 762.8
HOLD EVERYTHING
132.11
HOLD FAST
adhere 50.6
stand fast 142.12
navigation 274.79
be determined 622.9
persevere 623.4
restrain 758.7
hold 811.6
HOLD FORTH
expound 560.16
speak 592.11
declaim 597.9
offer 771.4
propound 771.5
HOLD GOOD
be reasonable
481.18
prove true 504.11
hold true 515.7
HOLD IN 758.7
HOLD IT AGAINST
927.9
HOLD OFF
delay 132.8
temporize 132.10
repulse 288.2

be unwilling 621.4
ward off 797.10
HOLD ON
adhere 50.5
endure 110.6
wait 132.11
continue 143.3
cease 144.13
persevere 623.4
retain 811.6
wait out the market
831.23
HOLD ONE'S OWN
stand fast 142.12
be determined 622.9
govern 739.12
resist 790.5
retain 811.5
HOLD ONE'S TONGUE
450.5
HOLD OUT
endure 110.6
stand fast 142.12
not weaken 158.9
extend 178.7
persevere 623.4
be obstinate 624.7
offer 771.4
refuse 774.3
resist 790.2,5
HOLD OUT FOR 787.9
HOLD OUT ON
keep secret 612.8
withhold 850.8
HOLD OVER 132.8
HOLD THE REINS
745.9
HOLD THE SCALES
weigh 351.10
judge 493.12
HOLD TOGETHER
be consistent 26.10
be joined 47.11
cohere 50.5
hold true 515.7
co-operate 784.4
HOLD UP
be consistent 26.10
keep waiting 132.6
delay 132.7,8
stand fast 142.12
not weaken 158.9
support 215.22
retard 269.9
raise up 315.5
buoy 352.8
stand the test
488.10
hold true 515.7
persevere 623.4
hinder 728.10
restrain 758.7
lend support 783.12
resist 790.2
rob 822.14
overcharge 846.7
display 902.17
HOLD WATER
be consistent 26.10
be reasonable
481.18

prove true 504.11
hold true 515.7
HOLD WITH
agree to 520.8
consent 773.3
approve of 966.9
HOLD YOUR HORSES
132.11
NOT HOLD A CANDLE
TO 37.4
NOT HOLD ONE'S
PUNCHES 755.5
NOT HOLD TOGETHER
517.7
interjs. 144.13
holdback 728.1,7
holder
receptacle 192.1
possessor 807.1
recipient 817.3
holding
nouns possession
806.1
property 808.4
retention 811.1
shares 832.3
adjs. supporting
215.24
obsessing 472.33
interesting 528.20
possessing 806.10
retentive 811.8
HOLDING TOGETHER
50.8
holding company
786.9; 831.15
holdings 808.1
hold-off 132.5
holdout 787.4
holdover 744.11
holdup delay 132.2
retardation 269.4
robbery 822.3
highwayman 823.5
overcharge 846.5
hold-up 348.11
holdup man 823.5
hole
nouns degree 29.1
place 183.1
hovel 190.10
lair 190.22
dive 190.24
compartment 191.2
nook 191.3
cellar 191.17
small place 195.3
cleft 200.2
pit 208.2
cavity 256.2
cave 256.5
opening 264.1
air pocket 277.38
hiding place 613.4
fault 676.2
filthy place 680.11
score 722.4
predicament 729.4
impasse 729.5
prison 759.7,9

den of iniquity
979.10
HOLE IN ONE 722.4
IN A HOLE 729.20
PUT IN A HOLE
729.14
verbs 264.15
HOLE UP
hide out 613.9
hibernate 710.14
hole-and-corner
612.14
holeproof 158.18
holey 264.19
Holi 876.4
holiday
nouns 709.4
verbs 709.9
adjs. 709.10
holidays 709.3
holier-than-thou
1027.5
Holiness 915.5
holiness divine
attribute 1011.15
sacredness 1024.1
godliness 1026.2
holistic theory 688.1
Hollander 417.9
holler
nouns 873.4
verbs object 520a.5
complain 873.13
hollo
nouns 458.1
verbs 458.6
interjs. 528.23
hollow
nouns compartment
191.2
pit 208.2
cavity 256.2
verbs be concave
256.12,13
dedicate 814.12
adjs. vacant 186.12
concave 256.16
deep-toned 453.10
specious 482.13
insincere 614.32
hungry 632.26
advs. 56.17
hollowed 256.16
hollowhearted 614.32
hollowing 814.4
hollowly
vacantly 186.15
insincerely 614.36
hollowness
vacancy 186.2
concavity 256.1
resonance 453.1
insincerity 614.5
hunger 632.7
holm island 385.2
marsh 399.1
holocaust 1030.7
Holocephali, Holo-
cephala, holo-
cephalans, holo-
cephalians 414.11

holograph
  nouns 568.4
  adjs. 600.24
holoproteide 307.6
Holothurioidea,
  holothurians 414.7
holotony 684.5
holt 410.12
holus-bolus
  hastily 707.12
  recklessly 892.11
holy sacred 1024.7
  godly 1026.9
  THE HOLY 1024.2
Holy Church 1022.4
Holy City 1016.4
Holy Communion
  1038.8
holyday, holy day
  1038.14
Holy Father
  God 1011.11
  pope 1036.8
Holy Ghost 1011.14
Holy Grail 1038.11
Holy Joe 1036.2
Holy Mary 1013.5
holy-minded 1026.9
holy of holies
  private room 191.8
  toilet 680.13
  sanctuary 1040.5
holy orders
  ministry 1035.10
  sacrament 1038.5
holy place 1040.4
Holy Scriptures
  1019.2
Holy Spirit 1011.14
holystone 679.18
holy terror
  violent person 161.9
  frightener 889.8
  hellion 941.3
Holy Thursday
  1038.15
holytide 1038.14
Holy Trinity 1011.10
holy water 1038.11
holy wedlock 931.1
Holy Week 1038.15
Holy Willie 1027.3
Holy Writ 1019.2
homage
  reverence 962.1,2
  allegiance 972.7
  worship 1030.1
  PAY HOMAGE TO
  do honor 962.5
  worship 1030.10
homaloid 213.3
homalcidal 213.8
homard 306a.25
hombre 419.5
home
  nouns the grave 121.2
  fatherland 180.2
  abode 190.3
  habitat 190.4
  madhouse 472.14
  infirmary 687.29

asylum 698.4
AT HOME
  at one's home
  187.18
  at ease 885.12
AT HOME IN
  versed in 474.19
  used to 640.17
  skilled in 731.25
AT HOME WITH
  925.16
BE AT HOME TO 923.7
DOWN HOME 187.18
FROM HOME 186.10
MAKE ONESELF AT
  HOME 885.8
  verbs 187.8
HOME ON 345.17
  adjs. domestic 188.8
  residential 190.27
homebody 922.6
home-bred 188.7
home-brew 994.20
homecoming 299.3
homecroft
  abode 190.6
  farm 412.8
home economics
  management 745.6
  economics 849.4
homefelt 853.25
homefolks 11.6
home-grown 188.8
homeland 180.2
homeless alone 89.8
  unplaced 184.9
  destitute 836.9
  forlorn 922.13
homelessness
  destitution 836.2
  forlornness 922.4
homelike
  homish 190.28
  comfortable 885.11
homeliness
  informality 645.1
  comfortableness
  885.2
  vulgarity 896.5
  ugliness 897.1
  simpleness 900.1
  humbleness 904.1
home-loving 188.8
homely
  domestic 188.8
  homelike 190.28
  plain-speaking 589.3
  informal 645.3
  comfortable 885.11
  vulgar 896.14
  uncomely 897.6
  simple 900.6
  humble 904.9
  plebeian 917.11
homemade
  handmade 166.27
  domestic 188.8
homemaker 747.2
homemaking
  nouns domesticity
  188.3

husbandry 745.6
  adjs. 188.8
homeopath 686.7
homeopathic 686.18
homeopathy 686.2
homer 722.4
Homeric epical 606.16
  poetic 607.21
Homeric laughter
  874.4
home roof 190.3
home rule
  autonomy 739.4
  self-determination
  760.4
home run 722.4
homesick 632.23
homesickness 632.5
homespun
  homemade 166.27
  rough 260.6
  coarse 350.6
  cloth 377.9
  plain-speaking 589.3
  vulgar 896.14
  plain 900.6
homestall 190.3
homestead
  home 190.3,6
  farm 412.8
homesteader 189.9
homestretch 70.3
home towner 189.5
homeward
  toward 289.28
  arriving 299.10
homeward bound
  274.67
homeward-bound
  299.10
homework
  lesson 560.6
  task 654.2
homey
  homelike 190.28
  comfortable 885.11
homeyness 885.2
homicidal
  ~ maniac 408.10
  murderous 408.24
homicide
  killing 408.2,4
  murderer 408.10
homiletic(al) 560.18
homiletics 597.1
homily lesson 560.6
  discourse 604.1
homing pigeon
  carrier 270.5
  mail carrier 559.6
hominy 306a.34
homish 190.28
homo mankind 416.1
  person 416.3
  homosexual 418.12
  man 419.5
homocentric(al)
  225.15
homocycle 325.7
homocyclic 325.17

homogeneity
  uniformity 17.1
  similarity 20.1
  no mixture 45.1
homogeneous
  uniform 17.5
  similar 20.10
  simple 45.5
homogenesis 166.6
homogenetic 166.24
homogenize 17.4
homoiousia 20.1
homoiousian 20.10
homologate,
  homologize 26.11
homologous
  related 9.6
  correlative 13.12
homology 9.1
homonuclear 325.18
homonym 580.3
homoousia 14.1
homoousian 14.6
homophonic
  phonic 449.16
  unisonant 461.50
homophony
  phonics 449.7
  music 461.21
homo sapiens 416.1
homosexual
  nouns 418.11
  adjs. perverted 418.23
  mannish 419.13
  effeminate 420.15
homosexualist 418.11
homosexuality
  sex abnormality
  418.10
  mannishness 419.1
  effeminacy 420.2
homunculus 195.6
hone 257.10
HONE FOR 632.16
honest
  genuine 515.13
  honorable 972.14
honestly
  genuinely 515.17
  honorably 972.21
honest-to-god 515.13
honesty
  genuineness 515.5
  integrity 972.1
honey
  nouns sweet 306a.39
  nectar 430.4
  good thing 672.7
  endearment 930.5
  verbs sweeten 430.5
  flatter 968.6
honeybee 413a.4
honeycomb
  nouns pits 256.6
  porousness 264.8
  verbs permeate 185.7
  perforate 264.15
honeycombed
  pitted 256.17
  riddled 264.19
honeydew 430.4

honeyed sweet 430.6
flattering 968.9
honeyed words
endearments 930.4
suaveness 934.5
flattery 968.1
honeyfogle 968.7
honeymoon
nouns 931.4
verbs 931.17
honeymooner 931.6
honeymouthed,
honey-tongued
suave 934.18
flattering 968.9
honeysweet 430.6
honied 430.6
honing
nouns 632.5
adjs. 632.23
honk
nouns 452.4
verbs toot 452.8
quack 459.5
honky-tonk 994.25
Honor 915.2
honor
nouns properties
808.7
repute 912.3
token of esteem 914
title 915.1
respect 962.1
praise 966.5
integrity 972.1
chastity 986.1
DO HONOR TO 962.5
IN HONOR OF 875.6
PLEDGE ONE'S HONOR
768.4
UPON MY HONOR
521.10
WITH HONOR 914.12
verbs ~ a bill 839.18
celebrate 875.3
distinguish 912.12
do honor 914.8
respect 962.4
worship 1030.10
HONOR BEFORE
635.14
honorable
reputable 912.16
honorary 914.11
venerable 962.12
upright 972.13
honorable mention
citation 914.4
commendation
966.3
honorableness 972.1
honorably
reputably 912.21
uprightly 972.21
honorarium
gratuity 816.5
extra pay 839.6
honorary
~ member 786.11
honorific 914.11
honored famed 912.17

given honor 914.10
revered 962.11
honorific
nouns 915.1
adjs. honorary 914.11
titular 915.7
deferential 962.8
honors 484.3
DO THE HONORS
entertain 923.8
introduce 925.13
hoo 459.5
hooch 994.13,21
hood
nouns 941.4
verbs cover 227.23
coif 230.39
hooded 230.44
hooden 190.9
hoodlum 941.4
hoodoo
nouns evil genius
673.4
voodooism 1033.1
voodoo 1034.5
verbs jinx 727.12
bewitch 1034.10
adjs. 1033.14
hoodwink
blindfold 440.6
deceive 616.16
hoodwinked 440.9
hooey
nouns 545.3
interjs. 469.12
hoof
nouns 211.5
verbs 877.5
HOOF IT 272.26
hoofbeat 272.13
hoofed 413.41
hoofer
pedestrian 273.6
dancer 877.3
hoofing 877.1
hook
nouns angle 250.2
curve 251.2
point of land 255.8
anchor 276.16
blow 282.5
snare 616.11
lure 648.2
BY HOOK OR BY CROOK
655.13
GIVE THE HOOK
308.12
ON ONE'S OWN HOOK
voluntarily 620.11
independently
760.30
verbs fasten 47.8
angle 250.5
curve 251.6
strike 282.14
snare 616.20
wangle into 646.23
catch 820.14
steal 822.13
HOOK IT 300.14
HOOK UP 47.10

HOOK UP WITH 52.4
hookah 433.7
hooked angular 250.6
aquiline 251.8
hooker 276.3
hooking 47.3
hook-nosed 251.8
hooks 811.4
hook-shaped 251.8
hookup joining 47.1
combination 52.1
radio ~ 343.11
affiliation 784.3
hooky 186.4
PLAY HOOKY 186.8
hooligan 941.4
hoop
nouns band 252.3
whoop 458.1
verbs 458.6
hoopdedoodle 545.3
hoopie 271.9
hoopla to-do 62.4
ballyhoo 557.4
hoople 252.3
hooray
nouns 874.2
verbs 874.7
interjs. 874.12
hoosegow 759.8
hoosier
nouns 917.9
adjs. 181.6
hoosierdom 181.1
hoot
nouns small amount
35.2
yell 458.1
trifle 671.5
boo 965.3
NOT GIVE A HOOT
634.4
NOT GIVE A HOOT FOR
671.11
verbs yell 458.6
hoo 459.5
boo 965.10
hooter
small amount 35.2
alarm 702.3
hootmalalie 375.4
hootnanny 375.4
Hooverism 849.2
Hooverize 849.7
hop
nouns journey 272.5
stride 272.13
flight 277.7
jump 317.1
narcotic 685.10
dance 877.2
ON THE HOP
on the move 272.41
busy 705.20
verbs walk 272.27
fly 277.42
jump 317.5
dance 877.5
HOP IN
enter 301.7
board 313.12

HOP OFF 277.44
HOP ON IT 705.13
HOP TO IT
hurry 707.6
set to work 714.15
HOP UP 38.5
hope
nouns trust 500.1
expectation 537
desire 632.1
hopefulness 886
virtue 978.5
GIVE UP HOPE 887.10
HOLD OUT HOPE
promise 542.10
give hope 886.10
NO HOPE 887.1
PAST HOPE 887.15
WITHOUT HOPE
887.12
verbs expect 537.4
desire 632.14,16
be hopeful 886.7
HOPE FOR THE BEST
886.8
HOPE IN
trust in 500.12
hope 886.7
HOPE TO 651.5
hope deferred
disappointment
539.1
hopelessness 887.5
hoped for 537.11
hoped-for 632.30
hopeful
nouns 125.1
adjs. probable 510.5
expectant 537.9
propitious 542.16
hoping 886.11
hopefully
expectantly 537.13
hopingly 886.14
hopefulness 886.1
hopeless futile 667.13
despondent 870.22
disconsolate 870.29
without hope
887.12
hopelessness
no chance 155.10
impossibility 509
inexpectation 538
futility 667.2
no hope 887
hoper 886.6
hoping 886.11
hopoff aviation 277.6
departure 300.3
hop-o'-my-thumb
195.6
hopped up
excited 855.21
drunk 994.40
ALL HOPPED UP 860.6
ALL HOPPED UP
ABOUT 633.11
hopper jumper 317.4
grasshopper 413a.5
hoppergrass 413a.5

hot-tempered
  949.25
angry 950.27
ALL HOT AND
  BOTHERED
bewildered 513.22
confused 530.12
anxious 888.6
HOT FOR 633.11
HOT OFF THE FIRE
  122.10
hot air heat 327.8
hot wind 402.7
nonsense 545.4
chatter 594.3
bombast 599.2
brag 908.2
hot-air artist
chatterer 594.5
braggart 908.5
hotbed source 152.8
productiveness
  164.6
nursery 412.11
hot blood lust 418.4
hot temper 949.3
IN HOT BLOOD 950.30
hot-blooded
warm-blooded
  327.29
lustful 418.20
thoroughbred
  916.12
hotbox 320.6
hotchpot, hotchpotch
  44.6
hot dog
nouns 306a.21.31
interjs. 863.17
hotel mansion 190.7
inn 190.13
hôtel des invalides
  687.29
hôtelier 807.2
hotelkeeper 807.2
hotfoot
verbs 268.11
advs. 707.12
hothead
violent person 161.9
sorehead 949.11
hotheaded
violent 161.21
excitable 855.30
impetuous 892.8
hot-tempered
  949.25
hothouse 412.11
hot iron 328.14
hot jazz 461.9
hotly 855.35
hotness heat 327.1
pepperiness 432.2
hot-press 259.6
hot seat
electrocution1008.7
electric chair 1009.5
hot-short 359.5
hot-shot 268.6
hot springs
hot water 327.9

spa 687.31
hotspur
violent person 161.9
daredevil 892.4
sorehead 949.11
hot-tempered 949.25
hot tip 555.2
hot war 795.1
hot water heat 327.9
predicament 729.4
IN HOT WATER 729.20
hot wave 327.6
Houdini 1033.6
hough 690.15
hound
nouns dog 413.27
devotee 633.6
scoundrel 984.6
verbs follow 292.3
hunt 653.9
HOUND ON 646.16
hound-dog 413.27
hounding 292.1
hour
period of time 107.1
period 107.2
the time 114.2
HOUR AFTER HOUR
long 110.14
constantly 135.7
HOUR BY HOUR
  137.11
IDLE HOURS
inactivity 706.2
leisure 708.1
ONE'S HOUR IS COME
  407.31
houri 898.9
hourly
adjs. 137.9
advs. 135.7
House, the 740.4
house
nouns race 11.4
family 11.6
lineage 169.4
dwelling 190.5
astrology 374.20
audience 447.6
theater 609.17,19
workplace 717.1
firm 786.9
market 830.1
HOUSE BUILT ON
  SAND 159.7
HOUSE DIVIDED
  AGAINST ITSELF
  793.4
LIKE A HOUSE AFIRE
  268.22
ON THE HOUSE 848.5
verbs reside 187.8
domicile 187.11
shelter 697.17
HOUSE IN 235.5
housebreak
domesticate 188.5
train 560.13
subdue 762.10
housebreaker 823.3
housebreaking

domestication 188.4
training 560.3
burglary 822.3
housebroken 188.9
housebug 413a.7
housed 187.15
house dick 779.10
house dog dog 413.24
watchdog 697.10
household
nouns family 11.6
home 190.3
adjs. common 84.8
domestic 188.8
home 190.27
well-known 474.27
plain 900.6
householder 189.7
householding 188.3
householdry 188.3
household troops
  798.32
household words
  589.1
housekeeper 747.2
housekeeping
nouns domesticity
  188.3
husbandry 745.6
adjs. 188.8
houseless 184.9
housemaid 748.8
housemistress 747.2
house of cards 159.7
House of Commons
  740.4
house of correction,
  house of detention
  759.9
house of God 1040.1
House of Lords 740.3
house of prostitution
  987.9
House of Representa-
  tives 740.4
house organ 603.11
house-raising 920.10
houseroom 187.3
housetop 227.6
house trailer 271.17
housewares 829.5
housewarming 920.10
housewife 747.2
housewifery
domesticity 188.3
husbandry 745.6
housing
domiciliation 187.3
lodging 190.2
covering 227.2
horsecloth 227.12
hanger 277.21
radio ~ 343.3
Houyhnhnm 413.21
hovel
nouns 190.10
verbs 187.11
hover
be imminent 151.2
drift 277.42
soar 313.10

float 352.9
be irresolute 625.7
HOVER OVER 199.12
how why 154.7;
  484.44
in what manner
  655.11
HOW ARE YOU!
  923.15
HOW GOES IT? 923.16
HOW IT GOES 7.2
THE HOW 655.1
howbeit 33.8
how-do-you-do
predicament 729.4
greeting 923.4
howe'er
whatsoever 29.9
nevertheless 33.8
however
advs. whatsoever 29.9
nevertheless 33.8
anyhow 655.12
conjs. 506.16
howl
nouns yell 458.1
objection 520a.2
success 722.3
plaint 873.3,4
verbs blow 402.24
yell 458.6
yowl 459.2
object 520a.5
wail 873.11,13
howler blunder 517.5
falsehood 614.12
howling
nouns 343.24
adjs. great 34.13
ululant 459.6
howsoever,
  howsomever 29.9
hoyden
nouns girl 125.6
tomboy 419.9
adjs. 419.13
huaca 1012.10
hub center 225.2
axle 320.5
hob 328.11
hubble 320.5
hubbub
commotion 62.4
turbulence 161.2
agitation 323.1
uproar 452.3
outcry 458.4
bustle 705.4
huckster
nouns advertiser
  557.9
vendor 828.6
verbs haggle 825.14
peddle 827.9
huckstering 827.2
huddle
nouns jumble 62.3
conference 595.6
GO INTO A HUDDLE
assemble 74.15
confer 595.10

IN A HUDDLE 753.7
verbs confuse 63.3
  assemble 74.15
  stay near 199.12
Hudibrastic 607.21
hue
  nouns 361.1
  verbs 361.13
hue and cry
  outcry 458.4
  search 484.2
  publicity 557.4
  chase 653.2
  alarm 702.2
hued 361.17
hueless 362.7
huff
  nouns 950.7
  IN A HUFF 950.28
  verbs expand 196.4
  puff 402.23,25
  bully 889.19
  anger 950.22
huff and puff 714.11
huff-duff 345.4
huffily 949.27
huffiness 949.2
huffy 949.19
huftymagufty 545.3
hug
  nouns clasp 811.2
  welcome 923.2
  greeting 923.4
  embrace 930.2
  verbs adhere 50.5
  stay near 199.12
  hold 811.6,7
  seize 820.12
  welcome 923.9
  embrace 930.16
  HUG ONESELF
  rejoice 874.6
  pride oneself 903.5
  boast 508.7
  HUG THE SHORE
  stay near 199.12
  sail 274.41
huge great 34.11
  mammoth 194.20
hugeness 194.7
hugeous 194.20
huggermugger
  verbs 612.9
  adjs. confused 62.15
  clandestine 612.14
  advs. in disorder
    62.16
  secretly 612.20
huggermuggery 612.1
hugging 630.1
huitre 306a.25
hula girl 877.3
hulk big thing 194.11
  ship 276.3
  body 375.3
  clumsy fellow
    732.9
ulkiness
  bulkiness 194.9
  unwieldiness 729.8
  clumsiness 732.3

hulking bulky 194.19
  clumsy 732.20
hulky bulky 194.19
  unwieldy 729.18
  clumsy 732.20
hull
  nouns saddle 215.19
  cover 227.17
  pod 410.28
  verbs husk 231.9
  shoot 284.13
hullabaloo
  uproar 452.3
  outcry 458.4
hum
  nouns radio ~ 343.24
  singing 461.12
  verbs drone 451.13
  sing 461.39
  deceive 616.13
  be active 705.12
  HUM AND HAW
  stammer 593.7
  vacillate 625.8
human
  nouns 416.3
  adjs. mortal 416.10
  kind 936.14
  merciful 942.7
human dynamo
  energizer 160.5
  hustler 705.8
humane kind 936.14
  merciful 942.7
human equation 416.6
humanism
  anthropology 416.8
  humanities 560.7
humanist 499.10
humanistic
  human 416.10
  philosophical 499.10
humanitarian
  nouns 936.8
  adjs. 936.16
humanitarianism
    936.4
humanities 560.7
humanity
  mankind 416.1
  humanness 416.6
  mercy 942.1
humanization 416.7
humanize 416.9
humankind 416.1
humanly
  as a human 416.14
  kindly 936.19
human nature 416.6
humanness 416.6
humanoid 416.11
human race 416.1
human wreck 984.2
humble
  verbs conquer 725.10
  subdue 762.9
  humiliate 904.4
  HUMBLE ONESELF
  confess 554.7
  repent 871.7

demean oneself
    904.6
  HUMBLE ONESELF
  BEFORE 1030.10
  adjs. inferior 37.6
  contrite 871.9
  lowly 904.9
  modest 906.9
  plebeian 917.11
humbled
  conquered 725.16
  subdued 762.14
  humiliated 904.11
humblehearted 904.10
humble-looking 904.9
humbleness
  humility 904.1
  modesty 906
humble-spirited
    904.10
humble-visaged 904.9
humbling 762.4
humbly
  contritely 871.12
  meekly 904.14
  modestly 906.14
humbug
  nouns nonsense
    545.2
  quackery 614.7
  fake 614.14
  hoax 616.7
  impostor 617.6
  verbs 616.13
  interjs. 469.12
humbugability 501.2
humbugable 501.8
humbugger 617.1
humbuggery
  quackery 614.7
  falseness 614.14
humdinger
  good thing 672.7
  hustler 705.8
humdrum
  nouns
  repetitiousness
    103.4
  tedium 882.1
  bore 882.4
  adjs. samely 17.6
  repetitious 103.15
  tedious 882.8
humdrumness 882.2
Humean
  philosophical 499.11
  skeptical 1029.20
humid sultry 327.28
  moist 391.15
humidification 391.2
humidify 391.12
humidity
  sultriness 327.5
  variable 348.9
  dampness 391.2
humidor
  humidity 391.10
  tobacco jar 433.3
humify 391.12
humiliate
  humble 904.4

affront 963.4
humiliated 904.12
humiliating
  mortifying 904.13
  disgraceful 913.11
humiliation
  subdual 762.4
  mortification 904.2
  disgrace 913.5
humility
  humbleness 904
  modesty 906
Humism 1029.6
Humist 1029.12
hummer speeder 268.6
  good thing 672.7
  hustler 705.8
humming
  nouns hum 451.7
  singing 461.12
  adjs. 451.20
hummock 206.5
humor
  nouns nature 5.3
  fluid 387.3
  blood 387.4
  mood 523.4
  caprice 627.1
  cheerfulness 868.2
  wit 879.1
  IN BAD HUMOR
  unhappy 870.21
  ill-humored 949.17
  IN THE HUMOR
  disposed 523.8
  willing 620.5
  OUT OF HUMOR
  unhappy 870.21
  ill-humored 949.17
  angry 950.26
  verbs 757.7
humoring 757.4
humorist
  comedian 609.38,39
  wit 879.12
humorous funny 878.5
  witty 879.15
  THE HUMOROUS 878.3
humorously
  amusingly 878.7
  wittily 879.18
humorsome 627.6
hump
  nouns mountain
    206.7
  protuberance 255.3
  verbs arch 251.6
  carry 270.11
  hurry 707.6
  HUMP IT
  hurry 707.6
  try hard 712.10
humpback 248.3
humpbacked 248.13
humped
  humpbacked 248.13
  bowed 251.10
humpty-dumpty
    194.12
humpy 251.10
Hun vandal 691.8

soldier 798.8

hunch
nouns piece 55.3
lump 194.10
hump 255.3
intuition 480.3
verbs hump 251.6
crouch 316.8
hunchback 248.3
hunchbacked 248.13
hunched 251.10
hundi 833.11
hundred number 99.8
district 179.5
A HUNDRED TO ONE
510.7
hundredfold 99.29
hundred-percenter
939.3
hundredth 99.29
hundred-to-one shot
small chance 155.9
long odds 514.5
hundred-weight 99.8
hung 214.9
hunger
nouns 632.6,7
verbs 632.19
hungering 632.25,26
hungrily 632.32
hungry 632.25,26
GO HUNGRY 993.4
hunk
large amount 34.4
piece 55.3
lump 194.10
Hunker 140.4
Hunkerism 140.3
hunkers, hunkies
240.4
GET DOWN ON ONE'S
HUNKERS 316.9
hunks 850.6
hunky 30.8
hunkydory 672.14
hunt
nouns search 484.2
chase 653.2
verbs seek 484.24,25
go hunting 653.9
HUNT DOWN
find 487.4
persecute 665.6
HUNT IN COUPLES
flock together 73.7
associate with
920.15
HUNT OUT
drive out 308.13
seek 484.28
hunted, the 653.7
hunter horse 413.18
dog 413.27
seeker 484.18
huntsman 653.5
hunting
automation 348.21
search 484.2
pursuit 653.2
huntsman 653.5

hurdle
nouns jump 317.1
obstacle 728.4
THE HURDLES 317.3
verbs 317.5
hurdler 317.4
hurdle race
jumping 317.3
race 794.12
hurdling 317.3
hurdy-gurdist 463.9
hurdy-gurdy 464.16
hurl
nouns 284.4
verbs put 183.13
throw 284.12
HURL AT 796.30
HURL FORTH 161.12
hurler 284.8
hurling 284.3
Hurlothrumbo 889.8
hurly-burly
agitation 323.1
excitement 855.3
hurrah
nouns 874.2
verbs 874.7
interjs. huzza! 874.12
hallelujah 1030.16
hurray
nouns 874.2
verbs 874.7
interjs. 874.12
hurricane 402.13
hurried
impulsive 628.9
hasty 707.9
rushed 707.11
reckless 892.8
hurriedly
impulsively 628.13
hastily 707.12
recklessly 892.11
hurry
nouns speed 268.1
haste 707.1
excitement 855.3
BE IN NO HURRY
708.3
IN A HURRY 707.14
verbs speed 268.10
~ away 300.12
hasten 707.4,5
HURRY ABOUT 705.11
HURRY ON
urge on 646.16
hasten 707.4,5
HURRY UP
accelerate 268.15
hasten 707.4,5
hurrying 707.3
hurry-scurry
nouns 855.3
advs. hastily 707.12
recklessly 892.11
hurst 410.12
hurt
nouns pain 423.1
disadvantage 669.2
harm 673.3
impairment 690.1,7

mental pain 864.5
verbs collide 282.13
pain 423.7,8
harm 673.6
impair 690.10,13
grieve 864.14
be distressed 864.22
offend 950.20
HURT FOR 632.16
HURT TO 632.15
adjs. ~ physically
423.9
impaired 690.27
grieved 864.26
hurtful painful 423.10
detrimental 673.12
hurtfulness 673.5
hurting
nouns pain 423.1
damage 690.1
adjs. in pain 423.9
painful 423.10
HURTING TO 632.22
hurtle jostle 282.12
collide 282.13
hurtless 672.22
hurtlessness 672.10
husband
nouns director 746.1
spouse 931.8
verbs be saving
658.12
economize 849.7
HUSBAND ONE'S
RESOURCES
be saving 658.12
prepare for 718.11
economize 849.7
husbandless 932.7
husbandly
adjs. 931.19
advs. 849.11
husbandman 412.5
husbandry
agriculture 412.1
management 745.6
economy 849.1
hush
nouns 450.1
HUSH OF NIGHT
midnight 134.6
silence 450.1
verbs calm 162.7
silence 450.7,8
keep secret 612.9
interjs. 450.16
hushcloth 450.4
hushed
subdued 162.11
quiescent 267.10
silent 450.11
hush-hush
verbs silence 450.8
keep secret 612.9
adjs. 612.12
hushing
nouns 162.2
adjs. 162.15
hush money
bribe 649.2
payment 839.5

hush-up 612.3
husk
nouns 227.17
verbs 231.9
huskiness
strength 158.1
hoarseness 457.2
husking 920.12
husky
nouns sledge dog
270.6
dog 413.24
adjs. strong 158.13
dry 392.7
hoarse 457.14
hussar 798.12
hussy
saucy girl 911.5
strumpet 987.14
hustings
platform 215.13
court 999.3
hustle
nouns jostle 282.2
activity 705.7
haste 707.1
verbs confuse 63.3
escort 73.8
jostle 282.12;
323.11
be active 705.12
hurry 707.4,5
work hard 714.13
court 930.19
hustler speeder 268.6
man of action 705.8
hustling 705.22
hut 190.9
hutch
nouns 190.9
verbs 658.10
huzoor 915.3
huzza
nouns 874.2
verbs 874.7
interjs. 874.12
H-war 795.4
Hyades, Hyads
1012.16
hyalescence 338.1
hyalescent 338.5
hyaline
nouns sky 374.2
ocean 396.1
adjs. 338.5
hyalinocrystalline
338.5
hybrid
nouns crossbreed
44.8
word 580.9
adjs. 44.16
hybridism
crossbreeding 44.4
word 580.9
hybridize 44.14
Hydra monster 85.20
productiveness
164.6
hydracid 378.1
Hydra-headed 168.15

hydrant 395.12
hydrargyrum 268.7
hydrate 378.6
hydration 378.5
hydraulic
~ power 156.4
aquatic 391.16
hydraulics 346.4
hydrodynamic 346.14
hydrodynamics 346.4
hydrodynamometer
394.15
hydroelectric 341.27
hydroelectricity
341.17
hydroelectric power
power 156.4
electricity 341.17
hydrogenate 378.6
hydrogenation 378.5
hydrogen blast 325.15
hydrogen bomb
799.15
hydroglider 276.10
hydrographer 396.6
hydrographic(al)
396.7
hydrography
hydraulics 346.4
ocean 396.5
hydrokinetics 346.4
hydrol 391.3
hydrologic(al) 346.14
hydrology 346.4
hydrolysis 53.2
hydrolyst 53.2
hydrolyte 53.2
hydrolytic
disintegrative 53.6
electrolytic 341.29
hydrolyze 53.4
hydromatic 347.6
hydromechanic(al)
346.14
hydromechanics 346.4
hydrometallurgy
382.10
hydrometer
densimeter 353.8
fluids 387.5
hydrometric(al)
346.14
hydrometeograph
394.16
hydrometry 346.4
hydropathic 686.18
hydropathist 686.7
hydropathy 687.4
hydrophobia 472.7
hydrophyte 410.3
hydropic(al) 684.46
hydroplane
nouns boat 276.10
airplane 279.8
verbs 277.42
hydroponics 411.1
hydropot 990.4
hydrosphere
waters 391.3
atmosphere 401.2
hydrostatic 346.14

hydrostatics
aviation 277.2
hydraulics 346.4
hydrotherapy 687.4
hydrous 391.16
hydroxylate 378.6
hydroxylation 378.5
Hydrozoa, hydrozoans
414.4
hyena animal 413.49
savage 941.6
scoundrel 984.6
hyetograph 393.7
hyetography,
hyetology 393.8
Hygeia 683.1
hygieist, hygeist 681.3
hygiene 681.2
hygienic
sanitary 679.25
healthful 681.5
hygienics 681.2
hygienist 681.3
hygienization 679.3
hygienize 679.22
hygiologist 681.3
hygiology 681.2
hygric 391.19
hygrodeik, hygrograph
391.10
hygrology 391.9
hygrometer
humidity 391.10
weather gauge 401.8
hygrometric 391.19
hygrometry 391.9
hygrophanous, hy-
grophilous 391.19
hygroscope 391.10
hygroscopic 391.19
hygrostat 391.10
hygrostatics 391.9
hygrothermal 391.19
hygrothermograph
391.10
hyle 375.2
hylic 375.9
hylicism, hylism 375.5
hylicist 375.6
hylotheism
materialism 375.5
religion 1018.5
hylotheist
materialist 375.6
religionist 1018.14
hylotheistic 375.11
hylozoism 376.3
hylozoist 376.4
hylozoistic 376.8
Hymen
marriage 931.14
god 1012.5
hymen 931.4
hymeneal
nouns song 461.13
wedding 931.4
adjs. 931.19
Hymir 194.13
hymn
nouns music 461.16

paean 1030.3
verbs 1030.11
hymnal
nouns 461.28
adjs. 461.51
hymnbook 461.28
hymner 463.13
hymnist 463.22
hymnody 461.16
hymnologist 463.22
hymnology 461.16
hyp
nouns psychosis
472.6
hypochondria 870.4
verbs 870.18
hypallage 219.3
hyperacid 431.7
hyperacidity 431.2
hyperbatic 219.7
hyperbaton 219.3
hyperbola 251.2
hyperbole figure of
speech 549.2
exaggeration 615.1
hyperbolic
exaggerated 615.4
exaggerating 615.5
hyperbolism 615.1
hyperbolize 615.3
hyperborean
northern 289.15
frigid 332.15
hypercathexis 688.44
hypercritical
overparticular
894.12
overcritical 967.24
hypercriticism
overparticularity
894.4
criticism 967.4
hyperdermatomy
687.25
hyperdulia 1030.1
Hyperion sun 374.11
beauty 898.9
god 1012.5
hypernormal 85.14
hyperorthodox
dogmatic 512.22
bigoted 525.10
puritanical 1022.9
hyperorthodoxy
dogmatism 512.6
bigotry 525
religion 1022.6
hyperphysical 85.14
hyperphysics
physics 324.1
metaphysics 1032.3
hypersensitive 421.13
hypersensitivity 421.3
hypersonic
fast 268.20
sonic 449.17
hypersonic speed
speed 268.3
aviation 277.37
hypertension 684.8
hypertensive 684.46

hypertrophy 661.7
hyphen 48.1
hyphenate 189.4
hypnoanalysis 688.5
hypnoidal 710.22
hypnology 710.8
Hypnos 710.11
hypnosis
psychotherapy 688.5
hypnotic sleep 710.7
hypnotherapist 688.13
hypnotic
nouns sedative
685.11
types of ~ 685.48
sleep-inducer 710.10
adjs. sedative 685.39
mesmeric 710.22
hypnotism
psychotherapy 688.5
mesmerism 710.8
hypnotist 710.9
hypnotization 710.8
hypnotize
fascinate 648.6
mesmerize 710.18
spellbind 1034.8
hypnotized 1034.13
hypnotizer 710.9
hypo psychotic 472.16
photography 575.15
hypochondriac
688.14
hypochondria
psychosis 472.6
neurosis 688.22,33
dejection 870.4
hypochondriac
nouns psychotic
472.16
neurotic 688.14
adjs. insane 472.26
neurotic 688.48
dejected 870.24
hypochondriasis
688.33
hypochondriast
688.14
hypochondry
neurosis 688.33
dejection 870.4
hypocrisy
falseness 614.6
sanctimony 1027
hypocrite fake 617.8
religious ~ 1027.3
hypocritic(al) 614.33
hypoderma, hypo-
dermis 228.4
hypodermal 228.6
hypodermic
nouns 687.20
adjs. 228.6
hypomania 472.3
hypostasis essence 5.2
foundation 215.6
matter 375.2
hypotenuse 241.1
hypothec, hypothe-
cation 770.5
hypothecate 770.12

idiosyncratic
  characteristic 80.13
  eccentric 473.4
idiot 470.8
idiotic feeble-minded
    468.22
  foolish 469.8
  crazy 472.24
idioticon 603.7
idiotism 583.1
idle
  verbs be inert 267.8
  loaf 706.10
  IDLE AWAY 852.5
  adjs. unwarranted
    482.12
  vain 667.13
  trivial 671.16
  inactive 706.16
  leisure 708.5
  LIE IDLE 706.14
  NEVER IDLE 705.21
idlehood 706.2
idleness
  triviality 671.3
  inactivity 706.2
idler hobo 273.3
  loafer 706.7
idle talk gossip 556.7
  chatter 594.3
idling 705.3
idol
  nouns desired one
    632.11
  darling 929.13
  god 1012.2
  fetish 1031.3
  verbs 1031.5
idolater, idolatress
    1031.4
idolatrize 1031.5
idolatrizer 1031.4
idolatrous 1031.7
idolatry love 929.1
  idol worship 1031
idolify 1031.5
idolism love 929.1
  idolatry 1031.1
idolist 1031.4
idolistic 1031.7
idolization love 929.1
  veneration 962.1
  idolatry 1031.2
idolize adore 929.18
  esteem 962.4
  idolatrize 1031.5
idolizer 1031.4
idoloclast
  destroyer 691.8
  iconoclast 1029.10
idolodulia,
    idolomancy 1031.1
idolthyte
  nouns 1030.7
  adjs. 1031.7
idolum
  illusion 518.4
  phantom 1015.1
idol worship 1031.1
idol worshiper 1031.4

idol-worshiping
    1031.7
Idun See Ithunn
idyl, idyll 607.4
idyllic 607.21
idyllist 607.15
if 506.14
  IF EVER 105.12
  IF NEED BE, IF
    NECESSARY 637.17
  IF NOT 506.16
  IF ONLY 506.14
  IF POSSIBLE 508.11
  IF YOU PLEASE
    submission 763.20
    obediently 764.6
    please 772.20
    by your leave 775.21
  NO IFS, ANDS OR BUTS
    no qualifications
      507.1
    certainly 512.23
iffy provisory 506.8
  doubtful 513.15
igloo 190.9
ignatz 476.9
igneous 327.26
igneous rock 383.1
ignis fatuus
  luminescence
    334.13
  illusion 518.1
ignite set fire 328.21
  become angry
    950.18
ignited 327.27
igniter 330.4
ignition fire 327.12
  lighting 328.4
ignobile vulgus 917.3
ignobility
  vulgarity 896.5
  infamy 913.4
ignoble menial 748.16
  vulgar 896.15
  disreputable 913.10
  plebeian 917.11
ignominious 913.10
ignominy
  infamy 913.4
  abomination 957.2
ignoramus
  dunce, fool 470
  know-nothing 476.9
ignorance
  unintelligence 468
  unknowingness 476
  inexperience 732.2
  KEEP IN IGNORANCE
    612.8
  PLEAD IGNORANCE
    1004.11
ignorant
  nouns 476.9
  adjs. unintelligent
    468.13
  unknowing 476.13
  inexperienced
    732.17
ignorantism,
  ignorantness 476.1

ignore
  be incredulous 503.3
  be open-minded
    524.7
  disregard 529.3
  neglect 532.6
  disobey 765.6
  condone 945.4
  snub 964.6
  IGNORE IT 671.22
ignored 532.14
ignorer 532.5
ileac 224.12
ileum 224.6
ilk 61.3
  OF THAT ILK 9.6
ill
  nouns 673.3
  TAKE ILL 950.13
  adjs. inauspicious
    542.15
  bad 673.7
  sick 684.41
  unkind 937.14
  GO ILL WITH 727.8
  ILL AT EASE 864.25
  adys. inauspiciously
    542.18
  inconveniently
    669.9
  badly 673.13
  unkindly 937.25
ill-adapted 27.8
ill-advised
  unwise 469.9
  impulsive 628.11
ill-affected
  malevolent 937.17
  ill-humored 949.18
ill-assorted 27.8
illation 493.4
illative 504.18
illaudable 967.25
ill-balanced 31.5
ill-conditioned
  discourteous 935.5
  malevolent 937.17
  ill-humored 949.18
ill-conducted 732.21
ill-considered
  unwise 469.9
  impulsive 628.11
ill-contrived
  unwise 469.9
  ill-managed 732.21
ill-defined
  indistinct 444.5
  vague 513.17
ill-devised
  unwise 469.9
  impulsive 628.11
  ill-managed 732.21
ill-digested 719.11
ill-disposed
  malevolent 937.17
  ill-humored 949.18
ill-dispositedness 937.4
illegal 997.6
illegality
  illicit business 824
  unlawfulness 997

offense 997.4
illegally 997.8
illegibility 547.4
illegible 547.17
illegibly 547.19
illegitimacy 997.2
illegitimate
  nouns 170.5
  adjs. spurious 614.27
  illegal 997.6,7
illegitimate child
    170.5
illegitimately 997.8
illegitimation 997.2
ill-fated 542.15
ill-fatedness 542.6
ill-favor 913.1
ill-favored 897.7
ill feeling 927.4
ill-fitted 27.8
ill-flavored 428.5
ill-founded 482.12
ill-furnished 660.10
ill-got, ill-gotten
    973.15
ill health 684.2
ill-humor
  discontent 867
  bad temper 949
  anger 950.5
ill-humored 949.18
illiberal
  nouns 525.5
  adjs. narrow-minded
    525.10
  stingy 850.11
  selfish 976.6
illiberality
  narrow-mindedness
    525.1
  stinginess 850.3
  selfishness 976.2
illicit
  adulterous 987.27
  illegal 997.6
illicitly 997.8
ill-imagined 469.9
illimitability 104.1
illimitable
  infinite 104.3
  unrestricted 760.24
ill-intentioned 937.17
illiteracy 476.5
illiterate
  nouns 476.9
  adjs. 476.15
illiterateness 476.5
illiterati 476.9
ill-judged 469.9
ill-lighted, ill-lit
    336.15
ill-looking 897.7
ill luck 727.5
ill-made
  deformed 248.12
  unshapely 897.8
ill-managed 732.21
ill-mannered 935.5
ill manners 935.1
ill-marked 444.5

clean·y 679.27
immanence 5.1
immanent 5.6
Immanuel 1011.12
immaterial
  supernatural 85.14
  incorporeal 376.7
  unimportant 671.15
immaterialism
  immateriality 376.3
  philosophy 499.3
immaterialist
  idealist 376.4
  spiritualist 1032.13,
  14
immateriality
  intangible 4.3
  supernaturalism
  85.7
  incorporeity 376.1,2
  illusion 518.2
  unimportance 671.1
  phantom 1015.1
immaterialization
  1032.21
immaterialize
  dematerialize 376.6
  spiritualize 1032.22
immaterially 671.20
immature
  unadult 124.10
  half-learned 476.16
  undeveloped 719.11
immaturity
  youth 124.3
  undevelopment
  719.4
immeasurability 104.1
immeasurable 104.3
immeasurably
  extremely 34.22
  infinitely 104.4
immediacy
  instantaneousness
  113.1
  punctuality 131.3
  closeness 199.1
immediate
  adjs. continuous 71.9
  instantaneous 113.4
  present 120.2
  prompt 131.9
  imminent 151.3
  adjoining 199.16
  nearest 199.19
  direct 289.13
  interjs. 707.16
immediately
  instantly 113.6
  promp-ly 131.15
immedicable 887.15
immelodious 460.4
immemorial
  old 123.10
  traditional 123.12
immense great 34.11
  infinite 104.3
  mammoth 194.20
  superb 672.18
immensely
  vastly 34.18

infinitely 104.4
  superbly 672.24
immensity
  greatness 34.1
  infinity 104.1
  hugeness 194.7
immerge 318.7
immergence 318.2
immerse
  submerge 318.7
  engross 528.13
  baptize 1038.19
immersed 208.12
  IMMERSED IN
  involved 175.4
  engrossed 528.17
immersible 318.9
immersion
  submergence 318.2
  engrossment 528.3
  baptism 1038.7
immethodical See
  unmethodical
immigrant
  migrant 273.5
  incomer 301.4
immigrate
  migrate 272.21
  enter 301.12
immigration
  migration 272.4
  entrance 301.3
imminence,
  imminency 151.1
imminent 151.3
immingle 44.11
immiscibility 51.1
immiscible 51.4
immission 305.2
immit 305.10
immix 44.11
immixture
  mixture 44.1
  compound 44.5
immobile
  immovable 142.16
  motionless 267.11
immobility
  stability 142.3
  motionlessness 267.2
  inflexibility 355.3
immobilization 142.3
immobilize 142.8
immoderacy
  excess 661.1
  intemperance 991.1
immoderate
  excessive 661.17
  exorbitant 846.12
  intemperate 991.7
immoderately
  excessively 661.23
  exorbitantly 846.16
  intemperately
  991.10
immodest 988.6
immodesty 988.2
immolate before
  1030.14
immolation 1030.7
immoral 979.15

immorality 979.2
immortal
  nouns celebrity 912.9
  god 1012.2
  adjs. 112.9
immortality
  deathlessness 112.3
  fame 912.7
immortalization
  perpetuation 112.4
  glorification 912.8
immortalize
  perpetuate 112.5
  glorify 912.13
immotile 142.16
immotive
  immovable 142.16
  unmoving 267.11
immovability
  stability 142.3
  obstinacy 624.2
  unfeeling 854.1
immovable
  stable 142.16
  inflexible 355.12
  obstinate 624.9
  unfeeling 854.9
immundity 680.1
immune
  verbs 687.37
  adjs. 760.27
immunity
  ~ from disease
  687.19
  exemption 760.7
  privilege 956.4
  impunity 1005.1
immunize 687.37
immunologist 686.7
immunology,
  immunotherapy
  687.19
immunotoxin 685.22
immuration 759.3
immure confine 235.6
  imprison 759.15
immured
  enclosed 235.10
  imprisoned 759.20
immurement
  enclosure 235.1
  imprisonment 759.3
immutability
  unchangeability
  142.4
  inflexibility 355.3
  obstinacy 624.2
  divine attribute
  1011.15
immutable
  unchangeable
  142.18
  inflexible 355.12
  obstinate 624.9
imp brat 125.4
  mischief maker
  736.3
  pixy 1014.8
impact
  nouns effect 153.3
  rocket ~ 280.10

collision 282.3
  meaning 543.1
MAKE AN IMPACT
  UPON 853.16
  verbs 142.10
impacted 142.17
impair
  break 49.11,12
  damage 690.10
impaired broken 49.23
  imperfect 676.4
  damaged 690.27
impairment 690
impale pierce 264.15
  stab 796.27
  torture 1008.18
impalement
  perforation 264.3
  stabbing 796.11
  punishment 1008.2
impalpability
  intangibility 4.1
  infinitesimalness
  195.2
  imponderability
  352.1
  immateriality 376.1
  unintelligibility
  547.1
impalpable
  nouns intangible 4.3
  imponderable 352.2
  adjs. intangible 4.4
  infinitesimal 195.13
  imponderable
  352.10
  fine 360.11
  immaterial 376.7
  unintelligible 547.11
impanation 1038.8
impanel list 88.7
  enroll 568.15
  ~ a jury 1002.15
impanelment
  enrollment 568.14
  ~ of jurors 1002.4
imparadise 863.8
imparadised 863.14
impart
  communicate 270.9
  convey 552.7
  inform 555.7
  say 592.14
  give 816.12
impartation
  communication
  552.2
  giving 816.1
impartial
  unprejudiced 524.12
  neutral 804.7
  just 974.10
impartiality
  unprejudice 524.5
  neutrality 804.1
  justice 974.4
impartially 974.11
impartibility
  communicability
  270.4
  solidity 353.2

conveyability
552.5
contagiousness
684.3
impartible
inseparable 47.15
communicable
270.17
solid 353.13
transferable 552.10
contagious 684.47
giveable 816.22
impartment
communication
552.2
giving 816.1
impassability
imperviousness
265.2
inaccessibility 509.3
impassable
impervious 265.13
inaccessible 509.8
impasse 729.5
AT AN IMPASSE 729.22
impassibility 854.1
impassible 854.9
impassion 855.11
impassionable 853.19
impassioned
vehement 598.13
zealous 633.10
passionate 853.22
excited 855.21
amorous 929.23
impassive
unfeeling 854.9
inexcitable 856.10
impassively 854.15
impatience
impetuousness 628.2
eagerness 633.1
impatientness 860
impatient
impetuous 628.9
eager 633.9
restive 860.6
BE IMPATIENT 860.4
impatiently
eagerly 633.13
restively 860.8
impatientness 860.1
impeach
arraign 1002.14
accuse 1003.7
impeachability 981.1
impeachable 967.26
impeacher 1003.5
impeachment
arraignment 1002.3
accusation 1003.1
impeccability
perfection 675.1
innocence 982.1
impeccable
faultless 675.6
innocent 982.7
impeccably 675.10
impecuniosity,
impecuniousness
836.1

impecunious 836.7
impedance
electric ~ 341.12
~ matching 348.7
impede delay 132.7
retard 269.9
hinder 728.10,11
restrict 758.9
impeded
retarded 269.12
restricted 758.15
impeder 728.8
impediment
obstruction 265.3
speech ~ 593.1,6
hindrance 728.1,6
impedimenta
equipment 657.4
impediments 728.6
belongings 808.3
impedimental,
impedimentary,
impeding 728.18
impel actuate 266.5
drive 282.11
propel 284.10
obsess 472.23
prompt 646.12
compel 754.4
impelled 646.30
impellent 282.22
impeller 646.10
impelling
obsessing 472.33
motivating 646.25
impelling force 282.1
impend
be imminent 151.2
overhang 214.7
impendent, impending
imminent 151.3
overhanging 214.11
impenetrability
impregnability 158.4
imperviousness
265.2
density 353.1
inaccessibility 509.3
unintelligibility
547.1
impenetrable
impregnable 158.17
impervious 265.13
dense 353.12
inaccessible 509.8
unintelligible 547.11
impenitence 872.2
impenitent 872.5
impenitently 872.7
imperative
nouns mood 584.9
command 750.2
adjs. necessary 637.12
urgent 670.23
authoritative 737.14
mandatory 750.13
compulsory 754.9
obligatory 960.14
imperatively
authoritatively
737.18

mandatorily 750.15
compulsorily 754.11
imperator 747.8
imperatorial 737.16
imperceptibility
infinitesimalness
195.2
invisibility 444.1
unintelligibility
547.1
imperceptible
infinitesimal 195.13
invisible 444.4
unintelligible 547.11
imperfect
defective 676.4
blemished 677.8
impaired 690.27
immature 719.11,12
imperfection
inferiority 37.1
defectiveness 676
impairment 690
immaturity 719.4
imperfectly
slightly 35.10
inadequately 676.5
imperforate 265.10
imperforation 265.2
imperial
nouns 229.8
adjs. imperious
737.15
sovereign 737.16
Imperial Diet 740.2
Imperial Highness,
etc. 915.2
imperialism 739.8
imperialistic 737.17
imperiality 737.7
imperil 695.6
imperiled 695.13
imperilment 695.1
imperious
urgent 670.23
masterful 737.15
imperial 737.16
compelling 754.9
arrogant 910.11
obligatory 960.14
imperiously
masterfully 737.19
compulsorily 754.11
arrogantly 910.15
imperishability
immortality 112.3
indestructibility
142.6
imperishable
immortal 112.9
indestructible
142.19
impermanence,
impermanency
111.1
impermanent 111.7
impermeability
imperviousness
265.2
density 353.1

impermeable
impervious 265.13
dense 353.12
impersonal
objective 6.3
unprejudiced 524.12
impartial 974.10
impersonality 6.1
impersonally 974.11
impersonate
represent 570.9
pose as 570.10
enact 609.34
impersonation
representation 570.2
acting 609.9
impersonator
actor 610.1
masquerader 617.7
imperspicuity 547.3
imperspicuous 547.13
impersuadability
172.2
impersuadable,
impersuasible
uninfluenceable
172.4
obstinate 624.13
impersuasibility
uninfluenceability
172.2
obstinacy 624.5
impertinence
irrelevance 10.1
impudence 911.2
impertinent
irrelevant 10.6
impudent 911.9
impertinently
irrelevantly 10.8
impudently 911.12
imperturbability 856.1
imperturbable 856.10
imperturbation 856.2
impervious
uninfluenceable
172.4
impenetrable 265.13
opaque 340.3
inaccessible 509.8
callous 854.12
IMPERVIOUS TO
158.18
imperviousness
unsusceptibility
172.2
impenetrability
265.2
opaqueness 340.1
inaccessibility 509.3
callousness 854.3
impetigo 684.27
impetrate 772.11
impetration
entreaty 772.2
prayer 1030.4
impetuosity
violence 161.1
impulsiveness 682.2
haste 707.2
recklessness 892.2

idealism 533.7

imprecate
entreat 772.11
curse 970.5

imprecation
entreaty 772.2
curse 970.1
prayer 1030.4

imprecatory
supplicatory 772.17
maledictory 970.8

impregnability 158.4

impregnable 158.17

impregnate
imbue 44.12
fertilize 168.11
steep 391.13
inculcate 560.12

impregnated 168.17

impregnation
imbuement 44.2
insemination 168.4
steeping 391.7
inculcation 560.2

impresario
theaterman 609.27
director 746.1

impress
nouns offprint 24.5
characteristic 80.3
effect 153.3
indentation 256.6
mark 566.6
engraving 576.6
printing 601.3
verbs fix 142.10
indent 256.14
~ the mind 477.18
fix in the mind
535.18
inculcate 560.12
engrave 576.13
print 601.12
conscript 778.14
commandeer 820.17
shanghai 822.18
affect 853.16
IMPRESS UPON 853.17

impressed
infixed 142.14
engraved 576.16
affected 853.24
IMPRESSED WITH
believing 500.18
affected 853.24
IMPRESSED WITH
ONESELF 907.12

impressibility
pliancy 356.2
sensibility 421.2
emotional ~ 853.4

impressible
pliant 356.9
sensible 421.12
emotionally ~
853.19

impression copy 24.5
characteristic 80.3
effect 153.3
form 245.1
indentation 256.6

sensation 421.1
appearance 445.3
idea 478.1
hunch 480.3
supposition 498.4
opinion 500.4
inculcation 560.2
mark 566.6
engraving 576.6
printing 601.3
edition 603.2
emotion 853.3
GET THE IMPRESSION
480.4
GIVE A FALSE
IMPRESSION 551.2
HAVE THE
IMPRESSION 480.4
LABOR UNDER A FALSE
IMPRESSION 517.9
MAKE AN IMPRESSION
be heard 447.13
~ on the mind
477.18
be remembered
535.15
affect 853.16
UNDER THE
IMPRESSION 500.18

impressionability
suggestibility 171.5
pliancy 356.2
sensibility 421.2
teachability 562.5
emotional ~ 853.4

impressionable
suggestible 171.15
pliant 356.9
sensible 421.12
teachable 562.18
emotionally ~
853.19

impressive
sensible 421.12
convincing 500.22
eloquent 598.11
dramatic 609.37
exciting 855.31
grandiose 902.21

impressively
eloquently 598.15
grandiosely 902.28

impressment
conscription 778.6
commandeering
820.4
shanghaiing 822.8

imprimatur 775.6

imprint
nouns indentation
256.6
title 483.2
mark 566.6
engraving 576.6
printing 601.3
edition 603.2
printer's ~ 603.13
verbs infix 142.10
indent 256.14
fix in the mind
535.18

engrave 576.13
print 601.12

imprison 759.15

imprisoned 759.20

imprisonment 759.3

improbability
small chance 155.9
unlikelihood 511

improbable 511.3

improbity
falseheartedness
614.4
untruthfulness
614.8
deceitfulness 616.3
dishonesty 973

impromptu
nouns musical ~
461.27
improvisation 628.5
adjs. 628.12
advs. 628.15

impromptuist 628.6

improper
unsuitable 27.7
ungrammatical
585.4
inelegant 588.2
inexpedient 669.5
naughty 736.5
vulgar 896.10
wrong 957.3
indecent 988.5

improperly
vulgarly 896.16
wrongfully 953.4

impropriate
monopolize 806.7
appropriate 820.16

impropriation
possession 806.4
appropriation 820.3

impropriator, impro-
priatrix 807.2

impropriety
inappropriateness
27.3
barbarism 580.6
solecism 585.2
inelegant style 588.1
inexpedience 669.1
misbehavior 736.1
vulgarity 896.1
wrong 957.1
indecency 988.1

improvability 692.9

improvable
ameliorable 689.17
emendable 692.25

improve
train 560.13
perfect 675.5
get better 689.7
better 689.9
recuperate 692.19
recover 692.20
IMPROVE ONE'S
MIND 560.10

improved 689.13

improvement
training 560.3

betterment 689
recovery 692

improvidence
negligence 532
thriftlessness 719.2
rashness 892.1

improvident
negligent 532.10,11
unpreparing 719.15
rash 892.7

improving 689.15

improvisate 628.12

improvisation
invention 166.5
musical ~ 461.27
extemporization
628.5

improvisator
singer 463.13
recitationist 597.7
bard 607.14
extemporizer 628.6

improvisatorial, im-
provisatory 628.12

improvise
invent 166.14
extemporize 628.8

improvisé 628.12

improvised, impro-
visional, improviso
628.12

improviser 628.6

improvvisatore
singer 463.13
recitationist 597.7
bard 607.14
extemporizer 628.6

imprudence
unwiseness 469.2,4
rashness 892.1

imprudent
unwise 469.9
rash 892.7

impudence 911.2

impudent 911.9

impudicity 988,2

impugn refute 505.5
deny 522.4
censure 967.13

impugnation, im-
pugnment 788.1

impugned 505.7

impulse impelling 282
~ of life 406.3
sudden thought 628
urge 646.6
GIVE AN IMPULSE TO
787.17
ON IMPULSE 628.14

impulsion
impulse 282.1
urge 646.6

impulsive
impelling 282.22
instinctive 480.6
impetuous 628.9
motivating 646.25
hasty 707.10

impulsively
on impulse 628.13
hastily 707.15

impunity 1005.1
WITH IMPUNITY
696.8
impure inelegant 588.2
unclean 680.22
unchaste 987.23
obscene 988.9
impurity
inelegant style 588.1
uncleanness 680.1
unchastity 987.1
imputable
attributable 154.5
culpable 967.26
imputation
attribution 154.1
stigma 913.6
criticism 967.4
aspersion 969.4
accusation 1003.1
imputative 1003.13
impute attribute 154.2
accuse 1003.7
IMPUTE TO 154.3
in
nouns influence 171.2
entranceway 301.5
stand-in 925.3
adjs. ingoing 301.13
~ favor 925.17
advs. inside 224.14
into 301.14
preps. at 183.28
within 224.17
into 301.14
BE IN FOR 637.10
BE IN FOR IT 1008.24
BE IN IT 155.13
HAVE IT IN FOR 927.9
IN BAD 913.13
IN BAD WITH 927.14
IN FOR IT 768.8
IN SO FAR AS 154.8
IN THAT 154.9
IN WITH
leagued 52.6
friendly with 925.17
inability
incapability 157.2
incompetence 732.1
inabstinence 991.1
inabstinent 991.7
inaccessibility
unattainability
509.3
reserve 611.3
unsociability 921.2
inaccessible
out-of-the-way 198.9
unattainable 509.8
reserved 611.8
unsociable 921.6
inaccordance
difference 16.1
disagreement 27.1
unconformity 83.1
inaccordant
differing 16.7
disagreeing 27.6
disaccordant 793.16

inaccuracy
uncorrectness 517.2
unmeticulousness
532.4
inaccurate
unmeticulous
532.13
incorrect 517.15
ungrammatical
585.4
inaccurately 532.19
inacquiescent 774.6
inaction
motionlessness
267.2
do-nothingism 704
inactivity 706.1
inactivate 157.9
inactive inert 267.12
idle 706.15
inactively 267.18
inactivity
motionlessness
267.2
inactiveness 706
inadept 732.15
inadeptly 732.22
inadequacy
inequality 31.1
inferiority 37.1
incompleteness 57.1
inability 157.2
insufficiency 660.1
imperfection 676.1
inferiority 678.3
psychological ~
688.15
incompetence 732.1
unsatisfactoriness
867.2
inadequate
unequal 31.4
deficient 57.4
short of 312.5
insufficient 660.7
imperfect 676.4
inferior 678.10
incompetent 732.19
unsatisfactory 867.6
inadequately
insufficiently 660.12
imperfectly 676.5
poorly 678.13
incompetently
732.22
unsatisfactorily
867.9
inadmissibility
inaptness 27.3
exclusion 77.1
inexpedience 669.1
unsatisfactoriness
867.2
inadmissible
irrelevant 10.6
inapt 27.7
exclusive 77.8
inexpedient 669.5
unsatisfactory 867.7
inadmissibly 867.9

inadvertence,
inadvertency
error 517.4
inattention 529.1
neglect 532.1
inadvertent
inattentive 529.6
negligent 532.10
inadvertently 532.17
inadvisability
unwiseness 469.2
inexpedience 669.1
inadvisable
unwise 469.9
inexpedient 669.5
inaffable 935.4
inalienable
inherent 5.6
incommunicable
811.10
inalienable right 956.3
inamorata 929.12
in and out
irregularly 138.4
variably 141.8
to and fro 322.20
in-and-out 253.11
inane
ineffectual 157.15
foolish 469.8
thoughtless 479.4
vain 667.13
trivial 671.16
sentimental 853.21
inanimate, inanimated
381.5
inanimation 381.2
inanition 186.2
inanity
unsubstantiality 4.1
ineffectualness 157.3
foolishness 469.1
thoughtlessness
479.1
uselessness 667.2
triviality 671.3
sentimentality 853.7
inappealable
unqualified 507.2
unquestionable
512.15
inappetence,
inappetency
undesirousness 643.3
apathy 854.4
inappetent 634.7
inapplicability
irrelevance 10.1
inaptness 27.3
inapplicable
irrelevant 10.6
inapt 27.7
inapposite
irrelevant 10.6
inapt 27.7
inappositely 10.8
inappreciability 195.2
inappreciable
infinitesimal 195.13
imperceptible 444.4
insignificant 671.15

inapprehensibility
547.1
inapprehensible
547.11
inapprehensibly
547.18
inapprehensive 468.14
inappropriate
irrelevant 10.6
inapt 27.7
untimely 130.7
inexpedient 669.5
inappropriately 669.8
inapt
inappropriate 27.7
unintelligent 468.13
inexpedient 669.5
unskillful 732.15
inaptitude
inappropriateness
27.3
inexpedience 669.1
unskillfulness 732.1
inaptly
inexpediently 669.8
unskillfully 732.22
inarch 303.5
inarticulate
tongue-tied 450.14
indistinct 547.13
inarticulated
indistinct 547.13
inarticulate 593.11
inarticulateness
muteness 450.2
speech defect 593.2
inarticulation 593.2
inartificial
genuine 515.13
natural 719.13
unaffected 734.6
simple 900.7
inartificiality
genuineness 515.5
naturalness 719.3
artlessness 734.2
simplicity 900.2
inartistic 897.10
inasmuch 29.8
INASMUCH AS, IN AS
MUCH AS 154.8
inattention
heedlessness 529
distraction 530
negligence 532
inattentive
heedless 529.6
distracted 530.10
negligent 532.10
inattentiveness 529.1
inaudibility 450.1
inaudible 450.11
inaudibly 450.15
inaugural
nouns address 597.2
ceremony 644.4
adjs. preceding 64.4
beginning 68.13
inaugural address
inauguration 68.4
speech 597.2

inaugurate begin 68.10
  admit 305.10
  instate 778.11
inauguration
  introduction 68.4
  initiator 166.10
  admission 305.2
  instatement 778.3
Inauguration Day
  137.12
inauguratory 68.13
inauspicious
  untimely 130.7
  ill-omened 542.15
inauspiciously 542.18
inbeing 5.1
inborn 5.7
inbound
  approaching 299.10
  ingoing 301.13
inbred innate 5.7
  endogamic 168.17
inbreed 168.9
inbreeding 168.2
Inca 747.9
incalculability
  infinity 104.1
  uncertainty 513.1
incalculable
  infinite 104.3
  uncertain 513.14
incalculably
  extremely 34.22
  infinitely 104.4
incandesce
  glow 327.21
  shine 334.23
incandescence
  heat glow 327.11
  light 334.2
incandescent
  glowing 327.27
  luminous 334.30
incandescent light
  334.18
incantation 1034.4
incantational, incanta-
  tory 1033.14
incapability
  inability 157.2
  unqualification
  719.1
  incompetence 732.1
incapable
  nouns impotent 157.6
  cripple 684.32
  incompetent 732.7
  adjs. unable 157.14
  unqualified 719.9
  incompetent 732.19
incapably 732.22
incapacious 204.13
incapaciousness 204.1
incapacitate
  disable 157.9
  invalid 684.37
incapacitated 157.16
incapacity
  inability 157.2
  unintelligence 468.1
  incompetence 732.1

incarcerate 759.15
incarcerated 759.20
incarceration 759.3
incarmined 367.7
incarnadine
  verbs 367.4
  adjs. 367.9
incarnate
  verbs 375.8
  adjs. 375.10
incarnation 375.7
THE INCARNATION
  1011.13
incase 235.9
incasement,
  encasement
  cover 227.18
  enclosure 235.2
incautious 892.7
incautiousness 892.1
incendiarism 328.7
incendiary
  nouns arsonist 328.8
  instigator 646.11
  adjs. inflammatory
  328.26
  incitive 646.28
incense
  nouns
  fragrance 435.1,4
  suaveness 934.5
  flattery 968.1
  oblation 1030.7
  thurification 1038.4
  verbs 435.8
incense 950.22
incense burner 435.6
incensed 950.25
incensory
  scenter 435.6
  thurible 1038.11
incentive
  nouns 646.7
  adjs. 646.28
incentor 646.11
inception
  beginning 68.3
  source 152.5
inceptor 564.6
incertitude 513.1
incessancy
  continuity 71.7
  perpetuity 112.1
  constancy 135.2
incessant
  continuous 71.9
  recurrent 103.13
  perpetual 112.7
  constant 135.5
incessantly
  continuously 71.11
  perpetually 112.10
  constantly 135.7
incest
  sex abnormality
  418.10
  illicit intercourse
  987.7
incestuous 987.27
inch
  nouns 199.2

IN AN INCH OF 199.20
INCH BY INCH
  gradually 29.6
  piecemeal 55.8
TO AN INCH, WITHIN
  AN INCH 515.21
  verbs go slow 269.6
  creep 272.25
  measure 489.11
inchmeal
  gradually 29.6
  piecemeal 55.8
inchoate
  verbs 68.9
  adjs. 68.13
inchoation 68.3
inchworm 413a.8
incidence 150.2
incident
  circumstance 8.1
  occurrence 150.2
  story action 606.9
INCIDENT TO
  liable to 174.5
  contingent 506.9
incidental
  nouns nonessential
  6.2
  note 462.14,18
  adjs. extrinsic 6.4
  circumstantial 8.6
  parenthetical 10.6
  occasional 129.12
  spare 136.3
  chance 155.15
  liable 174.6
INCIDENTAL TO 506.9
incidentally
  by the way 129.14
  by chance 155.18
incidentals 8.2
incinerate burn 328.24
  cremate 409.21
incinerated 328.29
incineration
  burning 328.5
  cremation 409.2
incinerator 328.12
incipience, incipiency
  68.3
incipient
  beginning 68.13
  embryonic 195.14
incise sever 49.10
  notch 261.4
  furrow 262.3
  open 264.11
  engrave 576.12
incised notched 261.5
  furrowed 262.4
  engraved 576.16
incision cleft 200.2
  gash 261.1
  furrow 262.1
  engraving 576.1
  surgical ~ 687.26
  injury 690.7
incisive
  energetic 160.11
  acrimonious 160.12
  caustic 937.21

incisiveness 937.8
incisor 257.7
incitation 646.4
Incitatus 413.21
incite 646.17
incitement 646.4,7
inciter 646.11
inciting, incitive
  646.28
incivility 935.1
inclemency
  violence 161.1
  cold 332.1
  harshness 937.9
  mercilessness 943.1
inclement cold 332.15
  harsh 937.22
  merciless 943.3
inclination
  tendency 173.1
  leaning 218.2
  incline 218.4
  direction 289.1
  declination 314.1
  disposition 523.3
  prejudice 525.3
  will 619.1
  desire 632.3
  intention 651.1
  aptitude 731.5
  obeisance 962.2
  partiality 975.3
inclinational,
  inclinatory
  tending 173.4
  inclining 218.15
incline
  nouns 218.4
  verbs influence 171.7
  tend 173.3
  lean 218.10
  bear 289.8
  gravitate 351.15
  be willing 620.3
  induce 646.22
INCLINE AN EAR TO
  528.7
INCLINE TOWARDS
  635.14
inclined
  leaning 218.15
  minded 523.8
  willing 620.5
  prompted 646.30
BE INCLINED TO
  THINK 498.9
INCLINED TO 173.6
INCLINED TO BELIEVE
  501.7
inclining 173.4
inclose, inclosure
  See enclose etc.
include
  comprise 76.3
  enclose 235.5
including
  adjs. 76.5
  preps. 40.11
inclusion
  comprisal 76
  enclosure 235.1

hopelessness 887.3
incorrigible
  ungovernable 624.12
  past hope 887.15
  wicked 979.22
incorruptibility
  immortality 112.3
  indestructibility
    142.6
  trustworthiness
    972.6
incorruptible
  immortal 112.9
  indestructible
    142.19
  trustworthy 972.19
incountry 224.3
incrassate
  verbs 353.10
  adjs. 196.12
incrassated 353.14
incrassation 353.4
increase
  nouns ~ in degree
    38.1
  addition 40
  expansion 196.1
  aggravation 883.1
  ON THE INCREASE
    38.8
  verbs make greater
    38.4
  become greater 38.6
  multiply 100.6
  expand 196.4,5
  grow 196.7
  aggravate 883.2
increased
  intensified 38.7
  expanded 196.10
  aggravated 883.4
increasing 38.8
increasingly 38.9
incredibility
  unusualness 85.2
  unbelievability 502.3
  improbability 511.1
incredible
  remarkable 34.10
  fantastic 85.12
  unbelievable 502.10
  improbable 511.3
  wonderful 918.9
incredulity
  skepticism 502.2
  ungullibility 503
  infidelity 1029.6
incredulous
  skeptical 502.9
  ungullible 503.4
  skeptical 1029.20
incredulousness 503.1
incremate 409.21
increment
  increase 38.1
  addition 41.1
incremental 38.8
increscent 374.8
incriminate 1003.10
incriminating 1003.14

incrimination 1003.2
incriminator 1003.5
incriminatory 1003.14
incrust 227.29
incrustation 227.15
incrusted 355.13
incubate 166.16
incubation 166.7
incubator 152.8
incubator baby 125.7
incubus burden 351.7
  hallucination 518.7
  dream 533.9
  ogre 889.8
  demon 1014.7
inculcate 560.12
inculcation 560.2
inculpability 982.3
inculpable 982.8
inculpate 1003.10
inculpation 1003.2
inculpative 1003.14
inculpatory 1003.14
incumbency
  burden 351.7
  office 654.5
  responsibility 960.2
  ecclesiastical ~
    1035.9
incumbent
  nouns resident 189.2
  political ~ 744.11
  clergyman 1036.7
  adjs. impending
    214.11
  overlying 227.38
  burdensome 351.17
  INCUMBENT ON,
  INCUMBENT UPON
    960.13
incumber, incum-
  brance See en-
  cumber etc.
incunabula
  beginning 68.3
  infancy 124.5
incunabular 68.13
incunabulum 603.3
incur contract 174.4
  sicken of 684.34
incurability 887.3
incurable
  nouns 684.31
  adjs. 887.15
incurably 887.18
incuriosity 527
incurious 527.3
incursion
  intrusion 237.1
  overstepping 311.3
  attack 796.4
incursive 796.31
incurvate
  verbs 251.6
  adjs. 251.7
incurvated 251.7
incurvation,
  incurvature
  curvature 251.1
  concavity 256.1

incurve
  nouns 284.4
  verbs 251.6
incurved, incurving
  curved 251.7
  concave 256.16
incus 447.7
indaba
  conference 595.6
  council 753.1
indagate 484.30
indagation 484.5
indagative 484.41
indagator 484.19
indebted 838.8
  INDEBTED TO
  grateful 947.5
  obliged to 960.15
indebtedness,
  indebtment 838.1
indecency
  unseemliness 669.1
  vulgarity 896.1
  unchastity 987
  indelicacy 988
indecent
  unclad 231.13
  inexpedient 669.5
  vulgar 896.10
  indelicate 988.5
indecently 896.16
indeciduous 112.8
indecipherability
    547.4
indecipherable 547.17
indecision
  uncertainty 513.1
  irresolution 625.1
indecisive
  formless 246.4
  inconclusive 505.8
  uncertain 513.16,17
  irresolute 625.9
indecisively
  uncertainly 513.26
  irresolutely 625.12
indecorous
  inelegant 588.2
  inexpedient 669.5
  vulgar 896.10
  wrong 957.3
  indecent 988.5
indecorously
  vulgarly 896.16
  wrongfully 953.4
indecorum
  vulgarity 896.1
  indecorousness 957.1
  indecency 988.1
indeed
  absolutely 34.21
  is that so? 484.48
  certainly 512.23
  truly 515.16
  yes 520.18
  affirmation 521.9
  really! 918.17
indefatigability
  perseverance 623.1
  industriousness
    705.6

indefatigable 623.7
indefeasibility
  unchangeability
    142.4
  inevitability 637.7
indefeasible
  unchangeable
    142.18
  unavoidable 637.15
  incommunicable
    811.10
indefectibility 675.1
indefectible,
  indefective 675.6
indefensibility 975.5
indefensible 975.12
indefinable
  vague 513.17
  inexpressible 545.13
  inexplicable 547.16
indefinite
  general 79.10
  infinite 104.3
  formless 246.4
  indistinct 444.5
  vague 513.17
  neutral 804.7
indefinite article 584.5
indefinitely
  immeasurably 34.22
  infinitely 104.4
  vaguely 513.26
indefiniteness
  formlessness 246.1
  indistinctness 444.2
  vagueness 513.4
  neutrality 804.2
indeliberate 628.11
indelibility 142.6
indelible
  ineradicable 142.19
  fast-dyed 361.18
  unforgettable 535.25
  deep-felt 853.25
indelicacy
  vulgarity 896.1
  indecency 988.1
indelicate
  vulgar 896.10
  indecent 988.5
indelicately 896.16
indemnification
  compensation 33.1
  restitution 821.2
  recompense 839.3
  atonement 1010.1
indemnificatory
  compensatory 33.6
  restitutive 821.7
indemnify
  compensate 33.4
  make restitution
    821.5
  recompense 839.10
indemnity
  compensation 33.1
  security 770.1
  recompense 839.3
  forgiveness 945.2
  amnesty 1005.1
  atonement 1010.1

indistinguishability
  indistinctness 444.2
  unintelligibility
    547.1
indistinguishable
  identical 14.7
  indistinct 444.5
  without distinction
    492.8
  unintelligible 547.11
indistinguishableness
    492.3
indisturbance 856.2
indite 600.21
inditement 600.2
inditer 600.15
individual
  nouns being 3.3
    integer 89.4
    organism 405.2
    person 416.3
  adjs. special 80.12
    one 89.7
    personal 416.12
individualism
  characteristic 80.3
  individuality 80.4
  disposition 523.3
  politics 743.8
  independence 760.4
  egoism 907.3
individualist
  nouns politics 743.8
    independent 760.11
    egoist 907.5
  adjs. individual 80.12
    nonsocialistic 743.21
individuality being 3.3
  identity 14.1
  selfness 80.4
  oneness 89.1
individualization
  differentiation 16.4
  particularization
    80.7
individualize
  differentiate 16.6
  particularize 80.10
indivisibility 353.2
indivisible
  impartible 47.15
  solid 353.13
indocile
  ungovernable 624.12
  disobedient 765.10
indocility
  ungovernability
    624.4
  disobedience 765.1
indoctrinate
  rehabilitate 145.10
  instruct 560.12
indoctrination
  rehabilitation 145.3
  instruction 560.2
Indo-Iranian 417.3
indolence 706.4
indolent
  nouns 706.6
  adjs. 706.17

indomitability
  invincibility 158.4
  ungovernability
    624.4
indomitable
  invincible 158.17
  ungovernable 624.12
indoors, indoor 224.16
indorse ratify 520.12
  guarantee 770.11
indorsement 520.4
indorser 520.7
Indra thunder 455.5
  god 1012.7
indraft, indraught
  influx 301.2
  inspiration 402.1
in dubio 513.15
indubious
  believing 500.18
  undoubted 512.16
indubitable 512.15
indubitably 512.25
induce cause 152.12
  elicit 304.12
  infer 493.10
  persuade 646.22
inducement 646.3,7
inducer 646.10
inducible 504.18
induct initiate 68.9
  bring in 305.14
  install 778.11
  conscript 778.14
inductance 341.14
inductee 798.17
inductile 355.12
inductility 355.3
induction
  electric ~ 341.14
  logic 481.3
  conclusion 493.4
  installation 778.3
  conscription 778.6
  holy orders 1035.10
inductive 481.22
inductive method, in-
  ductive reasoning
    481.3
inductivity 341.14
indulge humor 757.7
  cherish 811.7
  be intemperate
    991.4
INDULGE IN
  delight 863.10
  be intemperate
    991.4
INDULGE ONE'S
  APPETITES
  be intemperate
    991.4
  be gluttonous 992.5
INDULGE ONESELF
  be selfish 976.4
  be intemperate
    991.4
INDULGE WITH 816.15
indulged 757.11
indulgence
  tolerance 524.4

leniency 757.4
  permission 775.2
  patience 859.1
  considerateness
    936.3
  forgiveness 945.1
  privilege 956.4
  intemperance 991.1
indulgent
  tolerant 524.11
  lenient 757.10
  permissive 775.15
  patient 859.10
  considerate 936.17
  intemperate 991.7
induna 747.9
indurate
  verbs harden 355.7
  callous 854.6
  adjs. 355.13
indurated
  hardened 355.13
  callous 854.12
  hardened 979.21
induration
  hardness 355.1
  hardening 355.5
  callousness 854.3
  impenitence 872.2
indurative 355.14
industrial
  manufactural 166.21
  occupational 654.16
  commercial 825.17
industrial arts 572.3
industrialism 825.8
industrialist
  manufacturer
    166.10
  businessman 828.1
industrialization 825.9
industrialize 825.16
industrials 832.1
industrious
  indefatigable 623.7
  active 705.21
industriously 705.25
industry trade 654.6
  industriousness
    705.6
  work 714.4
  concern 786.9
  commerce 825.1
indwell inhere 5.5
  inhabit 187.8
indweller 189.2
indwelling
  nouns 5.1
  adjs. inherent 5.6
  inhabiting 187.14
inearth 409.20
inebriant
  nouns 994.12
  adjs. 994.45
inebriate
  nouns 994.10
  verbs 994.28
  adjs. 994.38
inebriated 994.38
inebriating 994.45
inebriation 994.1

inebrious 994.38
inedible 428.8
ineducation 476.5
ineffability
  inexpressibility
    545.6
  sacredness 1024.1
ineffable
  inexpressible 545.13
  wonderful 918.12
  sacred 1024.7
ineffaceability 142.6
ineffaceable 142.19
ineffective
  unable 157.14
  ineffectual 157.15
  uninfluential 172.3
  unsuccessful 723.17
  BE INEFFECTIVE 157.7
ineffectiveness
  ineffectualness 157.3
  uninfluentiality
    172.1
ineffectual
  of no force 157.15
  uninfluential 172.3
  unsuccessful 723.17
ineffectuality
  impotence 157.3
  forcelessness 172.1
  unimportance 671.1
inefficacious
  ineffectual 157.15
  uninfluential 172.3
  unsuccessful 723.17
inefficacy
  ineffectualness 157.3
  uninfluentiality
    172.1
inefficiency
  inability 157.2
  unskillfulness 732.1
inefficient
  unable 157.14
  unproficient 732.15
inefficiently 732.22
inelastic 355.12
inelasticity 355.3
inelegance
  linguistic ~ 588
  clumsiness 732.3
  vulgarity 896.1
  unbeautifulness
    897.1
  indecency 988.1
inelegancy
  inelegant style 588.1
  vulgarity 896.1
  indecency 988.1
inelegant speech 588.2
  clumsy 732.20
  vulgar 896.10
  unbeautiful 897.6
  indecent 988.5
ineligibility 669.1
ineligible
  nouns 635.9
  adjs. 669.5
ineluctability 637.7
ineluctable 637.15
inept inapt 27.7

unintelligent 468.13
foolish 469.8
inexpedient 669.5
unskilful 732.15
ineptitude
unintelligence 468.1
foolishness 469.1
ineptness 732.1
inequal 260.6
inequality
ununiformity 18.1
disagreement 27.1
disparity 31
unsmoothness 260.1
inequitable 975.9
inequitableness 975.1
inequity 975.1
ineradicability, in-
erasableness 142.6
ineradicable,
inerasable 142.19
inerrability 512.1
inerrable, inerrant
512.19
inert
motionless 267.12
inanimate 381.5
listless 706.18
inertia vegetation 1.6
immobility 142.3
inertness 267.4
indolence 706.4
inertly 267.18
inerudite 476.15
inerudition 476.5
inescapable 637.15
inescapably 637.19
inescutcheon 567.2
inestimable
invaluable 663.21
priceless 846.10
inevasible 637.15
inevasibly 637.19
inevitability
necessity 637.7
fate 638.2
inevitable
necessary 637.15
fated 638.9
THE INEVITABLE
637.7
inevitably
consequently 153.9
necessarily 637.19
inexact vague 513.17
inaccurate 517.15
unmeticulous
532.13
ungrammatical
585.4
inexactitude
inaccuracy 517.2
unmeticulousness
532.4
inexactly
inaccurately 517.19
unmeticulously
532.19
inexcitability
imperturbability 856
unnervousness 858

inexcitable 856.10
inexcusability 975.5
inexcusable 975.12
inexertion 706.4
inexhaustibility 104.1
inexhaustible 104.3
inexorability
obstinacy 624.2
strictness 755.2
inexorable
obstinate 624.9
strict 755.7
inexorably
obstinately 624.15
strictly 755.9
inexpectance,
inexpectancy 538.1
inexpectant 538.9
inexpectation 538
inexpedience
unwiseness 469.2
unfitness 669
mismanagement
732.6
inexpedient
untimely 130.7
unwise 469.9
unfitting 669.5
inexpensive 847.7
inexpensively 847.10
inexperience
immaturity 124.3
ignorance 476
unskillfulness 732.2
inexperienced
immature 124.10
ignorant 476.13
unpracticed 732.17
inexpert 732.15
inexpertly 732.22
inexpiable 975.12
inexpiableness 975.5
inexplicability 547.5
inexplicable 547.16
inexplicably 547.21
inexpressibility
ineffability 545.6
sacredness 1024.1
inexpressible
ineffable 545.13
wonderful 918.12
sacred 1024.7
inexpressibly
ineffably 545.16
wonderfully 918.15
inexpressive 545.11
inexpugnability 158.4
inexpugnable 158.17
inextensibility 355.3
inextensible 355.12
inextensile, inex-
tensional 355.12
inextension 376.1
in extenso
at length 8.11
throughout 56.18
inextinguishability
142.6
inextinguishable
142.19
in extremis 729.24

inextricability
complexity 46.1
immobility 142.3
insolvability 547.5
inextricable mazy 46.5
stuck 142.17
unsolvable 547.16
infallibilism 512.6
infallibilist 512.7
infallibility 512.1
infallible 512.19
infamous terrible 673.9
disreputable 913.10
wicked 979.17
infamousness
terribleness 673.2
disrepute 913.3
infamy disrepute 913.4
abomination 957.2
infancy
beginning 68.3
minority 124.3
babyhood 124.5
IN ITS INFANCY 68.13
infant
nouns minor 125.1
baby 125.7
childish person
470.10
novice 564.7
unsophisticate 734.3
adjs. rudimentary
68.13
babyish 124.12
infanta 916.9
infanticide
killing 408.4
sacrifice 1030.7
infantile
beginning 68.13
babyish 124.12
puerile 468.24
infantile paralysis
684.19
infantilism 468.11
infantine
babyish 124.12
puerile 468.24
infantry youth 125.2
army 798.26
infantryman 798.10
infarct 265.3
infarcted 265.10
infarction 265.3
infare 920.10
infatuate
nouns fanatic 472.17
enthusiast 633.5
lover 929.11
verbs stultify 469.7
obsess 472.23
enamor 929.20
adjs. 929.25
infatuated
obsessed 472.32
enthusiastic 633.11
enamored 929.25
infatuation
foolishness 469.1,5
craze 472.12
credulity 501.1

enthusiasm 633.3
love 929.4
infect
radioactivate 326.9
inspire 646.20
pollute 680.19
disease 684.38
corrupt 690.12
excite 855.11
infected
radioactive 326.10
impure 680.22
diseased 684.45
infection
inspiration 646.9
pollution 680.4
disease 684.3
infectious 684.47
infectiousness 684.3
infective 684.47
infecund 165.4
infecundity 165.1
infelicitous inapt 27.7
untimely 130.7
inexpedient 669.5
infelicity
inaptness 27.3
untimeliness 130.1
inexpedience 669.1
wretchedness 864.6
unhappiness 870.2
infer deduce 493.10
suppose 498.9
imply 544.4
construe 550.10
inferable 504.18
inference logic 481.3
deduction 493.4
supposition 498.2,3
implication 544.2
inferential
deducible 504.18
suggestive 544.6
construable 550.20
inferentialism 481.3
inferior
nouns 37.3
adjs. subordinate 37.6
lower 207.8
petty 671.17
poor 678.10
subject 762.12
inferiority
subordinacy 37.1
poorness 678.3
psychological ~
688.15
subjection 762.2
inferiority complex
inferiority 37.2
complex 688.30
inferiorness 678.3
infernal
execrable 673.10
cruel 937.24
cursed 970.10
wicked 979.18
hellish 1017.6
infernally 34.26
infernal machine
799.15

infernal pit 208.2
inferno 1017.1
inferred
  assumed 498.14
  implied 544.7
infertile 165.4
infertility 165.1
infest overrun 311.6
  torment 864.19
infestation
  pervasion 185.3
  overrunning 311.2
infested 311.11
infestive 870.21
infestivity 870.2
infestment 311.2
infidel
  nouns misbeliever
    1023.6
  unbeliever 1029.11
  adjs. misbelieving
    1023.10
  unbelieving 1029.19
infidelic
  misbelieving
    1023.10
  unbelieving 1029.19
infidelism
  misbelief 1023.3
  unbelief 1029.5
infidelity
  falseheartedness
    614.4
  unfaithfulness 973.5
  misbelief 1023.3
  unbelief 1029.5
infield 876.13
infielder 876.20
infiltrate imbue 44.12
  filter in 301.11
  absorb 305.13
  steep 391.13
infiltration
  imbuement 44.2
  ingress 301.1
  absorption 305.6
  steeping 391.7
infinite
  all-comprehensive
    79.13
  boundless 104.3
  eternal 112.7
  omnipresent 185.13
  divine 1011.20
  THE INFINITE, THE
  INFINITE BEING
    1011.2
infinitely
  extremely 34.22
  illimitably 104.4
  eternally 112.10
infiniteness 104.1
infinitesimal
  nouns 35.2
  adjs. 195.13
infinitesimalness 195.2
infinitive 584.4
infinitude 104.1
infinity
  boundlessness 104
  eternity 112.2

omnipresence **185.2**
  divine attribute
    1011.15
TO INFINITY 104.4
infirm aged 126.17
  weak 159.15
  feeble-minded
    468.21
  unreliable 513.18
  weak-willed 625.11
  unhealthy 684.40
  unsafe 695.11
  morally ~ 979.16
infirmary 687.29
infirmity
  old age 126.5
  weakness 159.3
  feeble-mindedness
    468.8
  unreliability 513.6
  weak will 625.4
  defect 676.2
  illness 684.1,2
  unsafeness 695.2
  moral ~ 979.9
infirmity of purpose
    625.1
infix establish 142.10
  fix in the mind
    535.18
  inculcate 560.12
infixed intrinsic 5.6
  established 142.14
  habitual 640.19
infixion fixity 142.2
  insertion 303.1
  inculcation 560.2
in flagrante delicto
    981.4
inflame ignite 328.21
  redden 367.4
  irritate 423.7
  incite 646.17
  excite 855.11
  anger 950.22
INFLAME WITH LOVE
    929.20
inflamed
  violent 161.21
  hot 327.27
  reddened 367.6
  sore 423.11
  feverish 684.43
  excited 855.21
inflamer 646.11
inflaming 328.26
inflammability 328.9
inflammable
  nouns 330.1
  adjs. 328.27
inflammation
  ignition 328.4
  soreness 423.4
  incitement 646.4
  sore 684.28
  excitement 855.10
inflammatory
  inflaming 328.26
  incitive 646.28
inflatable 196.9
inflate expand 196.4

talk big 599.6
overexpand 661.14
  ~ prices 846.9
  make conceited
    907.7
inflated
  distended 196.12
  bombastic 599.10
  pompous 902.22
  boastful 908.10
inflation
  distension 196.2
  grandiloquence
    599.1
  overexpansion 661.7
  high prices 846.3
  pompousness 902.7
inflationary
  expansive 196.9
  exorbitant 846.12
inflect bend 251.6
  sound 449.12
  grammaticize 584.12
inflection bend 250.2
  bending 251.3
  tone 449.2
  ~ of voice 449.4
  grammar 584.1
inflectional 584.13
inflective
  deflective 290.8
  inflectional 584.13
inflexibility
  immovability 142.3
  rigidness 355.3
  obstinacy 624.2
  strictness 755.2
inflexible
  immovable 142.16
  uninfluenceable
    172.4
  rigid 355.12
  obstinate 624.9
  strict 755.7
inflict do 703.6
  impose 961.5
INFLICT UPON
  impose upon 961.7
  punish 1008.10
infliction bane 674.1
  affliction 864.8
  imposition 961.1
  punishment 1008.1
inflictive 1008.25
inflorescence 410.24
inflorescent 410.36
inflow
  nouns influx 301.2
  inspiration 402.1
  verbs 301.10
inflowing 301.13
influence
  nouns sway 171.1
  influencer 171.6
  authority 737.3
  EXERCISE INFLUENCE,
  EXERT INFLUENCE
    171.9
  HAVE INFLUENCE
  OVER
  influence 171.11

dominate 739.14
UNDER THE INFLU-
  ENCE 994.38
verbs contribute to
    152.13
  sway 171.7
  prejudice 525.8
  induce 646.22,23
influenceability 171.5
influenceable 171.15
influenced
  prejudiced 525.12
  partial 975.11
influence peddling
  influence 171.3
  politics 742.30
influencer 171.6
influential
  powerful 171.13
  authoritative 737.14
  BE INFLUENTIAL
    171.10
influentiality 171.1
influenza 684.12
influenzal 684.46
influx mouth 264.6
  inflow 301.2
influxion 301.2
info 555.1
infold, enfold
  surround 232.6
  fold 263.5
  embrace 930.16
infolded 232.11
infolding
  nouns 263.4
  adjs. 232.9
infoldment,
  enfoldment
  surrounding 232.5
  folding 263.4
  embrace 930.2
inform
  verbs tell 555.7
  report 556.11
  instruct 560.10
  inspire 646.20
INFORM ON, INFORM
  AGAINST 555.11
  adjs. 246.4
informal
  unmethodical 62.11
  unconventional 83.8
  colloquial 578.16
  unceremonious
    645.3
informality
  unconventionality
    83.3
  unceremoniousness
    645
informalness 645.1
informant 555.5
information
  computer data
    348.19
  knowledge 474.1
  enlightenment 555
  informant 555.5
  news 556.1
  instruction 560

inquiring
nouns 484.1
adjs. questioning
484.14,39
curious 526.5
inquiring mind
inquiry 484.1
curiosity 526.1
inquiry
inquiring 484.13,16
trial 1002.5
INQUIRY INTO 484.5
MAKE INQUIRY 484.21
inquisition
nouns inquiry 484.1
tribunal 999.1
trial 1002.5
verbs 484.21
inquisitional 484.39
inquisitionist 484.17
inquisitive
nouns 526.2
adjs. meddlesome
237.9
curious 526.5
inquisitiveness
meddlesomeness
237.2
curiosity 526.1
inquisitor 484.17
inquisitorial 484.39
in re 9.10
inroad
nouns intrusion 237.1
overstepping 311.3
invasion 796.4
MAKE AN INROAD
796.21
verbs 796.21
inrun 301.2
inrush
nouns influx 301.2
inspiration 402.1
verbs 301.10
inrushing 301.13
ins 744.11
insalubrious
harmful 673.12
unwholesome 682.4
insalubrity
harmfulness 673.5
unwholesomeness
682
ins and outs
circumstances 8.2
vicissitudes 155.5
insane
mentally deficient
468.22
foolish 469.8
mad 472.24
BE INSANE 472.19
insane asylum 472.14
insanely 472.34
insanitary 682.4
insanity
mental deficiency
468.9
foolishness 469.1
lunacy 472

insatiability 632.8
insatiable, insatiate
632.28
insatiable desire 632.8
inscribe infix 142.10
fix in the mind
535.18
record 568.15
engrave 576.12
letter 579.9
write 600.23
address 602.14
inscribed
recorded 568.17
engraved 576.16
written 600.24
inscriber 577.8
inscript
engraving 576.1
inscription 600.3
inscription
epitaph 409.18
motto 516.4
engraving 576.1
lettering 579.8
writing 600.3
address 602.10
dedication 603.13
inscroll record 568.15
inscribe 600.23
inscrolled 600.24
inscrutability 547.1
inscrutable 547.11
insculpture
sculpture 573.6
engrave 576.12
insculptured 576.16
insect bug 413a.2
types of ~ 413a.11
wretch 984.6
Insecta insects 413a.1
zoology 414.8
insecticide 408.11
insectile 413a.9
Insectivora, insecti-
vores 414.12
insectivore 413.3
insectivorous 306.29
insectlike 413a.9
insects bugs 413a.1
zoology 414.8
insecure
uncertain 513.18,21
unsafe 695.11
insecurity
unreliability 513.6
unsafeness 695.2
inseminate
impregnate 168.11
sow 412.18
inseminated 168.17
insemination
impregnation 168.4
sowing 412.14
insensate
inanimate 381.5
insensitive 422.5
unintelligent 468.13
unwise 469.9
insensateness 381.2

insensibility
infinitesimalness
195.2
inanimateness 381.2
physical ~ 422
incognizance 476.3
neurosis 688.22
emotional ~ 854.2
insensible
inappreciable 195.13
inanimate 381.5
physically ~ 422.5
imperceptible 444.4
unaware 476.14
emotionally ~
854.10
INSENSIBLE TO THE
PAST 536.9
insensibly
unknowingly 476.19
unfeelingly 854.14
insensitive
physically ~ 422.5
callous 854.12
insensitivity
physical ~ 422.1
callousness 854.3
insentience
inanimateness 381.2
physical ~ 422.1
insentient
inanimate 381.5
insensitive 422.5
inseparability 353.2
inseparable
joined 47.15
solid 353.13
inseparables 926.7
insert
nouns 303.2
verbs infix 142.10
put in 303.3
register 568.15
INSERT IN 236.7
insertion
interjection 236.2
putting in 303
insert 303.2
registration 568.14
inset
nouns 303.2
verbs 303.4
inseverable 47.15
inshore
adjs. 224.10
advs. 224.15
inside
nouns inner nature
5.4
interior 224.2
adjs. interior 224.9
confidential 612.16
advs. 224.14
INSIDE AND OUT
throughout 56.18
everywhere 178.11
preps. 224.17
inside information
555.2
inside man 779.9

inside out
thoroughly 56.15
inverted 219.7
insider
informant 555.5
member 786.11
insides contents 193.1
internals 224.4
vitals 224.5
inside track
advantage 36.2
influence 171.2
HAVE THE INSIDE
TRACK
have advantage
36.11
have influence
171.10
insidious
deceitful 616.22
wily 733.12
dishonest 973.15
insidiously
deceitfully 616.24
cunningly 733.15
insight
discernment 466.4
intuition 480.1
clairvoyance 1032.8
insignia 567.1
insignificance
smallness 35.1
meaninglessness
545.1
unimportance 671.1
insignificancy
trifle 671.6
a nobody 671.7
insignificant
inconsiderable 35.7
meaningless 545.9
unimportant 671.15
insincere false 614.32
affected 901.15
insincerely 614.36
insincerity
falseness 614.5
affectation 901.1
insinuate
intrude 237.5
insert 303.3
hint 555.9
INSINUATE IN 236.7
INSINUATE ONESELF
enter 301.7
ingratiate 905.9
insinuated 544.7
insinuating 544.6
insinuation
interjection 236.2
intrusion 237.1
insertion 303.1
hint 555.4
ingratiation 905.2
aspersion 969.4
insinuative 544.6
insipid
wishy-washy 159.17
tasteless 429.2
prosaic 608.5
indifferent 634.5

mediocre 678.8
sentimental 853.21
dull 881.6
insipidity
tastelessness 429.1
indifference 634.1
dullness 881.1
insist urge 646.14
maintain 751.7
INSIST UPON
dwell on 103.9
stipulate 506.4
urge 646.14
insist 751.7
insistence
persistence 623.1
urging 646.5
urgency 670.4
demand 751.3
insistent
persistent 623.7
motivating 646.25
urgent 670.23
demanding 751.8
in situ 183.21
insnare See ensnare
insobriety 994.1
insociable 921.5
insolate sun 328.18
dry 392.6
insolation
heating 328.1
drying 392.3
sunstroke 684.20
insole 227.20
insolence
defiance 791.1
arrogance 910
impudence 911
insolent defiant 791.8
arrogant 910.9
disdainful 910.13
impudent 911.8
insulting 963.6
insolubility 353.2
insoluble
undissolvable 353.13
insolvable 547.16
insolvability 547.5
insolvable 547.16
insolvency 840.3
insolvent
nouns 840.4
adjs. 840.11
BECOME INSOLVENT
840.7
insomnia 711.1
insomniac 711.1
insomuch 29.8
INSOMUCH AS 154.8
insouciance
unconcern 634.2
apathy 854.4
insouciant
unconcerned 634.6
apathetic 854.13
inspect 484.31
inspection
automatic ~ 348.7
examination 484.4
inspectional 484.41

inspector
automatic ~ 348.35
examiner 484.19
police ~ 697.14
overseer 746.2
inspectoral, inspectorial 484.41
inspiration
reception 305.5
inhalation 402.1
respiration 402.19
genius 466.8
bright idea 478.9
intuition 480.1
creative thought
533.2
sudden thought
628.1
motivation 646.9
encouragement
891.9
unction 1011.18
divine ~ 1019.8
inspirational
instinctive 480.6
provocative 646.26
inspiratory 402.30
inspire inhale 305.12
breathe 402.25
prompt 646.20
cheer 868.6
encourage 891.16
INSPIRE HOPE
886.10
INSPIRE RESPECT
962.7
inspired
imaginative 533.18
elegant 587.7
prompted 646.31
scriptural 1019.9
inspirer 646.10
inspiring
eloquent 598.14
provocative 646.26
cheering 868.16
inspirit inspire 646.20
cheer 868.6
encourage 891.16
inspiriting
inspiring 646.26
cheering 868.16
inspissate 353.10
instability
changeableness
141.2
weakness 159.3
unreliability 513.6
irresolution 625.1
weak will 625.4
unsafeness 695.2
install
inaugurate 68.10
institute 166.13
put in 183.17
admit 305.10
instate 778.11
installation
inauguration 68.4
institution 166.4
installment 183.7

admission 305.2
instatement 778.3
holy orders 1035.10
installment part 55.1
inauguration 68.4
installation 183.7
investiture 778.3
payment 839.1
BY INSTALLMENTS
55.8
installment plan 837.1
instance
nouns circumstance
8.2
example 25.2
urging 646.5
suggestion 771.2
FOR INSTANCE 504.25
IN EVERY INSTANCE
79.16
verbs circumstantiate
8.5
cite 504.14
instant
nouns 113.3
AT WHICH INSTANT
105.7
IN AN INSTANT 113.7
IN THAT INSTANT
105.11
ON THE INSTANT
instantly 113.6
punctually 131.14
promptly 131.15
adjs. instantaneous
113.4
present 120.2
prompt 131.9
imminent 151.3
urgent 670.23
quick 705.17
insistent 751.8
adv. 113.6
instantaneity 113.1
instantaneous 113.4
instantaneously 113.6
instanter
instantly 113.6
promptly 131.15
instantly
instantaneously
113.6
promptly 131.15
quickly 705.24
instate admit 305.10
install 778.11
instatement
admission 305.2
installation 778.3
instauration 692.7
instead 148.11
instep 211.5
instigate 646.17
instigation 646.4
instigative 646.28
instigator 646.11
instill imbue 44.12
inculcate 560.12
instillation
imbuement 44.2
inculcation 560.2

instillment
imbuement 44.2
inculcation 560.2
instinct
intuition 480.2
involuntariness
637.5
id 688.39
talent 731.4
BY INSTINCT, ON
INSTINCT 480.7
INSTINCT WITH
806.10
instinctive innate 5.7
intuitive 480.6
involuntary 637.14
instinctively
intuitively 480.7
involuntarily 637.18
instinctual 5.7
institor 779.3
institute
nouns school 565.1
organization 786.8
verbs inaugurate
68.10
create 166.13
INSTITUTE AN
INQUIRY 484.21
institution
inauguration 68.4
creation 166.4
madhouse 472.14
custom 640.1
workplace 717.1
organization 786.8
law 996.3
holy orders 1035.10
rite 1038.3
institutional 565.18
institutionalize 759.17
institutive 152.15
institutor 166.10
instruct
inform 555.7
teach 560.10
order 750.9
advise 752.6
instructable 562.18
instructed 474.18
instruction
knowledge 474.4
information 555
teaching 560.1,6
precept 749.1
directive 750.3
advice 752.1
RECEIVE INSTRUCTION
562.11
instructional 560.18
instructions computer
data 348.12
directions 560.5
formula 749.3
instructive
informative 555.17
educational 560.18
preceptive 749.5
commanding 750.14
instructor
teacher 563.1,4

intensified
increased 38.7
aggravated 883.4
intensify
increase 38.5,6
aggravate 883.2
intensifying 38.8
intensity greatness 34.1
energy 160.1
violence 161.1
luminous power
334.21
colorfulness 361.3
intensive
nouns 584.2
adjs. increasing 38.8
thorough 56.10
intent
nouns meaning 543.2
intention 651.1
TO ALL INTENTS AND
PURPOSES
equally 30.12
on the whole 54.13
WITH BAD INTENT
937.28
adjs. attentive 528.17
zealous 633.10
INTENT UPON
determined upon
622.16
aspiring 632.29
intention
meaning 543.2
determination 622.1
motive 646.1
purpose 651
intentional 651.9
intentionally 651.11
intently
attentively 528.21
zealously 633.14
intentness
engrossment 528.3
zeal 633.2
inter 409.20
interact 13.7
interaction 13.3
interactive 13.11
interaffiliated 13.10
interaffiliation
interrelation 13.2
interconnection 47.2
interagency 803.1
interagent
medium 656.3
intermediary 779.4
mediator 803.3
inter alia 40.11
interallied 13.10
interassociate
interrelate 13.6
interjoin 47.6
interassociated 13.10
interassociation
interrelation 13.2
interconnection 47.2
interblend mix 44.11
combine 52.3
interbred 44.16
interbreed 44.14

interbreeding 44.4
intercalary
calendrical 114.15
interpolative 236.10
intercalate
calendar 114.14
interpose 236.7
intercalation 236.2
intercede 803.6
interceder 803.3
intercept 728.10
interception
radar ∼ 345.9
hindrance 728.1
interceptive 728.17
intercession
mediation 803.1
Christly function
1011.17
prayer 1030.4
intercessional 803.8
Intercessor
Christ 1011.12
Holy Ghost 1011.14
intercessor 803.3
intercessory 803.8
interchange
nouns exchange 149.1
intercommunication
552.1
∼ of speech 595.1
∼ of views 595.6
barter 825.2
retaliation 953.1
verbs exchange 149.4
intercommunicate
552.6
trade 825.10
interchangeability
149.3
interchangeable 149.5
intercollegiate
intercurrent 149.6
interscholastic
560.19
intercolumnar 236.12
intercom 558.8
intercommunicate
interconnect 47.11
communicate 552.6
intercommunicating
47.16
intercommunication
joining 47.1
communication
552.1
∼ system 558.8
social intercourse
920.4
intercommunion
intercommunication
552.1
social intercourse
920.4
interconnect
interrelate 13.6
interjoin 47.6
interconnected 13.10
interconnection
interrelation 13.2
interjoinder 47.2

bond 48.1
intercontinental
236.12
intercosmic 374.25
intercourse
copulation 168.3
communication
552.1
conversation 595.1
commerce 825.1
social ∼ 920.4
intercross 220.6
intercrossing 220.1,2
intercurrence 236.1
intercurrent
interchangeable
149.6
intervening 236.11
interdenominational
intercurrent 149.6
nonsectarian
1018.25
interdepend 13.6
interdependence 13.2
interdependent 13.10
interdict
nouns 776.1
verbs 776.3
interdiction 776.1
interdictive 776.6
interdigitate mesh 13.7
interjoin 47.6
interdigitation
interaction 13.3
interjoinder 47.2
interest
nouns relevance 9.2
concern 150.3
cause 152.10
influence 171.2
controversialists
481.14
curiosity 526.1
attention 528.2
motive 646.1
incentive 646.7
appeal 648.1
business 654.1
advantage 663.4
importance 670.1
good 672.4
aid 783.4
party 786.5
estate 808.4
share 814.5
premium 838.3
right 956.3
selfishness 976.1
IN ONE'S OWN
INTEREST 976.7
MAIN INTEREST 81.1
MAKE INTEREST
772.14
MAKE INTEREST FOR
783.13
OF CURRENT
INTEREST 483.6
TAKE NO INTEREST IN
be incurious 527.2
not care 634.4

TO ONE'S INTEREST
672.26
verbs relate 9.3
involve 175.2
excite ∼ 528.12
attract 648.5
INTEREST IN 646.22
interested
involved 175.3
prejudiced 525.12
attentive 528.16
partisan 786.18
partial 975.11
interestedly
attentively 528.21
partially 975.13
interest group 742.32
interesting
provocative 528.19
attractive 648.7
interests
capitalists 743.7
factions 786.5
LOOK AFTER ONE'S
OWN INTERESTS
976.4
interfacial 236.12
interfere
intrude 237.5
hinder 728.10
intervene 803.6
INTERFERE WITH
177.6
NOT INTERFERE
760.15
interference
counteraction 177.1
intrusion 237.1
radio ∼ 343.24
television ∼ 344.5
hindrance 728.1
intervention 803.1
RUN INTERFERENCE
FOR 783.13
interfering 237.8
interfold 263.5
interfuse
combine 52.3
intersperse 236.8
interfusion
mixture 44.1
interspersion 236.3
intergalactic matter
281.11
intergalactic space
374.3
interim
nouns interlude 109
respite 709.2
IN THE INTERIM
109.5
adjs. 109.4
interior
nouns
inside 224.2
inland 224.3
center 225.2
picture 572.13
secret 612.15
adjs. domestic 188.8
internal 224.9

interrogational 484.39
interrogative,
  interrogatory
  nouns 484.13
  adjs. 484.39
interrogator 484.17
interrupt stop 144.10
  intrude 237.6
  hinder 728.10
interrupted 72.4
interrupter 558.19
interrupting 728.17
interruption
  intermission 72.2
  interim 109.1
  pause 144.3
  interval 200.1
  intrusion 237.1
  hindrance 728.1
interruptive
  intrusive 237.8
  hindering 728.17
interscholastic
  intercurrent 149.6
  interschool 560.19
intersect 220.6
intersected 220.8
intersecting
  nouns 220.1
  adjs. 220.8
intersection
  interval 200.1
  crossing 220.1,2
intersectional
  crossing 220.8
  interjacent 236.12
interseptum 236.5
intersex 418.11
intersexual 418.17
intersexualism, inter-
  sexuality 418.10
intersidereal 374.25
intersow 236.8
interspace
  nouns 200.1
  verbs 200.4
interspaced 200.6
intersperse 236.8
interspersion 236.3
intersprinkle 236.8
interstate 149.6
interstellar
  interjacent 236.12
  celestial 374.25
interstice 200.1
interstitial
  intervallic 200.5
  interjacent 236.12
intertexture
  interlacing 221.1
  texture 350.1
interthread 221.7
interthreaded 221.8
interthreading 221.1
intertie
  interrelate 13.6
  interjoin 47.6
  interlace 221.7
intertied
  interrelated 13.10
  interlaced 221.8

intertieing 221.1
intertissue 221.7
intertissued 221.8
intertribal 149.6
intertwine 221.7
intertwined 221.8
intertwining
  nouns 221.1
  adjs. 221.9
intertwist
  nouns 46.2
  verbs 221.7
intertwisted 221.8
intertwisting 221.1
interurban
  nouns train 271.12
  railway 655.8
  adjs. intercurrent
    149.6
  between cities 182.9
interval
  nouns degree 29.1
  interruption 72.2
  period 107.1
  interim 109.1
  pause 144.3
  interspace 200
  musical ~ 462.20
  AT INTERVALS
  haphazardly 62.17
  intermittently 72.5
  occasionally 136.5
  irregularly 138.4
  verbs intervene 109.3
  interspace 200.4
intervale 256.9
intervaled 200.6
intervallic 200.5
intervene
  interlude 109.3
  come between 236.6
  intrude 237.5
  mediate 803.6
intervener 803.3
intervenience 236.1
intervenient
  intervening 236.11
  intrusive 237.8
intervening
  interjacent 236.11
  instrumental 656.6
intervention
  interposition 236.1
  intrusion 237.1
  mediation 803.1
interventional 803.8
interview
  nouns audition 447.2
  conference 595.6
  engagement 920.7
  verbs 484.22
interviewer 603.22
interweave 221.7
interweaving
  nouns 221.1
  adjs. 221.9
interwed 931.16
interwork 13.7
interworking
  nouns 13.3
  adjs. 13.11

interwoven 221.8
intestate 816.25
intestinal 224.12
intestinal fortitude
  891.5
intestinal juice
  digester 307.7
  secretion 310.2
intestine
  domestic 188.8
  internal 224.9
intestines 224.6
inthrall, inthralling
  etc. See enthrall
  etc.
intimacy coition 168.3
  secrecy 612.2
  sociability 920.1
  friendliness 925.5
intimate
  nouns shirt 230.15
  friend 926.1
  verbs hint 555.9
  announce 557.12
  adjs. joined 47.13
  personal 80.12
  homelike 190.28
  near 199.14
  innermost 224.9
  secret 612.15
  sociable 920.19
  friendly 925.18
intimated 544.7
intimately 925.21
intimates 230.22
intimation trace 35.4
  hunch 480.3
  supposition 498.4
  foreboding 542.1
  omen 542.2
  monition 555.1
  hint 555.4
  announcement
    557.2
  clue 566.8
intimidate cow 889.19
  threaten 971.2
intimidation 889.5
intinction 1038.8
intitle, intitlement
  See entitle etc.
into in 224.17
  to 301.14
intolerability 862.7
intolerable 862.16
intolerably 862.20
intolerance,
  intoleration
  bigotry 525.2
  impatience 860.2
intolerant
  nouns 525.5
  adjs. bigoted 525.11
  impatient 860.7
intonate sound 449.12
  sing 461.39
intonated 449.13
intonation tone 449.2
  ~ of voice 449.4
  singing 461.12
  expression 461.31

music 462.2
  accent 462.24
intone sound 449.12
  sing 461.39
intoned 449.13
intorsion 253.1
intort twine 221.7
  convolve 253.4
in toto 54.12
intoxation 684.23
intoxicant 994.12
intoxicate thrill 855.16
  inebriate 994.28
intoxicated
  fervent 853.22
  inebriated 994.38
intoxicating 994.45
intoxication
  poisoning 684.23
  elation 863.2
  inebriation 994
intoxicative 994.45
intracoastal 224.11
intractability
  inflexibility 355.3
  ungovernability
    624.4
intractable
  inflexible 355.12
  ungovernable 624.12
intractile 355.12
intrados 224.2
intragroupal 224.11
intramarginal 224.11
intramontane 224.11
intramundane 224.11
intramural
  internal 224.11
  scholastic 560.19
intransigeance
  conservatism 140.3
  uncompromisingness
    624.2
intransigeant
  conservative 140.4
  obstinate person
    624.6
intransigence
  conservatism 140.3
  uncompromisingness
    624.2
intransigent
  nouns conservative
    140.4
  obstinate person
    624.6
  adjs. conservative
    140.8
  uncompromising
    624.9
intransigentism
  conservatism 140.3
  uncompromisingness
    624.2
intransigentist 140.4
intransitive
  nouns 584.3
  adjs. 584.13
in transitu 270.20
intransmutability
  142.4

intransmutable 142.18
intransparency 340.1
intransparent 340.3
intraterritorial 224.11
intrathecal 687.21
intravenous 687.21
intreat 797.9
intrench, intrenchment
    etc. See entrench
    etc.
intrepid 891.17
intrepidity,
    intrepidness 891.1
intricacy 46.1
intricate 46.4
intrigant 652.8
intrigue
    nouns plot 652.6
    artifice 733.3
    love affair 929.6
    verbs fascinate 648.6
    plot 652.10
intrigued 863.12
intriguer
    schemer 652.8
    political ~ 744.6
intriguery 652.6
intrigues 171.3
intriguing
    alluring 648.7
    scheming 652.14
    delightful 861.6
intrinsic 5.6
introceptive 305.16
introduce
    place before 64.3
    inaugurate 68.10
    innovate 139.8
    insert 303.3
    bring in 305.14
    preinstruct 560.14
    submit 771.5
    acquaint 925.13
    INTRODUCE IN 236.7
introducer
    innovator 139.3
    originator 166.10
introduction
    prelude 66.2
    inauguration 68.4
    innovation 139.3
    interjection 236.2
    insertion 303.1
    bringing in 305.7
    musical ~ 461.26
    preinstruction 560.4
    theatrical ~ 609.8
    acquainting 925.4
    GIVE AN INTRODUC-
    TION 925.13
introductory
    beginning 68.13
    introductive 305.18
introgression 301.1
Introit psalm 1030.3
    rite 1038.10
introjection 688.43
intromission
    insertion 303.1
    admission 305.2
intromissive 305.16

intromit insert 303.3
    admit 305.10
intromittent 305.16
introspection, intro-
    spectionism 688.31
introspective 688.50
introversion
    inversion 219.1
    reticence 611.3
    psychological ~
    688.31
introversive 688.50
introvert
    nouns personality
    416.5
    psychology 688.31
    verbs 219.5
    adjs. 688.50
introverted
    inverted 219.7
    reticent 611.8
    introspective 688.50
intrude
    interlope 237.5
    overstep 311.9
intruder 237.3
intrusion
    interloping 237
    overstepping 311.3
intrusive
    interfering 237.8
    hindering 728.17
intrust See entrust
intuition 480
intuitional 480.5
intuitionism 955.2
intuitive 480.5
intuitivism 480.1
intumescence
    distension 196.2
    swelling 255.4
    tumescence 684.29
inundate
    submerge 318.7
    flood 391.4
    overflow 394.18
    oversupply 661.15
inundated
    underwater 208.12
    flooded 391.17;
    394.26
inundation
    submergence 318.2
    flooding 391.6
    overflow 394.6
inunderstandable
    547.11
inurbane 181.7
inurbanity
    rusticity 181.3
    impoliteness 935.1
inure accustom 640.10
    avail 663.17
    callous 854.6
inured
    habituated 640.19
    callous 854.12
    hardened 979.21
inuredness 854.3
inurement 640.7
inurn 409.20

inutility 667.1
invade intrude 237.5
    infest 311.6
    overstep 311.9
    attack 796.21
invader 796.13
invading 796.31
invalid
    nouns 684.31
    verbs 684.37
    adjs. ineffectual
    157.15
    illogical 482.10
    sickly 684.40
    void 777.3
invalidate
    disqualify 157.10
    neutralize 177.7
    disprove 505.4
    invalid 684.37
    annul 777.2
invalidated
    disabled 157.16
    disproved 505.7
invalidating 177.9
invalidation
    neutralization 177.2
    disproof 505.1
    annulment 777.1
invalided 684.44
invalidism
    helplessness 157.4
    sickliness 684.2
invalidity
    ineffectualness 157.3
    illogicalness 482.2
    sickliness 684.2
invaluable
    useful 663.21
    precious 846.10
invariability
    sameness 17.2
    stability 142.1
    tedium 882.1
invariable
    nouns 142.6
    adjs. uniform 17.5
    unchangeable
    142.18
invariably
    uniformly 17.8
    universally 79.16
    always 112.11
invasion
    intrusion 237.1
    infestation 311.2
    attack 796.4
invasive
    intrusive 237.8
    invading 796.31
invective
    nouns revilement
    967.8
    malediction 970.2
    adjs. 967.23
inveigh against 967.13
inveighing 967.23
inveigle
    ensnare 616.20
    lure 648.4
inveiglement 648.1

inveigler 648.3
invent originate 166.14
    trump up 614.18
invented made 166.28
    trumped-up 614.30
invention
    origination 166.5
    product 167.1
    originality 533.3
    figment 533.5
    falsehood 614.10
inventive 533.18
inventor
    originator 166.10
    imaginer 533.12
inventorial 88.8
inventory
    nouns 88.1
    verbs sum up 87.12
    index 87.14
    list 88.7
    take stock 843.9
inveracity 614.8
inverse
    nouns opposite 15.2
    opposite side 238.3
    verbs 219.5
    adjs. opposite 15.5
    reverse 238.5
inversed 219.7
inversely 15.7
inversion 219
invert 219.5
invertebracy 625.4
invertebrate
    nouns weakling 159.6
    animal 413.3; 414.4
    coward 890.5
    adjs. invertebral
    413.48
    weak-willed 625.11
inverted 219.7
invest empower 156.9
    wrap 227.22
    clothe 230.38
    surround 232.6
    provide 657.7
    instate 778.11
    besiege 796.20
    endow 816.17
    make investment
    834.16
invested
    clothed 230.44
    provided 657.12
    endowed 816.25
investigate
    discuss 481.16
    explore 484.30
investigation
    discussion 481.4
    research 484.5
    UP FOR INVESTIGA-
    TION 1002.21
investigational, investi-
    gative 484.41
investigator
    examiner 484.19
    detective 779.10
investiture
    covering 227.2

jenny
spinning wheel
205.5
ass 413.22
female animal
420.10
jeopard, jeopardize
695.6
jeopardized 695.13
jeopardous 695.9
jeopardy
nouns 695.1
IN JEOPARDY
in danger 695.13
on trial 1002.21
verbs 695.6
jeremiad plaint 873.3
berating 967.8
Jeremiah 1020.1
jerk
nouns yank 285.3
twitch 323.3
fool 470.2
verbs flip 284.12
yank 285.5
twitch 323.13
preserve 699.8
be excited 855.18
jerking
nouns twitching 323.5
preservation 699.2
adjs. 323.20
jerk line 657.5
jerks 688.24
BY JERKS
intermittently 72.5
irregularly 138.4
jerkily 323.24
THE JERKS 684.17
jerkwater 671.17
jerkwater town 182.3
jerky
nouns 306a.13
adjs. 323.20
Jerry German 417.9
soldier 798.8
jerry
nouns 680.14
adjs. flimsy 159.14
knowing 474.15
jerry-building 244.2
jerry-built 159.14
jerry shop 994.25
Jerry sneak
coward 890.6
knave 984.3
Jersey lightning 994.16
Jerusalem pony 413.22
Jesse James 823.12
jest
nouns trifle 671.5
joke 879.6
banter 880.1
jeer 965.2
laughingstock 965.7
IN JEST 879.19
verbs joke 879.13
banter 880.4
jestbook 879.6
jester clown 610.9
humorist 879.12

jesting
nouns 880.2
adjs. 879.15
jestingly 879.19
jestingstock 965.7
Jesuit casuist 482.6
religious 1036.17
jesuitic 482.14
Jesuitism, Jesuitry
482.1,4
Jesus, Jesus Christ
1011.12
jet
nouns gist 5.2
airplane 279.3
aeromotor 279.17
outpour 308.7
burner 328.10
black 364.4
spout 394.9
main point 670.6
verbs flow out 302.13
spew 308.23
spout 394.21
Jet Age 107.9
jet-black 364.8
jet d'eau 394.9
jet engineering 277.2
jet pilot 278.1
jet plane 279.3
jet power power 156.4
aviation 277.30
jet-propelled
aviation 277.56
propelled 284.17
jet propulsion
aviation 277.30
propulsion 284.2
jetsam castaway 631.4
discard 666.3
jettison
nouns castaway 631.4
discard 666.3
verbs 666.7
jetty
nouns buttress 215.4
pier 698.6
adjs. 364.8
jeu de mots 879.8
jeu d'esprit 879.7
jeu de théâtre 609.9
jeune premier 610.5
je veux bien 520.18
je vous prie 772.20
je vous remercie
beaucoup! 947.6
Jew, Jewess
Semite 417.3
Judaist 1018.19
jewel
nouns bearing 320.7
good thing 672.5
ornament 899.6
favorite 929.13
admirable person
983.1
verbs 899.8
jeweler 828.3
jewelled 899.10
jewelry 899.5
jewelry store 830.5

Jewish Semitic 417.11
Judaical 1018.28
Jewish calendar 114.8
Jewish Law 1019.3
Jewism 1018.10
Jewry ghetto 182.5
Jews 417.3
jew's-harp, jews'-harp
464.1
Jezebel vixen 941.8
strumpet 987.14,15
jheel 399.1
jib
nouns 239.4
verbs change 139.5
tack 274.32
recoil 283.7
jibber 593.4
jibber the kibber
signal ship 274.55
signal 566.21
jib boom 239.3
jibe agree 26.7
change 139.5
tack 274.32
jiff, jiffy 113.3
IN A JIFFY
instantly 113.7
quickly 268.23
jig
nouns jerk 285.3
twitch 323.3
fishhook 616.12
verbs jerk 285.5
twitch 323.13
dance 877.5
jigger
nouns bicycle 271.8
streetcar 271.14
thing 375.4
chigoe 413a.6
dram 994.6
verbs jerk 285.5
twitch 323.13
jiggerman, jiggers man
701.5
jiggers!
warning 701.11
beware! 893.14
jigget
nouns 323.3
verbs jerk 285.5
twitch 323.13
jiggety
unsteady 159.16
jerky 323.20
jiggle
nouns jerk 285.3
twitch 323.3
verbs jerk 285.5
twitch 323.13
jigsaw 49.10
jigsaw puzzle 547.7
jihad 795.8
Jill, jill girl 125.6
sweetheart 929.12
jillion
nouns number 99.13
a ~ 101.4
adjs. 101.7

jilt
nouns 617.1
verbs 631.5
jilted 865.11
jilter 617.1
Jim Crow 417.7
Jim Crow car 271.14
Jim Crow law 525.4
jim-dandy 672.7
jimjams creeps 425.4
delirium tremens
472.10
jitters 857.2
shivers 889.4
jimmed up 690.28
jimmies 857.2
jimmy
nouns pry 286.4
sheep's head 306a.15
verbs 286.8
jimp 59.8
jim up 690.11
jingle
nouns assonance 20.3
ringing 453.3
~ bell 453.4
fluster 530.3
poem 607.4
rhyme 607.10
verbs ring 453.8
fluster 530.7
versify 607.19
jingled 994.40
jinglejangle
nouns 453.3
verbs 453.8
jingler 833.4
jingles 857.2
jingling
nouns 453.3
adjs. 453.12
jingo, jingoist
nouns militarist 798.5
patriot 939.3
adjs. chauvinistic
795.27
overpatriotic 939.5
jingoism
militarism 795.16
overpatriotism 939.2
jingoistic 795.27
jinni, jinnee, jinniyeh
1014.7
jinrikisha 271.3
jint 47.4
jinx
nouns 673.4
verbs 727.12
jipper 329.4
jitneur, jitneuse 273.10
jitney
diminutive 195.4
bus 271.11
~ driver 273.10
coin 833.7
jitter 857.7
jitterbug
nouns music lover
463.23
dancer 877.3
verbs 877.5

jitterbugging 877.1
jitters 857.2
jittery 357.12
jiva, jivatma
  life force 406.3
  soul 1032.17
jive
  nouns hot jazz 461.9
    slang 578.6
    kidding 880.1
  verbs syncopate
    461.44
    dance 877.5
    tease 880.4
jivester 578.13
jo 929.12
job
  nouns affair 150.3
    swindle 616.8
    task 654.2
    function 654.3
    position 654.5
    act 703.3
    theft 822.10
  ON THE JOB
    attentive 528.15
    alert 531.14
    busy 705.20
  OUT OF A JOB 706.16
  PUT UP A JOB
    prearrange 639.3
    plot 652.10
    accuse falsely
      1003.12
  verbs let out 778.13
    trade in 825.11
jobation 967.6
jobber
  pieceworker 716.2
  intriguer 733.8
  stockbroker 831.10
jobbernowl 470.1
jobbery
  chicanery 616.4
  Machiavellianism
    733.2
  political ~ 742.35
jobbing
  barter 325.2
  stockbroking 831.18
jobholder
  wage earner 716.2
  political ~ 744.11
jobless 706.16
job lot 829.1
Job's comforter 887.7
Jock Scot 417.9
  soldier 798.8
jockey
  nouns saddle pad
    215.19
    racer 268.6
    horseman 273.8
    cheat 617.3
  verbs deceive 616.17
    maneuver 733.10
jockeyism 616.4
jocose 879.15
jocosity, jocoseness
  879.2
jocular merry 868.15

witty 879.15
jocularity
  merriment 868.5
  wittiness 879.2
jocund 868.15
jocundity 868.5
Joel 1020.1
jog
  nouns projection
    255.2
    notch 261.1
    slow motion 269.2
    gait 272.14
    push 282.2
    jerk 285.3
    shake 323.3
    routine 640.5
  verbs walk 272.27
    push 282.12
    jerk 285.5
    shake 323.11
  JOG ALONG 300.6
  JOG ON
    continue 143.3
    plod 269.7
    walk 272.26
    progress 293.3
  JOG THE MEMORY
    535.20
jogger 535.6
joggle
  nouns projection
    255.2
    notch 261.1
    jerk 285.3
    shake 323.3
  verbs jerk 285.5
    shake 323.11
joggly unsteady 159.16
  jolty 323.21
jogtrot
  repetitious 103.15
  tedious 882.8
jog trot dash 268.4
  slow motion 269.2
jog-trot
  verbs 269.6
  adjs. 17.6
Johannine Epistles
  1019.4
John 419.5
john 680.13
John Bull
  country 180.5
  the government
    739.3
John Doe name 581.7
  a nobody 671.7
John Hancock 581.10
  PUT ONE'S JOHN
    HANCOCK ON
    520.12
Johnny man 419.5
  soldier 798.8
johnnycake 306a.28
Johnny-come-lately
  784.4
Johnny on the spot
  prompt 131.9
  attentive 528.15

John Q. Public
  public 416.2
  the people 917.2
Johnsonese 599.1
Johnsonian 599.9
joie de vivre 863.1
join
  nouns 47.4
  verbs identify 14.5
    connect 47.5
    come together 47.11
    combine 52.3
    concur 176.2
    adjoin 199.9
    juxtapose 199.13
    side with 784.6
    ~ as a member
      786.14
    associate with
      920.15
    marry 931.15
  JOIN FORCES 52.4
  JOIN IN
    co-operate 784.4
    participate 813.5
  JOIN ISSUE
    argue 481.17
    quarrel 793.12
    fight 794.17
  JOIN ISSUE UPON
    522.4
  JOIN THE PARADE
    642.10
  JOIN TOGETHER
    league 52.4
    marry 931.15
  JOIN WITH
    add 40.3
    league 52.4
    side with 784.6
joinder 47.1
joined 47.13
joiner abutter 199.6
  member 786.11
joining
  nouns accession 40.1
    junction 47.1
    joint 47.4
    meeting 199.4
  adjs. 47.16
joint
  nouns junction 47.4
    member 55.4
    dive 190.24
    roast 306a.12
    gambling den
      514.14
    den of iniquity
      979.10
    brothel 987.9
  OUT OF JOINT
    out of place 27.7
    out of order 62.12
    dislocated 184.8
    in disrepair 690.36
  PUT OUT OF JOINT
    184.4
  verbs fasten 47.8
    disjoint 49.16
  adjs. mutual 13.13

joined 47.12
  combined 52.5
  accompanying 73.9
  concurrent 176.4
  mutual 813.9
joint committee 740.5
joint discussion 481.4
jointed 47.17
joint effort 784.1
jointly mutually 13.15
  concurrently 176.5
  co-operatively 784.9
joint operations 795.9
joint resolution 740.15
joint return 844.10
joint stock 832.2
joint-stock bank
  834.13
joint-stock company
  company 786.9
  stock company
    831.15
jointure 817.2
joke
  nouns trifle 671.5
    jest 879.6
    banter 880.1
    laughingstock 965.7
  IN JOKE 879.19
  NO JOKE
    reality 1.2
    importance 670.3
  PLAY A PRACTICAL
    JOKE UPON 616.14
  verbs jest 879.13
    banter 880.4
joker person 416.3
  man 419.5
  provision 506.2
  clause 740.19
  playing card 876.17
  humorist 879.12
joking
  nouns 880.2
  ALL JOKING ASIDE
    affirmation 521.9
    frankly 972.23
  adjs. 879.15
jokul 332.6
joky 879.15
jollies 798.28
jollification 876.3
jolliness 868.5
jollity
  merriment 868.5
  festivity 876.3
  conviviality 920.3
jolly
  nouns marine 275.4
    banter 880.1
  verbs make merry
    876.26
    banter 880.4
    flatter 968.6
  adjs. merry 868.15
    festive 876.30
    convivial 920.18
    drunk 994.38
  advs. 34.20
jollyer 880.3

IN JUXTAPOSITION
in conjunction
199.21
beside 241.11,12
juxtapositional 199.16
juxtapositive 199.16

K

kaama 413.5
Kabibonokka 402.3
kack 215.19
Kaffee-Klatsch 920.10
Kaffir 1023.6
kaffir beer 994.20
kahin 1036.12
kaid 747.9
Kaiser 747.9
kaiserdom, kaisership
737.7
kale 833.2
kaleidoscope 141.4
kaleidoscopic
changeable 141.6
variegated 373.9
kalends See calends
Kali 1012.7
Kalki 1012.8
Kalpa 107.5
Kama 929.8
kama 1032.20
kamaloka 1016.9
kamarupa 1032.19
kamavachara 1016.9
kame 206.6
kami 1011.3
kamic body 1032.19
kamikaze 279.9
kangaroo closure
stop 144.5
legislation 740.16
kangaroo court 999.3
Kantian 499.11
kaolin 574.3
Kapelle 463.12,18
Kapellmeister 463.19
kapok 356.4
kaput 691.27
Karaism, Karaitism
1018.10
Karaite 1018.19
Karma 1012.8
karroo, karoo 165.2
karyokinesis, karyomi-
tosis 405.15
karyoplasm 405.3
karyosome
nucleolus 405.10
chromosome 405.11
kasis 1036.12
katy 230.25
kayo See K. O.
keck retch 308.24
feel disgust 865.5
kedge 274.50
keel
nouns 276.26
ON AN EVEN KEEL
even 30.10
apoise 276.19
verbs tilt 218.10

careen 274.45
KEEL OVER
overturn 219.6
capsize 274.46
faint 422.4
keelhaul 1008.18
keelhauling 1008.2
keen
nouns 873.5
verbs 873.8
adjs. energetic 160.11
acrimonious 160.12
violent 161.15
sharp 257.11
cold 332.15
keenly sensitive
421.14
pungent 432.6
odorous 434.10
shrill 457.13
smart 466.14
alert 531.14
eager 633.9
good 672.14
fervent 853.22
deep-felt 853.25
penetrating 855.32
witty 879.15
caustic 937.21
KEEN ABOUT
enthusiastic 633.11
fond of 929.27
KEEN ON
interested 528.16
eager 632.22
enthusiastic 633.11
keen-edged 257.11
keener mourner 409.7
crafty person 733.6
keen interest 633.3
keenly
energetically 160.14
eagerly 633.13
fervently 853.27
keenness
acrimony 160.4
sharpness 257.1
cold 332.1
pungency 432.1
odorousness 434.2
smartness 466.2
alertness 531.5
eagerness 633.1
wittiness 879.2
causticity 937.8
keen-scented 434.13
keen-sighted 438.23
keen-witted
smart 466.14
witty 879.15
keep
nouns nourishment
306a.3
accommodations
657.3
custody 759.5
prison 759.7
support 783.3
stronghold 797.6
FOR KEEPS
forever 112.12

to keep 811.11
MAKE ONE'S KEEP
657.11
verbs endure 110.6
stet 142.20
maintain 143.4
reside 187.8
remember 535.14
reserve 658.12
preserve 699.7
restrain 758.7
obey 764.2
observe 766.2
sustain 787.11
retain 811.5,7
celebrate 875.3
∼ a rite 1038.17
KEEP AT IT
persevere 623.2
be industrious
705.14
KEEP BACK
delay 132.7
retard 269.9
keep secret 612.8
reserve 658.12
not use 666.5
hinder 728.10
restrain 758.7
KEEP BODY AND SOUL
TOGETHER
keep alive 406.9
support oneself
657.11
keep healthy 683.4
KEEP CLEAR OF
keep one's distance
198.7
avoid 629.6
KEEP COMPANY
930.26
KEEP COMPANY WITH
accompany 73.7
associate with
920.15
KEEP DOWN
oppress 739.15
suppress 758.8
subjugate 762.8
KEEP FAITH WITH
observe 766.2
be faithful 972.9
KEEP FROM
keep secret 612.8
avoid 629.6
refrain 704.3
prevent 728.14
restrain 758.7
abstain 990.7
KEEP HOUSE 183.18
KEEP IN
restrain 758.7
confine 759.12
KEEP IN WITH 925.9
KEEP IT UP 623.10
KEEP OFF
repulse 288.2
prevent 728.14
ward off 797.10
KEEP OFF AND ON
fluctuate 141.5

vacillate 625.8
be capricious 627.4
KEEP ON
endure 110.6
continue 143.3
persevere 623.2
be industrious
705.14
KEEP ONE POSTED
555.8
KEEP ONE'S HEAD
856.9
KEEP ONE'S OWN
COUNSEL
be uncommunicative
611.5
keep secret 612.8
KEEP ONE'S SHIRT ON
keep calm 856.9
be patient 859.4
KEEP OUT 77.4
KEEP TAB, KEEP TABS
87.13
KEEP TAB OF, KEEP
TABS OF 555.15
KEEP TAB ON, KEEP
TABS ON 697.18
KEEP THE FAITH
1026.6
KEEP THE GOLDEN
MEAN
be moderate 162.5
be neutral 804.6
KEEP THE MEMORY
ALIVE 535.14
KEEP THE POT
BOILING
persevere 623.2
be industrious
705.14
KEEP THE WOLF FROM
THE DOOR 657.11
KEEP THE WOUND
OPEN 954.5
KEEP TO ONESELF
be silent 450.5
be uncommunicative
611.5
keep secret 612.8
be unsociable 921.4
KEEP UNDER
oppress 739.15
suppress 758.8
subjugate 762.8
restrain oneself
856.8
KEEP UP
continue 143.4
not weaken 158.9
support 215.22
persevere 623.2
be fashionable
642.10
preserve 699.7
KEEP UP ON 555.15
KEEP UP WITH 268.18
KEEP UP WITH THE
JONESES 642.10
NOT KEEP 765.6
keeper guardian 697.5
preserver 699.4

K
L

speculate 831.23
adjs. deadly 408.23
  alluring 648.7
  exhausting 715.11
  exciting 855.31
  delightful 861.6
  amusing 876.29
  humorous 878.5
  beautiful 898.19
kill-joy marplot 728.9
  spoilsport 870.14
kiln
  nouns 574.5
  verbs 392.6
kilocalorie 327.18
kilocycle 99.10
kilocycles 343.15
kilogram 99.10
kilogram-calorie
  327.18
kilogrammeter 160.6
kiloliter 99.10
kilometer 99.10
kilowatt 341.35
kilowatt-hour 160.6
kilter, kelter 7.3
  OUT OF KILTER
  disorderly 62.12
  out of repair 690.36
kin 11.2
kind
  nouns race 11.4
  sort 61.3
  sex 418.1
  GIVE IN KIND 953.6
  IN KIND 20.18
  OF A KIND
  alike 20.11
  mediocre 678.7
  OF ANY KIND 61.9
  OF THAT KIND 9.6
  adjs. lenient 757.10
  benign 936.14
kind deed 936.7
kindergarten 565.4
kindergartner,
  kindergartener
  teacher 563.1
  student 564.3
kindhearted 936.14
kindle
  give birth 166.19
  ignite 328.21
  incite 646.18
  excite 855.11
  become angry
  950.18
kindliness
  indulgence 757.3
  kindness 936.1
kindling
  nouns ignition 328.4
  firewood 330.3
  adjs. 328.26
kindly
  adjs. indulgent
  757.10
  kind 936.14
  advs. heartily 853.27
  pleasantly 861.9

benignly 936.19
kindness
  indulgence 757.3
  benignity 936
  favor 936.7
kind of
  as though 20.19
  rather 29.7
kindred
  nouns kinship 11.1
  kinsmen 11.2
  adjs. related 9.6
  consanguineous 11.7
kine 413.8
kinematics
  aviation 277.2
  dynamics 346.3
kinematograph
  camera 575.13
  projector 575.14
  theater 609.18
kinesis 266.1
kinetic
  energetic 160.11
  dynamic 346.12
kinetic energy 160.1
kinetics aviation 277.2
  dynamics 346.3
kinfolk, kinfolks 11.2
king principal 670.10
  potentate 747.8
  industrialist 828.1
  playing card 876.17
  chessman 876.18
  prince 916.8
kingcraft 742.3
kingdom country 180.1
  class 61.4,5
kingdom come
  utopia 533.11
  heaven 1016.1
kingdom of God
  1016.1
kingdom of heaven
  1016.1
Kingdom of
  Micomicon 533.11
kingfish 747.3
kinghood 737.7
King James Version
  1019.2
kinglet 747.8
kinglike regal 737.16
  noble 916.11
kingliness 903.2
kingly regal 737.16
  dignified 903.12
  noble 916.11
kingmaker
  influence 171.6
  politician 744.7
king of beasts 413.4
King of Kings
  1011.2,12
King of the Jews
  1011.12
kingpin 747.3
King's Birthday
  137.12
king's English 578.3

MURDER THE KING'S
ENGLISH
  be ungrammatical
  585.3
  mispronounce
  593.10
king's evil 684.13
King's highway 655.6
kingship country 180.1
  sovereignty 737.7
king size 194.4
king-size 194.23
king's ransom 835.2
kink
  nouns complication
  46.2
  coil 253.2
  crinkle 263.6
  crick 423.2
  eccentricity 473.2
  caprice 627.1
  expedient 668.2
  verbs 253.5
kinked 253.9
kinky curly 253.9
  eccentric 473.4
  capricious 627.5
kinsmen, kinspeople
  11.2
kinship
  relationship 9.1
  consanguinity 11.1
kiosk pavilion 190.5
  arbor 190.11
kip
  lodginghouse 190.13
  bedroom 191.7
  bed 215.20
kipper
  nouns 306a.24
  verbs 699.8
kippered herring, kip-
  pered salmon
  306a.24
kippering 699.2
kirk 1040.1
kismet 638.2
kismetic 638.9
kiss
  nouns touch 424.1
  greeting 923.4
  osculation 930.3
  verbs touch 424.7
  greet 923.10
  osculate 930.17
  KISS AND MAKE UP
  802.10
  KISS GOOD-BY
  lose 810.5
  relinquish 812.3
  KISS ONE'S FEET
  905.6
  KISS THE ROD 763.11
kissable 929.22
kiss curl 229.5
kisser face 239.4
  mouth 264.5
kissing 930.1
kiss-me-quick 229.5
kiss of peace 1038.4
kist 409.11

Kiswahili 578.10
kit bunch 74.6
  set 74.11
  youngling 125.8
  basket 192.4
  kitten 413.28
  violin 464.6
  outfit 657.4
kit and caboodle 54.4
kitchen belly 192.3
  cookroom 329.3
kitchener 329.2
kitchenette 329.3
kitchenmaid 748.8
kitchenman 748.7
kitchenware 829.5
kite
  nouns aircraft 279.14
  bad check 833.10
  verbs glide 272.34
  soar 313.10
kiteflying 488.4
kites 276.14
kith and kin, kith and
  kind 11.2
kithless alone 89.8
  forlorn 922.13
kithlessness 922.4
kitling
  youngling 125.8
  kitten 413.28
kitten
  nouns child 125.3
  youngling 125.8
  cat 413.28
  verbs 166.19
kittenish infant 124.12
  catlike 413.38
kittle
  verbs 425.6
  adjs. 425.9
kittlish 425.9
kitty cat 413.28
  jack pot 514.4
kitty-cat 413.28
kittycorner, kitty-
  cornered 218.20
kit violin 464.6
kiver 227.2
kiwi 278.5
Klang, Klangfarbe
  449.3
Klavier 464.13
klaxon
  nouns horn 452.5
  alarm 702.3
  verbs 452.8
klepto 472.16
kleptomania
  craze 472.12
  thievishness 822.12
kleptomaniac
  nouns 472.16
  adjs. 472.26
klieg eyes 439.6
knack talent 731.6
  trinket 899.4
  GET THE KNACK OF
  562.9
  NOT HAVE THE KNACK
  732.10

knap 206.5
knave
  playing card 876.17
  rascal 984.3
knavery
  chicanery 616.4
  roguery 973.2
knavish 973.16
knavishness 973.2
knead mix 44.11
  form 245.6
  massage 349.6
  stroke 424.8
kneading
  massaging 349.3
  stroking 424.2
knee joint 47.4
  angle 250.2
  legs 272.16
ON ONE'S KNEES, ON
  BENDED KNEE
  submissive 763.16
  supplicatory 772.16
  humbled 904.11
  obsequious 905.13
  obeisant 962.10
  worshipful 1030.15
knee-deep deep 208.9
  shallow 209.5
knee-high 206.19
  KNEE-HIGH TO A
  GRASSHOPPER 207.6
kneel truckle 905.6
  make obeisance
  962.6
KNEEL TO
  submit 763.10
  entreat 772.11
kneeling 962.2
kneeling stool 1040.10
knell
  nouns death bell
  409.6
  tolling 453.3
  verbs 453.8
knelling 453.3
knez 916.3
knickknack trifle 671.5
  toy 876.16
  trinket 399.4
knickknacks 829.6
knife
  nouns cutter 347.2
  surgery 687.24
  verbs stab 796.27
  be treacherous
  973.12
knife-edge 257.2
knife-edged, knifelike
  257.11
knife pleat 263.2
knifing 796.11
knight
  nouns chessman
  876.18
  nobleman 916.6
  gallant 934.9
KNIGHT OF THE
  ELBOW 514.16
KNIGHT OF THE PEN
  600.14

KNIGHT OF THE ROAD
  tramp 273.3
  salesman 828.5
  verbs 780.3
knightage 916.2
knight-errant
  defender 797.7
  knight 916.6
knight-errantry
  knightly skill 795.11
  magnanimity 977.2
knight-errantship
  916.10
knighthood
  knightly skill 795.11
  nobility 916.10
knightliness
  courage 891.1
  gallantry 934.2
  magnanimity 977.2
knightly brave 891.17
  noble 916.11
  courteous 934.15
  magnanimous 977.6
knightly skill 795.11
knight service 806.1
knit
  verbs fasten 47.7
  grow together 47.11
  contract 197.7
  interlace 221.7
  wrinkle 263.6
  heal 692.21
KNIT THE BROW
  949.15
  adjs. 221.8
knitted 263.8
knitter 222.2
knitting
  contraction 197.1
  interlacing 221.1
knitting machine
  221.6
knives 347.3
knob hill 206.5
  head 210.5
  sphere 254.2
  protuberance 255.3
knobbed 255.16
knobby
  knobbed 255.16
  hilly 206.23
knobstick 626.6
knob twister
  radar man 345.14
  radio man 343.27
knock
  nouns blow 282.4
  bang 455.1
  criticism 967.4
  verbs collide 282.13
  strike 282.14
  pound 282.15
  bang 455.6
  criticize 967.14
  disparage 969.8
KNOCK ABOUT 665.5
KNOCK AROUND
  wander 272.22
  discuss 481.16

KNOCK DEAD
  delight 863.8
  amuse 876.23
  be beautiful 898.15
KNOCK DOWN
  fell 316.5
  raze 691.19
  auction off 827.11
  unnerve 857.10
  deject 870.18
KNOCKED SILLY
  530.14
KNOCK IN THE HEAD
  kill 408.18
  ruin 691.11
KNOCK INTO ONE'S
  HEAD 560.12
KNOCK IT OFF! 144.14
KNOCK OFF
  deduct 42.7
  stop 144.8
  die 407.16
  do offhand 532.9
  write 600.21
  improvise 628.8
  recess 709.8
  accomplish 720.4
KNOCK ONE'S EYES
  OUT 898.15
KNOCK ONESELF OUT
  712.10
KNOCK ONE'S HEAD
  AGAINST 282.12
KNOCK ON THE HEAD
  end 70.7
  kill 408.18
  defeat 725.6
KNOCK ON WOOD
  be superstitious
  501.6
  be hopeful 886.8
KNOCK OUT
  end 70.7
  render powerless
  157.11
  form 245.6
  knock unconscious
  422.3
  do carelessly 532.9
  write 600.21
  destroy 691.11
KNOCK THE BOTTOM
  OUT OF
  disqualify 157.10
  disprove 505.4
  thwart 728.15
KNOCK THE PROPS
  FROM UNDER
  render powerless
  157.11
  disprove 505.4
  disillusion 519.2
KNOCK TOGETHER
  532.9
KNOCK UNDER 763.6
KNOCK UP
  elevate 315.5
  waken 711.4
  fatigue 715.4
knockabout 161.19
knockdown 925.4

GIVE A KNOCKDOWN
  925.13
knock-down-drag-out
  nouns 794.5
  adjs 161.19
knocker 969.6
knocking 455.11
knock-knee 248.3
knock-kneed 248.12
knockout end-all 70.4
  unconsciousness
  422.2
  good thing 672.7
  victory 724.1
  beauty 898.8
knockout blow 70.4
knockout drops
  narcotic 685.10
  liquor 994.8
knoll hill 206.5
  hilltop 206.8
knot
  nouns complication
  46.2
  tie 48.3
  types of ~ 48.8
  hair 229.7
  distortion 248.1
  sphere 254.2
  bulge 255.3
  solid 353.6
  problem 547.7
  dilemma 729.6
  clique 786.7
  verbs tangle 46.3
  distort 248.5
  knit 263.6
  lump 353.10
KNOT THE SCORE 30.6
knothole 264.4
knotted complex 46.4
  gnarled 255.16
  rough 260.8
  knitted 263.8
  clotted 353.14
  abstruse 547.12
  difficult 729.16
knotty knobbed 255.16
  rough 260.8
  abstruse 547.12
  difficult 729.16
knout
  nouns 1009.1
  verbs 1008.14
know
  nouns 474.1
  IN THE KNOW 474.16
  THE KNOW 555.1
  verbs experience
  150.8
  sense 421.7
  have knowledge
  474.12,13
  be certain 512.9
  recognize 535.13
  be friends 925.9
  JUST KNOW
  intuition 480.4
  be certain 512.9
  foreknow 540.7

lamblikeness
  gentleness 763.5
  innocence 982.2
lame
  nouns 684.32
  verbs disable 157.9
  cripple 690.15
  adjs. crippled 690.29
  unsuccessful 723.17
  GO LAME 684.36
lame brains 472.2
lame duck
  politician 744.9
  speculator 831.11
  insolvent 840.4
lame-duck act 996.6
lame-duck congress
  740.1
lame excuse
  pretext 647.1
  excuse 1004.4
lamella 226.2
lamellar, lamellate
  226.6
lamellation 226.4
Lamellibranchia
  414.9
lamelliform 226.6
lament
  nouns 873.3
  verbs 873.8
lamentabile 461.54
lamentability 862.4
lamentable
  terrible 673.9
  grievous 862.11
  sorrowful 870.27
lamentably
  exceedingly 34.25
  terribly 673.14
  grievously 862.18
lamentation
  sorrow 870.10
  lamenting 873
lamenter 409.7
lamenting
  nouns 873.1
  adjs. 873.15
lamentive 873.16
lame verses 607.3
lamia monster 941.7
  fiend 1014.7
  witch 1033.8
lamina layer 226.2
  leaf 410.17
laminar flow 277.35
laminate
  verbs 226.5
  adjs. 226.6
laminated 226.6
laminated glass, lam-
  inated wood 226.2
laminates 377.7
lamination 226.4
laminous 226.6
Lammas 1038.15
lamp
  nouns light 335.1
  torch 335.3
  types of ~ 335.8

eye 438.9
  verbs 438.12
lampadedromy 794.12
lampblack
  nouns 364.6
  verbs 364.7
lampfly 335.5
lamp-hour 334.21
lamping 334.30
lamplight 334.18
lamplit 334.38
lampoon
  nouns 969.5
  verbs 969.12
lampooner, lampoonist
  969.7
lamp shade 337.3
lamp shell 414.6
lampwick 335.7
lanai 191.21
lanate, lanated 229.24
lance
  nouns 798.12
  verbs sever 49.10
  pierce 264.15
  throw 284.12
  stab 796.27
lance corporal 747.23
lance-flamme 799.5
lance Jack 747.23
lancelike 257.15
Lancelot 916.6
lancer 798.12
lance sergeant 747.23
lanciform 257.15
lancinate pain 423.7
  torture 864.20
lancinated 864.28
lancination 864.7
land
  nouns region 179.1
  country 180.1
  ground 384
  real estate 808.7
  MAKE LAND
  navigation 274.40
  land 299.8
  ON LAND, BY LAND
  384.11
  verbs ~ a plane
  277.49
  disembark 299.8
  alight 314.7
  wangle into 646.23
  catch 820.14
  LAND ON 1008.12
land agent 779.3
landed 808.9
landed gentry
  landowners 807.3
  gentry 916.3
landed interest 807.3
landfall
  airplane landing
  277.15
  arrival 299.2
landgrave 916.5
landholder 807.3
landholding
  nouns 806.2
  adjs. 806.10

landing stage 215.13
  aviation 277.15
  airport 277.19
  arrival 299.2
  stairs 313.3
  wharf 698.6
landing angle 277.23
landing crew 278.5
landing deck
  carrier ~ 276.8
  airstrip 277.20
landing field 277.19
landing place 698.6
landing run 277.15
landing speed 277.37
landing stage
  platform 215.13
  stairs 313.3
  wharf 698.6
landing strip 277.20
landless 836.9
landlocked 758.16
landlord owner 807.2
  proprietor 807.3
landlouper 273.3
landlouping 272.36
landlubber sailor 275.2
  landsman 384.3
landman 384.3
landmark
  boundary 234.3
  mark 566.9
  significant point
  670.6
land measure 489.5
landocracy
  government 739.6
  capitalists 743.7
Land of Beulah
  utopia 533.11
  heaven 1016.1
land-office business
  726.5
Land of Liberty 180.3
land of make-believe
  609.1
land of Nod 710.2
Land of Promise
  533.11
Land of the Leal
  1016.1
Land of the Rose
  180.4
landowner 807.3
  BECOME A LAND-
  OWNER 409.23
landowning
  nouns 806.2
  adjs. 806.10
land pirate
  swindler 617.4
  thief 823.1
land rat 823.1
landreeve 746.3
lands 808.7
landscape view 445.6
  picture 572.13
landscape architect,
  landscape gardener
  gardener 412.6
  artist 577.10

landscape architec-
  ture, landscape
  gardening
  gardening 412.2
  art 572.4
landscape painting
  572.5
land shark 617.4
landslide slide 314.4
  political ~ 742.22
landslip 314.4
landsman 384.3
Landsting 740.3
Landsturm 798.17
landward
  adjs. 181.6
  advs. coastward
  274.71
  toward 289.28
Landwehr 798.24
lane airway 277.39
  passageway 655.4
  road 655.6
langrage, langrel shot
  799.14
langspiel 464.3
langsyne 119.2
language speech 578
  linguistics 578.11
  diction 586.1
  utterance 592.1
  swearing 970.3
language classifications
  578.19
languages
  types of ~ 578.21
  international ~
  578.22
langue d'oc, langue
  d'oïl 578.8
langue du pays 578.4
languid weak 159.12
  inert 267.12
  slow 269.10
  listless 706.18
  sleepy 710.19
  weary 715.6
  apathetic 854.13
languidly
  inertly 267.18
  slowly 269.13
languidness
  languor 706.5
  apathy 854.4
languish decrease 39.6
  weaken 159.9
  sicken 684.35
  deteriorate 690.19
  despond 870.16
  LANGUISH FOR 632.16
languishing
  nouns 632.5
  adjs. decreasing 39.11
  lingering 110.11
  drooping 159.21
  longing 632.23
  deteriorating 690.43
  dejected 870.22
  lovelorn 929.24
languishment
  decline 39.1

weakness 159.1
enfeeblement 159.5
longing 632.5
sickliness 684.2
lassitude 706.5
sorrow 870.10
languor
  weakness 159.1
  inertness 267.4
  slowness 269.1
  listlessness 706.5
  drowsiness 710.1
  fatigue 715
languorous
  drooping 159.12
  inert 267.12
  slow 269.10
  langued 706.18
lanky
  nouns 204.8
  adjs. thin 204.16
  tall 206.21
lantern skylight 264.7
  light 335.1
lantern fly 335.5
lantern-jawed 204.18
lantern light 334.18
lanternlit 334.38
lantern of Diogenes
  484.2
lantern slide 575.5
Laodicean
  nouns 625.5
  adjs. irresolute 625.9
  indifferent 634.5
Laodiceanism
  irresolution 625.1
  indifference 634.1
Laotzu 1020.3
lap
  nouns appendage 41.2
  lamina 226.2
  overlap 227.4
  front 239.1
  drink 306.4
  circuit 319.2
  swash 394.8
  lick 424.1
  ~ of luxury 726.1
  liquor 994.13
LAY IN THE LAP OF
  THE GODS 859.6
ROLL IN THE LAP OF
  LUXURY
  prosper 726.10
  be rich 835.11
  verbs outdistance 36.9
  overlap 227.33
  drink 306.28
  swash 394.20
  lick 424.9
  ripple 451.11
  cuddle 930.15
  tipple 994.29
LAP OVER
  overlap 227.33
  fold over 263.5
LAP UP
  drink 306.28
  be credulous 501.5
  tipple 994.29

laparotomy 687.26
lap dog 413.24
lapel appendage 41.2
  fold 263.1
lapidary
  nouns 577.8
  adjs. 576.17
lapidate kill 408.18
  stone 796.29
lapidation
  killing 408.1
  stoning 796.12
lapideous hard 355.10
  stony 383.8
lapidification 355.5
lapidify 355.7
lapin 413.29
lappet appendage 41.2
  lobe 214.4
  fold 263.1
  ear lobe 447.7
lapping 227.38
lapse
  nouns decline 39.2
  close 70.3
  ~ of time 105.4
  pause 144.3
  conversion 145.1
  reversion 146.1
  sinkage 314.2
  error 517.4
  ~ of memory 536.2
  deterioration 690.3
  relapse 694.1
  moral ~ 980.2
  verbs expire 70.6
  elapse 105.5
  be converted 145.12
  revert 146.4
  sink 314.6
  err 517.8
  deteriorate 690.18
  relapse 694.4
  be sinful 979.13
lapsed 119.5
lapsing 694.5
lapstreak 227.38
Laputa 533.11
larboard
  nouns 243.1
  adjs. 243.5
  advs. leftward 243.7
  port 274.72
  interjs. 274.80
larcenist 823.1
larcenousness 822.12
larceny 822.2
lard
  nouns 306a.16
  verbs lubricate 379.8
  enhance 689.9
lardaceous 379.9
larder 658.1
lardy 379.9
lares 190.26; 1012.19
lares and penates
  1012.19
large spacious 178.9
  sizable 194.16
  exaggerated 615.4
  excessive 661.17

AT LARGE
  at length 8.11
  wholly 54.12
  in general 79.15
  diffusely 591.15
  free 760.19
LARGE AS LIFE 194.22
large calorie 327.18
large heart
  generosity 851.1
  magnanimity 977.2
largehearted
  tolerant 524.11
  generous 851.4
  benevolent 936.16
  magnanimous 977.6
largeheartedly
  generously 851.5
  magnanimously
  977.8
largeheartedness
  tolerance 524.4
  generosity 851.1
  benevolence 936.4
  magnanimity 977.2
large intestine 224.6
largely greatly 34.17
  on a large scale
  194.24
large-minded 524.8
largeness size 194.1
  bigness 194.6
large order
  hearty meal 306.8
  falsehood 614.12
  big undertaking
  713.2
  difficulty 729.2
larger 38.7
large-scale
  extensive 79.12
  large 194.16
large size 194.4
largess gratuity 816.5
  generosity 851.1
larghetto
  nouns 461.25
  advs. 461.55
largify increase 38.4
  enlarge 196.4
largish 194.16
largo
  nouns 461.25
  advs. 461.55
lariate 616.12
lark
  nouns ascent 313.7
  songbird 463.15
  revel 876.6
WITH THE LARK 133.8
  verbs ride 272.33
  frolic 876.26
larkish 876.31
larrikin 941.4
larrup hit 282.15
  whip 1008.15
larruping
  nouns 1008.5
  adjs. 427.8
larva chrysalis 125.9
  embryo 405.13

ghost 1015.1
larval 405.23
laryngismus 684.5
laryngitis 684.12
larynx 592.10
lascar 275.1
lascivious 987.29
lash
  nouns spank 282.8
  goad 646.8
  whip 1009.1
UNDER THE LASH
  754.12
  verbs fasten 47.9
  moor 274.16
  herd 415.7
  goad 646.15
  bind 758.10
  criticize 967.21
  flog 1008.14
LASH AND CARRY
  711.5
LASH INTO A FURY
  incite 646.17
  irritate 855.13
  enrage 950.23
LASH OUT AT 796.17
LASH THE WAVES
  667.8
lashes 229.12
lashing fastening 47.3
  flogging 1008.4
lashings 34.6
lass, lassie girl 125.6
  sweetheart 929.12
lassitude
  weakness 159.1
  languor 706.5
lasso
  nouns circle 252.2
  snare 616.12
  verbs 820.14
last
  nouns mold 25.6
  end 70.1
  graver 576.11
  verbs 110.6
  adjs. supreme 36.15
  final 70.10
  latest 122.15
  foregoing 119.8
  eventual 150.11
  parting 300.19
AT LAST, AT LONG
  LAST
  finally 70.11
  eureka! 487.11
ON ONE'S LAST LEGS
  aged 126.17
  dying 407.27
  worn out 690.35
  tired out 715.8
  advs. 70.11
Last Gospel 1038.10
lasting
  substantial 3.5
  durable 110.10
  lingering 110.11
  permanent 140.7
  unforgotten 535.23

lastingness
  durability 110.1
  permanence 140.1
Last Judgment 121.3
lastly 70.11
last name 581.5
last resort, last
  resource
  last expedient 668.2
  refuge 698.2
last rites
  last offices 409.14
  extreme unction
    1038.6
last roundup 407.1
last stop 299.5
last straw 152.3
  THE LAST STRAW
    860.3
Last Supper 1038.8
last will and testament
  816.10
last word
  a novelty 122.2
  ultimatum 771.3
  THE LAST WORD 642.4
lasty 110.10
Latakia 433.2
latch fasten 47.8
  close 265.6
latchkey 264.10
late
  adjs. former 119.7
  recent 122.13
  untimely 130.7
  tardy 132.15
  late-lamented 407.24
  advs. 132.18
  OF LATE 122.17
  TOO LATE 130.7
late-lamented 407.24
lately 122.17
late-model 122.9
latency
  dormancy 267.4
  hidden meaning 544
lateness
  recentness 122.1
  untimeliness 130
  tardiness 132
latent inert 267.12
  underlying 544.5
  hidden 613.12
latentness 544.1
later
  adjs. subsequent
    117.3
  future 121.8
  latter 122.13
  advs. subsequently
    117.5
  in the future 121.9
laterad 241.8
lateral
  nouns ~ pass 284.4
  consonant 449.5
  adjs. side 241.6
  phonetics 449.18
lateralize 241.5
laterally 241.8
lateritious 367.7

latest present 120.2
  newest 122.15
latest wrinkle, the
  a novelty 122.2
  novel idea 478.8
  the rage 642.4
latex 387.2
lath
  nouns thinness 204.7
  slat 205.4
  wood 377.3
  verbs 227.25
lathe conversion 145.7
  district 179.5
lathee 216.2
lather
  nouns sweat 309.7
  foam 404.2
  impatience 860.1
  GET ONESELF INTO A
    LATHER 860.4
  verbs foam 404.5
  soap 679.18
  whip 1008.15
lathering 1008.5
lathery 404.7
lathhouse 412.11
lathing 377.3
lath-legged lean 204.17
  lanky 206.21
lathwork 377.3
laticostate, latidentate
  203.7
latigo 215.19
Latinism 578.9
Latinist 475.3
Latin school 565.6
latish 132.15
latitude room 178.3
  zone 179.3
  liberality 524.2
  freedom 760.3
latitude and longitude
  location 183.1
  co-ordinates 489.6
latitudinarian
  nouns liberal 524.6
  freethinker 1029.13
  adjs. liberal 524.9
  freethinking 1029.21
latitudinarianism
  liberalism 524.2
  freethinking 1029.7
latrate 459.2
latria 1030.1
latrine 680.13
latrine rumor 556.6
latrocinium 822.12
latter
  foregoing 119.8
  recent 122.13
Latter-day Saint
  1018.20
latterly 122.17
lattice
  nouns trellis 220.3
  framework 244.4
  window 264.7
  atomic ~ 325.7
  verbs 220.7

latticed, latticelike
  220.11
latticework
  trelliswork 220.3
  framework 244.4
laud
  nouns praise 966.5
  glorification 1030.2
  paean 1030.3
  verbs praise 966.12
  glorify 1030.11
laudable 966.19
laudation praise 966.5
  glorification 1030.2
laudatory 966.15
lauder 966.8
lauds 1030.8
laugh
  nouns 874.4
  FOR LAUGHS 876.33
  verbs 874.9
  LAUGH AT
  defy 791.4
  ridicule 965.8
  LAUGH OFF 529.4
  LAUGH ON THE
    WRONG SIDE OF
    ONE'S MOUTH
  be disappointed
    539.4
  be sad 870.15
laughable 878.5
laughing
  nouns 874.4
  adjs. 868.10
  NO LAUGHING MATTER
    670.3
laughingly 868.19
laughingstock 965.7
laughter 874.4
laughter-loving
  868.15
launch
  inaugurate 68.10
  ~ a rocket 280.13
  throw 284.12
  set going 284.14
  LAUNCH AN ATTACK
    796.18
  LAUNCH FORTH 713.3
  LAUNCH INTO,
    LAUNCH UPON
  undertake 713.3
  set to work 714.15
  LAUNCH OUT AGAINST
    796.15
launcher
  rocket ~ 280.11
  projector 799.20
launching
  inauguration 68.4
  rocket ~ 280.10
launching base 281.5
launching platform
  280.11
launching way 277.20
launder 679.18
laundress 679.14
laundromat 679.9
laundry
  laundering 679.5

  washhouse 679.9
laundryman 679.14
laundry room 191.13
laureate
  nouns 607.15
  adjs. 914.10
laurel 914.3
lava residue 43.2
  slag 328.16
Lavabo 1038.10
lavabo washing 679.4
  washbasin 679.12
lavage washing 679.4
  enema 685.17
lavandera, lavandero
  679.14
lavanter 840.5
lavation 679.4
lavatory washing 679.4
  washroom 679.8
  washbasin 679.12
  water closet 680.13
lave drench 391.13
  wash 679.18
lavement 685.17
lavender
  nouns 435.2
  adjs. 372.3
lavender water 435.3
laving 679.4
lavish
  nouns 34.6
  verbs 852.3
  LAVISH UPON
  give to 816.15
  be generous 851.3
  adjs. plentiful 659.7
  superabundant
    661.20
  generous 851.4
  prodigal 852.8
lavishly
  plentifully 659.9
  superabundantly
    661.25
  generously 851.5
lavishment 659.2
lavishness
  abundance 659.2
  superabundance
    661.2
  prodigality 852.1
law
  nouns rule 84.4
  axiom 516.2
  bill 740.19
  precept 749.2
  decree 750.4
  statute 996.3
  jurisprudence 996.7
  AT LAW 1002.21
  BY LAW 996.12
  HAVE THE LAW ON
    1002.12
  MAKE LAWS 740.20
  PRACTICE LAW 1001.6
  TAKE THE LAW INTO
    ONE'S OWN HANDS
  have one's way 619.3
  be lawless 738.4
  violate 767.4

transgress 997.5
THE LAW 1019.3
WITHIN THE LAW
    996.10
verbs 1002.12
law-abiding
    obedient 764.3
    honorable 972.13
law and order 801.2
lawbreaker 984.9
lawbreaking 997.3
law court 999.2
law enforcement agent
    697.14
lawful valid 515.12
    permitted 775.16
    legal 996.10
lawfully
    permissibly 775.20
    legally 996.12
lawgiver 744.3
lawless
    anarchical 738.5
    disobedient 765.9
    illegal 997.6
lawlessness
    anarchy 738
    disobedience 765.1
    illicitness 997.1
lawlike 996.10
lawma 12.3
lawmaker 744.3
lawmaking
    nouns 740.15
    adjs. 740.21
law merchant 996.4
lawn 410.7
lawn party 920.10
law of the Medes and
    Persians rule 84.4
    maintenance 140.2
    stability 142.7
law school 565.7
lawsuit 1002
lawyer agent 779
    intercessor 803.3
    attorney 1001
lawyerlike, lawyerly
    1001.7
lax loose 51.5
    dilatory 132.16
    limp 355.10
    phonetics 449.18
    vague 513.17
    remiss 532.10
    ungrammatical
        585.4
    indolent 706.17
    improvident 719.15
    unstrict 756.4
    lenient 757.8
    unrestrained 760.22
    loose-moraled
        987.26
laxate slacken 51.3
    soften 356.6
laxation looseness 51.2
    limpness 356.3
    softening 356.5

laxative
    nouns cathartic
        685.15
    types of ~ 685.55
    adjs. 685.41
laxity looseness 51.2
    limpness 356.3
    vagueness 513.4
    remissness 532.1
    improvidence 719.2
    unstrictness 756.1
    moral ~ 987.4
laxly 532.17
laxness looseness 51.2
    dilatoriness 132.5
    limpness 356.3
    remissness 532.1
    improvidence 719.2
    unstrictness 756.1
    leniency 757
    unrestraint 760.2
lay
    nouns arrangement
        60.1
    posture 183.4
    direction 289.1
    song 461.13
    poem 607.4
    profession 654.6
GET THE LAY OF THE
    LAND 289.12
THE LAY OF THE LAND
    7.2
verbs allay 162.6
    ~ eggs 166.18
    place 183.14
    deposit 183.15
    level 213.6
    smooth down 259.5
    navigation 274.50
    bet 514.19
    pacify 802.7
    relieve 884.5
    impose 961.4
    exorcise 1033.12
LAY ABOUT ONE
    be active 705.12
    struggle 714.11
    besiege 796.20
LAY A COURSE FOR
    274.29
LAY A HAND ON
    molest 673.6
    attack 796.15
LAY A HEAVY HAND ON
    755.5
LAY ANCHOR 274.16
LAY AN EGG
    fail 723.9
    bomb 796.25
LAY ASIDE
    segregate 77.6
    postpone 132.8
    remove 270.10
    dismiss 529.4
    put aside 666.6
LAY AT 796.15
LAY AT ONE'S FEET
    771.4
LAY A TRAP FOR
    616.20

LAY AWAY
    store 658.10
    put away 666.6
LAY BACK 629.9
LAY BEFORE
    confront with 239.9
    inform 555.7
    propose 771.5
LAY BY
    postpone 132.8
    navigation 274.18
    reserve 658.12
    put aside 666.6
    lie idle 706.14
    prepare for 718.11
LAY BY THE HEELS
    defeat 725.7
    arrest 759.16
    capture 820.15
LAY DOWN
    deposit 183.15
    level 213.6
    careen 274.45
    postulate 498.12
    bet 514.19
    declare 521.4
    give up 631.7
    store 658.10
    prescribe 750.10
    stipulate 751.6
    pay 839.15
LAY DOWN ONE'S
    ARMS
    surrender 763.8
    make peace 802.11
LAY DOWN ONE'S LIFE
    407.15
LAY DOWN THE LAW
    dogmatize 512.10
    order 750.11
    demand 751.7
LAY EMPHASIS UPON
    emphasize 670.13
    insist 751.7
LAY FOR
    sail for 274.37
    head for 289.10
    ambush 613.11
LAY HANDS ON
    attack 796.15
    take possession
        809.8
    seize 820.12
    impose 961.4
    bless 1030.13
    confirm 1038.18
LAY IN
    sail for 274.37
    store 658.10
LAY IN PROVISIONS
    718.11
LAY IN RUINS 691.10
LAY INTO
    fight 794.15
    attack 796.15
LAY IT ON
    talk big 599.6
    exaggerate 615.3
    overdo 661.12
    overcharge 846.7
    flatter 968.6

LAY LOW
    weaken 159.10
    fell 316.5
    kill 408.18
LAY MONEY ON
    500.13
LAY OFF
    cease 144.6
    stop 144.8
    stop it! 144.14
    circumscribe 233.4
    dismiss 308.18
    shut up! 450.17
    measure 489.12
    plot 652.11
    put aside 666.6
    lie idle 706.14
    recess 709.8
    don't! 776.8
LAY ON
    cover 227.21
    impose 961.4,6
    flog 1008.14
LAY ONESELF OPEN TO
    be liable 174.3
    risk 695.7
LAY ONESELF OUT
    be active 705.13
    try hard 712.9,10
    exert oneself 714.9
LAY ONE'S HANDS ON
    487.2
LAY OPEN
    divest 231.5
    open 264.11
    disclose 554.4
    endanger 695.6
LAY OUT
    level 213.6
    knock down 316.5
    kill 408.14
    ~ the dead 409.22
    knock unconscious
        422.3
    measure 489.12
    plot 652.11
    exert 714.8
    expend 841.5
    ~ money 834.16
LAY OVER
    postpone 132.8
    cover 227.21
LAY PLANS 652.9
LAY SIEGE TO
    besiege 796.20
    woo 913.19
LAY TO
    attribute to 154.3
    navigation 274.18
    lie idle 706.14
    apply oneself 714.9
LAY TOGETHER 47.5
LAY TO REST 409.20
LAY UP
    navigation 274.18
    store up 658.11
    put away 666.6
    sicken 684.37
LAY UPON 961.4,6
LAY WITH 168.10
    adjs. 1037.3

electric circuit 341.4
  sharper 617.4
GIVE A LEG UP 783.11
NOT HAVE A LEG TO
  STAND ON
  be impotent 157.7
  reason ill 482.8
ON ONE'S LEGS
  erectly 212.12
  well 683.7
verbs 272.26
LEG IT
  walk 272.26
  hasten off 300.14
  flee 629.10
legacy 816.10
legal valid 515.12
  permitted 775.16
  legitimate 996.10
legal action 1002.1
legal adviser 1001.1
legal assessor 1000.4
legal authority 998.1
legal bond 832.4
legalese 578.7
legal holiday 709.4
legal instrument 568.4
legalism 996.1
legality
  permissibility 775.9
  legitimacy 996
legalization
  legislation 740.15
  legitimatization
    996.2
legalize
  legislate 740.20
  decree 750.9
  make legal 996.8
legally
  permissibly 775.20
  legitimately 996.12
legal medicine
  medicine 686.1
  jurisprudence 996.7
legal power
  authority 737.1
  jurisdiction 998.1
legal profession 1001.5
legal remedy 1002.1
legal right 998.1
legal tender 833.1
legate delegate 779.2
  diplomat 779.6
legatee 817.4
legation office 717.8
  commission 778.1
  diplomats 779.7
legato
  nouns 461.31
  adjs. 461.54
leg bail 629.4
legend tradition 123.2
  title 483.2
  inscription 600.3
  story 606.7
  mythology 1012.21
legendary
  traditional 123.12
  imaginary 533.21
  narrative 606.18

mythological
  1012.22
legerdemain 616.5
leggiero 461.54
leggings 230.62
leggy 206.21
legibility 546.3
legible 546.11
legibly 546.13
legion throng 74.4
  multitude 101.3
  military unit 798.19
légionnaire 798.6
legislate 740.20
legislation
  legislating 740.15
  act 996.3
legislative 740.21
legislative caucus
  742.9
legislative lobby
  742.33
legislator 744.3
legislatorial 740.21
legislature legislative
  body 740
  legislation 740.15
legist 1001.2
legit
  nouns legitimate
    drama 609.4
  legitimate theater
    609.17
  adjs. 996.10
legitimacy
  genuineness 515.5
  permissibility 775.9
  legality 996.1
  justifiability 1004.7
legitimate
  verbs 996.8
  adjs. logical 481.21
  genuine 515.13
  theatrical 609.37
  permitted 775.16
  legal 996.10
  justifiable 1004.14
legitimate actor 610.1
legitimately
  genuinely 515.17
  permissibly 775.20
  legally 996.12
legitimate stage 609.4
legitimate theater
  609.17
legitimatization 996.2
legitimize 996.8
leg man 603.22
legs velocity 268.2
  shanks 272.16
legume plant 410.4
  pod 410.28
  seed 410.29
legumen 410.28
légumes 306a.35
legumin 353.7
leguminiform, legumi-
  nose, leguminous
  410.34
legwork 272.10
lei 410.23

Leibnitzian 499.11
leisure
  nouns 708
AT ONE'S LEISURE
  132.19
  adjs. 706.16
leisureliness
  slowness 269.1
  unhurriedness 708.2
leisurely
  adjs. slow 269.10
  unhurried 708.6
  advs. tardily 132.19
  slowly 269.13
leitmotif, leitmotiv
  461.30
lemma bract 410.17
  premise 481.8
lemon
  nouns sour 431.3
  failure 723.2
  adjs. 369.4
lemures 1015.1
Lemuroidea 414.12
Lenard ray 326.3
lend
  nouns 818.2
  verbs 818.5
LEND A HAND
  navigation 274.79
  help 783.11
LEND AN EAR 447.11
LEND AN EAR TO
  528.7
LEND A WILLING EAR
  620.3
LEND ONESELF TO
  assent 520.8
  abet 783.14
  participate 813.5
lender 818.3
lending 818
lending library 603.18
lend-lease
  nouns lease 778.5
  lending 818.1
  verbs lease 778.13
  loan 818.5
length distance 198.1
  longness 201
  linear measures
    489.17
AT ARM'S LENGTH
  198.15
AT FULL LENGTH
  throughout 56.18
  horizontally 213.10
AT LENGTH
  in detail 8.11
  at last 70.11
  lengthwise 201.15
  diffusely 591.15
GO ALL LENGTHS
  be thorough 56.8
  persevere 623.5
  try hard 712.12
  do up brown 720.7
GO TO GREAT
  LENGTHS 531.7
length and breadth
  54.3

lengthen increase 38.4
  protract 110.9
  continue 143.4
  elongate 201.9
lengthened
  protracted 110.11
  prolonged 201.12
lengthening
  nouns protraction
    110.2
  continuance 143.1
  prolongation 201.5
  adjs. 38.8
lengthily 201.14
lengthiness 201.1
lengthwise
  along 201.15
  horizontally 213.10
lengthy
  nouns 206.12
  adjs. long 201.11
  tall 206.21
  diffuse 591.12
lenience
  tolerance 524.4
  indulgence 757
  patience 859.1
leniency
  tolerance 524.4
  laxness 756
  indulgence 757
  mercy 942.1
lenient
  softening 356.16
  tolerant 524.11
  lax 756.4
  indulgent 757.8
  patient 859.10
  merciful 942.7
lenitive
  nouns mitigator 162.3
  ointment 379.3
  medicine 685.8
  adjs. palliative 162.16
  softening 356.6
  lubricant 379.10
  qualifying 506.7
  remedial 685.35
  relieving 884.9
lenity 757.1
lens eye ~ 438.9
  optical ~ 442.1
l'ensemble 231.3
lens-shaped 251.14
Lent fast 993.3
  holy days 1038.15
lent 818.6
lenten 993.5
lenten diet 993.2
Lententide 1038.15
lenticular, lentiform
  251.14
lentiginous,
  lentiginose 680.25
lentigo mark 566.4
  freckle 677.1
lentitude
  slowness 269.1
  languor 706.5
lentitudinous 706.18
lento 461.55

Leo 413.4
leonine lionlike 413.38
  poetic 607.21
leopard 373.6
le pas precedence 64.1
  precession 291.1
leper 924.3
lepidodendraceae,
  lepidodendrids,
  lepidodendroids,
  lepidodendron
  411.7
lepidopterous, lepi-
  dopteran 413a.9
lepidote 226.7
leporide 413.29
leppy 413.8
lepra 684.9
leprechaun 1012.15
leprosy 684.9
leprous 684.46
Lesbian
  nouns 418.11
  adjs. 418.23
Lesbianism 418.10
lese majesty 973.7
lesion disease 684.1
  injury 690.7
less
  adjs. inferior 37.6
  reduced 39.10
  fewer 102.6
  advs. least 37.9
  decreasingly 39.12
  preps. minus 42.14
  without 660.11
  NO LESS THAN 28.7
lessee lodger 189.8
  tenant 807.4
lessen decrease 39.6
  reduce 39.7
  moderate 162.6
  relieve 884.5
lessening
  nouns decrease 39.1
  moderation 162.2
  relief 884.1
  adjs. decreasing 39.11
  mitigating 162.14
lesser inferior 37.6
  reduced 39.10
lesson teaching 560.6
  warning 701.1
  reproof 967.5
  GIVE A LESSON 560.16
  GIVE A LESSON TO
  teach 560.10
  punish 1008.10
lest 174.7
let
  nouns 778.5
  verbs tap 304.10
  suppose 498.9
  permit 775.10
  lease 778.13
  LET ALONE
  be conservative
  140.6
  leave undone 532.7
  avoid 629.6
  not use 666.5

do nothing 704.4
not interfere 760.15
abstain 990.7
LET BYGONES BE
  BYGONES 945.5
LET DOWN
  relax 162.9
  slow up 269.9
  lower 316.4
  disappoint 539.2
  desert 631.6
  deteriorate 690.17
  rest 709.7
  humiliate 904.4
  be unfaithful 973.11
LET DOWN EASY 519.2
LET FLY
  throw 284.12
  shoot 284.13
LET FLY AT
  796.17,30
LET GO
  demobilize 75.9
  dismiss 308.18
  neglect 532.6
  leave undone 532.7
  do nothing 704.5
  go unrestrained
  760.17
  free 761.5,11
  relinquish 812.4
  make merry 876.26
  acquit 1005.4
LET HAVE 816.12
LET HAVE IT
  strike 282.14
  punish 1008.12
LET IN
  admit 305.10
  deceive 616.13
  be hospitable 923.7
LET IN ON
  divulge 554.5
  tip 555.10
LET INTO
  disillusion 519.2
  divulge 554.5
LET IT GO
  stet 142.20
  disregard 529.4
  no matter 671.22
  forgive 945.5
LET OFF
  fire 161.13
  shoot 284.13
  discharge 308.18
  exempt 760.13
  free 761.5
  acquit 1005.4
LET OFF STEAM
  876.26
LET ON
  divulge 554.6
  pretend 614.22
LET ONESELF GO
  deteriorate 690.17
  go unrestrained
  760.17
  make merry 876.26
LET ONESELF IN FOR
  729.11

LET ONE'S HAIR DOWN
  645.2
LET OUT
  lengthen 201.9
  dismiss 308.18
  exhaust 308.22
  divulge 554.5,6
  say 592.14
  free 761.5
  lease 778.13
LET PASS
  disregard 529.3
  let go 704.5
  forgive 945.5
LET SLIP
  neglect 532.6
  divulge 554.6
  let go 704.5
  lose 810.5
LET THE AIR OUT OF
  deflate 197.10
  disillusion 519.2
LET THE CAT OUT OF
  THE BAG 554.6
LET TOMORROW TAKE
  CARE OF ITSELF
  719.7
LET UP
  decrease 39.6
  slacken 51.3
  pause 144.9
  cease 144.13
  relax 162.9
  slow up 269.9
  rest 709.7
LET WELL ENOUGH
  ALONE
  avoid 629.6
  do nothing 704.4
  be content 866.5
  abstain 990.7
NEVER LET GO 811.6
NOT LET GO 472.23
TO LET 778.19
  adjs. 778.17
let-alone 704.6
let-alone principle
  inaction 704.1
  noninterference
  760.8
letdown
  relaxation 162.2
  retardation 269.4
  disappointment
  539.1
  humiliation 904.2
lethal 408.23
lethal blow 408.9
lethal chamber 1009.5
lethality 408.8
lethargic, lethargical
  listless 706.18
  drowsy 710.19
  apathetic 854.13
lethargically 854.15
lethargy
  neurosis 688.22
  languor 706.5
  sleep 710.6
  apathy 854.4

Lethe
  forgetfulness 536.1
  Hades 1017.4
Lethean 1017.6
Letheian 536.9
lethologica 536.2
l'Etoile du Nord
  star 374.5
  guiding star 746.7
letter
  nouns speech sound
  449.5
  literalness 543.5
  written character
  579
  type 601.6
  epistle 602.2
  DROP A LETTER
  270.14
  TO THE LETTER
  543.15
  verbs 579.9
letter bag 602.5
letter box 602.7
letter card 602.4
letter carrier 559.5
letter drop 602.7
lettered learned 474.21
  literal 579.11
letter file 88.3
lettergram 558.16
letterhead
  heading 483.2
  address 602.10
lettering
  initialing 579.8
  inscription 600.3
letter of credit
  letter 602.3
  credit 837.3
letter of introduction
  identification 566.10
  recommendation
  966.4
letter-perfect 515.14
letter post 602.5
letterpress title 483.2
  print 601.3
letters
  scholarship 474.5
  alphabet 579.4
  literature 600.13
  mail 602.5
  autobiography 606.4
letter telegram 558.16
letterweight 351.6
letter writer 602.9
lettuce 833.6
letup decrease 39.1
  interruption 72.2
  pause 144.3
  relaxation 162.2
  retardation 269.4
  respite 709.2
leucocytes 387.4
leucocythemia 684.8
leucoderma 363.1
leucorrhea 387.3
leukemia 684.8
Levant 179.6

levant
nouns 402.9
verbs 629.10
levanter wind 402.9
fleer 629.5
levee assembly 74.2
porch 191.21
trench 262.2
reception 920.9
level
nouns degree 29.1
equality 30.1
draw 30.4
story 191.23
plane 213.3
layer 226.1
smoothness 259.3
plain 386.1
ON A LEVEL 213.10
ON THE LEVEL 972.14
verbs make uniform
17.4
equalize 30.7
flatten 213.6
smooth 259.5
fell 316.5
raze 691.19
LEVEL AT
aim 289.6
shoot at 796.23
LEVEL OFF 277.49
LEVEL WITH 972.10
adjs. uniform 17.5
even 30.8
horizontal 213.8
smooth 259.9
just 974.8
advs. 213.10
levelheaded
sensible 466.18
composed 856.13
levelheadedness
sensibleness 466.6
equanimity 856.3
levelness
horizontalness 213.1
smoothness 259.1
level-off 277.6
lever
nouns 286.4
verbs 286.8
leverage
influence 171.1
fulcrumage 286
leveret 413.29
leviable 844.17
leviathan
behemoth 194.14
ship 276.3
levigate 360.9
levigation 360.4
levigator 360.7
levirate, leviration
931.2
levitate 352.9
levitation
lightness 352.1
spiritualism 1032.6
levitative 352.14
Levite 1036.11

Levitic, Levitical
1035.13
levity lightness 352.1
fickleness 627.3
triviality 671.3
lightheartedness
868.3
gaiety 868.5
levoduction, levorota-
tion, levoversion
243.2
levorotatory 243.5
levy
nouns recruital 778.6
rally 795.13
recruits 798.17
seizure 820.4
tax 844.10
verbs recruit 778.14
rally 795.24
seize 820.17
assess 844.14
impose 961.4
lewd unchaste 987.29
obscene 988.9
lewdness
unchastity 987.5
obscenity 988.4
Lewis-Langmuir
theory 325.2
lex 996.3
lex domicilii 996.4
lexical 580.18
lexicographer,
lexicologist,
lexiconist 578.12
lexicographic, lexico-
graphical 580.18
lexicography 580.13
lexicon 603.7
lexigraphy
lexicology 580.13
writing 600.10
lexiphanicism 599.3
lex non scripta,
lex scripta 996.4
liabilities 843.1
liability
proneness 173.1
possibility 174.1
likelihood 510.1
disadavantage 669.2
exposure 695.3
debt 838.1
responsibility 960.2
liable likely 510.5
exposed 695.15
chargeable 838.9
responsible 960.16
BE LIABLE 174.3
LIABLE TO
likely to 173.6
subject to 174.5
liaison joining 47.1
bond 48.1
love affair 929.6
liar 617.9
libation drink 306.4
dram 994.6
oblation 1030.7

libel
nouns slander 969.3
legal declaration
1002.7
verbs 969.11
libelant 1003.5
libelee 1003.6
libeler 969.6
libelous 969.13
Liberal 742.28
liberal
nouns broad person
524.6
political ~ 743.10
adjs. extensive 79.12
broad-minded 524.9
plentiful 659.7
progressive 743.18
generous 851.4
hospitable 923.11
magnanimous 977.6
liberal arts 560.7
liberal education
learning 474.4
education 560.9
Liberalism 742.26
liberalism
broad-mindedness
524.2
political ~ 743.3
liberalist liberal 524.6
progressive 743.10
liberalistic
liberal 524.9
progressive 743.18
liberality
broad-mindedness
524.2
abundance 659.2
gift 816.4
generosity 851
hospitality 923.1
magnanimity 977.2
liberalize 760.12
liberally
plentifully 659.9
generously 851.5
magnanimously
977.8
liberalness
broad-mindedness
524.2
abundance 659.2
generosity 851.1
magnanimity 977.2
liberate rescue 700.2
free 761.4
liberated 761.10
liberation escape 630.1
rescue 700.1
freeing 761
liberator 940.2
libertine
nouns 987.10
adjs. 524.9
libertinism 987.3
liberty
opportunity 129.2
leave 709.3
freedom 760.1
exemption 760.7

permission 775.1
privilege 956.4
presumption 959.2
AT LIBERTY
unemployed 706.16
free 760.19
GO AT LIBERTY
escape 630.7
go free 761.9
TAKE THE LIBERTY
959.6
libidinal sexual 418.17
instinctive 480.6
libidinous
concupiscent 418.20
lascivious 987.29
libido sexuality 418.2
instinct 480.2
desire 632.1
psychology 688.39
Libra 128.7
librarian
bookman 603.21
manager 746.3
library room 191.6
newspaper ~ 601.9
bookery 603.18
librate 322.9
libration 322.1
libratory 322.14
librettist poet 607.15
dramatist 609.26
libretto music 461.28
playbook 609.25
license
lawlessness 738.1
freedom 760.1
exemption 760.7
permission 775.1
permit 775.6
authorization 775.12
commission 778.1
privilege 956.4
presumption 959.2
licensed lawless 738.5
lax 756.4
privileged 760.27
authorized 775.18
licensee 778.8
licentious
lawless 738.5
unrestrained 760.22
incontinent 987.25
debauched 991.8
licentiousness
lawlessness 738.1
unrestraint 760.2
profligacy 987.3
dissipation 991.2
lichen plant 410.4
disease 684.27
lich gate 409.15
lich-house 409.9
licit permitted 775.16
legal 996.10
licitly
permissibly 775.20
legally 996.12
lick
nouns small amount
35.4

velocity 268.2
blow 282.4
lap 424.1
taste 426.2
improvisation
461.27
attempt 712.2
stroke of work 714.4
NOT A LICK 2.3
verbs lap up 306.28
lap 424.9
baffle 513.13
medicate 687.33
defeat 725.6
whip 1008.15
LICK INTO SHAPE
shape 245.6
train 560.13
LICK ONE'S CHOPS
632.19
LICK THE DUST
be defeated 725.12
be submissive 763.11
humble oneself
904.6
grovel 905.6
lick and a promise
532.5
licked baffled 513.23
defeated 725.14
lickerish
concupiscent 418.20
greedy 632.28
lecherous 987.29
licking defeat 725.1
whipping 1008.5
lickpenny 850.6
lickspit, lickspittle
905.3 6
lictor 747.20
lid cover 227.5
hat 230.25
stopper 265.4
eyelid 438.9
PUT THE LID ON
end 70.7
silence 450.8
hush up 612.9
complete 720.6
suppress 758.8
lie
nouns posture 183.4
direction 289.1
falsehood 614.11
verbs extend 178.7
be situated 183.10
be present 185.6
recline 213.5
~ at anchor 274.17
~ in state 409.22
falsify 614.19
exaggerate 615.3
LIE ALONG 274.45
LIE AROUND 706.10
LIE BY
border on 199.9
stay near 199.12
navigation 274.18
lie idle 706.14
LIE DOWN
lie 213.5

shirk 629.9
rest 709.6
LIE IN
exist in 1.11
give birth 166.19
be situated 183.10
sail for 274.37
LIE LOW
be low 207.4
hide 613.9
LIE ON
rest on 215.23
weigh on 351.11
depend 506.6
oppress 727.8
LIE OVER
be imminent 151.2
cover 227.33
LIE STILL 267.7
LIE UNDER
be liable 174.3
be low 207.4
LIE UPON 960.6
lie-abed
lazybones 706.6
sleepyhead 710.12
lied 461.13
Liederkranz, Lieder-
tafel 463.18
lie detector 688.10
lief 620.9
liege
nouns ruler 747.8
subject 762.5
adjs. 762.12
lien 770.6
lientery 309.2
lieu 183.5
IN LIEU OF 148.12
lieutenancy, lieu-
tenantship 747.25
lieutenant
police ~ 697.14
officer 747.22,24
deputy 779.1
lieutenant governor
747.14
lieve 620.9
Life 1011.7
THE LIFE 1011.12
life existence 1
being 3.3
lifetime 110.5
~ after death 121.2
affairs 150.4
energy 160.3
animator 160.5
vitality 406
person 416.3
biography 606.4
career 654.6
liveliness 705.2
vivacity 868.4
COME TO LIFE 406.7
FOR LIFE
lifetime 110.13
always 112.13
FULL OF LIFE 705.16
GIVE LIFE TO 406.8
GIVE NEW LIFE TO
help 783.11

stimulate 855.12
LIFE OF THE PARTY
animator 160.5
humorist 879.12
NOT ON YOUR LIFE
by no means 522.8
I refuse 774.9
God forbid! 967.27
PUT NEW LIFE INTO
revive 692.16
refresh 693.2
THE LIFE OF RILEY
726.1
lifeboat escape 630.3
lifesaver 699.5
life buoy float 276.11
life preserver 699.5
life force 406.3
life-giving
procreative 168.16
animative 406.11
lifeguard 697.8
lifeless inert 267.12
lackluster 336.19
inanimate 381.5
dead 407.24
listless 706.18
dull 881.6
lifelessness
lackluster 336.6
inanimateness 381.2
languor 706.5
dullness 881.1
lifelike alike 20.16
descriptive 606.15
lifelikeness 20.6
life line escape 630.3
preserver 699.5
lifelong 110.13
life preserver 699.5
life principle
life force 406.3
spirit 1032.18,20
lifer 759.11
lifesaver
lifeguard 697.8
preserver 699.4
life size 194.3
life-sized 194.22
lifetime
nouns 110.5
adjs. 110.13
life-weary 882.10
lifework 654.6
lift
nouns height 206.2
ride 272.7
aviation 277.32
boost 315.2
elevator 315.5
heavens 374.2
atmosphere 401.2
inspiration 646.9
improvement 689.1
aid 783.2
theft 822.10
booty 822.11
thrill 855.2
GIVE A LIFT
help 783.11
cheer 868.6

verbs elevate 315.5
inspire 646.20
improve 689.9
steal 822.13
pay off 839.13
elate 868.7
LIFT A FINGER
act 703.5
attempt 712.5
LIFT A HAND AGAINST
796.15
LIFT UP
erect 212.8
raise up 315.5
LIFT UP THE EYES
438.13
LIFT UP THE VOICE
458.9
NOT LIFT A FINGER
704.2
lift component, lift
ratio 277.32
lifter lever 286.4
windlass 286.7
tackle 286.10
erector 315.3
thief 823.1
stove ~ 328.15
lifting
nouns elevation 315.1
theft 822.1
adjs. elevating 315.10
inspiring 646.26
lifts 276.31
ligament bond 48.1
tendon 48.4
cord 205.2
ligamental 205.7
ligation fastening 47.3
bond 48.1
cord 205.2
ligature bond 48.1
cord 205.2
music 462.12
type 601.6
light
nouns dawn 133.3
twilight 134.3
window 264.7
speed 268.7
lighter 330.4
illumination 334
luminous power
334.21
luminant 335.1
types of ~ 335.8
signal ~ 335.9
eyesight 438.1
viewpoint 438.7
aspect 445.3
opinion 500.4
attitude 523.2
interpretation 550.1
information 555.1
divine attribute
1011.15
COME TO LIGHT
appear 445.8
be found 487.9
be revealed 554.9
GIVE LIGHT 334.23

limit
nouns consummation
56.4
end 70.2
capacity 194.2
summit 210.2
termination 233.3
boundary 234.3
~ of patience 860.3
GO THE LIMIT
be thorough 56.8
persevere 623.5
do one's best 712.11
do up brown 720.7
HAVE NO LIMIT
be infinite 104.2
be eternal 112.6
TO THE LIMIT
utterly 56.17
to perfection 675.11
to completion
720.13
WITHOUT LIMIT 104.3
verbs specialize 81.4
restrict 233.5
qualify 506.3
restrain 758.9
LIMIT ONESELF 990.6
limitable 233.11
limitary 233.10
limitation
narrowness 204.1
circumscription
233.2
boundary 234.3
qualification 506.1
restriction 758.3
estate 808.4
limitative
limiting 233.10
qualifying 506.7
restraining 758.12
limited
nouns 271.12
adjs. specialized 81.5
moderate 162.11
local 179.9
cramped 195.9
narrow 204.13
circumscribed 233.8
topical 483.5
qualified 506.10
meager 660.8
restrained 758.15
limiting
restricting 233.10
qualifying 506.7
restraining 758.12
limitless infinite 104.3
unrestricted 760.24
limitlessly 104.4
limitlessness 104.1
limn 572.20
limner 577.2
limniad 1012.17
limoniad 1012.16
limp
nouns 272.14
verbs be weak 159.8
halt 272.27
adjs. weak 159.12

drooping 214.10
flaccid 356.10
limp-cover 603.1
limpet food 306a.25
shellfish 414.9
limpid
transparent 338.4
intelligible 546.10
limpidity
transparency 338.1
intelligibility 546.2
limpness 356.3
Limuloidea 414.8
linaloa 435.4
lincture 685.4
linctus 685.4
line
nouns race 11.4
keeping 26.1
series 71.2
procession 71.4
specialty 81.1
conformity 82.1
lineage 169.4
trend 173.2
equator 179.3
length 201.4
cord 205.2
boundary 234.3
direction 289.1
music staff 461.29
telephone ~ 558.20
mark 566.5
painting 572.10
engraving 576.1
note 602.2
~ of poetry 607.11
policy 652.5
vocation 654.6
way 655.1
railway 655.8
party ~ 742.4
army 798.22
merchandise 829.1
DROP A LINE 602.11
GET IN LINE
line up 71.7
conform 82.4
GIVE ONE LINE 760.14
IN A LINE
consecutively 71.12
straight 249.5
IN LINE WITH
in agreement 26.20
in conformity 82.7
directly 289.25
KEEP IN LINE 755.4
OUT OF LINE
erroneous 517.14
inaccurate 517.15
unconforming 83.7
OUT OF LINE WITH
dissimilar 21.4
in disagreement
27.10
verbs align 60.8
line up 71.6
interline 287.30
border 234.10
mark 566.18
engrave 576.12

outline 652.12
LINE UP
arrange 60.8
align 71.6
get in line 71.7
parallelize 217.5
schedule 639.4
plan 652.9
LINE UP WITH 784.6
lineage race 11.4
extraction 169.4
lineal racial 11.8
continuous 71.10
genealogical 169.14
linear 249.5
lineality 249.1
lineament
characteristic 80.3
appearance 445.3
lineaments
outline 234.2
face 239.4
features 445.4
linear
consecutive 71.10
straight 249.5
linear measure
489.5,17
linear tactics 795.10
lineation 566.5
line-bred 168.17
line-breed 168.9
lined 576.16
line engraver 577.8
line engraving 576.2
line letter 440.5
lineman
trainman 273.13
electrician 341.19
sportsman 876.20
linen 227.11
linen closet 191.15
line noise 343.24
linens 829.3
line of action 655.1
line of battle 800.2
line of business 654.6
line of circumvallation
234.3
line of credit 837.1
line of defense 798.22
line of demarcation
boundary 234.3
distinction 491.3
line of descent 169.4
line of direction 289.1
line of duty 960.1
line of flight 277.29
line of goods 829.1
line of sight 443.3
liner lining 227.20
ship 276.5
lines outline 234.2
lineaments 445.4
artistry 572.9
role 609.11
actor's ~ 609.25
way 655.1
reins 657.5
ALONG THESE LINES
655.11

BETWEEN THE LINES
544.5
lineup 652.1
line-up
arrangement 59.1
list 88.1
schedule 639.2
linga sharira
1032.19,20
linger
be protracted 110.7
procrastinate 132.10
tarry 132.11
continue 143.3
go slow 269.8
lag 292.4
idle 706.12
lingerer
slow goer 269.5
idler 706.7
lingerie 230.22
lingering
nouns protraction
110.2
delay 132.3
slowness 269.3
idling 706.3
adjs. protracted
110.11
dilatory 132.16
slow 269.11
lingo language 578.1
jargon 578.6
lingua tongue 426.5
language 578.1
jargon 578.6
linguadental 449.5
lingua franca 578.10
lingual
nouns 449.5
adjs. 426.10
linguiform 426.10
linguist, linguister,
lingster
interpreter 550.8
philologist 578.12
linguistic(al) 578.15
linguistic families
578.20
linguistics
semantics 543.7
language 578.11
lexicology 581.13
grammar 584
lingulate 426.10
liniment 685.9
lining contents 193.1
inner cover 227.20
link
nouns bond 48.1
member 55.4
intermediary 236.4
torch 335.3
verbs relate 9.4
join 47.5
linkage 47.1
linked 47.13
LINKED TO 40.12
linking 47.1
links 876.13

litterbug 62.7
litters 271.28
little
  nouns small amount
    35.2
    short time 111.3
    short distance 199.2
  A LITTLE AT A TIME
    29.6
  LITTLE BY LITTLE
    gradually 29.6
    piecemeal 55.8
    slowly 269.13
  adjs. small 195.9
    short 202.8
    narrow-minded
      525.10
    unimportant 671.15
    niggardly 850.10
    petty 913.12
    unmagnanimous
      976.6
  MAKE LITTLE OF
    underestimate 497.2
    deem unimportant
      671.11
    take it easy 730.10
  TOO LITTLE 660.7
  advs. slightly 35.10
    on a small scale
      195.15
little bugger 125.3
little devil
    mischief-maker
      736.3
    imp 1014.8
little fellow
    child 125.3
    insignificancy 671.7
    small businessmen
      828.1
    common man 917.7
little game
    scheme 652.6
    artifice 733.3
Little Italy, Little
    Hungary etc. 182.5
Little Joe 96.1
Little Lord Fauntleroy
      420.11
little Mary 192.3
little-minded 525.10
little-mindedness
      525.1
littleness
    inferiority 37.1
    diminutiveness 195
    shortness 202
    narrow-mindedness
      525.1
    unimportance 671.1
    niggardliness 850.2
    pettiness 913.3
    selfishness 976.2
little one 125.3
little people 1012.14
little person 525.5
littlest 37 8
little talk 595.4
little theater 609.17

littoral
  nouns 384.2
  adjs. bordering 234.11
    coastal 384.9
lit up
    illuminated 334.38
    drunk 994.40
liturgic(al) 1038.21
liturgics 1038.1
liturgist 1038.2
Liturgy 1038.9
liturgy 1038.3
lituus staff 216.2
    instrument 464.8
livability 187.6
livable 187.16
live
  verbs endure 110.6
    reside 187.8
    be alive 406.6
    be famous 912.10
  LIVE AGAIN 406.7
  LIVE ALONE
    seclude oneself 922.8
    be unmarried 932.5
  LIVE AND LET LIVE
    be open-minded
      524.7
    let alone 704.4
    not interfere 760.15
  LIVE BY ONE'S WITS
    cheat 616.18
    be cunning 733.9
    be dishonest 973.10
  LIVE DOWN 1010.4
  LIVE FAST 991.6
  LIVE FOR THE DAY
    719.7
  LIVE HIGH
    prosper 726.10
    be rich 835.11
    be intemperate
      991.4
  LIVE IN A GLASS
    HOUSE
    be exposed 443.5
    risk 695.7
    be rash 892.5
  LIVE OFF OF 905.11
  LIVE ON
    endure 110.6
    postexist 121.7
  LIVE OR DIE
    without fail 512.26
    come what may
      622.20
  LIVE OVER 609.34
  LIVE THROUGH
    endure 110.6
    win through 722.13
  LIVE TOGETHER
    931.18
  LIVE UP TO 766.2
    991.4
  adjs. burning 327.27
    electrified 341.31
    alive 406.10
    alert 531.14
    lively 705.16
  live circuit 341.4
  live coal 327.15

lived-in 885.11
livelihood 783.3
liveliness
    energy 160.3
    pungency 432.2
    eloquence 598.4
    activeness 705.2
    gaiety 868.4
livelong 110.13
lively
  adjs. energetic 160.11
    pungent 432.7
    topical 483.6
    interesting 528.19
    eloquent 598.12
    fresh 693.5
    active 705.16
    gay 868.14
  LOOK LIVELY
    pay attention 528.8
    be vigilant 531.8
    beware! 893.14
    hurry! 707.16
  advs. 705.23
lively imagination
    533.4
lively interest 526.1
lively market 831.2
lively pace 268.1
live man 705.8
liven energize 160.9
    cheer 868.6
liver vitals 224.5
    meat 306a.20
    digester 307.7
liveried 230.44
liverwort 410.4
liverwurst 306a.21
livery dress 230.2
    uniform 230.7
    insignia 567.1
liveryman 760.10
live show 344.2
livestock 413.1
live wire
    electricity 341.5
    hustler 705.8
livid black 364.12
    lead-gray 365.3
    purple 372.3
lividity blackness 364.1
    purpleness 372.1
lividness
    blackness 364.1
    purpleness 372.1
living
  nouns life 406.1
    livelihood 783.3
    benefice 1035.9
  AMONG THE LIVING
    406.10
  MAKE A LIVING 657.11
  THE LIVING 406.4
  adjs. existent 1.13
    lifelike 20.16
    energetic 160.11
    dwelling 187.14
    burning 327.27
    organic 405.18
    alive 406.10

topical 483.6
living being
    organism 405.2
    animal 413.2
living force
    force 156.5
    life force 406.3
living quarters 190.2
living room 191.5
lixiviate leach 302.15
    filter 354.6
lixiviation
    leaching 302.6
    filtration 354.3
lixiviator
    percolator 354.4
    cleanser 679.16
lixivium
    solution 390.3
    cleanser 679.16
lizard 413.30
lizardlike 413.43
llama 270.6
llano plain 386.1
    grassland 410.8
load
  nouns large amount
      34.3
    fill 56.3
    contents 193.2
    freight 270.7
    burden 351.7
    overload 661.3
    impediment 728.6
    gun charge 799.10
    care 864.8
    imposition 961.3
  A LOAD OFF ONE'S
    MIND 884.3
  verbs fill 56.7
    lade 183.16
    ~ a gun 284.13
    burden 351.13
    falsify 614.17
    prepare 718.9
load control 348.8
loaded fraught 56.13
    burdened 351.18
    drunk 994.40
  LOADED FOR BEAR
    searching 484.40
    in pursuit 653.12
    ready 718.16
loader 275.10
loading 183.6
load resistance 342.10
loads 34.4
loadstone 287.3
loaf
  nouns lump 194.10
    bread 306a.27
    loafing 706.3
    Eucharist 1038.8
  verbs 706.10
loafer vagabond 273.3
    idler 706.7
    beggar 772.8
loafing 706.3
loamy soft 356.12
    earthy 384.7

loan
nouns 818.2
verbs 818.5
lo and behold!
attention! 528.22
oh! 918.18
loan shark 818.3
loath reluctant 621.6
disliking 865.8
NOTHING LOATH
willing 620.6
consenting 773.5
loathe 928.4
loathing
nouns disgust 865.2
hatred 928.1
adjs. 928.6
loathsome nasty 428.7
odious 862.9
ugly 897.11
loaves and fishes
prosperity 726.1
godsend 809.6
lobar 214.12
lobar pneumonia
684.12
lobate 214.12
lobation 214.4
lobby
nouns influencers
171.6
vestibule 191.19
legislative ~ 742.33
verbs 171.9
LOBBY THROUGH
influence 171.9
legislate 740.20
lobbying, lobbyism
influence 171.3
political ~ 742.30
lobbyist
influencer 171.6
politics 742.33
lobe member 55.4
pendant 214.4
ear ~ 447.7
loblolly gruel 306a.34
semiliquid 388.5
mud puddle 388.9
lobo 413.4
lobotomy 687.26
lobscouser 275.1
lobster
nouns food 306a.25
clumsy fellow 732.9
adjs. 367.7
lobster trick 108.3
lobular 214.12
lobule member 55.4
lobe 214.4
ear lobe 447.7
local
nouns train 271.12
way car 271.13
organization 786.10
labor union 787.1
adjs. regional 179.9
topical 483.5
local anesthetic 685.13
local color color 361.1
fiction 606.9

locale 183.1
localism dialect 578.8
policy 742.4
locality
location 183.1
habitat 190.4
localization 183.6
localize 183.11
local room 601.9
local union 787.1
locate situate 183.11
settle 183.18
located 183.19
location region 179
situation 183
placement 183.6
farm 412.8
locational
regional 179.8
positional 183.20
locative 584.7
loc. cit. 504.26
loch lake 397.1
inlet 398.1
lock
nouns ~ of hair
229.5
deadlock 267.3
floodgate 395.11
fetter 758.5
hold 811.3
fence 824.6
UNDER LOCK AND KEY
imprisoned 759.20
safe 696.6
verbs fasten 47.8
close 265.6
barricade 728.12
LOCK HORNS
quarrel 793.12
fight 794.18
LOCK IN 759.15
LOCK ON 345.17
LOCK OUT
exclude 77.4
refuse work 787.10
LOCK THE DOOR 698.7
LOCK THE STABLE
DOOR AFTER THE
HORSE IS STOLEN
mistime 130.6
do in vain 667.8
mismanage 732.14
lock, stock and barrel
all 54.3
throughout 56.18
locked in 344.16
locker
refrigerator 333.6
strongbox 834.12
locker plant 333.6
locket 899.6
lock gate 395.11
lock hospital 687.30
**locking on, locking
signals** 345.8
lockjaw 684.8
lockout exclusion 77.1
shutout 787.8
locks 229.4
lock step 272.14

DO THE LOCK STEP
272.29
lockup 759.7
lock weir 395.11
loco
nouns 684.10
verbs 472.22
adjs. 472.24
loco citato 504.26
locomobile 348.26
locomote 272.17
locomotion 272.1
locomotive
mechanical 346.11
self-propelled 348.26
locomotives 272.16
locomotor 346.11
locomotor ataxia
684.8
locular 192.9
locum tenens
substitute 148.2
resident 189.2
doctor 686.5
deputy 779.1
locus locality 183.1
toilet 680.13
locus standi 215.5
locust 413a.5
locution
language 578.1
word 580.1
phrase 583.1
diction 586.1
utterance 592.3
lode mineral ~ 382.6
source of supply
658.4
lode claim 382.7
lodestar center of
attraction 225.4
magnet 287.3
star 374.5
guiding star 746.7
lodestuff 382.6
lodge
nouns house 190.5
den 190.22
society 786.10
verbs establish 142.10
stick 142.11
repose 183.14
deposit 183.15
reside 187.8
house 187.11
store 658.10
catch 820.14
LODGE A COMPLAINT
1003.7
lodger roomer 189.8
tenant 807.4
lodging
nouns habitation
187.1
housing 187.3
quarters 190.1,2
adjs. 187.14
lodginghouse 190.13
lodgment
placement 183.7
housing 187.3

abode 190.1
quarters 190.2
lodginghouse 190.13
loess residue 43.2
deposit 270.8
loft
nouns attic 191.16
head 210.5
stage ~ 609.20
verbs 315.5
loftily grandiloquently
599.13
ostentatiously
902.25
dignifiedly 903.14
arrogantly 910.15
loftiness
greatness 34.2
height 206.1
eloquence 598.6
grandiloquence
599.1
ostentation 902.1
dignity 903.2
arrogance 910.1
distinction 912.5
magnanimity 977.2
lofty great 34.9
high 206.19
airy 401.13
eloquent 598.14
grandiloquent 599.9
ceremonious 644.8
ostentatious 902.18
proud 903.11
arrogant 910.9
distinguished 912.19
magnanimous 977.6
log
nouns speedometer
268.8
firewood 330.3
wood 377.3
record 568.10
account book 843.4
verbs navigation
274.50
register 568.15
enter accounts 843.8
adjs. 377.8
**logan stone, loggan
stone** 322.8
logarithmic 86.8
logbook, log book
record book 568.10
account book 843.4
log cabin 190.8
loge 609.19
logger 412.7
loggerhead 470.4
AT LOGGERHEADS
at variance 27.10
at odds 793.17
at enmity 927.13
loggia 191.18
logging
lumbering 412.3
registration 568.14
logic
reasoning 481.2,10
manual 603.9

logical sensible 466.18
  reasonable 481.21
  credible 500.21
  plausible 510.6
logicality 481.10
logicalize 481.15
logically 481.23
logical result 493.4
logician, logicalist 481.12
logics, logistic 481.2
logistics 795.11
log line 268.8
logogram
  logogriph 547.8
  character 579.3
  anagram 879.8
logogrammatic 547.15
logograph 579.3
logographer 600.17
logographical(al) 600.28
logography 600.9
logomacher, logomachist 481.13
logomachic(al) 481.20
logomachy 481.5
logomania 594.2
logometric 86.8
logorrhea 594.2
logos, Logos 1011.8
logroll 740.20
logroller
  politics 742.31
  politician 744.6
logrolling
  legislation 740.16
  politics 742.30
logy 267.12
loin back 240.3
  meat cut 306a.17
loincloth 230.19
loiter linger 132.11
  go slow 269.8
  lag 292.4
  idle 706.12
loiterer
  slow goer 269.5
  idler 706.7
loitering
  nouns slowness 269.3
  idling 706.3
  adjs. dilatory 132.16
  slow 269.11
lokey man 273.12
Loki giant 194.13
  Norse gods 1012.6
  god of evil 1014.6
  gods 1017.5
loll
  nouns 213.2
  verbs sprawl 213.5
  repose 709.6
  LOLL AROUND 706.10
lollapaloosa 672.7
loller 706.7
lolling sprawling 213.9
  loafing 706.3
lolloper 194.11
lolloping 194.21
lolly 332 6

loma 206.5
Lombard Street 831.8
lone one 89.7
  alone 89.8
  lonely 922.12
loneliness, loneness
  aloneness 89.2
  lonesomeness 922.3
lonely, lonesome
  alone 89.8
  lonesome 922.12
lone prairie 386.1
lone wolf 932.3
lone woman 932.4
long
  nouns long time 110.4
  bull 831.13
  BE LONG OF THE MARKET 831.23
  ERE LONG 131.16
  GO LONG 831.24
  verbs 632.14
  LONG FOR 632.16
  adjs. protracted 110.11
  lengthy 201.11
  tall 206.21
  phonetics 449.18
  diffuse 591.12
  advs. 110.14
long account 831.13
long ago
  nouns 119.2
  advs. 119.13
longanimity
  patience 859.1
  forgiveness 945.1
longanimous
  patient 859.10
  forgiving 945.6
long bit 833.7
longbow 799.18
long-distance
  nouns phone girl 558.11
  phone call 558.15
  adjs. distant 198.8
  telephone 558.23
long dozen 99.7
long drink of water 206.12
longear 413.22
long-eared 447.16
longed-for 632.30
long-established
  traditional 123.12
  inveterate 142.14
  habitual 640.19
longevity 110.1
longevous 110.10
long face
  grimness 869.1
  sullen look 949.9
long-faced
  solemn 869.3
  sad 870.20
long green 833.6
longhair antiquated person 123.8
  conservative 140.4
long-haired 140.8

longhand
  nouns 600.5
  adjs. 600.24
longhead
  sagacity 466.4
  wise man 467.1
longheaded 466.16
longheadedness 466.4
long home 409.16
longhorn native 189.3
  veteran 731.14
long hundred 99.8
longiloquence 591.2
longiloquent 591.12
longing
  nouns 632.5
  adjs. 632.23
longing eye 632.4
long interest 831.13
longitude zone 179.3
  length 201.1
  celestial ~ 374.16
longitudinally 201.15
Long John Silver 823.8
long-lasting 110.10
long-legged 206.21
longlegs 206.12
long-limbed 206.21
long-lived 110.10
long-livedness 110.1
long-lost 810.7
long market 831.1
Long Melford 282.5
long million 99.12
longness 201.1
long odds
  small chance 155.9
  odds 514.5
longo intervallo
  intermittently 72.5
  irregularly 138.4
long-pending 110.11
long pig 407.13
long pull 714.1
long purse 835.1
long sea 394.14
long seller 831.13
longshanks
  tall person 206.12
  legs 272.16
longshoreman 275.10
long shot
  small chance 155.9
  long odds 514.5
  photograph 575.10
  BY A LONG SHOT 34.19
  NOT BY A LONG SHOT nowise 35.14
  by no means 522.8
long side 813.13
long-sighted
  presbyopic 439.11
  sagacious 466.16
  foreseeing 540.8
long-sightedness
  presbyopia 439.4
  sagacity 466.4
  foresight 540.1
long since 119.13,15

longsome 201.11
long-spun 591.12
long standing 110.1
long-standing
  durable 110.10
  traditional 123.12
long-suffering
  nouns tolerance 524.4
  patience 859.1
  forgiveness 945.1
  adjs. tolerant 524.11
  patient 859.10
  forgiving 945.6
long suit specialty 81.1
  forte 731.4
long time, long while 110.4
"long" wave 343.14
long way 198.2
longways 201.15
long-winded
  protracted 110.11
  prolix 591.12
  tedious 882.8
longwise 201.15
looby fool 470.1
  clumsy fellow 732.9
  boor 896.6
  rustic 917.9
look
  nouns small amount 35.4
  sight 438.3
  appearance 445.3
  THE NEW LOOK 642.1
  verbs see 438.13,16
  appear 445.10
  search 484.25
  heed 528.6
  LOOK ABOUT FOR 484.24
  LOOK ABOUT ONE be vigilant 531.8
  beware 893.7
  LOOK AFTER follow 438.14
  care for 697.18
  supervise 745.10
  serve 748.14
  LOOK A GIFT HORSE IN THE MOUTH 948.3
  LOOK AGOG 918.4
  LOOK AHEAD 540.6
  LOOK ALL OVER 484.27
  LOOK ALONG 201.10
  LOOK ANOTHER WAY 438.21
  LOOK ASQUINT look askance 438.19
  squint 439.9
  LOOK AT look 438.14
  examine 484.31
  LOOK AT IT 523.6
  LOOK AWAY 438.21
  LOOK BACK 535.11
  LOOK BACK UPON 967.10

love match 931.2
love nest abode 190.3
  rendezvous 920.8
lovepot 994.10
love potion 418.6
lover
  ~ of beauty 895.6
  sweetheart 929.11
  endearment 930.5
loverlike, loverly
  929.23
lovesick 929.24
lovesome
  lovable 929.22
  loving 929.24
loving 929.24
loving cup 914.3
lovingly 929.28
low
  nouns 347.6
  REACH A NEW LOW
    847.6
  verbs 459.2
  adjs. inconsiderable
    35.7
  inferior 37.6
  unelevated 207.6
  lowered 316.10
  phonetics 449.18
  faint-sounding
    451.16
  low-pitched 453.10
  inelegant 588.2
  menial 748.16
  low-priced 847.7
  dejected 870.22
  vulgar 896.15
  humble 904.9
  infamous 913.12
  plebeian 917.11
  unfavorable 967.22
  wicked 979.17
  indecent 988.8
  advs. near the ground
    207.10
  faintly 451.21
low-bodied 207.6
lowborn, lowbred
  917.11
lowbrow
  nouns personality
    416.5
  ignoramus 476.9
  adjs. 476.15
Low Church 1018.9
low class 678.4
low-class 678.10
low comedy 609.6
low-cut 207.7
low-down
  nouns 555.2
  adjs. 913.12
lower
  verbs reduce 39.7
  deepen 208.7
  excavate 256.15
  reduce sail 274.52
  sink 314.6
  depress 316.4
  forebode 542.8
  demote 780.4

cheapen 847.6
deject 870.18
humble 904.5
LOWER ONESELF
  condescend 904.7
  disgrace oneself
    913.7
  adjs. inferior 37.6
  reduced 39.10
  subjacent 207.8
lower, lour
  nouns 949.9
  verbs be imminent
    151.2
  be dark 336.13
  look sullen 949.15
  threaten 971.2
lower case letter 579.2
  type 601.6
lower-case
  small-lettered 579.11
  type 601.18
lower chamber 740.4
lower classes, lower
  cut 917.1
lowered reduced 39.10
  depressed 316.10
lower house 740.4
lowering
  nouns decrease 39.1
  deepening 208.6
  sinkage 314.2
  depression 316.1
  cheapening 847.4
  adjs. imminent 151.3
  ominous 542.13
lowering, louring
  dark 336.15
  sullen 949.24
  threatening 971.3
lowermost 211.7
lower side 211.1
lower world 1017.1
lowest least 37.8
  bottom 211.7
low fellow 896.6
low frequency
  343.15,31
Low German 578.8
low grade 678.4
low-grade 678.10
low house 409.16
low-hung 207.6
lowland
  nouns lowness 207.3
  plain 386.1
  adjs. 181.6
lowlands
  the country 181.1
  lowness 207.3
  plain 386.1
low-level, low-leveled
  207.6
lowlifer 984.2
lowliness 904.1
lowly inferior 37.6
  menial 748.16
  humble 904.9
  plebeian 917.11
low-lying 207.6

low-minded
  vulgar 896.15
  evil 979.20
lown dolt 470.5
  clumsy fellow 732.9
  rascal 984.3
low-necked 207.7
lowness squatness 207
  faint sound 451.1
  deep tone 453.1
  dejection 870.3
  vulgarity 896.5
  infamy 913.3
low pitch 462.4
low-pitched 453.10
low-pressure area
  277.38
low price 847.2
low-priced 847.7
low quality 678.4
low-quality 678.10
low-sized 207.6
low-sounding 451.16
low-spirited 870.22
low-tension 341.31
low-test 678.10
low tide
  low water 207.2
  tide 394.13
low-toned 453.10
low visibility 443.2
low voice 451.4
low-voiced 451.16
low water
  lowness 207.2
  low tide 394.13
  poverty 836.1
loyal obedient 764.3
  observant 766.4
  faithful 972.20
loyalty 972.7
Loyolite 1036.17
lozenge angle 250.2
  insignia 567.2
  tablet 685.6
lubber sailor 275.2
  dolt 470.5
  idler 706.7
  clumsy fellow 732.9
Lubberland 533.11
lubberly
  adjs. clumsy 732.20
  boorish 896.13
  advs. 732.23
lubricant
  nouns 379.2
  adjs. 379.10
lubricate 379.8
lubricated 994.40
lubrication 379.6
lubricative, lubricatory
  379.10
lubricator 379.2
lubricity oiliness 379.5
  lasciviousness 987.5
lubricous 987.29
lubritorium, lubritory
  379.7
Lucas's type 440.5
lucence, lucency
  luminousness 334.3

translucence 338.1
lucent shining 334.31
  translucent 338.4
lucid shining 334.31
  transparent 338.4
  sane 471.4
  intelligible 546.10
lucidity
  luminousness 334.3
  transparency 338.1
  sanity 471.1
  intelligibility 546.2
  clairvoyance 1032.8
lucidly 546.12
Lucifer
  heavenly body 374.5
  devil 1014.5
lucifer 330.5
Luck 155.2
luck chance 155.1
  good fortune 726.2
  misfortune 727.5
  BE IN LUCK 726.11
  IN LUCK 726.14
  LEAVE TO LUCK
    514.18
  OUT OF LUCK 727.14
luckily
  auspiciously 542.19
  fortunately 726.16
luckless 727.14
lucky timely 129.10
  auspicious 542.16
  fortunate 726.14
lucky bean, lucky piece
  1034.5
lucky strike
  mining 382.7
  discovery 487.1
  stroke of luck 726.3
lucrative 809.14
lucre gain 809.3
  money 833.1
  wealth 835.1
lucubrate
  study hard 562.12
  work late 714.13
lucubration
  thought 477.2
  study 562.3
  writing 600.11
  treatise 604.1
luculent 334.31
lucus naturae 85.6
ludicrous 878.5
  THE LUDICROUS 878.3
ludicrousness 878.1
luetic 684.46
luff
  nouns sail 276.14
  lieutenant 747.22
  verbs 274.27
lug
  nouns appendage 41.2
  fill 56.3
  load 193.2
  face 239.4
  freight 270.7
  pull 285.2
  ear 447.7
  verbs carry 270.11

madrigalist 463.22
madstone 1034.5
Maecenas 785.8
maelstrom
　turmoil 323.1
　whirlpool 394.12
maestro
　musician 463.1
　teacher 563.1
maestro di cappella
　463.20
Mae West 699.5
Mafia 984.10
maffick 875.3
mag
　nouns chatter 594.3
　chatterer 594.5
　verbs 594.6
magasin
　warehouse 658.6
　market 830.1
magazine
　periodical 603.11
　storehouse 658.6
　arsenal 799.2
magazinist, magaziny
　603.26
magazinist 600.15
Magdalen 871.5
mage 1033.6
magenta red 367.7
　purple 372.3
maggot larva 125.9
　eccentricity 473.2
　caprice 627.1
maggoty
　eccentric 473.4
　capricious 627.5
　filthy 680.25
　spoiled 690.40
Magi 467.5
magian
　nouns 1033.6
　adjs. 1033.14
magianism 1033.1
magic
　nouns 1033.1
　adjs. 1033.14
magic carpet 1034.7
magic circle 1033.3
magic formula 1034.4
magician 1033.6
magic lantern 575.14
magic spell 1034.1
magic wand 1034.6
magism 1033.1
magisterial
　dogmatic 512.22
　masterful 737.15
　dignified 903.12
　arrogant 910.11
　judicial 998.6
magisterialness
　imperiousness 737.2
　arrogance 910.3
magistracy
　district 179.5
　magistrateship
　　737.6
　jurisdiction 998.3

magistrate
　official 747.18
　judge 1000.1
magistrateship,
　magistrature
　authority 737.6
　jurisdiction 998.3
magma 44.5
Magna Charta, Magna
　Carta 769.2
magna cum laude
　914.12
magnanimity 977.2
magnanimous 977.6
magnanimousness
　977.2
magnate
　personage 670.8
　grandee 916.4
magnet
　nouns 287.3
　verbs 287.4
magnetic
　attractive 287.5
　electromagnetic
　　341.28
magnetic axis 341.8
magnetic elements
　341.7
magnetic field 341.3
magnetic needle 746.8
magnetics 341.7
magnetic units 341.36
magnetism 341.7
magnetite 287.3
magnetization 341.7
magnetize
　influence 171.9
　attract 287.4
　electromagnetize
　　341.24
　hypnotize 710.18
magnetod 710.8
magnetoelectricity
　341.1
magnetometer 281.7
magnetomotivity
　341.10
magnetotherapy 687.7
Magnificat 1030.3
magnification
　intensification 38.2
　enlargement 196.1
　exaggeration 615.1
　aggravation 883.1
　glorification 912.8
　worship 1030.2
magnificence
　superexcellence
　　672.2
　splendor 902.5
magnificent
　superb 672.18
　grandiose 902.21
magnifico 916.4
magnified
　exaggerated 615.4
　aggravated 883.4
magnifier 442.1
magnify intensify 38.5
　expand 196.4

exaggerate 615.3
　aggravate 883.2
　glorify 912.13
　praise 966.12
　worship 1030.11
magnifying glass
　442.1
magniloquence 599.1
magniloquent 599.9
magnitude
　amount 28.1
　greatness 34.1
　size 194.1
magnum opus 603.1
magnus Apollo 467.2
magpie 594.5
magsman 617.4
magus 1033.6
maharaja, maharajah
　747.10
maharani
　empress 747.12
　princess 916.9
maharao 747.10
mahat 1011.8
mahatma
　wise man 467.1
　expert 731.12
　occultist 1032.11
Mahavira 1020.3
mahogany 366.4
THE MAHOGANY
　215.15
mahout 273.9
maid
　nouns girl 125.6
　maidservant 748.8
　spinster 932.4
　verbs 748.14
maiden
　nouns girl 125.6
　spinster 932.4
　guillotine 1009.5
　adjs. first 68.15
　girlish 124.11
　unmarried 932.7
maidenhead
　girlhood 124.2
　membrane 228.3
　spinsterhood 932.1
maidenhood
　girlhood 124.2
　spinsterhood 932.1
maidenliness 124.4
maidenly girlish 124.11
　unmarried 932.7
maiden name 581.5
maiden speech 68.4
maid of honor 931.5
maidservant 748.8
mail
　nouns shell 227.16
　plumage 229.18
　letters 602.5
　armor 797.3
BY MAIL 270.19
　verbs dispatch 270.14
　post 602.13
　adjs. 602.15
mailable 270.17
mailbag 602.5

mailbox 602.7
mail carrier 559.5
mailclad 797.13
mail coach
　coach 271.11
　mail carrier 559.6
mailed 797.13
mailman 559.5
mail-order house 830.1
mail orderly 275.6
mail train 559.6
mail van 271.13
maim tear apart 49.13
　disable 157.9
　injure 690.13
　demolish 691.17
main
　nouns conduit 395.7
　ocean 396.1
IN THE MAIN
　essentially 5.10
　chiefly 36.19
　on the whole 54.13
　adjs. chief 36.16
　first 68.15
　most important
　　670.25
main body 54.5
main chance 155.8
main course, the
　173.2
main dish 306a.7
main drag 655.6
main feature 81.2
main features 234.2
main force
　power 156.1
　compulsion 754.2
mainland
　nouns 385.1
　adjs. 385.6
mainlander 385.3
main line 655.8
main office 225.6
mainpernor 770.8
main point 670.6
mainprise 770.2
mains abode 190.6
　farm 412.8
mainsail 276.30
mainspring 152.6
mainstay
　nouns support 215.2
　upholder 785.8
　verbs 215.22
Main Street 643.1
maintain endure 110.6
　continue 143.4
　support 215.22
　~ position 274.48
　affirm 521.4
　preserve 699.7
　insist 751.7
　lend support 783.12
　possess 806.5
　retain 811.5
　justify 1004.10
maintained 215.25
maintainer
　supporter 215.2
　backer 785.8

maintaining
nouns 751.3
adjs. 215.24
maintenance
durability 110.1
preservation 140.2
continuance 143.1
support 215.1
conservation 699.1
aid 783.3
retention 811.1
maintenance man
341.19
maintien 735.1
Maioli, Majoli 603.17
maire 747.19
maison de santé
687.29
mais si 520.18
maître d'hotel
steward 746.3
major-domo
748.6,11
proprietor 807.2
majestic great 34.9
sculpturesque 573.7
eloquent 598.14
ceremonious 644.8
regal 737.16
grandiose 902.21
dignified 903.12
majesty
greatness 34.2
eloquence 598.6
sovereignty 737.7
king 747.8
stateliness 902.5
dignity 903.2
title 915.2
divine attribute
1011.15
Majoli See **Maioli**
majolica painter 577.4
major
nouns adult 127.1
key 462.15
study 560.7
officer 747.22
adjs. superior 36.13
senior 126.18
major chord 462.17
major deities, the
1012.1
major-domo
steward 746.3
servant 748.11
major in specialize 81.4
study 562.15
majority
nouns superiority 36.1
main part 54.5
plurality 100.2
maturity 126.2
majorship 747.25
ATTAIN MAJORITY
126.9
IN THE MAJORITY
100.10
THE MAJORITY 917.3
adjs. 100.9
major key 462.15

major-league 670.16
major operations
795.9
major premise 481.8
Major Prophets
1019.3
majorship 747.25
majuscular 579.11
majuscule
letter 579.2
type 601.6
majuscule script 600.5
make
nouns character 5.3
composition 58.1
kind 61.3
amount made 167.4
structure 244.1
form 245.1
gain 809.3
receipts 842.1
ON THE MAKE 712.13
verbs compose 58.3
convert 145.8
cause 152.11
create 166.12
travel 272.18
arrive 299.6
consider 493.8
recognize 535.13
understand 546.8
do 703.6
accomplish 720.4
compel 754.4
execute 769.10
earn 809.7
MAKE AFTER 653.8
MAKE A MESS OF
spoil 690.11
botch 732.12
MAKE A MONKEY OF
469.7
MAKE A MOUNTAIN OF
A MOLEHILL 615.3
MAKE A NEW MAN OF
145.9
MAKE A PASS AT
attempt 712.5
strike at 796.17
MAKE A PIG OF
ONESELF 992.6
MAKE A PINCH 759.16
MAKE A PRODUCTION
OF 670.15
MAKE AS IF 614.22
MAKE AT
sail for 274.37
attack 796.15
MAKE A TOUCH
772.15
MAKE AWAY WITH
kill 408.13
destroy 691.12
MAKE BELIEVE 614.22
MAKE DO
make shift 668.3
get by 678.6
MAKE FOR
sail for 274.37
head for 289.10

MAKE IT
be able 156.10
succeed 722.11
MAKE MERRY 876.26
MAKE MERRY WITH
play a joke 879.14
banter 880.4
make fun of 965.8
MAKE MUCH OF
exaggerate 615.3
enthuse 633.8
rate highly 670.12
praise 966.12
MAKE NO BONES
ABOUT 622.10
MAKE NOTHING OF
underestimate 497.2
not understand
547.10
unimportant 671.11
MAKE OFF
decamp 300.11
flee 629.10
MAKE OFF WITH
822.13
MAKE ONE
identify 14.5
combine 52.3
unify 89.5
marry 931.15
MAKE ONE'S BLOOD
RUN COLD 889.14
MAKE ONE SEE
DOUBLE 994.28
MAKE ONESELF
SCARCE
absent oneself 186.7
leave 300.10
flee 629.11
MAKE ONESELF
UNDERSTOOD 546.6
MAKE ONE'S MARK
succeed 722.9
prosper 726.9
MAKE ONE'S MOUTH
WATER 648.5
MAKE ONE'S WAY
progress 293.4
support oneself
657.11
MAKE OUT
contrive 7.6
see 438.12
know 474.12
solve 486.2
detect 487.5
prove 504.11
recognize 535.13
understand 546.8
write out 568.15
draft 600.22
draw up 652.11
eke out 657.11
make shift 668.3
manage 722.11
execute 769.10
MAKE OUT LIKE
pretend 614.22
affect 901.12
MAKE OVER
convert 145.8

reproduce 168.8
enthuse 633.8
rate highly 670.12
remake 692.18
transfer 815.3
MAKE OVERTURES
influence 171.9
communicate with
552.8
MAKE PLAIN
explain 550.11
manifest 553.5
MAKE READY 718.6
MAKE SAIL 274.21
MAKE SENSE
be reasonable 481.18
be understandable
546.4
MAKE SHORT WORK OF
destroy 691.11
hasten 707.5
accomplish 720.4
win easily 724.5
MAKE STRIDES
progress 293.2
improve 689.7
MAKE THE WORST OF
overestimate 496.2
be pessimistic 887.9
MAKE TRACKS
go fast 268.11
hasten off 300.14
MAKE UP
complete 56.6
compose 58.3
assemble 74.17
manufacture 166.12
invent 166.14
compose print
601.14
trump up 614.18
improvise 628.8
prepare 718.7
settle 769.9
make peace 802.10
MAKE UP FOR
compensate 33.4
atone for 1010.4
MAKE UP FOR LOST
TIME
progress 293.2
improve 689.7
be active 705.12
hasten 707.5
MAKE UP ONE'S MIND
decide 493.11
convince oneself
500.16
resolve 622.7
decide upon 635.13
persuade oneself
646.24
MAKE UP TO
influence 171.9
head for 289.10
communicate with
552.8
address 592.18
curry favor 904.8
make friends 925.11

MAKE USE OF
  use 663.10,16
  borrow 819.4
  appropriate 820.16
MAKE WATER 309.12
MAKE WAY FOR
  substitute 148.4
  make room 264.13
  turn aside 290.6
  avoid 629.6
  facilitate 730.6
MAKE WHOOPEE
  876.25
MAKE WING 277.42
NOT BE ABLE TO
  MAKE HEAD OR
  TAIL OF
  be uncertain 513.9
  not understand
    547.10
NOT MAKE ANY
  DIFFERENCE
  671.10
NOT MAKE SENSE
  547.9
NOT MAKE THE GRADE
  cannot 157.8
  fall short 312.2
make-believe
  nouns 614.3
  adjs. theatrical 609.37
  sham 614.27
make-peace 803.5
maker producer 166.10
  doer 716.1
  types of ~ 716.12
THE MAKER 1011.2
makeshift
  nouns pretext 647.1
  temporary expedient
    668.2
  adjs. substitute 148.8
  expedient 668.6
make-up character 5.3
  composition 58.1
  structure 244.1
  book ~ 603.13
  theatrical ~ 609.21
  cosmetics 898.11
make-up man 609.27
make-up room 601.9
makeweight
  counterweight 33.2
  complement 56.5
  weight 351.4
making
  manufacture 166.3
  amount made 167.4
BE THE MAKING OF
  benefit 672.11
  make better 689.9
  help 783.11
IN THE MAKING
  718.23
makings
  component 58.2
  gains 809.3
  receipts 842.1
HAVE THE MAKINGS
  158.8
Malachi 1020.1

malacology 414.1
Malacostraca, mala-
  costracans 414.8
malade imaginaire
  688.14
maladie du pays 632.5
maladjusted 732.19
maladjustment
  psychological ~
    688.16
  inaptitude 732.1
maladminister 732.13
maladministration
  732.6
maladroit 732.20
maladroitness 732.3
malady 684.1
mala fides 973.5
malaise pain 423.1
  discomfort 864.1
malapert
  nouns 911.5
  adjs. 911.9
malaprop 517.6
malapropism, mala-
  propoism 517.6
malapropos,
  mal à propos
  inappropriate 27.7
  untimely 130.7
  inexpedient 669.5
malaria fume 400.1
  poison 674.4
  disease 684.9
malarial 684.46
malarial fever 684.9
malarkey 545.3
Malayan race 417.2,17
malconformation
  248.3
malcontent
  nouns rebel 765.5
  grumbler 867.3
  adjs. 867.5
malcontented 867.5
mal de mer 684.22
mal du pays 632.5
male
  nouns 419.4
  adjs. 419.11
malediction 970.1
maledictory 970.8
malefaction 980.2
malefactor
  evildoer 941.1
  wrongdoer 984.8
malefactory 980.4
malefic
  harmful 673.12
  malicious 937.18
maleficence 937.5
maleficent 937.18
male gamete 405.7
maleness sex 418.1
  masculinity 419.1
male variety 419.3
malevolence 937.4
malevolent
  nouns 941.1
  adjs. 937.17
malevolently 937.28

malfeasance
  mismanagement
    732.6
  wrongdoing 980.1,2
malfeasant
  nouns 941.1
  adjs. 980.4
malfeasor
  evildoer 941.1
  wrongdoer 984.8
malformation 248.3
malformed 248.12
malgré soi 621.8
mali 412.6
malice 937.5
WITH MALICE
  AFORETHOUGHT
  intentionally 651.11
  maliciously 937.28
malice prepense 937.5
malicious 937.18
malicious gossip 556.8
maliciously 937.28
maliciousness 937.5
malific 542.15
malign
  verbs 969.9
  adjs. deadly 408.23
  unpropitious 542.15
  harmful 673.12
  virulent 682.5
  malicious 937.18
malignance,
  malignancy
  deadliness 408.8
  harmfulness 673.5
  malice 937.5
malignant
  deadly 408.23
  inauspicious 542.15
  harmful 673.12
  virulent 682.5
  malicious 937.18
malignity
  deadliness 408.8
  harmfulness 673.5
  malice 937.5
malik 915.3
malikzadi 916.9
malinger 629.9
malingerer 629.3
malingering
  nouns 629.2
  adjs. 629.14
malingery 629.2
malism 887.6
malison 970.1
malist 887.7
malkin 62.7
mall 655.3
mallard 306a.22
malleability
  pliancy 356.2
  teachability 562.5
malleable pliant 356.9
  teachable 562.18
mallet 573.5
malleus 447.7
malnutrition dietary
  deficiency 307.11
  illness 684.8

malodor 436.1
malodorous fetid 436.5
  rotten 690.38
malodorousness
  smelliness 436.2
  rottenness 690.6
malpractice
  misuse 665.1
  wrongdoing 980.1
malt
  malted milk 306a.47
  beer 994.17
maltreat 665.5
maltreatment 665.2
malum 980.2
malversation 980.1
mam, mama 169.10
mama's boy
  mollycoddle 420.11
  spoiled child 757.5
mamelon, mamelo-
  nation 255.6
mamma
  mother 169.10
  breast 255.6
  gland 310.9
mammal 413.3
Mammalia 414.12
mammalian
  nouns 413.3
  adjs. bosom 255.18
  animal 413.47
mammalogy 414.1
mammals 414.12
mammary, mammate
  255.18
mammary gland 310.9
mammectomy 687.25
mammiform 255.18
mammilla, mammil-
  lation 255.6
mammillary 255.18
mammilloplasty
  687.27
mammon money 833.1
  wealth 835.1
mammoth
  nouns behemoth
    194.14
  animal 413.6
  adjs. 194.20
mammy
  mother 169.10
  Negro 417.7
  nursemaid 697.7
man
  nouns prehistoric ~
    123.25
  adult 127.1
  old ~ 169.11
  mankind 416.1
  person 416.3
  menfolk 419.3
  male 419.5
  servant 748.3
  chessman 876.18
  average ~ 917.7
  lover 929.11
  husband 931.8
A MAN 891.8
LIKE A MAN 622.18

PUT ON THE NEW
  MAN 145.9
TO A MAN 520.17
verbs equip 657.8
  fortify 797.9
interjs. 863.17
mana 1012.10
man about town
  sophisticate 731.15
  dandy 901.9
manacle
  nouns 758.4
  verbs 758.10
manage
  nouns 565.12
  verbs fare 7.6
  operate 163.5
  pilot 274.14
  eke out 657.11
  make use of 663.10
  make shift 668.3
  contrive 722.11
  govern 739.11
  direct 745.8
MANAGE ONESELF
  735.4
manageability
  wieldiness 730.2
  compliance 763.4
manageable
  wieldy 730.12
  compliant 763.14
management
  operation 163.1
  handling 663.2
  use 663.8
  guardianship 697.2
  government 739
  direction 745
  directorate 746.10
  husbandry 849.1
manager
  actor's ~ 609.29
  director 746.1
managerial 745.12
managership 745.4
managing 745.12
man among men, a
  983.4
mañana
  nouns 121.1
  advs. 121.9
man and wife 931.10
manas 1032.20
man-at-arms 798.7
manavel, manarvel
  822.13
man-bird 278.1
manciple 657.6
mandamus 750.6
mandarin 747.14,17
mandatary 180.1
mandate
  country 180.1
  referendum 740.18
  command 750.2
  commission 778.1
mandatory
  imperative 750.13
  obligatory 960.14
mandibles 264.5

mandibular 264.22
mandola, mandolin
  464.4
mandolinist 463.5
mandolute 464.4
mandore 464.2,4
mandrel 320.5
manducate 306.25
manducation 306.1
manducatory 306.30
mane 229.2,4
man-eater eater 306.13
  cannibal 408.10
  savage 941.6
man-eating 306.29
manège
  horsemanship 272.6
  horse training 415.1
  school 565.12
manes 1032.17
maneuver
  nouns action 703.3
  strategy 733.4
  military ~ 795.9
  verbs operate 163.5
  navigate 274.48
  intrigue 652.10
  manipulate 733.10
maneuverability 163.3
maneuverable 163.11
maneuverer
  schemer 652.8
  strategist 733.7
maneuvering
  nouns intrigue 652.6
  strategy 733.4
  military ~ 795.10
  adjs. 733.14
maneuvers
  navigation 274.7
  strategy 733.4
man fish 1012.17
man Friday
  servant 748.1
  assistant 785.7
man from Mars 281.8
manful manly 419.11
  courageous 891.17
manfully 622.18
manfulness
  masculinity 419.1
  courage 891.1
mange itch 425.3
  disease 684.10
manger 191.2
manger son blé en
  herbe 852.4
mangle
  tear apart 49.13
  press 259.6
  injure 690.13
  demolish 691.17
mangled torn 49.22
  mutilated 57.5
mangling
  laceration 49.2
  demolition 691.5
mangy itchy 425.10
  contemptible 913.12
manhandle
  move 270.10

maltreat 665.5
man-hater 938.2
man-hating 938.3
manhole 264.4
manhood
  maturity 126.2
  masculinity 419.1
  mankind 419.3
  courage 891.1
man-hour 107.2
man hunter 779.10
mania 472.1,12
maniac
  nouns 472.15
  adjs. 472.29
maniacal 472.29
manic 472.24
manic-depressive
  nouns 472.16
  adjs. 472.26
manichord, mani-
  chordon 464.13
manicure
  nouns 898.10
  verbs 679.19
manicurist 898.12
maniéré 901.15
manifest
  nouns train 271.12
  statement 843.3
  verbs demonstrate
    504.9
  exhibit 553.5
  disclose 554.4
  indicate 566.16
MANIFEST ITSELF
  445.8
  adjs. visible 443.6
  indubitable 512.15
  apparent 553.8
BE MANIFEST 553.7
manifestable 553.13
manifestation
  appearance 445.1
  evidence 504.1
  display 553
  disclosure 554
  indication 566.1
manifested 553.12
manifestly
  visibly 443.8
  apparently 553.14
manifestness
  visibility 443
  unmistakableness
    512.1
  apparentness 553.3
manifesto
  announcement
    557.2
  decree 750.4
manifold
  nouns 24.4
  verbs copy 22.8
  transcribe 600.19
  adjs. multiform 19.3
  multiple 100.8
manikin dwarf 195.6
  figure 570.4
man in the moon
  moon 374.8

fancy 533.5
man in the street
  a nobody 671.7
  common man 917.7
maniple 798.19
manipulatability 163.3
manipulatable 163.11
manipulate
  operate 163.5
  pilot 277.43
  handle 424.6
  falsify 614.17
  employ 663.10
  maneuver 733.10
  ~ the market
    831.25
manipulation
  operation 163.1
  automatic ~ 348.7
  handling 424.2
  intrigue 652.6
  using 663.8
  stratagem 733.4
  stock market ~
    831.20
manipulator
  operator 163.4
  strategist 733.7
manito 1012.10
mankind
  humankind 416
  menfolk 419.3
manlihood
  maturity 126.2
  masculinity 419.1
manlike
  anthropoid 416.11
  manly 419.11
manliness
  masculinity 419.1
  courage 891.1
manly
  masculine 419.11
  courageous 891.17
  honorable 972.13
man mountain 158.6
manna food 306a.8
  nectar 430.4
  sustenance 783.3
mannequin 570.4
manner mode 7.4
  kind 61.3
  appearance 445.3
  diction 586.2
  custom 640.1
  way 655.1
  behavior 735.1
ALL MANNER OF 19.4
IN A MANNER
  as it were 20.19
  to a degree 35.11
  theoretically 498.16
IN THE MANNER OF
  20.18
IN WHAT MANNER
  655.11
mannered
  elegant 587.9
  formal 644.7
  behaviored 735.7
  affected 901.15

mannerism
  elegance 587.3
  affectation 901.2
mannerist stylist 586.3
  affecter 901.7
mannerless 935.5
mannerliness 934.3
mannerly
  adjs. 934.16
  advs. 934.19
manner of speaking
  figure of speech
    549.1
  diction 586.2
  enunciation 592.6
manners
  etiquette 644.3
  behavior 735.1
  mannerliness 934.3
mannified 419.13
mannify 419.10
mannish 419.11,13
mannishness 419.1
man of action 705.8
man of all work 748.10
man of experience
  731.15
man of honor 972.8
man of iron 859.3
man of learning, man
  of letters 475.3
man of mark
  personage 670.8
  celebrity 912.9
man of means 835.6
man of science 474.11
Man of Sorrows, the
  1011.12
man of straw
  nonentity 4.2
  insignificancy 671.7
man of taste 895.6
man of the world
  fashionable person
    642.7
  sophisticate 731.15
man-of-war 276.7
manometer 400.6
manor 808.7
manor house 190.5
manorial 808.10
man power 156.4
manse 1040.7
manservant 748.3
mansion house 190.7
  astrology 374.20
mansional 90.27
man-sized 194.16
man-sized job 729.2
manslaughter 408.2
manslayer 408.10
mantel 215.14
mantelet, mantlet
  797.4
mantelpiece,
  mantelshelf 215.14
mantilla 230.26
mantle
  nouns cover 227.2
  garment 230.12
  ~ of snow 332.9

insignia 567.1
  clerical ~ 1039.2
  verbs spread out
    196.6
  cover 227.21
  cloak 230.39
  redden 367.5
  scum 404.5
  flush 855.20
  blush 906.8
  anger 950.14
mantled 227.34
mantling
  reddening 367.3
  blushing 906.5
mantrap 616.11
manual
  nouns book 603.5,8
  guidebook 746.9
  ritual 1038.12
  adjs. 656.7
manual alphabet 448.4
manual art 572.3
manual labor 714.4
manual training 560.3
manucure 898.12
manufactory 717.3
manufactural 166.21
manufacture
  nouns making 166.3
  product 167.1
  verbs make 166.12
  trump up 614.18
manufactured 166.27
manufacturer 166.10
manufacturing 166.21
manumission 761.1
manumit 761.4
manumitter 940.2
manure
  nouns fertilizer 164.4
  dung 309.4
  verbs 164.8
manure pile 680.10
manus 811.4
manuscript
  nouns writing
    600.4,11
  copy 601.4
  adjs. 600.24
Manvantara 107.5
man without a country
  924.3
many
  nouns 101.3
  THE MANY 917.3
  adjs. different 16.7
  various 19.4
  numerous 101.7
  frequent 135.4
  NOT MANY 102.4
many-colored, many-
  hued 373.9
manyness 101.1
manyplies 192.3
many-sided
  multiform 19.3
  changeable 141.6
  multilateral 241.7
  versatile 731.23
many-sidedness 731.3

many times
  adjs. 135.4
  advs. repeatedly
    103.16
  frequently 135.6
map
  nouns face 239.4
  chart 652.4
  verbs radar 345.17
  chart 652.11
maple sirup 430.3
mapping 345.8
maquereau 987.18
mar disfigure 248.7
  blemish 677.4
  impair 690.11
  botch 732.12
marabou 44.9
Marabout 922.5
marantic 204.19
marasmic 204.19
marasmus
  emaciation 204.6
  disease 684.14
marathon 794.12
maraud
  nouns 822.5
  verbs 822.15
marauder 823.6
marauding
  nouns 822.5
  adjs. 822.21
marble
  nouns smoothness
    259.3
  hardness 355.6
  variegation 373.6
  sculpture 573.2
  plaything 876.16
  HAVE ALL ONE'S
    MARBLES 466.10
  verbs 373.7
  adjs. hard 355.10
  white 363.8
marble city 409.15
marbled 373.12
marblehearted 937.23
marbleize 373.7
marblelike
  hard 355.10
  stone 383.7
marcel
  nouns 229.15
  verbs wave 229.22
  curl 253.5
marcescence 690.4
marcescent 690.43
march
  nouns boundary
    234.3
  frontier 234.5
  walk 272.12
  gait 272.15
  progress 293.1
  music 461.11
  route 655.2
  ON THE MARCH
    272.41
  verbs ~ with 199.9
  border 234.10
  walk 272.29

MARCH AGAINST
  796.18
MARCH OFF 300.6
MARCH PAST 71.8
Märchen 606.7
marches bounds 234.1
  frontier 234.5
marching 272.10
marchioness 916.7
marchland 234.5
march of time 105.4
marconigram 558.16
marconigraph 558.22
marconigraphy 558.3
Mardi gras 876.4
mare horse 413.12
  female animal
    420.10
maréchal 747.22
Marengo 413.21
mare's-nest 616.7
mare's-tail 403.1
marge 234.10
margin
  nouns room 178.3
  border 234.4
  free scope 760.3
  deposit 770.3
  stock market 832.9
  verbs 234.10
  MARGIN UP 831.23
marginal 234.11
marginate
  verbs 234.10
  adjs. 234.12
margined, marginated
  234.12
margrave, margravine
  916.5
mariage de
  convenance 931.2
marigold 833.8
marigraph 394.16
market garden 412.10
marimba 464.20
marimbaist 463.6
marina 698.6
marinate, marinade
  699.8
marination 699.2
marine
  nouns mariner 275.4
  ships 276.1
  navy 798.27
  adjs. nautical 274.60
  oceanic 396.7
marine animals 413.53
Marine Corps 798.28
marine painting 572.5
mariner 275
marines 798.28
Mariolatry, Mariology
  1018.7
marionette
  figure 570.4
  doll 876.16
marital 931.19
marital affinity 12.1
maritime
  nautical 274.60
  oceanic 396.7

mark
nouns degree 29.1
characteristic 80.3
boundary 234.3
notch 261.4
musical ~ 462.12
evidence 504.1
indication 566.2,7,9
marking 566.4
signature 581.10
dupe 618.1
objective 651.2
importance 670.1
blemish 677.3
coin 833.9
reputation 912.5
ABOVE THE MARK
36.20
AT LOW-WATER MARK
660.7
BELOW THE MARK
least 37.9
below 207.11
inferior 678.11
HIT THE MARK
succeed 722.8
impress 853.16
LEAVE ONE'S MARK
912.10
MISS THE MARK
fall short 312.4
be imperfect 676.3
fail 723.13
OF MARK
remarkable 34.10
important 670.18
famous 912.17
ON THE MARK 718.16
OVER THE MARK 36.20
TOE THE MARK 82.4
UP TO THE MARK
up to par 672.17
competent 731.22
verbs distinguish 16.6
specify 80.9
characterize 80.11
rate 493.9
show 504.9
heed 528.6
indicate 566.16,17
make a ~ 566.18
engrave 576.12
letter 579.9
punctuate 584.12
destine 638.7
emphasize 670.13
stain 677.6
MARK DOWN
record 568.15
cheapen 847.6
MARK MY WORDS
521.9
MARK OFF
characterize 80.11
circumscribe 233.4
measure 489.12
mark 566.18
plot 652.11
assign 814.10
markdown 847.4

marked
remarkable 34.10
superior 36.13
characteristic 80.13
engraved 576.16
destined 638.9
important 670.18,22
distinguished 912.17
MARKED DOWN
at a bargain 827.14
cheapened 847.9
marker
aviation 277.16
radio ~ 343.5
indication 566.9
monument 568.11
recorder 569.1
marker buoy 345.7
market
nouns square 182.7
trade 825.1
clientele 826.3
sale 827.1
mart 830
GO TO MARKET 712.5
IN THE MARKET FOR
searching 484.40
in pursuit 653.12
ON THE MARKET
827.14
PLAY THE MARKET
831.23
PUT ON THE MARKET
832.12
THE MARKET 831.1
verbs trade 825.11
shop 826.8
sell 827.8
marketability 827.7
marketable 827.12
marketer 826.5
market gardener 412.6
market hall 830.4
marketing
shopping 826.1
selling 827.2
GO MARKETING 826.8
market overt 830.2
IN MARKET OVERT
553.15
market place
square 182.7
mart 830.2
IN THE MARKET
PLACE 553.15
market price
stock market 832.8
price 844.2
AT THE MARKET
PRICE 832.14
marking mark 566.4
engraving 576.1
mark of Cain 913.6
marksman
shooter 284.9
proficient 731.11
marksmanship 731.1
marl 384.1
marlinespike 286.4
marly 384.7
marm 420.8

marmalade 306a.39
marmoreal 363.8
maroon
verbs 631.5
adjs. 367.7
marplot 728.9
marquee 609.22
marquetry 373.4
marquis 916.5
marquisate 916.10
marred
deformed 248.12
blemished 677.8
spoiled 690.28
marriable 126.12
marriage union 47.1
matrimony 931
wedding 931.4
CONTRACT MARRIAGE
768.6
GIVE IN MARRIAGE
931.15
marriageability 931.3
marriageable
mature 126.12
nubile 931.21
marriage bed 931.1
marriage broker 931.13
marriage contract
768.3
marriage of con-
venience 931.2
marriage portion 816.9
marriage song 931.4
marriage vow 768.3
married 931.19,22
married couple 931.10
married state 931.11
marrow essence 5.2
substance 193.4
center 225.2
marrowless
enervated 157.19
weak 159.12
marry join 47.5
wed 931.15,16
Mars planet 374.6
war-god 795.18
god 1012.5
marsh 399
marshal
nouns
constable 697.14
officer 747.22
M.C. 876.22
verbs arrange 60.8
escort 73.8
marshland 399.1
marshy 399.3
Mars ship 281.2
marsupial
nouns 413.3
adjs. vascular 192.9
animal 413.47
Marsupialia 414.12
marsupian 413.3
mart 830.1,2
martello, martello
tower tower 206.11
stronghold 797.6
martial 795.26

martiality 795.16
martial law
anarchy 738.2
government 739.4
force 754.3
martial music
music 461.11
militarism 795.17
Martian 281.8
martinet 747.15
martingale
harness 657.5
curb 728.7
Martinmas 1038.15
martyr
nouns 864.11
verbs 864.20
martyrdom
killing 408.1
torture 864.7
punishment 1008.2
martyrize 864.20
Marut 1012.7
marvel
nouns 918.2
verbs 918.4
marvelous
remarkable 34.10
extraordinary 85.13
superb 672.18
wonderful 918.9
marvelousness
unusualness 85.2
superexcellence
672.2
wonderfulness 918.3
Marxism 743.4
Marxist 743.11
Mary Baker Eddy
1020.3
mascara 898.11
mascle 567.2
mascot, mascotte
1034.5
masculine
nouns male 419.4
gender 584.8
adjs. 419.11
masculineness 419.1
masculinity 419
masculinize 419.10
mash
nouns mixture 44.6
jumble 62.3
feed 306a.4
pulp 389.2
infatuation 929.4
MASHED ON 929.27
verbs soften 356.6
pulverize 360.9
smash 389.5
masher
pulverizer 360.7
pulper 389.4
dandy 901.9
philanderer 930.11
mashiness 389.1
mashing 360.4
mash note 930.12
mashy 389.6
masjid 1040.2

mask
  nouns cover 227.2
    sculpture 573.3
    drama 609.4
    disguise 616.10
    pretext 647.1
    ball 877.2
    party 920.10
  verbs cover 227.21
    conceal 613.7
masked 227.34
masked ball 877.2
masker 617.7
masochism 688.32
masochist 688.14
masochistic 688.48
Mason 1032.11
Masonic, Masonical
  1032.24
Masonry 1032.1
Masora, Masorah
  1019.5
masque drama 609.4
  mask 616.10
  ball 877.2
  party 920.10
masquerade
  costume 230.9
  impersonation 570.2
  disguise 616.10
  dance 877.2
  party 920.10
masquerade as
  impersonate 570.10
  pose as 614.23
masquerader 617.7
Mass 1038.9
mass
  nouns substance 3.1
    quantity 28.1
    large amount 34.3
    main part 54.5
    accumulation 74.8
    majority 100.2
    size 194.1
    lump 194.10
    thickness 203.2
    solid 353.6
  IN THE MASS 54.12
  THE MASSES 917.3
  verbs accumulate
    74.17
    load 183.16
massacre
  nouns 408.3
  verbs 408.17
massacrer 408.10
massage
  nouns rubbing 349.3
    feeling 424.2
  verbs rub 349.6
    stroke 424.8
    therapy 687.33
massager, massageuse,
  massagist 349.4
massaging 349.3
Mass book 1038.12
massed 74.21
mass energy 325.14
masser, masseur,
  masseuse 349.4

massive substantial 3.5
  bulky 194.19
  thick 203.8
  ponderous 351.17
  compacted 353.12
massiveness
  bulkiness 194.9
  ponderousness 351.2
mass market 827.1
mass meeting 74.2
mass movement
  152.10
mass murder 408.3
mass-produce 166.11
mass-produced 166.25
massy 194.19
mast 276.13,29
mastaba 409.16
Master 419.7
  THE MASTER 1011.12
master
  nouns boy 125.5
    wise man 467.1
    teacher 563.1
    painting 572.11
    artist 577.1
    ~ craftsman
      716.6
    conqueror 724.2
    expert 731.12
    chief 747.24
    proprietor 807.2
    degree 915.6
    judge 1000.4
  BE MASTER OF
    know 474.13
    be skilled 731.16
  MASTER OF
    versed in 474.19
    skilled in 731.25
    possessed of 806.10
  verbs know well
    474.13
    learn 562.9
    conquer 725.10
    dominate 739.14
    subdue 762.9
    ~ one's feelings
      856.7
  adjs. main 36.16
    most important
      670.25
    governing 739.17
masterate 915.6
masterdom 737.6
mastered 725.16
masterful
  skillful 731.20
  imperious 737.15
  arrogant 910.11
masterfulness
  imperiousness 737.2
  arrogance 910.3
masterhood 737.6
master key 264.10
masterly
  adjs. 731.20
  advs. 731.28
mastermind
  nouns wise man 467.1

  expert 731.12
  verbs 745.8
master of ceremonies
  radio 343.26
  theaterman 609.27
  revel master 876.22
Master of the Rolls
  1000.5
masterpiece,
  masterwork
  work of art 572.11
  masterwork 731.10
master plan 652.1
master sergeant
  747.23
mastership
  proficiency 731.1
  mastery 737.6
  control 739.2
  directorship 745.4
master stroke 731.10
mastery
  influence 171.1
  vanquishment 725.1
  proficiency 731.1
  dominion 737.6
  control 739.2
  GET THE MASTERY OF
    171.12
  HAVE THE MASTERY
    OF 739.14
masthead
  nouns 483.2
  verbs 1008.10
mastic 388.6
masticate chew 306.25
  macerate 389.5
mastication
  chewing 306.1
  pulpification 389.3
masticatory 306.30
Mastigophora, mas-
  tigophorans 414.3
mastodon
  nouns prehistoric
    animal 123.26
    behemoth 194.14
    animal 413.6
  adjs. 194.20
mastoiditis 684.8
mastology 414.1
mastotomy 687.26
mat
  nouns bedding 215.21
    rug 227.9
    hair 229.4
    dullness 336.6
  verbs complicate 46.3
    interweave 221.7
    dull 336.11
  adjs. 336.19
matador killer 408.10
  bullfighter 798.4
mat-burn 690.7
match
  nouns counterpart
    20.5
    equal 30.5
    two 90.2
    lighter 330.5
    contest 794.3

  game 876.9
  marriage 931.1
  verbs coincide 14.4
    be alike 20.7
    correspond 26.7
    equal 30.6
    pair 90.5
    size 194.15
    parallel 217.4,5
    oppose 238.4
    compare 490.4,7
    ~ coins 514.17
    marry 931.15
    give in kind 953.6
matched 90.8
matching
  nouns 490.1
  adjs. analogous 20.11
    comparable 490.8
matchless 36.17
matchmaker 931.13
mate
  nouns counterpart
    20.5
    accompanier 73.4
    seaman 275.7
    officer 747.24
    confederate 785.2
    comrade 926.4
    spouse 931.7
  verbs pair 90.5
    copulate 168.10
mated 90.8
matelot 275.1
mater dolorosa 1013.5
materfamilias 169.10
material
  nouns substance 3.2
    covering ~ 227.46
    matter 375.2
    fabric 377.5
    types of ~
      377.13–19
    writing ~ 600.30
  adjs. substantial 3.4
    essential 5.8
    corporeal 375.9
    salient 670.20
    materialistic 1029.16
material assets 808.8
materialism
  physicism 375.5
  unspirituality 1029.2
materialist 375.6
materialistic
  naturalistic 375.11
  worldly 1029.16
materiality
  substantiality 3
  matter 375.2
  importance 670.1
materialization
  corporealization
    375.7
  appearance 445.1
  ghost 1015.1
  spirit ~1032.6
materialize
  occur 150.6
  corporealize 375.8
  appear 445.8

turn up 487.9
materialness 375.1
materials 377.1
material wealth 835.1
materia medica 686.1
materiate 375.9
matériel 657.4
maternal 169.13
maternal love 929.5
maternity, maternal-
  ness 169.3
maternity hospital,
  maternity ward
  687.29
mates 90.2
mat finish 336.6
math, mathematic 87.2
mathematical
  numerative 87.17
  exact 515.15
mathematical elements
  86.9
mathematical point
  195.7
mathematical precision
  515.3
mathematician 87.9
mathematics
  numbers 87.2
  types of ~ 87.18
matin, matinal 133.6
matinee 920.9
matinee idol
  actor 610.1
  darling 929.13
mating 168.3
matins morning 133.1
  devotions 1030.8
matman 798.3
matriarch 169.10
matriarchal 739.16
matriarchate 739.5
matriarchic 739.16
matriarchy 739.5
matricide 408.4
matriculate list 88.7
  register 568.15
matriculation
  listing 88.6
  registry 568.14
matrimonial 931.19
matrimonial agency
  931.13
matrimonial union
  931.1
matrimony
  marriage 931.1
  sacrament 1038.5
  CONTRACT MATRI-
  MONY 931.16
matrix mold 25.6
  womb 152.9
  gangue 382.6
matroclinous 169.15
matrocliny 169.6
matron woman 420.5
  housekeeper 747.2
  wife 931.9
matronage 420.1
matronal 420.14
matronhood 420.1

matronize 697.18
matronlike 420.14
matronly 420.14
matron of honor 931.5
matronship 420.1
Matsya 1012.8
matted complex 46.4
  uncombed 62.13
matter
  nouns circumstance
    8.2
  amount 28.1
  affair 150.3
  content 193.4
  pus 309.6
  material 375.2
  fluid 387.3
  topic 483.1
  printed ~ 601.4
  writing 600.11
  motive 646.1
  business 654.1
  importance 670.1
  trouble 729.3
  BE THE MATTER
    729.12
  IN THE MATTER OF
    9.10
  LITTLE MATTER, NOT
    MATTER 671.10
  OF NO MATTER 671.14
  verbs suppurate
    309.13
  be important 670.11
mattering
  nouns 309.6
  adjs. 309.19
matter of concern
  670.5
matter of course 640.4
matter of fact fact 1.3
  prosaicness 881.2
matter-of-fact
  practical 534.6
  plain-speaking 589.3
  prosaic 608.5
  dull 881.8
  plain 900.6
matter of indifference
  trifle 671.6
  mediocrity 678.1
matter of life and
  death
  necessity 637.4
  urgency 670.4
matter of no conse-
  quence 671.6
matters 150.4
matters in hand 654.2
matte shot 575.10
mattress 215.21
maturant 685.27
maturate
  suppurate 309.13
  ripen 720.8
maturation
  aging 126.6
  incubation 166.7
  suppuration 309.6
  development 321.2
  refinement 689.2

full development
  720.2
maturative
  nouns 685.27
  adjs. 309.19
mature
  verbs grow old 126.9
  be converted 145.12
  develop 321.6
  grow 689.10
  ripen 720.8
  fall due 838.7
  adjs. adult 126.12
  ready 718.16
  ripe 720.12
  due 838.10
mature age 126.2
maturescent 126.12
mature thought 477.5
Maturine 1036.17
maturity
  adulthood 126.2
  readiness 718.4
  full development
    720.2
  falling due 838.1
matutinal 133.6
matzoth 306a.27
maud, Maud 413.23
maudlin silly 469.8
  sentimental 853.21
  drunk 994.38
maul abuse 665.5
  bruise 690.14
Mau Mau 823.4
maund, maun 192.4
maunder digress 591.9
  mumble 593.8
maundering
  nouns discursiveness
    591.3
  mumbling 593.4
  adjs. 591.13
Maundy Thursday
  1038.15
mausoleum 409.16
mauvaise honte 901.6
mauvais goût 896.1
mauvais suject 984.2
mauve 372.3
Mauve Decade 107.7
maverick
  newcomer 78.4
  nonconformist 83.4
  calf 413.8
mavis 463.15
maw 192.3
mawkish
  nauseous 428.7
  sentimental 853.21
  disgusting 862.9
mawkishness
  sentimentality 853.7
  odiousness 862.2
Mawworm
  hypocrite 617.8
  pietist 1027.3
maxilla 264.5
maxillary 264.22
maxim belief 500.2
  aphorism 516

rule 749.2
maximal
  supreme 36.15
  highest 210.9
maximize 615.3
maximum
  nouns most 36.3
  consummation 56.4
  summit 210.2
  adjs. supreme 36.15
  highest 210.9
may be able 156.10
  be allowed 775.14
maybe 508.9
Mayfair 642.6
May fly 111.5
mayhem 690.1
mayonnaise 306a.37
mayor, mayoress
  747.19
mayoralty, mayorship
  998.3
Maypole 216.1
Mazda 1011.16
maze complication
  46.2
  confusion 530.3
mazed
  bewildered 513.22
  muddled 530.13
mazuma 833.2
mazy complex 46.4
  circuitous 319.7
M.C. radio 343.26
  master-of-ceremonies
    609.27
  congressman 744.3
  revel master 876.22
McCarthyism
  persecution 665.3
  policy 742.4
McCoy, the 515.6
me 80.5
mead, meadow 410.8
meadowy 410.40
meager
  verbs 204.12
  adjs. sparse 102.5
  narrow 204.13
  lean 204.16
  scanty 660.8
  trivial 671.16
meagerness
  fewness 102.1
  thinness 204.5
  scantiness 660.2
meal fodder 306a.4
  repast 306.5
  bran 360.5
mealie 410.27
mealiness 360.1
meal ticket 834.2,9
mealy powdery 360.11
  pale 362.9
mealymouthed
  hypocritical 614.33
  suave 934.18
  flattering 968.9
  sanctimonious
    1027.5

mealymouthedness
  hypocrisy 614.6
  suaveness 934.5
  flattery 968.2
  sanctimony 1027.1
mean
  nouns medium 32
  mid-course 804.3
  IN THE MEAN
  mediumly 32.4
  midway 69.5
  verbs signify 543.8
  intend 651.4
  MEAN NOTHING 545.7
  MEAN WHAT ONE
    SAYS 622.8
  adjs. medium 32.3
  middle 69.4
  intervening 236.11
  narrow-minded
    525.10
  paltry 671.18
  inferior 678.10
  squalid 680.27
  difficult 729.16
  menial 748.16
  niggardly 850.10
  vulgar 896.15
  humble 904.9
  servile 905.12
  infamous 913.12
  plebeian 917.11
  malicious 937.18
  ill-humored 949.19
  unmagnanimous
    976.6
meander
  nouns complication
    46.2
  convolution 253.1
  verbs convolve 253.4
  migrate 272.21
  deviate 290.4
meandering
  nouns 253.1
  adjs. complex 46.4
  winding 253.6
  wandering 272.36
  deviative 290.7
meaning
  nouns purport 543
  interpretation 550
  intention 651.1
  FULL OF MEANING
    543.10
  GIVE THE MEANING
    550.12
  adjs. meaningful
    543.10
  intentional 651.9
meaningful 543.10
meaningfulness 543.6
meaningless 545.9
  BE MEANINGLESS
    545.7
meaninglessness 545
meanness
  inferiority 37.1
  narrow-mindedness
    525.1
  paltriness 671.2

baseness 678.3
squalidness 680.3
niggardliness 850.2
vulgarity 896.5
humbleness 904.1
servility 905.1
infamy 913.3
malice 937.5
ill humor 949.2
ungenerousness
  976.2
means way 655.1
  agency 656
  expedient 668.2
  assets 808.8
  funds 833.14
  BY ALL MEANS
  certainly 512.23
  assent 520.19
  BY MEANS OF 656.8
  BY NO MEANS
  nowise 35.14
  on no account 522.8
  God forbid! 967.27
  KEEP WITHIN ONE'S
    MEANS 849.7
mean semitone 462.20
means of access 301.5
mean-spirited 525.10
meant implied 544.7
  intentional 651.9
meantime, meanwhile
  nouns 109.2
  advs. 109.5
measles 684.4
measly petty 671.17
  diseased 684.46
  mean 913.12
measurability 489.8
measurable 489.15
measure
  nouns quantity 28.1,2
  degree 29.1
  process 163.2
  extent 178.1
  size 194.1
  capacity 194.2
  distance 198
  length 201.1
  stratum 226.1
  melody 461.4
  musical ~ 461.24
  musical rest 462.21
  rhythm 462.22
  gauge 489.1,2,4
  linear ~ 489.17
  area ~ 489.18
  volume ~ 489.19
  poetry 607.8,9,11
  expedient 668.2
  act 703.3
  share 814.5
  enactment 996.3
  BEYOND MEASURE
  extremely 34.22
  superabundantly
    661.25
  HAVE ONE'S MEASURE
    487.8
  IN FULL MEASURE
  completely 56.15

amply 659.8
verbs adjust 26.13
  calculate 87.11
  size 194.15
  traverse 272.19
  gauge 489.11
  compare 490.4
  MEASURE SWORDS
    WITH 794.18
  MEASURE UP 718.15
  MEASURE UP TO
  be equal 30.6
  compare with 490.7
  NOT MEASURE UP
    676.3
  NOT MEASURE UP TO
    37.4
  NOT MEASURE UP TO
    EXPECTATION 539.3
measured uniform 17.5
  rhythmical 462.27
  deliberate 489.14
  metrical 607.22
  temperate 990.9
measure for measure
  compensation 33.1
  interchange 149.1
  reprisal 953.3
  justice 974.1
measureless 104.3
measurelessness 104.1
measurement
  quantity 28.1
  calculation 87.3
  size 194.1
  mensuration 489
measurer 489.4,10
measures means 656.1
  precaution 893.3
  TAKE MEASURES
  plan 652.9
  act 703.5
  take precautions
    893.6
measure signature
  462.12
measuring
  nouns measurement
    489.1
  comparison 490.1
  adjs. 489.13
measuring worm
  413a.8
meat
  nouns essence 5.2
  substance 193.4
  meal 306.5
  food 306a.1,12
  nut 306a.38
  food for thought
    483.1
  subsistence 783.3
  verbs 306.15
meat eater 306.13
meat-eating 306.29
meatiness 543.6
meatman 828.3
meat market 830.6
meatus 395.13
meaty 543.10
mecate 1009.5

mechanic
  machinist 346.7
  repairman 692.10
  artisan 716.6
mechanical
  machinal 346.11
  involuntary 637.14
mechanical bird 279.6
mechanical device
  347.4
mechanical drawing
  572.6
mechanical man
  348.12
mechanics
  mechanology 346
  technique 731.7
mechanism
  machinery 347.5
  servomechanism
    348.13,30
  control ~ 348.34
  materialism 375.5
  means 656.2
  technique 731.7
mechanistic
  mechanical 346.11
  philosophical 499.10
mechanization 346.8
mechanize make
  mechanical 346.9
  equip 657.8
mechanized 346.11
mechanology 346.1
med 686.5
Médaille Militaire
  914.6
medal 914.6
medalist, medallist
  731.13
medallion relief 573.3
  medal 914.6
meddle 237.7
meddler 237.4
meddlesome
  meddling 237.9
  inquisitive 526.5
meddlesomeness
  intrusiveness 237.2
  inquisitiveness
    525.1
meddling
  intrusion 237.2
  meddlesome 237.9
meden agan 162.1
medial medium 32.3
  middle 69.4
  intervening 236.11
median
  nouns 69.1
  adjs. middle 69.4
  intervening 236.11
mediant 462.15
mediary 236.4
mediate
  make peace 802.9
  intercede 803.6
mediating 803.8
mediation
  instrumentality
    656.2

intercession 803
Christly function
1011.17
mediative 803.8
mediator 803.3
mediatorial
instrumental 656.6
intercessory 803.8
mediatorship 803.2
mediatory 803.8
medic 686.5
medicable 692.25
medical
nouns 686.5
adjs. 686.18
medical center 225.8
Medical Corps 798.20
medicalese 578.7
medical examiner
686.5
medical instruments
687.39
medical jurisprudence
medicine 686.1
jurisprudence 996.7
medical man 686.5
medical practice
686.16
medical school 565.7
medical sciences
686.19
medical treatment
687.17
medicament 685.4
medicamentation
687.17
medicaster 686.6
medicate
adulterate 44.13
treat 687.34
medication
adulteration 44.3
therapy 687.17
medicative 685.34
medicinal
nouns 685.4
adjs. 685.34
medicine
nouns remedy 685.4
types of ～ 685.44–
56
materia medica 686
therapy 687
psychosomatic ～
688.4
liquor 994.13
PRACTICE MEDICINE
686.17
verbs 687.34
medicine man
doctor 686.6
witch doctor 1033.7
medico 686.5
medicopsychology
688.4
mediety 92.2
medieval 123.13
medieval history 606.4
medievalism
antiquarianism
123.4

ignorance 476.8
medievalist 123.5
medieval mode 462.10
mediocre
tolerable 672.20
middling 678.7
mediocreness 678.1
mediocrity
insignificancy 671.7
tolerableness 672.3
mediocreness 678
meditate contemplate
477.11,15
intend 651.7
MEDITATE OVER,
MEDITATE UPON
477.12
meditated
intentional 651.9
advised 752.11
meditating 477.20
meditation 477.2
meditative 477.20
mediterranean
middle 69.4
midland 224.10
Mediterranean race
417.2
medium
nouns mean 32.1
environment 232.4
intermediary 236.4
color 361.7
instrument 656.3
doer 716.1
interagent 779.4
mediator 803.3
mid-course 804.3
spiritualist 1032.13
THROUGH THE
MEDIUM OF 656.8
adjs. mean 32.3
middle 69.4
intervening 236.11
mediocre 678.7
mediumism 1032.5
mediumistic 1032.25
medium of exchange
833.1
medium of proof
504.1
medium shot 575.10
medius 424.5
medley
nouns mixture 44.6
miscellany 74.12
music 461.6
adjs. 44.15
medulla marrow 225.2
brain 465.5
medullary 356.11
Medusa 1033.9
medusae 414.4
meed share 814.5
recompense 839.3
～ of praise 966.5
meek
submissive 763.15
patient 859.11
humble 904.10
modest 906.9

meekness
submissiveness 763.5
patience 859.2
humility 904.1
modesty 906.1
meerschaum 433.7
meet
nouns assembly 74.2
meeting place
190.23
game 876.9
rendezvous 920.8
verbs join 47.11
assemble 74.15
conform 82.3
experience 150.8
encounter 199.11
confront 239.8
collide 282.13
converge 297.2
concur 520.9
satisfy 659.4
fulfill 766.2
oppose 788.6
brave 891.11
MEET HALFWAY
mediate 803.6
compromise 805.2
MEET ONE AT EVERY
TURN
pervade 185.7
superabound 661.9
MEET UP WITH
experience 150.8
encounter 199.11
find 487.3
adjs. timely 129.10
expedient 668.4
just 974.8
meeting
nouns joining 47.1
assembly 74.2
encounter 199.4
collision 282.3
convergence 297.1
conference 595.6
rendezvous 920.8
religious ～ 1030.8
HOLD A MEETING
74.16
adjs. joining 47.16
assembled 74.21
concurrent 176.4
in contact 199.17
converging 297.3
meetinghouse
building 190.15
church 1040.1
meeting of minds
agreement 26.3
unanimity 520.5
meeting place
resort 190.23
trysting place 920.8
meetness 129.1
megacosm 374.1
megacycles 343.15
megadeath 407.1
Megaera 1014.11
megagamete 405.6
megalith 568.11

megaloblast 405.5
megalomaniac 472.16
meganucleus 405.10
megaphone 447.8
Megarian 499.11
megascope 575.14
**megasporangium,
megaspore** 405.9
megrim
migraine 423.5
caprice 627.1
megrims disease 684.10
blues 870.6
mehtar 679.13
mein Herr 419.7
meiosis 405.15
Meistersinger
singer 463.13
bard 607.14
melancholia
psychosis 472.6
neurosis 688.22
sadness 870.5
melancholic 870.23
melancholiness 870.5
melancholy
nouns pensiveness
477.3
sadness 870.5
adjs. dark 336.15
sad 870.23
depressing 870.31
melange 44.6
Melba toast 306a.27
Melchior 467.5
**Melchizedek priest-
hood** 1036.10
meld 52.3
mêlée 794.3
melee commotion 62.4
contest 794.3
Melibean 607.21
melic 461.49
melinite 799.9
meliorate 689.7,9
melioration 689.1
meliorative 689.15
mellifluence 461.2
mellifluent, mellifluous
sweet 430.6
musical 461.49
mellisonant 461.49
mellophone 464.8,12
mellow
verbs mature 126.9
be converted 145.12
soften 356.6
ripen 720.8
adjs. mature 126.12
soft 356.8
soft-colored 361.22
resonant 453.9
melodious 461.49
ripe 720.12
drunk 994.38
mellowing
maturation 126.6
softening 356.5
mellowness
softness 356.1
resonance 453.1

mentally retarded
468.22
mentally sound 471.4
mental outlook 523.2
mental philosophy
499.1
mentals 465.2
mental shock
684.18; 688.19
mental strain 857.3
mental telepathy
1032.9
mentation 477.1
menticide 145.3
menticulture 689.3
mention
  nouns information
    555.1
  report 557.2
  remark 592.4
  citation 914.4
  verbs specify 80.9
  remark 592.16
  MENTION TO
  remind 535.20
  make known 555.7
  NOT TO MENTION
    40.11
Mentor 467.2
mentor wise man 467.1
  teacher 563.1
  adviser 752.4
mentum 239.6
menu list 88.4
  food 306.12
  schedule 639.2
menue viande 306a.12
meow 459.2
Mephistophelean,
  Mephistophelian
  979.18
Mephistopheles,
  Mephisto 1014.5
mephitic(al)
  malodorous 436.6
  poisonous 682.5
mephitis fume 400.1
  malodor 436.1
  poison 674.4
mercantile 825.17
mercantilism 825.8
mercenariness 850.2
mercenary
  nouns hireling 748.2
  soldier 798.16
  adjs. hired 778.17
  niggardly 850.10
  corruptible 973.22
mercer 230.32
mercerization 378.5
mercerize 378.6
merchandise
  nouns 829.1
  verbs 825.11
merchandiser 828.2
merchant
  nouns 828.2
  adjs. 825.17
merchantable 827.12
merchant marine
  ships 276.1

navy 798.27
merchantry
  commerce 825.1
  tradesmen 828.11
merci, merci
  beaucoup! 947.6
merciful
  lenient 757.8–10
  charitable 936.16
  compassionate 942.7
mercifulness 942.2
merciless 943.3
mercilessness 943.1
mercurial
  changeable 141.7
  fast 268.19
  metallic 382.16
  fickle 627.7
  active 705.15
mercurialness 627.3
mercurous 382.16
Mercury planet 374.6
  messenger 559.1
  commerce 825.8
  god 1012.5
mercury
  changeability 141.4
  speed 268.7
  temperature 327.19
  metal 382.3
  guide 746.6
mercy
  nouns leniency 757
  charity 936.4
  compassion 942.1
  AT THE MERCY OF
  liable 174.5
  be subject 762.11
  HAVE MERCY UPON
    942.4
  interjs. 942.10
mercy killing 408.1
mercy seat 999.8
mere
  nouns sea 396.1
  lake 397.1
  inlet 398.1
  adjs. sheer 35.9
  simple 45.5
mere show
  formality 644.1
  affectation 901.1
meretricious
  tawdry 902.20
  prostitute 987.28
meretrix 987.16
merge mingle 44.11
  combine 52.3
  be converted 145.12
  submerge 318.7
  MERGE IN 58.3
  MERGE INTO
  modulate 139.5
  be converted 145.12
merged 52.5
merger 786.9
merging 52.7
meridian
  nouns ~ of life 126.4
  midday 133.5
  latitude 179.3

summit 210.2
  celestial ~ 374.16
  adjs. noon 133.7
  top 210.9
meridiem 133.5
meridional 210.9
meringue 306a.39
merit
  nouns 672.1
  TAKE MERIT TO
    ONESELF 908.7
  verbs 958.5
merited
  warranted 958.9
  just 974.8
meriting 958.10
meritorious
  valid 515.12
  praiseworthy 966.19
meritoriousness
  validity 515.4
  praiseworthiness
    966.7
merits 958.3
Merlin 1033.6
merlon 797.4
mermaid, merman
  swimmer 274.12
  sea spirit 396.4
  sea nymph 1012.17
merogenesis 166.6
merogenetic 166.24
Merostomata 414.8
merriment
  gaiety 868.5
  laughter 874.4
  merrymaking 876.3
merry gay 868.15
  festive 876.30
  drunk 994.38
  MAKE MERRY 875.3
merry-andrew 610.9
Merry Christmas 137.5
merry dancers 334.16
merry-go-round
  whirl 320.2,4
  revelry 876.7
  carrousel 876.15
merrymaker 876.19
merrymaking
  nouns 876.3
  adjs. 876.30
merrythought 1034.7
mesa 386.1
mésalliance
  misalliance 10.2
  mismatch 27.3
  marriage 931.1
mesdames 420.8
mesencephalon 465.5
mesh
  nouns interaction
    13.3
  complex 46.2
  network 220.3
  IN MESH 13.11
  verbs interact 13.7
  crisscross 220.7
  ensnare 616.20
  catch 820.14
meshed 220.11

meshes network 220.3
  snare 616.12
  OUT OF THE MESHES
    696.6
meshing 13.3
meshwork 220.3
meshy 220.11
mesial 69.4
mesilla 386.1
mesmeric 710.22
mesmerism 710.8
mesmerist 710.9
mesmerization 710.8
mesmerize
  fascinate 648.6
  hypnotize 710.18
  spellbind 1034.8
mesmerized 1034.13
mesmerizer 710.9
mesne
  nouns 807.2
  adjs. 236.11
mesoblast, mesoderm
  405.5
mesogaster 224.6
mesogastric 224.12
mesomorph 416.5
meson, mesotron
  radioactivity 326.4
  electron 342.3
mesoplast 405.10
mesothorium 326.5
Mesozoic Era 107.10
Mess 1038.9
mess
  nouns quantity 28.2
  large amount 34.4
  mixture 44.6
  jumble 62.3
  meal 306.5
  failure 723.6
  predicament 729.4
  bungle 732.5
  share 814.5
  eyesore 897.4
  IN A MESS
  confused 62.15
  in disorder 62.16
  in trouble 729.20
  LOOK A MESS 897.5
  MAKE A MESS OF IT
    63.3
  verbs 680.19
  MESS AROUND 671.13
  MESS AROUND WITH
  tamper 237.7
  do carelessly 532.9
  MESS UP
  disarrange 63.2
  spoil 690.11
  botch 732.12
  MESS WITH
  tamper 237.7
  eat with 306.19
message
  computer data
    348.19
  dispatch 556.4
  telegram 558.16
  epistle 602.2
Messalina 987.15

messenger
  forerunner 66.1
  omen 542.3
  courier 559
  delegate 779.2
messenger of God
  1013.1
messengers cloud 403.1
  omen 542.4
  warning sign 701.3
mess hall
  dining room 191.11
  restaurant 306.14
Messiah, the 1011.12
Messieurs 419.7
messiness 62.6
messmate 926.4
mess sergeant 747.23
mess steward 275.6
messuage abode 190.6
  farm 412.8
  property 808.7
messy slovenly 62.14
  dirty 680.24
mestee, mestiza,
  mestizo 44.8
metabola, metabole
  139.2
metabolic 245.9
metabolism
  transformation
   139.2
  nutrition 307.9
metabolize
  transform 139.7
  assimilate 307.16
metacenter 225.2
metachronism 115.1
metage 489.1
metagenesis
  transformation
   139.2
  generation 166.6
metagenetic 166.24
metagram 879.8
metal
  nouns substance 3.2
  mineral 382.3
  verbs 227.28
  adjs. 382.15
metalcraft 572.3
metalepsis 549.2
metalleity 382.3
metallic metal 382.15
  harsh-sounding
   457.14
metallicity 382.3
metallics 382.3
metallide 382.4
metalliferous, metalli-
  form, metalline
  382.15
metallograph 575.3
metallography 382.10
metalloid
  nouns 382.3
  adjs. 382.15
metallophone 464.20
metallorganic 382.15
metallurgical 382.17
metallurgist 382.11

metallurgy 382.10
metals 382.20–22
metalware
  metal 382.3
  merchandise 829.4
metalwork 382.3
metalworker 716.7
metamer 378.1
metameric 378.7
metamorphic
  multiform 19.3
  changeable 141.6
metamorphism 139.2
metamorphose 139.7
metamorphosis 139.2
metamorphotic 19.3
metaphor 549.2
metaphorical 549.4
metaphrase 550.3
metaphrast 550.8
metaphrastic 550.19
metaphysic(al)
  1032.24
metaphysician, meta-
  physicist 1032.12
metaphysics
  existence 1.7
  esoterics 1032.3
metaplasm 405.3
metapsychic(al)
  1032.24
metapsychics 1032.4
metapsychist 1032.12
metapsychosis 1032.8
metasomatism, meta-
  somatosis 139.2
metastasis
  transformation
   139.2
  inversion 219.3
  transference 270.1
metastatic 270.17
metatheria 414.12
metathesis
  transformation
   139.2
  inversion 219.3
  transference 270.1
  figure of speech
   549.2
metathetic 270.17
métayage, métayer
  system 806.1
Metazoa 414.3
mete
  nouns 234.3
  verbs measure 489.11
  apportion 814.9
  give 816.12
metempiric(al) 547.14
metempsychosis
  transformation
   139.2
  reincarnation 375.7
metencephalon 465.5
meteor 374.15
meteoric
  transient 111.8
  flashing 334.34
  celestial 374.25
  atmospheric 401.13

meteoric particles
  281.11
meteorism 196.2
meteorite 374.15
meteorites 281.11
meteoritic 374.25
meteoritics 374.19
meteoroid, meteorolite
  374.15
meteorologic 401.14
meteorology
  aviation 277.2
  astronomy 374.19
  climatology 401.6
meteoroscopy 374.19
meteors 281.11
meter
  nouns light ~ 334.42
  electric ~ 341.40
  electronic ~ 342.21
  gas ~ 400.6
  spectrometers
   442.15
  rhythm 462.22
  gauge 489.4
  measurer 489.10
  poetry 607.8,9
  verbs 489.11
metes 234.1
methinks 500.26
method order 59.1
  plan 652.1
  way 655.1
methodic, methodical
  regular 17.5
  orderly 59.6
  regular 137.7
  formal 644.10
methodicalness 137.1
methodization 60.2
methodize 60.9
methodized 60.13
methodologist 82.2
Methuselah 127.2
metic 189.9
meticulous
  exacting 531.12
  observant 766.4
  fastidious 894.9
meticulousness
  carefulness 531.3
  fastidiousness 894.1
métier specialty 81.1
  vocation 654.6
métis, métisse 44.8
metonym 580.3
metonymical 549.4
metonymy 549.2
metoposcopy
  physiognomy 239.7
  interpretation 550.9
metric
  rhythmical 462.27
  measuring 489.13
  measured 489.14
  poetic 607.22
metrical foot 607.9
metrical romance
  607.4
metric system 489.1
metrocracy 739.5

metrology 489.9
metronome 464.26
metronomic 114.15
metropolis
  district 179.5
  town 182.1
  center 225.7
metropolitan
  nouns 1036.8
  adjs. 182.9
mettle
  temperament 523.4
  pluck 622.3
  courage 891.5
mettlesome
  plucky 622.14
  excitable 855.29
  resolute 891.18
mettlesomeness
  pluck 622.3
  excitability 855.9
  courage 891.4
mew
  nouns den 190.22
  hiding place 698.5
  verbs enclose 235.5
  miaow 459.2
  confine 759.12
mewed 235.10
mewl 459.2
mews 190.16
mezzanine 191.23
mezzo 69.4
mezzo cammin 126.4
mezzolith 123.6
mezzolithic 123.20
mezzo-relievo 573.3
mezzo staccato 461.31
mezzo termine 32.1
mezzotint
  nouns 576.2,9
  verbs 576.14
mian ruler 747.11
  title 915.3
miaow 459.2
miasm, miasma
  fume 400.1
  malodor 436.1
  poison 674.4
  contagion 684.3
miasmal, miasmic
  malodorous 436.6
  poisonous 682.5
miasmatic 682.5
micaceous 382.14
Micah 1020.1
Micawber 532.5
Micawberish 132.16
Micawberism 132.5
Michael 1013.4
Michaelmas, Michael-
  mastide 1038.15
mick 417.9
Mickey 345.2
mickey finn
  narcotic 685.10
  drink 994.8
microbe 195.7
microbial, microbic
  195.14

MILITATE AGAINST
  counteract 177.6
  oppose 788.5
militia 798.23
militiaman 798.6
milk
  nouns beverage
    306a.48
  white 363.2
  fluid 387.2,3
  verbs draw from
    304.10
  ~ cows 415.6
  exploit 663.16
  despoil 820.21
  adjs. 387.8
milk and honey 726.1
milk and water 159.7
milk-and-water
  weak 159.17
  insipid 429.2
  mediocre 678.8
milkiness
  semitransparency
    339.2
  whiteness 363.1
  fluidity 387.1
  semiliquidity 388.1
milking 304.2
milk leg 684.8
milk-livered 890.10
milkmaid 748.8
milkman 828.6
milk of human
  kindness 936.1
milk sickness 684.10
milksop weakling 159.6
  mollycoddle 420.11
  coward 890.5
milksopism
  effeminacy 420.2
  cowardice 890.1
milksoppish, milk-
  soppy 890.10
milk tooth 257.7
milky weak 159.17
  pearly 339.5
  white 363.8
  lacteal 387.8
  emulsive 388.11
Milky Way 374.13
mill
  nouns types of ~
    347.20
  workshop 717.3
  fight 794.9
  coin 835.7
  HAVE BEEN THROUGH
    THE MILL 731.18
  PUT THROUGH THE
    MILL 550.13
  verbs manufacture
    166.12
  serrate 261.4
  move around 320.12
  machine 346.10
  pulverize 360.9
  box 794.14
  beat 1003.14
milldam 728.5
millenary 99.31

millennial
  thousandth 99.31
  utopian 533.23
millennium
  thousand 99.10
  period 107.2
  utopia 533.11
  good times 726.4
millepede
  thousand 99.10
  insect 413a.2
miller 798.2
millesecond 107.2
millet 306a.34
millet seed 195.7
milliard 99.12
milligram, milliliter,
  millimeter 99.10
millimicron 195.8
milliner 230.36
millinery
  headdress 230.25
  garment making
    230.31
million
  nouns number 99.11
  the ~ 917.3
  LOOK LIKE A MILLION
    898.15
  adjs. 101.7
millionaire 835.6
millions 835.2
MILLIONS OF 101.7
millionth 99.32
millpond sea 396.1
  pond 397.1
millrace 394.4
mill run 394.4
millstone burden 351.7
  pulverizer 360.7
MILLSTONE ROUND
  ONE'S NECK
  impediment 728.6
  care 864.8
millstream 394.1
milord 915.2
milquetoast 159.6
milreis 833.9
milt 405.7
milzbrand 684.10
mime
  nouns mummer
    610.10
  masquerade 617.7
  verbs 22.6
mimeograph
  copy 22.8
  print 601.13
mimeography 22.3
mimer imitator 22.4
  mummer 610.10
  masquerader 617.7
mimetic 22.10
mimic
  nouns imitator 22.4
  mummer 610.10
  verbs 22.6
  adjs. 22.10
mimicker 22.4
mimicry 22.2
Mimir 194.13

mimographer 609.26
mimologist 610.10
Min 1012.9
minaret 206.11
minatory 971.3
minauderie 901.2
mince
  nouns 306a.12
  verbs shatter 49.12
  walk 272.27
  talk 593.6
  ~ the truth 614.20
  be affected 901.14
  extenuate 1004.12
mincemeat 306a.12
MAKE MINCEMEAT OF
  shatter 49.12
  injure 690.13
  demolish 691.17
mincing
  walking 272.35
  affected 901.18
Mind 1011.7
mind
  nouns intellect 465.1
  intelligence 466.9
  opinion 500.4
  mood 523.4
  heed 528.1
  recollection 535.1
  will 619.1
  desire 632.1
  intention 651.1
  subconscious 688.39
  psyche 1032.17,20
  ALL IN THE MIND
    533.19
  BE OF ANOTHER
    MIND 626.9
  BE OF TWO MINDS
    625.6
  COME TO MIND
  occur to 477.17
  be remembered
    535.16
  GIVE A PIECE OF
    ONE'S MIND 967.18
  GIVE THE MIND TO
  concentrate 477.9
  think about 477.10
  attend to 528.5
  HAVE A MIND TO
  will 619.2
  be willing 620.3
  desire 632.14
  intend 651.7
  HAVE IN MIND
  think of 477.15
  remember 535.14
  intend 651.7
  HAVE ON ONE'S MIND
    477.19
  IN ONE'S RIGHT MIND
  sane 471.4
  sober 995.3
  KEEP AN OPEN MIND
    524.7
  KEEP IN MIND
  think of 477.15
  take cognizance
    528.9

  remember 535.14
  OF ONE MIND
  in agreement 26.16
  unanimous 520.15
  accordant 792.3
  OUT OF ONE'S MIND
    472.24,30
  PAY NO MIND 529.3
  TO ONE'S MIND 500.25
  verbs heed 528.6
  care 531.6
  be careful 531.7
  remember 535.11
  remind 535.20
  rather not 621.3
  intend 651.4
  care for 697.18
  obey 764.2
  beware 893.7
  MIND ONE'S MANNERS
    934.11
  MIND ONE'S OWN
    BUSINESS
  be incurious 527.2
  not interfere 760.15
  MIND ONE'S P'S AND
    Q'S
  be careful 531.7
  behave oneself
    735.5
  be polite 934.11
  MIND OUT
  pay attention 528.8
  be vigilant 531.8
  beware 893.7
  be careful! 893.14
  MIND YOU 521.9
  NEVER MIND!
  who cares! 634.10
  no matter 671.22
  NOT MIND
  not care 634.4
  disobey 765.6
mind body 1032.19
mind culture 689.3
mind cure 688.5
mind-curist 688.13
minded disposed 523.8
  willing 620.5
  prompted 646.30
mindful aware 474.15
  attentive 528.15
  careful 531.10
  reminiscent 535.22
  cautious 893.8
  considerate 936.17
MINDFUL OF 474.16
mindfulness
  awareness 474.2
  attention 528.1
  care 531.1
  caution 893.1
  considerateness
    936.3
mind-healer 686.12
mindless
  unintelligent 468.13
  unaware 476.14
  incurious 527.3
  careless 532.11
  unconcerned 634.6

misstatement
  error 517.3
  misrepresentation
    571.1
  falsification 614.9
misstep 517.4
missy 125.6
mist
  nouns dimness 336.5
  rain 393.1
  cloud 403.1
  verbs dim 336.11
  opaque 340.2
  cloud 403.7
mistakable
  errable 513.20
  misunderstandable
    551.4
mistake
  nouns 517.3
  verbs 517.12
mistaken 517.16
  BE MISTAKEN
    err 517.9
    misbelieve 1023.8
  NOT TO BE MISTAKEN
    distinct 443.7
    manifest 553.8
mistaught 561.5
misteach 561.3
misteaching
  nouns 561
  adjs. 561.6
misted 336.18
Mister 419.7
misterm 581.12
misthink 495.2
mistime
  misdate 115.2
  ill-time 130.4
mistimed
  misdated 115.3
  untimely 130.7
mistiming 115.1
mistiness
  dimness 336.5
  opaqueness 340.1
  cloudiness 403.4
  indistinctness 444.2
misting 336.7
mistral 402.9
mistranslate 551.2
mistranslation 551.1
mistreat 665.5
mistreatment 665.2
Mistress 420.8
mistress
  instructress 563.2
  matron 747.2
  proprietor 807.2
  sweetheart 929.12
  kept woman 987.17
mistrial 1002.5
mistrust
  nouns doubt 502.2
  jealousy 951.2
  verbs doubt 502.6
  be jealous 951.3
mistrusted 502.12
mistrustful 502.9
misty dim 336.18

opaque 340.3
  rainy 393.10
  cloudy 403.8
  indistinct 444.5
  obscure 547.13
misunderstand
  mistake 517.12
  misinterpret 551.2
misunderstandable
  551.4
misunderstanding
  error 517.3
  misinterpretation
    551.1
  disagreement 793.2
misunderstood
  misinterpreted 551.3
  unappreciated
    865.10
misusage error 517.6
  solecism 585.2
  misuse 665.1
misuse
  nouns 665
  verbs misdo 517.11
  misemploy 665.4
misused 762.15
mite
  small amount 35.2
  child 125.3
  minute thing 195.7
  minuteness 195.8
  insect 413a.7
  animal 414.8
  coin 833.8
miter
  nouns joint 47.4
  insignia 567.4
  verbs 47.8
mitigate
  reduce 39.8
  moderate 162.6
  relax 162.9
  qualify 506.3
  relieve 884.5
  extenuate 1004.12
mitigated 506.10
mitigating
  alleviating 162.14
  qualifying 506.7
  relieving 884.9
mitigation
  decrease 39.1
  moderation 162.2
  relief 884.1
  extenuation 1004.5
mitigative
  qualifying 506.7
  relieving 884.9
mitigator
  modulator 162.3
  sedative 685.11
mitigatory 506.7
mitosis 405.15
mitraille 799.14
mitrailleur 798.11
mittimus
  dismissal 308.5
  writ 750.6
  judge 1000.1

mix
  nouns mixture 44.6
  jumble 62.3
  predicament 729.4
  verbs mingle 44.11
  combine 52.3
  be indiscriminate
    492.4
  MIX IT UP WITH
    794.18
  MIX UP
    mix 44.11
    complicate 46.3
    confuse 63.3
    fluster 530.7
  MIX WITH 920.15
mixable 44.17
mixblood 44.8
mixed composite 44.15
  combined 52.5
  phonetics 449.18
mixed up complex 46.4
  confused 62.15
  flustered 530.12
mixen 680.11
mixer blender 44.10
  control board
    343.10
  radioman 343.27
  sociable person
    920.14
mixing mixture 44.1
  radio 343.19
  television 344.3
mixture
  admixture 44
  compound 44.5
  combination 52
  solution 390.3
  preparation 718.3
mix-up mixture 44.6
  muddle 62.2
  contest 794.3
mizzle
  nouns 393.1
  verbs decamp 300.11
  drizzle 393.9
  flee 629.11
mizzly 393.10
mnemonic 535.22
mnemonics, mnemoni-
  zation, mnemo-
  techny 535.10
Mnemosyne 535.10
moan
  nouns 873.3
  verbs blow 402.24
  sough 451.14
  suffer 864.22
  wail 873.11
moaning 451.8
moat trench 262.2
  fortification 797.5
mob
  nouns company 74.3
  throng 74.4
  miscellany 74.12
  crowd 786.7
  THE MOB
  the masses 917.3

  criminals 984.10
  verbs 965.9
mobile
  nouns 572.11
  adjs. changeable
    141.6
  expressive 543.10
mobility
  changeableness
    141.1
  expressiveness 543.6
mobilization
  assemblage 74.1
  motion 266.1
  recruital 778.6
  rally 795.13
mobilize
  assemble 74.17
  make movable 266.5
  recruit 778.14
  rally 795.24
mobocracy 738.2
mobsman 823.4
mock
  nouns sham 614.13
  gibe 965.2
  verbs mimic 22.6
  deceive 616.13
  borrow 819.4
  ridicule 965.9
  adjs. imitation 22.9
  sham 614.27
mocker 22.4
mockery
  mimicry 22.2
  insincerity 614.5
  ridicule 965.1,6
  laughingstock 965.7
mock-heroic
  poetic 607.21
  comical 878.6
mocking
  nouns 819.2
  adjs. 965.12
mockingbird
  imitator 22.4
  songbird 463.15
mock-up 25.5
modal
  conditional 7.7
  formal 644.7
mode manner 7.4
  musical ~ 462.10
  logic 481.7
  grammar 584.9
  diction 586.2
  ~ of expression
    592.6
  fashion 642.1
  way 655.1
  BY WHAT MODE
    655.11
  IN THE LATEST MODE
    642.16
model
  nouns reproduction
    24.3
  pattern 25
  form 245.1
  idea 478.3
  measure 489.2

image 570.3
mannequin 570.4
standard 749.2
paragon 983.4
verbs ~ after 22.7
form 245.6
sculpture 573.6
adjs. exemplary 25.8
meritorious 966.19
modeler 577.6
modeling 573.1
modeling clay 573.5
modelled 573.8
model-T 123.16
moderate
nouns conservative 140.4
moderationist 162.4
verbs modulate 162.6
slow down 269.9
qualify 506.3
mediate 803.6
adjs. inconsiderable 35.7
conservative 140.8
temperate 162.10
slow 269.10
tolerable 672.20
mediocre 678.7
lenient 757.8
inexpensive 847.7
temperate 990.9
moderateness
moderation 162.1
mediocrity 678.1
leniency 757.1
inexpensiveness 847.1
moderation
conservatism 140.3
moderateness 162
temperance 990.1
IN MODERATION
palliative 162.16
temperately 990.12
moderationism
conservatism 140.3
moderation 162.1
moderationist
conservative 140.4
moderate 162.4
moderations 484.3
moderator
mitigator 162.3
mediator 803.4
judge 1000.1
modern
nouns 122.4
adjs. 122.14
modernism 122.3
modernist 122.4
modernistic 122.14
modernity, moderniza-tion 122.3
modernize 122.6
modernized 122.14
modernizer 122.4
modest
inconsiderable 35.7
humble 904.9
unpretentious 906.9

decent 986.5
modesty
humbleness 904
unpretentiousness 906
decency 986.2
modicum
small amount 35.2
share 814.5
modifiability 141.1
modifiable
changeable 141.6
convertible 145.13
modification
differentiation 16.4
change 139.1
tone 449.2
qualification 506.1
modificator 139.4
modificatory 506.7
modified
changed 139.9
qualified 506.10
modifier
alterant 139.4
part of speech 584.2
modify
differentiate 16.6
quantify 28.4
change 139.6
qualify 506.3
modifying 506.7
modish 642.12
modishness 642.2
modiste 230.35
mods 484.3
modulate
change 139.5,6
moderate 162.6
inflect 449.12
qualify 506.3
modulated 506.10
modulation
change 139.1
moderation 162.2
radio 343.17
music 462.2
tone 449.2
modulator 162.3
modulatory 506.7
module integer 89.4
diameter 203.3
modus operandi 655.1
modus vivendi 802.5
mofussil 179.5
mog 272.17
Mogul 747.9
mogul 670.8
Mohammed 1020.3
Mohammedan
nouns 1018.21
adjs. 1018.29
Mohammedanism 1018.11
mohur 833.5
moider bewilder 513.12
distract 530.7
moidore 833.5
moiety part 55.1
half 92.2

moil
nouns agitation 323.1
toil 714.4
verbs seethe 320.12
toil 714.12
moiler 716.2
Moirai 638.3
moist
verbs 391.12
adjs. damp 391.15
rainy 393.10
moisten 391.12
moistening
nouns 391.6
adjs. 391.18
moistness, moistiness 391.1
moisture
exudation 302.6
dampness 391
mistiness 403.4
moistureproof 392.11
moke network 220.3
donkey 413.22
molar
nouns 257.7
adjs. 257.17
molasses
adherent 50.3
semiliquid 388.5
sweetening 430.3
mold
nouns character 5.3
reproduction 24.6
form 25.6
kind 61.3
form 245.1
ground 384.1
plant 410.4
fungus 411.4
blight 674.2
verbs form 245.6
sculpture 573.6
deteriorate 690.23
moldability
pliancy 356.2
teachability 562.5
moldable pliant 356.9
teachable 562.18
molded 573.8
molder
nouns 577.6
verbs 690.23
moldering old 123.14
moldy 690.40
molding
reproduction 24.6
shaping 245.5
moldy, mouldy
old 123.14
tainted 690.40
mole tower 206.11
buttress 215.4
bulge 255.3
blindness 440.4
mark 566.4
blemish 677.1
growth 684.29
breakwater 698.6
barrier 728.5

fortification 797.4
molecular 195.13
molecular weight
weight 351.8
chemistry 378.4
molecule
small amount 35.2
minute thing 195.7
mole-eyed 439.13
molehill pile 74.9
mound 206.5
trifle 671.5
molest mistreat 665.5
harm 673.6
annoy 864.19
molestation
mistreatment 665.5
annoyance 864.2
moll 420.6
mollah 1000.3
mollescence 356.5
mollescent, mollient 356.16
mollification
tranquilization 162.2
softening 356.5
pacification 802.1
relief 884.1
mollifier 162.3
mollify calm 162.7
soften 356.6
pacify 802.7
relieve 884.5
mollifying
tranquilizing 162.15
softening 356.16
conciliatory 802.12
Mollusca 414.9
molluscan, molluscoid 413.48
Molluscoida 414.6
mollusk 414.9
Molly, molly
homosexual 418.12
mollycoddle 420.11
mollycoddle
nouns weakling 159.6
effeminate 420.11
spoiled child 757.5
verbs 757.7
mollycoddling 757.4
Moloch 1012.11
molt 231.10
molten melted 328.30
liquefied 390.6
mom 169.10
moment second 107.2
instant 113.3
influence 171.1
impetus 282.1
importance 670.1
authority 737.3
FOR THE MOMENT 111.9
IN A MOMENT
instantly 113.7
presently 131.16
momentariness
transience 111.1

instantaneousness
113.1
momentary
transient 111.7
instantaneous 113.4
momentous
eventful 150.10
influential 171.13
important 670.16
authoritative 737.14
momentum 282.1
mommick, mommix
63.3
mommixed 62.15
mommy 169.10
Momus 1012.5
momus 967.9a
monachal
celibate 932.6
monastic 1035.14
claustral 1040.15
monachism 932.1;
1035.4
monad
nouns one 89.3
minute thing 195.7
adjs. 89.11
monandrous 931.20
monandry 931.2
monarch 747.8
monarchal 737.16
monarchial, monarchic
sovereign 737.16
governmental
739.16
monarchism 739.8
monarchist 743.14
monarchistic 737.17
monarchy 739.4
monasterial
monastic 1035.14
claustral 1040.15
monastery 1040.6
monastic
nouns celibate 932.2
monk 1036.16
adjs. celibate 932.6
monkish 1035.14
claustral 1040.15
monasticism
monachism 932.1
monkhood 1035.4
monatomic
atomic 325.17
monovalent 378.8
monaural 449.16
Monday 105.6
monde 642.6
monetary 833.28
monetization 833.22
monetize 833.25
money legal tender 833
wealth 835.1
COME INTO MONEY
prosper 726.11
grow rich 835.9
FOR MONEY 809.15
GET ONE'S MONEY'S
WORTH 847.5
IN THE MONEY 835.13

MAKE MONEY
profit 809.10
grow rich 835.9
MONEY TO BURN
superabundance
661.2
wealth 835.1
POUR MONEY INTO
834.16
PUT ONE'S MONEY ON
THE LINE 839.17
PUT UP THE MONEY
834.15
moneybag 834.14
moneybags
wealth 835.1
rich man 835.6
moneybox 834.12
money broker
moneylender 818.3
broker 828.9
money-changer
834.10
money changer
broker 828.9
banker 834.10
money changing 834.4
moneyed 835.13
moneyer 833.24
moneygrub, money-
grubber 850.6
moneygrubbing
nouns acquisition
809.1
miserliness 850.4
adjs. 850.12
moneylender
lender 818.3
banker 834.10
moneyless 836.9
moneylessness 836.2
money-making 809.1
money matters 834.1
moneymonger
moneylender 818.3
banker 834.10
moneyocracy
government 739.6
capitalists 743.7
money order 833.11
money-raising 819.1
moneys 833.14
money's worth
benefit 663.4
worth 844.3
monger 828.2,6
Mongol, Mongolian,
Mongoloid 417.4
Mongolian monster
85.6
Mongolian race
417.2,14
mongrel
nouns crossbreed 44.8
dog 413.25
scoundrel 984.6
adjs. hybrid 44.16
inelegant 588.2
moniker, monicker
581.3

monilated, monili-
form, moniloid
254.10
monism
materialism 375.5
philosophy 499.5
monistic
materialistic 375.11
philosophical 499.10
monition
intimation 555.1
dissuasion 650.1
warning 701.1
summons 750.7
monitor
nouns
radioman 343.27
television ~ 344.13
informant 555.5
pupil teacher 563.5
student 564.1
recorder 569.1
warning 701.3
director 746.1
adviser 752.4
verbs 343.29
monitorial
warning 701.9
advisory 752.10
monitoring 344.3
monitory
nouns 602.3
adjs. ominous 542.13
informative 555.17
dissuasive 650.5
warning 701.9
advisory 752.10
monk ferret 413.4
monkey 413.4
celibate 932.2
religious 1036.16
monkery 1035.4
monkey
nouns imitator 22.4
animal 413.4
types of ~ 413.50
dupe 618.1
mortgage 770.5
money 833.8
temper 950.6
laughingstock
965.7
verbs 671.13
MONKEY WITH 237.7
monkey-doodle 545.3
monkeying 671.8
monkey-rigged 276.17
monkeys 327.6
monkeyshine 879.10
monkeyshines 879.5
monkhood 1035.4
monkish
celibate 932.6
monastic 1035.14
monochord
harmony 461.3
clavichord 464.13
music 464.26
monochordist 463.7
monochromatic
361.16

monochromatism
440.3
monochrome
nouns 361.6
adjs. monochromic
361.16
pictorial 572.22
monochromic 361.16
monochromist 577.4
monocle 442.2
monocled 442.10
monoclinous 418.23
Monocotyledones,
monocotyledons
411.8
monocracy 739.4
monocratic 739.16
monocular
poor-sighted 439.12
monocled 442.10
monodic 461.50
monodram, mono-
drama 609.4
monodramatic 609.37
monodramatist 609.26
monody music 461.21
poem 607.4
dirge 873.5
monogamist 931.12
monogamous 931.20
monogamy 931.2
monogenesis 166.6
monogenetic 166.24
monogram
device 579.1
signature 581.10
monograph
monogram 579.1
treatise 604.1
sketch 606.1
monographer
writer 600.15
dissertator 604.3
monogynist 931.12
monogynous 931.20
monogyny 931.2
monolith stone 383.1
monument 568.11
monolithic 383.8
monologian 596.2
monologic 596.4
monologist, mono-
loguist 596.2
monologize 596.3
monologue
soliloquy 596.1
drama 609.4
monomachy 794.7
monomania 472.13
monomaniac
nouns 472.17
adjs. 472.32
monometallism 833.20
monophonic 461.50
monophony 461.21
monoply 806.4
monopolist
restrictionist 758.6
hog 976.3
monopolistic, monop-
olitical 806.12

monopolization 806.4
monopolize
  engross 528.13
  possess 806.7
  corner 831.26
monopolized 528.17
monopolizing 806.12
monopoly
  syndicate 786.9
  corner 831.20
monopthong 449.5
monorail 655.8
monosome 405.11
monostich 607.5,11
monosyllable
  syllable 579.6
  word 580.1
monosyllabic 579.12
monotheism 1018.5
monotheist 1018.14
monotheistic 1018.23
monotone
  nouns repetitiousness
    103.4
  tone 449.2
  adjs. monotonous
    103.15
  monotonic 449.14
monotonous
  samely 17.6
  repetitious 103.15
  tedious 882.8
monotony
  sameliness 17.2
  repetitiousness 103.4
  monotone 449.2
  tedium 882.1
Monotremata, mono-
  tremes 414.12
monotype 601.13
Monroe Doctrine
  politics 742.5
  noninterference
    760.8
Monsieur 419.7
Monsignor 915.5
monsoon rains 393.4
  wind 402.10
monster
  nouns monstrosity
    85.6
  mythical ~ 85.20
  behemoth 194.14
  ugly person 897.4
  fiend 941.7
  adjs. 194.20
monstrance 1038.11
monstrosity
  oddity 85.3
  monster 85.6
  hugeness 194.7
  deformity 248.3
monstrous
  adjs. fantastic 85.12
  huge 194.20
  deformed 248.12
  absurd 469.10
  excessive 661.17
  ugly 897.8
  infamous 913.12

  wicked 979.17
  advs. 34.20
monstrousness
  oddity 85.3
  hugeness 194.7
  absurdity 469.3
  excess 661.1
  disreputability 913.3
montage
  picture 572.12
  photography 575.3
month 107.2
  MONTH AFTER MONTH
  long 110.14
  constantly 135.7
monthlies 309.9
monthlong 110.12
monthly
  nouns 603.11
  adjs. 137.9
monticle, monticule
  206.5
monticuline, monticu-
  lous, montiform,
  montigeneous
  206.23
montura 215.19
monument
  tower 206.11
  memorial 568.11
  figure 570.4
monumental
  great 34.11
  mammoth 194.20
  high 206.19
  sculptural 573.7
  notable 670.18
monumentalism 194.7
monumentalize 112.5
moo 459.2
mooch
  nouns 618.1
  verbs play truant
    186.8
  ~ over 266.4
  wander 272.22
  ~ off 629.12
  loaf 706.10
  beg 772.15
  steal 822.13
moocha 230.19
moocher idler 706.8
  beggar 772.8
  guest 923.6
mooching 772.6
mood nature 5.3
  humor 523.4
  grammar 584.9
  story ~ 606.9
  caprice 627.1
  IN THE MOOD
  disposed 523.8
  willing 620.5
  NOT IN THE MOOD
  621.5
moodiness
  capriciousness 627.2
  glumness 870.8
  sullenness 949.8
moodish, moody
  whimsical 627.6

  glum 870.26
  sulky 949.24
moon
  nouns month 107.2
  changeability 141.4
  heavenly body 374.8
  verbs 530.9
moonbeam 334.11
moon-blind, moon
  blindness, moon-
  blink 440.2
mooncalf 470.1
moon dog 334.14
moon-eyed 439.12
moonfaced 194.18
moonglade, moonglow
  334.11
moon goddess 374.9
moonless 336.14
moonlight
  nouns moonshine
    334.11
  illicit liquor 994.21
  verbs deal illicitly
    824.7
  moonshine 994.37
moonlighter
  illicit dealer 824.4
  moonshiner 994.24
moonlighting
  illicit business 824.1
  bootlegging 994.22
moonlike 251.15
moonlit 334.38
moonraker 276.14
moonraking
  nouns 530.2
  adjs. 530.11
moonsail 276.14
moonshade
  shade 336.3
  lamp shade 337.3
moon-shaped 251.15
moonshine
  nouns moonlight
    334.11
  false argument
    482.3
  nonsense 545.2
  humbug 614.14
  liquor 994.21
  verbs deal illicitly
    824.7
  bootleg 994.37
moonshiner
  illicit dealer 824.4
  bootlegger 994.24
moonshining
  illicit business 824.1
  bootlegging 994.22
moon-struck 472.24
moony 530.11
moor
  nouns hill 206.5
  plain 386.1
  marsh 399.1
  verbs secure 142.9
  settle 183.18
  ~ a ship 274.16
  tether 758.10
mooring buoy 276.16

mooring mast 277.21
moorings
  anchor 276.16
  harbors 698.6
moorish 399.3
moorland plain 386.1
  marsh 399.1
moorlander, moorman
  386.2
moory 399.3
moot
  verbs argue 481.17
  pose 498.12
  propose 771.6
  adjs. 502.12
moot case 484.13
moot court 999.3
mooted
  assumed 498.14
  disputed 502.12
mooter 481.13
moot point 484.13
mop
  nouns hair 229.4
  grimace 248.4
  verbs grimace 248.8
  scrub 679.18
mopboard 211.2
mope
  nouns idler 706.7
  sad person 870.13
  verbs walk 272.26
  grieve 870.17
  sulk 949.14
mope-eyed 439.11
moper 706.7
mopes blues 870.6
  sulks 949.10
mopiness, mopishness
  glumness 870.8
  sullenness 949.8
moping, mopish
  glum 870.26
  sullen 949.24
mopping 679.4
mopsy 987.14
mopus
  visionary 533.13
  money 833.2
mopy glum 870.26
  sulky 949.24
mora 607.9
moraine residue 43.2
  deposit 270.8
moral
  nouns likeness 20.6
  maxim 516.1
  lesson 560.6
  POINT A MORAL
  560.16
  adjs. virtual 5.8
  ethical 955.6
  upright 972.13
  virtuous 978.7
moral certainty 512.1
moral climate
  climate 523.5
  morality 955.3
moral deficiency
  688.15
morale 955.3

moral fiber 622.4
moralistic 955.6
morality lesson 560.6
  drama 609.4
  ethics 955.3
  virtue 978.1
morality play 609.4
moralization 560.6
moralize 560.16
MORALIZE UPON
  493.14
moral rectitude 978.1
morals 955.3
moral strength 972.1
moral turpitude 979.6
moral victory 724.1
morass 399.1
moratorium
  delay 132.2
  ~ of debts 840.2
moratory 132.15
morbid
  unhealthy 684.40
  diseased 684.45
  ghastly 889.29
morbidity, morbidness
  684.1,2
morbid psychology
  688.1
morbiferous, morbific
  682.4
morceau
  small amount 35.3
  treatise 604.1
mordacious
  acrid 160.12
  caustic 937.21
mordacity
  acridity 160.4
  causticity 937.8
mordancy
  acrimony 160.4
  acidity 431.2
  pungency 432.1
  causticity 937.8
mordant
  nouns 328.14
  adjs. acrimonious
    160.12
  acid 431.7
  pungent 432.6
  caustic 937.21
mordent 462.18
more
  nouns extra 41.4
  number 100.1
  adjs. additional 40.9
  plural 100.7
  advs. increasingly 38.9
  additionally 40.10
  ALL THE MORE 36.19
  MORE OR LESS
  some 28.6
  approximately
    199.26
  MORE THAN 36.20
  NO MORE
  nonexistent 2.10
  past 119.5
  dead 407.24
  vanished 446.4

NO MORE THAN 35.12
moreish 427.10
morendo 461.54
moreover 40.10
mores
  conventions 643.2
  etiquette 644.3
morganatic 931.20
morgue
  mortuary 409.9
  newspaper ~ 601.9
THE MORGUE
  judiciary committee
    740.5
  Library of Congress
    740.13
moribund 407.27
moribundity 407.11
Mormon
  polygamist 931.12
  religionist 1018.20
morn 133.1
Morning 133.2
morning
  nouns 133.1
IN THE MORNING
  133.8
ONE FINE MORNING
  once 119.11
  someday 121.12
  adjs. 133.6
morning devotions
  1030.8
morning, noon and
  night long 110.14
  constantly 135.7
mornings 133.8
morning star 374.5
morningtide, morning
  time, morntime
  133.1
moron 470.8
moronic 468.22
moronism, moronity
  468.9
morose glum 870.26
  sullen 949.24
moroseness
  glumness 870.8
  sullenness 949.8
morosis 468.9
morpheme 580.1
Morpheus 710.11
morphinism 640.8
morphologist 405.17
morphology
  anatomy 244.7
  linguistics 578.11
morphon 405.2
morphotic 245.8
morrow, the 121.1
Morse code 612.7
morsel
  small amount 35.3
  piece 55.3
  bite 306.2
  delicacy 306a.8
Morta 638.3
mortal
  nouns 416.3
  adjs. perishable 111.7

fatal 408.23
human 416.10
wearisome 715.11
irksome 882.9
  advs. 34.20
mortality
  perishability 111.1
  mortalness 407.11
  humanity 416.1
  human nature 416.6
mortals 416.1
mortal sin 980.2
mortar
  nouns 145.7
  verbs 227.27
mortarboard 567.1
mortgage 770.5,12
mortgage broker 828.9
mortgagee 838.4
mortgagor, mortgage
  holder 818.3
mortician 409.8
mortification
  gangrene 684.30
  decay 690.6
  chagrin 864.4
  humiliation 904.2
  asceticism 989.1
  penance 1010.3
mortified
  diseased 684.45
  decayed 690.38
  chagrined 864.25
  humiliated 904.12
mortify decay 690.23
  chagrin 864.16
  humiliate 904.4
MORTIFY ONESELF
  990.6
mortifying
  embarrassing 862.12
  humiliating 904.13
mortise
  nouns 47.4
  verbs 47.8
mortmain 808.6
mortuary
  nouns 409.9
  adjs. deathly 407.23
  funereal 409.25
mosaic
  nouns check 373.4
  picture 572.12
  ceramic 574.2
  adjs. varied 19.4
  checked 373.14
Mosaic Law, the
  1019.3
mosey go slow 269.6
  depart 300.6
Moslem
  nouns 1018.21
  adjs. 1018.29
Moslemism 1018.11
mosque 1040.2
mosquito 413a.7
mosquito fleet 798.27
moss morass 399.1
  plant 410.4
  types of ~ 410.49
  money 833.2

mossback
  antiquated person
    123.8
  conservative 140.4
mossbacked 126.17
mossgrown 123.14
moss-grown
  mossy 410.40
  moldy 690.40
mosstrooper 823.7
mossy 410.40
most
  nouns maximum 36.3
  main part 54.5
  majority 100.2
MAKE THE MOST OF
  overestimate 496.2
  exaggerate 615.3
  utilize 663.15
  compromise 805.2
  reconcile oneself
    859.6
THE MOST 36.18
  adjs. greatest 34.15
  maximum 36.15
  greatest number
    100.9
  advs. very 34.22
  almost 199.25
AT MOST 35.11
MOST ASSUREDLY
  certainly 512.23
  yes 520.18
MOST LIKELY 510.7
MOST OFTEN 84.9
Most Excellent, Most
  Honorable 915.8
mot maxim 516.1
  witticism 879.7
mot à mot 543.15
Motazilite 1018.21
mot de passe 566.11
mot d'ordre
  countersign 566.11
  command 750.1
mote
  small amount 35.2
  minute thing 195.7
  lightness 352.3
MOTE IN THE EYE
  dim-sightedness
    439.2
  narrow-mindedness
    525.1
motel 190.14
motet music 461.16
  hymn 1030.3
moth 674.2
moth-eaten old 123.14
  aged 126.17
  impaired 690.40
  trite 881.9
Mother 915.5
mother
  nouns cause 152.4
  producer 166.10
  genetrix 169.10
  verbs procreate 168.9
  adopt 635.12
  care for 697.18
  adjs. 169.13

mother country 180.2
mother earth 374.7
motherhood 169.3
mother-in-law 12.3
motherland 180.2
motherless
    helpless 157.18
    orphan 407.28
    forlorn 922.13
motherlike 169.13
motherliness 169.3
mother love 929.5
Mother Nature 1011.9
Mother of God 1013.5
mother-of-pearl
    nouns pearliness
        339.2
    iridescence 373.6
    adjs. 373.10
mothership 169.3
mother superior
    mistress 747.2
    nun 1036.18
mother tongue 578.4
mother wit 466.1
motif edging 234.7
    musical ~ 461.30
    topic 483.1
motile 266.6
motility 266.3
motion
    nouns process 163.2
    trend 173.2
    movement 266
    travel 272.1
    mechanism 347.5
    gesture 566.13
    activity 705.1
    legislative ~ 740.15
    proposal 771.2
    GO THROUGH THE
        MOTIONS 614.22
    IN MOTION 266.6
    MAKE A MOTION
        771.5
    PUT IN MOTION
    impel 282.11
    set going 284.14
    carry out 703.9
    verbs 566.20
motionless 267.11
motionlessness 267.2
motion picture 609.15
motion-picture camera
    575.13
motion-picture fan
    609.31
motion-picture pho-
    tography 575.1
motion-picture pro-
    jector 575.14
motivate 646.12
motivating 646.25
motivating force 160.5
motivation
    influence 171
    inducement 646.2
motive
    noun musical ~
        461.30
    topic 483.1

motivation 646
    intention 651
    adjs. 266.6
motive force 688.39
motivity 266.3
motley
    nouns costume 230.9
    variegation 373.1
    comedy 609.7
    verbs diversify 19.2
    variegate 373.7
    adjs. varied 19.4
    variegated 373.12
motocar 271.9
motocycle 271.8
motor
    nouns automobile
        271.9
    aircraft ~ 279.17
    engine 347.4
    types of ~ 347.23
    verbs 272.32
    adjs. 266.6
motorbike 271.8
motorboat 276.2
motorbus 271.11
motorcade 71.4
motorcar 271.9
motor coach 271.11
motor court 190.14
motorcycle
    nouns 271.8,27
    verbs 272.32
motorcycler, motor-
    cyclist 273.11
motorcycling 272.6
motor-driven 346.11
motoring 272.6
motorist 273.10
motorium 266.3
motorization 346.8
motorize 346.9
motorman 273.12
motor psychology
    688.2
motor vehicle 271.9
motte 410.13
mottle
    nouns colored spot
        373.3
    mark 566.4
    verbs variegate 373.7
    mark 566.18
mottled 373.12
motto title 483.2
    maxim 516.1,4
    device 567.2
    inscription 600.3
mouchard
    informer 555.6
    detective 779.10
mouillé 449.18
moujik 917.8
mouldy See moldy
mound
    nouns heap 74.9
    hill 206.5
    tomb 409.16
    barrier 728.5
    fortification 797.4
    verbs 74.18

mount
    nouns mountain
        206.7
    backing 215.10
    ascent 313.1
    horse 413.18
    verbs increase 38.6
    copulate 168.10
    be high 206.15,17
    fly 277.45
    ascend 313.8,11
    get on 313.12
    put on 315.7
    ~ an attack 796.18
    MOUNT A HOBBY
    dwell on 103.9
    be boresome 882.7
    MOUNT UP TO
    total 54.7
    cost 844.15
mountain
    large amount 34.3
    hill 206.7
    MOUNTAINS OF THE
        WORLD 206.28
mountain canary
    413.22
mountain climber
    313.6
mountain dew 994.21
mountain-dwelling
    206.22
mountained 206.23
mountaineer
    backsettler 189.10
    climber 313.6
mountain flax 331.5
mountain lion 413.4
mountainous
    huge 194.20
    hilly 206.23
mountainousness
    194.7
mountain range
    206.9,29
Mountain time 114.3
mountaintop
    pinnacle 206.8
    summit 210.2
mountebank
    buffoon 610.9
    charlatan 617.6
mountebankery,
    mountebankism
    614.7
Mounted Police,
    Mounties 697.15
mounting
    nouns setting 215.10
    ascent 313.1
    adjs. 313.16
Mount Olympus
    1016.10
mourn 873.8
mourner 409.7
mourners' bench
    1040.13
mournful
    grievous 862.11
    sorrowful 870.27
    plaintive 873.16

mournfulness 870.11
mourning
    nouns lamentation
        873.1
    garments 873.6
    GO INTO MOURNING
        873.14
    adjs. 873.15
mourning band,
    mourning ring
    873.6
MOUSE 281.6
mouse
    nouns diminutive
        195.4
    black eye 690.8
    timid person 906.6
    verbs 484.25
    MOUSE OVER
    ponder 477.12
    study 562.12
mouse-colored 365.3
mouse-eared 447.16
mousehole 264.4
mousehound 413.4
mouselike 413.40
mouser 413.28
mousetrap
    rocket launcher
        280.11
    trap 616.11
mousiness
    grayness 365.1
    timidity 906.4
mousse 306a.39
mousseux 404.6
mousy
    mouse-gray 365.3
    mouselike 413.40
    quiet 450.11
    timid 906.12
mouth
    nouns grimace 248.4
    anatomy 264.5
    orifice 264.6
    entranceway 301.5
    eater 306.13
    inlet 398.1
    verbs grimace 248.8
    chew 306.25
    touch 424.8
    lick 424.9
    speak 592.11
    mumble 593.8
    declaim 597.9
mouthful fill 56.3
    bite 306.2
    grandiloquence
        599.3
    YOU SAID A MOUTH-
        FUL 515.22
mouth harp 464.11
mouth honor
    hypocrisy 614.6
    sanctimony 1027.2
    GIVE MOUTH HONOR
    be hypocritical
        614.24
    be sanctimonious
        1027.4
mouthing 593.4

muffing 732.4
muffle
  nouns nose 255.7
    muffler 450.4
  verbs silence 450.9,10
    mumble 593.8
  MUFFLE UP 230.38
muffled 451.17
muffler 450.4
mufti
  civilian dress 230.8
  judge 1000.3
  priest 1036.12
mug
  nouns face 239.4
    grimace 248.4
    mouth 264.5
    man 419.5
    photograph 575.3
    ruffian 941.4
  verbs grimace 248.8
    photograph 575.16
    overact 609.35
mugginess
    327.5; 391.2
muggy 327.28; 391.15
mughouse 994.25
mugwump
  apostate 626.5
  personage 670.8
  nonpartisan 742.29
  independent 760.11
mugwumpery,
    mugwumpism
  nonpartisanism
    742.27
  neutralism 804.1
mugwumpian 742.49
Muharram 876.4
mulada 74.5
mulatto 44.9
mulberry 372.3
mulch 412.17
mulct
  nouns 1007.3
  verbs swindle 616.18
    fine 1007.5
mule crossbreed 44.8
  spinning jenny 205.5
  animal 413.23
  obstinate person
    624.6
mule-jenny 205.5
mule skinner, muleteer
    273.9
muley head 413.8
muliebrile 420.14
muliebrity 420.1
muliebrous 420.15
mulish asinine 413.41
  obstinate 624.8
mulishness 624.1
mull
  nouns promontory
    255.8
  failure 723.6
  verbs warm 328.17
  sweeten 430.5
  MULL OVER 477.12
mullah teacher 563.1
  priest 1036.12

mullet 99.1
mulligan stew 298.11
mulligatawny 306a.10
mulligrubs
  blues 870.6
  sulks 949.10
mullion 216.4
multiangular 250.12
multicellular 405.20
multicolor
  nouns 373.1
  adjs. 373.9
multicolored, multi-
    colorous 373.9
multifarious 19.3
multifariousness 19.1
multifid 55.6
multiflorous 410.36
multifold
  manifold 19.3
  multiple 100.8
multiform 19.3
multiformity 19
multigraph copy 22.8
  print 601.13
multilateral
  many-sided 241.7
  multiangular 250.12
multilateral trade
    825.1
multiloquence, mul-
    tiloquy 594.1
multiloquent, mul-
    tiloquous 594.9
multimillionaire 835.6
multinomial 100.8
multiparity 166.9
multiparous 168.16
multipartite 49.20
multiphase 19.3
multiple
  nouns 100.4
  adjs. 100.8
multiple personality
  psychosis 472.4
  dissociation 688.27
multiplex 19.3
multiplicand 100.4
multiplication
  mathematics 87.4
  multiplying 100.4
  proliferation 164.2
  procreation 168.2
multiplication table
    100.4
multiplicity 101.1
multiplied 100.8
multiplier 100.4
multiply increase 38.6
  calculate 87.11
  pluralize 100.6
  be productive 164.7
  procreate 168.9
multiplying
  nouns 100.4
  adjs. 38.8
multiprop 279.2
multitheism 1018.5
multitude
  large amount 34.3–6
  throng 74.4

large number 101.3
THE MULTITUDE
  917.3
multitudinal 101.7
multitudinousness
    101.1
multivalence 378.3
multivalent 378.8
mum
  nouns 450.1
  adjs. mute 450.14
  taciturn 611.7
KEEP MUM
  be silent 450.5
  keep secret 612.8
  interjs. 450.16
mumble
  nouns 593.4
  verbs chew 306.25
  say 592.17
  talk incoherently
    593.8
mumbling 593.4
Mumbo Jumbo
  god 1012.11
  bugbear 1014.10
  charm 1034.5
mumbo jumbo
  bugbear 1014.10
  incantation 1034.4
  charm 1034.5
mumbo-jumbo 545.4
mummer
  actor 610.1,10
  masquerader 617.7
mummery
  acting 609.9
  hypocrisy 614.6
  disguise 616.10
  ceremony 644.4
  sanctimony 1027.1
mummification
  drying 392.3
  mummy 407.13
  embalmment 409.3
  preservation 699.2
mummified 392.9
mummify dry 392.6
  embalm 409.22
  preserve 699.8
mummy
  mother 169.10
  dryness 392.2
  corpse 407.13
mump mumble 593.8
  deceive 616.17
  beg 772.15
mumper 772.8
mumpish glum 870.26
  sullen 949.24
mumpishness
  glumness 870.8
  sullenness 949.8
mumps disease 684.9
  blues 870.6
  sulks 949.10
mumsy 169.10
munch
  nouns 306.2
  verbs 306.25

mundane
  earthly 374.27
  unsacred 1025.3
  unspiritual 1029.16
THE MUNDANE 1025.2
mundaneness 1029.2
mundatory 679.16
mundunugu 1033.7
municipal 182.9
municipality
  town 182.1
  bureau 998.4
municipium 182.1
munificence 851.1
munificent 851.4
muniment 797.4
muniments 770.4
munition
  nouns 799.8
  verbs 657.8
munition plant 717.3
munitions
  equipment 657.4
  supplies 658.1
  weapons 799.1
munshi 563.1
mural
  nouns 572.12
  adjs. 236.13
murder
  nouns 408.2
  verbs kill 408.16
  botch 732.12
murder 408.10
murderous
  killing 408.24
  cruel 937.24
muricate 257.13
murk
  nouns darkness 336.4
  dark color 364.2
  verbs darken 336.10
  opaque 340.2
  blacken 364.7
  adjs. dark 336.16
  dark-colored 364.9
murkiness
  darkness 336.4
  opaqueness 340.1
  dark color 364.2
murky dark 336.16
  opaque 340.3
  dark-colored 364.9
  stained 677.9
murmur
  nouns trickle 394.7
  soft sound 451.4
  plaint 873.3
  verbs trickle 394.19
  blow 402.24
  sound faintly 451.10
  say 592.17
  complain 873.13
murmured 451.16
murmurer 867.3
murmuring
  nouns murmur 451.4
  complaining 873.4
  adjs. 451.18
murmurish,
    murmurous 451.18

murrain 684.4
Murray 746.9
murrey 367.7
murshid 1036.12
Musci 411.5
muscle
　nouns 158.2
　verbs 58.10
　MUSCLE IN 237.5
muscle-bound 758.16
muscle man
　strong man 158.6
　thug 941.4
muscular 158.14
muscularity,
　musculature 158.2
muse
　nouns reverie 530.2
　dream 533.9
　poetic ~ 607.12,13
　THE MUSES 463.24
　verbs ponder 477.11
　abstract oneself
　　530.9
　dream 533.17
　say 592.16
　MUSE ON, MUSE UPON,
　　MUSE OVER 477.12
museful
　thoughtful 477.20
　abstracted 530.11
　dreamy 533.25
musefulness
　abstraction 530.2
　dreaminess 533.8
musette 464.9,10
museum 558.9
mush
　nouns umbrella 227.7
　face 239.4
　mouth 264.5
　walk 272.12
　cereal 306a.34
　pulp 389.2
　sentimentality 853.7
　verbs 272.29
　MUSH THROUGH
　　277.46
mushiness
　pulpiness 389.1
　sentimentalism
　　853.7
mushroom
　nouns umbrella 227.7
　plant 410.4
　upstart 917.10
　verbs 196.7
　adjs. 917.13
mushroom cloud
　325.15
mushy weak 159.17
　pulpy 389.6
　sentimental 853.21
music melody 461.28
　types of ~ 461.57
　harmonics 462.1
　MUSIC OF THE
　　SPHERES
　order 59.1
　stars 374.4
　harmony 461.3

musical
　nouns 461.33
　adjs. 461.48,49
musical comedy
　music 461.35
　drama 609.6
musicale 461.33
musical instruments
　464
musicality 461.2
musicalize
　melodize 461.36
　harmonize 461.47
musicalness 461.2
musical review 609.4
musical score 461.28
musical sentence
　461.24
musica mensurata
　461.10
music box 464.17
music demy 461.28
music director 463.19
music drama 461.35
music festival 461.33
music hall 609.17
musician 463.1
musicianly 461.48
musicianship 461.32
musiclike 461.49
music lover 463.23
music-mad 461.48
music maker 463.1
musico 463.1
musicofanatic 463.23
musicology 462.1
musicomania 461.32
music paper 461.28
music roll 461.28;
　464.14
music school 565.9
music-tongued 461.49
music wire 464.24
musiker 463.1
musing
　nouns thought 477.2
　abstraction 530.2
　dreaming 533.8
　adjs. thoughtful
　　477.20
　abstracted 530.11
　dreaming 533.25
musk 435.2
musket 799.5
musketeer
　shooter 284.9
　soldier 798.11
musketry 799.1
muskiness 435.1
musky 435.9
muslin 276.14
musnud throne 737.10
　council 753.1
muss
　nouns 62.3
　verbs 63.2
mussal 330.4; 335.3
mussed up 62.13
mussel food 306a.25
　mollusk 414.9
Mussulman 1018.21

mussy slovenly 62.14
　dirty 680.24
must
　nouns rut 418.5
　malodor 436.2
　necessity 637.1
　blight 674.2
　obligation 960.1
　new wine 994.18
　IN MUST 418.21
　verbs 637.10
　IT MUST BE, IT NEEDS
　　MUST BE 637.20
　adjs. in heat 418.21
　necessary 637.12
　mandatory 750.13
　obligatory 960.14
mustache, mustachio
　229.11
mustang 413.14
mustard 164.6
mustard plaster 685.28
mustard seed 195.7
mustee 44.8
muster
　nouns assemblage
　　74.1
　roll 88.5
　schedule 639.2
　recruiting 778.6
　rally 795.13
　verbs assemble
　　74.15,17
　summon 750.12
　recruit 778.14
　rally 795.24
　MUSTER COURAGE
　　891.13
　MUSTER OUT 75.9
　MUSTER UP
　　summon up 646.13
　send for 750.12
mustiness
　malodor 436.2
　triteness 881.3
musty old 123.14
　in heat 418.21
　fetid 436.5
　moldy 690.40
　trite 881.9
mutability 141.1
mutable 141.6
mutate 139.5,6
mutation 139.2
mute
　nouns mourner 409.7
　deaf-mute 448.3
　speech sound 449.5
　dummy 450.3
　muffler 450.4
　actor 610.6
　verbs 450.9
　adjs. inanimate 381.5
　silent 450.12,14
　taciturn 611.7
muted
　phonetics 449.18
　muffled 451.17
mutedness 451.2
muteness deaf-and-
　dumbness 448.2

silence 450.2
taciturnity 611.2
mutilate cut off 42.10
　tear apart 49.13
　deform 248.7
　injure 690.13
　demolish 691.17
mutilated torn 49.22
　mangled 57.5
　deformed 248.12
mutilation
　excision 42.3
　laceration 49.2
　deformity 248.3
　injury 690.7
　demolition 691.5
mutilator 691.8
mutineer
　nouns 765.5
　verbs 765.8
mutineering
　nouns 765.4
　adjs. 765.12
mutinous 765.12
mutiny
　nouns 765.4
　verbs 765.8
mutism
　muteness 450.2
　neurosis 688.25
mutt dog 413.25
　fool 470.2
mutter
　nouns murmur 451.4
　mumble 593.4
　plaint 873.3
　verbs murmur 451.10
　say 592.17
　mumble 593.8
　complain 873.13
mutterer 867.3
muttering
　murmur 451.4
　mumbling 593.4
mutton meat 306a.15
　sheep 413.9
mutton chops 229.8
muttonhead 470.4
muttonheaded 468.17
mutual
　reciprocal 13.13
　joint 73.9
　interchangeable
　　149.5
　common 813.9
mutuality 13.1
mutual understanding
　agreement 26.2
　unanimity 520.5
mux
　nouns mixture 44.6
　jumble 62.3
　multiplex circuit
　　341.4
　verbs 63.2
muzhik 917.8
muzzle
　nouns nose 255.7
　mouth 264.5,6
　silencer 450.4

shackle 758.4
verbs render
powerless 157.11
silence 450.10
restrain 758.10
muzzler 402.12
muzzy muddleheaded
468.18
muddled 530.13
drunk 994.39
M.V.D. 697.15
my 806.13
mycologist 411.2
mycology 411.1
myelencephalon 465.5
My Lord 915.2
Mynheer 419.7
Mynheer Closh 417.9
myocarditis 684.16
myography, myology
244.7
myopia 439.3
myopic 439.11
myriad
nouns 99.10
adjs. 101.7
myriapod 413a.2
Myriapoda,
myriapods 414.8
myrmidon
retainer 748.1
henchman 785.7
myrrh 435.2
myself 80.5
mysteries 1038.5
mysterious
recondite 547.14
secret 612.12
occult 1032.24
mysteriousness 547.2
mystery enigma 547.7
drama 609.4
secret 612.5
mysticism 1032.1
sacrament 1038.3
mystes 1036.15
mystic
nouns 1032.11
adjs. philosophical
499.10
recondite 547.14
occult 1032.24
mysticism 1032.1
mystification 613.1
mystified 513.23
mystify 513.13
mystifying 513.24
mytacism 593.1
myth fancy 533.5
story 606.7
falsehood 614.10
mythical
imaginary 533.21
fictional 606.17
fictitious 614.30
mythological
1012.22
mythicism 1012.21
mythify 614.18
mythmaker
imaginer 533.12

storyteller 606.10
mythological
imaginary 533.21
mythical 1012.22
mythology 1012.21
mythomania 614.8
mythomaniac 617.9
Myxomycetes 411.4

N

nab arrest 759.16
capture 820.15
nabob personage 670.8
governor 747.14
rich man 835.6
nacre pearliness 339.2
iridescence 373.6
nacred, nacreous,
nacrous, nacry
373.10
nadir 211.2
nadiral 211.8
nag
nouns 413.12,13,16
verbs 967.16
nagara 464.21
Nagari 579.5
nagging
nouns 967.4
adjs. shrewish 949.21
faultfinding 967.24
naggy
nouns 413.13
adjs. 949.21
nagual 1012.10
Nahum 1020.1
naiad 1012.17
naïf See naïve
naik 747.23
nail
nouns 833.4
ON THE NAIL
instantly 113.6
now 120.3
cash down 839.25
verbs fasten 47.8
see 438.12
recognize 535.13
catch 820.14
nailery 717.3
nailhead 210.3
nail polish 898.11
nails strength 158.7
hardness 355.6
clutches 811.4
naïve, naïf
nouns 734.3
adjs. gullible 501.8
artless 734.5
naïvely 734.7
naïveté, naïvety
gullibility 501.2
artlessness 734.1
naked unmixed 45.6
nude 231.14
open 264.17
exposed 553.9
unprotected 695.15
unadorned 900.8
naked eye 438.9

nakedness
nudity 231.3
unadornment 900.3
naked truth 515.2
naker 464.21
namby-pamby
nouns weakling 159.6
sentimentality 853.7
adjs. weak 159.17
insipid 678.8
sentimental 853.21
overnice 901.18
namda 227.12
name
nouns appellation
581.3
personage 670.8
reputation 912.1
celebrity 912.9
BY NAME 581.16
GO UNDER THE NAME
OF 581.13
IN NAME ONLY
supposedly 498.17
nominal 581.15
alleged 647.4
IN THE NAME OF
by authority of
737.20
for 783.26
WITHOUT A NAME
582.3
verbs specify 80.9
cite 504.14
denominate 581.11
nominate 635.16
appoint 778.10
NAME OVER 87.10
adjs. 670.16
name and address
602.10
named aforesaid 64.5
called 581.14
nominated 635.23
name dropper 910.7
nameless
anonymous 582.3
unrenowned 913.14
namely
nominally 80.18
to wit 550.21
NAMELY IF 506.14
namesake 581.3
naming denomination
581.2
nomination 635.6
appointment 778.2
Nanak 1020.3
nance, Nancy, nancy
418.12
Nanna 1012.6
nanny
goat 413.10
female animal
420.10
nursemaid 697.7
nanoid 195.12
naos 1040.4
nap texture 350.1
sleep 710.3,13
Napaea 1012.16

nape 48.5
napery cloth 377.5
dry goods 829.3
napiform 251.20
napoleon 833.5
napoo
verbs 691.13
adjs. 2.10
napping
unaware 476.14
inattentive 529.8
bemused 530.11
nappy textural 350.7
sleepy 710.19
inebriated 994.38
Naraka 1017.1
narcissism 688.32
narcissist 688.14
Narcissus 898.9
narcoanalysis, narco-
hypnosis 688.5
narcosis 422.1
narcosynthesis 688.5
narcotherapist 688.13
narcotherapy 688.5
narcotic
nouns addict 640.9
drug 685.10
types of ~ 685.47
adjs. anesthetic 422.8
medicinal 685.39
narcotics traffic 824.1
narcotization 422.1
narcotize 422.3
nard 379.3
nares nostrils 255.7
olfactories 434.5
narghile, nargileh
433.7
nark
nouns 555.6
verbs 555.11
narrate 606.13
narratio 1002.7
narration 606.2,6
narrational 606.16
narrative
nouns narration
606.2,6
~ poetry 607.2
~ poem 607.4
adjs. 606.16
narrator 606.10
narrow
nouns strait 204.3
inlet 398.1
verbs specialize 81.4
contract 197.7
taper 204.10
limit 233.5
qualify 506.3
adjs. slender 204.13
limited 233.8
phonetics 449.18
narrow-minded
525.10
meticulous 531.12
meager 660.8
poor 836.7
strait-laced 901.19
narrow escape 630.2

narrow-gauge, narrow-
gauged
narrow 204.13
narrow-minded
525.10
narrowhearted 525.10
narrow house 409.16
narrowing
contraction 197.1
tapering 204.2
narrowish 204.13
narrowly 204.21
narrow means 836.1
narrow-minded 525.10
narrows strait 204.3
inlet 398.1
narrow squeak 630.2
narrowy 204.13
Narsinh 1012.8
narthex 191.19
nary one none 2.3
nobody 186.6
nasal
nouns 449.5
adjs. respiratory
402.30
phonetics 449.18
nasalization 593.1
nasalize 593.9
nasalized 449.18
nasal twang 593.1
nascency
beginning 68.3
birth 166.9
nascent 63.14
nastiness
unsavoriness 428.3
filthiness 680.2
odiousness 862.2
repugnance 865.2
obscenity 988.4
Nastrond 1017.3
nasty
verbs 680.19
adjs. unsavory 428.7
foul 680.25
odious 862.9
obscene 988.9
nasty blow
calamity 727.2
distress 364.5
nasty look 967.9
natal nascent 68.14
native 138.7
natal day 137.4
natant 274.61
natation
swimming 274.11
bathing 579.6
natator 274.12
natatorial, natatory
274.61
natatorium 679.11
nates 240.4
nation race 11.4
country 180.1
list of ~ 180.9
community 416.2
national
nouns 189.4
adjs. racial 11.8

communal 416.13
national anthem
song 461.13
militarism 795.17
National Assembly
parliament 740.2
senate 740.3
National Guard
798.23
nationalism
nationality 180.6
policy 742.5
collectivism 743.5
patriotism 939.2
nationalist 743.12
nationalistic
socialist 743.20
patriotic 939.5
nationalities 417.1,9
nationality race 11.4
nation 180.1
statehood 180.6
nativity 188.1
community 416.2
types of ~ 417.20
nationalism 939.2
nationalization
making national
180.7
naturalization 188.4
collectivization
813.3
nationalize
make national 180.8
domesticate 188.5
collectivize 813.7
national park 699.6
Nationalrat 740.4
national socialism
government 739.8
partisanism 742.26
nation-wide 79.13
native
nouns 189.3
adjs. innate 5.7
indigenous 188.7
genuine 515.13
natural 719.13
artless 734.5
unaffected 900.7
GO NATIVE 188.6
native-born 188.7
native environment
190.4
native heath 180.2
native land 180.2
native language 578.4
native stones 383.9
native tongue 578.4
native wit 466.1
nativity
beginning 68.3
birth 166.9
nativeness 188.1
horoscope 374.20
THE NATIVITY
Christmas 137.5
birth 166.9
NATO 769.2
nattily 642.17
natty 642.13

natural
nouns note 462.14
idiot 470.8
dice throw 514.9
sure success 722.2
expert 731.11
A NATURAL 84.3
adjs. innate 5.7
lifelike 20.16
normal 84.7
instinctive 480.6
genuine 515.13
typical 570.12
elegant 587.6
plain-speaking 589.3
informal 645.3
raw 719.13
artless 734.5
unaffected 900.7
natural child 170.5
natural death 407.1
naturalism
realism 84.1
materialism 375.5
naturalness 734.2
naturalist 405.17
naturalistic
natural 84.7
materialistic 375.11
philosophical 499.10
naturality 515.5
naturalization
domestication 188.4
habituation 640.7
naturalize
domesticate 188.5
accustom 640.10
naturalized
domesticated 188.9
accustomed 640.16
naturalized citizen
189.4
naturally
by nature 5.9
normally 84.9
consequently 153.9
genuinely 515.17
yes 520.18
plainly 589.4
informally 645.4
artlessly 734.7
unaffectedly 900.11
natural philosophy
324.1
natural science
physics 324.1
science 405.16;
474.10
natural selection 321.4
Nature 1011.9
nature essence 5.3
kind 61.3
characteristic 80.3
tendency 173
universe 374.1
temperament 523.3
natural state 719.3
naturalness 734.2
BY NATURE 5.9
NATURE IN THE RAW
nudity 231.3

natural state 719.3
THE NATURE OF THE
BEAST
nature 5.3
in character 80.13
typical 570.12
THE NATURE OF
THINGS 7.2
naturellement
naturally 153.9
yes 520.18
naturopathic 686.18
naturopathy
healing 686.2
therapy 687.3
naught, nought
nothing 2.2
trifle 671.6
COME TO NAUGHT 2.5
naughtiness
misbehavior 736.1
wickedness 979.5
naughty
misbehaving 736.5
bad 979.17
Naughty Nineties
107.7
nausea vomiting 308.8
nauseation 684.22
nauseant
nouns sickener 428.3;
865.3
cloyer 662.3
emetic 685.16
adjs. nasty 428.7
disgusting 862.9
nauseate 864.13
nauseated sick 684.42
disgusted 864.23
nauseating nasty 428.7
disgusting 862.9
nauseation 684.22
nauseous nasty 428.7
disgusting 862.9
nautch 877.2
nautch girl 877.3
nautical marine 274.60
oceanic 396.7
naval 274.60
naval vessels 276.24
naval warfare 795.4
navar aviation 277.4
radar 345.2
navarch
shipmaster 275.7
officer 747.24
nave center 225.2
hub 320.5
church ~ 1040.9
navel 225.2
navicert 568.5
navicular, naviform
251.12
navigability
navigation 274.1
accessibility 508.3
navigable
boatable 274.62
accessible 508.8
navigate sail 274.13
avigate 277.42

navigating 274.1
navigation sailing 274
  aerial ~ 277.4
  radar ~ 345.8
navigational 274.60
navigator
  mariner 275.1,6
  avigator 278.4
navvy
  steam shovel 256.10
  laborer 716.2
navy tobacco 433.8
  naval forces 798.27
nawab ruler 747.10,11
  title 915.3
nay
  nouns the negative
    481.14
  no 522.1
  vote 635.5
  advs. 522.7
  NAY RATHER 15.7
Nazarene
  Jesus 1011.12
  Christian 1018.15
naze 255.8
Nazi 742.28
nazification 145.3
nazify 145.10
Naziism, Nazism
  government 739.8
  partisanism 742.26
N.C.O. 747.23
neap
  nouns low water
    207.2
  tongue 216.1
  ~ tide 394.13
  adjs. 207.6
near
  verbs resemble 20.7
  ~ in time 121.6
  be imminent 151.2
  approach 295.3
  adjs. related 9.7
  approximative 20.14
  imitation 22.9
  imminent 151.3
  close 199.14
  nearer 199.18
  narrow 204.13
  left 243.5
  sham 614.27
  stingy 850.11
  intimate 925.18
  advs. about 35.13
  closely 199.24
  nearly 199.25
  BE NEAR 199.8
  GO NEAR 295.3
  NEAR ONE'S END
    407.27
  NEAR THE WIND
    274.70
  NEAR TO
  about 35.13
  about to 121.13
  nearly 199.25
  NEAR UPON
  about 35.13

approximately
  199.26
preps. at 183.28
  nigh 199.20
nearabout, nearabouts
  nearby 199.20
  nearly 199.25
near-at-hand
  imminent 151.3
  nearby 199.15
nearby
  adjs. 199.15
  advs. 199.20
near by near 199.20
  nearly 199.25
  beside 241.11
Near East 179.6
near go 630.2
nearing
  nouns 295.1
  adjs. future 121.8
  imminent 151.3
  approaching 295.4
nearly about 35.13
  almost 199.25
  narrowly 204.21
nearmost 199.19
nearness relation 9.1
  likeness 20.1
  closeness 199
  narrowness 204.1
  stinginess 850.3
  intimacy 925.5
near side 243.1
near-sight 439.3
nearsighted
  myopic 439.11
  undiscerning 468.14
  narrow-minded
    525.10
nearsightedness
  myopia 439.3
  unperceptiveness
    468.2
  narrow-mindedness
    525.1
neat
  verbs 60.11
  adjs. apt 26.18
  net 43.6
  unmixed 45.6
  trim 59.8
  well-shaped 247.6
  elegant 587.6,7
  plain-speaking 589.3
  concise 590.4
  spruce 642.13
  adroit 731.20
neaten 60.11
neat fingered, neat
  handed 731.21
neatherd 415.3
neb tip 70.2
  beak 255.7
  point 257.4
Nebiim 1019.3
nebulae 374.14
nebular 374.25
nebulose 374.25
nebulosity 403.4
nebulous dim 336.18

celestial 374.25
  cloudy 403.8
  obscure 547.13
necessarian
  nouns 638.5
  adjs. 638.10
necessarianism 638.4
necessaries 637.2
necessarily
  consequently 153.9
  of necessity 637.16
necessariness 637.1
necessary
  nouns requirement
    637.2
  toilet 680.13
  adjs. 637.12
  BE NECESSARY 637.10
necessism 638.4
necessist 638.5
necessitarian
  nouns 638.5
  adjs. 638.10
necessitarianism 638.4
necessitate
  require 637.8
  oblige 754.5
necessitation 637.1
necessitative 637.12
necessities 637.2
necessitous
  necessary 637.12
  needy 836.8
necessitude 637.1
necessity
  requirement 637.2
  fate 638.2
  neediness 836.2
  BE UNDER THE NECES-
    SITY OF 637.10
  OF NECESSITY
  consequently 153.9
  necessarily 637.16
  compulsively 754.11
neck
  nouns cervix 48.5
  narrow 204.3
  ~ of land 255.8
  GET IT IN THE NECK
    1008.22
  RUN NECK AND NECK
    268.14
  verbs make love
    930.13
  hang 1008.20
neck-and-neck race
  30.4
neckband 252.3
necker 929.11
necking 930.1
necklace band 252.3
  ornament 899.6
neck oil 994.13
neck or nothing 622.20
necktie party 1008.7
neckwear 230.64
necrology
  death 407.12
  biography 606.4
necromancer 1033.5
necromancy 1033.1

necromantic 1033.14
necrophilia 688.32
necropolis 409.15
necropsy 484.9
necroscopical 409.25
necroscopy 484.9
necrosis
  gangrene 684.30
  decay 690.6
nectar delicacy 306a.8
  sweetness 430.4
nectareous
  delicious 427.8
  sweet 430.6
nectar of the gods
  994.12
ned 833.5
neddy, Neddy 413.22
nee 166.26
nee 166.26
need
  nouns deficiency 57.2
  requirement 637.2
  lack 660.4
  poverty 836.2
  verbs require 637.9
  be obliged 637.10
  lack 660.6
  be poor 836.5
needed 637.13
needful
  nouns the necessary
    637.2
  money 833.2
  adjs. 637.13
neediness 836.2
needing deficient 57.4
  lacking 660.11
needle
  nouns types of ~
    222.8
  thorn 257.8
  magnetic ~ 287.3
  leaf 410.17
  phonograph ~
    464.18
  etching ~ 576.11
  compass ~ 746.8
  verbs sew 222.4
  pierce 264.15
  goad 646.15
  tease 864.19
needle bath
  sprinkler 391.8
  bath 679.7
needle in a haystack
  513.8
  LOOK FOR A NEEDLE
    IN A HAYSTACK
  be impossible 509.5
  do in vain 667.8
needlelike 257.12
needles 797.3
needless
  superfluous 661.18
  useless 667.10
needlessly
  superfluously 661.26
  uselessly 667.15
needlessness
  superfluity 661.4
  uselessness 667.1

needle valve 395.10
needle-witted 466.14
needlewoman 222.2
needlework
  sewing 222.1
  types of ~ 222.6
needleworker 222.2
needling 646.5
needy
  nouns 836.3
  adjs. 836.8
ne'er 106.4
ne'er a one none 2.3
  nobody 186.6
ne'er-do-well
  nouns idler 706.8
  wretch 984.2
  adjs. 706.17
nefarious terrible 673.9
  infamous 913.12
  wicked 979.17
negate disprove 505.4
  deny 522.3
  refuse 774.3
negated 505.7
negation
  nonexistence 2.1
  disproof 505.1
  denial 522
  refusal 774.1
negative
  nouns mold 25.6
  minus quantity 42.2
  negat on 522.1
  film 575.12
  engraving 576.6
  veto 776.2
  IN THE NEGATIVE
    522.6
  THE NEGATIVE 481.14
  verbs neutralize 177.7
  disprove 505.4
  negate 522.3
  refuse 774.3
  veto 776.5
  adjs. nonexistent 2.7
  mathematics 86.8
  electronegative
    341.32
  denying 522.5
  neuter 804.7
negativeness 2.1
negativism 688.34
negativity 2.1
negatory
  refutatory 505.6
  denying 522.5
negatron 342.3
neglect
  nouns inattention
    529
  negligence 532
  verbs ~ the
    opportunity 130.6
  slight 532.6
  snub 964.6
neglected 532.14
neglectful
  inattentive 529.6
  negligent 532.10
neglectfully 532.17

neglector, neglecter
  negligent 532.5
  trifler 671.9
  bungler 732.8
négligé 230.20
negligee 230.20
  IN NEGLIGEE 230.46
negligence
  slovenry 62.6
  procrastination
    132.5
  inattention 529
  neglect 532.1
  unconcern 634.2
negligent
  nouns 532.5
  adjs. slovenly 62.14
  procrastinating
    132.16
  inattentive 529.6
  neglectful 532.10
  unconcerned 634.6
negligibility 671.1
negligible slight 35.7
  insignificant 671.15
negotiability
  workability 163.3
  practicability 508.2
negotiable
  workable 163.11
  practicable 508.7
  transferable 815.5
negotiables 832.1
negotiant
  intermediary 779.4
  mediator 803.3
negotiate hurdle 317.5
  manage 722.11
  treat with 769.7
  ~ a peace 802.9
  mediate 803.6
  pass 815.3
  bargain 825.14
negotiation
  arbitration 803.2
  commerce 825.3,4
negotiator
  intermediary 779.4
  mediator 803.3
Negress 417.7
Negrillo 195.6
Negritic pygmy 195.12
  Negro 417.12
Negrito 195.6
Negro
  nouns mulatto 44.9
  colored person 417.7
  adjs. 417.12
negro 364.8
Negroid
  nouns 417.7
  adjs. 417.12
negroize 364.7
Negro race race 417.2
  types of ~ 417.18
Negus 747.9
neigh 459.2
neighbor
  nouns neighborer
    199.6
  friend 926.1

verbs adjoin 199.9
  juxtapose 199.13
  adjs. 199.16
neighborer 199.6
neighborhood
  region 179.1
  proximity 199.1
  environs 232.1
  IN THE NEIGHBOR-
    HOOD OF
  about 35.13
  near 199.14
  approximately
    199.26
  around 232.13
neighboring
  adjacent 199.16
  surrounding 232.9
neighborliness
  hospitality 923.1
  friendliness 925.1
neighborly
  hospitable 923.11
  friendly 925.14
neither 522.9
  NEITHER HERE NOR
    THERE
  irrelevant 10.7
  nowhere 186.16
  unimportant 671.15
  NEITHER HIDE NOR
    HAIR 2.3
  NEITHER HOT NOR
    COLD
  irresolute 625.9
  indifferent 634.5
  mediocre 678.8
  neutral 804.7
  NEITHER MORE NOR
    LESS
  equivalent 30.9
  exactly 515.19
  NEITHER ONE THING
    NOR THE OTHER
  insipid 429.2
  indifferent 634.5
  mediocre 678.8
  neutral 804.7
nekton 405.1
nektonic 405.25
Nemesis
  avenger 954.3
  Justice 974.5
nemesis justice 974.1
  retribution 1008.1
Neo-Darwinism 321.4
Neo-Fascism 739.8
Neo-Hegelian 499.11
Neo-Lamarckism
  321.4
neolith 123.6
neolithic 123.20
neologic 580.20
neologism
  innovation 139.3
  word 580.7
neologist
  modernist 122.4
  word-coiner 580.16
neologize 139.8
neology 580.7

neonate 125.7
neophyte
  convert 145.5
  novice 564.7
  religious ~ 1026.4
neoplasm 684.29
Neoplatonic 499.11
Neo-Pythagorean
  499.11
Neo-Scholastic 499.11
neoteric
  nouns 122.4
  adjs. new 122.7
  neological 580.20
neoterism 580.7
neoterist
  modernist 122.4
  neologist 580.16
Neph 1012.9
nephalism 990.2
nephalist 990.4
nephelognosy 403.5
nephelometer, neph-
  elorometer 403.6
nephesh 1032.17
nephew 11.3
nephological 403.11
nephologist,
  nephology 403.5
nephoscope 403.6
nephrectomy 687.25
nephritic 684.46
nephritis 684.8
nephrosis 684.8
nephrotomy 687.26
nephrotuberculosis
  684.13
Nephthys 1012.9
nepotism 975.3
Neptune planet 374.6
  sea god 396.4
  god 1012.5,17
Nereid sea god 396.4
  nymph 1012.17
nerval 421.11
nerve
  nouns organ 421.6
  courage 891.5
  impudence 911.3
  HAVE A NERVE 911.6
  HAVE THE NERVE
    891.10
  WITHOUT A NERVE IN
    ONE'S BODY 858.2
  verbs 891.16
  NERVE ONESELF
    891.13
nerve center
  center 225.5
  radar station 345.6
nerve-deaf 858.2
nerveless
  enervated 157.19
  unnervous 858.2
nerve-racking, nerve-
  rending, etc.
  857.15
nerves 857.1
  ALL NERVES 857.11
  GET ON ONE'S NERVES
  grate on 457.10

make nervous 857.9
annoy 864.18
NERVES ALL SHOT
857.14
NERVES OF STEEL
858.1
nerviness 891.4
nervous neural 421.11
eloquent 598.12
agitated 855.24
excitable 855.29
jittery 857.11
nervous breakdown
688.17
HAVE A NERVOUS
BREAKDOWN 857.8
nervous disorder
disease 684.17
neurosis 688.17
nervously 857.16
nervous prostration
collapse 684.7
neurosis 688.17
nervous system 421.6
nervous tension 857.3
nervous wreck
wreck 690.9
nervousness 857.6
nervy strong 158.13
nervous 857.11
bold 891.18
impudent 911.9
nescience 476.1
nescient 476.13
nese 255.7
ness 255.8
nest
nouns multitude
101.3
breeding place 152.8
lodging 190.1
abode 190.21
haunt 190.23
airport 277.19
verbs settle 183.18
reside 187.8
n'est-ce pas? 484.47
nest egg 658.3
KEEP AS A NEST EGG
save up 658.12
prepare 718.11
nester 189.9
nestle protect 697.17
snuggle 885.10
cuddle 930.15
nestling
youngling 125.8
cuddling 930.1
Nestor elder 127.2
sage 467.2
adviser 752.4
net
nouns network 220.3
porousness 264.8
~ weight 351.1
snare 616.12
~ profit 809.3
receipts 842.1
~ price 844.2
~ worth 844.3
verbs crisscross 220.7

weave 221.7
ensnare 616.20
gain 809.7
catch 820.14
adjs. 43.6
nether 207.8
nethermost 211.7
nether side 211.1
nether world 1017.1
netted 220.11
netting
network 220.3
radio network
343.11
nettle
nouns 257.8
verbs incite 646.17
annoy 864.17
anger 950.22
nettled
annoyed 864.24
provoked 950.25
nettle rash 684.27
netty 220.11
network
webwork 220.3
radio ~ 343.11
neural
posterial 240.9
nerval 421.11
neuralgia 684.17
neuralgic 684.46
neurasthenia 688.21
neurasthenic
ill 684.46
neurotic 688.48
neuritic 684.46
neuritis 684.8,17
neuro 688.14
neurological
neural 421.11
medical 686.18
neurologist
nerves 421.6
doctor 686.7
neurology 421.6
neuron 421.6
neuroparalysis 684.19
neuropath 688.14
neuropathy 684.17
neuroplasty 687.27
neuropsychiatric
688.47
neuropsychiatrist
688.13
neuropsychiatry 688.3
neuropsychology 688.1
neuropsychopathic
472.26
neuropsychopathy,
neuropsychosis
472.3
neurosis 688.17
neurotic
nouns 688.14
adjs. sedative 685.39
psychoneurotic
688.48
neuroticism 688.17
neurotomy 687.26

neuter
nouns gender 584.8
neutral 804.4
adjs. sexless 418.22
indifferent 634.5
mediocre 678.7
neutral 804.7
neutral
nouns ~ gear 347.6
nonpartisan 742.29
independent 760.11
~ person 804.4
adjs. achromatic
362.7
antacid 378.7
sexless 418.22
unbiased 524.12
indifferent 634.5
mediocre 678.7
nonpartisan 742.49
independent 760.20
neuter 804.7
neutralism
political ~ 742.5
nonpartisanism
742.27
neutrality 804.1
neutrality
sexlessness 418.9
impartiality 524.5
indifference 634.1
mediocrity 678.1
neutralism 804.1
neutralization 177.2
neutralize offset 33.5
cushion 162.8
nullify 177.7
neutralizer
counteractant 177.3
chemical 378.1
medicine 685.20
neutralizing 177.9
neutrodyne 343.31
neutrons 325.24
névé 332.6
never nowise 35.14
not ever 106.4
by no means 522.8
NEVER A ONE
none 2.3
nobody 186.6
NEVER OTHERWISE
invariably 17.8
universally 79.16
always 112.11
NEVER SAY DIE
not weaken 158.9
persevere 623.4,10
resist 790.5
cheer up! 868.20
NEVER SO
considerably 34.17
especially 36.19
NEVER TO BE
FORGOTTEN
unforgettable 535.25
notable 670.18
never-dying 112.9
never-ending
continuous 71.9
perpetual 112.7

nevermore 106.4
neverness 106.1
nevertheless
notwithstanding
33.8
anyhow 655.12
never-tiring 623.7
Nevison 823.12
nevus
protuberance 255.3
mark 566.4
blemish 677.1
growth 684.29
new
adjs. additional 40.9
recent 122.7
unused 666.12
NEW TO
unaccustomed 641.4
inexperienced
732.17
advs. again 91.6
anew 122.16
new beginning 143.2
new-begotten 122.9
new birth
conversion 145.2
revival 692.3
salvation 1024.4
newborn
newfledged 122.9
infant 124.12
born 166.26
newborn babe 982.4
new broom
man of action 705.8
officeholder 744.11
new-built 122.9
newcomer 78.4
New Deal 742.6
new departure 68.1
newel 216.4
New England 179.7
New Englander 189.11
New England Primer
603.8
newest 122.15
newfangle,
newfandangle
nouns 122.2
adjs. 122.12
newfangled, new-
fandangled 122.12
new-fashion,
new-fashioned
modern 122.14
fashionable 642.11
newfledged
newborn 122.9
immature 124.10
new high 36.3
New Jerusalem
utopia 533.11
heaven 1016.4
newly again 91.6
anew 122.16
newly come 122.13
newly-rich 917.10,13
newlywed 931.6
newlyweds 931.10
new-made 122.9

new-model
verbs convert 145.9
remodel 692.18
adjs. 122.9
new moon 374.8
newness freshness 122
unaccustomedness
641.2
news tidings 556
newspaper 603.12
news analyst 604.4
newsbill 556.5
newsboy 828.6
newscast
nouns 343.21
verbs 343.28
newscaster 343.26
newsdealer 828.3
news editor 603.22
news flash 558.16
newsful 556.13
news item 556.3
newsletter 556.5
newsman 603.22
newsmonger 556.9
newsmongery 556.7
newspaper 603.12
newspaperese 578.7
newspaperish 603.26
newspaperman 603.22
newsprint 572.19
newsreel 609.15
news report 556.5
newsstand 830.3
newsworthy 556.13
newsy
nouns 828.6
adjs. 556.13
New Testament
1019.4
New Thought 1018.12
New Thoughtist
1018.22
new twist 478.8
New World 179.6
new wrinkle
a novelty 122.2
novel idea 478.8
next
adjs. succeeding 65.5
nearest 199.19
aware 474.17
GET NEXT TO
become informed
555.13
ingratiate 905.9
make friends 925.12
advs. 117.5
next of kin 11.2
next world 121.2
nexus bond 48.1
series 71.2
Niagara 394.11
niagara 394.5
nib end 70.2
tongue 256.1
beak 255.7
point 257.4
nibble
nouns 306.2
verbs eat 306.24,25

be credulous 501.5
NIBBLE AT 967.16
Nibelung 195.6
nice detailed 8.7
savory 427.8
discriminative 491.8
precise 515.15
meticulous 531.12
suitable 668.4
good 672.13
pleasant 861.5
fastidious 894.11
tasteful 895.9
kind 936.14
proper 956.8
scrupulous 972.15
BE NICE 735.5
nice go 729.4
nicely
expediently 668.7
excellently 672.23
kindly 936.19
Nicene Creed 1021.2
Nicene Fathers 1020.2
nicety
fine distinction 16.2
finesse 491.1
preciseness 515.3
meticulousness
531.3
punctilio 749.4
fastidiousness 894.3
taste 895.1
TO A NICETY
just right 515.21
to perfection 675.11
niche nook 191.3
recess 256.7
~ in the hall of
fame 912.7
nick
nouns ~ of time
129.5
notch 261.1
dice throw 514.9
IN THE NICK OF TIME
opportunely 129.13
in time 131.12
verbs notch 261.4
swindle 616.18
steal 822.13
nicked 261.5
nickel
nouns element 378.11
metal 382.20
coin 833.7,19
adjs. 382.16
nickelic, nickeline,
nickelous 382.16
nickelodeon
juke box 464.18
theater 609.18
nickel plate 227.14
nicker 459.2
nicknack toy 876.16
trinket 899.4
nickname 581.7,11
nicotia tobacco 433.1
nicotine 433.10
nicotian tobacco 433.1
tobacco user 433.12

nicotine 433.10
nicotinism 433.16
nictitate 439.10
nictitation 439.7
nide 187.8
nidus
breeding place 152.8
abode 190.21
niece 11.3
Niflhel 1017.3
nifty
nouns 672.7
adjs. stylish 642.13
good 672.14
niggard
nouns 850.5
adjs. 850.10
niggardly
adjs. paltry 671.18
stingy 850.10
advs. 850.14
nigger capstan 286.7
light shield 337.3
Negro 417.7
niggerhead, negrohead
433.8
niggertoe 306a.38
niggle 965.9
niggling 671.17
nigh
adjs. near 199.14
left 243.5
advs. about 35.13
nearly 199.25
prep. 199.20
nigh side 243.1
night
nouns nighttime
134.4
black 364.4
AT NIGHT, BY NIGHT,
etc. nightly 134.11
darkling 336.21
adjs. 134.9
night and day 135.7
night-black
dark 336.14
black 364.8
night blindness 440.2
nightcap 994.8
night-clad, night-
cloaked 336.14
night clothes 230.21
night club 876.11
night-dark dark 336.14
black 364.8
nightdress 230.21
night-enshrouded
336.14
nightfall 134.2
night-fallen 134.9
night-filled 336.14
night float 686.13
nightgown 230.21
nighthawk taxi 271.11
dissipater 991.3
night-hid 336.14
nightie 230.21
nightingale 463.15
nightingale's tongue
306a.8

night letter 558.16
nightlong 110.12
nightly
adjs. 134.9
advs. 134.11
nightmare
hallucination 518.7
dream 533.9
horror 864.7
ogre 889.8
night owl 991.3
nights 134.11
night shift 108.3
nightshirt 230.21
night song 1030.8
night spot 876.11
nighttime
nouns 134.4
adjs. 134.9
night-veiled 336.14
nightwalker
noctambulist 273.7
earthworm 413a.8
nightwalking, night-
wandering
nouns 272.11
adjs. 272.37
night watchman 697.9
nightwear 230.21
nigrescence 364.1
nigrescent, nigricant
364.9
nigrify 364.7
nigrine black 364.8
negro 417.12
nigrities, nigritude
364.1
nigrous 364.8
nihil 2.2
nihilism anarchy 738.2
politics 743.4
nihilist destroyer 691.8
anarchist 738.3
radical 743.11
nihilistic
anarchical 738.6
radical 743.19
nihility
nonexistence 2.1
nonentity 4.2
insignificancy 671.6
Nike missile 280.15
goddess 1012.5
nil 2.2
Nilometer 394.16
nimble fast 268.19
smart 466.14
alert 531.14
quick 705.17
agile 731.21
nimble-fingered 731.21
nimble-footed
fast 268.19
agile 731.21
nimble-witted
smart 466.14
witty 879.15
nimbly actively 705.24
agilely 731.28
nimbose 403.8
nimbosity 403.4

nonage nine 99.5
　minority 124.3
nonagenarian 127.2
nonaggression 801.4
nonaggressive
　unenterprising
　　706.17
　peaceable 801.10
nonagon 99.5
nonagreement 520a.1
nonalcoholic
　~ beverage 306a.47
　unintoxicating 995.4
nonappearance
　absentation 186.4
　invisibility 444.1
nonary 99.21
nonassent 520a.1
nonattendance 186.4
nonattendant 186.9
nonbeing 2.1
nonbeliever 1029.11
nonbelligerent 801.5
nonbiological 381.4
nonbreakable 358.5
non-Catholic
　nouns 1018.18
　adjs. 1018.26
nonce 120.1
FOR THE NONCE
　meantime 109.5
　temporarily 111.9
　now 120.3
　once 136.6
nonce word 580.7
nonchalance
　unconcern 634.2
　imperturbability
　　856.5
nonchalant
　unconcerned 634.6
　imperturbable
　　856.15
non-Christian
　nouns 1023.6
　adjs. 1023.10
noncivilized
　savage 161.20
　uncultured 896.12
nonclerical 1037.3
noncoherent 51.4
noncohesion 51.1
noncohesive 51.4
noncollegiate 560.19
noncom 747.23
noncombatant
　nouns 801.5
　adjs. 801.10
noncombative 801.10
noncommissioned
　778.16
noncommissioned
　officer
　officer 747.23
　soldier 798.9
noncommittal 893.8
noncommunicable
　811.10
noncompetitive 784.7
noncompletion 721.1

noncompliance
　nonconformity 83.2
　disobedience 765.1
　refusal 774.1
noncompos 472.15
non compos mentis
　472.24
nonconcurrence
　nonconformity 83.2
　dissent 520a.1
nonconducting, non-
　conductive 341.33
nonconductor 341.13
nonconformance 83.2
nonconforming
　unconformable 83.6
　dissentient 520a.6
nonconformist
　original 83.4
　dissenter 520a.3
　heretic 1023.5
nonconformity
　nonobservance 83.2
　dissent 520a
　unorthodoxy 1023
nonconscious 381.5
nonconsent 774.1
nonconsenting 774.6
nonconstitutional
　997.6
noncontagious 811.10
noncontinuance 72.1
noncontinuous 72.4
noncontroversial
　512.15
noncreative 165.5
nondescript
　nouns 85.5
　adjs. 85.13
nondevelopment 719.4
nondivisible 353.13
nondurable 111.7
none
　nouns not any 2.3
　~ else 89.3
　~ to spare 660.1
　divine service 1030.8
　advs. 2.11
NONE THE LESS 33.8
nonecclesiastical
　1037.3
nonedible 428.8
nonelastic 355.12
nonelectrolyte 341.22
nonemotional 854.9
nonendurance 860.2
nonentity
　nonexistence 2.1
　nullity 4.2
　a nobody 671.7
nones 1030.8
nonessential
　nouns 6.2
　adjs. extrinsic 6.4
　incidental 8.6
　irrelevant 10.6
　superfluous 661.18
　needless 667.10
nonesuch oddity 85.5
　the best 672.8
　prodigy 918.2

nonetheless 655.12
nonexecution 721.1
nonexistence
　nonbeing 2
　vacuity 186.2
nonexistent
　unexisting 2.7
　vacuous 186.12
　imaginary 533.19
nonexpectation 538.1
nonextension 376.1
nonexteriority, non-
　externality 376.1
nonfeasance 980.2
nonfeasor 984.8
nonfertile 165.4
nonfiction
　nouns 608.1
　adjs. 608.4
nonfictional 608.4
nonflier 278.5
nonfulfillment
　noncompletion
　　721.1
　nonobservance 767.1
nonfunctional 667.14
nongregarious 921.5
nonhabitable 187.17
nonhuman 85.14
nonillion 99.13
noninfectious 811.10
noninflammable 331.9
noninhabitance 186.2
noninterference,
　nonintervention
　politics 742.4
　isolationism 760.8
nonintoned 450.12
nonintoxicating 995.4
non-Islamic 1023.10
non-Jew 1023.6
nonjuror 83.4
nonlegal 997.6
nonlicit 997.6
nonlinear system 348.5
nonliving 381.5
nonmalignant 672.22
nonmaterial 376.7
nonmelodious 460.4
nonmetal 382.3
nonmetallic 382.15
nonmilitant 801.10
nonministerial 1037.3
non-Mohammedan,
　non-Moslem
　nouns 1023.6
　adjs. 1023.10
nonmoral
　amoral 955.7
　immoral 979.15
nonmorality 979.2
non-Mormon
　nouns 1023.6
　adjs. 1023.10
nonny 470.1
nonobedience 765.1
nonobjective
　nouns 572.12
　adjs. abstract 4.8
　subjective 5.6
nonobjectivity 5.1

nonobservance
　nonconformity 83.2
　nonfulfillment 767
nonobservant
　unconformable 83.6
　unfaithful 767.5
nonoccupance 186.2
nonoccupation 186.2
nonoccupational
　654.17
nonoccurrence 2.1
nonodorous 437.5
nonofficial 513.19
nonorthodox 1023.9
nonpareil
　nouns 672.8
　adjs. 36.17
nonpartisan
　nouns political ~
　　742.29
　independent 760.11
　neutral 804.4
　adjs. ~ politics
　　742.49
　independent 760.20
　neutral 804.7
nonpartisanism
　political ~ 742.27
　neutralism 804.1
nonpastoral 1037.3
nonpayer 840.5
nonpaying 840.10
nonpayment 840
nonperformance
　nonaccomplishment
　　721.1
　nonobservance 767.1
nonperishable 142.19
nonpermanent 111.7
nonpermissible 776.7
nonphysical 376.7
nonplus
　nouns quandary 513.3
　impasse 729.5
　verbs baffle 513.13
　thwart 728.15
nonplusation 513.3
nonplused
　baffled 513.23
　at an impasse 729.22
nonpoetic 608.5
nonpoisonous 672.22
nonporous 353.12
nonpresence 186.1
nonprevalence 666.1
nonproducing, non-
　productive 165.4
nonprofessional 716.5
nonprogressive 140.8
nonprohibitive 775.15
non-pros 1002.14
nonreality 2.1
nonreligious 1037.3
nonremunerative
　667.12
nonrepentance 872.2
nonrepresentational
　4.8
nonresidence 186.2
nonresident 186.10

nonresistance
political ~ 742.5
noninterference
760.8
submission 763.1
patience 859.2
nonresistant
nouns 801.5
adjs. 763.12
nonreturnable 142.18
nonrevealing 613.17
nonreversible 142.18
nonrigid 356.8
nonsacred 1025.3
nonsalable 827.13
nonscholastic 560.19
nonscientific 482.10
nonsectarian 1018.25
nonsense
nouns absurdity 469.3
meaninglessness
545.2
interjs. 469.12
nonsense verse 607.3
nonsensical
absurd 469.10
meaningless 545.10
nonsensicality
absurdity 469.3
meaninglessness
545.1
nonsensification 469.5
nonsensify 469.7
non sequitur 493.4
nonsinusoidal circuit
342.8
nonsocialistic 743.21
nonsonant
nouns 449.5
adjs. 450.12
nonspecific
general 79.10
indefinite 513.17
nonspiritual 375.9
nonstop 71.9
nonstretchable 355.12
nonsubjective 6.3
nonsubjectivity 6.1
nonsubsistence 2.1
nonsubsistent 2.7
nonsubstantial 4.4
nonsuccess 723.1
nonsuit 1002.7
nonsymmetric 248.10
nonsystematic 62.11
nontoxic 672.22
nontranslucency 340.1
nontranslucent 340.3
nonunderstanding
nouns 468.2
adjs. undiscerning
468.14
intolerant 525.11
nonuple 99.21
nonuplet 99.5
nonuse 666.1
nonutilitarian 667.14
nonvenomous 672.22
nonvirulent 672.22
nonvocal 449.5
nonvocational 654.17

nonvoter 742.24
nonworker 706.9
noodle head 210.5
brain 465.4
fool 470.1
noodlehead 470.4
noodles 306a.32
nook room 191.3
angle 250.2
recess 256.7
noon
nouns midday 133.5
summit 210.2
adjs. 133.7
noonday
nouns 133.5
adjs. 133.7
no one 186.6
nooning 133.5
noonlight
midday 133.5
daylight 334.10
noonlit 133.7
noontide 133.5
noontime 133.5
noose
nouns circle 252.2
snare 616.12
hanging 1008.7
hangman's rope
1009.5
verbs loop 221.7
snare 616.20
catch 820.14
hang 1008.20
no-par stock 832.2
price 832.8
nope 522.7
nor 522.9
Nordic 417.3
norm standard 84.4
measure 489.2
norma 84.4
normal
nouns average 32.1
natural 84.3
vertical 212.2
school 565.7
adjs. average 32.3
orderly 59.6
natural 84.7
save 471.4
typical 570.12
normalcy
normal state 84.1
sanity 471.1
normality
normal state 84
sanity 471.1
normalization 84.5
normalize 84.6
normally 84.9
normal school 565.7
Norman 417.3
normoblast 405.5
Norn 194.13
Norns 638.3
Norse, Norseman
417.3
North 179.7

north
nouns 289.3
UP NORTH 313.16
verbs 289.9
adjs. 289.17
North America 385.1
North American 417.8
northbound 289.16
Northeast 179.7
northeast
nouns 289.3
adjs. 289.21
northeaster, nor'easter
402.9
northeastern 289.21
norther
nouns 402.9
verbs 289.9
northern
verbs 289.9
adjs. directional
289.15
north 289.17
northerner 189.11
northern lights 334.16
northernmost 289.17
northing 289.4
northland 179.7
northlander 189.11
Northman
inhabitant 189.11
Scandinavian 417.3
North Pole
opposites 238.2
cold place 332.5
North Star star 374.5
guiding star 746.7
northward
nouns 289.3
adjs. 289.17
Northwest 179.7
northwest
nouns 289.3
adjs. 289.22
northwester 402.9
northwestern 289.22
north wind 402.9
norward 289.17
nose
nouns prow 239.3
snout 255.7
nozzle 395.9
person 416.3
detective 779.10
A NOSE FOR NEWS
556.1
HOLD ONE'S NOSE IN
THE AIR
be proud 903.4
be arrogant 910.8
KEEP A NOSE TO THE
WIND 531.8
NOSE TO NOSE 238.6
ON THE NOSE 131.14
PUT ONE'S NOSE OUT
OF JOINT
excel 36.7
disappoint 539.2
defeat 725.6
thwart 728.15
humiliate 904.4

UNDER ONE'S NOSE
nearby 199.15
before 239.13
openly 553.15
defiantly 791.9
verbs meddle 237.7
push 282.12
nuzzle 424.8
smell 434.8
trace 484.29
pry 526.4
nasalize 593.9
NOSE AROUND 484.25
NOSE DOWN 277.46
NOSE INTO 274.43
NOSE OUT
trace 484.29
discover 487.6
defeat 725.6
NOSE UP
aviate 277.46
crash-land 277.49
nosebleed 309.8
nose count 88.5
nose dive
aviation 277.10
dive 318.1
failure 723.3
nose-dive
aviation 277.47
dive 318.6
nose-ender 402.12
nose finish 30.4
nosegay
bouquet 410.23
fragrance 435.1
nose-over 277.15
nose ring band 252.3
ornament 899.6
nose-up 277.15
no show 155.10
nosiness 526.1
nostalgia
wistfulness 632.4
homesickness 632.5
sentimentality 853.7
nostalgic
wistful 632.23
sentimental 853.21
nostology 126.8
nostrils nose 255.7
olfactories 434.5
nostrum 685.2
nosy
nouns 526.2
adjs. meddlesome
237.9
odorous 434.9
smelly 436.5
inquisitive 526.6
not 522.7
nota bene 528.6
notabilia 670.5
notability
greatness 34.2
obviousness 553.4
importance 670.2
personage 670.8
repute 912.5
celebrity 912.9

notable
nouns personage
670.8
celebrity 912.9
adjs. remarkable
34.10
obvious 553.11
important 670.18
famous 912.17
notarization 520.4
notarize 520.12
notary public 569.1
notation
mathematics 87.4
musical ~ 462.12
comment 550.6
note 568.3
account entry 843.5
notch
nouns degree 29.1
cleft 200.3
indentation 256.6
nick 251
UP TO THE NOTCH
672.17
verbs indent 256.14
nick 261.4
notched
indented 256.17
nicked 261.5
notching 261.2
note
nouns color 361.5
observation 438.2
tone 449.2
birdcall 459.1
melody 461.4
pitch 462.4
musical ~ 462.14,
20
attention 528.1
comment 550.6
sign 566.2
memorandum 568.3
certificate 568.5
remark 592.4
epistle 602.2
importance 670.1
money 833.6,11
account entry 843.5
reputation 912.5
OF NOTE
important 670.17
famous 912.17
verbs heed 528.6
indicate 566.16
record 568.15
remark 592.16
enter accounts 843.8
notebook 568.10
noted 912.17
noteworthy
remarkable 34.10
special 30.12
extraordinary 85.13
notable 670.18
nothing
nonexistence 2.2
void 185.3
trifle 671.6

COME TO NOTHING
cease to be 2.5
be unproductive
165.3
fall through 312.3
perish 691.22
fail 723.12
DO NOTHING
be conservative
140.6
refrain 704.2
idle 706.10
FOR NOTHING
gratuitous 848.5
gratuitously 848.6
HAVE NOTHING TO DO
706.14
HAVE NOTHING TO DO
WITH
be unrelated 10.3
ignore 529.3
reject 636.2
avoid 629.6
let alone 704.4
refuse 774.3
be inhospitable
924.4
abstain 990.7
LIKE NOTHING 730.13
NEXT TO NOTHING
35.6
NOTHING DOING
quiescent 267.10
by no means 522.8
I refuse 774.9
God forbid! 967.27
NOTHING ELSE BUT
really 1.16
certainly 512.23
truly 515.16
NOTHING OF THE
KIND, NOTHING OF
THE SORT
different thing 16.3
nothing like 21.5
no 522.7
NOTHING TO BRAG
ABOUT 678.7
NOTHING TO IT 730.11
nothingarian
nonpartisan 742.29
neutral 804.4
nothingness
nonexistence 2.1
unconsciousness
422.2
notice
nouns observation
438.2
critique 493.2
attention 528.1
information 555.1
announcement
557.2,6
commentary 604.2
warning 701.1
order 750.6
GIVE NOTICE
inform 555.7
announce 557.12
warn 701.6

WITHOUT NOTICE
538.14
verbs see 438.12
detect 487.5
heed 528.6
care 531.6
noticeability 553.4
noticeable
remarkable 34.10
visible 443.6
appreciable 489.15
obvious 553.8,11
notification
information 555.1
announcement
557.2
warning 701.1
order 750.6
notifier 555.5
notify remind 535.20
inform 555.7
announce 557.12
warn 701.6
notion idea 478.1
supposition 498.4
opinion 500.4
caprice 627.1
impulse 628.1
intention 651.1
HAVE NO NOTION
476.12
notional
ideational 478.11
fanciful 533.20
whimsical 627.5
notionalist 498.6
notion counter 830.11
notioned 478.12
notions 829.6
notoriety
publicity 557.4
fame 912.1
notorious
famous 912.17
infamous 913.10
Notre Dame 1013.5
Notus 402.3
notwithstanding 33.8
nought See **naught**
noumenon 478.2
noun 584.4
nourish feed 306.16
nutrify 307.15
encourage 646.21
nurture 783.16
nourishing 307.19
nourishment
nutriment 306a.3
nutrition 307.1
aid 783.3
nous mind 465.1
ready wit 466.2
world spirit 1011.8
nouveau riche 917.10
nouvelle 606.8
novate 139.8
novel
nouns book 603.1
story 606.8
adjs. original 23.3
new 122.11

novela, novella 606.8
novelet, novelette
606.8
novelist writer 600.15
storyteller 606.10
novelize write 600.21
fictionize 606.13
novelties 829.6
novelty originality 23.1
newness 122.1
innovation 122.2
novemdecillion 99.13
novena nine 99.5
divine service 1030.8
novenary 99.21
novice newcomer 78.4
ignoramus 476.9
tyro 564.7
nun 1036.18
novitiate 564.7
now
nouns 120.1
advs. at once 113.8
at present 120.3
AS OF NOW
as yet 120.3
henceforth 121.10
JUST NOW
instantly 113.6
now 120.3
recently 122.17
NOW AND FOREVER
112.12
NOW AND THEN 136.5
NOW OR NEVER
129.13
UNTIL NOW
since 119.14
to date 120.4
interjs. 502.14
nowadays 120.3
noway, noways
nowise 35.14
by no means 522.8
nowhere, nowheres
186.16
NOWHERE NEAR 35.14
NOWHERE TO BE
FOUND
nonexistent 2.7
absent 186.9
nowise 35.14
noxious nasty 428.7
harmful 673.12
insalubrious 682.4,5
odious 862.9
noxiousness
harmfulness 673.5
insalubrity 682.1,2
odiousness 862.2
nozzle nose 255.7
mouth 264.6
conduit 395.9
nth, the 56.4
TO THE NTH 56.17
nuance 16.2
nub gist 5.2
main point 670.6
nubbin
diminutive 195.4
pommel 215.19

lump 255.3
ear of corn 410.27
nubilate
darken 336.10
cloud 403.7
nubilation
obscuration 336.7
opaqueness 340.1
cloudiness 403.4
nubile mature 126.12
marriageable 931.21
nubility 931.3
nubilous dim 336.18
opaque 340.3
cloudy 403.8
nucha 48.5
nucleal central 225.13
nuclear 405.22
nuclear central 225.13
atomic 325.18
nucleal 405.22
nuclear atom 325.4
nuclear energy 325.14
nuclear complex
688.30
nuclear explosive
799.16
nuclear fission 325.8
nuclear fuel 325.10
nuclear fusion 325.9
nuclear physics 325.1
nuclear power
power 156.4
atomics 325.14
nuclear reactor 325.12
nucleary, nucleate
central 225.13
nuclear 405.22
nucleation 393.5
nucleization 325.8
nucleize 325.16
nucleolar, nucleolate,
nucleolated 405.22
nucleolus 405.10
nucleon 325.6
nucleonics 325.1
nucleoplasm 405.3
nucleus gist 5.2
rudiment 152.7
center 225.2
atomic ~ 325.6
biology 405.10
Nuda 414.4
nude
nouns nudity 231.3
picture 572.12
adjs. naked 231.14
unadorned 900.8
nudge
nouns prod 282.2
signal 566.14
verbs prod 282.12
remind 535.20
signal 566.21
nudism, nudist 231.3
nudity nakedness 231.3
unadornment 900.3
nugacious
ineffectual 157.15
vain 667.13
trivial 671.16

nugacity 667.2
nugatory
ineffectual 157.15
vain 667.13
trivial 671.16
nugget lump 194.10
gold 833.19
nuisance
annoyance 864.2
bore 882.4
null nonexistent 2.7
vacant 186.12
nullah ravine 200.3
watercourse 395.2
null and void
vacant 186.12
invalid 777.3
DECLARE NULL AND
VOID 777.2
nullification
neutralization 177.2
repeal 777.1
nullifidian
nouns 1029.11
adjs. unbelieving
502.8
irreligious 1029.19
nullifier 177.3
nullify
neutralize 177.7
annihilate 691.13
repeal 777.2
clear of debt 840.9
nullifying 177.9
nulli secundus 36.17
nullity
nonexistence 2.1
nonentity 4.2
insignificancy 671.6
nullius filius 170.5
numb
verbs freeze 332.11
benumb 422.3
~ emotionally 854.8
adjs. numbed 422.5
apathetic 854.13
number
nouns quantity 28.2
section 55.2
kind 61.3
numeral 86
sum 86.3
rhythm 462.22
edition 603.2,14
act 609.8
HAVE ONE'S NUMBER
487.8
NUMBERED WITH THE
DEAD 407.24
WITHOUT NUMBER
104.3
verbs amount to 54.7
numerate 87.10
limit 233.5
NUMBER AMONG 76.3
numberable 87.16
numbering 87.1
numberless
innumerable 101.11
infinite 104.3
number one 80.5

numbers quantity 28.1
arithmetic 87.2
multitude 101.3
rhythm 462.22
poetic meter 607.9
IN ROUND NUMBERS
on an average 32.5
approximately
199.26
numbers pool 514.10
numbing
freezing 332.15
deadening 422.8
anesthetic 685.40
numen 1012.19
numeral
nouns 86.1
adjs. 86.8
numerary 86.8
numerate 87.10
numeration 87
numerative
numeral 86.8
enumerative 87.15
numerical 86.8
numeric data 348.19
numerous many 101.7
abundant 659.7
numismatic 833.28
numismatics 833.21
nummary 833.28
numskull 470.3
nun 1036.18
nunciate 559.3
nuncio 779.6
nuncupative
evidential 504.17
oral 592.20
nunnery 1040.6
nuptial
verbs 931.15
adjs. 931.19
nuptials 931.4
nurse
nouns sister 686.13
nursemaid 697.7
verbs suckle 306.16
~ the sick 687.33
care for 697.18
nurture 783.16
cherish 811.7
nursemaid 697.7
nursery infancy 124.5
source 152.8
room 191.7
plantation 412.11
school 565.4
nurseryman 412.6
nursery rhyme 607.4
nursling 125.7
nurture
nouns nutriment
306a.3
training 560.3
aid 783.3
verbs feed 306.16
train 560.13
encourage 646.21
care for 697.18
foster 783.16
cherish 811.7

Nut 1012.9
nut
nouns fastener 48.7
head 210.5
food 306a.51
lunatic 472.15
fanatic 472.17
eccentric 473.3
enthusiast 633.5
overhead 841.3
seed 410.29
HARD NUT TO CRACK
enigma 547.7
dilemma 729.6
OFF ONE'S NUT
472.25
verbs 412.19
nut-brown 366.3
nuthouse
madhouse 472.14
Patent Office 740.13
nutrient
nouns food 306a
nutriment 307.3
adjs. 307.19
nutrify 307.15
nutriment food 306a.3
nutrition 307.3
nutrition 307.1
nutritionist 307.13
nutritious 307.19
nutritive
nouns 307.3
adjs. 307.19
nuts
nouns food 306a.38
list of ~ 306a.51
THE NUTS 672.7
adjs. 472.25
NUTS ABOUT
enthusiastic 633.11
enamored 929.27
interjs. 965.16
NUTS TO YOU!
by no means 522.8
I refuse 774.9
nutshell
nouns small amount
35.2
hull 410.28
IN A NUTSHELL
smally 195.15
in brief 590.6
PUT IT IN A NUTSHELL
605.5
verbs 605.5
nutting 412.15
nutty flavorful 427.9
spicy 432.7
foolish 469.8
insane 472.25
eccentric 473.4
nuzzle nose 424.8
cuddle 930.15
nyctalopia 440.2
nyctalopic 440.8
nymph
larva 125.9; 405.13
deity 1012.16
nympha 125.9

O
P

obscure
nouns 336.1
verbs darken 336.10
opaque 340.2
cloud 403.7
blind 440.6
conceal 613.7
adjs. formless 246.4
dark 336.14
dim 336.18
opaque 340.3
indistinct 444.5
vague 513.17
unintelligible 547.13
equivocal 548.3
unrenowned 913.14
obscured
blinded 440.9
concealed 613.12
obscurely
vaguely 513.26
unintelligibly 547.19
obscuring
obscurant 336.20
blinding 440.10
concealing 613.17
obscurity
nonentity 4.2
formlessness 246.1
darkness 336.1
opaqueness 340.1
indistinctness 444.2
vagueness 513.4
unintelligibility 547.3
insignificancy 671.6
obsecration
supplication 772.2
prayer 1030.4
obsequial 409.25
obsequies 409.4
obsequious 905.13
obsequiousness 905.2
observable
visible 443.6
manifest 553.8
observably 553.14
observance
conformity 82.1
watching 438.2
attention 528.1
vigilance 531.4
custom 640.1
ceremony 644.4
behavior 735.1
obedience 764.1
keeping 766
celebration 875.1
rite 1038.3
Observant 1036.17
observant
attentive 528.15
vigilant 531.13
faithful 766.4
observation
watching 438.2
idea 478.1
opinion 500.4
attention 528.1
remark 592.4
keeping 766

EXCHANGE
OBSERVATIONS
compare notes 490.6
confer 595.10
observation flight
277.8
observation post 438.8
observation tower
206.11
observatory
astronomy 374.17
lookout 438.8
observe conform 82.3
see 438.12
examine 484.31
heed 528.6
remark 592.16
obey 764.2
keep 766.2
celebrate 875.3
~ a rite 1038.17
NOT OBSERVE 765.6
OBSERVE THE
FORMALITIES 644.6
OBSERVE THE GOLDEN
RULE 977.4
observer aviator 278.3
spectator 441.1
observing 528.15
obsess possess 472.23
haunt 864.21
demonize 1014.17
bewitch 1034.10
obsessed
infatuated 472.32
haunted 1015.10
bewitched 1034.14
obsessing 472.33
obsession
mania 472.13
spirit control 1015.5
bewitchment 1034.2
obsessional 472.33
obsessive 472.33
obsolesce
superannuate 123.9
disuse 666.9
obsolescence
archaism 580.11
disuse 666.1
obsolescent 666.10
obsolete passé 123.15
disused 666.10
BECOME OBSOLETE
123.9
obsoletism
word 580.11
disuse 666.1
obstacle
obstruction 265.3
hindrance 728.4
obstacle race 794.12
obstetric(al) 686.18
obstetrician 686.10
obstetrics 686.2
obstinacy
opinionatedness
512.6
stubbornness 624
obstinate
opinionated 512.22

stubborn 624.8
obstipation 265.3
obstreperous
turbulent 161.18
blatant 452.11
vociferous 458.10
ungovernable 624.12
disobedient 765.11
obstreperously
ungovernably 624.17
disobediently 765.13
obstreperousness
turbulence 161.3
noisiness 452.2
ungovernability
624.4
disobedience 765.2
obstruct delay 132.7
clog 265.7
retard 269.9
hinder 728.12
obstructant 728.4
obstructed 265.11
obstructer 728.8
obstructing 728.17
obstruction clog 265.3
retardation 269.4
hindrance 728.1
obstacle 728.4
obstructionism 728.1
obstructionist
hinderer 728.8
oppositionist 789.3
obstructive
nouns obstacle 728.4
oppositionist 789.3
adjs. 728.17
obstruent 728.17
obtain exist 1.8
prevail 79.9
induce 152.12
fetch 270.15
elicit 304.12
acquire 809.7
receive 817.6
obtainable
accessible 508.8
available 809.12
obtainment 809.1
obtention 809.1
obtestation
supplication 772.2
prayer 1030.4
obtrude intrude 237.5
expel 308.12
OBTRUDE ON 816.19
OBTRUDE UPON 959.7
obtruncate 42.10
obtruncation 42.3
obtrusion 237.1
obtrusive
intrusive 237.8
hindering 728.17
garish 902.20
presumptuous 911.8
obtrusively
garishly 902.27
presumptuously
911.11
obtund
moderate 162.6

blunt 258.2
deaden 422.3
dull the feelings
854.7
obtundity
bluntness 258.1
unfeeling 854.1
obtuse blunt 258.3
insensitive 422.5
stupid 468.16
unfeeling 854.9
obtuseness
bluntness 258.1
stupidity 468.3
unfeeling 854.1
obverse
nouns opposite 15.2
counterpart 20.5
opposite side 238.3
adjs. opposite 15.5
reverse 238.5
front 239.1
obviate 728.14
obviation 728.2
obvious distinct 443.7
manifest 553.8
BE OBVIOUS 553.7
obviously
distinctly 443.8
manifestly 553.14
ocarina 464.9
occasion
nouns circumstance
8.1
opportunity 129.2
event 150.2
cause 152.1
motive 646.1
HAVE OCCASION FOR
637.9
verbs 152.11
occasional
incidental 129.12
infrequent 136.3
causal 152.15
contingent 174.6
occasionally 136.5
Occident 179.6
occident 289.3
Occidental
nouns 417.8
adjs. 417.10
occidental 289.15
occipital 240.9
occiput 240.1
occlude 265.6
occlusion 265.1
occlusive
nouns 449.5
adjs. 449.18
occult
verbs 613.7
adjs. recondite 547.14
esoteric 1032.24
occultate
eclipse 336.10
conceal 613.7
occultation
eclipse 336.9
concealment 613.1
occultism 1032

risqué 988.7
offcut 601.3
offence See offense
offend
~ the nostrils 436.4
~ the ear 457.10
displease 864.13
give umbrage 950.20
affront 963.4
do wrong 980.3
~ against the law 997.5
offended 864.23
BE OFFENDED 950.13
offender 984.8
offense
violation 767.2
attack 796.1
umbrage 950.2
provocation 950.11
indignity 963.2
misdeed 980.2
illegality 997.4
GIVE OFFENSE 864.13
offenseless 982.6
offensive
nouns 796.1
ON THE OFFENSIVE 796.32
adjs. nasty 428.7
malodorous 436.5
combative 795.26
aggressive 796.32
odious 862.9
vulgar 896.10
ugly 897.11
insulting 963.6
obscene 988.9
offensively
displeasingly 862.17
vulgarly 896.16
hideously 897.13
offensiveness
unsavoriness 428.3
malodorousness 436.2
odiousness 862.2
ugliness 897.2
obscenity 988.4
offer
nouns attempt 712.2
proffer 771.1
OFFER OF MARRIAGE 930.7
verbs occur 477.17
adduce 504.13
put to choice 635.18
attempt 712.5
proffer 771.4
bid 826.9
offering gift 816.4
oblation 1030.7
Offertory 1038.10
offertory music 461.23
donation 816.6
hymn 1030.3
offering 1030.7
off-guard 529.8
offhand
adjs. careless 532.11

extemporaneous 628.12
informal 645.3
nonchalant 856.15
advs. carelessly 532.18
extemporaneously 628.15
informally 645.4
offhandedness
informality 645.1
nonchalance 856.5
office operation 163.1
room 191.6
tip 555.3
signal 566.14
ceremony 644.4
job 654.3
post 654.5
warning 701.4
workplace 717.8
staff 748.12
commission 778.1
kindness 936.7
bureau 998.4
divine service 1030.8
rite 1038.3
office-bearer
politician 744.11
official 747.17
office boy 748.4
office force 748.12
officeholder
political ~ 744.11
official 747.17
office hunger 742.10
office hunter 744.9
officer
nouns ship's ~ 275.7
policeman 697.14
official 747.17
military ~ 747.21
verbs command 739.11
manage 745.8
officer of the day 747.22
officer of the deck 275.7
office seeker 744.9
official
nouns functional 654.16
officer 747.17
adjs. authentic 512.18
authoritative 737.14
officialdom 747.16
officialese
jargon 578.7
politics 742.40
officialism 742.39
officiate
do duty 654.13
minister 656.5
administer 745.11
perform a rite 1038.18
officinal 685.4
officious 237.9
offing
remote distance 198.3

horizon 213.4
IN THE OFFING 151.3
offish reserved 611.8
haughty 910.12
off-key 460.4
off limits 233.9
off-pitch 460.4
offprint copy 24.5
print 601.3
offscourings, offscum
remains 43.1
refuse 667.4
offal 680.9
riffraff 917.5
off season 128.1
offset
nouns contrast 15.2
compensation 33.2
descendant 170.4
neutralizer 177.3
automation 348.21
print 601.3
verbs go counter to 15.3
compensate 33.5
cushion 162.8
offsetting
nouns
counterbalancing 33.1
neutralization 177.2
adjs. compensating 33.6
neutralizing 177.9
offshoot
addition 41.1
member 55.4
effect 153.1
by-product 167.3
descendant 170.4
branch 298.4
foliage 410.18
organization 786.10
offshore 396.10
off side 242.1
offspring child 125.3
effect 153.1
product 167.1
posterity 170.1
descendant 170.3
off stage 609.40
offtake 42.6
off-tone
off-color 361.21
dissonant 460.4
oft 135.6
often
repeatedly 103.16
frequently 135.6
NOT OFTEN 136.4
oftens, oftentimes, ofttimes 135.6
oftentime 135.4
oft-repeated 135.4
ogam dialect 578.8
character 579.3
writing 600.10
ogdoad 99.4
ogham
character 579.3
writing 600.10

ogive 251.4
ogle
nouns eye 438.5
flirtation 930.8
verbs look at 438.15
make eyes at 930.18
O.G.P.U. 697.15
ogre, ogress
frightener 889.8
monster 941.7
fiend 1014.7
oh! ouch! 423.14
alas! 873.20
surprise 918.18
ohm 341.35
ohmage 341.11
oie 306a.22
oil
nouns illuminant 334.20
fat 379
mineral ~ 379.11
vegetable ~ 379.12
animal ~ 379.13
~ painting 572.15
balm 685.9
flattery 968.1
verbs lubricate 379.8
bribe 649.3
medicate 687.34
flatter 968.7
OIL THE TONGUE 968.5
oilcan 799.15
oiled 994.40
oiligarchy 739.6
oiliness
greasiness 379.5
hypocrisy 614.6
suaveness 934.5
flattery 968.2
oiling 379.6
oil of joy 994.13
oil of myrcia 435.2
oil of palms
bribe 649.2
tip 816.5
money 833.2
oil painter 577.4
oil painting 572.5
oil refinery 717.3
oiltight 265.12
oily greasy 379.9
hypocritical 614.33
suave 934.18
flattering 968.9
oily-tongued
suave 934.18
flattering 968.9
oinomania
See oenomania
ointment salve 379.3
balm 685.9
money 833.2
unction 1038.6
Oireachtas 740.2
oiseau 306a.22
O.K., okay
nouns 520.4
verbs 520.12
adjs. correct 515.14

good 572.14
satisfactory 866.12
advs. 520.18
olam infinity 104.1
eternity 112.2
universe 374.1
olamic infinite 104.3
eternal 112.7
old ancient 123.10
mature 126.12
elderly 126.15
disused 666.10
experienced 731.26
OF OLD 119.13
old Adam
evil nature 979.8
carnal nature 985.2
old age 126.5
old-age insurance
welfarism 743.6
pension 816.8
old campaigner
veteran 731.14
politician 744.1
soldier 798.18
Old Clootie 1014.4
old country
region 179.6
fatherland 180.2
old crony 926.4
old days 119.2
olden 123.10
older
nouns elder 127.2
senior 127.5
adjs. elder 123.19
senior 126.18
oldest eldest 123.19
senior 126.18
Old Faithful 327.9
oldfangled, old-
fashioned 123.16
Old Floorer 407.3
old fogy
nouns old-fashioned
person 123.8
conservative 140.4
dotard 470.9
adjs. 123.17
old-fogyish
old-fashioned 123.17
conservative 140.8
Old Gentleman
1014.4
Old Glory 567.6
old goat 987.11
old-gold 368.2
Old Gooseberry
1014.4
Old Harry 1014.4
old hat
nouns 516.3
adjs. out-of-date
123.16
trite 881.9
Old Lady of Thread-
needle Street
834.13
old-line
conservative 140.8
established 142.14

old maid
fuss-budget 894.7
prude 901.11
spinster 932.4
old-maidish
prim 901.19
spinsterish 932.7
old man elder 127.2
father 169.9
shipmaster 275.7
commander 747.22
husband 931.8
old master
painting 572.11
artist 577.1
oldness
ancientness 123
elderliness 126.5
Old Nick 1014.4
Old Probabilities, Old
Prob 401.7
old salt sailor 275.3
veteran 731.14
old saw 516.3
old school 140.4
Old Scratch 1014.4
old soldier
cigar butt 433.6
malingerer 629.3
veteran 731.14
soldier 798.18
old song cliché 516.3
trifle 671.5
old stager actor 610.1
veteran 731.14
old story 516.3
Old Testament 1019.3
old-time 123.10
old-timer native 189.3
veteran 731.14
old times 119.2
old wheeze 879.9
old wife crone 127.3
mollycoddle 420.11
dotard 470.9
old wives' tale 501.3
old woman fogy 123.8
elder 127.3
mother 169.10
dotard 470.9
fuss-budget 894.7
wife 931.9
old-womanish
effeminate 420.15
senile 468.23
Old World 179.6
old-world 123.13
ole 123.10
oleaginous, oleic
379.9
oleo 609.24
olericultural 412.21
olericulture 412.2
oleum 379.1
olfaction 434.3
olfactories nose 255.7
organs 434.5
olfactory
nouns 434.4
adjs. 434.12
olibanum 435.4

olid 436.5
oligarch 747.6
oligarchic(al) 739.16
oligarchy 739.4
olio mixture 44.6
stew 306a.11
olivaceous 370.4
olive brown 366.3
green 370.4
olive branch
offspring 170.3
peace offering 802.2
olla 306a.11
olla-podrida
mixture 44.6
stew 306a.11
ology 474.10
olycook, olykoek
306a.43
Olympiad 876.10
Olympian
magnificent 902.21
heavenly 1016.13
Olympus 1016.10
omasum 192.3
ombrometer 393.7
omega 70.1
omelet, omelette
306a.26
omen
nouns 542.2
OF GOOD OMEN
542.16
verbs 542.8
ominous 542.13
omission
deficiency 57.2
exclusion 77.1
error 517.4
neglect 532.1
want 660.4
nonobservance
767.1
sin of ∼ 980.2
omit exclude 77.4
leave undone 532.7
omitted 186.9
omitting 77.9
omnibus
nouns carrier 270.5
bus 271.11
book 603.4
adjs. 76.6
omnibus bill 740.19
omnifarious 19.5
omniform 19.5
omnigenous 19.5
Omnipotence,
Omnipotent, the
1011.2
omnipotence 156.3
omnipotent
almighty 156.12
divine 1011.20
omnipresence
ubiquity 185.2
divine attribute
1011.15
omnipresent
everywhere 178.11
ubiquitous 185.13

divine 1011.20
omnirange 277.4
Omniscience,
Omniscient, the
1011.2
omniscience 474.6
omniscient
all-knowing 474.15
divine 1011.20
omnium-gatherum
mixture 44.6
jumble 62.3
miscellany 74.12
omnivore 306.13
omnivorous
all-eating 306.29
greedy 632.28
gluttonous 992.7
omophagist 306.13
omophagous 306.29
ompa 408.11
omphalectomy 687.25
omphalic 225.12
omphalos 225.2
on
adjs. happening 150.9
willing 620.5
BE ON
agree 520.10
be a bargain 825.15
ON TO 474.16
advs. after which
117.6
toward 289.28
forward 293.7
ON AND OFF
irregularly 138.4
variably 141.8
ON AND ON
increasingly 38.9
continuously 71.11
constantly 135.7
preps.
concerning 9.12
at 183.28
against 199.23
atop 210.14
upon 227.40
by means of 656.8
once whenever 105.12
former 119.7
one time 136.6
AT ONCE
instantly 113.8
promptly 131.15
ONCE AND AGAIN
twice 91.6
occasionally 136.5
ONCE FOR ALL
finally 70.11
once 136.6
come what may
622.20
ONCE MORE
again 103.17
encore! 103.18
ONCE UPON A TIME
119.11
once-over 438.6
GIVE THE ONCE-OVER
scrutinize 438.15

skim over 484.34
oncoming
  nouns beginning 68.1
    approach 295.1
  adjs. progressive
    293.5
    approaching 295.4
on-dit 556.6
one
  nouns unit 89.3
    person 416.3
  AS ONE
    simultaneously
      118.6
    concurrently 176.5
    unanimously 520.17
    co-operatively 784.9
  AT ONE 26.16
  AT ONE WITH 176.4
  BE AT ONE WITH
    concur 520.9
    accord 792.2
  adjs. identical 14.6
    an 28.6
    combined 52.5
    whole 54.8
    single 89.7
    married 931.22
  ALL ONE TO
    indifferent 634.5
    unconcerned 634.6
  ONE AND THE SAME
    the same 14.3
    identical 14.6
  ONE BY ONE
    separately 49.26
    severally 80.19
    singly 89.13
one and all
  nouns all 54.3
    everyone 79.4
  adjs. 79.14
  advs. 520.17
one and indivisible
  54.8
one and only 89.9
one-arm bandit 830.9
one-eyed 439.12
one for the book
    importance 670.5
    wonder 918.2
one-horse little 195.9
    insignificant 671.17
one-horse town 182.3
one in a thousand
    oddity 85.5
    first-rater 672.6
    prodigy 918.2
    paragon 983.4
oneirocriticism 550.9
oneirology 550.9
one-megaton bomb
    799.16
oneness identity 14.1
    agreement 26.1
    unity 89.1
one-night stand 609.12
one-piece 89.11
oner 672.7
onerous
    ponderous 351.17

laborious 714.19
    impedimental
      728.18
    difficult 729.17
    oppressive 862.15
onerously
    burdensomely
      351.21
    laboriously 714.20
    difficultly 729.26
oneself 80.5
  BE ONESELF 645.2
  BE ONESELF AGAIN
    692.20
  BY ONESELF
    singly 89.13
    independently
      760.30
    in solitude 922.12
one-sided
    unipartite 89.11
    unilateral 241.7
    distorted 248.10
    prejudiced 525.12
    partial 975.11
one-star wonder
    747.22
one-step 877.5
one-step rocket 280.4
one-time 119.7
one-tracked mind
    472.13
one-two, the 272.14
one voice 520.5
one-way 289.13
one-way trip 281.1
on-go 293.1
ongoing
  nouns course 266.2
    progression 293.1
  adjs. progressive 293.5
    improving 689.15
oniomania 472.12
onion 436.3
onliest 89.9
onlooker 441.1
only
  adjs. 89.9
  advs. merely 35.11
    simply 45.9
    solely 89.14
Only-Begotten, the
    1011.12
only-begotten 89.9
onomasticon 603.7
onomatology 581.1
onomatope 580.15
onomatoplasm 580.15
onomatopoeia, onoma-
    topoësis figure of
    speech 549.2
    word form 580.15
onrush course 266.2
    flow 394.4
onset beginning 68.1
    attack 796.1
onshore 384.11
onslaught 796.1
ontogenesis 321.3
ontogeny
    evolution 321.3

biology 405.16
ontology 1.7
onus
    impediment 728.6
    duty 960.1
    imposition 961.3
onward, onwards
    adjs. 293.5
    advs. 293.7
    interjs. 293.8; 313.17
Onychophora 414.8
oöcyte 405.8
oodles, oodlins 34.5
oœcium 405.8
oof 833.2
oofless 836.10
ooftish 833.2
oofy 835.13
oögenesis 166.6
oögonium 405.8
oomph 418.3
oont beast of burden
    270.6
    camel 413.5
oophorectomy, oo-
    phorocystectomy
    687.25
oösperm, oösphere
    405.8
oöspore 405.9
ooze
  nouns seepage 302.6
    mud 388.8
  verbs seep 302.15
    be damp 391.11
ooziness 388.4
oozing 302.6
oozy muddy 388.14
    miry 399.3
opacity
    opaqueness 340.1
    stupidity 468.3
    obscurity 547.3
opal pearliness 339.2
    opalescence 373.6
opalesce 373.8
opalescence
    pearliness 339.2
    iridescence 373.2
opalescent
    pearly 339.5
    iridescent 373.10
opaline pearly 339.5
    opalescent 373.10
opalize 373.8
opaloid pearly 339.5
    opalescent 373.10
opaque
  nouns eyeshade 337.2
    opaqueness 340.1
  verbs 340.2
  adjs. intransparent
    340.3
    stupid 468.15
    obscure 547.13
opaqueness 340
op. cit. 504.26
ope 264.11
open, the 223.3
  IN THE OPEN
    outdoors 223.10

openly 553.15
open
  verbs unfasten 49.9
    begin 68.11
    convene 74.16
    spread 196.6
    unclose 264.11
    unfold 321.5
    disclose 554.4
    ~ an account
      825.13
  OPEN FIRE
    begin 68.11
    fire upon 796.23
  OPEN ONE'S EYES
    disillusion 519.2
    become informed
      555.13
    wake up 711.4
    wonder 918.4
  OPEN ONE'S MOUTH
    592.13
  OPEN THE DOOR TO
    begin 68.11
    induce 152.12
    be liable 174.3
    admit 305.10
    expose oneself 695.7
    prepare the way
      718.12
    facilitate 730.6
    allow freedom
      760.14
    be hospitable 923.7
  OPEN THE FLOOD-
    GATES 308.22
  OPEN THE PURSE
    spend 841.5
    be generous 851.3
  OPEN THE WAY
    prepare the way
      718.12
    facilitate 730.6
  OPEN UP
    begin 68.11
    spread 196.6
    open 264.11
    unfold 321.5
    disclose 554.4
    unbosom 554.8
    go unrestrained
      760.17
  adjs. persuasible
    171.15
    vacant 186.14
    spread 196.11
    unclosed 264.17
    flat 386.3
    in view 443.6
    phonetics 449.18
    accessible 508.8
    questionable 513.15
    open-minded
      524.10
    communicative
      552.9
    manifest 553.9
    public 557.17
    extroverted 688.51
    unprotected 695.15
    leisure 708.5

artless 734.5
unlimited 760.24
generous 851.4
hospitable 923.11
honest 972.14
candid 972.17
OPEN FOR DISCUSSION
484.42
OPEN TO
liable to 174.5
accessible 508.8
OPEN TO DOUBT
unbelievable 502.10
questionable 513.15
openable 264.21
open-air outdoor 223.7
airy 401.13
open and aboveboard
972.14
open-and-shut
assured 512.20
obvious 553.8
prearranged 639.5
open-and-shut case
certainty 512.2
prearrangement
639.1
open arms 923.2
open bet 514.3
opencast 382.6
open country
open space 178.4
plain 336.1
open cut 382.6
open discussion 481.4
open door
admission 305.3
policy 742.5
hospitality 923.1
open-door policy
742.5
open-eared
listening 447.15
attentive 528.15
opener
inauguration 68.4
key 264.10
open-eyed
curious 526.5
attentive 528.15
vigilant 531.13
expectant 537.9
open forum
discussion 481.4
forum 753.4
openhanded 851.4
openhearted
tolerant 524.11
artless 734.5
generous 851.4
hospitable 923.11
candid 972.17
open-heartedness
tolerance 524.4
artlessness 734.1
generosity 851.1
hospitality 923.1
candor 972.4
opening
beginning 68.1
opportunity 129.2

open space 178.4
vacancy 186.2
cleft 200.2
aperture 264
entranceway 301.5
outlet 302.9
admission 305.3
unfoldment 321.1
appearance 445.1
display 553.2
position 654.5
passageway 655.4
openly
obviously 553.15
artlessly 734.7
outright 760.29
open market 831.1
open mind 524.3
open-mindedness
persuadability 171.5
broad-mindedness
524.3
openmouthed
vociferous 458.10
attentive 528.15
expectant 537.9
greedy 632.28
astonished 918.8
open-mouthed 526.5
openness
persuadability 171.5
liability 174.2
open-mindedness
524.3
communicativeness
552.4
manifestness 553.3
publicity 557.4
~ to danger 695.3
artlessness 734.1
candor 972.4
open order 795.7
open primary 742.15
open question 513.8
open-sesame
key 264.10
password 566.11
incantation 1034.4
open shop 787.2
open space 178.4
open waggon 271.13
open war 795.1
opera music 461.28
theater 609.17
playbook 609.25
opéra ballet 461.35
operability
workability 163.3
practicability 508.2
operable
workable 163.11
practicable 508.7
opera glass 442.3
operagoer 463.23
opera house 609.17
operant operator 163.4
worker 716.1
opera score 461.28
operatable 163.11
operate run 163.5
function 163.8

pilot 274.14
use 663.10
act 703.4
speculate 831.23
OPERATE ON
work on 163.7
doctor 687.33
operatic choral 461.51
theatrical 609.37
operating
working 163.12
acting 703.11
operation
functioning 163
employment 663.8
surgical ~ 687.24
action 703.1
military ~ 795.9
transaction 825.4
IN OPERATION
operating 163.12
in use 663.24
PUT IN OPERATION
663.11
operational 163.10
operative
nouns operator 163.4
worker 716.1
detective 779.10
adjs. 163.10
operator handler 163.4
telephone ~ 558.11
surgeon 686.8
worker 716.1
speculator 831.11
operculum 227.5
opere citato 504.26
operetta 461.35
operose
painstaking 531.11
laborious 714.19
difficult 729.17
operosely
laboriously 714.20
difficultly 729.26
ophicleide 464.8
ophidian
nouns 413.31
adjs. 413.44
ophiologist 414.2
ophite 373.6
Ophiuroidea,
ophiurans 414.7
ophthalmic 438.22
ophthalmologist 686.7
opiate 685.10
opiatic 685.39
opine judge 493.8
suppose 498.9
think 500.9
remark 592.16
opinion belief 500.4
point of view 523.2
advice 752.1
BE OF THE OPINION
500.9
IN MY OPINION
500.26
opinionated 512.22
opinionist
dogmatist 512.7

obstinate person
624.6
opium 685.10
opossum 413.4
oppidan
nouns 189.6
adjs. 182.9
oppidum 182.2
opponent
nouns adversary 789
combatant 798
adjs. 788.9
opportune
appropriate 26.19
timely 129.10
expedient 668.4
opportunely
seasonably 129.13
expediently 668.7
opportuneness
timeliness 129.1
expedience 668.1
opportunism
opportunity 129.2
policy 742.4
opportunist
opportunity 129.2
vacillator 625.5
politician 744.1
opportunity turn 108.2
occasion 129.2
AT THE FIRST OPPOR-
TUNITY 131.16
HAVE AN OPPOR-
TUNITY 155.13
MISS AN OPPORTUNITY
130.6
oppose
go counter to 15.3
counteract 177.6
contrapose 238.4
compare 490.4
refute 505.5
deny 522.4
be against 788.3
resist 790.3
disapprove of 967.10
OPPOSE CHANGE
140.6
opposed contrary 15.5
~ to change 140.8
adverse 727.13
oppositional 788.9
BE OPPOSED TO 15.3
opposer 789.3
opposing
nouns comparison
490.1
opposition 788.1
adjs. contrary 15.5
counteractive 177.8
denying 522.5
adverse 727.13
oppositional 788.9
opposingly
counteractively
177.11
adversely 727.16
opposite contrary 15.5
contrapositive 238.5
adverse 727.13

PUT IN WORKING
ORDER 718.8
TO ORDER 750.16
UNDER ONE'S ORDERS
762.13
verbs arrange 60.7
influence 171.8
pass judgment
493.13
direct 745.8
command 750.9
ordered equable 17.5
arranged 60.13
regular 137.7
measured 489.14
AS ORDERED 750.16
ordering
arrangement 60.1
regulation 745.1
orderless
unarranged 62.11
formless 246.4
orderlessness 246.1
orderliness order 59.3
peacefulness 801.2
orderly
nouns hospital ~
686.14
attendant 748.4
adjs. uniform 17.5
well-ordered 59.6
arranged 60.13
regular 137.7
formal 644.10
peaceful 801.9
orderly officer 747.22
orderly room 225.6
order of the day
affairs 150.4
schedule 639.2
convention 643.1
command 750.3
Order of the Purple
Heart 914.6
orders
instructions 560.5
holy ~ 1035.10
ordinal
nouns number 86.2
ritual 1038.12
adjs. classificational
61.7
serial 71.10
ordinance decree 750.4
allotment 814.3
law 996.3
rite 1038.3
ordinarily
usually 84.9
frequently 135.6
plainly 900.10
ordinariness
usualness 84.2
mediocrity 678.2
vulgarity 896.5
plainness 900.1
ordinary
nouns usual 84.3
inn 190.13
table d'hote 306.11
insignia 567.2

judge 1000.4
IN ORDINARY 658.16
OUT OF THE ORDINARY
85.10
adjs. average 32.3
usual 84.8
frequent 135.4
prosaic 608.5
mediocre 678.9
vulgar 896.14
plain 900.6
plebeian 917.11
ordinary run 79.3
ORDINARY RUN OF
THINGS 640.4
ordinate 778.10
ordinate and abscissa
489.6
ordination
organization 60.2
appointment 778.2
allotment 814.3
ecclesiastical ~
1035.10
ordnance 799.1
ordonnance
decree 750.4
law 996.3
ordure
excrement 309.4
filth 680.7
ore mineral 382.2
metal 382.3
types of ~ 382.19
oread 1012.16
ore-bearing, ore-
forming 382.14
ore bed 382.6
Oregon boot 1009.4
Oregon Jargon 578.10
ore shoot 382.6
organ member 55.4
music 464.15
publication 603.11
implement 656.3
organization 786.10
organer 463.8
organ-grinder 463.9
organic innate 5.7
structural 244.9
vital 405.18
organic being 405.2
organic chemical 378.1
organic chemistry
405.16
organic matter 405.1
organic psychosis
472.3
organic remains 407.13
organic unity
whole 54.1
unity 89.1
organism being 3.3
living being 405.2
organist 463.8
organization
composition 58.1
arrangement 60.2
classification 61
establishment 166.4
structure 244.1

organism 405.2
association 786.8
sect 1018.3
organize arrange 60.9
classify 61.6
establish 166.13
organized
arranged 60.13
organic 405.18
drunk 994.40
GET ORGANIZED 856.7
organized labor 787.1
organized matter 405.1
organizer
founder 166.10
planner 652.7
organology, organ-
ography 244.7
organometallic 382.15
organophone 464.15
organotherapy 687.3
organ player 463.8
organ point 462.15
orgasm 161.5
orgastic 161.17
orgiastic 991.9
orgy revel 876.6
debauch 991.2
spree 994.5
oriel 264.7
Orient 179.6
orient
nouns 289.3
verbs 289.12
adjs. 334.30
Oriental
nouns 417.8
adjs. 417.10
oriental 289.15
orientate 289.12
orientation 289.5
orifice opening 264.1
inlet 301.5
outlet 302.9
orificial 264.22
oriflamme 567.6
origin beginning 68.3
source 152.5
etymology 580.14
original
nouns nonimitation
23.2
pattern 25.1
nonconformist 83.4
source 152.5
native 189.3
manuscript 600.11
adjs. fundamental 5.8
unimitated 23.3
beginning 68.13
characteristic 80.13
unconventional 83.8
new 122.7
novel 122.11
causal 152.16
native 188.7
basic 211.8
genuine 515.13
inventive 533.18
unused 666.12

originality
nonimitation 23
individuality 80.4
unconventionality
83.3
newness 122.1
genuineness 515.5
inventiveness 533.3
originally
intrinsically 5.9
first 68.16
originate
initiate 68.9
begin 68.12
cause 152.11
invent 166.14
author 600.21
ORIGINATE IN 153.6
origination
beginning 68.3
source 152.5
invention 166.5
product 167.1
writing 600.2
originative
causative 152.15
creative 166.23
inventive 533.18
originator cause 152.4
producer 166.10
oriole 463.15
orismological 581.17
orismology 581.1
orison 1030.4
orle 567.2
Ormazd 1011.6
ornament
nouns musical ~
462.18
ornate speech 599.4
decoration 899.1
honor 914.1
verbs 899.7
ornamental 899.9
ornamentalist 577.11
ornamentation
ornate speech 599.4
decoration 899.1
types of ~ 899.12,
13
ornamented 899.10
ornamentist 577.11
ornate grandiloquent
599.12
ornamented 899.11
ornateness
flowery speech 599.4
elegance 899.2
ornerily 937.28
orneriness
perversity 624.3
disobedience 765.2
malice 937.5
ill humor 949.2
ornery perverse 624.11
disobedient 765.11
malicious 937.18
ill-tempered 949.19
ornithologist 414.2
ornithology 414.1
ornithopter 279.6

ornithotomy 687.26
orotund
  bombastic 599.10
  pompous 902.22
orotundity
  grandiloquence
    599.1
  pompousness 902.7
orphan
  nouns 631.4
  verbs 407.22
  adjs. 407.28
orphanage 698.4
Orpheus 463.24
orrery 374.17
orthodiagonal
  vertical 212.2
  perpendicular
    212.11
  right-angled 250.7
orthodiagram 687.12
orthodiagraph 687.11
orthodiagraphy 326.7
orthodontics 686.4
orthodontist 686.9
orthodox
  nouns believer 500.7
    true believer 1022.5
  adjs. right-handed
    242.5
    conventional 643.7
    religiously ~ 1022.8
orthodox Christian
    1022.5
orthodoxical 1022.8
orthodoxy 1022
orthoëpist
  phonetist 449.10
  philologist 578.12
orthoëpy
  phonetics 449.9
  lexicology 580.13
  pronunciation 592.6
orthogamy 168.4
orthogenesis 166.6
orthogenetic 166.24
orthogonal
  perpendicular
    212.11
  right-angled 250.7
  rectangular 250.9
orthographic
  projection 572.7
orthography 579.7
orthology 543.7
orthometric 250.7
orthopedia,
    orthopedics 686.2
orthopedist 686.7
orthopraxis,
    orthopraxy 686.2
orthopsychiatry 688.3
orthopter 279.6
orts remains 43.1
  refuse 667.4
oscar pistol 799.5
  award 914.2
oscillate
  fluctuate 141.5
  vibrate 322.9
  shake 323.10–12

generate 341.23
vacillate 625.8
oscillating
  vibrating 322.14
  vacillating 625.10
oscillation
  changeableness
    141.3
  vibration 322
  vacillation 625.2
oscillator 322.8
oscillatory
  vibratory 322.14
  vacillating 625.10
oscillograph 322.7
oscillometer 322.7
oscilloscope
  oscillation 322.7
  types of ~ 345.22
  computer unit
    348.18
oscine 413.34
oscitance, oscitancy
  gaping 264.2
  lethargy 706.5
  sleepiness 710.1
oscitant gaping 264.18
  sleepy 710.19
oscitate 264.16
osculate come in
    contact 199.10
  kiss 930.17
osculation
  contact 199.5
  kiss 930.3
osculatory
  in contact 199.17
  pax 1038.11
Osiris 1012.9
osmose 305.13
osmosis 305.6
  GET BY OSMOSIS 562.7
osmotic 305.17
osseous bony 244.11
  hard 355.10
ossicle 244.6
ossicular 244.11
ossiferous 244.11
ossification 355.5
ossified bone 244.11
  hardened 355.7
ossify harden 355.7
  callous 854.6
ossuarium 409.16
ossuary
  funeral urn 409.12
  tomb 409.16
osteal 244.11
ostensibility 510.2
ostensible
  apparent 445.11
  plausible 510.6
  illusory 518.9
  apparent 553.8
  specious 614.28
  alleged 647.4
ostensibly
  apparently 445.12
  manifestly 553.14
  speciously 614.35
  allegedly 647.5

ostent
  appearance 445.3
  ostentation 902.1
ostentation
  grandiloquence
    599.1
  pretentiousness 902
ostentatious
  grandiloquent 599.9
  pretentious 902.18
ostentatiously
  grandiloquently
    599.13
  pretentiously 902.25
osteography, osteology
    244.7
osteopath 686.7
osteopathic 686.18
osteopathy 686.2
ostiary 697.11
ostium 395.13
ostler See hostler
ostracism,
    ostracization
  banishment 308.4
  ban 924.2
ostracize
  banish 308.16
  ban 924.5
Ostracodermi 414.11
otalgia 423.5
other
  nouns 16.3
  adjs. different 16.8
    additional 40.9
    new 122.8
  AMONG OTHER
    THINGS 40.11
  NO OTHER
    the same 14.3
    one 89.3
  OTHER THAN
    different 16.8
    otherwise 16.10
other-directed 82.5
otherways 16.10
otherwise
  contrarily 15.7
  other 16.8
  differently 16.10
otherworldliness
  supernaturalism 85.7
  godliness 1026.2
otherworldly
  supernatural 85.14
  transmundane
    374.26
  heavenly 1016.13
  unworldly 1026.9
otic 447.14
otiose futile 667.13
  idle 706.16
otiosity
  uselessness 667.2
  inactivity 706.2
otography 447.9
otologist
  autist 447.10
  doctor 686.7
otology, otopathy,
    otoplasty

hearing 447.9
surgery 687.27
otorhinolaryngologist
    447.10
otoscope 447.8
otoscopy 447.9
ottar 435.2
ottava 462.9
otto 435.2
ottoman 215.5
ought
  nouns nothing 2.2
    some 28.3
    anything 79.5
    must 637.1
    duty 960.1
  verbs 637.10
  OUGHT TO
    must 637.10
    should 960.3
ouija 1032.6
ouphe elf 1012.15
  goblin 1014.9
our 806.13
Our Father 1011.11
Our Lady 1013.5
ourselves 80.5
ousia 1032.18
oust eject 308.12
  evict 308.14
  depose 781.2
ouster eviction 308.2
  ejector 308.10
ousting ejection 308.1
  eviction 308.2
  deposal 781.1
out
  nouns outlet 302.9
    excuse 1004.4
  verbs extinguish 331.7
    be revealed 554.9
  OUT WITH
    divulge 554.5,8
    say 592.14
  adjs. unmatched 21.4
    odd 85.11
    dislocated 184.8
    exterior 223.6
    extinguished 331.11
    unconscious 422.7
    erroneous 517.14
    disused 666.10
    dead-drunk 994.43
  BE OUT OF IT 155.14
  BE OUT OF ONE'S
    MIND 472.19
  JUST OUT 122.10
  OUT AT THE ELBOWS,
    OUT AT THE HEELS
    slovenly 62.14
    shabby 690.31
    impoverished 836.8
  OUT FOR
    searching 484.40
    after 653.12
    trying for 712.13
  OUT OF IT 37.7
  OUT OF ORDER
    disorderly 62.12
    unconforming 83.7

exaggerate 615.3
overload 661.16
charge too much
846.7
overcloud
darker 336.10
cloud 403.7
overcoat
garment 230.13
types of ~ 230.53
overcolor 615.3
overcolored 615.4
overcomable 508.7
overcome
verbs persuade 646.23
surmount 724.6
defeat 725.7
unnerve 857.10
adjs. defeated 725.14
overwrought 855.27
unnerved 857.14
~ with grief 870.30
dead-drunk 994.43
BE OVERCOME 694.4
overcoming
nouns 725.1
adjs. victorious 724.8
overpowering 725.17
exciting 855.31
overcommend 968.8
overcompensation
688.34
overconfidence
overcredulity 501.1
oversureness 512.5
rashness 892.1
overconfident
credulous 501.7
oversure 512.21
rash 892.7
overconscientious
overfastidious
894.12
overscrupulous
972.15
overcooked 329.7
overcopious 661.20
overcount 496.2
overcredulity 501.1
overcredulous 501.7
overcritical
overparticular
894.12
hypercritical 967.24
overcriticalness
overparticularity
894.4
hypercriticism 967.4
overcrossing 220.2
overcurious 526.5
overdesirous 633.12
overdevelop
overelaborate 661.11
overexpand 661.14
overdeveloped 194.23
overdevelopment
oversize 194.5
overexpansion 661.7
overdevout 1026.11
overdistend 661.14

overdo
exaggerate 615.3
do too much 661.11
overindulge 991.5
overdoing excess 661.6
intemperance 991.1
overdone
overcooked 329.7
grandiloquent 599.9
exaggerated 615.4
excessive 661.22
affected 901.15
overdose
nouns
too much 661.2
satiation 662.3
verbs
oversupply 661.15
satiate 662.4
overdraw
misrepresent 571.3
exaggerate 615.3
overextend 661.14
~ one's account
852.7
overdrawing
misrepresentation
571.1
exaggeration 615.1
overstretching 661.7
overdrawn
exaggerated 615.4
overdone 661.22
overdress 230.41
overdrive
nouns 347.6
verbs overdo 661.11
overwork 714.16
overdue
mistimed 115.3
late 132.15
BE OVERDUE 695.8
overeager 633.12
overeat 992.6
overelaborate
verbs 661.11
adjs. 899.11
overelegance 899.2
overelegant 899.11
overemphasize 670.13
overenthusiasm
fanaticism 472.11
overeagerness 633.4
overenthusiastic
fanatical 472.31
overeager 633.12
overequip 661.15
overesteem
overestimate 496.2
overpraise 968.8
overestimate
nouns 496.1
verbs
overreckon 496.2
exaggerate 615.3
overesteem 968.8
overestimated
overrated 496.3
exaggerated 615.4
overestimation
overreckoning 496

exaggeration 615
overcommendation
968.3
overexcite 855.11
overexcited 855.27
overexercise
nouns 661.6
verbs 661.11
overexert
overdo 661.11
overstrain 714.10
overexertion
overdoing 661.6
overstrain 714.2
overexpand 661.14
overexpend 661.11
overexpenditure
661.6
overextend 661.14
overextension 661.7
overexuberant 661.20
overfastidious 894.12
overfat 194.23
overfatigue 715.4
overfatness 194.5
overfed
oversize 194.23
overfull 661.21
satiated 662.6
gluttonous 992.8
overfeed, overfill
overstuff 661.16
satiate 662.4
overfleshed 194.23
overflow
nouns
overflowing 394.6
abundance 659.2
superabundance
661.3
verbs
flow over 394.18
abound 659.5
superabound 661.9
OVERFLOW WITH
101.5
OVERFLOW WITH
GRATITUDE 947.3
overflowing
nouns 394.6
adjs. abundant 659.7
overfull 661.21
overfull
overloaded 661.21
satiated 662.6
overfullness
overload 661.3
satiety 662.2
overfurnish 661.15
overgarment
garment 230.12
types of ~ 230.50
overgenerous 661.20
overget 299.9
overgo overrun 311.4
exceed 661.10
overgoing
overrunning 311.1
overdoing 661.6
overgorge
satiate 662.4

overeat 992.6
overgorged
satiated 662.6
overfed 992.8
overgreat
exaggerated 615.4
excessive 661.17
overgreediness 632.8
overgreedy 632.28
overgrow spread 196.6
overrun 311.5
grow rank 410.31
superabound 661.9
overgrown
oversize 194.23
overrun 311.10
luxuriant 410.41
overgrowth
oversize 194.5
overrunning 311.1
overexpansion 661.7
overhang
nouns 214.3
verbs be imminent
151.2
hang over 214.7
overhanging
nouns 214.3
adjs. imminent 151.3
jutting 214.11
overhappiness 863.2
overhappy 863.14
overhastily 131.13
overhastiness
prematurity 131.2
impulsiveness 628.2
overhasty
premature 131.8
impulsive 628.9
overhaul
nouns inspection
484.4
reparation 692.6
verbs audit 87.14
overtake 299.9
examine 484.31
repair 692.14
take account 843.9
overhead
nouns 841.3
advs. 206.27
overhear hear 447.12
learn 555.14
overheat 328.17
overheated
overwarm 327.25
heated 328.28
overheaviness 194.5
overheavy 194.23
overhung 214.11
overindulge
be intemperate
991.5
overeat 992.6
overindulged 992.8
overindulgence
intemperance 991.1
gluttony 992.1
overindulgent 991.7
overjoyed 863.14

oversight error 517.4
  guardianship 697.2
  supervision 745.2
  neglect 532.1
  nonobservance
    767.1
oversize
  nouns 194.5
  adjs. 194.23
overskip 317.5
oversleep 710.13
overslight 532.8
oversmoke
  blacken 364.7
  cloud 403.7
oversoon
  adjs. 131.8
  advs. 131.13
oversoul 1011.8
oversow 75.5
overspeak 615.3
overspend
  overdo 661.11
  overpay 846.8
  squander 852.7
overspent 715.9
overspread
  verbs disperse 75.5
  pervade 185.7
  cover 227.21
  overrun 311.5
  infest 311.6
  superabound 661.9
  adjs. 311.10
overspreading
  pervasion 185.3
  covering 227.1
  overrunning 311.1
  infestation 311.2
oversqueamish 894.12
overstate
  misrepresent 571.3
  exaggerate 615.3
overstatement
  misrepresentation
    571.1
  exaggeration 615.1
overstay 132.14
  OVERSTAY THE
    MARKET 831.23
overstep overgo 311.4
  transgress 311.9
  exceed 661.10
overstock 661.15
overstore 661.15
overstory 226.1
overstout 194.23
overstrain
  nouns
    overdoing 661.6
    overstretching 661.7
    overexertion 714.2
  verbs
    overestimate 496.2
    overtax 661.11
    overdo 661.14
    overexert 714.10
overstress
  exaggerate 615.3
  overemphasize
    670.13

overstretch 661.14
overstretched 661.22
overstride
  overgo 311.4
  stride over 311.8
overstrung 857.11
overstudy
  nouns 661.6
  verbs 661.11
overstuff
  upholster 227.31
  overfill 661.16
  satiate 662.4
overstuffed
  upholstered 227.36
  overfull 661.21
  satiated 662.6
oversufficiency 661.2
oversufficient 661.20
oversupplied 661.21
oversupply
  nouns 661.5
  verbs 661.15
oversure
  overconfident
    512.21
  rash 892.7
overswarm
  pervade 185.7
  overrun 311.6
  superabound 661.9
overswarming
  pervasion 185.3
  infestation 311.2
oversweet 430.7
overt 553.9
overt act 703.3
overtake
  catch up with 299.9
  inebriate 994.28
overtaken 994.39
  BE OVERTAKEN 694.4
overtalkative 594.9
overtarry 132.14
overtask, overtax
  overdo 661.11
  overburden 714.16
overtaxing 661.6
overtell 615.3
overtender 421.13
overthrow
  nouns revolution
    147.1
  overturn 219.2
  destruction 691.3
  defeat 725.1
  deposal 781.1
  verbs revolutionize
    147.4
  overturn 219.6
  refute 505.5
  destroy 691.20
  defeat 725.7
  depose 781.2
overthrowal
  refutation 505.2
  deposal 781.1
overthrown
  disproved 505.7
  ruined 691.27
  defeated 725.14

overthwart
  adjs. transverse 220.9
  opposed 788.9
  advs. 220.13
overtime 108.3
overtimid 890.10
overtire 715.4
overtness 553.3
overtold 615.4
overtone tone 449.2
  music 462.16
overtop excel 36.5
  rise above 206.16
overtrusting 501.7
overture
  nouns prelude 66.2
  musical ~ 461.26
  offer 771.1
  peace offering 802.2
  verbs 771.8
overturn
  nouns revolution
    147.1
  inversion 219.2
  destruction 691.3
  defeat 725.1
  verbs revolutionize
    147.4
  turn over 219.6
  capsize 274.46
  refute 505.5
  destroy 691.20
  defeat 725.7
overturned
  disproved 505.7
  defeated 725.14
overuse
  nouns 661.6
  verbs 661.11
overvaluation 496.1
overvalue 496.2
overvalued 496.3
overwariness 893.4
overwarm 327.25
overwary 893.11
overwearied 715.9
overweary 715.4
overweening
  overconfident
    512.21
  excessive 661.17
  rash 892.7
  vain 907.8
  arrogant 910.10
overweeningly
  excessively 661.23
  arrogantly 910.16
overweigh excel 36.5
  weigh too much
    351.10
  outweigh 351.14
  overload 661.16
overweight
  nouns oversize 194.5
  overbalance 351.1
  overload 661.3
  verbs
    outweigh 351.14
    overload 661.16
  adjs.
    overheavy 194.23

  heavy 351.16
overweightage 351.1
overweighted 661.21
overwhelm
  submerge 318.7
  inundate 394.18
  refute 505.5
  superabound 661.9
  oversupply 661.15
  destroy 691.20
  defeat 725.8
  astonish 918.5
overwhelmed
  flooded 394.26
  overfull 661.21
  defeated 725.14
  overwrought 855.27
  astonished 918.8
overwhelming
  evidential 504.17
  overpowering 725.17
  exciting 855.31
  astounding 918.11
overwise 907.11
overwork
  nouns 661.6
  verbs overdo 661.11
  overtask 714.16
overworked 899.11
overwrought
  grandiloquent 599.9
  exaggerated 615.4
  overdone 661.22
  overexcited 855.27
  overelaborate 899.11
overzealous
  fanatical 472.31
  overeager 633.12
  overreligious
    1026.11
overzealousness
  fanaticism 472.11
  overeagerness 633.4
  overdevoutness
    1026.3
ovicell 405.8
ovicular 405.24
oviduct 395.13
oviform 252.11
oviparous 405.24
ovoid
  nouns 252.6
  adjs. 252.11
ovular 405.24
ovule oval 252.6
  seed 405.13
  egg 405.14
ovum 405.8
owe 838.5
  OWE A GRUDGE 927.9
  OWE IT TO 960.4
owed unpaid 838.10
  due 958.7
owelty 30.1
owing
  attributable 154.5
  unpaid 838.10
  due 958.7
  OWING TO
    resulting from 153.8
  because of 154.9

pampered 757.11
pamphlet 603.10
pamphleteer
  nouns 600.15
  verbs 600.21
Pan 1012.18
pan
  nouns
    types of ~ 192.14
    face 239.4
  verbs fry 329.4
    mine 382.13
    photograph 575.16
    ridicule 965.8
    criticize 967.14
  PAN OUT 153.5
panacea 685.3
panache 229.16
Panama Canal 395.2
Pan-American 79.14a
pan-broil 329.4
pancake
  nouns 306a.44
  verbs 277.49
Panchen Lama
  1036.14
panchromatic 575.19
pancratiast
  victor 724.2
  athlete 876.21
pancreas digester 307.7
  gland 310.9
pancreatectomy, pan-
  creatotomy 687.25
pandal 190.11
Pandean pipes 464.11
pandect digest 605.1
  code 996.5
pandemia 684.4
pandemic
  universal 79.13
  epidemic 684.47
pandemoniac
  uproarious 161.17
  hellish 1017.6
pandemonic 1017.6
Pandemonium 1017.1
pandemonium
  confusion 62.5
  uproar 452.3
  hell 1017.1
pander
  nouns 987.18
  verbs 987.21
  PANDER TO
    serve 748.14
    minister to 783.18
    toady to 905.7
pandiculation 264.2
pandora, pandore,
  pandura 464.4
Pandora's box 684.4
pandowdy 306a.40
pane lamina 226.2
  windowpane 264.7
  glass 338.2
panegyric 966.5
panegyric(al) 966.15
panegyrist 966.8
panegyrize 966.12

panel
  nouns list 88.5
    lamina 226.2
    partition 236.5
    schedule 639.2
    forum 753.4
    jury 1000.7
    litigants 1002.11
  verbs partition 236.9
    ~ a jury 1002.15
panelboard 348.15
panel den 987.9
panel game 616.9
panelist 597.4
panelling
  boarding 377.3
  types of ~ 377.14
pang pain 423.2
  mental pain 864.5
  ~ of conscience
    871.2
pangen 405.4
pangenesis 166.6
pangenetic 166.24
panhandle 772.15
panhandler 772.8
Panhellenic 79.14a
panic
  nouns success 722.3
    financial ~ 831.22
    fright 889.1
  verbs 889.15
panicle 410.25
panic-stricken, panic-
  struck 889.26
panisc, panisk 1012.18
panjandrum 670.8
panlogical, pan-
  logistical 499.10
panoplied
  protected 697.20
  armored 797.13
panoply
  nouns armor 797.3
    arms 799.1
  verbs 697.17
panorama view 445.6
  picture 572.13
panoramic 76.6
Pan-Pacific 79.14a
Panpipe, Panpipes
  464.11
panpsychism
  materialism 375.5
  immaterialism 376.3
  psychics 1032.4
panpsychist
  immaterialist 376.4
  psychist 1032.12
pansophic(al) 474.28
pansophy 474.6
pansy flower 410.45
  homosexual 418.12
pant
  nouns 402.19
  verbs breech 230.39
    pulsate 322.11
    be hot 327.21
    breathe 402.25
    say 592.17
    get tired 715.5

  ~ with emotion
    855.18
PANT FOR 632.16
pantaloon 610.9
pantalooned 230.44
pantaloons 230.18
pantelegraphy 558.3
pantheism
  philosophy 499.5
  religion 1018.5
pantheist 1018.14
pantheistic 1018.23
pantheistic(al) 499.10
pantheon gods 1012.1
  temple 1040.2
pantheonic 1040.14
panther
  spottiness 373.6
  animal 413.4
pantile 306a.29
panting
  breathlessness 715.3
  trepidation 855.4
pantisocracy 739.4
pantod 710.8
pantograph 601.13
pantologic(al) 474.28
pantometer 250.4
pantomime
  nouns gesture 566.13
    dumb show 609.4
  verbs 609.33
pantomimic
  nouns 610.1
  adjs. 566.23
pantomimist 610.1
pantophagist 306.13
pantophagous 306.29
pantophagy 306.1
pantry 658.8
pants 230.18
pantywaist
  weakling 159.6
  mollycoddle 420.11
panzer armored 797.13
  ~ division 798.20
pap father 169.9
  nipple 255.6
  soft diet 307.10
  semiliquid 388.5
  political ~ 742.37
papa father 169.9
  pope 1036.8
papacy
  jurisdiction 737.6
  government 739.4
  popedom 1035.6
papal 1035.15
papal brief 602.3
papality 1035.6
paper
  nouns thinness 204.7
    material 377.6
    types of ~ 377.17
    document 568.4
    writing 600.11
    stationery 600.30
    newspaper 603.12
    treatise 604.1
    negotiable ~ 833.11
  ON PAPER

    in theory 498.16
    in writing 600.24
  verbs 227.25
  PAPER THE HOUSE
    609.32
  adjs. 377.10
paperback 603.1
papers
  naturalization 188.4
  documents 568.4
paper war 481.5
paperweight 351.6
papery flimsy 159.14
  paperlike 377.10
Paphian
  nouns 987.16
  adjs. 987.26
papier 377.6
papilla 255.6
papillary, papillose
  255.18
papillote 253.3
papish
  Catholic 1018.27
  papal 1035.15
papism 1018.7
papist, Papist
  nouns 1018.17
  adjs.
    Catholic 1018.27
    papal 1035.15
papistry 1018.7
papoose 125.7
pappose 229.25
pappus down 229.8
  beard 229.9
pappy 169.9
papula, papule 684.28
papulous 255.18
papyrus 600.12
par
  nouns equality 30.1
    value 832.8
  ABOVE PAR
    exceeding 36.20
    superior 672.15
    of securities 832.14
  BELOW PAR
    below 207.11
    inferior 678.11
    ill 684.41
    of securities 832.14
    at a discount 845.3
  UNDER PAR 37.9
  UP TO PAR 672.17
  adjs. 30.8
parable
  figure of speech
    549.2
  story 606.7
parabola 251.2
parabolic(al)
  figurative 549.4
  fictional 606.17
paracasein 353.7
parachronism 115.1
parachronistic 115.3
parachute
  nouns 279.13
  verbs bail out 277.53
    descend 314.5

parachutist 278.8
Paraclete 1011.14
parade
  nouns
    procession 71.4
    promenade 272.28
    spectacle 445.7
    walkway 655.3
    ostentation 902.4
  verbs file 71.8
    promenade 272.12
    march 272.29
    flaunt 902.17
paradigm
    pattern 25.1
    grammar 584.1
paradigmatic 25.8
paradisaic(al)
    delightful 861.6
    heavenly 1016.13
paradise park 410.11
    garden 412.10
    top gallery 438.8
    utopia 533.11
    balcony 509.19
    preserve 699.6
    bliss 863.2
    pleasance 876.14
    heaven 1016.1
paradoctor 278.8
paradox
    self-contradiction 27.2
    dilemma 729.6
paradoxical 27.9
paraffin, paraffine 379.11
parafinnic 379.9
paragon
    ~ of beauty 898.8
    good person 983.4
paragraph
  nouns section 55.2
    phrase 583.1
    passage 603.14
    treatise 604.1
  verbs 583.5
parallel
  nouns similar 20.4
    equal 30.5
    ~ line 217.2
    entrenchment 797.5
  WITHOUT PARALLEL 36.17
  verbs relate 9.4
    be alike 20.7
    equal 30.5
    coextend 217.4
    compare 490.4,7
  adjs. analogous 20.11
    coextending 217.6
    comparable 490.8
parallelepiped, parallelepipedon 217.2
parallelepipedal 217.6
paralleler 217.2
parallelinervate 217.6
parallelism
    similarity 20.1,4
    correspondence 26.1

equality 30.1
coextension 217
comparison 490.1
parallelistic 490.8
parallelization
    parallelism 217.1
    comparison 490.1
parallelize relate 9.4
    equidistance 217.5
    compare 490.4
parallelodrome 217.6
parallelogram 217.2
parallelograph, parallelometer 217.3
parallelotropism 217.1
paralogia 688.23
paralogical 482.14
paralogician 482.6
paralogism logic 481.7
    sophistry 482.1,3
paralogist 482.6
paralogize 482.8
paralogy
    psychosis 472.3
    sophistry 482.1
paralysis 684.19
paralytic 684.46
paralyzation 684.19
paralyze
    render powerless 157.11
    deaden 422.3
    ~ emotionally 854.8
    terrify 889.16
    astound 918.5
paralyzed
    disabled 157.16
    terrified 889.25
paramagnet 287.3
paramagnetism 341.7
paramnesia 536.2
paramount
  nouns
    principal 670.10
    master 747.3,8
  adjs. chief 36.16
    top 210.9
    most important 670.25
    ruling 739.17
paramountcy 36.3
paramour lover 929.11
    kept woman 987.17
paranoia 472.5
paranoiac, paranoid
  nouns 472.16
  adjs. 472.26
paranomia
    psychosis 472.3
    neurosis 688.26
parapathia, parapathy 688.17
parapet barrier 728.5
    bulwark 797.4
paraphasia 688.25
paraphernalia
    equipment 657.4
    belongings 808.2
paraphilia 688.32

paraphrase
  nouns 550.3
  verbs 550.15
paraphrast 550.8
paraphrastic 550.19
paraphrenia 472.5
paraphrenitis 472.9
paraplegia 684.19
parapsychology
    psychology 688.1
    psychics 1032.4
paraselene 334.14
parasite insect 413a.7
    sycophant 905.4
parasitic(al)
    rapacious 820.23
    sycophantic 905.13
parasitism 905.2
parasol 227.7
parathyroid 310.9
paratrooper 278.8
Paratroops 798.30
paratuberculosis 684.13
parboil 329.4
Parcae 638.3
parcel
  nouns part 55.1
    bundle 74.7
  PARCEL OF LAND
    plot 179.4
    field 412.9
  verbs partition 49.18
    bundle 74.19
    package 235.9
    apportion 814.7
  PARCEL OUT
    dispose 60.8
    apportion 814.9
parcel post 602.5
parch shrivel 197.9
    be hot 327.21
    burn 328.23
    dry 392.6
parched
    withered 197.13
    burnt 328.29
    dried 392.9
    thirsty 632.27
parching
  nouns shrinking 197.3
    burning 328.5
  adjs. 327.25
parchment
    document 568.4
    writing 600.11
par cœur 535.27
pard, pardner
    confederate 785.2
    comrade 926.4
pardon
  nouns
    forgiveness 945.2
    acquittal 1005.1
  verbs forgive 945.3
    acquit 1005.4
pardonable 1004.14
pardoned 945.7
pare cut off 42.10
    peel 231.8

cut prices 847.6
paregoric 685.11
paregoric(al) 685.39
parent
  nouns cause 152.4
    progenitor 169.8
  adjs. 169.13
parentage 169.1
parental 169.13
parenthesis
    discontinuity 72.1
    inversion 219.3
    interjection 236.2
parenthesize
    enclose 235.8
    punctuate 584.12
parenthetical
    unessential 10.6
    incidental 129.12
    interjectional 236.10
parenthetically 129.14
parenthood 169.1
parentless 407.28
paresis 684.8,19
paresthesia
    tingling 425.1
    disease 684.17
    neurosis 688.21
par excellence 36.18
par exemple 129.14
parfait 306a.46
parfum 435.2
parget plaster 227.27
    paint 361.14
parhelic ring, parhelion 334.14
pariah
    commoner 917.7
    outcast 924.3
pariah dog 413.25
paries 236.5
pari mutuel 514.3,12
paring piece 55.3
    flake 226.3
parings remains 43.1
    refuse 667.4
parish district 179.5
    diocese 1035.8
    laity 1037.1
  GO ON THE PARISH 836.5
parishioner 1037.2
parish lantern 374.8
parity analogy 20.1
    equality 30.1
    price 832.8
park
  nouns valley 256.9
    grassland 410.7
    pasture 410.8
    woodland 410.11
    reservation 699.6
    artillery ~ 799.2
    pleasance 876.14
  verbs place 183.12
    settle 183.18
  PARK IN SPACE 281.15
Parkinson's disease 684.19
parkway 655.6

parlance
language 578.1
diction 586.1
parlando
nouns 461.31
adjs. 461.54
parlay
nouns 514.3
verbs increase 38.4
bet 514.19
parley
nouns
conference 595.6
arbitration 803.2
verbs speak 592.11
converse 595.8
confer 595.10
Parliament 740.2
parliament 740.1
parliamentarian
nouns 481.13
adjs. 739.16
parliamentarianism
739.8
parliamentary
nouns train 271.12
mediator 803.3
adjs. 740.21
parlor room 191.5
shop 717.1
parlor bolshevik
743.11
parlor car 271.13
parlormaid 748.8
parlous
adjs. shrewd 466.15
dangerous 695.9
advs. 34.20
Parnassian 607.13
Parnassus 607.12
parochial local 179.9
narrow-minded
525.10
parodic(al) 965.14
parodist 879.12
parody
nouns 965.6
verbs 965.11
parol 592.20
parole
nouns speech 592.1
freedom 761.2
promise 768.1
verbs 761.5
parolee, parolist
759.11
paroli 514.3,19
paronomasia
assonance 20.3
wordplay 879.8
paronychia 684.28
paronymous
related 9.6
etymological 580.19
parorexia 688.21
parotitis 684.9
paroxysm spasm 323.6
frenzy 472.8
illness 684.5
fit of anger 950.8
paroxysmal 161.22

parquet
flooring 211.3
check 373.4
theater ~ 609.19
parquetry 373.4
parricide 408.4
parrot
nouns 22.4
verbs 22.6
parrotry 22.2
parry
nouns 629.1
verb quibble 482.9
refute 505.5
evade 629.8
fend off 797.10
parrying 482.5
parse
analyze 484.32
~ sentences 584.12
parsec 374.3
Parshuram 1012.8
Parsi 1031.4
Parsiism 1031.1
parsimonious
frugal 849.9
sparing 850.9
parsimony
frugality 849.1
niggardliness 850
parsing 584.1
parson 1036.2
parsonage 1040.7
parsoness 1036.5
part
nouns capacity 7.5
portion 55
component 58.2
region 179.1
piece 201.3
musical ~
461.22,24,28
~ of a book 603.14
role 609.11
function 654.3
share 814.5
DO ONE'S PART
share 813.6
do one's duty 960.9
IN PART
to a degree 35.11
partly 55.7
ON THE PART OF
apropos 9.10
for 783.26
TAKE THE PART OF
783.13
verbs disjoin 49.8
separate 49.19
disband 75.9
interspace 200.4
open 264.11
die 407.15
portion 814.7
divorce 933.5
PART COMPANY WITH
793.11
PART WITH
discard 666.7
relinquish 812.3

give away 816.20
adjs. 55.6
advs.
to a degree 35.11
partly 55.7
partake
participate 813.5
take 820.11
PARTAKE OF
resemble 20.7
eat 306.17
participate 813.5
partaker
participator 813.4
taker 820.9
partaking
nouns 813.1
adjs. 813.8
parted 200.6
PARTED FROM 810.8
parterre level 213.3
theater ~ 609.19
parthenogenesis 166.6
Parthenope 648.3
partial
fractional 55.6
limited 233.8
prejudiced 525.12
imperfect 676.4
partisan 786.18
unjust 975.11
PARTIAL TO
desirous 632.22
fond of 929.27
partiality
prejudice 525.3
desire 632.3
preference 635.4
partisanism 786.13
injustice 975.3
partially
to a degree 35.11
partly 55.7
imperfectly 676.5
unjustly 975.13
partibility 49.1
partible 49.25
participant
nouns 813.4
adjs. 813.8
participate 813.5
participation 813
participative, par-
ticipatory 813.8
participator 813.4
participial 584.13
particle
small amount 35.2
piece 55.3
minute thing 195.7
alpha ~ 326.4
part of speech 584.2
NOT A PARTICLE 2.3
parti-color, party-color
nouns 373.1
adjs. 373.9
particular
nouns
circumstance 8.2
part 55.1
event 150.2

technicality 749.4
IN PARTICULAR
in detail 8.11
specially 80.16
THE PARTICULAR 80.2
adjs. detailed 8.7
special 80.12
topical 483.5
meticulous 531.12
respective 814.14
fastidious 894.9
particularity
circumstance 8.3
characteristic 80.3
individuality 80.4
meticulousness
531.3
fastidiousness 894.1
particularization
circumstantiation
8.4
differentiation 16.4
specialization 80.7
logic 481.3
particularize
circumstantiate 8.5
differentiate 16.6
specialize 80.10
reason 481.15
particularly
in detail 8.11
remarkably 34.23
chiefly 36.19
specially 80.16
singly 89.13
respectively 814.15
fastidiously 894.14
parting
nouns
disjunction 49.1
disbandment 75.3
departure 300.1,4
death 407.1
PARTING OF THE WAY
falling out 793.4
quarrel 793.11
divorce 933.5
adjs. separating 49.2
departing 300.19
parting cup 994.8
Partingtonism 517.6
partisan
nouns follower 292.2
political ~ 742.28
supporter 785.8
adjs.
prejudiced 525.12
politics 742.48
factional 786.18
partial 975.11
partisanism
political ~ 742.1,2
partisanship 786.13
partiality 975.3
sectarianism 1018.
partisanship
partisanism 786.13
partiality 975.3
apportionment
814.1

backer 785.8
custo ner 826.4
financer 834.9
patronage
  protection 697.2
  fosterage 783.4
  clientele 826.3
  condescension 904.3
patronize
  sponsor 783.15
  trade with 825.13
  finance 834.15
  be condescending
  904.7
patronizer 826.4
patronizing 910.4
patronymic 581.5
patter
  nouns pitter-patter
  454.1
  nonsense 545.4
  language 578.1
  jargon 578.6
  acting business
  609.9
  verbs pound 282.15
  pitter-patter 454.4
  twaddle 545.8
  talk 592.11
  chatter 594.6
  act 609.33
patterer talker 592.9
  chatterer 594.5
pattern model 25.1
  form 245.1
  musical ~ 462.11
  idea 473.3
  measure 489.2
  design 572.12
  habit 640.3
  diagram 652.3
  psychological ~
  688.41
  behavior 735.1
  paragon 983.4
pattern after 22.7
pattons 230.27
patty, patty-cake, patty
  shell 306a.40
patulous 196.11
pauciloquent 611.7
pauciloquy 611.2
paucity 660.3
Pauline Epistles
  1019.4
Paul Jones 823.8
Paul Pry
  meddler 237.4
  inquisitive 526.2
Paul-Pry meddle 237.7
  be inquisitive 526.4
Paul Revere 559.1
paunch 192.3
paunched 196.13
paunchiness 194.8
paunchy 196.13
pauper 836.4
pauperism 336.2
pauperize 836.6
Pauropoda 414.8

pause
  nouns interruption
  72.2
  interim 109.1
  delay 132.2
  cessation 144.3
  ~ for station
  identification
  343.22
  musical ~ 462.12,
  21
  demur 621.2
  respite 709.2
  verbs cease 144.9
  demur 621.4
  be irresolute 625.7
  rest 709.8
pave
  nouns floor 211.3
  pavement 655.7
  verbs 227.24
  PAVE THE WAY
  prepare 718.12
  facilitate 730.6
pavement floor 211.3
  base 215.6
  flooring 377.2
  road 655.7
paver 718.5
pavestones 655.7
pavilion house 190.5
  cover 227.2
  tent 227.8
pavior 718.5
Pavlov 688.12
pavonian, pavonine
  blue 371.3
  iridescent 373.10
paw
  nouns 211.5
  verbs 424.6
pawky shrewd 466.15
  cunning 733.12
pawn
  nouns
  necessitarian 638.5
  tool 656.3
  pledge 770.2
  pawnbroker 818.3
  pawnshop 818.4
  chessman 876.18
  IN PAWN 770.15
  verbs 770.12
pawnbroker 818.3
pawnbrokery 818.4
pawned 770.15
pawning 819.1
pawnshop 818.4
paws 811.4
Pax 1038.10
pax
  nouns peace 801.1
  kiss of peace 1038.4
  osculatory 1038.11
  interjs. 450.16
Pax Dei 802.5
pax vobiscum!
  farewell! 300.25
  best wishes! 726.17
  peace! 801.11

pay
  nouns payment 839.4
  punishment 1008.1
  IN ONE'S PAY 748.15
  verbs undergo 150.8
  do 703.6
  be profitable 809.11
  recompense 839.10
  yield 842.3
  retaliate 953.5
  punish 1008.11
  IT DOESN'T PAY
  669.10
  PAY AS YOU GO
  839.17
  PAY BACK
  interchange 149.4
  retaliate 953.5
  PAY COURT TO
  curry favor 905.8
  make friends 925.11
  court 930.19
  PAY FOR
  finance 834.15
  defray 839.18
  PAY OUT
  settle 839.13
  hand out 839.14
  expend 841.5
  retaliate 953.5
  punish 1008.11
  PAY THE PIPER
  pay for 839.18
  be punished 1008.23
  PAY THROUGH THE
  NOSE 846.8
  PAY UP 839.13
payable 838.10
pay dirt 382.6
payee 817.3
payer 839.9
paying
  nouns 839.1
  adjs. profitable 809.14
  remunerative 839.21
paying guest
  lodger 189.8
  tenant 807.4
payload load 193.2
  cargo 270.7
  aviation 277.27
  rockets 280.7
paymaster 834.11
payment pay 839
  remuneration 839.4
  punishment 1008.1
payoff 70.1
pay-off result 153.2
  payment 839.1
pay roll 839.4
PBX 558.10
pea plant 410.4
  seed 410.29
peace quiescence 267.1
  silence 450.1
  accord 792
  peacefulness 801
  truce 802.5
  comfortableness
  885.2
  AT PEACE 801.9

  KEEP THE PEACE
  be moderate 162.5
  be at peace 801.7
  MAKE PEACE
  make up 802.9
  mediate 803.6
peaceable
  quiescent 267.10
  concordant 792.3
  pacific 801.9
  amicable 925.14
peaceful
  homelike 190.28
  quiescent 267.10
  pacific 801.9
  inexcitable 856.12
  comfortable 885.11
peacefulness
  quiescence 267.1
  peace 801.2
  mental calm 856.2
  comfortableness
  885.2
peace lover, peace man
  801.6
peacemaker 803.5
peace offering
  conciliation 802.2
  offering 816.4
  oblation 1030.7
peace officer 697.14
peace of mind
  peace 801.3
  content 866.1
peace pipe 802.2
peacetime
  nouns 801.1
  adjs.: 801.9
peach
  nouns fruit 306a.50
  good thing 672.7
  beauty 898.8
  verbs blab 554.6
  inform on 555.11
  adjs. orangeish 368.2
  yellowish 369.4
peacher 555.6
peachery 412.11
peachy 672.14
peacock
  nouns
  variegation 373.6
  bird 413.34
  male animal 419.8
  swaggerer 902.10
  verbs pose 901.13
  strut 902.15
peacockery
  posing 901.3
  ostentation 902.8
peacockish
  ostentatious 902.23
  vain 907.11
Peacock throne 737.10
peag 833.3
peahen 420.10
peak
  nouns
  mountain 206.8
  mountain peaks
  206.28

transparent 338.4
intelligible 546.10
pellucidity 338.1
Pelmatozoa 414.7
pelt
nouns skin 228.1
types of ~ 228.8
velocity 268.2
blow 282.4
verbs strike 282.15
shoot 284.13
hurl at 796.29
peltate 251.32
peltry 228.1
pemmican 306a.12
pemphigus 684.27
pen
nouns abode 190.6
enclosure 235.3
pasture 410.8
farm 412.8
writing 600.1
hand 600.5
writer 600.14
penitentiary 759.9
verbs enclose 235.5
write 600.19
confine 759.12
penal 1008 25
penal institution 759.7
penalization 1007.1
penalize
handicap 1007.4
punish 1008.10
penal servitude 1008.2
penalty
handicap 728.6
penalization 1007
punishment 1008.1
penance
penalty 1007.1
atonement 1010.3
sacrament 1038.5
DO PENANCE 1010.6
penates
gods of the
household 190.26
familiar spirit
1012.19
pence 833.8
penchant
tendency 173.1
desire 632.3
pencil
nouns
~ of light 334.5
artistry 572.8
artistic style 572.9
drawing ~ 572.19
verbs mark 566.18
draw 572.20
write 600.19
pencraft 600.2,4
pend hang 214.6
be uncertain 513.11
pendant
counterpart 20.5
addition 41.1
hanging 214.4
types of ~ 214.13
pendeloque 214.4

pendency 214
pendent
hanging 214.9
sloping 218.16
uncertain 513.16
pendente lite 109.5
pending
adjs. pendent 214.9
overhanging 214.11
uncertain 513.16
preps. during 105.8
until 105.10
pendragon 747.9
pendulant, pendular
214.9
pendulate
fluctuate 141.5
oscillate 322.9
vacillate 625.8
pendulation
changeableness
141.3
oscillation 322.1
vacillation 625.2
penduline 214.9
pendulosity 214.1
pendulous
pendent 214.9
overhanging 214.11
oscillating 322.14
pendulum 322.8
penetrability
accessibility 508.3
intelligibility 546.1
vulnerability 695.4
penetrable
pervious 264.21
accessible 508.8
intelligible 546.9
pregnable 695.16
penetralia 224.2
penetrate imbue 44.12
pervade 185.7
perforate 264.15
enter 301.9
chill 332.11
see through 487.8
be remembered
535.15
be understood 546.5
understand 546.8
~ the feelings
853.15
penetrating
cold 332.15
odorous 434.10
shrill 457.13
discerning 466.16
searching 484.40
deep-felt 853.25
exciting 855.32
caustic 937.21
penetration
imbuement 44.2
pervasion 185.3
perforation 264.3
ingress 301.1
discernment 466.4
discrimination 491.2
penfold See pinfold

penguin
flight trainer 279.10
bird 413.56
penial 418.18
Penicillium 411.4
peninsula 255.8
penis 418.8
penitence
reformation 145.2
repentance 871.4
penance 1010.3
penitent
nouns 871.5
adjs. 871.9
penitentiary
nouns prison 759.9
confessor 1036.4
church dignitary
1036.8
adjs. 871.9
penman 600.14
penmanship 600.4
pen name 581.8
pennant 567.6
penned
enclosed 235.10
written 600.24
penniless 836.9
pennon 567.6
Pennsylvania Dutch
578.8
penny 833.7,8
penny dreadful 606.8
penny-pinching
nouns 850.4
adjs. 850.12
penny-wise 850.9
PENNY-WISE AND
POUND-FOOLISH
unwise 469.9
parsimonious 850.9
prodigal 852.8
pennyworth
worth 844.3
bargain 847.3
penology 1008.9
pen pal 602.9
penscript
handwriting 600.4
writing 600.11
penseroso 870.23
pensile 214.9
pensility 214.1
pension
nouns 816.8
verbs 816.18
PENSION OFF
retire 308.18
subsidize 816.18
pension
boardinghouse
190.13
pensionary
nouns hireling 748.2
dependent 762.6
stipendiary 817.4
adjs. 816.25
pensioner
student 564.5
dependent 762.6
stipendiary 817.4

pensive
thoughtful 477.20
melancholy 870.23
pensively
thoughtfully 477.22
melancholily 870.35
penstock trough 395.3
floodgate 395.11
pentachord 462.8
pentad
nouns 99.1
adjs. 99.17
Pentagon 740.13
pentagon 99.1
pentagonal 250.11
pentameter, penta-
pody, pentastich
five 99.1
verse 607.5
pentarchy 99.1
Pentateuch five 99.1
Bible 1019.3
pentathlon 99.1
pentatomic 325.17
pentavalent 99.17
Pentecost 1038.15,16
penthouse house 190.5
apartment 191.4
pentrough 395.3
pent-up
enclosed 235.10
confined 759.19
penultimate 70.10
penumbra 336.3
penurious 850.10
penury 836.2
peon messenger 559.1
serf 762.7
soldier 798.9
peasant 917.8
peonage, peonism
762.1
people
nouns kinsmen 11.2
race 11.4
family 11.6
population 189.1
persons 416.2
subjects 762.5
laity 1037.1
THE PEOPLE 917.2
verbs 187.10
peopled 187.13
peoples 417
pep 160.2
BE FULL OF PEP
683.4
FULL OF PEP
energetic 160.11
lively 705.16
pepless 706.18
pep meet 742.12
pepper
nouns energy 160.2
condiment 306a.54
verbs sprinkle 75.7
shoot 284.13
spot 373.7
season 427.7
bombard 796.23

sentence 583.1
periodic(al)
  recurrent 137.8
  rhythmical 462.27
periodical
  nouns 603.11
  adjs. 603.26
periodically 137.11
periodicity
  recurrence 137.2
  rhythm 462.22
Peripatetic 499.11
peripatetic
  nouns itinerant 273.2
  pedestrian 273.6
  adjs. 272.35
peripateticate 272.26
Peripateticism 499.2
peripateticism 272.12
periphera
  exterior 223.6
  outlinear 234.14
periphery 234.1
periphrase
  nouns 591.5
  verbs 591.10
periphrasis 591.5
periphrastic 591.14
periplus 274.1
periscope 318.5
perish
  cease to be 2.5
  die 407.15
  disappear 446.2
  be destroyed 691.22
perishability 111.1
perishable 111.7
peristyle
  corridor 191.18
  room 191.24
  colonnade 216.5
peritoneum 228.3
peritonitis 684.8
periwig 229.14
periwinkle 306a.25
perjure oneself 614.21
perjurer 617.9
perjury 614.9
perk
  verbs 163.3
  PERK UP
  raise up 315.5
  improve 689.7
  recuperate 692.19
  refresh 693.2
  cheer up 368.8
  adjs. 907.11
perks 816.5
perky 907.11
perlustrate 484.33
perlustration 484.4
permanence
  durability 110.1
  perpetualness 112.1
  changelessness 140
  stability 142
  unchangeability 142.4
permanent
  nouns 229.15
  adjs. durable 110.10

perpetual 112.7
  changeless 140.7
  stable 142.13
  unchangeable 142.18
permanently
  perpetually 112.10
  unchangingly 140.9
permeability
  perviousness 264.9
  magnetic ~ 341.7
permeable 264.21
permeate imbue 44.12
  pervade 185.7
  saturate 391.13
permeated 391.17
  PERMEATED WITH 640.18
permeation
  imbuement 44.2
  pervasion 185.3
  saturation 391.7
permissible 775.16
permissibly 775.20
permission
  consent 773
  allowance 775
permissive
  nouns 584.9
  adjs.
  consenting 773.5
  permitting 775.15
permissively 775.19
permit
  nouns 775.6
  verbs consent 773.3
  allow 775.10
  NOT PERMIT 776.4
permitted 775.17
permutability
  changeableness 141.1
  interchangeability 149.3
permutable
  changeable 141.6
  interchangeable 149.5
permutation
  mathematics 86.4
  transformation 139.2
  interchange 149.1
permute 149.4
pernicious
  deadly 408.23
  harmful 673.12
  ~ anemia 684.8
pernickety 894.10
perorate
  expatiate 591.8
  declaim 597.9
peroration sequel 67.1
  speech 597.2
peroxide 362.5
peroxidize 378.6
perpendicular
  adjs. vertical 212.2
  plumb 212.11
  advs. 212.13
perpendicularity 212.1

perpetrate 703.6
perpetration 703.2
perpetrator 716.1
perpetual 112.7
perpetually 112.10
perpetuate 112.5
perpetuation 112.4
perpetuity 112
perplex
  complicate 46.3
  fill with doubt 502.7
  bewilder 513.13
perplexed
  complex 46.4
  bewildered 513.23
perplexing
  intricate 46.4
  bewildering 513.24
perplexity
  complexity 46.1
  bewilderment 513.3
  problem 547.7
  dilemma 729.6
perquisite gain 809.3
  gratuity 816.5
  boodle 822.11
perquisites 808.2
perquisition 484.2,5
perquisitor 484.18
perron 313.3
per saltum
  intermittently 72.5
  at once 113.8
perscrutate 484.33
perscrutation 484.5
perscrutator 484.19
per se essentially 5.10
  singly 89.13
persecute
  oppress 665.6
  torment 864.19
persecution
  mistreatment 665.3
  torment 864.7
persecutor 864.10
**Persephone, Perse-
  phassa, Proserpine,
  Proserpina** 412.4
perseverance
  resolution 622
  persistence 623
perseverant
  resolute 622.11
  persistent 623.7
persevere 623.2
persevering 623.7
perseveringly
  resolutely 622.17
  persistently 623.8
persiflage 880.1
persist prevail 17.3
  endure 110.6
  persevere 623.2
  urge 646.14
  PERSIST IN 811.5
persistence
  steadiness 17.1
  durability 110.1
  permanence 140.1
  perseverance 623.1

persistent
  constant 17.5
  durable 110.10
  permanent 140.7
  persevering 623.7
  habitual 640.15
person being 3.3
  human form 245.4
  body 375.3
  human being 416.3
  grammar 584.6
  character 609.11
  IN PERSON
  bodily 80.17
  individually 185.15
personable 898.17
personage
  person 416.3
  character 609.11
  great man 670.8
persona grata 983.1
personal
  nouns 604.1
  adjs. special 80.12
  human 416.12
personal appearance 609.13
personality being 3.3
  individuality 80.4
  person 416.3
  personal remark 969.4
personalize
  individualize 80.10
  personify 549.3
personally
  individually 80.17
  in person 185.15
persona non grata 984.1
personate
  represent 570.9
  impersonate 570.10
  enact 609.34
personation
  representation 570.2
  acting 609.9
personator 617.7
personification
  embodiment 375.7
  figure of speech 549.2
  representation 570.2
personify
  embody 375.8
  figure 549.3
  typify 570.9
personnel staff 748.12
  membership 786.12
perspective
  distance 198.1
  field of view 443.3
  view 445.6
  art 572.10
perspicacious
  sagacious 466.16
  discriminative 491.9
perspicacity
  vision 438.1
  sagacity 466.4
  discrimination 491.2

perspicuity
sagacity 466.4
intelligibility 546.2
manifestness 553.3
perspicuous
sagacious 466.16
intelligible 546.10
manifest 553.8
perspiration 309.7
perspire 309.14
perspiring, perspiry
309.20
persuadability 171.5
persuadable
influenceable 171.15
open-minded 524.10
persuade
convert 145.11
convince 500.15
induce 646.23
PERSUADE ONESELF
convince oneself
500.16
be persuaded 646.24
persuasibility
persuadability 171.5
open-mindedness
524.3
persuasible
influenceable 171.15
open-minded 524.10
persuasion kind 61.3
conversion 145.2
sex 418.1
belief 500.3
inducement 646.3
school 786.6
sect 1018.3
persuasive
nouns 646.3
adjs. convincing
500.22
persuading 646.29
BE PERSUASIVE 171.10
persuasiveness 646.3
pert sprightly 705.16
gay 868.13
conceited 907.11
impertinent 911.9
pertaining to
relating to 9.5
relevant 9.8
pertain to relate to 9.3
belong to 806.8
pertinacious
persevering 623.7
obstinate 624.8
pertinacity
perseverance 623.1
obstinacy 624.1
pertinence 9.2
pertinent 9.8
PERTINENT TO 9.5
pertinently 9.9
pertness 907.4
perturb
discompose 63.4
agitate 323.10
bewilder 513.12
fluster 530.7
alarm 702.5

trouble 729.12
excite 855.14
distress 864.15
perturbate
agitate 323.10
excite 855.14
perturbation
disarrangement 63.1
agitation 323.1
bewilderment 513.3
fluster 530.3
alarm 702.1
excitement 855.3,10
anxiety 888.1
fearfulness 889.4
perturbed
agitated 323.17
bewildered 513.22
confused 530.12
alarmed 702.7
excited 855.24
distressed 864.25
anxious 888.6
pertussis 684.12
peruke 229.14
perusal
inspection 484.4
study 562.3
peruse
examine 484.31
study 562.12
pervade imbue 44.12
permeate 185.7
pervading 853.25
pervasion
imbuement 44.2
permeation 185.3
perverse wrong 517.14
obstinate 624.11
ill-humored 949.19
perversion
distortion 248.2
homosexuality
418.10
sophistry 482.1
error 517.1
misinterpretation
551.1
misrepresentation
571.1
falsification 614.9
apostasy 626.2
misuse 665.1
psychological ~
688.32
corruption 690.2
perversity
obstinacy 624.3
antisocialism 688.16
ill humor 949.2
pervert
nouns sex ~ 418.11
apostate 626.5
degenerate 984.5
heretic 1023.5
verbs distort 248.6
reason ill 482.8
misinterpret 551.2
misrepresent 571.3
falsify 614.16
misuse 665.4

corrupt 690.12
perverted
distorted 248.10
homosexual 418.23
erroneous 517.14
misinterpreted 551.3
morally ~ 979.19
pervestigate 484.33
pervigilium 711.1
pervious
influenceable 171.15
permeable 264.21
exudative 302.20
transparent 338.4
accessible 508.8
pes 211.5
Pesach 1038.16
peseta, peso 833.9
pesky 862.13
pessimism
uncheerfulness
870.2
cynicism 887.6
pessimist
nouns 887.7
adjs. 887.16
pessimistic
uncheerful 870.21
cynical 887.16
pest bane 674.1
plague 684.4
annoyance 864.2
pesterer 864.10
bore 882.4
pester
importune 772.12
torment 864.19
nag 967.16
pesthole 684.4
pesthouse 687.30
pesticide 408.11
pestiferous
contagious 684.47
annoying 862.13
pestilence bane 674.1
epidemic 684.4
pestilent 862.13
pestle 360.7
pet
nouns sore 684.28
darling 929.13
endearment 930.5
dudgeon 950.7
verbs make love
930.13
caress 930.14
adjs. 929.21
petal 410.17,26
petard 799.9
petcock 395.10
peteman, peterman
823.3
Peter Duff 828.8
Peter Funk 826.6
peter out
cease to be 2.5
weaken 159.9
tire 715.5
fail 723.12
Peter's pence 816.6

petiole, petiolule,
petiolus 410.19
petit 671.17
petite 195.9
petite noblesse 916.3
petition
nouns political ~
742.30
request 772.1
prayer 1030.4
verbs request 772.10
pray 1030.12
petitionary 772.16
petitioner
supplicant 772.7
solicitor 828.7
petit larceny 822.2
petit mal 684.5
petits fours 306a.40
petkins 930.5
petrification 123.6
petrifaction 355.5
petrifactive 355.14
petrified
hardened 355.13
terrified 889.25
petrify harden 355.7
terrify 889.16
astound 918.5
petrography 382.9
petroleum, petrol
illuminant 334.20
oil 379.4
petrology 382.9
petter 929.11
petticoat
nouns waistcoat
230.14
woman 420.6
adjs. 420.14
pettifog 481.17
pettifogger 1001.3
pettifoggery 616.4
pettifogging 671.17
pettiness narrow-
mindedness 525.1
unimportance 671.1
niggardliness 850.2
meanness 913.3
unmagnanimousness
976.2
petting 930.1
pettish 949.21
petty narrow-minded
525.10
trivial 671.17
niggardly 850.10
mean 913.12
unmagnanimous
976.6
petty cash 833.18
petty larceny 822.2
petty officer 747.22
petulant 949.21
petulance, petulancy
949.5
peu de chose 671.6
pew
compartment 191.2
church ~ 1040.13

pewter, pewtery
382.16
pfennig 333.9
Phaeoplyceae 411.4
Phaëthon sun 374.11
   god 1012.5
phalansterianism,
   phalansterism
   743.5
phalanx company 74.3
   military unit 798.19
phallic(al) 418.18
phallus 418.8
phantasize 533.14
phantasm, phantasma
   illusion 518.4
   phantom 1015.1
phantasmagoria 445.6
phantasmal
   illusory 518.9
   fanciful 533.22
phantasmic 518.9
phantast 533.12
phantasy
   illusion 518.4
   fancy 533.1,5
phantom
   nouns illusion 518.4
   specter 1015.1
   adjs. 1015.7
phantomic(al), phan-
   tomlike 1015.7
Pharaoh 747.9
pharisaic(al)
   hypocritical 614.33
   sanctimonious
   1027.5
Pharisaism 1018.10
pharisaism
   hypocrisy 614.6
   sanctimony 1027.1
Pharisee
   religionist 1018.19
   pietist 1027.3
pharisee
   hypocrite 617.8
   pietist 1027.3
pharmaceutic(al)
   685.43
pharmaceutics 685.29
pharmaceutist,
   pharmacist 685.30
pharmacology 685.29
pharmacon 685.4
pharmacopedia, phar-
   macopoeia 685.32
pharmacoposia 685.5
pharmacopsychosis
   472.3
pharmacotherapy
   687.3
pharmacy
   pharmacology
   685.29
   drugstore 685.31
pharos
   watchtower 438.8
   landmark 566.9
pharyngitis 634.12
pharyngoplasty 687.27
pharynx 395.15

phase aspect 445.3
   caprice 627.1
phasis 445.3
pheasant 306a.22
phelloderm 228.2
phenomenal
   extraordinary 85.13
   eventful 150.10
   wonderful 918.9
phenomenon
   event 150.2
   appearance 445.5
   wonder 918.2
pheon 567.2
philander
   nouns love-making
   930.9
   philanderer 930.11
   verbs 930.18
philanderer 930.11
philanthropic(al)
   936.16
philanthropism,
   philanthropy 936.4
philanthropist 936.8
philatelist 74.14
philharmonic
   nouns concert 461.34
   music lover 463.23
   adjs. 461.48
philippic 967.8
Philistine
   nouns conformist
   82.2
   enemy 927.6
   adjs. 476.15
Philistinism 476.6
philologer, philologian
   578.12
philologic(al) 578.15
philology 578.11
philomel 463.15
philosoph, phiosophe
   sophist 482.6
   philosopher 499.7
philosophaster 482.6
philosophastry 482.1
philosopheme 481.8
philosopher
   sophist 482.6
   philosophizer
   499.7,13
   names of ~ 499.14
philosophers' stone
   panacea 685.3
   wealth 835.4
philosophic(al)
   of philosophy 499.9
   unruffled 856.12
philosophical 466.18
Philosophical Pleiad
   467.4
philosophicohistorical,
   philosophicoju-
   ristic, philosophi-
   colegal, etc. 499.9
philosophism 482.1,3
philosophist 482.6
philosophistic(al)
   sophistical 482.14
   philosophical 499.9

philosophize 481.15
philosophizer 499.7
philosophling 482.6
philosophy
   sophistry 482
   thought 499
   types of ~ 499.12
   manual 603.9
   equanimity 856.3
philter
   aphrodisiac 418.6
   love charm 1034.5
phiz, phizog
   face 239.4
   physiognomy 445.4
phlebitis 684.8
phlebotomist 686.8
phlebotomy 687.28
Phlegethon 1017.4
phlegm mucus 387.3
   lethargy 706.5
   apathy 854.4
phlegmatic
   nouns 416.5
   adjs. 706.18
phlegmatic(al) 854.13
phobia fear 889.1
   types of ~ 889.34
Phoebe five 99.1
   moon 374.9
Phoebus, Phoebus
   Apollo sun 374.11
   god 1012.5
Phoenician 579.5
phoenix mythical
   monster 85.20
   a beauty 898.8
   paragon 983.5
Pholidota 414.12
phon 449.11
phonate 449.12
phonation
   sounding 449.6
   utterance 592.3
phone
   nouns types of ~
   447.18
   speech sound 449.5
   telephone 558.5
   syllable 579.6
   verbs 558.21
phone book
   telephone 558.14
   book 603.6
   directory 746.9
phone call 558.15
phoneme 449.5
phonemics 578.11
phoner 558.13
phonetic
   nouns 579.3
   adjs. phonic 449.18
   spoken 592.20
phonetician,
   phoneticist 449.10
phonetic law 449.9
phonetics
   phonics 449.9
   spelling 579.7
phonetism 449.9
phonetist 449.10

phonic
   auditory 447.14
   sounded 449.13
   acoustic(al) 449.16
   phonetic 449.18
   spoken 592.20
phonics 449.7,9
phonoglyph,
   phonogram 579.3
phonograph
   graphophone 464.18
   character 579.3
phonographer
   phonetist 449.10
   stenographer 600.17
phonographic(al)
   600.28
phonograph record
   464.19
phonography
   phonetics 449.9
   spelling 579.7
   stenography 600.9
phonologist 578.12
phonology
   phonetics 449.9
   lexicology 580.13
   pronunciation 592.6
phony
   nouns fake 614.13
   impostor 617.6
   hypocrite 617.8
   adjs. 614.27
Phoronidea 414.6
phosphate 164.4
phosphatize 378.6
Phosphor 374.5
phosphoresce 334.26
phosphorescence
   334.13
phosphorescent
   334.37
phosphoric, phos-
   phorous 382.16
Phosphorus 374.5
photic 334.40
photics 334.22
photo
   nouns 575.3
   verbs 575.16
   adjs. 575.19
photoactinic 334.40
photocell 342.12
photoconduction
   341.13
photodisintegration
   325.8
photodrama 609.15
photoelectricity
   electricity 341.1
   electronics 342.1
photoelectric tube
   electronics 342.12
   types of ~ 342.17
photoelectronics
   342.1
photoemission 344.4
photoengrave 576.14
photoengraver 577.8
photoengraving
   576.3,8

pigeon
  nouns fowl 306a.22
    dupe 618.1
  verbs 616.13
pigeon English 578.10
pigeonhearted 890.10
pigeonhole
  nouns class 61.2
    recess 191.3
    small place 195.3
    holes 264.4
  verbs classify 61.6
    file 88.7
    postpone 132.8
    put aside 666.6
    ~ a bill 740.20
pigeon post
  mail carrier 559.6
    mail 602.5
piggish porcine 413.41
    greedy 632.28
    filthy 680.26
    gluttonous 992.7
piggy 413.11
piggy bank 834.13
pigheaded
    stupid 468.17
    obstinate 624.8
pig in a poke
    uncertainty 513.8
    gamble 514.2
    bargain 825.5
  BUY A PIG IN A POKE
    chance 514.18
    mismanage 732.14
    be rash 892.5
pig Latin 578.6
pigman 415.3
pigment
  nouns color 361.7
    whites 363.12
    blacks 364.13
    grays 365.5
    browns 366.5,6
    reds, pinks 367.13, 14
    oranges 368.3
    yellows 369.7
    greens 370.6
    blues 371.4
    purples 372.4
  verbs 361.13
pigmentary 361.16
pigmentation 361.10
pignus 770.2
pignus judiciale,
    pignus legale 770.6
pigpen, pigsty
    hovel 190.10
    filthy place 680.11
pigs' feet, pigs'
    knuckles 306a.16
pigskin sphere 254.2
    football 876.16
pigsticker 347.2
pigtail hair 229.7
    tail 240.5
    tobacco 433.8
Pigwiggen 195.6

pike
  nouns mountaintop 206.8
    spike 257.4
    turnpike 655.6
  verbs leave 300.9
    gamble 514.19
    shirk 629.9
pikeman 798.7
piker tramp 273.3
    gambler 514.16
    shirker 629.3
pikestaff 216.2
pilaster tower 206.11
    pillar 216.5
pile
  nouns large amount 34.4
    heap 74.9
    stake 216.7
    hair 229.2
    awn 229.9
    down 229.19
    tower 244.2
    atomic ~ 325.12
    texture 350.1
    leaf 410.17
    insignia 567.2
    wealth 835.2
  verbs fill 56.7
    heap 74.18
    load 183.16
  PILE IN 313.12
  PILE IT ON
    talk big 599.6
    exaggerate 615.3
    overdo 661.12
  PILE OUT 711.5
  PILE UP
    heap 74.18
    shipwreck 274.44
    exaggerate 615.3
    store up 658.11
  PILE UP TO 54.7
pile dweller 397.2
pileous 229.24
piles
    large amount 34.4
    sore 684.28
pile-up 727.2
pilfer
  nouns 822.1
  verbs 822.13
pilferer 823.1
pilgarlic 984.2
pilgrim
  nouns traveler 273.1
    religious 1036.16
  verbs 272.20
pilgrimage
  nouns 272.5
  verbs 272.20
pill cigarette 433.5
    medicine 685.6
    bore 882.4
pillage
  nouns plundering 822.5
    booty 822.11
  verbs 822.15
pillager 823.6

pillar stability 142.7
    tower 206.11
    post 216.5
    cylinder 254.4
    monument 568.11
    protection 697.4
pillarist, pillar saint
    recluse 922.5
    religious 1036.16
pillar of society
    personage 670.8
    worthy 983.3
pillar of the church
    worthy 983.3
    pietist 1026.4
Pillars of Hercules 566.9
pillbox 797.6
pillory
  nouns 1009.3
  verbs stigmatize 913.9
    punish 1008.10
pillow
  nouns cushion 215.21
    softness 356.5
  verbs 215.22
pillowcase, pillow slip 227.11
pilon 816.5
pilose 229.24
pilosis, pilosism, pilosity 229.1
pilot
  nouns operator 163.4
    steersman 275.8
    aviator 278.1
    cowatcher 697.3
    guider 746.6
    clergyman 1036.2
  verbs operate 163.5
    navigate 274.14
    ~ a plane 277.43
    guide 745.9
pilotage
    navigation 274.4
    contact flying 277.1
    guidance 745.1
    fee 844.7
pilot biscuit 306a.29
pilot burner, pilot light 328.10
pilotship
    navigation 274.4
    airmanship 277.3
pilous 229.24
pilpul 481.5
pilpulist 481.13
pilpulistic 481.20
pily 350.7
pimp
  nouns 987.18
  verbs 987.21
pimple
    swelling 255.4
    boil 684.28
pin
  nouns fastener 48.7
    stopper 265.4
    axle 320.5
    trifle 671.5

    ornament 899.6
  verbs 47.8
  PIN DOWN 758.10
  PIN ON
    attribute to 154.3
    accuse 1003.7
pinafore 230.17
pinakotheke, pinacotheca 658.9
Pinales 411.8
pin and web 684.11
pinball 514.7
pince-nez 442.2
pincers 811.4
pinch
  nouns crisis 129.4
    small place 195.3
    squeeze 197.2
    pang 423.2
    exigency 637.4
    urgency 670.4
    strait 729.4
    crux 729.7
    arrest 759.6
    theft 822.10
  DO IN A PINCH 659.4
  verbs squeeze 197.8
    sail 274.27
    pain 423.7
    arrest 759.16
    steal 822.13
    scrimp 850.7
pinchbeck
  nouns sham 614.13
    frippery 899.3
  adjs. 614.27
pinched thin 204.19
    straitened 729.24
    poor 836.7
pinchfist, pinchgut 850.5
pinchgut money, pinchgut pay 660.5
pinch-hit 148.5
pinch hitter
    substitute 148.2
    deputy 779.1
pinching
  nouns theft 822.1
    parsimony 850.1
  adjs. cold 332.15
    niggardly 850.12
pin curl 229.5
Pindaric 607.21
pinder 306a.38
pindling puny 35.7
    delicate 159.14
    little 195.9
    piddling 671.17
pine
  nouns saddle 215.19
    needle 257.8
  verbs weaken 159.9
    sicken 684.35
    deteriorate 690.19
    grieve 870.17
  PINE FOR 632.16
pineapple
    fruit 306a.50
    bomb 799.15
pine cone cone 254.5

erect 212.8
slope 218.10
sail 274.58
throw 284.12
fall 314.5
topple 314.8
plunge 318.6
sway 322.9
flounder 323.15
PITCH IN
begin 68.6
eat 306.17
set to work 714.15
PITCH INTO
undertake 713.3
set to work 714.15
fight 794.15
attack 796.15
PITCH UPON
meet 199.11
arrive at 299.7
decide upon 635.13
pitch and toss 514.7
pitch-black, pitch-dark
dark 336.14
black 364.8
pitched 218.15
pitcher 284.8
pitchfork
nouns 347.9
verbs 284.12
pitchhole cavity 256.3
recess 256.7
pitchman 828.7
pitch pipe 464.26
pitchy
pitch-dark 336.14
black 364.8
resinous 380.3
piteous 862.11
piteously 34.25
pitfall 616.11
pith gist 5.2
substance 193.4
center 225.2
meaning 543.1
pluck 622.3
main point 670.6
courage 891.5
pithless
enervated 157.19
weak 159.12
pithy soft 356.11
pulpy 389.6
epigrammatic 516.6
meaningful 543.10
concise 590.4
pitiable terrible 673.9
grievous 862.10
pitiably 862.18
pitiful paltry 671.18
terrible 673.9
shameful 913.11
compassionate 942.7
pitiless 943.3
pit man
theaterman 609.27
stockbroker 831.10
pittance
small amount 35.2
insufficiency 660.5

share 814.5
allowance 814.6
donation 816.6
pitted 256.17
pitter-patter
nouns repetitiousness
103.4
pulsation 322.3
flutter 323.4
patter 454.1
trepidation 855.4
verbs flutter 323.12
patter 454.4
adjs. 454.7
pittites 447.6
pituitary 310.9
pituite 387.3
pituitous 388.13
pity
nouns compassion
942
abomination 957.2
HAVE PITY 942.4
verbs 942.3
pitying 942.7
pivot
nouns joint 47.4
center 225.2
fulcrum 286.3
axle 320.5
verbs turn round
294.9
turn 320.9
pivotal 225.12
pixilate 472.22
pixilated 472.27
pixilation 472.1
pixy mischief-maker
736.3
elf 1012.15
imp 1014.8
pizzicato
nouns 461.31
adjs. 461.54
P.J's 230.21
placability 802.1
placable
appeasable 802.14
forgiving 945.6
placard
nouns 557.7
verbs 557.15
placate 802.7
placation 802.1,2
placative, placatory
802.12
place
nouns state 7.1
rank 29.2
turn 108.2
opportunity 129.2
region 179
plaza 182.7
location 183.1
stead 183.5
abode 190.1
dive 190.24
job 654.3,5
street 655.6
trysting ~ 920.8

~ of torment
1017.1
~ of worship
1040.1
GIVE PLACE 294.6
GIVE PLACE TO
substitute 148.4
avoid 629.6
HAVE ITS PLACE 183.9
IN ALL PLACES 178.11
IN ITS PLACE 148.12
IN PLACE 183.21
IN PLACE OF 148.12
IN PLACES
scatteringly 75.13
sparsely 102.8
here and there
183.26
IN THE FIRST PLACE
chiefly 36.19
first 68.16
MAKE PLACE 264.13
NO PLACE 186.16
OUT OF PLACE
inapt 27.7
disorderly 62.12
unconforming 83.7
misplaced 184.10
inexpedient 669.5
PLACE WHERE ONE
HANGS HIS HAT
190.3
TAKE THE PLACE OF
148.6
verbs arrange 60.8
classify 61.6
attribute 154.2
locate 183.11
put 183.12
repose 183.14
recognize 535.13
instate 778.11
invest in 834.16
impose 961.4
PLACE AT ONE'S
DISPOSAL 771.4
PLACE A VALUE ON
assess 493.9
price 844.13
PLACE BEFORE 239.9
PLACE CONFIDENCE
IN 500.12
PLACE IN JUXTA-
POSITION 490.4
PLACE IN ONE'S WAY
771.4
PLACE IN STATU
QUO 692.11
PLACE ITSELF 59.4
PLACE UPON
attribute to 154.3
apply 961.6
placed arranged 60.13
classified 61.8
located 183.19
placeman 747.17
placement
classification 61.1
attribution 154.1
location 183.1
putting 183.6

recognition 535.5
instatement 778.3
placenta 67.3
Placentalia, placentals
414.12
placer 382.6
placid
quiescent 267.10
inexcitable 856.12
placidity
quiescence 267.1
mental ~ 856.2
placidly
quiescently 267.16
composedly 856.16
placing 183.6
placket 264.4
plafond 227.6
plagal cadence 462.22
plagal mode 462.10
plagiarism 822.7
plagiarist, plagiarizer
823.10
plagiarize 822.17
plagiarizing 822.7
plague
nouns infestation
311.2
bane 674.1
epidemic 684.4
A PLAGUE UPON!
970.11
verbs infest 311.6
importune 772.12
torment 864.19
harass 864.21
worry 888.4
plagued
infested 311.11
tormented 864.27
worried 888.7
plaguer 864.10
plaguesome 862.13
plaguily 34.26
plaguing
nouns 772.3
adjs. importunate
772.18
annoying 862.13
worrying 888.9
plaguy
adjs. difficult 729.17
annoying 862.13
advs. 34.26
plaid
nouns 373.4
adjs. 373.14
plaided 373.14
plaidoyer 481.6
plain
nouns desert 165.2
level land 386
adjs. mere 35.9
unmixed 45.5
absolute 56.11
homely 190.28
plane 213.8
champaign 386.3
clearly seen 443.7
audible 449.15
intelligible 546.10

optionally 635.24
  at command 764.4
WITH PLEASURE
  willingly 620.8
  happily 863.16
pleasure-giving 861.5
pleasure-loving
  nouns 863.4
  adjs. 863.15
pleasure-, pleasure
  seeker 876.19
pleasure trip 272.5
pleat
  nouns 263.2
  verbs braid 221.7
  fold 263.5
pleb 917.7
plebe, pleb 564.5
plebeian
  nouns 917.7
  adjs. vulgar
   896.10–15
  ignoble 917.11
plebeianism 896.5
plebiscite vote 635.5
  referendum 740.18
  politics 742.18
plectron, plectrum
  464.25
pledge
  nouns vow 521.3
  promise 768.1
  security 770.2
  toast 994.9
  joiner 786.11
HELD IN PLEDGE
  770.16
TAKE THE PLEDGE
  990.8
  verbs promise 768.4
  give security 770.12
  obligate 960.11
  toast 994.35
pledged
  promised 768.8
  as earnest 770.15
pledget 685.28
pledging 819.1
pleiad 325.5
Pleiades 1012.16
Pleistocene Age
  107.10
plenary great 34.8
  full 56.12
  unlimited 760.24
plenary council 753.5
plenilune 374.8
plenipotentiary
  nouns 779.6
  adjs. 156.12
plenitude fullness 56.2
  plenty 659.2
IN THE PLENITUDE
  OF POWER 158.19
plenteous fertile 164.9
  plentiful 659.7
plentiful
  abundant 101.9
  fertile 164.9
  plenteous 659.7

superabundant
  661.20
plentifully
  abundantly 659.9
  superabundantly
  661.25
plenty
  nouns large amount
  34.4
  abundance 659.2
  superabundance
  661.2
  adjs. 659.6,7
  advs. considerably
  34.17
  abundantly 659.9
plenum assembly 74.2
  universe 374.1
pleny 56.12
pleonasm
  reiteration 103.3
  diffuseness 591.1
pleonastic 591.11
plethora repletion 56.2
  overfullness 661.3
  satiety 662.1
plethoric
  inflated 196.12
  overfull 661.21
pleura 228.3
pleurisy, pleuritis
  684.12
pleuritic 684.46
pleuron 241.1
plexiform 220.11
plexure, plexus 220.3
pliability
  pliancy 356.2
  teachability 562.5
  compliance 763.3
pliable
  influenceable 171.15
  pliant 356.9
  teachable 562.18
  compliant 763.13
pliably 763.18
pliancy
  pliability 356.2
  unstrictness 756.2
  compliance 763.3
pliant
  influenceable 171.15
  pliable 356.9
  unstrict 756.5
  compliant 763.13
pliantly 763.18
plica 263.1
plicate
  verbs 263.5
  adjs. 263.7
plicated 263.7
plication, plicature
  fold 263.1
  folding 263.4
pliers 304.8
plight
  nouns condition 7.1
  predicament 729.4
  promise 768.1
  verbs 768.4
PLIGHT FAITH 768.6

PLIGHT ONE'S HONOR
  768.4
PLIGHT ONE'S TROTH
  768.4,6
plighted 768.8
plighted bride 931.6
plighted faith,
  plighted love
  768.3
Plimsoll mark 489.7
plinth 215.8
plod go slow 269.7
  walk 272.27
  persevere 623.3
  drudge 714.14
plodder 716.3
plodding
  drudging 714.18
  dull 881.6
plop
  verbs put 183.13
  come down 314.6
  plunge 318.6
  bubble 404.4
PLOP DOWN
  deposit 183.15
  come down 314.6
  advs. suddenly 113.9
  directly 289.26
plot
  nouns tract 179.4
  plain 386.1
  field 412.9
  story ∼ 606.9
  script 609.25
  scheme 652.3,6
  verbs partition 49.18
  scheme 652.10
  plan 652.11
plotted 652.13
plotter 652.8
plotting 652.6,14
plough 723.16
plow
  nouns 723.7
  verbs furrow 262.3
  aviate 277.46
  cultivate 412.17
PLOW THE DEEP
  274.57
plowboy 412.5
plow horse 413.18
plowing 412.13
plowman 412.5
pluck
  nouns jerk 285.3
  spunk 622.3
  flunk 723.7
  courage 891.5
  verbs divest 231.5
  jerk 285.5
  harvest 412.19
  strum 461.41
  swindle 616.18
  flunk 723.16
  fleece 820.21
PLUCK BY THE
  BEARD
  defy 791.3
  insult 963.4

PLUCK OUT 304.9
PLUCK UP BY THE
  ROOTS 691.14
PLUCK UP HEART
  891.13
pluckless
  spiritless 634.6
  apathetic 854.13
  uncourageous
  890.11
plucky resolute 622.14
  courageous 891.18
plug
  nouns stopper 265.4
  blow 282.4
  commercial 343.23
  hydrant 395.12
  horse 413.16
  tobacco 433.8
  publicity 557.4
  wreck 690.9
  commendation
  966.3
  verbs stop up 265.7
  trudge 269.7
  strike 282.14
  shoot 284.13
  publicize 557.15
  persevere 623.3
  drudge 714.14
  commend 966.11
PLUG IN 341.23
plugged 265.11
plugger 557.9
plugs 43.1
plug-ugly 941.4
plum
  nouns good thing
  672.5
  political ∼ 742.37
  dividend 832.7
  money 833.8
  adjs. 212.11
  advs. 212.13
plumage 229.18
plumate 229.28
plumb
  nouns vertical 212.2
  vertical gauge 212.6
  weight 351.6
  verbs take soundings
  208.8
  make perpendicular
  212.9
  seal 265.6
  delve into 484.30
  fathom 486.2
  measure 489.11
  adjs. utter 56.11
  perpendicular
  212.11
  advs. quite 56.16
  perpendicularly
  212.13
  directly 289.26
plumbago 379.2
plumb bob 212.6
plumbing 657.4
plumbless 208.10
plumb line 212.6

plumb-line
 take soundings
  208.8
 plumb 212.9
plumb rule 212.6
plumcot 44.8
plume
 nouns 229.16
 verbs preen 679.19
  decorate 899.8
 PLUME ONESELF ON
  903.5
plumed
 feathered 229.28
 ornamented 899.10
plumelike 229.27
plume of smoke 400.1
plummet
 nouns plumb 212.6
  weight 351.6
 verbs 318.6
plumose 229.28
plump
 nouns 451.3
 verbs put 183.13
  fatten 196.8
  come down 314.6
  plunge 318.6
  vote 635.15
 PLUMP DOWN
  deposit 183.15
  come down 314.6
 PLUMP UPON 199.11
 adjs. full 56.12
  corpulent 194.18
 advs. suddenly 113.9
  directly 289.26
plumper 635.5
plumpness 194.8
plumule
 feather 229.16
 bud 410.21
plumy 229.27
plunder
 nouns plundering
  822.5
  booty 822.11
 verbs fleece 820.21
  pillage 822.15
plunderbund
 graft 742.35
 league 786.1
plunderer 823.6
plundering
 nouns 822.5
 adjs. 822.21
plunderous 822.21
plunge
 nouns dash 268.4
  dive 318
  flounder 323.8
  gamble 514.1
  swimming pool
  679.11
  difficulty 729.4
  speculation 831.19
 verbs sail 274.58
  fall 314.5
  dive 318.6
  flounder 323.15
  gravitate 351.15

bet 514.19
 be precipitate 707.7
 speculate 831.23
PLUNGE IN
 insert 303.6
 stab 796.27
PLUNGE INTO
 begin 68.6
 study 562.12
 be willing 620.3
 be precipitate 707.7
 undertake 713.3
 set to work 714.15
plunger diver 318.4
 gambler 514.16
 speculator 831.11
plunging 318.3
plunk
 nouns blow 282.4
  thud 451.3
 verbs put 183.13
  strike 282.14
  plunge 318.6
  croak 459.5
  strum 461.41
 PLUNK DOWN 183.15
 advs. suddenly 113.9
  directly 289.26
plunks 833.2
pluperfect 119.6;
  584.10
plural 100.7
 THE PLURAL 100.1
pluralism
 plurality 100.1
 philosophy 499.6
plurality
 pluralness 100
 majority 100.2
 multitude 101.3
pluralization 100.3
pluralize 100.5
plural system 742.18
plural vote 635.5
plurative 100.7
plurification 100.3
plurify 100.5
plus
 nouns addition 40.2
  adjunct 41.1
  surplus 661.5
 verbs 40.3
 adjs. additional 40.9
  electropositive
  341.32
 advs. 40.10
plush 902.21
plushness 902.5
plushy 377.9
plus sign 40.2
Pluto planet 374.6
 Olympic gods
  1012.5
 gods 1017.5
plutocracy 835.5
plutocrat
 capitalist 743.13
 rich man 835.6
plutocratic 743.22
plutology 849.4

Plutonian, Plutonic
 1017.6
plutonium bomb
 799.16
Plutus 835.7
pluvial 393.10
**pluviograph, pluvi-
  ometer, pluvio-
  scope** 393.7
**pluviography, pluvi-
  ometry** 393.8
pluvious 393.10
ply
 nouns lamina 226.2
  fold 263.1
 verbs fold 263.5
  navigate 274.13
  sail 274.27,32
  handle 424.6
  urge 646.14
  employ 663.10
  exert 714.8
  urge upon 771.9
  importune 772.12
 PLY A TRADE 825.11
 PLY ONE'S TRADE
  654.12
plying urging 646.5
 importunity 772.3
plywood 226.2
P.M., p.m. 134.1
pneuma
 life force 406.3
 soul 1032.17
pneumatic tire 252.4
 pneumatological
  346.13
 airy 401.13
pneumatics
 aviation 277.2
 mechanics 346.5
pneumatogram 556.4
**pneumatology, pneu-
  matonomy** 346.5
pneumatometer 400.6
pneumatotherapy
 687.3
pneumonectomy
 687.25
pneumonia 684.12
pneumonic
 pulmonic 224.12
 diseased 684.46
pneumonotomy
 687.26
poach cook 329.4
 steal 822.13
poached
 bulged 255.15
 cooked 329.6
poacher 823.1
poaching
 cooking 329.1
 theft 822.1
poachy 399.3
pock
 nouns blemish 677.1
  pustule 684.28
 verbs 256.14
pocked 256.17

pocket
 nouns bag 192.2
  garment part 230.66
  hollow 256.2
  air ~ 277.38
  funds 833.14
  purse 834.14
 GO INTO ONE'S
  POCKET 817.8
 IN ONE'S POCKET
  762.13
 OUT OF POCKET
  lacking 660.11
  bereft 810.8
  poor 836.7
 verbs load 183.16
  hem in 235.5
  ~ a bill 740.20
  receive 817.6
  take 820.11
  tolerate 859.7
 POCKET THE AFFRONT
  tolerate 859.7
  forgive 945.4
 adjs. 195.11
pocketbook
 notebook 568.10
 book 603.10
 purse 834.14
pocket money 833.18
pocket-sized 195.11
pocket veto
 veto 740.17
 negative 776.2
pockmark
 nouns indentation
  256.6
 blemish 677.1
 verbs 256.14
pock-marked 256.17
**pococurante, poco-
  curantish** 634.6
pod
 nouns bag 192.2
  belly 192.3
  seedcase 410.28
 verbs 231.9
podagra, podagric
 684.8
podesta 1000.2
podex 240.4
podginess
 corpulence 194.8
 stubbiness 202.2
podgy stout 194.18
 stubby 202.10
podiatrist 686.7
podiatry 686.2
podites 272.16
podium 215.13
poecilonym
 synonym 14.3
 word 580.3
poecilonymic 14.7
poecilonymy 14.1
poem verse 607.4
 beauty 898.7
poesy
 nouns poetry 607.1
  poetic works 607.6

muse 607.12
verbs 607.19
poet, poetaster 607.13
poetastery, poetastry,
   poetcraft 607.7
poetastic(al) 607.21
poet-dramatist 607.16
poethood 607.18
poetic(al)
   fanciful 533.24
   lyrical 607.21
poetic imagination
   533.2
poeticize 607.19
poetic justice 974.1
poetic license 607.7
poetic prose 608.1
poetics poetry 607.1
   prosody 607.7
poeticule 607.13
poetic works 607.6
poetize 607.19
poetizer 607.13
poet-king 607.16
poet laureate 607.15
poet-laureateship
   607.18
poetry 607
poetryless 608.5
poet-warrior 607.16
poetwise 607.21
pogrom 408.3
poignancy
   acrimony 160.4
   pungency 432.1
   eloquence 598.4
poignant
   acrimonious 160.12
   sharp 257.11
   keenly sensitive
     421.14
   painful 423.10
   pungent 432.6
   eloquent 598.12
   deep-felt 853.25
poikilothermic 332.20
poilu 798.8
point
   nouns circumstance
     8.2
   degree 29.1
   small amount 35.2
   halfway ~ 69.2
   end 70.2
   integer 89.4
   ~ of time 107.1
   stop 144.4
   acrimony 160.4
   location 183.1
   minute thing 195.7
   mountaintop 206.8
   summit 210.2
   breakwater 215.4
   angle 250.2
   ~ of land 255.8
   sharp ~ 257.4
   types of ~ 257.19
   direction 289.1
   ~ of the compass
     289.3
   topic 483.1

significance 543.1
tip 555.3
dot 566.4
sculptor's ~ 573.5
etcher 576.11
punctuation 584.11
objective 651.2
salient ~ 670.6
~ of joke 879.6
AT ALL POINTS 56.18
AT THE POINT OF
   about to 121.13
   near 199.22
AT THE POINT OF A
   GUN 754.12
COME TO A POINT
   focus 225.11
   be sharp 257.9
   converge 297.2
COME TO THE POINT
   particularize 80.10
   speak plainly 589.2
   be brief 590.3
GIVE POINTS
   handicap 30.7
   give advantage
     36.12
GIVE POINTS TO
   555.10
IN POINT
   apropos 9.8
   apt 26.18
IN POINT OF FACT
   actually 1.16
   truly 515.16
MAKE A POINT OF
   stipulate 506.4
   resolve 622.7
   demand 751.6,7
   contend for 794.21
MAKE ONE'S POINT
   722.7
ON THE POINT 234.15
ON THE POINT OF
   about to 121.13
   near 199.22
TO THE POINT
   apropos 9.8
   apt 26.18
   plainly 589.4
   concise 590.4
   salient 670.20
   verbs tend 173.3
   sharpen 257.10
   direct 289.6,8
   gravitate 351.15
   punctuate 584.12
POINT AT
   direct to 528.10
   indicate 566.17
   ridicule 965.8
POINT OFF 566.18
POINT OUT
   specify 80.9
   direct to 528.10
   indicate 566.17
POINT OUT TO 289.7
POINT TO
   attribute to 154.3
   tend 173.3
   direct 289.6

evidence 504.9
foretoken 542.9
imply 544.4
indicate 566.17
POINT UP 670.13
point-blank
   adjs. 515.19
   advs. directly 289.26
   plainly 589.4
point d'appui 286.3
pointed
   remarkable 34.10
   angular 250.6
   sharp 257.12
   epigrammatic 516.6
   significant 543.10
   concise 590.4
   emphasized 670.22
pointedly
   remarkably 34.23
   concisely 590.5
   intentionally 651.11
pointedness
   sharpness 257.1
   conciseness 590.1
pointer dog 413.27
   tip 555.3
   sign 566.3
Point Four 742.6
point in question
   topic 483.1
   question 484.13
pointless blunt 258.3
   dull 881.6
point of departure
   300.5
point of etiquette
   644.3
point of honor 972.2
point of order 740.15
point of view
   viewpoint 438.7
   attitude 523.2
point tenses 584.10
point-to-point race
   794.12
poise
   nouns equality 30.1
   equanimity 856.3
   verbs equalize 30.7
   hover 313.10
   weigh 351.10
   ballast 351.12
   measure 489.11
poised
   equiponderant
     30.10
   composed 856.13
poison
   nouns venom 674.3
   types of ~ 674.6
   liquor 994.15
   verbs radioactivate
     326.9
   kill 408.13
   infect 684.39
   corrupt 690.12
poisoned
   radioactive 326.10
   infected 684.45

poisoning
   killing 408.1
   infection 684.23
   corruption 690.2
   execution 1008.7
poisonous 682.5
poisonousness 682.2
poisonous plants
   674.7
poison-pen letter
   602.3
poisson 306a.24
poitrine d'agneau
   306a.15
poitrine de veau
   306a.14
poke
   nouns bag 192.2
   slow goer 269.5
   prod 282.2
   blow 282.4
   yoke 657.5
   purse 834.14
   verbs yoke 47.10
   go slow 269.6
   prod 282.12
   strike 282.14
   search 484.25
   goad 646.15
   potter 706.12
POKE AROUND
   search 484.25
   grope 484.26
POKE AT 796.17
POKE INTO 484.30
POKE ONE'S NOSE IN
   237.7
POKE OUT 255.9
POKE UP THE FIRE
   328.21
poker 328.15
poker dice 514.8
pokerish 355.11
pokey, poky
   inconsiderable 35.7
   dowdy 62.14
   little 195.9
   slow 269.10
   petty 671.17
   shabby 690.31
   dull 881.6
   mean 913.12
pokily, pokingly
   269.13
pokiness
   littleness 195.1
   slowness 269.1
   pettiness 671.1
   dullness 881.1
   meanness 913.3
poking 269.10
pokunt 1012.10
polar opposite 238.5
   electropolar 341.28
polar data 348.19
polar front 332.4
polaric 238.5
Polaris star 374.5
   guiding star 746.7

polarity
oppositeness 15.1
duality 90.1
contraposition 238.1
electricity 341.8
polarization
contraposition 238.1
electricity 341.8
polarize 238.4
polar lights, polar ray 334.16
polar star star 374.5
guiding star 746.7
pole
nouns shaft 216.1
beam 216.3
opposite 238.2
tail 240.5
mast 276.13
oar 276.15
axle 320.5
electric ~ 341.8
verbs 284.10
polecat animal 413.4
stinker 436.3
scoundrel 984.6
pol-econ 742.2
polemic 481.13
polemic(al)
argumentative 481.20
contentious 949.26
polemicist, polemist 481.13
polemics 481.5
polestar
center of attraction 225.4
magnet 287.3
star 374.5
guiding star 746.7
pole vault 317.1
pole vaulter 317.4
pole vaulting 317.3
police
nouns 697.14,15
verbs tidy 60.11
guard 697.19
police court 999.3
policedom 697.16
police force 697.15
police magistrate 1000.4
policeman
constable 697.14
detective 779.10
police state 739.4
police station 759.9
police-up 60.5
police van 271.10
Polichinelle 610.9
policy
judiciousness 466.7
plan 652.5
political ~ 742.4
insurance ~ 769.3
policyholder 770.9
policy maker 744.7

polio, poliomyelitis 684.19
polish
nouns burnish 259.2,4
types of ~ 259.14
elegance 587.1
cultivation 689.3
refinement 895.1
good breeding 934.4
verbs burnish 259.7
rub 349.6
improve 689.10,11
POLISH OFF
end 70.7
kill 408.14
complete 720.4
POLISH THE APPLE 905.8
POLISH UP
refresh the memory 535.19
study up 562.14
improve 689.11
polished sleek 259.10
shiny 334.33
elegant 587.6
perfected 675.9
refined 895.9
well-bred 934.17
polishing 349.1
polisson 984.5
Politburo 743.4
polite 934.14
politeness 934.1
polite society 642.6
politic
judicious 466.19
tactful 491.8
cunning 733.12
political 742.47
cautious 893.8
political 742.47
political economy
politics 742.2
economics 849.4
political government 739.1
political science 742.2
politicaster 744.4
politician
crafty person 733.8
politico 744
politicize, politick 742.41
politicly 491.10
politico 744.1
politics
cunning 733.2
political affairs 742
polity state 180.1
community 416.2
policy 652.5
political ~ 742.4
polizia 697.15
polka 877.5
polka dot 566.4
poll
nouns roll 88.5
head 210.5
survey 484.16

vote 635.5
schedule 639.2
election 742.21,22
tax 844.11
verbs cut off 42.10
enumerate 87.10
canvass 484.38
enroll 568.15
vote 635.15
pollard
nouns 410.10
verbs prune 42.10
shorten 202.6
pollen
nouns 405.9
verbs 168.11
poller 484.17
pollex 424.5
pollinate 168.11
pollination, pollinization 168.4
pollinize 168.11
polliwog, pollyfrog
youngling 125.8
tadpole 413.32
poll-parrot, polly-parrot 22.4
polls 742.21
pollster 484.17
poll tax 844.11
pollute defile 680.19
corrupt 690.12
inebriate 994.28
pollution
defilement 680.4
infection 684.3
corruption 690.2
polly 22.4
Pollyanna 886.6
Pollyannaism 886.3
poloist 876.20
polonium 326.5
polo pony 413.13
poltergeist
spirit 1015.1
psychical 1032.6
poltroon
nouns 890.6
adjs. 890.12
poltroonery 890.3
polyandrist 931.12
polyandrium 409.15
polyandrous 931.20
polyandry 931.2
polychord 464.2
polychrest 685.3
polychromatic
chromatic 361.16
variegated 373.9
polychromatist 577.4
polychrome
nouns 373.1
verbs 373.7
adjs. variegated 373.9
pictorial 572.22
polychromize 373.7
polycoustic 449.16
polydipsia 632.7
polygamist 931.12
polygamous 931.20

polygamy 931.2
polyglot
nouns jargon 578.6
philologist 578.12
dictionary 603.7
adjs. 578.15
polyglottonist 578.12
polygon plaza 182.7
geometric figure 250.14
polygonal 250.12
polygonal numbers 86.2
polygraphic(al) 600.28
polygraphy 600.9
polygynist 931.12
polygynous 931.20
polygyny 931.2
polyhedral
many-sided 241.7
multiangular 250.12
polymer 377.7
Polymnia, Polyhymnia 463.24
polymorphic 19.3
polymorphism 19.1
polymorphous 19.3
Polynesian race 417.17
polynomial 100.8
polyp animal 414.4
sore 684.28
Polyphemus
strong man 158.6
giant 194.13
polyphonic
phonic 449.16
contrapuntal 461.53
polyphonism 461.20
polyphony
phonics 449.7
music 461.20
poly-sci 742.2
polysyllabic 579.12
polysyllabic profundity 599.1
polysyllable 579.6
polytechnic school 565.8
polytheism 1018.5
polytheist 1018.14
polytheistic 1018.23
polyvalence 378.3
polyvalent 378.8
polyvalent vaccine 685.23
Polyzoa 414.6
pom 413.24
pomade
nouns 379.3
verbs 379.8
pomander 435.6
pomato 44.8
pomatum 379.3
Pomeranian 413.24
pomme d'amour 306a.35
pomme de terre 306a.35

pommel
nouns 215.19
verbs strike 282.15
beat 1008.14

pommer 464.9

pomologist 411.2

pomology 411.1

Pomona 42.4

pomp parade 71.4
spectacle 445.7
ostentation 902.6

pompadour 229.22

**pomp and circum-
stance** 902.6

pomposity
grandiloquence
599.1
ostentatiousness
902.7

pompous
bombastic 599.10
ceremonious 644.8
ostentatious 902.22

pond sea 396.1
pool 397.1

ponder 477.11

ponderable
nouns tangible 3.2
weight 351.6
adjs. tangible 3.4
weighable 351.19

ponderation 351.9

pondering
nouns 477.2
adjs. 477.20

ponderous
bulky 194.19
weighty 351.17
inelegant 588.3
important 670.21
unwieldy 729.18
clumsy 732.20
dull 881.6

ponderously
heavily 351.21
unwieldily 729.27
clumsily 732.23
dully 881.10

pondlet 397.1

pondlike, pondly 397.4

pone 306a.28

poniard 796.27

ponies 272.16

pons 465.5

pons asinorum 729.6

pontiff 1036.8

pontifical
nouns 1038.12
adjs. 1035.15

pontificalia, pontificals
1039.1

pontificate
nouns 1035.6
verbs talk big 599.6
be pompous 902.14

pontification 902.7

Pontius Pilate 1000.6

pontoon float 276.11
bridge 655.10

pony
nouns diminutive
195.4
horse 413.13,19
translation 550.3
money 833.8
adjs. 195.11

pony up 839.16

pooch
nouns 413.24
verbs 255.10

pooh, pooh-pooh
nouns 965.3
verbs 965.9
interjs. nonsense!
469.12
ridicule! 965.16

pooh-pooh theory
580.15

pool pond 397.1
stakes 514.4
swimming ~ 679.11
cartel 786.9
stock market 831.17

pool hall 876.12

pool one's interests
league 52.4
co-operate 784.6

pool room
gambling 514.14
playroom 876.12

poonghie 1036.14

poop
nouns 240.6
verbs 715.4

POOP OUT
weaken 159.9
fatigue 715.4
tire 715.5
fail 723.12

pooped 715.8

poor feeble 159.15
thin 204.19
illogical 482.11
inauspicious 542.15
meager 660.8
paltry 671.18
inferior 678.10
sickly 684.40
unskillful 732.15
impoverished 836.7
humble 904.9
mean 913.12
unfavorable 967.22
POOR IN SPIRIT
904.10
THE POOR 836.3

poor bet 155.9

poor devil
poor man 836.4
sufferer 864.11
wretch 984.2

poor diction 588.1

poor excuse
pretext 647.1
excuse 1004.4

poor fist
writing 600.7
failure 723.1
bungle 732.5

poorhouse 698.4

poorish feeble 159.15
sickly 684.40

poorling 836.4

poor lookout
small chance 155.9
improbability 511.1

poorly
adjs. 684.40
advs. meagerly
660.13
inferiorly 678.13
unskillfully 732.22
meanly 913.17

poor man
beggar 772.8
poorling 836.4
bankrupt 840.4

poorness
thinness 204.5
paltriness 671.2
inferiority 678.3
poverty 836.1
humbleness 904.1
meanness 913.3

**Poor Richard's
Almanac** 114.7

poor-sighted 439.11

poor stick 732.7

poor whites 836.3

poose 257.7

pop
nouns father 169.9
beverage 306a.47
bang 455.3
popular music 461.8
concert 461.34
verbs bulge 255.10
bubble 404.4
bang 455.8
POP AT 796.23
POP IN
enter 301.7
insert 303.3
POP OFF 407.16
POP THE QUESTION
question 484.21
propose 930.22
POP UP
arrive 299.6
rise 313.9
appear 445.9
be unexpected 538.6
POP UPON 199.11
advs. 113.9

pope 1036.8

popedom 1035.6

popehood, popeship
737.6

popery, popeism
1018.7

pop-eyed 255.15

popinjay 901.9

popish
Catholic 1018.27
papal 1035.15

popliteal space 272.16

popover 306a.30

popping 455.11

poppycock
nouns 545.2
interjs. 469.12

poppycockish
absurd 469.10
nonsensical 545.10

pops 169.9

popskull 994.14

populace
inhabitants 189.1
people 416.2
THE POPULACE 917.2

popular
nouns 461.34
adjs. prevalent 79.11
usual 84.8
well-known 474.27
in demand 632.30
customary 640.14
fashionable 642.11
conventional 643.7
vulgar 896.14
famous 912.17
well-liked 929.21
secular 1037.3

popular belief
opinion 500.4
superstition 501.3

popular front 742.34

popularity
fashionableness
642.2
reputation 912.1
popular regard
929.1

popularization 896.8

popularize
explain 550.11
vulgarize 896.9

popular music 461.8

popular vote 635.5

populate 187.10

populated 187.13

population
peopling 187.2
inhabitants 189.1

populous
teeming 74.22
numerous 101.10
populated 187.13

porc 306a.16

porcelain 574.7

porch veranda 191.21
church ~ 1040.9

porcine 413.41

porcupine 413.4

pore opening 264.1
vent 302.9
duct 395.13

pore over
examine 484.31
study 562.12

porely 684.40

Porifera, poriferans
414.4

poriomania 472.12

pork meat 306a.16
pap 742.37

pork barrel
political ~ 742.38
boodle 822.11

pork-barrel legislation
742.35

pork chop 306a.19

porker 413.11
pornographic 988.9
pornography 988.4
porose 264.20
porosity 264.8
porous
  permeable 264.20
  exudative 302.20
porousness 264.8
porpoise
  nouns fat man
    194.12
  animal 413.33
  verbs 277.46
porraceous 370.4
porridge
  cereal 306a.34
  semiliquid 388.5
port
  nouns posture 183.4
  portside 243.1
  window 264.7
  airport 277.19
  destination 299.5
  mien 445.3
  haven 698.1,6
  demeanor 735.1
  IN PORT 696.6
  PORT OF EMBARKA-
    TION 300.5
  verbs 274.33
  adjs. 243.5
  advs. leftward 243.7
  larboard 274.72
  interjs. 274.80
portable 270.17
portage
  transportation 270.3
  charge 844.7
Portagee 417.9
portal
  vestibule 191.19
  entranceway 301.6
  AT THE PORTALS OF
    DEATH 407.27
portative 270.17
portcullis
  barrier 728.5
  fortification 797.4
  LET THE PORTCULLIS
    DOWN 698.7
porte-cochere 301.6
portemonnaie 834.14
portend 542.8
portent omen 542.2,5
  forewarning 701.2
portentous
  extraordinary 85.13
  ominous 542.13
porter bearer 270.5
  trainman 273.13
  doorkeeper 697.11
porterage 270.3
porter aux nues 966.12
portfire 330.4
portfolio
  bookholder 603.20
  authority 737.8
  securities 832.1
porthole holes 264.4
  window 264.7

portico
  vestibule 191.19
  colonnade 216.5
portion
  nouns quantity 28.2
  part 55.1
  piece 201.3
  fate 638.2
  dose 685.5
  share 814.5
  dowry 816.9
  verbs partition 49.18
  apportion 814.7
portly
  corpulent 194.18
  dignified 903.12
portmanteau 580.10
portrait
  lifelikeness 20.6
  picture 572.16
  description 606.1
portraitist 577.4
portraiture
  representation 570.1
  portrait 572.16
  description 606.1
portray
  represent 570.7,10
  picture 572.20
  describe 606.12
  enact 609.34
portrayal
  representation
    570.1,2
  portrait 572.16
  description 606.1
  drama 609.9
portrayer 577.2
portreeve 747.20
portside 243.1
portside flinger 243.3
portsider 243.4
port tack 243.1
Portuguese 417.9
posada 190.13
pose
  nouns position 183.4
  pretense 614.3
  affectation 901.3
  verbs put 183.12
  postulate 498.12
  puzzle 513.13
  propound 771.6
  attitudinize 901.13
POSE A QUESTION
    484.21
POSE AS
  impersonate 570.10
  pretend to be
    614.23
Poseidon
  sea god 396.4
  god 1012.5,17
poser puzzle 547.7
  attitudinarian 901.8
poseur 901.8
posit 498.12
posited 183.19
position state 7.1,5
  rank 29.2
  location 183.1

posture 183.4
  viewpoint 438.7
  premise 481.8
  supposition 498.2
  opinion 500.4
  affirmation 521.1
  mental attitude
    523.1,2
  remark 592.4
  job 654.3,5
  proposal 771.2
  prestige 912.4
IN POSITION 183.21
positional 183.20
positive
  nouns 575.5
  adjs. actual 1.15
  downright 34.14
  mathematics 86.8
  electropositive
    341.32
  convinced 500.18
  unqualified 507.2
  certain 512.13,21
  dogmatic 512.22
  exact 515.15
  assertive 521.7
  obstinate 624.13
  emphatic 670.22
  dictatorial 737.15
positively really 1.16
  absolutely 34.21
  certainly 512.23
  exactly 515.19
  yes 520.18
  affirmatively 521.8
positiveness
  certainty 512.1,5,6
  exactness 515.3
  obstinacy 624.5
positive pole 341.8
positivism
  materialism 375.5
  dogmatism 512.6
positivist
  materialist 375.6
  dogmatist 512.7
  obstinate person
    624.6
positivist(ic)
  philosophical 499.10
  dogmatic 512.22
positron 342.3
posologist 685.30
posology 685.29
posse company 74.3
  throng 74.4
  military unit 798.19
posse comitatus 74.3
possess dement 472.22
  obsess 472.23
  know 474.12
  have 806.5
  take 820.11
  demonize 1014.17
  haunt 1015.6
  bewitch 1034.10
POSSESS THE MIND
    500.17
possessed
  insane 472.27

obsessed 472.32
  owned 806.9
  haunted 1015.10
  bewitched 1034.14
BE POSSESSED OF THE
  DEVIL 949.13
LIKE ALL POSSESSED
  furiously 34.24
  swiftly 268.22
possession
  country 180.1
  insanity 472.1
  obsession 472.13
  self-possession 622.5
  possessing 806
  taking 820.1
  equanimity 856.3
  spirit control 1015.5
  bewitchment 1034.2
possessions
  property 808.1
  wealth 835.1
possessive
  nouns 584.7
  adjs. possessory
    806.11
  selfish 976.5
possessor 807
possessorship 806.2
possessory 806.11
possibility
  good ~ 155.7
  good chance 155.8
  bare ~ 155.9
  liability 174.1
  conceivability 470
  likelihood 510.1
  improbability 511.1
  latency 544.1
BY ANY POSSIBILITY
    508.10
WITHIN THE BOUNDS
  OF POSSIBILITY
  reasonably 481.23
  possible 508.6
possible
  nouns 508.1
  adjs. mathematical
    86.8
  liable 174.6
  conceivable 508.6
  likely 510.5
  plausible 510.6
  latent 544.5
HARDLY POSSIBLE
    511.3
NOT POSSIBLE 509.6
possibles 833.2
possibly 508.9
possum
  nouns 413.4
  verbs 529.3
post
  nouns station 183.3
  upright 216.4
  pillar 216.5
  messenger 559.1
  mail 602.5
  post office 602.8
  office 654.5
  society 786.10

potterer trifler 671.9
time waster 706.7
potter's clay, potter's earth 574.3
potter's field 409.15
potter's wheel
conversion 145.7
ceramics 574.4
pottery
ceramics 574.1,2
manufactory 717.3
potty
nouns 680.14
adjs. 472.25
pot-valiance, pot-valiancy, pot-valor 994.1
pot-valiant, pot-valorous 994.42
pot-walloper
dishwasher 679.14
scullion 748.7
pouch
nouns 192.2
verbs 255.10
poulard 413.35
poulardize 42.11
poule 987.16
poulet 306a.22
Poulsen arc 341.6
poulterer 828.3
poultice
nouns 685.28
verbs dress wounds 687.33
relieve 884.5
poultry fowl 413.35
breeds of ~ 413.57
pounce
nouns jump 317.1
dive 318.1
verbs jump 317.5
plunge 318.6
POUNCE UPON
jump 317.5
plunge 318.6
surprise 538.7
attack 796.15
seize 820.13
pounces 811.4
pound
nouns kennel 190.18
blow 282.4
drum 454.1
prison 759.7
coin 833.8
verbs repeat 103.10
hit 282.15
pulverize 360.9
drum 454.4
beat time 461.45
bruise 690.14
impound 759.12
POUND AWAY 714.14
POUND AWAY AT 623.3
POUND OUT 532.9
POUND THE EAR 710.13
POUND THE PAVEMENT 272.22

poundage
capacity 194.2
weight 351.1
charge 844.8
discount 845.1
poundal 160.6
pound-folly 852.1
pound-foolish 852.8
pounding
nouns pulverization 360.4
drum 454.1
adjs. 454.7
pound sovereign 833.5
pour
nouns rain 393.2
torrent 394.5
verbs flow out 302.13
disgorge 308.23
rain 393.9
flow 394.17
abound 659.5
POUR FORTH
say 592.14
chatter 594.6
POUR IN 301.10
POUR IT ON
speed 268.9
be active 705.13
work hard 714.13
POUR OIL ON 884.5
POUR OIL ON THE FIRE 646.17
POUR OIL ON THE TROUBLED WATERS
calm 162.7
pacify 802.7
POUR OIL UPON 379.8
POUR ON
wet 391.14
give to 816.15
pourboire 816.5
Pour le mérite 914.6
pourparler 595.6
pourquoi? 484.44
pousse-café 994.8
pout
nouns 949.9,10
verbs protrude 255.10
be petulant 949.15
pouts 949.10
poverty scarcity 660.3
indigence 836.1
poverty-stricken 836.8
POW 759.11
powder
nouns power 156.1
dust 360.5
flight 629.4
explosive 799.9
cosmetic 898.11
POWDER AND SHOT 799.8
TAKE A POWDER 629.11
verbs sprinkle 75.7
speed 268.9
pulverize 360.9
crumble 360.10
powderiness 360

powdering 360.4
powderman 382.8
powder puff
mollycoddle 420.11
cosmetics 898.11
powder room 680.13
powdery 360.11
power
large amount 34.6
potency 156.1
strength 158
energy 160
influence 171.1
country 180.1
electric ~ 341.17
eloquence 598.3
will ~ 622.4
magnate 670.8
~ of suggestion 688.6
faculty 731.4
authority 737.1,4
control 739.2
~ of attorney 778.1
right 956.3
BEYOND ONE'S POWER
beyond one 157.20
unachievable 509.7
GIVE POWER 775.12
IN ONE'S POWER
under one's control 739.19
subjugated 762.13
IN POWER 737.21
LIE IN ONE'S POWER 156.10
OUT OF ONE'S POWER 760.22
POWER BEHIND THE THRONE
influence 171.6
politician 744.7
THE POWERS THAT BE
the authorities 739.3
officeholders 744.11
officialdom 747.16
TO THE NTH POWER 56.17
UNDER ONE'S OWN POWER 760.30
powerboat 276.2
power braking 281.14
power dive
aviation 277.10
dive 318.1
power-dive 277.47
power-driven 346.11
powerful
adjs. great 34.8
potent 156.11
strong 158.13
influential 171.13
loud 452.9
eloquent 598.11
authoritative 737.14
advs. 34.20
powerfully very 34.20
potently 156.14

strongly 158.20
eloquently 598.15
authoritatively 737.18
powerhouse
strong man 158.6
power station 341.18
hustler 705.8
powerless
impotent 157.13
weak 159.12
uninfluential 172.3
powerlessness
impotence 157.1
uninfluentiality 172.1
power-packed 156.11
power plant
powerhouse 341.18
engine 347.4
power politics 742.1
power reactor 325.12
powers 1013.3
POWERS OF DARKNESS 1014.1
power station 341.18
power tools 347.1
power wheel 574.4
powwow
nouns conference 595.6
convention 742.8
verbs 595.10
pox 684.9,15
P-plane 280.3
practicability
workability 163.3
feasibility 508.2
utility 663.3
practicable
nouns 609.21
adjs. workable 163.11
feasible 508.7
useful 663.18
expedient 668.5
practical
nouns 609.21
adjs. virtual 5.8
operative 163.10
workable 163.11
practicable 508.7
realistic 534.6
businesslike 654.15
useful 663.18
expedient 668.5
practicality
feasibility 508.2
practicalness 534.2
utility 663.3
practical joke 879.10
practical knowledge
knowledge 474.1
experience 731.9
practically
essentially 5.10
approximately 199.26
usefully 663.25
practical nurse 686.13

practice
nouns mathematics
87.4
tryout 488.3
training 560.3
custom 640.1
ceremony 644.4
vocation 654.6
procedure 655.1
usage 663.2
action 703.1
exercise 714.6
experience 731.9
behavior 735.1
observance 766.1
rite 1038.3
IN PRACTICE
operating 163.12
in use 663.24
OUT OF PRACTICE
732.18
verbs specialize in
81.4
train 550.13
~ a play 609.36
use 663.10
do 703.7
observe 766.3
PRACTICE AT THE BAR
1001.6
PRACTICE UPON
experiment 488.8
exploit 563.16
impose upon 961.7
practiced used 663.23
skilled 731.24,26
practicing 703.11
practitioner 716.1
prad 413.12
prado 655 3
praedial 808.9
praefoliation 410.16
praenomen 581.6
praetor 1000.2
pragmatic(al)
meddlesome 237.9
dogmatic 512.22
practical 534.6
pragmatic logic 481.2
pragmatics 578.11
pragmatism
officiousness 237.2
dogmatism 512.6
matter-of-factness
534.2
pragmatist
busybody 237.4
realist 534.3
pragmatist(ic) 499.10
pragmatize 1004.9
prairie plain 386.1
grassland 410.8
prairie chicken 413.34
prairie schooner 271.2
prairie wolf 413.4
praise
nouns thanksgiving
947.2
approbation 966.5
flattery 963

worship 1030.2
BEYOND ALL PRAISE
perfect 675.6
praiseworthy 966.19
verbs laud 966.12
flatter 968.5
glorify God 1030.11
PRAISE BE! 874.12
PRAISE GOD
glorify 1030.11
hallelujah! 1030.16
praise meeting 1030.8
praiser 966.8
praiseworthiness 966.7
praiseworthy 966.19
pralltriller 462.18
pram 271.6
prana life force 406.3
spirit 1032.18,20
prance
nouns gait 272.14
caper 317.2
verbs walk 272.27
ride 272.33
caper 317.6
dance 877.5
swagger 902.15
prancer 413.12,20
prang 277.17
prank
nouns prance 317.2
caprice 627.1
joke 879.10
verbs dress up 230.41
prance 317.6
adorn 899.7
prankish, pranky
mischievous 736.6
facetious 879.17
prankster 879.12
prat 240.4
prate
nouns nonsense 545.4
chatter 594.3
verbs twaddle 545.8
gossip 556.12
chatter 594.6
pratfall 314.3
prattle
nouns nonsense 545.4
talk 592.1
chatter 594.3
chat 595.5
verbs twaddle 545.8
gossip 556.12
chatter 594.6
chat 595.9
prattler 594.5
pravity 979.6
prawn 306a.25
praxis grammar 584.1
custom 640.1
action 703.1
behavior 735.1
pray
verbs request 772.10,
11
worship 1030.12
interjs. 772.20
prayer request 772.2

worship 1030.4,8
PRAYER OF THANKS
947.2
prayer book 1038.12
prayerful 772.16
prayer mat, prayer rug
1040.10
prayer meeting 1030.8
prayers 1030.8
prayer wheel, prayer
machine
prayer 1030.4
ritualism 1038.11
preach
nouns 597.3
verbs expound 560.16
lecture 597.10
give advice 752.7
PREACH A FUNERAL
409.20
PREACH TO THE
WINDS 667.8
preacher
teacher 563.8
lecturer 597.5
clergyman 1036.3
preachify 597.10
preaching 597.3
preaching brother,
preaching friar
1036.17
preachment
lesson 560.6
lecture 597.3
preachy 752.10
preadamite
nouns 123.7
adjs. 123.11
preamble
nouns 66.2
verbs 64.3
preannounce 542.11
preannouncement
541.1
preapprehension
hunch 480.3
preconception 494.1
foresight 540.2
foreknowledge
540.3
foreboding 542.1
prearrange 639.3
prearranged 639.5
prearrangement 639
prebend 1035.8
prebendal stall 1035.8
prebendary 1036.8
prebendaryship 1035.8
precarious
unreliable 513.18
hazardous 695.12
precariousness
unreliability 513.6
hazardousness 695.2
precatory 772.17
precaution
nouns forewarning
701.2
caution 893.3
verbs 701.8

precautional,
precautionary
forewarning 701.10
cautious 893.10
precautions 893.3
precautious 893.10
precede take
precedence 36.10
come before 64.2
be prior 116.3
go before 291.2
precedence rank 29.2
priority 36.1
anteposition 64
precedency 116.1
precedent
nouns example 25.1
forerunner 66.1
decision 493.5
adjs. anterior 64.4
leading 291.3
precedential 25.8
preceding
nouns 291
adjs. ~ in order 64.4
prior 116.4
foregoing 119.8
leading 291.3
precentor
choirmaster 463.20
teacher 563.5
leader 746.5
choir chaplain
1036.9
precept belief 500.2
axiom 516.2
instruction 560.6
rule 749
order 750.3,6
preceptive
instructive 560.18
prescriptive 749.5
mandatory 750.14
preceptor 563.1
preceptoral 563.12
preceptorship 563.11
preceptress 563.2
precession
precedence 64
previousness 116.1
front 239
going before 291.1
precessional 291.3
précieuse
nouns 901.10
adjs. 901.18
precinct region 179.2
district 179.5
proximity 199.1
political ~ 742.16
precincts 232.1
preciosity
elegance 587.3
overniceness 901.5
precious
nouns 930.5
adjs. great 34.8
downright 34.14
thorough 56.10
elegant 587.9
valuable 846.10

purchase 826.2
preen groom 679.19
primp 899.7
PREEN ONESELF
903.5
pre-engage 778.12
pre-engagement
engagement 768.2
bespeaking 778.4
pre-establish 638.6
pre-estimate
nouns 494.1
verbs 494.2
pre-examine 484.36
pre-exist 116.3
pre-existence 116.1
pre-existent 116.4
prefab
nouns 244.2
verbs 166.12
adjs. 166.27
prefabricate 166.12
prefabricated
made 166.27
ready-built 718.20
prefabrication
fabrication 166.3
structure 244.2
Preface 1038.10
preface
nouns 66.2
verbs 64.3
prefatory 64.4
prefect student 564.1
executive 747.5
PREFECT OF STUDIES
565.17
prefectship,
prefecture 737.6
prefer choose 635.14
present 771.4
promote 780.3
be partial 975.8
PREFER A CLAIM
1002.14
PREFER A PETITION
772.10
PREFER CHARGES
1003.7
preferable 635.22
preferably 635.25
preference
priority 64.1
choice 635.4
favorite 929.13
favoritism 975.3
BY PREFERENCE
635.25
preference primary
742.15
preference share 832.3
preferential 635.22
preferential shop
787.2
preferential voting
742.18
preferment
improvement 689.1
promotion 780.1
holy orders 1035.10
preferred stock 832.2

prefiguration
omen 542.2
typification 570.6
prefigurative 542.14
prefigure
presume 498.11
foretoken 542.9
typify 570.9
prefix
nouns addition 41.1
prelude 66.2
syllable 579.6
verbs 64.3
prefixture 66.2
pregnable 695.16
pregnancy
productiveness
164.1
gestation 168.6
meaningfulness
543.6
pregnant full 56.12
productive 164.9
with young 168.18
meaningful 543.10
concise 590.4
significant 670.19
preheat 328.17
prehensile 811.9
prehensility 811.1
prehension
retention 811.1
seizure 820.2
prehistoric
primitive 123.11
~ men 123.25
~ animals 123.26
prehuman
nouns 123.6
adjs. 123.11
preindicate 542.9
preindication 542.2
preinstruct 560.14
preinstruction 560.4
prejudge 494.2
prejudgment
preconception 494
prejudice 525.3
prejudice
nouns partiality
525.3
preference 635.4
disadvantage 669.2
verbs bias 525.8
harm 673.6
prejudiced
opinionated 512.22
biased 525.12
prejudicial
predispositional
494.4
disadvantageous
669.6
detrimental 673.12
prelacy
ministry 1035.5
benefice 1035.9
clergy 1036.1
prelate 1036.8
prelatial, prelatic(al)
1035.13

prelature 1035.5
prelect 597.10
prelection
lesson 560.6
lecture 597.3
prelector
teacher 563.8
lecturer 597.5
prelibation 540.4
prelim 66.2
preliminary
nouns 66.2
SETTLE PRELIMI-
NARIES 718.6
adjs. 64.4
prelude
nouns preface 66.2
musical ~ 461.26
verbs 64.3
preludial, prelusive
64.4
premature
~ baby 125.7
untimely 130.7
too early 131.8
prematurely 131.13
prematurity
untimeliness 130
precocity 131.2
premaxilla 264.5
premeditate 651.8
premeditated 651.10
premeditation
forethought 540.2
predeliberation
651.3
WITHOUT PREMEDI-
TATION 628.14
WITH PREMEDITA-
TION 651.11
premier
nouns 747.7
adjs. 67.15
première
nouns 609.13
verbs 609.32
première danseuse
star performer 610.5
dancer 877.3
premier performance
609.13
premiership 737.6
premise
nouns prelude 66.2
antecedent 116.2
logic 481.8
verbs 64.3
premises 179.1
premium bonus 41.4
gratuity 816.5
interest 838.3
extra pay 839.6
AT A PREMIUM
scarce 660.9
expensively 846.13
premolar 257.7
premonition
hunch 480.3
foreboding 542.1
forewarning 701.2

HAVE A PREMONITION
540.7
premonitor
omen 542.2
warning 701.3
premonitory
predictive 541.11
ominous 542.14
Premonstratensian
1036.17
prenatal 68.14
prendre la balle au
bond 129.8
prenotation 541.1
prenotice
preconception 494.1
prediction 541.1
forewarning 701.2
prenotification 701.2
prenotify 701.8
prenotion
preconception 494.1
forethought 540.2
prentice
nouns 716.5
adjs. 778.18
preoccupancy 806.1
preoccupation
obsession 472.13
thoughtfulness
477.3
engrossment 528.3
abstraction 530.2
neurosis 688.22
appropriation 820.3
preoccupied
obsessed 472.32
~ in thought
477.21
engrossed 528.17
abstracted 530.11
preoccupy
obsess 472.23
~ the thoughts
477.19
engross 528.13
appropriate 820.16
preoption 635.4
preordain 638.6
preorder 639.3
preordination 638.1
prepaid 839.22
préparateur 718.5
preparation
manufacture 166.3
groundwork 215.6
dish 306a.7
music 462.2
training 560.3
writing 600.2
equipment 657
making ready 718
IN PREPARATION
718.23
IN PREPARATION FOR
718.25
preparationist,
preparator 718.5
preparative
nouns 718.3
adjs. 718.21

preparatory
nouns 718.3
adjs. preceding 64.4
~ school 565.6
~ act 718.1
preparative 718.21
prepare make 166.12
cook 329.4
train 560.13
write 600.21
equip 657.8
make ready 718.6
PREPARE FOR
prepare 718.11
take precautions 893.6
PREPARE ONESELF 718.13
PREPARE THE WAY
pave the way 718.12
facilitate 730.6
prepared
provided 657.12
well-prepared 657.13
ready 718.16
skilled 731.24
preparedness
readiness 718.4
military ~ 742.5
preparer 718.5
preparing
nouns 718.1
adjs. 151.3
prepay 839.10
prepayment 839.1
prepense 651.10
prepollence, prepollency 737.5
prepollent
influential 171.14
ruling 739.17
preponderance
superiority 36.1
majority 100.2
influence 171.1
dominion 737.5
preponderant
chief 36.16
influential 171.14
ruling 739.17
preponderate
excel 36.5
dominate 739.14
preposition 584.2
prepositional 584.13
prepossess
prejudice 525.8
appropriate 820.16
prepossessed
obsessed 472.32
prejudiced 525.12
prepossessing
alluring 648.7
delightful 861.6
prepossession
obsession 472.13
preconception 494.1
prejudice 525.3
preference 635.4
preoccupancy 806.1

appropriation 820.3
preposterous
absurd 469.10
unbelievable 502.10
impossible 509.6
fanciful 533.20
excessive 661.17
exorbitant 846.12
unwarranted 959.9
prepotence, prepotency
superiority 36.1
dominion 737.5
prepotent
influential 171.14
ruling 739.17
prep school 565.6
prepublication 541.1
Pre-Raphaelite 123.5
prerequire 637.9
prerequisite
nouns condition 506.2
requirement 637.2
adjs. 637.13
preresolution 651.3
preresolve
predetermine 638.6
premeditate 651.8
prerogative
authority 737.1
right 956.3
presa 462.12
presage
nouns foreknowledge 540.3
prediction 541.1
foreboding 542.1
omen 542.2
verbs predict 541.9
forebode 542.8
presageful
predictive 541.11
portentous 542.13
presagement 541.1
presager
prophet 541.4
omen 542.2
presbyopia 439.4
presbyopic 439.11
presbyter 1036.4
presbyterate 1035.5
presbytery
council 753.5
ministry 1035.5
clergy 1036.1
church ~ 1040.7,9
preschool
nouns 565.4
adjs. 565.18
prescience 540.3
prescient 540.8
prescribe direct 745.8
order 750.10
advise 752.6
~ laws 996.8
prescribed 749.5
prescribed form
rule 84.4
custom 640.4

prescript
nouns axiom 516.2
precept 749.1
directive 750.3
law 996.3
adjs. preceptive 749.5
mandatory 750.14
prescription
axiom 516.2
custom 640.1
remedy 685.1
precept 749.1,3
directive 750.3
monopolization 806.4
right 956.3
law 996.3
prescriptive
traditional 123.12
customary 640.14
conventional 643.7
preceptive 749.5
mandatory 750.14
presearch
nouns 484.11
verbs 484.36
presence
existence 1.1
posture 183.4
hereness 185
mien 445.3
appearance 445.5
phantasm 518.4
behavior 735.1
~ of mind 856.3
specter 1015.1
~ of God 1016.1
IN THE PRESENCE OF 185.16
presence chamber 191.20
presenile dementia 472.3
present
nouns now 120
tense 584.10
gift 816.4
AT PRESENT 120.3
verbs direct 289.6
adduce 504.13
exhibit 553.5
inform 555.7
expound 560.16
phrase 583.4
say 592.14
stage 609.32
put to choice 635.18
provide 657.7
offer 771.4
give 816.12
introduce 925.13
PRESENT A BOLD FRONT 891.11
PRESENT ARMS 962.5
PRESENT ITSELF
occur 150.6
appear 445.8
suggest itself 477.17
PRESENT ONESELF
report 185.11
volunteer 771.10

pay respects 934.12
PRESENT TO 239.9
adjs. existent 1.13
current 120.2
at hand 185.12
BE PRESENT
exist 1.8
be there 185.6
BE PRESENT AT 185.8
BE PRESENT IN 1.11
PRESENT TO THE MIND 535.23
presentable
revealable 553.13
tolerable 672.20
giveable 816.22
comely 898.17
presentation
appearance 445.1,7
exhibition 553.2
theatrical ~ 609.13
plan 652.2
offer 771.1
giving 816.1
gift 816.4
debut 920.13
introduction 925.4
holy orders 1035.10
UPON PRESENTATION
at sight 438.24
on demand 751.11
present-day, present-time present 120.2
modern 122.14
presented 583.6
presenter 816.11
presentiment
hunch 480.3
foreboding 542.1
HAVE A PRESENTIMENT 540.7
presently 131.16
presentment
exhibition 553.2
theatrical ~ 609.13
giving 816.1
arraignment 1002.3
present participle 584.2
preserval 699.1
preservation
perpetuation 112.4
maintenance 140.2
protection 697
conservation 699.1
retention 811.1
divine function 1011.16
preservative
nouns 699.3
adjs. conservative 140.8
protective 697.22
preservatory 699.10
preservatize 699.8
preservatory 699.10
preserve
nouns sweet 306a.39
reserve 699.6
verbs maintain 143.4
reserve 658.12

pretty lies 968.1
pretty much 34.17
pretty near
  about 35.13
  nearly 199.25
pretty penny
  large sum 835.2
  high price 846.3
pretty up
  dress up 230.41
  beautify 898.14
pretty well
  adjs. 672.20
  advs. 672.25
pretypify
  foretoken 542.9
  typify 570.9
pretzel 306a.29
prevail exist 1.8
  be uniform 17.3
  excel 36.5
  be prevalent 79.9
  endure 110.6
  succeed 722.6
  triumph 724.3
  dominate 739.14
PREVAIL UPON
  646.23
prevailing chief 36.16
  prevalent 79.11
  usual 84.8
  happening 150.9
  influential 171.14
  ~ taste 642.1
  abundant 659.7
  victorious 724.8
prevalence
  commonness 79.2
  usualness 84.2
  frequency 135.1
  customariness 640.6
  fashionableness
  642.2
  abundance 659.2
prevalent
  existent 1.13
  current 79.11
  frequent 135.4
  happening 150.9
  well-known 474.27
  customary 640.14
  fashionable 642.11
  abundant 659.7
  ruling 739.17
prevaricate
  quibble 482.9
  lie 614.20
prevarication
  quibbling 482.5
  falsehood 614.9,11
prevaricator
  quibbler 482.7
  liar 617.9
prévenance 934.5
prevenience 131.1
prevenient
  precedent 64.4
  early 131.7
prevent 728.14
preventable,
  preventible 629.13

preventative
  nouns antidote 177.3
  prophylactic 685.18
  adjs. 728.19
preventative
  treatment 687.18
prevention
  preconception 494.1
  hindrance 728.2
preventive
  nouns antidote 177.3
  prophylactic 685.18
  adjs. exclusive 77.8
  prophylactic 685.37
  hindering 728.19
preventive custody
  759.5
preventive measure
  893.3
preventive medicine
  686.1
preventive war 795.3
preview
  nouns view 438.3
  pre-examination
  484.11
  motion picture
  609.15
  verbs 484.36
previous prior 116.4
  past 119.7
  premature 131.8
PREVIOUS TO 116.6
previously 119.10
prevision 540.1
prewar 116.5
prewarn 701.8
prexy 747.5
prey quarry 653.7
  defeatee 725.5
  sufferer 864.11
prey on eat 306.25
  plunder 822.15
  torment 864.21
price
  nouns odds 514.5
  stock market ~
  832.8
  interest 838.3
  recompense 839.3
  cost 844
  penalty 1007.1
ASKING PRICE
  offer 771.1
  price 844.2
AT A HIGH PRICE
  846.13
AT A LOW PRICE
  847.10
AT ANY PRICE 622.20
AT WHAT PRICE
  655.11
BEYOND PRICE
  useful 663.21
  precious 846.10
FIX THE PRICE OF
  844.13
NOT AT ANY PRICE
  522.8
  verbs 844.13
price controls 844.6

price current
  stock market 832.8
  price 844.2
price cut 847.4
price fixing, price-
  freeze 844.6
price index 844.5
priceless
  invaluable 663.21
  precious 846.10
  amusing 878.5
price supports
  policy 742.4
  prices 844.6
price tag 566.12
prick
  nouns prickle 257.4
  pang 423.2
  goad 646.8
  verbs pierce 264.15
  herd 415.7
  pain 423.7
  prickle 425.5
  goad 646.15
  distress 864.14
PRICK THE BUBBLE
  519.2
PRICK UP THE EARS
  listen 447.11
  be curious 526.3
  heed 528.7
prick-eared 447.16
pricking
  prickly 257.13
  goading 646.5
pricking of conscience,
  pricking of heart
  871.2
prickle
  nouns adherent 50.3
  spike 257.4
  thorn 257.8
  prickling 425.1
  verbs 425.5
prickles 425.1
prickling
  nouns 425.1
  adjs. 425.8
prickly pointed 257.13
  tingly 425.8
prickly heat 684.27
prick song 461.20
pricky 257.13
pride
  ~ of lions 74.5
  good thing 672.5
  ostentation 902.6
  proudness 903
  vanity 907
  boastfulness 908
  arrogance 910.1
PUT ONE'S PRIDE IN
  ONE'S POCKET
  904.6
WITH PRIDE 903.13
pride oneself on 903.5
pride and joy 672.5
prie-dieu 1040.10
priest 1036.4,10,11
priestcraft 1035.2
priestery 1036.1

priestess 1036.5
priesthood
  ministry 1035.1,3
  clergy 1036.1
priestish, priestly,
  priest-ridden
  1035.13
priestism 1035.3
priestship 1035.1
prig
  nouns thief 823.1
  prude 901.11
  snob 910.7
  verbs 822.13
prigger 823.1
priggery 910.6
priggish
  thievish 822.20
  prudish 901.19
  snobbish 910.14
priggism
  thievishness 822.12
  snobbery 910.6
prim formal 644.9
  prudish 901.19
prima buffa 610.5
primacy
  supremacy 36.3
  dominion 737.5
  primateship 1035.5
prima donna
  singer 463.13
  star performer 610.5
  principal 670.10
prima facie
  at sight 438.24
  apparently 445.12
primal chief 36.16
  beginning 68.13
  original 152.16
  basic 211.8
primaries 229.18
primarily
  essentially 5.10
  chiefly 36.19
  first 68.16
primary
  nouns ~ color 361.6
  school 565.5
  election 742.15
  adjs. essential 5.8
  chief 36.16
  beginning 68.13
  original 152.16
  basic 211.8
  front 239.11
  most important
  670.25
primary cause 688.19
primary color 361.6
primary digestion
  307.7
primary education
  560.9
primary election
  742.15
primary electron 342.3
primary school 565.5
primary trainer 279.10
primate
  manlike ~ 123.25

bishop 1036.8
Primates 414.12
primates 413.50
primateship 1035.5
prime
nouns beginning 68.2
 spring 128.2
 dawn 133.3
 the best 672.8
 divine service
 1040.8
 IN ONE'S PRIME
 126.13
 PAST ONE'S PRIME
 126.14
verbs ~ a gun 284.13
 paint 361.14
 coach 560.11
 prepare 718.9
 PRIME UP 994.31
adjs. chief 36.16
 beginning 68.13
 mathematics 86.8
 primitive 123.11
 front 239.11
 most important
 670.25
 best 672.19
primed ready 718.16
 skilled 731.24
 drunk 994.40
 PRIMED FOR 718.19
prime interval 462.20
prime meridian 179.3
prime minister 747.7
prime mover
 cause 152.4
 originator 166.10
prime number 86.2
prime of life 124.1
prime of the year
 128.2
primer
 detonator 330.7
 paint 361.12
 textbook 603.8
prime song 1030.8
primeval
 primitive 123.11
 original 152.16
primigenia
 beginning 68.13
 primitive 123.11
priming
 detonator 330.7
 paint 361.11,12
 instruction 560.4
primitive
nouns ancient 123.7
 native 189.3
 word 580.2
adjs. fundamental 5.8
 beginning 68.13
 ancient 123.11
 original 152.16
 native 188.7
 basic 211.3
 uncivilized 896.12
primitive self
 instinct 480.2
 id 688.39

primogenitary 126.18
primogenitors 169.7
primogeniture
 seniority 126.3
 heirship 817.2
primoprimitive 123.11
primordial
 prototypal 25.9
 primitive 123.11
 original 152.16
primp dress up 230.41
 adorn 899.7
primrose pink 367.9
 yellowish 369.4
primum mobile 152.4
prince
 nobleman 916.8
 worthy 983.1
princedom
 princeship 737.6
 nobility 916.10
princelike regal 737.16
 noble 916.11
princeliness
 dignity 903.2
 magnanimity 977.2
princely regal 737.16
 generous 851.4
 magnificent 902.21
 dignified 903.12
 noble 916.11
 magnanimous 977.6
Prince of Darkness
 1014.3
Prince of Peace
 1011.12
Prince of Wales's
 feathers 567.3
prince regent
 ruler 747.13
 prince 916.8
princeship
 authority 737.6
 nobility 916.10
princess, princesse
 916.9
principal
nouns stop 464.23
 school ~ 563.9
 chief 670.10
 master 747.3
 capital 833.15
adjs. chief 36.16
 first 68.15
 most important
 670.25
principalities 1013.3
principality
 country 180.1
 angel 1013.1
principal keeper
 759.10
principally
 chiefly 36.19
 first 68.16
principate 180.1
principia
 rudiments 68.5
 precept 749.2
principium 516.2

principle
 essential 5.2
 rule 84.4
 cause 152.1,10
 foundation 215.6
 belief 500.2
 axiom 516.2
 precept 749.2
principled 972.13
principles
 rudiments 68.5
 policy 652.5
 ethics 955.1
 integrity 972.1
prink dress up 230.41
 adorn 899.7
 mince 901.14
print
nouns copy 24.5
 indentation 256.6
 mark 566.6
 picture 572.12
 photographic ~
 575.5
 engraving 576.6
 letter 579.2
 printing 601.3
 type 601.6
 edition 603.2
 IN PRINT 601.17
verbs fix 142.10
 impress 535.18
 publish 557.14
 ~ a photograph
 575.17
 engrave 576.13
 stamp 601.12
printed
 engraved 576.16
 in print 601.17
printed circuit 342.8
printed matter 601.4
printer press 601.8
 pressman 601.10
 publisher 603.21
printer's devil 601.10
printer's imprint
 603.13
printing
 engraving 576.5
 letter 579.2
 type ~ 601
 edition 603.2
printing equipment
 601.24
printing press 601.8
printing presses
 601.22
print shop 601.8
printworks 717.4
Prinz 916.8
prior
nouns 1036.16
adjs. ~ in order 64.4
 previous 116.4
 BE PRIOR 116.3
priorate 1040.6
prioress 1036.18
priority
nouns precedence
 36.1

prior time 116
 past time 119
 front 239.1
adjs. 64.1
priory 1040.6
prism 250.2
prismal angular 250.6
 variegated 373.9
prismatic
 angular 250.6
 chromatic 361.16
 variegated 373.9
prismoid 250.2
prison 759.7
 IN PRISON 759.20
prisoner
 convict 759.11
 accused 1003.6
prisonhouse 759.7
prissiness 420.2
prissy
nouns 420.11
adjs. 420.15
pristine
 primitive 123.11
 original 152.16
prithee 772.20
prittle-prattle
nouns chatter 594.3
 chitchat 595.5
verbs 595.9
privacy secrecy 612.2
 retreat 698.5
 seclusion 922.1
 IN PRIVACY
 in private 612.21
 in seclusion 922.14
Privatdocent, Privat-
 dozent 563.6
private
nouns 798.9
 IN PRIVATE 612.21
adjs. personal 80.12
 confidential 612.15
 secluded 922.10
private enterprise
 825.1
privateer
nouns 823.8
verbs 822.16
privateering 822.6
private eye 779.10
private information
 555.2
private instructor
 563.6
private line 558.20
privately
 personally 80.17
 in private 612.21
private matter 612.5
private school 565.2
privation loss 810.1
 divestment 820.5
 poverty 836.2
privative 820.22
privilege
nouns 956.4
verbs 775.12
privileged
 exempt 760.27

licensed 775.18
privileged communi-
cation 612.5
privileged question
740.15
privity bond 48.1
knowledge 474.1
privy
nouns 680.13
IN PRIVY 612.21
adjs. confidential
612.15
secluded 922.10
PRIVY TO 474.16
privy council 753.1
privy seal, privy
signet 567.3
prix fixe 844.2
prize
nouns leverage 286.1
lever 286.4
good thing 672.5,8
booty 822.11
award 914.2
verbs pry 286.8
measure 489.11
assess 493.9
rate highly 670.12
price 844.13
hold dear 929.18
respect 962.4
adjs. 672.19
prize court 999.3
prize fight 794.9
prize fighter 798.2
prizeman 731.13
prize ring 800.1
prize sap 470.2
pro
nouns 481.14
adjs. 654.16
advs. 966.20
pro and con 481.20
probabilism 510.1
probability
good chance 155.8
liability 174.1
likelihood 510
GO BEYOND THE
BOUNDS OF PROBA-
BILITY 511.2
probable 510.5
probably 510.7
probate
nouns 816.10
verbs 504.12
probate court 999.3
probate judge 1000.4
probation 488.2
ON PROBATION
on trial 488.14
probationary 564.11
probationary
experimental 488.11
on probation 564.11
probationer,
probationist
novice 564.8
nurse 686.13
probative
experimental 488.11

evidential 504.17
probatum est 504.27
probe
nouns examination
484.5,6
feeler 488.4
probationer 564.8
nurse 686.13
verbs explore 484.30
feel out 488.9
measure 489.11
probity 972
problem topic 483.1
question 484.13
enigma 547.7
problematic(al)
unbelievable 502.10
questionable 513.15
enigmatical 547.15
proboscis 255.7
procacious 911.8
procacity 911.1
procedure
process 163.2
custom 640.4
policy 652.5
method 655.1
usage 663.2
behavior 735.1
proceed
elapse 105.5
progress 293.2
act 703.4
PROCEED FROM 153.6
proceeding
nouns affair 150.3
process 163.2
procedure 655.1
act 703.3
behavior 735.1
adjs. 293.5
proceedings
affairs 150.4
minutes 568.6
activity 705.1
lawsuit 1002.1
proceeds
produce 167.2
gain 809.4
receipts 842.1
process
nouns operation
163.2
automation 348.21
procedure 655.1
writ 750.6
IN PROCESS
in operation 163.12
in preparation
718.23
IN THE PROCESS OF
105.8
verbs 718.6
process control 348.8
processing
automatic ~ 348.7
treatment 718.1
processing tax 844.11
procession
sequence 65.1

train 71.4
processional 1038.4
processional march
461.11
process lag 348.11
process loop 348.6
process of time 105.4
IN THE PROCESS OF
TIME 121.1
process server 750.8
process shot 575.10
process variables 348.9
procès-verbal
testimony 504.3
affidavit 568.5
law 1002.7
prochein ami 779.1
prochronism 115.1
proclaim
forerun 116.3
presage 542.11
announce 557.13
PROCLAIM THE BANNS
931.15
proclaimer 559.3
proclamation
announcement
557.2
decree 750.4
proclamatory 557.18
proclivity
tendency 173.1
disposition 523.3
desire 632.3
proconsul 779.6
procrastinate 132.10
procrastinating, pro-
crastinative 132.16
procrastination 132.5
procrastinator 532.5
procreant 168.16
procreate 168.9
procreation 168.2
procreative 168.16
procreator 169.8
Procrustean 755.6
Procrustean bed
1009.4
Procrustean law 84.4
proctor steward 746.3
agent 779.3
lawyer 1001.1
proctorship 745.4
procumbent 213.9
procurable 508.8
procuration
proxy 778.1
acquisition 809.1
procurator
steward 746.3
agent 779.3
lawyer 1001.1
procure induce 152.12
fetch 270.15
elicit 304.12
prompt 646.22
acquire 809.7
purchase 826.7
pimp 987.21
procurement 809.1

procurer, procuress
987.18
prod
nouns thrust 282.2
goad 646.8
verbs thrust 282.12
goad 646.15
prodigal
nouns 852.2
adjs. plentiful 659.7
superabundant
661.20
extravagant 852.8
unvirtuous 979.16
intemperate 991.7
prodigality
abundance 659.2
superabundance
661.2
extravagance 852
unvirtuousness
979.3
intemperance 991.1
prodigal son
prodigal 852.2
penitent 871.5
prodigious great 34.11
extraordinary 85.13
miraculous 85.15
huge 194.20
wonderful 918.9
prodigy oddity 85.5
miracle 85.8
first-rater 672.6
genius 731.12
wonder 918.2
prodrome 701.3
produce
nouns product 167.2
yield 809.4
merchandise 829.7
receipts 842.1
verbs cause 152.11
bring about 163.6
create 166.12
bear 166.17
lengthen 201.9
adduce 504.13
exhibit 553.5
author 600.21
stage 609.32
do 703.6
accomplish 720.4
producer
creator 166.10
theaterman 609.27
doer 716.1
producible
causable 166.29
revealable 553.13
product sum 86.3
production 167
types of ~ 167.5
yield 809.4
commodity 829.2
producible 166.29
production
creation 166
product 167.1
lengthening 201.5
musical ~ 461.5

exhibition 553.2
writing 600.2,11
book 603.1
theatrical ~ 609.13
execution 703.2
accomplishment
   720.1
IN PRODUCTION
under construction
   166.30
in preparation
   718.23
productional 166.21
production line
   assembly 74.13
   production 166.2
production tax 844.11
productive
   fruitful 164.9
   creative 166.23
   inventive 533.18
   gainful 809.14
productiveness 164
productivity
   productiveness
      164.1
   inventiveness 533.3
proem, proemium
   66.2
proemial 54.4
prof 563.4
profanation
   misuse 665.1
   desecration 1028.2
profanatory 1028.6
profane
   nouns 1025.2
   verbs misuse 665.4
      unhallow 1028.4
   adjs. blasphemous
      970.8
      unsacred 1025.3
      impious 1028.6
      unspiritual 1029.16
profane oath 970.4
profanity
   swearing 970.3
   unsacredness 1025.1
   blasphemy 1028.2
profanum vulgus
   917.3
profess affirm 521.4
   feign 614.22
   allege 647.3
profession
   ~ of faith 500.5
   testimony 504.3
   affirmation 521.1
   pretext 647.2
   vocation 654.6
THE PROFESSION
   716.4
professional
   nouns worker 716.4
      expert 731.11
   adjs. 654.16
professional ethics
   955.1
professionalism 654.8
professionally 654.18

professional mourner
   409.7
professor
   acceptor 520.6
   teacher 563.4
THE PROFESSOR
   348.16
professorate
   teachers 563.10
   professorship 563.11
professorial, professor-
   like 563.12
professorship 563.11
proffer
   nouns 771.1
   verbs 771.4
proficiency 731.1
proficient
   nouns 731.11
   adjs. 731.20
PROFICIENT IN
   731.25
profile
   nouns outline 234.2
      picture 572.16
      biography 606.4
      diagram 652.3
      psychogram 688.10
   verbs 234.9
profile drag 277.33
profit
   nouns avail 663.4
      good 672.4
      gain 809.3
   verbs avail 663.17
      benefit 672.11
      make money 809.10
PROFIT BY
   take advantage of
      129.9
   utilize 663.15
profitability
   utility 663.3
   expedience 668.1
   helpfulness 783.10
profitable
   useful 663.21
   expedient 668.4
   beneficial 672.21
   helpful 783.21
   remunerative 809.14
profitably
   usefully 663.25
   beneficially 672.26
   helpfully 783.24
   lucratively 809.15
profiteer
   nouns 820.10
   verbs 846.7
profiteering 846.5
profitless 667.12
profits gains 809.3
   receipts 842.1
profit sharing 813.2
profit-sharing 813.9
profit taking 831.19
profligacy
   extravagance 852.1
   turpitude 979.6
   dissoluteness 987.3

profligate
   nouns 987.10
   adjs. extravagant
      852.8
   wicked 979.19
   dissolute 987.25
profluence 394.4
profluent 394.25
pro forma 644.11
profound
   downright 34.14
   deep 208.9
   wise 466.17
   learned 474.21
   abstruse 547.14
   deep-felt 853.25
profound sleep 710.5
profound thought
   thoughtfulness
      477.3
   engrossment 528.3
profundity
   depth 208.1
   wisdom 466.5
   abstruseness 547.2
profuse
   numerous 101.10
   diffuse 591.11
   abundant 659.7
   generous 851.4
   prodigal 852.8
profuseness
   numerousness 101.1
   diffuseness 591.1
   abundance 659.2
   prodigality 852.1
profusion
   large amount 34.3
   numerousness 101.1
   diffuseness 591.1
   abundance 659.2
   prodigality 852.1
profusive
   abundant 659.7
   diffuse 591.11
prog tramp 273.3
   food 306a.2
progenitive 168.15
progenitor 169.8
progenitors 169.7
progenitorship 169.1
progenitress, pro-
   genitrix 169.7
progeny 170.1
prognathous 255.13
prognose 687.32
prognosis
   prediction 541.1
   interpretation 550.1
   medical ~ 687.16
prognostic
   nouns omen 542.2
   medical ~ 687.16
   adjs. predictive
      541.11
   interpretative
      550.16
prognosticate
   predict 541.9
   forebode 542.8

prognostication
   prediction 541.1
   omen 542.2
   medical ~ 687.16
prognosticator 541.4
prognostics
   interpretation 550.9
   medicine 687.14
program
   nouns guided missile
      ~ 280.7
   broadcast 343.21
   advertisement 557.8
   schedule 639.2
   policy 652.5
   political ~ 742.6
   platform 742.7
   verbs 639.4
programma 557.8
programme 639.2
programmer 343.26
programming 280.10
program music 461.5
progress
   nouns ~ of time
      105.4
   conversion 145.1
   velocity 268.2
   travel 272.1,5
   navigation 274.9
   progression 293.1
   development 321.2
   improvement 689.1
IN PROGRESS
   going on 293.6
   in preparation
      718.23
   verbs move 272.17
   advance 293.2
   develop 321.6
   improve 689.7
   prosper 726.7
progression
   sequence 65.1
   series 71.2
   mathematical ~
      86.7
   travel 272
   advance 293
   development 321.2
   improvement 689.1
progressive
   nouns reformer 689.6
   liberal 743.10
   adjs. gradual 29.5
   consecutive 71.10
   modern 122.14
   advancing 293.5
   improving 689.15
   liberal 743.18
progressively 71.12
progressiveness 293.1
progressive tax 844.10
progressive tense
   584.10
progressivism
   reform 689.5
   politics 743.3
progressivist 689.6
Progymnasium 565.6

pro hac vice
  now 120.3
  once 136.6
prohibit
  prevent 728.14
  forbid 776.3
prohibited 776.7
prohibition
  exclusion 77.1
  prevention 728.2
  forbiddance 776
  temperance 990.3
Prohibition Era 107.6
prohibitionism 990.3
Prohibitionist 742.28
prohibitionist 990.5
Prohibition Party
  742.25
prohibitive
  exclusive 77.8
  preventive 728.19
  prohibiting 776.6
project
  nouns
    guided missile ~
      280.7
    intention 651.1
    plan 652.2
    undertaking 713.1
  verbs protrude 255.9
    launch 280.13
    traject 284.11
    screen 575.18
    plan 652.9
  PROJECT OVER 214.7
projectile
  nouns trajectile 284.6
    missile 799.12
  adjs. 284.16
projectile rocket
  280.2
projecting
  overhanging 214.11
  protruding 255.13
projection
  overhanging 214.3
  protuberance 255.2
  jag 257.5
  trajection 284.3
  plan 652.2,3
  psychological ~
    688.34
  psychology 688.43
projector
  rocket launcher
    280.11
  photographic ~
    575.14
  planner 652.7
  launcher 799.20
projector tube 280.11
prolate 252.11
prolate spheroid 252.6
prolation 461.10
prolegomenon 66.2
prolepsis prelude 66.2
  false time 115.1
proletarian
  nouns 917.7
  adjs. 917.12
proletariat 917.1

proliferate
  multiply 100.6
  be productive 164.7
  procreate 168.9
proliferation
  multiplication
    100.4
  productiveness
    164.2
  procreation 168.2
proliferous 164.9
prolific
  productive 164.9
  inventive 533.18
prolificacy
  productiveness
    164.1
  inventiveness 533.3
prolificate
  increase 38.6
  make productive
    164.8
prolification 164.2
prolix wordy 591.12
  tedious 882.8
prolixity
  wordiness 591.2
  tediousness 882.2
prolocutor
  teacher 563.8
  spokesman 779.5
prologize 64.3
prologue prelude 66.2
  act 609.8
prolong protract 110.9
  postpone 132.8
  continue 143.4
  lengthen 201.9
  PROLONG THE AGONY
    torment 423.7
    torture 864.20
prolongate 201.9
prolongation
  sequence 65.1
  protraction 110.2
  postponement 132.4
  continuance 143.1
  lengthening 201.5
prolonged
  protracted 110.11
  lengthened 201.12
prom concert 461.34
  dance 877.2
promenade
  nouns parade 71.4
    walk 272.12
    walkway 655.3
    dance 877.2
  verbs parade 71.8
    walk 272.28
Promethean 406.11
Promethean spark
  406.3
prominence
  greatness 34.2
  height 206.1
  protuberance 255.2
  distinctness 443.2
  obviousness 553.4
  importance 670.2
  famousness 912.5

prominent
  great 34.9
  high 206.19
  protruding 255.13
  distinct 443.7
  obvious 553.11
  important 670.16
  famous 912.18
prominently
  remarkably 34.23
  to a high degree
    36.18
  distinctly 443.8
  obviously 553.16
  importantly 670.26
  famously 912.22
promiscuity
  haphazardness 62.1
  indiscrimination
    492.1
  carelessness 532.3
promiscuous
  mixed 44.15
  orderless 62.11
  haphazard 155.16
  indiscriminate 492.6
  careless 532.12
promiscuously
  haphazardly 62.17
  aimlessly 155.19
  carelessly 532.18
promise
  nouns oath, vow
    521.3
    prediction 541.1
    foretoken 542.2
    pledge 768
    contract 769
    hope 886.1
  KEEP ONE'S PROMISE
    fulfill 766.2
    keep faith with
      972.9
  OF PROMISE
    auspicious 542.16
    hopeful 886.13
  verbs seem likely
    510.3
    swear 521.5
    predict 541.9
    foretoken 542.10
    pledge 768.4
    contract 769.6
    give hope 886.10
  I PROMISE 521.10
  PROMISE IN MAR-
    RIAGE 768.6
  PROMISE ONESELF
    537.4
promised
  expected 537.11
  predicted 541.14
  portended 542.12
  pledged 768.8
  contracted 769.12
  AS PROMISED 769.13
Promised Land 533.11
  THE PROMISED LAND
    1016.1
promising
  probable 510.5

auspicious 542.16
  hopeful 886.13
promissory 768.7
promissory note
  833.11
promontory 255.8
promorphology 244.7
promote
  advertise 557.15
  actuate 646.12
  subserve 656.5
  improve 689.9
  prefer 780.3
  help 783.15
  further 783.17
  finance 834.15
promoter
  publicist 557.9
  planner 652.7
  backer 785.8
  financer 834.9
  PROMOTER OF THE
    FAITH 1036.8
promotion
  advertising 557.5
  improvement 689.1
  preferment 780
  furtherance 783.5
  financing 834.2
  GIVE AN IRISH PRO-
    MOTION 780.4
prompt
  nouns 535.6
  verbs influence 171.7
    remind 535.20
    hint 555.9
    move 646.13,22
    advise 752.7
  adjs. punctual 131.9
    alert 531.14
    willing 620.5
    businesslike 654.15
    quick 705.17
  advs. 131.15
promptbook
  notebook 568.10
  playbook 609.25
prompted 646.30
  PROMPTED BY THE
    OCCASION 120.3
prompter
  reminder 535.6
  theaterman 609.27
  inducer 646.10
prompting
  nouns reminder
    535.6
    motivation 646.2
  adjs. 646.27
promptitude
  punctuality 131.3
  alertness 531.5
  quickness 705.3
promptly
  at once 131.15
  willingly 620.8
  quickly 705.24
promptness
  punctualness 131.3
  alertness 531.5
  willingness 620.1

clairvoyance 1032.8
psychoneurosis 688.17
psychoneurotic
 688.14,48
psychonomics,
 psychonomy 688.1
psychoorganic 688.46
psychopath
 psychotic 472.16
 psychopathist
 688.13
psychopathia 472.3
psychopathia sexualis
 psychosis 472.3
 perversion 688.32
psychopathic
 psychotic 472.26
 psychopathological
 688.46
psychopathic
 hospital 472.14
psychopathic
 personality
 psychosis 472.3
 psychotic 472.16
psychopathologist
 688.13
psychopathology
 688.3
psychopathy 472.3
psychophysicist
 688.12
psychophysics
 physics 324.1
 psychology 688.1
psychophysiologist
 688.12
psychophysiology
 688.1
psychorhythmia 472.3
psychorrhagy 1032.6
psychosensory 1032.25
psychosexuality
 psychosis 472.3
 perversion 688.32
psychosis
 insanity 472.3
 neurosis 688.17
 dipsomania 994.3
psychosocial 688.46
psychosomatic 688.46
psychosomatic
 medicine 688.4
psychosophy 1032.4
psychostatics
 mechanics 346.2
 psychology 688.1
psychosthenic 688.48
psychosurgery
 operation 687.26
 psychotherapy 688.5
psychosynthesis
 688.38
psychotaxia 688.23
psychotaxis 688.34
psychotechnician, psy-
 chotechnologist
 688.12
psychotechnics, psy-
 chotechnology
 688.1

psychotherapeutics,
 psychotherapy
 688.5
psychotherapeutist,
 psychotherapist
 688.13
psychotic
 nouns 472.16
 adjs. psychopathic
 472.26
 neurotic 688.48
psychrometer 391.10
psychrometry 391.9
Ptah 1012.9
pteridophyta, pterido-
 phytes 411.6
ptisan 685.4
ptyalism 310.3
ptyalize 310.6
pub public house
 190.13
 barroom 994.25
puberty 124.6
pubes 229.2
pubescence
 adolescence 124.6
 hairiness 229.1
 hair 229.2
pubescent
 nouns 125.1
 adjs. adolescent
 124.13
 hairy 229.24
pubigerous 229.24
public
 nouns population
 189.1
 people 416.2
 clientele 826.3
 the people 917.2
 barroom 994.25
 adjs. of people 416.13
 made ~ 557.17
 communal 813.9
 vulgar 896.14
 IN PUBLIC
 openly 553.15
 publicly 557.19
public address 597.2
public-address system
 343.7
publican 994.23
publication
 promulgation 557
 printing 601.1
 book 603.1
 NOT FOR PUBLICA-
 TION 612.16
public charge 762.6
public crib
 politics 742.38
 treasury 834.12
public defender
 1001.4
public enemy
 enemy 927.6
 criminal 984.9
public functionary
 747.18
public house
 inn 190.13

barroom 994.25
publicist
 publicizer 557.9
 journalist 603.22
 commentator 604.4
 lawyer 1001.4
publicity 557.4
publicity agent,
 publicity man
 publicist 557.9
 theater 609.29
publicize 557.15
publicizing 557.5
public law 996.4
publicness 557.4
public official 747.18
public opinion
 opinion 500.4
 influence 742.30
public school 565.2,6
public servant 747.18
public speaking 597
public spirit 939
public utility 786.9
publish divulge 554.5
 promulgate 557.10
 print 601.12
PUBLISH THE BANNS
 betroth 768.6
 marriage 931.15
publisher 603.21
publishers 601.8
publishing
 publication 557.1
 printing 601.1
puce brown 366.3
 reddish 367.7
Puck 1014.8
puck brat 125.4
 mischief-maker
 736.3
 imp 1014.8
pucka 515.12
pucker
 nouns perplexity
 513.3
 fluster 530.3
 trepidation 855.5
 anxiety 888.1
 dudgeon 950.7
 verbs contract 197.7
 wrinkle 263.3,6
puckered
 contracted 197.12
 wrinkled 263.8
puckering 197.1
puckery 263.8
puckish
 mischievous 736.6
 impish 1014.19
puckishness 736.2
pud 211.5
pudder 62.4
pudding
 food 306a.45
 softness 356.4
 semiliquid 388.5
puddings 224.6
puddle mud ~ 388.9
 pool 397.1

puddle jumper 279.5
pudge 194.12
pudginess
 corpulence 194.8
 stubbiness 202.2
pudgy
 nouns 194.12
 adjs. corpulent
 194.18
 stubby 202.10
pudicity 986.2
pueblo 182.2
puerile young 124.11
 simple-minded
 468.24
puerilism 468.11
puerility youth 124.4
 simple-mindedness
 468.11
puff
 nouns swelling 196.2
 pastry 306a.40
 softness 356.4
 ~ of smoke 400.1
 wind 402.4
 breath 402.19
 smoke 433.11
 publicity 557.4
 powder ~ 898.11
 commendation
 966.3
 verbs expand 196.4
 blow 402.23
 breathe 402.25
 smoke 433.15
 get tired 715.5
 boast 908.6
 praise 966.12
PUFF UP
 expand 196.4,5
 make conceited
 907.7
 praise 966.12
puffball 410.4
puffer 966.8
puffiness, puffing
 196.2
puffy 196.12
pug
 nouns footprint
 566.6
 pugilist 798.2
 adjs. 202.10
pugged 202.10
pugilism 794.9
pugilist 798.2
pugnacious 795.26
pugnacity 795.16
pug-nosed
 pugged 202.10
 deformed 248.12
puisne 124.15
puisne judge, puisne
 justice 1000.4
puissance power 156.1
 authoritativeness
 737.2
puissant potent 156.11
 authoritative 737.14
pujari 1036.13

puke
nouns 308.8
verbs 308.24
pukes 684.22
pukish, puky 684.42
pulchritude 898.1
pulchritudinous
898.16
Pulcinella 610.9
pule ululate 459.2
whimper 873.12
puling howling 459.6
whimpering 873.16
Pulitzer Prize 914.2
pull
nouns influence 171.2
pulling 285.2
attraction 287.1
drink 306.4
proof 601.5
effort 714.2
dram 994.6
PULL OVER 36.2
verbs row 274.56
draw 285.4
attract 287.4
extract 304.9
smoke 433.15
~ a proof 601.12
~ around 692.20
commit 703.6
~ for 712.7
strain 714.10
arrest 759.16
~ apart 967.15
PULL BACK
recoil 283.7
retract 296.3
demur 621.4
PULL DOWN
dismantle 49.14
fell 316.5
raze 691.19
receive 817.6
draw wages 839.20
PULL IN
draw in 286.9
retract 296.3
arrive 299.6
restrain 758.7
arrest 759.16
PULL OFF
commit 703.6
accomplish 720.5
succeed with 722.10
PULL ONESELF
TOGETHER 885.7
PULL ONE'S LEG
deceive 616.13
joke 879.14
make fun of 965.8
flatter 968.6
PULL OUT
aviate 277.46
leave 300.6
extract 304.9
secede 631.6
eradicate 691.14
PULL THE STRINGS
influence 171.9
control 739.12

PULL THE WOOL
OVER ONE'S EYES
616.16
PULL THROUGH
692.20
PULL TOGETHER
784.4
PULL TO PIECES
disjoin 49.13
demolish 691.17
find fault 967.15
PULL UP
stop 144.8,11
aviate 277.46
extract 304.9
arraign 1002.14
PULL UP STAKES
300.16
pullet child 125.3
younglet 125.8
pulling
nouns drawing 285.1
extraction 304.1
adjs. drawing 285.6
attracting 287.5
pulling power 287.1
Pullman, Pullman
car 271.13
pull-out 277.10
pullulate
be productive 164.7
grow 196.7
germinate 410.31
pullulation
proliferation 164.2
growth 196.3
germination 410.30
pull-up 277.10
pulmonary 402.30
pulmonary artery
395.14
pulmonic
pneumonic 224.12
diseased 684.46
pulp
nouns mash 389.2
magazine 603.11
verbs 389.5
**pulpefaction, pulpifi-
cation** 389.3
pulper, pulpifier 389.4
pulpify 389.5
pulpiness 389
pulpit
platform 215.13
ministry 1035.1
church 1040.12
pulpiter, pulpiteer
1036.3
pulpous 389.6
pulpousness 389.1
pulpwood 389.2
pulpy squashy 356.13
mushy 389.6
pulsate throb 322.11
drum 454.4
pulsatile 322.17
**pulsating, pulsative,
pulsatory**
throbbing 322.17
rhythmical 462.27

pulsation throb 322.3
drumming 454.1
rhythm 462.25
pulse
nouns pulsation
322.3
television ~ 344.4
radar ~ 345.10
plant 410.4
rhythm 462.25
verbs throb 322.11
resonate 453.6
pulsejet 279.3
pulsing
throbbing 322.17
resonating 453.9
rhythmical 462.27
pulsion 284.1
pulsive
impulsive 282.22
propulsive 284.15
pulverable 360.13
pulveraceous
powdery 360.11
pulverable 360.13
pulverization
abrasion 349.2
comminution 360.4
pulverize abrade 349.7
powder 360.9
pulverized 360.11
pulverizer mill 347.20
instrument 360.7
pulverous, pulvereous
360.11
pulverulence 360.1
pulverulent 360.11,13
puma 413.4
pumice 259.8
pummel strike 282.15
beat 1008.14
pump
nouns 347.22
verbs expand 196.4
extract 304.10
move up and down
322.13
interrogate 484.22
PUMP FULL OF LEAD
284.13
PUMP OUT 304.10
PUMP UP 196.4
pumped 715.10
pumping 304.2
pumpkin head 470.4
pumpkin-headed
468.17
pump room 687.31
pun
nouns assonance 20.3
witticism 879.8
verbs assonate 20.9
joke 879.13
punch
nouns die 25.6
energy 160.2
poke 282.2
blow 282.4
pungency 432.2
graver 576.11
eloquence 598.4

liquor 994.19
verbs perforate
264.15
poke 282.12
strike 282.14
~ cattle 415.7
PUNCH IN 114.12
PUNCH OUT
time out 114.12
leave 300.15
Punch and Judy 610.9
Punch-and-Judy show
609.14
punch bowl 994.12
**punch-cards, punched
cards** 348.18
punch-drunk 530.14
puncheon 377.3
puncher, cowpuncher
horseman 273.8
cowkeeper 415.3
Punchinello 610.9
punchy 202.10
punctate, punctated
373.13
punctilio
formalism 644.2
etiquette 644.3
technicality 749.4
fastidiousness 894.1
point of honor
972.2
punctilious
meticulous 531.12
formal 644.10
observant 766.4
fastidious 894.9
scrupulous 972.15
punctiliousness
meticulousness
531.3
precisianism 642.2
fastidiousness 894.1
punctual
prompt 131.9
meticulous 531.12
observant 766.4
scrupulous 972.15
**punctuality, punc-
tualness** 131.3
punctuate
~ a sentence 584.12
emphasize 670.13
punctuated 670.22
punctuation
grammar 584.11
types of ~ 584.14
puncture
nouns perforation
264.3
injury 690.7
verbs deflate 197.10
perforate 264.15
disprove 505.4
punctured 505.7
punctureproof
proof 158.18
impervious 265.13
puncturer 347.2
pundit
learned man 475.3

teacher 563.1
religious 1036.13
pundita 563.2
pungency
  bitterness 428.2
  sourness 431
  piquancy 432
  odorousness 434.2
  eloquence 598.4
  wittiness 879.2
pungent
  painful 423.10
  bitter 428.6
  sour 431.6
  piquant 432.6
  odorous 434.10
  eloquent 598.12
  witty 879.15
puniness
  inconsiderableness
    35.1
  littleness 195.1
  meagerness 660.2
  pettiness 671.1
punish 1008.10
punishing 1008.25
punishment
  deserts 958.3
  chastisement 1008
punitive, punitory
  revengeful 954.6
  penal 1008.25
punk
  nouns child 125.3
  lighter 330.6
  adjs. bad 673.8
  inferior 678.10
punkah 402.22
punkie 413a.7
punner, punster
  879.12
punning 879.8
punt
  nouns 282.9
  verbs row 274.56
  kick 282.20
  bet 514.19
punter 514.16
puny
  inconsiderable 35.7
  delicate 159.14
  little 195.9
  meager 660.8
  petty 671.17
pup
  nouns boy 125.5
  youngling 125.8
  tributary 394.3
  dog 413.24
  verbs 166.19
pupa 125.9
pupil eye 438.9
  student 564.1
puppet nonentity 4.2
  miniature 195.5
  figure 570.4
  cat's-paw 656.3
  figurehead 747.4
  doll 876.16
puppet show 609.14

puppy boy 125.5
  youngling 125.8
  dog 413.24
  fop 901.9
puppyism 901.4
puppy love 929.4
purana 1019.7
purblind
  dim-sighted 439.13
  undiscerning 468.14
  narrow-minded
    525.10
purblindness
  dim-sightedness
    439.2
  unperceptiveness
    468.2
  narrow-mindedness
    525.1
purchasable 973.22
purchase
  nouns influence 171.1
  foothold 215.5
  leverage 286.2
  tackle 286.6
  bribery 649.1
  hold 811.2
  buying 826
  verbs bribe 649.3
  buy 826.7
purchased 826.11
purchaser 826.5
purchasing
  nouns 826.1
  adjs. 826.10
purdah shade 337.1
  harem 931.11
pure simple 45.5
  utter 56.11
  genuine 515.13
  elegant 587.6
  plain-speaking 589.3
  perfect 675.6
  clean 679.23
  fresh 693.5
  tasteful 895.8
  simple 900.6
  innocent 982.7
  chaste 986.4
  godly 1026.9
pure-blooded,
  purebred 916.12
purée soup 306a.10
  semiliquid 388.5
pure-hearted
  chaste 986.4
  godly 1026.9
purely
  absolutely 34.21
  merely 35.11
  simply 45.9
  perfectly 675.10
  cleanly 679.27
purfle 234.10
purgation
  defecation 309.2
  cleansing 679.2
  psychological ∼
    688.36
  penance 1010.3

purgative
  nouns 685.15
  adjs. cleansing 679.26
  cathartic 685.41
purgatory
  torment 864.7
  penance 1010.3
  hell 1017.1
purge
  nouns elimination
    77.2
  catharsis 309.2
  killing 408.2
  purgation 679.2
  cathartic 685.15
  extermination 691.6
  deposal 781.1
  verbs get rid of 77.5
  do away with
    308.19
  evacuate 308.20
  kill 408.16
  cleanse 679.17
  physic 687.33
  exterminate 691.14
  depose 781.2
  absolve 1005.4
purged 679.24
purging
  nouns killing 408.2
  cleansing 679.2
  adjs. 679.26
purification
  refinement 354.3
  cleansing 679.2
  sanctification
    1024.3
purificator 679.16
purificatory 679.26
purified 679.24
purifier 679.16
purify refine 354.6
  cleanse 679.17
  sanctify 1024.5
purifying
  cleansing 679.26
  cathartic 685.41
Purim 1038.16
purism 901.5
purist classicist 587.4
  affecter 901.7
puritan prude 901.11
  ascetic 989.2
puritanical
  strait-laced 901.19
  ascetic 989.3
  hyperorthodox
    1022.9
puritanism
  asceticism 989.1
  hyperorthodoxy
    1022.6
purity no mixture 45.1
  elegant style 587.1
  cleanness 679.1
  innocence 982.1
  chastity 986.1
  godliness 1026.2
purl
  nouns 394.7
  verbs border 234.10

trickle 394.19
  eddy 394.22
  ripple 451.11
purlieu 190.23
purlieus region 179.1
  environs 232.1
purling 451.19
purloin 822.13
purloiner 823.1
purloining 822.1
purohit 1036.13
purpie 372.3
purple
  nouns color 372.1
  colors, pigments
    372.4
  robe of state 567.3
  sovereignty 737.7
  verbs 372.2
  adjs. purple-colored
    372.3
  royal 737.16
purple and fine linen
  726.1
purple passages, pur-
  ple patches 599.4
purplescent 372.3
purplish 372.3
purplure 372.1
purport
  nouns 543.1
  verbs mean 543.8
  allege 647.3
purported 647.4
purportless 545.9
purpose
  nouns meaning 543.2
  resolution 622.1
  intention 651.1
  function 663.5
  OF NO PURPOSE 667.9
  ON PURPOSE 651.11
  TO GOOD PURPOSE
    effectively 156.14
    successfully 722.14
  TO NO PURPOSE
    amiss 312.7
    uselessly 667.15
    unsuccessfully
      723.18
  TO THE PURPOSE
    apropos 9.8
    apt 26.18
  verbs resolve 622.7
  intend 651.4
purposed 651.9
purposeful
  determined 622.11
  intentional 651.9
purposefulness 622.1
purposeless
  aimless 155.16
  meaningless 545.9
  useless 667.9
purposelessness
  aimlessness 155.3
  uselessness 667.1
purposely 651.11
purr 451.13

purring
  nouns 451.7
  adjs. 451.20
pur sang 916.12
purse
  nouns funds 833.14
    wallet 834.14
  verbs pucker 197.7
    wrinkle 263.6
purse bearer 834.11
pursed
  puckered 197.12
  wrinkled 263.8
purser seaman 275.6
  provider 657.6
  bursar 834.11
purse race 794.13
purse snatcher 823.2
purse strings 834.14
pursing 197.1
pursuance
  continuance 143.1
  pursuit 653.1
  IN PURSUANCE OF
  for 651.12
  after 653.12
pursuant
  nouns 653.4
  adjs. 653.11
  PURSUANT TO 651.12
pursue specialize 81.4
  follow 292.3
  seek 484.24
  run after 653.8
  persecute 665.6
  carry on 703.7
  court 930.19
pursuer
  follower 292.2
  devotee 633.6
  chaser 653.4
  lover 929.11
pursuing
  nouns 653.1
  adjs. 653.11
pursuit specialty 81.1
  objective 651.2
  pursuing 653
  occupation 654.6
  IN PURSUIT 653.11
  IN PURSUIT OF 653.12
pursuivant 292.2
pursy puffy 196.12
  wrinkled 263.8
purulence 309.6
purulent pussy 309.19
  serous 387.7
purusha 1032.17
purvey 657.9
purveyance 657.1
purveyancer, purveyor
  657.6
purview 651.1
purwannah 775.5
pus matter 309.6
  fluid 387.3
push
  nouns company 74.3
  crowd 74.4
  crisis 129.4
  energy 160.2

shove 282.2
propulsion 284.1
urge 646.6
pushfulness 705.7
gang 786.7
attack 796.1
verbs shove 282.12
propel 284.10
press forward 293.4
urge 646.14
be active 705.12
hasten 707.4
try hard 712.10
importune 772.12
sell illicitly 824.7
PUSH ASIDE
postpone 132.8
dismiss 529.4
reject 636.2
put aside 666.6
PUSH BACK
repulse 288.2
ward off 797.10
PUSH DOWN
aviate 277.46
depress 316.4
PUSH FORWARD
forge ahead 293.4
further 783.17
PUSH IN
intrude 237.5
enter 301.7
thrust in 303.6
PUSH OFF 300.7
PUSH THE PEN, PUSH
  THE PENCIL 600.19
PUSH UP DAISIES
  409.23
PUSH UPON
urge upon 771.9
thrust upon 816.19
push car 271.15
push-down 277.10
pushed 707.11
pusher 279.2
pushful 705.22
pushfulness 705.7
pushing
  nouns 284.1
  adjs. meddlesome
    237.9
  propulsive 284.15
  enterprising 705.22
push-over
  weakling 159.6
  easy mark 618.1
  easy thing 730.3
pusillanimity, pusil-
  lanimousness 890.3
pusillanimous 890.12
puss girl 125.6
  face 239.4
  cat 413.28
pussiness 309.6
pussy girl 125.6
  cat 413.28
pussy purulent 309.19
  serous 387.7
pussyfoot
  nouns 482.7
  verbs creep 272.25

hedge 482.9
sneak 613.10
hedge 629.8
be cautious 893.5
pussyfooter 482.7
pussyfooting
  nouns politics 742.40
  quibbling 482.5
  adjs. 482.15
pustule
  swelling 255.4
  fester 684.28
put
  nouns throw 284.4
  fool 470.1
  dupe 618.1
  option 831.21
  rustic 917.9
  verbs attribute 154.2
  place 183.12
  repose 183.14
  sail 274.30
  butt 282.12
  throw 284.12
  hasten off 300.14
  vomit 308.24
  phrase 583.4
  administer 663.11
  invest in 834.16
  impose 961.4
  PUT ABOUT
  tack 274.32
  turn round 294.9
  publish 557.10
  excite 855.14
  PUT ACROSS
  make clear 546.6
  accomplish 720.5
  succeed with 722.10
  PUT ALL ONE'S EGGS
    IN ONE BASKET
    892.5
  PUT ASIDE
  segregate 77.6
  postpone 132.8
  remove 270.10
  dismiss 529.4
  reserve 658.12
  put away 666.6
  PUT A STOP TO
  stop 144.11
  prevent 728.13
  PUT AWAY
  eat 306.20
  kill 408.14
  reject 636.2
  store 658.10
  lay away 666.6
  dispose of 720.4
  divorce 933.5
  PUT BACK
  about-ship 274.32
  repulse 288.2
  turn back 294.8
  impair 690.10
  restore 692.11
  refuse 774.4
  ward off 797.10
  return 821.4
  PUT BEFORE
  confront 239.9

inform 555.7
propose 771.5
PUT DOWN
deposit 183.15
record 568.15
extinguish 691.15
suppress 758.8
pay 839.15
PUT FORTH
extend 178.7
grow 196.7
set forth 300.7
burgeon 410.32
publish 557.14
say 592.14
exert 714.8
offer 771.4
propose 771.5
display 902.17
PUT IN
spend time 105.6
install 183.17
internalize 224.8
interrupt 237.6
sail for 274.37
land 299.8
enter 301.7
insert 303.3
plant 412.18
spend 663.13
instate 778.11
PUT IN A SPOT 729.14
PUT IN A WORD FOR
  966.11
PUT IN FOR 772.9
PUT IN ONE'S HEAD
  555.9
PUT IN PLACE 183.11
PUT IN PRACTICE
apply 663.11
carry out 703.9
PUT OFF
postpone 132.8
doff 231.6
sail 274.20
sail from 274.38
evade 629.8
PUT ON
cover 227.21
don 230.42
obtrude 237.5
accelerate 268.15
help up 315.7
stage 609.32
feign 614.22
discommode 669.4
perform 703.8
hire 778.12
affect 901.12
be ostentatious
  902.14
impose 961.4,6,7
PUT ONE IN HIS
  PLACE 964.5
PUT ONESELF FOR-
  WARD 902.12
PUT ONESELF IN
  ANOTHER'S SHOES
  22.7
PUT ONESELF OUT
make an effort 712.9

queen's English 578.3
  MURDER THE QUEEN'S
    ENGLISH
  be ungrammatical
    585.3
  mispronounce
    593.10
queenship 737.7
queer
  nouns homosexual
    418.12
  courterfeit 833.10
  verbs disable 157.9
  spoil 690.11
  thwart 728.16
  adjs. odd 85.11
  homosexual 418.23
  insane 472.24
  eccentric 473.4
  false 514.27
queered 690.28
queer fish 85.4
queerly 85.18
queerness oddity 85.3
  insanity 472.1
  eccentricity 473.1
Queer Street 836.1
quell calm 162.7
  extinguish 691.15
  suppress 758.8
  subdue 762.9
quelled
  tempered 162.11
  subdued 762.14
quelling
  suppression 758.2
  subdual 762.4
quench
  extinguish 331.7
  discourage 650.4
  destroy 691.15
  suppress 758.8
  gratify 863.6
quenched 331.11
quenching
  extinguishment
    331.2
  suppression 758.2
quenchless
  inextinguishable
    142.19
  greedy 632.28
querier, querist
  inquirer 484.17
  inquisitive 526.2
quern, quernstone
  360.7
querulous
  plaintive 873.16
  peevish 949.21
querulously
  plaintively 873.19
  peevishly 949.28
query
  nouns 484.13
  verbs question
    484.21,22
  doubt 502.6
querying
  nouns 484.14
  adjs. 484.39

quest
  nouns 484.2
  IN QUEST OF 484.40
  verbs 484.24
question
  nouns topic 483.1
  query 484.13
  doubt 502.2
  uncertainty 513.8
  problem 547.7
  legislative ~ 740.15
  BEYOND QUESTION
  undoubted 512.16
  certainly 512.25
  IN QUESTION
  at issue 484.42
  questionable 513.15
  OUT OF THE QUESTION
  impossible 509.6
  rejected 636.3
  refused 774.7
  prohibited 776.7
  hopeless 887.14
  PUT TO THE QUESTION
  interrogate 484.22
  torture 1008.18
  WITHOUT QUESTION
    500.18
  verbs query 484.21,22
  doubt 502.6
  be uncertain 513.9
questionable
  unbelievable 502.10
  improbable 511.3
  doubtful 513.15
  deceptive 616.21
  dishonest 973.15
questionably 513.25
questionary 484.16
questioned 502.12
questionee 484.20
questioner
  inquirer 484.17
  inquisitive 526.2
questioning
  nouns 484.14
  adjs. inquiring 484.39
  doubtful 502.9
questionist
  inquirer 484.17
  student 564.5
questionless
  believing 500.18
  certain 512.16
question mark
  question 484.13
  problem 547.7
question-mark 484.22
questionnaire
  nouns 484.16
  verbs 484.38
queue
  nouns afterpart 67.2
  series 71.2
  hair 229.7
  tail 240.5
  waiting line 609.31
  verbs 71.7
quibble
  nouns cavil 482.4

ambiguity 548.2
  verbs 482.9
quibbler 482.7
quibbling
  nouns 482.5
  adjs. 482.15
quiblet 482.4
quick
  nouns vital part 5.4
  sore spot 421.4
  THE QUICK 406.4
  TO THE QUICK 421.15
  adjs. transient 111.8
  sudden 113.5
  prompt 131.9
  fast 268.19
  living 406.10
  smart 466.14
  alert 531.14
  teachable 562.18
  impulsive 628.9
  lively 705.17
  hasty 707.9
  dexterous 731.20
  hot-tempered
    949.25
  advs. 268.21
quick ear 447.3
quicken energize 160.9
  accelerate 268.15
  be born 406.7
  vivify 406.8
  sensitize 421.8
  refresh 693.2
  hasten 707.4
  facilitate 730.6
  further 783.17
  stimulate 855.12
quickening
  nouns invigoration
    160.7
  acceleration 268.5
  vivification 406.5
  hastening 707.3
  facilitation 730.4
  adjs. energizing
    160.13
  life-giving 406.11
quick-freeze
  freeze 333.11
  preserve 699.8
quick-freezer 333.5
quick freezing 333.1
quick-freezing
  freezing 333.12
  preservation 699.2
quick-froze, quick-
    frozen 333.14
quickie 787.7
quickly briefly 111.10
  promptly 131.15
  swiftly 268.21
  impulsively 628.13
  lively 705.24
  hastily 707.12
quickness
  promptness 131.3
  velocity 268.1
  smartness 466.2
  alertness 531.5
  teachability 562.5

impulsiveness 628.2
alacrity 705.3
haste 707.2
dexterousness 731.1
quick parts 466.2
quicksand 399.1
quicksands 695.5
quick-scented 434.13
quicksilver
  nouns changeability
    141.4
  speed 268.7
  metal 382.3
  adjs. 705.16
quickstep march
  gait 272.15
  music 461.11
quick-tempered
  949.25
quick-witted
  smart 466.14
  witty 879.15
quick-wittedness
  smartness 466.2
  wittiness 879.2
quid
  nouns essence 5.2
  cud 306.2
  tobacco 433.8
  coin 833.8
  verbs 433.15
quiddity essence 5.2
  quibble 482.4
quidnunc
  inquisitive 526.2
  gossip 556.9
quid pro quo
  equivalent 33.2
  interchange 149.1
quiescence, quies-
    cency 267.1
quiescent still 267.10
  silent 450.12
quiet
  nouns quiescence
    267.1
  silence 450.1
  peace 801.2
  mental calm 856.2
  ON THE QUIET 612.20
  verbs calm 162.7
  hush 450.7,8
  adjs. quiescent 267.10
  silent 450.11
  gentle 763.15
  peaceful 801.9
  inexcitable 856.12
  tasteful 895.8
  modest 906.11
  KEEP QUIET
  be quiescent 267.7
  silence! 450.16
  interjs. 450.16
quieten 450.7,8
quietener
  silencer 450.4
  sedative 685.11
quietening
  nouns 162.2
  adjs. tranquilizing
    162.15

sedative 685.39
quieting 162.2
quietism 859.2
quietlike 450.15
quietly
  quiescently 267.16
  silently 450.15
  gently 763.19
  composedly 856.16
  tastefully 895.11
  modestly 906.14
quietness
  quiescence 267.1
  silence 450.1
  gentleness 763.5
  peace 801.2
  tastefulness 895.4
quietsome 450.11
quietude
  quiescence 267.1
  silence 450.1
  peace 801.2
  mental calm 856.2
quietus end-all 70.4
  death 407.1
  deathblow 408.9
  defeat 725.1
  acquittal 1005.1
  GIVE THE QUIETUS
  end 70.7
  kill 408.18
  destroy 691.11
quill
  nouns 229.16,17
  GET ONE'S QUILLS UP
  950.17
  verbs 263.5
quill driver 600.14
quill driving 600.1
quilled 263.7
quill pig 413.4
quilt 227.11
quilting bee 920.12
quinary 99.17
quincentenary 137.4
quincentennial 137.4
quincuncial 99.17
quincunx 99.1
**quindecennial, quin-
decim, quinde-
cima, quindene**
  99.7
quindecillion 99.13
quinine 99.5
quinquefid 99.17
quinquennial 137.4
quinquennium 107.2
quinquepartite 99.17
quinquepartition
  99.14
quinquesect 99.15
quinquesection 99.14
quinsy 684.12
quint 99.1
quintain 651.2
quintessence
  essence 5.2
  extract 304.7
  the best 672.8
  perfection 675.3

quintessential
  distinctive 80.13
  extracted 304.16
  typical 570.12
  best 672.19
quintet, quintette
  five 99.1
  music 461.17
quintillion 99.13
quintroon 44.9
**quintuple,
quintuplicate**
  verbs 99.16
  adjs. 99.17
quintuplet 99.1
quip
  nouns eccentricity
  473.2
  quibble 482.4
  caprice 627.1
  witticism 879.7
  gibe 965.2
  verbs 879.13
quipster 879.12
quire 377.6
quirk twist 248.1
  eccentricity 473.2
  quibble 482.4
  caprice 627.1
  witticism 879.7
  mannerism 901.2
quirt 1009.1
quisle 973.14
Quisling, quisling
  617.10
quit
  nouns 77.2
  verbs separate 49.19
  cease 144.6
  depart 300.8
  abandon 631.5
  disuse 666.4
  resign 782.2
  repay 839.11
  adjs. 760.28
  GET QUIT OF
  get rid of 77.5
  dispose of 308.19
  discard 666.7
  free oneself 761.8
  QUIT OF 760.28
quitclaim
  nouns 812.2
  verbs 812.3
quite somewhat 29.7
  very 34.20
  positively 34.21
  absolutely 56.16
  that's right 515.22
  yes 520.18
  NOT QUITE
  comparative 490.8
  almost 199.25
quitrent 844.9
quits 30.8
  BE QUITS 953.7
  GET QUITS WITH
  839.12
quittance
  payment 839.1,3

receipt 842.2
  reprisal 953.2
  acquittal 1005.1
  atonement 1010.1
quitter 629.3
quiver
  nouns sheath 192.19
  agitation 323.3,4
  flicker 334.8
  tremolo 462.19
  excitement 855.2
  trepidation 855.4
  IN A QUIVER
  excited 855.24
  nervous 857.12
  verbs shake 323.11,12
  shiver 332.10
  flicker 334.25
  be excited 855.18
  be afraid 889.13
quivering
  nouns agitation 323.2
  flickering 334.8
  trepidation 855.4
  adjs. shaking 323.18
  flickering 334.36
  nervous 857.12
quivery shaky 323.18
  flickery 334.36
  nervous 857.12
qui vive
  ON THE QUI VIVE
  alert 531.14
  excited 855.21
Quixote 533.13
quixotic(al) 533.24
quixotism, quixotry
  533.7
quixotize 533.16
quiz
  nouns examination
  484.3,14
  quizzer 484.17
  inquisitive 526.2
  joke 879.7,10
  banter 880.1
  laughingstock
  965.7
  verbs interrogate
  484.22
  banter 880.4
quizz 965.9
quizzee 484.20
quizzer 484.17
quizzical
  inquiring 484.39
  inquisitive 526.5
  amusing 878.5
  bantering 880.5
quizzically 878.7
quizzing
  nouns questioning
  484.14
  banter 880.2
  adjs. 484.39
quizzing glass 442.2
quoad hoc 9.11
quod 759.8
**quod erat demon-
strandum** 504.27

quoil
  nouns 253.2
  verbs 253.5
quoin
  cornerstone 215.7
  corner 250.2
quoit 284.6
quondam 119.7
Quonset hut 190.9
quorum 74.2
quota ratio 86.6
  share 814.5
quotation
  repetition 103.1
  citation 504.6
  stock ~ 832.8
  price 844.2
quote repeat 103.7
  cite 504.14
  ~ a price 844.13
quotidian 137.9
quotient 86.9
quotum 86.6
q.v. 504.26

R

Ra, Amen-Ra
  sun 374.11
  god 1012.9
rabbet
  nouns 47.4
  verbs 47.8
rabbi, rabbin 1036.11
rabbinic(al) 1035.13
rabbinism 1018.10
rabbinist 1018.19
rabbit
  productiveness
  164.6
  animal 413.29
rabbit-foot 1034.5
rabble mob 74.4
  the masses 917.4
rabble rouser 646.11
rabble-rousing
  nouns incitement
  646.4
  electioneering
  742.12
  adjs. 646.28
Rabelaisian 965.13
rabid mad 472.29
  fanatical 472.31
  overwrought 855.26
  infuriated 950.29
rabidly 855.36
rabidness
  insanity 472.1
  fanaticism 472.11
rabies 472.7
race
  nouns people 11.4;
  417
  prehistoric ~
  123.25
  speed 268.4
  stream 394.1
  flow 394.4
  watercourse 395.2

promotion 780.1
verbs increase 38.4
assemble 74.17
rear 166.11
construct 166.12
erect 212.8
emboss 255.11
elevate 315.5
leaver 352.7
grow 412.16
train 560.13
utter 592.14
provoke 646.19
recruit 778.14
promote 780.3
excite 855.11
glorify 912.13
conjure 1033.11
RAISE A BREEZE
create a disturbance
  62.9
brawl 793.13
RAISE A CRY 566.21
RAISE A HOWL
object 520a.5
complain 873.13
RAISE A HUE AND
  CRY 458.8
RAISE A HUE AND CRY
  AGAINST 967.13
RAISE A LAUGH
  876.23
RAISE AN ALARM
  702.6
RAISE A QUESTION
  502.6
RAISE CAIN
create a disturbance
  62.9
be noisy 452.7
vociferate 458.8
be angry 950.15
RAISE EXPECTATIONS
  886.10
RAISE FROM THE
  DEAD 692.16
RAISE GHOSTS
  1033.11
RAISE MONEY 819.3
raised
produced 166.25
in relief 255.17
elevated 315.9
raiser
producer 166.10
farmer 412.5
raising
nouns erect on 212.4
elevation 315.1
growing 412.12
upbringing 560.3
adjs. 352.16
raison d'être 551.2
raja, rajah 747.10
raj-gaddi 737.10
raj-kumari 915.9
Rajput 798.5
rake
nouns thinness 204.7
slope 218.2
teeth 257.5

libertine 987.10
verbs slope 218.10
cultivate 412.17
search 484.27
comb 679.20
enfilade 796.23
debauch 987.19
RAKE OVER THE
  COALS 967.18
RAKE UP
collect 74.17
procure 809.9
RAKE UP THE PAST
  535.12
rakehell, rakehellish
  987.25
rake-off profit 809.3
commission 814.5
pay 839.7
raking 218.15
raking-down 967.6
rakish 987.25
rakishness 987.3
rallentando
nouns 461.25
adjs. 461.55
rally
nouns assemblage
  74.2
recovery 692.8
political ~ 742.12
call to arms 795.13
stock market ~
  832.8
verbs arrange 60.8
assemble 74.15,17
improve 689.8
recover 692.19,20
call to arms 795.24
banter 880.4
ridicule 965.9
RALLY ROUND
form 59.4
assemble 74.15
side with 784.6
rallying cry
call 566.15
rally 795.13
ram
nouns sheep 413.9
male animal 419.8
verbs 282.12
RAM DOWN 353.9
RAM DOWN ONE'S
  THROAT 816.19
RAM IN
fill 56.7
thrust in 303.6
Rama 1012.8
Ramadan 993.3
ramage 410.16
Ramanandi 1036.13
ramark 345.7
ramble
nouns wandering
  272.3
walk 272.12
verbs wander 272.22
deviate 290.4
be insane 472.19
digress 591.9

RAMBLE ON 594.6
rambler 273.2
ramble-scramble
adjs. 62.15
advs. in disorder
  62.16
carelessly 532.18
recklessly 892.11
rambling
nouns wandering
  272.3
deviation 290.1
discursiveness 591.3
adjs. desultory 141.7
wandering 272.36
deviative 290.7
circuitous 319.7
delirious 472.30
distracted 530.10
discursive 591.13
rambunctious 161.19
ramification
member 55.4
branching 298.3
branch 298.4
ramify 298.7
Ramillie 229.14
ramjet 279.3
ram-jet propulsion
aviation 277.30
propulsion 284.2
ramous 298.10
ramp
nouns incline 218.4
take-off ~ 280.11
swindle 616.8
verbs rampage 161.10
climb 313.11
romp 317.6
swindle 616.18
steal 822.13
rampacious 161.19
rampage
nouns 62.4
GO ON A RAMPAGE
create a disturbance
  62.8
become violent
  161.14
verbs 161.10
rampageous 161.19
rampant
prevalent 79.11
unruly 161.18
perpendicular
  212.11
upreared 315.9
abundant 659.7
unrestrained 760.22
rampart
buttress 215.4
barrier 728.5
fortification 797.4
ramroddy 355.11
ramshackle 690.32
Ramwat 1036.13
Ran 194.13
rana 747.10
ranch
nouns 412.8
verbs 412.16

rancher farmer 412.5
cattleman 415.2
rancheria 412.8
ranchero 415.3
ranch house 190.5
ranchman
farmer 412.5
cattleman 415.2
rancho village 182.2
hut 190.9
ranch 412.8
rancid fetid 436.5
tainted 690.39
rancidness 436.2
rancor animosity 927.4
malevolence 937.7
resentment 950.3
revengefulness
  954.2
rancorous
malevolent 937.20
resentful 950.24
revengeful 954.6
randan
commotion 62.4
revel 876.6
spree 994.5
randem 271.5
random
nouns 155.4
AT RANDOM
haphazardly 62.17
casually 155.19
adjs. orderless 62.11
haphazard 155.16
random data 348.19
random shot
chance 155.4
gamble 514.2
randy revel 876.6
spree 994.5
range
nouns rank 29.1
series 71.2
compass 178.2
habitat 190.4
size 194.1
distance 198.1
mountain ~ 206.9
list of mountain
  ranges 206.29
direction 289.1
pasture 410.8
~ of vision 443.3
earshot 447.4
scale 462.6
scope 760.3
OUT OF RANGE 198.22
WITHIN RANGE
  199.20
verbs arrange 60.8
line up 71.6
extend 178.7
size 194.15
wander 272.22
search 484.25
RANGE ITSELF 59.4
RANGE WITH 784.6
range finding 345.8
rangeman 697.5
Ranger 798.6

ranger forester 412.7
    guardian 697.5
range rider 697.5
ranging
    nouns 345.9
    adjs. 272.36
rangy 206.21
rani empress 747.12
    princess 916.9
rank
    nouns character 7.5
    grade 29.2
    class 61.2
    series 71.2
    military 798.19
    prestige 912.4
    nobility 916.1
    verbs outrank 36.8
    arrange 60.8
    classify 61.6
    precede 64.2
    range 71.6
    size 194.15
    assess 493.9
    be regarded 493.15
    adjs. downright
        34.14
    coarse 260.6
    luxuriant 410.41
    unsavory 428.7
    strong-flavored
        432.8
    malodorous 436.5
    bad 673.9
    foul 680.25
    tainted 690.39
    infamous 913.12
    wicked 979.17
    indecent 988.8
rank and file
    army 798.22
    commonalty 917.1
ranked 60.13
ranking
    nouns 61.1
    adjs. 36.16
ranking member
    744.3
rankle
    suppurate 309.13
    make sore 423.7
    be remembered
        535.15
    putrefy 690.23
    prey on 864.21
rankling
    nouns festering 309.6
    soreness 423.4
    resentment 950.3
    adjs. festering 309.19
    sore 423.11
rankness
    strong flavor 432.3
    malodorousness
        436.2
    terribleness 673.2
    filthiness 680.2
    infamousness 913.3
    indecency 988.3
ranks 798.22

ransack
    rummage 484.27
    plunder 822.15
ransacking
    search 484.2
    pillage 822.5
ransom
    nouns rescue 700.1
    recovery 821.3
    verbs redeem 692.12
    rescue 700.2
    recover 821.6
rant
    nouns bombast 599.2
    bluster 909.1
    verbs be violent
        161.10
    be insane 472.19
    declaim 597.9
    overact 609.35
    get excited 855.17
    bluster 909.3
    rage angrily 950.15
rantan, ran-tan
    commotion 62.4
    drum 454.1
    revel 876.6
    spree 994.5
ranter speaker 597.4
    blusterer 909.2
    pietist 1027.3
ranting
    nouns 472.9
    adjs. rabid 472.29,30
    overwrought 855.26
    blustering 909.4
    infuriated 950.29
rantipole 892.4
rao 747.10
rap
    nouns knock 282.4
    blow 282.6
    bang 455.1
    trifle 671.5
    gibe 965.2
    criticism 967.4
    rascal 984.3
    sentence 1006.1
    RAP ON THE
        KNUCKLES
    reprimand 967.5,17
    punishment 1008.3
    verbs knock 282.15
    hit 282.16
    bang 455.6
    criticize 967.14
    RAP OUT
    exclaim 458.7
    ~ an oath 970.6
rapacious
    greedy 632.28
    grasping 820.23
rapacity greed 632.8
    predacity 820.7
rape
    nouns theft 822.5
    debauchment 987.6
    verbs seize 820.12
    debauch 987.20
raper 987.12
Raphael 1013.4

raphe 47.4
rapid
    nouns 394.10
    adjs. steep 218.18
    fast 268.19
rapidity 268.1
rapidly 268.21
rapids 394.10
rapine 822.5
rapist 987.12
rapparee 823.7
rappee 433.9
rapper
    falsehood 614.12
    oath 970.4
rapping 455.11
rapport relation 9.1
    agreement 26.1
    empathy 688.43
    accord 792.1
    IN RAPPORT
    in agreement 26.14
    in accord 792.3
rapprochement
    accord 792.1
    reconciliation 802.3
rapscallion 984.3
rapt
    preoccupied 477.21
    interested 528.18
    overjoyed 863.14
raptorial 811.9
rapture delight 863.2
    trance 1034.3
rapturous 863.14
rapturously 863.16
rara avis oddity 85.5
    celebrity 912.9
rare
    nouns 55.5
    adjs. unsubstantial
        4.5
    unusual 85.10
    sparse 102.5
    infrequent 136.2
    thin 204.15
    undercooked 329.8
    rarefied 354.7
    scarce 660.9
    notable 670.18
raree show 609.14
rarefaction
    expansion 196.1
    rarity 354.2
rarefactive 354.8
rarefication 196.1
rarefied
    unsubstantial 4.5
    diluted 159.19
    thin 204.15
    rare 354.7
rarefy dilute 159.11
    expand 196.4
    thin 204.11
    attenuate 354.5
rare gas 400.1
rarely unusually 85.16
    infrequently 136.4
    scarcely 660.14
rare metals 382.3
rarifaction 354.2

rarify 354.5
rarity unusualness 85.2
    oddity 85.5
    fewness 102.1
    infrequency 136.1
    thinness 204.4
    tenuity 354
    scarcity 660.3
    prodigy 918.2
rascal 984.3
rascality 973.2
rascally 973.16
rase See **raze**
rash
    nouns 684.27
    adjs. hasty 707.10
    incautious 892.7
rasher piece 55.3
    slice 226.2
    ~ of bacon 306a.16
rashly hastily 707.15
    incautiously 892.10
rasorial 413.45
rasp
    nouns 457.3
    verbs abrade 349.7
    chafe 423.7
    sound harshly 457.9
    irritate 864.18
raspberry 965.3
    GIVE THE RASPBERRY
        965.10
raspiness 457.2
rasping
    nouns 349.2
    adjs. grinding 349.10
    chafing 423.13
    harsh-sounding
        457.15
raspings remains 43.1
    filings 360.5
    refuse 667.4
raspy 457.15
rassle, rastle 794.14
rassler, rastler 798.3
rassling, rastling
    794.10
rat
    nouns hairpiece
        229.13
    traitor 617.10
    deserter 626.5,6
    strikebreaker 787.6
    scoundrel 984.6
    verbs inform on
        555.11
    desert 631.6
    scab 787.11
rataplan, rat-a-tat
    nouns 454.1
    verbs 454.4
ratchet 257.5
rate
    nouns rank 29.2
    ratio 86.6
    velocity 268.2
    interest 838.3
    price 844.1,3
    AT A GREAT RATE
    swiftly 268.21
    dearly 846.13

AT ANY RATE
notwithstanding
33.8
at least 35.11
certainly 512.23
anyhow 655.12
verbs quantify 28.4
classify 61.6
measure 489.11
assess 493.9
be regarded 493.15
price 844.13
deserve 958.5
berate 967.20
RATE HIGHLY 670.12
rated 844.16
rated man 747.21
ratepayer 839.9
rath 797.6
rather
nouns 635.4
verbs 635.14
advs. contrarily 15.7
somewhat 29.7
however 33.8
instead 148.11
preferably 635.25
tolerably 672.25
interjs. that's right
515.22
yes! 520.18
ratherish 29.7
rathskeller 994.25
ratification
confirmation 504.5
endorsement 520.4
ratifier 520.7
ratify confirm 504.12
endorse 520.12
rating rank 29.2
classification 61.1
class 61.2
measurement 489.1
estimate 493.3
officer 747.21
credit ~ 337.1
worth 844.4
berating 967.8
ratio degree 29.1
mathematical ~
86.6
comparability 490.3
ratiocination
thought 477.1
reasoning 481.1
ratiocinative 481.19
ratiocinator 481.12
ration
nouns 814.6
verbs provision 657.9
budget 814.11
rational
nouns 152.2
adjs. mathematics
86.8
mental 465.6
intelligent 466.12,
18
sane 471.4
reasonable 481.19,
21

practical 534.6
rationale reason 152.2
explanation 550.4
rationalism
reasoning 481.1
theology 1021.1
rationalist 481.12
rationalistic(al)
499.10
rationality
intelligence 466.1
sensibleness 466.6
sanity 471.1
reasonableness
481.1,10
practicalness 534.2
rationalization
reasoning 481.1
psychological ~
688.34
justification 1004.1
rationalize
reason 481.15
justify 1004.9
rationalizer 481.12
rationalizing 481.1
rationally
intelligently 466.20
reasonably 481.23
rationing 814.6
rations
provisions 306a.6
half ~ 660.5
ratlike 413.40
rat poison
pesticide 408.11
liquor 994.15
rat race 667.2
rat's-tail, rattail
hair 229.7
tail 240.5
rattan cane 377.4
whip 1009.2
ratter 626.5
ratting 631.2
rattle
nouns racket 452.3
noisemaker 452.5
clatter 454.3
percussive 464.20
fluster 530.3
nonsense 545.4
chatterer 594.5
predicament 729.4
prison 759.8
verbs clatter 454.6
fluster 530.7
twaddle 545.8
chatter 594.6
rattleboned 204.16
rattlebones
thin person 204.8
music 464.20
rattlebox 452.5
rattlebrain, rattlehead,
rattlepate 470.7
rattlebrained, rattle-
headed, rattlepated
empty-headed
468.19

scatterbrained
530.16
rattled 530.12
rattler train 271.12
railway car 271.13
rattletrap
chatterer 594.5
wreck 690.9
rattletraps 808.2
rattling
nouns 454.3
adjs. 454.8
rattly 454.8
rattrap 616.11
ratty infested 311.11
ratlike 413.40
shabby 690.31
raucity 457.2
raucous 457.14
raucousness 457.2
ravage
nouns infestation
311.2
devastation 691.1
pillage 822.5
debauchment 987.6
verbs infest 311.6
devastate 691.10
plunder 822.15
debauch 987.20
ravaged
infested 311.11
ruined 691.27
ravagement 822.5
ravager
plunderer 823.6
debaucher 987.12
ravages of time
disintegration 53.1
time 105.3
deterioration 690.5
ravaging
nouns 822.5
adjs. destructive
691.25
plunderous 822.21
rave be violent 161.10
be insane 472.19
enthuse 633.8
get excited 855.17
bluster 909.3
rage angrily 950.15
RAVE AGAINST 967.20
ravel
nouns 46.2
verbs disinvolve 45.4
complicate 46.3
solve 486.2
ravelin 797.4
raven
nouns 364.4
verbs plunder 822.15
eat greedily 992.5
RAVEN FOR 632.18
adjs. 364.8
ravening
turbulent 161.17
desirous 632.25
greedy 632.28
rapacious 820.23

ravenous
greedy 632.26,28
rapacious 820.23
gluttonous 992.7
ravenously
greedily 632.33
gluttonously 992.9
raver 909.2
ravine 200.3
raving
nouns 472.9
adjs. turbulent
161.17
rabid 472.29,30
overwrought 855.26
beautiful 898.19
blustering 909.4
infuriated 950.29
ravioli 306a.32
ravish seize 820.12
plunder 822.15
delight 863.8
debauch 987.20
ravished 863.14
ravisher
plunderer 823.6
debaucher 987.12
ravishing
alluring 648.7
delightful 861.6
beautiful 898.19
ravishment
pillage 822.5
delight 863.2
debauchment 987.6
raw
nouns 421.4
IN THE RAW 231.14
adjs. immature
124.10
naked 231.14
cold 332.15
wind-swept 402.28
sore 423.11
ignorant 476.13
undeveloped 719.10
unprepared 719.11
inexperienced
732.17
vulgar 896.11
indecent 988.8
rawal, rawat 747.10
rawboned 204.16
raw deal 975.4
rawhide
nouns skin 228.1
whip 1009.1
verbs 1008.14
rawhiding 1008.4
raw material
material 377.1
undevelopment
719.5
rawness
immaturity 124.3
cold 332.1
ignorance 476.1
unpreparedness
719.4
unskillfulness 732.2
vulgarity 896.2

indecency 988.3
raw recruit
  novice 564.7
  recruit 798.17
ray
  nouns radius 203.3
  radiation 298.2
  radiorays 326.3
  ~ of light 334.5
  ~ of sunshine
    334.10; 886.6
  ~ of hope 886.4
  verbs 298.6
  interjs. 874.12
rayless 440.8
raze, rase level 213.6
  fell 316.5
  graze 349.7
  obliterate 691.16
  demolish 691.19
razoredge 257.2
razor-edged 257.11
razor strap 1009.1
razz
  nouns 965.3
  verbs banter 880.4
  ridicule 965.8
razzia raid 796.4
  pillage 822.5
razzing 880.2
razzle-dazzle
  nouns commotion
    62.4
  noisemaker 452.5
  confusion 530.3
  verbs 530.7
re
  nouns 462.7
  preps. 9.10
reabsorb 305.15
reabsorption 305.8
reach
  nouns degree 29.1
  compass 178.2
  distance 198.1
  length 201.1
  wagon ~ 216.1
  plain 386.1
  inlet 398.1
  earshot 447.4
  OUT OF REACH
    out-of-the-way
      198.9
    out of range 198.22
    inaccessible 509.8
  WITHIN REACH
    present 185.12
    near 199.20
    accessible 508.8
  verbs equal 30.6
  influence 171.9
  extend 178.7
  arrive 299.6
  arrive at 299.7
  overtake 299.9
  be heard 447.13
  communicate with
    552.8
  bribe 649.3
  go around 659.4
  deliver 816.13

NOT ABLE TO REACH
    37.7
NOT REACH 312.2
REACH A COMPROMISE
    805.2
REACH OUT
    extend 178.7
    be distant 198.5
    be long 201.8
TRY TO REACH
    632.20
reachable 508.8
reaching 299.1
reach-me-down
    123.18
react respond 283.5
  ~ emotionally
    853.11
  REACT TO 485.6
reactance 341.12
reacting 283.9
reaction effect 153.3
  aviation 277.30
  response 283
  opinion 500.4
  resistance 790.1
  emotional ~ 853.5
reactionary
  nouns conservative
    140.4
  recalcitrant 283.4
  malcontent 867.3
  adjs. conservative
    140.8
  reversionary 146.7
  counteractive 177.8
  reactive 283.9
  apostate 626.11
reactionaryism
  conservatism 140.3
  apostasy 626.2
reactionism 626.2
reactionist
  nouns conservative
    140.4
  recalcitrant 283.4
  malcontent 867.3
  adjs. conservative
    140.8
  apostate 626.11
reactivate
  energy 160.10
  restore 692.11
  remilitarize 795.25
reactivation
  activation 160.8
  restoration 692.1
  remilitarization
    795.15
reactive 283.9
reactology 688.1
reactor 325.12
read understand 546.7
  interpret 550.10
  peruse 562.12
  recite 597.9
  proofread 601.15
READ BETWEEN THE
    LINES 550.10
READ LAW 562.15

READ ONESELF IN
    1035.11
READ OUT OF
    expel from 308.18
    depose 781.2
READ THE RIOT ACT
    order 750.11
    reprove 967.17
READ UP ON 562.14
readability 546.3
readable 546.11
readapt 26.13
readaptation 26.4
reader computer unit
    348.18
  reading glass 442.1
  advertisement 557.6
  teacher 563.8
  speaker 597.5,7
  proofreader 601.11
  textbook 603.8
  newspaperman
    603.22
  churchman 1036.9
readers 442.2
readership 563.11
readily willingly 620.8
  eagerly 633.13
  availably 663.26
  quickly 705.24
  easily 730.13
readiness
  promptness 131.3
  tendency 173.1
  alertness 531.5
  teachability 562.5
  willingness 620.1
  eagerness 633.1
  quickness 705.3
  preparedness 718.4
  dexterousness 731.1
reading
  radar signal 345.11
  scholarship 474.5
  version 550.2
  perusal 562.3
  recitation 597.2
READING IN 1035.10
reading desk
  desk 215.16
  lectern 1040.12
reading glass 442.1
reading matter 601.4
readjust
  readapt 26.13
  rearrange 60.12
  restore 692.11
readjustment
  readaptation 26.4
  rearrangement 60.6
  rehabilitation 145.3
  psychological ~
    688.38
  restoration 692.1
readmission 305.8
readmit 305.15
ready
  nouns 718.1
  THE READY 833.17
  verbs train 560.13
  fix 692.14

prepare 718.6
READY UP
  plan 652.9
  prepare 718.6
  adjs. prompt 131.9
  alert 531.14
  teachable 562.18
  willing 620.5
  eager 633.9
  handy 663.19
  quick 705.17
  prepared 718.16
  dexterous 731.20
NOT BE READY 719.6
READY FOR
  liable to 174.5
  prepared for 718.19
READY TO 173.6
  interjs. 718.26
**ready-built, ready-
  cooked, ready-cut,
  etc.** 718.20
readying
  training 560.3
  preparation 718.1
**ready-made, ready-to-
  wear**
  made 166.27
  ready-prepared
    718.20
ready-mades 230.4
ready money 833.17
ready pen 600.2
ready reply 485.1
ready wit
  smartness 466.2
  wit 879.1
reaffirm 103.8
reaffirmation 103.2
reagent
  chemical 378.1
  test 488.5
real
  adjs. actual 1.15
  substantial 3.4
  mathematical 86.8
  true 515.11,13
  literal 543.12
  of property 808.10
  NOT REAL 2.8
  advs. 34.20
real estate 808.7
Realgymnasium 565.6
realism
  naturalism 84.1
  practicalness 534.2
realist
  nouns 534.3
  adjs. 534.6
realistic lifelike 20.16
  naturalistic 84.7
  philosophical
    499.10
  practical 534.6
  descriptive 606.15
reality actuality 1.2
  truth 515
  genuineness 515.5
  IN REALITY
    really 1.16
    truly 515.16

realization
cognizance 474.2
accomplishment
720.1
realize know 474.12
understand 546.7
achieve 720.4
~ a profit 809.10
sell for 827.8
realized known 474.26
accomplished 720.9
really
advs. actually 1.16
positively 34.21
is that so? 484.48
truly 515.16,17
yes 520.18
literally 543.15
interjs. 918.17
realm region 179.2
country 180.1
sphere of work
654.4
realness 515.5
Realpolitik 742.1
real presence 1038.8
realtor 828.9
realty 808.7
ream
nouns 277.6
verbs 264.15
reanimate
revive 692.16
refresh 693.2
reanimation 692.3
reap harvest 412.19
acquire 809.7
REAP THE BENEFIT
OF
utilize 663.15
profit 663.17
get one's deserts
958.6
Reaper 407.3
reaper 412.5
reaping 412.15
reappear repeat 103.11
recur 137.6
rise again 406.7
reappearance
repetition 103.1
periodicity 137.2
reappearing
recurrent 103.13
reproductive 168.15
renascent 692.24
rear
nouns background
232.2
hinder part 240
~ guard 240.2
rump 240.4
verbs loom 34.7
produce 166.11
construct 166.12
be high 206.15
rise 212.7
erect 212.8
sail 274.58
raise 315.5
grow 412.16

train 560.13
adjs. 240.8
rear admiral 747.24
rear end 240.1
rear guard rear 240.2
guard 697.8
rearing erection 212.4
elevation 315.1
growing 412.12
upbringing 560.3
rearmost 240.8
rearrange 60.12
rearrangement 60.6
rearward
adjs. 240.8
advs. hindward
240.14
backwards 294.13
reasiness See
reastiness
reason
nouns cause 152.2
intellect 465.1
sensibleness 466.6
sanity 471.1
logic 481.6,10
solution 486.1
explanation 550.4
motive 646.1
justification 1004.6
BY REASON OF
hence 154.6
because of 154.9
GO BEYOND REASON
511.2
IN REASON
palliative 162.16
reasonably 481.23
rightfully 956.9
in justice 974.12
OUT OF ALL REASON
482.16
REASON WHY 152.2
STAND TO REASON
be reasonable
481.18
be certain 512.9
be manifest 553.7
WITHIN REASON
481.23
WITHOUT REASON
482.10
verbs rationalize
481.15
discuss 481.16
deduce 493.10
REASON IN A CIRCLE
482.8
REASON OUT 477.10
REASON WITH 595.10
reasonability
logicality 481.10
plausibility 510.2
justifiability 1004.7
reasonable
moderate 162.12
intelligent 466.12,
18
sane 471.4
logical 481.21

practical 534.6
inexpensive 847.7
justifiable 1004.14
reasonableness
judgment 466.6
logicalness 481.10
practicalness 534.2
inexpensiveness
847.1
reasonably
intelligently 466.20
logically 481.23
inexpensively
847.10
reasoner
rationalist 481.12
sophist 482.6
philosopher 499.7
reasoning
nouns rationalizing
481
specious ~ 482.1
adjs. mental 465.6
rational 481.19
reasonless
unintelligent 468.13
unwise 469.9
insane 472.24
illogical 482.10
impulsive 628.10
reassemble 74.20
reassembly 74.1
reassert 103.8
reassertion 103.2
reassurance
sureness 512.8
comfort 885.4
emboldening 891.9
reassure assure 512.11
comfort 885.6
give hope 886.10
embolden 891.16
reassured 512.21
reassurement 512.8
reassuring
auspicious 542.16
comforting 885.13
hopeful 886.13
reassuringly 542.19
reastiness, reasiness
436.2
reasty, reasy
fetid 436.5
rancid 690.39
rebate
nouns deduction
42.6
discount 845.1
verbs 845.2
rebatement
deduction 42.6
discount 845.1
rebec, rebeck 464.5
rebegin 143.6
rebeginning 143.2
rebehold 484.35
rebeholding 484.10
rebel
nouns revolutionist
147.3

insurgent 765.5
verbs 765.8
adjs. 765.12
rebellion 765.4
rebellious
revolutionary 147.5
mutinous 765.12
rebelliousness 765.3
rebirth
conversion 145.2
revival 692.3
salvation 1024.4
reborn 1026.10
rebound
nouns recoil 283.2
reverberation 453.2
ON THE REBOUND
283.11
verbs recoil 283.6
reverberate 453.7
rebounding
recoiling 283.10
reverberating 453.11
rebroadcast 343.21
rebuff
nouns recoil 283.2
repulse 288.1
rejection 636.1
defeat 725.2
refusal 774.2
resistance 790.1
snub 964.2
verbs repulse 288.2
reject 636.2
refuse 774.5
drive back 797.10
snub 964.5
rebuffed 636.3
rebuild
reproduce 168.8
remake 692.18
rebuilding
reconstruction 168.1
recreation 692.5
rebuke
nouns 967.5
verbs 967.17
rebus 547.8
rebut reply 485.5
refute 505.5
rebuttal answer 485.2
refutation 505.2
IN REBUTTAL 485.8
rebutter 485.2
rebuy 826.7
rebuying 826.1
recalcitrance, recal-
citrancy ungovern-
ability 624.4
disobedience 765.2
resistance 790.1
recalcitrant
nouns 283.4
adjs. recoiling 283.10
ungovernable
624.12
disobedient 765.11
resistant 790.6
recalcitrate
recoil 283.6
resist 790.3

recalcitration
recoil 283.2
resistance 790.1
recall
nouns recollection
535.4
recantation 626.3
repeal 777.1
~ of ambassadors
793.4
BEYOND RECALL
887.15
verbs remember
535.11
recant 626.9
summon 750.12
repeal 777.2
recalled 535.23
recalling
recollection 535.4
recantation 626.3
recant 626.9
recantation 626.3
recap
nouns recapitulation
103.2
tire 252.4
verbs re-cover 227.32
repair 692.14
recapitulate
sum up 87.12
reiterate 103.8
recapitulation
summation 87.5
reiteration 103.2
compendium 605.2
recapitulatory 103.14
recapture
nouns 821.3
verbs 821.6
recast
nouns 692.5
verbs 692.18
recce, recco 484.12
recede regress 294.5
move away 296.2
recedence
recession 296.1
surrender 763.2
recedent 296.4
receding 296.5
receipt taking in 305.1
answer 485.1
axiom 516.2
prescription 685.1
formula 749.3
receival 817.1
receipts 842.1
acknowledgment
842.2
receipts gains 809.3
income 842.1
accounts 843.1
receival 817.1
receive include 76.3
take in 305.10
~ radar 345.17
believe 500.8
assent 520.8
get 817.6
~ hospitably 923.7

REFUSE TO RECEIVE
refuse 774.5
be inhospitable
924.4
received
traditional 123.12
known 474.26
believed 500.20
authoritative 512.18
recognized 520.14
conventional 643.7
accepted 817.10
approved 966.18
orthodox 1022.8
BE RECEIVED
arrive 299.6
find credence
500.17
come to hand 817.8
receiver
receptacle 192.1
radio ~ 343.3
television ~ 344.11
believer 500.7
telephone ~ 558.5
telegraph ~ 558.19
recipient 817.3
fence 824.6
treasurer 834.11
religionist 1026.4
receiver units
radio ~ 343.33
television ~ 344.17
receiving
nouns 817
adjs. 817.9
recency 122.1
recent former 119.7
new 122.13
recently 122.17
recept 478.1
receptacle
container 192
types of ~ 192.11–
24
reception
inclusion 76.1
taking in 305
radio ~ 343.24
television ~ 344.5
interview 595.6
receiving 817.1
sociable 920.9
welcome 923.2
receptionist 923.5
receptive
persuasible 171.15
admissive 305.16
pliant 356.9
sensory 421.10
sensible 421.12
open-minded
524.10
teachable 562.18
receiving 817.9
emotionally ~
853.19
hospitable 923.11
receptiveness
persuadability 171.5
receptivity 305.9

pliancy 356.2
sensibility 421.2
open-mindedness
524.3
hospitality 923.1
receptivity
receptiveness 305.9
sensibility 421.2
teachability 562.5
receptor 421.5
recess
nouns pause 144.3
nook 191.3
indentation 256.7
~ of the memory
535.1
hiding place 613.4
refuge 698.5
respite 709.2
seclusion 922.1
verbs adjourn 132.9
pause 144.9
indent 256.14
rest 709.8
recesses 224.2
recession recess 256.7
motion from 296
depression 727.6
surrender 763.2
business ~ 825.7
recessional
nouns 461.5,16
adjs. 296.4
recessive
reversionary 146.7
regressive 294.11
receding 296.4
Rechabite 990.4
Rechabitism 990.2
réchauffé
nouns cliché 516.3
old joke 879.9
adjs. twice-told
103.12
warmed-over 328.28
recheck
nouns 484.10
verbs re-examine
484.35
verify 512.12
recherché
unusual 85.10
stylish 642.13
recidive 694.4
recidivism 694.2
recidivist
apostate 626.5
backslider 694.3
recidivous 694.5
recipe axiom 516.2
prescription 685.1
formula 749.3
recipience
taking in 305.1
receiving 817.1
recipient
nouns receptacle
192.1
receiver 817.3
adjs. receptive 305.16
receiving 817.9

reciprocal
nouns 20.5
adjs. correlative
13.12
mathematics 86.8
interchangeable
149.5
alternate 322.18
retaliatory 953.8
reciprocality
correlation 13.1
interchange 149.1
reciprocally
mutually 13.14
interchangeably
149.7
reciprocate
correspond 13.8
interchange 149.4
alternate 322.12
concur 520.9
accord 792.2
retaliate 953.4
reciprocation
correlation 13.1
interchange 149.1
alternation 322.4
retaliation 953.1
IN RECIPROCATION
953.9
reciprocative
correlative 13.12
interchangeable
149.5
alternate 322.18
reciprocator 13.4
reciprocity
correlation 13.1
interchange 149.1
recital
reiteration 103.2
concert 461.34
lesson 560.6
speech 597.2
narration 606.2
recitalist 463.1
recitation
lesson 560.6
speech 597.2
recitative 461.13
recite sum up 87.12
reiterate 103.8
state 592.15
declaim 597.9
narrate 606.13
~ the rosary
1030.12
reciter
speaker 597.7
narrator 606.10
reckless
careless 532.11
unconcerned 634.6
rash 892.8
recklessly
carelessly 532.18
unconcernedly
634.9
rashly 892.11
recklessness
carelessness 532.2

rescue 700.2
regain 821.6
re-cover 227.32
recoverability 692.9
recoverable 692.25
recovery
restoration 692.2,8
rescue 700.1
retrieval 821.3
business ~ 825.7
recreancy
apostasy 626.2
perfidy 973.5
recreant
nouns apostate 626.5
coward 890.6
reprobate 984.5
adjs. apostate 626.11
cowardly 890.12
knavish 973.16
unfaithful 973.19
recreate
reproduce 168.8
remake 692.18
amuse 876.23
recreation
reproduction 168.1
reconstruction
692.5
amusement 876.1
recreational 876.29
recreative
reproductive 168.15
amusing 876.29
recrement 43.2
recriminate 1003.11
recrimination 1003.3
recriminatory 1003.13
recrudescence 694.1
recrudescent 694.5
recruit
nouns newcomer 78.4
novice 564.7
conscript 798.17
verbs reinforce 40.4
replenish 657.7
restore 692.11
recuperate 692.19
conscript 778.14
RECRUIT ONE'S
STRENGTH
strengthen 158.11
recuperate 692.19
recruiting, recruital,
recruitment
recovery 692.8
conscription 778.6
recruits
reinforcements
783.8
conscripts 798.17
rectal 224.12
rectangle 250.14
rectangular
oblong 201.13
quadrangular 250.9
rectangularity 250.1
rectifiable 692.25
rectification
revision 689.4
reparation 692.6

rectify adjust 26.13
straighten 249.4
refine 354.6
emend 689.12
remedy 692.13
rectilinear, rectilineal
249.5
rectilinearity 249.1
rectitude 972.1
recto
right side 242.1
page 603.13
rector director 746.1
churchman 1036.8
rectorate 1035.5
rectoress, rectress
747.2
rectorship 1035.5
rectory benefice 1035.9
parsonage 1040.7
rectum 224.6
reculade 294.2
recumbency 213.2
recumbent prone 213.9
leaning 218.15
recuperate
improve 689.7
restore 692.15
get better 692.19
recover 821.6
recuperation
recovery 692.8
retrieval 821.3
recuperative, recu-
peratory 692.23
recur repeat 103.11
~ periodically 137.6
be remembered
535.16
RECUR TO
revert to 146.6
resort to 663.14
recure 692.15
recurrence
repetition 103.1
periodicity 137.2
recurrent
repeated 103.13
frequent 135.4
periodic 137.8
habitual 640.15
recurrently 137.11
recurring
repeated 103.13
periodic 137.8
habitual 640.15
recurvate 251.7
recurve 251.6
recurved 251.7
recusance, recusancy
nonconformity 83.2
dissent 520a.1
recusant
nouns dissenter
520a.3
apostate 626.5
adjs. unconformable
83.6
dissentient 520a.6
Red 147.3

red
nouns revolutionist
147.3
red head 361.8
color 367.1
colors, pigments
367.13,14
reformer 689.6
radical 743.11
IN THE RED 810.9
adjs. reddish-brown
366.4
red-colored 367.6
sore 423.11
radical 743.19
blushing 906.13
GET RED IN THE
FACE 906.8
redact 689.12
redaction 689.4
redan 797.4
redbait 525.7
redbaiting 525.4
red-baiting 743.4
red blindness 440.3
Red Book 568.8
red book 568.7
redcap porter 270.5
trainman 273.13
red cent trifle 671.5
coin 833.7
redcoat 798.8
red-complexioned
367.10
red corpuscles 387.4
red-crested, red-
crowned 367.11
Red Cross 687.29
redden
make red 367.4
become red 367.5
blush 906.8
anger 950.14
reddened 367.6
reddening
nouns coloring 367.3
blushing 906.5
adjs. 367.12
reddishness 367.1
reddition
rendition 550.2
restitution 821.1
reddness 366.6
redeem convert 145.9
substitute 148.4
reclaim 692.12
rescue 700.2
recover 821.6
pay 839.18
atone for 1010.4
give salvation 1024.6
REDEEM ONE'S PLEDGE
fulfill 766.2
do one's duty 960.10
keep faith with
972.9
redeemability 692.9
redeemable
recoverable 692.25
rescuable 700.3
payable 838.10

Redeemer, the
1011.12
redeemer 940.2
redemption
conversion 145.2
reclamation 692.2
rescue 700.1
recovery 821.3
atonement 1010.1
Christly function
1011.17
religious ~ 1024.4
redemptive 821.7
red flag 701.3
red-hand 981.4
red-handed
murderous 408.24
in the act 981.4
red hands 981.1
redhead 361.8
red heat 327.4
red herring
fish 306a.24
ruse 733.3
red-hot violent 161.21
hot 327.25
fervent 853.22
excited 855.23
red-ink 367.4
redintegration 692.1
redivivus 692.24
red-letter day 709.4
red light
traffic light 335.4
signal 566.14
warning 701.3
red-light district
city district 182.5
brothels 987.9
red man 417.5
redness
heat glow 327.11
color 367
redo 692.18
redolence odor 434.1
fragrance 435.1
redolent
odorous 434.9
fragrant 435.9
reminiscent 535.22
redouble intensify 38.5
reduplicate 91.2
repeat 103.7
REDOUBLE ONE'S
EFFORTS 712.9
redoubled 103.12
redoubling
intensification 38.2
repetition 103.1
redoubt 797.4
redoubtable 889.29
redound to
contribute 152.13
conduce 173.3
REDOUND TO ONE'S
HONOR 912.15
REDOUND TO THE
HONOR 966.14
red rag tongue 426.5
provocation 950.11

redress
nouns reparation
692.6
restitution 821.2
recompense 839.3
reprisal 953.2
atonement 1010.1
verbs remedy 692.13
atone for 1010.4
red scare 743.4
redshort 359.5
redskin Indian 417.5
savage 941.6
red tape delay 132.2
routine 640.5
officialism 742.39
red-tapist 747.17
reduce decrease 39.7
weaken 159.10
dilute 159.11
moderate 162.6
shorten 202.6
slenderize 204.12
~ sail 274.52
lower 316.4
analyze 484.32
qualify 506.3
sicken 684.37
conquer 725.10
subdue 762.9
demote 780.4
impoverish 836.6
discount 845.2
cheapen 847.6
relieve 884.5
abase 904.5
REDUCE TO
~ order 60.7
convert 145.8
~ ashes 328.24;
409.21
~ dust 360.9
~ silence 505.5
~ writing 568.15
reduced
diminished 39.10
diluted 159.19
lowered 316.10
sickly 684.40
conquered 725.16
subdued 762.14
poor 836.7
depreciated 847.9
humbled 904.11
reducing
nouns 204.9
adjs. mitigating
162.14
slenderizing 204.20
reduct 42.7
reductio ad absurdum
505.1
reduction decrease 39.1
mathematics 87.4
conversion 145.1
weakening 159.5
moderation 162.2
abridgment 202.3
lowering 316.1
subdual 762.4
demotion 780.2

discount 845.1
cheapening 847.4
relief 884.1
reductive 39.11
redundancy
repetition 103.3
diffuseness 591.1
superfluity 661.4
redundant
repetitious 103.14
diffuse 591.11
superfluous 661.18
red-up 60.5
reduplicate copy 22.8
redouble 91.2
repeat 103.7
reduplicated 103.12
reduplication
reproduction 22.3
doubling 91.1
repetition 103.1
reduplicative 103.14
re-echo
nouns repetition
103.1
reverberation
453.2
reply 485.1
verbs imitate 22.5
repeat 103.7
reverberate 453.7
reply 485.4
re-echoing
repetitious 103.14
reverberating 453.11
replying 485.7
reechy fetid 436.5
rancid 690.39
reed weakness 159.7
tube 395.6
plant 410.5
stem 410.19
arrow 799.17
reediness 457.1
reed instruments, reeds
464.9
reed organ 464.15
re-educate 145.10
reeducation 688.37
re-education 145.3
reedy 457.13
reef
nouns shoal 209.2
point of land 255.8
sail 276.30
island 385.2
TAKE A REEF 849.8
verbs retard 269.9
reduce sail 274.52
reefer
refrigerator car
271.13
refrigerator 333.4
reefs 695.5
reefy 209.6
reek
nouns smoke 328.16
fume 400.1
malodor 436.1
verbs exude 302.15
smoke 327.22

be damp 391.11
vaporize 400.7
smell 434.6
smell bad 436.4
reeking
nouns 436.1
adjs. smoking 327.27
soaked 391.17
vaporous 400.8
odorous 434.10
malodorous 436.6
reeky vaporous 400.8
maladorous 436.6
reel
nouns windlass 286.7
whirl 320.2
sway 322.5
flounder 323.8
peal 455.4
verbs sail 274.58
whirl 320.11
swing 322.9
flounder 323.15
eddy 394.22
be drunk 994.33
REEL BACK 283.7
REEL IN 286.9
REEL OFF 594.6
reeling
nouns 320.1
adjs. rotating 320.14
swaying 322.16
drunk 994.38
re-embodiment 375.7
re-embody
combine 52.3
reincarnate 375.8
re-enact 609.34
re-enliven 693.2
re-enter 143.6
re-entrance
resumption 143.2
return 299.3
re-entry 299.3
re-establish
reproduce 168.8
restore 692.11
re-establishment
reproduction 168.1
restoration 692.1
re-estate 692.11
reeve 747.20
re-examination
reconsideration
477.5
reinquiry 484.10
re-examine
reconsider 477.14
reinquire 484.35
refashion convert 145.9
reproduce 168.8
remake 692.18
refashioning
reproduction 168.1
reconstruction 692.5
refection repast 306.5
food 306a.3
refreshment 693.1
refectory 191.11
referable 154.5
REFERABLE TO 9.5

referee
nouns mediator 803.4
judge 1000.1
verbs 803.6
reference
nouns relevance 9.2
aspect 445.3
citation 504.6
reference mark
584.11
recommendation
966.4
REFERENCE TO 154.1
WITHOUT REFERENCE
TO 10.8
WITH REFERENCE TO
9.10
verbs 504.15
reference book 603.6
reference mark
sign 584.11
types of ~ 584.14
referendum vote 635.5
political ~ 740.18
politics 742.18
referential
suggestive 544.6
figurative 549.4
refer to relate to 9.3
attribute to 154.3
cite 504.15
indicate 566.17
consult 595.10
refill 56.6
refinance 834.17
refine rarefy 354.6
sensitize 421.8
improve 689.10
REFINE UPON 689.9
refined fine 350.8
rare 354.7
discriminative 491.8
precise 515.15
meticulous 531.12
elegant 587.6
perfected 675.9
purified 679.24
fastidious 894.11
tasteful 895.9
well-bred 934.17
refinement
fine distinction 16.2
fineness 350.3
rarefaction 354.3
finesse 491.1
preciseness 515.3
meticulousness 531.3
elegant style 587.1
improvement 689.2
cultivation 689.3
fastidiousness 894.3
taste 895.1
good breeding 934.4
refiner 354.4
refinery refiner 354.4
plant 717.3
refit 692.11
reflect mirror 22.5
bend 251.6
radar 345.16
reverberate 453.7

deposal 781.1
relief 884.2
remove
nouns degree 29.1
food 306.10
class 564.9
verbs deduct 42.7
disjoin 49.8
eliminate 77.5
interspace 200.4
divest 231.5
doff 231.6
transfer 270.10
depart 300.8
extract 304.9
eject 308.12
dismiss 308.18
evacuate 308.20
assassinate 408.16
discard 666.7
eradicate 691.14
obviate 728.14
depose 781.2
relieve 884.6
removed
unrelated 10.5
unjoined 49.20
alone 89.8
distant 198.8
intervaled 200.6
reserved 611.8
unsociable 921.6
secluded 922.9
removement 270.2
remunerate
profit 663.17
pay 839.10
remuneration 839.3,4
remunerative
valuable 663.21
profitable 809.14
paying 839.21
remunerator 839.9
renaissance,
renascence 692.3
renascent
reproductive 168.15
renewed 692.24
rencontre 199.4
rencounter
meeting 199.4
contest 794.3
rend sever 49.10
extract 304.13
wound 690.13
wrest from 820.19
REND THE AIR
be loud 452.6
cry 458.9
REND THE HEART
870.19
render convert 145.8
extract 304.14
~ music 461.40
translate 550.14
communicate 552.7
narrate 606.13
do 703.6
execute 769.10
give 816.12
pay 839.10

~ a service 936.13
RENDER UP 812.3
renderable 550.20
rendering
extraction 304.6
musical ~ 461.31
interpretation 550.2
account 606.3
execution 769.5
rendezvous
nouns meeting 74.2
tryst 920.8
verbs 74.15
rending
nouns severance 49.2
extraction 304.5
adjs. 862.14
rendition
extraction 304.6
musical ~ 461.31
interpretation 550.2
account 606.3
restitution 821.1
renegade
nouns apostate 626.5
fugitive 629.5
adjs. 626.11
renege, renig
nouns 777.1
verbs withdraw 631.5
revoke 777.2
renew resume 143.6
convert 145.9
remember 535.11
restore 692.16,17
RENEW ONE'S
STRENGTH
recuperate 692.19
refresh 693.2
renewal
resumption 143.2
conversion 145.2
restoration 692.3,4
relapse 694.1
renewed new 122.8
revived 692.24
reniform 251.19
renig See renege
renitence, renitency
counteraction 177.1
rigidity 355.2
elasticity 357.1
reluctance 621.1
resistance 790.1
renitent
counteractive 177.8
rigid 355.11
elastic 357.7
reluctant 621.6
resistant 790.6
rennet bag 192.3
renounce deny 522.4
recant 626.9
abandon 631.7
reject 636.2
relinquish 812.3
swear off 990.8
renounced 636.3
renouncement
recantation 626.3
abandonment 631.3

rejection 636.1
temperance 990.1
renovate 692.17
renovation 692.4
renovator 692.10
renovize 692.17
renown 912.1
renowned 912.17
renownless 913.14
rent
nouns break 49.3
tenement 190.12
cleft 200.2
hire 778.5
dues 844.9
verbs open 264.11
hire 778.13
adjs. torn 49.22
cleft 200.7
tattered 690.31
rental hire 778.5
dues 844.9
rentee 807.4
renter lodger 189.8
tenant 807.4
renunciation
recantation 626.3
renouncement 631.3
rejection 636.1
surrender 763.2
relinquishment
812.1
temperance 990.1
renunciative
repudiative 626.12
rejective 636.4
renunciatory 626.12
reoccupation 821.3
reoccupy 821.6
reoccur repeat 103.11
recur 137.6
reoccurrence
repetition 103.1
periodicity 137.2
reopen 143.6
reopening 143.2
reorganization
rearrangement 60.6
reproduction 168.1
restoration 692.1
reorganize
rearrange 60.12
reproduce 168.8
restore 692.11
reorientation 688.37
rep 984.5
repair
nouns condition 7.3
reparation 692.6
OUT OF REPAIR
690.36
verbs fix 692.14
atone for 1010.4
REPAIR TO 272.24
repairable 692.25
repairing 692.6
repairman 692.10
repair shop 717.6
reparability 692.9
reparable 692.25

reparation
remedy 685.1
repair 692.6
restitution 821.2
recompense 839.3
reprisal 953.2
atonement 1010.1
MAKE REPARATION
make restitution
821.5
repay 839.11
atone for 1010.4
reparative
compensatory 33.6
restorative 692.22
restitutive 821.7
retributive 839.21
retaliatory 953.8
repartee retort 485.1
wit 879.7
reparteeist 879.12
repartition 814.1
repast 306.5
repatriate 145.10
repatriation 145.3
repay
reimburse 839.11
retaliate 953.5
repaying 839.21
repayment
reimbursement
839.2
reprisal 953.2
repeal
nouns 777
verbs 777.2
repeat
nouns 103.5
verbs copy 22.5
reiterate 103.7
recur 103.11
remember 535.17
repeated 103.12
repeatedly 103.16
repeater voter 742.24
revolver 799.5
repeating 103.14
repel repulse 288.2
reject 636.2
disincline 650.4
avert 728.14
refuse 774.5
resist 790.2
drive back 797.10
offend 864.13
repelled 864.23
repellence, repellency
repulsion 288.1
resistance 790.1
repellent
repulsive 288.3
nasty 428.7
resistant 790.6
odious 862.9
repelling
nouns 288.1
adjs. repulsive 288.3
ugly 897.11
repent
reform 145.9
be penitent 871.7

reptilian
nouns 413.30
adjs. reptile 413.43
obsequious 905.13
base 913.12

reptiliform, reptiloid
413.43

republic country 180.1
government 739.4

Republican 742.28

republican
nouns 917.7
adjs. 739.16

Republicanism 742.26

republicanism 739.8

republicanize 743.15

Republican Party
742.25

repudiate exclude 77.4
deny 522.4
recant 626.9
reject 636.2
not pay 840.6

repudiation
exclusion 77.1
recantation 626.3
rejection 636.1
nonpayment 840.1

repudiative
abjuratory 626.12
rejective 636.4

repugnance
contrariety 15.1
disagreement 27.1
counteraction 177.1
opposition 788.2
resistance 790.1
aversion 865.2
hostility 927.3

repugnant
contrary 15.5
disagreeing 27.6
counteractive 177.8
nasty 428.7
denying 522.5
opposed 788.9
resistant 790.6
odious 862.9
ugly 897.11
hostile 927.11

repulse
nouns recoil 283.2
repelling 288.1
defeat 725.2
refusal 774.2
resistance 790.1
snub 964.2
verbs repel 288.2
reject 636.2
refuse 774.5
resist 790.2
drive back 797.10
snub 964.5

repulsed 636.3

repulsion
repelling 288
electric ~ 341.9
rejection 636.1
resistance 790.1
repugnance 865.2

repulsive
repelling 288.3
nasty 428.7
malodorous 436.5
resistant 790.6
odious 862.9
ugly 897.11

repulsiveness
unsavoriness 428.3
malodorousness
436.2
odiousness 862.2
ugliness 897.2

repulsor
rocket plane 279.4
rocket 280.1

repurchase
nouns 826.1
verbs 826.7

reputability
repute 912.2
probity 972.1

reputable
well-thought-of
912.16
honorable 972.13

reputably 912.21

reputation 912.1

repute
nouns 912
verbs 498.9

reputed 498.14

reputedly 498.17

request
nouns demand 751
petition 772
verbs demand 751.4
ask 772.9

requiem
last rites 409.4
dirge 873.5
Mass 1038.9

requiescat in pace
409.27

require entail 76.4
necessitate 637.9
lack 660.6
demand 751.4
oblige 754.5
charge 844.14
obligate 960.11

required 637.13
AS REQUIRED 750.16

requirement
necessity 637.2
demand 751.1

requisite
nouns condition
506.2
requirement 637.2
adjs. 637.13

requisition
nouns requirement
637.2
demand 751.1
request 772.1
verbs demand 751.4
request 772.9

requisitory 751.9

requital
restitution 821.2

recompense 839.3
reprisal 953.2
revenge 954
IN REQUITAL
in restitution 821.8
in reward 839.24
in reprisal 953.9

requite
interchange 149.4
make restitution
821.5
repay 839.11
retaliate 953.5

requitement 839.3

reredos 1040.10

rerun 343.21

rescind 777.2

rescindment 777.1

rescission 777.1

rescript answer 485.1
epistle 602.2
revision 689.4
command 750.2

rescuable 700.3

rescue
nouns 700
verbs 700.2

rescuer 940.2

research
nouns missile ~
280.7
investigation 484.5
verbs 484.25

researcher, researchist
484.18

resection
disjunction 49.1
surgical ~ 687.24

resell 827.8

resemblance
similarity 20.1
copy 24.1
image 570.3

resemble 20.7
NOT RESEMBLE 16.5

resembling 20.10

resene 380.1

resent 950.12

resentful 950.24

resentfulness 950.1

resenting 950.24

resentment 950

reservation
qualification 506.1
reticence 611.3
preserve 699.6
engagement 778.4
HAVE NO RESER-
VATIONS 500.11
NO RESERVATIONS
507.1
WITH RESERVATIONS
502.13

reserve
nouns reticence 611.3
~ supply 658.3
sanctuary 698.1
preserve 699.6
modesty 906.3
IN RESERVE
imminent 151.3

in store 658.17
in readiness 718.22
WITHOUT RESERVE
507.2
verbs postpone 132.8
save 658.12
not use 666.5
engage 778.12
allot 814.10

reserved
reticent 611.8
saved 658.15
modest 906.11

reserves
~ supply 658.3
military ~ 798.24

reservoir
nouns pool 397.1
store 658.3,6
verbs 658.10

reset readjust 26.13
sharpen 257.10
transplant 412.18

resetting 412.14

reshape 145.9

reside 187.8
RESIDE IN 1.11

residence
nouns habitation
187.1
abode 190.1
IN RESIDENCE 187.14
verbs 183.18

resident
nouns inhabitant
189.2
intern 686.5
diplomat 779.6
tenant 807.4
clergyman 1036.7
adjs. inherent 5.6
residing 187.14

residential 190.27

residentiary
nouns inhabitant
189.2
clergyman 1036.7
adjs. resident 187.14
residential 190.27

resider 189.2

residing
nouns 187.1
adjs. 187.14

residual
nouns 43.1
adjs. 43.7

residuary 43.7

residue, residuum 43.1

resign waive 631.7
submit 763.6
~ from office 782.2
relinquish 812.3
deliver 816.13

resignation
abandonment 631.3
submission 763.1
demission 782
relinquishment
812.1
patience 859.2

resigned
submissive 763.12
patient 859.11
resignedly
submissively 763.17
patiently 859.13
resile 283.6
resilience recoil 283.2
elasticity 357.1
lightheartedness
868.3
resilient
recoiling 283.10
elastic 357.7
recuperative 692.23
cheerful 868.11
resin
nouns substance 380
types of ~ 380.4
verbs 380.2
resina 380.1
resinate
nouns 380.1
verbs 380.2
**resinic, resinous,
resiny** 380.3
resinize 380.2
resinoid
noun 380.1
adjs. 380.3
resist counteract 177.6
oppose 788.3
withstand 790.2
resistance
counteraction 177.1
aviation 277.33
electric ~ 341.12
electronic ~ 342.10
friction 349.5
toughness 358.1
inhibition 688.35
opposition 788
withstanding 790
military 798.15
resistant proof 158.18
counteractive 177.8
tough 358.4
unyielding 624.9
resisting 790.6
resisting 790.6
resistless
impregnable 158.17
necessary 637.12
resolute
determined 622.11
perseverant 623.7
obstinate 624.8
unyielding 624.9
bold 891.18
resolutely
determinedly 622.17
perseveringly 623.8
courageously 891.22
resoluteness
determination 622.1
unyieldingness
624.2
courage 891.4
resolution
dissection 49.4
disintegration 53.1

conversion 145.1
music 462.2
analysis 484.8
solution 486.1
verdict 493.5
determination 622
perseverance 623
obstinacy 624
decay 690.5
legislative ~ 740.15
motion 771.2
courage 891.4
resolutive
nouns 390.4
adjs. 390.8
resolve
nouns 622.1
verbs transform
139.7
analyze 484.32
solve 486.2
decide 493.11
determine 622.7
RESOLVE INTO 145.8
resolvable 486.3
resolved 622.11
resolvent
nouns 390.4
adjs. disintegrative
53.5
solvent 390.8
resolving 486.1
resonance 453
resonant 453.9
resonate 453.6
resonating 453.9
resonator 453.5
resorb 305.15
resorbence 305.8
resorbent 305.17
resort haunt 190.23
use 663.1
expedient 668.2
health ~ 687.31
refuge 698.2
resort to
frequent 185.10
go to 272.24
avail oneself of
663.14
resound
nouns 453.2
verbs be loud 452.6
reverberate 453.7
resounder 453.5
resounding
nouns 453.2
adjs. loud 452.9
reverberating
453.11
resoundingly 452.12
resource supply 658.2
expedient 668.2
refuge 698.2
skill 731.1
resourceful 731.20
resourcefulness 731.1
resources means 656.1
supply 658.2
assets 808.8
funds 833.14

respect
nouns particular 8.2
relevance 9.2
viewpoint 438.7
aspect 445.3
attitude 523.2
attention 528.1
repute 912.3
politeness 934.1
deference 962
IN NO RESPECT
nowise 35.14
by no means 522.8
WITH DUE RESPECT
962.13
WITHOUT RESPECT TO
33.9
WITH RESPECT TO
9.10
verbs relate to 9.3
acknowledge 520.11
observe 766.2
be considerate
936.11
revere 962.4
respectability 972.1
respectable
tolerable 672.20
reputable 912.16
honorable 972.13
respectably 912.21
respected 962.11
respectful
polite 934.14
deferential 962.8
respecting 9.11
respective
mutual 13.13
special 80.12
distributive 814.14
respectively
mutually 13.15
each 80.19
distributively
814.15
respectless
impartial 524.12
careless 532.11
inconsiderate
937.16
respects
compliments 934.8
regards 962.3
IN ALL RESPECTS
on the whole 54.13
throughout 56.18
exactly 515.19
IN OTHER RESPECTS
16.10
PAY ONE'S RESPECTS
TO 934.12
respiration 402.19
respirators 687.40
respiratory 402.30
respire 402.25
respite
nouns delay 132.2
pause 144.3
rest 709.2
reprieve 1005.3
verbs 1005.5

**resplendence,
resplendency**
brightness 334.4
illustriousness 912.6
resplendent
bright 334.32
beautiful 898.19
illustrious 912.20
respond
correspond 26.7
reciprocate 149.4
react 283.5
~ to stimuli 421.7
answer 485.4
accord 792.2
~ emotionally
853.11
respondence
reaction 283.1
answer 485.1
respondent
nouns responder
485.3
accused 1003.6
adjs. reactive 283.9
answering 485.7
responder 485.3
responding
reactive 283.9
answering 485.7
response
reaction 283.1
sensation 421.1
music 461.23,24
answer 485.1
rapport 792.1
emotional ~ 853.5
anthem 1030.3
responsibility
solvency 834.6
duty 960.2
trustworthiness
972.6
FIX THE RESPONSI-
BILITY FOR
attribute to 154.3
accuse 1003.8
TAKE THE RESPONSI-
BILITY
volunteer 620.4
answer for 960.8
responsible
solvent 834.17
liable 960.16
trustworthy 972.19
responsions 484.3
responsive
persuasible 171.15
reactive 283.9
pliant 356.9
elastic 357.7
sensitive 421.13
answering 485.7
open-minded
524.10
teachable 562.18
emotionally ~
853.19
responsiveness
persuadability 171.5
pliancy 356.1

elasticity 357.1
sensitivity 421.3
open-mindedness 524.3
teachability 562.5
responsory,
responsary
music 461.23
anthem 1030.3
ressaidar, ressaldar
747.22
rest
nouns remainder 43.1
pause 144.3
support 215.2
quiescence 267.1
fulcrum 286.3
stair 313.5
death 407.1
silence 450.1
musical ~ 462.21
repose 709.2
AT REST
quiescent 267.10
dead 407.24
buried 409.26
abed 709.11
at ease! 709.13
comfortable 885.12
verbs pause 144.9
calm 162.7
be situated 183.10
place 183.14
be quiescent 267.7
~ at anchor 274.17
trust 500.14
depend 506.6
take ~ 709.6
~ a law case 1002.18
REST ASSURED
believe 500.11
believe me 500.27
be certain 512.9
hope 886.7
REST EASY 646.24
REST IN
exist in 1.11
put trust in 500.12
REST IN PEACE
409.27
REST ON
lie on 215.23
weigh on 351.11
rely on 500.13
be contingent 506.6
REST ON ONE'S OARS
pause 144.9
be quiescent 267.7
REST UPON ONE'S
OARS
shirk 629.9
do nothing 704.2
idle 706.13
REST WITH
depend on 506.6
be one's duty 960.6
restate reiterate 103.8
paraphrase 550.15
restatement
reiteration 103.2

paraphrase 550.3
restaurant 306.14
restaurateur 807.2
restful
soothing 162.15
quiescent 267.10
comfortable 885.11
restfulness
quiescence 267.1
comfortableness 885.2
resthouse 190.13
resting place
quarters 190.2
support 215.2
tomb 409.16
restitution
restoration 692.1
return 821
repayment 839.2,3
atonement 1010.1
MAKE RESTITUTION
make amends 821.5
repay 839.11
restitutive, restitutory
reparative 692.22
compensatory 821.7
restive stickling 621.7
stubborn 624.12
disobedient 765.11
restless 855.28
impatient 860.6
restiveness
ungovernability 624.4
disobedience 765.2
impatience 860.1
restless
changeable 141.7
agitated 323.17
bustling 705.19
wakeful 711.6
fidgety 855.28
impatient 860.6
restlessness
agitation 323.1
bustle 705.4
wakefulness 711.1
excitement 855.4
impatience 860.1
restorable 692.25
restoration
vitaminization 307.12
improvement 689
re-establishment 692.1
restitution 821.1
restorative
nouns 685.1
adjs. remedial 685.34
reparative 692.22
compensatory 821.7
restore
vitaminize 307.18
make sane 471.3
put back 692.11
make restitution 821.4
restrain
moderate 162.6

limit 233.5
qualify 506.3
hinder 728.10
constrain 758.7
confine 759.13
simplify 900.5
RESTRAIN ONESELF
compose oneself 856.7
be temperate 990.6
restrainable 763.14
restrained
moderate 162.11
elegant 587.6
reserved 611.8
constrained 758.13
tasteful 895.8
modest 906.11
temperate 990.9
restraining 758.11
restraint
moderation 162.1
limitation 233.2
elegant style 587.1
reserve 611.3
self-control 622.5
inhibition 688.35
hindrance 728
constraint 758
confinement 759.1
~ of trade 825.1
equanimity 856.3
tastefulness 895.4
modesty 906.3
temperance 990.1
WITHOUT RESTRAINT
freely 760.29
intemperately 991.10
restrengthen
add to 40.4
strengthen 158.11
restrengthening 158.5
restrict specialize 81.4
limit 233.5
qualify 506.3
restrain 758.9
restricted
specialized 81.5
narrow 204.13
limited 233.8,9
topical 483.5
qualified 506.10
restrained 758.15
restricting
limiting 233.10
qualifying 506.7
restraining 758.12
restriction
narrowness 204.1
limitation 233.2
qualification 506.1
restraint 758.3
restrictionist 758.6
restrictive
limiting 233.10
qualifying 506.7
restraining 758.12
rest room 680.13
resty stubborn 624.12
disobedient 765.11

result
nouns effect 153.1
product 167.1
solution 486.1
deduction 493.4
verbs ensue 117.2
turn out 153.5
resultant
nouns 153.1
adjs. 153.7
resume reiterate 103.8
recur 103.11
recommence 143.6
recover 821.6
résumé
reiteration 103.2
compendium 605.2
resumption
recommencement 143.2
revival 692.3
repossession 821.3
resupinate 219.7
resupination 219.1
resupine 213.9
resurge 406.7
resurgence 692.3
resurgent
reproductive 168.15
renascent 692.24
resurrect 692.16
resurrection
revival 692.3
apotheosis 1016.12
resuscitate 692.16
resuscitation 692.3
retable shelf 215.14
predella 1040.11
retail
nouns 827.1
verbs disperse 75.5
reiterate 103.8
sell 827.8
adjs. 825.17
retailer 828.2
retain stet 142.20
maintain 143.4
remember 535.14
reserve 658.12
employ 778.12
keep 811.5
retained
remembered 535.23
reserved 658.15
retainer
bodyguard 697.13
servant 748.1
fee 839.5
retainment
engagement 778.4
retention 811.1
retake
nouns photograph 575.10
retaking 821.3
verbs 821.6
retaliate
make requital 953.4
take revenge 954.4
retaliation
requital 953

reub See rube
reune
 nouns 47.1
 verbs join 47.5
 reassemble 74.20
reunion joining 47.1
 assemblage 74.1
 reconciliation 802.3
 sociable 920.9
reunite join 47.5
 reassemble 74.20
 reconcile 802.8
rev 268.15
revamp
 transform 139.7
 revise 689.12
 remake 692.18
reveal open 264.12
 ~ itself 445.8
 discover 487.4
 manifest 963.5
 disclose 554.4,5
 indicate 566.16
revealable 553.13
revealed visible 443.6
 unhidden 553.9
 scriptural 1019.9
 BE REVEALED
 be seen 443.4
 be disclosed 554.9
revealing
 nouns 554.1
 adjs. 554.11
revealment 554.1
reveille 566.15
revel
 nouns 875
 verbs rejoice 874.6
 frolic 876.6
 make merry 876.26
 wassail 994.34
 REVEL IN 863.10
Revelation 1019.4
revelation
 appearance 445.1
 discovery 487.1
 vision 533.9
 manifestation 553
 disclosure 554.1
 divine ~ 1019.8
revelational
 revealing 554.11
 scriptural 1019.9
reveler
 pleasure seeker
 876.19
 tippler 994.10
reveling, revelment,
 revelry, revels
 876.3
revenant 1015.1
revenge
 nouns reprisal 953
 vengeance 954
 TAKE REVENGE
 953.4–7
 verbs 954.4
revengeful 954.6
revengefulness 954.2
revenue income 842.1
 tax 844.10

reverberate
 resound 453.7
 reply 485.4
reverberating 453.11
reverberation
 resounding 453.2
 reply 485.1
reverberator 453.5
revere
 hold dear 929.18
 respect 962.4
 worship 1030.10
revered
 adored 929.21
 respected 962.11
Reverence 915.2
reverence
 nouns respect 962.1,2
 piety 1026.1
 worship 1030.1
 verbs respect 962.4
 worship 1030.10
reverenced 962.11
Reverend
 nouns ecclesiastical
 titles 915.5
 clergyman 1036.2
 adjs. 915.8
reverend
 nouns 1036.2
 adjs. 962.12
reverent, reverential
 respectful 962.9
 pious 1026.8
 worshipful 1030.15
reverie
 brown study 530.2
 dream 533.9
 IN A REVERIE 530.11
reversal
 reversion 146.1
 inversion 219.1
 reverse 294.3
 tergiversation 626.1
 relapse 694.1
 defeat 725.2
 ~ of fortune 727.3
 repeal 777.1
reverse
 nouns opposite 15.2
 reversion 146.1
 inversion 219.1
 opposite side 238.3
 back 240.1
 backup 294.3
 ~ gear 347.6
 tergiversation 626.1
 relapse 694.1
 defeat 725.2
 ~ of fortune 727.3
 verbs revert 146.4
 invert 219.5
 back up 294.7
 repeal 777.2
 adjs. contradictory
 15.5
 opposite 238.5
reversed
 inverted 219.7
 backward 294.12
reversement 277.13

reversible 146.8
reversion
 backward change
 146.1
 inversion 219.1
 regression 294.3
 revival 692.3
 relapse 694
 estate 808.5
 transfer 815.2
 inheritance 817.2
reversionary
 regressive 146.7
 restitutive 821.7
reversioner
 reversionist 146.3
 apostate 626.5
 heir 817.5
reversionist
 reversioner 146.3
 apostate 626.5
 backslider 694.3
reverso 603.13
revert recur 103.11
 change back 146.4
 regress 294.5
 relapse 694.4
revertible
 returnable 146.8
 restitutive 821.7
reverting 146.1
revest 692.11
review
 nouns parade 71.4
 reiteration 103.2
 reconsideration
 477.5
 discussion 481.4
 inspection 484.4,10
 critique 493.2
 recollection 535.4
 magazine 603.11
 commentary 604.2
 compendium 605.2
 relation 606.2
 drama 609.4
 verbs reiterate 103.8
 reconsider 477.14
 discuss 481.16
 examine 484.31
 re-examine 484.35
 criticize 493.14
 remember 535.11
 write upon 604.5
 relate 606.13
reviewer critic 493.7
 writer 600.15
 commentator 604.4
revile ridicule 965.9
 berate 967.20
 curse 970.7
revilement
 berating 967.8
 abuse 970.2
reviling 967.23
revindicate 821.6
revindication 821.3
revisal 689.4
revise
 nouns press ~ 601.5

revision 689.4
 verbs rewrite 600.19
 emend 689.12
Revised Version
 1019.2
reviser 603.22
revision
 re-examination
 484.10
 emendation 689.4
 UNDER REVISION
 718.23
revisional 689.16
revisit 185.9
revisory 689.16
revival
 restoration 692.3
 relapse 694.1
 religious ~ 1030.8
revivalist 1036.6
revivatory 692.23
revive come to 406.7
 remember 535.11
 restore 692.16
 recover 692.20
 refresh 693.2
revived 692.24
reviver
 stimulant 685.7
 pick-me-up 994.7
revivification
 restrengthening
 158.5
 revival 692.3
 refreshment 693.1
revivify revive 692.16
 refresh 693.2
reviviscent 692.23
revocation
 recantation 626.3
 repeal 777.1
revocatory 626.12
revoke recant 626.9
 repeal 777.2
revokement
 recantation 626.3
 repeal 777.1
revolt
 nouns revolution 147
 rebellion 765.4
 strike 787.7
 verbs revolutionize
 147.4
 rebel 765.8
 strike 787.9
 offend 864.13
 REVOLT AT 865.6
revolted 864.23
revolter 765.5
revolting nasty 428.7
 odious 862.9
 ugly 897.11
revolute 147.4
revolution
 nouns round 137.3
 radical change 147
 circuit 319.2
 rotation 320.1
 revolt 765.4
 verbs 147.4
revolutional 147.5

revolutionary
nouns revolutionist
147.3
radical 743.11
adjs. catastrophic
147.5
radical 743.19
insurrectionary
765.12
revolutionary war
795.3
revolutionism
revolution 147.2
politics 743.4
revolutionist
nouns revolutionary
147.3
radical 743.11,19
rebel 765.5
adjs. 147.6
revolutionize
overthrow 147.4
revolt 765.8
revolutionizer 147.3
revolutions 320.3
revolutions per minute
velocity 268.2
rotation 320.3
revolve recur 137.6
rotate 320.9
ponder 477.12
REVOLVE ON 506.6
revolver 799.5
revolving
nouns 477.2
adjs. 320.14
revs 320.3
revue 609.4
revulsion
reversion 146.1
revolution 147.1
inversion 219.1
reaction 283.1
revulsionary
reversionary 146.7
revolutionary 147.5
apostate 626.11
revulsive
revolutionary 147.5
reactive 283.9
apostate 626.11
reward
nouns recompense
839.3
award 914.2
reprisal 953.2
IN REWARD 839.24
verbs 839.10
rewarding 839.21
rewardless 667.12
rewarm 692.16
rewed 931.16
reword reiterate 103.8
paraphrase 550.15
rewording 550.3
rework 689.12
rewrite
nouns 689.4
verbs write 600.19
revise 689.12
rewrite man 603.22

rewriting 689.4
reynard 413.4
R. F. D. 602.5
Rhadamanthus
Justice 974.5
judge 1000.6
god 1017.5
rhamphoid 251.9
rhapsode 607.15
rhapsodic(al)
poetic 607.21
ecstatic 863.14
rhapsodist
minstrel 463.16
visionary 533.13
poet 607.15
enthusiast 633.5
rhapsodize
idealize 533.16
enthuse 633.8
rhapsody medley 44.6
poem 607.4
Rhea 1012.5
rheostatics 346.2
rhetor 597.6
rhetoric diction 586.1
oratory 597.1
eloquence 598.1
grandiloquence
599.1
manual 603.9
rhetorical
oratorical 597.11
eloquent 598.8
grandiloquent 599.9
rhetorical question
484.13
rhetorician
orator 597.6
phrasemonger
599.5
rheum fluid 387.3
disease 684.12
rheumatic
nouns 684.31
adjs. 684.46
rheumatism 684.8
rheumy 387.7
Rh factor 387.4
rhinal 402.30
rhinarium 255.7
rhinestone 899.6
rhinitis 684.8
rhino rhinoceros 413.6
money 833.2
**rhinoceroid, rhinoc-
erotic** 413.42
rhinoceros 413.6
rhinoplasty 687.27
rhipidate 196.11
rhizanthous 410.36
rhizoid 410.34
rhizome 410.20
Rhizopoda, rhizopods
414.3
Rhodophyceae 411.4
rhombencephalon
465.5
**rhombic(al), rhom-
boidal** 250.9
rhombohedral 250.11

rhonchus 456.1
rhubarb
vegetable 306a.35
controversy 481.5
quarrel 793.5
rhumb 289.3
rhumba See **rumba**
rhyme, rime
nouns assonance 20.3
poetry 607.1,10
poem 607.4
WITHOUT RHYME OR
REASON
illogical 482.10
meaningless 545.9
capriciously 627.8
verbs assonate 20.9
make rhymes 607.20
rhymeless, rimeless
608.5
rhymery, rimery 607.7
rhymester, rimester
607.13
rhymic, rimic 607.23
rhyming
nouns 607.7
adjs. assonant 20.17
poetic 607.23
rhythm swing 322.5
cadence 462.22
euphony 587.2
meter 607.9
IN RHYTHM 462.27
rhythmic(al)
cadent 462.27
measured 489.14
metrical 607.22
rhythmics 462.1
rhythmometer 464.26
rial 833.9
rialto 830.2
riant 868.10
rib
nouns ridge 255.3
wife 931.9
verbs 880.4
ribald
nouns 896.6
adjs. vulgar 896.11
obscene 988.9
ribaldry
vulgarity 896.2
swearing 970.3
obscenity 988.4
riband 914.5
ribband 205.4
ribbed 262.4
ribber 880.3
ribbing 880.2
ribbon
nouns strip 205.4
decoration 914.5
verbs 899.8
ribbons 657.5
ribby 204.16
rich
nouns 835.5
adjs. fertile 164.9
colorful 361.19
rich-flavored 427.9
oversweet 430.7

resonant 453.9
melodious 461.49
interesting 528.19
grandiloquent
599.12
abundant 659.7
wealthy 835.13
valuable 846.10
expensive 846.11
humorous 878.5
ornate 899.11
GROW RICH 835.9
richen 835.8
richening 164.11
riches 835.1
richling 835.6
richly
grandiloquently
599.14
abundantly 659.9
expensively 846.15
richness
productiveness
164.1
colorfulness 361.3
sweetness 430.1
resonance 453.1
abundance 659.2
wealth 835.1
expensiveness 846.2
humorousness
878.1
ornateness 899.2
rick
nouns heap 74.9
garner 658.7
verbs 74.18
ricketiness 159.3
ricketish 159.16
rickets 684.8
rickety
unsteady 159.16
diseased 684.46
rickrack 261.2
ricksha 271.3
ricochet
nouns 283.2
verbs 283.6
ricochet fire 796.9
rid 760.28
GET RID OF
eliminate 77.5
dispose of 308.19
kill 408.16
discard 666.7
destroy 691.12
free oneself 761.8
riddance
elimination 77.2
escape 630.1
discard 666.3
relinquishment
812.1
riddle
nouns sorter 60.4
network 220.3
porousness 264.8
sifter 354.4
enigma 547.8
verbs sort 60.10
segregate 77.6

perforate 264.15
shoot 284.13
sift 354.6
speak in riddles
547.9
riddled 264.19
riddling
nouns 354.3
adjs. 547.15
ride
nouns 272.7
TAKE FOR A RIDE
408.16
verbs sit on 215.23
carry 270.11
travel 272.32
~ at anchor 274.17
~ a storm 274.42
float 274.57
pester 864.19
twit 880.4
ridicule 965.8
LET IT RIDE
neglect 532.6
let go 704.5
RIDE AND TIE
ride 272.32
alternate 322.12
RIDE FOR A FALL
892.6
RIDE HARD
speed 268.9
ride 272.33
RIDE HERD ON
herd 415.7
look after 697.18
direct 745.9
RIDE OUT
~ a storm 274.42
weather 696.2
RIDE ROUGHSHOD
OVER
run over 311.7
tyrannize 739.15
be severe 755.5
RIDE THROUGH
142.12
rider addition 41.1
horseman 273.8
horse 413.18
clause 740.19
ridge
nouns hill 206.6
back 240.3
bulge 255.3
wrinkle 263.3
verbs raise 255.11
wrinkle 263.6
ridged 263.8
ridge-runner 189.10
ridicule
nouns banter 880
derision 965
verbs 965.8
ridiculing 965.12
ridiculous
nouns 878.3
adjs. absurd 469.10
unbelievable 502.10
impossible 509.6
ludicrous 878.5

ridiculousness
absurdity 469.3
ludicrousness 878.1
riding district 179.5
travel 272.6
rife prevalent 79.11
numerous 101.10
rumored 556.15
abundant 659.7
rifeness
prevalence 79.2
numerousness 101.1
riff rapids 394.10
improvisation
461.27
riffle
nouns rapids 394.10
wavelet 394.14
verbs 63.3
riffraff
nouns refuse 667.4
offal 680.9
rabble 917.5
adjs. 671.18
rifle
nouns soldier 798.7
gun 799.5
verbs search 484.27
plunder 822.15
rifleman shooter 284.9
soldier 798.11
rifler 823.6
rifles 798.26
rifling 822.5
rift
nouns break 49.3
cleft 200.2
falling-out 793.4
verbs 264.11
adjs. 200.7
rig
nouns dress 230.2
suit 230.6
vehicle 271.5
rigging 276.12
equipment 657.4
frolic 876.5
verbs costume 230.40
equip 657.8
~ the market
831.25
rigged decked 276.17
equipped 657.12
rigger
aircraftsman 278.6
lineman 341.19
rigging clothes 230.2
ship's ~ 276.12,31
equipment 657.4
stock market ~
831.20
right
nouns ~ side 242.1
truth 515.1
authority 737.1
estate 808.4
propriety 956.1
privilege 956.3
justice 974.1
justification 1004.6
BY RIGHT 956.9

DO RIGHT BY 936.10
HAVE A RIGHT TO
958.4
HAVE NO RIGHT TO
959.5
RIGHT OF WAY 36.1
verbs adjust 26.13
put in order 60.7
remedy 692.13
adjs. right-hand
242.4
straight 249.5
sane 471.4
correct 515.14
conventional 643.7
expedient 668.4
proper 956.8
honorable 972.13
just 974.8
orthodox 1022.8
NOT RIGHT
insane 472.24
erroneous 517.14
RIGHT OF CENTER
140.8
advs. very 34.20
quite 56.16
rightwardly 242.7
directly 289.25,26
exactly 515.19
yes 520.18
rightfully 956.9
RIGHT ALONG
regularly 17.8
constantly 135.7
RIGHT AWAY
at once 113.8
promptly 131.15
RIGHT WITH 26.20
interjs. 274.80
rightabout-face
nouns about-face
294.3
tergiversation 626.1
verbs 294.10
right-and-left
extensively 178.10
all around 232.14
laterally 241.8
right angle 212.2
**right-angle, right-
angular**
perpendicular
212.11
right-angled 250.7
right-angularity
perpendicularity
212.1
angularity 250.1
righteous
nouns good persons
983.6
believers 1026.5
adjs. virtuous 978.7
Godly 1026.9
righteousness
virtue 978.1
godliness 1026.2
rightful
genuine 515.13
right 956.8

just 974.8
legal 996.10
rightfully
genuinely 515.17
by rights 956.9
duely 958.11
justly 974.11
rightfulness
propriety 956.1
justice 974.1
legality 996.1
right hand
right side 242.1
assistant 785.7
right-hand 242.4
right-handed 242.5
right-handedness
242.2
Right Honorable
915.8
rightist 140.4
rightly
correctly 515.18
expediently 668.7
by rights 956.9
right mind 471.1
right-minded
sane 471.4
honorable 972.13
virtuous 978.7
rightness
dextrality 242.2
correctness 515.3
expedience 668.1
righto
that's right 515.22
yes 520.18
rightward, rightwards
242.7
right wing 140.4
right-wing 140.8
right-winger 140.4
right-wingism 140.3
rigid hard 355.11
exact 515.15
meticulous 531.12
obstinate 624.9
formal 644.9
strict 755.7
rigidify 355.9
rigidity hardness 355.2
exactness 515.3
obstinacy 624.2
strictness 755.2
rigidly exactly 515.19
obstinately 624.15
formally 644.12
strictly 755.9
rigmarole 594.4
rigor violence 161.1
cold 332.1
rigidity 355.2
exactness 515.3
strictness 755.2
rigor mortis 407.1
rigorous
violent 161.15
cold 332.15
rigid 355.11
exact 515.15
meticulous 531.12

obstinate 624.9
strict 755.7
rigorously
  violently 161.24
  obstinately 624.15
  strictly 755.9
rig-out 230.2
Rigsdag 740.2
Rig-Veda 1019.7
Riksdag 740.2
rildy 227.11
rile agitate 323.10
  muddy 680.17
  annoy 864.17
  anger 950.22
riled 864.24
  RILED UP 950.26
rill, rillet 394.1
rim
  nouns border 234.4
  band 252.4
  verbs 234.10
rime
  nouns assonance 20.3
  cleft 200.2
  frost 332.8
  poetry 607.1,10
  poem 607.4
  verbs assonate 20.9
  ream 264.15
  make rhymes
    607.20
rime-frosted 332.17
rimming 234.11
rimose 200.7
rimple 263.3,6
rimpled 263.8
rimulose 200.7
rind 228.1,2
rinderpest 684.10
rindle 394.1
ring
  nouns circle 252.2,3
  atomic ~ 325.7
  halo 334.14
  ringing 453.3
  phone call 558.15
  insignia 567.4
  association 786.1,7
  arena 800.1
  ornament 899.6
  THE RING 794.9
  verbs encircle 232.7
  resound 452.6
  peal 453.8
  telephone 558.21
  NOT RING ANY BELLS
    545.7
  NOT RING TRUE
    614.15
  RING DOWN 609.32
  RING DOWN ON 70.7
  RING FALSE 614.15
  RING IN
  inaugurate 68.10
  time in 114.12
  substitute 148.4
  RING OFF
  shut up! 450.17
  ~ the phone 558.21

RING OUT
  time out 114.12
  leave 300.15
RING THE BELL 722.8
RING TRUE 515.7
RING UP
  telephone 558.21
  drama 609.32
ringdove 463.15
ringed circled 232.12
  ~ about 233.7
ringent 264.18
ringer similar 20.6
  substitute 148.2
  bell 453.4
  sharper 617.4
ring-in 148.2
ringing
  nouns 453.3
  adjs. resounding
    452.9
  pealing 453.12
ringleader 646.11
ringlet
  ~ of hair 229.5
  circlet 252.5
ringlike 252.10
ringside 438.8
ring-tailed roarer
  violent person 161.9
  hellion 941.3
ringworm 684.27
rink 876.13
rinse
  nouns 679.4
  verbs 679.18
rinsing 679.4
rinsings 667.4
riot
  nouns commotion
    62.4
  violence 161.3
  success 722.3
  revolt 765.4
  brawl 793.7
  verbs 765.8
  RIOT IN 863.10
rioter 765.5
rioting 161.3
riotous violent 161.18
  unrestrained 760.22
  seditious 765.12
  dissolute 991.8
rip
  nouns break 49.3
  riptide 394.13
  horse 413.16
  reprobate 984.5
  libertine 987.10
  verbs 264.11
riparial, riparian,
  riparious 384.9
rip cord 279.13
ripe
  verbs 720.8
  adjs. mature 126.12
  ready 718.16
  fully developed
    720.12
ripen mature 126.9
  suppurate 309.13

develop 321.6
reach completion
  720.8
RIPEN INTO 145.12
ripeness
  readiness 718.4
  full development
    720.2
ripening
  maturation 126.6
  development 321.2
riposte, ripost
  nouns answer 485.1
  repartee 879.7
  verbs 485.4
ripping 672.14
ripple
  nouns corrugation
    260.3
  crinkle 263.3
  trickle 394.7
  rapids 394.10
  wavelet 394.14
  ~ of applause 451.5
  verbs crinkle 263.6
  disturb 323.10
  trickle 394.19
  murmur 451.11
rippled 263.8
rippling 451.19
riprap 215.6
ripraps 394.10
riproaring 161.17
riptide 394.13
rise
  nouns increase 38.1
  source 152.5
  height 206.2
  uprise 212.5
  acclivity 218.6
  reaction 283.1
  ascent 313.1
  development 321.2
  improvement 689.1
  GET A RISE OUT OF
    283.8
  GIVE RISE TO
  cause 152.11
  generate 166.15
  verbs increase 38.6
  originate 68.12
  be high 206.15
  get up 212.7
  slope 218.10
  ascend 313.8
  raise 315.5
  levitate 352.9
  appear 445.8
  get louder 452.6
  ~ from bed 711.5
  succeed 722.9
  revolt 765.8
  RISE ABOVE
  loom 34.7
  surmount 206.16
  triumph over 724.6
  RISE ABOVE IT 859.6
  RISE AND SHINE
  navigation 274.79
  arise 711.5
  RISE FROM 153.6

RISE TO THE
  OCCASION
  speak 592.13
  be impulsive 628.7
Risen, the 1011.12
riser 313.5
risibilities, risibility
  879.11
risible laughter-
  loving 868.15
  laughable 878.5
risibles 879.11
rising
  nouns uprising 212.5
  acclivity 218.6
  swelling 255.4
  ascent 313.1
  appearance 445.1
  inflammation
    684.28
  revolt 765.4
  adjs. sloping 218.17
  ascending 313.14
risk
  nouns gamble 514.1
  danger 695.1
  investment 834.3
  DO AT ONE'S OWN
    RISK 960.8
  RUN THE RISK 695.7
  verbs chance 514.18
  endanger 695.6,7
  invest in 834.16
risk capital
  speculation 831.19
  capital 833.15
riskful 695.10
riskily 695.17
riskiness 695.2
risky hazardous 695.10
risqué 988.7
risqué 988.7
ritardando
  nouns 461.25
  advs. 461.55
rite ceremony 644.4
  religious ~ 1038.3
ritornel, ritornelle,
  ritornello
  prelude 66.2
  refrain 103.5
  music 461.24
Ritter 916.6
ritual
  nouns ceremony
    644.1,4
  religious 1038.3
  rituale 1038.12
  adjs. ceremonious
    644.8
  ritualistic 1038.21
ritualism
  formalism 644.2
  religious ~ 1038.1
ritualist 1038.2
ritualistic
  ceremonious 644.8
  ritual 1038.21
rituality
  ceremony 644.1
  ritualism 1038.1,3

ritualize 644.5
ritzy 902.18
rival
 nouns equal 30.5
 opponent 789.2
 verbs equal 30.6
 excel 36.5
 emulate 672.12
 compete with
  794.19
 adjs. 794.24
rivaling
 surpassing 36.14
 competitive 794.24
rivalry
 competition 794.2
 envy 952.1
rive sever 49.10
 open 264.11
river stream 394.1
 torrent 394.5
riverain 384.9
riverhead source 152.6
 stream 394.2
river horse
 behemoth 194.14
 hippopotamus
  413.6
riverine coastal 384.9
 fluvial 394.24
riverscape view 445.6
 picture 572.13
riverside 384.2
riverway 395.2
rivery 394.24
rivet
 nouns 47.7
 verbs 47.8
 ~ one's attention
  528.11
riveted 142.15
rivose, rivulose 253.6
rivulation 253.1
rivulet 394.1
roach 229.22
road inlet 398.1
 way 655.3,6
 roadstead 698.6
 GO ON THE ROAD
  272.20
 HIT THE ROAD 272.22
 ON THE ROAD
  absent 186.10
  on the way 270.20
  toward 289.28
  forward 293.7
road agent 823.5
roadblock 728.5
roadbook 746.9
road hog
 motorist 273.10
 monopolist 976.3
roadhop 277.48
roadhopping 277.14
road horse 413.18
roadhouse inn 190.13
 cabaret 876.11
road map map 652.4
 directory 746.9
roads, roadstead
 inlet 398.1

 port 698.6
roadster 413.18
road-test 488.8
roadway 655.6
roam
 nouns 272.3
 verbs 272.22
roamer 273.2
roaming
 nouns 272.3
 adjs. 272.36
roan
 nouns 413.15
 adjs. 366.4
Roan Barbary 413.21
roanoke 833.3
roar
 nouns uproar 452.3
  boom 455.4
  shout 458.1
  ~ of laughter 874.4
 verbs be violent
  161.10
  blow 402.24
  be noisy 452.7
  boom 455.9
  shout 458.6
  ululate 459.2
  say 592.17
  laugh 874.9
roarer
 strong man 158.6
 violent person 161.9
 horse 413.16
 hellion 941.3
roaring great 34.13
 booming 455.12
Roaring Twenties
  107.8
roast
 nouns 306a.7,12
 verbs be hot 327.21
  cook 329.4
  interrogate 484.23
  banter 880.4
  criticize 967.21
 adjs. 329.6
roasted 329.6
roaster fowl 306a.22
 hot day 327.7
roasting
 nouns cooking 329.1
  interrogation 484.15
  banter 880.2
  reproof 967.6
 adjs. 327.25
rob
 nouns 388.5
 verbs 822.14
 ROB PETER TO PAY
  PAUL
  compensate 33.4
  rob 822.14
robber 823.1
robbery 822.3,10
robbing 822.3
robe
 nouns cover 227.10
  garment 230.3,12
  ~ of state 567.3

 clerical ~ 1039.2
 verbs 230.38
robed 230.44
robing 230.1
Robin Goodfellow
  1014.8
Robin Hood
 thief 823.12
 altruist 936.8
robomb 280.3
roborant
 nouns 685.7
 adjs. 685.38
robot
 automaton 348.12
 necessitarian 638.5
robot bomb 280.3
robot control 348.3
robotize 348.23
robot rocket 281.2
robot satellite 281.6
robust, robustious
 strong 158.13
 healthy 683.9
robustness
 strength 158.1
 healthiness 683.3
rock
 nouns stability 142.7
  strength 158.7
  sway 322.5
  flounder 323.8
  hardness 355.6
  stone 383
  refuge 698.1
  missile 799.12
  coin 833.4
 verbs sail 274.58
  sway 322.9
  flounder 323.15
  stone 796.29
 adjs. 383.7
rock-and-roll 461.9
rock bottom
 bottom 211.1
 foundation 215.6
rock-bottom 211.7
 HIT ROCK-BOTTOM
  degenerate 690.18
  be unfortunate
   727.11
  despond 870.16
rock-bound
 rugged 260.7
 bound 758.16
Rockefeller 835.7
rocker oscillator 322.8
 sieve 354.4
 OFF ONE'S ROCKER
  472.25
rocket
 nouns speed 268.7
  aircraft 280.1
  types of ~ 280.14
  rocket names 280.15
  spaceship 281.2
  ascent 313.7
  signal 566.14
 verbs skyrocket
  280.12
  ascend 313.9

 rocket bomb 280.3
rocketborne 281.16
rocketeer
 rocket man 280.6
 astronaut 281.8
rocket engine 281.4
rocket engineer 280.6
rocket engineering
 aviation 277.2
 rockets 280.7
rocketer, rocketor
  280.6
rocket gun 280.11
rocket pilot 281.8
rocket plane 279.4
rocket power
 power 156.4
 aviation 277.30
rocket-propelled
 aviation 277.56
 propelled 284.17
rocket propulsion
 aviation 277.30
 propulsion 284.2
rocketry 280.7
rocket ship 281.2
rock garden 412.10
rockiness 684.1
rocking 322.16
rocking chair 322.8
rocking horse 876.16
rockman 382.8
rock pile 1008.2
rocks
 hidden danger 695.5
 money 833.2
 GO ON THE ROCKS
  fail 723.9
  come to grief
   727.10
  go bankrupt 840.7
 ON THE ROCKS
  aground 274.77
  stranded 729.25
  bankrupt 840.11
rockweed 410.4
rocky unsteady 159.16
 rugged 260.7
 hard 355.10
 stony 383.8
 sickish 684.41
rococo 85.12
rod shaft 216.1
 insignia 567.3
 ~ and reel 653.3
 scepter 737.8
 gun 799.5
 whip 1009.2
 wand 1034.6
rodent
 nouns 413.3
 adjs. 413.40
Rodentia 414.12
rodenticide 408.11
rodents 414.12
rodeo roundup 74.1
 show 609.14
rodlike 355.11
rodman 941.4
Rodomont 908.5

ROOT ON 646.16
ROOT OUT
eliminate 77.5
extract 304.9
seek 484.28
eradicate 691.14
rooted
traditional 123.12
established 142.14
habitual 640.19
rooter 633.6
rootlet 410.20
rootlike 410.34
rootstock 410.20
rope
nouns cord 205.2
ship's ropes 276.31
cigar 433.4
free scope 760.3
hangman's ~
1009.5
GIVE ONE ROPE
760.14
ROPE OF SAND
incoherence 51.1
weakness 159.7
THE ROPE 1008.7
verbs tie 47.9
bind 758.10
lasso 820.14
ROPE IN 648.4
ROPE OFF 233.4
ropedancer 876.21
ropes influence 171.3
rigging 276.31
HAVE ON THE ROPES
729.15
rope's end 1009.1
ropewalker 876.21
ropeway 655.9
ropework, roping
cordage 205.3
rigging 276.12
ropiness
toughness 358.1
viscidity 388.2
ropy stringy 205.7
tough 358.4
viscid 388.12
roric, rorulent 391.15
Rorschach test 688.11
rory-tory, rory-cum-
tory 902.19
Rosary 1038.9
rosary prayer 1030.4
beadroll 1038.11
Roscius 610.1
rose
nouns 395.9
UNDER THE ROSE
612.19
adjs. 367.9
rosebud 410.21
rose-colored, roseate
pink 367.9
auspicious 542.16
optimistic 886.12
rosehead 395.9
rose oil 435.2
Rosetta stone
hieroglyphics 579.3

writing 600.12
rose water 435.3
rose-water 435.8
Rosh Hashana
1038.16
Rosicrucian
nouns 1032.11
adjs. 1032.24
rosin
nouns 380.1
verbs 380.2
Rosinante 413.16,21
rosiny 380.3
roster roll 88.5
schedule 639.2
rostrate, rostriform
251.9
rostrum
platform 215.13
prow 239.3
pulpit 1040.12
rosy pink 367.9,10
auspicious 542.16
optimistic 886.12
rot
nouns nonsense
545.3
blight 674.2
disease 684.10
putrefaction 690.6
verbs 690.23
Rota 999.6
rota 88.5
rotary
nouns 220.2
adjs. 320.15
rotate recur 137.6
revolve 320.9
rotating 320.14
rotation
sequence 65.1
round 137.3
turning 320
IN ROTATION 137.12
rotational, rotative
320.15
rotator 320.4
rotators 320.17,18
rotatory 320.15
rote
BY ROTE 535.27
rotgut 994.15
rotifers 414.5
rotocraft 279.5
rotograph
nouns engraving
576.8
newspaper 603.12
verbs 576.14
rotogravure
engraving 576.3,8
newspaper 603.12
rotor 320.4
rotten unsound 159.15
bad 673.8
decayed 690.38
dishonest 973.15
wicked 979.19
rottenness
putridity 690.6
turpitude 979.6

rotter 984.7
rotund
verbs 254.6
adjs. corpulent
194.18
round 254.8
rotunda 190.5
rotundity
corpulence 194.8
roundness 254
rotundness 254.1
roturier 917.7
roué 987.10
rouge
nouns red 367.1
radical 743.11
cosmetic 898.11
verbs 367.4
rough
nouns ~ ground
260.2
drawing 572.14
draught 652.3
vulgarian 896.6
ruffian 941.4
IN THE ROUGH
roughly 260.11
unfinished 719.12
THE ROUGH 719.4
verbs roughen 260.4
treat roughly 665.5
ROUGH IN 652.12
ROUGH IT 187.12
ROUGH OUT
form 245.6
do carelessly 532.9
adjs. acrimonious
160.12
violent 161.15
rowdy 161.19
unsmooth 260.6
jolting 323.21
bitter 428.6
pungent 432.6
harsh-sounding
457.14
unfinished 719.12
difficult 729.16
vulgar 896.11
gruff 935.7
harsh 937.22
advs. 260.11
rough-and-ready
ready 718.16
unpolished 896.12
rough-and-tumble
nouns 62.4
adjs. 161.19
roughcast
verbs plaster 227.27
form 245.6
do carelessly 532.9
adjs. rough 260.6
unfinished 719.12
rough diamond
unfinish 719.5
good person 983.1
roughen rough 260.4
agitate 323.10
rough-grained 260.6
roughhew form 245.6

do carelessly 532.9
roughhewn
rough 260.6
unfinished 719.12
roughhouse
nouns rough-and-
tumble 62.4
rowdiness 736.1
verbs be disorderly
62.9
cut up 736.4
roughly approximately
199.26
unsmoothly 260.11
vulgarly 896.16
harshly 937.29
roughneck
nouns vulgarian
896.6
ruffian 941.4
adjs. 896.13
roughness
acrimony 160.4
unsmoothness 260
pungency 432.1
raucousness 457.2
unfinish 719.4
vulgarity 896.2
gruffness 935.3
harshness 937.9
roughrider 273.8
roughscuff 917.4
roulade
nouns 461.24; 462.18
verbs 461.39
rouleau bundle 74.7
cylinder 254.4
coins 833.4
roulette 514.7
roulette wheel 514.11
round
nouns degree 29.1
series 71.2
turn 108.2
cycle 137.3
sphere 179.2
circle 252.2
meat cut 306a.17
rung 313.5
circuit 319.2
whirl 320.2
rondo 461.19
routine 640.5
walk of life 654.4
route 655.2
cards 876.17
~ of applause 966.2
GO THE ROUNDS
wander 272.22
be published 557.16
THE ROUNDS 876.7
verbs circle 252.9
rotund 254.6
turn around 294.9
go around 319.5
rotate 320.9
ROUND IN 74.15
ROUND OUT
complete 56.6
round 254.6
bulge 255.10

finish 720.6

ROUND UP
drive together **74.17**
herd 415.7
procure 809.9
adjs. full 56.12
circular 252.10
rotund 254.8
unqualified 507.2
advs. around 232.13
in a circle 320.16

ROUND ABOUT
exterior 223.6
around 232.13
circuitously 319.9
in a circle 320.16

ROUND AND ROUND
by turns 137.12
variably 141.8
windingly 253.11
in circles 320.16
back and forth
  322.20

roundabout
nouns circuit 319.3
whirligig 320.4
merry-go-round
  876.15
adjs. surrounding
  232.9
circuitous 319.7
circumlocutory
  591.14
preps. over 183.29
through 289.29

rounded
circular 252.10
round 254.8
phonetics 449.18

roundel circle 252.2
poem 607.4

roundelay
rondo 461.19
poem 607.4

rounder
libertine 987.10
dissipater 999.3

round-faced 194.18

roundhouse
building 190.17
blow 282.5
toilet 680.13
repair shop 717.6

roundlet 252.5

round lot 832.3

roundly
completely 56.15
approximately
  199.26

roundness
circularity 252.1
rotundity 254.1

round robin
letter 602.3
request 772.1

SIGN A ROUND ROBIN
924.5

round-shouldered
248.12

roundsman 697.14

round table 588.3

round-the-clock 71.9

round top 227.8

round trip
journey 272.5
space flight 281.1

roundup 74.1

roup
nouns hoarseness
  457.2
auction 827.4
verbs 827.11

rouper 828.8

roupiness 457.2

roupingwife 828.2

roupy 457.14

rouse elicit 304.12
incite 646.19
awaken 711.4
excite 855.11

rouser surprise 538.2
instigator 646.11

rousing
nouns 711.2
adjs. great 34.13
provocative 646.27

roustabout
longshoreman
  275.10
laborer 716.2

rout
nouns attendance
  73.6
mob 74.4
agitation 323.1
defeat 725.2
rabble 917.4
verbs defeat 725.9
put to flight 797.10

ROUT OUT
eject 308.13
clean 679.17

route 655.2

routine
nouns order 59.1
habit 640.5
adjs. 640.15

rove
nouns 272.3
verbs wander 272.22
deviate 290.4

rover wanderer 273.2
bandit 823.4
robber 823.8

roving
nouns wandering
  272.3
discursiveness 591.3
adjs. desultory 141.7
wandering 272.36
deviative 290.2
discursive 591.13

row
nouns series 71.2
street 655.6
~ of pins 671.5
quarrel 793.6
verbs line-up 71.6
paddle 274.56

row
nouns commotion
  62.4

verbs quarrel 793.7

rowdiness 736.1

rowdy
nouns cutup 736.3
vulgarian 896.6
ruffian 941.4
adjs. boisterous
  161.19
disorderly 736.5
boorish 896.13

rowdydow
commotion 62.4
uproar 452.3

rowdyism
misbehavior 736.1
boorishness 896.4

rowel 646.8

rowen 67.3

rower 275.5

rowlock fulcrum 286.3
pivot 320.5

royal
nouns 747.8
adjs. excellent 672.13
sovereign 737.16
dignified 903.12

Royal Highness 915.2

royal highness 747.8

royalist 737.17

royalistic 737.17

royally
excellently 672.23
dignifiedly 903.14

royal road road 655.6
facility 730.1

royalty
sovereignty 737.7
potentate 747.8
payment 839.7
nobility 916.2

r.p.m. velocity 268.2
revolutions 320.3

R.S.V.P. 602.12

ruach 1032.17

rub
nouns crisis 129.4
friction 349.1
touch 424.1
hindrance 728.4
crux 729.7
verbs graze 199.10
polish 259.7
frictionize 349.6
chafe 423.7
stroke 424.8
treat 687.33

RUB DOWN
massage 349.6
groom 415.6

RUB OFF
remove 42.10
wear 690.21

RUB ON
plod 269.7
progress 293.3

RUB ONE'S EYES 918.4

RUB OUT
excise 42.8
obliterate 691.16

RUB THE WRONG WAY
ruffle 260.5

irritate 864.18

RUB UP
rub 349.6
refresh the memory
  535.19
study up 562.14
touch up 689.11

rub-a-dub
nouns 454.1
verbs 454.4

rubber
nouns massager 349.4
elastic 357.3
types of ~ 357.9
eraser 691.9
cards 876.17
verbs rubberize 357.6
stare 438.16
sight-see 441.6
be curious 526.3
adjs. 357.8

rubber check 833.10

rubberize 357.6

rubberized 357.8

rubberneck
nouns excursionist
  273.1
sight-seer 441.3
inquisitive 526.2
verbs stare 438.16
sight-see 441.6
be curious 526.3
adjs. sight-seeing
  441.7
curious 526.5

rubbernecked 526.5

rubber-stamp 520.12

rubbery 357.8

rubbing
nouns friction 349.1
stroking 424.2
adjs. 349.9

rubbish
nouns nonsense 545.2
refuse 667.5
trumpery 671.4
riffraff 917.5
interjs. 469.12

rubbishy
nonsensical 545.10
paltry 671.18

rubble stone 383.1
trash 667.5

rubblestone 383.1

rubdown 349.3

rube
nouns dolt 470.5
clumsy 732.9
rustic 917.9
adjs. 181.6

rubefaction 367.3

rubelle 367.1

rubeola 684.9

rubescence
redness 367.1
reddening 367.3

rubescent 367.12

rubiate 367.6

rubicund 367.6,10

rubicundity
heat glow 327.11

redness 367.1
rubification 367.3
rubificative 367.12
rubiginous 366.4
ruble 833.9
rubric title 483.2
 law 996.3
 ritual 1038.12
rubric(al) 367.6
rubricate
 verbs 367.4
 adjs. 367.6
rubrication 367.3
rubricity 367.1
rubricize 367.4
rubricose 367.6
rubrific 367.12
ruby 367.7
ruck
 nouns generality 79.3
 rut 262.1
 THE RUCK 917.4
 verbs 263.3,6
ruckle
 nouns 454.3
 verbs crumple 263.6
 rattle 454.6
ruckus
 commotion 62.4
 uproar 452.3
 row 793.6
ructation 308.9
ruction
 commotion 62.4
 uproar 452.3
 row 793.6
rudder
 plane part 279.16
 guide 745.5
rudderless 157.13
rudderpost 240.6
ruddied 367.6
ruddiness 367.1
ruddle 367.4
ruddy red 367.6,10
 execrable 673.10
 blushing 906.13
 blasted 970.10
rude harsh-sounding
 457.14
 unlearned 476.15
 inelegant 588.2
 healthy 683.9
 unfinished 719.12
 vulgar 896.11
 impudent 911.9
 discourteous 935.4
rude awakening
 disillusionment
 519.1
 rousing 711.2
rudeness
 raucousness 457.2
 inelegant style 588.1
 unfinish 719.4
 vulgarity 896.2
 impudence 911.2
 impoliteness 935.1
rudiment origin 152.7
 foundation 215.6
 embryo 405.13

rudimental
 beginning 68.13
 embryonic 195.14
 undeveloped 719.12
rudimentary
 beginning 68.13
 original 152.16
 embryonic 195.14
 basic 211.8
 fetal 405.23
 undeveloped 719.12
rudiments 68.5
rue 871.6
rueful grievous 862.11
 sorrowful 870.27
 regretful 871.8
ruefulness 870.11
ruff
 nouns drumbeat
 454.1
 trump 876.17
 verbs 263.5
ruffian rowdy 736.3
 vulgarian 896.6
 tough 941.4
ruffianism
 misbehavior 736.1
 boorishness 896.4
ruffle
 nouns muddle 62.2
 edging 234.7
 fold 263.1
 drumbeat 454.1
 fluster 530.3
 expedient 668.2
 excitement 855.3
 verbs disarrange 63.2
 rumple 260.5
 fold 263.5
 agitate 323.10
 drum 454.4
 beat time 461.45
 fluster 530.7
 excite 855.14
 annoy 864.17
 anger 950.22
ruffled
 disheveled 62.13
 convolutional 253.6
 rough 260.6
 agitated 323.17
 confused 530.12
 excited 855.24
 annoyed 864.24
rufous
 reddish-brown 366.4
 reddish 367.6
rufulous 367.6
rug bedding 215.21
 carpet 227.9,44
 coverlet 227.10
Rugby 876.8
rugged substantial 3.5
 strong 158.13
 rough 260.7
 wrinkled 263.8
 healthy 683.9
 difficult 729.16
 stern 755.6
 harsh 937.22

rugged individualism
 760.4
rugged individualist
 politics 743.8
 independent 760.11
ruggedness
 strength 158.1
 roughness 260.1
 healthiness 683.3
 difficulty 729.1
 sternness 755.1
Rugger 876.8
rugose, rugous 263.8
rugosity 260.1
ruin
 nouns ruins 690.9
 destruction 691.1
 defeat 725.1
 loss 810.1
 gin 994.16
 verbs spoil 690.11
 destroy 691.10
 defeat 725.6
 frustrate 728.15
 bankrupt 840.8
 debauch 987.20
ruinate 691.10
ruination 691.1
ruined spoiled 690.28
 destroyed 691.27
 defeated 725.14
 bankrupt 840.11
 irremediable 887.15
ruiner 691.8
ruining 691.25
ruinous
 destructive 691.25
 in ruins 691.27
 disastrous 727.15
ruins remains 43.1
 relic 123.6
 wreck 690.9
 IN RUINS 691.27
rule
 nouns criterion 25.1
 average 32.1
 principle 84.4
 influence 171.1
 measure 489.2
 belief 500.2
 axiom 516.2
 habit 640.4
 jurisdiction 737.4
 sway 739.1
 precept 749.2
 decree 750.4
 law 996.3
 verbs prevail 79.9
 influence 171.8
 pass judgment
 493.13
 govern 739.13
 decree 750.9
RULE OFF 489.12
RULE OUT
 excise 42.8
 cancel 691.16
 obviate 728.14
RULE THE ROOST
 739.14
rule of thumb 488.1

ruler governor 747.6,8
 paddle 1009.2
ruling
 nouns verdict 493.5
 decree 750.4
 law 996.3
 adjs. chief 36.16
 prevalent 79.11
 influential 171.14
 most important
 670.25
 governing 739.17
rum
 nouns 994.12
 adjs. odd 85.11
 good 672.14
rumba, rhumba 877.5
rumble
 nouns boom 455.4
 rumor 556.6
 verbs ripple 451.11
 boom 455.9
rumbling 455.12
rumbumptious, rum-
 bustious 161.19
rumen 192.3
ruminant
 nouns 413.3
 adjs. cud-chewing
 306.30
 animal 413.41
 thoughtful 477.20
ruminants 414.12
ruminate chew 306.25
 ponder 477.11
Ruminatia 414.12
ruminating
 cud-chewing 306.30
 thoughtful 477.20
rumination
 chewing 306.1
 thought 477.2
rummage
 nouns litter 62.3
 search 484.2
 junk 667.5
 verbs 484.27
rummy oddity 85.4
 drunkard 994.11
 liquor dealer 994.23
rumor
 nouns 556.6
 verbs 557.10
rumored 556.15
rumormonger 556.9
rump remainder 43.1
 buttocks 240.4
 meat cut 306a.17
rumple disarrange 63.2
 ruffle 260.5
 crumple 263.3,6
rumpled
 disheveled 62.13
 crumpled 263.8
rumpus
 commotion 62.4
 uproar 452.3
 row 793.6
rumpus room
 room 191.12
 amusement 876.12

rumrunner
  smuggler 824.5
  bootlegger 994.24
rumrunning
  smuggling 824.2
  bootlegging 994.22
rumshop 994.25
run
  nouns average 32.1
  succession 71.2
  prevalence 79.2
  generality 79.3
  continuance 143.1
  trend 173.2
  burrow 190.22
  piece 201.3
  course 266.2
  speed 268.4
  migration 272.4
  journey 272.5
  voyage 274.6
  flight 277.7
  direction 289.1
  stream 394.1
  flow 394.4
  music 462.18
  routine 640.5
  customariness 640.6
  path 655.2,3
  freedom 760.1
  race 794.12
HAVE A RUN 642.9
HAVE THE RUN OF
  760.16
IN THE LONG RUN
  on an average 32.5
  on the whole 54.13
  generally 79.15
  in time 121.1
  eventually 150.12
ON THE RUN
  on the move 272.41
  busy 705.20
RUN OF LUCK 726.3
verbs elapse 105.5
  endure 110.6
  operate 163.5
  be operative 163.8
  incur 174.4
  extend 178.7
  speed 268.11
  course 272.17
  migrate 272.21
  pilot 274.14
  sail 274.24,57
  thrust 282.12
  suppurate 309.13
  melt 328.20
  liquefy 390.5
  flow 394.17
  trace 484.29
  publish 601.12
  flee 629.10
  nominate 635.16
  pursue 653.8,9
  ~ for office 742.42
  direct 745.8,9
  smuggle 824.8
RUN A BLOCKADE
  274.13

RUN A CHANCE
  514.18
RUN ACROSS
  encounter 199.11
  find 487.3
RUN AFOUL OF
  sail into 274.43
  collide 282.13
  contend with
    794.16
RUN AFTER
  fetch 270.15
  pursue 653.8
  toady 905.8
  lionize 912.14
  make friends 925.11
RUN AGAINST
  counteract 177.6
  oppose 788.3
RUN AGROUND 727.10
RUN CIRCLES AROUND
  36.8
RUN COUNTER TO
  counter 15.3
  counteract 177.6
  oppose 788.3
RUN DOWN
  sail into 274.43
  run over 311.7
  trace 484.29
  find 487.4
  decline in health
    684.35
  deteriorate 690.18
  disparage 969.8
RUN DRY 664.4
RUN FOR IT 629.10
RUN IN
  foist in 10.4
  interpose 236.7
  sail into 274.43
  thrust in 303.6
  arrest 759.16
  visit 920.16
RUN INTO
  amount to 54.7
  be converted 145.12
  encounter 199.11
  sail into 274.43
  collide 282.13
  discover 487.3
  ~ the ground
    661.11
  cost 844.15
RUN ITS COURSE
  end 70.6
  elapse 105.5
  be past 119.4
RUN OFF
  hasten off 300.14
  print 601.12
  flee 629.10
  depreciate 847.6
RUN OFF AT THE
  MOUTH
  twaddle 545.8
  chatter 594.6
RUN ON
  endure 110.6
  continue 143.3
  chatter 594.6

RUN OUT
  end 70.6
  elapse 105.5
  emerge 302.13
  eject 308.13
  expatiate 591.8
  escape 630.9
  be used up 664.4
  perish 691.22
  fatigue 715.5
RUN OUT ON 631.6
RUN OVER
  number 87.10
  reiterate 103.8
  trample on 311.7
  overflow 394.18
  ponder 477.12
  examine 484.31
  browse 562.13
RUN RIOT
  create a disturbance
    62.8
  become violent
    161.14
  overrun 311.5
  exaggerate 615.3
  superabound 661.9
  riot 765.8
  dissipate 991.6
RUN ~ THE RISK
  be liable 174.3
  chance 514.18
RUN THROUGH
  be uniform 17.3
  pervade 185.7
  pierce 264.15
  browse 562.13
  superabound 661.9
  stab 796.27
  squander 852.3
RUN TO EARTH
  trace 484.29
  find 487.4
RUN TOGETHER 297.2
RUN TO PATTERN
  640.12
RUN TO SEED
  go to waste 664.5
  deteriorate 690.20
RUN UP
  increase 38.6
  construct 166.12
  ~ a bill 838.6
RUN UP AGAINST
  experience 150.8
  encounter 199.11
  find 487.3
runabout 273.2
runagate
  apostate 626.5
  fugitive 629.5
run-around
  evasion 629.1
  circumvention
    733.5
runaway
  nouns deserter 626.5
  fugitive 629.5
  adjs. 629.15
rundle rung 313.5
  roller 320.4

  stream 394.1
rundown 605.2
run-down
  nouns 277.8
  adjs. weakened
    159.18
  sickly 684.40
  deteriorated
    690.32,35
  tired 715.6
rune character 579.3
  magic 1033.1
runer minstrel 463.16
  bard 607.14
runes writing 600.10
  poetry 607.2
runesmith 607.14
rung degree 29.1
  step 313.5
runic
  ~ alphabet 579.4
  ~ writing 600.27
  poetic 607.21
run-in quarrel 793.5
  fight 794.3
runlet, runnel 394.1
runner member 55.4
  operator 163.4
  racer 268.6
  sled ~ 271.18
  trough 395.4
  tendril 410.18
  messenger 559.1
  smuggler 824.5
  salesman 828.5
  solicitor 828.7
  procurer 987.18
runner-up 724.2
running
  nouns operation
    163.1
  festering 309.6
  melting 328.3
  liquefaction 390.1
BE IN THE RUNNING
  155.13
OUT OF THE RUNNING
  not comparable 37.7
  disabled 157.17
  adjs. continuous 71.9
  prevalent 79.11
  present 120.2
  operating 163.12
  flowing 394.25
  cursive 600.24
  advs. 71.12
running account
  843.2
running commentary
  604.2
running head 483.2
running mate 744.9
runoff 302.4
run-off 876.9
runout 629.4
run-out 715.8
runt diminutive 195.4
  dwarf 196.6
  insignificancy 671.7
run-through
  perusal 484.4

summary 605.2
runty 195.12
runway
  flight deck 276.8
  airstrip 277.20
  path 655.3
rupee 833.9
rupia 684.27
rupture
  nouns break 49.3
  breach 200.2
  sickness 684.8
  injury 690.7
  falling-out 793.4
  verbs break 49.11
  breach 264.14
ruptured 49.23
rural rustic 181.6
  agricultural 412.20
rural district 181.1
ruralism 181.3
ruralization 181.4
ruralize 181.5
ruse trick 616.6
  artifice 733.3
ruse de guerre 733.4
rush
  nouns outburst 161.6
  course 266.2
  dash 268.4
  flow 394.4
  jet 394.9
  plant 410.5
  trifle 671.5
  haste 707.1
  demand 751.1
  attack 796.1
  verbs speed 268.10
  flow 394.17
  hasten 707.4,5
  charge 796.19
  interjs. 707.16
rushed 707.11
rushing 394.25
rushlight light 334.18
  candle 335.2
rusk 306a.29
russet 366.4
Russian 579.5
Russianism 180.6
Russianization 188.4
Russianize 188.5
rust
  nouns plant 410.4
  blight 674.2
  decay 690.5
  verbs color 366.2
  redden 367.4
  corrode 690.22
  adjs. 366.4
rust-cankered, rust-
  eaten 690.41
rustic
  nouns farmer 412.5
  countryman 917.9
  adjs. 181.6
rusticate
  ruralize 181.5
  banish 308.16
  seclude oneself
    922.8

rustication
  ruralization 181.4
  banishment 308.4
  retirement 922.1
rusticity 181.3
rustle
  sound softly 451.12
  hustle 705.12
  steal 822.13
rustler
  hustler 705.8
  thief 823.9
rustling
  nouns 451.6
  adjs. 451.18
rustre 567.2
rust-worn 690.41
rusty old 123.14
  aged 126.17
  rust-colored 366.4
  corroded 690.41
  unpracticed 732.18
  surly 949.24
rut
  nouns furrow 262.1
  sexual heat 418.5
  routine 640.5
  track 655.3
  IN A RUT
  samely 17.7
  habituated 640.18
  verbs furrow 262.3
  be in heat 418.15
ruth 942.1
ruthful 942.7
ruthfulness 942.2
ruthless
  cruel 937.23,24
  merciless 943.3
ruthlessness
  cruelty 937.11
  mercilessness 943.1
rutilant, rutilous
  334.30
rutted 262.4
rutting, ruttish, rutty
  418.21
rye 410.29
ryot 917.8

S

Sabaism 1031.1
Sabaist 1031.4
Sabaoth 798.22
sabbat 1033.3
Sabbatarian
  nouns ascetic 989.2
  ritualist 1038.2
  adjs. 989.3
Sabbatarianism
  asceticism 989.1
  hyperorthodoxy
    1022.6
  ritualism 1038.1
Sabbath
  day of rest 709.5
  holyday 1038.14
Sabbath-breaker
  1028.3
Sabbath school 565.10

sabbatical
  nouns 709.3
  adjs. 709.10
sabbatism
  hyperorthodoxy
    1022.6
  ritualism 1038.1
sabbatist 1038.2
sabe
  nouns intelligence
    466.1
  understanding 474.3
  verbs 474.12
saber
  nouns 799.22
  verbs 796.27
Sabir 578.10
sable
  nouns fur 228.8
  black 364.1
  animal 413.49
  adjs. 364.8
sabotage
  nouns 690.1
  verbs 690.16
saboteur
  subversive 617.11
  destroyer 691.8
sabreur 798.1
sabuline, sabulose
  360.12
sabulosity 360.2
sabulous 360.12
SAC 798.30
sac 192.2
sacatra 44.9
saccharide 307.5
saccharin 430.3
saccharine 430.6
saccharinity 430.1
saccular 192.9
sacellum 1040.3
sacerdotal 1035.13
sacerdotalism 1035.3
sachem
  personage 670.8
  politician 744.7
  chief 747.3,9
sachet 435.6
sack
  nouns bag 192.2
  pillage 822.5
  THE SACK 308.5
  verbs load 183.16
  bag 235.9
  discharge 308.18
  secure 809.7
  catch 820.14
  plunder 822.15
  SACK UP 710.16
sackbut 464.8
sackcloth and ashes
  mourning 873.6
  penance 1010.3
sacker 823.6
sacking 822.5
sack race 794.12
Sacrament, the 1038.8
sacrament 1038.3

sacramental
  nouns 1038.3,11
  adjs. 1038.21
sacramentalism 1038.1
sacramentalist 1038.2
sacrarium 1040.3,4,5,9
sacred 1024.7
Sacred College 1036.1
sacrifice
  nouns loss 810.1
  giving up 812.1
  self-sacrifice 977.1
  oblation 1030.7
  AT ANY SACRIFICE
    622.20
  verbs lose 810.5
  give up 812.3
  give away 816.20
  sell 827.8
  be sacrificing 977.3
  offer ~ 1030.14
sacrificial 812.5
sacrificing
  nouns 977.5
  adjs. 812.5
sacrilege 1028.2
sacrilegious 1028.6
sacrilegist 1028.3
sacring bell 1038.11
sacrist, sacristan
  1036.9
sacristy 1040.9
sacrosanct 1024.7
sad great 34.8
  undercooked 329.8
  dark 364.9
  gray 365.3
  paltry 671.18
  terrible 673.9
  unfortunate 727.14
  grievous 862.11
  unhappy 870.20
  depressing 870.31
  shameful 913.11
sad case 984.2
sadden 870.18
saddened 870.20
saddle
  nouns ridge 206.6
  seat 215.19
  types of ~ 215.32
  ~ of mutton
    306a.15
  meat cut 306a.17
  seat of power 737.9
  IN THE SADDLE
  prepared 718.16
  in charge 737.21
  verbs harness 47.10
  burden 351.13
  SADDLE WITH
  affix 40.3
  attribute to 154.3
  hamper 728.11
  obligate 960.11
  impose 961.4
  accuse of 1003.9
  interjs. 300.24
saddleback 206.6
saddle blanket, saddle-
  cloth 227.12

saddle horse 413.18
saddler horse 413.18
  merchant 828.3
saddlery 830.5
saddling 154.1
Sadducee 1018.19
sadism 688.32
sadist 688.14
sadistic 688.48
sadness 870
sad sack
  weakling 159.6
  wretch 984.2
safari 272.5
safe
  nouns 834.12
  adjs. secure 696.4
  protected 697.20
  cautious 893.8
safe and sound 696.4
safeblowing, safe-
  breaking, safe-
  cracking 822.3
safe-conduct
  escort 73.5
  guard 697.13
  passport 775.7
safe-deposit box
  834.12
safeguard
  nouns protection
  697.3,13
  passport 775.7
  precaution 893.3
  verbs 697.17
safehold refuge 698.1
  stronghold 797.6
safekeeper
  protector 697.4
  preserver 699.4
safekeeping
  protection 697.1
  preservation 699.1
safely 696.8
safety security 696
  protection 697
safety belt, safety buoy
  699.5
safety first 893.1
safety glass 226.2
safety match 330.5
safety valve 697.3
safety zone 698.3
saffron 369.4
sag
  nouns hang 214.2
  droop 314.2
  market slump 831.5
  depreciation 847.4
  verbs hang 214.6
  bend 251.6
  drift 274.31
  droop 314.6
  depreciate 847.6
saga 506.6
sagaciate 7.6
sagacious 466.16
sagacity 466.4
sagaman 606.10
sagamore 747.9

sage
  nouns 467.1
  adjs. 466.17
sagging
  hanging 214.10
  drooping 314.11
sagittal, sagittate
  257.14
Sahara 165.2
sahib man 419.5
  title 915.3
Sahibah lady 420.5
  mistress 420.8
said aforesaid 64.5
  spoken 592.20
ALL SAID AND DONE
  720.10
IT IS SAID 556.16
sail
  nouns voyage 274.6
  ship 276.6
  ship's ~ 276.14
  types of ~ 276.30
IN FULL SAIL 268.24
IN SAIL 274.66
PUT ON SAIL
  speed 268.16
  set sail 274.22
UNDER PRESS OF SAIL
  swiftly 268.21
  sailing 274.67
UNDER SAIL
  moving 266.7
  sailing 274.67
  verbs move smoothly
  272.34
  navigate
  274.13,20,57
  float 352.9
  go easily 730.8
SAIL AWAY FROM
  274.38
SAIL INTO
  navigation 274.43
  set to work 714.15
  fight 794.15
  attack 796.15
SAIL THE HEAVENS
  281.15
SAIL TOO NEAR THE
  WIND
  risk 695.7
  be rash 892.5
SAIL UNDER FALSE
  COLORS 614.23
sailboat 276.6
sailer 276.6
sailing
  nouns gliding 272.8
  navigation 274.1,2
  adjs. 274.63
sailing master 275.7
sailing vessels 276.23
sailor voyager 273.1
  mariner 275.1
  navy 798.27
sailor's blessing 970.4
sailplane 279.12
saint
  nouns good person
  983.6

angel 1013.1
apostle 1020.2
pietist 1026.4
WITH THE SAINTS
  407.24
verbs sanctify 1024.5
  canonize 1035.12
St. Anthony's fire
  684.27
sainted 1024.8
St. Elmo's fire 334.13
sainthood 1026.2
sainting 1024.3
saintly, saintlike
  virtuous 978.7
  godly 1026.9
Saint Nicholas
  1012.20
saint's day
  anniversary 137.4
  holyday 1038.14
saintship 1026.2
Saint-Simonian
  743.12,20
St. Tib's Eve 106.2
St. Vitus's dance
  684.17
sake motive 646.1
  purpose 651.1
FOR THE SAKE OF
  because of 154.9
  for 651.12; 783.26
salaam
  nouns 962.2
  verbs 962.6
salaams 923.3
salability 827.7
salable 827.12
salacious
  concupiscent 418.20
  unchaste 987.29
  obscene 988.9
salacity
  lasciviousness 987.5
  obscenity 988.4
salad mixture 44.6
  food 306a.36
salad dressing 306a.37
salamander
  poker 328.15
  spirit 1012.13
salamandrian 413.43
salami 306a.21
salaried 839.22
salary
  nouns 839.4
  verbs 839.10
sale 827
FOR SALE 827.14
MAKE A SALE 827.8
PUT UP FOR SALE
  827.10
sales agent
  agent 779.3
  salesman 828.4
sales campaign 827.2
salesclerk 828.4
salesman 828.4
sales manager 828.4
salesmanship 827.2
sales resistance 827.6

salesroom 830.10
sales talk 827.5
salience
  protuberance 255.2
  obviousness 553.4
  importance 670.1
salient
  nouns 255.2
  adjs. protruding
  255.13
  obvious 553.11
  important 670.20
salient fact 1.3
salient point 670.6
salina 397.1
saline 432.9
salinity 432.4
saliva digester 307.7
  spittle 310.3
salivant, salivary 310.7
salivary glands 307.7
salivate 310.6
salivation 310.3
salivous 310.7
sallow
  verbs 369.3
  adjs. pale 362.9
  yellowish 369.4
sally
  nouns journey 272.5
  attack 796.1
  witticism 879.7
  verbs set forth 300.7
  issue 302.12
sally port outlet 302.9
  covert way 613.5
  escape 630.3
  fortification 797.4
salmagundi
  mixture 44.6
  stew 306a.11
salmi 306a.11
salmon
  nouns color 367.14
  fish 413.55
  adjs. 367.9
salon
  drawing room 191.5
  gallery 658.9
  reception 920.9
saloon
  drawing room 191.5
  room 191.10
  gallery 658.9
  barroom 994.25
salt
  nouns mariner 275.1
  saltiness 432.4
  preservative 699.3
  veteran 731.14
  money 833.2
  wit 879.1
BELOW THE SALT
  917.11
SALT OF THE EARTH
  the best 672.8
  commonalty 917.1
  worthy 983.3
  verbs season 427.7
  falsify 614.17
  preserve 699.8

scientific
  nouns 474.11
  adjs. technical 474.28
    exact 515.15
    realistic 534.6
scientist 474.11
scilicet, scil., sc.
    namely 80.18
    to wit 550.21
scintilla
    modicum 35.4
    spark 327.14
    sparkle 334.7
scintillant 334.35
scintillate
    sparkle 334.24
    be smart 466.11
    be eloquent 598.7
    be witty 879.13
scintillating
    sparkling 334.35
    witty 879.15
scintillation
    spark 327.14
    sparkle 334.7
    TV interference
      344.5
    witticism 879.7
scintillescent 334.35
sciolism 476.6
sciolist 475.7
sciolistic 476.16
scion member 55.4
    offspring 170.3
sciotheism 1018.5
scissile separable 49.25
    atomics 325.19
    brittle 359.4
scission 49.2
scissor 49.10
scissorbill 787.6
scissor-legs 272.16
scissors 811.3
scissure break 49.3
    cleft 200.2
sclerosis 684.8
sclerotomy 687.26
scobs remains 43.1
    filings 360.5
scoff
  nouns meal 306.5
    food 306a.2
    gibe 965.2
  verbs eat 306.18
    jeer 965.9
scoffer 1029.12
scoffing
  nouns 965.1
  adjs. 965.12
scofflaw 984.9
scold
  nouns shrew 949.12
    chider 967.9a
  verbs 967.17
scolding 967.5
sconce
  nouns head 210.5
    brain 465.4
    fortification 797.4
    fine 1007.3
  verbs 1007.5

scone 306a.30
scoop
  nouns ladle 192.7
    hollow 256.2
    news 556.3
  THE SCOOP
    the facts 1.4
    information 555.1
  verbs excavate 256.15
    ladle 270.16
  SCOOP THE MARKET
    831.23
scoot speed 268.10
    decamp 300.11
scop 607.13
scope degree 29.1
    opportunity 129.2
    compass 178.2
    size 194.1
    types of ~ 442.12–
      15
    ~ of vision 443.3
    freedom 760.3
scophony 344.1
scopic 442.9
scopophilia 688.32
scorbutic 684.46
scorch
  nouns run 268.4
    burn 328.6
  verbs speed 268.9
    be hot 327.21
    burn 328.23
    dry 392.6
    discolor 677.6
    criticize 967.21
scorched burnt 328.29
    dried 392.9
scorcher speeder 268.6
    hot day 327.7
scorching
  nouns 328.5
  adjs. violent 161.21
    hot 327.25
    caustic 937.21
score
  nouns sum 86.3
    twenty 99.7
    notch 261.1
    furrow 262.1
    musical ~ 461.28
    mark 566.4
    playbook 609.25
    motive 646.1
    success 722.4
    debt 838.1
    account 843.2,3
    price 844.1
  ON THE SCORE OF
    apropos 9.10
    because of 154.9
  PAY OFF OLD SCORES
    953.7
  THE SCORE 1.4
  verbs calculate 87.11
    list 88.7
    notch 261.4
    furrow 262.3
    ~ music 461.47
    mark 566.18
    succeed 722.8

gain 809.7
SCORE A BULL'S EYE
    515.8
scoreboard 568.9
scored notched 261.5
    furrowed 262.4
scorekeeper 569.1
scores 101.3
scoria residue 43.2
    slag 328.16
    volcanic rock 383.1
scorification 328.5
scorify 328.23
scorn
  nouns 964.1
  verbs reject 636.2
    defy 791.4
    be fastidious 894.8
    disdain 964.3
scorned 636.3
scornful 964.8
scorning 636.1
scorpion 414.8
Scot 417.9
scot fee 839.5
    charges 844.7
scotch
  nouns notch 261.1
    mark 566.4
    hindrance 728.7
  verbs notch 261.4
    mark 566.18
    wound 690.13
    thwart 728.15
scotched 261.5
Scotchman Scot 417.9
    niggard 850.5
scot-free free 760.19
    gratuitous 848.5
  GO SCOT FREE
    escape 630.7
    go free 761.9
Scotistic 499.11
Scotland Yard 697.15
scotograph 575.8
scotomy, scotoma
    530.4
Scotsman 417.9
Scotticism 578.9
scoundrel 984.3
scour
  nouns 268.4
  verbs polish 259.7
    speed 268.10
    rub 349.6
    search 484.27
    scrub 679.18
  SCOUR THE COUNTRY
    272.19
scourge
  nouns bane 674.1
    punishment 1008.1
    whip 1009.1
  verbs 1008.14
scourging 1008.4
scouring
    rubbing 349.1
    scrubbing 679.4
scourings remains 43.1
    refuse 667.4

scout
  nouns forerunner
      66.1
    aviator 278.3
    person 416.3
    man 419.5
    servant 748.9
    spy 779.9
  verbs reconnoiter
      484.37
    reject 636.2
    defy 791.4
    spurn 964.4
    ridicule 965.9
  SCOUT OUT
    hunt out 484.28
    spy out 484.37
scouted 636.3
scowl
  nouns sullen look
      949.9
    reproving look
      967.9
  verbs 949.15
scowling 949.24
scrabble
  nouns crawl 272.9
    scrawl 600.8
  verbs scramble
      272.25
    scribble 600.20
  SCRABBLE UP 313.11
scrag
  nouns neck 48.5
    thin person 204.8
    horse 413.17
  verbs 1008.20
scraggly 260.7
scraggy stunted 195.12
    thin 204.16
    rugged 260.7
scram
  nouns 629.4
  verbs leave 300.10
    flee 629.11
  interjs. 308.29
scramble
  nouns mixture 44.6
    jumble 62.3
    commotion 62.4
    crawl 272.9
    pursuit 653.1
    haste 707.1
    predicament 729.4
    contest 794.3
  verbs mix 44.11
    speed 268.10
    crawl 272.25
    hustle 705.12
    hasten 707.5
    contend 794.14
  SCRAMBLE FOR
    820.13
  SCRAMBLE UP 313.11
scramblebrained
    stupid 468.18
    scatterbrained
      530.16
scrambled 44.15
scrambled eggs
    306a.26

scranch
 nouns 457.3
 verbs chew 306.25
  grind 349.8
  pulverize 360.9
  sound harshly 457.9
scrap
 nouns small amount
  35.3
  piece 55.3
  child 125.3
  minute thing 195.7
  waste 667.5
  quarrel 793.5
  fight 794.3
 verbs discard 666.8
  quarrel 793.12
  fight 794.14
 adjs. 666.11
scrapbook 568.10
scrape
 nouns scraping 349.2
  harsh sound 457.3
  abrasion 690.7
  predicament 729.4
  obeisance 962.2
 verbs graze 199.10
  abrade 349.7
  touch 424.7
  sound harshly 457.9
  fiddle 461.42
  engrave 576.12
  injure 690.13
  economize 849.7
  make obeisance
   962.6
 SCRAPE ALONG
  eke out 657.11
  manage 722.11
 SCRAPE TOGETHER
  collect 74.17
  procure 809.9
scrap-heap 666.8
scraping
 nouns abrasion 349.2
  economizing 849.2
 adjs. 457.15
scrap iron 667.4
scrapper 798.1
scrapple 306a.12
scrappy
  fragmentary 55.6
  disconnected 72.4
  irregular 138.3
  pugnacious 795.26
  contentious 949.26
scraps remains 43.1
  waste 667.4
scrapworks 717.4
scrapy 457.15
scratch
 nouns nothing 2.2
  crisis 129.5
  shallowness 209.1
  furrow 262.1
  feed 306a.4
  scrape 349.2
  grating sound 457.3
  mark 566.4
  bad likeness 571.2
  engraving 576.1

scribble 600.8
  blemish 677.1
  injury 690.7
 verbs furrow 262.3
  scrape 349.7
  itch 425.5
  sound harshly 457.9
  mark 566.18
  misdraw 571.4
  draw 572.20
  engrave 576.12
  scribble 600.20
  injure 690.13
  work hard 714.13
 SCRATCH OUT
  excise 42.8
  cancel 691.16
 SCRATCH THE
  SURFACE 209.4
 adjs. 155.15
scratched
  furrowed 262.4
  scribbled 600.25
scratches 343.24
scratch hit
  accident 155.6
  stroke of luck 726.3
scratch pad 568.10
scratch test 687.19
scratchy itchy 425.10
  harsh-sounding
   457.15
  scribbly 600.25
scrawl
 nouns 600.8
 verbs 600.20
scrawny 204.16
screak
 nouns 457.4
 verbs screech 457.7
  squeal 459.2
screaky 457.13
scream
 nouns screech 457.4
  yell 458.1
  blunder 517.5
  success 722.3
  plaint 873.3
 verbs blow 402.24
  screech 457.7
  yell 458.6
  squeal 459.2
  say 592.17
  wail 873.11
screamer
  headline 483.2
  blunder 517.5
screaming
  vociferous 458.10
  humorous 878.5
  garish 902.20
screaming meemies
  472.10
screech
 nouns shrill 457.4
  yell 458.1
 verbs shrill 457.7
  yell 458.6
  squeal 459.2
  say 592.17

screeching, screechy
  457.13
screed
  small amount 35.3
  list 88.1
  lecture 597.3
  dissertation 604.1
  tirade 967.8
screen
 nouns sorter 60.4
  net 220.3
  cover 227.2
  porousness 264.8
  shade 337.1
  sifter 354.4
  the cinema 609.16
  stage ~ 609.24
  safeguard 697.3
 verbs sort 60.10
  segregate 77.6
  cover 227.21
  shade 337.5
  sift 354.6
  discriminate 491.6
  project 575.18
  conceal 613.7
  protect 697.17
  defend 797.8
screened
  covered 227.34
  shaded 337.7
  protected 697.20
screening
 nouns sorting 60.3
  netting 220.3
  covering 227.1
  sifting 354.3
 adjs. covering 227.37
  shading 337.6
  protecting 697.22
  defensive 797.11
screenwriter 609.26
screw
 nouns distortion
  248.1
  coil 253.2
  key 264.10
  propeller 284.7
  horse 413.16
  turnkey 759.10
  skinflint 850.5
  torture 1009.4
 A SCREW LOOSE
  insanity 472.2
  fault 676.2
 PUT THE SCREWS TO
  grill 484.23
  compel 754.6
 verbs fasten 47.8
  distort 248.5
  twist 253.4
  rotate 320.9
  force 754.6
  extort 822.19
  scrimp 850.7
 SCREW UP
  fasten 47.7
  strengthen 158.11
  tighten 355.9
  prepare 718.9

 SCREW UP ONE'S
  COURAGE 891.13
screwball
 nouns pitch 284.4
  lunatic 472.15
  eccentric 473.3
 adjs. insane 472.25
  eccentric 473.4
screwed 994.40
 SCREWED UP 62.15
screwy askew 218.14
  winding 253.6
  spiral 253.8
  foolish 469.8
  insane 472.25
  eccentric 473.4
scribblage 600.8
scribble
 nouns 600.8
 verbs 600.20
scribblemania 600.2
scribblement 600.8
scribbler 600.14,16
scribbling 600.8
scribbly 600.25
scribe
 nouns recorder 569.1
  writer 600.14,15
  churchman 1036.11
 verbs 600.19,23
scribes and Pharisees
  1027.3
scrimmage 794.3
scrimp
 nouns 850.6
 verbs economize
  849.7
  stint 850.7
 adjs. sparse 102.5
  scanty 660.9
 advs. 102.8
scrimping
 nouns economizing
  849.2
  parsimony 850.1
 adjs. economical
  849.9
  parsimonious 850.9
scrimption
  small amount 35.2
  few 102.2
  pittance 660.5
scrimpy sparse 102.5
  scanty 660.9
scrip document 568.4
  writing 600.11
  money 833.6,12
script document 568.4
  letter 579.2
  writing 600.1,4,5,11
  playbook 609.25
scription 600.1
scriptorial 600.24
scriptural
  written 600.24
  Biblical 1019.9
  orthodox 1022.8
Scripture 1019.2
scripture truth 515.2
  Bible 1019.1
scriptwriter 609.26

seam
nouns joint 47.4
   stratum 226.1
  verbs 566.18
sea-maid 1012.17
seaman mariner 275.1
   sea spirit 396.4
seamanship
   navigation 274.3
   skill 731.1
seamark 566.9
sea moss plant 410.4
   animal 414.6
seam squirrel 413a.6
seamstress
   sewer 222.2
   garmentmaker
    230.33–35
séance session 74.2
   spiritualistic ~
    1032.5
sea nymph 1012.17
seapiece 572.13
sea pig 413.33
Seapin 617.9
seaplane 279.8
seaport 698.6
sear
nouns 328.6
verbs shrivel 197.9
   burn 328.23
   cook 329.4
   dry 392.6
   deteriorate 690.19
   callous 854.6
adjs. withered 197.13
   dried 392.9
search
nouns 484.2
IN SEARCH OF
   searching 484.40
   after 653.12
verbs 484.25
SEARCH FOR 484.24
SEARCH INTO 484.30
SEARCH OUT 484.28
searcher 484.18
searching
nouns 484.2
adjs. 484.40
search mission 277.8
search warrant 750.6
seared burnt 328.29
   cooked 329.6
   dried 392.9
   callous 854.12
   hardened 979.21
searing
nouns shrinking
   197.3
   burning 328.5
adjs. 327.25
seascape view 445.6
   picture 572.13
seashore 384.2
seasick 684.42
  BE SEASICK 308.24
seasickness 684.22
seaside
nouns 384.2
adjs. 384.9

season
nouns period of time
   107.1
  ~ of year 128
OUT OF SEASON
   inapt 27.7
   outmoded 123.16
   seasonal 128.8
verbs imbue 44.12
   mature 126.9
   flavor 427.7
   qualify 506.3
   accustom 640.10
   preserve 699.8
seasonable
   appropriate 26.19
   timely 129.10
   expedient 668.4
seasonal
   of the seasons 128.8
   periodic 137.8
seasoned spiced 432.7
   qualified 506.10
   accustomed 640.16
   experienced 731.26
seasoning tinge 44.7
   maturation 126.6
   flavoring 427.3
   habituation 640.7
   preservation 699.2
seat
nouns capital 182.4
   station 183.3
   abode 190.1
   base 215.6
   chair 215.18
   types of ~ 215.31
   headquarters 225.6
   center 225.7
   rump 240.4
  ~ of thought 465.4
  ~ of authority
   737.9
  ~ of justice 999.8
verbs fix 142.10
   place 183.12
   establish 183.17
  ~ oneself 316.9
seated
   established 142.14
   situated 183.19
  BE SEATED 316.9
sea urchin 414.7
sea wall 215.4
seaward toward 289.28
   oceanward 396.10
seaway room 178.3
   waterway 274.10
seaweed 410.4
seaworthy
   fit for sea 276.18
   safe 696.7
sebaceous 379.9
sebkha 386.1
sec 113.3
secant
nouns 249.2
adjs. separating 49.24
   crossing 220.8
secede 631.6
seceder 626.5

secern 310.5
secernment 310.1
secession 631.2
secessioner,
   secessionist 626.5
seclude separate 77.6
   quarantine 759.14
  ~ oneself 922.8
secluded secret 612.15
   concealed 613.12
   retired 922.9
seclusion
   separation 77.3
   privacy 612.2
   retreat 698.5
   quarantine 759.2
   retirement 922
seclusive
   exclusive 77.8
   unsociable 921.6
second
nouns moment 107.2
   instant 113.3
   assistant 785.6,8
IN A SECOND 113.7
verbs 783.13
adjs. ~ to none 36.17
   inferior 37.6
   double 91.3
advs. 91.5
secondaries 224.18
secondary
nouns nonessential
   6.2
   inferior 37.3
   substitute 148.2
  ~ color 361.6
   deputy 779.1
adjs. unessential 6.4
   inferior 37.6
   double 91.3
   substitute 148.8
   contingent 150.11
   second-rate 678.10
second best 678.4
second-best 678.10
second childhood
   468.10
second-class 678.10
seconder 785.8
second fiddle 37.1,3
secondhand
   borrowed 22.9
   used 123.18
second helping 306.10
secondly 91.5
second nature 640.3
second person 584.6
second-rate 678.10
second-rater 678.5
seconds tobacco 433.2
   commodity 829.2
   bond 832.4
second self 20.5
second sight
   intuition 480.1
   clairvoyance 1032.8
second-stringer 37.3
second thought
   sequel 67.1
   afterthought 477.5

secpar 374.3
secrecy
   secretness 612.1
   concealment 613
   seclusion 922.1
secret
nouns key 566.8
   confidence 612.5
IN SECRET 612.19
IN THE SECRET
   474.16
adjs. mysterious
   547.14
   covert 612.12
   secretive 612.17
   hidden 613.12
   secluded 922.10
KEEP SECRET
   keep dark 612.8
   conceal 613.7
Secreta 1038.10
secreta 310.1
secret agent 779.9
secrétaire 215.16
secretarial 600.29
Secretariat 741.2
secretariat 998.4
secretary desk 215.16
   recorder 569.1
   scribe 600.14
   agent 779.3
Secretary of Agricul-
   ture, Secretary of
   Commerce, etc.
   740.8
secrete excrete 309.10
   secern 310.5
   keep secret 612.8
   conceal 613.8
secret ink 612.6
secretion
   excretion 309
   secernment 310
   concealment 613.1
secretional,
   secretionary 310.7
secretive
   secretional 310.7
   uncommunicative
   611.6,7
   secret 612.17
secretory
   excretory 309.17
   secretional 310.7
Secret Service 740.12
secret service 779.11
sect party 786.5,6
   religious ~ 1018.3
sectarial 61.7
sectarian
nouns nonconformist
   83.4
   dissenter 520a.3
   religious ~ 1018.16
adjs. classificational
   61.7
   dissentient 520a.6
   partisan 786.18
   denominational
   1018.24

sectarianism
 partisanism 786.13
 denominationalism
  1018.4
sectarism 1018.3,4
Sectary 1018.21
sectary
 nouns nonconformist
  83.4
 follower 292.2
 dissenter 520a.3
 partisan 785.8
 religious 1018.16
 types of Christian ~
  1018.34
 adjs. classificational
  61.7
 dissentient 520a.6
 partisan 786.18
 sectarian 1018.24
section
 nouns disjunction
  49.1
 part 55.1,2
 class 61.5
 region 179.1
 plot 179.4
 musical ~ 461.24
 book ~ 603.14
 surgical ~ 687.24
 military 798.19
 verbs 49.18
sectional partial 55.6
 regional 179.8
 partisan 786.18
sectionalism
 policy 742.4
 partisanism 786.13
sector part 55.1
 semicircle 252.8
secular
 nouns 1037.2
 adjs. centuried 99.29
 centennial 137.9
 profane 1025.3
 worldly 1029.16
 lay 1037.3
secularism
 theology 1021.1
 irreligion 1029.5
secularist
 nouns 1029.11
 adjs. 1037.3
secularization 781.1
secularize 781.2
secundines 67.3
securable 508.8
secure
 verbs fasten 47.7
 make fast 142.9
 close 265.6
 fetch 270.15
 elicit 304.12
 preserve 699.7
 bind 758.10
 guarantee 770.11
 defend 797.8
 acquire 809.7
 hold 811.6
 receive 817.6
 adjs. fast 47.14

stable 142.13
sure 512.17,20,21
safe 696.4
securement
 acquisition 809.1
 receival 817.1
securities 832
security
 stability 142.1
 sureness 512.4,5
 safety 696.1
 guaranty 770
 hope 886.1
 ON SECURITY 818.7
security risk
 subversive 617.11
 radical 743.11
sedate
 composed 856.14
 solemn 869.3
 dignified 903.12
sedative
 nouns mitigator
  162.3
 medicine 685.11
 types of ~ 685.48
 adjs. palliative 162.16
 calmative 685.39
sedentary 706.15
sedge 410.5
sedilia 1040.13
sediment dregs 43.2
 deposit 270.8
sedimental, sedi-
  mentary 43.7
sedition revolt 765.4
 treason 973.7
seditionary
 nouns 646.11
 adjs. 765.12
seditionist 646.11
seditious 765.12
seduce lure 648.4
 enamor 929.20
 debauch 987.20
seducement
 allurement 648.1
 debauchment 987.6
seducer tempter 648.3
 debaucher 987.12
seducing 648.7
seduction
 allurement 648.1
 debauchment 987.6
seductive
 desirable 632.31
 alluring 648.7
seductor, seductress
  648.3
sedulous
 persevering 623.7
 industrious 705.21
see
 nouns 1035.8
 verbs behold 438.12
 know 474.12
 contemplate 477.16
 detect 487.5
 meet a bet 514.19
 heed 528.6
 visualize 533.15

understand 546.8
visit 920.16
NOT SEE 440.7
NOT SEE AN INCH BE-
  YOND ONE'S NOSE
 be unintelligent
  468.12
 be prejudiced 525.6
 mismanage 732.14
NOT SEE FOR LOOKING
 be blind 440.7
 disregard 529.3
 not understand
  547.10
SEE AFTER
 seek 484.24
 care for 697.18
SEE DOUBLE
 be dim-sighted
  439.8
 be drunk 994.33
SEE EYE TO EYE 520.9
SEE FIT
 will 619.2
 be willing 620.3
 prefer 635.14
SEE HOW THE LAND
  LIES
 feel out 488.9
 foresee 540.6
 take precautions
  893.6
SEE IT THROUGH
 be thorough 56.8
 persevere 623.5
SEE ONE'S WAY 540.6
SEE ONE THROUGH
  783.11
SEE RED 950.17
SEE THE LIGHT
 quicken 406.7
 appear 445.8
 understand 546.8
 be published 557.16
SEE THE LIGHT OF
  DAY
 originate 68.12
 appear 445.8
SEE THROUGH
 detect 487.8
 understand 546.8
 persevere 623.5
SEE TO
 attend to 528.5
 look after 697.18
 overlook 745.10
SEE TO IT 512.11
 interjs. attention!
  528.22
 I told you so 537.14
SEE YOU LATER!
  300.25
seeable visible 443.6
 manifest 553.8
seed
 nouns rudiment
  152.7
 lineage 169.4
 posterity 170.1
 sperm 405.7
 plant ~ 410.29

GONE TO SEED
 old 123.14
 unpractical 732.18
GO TO SEED 664.5
 verbs 412.18
seeder 75.4
seeding 412.14
CLOUD SEEDING
 aviation 277.1
 rain making 393.5
seedling 410.3,10
seedtime
 ~ of life 124.1
 spring 128.2
seedy slovenly 62.14
 sickish 684.41
 shabby 690.31
 tired-looking 715.7
seeing
 nouns 438.1
 adjs. 438.22
SEEING AS HOW 154.8
Seeing Eye dog 413.24
seek search 484.24
 endeavor 712.4
 solicit 772.14
 ~ in law 1002.12
seeker searcher 484.18
 aspirant 632.12
 applicant 772.7
seek-sorrow 887.7
seem 445.10
SEEM LIKE
 resemble 20.7
 appear 445.10
SEEM LIKELY 510.3
seeming
 nouns appearance
  445.3
 illusion 518.2
 pretense 614.3
 IN SEEMING 498.17
 adjs. apparent 445.11
 illusory 518.9
 specious 614.28
seemly
 nouns 956.1
 adjs. elegant 587.7
 expedient 668.4
 tasteful 895.10
 proper 956.8
 decent 986.5
 advs. 895.11
seen 443.1
seep
 nouns 302.6
 verbs ooze 302.15
 be damp 391.11
SEEP IN
 filter in 301.11
 absorb 305.13
 learn 562.7
seepage oozing 302.6
 absorption 305.6
seer spectator 441.1
 visionary 533.13
 prophet 541.4
seesaw
 nouns oscillation
  322.4,8

plaything 876.15
verbs fluctuate 141.5
  alternate 322.12
  vacillate 625.8
adjs. 322.18
advs. 322.20
seethe
nouns 323.1
verbs be violent
  161.11
  move around 320.12
  be hot 327.21
  boil 328.19
  steep 391.13
  bubble 404.4
• ~ with excitement
  855.19
  be angry 950.15
segment
nouns 55.1
verbs 49.18
segmental, segmentary
  55.6
segno 462.12
segregate
verbs differentiate
  16.6
  separate 77.6
  distinguish 491.6
  select 635.11
  quarantine 759.14
adjs. unrelated 10.5
  segregated 51.4
segregation
  differentiation 16.4
  separation 77.3
  discrimination 491.3
  prejudice 525.4
  quarantine 759.2
seigneur
  master 747.1
  nobleman 916.4
seigneurial 808.10
seigneury
  See seigniory
seignior mister 419.7
  master 747.1
  nobleman 916.4
seignioral 808.10
seignioralty, seigniory,
  seigneury
  authority 737.6
  proprietorship 806.2
  nobility 916.10
seine
nouns 616.12
verbs 653.10
seisin See seizin
seismic 322.19
seismicity, seismism
  322.6
seismograph 322.7
seismography 322.6
seismology 322.6
seismometer 322.7
seismometry 322.6
seismoscope 322.7
seize understand 546.7
  usurp command
  737.13
  arrest 759.16

lay hold of 820.12
seized of 806.10
seized with 853.24
seizin, seisin 806.1
seizure spasm 323.6
  frenzy 472.8
  ~ of illness 684.5
  ~ of power 737.11
  arrest 759.6
  hold 811.2
  taking 820.2,8
  booty 822.11
selachian 413.46
selachians 414.11
Selachii 414.11
Selaginellaceae 411.6
seldom 136.4
NOT SELDOM 135.6
SELDOM SEEN
  sparse 102.5
  infrequent 136.2
select
nouns 672.8
verbs specify 80.9
  choose 635.11
  appoint 778.10
  draft 778.14
adjs. exclusive 77.8
  chosen 635.23
  choice 672.19
  exclusive 894.13
selected 635.23
selectee
  appointee 778.8
  recruit 798.17
selection
  specification 80.6
  excerpt 605.3
  choice 635.1
  appointment 778.2
selective
  exclusive 77.8
  discriminative 491.8
  choosing 635.20
  particular 894.9,13
Selective Service 778.6
selectivity 635.8
selectman 747.19
Selene 374.9
self ego 80.5
  psyche 1032.17
OTHER SELF 926.1
self-abasement 977.1
self-abasing 977.5
self-abnegation 977.1
self-absorption 976.1
self-accusation 871.3
self-acting
  automatic 348.25
  voluntary 620.7
self-action 348.1
self-adjusting 348.25
self-admiration 907.1
self-advancement
  976.1
self-annulling 482.10
self-applause 908.3
self-approbation 908.3
self-assertion 622.6
self-assuming 907.8
self-assumption 907.1

self-assurance
  self-confidence
  512.5
  poise 856.3
self-besot 976.5
self-called 581.15
self-centered
  egotistic 907.10
  selfish 976.5
self-christened 581.15
self-closing 348.25
self-command
  self-control 622.5
  equanimity 856.3
self-communion 477.6
self-complacence
  complacence 866.2
  vanity 907.1
self-conceit 907.4
self-condemnation
  871.3
self-confidence
  self-assurance 512.5
  poise 856.3
self-conquest 622.5
self-conscious 906.12
self-consequence
  903.1
self-consideration
  976.1
self-consistency 26.1
self-consultation 477.6
self-containment
  independence 760.4
  unsociability 921.1
self-content
nouns
  complacence 866.2
  vanity 907.1
adjs.
  complacent 866.10
  vain 907.8
self-contradiction 27.2
self-control
nouns
  automation 348.1
  self-command 622.5
  equanimity 856.3
  stoicism 859.1
  temperance 990.1
verbs 348.24
self-conviction
  conviction 500.3
  self-reproach 871.3
self-counsel 477.6
self-cremation 328.5
self-deceit, self-
  deception 518.1
self-defense 797.1
self-delusion 518.1
self-denial
  self-control 622.5
  unselfishness 977.1
  temperance 990.1
self-depreciation 906.2
self-destruction 408.5
self-determination
  voluntariness 620.2
  autonomy 739.4
  independence 760.4
self-detraction 906.2

self-devotion
  selfishness 976.1
  self-sacrifice 977.1
self-direct 348.24
self-direction
  automation 348.1
  self-control 622.5
  independence 760.4
self-discipline
  self-control 622.5
  temperance 990.1
self-doubt 502.2
self-educated 474.24
self-education 562.1
self-effacement 906.2
self-endearment 907.1
self-esteem pride 903.1
  vanity 907.1
self-evidence 553.3
self-existence 1.5
self-existent
  existent 1.14
  the ~ 478.4
self-explanatory 553.8
self-expression 622.6
self-fertilization 168.4
self-flattering 908.9
self-forgetful 977.5
self-glorification 908.3
self-govern 348.24
self-government
  automation 348.1
  self-control 622.5
  government 739.4
  independence 760.4
self-gratulation 908.3
self-help 783.6
self-humiliation 871.3
self-hypnosis 710.7
self-identity
  identity 14.1
  individuality 80.4
self-immolation
  burning 328.5
  self-sacrifice 977.1
  sacrifice 1030.7
self-importance 907.1
self-improvement
  783.6
self-induction 341.14
self-indulgence
  selfishness 976.1
  intemperance 991.1
self-instruction 562.1
self-interest
  egotism 907.3
  selfishness 976.1
selfish
  egotistical 907.10
  self-seeking 976.5
selfism 976.1
self-jealousy 976.1
self-knowledge 474.1
selfless 977.5
self-love 907.1
self-luminous 334.37
selfmade 166.27
self-made 474.24
self-mastery 622.5
self-moved 348.26
self-movement 348.1

senility, senile
dementia
feeble-mindedness
458.10
dementia 472.3
senior
nouns superior 36.4
elder 127.5
student 564.5
chief 747.3
adjs 126.18
seniority
superiority 36.1
eldership 126.3
señor mister 419.7
nobleman 916.4
señora 420.8
señorita 420.9
sensation sense 421
great success 722.3
emotion 853.3
thrill 855.2
wonder 918.2
sensational
eloquent 598.11
dramatic 609.37
superb 672.18
exciting 855.33
sensationalistic 499.10
sensationless
oratory 597.1
dramatics 609.2
emotionalism 853.8
sensatory 421.10
sense
nouns
sensation 421.1
~ of smell 434.4
~ of hearing 447.1
intelligence 466.1,6
reasonableness
481.10
meaning 543.1
~ cf humor 879.11
~ cf relief 884.4
IN A SENSE 498.16
verbs feel 421.7
~ intuitively 480.4
understand 546.7
senseless
inanimate 381.5
unconscious 422.7
unintelligent 468.13
foolish 469.8
insane 472.24
illogical 482.10
meaningless 545.9
sense organ 421.5
senses sensation 421.5
wits 465.2
sanity 471.1
COME TO ONE'S
SENSES 471.2
sensibilities 853.1
sensibility
physical ~ 421.2
awareness 474.2
discrimination 491.1
emotional ~ 853.4
sensible tangible 3.4
ponderable 351.19

physically ~ 421.12
intelligent 466.12,18
sane 471.4
cognizant 474.15
logical 481.21
practical 534.6
emotionally ~
853.19
appreciative 947.5
sensibleness
sensibility 421.2
judgment 466.6
reasonableness
481.10
practicalness 534.2
sensibly
intelligently 466.20
reasonably 481.23
sensing 480.5
sensitive pliant 356.9
sensory 421.10
sensible 421.13
discriminating 491.8
emotionally ~
853.19
touchy 949.20
sensitivity
sensibility 421.3
discrimination 491.1
emotional ~ 853.4
sensitize 421.8
sensorial 421.10
sensorium 465.4
sensory
nouns 465.4
adjs. 421.10
sensual sexual 418.17
carnal 985.5
lascivious 987.29
sensualism 985.1
sensualist 985.3
sensuality
sexuality 418.2
carnality 985
lasciviousness 987.5
sensualize 985.4
sensuist 985.3
sensuous
sensory 421.10
sensual 985.5
sentence
nouns verdict 493.5
saying 516.1
phrase 583.1
remark 592.4
condemnation
1006.1
verbs pass judgment
493.13
syllable 583.5
condemn 1006.3
sententious
epigrammatic 516.6
concise 590.4
grandiloquent 599.9
laconic 611.7
sentience, sentiency
421.2
sentient 421.12
sentiment idea 478.1
opinion 500.4

attitude 523.1
emotion 853.3,7
sentimental
emotional 853.21
loving 929.24
sentimentality
sentiment 853.7
affectionateness
929.3
sentimentalize 853.14
sentiments 853.1
sentinel, sentry
guard 697.9
lookout man 701.5
STAND SENTINEL
697.19
sepal 410.17
separability 49.1
separable 49.25
separate
verbs
differentiate 16.6
disjoin 49.8
part company 49.19
sort 60.10
disband 75.9
segregate 77.6
interspace 200.4
partition 236.9
open 264.11
diverge 298.5
sift 354.6
analyze 484.32
distinguish 491.6
select 635.11
quarantine 759.14
quarrel 793.11
alienate 793.15
divorce 933.5
adjs. unrelated 10.5
different 16.7
unjoined 49.20
alone 89.8
respective 814.14
secluded 922.9
separated
unrelated 10.5
unjoined 49.20
alone 89.8
distant 198.8
intervaled 200.6
secluded 922.9
alienated 927.12
separately apart 49.26
singly 89.13
separating 49.24
separation
differentiation 16.4
disjunction 49.1
disbandment 75.3
segregation 77.3
partition 236.5
divergence 298.1
sifting 354.3
discrimination 491.3
quarantine 759.2
alienation 793.4
seclusion 922.1
divorce 933.1
separation center
778.6

separatism 49.1
separatist
dissenter 520a.3
apostate 626.5
separative
differentiative 16.9
separating 49.24
disintegrative 53.5
exclusive 77.8
separator
separation 49.6
extractor 304.8
sepia 366.4
sepian 44.9
sepoy 798.8
seppuku 408.5
sepsis 684.23
sept class 61.2
lineage 169.4
septal 236.13
septenary 99.19
septennate 99.3
septennial 137.4
septet seven 99.3
music 461.17
septic diseased 684.45
putrefactive 690.37
septicemia, septicity
684.23
septic poisoning
684.23
septic tank 680.12
septillion 99.13
septimal 99.19
septuagenary, septua-
gesimal 99.28
Septuagint 1019.2
septulum, septum
236.5
septuor seven 99.3
music 461.17
septuple
sevenfold 99.19
~ time 462.23
sepulcher 409.16
sepulchral
funereal 409.25
deep-toned 453.10
sepulture
nouns 409.1
verbs 409.20
sequacious
succeeding 65.5
pliant 356.9
sequacity 356.2
sequel, sequelant 67
sequence
succession 65
series 71.2
posteriority 117.1
effect 153.1
IN SEQUENCE 59.10
sequent
nouns sequel 67.1
effect 153.1
adjs. succeeding 65.5
consecutive 71.10
subsequent 117.3
resultant 153.7
sequential
succeeding 65.5

consecutive 71.10
resultant 153.7
deducible 504.18
sequester 820.17
sequestered
secret 612.15
concealed 613.12
recluse 922.11
sequestrate 820.17
sequestration
confiscation 820.4
seclusion 922.1
sequitur 67.1
seraglio, serai 931.11
seraph
good person 983.6
angel 1013.1
seraphic
lovable 929.22
virtuous 978.7
angelic 1013.6
godly 1026.9
seraphim 1013.3
seraphine, seraphina
464.15
sere See sear
serenade
nouns music 461.13
celebration 875.2
courtship 930.6
verbs sing 461.39
celebrate 875.4
court 930.19
serenader 463.16
serenata 461.13
serene
luminous 334.31
peaceful 801.9
inexcitable 856.12
serenely 856.16
serenity
quiescence 267.1
peace 801.2
mental ∼ 856.2
serf 762.7
serfdom, serfhood
762.1
sergeancy 747.25
sergeant
police ∼ 697.14
officer 747.23
sergeant-at-arms
747.20
sergeant-at-law 1001.4
serial
nouns section 55.2
radio ∼ 343.21
publication
603.11,14
adjs.
consecutive 71.10
periodic 137.8
periodical 603.26
serial number 86.2
seriatim in order 59.10
consecutively 71.12
sericeous 356.15
series class 61.5
succession 71.2
set 74.11

mathematical ∼
86.7
round 137.3
IN A SERIES 71.12
IN SERIES 59.10
seriocomic(al) 878.6
serious great 34.8
thoughtful 477.20
earnest 622.11
zealous 633.10
important 670.21
solemn 869.3
seriously
decidedly 34.21
affirmation 521.9
earnestly 622.17
zealously 633.14
solemnly 869.4
seriousness
resoluteness 622.1
zeal 633.2
importance 670.3
earnestness 869.1
IN ALL SERIOUSNESS
affirmation 521.9
resolutely 622.17
frankly 972.23
sermon lesson 560.6
lecture 597.3
reproof 967.5
sermoner, sermonist
lecturer 597.5
preacher 1036.3
sermonet 597.3
sermonize
expound 560.16
lecture 597.10
serologist 686.7
seroon 74.7
serosa 228.3
serosity 387.1
serotherapy 687.19
serous 387.7
serpent coil 253.2
snake 413.31
horn 464.9
instrument 464.23
deceiver 617.1
scoundrel 984.6
THE SERPENT 1014.3
serpentiform,
serpentile
sinuous 253.7
snakelike 413.44
serpentine
verbs 253.4
adjs. sinuous 253.6,7
circuitous 319.7
snakelike 413.44
serrate
verbs 261.4
adjs. 261.5
serrated 261.5
serration 261.2
serried crowded 74.22
dense 353.12
serum fluid 387.3
blood ∼ 387.4
antitoxin 685.22
∼ therapy 687.19

servant
instrument 656.3
retainer 748
slave 762.7
assistant 785.6
∼ of God 1036.2
servantry 748.12
serve
nouns 284.4
verbs suit 26.8
copulate 168.10
conduce 173.3
propel 284.12
officiate 654.13
be instrumental
656.5
suffice 659.4
avail 663.17
benefit 672.11
act 703.4
work for 748.14
summons 750.12
help 783.18
bear arms 795.23
help to 816.12
SERVE AN APPREN-
TICESHIP 562.11
SERVE AS
pass for 570.8
act as 656.5
SERVE IN ONE'S
STEAD 779.13
SERVE NOTICE 555.7
SERVE ONE RIGHT
get one's deserts
958.6
be fair 974.6
punish 1008.10
SERVE TIME 759.18
service
nouns cordage 205.3
ship's ∼ 276.12
propulsion 284.4
serving 306.10,11
ceremony 644.4
job 654.5
use 663.4
governmental ∼
740.12
employment 748.13
aid 783.1
military ∼ 795.14
military arm 798.21
favor 936.7
divine ∼ 1030.8
rite 1038.3
AT ONE'S SERVICE
783.21
AT YOUR SERVICE
764.7
BE OF SERVICE TO
663.17
DO A SERVICE 783.19
DO SERVICE
serve 748.14
toady to 905.7
pay respects 934.12
worship 1030.10
IN SERVICE 663.24
IN THE SERVICE OF
783.26

OF SERVICE 663.18
verbs 692.14
serviceability
utility 663.3
helpfulness 783.10
serviceable
instrumental 656.6
useful 663.18
helpful 783.21
service call 795.13
serviceman
navy man 275.4
air ∼ 278.3
military man 798.6
service station 830.8
servile faithful 24.8
exact 515.15
literal 543.12
submissive 763.12
obsequious 905.12
servility
submissiveness 763.3
obsequiousness 905
serving
nouns ship's ∼
276.12
∼ of food 306.10
manner of ∼
306a.56
adjs. acting 703.11
ministering 748.15
helping 783.20
servitor
student 564.5
servant 748.1
servitorship 748.13
servitrix 748.8
servitude
service 748.13
slavery 762.1
servo 348.13
servo control
automation 348.3
mechanism 348.14
servo-control 348.23
servo engineering
348.2
servo instrumentation
instrumentation
347.7
automation 348.1
servolab
automation 348.5
laboratory 717.7
servomechanization
automation 348.13
types of ∼ 348.30
sesquicentennial
number 99.30
anniversary 137.4
sesquipedal
long 201.11
grandiloquent
599.11
sesquipedalian
nouns 599.3
adjs. long 201.11
grandiloquent
599.11
session assembly 74.2
council 753.5

SET TO WORK 714.15
SET UP
  inaugurate 68.10
  cause 152.11
  strengthen 158.11
  construct 166.12
  institute 166.13
  install 183.17
  erect 212.8
  raise up 315.5
  print 601.14
  prearrange 639.3
  plan 652.9
  remedy 692.13
  refresh 693.2
  propose 771.5
  help 783.11
  finance 834.15
  treat 839.19
  exalt 912.13
  anger 950.22
SET UP HOUSEKEEPING
  183.18
SET UP IN BUSINESS
  settle 183.18
  do business 654.12
  finance 834.15
SET UPON
  importune 772.12
  attack 796.15
  adjs. fast 47.14
  established 142.14
  fixed 142.15
  located 183.19
  sharpened 257.11
  solidified 355.13
  assured 512.20
  determined 622.12
  obstinate 624.8
  customary 640.14
  habituated 640.19
  formal 644.9
  ready 718.16
  prepared for 718.19
  trite 881.9
GET SET 718.13,26
SET AGAINST 927.11
SET APART
  destined 638.9
  consecrated 1024.8
SET AT REST
  ended 70.8
  accomplished 720.9
SET IN ONE'S WAYS
  obstinate 624.8
  habituated 640.19
SET ON
  determined upon
    622.16
  aspiring 632.29
SET UP
  victorious 724.8
  prosperous 726.12
  wealthy 835.13
  conceited 907.11
seta hair 229.2
  feather 229.16
  bristle 260.3
setaceous 260.9
setarious 260.10

setback
  retardation 269.4
  regression 294.1
  relapse 694.1
  defeat 725.2
  misfortune 727.3
  hindrance 728.1
setdown
  humiliation 904.2
  reproof 967.6
set form rule 84.4
  custom 640.4
set gun 616.11
setiform 260.10
setoff contrast 15.2
  compensation 33.2
  departure 300.2
  print 601.3
  discount 845.1
setose 260.9
setout beginning 68.1
  departure 300.2
set square 212.6
setter 413.27
setting
  nouns mounting
    215.10
  background 232.2
  congelation 353.4
  solidification 355.5
  planting 412.14
  adjs. 314.11
setting apart 1024.3
settle
  nouns 215.14
  verbs organize 60.9
  conform 82.3
  fix 142.10
  establish 183.17
  fix residence 183.18
  colonize 187.10
  sink 314.6
  alight 314.7
  gravitate 351.15
  kill 408.14
  decide 493.11
  prove 504.11
  refute 505.5
  assure 512.11
  resolve 622.7
  ruin 691.11
  defeat 725.6
  arrange 769.9
  reconcile 802.8
  mediate 803.7
  pay off 839.13
  punish 1008.11
SETTLE ACCOUNTS
  pay 839.13
  retaliate 953.7
  punish 1008.10
SETTLE DOWN
  be moderate 162.5
  fix residence 183.18
  land 277.49
  sink 314.6
SETTLE FOR 866.5
SETTLE INTO 145.12
SETTLE ON
  light on 314.10
  endow 816.17

SETTLE ONE'S HASH
  ruin 690.11
  defeat 725.6
  punish 1008.11
SETTLE THE SCORE
  retaliate 953.7
  punish 1008.11
SETTLE UPON
  attribute to 154.3
  decide upon 635.13
SETTLE WITH
  settle 769.9
  pay 839.12
  retaliate 953.7
  punish 1008.10
settled ended 70.8
  established 142.14
  fixed 142.15
  located 183.19
  proved 504.22
  assured 512.20
  resolute 622.12
  habitual 640.19
  defeated 725.14
  contracted 769.12
  paid 839.22
settled principle
  axiom 516.2
  precept 749.2
settlement
  sediment 43.2
  colony 180.1
  establishment 183.7
  colonization 187.2
  proof 504.4
  arrangement 769.4
  community 786.3
  conciliation 802.4
  estate 808.4
  endowment 816.9
  payment 839.1
settler end-all 70.4
  inhabitant 189.9
  clincher 505.3
settlings 43.2
settlor 816.11
set-to argument 481.5
  quarrel 793.5
  contest 794.3
setula, setule
  hair 229.2
  bristle 260.3
setup
  composition 58.1
  arrangement 59.1
  structure 244.1
  prearrangement
    639.1
  plan 652.1
  easy thing 730.3
set-up 639.5
seven, sevener 99.3
sevenfold 99.19
seven-league boots
  1034.7
seven-out 99.3
seven sacraments
  1038.5
Seven Sages 467.4
seven seas 396.1
seventh 99.19

seventh heaven
  bliss 863.2
  heaven 1016.5
seventieth 99.28
seventy 99.7
sever
  differentiate 16.6
  cut 49.10
  distinguish 491.6
severable
  separable 49.25
  apportionable
    814.13
several
  nouns 101.2
  adjs. different 16.7
  various 19.4
  special 80.12
  many 101.8
  respective 814.14
severalization 16.4
severalize
  differentiate 16.6
  distinguish 491.6
severally
  variously 19.6
  separately 49.26
  each 80.19
  singly 89.13
  respectively 814.15
several times 103.16
severance
  differentiation 16.4
  sunderance 49.2
severance pay 839.4
severe
  acrimonious 160.12
  violent 161.15
  cold 332.15
  painful 423.10
  pungent 432.6
  exact 515.15
  plain-speaking 589.3
  strict 755.6
  simple 900.9
  gruff 935.7
  harsh 937.22
severed 49.22
severely
  exceedingly 34.24
  violently 161.24
  strictly 755.8
  harshly 937.29
severity
  acrimony 160.4
  violence 161.1
  cold 332.1
  pungency 432.1
  exactness 515.3
  plain speech 589.1
  strictness 755.1
  simplicity 900.4
  gruffness 935.3
  harshness 937.9
sew fasten 47.8
  stitch 222.4
SEW UP
  sew 222.4
  prearrange 639.3
  mend 692.14

sharp practice 616.4
sharp-set 632.26
sharpshooter
  shooter 284.9
  gambler 514.16
  soldier 798.11
sharp-sighted 438.23
sharp-witted 466.14
shastra 1019.7
shatter fragment 49.12
  madden 472.22
  confuse 530.7
  ~ one's hopes
   887.11
shatterable 359.4
shatterbrain 470.7
shatterbrained
  insane 472.24
  scatterbrained
   530.16
shattered
  severed 49.23
  flustered 530.12
shattery fragile 159.14
  brittle 359.4
shave cut off 42.10
  smooth 259.5
  swindle 616.18
  cut prices 847.6
shaven 231.17
shaver 125.3
shavetail 747.22
shaving piece 55.3
  thinness 204.7
  flake 226.3
shavings
  remains 43.1
  refuse 667.4
shaw 410.12
Shawondasee 402.3
shay 271.4
she
  nouns self 80.5
  female 420.4
  adjs. 420.14
sheaf 74.7
shear cut off 42.10
  divest 231.5
  fleece 820.21
sheath 227.18
sheathe wrap 227.22
  cover 227.25
  clothe 230.38
  ~ the sword 802.11
sheathed 227.34
sheathing
  nouns covering
   227.1,18
  board 377.3
  adjs. 227.37
shebang, the 54.4
she-bear 420.10
shebeen 994.26
shed
  nouns hut 190.9
  hangar 277.21
  verbs slough 231.10
  radiate 298.6
  ~ tears 873.10
SHED BLOOD
  bleed 309.15

kill 408.15
SHED LIGHT UPON
  illuminate 334.28
  explain 550.11
shedu 1014.7
shee 1012.14
sheen 334.2
sheeny 334.33
sheep animal 413.9
  breeds of ~ 413.60
  laity 1037.1
sheepherding 415.1
sheepherder 415.3
sheep in wolf's
  clothing 889.7
sheepish
  sheeplike 413.41
  shamefaced 906.13
sheepman 415.2,3
sheep rot 684.10
sheep's eyes
  wistfulness 632.4
  flirtation 930.8
sheepskin 568.5
sheer
  nouns obliquity 218.3
  deviation 290.1
  verbs oblique 218.9
  sail 274.32
  deviate 290.3
SHEER OFF
  recoil 283.7
  dodge 629.8
  adjs. mere 35.9
  unmixed 45.6
  utter 56.11
  perpendicular
   212.11
  steep 218.18
  diaphanous 338.4
  advs. quite 56.16
  perpendicularly
   212.13
sheerness 338.1
sheet leaf 226.2
  white 363.2
  paper 377.6
  poster 557.7
  newspaper 603.12
sheeting
  bed linen 227.11
  boarding 377.3
sheet metal 382.5
sheet music 461.28
sheets 227.11
sheetwork 601.2
she-goat goat 413.10
  female animal
   420.10
sheik, sheikh
  chief 747.9
  prince 916.8
  priest 1036.12
sheitan See shaitan
shekel 833.9
shekels 833.2
shelf shoal 209.2
  ledge 215.14
  stratum 226.1
PUT ON THE SHELF
  postpone 132.8

put aside 666.6
shelfworn 690.30
she-lion 420.10
shell
  nouns covering
   227.15,16,17
  types of ~ 227.45
  atomic ~ 325.6
  coffin 409.11
  pod 410.28
  ear 447.7
  cartridge 799.11
  missile 799.14
  verbs husk 231.9
  bombard 796.23
SHELL OUT
  give 816.12
  pay out 839.14
  expend 841.5
shellac
  nouns 994.15
  verbs paint 361.14
  defeat 725.8
shellacked 994.40
shellacking
  painting 361.11
  utter defeat 725.3
shellback
  sailor 275.3
  veteran 731.14
shellfire 796.9
shellfish food 306a.25
  animal 414.8
shell game 616.9
shellproof 158.18
shell-shaped 251.21
shellshock
  illness 684.18
  neurosis 688.17
shelter
  nouns quarters 190.2
  cover 227.2
  shade 337.1
  protection 697.1
  refuge 698.3
IN SHELTER
  verbs house 187.11
  shade 337.5
  protect 697.17
sheltered
  shaded 337.7
  protected 697.20
sheltering
  shading 337.6
  protecting 697.22
shelty 413.13
shelve
  nouns 215.14
  verbs postpone 132.8
  slope 218.10
  put aside 666.6
shelving 218.15
shenanigan 879.10
shenanigans 879.5
Sheol 1017.1
shepherd
  nouns escort 73.5
  herder 415.3
  guide 746.6
  clergyman 1036.2
  verbs escort 73.8

herd 415.7
take care of 697.18
direct 745.8
sherbet 306a.46
sherif chief 747.9
  prince 916.8
sheriff 697.14
sheriffdom 697.16
sheriffry, sheriffwick
  constableship
   697.16
  bureau 998.4
Sherlock Holmes
  779.10
Shetland 413.13
shew evidence 504.9
  manifest 553.5
she-wolf
  violent person
   161.9
  vixen 941.8
  shrew 949.12
Shiah 1018.21
shibboleth 580.8
shield
  nouns cover 227.2
  shell 227.16
  shade 337.1
  insignia 567.2
  protection 697.3
  verbs cover 227.21
  shade 337.5
  protect 697.17
  defend 797.8
shielded
  covered 227.34
  shaded 337.7
  protected 697.20
shielding
  nouns 227.1,37
  adjs. covering 227.37
  shading 337.6
  protecting 697.22
  defensive 797.11
shieldlike, shield-
  shaped 251.22
shift
  nouns spell 108.3
  change 139.1
  conversion 145.1
  waist 230.15
  removal 270.2
  deviation 290.1
  picture ~ 344.5
  quibble 482.4
  trick 616.6
  subterfuge 629.1
  pretext 647.1
  expedient 668.2
  artifice 733.3
  verbs change 139.5
  fluctuate 141.5
  be converted 145.12
  move 266.4
  remove 270.10
  tack 274.32
  deviate 290.3
  quibble 482.9
  vacillate 625.8
SHIFT FOR ONESELF
  760.18

SHIFT THE BLAME
960.8
shiftiness stealth 612.4
deceit 616.3
craftiness 733.1
shifting
nouns changeableness
141.3
deviation 290.1
quibbling 482.5
vacillation 625.2
adjs. changeable
141.7
wandering 272.36
deviative 290.7
vacillating 625.10
shiftless
indolent 706.17
improvident 719.15
shiftlessness
indolence 706.4
improvidence 719.2
shifty
furtive 612.14,17
deceitful 616.22
evasive 629.14
makeshift 668.6
crafty 733.12
treacherous 973.20
Shiite 1018.21
shikar 653.2,9
shikari, shikaree 653.5
shilling 833.8
shilly-shally
nouns vacillation
625.2
shilly-shallyer 625.5
verbs 625.8
adjs. 625.10
advs. 625.12
shimmer
nouns 334.7
verbs 334.24
shimmering
nouns 334.7
adjs. 334.35
shimmery 334.35
shimmy 877.5
shin
nouns 272.16
verbs 313.11
shindig dance 877.2
party 920.10
shindy
commotion 62.4
row 793.6
festivity 876.6
dance 877.2
party 920.10
shine
nouns commotion
62.4
polish 259.2
light 334.2,10
prank 879.10
splurge 902.4
fancy 929.1
bootleg 994.21
TAKE THE SHINE OUT
OF
excel 36.7

humiliate 904.4
verbs polish 259.7
give light 334.23
be smart 466.11
be eloquent 598.7
furbish 689.11
be beautiful 898.15
be illustrious 912.10
SHINE IN, SHINE AT
731.16
SHINE UPON
illuminate 334.28
abet 783.14
SHINE UP TO
curry favor 905.8
make friends 925.11
shined 334.33
shiner black eye 690.8
coin 833.4
shingle
nouns hairdo 229.15
grain 360.6
wood 377.3
stone 383.3
verbs cover 227.25
overlap 227.33
coiffure 229.22
spank 1008.15
shingled 227.38
shingles 684.27
shingling 1008.5
shingly 383.8
shininess 334.2
shining
luminous 334.30
shiny 334.33
gorgeous 898.19
illustrious 912.20
shining example
example 25.4
paragon 983.4
Shinjuku 987.9
shinplaster 833.6
Shintoist 1018.30
shiny luminous 334.30
shining 334.33
ship
nouns watercraft
276.3
aircraft 279.1,11
GO BY SHIP 274.13
SHIP OF THE DESERT
beast of burden
270.6
camel 413.5
SHIP OF THE LINE,
SHIP OF WAR 276.7
verbs load 183.16
transport 270.12
freight 270.14
SHIP OARS
row 274.56
navigation 274.79
shipboard 276.3
shipload 193.2
shipman 275.1
shipmaster 275.7
shipmate 926.4
shipment
transportation 270.3
freight 270.7

ship parts 276.26
shipping
transportation 270.3
ships 276.1
shippon 190.16
ships marine 276.1
types of ~ 276.22
navy 798.27
shipshape trim 59.8
navigation 276.20
shipwreck
nouns ruin 691.4
accident 727.2
verbs navigation
274.44
destroy 691.10
shipwrecked 729.25
shipyard
anchorage 698.6
repair shop 717.6
shire 179.5
shirk
nouns 629.3
verbs 629.9
SHIRK OFF 629.12
SHIRK OUT OF
shirk 629.9
not pay 840.6
shirker 629.3
shirking
nouns 629.2
adjs. 629.14
shirr wrinkle 263.6
cook 329.4
shirred 329.6
shirred eggs 306a.26
shirring 329.1
shirt
nouns waist 230.15
types of ~ 230.54
hair ~ 1010.3
verbs 230.39
shirtwaist 230.15
shish kabab 306a.12
Shiva See Siva
shivaree
nouns noise 452.3
serenade 875.2
verbs 875.4
shive
small amount 35.3
flake 226.3
shiver
nouns small amount
35.3
piece 55.3
shake 323.3
trepidation 855.4
verbs shatter 49.12
shake 323.11
be cold 332.10
be excited 855.18
be afraid 889.13
shivereen
nouns small amount
35.3
piece 55.3
verbs 49.12
shivering
nouns agitation 323.2

chilliness 332.2
adjs. shaking 323.18
cold 332.16
nervous 857.12
shivers shivering 323.2
chilliness 332.2
creeps 425.4
restlessness 855.4
nervousness 857.2
trepidation 889.4
shivery shaky 323.18
cold 332.16
crumbly 360.13
nervous 857.12
brittle 359.4
fearful 889.22
shizoku 916.3
shoal
nouns flock 74.5
multitude 101.3
shallow 209.2
verbs 209.3
adjs. 209.5
shoaliness, shoalness
209.1
shoals 695.5
shoaly 209.6
shoat 413.11
shock
nouns bunch 74.6
concussion 161.8
hair 229.4
collision 282.3
electric ~ 341.6
start 538.3
trauma 684.18
stroke 684.19
calamity 727.2
distress 864.5
verbs electrify 341.23
startle 538.8
offend 864.13
frighten 889.16
shock absorber 162.3
shocked
startled 538.13
appalled 864.23
shocker
surpriser 538.2
story 606.7
shocking
startling 538.11
terrible 673.9
appalling 862.10
frightful 889.29
disgraceful 913.11
shock reaction 688.20
shock treatment
therapy 687.18
psychotherapy 688.7
shock troops 798.22
shod 230.44
shoddiness
slovenry 62.6
baseness 913.3
shoddy
nouns sham 614.13
refuse 667.4
adjs. dowdy 62.14
cloth 377.9
false 614.27

paltry 671.18
shabby 690.31
base 913.12
shoe 230.39
shoed 230.44
shoemaker 230.37
shoemaking 230.31
shoes footwear 230.27
types of ~ 230.60
IN ONE'S SHOES
148.12
shogun 747.9
shoot
nouns descendant
170.4
weft 221.4
rocket fire 280.10
ore ~ 382.6
rapid 394.10
channel 395.3
branch 410.18
shooting pain 423.2
verbs discharge
161.13
grow 196.7
speed 268.10
~ ballast 274.51
row 274.56
sail 274.57
launch rocket
280.13
~ into space 281.15
fire 284.13
kill 408.18
sprout 410.32
hurt 423.8
~ craps 514.17
photograph 575.16
vaccinate 687.37
execute 1008.19
SHOOT AHEAD OF
distance 36.9
pass 311.8
SHOOT AT 796.23
SHOOT FULL OF
HOLES 505.4
SHOOT OFF ONE'S
MOUTH 594.6
SHOOT ONE'S BOLT
852.7
SHOOT OUT 255.9
SHOOT STRAIGHT
be honest 972.10
be fair 974.6
SHOOT THE BREEZE
talk 592.12
converse 595.8
SHOOT THE WORKS
do one best 712.11
do thoroughly 720.7
SHOOT UP
increase 38.6
grow 196.7
stick up 255.9
ascend 313.9
vegetate 410.31
shooter gunner 284.9
Nimrod 653.5
artilleryman 798.11
gun 799.5

shooting
nouns firing 284.3
killing 408.1
pain 423.2
hunting 653.2
gunfire 796.9
execution 1008.7
adjs. 423.10
shooting iron 799.5
shooting match, the
54.4
shooting star
meteor 374.15
omen 542.4
shop
nouns workshop
717.1,8
store 830.1
KEEP SHOP 654.12
verbs ~ for 484.24
market 826.8
shopboard 830.11
shopkeeper 828.2
shoplifter 823.1
shoplifting 822.1
shopman 828.2
shopmate 785.5
shopper 826.5
shopping 826.1
shopping center
city district 182.5
center 225.8
shopping spree 826.1
shopworn 690.30
shore
nouns 384.2
verbs 215.22
shore bird 413.34
shore leave 709.3
shoreless 104.3
shoreline 384.2
shore patrol 697.15
shoreward
adjs. 384.9
advs. 384.11
short
nouns shortage 57.2
~ circuit 341.4
want 660.4
bear 831.12
IN SHORT 590.6
verbs 341.23
adjs. inconsiderable
35.7
deficient 57.4
transient 111.8
little 195.9
brief 202.8
low 207.6
short of 312.5
brittle 359.5
friable 360.13
phonetics 449.18
concise 590.4
lacking 660.11
curt 935.7
AT SHORT NOTICE
briefly 111.10
extemporaneously
628.15

IN SHORT ORDER
268.23
RUN SHORT
fall short 312.2
want 660.6
SHORT OF
under 37.9
minus 42.14
deficient 57.4
inadequate 312.5
lacking 660.11
imperfect 676.4
~ breath 715.10
~ money 836.7
advs. 202.13
shortage
deficiency 57.2
shortcoming 312.1
want 660.4
shortbread, shortcake
306a.41
short-breathed 715.10
short-change 616.18
short-changer 617.4
short circuit 341.4
short-circuit 341.23
shortcoming
inequality 31.1
deficiency 57.1
falling short 312
want 660.4
imperfection 676.1
fault 676.2
short commons 306a.6
short-commons
short allowance
660.5
fast 993.2
short cut 202.5
short-cut
verbs 202.7
adjs. 202.9
short distance 199.2
shorten reduce 39.7
abbreviate 202.6
shortened 202.9
shortening
reduction 39.1
abbreviation 202.3
shorter 39.10
shortest 37.8
shortfall 312.1
shorthand
nouns 600.9
verbs 600.19
adjs. 600.28
shorthanded 660.10
shorthander 600.17
shorthorn
newcomer 78.4
native 189.3
short-legged 202.11
short-lived 111.7
short-livedness 111.1
short memory 536.1
shortness
briefness 111.2
littleness 195
briefness 202
lowness 207.1
conciseness 590.1

~ of breath 715.3
curtness 935.3
short ribs 306a.13
shorts bears 831.12
securities 832.1
short shrift
pause 144.3
little mercy 943.1
GIVE SHORT SHRIFT TO
755.5
short sight 439.3
shortsighted
myopic 439.11
undiscerning 468.14
narrow-minded
525.10
shortsightedness
myopia 439.3
unperceptiveness
468.2
narrow-mindedness
525.1
shortstop 876.20
shortstop bath 575.15
short story 606.8
short supply 660.1
IN SHORT SUPPLY
deficient 57.4
scarce 660.9
short temper 949.3
short-tempered 949.25
short-term, short-
termed 111.8
short time 111.3
IN A SHORT TIME
briefly 111.10
soon 131.16
short wave 343.14
short-wave
verbs 343.28
adjs. 343.31
short-winded 715.10
short-windedness
715.3
short-winged 202.11
short-witted 468.13
shot
nouns speed 268.7
rocket fire 280.10
discharge 284.5
shooter 284.9
detonation 455.3
guess 498.3
gamble 514.3,9
photograph
575.3,10
vaccination 687.20
attempt 712.2
gunfire 796.9
bullet 799.14
fee 839.5
charges 844.7
parting ~ 965.2
dram 994.6
A SHOT IN THE
LOCKER
reserves 658.3
last resort 668.2
HAVE A SHOT AT
155.13

LIKE A SHOT
  instantly 113.7
  swiftly 268.22
SHOT IN THE DARK
  wild guess 498.3
  gamble 514.2
TAKE A SHOT AT
  796.23
adjs. variegated 373.9
  unnerved 857.14
SHOT THROUGH 373.9
SHOT TO PIECES
  857.14
shote See shoat
shot-free 848.5
shot-put 284.4
shot-putter 284.8
should must 637.10
  ought to 960.3
shoulder
  nouns support 215.2
  buttress 215.4
  shelf 215.14
  meat cut 306a.17
GIVE THE SHOULDER
  964.5
ON THE SHOULDERS
  OF 206.27
PUT ONE'S SHOULDER
  TO THE WHEEL
  be determined 622.8
  undertake 713.3
  set to work 714.15
SHOULDER TO
  SHOULDER
  with 73.10
  concurrently 176.5
  side by side 241.12
  co-operatively 784.9
  verbs support 215.22
  carry 270.11
  thrust 282.12
  ∼ one's way 293.4
  ∼ arms 718.13
shoulders 255.2
shout
  nouns yell 458.1
  treat 839.8
  cheer 874.2
  laughter 874.4
  verbs yell 458.6
  ∼ out 458.8
  treat 839.19
  cheer 874.7
  laugh 874.9
SHOUT FROM THE
  HOUSETOPS 557.13
shouting 458.10
shove
  nouns company 74.3
  crowd 74.4
  shive 226.3
  push 282.2
  propulsion 284.1
  verbs push 282.12
  propel 284.10
  ∼ aside 290.6
  ∼ away 636.2
  sell illicitly 824.7
SHOVE OFF
  sail 274.20,38

set forth 300.7
  die 407.16
SHOVE ON
  go 272.17
  depart 300.6
shovel
  nouns 347.12
  verbs 270.16
shoving
  nouns 284.1
  adjs. 284.15
show
  nouns opportunity
    129.2
  chance 155.8
  appearance 445.3,7
  possibility 508.1
  illusion 518.2
  manifestation
    553.2
  indication 566.1
  theatrical ∼ 609.13
  false ∼ 614.3
  ∼ of hands 635.5
  formality 644.1
  pretext 647.1
  affectation 901.1
  ostentation 902.4
FOR SHOW 901.20
GET THE SHOW ON
  THE ROAD 68.6
MAKE A SHOW OF
  pretend 614.22
  affect 901.12
  verbs direct 289.7
  be seen 443.4
  appear 445.8
  evidence 504.9
  prove 504.11
  explain 550.11
  manifest 553.5
  disclose 554.4
  teach 560.10
  indicate 566.16
  screen 575.18
SHOW FIGHT 791.3
SHOW FORTH
  manifest 553.5
  publish 557.11
SHOW OFF 902.16
SHOW ONE HIS PLACE
  964.5
SHOW ONE'S COLORS
  navigation 274.55
  manifest oneself
    553.6
  signal 566.21
SHOW ONE'S FACE
  185.8
SHOW ONE'S TEETH
  snarl 459.4
  be defiant 791.3
  be angry 950.14
SHOW SIGNS OF LIFE
  revive 406.7
  recover 692.20
SHOW THE DOOR
  308.17
SHOW THROUGH
  338.3

SHOW UP
  excel 36.7
  occur 150.6
  attend 185.8
  arrive 299.6
  be seen 443.4
  appear 445.8
  be found 487.9
  disprove 505.4
  expose 554.4
showboat 609.17
show business 609.1
showcase 830.11
showdown 554.1
shower
  nouns throng 74.4
  sprinkle 391.5
  sprinkler 391.8
  rain 393.1
  bath 679.7
  donation party
    920.10
  verbs rain 393.9
  abound 659.5
SHOWER DOWN UPON
  give 816.15
  be generous 851.3
showery 393.10
showiness
  grandiloquence
    599.1
  ostentation 902.3
showing
  nouns display 553.2
  indication 566.1
  adjs. 554.11
showing-off 902.4
showman 609.27
showmanship 609.3
shown
  proved 504.22
  ∼ up 505.7
  manifested 553.12
show-off 902.11
showroom 830.10
showup
  arrival 299.1
  appearance 445.1
  exposure 554.1
showy
  grandiloquent 599.9
  ostentatious 902.19
shrapnel 799.14
shred
  nouns small amount
    35.3
  piece 55.3
  strip 205.4
TO SHREDS 49.27
  verbs 205.6
shredding 343.24
shrew 949.12
shrewd
  smart 466.15
  crafty 733.12
shrewdness
  smartness 466.3
  craftiness 733.1
shrewish 949.21
shrewishness 949.5

shriek
  nouns screech 457.4
  yell 458.1
  laughter 874.4
  verbs screech 457.7
  yell 458.6
  say 592.17
  laugh 874.9
shrieking, shrieky
  457.13
shrievalty
  constableship
    697.16
  bureau 998.4
shrieve 697.14
shrift 554.3
shriftless
  graceless 979.22
  unregenerate
    1029.18
shriftlessness 1029.4
shrill
  nouns 457.4
  verbs 457.7
  adjs. 457.13
shrillness 457.1
shrimp
  nouns diminutive
    195.4
  dwarf 195.6
  food 306a.25
  crustacean 414.8
  verbs 653.10
shrine
  nouns coffin 409.11
  tomb 409.16
  monument 568.11
  holy place 1040.4
  verbs 235.5
shrink
  shrivel 197.9
  recoil 283.7
  wince 423.8
  fight shy 621.4
  ∼ from 865.6
  flinch 889.12
shrinkage
  decrement 39.3
  shrinking 197.3
  loss 810.2
shrinking
  nouns
  shriveling 197.3
  unwillingness 621.2
  adjs. reticent 611.8
  unwilling 621.7
  fearful 889.22
  modest 906.11
shrinking violet 906.6
shrive
  absolve 1005.4
  ∼ oneself 1010.6
  hear confession
    1038.20
shrivel age 126.10
  shrink 197.9
  dry 392.6
  deteriorate 690.19
shriveled
  shrunk 197.13
  thin 204.19

dried 392.9
wasted 690.34
shriveling
nouns 197.3
adjs. 690.43
shroud
nouns cover 227.2
rigging 276.31
graveclothes 409.14
verbs wrap 227.22
clothe 230.38
conceal 613.7
protect 697.17
shrouded
covered 227.34
protected 697.20
shrouding
nouns 227.1
adjs. 227.37
shrub
bush 410.9
types of ~ 410.50
shrubbery
shrubs 410.9
nursery 412.11
shrubby 410.37,38
shrubland 410.11
shrubwood 410.14
shrug
nouns 566.13
verbs 566.20
SHRUG OFF
depreciate 497.2
ignore 529.4
SHRUG THE
SHOULDERS
negate 522.3
gesture 566.20
show dislike 865.6
disapprove of
967.10
shrunk, shrunken
197.13
shuck 227.17
shucks 671.5
shudder 332.10
SHUDDER AT
show dislike 865.6
loathe 928.4
shuddering 865.2
shuffle
nouns slow motion
269.2
gait 272.14
quibble 482.4
trick 616.6
subterfuge 629.1
artifice 733.3
verbs mix 44.11
mix up 63.3
fluctuate 141.5
walk 272.27
quibble 482.9
vacillate 625.8
dance 877.5
SHUFFLE ALONG
go slow 269.6
walk 272.26
SHUFFLE OFF 629.7
SHUFFLE THE CARDS
139.6

shuffler
quibbler 482.7
cheat 617.3
vacillator 625.5
shuffling
nouns changeableness
141.3
quibbling 482.5
chicanery 616.4
vacillation 625.2
adjs.
changeable 141.7
quibbling 482.15
vacillating 625.10
shun avoid 629.6
snub 964.7
abstain 990.7
shunning 629.1
shunt
nouns 284.1
verbs move 270.10
push 284.10
turn aside 290.6
put aside 666.6
shush
nouns 450.1
verbs hush 450.7,8;
450.16
keep secret 612.9
shut
nouns 77.2
verbs stop 144.12
close 265.6
SHUT DOWN, SHUT UP
SHOP
stop 144.8
close 265.8
SHUT DOWN ON,
SHUT DOWN UPON
silence 450.8
suppress 758.8
SHUT OFF
turn off 144.12
obstruct 728.12
SHUT ONE'S EYES TO
be incredulous
503.3
be open-minded
524.7
disregard 529.3
suffer 775.11
condone 945.4
SHUT OUT
exclude 77.4
defeat 725.8
obstruct 728.12
prohibit 776.3
lock out 787.10
SHUT UP
pen in 235.5
close 265.6,8
be silent 450.5
refute 505.5
confine 759.12
adjs. closed 265.9
~ of 760.28
shutdown
cessation 144.1
closure 265.1
shut-eye 710.2

shut-in
nouns
sick person 684.31
recluse 922.5
adjs. enclosed 235.10
confined 759.19
shutout
utter defeat 725.3
lockout 787.8
shutter shut 265.8
curtain 337.5
shutting 265.1
shuttle
nouns train 271.12
aviation 277.7
oscillator 322.8
verbs
alternate 322.12
vacillate 625.8
shuttlecock
nouns 625.5
verbs 322.12
shuttlewise 322.20
shuttle-witted 530.16
shy
nouns recoil 283.3
throw 284.4
dodge 629.1
attempt 712.2
verbs recoil 283.7
throw 284.12
quibble 482.9
be startled 538.5
fight ~ 621.4
dodge 629.8
take fright 889.11
adjs.
deficient 57.4
evasive 629.14
lacking 660.11
fearful 889.22
bashful 906.12
SHY OF
demurring 621.7
lacking 660.11
disliking 865.8
chary 893.9
Shylock 818.3
shyness
timidity 889.2
bashfulness 906.4
shyster rogue 984.3
lawyer 1001.3
sí 520.18
Siamese twins 90.4
sib
nouns 11.2
adjs. 11.7
Siberia 332.5
Siberian 332.15
sibilance, sibilancy
456.1
sibilant 456.3
sibilate 456.2
sibilation 456
sibling
nouns 11.2
adjs. 11.7
sibship 11.1
sibyl 541.6

sibyllic, sibylline
541.11
Sibylline Books,
Sibylline Oracles
541.7
siccant 392.10
siccation 392.3
siccative
nouns 392.4
adjs. 392.10
sick
nouns 684.31
adjs. ill 684.41
nauseated 684.42
sad 870.29
weary 882.10
SICK OF
satiated 662.6
disgusted 864.23
disliking 865.8
tired of 882.10
sick bay 687.29
sickbed 687.29
sicken
take sick 684.34
afflict 684.37
disgust 864.13
SICKEN AT 865.5
SICKEN OF 684.34
sickened 864.23
sickener
foulness 428.3
cloyer 662.3
nauseant 865.3
sickening
nasty 428.7
disgusting 862.9
sickish 684.41
sickishness 684.1
sickle 250.2
sicklelike, sickle-
shaped 251.13
sickle of Death 407.3
sickliness
paleness 362.2
unhealthiness
684.2
sickling 684.31
sick list 88.1
ON THE SICK LIST
684.41
sickly
weakly 159.12–21
haggard 204.19
pale 362.9
unhealthy 684.40
sickness menses 309.9
illness 684.1
IN SICKNESS AND IN
HEALTH 623.9
sickroom 687.29
side
nouns lineage 169.4
hillside 218.4
edge 234.4
flank 241
aspect 445.3
~ of controversy
481.14
actor's lines 609.25
party 786.5

SIGN UP
  enlist 778.12,14
  join 736.14
signal
 nouns
  radio ~ 343.13
  radar ~ 345.11
  sign 556.2,14
  code 612.7
  alarm 702
 verbs
  navigation 274.55
  sign 566.21
 adjs.
  remarkable 34.10
  important 670.20
signaler 701.5
signalize
  signal 566.21
  celebrate 875.3
  distinguish 912.12
signal light
  types of ~ 335.9
  signal 566.14
signalman 701.5
signals 348.19
signator, signatory
  520.7
signature radio 343.22
  musical ~ 462.12
  endorsement 520.4
  sign 566.2
  lettering 579.8
  autograph 581.10
  book ~ 603.13
signboard
  billboard 557.7
  sign 566.3
signed 769.12
signer 520.7
signet
  endorsement 520.4
  seal 566.12
  insignia 567.3
  signature 581.10
significance
  meaning 543.1,6
  importance 670.1
  distinction 912.5
significant
  evidential 504.17
  ominous 542.13
  meaningful 543.10
  indicative 566.22
  important 670.19
  distinguished 912.18
signification
  specification 80.6
  meaning 543.1
  indication 566.1
significative
  meaningful 543.10
  indicative 566.22
signify specify 80.9
  evidence 504.9
  foretoken 542.9
  mean 543.8
  hint 555.9
  indicate 566.16,17
  be important 670.11

SIGNIFY NOTHING
  be meaningless
   545.7
  be unimportant
   671.10
signior mister 419.7
  nobleman 916.4
sign language 566.13
sign manual 581.10
sign of the cross
  benediction 1030.5
  ritual 1038.4
MAKE THE SIGN OF
  THE CROSS OVER
  1030.13
signor, signore 419.7
signora 420.8
signorina 420.9
signorino 419.7
signpost 566.3
Sigyn 1012.6
sike 394.1
sikhara 206.11
silage 306a.4
silence
 nouns
  soundlessness 450
  taciturnity 611.2
 IN SILENCE
  silently 450.15
  secretly 612.19
 KEEP SILENCE 450.5
 verbs render
  powerless 157.11
  kill 408.18
  hush 450.8
  refute 505.5
  defeat 725.6
 interjs. 450.16
silence cloth, silencer
  450.4
silent soundless 450.11
  unexpressed 544.9
  taciturn 611.7
silently quietly 450.15
  tacitly 544.12
silent partner 785.2
silenus 1012.18
silhouette
 nouns outline 234.2
  shadow 336.3
  picture 572.16
 verbs 234.9
silicic 382.14
silique 410.28
siliquose 192.9
silk smoothness 259.3
  light filter 337.4
  softness 356.4
  attorney 1001.4
silk gown, silk-
  gownsman 1001.4
silk-stocking 916.4
silkworm 205.5
silky filamentary 205.7
  glossy 259.10
  soft 356.15
  cloth 377.9
sill base 215.6,9
  seat 215.18
  fool 470.6

silliness
  foolishness 469.1
  triviality 671.3
silly
 nouns 470.6
 adjs. foolish 469.8
  dazed 530.14
  trivial 671.16
silo 658.7
silt residue 43.2
  deposit 270.8
silt up 209.3
silvan 181.8
silver
 nouns
  silverware 347.3
  white 363.2
  money 833.1,19
 verbs plate 227.28
  whiten 363.6
  gray 365.2
 adjs. white 363.8
  gray 365.3
  metallic 382.16
  eloquent 598.8
silver-headed 365.4
silvering 363.4
silver lining 886.3
silver plate 227.14
silver-plate 227.28
silver-plated
  plated 227.35
  metallic 382.16
silver screen, the
  609.16
silver-tongued
  musical 461.49
  eloquent 598.8
silverware
  tableware 347.3
  merchandise 829.4
silvery white 363.8
  gray 365.3
  metallic 383.16
  musical 461.49
silvicultural 412.21
silviculture 412.2
silviculturist 412.6
Simhath Torah
  1038.16
similar
 nouns 20.4
 adjs. identical 14.6
  like 20.10
similarity
  identicalness 14
  likeness 20
similarize
  make alike 20.8
  harmonize 26.11
similarly thus 8.8
  identically 14.8
  likewise 20.18
  furthermore 40.10
simile 549.2
similitude
  similarity 20.1,5
  copy 24.1
  comparison 490.1
  simile 549.2
  image 570.3

similitudinize 549.3
similize liken 490.4
  figure 549.3
simmer
 nouns 328.2
 verbs
  be violent 161.11
  be hot 327.21
  boil 328.19
  cook 329.4
  bubble 404.4
  ~ with excitement
   855.19
  be angry 950.15
SIMMER DOWN 856.7
simmering
 nouns 328.2
 adjs. hot 327.25
  passionate 855.30
  angry 950.27
simoleons 833.2
Simon Legree
  villain 610.1
  tyrant 747.15
simon-pure pure 45.5
  genuine 515.13
simoom, simoon
  402.7,14
simous 248.12
simp 470.8
simper
 nouns 874.3
 verbs grin 874.8
  be affected 901.14
simpering 901.18
simple
 nouns 685.4
 adjs. mere 35.9
  unmixed 45.5
  homely 190.28
  simple-minded
   468.22
  ignorant 476.13
  gullible 501.8
  elegant 587.6
  plain-speaking 589.3
  informal 645.3
  easy 730.11
  artless 734.5
  plain 900.6
  humble 904.9
simplehearted 734.5
simple-minded
  feeble-minded
   468.22
  artless 734.5
Simple Simon
  simpleton 470.8
  dupe 618.1
simpleton 470.8
simpletonian, simple-
  witted 468.22
simplicity
  no mixture 45
  simple-mindedness
   468.9
  ignorance 476.1
  gullibility 501.2
  elegant style 587.1
  plain speech 589.1
  informality 645.1

artlessness 734.1
unornamentation
900
simplification
disentanglement
45.2
explanation 550.4
simplified 45.8
simplify
disinvolve 45.3
explain 550.11
make simple 900.5
simply merely 35.11
purely 45.9
solely 89.14
in plain words 589.4
informally 645.4
easily 730.13
artlessly 734.7
plainly 900.10
simulacrum
image 24.1
sham 614.13
simulate sham 614.22
borrow 819.4
affect 901.12
simulated sham 614.27
affected 901.16
simulation sham 614.3
borrowing 819.2
simulative
imitative 22.10
sham 614.27
simulcast 344.2
simultaneous 118.4
simultaneousness 118
sin
nouns 980.1,2
verbs 980.3
Sinaean 417.9
Sinaitic 579.5
sinapism 685.28
since
advs. afterwards 117.5
ago 119.2
until now 119.14
conjs. 154.8
sincere
genuine 515.13
zealous 633.10
candid 972.17
sincerely
zealously 633.14
frankly 972.23
sincerity
genuineness 515.5
zeal 633.2
candor 972.4
sinecure 730.3
sine qua non
condition 506.2
salient point 670.6
sinew tendon 48.4
muscle 158.2
sinewless
enervated 157.19
weak 159.12
sinewy 158.14
sinful 979.17
sinfully 979.23
sinfulness 979.5

sing
nouns 461.33
verbs blow 402.24
warble 459.5
vocalize 461.39
confess 554.7
say 592.17
poetize 607.19
rejoice 874.6
SING A DIFFERENT
TUNE 626.7
SING A FAMILIAR
TUNE 881.5
SING OUT 458.8
SING SMALL 904.6
SING THE SAME OLD
SONG
dwell on 103.9
be boresome 882.7
singe
nouns 328.6
verbs burn 328.23
discolor 677.6
singer 463.13
singing
nouns 461.12,33
adjs. 461.51
single
nouns 240.5
adjs. simple 45.5
one 89.7
unmarried 932.7
single blessedness
932.1
single file 71.2
single-foot
nouns 272.14
verbs 272.27
single-footer 413.20
singlehanded
adjs. 89.8
advs. 730.13
singlehearted
artless 734.5
honest 972.14
single-minded 734.5
singleness
no mixture 45.1
unity 89.1
~ of purpose 623.1
~ of heart 734.1
celibacy 932.1
single out 635.11
single-prop 279.2
singles 876.9
singleton integer 89.4
playing card 876.17
singletree 220.5
singly simply 45.9
alone 89.13
singsong
nouns
repetitiousness
103.4
musicale 461.33
adjs. samely 17.6
repetition 103.15
tedious 882.8
Singspiel 461.35
singular special 80.12
characteristic 80.13

odd 85.11
one 89.7
unique 89.9
singularity
characteristic 80.3
individuality 80.4
oddity 85.3
oneness 89.1
singularly
remarkably 34.23
oddly 85.18
singly 89.13
sinister
oblique 218.13
left 243.5
ominous 542.13
evil 673.7
adverse 727.13
dishonest 973.15
sinistra 243.3
sinistrad 243.7
sinistral
nouns 243.4
adjs. left 243.5
left-handed 243.6
sinistrality, sinistration
243.2
sinistrally 243.7
sinistrocerebral,
sinistrocular 243.5
sinistrodextral
ambidextrous 242.6
left-handed 243.6
sinistrogyrate 243.5
sinistrogyration 243.2
sink
nouns cavity 256.2
drain 395.5
washbasin 679.12
sump 680.12
~ of iniquity 979.10
IN SINK 461.50
verbs
be transient 111.6
age 126.10
weaken 159.9
deepen 208.7
excavate 256.15
capsize 274.46
recede 296.2
go down 314.6
lower 316.4
submerge 318.7,8
gravitate 351.15
mire 399.2
disappear 446.2
ignore 529.4
conceal 613.8
sicken 684.35
deteriorate 690.18
tire 715.5
fail 723.10
come to grief 727.10
be unfortunate
727.11
invest in 834.16
despond 870.16
deject 870.18
SINK BACK 694.4
SINK IN
mire 399.2

penetrate the mind
477.18
be remembered
535.15
be understood 546.5
be impressed 853.16
sinkage draft 208.5
deepening 208.6
decline 314.2
sinker
dumpling 306a.33
doughnut 306a.43
weight 351.6
sinkhole 256.3
sinking fund 834.3
sink or swim
without fail 512.26
come what may
622.20
sinless
virtuous 978.9
innocent 982.6
sinner 984.8
sinner it 980.3
Sinn Feiner 147.3
Sinologist 578.12
sinter residue 43.2
deposit 270.8
sinuate 253.6
sinuation, sinuosity
253.1
sinuous winding 253.6
circuitous 319.7
sinus curve 251.2
cavity 256.2
sinusitis 684.8
sip
nouns small amount
35.3
drink 306.4
taste 426.2
dram 994.6
verbs drink 306.27
taste 426.7
tipple 994.29
siphon
nouns 395.6
verbs pipe 270.13
channel 395.19
SIPHON OFF 304.10
Sir 915.3
sir 419.7
sircar 739.3
sirdar ruler 747.10
officer 747.22
title 915.3
sire
nouns cause 152.4
creator 166.10
father 169.9
man 419.5
title 915.3
verbs originate
152.11
father 168.9
Siren music 463.24
temptress 648.3
siren
nouns sea spirit 396.4
noisemaker 452.5
temptress 648.3

annoy 864.17
verbs excel 36.6
peel 231.8
abrade 349.7
injure 690.13
defeat 725.6
fleece 820.21
overcharge 846.7
SKIN OVER 692.21
skin and bones 204.5
skin-deep slight 35.7
shallow 209.5
skin-dive 318.6
skinflint 850.5
skinful fill 56.3
satiety 662.1
skin game 616.9
skinned 725.14
skinny
nouns 204.8
adjs. thin 204.16
skinlike 228.6
skip
nouns step 272.13
jump 317.1
servant 748.9
verbs play truant
186.8
walk 266.16
decamp 300.11
caper 317.6
leave undone 532.7
evade 629.7
flee 629.10
escape 630.6
rejoice 874.6
frolic 876.25
dance 877.5
SKIP IT 671.22
SKIP OVER
skim over 484.34
slight 532.8
skip-bomb 796.25
skipjack 917.10
skipper
shipmaster 275.7
master 747.24
skipper's daughters
394.14
skippet 192.4
skippingly 72.5
skirmish
nouns 794.3
verbs 794.14
skirt
nouns appendage
41.2
dress 230.16
types of ∼ 230.55
border 234.4
woman 420.6
verbs border 234.10
go round 319.4
SKIRT THE SHORE
274.41
skirt chaser
philanderer 930.11
libertine 987.10
skirting
nouns 234.7
adjs. 234.11

skirts 234.1
ON THE SKIRTS OF
199.22
skis 271.18
skit 609.8
skittery
nervous 857.12
skittish 889.22
skittish fickle 627.7
excitable 855.29
frisky 868.14
jumpy 889.22
shy 906.12
skive 42.10
Skuld 638.3
skulduggery 616.4
skulk sneak 613.10
cower 890.9
skulking furtive 612.14
cowering 890.13
skull 210.6
skull and crossbones
cross 220.4
death 407.14
danger sign 701.3
skunk animal 413.4
stinker 436.3
scoundrel 984.6
sky
nouns 374.2
TO THE SKIES 34.17
verbs 315.5
sky-high 206.20
skylark
nouns 313.7
verbs 876.26
skylight 264.7
sky line 213.4
skyriding 277.1
skyrocket
nouns 313.7
verbs rocket 280.12
ascend 313.9
skysail 276.14
skyscape view 445.6
picture 572.13
skyscraper
tower 206.11
structure 244.2
skysail 276.14
skyscraping 206.20
skysweeper 799.7
skyward aloft 206.27
upward 313.16
skyway 277.39
skywriting 557.5
sky writing 277.1
slab
nouns lamina 226.2
board 377.3
mud 388.8
mud puddle 388.9
puddle 397.1
adjs. viscid 388.12
monument 568.11
slime 680.8
muddy 388.14
slabber
nouns 310.3
verbs 310.6
slab-sided 204.16

slack
nouns 330.2
verbs make slack 51.3
relax 162.9
extinguish 331.7
shirk 629.9
let up 709.7
adjs. loose 51.5
dilatory 132.16
weak 159.12
inert 267.12
slow 269.10
remiss 532.10
reluctant 621.6
inadequate 660.7
indolent 706.17
improvident 719.15
lax 756.4
loose-moraled
987.26
slacken reduce 39.8
loosen 51.3
delay 132.7
relax 162.9
slow down 269.9
let up 709.7
hinder 728.10
relieve 884.5
slacker 629.3
slackness
looseness 51.2
dilatoriness 132.5
slowness 269.1
remissness 532.1
improvidence 719.2
laxness 756.1
slack-off, slack-up
269.4
slag residue 43.2
scoria 328.16
slake slacken 162.9
gratify 863.6
relieve 884.5
SLAKE ONE'S THIRST
994.29
slam
nouns blow 282.4
bang 455.1
score 722.4
gibe 965.2
criticism 967.4
verbs shut 265.6
strike 282.14
bang 455.6
criticize 967.14
SLAM INTO 282.13
SLAM THE DOOR IN
ONE'S FACE
avoid 629.6
refuse 774.5
snub 964.5
slam-bang
verbs 455.6
advs. bang 455.13
recklessly 892.11
slammock, slummock
62.7
slander
nouns 969.3
verbs 969.11
slanderer 969.6

slanderous 969.13
slang
nouns 578.6
adjs. 578.17
slangster 578.13
slangy 578.17
slant
nouns slope 218.2
glance 438.4
viewpoint 438.7
aspect 445.3
attitude 523.2
bias 523.3
story angle 606.9
verbs slope 218.10
angle 525.9
adjs. 218.15
slantways, slantwise
adjs. 218.15
advs. 218.24
slap
nouns blow 282.8
sound 455.1
attempt 712.2
gibe 965.2
chastisement 1008.3
verbs put 183.13
hit 282.18
crack 455.6
chastise 1008.13
SLAP DOWN 183.15
SLAP ON 40.3
SLAP OUT 532.9
advs. 113.9
slapbang
adjs. 892.8
advs. 892.11
slap-bang
verbs 455.6
adjs. 707.9
advs. suddenly 113.9
bang 455.13
hastily 707.12
slapdash
nouns 532.3
verbs paint 361.14
do carelessly 532.9
adjs. hasty 707.9
reckless 892.8
advs. suddenly 113.9
carelessly 532.18
hastily 707.12
recklessly 892.11
slaphappy
crazy 472.25
groggy 530.14
slapper 194.11
slapping great 34.13
huge 194.21
banging 455.11
slapstick
nouns 609.6,9
verbs 609.33
adjs. 609.39
slash
nouns slit 49.3
price cut 847.4
verbs sever 49.10
cut prices 847.6
criticize 967.21

slat thinness 204.7
  strip 205.4
  slab 225.2
  wood 377.3
slate
  nouns writing
    material 600.30
    schedule 639.2
    ballot 742.20
  verbs cover 227.25
    schedule 639.4
slather, slathers 34.5
slattern 62.7
slatternly 62.14
slaty gray 365.3
  stone 333.7
slaughter
  nouns 408.1,3
  verbs 408.17
slaughterer 408.10
slaughterhouse 408.12
slaughterous 408.24
slaunchways, slaunch-
  wise 218.24
slave
  nouns instrument
    656.3
    drudge 716.3
    serf 762.7
  A SLAVE TO 762.13
  verbs 714.13
slave driver
  supervisor 746.2
  taskmaster 747.15
slaver
  nouns slobber 310.3
    nonsense 545.4
  verbs slobber 310.6
    be insane 472.19
    talk nonsense 545.8
    flatter 968.5
laverer 968.4
slavery drudgery 714.4
  bondage 762.1
slave trade 825.1
lavey 748.1,10
Slavic race 417.15
lavish 905.12
lavishness 905.1
law 306a 36
lay kill 408.13
  delight 863.8
  amuse 876.23
layer 408.10
leave 46.2
leazy 159.14
led
  nouns sleigh 271.18
    types of ~ 271.29
  verbs haul 270.12
    slide 272.34
ledding 272.8
ledge
  nouns 271.18
  verbs 270.12
ledge dog 270.6
leek
  verbs 259.7
  adjs. trim 59.8
    smooth 259.10
    unctuous 379.9

spruce 642.13
sleep
  nouns death 407.1
    unconsciousness
     422.2
    slumber 710.2
    hypnotic ~ 710.7
  GO TO SLEEP 710.15
  PUT TO SLEEP
    anesthetize 422.3
    make sleep 710.18
  verbs be inert 267.8
    slumber 710.13
  SLEEP AT ONE'S POST
    706.10
  SLEEP IT OFF
    recuperate 692.19
    sober up 995.2
  SLEEP OUT 187.12
  SLEEP UPON
    postpone 132.8
    consider 477.13
  SLEEP WITH 168.10
sleeper
  railway car 271.13
  wager 514.3
  slumberer 710.12
sleep-inducer
  sedative 685.11
  sleep-provoker
    710.10
sleepiness
  languor 706.5
  drowsiness 710.1
sleeping inert 267.12
  dead 407.24
  inattentive 529.8
  asleep 710.20
  LET SLEEPING DOGS
    LIE 760.15
sleeping beauty
  710.12
sleeping car 271.13
sleeping pills 685.11
sleeping sickness 684.9
sleepless alert 531.14
  industrious 705.21
  wakeful 711.6
sleeplessness
  alertness 531.5
  wakefulness 711.1
sleep-producer, sleep-
  provoker 710.10
sleep treatment 688.6
sleepwalk
  nouns 272.11
  verbs 272.31
sleepwalker 273.7
sleepwalking
  nouns somnambulism
    272.11
    neurosis 688.26
  adjs. 272.37
sleepy
  nouns 710.12
  adjs. languid 706.18
    drowsy 710.19
sleepyhead
  lazybones 706.6
  sleeper 710.12

sleet
  nouns 332.6
  verbs 332.12
sleeve 230.66
  UP ONE'S SLEEVE
    612.19
sleeveless 667.9
sleigh
  nouns sled 271.18
    types of ~ 271.29
  verbs 272.34
sleight trick 616.6
  knack 731.6
  artifice 733.3
sleight of hand 616.5
Sleipnir 413.21
slender
  inconsiderable 35.7
  narrow 204.13
  thin 204.15
  meager 660.8
  trivial 671.16
slenderize 204.12
sleuth, sleuthhound
  779.10
slew, slews 34.4
slice
  nouns piece 55.3
    rasher 226.2
  verbs 49.10
slick
  nouns 603.11
  verbs sleek 259.7
    paint 361.14
    lubricate 379.8
  SLICK UP 230.41
  adjs. sleek 259.10
    slippery 259.11
    unctuous 379.9
    shrewd 466.15
    alert 531.14
    clever 731.20
    cunning 733.12
  SLICK AS A WHISTLE
    730.13
  advs. 733.15
slicker smoother 259.4
  sharper 617.4
  crafty person 733.6
slidder
  nouns 314.4
  verbs 314.9
sliddery 259.11
slide
  nouns smoothness
    259.3
    glide 272.8
    slip 314.4
    lantern ~ 575.5
  verbs elapse 105.5
    glide 272.34
    slip 314.9
    deteriorate 690.18
    go easily 730.8
  SLIDE BACK 694.4
  SLIDE INTO 145.12
sliding scale 839.4
slight
  nouns neglect 532.1
    nonobservance
     767.1

  snub 964.2
  verbs disregard 529.3
    neglect 532.8
    defy 791.4
    snub 964.6
  adjs. inconsiderable
    35.7
    frail 159.14
    little 195.9
    thin 204.15
    shallow 209.5
    rare 354.7
    meager 660.8
    trivial 671.16
slighted 532.14
slightest 37.8
slightly in a small
  degree 35.10
  smally 195.15
  meagerly 660.13
slim
  nouns 204.8
  verbs 204.12
  adjs. sparse 102.5
    thin 204.15
    meager 660.8
    sly 733.12
slime
  nouns mud 388.8
    filth 680.8
  verbs 680.17
slimy clammy 388.13
  filthy 680.25
sling
  nouns throw 284.4
    bandages 685.28
    weapon 799.19
  verbs miscarry 166.19
    suspend 214.8
    throw 284.12
  SLING AT 796.30
  SLING THE LEAD
    208.8
slingshot 799.19
slink
  nouns 890.6
  verbs miscarry 166.19
    sneak 613.10
    cower 890.9
  SLINK OFF 629.12
  adjs. 204.16
slinky thin 204.16
  furtive 612.14
  cowering 890.13
slip
  nouns small amount
    35.3
    youngling 125.1
    diminutive 195.4
    thinness 204.7
    strip 205.4
    pillow slip 227.11
    aviation 277.22
    slide 314.4
    error 517.4
    proof 601.5
    dock 698.6
    failure 723.4
    bungle 732.5
    misdeed 980.2

GIVE ONE THE SLIP
630.8
GIVE THE SLIP 629.7
verbs elapse 105.5
  glide 272.34
  slide 314.9
  err 517.8
  deteriorate 690.18
  fail 723.13
  bungle 732.11
  give 816.12
  be sinful 979.13
LET SLIP THROUGH
  THE FINGERS
  mistime 130.6
  lose 810.5
SLIP AWAY
  absent oneself 186.7
  avoid 629.12
  escape 630.8
SLIP BACK 694.4
SLIP IN 301.7
SLIP ON 230.42
SLIP ONE OVER ON
616.13
SLIP ONE'S BREATH
407.16
SLIP OVER
  skim over 484.34
  slight 532.8
SLIP THE MEMORY
536.5
SLIP UP
  err 517.8
  fail 723.13
slip case, slip cover
603.16
slippage 314.4
slippery slick 259.11
  unctuous 379.9
  unreliable 513.18
  evasive 629.14
  precarious 695.12
  cunning 733.12
  treacherous 973.20
slippy slippery 259.11
  alert 531.14
  precarious 695.12
slipshod slovenly 62.14
  careless 532.12
  ungrammatical
  585.4
slipslap 545.4
slipslop
  nouns 517.6
  adjs. 585.4
slipstream 277.36
slip-up error 517.4
  failure 723.4
slish 49.10
slit
  nouns split 49.3
  cleft 200.2
  furrow 262.1
  verbs sever 49.10
  furrow 262.3
  open 264.11
  adjs. severed 49.22
  cleft 200.7
  furrowed 262.4

slither
  nouns glide 272.8
  slide 314.4
  verbs glide 272.34
  slide 314.9
slithering
  gliding 272.8
  reptile 413.43
slithery slippery 259.11
  clammy 388.13
sliver
  small amount 35.3
  splinter 55.3
slob slattern 62.7
  ice 332.6
  clumsy fellow 732.9
slobber
  nouns 310.3
  verbs salivate 310.6
  slop 391.12
sloe
  nouns 364.4
  adjs. 364.8
slog
  nouns 282.4
  verbs trudge 272.27
  strike 282.14
slogan motto 516.4
  catchword 580.8
  rallying cry 795.13
slop
  nouns mud 388.8
  mud puddle 388.9
  filth 680.8,9
  sentimentality 853.7
  verbs moisten 391.12
  spill 394.18
slope
  nouns 218.2,4
  verbs slant 218.10
  decamp 300.11
  flee 629.11
sloping 218.15
sloppy slovenly 62.14
  muddy 388.14
  wet 391.16
  miry 399.3
  careless 532.12
  ungrammatical
  585.4
  sentimental 853.21
slops
  ready-mades 230.4
  feed 306a.4
  offal 680.9
slosh
  nouns snow 332.9
  mud 388.8
  splash 391.5
  swash 394.8
  slime 680.8
  verbs splash 391.12
  spill 394.18
  swash 394.20
  ripple 451.11
sloshy 388.14
slot 264.1
sloth 706.4
slothful 706.17
slot machine
  gambling 514.11

  vender 830.9
slouch
  nouns slow motion
  269.2
  gait 272.14
  clumsy fellow 732.9
NO SLOUCH
  proficient 731.11
  worthy 983.2
  verbs 272.27
slouchy 62.14
slough
  nouns cast skin 228.5
  marsh 399.1
  offal 680.9
  gangrene 684.30
  predicament 729.4
  verbs shed 231.10
  discard 666.7
sloughy 231.18
sloven 62.7
slovenly untidy 62.14
  careless 532.12
  ungrammatical
  585.4
slovenry
  untidiness 62.6
  carelessness 532.3
slow
  verbs 269.9
SLOW DOWN
  delay 132.7
  moderate 162.6
  retard 269.9
  relax 709.7
  adjs. late 132.15
  dilatory 132.16
  slow-moving 269.10
  stupid 468.16
  dull 881.6
SLOW TO 621.6
  advs. behindhand
  132.18
  slowly 269.13
GO SLOW
  dawdle 269.6
  beware! 893.14
slow coach 269.5
slowdown 787.7
slow-down 269.4
slowing, slowing down
  269.4
slowly gradually 29.6
  tardily 132.19
  leisurely 269.13
  dully 881.10
slow motion 269.2
slow-moving 269.10
slowness
  dilatoriness 132.5
  leisureliness 269
  stupidity 468.3
  dullness 881.1
slowpoke 269.5
slow time 272.15
slow-up 269.4
slow-witted 468.16
sloyd 560.3
slubber
  nouns 680.8
  verbs stain 677.6

  dirty 680.17
  bungle 732.11
slubberdegullion 62.7
slubberer slattern 62.7
  bungler 732.8
sludge ice 332.6
  mud 388.8
  slime 680.8
sludgy 388.14
slue
  nouns 218.3
  verbs 218.9
slug
  nouns dose 55.5
  slow goer 269.5
  animal 414.9
  type ~ 601.7
  idler 706.7
  bullet 799.14
  gold piece 833.5
  token 833.12
  nugget 833.19
  verbs 269.6
sluggard
  slow goer 269.5
  idler 706.7
sluggish
  dilatory 132.16
  inert 267.12
  slow 269.10
  stupid 468.16
  listless 706.18
  apathetic 854.13
sluggishness
  weakness 159.1
  slowness 269.1
  stupidity 468.3
  languor 706.5
  apathy 854.4
sluice stream 394.5
  channel 395.5
  floodgate 395.11
slum
  nouns 680.11
  verbs 441.6
slumber
  nouns 710.2
  verbs be inert 267.8
  sleep 710.13
slumberer 710.12
slumbering
  inert 267.12
  sleeping 710.20
slumberland 710.2
slumberless 711.6
slumberous, slumbery
  710.19
slumming 441.4
slummock, slummocky
  See slammock, etc.
slump
  nouns decline 39.2
  shortcoming 312.1
  sinkage 314.2
  deterioration 690.3
  stock market ~
  831.5
  depreciation 847.4
  verbs fall short 312.2
  descend 314.6
  deteriorate 690.18

snarl
nouns tangle 46.2
  harsh sound 457.3
  quarrel 793.5
verbs tangle 46.3
  blow 402.24
  sound harshly 457.8
  growl 459.4
  say 592.17
  be angry 950.14
SNARL UP
  complicate 46.3
  confuse 63.3
snarled 46.4
GET ALL SNARLED UP
  729.11
snarleyyow 413.24
snatch
nouns
  small amount 35.3
  piece 55.3
  seizure 820.2
BY SNATCHES
  piecemeal 55.8
  haphazardly 62.17
  intermittently 72.5
  irregularly 138.4
  jerkily 323.24
verbs jerk 285.5
  seize 820.12,14
  steal 822.13,18
snatchy
  disconnected 72.4
  irregular 138.3
sneak
nouns coward 890.6
  knave 984.3
verbs creep 272.25
  lurk 613.10
  smuggle 824.8
  cower 890.9
SNEAK OFF 629.12
SNEAK OUT OF
  shirk 629.9
  escape 630.8
sneak attack
  deceit 616.3
  attack 796.2
sneak thief 823.1
sneak thievery 822.1
sneaky furtive 612.14
  cowering 890.13
sneer
nouns 955.4
WITH A SNEER 964.9
verbs sail 274.22
  scoff 965.9
sneering
  scornful 964.8
  derisive 965.12
sneeze
nouns
  exhalation 402.19
  sibilation 456.1
verbs exhale 402.25
  sibilate 456.2
NOT TO BE SNEEZED
  AT 670.17
SNEEZE AT
  ignore 529.4
  disdain 964.3

sneezy 402.31
snick 35.3
snicker, snigger
nouns laughter 874.4
  scornful laugh 965.4
verbs 874.9
SNICKER AT 965.8
snide
nouns 833.10
adjs. false 614.27
  base 673.8
  scurvy 913.12
sniff
nouns sniffle 402.19
  sibilation 456.1
  dudgeon 950.7
verbs inhale 402.25
  smell 434.8
  sibilate 456.2
  detect 487.6
SNIFF OUT
  trace 484.29
  discover 487.6
sniffer 345.4
sniffle
nouns sniff 402.19
  sibilation 456.1
verbs sniff 402.25
  sibilate 456.2
sniffles 684.12
sniffy 910.14
snifter 994.6
snifting valve 697.3
snigger See snicker
sniggle
nouns 616.12
verbs ensnare 616.20
  catch 820.14
snip
nouns
  small amount 35.3
  piece 55.3
  minute thing 195.7
  tailor 230.34
  ship's tailor 275.6
verbs 49.10
snipe
nouns 433.6
verbs shoot 284.13
  shoot at 796.23
sniper 798.11
snippet
  small amount 35.3
  minute thing 195.7
snippy
  fragmentary 55.6
  snobbish 910.14
  curt 935.7
snitch
nouns
  small amount 35.2
  informer 555.6
verbs tattle 555.11
  steal 822.13
snivel
nouns
  hypocrisy 614.6
  sanctimony 1027.1
verbs
  be hypocritical
    614.24

weep 873.10
  be sanctimonious
    1027.4
sniveler canter 617.8
  pietist 1027.3
snivelling
nouns 873.2
adjs. weeping 873.17
  obsequious 905.13
  sanctimonious
    1027.5
snivy 624.11
snob
  shoemaker 230.37
  deserter 626.6
  sycophant 905.3
  prig 910.7
snobbery
  exclusiveness 894.5
  haughtiness 910.6
snobbish, snobby
  exclusive 894.13
  haughty 910.14
snookums 930.5
snoop
nouns meddler 237.4
  inquisitive 526.2
verbs meddle 237.7
  pry 526.4
snoopy
  meddlesome 237.9
  inquisitive 526.6
snoot 255.7
snooty 910.14
snooze, snoozle
nouns 710.3
verbs 710.13
snoozy 710.19
snore
nouns
  sibilation 456.1
  harsh sound 457.3
verbs sibilate 456.2
  sound harshly 457.8
  sleep 710.13
snork
nouns 456.1
verbs sibilate 456.2
  grunt 459.3
snorkel
  submarine 276.9
  diving 318.5
  tube 395.6
snort
nouns
  sibilation 456.1
  snicker 874.4
  ~ of scorn 965.4
  dram 994.6
verbs sibilate 456.2
  grunt 459.3
  say 592.17
  snicker 874.9
snorter 158.6
snot 387.3
snotty mucous 388.13
  snobbish 910.14
snout nose 255.7
  nozzle 395.9
snow
nouns

frozen water 332.9
  TV interference
    344.5
  white 363.2
  narcotic 685.10
verbs 332.12
SNOW UNDER
  snow 332.12
  overwhelm 725.8
snowball
nouns
  accumulation 74.8
  snow 332.9
verbs increase 38.6
  ball 254.7
snowbank 332.9
snow-blind
verbs 440.6
adjs. 440.9
snow blindness 440.1
snowblink 334.9
snowbound 332.19
**snow-capped, snow-
  clad** 332.18
snowdrift heap 74.9
  snow 332.9
snowfall 332.9
snowflake flake 226.3
  snow 332.9
snowshoes 271.18
snowslide, snowslip
  slide 314.4
  snow 332.9
snowstorm snow 332.9
  TV interference
    344.5
snowy snowlike 332.18
  white 363.8
snub
nouns 964.2
verbs cut off 42.10
  shorten 202.6
  check 728.10
  restrain 758.7
  rebuff 964.5
adjs. 202.10
snubbed, snubby
  202.10
snubbing post 216.4
snub-nosed
  pugged 202.10
  deformed 248.12
snuff
nouns
  inhalation 305.5
  sniff 402.19
  tobacco 433.9
  sibilation 456.1
verbs inhale 305.12
  extinguish 331.7
  sniff 402.25
  smell 434.8
  sibilate 456.2
SNUFF OUT
  extinguish 331.7
  destroy 691.15
snuff bottle, snuffbox
  433.9
snuff dipper, snuffer
  433.12

snuffle
nouns
inhalation 305.5
sniff 402.19
sibilation 456.1
hypocrisy 614.6
sanctimony 1027.1
verbs inhale 305.12
sniff 402.25
sibilate 456.2
nasalize 593.9
be hypocritical
614.24
be sanctimonious
1027.4
snuffler canter 617.8
pietist 1027.3
snuffman 433.13
snuffy tobacco 433.16
dirty 680.24
snug
verbs make
comfortable 885.9
snuggle 885.10
adjs. trim 59.8
homelike 190.28
close 265.12
seaworthy 276.18
safe 696.7
comfortable 885.11
unsociable 921.5
snuggle nestle 885.10
cuddle 930.15
snugness 885.2
so
adjs. 20.12
advs. thus 8.8
likewise 20.18
insomuch 29.8
as 30.12
very much 34.17
very 34.20
how 655.11
NOT SO 522.7
SO BE IT 520.19
SO FAR
thus far 35.11
until now 120.4
SO TO SPEAK
as it were 20.19
figuratively 549.5
conjs.
provided 506.15
so that 651.12
soak
nouns blow 282.4
soaking 391.7
spree 994.5
drunkard 994.11
verbs strike 282.14
extract 304.14
drench 391.13
saturate 661.16
overcharge 846.7
tipple 994.29
SOAK IN
absorb 305.13
be understood 546.5
learn 562.7
soakage 391.7

soaked
drenched 391.17
saturated 661.21
drunk 994.40
SOAKED IN 640.18
soaker rain 393.2
drunkard 994.10
soaking
nouns
extraction 304.6
drenching 391.7
adjs.
absorbent 305.17
soaked 391.17
drenching 391.18
soaky 391.17
so-and-so 582.2
soap
nouns bribe 649.2
cleanser 679.16
types of ~ 679.29
slush fund 742.38
flattery 968.1
verbs wash 679.18
flatter 968.7
SOAP THE WAYS 379.8
soapbox
nouns 215.13
verbs 597.8
soapbox orator
orator 597.6
electioneerer 744.10
soap bubble 404.1
soapiness 379.5
soap opera 343.21
soapsuds 404.2
soapy unctuous 379.9
sudsy 404.7
suave 934.18
flattering 968.9
soar be high 206.15
fly 277.42
rise 313.10
float 352.9
SOAR THROUGH SPACE
281.15
soaring
nouns 277.1
adjs. 206.19
sob
nouns 873.3
verbs sop 391.13
blow 402.24
sough 451.14
weep 873.10
sobbing
nouns sough 451.8
weeping 873.2
adjs. 873.17
sobby 391.17
sober
verbs moderate 162.6
make sane 471.3
SOBER DOWN
moderate 162.6
calm down 856.7
SOBER UP 995.2
adjs. moderate
162.10
dark 364.9
gray 365.3

sensible 466.18
sane 471.4
thoughtful 477.20
plain-speaking 589.3
ceremonious 644.8
important 670.21
composed 856.14
solemn 869.3
dignified 903.12
temperate 990.9
unintoxicated 995.3
soberly
palliative 162.16
solemnly 869.4
dignifiedly 903.14
sober-minded
sensible 466.18
sane 471.4
composed 856.14
serious 869.3
soberness
dark color 364.2
grayness 365.1
levelheadedness
466.6
plain speech 589.1
composure 856.4
sobriety 869.1
unintoxicatedness
995.1
IN ALL SOBERNESS
affirmation 521.9
frankly 972.23
sobriety
moderation 162.1
levelheadedness
466.6
sanity 471.1
composure 856.4
soberness 869.1
dignity 903.2
temperance 990.1
unintoxicatedness
995
sobriquet, soubriquet
581.7
sob story 853.7
socage 806.1
so-called
nominal 581.15
spurious 614.27
alleged 647.4
soccer 876.8
sociability
communicativeness
552.4
gregariousness 920
friendliness 925
sociable
nouns 920.9
adjs. communicative
552.9
gregarious 920.17
friendly 925.14
sociably 920.20
social
nouns 920.9
adjs. public 416.13
associational 786.16
sociable 920.17
social affair 920.9

social approval 688.19
social call 920.6
social circle 642.6
social climber 917.10
Social Commission
741.5
social conduct 644.3
social consciousness
939.1
social democracy
739.4
social discrimination
525.4
social economy 849.4
social ethics 955.1
social evil 987.8
social gathering 920.9
social graces 644.3
social insurance 743.6
social intercourse
920.4
socialism 743.5
Socialist 742.28
socialist
nouns 743.12
adjs. 743.20
Socialist Party 742.25
socialite 642.7
sociality 920.1
socialization 813.3
socialize 813.7
socialized medicine
medicine 686.1
welfarism 743.6
social legislation
740.15
social lion 912.9
social lubricant
994.12
socially 920.20
social maladjustment
688.16
social-minded 920.17
social outcast 924.3
social pathology
688.41
social pressure 742.30
social procedures
644.3
social register
register 568.8
society 642.6
social relations 920.4
social season 128.1
social security 743.6
social service 936.5
social usage 643.1
social worker 936.8
societal 416.13
society
nouns company 73.2
community 189.1
populace 416.2
polite ~ 642.6
association 786.1
commonwealth
786.3
fellowship 786.4
companionship
920.5
sect 1018.3

foot 211.5
adjs. one 89.7
unique 89.9
unmarried 932.7
solecism
sophism 482.3
error 517.5,6
ungrammaticism 585.2
solecistic(al) 585.4
sole frite 306a.24
solely simply 45.9
singly 89.14
solemn silent 450.11
ceremonious 644.8
important 670.21
sober 869.3
gloomy 870.25
celebrative 875.5
dignified 903.12
reverential 962.9
pious 1026.8
devotional 1030.15
solemn declaration
oath 521.3
promise 768.1
solemn entreaty 772.2
solemn mockery 1027.2
solemnness 869.1
solemnity
formality 644.1,4
importance 670.3
soberness 869
sadness 870.7
pomp 902.6
dignity 903.2
religious rite 1038.3
solemnize
dignify 644.5
celebrate 875.3
~ a rite 1038.17
solemnly soberly 869.4
gloomily 870.32
dignifiedly 903.14
solemn silence 450.1
solemn word
oath 521.3
promise 768.1
sol-fa
nouns solmization 461.12
scale 462.7
verbs 461.39
sol-faist 463.13
solfeggio 461.12
solicit canvass 742.43
request 772.14
solicitant
aspirant 632.12
applicant 772.7
solicitation
canvass 742.13
request 772.5
solicitor
canvasser 828.7
lawyer 1001.1
solicitor general 1001.4
solicitous
careful 531.10

eager 633.9
supplicatory 772.16
concerned 888.6
considerate 936.17
solicitude care 531.1
eagerness 633.1
anxiety 888.1
caution 893.1
considerateness 936.3
solid
nouns 353.6
adjs. substantial 3.4,5
complete 56.9
crowded 74.22
stable 142.13
strong 158.16
dense 353.12
hard 355.10
sensible 466.18
reliable 512.17
valid 515.12
unanimous 520.15
resolute 622.12
good 672.14
solvent 834.17
solidarity
completeness 56.1
unity 89.1
solidification
coherence 50.1
combination 52.1
hardening 355.5
solidified 355.13
solidify combine 52.3
condense 353.9
thicken 353.10
harden 355.8
solidity
substantiality 3.1
completeness 56.1
unity 89.1
stability 142.1
strength 158.3
density 353.1
hardness 355.1
levelheadedness 466.6
reliability 512.4
validity 515.4
solvency 834.6
soliloquist 596.2
soliloquize 596.3
soliloquizing 596.4
soliloquy 596
solitaire 922.5
solitariness
aloneness 89.2
solitude 922.3
solitary
nouns 922.5
adjs. one 89.7
alone 89.8
in solitude 922.12
solitude aloneness 89.2
seclusion 922.3
solitudinarian 922.5
solmizate 461.39
solmization 461.12
solo
nouns ~ flight 277.7

music 461.17
verbs 277.43
adjs. 89.8
soloist 463.1
Solomon sage 467.2
judge 1000.6
NO SOLOMON 470.1
WISE AS SOLOMON 466.17
Solon sage 467.4
statesman 744.2
solstice 128.7
solstitial 128.8
solstitial colure 374.16
solubilization 390.1
solubilize 390.5
soluble
dissolvable 390.9
solvable 486.3
solus 89.8
solution
nouns dissolution 390.1,3
music 462.2
solving 486
photographic ~ 575.15
verbs 50.7
solvent
nouns 679.16
adjs. 839.23
Soma 1012.7
soma 375.3
Somascope 687.11
somatic(al) 375.9
somatism 375.5
somatist
materialist 375.6
psychiatrist 688.13
somatization reaction 688.20
somatology 405.16
somber
nouns 336.2
verbs 336.10
adjs. dark 336.15
lackluster 336.19
dark-colored 364.9
gray 365.3
foreboding 542.13
important 670.21
solemn 869.3
sad 870.25
sombrous dark 336.15
dark-colored 364.9
sad 870.25
some
nouns 28.3
adjs. certain 28.6
plural 100.7
advs. 29.7
somebody
person 416.3
personage 670.8
celebrity 912.9
someday 121.12
somehow, somegate 655.13
some one, someone 416.3
someplace 183.27

somersault 219.2
somerset 219.2
something
nouns thing 3.3
some 28.3
object 375.4
personage 670.8
BE SOMETHING
be important 670.11
be famous 912.10
HAVE SOMETHING ON 504.16
LOOK LIKE SOME-
THING THE CAT
BROUGHT IN 897.5
SOMETHING TO
CHEW ON 483.1
SOMETHING TO WRITE
HOME ABOUT 918.2
advs. somewhat 29.7
in future 121.12
something else 16.3
something else again
irrelevant 10.7
different thing 16.3
something for
something 149.1
something like
related 9.7
similar 20.10
somewhat 29.7
something or other
thing 375.4
uncertainty 513.8
sometime 119.7
SOMETIME OR OTHER 121.12
sometimes 136.5
someway 655.13
somewhat
nouns 28.3
advs. 29.7
somewhere 183.27
somewhere about,
somewhere near
about 35.13
hereabout 183.24
approximately 199.26
somewhere else
elsewhere 186.17
abstracted 530.11
somnambulant, som-
nambular 272.37
somnambulate 272.31
somnambulation 272.11
somnambulator, som-
nambule, somnam-
bulist 273.7
somnambulism
sleepwalking 272.11
neurosis 688.26
somnambulistic
hypnosis 710.7
somnifacient
nouns hypnotic 685.11
sleep-inducer 710.10
adjs. sedative 685.39

sorry plight 729.4
sort
  nouns 61.3
  ALL SORTS 44.6
  ALL SORTS OF
  divers 19.4
  multitude 101.3
  OF SORTS
  of different kinds
    16.8
  varied 19.4
  mediocre 678.7
  OF THAT SORT 9.6
  OUT OF SORTS
  disorderly 62.12
  ill 684.41
  in disrepair 690.36
  unhappy 870.21
  out of humor
    949.17
  SORT OF
  as though 20.19
  rather 29.7
  verbs assort 60.10
  classify 61.6
  size 194.15
  SORT OUT 77.6
  SORT WITH
  agree 26.9
  accompany 73.7
  fraternize 920.15
sortable
  appropriate 26.19
  timely 129.10
  expedient 668.4
sortal 61.7
sorted ordered 60.13
  classified 61.8
sorter 60.4
sortie aviation 277.8
  attack 796.1
sortilege 1033.1
sorting sifting 60.3
  classification 61.1
  automation 348.20
sortition 514.6
sorty varied 19.4
  classificational 61.7
soso 678.7
so-so 678.12
sossinger 306a.21
sossle 680.8
sot fool 470.1
  drunkard 994.10
soteriology 1021.1
sottise 469.4
sottish stupid 468.15
  bibulous 994.44
sotto voce under the
  breath 451.22
  secretly 612.19
sou trifle 671.5
  coin 833.9
  WITHOUT A SOU
    836.9
soubrette actor 610.1
  maidservant 748.8
soubriquet See
  sobriquet
sou'easter 402.9
soufflé 306a.26

sough
  nouns drain 395.5
  sump 680.12
  verbs blow 402.24
  moan 451.14
soul essence 5.2,4
  substance 193.4
  life 406.1
  person 416.3
  inmost ~ 465.3
  genius 466.8
  affections 853.2,9
  ~ in hell 1014.1
  ~ of the dead
    1015.1
  spirit 1032.17,20
  NOT A SOUL 186.6
soulful 853.18
soulless
  inanimate 381.5
  unfeeling 854.9
soullessness 854.1
soulmate 929.14
Soul Principle 1011.7
soul-sick 870.29
soul-stirring 855.31
sound
  nouns bladder 192.2
  depth 208.4
  strait 398.1
  earshot 447.4
  tone 449
  ~ of trumpets
    452.4
  report 455.1
  probe 488.4
  ~ of trumpet 702.2
  verbs take soundings
    208.8
  dive 318.6
  seem 445.10
  make a ~ 449.12
  toot 452.8
  resound 453.7
  ring 453.8
  ~ a sour note 460.3
  ~ a horn 461.43
  probe 484.30
  feel out 488.9
  measure 489.11
  ~ true 515.7
  ~ a trumpet 557.13
  ~ an alarm 566.21
  utter 592.14
  ~ the alarm 702.6
  ~ a fanfare 875.3
  SOUND A TATTOO
  toot 452.8
  drum 454.4
  beat time 461.45
  SOUND LIKE
  resemble 20.7
  seem 445.10
  SOUND THE PRAISES
    OF
  praise 966.12
  glorify 1030.11
  adjs. substantial 3.5
  fast 47.14
  stable 142.13

  strong 158.16
  sensible 466.18
  sane 471.4
  logical 481.21
  reliable 512.17
  valid 515.12
  practical 534.6
  perfect 675.6
  healthy 683.8
  safe 696.5
  solvent 834.17
  orthodox 1022.8
sound barrier
  aviation 277.37
  sonics 449.8
sound control 343.19
sounded
  phonic 449.13
  spoken 592.20
sound effects 343.21
sounder
  types of ~ 208.17
  resonator 453.5
  probe 488.4
  telegraph ~ 558.19
sounding
  nouns depth ~ 208.4
  sonation 449.6
  adjs. sonant 449.14
  resounding 453.11
  ringing 453.12
sounding board 488.4
sound law 449.9
soundless deep 208.10
  silent 450.11
soundlessness 450.1
sound man
  radio ~ 343.26
  television ~ 344.13
soundness
  substantiality 3.1
  stability 142.1
  strength 158.3
  sensibleness 466.6
  sanity 471.1
  reasonableness
    481.10
  reliability 512.4
  validity 515.4
  perfectness 675.2
  healthiness 683.2
  solvency 834.6
  orthodoxy 1022.1
sound-on-film 575.12
soundproof
  verbs 158.12
  adjs. 158.18
sound shifting 449.9
sound track 575.12
sound truck 343.8
sound waves 449.1
soup power 156.1
  overcast 277.38
  food 306a.10
  semiliquid 388.5
  fog 403.3
  developer 575.15
  IN THE SOUP 729.20
  SOUP'S ON! 306.33
  soup-and-fish 230.11

soupbone 286.5
soupçon 35.4
souper watch 114.6
souper supper 306.6
soup-strainer 229.11
soup up 38.5
soupy 403.10
sour
  nouns acid 378.1,13
  sourness 431.1,3
  verbs turn ~ 431.5
  ~ the temper
    949.16
  adjs. bitter 428.6
  tart 431.6
  pungent 432.6
  off-key 460.4
  tainted 690.39
  unpleasant 862.8
  ~ tempered 949.23
sourbelly 870.13
sourbread, sourcake
    306a.27
source cause 152.5
  ~ of supply 658.4
sourdine
  nouns 450.4
  adjs. 451.17
sourdook 306a.47
sourdough
  native 189.3
  prospector 382.8
soured sour 431.6
  tainted 690.39
  sour-tempered
    949.23
souren 431.5
sour grapes sour 431.3
  impossibility 509.1
souring 431.3,4
sourness
  bitterness 428.2
  tartness 431
  pungency 432
  dissonance 460.1
  ill humor 949.1
sourpuss 870.13
sour-sweet 430.6
sousaphone 464.8
souse
  nouns plunge 318.2
  drench 391.7
  spree 994.5
  drunkard 994.11
  verbs dip 318.7
  drench 391.13
  inebriate 994.28
  tipple 994.31
sous tous les rapports
    56.18
souter 230.37
South 179.7
south
  nouns 289.3
  DOWN SOUTH 314.13
  verbs 289.9
  adjs., advs. 289.18
South America 385.1
South American 417.8
southbound 289.16
Southeast 179.7

specious
  fallacious 482.13
  plausible 510.6
  illusory 518.9
  false 614.28
  alleged 647.4
specious reasoning
  482.1
speck
  nouns
  small amount 35.2
  minute thing 195.7
  fleck 373.3
  mark 566.4
  blemish 677.3
  NOT A SPECK
  none 2.3
  nowise 35.14
  verbs sprinkle 75.7
  speckle 373.7
  mark 566.18
  spot 677.5
specked, speckled
  sprinkled 75.11
  speckled 373.13
speckle
  nouns fleck 373.3
  mark 566.4
  blemish 677.3
  verbs sprinkle 75.7
  fleck 373.7
  mark 566.18
  spot 677.5
specs 442.2
spectacle sight 445.7
  drama 609.4
  wonder 918.2
spectacled 442.10
spectacles 442.2
spectacular
  dramatic 609.37
  ostentatious 902.24
spectate 441.5
spectator
  attender 185.5
  observer 441
  audience 447.6
  theatergoer 609.42
specter
  illusion 518.4
  ghost 1015
specterlike 1015.7
spectral ethereal 4.5
  supernatural 85.14
  ~ color 361.6
  incorporeal 376.7
  ghostly 1015.7
**spectrogram, spectro-
  graph, spectro-
  heliogram** 575.9
spectrology 361.9
spectrometers 442.15
spectrometry 442.6
**spectrophotometry,
  spectroradiometry**
  342.1
spectroscopy 442.6
spectrum
  frequency ~ 343.15
  color 361.6
  variegation 373.6

aftermirage 518.6
spectrum analysis
  361.9
speculate
  consider 477.11
  theorize 498.8
  gamble 514.17
  ~ in the market
  831.23
speculation
  thought 477.2
  theory 498.1
  gamble 514.1
  gambling 514.6
  stock market ~
  831.19
speculative
  thoughtful 477.20
  experimental 488.11
  theoretical 498.13
  uncertain 513.14
  risky 695.10
speculator
  theorist 498.6
  gambler 514.16
  stock market ~
  831.11
speculum
  plumage 229.15
  mirror 442.5
speech
  language 578.1
  diction 586.1
  talking 592
  chatter 594.3
  conversation 595
  palaver 595.3
  elocution 597
  address 597.2
speechcraft
  linguistics 578.11
  elocution 597.1
speech defect 593.1
speechification
  speechmaking 597.1
  speech 597.2
speechify 597.8
speechmaker 597.4
speechmaking 597.1
speechless
  mute 450.14
  taciturn 611.7
speech sound 449.5
speed
  nouns velocity 268.1
  aviation 277.37
  WITH ALL SPEED
  promptly 131.15
  swiftly 268.24
  verbs go fast 268.9
  hasten 707.4
  facilitate 730.6
  further 783.17
  SPEED UP
  accelerate 268.15
  hasten 707.4
speed demon
  speeder 268.6
  motorist 273.10
speeder
  runner 268.6

motorist 273.10
speedily
  promptly 131.15
  swiftly 268.21
speed of sound
  speed 268.3
  aviation 277.37
speedometer 268.8
speed tools 347.1
speed-up 268.5
speedway 655.6
speed writing 600.9
speedy
  sudden 113.5
  prompt 131.9
  fast 268.19
spell
  nouns turn 108
  bout 108.2
  distance 198.1
  short distance 199.2
  respite 709.2
  magic ~ 1034
  UNDER A SPELL
  1034.13
  verbs
  take turns 108.4
  substitute for 148.5
  mean 543.8
  form words 579.10
  spellbind 1034.8
  SPELL OUT
  itemize 8.5
  explain 550.11
  spell 579.10
spellbind orate 597.9
  cast a spell 1034.8
spellbinder
  orator 597.6
  charmer 1033.9
spellbinding
  interesting 528.20
  bewitching 1034.12
spellbound
  interested 528.18
  astonished 918.8
  under a spell
  1034.13
spellcraft 1033.1
**spelldown, spelling-
  down, spelling,**
  etc. 579.7
speller, spelling book
  603.8
spelling bee
  spelling 579.7
  bee 920.12
spell-struck 1034.13
spence
  dining room 191.11
  larder 658.8
Spencerian 499.11
Spencerianism 321.4
Spencerian writing
  600.5
spend
  ~ time 105.6
  undergo 150.8
  employ 654.9
  use 663.11,13
  consume 664.2

expend 841.5
  waste 852.4
spendable 663.22
spend-all 852.2
spender
  expender 841.4
  spendthrift 852.2
spending
  consumption 664.1
  expenditure 841.1
spending money
  833.18
spendings 841.2
spendthrift
  nouns 852.2
  adjs. 852.8
Spenser 607.17
spent used up 664.6
  worn out 690.35
  tired out 715.8
  paid 839.22
  wasted 852.9
sperm 405.7
spermary gland 310.9
  genitals 418.8
spermatia 405.7
spermatic
  procreative 168.16
  seminal 405.21
  testicular 418.18
spermatic cord 48.4
spermatic fluid 405.7
spermatiophore 405.9
spermatize 168.11
**spermatocyte, sperm-
  atogonium** 405.7
**spermatophyta, sperm-
  atophytes** 411.8
spermatophyte 410.3
**spermatozoa, sperm-
  atozoid, spermato-
  zoon** 405.7
**spermatozoal, sperm-
  atozoam, sperm-
  atozoic, spermic**
  405.21
sperm cell 405.7
spermogonium 405.9
spew
  nouns 308.8
  verbs erupt 161.12
  disgorge 308.23,24
  spit 310.6
sphacelate
  verbs 690.23
  adjs. diseased 684.45
  decayed 690.38
sphacelation
  gangrene 684.30
  decay 690.6
sphacelus 690.6
sphere
  nouns rank 29.2
  ~ of influence 171.4
  extent 178.1
  realm 179.2
  ball 254.2
  star 374.5
  earth 374.7
  atmosphere 401.2
  ~ of work 654.4

spiritual wife 987.17
spirituosity 376.1
spirituous 994.46
spiritus 1032.17
spirit world 376.1
spirit writing 1032.6
spiroid 253.8
spirometer 400.6
spissitude
  density 353.1
  viscidity 388.2
spit
  nouns
    spitting image 20.6
    point of land 255.8
    saliva 310.3
    turnspit 328.15
    hissing 456.1
  verbs pierce 264.15
    expectorate 310.6
    rain 393.9
    hiss 456.2
    transfix 796.27
SPIT IT OUT 554.8
SPIT UPON 964.4
spit and image 20.6
spit-and-run 433.8
spite 937.6
IN SPITE OF 33.9
IN SPITE OF ONESELF
  621.8
spiteful 937.19
spitfire
  violent person 161.9
  irascible person
    949.11
spitnew 122.10
spitting distance
  199.2
spitting image 20.6
spittle 310.3
splanchnic 224.12
splanchnology
  enterology 224.7
  organology 244.7
splash
  nouns blotch 373.3
    splatter 391.5
    swash 394.8
    mark 566.4
    blotch 677.3
    splurge 902.4
  verbs wet 391.12
    swash 394.20
    ripple 451.11
    spatter 677.5
    dirty 680.20
    splurge 902.13
MAKE A SPLASH
  splurge 902.13
  be famous 912.10
splashing 391.6
splashy muddy 388.14
  wet 391.16
  miry 399.3
  showy 902.19
splat 377.3
splatter
  nouns 391.5
  verbs wet 391.12
    spot 677.5

dirty 680.20
splattering 391.6
splay
  nouns 196.1
  verbs 196.6
  adjs. 196.11
splayed 196.11
splayfoot
  nouns foot 211.5
    deformity 248.3
  adjs. 248.12
splaying 196.11
spleen gland 310.9
  ill humor 949.1
  resentment 950.3
spleeny 949.19
splendacious 902.21
splendent
  bright 334.32
  illustrious 912.20
splendid
  bright 334.32
  excellent 672.13
  beautiful 898.19
  grandiose 902.21
  illustrious 912.20
splendidness 898.6
splendor
  brightness 334.4
  beauty 898.6
  magnificence 902.5
  illustriousness 912.6
splendorous
  beautiful 898.19
  illustrious 912.20
splendrous
  bright 334.32
  beautiful 898.19
  illustrious 912.20
splenetic
  glandular 310.8
  ill-humored 949.19
splenic fever 684.10
splice tie 47.9
  interlace 221.7
  marry 931.15
splint
  nouns 685.28
  verbs 687.33
splinter
  nouns
    small amount 35.3
    piece 55.3
    thinness 204.7
TO SPLINTERS 49.27
  verbs 49.12
splinter group 786.5
splintery 359.4
split
  nouns break 49.3
    cleft 200.2
    falling-out 793.4
  verbs sever 49.10
    crack 49.11
    partition 49.18
    bisect 92.3
    open 264.11
    ~ the atom 325.16
    blab 554.6
    inform on 555.11
    quarrel 793.11

apportion 814.7
  laugh 874.9
SPLIT HAIRS
  differentiate 16.6
  quibble 482.9
  discriminate 491.6
SPLIT THE DIFFER-
  ENCE
  average 32.2
  compromise 805.2
  share 813.6
SPLIT THE EARS
  deafen 448.6
  be loud 452.6
  grate on 457.10
SPLIT UP
  partition 49.18
  separate 49.19
  disband 75.9
  apportion 814.7
  divorce 933.5
  adjs. severed 49.22
  divided 92.4
  cleft 200.7
split infinitive 584.4
split-level 190.5
split personality
  psychosis 472.4
  dissociation 688.27
split schedule 108.3
split second 113.3
split ticket 742.20
splitting
  nouns severance 49.2
  apportionment
    814.1
  adjs. violent 161.15
  dashing 268.19
split-up 75.3
splotch
  nouns color 373.3
    blotch 677.3
  verbs color 373.7
    spot 677.5
splurge
  nouns 902.4
  verbs 902.13
splurgy 902.19
splutter
  nouns flutter 323.4
    bustle 705.4
    bluster 909.1
  verbs flutter 323.12
    mumble 593.8
    bluster 909.3
spoil
  nouns 822.11
  verbs impair 690.11
    go bad 690.23
    frustrate 728.15
    botch 732.12
    pamper 757.7
    plunder 822.15
SPOIL FOR 632.16
spoilage 690.5
spoilation 822.5
spoiled
  deteriorated
    690.28,38
  pampered 757.11

spoiled child
  mama's boy 757.5
  favorite 929.13
spoiler 823.6
spoils
  ~ of office 742.36
  booty 822.11
spoilsport
  marplot 728.9
  kill-joy 870.14
spoils system 742.36
spoke radius 203.3
  rung 313.5
  hindrance 728.7
PUT A SPOKE IN ONE'S
  WHEELS
  disable 157.9
  thwart 728.15
spoken 592.20
spoken language 578.4
spoken word 592.3
spokesman
  informant 555.5
  speaker 597.4
  deputy 779.5
  mediator 803.3
spoliate 822.15
spoliation 822.5
spoliative 822.21
spoliator 823.6
spondaic 607.22
spondee 607.9
spondulics, spondulix
  833.2
sponge
  nouns
    porousness 264.8
    absorbent 305.6
    animal 414.4
    bath 679.4,7
    dressing 685.28
    eraser 691.9
    sycophant 905.4
    drunkard 994.11
  verbs absorb 305.13
    moisten 391.12
    dry 392.6
    wash 679.18
    obliterate 691.16
    extort 822.19
    clear of debt 840.9
    be a parasite 905.11
spongeous 305.17
sponger 905.4
Spongiae 414.4
sponging
  nouns
    absorption 305.6
    washing 679.4
    clearing debt 840.2
  adjs. 905.13
sponging house 759.9
Spongiozoa 414.4
spongy
  porous 264.20
  absorbent 305.17
  soft 356.11
  pulpy 389.6
  miry 399.3
sponsion 770.10

sponsor
nouns
  guarantor 770.8
  financer 834.9
verbs
  guarantee 770.11
  patronize 783.15
  finance 834.15
  accept responsibility
    960.8
sponsorship
  guarantorship
    770.10
  patronage 783.4
  financing 834.2
spontaneity
  automation 348.1
  voluntariness 620.2
  involuntariness
    637.5
spontaneous
  automatic 348.25
  instinctive 480.6
  voluntary 620.7
  involuntary 637.14
spontaneous com-
  bustion 328.5
spoof
nouns 616.1,7
verbs
  jam radar 345.18
  fool 616.14
spoofery 616.1
spook
nouns 1015.1
verbs 1015.6
spooked 1015.10
spooky ghostly 1015.9
  haunted 1015.10
spoon
nouns 347.3
verbs ladle 270.16
  fish 653.10
  make love 930.13
spoondrift 404.2
spooner 929.11
spoonerism
  malapropism 517.6
  word 580.3
spoon food 307.10
spoonful 35.2
spooning 930.1
spoony
nouns 470.6
adjs. silly 469.8
  affectionate 929.24
spoor 566.7
sporadic
  dispersed 75.10
  irregular 138.3
  epidemic 684.47
sporal 405.21
spore 405.9
sporogenesis 166.6
sporogenous
  genetic 166.24
  sporal 405.21
sporoid 405.21
sporophore, sporo-
  phyte 405.9
sporous 405.21

Sporozoa 414.3
sport
nouns
  gambler 514.16
  hunting 653.2
  ~ of fortune 727.7
  ~ of kings 794.11
  good loser 810.4
  amusement 876.2,9
  plaything 876.16
  sportsman 876.20
  jest 879.6
  banter 880.1
  dandy 901.9
verbs wear 230.43
  gamble 514.17
  hunt 653.9
  play 876.25
  flaunt 902.17
SPORT ONE'S OAK
  924.4
sporting
nouns
  gambling 514.6
  hunting 653.2
adjs. sportive 876.32
  fair 974.9
sportive
  mischievous 736.6
  gay 868.14
  playful 876.31
  facetious 879.17
sports
nouns games 876.8
  types of ~ 876.34
adjs. 876.32
sportscast
nouns 343.21
verbs 343.28
sportscaster 343.26
sportsman
  gambler 514.16
  hunter 653.5
  gamester 876.20
sportsmanship 974.3
sportswear
  clothing 230.1
  merchandise 829.3
sportula 816.5
sporty dressy 642.13
  showy 902.19
sporule 405.9
sposh mud 388.8
  slime 680.8
sposhy muddy 388.14
  miry 399.3
spot
nouns location 183.1
  short distance 199.2
  radar signal 345.11
  fleck 373.3
  mark 566.4
  limelight 609.22
  blemish 677.3
  soil 680.5
  predicament 729.4
  stigma 913.6
HIT THE HIGH SPOTS
  speed 268.9
  skim over 484.34
  slight 532.8

  summarize 605.5
HIT THE SPOT 26.8
IN A SPOT 729.20
IN SPOTS
  haphazardly 62.17
  intermittently 72.5
  scatteringly 75.13
  sparsely 102.8
  irregularly 138.4
  here and there
    183.26
ON THE SPOT
  instantly 113.6
  now 120.3
  promptly 131.15
  here 183.24
  at sight 438.24
  in danger 695.13
verbs sprinkle 75.7
  locate 183.11
  radar 345.17
  speckle 373.7
  see 438.12
  detect 487.5
  recognize 535.13
  mark 566.18
  stain 677.5
spot check 484.7
spotless
  faultless 675.6
  clean 679.23
  innocent 982.7
  chaste 986.4
spotlight
nouns light 334.18
  publicity 557.4
  limelight 609.22
verbs
  illuminate 334.28
  emphasize 670.13
spots 832.10
spotted
  diversified 19.4
  sprinkled 75.11
  speckled 373.13
  soiled 680.23
spotted fever 684.9
spotter aviator 278.3
  informer 555.6
  spy 779.9
spotty varied 19.4
  intermittent 72.4
  irregular 138.3
  speckled 373.13
spousal 931.19
spousals 931.4
spouse 931.7
spouseless 932.7
spout
nouns outpour 308.7
  waterspout 393.2
  jet 394.9
  conduit 395.8
  pawnshop 818.4
verbs erupt 161.12
  flow out 302.13
  spew 308.23
  jet 394.21
  chatter 594.6
  declaim 597.9
  overact 609.35

  pawn 770.12
spouter geyser 394.9
  speaker 597.4
sprain
nouns 690.7
verbs 690.13
sprawl
nouns lying 213.2
  fall 314.3
verbs spread 196.6
  be long 201.8
  lie 213.5
  fall 314.8
  repose 709.6
sprawling
  spreading 196.11
  lying 213.9
spray
nouns member 55.4
  shots 284.5
  sprinkle 391.5
  sprayer 391.8
  jet 394.9
  atomizer 400.5
  foam 404.2
  foliage 410.16
  flowers 410.23
  perfumer 435.6
  gunfire 796.10
verbs sprinkle 391.12
  squirt 394.21
  atomize 400.7
sprayer 391.8
spray gun 572.19
spread
nouns dispersion 75.1
  multiplication 100.4
  extent 178.1
  size 194.1
  expansion 196.1
  breadth 203.1
  cover 227.10
  divergence 298.1
  meal 306.5,9
  heading 483.2
  publication 557.1
  advertisement 557.6
  option 831.21
  price 832.9
verbs increase 38.6
  disperse 75.5
  generalize 79.8
  multiply 100.6
  extend 178.7
  expand 196.6
  sprawl 201.8
  widen 203.4
  open 264.11
  diverge 298.5
  radiate 298.6
  publish 557.10
  be published 557.16
SPREAD ON 227.26
SPREAD ONESELF
  brag 908.6
  be hospitable 923.8
SPREAD OVER
  cover 227.21
  overrun 311.5
SPREAD SAIL 274.21
adjs. dispersed 75.10

yell 458.1
row 793.6
verbs blow 402.23
yell 458.6
squeal 459.2
wail 873.11
squally 402.26
squalor
slovenry 62.6
dirtiness 680.3
squamous 226.7
squander 852.3
squandered 852.9
squandering 852.1
squantum 876.4
square
nouns old fogy 123.8
plot 179.4
city block 182.6
plaza 182.7
T ~ 212.6
yard 235.3
geometric figure
250.14
meal 306.8
unsophisticate
734.3
ON THE SQUARE
972.14
verbs fit 26.12
equalize 30.7
compensate 33.5
quadrate 96.3
make perpendicular
212.9
bribe 649.3
GET SQUARED AWAY
68.7
SQUARE ACCOUNTS
pay 839.13
retaliate 953.7
punish 1008.10
SQUARE OFF 794.15
SQUARE WITH 26.9
adjs. even with 30.8
rectangular 250.9
exact 515.15
honest 972.14
just 974.8
advs.
perpendicularly
212.13
directly 289.26
exactly 515.19
square dance 877.2
square deal 974.3
square-dealing
honest 972.14
just 974.9
squarehead 470.4
squarely
directly 289.26
exactly 515.19
square meal 306.8
square peg in a round
hole 27.4
square-rigged 276.17
square shooter 972.8
square-shooting
honest 972.14

just 974.9
squash
nouns blow 282.4
mud 388.8
pulp 389.2
hissing 456.1
verbs soften 356.6
mash 360.9
pulp 389.5
silence 450.8
hiss 456.2
refute 505.5
hush up 612.9
extinguish 691.15
suppress 758.8
squashing 758.2
squashy
soft 356.13
muddy 388.14
pulpy 389.6
miry 399.3
squat
nouns 316.3
verbs settle 183.18
crouch 207.4
cower 316.8
sit down 316.9
adjs. squatty 202.10
low 207.6
squatter
nouns 189.9
verbs 75.7
squattiness
stubbiness 202.2
lowness 207.1
squattish 202.10
squatty stubby 202.10
low 207.6
squaw woman 420.5
wife 931.9
squawk
nouns screech 457.4
objection 520a.2
complaint 873.4
verbs screech 457.7
croak 459.5
object 520a.5
confess 554.7
say 592.17
complain 873.13
squawking
nouns 873.4
adjs. 457.14
squawky 457.14
squdgy squashy 356.13
squishy 389.6
squeak
nouns 457.4
verbs screech 457.7
squeal 459.2
confess 554.7
squeaker 555.6
squeakiness 457.1
squeaky 457.13
squeal
nouns radio
interference 343.24
screech 457.4
yell 458.1
verbs screech 457.7

yell 458.6
howl 459.2
inform on 555.11
say 592.17
squealer 555.6
squeamish
nauseated 684.42
fastidious 894.10
squeamishness
nausea 684.22
fastidiousness 894.2
squeeze
noun facsimile 24.6
crowd 74.4
crisis 129.4
compression 197.2
narrow escape 630.2
crux 729.7
embrace 930.2
verbs facsimile 22.8
compress 197.8
cram 353.9
compel 754.6
wrest from 820.19
extort 822.19
hug 930.16
SQUEEZE IN
intrude 237.7
enter 301.7
thrust 303.6
SQUEEZE OUT 304.14
squeezing
compression 197.2
extraction 304.6
squelch
nouns 456.1
verbs silence 450.8
hiss 456.2
refute 505.5
extinguish 691.15
repress 758.8
squelcher 505.3
squelching 758.2
squelchy
squashy 356.13
muddy 388.14
pulpy 389.6
miry 399.3
squib fuse 330.7
lampoon 969.5
squiffer 464.12
squiffy 994.40
squinch
nouns 439.5
verbs 439.9
squint
nouns 439.5
verbs look askance
438.19
close eyes 439.9
squinting, squinty
439.11
squire
nouns escort 73.5
attendant 748.4
nobleman 916.5
lover 929.11
judge 1000.4
verbs escort 73.8
court 930.20
squirearchy 916.3

squireen 916.5
squirm
nouns 323.7
verbs wriggle 323.15
be excited 855.18
SQUIRM OUT OF
630.8
squirrel cage 640.5
squirt
nouns outpour 308.7
jet 394.9
verbs spew 308.23
spurt 394.21
squish
nouns 306a.39
verbs 389.5
squishy
squashy 356.13
pulpy 389.6
S.R.O. 185.4
sruti 1019.7
stab
nouns pang 423.2
guess 498.3
injury 690.7
attempt 712.2
thrust 796.3
verbs pierce 264.15
pain 423.7
wound 690.13
attack 796.27
grieve 864.14
STAB IN THE BACK
slander 969.11
be treacherous
973.12
stabbing
nouns 796.11
adjs. acrimonious
160.12
painful 423.10
penetrating 855.32
caustic 937.21
stabile 572.11
stabilitate 142.8
stability
substantiality 3.1
permanence 140
firmness 142
strength 158.3
reliability 512.4
stabilization 142.2
stabilize 142.8
stabilized 142.14
stabilizer
types of ~ 142.21
plane part 279.16
stable
nouns barn 190.16
~ of horses 413.19
filthy place 680.11
verbs lodge 187.11
enclose 235.5
adjs. substantial 3.5
firm 142.13
strong 158.16
reliable 512.17
safe 696.5
stable boy, stableman
415.2

staccato
  nouns music 461.25,
    31
  note 462.14
  adjs. 461.54
stack
  nouns large amount
    34.4
  heap 74.9
  book ~ 603.20
  verbs pile 74.18
  load 183.16
  STACK THE CARDS
  cheat 616.18
  prearrange 639.3
  STACK UP
  fare 7.6
  heap 74.18
  STACK UP WITH
  be like 20.7
  compare with 490.7
stacked
  accumulated 74.21
  prearranged 639.5
stacks 34.4
stack-up 244.1
stadholder,
    stadtholder 747.14
stadium amphitheater
    609.17
  arena 800.1
staff
  nouns support 215.2
  stave 276.2
  ~ of life 306a.27
  music ~ 461.29
  insignia 567.4
  scepter 737.8
  personnel 748.12
  committee 753.3
  pastoral ~ 1039.3
  verbs 657.8
staff officer 747.22
stag
  nouns deer 413.7
  male animal 419.8
  stockbroker 831.10
  party 920.10
  verbs 831.23
stag dance 877.2
stage
  nouns degree 29.2
  period 107.1
  scaffold 215.12
  platform 215.13
  tier 226.1
  scene 232.2
  stagecoach 271.11
  theater ~ 609.20
  arena 800.1
  ON STAGE 609.40
  THE STAGE 609.1
  verbs dramatize
    609.32
  perform 703.8
stagecoach 271.11
stagecraft 609.3
stage direction 749.1
stage director 609.27
stage fright
  nervousness 857.1

fear 889.4
stagehand 609.28
stage manager 609.27
stage name 581.8
stage play 609.4
stage player 610.1
stage presentation
    609.13
stagese 578.7
stage-set, stage setting
  setting 232.2
  theater 609.23
stage-struck 609.37
stage whisper 451.4
stageworthy 609.37
stagewright 609.26
stagger
  nouns gait 272.14
  aviation 277.22
  flounder 323.8
  attempt 712.2
  verbs fluctuate 141.5
  zigzag 218.12
  walk 272.27
  flounder 323.15
  ~ belief 502.7
  startle 538.8
  be irresolute 625.6
  excite 855.14
  frighten 889.14
  astonish 918.5
  be drunk 994.33
  STAGGER ALONG
  go slow 269.6
  depart 300.6
staggered
  zigzag 218.21
  startled 538.13
  astonished 918.8
staggerer
  surprise 538.2
  puzzle 547.7
staggering
  unbelievable 502.10
  startling 538.11
  astounding 918.11
staggers 684.10
staging 215.12
stagnancy 267.4
stagnant 267.12
stagnate vegetate 1.10
  be inert 267.8
stagnation
  vegetation 1.6
  inertness 267.4
stagy theatrical 609.37
  affected 901.15
  pretentious 902.24
staid sensible 466.18
  unimaginative 534.5
  composed 856.14
  solemn 869.3
staidness
  levelheadedness
    466.6
  unimaginativeness
    534.1
  composure 856.4
  decorousness 869.1
stain
  nouns color 361.1,7

blemish 677.3
stigma 913.6
  verbs color 361.13
  blemish 677.6
  soil 680.18
  stigmatize 913.9
stained colored 361.17
  spotted 373.13
  discolored 677.9
  soiled 680.23
stained glass window
    572.12
staining 361.10
stainless
  faultless 675.6
  clean 679.23
  innocent 982.7
  chaste 986.4
stair degree 29.1
  step 313.5
staircase, stairs,
    stairway 313.3
stake
  nouns post 216.7
  burning 328.5
  wager 514.3
  pledge 770.3
  estate 808.4
  financing 834.2
  execution 1009.5
  AT STAKE 770.15
  verbs bet 514.19
  pledge 770.12
  finance 834.15
  STAKE ON 500.13
  STAKE OUT 758.10
staked 770.15
stake horse 413.19
stakeout 820.2
staker
  race horse 413.19
  financer 834.9
stake race 794.13
stakes 514.4
staking 514.6
stalactite, stalagmite
    227.15
stale
  nouns 309.5
  verbs 309.12
  adjs. old 123.14
  insipid 429.2
  disused 666.10
  spoiled 690.39
  trite 881.9
stalemate 729.5
staleness
  antiquation 123.3
  insipidness 429.1
  triteness 881.3
stalk
  nouns shaft 216.1
  gait 272.14
  stem 410.19
  verbs ~ about 79.9
  walk 272.27
  hunt 653.9
  strut 902.15
stalker 653.5
stalking 612.4

stalking-horse
  horse 413.18
  blind 613.3
  candidate 744.9
stall
  nouns procrastination
    132.5
  hut 190.9
  stable 190.16
  compartment 191.2
  aviation 277.10
  theater ~ 609.19
  store 830.3
  diocese 1035.8
  church ~ 1040.13
  verbs temporize
    132.10
  stick 144.7
  stop 144.11
  ~ a plane 277.51
  fail 723.15
  hinder 728.13
stallion
  studhorse 413.12
  male animal 419.8
stalwart
  nouns strong man
    158.6
  partisan 742.28
  brave man 891.8
  adjs. strong 158.13
  corpulent 194.18
  courageous 891.17
stalwartness
  strength 158.1
  courage 891.1
stamen 410.26
stamina strength 158.1
  pluck 622.3
  courage 891.5
stammel 367.7
stammer
  nouns 593.3
  verbs 593.7
stammering
  nouns stuttering
    593.3
  neurosis 688.25
  adjs. 593.12
stamp
  nouns nature 5.3
  die 25.6
  kind 61.3
  characteristic 80.3
  form 245.1
  beat 282.10
  endorsement 520.4
  sign 566.2
  imprint 566.6
  label 566.12
  graver 576.11
  type 601.3,6
  postage ~ 602.6
  verbs infix 142.10
  form 245.6
  walk 272.27
  ~ the feet 282.2
  impress 535.18
  mark 566.19
  engrave 576.13
  letter 579.9

print 601.12
impress upon
853.17
STAMP OUT
extinguish 331.7
exterminate 691.15
stamp collector 74.14
stampede
nouns 889.1
verbs 889.15
stamping ground
190.23
stance 215.5
stanch
verbs 265.7
adjs. strong 158.16
close 265.12
dependable 512.17
resolute 622.12
devoted 925.20
faithful 972.20
stanchel, stancher,
stanchion 216.4
stanchness
strength 158.3
dependability 512.4
resoluteness 622.2
devotedness 925.7
fidelity 972.7
stand
nouns set 74.11
stop 144.2
position 183.3
footing 215.5
pedestal 215.8
table 215.15
standstill 267.3
growth 410.2
playing engagement
609.12
impasse 729.5
resistance 790.1
store 830.3
MAKE A STAND
AGAINST
oppose 788.3
resist 790.3
verbs exist 1.8
endure 110.6
be present 185.6
be quiescent 267.7
~ around 706.10
withstand 790.2,3
afford 841.6
tolerate 859.5
HAVE ALL ONE CAN
STAND 662.5
NOT STAND FOR
not permit 776.4
discountenance
967.11
NOT STAND UP 517.7
STAND A CHANCE
have a chance
155.13
be liable 174.3
be possible 508.4
STAND ALOOF
keep one's distance
198.7

be uncommunicative
611.5
avoid 629.6
let alone 704.4
refuse 774.3
be unsociable 921.4
snub 964.7
abstain 990.7
STAND APART
differ 16.5
stand alone 89.6
STAND BEHIND
sponsor 770.11
back up 783.13
STAND BY
border on 199.9
stay near 199.12
second 783.13
navigation 274.79
STAND FAIR TO
have a chance
155.13
be liable 174.3
be possible 508.4
seem likely 510.3
promise 542.10
STAND FAST
remain firm 142.12
be quiescent 267.7
be determined 622.9
persevere 623.10
resist 790.5
STAND FOR
sail for 274.37
typify 570.8
be a candidate
742.42
sponsor 770.11
volunteer 771.10
permit 775.11
be deputy 779.13
tolerate 859.5
STAND IN WITH
have influence
171.10
side with 784.6
be friends 925.9
STAND NO
NONSENSE
be determined 622.9
insist 751.7
STAND OFF
temporize 132.10
keep one's distance
198.7
sail from 274.38
recede 296.2
STAND ON
rest on 215.23
rely on 500.13
depend on 506.6
insist upon 751.7
be incumbent on
960.5
STAND ON CEREMONY
644.6
STAND ONE'S GROUND
stand fast 142.12
be determined 622.9
resist 790.5

STAND ON ONE'S
OWN LEGS
volunteer 620.4
be independent
760.18
STAND OUT
loom 34.7
project 255.9
be seen 443.4
be obvious 553.7
be obstinate 624.7
STAND OVER
postpone 132.8
watch over 697.18
govern 739.11
supervise 745.10
STAND PAT
be conservative
140.6
stand fast 142.12
gambling 514.19
STAND TOGETHER
be consistent 26.10
league 52.4
co-operate 784.4
STAND UP
keep one waiting
132.6
not weaken 158.9
rise 212.7
straighten 249.4
stand the test
488.10
hold true 515.7
persevere 623.4
withstand 790.2
treat 839.19
STAND UP FOR
guarantee 770.11
plead for 1004.10
STAND UP TO
resist 790.3
brave 891.11
meet an obligation
960.10
standard
nouns model 25.1
grade 29.1
principle 84.4
pedestal 215.8
post 216.4
measure 489.2
flag 567.6
precept 749.2
paragon 983.4
adjs. average 32.3
usual 84.8
authoritative 512.18
customary 640.14
regulation 749.5
orthodox 1022.8
UP TO STANDARD
672.17
standardbearer
politician 744.7
leader 746.5
officer 747.23
standardize 84.6
standard of living
849.5
standards 955.1

standard time 114.3
stand-by actor 610.6
mainstay 785.8
standee 609.31
Ständerat 740.3
stand-in
substitute 148.2
influence 171.2
deputy 779.1
good terms 925.3
standing
nouns state 7.1
rank 29.2
durability 110.1
permanence 140.1
position 183.3
footing 215.5
reputation 912.4
OF LONG STANDING
durable 110.10
traditional 123.12
adjs. 267.12
standing army 798.23
standing order
rule 84.4
law 996.3
standing ovation 966.2
standoff
nouns tie 30.4
procrastination
132.5
TO A STANDOFF 30.13
adjs. reserved 611.8
haughty 910.12
unsociable 921.6
standoffishness
reserve 611.3
haughtiness 910.4
unsociability 921.2
standpat
nouns conservative
140.4
obstinate person
624.6
adjs. conservative
140.8
immovable 142.16
standpattism
conservation 140.3
inaction 704.1
standpipe 395.6
standpoint
position 183.3
viewpoint 438.7
attitude 523.2
standstill
nouns stop 144.2
motionlessness
267.3
impasse 729.5
AT A STANDSTILL
in statu quo 140.10
immovable 142.16
motionless 267.11
doing nothing 704.7
at an impasse
729.22
COME TO A
STANDSTILL 144.7
adjs. 140.8

standstillism
  conservatism 140.3
  inaction 704.1
stand-up 212.10
stanza
  musical ~ 461.24
  verse 607.11
  act 609.8
stapes 447.7
staple
  nouns main part 54.5
  raw material 377.1
  supply 658.2,4
  storehouse 658.6
  commodity 829.2
  market 830.2
  verbs 47.8
  adjs. 142.15
staples 829.1
star
  nouns heavenly body
    374.4
  insignia 567.5
  actor 610.5
  principal 670.10
  decoration 914.5
  verbs headline 609.32
  act 609.33
  emphasize 670.13,
    14
  adjs. 36.16
starboard
  nouns 242.1
  verbs 274.33
  adjs. 242.4
  advs. rightward 242.7
  ships 274.72
starboard tack 242.1
starbright 334.30
starch
  nouns energy 160.2
  semiliquid 388.5
  TAKE THE STARCH
    OUT OF 904.4
  adjs. 644.9
starched stiff 355.11
  formal 644.9
starchiness
  stiffness 355.2
  formality 644.1
starchy stiff 355.11
  viscid 338.12
stardom 609.1
stare
  nouns 438.5
  verbs gaze 438.16
  be curious 526.3
  wonder 918.4
  STARE ONE IN THE
    FACE
  come 121.6
  be imminent 151.2
  be seen 443.4
  be obvious 553.7
starfish 414.7
stargazer 374.22,23
stargazing 374.19,20
staring distinct 443.7
  obvious 553.11
stark
  adjs. downright 34.14

mere 35.9
  rigid 355.11
  advs. 56.16
stark-blind 440.8
stark-mad 472.28
stark-naked 231.14
stark-staring
  downright 34.14
  distinct 443.7
  obvious 553.11
starless 336.14
starlessness 336.1
starlight 334.12
starlit 334.38
Star of the Sea 1013.5
starry starlike 257.18
  luminous 334.30
  celestial 374.25
starry-eyed 533.24
stars
  heavenly body 374.4
  fate 638.2
  UNDER THE STARS
    374.29
Stars and Stripes 567.6
star-shaped 257.18
starshine 334.12
star-spangled
  starlit 334.38
  starry 374.25
Star-Spangled Banner
  567.6
star-studded
  starlit 334.38
  starry 374.25
start
  nouns advantage 36.2
  beginning 68.1
  jerk 285.3
  departure 300.2,5
  ~ of surprise 538.3
  GET A HEAD START
  anticipate 131.6
  precede 291.2
  HEAD START
  advantage 36.2
  earliness 131.1
  MAKE A FRESH START
    143.6
  verbs come apart 49.7
  begin 68.6
  set going 284.14
  set forth 300.7
  jump 317.5
  be startled 538.5
  startle 538.8
  touch off 646.18
  ~ game 653.9
  break open 690.24
  broach 771.5
  take fright 889.11
  START ALL OVER
    143.6
  START GOING
  inaugurate 68.10
  set going 284.14
  START IN
  begin 68.6
  set to work 714.15
  START UP
  begin 68.7

inaugurate 68.10
  stick up 255.9
  set going 284.14
  ascend 313.9
  jump 317.5
  appear 445.9
starter 413.19
starting 300.2
starting point
  beginning 68.1
  departure 300.5
startle start 538.5
  surprise 538.8
  take fright 889.11
  frighten 889.14
  astonish 918.5
startled 538.13
startling
  surprising 538.11
  alarmed 702.7
  frightening 889.27
  astonishing 918.11
startlish
  excitable 855.29
  skittish 889.22
startlishness
  excitability 855.9
  skittishness 889.2
start-off
  beginning 68.1
  departure 300.2
starvation 660.4
starvation treatment
  687.18
starve be cold 332.10
  freeze 333.11
  die 407.19
  kill 408.13
  crave 632.18
  feel hungry 632.19
  be poor 836.5
  scrimp 850.7
starved thin 204.19
  frozen 332.16
  hungry 632.26
starveling
  nouns 836.4
  adjs. 204.19
starving 632.26
star worship 1031.1
stash
  nouns 613.4
  verbs cache 613.8
  store 658.10
stasis 267.4
stat photostatic copy
  24.5
  photostat 575.6
state
  nouns condition 7
  district 179.5
  country 180.1
  community 416.2
  ~ of mind 523.4
  pomp 902.6
  verbs specify 80.9
  postulate 498.12
  affirm 521.4
  announce 557.12
  expound 560.16
  remark 592.15

propound 771.6
  adjs. 416.13
statecraft 742.3
stated uniform 17.5
  fixed 142.15
  measured 489.14
  conditional 506.8
  certain 512.20
statehood 180.6
Statehouse 740.14
stateliness
  eloquence 598.6
  grandeur 902.5
  dignity 903.2
stately
  adjs. eloquent 598.14
  ceremonious 644.8
  grandiose 902.21
  dignified 903.12
  advs. 903.14
statement
  capitulation 87.5
  list 88.4
  premise 481.8
  topic 483.1
  testimony 504.3
  declaration 521.1
  information 555.1
  announcement
    557.2
  accounting 568.6
  remark 592.4
  narration 606.3
  proposal 771.2
  bill 843.3
  legal declaration
    1002.7
statemonger 744.4
stateroom
  room 191.9,10
  cabin 276.27
States, the 180.3
States-General 740.2
statesman, states-
  woman 744.2
statesmanlike,
  statesmanly 744.12
statesmanship 742.3
Statesman's Yearbook
  568.7
state-wide 79.13
static
  nouns 343.24
  adjs. inert 267.12
  electric 341.27
static condition 140.2
statics force 156.7
  mechanics 346.2
station
  nouns state 7.1
  rank 29.2
  position 183.3
  visual tracking ~
    280.8
  radio ~ 343.9
  office 654.5
  health ~ 687.29
  police ~ 759.9
  prestige 912.4
  verbs 183.12

stationary
  immovable 142.16
  motionless 267.11
station break 343.22
stationed 183.19
stationer 828.3
stationers 830.5
stationery 377.6;
  600.30
station house railroad
  station 183.3
  prison 759.9
stationmaster 273.13
statism 739.8
statistic(al) 87.15
statistics, statistology
  87.7
statuary
  nouns figure 570.4
  sculpture 573.1
  sculptor 577.6
  adjs. 573.7
statue 570.4
statuelike
  motionless 267.11
  sculptural 573.7
statuesque 573.7
stature 206.1
status state 7.1,5
  rank 29.2
  class 61.2
  position 183.3
  prestige 912.4
status quo 140.2
status seeker 917.10
statute 996.3
statutory 996.10
staunch
  verbs 265.7
  adjs. strong 158.16
  dependable 512.17
  resolute 622.12
  devoted 925.20
staunchness
  strength 158.3
  dependability 512.4
  resoluteness 622.2
  devotedness 925.7
stave
  nouns support 215.2
  staff 216.2
  rung 313.5
  stick 377.3
  music staff 461.29
  stanza 607.11
  verbs
  STAVE IN 264.14
  STAVE OFF
  postpone 132.8
  prevent 728.14
  fend off 797.10
staving 34.13
stay
  nouns tenacity 50.2
  ~ of execution
    132.2
  stop 144.2
  pause 144.3
  sojourn 187.5
  support 215.2

perseverance 623.1
respite 709.2
prevention 728.2,7
verbs adhere 50.5
endure 110.6
delay 132.7
postpone 132.8
wait 132.11
continue 143.3
cease 144.6
stop 144.11
~ away 186.7
reside 187.8
sojourn 187.9
support 215.22
be quiescent 267.7
retard 269.9
persevere 623.4
cure 692.15
prevent 728.13
~ at home 922.8
STAY FOR 537.6
STAY IT OUT
  not weaken 158.9
  persevere 623.4
  resist 790.5
STAY ONE'S HAND
  cease 144.6
  give up 631.7
STAY PUT
  adhere 50.5
  stand fast 142.12
  be quiescent 267.7
stay-at-home
  nouns 922.6
  adjs. untraveled
    267.13
  recluse 922.11
staying durable 110.10
  permanent 140.7
  dwelling 187.14
staying power 623.1
stays corset 230.23
  rigging 276.31
stead position 183.1
  place 183.5
  advantage 663.4
  IN STEAD OF 148.12
steadfast uniform 17.5
  durable 110.10
  constant 135.5
  stable 142.13
  reliable 512.17
  persevering 623.7
  faithful 972.20
steadfastness
  uniformity 17.1
  durability 110.1
  constancy 135.2
  stability 142.1
  reliability 512.4
  perseverance 623.1
  fidelity 972.7
steadily regularly 17.8
  constantly 135.7
  perseveringly 623.8
  faithfully 972.24
steadiness
  substantiality 3.1
  uniformity 17.1
  constancy 135.2

stability 142.1
reliability 512.4
perseverance 623.1
inexcitability 856.1
unnervousness 858.1
steading 412.8
steady
  nouns 929.10
  verbs 142.8
  adjs. substantial 3.5
  uniform 17.5
  constant 135.5
  stable 142.13
  reliable 512.17
  persevering 623.7
  safe 696.5
  inexcitable 856.10
  unnervous 858.2
  faithful 972.20
steak 306a.18
steal
  nouns theft 822.10
  booty 822.11
  bargain 847.3
  verbs creep 272.25
  sneak 613.10
  thieve 822.13
STEAL A MARCH UPON
  get ahead of 36.9
  anticipate 131.6
  precede 291.2
  evade 629.7
  circumvent 733.11
STEAL AWAY 629.12
STEAL ONE'S STUFF
  copy 22.5
  borrow 819.4
STEAL ONE'S THUNDER
  728.15
STEAL UPON 538.6
stealage theft 822.1
  booty 822.11
stealer 823.1
stealing creeping 272.9
  theft 822.1
stealth 612.4
stealthily 612.20
stealthy 612.14
stealy 822.20
steam
  nouns power 156.1
  hot water 327.9
  water 391.3
  vapor 400.1
  GET UP STEAM 718.9
  GO FULL STEAM
    AHEAD 705.12
  PUT ON STEAM 268.15
  UNDER STEAM 274.67
  verbs navigate 274.13
  be hot 327.21
  heat 328.17
  cook 329.4
  vaporize 400.7
steam bath 679.7
steamboat
  nouns 276.4
  verbs 274.13
steam cleaning 679.2
steamer
  nouns 276.4

BY STEAMER 270.19
  verbs 274.13
steam heat 327.1
steam-heat 328.17
steam-heated 328.28
steam heating 328.1
steaming
  nouns 400.4
  adjs. 400.8
steam roller
  pulverizer 360.7
  force 754.2
steamship 276.4
steam shovel 256.10
steam whistle 452.5
steamy 400.8
steed 413.12
steel
  nouns strength 158.7
  knife 347.2
  hardness 355.6
  sword 799.4
  verbs strengthen
    158.11
  plate 227.28
  callous 854.6
STEEL ONESELF
  be determined 622.8
  be impenitent 872.3
  nerve oneself 891.13
  adjs. 382.16
Steel Age 107.6
steel-nerved 858.2
steel plate 576.7
steels 832.2
steelworks 717.4
steely 382.16
steep
  nouns height 206.2
  precipice 212.3
  verbs imbue 44.12
  extract 304.14
  soak 391.13
  adjs. high 206.19
  precipitous 218.18
  abstruse 547.12
  excessive 661.17
  difficult 729.16
  expensive 846.11
steeped 391.17
steeping
  extraction 304.6
  soaking 391.7
steeple 206.11
steeplechase
  jumping 317.3
  race 794.13
steeplechaser 413.19
steepness
  precipitousness
    218.6
  expensiveness 846.2
steer
  nouns bovine 413.8
  male animal 419.8
  tip 555.3
  verbs operate 163.5
  pilot 274.14
  guide 745.9
STEER A MIDDLE
  COURSE 804.6

stunning
  stupefying 422.8
  terrifying 889.28
  beautiful 898.19
  astounding 918.11
stunt
  nouns
    theatrical ~ 609.9
    feat 703.3
  verbs shorten 202.6
    do aerobatics
      277.46
stunted 195.12
stunting 277.10
stunt man 278.1
stupa tomb 409.16
  monument 568.11
  shrine 1040.4
stupe
  nouns tower 206.11
    dressing 685.28
  verbs 884.5
stupefaction
  lethargy 706.5
  apathy 854.4
stupefied
  stunned 422.6
  apathetic 854.13
  terrified 889.25
stupefy stun 422.3
  ~ emotionally
    854.8
  terrify 889.16
  astound 918.5
stupefying
  stunning 422.8
  terrifying 889.28
stupendous
  great 34.11
  extraordinary
    85.13
  huge 194.20
  wonderful 918.9
stupid
  nouns 470.3
  adjs.
    unintelligent 468.15
    foolish 469.8
    gullible 501.8
    express onless
      545.11
stupidity
  unintelligence 468.3
  foolishness 469.1,4
stupor
  unconsciousness
    422.2
  neurosis 688.22
  lethargy 706.5
  sleep 710.6
  apathy 854.4
stupration 987.6
sturdiness
  substantiality 3.1
  strength 158.1,3
sturdy
  substantial 3.5
  strong 158.13,16
stutter
  nouns 593.3
  verbs 593.7

stuttering
  nouns
    stammering 593.3
    neurosis 688.25
  adjs. 593.12
sty hovel 190.10
  filthy place 680.11
  swelling 684.28
Stygian dark 336.15
  hellish 1017.6
Stygian shore 407.4
style
  nouns mode 7.4
    kind 61.3
    calendar 114.8
    form 245.1
    flower part 410.26
    appearance 445.3
    ant ~ 572.9
    types of art
      ~ 572.24
    types of architectural
      ~ 572.26
    graver 576.11
    name 581.3
    diction 586.2
    fashion 642.1
    way 655.1
    IN STYLE 642.11
  verbs name 581.11
    phrase 583.4
styled called 581.14
  phrased 583.6
styleless 123.16
stylish 642.12
stylishness 642.2
stylist
  types of ~ 577.12
  mannerist 586.3
stylite recluse 922.5
  religious 1036.16
stylization 643.4
stylize 643.5
stylized 643.8
stylobate 215.6
stylus 464.18
stymie 728.13
styptic 197.6,11
Styx death 407.4
  Hades 1017.4
Styxian 1017.6
suasible 171.15
suasion 646.3
suasive 646.29
suave 934.18
suaveness, suavity
  934.5
sub
  nouns inferior 37.3
    substitution 148.2
    submarine 276.9
    subaltern 747.22
  adjs. 37.6
subacid, sub-
  acidulous 431.7
subacidity 431.2
subahdar
  viceroy 747.14
  captain 747.22
subalpine 206.23

subaltern
  nouns inferior 37.3
    officer 747.22
  adjs. 37.6
subaqueous 208.12
subastral 374.27
subbase 215.8
subchaser 276.7
subclass 61.5
subcommittee
  legislature 740.5
  council 753.3
  commission 779.12
subconscious
  nouns 688.39
  adjs. 688.52
subcutaneous 228.6
subdean 1036.8
subdeb girl 125.6
  socialite 642.7
subdivide
  partition 49.18
  classify 61.6
  bisect 92.3
subdivision
  disjunction 49.1
  part 55.1
  classification 61.1
  class 61.2
  bisection 92.1
  housing
    development 187.3
  military ~ 798.19
subdivisional, sub-
  divisive 61.7
subdominant 462.15
subdual
  conquering 725.1
  suppression 758.2
  subjugation 762.4
subduct 42.7
subduction 42.1
subdue
  moderate 162.6
  calm 162.7
  soften 356.6
  muffle 450.9
  conquer 725.10
  suppress 758.8
  subjugate 762.9
  relieve 884.5
subdued
  tempered 162.11
  soft-colored 361.22
  muffled 451.17
  conquered 725.16
  suppressed 758.14
  subjugated 762.14
  meek 763.15
  tasteful 895.8
subduement
  moderation 162.2
  relief 884.1
subduer 724.2
subduing
  mitigating 162.14
  softening 356.16
  relieving 884.9
subeditor 603.22
subfamily 61.5
subgenus 61.5

subgroup 61.2
subhead
  nouns 483.2
  verbs 483.3
subheading 483.2
subito 113.6
subjacency 207.1
subjacent 207.8
subject
  nouns topic 483.1
    experimentee 488.7
    study 560.7
    part of speech 584.2
    plot 606.9
    vassal 762.5
  GET OFF THE
    SUBJECT 591.9
  verbs 762.8
  adjs. subjugated
    762.12
    submissive 763.12
  SUBJECT TO
    liable to 174.5
    contingent 506.9
    provided 506.12
    impose 961.4
subjected 762.13
  BE SUBJECTED TO
    undergo 150.8
    be liable 174.3
subjection
  inferiority 37.2
  subjugation 762
  submission 763.1
subjective
  intrinsic 5.6
  mental 465.6
  topical 483.4
  introverted 688.50
subjectivity
  intrinsicality 5.1
  introversion 688.31
subjoin add 40.3
  place after 65.4
subjoinder 592.4
sub Jove 374.29
sub judice 484.42
subjugate
  conquer 725.10
  subdue 762.8
subjugated
  conquered 725.16
  subjected 762.13
subjugation
  conquering 725.1
  subjection 762.1
subjugator 724.2
subjunctive 584.9
subkingdom 61.5
sublease, sublet
  778.13
sublessee 807.4
sublevate 315.5
sublevation 315.1
sublimate
  nouns 43.2
  verbs elevate 315.6
    refine 354.6
    vaporize 400.7
sublimated 315.9

sublimation
elevation 315.1
refinement 354.3
vaporization 400.4
psychology 688.34

sublime
verbs refine 354.6
vaporize 400.7
adjs. great 34.9
eloquent 598.14
delightful 861.6
beautiful 898.19
exalted 912.19
magnanimous 977.6

Sublime Porte 739.3

subliminal
nouns self 80.5
subconscious 688.39
adjs. 688.52

sublimity
greatness 34.2
eloquence 598.6
beauty 898.6
distinction 912.5
magnanimity 977.2

sublineation 566.5
sublingual 687.21
sublunar 374.27
submarine
nouns ship 276.9
bedpan 680.14
verbs 796.23
adjs. 208.12

submediant 462.15
submerge
~ a submarine
274.49
immerse 318.7

submerged 208.12
SUBMERGED IN
involved 175.4
engrossed 528.17

submergence
draft 208.5
navigation 274.8
immersion 318.2

submergible 318.9
submerse 318.7
submersed 208.12
submersible
nouns 276.9
adjs. 318.9

submersion draft 208.5
submergence 318.2
engrossment 528.3

subminiature
nouns 195.5
adjs. 195.11

submission plan 652.2
compliance 763
obedience 764
offer 771.1
patience 859.2

submissive
conformable 82.5
acquiescent 520.13
compliant 763.12
obedient 764.3
patient 859.11
humble 904.9

submissiveness
compliance 763.3
patience 859.2
humility 904

submit
postulate 498.12
yield 763.6
obey 764.2
offer 771.4,5
SUBMIT TO
acknowledge 520.11
yield to 763.9
endure 859.6

submittal 763.1
submultiple 86.8
subnormal
abnormal 85.9
mentally deficient
468.22

subnormality
abnormality 85.1
mental deficiency
468.9

suborder 61.2,5
subordinacy
inferiority 37.1
subjection 762.2

subordinary 567.2
subordinate
nouns inferior 37.3
servant 748.1
adjs. inferior 37.6
subject 762.12,16

subordination
inferiority 37.1
subjection 762.2

suborn 649.3
subornation 649.1
subpanation 1038.8
subpoena
nouns 750.7
verbs 750.12

subrent 778.13
subrogate 148.4
subrogation 148.1
sub rosa 612.19
subscribe 816.14
SUBSCRIBE TO
assent 520.8,12
guarantee 770.11
support 783.14

subscriber
endorser 520.7
contributor 816.11

subscript addition 41.1
sequel 67.1

subscription
endorsement 520.4
signature 581.10
contribution 816.1,6

subsequence 117.1
subsequent
succeeding 65.5
later 117.3
SUBSEQUENT TO 117.7

subserve
contribute to 152.13
be instrumental
656.5

subservience,
subserviency
inferiority 37.2
instrumentality
656.2
subjection 762.2
submission 763.1
servility 905.1

subservient
instrumental 656.6
subject 762.12
submissive 763.16
assistant 783.20
servile 905.12

subset 558.5
subside decrease 39.6
sink 314.6
gravitate 351.15
deteriorate 690.18

subsidence
decline 39.2
sinkage 314.2

subsidiary
nouns nonessential
6.2
inferior 37.3
adjs. extrinsic 6.4
assistant 783.20
stipendiary 816.25

subsiding
decreasing 39.11
sinking 314.11
deteriorating 690.43

subsidization 816.8
subsidize bribe 649.3
endow 816.18

subsidy 816.8
subsist exist 1.8
survive 43.4
prevail 79.9
endure 110.6

subsistence
existence 1.1
accommodations
657.3
aid 783.3

subsistent 1.13
subsisting 1.13
subsoil 384.1
subsonic 449.17
subsonics 449.8
subspecies 61.5
substance
substantiality 3.1,2
essence 5.2
quantity 28.1
content 193.4
matter 375.2
food for thought
483.1
meaning 543.1
summary 605.2
funds 833.14
wealth 835.1
~ of life 1032.18
IN SUBSTANCE
essentially 5.10
in brief 590.6

substances 377.1
substandard 578.16
substantial real 1.15

tangible 3.4
essential 5.8
stable 142.13
influential 171.13
large 194.16
solid 353.12
material 375.9
reliable 512.17
valid 515.12
meaningful 543.10
important 670.16
authoritative 737.14
solvent 834.17

substantialism 375.5
substantialist 375.6
substantiality
tangibility 3
stability 142.1
materiality 375
reliability 512.4
validity 515.4

substantialization
375.7

substantiatable 504.21
substantiate
substantialize 375.8
confirm 504.12

substantiated 504.22
substantiation
substantialization
375.7
confirmation 504.5

substantify 375.8
substantive
nouns 584.4
adjs. substantial 3.4
essential 5.8
nominal 584.13

substituent 148.2
substitutable 148.10
substitute
nouns replacement
148.2
understudy 610.6
deputy 779.1
verbs 148.4
SUBSTITUTE FOR
replace 148.5
be deputy 779.13
adjs. 148.8

substitution
compensation 33.1
replacement 148.1,2
atomic ~ 325.8
psychological ~
688.34

substitutional,
substitutionary,
substitutive 148.9

substratosphere
aviation 277.38
atmosphere 401.3

substratum
foundation 215.6
underlayer 226.1
substance 375.2

substruction,
substructure
foundation 215.6
understructure 244.3

substructural 244.9

subsultus 684.17
subsume 76.3
subtenant 807.4
subtend 238.4
subterfuge
  quibbling 482.5
  secretiveness 612.1
  hiding place 613.4
  trick 616.6
  avoidance 629.1
  pretext 647.1
  expedient 668.2
  refuge 698.2
  artifice 733.3
subterrane 256.5
subterranean, subterra-
  neous 208.11
subtile
  unsubstantial 4.5
  delicate 35.8
  fine 350.8
  rare 354.7
  cunning 733.12
subtility
  unsubstantiality 4.1
  thinness 204.4
  fineness 350.3
  rarity 354.1
  shrewdness 466.3
subtilty rarity 354.1
  shrewdness 466.3
  cunning 733.1
subtitle
  nouns title 483.2
  book ~ 603.13
  verbs 483.3
subtle
  unsubstantial 4.5
  delicate 35.8
  thin 204.15
  fine 350.8
  rare 354.7
  shrewd 466.15
  discriminative 491.8
  precise 515.15
  meticulous 531.12
  cunning 733.12
subtleness 733.1
subtlety
  unsubstantiality 4.1
  fine distinction 16.2
  fineness 350.3
  rarity 354.1
  shrewdness 466.3
  finesse 491.1
  preciseness 515.3
  meticulousness
    531.5
  cunning 733.1
  punctilio 749.4
subtonic 462.15
subtract deduct 42.7
  calculate 87.11
subtraction
  deduction 42.1,2
  mathematics 87.4
subtractive 42.12
subtrahend 42.2
subtribe 61.5
subtropical 327.24
subtropics zone 179.3

hot place 327.10
suburb 182.1
suburban urban 182.9
  environing 232.9
suburbanite 189.6
suburbia 182.5
suburbs
  city district 182.5
  environs 232.1
subvention 816.8
subversal 219.2
subversion
  revolution 147.1
  overturn 219.2
  refutation 505.2
  destruction 691.3
subversionary 691.25
subversive
  nouns 617.11
  adjs. 691.25
subvert overturn 219.6
  refute 505.5
  destroy 691.20
subway tunnel 256.5
  train 271.12
  railway 655.8
subzero 332.15
succedaneum 148.2
succeed
  come next 65.3
  be subsequent 117.2
  supplant 148.6
  achieve 720.4
  be successful 722.6
  triumph 724.3
  prosper 726.7
  devolve 815.4
  ~ to 817.7
succeeding
  following 65.5
  subsequent 117.3
  successful 722.13
succentor 1036.9
success
  accomplishment
    720
  successfulness 722
  victory 724
  prosperity 726
  MEET WITH SUCCESS
    722.6
  WITHOUT SUCCESS
    723.18
successful
  succeeding 722.13
  triumphant 724.8
  prosperous
    726.12–14
succession
  sequence 65.1
  series 71.2
  posteriority 117.1
  lineage 169.4
  posterity 170.1
  transfer 815.2
  IN QUICK SUCCESSION
    135.6
  IN SUCCESSION
    in order 59.10
    consecutively 71.12

successive
  succeeding 65.5
  consecutive 71.10
  subsequent 117.3
successiveness
  sequence 65.1
  continuity 71.1
successless 723.17
successor 292.2
succinct short 202.8
  sententious 516.6
  concise 590.4
succinctness
  shortness 202.1
  conciseness 590.1
succor
  nouns 783.1
  verbs 783.11
succorer 940.1
succors 783.8
succubus 1014.7
succulence
  juiciness 387.1
  pulpiness 389.1
succulent
  nouns 410.4
  adjs. juicy 387.6
  pulpy 389.6
  interesting 528.19
succumb die 407.15
  faint 422.4
  perish 691.22
  get tired 715.5
  be defeated 725.12
  submit 763.6
succussation,
  succussion 323.2
succussatory,
  succussive 323.18
such 20.4
  SUCH AS 20.12
such-and-such 582.2
suchness 5.3
suck
  nouns suction 305.5
  drink 306.4
  dram 994.6
  verbs draft off 304.10
  draw in 305.12
  drink 306.27
  ~ dry 820.21
  SUCK UP TO 905.8
sucker
  plant shoot 410.18
  dupe 618.1
  customer 826.4
  sycophant 905.4
  PLAY FOR A SUCKER
  stultify 409.7
  use 663.16
sucking drafting 304.2
  suction 305.5
sucking pig 306a.16
suckle suck 305.12
  nurse 306.16
  drink 306.27
  nurture 783.16
suckling 125.7
suction influence 171.2
  drafting 304.2
  sucking 305.5

sud 404.5
sudarium
  bathroom 679.8
  talisman 1034.5
sudatorium 679.8
sudatory 309.20
sudden
  nouns 113.2
  ALL OF A SUDDEN
  suddenly 113.9
  short 202.13
  adjs. abrupt 113.5
  impulsive 628.9
  hasty 707.10
  advs. 113.9
suddenness
  abruptness 113.2
  impulsiveness 628.2
  haste 707.2
suddenty 113.2
  ON A SUDDENTY 113.9
suddy 404.7
sudor, sudoresis 309.7
sudoric 309.20
sudorific
  nouns 685.25
  adjs. 309.20
suds
  nouns foam 404.2
  beer 994.17
  IN THE SUDS 729.20
  verbs 404.5
sudsy 404.7
sue request 772.10,14
  court 930.19
  prosecute 1002.12
suety 379.9
Suez Canal 395.2
suffer undergo 150.8
  feel pain 423.8
  be ill 684.33
  permit 775.11
  ~ loss 810.5
  endure 859.5
  ~ mentally 864.22
  be punished 1008.22
  NOT SUFFER
  not permit 776.4
  discountenance
    967.11
sufferable 866.12
sufferance
  permission 775.2
  forbearance 859.1
  ON SUFFERANCE
    775.17
sufferer
  sick person 684.31
  wretch 864.11
suffering
  nouns physical ~
    423.1
  mental ~ 864.5
  adjs. ~ physically
    423.9
  permissive 775.15
suffice
  be sufficient 659.4
  avail 663.17
sufficiency
  ability 156.2

validity 515.4
adequacy 659
satisfactoriness
866.3
sufficient valid 515.12
enough 659.6
satisfactory 866.11
sufficing
sufficient 659.6
satisfactory 866.11
suffix
nouns addition 41.1
sequel 67.1
syllable 579.6
verbs 65.4
sufflation
distension 196.2
inspiration 402.1
suffocate
be hot 327.21
strangle 408.19
suffocation 408.6
suffocating
airless 267.14
sultry 327.28
odorous 434.10
suffragan 1036.8
suffrage vote 635.5
political ~ 742.17
suffragette
suffragist 742.17
feminist 956.7
suffragettism
suffrage 742.17
feminism 956.6
suffragist
nouns politics 742.17
feminist 956.7
adjs. 742.47
suffuse imbue 44.12
pervade 185.7
suffusion
imbuement 44.2
pervasion 185.3
blush 906.5
Sufi 1018.21
Sufism 1018.11
sugar
nouns carbohydrate
307.24
sweetening 430.2
money 833.2
endearment 930.5
verbs sweeten 430.5
bribe 649.3
sugar-coat 430.5
sugar-coating 430.1
sugariness 430.1
sugar-water 430.4
sugary 430.6
suggest promise 542.10
mean 543.8
imply 544.4
hint 555.9
indicate 566.16
advise 752.6
SUGGEST ITSELF
477.17
SUGGEST TO 535.20
suggested
portended 542.12

implied 544.7
suggestibility
influenceability
171.5
psychology 688.6
suggestible 171.15
suggestio falsi 614.11
suggestion
small amount 35.4
tinge 44.7
supposition 498.4
reminder 535.6
implication 544.2
hint 555.4
indication 566.1
clue 566.8
plan 652.2
advice 752.1
proposal 771.2
HYPNOTIC
SUGGESTION
psychiatry 688.6
hypnotism 710.8
suggestive
reminiscent 535.22
ominous 542.13
meaningful 543.10
allusive 544.6
indicative 566.22
eloquent 598.10
descriptive 606.15
risqué 988.7
suggestiveness
ominousness 542.5
meaningfulness
543.6
suggestum 215.13
suicidal 408.24
suicide
nouns 408.5
verbs 408.22
sui generis 85.10
suisse 1036.9
suit
nouns set 74.11
~ of clothes 230.6
types of clothing
230.48
request 772.1,5
courtship 930.6
lawsuit 1002.1
prayer 1030.4
verbs fit 26.8,12
conform 82.3
costume 230.40
adjust 718.8
SUIT ONESELF
760.18
SUIT THE OCCASION
129.7
suitability fitness 26.5
timeliness 129.1
eligibility 635.9
expedience 668.1
qualification 718.4
suitable fit 26.19
timely 129.10
eligible 635.21
adequate 659.6
expedient 668.4
suite attendance 73.6

set 74.11
apartment 191.4
music 461.5
suited fitted 26.19
qualified 718.18
competent 731.22
suiting 26.19
suitor petitioner 772.7
lover 929.11
litigant 1002.11
plaintiff 1003.5
sukkoth 1038.16
sulcate, sulcated 262.4
sulcation, sulcus 262.1
sulfa 685.24
sulfur, sulphur 382.1
sulfurous 1017.6
sulk 949.14
sulkiness
obstinacy 624.3
sullenness 949.8
sulks 949.10
sulky obstinate 624.11
sullen 949.24
sullen obstinate 624.11
glum 870.26
sulky 949.24
sullenness
obstinacy 624.3
glumness 870.8
sulkiness 949.8
sullens 949.10
sullied soiled 680.23
unchaste 987.23
sully dirty 680.17
stigmatize 913.9
vilify 969.10
corrupt 979.14
debauch 987.20
sulphacid 378.1
sulpha drugs 685.54
sulphate, sulphatize
378.6
sulphation, sulphatiza-
tion 378.5
sulphidic, sulphitic
83.8
sulphite original 23.2
nonconformist 83.4
sulphitic, sulphidic
23.3
sulphur bath 679.2
sulphur-colored 369.4
sulphuric, sulfuric,
sulphurous,
sulfurous 382.14
Sultan 747.11
sultana 747.12
sultanate, sultanship
737.7
sultriness 327.5
sultry hot 327.28
obscene 988.9
sum
nouns quantity 28.1,2
total 54.2
number 86.3
summary 605.2
~ of money 833.13
SUM AND SUBSTANCE ·
content 193.4

summary 605.2
verbs 87.12
SUM UP
calculate 87.12
reiterate 103.8
sumless 104.3
summa cum laude
914.12
summariness
promptness 131.3
shortness 202.1
conciseness 590.1
summarize
sum up 87.12
reiterate 103.8
brief 605.5
summary
nouns enumeration
87.5
reiteration 103.2
compendium 605.2
adjs. prompt 131.9
short 202.8
concise 590.4
summate 87.12
summation sum 86.3
enumeration 87.5
summer
nouns season 128.3
hot weather 327.6
verbs 105.6
adjs. 128.8
summer day 327.7
summerhouse
house 190.11
nursery 412.11
summerlike,
summerly 128.8
summer school 565.2
summertide,
summertime 128.3
summery
summer 128.8
warm 327.24
summit
mountaintop 206.8
top 210.2
perfection 675.3
summital 210.9
summon
convoke 74.16
call for 750.12
invite 772.13
conscript 778.14
conjure 1033.11
SUMMON UP
elicit 304.12
visualize 533.15
remember 535.11
prompt 646.13
call up 750.12
excite 855.11
summoner 750.8
summons
nouns call 566.15
bidding 750.5
writ 750.7
invitation 772.4
recruital 778.6
verbs 750.12
sumo 794.10

sump drain 395.5
  puddle 397.1
  marsh 399.1
  cesspool 680.12
sumpter
  beast of burden
    270.6
  horse 413.18
  mule 413.23
sumption 481.8
sumptuary 833.28
sumptuous
  costly 846.11
  grandiose 902.21
sumptuousness
  costliness 846.2
  grandeur 902.5
sun
  nouns year 107.2
  heavenly body
    374.10
  sunstroke 684.20
  UNDER THE SUN
  existent 1.13
  earthly 374.27
  on earth 374.29
  verbs insolate 328.18
  sun-dry 392.6
sunbath 687.5
sunbeam 334.10
sunburn
  nouns 328.6
  verbs 366.2
sunburned, sunburnt
  burnt 328.29
  reddish-brown 366.4
  red 367.10
sunburst 334.10
sundae 306a.46
Sunday
  nouns day of rest
    709.5
  holyday 1038.14
  verbs 105.6
Sunday best 230.10
Sunday driver 273.10
Sunday school 565.10
sunder 49.10
sunderance 49.2
sundown 134.2
sundowner
  tramp 273.3
  drink 994.8
sundries
  assortment 74.12
  merchandise 829.6
sundry various 19.4
  several 101.8
sun-dry insolate 328.18
  dry 392.6
sunfisher
  buckjumper 317.4
  bronco 413.14
sunglass 442.1
sunglasses
  eyeshade 337.2
  spectacles 442.2
sun god 374.11
sunk concave 256.16
  lowered 316.10
  baffled 513.23

dejected 870.22
sunless 336.14
sunlight 334.10
sunlit 334.38
Sunna 123.2
sunniness
  pleasantness 861.3
  cheerfulness 868.1
Sunnite 1018.21
sunny warm 327.24
  shining 334.30
  auspicious 542.16
  pleasant 861.8
  cheerful 868.10
  optimistic 886.12
sunny side 861.3
sunrise dawn 133.3
  east 289.3
  AT SUNRISE 133.8
sunscald 328.6
sunset evening 134.2
  west 289.3
sunshade 227.7
sunshine light 334.10
  fair weather 726.4
  happiness 863.2
sunshiny warm 327.24
  shining 334.30
sunstroke 684.20
suntan 366.2
sun-tanned 366.3
sunup 133.3
sun worship 1031.1
sun worshiper 1031.4
sup
  nouns small amount
    35.4
  drink 306.4
  taste 426.2
  dram 994.6
  verbs dine 306.19
  drink 306.27
  taste 426.7
  tipple 994.29
supawn 306a.34
supe 610.6
super
  nouns extra 41.4
  supernumerary
    610.6
  superintendent
    746.2
  adjs. 672.18
superability 508.2
superable 508.7
superabound 661.9
superabundance
  plenty 659.2
  excess 661.2
superabundant
  plentiful 659.7
  oversufficient 661.20
superadd 40.3
superaddition 40.1
superaltar shelf 215.14
  predella 1040.11
superannuate
  antiquate 123.9
  pension off 308.18
superannuated 123.13
superannuation 123.3

superb
  superexcellent
    672.18
  magnificent 902.21
superbness 672.2
supercargo 746.1
supercharge fill 56.7
  overfill 661.16
supercherie 616.4
supercilious 910.13
superciliousness 910.5
superclass 61.5
superconductor 341.13
superconscious 688.52
super-duper 345.4
superego self 80.5
  psyche 688.39
  conscience 955.5
supereminence 672.2
supereminent 36.16
supererogate 661.11
supererogation 661.6
supererogatory 661.18
superexcellence 672.2
superexcellent 672.18
superfamily 61.5
superfetate
  verbs 168.12
  adjs. 168.18
superfetation
  addition 40.1
  conception 168.5
superficial slight 35.7
  shallow 209.5
  surface 223.6
  apparent 445.11
  shallow-witted
    468.20
  half-learned 476.16
  insincere 614.32
  frivolous 627.7
  formal 644.7
  trivial 671.16
  hasty 707.9
superficiality
  shallowness 209.1
  shallow-wittedness
    468.7
  half-learning 476.6
  insincerity 614.5
  frivolousness 627.3
  formality 644.1
  triviality 671.3
superficies
  shallowness 209.1
  surface 223.2
superfine 672.18
superfluent 352.13
superfluity
  excess 661.4
  frippery 899.3
superfluous 661.18
superfluousness 661.4
superheat 328.17
superhighway 655.6
superhuman 85.14
superimpose add 40.3
  cover 227.21
superimposed 227.38
superimposition 227.1

superimpregnated
  168.18
superimpregnation
  168.5
superincumbence
  227.1
superincumbency
  351.7
superincumbent
  overhanging 214.11
  overlying 227.38
  burdensome 351.17
superinduce 152.12
superintend 745.10
superintendence,
  superintendency
  supervision 745.2
  directorship 745.4
superintendent
  nouns police ~
    697.14
  supervisor 746.2
  adjs. 745.13
superior
  nouns higher-up 36.4
  chief 747.3
  adjs. greater 36.13
  higher 206.24
  excellent 672.15
superior court 999.3
superiores 1036.18
superiority
  pre-eminence 36.1
  goodness 672.1
superiority complex
  688.30
superjunction 401
superlative
  nouns exaggeration
    615.1
  the best 672.8
  adjs. supreme 36.15
  exaggerated 615.4
  extreme 661.17
superman 36.4
supermarket 830.1
supernal
  towering 206.19
  heavenly 1016.13
supernatant 352.13
supernational 416.13
supernatural
  nouns supernat-
    uralism 85.7
  the superphysical
    1032.2
  adjs. 85.14
supernatural being
  1012.12
supernaturalism
  supernormalness
    85.7
  religion 1032.2
supernaturalist
  1032.11
supernaturalistic 85.14
supernaturality, super-
  naturalness,
  supernature 85.7
supernormal 85.14
supernormalness 85.7

swimmer
  bather 274.12
  diver 318.4
swimming
  nouns aquatics
      274.11
  dizziness 530.4
  adjs. aquatic 274.61
  dizzy 530.15
swimming belt 699.5
swimming hole,
      swimming pool
      679.11
swimmingly
  successfully 722.14
  prosperously 726.15
  easily 730.13
swim suit 230.29
swindle
  nouns 616.8
  verbs 616.18
swindler 617.3
swine slattern 62.7
  pig 413.11
  breeds of ~ 413.61
  dirty person 680.15
  scoundrel 984.6
swineherd 415.3
swing
  nouns shift 108.3
  influence 171.1
  trend 173.2
  room 178.3
  hang 214.2
  gait 272.14
  blow 282.5
  oscillation 322.5
  pendulum 322.8
  flounder 323.8
  music 461.9
  rhythm 462.22
  poetic ~ 607.9
  operation 703.1
  free scope 760.3
  thrust 796.3
  plaything 876.15
  IN FULL SWING
  unweakened 158.19
  astir 705.18
  actively 705.23
  prospering 726.13
  verbs fluctuate 141.5
  dangle 214.6
  walk 272.27
  sail 274.58
  turn around 294.9
  wheel 320.9
  oscillate 322.9
  wave 322.10
  alternate 322.12
  flounder 323.15
  syncopate 461.44
  manage successfully
      722.11
  be hanged 1008.21
  SWING AT
  be credulous 501.5
  strike at 796.17
  SWING IN WITH 784.6
swinge singe 328.23
  whip 1008.14

swingeing
  nouns 1008.4
  adjs. 34.13
swinging
  nouns 320.1
  adjs. pendent 214.9
  oscillating 322.16
swingletree 220.5
swings 832.8
swing shift 108.3
swingster 463.2
swingy 462.28
swinish porcine 413.41
  greedy 632.28
  filthy 680.26
  carnal 985.6
  gluttonous 992.7
swinishness
  greed 632.8
  filthiness 680.2
  carnality 985.2
  gluttony 992.1
swipe
  nouns 419.5
  verbs 822.13
swipes 994.17
swiping 822.1
swirl
  nouns whirl 320.2
  eddy 394.12
  verbs whirl 320.11
  eddy 394.22
swirling
  nouns 320.1
  adjs. 320.14
swirly 320.15
swish
  nouns 456.1
  verbs sound softly
      451.12
  whish 456.2
Swiss 417.9
Swiss Guards 798.32
Swiss plan 114.8
Swiss steak 306a.18
switch
  nouns member 55.4
  substitution 148.1
  exchange 149.2
  hairpiece 229.13
  branch 410.18
  whip 1009.2
  verbs substitute 148.4
  exchange 149.4
  turn aside 290.6
  trade 825.10
  whip 1008.14
  SWITCH ON, SWITCH
      OFF 341.23
switchback 655.8
switchboard 558.10
switching
  television 344.3
  whipping 1008.4
switchman 273.13
swivel
  nouns 320.5
  verbs turn round
      294.9
  turn 320.9
swiveling 320.1

swizzle 994.29
swollen
  distended 196.12
  bombastic 599.10
  pompous 902.22
  proud 903.10
  boastful 908.10
swollenness
  bloating 196.2
  swelling 255.4
swoon
  nouns faint 422.2
  heavy sleep 710.6
  verbs 422.4
swoop
  nouns 318.1
  AT ONE SWOOP 113.8
  verbs 318.6
  SWOOP DOWN UPON
      820.13
sword
  nouns 799.4
  AT SWORDS' POINTS
      795.29
  PUT TO THE SWORD
  kill 408.18
  attack 796.27
  THE SWORD
  coercion 754.3
  war 795.1
  attack 796.11
  verbs 796.27
sword-in-hand
  prepared 718.16
  warring 795.28
  armed 797.14
swordlike 257.16
swordplay 794.8
swordplayer, swords-
      man 798.1
sybarite 985.3
sybaritic(al) 985.5
sybaritism 985.1
sycophancy 905.2
sycophant 905.3
sycophantic(al)
      905.13
syllabary 579.6
syllabic 579.12
syllabicate, syllabify,
      syllabize 583.5
syllabication, syllab-
      ification 583.2
syllabized 579.12
syllable
  nouns letters 579.6
  word 580.1
  poetic ~ 607.11
  verbs 583.5
syllabus 605.1
syllepsis 584.1
syllogism 481.3,7
syllogistic(al) 481.22
syllogize 481.15
syllogizer 481.12
sylph spirit 1012.13
  fairy 1012.15
sylphid 1012.15
sylphine, sylphlike,
      etc. 1012.23
sylvan 410.38

sylvan deity 1012.18
symbol
  nouns prototype 25.2
  number 86.1
  musical ~ 462.12
  emblem 566.2
  letter 579.1
  verbs 570.9
symbolic(al)
  figurative 549.4
  typical 570.12
symbolic logic 481.2
symbolics
  mysticism 1032.1
  ritualism 1038.1
symbolism
  symbol 566.2
  representation 570.6
  writing 600.10
  mysticism 1032.1
  ritualism 1038.1
symbolistic 570.12
symbolization 570.6
symbolize
  figure 549.3
  typify 570.9
symbolizing 570.11
symbolography 600.10
symbology
  representation 570.6
  writing 600.10
symbols 567.1
symmetric(al)
  balanced 30.10
  orderly 59.6
  uniform 247.5
  euphonious 587.8
symmetrization 247.3
symmetrize
  uniformize 17.4
  regularize 247.4
symmetry
  equality 30.1
  order 59.1
  proportion 247.1
  euphony 587.2
sympathetic
  sensitive 421.13
  tolerant 524.11
  understanding 792.3
  emotionable 853.19
  kind 936.14
  pitying 942.7
  condolent 944.3
sympathetic chord,
      sympathetic
      response 853.5
sympathies 853.1
sympathize
  accord 792.2
  pity 942.3
  SYMPATHIZE WITH
  commiserate 942.3
  condole with 944.2
sympathizer
  traitor 617.11
  fellow traveller
      743.11
  supporter 785.8
  friend 926.1

tabor pipe 464.9
tabular classified 61.8
  laminated 226.6
tabula rasa 186.3
tabulate
  verbs classify 61.6
  list 88.7
  record 568.15
  adjs. 61.8
tabulation listing 88.6
  registration 568.14
tabulator 87.19
tachometer 277.59
tachygrapher 600.17
tachygraphic(al)
  600.28
tachygraphy 600.9
tacit silent 450.13
  implicit 544.8
taciturn 611.7
taciturnity 611.2
tack
  nouns cordage 205.3
  direction 289.2
  deviation 290.1
  route 655.2
  gear 657.4,5
  GO UPON ANOTHER
    TACK 626.7
  verbs ~ on 40.3
  ~ together 47.5
  fasten 47.8
  change 139.5
  sail 274.32
tackiness tenacity 50.2
  stickiness 388.2
tackle
  nouns cordage 205.3
  rigging 276.12
  purchase 286.6
  types of ~ 286.10
  gear 657.4,5
  footballer 876.20
  verbs undertake
    713.3
  set to work 714.15
tackling 276.12
tacky
  nouns 690.9
  adjs. adhesive 50.9
  dowdy 62.14
  sticky 388.12
  shabby 690.31
tact 491.1
tactful 491.8
  BE TACTFUL 491.5
tactical 733.14
tactical maneuvers
  navigation 274.7
  aviation 277.10
  strategy 733.4
tactical unit 798.19
tactician 733.7
tactics
  navigation 274.7
  strategy 733.4
  military ~ 795.10
tactile tactual 424.10
  touchable 424.11

tactile hair, tactile
  process
  vibrissa 229.10
  feeler 424.4
tactile organ 424.4
tactility 424.3
taction contact 199.5
  touch 424.1
tactless 492.7
tactual 424.10
tactus 424.1
tad 125.3
tadpole
  youngling 125.8
  frog 413.32
taenia 205.4
taeniate, taeniform
  205.7
taffrail log 268.8
Taffy 417.9
taffy 968.1
tag
  nouns
  small amount 35.3
  appendage 41.2
  sequel 67.1
  afterpart 67.2
  end 70.2
  sheep 413.9
  label 566.12
  name 581.3
  token 833.12
  verbs add 40.3
  follow 292.3
  label 566.19
  name 581.11
tag end 70.2
tagtail
  follower 292.2
  hanger-on 905.5
tail
  nouns afterpart 67.2
  end 70.2
  hair 229.7
  rear 240.1
  rump 240.4
  caudal appendage
    240.5
  follower 292.2
  corner of eye 438.9
  waiting line 609.31
  WITH ONE'S TAIL
    BETWEEN ONE'S
    LEGS 904.14
  verbs 292.3
  TAIL OFF 39.6
  adjs. 240.8
tailed 240.10
tail end end 70.2
  rear 240.1
  stern 240.6
tail force 277.22
tail gunner 278.4
tailing 292.1
tailleur 230.34
taillike 240.10
tailor
  nouns 230.34
  verbs fit 26.12
  sew 222.4
  form 245.6

tailoring 230.31
tailor-made 166.27
tailpiece afterpart 67.2
  latter part 240.1
  tail 240.5
  coda 461.24
  engraving 576.6
tailrace 395.2
tails full dress 230.11
  opposite side 238.3
  IN TAILS 230.45
tailspin 723.3
  GO INTO A TAILSPIN
    950.19
tail spin 277.12
tailwagger 413.24
tailward, tailwards
  240.14
tail wind 277.38
taint
  nouns tinge 44.7
  characteristic 80.3
  blemish 677.3
  infection 684.3
  stigma 913.6
  verbs stain 677.6
  defile 680.19
  infect 684.38
  corrupt 690.12
  stigmatize 913.9
tainted stained 677.9
  soiled 680.23
  diseased 684.45
  spoiled 690.39
  vice-corrupted
    979.19
taintless
  flawless 675.6
  clean 679.23
  innocent 982.7
  chaste 986.4
tais-toi! 450.16
take
  nouns
  photograph 575.10
  gain 809.3
  catch 820.8
  booty 822.11
  receipts 842.1
  verbs entail 76.4
  convey 270.11
  eat 306.17
  catch fire 328.22
  suppose 498.9
  deem 500.9
  understand 546.7
  sicken of 684.34
  succeed 722.6
  get 809.7
  receive 817.6
  borrow 819.4
  ~ possession 820.11
  steal 822.13
  tolerate 859.7
  HAVE ALL ONE CAN
    TAKE 662.5
  NOT TAKE 157.7
  NOT TAKE ANY MORE
    OF 662.5
  NOT TAKE CARE OF
    532.6

NOT TAKE KINDLY TO
  967.10
TAKE ABACK
  startle 538.8
  dismay 889.18
TAKE A BACK SEAT
  be inferior 37.4
  be modest 906.7
TAKE ABOUT 697.18
TAKE A BOW!
  congratulations!
    946.4
  bravo! 966.21
TAKE A BREAK 709.8
TAKE ACCOUNT OF
  allow for 506.5
  note 528.9
  take stock 843.9
TAKE A DARE 791.7
TAKE A DIM VIEW OF
  967.10
TAKE A DROP
  tipple 994.29
  get drunk 994.32
TAKE A FAVORABLE
  TURN
  improve 689.8
  recuperate 692.19
  prosper 726.7
TAKE A FLIER 831.23
TAKE A FLING AT
  796.17
TAKE A FLYER 514.19
TAKE AFTER
  resemble 20.7
  emulate 22.7
TAKE A LEAP IN THE
  DARK
  chance 514.18
  be rash 892.5
TAKE A LIBERTY
  presume on 959.7
  show disrespect
    963.3
TAKE A LIKING TO
  929.19
TAKE AMISS 950.13
TAKE A NEW LEASE
  ON LIFE 692.19
TAKE AN INTEREST
  531.6
TAKE AN INTEREST
  IN
  be curious 526.3
  care for 929.17
TAKE APART
  disassemble 49.14
  demolish 691.17
TAKE AT ONE'S WORD
  500.8
TAKE AWAY
  deduct 42.7
  remove 270.10
  away with 636.5
  steal 822.13
TAKE AWAY FROM
  820.18
TAKE BACK
  recant 626.9
  repeal 777.2
  return 821.4

Talmudism 1018.10
Talmudist 1018.19
taloned 811.9
talons 811.4
talus 218.4
tamanoas 1012.10
tambo
  drummer 463.10
  minstrel 463.16
tamboura, tambura
  464.4
tambour de basque
  464.21
tambourgi 463.10
tambourin 464.21
tambourine
  drummer 463.10
  minstrel 463.16
  timbrel 464.21
tame
  verbs moderate 162.6
  domesticate 188.5
  subdue 762.10
  adjs.
  temperate 162.10
  domesticated 188.9
  inert 267.12
  meek 763.15
tameable 763.14
tame cat, tame pussy
  420.11
tamed
  domesticated 188.9
  gentle 763.15
tameless 161.20
tamely 763.19
tameness 763.5
taming
  domestication 188.4
  subdual 762.4
Tammany Hall 742.25
Tammany man 744.1
tamp 282.15
tamper with
  adulterate 44.13
  meddle 237.7
  falsify 614.17
  bribe 649.3
tampon, tampion
  685.28
tam-tam 464.21
tan
  nouns 366.5
  verbs suntan 366.2
  whip 1008.15
  adjs. 366.3
tanbur 464.4
tandem
  nouns 271.5
  advs. 240.12
tandle 327.12
tang
  characteristic 80.3
  tine 257.4
  fang 257.7
  taste 426.1
  pungency 432.2
  poison 674.5
tangelo 44.8
tangency 199.5

tangent
  nouns 199.6
  GO OFF AT A TANGENT
  deviate 290.6
  diverge 298.5
  get excited 855.17
  GO OFF ON A TANGENT
  angle 250.5
  digress 591.9
  adjs. 199.17
tangential 199.17
tangibility
  substantiality 3.1
  touchableness 424.3
tangible
  nouns 3.2
  adjs. substantial 3.4
  touchable 424.11
tangibles 808.8
tanginess 432.2
tangle
  nouns 46.2
  verbs complicate 46.3
  involve 175.2
  ensnare 616.20
  catch 20.14
  TANGLE WITH 794.18
tangled 46.4
  GET ALL TANGLED
  729.11
  TANGLED IN 175.4
tangle-legs 994.13
tanglement 46.1
tango 877.5
tangy 432.7
tank
  nouns ~ car 271.13
  pool 397.1
  drunkard 994.11
  verbs 235.9
  TANK UP 994.31
tankage 194.2
tank car 271.13
Tank Corps 798.20
tanked 994.40
tanker ship 281.2
tanner 833.8
tannery 717.3
tanning 1008.5
tan-skinned 366.3
tant soit peu 35.10
tantalization 648.1
tantalize
  interest 528.12
  tempt 648.5
  tease 864.19
  seduce 929.20
tantalized 528.16
tantalizer 648.3
tantalizing
  appetizing 427.10
  interesting 528.19
  desirable 632.31
  tempting 648.7
tantalizingly 648.8
tantamount 30.9
tantara, tantarara
  452.4
tantra 1019.7
tantrum 950.8
Taoist(ic) 1018.30

Tao Te Ching 1019.6
tap
  nouns kind 61.3
  stopper 265.4
  blow 282.6
  siphon 395.6
  faucet 395.10
  taproot 410.20
  bang 455.1
  taproom 994.25
  ON TAP 663.19
  verbs open 264.11
  perforate 264.15
  hit 282.16
  draft off 304.10
  bang 455.6
tap-dance 877.5
tap dancer 877.3
tape
  nouns strip 205.4
  recording 568.9
  dressing 685.28
  liquor 994.13
  verbs 47.9
tapeline 205.4
taper
  nouns
  narrowing 204.2
  lighter 330.4
  light 335.1
  candle 335.2
  wick 335.7
  verbs 204.10
  adjs. 204.14
tape recorder 464.18
tape recording 464.19
tapered
  narrowed 204.14
  pointed 257.12
tapering
  nouns 204.2
  adjs.
  narrowing 204.14
  pointed 257.12
tapestry 572.12
tapeworm 632.7
  HAVE A TAPEWORM
  632.19
tapis
  ON THE TAPIS
  in question 484.42
  planned 652.13
tapping
  nouns 304.2
  adjs. 455.11
taproom 994.25
taproot 410.20
taps
  trumpet call 452.4
  call 566.15
tapster 994.23
tar
  nouns mariner 275.1
  black 364.4
  pavement 655.7
  verbs pave 227.24
  coat 227.26
  TAR AND FEATHER
  1008.18
  TARRED WITH THE
  SAME BRUSH 20.13

taradiddle, taradiddler
  617.9
tarantara 452.4
tardily 132.19
tardiness 132.1
tardy 132.15
tare deduction 42.6
  discount 845.1
tares 667.4
target
  atomic fission 325.8
  goal 651.2
  laughingstock 965.7
target date 233.3
target day 796.14
target image 345.11
target planet 281.1
target values 348.10
Targu 579.5
Targum 550.3
tariff 844.10
tarn 397.1
Tarnhelm 1034.7
tarnish
  nouns blemish 677.3
  stigma 913.6
  verbs dim 362.5
  stain 677.6
  taint 680.19
  stigmatize 913.9
  vilify 969.10
tarnished
  stained 677.9
  soiled 680.23
Tarnkappe 1034.7
tarradiddle
  nouns 614.11
  verbs 614.19
tarriance 132.3
tarry
  verbs remain 110.7
  wait 132.11
  continue 143.3
  be quiescent 267.7
  dawdle 269.8
  TARRY FOR 537.6
  adjs. 380.3
tarrying
  nouns delay 132.3
  slowness 269.3
  adjs. 269.11
tarsus 272.16
tart
  nouns pastry 306a.40
  strumpet 987.14
  adjs.
  acrimonious 160.12
  sour 431.6
  caustic 937.21
tartan 373.4
tartar 949.11
Tartarean
  cruel 937.24
  hellish 1017.6
Tartareous 1017.6
Tartarus 1017.3
tartness
  acrimony 160.4
  sourness 431.1
  causticity 937.8

television technician
  344.13
televisual 344.16
televox 348.12
tell
  ~ apart 21.2
  number 87.10
  have influence
    171.10
  evince 504.9
  recognize 535.13
  ~ fortunes 541.9
  ~ how 550.11
  divulge 554.5
  inform 555.7
  report 556.11
  say 592.14
  narrate 606.13
  be important 670.11
  be impressed 853.16
  NOT TELL 612.8
  TELL A THING OR
    TWO 967.18
  TELL IN ADVANCE
    701.8
  TELL IT TO THE
    MARINES!
  nonsense! 469.12
  disbelief 502.14
  TELL OFF
  number 87.10
  reprove 967.18
  TELL ON 555.11
  TELL ONE TO ONE'S
    FACE 239.9
  TELL TALES 554.6
  TELL THE WORLD
    521.5
  TELL WHERE TO GET
    OFF 967.19
teller
  informant 555.5
  ~ of tales 606.10
  banker 834.10
telling
nouns
  numeration 87.1
  narration 606.2
adjs. potent 156.11
  influential 171.13
  evidential 504.17
  meaningful 543.10
  eloquent 598.11
  significant 670.19
  exciting 855.31
telltale
nouns hint 555.4
  informer 555.6
  gossip 556.9
  clue 566.8
adjs. 555.18
tellurian, telluric
  earthly 374.27
  terrestrial 384.6
telpher, telpherway
  655.9
telpherage 270.3
Tellus 1012.5
temblor 161.5
temeritous 892.7
temerity 892.1

temper
nouns nature 5.3
  hardness 355.4
  disposition 523.3,4
  bad ~ 949.3
  anger 950.6
  HAVE A TEMPER
    949.13
  IN A TEMPER 950.28
  OUT OF TEMPER
    949.17
verbs moderate 162.6
  harden 355.7
  qualify 506.3
tempera color 361.7
  painting 572.15
temperament
  nature 5.3
  disposition 523.3
  artistic ~ 572.8
temperamental
  constitutional 5.7
  dispositional 523.7
  moody 627.6
  sensitive 949.20
temperamentalness
  capriciousness 627.2
  sensitiveness 949.4
temperance
  moderation 162.1
  virtue 978.5
  abstemiousness 990
temperate
  moderate 162.10
  warmish 327.24
  abstemious 990.9
temperateness
  moderation 162.1
  temperance 990.1
Temperate Zones
  179.3
temperature
  heat 327.2
  variable 348.9
  RUN A TEMPERATURE
  sicken 684.34
  get excited 855.17
tempered
  moderate 162.11
  metallic 382.15
  qualified 506.10
  disposed 523.8
temperer 162.3
tempering
nouns moderation
  162.2
  hardening 355.5
adjs. 162.14
tempest storm 161.4
  windstorm 402.13
  excitement 855.8
  TEMPEST IN A TEAPOT
  exaggeration 615.2
  triviality 671.3
tempestuous
  turbulent 161.17
  windy 402.27
  excited 855.25
tempestuousness
  161.2
Templar 1036.17

template 25.6
temple side 241.1
  church 1040.2
templelike 1040.14
tempo 462.23
  IN TEMPO
  synchronous 118.5
  in time 462.29
temporal
nouns 1025.2
adjs. temporary 111.7
  chronological
    114.15
  earthly 374.27
  unsacred 1025.3
  mundane 1029.16
  secular 1037.3
temporariness 111.1
temporary
  interim 109.4
  transient 111.7
  substitute 148.8
  makeshift 668.6
temporization 132.5
temporize 132.10
temporizer 976.3
tempt
  ~ the appetite
    427.4
  lure 648.5
  seduce 929.20
temptation 648.1
tempter 648.3
  THE TEMPTER
    1014.3
tempting
  appetizing 427.10
  alluring 648.7
temptress 648.3
tempus fugit 105.14
ten 99.6
tenability 500.6
tenable
  believable 500.21
  defensible 797.15
tenacious
  adhesive 50.9
  viscid 388.12
  persevering 623.7
  obstinate 624.8
  retentive 811.8
tenacity
  adhesiveness 50.2
  viscidity 388.2
  perseverance 623.1
  obstinacy 624.1
tenaille, tenail 797.4
tenancy 806.1
tenant
nouns inhabitant
  189.2
  holder 807.4
verbs 187.8
tenantable 187.16
tenanted 187.13
tenantless 186.13
tenantry 806.1
ten-cent store 830.1
Ten Commandments
  955.1
tend incline 173.3

bear 289.8
  gravitate 351.15
  ~ stock 415.6
  heed 528.6
  look after 697.18
  serve 748.14
tendance 748.13
tendency
  inclination 173
  direction 289.1
  disposition 523.3
  psychological ~
    688.41
  aptitude 731.5
tendent, tendential,
  tendentious 173.4
tender
nouns railway car
  271.13
  attendant 748.4
  offer 771.1
verbs administer
  663.11
  offer 771.4
  give 816.12
  pay 839.10
  TENDER ONE'S
    RESIGNATION 782.2
adjs. delicate 35.8
  young 124.10
  light 352.11
  soft 356.8
  soft-colored 361.22
  sensitive 421.13
  emotionally ~
    853.20
  affectionate 929.24
  kind 936.14
  merciful 942.7
tender age 124.1
tender-conscienced
  972.15
tenderfoot
  newcomer 78.4
  novice 564.7
  raw recruit 798.17
tenderhearted
  tender 853.20
  kind 936.14
  merciful 942.7
tenderheartedness
  tender feeling 853.6
  kindness 936.1
tenderling 420.11
tenderloin
  city district 182.5
  meat 306a.17,18
  brothels 987.9
tenderness
  youth 124.1
  lightness 352.1
  softness 356.1
  sensitiveness 421.3
  tender feeling 853.6
  pity 942.2
tending 173.4
tendon 48.4
tendril member 55.4
  filament 205.1
  coil 253.2
  plant ~ 410.18

tenebrious, tenebrose,
　tenebrous 336.14
tenebrity, tenebrous-
　ness 336.1
tenement
　house 190.12
　apartment 191.4
　property 808.7
tenet 500.2
tenez! 144.13
tenfold 99.22
tenigue 715.1
tenner ten 99.6
　money 833.7,8
tennis court 876.13
Tenno 747.9
tenor
　nouns character 5.3
　mode 7.4
　transcript 24.4
　trend 173.2
　direction 289.1
　tone 449.2
　voice part 461.22
　voice 462.5
　singer 463.14
　instrument 464.1
　meaning 543.1
　adjs. high-pitched
　　457.12
　vocal 461.51
tenoroon 464.9
ten-percenter 609.29
tense
　nouns 584.10
　verbs stretch 201.9
　stiffen 355.9
　strain 714.10
　adjs. stretched 201.12
　rigid 355.11
　phonetics 449.18
　nervous 857.13
tenseness
　rigidity 355.2
　nervousness 857.3
tensibility, tensility
　357.1
tensible, tensile 357.7
tension stretch 201.5
　stiffness 355.2
　stretching 357.2
　strain 714.2
　disaccord 793.1
　nervous ~ 857.3
tensity 355.2
tensor 158.2
ten spot 833.7
ten-strike
　success 722.3,4
　stroke of luck 726.3
tent
　nouns cover 227.2,8
　types of ~ 227.43
　dossil 685.28
　verbs 137.12
tentacles, tentacula
　811.4
Tentaculata 414.4
tentage 227.8
tentative
　nouns ~88.1

adjs. temporary 109.4
　substitute 148.8
　experimental 488.11
　makeshift 668.6
tented 227.34
tenterhooks
　ON TENTERHOOKS
　uncertain 513.23
　expectant 537.10
　anxious 888.6
tenth
　nouns 99.14
　adjs. 99.22
tenths 844.10
tenting 187.4
ten to one 510.7
ten-to-one shot 514.5
tenuity
　unsubstantiality 4.1
　delicacy 35.1
　thinness 204.4
　rarity 354.1
tenuous
　unsubstantial 4.5
　delicate 35.8
　thin 204.15
　rare 354.7
tenuousness
　unsubstantiality 4.1
　rarity 354.1
tenure term 107.3
　possession 806.1
téorbe 464.4
tepefaction 328.1
tepefy 328.17
tepid 327.24
tepidarium 679.8
tepidity, tepidness
　327.3
teratism
　abnormality 85.1
　monstrosity 85.6
teratogenic 85.12
teratogeny 85.6
teratoid 85.12
teratology
　monstrosity 85.6
　deformity 248.3
tercentenary
　nouns number 99.8
　anniversary 137.4
　adjs. 99.30
tercentennial
　number 99.8
　anniversary 137.4
tercet three 93.1
　notes 462.14
　verse 607.5
terebration 264.3
tergal 240.9
tergiversant
　nouns 626.4
　adjs. 626.10
tergiversate
　equivocate 482.9
　apostatize 626.7
tergiversating
　nouns 626.1
　adjs. 626.10
tergiversation
　equivocation 482.5

apostasy 626
tergiversator 626.4
tergum 240.3
term
　nouns end 70.1
　time 105.1
　tenure 107.3
　premise 481.8
　word 580.1
　estate 808.4
　verbs 581.11
termagant
　violent person 161.9
　vixen 941.8
　scold 949.12
termed 581.14
terminable 233.11
terminal
　nouns end 70.1
　railroad station
　　183.3
　limit 233.3
　destination 299.5
　railway 655.8
　adjs. final 70.10
　limital 233.11
terminate end 70.5
　result 153.5
　complete 720.6
terminating 70.9
termination end 70.1
　result 153.2
　limit 233.3
　completion 720.2
terminational,
　terminative 70.10
terminological 581.17
terminology 581.1
terminus end 70.1
　railroad station
　　183.3
　limit 233.3
　destination 299.5
　railway 655.8
termite 413a.3
termless 104.3
terms
　stipulations 506.2
　conciliation 802.4
　BE ON GOOD TERMS
　　925.9
　IN GENERAL TERMS
　　513.26
　IN GLOWING TERMS
　　598.15
　IN PLAIN TERMS
　　546.12
　MAKE TERMS
　　negotiate 769.7
　　mediate 803.6
　ON BAD TERMS 927.14
　ON EVEN TERMS 30.8
　ON TERMS 837.10
tern, ternal 94.3
ternary, ternion 93.1
ternary, ternate 94.3
Terpsichore 463.24
terpsichore
　dancing 877.1
　dancer 877.3

terpsichorean
　nouns 877.3
　adjs. 877.6
terra earth 374.7
　land 384.1
terrace 215.13
terra cotta
　sculpture 573.2
　ceramics 574.3
terra-cotta 366.4
terra firma base 211.3
　foundation 215.6
　land 384.1
　ON TERRA FIRMA
　　on land 384.11
　safe 696.6
terrain region 179.1
　land 384.1
terraqueous 384.6
terrene
　nouns 384.1
　adjs. earthly 374.27
　terrestrial 384.6
terrestrial
　earthly 374.27
　terrene 384.6
　mundane 1029.16
terrible
　adjs. great 34.12
　very bad 673.9
　unpleasant 862.10
　horrible 889.29
　hideous 897.11
　advs. 34.25
terribleness
　badness 673.2
　unpleasantness
　　862.3
　hideousness 897.2
terrier list 88.1
　account 843.2
terrific great 34.12
　superb 672.18
　terrible 889.29
terrified 889.25
terrify 889.16
terrifying 889.28
territorial 179.8
territory region 179.1
　province 180.1
terror
　violent person 161.9
　horror 889.1
　frightener 889.8
　hellion 941.3
　IN TERROR 889.32
terrorism anarchy
　738.2
　despotism 739.10
　fear 889.6
terrorist
　anarchist 738.3
　alarmist 889.7
terroristic 738.6
terrorization 889.6
terrorize 889.19
terror-stricken 889.25
Tersanctus 1038.10
terse
　epigrammatic 516.6
　concise 590.4

terseness 590.1
tertian 137.9
tertiaries 229.18
tertiary
 nouns 361.6
 adjs. 94.4
tertium quid 16.3
terzet 461.17
terzetto three 93.1
 music 461.17
tessellate
 verbs 373.7
 adjs. 373.14
tessellated 373.14
tessellation 373.4
tessera 566.11
tesserae 373.4
test
 nouns shell 227.16
 examination 484.3
 experiment 488.2
 road ~ 488.3
 measure 489.2
 association ~
  688.11
 verbs examine 484.22
 experiment 488.8
 adjs. 488.11
testa 227.16
testaceous 228.6
Testament 1019.2
testament
 testimony 504.3
 will 816.10
testamentary 816.25
testamur 568.5
testate
 nouns 816.11
 adjs. 816.25
testator 816.11
testatory 504.17
tested 488.12
testee 488.7
tester 488.6
testes 418.8
test flight 277.7
testicle gland 310.9
 genitals 418.8
testicular 418.18
testification 504.3
testifier 504.7
testify give evidence
  504.10
 ~ against 555.11
 indicate 566.16
testimonial
 testimony 504.3
 certificate 568.5
 memorial 568.11
 reference 966.4
testimonium 504.3
testimony 504.3
testiness 949.2
testing
 nouns 488.1
 adjs. 488.11
testis 310.9
teston 833.8
test pattern 344.5
test pilot 278.1
test rocket 280.5

testy 949.19
tetanus 684.5,8
tetched, tetchiness See
 teched etc.
tête à tête 241.12
tête-à-tête
 nouns 595.4
 adjs. dual 90.6
 conversational
  595.11
 sociable 920.19
tête de veau 306a.14
tether
 nouns 758.4
 verbs 758.10
tetrachord 462.8
tetractinal 96.4
tetrad
 nouns 96.1
 adjs. 96.4
tetradic 96.4
tetragonal 250.9
tetragram, tetra-
 grammaton 96.1
tetrahedral
 four-sided 241.7
 quadrangular 250.9
tetralogy 96.1
tetrameter 607.5
tetraphony 96.1
tetraploid 97.3
tetrapody four 96.1
 verse form 607.5
tetrarch 747.14
tetrarchic(al) 737.16
tetraseme 607.9
tetrastich 607.5
tetratomic 325.17
tetravalence 378.3
tetravalent
 quarternary 96.4
 valent 378.8
tetter 684.27
Teufel 1014.2
Teutonic race 417.2
tewel 328.10
text musical ~ 461.28
 topic 483.1
 letterpress 601.4
 textbook 603.8
 book ~ 603.13
 playbook 609.25
textile
 nouns 377.5
 adjs. woven 221.8
 textural 350.5
 cloth 377.9
textual topical 483.4
 literal 543.12
 scriptural 1019.9
 orthodox 1022.8
textualism 543.5
textualist 1022.5
textuary
 scriptural 1019.9
 orthodoxist 1022.5
textural
 structural 244.9
 textured 350.5
texture web 220.3
 weaving 221.1

structure 244.1
smoothness 259
roughness 260
surface quality 350
textile 377.5
textured 350.5
Thais 987.15
thakur ruler 747.10
 idol 1031.3
Thales 467.4
Thalia 609.30
thallogens, Thallo-
 phyta, thallo-
 phytes 411.4
than other ~ 16.10
 barring 77.9
 compared to 490.10
thana 759.9
thanatosis 710.7
thank 947.4
THANK ONE'S STARS
 rejoice 874.6
 be thankful 947.3
thankful 947.5
thankfulness 947.1
thankless
 unappreciated
  865.10
 ungrateful 948.4
thanks
 nouns
 thanksgiving 947.2
 prayer 1030.4
RETURN THANKS
 thank 947.4
 pray 1030.12
THANKS TO 154.9
 interjs. 947.6
thanksgiving
 gratitude 947.2
 prayer 1030.4
thank-you 947.2
that ~ one 80.15
 when 105.7
 lest 174.7
AT THAT
 additionally 40.10
 even so 506.15
THAT BEING SO 8.9
THAT GOES WITHOUT
 SAYING 512.27
THAT IS TO SAY
 namely 80.18
 i.e. 550.21
THAT'S FINAL, THAT'S
 THAT 70.13
thatch
 nouns 229.4
 verbs 227.25
thaumaturge 1033.5
thaumaturgia 1033.1
thaumaturgic(al)
 miraculous 85.15
 sorcerous 1033.14
thaumaturgics, thau-
 maturgism, thau-
 maturgy 1033.1
thaumaturgist 1033.5
thaw
 nouns 328.3
 verbs melt 328.20

have pity 942.4
thawer 402.7
thawing 328.3
thearchy 739.4
theater audience 447.6
 schoolroom 565.16
 drama 609.1
 playhouse 609.17
 arena 800.1
 battlefield 800.2
theatercraft 609.3
theatergoer 609.31
theaterlike 609.37
theaterman 609.27
theater of operations,
 theater of war
 800.2
theatricable 609.37
theatrical
 nouns 610.1
 adjs. dramatic 609.37
 affected 901.15
 showy 902.24
theatricalism 609.2
theatricalize 609.32
theatricals
 costume 230.9
 dramatics 609.2
theatrical season
 128.1
theatrician 609.27
theatricism, theatrics
 609.2
theatromania, theatro-
 phobia 609.1
theatron 609.17
theca 410.28
thecal 227.39
theft 822.1,10
their, theirs 806.13
theism 1018.5
theist 1018.14
theistic philosophical
 499.10
 religious 1018.23
them 80.5
thematic(al) 483.4
theme
 musical ~ 461.30
 topic 483.1
 essay 604.1
theme song
 radio 343.22
 song 461.13
themselves 80.5
then
 adjs. 119.7
 advs. also 40.10
 when 105.7
 at that time 105.11
 subsequently 117.5
 formerly 119.10
 hence 154.6
 JUST THEN 113.6
 THEN AND THERE
  113.8
 conjs. 16.10
thence
 henceforth 121.10
 hence 154.6
 elsewhere 186.17

awa▼ 300.21
thenceforth 121.10
theocracy
  government 739.4
  hierarchy 1035.7
theocratic(al)
  governmental
    739.16
  hierarchical 1035.16
theocratist 1035.16
theodolite 250.4
theogony 1012.1
theologian, theologist
  1021.3
theological
  nouns 1021.3
  adjs. 1021.4
theologism 1021.1
theology 1021.1
theopantism 1018.5
theophania 1019.8
theophany
  apparition 1015.1
  religion 1019.8
theopneustia, theo-
  pneusty 1019.8
theopneustic 1019.9
theorbist 463.5
theorbo 464.4
theorem
  premise 481.8
  topic 483.1
  supposition 498.2
  axiom 516.2
theoretic 498.6
theoretical 498.13
theoretician 498.6
theoretics, theorics
  498.1
theorist 498.6
theorization 498.1
theorize reason 481.15
  hypothesize 498.8
theorizer 498.6
theory
  supposition 498.1
  opinion 500.4
  IN THEORY 498.16
theory of evolution
  321.4; 498.1
theory of relativity
  178.6; 498.1
Theos 1011.3
theosophic(al)
  1032.24
theosophist
  nouns 1032.11
  adjs. 1032.24
theosophy 1032.1
theotherapy 1018.12
Theotokos 1013.5
theow 762.7
therapeusis 687.1
therapeutic
  nouns 685.4
  adjs. 685.34
therapeutics 687.1
therapeutist, therapist
  636.5
therapy
  dietetics 307.14

medicines 685
  healing arts 686
  therapeutics 687
  psychotherapy
    688.5–7
  faith healing
    1018.12
there
  nouns 183.2
  adjs. alert 531.14
  competent 731.22
  advs. thereat 183.25
  present 185.14
thereabout, there-
  abouts about 35.13
  there 183.25
  approximately
    199.26
thereafter
  subsequently 117.5
  henceforth 121.10
there at 731.25
thereat then 105.11
  hence 154.6
  there 183.25
thereby 9.11; 656.8
therefor hence 154.6
  for that 651.12
therefore hence 154.6
  this being so 493.17
therein thereof 9.11
  in 224.14
thereness 185.1
thereof of that 9.11
  from 300.21
thereon, thereupon
  of that 9.11
  subsequently 117.5
theretofore 116.6
therewith
  advs. with 73.10
  then 117.5
  preps. including
    40.11
  by means of 656.8
Theria 414.12
theriaca, theriac
  685.21
theriacal, therial
  685.34
theriotheism 1018.5
therm 327.18
thermae
  hot springs 327.9
  spa 687.31
thermal 327.24,30
thermal unit 327.18
thermantidote 402.22
thermic 327.30
thermic fever 684.20
thermion 341.22;
  342.3
thermionic 341.29;
  342.15
thermionics 342.1
thermodynamic(al)
  327.32
thermodynamics
  327.20
thermogenesis 328.5
thermology 327.20

thermoluminescence
  334.13
thermoluminescent
  334.37
thermolysis 53.2
thermolytic 53.6
thermolyze 53.4
thermometer 327.19
thermoneurosis
  688.17
thermonuclear 325.18
thermonuclear bomb
  799.16
thermonuclear fusion
  325.9
thermonuclear power
  power 156.4
  atomics 325.14
  types of ~ 327.34
thermostatics 346.2
thermotherapy 687.5
thermotics 327.20
theroid 985.6
thesaurus 603.7
these 80.14
Theseus and Pirithoüs
  926.8
thesis premise 481.8
  topic 483.1
  supposition 498.2
  essay 604.1
  accent 607.9
Thesmophoros 412.4
Thespian
  nouns 610.1
  adjs. 609.37
Thespian art 609.2
Thespis 609.30
Thetis sea god 396.4
  sea nymph 1012.17
theurgist 1033.5
theurgy 1033.1
thew sinew 48.4
  muscle 158.2
thewy 158.14
they 80.5
thick
  nouns 69.1
  IN THE THICK OF
  among 44.18
  midway 69.5
  between 236.14
  THROUGH THICK AND
  THIN
  throughout 56.18
  to the end 70.12
  perseveringly 623.9
  verbs thicken 203.5
  densify 353.10
  adjs. numerous
    101.10
  broad 203.8
  opaque 340.3
  dense 353.12
  viscid 388.12
  luxuriant 410.41
  guttural 449.18
  husky 457.14
  stupid 468.15
  incredible 502.10
  ~ voice 593.11

friendly 925.18
  advs. 353.15
thick-bodied
  big-bellied 196.13
  thick 203.8
thick-brained 468.16
thick-coming
  numerous 101.10
  recurrent 103.13
  frequent 135.4
  dense 353.12
thicken increase 38.4
  broaden 203.5
  densify 353.10
thickened 353.14
thickening 353.4
thicket clump 74.6
  grove 410.13
thick-girthed
  big-bellied 196.13
  thick 203.8
thick-growing 353.12
thickhead 470.4
thick-headed 468.16
thick-headedness
  468.3
thickness
  breadth 203.2
  layer 226.1
  opaqueness 340.1
  density 353.1
  viscidity 388.2
  raucousness 457.2
  intimacy 925.5
thickset stout 194.18
  stubby 202.10
  thick 203.8
  dense 353.12
thick-set 410.13
thick skin protective
  covering 227.16
  armor 797.3
  callousness 854.3
thick-skinned 854.12
thick-spread, thick-
  spreading 353.12
thickwit 470.3
thick-witted 468.16
thick-wittedness 468.3
thief 823.1
  LIKE A THIEF IN THE
  NIGHT
  unexpectedly 538.14
  surreptitiously
    612.20
  deceitfully 616.24
  dishonestly 973.23
Thief of Bagdad
  823.12
thieve 822.13
thievery 822.1
thieving
  nouns 822.1
  adjs. 822.20
thievish 822.20
thievishness 822.12
thigh 272.16
thill 216.1
thiller 413.18
thimbleful 35.2

THROW A WRENCH IN
 THE MACHINERY
disable 157.9
thwart 728.15
THROW COLD WATER
 ON
moderate 162.6
discourage 650.4
THROW DOWN
fell 316.5
demolish 691.19
destroy 691.20
THROW IN
interpose 236.7
insert 303.3
THROW IN ONE'S
 TEETH
confront with
 239.9
accuse of 1003.9
THROW IN THE
 TOWEL 763.8
THROW IN WITH
league 52.4
side with 784.6
THROW OFF
unhorse 184.6
doff 231.6
shed 231.10
get rid of 308.19
eject 308.22
do offhand 532.9
say 592.14
improvise 628.8
break a habit 641.3
free oneself 761.8
THROW ONESELF AT
 THE FEET OF
submit 763.10
entreat 772.11
grovel 905.6
beg mercy 942.6
THROW ONE'S HAT IN
 THE RING
be a candidate
 742.42
challenge 791.3
THROW ONE'S WEIGHT
 AROUND 737.12
THROW OPEN TO
 305.10
THROW OUT
eject 308.12,23
discard 666.7
THROW OVER
eliminate 77.5
refute 505.5
jilt 631.5
give up 631.7
discard 666.7
destroy 691.20
THROW THE BULL
 545.8
THROW TOGETHER
mix 44.11
do carelessly 532.9
THROW UP
vomit 308.24
elevate 315.5
give up 631.7
relinquish 812.3

throwaway
handbill 557.8
discard 666.3
throwback
reversion 146.2
regression 294.1
misfortune 727.3
thrower 284.8
throwing 284.3
thrown
~ together 44.15
baffled 513.23
~ for a loss 725.14
thrum
nouns 454.1
verbs hum 451.13
drum 454.4
play music 461.41,
 45
thrummer 463.5
thrumming
nouns 451.7
adjs. humming
 451.20
drumming 454.7
thrush
songbird 463.15
disease 684.12
thrust
nouns aviation
 277.29
rocket ~ 280.9
push 282.2
attack 796.3
verbs put 183.13
push 282.12
THRUST AND PARRY
 794.14
THRUST ASIDE 529.4
THRUST AT 796.17
THRUST BACK 288.2
THRUST IN
interpose 236.7
intrude 237.5
enter 301.7
insert 303.6
THRUST OUT
extend 178.7
eject 308.12
THRUST UPON
urge upon 771.9
force upon 816.19
Thruthvang, Thruth-
 leim 1016.11
thruway 655.6
Thrymheim 1016.11
thud
nouns 451.3
verbs 451.15
thug assassin 408.10
ruffian 941.4
thuggee, thuggery,
 thuggism 408.2
thumb
nouns 424.5
ALL THUMBS 732.20
KEEP UNDER ONE'S
 THUMB
have influence over
 171.11
dominate 739.14

subjugate 762.8
verbs 424.6
THUMB A RIDE
 272.30
THUMB DOWN
refuse 774.3
disapprove of
 967.10
THUMB ONE'S NOSE
 AT 791.4
THUMB OVER
skim over 484.34
browse 562.13
thumb index 88.2
thumbmark, thumb-
 print 566.6
thumbnail 811.4
thumbscrew 1009.4
thump
nouns blow 282.4
thud 451.3
drum 454.1
verbs strike 282.14,15
drum 454.4
beat time 461.45
chastise 1008.14
THUMP IN 277.49
thumper 194.11
thumping
nouns 454.1
adjs. great 34.13
huge 194.21
drumming 454.7
thunder
nouns thunderstorm
 393.3
boom 455.5
verbs boom 455.9
say 592.17
THUNDER AGAINST
 967.20
THUNDER FORTH
 557.13
thunderball 334.17
thunderblast 455.5
thunderbolt
speed 268.7
lightning 334.17
surprise 538.2
LIKE A THUNDERBOLT
 113.9
thunderclap
thunder 455.5
surprise 538.2
thundercloud,
 thunderhead
cloud 403.1
omen 542.4
warning 701.3
thunder-gust
rain 393.3
windstorm 402.13
thunderheaded 403.8
thundering
nouns 455.5
adjs. great 34.13
huge 194.21
booming 455.12
thunderlike,
 thunderous 455.12
thunder mug 680.14

thunder of applause
 966.2
thunderpeal 455.5
thundershower 393.3
thundersquall
rain 393.3
windstorm 402.13
thunderstorm 393.3
thunderstroke
lightning 334.17
thunder 455.5
thunderstruck 918.8
thunder tube 799.9
thundery 455.12
thurible scenter 435.6
church ~ 1038.11
thurifer
censer bearer 435.5
churchman 1038.11
thurification 1038.4
thurify 435.8
thus this way 8.8
similarly 20.18
hence 154.6
for instance 504.25
so 655.11
thusly this way 8.8
hence 154.6
thwack
nouns blow 282.4
bang 455.1
verbs strike 282.14
bang 455.6
thwart
verbs disappoint
 539.2
frustrate 728.15
adjs. 220.9
advs. 220.13
thwarted 539.5
thwarter 728.8
thwarting 728.3
thwartways 220.13
thymic 310.8
thymus 310.9
thyroid 310.9
thyrotomy 687.26
thyroxin 310.2
thyrsus staff 216.2
ti 462.7
tiara insignia 567.3,4
ornament 899.6
Tiburtine sibyl 541.6
tic 684.17
tick
nouns instant 113.3
insect 413a.7
animals 414.8
ticktock 454.2
mark 566.4
credit 837.1
verbs function 163.8
ticktock 454.5
mark 566.18
extend credit 837.6
TICK OFF
specify 80.9
indicate 566.17
mark 566.18
ticker timepiece 114.6

advice 752.2
gratuity 816.5
verbs top 210.8
tilt 218.10
~ over 219.6
cover 227.23
careen 274.45
inform 555.10
give 816.12
TIP OFF
inform 555.10
warn 701.7
tip-crowning 210.9
tip-off tip 555.3
warning 701.4
tipped topped 210.11
tilted 218.15
tipper 555.5
tipping 218.15
tipple
nouns 994.12
verbs 994.29
tippler 994.10
tippling
nouns 994.4
adjs. 994.44
tippybob 835.6
tipsification 994.1
tipsify 994.28
tipsiness 994.1
tipstaff
constable 697.14
bailiff 747.20
tipster
predictor 541.5
informant 555.5
tipsy 994.38
tiptoe
nouns 272.9
ON TIPTOE
on high 206.27
creeping 272.38
expectant 537.10
verbs creep 272.25
be cautious 893.5
adjs. 272.38
advs. 206.27
tiptoeing
nouns 272.9
adjs. 272.38
tiptop supreme 36.15
top 210.9
first-rate 672.16
tip-top 210.2
tirade lecture 597.3
berating 967.8
tirailleur 798.11
tire
nouns rim 252.4
fatigue 715.1
verbs fatigue 715.4,5
bore 882.5
tired fatigued 715.6
bored 882.10
TIRED OF
satiated 662.6
sick of 882.10
tiredness fatigue 715.1
boredom 882.3
tireless 623.7
tirer d'affaire 700.2

Tiresias 541.4
tiresome
fatiguing 715.11
vexatious 862.13
tedious 882.9
tiresomeness
vexatiousness 862.5
tediousness 882.2
tiring fatiguing 715.11
boring 882.9
tisane 685.4
Tishah b'ab, Tishah
bov 1038.16
Tisiphone 1014.11
tissue
nouns main part 54.5
network 220.3
fabric 377.5
verbs 221.7
tit diminutive 195.4
teat 255.6
TIT FOR TAT
interchange 149.1
reprisal 953.3
Titan
strong man 158.6
giant 194.13
sun 374.11
Titania 1012.15
titanic strong 158.15
huge 194.20
tithable 844.17
tithe
nouns part 55.1
tenth 99.14
tax 844.10
verbs 844.14
adjs. 99.22
tithing 179.5
tithingman 74.14
Titian, titian
reddish-brown 366.4
red 367.7
red-haired 367.11
titillate tickle 425.6
interest 528.12
tempt 648.5
thrill 855.16
delight 863.8
amuse 876.23
titillated
interested 528.16
amused 876.28
titillating
interesting 528.19
tempting 648.7
amusing 876.29
titillation
tickling 425.2
thrill 855.2
pleasure 863.1
titillative
ticklish 425.9
tempting 648.7
delightful 861.6
amusing 876.29
titivate, tittivate
dress up 230.41
smarten up 899.7
title
nouns caption 483.2

name 581.3
book ~ 603.13
estate 808.4
~ of honor 915.1
right 956.3
HAVE A TITLE TO
958.4
HAVE NO TITLE TO
959.5
verbs caption 483.3
name 581.11
titled named 581.14
noble 916.11
title page title 483.2
book 603.13
title role 609.11
titmouse 195.4
titrate 484.32
titration 484.8
titter
nouns 874.4
verbs 874.9
tittle
nouns
small amount 35.2
minute thing 195.7
dot 566.4
mark 584.11
TO A TITTLE 515.21
verbs 556.12
tittle-tattle
nouns gossip 556.7
chatter 594.3
chitchat 595.5
verbs gossip 556.12
prate 594.6
chat 595.9
tittle-tattler 556.9
titty 255.6
titubancy 593.3
titubant 593.11
titubation 593.3
titular nominal 581.15
of a title 915.7
titulary 915.7
Tiu See Tyr
tizzy dither 855.5
dudgeon 950.7
IN A TIZZY
in a dither 855.22
angry 950.28
tmesis 219.3
TNT, T.N.T. 799.9
to until 105.10
at 183.28
as far as 198.20
toward 198.28
into 301.14
for 651.12
TO AND FRO
reciprocally 13.14
variably 141.8
interchangeably
149.7
back and forth
322.20
TO A T
exactly 515.21
to perfection 675.11
toad animal 413.32
toady 905.3

toadeating
nouns 905.2
adjs. 905.13
toad stabber 347.2
toadstool 410.4
toady
nouns 905.3
verbs 905.6
toadying
nouns 905.2
adjs. 905.13
toadyism 905.2
to-and-fro
nouns 322.4
verbs 322.12
adjs. 322.18
toast
nouns bread 306a.27
fine lady 901.10
pledge 994.9
verbs be hot 327.21
cook 329.4
drink to 994.35
adjs. 366.3
toasted 329.6
toasting
nouns 329.1
adjs. 327.25
toastmaster 876.22
toasty 327.24
tobacco
nouns 433
adjs. 433.16
tobacco belt 181.1
tobacco camphor
433.10
tobaccoism 433.11
tobaccoite 433.12
tobaccolike 433.16
tobacconist
tobacco 433.13
merchant 828.3
tobacconists 830.5
tobaccophile 433.12
to-be 121.8
toboggan 272.34
GO ON THE TOBOGGAN
weaken 159.9
deteriorate 690.18
tobogganing 272.8
toby 433.4
tocogeny, tocology
686.2
tocsin 702.3
today
nouns 120.1
advs. 120.3
toddle
nouns 272.14
verbs go slow 269.6
walk 272.27
TODDLE ALONG
go slow 269.6
depart 300.6
toddler 125.7
to-do commotion 62.4
excitement 855.3
toe 211.5
ON ONE'S TOES 531.14
toehold
foothold 215.5

GO ON A TOOT
make merry 876.26
spree 994.34
verbs blare 452.8
~ a horn 461.43
TOOT ONE'S OWN
HORN 908.6
tooter
musician 463.4
horn 464.7
tooth
nouns cog 257.5
anatomy 257.7
texture 350.1
taste 426.1
TOOTH AND NAIL
fiercely 161.26
resolutely 622.17
laboriously 714.20
verbs notch 261.4
give texture 350.4
toothache 423.5
toothdrawer 686.9
toothed dental 257.17
notched 261.5
toothful 994.6
toothless 258.4
toothlike 257.17
tooth paste
cleanser 679.16
prophylactic 685.18
toothsome, toothy
427.8
tootle
nouns 452.4
verbs toot 452.8
~ a horn 461.43
tootsy 211.5
top
nouns topside 210
summit 210.2
head 210.5
surface 223.2
lid 227.5
roof 227.6
tent 227.8
toy 376.16
AT THE TOP OF THE
LADDER 210.14
GO OVER THE TOP
795.19
ON TOP 722.13
ON TOP OF
add tionally 40.10
atop 210.14
on 227.40
ON TOP OF THE HEAP
successful 722.13
prosperous 726.12
verbs excel 36.5
overtop 206.16
crown 210.8
cover 227.23
TOP OFF 720.6
adjs. supreme 36.15
topmost 210.9
toparchy 180.1
topcoat 230.13
tope
nouns tower 206.11
tomb 409.16

grove 410.12
monument 568.11
shrine 1040.4
verbs 994.30
toper 994.10
topflight chief 36.16
first-rate 672.16
topfull 56.12
topgallant
nouns 210.2
adjs. 210.9
top-heavy 31.5
Tophet 1017.1
top-hole
supreme 36.15
first-rate 672.16
topic subject 483
plot 606.9
topical local 179.9
thematic 483.4
toping
nouns 994.4
adjs. 994.44
top kick 747.23
topknot top 210.3
hair 229.7
feathers 229.16
topknotted 229.29
topless high 206.19
headless 210.12
toploftily 910.15
toplofty 910.9
topmost
supreme 36.15
top 210.9
top-notch
supreme 36.15
first-rate 672.16
topnotcher 731.11
top-notcher 672.6
topographer
surveyor 489.10
map maker 652.4
topographic(al)
regional 179.8
measuring 489.13
topography
location 183.8
surveying 489.9
mapping 652.4
toponymy 581.1
topped 210.11
topper 230.13
topping
nouns 210.7
adjs. surpassing 36.14
crowning 210.10
toppings 210.15
topple fall 314.8
break down 690.25
be destroyed 691.21
TOPPLE OVER
overturn 219.6
fall 314.8
break down 690.25
top priority 64.1
tops 672.16
THE TOPS 672.8
topsail 276.30
top sawyer
principal 670.10

chief 747.3
top secret 612.5
top-secret 612.12
top sergeant 747.23
topside
nouns 210.1
advs. atop 210.14
on deck 274.66
topsided 31.5
topsman 1008.8
topsoil 384.1
topsy-turvify 219.6
topsy-turvy
nouns disorder 62.1
inversion 219.1
verbs 219.6
adjs. confused 62.15
upside-down 219.7
advs. 219.8
topsy-turvydom
disorder 62.1
inversion 219.1
tor 206.8
Torah 1019.3
torah 1019.8
torch
nouns
blowtorch 328.13
lighter 330.4
light 335.1,3
verbs 653.10
torchlight 334.18
torchlit 334.38
torch race 794.12
torch singer 463.13
torch song 461.13
toreador, torero 798.4
torment
nouns pain 423.6
bane 674.1
distress 864.7
tormentor 864.10
worry 888.2
punishment 1008.2
verbs pain 423.7
persecute 665.6
harass 864.19
harrow 864.20
obsess 864.21
worry 888.4
tormented
in pain 423.9
harassed 864.27
worried 888.7
tormenting
painful 423.10
harassing 862.13,14
worrying 888.9
tormentor
stage wing 609.24
harasser 864.10
tormina 423.5; 684.21
terminal 423.12
torn severed 49.22
alienated 927.12
tornado
outburst 161.6
wind 402.13,15
torose 255.16
torpedo
nouns assassin 408.10

missile 799.14
types of ~ 799.27
gunman 941.4
verbs shoot 284.13
fire upon 796.23
torpedoman 275.6
torpescence 706.5
torpid inert 267.12
listless 706.18
apathetic 854.13
torpidity
languor 706.5
apathy 854.4
Torpids 794.12
torpor
inertness 267.4
languor 706.5
apathy 854.4
torque
aviation 277.28
ornament 899.6
torrefaction 328.1
torrefy burn 328.23
dry 392.6
torrent outburst 161.6
speed 268.7
stream 394.5
torrid 327.25
torridity 327.4
Torrid Zone
latitude 179.3
hot place 327.10
torsion
convolution 253.1
aviation 277.28
torsional 253.6
torso 375.3
tort misdeed 980.2
offense 997.4
torticollis 684.8
tortile 253.6
tortility 253.1
tortilla 306a.28
tortoise
slow goer 269.5
turtle 413.30
tortoiselike 269.10
tortoise shell 373.6
tortoise-shell 373.6
tortuosity 253.1
tortuous
twisting 253.6
circuitous 319.7
torture
nouns pain 423.6
torment 864.7
punishment 1008.2
verbs twist 248.5
pain 423.7
torment 864.20
punish 1008.18
tortured in pain 423.9
anguished 864.28
torturous
painful 423.10
agonizing 862.14
Tory
conservative 140.4
partisan 742.28
Toryism
conservatism 140.3

partisanism 742.26
tosh 545.3
toss
nouns
even chance 155.7
throw 284.4
flounder 323.8
gamble 514.2
verbs
discompose 63.4
put 183.13
sail 274.58
throw 284.12
sway 322.9
flounder 323.15
billow 394.23
be excited 855.18
TOSS AND TURN
flounder 323.15
vacillate 625.8
not sleep 711.3
be excited 855.18
TOSS OFF
drink 306.27
do offhand 532.9
improvise 628.8
tipple 994.29
TOSS ONE'S HAT IN
THE RING
be a candidate
742.42
challenge 791.3
TOSS OUT
eject 308.12
improvise 628.8
TOSS THE HEAD
dismiss 529.4
be arrogant 910.8
TOSS UP 514.17
tossing 322.16
tosspot 994.10
tossup
even chance 155.7
uncertainty 513.8
gamble 514.2
tot total 54.2
child 125.3
total
nouns 54.2
verbs amount to 54.7
sum up 87.12
adjs. whole 54.8
utter 56.11
unqualified 507.2
totaling 87.3
totalitarian 739.16
totaliarianism 739.9
totality whole 54.1
completeness 56.1
totalizator, totalizer
514.12
totally wholly 54.12
completely 56.16
tote
nouns total 54.2
freight 270.7
verbs total 54.7
escort 73.8
carry 270.11
TOTE FAIR 974.7
totem symbol 566.2

guardian spirit
1012.19
totem pole pole 216.1
symbol 566.2
toting 270.3
totitive 86.8
totter
nouns gait 272.14
stagger 323.8
verbs fluctuate 141.5
be weak 159.8
walk 272.27
stagger 323.15
vacillate 625.8
break down 690.25
TOTTER ALONG 269.6
TOTTER ON THE
BRINK 695.8
tottering
nouns changeableness
141.3
alternation 322.4
adjs. aged 126.17
unsteady 159.16
deteriorating 690.44
tottery aged 126.17
unsteady 159.16
precarious 695.11
tottle
nouns 54.2
verbs total 54.7
sum up 87.12
tottlish 159.16
tot up 87.12
touch
nouns
small amount 35.4
tinge 44.7
contact 199.5
sense 421.5
sensation 424.1
musical ~ 461.31
communication
552.3
nudge 566.14
act 703.3
request 772.1
~ of conscience
871.2
IN TOUCH WITH
related 9.6
adjacent 199.16
KEEP IN TOUCH!
300.25
verbs relate to 9.3
equal 30.6
come in contact
199.10
feel 424.6
interest 528.12
nudge 566.21
beg 772.15
borrow 819.3
affect 853.13
excite pity 942.5
NOT ABLE TO TOUCH
37.7
NOT TOUCH
not use 666.5
abstain 990.7

TOUCH A SOFT SPOT
sensitivity 421.9
grieve 864.14
TOUCH BOTTOM
degenerate 690.18
be unfortunate
727.11
despond 870.16
TOUCH OFF
fire 161.13
incite 646.18
TOUCH SHOULDERS
WITH 920.15
TOUCH THE HAT
923.10
TOUCH UP
furbish 689.11
repair 692.14
TOUCH UPON
deal with 9.3
be superficial 209.4
touch 424.7
skim over 484.34
slight 532.8
write upon 604.5
touchable 424.11
touch and go
even chance 155.7
uncertainty 513.8
gamble 514.2
touch-and-go 513.14
touchdown 722.4
touched insane 472.24
tainted 690.39
affected 853.24
contrite 871.9
touchhole 395.17
touchiness
sensitiveness 421.3
ticklishness 425.2
precariouness 695.2
irascibility 949.4
touching
nouns contact 199.5
feeling 424.2
adjs. in contact
199.17
interesting 528.19
affecting 853.23
pathetic 862.11
preps. 9.11
touchstone 489.2
touchwood 330.6
touchy
sensitive 421.13
ticklish 425.9
precarious 695.12
irascible 949.20
tough
nouns 941.4
adjs. adhesive 50.9
violent 161.15
hard 355.10
unyielding 355.12
resistant 358.4
viscid 388.12
abstruse 547.12
obstinate 624.10
laborious 714.19
difficult 729.16
strict 755.6

hardened 979.21
toughen harden 355.7
make tough 358.3
tough luck 727.5
toughness
tenacity 50.2
hardness 355
inflexibility 355.3
resistance 358
viscidity 388.2
obstinacy 624.1
difficulty 729.1
strictness 755.1
toupee 229.14
tour
nouns shift 108.3
journey 272.5
circuit 319.2
ON TOUR
absent 186.10
touring 272.35
verbs 272.20
tour de force 731.10
tourer 273.1
touring 272.35
tourism 272.1
tourist
nouns 273.1
verbs 272.20
tourist camp 190.25
touristic(al) 272.35
touristry 272.1
touristy 272.35
tournament
battle 794.3
games 876.10
tourney
nouns battle 794.3
tournament 876.10
verbs 794.14
tourniquet 685.28
tournure
outline 234.2
form 245.2
touse
nouns commotion
62.4
row 793.6
verbs 63.2
tousle 63.2
tousled 62.13
tout
nouns lookout 531.4
predictor 541.5
tipster 555.5
scout 779.9
solicitor 828.7
KEEP TOUT
keep watch 531.8
keep guard 697.19
verbs spy out 484.37
keep guard 697.19
solicit 772.14
tout à fait 56.15
tout à l'heure 131.16
tout au contraire
contrarily 15.7
by no means 522.8
tout ensemble all 54.3
the nude 231.3
touter predictor 541.5

tipster 555.5
solicitor 828.7
tout le monde 79.4
tow 285.4
towage towing 285.1
charge 844.7
toward
adjs. 763.14
preps. at 183.28
facing 238.6
in the direction of
289.28
towardness 763.4
towel 1008.16
tower
nouns stability 142.7
chateau 190.7
height 206.11
structure 244.2
meteorological ~
280.8
watchtower 438.8
protection 697.4
stronghold 797.6
verbs loom 34.7
be high 206.15
soar 313.10
towering huge 194.20
lofty 206.19
tower of silence
409.16
tower of strength
strong man 158.6
protector 697.4
stronghold 797.6
towery 206.19
towheaded 363.10
towing
nouns 285.1
adjs. 285.6
town
nouns 182
GO TO TOWN 722.9
ON THE TOWN 987.28
adjs. 182.9
towner 189.6
**townfolk, townsman,
townspeople** 189.6
town hall hall 190.15
courthouse 999.9
townhouse
poorhouse 698.4
courthouse 999.9
town house 190.5
townscape view 445.6
picture 572.13
township
district 179.5
town 182.1
towny, townee 189.6
towpath 655.3
tow-row 793.5
toxemia 684.23
toxic
nouns 674.3
adjs. 682.5
toxicant
nouns poison 674.3
intoxicant 994.12
adjs. 582.5
toxicity 682.2

toxicology 674.3
toxiferous 682.5
toxin 674.3
toxophilite
archer 284.9
sportsman 876.20
toy
nouns dupe 618.1
cat's-paw 656.3
trifle 671.5
plaything 876.16
trinket 899.4
laughingstock 965.7
verbs dally 671.13
make love 930.13
TOY WITH
consider 477.11
trifle with 671.13
toying 671.8
trace
nouns small amount
35.4
vestige 43.1
tinge 44.7
radar signal 345.11
track 566.7
record 568.1
tug 657.5
engram 688.40
NOT A TRACE 2.3
verbs copy 22.8
seek 484.29
mark 566.18
draw 572.20
write 600.19
outline 652.12
TRACE DOWN
derive from 154.4
trace 484.29
find 487.4
TRACE OUT 579.10
traceable 154.5
tracer atom 325.4
radiator 326.5
isotope 687.10
tracery network 220.3
curves 251.2
trachea 395.16
tracheal 395.20
Tracheata 414.8
tracheocele 684.8
trachoma 684.11
tracing
reproduction 22.3
copy 24.4
picture 572.14
track
nouns spoor 566.7
routine 640.5
path 655.3
sport 876.8
playground 876.13
KEEP TRACK OF
keep account of
87.13
keep informed
555.15
OFF THE BEATEN
TRACK 85.10
OFF THE TRACK
insane 472.25

bewildered 513.22
mistaken 517.16
PUT ON THE RIGHT
TRACK 289.7
verbs traverse 272.19
walk 272.26
trace 484.29
TRACK DOWN
derive from 154.4
trace 484.29
find 487.4
tracking 345.8
tracking station 345.6
trackless 265.10
track meet 876.10
tract area 178.1
plot 179.4
subdivision 187.3
field 412.9
booklet 603.10
tractability
pliancy 356.2
compliance 763.3
tractable
conformable 82.5
pliant 356.9
compliant 763.13
tractably 763.18
tractate 604.1
tractile 356.9
tractility 356.2
traction pulling 285
attraction 287.1
tractional, tractive
285.6
tractor vehicle 271.16
types of ~ 271.25
airplane 279.2
trade
nouns exchange
149.2
vocation 654.6
commerce 825.1
barter 825.2,5
verbs exchange 149.4
barter 825.10
TRADE ON 663.15
trade-in 825.5
trade-last 966.6
trademark 566.12
trader 828.2
trades 402.10
**tradesfolk, tradesmen,
tradespeople**
828.11
trade union 787.1
trade wind 402.10
trading
nouns exchange
149.2
barter 825.2
adjs. 825.17
trading post 830.1
tradition immemorial
usage 123.2
superstition 501.3
traditional old 123.12
historical 606.18
conventional 643.7
traditionalism 123.2
traditionalistic 499.10

traditional logic 481.2
traditive 123.12
traduce 969.11
traducement 969.3
traducer 969.6
traffic
nouns intercourse
552.1
commerce 825.1
verbs 825.10
TRAFFIC IN 825.12
TRAFFIC WITH
communicate 552.6
trade with 825.13
trafficker 828.2
trafficking 825.2
traffic lights
lights 335.4
signal 566.14
tragedian
dramatist 609.26
actor 610.7
tragédie 609.5
tragedy drama 609.5
calamity 727.2
tragic(al)
tragicodramatic
609.38
disastrous 727.15
tragically 727.18
tragicodramatic
609.38
tragicomedy 609.6
tragicomic
dramatic 609.39
humorous 878.6
trail
nouns afterpart 67.2
attendance 73.6
odor 434.1
spoor 566.7
path 655.3
HIT THE TRAIL
journey 272.20
travel 272.22
set forth 300.7
ON THE TRAIL 653.12
ON THE TRAIL OF
487.10
verbs draggle 214.6
be behind 240.7
lag 269.8
draw 285.4
follow 292.3
lag behind 292.4
trace 484.29
trail blazer 718.5
trailer vehicle 271.17
motion picture
609.15
trailer court 190.14
trailing
nouns 292.1
adjs. 292.5
train
nouns afterpart 67.2
series 71.2
procession 71.4
attendance 73.6
tail 240.5
railroad ~ 271.12

military ~ 798.19
IN THE TRAIN OF
behind 292.6
serving 748.15
TRAIN OF THOUGHT
477.4
verbs transport
270.12
draw 285.4
direct 289.6
teach 560.13
trainable 562.18
trainband 798.23
trainbearer
follower 292.2
attendant 748.4
trainboy 273.13
trained 731.24
trainee student 564.1
recruit 798.17
trainer aircraft 279.10
horse ~ 415.2
teacher 563.7
school 565.13
training 560.3
trainload 193.2
trainman, trainmaster
273.13
traipse, trapes
nouns slattern 62.7
walk 272.12
verbs go slow 269.6
gad 272.22
walk 272.26,27
traipsing, trapesing
nouns 272.3
adjs. 272.36
trait
characteristic 80.3
habit 640.3
traitor informer 555.6
treasonist 617.10
turncoat 626.5
traitorous 973.21
traits 445.4
traject 284.11
trajectile
nouns projectile
284.6
missile 799.12
adjs. 284.16
trajection 284.3
trajectory
rocket 280.10
celestial ~ 374.16
route 655.2
tralatition 549.2
tralatitious 549.4
tram
nouns streetcar
271.14
railway 655.8
verbs 272.32
tramline 655.8
trammel
nouns 758.3,4
verbs hamper 728.11
restrain 758.9,10
trammeled 758.15,16
tramontane
nouns alien 78.3

wind 402.9
adjs. 198.11
tramontanta 402.9
tramp
nouns walk 272.12
vagabond 273.3
pedestrian 273.6
verbs wander 272.22
walk 272.29
tramping 272.10
trample 311.7
TRAMPLE DOWN
conquer 725.10
tyrannize 739.15
TRAMPLE IN THE
DUST
conquer 725.10
subdue 762.9
TRAMPLE ON
run over 311.7
violate 767.4
TRAMPLE OUT 691.15
tramroad, tramway
655.8
trance
nouns brown study
530.2
dream 533.9
catalepsy 688.26
sleep 710.6
hypnosis 710.7
spell 1034.3
IN A TRANCE
dreaming 533.25
spellbound 1034.13
verbs hypnotize
710.18
spellbind 1034.8
tranced 533.25
trance writing 1032.6
tranquil
quiescent 267.10
peaceful 801.9
inexcitable 856.12
tranquilization 162.2
tranquilize 162.7
tranquilizer
pacifier 162.3
sedative 685.11
tranquilizing
pacifying 162.15
sedative 685.39
tranquillity
quiescence 267.1
peace 801.2
mental ~ 856.2
trans- 198.11
transact
~ business 654.12
do 703.8
execute 769.10
transaction
affair 150.3
action 703.2,3
execution 769.5
business ~ 825.4
transanimation 139.2
transcalency 327.17
transcalent 327.31
transcend excel 36.5

go beyond 661.10
transcendence, trans-
cendency 36.1
transcendent
surpassing 36.14
recondite 547.14
transcendental
surpassing 36.14
supernatural 85.14
transmundane
374.26
recondite 547.14
heavenly 1016.13
transcendentalism
supernaturalism
85.7
philosophy 499.3
religion 1032.2
transcendentalist
1032.11
transcending 36.14
transconductance
342.9
transcontinental
198.11
transcribe copy 22.8
~ music 461.47
translate 550.14
write 600.19
transcript copy 24.4
music score 461.28
transcription
reproduction 22.3
copy 24.4
record 464.19
translation 550.3
transept 1040.9
transequational
198.11
transeunt 111.7
transfer
nouns transcript 24.4
removal 270.1
communication
552.2
~ of property 815
delivery 816.1
BY TRANSFER 270.19
verbs remove 270.9
communicate 552.7
~ property 815.3
deliver 816.13
transferability
transmissibility
270.4
communicability
552.5
transferable
removable 270.17
communicable
552.10
assignable 815.5
transference
removal 270
communication
552.2
psychological ~
688.43
~ of property 815.1
delivery 816.1

transfiguration
transformation
139.2
rite 1038.4
transfigure 139.7
transfix stick 142.8
pierce 264.15
impale 796.27
transfixation,
transfixion
perforation 264.3
impalement 796.11
transfixed 142.17
transforation 264.3
transform 139.7
transformable 145.13
transformation
change 139.2
stage scene 609.24
transformed 139.9
transformer 139.4
transformism 139.2
transfuse imbue 44.12
pervade 185.7
transfer 270.9
give transfusion
687.36
transfusion
imbuement 44.2
pervasion 185.3
transference 270.1
blood ~ 687.22
transgress
overstep 311.9
violate 767.4
sin 980.3
trespass 997.5
transgression
overstepping 311.3
violation 767.2
sin 980.2
lawbreaking 997.3
transgressive 765.9
transgressor 984.8
transience, transiency
111
transient
nouns transience
111.4
lodger 189.8
traveler 273.1
adjs. short-lived 111.7
migratory 272.36
transilience 147.1
transilient 147.5
transistor 342.13
transit
conversion 145.1
transference 270.1
travel 272.1
IN TRANSIT 270.20
transition
conversion 145.1
transference 270.1
transitional
convertible 145.13
moving 266.6
transitive
nouns 584.3
adjs. transient 111.7
verbal 584.13

footstep 272.13
gait 272.14
stair 313.5
verbs 272.26
TREAD DOWN 739.15
TREAD ON ONE'S TOES
950.20
TREAD ON THE HEELS
OF
stay near 199.12
follow 292.3
approach 295.3
TREAD UNDERFOOT
725.10
TREAD UNDER FOOT
tyrannize 739.15
subdue 762.9
TREAD UPON
run over 311.7
tyrannize 739.15
treadle
nouns pedal 284.7
lever 286.4
verbs 284.10
treadmill
routine 640.5
punishment 1009.3
treason 973.7
treasonable 973.21
treasonist 617.10
treasonous 973.21
treasure
nouns store 658.1
good thing 672.5
funds 833.14
wealth 835.1
verbs remember
535.14
hoard 658.11
rate highly 670.12
cherish 811.7
hold dear 929.18
treasured
hoarded 658.14
cherished 929.21
treasure house
storehouse 658.6
treasury 834.12
treasurer 834.11
treasure-trove 809.5
treasury
~ of words 603.7
storehouse 658.6
depository 834.12
treat
nouns repast 306.5
standing ~ 839.8
delight 863.3
verbs operate on
163.7
discuss 481.16
deal with 663.12
doctor 687.33
process 718.6
behave toward
735.6
~ to 839.19
TREAT OF
deal with 9.3
write upon 604.5

TREAT WITH
negotiate 769.7
~ contempt 791.4
mediate 803.6
~ disrespect 963.3
treatise 604
treatment
discussion 481.4
art 572.10
treatise 604.1
usage 663.2
medical ~ 687.17
processing 718.1
treaty compact 769.2
~ of peace 802.5
treble
nouns voice part
461.22
voice 462.5
~ clef 462.13
verbs 94.2
adjs. triple 94.3
high-pitched 457.12
vocal 461.51
trebly 94.5
trebuchet, trebucket
catapult 799.19
cucking stool 1009.3
tree
nouns genealogy
169.5
mast 276.13
plant 410.10
~ types of 410.51
gallows 1009.5
UP A TREE
baffled 513.23
cornered 729.23
verbs baffle 513.13
corner 729.15
treelike
branching 298.10
arboreal 410.37
treelikeness 298.3
tree of knowledge
474.8
tree of life 465.5
tree-shaped 298.10
trefoil 93.1
trek
nouns migration
272.4
journey 272.5
verbs journey 272.20
migrate 272.21
draw 285.4
trekker
traveler 273.1
migrant 273.5
trellis
nouns 220.3
verbs 220.7
trelliswork 220.3
Trematoda 414.5
tremble
nouns shake 323.3
tremolo 462.19
trepidation 855.4
verbs be weak 159.8
shake 323.11
shiver 332.10

be excited 855.18
be afraid 889.13
trembles 857.2
trembling
nouns 323.2
adjs. shaking 323.18
nervous 857.12
fearful 889.22
trembly shaky 323.18
nervous 857.12
tremellose 388.12
tremendous
great 34.12
huge 194.20
superb 672.18
terrifying 889.29
tremendously
vastly 34.18
superbly 672.24
frightfully 889.33
tremolando
music 461.54
tremolo 462.19
tremolant 462.19
tremolo
nouns 462.19
verbs 461.39
tremoloso 461.54
tremor quiver 323.3
tremolo 462.19
excitement 855.2
trepidation 855.4
tremors 688.24
tremulant
excited 855.24
nervous 857.12
tremulous
trembling 323.18
~ voice 593.11
excited 855.24
nervous 857.12
trembling 889.22
trench
nouns furrow 262.2
aqueduct 395
entrenchment 797.5
verbs intrude 237.5
canal 262.3
TRENCH ON
adjoin 199.9
overstep 311.9
violate 767.4
trenchancy
acrimony 160.4
conciseness 590.1
causticity 937.8
trenchant
energetic 160.11
acrimonious 160.12
concise 590.4
significant 670.19
caustic 937.21
trencherman
eater 306.13
gourmand 992.3
trend
nouns tendency 173.2
direction 289.1
verbs tend 173.3
bear 289.8
deviate 290.3

trepan, trapan
nouns deception
616.6
trap 616.11
deceiver 617.1
instrument 687.39
verbs perforate 264.15
cheat 616.18
trap 616.20
trephine
nouns 687.39
verbs 264.15
trepidation
agitation 323.1
alarm 702.1
excitement 855.4
fear 889.4
trepidity
agitation 323.1
excitement 855.4
fear 889.4
très bien 520.18
très bon 672.13
trespass
nouns overstepping
311.3
violation 767.2
sin 980.2
lawbreaking 997.3
verbs intrude 237.5
overstep 311.9
violate 767.4
sin 980.3
transgress 997.5
trespasser 237.3
trespassing 997.3
tress 229.5
tresses 229.4
tressure 567.2
trest 215.17
**trestle, trestlework,
trestling** 215.17
trews 230.18
trey 93.2
triad three 93.1
chord 462.17
triadelphous 95.4
triadic(al) 93.4
tria juncta in uno 93.4
trial
nouns examination
484.3
experiment 488.1,2
attempt 712.2
tribulation 864.9
court ~ 1002.5
ON TRIAL
experiment 488.14
in litigation 1002.21
adjs. three 93.4
experimental 488.11
trial and error 488.11
trial-and-error 488.11
trialogue 595.3
triangle three 93.1
geometric figure
250.14
gong 453.4
orchestral ~ 464.20
love 929.6
punishment 1009.3

triangular
three-parted 95.4
trilateral 250.8
triangulate
verbs 95.3
adjs. 95.4
triangulation
trisection 95.1
radar ~ 345.8
triarch 95.4
triarchy 739.4
triatomic 325.17
tribal 11.8
tribasic 325.17
tribe race 11.4
kind 61.3
class 61.5
company 74.3
flock 74.5
tribesman 11.5
tribofluorescence
334.13
tribofluorescent
334.37
triboluminescence
334.13
triboluminescent
334.37
tribulation 864.9
tribunal
nouns platform
215.13
council 753
court 999
adjs. 999.10
tribune
platform 215.13
judge 1000.2
tributary
nouns 394.3
adjs. 816.24
tribute
contribution 816.6
fee 839.5
tax 844.10
praise 966.5
PAY TRIBUTE 966.12
PAY TRIBUTE TO
962.5
trice 113.3
IN A TRICE 113.7
tricennial 137.4
triceps 158.2
trice up fasten 47.7
tighten 355.9
trichi 433.4
trichinopoly 433.4
trichinosis 684.8
trichoid 229.23
trichotomize 95.3
trichotomous 95.4
trichotomy
trisection 95.1
operation 687.26
trichroism 373.1
trichromatic,
trichomic 373.9
trick
nouns characteristic
80.3
enlistment 107.3

shift 108.3
foolish act 469.4
illusion 518.1
deception 616.6
habit 640.3
knack 731.6
artifice 733.3
cards 876.17
prank 879.10
mannerism 901.2
DO THE TRICK
effectuate 720.4
succeed 722.11
verbs deceive 616.13
play pranks 879.14
TRICK UP
dress up 230.41
adorn 899.7
adjs. 22.9
tricker 617.2
trickery
deception 616.4,5
prankishness 879.4
ornament 899.3
trickiness
deception 616.1
cunning 733.1
prankishness 879.4
trickle
nouns drip 302.5
flow 394.7
verbs leak 302.14
flow 394.19
trickster
deceiver 617.2
crafty person 733.6
tricksy
deceptive 616.21
spruce 642.13
crafty 733.12
mischievous 736.6
prankish 879.17
tricky
deceptive 616.21
deceitful 616.22
evasive 629.14
crafty 733.12
mischievous 736.6
prankish 879.17
treacherous 973.20
tricolor
nouns 567.6
adjs. 373.9
tricorn, tricornered,
tricuspid 95.4
tricycle 271.8
trident
nouns 93.1
adjs. 95.4
tridental, tridentate,
tridentated 95.4
tried tested 488.12
devoted 925.20
trustworthy 972.19
tried-and-trueness
925.7
triennial
anniversary 137.4
plant 410.3
triennium 93.1
trifid 95.4

trifle
nouns food 306a.40
bagatelle 671.5
verbs fool 469.6
treat lightly 671.13
make love 930.13
TRIFLE WITH
do carelessly 532.9
~ the truth 614.20
show disrespect
963.3
trifler dilettante 475.7
dallier 671.9
trifles 671.4
trifling
nouns 671.8
adjs. 671.16
trifloral, triflorate,
trifoliate 95.4
triforium 1040.9
triform 93.4
trifurcate 95.4
trig
nouns 87.2; 250.3
adjs. trim 59.8
spruce 642.13
trigamist 931.12
trigamy 931.2
trigger radar 345.17
touch off 646.18
trigger man
assassin 408.10
hoodlum 941.4
trigonal
three-parted 95.4
triangular 250.8
trigonoid 95.4
trigonometric(al)
87.17
trigonometrician 87.9
trigonometry
mathematics 87.2
goniometry 250.3
trigrammatic 95.4
trigraph 449.5
trihedral 241.7
trihedron 93.1
trihydrol 391.3
trike 271.8
trilateral
three-parted 95.4
three-sided 241.7
triangular 250.8
triliteral 95.4
trill
nouns trickle 394.7
tremolo 462.19
verbs leak 302.14
trickle 394.19
ripple 451.11
warble 459.5
sing 461.39
trillando 461.54
trillet, trilleto 462.19
trilling 451.19
trillion 99.13
trillo 462.19
Trilobita, trilobites
414.8
trilogic(al) 94.3
trilogy 93.1

trim
nouns fettle 7.3
clothing 230.1
decoration 899.1
IN TRIM
in order 59.7
shipshape 276.19
PUT IN TRIM
tidy 60.11
prepare 718.8
verbs tidy 60.11
border 234.10
~ ship 274.51
vacillate 625.8
defeat 725.6
be neutral 804.5
reduce 847.6
decorate 899.7
reprove 967.18
whip 1008.15
TRIM SAIL 274.21
adjs. orderly 59.8
well-shaped 247.6
shipshape 276.19
spruce 642.13
trimerous 95.4
trimetallic 382.15
trimeter 607.5
trimly 642.17
trimmed rigged 276.17
defeated 725.14
ornamented 899.10
trimmer
vacillator 625.5
politician 744.1
trimming
nouns edging 234.7
chicanery 616.4
vacillation 625.2
decoration 899.1
adjs. vacillating
625.10
tergiversating
626.10
trimness
orderliness 59.3
spruceness 642.3
trim-up 60.5
Trimurti 1011.10
trinal three 93.4
threefold 94.3
trinely 94.5
trinitrotoluene, trini-
trotoluol 799.9
Trinity 1011.10
trinity triad 93.1
threeness 93.3
Trinity Sunday
1038.15
trinket trifle 671.5
toy 876.16
gewgaw 899.4
trinomial 93.1
trio three 93.1
music 461.17
triolet 607.4
triologue 609.4
trionym 93.1
trip
nouns journey 272.5
flight 277.7

stumble 314.3
error 517.4
bungle 732.5
misdeed 980.2
verbs speed 268.11
walk 272.27
stumble 314.8
caper 317.6
err 517.8
trap 616.20
bungle 732.11
frolic 876.25
dance 877.5
be sinful 979.13
TRIP UP
catch 487.7
trap 616.20
defeat 725.7
triparted, tripartite
95.4
tripe nonsense 545.3
rubbish 667.5
tripedal 95.4
tripes 224.6
triphibian 279.8
triphthong 449.5
Tripitaka 1019.6
triple
verbs intensify 38.5
treble 94.2
adjs. 94.3
triplet three 93.1
notes 462.14
verse 607.5
triple time 462.23
triplex 94.3
triplicate
nouns copy 24.3
triplication 94.1
verbs copy 22.8
triple 94.2
adjs. 94.3
triplicity
threeness 93.3
triplication 94.1
triplopy 93.1
tripod three 93.1
fire iron 328.15
tripodic 95.4
tripody 607.5
tripos 484.3
tripot 514.14
tripper 273.1
tripping elegant 587.8
eloquent 598.9
trippingly
swiftly 268.21
~ on the tongue
598.15
tripsis 360.4
**Triptolemus,
Triptolemos** 412.4
triptych 568.10
triquetral 95.4
triquetrous
three-parted 95.4
three-sided 241.7
trireme 93.1
Trisagion 1030.3
trisect 95.3
trisected 95.4

trisection 95
triseme three 93.1
poetry 607.9
triskelion 93.1
trismus 684.8
triste 870.25
tristful 870.23
tristfulness 870.5
tristich 607.5
trisubstitution 325.8
trisul 93.1
tritanopia 440.3
trite
well-known 474.27
stereotyped 881.9
triteness cliché 516.3
banality 881.3
tritheism 1018.5
tritheist 1018.14
tritheistic 1018.23
triticism 516.3
tritium 325.5
Triton sea god 396.4
god 1012.17
tritons 325.6
triturable 360.13
triturate 360.9
trituration 360.4
triturator 360.7
triumph
nouns victory 724.1
exultation 874.1
ovation 875.1
elation 908.4
verbs succeed 722.6
be victorious 724.3
exult 908.8
triumphal 724.8
triumphant
successful 722.13
victorious 724.8
exultant 908.11
triumvirate three 93.1
government 739.4
Triune 1011.10
triune 93.4
triunity 93.3
trivalence 378.3
trivalent 378.8
trivet tripod 93.1
fire iron 328.15
trivia 671.4
trivial shallow 209.5
trifling 671.16
triviality
shallowness 209.1
insignificance
671.3,5
troat 459.2
trochaic 607.22
troche 685.6
trochee 607.9
Trochelminthes 414.5
trochilic 320.15
trochilics 320.8
Trojan horse
fifth column 617.11
saboteur 691.8
troll
nouns rondo 461.19

mythical being
1014.7
verbs propel 284.10
draw 285.4
roll 320.10
sing 461.39
fish 653.10
troller 653.6
trolley
nouns streetcar 271.4
push car 271.15
OFF THE TROLLEY
472.25
verbs 272.32
trolling
nouns rotation 320.1
fishing 653.3
adjs. 320.14
trollop slattern 62.7
strumpet 987.14
tromba 464.8
tromba marina 464.5
trombone 464.8,23
troop company 74.3
military unit 798.19
trooper
cavalryman 798.12
war horse 798.33
troops 798.22
trope 549.2
trophoplasm 405.3
trophy
memento 535.7
award 914.3
tropical warm 327.24
figurative 549.4
Tropics 179.3
tropics 327.10
**tropopause,
troposphere**
aviation 277.38
atmosphere 401.3
trot
nouns old woman
127.3
run 268.4
translation 550.3
routine 640.5
verbs run 268.11
ride 272.33
TROT ALONG 300.6
TROT OUT 553.5
troth belief 500.1
promise 768.1,3
fidelity 972.7
trots 309.2
trotter foot 211.5
horse 413.20
trotters legs 272.16
pig's feet 306a.16
troubadour
minstrel 463.16
bard 607.14
trouble
nouns commotion
62.4
inconvenience 669.3
effort 714.1
adversity 727.1
difficulty 729.3
annoyance 864.2

affliction 864.8
anxiety 888.1
IN TROUBLE 729.19
verbs discompose
63.4
agitate 323.10
discommode 669.4
give ~ 729.12
excite 855.14
distress 864.15
torment 864.19
concern 888.3
NOT TROULE ONE'S
HEAD ABOUT 529.3
TROUBLE ONESELF
712.9
troubled
agitated 323.17
excited 855.24
annoyed 864.24
distressed 864.25
anxious 888.6
troublemaker
agitator 646.11
mischief-maker
941.2
trouble shooter
electrician 341.19
repairman 692.10
troublesome
perverse 624.11
inconvenient 669.7
laborious 714.19
difficult 729.17
annoying 862.13
troubling 862.13
troublous
turbulent 161.17
agitated 323.17
trough
nouns trench 262.2
aviation 277.38
conduit 395.3
verbs 262.3
troughed 262.4
troughing, troughway
395.3
trounce
criticize 967.21
chastise 1008.14
trouncing 1008.4
troupe
nouns company 74.3
theatrical ~ 610.11
verbs 609.33
trouper 610.1
trousers
breeches 230.18
types of ~ 230.56
trousseau 230.2
**trouvère, trouveur,
trouvere,** trovatore 607.14
trove 809.5
trover find 809.5
reclamation 821.3
trowel 347.13
truancy 186.4
truant
nouns absentee 186.5
shirker 629.3
adjs. 186.11

PLAY TRUANT 186.8
truantism 186.4
truce pause 144.3
armistice 802.5
truck
nouns flatcar 271.13
types of ~ 271.24
vegetables 306a.35
nonsense 545.2
intercourse 552.1
trash 667.5
trumpery 671.4
commerce 825.1
groceries 829.7
HAVE NO TRUCK WITH
ignore 529.3
avoid 629.6
be inhospitable
924.4
snub 964.7
verbs haul 270.12
trade 825.10
dance 877.5
truckage 270.3
truck driver, trucker
273.10
truck farm 412.8
truckle 905.6
TRUCKLE TO
be submissive
762.10
toady to 905.7
truckler 905.3
truckling
nouns 905.2
adjs. 905.13
truckload 193.2
truculence 937.11
truculent 937.24
trudge go slow 269.7
walk 272.27
true
nouns 515.1
verbs 26.13
adjs. straight 249.5
certain 512.13
unerroneous 515.11
literal 543.12
observant 766.4
devoted 925.20
veracious 972.16
trustworthy 972.19
faithful 972.20
orthodox 1022.8
NOT TRUE
erroneous 517.14
false 614.26
NOT TRUE TO 973.19
RUN TRUE TO FORM
be uniform 17.3
be characteristic
80 11
be wont 640.12
TRUE TO LIFE
lifelike 20.16
descriptive 606.15
true bill 1002.3
true blue 972.7
true-blue
man of honor 972.8
faithful 972.20

orthodox 1022.8
truelove love 929.1
sweetheart 929.12
trueness truth 515.1
devotedness 925.7
faithfulness 972.7
truepenny 972.8
true-speaking
speaking 592.21
veracious 972.16
true-spirited 972.13
true-tongued 972.16
truism 516.2
trull 987.14
truly positively 34.21
certainly 512.23–25
verily 515.16
yes 520.18
literally 543.15
truthfully 972.22
trump
nouns good thing
672.7
master stroke
731.10
cards 876.17
admirable person
983.2
verbs cap 36.5
~ up 614.18
trump card 731.10
trumped-up 614.30
trumpery
nouns nonsense 545.2
trifles 671.4
ornament 899.3
adjs. 671.18
trumpet
nouns toot 452.4
instrument 464.8
verbs toot 452.8
play a ~ 461.43
proclaim 557.13
trumpet call
toot 452.4
call 566.15
trumpeter
musician 463.4
messenger 559.3
truncate cut off 42.10
deform 248.7
truncated
mutilated 57.5
deformed 248.12
truncation
excision 42.3
deformity 248.3
truncheon
nouns 737.8
verbs 1008.14
truncheoning 1008.4
trundle propel 284.10
roll 320.10
trundling 320.1
trunk proboscis 255.7
torso 375.3
stalk 410.19
~ line 558.20
railway 655.8
trunks 230.29
trunnion 320.5

truss
nouns 74.7
verbs fasten 47.9
bundle 74.19
trussing 47.3
trust
nouns belief 500.1
dependent 762.6
commission 778.1
syndicate 786.9
estate 808.4
investment ~
831.16
credit 837.1
hope 886.1
IN TRUST 770.16
ON TRUST
with confidence
500.24
on credit 837.10
verbs believe
500.8,14
consign 816.16
extend credit 837.6
hope 886.7
TRUST IN 500.12
TRUST TO 500.13
trustability 972.6
trustable 972.19
trusted 500.20
NOT TO BE TRUSTED
973.18
trustee
depository 807.5
treasurer 834.11
truster believer 500.7
religionist 1026.4
trustful
trusting 500.19
credulous 501.7
artless 734.5
trustfulness
credulity 501.1
artlessness 734.1
trustiness 972.6
trusting
trustful 500.19
credulous 501.7
artless 734.5
trusting soul
credulity 501.4
dupe 618.1
trustless 973.18
trustworthiness
dependability 512.4
trustability 972.6
trustworthy
dependable 512.17
safe 696.5
trustable 972.19
trusty
nouns prisoner
759.11
man of honor 972.8
adjs. trusting 500.19
dependable 512.17
trustworthy 972.19
Truth 1011.7,12
truth reality 1.2
fact 1.3
trueness 515

axiom 516.2
veracity 972.3
orthodoxy 1022.1
TO TELL THE TRUTH
truly 515.16
truthfully 972.22
truthful 972.16
truthfulness 972.3
truthless 614.26,34
truthlessness 614.1,8
truth-loving, truth-
speaking
nouns 972.3
adjs. 972.16
truth serum 688.5
try
nouns test 488.2
attempt 712.2
verbs experiment
488.8
attempt 712.5
prosecute 1002.17
TRY CONCLUSIONS
reason 481.15
fight 794.17
TRY FOR 712.7
TRY HARD 712.10
TRY ON 488.8
TRY ONE 727.9
TRY ONE'S LUCK
gamble 514.17
attempt 712.8
TRY ONE'S TEMPER
855.13
TRY OUT 488.8
TRY THE PATIENCE
864.17
TRY TO 712.6
tryer-out 488.6
trying
nouns 488.1
adjs. testing 488.11
difficult 729.17
tryout hearing 447.2
trial 488.3
try square 212.6
tryst, trysting place
920.8
tryworks 717.4
tsar 749.9
tsarina 747.12
tub
nouns automobile
271.9
ship 276.3
bath 679.7
washtub 679.12
verbs 679.18
tuba 464.8,23
tubate 395.20
tubbiness 194.8
tubbing 679.5
tubby
nouns 194.12
adjs. corpulent
194.18
stubby 202.10
tube
nouns inner ~ 252.4
tunnel 256.5
firing ~ 280.11

electron ~ 342.11,
16–18
camera ~ 344.19
pipe 395.6
railway 655.8
verbs 270.13
tubed, tubelike 395.20
tuber, tubercle
root 410.20
growth 684.29
tubercular,
tuberculous
nodular 255.16
diseased 684.46
tuberculosis 684.13
tuberose 255.16
tuberosity 255.2
tuberous
knobbed 255.16
vegetable 410.34
tuberousness 255.2
tubiform 395.20
tubing 395.6
tubular 395.20
tubulation, tubule,
tubulet, tubulure
395.6
tuck
nouns appendage
41.2
fold 263.1
feast 306.9
sweets 306a.39
vital spirit 406.3
appetite 632.7
verbs 263.5
TUCK IN
insert 303.3
eat 306.20
put to bed 710.17
snug 885.9
TUCK ON 40.3
TUCK UP
tire 715.4
hang 1008.20
tucked 263.7
tucker
nouns food 306a.1,6
fatigue 715.1
verbs 715.4
tuck-in, tuck-out 306.9
tuft bunch 74.6
hair 229.6
goatee 229.8
feathers 229.16
growth 410.2
tufted 229.29
tufthunter
sycophant 905.3
self-seeker 976.3
tufthunting 905.2
tug
nouns pull 285.2
trace 657.5
effort 714.2
verbs pull 285.4
strain 714.10
tugging
nouns 285.1
adjs. 285.6
tug of war 794.4

tuition 560.1
tuitional, tuitionary
educational 560.18
pedagogical 563.12
tularemia 684.9
Tullian 598.8
tumble
nouns jumble 62.3
fall 314.3
flounder 323.8
verbs confuse 63.3
sail 274.58
fall 314.8
wallow 320.13
flounder 323.15
be indiscriminate
492.4
be destroyed 691.21
be excited 855.18
TUMBLE FOR 501.5
tumble-down 690.32
tumbler 876.21
tumefaction,
tumescence
distention 196.2
swelling 255.4
growth 684.29
tumid
distended 196.12
bombastic 599.10
pompous 902.22
tumidity, tumidness
distention 196.2
grandiloquence
599.1
tummock 206.5
tummy 192.3
tumor swelling 255.4
growth 684.29
tumorous 684.46
tump 206.5
tumult
commotion 62.4
turbulence 161.2
agitation 323.1
uproar 452.3
excitement 855.3
tumultuous
turbulent 161.17
noisy 452.11
excited 855.25
tumulus 409.16
tun
nouns belly 192.3
drunkard 994.10
verbs 994.29
tunable 461.49
tundra plain 386.1
grassland 410.8
tune
nouns music 461.2,3
melody 461.4
pitch 462.4
IN TUNE 461.50
OUT OF TUNE
inaccordant 27.7
out of order 62.12
unconforming 83.7
dissonant 460.4
in disrepair 690.36

TO THE TUNE OF
to the amount of
28.7
at a price 844.19
verbs adjust 26.13
harmonize
461.36,37,40
fit 718.8
TUNE DOWN
reduce 39.7
moderate 162.6
radio 343.30
soften 356.6
TUNE IN
radio 343.30
radar 345.17
TUNE UP
radio 343.30
tune 461.37
begin to play 461.38
tuned 461.50
tuneful
musical 461.49
poetic 607.21
tunefulness 461.2
tuneless 460.4
tunelessness 460.1
tunester 463.1
tuning fork 464.26
tunnel
nouns burrow 190.22
cave 256.5
verbs 256.15
tunneler 256.10
tuny 461.49
tup ram 413.9
male animal 419.8
tupek 190.9
Turbellaria 414.5
turbid opaque 340.3
muddy 388.14
turbidity
agitation 323.1
cloudiness 340.1
muddiness 388.4
turbinal, turbinate
253.8
turbination 320.1
turbine 284.7
turbojet 279.3
turboprop 279.17
turbulence
turmoil 161.2
agitation 323.1
excitement 855.3
turbulent
tumultuous 161.17
noisy 452.11
excited 855.25
turd 309.4
turf peat 330.1
greenward 410.6
horse racing 794.11
racecourse 876.13
turflike, turfy 410.40
turfman 268.6
turgescence 196.2
turgid distended
196.12
bombastic 599.10
pompous 902.22

turgidity
distention 196.2
grandiloquence
599.1
Turk 931.12
turkey food 306a.22
fowl 413.35
failure 723.2
turkey draw 514.10
turkey gobbler
fowl 413.35
male animal 419.8
turkey-trot 877.5
Turkish bath 679.7
turmeric paper 488.5
turmoil
commotion 62.4
turbulence 161.2
agitation 323.1
excitement 855.3
turn
nouns mode 7.4
spell 108.2
shift 108.3
crisis 129.4
round 137.3
change 139.1
reversion 146.1
tendency 173.1
obliquity 218.3
form 245.1
contortion 248.1
bend 251.3
tour 272.5
walk 272.12
deviation 290.1
circuity 319.2
whirl 320.2
appearance 445.3
musical ~ 462.18
~ of the wheel
514.2
disposition 523.3
start 538.3
act 609.8
desire 632.3
deed 703.3
aptitude 731.5
transaction 825.4
round trade 831.19
favor 936.7
AT EVERY TURN 17.8
GIVE A TURN
change 139.6
startle 538.8
scare 889.14
IN TURN
in order 59.10
consecutively 71.12
by turns 137.12
interchangeably
149.7
OUT OF TURN 83.7
TO A TURN
exactly 515.21
to perfection 675.11
verbs change 139.5
tend 173.3
oblique 218.9
contort 248.5
curve 251.6

convolve 253.4
blunt 258.2
tack 274.32
direct 289.6,8
deviate 290.3
deflect 290.5
~ back 294.9
round 319.5
rotate 320.9
~ a pot 574.6
induce 646.22
TURN A DEAF EAR
 be deaf 448.5
 be incredulous 503.3
 disregard 529.3
 refuse 774.3
 be merciless 943.2
TURN AGAINST 973.14
TURN ASIDE
 change 139.5
 deviate 290.3,6
 digress 591.9
 avert 728.14
TURN AWAY FROM
 look away 438.21
 ignore 529.4
 avoid 629.6
 snub 964.5
TURN BACK
 recur 103.11
 revert 146.5
 about-ship 274.32
 head off 290.6
 go back 294.8
TURN DOWN
 invert 219.5
 refuse 774.3
TURN IN 710.16
TURN INSIDE OUT
 invert 219.5
 ransack 484.27
 confess 554.7
TURN INTO
 convert 145.8
 be converted 145.12
 translate 550.14
TURN LOOSE 761.5
TURN OFF
 shut off 144.12
 dismiss 308.17,18
 extinguish 336.12
 ~ electricity 341.23
 accomplish 720.5
 execute 1008.20
TURN ONE'S BACK
  UPON
 turn back 294.8
 ignore 529.4
 avoid 629.6
 flee 629.10
 abandon 631.5,6
 reject 636.2
 refuse 774.3
 oppose 788.3
 be inhospitable
  924.4
 snub 964.5
TURN ONE'S HAND TO
 do 703.7
 undertake 713.3

TURN ONE'S HEAD
 derange 472.21
 dizzy 530.8
 induce 646.22
 excite 855.14
 make proud 903.6
 make vain 907.7
 astonish 918.6
 enamor 929.20
TURN OUT
 fare 7.6
 result 153.5
 invert 219.5
 costume 230.40
 navigation 274.79
 eject 308.12,14
 dismiss 308.18
 extinguish 336.12
 prove to be 515.7
 come true 515.10
 equip 657.8
 arise 711.5
 accomplish 720.5
 strike 787.9
TURN OUT TO BE
 become 1.12
 eventuate 153.5
TURN OVER
 overturn 219.6
 fold over 263.5
 transfer 270.9
 capsize 274.46
 ponder 477.12
 assign 815.3
 hand over 816.13
TURN OVER A NEW
  LEAF
 change 139.6
 reform 145.9
TURN TAIL 629.10
TURN THE OTHER
  CHEEK 859.7
TURN THE SCALE
 unbalance 31.3
 have advantage
  36.11
 change 139.6
 induce 152.12
 gain influence
  171.12
 invert 219.5
TURN THE STOMACH
 864.13
TURN THE TABLES
 have advantage
  36.11
 change 139.6
 gain influence
  171.12
 invert 219.5
 retaliate 953.4
TURN THE TRICK
 effectuate 720.4
 succeed 722.11
TURN THUMBS
  DOWN ON
 refuse 774.3
 disapprove of 967.10
TURN TO
 begin 68.6
 be converted 145.12

resort to 663.14
undertake 713.3
set to work 714.15
TURN UP
 occur 150.6
 chance 155.11
 attend 185.8
 arrive 299.6
 upturn 313.13
 appear 445.8
 find 487.4
 be found 487.9
 be unexpected 538.6
TURN UP ONE'S
  NOSE AT
 ignore 529.4
 be fastidious 894.8
 disdain 964.4
TURN UPSIDE DOWN
 overturn 219.6
 ransack 484.27
turnabout 146.1
turnaround 294.3
turnback 626.5
turncoat traitor 617.10
 apostate 626.5
turned-up
 pugged 202.10
 upturned 313.15
Turnerfest 876.10
turning
 nouns bending 251.3
 convolution 253.1
 deviation 290.1
 rotation 320.1
 adjs. crooked 248.11
 winding 253.6
 deviating 290.7
 circuitous 319.7
 rotating 320.14
turning point 129.4
turnip 114.6
turniplike, turnip-
  shaped 251.20
turnkey 759.10
turnout assembly 74.2
 attendance 185.4
 wardrobe 230.2
 rig 271.5
 R. R. siding 655.8
 strike 787.7
turnover
 overturn 219.2
 pastry 306a.40
 sales 827.1
turnpike gate 301.6
 road 655.6
turnpiker 273.3
turnspit 328.15
turnstile 301.6
turntail 626.5
turnup 445.1
turp 361.14
turpentine
 nouns 361.7
 verbs 361.14
turpitude 979.6
turps 361.7
turquoise 371.3
turret 206.11
turtle 413.30

AT A TURTLE'S PACE
 269.13
turtledoves 929.16
turtlelike 269.10
turtle soup 306a.10
tusk
 nouns 257.7
 verbs 796.28
tusked 257.17
tussle
 nouns struggle 714.3
 contest 794.3
 verbs struggle 714.11
 contend 794.14
tussler 798.1
tussock tuft 74.6
 growth 410.2
tut! silence! 450.16
 pooh! 965.16
tutelage
 instruction 560.1
 tutorship 563.11
 protection 697.2
 patronage 783.4
tutelary
 nouns 1012.19
 adjs. 697.22
tutor
 nouns 563.4,6
 verbs 560.11
tutorage
 instruction 560.1
 tutorship 563.11
tutorial 563.12
tutoring 560.1
tutti 461.24
tutti-frutti 306a.39
Tux, Tuxedo 230.11
tuyère 328.10
TV 344.1
twaddle
 nouns
  nonsense 545.4
  chatter 594.3
 verbs
  talk nonsense 545.8
  chatter 594.6
 interjs. 469.12
twaddler 882.4
twaddling, twaddly
  545.10
twain
 nouns 90.2
 adjs. 90.6
IN TWAIN
 separately 49.26
 halved 92.4
twang
 nouns tang 426.1
 pungency 432.2
 harsh sound 457.3
 dialect 578.8
 accent 592.7
 nasalization 593.1
 verbs sound harshly
  457.8
 strum 461.41
twangy
 nasalized 449.18
 ~ voice 593.11
twank twang 457.8

strum 461.41
twattle
  nouns nonsense 545.4
    chatter 594.3
  verbs talk nonsense
    545.8
    chatter 594.6
tweak
  nouns pinch 197.2
    jerk 285.3
    pain 423.2
  verbs pinch 197.8
    jerk 285.5
    pain 423.7
  TWEAK THE NOSE
    864.19
tweedle
  nouns 452.4
  verbs finger 424.6
    whistle 452.8
    sing 461.39
    play music 461.43
    toy with 671.13
tweedledee
  nouns violinist 463.5
    instrument 464.1
  verbs whistle 452.8
    sing 461.39
tweedledum 464.1
tweedy 377.9
tweet 459.5
tweeter 343.4
twelfth 99.24
**Twelfth-day, Twelfth-
night, Twelfthtide**
    1038.15
twelve 99.7
twelvemonth 107.2
twentieth 99.26
twentieth-century
    122.14
twenty 99.7
twenty-four-hour 71.9
twice 91.4
  TWICE OVER 103.17
twice-told 103.12
twice-told tale
    cliché 516.3
    old joke 879.9
twiddle finger 424.6
    toy with 671.13
  TWIDDLE ONE'S
    THUMBS
    do nothing 704.2
    idle 706.11
twiddle-twaddle 545.4
twig
  nouns member 55.4
    branch 410.18
  verbs see 438.12
    discover 487.5
twilight
  nouns foredawn
    133.4
    dusk 134.3
  adjs. 134.8
twill weave 221.7
    flute 263.5
twilled 263.7
twin
  nouns 20.5

adjs. identical 14.6
  matching 20.11
  accompanying 73.9
  double 91.3
twine
  nouns 205.2
  verbs interlace 221.7
    convolve 253.4
twined 221.8
twinge
  nouns 423.2
  verbs 423.8
twining
  nouns 221.1
  adjs. 221.9
twink 113.3
twinkle
  nouns instant 113.3
    glitter 334.7
  verbs 334.24
twinkling
  nouns instant 113.3
    twinkle 334.7
  IN A TWINKLING
    instantly 113.7
    quickly 268.23
  adjs. 334.35
twins 90.4
twirl
  nouns coil 253.2
    whirl 320.2
    eddy 394.12
  verbs convolve 253.4
    whirl 320.10
twirling 320.14
twist
  nouns
    complication 46.2
    tendency 173.1
    braid 205.2
    obliquity 218.3
    hair 229.7
    distortion 248.1
    coil 253.2
    tobacco 433.8
    aspect 445.3
    eccentricity 473.2
    disposition 523.3
    prejudice 525.3
    story angle 606.9
    appetite 632.7
  verbs oblique 218.9
    interlace 221.7
    distort 248.5
    convolve 253.4
    deviate 290.4
    deflect 290.5
    turn 320.9
    prejudice 525.8
    misrepresent 571.3
    falsify 614.16
  TWIST AND TURN
    convolve 253.4
    deviate 290.4
    wriggle 323.15
    be excited 855.18
  TWIST AROUND ONE'S
    LITTLE FINGER
    have influence over
    171.11

subdue 762.9
TWIST ONE'S ARM
  urge 646.14
  persuade 646.23
  compel 754.6
twisted
  complex 46.4
  distorted 248.10
  crooked 248.11
  circuitous 319.7
  eccentric 473.4
twister
  friedcake 306a.43
  cyclone 402.15
  falsehood 614.11
twisting
  nouns
    interlacing 221.1
    convolution 253.1
    misrepresentation
    571.1
  adjs. winding 253.6
    deviative 290.7
    circuitous 319.7
twit
  nouns banter 880.1
    gibe 965.2
  verbs tweet 459.5
    sing 461.39
    banter 880.4
    ridicule 965.9
    reproach 1003.7
twitch
  nouns jerk 285.3
    shake 323.3
    twinge 423.2
    start 538.3
  verbs jerk 285.5
    vellicate 323.13
    hurt 423.8
    be excited 855.18
twitching
  nouns jerking 323.5
    neurosis 688.24
    nervousness 857.1
  adjs. 323.20
twitchy, twitchety
    jerky 323.20
    nervous 857.12
twitter
  nouns shake 323.3
    trepidation 855.4
    excitement 855.5
    banterer 880.3
  ALL OF A TWITTER
    agitated 323.17
    excited 855.24
    nervous 857.12
  IN A TWITTER 855.22
  verbs shake 323.11
    warble 459.5
    sing 461.39
    be excited 855.18
twittery 857.12
twitting
  nouns banter 880.2
    ridicule 965.1
  adjs. bantering 880.5
    derisive 965.12
'twixt 236.14

two
  nouns 90.2
  adjs. 90.6
  IN TWO
    unjoined 49.20
    asunder 49.26
    halved 92.4
  NO TWO WAYS ABOUT
    IT 512.23
  TWO OF A KIND
    counterparts 20.5
    friends 926.7
two bits 833.7
two-by-four
  nouns 377.3
  adjs. little 195.9
    insignificant 671.17
two cents 671.5
two-dimensional 178.8
two-edged 257.11
two-faced double 91.3
    falsehearted 614.31
    deceitful 616.13
two-fisted 419.12
twofold
  adjs. 91.3
  advs. 91.4
two-handed 731.23
two-horned 251.11
twoness 90.1
twopence 833.8
twopenny-halfpenny
    paltry 671.18
    cheap 847.8
two-ply 91.3
twoscore 99.7
two shakes 111.3
two-sided double 91.3
    bilateral 241.7
twosome two 90.2
    game 876.9
two-step 877.5
two-time 973.13
two-wheeler 271.3
tycoon
    personage 670.8
    shogun 747.9
    industrialist 828.1
    financier 834.8
tyke, tike dog 413.24
    peasant 917.8
tyler See tiler
tymbal See timbal
tympan 464.21
tympanic membrane
    membrane 228.3
    eardrum 447.7
**tympanism, tym-
panites** 196.2
tympanist 463.10
tympanon 464.21
tympanum
    membrane 228.3
    ear 447.7
    drum 464.21
tympany
    distention 196.2
    drum 464.21
typal 61.7

type
 nouns prototype 25.2
  kind 61.3
  characteristic 80.3
  form 245.1
  measure 489.2
  sign 566.2
  representative 570.5
  print 601.6
  kinds of ~ 601.19
  sizes of ~ 601.20
  styles of ~ 601.21
 OF A TYPE 20.15
 verbs 600.19
typescript
  writing 600.11
  copy 601.4
typeset 601.17
typesetter 601.10
typesetting 601.2
typewrite 600.19
typewriter
  typist 600.18
  types of ~ 600.31
typewriting 600.1
typewritten 600.24
typhobacterin 685.23
typhoid, typhoid fever
  684.9
Typhon 1014.6
typhonic, typhoonish
  402.27
typhoon 402.15
typhus 684.9
typical
  precedental 25.8
  classificational 61.7
  characteristic 80.13
  normal 84.7
  figurative 549.4
  representative
   570.12
typification 570.6
typify prefigure 542.9
  figure 549.3
  symbolize 570.9
typifying 570.11
typing 600.1
typist 600.18
typographer 601.10
typographic(al)
  601.18
typographical error
  517.3
typography 601.1
typotelegraphy 558.3
Tyr war-god 795.18
  god 1012.6
tyrannical 737.15
tyrannize 739.15
tyrannous 737.15
tyranny 739.10
tyrant 747.15
tyro 564.7

U

uberous 164.9
ubiety 185.1
ubiquitous
  omnipresent 185.13

divine 1011.20
ubiquity
  omnipresence 185.2
  divine attribute
   1011.15
U-boat 276.9
udometer, udomo-
  graph 393.7
ugh yes 520.18
  phew! 865.13
ugliness
  uncomeliness 897
  ill humor 949.2
ugly uncomely 897.6
  ill humored 949.19
ugly customer
  violent person 161.9
  ruffian 941.4
  sorehead 949.11
ugly duckling 897.4
uhlan 798.12
uitlander 78.3
ukase 750.4
ukulele 464.4
ulcer 684.28
ulcerate 690.12
ulcerated
  diseased 684.45
  decayed 690.38
ulceration 684.28
ulcerous 684.45
ulema 1000.3
uliginose, uliginous
  muddy 388.14
  swampy 399.3
Ull, Ullr 1012.6
ullage 57.2
ulotrichous 229.24
ulterior
  additional 40.9
  extraneous 78.5
  thither 198.10
ulterior motive 646.1
ultimate
  nouns 675.3
  adjs. final 70.10
  future 121.8
  eventual 150.11
ultimately
  finally 70.11
  in time 121.11
  eventually 150.12
ultimatum
  final condition 506.2
  final objective 651.2
  demand 751.1
  offer 771.3
ultimogeniture 817.2
ultra extreme 34.15
  fanatical 472.31
  radical 743.19
ultra- 198.11
ultrahigh frequency
  343.15
ultraism 743.4
ultramarine 198.11
ultramontane
  nouns alien 78.3
  Catholic 1018.17
  adjs. beyond 198.11
  Catholic 1018.27

ecclesiastical
  1035.13
ultramundane 198.11
ultrasonic fast 268.20
  sonic 449.17
ultrasonics
  automation 348.2
  sound 449.8
ultrasonic speed
  speed 268.3
  aviation 277.37
ultraviolet ray 334.5
ululant howling 459.6
  wailful 873.16
ululate howl 459.2
  wail 873.11
ululation, ululu
  howling 459.1
  wail 873.3
Uma 1012.7
umbel 410.25
umber 366.3
umbilical 225.12
umbilical cord 48.4
umbilicus 225.2
umbra 336.3
umbrage 950.2
 GIVE UMBRAGE
  950.20
umbrageous 336.17
umbrella cover 227.7
  aviation 277.8
  parachute 279.13
umpirage 803.2
umpire
  nouns mediator 803.4
  judge 1000.1
  verbs 803.6
umpteen 101.2
umpteenth 99.25
unabashed
  unafraid 891.20
  impudent 911.10
  immodest 988.6
unabated 34.16
unabetted 89.8
unabject 872.5
unable
  incapable 157.14
  incompetent 732.19
unabridged 54.11
unaccented 449.13
unacceptable
  unsatisfactory 867.7
  unwelcome 924.7
  objectionable
   967.25
unaccepted 1023.9
unaccessible 509.8
unaccommodating
  discourteous 935.4
  inconsiderate
   937.16
unaccompanied 89.8
unaccomplished
  unachieved 721.3
  unskilled 732.16
unaccountable
  fantastic 85.12
  unpredictable
   513.14

inexplicable 547.16
  lawless 738.5
  exempt 760.27
unaccustom 641.2
unaccustomed
  unused to 641.4
  inexperienced
   732.17
unachievable 509.7
unachieved 721.3
unacknowledged
  anonymous 582.3
  unthanked 948.5
unacquaintance
  ignorance 476.1
  unaccustomedness
   641.1
  unskillfulness 732.2
unacquainted 476.13
 UNACQUAINTED WITH
  unaccustomed 641.4
  inexperienced
   732.17
unacquirable 509.8
unactive 706.15
unactual unreal 2.8
  illusory 518.9
  imaginary 533.19
unadaptable 83.6
unadapted
  unsuited 27.8
  unfitted 719.9
  incompetent 732.19
unadhesive 51.4
unadjustable 83.6
unadjusted 732.19
unadmonished 538.9
unadorned
  plain-speaking 589.3
  unornamented
   900.8
unadult 124.10
unadulterated 45.6
unadvantageous 669.6
unadventurous 893.8
unadverse 620.6
unadvised
  unwise 469.9
  inexpectant 538.9
  unpremeditated
   628.11
unaesthetic 897.10
unaffable 611.8
unaffected
  uninfluenced 172.5
  genuine 515.13
  elegant 587.6
  plain-speaking 589.3
  obstinate 624.9
  informal 645.3
  artless 734.6
  unmoved 854.11
  natural 900.7
  undeceptive 972.18
unaffiliated 10.5
unafraid
  confident 512.21
  fearless 891.19
unagitated
  quiescent 267.10
  unexcited 856.11

unagreeable 924.7
unaided 89.8
unailing 683.7
unalarmed 891.19
unalert 529.8
unalike 21.4
unallayed
  unweakened 158.19
  unmitigated 161.16
unallied 10.5
unallowable 975.12
unallowed
  prohibited 776.7
  illegal 997.6
unalluring 862.8
unalterable
  unchangeable
    142.18
  inflexible 355.12
  obstinate 624.9
unaltered 140.7
unaltruistic 937.15
unamazed 919.3
unambiguous 546.10
unambitious
  unaspiring 634.7
  modest 906.9
unamenable 172.4
unamiable
  unfriendly 927.10
  unkind 937.14
unamicable 927.10
unamusing 881.7
unanchored
  unfastened 49.21
  adrift 274.65
unangelic
  unvirtuous 979.16
  ungodly 1029.17
unanimated
  inanimate 381.5
  unaffected 854.11
unanimity 520.5
unanimous 520.15
unanswerable
  proved 504.23
  unquestionable
    512.15
  lawless 738.5
  exempt 760.27
unanswered 504.23
unanticipated
  sudden 113.5
  unexpected 538.10
unappalled 891.20
unapparent
  invisible 444.4
  unknown 476.18
  unrevealed 613.13
unappetizing
  unsavory 428.5
  unpleasant 862.8
unappreciative
  ungrateful 948.4
  disapprobatory
    967.22
unapprehended
  476.18
unapprehensive
  891.19
unapprized 476.13

unapproachable
  out-of-the-way 198.9
  inaccessible 509.8
  reserved 611.8
  unsociable 921.6
unapproved 1023.9
unapproving 967.22
unapt
  unappropriate 27.7
  unskillful 732.15
unarmed
  unprotected 695.14
  unequipped 719.9
unarranged
  orderless 62.11
  unprepared 719.8
unarticulated 450.12
unartificial
  unaffected 734.6
  simple 900.7
unartistic 897.10
unascertainable
  547.11
unashamed 988.6
unasked
  voluntary 620.7
  unwelcome 865.12
  uninvited 924.7
unaspiring
  unambitious 634.7
  modest 906.9
unassailable 158.17
unassertive 763.12
unassisted 89.8
unassociated
  unrelated 10.5
  unjoined 49.20
unassuming
  genuine 515.13
  informal 645.3
  artless 734.6
  natural 900.7
  modest 906.9
  undeceptive 972.18
unassured 513.21
unattached 49.20
unattackable 158.17
unattainable
  nouns 509.1
  adjs. 509.7,8
unattained 721.3
unattended
  alone 89.8
  neglected 532.14
unattested 505.8
unattired 231.13
unattracted 634.7
unattractive
  undesirable 862.8
  ugly 897.6
unauthentic
  illogical 482.10
  unauthoritative
    513.19
  erroneous 517.17
  illusory 518.9
  false 614.27
  unorthodox 1023.9
unauthoritative
  uninfluential 172.3
  unreliable 513.19

unorthodox 1023.9
unavailable 509.8
unavailing
  ineffectual 157.15
  useless 667.9
unavenged 945.7
unavoidable
  nouns 637.7
  adjs. 637.15
unawakened 710.20
unaware
  ignorant 476.14
  inexpectant 538.9
unawares
  suddenly 113.9
  unknowingly 476.19
  unexpectedly 538.14
  innocently 982.9
unawed
  unafraid 891.20
  unastonished 919.3
unbalance
  nouns inequality 31.1
  insanity 472.1
  verbs
  overbalance 31.3
  madden 472.22
unbalanced
  unequal 31.5
  off center 225.16
  insane 472.24
  unjust 975.9
unbar unfasten 49.9
  unlock 761.6
unbased 482.12
unbashful 891.19
unbathed 680.22
unbearable
  odorous 434.10
  insufferable 862.16
unbeatable
  peerless 36.17
  unconquerable
    158.17
unbeaten new 122.7
  unused 666.12
  undefeated 724.9
unbecoming
  inapt 27.7
  inexpedient 669.5
  indecent 988.5
unbefitting
  unsuitable 27.7
  untimely 130.7
  inexpedient 669.5
unbegotten
  self-existent 1.14
  nonexistent 2.9
unbeguiling 972.18
unbegun 719.8
unbeheld 444.4
unbelief disbelief 502
  incredulity 503
  misbelief 1023.2
  irreligion 1029.5
unbelievable
  incredible 502.10
  unreliable 513.18
unbeliever 1029.11
unbellicose 801.10
unbeloved 865.11

unbend relax 162.9
  straighten 249.4
  be pliant 356.7
  set at ease 709.7
  condescend 904.7
unbenevolent 937.15
unbenign 937.14
unbent 249.5
unbesought 620.7
unbias
  unprejudice 524.5
  impartiality 974.4
unbidden
  voluntary 620.7
  unwelcome 865.12
  uninvited 924.7
unbind unfasten 49.9
  free 761.6
unblamable 982.8
unblemished
  faultless 675.6
  clear 679.23
unblended 45.6
unblest
  lacking 660.11
  unfortunate 727.14
unblinking
  unnervous 858.2
  unafraid 891.20
unblock 264.12
unboastful 906.9
unborn 2.9
unbosom oneself
  554.8
unbought
  unsold 827.13
  free 848.5
unbound
  unfastened 49.21
  free 760.24,25
unbounded
  infinite 104.3
  unrestricted 760.24
unbowed
  unbent 249.5
  undefeated 724.9
unbrace relax 162.9
  unnerve 857.10
unbreakable 358.5
unbridle 761.6
unbridled
  lawless 738.5
  unrestrained 760.22
unbroken even 17.5
  continuous 71.9
  constant 135.5
  straight 249.5
  smooth 259.9
  direct 289.13
  undamaged 675.8
unbuckle 49.9
unbuild
  disassemble 49.14
  demolish 691.17
unburden
  unload 308.21
  lighten 352.6
  ~ one's heart 554.8
unburnable 331.9
unbury 409.24
unbusinesslike 654.17

unconstitutional 997.6
unconstitutionality
997.1
unconstrained
communicative
552.9
informal 645.3
unrestrained 760.22
candid 972.17
unconstraint
communicativeness
552.4
informality 645.1
freedom 760.2
candor 972.4
unconsumed 43.6
unconsummated 721.3
uncontentious 801.10
uncontested
believed 500.20
undoubted 512.16
uncontinent 987.24
uncontradicted 512.16
uncontrite 872.5
uncontrived 719.8
uncontrol
lawlessness 738.1
unrestraint 760.2
intemperance 991.1
uncontrollable
ungovernable
624.12
inevitable 637.15
uncontrolled
changeable 141.7
capricious 627.5
impulsive 628.9
lawless 738.5
unrestrained 760.22
uncontroverted
512.16
unconventional 83.8
unconversant
ignorant 476.13
unaccustomed
641.4
inexperienced
732.17
unconversational
611.6
unconverted
unconvinced 502.8
irreligious 1029.18
unconvinced 502.8
unconvincible 503.4
unconvincing 502.10
uncooked 719.10
uncooperative 624.11
uncopied
unimitated 23.4
genuine 515.13
uncordial
inhospitable 924.6
unfriendly 927.10
unamiable 937.14
uncork 264.12
uncorroborated 505.8
uncorrupted
unadulterated 45.6
honorable 972.13
virtuous 978.9

uncounted
innumerable 101.11
undetermined
513.16
uncouple 49.8
uncourageous 890.11
uncourteous 935.4
uncourtly
inelegant 588.2
discourteous 935.4
uncouth rustic 181.7
inelegant 588.2
clumsy 732.20
vulgar 896.12
indecent 988.8
uncover divest 231.5
unclose 264.12
find 487.4
disclose 554.4
tip the hat 923.10
uncovered
open 264.17
unhidden 553.10
unprotected 695.14
uncreated
self-existent 1.14
nonexistent 2.9
uncreative 165.5
uncredulous 503.4
uncringing 891.20
uncritical
undiscriminating
492.6
unmeticulous
532.13
uncensorious 966.17
uncropped 54.10
uncrown 781.2
unction
ointment 379.3
anointment 379.6
balm 685.9
fervor 853.9
flattery 968.2
divine ~ 1011.18
rite 1038.6
unctional, unctious
379.9
unctuous oily 379.9
hypocritical 614.33
suave 934.18
flattering 968.9
sanctimonious
1027.5
uncultivated
countrified 181.7
unlearned 476.15
undeveloped
719.12,14
uncouth 896.12
uncultured
countrified 181.7
unlearned 476.15
undeveloped 719.12
uncouth 896.12
uncurbed
lawless 738.5
unrestrained 760.22
uncurl 249.4
uncurtain open 264.12
disclose 554.4

uncurtained 553.10
uncurved 249.5
uncustomary 85.10
undamaged 675.8
undamped 392.7
undangerous 696.5
undaring
uncourageous
890.11
cautious 893.8
undaunted
persevering 623.7
unafraid 891.20
undazed 919.3
undazzled
unprejudiced
524.12
unamazed 919.3
undebauched
virtuous 978.9
chaste 986.7
undeceitful 972.18
undeceivable 503.5
undeceived
cognizant of 474.16
disillusioned 519.5
undeceiving
disabusing 519.4
undeceptive 972.18
undecennary,
undecennial 99.23
undeception 519.1
undeceptive 972.18
undecided
unproved 505.8
uncertain 513.16
irresolute 625.9
undecillion 99.13
undecipherable
547.17
undecorated 900.8
undecorative 897.10
undefaced
undamaged 675.8
unbeaten 724.9
undefended 695.14
undefiled clean 679.23
innocent 982.7
chaste 986.4
undefinable
inexpressible 545.13
inexplicable 547.16
undefined
formless 246.4
indistinct 444.5
vague 513.17
anonymous 582.3
undeflectable
unchangeable
142.18
resolute 622.12
undeformed 675.8
undeft 732.15
undegenerate 978.9
undelectable, undeli-
cious
unsavory 428.5
unpleasant 862.8
undeliberate, unde-
liberated 628.11

undeludable 503.5
undemolished 675.8
undemonstrable
unprovable 505.9
questionable 513.15
undemonstrated 505.8
undemonstrative
611.8
undemoralized 978.9
undeniable
proved 504.23
unquestionable
512.15
undenied
proved 504.23
true 515.11
undenominational
1018.25
undependable
changeable 141.7
uncertain 513.18
fickle 627.7
unsafe 695.11
untrustworthy
973.18
undepraved 978.9
under
adjs. 207.8
preps. least 37.9
below 207.11
in subjection 762.16
underage 124.10
underagent 779.3
underbelly belly 192.3
bottom 211.1
underbid 825.14
underboard 612.19
underbody 230.23
underbreath 451.4
underbrush 410.15
underbuilding
foundation 215.6
understructure
244.3
undercast
aviation 277.38
clouds 403.4
undercoat
nouns 361.12
verbs 361.14
undercolor 361.1
undercooked 329.8
undercover 612.14
undercover man
informer 555.6
spy 779.9
undercovert 613.4
undercrossing 220.2
undercurrent
counterforce 177.4
current 394.4
air current 402.1
latency 544.1
hidden danger
695.5
opposition 788.1
undercut 827.8
underdog 725.5
underdone 329.8
underdraw 571.3

underestimate
  nouns 497.1
  verbs 497.2
underfed 204.19
underfoot 207.11
undergarments
  underclothes 230.22
  types of ~ 230.58
undergo
  experience 150.8
  afford 841.6
undergraduate 564.5
underground
  nouns cellar 191.17
  tunnel 256.5
  train 271.12
  grapevine 556.10
  covert way 613.5
  subversives 617.11
  railway 655.8
  military 798.15
  GO UNDERGROUND
    613.9
  adjs. subterranean
    208.11
  surreptitious 612.14
  concealed 613.12
  advs. buried 409.26
  secretly 612.19
underground railroad
  613.5
underground route
  grapevine 556.10
  covert way 613.5
undergrowth 410.15
underhand,
  underhanded
  clandestine 612.14
  deceitful 616.22
  dishonest 973.15
underived 23.3
underlayer 226.1
underlessee
  lodger 189.8
  tenant 807.4
underlet 778.13
underlie be low 207.4
  rest on 215.23
  be latent 544.3
underline
  nouns 566.5
  verbs mark 566.18
  emphasize 670.13
underling
  inferior 37.3
  servant 748.1
underlining 566.5
underlying
  fundamental 5.8
  basic 211.8
  latent 544.5
undermine 690.16
undermost 211.7
underneath
  nouns 211.1
  preps. below 207.11
  in subjection 762.16
undernourished
  204.19
underpass 655.4
underpin 215.22

underpinning 215.6
underpinnings 272.16
underplot 652.6
underprivileged
  nouns unfortunates
    727.7
  the masses 917.6
  adjs. 727.14
underprize 497.2
underprop 215.22
underrate 497.2
underrating 497.1
underscore
  nouns 566.5
  verbs mark 566.18
  emphasize 670.13
undersea 208.12
undersell 827.8
underset 215.22
undersexed 418.17
undershoot 277.49
underside 211.1
undersign
  endorse 520.12
  guarantee 770.11
undersize
  nouns 195.1
  adjs. 195.12
undersong
  refrain 103.5
  divine service
    1030.8
understand
  know 474.12
  suppose 498.9
  imply 544.4
  comprehend 546.7
  interpret 550.10
  GIVE ONE TO
    UNDERSTAND 555.7
  NOT UNDERSTAND
    547.10
  UNDERSTAND ONE
    ANOTHER 792.2
understandability
  546.1
understandable
  knowable 474.25
  intelligible 546.9
understanding
  nouns agreement
    26.2
  intellect 465.1
  intelligence 466.1
  the wise 467.3
  comprehension
    474.3
  unanimity 520.5
  tolerance 524.4
  compact 769.1
  accord 792.1
  BEYOND UNDERSTAND-
    ING 547.11
  COME TO AN
    UNDERSTANDING
  agree 520.10
  make peace 802.10
  PASS UNDERSTANDING
    547.9
  WITH THE UNDER-
    STANDING 506.12

adjs. intelligent
  466.12,16
  knowing 474.15
  tolerant 524.11
  accordant 792.3
understate 571.3
understood
  traditional 123.12
  known 474.26
  assumed 498.14
  tacit 544.8
understory 226.1
understrapper 37.3
understratum 226.1
understructure
  foundation 215.6
  substructure 244.3
understudy
  substitute 148.2
  actor 610.6
undertake
  carry on 703.7
  attempt 712.5
  set about 713.3
  promise 768.5
undertaker 409.8
undertaking
  business 654
  attempt 712.2
  enterprise 713
  promise 768.2
under-the-counter,
  under-the-table
  surreptitious 612.14
  illicit 997.6
undertone tone 449.2
  murmur 451.4
  IN AN UNDERTONE
    451.22
undertow
  undercurrent 394.4
  hidden danger 695.5
undervalue 497.2
underwater 208.12
under way
  moving 266.7
  sailing 274.67
underwear 230.22
underweight
  nouns thinness 204.5
  weight 351.1
  adjs. thin 204.16
  light 352.12
underworld
  gangland 984.10
  hell 1017.1
underwrite
  endorse 520.12
  guarantee 770.11
underwriter
  endorser 520.7
  insurer 770.8
undeserved
  undue 959.9
  unjust 975.9
undesignated 582.3
undesigned
  unintentional
    155.17
  unpremeditated
    628.11

undesigning
  artless 734.6
  undeceptive 972.18
undesirable
  inexpedient 669.5
  unpleasant 862.8
  unsatisfactory 867.7
  unwanted 924.7
undesired 865.12
undesirous 634.7
undespairing 886.11
undestroyable 142.19
undestroyed
  unchanged 140.7
  undamaged 675.8
undetached
  prejudiced 525.12
  partial 975.11
undetected 613.13
undetermined
  chance 155.15
  unproved 505.8
  uncertain 513.16
  irresolute 625.9
undeveloped
  immature 124.10
  unprepared 719.12
undeviating
  uniform 17.5
  unchangeable
    142.18
  straight 249.5
  direct 289.13
  exact 515.15
undevised 719.8
undevoted 641.4
undevout 1029.15
undexterous,
  undextrous 732.15
undies 230.22
undifferent 14.6
undiffident 891.19
undigested 719.11
undignified
  colloquial 578.16
  inelegant 588.2
  informal 645.3
  unworthy 669.5
  vulgar 896.10
undiluted 45.6
undiminished
  unreduced 34.16
  whole 54.10
  unweakened 158.19
undine 1012.13,17
undiplomatic 492.7
undirected
  orderless 62.11
  purposeless 155.16
  deviative 290.7
undiscernible 444.4
undiscerning
  blind 440.8
  nonunderstanding
    468.14
  inattentive 529.6
undisciplined
  changeable 141.7
  capricious 627.5
  lawless 738.5
undisclosable 612.12

certainly 512.23
explicitly 546.12
unerring
infallible 512.19
exact 515.15
virtuous 978.9
unerroneous 515.11
unerudite 476.15
unessayed 666.12
unessential
nouns 6.2
adjs. extrinsic 6.4
irrelevant 10.6
superfluous 661.18
needless 667.10
insignificant 671.15
unestablished
unplaced 184.9
unproved 505.8
unethical 973.15
uneven
ununiform 18.2
unequal 31.4
irregular 138.3
rough 260.6
unjust 975.9
unevenness
ununiformity 18.1
inequality 31.1
irregularity 138.1
roughness 260.1
unexacting
undiscriminating
492.6
unmeticulous
532.13
unstrict 576.5
unexaggerated 515.13
unexamined 532.16
unexampled
unimitated 23.4
peerless 36.17
extraordinary 85.13
unexcelled 36.17
unexceptionable
tolerable 672.20
satisfactory 866.12
inculpable 982.8
unexceptional
normal 84.7
ordinary 678.9
unexcessive 162.12
unexcited 856.11
unexciting 881.7
unexecuted 721.3
unexempt from
960.16
unexercised 666.12
unexhausted
unweakened 158.19
unwearied 693.7
unexisting 2.7
unexpansive 611.8
unexpected
unusual 85.10
sudden 113.5
chance 155.15
unanticipated
538.10

BE UNEXPECTED
538.6
unexpectedly
unusually 85.16
suddenly 113.9
unintentionally
155.20
unawares 538.14
unexpecting 538.9
unexpedience 130.1
unexpensive 847.7
unexperienced 732.17
unexplainable 547.16
unexplained
unknown 476.18
unrevealed 613.13
unexploitable 503.5
unexplored
unknown 476.18
unexamined 532.16
unrevealed 613.13
unexposed
unknown 476.18
hidden 613.13
unexpressed
tacit 450.13
implied 544.9
unexpressive 545.11
unextensible 355.12
unextinguished
unmitigated 161.16
burning 327.27
unextravagant 162.12
unextreme 162.12
unfabricated 515.13
unfacile 732.15
unfaded
unweakened 158.19
undamaged 675.8
unfading
immortal 112.9
permanent 140.7
fast-dyed 361.18
unfailing
permanent 140.7
sure 512.17
faithful 972.20
unfair 975.10
unfaithful
apostate 626.11
nonobservant 767.5
inconstant 973.19
unfaithworthy
undependable
513.18
untrustworthy
973.18
unfaked 515.13
unfallacious 515.11
unfallen 978.9
unfalse true 515.11
trustworthy 972.19
unfaltering
sure 512.21
resolute 622.13
persevering 623.7
unfamed 913.14
unfamiliar
unusual 85.10
new 122.11
unconversant 476.13

UNFAMILIAR WITH
unaccustomed
641.4
inexperienced
732.17
unfamiliarity 122.1
ignorance 476.1
unaccustomedness
641.1
unskillfulness 732.2
unfanatical 524.13
unfanciful 534.5
unfancy 900.9
unfashionable
unconventional
83.8
outmoded 123.16
unfashioned
unformed 246.5
unprepared 719.12
unfasten 49.9
unfastened 49.21
unfastidious 492.6
unfathomable
infinite 104.3
deep 208.10
unintelligible
547.11
unfatigued 693.7
unfavorable
untimely 130.7
inauspicious 542.15
disadvantageous
669.6
adverse 727.13
opposed 788.9
disapprobatory
967.22
unfearful, unfearing
891.19
unfeasible 509.7
unfed
unprovided 660.10
fasting 993.5
unfeeling
nouns
physical ∼ 422.1
emotional ∼ 854.1
heartlessness 937.10
adjs.
inanimate 381.5
physically ∼ 422.5
unemotional 854.9
heartless 937.23
unfeigned
genuine 515.13
undeceptive 972.18
unfeigning
genuine 515.13
artless 734.6
natural 900.7
undeceptive 972.18
unfelt numb 422.5
unaffected 854.11
unfeminine
mannish 419.13
discourteous 935.6
unfertile 165.4
unfetter 761.6
unfictitious 515.13
unfigurative 543.12

unfilled
unoccupied 186.13
vacant 186.14
unfinical 532.13
unfinish 719.4
unfinished
imperfect 676.4
unprepared 719.12
uncompleted 721.3
unskilled 732.16
unfit
verbs 157.10
adjs. unsuitable 27.7
unable 157.14
inexpedient 669.5
unqualified 719.9
incompetent 732.19
UNFIT TO LIVE IN
187.17
unfitting
unsuitable 27.7
untimely 130.7
inexpedient 669.5
unfix 49.9
unfixed
unfastened 49.21
changeable 141.7
unconfirmed 505.8
uncertain 513.16
unflagging
unweakening 158.19
persevering 623.7
unflattering
genuine 515.13
undeceptive 972.18
unflavored 429.2
unfledged 124.10
unflexible 355.12
unflinching
resolute 622.13
persevering 623.7
unnervous 858.2
unafraid 891.20
unflustered 856.11
unfold spread 196.6
straighten 249.4
open 264.12
evolve 321.5
explain 550.11
display 553.5
disclose 554.4
UNFOLD A TALE
606.13
unfolded 196.11
unfolding
nouns
evolution 321.1
blossoming 410.24
appearance 445.1
display 553.2
disclosure 554.1
adjs. 321.7
unfool 519.2
unfoolable 503.5
unforbearing
intolerant 525.11
impatient 860.7
unforbidden 775.17
unforbidding 756.5
unforced
voluntary 620.7

unrestrained 760.22
unforeseeable 538.10
unforeseen
 nouns 538.1
 adjs. sudden 113.5
  chance 155.15
  unexpected 538.10
unforgettable
  remembered 535.25
  notable 670.18
unforgivable 975.12
unforgotten 535.23
unform 246.3
unformed
  immature 124.10
  formless 246.5
  undeveloped 719.12
unfortified
  unadulterated 45.6
  unprotected 695.14
unfortunate
 nouns 727.7
 adjs. untimely 130.7
  inauspicious 542.15
  inexpedient 669.5
  unlucky 727.14
unfounded 482.12
unfrank 614.32
unfree 762.13
unfreeze 328.20
unfrequent 136.2
unfrequented 922.9
unfriended
  helpless 157.18
  forlorn 922.13
unfriendly
  opposed 788.9
  unsociable 921.5
  inhospitable 924.6
  inimical 927.10
unfrightened 891.19
unfrock 781.2
unfrozen 327.24
unfruitful 165.4
unfulfilled 721.3
unfunny 881.7
unfurbished 900.8
unfurl ~ sail 274.21
  ~ an ensign 274.55
  unroll 321.5
  ~ a flag 566.21
unfurnish 49.14
unfurnished 719.9
unfussy
  unmeticulous 532.13
  inornate 900.9
ungag 761.6
ungainly 732.20,23
ungallant
  unheroic 890.11
  discourteous 935.4
ungarbed 231.13
ungarnished 900.8
ungenerous
  intolerant 525.11
  stingy 850.11
  unbenevolent
   937.15
  selfish 976.6
ungenial
  unfriendly 927.10

unamiable 937.14
ungenteel
  vulgar 896.10
  plebeian 917.11
  ill-bred 935.6
ungentle
  savage 161.20
  ill-bred 935.6
ungentlemanly 935.6
ungenuine 614.27
ungettable 509.8
ungifted 732.16
ungiven to 641.4
unglorified 913.14
unglue 49.9
ungodliness
  unvirtuousness
   979.3
  impiety 1029.3
ungodly
  execrable 673.10
  unvirtuous 979.16
  impious 1029.17
ungood 979.16
ungovernable 624.12
ungoverned
  impulsive 628.9
  lawless 738.5
  free 760.22,26
ungraceful
  untactful 492.7
  inelegant 588.2
  clumsy 732.20
  unbeautiful 897.9
ungracious
  inhospitable 924.6
  discourteous 935.4
  unkind 937.14
ungrammatic(al)
   585.4
ungrammaticism
   585.2
ungrateful 948.4
ungratified 867.5
ungratifying 867.6
ungregarious 921.5
ungrieving 872.4
unground
  unsubstantial 4.7
  unfounded 482.12
ungrudging
  willing 620.6
  consenting 773.5
  generous 851.4
unguarded
  unintentional
   155.17
  unalert 529.8
  unpremeditated
   628.11
  unprotected 695.14
  IN AN UNGUARDED
   MOMENT 538.14
unguent
 nouns
  ointment 379.3
  balm 685.9
 verbs 379.8
 adjs. 379.9
unguentary, un-
  guentous 379.9

unguentum
  ointment 379.3
  balm 685.9
ungues 811.4
unguided
  unintentional
   155.17
  unlearned 476.15
  unpremeditated
   628.11
unguiform 251.8
unguilty 982.6
unguinous 379.9
ungula 211.5
ungulae 811.4
Ungulata, ungulates
   414.12
ungulate
 nouns 413.3
 adjs. 413.41
ungullible 503.5
unhabitable 187.17
unhabituated 641.4
unhallow 1028.4
unhallowed 1025.3
unhamper 730.7
unhampered
  communicative
   552.9
  untrammeled
   760.23
unhampering 730.5
unhand free 761.5
  relinquish 812.4
unhandicapped 760.23
unhandled
  new 122.7
  unused 666.12
unhandsome
  unbecoming 669.5
  ugly 897.6
unhandy
  inopportune 130.7
  inconvenient 669.7
  unwieldy 729.18
  clumsy 732.20
unhappiness
  displeasure 864
  discontent 867
  sadness 870.2
unhappy
  untimely 130.7
  inexpedient 669.5
  unfortunate 727.14
  displeased 864.23
  discontented 867.5
  sad 870.21
UNHAPPY ABOUT
  displeased 864.23
  regretful 871.8
unharbored 184.9
unhardened 159.12
unharmed 675.8
unharmonious
  disagreeing 27.6
  unmelodious 460.4
  disaccordant 793.16
unharness 761.16
unharsh 756.5
unhasty 708.6
unhatched 719.8

unhazardous 696.5
unhealthy
  unhealthful 682.4
  sickly 684.40
  unsafe 695.11
unhearable 450.11
unheard
  silent 450.11
  unknown 476.18
unheard-of
  unusual 85.10
  new 122.11
  unknown 476.18
  impossible 509.6
  unrenowned 913.14
unhearing 448.7
unheated 332.14
unheavy 352.10
unheeded 532.15
unheedful
  inattentive 529.6
  careless 532.11
  inconsiderate
   937.16
unhelpful
  unco-operative
   624.11
  unserviceable
   667.14
unhep 476.13
unheroic 890.11
unhesitant 622.13
unhesitating
  undoubting 500.18
  implicit 507.2
  sure 512.21
  resolute 622.13
unhewn
  unformed 246.5
  unfinished 719.12
unhidden
  visible 443.6
  unconcealed 553.10
unhide 554.4
unhidebound 524.8
unhindered 760.23
unhinge
  disjoint 49.16
  dislocate 184.4
  madden 472.22
unhinged
  dislocated 184.8
  insane 472.24
unhitch 49.9
unhobble 761.6
unholy
 nouns 1025.2
 adjs. unsacred 1025.3
  ungodly 1029.17
unhonored
  unrenowned
   913.14
  unrespected 963.7
unhook 49.9
unhoped for 538.10
unhorse
  unseat 184.5
  dismount 314.7
unhospitable 924.6
unhostile
  peaceable 801.10

frighten 889.14
unnerved
  enervated 157.19
  unmanned 857.14
unnotable 913.14
unnoted
  unnoticed 532.15
  unrenowned 913.14
unnoteworthy
  unimportant 671.15
  ordinary 678.9
unnoticed
  invisible 444.4
  unheeded 532.15
  unrenowned 913.14
unnumbered 104.3
unobjectionable
  desirable 632.31
  tolerable 672.20
  satisfactory 866.12
  inculpable 982.8
  justifiable 1004.14
unobliging 937.16
unobscured
  light 334.31
  unhidden 553.10
unobservant
  inattentive 529.6
  nonobservant 767.5
unobserved
  invisible 444.4
  unheeded 532.15
unobserving
  blind 440.8
  inattentive 529.6
unobstructed
  open 264.17
  unhampered 760.23
unobtainable 509.8
unobtrusive
  clandestine 612.14
  tasteful 895.8
  modest 906.9
unoccupiable 187.17
unoccupied
  vacant 186.13,14
  empty-headed
    463.19
  thoughtless 479.4
  unemployed 706.16
  leisured 708.5
unofficial
  unauthoritative
    513.19
  informal 645.3
  illegal 997.6
unoften 136.4
unopen, unopened
  265.9
unopinionated, un-
  opinioned 524.13
unordered
  orderless 62.11
  formless 246.4
unordinary 85.10
unorganic 381.4
unorganized
  orderless 62.11
  formless 246.4
  inorganic 381.4
  unprepared 719.8

unoriginal
  uninventive 165.5
  unimaginative 534.5
unoriginated 1.14
unornamental 897.10
unornamented 900.8
unornate 900.9
unorthodox
  unconventional 83.8
  left-handed 243.6
  fallacious 517.4
  heretical 1023.9
unorthodoxy
  nonconformity 83.2
  unconventionality
    83.3
  fallacy 517
  heresy 1023
unostentatious 906.9
unowed paid 839.23
undue 959.9
unpack 308.21
unpaid
  owing 838.10
  unremunerated
    840.12
unpalatable
  unsavory 428.5
  unpleasant 862.8
unparalleled
  peerless 36.17
  extraordinary 85.13
unpardonable 975.12
unpardonable sin
  980.2
unparticular
  undiscriminating
    492.6
  unmeticulous 532.13
unpassable 265.13
unpassionate
  unemotional 854.9
  inexcitable 856.10
unpatriotic 938.3
unpayable 840.13
unpeaceful
  unquiet 323.17
  combative 795.26
unpeered 36.17
unpeople 308.15
unpeopled 186.13
unperceivable 444.4
unperceived
  invisible 444.4
  unknown 476.18
  unheeded 532.15
  hidden 613.13
unperceiving
  blind 440.8
  inattentive 529.6
unperceptive 468.14
unperforated 265.10
unperformable 509.7
unperformed 721.3
unpersuadable
  uninfluenceable
    172.4
  obstinate 624.13
unperturbed 856.11
unphilanthropic(al)
  937.15

unphilosophical
  482.10
unphysical 376.7
unpierceable 265.13
unpin 49.9
unpinion 761.6
unpitying 943.3
unplace 184.5
unpleasant,
  unpleasing
  unsavory 428.5
  unenjoyable 862.8
unpleasantness 862
unpliable
  uninfluenceable
    172.4
  inflexible 355.12
unplug 264.12
unplumbed 104.3
unpoetic(al)
  matter-of-fact 534.5
  plain-speaking 589.3
  prosaic 608.5
unpointed 258.3
unpolished
  countrified 181.7
  rough 260.6
  inelegant 588.2
  unfinished 719.12
  uncouth 896.12
unpolite 935.4
unpolitic 492.7
unpolluted 679.23
unpopular
  uncared-for 865.10
  unrenowned 913.14
unpopulated 186.13
unpossessed of 660.11
unpracticability 509.2
unpractical 533.24
unpracticed 732.16,17
unpragmatic(al)
  524.13
unpraiseworthy 967.25
unprecedented
  unimitated 23.4
  extraordinary 85.13
unprecise
  inaccurate 517.15
  unmeticulous
    532.13
unpredictable
  uncertain 513.14
  fickle 627.7
unprejudiced 524.12
unpremeditated
  premature 131.8
  unintentional
    155.17
  impulsive 628.11
unprepared
  premature 131.8
  unwary 529.8
  unready 719.8
  unskilled 732.16
  BE UNPREPARED
    719.6
unprepossessing 897.7
unpresuming, unpre-
  sumptuous 906.9

unpretending
  homely 190.28
  genuine 515.13
  artless 734.6
  natural 900.7
  modest 906.9
  undeceptive 972.18
unpretentious
  artless 734.6
  natural 900.7
  modest 906.9
unpreventable 637.15
unprevented 760.23
unprimed
  unprepared 719.8
  unskilled 732.16
unprincipled 973.15
unprintable 988.9
unprized 497.3
unprocessed 719.12
unproclaimed 544.9
unprocurable 509.8
unproduced 2.9
unproductive
  ineffectual 157.15
  unfruitful 165.4
  BE UNPRODUCTIVE
    165.3
unprofessional 654.17
unproficient 732.15
unprofitable 667.12
unprofitably 810.9
unprofound
  shallow 209.5
  shallow-witted
    468.20
unprogressive
  nouns 140.4
  adjs. 140.8
unprohibited 775.17
unpromising 542.15
unprompted
  unintentional
    155.17
  unpremeditated
    628.11
unpronounced
  silent 450.12
  unexpressed 544.9
unpropitious
  untimely 130.7
  inauspicious 542.15
  opposed 788.9
unprosperous
  unfortunate 727.14
  poor 836.7
unprotected
  helpless 157.18
  defenseless 695.14
unprovable 505.9
unprovided
  unsupplied 660.9
  unequipped 719.9
unprovidential 727.14
unproviding 719.15
unprovincial 524.8
unpublishable 612.16
unpublished 544.9
unpunctual 132.15
unpure 680.22

unqualified
downright 34.14
thorough 56.10
unable 157.14
unconditional 507.2
genuine 515.13
ineligible 669.5
unfitted 719.9
incompetent 732.19
unlimited 760.24
unquelled
unmitigated 161.16
undefeated 724.9
unrestrained 760.26
unquenchable
inextinguishable 142.19
greedy 632.28
unquenched
unmitigated 161.16
burning 327.27
unquestionable 512.15
unquestioned
believed 500.20
undoubted 512.16
unquestioning
believing 500.18
implicit 507.2
unquiet
nouns 705.4
adjs. agitated 323.17
bustling 705.19
restless 855.28
unquotable 612.16
unravel disinvolve 45.4
solve 486.2
unreachable 509.8
unread 476.15
unreadable 547.17
unready late 132.15
unalert 529.8
unprepared 719.8
unreal unactual 2.8
unsubstantial 4.4,5
illusory 518.9
fanciful 533.19–22
false 614.27
unrealistic unreal 2.8
impractical 533.24
unreality
unactuality 2.1
unsubstantiality 4.1
illusion 518.2
idealism 533.7
falseness 614.2
unrealized 721.3
unreasonable
unwise 469.9
fanatical 472.31
illogical 482.10
impractical 533.24
capricious 627.5
excessive 661.17
exorbitant 846.12
unjustifiable 975.12
unreasoning
unintelligent 468.13
thoughtless 479.4
impulsive 628.10
unrecalled 536.8

unreceptive
uninfluenceable 172.4
inhospitable 924.6
unrecognizable
indistinct 444.5
unintelligible 547.11
unrecorded 544.9
unreduced
undiminished 34.16
whole 54.10
unreel 321.5
unrefined
countrified 181.7
rough 260.6
coarse-grained 350.6
unlearned 476.15
inelegant 588.2
unfinished 719.12
vulgar 896.12
unreflecting
injudicious 469.9
inattentive 529.6
impulsive 628.10
unrefreshed 715.6
unrefutable
proved 504.23
unquestionable 512.15
unrefuted
proved 504.23
true 515.11
unregarded
unheeded 532.15
unrespected 963.7
unregenerate 1029.18
unregretful,
unregretting 872.4
unregular 138.3
unrehearsed 628.12
unrelated 10.5
unrelaxed rigid 355.11
nervous 857.13
unrelenting
persevering 623.7
unyielding 624.9
strict 755.7
unreliability
changeableness 141.2
uncertainty 513.6
fickleness 627.3
unsafeness 695.2
untrustworthiness 973.4
unreliable
changeable 141.7
uncertain 513.18
tergiversating 626.10
fickle 627.7
unsafe 695.11
untrustworthy 973.18
unreliant 513.21
unreligious 1029.15
unreluctant
willing 620.6
consenting 773.5
unremarkable 678.9

unremarked 532.15
unrememberable 536.10
unremitting
continuous 71.9
perpetual 112.7
constant 135.5
persevering 623.7
unremorseful
unregretful 872.4
unmerciful 943.3
unremunerated 840.12
unremunerative 667.12
unrenowned 913.14
unrepatriate 626.5
unrepeated 89.9
unrepentant,
unrepenting 872.5
unreplenished 660.10
unrepressed
communicative 552.9
unrestrained 760.22
unreproachful 966.17
unrequested 620.7
unrequired
voluntary 620.7
needless 667.10
unrequited
unpaid 840.12
unthanked 948.5
unresemblance 21.1
unresentful 945.6
unreserved
thorough 56.10
unqualified 507.2
communicative 552.9
unrestricted 760.22
candid 972.17
unresigned 765.10
unresisting
submissive 763.12
patient 859.11
unresolved 625.9
unrespectable 913.10
unrespected 963.7
unresponsive
uninfluenceable 172.4
unfeeling 854.9
unresponsiveness
uninfluenceability 172.2
neurosis 688.22
unfeeling 854.1
unrest agitation 323.1
excitement 855.4
unrestful 855.28
unrestorable 142.18
unrestrained
changeable 141.7
communicative 552.9
capricious 627.5
lawless 738.5
lax 756.4
free 760.22
candid 972.17

unrestraint
communicativeness 552.4
lawlessness 738.1
laxness 756.
freedom 760.2
candor 972.4
intemperance 991.1
unrestricted
undiminished 34.16
thorough 56.10
open 264.17
unqualified 507.2
communicative 552.9
unlimited 760.24
unretained 536.8
unretarded 34.16
unreticent 552.9
unreturnable 142.18
unrevealable 612.12
unrevealed
unknown 476.18
hidden 613.13
unrevengeful 945.6
unrevered 963.7
unrewarded
unpaid 840.12
unthanked 948.5
unrewarding 667.12
unrhymed, unrimed 608.5
unriddle 486.2
unrig 49.14
unrighteous
unvirtuous 979.16
ungodly 1029.17
THE UNRIGHTEOUS 984.11
unrightful 975.9
unripe
immature 124.10
premature 131.8
sour 431.6
ignorant 476.13
unprepared 719.11
inexperienced 732.17
unrivaled 36.17
unroll open 264.12
unfold 321.5
disclose 554.4
unromantic
practical 534.6
prosaic 608.5
unroot 304.9
unrooted 524.13
unrough, unroughened 259.9
unrueful 872.4
unruffled
smooth 259.9
quiescent 267.10
unaffected 854.11
unexcited 856.11
unruly
disorderly 161.18
ungovernable 624.12
lawless 738.6

weak-willed 625.11
unsafe 695.11
unstaid 141.7
unstained clean 679.23
chaste 986.4
unsteadfast
changeable 141.7
unreliable 513.18
unfaithful 973.19
unsteady uneven 18.2
ill-balanced 31.5
irregular 138.3
changeable 141.7
infirm 159.16
wavering 323.19
unreliable 513.18
weak-willed 625.11
precarious 695.11
unstern 756.5
unstick 49.9
unstinting 851.4
unstirred
unaffected 854.11
unexcited 856.11
unstirring 267.10
unstop 264.12
unstopped
continuous 71.9
constant 135.5
open 264.17
unstored 660.10
unstrain 162.9
unstrained 858.2
unstrap unfasten 49.9
free 761.6
unstrengthen 159.10
unstressed 449.13
unstring
weaken 159.10
relax 162.9
unnerve 857.10
unstrict 756.5
unstrong 159.12
unstruck 854.11
unstrung 857.14
unstudied
unexamined 532.16
colloquial 578.16
unpremeditated 628.11
informal 645.3
unstudious 476.15
unsturdy 159.15
unsubduable 158.17
unsubdued
unmitigated 161.16
undefeated 724.9
unrestrained 760.26
unsubject free 760.26
exempt 760.27
unsubmissive
uncomfortable 83.6
ungovernable 624.12
disobedient 765.10
unsubstantial
intangible 4.4
flimsy 159.14–16
weightless 352.10
rare 354.7
immaterial 376.7

illogical 482.11
unreliable 513.18
illusory 518.9
unsubstantiality
intangibility 4
flimsiness 159.2
weakness 159.3
rarity 354.1
immateriality 376
unreliability 513.6
illusion 518.2
phantom 1015.1
unsubstantiated 505.8
unsuccessful
successless 723.17
unfortunate 727.14
BE UNSUCCESSFUL 723.9
unsuccessive 72.4
unsufficing 660.7
unsuggested 545.12
unsuggestible 172.4
unsuitability
unfitness 27.3
untimeliness 130.1
inexpedience 669.1
unpreparedness 719.1
unsatisfactoriness 867.2
unsuitable
unfit 27.7
untimely 130.7
inexpedient 669.5
unsatisfactory 867.7
unsuited
unfitted 27.8
unadapted 719.9
unsullied
clean 679.23
virginal 719.13
innocent 982.7
chaste 986.4
unsung 544.9
unsupplied
unprovided 660.10
unequipped 719.9
unsupported
unaided 89.8
unfounded 482.12
unproved 505.8
unsuppressed
communicative 552.9
unrestrained 760.22
unsure
uncertain 513.14,18,21
precarious 695.11
untrustworthy 973.18
unsurmountable
impregnable 158.17
unachievable 509.7
unsurpassable, un-
surpassed 36.17
unsurprised
expectant 537.9
unastonished 919.3

unsusceptible
unchangeable 142.18
unsuggestible 172.4
unfeeling 854.9
unsuspected
unknown 476.18
believed 500.20
unsuspecting
unaware 476.14
trusting 500.19
credulous 501.7
inexpectant 538.9
unsuspicious
trusting 500.19
credulous 501.7
artless 734.5
unsustainable
unreasonable 482.12
unprovable 505.9
questionable 513.15
unsustained
unfounded 482.12
unproved 505.8
unswallow 308.24
unswayable 172.4
unswayed
uninfluenced 172.5
unprejudiced 524.12
impartial 974.10
unsweet, un-
sweetened 431.6
unswept 680.22
unswerving
straight 249.5
direct 289.13
resolute 622.13
persevering 623.7
unsymmetric(al) 248.10
unsymmetry
disorder 62.1
distortion 248.1
unsympathetic
intolerant 525.11
unkind 937.14
pitiless 943.3
unsympathetic(al) 854.9
unsynthetic 515.13
unsystematic
orderless 62.11
irregular 138.3
untaciturn 552.9
untactful 492.7
untainted
faultless 675.6
clean 679.23
preserved 699.11
innocent 982.7
chaste 986.4
untaken 186.14
untalented 732.16
untalkative 611.7
untalked-of 544.9
untamed
savage 161.20
uncivilized 896.12
untangle
disentangle 45.4

solve 486.2
untarnished
clean 679.23
chaste 986.4
untasteful
unsavory 428.5
unpleasant 862.8
vulgar 896.10
untasty 428.5
untaught 476.15
untaxed 848.5
unteachable 468.15
untellable 612.12
untempered 161.16
untenable
unreasonable 482.12
unbelievable 502.10
untenacious 51.4
untenantable 187.17
untenanted 186.13,14
unterrified 891.19
Unterseeboot 276.9
untested 505.8
untether 761.6
unthankful 948.4
unthawed 332.14
unthinkable
unbelievable 502.10
impossible 509.6
unthinking
unintentional 155.17
unintelligent 468.13
injudicious 469.9
thoughtless 479.4
careless 532.11
impulsive 628.10
involuntary 637.14
inconsiderate 937.16
unthoughtful
injudicious 469.9
impulsive 628.10
inconsiderate 937.16
unthought-of
unusual 85.10
unintentional 155.17
unconsidered 479.5
unheeded 532.15
unthread 45.4
unthreatened 696.4
unthrifty 719.15
unthrone 781.2
untidy 62.14
untie unfasten 49.9
free 761.6
UNTIE THE PURSE STRINGS 851.3
until 105.10
UNTIL WE MEET AGAIN! 300.25
untilled 719.14
untimeliness
unseasonableness 130.1
prematurity 131.2
lateness 132
untimely
inapt 27.7

unworthy
nouns 984.1
adjs.
inexpedient 669.5
unimportant 671.19

unwrap
remove 231.6
straighten 249.4
open 264.12

unwrinkled 259.9

unwritten
traditional 123.12
unexpressed 544.9
oral 592.20

unwritten constitution 996.6

unwritten law 996.4

unwrought 719.12

unyielding
immovable 142.16
uninfluenceable 172.4
inflexible 355.12
obstinate 624.9
strict 755.7

unyoke
disjoin 49.8
free 761.6

up
nouns increase 38.1
improvement 689.1
verbs increase 38.4
~ and go 300.6
~ and do 703.6
UP AND AT THEM!
796.34
UP OARS! 274.79
adjs. up-to-date
122.14
foamy 404.7
fashionable 642.11
KEEP UP TO DATE
555.15
KEEP UP TO
STANDARD 82.4
NOT UP TO 732.19
NOT UP TO EX-
PECTATION 867.6
NOT UP TO SNUFF
678.11
ONE UP ON 36.14
UP IN
versed in 474.19
skilled in 731.25
UP TO
able 156.13
cognizant of 474.16
scheming 652.14
prepared for 718.19
competent 731.22
incumbent on
960.13
UP TO ONE'S EARS IN
involved 175.4
busy 705.20
~ debt 838.8
UP TO SNUFF
in order 59.7
up to par 672.17
competent 731.22

UP TO THE EARS
56.18
advs. aloft 206.27
vertically 212.12
upward 313.16
BE ALL UP WITH
perish 691.22
fail 723.12
BE UP AGAINST IT
727.9
UP AGAINST IT
baffled 513.23
straitened 729.24
UP AND ABOUT 683.7
UP IN ARMS
prepared 718.16
opposing 788.10
resistant 790.6
at odds 793.17
UP IN THE AIR
513.16,23
UP IN THE WORLD
726.12
UP TO 105.10
preps. 289.28
UP THE SPOUT 770.15
UP THE WIND 274.69
up-a-daisy! 313.17
upalong 313.16
up-anchor 274.19
up-and-coming 705.22
up-and-down
perpendicular
212.11
seesaw 322.18
up and down
perpendicularly
212.13
to and fro 322.20
up-and-up 972.14
Upanishad 1019.7
upbear
support 215.22
buoy 352.8
lend support 783.12
upbeat 462.25
upbend
nouns 313.2
verbs 313.13
upborne 215.25
upbraid 967.17
upbraiding 967.5
upbring 560.13
upbringing 560.3
upcast
nouns upturn 313.2
elevation 315.1
verbs upturn 313.13
raise 315.5
adjs. upturned 313.15
raised 315.9
upchuck 308.24
upclimb
nouns
acclivity 218.6
ascent 313.1
verbs 313.11
upcome
nouns 313.1
verbs 313.8

upcoming
nouns 313.1
adjs.
forthcoming 151.3
approaching 295.4
ascending 313.14
expected 537.11

upcountry
nouns
hinterland 181.2
interior 224.3
adjs.
hinterland 181.8
inland 224.10

upcurve 284.4

update date 114.13
modernize 122.6

updive 317.5

updraft 313.1

upend 212.8

upended 212.10

upflung 315.9

upgang 313.1

upgo
nouns
acclivity 218.6
ascent 313.1
verbs 313.8

upgoing
nouns 313.1
adjs. 313.14

upgrade
nouns 218.6
ON THE UPGRADE
689.15
verbs improve 689.9
promote 780.3
adjs. 218.17
advs. 218.24

upgrading 780.1

upgrow
become higher
206.17
uprise 313.8

upgrowth
growth 196.3
rise 313.1

upheaval
convulsion 161.5
elevation 315.1
outburst of passion
855.8

upheave rise 212.7
erect 212.8
raise 315.5

upheaving 161.22

upheld 215.25

uphelm 274.26

uphill
nouns 218.6
adjs. upgrade 218.17
ascending 313.14
laborious 714.19
difficult 729.16
advs.
slantingly 218.24
upward 313.16

uphoist 315.5

uphold
support 215.22
raise 315.5

buoy 352.8
corroborate 504.12
preserve 699.7
lend support 783.12
approve of 966.9
defend 1004.10

upholder
supporter 215.2
backer 785.8
defender 797.7

upholding
nouns 215.1
adjs. 215.24

upholster 227.31

upholstery
covering 227.1
furniture 657.4

upkeep
nouns
support 215.1
aid 783.3
verbs support 215.22
sustain 783.12

upland
nouns 206.3
adjs. rural 181.6
highland 206.22

uplands
the country 181.1
highlands 206.3

upleap
nouns 317.1
verbs 317.5

uplift
nouns acclivity 218.6
elevation 315.1
inspiration 646.9
improvement 689.1
verbs erect 212.8
raise 315.5
buoy 352.8
inspire 646.20
improve 689.9
elate 868.7
glorify 912.13

uplifted
upturned 313.15
raised 315.9
inspired 646.31

uplifting
nouns 212.4
adjs. elevating 315.10
inspiring 646.26

uplong 313.16

upmost 210.9

upon
advs.
after which 117.6
toward 289.28
UPON WHICH 105.7
preps. concerning
9.12
against 199.23
atop 210.14
on 227.40
by means of 656.8

uppard
adjs. 313.14
advs. 313.16

upper
superior 36.13

higher 206.24

upper case
capital 579.2
type 601.6
upper-case
large-lettered 579.11
type 601.18
upper chamber,
upper house 740.3
upper circles, upper
classes 916.2
upperclassman 564.5
upper crust,
upper cut
society 642.6
aristocracy 916.2
upper-cruster 916.4
uppercut 282.5
upper frequencies
343.15
upper hand
advantage 36.2
influence 171.1
dominion 737.5
HAVE THE UPPER
HAND
have advantage
36.11
dominate 739.14
uppermost
supreme 36.15
higher 206.24
top 210.9
BE UPPERMOST IN
ONE'S THOUGHTS
472.23
BE UPPERMOST IN
THE MIND 477.19
uppers and lowers
257.6
upper side 210.1
upper story
top side 210.1
head 210.5
brain 465.4
upper ten, upper
ten-thousand
society 642.6
aristocracy 916.2
uppish, uppity 910.9
upraisal 212.4
upraise erect 212.8
raise 315.5
buoy 352.8
uprear rise 212.7
erect 212.8
raise 315.5
upright
nouns vertical 212.2
post 216.4
piano 464.13
verbs 212.8
adjs. vertical 212.10
honorable 972.13
advs. 212.12
uprighteous 972.13
uprightness
verticalness 212.1
probity 972.1
uprisal rising 212.5
ascent 313.1

uprise
nouns height 206.2
rise 212.5
acclivity 218.6
ascent 313.1
verbs be high 206.15
become higher
206.17
rise 212.7
slope 218.10
ascend 313.8
uprising
nouns rising 212.5
acclivity 218.6
ascent 313.1
revolt 765.4
adjs. sloping 218.17
ascending 313.14
uproar
commotion 62.4
turbulence 161.2
noise 452.3
outcry 458.4
uproarious
turbulent 161.17
noisy 452.11
excited 855.25
uproot extract 304.9
eradicate 691.14
uprush 313.1
ups and downs
vicissitudes 155.5
alternation 322.4
UPS AND DOWNS OF
LIFE
vicissitudes 155.5
adversity 727.1
upset
nouns
revolution 147.1
overturn 219.2
refutation 505.2
ruin 691.3
frustration 728.3
verbs
discompose 63.4
revolutionize 147.4
overturn 219.6
capsize 274.46
refute 505.5
fluster 530.7
startle 538.8
spoil 690.11
destroy 691.20
defeat 725.7
thwart 728.15
excite 855.14
unnerve 857.10
distress 864.15
adjs. disproved 505.7
confused 530.12
startled 538.13
defeated 725.14
overwrought 855.27
unnerved 857.14
distressed 864.25
upshot 153.1
upside 210.1
upside down 219.8
upside-down
confused 62.15

topsy-turvy 219.7
upspear grow 196.7
upshoot 313.9
vegetate 410.31
upspin 313.8
upspring
nouns 317.1
verbs grow 196.7
upshoot 313.9
jump 317.5
upsprout grow 196.7
vegetate 410.31
upstage
verbs 964.5
adjs. 910.9
advs. 609.40
upstairs aloft 206.27
upward 313.16
upstairs and
downstairs 178.11
LOOK UPSTAIRS AND
DOWNSTAIRS 484.27
upstanding
erect 212.10
honorable 972.13
upstart
nouns 917.10
verbs 313.9
adjs. 917.13
upstream
verbs 313.8
advs. 313.16
upsurge 313.8
upsurgence 313.1
upswarm 313.8
upsweep
nouns 313.2
verbs 313.13
upswing
increase 38.1
ascent 313.1
improvement 689.1
upthrow
nouns 315.1
verbs 315.5
upthrown 315.9
upthrust 315.1
up-to-date
modern 122.14
informed 474.18
topical 483.6
fashionable 642.11
up-to-the-minute
modern 122.14
fashionable 642.11
uptown
nouns 182.5
adjs. 182.9
advs. 313.16
uptrend
increase 38.1
upturn 313.2
upturn
nouns increase 38.1
overturn 219.2
uptrend 313.2
verbs overturn 219.6
turn up 313.13
upward, upwards
adjs. 313.14
advs. aloft 206.27

up 313.16
UPWARDS OF
about 35.13
several 101.8
approximately
199.26
upward strabismus
439.5
upwind 313.8
up-wind 277.49
upwith
nouns 218.6
advs. 313.16
uraeus 567.3
uranic 374.25
uranographer,
uramologist 374.22
uranography, urano-
ogy, uranometry
374.19
Uranus 374.6
urban 182.9
urbane 934.14
urbanite 189.6
urbanity 934.1,6
urceole 1038.11
urchin 125.3
urea 309.5
uredo 684.27
ureter 395.13
ureterectomy 687.25
ureterotomy 687.26
urethra 395.13
urethrotomy 687.26
urge
nouns desire 632.1
inducement 646.6
libido 688.39
verbs incite 646.14
advise 752.7
importune 772.12
URGE ON THE MIND
560.12
URGE REASONS FOR
1004.10
URGE UPON 771.9
urgency
necessity 637.4
urge 646.6
importance 670.4
urgent
adjs.
necessary 637.12
motivating 646.25
important 670.23
insistent 751.8
interjs. 707.16
uric 309.18
Uriel 1013.4
urinal 680.14
urinalysis 687.15
urinary 309.18
urinate 309.12
urination 309.5
urine 309.5
urinometer 353.8
urn funeral ~ 409.12
ceramic 574.2
uroscopy 687.15
urp 308.24
ursine 413.39

varicose veins,
  varicosis 684.8
varicotomy 687.26
varied different 16.7
  diversified 19.4
  mixed 44.15
variegate
  diversify 19.2
  dapple 373.7
variegated
  diversified 19.4
  many-colored 373.9
variegation
  variety 19.1
  multicolor 373
variety difference 16.1
  multiformity 19.1
  kind 61.3
  class 61.5
  assortment 74.12
  change 139.1
  drama 609.13
Varietyese 578.7
variety performance
  609.13
variety store 830.1
variola 684.9
variolar 684.46
various different 16.7
  diversified 19.4
  several 101.8
AT VARIOUS TIMES
  136.5
variously
  differently 16.10
  severally 19.6
varmint animal 413.2
  scoundrel 984.6
varnish
  nouns pretext 647.1
  extenuation 1004.5
  verbs distort 248.6
  paint 361.14
  ~ speech 599.8
  falsify 614.16
  extenuate 1004.12
varnishing 361.11
varsity 565.7
Varuna sea god 396.4
  god 1012.7
vary differ 16.5
  differentiate 16.6
  diversify 19.2
  disagree 27.5
  change 139.5
  modify 139.6
  fluctuate 141.5
  deviate 290.3
  vacillate 625.8
varying different 16.7
  ununiform 18.2
  vacillating 625.10
vascular
  vesicular 192.9
  tubular 395.21
vase 574.2
vassal
  nouns 762.7
  adjs. 762.12
vassalism 762.1
vast great 34.11

mammoth 194.20
vastly 34.18
vastness greatness 34.1
  hugeness 194.7
Vatican
  papacy 1035.6
  palace 1040.8
vaticide 408.4
vaticinal, vaticinatory
  541.11
vaticinate 541.9
vaticination 541.1
vaudeville 609.4
vaudevillian
  nouns 610.1
  adjs. 609.37
vault
  nouns compartment
  191.2
  arch 251.4
  jump 317.1
  sky 374.2
  tomb 409.16
  hiding place 613.4
  coffer 834.12
  verbs arch 251.6
  jump 317.5
vaulted 251.10
vaulter 317.4
vaulting
  nouns curvature
  251.1
  arch 251.4
  jumping 317.3
  adjs. 632.29
vaunt
  nouns 908.1
  verbs 908.6
vaunting 908.9
Vayu wind 402.3
  god 1012.7
V.D. 684.15
veal 306a.14
vector compass course
  277.40
  direction 289.2
Veda 1019.7
Vedantic 1018.30
vedette 697.9
Vedic 1018.30
vee 99.1
Veep, the 747.7
veer
  nouns obliquity 218.3
  deviation 290.1
  verbs change 139.5
  oblique 218.9
  sidle 241.5
  wear ship 274.32
  deviate 290.3
  turn 294.9
vega plain 386.1
  grassland 410.8
vegetable
  nouns food 306a.35
  types of ~ 306a.49
  plant 410.3
  adjs. 410.34
vegetable kingdom
  class 61.4
  plant life 410.1

vegetal 410.34
vegetarian
  nouns eater 306.13
  abstainer 990.4
  adjs. vegetable-eating
  306.29
  vegetable 410.34
  abstinent 990.10
vegetarianism
  eating 306.1
  abstinence 990.2
vegetate exist 1.10
  be inert 267.8
  grow 410.31
vegetation
  existence 1.6
  stagnation 267.4
  plants 410.1
  growth 410.30
Vegliantino,
  Veillantif 413.21
vehemence
  violence 161.1
  loudness 452.1
  eloquence 598.5
  zeal 633.2
  fervor 853.9
  anger 950.10
vehement
  violent 161.15
  loud 452.9
  eloquent 598.13
  zealous 633.10
  passionate 855.30
vehemently
  violently 161.24
  eloquently 598.15
  zealously 633.14
vehicle
  nouns conveyance
  271.1
  types of ~ 271.21–
  29
  color 361.7
  photographic ~
  575.15
  drama 609.4
  medium 656.3
  verbs 270.12
vehicular 271.20
veil
  nouns cover 227.2
  garment 230.26
  shade 337.1
  secrecy 612.3
  pretext 647.1
TAKE THE VEIL
  seclude oneself
  922.8
  take holy orders
  1035.11
  verbs superimpose
  227.21
  shade 337.5
  conceal 613.7
veiled covered 227.34
  shaded 337.7
  vague 513.17
veiling
  nouns covering 227.1
  veil 230.26

adjs. covering 227.37
  shading 337.6
Veillantif See
  Vegliantino
vein
  nouns nature 5.3
  thinness 204.7
  mineral ~ 382.6
  vessel 395.14
  tone 449.2
  mood 523.4
  diction 586.2
  source of supply
  658.4
IN THE VEIN
  in the mood 523.8
  willing 620.5
  verbs 373.7
veined 373.15
veinous 395.21
veinstone 382.6
velar
  nouns 449.5
  adjs. guttural 449.18
  throaty 593.11
veld, veldt plain 386.1
  grassland 410.8
veldman, veldtsman
  386.2
velleity 619.1
vellicate
  twitch 323.13
  tickle 425.6
vellication
  twitching 323.5
  tickling 425.2
  nervousness 857.1
vellicative
  jerky 323.20
  ticklish 425.9
veloce 461.56
velocimeter 268.8
velocity 268
velutinous
  nappy 350.7
  soft 356.15
velvet
  smoothness 259.3
  softness 356.4
  prosperity 726.1
  comfort 885.1
velvety glossy 259.10
  nappy 350.7
  soft 356.15
  cloth 377.9
venal hired 778.17
  vendible 827.12
  niggardly 850.10
  corruptible 973.22
venality
  vendibility 827.7
  niggardliness 850.2
  corruptibility 973.9
vend 827.9
vendee 826.5
vendetta 793.5
vendibility 827.7
vendible
  nouns 829.2
  adjs. 827.12
vending 827.2

vending machine
830.9
vendor, vender
peddler 828.6
vending machine
830.9
vendue 827.4
venectomy 687.25
veneer
nouns shallowness
209.1
lamina 226.2
coating 227.13
verbs 227.25
venenation 684.23
venerability
dignity 903.2
sacredness 1024.1
venerable
ancient 123.10
elderly 126.15
dignified 903.12
revered 962.12
sacred 1024.7
venerate
respect 962.4
worship 1030.10
veneration
respect 962.1
piety 1026.1
worship 1030.1
venerational, venerative
respectful 962.9
pious 1026.8
worshipful 1030.15
venereal sexual 418.17
aphrodisiac 418.19
venereal disease
684.15
venery coition 168.3
hunting 653.2
profligacy 987.3
venesection 687.28
vengeance 954.1
WITH A VENGEANCE
exceedingly 34.24
utterly 56.17
effectively 156.14
violently 161.24
vengeful 954.6
venial 1004.14
venin 674.3
venire 750.7
venison 306a.12
vennel 655.6
venom poison 674.3
animosity 927.4
virulence 937.7
venomous
poisonous 682.5
virulent 937.20
venose, venous 395.21
venotomy 687.26
vent
nouns holes 264.4
parachute ~ 279.13
egress 302.2
outlet 302.9
air passage 395.17
escape 630.1

GIVE VENT
let out 308.22
divulge 554.5
verbs divulge 554.5
publish 557.14
~ one's spleen
950.16
ventage outlet 302.9
air duct 395.17
venter belly 192.3
womb 418.8
venthole holes 264.4
outlet 302.9
air duct 395.17
ventiduct 395.17
ventilate air 401.12
discuss 481.16
publish 557.11
write upon 604.5
refresh 693.3
ventilation
airing 401.10
discussion 481.4
publication 557.1
refreshment 693.1
ventilator
airway 395.17
aerator 401.11
fan 402.22
ventose 196.12
ventral 192.10
ventre à terre 268.21
ventricose 255.15
ventricular 192.10
ventriloquial, ventriloquistic 592.22
ventriloquism, ventriloquist, ventriloquy 592.8
venture
nouns gamble 514.1
undertaking 713.1
speculation 831.19
investment 834.3
verbs ~ a guess
498.10
~ to say 510.4
chance 514.18
attempt 712.5
speculate 831.23
invest in 834.16
dare 891.10
presume 959.6
venturer 514.16
venturesome, venturous risky 695.10
enterprising 705.22
daring 891.21
venue position 183.3
viewpoint 438.7
Venus planet 374.5,6
beauty 898.9
love 929.8
goddess 1012.5
Venus's flytrap 616.11
veracious 972.16
veraciously 972.22
veracity 972.3
veranda 191.21
verb 584.3

verbal
nouns 584.3
adjs. verbatim 543.12
vocabular 580.17
of verbs 584.13
oral 592.20
verbal amnesia
amnesia 536.2
neurosis 688.26
verbal contest 481.5
verbal intercourse
595.1
verbalism word 580.1
phrase 583.1
wordiness 591.2
verbalize phrase 583.4
say 592.14
verbal thrust 965.2
verbatim
adjs. 543.12
advs. 543.15
verbatim et literatim
543.15
verbiage
vocabulary 580.12
diction 586.1
wordiness 591.2
verbigeration 688.25
verbose 591.12
verboten 776.7
verdancy
greenness 370.1
ignorance 476.1
verdant green 370.4
verdurous 410.40
ignorant 476.13
inexperienced
732.17
verdict 493.5
verdigris
nouns 370.2
verbs 370.3
verdigrisy 370.5
verdure
greenness 370.1
plants 410.1
verdurous green 370.4
verdured 410.40
Verein 786.1
verge
nouns 234.4
ON THE VERGE 234.15
ON THE VERGE OF
about to 121.13
near 199.22
verbs tend 173.3
border 234.10
bear for 289.8
VERGE UPON 199.9
verger, vergeress
1036.9
veridical
genuine 515.13
veracious 972.16
verifiable 504.21
verification test 488.2
collation 490.2
confirmation 504.5
ascertainment 512.8
verificative 504.20
verify test 488.8

collate 490.5
confirm 504.12
certify 512.12
verily positively 34.21
truly 515.16
verisimilar 510.5
verisimilitude 510.1
veritable real 1.15
utter 56.11
true 515.11
verity 515.1
verjuice 431.1,3
vermeology 414.1
Vermes 414.5
vermicelli 306a.32
vermicide
exterminator 408.11
medicine 685.19
vermicular 413a.10
vermiform
sinuous 253.7
wormlike 413a.10
vermifugal 685.37
vermifuge 685.19
vermilion
verbs 367.4
adjs. 367.7
vermin animals 413.3
insects 413a.6
riffraff 917.5
verminous
rodent 413.40
buggy 413a.9
vernacular
nouns 578.6
THE VERNACULAR
578.4
adjs. common 84.8
local 179.9
native 188.7
colloquial 578.16
vulgar 896.14
vernal new 122.7
immature 124.10
springlike 128.8
vernal equinox
season 128.7
astronomy 374.16
vernation 410.16
Verner's law 449.9
Vernunft 465.1
veronica
talisman 1034.5
icon 1038.11
verruca wart 255.3
blemish 677.1
growth 684.29
verrucated, verrucose
255.14
versatile 731.23
versatility 731.3
vers de société 607.2
verse section 55.2
musical ~ 461.24
passage 603.14
poetry 607.1
poem 607.4
metrical pattern
607.8
measure 607.11
versecraft 607.7

versemaker 607.13
verseman 607.13
versemongering, verse-
    mongery 607.7
versicle poem 607.4
    chant 1030.3
versicolor, versicolor-
    ate, versicolored,
    versicolorous
    373.9
versifiaster 607.13
versification 607.7
versifier 607.13
versify 607.19
version 550.2
vers libre 607.2
verso left side 243.1
    page 603.13
Verstand 466.1
versus
    opposite to 238.6
    against 788.11
verte 370.1
vertebral 413.47
vertebrate
    nouns 413.3
    adjs. 413.47
vertex 210.2
Verthandi 638.3
vertical
    nouns 212.2
    adjs. top 210.9
    upright 212.10
verticality 212.1
vertically 212.12
verticillaster 410.25
vertiginous
    rotary 320.15
    dizzy 530.15
vertigo 530.4
verve energy 160.2
    resilience 357.1
    imagination 533.4
    eloquence 598.5
    eagerness 633.1
    liveliness 705.2
    fervor 853.9
very 34.20
Very Reverend, the
    titular 915.8
    clergyman 1036.2
vesicant 685.26
vesicate 328.23
vesication 328.5
vesicatory 685.26
vesicle blister 255.3
    bubble 404.1
    blemish 677.1
vesicular
    capsular 192.9
    vascular 395.21
vesper
    nouns evening 134.2
    devotions 1030.8
    adjs. 134.8
vespertine 134.8
vespiary 190.21
vessel receptacle 192.1
    drinking ~ 192.15
    boat 276.2
    armored ~ 276.7

duct 395.13
vest 230.14
vest in repose 183.14
    belong to 806.8
    endow 816.17
Vesta gods of the
    household 190.26
    goddess 1012.5
vesta 330.5
vestal, vestal virgin
    virgin 932.4
    good woman 983.7
vested 142.14
vested interests
    capitalists 743.7
    estate 808.4
    right 956.3
vestibule
    portal 191.19
    cochlea 447.7
vestige remains 43.1
    tinge 44.7
    relic 123.6
    trace 566.7
    record 568.1
vestiture 227.2
vestment
    covering 227.2
    clothing 230.1
    garment 230.3
    types of ~ 1039.5
vestmental
    sartorial 230.47
    vestmentary 1039.4
vestments 1039.1
vestry council 753.5
    church ~ 1040.9
vesture clothing 230.1
    garment 230.3
    canonicals 1039.1
vesuvian 330.5
vet veterinary 686.11
    veteran 731.14
    soldier 798.18
vetch 410.4
veteran
    nouns old hand
    731.14
    soldier 798.18
    adjs. 731.26
veterinarian,
    veterinary 686.11
veto
    nouns legislative ~
    740.17
    prohibition 776.2
    verbs 776.5
vex annoy 864.17
    worry 888.4
    anger 950.22
vexation evil 673.3
    annoyance 864.2
    anxiety 888.1
    resentment 950.1
vexatious 862.13
vexatiously 862.19
vexed annoyed 864.24
    worried 888.7
    provoked 950.25
vexillum 567.6
via 289.29

viability 406.1
viable 406.10
viaduct 655.10
Via Lactea 374.13
vials of wrath, vials of
    hate hatred 928.1
    anger 950.5
viands 306a.1
viaticum
    provisions 306a.5
    last rites 409.4
    extreme unction
    1038.6
vibes 464.20
vibrancy 453.1
vibrant
    energetic 160.11
    resonant 453.9
vibraphone 464.20
vibrate oscillate 322.9
    shake 323.11
    resonate 453.6
vibratile 322.14
vibratility 322.1
vibrating
    oscillating 322.14
    shaking 323.18
    resonating 453.9
vibration
    oscillation 322.1
    shaking 323.2
    resonance 453.1
vibrato 462.19
vibrator
    oscillator 322.8
    agitator 323.9
vibratory 322.14
vibrissa
    tactile hair 229.10
    feather 229.16
    feeler 424.4
vibrograph,
    vibroscope 322.7
vicar deputy 779.1,8
    churchman 1036.8
vicarage
    benefice 1035.9
    parsonage 1040.7
vicariate 1035.5
vicarious 148.8
vicarship 1035.5
vice
    nouns fault 676.2
    vice-agent 779.8
    wickedness 979
    wrongdoing 980
    adjs. 779.14
    preps. 148.12
vice-admiral
    officer 747.24
    deputy 779.8
vice-agent 779.8
vice-bishop, vice-
    caliph 779.8
vice-chairman 779.8
vice-chancellor 1000.4
vice-consul 779.6
vice-corrupted 979.19
vice-dean, vice-
    director 779.8

vice-general, vice-
    governor 779.8
vicegerent
    nouns 779.8
    adjs. 779.14
vice-king
    regent 747.13
    deputy 779.8
vice-legate 779.6
vice-master 779.8
vicenary, vicennial
    99.26
vice-pope, vice-prefect
    779.8
vice-president
    executive 747.5,7
    deputy 779.8
vice-priest, vice-prior,
    vice-provost 779.8
vice-queen, vicereine
    779.8
viceroy
    governor 747.14
    deputy 779.8
vicesimal 99.26
vice-sultan 779.8
vice versa 15.7
vice-warden 779.8
vicinage region 179.1
    proximity 199.1
    environs 232.1
vicinal 199.14
vicinity region 179.1
    proximity 199.1
    environs 232.1
IN THE VICINITY OF
    about 35.13
    near 199.14
    approximately
    199.26
    around 232.13
vicious savage 161.20
    cruel 937.24
    wicked 979.17
vicious circle
    vicissitudes 155.5
    sophistry 482.1
    futility 667.2
    psychology 688.20
viciousness
    fierceness 161.1
    cruelty 937.11
    wickedness 979.5
vicissitude 141.3
vicissitudes 155.5
vicissitudinary, vicis-
    situdinous 141.7
victim dupe 618.1
    prey 653.7
    patient 684.31
    defeatee 725.5
    sufferer 864.11
    laughingstock 965.7
victimization 616.1
victimize
    murder 408.16
    deceive 616.13
victor 724.2
Victoria Cross 914.6
Victorian
    nouns 901.11

adjs. antiquated
  123.13
 stra t-laced 901.19
victorious 724.8
victory success 722
 triumph 724.1
victress 724.2
Victrola 464.18
victual 657.9
victuals 306a.1
Vidar See Vitharr
videlicet namely 80.18
 to wit 550.21
video
 nouns 344.1
 adjs. 344.16
videogenic 344.16
video transmitter
  344.8
viduage, viduation
  933.3
vie
 compare with 490.7
 rival 672.12
 VIE FOR 794.21
 VIE WITH
 compare with 490.7
 compete with
  794.19
vielle viol 464.5
 hurdy-gurdy 464.16
view
 nouns look 438.3
 field of ~ 443.3
 appearance 445.3
 scene 445.6
 opinion 500.4
 attitude 523.2
 picture 572.13
 intention 651.1
 COME IN VIEW 445.8
 HAVE IN VIEW
 expect 537.4
 intend 651.7
 IN VIEW
 imminent 151.3
 present 185.12
 visible 443.6
 expected 537.11
 planned 652.13
 IN VIEW OF 154.8
 KEEP IN VIEW
 look at 438.14
 take cognizance
  528.9
 be vigilant 531.8
 remember 535.14
 expect 537.4
 WITH A VIEW TO
  651.12
 verbs see 438.12,14
 contemplate 477.16
 take an attitude
  523.6
 heed 528.6
 VIEW AS 500.9
viewer 441.1
viewing 438.2
viewpoint
 standpoint 438.7
 attitude 523.2

viewy visionary 533.24
 notional 627.5
vigesimal 99.26
vigil 531.4
 KEEP VIGIL
 keep watch 531.8
 keep guard 697.19
vigilance 531.4
vigilant 531.13
vigilantes, vigilance
  committee 697.15
vigils 1030.8
vigintillion 99.13
vignette
 engraving 576.6
 sketch 606.1
vigor power 156.1
 strength 158.1
 energy 160.1
 eloquence 598.3
 health 683.3
vigorous potent 156.11
 strong 158.13
 energetic 160.11
 tough 358.4
 eloquent 598.11
 healthy 683.9
 fresh 693.5
 flourishing 726.13
vigorously
 powerfully 156.14
 strongly 158.20
 energetically 160.14
 eloquently 598.15
Viking 417.3
viking 823.8
vile nasty 428.7
 malodorous 436.5
 paltry 671.18
 very bad 673.9
 filthy 680.25
 odious 862.9
 vulgar 896.15
 infamous 913.12
 wicked 979.17
 obscene 988.9
vileness
 unsavoriness 428.3
 malodorousness
  436.2
 paltriness 671.2
 badness 673.2
 filthiness 680.2
 odiousness 862.2
 disreputability
  913.3
 wickedness 979.5
 obscenity 988.4
vilification
 defamation 969.2
 malediction 970.2
vilify stigmatize 913.9
 defame 969.10
 curse 970.7
vilifying 969.13
vilipend 969.10
villa 190.7
village
 nouns 182.2
 adjs. 182.9
village green 410.7

villager 189.6
villain actor 610.1
 serf 762.7
 rascal 984.3
villainous
 terrible 673.9
 knavish 973.16
 wicked 979.17
villainy 973.2
villein
 townsman 189.6
 householder 189.7
 serf 762.7
villenage
 serfhood 762.1
 possession 806.1
villeinhood 762.1
villeinhold 806.1
villose, villous 229.24
villus 229.2
vim 160.2
vimana 206.11
vin 994.18
vina 464.2
vinaceous 367.7
vinaigrette 435.6
vincibility 695.4
vincible 695.16
vinculum bond 48.1
 music 462.12
vindicable 1004.14
vindicate
 ~ a claim 751.5
 justify 1004.9
 exculpate 1005.4
vindication
 justification 1004.1
 exculpation 1005.1
vindicative 1004.13
vindicator
 defender 797.7
 avenger 954.3
 justifier 1004.8
vindicatory
 avenging 954.6
 justifying 1004.13
vindictive 954.6
vindictiveness 954.2
vine plant 410.4
 types of ~ 410.52
 THE VINE 1011.12
vinegar sour 431.3
 preservative 699.3
vinegarish sour 431.6
 sour-tempered
  949.23
vinegary 431.6
vinegrower 412.6
vinery 412.11
vineyard 412.10
Vingolf 1016.11
viniculture 412.2
vino 994.18
vinous 994.46
vintage 809.4
vintner 994.23
viol 464.5
viola violist 463.5
 instrument 464.5
violaceous 372.3
violate break 767.4

debauch 987.20
 ~ the law 997.5
violation
 infraction 767.2
 ~ of chastity 987.6
 ~ of law 997.3
 offense 997.4
violative 765.9
violator 987.12
violence
 vehemence 161
 coercion 754.3
 cruelty 937.11
 anger 950.10
 DO VIOLENCE 665.5
violent
 nouns 161.9
 adjs. vehement
  161.15
 rabid 472.29
 coercive 754.10
 overwrought 855.26
 passionate 855.30
violently
 exceedingly 34.24
 with violence
  161.24
 excitedly 855.36
violet 372.3
violette 464.5
violin
 nouns 464.6
 verbs 461.42
violinette, violino
  piccolo, violotta
  464.6
violinist, violist 463.5
violoncello, violon-
  cello piccolo,
  violone 464.5
viper coil 253.2
 serpent 413.31
 scoundrel 984.6
viperous, vipery
  413.44
virago
 violent person 161.9
 vixen 941.8
 shrew 949.12
vire 799.17
virelay 607.4
virescence 370.1
virescent 370.4
virgate 355.11
virgin
 nouns girl 125.6
 spinster 932.4
 good woman 983.7
 adjs. new 122.7
 unmarried 932.7
 chaste 986.6
virginal
 nouns piano 464.13
 ritual 1038.12
 adjs. new 122.7
 natural 719.13
 unmarried 932.7
 chaste 986.6
virgin forest 410.11
virginity
 spinsterhood 932.1

chastity 986.3
Virgin Mary 1013.5
virgin soil
unknown 476.7
undevelopment 719.5
viridescence 370.1
viridity 370.1
virify 419.10
virile 419.12
virileness 419.2
virilify 419.10
virility 419.2
viripotent 419.12
virtu artistry 572.8
work of art 572.11
artistic taste 895.5
virtual essential 5.8
potential 544.5
virtually
practically 5.10
potentially 544.10
virtue potency 156.1
excellence 672.1
valor 891.1
virtuousness 978
innocence 982
chastity 986.1
godliness 1026.2
BY VIRTUE OF
because of 154.9
by dint of 156.17
by authority of 737.20
virtueless 979.16
virtues 1013.3
virtuosic 461.48
virtuosity 895.5
virtuoso
musician 463.1
connoisseur 895.7
virtuous good 978.7
innocent 982.6
chaste 986.4
godly 1026.9
virulence
acrimony 160.4
deadliness 408.8
poisonousness 682.2
animosity 927.4
malevolence 937.7
resentment 950.3
virulency 682.2
virulent
acrimonious 160.12
deadly 408.23
poisonous 682.5
hostile 927.11
malevolent 937.20
virus poison 674.3
infection 684.3
visa, visé
nouns endorsement 520.4
certificate 568.5
signature 581.10
verbs 520.12
visage face 239.4
countenance 445.4
visagraph 440.5

vis-á-vis
nouns 15.2
advs. 238.6
viscera insides 224.4
vitals 224.5
visceral 224.12
viscid adhesive 50.9
mucilaginous 388.12
viscidity tenacity 50.2
mucilaginousness 388.2
viscose 388.12
viscosity tenacity 50.2
viscidity 388.2
viscount 916.5
viscous 388.12
viselike 811.8
Vishnu 1011.4
visibility
aviation 277.38
perceptibility 443
visible
nouns 443.1
adjs. perceptible 443.6
manifest 553.8
BECOME VISIBLE 445.8
visibly
perceptibly 443.8
manifestly 553.14
vis inertia 267.4
vision
nouns sight 438
apparition 445.5
illusion 518.4
visual image 533.6
dream 533.9
figure of speech 549.2
beauty 898.7
specter 1015.1
verbs 533.15
visional 533.24
visionariness 533.7
visionary
nouns 533.13
adjs. 533.24
visioned 533.18
visionless 440.8
visit
nouns chat 595.4
social call 920.6
verbs attend 185.8
go to 272.24
chat 595.9
call on 920.16
VISIT UPON 1008.10
VISIT WITH 595.8
visitant incomer 301.4
visitor 923.6
visitation bane 674.1
illness 684.5
visiting 920.6
visiting 920.6
ON VISITING TERMS 925.17
visiting card 566.10
visiting fireman 273.1
visitor attender 185.5

incomer 301.4
overseer 746.2
guest 923.6
visor 616.10
vista
field of view 443.3
view 445.6
vista of time 110.3
visual ocular 438.22
visible 443.6
visual image 533.6
visualization 533.6
visualize 533.15
vital organic 405.18
living 406.10
needful 637.13
important 670.24
vital force
life force 406.3
spirit 1032.18
theosophy 1032.20
vital impulse
instinct 480.2
libido 688.39
vitalistic 499.10
vitality strength 158.1
life 406.1
vitalization
invigoration 160.7
vivification 406.5
vitalize energize 160.9
vivify 406.8
vitalizing 160.13
vitalness 637.3
vital principle
inner nature 5.4
life force 406.3
spirit 1032.18
vitals
essential parts 5.4
stomach 192.3
insides 224.4
vital organs 224.5
vital spirit
life force 406.3
spirit 1032.18
vital statistics 87.7
vitamer 307.4
vitaminization 307.12
vitaminize 307.18
vitaminologist 307.13
vitaminology 307.14
vitamins 307.23
vitascope 575.14
Vitharr, Vidar 1012.6
Vithi 1016.11
vitiate
neutralize 177.7
corrupt 690.12
demoralize 979.14
vitiated
diseased 684.45
wicked 979.19
vitiating 177.9
vitiation
neutralization 177.2
corruption 690.2
viticultural 412.21
viticulture 412.2
viticulturist 412.6

**vitreal, vitrean,
vitreous** 338.5
vitreosity 338.1
vitrics 338.2
**vitrifaction, vitri-
fication** 355.5
vitrified 355.13
vitriform 338.5
vitrify 355.7
vitriol
animosity 927.4
virulence 937.7
vitriolic
acrimonious 160.12
acid 431.7
virulent 937.20
vittles 306a.1
vituperate
revile 967.20
curse 970.7
vituperation
revilement 967.8
malediction 970.2
vituperative
reviling 967.23
maledictory 970.8
viva! 966.22
vivace 461.56
vivacious
energetic 160.11
lively 705.16
gay 868.14
vivaciously
energetically 160.14
briskly 705.23
gayly 868.18
vivaciousness 705.2
vivacity energy 160.3
~ of imagination 533.4
liveliness 705.2
gaiety 868.4
vivarium 415.5
viva-voce
nouns 635.5
advs. 592.23
vivid energetic 160.11
brilliant 334.32
colorful 361.19
keenly sensitive 421.14
unforgotten 535.23
meaningful 543.10
eloquent 598.10
descriptive 606.15
dramatic 609.37
vividly
meaningfully 543.14
eloquently 598.15
descriptively 606.19
vividness
brightness 334.4
colorfulness 361.3
meaningfulness 543.6
eloquence 598.1
vivification
vitalization 406.5
refreshment 693.1
vivify vitalize 406.8

vouch
nouns 521.2
verbs
  bear witness 504.10
  depose 521.5
  promise 768.4
voucher
  witness 504.7
  credential 568.5
  money order 833.11
  receipt 842.2
  recommendation
    966.4
vouching 521.2
vouchsafe
  deign 773.4
  permit 775.10
  give 816.12
  condescend 904.7
vouchsafement
  permission 775.1
  giving 816.1
  gift 816.4
vow
nouns oath 521.3
  promise 768.1
TAKE THE VOWS
  768.6
TAKE VOWS 1035.11
verbs vouch 521.5
  promise 768.4
vowel
nouns 449.5
adjs. 449.18
vowellike
nouns 449.5
adjs. 449.18
vox populi 500.4
voyage
nouns 274.6
verbs 274.13
voyager, voyageur
  273.1
voyeur 688.14
voyeurism 688.32
V.P. 747.7
vs. versus 238.6
  against 788.11
V-shaped
  angular 250.6
  forked 298.10
vug, vugg, vugh 256.2
Vulcan smith 716.7
  god 1012.5
vulcanize 357.6
vulgar
  inelegant 588.2
  unrefined 896.10
  garish 902.20
  plebeian 917.11
  indecent 988.8
vulgarian 896.6
vulgarism word 580.6
  inelegant style 588.1
  vulgarity 896.1
vulgarity
  inelegant style 588.1
  bad taste 896
  indecency 988.3
vulgarize 896.9
vulgarly 896.16

vulgarness
  vulgarity 896.1
  garishness 902.3
Vulgate 1019.2
vulgate 578.4
vulnerable 695.16
vulnerable point
  weakness 159.4
  vulnerability 695.4
vulnerary 685.9
vulpine
  foxlike 413.37
  cunning 733.12
vulture 820.10
vulturous 820.23
vulva 418.8
vulval 418.18
vulvar 418.18
vying 794.24

W

wabble See wobble
Wabun 402.3
wackiness
  foolishness 469.1
  insanity 472.2
wacky foolish 469.8
  insane 472.25
  eccentric 473.4
wad
nouns
  large amount 34.4
  lump 194.10
  bankroll 833.16
  wealth 835.2
verbs fill 56.7
  line 227.30
wadding
  contents 193.1
  lining 227.20
  stopping 265.5
  padding 356.5
waddle 272.27
Wade 194.13
wade 274.59
WADE INTO
  set to work 714.15
  attack 796.15
WADE THROUGH
  study 562.12
  drudge 714.14
wadi ravine 200.3
  valley 256.9
  river 394.1
  watercourse 395.2
wading 274.11
wads 34.4
wafer thinness 204.7
  lamina 226.2
  food 306a.29
  Eucharistic ~
    1038.8
waffle 306a.44
waft convey 270.11
  float 352.9
  blow 402.23
waftage 270.3
wag
nouns
  oscillation 322.5

wiggle 323.7
mischief-maker
  736.3
  humorist 879.12
verbs leave 300.9
  oscillate 322.9
  wave 322.10
  wiggle 323.15
WAG THE TONGUE
  592.11
wage
nouns 839.4
verbs 703.7
waged 839.22
wage earner
  wageworker 716.2
  employee 748.2
wager
nouns 514.3
verbs 514.19
wagering 514.6
wages 839.4
wage scale 839.4
waggery, waggishness
  mischievousness
    736.2
  facetiousness 879.4
waggish
  mischievous 736.6
  facetious 879.17
waggle
nouns
  oscillation 322.5
  wiggle 323.7
verbs oscillate 322.9
  wiggle 323.15
waggon wagon 271.2
  freight car 271.13
wagon
nouns vehicle
  271.2,6,21
  police van 271.10
ON THE WAGON
  990.10
verbs 270.12
wagoner 273.9
wagonload 193.2
wagwit 879.12
Wahabi 1018.21
waif
  vagabond 273.3
  derelict 631.4
wail
nouns screech 457.4
  plaint 873.3
verbs blow 402.24
  sigh 451.14
  screech 457.7
  ululate 459.2
  say 592.17
  lament 873.11
wailful 873.16
wailing
nouns sough 451.8
  lamentation 873.1
adjs. howling 459.6
  lamenting 873.15
wain 271.2
wainscot
nouns base 211.2

lining 227.20
verbs 227.30
waist middle 69.1
  shirt 230.15
  types of ~ 230.54
waistband
  types of ~ 230.65
  band 252.3
waistcloth 230.19
waistcoat 230.14
waistline 69.1
wait
nouns delay 132.2
  singer 463.16
LIE IN WAIT 613.10
verbs postpone 132.8
  tarry 132.11
  await 537.6
  be patient 859.4
WAIT ON
  accompany 73.7
  escort 73.8
  await 537.6
  serve 748.14
  help 783.18
  toady to 905.7
  pay respects 934.12
waiter tray 192.8
  attendant 748.4,6
waiting
nouns delay 132.3
  expectancy 537.3
adjs. expectant 537.9
  serving 748.15
waiting room 191.20
waitress 748.6
waits 463.12
waive postpone 132.8
  give up 631.7
  not use 666.5
  relinquish 812.3
waiver 812.2
wakan 1012.10
wake
nouns afterpart 67.2
  airplane ~ 277.36
  death watch 409.4
  track 566.7
  sociable 920.9
IN THE WAKE OF
  292.6
verbs awaken 711.4
  excite 855.11
WAKE UP
  disillusion 519.2
  provoke 646.19
  awake 711.4
  excite 855.11
adjs. 711.7
wakeful alert 531.14
  sleepless 711.6
wakeless 710.20
waken provoke 646.19
  excite 855.11
wakening 711.2
waldgrave 916.5
wale
nouns welt 255.3
  texture 350.1

market 830.1
verbs 658.10
wareroom
storehouse 658.6
market 830.1,10
wares 829.1
warfare 795
warfarer 798.7
war-god, war goddess
795.18
warhead 280.2
war head 799.10
war horse
old woman 127.3
veteran 731.14
politician 744.1
soldier 798.18
charger 798.33
warily 893.13
wariness 893.2
warlike 795.26
warlock 1033.5
warm
verbs heat 328.17
redden 367.4
excite 855.11
whip 1008.15
WARM OVER
reheat 328.17
revive 692.16
adjs. near 199.14
calid 327.24
warm-colored
361.16
red 367.6
near discovery
487.10
eloquent 598.13
fervent 853.22
excited 855.23
comfortable 885.11
friendly 925.15
BE WARM
be near 199.8
detect 487.6
warm-blooded 327.29
warm color 361.2
warm-complexioned
367.10
warmed 328.28
warmed-over
twice-told 103.12
reheated 328.28
trite 881.9
warmer 328.10
warmhearted
tender 853.20
friendly 925.15
kind 936.14
sympathetic 942.7
warmheartedness
tender feeling 853.6
friendliness 925.6
kindness 936.1
warning
nouns 328.1
adjs. 328.25
warmish 327.24
warmly
eloquently 598.15
fervently 853.27

excitedly 855.35
amicably 925.21
warmness
warmth 327.1
comfortableness
885.2
friendliness 925.6
warmonger 798.5
warmongering
nouns 795.16
adjs. 795.27
warm springs
hot water 327.9
spa 687.31
warmth
warmness 327.1
color 361.2
eloquence 598.5
fervor 853.9
warn remind 535.20
forebode 542.8
caution 701.6
sound the alarm
702.6
threaten 971.2
WARN OFF 776.3
warner 701.5
warning
nouns reminder 535.6
omen 542.2
caution 701
alarm 702
threat 971
WITHOUT WARNING
538.14
adjs. 701.9
warp
nouns tendency 173.1
obliquity 218.3
weaving 221.4
distortion 248.1
disposition 523.3
prejudice 525.3
WARP AND WOOF
350.1
verbs change 139.5
tend 173.3
shrink 197.9
distort 248.5
navigation 274.50
deflect 290.5
prejudice 525.8
misrepresent 571.3
falsify 614.16
corrupt 690.12
war paint
clothes 230.10
cosmetics 898.11
warpath 795.16
GO ON THE WARPATH
795.21
warped
distorted 248.10
partial 975.11
morally ~ 979.19
warplane 279.9
warrant
nouns oath 521.3
credential 568.5
writ 750.6
promise 768.1

security 770.1
sanction 775.3,6
commission 778.1
money order 833.11
receipt 842.2
justification 1004.6
verbs attest 504.10,12
acknowledge 520.11
vouch 521.5
promise 768.4
guarantee 770.11
authorize 775.12
justify 1004.9
warrantable
permissible 775.16
justifiable 1004.14
warranted
acknowledged
520.14
guaranteed 770.14
authorized 775.18
due 958.9
warrantee 770.9
warrant officer
747.23,24
warranty
promise 768.1
security 770.1
authorization 775.3
warren 164.6
warring
contending 794.23
militant 795.26
warrior 798.7
warriorlike 795.26
warship ship 276.7
navy 798.27
war song 461.13
militarism 795.17
wart
diminutive 195.4
dwarf 195.6
bulge 255.3
blemish 677.1
growth 684.29
warty 255.14
war whoop
alarm 702.2
rally 795.13
wary 893.9
wash
nouns
airplane ~ 277.36
paint 361.12
swash 394.8
marsh 399.1
photography 575.15
washing 679.4,5
cleanser 679.16
verbs
be consistent 26.10
paint 361.14
drench 391.13
swash 394.20
ripple 451.11
hold true 515.7
clean 679.18
NOT WASH 517.7
WASH DOWN 306.27
WASH ONE'S HANDS OF
give up 631.7

discord 666.7
refuse 774.3
relinquish 812.3
WASH OUT
fade 362.5
clean 679.18
flunk 723.16
WASH UP 70.7
washbasin, washbowl
679.12
washboard 260.2
washday 679.5
washdish 679.12
washed-out
faded 362.8
impaired 690.33
washed up 70.8
washed-up
fatigued 715.8
finished 720.10
washer circle 252.2
cleaner 679.14
washerwife, washer-
woman 679.14
washery, washhouse
679.9
washing
cleaning 679.4
cleansing 679.5
speculation 831.19
Washingtonese
jargon 578.7
officialese 742.40
washout
aviation 277.3
overflow 394.6
washing 679.4
debacle 691.4
failure 723.2,7,8
washpot 679.12
washroom 679.8
washshed 679.9
washstand 679.12
washtub 679.12
wash-up 679.4
washwoman 679.14
washwork 679.5
washy
wishy-washy 159.17
insipid 429.2
waspish 949.19
wassail
nouns 994.5
verbs 994.34
wassailer 994.10
wastage
consumption 664.1
refuse 667.4
deterioration 690.4
loss 810.2
waste
nouns
decrement 39.3
wasteland 165.2
excrement 309.3
consumption 664.1
refuse 667.4
deterioration 690.4
devastation 691.1
loss 810.2
prodigality 852.1

dam 728.5
weird
  nouns 1034.1
  adjs. odd 85.11
    deathlike 407.23
    creepy 889.30
    spooky 1015.9
    sorcerous 1033.14
Weird Sisters
  Fates 638.3
  witches 1033.8
Weismannism
  heredity 169.6
  evolution 321.4
welcome
  nouns 923.2
  verbs 923.9
  adjs. pleasant 861.5
    agreeable 923.12
  interjs. 923.4
weld
  nouns 47.4
  verbs 50.7
welder
  blowtorch 328.13
  types of ∼ 347.21
welfare good 672.4
  prosperity 726.1
  ∼ work 936.5
welfare state
  government 739.4
  welfarism 743.6
welfare work 936.5
welfarism
  socialism 743.6
  philanthropy 936.4
welkin 374.2
well
  nouns source 152.6
    depth 208.2
    pit 256.4
    pool 397.1
    source of supply
      658.4
  verbs flow out 302.13
    gush 394.21
  adjs. 683.7
  ALL'S WELL! 696.9
  GET WELL 692.20
  advs. ably 156.15
    auspiciously 542.19
    excellently 672.23
    successfully 722.14
    skillfuly 731.28
    kindly 936.19
  WELL DONE! 966.21
  WELL OUT OF 630.10
  interjs. imagine!
    533.27
    astonishment 918.20
well-advised 466.19
well-affected
  favorable 783.22
  friendly 925.14
  kind 936.18
well-appointed 657.13
well-armed
  well-equipped
    657.13
  well-prepared
    718.16

armed 797.14
well-arranged 572.21
well-balanced
  symmetrical 247.5
  sensible 466.18
  self-possessed 856.13
well-behaved 934.16
well-being good 672.4
  health 683.1
  prosperity 726.1
  comfort 885.1
well-beloved
  nouns 929.12
  adjs. 929.21
well-bred
  well-born 916.12
  well-mannered
    934.17
well-built
  substantial 3.5
  able-bodied 158.14
  made 166.27
well-chosen 587.7
well-composed 572.21
well-conned 474.20
well-considered
  731.27
well-cooked 329.7
well-defined
  distinct 443.7
  precise 515.15
  clear 546.10
well-designed, well-
  devised 731.27
well-disposed
  willing 620.5
  favorable 783.22
  friendly 925.14
  kind 936.18
  approving 966.16
well-done
  well-cooked 329.7
  skillful 731.20
well-drawn 606.15
well-educated 474.20
well-equipped 657.13
well-expressed 587.7
well-favored
  shapely 247.6
  comely 898.17
well-fed 194.18
well-fitted
  well-equipped
    657.13
  well-qualified
    718.18
  competent 731.22
well-fixed
  prosperous 726.12
  wealthy 835.13
well-formed 247.6
well-founded
  substantial 3.5
  established 142.14
  logical 481.21
  plausible 510.6
  reliable 512.17
  valid 515.12
well-furnished 657.13
well-groomed
  trim 59.8

well-dressed 642.13
well-grounded
  substantial 3.5
  established 142.14
  well-informed
    474.20
  logical 481.21
  plausible 510.6
  reliable 512.17
  valid 515.12
wellhead 152.6
well-heeled
  well-equipped
    657.13
  well-armed 797.14
  wealthy 835.13
well-informed 474.20
  BE WELL-INFORMED
    474.13
well-intentioned
  favorable 783.22
  friendly 925.14
  kind 936.18
well-invented
  plausible 510.6
  well-devised 731.27
well-kept trim 59.8
well-preserved
  699.11
well-known
  known 474.27
  famous 912.17
well-laid 731.27
well-made
  substantial 3.5
  made 166.27
  shapely 247.6
well-mannered 934.16
well-marked 443.7
well-meaning, well-
  meant favorable
    783.22
  friendly 925.14
  kind 936.18
well-off
  prosperous 726.12
  wealthy 835.13
well-ordered 59.6
well-paying 809.14
well-planned 731.27
well-posted 474.20
well-prepared 657.13
well-preserved 699.11
well-proportioned
  247.6
well-provided 657.13
well-put 587.7
well-rated 837.8
well-read 474.20
well-regulated 59.6
well-rooted 142.14
well-rounded 56.9
well-set
  established 142.14
  able-bodied 158.14
  symmetrical 247.5
well-shaped 247.6
well-situated
  prosperous 726.12
  wealthy 835.13

well-spent 663.21
well-spoken
  spoken 592.21
  eloquent 598.8
  mannerly 934.16
wellspring
  source 152.6
  source of supply
    658.4
well-stocked, well-
  supplied 657.13
well-suited
  well-qualified
    718.18
  competent 731.22
well-thought-of
  reputable 912.16
  respected 962.11
well-thought-out
  731.27
well-timed 129.10
well-to-do
  prosperous 726.12
  wealthy 835.13
well-trodden 640.15
well-varied 572.21
well-versed 474.20
  BECOME WELL-
    VERSED IN 562.9
well-wisher 785.8
well-worked-out
  731.27
well-worn worn 690.30
  trite 881.9
welsh
  shirk out of 629.9
  not pay 840.6
welsher shirker 629.3
  defaulter 840.5
Welshman 417.9
welt
  nouns edging 234.7
    ridge 255.3
    sore 684.28
  verbs 1008.15
welter
  nouns 323.8
  verbs sail 274.58
    grovel 316.8
    wallow 320.13
    flounder 323.15
welterweight
  weight 351.3
  pugilist 798.2
wen 684.29
wench girl 125.6
  strumpet 987.14
wenching 987.3
wend 272.17
werefolk, werewolf
  1014.13
werowance 747.9
weskit 230.14
West 179.6,7
west
  nouns 289.3
  verbs 289.9
  adjs., advs. 289.20
westbound 289.16
West End 182.5

wester
 nouns 402.9
 verbs 289.9
westerly
 nouns 402.9
 adjs., advs. 289.20
Western 417.10
western
 nouns ~ story 606.7
 motion picture
  609.15
 verbs 289.9
 adjs. directional
  289.15
 west 289.20
 advs. 289.20
Westerner 417.8
westerner
 inhabitant 189.11
 western story 606.7
westing 289.4
westland 179.7
westlander 189.11
West Point 565.13
West Side 182.5
westward
 nouns 289.3
 adjs., advs. 289.20
wet
 nouns moistness
  391.1
 rain 393.1,4
 dram 994.6
 verbs urinate 309.12
 sweat 309.14
 moisten 391.12
 rain 393.9
 drink to 994.35
 WET ONE'S WHISTLE
  994.30
 adjs. 391.15
wetback 273.5
wet blanket
 extinguisher 331.3
 discouragement
  650.2
 marplot 728.9
 saddener 870.14
 bore 882.4
 THROW A WET
  BLANKET ON
  moderate 162.6
  discourage 650.4
wether ram 413.9
 male animal 419.8
wetness 391.1
wet nurse 697.7
wet-nurse
 suckle 306.16
 nurture 783.16
wetting
 nouns 391.6
 adjs. 391.18
wettish 391.15
whack
 nouns fettle 7.3
 piece 55.3
 turn 108.2
 blow 282.4
 bang 455.1
 attempt 712.2

share 814.5
 GET OUT OF WHACK
  690.26
 IN WHACK 59.7
 verbs sever 49.10
 strike 282.14
 bang 455.6
 WHACK DOWN 316.5
 WHACK UP
 partition 49.18
 apportion 814.7
whacker 194.11
whacking great 34.13
 huge 194.21
whacks 813.1
whacky insane 472.25
 eccentric 473.4
whale
 nouns big thing
  194.11
 behemoth 194.14
 types of ~ 413.54
 verbs fish 653.10
 whip 1008.15
whalebone 357.3
whaler
 big thing 194.11
 fisherman 653.6
whaling
 nouns fishing 653.3
 whipping 1008.5
 adjs. great 34.13
 huge 194.21
whang piece 55.3
 chunk 194.10
 thong 205.2
whap See whop
whapper
 big thing 194.11
 falsehood 614.12
wharf 698.6
wharfage 844.7
what
 nouns 79.6
 AND WHAT NOT
 et cetera 40.13
 numerous 101.12
 WHAT IT TAKES
 ability 156.2
 talent 731.4
 advs. 484.43
 interjs. 918.17
whatever
 nouns 79.6
 advs. however 29.9
 of any kind 61.9
what for 154.7
what-for reproof 967.7
 punishment 1008.1
whatsoever
 nouns 79.6
 advs. however 29.9
 of any kind 61.9
what's what fact 1.3
 truth 515.1
wheal 684.28
wheat food 306a.4
 grain 410.29
wheedle coax 646.14
 importune 772.12
 flatter 968.5

wheedler
 coaxer 646.10
 flatterer 968.4
wheedling
 nouns coaxing 646.3
 importunity 772.3
 flattery 968.1
 adjs. importunate
  772.18
 flattering 968.9
wheel
 nouns vehicle 271.8
 whirl 320.2
 rotator 320.4
 gambling ~ 514.11
 potter's ~ 574.4
 personage 670.9
 torture 1009.4
 AT THE WHEEL
  737.21
 verbs ride 272.32
 turn round 294.9
 rotate 320.9,11
 drive 745.9
 WHEEL AROUND
  137.6
wheelbarrow
 nouns 271.26
 verbs 270.12
wheel chair 271.7
wheeler 413.18
wheel horse
 horse 413.18
 politician 744.1
wheeling
 nouns 320.1
 adjs. 320.14
wheel of fortune
 changeability 141.4
 gambling 514.11
 fate 638.2
wheels
 types of ~ 320.18
 machinery 347.5
 HAVE WHEELS IN THE
  HEAD 472.19
 ON WHEELS
 smoothly 259.12
 easily 730.13
 WHEELS WITHIN
  WHEELS
 complication 46.2
 mechanism 347.5
wheelsman 275.8
wheelwork,
 wheelworks 347.5
wheeze
 nouns respiration
  402.19
 sibilation 456.1
 trick 616.6
 joke 879.6
 verbs breathe 402.25
 sibilate 456.2
wheezing, wheezy
  456.3
whelk food 306a.25
 pustule 684.28
whelm
 submerge 318.7
 oversupply 661.15

whelp
 nouns boy 125.5
 youngling 125.8
 welt 255.3
 dog 413.24
 sore 684.28
 scoundrel 984.6
 verbs 166.19
when although 33.8
 at which time 105.7
 at what time?
  484.45
whence hence 154.6
 away 300.21
 where? 484.46
whenever when 105.7
 whensoever 105.12
where
 nouns 183.2
 advs. whither 183.22
 whereabouts?
  484.46
whereabouts
 nouns 183.2
 advs. where 183.22
 where? 484.46
whereas while 105.9
 since 154.8
whereat 117.6
whereaway
 where 183.22
 whereabouts?
  484.46
whereby 656.8
where'er, wherever
  183.23
wherefore
 after which 117.6
 hence 154.6
 why 154.7
 why? 484.44
 this being so 493.17
wherefore, the 152.2
wherefrom 154.6
wherein of which 9.11
 in 224.14
whereof 9.11
whereon of which 9.11
 after which 117.6
whereto of which 9.11
 after which 117.6
 where? 484.46
whereunto
 of which 9.11
 after which 117.6
whereupon
 of which 9.11
 when 105.7
 after which 117.6
wherewith
 nouns means 656.1
 money 833.1
 advs. 117.6
 preps. 656.8
wherewithal
 nouns means 656.1
 money 833.1
 HAVE THE WHERE-
  WITHAL 835.10
 preps. 656.8

windowpane
window 264.7
glass 338.2
window-rattling 452.9
window-shop 826.8
window shopper 826.5
window shopping
825.1
window sill 215.9
windpipe 395.16
windrow 71.2
winds 464.7
TO THE FOUR WINDS
everywhere 178.12
everywhither 289.27
windscreen,
windshield 697.3
windstorm 402.13
wind-swept 402.28
windtight 265.12
windup end 70.1
completion 720.2
windward
nouns 241.3
adjs. 241.6
advs. 241.9
windwayward 402.26
windy
nouns 908.5
adjs. unsubstantial
4.5
flatulent 196.12
rare 354.7
breezy 402.26
diffuse 591.12
talkative 594.9
bombastic 599.10
boastful 908.10
wine
nouns beverage
994.18
types of ~ 994.49
adjs. 367.7
winebibbing
nouns 994.4
adjs. 994.44
wine-colored 367.7
wine cooler 333.3
wine-red 367.7
winery 994.27
wing
nouns addition 41.3
member 55.4
plane part 279.16
arm 286.5
~ of fowl 306a.23
stage ~ 609.24
flight 629.4
protection 697.2
faction 786.5,10
military 798.19
air force 798.29
ON THE WING
on the way 270.20
on the move 272.41
flying 277.57
UNDER THE WING
697.21
verbs disable 157.9
convey 270.11
fly 277.42

wound 690.15
wing and wing 274.68
wingcut 609.24
winged alate 41.5
fast 268.19
winging
nouns 277.1
adjs. 277.56
wingman 278.1
wing-over
nouns 277.13
verbs 277.46
wings insignia 567.5
stage ~ 609.20
LEND WINGS TO
783.17
wink
nouns instant 113.3
glance 438.4
signal 566.14
nap 710.3
verbs blink 439.10
signal 566.21
WINK AT
be blind to 440.7
be open-minded
524.7
disregard 529.3
suffer 775.11
condone 945.4
winker eye 438.9
blinkard 439.7
winkers 229.12
winking
nouns 439.7
adjs. 439.11
winner
good thing 672.7
victor 724.2
winning
nouns 724.1
adjs. alluring 648.7
victorious 724.8
delightful 861.6
lovable 929.22
winningly 861.10
winnings 809.3
winnow
nouns 354.4
verbs segregate 77.6
sift 354.6
fan 401.12
analyze 484.32
select 635.11
winnower 354.4
winnowing
sifting 354.3
analysis 484.8
wino 994.10
winsome
alluring 648.7
delightful 861.6
cheerful 868.10
lovable 929.22
winter
nouns old age 126.5
season 128.6
coldness 332.3
verbs pass the ~
105.6

hibernate 710.14
adjs. 128.8
wintertide, wintertime
128.6
wintery, wintry
winter 128.8
cold 332.15
winy 994.46
wipe
nouns blow 282.4
gibe 965.2
verbs strike 282.14
dry 392.6
clean 679.17,21
whip 1008.14
WIPE OUT
excise 42.8
kill 408.14
destroy 691.14,16
clear of debt 840.9
WIPE THE SLATE
CLEAN
clear of debt 840.9
forgive 945.3
absolve 1005.4
WIPE UP 691.14
wire
nouns cord 205.2
electric ~ 341.41
telegram 558.16
pickpocket 823.2
GET UNDER THE WIRE
724.4
verbs fasten 47.9
wireless 558.22
wiredrawn
finespun 204.15
fine 350.8
wireless
nouns radio 343.1,3
telegraphy 558.4,6
telegram 558.16
verbs radiocast 343.28
telegraph 558.22
adjs. radio 343.31
telegraphic 558.24
wireman 558.18
wirephoto
telegram 558.17
photograph 575.3
wirepull 171.9
wirepuller
influencer 171.6
machinator 652.8
strategist 733.7
political ~ 742.31;
744.6
wirepulling
influence 171.3
intrigue 652.6
stratagem 733.4
political ~ 742.30
wires 171.3
wireway 655.9
wireworks 717.4
wiry muscular 158.14
stringy 205.7
wisdom sagacity 466.5
erudition 474.4,5
wise
nouns 655.1

IN NO WISE 35.14
IN SUCH WISE
thus 8.8
insomuch 29.8
so 655.11
THE WISE 467.3
adjs. sagacious 466.17
hep 474.17
learned 474.21
ungullible 503.5
GET WISE TO
see through 487.8
become informed
555.13
GET WISE TO
YOURSELF 469.13
wiseacre
wiseling 467.6
dunce 470.1
wisecrack
nouns 879.7
verbs 879.13
wisecracker 879.12
wise guy
wiseacre 467.6
impudent person
911.5
wisehead 467.1
wiseling 467.6
Wise Lord 1011.6
wiseman, wise man
467.1
Wise Men 467.4
wisenheimer 467.6
Wise One 1011.6
wise up 555.7
wish
nouns will 619.1
desire 632.1
request 772.1
verbs will 619.2
desire 632.14
request 772.9
wishbone
food 306a.23
wish-bringer 1034.7
wish-bringer 1034.7
wished-for 632.30
wisher 632.12
wishful 632.23
wish fulfillment 632.1
wishfulness 632.4
wishful thinking
idealism 533.7
wishing 632.4
wish-giver 1034.7
wishing 632.21
wishing cap 1034.7
wishing well 1034.7
wish-wash 545.4
wishy-washy
namby-pamby
159.17
insipid 429.2
indifferent 634.5
mediocre 678.8
wisket, whisket 192.4
wisp bunch 74.6
diminutive 195.4
will-o'-the-wisp
334.13

wistful
  pensive 477.20
  desirous 632.23
  melancholy 870.23
wistfully
  thoughtfully 477.22
  desirefully 632.32
  melancholily 870.35
wistfulness
  pensiveness 477.3
  wishing 632.4
  melancholy 870.5
wit intelligence 466.1
  savoir-faire 731.9
  humor 879
  humorist 879.12
  AT ONE'S WIT'S END
  perplexed 513.23
  at an impasse
    729.22
  TO WIT
  namely 80.18
  that is 550.21
witch
  nouns old woman
    127.3
  violent person 161.9
  ugly person 897.4
  vixen 941.8
  shrew 949.12
  sorceress 1033.8
  verbs fascinate 648.6
  bewitch 1034.10
  adjs. 1033.14
witchcraft 1033.1
witch doctor 1033.7
witched 1034.14
witchery
  allurement 648.1
  sorcery 1033.1
  spell 1034.2
witch-held 1034.14
witch hunt 743.4
witch-hunt 665.3
witch-hunter 1033.7
witch-hunting 665.3
witching
  alluring 648.7
  bewitching 1034.12
witchman 1033.7
witch of Endor
  spiritualist 1032.13
  witch 1033.8
witch-ridden, witch-
  struck 1034.14
witch stick 541.3
witch-wiggler 1033.5
witchwork 1033.1
witchy 1033.14
with
  advs. concurrently
    176.5
  co-operatively 784.9
  preps. in agreement
    26.20
  in spite of 33.9
  including 40.11
  among 44.18
  in company with
    73.10

  by means of 656.8
  having 806.14
  GET WITH IT 714.15
withdraw deduct 42.7
  retreat 294.6
  recede 296.2
  draw back 296.3
  depart 300.8
  extract 304.9
  recant 626.9
  abandon 631.5
  repeal 777.2
withdrawal
  elimination 77.2
  retreat 294.2
  recession 296.1
  departure 300.1
  extraction 304.1
  recantation 626.3
  abandonment 631.1
  escapism 688.34
  repeal 777.1
  resignation 782.1
  seclusion 922.1
withdrawn
  secret 612.15
  secluded 922.9
wither age 126.10
  shrink 197.9
  dry 392.6
  sicken 684.35
  deteriorate 690.19
withered
  shriveled 197.13
  thin 204.19
  dried 392.9
  wasted 690.34
withering
  nouns
  shrinking 197.3
  waste 690.4
  adjs.
  deteriorating 690.43
  destructive 691.25
  caustic 937.21
  contemptuous 964.8
withers 255.2
withheld 658.15
withhold
  keep secret 612.8
  reserve 658.12
  restrain 758.7
  refuse 774.4
  prohibit 776.3
  be stingy 850.8
  abstain 990.7
withholding tax
    844.11
within
  advs. 224.14
  preps. 224.17
withindoors 224.16
withinside 224.14
without
  advs. 223.9
  preps. minus 42.14
  barring 77.9
  lacking 660.11
  conjs. 506.16
withstand 790.2,3

withstanding
  nouns 790.1
  adjs. 790.6
witless
  unintelligent 468.13
  foolish 469.8,9
  insane 472.24
  unaware 476.14
  giddy 530.16
witlessly
  foolishly 469.11
  unknowingly 476.19
witlessness
  unintelligence 468.1
  foolishness 469.1
  indiscretion 469.2
  insanity 472.1
  giddiness 530.5
witling wiseacre 476.6
  fool 470.1
  humorist 879.12
witness
  nouns spectator 441.1
  testimony 504.3
  deponent 504.7
  informant 555.5
  voucher 568.5
  verbs attend 185.8
  see 438.12
  testify 504.10
  interjs. 528.22
witnessing 438.2
witness stand 999.9
wits 465.2
  HAVE ALL ONE'S WITS
    ABOUT ONE
  be intelligent 466.10
  be vigilant 531.8
  be experienced
    731.18
  OUT OF ONE'S WITS
  insane 472.24
  overwrought 855.26
witticism joke 879.7
  persiflage 880.1
wittily 879.18
wittiness 879.2
witting 651.9
wittingly
  knowingly 474.29
  intentionally 651.11
witty 879.15
wive 931.16
wizard expert 731.12
  sorcerer 1033.5
wizardlike, wizardly
    1033.14
wizardry 1033.1
wizen
  nouns gullet 395.15
  windpipe 395.16
  verbs age 126.10
  shrink 197.9
  dry 392.6
  deteriorate 690.19
  adjs. shrunk 197.13
  thin 204.19
wizened
  shrunk 197.13
  thin 204.19
  dried 392.9

  wasted 690.34
wizzen
  verbs shrink 197.9
  dry 392.6
  deteriorate 690.19
  adjs. 204.19
wobble
  nouns 323.3
  verbs fluctuate 141.5
  walk 272.27
  oscillate 322.9
  shake 323.11
  vacillate 625.8
wobbly
  unsteady 159.16
  shaky 323.18
  vacillating 625.10
Woden See **Odin**
woe evil 673.3
  bane 674.1
  anguish 864.6,8
  grief 870.10
  WOE BETIDE! 942.10
  WOE'S ME! 873.20
woebegone
  wretched 864.29
  sad 870.22
woeful terrible 673.9
  grievous 862.11
  wretched 864.29
  sad 870.27
woefully
  exceedingly 34.25
  terribly 673.14
  grievously 862.18
  sadly 870.37
wog 189.3
wold 386.1
wolf
  nouns animal 413.49
  philanderer 930.11
  libertine 987.10
  WOLF AT THE DOOR
    836.2
  WOLF IN SHEEP'S
    CLOTHING 617.6
  verbs devour 306.21
  eat greedily 992.5
wolfish wolflike 413.37
  rapacious 820.23
wolverine 413.4
woman girl 125.6
  adult 127.1
  old ~ 169.12
  womankind 420.3
  female 420.5
  mollycoddle 420.11
  wife 931.9
  bad ~ 987.14,16
  paramour 987.17
woman chaser
  philanderer 930.11
  libertine 987.10
womanfolk 420.5
woman-hater 938.2
womanhood
  maturity 126.2
  femininity 420.1,3
womanish 420.14,15
womanism 956.6
womanist 956.7

womanization 420.12
womanize 420.13
womankind 420.3
womanliness 420.1
womanly 420.14
woman of the world
642.7
woman suffrage
franchise 742.17
feminism 956.6
woman-suffragist
politics 742.17
feminist 956.7
womb source 152.9
genitals 418.8
women 799.19
wonder
nouns miracle 85.8
first-rater 672.6
astonishment 918
marvel 918.2
NO WONDER! 919.4
verbs not know
476.12
be uncertain 513.9
marvel 918.4
wonder drugs 685.24
wonderful
adjs. remarkable
34.10
extraordinary 85.13
superb 672.18
marvelous 918.9
advs. 34.23
wonderfully
remarkably 34.23
extraordinarily
85.17
superbly 672.24
marvelously 918.13
wonderland 533.11
wonderless 919.3
wonderment
astonishment 918.1
wonder 918.2
wonder-stricken,
wonder-struck
918.8
wonderwork 85.8
wonder-worker 1033.5
wonder-working 85.15
wondrous
adjs. 918.9
advs. 34.23
wont
nouns 640.1
verbs 640.12
adjs. 640.16
wonted usual 84.8
accustomed
640.14,16
wonting 640.1
woo solicit 772.14
court 930.19
wood
nouns saddle 215.19
firewood 330.3
lumber 377.3
types of ~ 377.13
woodland 410.11
adjs. 377.8

woodbine 433.4
wood carving
figure 570.4
sculpture 573.1
woodchuck 413.4
woodcraft
forestry 412.3
art 572.3
woodcut
engraving 576.6
stage ~ 609.24
woodcutter 412.7
wooded 410.38
wooden wood 377.8
stupid 468.16
expressionless
545.11
wood engraving
576.2,6
woodenhead 470.4
woodenheaded 468.17
wooden horse 1009.3
woodland
nouns 410.11
adjs. hinterland 181.8
sylvan 410.38
woodman
woodlander 189.10
forester 412.7
woodmote 999.5
wood-note 459.1
woodpecker 413.34
woodprint 576.6
woods
hinterland 181.2
woodland 410.11
wood winds 464.9
woodsman
backwoodsman
189.10
forester 412.7
woodsy 410.38
woodwind, woodwinds
463.12
wood winds 464.9
woody wooden 377.8
wooded 410.38
wooer 929.11
woof weft 221.4
texture 350.1
fabric 377.5
woofer 343.4
wooing
solicitation 772.5
courtship 930.6
wool hair 229.2
softness 356.4
woolen 377.9
woolens 230.22
woolgathering
nouns 530.2
adjs. 530.11
woolly
fleecy 229.24
downy 356.14
cloth 377.9
woolly-headed 229.24
woolpack 403.1
woolsack
official seat 737.9
judgment seat 999.8

woomping 343.24
woon 747.14
woozy 530.14
word
nouns
testimony 504.3
maxim 516.1
declaration 521.1
oath 521.3
information 555.1
news 556.1,4
term 580.1
utterance 592.3,4
account 606.3
command 750.1
promise 768.1
AS GOOD AS ONE'S
WORD
observant 766.4
trustworthy 972.19
GIVE ONE'S WORD
testify 504.10
promise 768.4
GIVE WORD 555.7
HAVE A GOOD WORD
FOR 966.11
HAVE A WORD WITH
595.8
HAVE THE LAST WORD
induce 152.12
have one's way
619.3
insist 751.7
IN A WORD 590.6
IN OTHER WORDS
550.21
KEEP ONE'S WORD
fulfill 766.2
keep faith with
972.9
ON ONE'S WORD
768.7
THE WORD
Logos 1011.13
Bible 1019.2
UPON MY WORD
521.10
WORD TO THE WISE
reminder 535.6
tip 555.3
warning 701.1
advice 752.2
verbs phrase 583.4
say 592.14
wordage
vocabulary 580.12
diction 586.1
word blindness, word
deafness
amnesia 536.2
neurosis 688.26
wordbook 603.7
word-bound 611.7
word-coiner 580.16
wordcraft 597.1
worded 583.6
word for word 543.15
GIVE WORD FOR WORD
repeat 103.7
memorize 535.17
word-for-word 543.12

word history 580.14
wordiness 591.2
wording 586.1
wordless
silent 450.13,14
unexpressed 544.9
taciturn 611.7
word of mouth 592.3
BY WORD OF MOUTH
592.23
word painter
writer 600.15
storyteller 606.10
word painting, word
picture 606.1
wordplay 879.8
words
vocabulary 580.12
talk 592.1
conversation 595.3
quarrel 793.5
HAVE WORDS WITH
quarrel 793.12
reprove 967.17
IN PLAIN WORDS
intelligibly 546.12
plainly 589.4
frankly 972.23
PUT WORDS IN ONE'S
MOUTH
attribute to 154.3
suggest 555.9
word-seller 600.15
wordy 591.12
work
nouns
operation 163.1
product 167.1
musical ~ 461.5
~ of art 572.11
writing 600.11
book 603.1
business 654.1,2,6
action 703.1
labor 714.4
AT WORK
operating 163.12
busy 705.20
OUT OF WORK 706.16
verbs mix 44.11
cause 152.11
operate 163.5,6
be operative 163.8
influence 171.7
form 245.6
ferment 378.6
effervesce 404.4
cultivate 412.17
solve 486.2
busy oneself
654.9,10
overwork 661.11
use 663.10
exploit 663.16
act 703.4
labor 714.12
~ hard 714.13
busy 714.16
accomplish 720.4
WORK AGAINST TIME
spend time 105.6

repute 912.3
adjs.
possessing 806.10
valued at 844.16
NOT WORTH A RAP
836.7
NOT WORTH HAVING
667.11
NOT WORTH SAVING
666.10
WORTH ONE'S SALT
663.21
worthless
useless 667.11
paltry 671.19
worth-while
useful 663.21
expedient 668.4
profitable 809.14
worthy
nouns
personage 670.8
celebrity 912.9
reputable person
983.1
adjs. eligible 635.21
fit 668.4
qualified 731.22
valuable 846.10
reputable 912.16
praiseworthy 966.19
honorable 972.13
WORTHY OF 958.10
**would as leave, would
as lief**
be willing 620.3
prefer 635.14
would-be
nouns 917.10
adjs. nominal 581.15
presumptuous
910.10
wound
nouns sore 684.28
injury 690.7
mental pain 864.5
verbs pain 423.7
harm 673.6
injure 690.13
irritate 855.13
grieve 864.14
offend 950.20
wounded
pained 423.9
grieved 864.26
wound up 70.8
ALL WOUND UP IN
175.4
GET ALL WOUND UP
729.11
woven
interwoven 221.8
cloth 377.9
wow
nouns 722.3
verbs delight 863.8
amuse 876.23
interjs. goody! 863.17
hurrah! 874.12
oh! 918.18
wrack plant 410.4

ruin 691.1
GO TO WRACK AND
RUIN 691.23
wraith illusion 518.4
specter 1015.1,3
wraithlike, wraithy
1015.7
wrangle
nouns 793.5
verbs herd 415.7
argue 481.17
quarrel 793.12
~ over 794.22
wrangler herder 415.3
arguer 481.13
student 564.5
disputant 789.3
combatant 798.1
wrangling
argument 481.5
contention 794.1
wrap
nouns wrapper 227.19
garment 230.12
UNDER WRAPS
secret 612.12
restrained 758.13
verbs bind 47.9
cover 227.22
clothe 230.38
surround 232.6
wrapped
covered 227.34
surrounded 232.11
WRAPPED UP IN
involved in 175.4
engrossed 528.17
habituated 640.18
devoted to 929.27
WRAPPED UP IN
ONESELF
conceited 907.12
selfish 976.5
wrapper cover 227.19
garment 230.12
wrapping
nouns covering 227.1
wrapper 227.19
adjs. covering 227.37
surrounding 232.9
wrath 950.5
wrathful 950.26
wreak do to 703.6
inflict 961.5
WREAK ONE'S VENGE-
ANCE 954.4
wreath
nouns braid 221.3
circle 252.2
flowers 410.23
trophy 914.3
verbs 221.7
wreathe
encircle 232.7
decorate 899.8
wreathed
woven 221.8
ornamented 899.10
wreathing 221.1
wreathlike 253.6
wreathwork 221.3

wreck
nouns jalopy 271.9
ruins 690.9
destruction 691.1
crash 691.4
accident 727.2
nervous ~ 857.6
verbs
shipwreck 274.44
destroy 691.10
demolish 691.17
wreckage 691.5
wrecked
ruined 691.27
stranded 729.25
wrecker
destroyer 691.8
plunderer 823.6
wrench
nouns twist 248.1
jerk 285.3
extraction 304.5
types of ~ 347.17
pang 423.2
sprain 690.7
mental pain 864.5
verbs distort 248.5
jerk 285.5
extract 304.13
misrepresent 571.3
sprain 690.13
wrest 820.19
wrenching 304.5
wrest
nouns twist 248.1
extraction 304.5
verbs distort 248.5
extract 304.13
usurp command
737.13
seize 820.19
wresting 304.5
wrestle
nouns 714.3
verbs struggle 714.11
scuffle 794.14
~ with 794.18
wrestler 798.3
wrestling 794.10
wretch sufferer 864.11
good-for-nothing
984.2
wretched paltry
671.18
terrible 673.9
squalid 680.27
miserable 864.29
unhappy 870.21
disreputable 913.12
wretchedness
paltriness 671.2
terribleness 673.2
distress 864.6
unhappiness 870.2
disreputability 913.3
wrick
nouns 690.7
verbs 690.13
wriggle
nouns 323.7
verbs wiggle 323.15

be excited 855.18
WRIGGLE INTO 301.7
WRIGGLE OUT OF
630.8
wriggler 125.9
wriggling, wriggly
323.22
wright artisan 716.6
types of ~ 716.11
wring
nouns contortion
248.1
extraction 304.5
verbs distort 248.5
convolve 253.4
extract 304.13,14
pain 423.7
wrest 820.19
torture 864.20
WRING FROM
wrest from 820.19
extort 822.19
WRING ONE'S HANDS
873.9
wringer 304.8
wringing 304.5
wrinkle
nouns corrugation
263.3
fad 642.5
verbs age 126.10
contract 197.7
corrugate 263.6
wrinkled aged 126.15
corrugated 263.8
wrinkling 197.1
wrinkly 263.8
wrist joint 47.4
arm 286.5
wristband, wristlet
band 252.3
bracelet 899.6
writ 750.6
write ~ music 461.47
record 568.15
pen 600.19
~ poetry 607.19
~ prose 608.3
WRITE OFF
cancel 42.8
repeal 777.2
~ a debt 840.9
discount 845.2
forgive 945.5
WRITE ONE'S OWN
TICKET 619.3
WRITE OUT
record 568.15
spell out 579.10
draw up 600.22
WRITE TO 602.11
WRITE UP
report 556.11
publicize 557.15
record 568.15
write upon 604.5
write-off
cancellation 777.1
moratorium 840.2
discount 845.1
writer penman 600.14

yegg, yeggman 823.3

yell
 nouns shout 458.1
  cheer 874.2
 verbs shout 458.6
  wail 873.11
  cheer 874.7
  ~ at 967.20

yelling 458.10

yellow
 nouns color 369.1
  pigments 369.7
  yolk 405.14
 verbs shone 369.3
 adjs. yellow-colored
  369.4
  sensational 855.33
  cowardly 890.10
  jealous 951.4

yellow book 568.7
yellow boy 833.5,6
yellow fever 684.9
yellow flag
 warning 701.3
 quarantine 759.2
yellowish 369.4
yellow jack
 disease 684.9
 warning 701.3
 quarantine 759.2
yellow jaundice
 yellowness 369.2
 disease 684.8
yellow journalism
 853.8
yellowness color 369
 cowardice 890.1
Yellow Nineties 107.7
yellow peril 417.4
yellow race 417.2
yellow streak 890.4

yelp
 nouns 458.1
 verbs yell 458.6
  bark 459.2
  say 592.17
  complain 873.13
  ~ at 967.20
yelping 458.10

yen
 nouns desire 632.5
  coin 833.9
 verbs 632.16

yeoman seaman 275.6
 farmer 412.5
 guard 697.8
 attendant 748.4
 soldier 798.14
yeomanly
 adjs. 972.13
 advs. 891.22
yeomanry 798.27
yep 520.18
yerk
 nouns blow 282.4
  jerk 285.3
 verbs strike 282.14
  jerk 285.5
  ~ out 461.38
yes
 nouns assent 520.2

vote 635.5
 verbs 520.8
 advs. 520.18
yes man 905.3
yesterday, yesteryear
 119.1
yet
 notwithstanding
  33.8
 in addition 40.10
 prior to 116.6
 until now 120.4
Yiddish 417.11
yield
 nouns produce 167.2
  gain 809.4
 verbs produce 166.17
  be pliant 356.7
  acknowledge 520.11
  give up 631.7
  provide 657.7
  submit 763.7
  consent 773.4
  relinquish 812.3
  give 816.12
  bring in 842.3
  sell for 844.15
YIELD THE PALM
 concede superiority
  37.5
 surrender 763.8
YIELD TO
 acknowledge 520.11
 indulge 757.7
 submit to 763.9
 accept 859.6
NOT YIELD AN INCH
 624.7
yielding
 nouns bearing 166.8
  abandonment 631.3
  submission 763.1
  relinquishment
   812.1
 adjs. bearing 164.10
  pliant 356.9
  unstrict 756.5
  submissive 763.13
yip 459.2
Ymir giant 194.13
 god 1012.6
yodel
 nouns 461.12
 verbs 461.39
yodeler 463.13
yodeling 461.12
Yoga 989.1
yoga, yogeeism 1032.1
yogi, yogin
 ascetic 989.2
 occultist 1032.11
 religious 1036.13
yogism 1032.1
yogist 1032.11
yo-ho
 nouns 458.1
 verbs call 458.6
  attention! 528.23
yoick 458.6
yoicks 458.3; 653.13

yoke
 nouns two 90.2
  harness 657.5
  shackle 758.4
 verbs join 47.5
  fasten 47.10
  pair 90.5
yoked 90.8
yokefellow
 co-worker 785.5
 companion 926.4
yokel
 nouns dolt 470.5
  clumsy fellow 732.9
  country bumpkin
   917.9
 adjs. 181.7
yokeldom 181.1
yokemate
 co-worker 785.5
 companion 926.4
 spouse 931.7
yolk 405.14
yolked, yolky 405.24
yom Kippur 1038.16
yon, yond, yonder
 adjs. that 80.15
  thither 198.10
 advs. 198.13
 preps. 198.21
yore
 nouns 119.2
 adjs. 123.10
Yorkshire pudding
 306a.45
you 80.5
YOU BET 520.18
YOU CAN BET ON IT
 510.11
YOU DON'T SAY!
 indeed! 484.48
 astonishment
  918.20
YOU HAVE ANOTHER
 GUESS COMING
 you're wrong 517.20
 I refuse 774.9
YOU SAID IT 515.22
YOU SHOULD LIVE SO
 LONG!
 not likely 511.4
 I refuse 774.9
you-all 80.5
you-know-who 582.2
young
 nouns youth 125.2
  brood 170.2
 HAVE YOUNG 166.19
 WITH YOUNG 168.18
 adjs. new 122.7
  youthful 124.9
young blood 125.2
younger
 nouns 125.1
 adjs. 124.15
younger generation
 125.2
youngling
 nouns 125
 adjs. 124.9

young man 929.11
youngness 124.1
youngster 125.1
younker 125.1
your, yours 806.13
Your Majesty, Your
 Excellency, etc.
 915.2
yourself, yourselves
 80.5
yours truly 80.5
youth youngness 124
 youngling 125.1
 young people 125.2
 boy 125.5
youthen 124.8
youthful 124.9
youthfulness, youth-
 head, youthhood
 124.1
youthify 124.8
youthlike, youthsome,
 youthy 124.9
yowl
 nouns yell 458.1
  plaint 873.3
 verbs yell 458.6
  howl 459.2
  wail 873.11
yowling 459.6
Y-shaped
 angular 250.6
 forked 298.10
yucca 257.8
Yuga 107.5
Yuit 417.6
Yule, Yuletide 137.5
yule log 330.3
yummy 427.8

Z

Z 70.1
Zadkiel 1013.4
zag
 nouns zigzag 218.8
  angle 250.2
 verbs zigzag 218.12
  angle 250.5
zambo 44.9
zamindar 807.3
zamindari 808.7
zany fool 470.1
 clown 610.9
 wag 879.12
zeal eagerness 633.2
 piety 1026.1
zealot fanatic 472.17
 enthusiast 633.5
 pietist 1026.4
zealotic(al)
 fanatical 472.31
 pious 1026.8
zealotism, zealotry
 fanaticism 472.11
 zeal 633.4
 piety 1026.1
zealous eager 633.10
 industrious 705.21

pious 1026.8
zealousness
industriousness
705.6
piety 1026.1
zebra 373.6
zebrass, zebrule 44.8
Zechariah 1020.1
zemi 1012.10
zenana 931.11
Zend-Avesta 1019.6
zendician, zendik,
zendikite 1023.6
zenith 210.2
zenithal 210.9
Zephaniah 1020.1
Zephyr, Zephyrus
402.3
zephyr 402.5
zeppelin 279.11
zero 2.2
BELOW ZERO 332.15
zero hour crucial
moment 129.6
attack 796.14
zest savor 427.2
pungency 432.2
eagerness 633.1
pleasure 863.1
WITH ZEST
willingly 620.8
eagerly 633.13
cheerfully 868.18
zestful piquant 432.7
eager 633.9
vivacious 868.14
zestfulness
pungency 432.2

eagerness 633.1
gaiety 868.4
zetetic 484.18
Zeus 1012.5
zig
nouns zigzag 218.8
angle 250.2
verbs zigzag 218.12
angle 250.5
zigzag
nouns obliquity 218.8
angle 250.2
verbs stagger 218.12
angle 250.5
alternate 322.12
adjs. 218.21
zillion
nouns number 99.13
multitude 101.4
adjs. 101.7
zinc 227.28
zincograph 576.7
zincographer 577.8
zincography 576.2
zinc plate 576.7
zing 160.2
zingaro 273.4
Zion 1016.4
zip
nouns energy 160.2
pungency 432.2
sibilation 456.1
verbs speed 268.9
sibilate 456.2
ZIP UP
energize 160.9
close 265.6
zipper fasten 47.8

close 265.6
zippy energetic 160.11
pungent 432.7
gay 868.14
zircon light 334.18
zither 464.3
zitherist 463.5
zizz 160.2
zodiac belt 252.3
stars 374.16
astrology 374.20
zodiacal 374.25
zodiacal light 334.15
zoetic organic 405.18
living 406.10
zoic 413.36
Zollverein 786.1
zombi 470.8
zonal 179.8
zone
nouns region 179.1
latitude 179.3
stratum 226.1
belt 252.3
celestial ∼ 374.16
verbs 49.18
zone time 114.3
zoo 415.5
zoogeography,
zoography 414.1
zoographer 414.2
zooid 405.2
zooidal 413.36
zoolater 1031.4
zoolatrous 1031.7
zoolatry 1031.1
zoologic(al) 413.36;
414.13

zoological garden
415.5
zoologist
biologist 405.17
scientist 414.2
zoology
anatomy 244.7
biology 405.16
animals 414
anthropology 416.8
manual 603.9
zoom
nouns 277.10
verbs speed 268.9
fly 277.45
zoon 405.2
zoonomy 414.1
zoophysical 324.3
zoophysics 324.1
zoophyte 414.4
zooplasty 687.27
zoospore 405.9
zootheism 1018.5
zootheist 1018.14
zootomy 244.7
zoril animal 413.4
stinker 436.3
Zoroaster, Zarathustra
1020.3
Zoroastrian
nouns 1031.4
adjs. 1018.30
Zouave 798.10
zounds! 918.19
zwieback 306a.29
zygospore 405.9
zygote 405.8
zymic 352.16
zymotic 684.47

ABBREVIATIONS USED
IN THIS BOOK

abbr.	. .	abbreviation	F.	. . .	French
ADJS.	. .	adjectives	fem.	. . .	feminine
ADVS.	. .	adverbs	fig.	. . .	figurative
aero.	. .	aeronautics, aeronautical	Fin., Finn.		Finland, Finnish
alg.	. . .	algebra	fort.	. .	fortification
Amer.	. .	America, American	G.	. . .	German
anat.	. .	anatomy	geol.	. .	geology
anon.	. .	anonymous	geom.	. .	geometry
antiq	. .	antiquity	Gr.	. . .	Greece, Greek
Arab.	. .	Arabian	gram.	. .	grammar, grammatical
arch.	. .	archaic	Heb.	. .	Hebrew
archaeol.	.	archaeology	her.	. . .	heraldry, heraldic
astrol.	. .	astrology	Hind.	. .	Hindustani
astron.	. .	astronomy	hist.	. . .	history, historical
Austral.	.	Australia, Australian	ibid.	. . .	ibidem (L., in the same
biol.	. .	biology			place)
bot.	. . .	botany	illit.	. . .	illiterate
Brit.	. . .	Britain, British	Ind.	. . .	India, Indian
Calif.	. .	California	INTERJS.	. .	interjections
Can.	. .	Canada, Canadian	INTERROGS.		interrogatives
Cath.	. .	Catholic	Ir.	. . .	Ireland, Irish
ch.	. . .	church	iron.	. .	irony, ironical
chem.	. .	chemistry, chemical	It.	. . .	Italy, Italian
Chin.	. .	China, Chinese	Jap.	. . .	Japan, Japanese
coll.	. . .	colloquial	joc.	. . .	jocose, jocular
com.	. .	commerce, commercial	journ.	. .	journalistic
CONJS.	. .	conjunctions	L.	. . .	Latin
Conn.	. .	Connecticut	mach.	. .	machinery
crim.	. .	criminal	masc.	. .	masculine
criminol.	.	criminology	Mass.	. .	Massachusetts
derog.	. .	derogatory	math.	. .	mathematics, mathematical
dial.	. . .	dialect	meas.	. .	measure
Du.	. . .	Dutch	mech.	. .	mechanics, mechanical
E.	. . .	East, Eastern	med.	. .	medicine, medical
eccl.	. .	ecclesiastical	metal.	. .	metallurgy
econ.	. .	economics	meteorol.	. .	meteorology
elec.	. .	electricity, electrical	Mex.	. .	Mexico, Mexican
Eng.	. .	England, English	mfg.	. . .	manufacturing
erron.	. .	erroneous	mil.	. . .	military
esp.	. . .	especially	min.	. . .	mining, mineralogy
etc.	. . .	et cetera	ML.	. .	Medieval Latin
exc.	. . .	except	Moham.	. .	Mohammedan

Mongol.	.	Mongolia, Mongolian	R.R. . .	railroading
mus.	. .	music, musical	Russ. . .	Russia, Russian
myth.	. .	mythology	S. . . .	South, Southern
N.	. . .	North, Northern	S. Afr. . .	South Africa
N. Afr.	.	North Africa	S. Amer. .	South America
N. Amer.	.	North America	Scot. . .	Scotland, Scotch, Scottish
naut.	. .	nautical	sing. . . .	singular
neurol.	. .	neurology	Southwest.	Southwestern
NL.	. . .	New Latin	Sp. . . .	Spain, Spanish
N.Y.C. .	.	New York City	spec. . .	special, specially
obs.	. . .	obsolete	surg. . .	surgery
Per.	. . .	Persia, Persian	tech. . .	technology, technical
petrog.	. .	petrography	teleg. . .	telegraphy
Pg.	. . .	Portugal, Portuguese	Teut. . .	Teuton, Teutonic
pharm.	. .	pharmacy, pharmaceutical	theat. . .	theatrical
philos.	. .	philosophy	theol. . .	theology
phonet.	. .	phonetics	Theos. . .	Theosophy
PHRS.	. .	phrases	Turk. . .	Turkey, Turkish
phys.	. .	physics	TV . . .	television
physiol.	.	physiology	U. . . .	Union
P.I. . . .		Philippine Islands	U.N. . .	United Nations
pl.	. . .	plural	univ. . .	university
polit.	. .	politics, political	U.S. . . .	United States
Pr.	. . .	Provence, Provençal	U.S.S.R. .	Union of Soviet Socialist Republics
PREPS.	. .	prepositions		
print.	. .	printing	usu. . . .	usually
pros.	. .	prosody	vulg. . .	vulgar
psychol.	.	psychology	W. . . .	West, Western
R.C.Ch.	.	Roman Catholic Church	W. Ind. .	West Indies
rel.	. . .	religion	zool. . .	zoology
Rom.	. .	Rome, Roman		

evil-faced, evil-headed, evil-eyed, evil-savored, evil-affected, evil-gotten.

12. **harmful, hurtful,** scatheful *or* scathful [dial.], **baneful,** baleful, **injurious, damaging, detrimental,** deleterious, pernicious, mischievous, noxious, noisome; **malignant,** malign, malefic(al); prejudicial, disadvantageous, disserviceable; corrosive, corroding; insalubrious 682.4.

ADVS. 13. **badly,** bad [coll.], **ill,** wrong, evil, evilly, wrongly, amiss, to one's cost.

14. **terribly, dreadfully, horribly,** horridly, **awfully** [coll.], **atrociously** [coll.], **deplorably,** lamentably, regrettably, pitifully, woefully, grievously, sadly, grossly, flagrantly, **outrageously,** scandalously, shamefully, shockingly, infamously, egregiously, execrably, **vilely, wretchedly, basely,** odiously, obnoxiously, abominably, detestably, despicably, contemptibly, foully; awful, dreadful [both dial. & coll.]; something fierce *or* terrible [slang].

674. BANE

NOUNS 1. **bane, curse, affliction,** in~~fec~~tion, visitation, **plague,** pestilence, ~~scourge, torment, grievance, woe, sore,~~ in

Cross-references suggest additional meanings.

rot; worm, worm in the apple *or* rose; ~~moth,~~ "moth and rust" [Bible].

3. **poison, venom,** venin, **virus, toxic,** toxin, toxicant, leaven; deliriant, delirifacient; pesticide 408.11; toxicology.

4. **miasma,** miasm, **mephitis,** effluvium, malaria; coal gas, chokedamp, blackdamp.

5. **sting, stinger,** dart; **fang,** tang [dial.]; bee sting, snake bite.

6. poisons

aconite	cyanide of
antimony	potassium
arsenic	D.D.T.
arsenious acid	hemlock
arsenious oxide	hydrocyanic acid
bichloride of	hydrocyanide
mercury	nicotine
carbolic acid	nitrogen
carbon dioxide	Paris green
carbon monoxide	poison gas
carbonic acid	prussic acid
carbonic gas	ptomaine
chlorine	rat poison
chlorine dioxide *or*	strychnine
peroxide	tannic acid
	tannin
corrosive sublimate	tartar emetic

poisonous plants

~~Banewort~~   ~~nightshade~~

Boldface type pinpoints the most commonly used words.

de~~ath camass~~   ~~poison grass~~
death cup   poison hemlock
foxglove   poison ivy
Gastrolobium   poison laurel
greyana   poison oak
hellebore   poison rhubarb
hemp   poison sumac
henbane   poison tobacco
Indian hemp   poisonweed
Jimson weed   pokeweed
locoweed   sheep laurel
May apple   Swainsona
mescal   upas
monkshood   water hemlock
mushroom

675. PERFECTION

NOUNS 1. **perfection,** finish; **faultlessness, flawlessness,** defectlessness, indefectibility; spotlessness, stainlessness, taintlessness; immaculateness, impeccability.

2. **soundness, intactness, wholeness,** entireness, completeness, **integrity.**

3. **acme of perfection, pink, pink of perfection,** height, acme, ultimate, summit, culmination, consummation, quintessence, *ne plus ultra* [L., no more beyond].

4. ideal 25.4; paragon 983.4.

VERBS 5. **perfect,** develop, improve 689.10; complete 720.6.

ADJS. 6. **perfect,** pure, ideal; **faultless, flawless,** defectless; spotless, stainless, taintless, unblemished, untainted, unspotted; immaculate, impeccable; indefective, indefectible; beyond all praise, irreproachable, *sans peur et sans reproche* [F., without fear and without reproach].

7. **sound, intact, whole, entire, complete;** sound as a roach, right as a trivet.

8. **undamaged, unharmed, unhurt, uninjured,** unscathed, **unspoiled,** unim**paired;** harmless, scatheless; **unmarred,** ~~unma~~rked, unscarred, unscratched, unde~~faced,~~ ~~un~~bruised; **unbroken,** unshattered, unto~~rn~~

Word lists help you recall names of specific things.

~~fo~~

~~w~~

elabor~~ate, high-wrought.~~

ADVS. 10. **perfectly,** purely, ideally; **faultlessly, flawlessly,** spotlessly; immaculately, impeccably; **wholly, entirely, completely;** clean, clean as a whistle.

11. **to perfection, to a turn, to a T,** to